Glencoe
Literature
The Reader's Choice

American Literature

INDIANA EDITION

PROGRAM CONSULTANTS

Jeffrey D. Wilhelm, PhD

Douglas Fisher, PhD

Beverly Ann Chin, PhD

Jacqueline Jones Royster, DA

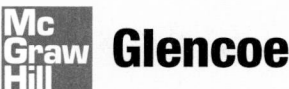
McGraw Hill Glencoe

New York, New York Columbus, Ohio Chicago, Illinois Woodland Hills, California

ACKNOWLEDGMENTS

Grateful acknowledgment is given authors, publishers, photographers, museums, and agents for permission to reprint the following copyrighted material. Every effort has been made to determine copyright owners. In case of any omissions, the publisher will be pleased to make suitable acknowledgments in future editions.

Acknowledgements continued on page R104.

Image Credits:
IN5 age fotostock/SuperStock; **IN21** Robert Glusic/CORIS.

 Glencoe

The *McGraw-Hill* Companies

Send all inquiries to:
Glencoe/McGraw-Hill
8787 Orion Place
Columbus, OH 43240-4027

ISBN: (student edition) 978-0-07-878182-7
MHID: (student edition) 0-07-878182-5
ISBN: (teacher edition) 978-0-07-878186-5
MHID: (teacher edition) 0-07-878186-8

Printed in the United States of America.

1 2 3 4 5 6 7 8 9 027/043 12 11 10 09 08 07

Senior Program Consultants

Jeffrey D. Wilhelm, PhD, a former middle and secondary school English and reading teacher, is currently Professor of Education at Boise State University. He is the author or coauthor of numerous articles and several books on the teaching of reading and literacy, including award-winning titles such as *You Gotta BE the Book* and *Reading Don't Fix No Chevys*. He also works with local schools as part of the Adolescent Literacy Project and recently helped establish the National Writing Project site at Boise State University.

Douglas Fisher, PhD, is Professor of Language and Literacy Education and Director of Professional Development at San Diego State University, where he teaches English language development and literacy. He also serves as Director of City Heights Educational Pilot, which won the Christa McAuliffe Award from the American Association of State Colleges and Universities. He has published numerous articles on reading and literacy, differentiated instruction, and curriculum design. He is coauthor of the book *Improving Adolescent Literacies: Strategies That Work* and coeditor of the book *Inclusive Urban Schools*.

Program Consultants

Beverly Ann Chin, PhD, is Professor of English, Director of the English Teaching Program, former Director of the Montana Writing Project, and former Director of Composition at the University of Montana in Missoula. She currently serves as a Member at Large of the Conference of English Leadership. Dr. Chin is a nationally recognized leader in English language arts standards, curriculum, and assessment. Formerly a high school teacher and an adult education reading teacher, Dr. Chin has taught in English language arts education at several universities and has received awards for her teaching and service.

Jacqueline Jones Royster, DA, is Professor of English and Senior Vice Provost and Executive Dean of the Colleges of Arts and Sciences at The Ohio State University. She is currently on the Writing Advisory Committee of the National Commission on Writing and serves as chair for both the Columbus Literacy Council and the Ohioana Library Association. In addition to the teaching of writing, Dr. Royster's professional interests include the rhetorical history of African American women and the social and cultural implications of literate practices. She has contributed to and helped to edit numerous books, anthologies, and journals.

Special Consultant

FOLDABLE **Dinah Zike, MEd,** was a classroom teacher and a consultant for many years before she began to develop Foldables™—a variety of easily created graphic organizers. Zike has written and developed more than 150 supplemental books and materials used in classrooms worldwide. Her *Big Book of Books and Activities* won the Teachers' Choice Award.

Glencoe National Reading and Language Arts Advisory Council

Mary A. Avalos, PhD
Assistant Department Chair,
  Department of Teaching
  and Learning
Research Assistant Professor,
  Department of Teaching
  and Learning
University of Miami
Coral Gables, Florida

Wanda J. Blanchett, PhD
Associate Dean for Academic
  Affairs and Associate
  Professor of Exceptional
  Education
School of Education
University of Wisconsin–
  Milwaukee
Milwaukee, Wisconsin

William G. Brozo, PhD
Professor of Literacy
Graduate School of Education
College of Education and
  Human Development
George Mason University
Fairfax, Virginia

Nancy Drew, EdD
LaPointe Educational
  Consultants
Corpus Christi, Texas

Susan Florio-Ruane, EdD
Professor
College of Education
Michigan State University
East Lansing, Michigan

Sharon Fontenot O'Neal, PhD
Associate Professor
Texas State University
San Marcos, Texas

Nancy Frey, PhD
Associate Professor of Literacy
  in Teacher Education
School of Teacher Education
San Diego State University
San Diego, California

Victoria Gentry Ridgeway, PhD
Associate Professor
Reading Education
Clemson University
Clemson, South Carolina

Kimberly Lawless, PhD
Associate Professor
Curriculum, Instruction
  and Evaluation
College of Education
University of Illinois
  at Chicago
Chicago, Illinois

William Ray, MA
Lincoln-Sudbury Regional
  High School
Sudbury, Massachusetts

Janet Saito-Furukawa, MEd
Literacy Coach
Washington Irving
  Middle School
Los Angeles, California

Bonnie Valdes, MEd
Independent Reading
  Consultant
CRISS Master Trainer
Largo, Florida

Heather Bontratger
Language Arts Teacher
NorthWood Middle School
Wakarusa, Indiana

Heather Coy
Language Arts
   Department Chair
Harrison High School
Evansville, Indiana

Kristin Cramer
Language Arts Teacher
NorthWood Middle School
Wakarusa, Indiana

Judith Ann Gibson
English Teacher
Lawrence North High School
Indianapolis, Indiana

Fred Fox
Language Arts Teacher
Doe Creek Middle School
New Palestine, Indiana

John Houser
Language Arts
   Department Chair
Snider High School
Fort Wayne, Indiana

Dina Koble
Language Arts Teacher
NorthWood Middle School
Wakarusa, Indiana

Sherri Pankratz
English Teacher
Carmel High School
Carmel, Indiana

Madelyn Russell
Literature Teacher
Thompkins Middle School
Evansville, Indiana

Correlation to the Indiana Academic Standards

Indiana Academic Standards	*Glencoe Literature*, American Literature
Standard 1 READING: Word Recognition, Fluency, and Vocabulary Development	
11.1 Word Recognition involves the understanding of the basic features of words: word parts, patterns, relationships, and origins. Students use phonics, context clues, and a growing knowledge of English and other languages to determine the meaning of words and become fluent readers.	
Vocabulary and Concept Development	
11.1.1 Understand unfamiliar words that refer to characters or themes in literature or history.	Building Background 218, 679, 787, 1330 Literary Element 789 Reading Strategy 111 Responding and Thinking Critically 663
11.1.2 Apply knowledge of roots and word parts from Greek and Latin to draw inferences about the meaning of vocabulary in literature or other subject areas.	Vocabulary Practice 101, 262, 607, 804, 956, 1011, 1297 Vocabulary Workshop 121, 973
11.1.3 Analyze the meaning of analogies encountered, analyzing specific comparisons as well as relationships and inferences.	Literary Criticism 128 Literary Element 86, 209, 492, 829 Literary Element Review 290 Reading Strategy 703, 1229 Responding and Thinking Critically 93, 199, 427, 590, 710 Vocabulary Practice 526, 681, 698, 773, 798, 899, 966, 1066, 1152, 1187, 1219, 1229, 1245, 1256 Vocabulary Workshop 94 Writing About Literature 128, 526, 977

Standard 2 READING: Comprehension and Analysis of Nonfiction and Informational Text	
11.2 Comprehension involves understanding grade-level-appropriate material. Students develop strategies such as asking questions; making predictions; and identifying and analyzing structure, organization, perspective, and purpose. After Grade 5, the focus is on informational texts.	
Structural Features of Informational and Technical Materials	
11.2.1 Analyze both the features and the rhetorical (persuasive) devices of different types of public documents, such as policy statements, speeches, or debates, and the way in which authors use those features and devices.	Comparing Literature 224 Interdisciplinary Activity 989 Literary Element 93, 111, 117, 127, 357, 389, 972 Reading Strategy 111, 117, 357, 1201 Responding and Thinking Critically 52, 93, 111, 117, 127, 185, 357, 389, 728, 972, 1152 Writing About Literature 111, 117, 128, 357, 389 Writing Workshop 147–148

Indiana Academic Standards	Glencoe Literature, American Literature
Analysis of Grade-Level-Appropriate Nonfiction and Informational Text	
11.2.2 Analyze the way in which clarity of meaning is affected by the patterns of organization, repetition of the main ideas, organization of language, and word choice in the text.	Author's Language and Style 821, 1012 Literary Element 65, 103, 140, 185, 372, 542, 791, 820, 907, 1152, 1168, 1296, 1307 Literary Element Review 185, 1168, 1307 Reading Strategy 59, 101, 493, 798, 888, 1144, 1308 Responding and Thinking Critically 73, 185, 1146, 1232, 1265, 1296 Writing About Literature 59, 385, 989 Writing Workshop 615–617 You're the Critic 383
11.2.3 Verify and clarify facts presented in several types of expository texts by using a variety of consumer, workplace, and public documents.	Internet Connection 263, 440, 698, 1267 Writing About Literature 1012 Writing Workshop 444–453
11.2.4 Make reasonable assertions about an author's arguments by using elements of the text to defend and clarify interpretations.	Literary Element 111, 217, 357 Reading Strategy 117, 217, 357, 1201 Responding and Thinking Critically 185, 217, 357 Writing About Literature 111, 117, 128, 357
11.2.5 Analyze an author's implicit and explicit assumptions and beliefs about a subject.	Literary Element 199 Quickwrite 219 Reading Strategy 59, 725, 972, 1011, 1192
Expository (Informational) Critique	
11.2.6 Critique the power, validity, and truthfulness of arguments set forth in public documents, speeches, or essays; their appeal to both friendly and hostile audiences; and the extent to which the arguments anticipate and address reader concerns and counterclaims.	Comparing Literature 224 Interdisciplinary Activity 972 Literary Element 111, 217, 357 Reading Strategy 217 Responding and Thinking Critically 93, 111, 127, 217, 357, 728, 972, 1152, 1232 Writing About Literature 111, 128, 357

Indiana Academic Standards	Glencoe Literature, American Literature
Standard 3 READING: Comprehension and Analysis of Literary Text	

11.3 Response to grade-level-appropriate literature includes identifying story elements such as character, theme, plot, and setting, and making connections and comparisons across texts. Literary response enhances students' understanding of history, culture, and the social sciences.

Structural Features of Literature

11.3.1 Analyze characteristics of subgenres, types of writings such as satire, parody, allegory, and pastoral that are used in poetry, prose, plays, novels, short stories, essays, and other basic genres. • Satire: using humor to point out weaknesses of people and society. • Parody: using humor to imitate or mock a person or situation. • Allegory: using symbolic figures and actions to express general truths about human experiences. • Pastoral: showing life in the country in an idealistic— and not necessarily realistic—way.	Literary Criticism 1275 Literary Element 73, 405, 1168, 1244, 1322 Responding and Thinking Critically 80, 239, 276, 344 Writing About Literature 80

Analysis of Grade-Level-Appropriate Literary Text

11.3.2 Analyze the way in which the theme or meaning of a selection represents a view or comment on life, using textual evidence to support the claim.	Comparing Literature 46, 224, 998, 1181 Listening and Speaking 1191, 1297 Literary Criticism 566, 988 Literary Element 182, 217 Quickwrite 41, 219, 687, 994 Reading Strategy 87, 186, 209, 277, 1011 Responding and Thinking Critically 26, 32, 52, 73, 86, 93, 101, 103, 117, 127, 140, 182, 185, 188, 199, 209, 217, 239, 249, 261, 276, 290, 335, 344, 357, 366, 372, 383, 389, 398, 401, 405, 413, 427, 430, 433, 438, 503, 515, 525, 530, 566, 571, 590, 663, 676, 681, 693, 698, 703, 710, 712, 722, 728, 739, 759, 783, 789, 804, 813, 819, 825, 829, 833, 873, 898, 907, 933, 966, 972, 977, 988, 1010, 1018, 1045, 1066, 1088, 1105, 1146, 1152, 1157, 1168, 1176, 1186, 1191, 1195, 1206, 1214, 1219, 1229, 1232, 1244, 1255, 1265, 1274, 1279, 1289, 1296, 1322, 1333 Visual Literacy 759 Writing About Literature 26, 182, 199, 278, 372, 430, 440, 503, 543, 740, 773, 833, 925, 989, 1187, 1229, 1250, 1279

Indiana Academic Standards	*Glencoe Literature,* American Literature
11.3.3 Analyze the ways in which irony, tone, mood, the author's style, and the "sound" of language achieve specific rhetorical (persuasive) or aesthetic (artistic) purposes or both.	Literary Element 127, 530, 571, 739, 825, 1176, 1214, 1224 Literary Element Review 185, 492, 873, 933, 1200, 1274, 1322, 1333 Reading Strategy 389, 530, 681, 698, 804 Responding and Thinking Critically 249, 435, 438, 542, 712, 714, 773, 789, 923, 977, 1244, 1301 Writing About Literature 263, 655, 977, 1201, 1267, 1323 Writing Workshop 1340
11.3.4 Analyze ways in which poetry or prose uses imagery, personification, figures of speech, and sounds to evoke readers' emotions.	Literary Element 86, 93, 185, 209, 249, 427, 435, 439, 655, 829, 977, 1186, 1219, 1229, 1289, 1301 Literary Element Review 290, 439, 1224 Reading Strategy 111, 427, 435, 439, 676, 703, 789, 1200, 1219, 1229, 1301 Responding and Thinking Critically 185, 249, 427, 590, 655, 703, 829, 1186, 1219 Writing About Literature 592, 655, 804, 934, 1201
11.3.5 Analyze or evaluate works of literary or cultural significance in history (American, English, or world) that: • reflect a variety of genres in each of the respective historical periods. • were written by important authors in the respective major historical periods. • reveal contrasts in major themes, styles, and trends. • reflect or shed light on the seminal philosophical, religious, social, political, or ethical ideas of their time.	Comparing Literature 46, 224, 347, 561, 688, 998, 1181 Reading Strategy 80, 292, 335, 909 Responding and Thinking Critically 26, 32, 36, 52, 59, 65, 73, 80, 86, 93, 101, 103, 111, 117, 127, 133, 140, 182, 185, 188, 199, 201, 209, 217, 239, 249, 261, 276, 290, 335, 344, 357, 366, 372, 383, 389, 398, 401, 405, 413, 427, 430, 433, 435, 438, 489, 492, 503, 515, 525, 530, 542, 551, 566, 571, 590, 606, 663, 670, 676, 681, 693, 698, 703, 710, 712, 714, 722, 728, 739, 759, 773, 783, 789, 797, 804, 813, 819, 825, 829, 833, 873, 887, 898, 907, 912, 923, 933, 939, 955, 966, 972, 977, 988, 1010, 1018, 1045, 1066, 1088, 1105, 1152, 1157, 1168, 1176, 1186, 1191, 1195, 1200, 1206, 1214, 1219, 1224, 1229, 1232, 1244, 1250, 1255, 1265, 1274, 1279, 1284, 1289, 1296, 1301, 1307, 1322, 1328, 1333
11.3.6 Analyze the way in which authors have used archetypes (original models or patterns, such as best friend, champion, crusader, free spirit, nurturer, outcast, tyrant, and others) drawn from myth and tradition in literature, film, political speeches, and religious writings.	Literary Element 26 Literary Element Review 240, 898 Responding and Thinking Critically 21

Indiana Academic Standards	*Glencoe Literature*, American Literature
Literary Criticism	
11.3.7 Analyze the clarity and consistency of political assumptions (statements that take for granted something is true), beliefs, or intentions in a selection of literary works or essays on a topic.	Listening and Speaking 1191 Literature Groups 1187 Reading Check 1137 Reading Strategy 390, 1191, 1192 Responding and Thinking Critically 353, 392, 1146, 1157, 1176, 1186, 1191, 1195, 1200 Writing About Literature 1201
11.3.8 Analyze the philosophical arguments presented in literary works to determine whether the authors' positions have contributed to the quality of each work and the credibility of the characters.	Comparing Literature 224, 1181 Literary Criticism 87 Literary Element 217, 357 Quickwrite 219 Reading Check 1139, 1141 Reading Strategy 87, 117, 186, 357, 725, 1011, 1088 Responding and Thinking Critically 117, 185, 217, 357, 728, 808, 1010, 1152, 1168, 1206 Writing About Literature 1176

Standard 4 WRITING: Processes and Features	
11.4 The writing process includes prewriting, drafting, editing, and revising. Students progress through these stages to write clear, coherent, and focused paragraphs and essays.	
Organization and Focus	
11.4.1 Discuss ideas for writing with classmates, teachers, and other writers.	Writing Workshop 149, 299, 1113, 1337
11.4.2 Demonstrate an understanding of the elements of discourse, such as purpose, speaker, audience, and form, when completing narrative, expository, persuasive, or descriptive writing assignments.	Comparing the Big Idea 46 Quickwrite 45 Writing About Literature 87, 117, 263, 385, 516, 712, 1088, 1219, 1245, 1267 Writing Workshop 149, 299, 617–618, 837, 1113, 1338
11.4.3 Use point of view, characterization, style, and related elements for specific narrative and aesthetic (artistic) purposes.	Creative Writing 87 Writing About Literature 405, 516, 784, 1088, 1245, 1267, 1284 Writing Workshop 299, 1113

Indiana Academic Standards	*Glencoe Literature,* American Literature
11.4.4 Structure ideas and arguments in a sustained and persuasive way and support them with precise and relevant examples.	Learning for Life 956 Literary Criticism 291, 1275 Quickwrite 219, 345, 994 Test Preparation and Practice 161 Unit Introduction 176, 328 Writing About Literature 26, 52, 140, 182, 199, 773, 925 Writing Workshop 146–153, 1334–1341
11.4.5 Enhance meaning using rhetorical devices, including the extended use of parallelism, repetition, and analogy and the issuance of a call for action.	Writing About Literature 111, 217, 347, 389 Writing Workshop 149, 153, 1338
11.4.6 Use language in creative and vivid ways to establish a specific tone.	Creative Writing 87 Revising Check 241, 263, 278, 1012 Writing About Literature 101, 103, 140, 241, 1219 Writing Workshop 302, 347, 445, 840, 1340
Research Process and Technology	
11.4.7 Develop presentations using clear research questions and creative and critical research strategies, such as conducting field studies, interviews, and experiments; researching oral histories; and using Internet sources.	Comparing Literary Trends 688 Internet Connection 939 Learning for Life 813, 829, 1245 Unit Introduction 866 Writing About Literature 1012, 1187 Writing Workshop 444–453
11.4.8 Use systematic strategies to organize and record information, such as anecdotal scripting or annotated bibliographies.	Writing About Literature 440, 740, 761, 784, 874, 889, 899, 934, 1012, 1107, 1225, 1275, 1297, 1323 Writing Workshop 149, 299, 445–446, 451, 618, 837, 1113, 1337–1338
11.4.9 Use a computer to integrate databases, pictures and graphics, and spreadsheets into word-processed documents.	Writing Workshop 296–303
11.4.13 Integrate quotations and citations into a written text while maintaining the flow of ideas.	Writing Workshop 152, 445–453, 618

Indiana Academic Standards	*Glencoe Literature,* American Literature
Evaluation and Revision	
11.4.10 Review, evaluate, and revise writing for meaning, clarity, achievement of purpose, and mechanics.	Revising Check 385, 724, 889, 925 Test Preparation and Practice 851 Writing About Literature 241, 263, 278, 291, 385, 415, 526, 543, 592, 607, 655, 724, 740, 761, 784, 798, 821, 874, 899, 908, 925, 934, 966, 989, 1012, 1169, 1187, 1225, 1256, 1267, 1275, 1297, 1308, 1323 Writing Workshop 152–153, 302–303, 452–453, 622–623, 840–841, 1116–1117, 1340–1341
11.4.11 Edit and proofread one's own writing, as well as that of others, using an editing checklist.	Writing Workshop 152, 302, 452, 622, 840, 1116, 1340
11.4.12 Revise text to highlight the individual voice, improve sentence variety and style, and enhance subtlety of meaning and tone in ways that are consistent with the purpose, audience, and form of writing.	Revising Check 592, 655, 761, 821, 1012, 1107, 1267 Writing About Literature 1245 Writing Workshop 153, 302–303, 452–453, 622–623, 840, 1116–1117, 1340

Standard 5 WRITING: Applications (Different Types of Writing and Their Characteristics)

11.5 Through the exploration of different types of writing and the characteristics of each, students become proficient at narrative (stories), expository (informational), descriptive (sensory), persuasive (emotional appeal), argumentative (logical defense), and technical writing. Writing demonstrates an awareness of the audience (intended reader) and purpose for writing.	
11.5.1 Write fictional, autobiographical, or biographical narratives that: • narrate a sequence of events and communicate their significance to the audience. • locate scenes and incidents in specific places. • describe with specific details the sights, sounds, and smells of a scene and the specific actions, movements, gestures, and feelings of the characters; in the case of autobiography or fiction, use interior monologue (what the character says silently to self) to show the character's feelings. • pace the presentation of actions to accommodate changes in time and mood.	Writing About Literature 405, 516 Writing Workshop 296–303, 1110–1117

Indiana Academic Standards	*Glencoe Literature,* American Literature
11.5.2 Write responses to literature that: • demonstrate a comprehensive understanding of the significant ideas in works or passages. • analyze the use of imagery, language, universal themes, and unique aspects of the text. • support statements with evidence from the text. • demonstrate an understanding of the author's style and an appreciation of the effects created. • identify and assess the impact of perceived ambiguities, nuances, and complexities within the text.	Comparing Literature 998 Quickwrite 559, 560, 685, 687, 1177 Test Preparation and Practice 1351 Writing About Literature 117, 263, 278, 415, 430, 489, 503, 526, 543, 551, 592, 607, 655, 665, 670, 676, 681, 703, 724, 761, 798, 804, 821, 833, 874, 899, 908, 934, 966, 989, 1045, 1066, 1176, 1215, 1225, 1275, 1297, 1323 Writing Workshop 614–623, 834–841
11.5.9 Write academic essays, such as an analytical essay, a persuasive essay, a research report, a summary, an explanation, a description, or a literary analysis that: • develops a thesis. • creates an organizing structure appropriate to purpose, audience, and context. • includes accurate information from primary and secondary sources and excludes extraneous information. • makes valid inferences. • supports judgments with relevant and substantial evidence and well-chosen details. • uses technical terms and notations correctly. • provides a coherent conclusion.	Comparing Literature 347 Test Preparation and Practice 851 Writing About Literature 241, 291, 440, 740, 889, 1019, 1169, 1201, 1256, 1308 Writing Workshop 146–153, 444–453, 614–623, 834–841, 1334–1341
11.5.3 Write reflective compositions that: • explore the significance of personal experiences, events, conditions, or concerns by using rhetorical strategies, including narration, description, exposition, and persuasion. • draw comparisons between specific incidents and broader themes that illustrate the writer's important beliefs or generalizations about life. • maintain a balance in describing individual events and relating those events to more general and abstract ideas.	Literary Criticism 1169 Test Preparation and Practice 313, 478, 633, 1127 Unit Introduction 648 Writing About Literature 1107, 1157, 1229, 1279 Writing Workshop 296–303

Indiana Academic Standards	*Glencoe Literature,* American Literature
11.5.4 Write historical investigation reports that: • use exposition, narration, description, argumentation, or some combination of rhetorical strategies to support the main argument. • analyze several historical records of a single event, examining critical relationships between elements of the topic. • explain the perceived reason or reasons for the similarities and differences in historical records with information derived from primary and secondary sources to support or enhance the presentation. • include information from all relevant perspectives and take into consideration the validity and reliability of sources. • include a formal bibliography.	Writing Workshop 444–453
11.5.5 Write job applications and résumés that: • provide clear and purposeful information and address the intended audience appropriately. • use varied levels, patterns, and types of language to achieve intended effects and aid comprehension. • modify the tone to fit the purpose and audience. • follow the conventional style for that type of document (a résumé or cover letter of application) and use page formats, fonts (typeface), and spacing that contribute to the readability and impact of the document.	Writing Handbook R42–45 Writing Workshop 297, 1111
11.5.6 Use varied and extended vocabulary, appropriate for specific forms and topics.	Learning for Life 956 Literary Criticism 988 Unit Introduction 866 Writing About Literature 372, 592, 977, 1012, 1088, 1187, 1219, 1267, 1279
11.5.7 Use precise technical or scientific language when appropriate for topic and audience.	Interdisciplinary Activity 493, 592 Learning for Life 889 Unit Introduction 866

Indiana Academic Standards	*Glencoe Literature,* American Literature
11.5.8 Deliver multimedia presentations that: • combine text, images, and sound and draw information from many sources, including television broadcasts, videos, films, newspapers, magazines, CD-ROMs, the Internet, and electronic media-generated images. • select an appropriate medium for each element of the presentation. • use the selected media skillfully, editing appropriately, and monitoring for quality. • test the audience's response and revise the presentation accordingly.	Interdisciplinary Activity 821 Performing 1215
Research Application	
11.5.10 Write or deliver a research report that has been developed using a systematic research process (defines the topic, gathers information, determines credibility, reports findings) and that: • uses information from a variety of sources (books, technology, multimedia), distinguishes between primary and secondary documents, and documents sources independently by using a consistent format for citations. • synthesizes information gathered from a variety of sources, including technology and one's own research, and evaluates information for its relevance to the research questions. • demonstrates that information that has been gathered has been summarized, that the topic has been refined through this process, and that conclusions have been drawn from synthesizing information. • demonstrates that sources have been evaluated for accuracy, bias, and credibility. • incorporates numeric data, charts, tables, and graphs. • organizes information by classifying, categorizing, and sequencing, and demonstrates the distinction between one's own ideas from the ideas of others, and includes a bibliography (Works Cited).	Writing Workshop 444–453

Indiana Academic Standards	Glencoe Literature, American Literature
Standard 6 WRITING: English Language Conventions	
11.6 Conventions include the grade-level-appropriate mechanics of writing, such as penmanship, spelling, grammar, capitalization, punctuation, sentence structure, and manuscript form.	
11.6.1 Demonstrate control of grammar, diction, paragraph and sentence structure, and an understanding of English usage.	Author's Language and Style 241, 263, 278, 440, 592, 761, 821, 889, 925, 1012, 1107, 1267 Grammar Workshop 367, 741, 1170 Test Preparation and Practice 160–161, 312–313, 462–463, 850–851, 1126–1127, 1349–1351 Writing Workshop 153, 452, 622, 623, 840, 1116, 1117, 1340, 1341
11.6.2 Produce writing that shows accurate spelling and correct punctuation and capitalization.	Test Preparation and Practice 851 Writing About Literature 241, 263, 278, 291, 385, 415, 526, 543, 592, 607, 655, 724, 740, 761, 784, 798, 821, 874, 899, 908, 925, 934, 966, 989, 1012, 1169, 1187, 1225, 1256, 1267, 1275, 1297, 1308, 1323 Writing Workshop 303, 453, 841
11.6.3 Apply appropriate manuscript conventions in writing – including title page presentation, pagination, spacing, and margins – and integration of source and support material by citing sources within the text, using direct quotations, and paraphrasing.	Writing Workshop 153, 303, 444–453, 623, 841, 1117, 1341
11.6.4 Identify and correctly use clauses, both main and subordinate; phrases, including gerund, infinitive, and participial; and the mechanics of punctuation, such as semicolons, colons, ellipses, and hyphens.	Author's Language and Style 385, 665, 724 Grammar Workshop 81, 141, 279, 517, 926, 1246

Indiana Academic Standards	Glencoe Literature, American Literature
Standard 7 LISTENING AND SPEAKING: **Skills, Strategies, and Applications**	
11.7 Response to oral communication includes careful listening and evaluation of content. Speaking skills, such as phrasing, pitch, and tone are developed in conjunction with such strategies as narration, exposition, description, and persuasion and are applied to students' delivery of oral presentations.	
Comprehension	
11.7.1 Summarize a speaker's purpose and point of view and ask questions to draw interpretations of the speaker's content and attitude toward the subject.	Interdisciplinary Activity 972 Learning for Life 829 Listening and Speaking 1012, 1297 Literature Groups 1019 Speaking, Listening, and Viewing Workshop 625, 1343
Organization and Delivery of Oral Communication	
11.7.2 Use rhetorical questions (questions asked for effect without an expected answer), parallel structure, concrete images, figurative language, characterization, irony, and dialogue to achieve clarity, force, and artistic effect.	Listening and Speaking 209, 344, 784, 1191 Performing 65 Speaking, Listening, and Viewing Workshop 154–155, 843, 1342–1343 Writing About Literature 111 Writing Workshop 146–153
11.7.3 Distinguish between and use various forms of logical arguments, including: • inductive arguments (arguments that demonstrate something that is highly likely, such as *All of these pears are from that basket and all of these pears are ripe, so all of the pears in the basket are ripe.*) and deductive arguments (arguments that draw necessary conclusions based on the evidence, such as *If all men are mortal and he is a man, then he is mortal.*). • syllogisms and analogies (assumptions that if two things are similar in some ways then they are probably similar in others).	Reading Handbook R24–R25 Reading Strategy 113, 117
11.7.4 Use logical (causality, appeal to authority), ethical, and emotional appeals that enhance a specific tone and purpose.	Listening and Speaking 209, 784, 1012 Speaking, Listening, and Viewing Workshop 154–155, 1342–1343 Writing Workshop 146–153, 1339–1340

Indiana Academic Standards	*Glencoe Literature,* American Literature
11.7.5 Use appropriate rehearsal strategies to pay attention to performance details, achieve command of the text, and create skillful artistic staging.	Performing 93, 415, 665, 714, 825, 1107, 1328 Speaking, Listening, and Viewing Workshop 155, 305, 455, 625, 843, 1343
11.7.6 Use effective and interesting language, including informal expressions for effect, Standard English for clarity, and technical language for specificity.	Learning for Life 889, 1245 Listening and Speaking 784, 1012, 1191, 1297 Literary Criticism 566 Performing 65 Speaking, Listening, and Viewing Workshop 154–155, 304–305, 454–455, 624–625, 842–843, 1118–1119, 1342–1343
11.7.7 Use research and analysis to justify strategies for gesture, movement, and vocalization, including pronunciation, enunciation, and the use of dialect.	Learning for Life 1245 Listening and Speaking 344, 433 Performing 93, 249, 415, 665, 714, 825, 1328 Speaking, Listening, and Viewing Workshop 155, 305, 455, 625, 843, 1119
11.7.8 Evaluate when to use different kinds of effects (including visuals, music, sound, and graphics) to create effective productions.	Learning for Life 889 Listening and Speaking 1297 Performing 249, 1107, 1215, 1328 Speaking, Listening, and Viewing Workshop 155, 305, 455, 843, 1118–1119
Analysis and Evaluation of Oral and Media Communications	
11.7.9 Analyze strategies used by the media to inform, persuade, entertain, and transmit culture (including advertising; perpetuating of stereotypes; and using visual representations, special effects, and language).	Analyzing Political Cartoons 105 Interdisciplinary Activity 989 Internet Connection 73, 263, 440, 698, 939, 1267, 1301, 1287 Unit Introduction 648
11.7.10 Analyze the impact of the media on the democratic process (including exerting influence on elections, creating images of leaders, and shaping attitudes) at the local, state, and national levels.	Analyzing Political Cartoons 105 Interdisciplinary Activity 989 Unit Introduction 866

Indiana Academic Standards	*Glencoe Literature,* American Literature
11.7.11 Interpret and evaluate the various ways in which events are presented and information is communicated by visual image-makers (such as graphic artists, documentary filmmakers, illustrators, and news photographers).	Analyzing Political Cartoons 105 Interdisciplinary Activity 821 Primary Visual Artifact 261 Responding and Thinking Critically 1311 Speaking, Listening, and Viewing Workshop 1118–1119 Unit Introduction 866, 1142 Viewing the Art 21, 31, 39, 40, 58, 69, 71, 91, 99, 104, 115, 126, 139, 181, 196, 206, 215, 233, 234, 237, 254, 257, 270, 286, 347, 365, 380, 408, 412, 429, 487, 491, 509, 522, 533, 581, 587, 599, 651, 692, 706, 720, 736, 746, 750, 753, 755, 780, 795, 894, 897, 906, 964, 1035, 1042, 1044, 1048, 1059, 1062, 1064, 1073, 1085, 1094, 1096, 1194, 1237, 1238, 1319 Visual Literacy 590, 663 You're the Critic 276
11.7.12 Critique a speaker's use of words and language in relation to the purpose of an oral communication and the impact the words may have on the audience.	Comparing Literature 224 Interdisciplinary Activity 530 Literary Element 93, 111, 357, 389, 530, 972 Reading Strategy 93, 111, 357, 389, 530, 972 Responding and Thinking Critically 93, 105, 111, 357, 389, 530, 728, 972 Writing About Literature 111 Writing Workshop 147–148, 150–151
11.7.13 Identify rhetorical and logical fallacies used in oral addresses including *ad hominem* (appealing to the audience's feelings or prejudices), false causality (falsely identifying the causes of some effect), red herring (distracting attention from the real issue), overgeneralization, and the bandwagon effect (attracting the audience based on the show rather than the substance of the presentation).	Reading Handbook R25 Responding and Thinking Critically 105 Writing Workshop 1335–1337
11.7.14 Analyze the four basic types of persuasive speech (propositions of fact, value, problem, and policy) and understand the similarities and differences in their patterns of organization and the use of persuasive language, reasoning, and proof.	Reading Strategy 217 Responding and Thinking Critically 105 Writing Workshop 152
11.7.15 Analyze the techniques used in media messages for a particular audience and evaluate their effectiveness (for example, Orson Welles' radio broadcast *War of the Worlds* by H.G. Wells).	Writing Workshop 147–148, 1335–1337

Indiana Academic Standards	*Glencoe Literature,* American Literature
Speaking Applications	
11.7.16 Deliver reflective presentations that: • explore the significance of personal experiences, events, conditions, or concerns, using appropriate speech strategies, including narration, description, exposition, and persuasion. • draw comparisons between the specific incident and broader themes to illustrate beliefs or generalizations about life. • maintain a balance between describing the incident and relating it to more general, abstract ideas.	Speaking, Listening, and Viewing Workshop 154–155, 304–305, 1342–1343
11.7.17 Deliver oral reports on historical investigations that: • use exposition, narration, description, persuasion, or some combination of those to support the thesis (the position on the topic). • analyze several historical records of a single event, examining each perspective on the event. • describe similarities and differences between research sources, using information derived from primary and secondary sources to support the presentation. • include information on all relevant perspectives and consider the validity (accuracy and truthfulness) and reliability (consistency) of sources.	Speaking, Listening, and Viewing Workshop 454–455 Unit Introduction 866
11.7.18 Deliver oral responses to literature that: • demonstrate a comprehensive understanding of the significant ideas of literary works and make assertions about the text that are reasonable and supportable. • present an analysis of the imagery, language, universal themes, and unique aspects of the text through the use of speech strategies, including narration, description, persuasion, exposition, or a combination of those strategies. • support important ideas and viewpoints through specific references to the text and to other works. • demonstrate an awareness of the author's style and an appreciation of the effects created. • identify and assess the impact of ambiguities, nuances, and complexities within the text.	Listening and Speaking 1191 Speaking, Listening, and Viewing Workshop 624–625, 842–843

Indiana Academic Standards	*Glencoe Literature*, American Literature
11.7.19 Deliver multimedia presentations that: • combine text, images, and sound by incorporating information from a wide range of media, including films, newspapers, magazines, CD-ROMs, online information, television, videos, and electronic media-generated images. • select an appropriate medium for each element of the presentation. • use the selected media skillfully, editing appropriately and monitoring for quality. • test the audience's response and revise the presentation accordingly.	Interdisciplinary Activity 821, 925, 1206 Learning for Life 889 Listening and Speaking 1297 Performing 249, 1107, 1215, 1328 Speaking, Listening, and Viewing Workshop 154–155, 304–305, 454–455, 842–843, 1118–1119 Unit Introduction 176, 648, 866, 1142
11.7.20 Recite poems, selections from speeches, or dramatic soliloquies with attention to performance details to achieve clarity, force, and aesthetic effect and to demonstrate an understanding of the meaning (for example, stage a presentation of Hamlet's soliloquy "To Be or Not to Be").	Listening and Speaking 433, 1191 Performing 93, 249, 415, 665, 714, 825, 1107, 1215, 1328 Speaking, Listening, and Viewing Workshop 842–843 Unit Introduction 328

BOOK OVERVIEW

Reference Section

CONTENTS

"*There is another world under this, and it is like ours in everything . . .*"

—Cherokee Myth

> *"I had never seen among any people such instances of brutal cruelty . . ."*
>
> —Olaudah Equiano

"... the harder the conflict, the more
glorious the triumph."

—Thomas Paine

"*All men are privately influenced by women.*"
—Margaret Fuller

PART 2   The Dark Side of Romanticism

> "He looked not unlike the weather
> horizon when a storm is coming up . . ."
> —Herman Melville

"Oppressed so hard they could not stand,
Let my people go."

—from "Go Down, Moses"

"I am of old and young, of the foolish as much
as the wise . . ."

—Walt Whitman

*"Parting is all we know of heaven,
And all we need of hell."*

—Emily Dickinson

"White waves paced to and fro
in the moonlight."

—Stephen Crane

UNIT FIVE BEGINNINGS OF THE MODERN AGE
1910–1930s 634

PART 1 MODERN POETRY 649

"*Forgive me
they were delicious
so sweet
and so cold*"

—William Carlos Williams

PART 7   MODERN FICTION

> "Your grief and mine must intertwine
> like sea and river."
> —Countee Cullen

UNIT SIX FROM DEPRESSION TO COLD WAR

1930s-1960s ... 852

PART 1 The New Regionalism and the City ... 867

"There was some element of great beauty there that makes the rush of warmth."

—John Steinbeck

Vocabulary Workshop:
Word Parts: Understanding Roots, Prefixes, and Suffixes ... 875

> "He had a look of composed
> dissatisfaction as if he understood
> life thoroughly."
>
> —Flannery O'Connor

"The rumor of witchcraft is all about . . ."
—Arthur Miller

> "I saw ten thousand talkers whose tongues were all broken . . ."
>
> —Bob Dylan

PART 2   Nature and Technology 1207

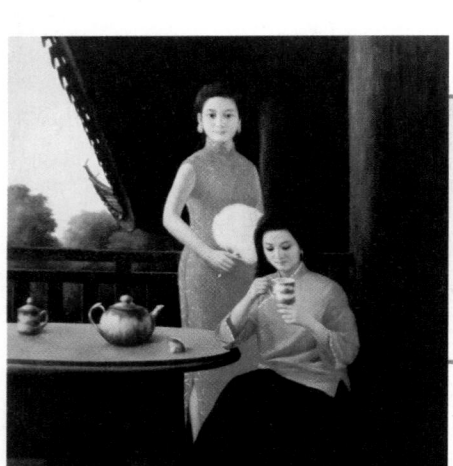

*"Finally Brave Orchid's children
quit wandering
and drooped on a railing."*

—Maxine Hong Kingston

Reference Section

SELECTIONS BY GENRE

Graphic Novel

Poetry

Song

Letter, Journal, or Diary

Speech or Public Document

PERSPECTIVES

*Award-winning nonfiction book excerpts
and primary source documents*

TIME

High-interest, informative magazine articles

LITERARY HISTORY

LITERATURE OF THE TIME

For Independent Reading

TEST PREPARATION AND PRACTICE

SKILLS WORKSHOPS

Why do I need this book?

Glencoe Literature, The Reader's Choice is more than just a collection of stories, poems, nonfiction articles, and other literary works. Every unit is built around **Big Ideas,** concepts that you will want to think about, talk about, and maybe even argue about. Big Ideas help you become part of an important conversation. You can join in lively discussions about who we are, where we have been, and where we are going.

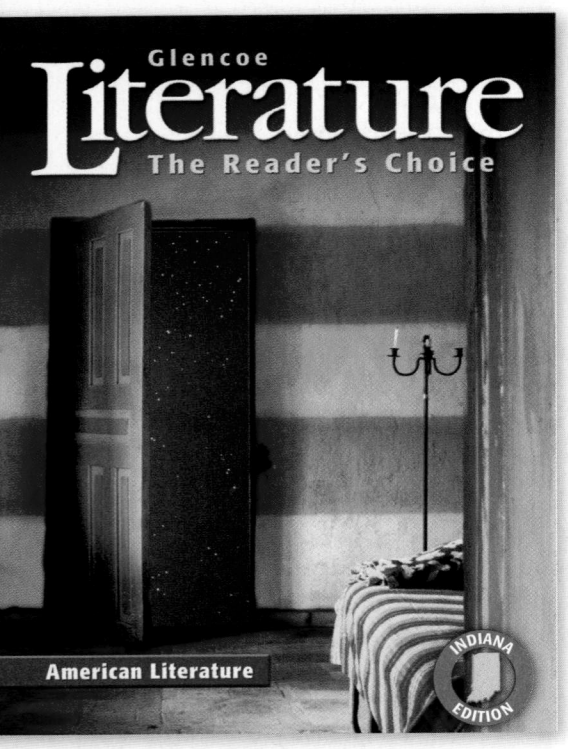

Organization

The literature selections you will read are organized chronologically into seven units spanning early America to the present.

Each unit contains the following:

A **UNIT INTRODUCTION** provides you with the background information to help make your reading experience more meaningful.

- The **TIMELINE** helps you keep track of major literary and historical events.

- **BY THE NUMBERS** shows you figures and key data at a glance.

- **BEING THERE** gives you a glimpse of the geography related to the literary period.

- **HISTORICAL, CULTURAL, AND SOCIAL FORCES** explains the influences that shape a specific literary period.

- **BIG IDEAS** targets three concepts that you can trace as you read the literary selections.

- **LITERATURE SELECTIONS** follow each Unit Introduction. The selections are organized as follows.

Reading and Thinking

Each of the main selections in your textbook is arranged in three parts.

• Start with **BEFORE YOU READ.** Learn about the context that sets the stage for the selection and preview the skills and strategies that will guide your reading.

MEET THE AUTHOR introduces you to the real-life story of the writer whose work you will read and analyze.

LITERATURE PREVIEW and **READING PREVIEW** list the basic tools you will use to read and analyze the selection.

• Next, read the **LITERATURE SELECTION** from beginning to end. As you flip though most of the selections, you will see that parts of the text are highlighted in different colors. At the bottom of the page are color-coded questions that help you think about and understand the highlighted text.

RESPONDING AND THINKING CRITICALLY

Respond
1. What ideas in this speech will you remember? Why?

Recall and Interpret
2. (a)Why did the author choose "to keep and to embrace" the name Walker? (b)In what ways is this name more than just a name to her?

3. (a)What circumstances kept Walker's family from owning land? (b)How did the circumstances affect her family history?

4. (a)According to Walker, what was the most important thing Dr. King did for African Americans? (b)From her description of this contribution, what can you infer about Walker and what she values?

Analyze and Evaluate
5. (a)What is the connection between Walker's story about her brothers and sisters leaving the land and what she calls Dr. King's great achievement? (b)If you had been in the audience the day Walker delivered this speech, how do you think this argument would have affected you?

6. (a)How does Walker describe Dr. King to make him seem more than a human being? (b)In your opinion, does she prove that he lived up to this super-human introduction? Explain.

Connect
7. **Big Idea** **An Era of Protest** On the basis of this speech, how important would you say individual leadership was to the Civil Rights movement? Explain.

LITERARY ANALYSIS

Literary Element Anecdote

Typically, writers use an **anecdote** to entertain, to explain an idea, or to reveal the personality of a character. In this speech, Walker tells an anecdote about seeing Dr. King for the first time.

1. What does this anecdote tell you about Walker as a child?

2. What does it tell you about why Dr. King became a hero to African Americans?

Writing About Literature

Analyze Genre Elements Many speeches reference or celebrate the lives of famous men and women. Compose a speech about a person who has influenced your life. Identify your audience. Then focus on the most important aspects of your subject and grab your listeners' attention with one or two interesting anecdotes.

Literature Online **Web Activities** For eFlashcards, Selection Quick Checks, and other Web activities, go to www.glencoe.com.

READING AND VOCABULARY

Reading Strategy Activating Prior Knowledge

A reader typically brings two types of knowledge to a piece of writing: hard facts and personal experiences.

1. Identify a passage from Walker's speech that interests you. What factual or personal knowledge can you bring to it?

2. Walker's anecdote begins with the purchase of a television set in 1960. List one factual and one personal piece of information that helped you understand this part of the anecdote.

Vocabulary Practice

Practice with Antonyms Identify the antonym for each vocabulary word.

1. ancestral   a. modern   b. intelligent
2. colossal   a. minuscule   b. statuary
3. continuity   a. lawlessness b. impermanence
4. ephemeral   a. dull   b. permanent

ALICE WALKER **1157**

LITERARY ANALYSIS

Literary Element Suspense

Suspense generally increases as the plot of a story moves toward its climax. In "The Pit and the Pendulum," Poe generates tension and uncertainty by pitting the narrator against one horror after another. The reader becomes more and more involved in the story, concerned about what will happen to the narrator.

1. The narrator undergoes moments of both physical and psychological torment. Give two examples of each. Describe the event, and tell how each event heightens the story's suspense.

2. In your opinion, what is the most suspenseful moment in the story? Explain your choice.

Review: Point of View

As you learned in Unit One, point of view refers to the perspective from which a story is told. Poe's story is told in the first-person point of view. The narrator is a character in the story who uses the pronouns *I*, *me*, and *my*. Everything that the reader learns is filtered through the eyes, ears, and thoughts of the narrator.

Partner Activity With another classmate discuss how the story's point of view helps create suspense. With your partner, design a web diagram. List examples in which the first-person point of view limits your knowledge of events, characters, and setting.

READING AND VOCABULARY

Reading Strategy Identifying Sequence

In their stories, writers need not always present the **sequence**, or the logical order of ideas or events, in the same way. In addition to using chronological, or time, order to retell events, authors can also use flashbacks or flash-forwards to show events that happened earlier or later in the sequence.

1. What method does the narrator use to retell the events of his tale in "The Pit and the Pendulum"?

2. The term *deus ex machina* originally meant a god that suddenly appeared in a Greek tragedy—sometimes lowered from a crane—to resolve a situation too complex for humans. Today, the term refers to an improbable, contrived, or artificial solution to a problem in a piece of fiction. Do you think that the ending of "The Pit and the Pendulum" is a *deus ex machina* or a part of the story's logical sequence? Explain.

Vocabulary Practice

Practice with Word Origins Match each vocabulary word from "The Pit and the Pendulum" with the word that has the same origin. Use a dictionary if necessary.

1. deduce   a. pedometer
2. impede   b. approximate
3. lethargy   c. introduce
4. proximity   d. effusive
5. diffuse   e. lethe

Academic Vocabulary

Here are two vocabulary words from the vocabulary list on page R86.

environment (en vī' rən mant, -vī' ərn-) n. surroundings; the cultural and social conditions affecting an individual or community

maximize (mak'sə mīz') v. to make as great as possible; increase to the maximum

Practice and Apply
1. Which details in the narrator's **environment** are Gothic?
2. How does Poe **maximize** suspense?

- Wrap-up the selection with **AFTER YOU READ.** Explore what you have learned through a wide range of reading, thinking, vocabulary, and writing activities.

Vocabulary

VOCABULARY WORDS that may be new or difficult to you are chosen from each selection. They are introduced on the **BEFORE YOU READ** page. Each word is accompanied by its pronunciation, its part of speech, its definition, and the page number on which it appears. The vocabulary word is also used in a sample sentence. Vocabulary words are highlighted in the Literature Selection.

VOCABULARY PRACTICE On the **AFTER YOU READ** pages, you will be able to practice using the vocabulary words in an exercise. This exercise will show you how to apply a vocabulary strategy to understand new or difficult words.

ACADEMIC VOCABULARY Many of the **AFTER YOU READ** pages will also introduce you to two words that are frequently used in academic work. You will be prompted to apply the definitions of these words to answer questions about the selection that you have just read.

Writing Workshops

Each unit in *Glencoe Literature, The Reader's Choice* includes a Writing Workshop. The workshop walks you through the writing process as you work on an extended piece of writing related to the unit.

- You will create writing goals and apply strategies to meet them.
- You will pick up tips and polish your critical skills as you analyze professional and workshop models.
- You will focus on mastering specific aspects of writing, including organization, grammar, and vocabulary.
- You will use a rubric to evaluate your own writing.

Revising

Use the rubric below to evaluate your writing.

Rubric: Writing an Effective Persuasive Speech

☑ Does your issue have opposing viewpoints?
☑ Do you choose one side of the debate and clarify your position?
☑ Do you present your reasons and supporting evidence in a logical order?
☑ Do you use rhetorical devices to strengthen your argument?
☑ Do you use appeals to logic, ethics, and emotion?
☑ Do you present and respond to counterarguments in a respectful tone?
☑ Do you persuade your audience to act?

Indiana Test Preparation and Practice

Following each unit, you will be tested on the literature, reading, and vocabulary skills you have just learned. Designed to simulate Indiana's standardized tests, this test will give you the practice you need to succeed while providing an assessment of how well you have met the unit objectives.

Organizing Information

Graphic organizers—such as Foldables, diagrams, and charts—help you keep your information and ideas organized.

Test Preparation and Practice

English Language Arts

Indiana Test Practice

Reading: Vocabulary, Comprehension, and Analysis

Carefully read the following passage. Use context clues to help you define any words with which you are unfamiliar. Pay close attention to the author's main idea and use of rhetorical devices. Then, on a separate sheet of paper, answer the questions on pages 309–310.

from *Self-Reliance* by Ralph Waldo Emerson

THREE-POCKET BOOK

FOLDABLES Study Organizer

Big Idea 1 | Big Idea 2 | Big Idea 3

You might try using this graphic organizer to keep track of the three big ideas in this unit.

LITERARY MAP OF THE UNITED STATES

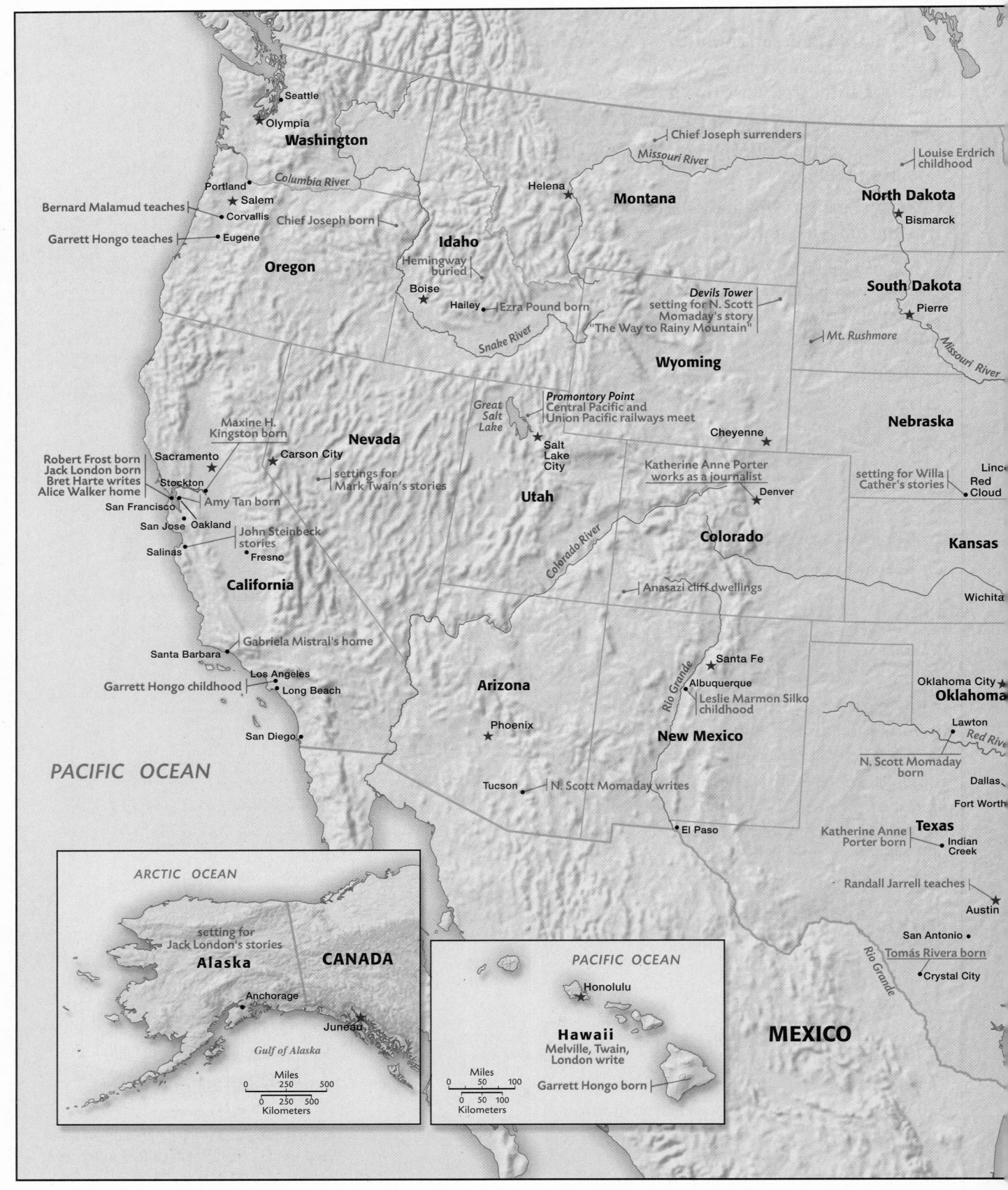

Seattle

★ Olympia

Washington

Chief Joseph surrenders

Missouri River

Louise Erdrich childhood

Portland •
★ Salem

Helena ★

Montana

North Dakota

★ Bismarck

Columbia River

Bernard Malamud teaches

• Corvallis

Chief Joseph born

Garrett Hongo teaches

• Eugene

Oregon

Idaho

Hemingway buried

★ Boise

Hailey •

Ezra Pound born

Snake River

Devils Tower
setting for N. Scott
Momaday's story
"The Way to Rainy Mountain"

South Dakota

★ Pierre

Mt. Rushmore

Missouri River

Wyoming

Maxine H. Kingston born

Great Salt Lake

Promontory Point
Central Pacific and
Union Pacific railways meet

Cheyenne •

Nebraska

Robert Frost born
Jack London born
Bret Harte writes
Alice Walker home

Sacramento ★

Carson City •

Nevada

Salt Lake City ★

Katherine Anne Porter
works as a journalist

setting for Willa
Cather's stories

Linc •
Red
• Cloud

Stockton •

Amy Tan born

Utah

Denver ★

San Francisco
San Jose •
Oakland •

John Steinbeck stories

Colorado

Kansas

Salinas •

• Fresno

Colorado River

California

Anasazi cliff dwellings

Wichita •

Gabriela Mistral's home

Santa Barbara •

Los Angeles •
• Long Beach

Garrett Hongo childhood

Arizona

Rio Grande

Santa Fe ★

• Albuquerque

Leslie Marmon Silko childhood

Oklahoma City ★

Oklahoma

Lawton •

Red Rive

PACIFIC OCEAN

Phoenix ★

San Diego •

Tucson • N. Scott Momaday writes

New Mexico

N. Scott Momaday born

Dallas •

Fort Worth

• El Paso

Katherine Anne
Porter born

Texas

• Indian
Creek

Randall Jarrell teaches

Austin

ARCTIC OCEAN

setting for
Jack London's stories

Alaska

CANADA

San Antonio •

Tomás Rivera born

• Crystal City

Anchorage •

PACIFIC OCEAN

Juneau •

Gulf of Alaska

Honolulu ★

Miles
0   250   500
0   250 500
Kilometers

Miles
0   50   100
0   50 100
Kilometers

Hawaii
Melville, Twain,
London write

Garrett Hongo born

MEXICO

Rio Grande

CANADA

Bob Dylan born

Hibbing

Louise Erdrich born

F. Scott Fitzgerald childhood

St. Paul

esota

O'Brien born

Austin

Lake Superior

Mississippi River

Wisconsin

Eudora Welty studies

Michigan

Lansing

Battle Creek

Milwaukee

Madison

Lake Michigan

Lake Huron

Detroit

Robert Hayden writes

Lake Erie

Buffalo

Lake Ontario

Albany

New York

Maine

Augusta

Gardiner

Vermont

Montpelier

Lake Champlain

Concord

New Hampshire

Massachusetts

Boston

Providence

Rhode Island

Hartford

Connecticut

Iowa

Des Moines

Iowa City

Sandra Cisneros childhood

Archibald MacLeish born

Glencoe

Chicago

Oak Park

Hemingway born

Ambrose Bierce childhood

Warsaw

Toledo

Cleveland

Lorain

Akron

Toni Morrison born

Ohio

Columbus

Dayton

1851 Women's Rights Convention

Pennsylvania

Harrisburg

Pittsburgh

Philadelphia

Trenton

New York

New Jersey

Dover

Delaware

Baltimore

Annapolis

Washington, D.C.

Maryland

see inset on next page

Iowa Writer's Workshop

Galesburg

Carl Sandburg born

Illinois

Indianapolis

Edgar Lee Masters childhood

Indiana

Paul Laurence Dunbar born

Twain childhood

Gwendolyn Brooks born

Hannibal

Lewistown

New Salem

Springfield

Abraham Lincoln studies

Cincinnati

Ohio R.

Frankfort

Louisville

West Virginia

Charleston

Lexington

Richmond

Kansas City

Jefferson City

St. Louis

T. S. Eliot, Kate Chopin born

Edgar Lee Masters born

Missouri

Robert Penn Warren born

Guthrie

Paul Laurence Dunbar childhood

Kentucky

Virginia

Randall Jarrell teaches

Great Smoky Mtns.

Cherokee myths

Greensboro

Flat Rock

Raleigh

Langston Hughes born

Joplin

Randall Jarrell born

Robert Hayden teaches

Nashville

Tennessee

North Carolina

Charlotte

Carl Sandburg's last home

Arkansas

Arkansas R.

Little Rock

setting for William Faulkner's stories

Memphis

Oxford

Martin Luther King Jr. born

Atlanta

Columbia

South Carolina

Charleston

Ft. Sumter

First Civil War battle

Mary Chesnut lives

ATLANTIC OCEAN

Alabama

M. L. King Jr. jailed

Birmingham

Eatonton

Alice Walker born

Georgia

Mississippi

Zora Neale Hurston born

Notasulga

Montgomery

Savannah

Flannery O'Connor born

Eudora Welty home

Jackson

Louisiana

Bontemps born

Roxie

Richard Wright born

Tallahassee

Alexandria

Baton Rouge

Toni Morrison teaches

New Orleans

Jacksonville

setting for Stephen Crane's story "The Open Boat"

James Weldon Johnson born

Zora Neale Hurston childhood

Eatonville

Florida

setting for Kate Chopin's stories

William Faulkner meets Sherwood Anderson

Cabeza de Vaca lands

Gulf of Mexico

Lake Okeechobee

Miami

Elizabeth Bishop writes

Hemingway writes

Key West

N

W   E

S

Miles

0   50   100   150   200

0   100   200

Kilometers

Puerto Rico

Aurora Levins Morales childhood

Judith Ortiz Cofer born

Miles

0   25

0   25

Kilometers

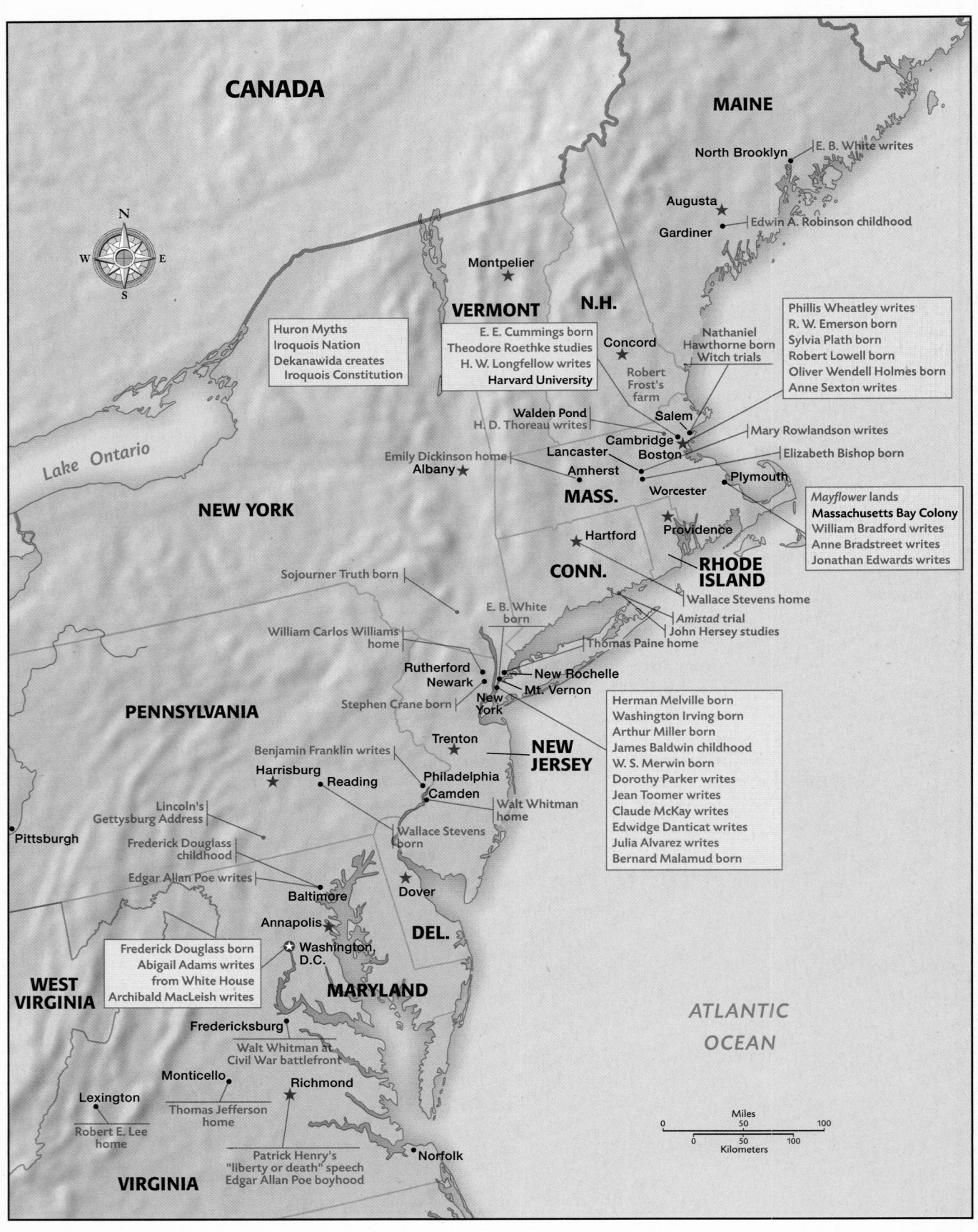

CANADA

MAINE

North Brooklyn · — E. B. White writes

Augusta ★
Gardiner · — Edwin A. Robinson childhood

Montpelier ★

VERMONT   N.H.

Huron Myths
Iroquois Nation
Dekanawida creates
Iroquois Constitution

E. E. Cummings born
Theodore Roethke studies
H. W. Longfellow writes
Harvard University

Concord ·

Nathaniel
Hawthorne born
Witch trials

Phillis Wheatley writes
R. W. Emerson born
Sylvia Plath born
Robert Lowell born
Oliver Wendell Holmes born
Anne Sexton writes

Robert
Frost's
farm

Walden Pond
H. D. Thoreau writes

Salem ·

Cambridge ·
Boston

— Mary Rowlandson writes

Emily Dickinson home |
Albany ★

Lancaster ·
Amherst ·

Worcester ·

— Elizabeth Bishop born

Plymouth ·

Lake Ontario

NEW YORK

MASS.

Hartford ★

Providence ★

RHODE
ISLAND

Mayflower lands
Massachusetts Bay Colony
William Bradford writes
Anne Bradstreet writes
Jonathan Edwards writes

CONN.

Sojourner Truth born |

Wallace Stevens home

E. B. White
born

— Amistad trial
— John Hersey studies

William Carlos Williams
home

— Thomas Paine home

Rutherford ·
Newark ·

New Rochelle
Mt. Vernon

PENNSYLVANIA

Stephen Crane born —

New
York

Herman Melville born
Washington Irving born
Arthur Miller born
James Baldwin childhood
W. S. Merwin born
Dorothy Parker writes
Jean Toomer writes
Claude McKay writes
Edwidge Danticat writes
Julia Alvarez writes
Bernard Malamud born

Trenton ★

NEW
JERSEY

Benjamin Franklin writes |
Harrisburg ★

Reading ·

Philadelphia ·
Camden ·

Walt Whitman
home

Lincoln's
Gettysburg Address |

Wallace Stevens
born

Frederick Douglass
childhood

Pittsburgh ·

Edgar Allan Poe writes |

Baltimore ·

Dover ★

DEL.

Annapolis ★

Frederick Douglass born
Abigail Adams writes
from White House
Archibald MacLeish writes

◎ Washington,
D.C.

WEST
VIRGINIA

MARYLAND

ATLANTIC

OCEAN

Fredericksburg ·

Walt Whitman at
Civil War battlefront

Monticello ·

Richmond ★

Lexington ·

Thomas Jefferson
home

Robert E. Lee
home

Patrick Henry's
"liberty or death" speech
Edgar Allan Poe boyhood

Norfolk ·

VIRGINIA

Miles
0   50   100

0   50   100
Kilometers

SCAVENGER HUNT

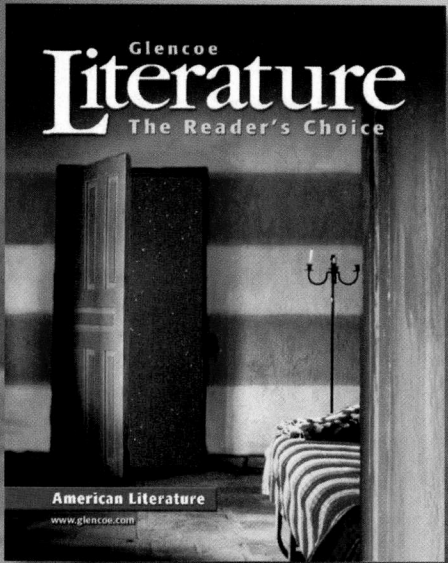

American Literature
www.glencoe.com

Glencoe's *Reader's Choice* contains a wealth of information. The trick is to know where to look to access all of that information. If you go through this scavenger hunt, either alone or with teachers or parents, you will quickly learn how the textbook is organized and how to get the most out of your reading and study time.

Let's get started!

1. How many units and parts are there in this book?

2. What is the difference between the glossary and the index?

3. There is a section on Test-Taking Strategies in the Reference Section in the back of the textbook. Where else in the book can you find help for test preparation?

4. In what special feature can you find historical information about the time in which a certain author lived?

5. If you want to quickly find all of the public documents pertaining to colonial America, where would you look?

6. If you wanted to find a definition of the term *psychological realism*, where would you look?

7. What are the Big Ideas for Unit 2, and how can you find them in the text?

8. The Web site for the book is referred to throughout the book. What sort of information does the Web site contain that might help you?

9. Which of the book's main features will provide you with the strategies for developing your writing skills?

After you answer all the questions, meet with a partner or a small group to compare answers.

The First Harvest in the Wilderness, 1855, Asher Brown Durand. Oil on canvas, 32 x 47½ in. Brooklyn Museum of Art, NY.

Early America

BEGINNINGS—1800

Looking Ahead

The roots of American literature display a rich, complex mixture of cultures and eras. Through oral tradition, the Native American peoples preserved their myths, tales, songs, and other lore from long ago. When Europeans reached the Americas, their writings recorded their experiences of exploration and settlement. Africans who were brought to the Americas by force wrote of the conditions of slavery. American literature developed further as writers played an important role in the colonial struggle for independence from Great Britain.

Keep the following questions in mind as you read:

⟫⟫⟫ How did Native Americans view their relationship to the world around them?

⟫⟫⟫ What were the major cultural features that the Puritans brought with them to New England?

⟫⟫⟫ How did the development of society in colonial America lead to the Revolution?

INDIANA ACADEMIC STANDARDS (pages 4–17)

11.3.5 Analyze or evaluate works of literary or cultural significance in history (American…) that reflect a variety of genres in each of the respective historical periods; were written by important authors in the respective major historical periods; reveal contrasts in major themes, styles, and trends; reflect or shed light on the seminal philosophical, religious, social, political, or ethical ideas of their time.

Timeline
1500-1800

American flag, c. 1781

1500

1542
La Relación by Álvar Núñez Cabeza de Vaca is published

1600

1630
William Bradford begins *Of Plymouth Plantation* ▼

Pilgrims going to Church, 1867. George Henry Boughton. Oil on canvas, 29 x 52 in. New York Historical Society, NY.

1640
Bay Psalm Book is published

1650
Anne Bradstreet's poems are published in London

1682
A Narrative of the Captivity and Restoration of Mrs. Mary Rowlandson is published

1500

1492
Columbus makes his first voyage to the Americas

1521
Cortés conquers the Aztec empire

Aztec calendar stone ▶

1528–1536
Cabeza de Vaca wanders the American Southwest

1600

1607
Jamestown, first permanent English colony in America, is founded in Virginia

1619
First Africans arrive in Virginia

1620
Pilgrims aboard the *Mayflower* arrive at Cape Cod

1630
Massachusetts Bay Colony is founded

1637
Anne Hutchinson is banished for religious dissent

1675–1676
King Philip, chief of the Wampanoags, wages war in New England

1681
William Penn founds the Pennsylvania colony

1692
Witchcraft trials begin in Salem, Massachusetts

1500

Martin Luther ▲

1517
Protestant Reformation begins in Germany

1522
What is left of Magellan's ships and crew complete circumnavigation of the globe

1558
Elizabeth I becomes queen of England

1588
English fleet defeats the Spanish Armada

1600

1600
Edo (Tokyo) becomes the capital of Japan

1632
Shah Jahan begins the Taj Mahal as tomb for his wife Mumtaz

Taj Mahal ▶

1642
English Civil War begins

1649
King Charles I of England is executed; Puritan Commonwealth is established

1660
English monarchy is restored under Charles II

1688
Glorious Revolution establishes limited monarchy in England

Benjamin Franklin ▶

1700

1704
First colonial newspaper is published

1732
Benjamin Franklin's first *Poor Richard's Almanack* is published

1771
Benjamin Franklin begins his *Autobiography*

1773
Phillis Wheatley's poems are published in London

1776
Thomas Paine's *Common Sense* is published

1776
Thomas Paine begins *The Crisis* series

1782
Letters from an American Farmer by Michel Guillaume Jean de Crèvecoeur is published

1783 ▲
Noah Webster's *American Speller* is published

1787
Thomas Jefferson's *Notes on the State of Virginia* is published

1789
Interesting Narrative of the Life of Olaudah Equiano is published in London

1700

1735
John Peter Zenger trial helps establish freedom of the press

1736
Great Awakening religious revival begins in Massachusetts

1739
Africans attack slaveholders in the Stono Rebellion

1754–1763
French and Indian War is fought

1765 ▲
Stamp Act triggers protest throughout colonies

1770
British troops fire on colonists in Boston Massacre

1775
Battles of Lexington and Concord are fought

1776
Declaration of Independence is signed

1781
British surrender at Yorktown, ending the Revolutionary War

1783
Treaty of Paris is signed, confirming independence of United States

1788
U.S. Constitution is ratified

1789
George Washington becomes first president

◀ Revolutionary War drum

1700

1726
Jonathan Swift's *Gulliver's Travels* is published

1760
George III becomes king of Great Britain

1778
James Cook lands on Hawaii

1789
French Revolution begins in Paris

1793
French rulers Louis XVI and Marie Antoinette are executed

Literature Online Timeline Visit www.glencoe.com for an interactive timeline.

Reading Check

Analyzing Graphic Information What was the history of the English monarchy between 1642 and 1688?

By the Numbers

The Columbian Exchange

Following the arrival of European explorers and settlers in the Western Hemisphere, many plants and animals were carried between the Americas and Europe, Africa, and Asia. This complex interaction, called the Columbian Exchange, permanently altered Earth's ecosystems and changed many cultures around the world.

The results of the Columbian Exchange were mixed. The introduction to Europe of staple crops from the Americas, such as the potato, contributed to a European population explosion. However, Europeans unintentionally brought with them many diseases to which Native Americans had no immunity.

Devastating epidemics resulted, with some Native American groups suffering a 90 percent population loss in the first century after European contact.

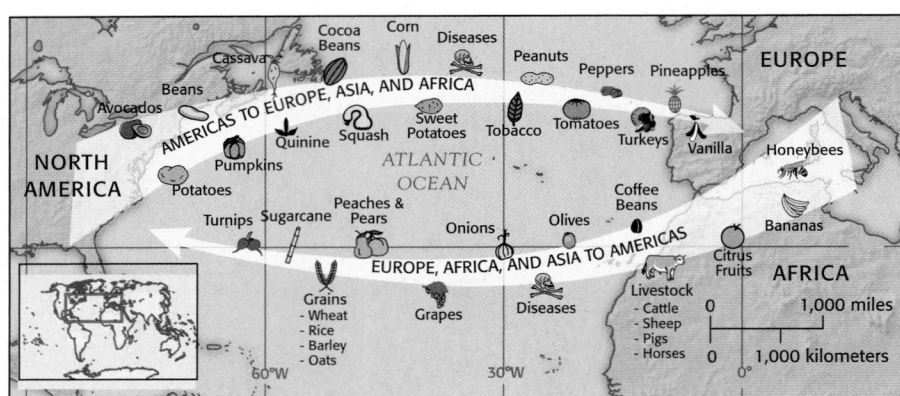

RELIGION IN THE COLONIES 1700s

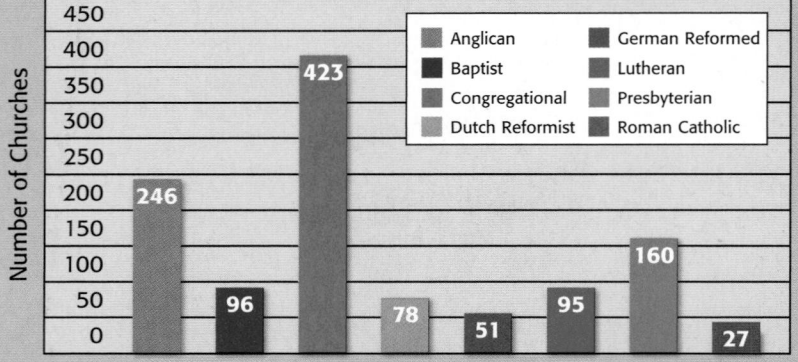

Legend:
- Anglican
- Baptist
- Congregational
- Dutch Reformist
- German Reformed
- Lutheran
- Presbyterian
- Roman Catholic

Values shown: 246, 96, 423, 78, 51, 95, 160, 27

Number of Churches (y-axis: 0–450)

Source *Historical Atlas of Religion in America*, by Edwin Scott Gaustad

REVOLUTIONARY WAR CASUALTIES

American
- 7,200 battlefield deaths
- 8,200 battlefield wounded
- 1,400 missing in action
- 10,000 deaths from disease and other causes
- 8,500 deaths in British prisons

British
- 10,000 dead from all causes

SLAVERY

- From 8 to 10 million enslaved Africans were taken to the Americas.
- Some 3.5 million were taken to the Portuguese colony of Brazil.
- About 1.5 million were taken to Spanish colonies.
- Nearly 4 million were taken to British, French, and Dutch colonies in the Caribbean.
- Approximately 500,000 were taken to Britain's North American colonies.

NATIVE AMERICAN DIVERSITY

Native American cultures were extraordinarily diverse. Experts estimate that at least 300 distinct languages were spoken in North America when Columbus arrived. The number may have been as high as 1,000. There were 20 language groups in California alone.

Being There

The Cherokee, Iroquois, and Huron peoples lived in what is now the eastern United States. Great Britain's American colonies extended from present-day Maine to Georgia.

A *Town of Secota,* 16th century, Theodore de Bry. Engraving. Musée de la Marine, Paris.

B *Residence of David Twining,* 1845–1847, Edward Hicks. Oil on canvas. Private collection.

C *Tontine Coffee House,* c. 1797, Francis Guy. Oil on linen. New York Historical Society, NY.

Literature Online **Maps in Motion** Visit www.glencoe.com for an interactive map.

Reading Check

Analyzing Graphic Information:

1. What animals were introduced into the Americas from Europe? What animal was taken from the Americas to Europe?

2. How do American Revolutionary War casualties compare with those of the British?

3. Where were most of colonial America's large cities located?

Early America

Historical, Social, and Cultural Forces

Pulling Down the Statue of George III, 1857. William Walcutt. Oil on canvas. Lafayette College Art Collection, Easton, PA.

The Native Americans

When Europeans arrived in the Western Hemisphere in the 1490s, it was already home to hundreds of Native American peoples with different languages, cultures, and social values. The ancestors of these Native Americans had come to the Western Hemisphere from Asia thousands of years before. Most of these peoples reached North America by a land bridge that once linked Siberia and Alaska across the Bering Strait, but some may have used sea routes.

For thousands of years, the descendants of these peoples spread throughout the forests, plains, deserts, and mountains of the Americas. The Native Americans responded to these varied environments with differ-ent types of social organization. Some peoples, such as the Maya and the Aztecs of Mexico and Central America, created complex societies with great cities, large-scale farming, and elaborate record keeping based on systems of writing. Other Native Americans, such as the Plains Indians, who hunted the great herds of buffalo, lived in simple, portable dwellings and passed on their knowledge through oral tradition.

European Contact

Beginning about 1400, a number of forces prompted Europeans to start exploring the rest of the world. These forces included the growth of trade between Europe and Asia and advances in navigation and shipbuilding. Led by the Portuguese and the Spanish, European explorers brought many parts of the world into meaningful contact with one another for the first time in history. One of these explorers was Christopher Columbus, an Italian who commanded a Spanish fleet. In 1492 he made the first of four voy-ages from Spain to the Americas, opening the era of cultural contact between Europe and the Western Hemisphere.

"Why will you take by force what you may obtain by love? Why will you destroy us who supply you with food?"

—Powhatan to Captain John Smith

This cultural contact had enormous effects on world history. The European exploration, conquest, and set-tlement of the Americas led to the founding of many new nations—including the United States—that would play a large role in world affairs. For the Native Americans, however, it was the beginning of an immense tragedy during which many of their societies were destroyed by war and disease.

Religious Belief

Religion was a major factor in American colonial culture. This was particularly true in the New England colonies, where groups of Protestants from England, such as the Pilgrims and Puritans, founded settlements beginning in 1620. Other groups seeking religious freedom followed, including the Quakers led by William Penn, who settled in Pennsylvania in 1670. In the 1730s and 1740s, a religious revival called the Great Awakening, which began in New England, spread throughout the American colonies. Two results of this movement were increased feelings of responsibility for Native Americans and enslaved Africans and a more tolerant spirit toward other faiths.

The Slave Trade

From their beginnings, the American colonies suffered from a severe labor shortage. This was particularly true in the South, where large tobacco and rice plantations required hundreds of workers. Despite protests from some groups (such as the Quakers), many colonists participated in the slave trade. By 1750 there were more than 200,000 enslaved Africans in Britain's North American possessions, most of them in the Southern colonies. These colonies developed slave codes—sets of laws that formally regulated slavery and defined the relationship between enslaved Africans and free people. Over time these slave codes became increasingly strict.

The American Revolution

In the mid-1760s, unrest began to develop in Great Britain's American colonies. A long war with France had left Britain in debt. To raise money, the British government passed a series of unpopular laws, including taxes on a variety of everyday items. By the mid-1770s, resentment over these taxes was leading to political violence and calls for colonial self-rule.

> *"The war is inevitable—and let it come!"*
>
> —Patrick Henry

In April 1775, the British colonial government in Massachusetts ordered troops to the towns of Lexington and Concord to control unrest. The first battles of the Revolutionary War were fought there between American militiamen and British soldiers. On July 4, 1776, the Second Continental Congress adopted the Declaration of Independence, asserting the colonists' right to self-government and establishing the United States of America. To defend their independence, the Americans fought a long war with the British, who finally accepted American independence in 1783.

PREVIEW **Big Ideas** of Early America

1 The Sacred Earth and the Power of Storytelling

Much of Native American oral literature expressed a reverence for the natural world. Native American life was organized around the cycles of nature, and many myths and folktales told of the origins of various aspects of the universe and of human relationships with the natural world.

See pages 12–13.

2 Life in the New World

European explorers and settlers left accounts of endurance and religious faith as they struggled to adapt to life in an unfamiliar world. Victims of the slave trade, Africans recorded their fight to survive.

See pages 14–15.

3 The Road to Independence

British taxes, regulations, and soldiers on American soil aroused annoyance, irritation, and finally revolt. American writers provided ideas and inspiration to the cause of American freedom.

See pages 16–17.

The Sacred Earth and the Power of Storytelling

We often have a strong feeling for the land where we live—its shapes and colors, its sounds and smells. For Native Americans, this feeling for the natural world around them ran very deep. To them, the entire earth and all of the living things that inhabited it were sacred. In Native American cultures, this reverence for the earth and its creatures was passed down orally from generation to generation. Speakers and storytellers were valued members of Native American communities.

The Cycle of Life

This attitude toward the natural world shaped the religious beliefs of Native Americans. They saw animals, plants, and the forces of nature as part of a great sacred cycle of life that human beings must treat with deep respect. The religious ceremonies of Native American peoples were organized around the events of this natural cycle, such as the changing seasons and the birth, growth, and death of living things. Native Americans saw spiritual values in the natural world. Through dreams and visions, they sought contact with the spirits they believed to inhabit all living things. Through their tales and songs, Native Americans expressed their view of the sacredness of the natural world.

> "Sell a country! Why not sell the air, the great sea, as well as the earth? Did not the Great Spirit make them all for the use of his children?"
>
> —Tecumseh, Shawnee leader

Owning the Land

The Native Americans' belief that the natural world is sacred affected their attitude toward land-ownership. In their view, no one person could own land, which instead belonged in common to all people—and other living things—that inhabited it.

This concept of common ownership contrasted sharply with that of the Europeans, who in the early 1600s began settling North America. These settlers had a fierce desire to own their own land. Violent conflicts often resulted when Native American leaders signed treaties—which they usually did not understand—that opened lands to white settlement.

> "American literature begins with the first human perception of the American landscape expressed and preserved in language."
>
> —N. Scott Momaday

A Legacy of Stories

The Native American oral tradition began approximately forty thousand years ago when the first Native Americans crossed from Asia to Alaska via a land bridge that has since been covered by the waters of the Bering Strait. As populations migrated south, unique cultures and languages developed in response to a variety of environments. When European explorers first arrived in the New World, thousands of languages, some of them as different from one another as English is from Chinese, were spoken in the Americas. Each of these cultures developed its own stories and mythology.

No one knows what the earliest stories were about, but it is likely that many dramatized the precarious day-to-day existence of the first Native Americans. Stone Age hunters may have related tales of the hunt to groups sitting around campfires. Sacred stories were often at the heart of religious ceremonies, and in societies where myth and reality merged, rituals were thought to link the spirits of hunters and animals. Versions of the earliest stories have evolved through hundreds of generations and are still a living part of Native American traditions.

Mimbres style pottery bowl painted with the guardians of the four seasons, Mogollon culture, A.D. 10th century. Maxwell Museum of Anthropology, Albuquerque, NM.

I Have Killed the Deer
Taos Pueblo Song

I have killed the deer.
I have crushed the grasshopper
And the plants he feeds upon.
I have cut through the heart
Of trees growing old and straight.
I have taken fish from water
And birds from the sky.
In my life I have needed death
So that my life can be.

When I die I must give life
To what has nourished me.
The earth receives my body
And gives it to the plants
And to the caterpillars
To the birds
And to the coyotes
Each in its own turn so that
The circle of life is never broken.

Reading Check
Analyzing Cause and Effect How did Native Americans' religious views lead to conflict with Europeans?

Big Idea 2

Life in the New World

Even under favorable circumstances, adjusting to a new home and a new way of life is often hard. For the Europeans who explored and settled North America, this experience was frequently a struggle to endure and subdue a wilderness and was marked by fierce conflicts with Native Americans. For the Africans seized from their homes and enslaved in the Americas, the experience was a battle first to survive and then to hold on to their cultural identity under slavery.

A Collision of Cultures

Europeans began to explore North America in the early 1500s. Many of these explorers wrote grim reports of the hardships they encountered in the wilderness. The first arrivals were followed by other Europeans, settlers who built towns and started farms. As European settlement spread, conflict developed between the newcomers and Native Americans that often led to brutal wars. Their superior weapons enabled the Europeans to overcome their enemies. Even more destructive to the Native Americans were the diseases the newcomers brought with them. As a result of war and disease, few Native Americans survived beyond the end of the 1600s.

Puritan Style

The Puritans were European settlers who had the greatest influence on early American literature. They began to establish communities in New England in the 1620s after leaving England to escape what they saw as signs of corruption in the Church of England. These included elaborate rituals, a richly dressed clergy, and fine churches. In opposition to this, Puritans dressed in a plain style and held their simple religious services in undecorated meeting-houses. They also believed that they had a God-given responsibility to establish an ideal way of life in America.

The Puritans' plainness and piety showed in their writing, which employed straightforward language and often focused on their faith. William Bradford (see pages 60–65) was a member of the Puritan group known as the Pilgrims, who settled Plymouth Colony in 1620. Bradford viewed writing primarily as a practical tool. At the beginning of his history of the Plymouth Colony, he said that he intended to produce a record of events in "a plain style, with singular regard unto the simple truth in all things."

> "For we must consider that we shall be as a city upon a hill. The eyes of all people are upon us."
>
> —John Winthrop

In 1734 Jonathan Edwards (see pages 88–93), a Congregational minister who was the greatest spokesman of Puritanism, began a series of religious revivals among the young people in his community of Northampton, Massachusetts. His powerful sermons, such as "Sinners in the Hands of an Angry God," helped start and sustain the Great Awakening, a widespread religious revival throughout the American colonies. Edwards maintained that a person had to repent and convert in order to be "born again." This idea of having an internal emotional experience that brings one to God was a central idea of the Great Awakening.

Surviving Slavery

The first enslaved Africans were brought to Virginia in 1619. By the 1700s, slave ships arrived regularly in the American colonies full of African men, women, and children to be bought and sold. Most of these people, like Olaudah Equiano (see pages 63–73), had been taken from their homes in West Africa by slave traders. After enduring the horrors of the "Middle Passage," the long sea voyage across the Atlantic, they reached the slave markets of the Americas. Despite brutal living conditions, these Africans struggled to preserve parts of their heritage—the social values and cultural traditions of their homelands—but usually without success.

Quaker Meeting, late 18th century. Anonymous. Oil on canvas, 25¼ x 30 in. Museum of Fine Arts, Boston, MA.

from *Of Plymouth Plantation* by William Bradford

September 6. These troubles being blown over, and now all being compact together in one ship [the *Mayflower*], they put to sea again with a prosperous wind, which continued divers days together, which was some encouragement unto them; yet, according to the usual manner, many were afflicted with sea sickness. And I may not omit here a special work of God's providence. There was a proud and very profane young man, one of the seamen, of a lusty, able body, which made him the more haughty; he would always be condemning the poor people in their sickness, and cursing them daily with grievous execrations, and did not let to tell them that he hoped to help to cast half of them overboard before they came to their journey's end, and to make merry with what they had; and if he were by any gently reproved, he would curse and swear most bitterly. But it pleased God before they came half seas over, to smite this young man with a grievous disease, of which he died in a desperate manner, and so was himself the first that was thrown overboard. Thus his curses light on his own head, and it was an astonishment to all his fellows, for they noted it to be the just hand of God upon him.

Reading Check

Evaluating Why did the Puritans adopt a plain style in their writing?

As human beings grow, they experience the challenges and rewards of becoming independent. Maturity brings both greater responsibilities and greater rights. Separated by a long, dangerous sea voyage from Britain, the American colonists became used to managing their own affairs. As colonial society developed, many Americans came to believe that this growth in responsibility should be matched with an increase in political and economic rights. In time, this belief would lead to revolution—resulting in a break with Britain, a long war, and full independence.

A "Natural Aristocracy"

The culture of the American colonies was shaped by the practical, self-reliant, pioneer spirit of settlers who had left their homelands to seek a better life. As the French-born American Michel Guillaume Jean de Crèvecoeur observed, "*He* is an American who, leaving behind him all his ancient prejudices and manners, receives new ones from the mode of life he has embraced, the new government he obeys, and the new rank he holds." The career of Benjamin Franklin (see pages 96–103) reflected the American colonists' ability to rise in the world. He began life as one of seventeen children in a poor family. He ended as a successful businessman, an influential politician, and a famous writer and scientist.

> "Sloth, like rust, consumes faster than labor wears, while the used key is always bright."
>
> —Benjamin Franklin

Another important factor in the maturing of American colonial society was an emphasis on self-improvement through education. New England's Puritans, for example, established a system of public schools, believing that learning was a defense against evil. The combined effect of a bold, enterprising spirit coupled with education was the emergence in the American colonies of an outstanding political leadership, which one of these leaders, Thomas Jefferson (see pages 112–117), called a "natural aristocracy" of virtue and talent.

Political Rights

Philosophical ideas helped to direct the American colonists' moves toward revolution. During the 1700s, America came under the influence of the European cultural movement known as the Enlightenment. Enlightenment thinkers believed that natural laws applied to social, political, and economic relationships. Among the ideas of the Enlightenment was the concept that human beings possessed certain natural, or "inalienable" rights, basic rights that could never be taken away. Thomas Jefferson believed that the colonists had a natural right to be free. He also believed that they had a right—indeed a duty—to end what he saw as Britain's tyrannical rule of the colonies by establishing their own independent government. In the Declaration of Independence, Jefferson eloquently expressed the fundamental ideas behind the American Revolution and fiercely denounced British injustice.

Women's Lives

In colonial America, law and custom gave men greater authority and importance than women in politics and in the household. A married woman, in particular, had few legal rights and was almost completely under her husband's control. Despite their legal limitations, many colonial women worked outside their homes, running farms and businesses. Women also played a vital role in the movement for American independence by organizing boycotts of British goods. During the Revolutionary War, women continued to make important contributions to the American cause, both on the home front and on the battlefront. However, the full exercise of the political rights they helped win would be denied them for another 140 years.

Midnight Ride of Paul Revere, 1815. Artist Unknown.

from *The Autobiography* by Benjamin Franklin

1. **Temperance.** Eat not to dullness; drink not to elevation.
2. **Silence.** Speak not but what may benefit others or yourself; avoid trifling conversation.
3. **Order.** Let all your things have their places; let each part of your business have its time.
4. **Resolution.** Resolve to perform what you ought; perform without fail what you resolve.
5. **Frugality.** Make no expense but to do good to others or yourself; *i.e.,* waste nothing.
6. **Industry.** Lose no time; be always employed in something useful; cut off all unnecessary actions.
7. **Sincerity.** Use no hurtful deceit; think innocently and justly, and, if you speak, speak accordingly.
8. **Justice.** Wrong none by doing injuries or omitting the benefits that are your duty.
9. **Moderation.** Avoid extremes; forbear resenting injuries so much as you think they deserve.
10. **Cleanliness.** Tolerate no uncleanliness in body, clothes, or habitation.
11. **Tranquility.** Be not disturbed at trifles or at accidents common or unavoidable.
12. **Chastity.** Rarely use venery but for health or offspring, never to dullness, weakness, or the injury of your own or another's peace or reputation.
13. **Humility.** Imitate Jesus and Socrates.

Reading Check

Analyzing Cause and Effect How did the American colonies come to have an effective group of leaders at the time of the Revolution?

Wrap-Up

Why It Matters

American literature began with the oral tradition of the Native Americans. This ancient legacy of stories, songs, prayers, history, and other lore enabled the Native Americans to preserve the outlines of a world that largely vanished. Disease and war followed the arrival of Europeans in the Western Hemisphere. In recent years, new generations of Native American writers have reinterpreted, in modern terms, the literary themes and forms of this tradition, as part of a continuing effort to explore Native American cultural identity.

The writings of the Puritans are part of a cultural tradition stretching back to the time of Martin Luther and the beginnings of the Protestant Reformation. As interpreted by the Puritans, some of the most important features of this tradition became central to the American cultural tradition. Central to this Puritan legacy is the belief in a God-given mission to offer an example to the world of an ideal community. Another influential feature of Puritan culture is its emphasis on simplicity and practicality.

Puritanism inspired the religious revival of the Great Awakening, which in turn inspired a desire for democracy and equality in its followers. To many Americans, this sense of equality applied not only to religion but to society as well. It encouraged in them a willingness to criticize established authority—including the authority of the British government.

Cultural Links

>>> Native American literature has been flourishing since the late 1960s. Among the major writers contributing to this literary renaissance are N. Scott Momaday, Louise Erdrich, Leslie Marmon Silko, and Sherman Alexie.

>>> The writings of Benjamin Franklin, particularly his *Autobiography*, have inspired both Americans and people around the world to implement programs of self-improvement. Frederick Douglass was among those who used Franklin's writing as a model.

>>> In 1848, at the first women's rights convention in the United States, Elizabeth Cady Stanton modeled her "Declaration of Rights and Sentiments" on Jefferson's Declaration of Independence.

You might try using this study organizer to keep track of the literary elements you learn in this unit.

FOLDABLES Study Organizer

BOUND BOOK

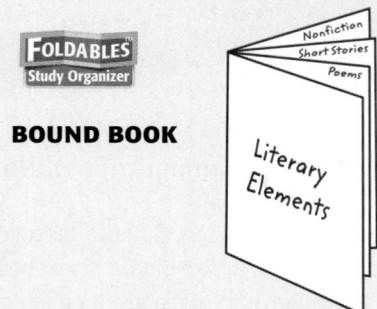

Nonfiction / Short Stories / Poems / Literary Elements

 Big Ideas Link to Web resources to further explore the Big Ideas at www.glencoe.com.

Connect to Today >>>
Use what you have learned about the period to do one of these activities.

1. **Speaking/Listening** Divide into two groups and debate the following statement: "The influence of Puritanism on modern American culture has been generally positive."

2. **Visual Literacy** Alone or with other students, create a design expressing the Native American concept of the unending cycle of life.

3. **Writing** Write a brief essay exploring how Jefferson's "natural aristocracy" of virtue and talent that formed the leadership of the American Revolution would regard those governing the United States today?

INDIANA ACADEMIC STANDARDS (page 18)
11.3.8 Analyze...philosophical arguments...
11.5.3 Write reflective compositions that...draw comparisons between specific incidents and broader themes...

Literature Online **Study Central** Visit www.glencoe.com and click on Study Central to review Early America.

THE SACRED EARTH AND THE POWER OF STORYTELLING

Crossing the Ford, Platte River, Colorado, 1867–1870, Thomas Worthington Whittredge. Oil on canvas. Century Association, New York.

> *"Let us tell the old stories,*
> *Let us sing the sacred songs."*
>
> —N. Scott Momaday, "Carriers of the Dream Wheel"

Native American Mythology

CENTURIES BEFORE THE FIRST Europeans arrived on the shores of North America, Native Americans had established hundreds of thriving nations, each with a unique culture and heritage. Each nation had its own tradition of **oral literature**—stories that were passed down from one generation to the next as they were told and retold in the privacy of households and in tribal ceremonies. These stories embodied the tribe's past and told of its close relationship with the natural world. The result is a literature that is timeless, a literature created by no one author but by the people as a whole.

> *"You know, everything had to begin, and this is how it was: the Kiowas came one by one into this world through a hollow log."*
>
> —N. Scott Momaday
> from *The Way to Rainy Mountain*

Creation Myths

An important part of the oral tradition of each culture was its myths. A **myth** is an anonymous, traditional story that relies on the supernatural to explain a natural phenomenon, an aspect of human behavior, or a mystery of the universe. Myths try to explain why the world is the way it is. They provide imaginative ways to help people feel at home in the world and make sense of it. **Creation myths** tell how the world and human beings came to exist. Some myths, called **origin myths,** explain how natural phenomena, such as the stars, moon, and mountains, came to be or why a society has certain beliefs and customs. Often, elements of both creation myths and origin myths appear in one story, as in this myth of the Taos Pueblo people:

"When earth was still young and giants still roamed the land, a great sickness came upon them. All of them died except for one small boy. One day while he was playing, a snake bit him. The boy cried and cried. The blood came out, and finally he died. With his tears our lakes became. With his blood the red clay became. With his body our mountains became, and that was how earth became."

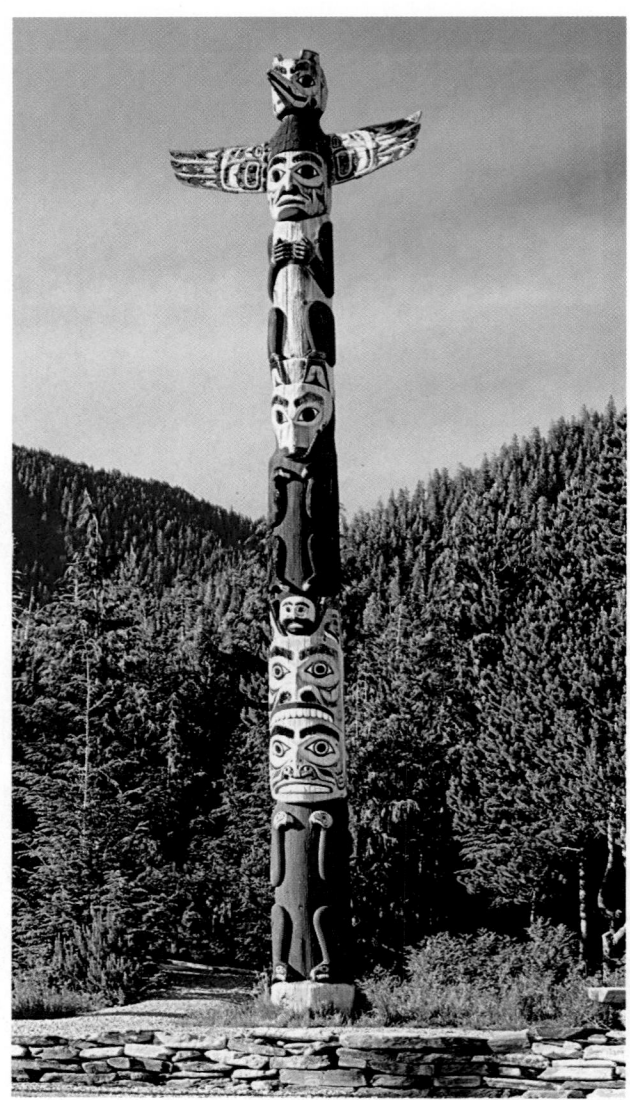

Totem Pole at Saxman Totem Park, Ketchikan. Tlingit. Wood sculpture. Ketchikan, Alaska, USA.

Archetypes

The myths told by peoples around the world share common elements known as archetypes. An **archetype** (är′ kə tīp′) is a symbol, story pattern, or character type that is found in the literature of many cultures. An example of an archetype is children with opposite qualities who are born of the same parent. In Iroquois myth, Sky Woman gives birth to twins, one good and one evil. This event explains the eternal struggle between light and dark and between order and chaos.

Tricksters

Another archetype found in Native American mythology is the **trickster.** This character type, frequently an animal—such as a coyote, a raven, or a mink—that speaks and displays other human traits, has two sides to its personality. Tricksters are rebels who defy authority and frequently cause trouble, but they are also clever and creative figures who can unexpectedly reveal wisdom. For example, in one Native American myth, the coyote brought death into the world when he realized that the earth would become too crowded if people were to live forever. In a Navajo myth, the Holy People were gathered to place the stars in the sky. This process was taking so long that Coyote grew impatient, snatched the bag of stars, and hurled it into the heavens, forming the Milky Way. A Kiowa myth explains how a trickster stole the sun from those who lived on the other side of the earth so that all people could share day and night equally.

The Function of Myths

Native American myths told by various tribes have several things in common. Many emphasize a strong

Round rattle, raven/halibut design. Seattle Art Museum, Gift of John H. Hauberg.
Viewing the Artifact: What feature does this artifact contain that reflects Native American beliefs?

spiritual bond between the Creator, humanity, and the entire natural world. They emphasize that it is the duty of human beings to maintain a balance within the natural world.

In many Native American cultures, each family group, or clan, believed it descended from a particular animal or other natural object, called the **totem.** Members of the bear clan, for example, honored the bear as their clan ancestor. The bear in turn served as the clan's guardian spirit, helping and protecting its members. The bear clan was responsible for preserving the myths of the bear.

Myths and rituals continue to play a central role in traditional Native American cultures. They are used to give people a sense of order and identity, to heal the sick, to ensure a plentiful supply of food, to teach moral lessons, and to initiate young people into adulthood and the wisdom of the tribal past.

Literature Online **Literary History** For more about Native American mythology, go to www.glencoe.com.

RESPONDING AND THINKING CRITICALLY

1. In your opinion, what is the most vital role of mythology in a culture?

2. How do Native American myths express a dual view of reality?

3. What are some archetypes that can be found in such forms of popular culture as comic books, movies, and video games?

INDIANA ACADEMIC STANDARDS (pages 20–21)
11.3.5 Analyze or evaluate works of literary or cultural significance in history…

11.3.6 Analyze the way in which authors have used archetypes…drawn from myth and tradition…

How the World Was Made

MEET THE CHEROKEE

Their neighbors, the Creek, called them *Cherokee*, meaning "people with another language." They called themselves *Aniyunwiya*, "the real people." Hundreds of years ago, the Cherokee were the largest Native American nation in what is now the southeastern United States. Like most other Native American peoples, the Cherokee possessed a vibrant oral culture. Myths helped the Cherokee understand the world around them, live in harmony with nature, and pass on their beliefs and values to their descendants.

In the mid-1500s, the Cherokee used stone tools and hunted bears, elk, and deer. They lived in log cabins with bark roofs, no windows, and a smoke hole in the roof, in towns of about 200 people. At any given time, the Cherokee were in either peace mode or war mode. Because they lived in an alternating state, the Cherokee government was made up of two sets of officials: a white chief, who ruled during peacetime, and a red chief, who ruled during wartime.

Treaty of Augusta In the frenzy of activity surrounding the American Revolution, Cherokee land-holdings were drastically reduced. The Cherokee had been friendly trading partners with the British throughout the 1700s but had fallen into debt. In the Treaty of Augusta in 1773, the Cherokee and Creek were forced to cede vast swaths of their tribal lands in Georgia to repay these debts to the British. Hoping to regain their traditional hunting grounds, the Cherokee pledged their support for the British at the beginning of the American Revolution. In the 1770s and 1780s, the Cherokee engaged in a flurry of skirmishes with the American army. They lost each time and were forced to surrender more lands.

Assimilation In the 1800s, the Cherokee learned to adapt by assimilating elements of white culture.

Literature Online **Author Search** For more about the Cherokee, go to www.glencoe.com.

They learned new farming, weaving, and construction methods. In 1821, Sequoyah, a half-Cherokee who had served in the U.S. Army, developed a system of writing the Cherokee language called a syllabary, a set of written characters in which each character represents a syllable. When Sequoyah pitched the syllabary to the tribal council, the chiefs marveled at its prospects and immediately accepted the new technology. Within a few years, almost the entire Cherokee nation was literate. In 1828, the Cherokee used their syllabary to publish *The Cherokee Phoenix*, the first Native American newspaper. But adopting white cultural practices did nothing to disarm the westward expansion. In 1830, the Cherokee were forcibly removed from their land under the Indian Removal Act. Some 15,000 Cherokee were placed in internment camps. Meanwhile, settlers pillaged and burned Cherokee homes.

Trail of Tears In 1838–1839, the Cherokee were exiled from their ancestral home and forced to march 1,000 miles to present-day Oklahoma, then known as Indian Territory. As many as 4,000 Cherokee died during the grueling 116-day journey. The soldiers refused to slow down for the sick and exhausted. Today, most Cherokee still live in Oklahoma, while several thousand, the descendants of those who escaped the Trail of Tears, still live in North Carolina.

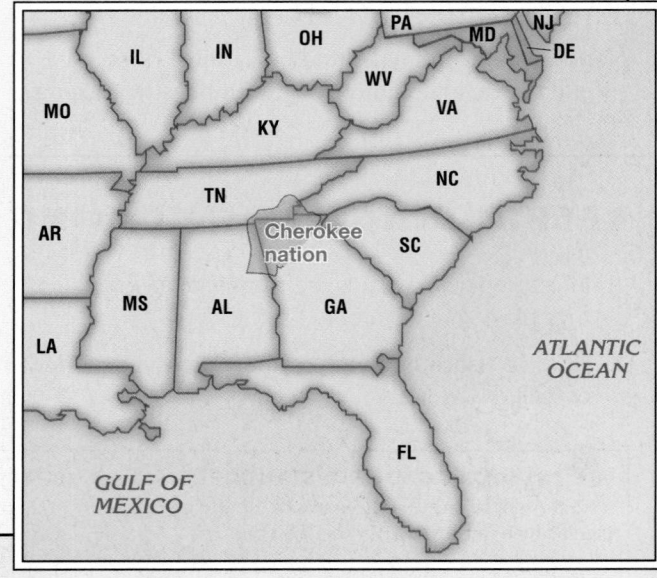

Connecting to the Myth

The natural world was an endless source of mystery for storytellers of the past. "How the World Was Made" is a creation myth, or a story that explains how the world began. Stories have also been written to explain other natural phenomena. As you read, think about the following questions:

- What other events or characteristics in the natural world might be explained through a story?
- In what ways might a story reflect the storyteller's own view of the world?

Building Background

Between 1887 and 1890, James Mooney, an anthropologist for the Smithsonian Institution in Washington, D.C., lived with the Cherokee in North Carolina. He won their trust and was able to collect a number of firsthand accounts of Cherokee rituals and stories, including the myth "How the World Was Made," which he published in 1900 in *Myths of the Cherokee*.

Setting Purposes for Reading

Big Idea **The Sacred Earth and the Power of Storytelling**

As you read "How the World Was Made," notice what it reveals about the Cherokees' relationship with nature.

Literary Element Archetype

An **archetype** is a character type, a descriptive detail, an image, or a story pattern that recurs frequently in the literature from many cultures and evokes strong emotional responses. As you read "How the World Was Made," look for archetypal elements.

- See Literary Terms Handbook, p. R2.

Literature Online **Interactive Literary Elements Handbook** To review or learn more about the literary elements, go to www.glencoe.com.

Reading Strategy Identifying Sequence

Identifying sequence is finding the logical order of ideas or events. Common forms of sequencing include time order, spatial order, and order of importance. Often, two or more types of sequencing are used in one literary work. In fact, time order, spatial order, and order of importance are all employed in this Cherokee genesis myth.

Reading Tip: Taking Notes Use a chart to record an example of each type of sequencing.

Detail	Type of Sequencing	Why
p. 25 "Men came after the animals and plants"	Order of Importance (also time order)	Animals and plants were created before men so that men would be able to survive

Vocabulary

vault (vôlt) *n.* an arched structure forming a roof or ceiling; p. 24 *The church's vault arched high over our heads.*

alight (ə līt′) *v.* to descend and come to rest; p. 24 *The cat watched the pigeon alight on the roof.*

conjurer (kon′jər ər) *n.* one who performs magic; sorcerer; p. 25 *The conjurer amused the audience with his tricks.*

Vocabulary Tip: Synonyms Synonyms are words that have the same or similar meanings. Note that synonyms are always the same part of speech.

INDIANA ACADEMIC STANDARDS (pages 23–26)
11.3.6 Analyze…archetypes…from myth and tradition…
11.2.2 Analyze…patterns of organization…

11.5.2 Write responses to literature that…analyze universal themes and unique aspects of the text…

HOW the World Was Made

(Cherokee–Great Smoky Mountains)
Retold by James Mooney

The earth is a great island floating in a sea of water, and suspended at each of the four cardinal points[1] by a cord hanging down from the sky **vault,** which is of solid rock. When the world grows old and worn out, the people will die and the cords will break and let the earth sink down into the ocean, and all will be water again. The Indians are afraid of this.

When all was water, the animals were above in Gălûñ′lătĭ (go lun(g) lot′ i), beyond the arch; but it was very much crowded, and they were wanting more room. They wondered what was below the water, and at last Dâyuni′sĭ (dô yun ē′ si), "Beaver's Grandchild," the little Water-beetle, offered to go and see if it could learn. It darted in every direction over the surface of the water, but could find no firm place to rest. Then it dived to the bottom and came up with some soft mud, which began to grow and spread on every side until it became the island which we call the earth.

It was afterward fastened to the sky with four cords, but no one remembers who did this.

At first the earth was flat and very soft and wet. The animals were anxious to get down, and sent out different birds to see if it was yet dry, but they found no place to **alight** and came back again to Gălûñ′lătĭ. At last it seemed to be time, and they sent out the Buzzard and told him to go and make ready for them. This was the Great Buzzard, the father of all the buzzards we see now. He flew all over the earth, low down near the ground, and it was still soft. When he reached the Cherokee country, he was very tired, and his wings began to flap and strike the ground, and wherever they struck the earth there was a valley, and where they turned up again there was a mountain. When the animals above saw this, they were afraid that the whole world would be mountains, so they called him back, but the Cherokee country remains full of mountains to this day.

When the earth was dry and the animals came down, it was still dark, so they got the sun and

---

1. The *four cardinal points* are the four main directions on a compass (north, south, east, and west).

Big Idea The Sacred Earth and the Power of Storytelling *What does Water-beetle's role in the story reveal about the Cherokees' relationship with animals?*

Vocabulary

vault (vôlt) *n.* an arched structure forming a roof or ceiling

Literary Element Archetype *What traits does the Great Buzzard share with characters you know from other stories?*

Vocabulary

alight (ə līt′) *v.* to descend and come to rest

set it in a track to go every day across the island from east to west, just overhead. It was too hot this way, and Tsiska′gĭlĭ′ (chēs kä′ gi li′) the Red Crawfish, had his shell scorched a bright red, so that his meat was spoiled; and the Cherokee do not eat it. The **conjurers** put the sun another hand-breadth[2] higher in the air, but it was still too hot. They raised it another time, and another, until it was seven handbreadths high and just under the sky arch. Then it was right, and they left it so. This is why the conjurers call the highest place Gûlkwâ′gine Di′gălûñ′lătiyûñ′ (gul kwô′ gē nā   dē′ gol un(g) lot ē yun(g′)), "the seventh height," because it is seven hand-breadths above the earth. Every day the sun goes along under this arch, and returns at night on the upper side to the starting place.

There is another world under this, and it is like ours in everything—animals, plants, and people—save that the seasons are different. The streams that come down from the mountains are the trails by which we reach this underworld, and the springs at their heads are the doorways by which we enter it, but to do this one must fast and go to water and have one of the underground people for a guide. We know that the seasons in the underworld are different from ours, because the water in the springs is always warmer in winter and cooler in summer than the outer air.

When the animals and plants were first made—we do not know by whom—they were told to watch and keep awake for seven nights, just as young men now fast and keep awake when they pray to their medicine.[3] They tried to do this, and

---

2. A *hand-breadth* is a unit of measurement based on the width of a hand. It varies from 2½ to 4 inches.
3. Many Native American cultures believe that each plant, animal, and human has its own natural spirit that gives it power. *Medicine,* in this instance, refers to this spirit.

Reading Strategy   Identifying Sequence *When do the following events take place in relation to those you have already read about?*

Vocabulary

conjurer (kon′ jər ər) *n.* one who performs magic; sorcerer

nearly all were awake through the first night, but the next night several dropped off to sleep, and the third night others were asleep, and then others, until, on the seventh night, of all the animals only the owl, the panther, and one or two more were still awake. To these were given the power to see and to go about in the dark, and to make prey of the birds and animals which must sleep at night. Of the trees only the cedar, the pine, the spruce, the holly, and the laurel were awake to the end, and to them it was given to be always green and to be greatest for medicine, but to the others it was said: "Because you have not endured to the end you shall lose your hair every winter."

Men came after the animals and plants. At first there were only a brother and sister until he struck her with a fish and told her to multiply, and so it was. In seven days a child was born to her, and thereafter every seven days another, and they increased very fast until there was danger that the world could not keep them. Then it was made that a woman should have only one child in a year, and it has been so ever since. ∾

RESPONDING AND THINKING CRITICALLY

Respond

1. Which events in this myth do you find most memorable and why?

Recall and Interpret

2. (a)What is the little Water-beetle's role in the creation of Earth? (b)What does this tell you about Cherokee reverence for all creatures?

3. (a)What do the "conjurers" do? (b)Who do you think the conjurers are? Explain.

4. (a)Which animals and plants are able to keep awake for seven nights? (b)What moral lesson might this episode teach?

Analyze and Evaluate

5. (a)What does the narrator say when Cherokee tradition has no answer or explanation for an occurrence? (b)How does the narrator's phrasing enhance the myth? Explain.

6. For the Cherokee, are humans more important than plants or animals or equal to them? Support your view with examples from the myth.

Connect

7. **Big Idea** The Sacred Earth and the Power of Storytelling (a)Why do the Cherokee people explain natural phenomena, such as mountains, underground springs, nocturnal predators, or evergreen trees, in story terms? (b)What do these explanations suggest about the Cherokee relationship with nature?

LITERARY ANALYSIS

Literary Element Archetype

One example of an archetype found in myths and folktales from many cultures is a daunting challenge or test that only heroic characters can overcome.

1. How does this archetype appear in "How the World Was Made"?

2. What examples of this archetype can you recall from other myths and folktales?

Writing About Literature

Explore Purpose of Myth Traditional societies preserve and retell their myths for a variety of reasons. For example, myths often express basic religious beliefs and explain social customs. In a paragraph, explain why you think the Cherokee storytellers retold and passed on "How the World Was Made."

READING AND VOCABULARY

Reading Strategy Identifying Sequence

In a myth, such as "How the World Was Made," events usually occur in chronological, or time order.

1. List the sequence of events in the myth.

2. Which detail is an exception to the time order?

Vocabulary Practice

Practice with Synonyms Find the synonym for each vocabulary word from the myth listed in the first column.

1. vault
   a. dome   **b.** universe

2. alight
   a. land   **b.** arise

3. conjurer
   a. chief   **b.** magician

Literature Online **Web Activities** For eFlashcards, Selection Quick Checks, and other Web activities, go to www.glencoe.com.

from

THE WAY TO RAINY MOUNTAIN

N. Scott Momaday

Pulitzer Prize Winner

Building Background

In the 1700s, the Kiowa (kī´ə wä) Indians began a long migration from southwestern Montana to the southern Great Plains. Along the way, they made contact with the Crow Indians of southeastern Montana, whose nomadic way of life greatly influenced the Kiowa. Their travels came to an end in 1868 when they were forced to settle on an Oklahoma reservation. Kiowa author N. Scott Momaday (mom´ə dā) frequently writes about the Kiowas' rich history. In the following selection, he describes their connection to the natural world and the end of the tribe's golden age.

Set a Purpose for Reading

Read to learn about the Kiowas' culture and their relationship with the land.

Reading Strategy

Analyzing Cultural Traditions

In the selection, Momaday presents his understanding of Kiowa culture. Examine the elements that make up the selection, such as the descriptions of the land, of Kiowa history, and of Momaday's grandmother. Think about what all of these elements, taken together, suggest about the Kiowa.

A single knoll rises out of the plain in Oklahoma, north and west of the Wichita Range. For my people, the Kiowas, it is an old landmark, and they gave it the name Rainy Mountain. The hardest weather in the world is there. Winter brings blizzards, hot tornadic winds arise in the spring, and in summer the prairie is an anvil's edge. The grass turns brittle and brown, and it cracks beneath your feet. There are green belts along the rivers and creeks, linear groves of hickory and pecan, willow and witch hazel. At a distance in July or August the steaming foliage seems almost to writhe[1] in fire. Great green and yellow grasshoppers are everywhere in the tall grass, popping up like corn to sting the flesh, and tortoises crawl about on the red earth, going nowhere in the plenty of time. Loneliness is an aspect of the land. All things in the plain are isolate;[2] there is no confusion of objects in the eye, but *one* hill or *one* tree or *one* man. To look upon that landscape in the early morning, with the sun at your back, is to

---

1. *Writhe* means "to twist as in great pain."
2. *Isolate* means "solitary."

lose the sense of proportion. Your imagination comes to life, and this, you think, is where Creation was begun.

I returned to Rainy Mountain in July. My grandmother had died in the spring, and I wanted to be at her grave. She had lived to be very old and at last infirm.[3] Her only living daughter was with her when she died, and I was told that in death her face was that of a child.

I like to think of her as a child. When she was born, the Kiowas were living the last great moment of their history. For more than a hundred years they had controlled the open range from the Smoky Hill River to the Red, from the headwaters of the Canadian to the fork of the Arkansas and Cimarron. In alliance with the Comanches, they had ruled the whole of the southern Plains. War was their sacred business, and they were among the finest horsemen the world has ever known. But warfare for the Kiowas was preeminently[4] a matter of disposition rather than of survival, and they never understood the grim, unrelenting advance of the U.S. Cavalry. When at last, divided and ill-provisioned, they were driven onto the Staked Plains in the cold rains of autumn, they fell into panic. In Palo Duro Canyon they abandoned their crucial stores to pillage[5] and had nothing then but their lives. In order to save themselves, they surrendered to the soldiers at Fort Sill and were imprisoned in the old stone corral that now stands as a military museum. My grandmother was spared the humiliation of those high gray walls by eight or ten years, but she must have known from birth the affliction of defeat, the dark brooding of old warriors.

Her name was Aho, and she belonged to the last culture to evolve in North America. Her forebears came down from the high country in western Montana nearly three centuries ago. They were a mountain people, a mysterious tribe of hunters whose language has never been positively classified in any major group. In the late seventeenth century they began a long migration to the south and east. It was a journey toward the dawn, and it led to a

golden age. Along the way the Kiowas were befriended by the Crows, who gave them the culture and religion of the Plains. They acquired horses, and their ancient nomadic spirit was suddenly free of the ground. They acquired Tai-me,[6] the sacred Sun Dance doll, from that moment the object and symbol of their worship, and so shared in the divinity of the sun. Not least, they acquired the sense of destiny, therefore courage and pride. When they entered upon the southern Plains they had been transformed. No longer were they slaves to the simple necessity of survival; they were a lordly and dangerous society of fighters and thieves, hunters and priests of the sun. According to their origin myth, they entered the world through a hollow log. From one point of view, their migration was the fruit of an old prophecy, for indeed they emerged from a sunless world.

Although my grandmother lived out her long life in the shadow of Rainy Mountain, the immense landscape of the continental interior lay like memory in her blood. She could tell of the Crows, whom she had never seen, and of the Black Hills, where she had never been. I wanted to see in reality what she had seen more perfectly in the mind's eye, and traveled fifteen hundred miles to begin my pilgrimage.

Yellowstone, it seemed to me, was the top of the world, a region of deep lakes and dark timber, canyons and waterfalls. But, beautiful as it is, one might have the sense of confinement there. The skyline in all directions is close at hand, the high wall of the woods and deep cleavages of shade. There is a perfect freedom in the mountains, but it belongs to the eagle and the elk, the badger and the bear. The Kiowas reckoned their stature by the distance they could see, and they were bent and blind in the wilderness.

Descending eastward, the highland meadows are a stairway to the plain. In July the inland slope of the Rockies is luxuriant[7] with flax and buckwheat, stonecrop and larkspur.[8] The earth

---

3. *Infirm* means "physically weak" or "feeble."
4. *Preeminently* means "primarily."
5. *Pillage* means "to loot" or "to plunder."

6. *Tai-me* (tī′ mā), the Sun Dance doll, wears a robe of white feathers.
7. *Luxuriant* means "marked by rich or plentiful growth."
8. *Flax* is a flowering plant whose fibers are spun to make cloth. *Buckwheat* is a plant whose seeds are used as a cereal grain. *Stonecrop* is a flowering plant found on rocks and walls. *Larkspur* is known for its showy flower stalks.

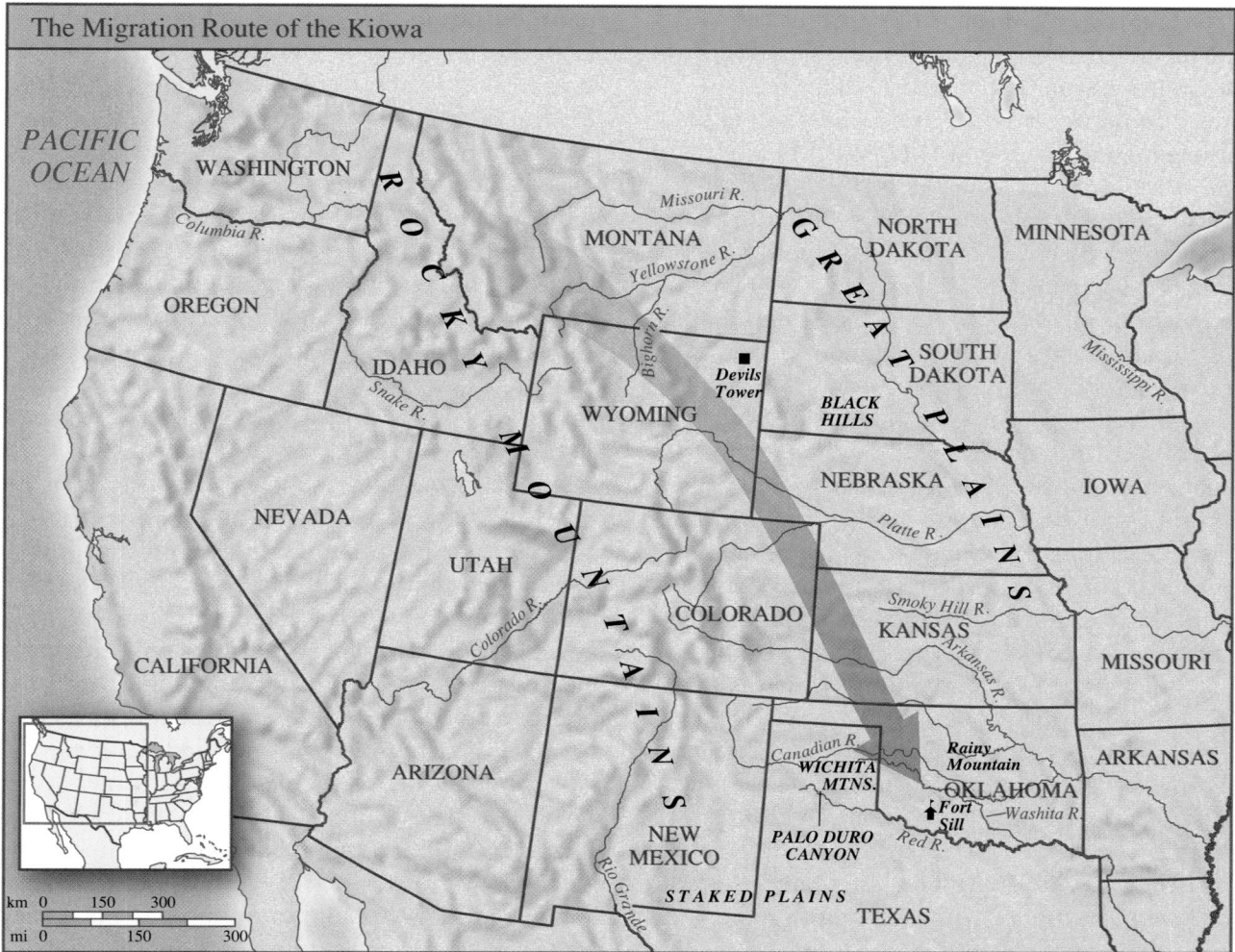

The Migration Route of the Kiowa

unfolds and the limit of the land recedes. Clusters of trees, and animals grazing far in the distance, cause the vision to reach away and wonder to build upon the mind. The sun follows a longer course in the day, and the sky is immense beyond all comparison. The great billowing clouds that sail upon it are shadows that move upon the grain like water, dividing light. Farther down, in the land of the Crows and Blackfeet, the plain is yellow. Sweet clover takes hold of the hills and bends upon itself to cover and seal the soil. There the Kiowas paused on their way; they had come to the place where they must change their lives. The sun is at home on the plains. Precisely there does it have the certain character of a god. When the Kiowas came to the land of the Crows, they could see the dark lees[9] of the hills at dawn across the Bighorn River, the profusion of light on the grain shelves, the

oldest deity ranging after the solstices.[10] Not yet would they veer southward to the caldron of the land that lay below; they must wean their blood[11] from the northern winter and hold the mountains a while longer in their view. They bore Tai-me in procession to the east.

A dark mist lay over the Black Hills, and the land was like iron. At the top of a ridge I caught sight of Devil's Tower[12] upthrust against the gray sky as if in the birth of time the core of the earth had broken through its crust and the motion of the world was begun.

---

9. *Lees* are the sides of hills that are away from the wind.

10. *Solstices* are days when the earth and the sun are in a certain alignment. In the Northern Hemisphere, the summer and winter solstices are the longest and shortest days of the year.

11. *Wean their blood* means "to become acclimated by removing themselves gradually."

12. *Devils Tower,* an 865-foot-high column of volcanic rock in Wyoming, was designated as a national monument in 1906.

There are things in nature that engender[13] an awful quiet in the heart of man; Devil's Tower is one of them. Two centuries ago, because they could not do otherwise, the Kiowas made a legend at the base of the rock. My grandmother said:

Eight children were there at play, seven sisters and their brother. Suddenly the boy was struck dumb; he trembled and began to run upon his hands and feet. His fingers became claws, and his body was covered with fur. Directly there was a bear where the boy had been. The sisters were terrified; they ran, and the bear after them. They came to the stump of a great tree, and the tree spoke to them. It bade them climb upon it, and as they did so it began to rise into the air. The bear came to kill them, but they were just beyond its reach. It reared against the tree and scored the bark all around with its claws. The seven sisters were borne into the sky, and they became the stars of the Big Dipper.[14]

From that moment, and so long as the legend lives, the Kiowas have kinsmen in the night sky. Whatever they were in the mountains, they could be no more. However tenuous their well-being, however much they had suffered and would suffer again, they had found a way out of the wilderness.

My grandmother had a reverence for the sun, a holy regard that now is all but gone out of mankind. There was a wariness in her, and an ancient awe. She was a Christian in her later years, but she had come a long way about, and she never forgot her birthright. As a child she had been to the Sun Dances; she had taken part in those annual rites, and by them she had learned the restoration of her people in the presence of Tai-me. She was about seven when the last Kiowa Sun Dance was held in 1887 on the Washita River above Rainy Mountain Creek. The buffalo were gone. In order to consummate[15] the ancient sacrifice—to impale the head of a buffalo bull upon the medicine tree—a delegation of old men journeyed into Texas, there to beg and barter for an animal from the Goodnight herd. She was ten when the Kiowas came together for the last time as a living Sun Dance culture. They could find no buffalo; they had to hang an old hide from the sacred tree. Before the dance could begin, a company of soldiers rode out from Fort Sill under orders to disperse the tribe. Forbidden without cause the essential act of their faith, having seen the wild herds slaughtered and left to rot upon the ground, the Kiowas backed away forever from the medicine tree. That was July 20, 1890, at the great bend of the Washita. My grandmother was there. Without bitterness, and for as long as she lived, she bore a vision of deicide.[16]

Now that I can have her only in memory, I see my grandmother in the several postures that were peculiar to her: standing at the wood stove on a winter morning and turning meat in a great iron skillet; sitting at the south window, bent above her beadwork, and afterwards, when her vision failed, looking down for a long time into the fold of her hands; going out upon a cane, very slowly as she did when the weight of age came upon her; praying. I remember her most often at prayer. She made long, rambling prayers out of suffering and hope, having seen many things. I was never sure that I had the right to hear, so exclusive were they of all mere custom and company. The last time I saw her she prayed standing by the side of her bed at night, naked to the waist, the light of a kerosene lamp moving upon her dark skin. Her long, black hair, always drawn and braided in the day, lay upon her shoulders and against her breasts like a shawl. I do not speak Kiowa, and I never understood her prayers, but there was something inherently sad in the sound, some merest hesitation upon the syllables of sorrow. She began in a high and descending pitch, exhausting her breath to silence; then again and again—and always the same intensity of effort, of something that is, and is not, like urgency in the human voice. Transported so in the dancing light among the shadows of her room, she seemed beyond the reach of time.

---

13. *Engender* means "to give rise to" or "to produce."
14. The *Big Dipper* is part of a larger constellation called Ursa Major, the Great Bear.
15. *Consummate* means "to bring to completion."

16. *Deicide* is the killing of a god.

Viewing the Photograph: Why do you think the sight of Devil's Tower (see pages 29–30) might have inspired the Kiowa to create a legend?

But that was illusion; I think I knew then that I should not see her again.

Houses are like sentinels in the plain, old keepers of the weather watch. There, in a very little while, wood takes on the appearance of great age. All colors wear soon away in the wind and rain, and then the wood is burned gray and the grain appears and the nails turn red with rust. The windowpanes are black and opaque;[17] you imagine there is nothing within, and indeed there are many ghosts, bones given up to the land. They stand here and there against the sky, and you approach them for a longer time than you expect. They belong in the distance; it is their domain.[18]

Once there was a lot of sound in my grand-mother's house, a lot of coming and going, feasting and talk. The summers there were full of excitement and reunion. The Kiowas are a summer people; they abide the cold and keep to themselves, but when the season turns and the land becomes warm and vital they cannot hold still; an old love of going returns upon them. The aged visitors who came to my grandmother's house when I was a child were made of lean and leather, and they bore them-selves upright. They wore great black hats and bright ample shirts that shook in the wind. They rubbed fat upon their hair and wound their braids with strips of colored cloth. Some of them painted their faces and carried the scars of old and cherished enmities.[19] They were an old council of warlords, come to remind and be reminded of who they were. Their wives and daughters served them well. The women might indulge themselves; gossip was at once the mark and compensation of their servitude. They made loud and elaborate talk among themselves, full of jest and gesture, fright and false alarm. They went abroad[20] in fringed and flowered shawls, bright beadwork and German silver.[21] They were at home in the kitchen, and they prepared meals that were banquets.

There were frequent prayer meetings, and great nocturnal feasts. When I was a child I played with my cousins outside, where the lamplight fell upon the ground and the sing-ing of the old people rose up around us and carried away into the darkness. There were

---

17. *Opaque* means "unable to let light through."
18. A *domain* is "a territory over which control is exercised."
19. *Enmities* means "deep-seated hatreds."
20. Here, *abroad* means "away from one's home."
21. *German silver* is an alloy that resembles real silver.

a lot of good things to eat, a lot of laughter and surprise. And afterwards, when the quiet returned, I lay down with my grandmother and could hear the frogs away by the river and feel the motion of the air.

Now there is a funeral silence in the rooms, the endless wake of some final word. The walls have closed in upon my grandmother's house. When I returned to it in mourning, I saw for the first time in my life how small it was. It was late at night, and there was a white moon, nearly full. I sat for a long time on the stone steps by the kitchen door. From there I could see out across the land; I could see the long row of trees by the creek, the low light upon the rolling plains, and the stars of the Big Dipper. Once I looked at the moon and caught sight of a strange thing. A cricket had perched upon the handrail, only a few inches away from me. My line of vision was such that the creature filled the moon like a fossil. It had

gone there, I thought, to live and die, for there, of all places, was its small definition made whole and eternal. A warm wind rose up and purled[22] like the longing within me.

Visual Vocabulary
A *scissortail,* a type of flycatcher, is a small gray and pink bird with a forked tail.

The next morning I awoke at dawn and went out on the dirt road to Rainy Mountain. It was already hot, and the grasshoppers began to fill the air. Still, it was early in the morning, and the birds sang out of the shadows. The long yellow grass on the mountain shone in the bright light, and a scissor-tail hied[23] above the land. There, where it ought to be, at the end of a long and legendary way, was my grandmother's grave. Here and there on the dark stones were ancestral names. Looking back once, I saw the mountain and came away.

22. *Purled* means "rippled with a murmuring sound."
23. *Hied* means "went quickly."

RESPONDING AND THINKING CRITICALLY

Respond

1. How did you react to the description of the end of the Kiowas' old way of life?

Recall and Interpret

2. (a)What is the importance of Rainy Mountain? (b)Why, do you think, does Momaday feel that Rainy Mountain is "where Creation was begun"?

3. Summarize what you learned about the Kiowa surrender and the last Sun Dance. Then explain Momaday's attitude toward these events, supporting your answer with details from the selection.

4. (a)What elements of Kiowa traditional beliefs were part of the grandmother's life? (b)What do you learn about the Kiowa people from the way that they respond to the end of their traditional lifestyle?

Analyze and Evaluate

5. (a)Explain why Momaday considers his grandmother a living embodiment of Kiowa history. (b)Did you find this description convincing? Why or why not?

6. Momaday watches a cricket that he says came to Rainy Mountain to die, "for there, of all places, was its small definition made whole and eternal." He also describes his grandmother's grave. Which of these works best for you as a symbol? Explain.

Connect

7. Momaday once said, "I don't see any validity in the separation of man and landscape." He has also called human alienation from nature "one of the great afflictions of our time." How are these ideas embodied in the selection? Support your answer.

INDIANA ACADEMIC STANDARDS (pages 27–32)
11.3.5 Analyze or evaluate works of literary or cultural significance in history…

11.2.5 Analyze an author's…beliefs about a subject.

Comparing Literature Across Time and Place

Connecting to the Reading Selections

Oral cultures use storytelling to pass on ancient traditions. The four literary works compared here—a Huron myth, a West African folktale, and two Native American poems—reflect this tradition of storytelling in different ways.

COMPARING THE `Big Idea` The Sacred Earth and the Power of Storytelling

Storytellers played a vital role in oral cultures. They both preserved ancient myths and traditions and made them live for new generations.

COMPARING Mythic Elements

A **myth** is a traditional story that explains a belief, a custom, or a force of nature. Certain mythic elements, such as creation or journeys, are used by storytellers in many different cultures.

COMPARING Cultures

The writers featured here each reflect their times and places, as well as transmit the heritage and belief systems of their cultures.

The Sky Tree

MEET THE HURON

The Huron people believed that Earth was an island resting on the back of the Great Turtle that swam in the primal waters. So their name for themselves, *Wendat*, in their own language means "islanders." The name *Huron*, meaning "boar's head" or "rough hair," was given to them by the French explorers with whom they traded furs. In the 1600s, the Huron were members of a confederacy of tribes living northeast of the Great Lakes in what is now southern Canada. Even before the French arrived, the Huron were great traders. In the mid-1600s, their long conflict with the Iroquois nations (see page 47) reached a climax when the Iroquois seized control of the fur trade and forced the Huron to flee their homelands.

LITERATURE PREVIEW

Connecting to the Myth

What would you risk to save the person you love most? As you read "The Sky Tree," see how Aataentsic, the Earth-mother, responds to this challenge.

Building Background

"The Sky Tree" is an example of a type of creation story known as an earth-diver myth. In this type of myth a being dives into the primal waters to retrieve mud. This mud is spread on the back of the Great Turtle, eventually growing to form an island that becomes Earth.

Setting Purposes for Reading

Big Idea The Sacred Earth and the Power of Storytelling

Notice how this myth conveys the Huron belief in the relationship between human beings and the natural world.

Literary Element Oral Tradition

Oral tradition is literature that passes by word of mouth from one generation to the next. Consider why the Huron created and preserved "The Sky Tree."

• See Literary Terms Handbook, p. R12.

READING PREVIEW

Reading Strategy Questioning

Questioning is asking yourself at regular intervals whether you have understood what you have read.

....

Reading Tip: Taking Notes As you read "The Sky Tree," write down questions that puzzle you in the left-hand column of a double-entry journal. See the example below.

Question	Answer
What is the meaning of Aataentsic's act in cutting down the Sky Tree?	

Literature Online **Interactive Literary Elements Handbook** To review or learn more about the literary elements, go to www.glencoe.com.

The Sky Tree

Huron—Eastern Woodland
Retold by Joseph Bruchac

In the beginning, Earth was covered with water. In Sky Land, there were people living as they do now on Earth. In the middle of that land was the great Sky Tree. All of the food which the people in that Sky Land ate came from the great tree. The old chief of that land lived with his wife, whose name was Aataentsic,[1] meaning "Ancient Woman," in their longhouse[2] near the great tree. It came to be that the old chief became sick and nothing could cure him. He grew weaker and weaker until it seemed he would die. Then a dream came to him and he called Aataentsic to him.

"I have dreamed," he said, "and in my dream I saw how I can be healed. I must be given the fruit which grows at the very top of Sky Tree. You must cut it down and bring that fruit to me."

Aataentsic took her husband's stone ax and went to the great tree. As soon as she struck it, it split in half and toppled over. As it fell a hole opened in Sky Land and the tree fell through the hole. Aataentsic returned to the place where the old chief waited.

"My husband," she said, "when I cut the tree it split in half and then fell through a great hole. Without the tree, there can be no life. I must follow it."

Then, leaving her husband she went back to the hole in Sky Land and threw herself after the great tree.

As Aataentsic fell, Turtle looked up and saw her. Immediately Turtle called together all the water animals and told them what she had seen.

"What should be done?" Turtle said.

Beaver answered her. "You are the one who saw this happen. Tell us what to do."

"All of you must dive down," Turtle said. "Bring up soil from the bottom, and place it on my back."

Immediately all of the water animals began to dive down and bring up soil. Beaver, Mink, Muskrat, and Otter each brought up pawfuls of wet soil and placed the soil on the Turtle's back until they had made an island of great size. When they were through, Aataentsic settled down gently on the new Earth and the pieces of the great tree fell beside her and took root. ◔

---

1. *Aataentsic* was the Earth-mother in Huron mythology. The Huron believed themselves to be the children of Aataentsic.
2. A *longhouse* was a bark-covered Native American communal dwelling that could have space for multiple families as well as rooms for tribal ceremonies.

Reading Strategy Questioning *Why is the old chief's dream important to the story?*

Big Idea The Sacred Earth and the Power of Storytelling *How does this part of the story reflect a Native American attitude toward the natural world?*

RESPONDING AND THINKING CRITICALLY

Respond

1. Would you describe Aataentsic's actions as heroic? Why or why not?

Recall and Interpret

2. (a)What is the Sky Tree? (b)Why is it important to the people in Sky Land?

3. (a)Why does Aataentsic cut down the Sky Tree? (b)What does this action reveal about her relationship with her husband?

4. (a)Which animal observes Aataentsic's fall? (b)What role does this animal assume?

Analyze and Evaluate

5. (a)What is the function of the old chief's dream in "The Sky Tree"? (b)What does this myth suggest about the importance that Native Americans attribute to knowledge gained from dreams?

6. (a)What motivates Aataentsic to follow the Sky Tree into the hole? (b)How do you view her actions?

Connect

7. **Big Idea** **The Sacred Earth and the Power of Storytelling** What does the role of the water animals in the creation of Earth suggest about Native American attitudes toward other living creatures?

LITERARY ANALYSIS

READING AND VOCABULARY

Literary Element Oral Tradition

Oral tradition is a way of recording the past, glorifying leaders, and teaching moral values.

1. Why do you think the Huron preserved and perpetuated a myth such as "The Sky Tree"?

2. How might this myth have been used by the Huron to teach a moral lesson?

Literature Groups

Comparing Creation Myths Creation myths such as "The Sky Tree" are closely tied to Native Americans' religious beliefs and their reverence for the natural world. What other creation stories have you read or heard? How are these stories like and unlike "The Sky Tree"? What different values do these stories teach? Discuss these questions in your group and report the results to the class.

Reading Strategy Questioning

Review the questions that you wrote in your double-entry journal and answer them now.

Academic Vocabulary

Here are two words from the vocabulary list on page R86. These words will help you think, write, and talk about the selection.

function (fungk´shən) n. the action or purpose for which something is intended

tradition (trə dish´ən) n. an inherited pattern of belief or custom

Practice and Apply

1. What is the **function** of the Great Turtle in Huron mythology?
2. What **tradition** do the Huron preserve about the Earth-mother Aataentsic?

Literature Online **Web Activities** For eFlashcards, Selection Quick Checks, and other Web activities, go to www.glencoe.com.

How the Leopard Got His Claws

Retold by Chinua Achebe and John Iroaganachi

BEFORE YOU READ

Building Background

West African writer Chinua Achebe has used the English language to challenge many of the racist attitudes he observed as a young man. Born in 1930, Achebe grew up in an Ibo (also spelled *Igbo*) village in eastern Nigeria. His acclaimed 1958 novel, *Things Fall Apart,* gained him an international reputation. The novel depicts a cultural clash between traditional Ibo values and laws imposed by British colonialists. Speaking of the influence of colonialism, Achebe said that his nation has been confronted with "a crisis in the soul" in which "we have accepted everything alien as good and practically everything local or native as inferior." One of Achebe's goals has been to "help [his] society regain belief in itself."

Achebe's myth is an adaptation of a children's story by teacher and writer John Iroaganachi. Achebe's version is full of dark undertones that suggest an allegorical link to the British colonial era and the Nigerian Civil War, which lasted from 1967 to 1970. Various military regimes, representing hostile ethnic groups, have periodically seized power in Nigeria since it declared its independence from Britain in 1960. Today, continued political corruption and ethnic struggles have stalled the progress of Nigeria toward unity, peace, and stability.

Literature Online **Author Search** For more about Chinua Achebe and John Iroaganachi, go to www.glencoe.com.

If you look at the world in terms of storytelling, you have, first of all, the man who agitates, the man who drums up the people—I call him the drummer. Then you have the warrior, who goes forward and fights. But you also have the storyteller who recounts the event, and this is the one who survives, who outlives all the others. It is the storyteller who makes us what we are, who creates history. The storyteller creates the memory that the survivors must have; otherwise, their surviving would have no meaning.

—Chinua Achebe

In the beginning . . . all the animals in the forest lived as friends. Their king was the leopard. He was strong, but gentle and wise. He ruled the animals well, and they all liked him.

At that time the animals did not fight one another. Most of them had no sharp teeth or claws. They did not need them. Even King Leopard had only small teeth. He had no claws at all.

Only the dog had big, sharp teeth. The other animals said he was ugly, and they laughed at him.

"It is foolish to carry sharp things in the mouth," said the tortoise.

"I think so, too," said the goat.

The monkey jumped in and began to tease the dog.

"Don't worry, my dear friend," said the monkey. "You need your teeth to clear your farm."

The animals laughed at the monkey's joke.

When the farming season came round, King Leopard led the animals to their farmland. They all worked hard to prepare their plots. At the end of the day they returned home tired. They sat on log benches in the village square. As they rested they told stories and drank palm wine.[1]

But soon it would be the rainy season, and the animals would have no shelter from the rain.

The deer took this problem to King Leopard. They talked about it for a long time. King Leopard decided to call the animals together to discuss it.

One bright morning . . . King Leopard beat his royal drum. When the animals heard the drum, they gathered at the village square. The tortoise was there. The goat was there, too. The sheep, the grass-cutter,[2] the monkey, the hedgehog,[3] the baboon, the dog and many others were there.

King Leopard greeted them and said, "I have called you together to plan how we can make ourselves a common shelter."

"This is a good idea," said the giraffe.

"Yes, a very good idea," said many other animals.

"But why do we need a common house?" said the dog. He had never liked King Leopard.

"The dog has asked a good question," said the duck. "Why do we need a common shelter?"

"We do need somewhere to rest when we return from our farms," replied King Leopard.

"And besides," said the goat, "we need a shelter from the rain."

"I don't mind being wet," said the duck. "In fact, I like it. I know that the goat does not like water on his body. Let him go and build a shelter."

"We need a shelter," said the monkey, jumping up and down in excitement.

"Perhaps we need one, perhaps we don't," said the lazy baboon sitting on the low fence of the square.

---

1. *Palm wine* is created from the sap of a palm tree.
2. The *grass-cutter* is a type of rodent.
3. A *hedgehog* is a small, hairy mammal; some varieties have quills.

The dog spoke again. "We are wasting our time. Those who need a shelter should build it. I live in a cave, and it is enough for me." Then he walked away. The duck followed him out.

"Does anyone else want to leave?" asked King Leopard. No one answered or made a move to go.

"Very well," said King Leopard. "Let the rest of us build the village hall."

The animals soon scattered about to find building materials. The tortoise copied the pattern on his back and made the plan of the roof. The giant rat and mouse dug the foundations. Some animals brought sticks, some ropes, others made roof-mats.

As they built the house, they sang many happy songs. They also told many jokes. Although they worked very hard, everyone was merry.

After many weeks they finished the building.

It was a fine building. The animals were pleased with it. They agreed to open it with a very special meeting.

On the opening day the animals, their wives and children gathered in the hall. King Leopard then made a short speech. He said: "This hall is yours to enjoy. You worked very hard together to build it. I am proud of you."

The animals clapped their hands and gave three cheers to their king.

From that day they rested in their new hall whenever they returned from their farm.

But the dog and the duck kept away from the hall.

One morning the animals went to their farms as usual. King Leopard went to visit a chief in another village.

At first the sun was shining. Then strong winds began to blow. Dark clouds hid the sun. The first rain was coming. The songbirds stopped their singing. The humming insects became quiet. Lightning flashed across the dark clouds. Claps of thunder sounded. The rain poured and poured.

The animals in their farms saw the rain coming and began to hurry to the village hall.

The dog also saw the rain coming and returned to his cave. But it was a very, very heavy rain. Water began to enter the cave. Soon it was flooded.

The dog ran from one end of his cave to the other. But the water followed him everywhere. At last he ran out of the cave altogether and made straight for the hall of the animals.

The deer was already there. He was surprised to see the dog enter the hall.

"What do you want here?" said the deer to the dog.

"It is none of your business," replied the dog.

"It is my business," said the deer. "Please go out, this hall is for those who built it."

Then the dog attacked the deer and bit him with his big, sharp teeth. The deer cried with pain. The dog seized him by the neck and threw him out into the rain.

The other animals came in one after the other.

The dog barked and threw each of them out. They stood together shivering and crying in the rain. The dog kept barking and showing his teeth.

Then the deer cried out:

> O Leopard our noble king,
> Where are you?
> Spotted king of the forest,
> Where are you?
> Even if you are far away
> Come, hurry home:

Baboon, 1978. Felipe Benito Archuleta. Carved and painted cottonwood and pine with glue and sawdust. Smithsonian American Art Museum, Washington, DC.

Viewing the Art: Does this sculpture of a baboon resemble any of the animals in the story? Explain.

> The worst has happened to us
> The worst has happened to us . . .
> The house the animals built
> The cruel dog keeps us from it,
> The common shelter we built
> The cruel dog keeps us from it,
> The worst has happened to us
> The worst has happened to us . . .

The cry of the deer rang out loud and clear. It was carried by the wind. King Leopard heard it on his way back from his journey and began to run toward the village hall.

As he got near, he saw the animals, wet and sheltering under a tree. They were all crying. As he got nearer still, he could see the dog walking up and down inside the hall.

King Leopard was very angry. "Come out of the hall at once," he said to the dog. The dog barked and rushed at him. They began to fight. The dog bit the leopard and tore his skin with his claws. King Leopard was covered with blood. The dog went back to the hall. He stood at the door barking and barking. "Who is next? Who! Who!" he barked.

King Leopard turned to the animals and said: "Let us go in together and drive out the enemy. He is strong, but he is alone. We are many. Together we can drive him out of our house."

But the goat said: "We cannot face him. Look at his strong teeth! He will only tear us to pieces!"

"The goat is right," said the animals. "He is too strong for us."

The tortoise stood up and said: "I am sure we are all sorry about what has happened to the leopard. But he was foolish to talk to the dog the way he did. It is foolish to annoy such a powerful person as the dog. Let us make peace with him. I don't know what you others think. But I think he should have been our king all along. He is strong; he is handsome. Let us go on our knees and salute him."

"Hear! Hear!" said all the animals. "Hail the dog!"

Tears began to roll down the face of the leopard. His heart was heavy. He loved the animals greatly. But they had turned their backs on him. Now he knew they were cowards. So he turned his back on them and went away. Because of his many wounds

CHINUA ACHEBE AND JOHN IROAGANACHI **39**

Aquamanile (Water Jug) *in the Shape of a Leopard,* Benin.
British Museum, London.
Viewing the Art: In what ways does this sculpture remind you
of the leopard in the story?

he was weak and tired. So he lay down after a while
to rest under a tree, far from the village.

The animals saw him go. But they did not care.
They were too busy praising their new king, the
dog. The tortoise carved a new staff for him. The
toad made a new song in his praise:

> The dog is great
> The dog is good
> The dog gives us our daily food.
> We love his head, we love his jaws
> We love his feet and all his claws.

The dog looked round the circle of animals
and asked, "Where is the leopard?"

"We think he has gone away, O King," said
the goat.

"Why? He has no right to go away," said the
dog. "Nobody has a right to leave our village and
its beautiful hall. We must all stay together."

"Indeed," shouted the animals. "We must stay
together! The leopard must return to the village!
Our wise king has spoken! It is good to have a
wise king!"

The dog then called out the names of six
strong animals and said to them: "Go at once
and bring back the leopard. If he should refuse
to follow you, you must drag him along. If we
let him go, others may soon follow his wicked
example until there is no one left in our village.

That would be a very bad thing
indeed. It is my duty as your king
to make sure that we all live
together. The leopard is a wicked
animal. That is why he wants to go
away and live by himself. It is our duty
to stop him. Nobody has a right to go
away from our village and our beautiful
hall."

"Nobody has a right to go away from the
village," sang all the animals as the six messengers went to look for the leopard.

They found him resting under the tree
beyond the village. Although he was wounded
and weak he still looked like a king. So the six
messengers stood at a little distance and spoke to
him.

"Our new king, the dog, has ordered you to
return to the village," they said.

"He says that no one has a right to leave the
village," said the pig.

"Yes, no one has a right to leave our village
and its beautiful hall," said the others.

The leopard looked at them with contempt.
Then he got up slowly. The six animals fell back.
But the leopard did not go toward them. He
turned his back on them and began to go away—
slowly and painfully. One of the animals picked
up a stone and threw it at him. Then all the others immediately picked up stones and began to
throw. As they threw they chanted: "No one has
a right to leave our village! No one has a right to
leave our village!"

Although some of the stones hit the leopard
and hurt him, he did not turn round even once.
He continued walking until he no longer heard
the noise of the animals.

The leopard traveled seven days and seven
nights. Then he came to the house of the
blacksmith. The old man was sitting at his
forge. The leopard said to him: "I want the
strongest teeth you can make from iron. And I
want the most deadly claws you can make from
bronze."

The blacksmith said: "Why do you need such
terrible things?" The leopard told his story. Then
the blacksmith said: "I do not blame you."

The blacksmith worked a whole day on the
teeth, and another full day on the claws. The
leopard was pleased with them. He put them on

and thanked the blacksmith. Then he left and went to the house of Thunder.

The leopard knocked at the door and Thunder roared across the sky.

"I want some of your sound in my voice," said the leopard. "Even a little bit."

"Why do you want my sound in your voice?" asked Thunder. "And why have you got those terrible teeth and claws?"

The leopard told his story. "I do not blame you," said Thunder. He gave the sound to the leopard. "Thank you for the gift," said the leopard. And he began his journey home.

The leopard journeyed for seven days and seven nights and returned to the village of the animals. There he found the animals dancing in a circle round the dog. He stood for a while watching them with contempt and great anger. They were too busy to notice his presence. He made a deep, terrifying roar. At the same time he sprang into the center of the circle. The animals stopped their song. The dog dropped his staff. The leopard seized him and bit and clawed him without mercy. Then he threw him out of the circle.

All the animals *trembled*.

But they were too afraid to run. The leopard turned to them and said:

"You miserable worms. You shameless cowards. I was a kind and gentle king, but you turned against me. From today I shall rule the forest with terror. The life of our village is ended."

"What about our hall?" asked the tortoise with a trembling voice.

"Let everyone take from the hall what he put into it," said the leopard.

The animals began to weep as they had wept long ago in the rain. "Please forgive us, O Leopard," they cried.

"Let everyone take from the hall what he put into it," repeated the leopard. "And hurry up!" he thundered.

So the animals pulled their hall apart. Some carried away the wood, and some took the roof-mats. Others took away doors and windows. The toad brought his talking drum and began to beat it to the leopard and to sing:

Alive or dead the leopard is king.
Beware my friend, don't twist his tail.

But the leopard roared like thunder and the toad dropped his drum and the animals scattered in the forest.

The dog had already run a long way when the leopard roared. Now he ran faster and faster. His body was covered with blood, and he was very, very weak. He wanted to stop and rest a little. But the fear of the leopard was greater than his weakness. So he staggered and fell and got up and staggered on and on and on. . . .

After many days the dog came to the house of the hunter.

"Please protect me from the leopard," he cried.

"What will you do for me in return?" asked the hunter.

"I will be your slave," said the dog. "Any day you are hungry for meat I shall show you the way to the forest. There we can hunt together and kill my fellow animals."

"All right, come in," said the hunter.

Today the animals are no longer friends, but enemies. The strong among them attack and kill the weak. The leopard, full of anger, eats up anyone he can lay his hands on. The hunter, led by the dog, goes to the forest from time to time and shoots any animals he can find. Perhaps the animals will make peace among themselves someday and live together again. Then they can keep away the hunter who is their common enemy. ◁

Quickwrite

The animal leaders in Achebe's myth use violence to seize and wield power. What lessons do you think Achebe suggests through his depiction of the animals and their encounters with the hunter? Write a paragraph explaining your views.

Prayer to the Pacific

Leslie Marmon Silko

Our Life on His Back, 1993. Julie Lankford Olds. Oil on canvas, 12 x 16 in. Minnetrista Cultural Center & Oakhurst Gardens, Muncie, IN.

BEFORE YOU READ

Building Background

Leslie Marmon Silko grew up hearing traditional Native American stories and myths at the Laguna Pueblo Reservation near Albuquerque, New Mexico. Silko's writing emphasizes the vital function of the audience in the oral tradition as well as the importance of nature and ritual in Pueblo culture. Silko writes, "Storytelling always includes the audience and the listeners, and, in fact, a great deal of the story is believed to be inside the listener, and the storyteller's role is to draw the story out of the listeners."

Silko's poem uses myth to draw a comparison between the west-to-east movement of rain clouds and the migration of early peoples to America. Historians have theorized that tens of thousands of years ago these migrants arrived in America from Asia. They most likely traveled across a land bridge where the Bering Strait now separates Asia and North America.

Literature Online **Author Search** For more about Leslie Marmon Silko, go to www.glencoe.com.

I traveled to the ocean
          distant
                from my southwest land of sandrock
            to the moving blue water
5   Big as the myth of origin.

    Pale
pale water in the yellow-white light of
              sun   floating west
                  to China
10   where ocean herself was born.
Clouds that blow across the sand are wet.

Squat in the wet sand and speak to the Ocean:
        I return to you   turquoise   the red coral you sent us,
           sister spirit of Earth.
15 Four round stones in my pocket   I carry back the ocean
           to suck and to taste.

Thirty thousand years ago
          Indians came riding across the ocean
          carried by giant sea turtles.
20 Waves were high that day
        great sea turtles waded   slowly out
                  from the gray sundown sea.
Grandfather Turtle rolled in the sand   four times
        and disappeared
25   swimming into the sun.

And so   from that time
      immemorial,[1]
          as the old people say,
rain clouds drift from the west
30   gift from the ocean.

Green leaves in the wind
Wet earth on my feet
      swallowing raindrops
          clear from China.

---

1. *Immemorial* means "extending back beyond memory or record."

Discussion Starter

How does the speaker's explanation of the origin of rain in "Prayer to the Pacific" illustrate the Native American attitude toward nature? Discuss this question in your group. Use specific details from the poem to support your opinions. Then share your conclusions with the class.

The Summer of Black Widows

Sherman Alexie

BEFORE YOU READ

Building Background

Poetry slam champion Sherman Alexie has attracted attention for the variety of his literary skills. Born in 1966, Alexie grew up on the Spokane Indian Reservation in Washington State. He is a three-time winner of the World Heavyweight Championship Poetry Bout and wrote the screenplay for *Smoke Signals,* the first movie entirely produced, directed, and acted by Native Americans. Alexie adapted the screenplay from a short story from his collection *The Lone Ranger and Tonto Fistfight in Heaven.* The film won both the Audience Award and the Filmmakers Trophy at the 1998 Sundance Film Festival. He compared his role in making the film to that of African American filmmaker Spike Lee. "Spike didn't necessarily get films made as much as he inspired filmmakers to believe in themselves.

That's what's going to happen here. These 13-year-old Indian kids who've been going crazy with their camcorders will finally see the possibilities."

Alexie has been recognized for his ability to infuse his writing about the difficulties of life on Indian reservations with humorous insights. Of his writing, he once said, "I write about the kind of Indian I am: kind of mixed up, kind of odd, not traditional. I'm a rez kid who's gone urban." At the same time, Alexie's work draws upon many traditional Native American themes, such as the cultural significance of storytelling.

Literature Online **Author Search** For more about Sherman Alexie, go to www.glencoe.com.

The spiders appeared suddenly
after that summer rainstorm.

Some people still insist the spiders fell with the rain
while others believe the spiders grew from the damp soil like weeds
    with eight thin roots.

5   The elders knew the spiders
carried stories in their stomachs.

We tucked our pants into our boots when we walked through fields
    of fallow[1] stories.
An Indian girl opened the closet door and a story fell into her hair.
We lived in the shadow of a story trapped in the ceiling lamp.
10 The husk of a story museumed on the windowsill.
Before sleep, we shook our blankets and stories fell to the floor.
A story floated in a glass of water left on the kitchen table.
We opened doors slowly and listened for stories.
The stories rose on hind legs and offered their red bellies to the
    most beautiful Indians.
15 Stories in our cereal boxes.
Stories in our firewood.
Stories in the pockets of our coats.
We captured stories and offered them to the ants, who carried the
    stories back to their queen.
A dozen stories per acre.
20 We poisoned the stories and gathered their remains with broom
    and pan.

The spiders disappeared suddenly
after that summer lightning storm.
Some people still insist the spiders were burned to ash
while others believe the spiders climbed the lightning bolts and
    became a new constellation.

25 The elders knew the spiders
had left behind bundles of stories.

Up in the corners of our old houses
we still find those small, white bundles
and nothing, neither fire
30 not water, neither rock nor wind,
can bring them down.

---

1. *Fallow* means "unseeded, idle, or burned-out."

Quickwrite

In this poem, the speaker uses a metaphor that compares stories with spider webs. What does the speaker's use of this metaphor suggest about the nature of stories? How does the attitude of the elders toward stories differ from the attitude of the majority of the people in the poem? Write a paragraph in which you address these questions.

Wrap-Up: Comparing Literature *Across Time and Place*

- ### The Sky Tree
  Huron—Eastern
  Woodland

- ### How the Leopard Got His Claws
  Chinua Achebe and
  John Iroaganachi

- ### Prayer to the Pacific
  Leslie Marmon
  Silko

- ### The Summer of Black Widows
  Sherman Alexie

COMPARING THE `Big Idea` The Sacred Earth and the Power of Storytelling

Writing Read the following quotations from the selections. Write a brief essay in which you compare two or more of the quotations. Base your comparison on the way the quotations exemplify the power of storytelling and the tradition of the creation myth in oral cultures. Cite evidence from the selections to support your main ideas.

> "My husband," she said, "when I cut the tree it split in half and then fell through a great hole. Without the tree, there can be no life. I must follow it."
>
> —Huron, "The Sky Tree"

> "Perhaps the animals will make peace among themselves someday and live together again. Then they can keep away the hunter who is their common enemy."
>
> —Chinua Achebe and John Iroaganachi "How the Leopard Got His Claws"

> "And so   from that time
>   immemorial,
>   as the old people say,
> rain clouds drift from the west
>   gift from the ocean."
>
> —Leslie Marmon Silko, "Prayer to the Pacific"

> "The elders knew the spiders carried stories in their stomachs."
>
> —Sherman Alexie "The Summer of Black Widows"

COMPARING Mythic Elements

Group Activity Personification, supernatural occurrences, and stories about the origin of the universe are features of myths in a variety of cultures. The Huron myth, Achebe's myth, Silko's poem, and Alexie's poem use these elements for a variety of purposes. In a small group, discuss the following questions. Cite evidence from the selections to support your points.

1. How does each writer describe different aspects of the origin of the universe?
2. What is the importance of the writer's cultural background in each of these selections?
3. How does the personification of animals contribute to each of the selections?
4. What insights about life offered by the writer do you find most compelling?

COMPARING Cultures

Speaking and Listening Before the writers in various cultures recorded their stories in books, storytellers recounted tales orally. Research one or more of the cultures represented by the selections: Huron (also called Wyandot), Nigerian, Pueblo, or Spokane. As you investigate, compare and contrast the belief systems of these cultures. Then compose a mythic story that describes the origin of some aspect of life. Tell your story to the class in the oral tradition of one of the cultures you have investigated.

INDIANA ACADEMIC STANDARDS (page 46)
11.3.2 Analyze the way in which the theme...represents a view...on life, using textual evidence to support the claim.

11.3.5 Analyze...works...that reflect or shed light on... philosophical [and] religious...ideas of their time.

from *The Iroquois Constitution*

MEET DEKANAWIDA

When Iroquois tribes in present-day New York State were torn apart by fighting, one man stepped in to instill peace. Dekanawida (dək uhn ä wē´ dä) believed from an early age that he was predestined to unite the Iroquois nation. "It is my business to stop the shedding of blood among human beings," he said.

Traditional accounts of his life vary. He was thought to be a Huron born around 1550 near what is now Kingston, Ontario. In one account, Dekanawida was the son of a virgin mother who, in the months leading up to his birth, observed omens that told Dekanawida would be a source of evil and destruction for the Huron people. To save her tribe, Dekanawida's mother tried three times to drown her infant son in an icy river, but to her disbelief, woke up each of the following mornings with the child resting softly in her arms. His mother interpreted this as a sign that he was fated to live and began to rear the boy.

> *"The Word I bring is that all peoples shall love one another and live together in peace."*
>
> —Dekanawida

A Quest for Peace As a young man, Dekanawida trekked southward on a spiritual quest to perform his destined work. He forged a strong friendship with Hiawatha, an Onandaga tribal leader. Both men agreed that continual warring was making the tribes vulnerable to outside attack. Legend has it that Dekanawida was the laconic mastermind of the Iroquois Constitution. Because Dekanawida may have had a speech impediment, Hiawatha, a charismatic leader and great orator, was his spokesman and interlocutor. Dekanawida was highly esteemed by the Iroquois people. In fact, he was the first "pine tree chief," or chief chosen on the basis of merit rather than by heredity.

In 1570, the two leaders established an alliance among the five nations of the Iroquois—the Seneca, Cayuga, Oneida, Onondaga, and Mohawk. Dekanawida created the alliance's constitution, which established rules for decision making and debate. Around 1600, after Dekanawida had completed the task of establishing the confederacy, he mysteriously vanished. But thanks to the peaceful government he had helped create, the confederacy was able to resist outside pressures for almost two hundred years.

Dekanawida was born around 1550 and vanished around 1600.

Literature Online **Author Search** For more about Dekanawida, go to www.glencoe.com.

The Five Iroquois Tribes and the Hurons

CANADA

Huron

Lake Ontario

Seneca
Cayuga
Onondaga
Oneida
Mohawk

UNITED STATES

Connecting to the Text

Think of times when you have worked with others to make a decision or to achieve a common goal. In the Iroquois Constitution, Dekanawida ensures peaceful decision making by the five nations. As you read, think about the following questions:

- How might the language someone uses help or hinder a common decision?
- How have groups that you have been involved in finally reached a consensus?

Building Background

After the Iroquois Confederacy was founded around 1570, there was peace, and the tribes prospered. Together the five tribes prevented French, English, and Dutch colonists from annexing their lands. The Revolutionary War, however, caused deep rifts between the tribes of the Iroquois Confederacy, resulting in its end. But its legacy was a lasting one. Dekanawida's system was so effective that Benjamin Franklin urged fellow colonists to view it as a model.

Setting Purposes for Reading

Big Idea The Power of Storytelling

Notice the ways in which the Iroquois Constitution reflects the Native Americans' use of language to describe their reverence for the natural world.

Literary Element Author's Purpose

The **author's purpose** is the author's intent in creating a work. As you read the constitution, carefully examine its provisions to see how they support Dekanawida's goals.

- See Literary Terms Handbook, p. R2.

Literature Online **Interactive Literary Elements Handbook** To review or learn more about the literary elements, go to www.glencoe.com.

Reading Strategy Drawing Conclusions About Culture

When you **draw a conclusion,** you use a number of pieces of information to make a general statement about people, places, events, or ideas. As you read, draw conclusions about Iroquois society by looking at the values expressed in the constitution.

Reading Tip: Conclusions Diagram Use a diagram to record details from the selection as well as your conclusions about the Iroquois.

Detail	Detail	Detail
The tribes' meeting place is called the Tree of the Great Peace.	Any man or nation that obeys the laws is welcome to shelter beneath the tree.	

The Iroquois want their government to be peaceful.

Conclusion

Vocabulary

disposition (dis´ pə zish´ən) *n.* one's general way of thinking or feeling; p. 49 *Julia had a cheerful disposition.*

convene (kən vēn´) *v.* to come together; assemble; p. 50 *Congress will convene to hear the president's speech tonight.*

posterity (pos ter´ ə tē) *n.* generations of the future; all of one's descendants; p. 50 *Mr. Norris requires students to create a record of their thoughts for posterity.*

temper (tem´ pər) *v.* to modify or moderate; soften; p. 50 *Alvaro tempers his anger by counting to ten.*

deliberation (di lib´ ə rā´ shən) *n.* careful consideration; p. 51 *After long deliberation, the city council voted to build a new library.*

INDIANA ACADEMIC STANDARDS (pages 48–52)
11.2 Develop strategies such as [analyzing]...purpose...
11.5.9 Write...a literary analysis...

11.2.4 Make reasonable assertions about an author's arguments by using elements of the text...

from The Iroquois Constitution

Dekanawida

The Tree of the Great Peace

I am Dekanawida and with the Five Nations' Confederate Lords I plant the Tree of the Great Peace. I plant it in your territory, Adodarho,[1] and the Onondaga Nation, in the territory of you who are Firekeepers.[2]

I name the tree the Tree of the Great Long Leaves. Under the shade of this Tree of the Great Peace we spread the soft white feathery down of the globe thistle[3] as seats for you, Adodarho, and your cousin Lords.

We place you upon those seats, spread soft with the feathery down of the globe thistle, there beneath the shade of the spreading branches of the Tree of Peace. There shall you sit and watch the Council Fire of the Confederacy of the Five Nations, and all the affairs of the Five Nations shall be transacted at this place.

Roots have spread out from the Tree of the Great Peace, one to the north, one to the east, one to the south, and one to the west. The name of these roots is the Great White Roots and their nature is Peace and Strength.

If any man or any nation outside the Five Nations shall obey the laws of the Great Peace and make known their **disposition** to the Lords of the Confederacy, they may trace the Roots to the Tree and if their minds are clean and they are obedient and promise to obey the wishes of the Confederate Council, they shall be welcomed to take shelter beneath the Tree of the Long Leaves.

We place at the top of the Tree of the Long Leaves an Eagle who is able to see afar. If he sees in the distance any evil approaching or any danger threatening, he will at once warn the people of the Confederacy.

The Care of the Fire

The Smoke of the Confederate Council Fire shall ever ascend and pierce the sky so that other nations who may be allies may see the Council Fire of the Great Peace.

You, Adodarho, and your thirteen cousin Lords shall faithfully keep the space about the Council Fire clean and you shall allow neither dust nor dirt to accumulate. I lay a Long Wing before you as a broom. As a weapon against a crawling creature I lay a staff with you so that you may thrust it away from the Council Fire.

The Laws of the Council

Whenever the Confederate Lords shall assemble for the purpose of holding a council, the Onondaga Lords shall open it by expressing their gratitude to their cousin Lords and greeting them, and they shall make an address and offer thanks to the earth where men dwell, to the

---

1. *Adodarho* was an Onondaga chief who enjoyed a position of honor in the Confederate Council. His name became an honorific, or traditional title, for Iroquois leaders.
2. *Firekeepers* were important chiefs who oversaw the Council Fire, which symbolized the confederacy.
3. *Globe thistle* is a plant that has prickly leaves and blue flowers. Like a dandelion, the flower becomes a mass of white, silky fuzz, or down, when it goes to seed.

Literary Element Author's Purpose *Based on this statement, what do you think is Dekanawida's purpose in writing this piece?*

Vocabulary

disposition (dis′ pə zish′ ən) *n.* one's general way of thinking or feeling

Reading Strategy Drawing Conclusions About Culture *What can you conclude about the Iroquois attitude toward strangers or outsiders?*

Big Idea The Power of Storytelling *How does the opening of a council meeting reflect the importance of storytelling in Native American culture?*

streams of water, the pools, the springs and the lakes, to the maize[4] and the fruits, to the medicinal herbs and trees, to the forest trees for their usefulness, to the animals that serve as food and give their pelts for clothing, to the great winds and the lesser winds, to the Thunderers, to the Sun, the mighty warrior, to the moon, to the messengers of the Creator who reveal his wishes and to the Great Creator who dwells in the heavens above, who gives all the things useful to men, and who is the source and the ruler of health and life.

All the business of the Five Nations' Confederate Council shall be conducted by the two combined bodies of Confederate Lords. First the question shall be passed upon by the Mohawk and Seneca Lords; then it shall be discussed and passed by the Oneida and Cayuga Lords. Their decisions shall then be referred to the Onondaga Lords (Firekeepers) for final judgment.

When the Council of the Five Nation Lords shall convene, they shall appoint a speaker for the day. He shall be a Lord of either the Mohawk, Onondaga, or Seneca Nation.

No individual or foreign nation interested in a case, question, or proposition shall have any voice in the Confederate Council except to answer a question put to him or them by the speaker for the Lords.

If the conditions which shall arise at any future time call for an addition to or change of this law, the case shall be carefully considered, and if a new beam seems necessary or beneficial, the proposed change shall be voted upon and, if adopted, it shall be called, "Added to the Rafters."[5]

---

4. *Maize* is corn.
5. The Iroquois leaders thought of their confederacy of five nations as a longhouse, a communal Iroquois dwelling with an east door, a west door, and a central fire. The terms *beam* and *Added to the Rafters* continue this comparison.

The Clans

Among the Five Nations and their posterity there shall be the following original clans: Great Name Bearer, Ancient Name Bearer, Great Bear, Ancient Bear, Turtle, Painted Turtle, Standing Rock, Large Plover, Little Plover, Deer, Pigeon Hawk, Eel, Ball, Opposite-Side-of-the-Hand, and Wild Potatoes. These clans, distributed through their respective Nations, shall be the sole owners and holders of the soil of the country, and in them is it vested as a birthright.

People of the Five Nations [who are] members of a certain clan shall recognize every other member of that clan, irrespective of the Nation, as relatives.

The lineal descent of the people of the Five Nations shall run in the female line. Women shall be considered the progenitors[6] of the Nation. They shall own the land and the soil. Men and women shall follow the status of the mother.

The Leaders

The Lords of the Confederacy of the Five Nations shall be mentors[7] of the people for all time. The thickness of their skin shall be seven spans—which is to say that they shall be proof against anger, offensive actions, and criticism. Their hearts shall be full of peace and good will and their minds filled with a yearning for the welfare of the people of the Confederacy. With endless patience they shall carry out their duty, and their firmness shall be tempered with a tenderness for their people. Neither anger nor fury shall find

---

6. *Progenitors* are direct ancestors or originators of an ancestral line.
7. *Mentors* are wise and trusted advisers.

Reading Strategy Drawing Conclusions About Culture *What shift in traditional attitudes toward the land is shown here and what conclusion might you draw from it?*

lodgment in their minds, and all their words and actions shall be marked by calm **deliberation**.

The Festivals

The rites and festivals of each Nation shall remain undisturbed and shall continue as before because they were given by the people of old times as useful and necessary for the good of men.

The recognized festivals of Thanksgiving shall be the Midwinter Thanksgiving, the Maple or Sugar Making Thanksgiving, the Raspberry Thanksgiving, the Strawberry Thanksgiving, the Corn Planting Thanksgiving, the Corn Hoeing Thanksgiving, the Little Festival of Green Corn, the Great Festival of Ripe Corn, and the complete Thanksgiving for the Harvest.

Literary Element   Author's Purpose *How does Dekanawida's lengthy description of the traits of the Lords of the Confederacy reinforce his purpose for writing the constitution?*

Vocabulary

deliberation (di lib′ ə rā′ shən) *n.* careful consideration

The Symbols

A large bunch of shell strings, in the making of which the Five Nations' Confederate Lords have equally contributed, shall symbolize the completeness of the union and certify the pledge of the Nations represented by the Confederate Lords of the Mohawk, the Oneida, the Onondaga, the Cayuga, and the Seneca, that all are united and formed into one body or union called the Union of the Great Law, which they have established.

Five arrows shall be bound together very strong, and each arrow shall represent one nation. As the five arrows are strongly bound, this shall symbolize the complete union of the nations. Thus are the Five Nations united completely and enfolded together, united into one head, one body, and one mind. Therefore they shall labor, legislate, and council together for the interest of future generations. ∾

RESPONDING AND THINKING CRITICALLY

Respond

1. What is your opinion of Dekanawida's abilities as a peacemaker? Explain.

Recall and Interpret

2. (a)What does Dekanawida say is the nature of the roots of the Tree of the Great Peace? (b)What is placed at the top of the tree? Explain what this suggests about the purpose behind the Iroquois Confederacy's formation.

3. (a)Describe the rules Dekanawida includes about making changes to the law. (b)Given these rules, how would you characterize Dekanawida's skills as a planner?

4. Explain the symbols of the confederacy described on page 51. In what way, do you think, does the design of the symbols reflect Dekanawida's vision for the confederacy?

Analyze and Evaluate

5. (a)How does the Iroquois Constitution divide authority among the five nations? (b)What benefits did the Iroquois stand to gain by structuring decision making this way?

6. (a)Judging by the provision about the leaders, what were important leadership qualities in the confederacy? (b)Do you think Dekanawida was right to stress these qualities? Explain.

Connect

7. **Big Idea** The Power of Storytelling (a)Native American life was organized around the cycles of nature. How is this fact reflected in the Iroquois Constitution? (b)Explain in what other ways the constitution displays the Iroquois reverence for nature. Then tell how you think such a reverence strengthened the Iroquois.

LITERARY ANALYSIS

Literary Element Author's Purpose

The **author's purpose** may be to entertain, to inform, to explain, to persuade, or to describe. After forming your initial idea of the author's purpose, double-check your notion against the information in the piece.

1. What is Dekanawida's basic purpose in creating the Iroquois Constitution?

2. What different comparisons does he introduce to convey his ideas of peace and unity?

Writing About Literature

Analyze Cultural Context The Iroquois Constitution describes rituals associated with the functioning of the Confederate Council. What was the point of these rituals? What do they indicate about the values of Iroquois society? In two paragraphs, analyze and evaluate the rituals.

Literature Online **Web Activities** For eFlashcards, Selection Quick Checks, and other Web activities, go to www.glencoe.com.

READING AND VOCABULARY

Reading Strategy Drawing Conclusions

To **draw conclusions** about the Iroquois, think about how the details tell you something about Iroquois society. Then make a general statement expressing your insight. Review the passage on page 50 that describes how women are to be considered and what women shall own. What conclusions do you draw about the importance of women in Iroquois society?

Vocabulary Practice

Practice with Analogies Choose the word pair that best completes the analogy.

1. convene : gather ::
   a. soar : fall
   b. build : erect
   c. save : spend

2. posterity : ancestors ::
   a. lair : den
   b. lane : path
   c. kindness : cruelty

Part 2

LIFE IN THE NEW WORLD

Self-portrait, c. 1680. Thomas Smith. Oil on canvas, 24³/₄ x 23³/₄ in. Worcester Art Museum, Worcester, MA.

"For we must consider that we shall be as a city upon a hill. The eyes of all people are upon us."

—John Winthrop, *A Model of Christian Charity*

from *La Relación*

MEET ÁLVAR NÚÑEZ CABEZA DE VACA

Few adventurers have faced greater odds than the Spanish explorer Álvar Núñez Cabeza de Vaca (äl′ vär noo′ nyez kä bä′ zä dä bä′ kä). Stranded and defenseless in the vast wilderness of the New World, he had only a slim chance of surviving. His tale of the journey, *La Relación*, was the first European account of the interior of what is now the United States.

In 1527, Cabeza de Vaca left Spain as a career soldier on an expedition to occupy North America and discover riches for the king. The expedition, which landed in 1528 at what is today Tampa Bay, Florida, was a disaster. Boat accidents, faulty judgment, and disease led to the deaths of many of the 600 men. The survivors developed a fruitful relationship with the Apalachee tribe, but the situation soured when the Spaniards took the tribe's leader hostage. The Spaniards ended up cowering in a coastal swamp, eating horseflesh to survive. Finally, led by Cabeza de Vaca, the explorers constructed basic rafts from horsehide and trees and set sail, praying they could reach Cuba. Wracked by starvation and thirst, the 80 men who managed to cling to the rafts were buffeted by a hurricane and deposited near present-day Galveston, Texas, on the Gulf of Mexico.

By the following spring, there were 15 men alive. Eventually, Cabeza de Vaca and three others were the only survivors. Cabeza de Vaca lived among the nomadic Native Americans in east Texas—the Karankawa, the Mariames, the Yguazes—for four years, adapting to their ways of life and morphing from conquistador to trader and physician in order to survive. The Native Americans were not as lucky. Many perished as a result of a stomach virus that the Spaniards unwittingly carried with them.

Trailblazer Cabeza de Vaca then traveled south and west, hoping to find a Spanish outpost. He was the first European to trek through present-day Texas. He may have passed through Arizona and New Mexico, but details about his precise route are scarce. He continued west through the Sierra Madre and the Sonoran Desert in northern Mexico, may have reached the Pacific Ocean, and then turned south, finally running into a band of Spanish slave traders in the present-day Mexican state of Sinaloa on Mexico's west coast. His countrymen were flabbergasted when Cabeza de Vaca stood before them naked and filthy, with a number of Native Americans at his side. Eight years had passed since he had landed in Florida. During that time, he had traveled approximately 2,500 miles, mostly on foot.

During his travels, Cabeza de Vaca proved to be a masterful ethnologist. He lived among Native Americans before they had been influenced by European culture. His writings detail the unique customs of many tribes. Unlike other early explorers, he called for tolerance and justice for Native Americans.

Álvar Núñez Cabeza de Vaca was born around 1490 and died around 1556.

> "We were entering a land for which we had no description, without knowing what kind of place it was, nor by what people it was inhabited, nor in which part of it we were."
>
> —Álvar Núñez Cabeza de Vaca
> from *La Relación*

Literature Online **Author Search** For more about Álvar Núñez Cabeza de Vaca, go to www.glencoe.com.

Adaptation The expedition landed in November.

Connecting to the Narrative

How does Cabeza de Vaca react when his group washes up on a foreign shore? In his narrative, Cabeza de Vaca professes his fear of the Native Americans because he knows nothing about them. As you read, think about the following questions:

- What motivates Cabeza de Vaca to try to set sail once the Spaniards have landed?
- As the Native Americans lead Cabeza de Vaca and his group to their lodges, the Spaniards do not know if they are going to be saved or sacrificed. How do you think you would react if you were in this situation?

Building Background

In the early 1500s, Spanish conquistadores began exploring and invading Central and South America, searching for gold and other riches. In 1520, Hernán Cortés defeated the Aztecs and sacked Tenochtitlán, the site of present-day Mexico City. In 1534, Francisco Pizarro conquered the Incas in Peru. The indigenous people were baffled and frightened by the sudden appearance of the Spanish. The Spanish had weapons that ensured victory in war: horses, war dogs, guns, cannons, as well as their greatest weapon, the smallpox virus. As a result of Spanish occupation, indigenous societies and cultures were in shambles. Indigenous peoples and the Spanish began to intermarry, creating a mixed race.

Setting Purposes for Reading

Big Idea Life in the New World

As you read, think about what the narrative implies about the Spaniards' view of their own culture in comparison with that of the indigenous people they encountered in the New World.

Literary Element Point of View

Point of view is the relationship of the narrator to the story. In a narrative with a first-person point of view, the narrator is a character in the story and uses the words *I* and *me*. As you read, be aware of how Cabeza de Vaca's first-person point of view affects his description of people and events.

- See Literary Terms Handbook, p. R14.

Reading Strategy Recognizing Bias

Bias refers to an author's inclination toward a particular opinion or position. Look for examples of the author's bias in his descriptions of himself, his fellow explorers, and the Native Americans he encounters.

Reading Tip: Taking Notes Use a chart to record instances of bias and what they tell about Cabeza de Vaca.

Quote	Bias
p. 58 "Crude and untutored people, who were like brutes"	Cabeza de Vaca assumes that the indigenous people are unintelligent and unschooled before he knows anything about their culture and way of life.

Vocabulary

ration (rash′ən) *n.* fixed portion or share; p. 56 *The campers ate their entire day's ration and were still hungry.*

rouse (rouz) *v.* to awaken from sleep; p. 56 *They had gone to bed late, and it was difficult to rouse them.*

revive (ri vīv′) *v.* to give new strength and vitality, or bring back to consciousness; p. 56 *The lifeguard was able to revive the unconscious swimmer.*

embark (em bärk′) *v.* to set out on a venture; p. 57 *The hunting party mounted their horses and prepared to embark.*

Literature Online **Interactive Literary Elements Handbook** To review or learn more about the literary elements, go to www.glencoe.com.

INDIANA ACADEMIC STANDARDS (pages 55–59)
11.2.5 Analyze an author's implicit and explicit assumptions and beliefs about a subject.

11.3.8 Analyze...credibility...
11.5.9 Write...an analytical essay...

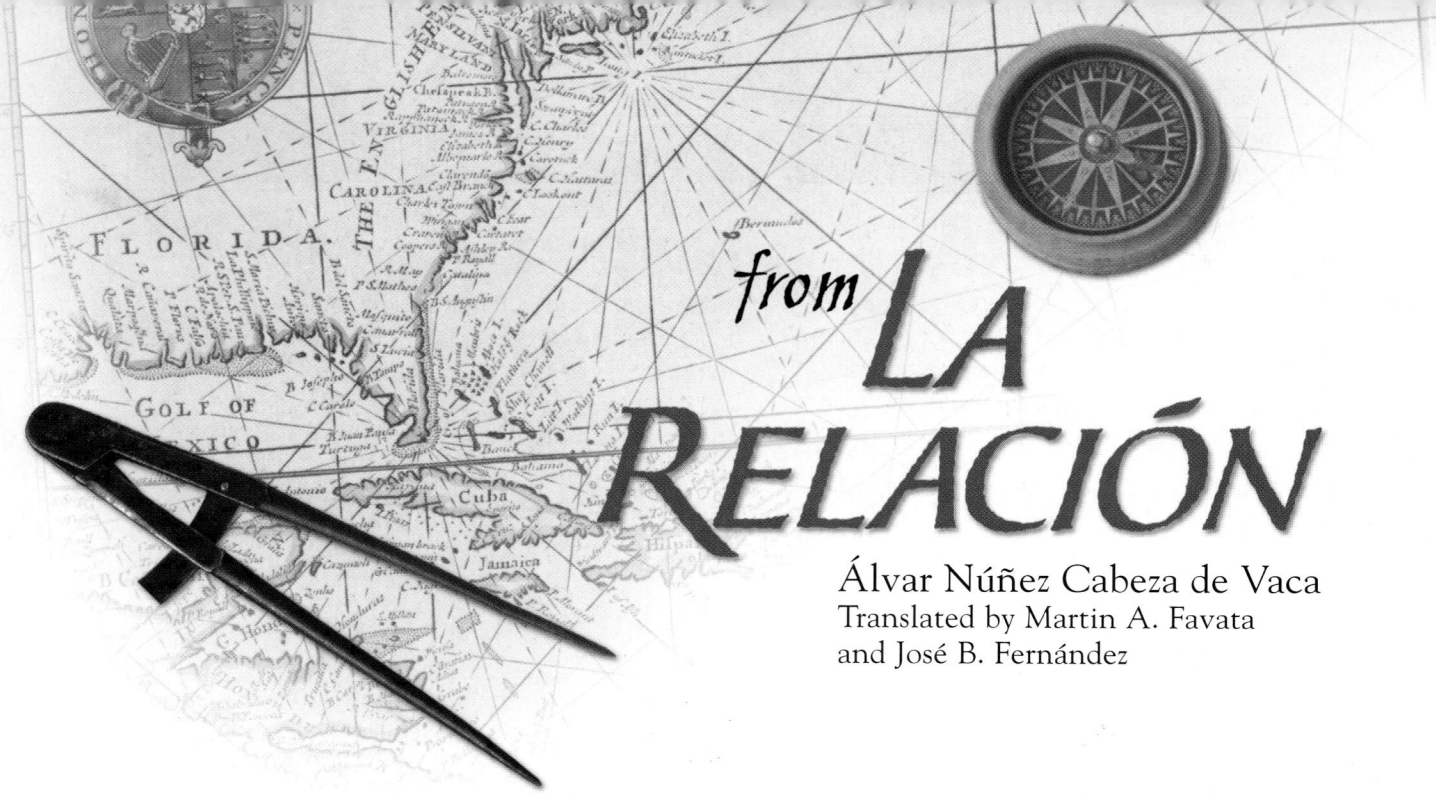

from LA RELACIÓN

Álvar Núñez Cabeza de Vaca
Translated by Martin A. Favata
and José B. Fernández

We sailed in this manner together for four days, eating a daily **ration** of half a handful of raw corn. After four days a storm came up and caused the other boat to be lost. We did not sink because of God's great mercy. The weather was rough, very cold, and wintery. We had been suffering from hunger for many days and had been pounded so much by the sea that the following day many men began to faint. By nightfall all the men in my boat had passed out, one on top of another, so near death that few of them were conscious and fewer than five were still upright. During the night only the sailing master and I were left to sail the boat. Two hours after nightfall he told me I should take over because he was in such a condition that he thought he would die that very night; so I took the tiller. In the middle of the night, I went to see if the sailing master had died, but he told me that he was better and that he would steer until daybreak. At that time I certainly would have rather died than see so many people before me in that condition. After the sailing master

took over the boat, I tried to rest some but could not, and sleep was the furthest thing from my mind.

Near dawn I thought I heard the roar of the breakers[1] near shore, which was very loud because the coast was low. Surprised by this, I **roused** the sailing master, who said he thought we were near land. We took a sounding and found that the water was seven fathoms[2] deep. He thought that we should stay out until dawn. So I took an oar and rowed along the coast, which was a league[3] distant. Then we set our stern[4] to sea.

Near land a great wave took us and cast the boat out of the water as far as a horseshoe can be tossed. The boat ran aground with such force that it **revived** the men on it who were almost dead. When they saw they were near land they pushed themselves overboard and crawled on their hands and knees. When they got to the beach, we lit a

1. *Breakers* are waves that foam as they break on rocks or a shoreline.
2. A *fathom* is a linear measure equal to six feet, used mainly in measuring the depth of water.
3. A *league* is a measure of distance equal to some three miles.
4. The *stern* is the rear part of a boat or ship.

Literary Element Point of View *How might another person on the boat have described this scene?*

Vocabulary

ration (rash´ ən) *n.* fixed portion or share

Vocabulary

rouse (rouz) *v.* to awaken from sleep
revive (ri vīv´) *v.* to give new strength and vitality, or bring back to consciousness

fire by some rocks and toasted some of the corn we had and found rain water. With the warmth of the fire, the men revived and began to regain some of their strength. We arrived at this place on the sixth of November.

Once our people had eaten, I sent Lope de Oviedo, who was stronger and fitter than the rest of us, to climb one of the trees nearby to sight the land and find out something about it. He did this and saw that we were on an island, and that the land appeared to have been trampled by livestock. He thought for this reason that it must be a country of Christians, and told us so. I told him to look again very carefully to see if there were any paths that could be followed, but not to go too far because of possible danger. He found a path and followed it for half a league and found some unoccupied Indian huts, for the Indians had gone into the fields. He took a pot from one of them, a small dog and some mullet[5] and started back.

We thought he was taking a long time to return, so I sent two other Christians to look for him and find out what had happened to him. They found him near there, pursued by three Indians with bows and arrows. They were calling out to him and he was trying to speak to them through sign language. He got to where we were and the Indians stayed back a bit seated on the same shore. Half an hour later another one hundred Indian bowmen appeared. We were so scared that they seemed to us to be giants, whether they were or not. They stopped near us, where the first three were. We could not even think of defending ourselves, since there were scarcely six men who could even get up from the ground. The Inspector and I went towards them and called them, and they approached us. As best we could we tried to reassure them and ourselves, and gave them beads and little bells. Each of them gave me an arrow, which is a sign of friendship. In sign language they told us that they would return in the morning and bring us food, since they did not have any at the time.

The following day at sunrise, at the time the Indians had indicated, they came to us as promised, bringing us much fish, some roots which they eat, the size of walnuts, some larger or smaller. Most of these are pulled with great difficulty from under the water. In the evening they returned to bring us more fish and the same kind of roots. They had their women and children come to see us and they considered themselves rich with little bells and beads that we gave them. The following days they returned to visit with the same things as before.

Seeing that we were provisioned with fish, roots, water, and the other things we requested, we agreed to **embark** on our voyage once again. We dug up the boat from the sand. We had to strip naked and struggle mightily to launch it, because we were so weak that lesser tasks would have been enough to exhaust us. Once we were out from the shore the distance of two crossbow shots, a wave struck us quite a blow and got us all wet. Since we were naked and it was very cold, we let go of the oars. Another strong wave caused the boat to capsize. The Inspector and two other men held on to it to survive, but quite the opposite occurred because the boat pulled them under and they drowned. Since the surf was very rough, the sea wrapped all the men in its waves, except the three that had been pulled under by the boat, and cast them on the shore of the same island. Those of us who survived were as naked as the day we were born and had lost everything we had. Although the few things we had were of little value, they meant a lot to us.

It was November then and the weather was very cold. We were in such a state that our bones could easily be counted and we looked like the picture of death. I can say for myself that I had not eaten anything but parched corn since the previous May, and sometimes I had to eat it raw. Although the horses were slaughtered while we were building the boats, I was never able to eat them, and I had eaten fish fewer than ten times. This is but a brief comment, since anyone can

---

5. A *mullet* is a type of fish.

Big Idea Life in the New World *How does Lope de Oviedo's assumption reflect the Spaniards' expectations of the New World?*

Literary Element Point of View *How does Cabeza de Vaca use his own experience to illustrate the state of his crew?*

Vocabulary

embark (em bärk′) *v.* to set out on a venture

imagine what shape we were in. On top of all this, the north wind began to blow, and so we were closer to death than to life. It pleased our Lord to let us find some embers among the coals of the fire we had made, and we made large fires. In this way we asked our Lord's mercy and the forgiveness of our sins, shedding many tears, with each man pitying not only himself but all the others who were in the same condition.

At sunset the Indians, thinking that we had not gone, looked for us again and brought us food. When they saw us in such a different state of attire and looking so strange, they were so frightened that they drew back.

Viewing the Art: How would you describe the mood of Cabeza de Vaca and the three other surviving members of his crew in this depiction?

I went out to them and called them and they returned very frightened. I let them know through sign language that one of our boats had sunk and that three of our men had drowned. And there before their very eyes they saw two of the dead men, and those of us who were alive seemed as if we would soon join them.

The Indians, seeing the disaster that had come upon us and brought so much misfortune and misery, sat down with us. They felt such great pain and pity at seeing us in such a state that they all began to cry so loudly and sincerely that they could be heard from afar. This went on for more than half an hour. In fact, seeing that these crude and untutored people, who were like brutes, grieved so much for us, caused me and the others in my company to suffer more and think more about our misfortune. When their crying ceased, I told the Christians that, if they agreed, I would ask those Indians to take us to their lodges. And some who had been in New Spain[6] responded that we should not even think about it, because if they took us to their lodges they would sacrifice us to their idols.[7] But seeing that we had no other recourse and that any other action would certainly bring us closer to death, I did not pay attention to what they

were saying and I asked the Indians to take us to their lodges. They indicated that they would be very pleased to do this. They asked us to wait a bit and then they would do what we wanted. Then thirty of them loaded themselves with firewood and went to their lodges, which were far from there. We stayed with the others until nearly nightfall, when they held on to us and took us hastily to their lodges. Since it was so cold and they feared that someone might faint or die on the way, they had provided for four or five large fires to be placed at intervals, and they warmed us at each one. Once they saw that we had gained some strength and gotten warmer, they took us to the next one so rapidly that our feet scarcely touched the ground. In this way we went to their lodges and found that they had one ready for us with many fires lighted in it. Within an hour of our arrival they began to dance and have a great celebration that lasted all night. For us there was no pleasure nor celebration nor sleep because we were waiting to see when they would sacrifice us. In the morning they again gave us fish and roots and treated us so well that we were a little reassured and lost some of our fear of being sacrificed. ✄

---

6. *New Spain* was a part of the Spanish Empire in the 1500s. It included Venezuela, Florida, Mexico, Central America, and other territory. Mexico City was its capital.

7. *Idols* are images of gods used as objects of worship.

Big Idea Life in the New World *What does this passage imply about the Spaniards' ideas about people in the New World?*

RESPONDING AND THINKING CRITICALLY

Respond

1. After reading Cabeza de Vaca's account, what questions might you ask him?

Recall and Interpret

2. (a)How do Cabeza de Vaca and his men reach the island? (b)Why might their landing seem like a miracle to them?

3. (a)Why do the Native Americans chase Lope de Oviedo? (b)How does the behavior of Oviedo and his pursuers reveal each group's assumptions about the other?

4. (a)In what ways do the Native Americans help Cabeza de Vaca and his companions? (b)What do you think prompts them to give assistance?

Analyze and Evaluate

5. How do Cabeza de Vaca's descriptions of his own and his men's suffering contribute to the effectiveness and emotional impact of this account?

6. How do Cabeza de Vaca's references to God's mercy affect your impressions of him and his mission?

7. In your opinion, were the explorers sufficiently prepared for their journey?

Connect

8. **Big Idea** **Life in the New World** What does Cabeza de Vaca's narrative indicate about the difficulties of first encounters between Native Americans and Europeans?

LITERARY ANALYSIS

Literary Element Point of View

The narrator tells what happens in a story from his or her **point of view.** Keep in mind that a first-person narrator in a nonfiction account will recall what he or she considers important and relate it in a way that suits his or her purpose. Narratives of the same events written with a third-person omniscient point of view, or by a different "first person," may reflect different details, feelings, and ideas.

1. How might the story told in *La Relación* have been different if one of Cabeza de Vaca's men or one of the Native Americans had told it?

2. Cabeza de Vaca portrays himself as a heroic character. What details create this image?

READING AND VOCABULARY

Reading Strategy Recognizing Bias

Although Cabeza de Vaca wrote his account to give the king useful information about the New World, it still contains considerable **bias.** To detect bias, look for oversimplification and stereotyping; analyze the writer's reasoning; and identify emotionally charged language.

1. Refer to the chart you made and identify two examples of bias in Cabeza de Vaca's narrative.

2. Write the strategy that helped you recognize the bias and the word clues that helped you make your decision.

Writing About Literature

Evaluate Author's Craft Choose a passage in *La Relación,* and examine Cabeza de Vaca's choice of descriptive words. Evaluate the effectiveness of his descriptions and how they add to the value of the work. Organize your comments in a one-page paper.

Literature Online **Web Activities** For eFlashcards, Selection Quick Checks, and other Web activities, go to www.glencoe.com.

from *Of Plymouth Plantation*

MEET WILLIAM BRADFORD

It was 1620, and the passengers aboard the *Mayflower* were traveling to the Americas. Violent storms tossed the creaking ship and blew it far off course. Among the passengers was thirty-year-old William Bradford.

Born in Yorkshire, England, in 1590, Bradford was orphaned as an infant and brought up by relatives. As a youth, he studied the Bible and became a Separatist. Like the Puritans, Separatists sought reforms in the Church of England. Rather than try to "purify" it, however, the Separatists broke away. In 1609, Bradford expatriated, moving to Leiden in Holland with the congregation and its leader, John Robinson. Fearing they might become assimilated into Dutch culture and lose their identity, the Separatists decided to go to the Americas. John Carver, a successful businessman, attained financial backing and chartered the *Mayflower*. Nearly 500 miles northeast of their intended destination, the Separatists landed in Provincetown, Massachusetts, on Cape Cod on November 21, 1620. On December 26, the 102 settlers disembarked nearby at a site they named Plymouth, after the town where they had set sail. Before leaving the *Mayflower,* the men in the group drafted and signed the historic Mayflower Compact, the colony's rules of government.

> *"All great and honorable actions are accompanied with great difficulties, and must be both enterprised and overcome with answerable courage."*
>
> —William Bradford

The First Winter The group of about 100 settlers, known today as the Pilgrims, elected Bradford leader after John Carver, the first governor, died. The voyage had been harsh. They arrived with little or no food at the onset of winter and had no wilderness survival skills. They constructed crude shelters, hoping to make it through the winter. Nearly half the colonists died of scurvy, pneumonia, fever, or starvation.

Governor The colony survived and in time grew into a thriving community under Bradford's leadership. He was reelected governor for thirty one-year terms between 1622 and 1656. In his gubernatorial years, he served as chief magistrate, high judge, and treasurer. He also presided over the community's legislature, known as the General Court. Unlike the Massachusetts Bay Colony, which was a Bible commonwealth, Plymouth was fairly egalitarian for its day, allowing Presbyterians and maverick nonbelievers to live in the community without forcing them to practice in Congregationalist or Separatist churches. To ensure a peaceable, organized society, Bradford distributed parcels of land equally to all settlers, even nonbelievers. This organizational principle facilitated the private subsistence farming that drove Plymouth's economy in its early years.

In 1630, Bradford started to compile *Of Plymouth Plantation, 1620–1647,* one of the most important narratives of early colonial life. The chronicle is unique in that it separates religious commentary from historical commentary. Certain narratives published by Puritans who had arrived during the Great Migration deemed colonial life as God's plan. Bradford made no such doctrinaire claims. Instead, he steered a middle course between a Bible commonwealth and a secular society that made for a prosperous Plymouth.

William Bradford was born in 1590 and died in 1657.

Literature Online **Author Search** For more about William Bradford, go to www.glencoe.com.

Connecting to the History

How important is it to be able to openly express your own beliefs? In his narrative, William Bradford tells harrowing stories of the settlers' first winter in New England, a difficult step in the path to religious freedom. As you read the text, think about the following questions:

- Have you ever been in a situation where you felt you were not allowed or able to share your beliefs?
- Would you put everything on the line for your beliefs?

Building Background

Sea voyages were extremely dangerous in the 1600s. The wooden ships were easily damaged when they hit shoals (sandbars or shallow spots in the water). Sometimes, strong waves caused ships to "seele," or lurch suddenly from side to side. In fierce winds, sails were lowered by heavy ropes called "halyards," and ships would have to "hull" or drift at sea.

Setting Purposes for Reading

Big Idea Life in the New World

As you read William Bradford's description of Plymouth Plantation, notice how the colonists demonstrate their values in their daily effort to survive and flourish in a harsh environment.

Literary Element Diction

Diction is a writer's choice of words, an important element of the writer's voice or style. As you read, consider how Bradford's diction expresses the values of his time.

- See Literary Terms Handbook, p. R5.

Literature Online **Interactive Literary Elements Handbook** To review or learn more about the literary elements, go to www.glencoe.com.

Reading Strategy Monitoring Comprehension

Bradford's writing style, while typical of his time, can be hard to understand today becuse he uses archaic idioms and vocabulary and long, complex sentences. When you encounter a difficult passage, try breaking long sentences into smaller parts as you read.

Reading Tip: Taking Notes Choose three of Bradford's sentences that are difficult to understand and rewrite them using everyday contemporary words.

Sentence	Revision
"At length they understood by discourse with him, that he was not of these parts, but belonged to the eastern parts where some English ships come to fish."	"After talking with him for a while, they found out that he lived in the east near the ocean where the English had come to fish."

Vocabulary

resolve (ri zolv´) v. to decide; determine; p. 62 *After failing two driving tests, Candy resolved to pass her third.*

providence (prov´ ə dəns) n. divine care or guidance; foresight; p. 63 *We trusted to providence that it would not rain on graduation day.*

procure (prə kyoor´) v. to obtain by care or effort; p. 64 *Sam set out to procure some dry wood for the campfire.*

commodity (kə mod´ ə te) n. a product or economic good; an article of trade; p. 64 *Our town's most important commodity is cranberries.*

feigned (fānd) adj. fictitious; not genuine; p. 64 *The actress was so convincing that it was hard to believe her emotions were feigned.*

INDIANA ACADEMIC STANDARDS (pages 61–65)
11.2.2 Analyze the way in which clarity of meaning is affected by…word choice in the text.

11.1.2 Draw inferences about the meaning of vocabulary in literature or other subject areas.

from

OF PLYMOUTH PLANTATION

William Bradford

from Chapter 9
Of Their Voyage, and How They Passed the Sea; and of Their Safe Arrival at Cape Cod

In sundry[1] of these storms the winds were so fierce and the seas so high, as they could not bear a knot of sail, but were forced to hull for divers[2] days together. And in one of them, as they thus lay at hull in a mighty storm, a lusty[3] young man called John Howland, coming upon some occasion above the gratings was, with a seele of the ship, thrown into sea; but it pleased God that he caught hold of the topsail halyards which hung overboard and ran out at length. Yet he held his hold (though he was sundry fathoms under water) till he was hauled up by the same rope to the brim of the water, and then with a boat hook and other means got into the ship again and his life saved. And though he was something ill with it, yet he lived many years after and became a profitable member both in church and commonwealth. In all this voyage there died but one of the passengers, which was William Butten, a youth, servant to Samuel Fuller, when they drew near the coast.

But to omit other things (that I may be brief) after long beating at sea they fell with that land which is called Cape Cod; the which being made and certainly known to be it, they were not a little joyful. After some deliberation had amongst themselves and with the master of the ship, they tacked about and **resolved** to stand for the southward (the wind and weather being fair) to find some place about Hudson's River for their habitation. But after

---

1. *Sundry* refers to an indefinite number.
2. *Divers* means "several."
3. *Lusty* here means "strong."

Reading Strategy Monitoring Comprehension *How would you rephrase this passage in modern English?*

Vocabulary

resolve (ri zolv′) *v.* to decide; determine

they had sailed that course about half the day, they fell amongst dangerous shoals and roaring breakers, and they were so far entangled therewith as they conceived themselves in great danger; and the wind shrinking upon them withal,[4] they resolved to bear up again for the Cape and thought themselves happy to get out of those dangers before night overtook them, as by God's good **providence** they did. And the next day they got into the Cape Harbor where they rid[5] in safety. . . .

Being thus arrived in a good harbor, and brought safe to land, they fell upon their knees and blessed the God of Heaven who had brought them over the vast and furious ocean, and delivered them from all the perils and miseries thereof, again to set their feet on the firm and stable earth, their proper element. And no marvel if they were thus joyful, seeing wise Seneca[6] was so affected with sailing a few miles on the coast of his own Italy, as he affirmed, that he had rather remain twenty years on his way by land than pass by sea to any place in a short time, so tedious and dreadful was the same unto him.

But here I cannot but stay and make a pause, and stand half amazed at this poor people's present condition; and so I think will the reader, too, when he well considers the same. Being thus passed the vast ocean, and a sea of troubles before in their preparation (as may be remembered by that which went before), they had now no friends to welcome them nor inns to entertain or refresh their weatherbeaten bodies; no houses or much less towns to repair to, to seek for succor.[7] It is recorded in Scripture[8] as a mercy to the Apostle and his shipwrecked company, that the barbarians showed them no small kindness in refreshing them, but these savage barbarians, when they met with them (as after will appear) were readier to fill their sides full of arrows than otherwise. And for the season it was winter, and they that know the winters of that country know them to be sharp and violent, and subject to cruel and fierce storms, dangerous to travel to known places, much more to search an unknown coast.

from Chapter 11
The Starving Time

But that which was most sad and lamentable was, that in two or three months' time half of their company died, especially in January and February, being the depth of winter, and wanting houses and other comforts; being infected with the scurvy[9] and other diseases which this long voyage and their inaccommodate condition had brought upon them. So as there died some times two or three of a day in the foresaid time, that of 100 and odd persons, scarce fifty remained. And of these, in the time of most distress, there was but six or seven sound persons who to their great commendations, be it spoken, spared no pains night nor day, but with abundance of toil and hazard of their own health, fetched them wood, made them fires, dressed them meat, made their beds, washed their loathsome clothes, clothed and unclothed them. In a word, did all the homely[10] and necessary offices for them which dainty and queasy stomachs cannot endure to hear named; and all this willingly and cheerfully, without any grudging in the least, showing herein their true love unto their friends and brethren; a rare example and worthy to be remembered. Two of these seven were Mr. William Brewster, their reverend Elder, and Myles Standish, their Captain and military commander, unto whom myself and many others were much beholden in our low and sick condition. And yet the Lord so upheld these persons as in this general calamity they were not at all infected either with sickness or lameness. . . .

---

4. *Also* is another word for *withal.*
5. *Rid* means "rode."
6. *Seneca* was a Roman philosopher and writer.
7. *Succor* means "assistance in a time of need; relief."
8. The reference here to *Scripture,* or the Bible, is Acts of the Apostles 28, which tells of the kindness shown to St. Paul and his companions by the natives of Malta after they were shipwrecked on that island.

Literary Element Diction *How does this phrase reflect Bradford's beliefs?*

Vocabulary

providence (prov′ ə dəns) *n.* divine care or guidance; foresight

---

9. A severe lack of vitamin C causes a disease called *scurvy.*
10. *Homely* here means "domestic."

Literary Element Diction *What idea about life in the New World is reinforced by the adjectives in this passage?*

Indian Relations

All this while the Indians came skulking about them, and would sometimes show themselves aloof off, but when any approached near them, they would run away; and once they [the Indians] stole away their [the colonists'] tools where they had been at work and were gone to dinner. But about the 16th of March, a certain Indian came boldly amongst them and spoke to them in broken English, which they could well understand but marveled at it. At length they understood by discourse with him, that he was not of these parts, but belonged to the eastern parts where some English ships came to fish, with whom he was acquainted and could name sundry of them by their names, amongst whom he had got his language. He became profitable to them in acquainting them with many things concerning the state of the country in the east parts where he lived, which was afterwards profitable unto them; as also of the people here, of their names, number and strength, of their situation and distance from this place, and who was chief amongst them. His name was Samoset. He told them also of another Indian whose name was Squanto, a native of this place, who had been in England and could speak better English than himself.

Being, after some time of entertainment and gifts dismissed, a while after he came again, and five more with him, and they brought again all the tools that were stolen away before, and made way for the coming of their great Sachem, called Massasoit. Who, about four or five days after, came with the chief of his friends and other attendance, with the aforesaid Squanto. With whom, after friendly entertainment and some gifts given him, they made a peace with him (which hath now continued this 24 years) in these terms:

1. That neither he nor any of his should injure or do hurt to any of their people.

2. That if any of his did hurt to any of theirs, he should send the offender, that they might punish him.

3. That if anything were taken away from any of theirs, he should cause it to be restored; and they should do the like to his.

4. If any did unjustly war against him, they would aid him; if any did war against them, he should aid them.

5. He should send to his neighbors confederates to certify them of this, that they might not wrong them, but might be likewise comprised in the conditions of peace.

6. That when their men came to them, they should leave their bows and arrows behind them.

After these things he returned to his place called Sowams, some 40 miles from this place, but Squanto continued with them and was their interpreter and was a special instrument sent of God for their good beyond their expectation. He directed them how to set their corn, where to take fish, and to **procure** other **commodities,** and was also their pilot to bring them to unknown places for their profit, and never left them till he died.

from Chapter 12
First Thanksgiving

They began now to gather in the small harvest they had, and to fit up their houses and dwellings against winter, being all well recovered in health and strength and had all things in good plenty. For as some were thus employed in affairs abroad, others were exercised in fishing, about cod and bass and other fish, of which they took good store, of which every family had their portion. All the summer there was no want; and now began to come in store of fowl, as winter approached, of which this place did abound when they came first (but afterward decreased by degrees). And besides waterfowl there was great store of wild turkeys, of which they took many, besides venison, etc. Besides they had about a peck of meal a week to a person, or now since harvest, Indian corn to that proportion. Which made many afterwards write so largely of their plenty here to their friends in England, which were not **feigned** but true reports. ∞

Big Idea Life in the New World *How did life for the settlers change so drastically since their bleak arrival in the New World?*

Vocabulary

procure (prə kyoor′) *v.* to obtain by care or effort

commodity (kə mod′ə tē) *n.* a product or economic good; an article of trade

feigned (fānd) *adj.* fictitious; not genuine

Reading Strategy Monitoring Comprehension *What does this passage say about this "certain Indian"?*

RESPONDING AND THINKING CRITICALLY

Respond

1. If you had been a Plymouth settler, what do you think would have been your greatest challenge?

Recall and Interpret

2. (a)What hardships did the Pilgrims face aboard the *Mayflower* and in Plymouth? (b)In your opinion, were the Pilgrims skilled in adapting to unexpected conditions in the New World? Explain.

3. (a)What caused the Pilgrims to land on Cape Cod, in Massachusetts, instead of farther south, near the Hudson River? (b)How did this event affect the expedition?

4. (a)What enabled the Pilgrims to survive "the Starving Time"? (b)What do Bradford's comments reveal about the Pilgrims' character?

5. (a)What are some examples of Samoset's and Squanto's accomplishments? (b)What do you think might have happened to the Pilgrims without Squanto's help?

Analyze and Evaluate

6. (a)What were the six terms of peace meant to accomplish? (b)In your opinion, was this plan a good one? Explain.

7. (a)What enabled the Pilgrims to survive and celebrate their "First Thanksgiving"? (b)How much credit do you give the Pilgrims for this success?

Connect

8. **Big Idea** **Life in the New World** Do the experiences of the Pilgrims have any connection to our society today? Explain.

LITERARY ANALYSIS

Literary Element Diction

Diction is a writer's choice of words. Diction contributes to what we recognize as a writer's voice or style.

1. Paraphrase the first sentence on page 63, paragraph 1, which begins "Being thus arrived . . . "

2. How would you describe the style of this sentence?

Performing

You Are There Choose an event from Bradford's narrative and recast it in the form of a dramatic monologue. Speaking as if you were Bradford, address one or more of the Plymouth settlers during or after one of their experiences. Use modern language instead of Bradford's archaic diction.

Literature Online **Web Activities** For eFlashcards, Selection Quick Checks, and other Web activities, go to www.glencoe.com.

READING AND VOCABULARY

Reading Strategy Monitoring Comprehension

Bradford's writing style involves obscure idioms, archaic vocabulary, and long, complex sentences. In the description of the sea journey, he also uses jargon. You learned several of these words in Building Background. Now figure out a few on your own.

Vocabulary Practice

Jargon is vocabulary that is specific to a profession or a social group. Locate instances of jargon on page 62 and try to determine their meanings from the context.

Practice and Apply Choose the best meaning for each phrase.

1. they *tacked about*
   a. changed direction   **c.** stayed where they were
   b. could not decide   **d.** returned

2. they decided to *stand for* the southward
   a. avoid   **c.** head for
   b. represent   **d.** object to

The Life of Olaudah Equiano

MEET OLAUDAH EQUIANO

The life of Olaudah Equiano (ō lau′ dä e kwē ä′ nō) was a mixture of tragedy, struggle, and great achievement. The son of an Ibo chieftain, Equiano was born in Essaka, a village in what is now Nigeria. His village was a considerable distance from the coast, and as a child Equiano had never heard of the sea or of the people who lived beyond it. When he was eleven, he had a terrifying introduction to both when he and his sister were kidnapped by slave traders. They were separated, and Equiano was sold to Europeans and packed onto a slave ship headed for the Caribbean island of Barbados. The horrors Equiano witnessed on the ship haunted him for the rest of his life.

". . . I might say my sufferings were great; but when I compare my lot with that of most of my countrymen, I regard myself as a particular favorite of heaven. . . ."

—Olaudah Equiano

In the years after being captured, Equiano spent time in Virginia and England, where he was owned by an officer of the British Royal Navy. Equiano served in the British navy with this officer from 1758 to 1762, during the French and Indian War. Over the years, the officer baptized him, renamed him Gustavus Vassa, and taught him seafaring skills as well as how to read and write. These skills would serve Equiano well after the officer sold him to a merchant in the West Indies in 1763.

Sailor and Trader As a slave to the merchant, Equiano worked on trading ships between the West Indies and mainland American colonies and also did some trading on the side for which he was paid. In 1766, at the age of 21, he used money he had made to buy his freedom. He spent the next several years working on ships, traveling to Turkey, Italy, and Jamaica.

While sailing, Equiano realized that life as a free man was in many respects no easier than his life as a slave had been. Freed slaves in the British colonies had no legal rights and were often treated miserably. Equiano described his disappointment with the so-called freedom he was allowed to enjoy. Soon after he was freed, he wrote, "Hitherto I had thought only slavery dreadful; but the state of the free negro appeared to me now equally so at least, and in some respects even worse."

Freedom Fighter In 1776 Equiano settled in England to campaign against slavery. He helped organize several antislavery organizations in London and, along with other abolitionists, petitioned the British parliament to end the slave trade. Equiano was also part of the Committee for Relief of the Black Poor in London and a leader in the Sierra Leone recolonization project, a failed attempt to bring former slaves back to Africa. His greatest contribution to the abolitionist cause, however, was his 1789 autobiography, *The Interesting Narrative of the Life of Olaudah Equiano, or Gustavus Vassa, the African*. It was one of the first books published by a former slave and became one of the most influential slave narratives. Its graphic and powerful descriptions of the inhumanity Equiano and other slaves suffered helped further the abolitionist cause throughout Europe and the United States.

Olaudah Equiano was born in 1745 and died in 1797.

Literature Online **Author Search** For more about Olaudah Equiano, go to www.glencoe.com.

Connecting to the Autobiography

Imagine how you would feel if a group of people thought they had the right to deprive you of your freedom. In this excerpt from his narrative, Olaudah Equiano details the horrors he experienced as a slave. As you read, think about the following questions:

- How would you feel if someone tried to take away your freedom?
- What is a cause you care deeply about?

Building Background

From the 1500s to the 1800s, approximately ten million Africans suffered miserable treatment on the forced journey from their homes to enslavement in the Western Hemisphere. The most arduous portion of the journey, known as the Middle Passage, was a two-month voyage from West Africa to the West Indies. Some two million Africans died from malnutrition, disease, suffocation, beatings, and despair during the journey.

Setting Purposes for Reading

Big Idea Life in the New World

As you read, notice what the selection reveals about the suffering endured by many of the Africans who helped build the United States.

Literary Element The Slave Narrative

A **slave narrative** is an autobiographical account of a formerly enslaved person's life. Slave narratives helped abolitionists expose slavery's cruelty. As you read, evaluate Equiano's success in making readers aware of slavery's injustice.

- See Literary Terms Handbook, p. R16–R17.

Reading Strategy Responding

Responding is explaining what you think about a selection and how it affects you. Responding personally includes describing what you like, dislike, or find interesting in a selection and how these aspects of the work relate to your own life. More analytical responses deal with giving your opinion on aspects such as the behavior of the characters or stylistic techniques used by the author. As you read, consider the thoughts and feelings that the selection evokes and what factors contribute to your response.

Reading Tip: Taking Notes As you read the selection, jot down quick notes about the passages you think are especially moving or intense.

Vocabulary

apprehension (ap′ ri hen′ shən) n. fear of what may happen in the future; anxiety; p. 70 *Sam thought of his upcoming speech with apprehension.*

copious (kō′ pē əs) *adj.* large in quantity; plentiful; p. 70 *Copious amounts of food were served at the banquet.*

gratify (grat′ ə fī′) *v.* to satisfy or indulge; p. 71 *Our walks outside gratify my craving for sunlight.*

clamor (klam′ ər) n. confused, insistent shouting; p. 72 *The clamor woke Kim from her sleep.*

scruple (skroo′ pəl) n. moral principle that restrains action; p. 72 *Without a scruple, Nina stole the bike.*

Vocabulary Tip: Antonyms Antonyms are words that have opposite or nearly opposite meanings. For example, *joyful* and *mournful* are antonyms. Note that antonyms are always the same part of speech.

Literature Online Interactive Literary Elements Handbook To review or learn more about the literary elements, go to www.glencoe.com.

INDIANA ACADEMIC STANDARDS (pages 67–73)
11.3.5 Analyze...works of...cultural significance... that...shed light on...ethical ideas of their time.

11.3 [Respond] to grade-level-appropriate literature...

11.4.7 Develop presentations using...Internet sources.

from The Life of Olaudah Equiano

Olaudah Equiano

The first object which saluted[1] my eyes when I arrived on the coast, was the sea, and a slave ship, which was then riding at anchor, and waiting for its cargo. These filled me with astonishment, which was soon converted into terror, when I was carried on board. I was immediately handled, and tossed up to see if I were sound, by some of the crew; and I was now persuaded that I had gotten into a world of bad spirits, and that they were going to kill me. Their complexions, too, differing so much from ours, their long hair, and the language they spoke, (which was very different from any I had ever heard) united to confirm me in this belief. Indeed, such were the horrors of my views and fears at the moment, that, if ten thousand worlds had been my own, I would have freely parted with them all to have exchanged my condition with that of the meanest[2] slave in my own country. When I looked round the ship too, and saw a large furnace of copper boiling, and a multitude of black people of every description chained together, every one of their countenances[3] expressing dejection and sorrow, I no longer doubted of my fate; and, quite overpowered with horror and anguish, I fell motionless on the deck and fainted. When I recovered a little, I found some black people about me, who I believed were some of those who had brought me on board, and had been receiving their pay; they talked to me in order to cheer me, but all in vain.[4] I asked them if we were not to be eaten by those white men with horrible looks, red faces, and long hair. They told me I was not: and one of the crew brought me a small portion of spirituous liquor in a wine glass, but, being afraid of him, I would not take it out of his hand. One of the blacks, therefore, took it from him and gave it to me, and I took a little down my palate,[5] which, instead of reviving me, as they thought it would, threw me into the greatest consternation[6] at the strange feeling it produced, having never tasted any such liquor before. Soon after this, the blacks who brought me on board went off, and left me abandoned to despair.

I now saw myself deprived of all chance of returning to my native country, or even the least glimpse of hope of gaining the shore, which I now considered as friendly; and I even wished for my former slavery[7] in preference to my present situation, which was filled with horrors of every kind, still heightened by my ignorance of what I was to undergo. I was not long suffered[8] to indulge my grief; I was soon put down under the decks, and there I received such a salutation in my nostrils as I had never experienced in my life: so that, with the loathsomeness of the stench, and crying

---

1. Here, *saluted* means "became noticeable to" or "struck."
2. Here, *meanest* means "of the lowest social position or rank."
3. *Countenance* means "face" or "facial expression."

Literary Element Slave Narrative *Why might Equiano have included these details?*

Reading Strategy Responding *What about this passage makes it striking or memorable?*

4. Something done *in vain* is done without effect or success.
5. The *palate,* here, is the mouth and throat.
6. *Consternation* is paralyzing dismay or fear.
7. Equiano refers to a brief period of time he spent as a slave to the Africans who kidnapped him and eventually sold him. In his experience, slavery in Africa was far less brutal than slavery in the New World.
8. Here, *suffered* means "allowed."

The Slavedeck of the Albaroz, Prize to the H.M.S. Albatross, 1846. Francis Meynell. Watercolor. National Maritime Museum, London.
Viewing the Art: How do you think this image compares with Olaudah Equiano's description of conditions in the hold of a slave ship?

together, I became so sick and low that I was not able to eat, nor had I the least desire to taste any thing. I now wished for the last friend, death, to relieve me; but soon, to my grief, two of the white men offered me eatables; and, on my refusing to eat, one of them held me fast by the hands, and laid me across, I think the windlass,⁹ and tied my feet, while the other flogged me severely. I had never experienced any thing of this kind before, and although not being used to the water, I naturally feared that element the first time I saw it, yet, nevertheless, could I have got over the nettings,¹⁰ I would have jumped over the side, but I could not; and besides, the crew used to watch us very closely who were not chained down to the decks, lest we should leap into the water; and I have seen some of these poor African prisoners most severely cut, for attempting to do so, and hourly whipped for not eating. This indeed was often the case with myself. In a little time after, amongst the poor chained men, I found some of my own nation, which in a small degree gave ease to my mind. I inquired of these what was to be done with us? They gave me to understand, we were to be carried to these white people's country to work for them. I then was a little revived, and thought, if it were no worse than working, my situation was not so desperate; but still I feared I should be put to death, the white people looked and acted, as I thought, in so savage a manner; for I had never

---

9. A *windlass* is a type of crank with a handle. It is used to raise or lower a heavy object such as an anchor.
10. *Nettings* were networks of small ropes on the sides of a ship. On slave ships, nettings were used to prevent captives from jumping overboard.

Literary Element   Slave Narrative *How does the point of view affect the message of this selection?*

Big Idea   Life in the New World *What kind of mood does Equiano create here?*

seen among any people such instances of brutal cruelty; and this not only shown towards us blacks, but also to some of the whites themselves. One white man in particular I saw, when we were permitted to be on deck, flogged so unmercifully with a large rope near the foremast, that he died in consequence of it; and they tossed him over the side as they would have done a brute. This made me fear these people the more; and I expected nothing less than to be treated in the same manner. I could not help expressing my fears and **apprehensions** to some of my countrymen; I asked them if these people had no country, but lived in this hollow place? (the ship) they told me they did not, but came from a distant one. "Then," said I, "how comes it in all our country we never heard of them?" They told me because they lived so very far off. I then asked where were their women? had they any like themselves? I was told they had. "And why," said I, "do we not see them?" They answered, because they were left behind. I asked how the vessel could go? they told me they could not tell; but that there was cloth put upon the masts by the help of the ropes I saw, and then the vessel went on; and the white men had some spell or magic they put in the water when they liked, in order to stop the vessel. I was exceedingly amazed at this account, and really thought they were spirits. I therefore wished much to be from amongst them, for I expected they would sacrifice me; but my wishes were vain—for we were so quartered that it was impossible for any of us to make our escape.

While we stayed on the coast I was mostly on deck; and one day, to my great astonishment, I saw one of these vessels coming in with the sails up. As soon as the whites saw it, they gave a great shout, at which we were amazed; and the more so, as the vessel appeared larger by approaching nearer. At last, she came to an anchor in my sight, and when the anchor was let go, I and my countrymen who saw it, were lost in astonishment to observe the vessel stop—and

were now convinced it was done by magic. Soon after this the other ship got her boats out, and they came on board of us, and the people of both ships seemed very glad to see each other. Several of the strangers also shook hands with us black people, and made motions with their hands, signifying I suppose, we were to go to their country, but we did not understand them.

At last, when the ship we were in, had got in all her cargo, they made ready with many fearful noises, and we were all put under deck, so that we could not see how they managed the vessel. But this disappointment was the least of my sorrow. The stench of the hold while we were on the coast was so intolerably loathsome, that it was dangerous to remain there for any time, and some of us had been permitted to stay on the deck for the fresh air; but now that the whole ship's cargo were confined together, it became absolutely pestilential.[11] The closeness of the place, and the heat of the climate, added to the number in the ship, which was so crowded that each had scarcely room to turn himself, almost suffocated us. This produced **copious** perspirations, so that the air soon became unfit for respiration, from a variety of loathsome smells, and brought on a sickness among the slaves, of which many died—thus falling victims to the improvident[12] avarice,[13] as I may call it, of their purchasers. This wretched situation was again aggravated by the galling[14] of the chains, now became insupportable; and the filth of the necessary tubs,[15] into which the children often fell, and were almost suffocated. The shrieks of the women, and the groans of the dying, rendered[16] the whole a scene of horror

---

11. *Pestilential* means "poisonous" or "likely to cause disease or death."
12. *Improvident* means "lacking foresight" or "not providing for the future."
13. *Avarice* is greed.
14. *Galling* is the chafing or rubbing that causes irritation of the skin.
15. *Necessary tubs* are containers for bodily waste.
16. *Render* means "to cause to be" or "to make."

Big Idea Life in the New World *Why might Equiano have included a description of this event?*

Vocabulary

apprehensions (ap′ ri hen′ shən) *n.* fears of what may happen in the future; anxieties

Reading Strategy Responding *What is significant about Equiano's use of the word* cargo *here?*

Vocabulary

copious (kō′ pē əs) *adj.* large in quantity; plentiful

The Slave Ship, 1840. Joseph Mallord William Turner. Oil on canvas. Museum of Fine Arts, Boston.
Viewing the Art: What does this painting tell you about the voyages of slave ships in Equiano's time?

and the attempt procured them some very severe floggings. One day, when we had a smooth sea and moderate wind, two of my wearied countrymen who were chained together, (I was near them at the time,) preferring death to such a life of misery, somehow made through the nettings and jumped into the sea: immediately, another quite dejected fellow, who, on account of his illness, was suffered to be out of irons, also followed their example; and I believe many more would very soon have done the same, if they had not been prevented by the ship's crew, who were instantly alarmed. Those of us that were the most active, were in a moment put down under the deck, and there was such a noise and confusion amongst the people of the ship as I never heard before, to stop her, and get the boat out to go after the slaves. However, two of the wretches were drowned, but they got the other, and afterwards flogged him unmercifully, for thus attempting to prefer death to slavery. In this manner we continued to undergo more hardships than I can now relate, hardships which are inseparable from this accursed trade. Many a time we were near suffocation from the want of fresh air, which we were often without for whole days together. This, and the stench of the necessary tubs, carried off many.

During our passage, I first saw flying fishes, which surprised me very much; they used frequently to fly across the ship, and many of them fell on the deck. I also now first saw the use of the quadrant; I had often with astonishment seen the mariners make observations with it, and I could not think what it meant. They at last took notice of my surprise; and one of them, willing to increase it, as well as to **gratify** my curiosity, made me one day look through it. The clouds appeared to me to be land, which

almost inconceivable. Happily perhaps, for myself, I was soon reduced so low here that it was thought necessary to keep me almost always on deck; and from my extreme youth I was not put in fetters.[17] In this situation I expected every hour to share the fate of my companions, some of whom were almost daily brought upon deck at the point of death, which I began to hope would soon put an end to my miseries. Often did I think many of the inhabitants of the deep much more happy than myself. I envied them the freedom they enjoyed, and as often wished I could change my condition for theirs. Every circumstance I met with, served only to render my state more painful, and heightened my apprehensions, and my opinion of the cruelty of the whites.

One day they had taken a number of fishes; and when they had killed and satisfied themselves with as many as they thought fit, to our astonishment who were on deck, rather than give any of them to us to eat, as we expected, they tossed the remaining fish into the sea again, although we begged and prayed for some as well as we could, but in vain; and some of my countrymen, being pressed by hunger, took an opportunity, when they thought no one saw them, of trying to get a little privately; but they were discovered,

Reading Strategy Responding *How does this passage illustrate the illogical nature of punishments on the ship?*

Vocabulary

gratify (grat′ ə fī′) *v.* to satisfy or indulge

17. *Fetters* are leg irons.

disappeared as they passed along. This heightened my wonder; and I was now more persuaded than ever, that I was in another world, and that every thing about me was magic. At last, we came in sight of the island of Barbadoes, at which the whites on board gave a great shout, and made many signs of joy to us. We did not know what to think of this; but as the vessel drew nearer, we plainly saw the harbor, and other ships of different kinds and sizes, and we soon anchored amongst them, off Bridgetown.[18] Many merchants and planters now came on board, though it was in the evening. They put us in separate parcels,[19] and examined us attentively. They also made us jump, and pointed to the land, signifying we were to go there. We thought by this, we should be eaten by these ugly men, as they appeared to us; and, when soon after we were all put down under the deck again, there was much dread and trembling among us, and nothing but bitter cries to be heard all the night from these apprehensions, insomuch, that at last the white people got some old slaves from the land to pacify us. They told us we were not to be eaten, but to work, and were soon to go on land, where we should see many of our country people. This report eased us much. And sure enough, soon after we were landed, there came to us Africans of all languages.

We were conducted immediately to the merchant's yard, where we were all pent up together, like so many sheep in a fold, without regard to sex or age. As every object was new to me, every thing I saw filled me with surprise. What struck me first, was, that the houses were built with bricks and stories, and in every other respect different from those I had seen in Africa; but I was still more astonished on seeing people on horseback. I did not know what this could mean; and, indeed, I thought these people were full of nothing but magical arts. While I was in this astonishment, one of my fellow-prisoners spoke to a countryman of his, about the horses, who said they were the same kind they had in their country. I understood them, though they were from a distant part of Africa; and I thought it odd I had not seen any horses there; but afterwards, when I came to converse with different Africans, I found

they had many horses amongst them, and much larger than those I then saw.

We were not many days in the merchant's custody, before we were sold after their usual manner, which is this:—On a signal given, (as the beat of a drum,) the buyers rush at once into the yard where the slaves are confined, and make choice of that parcel they like best. The noise and **clamor** with which this is attended, and the eagerness visible in the countenances of the buyers, serve not a little to increase the apprehension of terrified Africans, who may well be supposed to consider them as the ministers of that destruction to which they think themselves devoted. In this manner, without **scruple,** are relations and friends separated, most of them never to see each other again. I remember, in the vessel in which I was brought over, in the men's apartment, there were several brothers, who, in the sale, were sold in different lots; and it was very moving on this occasion, to see and hear their cries at parting. O, ye nominal[20] Christians! might not an African ask you—Learned you this from your God, who says unto you, Do unto all men as you would men should do unto you?[21] Is it not enough that we are torn from our country and friends, to toil for your luxury and lust of gain? Must every tender feeling be likewise sacrificed to your avarice? Are the dearest friends and relations, now rendered more dear by their separation from their kindred, still to be parted from each other, and thus prevented from cheering the gloom of slavery, with the small comfort of being together, and mingling their sufferings and sorrows? Why are parents to lose their children, brothers their sisters, or husbands their wives? Surely, this is a new refinement in cruelty, which, while it has no advantage to atone[22] for it, thus aggravates distress, and adds fresh horrors even to the wretchedness of slavery. ∾

---

18. *Bridgetown* is the capital of Barbados.
19. Here, *parcels* means "groups."

Reading Strategy Responding *Why might Equiano have chosen to describe the slaves as sheep?*

20. *Nominal* means "in name only."
21. "Therefore all things whatsoever ye would that men should do to you, do ye even so to them." (Matthew 7:12)
22. *Atone* means "to make amends" or "to compensate for."

Literary Element Slave Narrative *How is this section different from the rest of the work? Why does Equiano make this change?*

Vocabulary

clamor (klam′ ər) *n.* confused, insistent shouting
scruple (skrōō′ pəl) *n.* moral principle that restrains action

RESPONDING AND THINKING CRITICALLY

Respond

1. What was your reaction to the description of life on a slave ship?

Recall and Interpret

2. (a)What does Equiano fear will happen to him when he is taken aboard the ship? (b)Why might he be so afraid?

3. (a)In spite of his fear, Equiano displays great curiosity. Relate an incident that reveals this curiosity. (b)What might the incident reveal about his character?

4. (a)What phrases does Equiano use to describe his feelings about slavery's separation of loved ones? (b)Why does he regard it as he does?

Analyze and Evaluate

5. The **tone** of a work is the attitude the author conveys toward his or her subject matter through elements such as word choice. (a)Review the last paragraph. How does Equiano's tone shift here from what came before? (b)Why does it shift? Explain how this shift in tone affected you.

6. Equiano's book was a best seller in its time. (a)Why do you think his story was so successful at capturing the public's interest? (b)Why would his story have been useful to the cause of abolition?

Connect

7. **Big Idea** **Life in the New World** How has reading this work affected your attitudes about personal freedom, human nature, or our nation's history of enslavement of Africans? Explain, using details from the selection.

LITERARY ANALYSIS

Literary Element The Slave Narrative

Equiano's account created a hunger for more information about slaves' lives. In the years that followed, many African Americans published their own slave narratives. Some authors expressed their opposition to slavery through direct statements of opinion. Why might Equiano's narrative have been more successful at reaching some people than an opinion piece? Include details from the narrative in your answer.

Internet Connection

Firsthand Accounts Go to the Library of Congress's home page at www.loc.gov. Search for the "African American History and Culture" page. Download and print a story or a photograph you find interesting and share it with your class.

Literature Online **Web Activities** For eFlashcards, Selection Quick Checks, and other Web activities, go to www.glencoe.com.

READING AND VOCABULARY

Reading Strategy Responding

Responding to literature is reacting in a personal way to what you read. To which aspects of slavery did you react most strongly? Explain.

Vocabulary Practice

Practice with Antonyms Choose the best antonym for each vocabulary word listed below.

1. apprehension
  a. nervousness   **c.** restlessness
  b. fearlessness   **d.** exhaustion

2. copious
  a. inadequate   **c.** sufficient
  b. ample   **d.** plentiful

3. gratify
  a. satisfy   **c.** neglect
  b. suggest   **d.** indulge

4. clamor
  a. silence   **c.** tumult
  b. outcry   **d.** insistence

from *A Narrative of the Captivity and Restoration of Mrs. Mary Rowlandson*

MEET MARY ROWLANDSON

In 1675, a long period of relative peace between the Native Americans and Europeans in New England ended in the bloody conflict known as King Philip's War. King Philip was the white settlers' name for Metacom, the *Sachem* or leader of the Wampanoag people, who vowed to halt European expansion into his lands. The war began as a series of Native American sieges on colonial towns in present-day Massachusetts, Connecticut, and Rhode Island. Lancaster, a frontier town in central Massachusetts, was one of the last to be ransacked.

> *"I had often before this said, that if the Indians should come, I should choose rather to be killed by them than taken alive; but when it came to the trial my mind changed. . . ."*
>
> —Mary Rowlandson

At dawn on February 10, 1676, a party of Wampanoag warriors took 24 prisoners from Lancaster, including Mary Rowlandson, her six-year-old daughter, and her older son and daughter. Rowlandson was the wife of Reverend Joseph Rowlandson, the first minister in Lancaster, and many of the townspeople had been using their home as a safe haven. But the Wampanoag quickly overwhelmed the defenders of this makeshift garrison. Both Rowlandson and her six-year-old daughter were wounded during the fray, and the child died eight days later. After being captured, Rowlandson was separated from her two surviving children and allowed only short, sporadic contact with them.

Survival as a Prisoner The Wampanoag killed many of the prisoners, but Rowlandson was spared because she was adept at sewing and knitting. She was held captive for three months. Her wounds healed, and she adapted to the Wampanoags' meager diet. She often bartered her skills as a seamstress for food, knitting a pair of socks for a quart of peas or making a shirt for a hunk of bear meat. The Wampanoag were constantly on the move, traveling as far north as New Hampshire while Rowlandson was being held captive. She had become disoriented early on, and fleeing was not an option, especially because she could not bear to leave her surviving children in the hands of the Wampanoag. A stolen Bible one of the Wampanoag had given her and the small portions of food she managed to procure were all that sustained her.

Reunited with Family In May 1676, Reverend Joseph Rowlandson paid a £20 ransom for the release of his wife and children, and Rowlandson was finally reunited with her family. Looking back on her life as a prisoner, she wrote, "I have been in the midst of those roaring lions, and savage bears, that feared neither God, nor man, nor the devil."

Mary Rowlandson's account of her ordeal was published in 1682. It received high acclaim and prompted many imitations. Written in a plain, vigorous style, *A Narrative of the Captivity and Restoration of Mrs. Mary Rowlandson* presented a realistic, if biased, account of Native Americans. Her memoir is the first—and widely considered the best—example of an American literary form, the so-called Indian-captivity narrative.

Mary Rowlandson was born around 1636 and died around 1710.

Literature Online Author Search For more about Mary Rowlandson, go to www.glencoe.com.

Connecting to the Narrative

In her narrative, Mary Rowlandson tells how, after being captured, she eked out a living among the Wampanoag, whose culture, language, diet, and nomadism were utterly foreign to her. As you read this narrative, think about the following questions:

- How do people deal with traumatic experiences? What effects do such experiences have on people?
- How does Rowlandson adapt mentally, physically, and emotionally from the day of her capture to the day of her release?

Building Background

As a child, the Wampanoag chief Metacom had watched his father, Massasoit, help the Pilgrims who arrived on the *Mayflower*. By 1675, there were about 50,000 Puritans in the Massachusetts Bay Colony. With each passing year, more Puritans arrived, encroaching on the Native Americans' land and disrupting their way of life. Forseeing the destruction of his tribe and other tribes, Metacom began forming alliances against the settlers. In 1675, after three Wampanoag were executed by the Puritans, a swift, desperate war broke out.

Setting Purposes for Reading

Big Idea Life in the New World

As you read Rowlandson's narrative, be aware of how the deep cultural conflict between New England's Native American and European inhabitants affected the lives of both groups.

Literary Element Allusion

An **allusion** is a reference to a well-known character, place, or situation from history or from music, art, or another literary work. As you read Rowlandson's narrative, notice her use of allusions.

- See Literary Terms Handbook, p. R1.

Literature Online Interactive Literary Elements **Handbook** To review or learn more about the literary elements, go to www.glencoe.com.

Reading Strategy · Analyzing Historical Context

Analyzing historical context involves gathering background information and exploring social forces that influenced the writing of a literary work. As you read Rowlandson's account, gather information about the cultural conflicts between Native Americans and Europeans that caused King Philip's War.

Reading Tip: Taking Notes Use a timeline like the one started below to record the sequence of events that led to King Philip's War.

Vocabulary

desolation (des´ə lā´ shən) *n.* devastation; misery; sadness; p. 76 *The survivors of the hurricane in Florida experienced great desolation when they found their homes destroyed.*

daunt (dônt) *v.* to overcome with fear; intimidate; p. 76 *A visit to the dentist would always daunt her.*

compassion (kəm pash´ ən) *n.* deep awareness of another's suffering with a desire to help; p. 76 *The compassion of the doctor earned the gratitude of his patients.*

discern (di sərn´, -zərn´) *v.* to recognize as different and distinct; distinguish; p. 77 *He could barely discern the boat on the horizon.*

lament (lə ment´) *v.* to express deep sorrow or grief; p. 78 *The dead child's mother began to weep and lament.*

from
A Narrative of the Captivity and Restoration of Mrs. Mary Rowlandson

Mary Rowlandson

Oh the doleful sight that now was to behold at this house! *Come, behold the works of the Lord, what* **desolation** *he has made in the earth.*[1] Of thirty seven persons who were in this one house, none escaped either present death or a bitter captivity, save only one, who might say as he, *Job*[2] i. 15, *And I only am escaped alone to tell the news.* There were twelve killed, some shot, some stabbed with their spears, some knocked down with their hatchets. When we are in prosperity, oh, the little that we think of such dreadful sights; and to see our dear friends and relations lie bleeding out their heart-blood upon the ground! . . .

I had often before this said, that if the Indians should come, I should choose rather to be killed by them than taken alive; but when it came to the trial my mind changed; their glittering weapons so **daunted** my spirit, that I chose rather to go . . . than that moment to end my days. And that I may the better declare what happened to me during that grievous captivity, I shall particularly speak of the several removes[3] we had up and down the wilderness.

There remained nothing to me but one poor wounded babe, and it seemed at present worse than death that it was in such a pitiful condition, bespeaking **compassion,** and I had no refreshing for it, nor suitable things to revive it . . .

The second remove.—But now (the next morning) I must turn my back upon the town, and travel with them into the vast and desolate wilderness, I know not whither.[4] It is not my tongue or pen

---

1. The author is quoting Psalms 46:8.
2. In the Bible, *Job* is a good man. His faith in God is tested by many afflictions. Messengers bring word of catastrophes affecting his possessions and family members. Each messenger tells Job that he alone has escaped to tell the news.

Literary Element Allusion *What does this allusion reveal immediately about the writer?*

Vocabulary

desolation (des′ ə lā′ shən) *n.* devastation; misery; sadness

---

3. Here, *removes* means "changes of residence"; we would say *moves* today.
4. *Whither* means "to what place."

Reading Strategy Analyzing Historical Context *What clues does this statement offer about the historical context?*

Vocabulary

daunt (dônt) *v.* to overcome with fear; to intimidate
compassion (kəm pash′ ən) *n.* deep awareness of another's suffering with a desire to help

can express the sorrows of my heart and bitterness of my spirit that I had at this departure: but God was with me in a wonderful manner, carrying me along, and bearing up my spirit, that it did not quite fail. One of the Indians carried my poor wounded babe upon a horse: it went moaning all along, I shall die, I shall die! I went on foot after it, with sorrow that cannot be expressed. At length I took it off the horse, and carried it in my arms, till my strength failed, and I fell down with it. Then they set me upon a horse, with my wounded child in my lap. . . .

Thus nine days I sat upon my knees, with my babe in my lap, till my flesh was raw again. My child, being even ready to depart this sorrowful world, they bid me carry it out to another wigwam; (I suppose because they would not be troubled with such spectacles;) whither I went with a very heavy heart, and down I sat with the picture of death in my lap. About two hours in the night, my sweet babe, like a lamb, departed this life, on Feb. 18, 1675 [1676] it being about six years and five months old. It was nine days (from the first wounding) in this miserable condition, without any refreshing of one nature or other, except a little cold water. I cannot but take notice how, at another time, I could not bear to be in the room where any dead person was; but now the case is changed; I must and could lie down by my dead babe, side by side, all the night after. I have thought since of the wonderful goodness of God to me, in preserving me so in the use of my reason and senses in that distressed time, that I did not use wicked and violent means to end my own miserable life. In the morning, when they understood that my child was dead, they sent for me home to my master's wigwam; (by my master, in this writing, must be understood Quannopin, who was a Saggamore,[5] and married King Philip's wife's sister; not that he first took me, but I was sold to him by another Narrhaganset Indian, who took me when first I came out of the garrison).[6] I went to take up my dead child in my arms to carry it with me, but they bid me let it alone; there was no resisting,

but go I must and leave it. When I had been a while at my master's wigwam, I took the first opportunity I could get to go look after my dead child. When I came, I asked them what they had done with it. They told me it was upon the hill; then they went and shewed me where it was, where I saw the ground was newly dug, and there they told me they had buried it; there I left that child in the wilderness, and must commit it, and myself also, in this wilderness condition, to Him who is above all.

. . . During my abode in this place Philip spake to me to make a shirt for his boy, which I did; for which he gave me a shilling;[7] I offered the money to my master, but he bade me keep it; and with it I bought a piece of horse flesh. Afterwards I made a cap for his boy, for which he invited me to dinner; I went, and he gave me a pancake about as big as two fingers; it was made of parched wheat, beaten and fried in bear's grease, but I thought I never tasted pleasanter meat in my life. There was a squaw who spake to me to make a shirt for her sannup; for which she gave me a piece of bear. Another asked me to knit a pair of stockings, for which she gave me a quart of peas. I boiled my peas and bear together, and invited my master and mistress to dinner; but the proud gossip, because I served them both in one dish, would eat nothing, except one bit that he gave her upon the point of his knife. Hearing that my son was come to this place, I went to see him, and found him lying flat upon the ground; I asked him how he could sleep so? he answered me, that he was not asleep, but at prayer; and lay so, that they might not observe what he was doing. I pray God he may remember these things, now he is returned in safety. At this place (the sun now getting higher) what with the beams and heat of the sun, and the smoke of the wigwams, I thought I should have been blind; I could scarce **discern** one wigwam from another.

---

5. A *Saggamore* was a subordinate chief in the hierarchy of various Native American peoples.
6. A *garrison* is a military post.

7. A *shilling* was an English or early American coin, whose value was 20 pence (pennies) or 1/20 pound.

Big Idea Life in the New World *How does this short passage illustrate the cultural differences between the Native Americans and the European settlers?*

Reading Strategy Analyzing Historical Context *Why does the author include this information?*

Vocabulary

discern (di surn′) *v.* to recognize as different and distinct; distinguish

There was here one Mary Thurston of Medfield, who, seeing how it was with me, lent me a hat to wear; but as soon as I was gone, the squaw (who owned that Mary Thurston) came running after me, and got it away again. Here there was a squaw who gave me one spoonful of meal;[8] I put it in my pocket to keep it safe; yet, notwithstanding, somebody stole it, but put five Indian corns in the room of it; which corns were the greatest provision I had in my travel for one day.

The Indians returning from Northampton, brought with them some horses and sheep, and other things which they had taken; I desired them that they would carry me to Albany upon one of those horses, and sell me for powder; for so they had sometimes discoursed.[9] I was utterly hopeless of getting home on foot the way that I came. I could hardly bear to think of the many weary steps I had taken to come to this place.

. . . My son being now about a mile from me, I asked liberty to go and see him; they bade me go, and away I went; but quickly lost myself, travelling over hills and through swamps, and could not find the way to him. And I cannot but admire at the wonderful power and goodness of God to me, in that though I was gone from home, and met with all sorts of Indians, and those I had no knowledge of, and there being no Christian soul near me; yet not one of them offered the least imaginable miscarriage to me. I turned homeward again, and met with my master; he showed me the way to my son: when I came to him I found him not well; and withal he had a boil on his side, which much troubled him; we bemoaned one another a while, as the Lord helped us, and then I returned again. When I was returned, I found myself as unsatisfied as I was before. I went up and down moaning and **lamenting;** and my spirit was

---

8. *Meal* is coarsely ground grain.
9. *Discoursed* means "discussed."

Vocabulary

lament (lə ment′) v. to express deep sorrow or grief

ready to sink with the thoughts of my poor children; my son was ill, and I could not but think of his mournful looks; and no Christian friend was near him to do any office of love for him, either for soul or body. And my poor girl, I knew not where she was, nor whether she was sick or well, or alive or dead. I repaired under these thoughts to my Bible (my great comforter in that time) and that scripture came to my hand, *Cast thy burden upon the Lord, and he shall sustain thee*. Psal. lv. 22.

But I was fain[10] to go and look after something to satisfy my hunger; and going among the wigwams, I went into one, and there found a squaw who showed herself very kind to me, and gave me a piece of bear. I put it into my pocket, and came home; but could not find an opportunity to broil it, for fear they would get it from me, and there it lay all that day and night in my stinking pocket. In the morning I went again to the same squaw, who had a kettle of ground nuts boiling; I asked her to let me boil my piece of bear in her kettle, which she did, and gave me some ground nuts to eat with it, and I cannot but think how pleasant it was to me. I have seen bear baked very handsomely amongst the English, and some liked it, but the thoughts that it was bear made me tremble: but now that was savory to me that one would think was enough to turn the stomach of a brute creature.

One bitter cold day I could find no room to sit down before the fire; I went out, and could not tell what to do, but I went into another wigwam where they were also sitting round the fire; but the squaw laid a skin for me, and bid me sit down; and gave me some ground nuts, and bade me come again; and told me they would buy me if they were able; and yet these were strangers to me that I never knew before.

. . . *The fourteenth remove.*—Now must we pack up and be gone from this thicket, bending our course towards the bay-towns. I having nothing to eat by the way this day, but a few crumbs of cake, that an Indian gave my girl the same day we were taken. She gave it me, and I put it into my pocket; there it lay till it was so moldy (for want of good baking) that one could not tell what it was made of; it fell all to crumbs, and grew so dry and hard, that it was like little flints;[11] and this refreshed me many times when I was ready to faint. It was in my thoughts when I put it into my mouth; that if ever I returned, I would tell the world what a blessing the Lord gave to such mean food. As we went along, they killed a deer, with a young one in her; they gave me a piece of the fawn, and it was so young and tender, that one might eat the bones as well as the flesh, and yet I thought it very good. When night came on we sat down; it rained, but they quickly got up a bark wigwam, where I lay dry that night. I looked out in the morning, and many of them had lain in the rain all night. I saw by their reeking.[12] Thus the Lord dealt mercifully with me many times; and I fared better than many of them.

. . . O the wonderful power of God that I have seen, and the experiences that I have had! I have been in the midst of those roaring lions and savage bears, that feared neither God nor man, nor the devil, by night and day, alone and in company, sleeping all sorts together; and yet not one of them ever offered the least abuse of unchastity to me in word or action. Though some are ready to say I speak it for my own credit; but I speak it in the presence of God, and to His glory.

. . . If trouble from smaller matters begins to arise in me, I have something at hand to check myself with, and say when I am troubled, it was but the other day, that if I had had the world, I would have given it for my freedom. . . . I have learned to look beyond present and smaller troubles, and to be quieted under them, as *Moses* said, *Exod.* xiv. 13, *Stand still, and see the salvation of the Lord.* FINIS[13]

---

10. In this instance, *fain* means "obliged."

Big Idea Life in the New World *Why is it important to Rowlandson that her son have a "Christian friend" near him?*

Literary Element Allusion *Why do these words help Rowlandson feel better about her son and daughter?*

Big Idea Life in the New World *How does Rowlandson suggest that life in the New World has changed her?*

---

11. *Flints* refers to pieces of flint, a very hard type of quartz.
12. *Reeking* here means "steaming"; that is, water was evaporating from their hair and clothing.
13. *Finis* means "The End."

RESPONDING AND THINKING CRITICALLY

Respond

1. What incident or observation in Rowlandson's account surprised or moved you most?

Recall and Interpret

2. (a)What does Rowlandson say that she always intended to do if Native Americans attacked? (b)Why do you think she changes her mind?

3. (a)What experience does Rowlandson have with Metacom (Philip)? (b)What impression of him does this episode convey?

4. (a)When Rowlandson first visits her son, what does she find him doing? (b)What might this episode suggest about the attitude of the Wampanoag?

Analyze and Evaluate

5. (a)How does Rowlandson portray her captors? (b)In your opinion, is this portrayal fair?

6. (a)What qualities or behaviors help Rowlandson survive her ordeal? (b)What did you find most puzzling about her behavior? Put your thoughts in the form of a question.

Connect

7. **Big Idea** **Life in the New World** Captivity narratives such as Rowlandson's were among the most popular literary genres in early America. What effect do you think this type of literature might have had on the colonists' attitudes and policies regarding Native Americans?

LITERARY ANALYSIS

Literary Element **Allusion**

The Bible shaped the Puritan culture of early New England. Rowlandson's biblical **allusions** would be readily understood by the first readers of her account.

1. What are some reasons for her biblical allusions?

2. What is the effect of her allusion to the Book of Job?

Writing About Literature

Analyze Genre Elements Like any other literary genre, the Indian-captivity narrative has characteristic elements. These include sudden, fierce Native American attacks on frontier settlements; innocent, defenseless prisoners (usually women and children); hardship as the Indians move from camp to camp; and eventual rescue of the captives. In two paragraphs, explain which of these elements are present in *A Narrative of the Captivity and Restoration of Mrs. Mary Rowlandson* and evaluate their overall literary effect.

Literature Online **Web Activities** For eFlashcards, Selection Quick Checks, and other Web activities, go to www.glencoe.com.

READING AND VOCABULARY

Reading Strategy **Analyzing Historical Context**

Mary Rowlandson's account provides historical context for both Native American and colonial life in seventeenth-century New England.

1. What does her account suggest about King Philip's War and about the position of the settlers?

2. What does her account of her time as a prisoner show about the life of the Wampanoag?

Vocabulary **Practice**

Practice with Synonyms Find the synonym for each vocabulary word. Use a dictionary or a thesaurus if you need help.

1. desolation   a. ruin   b. jungle
2. daunt   a. soothe   b. discourage
3. compassion   a. mercy   b. pleasure
4. discern   a. ignore   b. perceive
5. lament   a. bellow   b. mourn

Grammar Workshop

Sentence Structure

Using Adverb Clauses

"When I had been a while at my master's wigwam, I took the first opportunity I could get to go look after my dead child."

> —Mary Rowlandson, from *A Narrative of the Captivity and Restoration of Mrs. Mary Rowlandson*

Connecting to Literature In the quotation above, the sentence is made up of two clauses, a main (independent) clause and a subordinate (dependent) clause. The main clause, *I took the first opportunity I could get to go look after my dead child,* includes a subject and a predicate, and it expresses a complete thought. The subordinate clause, *When I had been a while at my master's wigwam,* also includes a subject and a predicate, but this clause depends on the main clause to complete its meaning.

One type of subordinate clause is the **adverb clause,** which may modify a verb, an adjective, or an adverb. An adverb clause answers a question—how? when? where? why? to what extent? or under what conditions?

Examples

- When Europeans came to the United States, they often brought disease. [The underlined adverb clause answers the question *when?* and modifies the verb *brought.*]

- Rowlandson was brave even though she was taken captive. [The underlined adverb clause answers the question *under what conditions?* and modifies the adjective *brave.*]

Exercise

Revise for Clarity Write a sentence for each pair of clauses below. If provided, use the subordinating conjunction. Underline the adverb clause, tell which question it answers about the main clause, and identify what it modifies.

1. **Clause:** many of them wrote about their experiences
   Clause: the captives were freed or escaped
   Subordinating conjunction: after
2. **Clause:** enslavement of Africans increased
   Clause: Quakers and other antislavery groups protested loudly
   Subordinating conjunction: until
3. **Clause:** than others did
   Clause: some early American settlers became more tolerant
4. **Clause:** he was white
   Clause: Cabeza de Vaca was accepted by most native people he encountered
   Subordinating conjunction: although

▶ **Punctuating Subordinate Clauses**

A subordinate clause can appear before, after, or in the middle of the main clause. When it introduces a sentence, it is set off from the main clause with a comma. In other positions it may not always be set off with punctuation.

▶ **Test-Taking Tip**

Subordinating conjunctions often introduce adverb clauses. Identify these conjunctions to help locate adverb clauses.

▶ **Subordinating Conjunctions**

after	if
although	since
as	so long as
as though	unless
because	until
before	when

▶ **Language Handbook**

For more on subordinate clauses, see Language Handbook, p. R46.

Literature Online
eWorkbooks To link to the Grammar and Language eWorkbook, go to www.glencoe.com.

ACADEMIC STANDARDS (page 81)
11.6.4 Identify and correctly use clauses, both main and subordinate...and the mechanics of punctuation...

Upon the Burning of Our House and To My Dear and Loving Husband

MEET ANNE BRADSTREET

"[Anne Bradstreet wrote] . . . the first good poems in America, while rearing eight children, lying frequently sick, keeping house at the edge of the wilderness, [and] managed a poet's range and extension within confines as severe as any American poet has confronted."

—Adrienne Rich

Anne Bradstreet was the first published poet in America—a remarkable accomplishment considering that writing was thought improper for a woman at that time. In fact, the title page of her first book assures readers that she did not shirk her responsibilities as a wife and mother in order to write poetry. The poems were said to be "the fruit of some few hours, curtailed from sleep and other refreshments."

From England to the New World Anne Bradstreet (born Dudley) was born and raised in England. At age 16, Anne married Simon Bradstreet, a friend of the family. Two years later, Anne, her husband, and her parents boarded the *Arbella* as members of John Winthrop's party and sailed to the Massachusetts Bay Colony to join the Puritan community there. At first, Bradstreet was appalled by the crude life of the settlement, but she soon adjusted. She wrote, "I changed my condition and was married, and came into this country, where I found a new world and new manners, at which my heart rose [reacted angrily]. But after I was convinced it was the way of God, I submitted to it and joined to the church at Boston."

Literature Online **Author Search** For more about Anne Bradstreet, go to www.glencoe.com.

In Massachusetts, Bradstreet began to write poetry. She wrote while caring for teething infants, while mending clothes by the fire at night, while struggling through bouts of tuberculosis and smallpox, and while maintaining a house in the wilderness of the New World. At first, Bradstreet imitated the lofty style of the established male poets. As a result, her early poems contain many wooden lines and forced rhymes, and they do not reveal her deeper emotions.

Bradstreet wrote for her own satisfaction and shared her poems only with her family and friends in the new colony. Nonetheless, her brother-in-law, the Reverend John Woodbridge, took fifteen of her poems to England without her knowledge and had them published under the title *The Tenth Muse Lately Sprung Up in America*. (The title alludes to the nine Muses of ancient Greek mythology, goddesses who inspired poets and other artists.)

A Change of Style When Bradstreet saw *The Tenth Muse* in print, she was dissatisfied with her work and stopped writing imitative verse. Instead, she started writing warm, natural poetry about her experiences as a wife, mother, and woman in seventeenth-century New England. Bradstreet's best poems explore her love for her husband, her sadness at the death of her parents and other family members, and her struggle to accept as God's will the losses she suffered. Six years after Bradstreet's death, an American edition of *The Tenth Muse*, which included some of her later poems as well as her revisions of her earlier work, appeared under the new title *Several Poems Compiled with Great Variety of Wit and Learning*.

Anne Bradstreet was born in 1612 and died in 1672.

ANNE BRADSTREET

Connecting to the Poems

What would it be like to lose most of the things you owned? How would you feel if you knew you were going to lose someone you love? In her poems, Bradstreet deals with loss and with the expectation of loss. As you read the poems, think about the following questions:

- How would you feel if you lost your home or a possession you treasure?
- What would you like to say to someone you love?

Building Background

Bradstreet's husband and father were both governors of the Massachusetts Bay Colony. Their prominence resulted in frequent moves and separations. This instability, along with the daily tragedies of colonial life and Bradstreet's Puritan beliefs, likely influenced her sense of impermanence.

Setting Purposes for Reading

Big Idea Life in the New World

In seventeenth-century New England, poetry was acceptable reading for Puritans only if it was religious. However, as a Puritan, Bradstreet viewed all events within the context of God's divine plan. She found similarities between the domestic details of daily life and the spiritual details of her religious life. Unlike the traditional verse of her day, Bradstreet's poems speak of everyday occurrences and personal emotions. As you read, consider how Bradstreet's religious beliefs affected her relationships and her interactions with the harsh circumstances of early American life.

Literary Element Metaphor

A **metaphor** is a figure of speech that compares or equates two seemingly unlike things. As you read these poems, notice how Bradstreet uses metaphors.

- See Literary Terms Handbook, p. R11.

Literature Online **Interactive Literary Elements Handbook** To review or learn more about the literary elements, go to www.glencoe.com.

Reading Strategy Drawing Conclusions About Author's Beliefs

When you **draw a conclusion,** you make a general statement based on the information in a text. For example, you might conclude that the author of an essay about the beauty of a prairie would support prairie conservation efforts. As you read Bradstreet's poems, use the details from the text as the basis for drawing conclusions about her personal and religious beliefs.

Reading Tip: Graphic Organizer Use a two-column chart to record details from the poems and the conclusions you draw from them.

Detail	Conclusion
p. 84, lines 53–54 "The world no longer let me love, My hope and treasure lies above."	Bradstreet believed in the afterlife, which she valued more than her earthly existence.
p. 85, lines 5–6 "I prize thy love more than whole mines of gold…"	

Vocabulary

bereft (bi reft´) *adj.* deprived of the possession or use of something; p. 84 *The foul weather left him bereft of his usual good mood.*

chide (chīd) *v.* to find fault with or to blame; p. 84 *The teacher chided the class for not completing their homework.*

recompense (rek´ əm pens´) *n.* something given in return for something else; compensation; p. 85 *When the soles of his new shoes came apart, the athlete requested recompense from the shoe company.*

INDIANA ACADEMIC STANDARDS (pages 83–87)
11.3.4 Analyze…figures of speech…
11.2.5 Analyze an author's…beliefs about a subject.

11.5.2 Write responses to literature that…analyze the use of imagery…

Upon the Burning of Our House
July 10th, 1666

Anne Bradstreet

In silent night when rest I took
For sorrow near I did not look
I wakened was with thund'ring noise
And piteous shrieks of dreadful voice.
5   That fearful sound of "Fire!" and "Fire!"
Let no man know is my desire.
I, starting up, the light did spy,
And to my God my heart did cry
To strengthen me in my distress
10 And not to leave me succorless.[1]
Then, coming out, beheld a space
The flame consume my dwelling place.
And when I could no longer look,
I blest His name that gave and took,[2]
15 That laid my goods now in the dust.
Yea, so it was, and so 'twas just.
It was His own, it was not mine,
Far be it that I should repine;[3]
He might of all justly **bereft**
20 But yet sufficient for us left.
When by the ruins oft I past
My sorrowing eyes aside did cast,
And here and there the places spy
Where oft I sat and long did lie:
25 Here stood that trunk, and there that
     chest,
There lay that store I counted best.

My pleasant things in ashes lie,
And them behold no more shall I.
Under thy roof no guest shall sit,
30 Nor at thy table eat a bit.
No pleasant tale shall e'er be told,
Nor things recounted done of old.
No candle e'er shall shine in thee,
Nor bridegroom's voice e'er heard
     shall be.
35 In silence ever shall thou lie,
Adieu, Adieu,[4] all's vanity.[5]
Then straight I 'gin my heart to **chide,**
And did thy wealth on earth abide?
Didst fix thy hope on mold'ring dust?
40 The arm of flesh didst make thy trust?
Raise up thy thoughts above the sky
That dunghill mists away may fly.
Thou hast an house on high erect,
Framed by that mighty Architect,
45 With glory richly furnished,
Stands permanent though this be fled.
It's purchased and paid for too
By Him who hath enough to do.
A price so vast as is unknown
50 Yet by His gift is made thine own;
There's wealth enough, I need no more,
Farewell, my pelf,[6] farewell my store.
The world no longer let me love,
My hope and treasure lies above.

---

1. *Succorless* means "without assistance" or "helpless."
2. This is a biblical reference to Job 1:21, ". . . the Lord gave, and the Lord hath taken away; blessed be the name of the Lord."
3. *Repine* means "to express unhappiness" or "to complain."

4. *Adieu* (ə dōō) is French for "good-bye."
5. *All's vanity* is a biblical reference to Ecclesiastes 1:2 and 12:8, "Vanity of vanities: all is vanity."
6. *Pelf* is a term for money or wealth, often used disapprovingly.

Reading Strategy Drawing Conclusions About Author's Beliefs *What conclusions can you draw about Bradstreet's faith in God from these lines?*

Vocabulary

bereft (bi reft´) *adj.* deprived of the possession or use of something

Literary Element Metaphor *Who is the "mighty Architect" in this metaphor?*

Vocabulary

chide (chīd) *v.* to find fault with or to blame

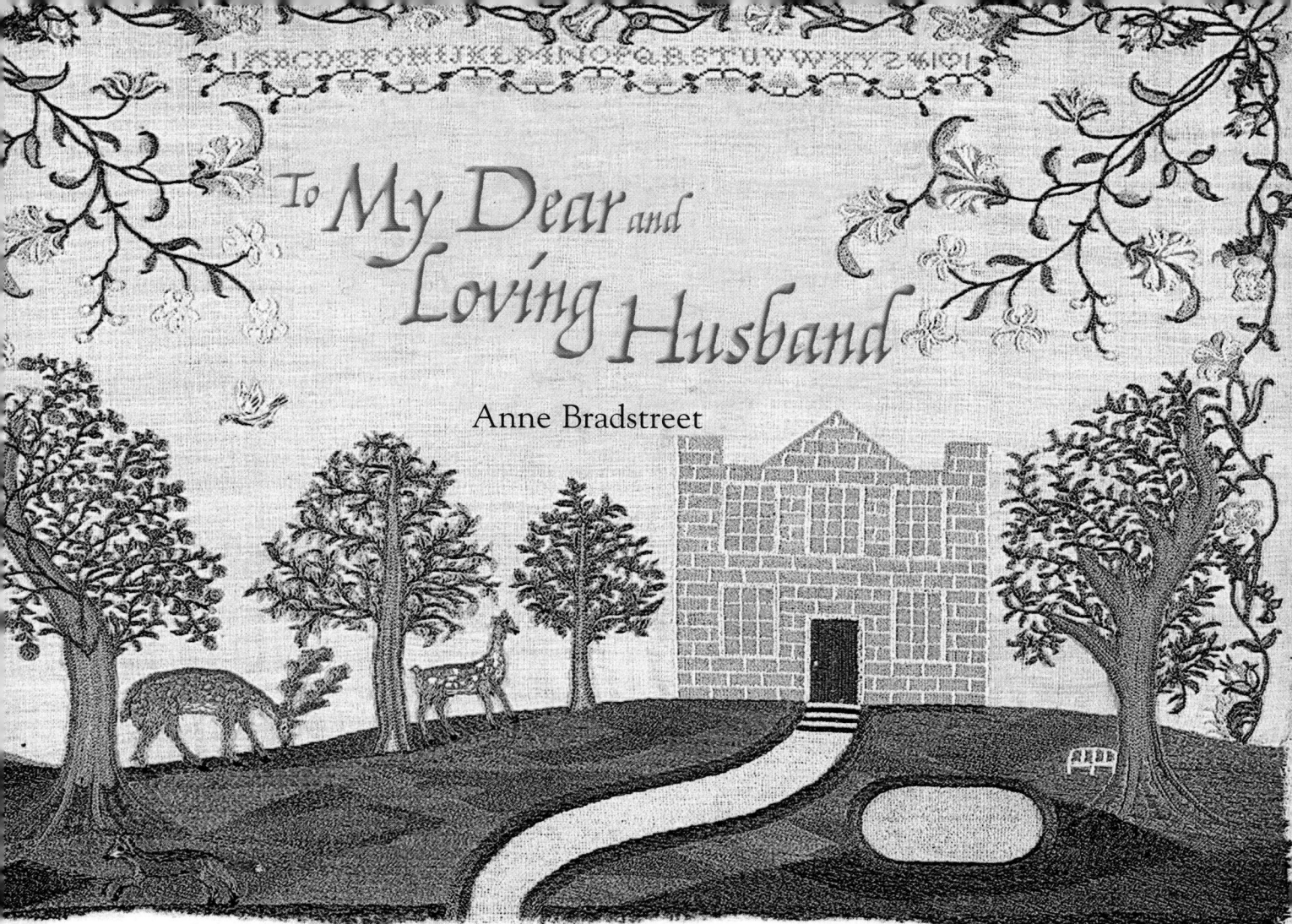

To My Dear and Loving Husband

Anne Bradstreet

If ever two were one, then surely we.
If ever man were loved by wife, then thee;
If ever wife was happy in a man,
Compare with me, ye women, if you can.
5   I prize thy love more than whole mines of gold
Or all the riches that the East doth hold.
My love is such that rivers cannot quench,
Nor ought[1] but love from thee, give
     recompense.

Thy love is such I can no way repay,
10   The heavens reward thee manifold,[2] I pray.
Then while we live, in love let's so persevere[3]
That when we live no more, we may live ever.

---

1. *Ought* means "anything."
2. Here, *manifold* means "in many different ways."

3. In the 1600s, the word *persevere* was pronounced *per sé ver*, with the accent on the second syllable. Therefore, it rhymes with *ever* in the following line.

Big Idea   Life in the New World   *How does Bradstreet's description of her love for her husband reflect her religious beliefs?*

RESPONDING AND THINKING CRITICALLY

Respond

1. Which Bradstreet poem did you find more poignant? Explain.

Recall and Interpret

2. (a)How did the speaker in "Upon the Burning of Our House" feel about her possessions before the fire? How does she feel afterward? (b)What do you think brought about the change in her perspective?

3. (a)In the final line, where does the speaker say her "hope and treasure" are? (b)What does this suggest about the speaker's home and possessions?

4. (a)In "To My Dear and Loving Husband," what does the speaker prize "more than whole mines of gold"? (b)Why do you think she compares the way she feels to mines of gold?

5. (a)What is the seeming contradiction in the last line of the poem? (b)What do you think this line means?

Analyze and Evaluate

6. (a)In "Upon the Burning of Our House," what effect do Bradstreet's frequent references to her faith have on the poem's meaning? (b)Do you think that she is successful in conveying her meaning? Explain.

7. (a)What purpose does the repetition in the opening lines of "To My Dear and Loving Husband" serve? (b)How well does repetition serve this purpose? Explain.

Connect

8. Big Idea **Life in the New World** How do Bradstreet's Puritan beliefs affect her perception of the world as represented by these poems?

Literary Element Metaphor

A **metaphor** is a figure of speech that compares two things by saying that one is another. For example, in the sentence "the desert became a sweltering oven," the desert is said to be an oven—a fitting comparison because they are both hot. Occasionally, a writer will use an **extended metaphor,** developing a metaphor beyond a single line. This is what Bradstreet does, beginning with line 43 of "Upon the Burning of Our House." Reread lines 43–50.

1. In your own words, summarize what you think the speaker is describing in the extended metaphor.

2. How do you think this extended metaphor relates to the speaker's description in lines 21–30?

Review: Author's Purpose

As you learned on page 48, an **author's purpose** is his or her intent in writing a literary work. Authors typically write for one or more of the following purposes: to persuade, to inform, to explain, to entertain, or to describe.

Partner Activity Meet with a classmate and discuss Bradstreet's purpose. Work with your partner to infer what Bradstreet's purpose was for writing each poem. To help you get started, fill out a chart like the one below for each poem. Include details from the poem that you think reveal information about her purpose. Then fill in the purpose you infer from those details.

Details	Purpose

Literature Online **Web Activities** For eFlashcards, Selection Quick Checks, and other Web activities, go to www.glencoe.com.

Reading Strategy Drawing Conclusions
About Author's Beliefs

Authors often incorporate their own beliefs into their writing. Sometimes they state these beliefs explicitly. Other times it might be possible to infer the author's beliefs only by examining their word choice, use of figurative language, or rhetorical techniques.

1. How does Bradstreet feel about worldly things?

2. List three pieces of evidence to support your opinion.

Vocabulary Practice

Practice with Synonyms Read the following sentences. Choose the best synonym for the underlined word. Use a dictionary if you need help.

1. The team's loss left the coach <u>bereft</u> of her usual enthusiasm.
   a. deprived   **b.** satisfied   **c.** comforted

2. Angela hated it when her older sister <u>chided</u> her.
   a. praised   **b.** criticized   **c.** teased

3. After we broke our neighbor's mailbox, we raked her yard as <u>recompense</u>.
   a. punishment   **b.** prize   **c.** compensation

Academic Vocabulary

Here are two vocabulary words from the vocabulary list on page R86. The words will help you think, write, and talk about the selection.

site (sīt) *n.* the location of a building or structure

aspect (as′ pekt) *n.* a trait or characteristic to be viewed, analyzed, or evaluated; an element of something being examined

Practice and Apply
1. What objects does the speaker recall while on the **site** of her destroyed home?
2. What **aspect** of Bradstreet's poems do you find most interesting?

Literature Online **Web Activities** For eFlashcards, Selection Quick Checks, and other Web activities, go to www.glencoe.com.

Writing About Literature

Responding to Theme Write a review of either "Upon the Burning of Our House" or "To My Dear and Loving Husband." Discuss what you liked or disliked about either of the two poems or whether you agreed with the speaker's views. You might also want to explain the effect of such devices as rhyme, rhythm, and metaphor. Use lines from the poems to support your opinions.

As you draft your review, be sure to

- create a clear, focused thesis statement that is supported by textual evidence and personal experience

- include topic sentences in paragraphs that are fully developed and logically organized and that handle a single aspect of your argument

- craft concise and effective opening and concluding paragraphs that introduce and reinforce your thesis

After completing your draft, meet with a peer reviewer to evaluate each other's work and to suggest revisions. Then proofread your draft for errors in spelling, grammar, and punctuation and make the appropriate edits.

Literary Criticism

Kenneth B. Murdock writes that, even in her best poems, Anne Bradstreet "conforms to the Puritan utilitarian view of art and to [the Puritans'] distrust of the frankly sensuous." Do you think the Bradstreet poems you have read show evidence of the "utilitarian view of art" or of her drawing back from the "frankly sensuous"? Write a paragraph citing evidence from the poems to support your opinion of Murdock's judgment.

Creative Writing

Bradstreet describes her response to losing her possessions. Think about something you own that you treasure. Then imagine how you would feel if you lost that cherished object. Quickly write a few words and phrases that describe the object and your possible reaction to its loss. Use these words and phrases to write your own poem. If you wish, you might try using **rhyme, repetition,** or **metaphor,** as Bradstreet does in her poems.

from *Sinners in the Hands of an Angry God*

MEET JONATHAN EDWARDS

Jonathan Edwards was a Puritan theologian, preacher, and philosopher who captivated congregations with his "preaching of terror," a brand of sermonizing aimed at shaking the faith of unrepentant sinners and saving them from eternal damnation. His sermons hinge on fire-and-brimstone depictions of hell and visions of churchgoers dangling by tenuous threads over the depths of hell, held by the hand of an angry God. "I think it is a reasonable thing to fright persons away from hell," Edwards explained. "Is it not a reasonable thing to fright a person out of a house on fire?"

As a child, the precocious Edwards used his vivid imagination and shrewd, analytical mind to write scientific essays on insects, colors, and rainbows. At 13, he matriculated at Yale. He intended to use his education to publish works refuting natural philosophy and its key doctrines of materialism and atheism.

> "O sinner! consider the fearful danger you are in: it is a great furnace of wrath, a wide and bottomless pit, full of the fire of wrath, that you are held over in the hand of that God…"
>
> —Jonathan Edwards

Conversion Edwards was a religious young man, due to his Puritan upbringing, but he had qualms about predestination, the doctrine that claims it is predetermined whether an individual will go to heaven or hell. But in 1721, while studying divinity, he underwent a religious conversion that confirmed his belief in God as omnipotent, total, and in control of all things, including human destiny. Edwards subsequently thought of the revelation of God in intuitive terms— God the divine conveyed directly to the individual soul.

In 1729, Edwards succeeded his grandfather at the pulpit in Northampton, Massachusetts. In his sermons, he attributed New England's ailing morality to its moral and religious independence and its incomplete acceptance of faith as the sole means to salvation. In the early 1730s, Edwards lambasted Arminianism, a movement in the Anglican Church that was gaining popularity among New England colonists. His sermons on the subject incited a religious revival in the Connecticut River valley in 1734–1735.

Great Awakening Between 1730 and 1750, a religious revival known as the Great Awakening swept through the colonies. Preachers attracted people in droves and brought about ecstatic emotional reactions and frenzied mass conversions with their sermons. Edwards sought to keep his audiences calm, but his sermons were equally effective. His sermons were reproduced and read across Britain and other regions in America. However, by 1750 some of Northampton's Puritans objected to Edwards's extreme teachings and removed him from his post. He went into exile for several years, during which he served as a missionary to Native Americans in the frontier village of Stockbridge. He then became president of what is now Princeton University but died of smallpox shortly thereafter. Edwards is widely considered the most influential American writer before Benjamin Franklin.

Jonathan Edwards was born in 1703 and died in 1758.

Literature Online Author Search For more about Jonathan Edwards, go to www.glencoe.com.

Connecting to the Sermon

If you were trying to convert someone to your way of thinking about an issue, would you use a gentle approach, scare tactics, or something in-between? What tone would you take? In this sermon, Edwards uses a stern tone and relies on scare tactics to motivate his audience. As you read the sermon, think about the following questions:

- Does Edwards at any point deviate from his tone? Do you think a consistent or a varied tone would work better for a sermon of this sort?
- How do you think Edwards would have recited or performed this sermon?

Building Background

This sermon, which Jonathan Edwards delivered in 1741, remains the most famous literary monument to the Great Awakening. Edwards upheld strict Calvinism, which taught that human nature is essentially evil and that God predestines only a select few to be saved from eternal punishment.

Setting Purposes for Reading

Big Idea Life in the New World

As you read Edwards's sermon, consider what it reveals about the importance of religion in colonial America.

Literary Element Imagery

Imagery refers to the set of mental pictures that writers create by using **sensory details,** or descriptions that appeal to one or more of the senses. As you read this sermon, look for the images Edwards uses to stir fear in the hearts of his audience.

- See Literary Terms Handbook, p. R9.

Literature Online **Interactive Literary Elements Handbook** To review or learn more about the literary elements, go to www.glencoe.com.

Reading Strategy Examining Connotation

Connotation refers to the implied or suggested meanings associated with a word beyond its denotation, or literal meaning. For example, the words *statesman* and *politician* have similar denotations but very different connotations. Connotation is subtle, but often very potent in its emphasis of the writer's points. Notice instances when connotation changes or heightens the impact of Edwards's message.

Reading Tip: Taking Notes Use a chart to record the denotations and connotations of three words Edwards uses to describe the plight of sinners.

Word	Denotation	Connotation
p. 90 sentenced	having had a sentence imposed, as in a trial	The word sentenced suggests the finality of a court trial.

Vocabulary

appease (ə pēz´) *v.* to bring to a state of peace or quiet; soothe; p. 90 *He tried to appease the sobbing child with a toy.*

abate (ə bāt´) *v.* to lessen or reduce in force or intensity; p. 90 *Did the storm abate after the sun came out?*

prudence (prood´ əns) *n.* exercise of good and cautious judgment; p. 91 *Showing prudence, the motorist slowed as she neared the school zone.*

abhor (ab hôr´) *v.* to regard with disgust; p. 91 *After working in a candy store, she began to abhor sweets.*

abominable (ə bom´ ə nə bəl) *adj.* disgusting; detestable; p. 91 *Stealing from the poor is an abominable crime.*

◾ **INDIANA ACADEMIC STANDARDS (pages 89–93)**
11.3.4 Analyze…imagery…[used] to evoke…emotions.
11.2.2 Analyze the way in which clarity of meaning is affected by…word choice in the text.
11.7.5 Use appropriate rehearsal strategies…

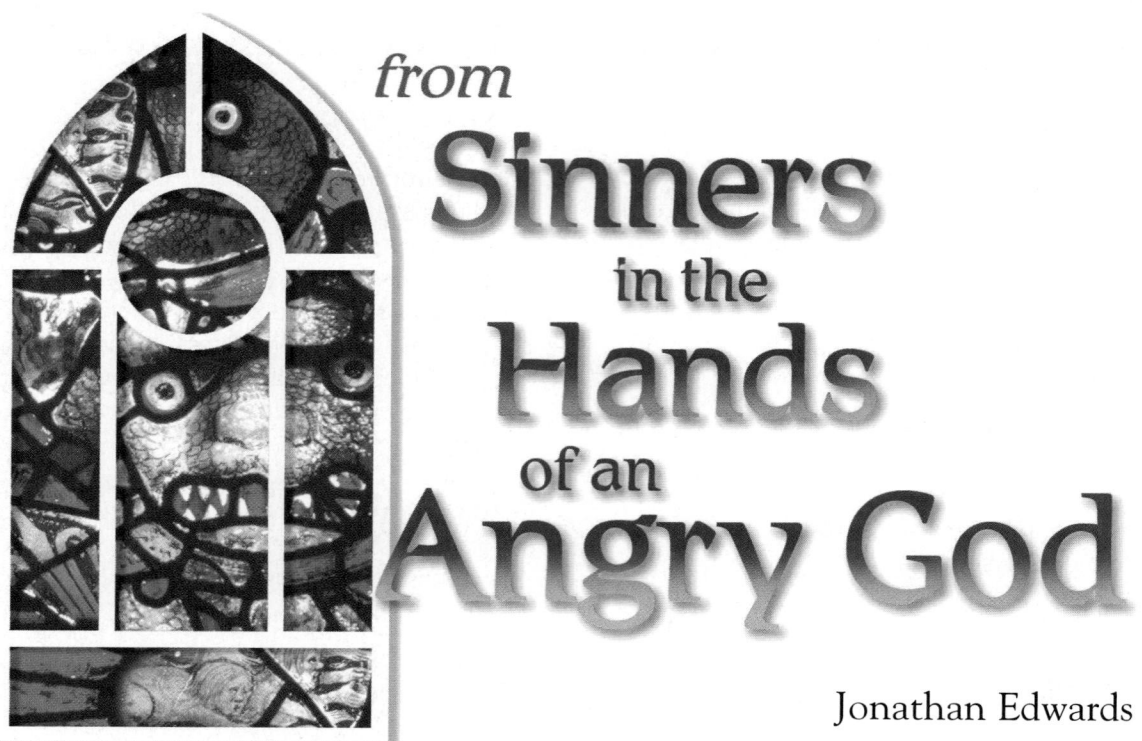

from Sinners in the Hands of an Angry God

Jonathan Edwards

So that thus it is, that natural men[1] are held in the hand of God over the pit of hell; they have deserved the fiery pit, and are already sentenced to it; and God is dreadfully provoked, his anger is as great towards them as to those that are actually suffering the executions of the fierceness of his wrath in hell, and they have done nothing in the least, to **appease** or **abate** that anger, neither is God in the least bound by any promise to hold them up one moment; the devil is waiting for them, hell is gaping for them, the flames gather and flash about them, and would fain[2] lay hold on them and swallow them up; the fire pent up in their own hearts is struggling to break out; and they have no interest in any Mediator, there are no means within reach that can be any security to them. In short, they have no refuge, nothing to take hold of; all that preserves them every moment is the mere arbitrary will, and uncovenanted, unobliged forbearance of an incensed God.

Application

The use may be of awakening to unconverted persons in this congregation. This that you have heard is the case of every one of you that are out of Christ.[3] That world of misery, that lake of burning brimstone, is extended abroad under you. There is the dreadful pit of the glowing flames of the wrath of God; there is hell's wide gaping mouth open; and you have nothing to stand upon, nor any thing to take hold of. There is nothing between you and hell but the air; it is only the power and mere pleasure of God that holds you up.

You probably are not sensible of this; you find you are kept out of hell, but do not see the hand of God in it; but look at other things, as the good state of your bodily constitution, your care of your own life, and the means you use for your

---

1. *Natural men* are those who have not been "born again" or received God's grace.
2. Here, *fain* means "willingly" or "gladly."

3. Those who are *out of Christ* are not in God's grace.

own preservation. But indeed these things are nothing; if God should withdraw his hand, they would avail no more to keep you from falling, than the thin air to hold up a person that is suspended in it.

Your wickedness makes you as it were heavy as lead, and to tend downwards with great weight and pressure towards hell; and if God should let you go, you would immediately sink and swiftly descend and plunge into the bottomless gulf, and your healthy constitution, and your own care and **prudence,** and best contrivance,[4] and all your righteousness, would have no more influence to uphold you and keep you out of hell, than a spider's web would have to stop a falling rock.

The bow of God's wrath is bent, and the arrow made ready on the string, and justice bends the arrow at your heart, and strains the bow, and it is nothing but the mere pleasure of God, and that of an angry God, without any promise or obligation at all, that keeps the arrow one moment from being made drunk with your blood.

Thus are all you that never passed under a great change of heart, by the mighty power of the Spirit of God upon your souls; all that were never born again, and made new creatures, and raised from being dead in sin, to a state of new, and before altogether unexperienced light and life, (however you may have reformed your life in many things, and may have had religious affections, and may keep up a form of religion in your families and closets,[5] and in the houses of God, and may be strict in it) you are thus in the hands of an angry God; it is nothing but his mere pleasure that keeps you from being this moment swallowed up in everlasting destruction.

---

4. A *contrivance* is a clever scheme or plan.
5. Here, *closets* refers to small rooms used especially for prayer and meditation.

Literary Element Imagery *Why does Edwards introduce this image?*

Big Idea Life in the New World *What does Edwards's observation indicate about the place of religion in the American colonies?*

Vocabulary

prudence (pro͞od′əns) *n.* exercise of good and cautious judgment

George Whitefield, c. 1742. John Wollaston. Oil on canvas, 32⅝ x 26 in. National Portrait Gallery, London.
Viewing the Art: Does the painting capture the tone of Jonathan Edwards's sermon? Support your opinion.

The God that holds you over the pit of hell, much as one holds a spider, or some loathsome insect, over the fire, **abhors** you, and is dreadfully provoked; his wrath towards you burns like fire; he looks upon you as worthy of nothing else, but to be cast into the fire; he is of purer eyes than to bear to have you in his sight; you are ten thousand times so **abominable** in his eyes, as the most hateful and venomous serpent is in ours.

O sinner! consider the fearful danger you are in: it is a great furnace of wrath, a wide and bottomless pit, full of the fire of wrath, that you are held over in the hand of that God, whose wrath

Vocabulary

abhor (ab hôr′) *v.* to regard with disgust
abominable (ə bom′ ə nə bəl) *adj.* disgusting; detestable

is provoked and incensed as much against you, as against many of the damned in hell: you hang by a slender thread, with the flames of divine wrath flashing about it, and ready every moment to singe it, and burn it asunder;[6] and you have no interest in any Mediator, and nothing to lay hold of to save yourself, nothing to keep off the flames of wrath, nothing of your own, nothing that you ever have done, nothing that you can do, to induce God to spare you one moment.

There is reason to think, that there are many in this congregation now hearing this discourse, that will actually be the subjects of this very misery to all eternity. We know not who they are, or in what seats they sit, or what thoughts they now have. It may be they are now at ease, and hear all these things without much disturbance, and are now flattering themselves that they are not the persons; promising themselves that they shall escape. If we knew that there was one person, and but one, in the whole congregation, that was to be the subject of this misery, what an awful thing it would be to think of! If we knew who it was, what an awful sight would it be to see such a person! How might all the rest of the congregation lift up a lamentable and bitter cry over him! But alas! Instead of one, how many is it likely will remember this discourse in hell! And it would be a wonder, if some that are now present should not be in hell in a very short time, before this year is out. And it would be no wonder if some persons, that now sit here in some seats of this meeting-house in health, and quiet and secure, should be there before to-morrow morning.

Those of you that finally continue in a natural condition, that shall keep out of Hell longest, will be there in a little time! Your damnation does not slumber; it will come swiftly, and in all probability very suddenly upon many of you. You have reason to wonder that you are not already in Hell. 'Tis doubtless the case of some that

heretofore you have seen and known, that never deserved Hell more than you, and that heretofore appeared as likely to have been now alive as you: Their case is past all hope. They are crying in extreme misery and perfect despair. But here you are in the land of the living, and in the house of God, and have an opportunity to obtain salvation. What would not those poor damned, helpless souls give for one day's such opportunity as you now enjoy!

And now you have an extraordinary opportunity, a day wherein Christ has flung the door of mercy wide open, and stands in the door calling and crying with a loud voice to poor sinners; a day, wherein many are flocking to him, and pressing into the kingdom of God. Many are daily coming from the east, west, north and south; many that were very lately in the same miserable condition that you are in, are in now a happy state, with their hearts filled with love to Him that has loved them and washed them from their sins in His own blood, and rejoicing in hope of the Glory of God.[7] How awful is it to be left behind at such a day! To see so many others feasting, while you are pining and perishing! To see so many rejoicing and singing for joy of heart, while you have cause to mourn for sorrow of heart and howl for vexation of spirit! How can you rest one moment in such a condition? . . .

Therefore let everyone that is out of Christ now awake and fly from the wrath to come. The wrath of Almighty God is now undoubtedly hanging over a great part of this congregation: Let everyone fly out of Sodom![8] *Haste and escape for your lives, look not behind you, escape to the mountain, lest you be consumed.* ❧

---

6. *Asunder* means "into separate pieces."

Literary Element   Imagery *Which senses does this image appeal to? What emotions does it stir?*

7. The author is referring to the many people who were part of the Great Awakening, a movement that urged people to experience religion on a personal, emotional level.
8. In Genesis 19:15–17, angels warn Lot, the only virtuous inhabitant of the sinful city of Sodom, to flee the city before it is destroyed.

Reading Strategy   Examining Connotation *How does the connotation of the word* flocking *contribute to Edwards's point?*

RESPONDING AND THINKING CRITICALLY

Respond

1. Imagine that you are in the congregation, listening to Edwards's sermon. How might you respond?

Recall and Interpret

2. (a)In the first paragraph, what generalization does Edwards make about all people? (b)Why do you think Edwards makes this statement?

3. (a)To what does Edwards compare the unrepentant sinner in paragraph seven? (b)What is the effect of this comparison?

4. (a)Near the end of the sermon, what does Edwards say Christ has done? (b)How would you describe Edwards's view of the relationship between God and humanity?

Analyze and Evaluate

5. An **allusion** is a reference to a well-known person, character, place, or situation. (a)What allusion does Edwards introduce in the last paragraph? (b)Why does he make this reference?

6. (a)What is the effect of Edwards's repetition of the word *you*? (b)How would the effect have been different if Edwards had replaced *you* with *a sinner*?

7. (a)What effect do you think Edwards intended his sermon to have on his congregation? (b)In what other ways might a person have reacted?

Connect

8. **Big idea** **Life in the New World** Life in the American colonies was difficult and dangerous. How do the conditions of colonial life contribute to the impact of Edwards's message?

LITERARY ANALYSIS

Literary Element **Imagery**

Visual images are the most common type of imagery, but a writer can also use other **sensory details** that appeal to the reader's sense of hearing, taste, smell, or touch.

1. What frightening images occur in the first two paragraphs? To which senses do they appeal?

2. List five additional images that Edwards uses in the sermon to make his arguments convincing.

Performing

Dramatic Reading Deliver a dramatic reading of a portion of "Sinners in the Hands of an Angry God." Use appropriate rehearsal strategies to focus on the following performance details:

- adjusting the level of your voice to convey emphasis
- using facial expressions and gestures to help reinforce the sermon's imagery

Literature Online **Web Activities** For eFlashcards, Selection Quick Checks, and other Web activities, go to www.glencoe.com.

READING AND VOCABULARY

Reading Strategy **Examining Connotation**

Words may have negative or positive associations, or **connotations.** For example, in describing sinners, Edwards uses the word *howl,* which has a negative connotation, suggesting an animal in distress.

1. Identify negative connotations in this passage: "you are ten thousand times so abominable in his eyes, as the most hateful and venomous serpent is in ours."

2. How do these connotations reinforce Edwards's message?

Vocabulary **Practice**

Practice with Analogies Choose the word pair that best completes each analogy:

1. appease : inflame ::
   a. defend : protect   c. injure : harm
   b. climb : scale   d. raise : lower

2. prudence : wisdom ::
   a. palace : hut   c. robbery : theft
   b. peak : canyon   d. stupidity : cunning

Vocabulary Workshop

Analogies

▶ **Vocabulary Terms**

An **analogy** is a type of comparison based on the relationships between pairs of things or ideas.

▶ **Test-Taking Tip**

When you encounter word analogies on a test, a good strategy is to keep in mind the word *relationship*. Ask yourself, "How is the first word related to the second?" Familiarize yourself with some of the most common word relationships, such as those listed in the chart on this page.

▶ **Literary Terms Handbook**

For more about analogies, see Literary Terms Handbook, p. R1.

eFlashcards For eFlashcards and other vocabulary activities, go to www.glencoe.com.

🔲 **ACADEMIC STANDARDS (page 94)**

11.1.3 Analyze the meaning of analogies encountered, analyzing specific comparisons as well as relationships and inferences.

Understanding Relationships Between Words

"God is dreadfully provoked, his anger is as great towards them as to those that are actually suffering the executions of the fierceness of his wrath in hell."

—Jonathan Edwards, from "Sinners in the Hands of an Angry God"

Connecting to Literature The definition of *wrath* tells you that the word means "extreme anger." One way to keep that information in your long-term memory is to relate it to a pair of words you know well. You can form an **analogy**—a way of showing that two relationships are the same—to remember the meaning of *wrath*.

wrath : anger :: starvation : hunger

This analogy is "Wrath is to anger as starvation is to hunger." Most analogy test questions ask you to identify the pair of words that best represents the relationship expressed by another pair of words.

glowing : flames ::

a. burning : freezing   **b.** fierce : lion   **c.** wren : bird   **d.** sailor : ship

To complete an analogy, use these tips:

- Describe the relationship of the first pair of words. ("*Glowing* is a characteristic of *flames*.") Then use that relationship to describe the relationship between the words in each answer choice. The one that fits best is the right answer. ("*Fierce* is a characteristic of a *lion*.")
- The words in the second pair should be the same parts of speech as the corresponding words in the first pair.
- If no choice makes sense, try another relationship between the first pair.

Analogies can be based on a variety of relationships.

Association or Usage	An *archer* is associated with or uses a *bow*.
Part/Whole	A *quart* is one-fourth of a *gallon*.
Example/Class	A *wigwam* is a type of *dwelling*.
Synonym or Antonym	*Miserable* is the opposite of *happy*.

Exercise

Choose the pair that best completes each analogy.

1. doleful : joyful ::
   a. icy : scalding   **b.** expensive : costly   **c.** month : year

2. globe : round ::
   a. fiery : blazing   **b.** student : class   **c.** box : rectangular

Part 3

THE ROAD TO INDEPENDENCE

Spirit of '76, 1891. Archibald M. Willard. Lithograph. 36 x 50 in. Private Collection.

"These are the times that try men's souls."

—Thomas Paine, *The Crisis,* No. 1

from *The Autobiography of Benjamin Franklin* and from *Poor Richard's Almanack*

MEET BENJAMIN FRANKLIN

Imagine that your senator invented the Internet and a new kind of electric guitar, spoke many languages, wrote poetry, started a successful corporation, founded a college, and helped write some of the world's most important political documents. If you can imagine such an extraordinary person today, then you are beginning to understand just how remarkable Benjamin Franklin was in his time.

> *"Dost though love life? Then do not squander time; for that's the stuff life is made of."*
>
> —Benjamin Franklin
> from *Poor Richard's Almanack*

Printer and Scientist Franklin was born into a poor Boston family, the tenth of seventeen children. His formal education ended when he was only ten years old. By the age of twelve, Franklin was an apprentice in his brother James's print shop. Over the next five years, Franklin mastered this trade, which eventually provided him with financial security. By the age of twenty-six, he was operating his own printing firm in Philadelphia and was writing and publishing *Poor Richard's Almanack*, one of the most popular and influential works of its time, under the pen name Richard Saunders.

As he moved into middle age, Franklin became more involved in civic affairs and scientific research. It was during this period of his life that he helped to found both the first public library in America and the Academy of Philadelphia, which evolved into the University of Pennsylvania. In 1746 and 1747, Franklin made groundbreaking investigations of electrical phenomena and lightning that brought him international fame. Franklin was also responsible for such diverse inventions as bifocal glasses, the Franklin stove, daylight saving time, and the lightning rod.

Diplomat and Revolutionary As a representative of the Pennsylvania Assembly, Franklin spent much of the period from 1757 to 1775 in London. He also acted as an agent for the colonies and argued against the hated Stamp Act. While Franklin had always opposed this tax, he did not, at first, support American independence. Instead, Franklin imagined a British empire made up of many self-governing nations. By 1775, however, his hopes for reconciliation had vanished. Franklin left Britain for Philadelphia, in preparation for the coming war. Upon his arrival, Franklin learned that the battles of Lexington and Concord had already been fought. Within days, Franklin was made a delegate to the Continental Congress for which he helped draft the Declaration of Independence.

Franklin's greatest contribution to the Revolution took place from 1776 to 1785, during his diplomatic mission to France. Franklin, whose charm and wit were famous, became a celebrity almost immediately. The American cause was soon adopted by the French government, which pledged funds and more than 40,000 troops. French support, secured by Franklin's diplomacy, was vital in achieving American independence. Franklin's role as a founder of the United States brought him fame, while his brilliant independent thinking and scientific rationalism assured him a high position among the major figures of the eighteenth-century Enlightenment.

Benjamin Franklin was born in 1706 and died in 1790.

Literature Online **Author Search** For more about Benjamin Franklin, go to www.glencoe.com.

Connecting to the Autobiography

In *The Autobiography of Benjamin Franklin,* Franklin discusses his arrival in Philadelphia. The excerpt from *Poor Richard's Almanack* contains some of Franklin's sayings. As you read, think about the following questions:

- How do you think you would react to moving to a new place where you didn't know anyone?
- When taking trips, have you found that most people are friendly and helpful to travelers? Explain.

Building Background

The passage from Franklin's autobiography begins with his arrival in Philadelphia in the 1720s. This bustling community of 5,000 people was the second-largest city in the colonies. Franklin published *Poor Richard's Almanack* in Philadelphia every year for the 25 years between 1733 and 1758. Almanacs were one of the earliest types of reading material to be published and were the forerunners of today's magazines. Colonial almanacs provided a wide variety of material, including puzzles, both serious and humorous articles, and common-sense aphorisms, or witty sayings, of the type that made Franklin famous.

Setting Purposes for Reading

Big Idea The Road to Independence

Read the excerpts from *The Autobiography of Benjamin Franklin* and *Poor Richard's Almanack* to learn how Franklin played a key role in the colonists' struggle for independence.

Literary Element Autobiography

An **autobiography** is a nonfiction narrative in which the author tells the story of his or her own life. As you read Franklin's autobiography, think about how his experience in Philadelphia helped to shape the person he was to become.

- See Literary Terms Handbook, p. R2.

Literature Online **Interactive Literary Elements Handbook** To review or learn more about the literary elements, go to www.glencoe.com.

Reading Strategy Analyzing Voice

Voice is the distinctive use of language that conveys the author's or narrator's personality. Word choice, tone, and sentence structure contribute to voice.

....

Reading Tip: Taking Notes In a chart, describe the effect of Franklin's word choice, tone, and sentence structure on voice.

Example	Effect
"ambulatory quack doctor"	vivid, humorous observation

Vocabulary

indentured (in den′ chərd) *adj.* bound by contract to serve someone for a time; p. 98 *The indentured servant completed a six-year term.*

ambulatory (am′ byə lə tôr′ ē) *adj.* moving from place to place; p. 98 *The ambulatory news correspondent traveled all over Europe and Africa.*

ingenious (in jēn′ yəs) *adj.* exhibiting creative ability; inventive; p. 98 *Shawn created an ingenious new device that mowed the lawn and raked the leaves at the same time.*

infidel (in′ fə del′) *n.* an unbeliever; p. 98 *In Puritan times, anyone who did not regularly attend church was considered an infidel.*

mortification (môr′ tə fi kā′ shən) *n.* feeling of shame, humiliation, or embarrassment; p. 98 *I experienced complete mortification when I realized I was sitting in a wad of gum.*

....

Vocabulary Tip: Word Roots The word *ingenious* contains the Latin root *gen,* which means "to give birth to" or "to produce."

INDIANA ACADEMIC STANDARDS (pages 97–101)
11.3.5 Analyze or evaluate works...written by important authors in the respective major historical periods.

11.2.2 Analyze...word choice in the text.
11.5.9 Write...a description...

from *The Autobiography of Benjamin Franklin*

Benjamin Franklin

In the evening I found myself very feverish and went to bed; but having read some where that cold water drunk plentifully was good for fever, I followed the prescription and sweat plentifully most of the night. My fever left me, and in the morning, crossing the ferry, I proceeded on my journey on foot, having fifty miles to go to Burlington,[1] where I was told I should find boats that would carry me the rest of the way to Philadelphia.

It rained very hard all the day; I was thoroughly soaked, and by noon a good deal tired; so I stopped at a poor inn, where I stayed all night, beginning now to wish I had never left home. I made so miserable a figure, too, that I found, by the questions asked me, I was suspected to be some runaway **indentured** servant and in danger of being taken up on that suspicion. However, I proceeded next day and got in the evening to an inn within eight or ten miles of Burlington, kept by one Dr. Brown. He entered into conversation with me while I took some refreshment, and finding I had read a little, became very obliging and friendly. Our acquaintance continued all the rest of his life. He had been, I imagine, an **ambulatory** quack doctor, for there was no town in England nor any country in Europe of which he could not give a very particular account. He had some letters,[2] and was **ingenious,** but he was an **infidel,** and wickedly undertook, some years after, to turn the Bible into doggerel[3] verse, as Cotton had formerly done with Virgil. By this means he set many facts in a ridiculous light, and might have done mischief with weak minds if his work had been published; but it never was.

At his house I lay that night, and arrived the next morning at Burlington, but had the **mortification** to find that the regular boats were gone a little before, and no other expected to go before Tuesday, this being

---

1. Burlington, New Jersey, is not far from Philadelphia, on the opposite side of the Delaware River.

Literary Element   Autobiography *What does Franklin reveal about himself in this passage?*

Vocabulary

indentured (in den´ chərd) *adj.* bound by contract to serve someone for a time

---

2. Here, *letters* means "education or knowledge, especially of literature."
3. English poet Charles Cotton (1630–1687) wrote a *doggerel* version, or parody, of Virgil's epic poem the *Aeneid*.

Reading Strategy   Analyzing Voice *What do Franklin's word choice and tone suggest about his attitude toward his new friend?*

Vocabulary

ambulatory (am´ byə lə tôr´ē) *adj.* moving from place to place

ingenious (in jēn´ yəs) *adj.* exhibiting creative ability; inventive

infidel (in´ fə del´) *n.* an unbeliever

mortification (môr´ tə fi kā´ shən) *n.* feeling of shame, humiliation, or embarrassment

Benjamin Franklin, Printer, c. 1928. John Ward Dunsmore. Oil on canvas, 28 x 36 in. The New York Historical Society, New York.

Viewing the Art: What might Benjamin Franklin have been discussing with the other people in this scene?

Saturday. Wherefore I returned to an old woman in the town, of whom I had bought some gingerbread to eat on the water, and asked her advice. She proposed to lodge me till a passage by some other boat occurred. I accepted her offer, being much fatigued by traveling on foot. Understanding I was a printer, she would have had me remain in that town and follow my business, being ignorant what stock was necessary to begin with. She was very hospitable, gave me a dinner of oxcheek with great good-will, accepting only of a pot of ale in return; and I thought myself fixed till Tuesday should come. However, walking in the evening by the side of the river, a boat came by, which I found was going toward Philadelphia with several people in her.

They took me in, and as there was no wind we rowed all the way; and about midnight, not having yet seen the city, some of the company were confident we must have passed it and would row no further; the others knew not where we were, so we put toward the shore, got into a creek, landed near an old fence, with the rails of which we made a fire, the night being cold, in October, and there we remained till daylight. Then one of the company knew the place to be Cooper's Creek, a little above Philadelphia, which we saw as soon as we got out of the creek, and arrived

---

Big Idea The Road to Independence *How does this description reveal the spirit of people who will fight for independence?*

there about eight or nine o'clock on the Sunday morning and landed at Market Street wharf.

I have been the more particular in this description of my journey, and shall be so of my first entry into that city, that you may in your mind compare such unlikely beginnings with the figure I have since made there. I was in my working dress, my best clothes coming round by sea. I was dirty, from my being so long in the boat. My pockets were stuffed out with shirts and stockings, and I knew no one nor where to look for lodging. Fatigued with walking, rowing, and the want of sleep, I was very hungry; and my whole stock of cash consisted in a single dollar, and about a shilling[4] in copper coin, which I gave to the boatmen for my passage. At first they refused it, on account of my having rowed; but I insisted on their taking it. Man is sometimes more generous when he has little money than when he has plenty; perhaps to prevent his being thought to have but little.

I walked toward the top of the street, gazing about till near Market Street, when I met a boy with bread. I had often made a meal of dry bread, and inquiring where he had bought it, I went immediately to the baker's he directed me to. I asked for biscuits, meaning such as we had at Boston; that sort, it seems, was not made at Philadelphia. I then asked for a threepenny loaf and was told they had none. Not knowing the different prices nor the names of the different sorts of bread, I told him to give me threepenny worth of any sort. He gave me accordingly three great puffy rolls. I was surprised at the quantity, but took it, and having no room in my pockets, walked off with a roll under

4. A *shilling* is a British coin equal to one-twentieth of a pound.

each arm and eating the other. Thus I went up Market Street as far as Fourth Street, passing by the door of Mr. Read, my future wife's father; when she, standing at the door, saw me, and thought I made, as I certainly did, a most awkward, ridiculous appearance. Then I turned and went down Chestnut Street and part of Walnut Street, eating my roll all the way; and coming round found myself again at Market Street wharf, near the boat I came in, to which I went for a draught[5] of the river water; and being filled with one of my rolls, gave the other two to a woman and her child that came down the river in the boat with us and were waiting to go further.

Thus refreshed I walked again up the street, which by this time had many clean-dressed people in it, who were all walking the same way. I joined them, and thereby was led into the great meeting-house of the Quakers,[6] near the market. I sat down among them, and after looking round a while and hearing nothing said,[7] being very drowsy through labor and want of rest the preceding night, I fell fast asleep and continued so till the meeting broke up, when some one was kind enough to rouse me. This, therefore, was the first house I was in, or slept in, in Philadelphia. ∾

---

5. Here, *draught* means "a gulp" or "a swallow."
6. *Quakers* are members of the Society of Friends, a Christian religious group founded in the seventeenth century.
7. Quaker religious meetings often include long periods of silence.

Reading Strategy Analyzing Voice *What does Franklin reveal about his personality with this passage?*

Literary Element Autobiography *Why might have Franklin chosen to include this detail in his autobiography?*

RESPONDING AND THINKING CRITICALLY

Respond

1. How would you have felt if, like Franklin, you arrived in an unfamiliar city with little money, no job, and no place to live?

Recall and Interpret

2. (a)What people does Franklin meet before he takes the boat to Philadelphia? (b)What do you learn about Franklin from these encounters?

3. (a)Why do the boatmen at first refuse to accept money from Franklin? (b)Why do you think he offers to pay?

4. (a)What does Franklin do during the Quakers' meeting? (b)What do you think the last sentence of this selection reveals about Franklin?

Analyze and Evaluate

5. (a)How does an autobiography differ from a biography? (b)How should a reader evaluate Franklin's autobiography differently from a biography or a piece of fiction?

6. (a)Why do you think Franklin emphasizes the importance of self-reliance? (b)Explain whether you think self-reliance is as important today as it was in Franklin's time.

Connect

7. **Big Idea** **The Road to Independence**
(a)Describe the colonists' reaction to Franklin when he arrives in Philadelphia. How likely are they to have had an experience similar to Franklin's? (b)How might the colonists' reaction be an indication of their desire for independence?

LITERARY ANALYSIS

Literary Element Autobiography

An **autobiography** is the story an author writes about his or her own life; therefore, an autobiography should be evaluated differently from other genres, such as biography or fiction.

1. Why do you think Franklin thought it was important to write his autobiography? Explain.

2. Do you think that Franklin presented himself as he really was, or did he present a biased, or one-sided, self-portrait? Support your response with details from the selection.

Writing About Literature

Analyze Character What have you learned about Benjamin Franklin from his autobiography? What personal characteristics does Franklin reveal? Use the personal details and experiences that Franklin presents to write a brief personality profile of Franklin as a young man. Use vivid language and quotes from the selection to enliven your profile of Franklin.

Literature Online Web Activities For eFlashcards, Selection Quick Checks, and other Web activities, go to www.glencoe.com.

READING AND VOCABULARY

Reading Strategy Analyzing Voice

Voice is determined by sentence structure, tone, and word choice. A writer may use short, simple sentences with familiar words or long, complex sentences with difficult words. A writer's tone may be serious, humorous, ironic, or somber.

1. According to your notes, what are some of the features of Franklin's voice?

2. Judging by Franklin's literary voice, what sort of personality do you imagine he possessed?

Vocabulary Practice

Word Origins Use your knowledge of the root *gen* (see page 97) and these clues to match each word to its meaning.

Clues: *con-* means "with"; *de-* means "away from"; *-ology* means "the study of"

1. congenital   **a.** recorded history of one's ancestry

2. degenerate   **b.** acquired at birth

3. genealogy   **c.** to fall away from a former condition

from

Poor Richard's Almanack

Benjamin Franklin

If you would keep your secret from an
     enemy, tell it not to a friend.
The worst wheel of the cart makes the
     most noise.
He that cannot obey, cannot command.
No gains without pains.
'Tis easier to prevent bad habits than to
     break them.
A rolling stone gathers no moss.
Today is yesterday's pupil.
Most fools think they are only ignorant.[1]
An empty bag cannot stand upright.
Well done is better than well said.

What you would seem to be, be really.
Honesty is the best policy.
Dost thou love life? Then do not squander
     time; for that's the stuff life is made of.
Beware of little expenses, a small leak will
     sink a great ship.
A penny saved is a penny earned.
Don't count your chickens before they are
     hatched.
Buy what thou hast no need of; and e'er
     long thou shalt sell thy necessaries.
Not to oversee workmen, is to leave them
     your purse open.
Fish and visitors smell in three days.
Quarrels never could last long, if on one
     side only lay the wrong.
Love thy neighbor; yet don't pull down your
     hedge.

---

1. *Ignorant* means "uneducated" or "uninformed."

Reading Strategy Connecting *What is a real-life example of this aphorism?*

RESPONDING AND THINKING CRITICALLY

Respond

1. (a)Which of the aphorisms from *Poor Richard's Almanack* were your favorites? (b)Which did you dislike?

Recall and Interpret

2. (a)According to Franklin, how can a secret be kept from an enemy? (b)Describe in your own words the advice given in the second aphorism.

3. (a)What does Franklin say will sink a great ship? (b)What do you think he means by this aphorism?

4. (a)In the final aphorism, what does Franklin say about "thy neighbor"? (b)What might he mean by "don't pull down your hedge"?

Analyze and Evaluate

5. (a)Which of Franklin's aphorisms gives the most valuable advice? Why? (b)Describe a situation where your chosen aphorism might apply.

6. The colonists found useful advice in the aphorisms of the *Almanack*. (a)Which of Franklin's aphorisms do you think would be most relevant in today's society? (b)Would any be irrelevant in today's society? Explain.

Connect

7. **Big Idea** **The Struggle for Independence** Which of these aphorisms would be most relevant to the colonists' struggle for independence? Explain.

LITERARY ANALYSIS

Literary Element Aphorism

Aphorisms are short, memorable statements that convey a general truth or observation about life. The aphorisms that Franklin wrote in *Poor Richard's Almanack* reflect his clever use of language. For example, when Franklin says, "An empty bag cannot stand upright," he presents a humorous metaphor for a spineless person who can't stand up for his or her own beliefs.

1. Choose one of Franklin's aphorisms. Explain how Franklin's word choice helps make the aphorism easy to remember.

2. Using modern language and references to contemporary life, reword one of Franklin's aphorisms.

Learning for Life

Advice by Aphorism The colonists found advice in the aphorisms of the *Almanack*, while today we read advice columns in the newspaper. Select a letter written to a newspaper advice columnist and compose an aphorism that sums up your advice to the letter writer.

Literature Online **Web Activities** For eFlashcards, Selection Quick Checks, and other Web activities, go to www.glencoe.com.

READING AND VOCABULARY

Reading Strategy Connecting

You can recall ideas from a reading selection better by **connecting** the literature to your own life. Ask yourself: Do I know someone like this? Have I ever felt this way? With a partner, discuss these questions as they pertain to *Poor Richard's Almanack*.

Academic Vocabulary

Here are two words from the vocabulary list on page R86. These words will help you think, write, and talk about the selection.

indicate (in′ di kāt′) *v.* to point out

emphasis (em′ fə sis) *n.* a stress on the importance of something

Practice and Apply
1. What did Franklin **indicate** is the best policy?
2. Why did Franklin place so much **emphasis** on saving money?

The Rhetoric of Revolution

> "Without the pen of Paine, the sword of Washington would have been wielded in vain."
>
> —John Adams

Patrick Henry's Famous Speech, 1915. Clyde DeLand. Oil on canvas.
Viewing the Art: How do you think this depiction of Patrick Henry compares with the tone of his famous speech?

THAT THE UNITED STATES WON independence from British colonial rule is as much a result of effective writers and powerful speakers as of General Washington and his brave army. Patrick Henry, Thomas Paine, and Thomas Jefferson were all highly skilled in rhetoric, the art of persuasion. Persuasion is often based on three types of appeal:

- appeal to reason, logic, and evidence
- appeal to emotions, such as fear, pride, or hate
- ethical appeal, or persuasion based on what we ourselves, moral philosophers, or the majority of people in our culture think is right

No matter what kinds of appeals speakers and writers focus on, they rely on a number of **rhetorical devices.** For example, making an ethical and emotional appeal in his pamphlet *The Crisis, No. 1,* Thomas Paine uses **figurative language,** or language that is used for descriptive effect. Figurative language expresses meaning beyond the literal level. In the following quotation, Paine uses imagery, a type of figurative language, to point out the difference between colonists who were unwilling to endure hardship and those who were willing to carry on despite bitter winters and military defeats.

"The summer soldier and the sunshine patriot will, in this crisis, shrink from the service of his country; but he that stands it now, deserves the love and thanks of man and woman."

Another common device is **hyperbole,** a figure of speech that uses exaggeration to express strong emotion, to make a point, or to evoke humor. In the following quotation, Thomas Paine uses hyperbole to enhance an emotional appeal when explaining the momentous opportunity the Revolution presented for freedom and human progress.

"The heart that feels not now is dead . . ."

Many speakers use **rhetorical questions,** or questions to which no answer is expected. A rhetorical question emphasizes the obvious answer to what is asked. Patrick Henry's "Speech to the Second Virginia Convention" contains more than twenty rhetorical questions. This technique builds to an emotional climax and makes a strong impression on the listeners. The following example presents an appeal to reason.

"They tell us, sir, that we are weak; unable to cope with so formidable an adversary. But when shall we be stronger? Will it be the next week, or the next year? Will it be when we are totally disarmed, and when a British guard shall be stationed in every house?"

"Not only do I want a cracker—we all want a cracker!"

Analyzing Political Cartoons What message does the cartoon convey about a speaker's ability to sway audiences?

In the following passage, Patrick Henry uses the rhetorical device **parallelism** for emphasis. Parallelism is the use of a series of words, phrases, or sentences that have similar grammatical form. Henry's series reaches a powerful climax with a reference to the English king. The appeal is to reason and emotion.

"Our petitions have been slighted; our remonstrances have produced additional violence and insult; our supplications have been disregarded; and we have been spurned, with contempt, from the foot of the throne."

Thomas Jefferson also uses parallelism in the Declaration of Independence to list the colonial grievances against King George III. Additionally, in the following excerpt, Jefferson uses another powerful rhetorical device, **connotative language,** to make an emotional and ethical appeal.

"He has plundered our seas, ravaged our coasts, burned our towns, and destroyed the lives of our people."

Connotation refers to the suggested or implied meanings that are associated with a word beyond its dictionary, or denotative, definition. Here, Jefferson uses verbs with strong negative connotations. *Plundered, ravaged, burned,* and *destroyed* all produce a strong emotional effect.

Earlier in the Declaration, Jefferson refers to "swarms of officers" sent to "harass our people." How different the statement would have been had he written, "A lot of soldiers were sent to bother us"!

While Thomas Paine, Patrick Henry, and Thomas Jefferson did not cause the American Revolution with their rebellious rhetoric, they did rally the colonists to their side. In fact, Paine's pamphlet *Common Sense* sold 100,000 copies in three months. A few months before its publication, Benjamin Franklin observed that he had heard no American speaking in favor of independence. Six months after *Common Sense* was published in Philadelphia, the Declaration of Independence was signed there.

Literature **Online** **Literary History** For more about the rhetoric of revolution, go to www.glencoe.com.

RESPONDING AND THINKING CRITICALLY

1. What answers is Patrick Henry expecting to his rhetorical questions quoted on the bottom of page 104? Explain.

2. What connotation is suggested by Thomas Jefferson's phrase "swarms of officers"?

3. Which type of persuasive appeal—appeal to reason, appeal to emotion, or appeal based on ethics—most influences your political views? Explain.

INDIANA ACADEMIC STANDARDS (pages 104–105)
11.2.1 Analyze...rhetorical (persuasive) devices...
11.7.14 Analyze the four basic types of persuasive speech...
11.7.12 Critique a speaker's use of words and language...
11.7.11 Interpret...information...by...illustrators...

Speech to the Second Virginia Convention

MEET PATRICK HENRY

On March 23, 1775, Patrick Henry stood before fellow delegates at the Second Virginia Convention and thundered his famous challenge, "Give me liberty, or give me death!" Thomas Marshall, a delegate to the convention, recalled that Henry's speech was "one of the most bold, vehement, and animated pieces of eloquence that had ever been delivered."

Henry was born in Hanover County, Virginia. After a series of unsuccessful ventures as a storekeeper and farmer, he began to study law. Henry was admitted to the bar in 1760 and within several years began to prosper. In 1765, at the age of twenty-nine, he became a member of the House of Burgesses, the representative assembly in colonial Virginia. That same year, England passed the Stamp Act, an extremely unpopular tax. When Henry attacked the act in a fiery speech in the House of Burgesses, several members interrupted him with accusations of treason. Henry replied, "If this be treason, make the most of it."

> "I know not what course others may take; but as for me, give me liberty, or give me death."
>
> —Patrick Henry

Governor and Legislator In 1776, as the battles of the Revolution raged around them, the citizens of Virginia elected Henry to be the first governor of the commonwealth under its new constitution. He served three consecutive one-year terms as governor from 1776 through 1778. As wartime governor, Henry vigorously supported General George Washington and his army. Afterward, he continued to play a prominent role in Virginia politics. He was the principal figure in the Virginia state legislature from 1780 to 1784 and again from 1787 to 1790. Between these two stints in the legislature, Henry again served as governor.

High Standards In 1787, Henry turned down an offer to attend the Philadelphia Constitutional Convention. Although he had toiled as a lawyer, legislator, and governor to uphold inalienable rights and protect the American colonists from British intervention, Henry initially opposed the ratification of the U.S. Constitution. What seemed a contradiction, even an insult, to his critics was really Henry's unwillingness to compromise his high ethical standards. Henry championed American independence, but he believed that the Constitution as written did not sufficiently secure the rights of states or those of individuals. Economics also played a role in his decision, for Henry feared that under the Constitution, Spain might retain control of the Mississippi River and the lucrative business of floating commerce up and down its waters.

The Constitution was published in 1787, but the nation remained divided in two camps. The Federalists supported the Constitution, and the Anti-Federalists did not. Henry was the nation's leading Anti-Federalist, and he and his supporters lobbied for amendments. The Constitution was ratified in Virginia in 1788 by the narrow margin of 89 to 79. The strong arguments that Henry and his faction of Anti-Federalists made during the debate eventually led to the Bill of Rights. Henry refused several high positions in the new federal government due to his ailing health and family responsibilities. He died at the age of 63 and was interred at Red Hill, his Virginia home.

Patrick Henry was born in 1736 and died in 1799.

Literature Online **Author Search** For more about Patrick Henry, go to www.glencoe.com.

Connecting to the Speech

What does liberty mean to you? In this speech, Patrick Henry invokes liberty as a battle cry against British meddling in colonial affairs. As you read the speech, think about the following questions:

- What are some liberties you enjoy? Would you risk your life to preserve one of these freedoms?
- What does the phrase "give me liberty, or give me death" mean to you?

Building Background

The British parliament passed a series of taxes on its colonies. American colonists protested these taxes, and thousands of British troops were sent to Boston to preserve order. Patrick Henry was one of the leaders of the growing opposition to British rule. The speech you are about to read would firmly establish Henry's reputation as a forceful proponent of liberty.

Setting Purposes for Reading

Big Idea The Road to Independence

As you read Henry's speech, notice what he implies about the disagreement among the American colonists over the issue of independence from British rule.

Literary Element Rhetorical Question

A **rhetorical question** is one to which no answer is expected or to which the answer is already known. It is used to emphasize the obvious answer to what is asked. As you read Henry's speech, notice how he uses rhetorical questions.

- See Literary Terms Handbook, p. R15.

Literature Online **Interactive Literary Elements Handbook** To review or learn more about the literary elements, go to www.glencoe.com.

Reading Strategy Analyzing Figures of Speech

Figurative language is used for descriptive effect, in order to convey ideas or emotions. Figurative expressions are not literally true but express some truth beyond the literal level. A **figure of speech** is a specific device or kind of figurative language, such as allusion, assonance, hyperbole, metaphor, metonymy, personification, simile, or symbol. As you read, notice how Patrick Henry uses figures of speech.

Reading Tip: Taking Notes Use a chart to record examples of figures of speech and to restate them in your own words.

Figure of Speech	Restatement
"Suffer not yourselves to be betrayed with a kiss."	

Vocabulary

arduous (är´ jōō əs) *adj.* requiring great exertion or endurance; difficult; p. 109 *Running the marathon was too arduous for eight of the contestants.*

insidious (in sid´ ē əs) *adj.* slyly treacherous and deceitful; deceptive; p. 109 *The candidate used insidious methods, such as bribery, to get elected.*

subjugation (sub´ jə gā´ shən) *n.* act of bringing under control; domination; p. 109 *No one liked being under the subjugation of an evil ruler.*

remonstrate (ri mon´ strāt) *v.* to object; to protest; p. 110 *The whole country will remonstrate if taxes are raised again.*

spurn (spurn) *v.* to reject with disdain; p. 110 *Would you spurn an offer of dinner in Paris?*

INDIANA ACADEMIC STANDARDS (pages 107–111)

11.2.1 Analyze both the features and the rhetorical (persuasive) devices of...speeches...

11.3.4 Analyze...figures of speech [used] to evoke...emotions.

11.5.9 Write...a literary analysis...

11.2.2 Analyze [how] meaning is affected by...repetition...

Patrick Henry Arguing the Parson's Cause at the Hanover County Courthouse, 1834.
George Cooke. Oil on canvas. Virginia Historical Society, Richmond.

Speech to the Second Virginia Convention

Patrick Henry

Mr. President:[1] No man thinks more highly than I do of the patriotism, as well as abilities, of the very worthy gentlemen who have just addressed the house. But different men often see the same subject in different lights; and, therefore, I hope it will not be thought disrespectful to those gentlemen, if, entertaining,[2] as I do, opinions of a character very opposite to theirs, I shall speak forth my sentiments freely and without reserve. This is no time for ceremony.

The question before the house is one of awful moment[3] to this country. For my own part, I

---

1. *Mr. President* refers to Peyton Randolph, president of the Virginia Convention.
2. In this case, *entertaining* means "having in mind."
3. The phrase *of awful moment* means "of great consequence."

consider it as nothing less than a question of freedom or slavery. And in proportion to the magnitude of the subject ought to be the freedom of the debate. It is only in this way that we can hope to arrive at truth, and fulfill the great responsibility which we hold to God and our country. Should I keep back my opinions at such a time, through fear of giving offense, I should consider myself as guilty of treason toward my country, and of an act of disloyalty toward the Majesty of Heaven, which I revere above all earthly kings.

Mr. President, it is natural for man to indulge in the illusions of hope. We are apt to shut our eyes against a painful truth, and listen to the song of that siren, till she transforms us into beasts. Is this the part of wise men, engaged in a great and **arduous** struggle for liberty? Are we disposed to be of the number of those who, having eyes, see not, and having ears, hear not, the things which so nearly concern their temporal[4] salvation? For my part, whatever anguish of spirit it may cost, I am willing to know the whole truth; to know the worst and to provide for it.

I have but one lamp by which my feet are guided; and that is the lamp of experience. I know of no way of judging of the future but by the past. And judging by the past, I wish to know what there has been in the conduct of the British ministry for the last ten years to justify those hopes with which gentlemen have been pleased to solace themselves and the House? Is it that **insidious** smile with which our

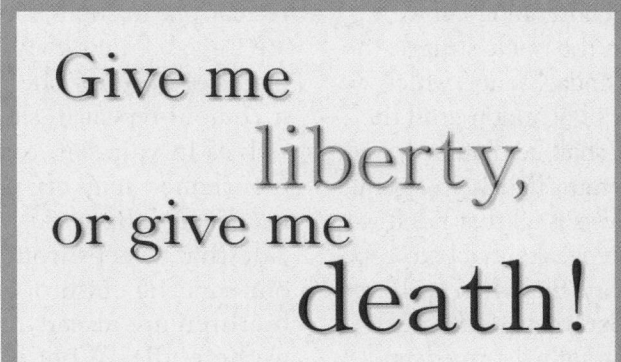

Give me liberty, or give me death!

petition has been lately received? Trust it not, sir; it will prove a snare to your feet. Suffer not yourselves to be betrayed with a kiss. Ask yourselves how this gracious reception of our petition comports with these warlike preparations which cover our waters and darken our land. Are fleets and armies necessary to a work of love and reconciliation? Have we shown ourselves so unwilling to be reconciled, that force must be called in to win back our love? Let us not deceive ourselves, sir. These are the implements of war and **subjugation;** the last arguments to which kings resort. I ask gentlemen, sir, what means this martial array,[5] if its purpose be not to force us to submission? Can gentlemen assign any other possible motives for it? Has Great Britain any enemy, in this quarter of the world, to call for all this accumulation of navies and armies? No, sir, she has none. They are meant for us; they can be meant for no other. They are sent over to bind and rivet upon us those chains which the British ministry have been so long forging. And what have we to oppose to them? Shall we try argument? Sir, we have been trying that for the last ten years. Have we anything new to offer on the subject? Nothing. We have held the subject up in every light of which it is capable; but it has been all in vain. Shall we resort to entreaty[6] and humble supplication?[7] What terms shall we find which have not been already exhausted? Let us not, I beseech you, sir, deceive ourselves longer.

---

5. A *martial array* is a military display.
6. An *entreaty* is a plea or request.
7. Here, *supplication* means "begging."

Literary Element Rhetorical Question *How does Henry build on this rhetorical question several sentences later?*

Reading Strategy Analyzing Figures of Speech *Explain Henry's use of metaphor in this sentence.*

Vocabulary

subjugation (sub´ jə gā´ shən) *n.* act of bringing under control; domination

---

4. The word *temporal* means "in time; relating to life on earth."

Reading Strategy Analyzing Figures of Speech *What is being compared in this metaphor?*

Vocabulary

arduous (är´ jōō əs) *adj.* requiring great exertion or endurance; difficult

insidious (in sid´ē əs) *adj.* slyly treacherous and deceitful; deceptive

Sir, we have done everything that could be done to avert the storm which is now coming on. We have petitioned; we have **remonstrated;** we have supplicated; we have prostrated[8] ourselves before the tyrannical hands of the ministry and parliament. Our petitions have been slighted; our remonstrances have produced additional violence and insult; our supplications have been disregarded; and we have been **spurned**, with contempt, from the foot of the throne. In vain, after these things, may we indulge the fond[9] hope of peace and reconciliation. There is no longer any room for hope. If we wish to be free—if we mean to preserve inviolate[10] those inestimable privileges for which we have been so long contending—if we mean not basely[11] to abandon the noble struggle in which we have been so long engaged, and which we have pledged ourselves never to abandon until the glorious object of our contest shall be obtained, we must fight! I repeat it, sir, we must fight! An appeal to arms and to the God of Hosts is all that is left us!

They tell us, sir, that we are weak; unable to cope with so formidable an adversary. But when shall we be stronger? Will it be the next week, or the next year? Will it be when we are totally disarmed, and when a British guard shall be stationed in every house? Shall we gather strength by irresolution and inaction? Shall we acquire the means of effectual resistance by lying supinely on our backs, and hugging the delusive phantom of hope, until our enemies shall have bound us hand and foot? Sir,

we are not weak, if we make a proper use of the means which the God of nature hath placed in our power. Three millions of people, armed in the holy cause of liberty, and in such a country as that which we possess, are invincible by any force which our enemy can send against us. Besides, sir, we shall not fight our battles alone. There is a just God who presides over the destinies of nations; and who will raise friends to fight our battles for us. The battle, sir, is not to the strong alone; it is to the vigilant, the active, the brave. Besides, sir, we have no election.[12] If we were base enough to desire it, it is now too late to retire from the contest. There is no retreat but in submission and slavery! Our chains are forged! Their clanking may be heard on the plains of Boston! The war is inevitable—and let it come! I repeat it, sir, let it come!

It is in vain, sir, to extenuate[13] the matter. Gentlemen may cry peace, peace—but there is no peace. The war is actually begun! The next gale that sweeps from the North will bring to our ears the clash of resounding arms![14] Our brethren are already in the field! Why stand we here idle? What is it that gentlemen wish? What would they have? Is life so dear, or peace so sweet, as to be purchased at the price of chains and slavery? Forbid it, Almighty God! I know not what course others may take; but as for me, give me liberty, or give me death! ∾

---

8. *Prostrated* means "bowed down."
9. Here, *fond* means "foolish."
10. The word *inviolate* means "unharmed and intact."
11. Here, *basely* means "dishonorably."

Big Idea The Road to Independence *Why does Henry refer to these past events?*

Literary Element Rhetorical Question *Why does Henry use so many rhetorical questions in this paragraph?*

Vocabulary

remonstrate (ri mon′ strāt) *v.* to object; to protest
spurn (spurn) *v.* to reject with disdain

---

12. In this instance, *election* means "choice."
13. To *extenuate* means "to make a situation seem less serious by offering excuses."
14. *[The next gale . . . arms!]* Colonists in Massachusetts were already engaged in open opposition to the British.

Reading Strategy Analyzing Figures of Speech *How does Henry extend the meaning of this metaphor that he has used earlier?*

Big Idea The Road to Independence *How does Henry's powerful conclusion limit the choices available to the American colonists?*

RESPONDING AND THINKING CRITICALLY

Respond

1. Imagine that you were a delegate at the Second Virginia Convention. How do you think you would have reacted to Henry's speech?

Recall and Interpret

2. (a)According to Henry, what is the question "of awful moment" to the country? (b)Why do you think Henry gives several reasons to support his need to speak out?

3. (a)What does Henry say about Britain's military and naval forces? (b)Why does he introduce this point?

4. (a)According to Henry, what makes Americans "invincible"? (b)Why does Henry say that God is on the side of the colonists?

Analyze and Evaluate

5. (a)Which emotions are expressed in the speech? (b)In your opinion, does Henry's passion add to his effectiveness? Explain.

6. (a)Why does Henry suggest that the colonists have only two choices—liberty or death? (b)In your opinion, are these the only options? Explain.

Connect

7. **Big Idea** **The Road to Independence** (a)What was Henry's immediate purpose in giving this speech? (b)What do you think he would have viewed as Virginia's next step?

LITERARY ANALYSIS

Literary Element **Rhetorical Question**

A rhetorical question presumes that listeners agree with the speaker. The speaker can use this persuasive technique as an emotional appeal designed to achieve solidarity with his or her audience or as a device to lead the audience to accept the speaker's beliefs.

1. What is the effect of the rhetorical questions in the last paragraph of Henry's speech?

2. Name one idea or belief that Henry wants his audience to accept.

Writing About Literature

Analyze Rhetorical Devices Parallelism is the use of a series of words, phrases, or sentences that have similar grammatical form. For example, in the next-to-last paragraph of his speech, Henry uses four rhetorical questions that consist of interrogative sentences beginning with the words *Will* or *Shall*. In a short essay, analyze Henry's uses of parallelism and explain how they support his purpose.

Literature Online **Web Activities** For eFlashcards, Selection Quick Checks, and other Web activities, go to www.glencoe.com.

READING AND VOCABULARY

Reading Strategy **Analyzing Figures of Speech**

In classical mythology, a siren was a sea goddess who lured sailors to their doom with her beautiful song.

1. What does Henry compare to the siren's song?

2. Why do you think he uses this metaphor?

Vocabulary **Practice**

Practice with Antonyms Find the antonym for each vocabulary word from "Speech to the Second Virginia Convention." Use a dictionary or thesaurus if you need help.

1. arduous   **a.** high   **b.** effortless

2. insidious   **a.** obvious   **b.** ugly

3. subjugation   **a.** fate   **b.** freedom

4. remonstrate   **a.** recall   **b.** approve

5. spurn   **a.** accept   **b.** dislike

Declaration of Independence

MEET THOMAS JEFFERSON

Honoring Nobel Prize winners at the White House in 1962, President John F. Kennedy observed, "I think this is the most extraordinary collection of talent, of human knowledge, that has ever been gathered together at the White House, with the possible exception of when Thomas Jefferson dined alone." The reference was to Jefferson's amazing mastery of at least a dozen different endeavors. He was an architect, inventor, lawyer, surveyor, musician, and botanist, to name but six professions in which Jefferson excelled. Ultimately he became president of the United States.

Thomas Jefferson was born in 1743, in Albemarle County in central Virginia, to Peter and Jane Randolph Jefferson. In 1760 he enrolled in the College of William and Mary in Williamsburg, where he studied mathematics, science, and law. He began his law practice in 1767 and was elected to the Virginia House of Burgesses in 1769. In 1772 he married a young widow, Martha Wayles Skelton. They had six children, but only two survived, and Martha died in 1782, after the birth of their last child.

> "The spirit of resistance to government is so valuable on certain occasions that I wish it to be always kept alive. . . . I like a little rebellion now and then."
>
> —Thomas Jefferson,
> from a letter to Abigail Adams, 1787

Jefferson the Writer As a delegate to the Second Continental Congress in 1776, Jefferson drafted what many believe is the most powerful argument for freedom ever written. When the delegates debated breaking away from Britain, they turned to Jefferson to commit their ideas about liberty and freedom to writing. He expressed those ideas in the Declaration of Independence. Although members of the congress edited, revised, and deleted portions of the draft, the final version was basically Jefferson's.

Jefferson the Leader Jefferson succeeded Patrick Henry as governor of Virginia but returned to serve in the congress from 1783 to 1784. After his appointment as U.S. ambassador to France, he became George Washington's secretary of state and then vice president under John Adams. In 1803, during the first of his two terms as president, Jefferson made a decision that changed the nation forever. He arranged to purchase the Louisiana Territory from France. The Louisiana Purchase cost the nation $11.25 million plus $3.75 million in French debts it agreed to pay—a transaction that doubled the size of the United States. Jefferson then sent a scientific expedition headed by Meriwether Lewis and William Clark to explore these new lands and continue on to the Pacific Ocean.

Jefferson's last years were spent at the Virginia home he designed, built, and rebuilt—Monticello. In 1819 he founded the University of Virginia at Charlottesville near his home. He died on July 4, 1826, exactly fifty years after the signing of the Declaration of Independence. A man of contradictions, he opposed slavery in principle but nonetheless owned slaves. His epitaph, which he composed himself, cited his writing of the Declaration of Independence among his achievements but made no reference to his presidency.

Thomas Jefferson was born in 1743 and died in 1826.

Literature Online Author Search For more about Thomas Jefferson, go to www.glencoe.com.

Connecting to the Text

How important is your freedom to you? If your freedoms were severely limited by the government, what do you think you would do? Jefferson's Declaration of Independence addresses such questions.

Building Background

In June 1776, Thomas Jefferson wrote the first draft of the Declaration of Independence in Philadelphia, where the Second Continental Congress had convened. On June 11, the delegates had appointed a five-member committee to draft a statement declaring independence from Britain. The committee included Benjamin Franklin, John Adams, and Jefferson, but Jefferson was called upon to do the writing. Some of his ideas about independence were not new. According to John Locke's theory of "natural law," which Jefferson had studied, human beings are "by nature free, equal and independent." Following Locke's lead, Jefferson stressed that the American Revolution was a struggle for the basic rights of all people.

Setting Purposes for Reading

Big Idea The Road to Independence

As you read the Declaration of Independence, notice how Jefferson details the hardships faced by colonists in their struggle for independence.

Literary Element Parallelism

Parallelism (sometimes called "matching parts") is the phrasing of similar ideas or elements—words, phrases, or sentences—in the same grammatical form. For example, notice the parallel phrases that begin this saying from Benjamin Franklin's *Poor Richard's Almanack:* "Early to bed, and early to rise, make a man healthy, wealthy, and wise." As you read the Declaration of Independence, notice Jefferson's effective use of parallelism.

- See Literary Terms Handbook, p. R13

Literature Online **Interactive Literary Elements Handbook** To review or learn more about the literary elements, go to www.glencoe.com.

Reading Strategy Evaluating Argument

To **evaluate arguments,** you need to understand how a writer organizes his or her thoughts. In **deductive reasoning,** a writer argues from general principles to specific conclusions. One type of deductive reasoning is the **syllogism,** a formula that presents an argument logically. A syllogism has three parts: a major premise, a minor premise, and a conclusion. In a valid syllogism, the conclusion follows logically from the premises. Here is an example:

- Major premise: All human beings are mortal.
- Minor premise: Jefferson is a human being.
- Conclusion: Jefferson is mortal.

As you read the Declaration of Independence, notice Jefferson's use of deductive reasoning.

Vocabulary

usurpation (ū´ sər pā´ shən) *n.* the act of seizing power without legal right or authority; p. 114 *The civil disorder led to usurpation of power by a group of military leaders.*

endeavor (en dev´ ər) *v.* to make an effort; to try; p. 115 *The student endeavored to finish his paper on time.*

tenure (ten´yər) *n.* conditions or terms under which something is held; p. 115 *Her tenure as judge depends on her effectiveness in the position.*

acquiesce (ak´ wē es´) *v.* to consent or agree silently, without objections; to comply passively; p. 116 *Belinda decided to acquiesce to her friend's plans for the evening.*

rectitude (rek´ tə tōōd´) *n.* uprightness of moral character; honesty; p. 116 *Known for his rectitude, Thomas was put in charge of the organization's funds.*

Vocabulary Tip: Synonyms Synonyms are words that have the same or similar meanings. The words *consent* and *agreement,* for example, are synonyms. Synonyms are always the same part of speech.

INDIANA ACADEMIC STANDARDS (pages 113–117)
11.2.2 Analyze...organization [and] repetition...
11.7.3 Distinguish between...forms of logical arguments, including...deductive arguments [and] syllogisms...

11.5.9 Write...a literary analysis...

Declaration of Independence

In Congress, July 4, 1776

Thomas Jefferson

When, in the course of human events, it becomes necessary for one people to dissolve the political bands which have connected them with another, and to assume, among the powers of the earth, the separate and equal station to which the laws of nature and nature's God entitle them, a decent respect to the opinions of mankind requires that they should declare the causes which impel them to the separation.

We hold these truths to be self-evident: that all men are created equal, that they are endowed by their Creator with certain unalienable rights;[1] that among these are life, liberty, and the pursuit of happiness; that to secure these rights, governments are instituted among men, deriving their just powers from the consent of the governed; that whenever any form of government becomes destructive of these ends, it is the right of the people to alter or to abolish it, and to institute new government, laying its foundation on such principles, and organizing its powers in such form, as to them shall seem most likely to effect their safety and happiness. Prudence,[2] indeed, will dictate that governments long established should not be changed for light and transient causes; and accordingly all experience hath shown that mankind are more disposed to suffer, while evils are sufferable, than to right themselves by abolishing the forms to which they are accustomed. But when a long train of abuses and **usurpations,** pursuing invariably the same object, evinces[3] a design to reduce them under absolute despotism,[4] it is their right, it is their duty, to throw off such government, and to provide new guards for their future security.

Such has been the patient sufferance of these colonies; and such is now the necessity which constrains[5] them to alter their former systems of government. The history of the present King of Great Britain is a history of repeated injuries and usurpations, all having in direct object the establishment of an absolute tyranny[6] over these states. To prove this, let facts be submitted to a candid world.

---

1. *Unalienable rights* cannot be taken away.
2. The exercise of good judgment is called *prudence.*

3. *Evinces* means "makes clear or evident."
4. *Despotism* is government by a ruler of absolute authority.
5. *Constrains* means "forces."
6. The arbitrary or oppressive exercise of power is *tyranny.*

Reading Strategy Evaluating Argument *Which of the basic principles stated earlier support this argument?*

Big Idea The Road to Independence *In what way does this statement shed light on what the colonists have endured in their struggle for independence?*

Vocabulary

usurpation (yū′ sər pā′ shən) *n.* the act of seizing power without legal right or authority

He has refused his assent[7] to laws, the most wholesome and necessary for the public good.

He has forbidden his governors to pass laws of immediate and pressing importance, unless suspended in their operation till his assent should be obtained; and when so suspended, he has utterly neglected to attend to them.

He has refused to pass other laws for the accommodation of large districts of people, unless those people would relinquish the right of representation in the legislature, a right inestimable to them, and formidable to tyrants only.

He has called together legislative bodies at places unusual, uncomfortable, and distant from the depository of their public records, for the sole purpose of fatiguing them into compliance with his measures.

He has dissolved representative houses repeatedly, for opposing, with manly firmness, his invasions on the rights of the people.

He has refused, for a long time after such dissolutions, to cause others to be elected; whereby the legislative powers, incapable of annihilation, have returned to the people at large for their exercise; the state remaining, in the meantime, exposed to all the dangers of invasion from without and convulsions within.

He has **endeavored** to prevent the population of these states; for that purpose obstructing the laws for naturalization[8] of foreigners, refusing to pass others to encourage their migrations hither, and raising the conditions of new appropriations of lands.

He has obstructed the administration of justice, by refusing his assent to laws for establishing judiciary powers.

He has made judges dependent on his will alone for the **tenure** of their offices, and the amount of payment of their salaries.

He has erected a multitude of new offices, and sent hither swarms of officers to harass our people and eat out their substance.

Drafting of the Declaration of Independence, c. 1900. Jean-Léon Gérome Ferris.
Viewing the Art: Do you think the artist convincingly depicts the importance of the event?

He has kept among us, in times of peace, standing armies, without the consent of our legislatures.

He has affected to render the military independent of, and superior to, the civil power.

He has combined with others to subject us to a jurisdiction foreign to our constitution and unacknowledged by our laws, giving his assent to their acts of pretended legislation:

For quartering[9] large bodies of armed troops among us;

For protecting them, by a mock trial, from punishment for any murders which they should commit on the inhabitants of these states;

For cutting off our trade with all parts of the world;

For imposing taxes on us without our consent;

For depriving us, in many cases, of the benefits of trial by jury;

For transporting us beyond seas, to be tried for pretended offenses;

---

7. *Assent* is agreement.
8. *Naturalization* is the process by which foreigners become citizens of another country.

Vocabulary

endeavor (en dev′ ər) *v.* to make an effort to; to try
tenure (ten′ yər) *n.* conditions or terms under which something is held

---

9. Here, *quartering* means "providing with living accommodations; lodging."

For abolishing the free system of English laws in a neighboring province,[10] establishing therein an arbitrary government, and enlarging its boundaries, so as to render it at once an example and fit instrument for introducing the same absolute rule into these colonies;

For taking away our charters, abolishing our most valuable laws, and altering fundamentally the forms of our governments;

For suspending our own legislatures, and declaring themselves invested with power to legislate for us in all cases whatsoever.

He has abdicated government here, by declaring us out of his protection and waging war against us.

He has plundered our seas, ravaged our coasts, burned our towns, and destroyed the lives of our people.

He is at this time transporting large armies of foreign mercenaries[11] to complete the works of death, desolation, and tyranny already begun with circumstances of cruelty and perfidy[12] scarcely paralleled in the most barbarous ages, and totally unworthy the head of a civilized nation.

He has constrained our fellow-citizens, taken captive on the high seas, to bear arms against their country, to become the executioners of their friends and brethren, or to fall themselves by their hands.

He has excited domestic insurrections among us, and has endeavored to bring on the inhabitants of our frontiers, the merciless Indian savages, whose known rule of warfare is an undistinguished destruction of all ages, sexes, and conditions.

In every stage of these oppressions we have petitioned for redress[13] in the most humble terms; our repeated petitions have been answered only by repeated injury. A prince whose character is thus marked by every act which may define a tyrant is unfit to be ruler of a free people.

Nor have we been wanting in our attentions to our British brethren. We have warned them, from time to time, of attempts by their legislature to extend an unwarrantable jurisdiction over us. We have reminded them of the circumstances of our emigration and settlement here. We have appealed to their native justice and magnanimity;[14] and we have conjured[15] them, by the ties of our common kindred, to disavow these usurpations, which would inevitably interrupt our connections and correspondence. They, too, have been deaf to the voice of justice and consanguinity.[16] We must, therefore, **acquiesce** in the necessity which denounces[17] our separation, and hold them, as we hold the rest of mankind, enemies in war, in peace, friends.

We, therefore, the representatives of the United States of America, in General Congress assembled, appealing to the Supreme Judge of the world for the **rectitude** of our intentions, do, in the name and by the authority of the good people of these colonies, solemnly publish and declare that these United Colonies are, and of right ought to be, free and independent states; that they are absolved from all allegiance to the British crown, and that all political connection between them and the state of Great Britain is, and ought to be, totally dissolved; and that, as free and independent states, they have full power to levy war, conclude peace, contract alliances, establish commerce, and do all other acts and things which independent states may of right do. And for the support of this declaration, with a firm reliance on the protection of Divine Providence, we mutually pledge to each other our lives, our fortunes, and our sacred honor. ∞

---

10. The *neighboring province* is Quebec, Canada.
11. *Mercenaries* are paid soldiers in a foreign army.
12. *Perfidy* means "a deliberate betrayal of trust."
13. A compensation for a wrong done is a *redress*.

Literary Element Parallelism *What does this use of parallelism emphasize?*

14. *Magnanimity* means "nobility of mind and heart."
15. Here, *conjured* means "solemnly appealed to."
16. *Consanguinity* is a relationship based on having ancestors in common; a blood relationship.
17. Here, *denounces* means "announces" or "proclaims."

Big Idea The Road to Independence *How does this sentence show the seriousness of declaring independence?*

Vocabulary

acquiesce (ak′ wē es′) *v.* to consent or agree silently, without objections; to comply passively

rectitude (rek′ tə tōōd′) *n.* uprightness of moral character; honesty

RESPONDING AND THINKING CRITICALLY

Respond

1. How has reading the Declaration of Independence affected your ideas about freedom?

Recall and Interpret

2. (a)What is the purpose of the document? (b)To which "opinions of mankind" might Jefferson be referring?

3. (a)According to Jefferson, which human rights are "unalienable"? (b)How do you interpret the phrase "pursuit of happiness"?

4. (a)How have the colonists met with "these oppressions"? (b)Why might the king have ignored the colonists' petitions for redress?

Analyze and Evaluate

5. (a)In what ways does Jefferson emphasize that the colonists' complaints are against the king of England, not against the British people? (b)Why do you think Jefferson went to such lengths to emphasize this distinction?

6. (a)What method of organization did Jefferson use in creating this document? (b)How effective is this method of organization?

Connect

7. What points that Jefferson made in the Declaration of Independence do you think remain the most important today?

8. **Big Idea** **The Road to Independence** (a)What does the Declaration of Independence stress about the dangers of changing a form of government? (b)What does this indicate about the process that led to the American Revolution?

LITERARY ANALYSIS

Literary Element **Parallelism**

Parallelism emphasizes the items that are arranged in similar structures.

1. How does Jefferson use parallelism in detailing the "self-evident" truths in the second paragraph of the Declaration of Independence?

2. What is the effect of the parallel use of the word *our* in the last sentence of the Declaration?

Writing About Literature

Evaluate Author's Craft Jefferson's presentation of the rights of all people proved so effective that the Declaration of Independence is universally admired. Identify at least three elements in the Declaration that, in your opinion, give it strength. Explain how each contributes to the power of the whole.

Literature Online **Web Activities** For eFlashcards, Selection Quick Checks, and other Web activities, go to www.glencoe.com.

READING AND VOCABULARY

Reading Strategy **Evaluating Argument**

Remember that deductive reasoning moves from general principles to specific conclusions.

1. How does the Declaration of Independence exhibit deductive reasoning?

2. Construct a syllogism based on one of the "self-evident" truths that Jefferson presents in the Declaration of Independence.

Vocabulary **Practice**

Practice with Synonyms Find the synonym for each vocabulary word. Use a dictionary or a thesaurus if you need help.

1. usurpation   **a.** takeover   **b.** release

2. endeavor   **a.** surrender   **b.** attempt

3. tenure   **a.** strength   **b.** hold

4. acquiesce   **a.** protest   **b.** comply

5. rectitude   **a.** integrity   **b.** ruin

Media Link to the Road to Independence

Preview the Article

Even the Founding Fathers had to revise their writing. In "How They Chose These Words," a historian describes the role of the writing process in drafting the Declaration of Independence.

1. From the title, what do you think this article will be about? What do you already know about this subject?

2. Read the *deck,* or the sentence in large type that appears below the title. How does the author feel about Franklin's edits?

Set a Purpose for Reading

Read to learn about the writing of the Declaration of Independence and the roles of Franklin and Jefferson in the struggle for American independence.

Reading Strategy

Determining the Main Idea and Supporting Details

The *main idea* of a text is the most important thing that the writer wants to convey about his or her subject. The main idea is not always obvious; you may have to identify it from details in the text.

As you read, create a graphic organizer like the one shown below.

Main Idea:
• Supporting detail 1: Benjamin Franklin made important changes to the document.
• Supporting detail 2:

■ **INDIANA ACADEMIC STANDARDS (pages 118–120)**

11.2 Develop [reading] strategies...

11.3.5 Analyze or evaluate works of literary or cultural significance in history...that... shed light on seminal philosophical...ideas of their time.

TIME

How They Chose These WORDS

Jefferson wrote the Declaration's first draft, but it was Franklin's editing that made a phrase immortal.

By WALTER ISAACSON

AS THE CONTINENTAL CONGRESS PREPARED TO VOTE on the question of American independence in 1776, it appointed a committee for a job that no one at the time thought was very important. The task, however, would turn out to be a momentous one: drafting a declaration that explained the decision. The committee included Benjamin Franklin, of course, and Thomas Jefferson and John Adams, as well as Connecticut merchant Roger Sherman and New York lawyer Robert Livingston.

How was it that Jefferson, at age 33, got the honor of drafting the document? His name was listed first on the committee, signifying that he was the chairman, because he had gotten the most votes and because he was from Virginia, the colony that had proposed the resolution. His four colleagues had other committee assignments that they considered to be more important. None of them realized that the document would eventually come to be viewed as a cornerstone of American politics. As for Franklin, he was still laid up in bed with boils and gout when the committee first met.

And thus it fell to Jefferson to compose, on a little lap desk he had designed, some of the most famous phrases in history while sitting alone in a second-floor room of a house on Market Street in Philadelphia just a block from Franklin's house. "When, in the course of human events . . . ," he famously began.

Taking a Page from Franklin

The document Jefferson drafted was in some ways similar to what Franklin would have written. It contained a highly specific bill of particulars against the British. It also recounted, as Franklin had often done, the details of America's attempts to make peace despite England's unbending attitude. Indeed, Jefferson's words echoed some of the language that Franklin had used, earlier that year, in a draft resolution that he never published: "Whereas, whenever kings, instead of protecting the lives and properties of their subjects, as is their bounden duty, do endeavor to perpetrate the destruction of either, they thereby cease to be kings, become tyrants, and dissolve all ties of allegiance between themselves and their people."

Jefferson's writing style, however, was different from Franklin's. It was graced with rolling rhythms and smooth phrases, soaring in their poetry and powerful despite their polish. In addition, Jefferson drew on a depth of philosophy not found in Franklin. He echoed both the language and grand theories of English and Scottish Enlightenment thinkers. Having read John Locke's *Second Treatise on Government* at least three times, Jefferson was most notably influenced by Locke's concept of natural rights. And Jefferson built his case, in a manner more sophisticated than Franklin would have, on a contract between government and the governed that was founded on the consent of the people. Jefferson also, it should be noted, borrowed freely from the phrasings of others, including the resounding Declaration of Rights in the new Virginia constitution. Today, this kind of borrowing might lead to accusations of plagiarism, but back then it was considered not only proper but learned.

When he had finished a draft and included some changes from Adams, Jefferson sent it to Franklin on the morning of Friday, June 21. "Will Doctor Franklin be so good as to peruse it," he wrote in his cover note, "and suggest such alterations as his more enlarged view of the subject will dictate?" People were much more polite to editors back then.

Change for the Better?

Franklin made only a few changes, some of which can be viewed written in his hand on what Jefferson referred to as the "rough draft" of the Declaration. The most important of his edits was small but significant. He crossed out, using the heavy backslashes that he often employed, the last three words of Jefferson's phrase "We hold these truths to be sacred and undeniable." Franklin changed them to the words now enshrined in history: "We hold these truths to be self-evident."

The idea of "self-evident" truths drew on the rational view of the world held by Isaac Newton and Franklin's close friend David Hume. The great Scottish philosopher Hume had developed a theory that distinguished between truths that describe matters of fact (such as "London is bigger than Philadelphia") and truths that are declared so through reason and definition ("the angles of a triangle total 180 degrees"; "all bachelors are unmarried"). He referred to the latter type of axioms as "self-evident" truths. By using the word sacred, Jefferson had implied, intentionally or not, that the principle in question—the equality of men and their endowment by their creator with inalienable rights—was a matter of religion. Franklin's edit turned it instead into a matter of reason and rationality.

DEFT TOUCH Franklin changed the phrase "sacred and undeniable" to "self-evident," an assertion of rationality.

National Archives

Franklin's other edits were less suitable. He changed Jefferson's "reduce them to arbitrary power" to "reduce them under absolute despotism," and he took out the literary flourish in Jefferson's "invade and deluge us in blood" to make it more sparse: "invade and destroy us." And a few of his changes seemed stodgy and unnecessary. "Amount of their salaries" became "amount and payment of their salaries."

Congress Makes Cuts

After the Continental Congress voted for independence from England, it formed itself into a committee to consider Jefferson's draft Declaration. The members were not so light in their editing as Franklin had been. Large sections were sliced out, most notably the one that criticized the king for continuing the slave trade. Congress also, to its credit, cut by

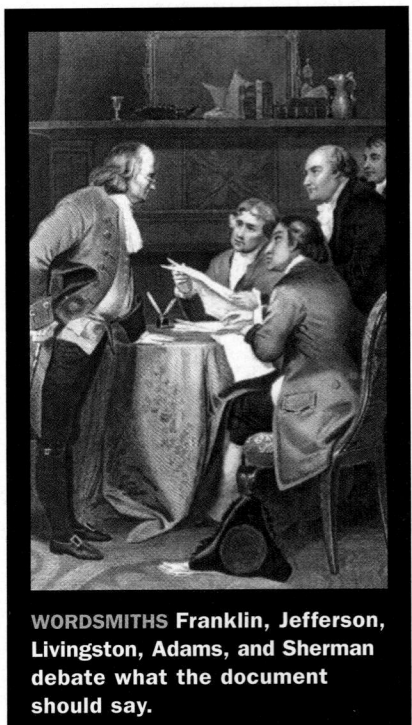

WORDSMITHS **Franklin, Jefferson, Livingston, Adams, and Sherman debate what the document should say.**

Archive Photos/NewsCom

more than half the draft's final five paragraphs, in which Jefferson had begun to ramble in a way that detracted from the document's power. Jefferson was upset. "I was sitting by Dr. Franklin," he recalled, "who perceived that I was not insensible to these mutilations." Franklin did his best to console him.

At the official signing of the parchment copy on August 2, John Hancock, the president of the Congress, penned his name with his famous flourish. "There must be no pulling different ways," he declared. "We must all hang together." Supposedly, Franklin replied, "Yes, we must, indeed, all hang together, or most assuredly we shall all hang separately." Their lives, as well as their sacred honor, had been put on the line.

—**Updated 2005, from TIME, July 7, 2003**

RESPONDING AND THINKING CRITICALLY

Respond

1. Imagine that you had assisted Thomas Jefferson in drafting the Declaration of Independence. What would you think of the revisions it underwent?

Recall and Interpret

2. (a)What book influenced Thomas Jefferson as he drafted the Declaration? (b)How did this book shape Jefferson's political beliefs?

3. (a)What criticism of the king of England did the Continental Congress delete from the draft Declaration? (b)What does this tell you about society during this time period?

Analyze and Evaluate

4. (a)Choose the sentence that best describes the main idea of the reading selection:

    i Editing is an important part of any writing assignment.

    ii The writing process played a notable role in crafting an important piece of American history.

    iii The authors of the Declaration had to work together in order to gain America's independence.

    (b)Explain why you think that your choice is the best possible answer.

5. (a)Identify at least two of Benjamin Franklin's revisions to Thomas Jefferson's draft. In what ways do you think these revisions affected the Declaration? (b)What does the article say about the importance of the revision process?

Connect

6. When Benjamin Franklin signed the Declaration of Independence, he believed that its creators were risking their lives. Explain why Franklin may have thought this and discuss how the written word influenced America's struggle for independence.

Vocabulary Workshop

Word Origins

Understanding Political Terms

"Whenever any form of government becomes destructive of these ends, it is the right of the people to alter or to abolish it."

—Thomas Jefferson, from the Declaration of Independence

Connecting to Literature Thomas Jefferson's words helped to "dissolve the political bands" between England and its American colonies. But do you know where the words he chose came from? Much of the political language Jefferson used, and that we still use today, traces its origins to ancient Greek and Latin.

Understanding a political term is easier if you know its origins. To understand the *etymology* of a word, or its origin and history, analyze the prefix, suffix, or root of the word. Many dictionaries display the etymology of a word in brackets before or after giving its definition. You may want to check the front of the dictionary for a guide to understanding the etymologies and abbreviations that appear in entries.

For example, the following entry gives the etymology of the word *govern*. Note that the symbol < means "comes from."

govern (guv´ ərn) *v.* to exercise political authority over: *to govern a nation.* [ME < OF *gouverner* < L *gubernāre* to steer (a ship) < Gk *kybernān* to steer]

The entry indicates that the word *govern* comes from a Middle English (ME) word, which comes from the Old French (OF) word *gouverner*, which comes from the Latin word *gubernāre*, which comes from the Greek *kybernān*, meaning "to steer." Knowing the etymology of the word *govern* not only enhances your understanding of the word's origins but may also help you understand other related words, such as *government* and *governor*.

Exercise

Use a dictionary to research the origins of the following political terms that appear in the Declaration of Independence. In a chart, copy the etymology for each word and write an explanation, similar to the one above, of what the etymology means. How might knowing a word's etymology help you understand the meanings of other words?

Word	Etymology	Explanation	
liberty			
jurisdiction			
usurp			
justice			

▶ **Vocabulary Terms**

A **prefix** is attached to the *beginning* of a word. It adds to or changes the word's meaning.

A **suffix** is attached to the *end* of a word. It adds to or changes the word's meaning.

A **root word** is the base word, or original word, to which a prefix or suffix can be added.

▶ **Test-Taking Tip**

Analyzing word parts can help you determine the meanings of words and increase your vocabulary. If you memorize common prefixes and suffixes, you will be more prepared when taking standardized tests.

▶ **Reading Handbook**

For more about understanding word origins, see Reading Handbook, p. R20.

Literature Online
For eFlashcards and other vocabulary activities, go to www.glencoe.com.

ACADEMIC STANDARDS (page 121)
11.1.2 Apply knowledge of roots and word parts from Greek and Latin to draw inferences about the meaning of vocabulary...

11.4.8 Use systematic strategies to organize and record information...

from *The Crisis, No. 1*

MEET THOMAS PAINE

Corset maker, cobbler, teacher, tax collector—
Thomas Paine failed miserably at every
line of work he attempted in his native
England. Finally, at age thirty-seven, Paine set
sail for the colonies to start a new life. It was
1774, and the colonists were weighing the pros
and cons of a break with England. Always a
friend of the "little guy," Paine sympathized with
the revolutionary forces.

> *"Had it not been for America, there
> had been no such thing as freedom left
> throughout the whole universe."*
>
> —Thomas Paine
> from *The Crisis, No. 5*

Success in America In January 1776, Paine
anonymously published the pamphlet *Common
Sense*, a cry for complete independence from
Britain. Paine argued that England was a mother
country "devouring her young." The pamphlet
quickly sold more than 100,000 copies. Paine
enlisted in Washington's army and began to write
the first pamphlet of a series of sixteen called *The
Crisis*. Washington ordered that this first pamphlet
be read aloud at every military campground. From
1777 to 1779, Paine served as secretary to the
Committee on Foreign Affairs of the Continental
Congress. After American independence was won,
Paine returned to private life.

Troubles in England and France Paine eventually returned to Europe—and to trouble. In the
early 1790s, he wrote a defense of the French
Revolution called *The Rights of Man*, in which he
argued against the rule of kings and for legislation
to help the poor. Although Paine had already
escaped to France, he was tried for treason and
outlawed by the British. After he was made a citizen by the French assembly, he became an elected
official. Unfortunately, he associated with the
wrong political party. When that party fell during
the French Revolution, he was thrown into prison
and stripped of citizenship. After almost a year,
and with the help of James Monroe, U.S. minister
to France, he was released. Paine returned to the
United States in 1802, but he received no hero's
welcome. Many Americans misunderstood his
later writings and branded him an atheist,
although Thomas Jefferson remained a good
friend.

When Paine's life ended, he was poor, alone, and
swollen with dropsy, a disease of the body's con-
nective tissue. Even after his death, the insults
continued. He was buried on his farm in New
Rochelle, New York. Ten years later, William
Cobbett, a British admirer of Paine, dug up his
remains and transported them to England, after
which they disappeared. (Cobbett apparently
intended a memorial that never came to pass.)
Paine achieved his successes with a pen only, but
his contribution to the cause of freedom is incalculable. *Common Sense* inspired even the most reluctant to rebel against what Paine called the
"tyranny of Britain."

Thomas Paine was born in 1737 and died in 1809.

Literature Online **Author Search** For more about
Thomas Paine, go to www.glencoe.com.

Connecting to the Essay

What should people expect from their government? If they think their government is unfair, should they speak up or keep quiet for fear of punishment? In his pamphlet *The Crisis, No. 1*, Paine calls upon his fellow colonists to rid themselves of tyranny. As you read the essay, think about the following questions:

- Under what circumstances do you think you would be forced to declare, "Enough is enough!"
- Is freedom worth risking one's life for?

Building Background

In *The Crisis*, Paine was not expressing new or original thoughts. Since about 1630, certain ideas had been developing in Europe, in what is now called the Age of Enlightenment. Among these were the beliefs that human beings have "natural rights" and that government is a social contract, drawing its power from (in Jefferson's words) "the consent of the governed." In other words, people voluntarily come together for trade and for protection, and they voluntarily submit to a government because that helps to keep things running smoothly. But if that government goes beyond its bounds, people can voluntarily end it. In his writing, Paine applied these popular views to a specific time and place, the Revolution in America.

Setting Purposes for Reading

Big Idea The Road to Independence

In their struggle with the British, the American colonists were fighting for a cause. As you read Paine's pamphlet, see how he encourages his readers' devotion to that cause.

Literary Element Tone

An author's attitude toward his or her subject matter or toward the audience is conveyed through **tone**. Tone consists of such elements as word choice, sentence structure, and figures of speech. As you read, notice how Paine's tone conveys his attitude.

- See Literary Terms Handbook, p. R19.

Reading Strategy Summarizing

To **summarize** what you have read is to state the main ideas in your own words and in a logical sequence. A summary is much shorter than the original. Summarizing can help you focus your understanding and remember what you have read.

Reading Tip: Outlining Look for main ideas and supporting details as you read. Putting them in a simple outline form will help you construct a summary after you read.

> 1. Britain's actions are tyrannical.
>   a. Britain has declared a right to tax us.
>   b.
>   c.

Vocabulary

tyranny (tir′ə nē) *n.* cruel use of authority; oppressive power; p. 124 *In order to regain their rights, the villagers rebelled against the tyranny of the king.*

resolution (rez′ə loo′shən) *n.* firmness of purpose; p. 125 *My resolution to study harder resulted in better grades.*

petrified (pet′rə fīd) *adj.* paralyzed with fear; p. 125 *Caught in our headlights, the deer seemed petrified and unable to move.*

exploit (eks′ ploit) *n.* notable, heroic deed; feat; p. 125 *Reading about superheroes can be fun, but I prefer learning about the exploits of real people.*

hypocrisy (hi pok′rə sē) *n.* an expression of feelings or beliefs not actually possessed or held; p. 125 *The politician revealed his hypocrisy when he did not fulfill his campaign promises.*

Literature Online Interactive Literary Elements Handbook To review or learn more about the literary elements, go to www.glencoe.com.

 INDIANA ACADEMIC STANDARDS (pages 123–128)
11.3.3 Analyze the ways in which…tone…achieve[s] specific rhetorical…purposes…
11.2 Develop [reading] strategies…
11.5.9 Write…a literary analysis…

from
The Crisis, No. 1

Thomas Paine

These are the times that try men's souls. The summer soldier and the sunshine patriot will, in this crisis, shrink from the service of his country; but he that stands it now, deserves the love and thanks of man and woman. **Tyranny,** like hell, is not easily conquered; yet we have this consolation with us, that the harder the conflict, the more glorious the triumph. What we obtain too cheap, we esteem[1] too lightly: it is dearness only that gives everything its value. Heaven knows how to put a proper price upon its goods; and it would be strange indeed if so celestial an article as freedom should not be highly rated. Britain, with an army to enforce her tyranny, has declared that she has a right (not only to tax) but "to bind us in all cases whatsoever";[2] and if being bound in that manner is not slavery, then is there not such a thing as slavery upon earth. Even the expression is impious;[3] for so unlimited a power can belong only to God.

Whether the independence of the continent was declared too soon, or delayed too long, I

---

1. *Esteem* means "to value" or "to appreciate."

---

2. In March 1766, the British parliament repealed the Stamp Act but also passed the Declaratory Act, which extended its right to impose taxes on the colonies and *"to bind [the colonies] in all cases whatsoever."*

3. *Impious* (im′ pē əs) means "lacking in reverence for God."

Big Idea The Road to Independence *Why does Paine compare taxation without representation to slavery?*

will not now enter into as an argument; my own simple opinion is, that had it been eight months earlier it would have been much better. We did not make a proper use of last winter; neither could we, while we were in a dependent state. However, the fault, if it were one, was all our own; we have none to blame but ourselves. But no great deal is lost yet. All that Howe[4] has been doing for this month past is rather a ravage than a conquest, which the spirit of the Jerseys[5] a year ago would have quickly repulsed, and which time and a little **resolution** will soon recover.

> . . . *he whose heart is firm, and whose conscience approves his conduct, will pursue his principles unto death.*

I have as little superstition in me as any man living; but my secret opinion has ever been, and still is, that God Almighty will not give up a people to military destruction, or leave them unsupportedly to perish, who have so earnestly and so repeatedly sought to avoid the calamities of war, by every decent method which wisdom could invent. Neither have I so much of the infidel[6] in me as to suppose that He has relinquished the government of the world, and given us up to the care of devils; and as I do not, I cannot see on what grounds the king of Britain can look up to heaven for help against us: a common murderer, a highwayman,[7] or a housebreaker, has as good a pretense as he.

It is surprising to see how rapidly a panic will sometimes run through a country. All nations and ages have been subject to them: Britain has trembled like an ague[8] at the report of a French fleet of flat-bottomed boats; and in the fourteenth century the whole English army, after ravaging the kingdom of France, was driven back like men **petrified** with fear; and this brave **exploit** was performed by a few broken forces collected and headed by a woman, Joan of Arc. Would that heaven might inspire some Jersey maid to spirit up her countrymen, and save her fair fellow sufferers from ravage and ravishment! Yet panics, in some cases, have their uses; they produce as much good as hurt. Their duration is always short; the mind soon grows through them, and acquires a firmer habit than before. But their peculiar advantage is, that they are the touchstones[9] of sincerity and **hypocrisy,** and bring things and men to light, which might otherwise have lain forever undiscovered. In fact, they have the same effect on secret traitors which an imaginary apparition[10] would have upon a private murderer. They sift out the hidden thoughts of man, and hold them up in public to the world. Many a disguised tory has lately shown his head, that shall penitentially solemnize[11] with curses the day on which Howe arrived upon the Delaware.

. . . Quitting this class of men, I turn with the warm ardor of a friend to those who have nobly stood, and are yet determined to stand the

---

8. An *ague* is a fit of shivering.
9. A *touchstone* is anything that tests the quality or genuineness of something.
10. An *apparition* is a ghost.
11. A colonist who supported British rule was a *tory*. *Penitentially solemnize* means "to celebrate formally with sorrow and regret."

Big Idea The Road to Independence *What does Paine feel is missing from the colonists' struggle?*

Reading Strategy Summarizing *Briefly, what does Paine say about the effect of panics on British sympathizers?*

Vocabulary

petrified (pet′ rə fīd) *adj.* paralyzed with fear; stiff or like stone

exploit (eks′ ploit) *n.* notable, heroic deed; feat

hypocrisy (hi pok′ rə sē) *n.* an expression of feelings or beliefs not actually possessed or held

---

4. Major General Sir William *Howe* was commander in chief of the British forces in America during part of the Revolutionary War.
5. At one time New Jersey was divided into two sections, East Jersey and West Jersey. The two parts were reunited as a royal colony in 1702.
6. Here, *infidel* means "someone who does not believe in God."
7. A thief who stole from travelers on a public road was a *highwayman*.

Literary Element Tone *Does Paine seem objective and removed here, or subjective and emotional? Explain.*

Vocabulary

resolution (rez′ ə l$\overline{oo}$′ shən) *n.* firmness of purpose

THOMAS PAINE **125**

Valley Forge soldier on picket duty, year unknown. Hand-tinted lithograph.

Viewing the Art: What does this image tell you about what the American colonists can expect in their struggle against the British?

matter out: I call not upon a few, but upon all: not on *this* State or *that* State, but on every State: up and help us; lay your shoulders to the wheel; better have too much force than too little, when so great an object is at stake. Let it be told to the future world that in the depth of winter, when nothing but hope and virtue could survive, that the city and the country, alarmed at one common danger, came forth to meet and to repulse it. Say not that thousands are gone—turn out your tens of thousands; throw not the burden of the day upon Providence, but *"show your faith by your works,"*[12] that God may bless you. It matters not where you live, or what rank of life you hold, the evil or the blessing will reach you all. The far and the near, the home ties and the back, the rich and poor, will suffer or rejoice alike. The heart that feels not now is dead; the blood of his children will curse his cowardice who shrinks back at a time when a little might have saved the whole, and made them happy. I love the man that can smile in trouble, that can gather strength from distress and grow brave by reflection. It is the business of little minds to shrink; but he whose heart is firm, and whose conscience approves his conduct, will pursue his principles unto death. My own line of reasoning is to myself as straight and clear as a ray of light. Not all the treasures of the world, so far as I

believe, could have induced[13] me to support an offensive war, for I think it murder; but if a thief breaks into my house, burns and destroys my property, and kills or threatens to kill me or those that are in it, and to *"bind me in all cases whatsoever"* to his absolute will, am I to suffer[14] it? What signifies[15] it to me, whether he who does it is a king or a common man; my countryman or not my countryman; whether it be done by an individual villain, or an army of them? If we reason to the root of things we shall find no difference; neither can any just cause be assigned why we should punish in the one case and pardon in the other. . . . ❧

---

12. Here, *Providence* means "God." *["show . . . your works"]* This phrase is a reference to the Book of James in the Bible.

Literary Element Tone *What does Paine imply about those people who do not act? How does this contribute to his tone?*

Reading Strategy Summarizing *Summarize the passage beginning "Not all the treasures of the world . . ."*

---

13. *Induced* means "persuaded."
14. Here, *suffer* means "to put up with."
15. Here, *signifies* means "makes important."

RESPONDING AND THINKING CRITICALLY

Respond

1. Suppose you were going to choose a sentence from Thomas Paine's essay to put on a bulletin board as a memorable quotation. Which sentence would you choose? Why?

Recall and Interpret

2. Which Americans does Paine criticize in his essay? Which does he praise?

3. (a)To whom does Paine compare the English king? (b)What emotions does Paine appeal to when describing the king?

4. What connection do you think Paine sees between the panics in European history Paine describes and the experience the colonists were facing?

5. (a)Paine suggests that this is not an "offensive" war. Why does he feel this way? (b)Why do you think Paine might have chosen this analogy as his final argument?

Analyze and Evaluate

6. Thomas Paine said that his goal as a writer was to use plain language. Cite some sentences from *The Crisis* that you think achieve his goal and some that do not.

7. (a)How does Paine use religion as part of his argument? (b)How effective is this approach in persuading the reader?

8. (a)In what ways does Paine express the Enlightenment idea that government should operate by "the consent of the governed"? (b)Do you agree with this idea?

Connect

9. **Big Idea** **The Road to Independence** Paine encourages his fellow citizens to defend themselves against British tyranny. (a)What kinds of qualities does Paine encourage the colonists to have? (b)How might these qualities help to define the new nation?

LITERARY ANALYSIS

Literary Element Tone

Tone is an author's attitude toward his or her subject matter or toward the audience, conveyed through elements such as word choice, sentence structure, and figures of speech. A writer's tone might convey a variety of attitudes such as sympathy, objectivity, or humor.

1. Find passages in Paine's essay that seem to have an objective tone.

2. Find examples of Paine's use of language that are emotional or even inflammatory.

3. From the overall tone in this essay, what do you infer about Paine's attitude toward his audience, the targeted readers of this essay?

Review: Diction

Diction is a writer's choice of words, an important element in the writer's voice or style.

Partner Activity With a classmate, choose two or three sentences that seem typical of Paine's writing. Analyze the sentences, paraphrasing them where appropriate and substituting your own words. Working with your partner, create a chart like the one below. Then write a paragraph describing Paine's diction.

Sentence	Paraphrase

Reading Strategy Summarizing

To summarize is to put the main ideas of a reading in your own words and in a logical sequence. Here is a useful way to think about summarizing a persuasive essay. Since most persuasion encourages people to act or think in a certain way, you can write your summary in three parts:

1. What is the problem?

2. What are the reasons for it?

3. What does the writer want you to do or think about it?

Write a very brief summary (two or three sentences) of this excerpt from Paine's *The Crisis, No. 1*. Be sure to include answers to the three questions mentioned above.

Vocabulary Practice

Practice with Multiple-Meaning Words Use a dictionary to locate at least one other meaning for each of these vocabulary words. List both the meaning of the word as it is used by Paine and the other meaning you have found.

Word	Paine's Meaning	Other Meaning
1. resolution		
2. petrified		
3. exploit		

Academic Vocabulary

Here are two vocabulary words from the vocabulary list on page R86.

philosophy (fə los′ ə fē) *n.* a particular system of thought or principles for the conduct of life

issue (ish′ yōō) *n.* a point or question to be discussed or decided

Practice and Apply

1. Describe Thomas Paine's **philosophy** regarding offensive and defensive warfare.

2. In the essay, why does Paine make an **issue** of Britain's declaration to extend its rights "to bind us in all cases whatsoever"?

Writing About Literature

Evaluate Author's Craft Thomas Paine wrote to persuade his fellow colonists to fight the British. To do so, he used a number of persuasive techniques, including logical argument, emotional appeals, name-calling, analogy, and allusions to history and the Bible. Write a brief essay in which you first state what you understand his purpose to be and then give examples of his use of persuasive devices to achieve his purpose. Finally, tell how well you think he has succeeded. Follow the writing path shown here to help you organize your essay.

After you complete a first draft, meet with a peer reviewer to evaluate each other's work and suggest revisions. Then proofread and edit your draft for errors in spelling, grammar, and punctuation.

Literary Criticism

Group Activity Thomas Paine has been described as "the sparkplug of the American Revolution." Meet with a few of your classmates to discuss the meaning of this metaphor. After you have discussed it, individually write statements that begin: "Thomas Paine was the sparkplug of the American Revolution because . . . " Then regroup to compare notes.

Literature Online **Web Activities** For eFlashcards, Selection Quick Checks, and other Web activities, go to www.glencoe.com.

To His Excellency, General Washington

MEET PHILLIS WHEATLEY

"We whose Names are underwritten, do assure the World, that the Poems . . . were (as we verily believe) written by Phillis, a young Negro Girl, who . . . [is] under the Disadvantage of serving as a Slave. . . ."

—Phillis Wheatley

In 1773 most readers would have doubted that an enslaved woman had written a book of poetry. The above statement was taken from the introduction to Phillis Wheatley's book of poetry, *Poems on Various Subjects, Religious and Moral,* published when Wheatley was only nineteen or twenty years old. Signed by eighteen of "the most respectable characters in Boston," including John Hancock and the royal governor, the statement was testimony to the authenticity of the poems. Wheatley was the first African American to publish a book of poetry.

Wheatley was born in the Senegal/Gambia region on the west coast of Africa around 1753. In 1761, when she was just seven or eight, she was captured by slave traders and brought to New England on the slave ship *Phillis.* John and Susanna Wheatley, wealthy Bostonians, purchased her to be a personal attendant for Mrs. Wheatley. They gave the child the family name Wheatley and the first name Phillis (the name of the ship she arrived on).

Early Promise Before long, the young girl was often seen trying to form letters on the wall with a piece of chalk or charcoal. When the Wheatley family recognized her intelligence, they did not give her menial tasks or allow her to associate with their other domestic slaves. Instead, Phillis was taught to read and write by Mrs. Wheatley's daughter. She gained free use of the home library and was supported and encouraged in her studies and writing. She mastered English and Latin, read many of the ancient Greek and Latin classics, and studied the Bible.

Wheatley first published a poem in 1767, when she was thirteen years old. Three years later, she published a poem honoring the famous evangelist Reverend George Whitefield. The poem resulted in favorable publicity for the young writer.

Book Published In May of 1773, the Wheatleys sent Phillis to London. A doctor had recommended a sea voyage for Phillis's health, and the Wheatleys' son Nathaniel was bound for London on business. There Wheatley was able to publish her first and only volume of poetry. Many of the poems contained pleas for justice, as shown in these lines from her poem "To the Right Honourable William, Earl of Dartmouth": "That from a father seiz'd his babe belov'd: / Such, such my case. And can I then but pray / Others may never feel tyrannic sway?"

Freedom When Phillis returned from England, the family freed her from enslavement. However, she remained in the Wheatley household until John Wheatley died in 1778. In April of that same year, she married John Peters, a freed African American. Her husband's business failed, and their two children died as infants. In 1784, alone and working as a servant, she wrote her last poem. Her husband died in debtor's prison, and on December 5, she died of malnutrition when she was only thirty-one. A brief announcement in Boston's *Independent Chronicle* read, "Last Lord's Day, died Mrs. Phillis Peters (formerly Phillis Wheatley), aged thirty-one, known to the world by her celebrated miscellaneous poems."

Phillis Wheatley was born around 1753 and died in 1784.

Author Search For more about Phillis Wheatley, go to www.glencoe.com.

Connecting to the Poem

Have you ever sent a letter to a U.S. president or another leader? In her letter and poem to George Washington, Wheatley expresses her admiration for him. Think about what you would write in a letter to the current president or another leader.

- What accomplishments would you thank the leader for?
- What solutions would you propose to local or national problems?

Building Background

When General George Washington traveled to Boston in 1775 to assume leadership of the Continental Army and to rid the city of occupying British soldiers, Phillis Wheatley wrote to him. Her letter and poem to the general were sent to his headquarters in nearby Cambridge. Washington was so impressed by Wheatley's poem that he invited her to visit him. The two met at his Cambridge headquarters.

Setting Purposes for Reading

Big Idea The Road to Independence

The "Columbia" that Phillis Wheatley speaks of in her poem is the United States of America, personified as a goddess of liberty. Phillis Wheatley herself, however, had not yet attained her own freedom in the United States. Critics have ridiculed Wheatley for writing a poem in which she glorifies our nation's freedom yet never speaks out against slavery. Others, however, see Wheatley as a woman who was painfully aware of the need to ingratiate herself with her supporters and patrons. Think about how Wheatley's experience as a slave might have affected her reaction to the American Revolution.

Literary Element Couplet

A couplet is two consecutive, paired lines of poetry, usually rhyming and often forming a stanza. Notice how Wheatley uses the couplet in this poem.

- See Literary Terms Handbook, p. R4

Reading Strategy Analyzing Structure

Poets often use inversion, or reversal of the usual word order, for emphasis or variety or to maintain a rhyme scheme. For example, look at this line in Wheatley's poem: "Thy ev'ry action let the goddess guide." In normal word order, this line would be "Let the goddess guide thy ev'ry action." Look for other examples of inversion.

....

Reading Tip: Understanding Inverted Sentences
To better understand the meaning of the poem, copy it onto a sheet of paper, changing each inversion to a more natural word order. Then compare the rhyme, rhythm, and emphasis in your modified version with the rhyme, rhythm, and emphasis in Wheatley's original poem.

George Washington. Artist unknown, after Charles Wilson Peale. Oil on canvas. Chateau de Versailles, France.

Literature Online **Interactive Literary Elements Handbook** To review or learn more about the literary elements, go to www.glencoe.com.

■ **INDIANA ACADEMIC STANDARDS (pages 130–133)**
11.2.2 Analyze the way in which clarity of meaning is affected by the…organization of language…

11.2 Develop strategies such as…identifying and analyzing structure…

To His Excellency, General Washington

Phillis Wheatley

Sir.

I Have taken the freedom to address your Excellency in the enclosed poem, and entreat your acceptance, though I am not insensible of its inaccuracies. Your being appointed by the Grand Continental Congress to be Generalissimo of the armies of North America, together with the fame of your virtues, excite sensations not easy to suppress. Your generosity, therefore, I presume, will pardon the attempt. Wishing your Excellency all possible success in the great cause you are so generously engaged in. I am,

> *Your Excellency's most obedient humble servant,*
> *Phillis Wheatley.*

Providence, Oct. 26, 1775.

His Excellency Gen. Washington.

> Celestial choir! enthron'd in realms of light,
>   Columbia's scenes of glorious toils I write.
> While freedom's cause her anxious breast alarms,
> She flashes dreadful in refulgent[1] arms.
> 5 See mother earth her offspring's fate bemoan,
> And nations gaze at scenes before unknown!

---

1. *Refulgent* means "radiant."

Reading Strategy   Analyzing Structure *How would you change the inversion in this passage to a more natural word order?*

See the bright beams of heaven's revolving light
Involved in sorrows and the veil of night!
    The goddess comes, she moves divinely fair,
10   Olive and laurel binds her golden hair:
Wherever shines this native of the skies,
Unnumber'd charms and recent graces rise.
    Muse![2] bow propitious[3] while my pen relates
How pour her armies through a thousand gates,
15   As when Eolus[4] heaven's fair face deforms,
Enwrapp'd in tempest and a night of storms;
Astonish'd ocean feels the wild uproar,
The refluent[5] surges beat the sounding shore;
Or thick as leaves in Autumn's golden reign,
20   Such, and so many, moves the warrior's train.
In bright array they seek the work of war,
Where high unfurl'd the ensign[6] waves in air.
Shall I to Washington their praise recite?
Enough thou know'st them in the fields of fight.
25   Thee, first in peace and honours,—we demand
The grace and glory of thy martial band.
Fam'd for thy valour, for thy virtues more,
Hear every tongue thy guardian aid implore!
    One century scarce perform'd its destined round,
30   When Gallic[7] powers Columbia's fury found;
And so may you, whoever dares disgrace
The land of freedom's heaven-defended race!
Fix'd are the eyes of nations on the scales,
For in their hopes Columbia's arm prevails.
35   Anon[8] Britannia[9] droops the pensive head,
While round increase the rising hills of dead.
Ah! cruel blindness to Columbia's state!
Lament thy thirst of boundless power too late.
    Proceed, great chief, with virtue on thy side,
40   Thy ev'ry action let the goddess guide.
A crown, a mansion, and a throne that shine,
With gold unfading, WASHINGTON! be thine.

---

2. The poet asks for aid from a *Muse.* In Greek mythology, the
Muses (goddesses) preside over arts and sciences.
3. Here, *propitious* means "favorably."
4. In Greek mythology, *Eolus* is the god of the winds.
5. *Refluent* means "back-flowing."
6. The *ensign* here is a flag.
7. *Gallic* means "French." Washington had fought the French during the
French and Indian War (1754–1763).
8. *Anon* means "soon."
9. *Britannia* is Great Britain, personified as a goddess.

Literary Element Couplet *How does this couplet work to form one complete idea?*

Big Idea The Road to Independence *What does the speaker mean by the "rising hills of dead"?*

RESPONDING AND THINKING CRITICALLY

Respond

1. What is your impression of Phillis Wheatley from reading her letter and poem?

Recall and Interpret

2. (a)In your own words, restate the message in Wheatley's letter to General Washington. (b)Based on the letter, what can you infer about her opinion of Washington?

3. (a)In the poem, what image of Columbia is described in lines 9–12? (b)What does that image convey about the speaker's view of America?

4. (a)In lines 13–22, to what things does the speaker compare the colonial army? (b)In your opinion, why might Wheatley have chosen to use these images?

Analyze and Evaluate

5. (a)To whom are lines 29–38 addressed? (b)How does this section of the poem differ from the rest?

6. How do Wheatley's allusions to mythology strengthen or weaken the meaning of the poem? Explain.

Connect

7. [Big Idea] **The Road to Independence** How do you think Wheatley's experience of being enslaved affected her attitude toward the colonial cause of freedom?

[Literary Element] Couplet

A **couplet** is two consecutive lines of poetry that rhyme. A **heroic couplet** (commonly used in epics that tell of heroes) has a specific rhythm, or meter, called **iambic pentameter.** In this meter, each line consists of five units, or feet, and each foot consists of two syllables, an unstressed one followed by a stressed one.

1. Read aloud three heroic couplets from the poem. In your opinion, does the heroic couplet form add to or detract from the meaning of the poem?

2. Why do you think Wheatley might have chosen to write this poem in heroic couplets?

Interdisciplinary Activity

Art: Choose one of the images from Wheatley's poem to illustrate. Then, in a drawing, painting, collage, or computer-generated image, express your own visual interpretation of the poem. Remember to give your work an appropriate title.

Literature Online **Web Activities** For eFlashcards, Selection Quick Checks, and other Web activities, go to www.glencoe.com.

[Reading Strategy] Analyzing Structure

Wheatley uses inversion in each of the following lines. Rewrite each without the use of inversion.

1. How pour her armies through a thousand gates, As when Eolus heaven's fair face deforms . . .

2. Shall I to Washington their praise recite?

Academic Vocabulary

Here are two vocabulary words from the vocabulary list on page R86.

dominate (däm′ ə nāt) *v.* to rule or control

structure (struk′ shər) *n.* something arranged in a definite pattern of organization

Practice and Apply

1. According to the poem, what is the result of Great Britain's effort to **dominate** the colonies?

2. How does Wheatley's sentence **structure** in this poem differ from that of ordinary prose?

Letter to John Adams and *Letter to Her Daughter*

MEET ABIGAIL ADAMS

In her day, Abigail Adams was known to the world as the loyal wife of John Adams, second president of the United States. Today she is just as famous for her brilliant mind. Adams participated in the events of some of the most tumultuous years of the nation, writing about them with sparkling wit.

A Happy Childhood The daughter of an accomplished Massachusetts minister, Adams grew up surrounded by people who valued strong principles and enjoyed defending them. Adams was passionate for knowledge and pursued her education in secret. She gained a wide knowledge of literature, but lamented what she felt was her ignorance. In letters to her husband, she argued that women deserved education and the right to own property.

> *"I desire you would remember the ladies, and be more generous and favorable to them than your ancestors."*
>
> —Abigail Adams, Letter to John Adams

Wife and Mother Adams met John Adams, a Harvard-trained lawyer, when she was fifteen. In 1764 the two married and went to live on John's farm at Braintree (later Quincy), Massachusetts. John Adams soon rose to prominence as a believer in American independence, requiring him to spend years in Philadelphia at the Continental Congress. Abigail, deeply supportive of the cause, stayed in Braintree to raise their five children. Outwardly cheerful, she felt, but rarely expressed, deep pain at being separated from her husband. After some months spent without a word from him, she finally wrote: "I pray my guardian generous to waft me the happy tidings of your safety and welfare . . . Difficult as the day is, cruel as this war has been, separated as I am on account of it

from the dearest connection in life, I would not exchange my country for the wealth of the Indies, or be any other than an American."

Later Years After the war, John Adams was selected as the first U.S. ambassador to England, later became the first vice president of the United States, and succeeded George Washington as president from 1797 to 1801. After John Adams lost the presidency, he and Abigail retired to Quincy. Their eldest son, John Quincy, went on to become the sixth president of the United States in 1825.

Letters That Endure Abigail Adams's letters vibrate with personality. She could be unapologetically opinionated, seeking to enlarge her husband's sense of morality: "You know my mind upon this subject," she wrote him regarding slavery. "I wish most sincerely there was not a slave in the province. It always appeared a most iniquitous scheme to me— fight ourselves for what we are daily robbing and plundering from those who have as good a right to freedom as we have." Her most famous observations relate to women, who she felt needed expanded legal rights and education. "If we mean to have heroes, statesmen, and philosophers, we should have learned women," she said.

Abigail Adams was born in 1744 and died in 1818.

Literature Online Author Search For more about Abigail Adams, go to www.glencoe.com.

Connecting to the Letters

When you need to communicate with someone far away, you may use a telephone or e-mail. Imagine how much letters meant to people living before the days of instant communication. As you read, think about how writing letters can help a person deal with separation from a loved one.

Building Background

The Continental Congress met in 1774 in Philadelphia. With the onset of war in 1775, the Congress became the provisional government for the American side. While John Adams labored at the Congress, war raged in Massachusetts. Troops occupied Boston for nearly a year, forcing Bostonians to house them. The British retreated just a few days before Abigail wrote her March 31, 1776, letter to her husband.

Twenty-four years later, President John Adams and First Lady Abigail Adams moved into the still-unfinished President's House in the District of Columbia, the new nation's capital. (The building was not officially known as the White House until 1902.) Adams's November 21, 1800, letter to her daughter describes her life there.

Setting Purposes for Reading

Big Idea The Road to Independence

As you read these letters, consider what Adams reveals about life during the Revolutionary War and the first years of this country. Also consider how the letters reflect ideals of the time, such as self-reliance and human rights.

Literary Element Description

Description is the use of details that appeal to the five senses to give the reader a vivid impression of a person, place, or thing. Good descriptive writing contributes to the overall purpose of a piece and avoids irrelevant details. As you read, notice details that give you a sense of being in colonial Boston and Washington, D.C.

• See Literary Terms Handbook, p. R4.

Literature Online Interactive Literary Elements **Handbook** To review or learn more about the literary elements, go to www.glencoe.com.

Reading Strategy Recognizing Author's Purpose

The **author's purpose** is the author's intent in writing a work. Authors usually write to persuade, to inform, to explain, to entertain, or to describe. As you read, consider what Adams describes and what opinions she expresses. What does her inclusion of these details tell you about her purpose for writing?

Reading Tip: Double-Entry Journal Use a double-entry journal to help you discover Adams's purpose.

Questions to ask	Answers
What does Adams's word choice suggest about her attitude toward her readers?	

Vocabulary

deprive (di prīv′) v. to take away from; to keep from enjoying or having; p. 136 *Students should not deprive themselves of education.*

tyrant (tī′rənt) n. a ruler who exercises power or authority in an unjust manner; one who has absolute power; p. 137 *Many colonists felt that King George was a tyrant.*

extricate (eks′ trə kāt′) v. to set free from; to remove; p. 138 *We need a plan to extricate ourselves from this dire situation.*

accommodate (ə kom′ə dāt′) v. to provide room or facilities for; p. 138 *The hotel will accommodate fifty people.*

recourse (rē′ kôrs′) n. resorting to a person or thing for help; p. 139 *Without a car, her only recourse was to phone her mother for a ride.*

INDIANA ACADEMIC STANDARDS (pages 135–140)

11.2.2 Analyze...word choice in the text.

11.2 Develop strategies such as...identifying and analyzing... purpose...

11.5.9 Write...a description...

Letter to John Adams

Abigail Adams

Birthplaces of John Adams and John Quincy Adams, 1849. G. N. Frankenstein.
Watercolor. Courtesy of the Adams National Historic Site, National Park Service.

Braintree, March 31, 1776

I wish you would ever write me a letter half as long as I write you; and tell me if you may where your fleet are gone? What sort of defense Virginia can make against our common enemy? Whether it is so situated as to make an able defense? Are not the gentry[1] lords and the common people vassals?[2] Are they not like the uncivilized natives Britain represents us to be? I hope their rifle men,[3] who have shown themselves very savage and even bloodthirsty, are not a specimen of the generality of the people.

I am willing to allow the colony great merit for having produced a Washington, but they have been shamefully duped by a Dunmore.[4]

I have sometimes been ready to think that the passion for liberty cannot be equally strong in the breasts of those who have been accustomed to **deprive** their fellow creatures of theirs. Of this I am certain: that it is not founded upon the generous and Christian principle of doing to others as we would that others should do unto us.

Do not you want to see Boston; I am fearful of the small pox, or I should have been in before this time. I got Mr. Crane to go to our house and see what state it was in. I find it has been occupied by one of the doctors of a regiment, very dirty, but no other damage has been done to it. The few things which were left in it are all gone. Crane has the key, which he never delivered up.

---

1. *Gentry* means the "upper," or "ruling," class.
2. Here, a *vassal* is someone in a subordinate or inferior position.
3. *Rifle men* refers to British soldiers and Loyalists fighting pro-independence forces.
4. The Earl of *Dunmore* was Virginia's last royal governor. He promised freedom to slaves who would fight against the Continental Congress and for England's king, thus angering American patriots.

Big Idea The Road to Independence *How does Adams's criticism reflect her belief in human rights?*

Vocabulary

deprive (di prīv′) *v.* to take away from; to keep from enjoying or having

I have wrote to him for it and am determined to get it cleaned as soon as possible and shut it up. I look upon it a new acquisition of property, a property which one month ago I did not value at a single shilling, and could with pleasure have seen it in flames.

The town in general is left in a better state than we expected, more owing to a precipitate[5] flight than any regard to the inhabitants, though some individuals discovered a sense of honor and justice and have left the rent of the houses in which they were for the owners and the furniture unhurt, or if damaged sufficient to make it good.

Others have committed abominable ravages. The mansion house of your president[6] is safe and the furniture unhurt, whilst both the house and the furniture of the Solicitor General have fallen a prey to their own merciless party. Surely the very fiends feel a reverential awe for virtue and patriotism, whilst they detest the parricide[7] and traitor.

I feel very differently at the approach of spring to which I did a month ago. We knew not then whether we could plant or sow with safety, whether when we had toiled we could reap the fruits of our own industry, whether we could rest in our own cottages, or whether we should not be driven from the sea coasts to seek shelter in the wilderness, but now we feel as if we might sit under our own vine and eat the good of the land.

I feel a gaieté de coeur[8] to which before I was a stranger. I think the sun looks brighter, the birds sing more melodiously, and nature puts on a more cheerful countenance. We feel a temporary peace, and the poor fugitives are returning to their deserted habitations.

Though we felicitate ourselves, we sympathize with those who are trembling lest the lot of Boston should be theirs. But they cannot be in similar circumstances unless pusillanimity[9] and cowardice should take possession of them. They have time and warning given them to see the evil and shun it.—I long to hear that you have declared an independency—and by the way, in the new Code of Laws which I suppose it will be necessary for you to make, I desire you would remember the ladies, and be more generous and favorable to them than your ancestors. Do not put such unlimited power into the hands of the husbands. Remember, all men would be **tyrants** if they could. If particular care and attention is not paid to the ladies, we are determined to foment a rebellion, and will not hold ourselves bound by any laws in which we have no voice, or representation.

That your sex are naturally tyrannical is truth so thoroughly established as to admit no dispute, but such of you as wish to be happy willingly give up the harsh title of master for the more tender and endearing one of friend. Why, then, not put it out of the power of the vicious and the lawless to use us with cruelty and indignity with impunity. Men of sense in all ages abhor those customs which treat us only as the vassals of your sex. Regard us then as beings placed by providence under your protection, and in imitation of the Supreme Being, make use of that power only for our happiness.

Abigail ∾

---

5. *Precipitate* means "sudden" or "hasty."
6. John Hancock was the president of the Continental Congress. When the British occupied Boston, General William Howe took Hancock's house as his headquarters.
7. Here, *parricide* means "a person who commits the crime of treason."
8. *Gaieté de coeur* (gā ə tā də   koer) is a French idiom meaning "lightheartedness" or "playfulness."

Reading Strategy Recognizing Author's Purpose *Why might Adams have included this information?*

Literary Element Description *How do these details express the emotional pitch of Adams's situation?*

9. *Pusillanimity* (pū´sə lə nim´ə tē) means "cowardliness" or "faintheartedness."

Big Idea The Road to Independence *How does this comment reflect Adams's support for the Revolution?*

Vocabulary

tyrant (tī´rənt) *n.* a ruler who exercises power or authority in an unjust manner; one who has absolute power

Letter to Her Daughter
from the New and Unfinished White House

Abigail Adams

Washington, 21 November, 1800.

My Dear Child,

I arrived here on Sunday last, and without meeting with any accident worth noticing, except losing ourselves when we left Baltimore, and going eight or nine miles on the Frederick road, by which means we were obliged to go the other eight through woods, where we wandered two hours without finding a guide, or the path. Fortunately, a straggling black came up with us, and we engaged him as a guide, to **extricate** us out of our difficulty; but woods are all you see, from Baltimore until you reach *the city*, which is only so in name. Here and there is a small cot,[1] without a glass window, interspersed amongst the forests, through which you travel miles without seeing any human being.

In the city there are buildings enough, if they were compact and finished, to **accommodate** Congress and those attached to it; but as they are, and scattered as they are, I see no great comfort for them. The river, which runs up to Alexandria, is in full view of my window, and I see the vessels as they pass and repass. The house is upon a grand and superb scale, requiring about thirty servants to attend and keep the apartments in proper order, and perform the ordinary business of the house and stables; an establishment very well proportioned to the President's salary. The lighting of the apartments, from the kitchen to parlors and chambers, is a tax indeed; and the fires we are obliged to keep to secure us from daily agues is another very cheering

Building the First White House, N. C. Wyeth. Location unknown.

comfort. To assist us in this great castle, and render less attendance necessary, bells are wholly wanting, not one single one being hung through the whole house, and promises are all you can obtain. This is so great an inconvenience, that I know not what to do, or how to do. The ladies from Georgetown and in the city have many of them visited me. Yesterday I returned fifteen visits,—but such a place as Georgetown appears,—why, our Milton is beautiful. But no comparisons;—if they will put me up some bells, and let me have wood enough to keep fires, I design to be pleased. I could content myself almost anywhere three months; but, surrounded with forests, can you believe that wood is not to be had, because people cannot be found to cut and cart it! Briesler entered into a contract with a man to supply him with wood. A small part, a few

---

1. A *cot* is a small house.

Vocabulary

extricate (eks′ trə kāt′) *v.* to set free from; to remove
accommodate (ə kom′ə dāt′) *v.* to provide room or facilities for

Literary Element Description *What does this detail tell you about the District of Columbia at the turn of the eighteenth century?*

Abigail Adams Hanging Laundry in the East Wing of the Unfinished White House.
Gordon Phillips. Oil on canvas. Collection of the White House Historical Association.
Viewing the Art: What does this painting tell you about Abigail's character?

cords[2] only, has he been able to get. Most of that was expended to dry the walls of the house before we came in, and yesterday the man told him it was impossible for him to procure it to be cut and carted. He has had **recourse** to coals; but we cannot get grates made and set. We have, indeed, come into a *new country*.

You must keep all this to yourself, and, when asked how I like it, say that I write you the situation is beautiful, which is true. The house is made habitable, but there is not a single apartment finished, and all withinside, except the plastering, has been done since Briesler came. We have not the least fence, yard, or other convenience, without, and the great unfinished audience-room I make a drying-room of, to hang up the clothes in. The principal stairs are not up, and will not be this winter. Six chambers are made comfortable; two are occupied by the President and Mr. Shaw; two lower rooms, one for a common parlor, and one for a levee-room.[3] Upstairs there is the oval room, which

is designed for the drawing-room, and has the crimson furniture in it. It is a very handsome room now; but, when completed, it will be beautiful. If the twelve years, in which this place has been considered as the future seat of government, had been improved, as they would have been if in New England, very many of the present inconveniences would have been removed. It is a beautiful spot, capable of every improvement, and, the more I view it, the more I am delighted with it.

Since I sat down to write, I have been called down to a servant from Mount Vernon[4], with a billet[5] from Major Custis, and a haunch of venison, and a kind, congratulatory letter from Mrs. Lewis, upon my arrival in the city, with Mrs. Washington's love, inviting me to Mount Vernon, where, health permitting, I will go, before I leave this place. . . .

Thomas comes in and says a House[6] is made; so to-morrow, though Saturday, the President will meet them. Adieu, my dear. Give my love to your brother, and tell him he is ever present upon my mind.

Affectionately your mother,
A. Adams ❧

---

2. A *cord* is a quantity of wood equal to 128 cubic feet.
3. A *levee-room* is a room for holding formal receptions.

Reading Strategy Recognizing Author's Purpose *Why might Adams have made this request?*

Vocabulary

recourse (rē´kôrs´) *n.* resorting to a person or thing for help

---

4. *Mount Vernon,* located near Washington, D.C., was the home of George Washington and his wife, Martha.
5. Here, *billet* means "a short letter."
6. Enough members of the *House* of Representatives had arrived for a session of Congress to take place.

RESPONDING AND THINKING CRITICALLY

Respond

1. Would you like to have known Abigail Adams? Why or why not?

Recall and Interpret

2. (a)From reading the first letter, what details did you learn about the British occupation of Boston, the role of Dunmore, and "those who are trembling lest the lot of Boston should be theirs"? (b)What are Abigail Adams's attitudes toward the conflict and the various people mentioned? Explain.

3. (a)What does Adams urge her husband to consider as he creates a new code of laws? (b)What reasons does she give for urging this consideration?

4. (a)In her letter to her daughter, what domestic problems does Adams discuss? (b)Why do you think she instructs her daughter not to reveal her feelings about these problems?

Analyze and Evaluate

5. Adams expresses herself openly in her letter to her husband. What does this tell you about their relationship?

6. Adams says that "all men would be tyrants if they could." (a)What do you think she means by this? (b)Are you convinced by her arguments?

7. (a)How can you tell that Adams is well informed about current events? (b)Do Adams's opinions seem fair to you? Explain.

8. What character traits could you attribute to Abigail Adams based solely on her letter to her daughter?

Connect

9. **Big Idea** **The Road to Independence** What do these letters tell you about life before and after the American Revolution?

LITERARY ANALYSIS

Literary Element **Description**

Good descriptive writing gives the reader a picture of a person, place, or thing.

1. Did Adams's descriptions bring war-torn Boston to life for you? Explain why or why not. If so, be sure to include specific examples of details that appealed to your senses.

2. Which descriptions in the second letter were most surprising or memorable to you? Explain.

Writing About Literature

Apply Form and Theme Imagine you're corresponding with someone who is about to move to your area. Write this person a letter giving an accurate description of the area, including the pros and cons of living there. Adding details that appeal to the senses will help you create a vivid description.

Literature Online **Web Activities** For eFlashcards, Selection Quick Checks, and other Web activities, go to www.glencoe.com.

READING AND VOCABULARY

Reading Strategy **Recognizing Author's Purpose**

You can get a sharper idea of Abigail Adams's purposes for writing by considering the context in which she wrote. Think of what you know about John Adams's responsibilities as well as the issues faced by colonists.

1. After considering the context, what would you say is one purpose of Adams's letter to her husband?

2. What was the purpose of the second letter? How well do you think it achieves its purpose?

Vocabulary **Practice**

Practice with Analogies Choose the word pair that best completes each analogy below.

1. tyrant : abuse ::
   a. manager : mislead   **c.** benefactor : aid
   b. expert : speculate   **d.** mentor : learn

2. accommodate : house
   a. wound : bandage   **c.** build : village
   b. crawl : stroller   **d.** transport : car

Grammar Workshop

Mechanics

Using Commas with Nonessential Elements

A **nonessential element** in a sentence is one that could be omitted without changing the basic meaning of the sentence. Such elements should be set off by one comma if the element appears at the beginning or the end of the sentence and by two commas if the element appears within the sentence. Examples of nonessential elements are underlined in the sentences below.

Participle:	He walked along, <u>singing</u>.
Infinitive:	<u>To begin</u>, he prepared himself for opposition.
Participial phrase:	Abigail, <u>disapproving of John's short letters</u>, gently scolded him.
Infinitive phrase:	<u>To be fair</u>, John Adams was unusually busy in Philadelphia.
Adjective clause:	Abigail, <u>who had been denied the advantages of a formal education</u>, was a great reader and tireless correspondent.
Appositive:	Abigail, <u>a wise woman</u>, often advised her husband.
Interjection:	<u>Alas</u>, one of John and Abigail's children died young.
Parenthetical expression:	Mrs. Adams was, <u>essentially</u>, able to adjust to any circumstance.

Exercise

Revise for Clarity Rewrite the sentences, adding commas where needed.

1. People who lived in the 1800s if alive today would I feel certain be astonished at the traffic between Baltimore and Washington, D.C.
2. To be sure Abigail's letter to her daughter is full of details that express her difficulties.
3. The First Lady faced with the lack of wood was somewhat perturbed.
4. The audience-room which was unfinished and empty was where clothes were dried.
5. An invitation from Mount Vernon Martha Washington's home would have been welcomed.
6. Heavens what a primitive place Washington seemed to be in 1800!

▶ **Nonessential Elements**

To determine whether a word, a phrase, or a clause is essential, try reading the sentence without it. Here's another tip: when you read the sentence aloud, you may notice that you drop your voice slightly when reading nonessential clauses and phrases.

▶ **Test-Taking Tip**

When looking over a test essay, check to see that no commas are missing. The meaning of a sentence may seem clear to you, but missing commas may make it unclear to a reader.

▶ **Language Handbook**

For more on Missing Commas with Nonessential Elements, see Language Handbook, p. R55.

Literature Online
eWorkbooks To link to the Grammar and Language eWorkbook, go to www.glencoe.com.

ACADEMIC STANDARDS (page 141)

11.6.1 Demonstrate control of... sentence structure...

11.6.4 Identify and correctly use... the mechanics of punctuation...

from *John Adams*

Winner of the Pulitzer Prize

David McCullough

Building Background

Letters between John and Abigail Adams reveal their personal thoughts and feelings, providing insights into their lives, the Revolutionary War, and the career of the second president of the United States. The following selection, from historian David McCullough's biography *John Adams,* frequently refers to the correspondence of the Adamses.

Set a Purpose for Reading

Read to discover biographical information about Abigail and John Adams.

Reading Strategy

Analyzing a Biographical Narrative

Analyzing a **biographical narrative** involves looking closely at parts of a selection to determine what they reveal about a person's life and character. As you read, take notes about what the selection reveals about Abigail and John. Use word webs like the one below to help you.

nicknamed Diana

Abigail's life and character

O f the courtship Adams had said not a word in his diary. Indeed, for the entire year of 1764 there were no diary entries, a sure sign of how preoccupied he was.

At their first meeting, in the summer of 1759, Abigail had been a shy, frail fifteen-year-old. Often ill during childhood and still subject to recurring headaches and insomnia, she appeared more delicate and vulnerable than her sisters. By the time of her wedding, she was not quite twenty, little more than five feet tall, with dark brown hair, brown eyes, and a fine, pale complexion. For a rather stiff pastel portrait, one of a pair that she and John sat for in Salem a few years after their marriage, she posed with just a hint of a smile, three strands of pearls at the neck, her hair pulled back with a blue ribbon. But where the flat, oval face in her husband's portrait conveyed nothing of his bristling intelligence and appetite for life, in hers there was a strong, unmistakable look of good sense and character. He could have been almost any well-fed, untested young man with dark, arched brows and a grey wig, while she was distinctly attractive, readily identifiable, her intent dark eyes clearly focused on the world.

One wonders how a more gifted artist might have rendered Abigail. Long years afterward, Gilbert Stuart,[1] while working on her portrait, would exclaim to a friend that he wished to God he could have painted Mrs. Adams when she was young; she would have made "a perfect Venus,"[2] to which her husband, on hearing the story, expressed emphatic agreement.

Year after year through the long courtship, John trotted his horse up and over Penn's Hill[3] by the coast road five miles to Weymouth[4] at every chance and in all seasons. She was his Diana, after the Roman goddess of the moon. He was her Lysander, the Spartan hero. In the privacy of correspondence, he would address her as "Ever Dear Diana" or "Miss Adorable." She nearly always began her letters then, as later, "My Dearest Friend." She saw what latent abilities and strengths were in her ardent suitor and was deeply in love. Where others might see a stout, bluff[5] little man, she saw a giant of great heart, and so it was ever to be.

Only once before their marriage, when the diary was still active, did Adams dare mention her in its pages, and then almost in code:

Di was a constant feast. Tender, feeling, sensible, friendly. A friend. Not an imprudent, not an indelicate, not a disagreeable word of action. Prudent, soft, sensible, obliging, active.

She, too, was an avid reader and attributed her "taste for letters" to Richard Cranch,[6] who, she later wrote, "taught me to love the poets and put into my hands, Milton, Pope, and Thompson,[7] and Shakespeare." She could quote poetry more readily than could John Adams, and over a lifetime would quote her favorites again and again in correspondence, often making small, inconsequential mistakes, an indication that rather than looking passages up, she was quoting from memory.

Intelligence and wit shined in her. She was consistently cheerful. She, too, loved to talk quite as much as her suitor, and as time would tell, she was no less strong-minded.

Considered too frail for school, she had been taught at home by her mother and had access to the library of several hundred books accumulated by her father. A graduate of Harvard, the Reverend Smith[8] was adoring of all his children, who, in addition to the three daughters, included one son, William. They must never speak unkindly of anyone, Abigail remembered her father saying repeatedly. They must say only "handsome things," and make topics rather than persons their subjects—sensible policy for a parson's family. But Abigail had views on nearly everything and persons no less than topics. Nor was she ever to be particularly hesitant about expressing what she thought.

Open in their affections for one another, she and John were also open in their criticisms. "Candor is my characteristic," he told her, as though she might not have noticed. He thought she could improve her singing voice. He faulted her for her "parrot-toed" way of walking and for sitting cross-legged. She told him he was too severe in his judgments of people and that to others often appeared haughty.[9] Besides, she chided[10] him, "a gentleman has no business to concern himself about the legs of a lady."

During the terrible smallpox epidemic of 1764, when Boston became "one great hospital," he went to the city to be inoculated, an often harrowing, potentially fatal ordeal extending over many days. Though he sailed through with little discomfort, she worried excessively, and they corresponded nearly every day, Adams reminding her to be sure to have his letters "smoked," on the chance they carried contamination.

The rambling, old-fashioned parsonage at Weymouth and its furnishings were a step removed from the plain farmer's cottage of John's

---

1. Born in Rhode Island, *Gilbert Stuart* (1755–1828) was the most highly regarded American portrait painter of his time.
2. *Venus* was the Roman goddess of love and beauty, associated with the Greek goddess Aphrodite.
3. *Penn's Hill* is a hill near Boston.
4. *Weymouth,* a town in eastern Massachusetts, was Abigail Adams's birthplace.
5. Here, *bluff* means "outspoken and frank."
6. *Richard Cranch* was Abigail Adams's brother-in-law.
7. John *Milton* (1608–1674), Alexander *Pope* (1688–1744), and James *Thomson* (1700–1748)—whose name Abigail misspells—were all prominent British poets.
8. *The Reverend William Smith* was Abigail's father.
9. *Haughty* means "disdainfully proud."
10. *Chided* means "scolded constructively."

boyhood or the house Abigail would move to once they were married. Also, two black slaves were part of the Smith household.

According to traditional family accounts, the match was strongly opposed by Abigail's mother. She was a Quincy, the daughter of old John Quincy, whose big hilltop homestead, known as Mount Wollaston, was a Braintree[11] landmark. Abigail, it was thought, would be marrying beneath her. But the determination of both Abigail and John, in combination with their obvious attraction to each other—like steel to a magnet, John said—were more than enough to carry the day.

A month before the wedding, during a spell of several weeks when they were unable to see one another because of illness, Adams wrote to her:

> Oh, my dear girl, I thank heaven that another fortnight[12] will restore you to me— after so long a separation. My soul and body have both been thrown into disorder by your absence, and a month or two more would make me the most insufferable cynic in the world. I see nothing but faults, follies, frailties and defects in anybody lately. People have lost all their good properties or I my justice or discernment.
>
> But you, who have always softened and warmed my heart, shall restore my benevolence as well as my health and tranquility of mind. You shall polish and refine my sentiments of life and manners, banish all the unsocial and ill natured particles in my composition, and form me to that happy temper that can reconcile a quick discernment with a perfect candor.
>
> Believe me, now and ever your faithful
> Lysander

His marriage to Abigail Smith was the most important decision of John Adams's life, as would become apparent with time. She was in all respects his equal, and the part she was to play would be greater than he could possibly have imagined, for all his love for her and

what appreciation he already had of her beneficial, steadying influence.

Bride and groom moved to Braintree the evening of the wedding. There was a servant to wait on them—the same Judah who had been the cause of the family row years before—who was temporarily on loan from John's mother.[13] But as the days and weeks passed, Abigail did her own cooking by the open hearth, and while John busied himself with his law books and the farm, she spun and wove clothes for their everyday use.

Her more sheltered, bookish upbringing notwithstanding, she was to prove every bit as hardworking as he and no less conscientious about whatever she undertook. She was and would remain a thoroughgoing New England woman who rose at five in the morning and was seldom idle. She did everything that needed doing. All her life she would do her own sewing, baking, feed her own ducks and chickens, churn her own butter (both because that was what was expected and because she knew her butter to be superior). And for all her reading, her remarkable knowledge of English poetry and literature, she was never to lose certain countrified Yankee patterns of speech, saying "Canady" for Canada, as an example, using "set" for sit, or the old New England "aya," for yes.

To John's great satisfaction, Abigail also got along splendidly with his very unbookish mother. For a year or more, until Susanna Adams was remarried to an older Braintree man named John Hall, she continued to live with her son Peter in the family homestead next door, and the two women grew extremely fond of one another. To Abigail her mother-in-law was a cheerful, open-minded person of "exemplary benevolence," dedicated heart and soul to the welfare of her family, which was more than her eldest son ever committed to paper, even if he concurred.

John and Abigail's own first child followed not quite nine months after their marriage, a baby girl, Abigail or "Nabby," who arrived July 14, 1765, and was, her mother recorded, "the dear image of her still dearer Papa."

---

11. *Braintree*, a town in eastern Massachusetts, was John Adams's birthplace.
12. A *fortnight* is two weeks.

13. *Judah* was a homeless woman who, being unable to care for herself, had been brought to the Adamses' household by Braintree officials. Her arrival had caused a family argument.

A second baby, John Quincy, was born two years later, in 1767, also in mid-July, and Adams began worrying about college for Johnny, fine clothes for Nabby, dancing schools, "and all that." To Abigail, after nearly three years of marriage, her John was still "the tenderest of husbands," his affections "unabated."[14]

For Adams, life had been made infinitely fuller. All the ties he felt to the old farm were stronger now with Abigail in partnership. She was the ballast[15] he had wanted, the vital center of a new and better life. The time he spent away from home, riding the court circuit, apart from

14. *Unabated* means "at full strength."
15. Here, *ballast* means "something that provides stability."

her and the "little ones," became increasingly difficult. "God preserve you and all our family," he would write.

But in 1765, the same year little Abigail was born and Adams found himself chosen surveyor of highways in Braintree, he was swept by events into sudden public prominence. His marriage and family life were barely under way when he began the rise to the fame he had so long desired. "I never shall shine 'til some animating occasion calls forth all my powers," he had written, and here now was the moment.

"I am . . . under all obligations of interest and ambition, as well as honor, gratitude and duty, to exert the utmost of abilities in this important cause," he wrote, and with characteristic honesty he had not left ambition out.

RESPONDING AND THINKING CRITICALLY

Respond

1. In what ways do you think that the relationship between John and Abigail Adams is like relationships between married people today? How is it different?

Recall and Interpret

2. (a)What nicknames taken from the classical world did John and Abigail give each other? (b)How do these names reveal the perceptions each had of the other?

3. At the beginning of this excerpt, what inferences does McCullough draw about John's and Abigail's characters from their portrait? How do these inferences contribute to his portrayal of the couple?

Analyze and Evaluate

4. (a)Why does McCullough call Adams's marriage to Abigail the "most important decision of John Adams's life"? (b)Do you agree with his assessment? Explain.

5. McCullough writes that "life had become infinitely fuller" for John Adams after his marriage and the birth of his children. Do you think that Adams considered his marriage more fulfilling than his career? Why or why not?

Connect

6. Abigail's letters are notable partly because of their plea for protections for women's rights in the new American government. How does her reasoning resemble the views of other writers involved in the struggle for American independence?

7. Do you think that the marriage of John and Abigail Adams represents a good model for a modern marriage? Why or why not?

INDIANA ACADEMIC STANDARDS (pages 142–145)
11.2 Develop strategies such as…identifying and analyzing structure, organization, perspective, and purpose…

DAVID McCULLOUGH **145**

Writing Workshop

Persuasive Speech

 Supporting Your Opinion

> "Is life so dear, or peace so sweet, as to be purchased at the price of chains and slavery?"
>
> —Patrick Henry, from "Speech to the Second Virginia Convention"

Connecting to Literature Patrick Henry's direct and passionate "Speech to the Second Virginia Convention" is an example of persuasive writing. To write a successful persuasive speech, focus on the goals of persuasive writing and the strategies for achieving those goals. (For a review of persuasive strategies, see "The Rhetoric of Revolution" on pages 104–105.) The list below highlights the core features of effective persuasive writing.

Rubric: Features of Persuasive Writing

Goals	Strategies
To present a clearly stated opinion	☑ Choose an issue that has opposing viewpoints ☑ State your opinion in a single sentence in the introduction
To present a logically organized argument	☑ Give reasons for your opinion ☑ Use relevant evidence to support your reasons ☑ Analyze evidence to show how it supports your reasons ☑ Use transitions between ideas
To anticipate and address audience concerns and counterarguments	☑ Identify your audience ☑ Put yourself in the shoes of someone who disagrees with your opinion
To convince an audience that a particular point of view is correct	☑ Use appeals to logic, ethics, and emotion ☑ Employ rhetorical devices to strengthen your argument ☑ Maintain a respectful tone

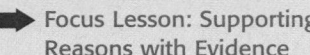

The Writing Process

In this workshop, you will follow the stages of the writing process. At any stage, you may think of new ideas to include and better ways to express them. Feel free to return to earlier stages as you write.

Prewriting

- - - - - - - - - - - - - - - -

Drafting

- - - - - - - - - - - - - - - -

Revising

- - - - - - - - - - - - - - - -

➤ Focus Lesson: Supporting Reasons with Evidence

Editing and Proofreading

➤ Focus Lesson: Parallelism

Presenting

- - - - - - - - - - - - - - - -

Writing Models For models and other writing activities, go to www.glencoe.com.

ACADEMIC STANDARDS (pages 146–153)
11.4.4 Structure ideas and arguments in a sustained and persuasive way and support them with precise and relevant examples.

> **Assignment**

Write a persuasive speech about a situation in your school or community that you wish to change. As you move through the stages of the writing process, keep your audience and purpose in mind.

Audience: your school or community

Purpose: to persuade others to improve a situation in the school or the community

Analyzing a Professional Model

In her persuasive speech, Becky Cain, the president of the League of Women Voters, urges members of the House of Representatives to abolish the Electoral College. As you read the following passage, notice how Cain clearly presents the debate and her position, supports her position with strong evidence, and urges her audience to act. Pay close attention to the comments in the margin. They point out features that you may want to include in your own persuasive speech.

From *"Proposals for Electoral College Reform"* by Becky Cain, President, League of Women Voters

I am pleased to be here today to express the League's support for a constitutional amendment to abolish the electoral college and establish the direct election of the President and Vice President of the United States by popular vote of the American people.

The electoral college system is fundamentally unfair to voters. In a nation where voting rights are grounded in the one-person, one-vote principle, the electoral college is a hopeless anachronism.

The current system is unfair for two reasons.

First, a citizen's individual vote has more weight if he or she lives in a state with a small population than if that citizen lives in a state with a large population.

For example, each electoral vote in Alaska is equivalent to approximately 112,000 people. Each electoral vote in New York is equivalent to approximately 404,000 eligible people (based on 1990 census data). And that's if everyone votes!

Real-World Connection

Much writing is persuasive. Think about all the texts you encounter in a day. Do those texts seek to change your thoughts or actions? Letters to Congress, editorials, advertisements, and movie trailers all use persuasive techniques. As you work on your persuasive speech, use relevant evidence and the techniques you see every day to encourage others to consider your position.

Introduction

Identify and explain the problem or the situation you are addressing, and propose a solution. Clarify your position in your thesis statement at the end of the introduction.

Reasons

Support your thesis statement with reasons. Reasons focus your arguments around central ideas. Appeal to your audience's logic, ethics, and emotions.

Supporting Evidence/ Statistics

Support your reasons with strong evidence, including examples and statistics.

The system is also unfair because a citizen's individual vote has more weight if the percentage of voter participation in the state is low. For example, if only half of all people in Alaska vote, then each electoral vote is equivalent to roughly 56,000 people.

Moreover, the electoral vote does not reflect the volume of voter participation within a state. If only a few voters go to the polls, all the electoral votes of the state are still cast.

Finally, the electoral college system is flawed because the Constitution does not bind presidential electors to vote for the candidates to whom they have been pledged. For example, in 1948, 1960, and 1976, individual electors pledged to the top two vote getters cast their votes for third-place finishers and also-rans. Defecting electors in a close race could cause a crisis of confidence in our electoral system.

For all these reasons, the League believes that the presidential election method should incorporate the one-person, one-vote principle. The President should be directly elected by the people he or she will represent, just as the other federally elected officials are in this country. Direct election is the most representative system. It is the only system that guarantees the President will have received the most popular votes. It also encourages voter participation by giving voters a direct and equal role in the election of the President. . . .

The time has come to take the next step to ensure a broad-based, representative democracy. Fairness argues for it. Retaining the fragile faith of American voters in our representative system demands it. We urge the House and the Senate to pass a constitutional amendment abolishing the electoral college system and establishing the direct popular election of our President and Vice President.

Supporting Evidence/Facts

Support your reasons with facts to appeal to your audience's sense of logic.

Appeals to Emotion

Create an emotionally appealing viewpoint by inviting your audience to identify and empathize with the negative consequences of inaction.

Conclusion

End your argument with a call to action. Persuade your audience to agree or take sides with your position.

Reading-Writing Connection Think about the writing techniques that you have just encountered and try them out in the persuasive speech you write.

Prewriting

Choose an Issue Think of a situation you would like to change. Have you noticed a rule or policy that is ineffective or unfair? Enacting change requires you to persuade others that a situation can and should be improved, and that your solution is the right one.

▶ The **purpose** of a persuasive speech is to inform and influence.

▶ Determine your **audience.** Your audience should include people who have the power to improve the situation you describe. As you write, think about the background your audience will need in order to understand the issue and which tone and types of evidence will help persuade them.

Clarify Your Position What is your opinion about the issue? In one or two sentences, clearly state the issue and your opinion about it. This is your **thesis.**

Support Your Position To persuade your audience that your position is valid, you need to provide reasons and support them with relevant evidence. You should make appeals to logic, ethics, and emotions. Defend your reasons with precise and accurate evidence, such as facts, expert opinions, statistics, and examples.

Outline Your Argument Before drafting your persuasive speech, create an outline to organize your reasons and evidence. Your introduction should describe the issue and propose your opinion. (For more information on types of proposals, see "Delivering a Persuasive Speech" on page 154.) In each body paragraph, include a reason and relevant evidence. In your conclusion, summarize your position and end with a call to action.

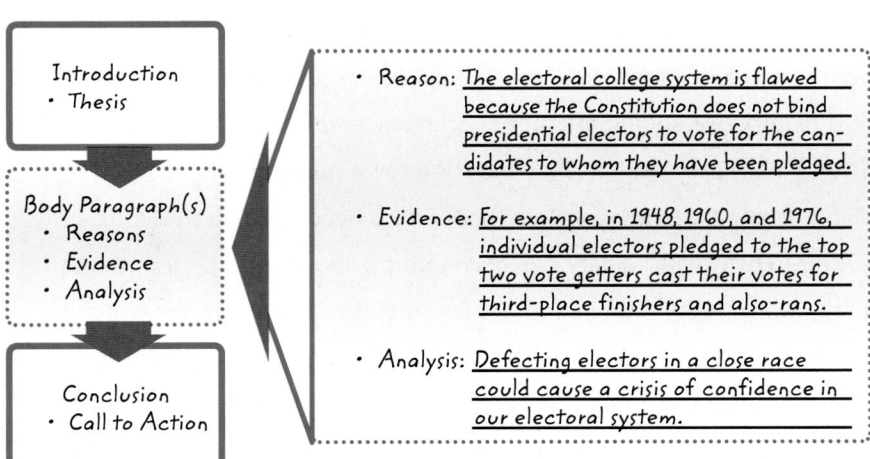

- Reason: The electoral college system is flawed because the Constitution does not bind presidential electors to vote for the candidates to whom they have been pledged.

- Evidence: For example, in 1948, 1960, and 1976, individual electors pledged to the top two vote getters cast their votes for third-place finishers and also-rans.

- Analysis: Defecting electors in a close race could cause a crisis of confidence in our electoral system.

Discuss Your Ideas Once you finish outlining your persuasive speech, share your ideas with a partner. To develop your writing voice and to become more comfortable speaking in front of an audience, read your thesis and reasons. Make sure that each part is clear and that your tone is engaging and respectful.

Address Counterarguments

Be sure your persuasive speech considers both sides of an issue. Anticipate and respond briefly to objections to your position. Use a pro-and-con scale to help you to separate the reasons for your argument (pros) from one or two counterarguments (cons).

Test Prep

Many tests include persuasive essays. As with a persuasive speech, clarify your position (thesis) and before writing briefly organize your reasons in an outline. For timed tests, spend only a few minutes prewriting and the majority of your time writing.

Drafting

Don't Get Stuck Writers often modify their original thesis after developing the rest of their argument. Keep in mind that it may be easier to start with a very general thesis, to draft your body paragraphs, and to go back to clarify your thesis afterward. Whichever order you choose, you will be able to revise your thesis later to make your position clear.

Analyzing a Workshop Model

Here is a final draft of a persuasive speech. Read the speech and answer the questions in the margin. Use the answers to these questions to guide you as you write your own speech.

Haunted House or Historical Attraction?

Hauntingly beautiful, perhaps—but not a haunted house!

Some neighbors claim that they hear strange sounds at night from the old Dillard mansion at the end of Briar Street. Others complain that with the sprawling weeds, teetering fence, and peeling paint, the house might just as well be haunted. Now the Briar Street Neighborhood Association is pressuring the city government to bulldoze the old house.

The Dillard mansion has been empty since 1971, and no doubt the neglect has made it quite an eyesore. Still, the house remains one of the town's oldest standing structures, and a decision to tear it down should not be made without considering other options. Instead of destroying an important part of Dillard history, we should attempt to renovate and restore it. The renovated mansion would serve as an ideal site for a town museum.

Many of our citizens recognize that Dillard needs a town museum. In fact, the Dillard Historical Society has been talking about building a museum for some time now. As historian and Society member Adam Frasier explains, "With no central location, Dillard's historic objects risk being damaged or lost. There is no systematic organization in place. The longer we postpone the decision, the worse it will get." In July 2004, the *Dillard Post* noted that an estimated 65 percent of archived material is currently in storage, unavailable to the public or even most researchers. Why not solve this need for a public museum by restoring the Dillard mansion?

Some critics may argue that the cost of restoring the old house would outweigh the benefits. The town would need to replace the existing plumbing

Introduction
Will the opening grab the audience's attention? Why or why not?

Background
How does citing this information help the audience?

Issue/Thesis Statement
What is the issue, or problem, according to the writer? What is the writer's solution to the problem?

Supporting Evidence/ Expert Opinion
How might this evidence help persuade a reluctant audience?

Rhetorical Question
How does this rhetorical question contribute to the writer's argument?

and electricity to bring it up to safety codes. A complete restoration would require expensive specialists and hours of costly research. However, the cost of building a new museum from the ground up would probably be more expensive overall. The town would need not only to purchase all new materials, fixtures, and labor, but also to pay for an architect and for land to build on. Moreover, a newer building could not achieve the look and atmosphere of an authentically historic space.

Records at Dillard City Hall indicate that the town's founder, Evan Dillard, built the house in 1798. Not only is the house more than 200 years old, it includes a number of architectural features that cannot be found anywhere else in the city. A hidden staircase leads to a secret room, and rare amethyst-glass windows and unexpected gables decorate the roof. Such a unique museum would appeal to both experts and amateurs, and it would probably draw tourists from all over the state.

Let's preserve the cultural heritage, deep history, and unique architecture of our town. Let's turn the Dillard eyesore into a historical attraction. Renovating—not bulldozing—the Dillard mansion is the first step.

Counterarguments

How might including a counterargument help persuade the audience? What is the effect of addressing the counterargument?

Appeals to Logic

What logical evidence does the writer provide? How does this evidence invite the audience to come to the same conclusions as the writer?

Reasons and Supporting Evidence

Why might the writer have chosen to give supporting evidence before the proposed action?

Parallelism

How is this an example of parallelism? What is the effect of using this rhetorical device in the conclusion?

Conclusion

How does the writer appeal to the audience and persuade the group to act?

Revising

Use the rubric below to evaluate your writing.

Traits of Strong Writing

Ideas message or theme and the details that develop it

Organization arrangement of main ideas and supporting details

Voice writer's unique way of using tone and style

Word Choice vocabulary a writer uses to convey meaning

Sentence Fluency rhythm and flow of sentences

Conventions correct spelling, grammar, usage, and mechanics

Presentation the way words and design elements look on a page

For more information on using the Traits of Strong Writing, see pages R33–R34 of the Writing Handbook.

Rubric: Writing an Effective Persuasive Speech

☑ Does your issue have opposing viewpoints?

☑ Do you choose one side of the debate and clarify your position?

☑ Do you present your reasons and supporting evidence in a logical order?

☑ Do you use rhetorical devices to strengthen your argument?

☑ Do you use appeals to logic, ethics, and emotion?

☑ Do you present and respond to counterarguments in a respectful tone?

☑ Do you persuade your audience to act?

▶ **Focus Lesson**

Supporting Reasons with Evidence

A well-supported reason will demonstrate that you are informed about your subject and that your argument is logical and valid. Make sure to support your reasons with convincing evidence from reliable sources. Here is a sentence from the Workshop Model followed by three kinds of supporting evidence—example, expert opinion, statistic—that you may want to use in your persuasive speech.

Draft:

Many of our citizens recognize that Dillard needs a town museum.

Revision:

Many of our citizens recognize that Dillard needs a town museum. In fact, the Dillard Historical Society has been talking about building a museum for some time now.[1] As historian and Society member Adam Frasier explains, "With no central location, Dillard's historic objects risk being damaged or lost. There is no systematic organization in place. The longer we postpone the decision, the worse it will get."[2] In July 2004, the Dillard Post noted that an estimated 65 percent of archived material is currently in storage, unavailable to the public or even most researchers.[3]

1: **Example**   2: **Expert Opinion**   3: **Statistic**

Editing and Proofreading

Get It Right When you have completed the final draft of your speech, proofread for errors in grammar, usage, mechanics, and spelling. Refer to the Language Handbook, pages R45–R59, as a guide.

> **Focus Lesson**

Parallelism

Parallelism is the use of a series of words, phrases, or sentences that have similar grammatical form. It is a rhetorical device, or a technique writers use to give their arguments more impact and to effectively express and emphasize ideas. To write a parallel sentence, balance each item in a series by using the same grammatical construction. For example, a noun should be matched with a noun, an adjective with an adjective, and a phrase with a phrase.

Original: In this sentence, similar ideas are not connected or emphasized.

Let's preserve <u>the cultural heritage</u> and <u>the deep history</u> of our town, as well as <u>its architecture</u>, which is unique.

Improved: Create parallel phrases to reflect the parallel meaning.

Let's preserve the <u>cultural heritage</u>, <u>deep history</u>, and <u>unique architecture</u> of our town.

Original: In this sentence, the series does not use parallel grammatical forms.

Others complain that with <u>the weeds</u>, <u>teetering fence</u>, and <u>the paint that is cracked and peeling</u>, the house might just as well be haunted.

Improved: Edit the sentence so that all items are parallel in form.

Others complain that with the <u>sprawling weeds</u>, <u>teetering fence</u>, and <u>peeling paint</u>, the house might just as well be haunted.

Rhetorical Devices

Here are some other rhetorical devices you may want to use in your speech. To be most effective, vary your use of these devices.

Repetition

Repeat a word, phrase, or clause for emphasis. *"I came, I saw, I conquered."*
—Julius Caesar

Rhetorical Question

These questions are not meant to be answered, but are asked to emphasize the obvious. *"If you wrong us, shall we not revenge?"*
—William Shakespeare

Metaphor

Metaphors compare two seemingly unlike things. *"No man is an island."*
—John Donne

Presenting

Preparing Your Persuasive Speech Once you have finished writing, revising, and editing your persuasive speech, you should think about how you'll present it to your audience. Many speakers read from note cards instead of from the paper itself. If you would rather read from your paper, you may wish to increase the type size and spacing, or add notes in the margins. Your teacher may ask for a clean copy of your speech to grade, so be sure to check the presentation guidelines.

Writer's Portfolio

Place a copy of your persuasive speech in your portfolio to review later.

Speaking, Listening, and Viewing Workshop

Delivering a Persuasive Speech

Connecting to Literature In 1799, George Washington needed help. Supporters of state independence were resisting the federal union. Fearing that "the tranquility of the Union [was] hastening to an awful crisis," Washington turned to Patrick Henry, who came out of retirement to speak passionately for the inviolability of the Union. Henry's last speech turned sullen opponents into cheering supporters.

Assignment Deliver a persuasive speech to an audience.

Planning Your Presentation

You have written your speech about a topic you care about, which is good, since it's easier to be persuasive when expressing real conviction. You have researched your topic and considered your audience as you wrote. Now it is time to work on communicating your points directly to the audience.

- Review your speech for clarity and logic. Find out how much time you will be allotted to speak. If necessary, shorten your speech while preserving your main points and key evidence.
- Thoroughly familiarize yourself with your speech and research. This will increase your confidence, help you speak fluently, and enable you to speak spontaneously should the need arise.
- Think again about your audience—who they are, what they know about your topic, and what their opinions might be. This will help you anticipate their reactions and prepare for the questions they may ask.
- Consider what tone would be appropriate for the occasion.

—remember to modulate the tone of your voice
—make eye contact with audience members

Creating Your Visual Media

Visual media or aids heighten the interest of a presentation and also help make evidence easier to grasp. As you review your speech, think about how media such as diagrams, photographs, or charts might support your points. Use the chart below to brainstorm ideas for visuals with a partner.

Important Points	Ideas for Visual Aids	What Visual Aid Will Demonstrate
The town garbage landfills are filling up at a record rate.	Photograph of landfill	The urgency of acting to prevent landfills from overflowing.

Rehearsing

Rehearse your speech both in private and in front of friends and family. Rehearsal helps you identify any grammar or spelling flaws that you may have missed—you don't want to stumble over them when it comes time to speak. Rehearsal will also help you present visual aids skillfully. Finally, rehearsal will help you refine your delivery until it is smooth and effective.

Ask your listeners for feedback on your pronunciation, pacing, and volume. If you will be fielding questions from your audience, ask your listeners for practice questions. Keep your answers focused and to the point. As you practice, you will grow more comfortable speaking.

Use some of the verbal and nonverbal techniques below.

Rubric: Techniques for Delivering a Presentation

Verbal Techniques	Nonverbal Techniques
☑ **Volume** Speak loudly enough so that everyone can hear you.	☑ **Posture** Stand up tall with your head straight.
☑ **Pronunciation** Speak clearly, pronouncing all the words.	☑ **Eye Contact** Make eye contact with people throughout your audience.
☑ **Pace** Speak at a moderate speed but vary the rate and use pauses.	☑ **Facial Expressions** Vary your facial expressions to reflect what you are saying.
☑ **Tone** Speak in an animated voice.	☑ **Gestures** Use natural gestures to reinforce your ideas.
☑ **Emphasis** Stress important words and ideas.	☑ **Visual Aids** Use photographs or other visuals to enhance your presentation.

Use a Mirror

Practice your gestures in front of a mirror until your body language looks natural.

Sound Check

Record your presentation and play it back to check on whether your voice expresses the right mood and your words are understandable.

Videotape

Videotape your performance and provide your own critique.

ACADEMIC STANDARDS (pages 154–155)
11.7.19 Deliver multimedia presentations that...select an appropriate medium for each element...
11.7.3 Use various forms of logical arguments...
11.7.5 Use appropriate rehearsal strategies...

Test Preparation and Practice

English Language Arts

Indiana Test Practice
Reading: Vocabulary, Comprehension, and Analysis

Carefully read the following passage. Use context clues to determine the meaning of words that you are unfamiliar with. Pay close attention to the author's main idea and use of rhetorical devices. Then answer the questions on pages 157–158.

from *The Whistle* by Benjamin Franklin

line

When I was a child of seven years old, my friends, on a holiday, filled my pocket with coppers. I went directly to a shop where they sold toys for children; and being charmed with the sound of a *whistle,* that I met by the way in the hands of another boy, I voluntarily offered and gave all my money for one. I then came home, and went whistling all over the house, much pleased with my

5 *whistle,* but disturbing all the family. My brothers, and sisters, and cousins, understanding the bargain I had made, told me I had given four times as much for it as it was worth; put me in mind what good things I might have bought with the rest of the money; and laughed at me so much for my folly, that I cried with vexation; and the reflection gave me more chagrin than the *whistle* gave me pleasure.

This, however, was afterwards of use to me, the impression continuing on my mind; so that

10 often, when I was tempted to buy some unnecessary thing, I said to myself, *Don't give too much for the whistle;* and I saved my money.

As I grew up, came into the world, and observed the actions of men, I thought I met with many, very many, *who gave too much for the whistle.*

When I saw one too ambitious of court favor, sacrificing his time in attendance on levees, his

15 repose, his liberty, his virtue, and perhaps his friends, to attain it, I have said to myself, *This man gives too much for his whistle.*

When I saw another fond of popularity, constantly employing himself in political bustles, neglecting his own affairs, and ruining them by that neglect, *He pays, indeed,* said I, *too much for his whistle.*

If I knew a miser, who gave up every kind of comfortable living, all the pleasure of doing good to

20 others, all the esteem of his fellow-citizens, and the joys of benevolent friendship, for the sake of accumulating wealth, *Poor man,* said I, *you pay too much for your whistle.*

When I met with a man of pleasure, sacrificing every laudable improvement of the mind, or of his fortune, to mere corporeal sensations, and ruining his health in their pursuit, *Mistaken man,* said I, *you are providing pain for yourself, instead of pleasure; you give too much for your whistle.*

from *The Whistle* by Benjamin Franklin *(continued)*

25   If I see one fond of appearance, or fine clothes, fine houses, fine furniture, fine equipages, all above his fortune, for which he contracts debts, and ends his career in a prison, *Alas!* say I, *he has paid dear, very dear, for his whistle.*

When I see a beautiful sweet-tempered girl married to an ill-natured brute of a husband, *What a pity,* say I, *that she should pay so much for a whistle!*

30   In short, I conceive that great part of the miseries of mankind are brought upon them by the false estimates they have made of the value of things, and by their giving too much for their whistles.

1. According to the passage, Franklin obtained the whistle from:
A. a shop.
B. friends on a holiday.
C. another boy.
D. a peddler.

2. Which of the following rhetorical devices is most evident in the sentence beginning in line 5?
F. Hyperbole
G. Rhetorical question
H. Connotative language
J. Parallelism

3. As it is used in line 7, the word *folly* most nearly means:
A. a great deal.
B. an agreement.
C. a mistake.
D. good sense.

4. As it is used in line 8, the word *reflection* most nearly means:
F. likeness.
G. mirror image.
H. possibility.
J. thought.

5. The use of the word *whistle* in line 11 is an example of the rhetorical device of:
A. connotative language.
B. hyperbole.
C. parallelism.
D. figurative language.

6. According to the narrator, if people neglect their affairs:
F. their affairs will suffer.
G. they will succeed in politics.
H. they will become popular.
J. they will no longer be able to live comfortably.

7. The literary device that is exemplified by the phrase "said I" in line 17 is:
A. allusion.
B. aphorism.
C. inversion.
D. meter.

8. In the paragraph beginning in line 19, one example of connotative language is the word:
F. pleasure.
G. miser.
H. wealth.
J. friendship.

9. As it is used in line 25, the word *fine* most nearly means:
  A. penalty.
  B. satisfactory.
  C. elegant.
  D. thin.

10. According to the narrator, how will a person who is fond of appearance end his career?
  F. With a fine house
  G. Without benevolent friendship
  H. In ruined health
  J. In prison

11. The narrator claims that most of the miseries of mankind are the result of:
  A. false estimates of value.
  B. the high costs of commodities.
  C. ill-natured brutes.
  D. the contracting of debts.

12. After the first paragraph, what literary or rhetorical device does the narrator employ at the end of each paragraph?
  F. Allusion
  G. Hyperbole
  H. Connotative language
  J. Repetition

13. On the basis of this passage, it might reasonably be concluded that the overall tone of "The Whistle" is:
  A. aphoristic.
  B. ironic.
  C. angry.
  D. formal.

14. It can reasonably be inferred that the author's main purpose for writing this passage was:
  F. to explain.
  G. to persuade.
  H. to entertain.
  J. to describe.

15. The main idea of this passage concerns:
  A. the foolishness of spending money on things one cannot afford.
  B. the results of wasting time.
  C. the need to be aware of the true cost of one's desires.
  D. the profit to be gained from listening to the advice of family members.

Reading: Word Recognition

For each item in this section, choose the word or words that best complete the sentence.

1. In the end, England's attempts to _____ the colonists' demand for representation were unsuccessful.
   A. abate
   B. rouse
   C. convene
   D. lament

2. The _____ in Boston Harbor frightened soldiers and woke many people.
   F. commodity
   G. ration
   H. clamor
   J. scruple

3. There were no _____ reactions to Patrick Henry's powerful speech to the Second Virginia Convention, which greatly _____ the delegates.
   A. petrified . . . alighted
   B. obliging . . . deprived
   C. feigned . . . roused
   D. ingenious . . . gratified

4. Jonathan Edwards believed that his sermons could help repair the _____ in people's souls.
   F. desolation
   G. prudence
   H. vault
   J. conjurer

5. Persecution in England motivated the Pilgrims to _____ on a very _____ voyage across the Atlantic Ocean.
   A. temper . . . abominable
   B. embark . . . arduous
   C. revive . . . copious
   D. abhor . . . insidious

6. The Native Americans viewed the Pilgrims with a great deal of _____, especially after so many began to arrive.
   F. apprehension
   G. compassion
   H. subjugation
   J. providence

7. The Native American oral tradition is populated with powerful _____, animals, and ancestral spirits.
   A. vaults
   B. mortifications
   C. scruples
   D. conjurers

8. According to Olaudah Equiano, the Africans, who were shown no _____ during the Middle Passage, were _____ by their captors' use of violence.
   F. mischief . . . appeased
   G. hypocrisy . . . daunted
   H. tyranny . . . spurned
   J. compassion . . . petrified

9. Thomas Jefferson hoped to protect America's _____ from tyranny when he drafted the Declaration of Independence.
   A. resolutions
   B. infidels
   C. rations
   D. posterity

10. During his lifetime, Benjamin Franklin created many _____ things.
    F. copious
    G. petrified
    H. ingenious
    J. insidious

Writing: Process and Language Conventions

In the following passage from the draft of an essay, there are underlined phrases and sentences. The numbers beneath the underlined words correspond to numbered test items. For each item, choose the alternative that is the best replacement for the underlined words. If you think the original should not be changed, choose "NO CHANGE."

The numbers in brackets identify the order of sentences and paragraphs. A boxed number refers to a question about a specific paragraph or about the essay as a whole.

Both the boxed numbers and the numbers that appear beneath underlined phrases and sentences refer to test-item numbers, not to the sequence of sentences or paragraphs.

[1]

[1] *Of all of those who signed this document, though, Benjamin Franklin was certainly the most important.* [2] *There are many important Americans whose names appear on the Declaration of Independence.* [3] *No other figure from this period is as interesting or as consistently relevant as Franklin continues to be.* [1]

[2]

Unlike many of the other founders Franklin was from a modest background and was largely self-educated. *He did not have the kinds of advantages that Jefferson, and Washington took for granted.*
2 ... 3

[3]

Franklin's background is startling when one considers his accomplishments. No other founder can claim the same number of achievements

in so many different fields of study. Franklin was a great scientist, writer, politician, philosopher, and diplomat. Amazingly, his formal education ended when he was only ten years old.
4

[4]

5 *What is truly incredible, though, is that so many of his inventions and concepts are still useful today. For example, Franklin was responsible for bifocal glasses, the lightning rod, the Franklin stove the first North American volunteer fire department, and the first North American public library.*
6 ... 6 ... 6

[5]

While the other founders were important figures who played prominent roles in the shaping of this country, none was as exciting, were as diverse in talents, or had as much foresight as Benjamin Franklin. 8
7 ... 7

1. Which of the following sequences of sentences will make paragraph 1 most logical?
   A. 2, 3, 1
   B. 3, 1, 2
   C. 2, 1, 3
   D. 3, 2, 1

2. F. NO CHANGE
   G. Unlike many of the other founders, Franklin was from a modest background
   H. Unlike other founders Franklin was from a modest background
   J. Many of the other founders came from modest backgrounds

3. A. NO CHANGE
   B. Washington, and Jefferson
   C. Jefferson and Washington
   D. Jefferson, Washington

4. F. NO CHANGE
   G. Franklin was a great scientist, writer, politician and philosopher, diplomat.
   H. Franklin was a great scientist and diplomat.
   J. Franklin was a scientist and writer and a politician, and philosopher, and diplomat.

5. Which of the following sentences, if inserted at this point, would provide the most effective transition to this paragraph?
   A. Benjamin Franklin was a good inventor.
   B. Franklin's inventions and scientific findings were groundbreaking in the 1700s.
   C. There were many things that Franklin knew, even without a strong formal education.
   D. In the long run, Franklin's formal education wasn't that important.

6. F. NO CHANGE
   G. the Franklin stove the first North American volunteer fire department and the first public library in North America.
   H. the Franklin stove and the first volunteer fire department and public library.
   J. the Franklin stove, the first North American volunteer fire department, and the first North American public library.

7. A. NO CHANGE
   B. was as diverse in talents, or had as much foresight
   C. is as diverse in talents, or had as much foresight
   D. that could be as diverse in talents, or have as much insight

8. What could have been added to the last paragraph to make it stronger?
   F. A summary of the key points
   G. New information
   H. Opposing viewpoints
   J. A visual aid

> Questions 9 and 10 ask about the essay as a whole.

9. The writer intends to add a paragraph concerning Franklin's contribution to the Revolutionary War. The most logical place to insert this paragraph is:
   A. before the third paragraph.
   B. after the last paragraph.
   C. before the second paragraph.
   D. after the fourth paragraph.

10. What information could have been added to this essay to make it more convincing?
   F. Rebuttals of specific arguments against the author's position
   G. Further examples of Franklin's inventions
   H. A thorough description of everyday life in America during the 1700s
   J. An account of Franklin's time in Paris

Writing: Applications

Benjamin Franklin wrote, "Those who would give up essential Liberty, to purchase a little temporary Safety, deserve neither Liberty nor Safety." Do you agree with this statement? Write a short persuasive essay in which you argue for or against Franklin's claim. As you write, keep in mind that your essay will be checked for **ideas, organization, voice, word choice, sentence fluency, conventions,** and **presentation.**

Literature Online **Unit Assessment** To prepare for the unit test, go to www.glencoe.com.

Independence (Squire Jack Porter), 1858. Frank Blackwell Mayer. Oil on paperboard. Smithsonian American Art Museum, Washington, DC.

AMERICAN ROMANTICISM

1800-1860

Looking Ahead

Powerful forces marked the period that produced the first great American literature. The arrival of the European cultural movement known as Romanticism strongly influenced many American writers of this time. These writers also responded to social forces, including an outburst of reform movements, the spread of industry, and the increasing sectional strife that would soon bring the Civil War.

Keep the following questions in mind as you read:

⇨ How do you think the big ideas that shaped this period continue to affect American culture today?

⇨ Which of the writers of this period reflect the positive side of Romanticism? Which reflect its dark side?

⇨ In what ways does the Romantic period seem better than the contemporary American period? In what ways does it seem worse?

INDIANA ACADEMIC STANDARDS (pages 162–175)
11.3.5 Analyze or evaluate works of literary or cultural significance in history (American...) that reflect a variety of genres in each of the respective historical periods; were written by important authors in the respective major historical periods; reveal contrasts in major themes, styles, and trends; reflect or shed light on the seminal philosophical, religious, social, political, or ethical ideas of their time.

TIMELINE 1800-1860

AMERICAN LITERATURE

1800	1810	1820	1830

1800
Library of Congress founded

1805
Red Jacket, a Seneca chief, gives a speech defending Native American beliefs

Chief Red Jacket ▶

1819
The Sketch Book by Washington Irving (which includes tales such as "Rip Van Winkle")

1828
Noah Webster's first dictionary of American English ▼

AN
AMERICAN DICTIONARY
OF THE
ENGLISH LANGUAGE:

1831
Ralph Waldo Emerson resigns from the ministry

1836
Transcendental Club founded

1837
Sarah Josepha Hale is made editor of *Godey's Lady's Book*; it becomes one of the most influential literary magazines of the century

UNITED STATES EVENTS

1800	1810	1820	1830

1803
United States buys Louisiana Territory from France, more than doubling the country's size

1807
Robert Fulton builds the *Clermont*, the first successful steamboat

1812–1815
United States and Great Britain fight War of 1812

1814
Francis Scott Key writes "The Star-Spangled Banner"

1815
Victory over British at New Orleans makes Andrew Jackson a national hero

1820
Missouri Compromise preserves balance of slave and free states

1825
Erie Canal opens, linking Atlantic Ocean and Great Lakes

1828
Andrew Jackson elected president

1831
Cyrus H. McCormick invents the mechanical reaper

1833
The American Anti-Slavery Society is founded in Philadelphia; by 1838 there are 250,000 members

1838
Cherokees are driven west along the Trail of Tears

WORLD EVENTS

1800	1810	1820	1830

1804
Napoleon crowned emperor of France

1805
Reign of Muhammad Ali begins in Egypt

1810
Miguel Hidalgo begins revolution in Mexico

1813
Simón Bolívar seizes Venezuela from Spain

1815
Napoleon defeated at the Battle of Waterloo

◀

The Mosque of Muhammad Ali

1821
Mexico declares independence from Spain

1825
World's first railway line opens in England

1829
Greece wins independence from Turkey

1837
Victoria crowned queen of Great Britain ▼

Literature Online **Timeline** Visit www.glencoe.com for an interactive timeline.

Masthead from the *North Star* newspaper

1840

1850

1840
Tales of the Grotesque and Arabesque by Edgar Allan Poe

1841
Social reformers establish Brook Farm, an experiment in communal living

1841
Essays by Ralph Waldo Emerson

1845
The Raven and Other Poems by Edgar Allan Poe

1845
Henry David Thoreau goes to live at Walden Pond

1845
Woman in the Nineteenth Century, an early work of feminism, by Margaret Fuller

1847
Frederick Douglass begins publishing the *North Star,* an abolitionist newspaper

1850
The Scarlet Letter by Nathaniel Hawthorne

1851
Moby-Dick by Herman Melville

1852
Uncle Tom's Cabin by Harriet Beecher Stowe

1854
Walden by Henry David Thoreau

1855
The Song of Hiawatha by Henry Wadsworth Longfellow

1855
Leaves of Grass by Walt Whitman

1840

1850

1844
Samuel Morse demonstrates the first telegraph by sending a message from Washington, D.C., to Baltimore

American gold coin ▼

1846–1848
Mexican-American War fought; Mexico cedes territory in Southwest to United States

1848
First women's rights convention held in Seneca Falls, New York

1849
California gold rush begins

1850
Fugitive Slave Act, forcing return of escaped slaves to their owners, inflames sectional conflict

1857
In *Dred Scott* case, Supreme Court rules that slaves and former slaves are not U.S. citizens

1859
Antislavery activist John Brown is hanged for raiding federal arsenal at Harpers Ferry, Virginia

1840

1850

1845
Potato famine begins in Ireland, leading to mass immigration to America

1848
Revolutions sweep Europe; Karl Marx and Friedrich Engels publish the *Communist Manifesto*

◄ Irish famine victims

1850
Taiping Rebellion begins in China

1855
Coronation of Czar Alexander II, who later frees the Russian serfs

▲
1859
Charles Darwin publishes his theory of evolution

Reading Check

Analyzing Graphic Information What relationship can you see between the events in U.S. history in 1815 and 1828 as they are related to the career of Andrew Jackson?

BY THE NUMBERS

URBAN AND RURAL POPULATIONS IN THE UNITED STATES, 1810–1870

Millions of People

— Rural Population
— Urban Population

Source *Historical Statistics of the United States: Colonial Times to 1970*

Purchasing Power

In 1851, a male textile worker earned $6.50 a week, a shoemaker or printer between $4 and $6 a week, and an unskilled laborer about $1 a week. Only a small group of skilled workers, such as blacksmiths, machinists, and carpenters, were able to make at least $10.38 per week. This is the amount that reformer Horace Greeley calculated as the weekly income that a family of five needed to make ends meet (see list below).

Weekly Needs

Flour	.63
Sugar	.32
Butter	.63
Milk	.14
Butcher's meat	$1.40
Potatoes	.50
Tea and coffee	.25
Candles and oil	.14
Fuel	.40
Sundries	.40
Household articles	.25
Bedding	.20
Rent	$3.00
Wearing apparel	$2.00
Newspapers	.12
TOTAL	**$10.38**

BIG CITIES OF 1830

City	Population
New York	200,000
Baltimore	80,000
Philadelphia	80,000
Boston	60,000

IMMIGRATION

- Between 1821 and 1840, 751,000 immigrants entered the United States.

- Between 1841 and 1860, more than four million immigrants came to the United States (most from Great Britain, Ireland, and Germany).

EDUCATION

- In 1850, 64.9 percent of white children and 31.3 percent of African American children attended school.

- In 1860, more than half of the country's 321 high schools were in Massachusetts, New York, and Ohio.

RAILROAD

- In 1833, there were 380 miles of rails in the United States. By 1860, there were more than 30,000 miles of rails in the United States.

FACTORIES

In 1840, U.S. factories and mills produced goods valued at less than $500 million. In 1850, they produced goods valued at more than $1 billion.

VOTER PARTICIPATION, 1824–1840

Percentage of Eligible Voters Who Voted

26.9% (1824), 57.6% (1828), 55.4% (1832), 57.8% (1836), 80.2% (1840)

Presidential Election Years

Source *Historical Statistics of the United States: Colonial Times to 1970*

BEING THERE

The major American writers of the period 1800–1860 lived in the northeastern United States, roughly the area from Maryland to New England. These images provide a glimpse of this area.

A *Boston as the Eagle and the Wild Goose See It*, 1860, James Wallace Black. Photograph. This photo of Boston is the first aerial photograph taken in the United States.

B *Market Street, Baltimore,* 1850. Unknown artist. Colored lithograph. Enoch Pratt Free Library, Baltimore MD. Painting of downtown Baltimore.

C *Brook Farm,* 1844. Josiah Wolcott. Oil on panel. Massachusetts Historical Society, Boston MA. Painting of a Transcendentalist community outside Boston.

Literature Online **Maps in Motion** Visit www.glencoe.com for an interactive map.

Reading Check

Analyzing Graphic Information

1. In which presidential election year during this period did voter participation increase the most from the previous one?

2. How many more U.S. citizens lived in rural areas than in urban areas in 1850?

3. What large cities are located in the area shown on the map? Judging by the images, how were the cities of the period like and unlike big U.S. cities today?

AMERICAN ROMANTICISM 1800-1860

Historical, Social, and Cultural Forces

The Industrial Revolution

In the mid-1700s, a huge economic change known as the Industrial Revolution began in Britain. Manufacturing shifted from skilled workers using hand tools to unskilled laborers tending large, complex machines. Factories, some housing hundreds of machines and workers, replaced home-based workshops. Manufacturers sold their goods nationwide or abroad instead of just locally.

The Industrial Revolution soon spread to the United States, where it caused tremendous economic growth and transformed American society. Hundreds of new factories were built. Francis C. Lowell, for example, opened a series of mills in northeastern Massachusetts beginning in 1814. His Boston Manufacturing Company employed thousands of women and children, who worked for lower wages than men and in often dangerous conditions. An expanding network of roads and canals united different sections of the country. Two new inventions—the steamboat and the railroad—revolutionized transportation.

Sectional Strife

The Industrial Revolution brought economic growth to the United States, but it was also one of several factors that were dividing Americans into two nations, the North and the South. The northern states had large cities and an economy based on manufacturing. The southern states had few large cities, and their farming economy was dominated by a single crop—cotton. Much of this cotton was grown on large plantations worked by slaves. The more fiercely northern reformers agitated to end slavery, the more stubbornly southerners defended the "peculiar institution" they saw as necessary to their way of life. In time, these divisions would bring the Civil War.

The Age of Reform

In the 1820s, idealistic Americans began an eager rush to improve American society, producing an outburst of reform movements. Many of these reformers were inspired by the Second Great Awakening, a major religious movement that reached its peak in the 1820s and 1830s. During the Age of Reform, Americans banded together in dozens of organizations to end slavery, stop drunkenness, secure women's rights, provide better care for the mentally ill, and improve prisons.

In the 1840s, railroads reduced the travel time from New York to Boston from a week (by stagecoach) to less than 12 hours.

Roots of Romanticism

Optimism and Individualism

Toward the end of the 1700s, bold new ideas began to transform European civilization. In time, many of these ideas would become part of Romanticism, a movement in art and thought that dominated Europe and the United States throughout much of the 1800s. Although Romanticism was not an organized cultural movement, Romantic writers did share two important attitudes. They valued imagination and feeling over intellect and reason. Some celebrated individualism and freedom; they believed in the basic goodness and equality of human beings and in their right to govern themselves. Others took a more pessimistic view of human life. Overall, Romanticism reflected a division between a "bright" and a "dark" vision of the world.

Kinship with Nature

Another attitude that the Romantics shared was a belief in the importance of nature. In the 1700s, many European thinkers had believed that nature was merely a wilderness to be tamed. In opposition to this view, the Romantics celebrated the beauty, power, and wonder of the natural world. They also stressed the value of nature as a spiritual and moral guide for humanity. The Romantics' reverence for nature also caused them to fear the destructive effects of industry.

The spread of factories and new inventions such as the railroad were changing the natural world.

> "A man should learn to detect and watch that gleam of light which flashes across his mind from within."
>
> —Ralph Waldo Emerson

The Power of Darkness

There was also a dark side to Romanticism that included a fascination with disease, madness, death, evil, the supernatural, and the destructive aspects of nature. Many Romantics were drawn to the nonrational side of human nature, such as the emotions, imagination, intuition—even evil and insanity. They were also fascinated by remote periods of history and exotic places. All these interests came together in the type of writing known as Gothic literature. In literature the word *Gothic* applies to works with a brooding atmosphere that emphasize the unknown and inspire fear. Gothic novels typically feature wild and remote settings, such as haunted castles or wind-blasted moors, and their plots involve violent or mysterious events.

PREVIEW Big Ideas of American Romanticism

1 Optimism and Individualism

Optimism is the belief that the world around us is always improving. Some American Romantics presented an optimistic view of the possibility of human progress, based in part on a democratic confidence in the ability of ordinary individuals to better themselves, their political system, and society.

See pages 170–171.

2 Kinship with Nature

Many American Romantics believed in the beneficial effects of a close link between humanity and nature. This belief coexisted with a concern that the spread of industry and new technology threatened the natural world and isolated people from it.

See pages 172–173.

3 The Power of Darkness

There was a dark underside to American Romanticism. It took a variety of forms, including a fascination with disease, madness, death, evil, the supernatural, and the destructive aspects of nature.

See pages 174–175.

Each of us has ambitions and plans, hopes and dreams. Our beliefs affect how we feel about what we can achieve as individuals and citizens. Optimists believe they can reach their goals in life. Ralph Waldo Emerson (see pages 178–188) was a lifelong optimist. He also celebrated the individual, proclaiming that by being true to their innermost selves, people could accomplish great things.

Rise of the Common People

Beginning in the 1820s, the American belief in the power of the ordinary citizen had a huge impact on both political and social life. Changes in voting laws expanded the electorate to include nearly all white males. In 1828, these voters elected frontiersman Andrew Jackson as president, marking the arrival of the common people in American politics. "Well, if Andrew Jackson can be president," observed one outraged North Carolina woman, "then anybody can!" Americans of this period also became involved in a broad range of reform movements. These ordinary citizens formed associations, raised money, wrote pamphlets, held rallies, gave speeches, and worked to pass laws designed to improve American society.

> "All that Adam had, all that Caesar could, you have and can do."
>
> —Ralph Waldo Emerson

Transcendentalism

Emerson's belief in the value of the individual was shaped by the era in which he lived. In the 1830s, the influence of Romanticism began to be felt in the United States. One result was Transcendentalism, a loosely organized movement that embodied the ideas of thinkers who were active in New England in the 1830s and 1840s. Emerson was a leading figure in this group, which began as an informal discussion club. Among those who participated in the talks at the Transcendental Club were Margaret Fuller, Henry David Thoreau, and Nathaniel Hawthorne.

The essence of Transcendentalism was the philosophy known as Idealism. For Idealists, such as the German philosopher Immanuel Kant, reality is not "out there" in material objects but instead exists in our ideas about those objects. The Transcendentalists believed that intuition is a more valuable guide than sensory experience in grasping what nature really is. As Emerson exulted in his essay "Nature," "I see the spectacle of morning from the hilltop over against my house, from daybreak to sunrise, with emotions which an angel might share."

Emerson's Outlook

Emerson's optimism convinced him that the universe existed for humanity's benefit. He told people that they simply needed to look within themselves to awaken a sense of wonder and recover their oneness with the universe: "Every spirit builds itself a house, and beyond its house a world, and beyond its world a heaven. Know then that the world exists for you." He believed that ordinary human beings had limitless potential. His avid reading of mystical Hindu philosophy influenced his conviction that humans are divine because they share in the Over-soul, Emerson's name for the spirit that pervades the universe. Emerson summed up his ideas by saying that he had really taught only one thing, that every person was infinite.

Emerson's Essays

Emerson is best known for his essays, such as "Self-Reliance." An essay is a short piece of nonfiction writing on any topic. Essays can range from serious, formal analyses to light, personal reflections. Although Emerson's essays are formal, they are not tightly unified around a single topic. Instead, he presented his thoughts in a loosely organized series of striking sentences. "The maker of a sentence," he observed, "launches out into the infinite."

The Jolly Flatboatmen, 1877–78. George Caleb Bingham. Oil on canvas, 26¹/₁₆ x 36³/₈ in. Daniel J. Terra Acquisition Endowment Fund, 1992. Terra Foundation for American Art, Chicago, IL.

from *Self-Reliance* by Ralph Waldo Emerson

Our houses are built with foreign taste; our shelves are garnished with foreign ornaments; our opinions, our tastes, our faculties, lean, and follow the Past and the Distant. The soul created the arts wherever they have flourished. It was in his own mind that the artist sought his model. It was an application of his own thought to the thing to be done and the conditions to be observed. And why need we copy the Doric or the Gothic model? Beauty, convenience, grandeur of thought, and quaint expression are as near to us as to any, and if the American artist will study with hope and love the precise thing to be done by him, considering the climate, the soil, the length of the day, the wants of the people, the habit and form of the government, he will create a house in which all these will find themselves fitted, and taste and sentiment will be satisfied also.

Insist on yourself; never imitate. Your own gift you can present every moment with the cumulative force of a whole life's cultivation; but of the adopted talent of another, you have only an extemporaneous, half possession. That which each can do best, none but his Maker can teach him. No man yet knows what it is, nor can, till that person has exhibited it. Where is the master who could have taught Shakespeare?

Reading Check

Analyzing Cause and Effect Why would Emerson's optimism have made him a reformer?

Big Idea 2
Kinship with Nature

Today, many people are concerned about the effects of civilization on the wilderness. Conflicts between environmentalists and commercial interests are widespread. How important is nature, and what can we learn from it? In the 1800s, Henry David Thoreau (see pages 202–217) revealed his thoughts about this question in his journal. Thoreau believed that contact with wild nature refreshed the human spirit. Other writers have described the benefits of nature's beauty and the feelings of peace that result from being out-of-doors. Nature can also teach us respect for its destructive ways and remind us that, though we try, we can never wholly subdue its powerful forces.

> *"I would rather sit on a pumpkin, and have it all to myself, than be crowded on a velvet cushion."*
>
> —Henry David Thoreau

America—Garden or Wilderness?

The natural environment of America has produced very different responses in different people. Luther Standing Bear, a Teton Sioux, explained the Native American view: "We did not think of the great open plains, the beautiful rolling hills, and winding streams with tangled growth as 'wild.' Only to the white man was nature a 'wilderness,' and only to him was the land 'infested' with 'wild' animals and 'savage' people. To us it was tame."

The first European explorers and settlers viewed America as both a paradise to be enjoyed and a wilderness to be tamed. Many Europeans were amazed and delighted at the number of animals and plants that were unknown in Europe. But to others, such as William Bradford, a leader of the Pilgrims who reached New England in 1620, America was a place to be feared: "What could they see but a hideous and desolate wilderness, full of wild beasts and wild men?"

Thoreau and Nature

Another New Englander, Emerson's friend Thoreau, also rejected a conventional life. Like Emerson, Thoreau championed American individualism. He spent two years in a cabin he built at Walden Pond near his home of Concord, Massachusetts. Thoreau sharply observed the natural surroundings there. "For many years," he wrote, "I was self-appointed inspector of snow storms and rain storms and did my duty faithfully." Thoreau was not fond of luxuries and not afraid of striking out on his own.

Emerson's and Thoreau's concept of the natural world had much in common with the Native American viewpoint. Both traditions found harmony and purpose in the unspoiled earth. At Walden, Thoreau communed with nature. He wrote, "You only need sit still long enough in some attractive spot in the woods that all its inhabitants may exhibit themselves to you by turns." Leslie Marmon Silko, a contemporary Native American author, expresses a similar view. She writes, "I never feel lonely when I walk alone in the hills: I am surrounded with living beings, with these sandstone ridges and lava rock hills full of life."

Thoreau and Politics

Thoreau's extreme individualism led him to take certain radical political positions. In the 1840s, as the southern states became more determined to protect and extend slavery, he came to regard all government as a threat to liberty. During the Mexican-American War (1846–1848), which many opponents of slavery believed was being fought to establish slavery in the West, Thoreau wrote his essay "Civil Disobedience." He argued that the individual conscience is more important than the law: "Law never made men a whit more just; and by means of their respect for it, even the well-disposed are daily made the agents of injustice."

Thoreau was even willing to spend time in jail for refusing to pay a tax that would have been used to finance the war. He later wrote that, behind bars, he felt freer than his townspeople who stood outside the prison walls but lived in subjugation to the state.

Cathedral Forest, Albert Bierstadt. Private collection.

Thoreau's Journals

Many of Thoreau's writings, including *Walden*, are based on his journal entries. A journal is a daily record of events kept by a writer. Thoreau kept a journal from the time he was twenty and reshaped and revised it throughout his life. When he died at forty-four, the journal ran to 7,000 manuscript pages containing nearly two million words.

Thoreau's journal provides insights into the extraordinary richness of his mind. In one entry, he observed, "My Journal is that of me which would else spill over and run to waste, gleanings from the field which in action I reap. I must not live for it, but in it for the gods."

from *The Journal*
by Henry David Thoreau

March 5. [1858] . . . We would fain know something more about these animals and stones and trees around us. We are ready to skin the animals alive to come at them. Our scientific names contain a very partial information only. It does not occur to me that there are other names for most of these objects, given by a people who stood between me and them, who had better senses than our race. . . . No science does more than arrange what knowledge we have of any class of objects. But, generally speaking, how much more conversant was the Indian with any wild animal or plant than we are, and in his language is implied all that intimacy, as much as ours is expressed in our language. How many words in his language about moose, or birch bark, and the like! The Indian stood nearer to wild nature than we. The wildest and noblest quadrupeds, even the largest freshwater fishes, some of the wildest and noblest birds and fairest flowers have actually receded as we advanced, and we have but the most distant knowledge of them. A rumor has come down to us that the skin of a lion was seen and his roar heard here by an early settler. But there was a race here that slept on his skin. It was a new light when my guide gave me Indian names for things for which I had only scientific ones before. In proportion as I understood the language, I saw them from a new point of view.

Reading Check

Interpreting How did Thoreau's individualism affect his attitude toward nature and politics?

The Power of Darkness

Our experience of life and the world has a dark side. We fear the evils we know—poverty, violence, disease, madness, death—and are troubled by nameless terrors that might lurk in the shadows beyond our knowledge. Not all the important American writers of Emerson's time shared his optimism. Nathaniel Hawthorne (see pages 265–278) admired Emerson but thought him unrealistic. To Herman Melville (see pages 280–291), Emerson's optimism was "nonsense" that ignored the "disagreeable facts" of life.

Hawthorne and Melville

Almost all of Hawthorne's fiction is based on stories of the past, particularly the history and legends of his Puritan ancestors in New England. Hawthorne was drawn to the Puritan past as Gothic writers were drawn to the Middle Ages. In Puritan New England, he found a strange, stark world that provided a richly textured background for the explorations of the nature of good and evil in his fiction. Hawthorne's friend Melville first gained a literary reputation for romantic tales of adventure in the South Seas. In succeeding books, he used his sea stories to explore the mystery of the evil that he saw in both human life and the forces of nature. In Melville's masterpiece, *Moby-Dick*, Ahab, the crazed captain of a whaling ship, sees evil personified in a huge white whale.

Gothic Horror

The dark side of European Romanticism can be seen in the tradition of Gothic literature. A classic example from nineteenth-century England is Mary Shelley's *Frankenstein*, a novel about a monster that destroys its creator. The American Romantics also recognized the power of darkness. Gothic horror relies chiefly on atmosphere, or mood, to achieve its effects. Writers create an atmosphere of horror through plot, characters, and settings that most people find chilling. Plots often focus on mysterious happenings, tragic events, and hideous outcomes. Characters are often mad, half-mad, or frightened to death. They may exhibit strange behavior and physical traits.

Settings are dark and often contain decayed dwellings with shadowy passageways, haunting sounds, and damp rooms.

Poe and the Terror of the Soul

A European tradition of Gothic literature existed long before Edgar Allan Poe (see pages 242–263), but he was the first American master of this type of horror. In his poems and stories, Poe often bettered earlier Gothic writers in achieving spine-tingling effects. Most of his stories and poems deal with loss and sorrow, ruin and revenge, disease and death. Poe's literary works reflected his own troubles and fears, but many readers responded favorably to his subject matter and the mood of his works, thus confronting their own fears. Emerson and the Transcendentalists believed that humans are inherently good. By contrast, Poe seems to have had an instinctive feel for the dark impulses of human nature. Poe observed, "The terror of which I write is not of Germany [the setting of much Gothic fiction], but of the soul." He expressed this spiritual terror in haunting literary works.

Poe's Short Stories

Poe was a master of the brief fictional narrative known as the short story. In addition to writing many Gothic tales of terror, he invented a new type of short fiction, the detective story. His first detective story, "The Murders in the Rue Morgue," combines Gothic horror with solid reasoning by Poe's fictional detective, Dupin.

Poe's stories illustrate his idea that any artistic composition should have a single, unique effect. This effect is evident in the gloomy, ominous beginning of his short story "The Fall of the House of Usher," guaranteed to make the reader long for sunshine or the comfort of his or her own room.

Abbey in an Oak Forest, 1810. Caspar David Friedrich. Oil on canvas. Nationalgalerie, Staatliche Museen zu Berlin, Berlin, Germany.

from *The Fall of the House of Usher* by Edgar Allan Poe

During the whole of a dull, dark, and soundless day in the autumn of the year, when the clouds hung oppressively low in the heavens, I had been passing alone, on horseback, through a singularly dreary tract of country; and at length found myself, as the shades of the evening drew on, within view of the melancholy House of Usher. I know not how it was—but, with the first glimpse of the building, a sense of insufferable gloom pervaded my spirit. I say insufferable; for the feeling was unrelieved by any of that half-pleasurable, because poetic, sentiment, with which the mind usually receives even the sternest natural images of the desolate or terrible. I looked upon the scene before me—upon the mere house, and the simple landscape features of the domain—upon the bleak walls—upon the vacant eye-like windows—upon a few rank sedges—and upon a few white trunks of decayed trees—with an utter depression of soul . . .

Reading Check

Comparing and Contrasting In what sense were Poe and Emerson both Romantics (see pages 170–174)? How did their Romanticism differ?

WRAP-UP

Why It Matters

Some of the most important characteristics of American Romanticism—such as optimism, individualism, and the impulse to reform—shaped American experience from the time of the first explorers and settlers. The New England colonists saw their communities as models for the rest of the world to imitate. As John Winthrop of Massachusetts put it, "We shall be as a city upon a hill." This sense of the United States as a nation with a reforming mission—what Abraham Lincoln described as "the last, best hope of earth"—continues today.

The Romantic view of human kinship with nature has had a limited influence on American culture. Beginning with a need to survive in a wilderness, Americans have typically viewed the land as something to be "tamed." This attitude has too often led to exploitation that damaged or destroyed natural environments. However, the modern environmental movement is an important legacy of Romanticism, which is also reflected in the nature writing of authors such as Gary Snyder, N. Scott Momaday, John McPhee, and Annie Dillard.

 Big Ideas Link to Web resources to further explore the Big Ideas at www.glencoe.com.

Cultural Links

➡ Emerson's essays had a great influence on Walt Whitman, who later said, "I was simmering, simmering, simmering. Emerson brought me to a boil."

➡ Thoreau's writings are among the basic texts of the American environmental movement. John Muir, founder of the Sierra Club, shared the basic outlook that Thoreau famously expressed: "In wildness lies the preservation of the world."

➡ As a pioneer of detective, horror, and science fiction writing, Poe has had a huge impact on popular culture worldwide.

FOLDABLES Study Organizer **THREE-POCKET BOOK**

Big Idea 1 Big Idea 2 Big Idea 3

You might try using this graphic organizer to keep track of the three big ideas in this unit.

Connect to Today

Use what you have learned about the period to do one of these activities.

1. Speaking/Listening Working with several other students, create a brief presentation for your class about how one of this period's big ideas affects American culture today. You can use examples from literature, fine art, music, movies, or other kinds of expression.

2. Visual Literacy Create an illustrated diagram showing the bright and dark sides of Romanticism. For example, you might present your diagram in the form of a color spectrum on which you position cultural ideas and values, works of art, and writers associated with Romanticism's two aspects.

3. Writing Taking into account the political, social, economic, and cultural characteristics of this period, do you think the United States was a better place to live in then or now? Write a brief essay exploring this question.

 INDIANA ACADEMIC STANDARDS (page 176)
11.7.17 Deliver oral reports on historical investigations...
11.5.3 Write reflective compositions that...draw comparisons between specific incidents and broader themes...

Literature Online Study Central Visit www.glencoe.com and click on Study Central to review American Romanticism.

PART 1
Individualism and Nature

Kindred Spirits, 1849. Asher Durand. Oil on canvas. The New York Public Library.

"We see the world piece by piece, as the sun, the moon, the animal, the tree; but the whole, of which these are the shining parts, is the soul."

—Emerson, "The Over-Soul"

from *Nature*, from *Self-Reliance*, and *Concord Hymn*

MEET RALPH WALDO EMERSON

Ralph Waldo Emerson was the central figure of American Romanticism. His ideas about the individual, claims about the divine, and attacks on society were revolutionary.

Emerson's father was a Unitarian minister and his mother a devout Anglican. When Emerson was only eight years old, his father died, and Mrs. Emerson was forced to open a boarding-house. At the age of 14, Emerson entered Harvard College. After graduation, he studied at Harvard Divinity School. By 1829, Emerson had been ordained a Unitarian minister and was preaching in Boston's Second Church.

In 1831 Ellen Tucker, Emerson's wife, died suddenly. Emerson had already been questioning his religious convictions, and after Ellen's death, he experienced intense grief that further eroded his faith. Eventually, Emerson left the church to embark on a career as a writer.

A Controversial Career In 1833 Emerson settled in Concord, Massachusetts, and began writing *Nature*. This slim book was to become one of Emerson's most influential works. Two years later, Emerson married Lydia Jackson, whom he called "Lidian." Emerson and Lydia had four children.

During the late 1830s, Emerson gained fame for his lectures—notably "The American Scholar" and the divinity school *Address*. These speeches, both delivered at Harvard, rejected organized religion and undue reverence for the past. Harvard's conservative administration was outraged. As a result, he was not invited to speak at the college for the next 30 years.

While Emerson's ideas enraged some, they excited many others and helped create the transcendentalist movement, of which Emerson was the spokesperson. Optimism, self-reliance, intuition, and idealism formed the core of transcendentalist thought. Idealism is a philosophy that maintains the belief that reality is created by the mind.

Challenges to Optimism Emerson's own optimism was challenged when his son Waldo died of scarlet fever in 1842. Two years later, Emerson's essay "The Tragic" appeared in *The Dial*, a transcendentalist magazine he had co-founded. In this essay, Emerson claimed that the arts and the intellect can "ravish us into a region whereinto these passionate clouds of sorrow cannot rise."

After 1870, his memory began to fail and the quality of his essays diminished. He stayed in Concord and wrote little in his last years; he died of pneumonia at the age of 79.

Emerson influenced writers as diverse as essayist Henry David Thoreau (page 202), novelist Louisa May Alcott, and poets Robert Frost (page 704), Wallace Stevens (page 689), and Hart Crane. Emerson was a radical individualist, and his impact on American thought can still be felt today. As modern critic Harold Bloom wrote, ". . . no single sage, not Dr. Johnson nor Coleridge, is as inescapable as Emerson goes on being for American poets and storytellers."

Ralph Waldo Emerson was born in 1803 and died in 1882.

Literature Online **Author Search** For more about Ralph Waldo Emerson, go to www.glencoe.com.

Connecting to the Essay

The following essay is a declaration of Emerson's belief in the power of nature. Emerson makes some startling claims about how people relate to the natural world and how nature responds to the individual. As you read these essays, think about the following questions:

- How do I interact with nature in my daily life?
- How does my mood affect the way I see the world?

Building Background

The Romantics tended to emphasize two aspects of nature—beauty and power. The darker Romantics, such as the Melville of *Moby-Dick,* stressed nature's destructive power. Although Emerson was sensitive to the power of the untamed American wilderness, he chose to dwell on the beauty of nature.

Nature is now recognized as one of Emerson's most important works. At the time of its anonymous publication, however, it received little attention. In fact, during his lifetime, Emerson was better known as an orator than as an essayist. Nevertheless, all of the ideas found in Emerson's later work are an extension or reevaluation of those initially expressed in *Nature.*

Setting Purposes for Reading

Big Idea Kinship with Nature

As you read this selection from *Nature,* notice how Emerson links nature to optimism and individualism.

Literary Element Theme

Theme is the central message of a work of literature that readers can apply to life. As you read, try to determine the central theme of Emerson's essay.

- See Literary Terms Handbook, p. R18.

Literature Online Interactive Literary Elements Handbook To review or learn more about the literary elements, go to www.glencoe.com.

Reading Strategy Recognizing Author's Purpose

The **author's purpose** is the author's intent in writing a piece of literature. Authors typically write to persuade, to inform, to explain, to entertain, or to describe. While reading this essay, try to determine Emerson's purpose.

Reading Tip: Asking Questions It might be useful to ask yourself questions as you read, such as the following:

- What is the thesis or main idea statement?
- How do the details support the thesis statement?
- What are Emerson's special concerns? Does he show any biases or prejudices? If so, what are they?

Vocabulary

perpetual (pər pech′ ōō əl) *adj.* lasting forever; eternal; p. 180 *The leaders of the American Revolution had hoped to create a perpetual union of states.*

integrate (in′ tə grāt′) *v.* to bring all parts together into a whole; p. 180 *Can we integrate the process by having all the committees report to one chairperson?*

perennial (pə ren′ ē əl) *adj.* continuing year after year; enduring; p. 181 *Water pollution is a perennial problem around factories and farms.*

blithe (blīth) *adj.* lighthearted and carefree; cheerful; p. 181 *The old man was always blithe in the company of his grandchildren.*

occult (ə kult′) *adj.* beyond human understanding; mysterious; p. 181 *The old doctor was interested in strange, occult research.*

Vocabulary Tip: Synonyms Words that have the same meaning are called synonyms. The words *ragged* and *shabby,* for example, are synonyms. Note that synonyms are always the same part of speech.

INDIANA ACADEMIC STANDARDS (pages 179–182)

11.3.2 Analyze the way in which the theme or meaning of a selection represents a view or comment on life, using textual evidence to support the claim.

11.2 Develop strategies such as...identifying and analyzing... purpose...

11.5.2 Write responses to literature that...support statements with evidence from the text.

from Nature

Ralph Waldo Emerson

To go into solitude, a man needs to retire as much from his chamber as from society. I am not solitary whilst I read and write, though nobody is with me. But if a man would be alone, let him look at the stars. The rays that come from those heavenly worlds will separate between him and what he touches. One might think the atmosphere was made transparent with this design, to give man, in the heavenly bodies, the **perpetual** presence of the sublime. Seen in the streets of cities, how great they are! If the stars should appear one night in a thousand years, how would men believe and adore; and preserve for many generations the remembrance of the city of God which had been shown! But every night come out these envoys[1] of beauty, and light the universe with their admonishing[2] smile.

The stars awaken a certain reverence, because though always present, they are inaccessible; but all natural objects make a kindred impression, when the mind is open to their influence. Nature never wears a mean[3] appearance. Neither does the wisest man extort her secret, and lose his curiosity by finding out all her perfection. Nature never became a toy to a wise spirit. The flowers, the animals, the mountains, reflected the wisdom of his best hour, as much as they had delighted the simplicity of his childhood.

When we speak of nature in this manner, we have a distinct but most poetical sense in the mind. We mean the integrity of impression made by manifold[4] natural objects. It is this which distinguishes the stick of timber of the wood-cutter from the tree of the poet. The charming landscape which I saw this morning is indubitably[5] made up of some twenty or thirty farms. Miller owns this field, Locke that, and Manning the woodland beyond. But none of them owns the landscape. There is a property in the horizon which no man has but he whose eye can **integrate** all the parts, that is, the poet. This is the best part of these men's farms, yet to this their warranty-deeds[6] give no title.

To speak truly, few adult persons can see nature. Most persons do not see the sun. At least they have a very superficial seeing. The sun illuminates only the eye of the man, but shines into the eye and the heart of the child. The lover of nature is he whose inward and outward senses are still truly adjusted to each other; who has retained the spirit of infancy even into the era of manhood. His intercourse with heaven and earth becomes part of his daily food. In the presence of nature a wild delight runs through the man, in spite of real sorrows. Nature says,—he is my creature, and

---

1. *Envoys* are those sent as representatives of another.
2. *Admonishing* means "gently warning" or "scolding."
3. Here, *mean* means "poor," "inferior," or "shabby."

Big Idea Kinship with Nature *How does Emerson's statement relate nature to his belief in individualism?*

Vocabulary

perpetual (pər pech′oo əl) *adj.* lasting forever; eternal

---

4. *Manifold* means "many kinds or varieties."
5. *Indubitably* means "without a doubt" or "certainly."
6. *Warranty-deeds* are legal documents that state ownership of property.

Reading Strategy Recognizing Author's Purpose *What does this statement suggest to you about Emerson's purpose?*

Vocabulary

integrate (in′ tə grāt′) *v.* to bring all parts together into a whole maugre[7] all his impertinent[8] griefs, he shall be glad with me. Not the sun or the summer alone, but every hour and season yields its tribute of delight; for every hour and change corresponds to and authorizes a different state of the mind, from breathless noon to grimmest midnight. Nature is a setting that fits equally well a comic or a mourning piece. In good health, the air is a cordial[9] of incredible virtue. Crossing a bare common,[10] in snow puddles, at twilight, under a clouded sky, without having in my thoughts any occurrence of special good fortune, I have enjoyed a perfect exhilaration. I am glad to the brink of fear. In the woods, too, a man casts off his years, as the snake his slough, and at what period soever of life is always a child. In the woods is perpetual youth. Within these plantations of God, a decorum and sanctity reign, a **perennial** festival is dressed, and the guest sees not how he should tire of them in a thousand years. In the woods, we return to reason and faith. There I feel that nothing can befall me in life,—no disgrace, no calamity (leaving me my eyes), which nature cannot repair. Standing on the bare ground,—my head bathed by the **blithe** air and uplifted into infinite space,—all mean egotism vanishes. I become a transparent eyeball; I am nothing; I see all; the currents of the Universal Being circulate through me; I am part or parcel of God. The name of the nearest friend sounds then foreign and accidental: to be brothers, to be acquaintances, master or servant, is then a trifle and a disturbance. I am the lover of uncontained and immortal beauty. In the wilderness, I find something more dear and connate[11] than in streets or villages. In the tranquil landscape, and especially in the distant line of the horizon, man beholds somewhat as beautiful as his own nature.

View from Mount Holyoke, Northampton, Massachusetts, after a Thunderstorm—The Oxbow, 1836. Thomas Cole. Oil on canvas. Metropolitan Museum of Art, New York.
Viewing the Art: What elements in this painting reflect the characteristics Emerson attributes to nature?

The greatest delight which the fields and woods minister is the suggestion of an **occult** relation between man and the vegetable. I am not alone and unacknowledged. They nod to me, and I to them. The waving of the boughs in the storm is new to me and old. It takes me by surprise, and yet is not unknown. Its effect is like that of a higher thought or a better emotion coming over me, when I deemed I was thinking justly or doing right.

Yet it is certain that the power to produce this delight does not reside in nature, but in man, or in a harmony of both. It is necessary to use these pleasures with great temperance. For nature is not always tricked[12] in holiday attire, but the same scene which yesterday breathed perfume and glittered as for the frolic of the nymphs is overspread with melancholy today. Nature always wears the colors of the spirit. To a man laboring under calamity, the heat of his own fire hath sadness in it. Then there is a kind of contempt of the landscape felt by him who has just lost by death a dear friend. The sky is less grand as it shuts down over less worth in the population. ∾

---

7. *Maugre* means "in spite of."
8. *Impertinent* means "irrelevant."
9. A *cordial* is a stimulant, such as a drink or medicine.
10. A *common* is community property, such as a park, owned or used by the public.
11. *Connate* means "being in harmony or sympathy."

Literary Element Theme *What does this statement tell you about Emerson's theme?*

Vocabulary

perennial (pə ren′ ē əl) *adj.* continuing year after year; enduring
blithe (blīth) *adj.* lighthearted and carefree; cheerful

---

12. Here, *tricked* means "dressed."

Literary Element Theme *Why does Emerson hold this belief?*

Vocabulary

occult (ə kult′) *adj.* beyond human understanding; mysterious

RESPONDING AND THINKING CRITICALLY

Respond

1. (a)Which of Emerson's ideas do you think are true in light of your own experience? (b)With which ideas do you disagree?

Recall and Interpret

2. (a)What does Emerson say would happen if the stars appeared only one night in a thousand years? (b)What does his comment suggest about human nature?

3. (a)In Emerson's view, how do adults and children differ in the way they view nature? (b)What does Emerson suggest accounts for this difference?

4. (a)According to Emerson, what effect does the experience of nature have on him? (b)What conclusion does he draw from that effect?

Analyze and Evaluate

5. (a)In this essay, how does Emerson personify, or give human traits to nature? (b)Does Emerson's personification of nature strengthen or weaken his arguments? Explain.

6. (a)How does Emerson show his idealism in this essay? (b)How does idealism affect the theme of *Nature?*

7. Emerson claims that the individual becomes childlike while immersed in nature. (a)What evidence does he use to support this statement? (b)Do you agree with this claim? Why or why not?

Connect

8. **Big Idea** **Kinship with Nature** How do your feelings about nature compare with those of Emerson?

LITERARY ANALYSIS

Literary Element Theme

Some works of literature have a **stated theme,** which is expressed directly. More works have an **implied theme,** which is revealed gradually through events, dialogue, or description. A literary work may have more than one theme.

1. What is the central theme in *Nature?* Is this theme stated or implied? Explain.

2. How is the theme of this essay consistent with Emerson's transcendentalism?

Writing About Literature

Respond to Theme Emerson states, "Nature always wears the colors of the spirit." Write a one-page response explaining why you agree or disagree with this statement. Use evidence from this essay and your personal experience to defend your position.

Literature Online **Web Activities** For eFlashcards, Selection Quick Checks, and other Web activities, go to www.glencoe.com.

READING AND VOCABULARY

Reading Strategy Recognizing Author's Purpose

Sometimes an author will have more than one purpose for writing. However, authors generally consider one purpose more important than the others.

1. What do you think Emerson's main purpose was for writing *Nature?*

2. In support of your opinion, list three details from the essay.

Vocabulary Practice

Practice with Synonyms Find the synonym for each vocabulary word from *Nature* listed in the first column. Use a dictionary or a thesaurus if you need help.

1. blithe	a. happy	b. reckless
2. integrate	a. dismantle	b. synthesize
3. occult	a. secret	b. unhealthy
4. perennial	a. long lasting	b. frequent
5. perpetual	a. unending	b. stubborn

from Self-Reliance

Ralph Waldo Emerson

Literary Element Figurative Language

Figurative language is descriptive language used to convey ideas or emotions. Figurative expressions are not literally true. They express some truth that reaches beyond the literal level. As you read the essay, examine how Emerson uses figurative language to help his readers understand his abstract ideas.

Reading Strategy Drawing Conclusions

Drawing a conclusion is using details from the text to arrive at a general statement. As you read "Self-Reliance," use the details Emerson presents as the basis for drawing a conclusion about his beliefs.

I read the other day some verses written by an eminent[1] painter which were original and not conventional. Always the soul hears an **admonition** in such lines, let the subject be what it may. The sentiment they instill is of more value than any thought they may contain. To believe your own thought, to believe that what is true for you in your private heart, is true for all men,—that is genius. Speak your **latent** conviction and it shall be the universal sense; for always the inmost becomes the outmost,—and our first thought is rendered back to us by the trumpets of the Last Judgment. Familiar as the voice of the mind is to each, the highest merit we ascribe to Moses, Plato, and Milton is that they set at naught books and traditions, and spoke not what men, but what they thought. A man should learn to detect and watch that gleam of light which

flashes across his mind from within, more than the lustre of the firmament of bards[2] and sages. Yet he dismisses without notice his thought, because it is his. In every work of genius we recognize our own rejected thoughts: they come back to us with a certain alienated majesty. Great works of art have no more affecting lesson for us than this. They teach us to abide by our spontaneous impression with good humored inflexibility then most when the whole cry of voices is on the other side. Else, tomorrow a stranger will say with masterly good sense precisely what we have thought and felt all the time, and we shall be forced to take with shame our own opinion from another.

There is a time in every man's education when he arrives at the conviction that envy is ignorance; that imitation is suicide; that he must take himself for better, for worse, as his portion; that though the wide universe is full

---

1. *Eminent* means "distinguished" or "prominent."

Vocabulary

admonition (ad′ mə nish′ ən) *n.* a warning; cautionary advice

latent (lā′ tənt) *adj.* present but not evident; hidden

---

2. *Bards* are poets.

Reading Strategy Drawing Conclusions *What does Emerson mean by this statement?*

of good, no kernel of nourishing corn can come to him but through his toil bestowed on that plot of ground which is given to him to till. The power which resides in him is new in nature, and none but he knows what that is which he can do, nor does he know until he has tried. Not for nothing one face, one character, one fact makes much impression on him, and another none. It is not without preëstablished harmony, this sculpture in the memory. The eye was placed where one ray should fall, that it might testify of that particular ray. Bravely let him speak the utmost syllable of his confession. We but half express ourselves, and are ashamed of that divine idea which each of us represents. It may be safely trusted as proportionate and of good issues, so it be faithfully imparted, but God will not have his work made **manifest** by cowards. It needs a divine man to exhibit any thing divine. A man is relieved and gay when he has put his heart into his work and done his best; but what he has said or done otherwise, shall give him no peace. It is a deliverance which does not deliver. In the attempt his genius deserts him; no muse[3] befriends; no invention, no hope.

Trust thyself: every heart vibrates to that iron string. Accept the place the divine Providence[4] has found for you; the society of your contemporaries, the connection of events. Great men have always done so and confided themselves childlike to the genius[5] of their age, betraying their perception that the Eternal was stirring at their heart, working through their hands, predominating[6] in all their being. And we are now men, and must accept in the highest mind the same transcendent[7] destiny; and not pinched in a corner, not cowards fleeing before a revolution, but redeemers and **benefactors,** pious aspirants[8] to be noble clay plastic under the Almighty effort, let us advance and advance on Chaos and the Dark. . . .

Society everywhere is in conspiracy against the manhood of every one of its members. Society is a joint-stock company in which the members agree for the better securing of his bread to each shareholder, to surrender the liberty and culture of the eater. The virtue in most request is conformity. Self-reliance is its aversion. It loves not realities and creators, but names and customs.

Whoso would be a man must be a nonconformist. He who would gather immortal palms[9] must not be hindered by the name of goodness, but must explore if it be goodness. Nothing is at last sacred but the **integrity** of your own mind. . . .

What I must do, is all that concerns me, not what the people think. This rule, equally arduous[10] in actual and in intellectual life, may serve for the whole distinction between greatness and meanness.[11] It is the harder, because you will always find those who think they know what is your duty better than you know it. It is easy in the world to live after the world's opinion; it is easy in solitude to live after our own; but the great man is he who in the midst of the crowd keeps with perfect sweetness the independence of solitude. ◦◦

---

3. In Greek mythology, the Muses were goddesses who presided over the arts and sciences. Here, *muse* is used to mean "a source of genius or inspiration."
4. The *divine Providence* is God.
5. Here, *genius* means "the distinctive character" or "predominant spirit."

6. *Predominating* means "having controlling power or influence."
7. *Transcendent* means "concerned with a spiritual reality that is beyond the limits of experience and knowable only through intuition."
8. *Aspirants* are those who seek, or aspire to, advancement or honors.
9. *Palm* leaves are a traditional symbol of victory or success.
10. *Arduous* means "difficult."
11. Here, *meanness* means "the state of having little importance, worth, or consequence."

Literary Element Figurative Language *What comparison is Emerson making here?*

Reading Strategy Drawing Conclusions *According to Emerson, what is the cause of our shame?*

Vocabulary

manifest (man′ ə fest′) *adj.* apparent to the eye or the mind; evident; obvious

Big Idea Optimism and Individualism *What does Emerson think about relationships between individuals?*

Vocabulary

benefactor (ben′ ə fak′ tər) *n.* one who gives help or financial aid
integrity (in teg′ rə tē) *n.* moral uprightness; honesty

RESPONDING AND THINKING CRITICALLY

Respond

1. (a)What was your reaction to Emerson's discussion of nonconformity? (b)In your experience, how valuable a trait is the type of nonconformity that Emerson recommends?

Recall and Interpret

2. (a)According to Emerson, what is genius? (b)How does his definition of genius relate to his belief in individualism?

3. (a)According to Emerson, in what way should a person approach his or her work? (b)What kind of "work" do you think he is describing?

4. (a)To what does Emerson compare society? (b)How does society affect what people value?

Analyze and Evaluate

5. Emerson uses many religious references throughout the essay. (a)Why do you think he does so? (b)How do they affect the essay's meaning and tone?

6. (a)What kinds of figurative language does Emerson use to describe both society and the individual? (b)How effective is his use of figurative language?

7. (a)What parts of Emerson's essay did you find most persuasive? (b)What techniques did he use to convince you of his arguments?

Connect

8. **Big Idea** **Optimism and Individualism** Do you think it is possible for people to live as individuals and nonconformists in modern society? Why or why not?

LITERARY ANALYSIS

Literary Element Figurative Language

There are many different kinds of **figurative language.** Examples include imagery, personification, metaphor, metonymy, simile, and symbol. An author can use each of these devices to generate various moods, effects, or ideas. For example, when Emerson says that a person "should learn to detect and watch that gleam of light which flashes across the mind from within," he is using a metaphor that compares a sudden idea to a flash of lightning.

1. When Emerson writes, "Trust thyself: every heart vibrates to that iron string," what kind of figurative language is he using?

2. Find at least two other examples of figurative language in the excerpt from "Self-Reliance." Tell how each helps to explain an idea or make it more concrete.

Review: Tone

As you learned in a previous lesson, **tone** is the reflection of a writer's attitude toward his or her subject matter, as conveyed through word choice, punctuation, sentence structure, and figures of speech.

Partner Activity Pair up with a classmate and discuss the tone of "Self-Reliance." Working with your partner, create a two-column chart similar to the one below. Fill in the left-hand column with examples from the text that demonstrate a particular tone. In the right-hand column, label each example with an adjective that describes the tone.

Examples	Tone
"It is a deliverance which does not deliver."	Resolute

Reading Strategy Drawing Conclusions

Authors often incorporate their own beliefs into their writing. Sometimes they state these beliefs explicitly. In other cases, they merely imply, or hint at, their beliefs. The reader can infer an author's beliefs by examining his or her word choice, figurative language, or rhetorical techniques. What do you think Emerson believes about the relationship between the individual and society? Is his belief stated or implied? List three details that support your opinion.

Vocabulary Practice

Practice with Antonyms Choose the best antonym for each vocabulary word from "Self-Reliance." Use a dictionary if you need help.

1. **admonition**
   a. betrayal
   b. encouragement
   c. adversary
2. **latent**
   a. punctual
   b. tardy
   c. obvious
3. **manifest**
   a. celebration
   b. hidden
   c. humane
4. **benefactor**
   a. detractor
   b. critic
   c. donor

Academic Vocabulary

Here are two vocabulary words from the vocabulary list on page R86. These words will help you think, write, and talk about the selection.

approach (ə prōch′) *n.* a method used to make advances toward a full understanding or accomplishment

evident (ev′ ə dənt) *adj.* clear; obvious

Practice and Apply
1. What was Emerson's **approach** to the issue of conformity in "Self-Reliance"?
2. What do you believe was **evident** to Emerson before he began writing this essay?

Writing About Literature

Compare and Contrast Theme In many of his essays, Emerson treats related topics, arguments, and themes. How are the themes of "Self-Reliance" and *Nature* similar? How are they different? Write a one- or two-page analysis, in which you compare and contrast the themes of these essays. Use evidence from Emerson's essays to defend your position.

Before you begin drafting, take notes on the similarities and differences in the two essays' themes in a Venn diagram, such as the one below:

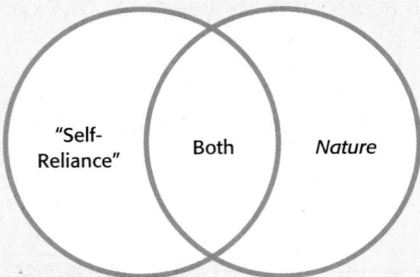

Include quotes from the texts related to the themes of each essay, as well as any impressions or ideas that struck you as you read. Once you have completed the diagram, begin drafting.

After completing your draft, meet with a peer reviewer to evaluate each other's work and suggest revisions. Then proofread and edit your draft for errors in spelling, grammar, and punctuation.

Literature Groups

Being Courageous In what ways would it take courage for students today to trust themselves and live according to their own convictions? Discuss this question in your group. Was Emerson courageous in expressing his beliefs? What might he have risked, if anything? What might he have gained? Share your ideas with the class.

Literature Online **Web Activities** For eFlashcards, Selection Quick Checks, and other Web activities, go to www.glencoe.com.

Concord Hymn

Ralph Waldo Emerson

BEFORE YOU READ

Building Background

On July 4, 1837, a monument was unveiled in Concord, Massachusetts. There, on April 20, 1775, American Minutemen fought the British in one of the first battles of the Revolutionary War. At the request of the Monument Committee, Emerson wrote the lyrics to "Concord Hymn," which was sung at the memorial ceremony.

Literary Element Metonymy

Metonymy, a type of figurative language, is the use of one word to stand for a related term. For example, in the aphorism "The pen is mightier than the sword," the word *pen* stands for words or writing, and *sword* stands for force or violence. Like other types of figurative language, metonymy is often used for descriptive effect or to convey a truth beyond the literal level.

Sung at the completion of Concord Monument, July 4, 1837.

By the rude bridge that arched the flood,
Their flag to April's breeze unfurled,
Here once the embattled farmers stood,
And fired the shot heard round the world,

5   The foe long since in silence slept,
Alike the Conqueror silent sleeps,
And Time the ruined bridge has swept
Down the dark stream which seaward creeps.

    On this green bank, by this soft stream,
10 We set to-day a votive stone,
That memory may their deed redeem,
When like our sires our sons are gone.

    Spirit! who made those freemen dare
To die, or leave their children free,
15 Bid time and nature gently spare
The shaft we raise to them and Thee.

Literary Element   Metonymy *How does Emerson use metonymy in this line?*

RESPONDING AND THINKING CRITICALLY

Respond

1. What were your reactions to the poem?

Recall and Interpret

2. (a)What did the farmers do at the bridge in Concord? (b)What does the speaker imply about the impact of their activities?

3. (a)Where are the battle's participants now? (b)What has happened to the bridge?

4. (a)What wish do the last two lines express? (b) Why do you think the speaker wishes for this?

Analyze and Evaluate

5. (a)A hymn is a song of praise or thanksgiving. What is Emerson praising or being thankful for in this poem? (b)Do you think this hymn is a fitting dedication for a war monument? Explain.

6. (a)What is the effect of the rhyme and rhythm of this poem? (b)Do think the use of rhyme is appropriate to the subject matter? Explain.

Connect

7. **Big Idea** **Optimism and Individualism** How does this poem relate to Emerson's optimism and belief in the individual?

LITERARY ANALYSIS

Literary Element Metonymy

Metonymy is a type of figurative language in which one word is used to stand for a related term. When Emerson writes that the "sun shines into a child's heart," he uses *heart* to stand for soul, or deep emotions.

1. To what is Emerson referring when he speaks of "the shot heard round the world"?

2. What kind of emotional response does the metonymy "the shot heard round the world" create?

Literature Groups

Why a Poem? Should Emerson have written a speech instead of a poem? Which form do you think would have been more effective? In your group, discuss these questions and use evidence from the poem to support your ideas. Summarize your ideas and share them with the class.

Literature Online **Web Activities** For eFlashcards, Selection Quick Checks, and other Web activities, go to www.glencoe.com.

READING AND VOCABULARY

Reading Strategy Applying Background Knowledge

Applying **background knowledge** can aid in evaluating a literary work. For example, apply background knowledge you learned in your American history classes to evaluate the accuracy of Emerson's poem.

1. Is Emerson's portrayal of the battle accurate?

2. In support of your opinion, provide at least three pieces of evidence from "Concord Hymn" and from your background knowledge.

Academic Vocabulary

Here are two words from the vocabulary list on page R86. These words will help you think, write, and talk about the selection.

communicate (kə mū′ ni kāt′) *v.* to pass along information or knowledge

period (pēr′ e əd) *n.* a division of time

Practice and Apply

1. What ideas did Emerson most successfully **communicate** in "Concord Hymn"?

2. How well did Emerson's first stanza capture the mood of the Revolutionary War **period**?

Preview the Article

Not only did Emerson's optimism inspire his writing, it may have helped him live longer. New research shows that people with a positive attitude are more likely to lead longer, happier lives.

1. Analyze the photos of the monk on page 190 and the babies on page 191. What might these tell you about the nature of the article?

2. Skim the first paragraph. What connection do you think the writer is going to make between biology and joy?

Set a Purpose for Reading

Read to discover the biological roots of positive emotion and to connect the article's ideas with the optimism of Emerson and Thoreau.

Reading Strategy

Analyzing Cause and Effect Relationships
Cause and effect describes the relationship between an action and its consequence. The cause, or action, directly results in the effect, or consequence.

While you read, record cause-and-effect situations presented in "The Biology of Joy" in a chart like the one below. Share your findings with the class.

Cause	Effect

ACADEMIC STANDARDS
(pages 189–192)
11.2.1 Analyze...the features...of different types of public documents...
11.2.2 Analyze the way in which clarity of meaning is affected by the patterns of organization...in the text.

TIME

The Biology of JOY

Scientists know plenty about depression. Now they are starting to understand the roots of positive emotion.

By **MICHAEL D. LEMONICK**

IT ALL BEGAN WITH RICHARD DAVIDSON, A PROFESSOR OF psychology and psychiatry at the University of Wisconsin. Davidson was in a lab observing a Buddhist monk sink deep into blissful meditation when he noticed something that sent his own pulse racing. Davidson checked the data streaming to his computer from electrodes attached to the monk's skull. Electrical activity in the left prefrontal lobe of the monk's brain was shooting up at a tremendous rate. "It was exciting," Davidson recalls. "We didn't expect to see anything that dramatic."

When Davidson made his discovery, he had been studying the link between prefrontal-lobe activity and the bliss deep meditators experience. But even for someone with his experience, watching the brain crackle with activity as a person entered a trancelike state was something never seen before. It made clear, says Davidson, that happiness isn't just a vague feeling. Instead it's a physical state of the brain—one that you can bring on deliberately.

That's not all. As researchers have gained an understanding of the physical characteristics of a happy brain, they have come to see that those traits have a powerful influence on the rest of the body. Scientists have discovered that happiness or feelings of hopefulness, optimism, and contentment appear to lessen the risk or limit the severity of cardiovascular disease, lung disease, diabetes, high blood pressure, and colds. According to a Dutch study of elderly patients, those upbeat mental states reduced an individual's risk of death 50%.

Doctors have known for years that clinical depression—the extreme opposite of happiness—can worsen heart disease and other illnesses. But the neurochemistry of depression is much better known than that of happiness, mostly because depression has been studied more intensively and for much longer. Until about 10 years ago, says Dacher Keltner, a psychologist at the University of California, Berkeley, "90% of emotion research focused on the negative. There still are all of these interesting questions about the positive state."

Happiness on the Brain

A growing number of researchers exploring the physiology and neurology of happiness are starting to answer those questions. Perhaps most basic of all is what happiness is, in a clinical sense. At this point, nobody can say exactly. The word happiness, Davidson observes, "is kind of a placeholder for a group of positive emotional states. It's a state of well-being where individuals are usually not motivated to change the way they are feeling. They're motivated to preserve it." But, Davidson notes, there is much more that scientists must learn about the qualities and effects of happiness in humans. Much of that information lies in a part of the brain called the left prefrontal cortex, the brain's major center of happiness.

Scientists want to know if the prefrontal cortex creates the sensation of happiness or whether it merely reflects a person's more general emotional state. Davidson thinks the answer is both: "We're confident that this part of the brain is the cause of at least certain kinds of happiness." That suggests some people are genetically predisposed to be happy by virtue of their busy prefrontal cortexes, and research in infants confirms it. Davidson first measured left prefrontal activity in babies less than a year old. Then he gave them a test in which their mothers left the room briefly. "Some babies will cry hysterically the instant the mom leaves," he says. "Others are more resilient." It turns out that the babies with the higher left prefrontal activity are the ones who don't cry. "We were actually able to predict which infants would cry in response to that brief but significant stress."

In short, some babies are just born happy. But neuroscientists have also learned that the brain is highly adaptable. It rewires itself in response to experience, and that's especially true before the age of puberty. One might assume, therefore, that negative experiences might destroy a happy personality—and if they're extreme and frequent enough, that might be true. Davidson has learned, however, that mild to moderate doses of negative experience are helpful. The reason, he believes, is that stressful events give us practice at bouncing back from unpleasant emotions. They're like an exercise to strengthen our happiness muscles.

The Chemistry of Happiness

Exactly what is the physical difference, though, between a left prefrontal cortex that leans towards happiness and one that doesn't? It almost certainly has in part to do with neurotransmitters. These chemicals ferry signals from one neuron to the next. Davidson believes that one of these chemicals, dopamine, may be significant. Researchers are studying the relationship of dopamine levels to feelings of extreme happiness and depression.

NIRVANA CHECK Davidson, right, prepares to record the brain activity of a Buddhist monk entering a state of blissful meditation.

James Schnepf for TIME

> ❝We're just beginning to apply a lens to all those parts of the nervous system in which the positive emotions are embodied. This is really neat territory.❞
>
> —DACHER KELTNER,
> University of California, Berkeley

ROBERT FROST ▶

"Happiness makes up in height for what it lacks in length."

Bettmann/Corbis

BENJAMIN FRANKLIN

"Happiness consists more in small conveniences or pleasures that occur every day, than in great pieces of good fortune that happen but seldom to a man in the course of his life."

Dopamine pathways may be especially important in aspects of happiness associated with moving toward some sort of goal such as monks achieving a meditative state. "People have made progress telling the difference between the positive feeling you get when you approach a goal, which maps onto dopamine, and the sensory pleasure of enjoying something, which maps onto the opioid system," says Berkeley's Keltner. "This is really neat territory."

Among those exploring that territory is Brian Knutson, an assistant professor of psychology and neuroscience at Stanford, who monitors the brains of test subjects. The mental mode he studies is anticipation. "When people think of happiness," says Knutson, "they think of feeling good. But a big part of happiness is also looking forward to something." Knutson's research was inspired by the classic work of Ivan Pavlov, who trained dogs to salivate at the sound of a bell, which they associated with mealtime.

Instead of food, Knutson used money—a small cash payoff if subjects won a video game. "When we looked at their brains just before they got the reward," he says, "we saw this spark that clearly had to do with how positive the idea of making money was." The spark showed up not in the left prefrontal cortex but in the nucleus accumbens, located in the subcortex, at the bottom of the brain. The bigger the prize, Knutson found, "the more activation." Knutson believes he is looking at the

Is happiness wired in from the beginning?

A cheerful outlook may be inborn. Babies with less activity in the left prefrontal cortex tend to cry when their mothers leave the room; those with more activity stay content. By looking at brain scans, researchers could predict which infants would cry.

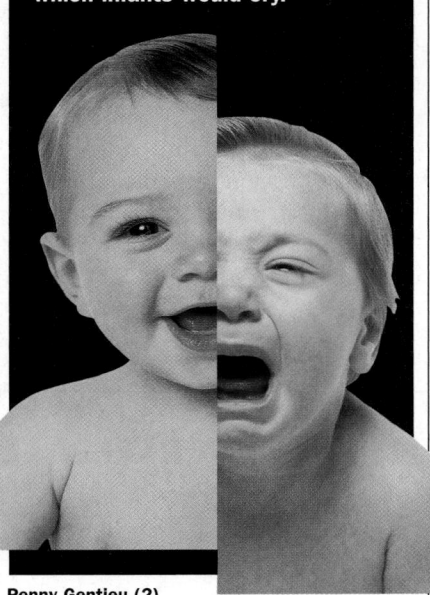

Penny Gentieu (2)

kind of happy feelings we experience as excitement. The primary focus of his work is to understand how emotion and reason work together as people make choices. But it could also be a key to mapping out the brain's broader happiness circuitry.

Happiness and Physical Health
Understanding brain changes when a person feels good is one aspect of happiness research. Another is understanding how positive emotion

affects the rest of the body. As with the brain studies, researchers tend to focus on specific aspects of happiness. Harvard psychologist Laura Kubzansky is studying optimism. In a large study she tracked 1,300 men for 10 years and found that heart-disease rates among men who called themselves optimistic were half the rates for men who didn't.

"It was a much bigger effect than we expected," she says. Kubzansky also looked at pulmonary function, since poor pulmonary function can signal a range of problems, including early death and cardiovascular disease. Again, optimists did much better. "I'm an optimist," she says, "but I didn't expect results like this."

In a separate study, Kubzansky, working with Duke psychologist Laura Richman, looked at hopefulness and curiosity—mental states that overlap with optimism in some ways. "We found them to be protective against hypertension, diabetes, and upper-respiratory infection," she says. Such protective effects may explain the longevity advantage found in that Dutch study of the elderly—an advantage for happy optimists that persisted even when researchers corrected for diet, education, and other factors.

Exactly how states of mind affect the body's biochemistry is still far from clear. Optimists may simply feel less stress than pessimists and so they can avoid the noxious biochemical cascades that stress is known to trigger. Another likely factor: optimistic, happy types seem to take better

◄ EDITH WHARTON

"If only we'd stop trying to be happy we'd have a pretty good time."

◄ MARK TWAIN

"Happiness ain't a thing in itself—it's only a contrast with something that ain't pleasant."

care of themselves than sad sacks do. Many studies—and common sense—suggest that to be the case.

In a series of studies begun in 1998, psychologist Robert Emmons of the University of California at Davis has found further evidence that happy people are better at keeping themselves in good shape. Emmons randomly assigned 1,000 adults to one of three groups. The first group kept daily journals of their moods and rated them on a scale of 1 to 6. The second group did that and listed the things that annoyed or hassled them throughout their day. The third group kept a journal but added an activity that has repeatedly been shown to improve one's sense of satisfaction with life: they were asked to write down every day all the things for which they were grateful.

Despite being assigned randomly, the last group not only had the predicted jump in their overall feelings of happiness, says Emmons, but were also found to spend more time exercising, be more likely to have regular medical checkups, and routinely take preventive health actions like wearing sunscreen. Overall, the "gratitude" group were promoting better health. "They rate themselves as more energetic, more enthusiastic, more alert," Emmons reports. In short, keeping the diaries contributed to their physical and emotional well-being.

Not surprisingly, the advantages were greatest when compared with the group that focused on life's hassles. "People who are grateful tend to view their body a certain way," says Emmons. "They see life as a gift, health as a gift. So they want to take certain measures to preserve it." Reminding yourself of what you're grateful for is a technique open to anyone, but more sophisticated methods of manipulating happiness are showing promise as well. Behavior therapy and medication, for example, are used mostly to fight depression, but they may also be useful in enhancing happiness.

Such positive results gratify happiness scientists. Thanks to Keltner, Davidson, and others, those findings have gained the field a degree of respectability that's long overdue—and that ultimately could make all of us a whole lot happier.

—From TIME, January 17, 2005

RESPONDING AND THINKING CRITICALLY

Respond

1. Were you surprised at the findings of the scientists? Why or why not?

Recall and Interpret

2. What are some reasons given in the article for why happier people live longer?

3. (a)Why did Davidson use a monk for his study? (b)What other professions or types of people would also be suitable for his experiment?

Analyze and Evaluate

4. (a)What kinds of evidence does the writer use to support his point? (b)Why is the writer's choice of evidence appropriate to his purpose?

5. How is your appreciation of Emerson and Thoreau affected by the possibility that their optimism may have been biologically determined?

Connect

6. Pretend that you are either Emerson or Poe and write a letter to the editor agreeing or disagreeing with the findings in "The Biology of Joy." Try to imitate the tone and language of the author you choose, using the excerpts from "Self-Reliance" on pages 183–184 and "The Pit and the Pendulum" on pages 251–260 as guidelines. Be sure to support your conclusions with evidence from the article.

from *Woman in the Nineteenth Century*

MEET MARGARET FULLER

New England socialite, expatriate revolutionary, transcendentalist, author, feminist—all of these labels describe Margaret Fuller. Born in Cambridgeport, Massachusetts, Fuller received an extensive education in literature, languages, and the arts from her father, Timothy Fuller Jr., a congressman from Massachusetts. She was a very precocious child and continued to educate herself after attending several local academies. After her father's sudden death in 1835, she became responsible for the education of her eight younger siblings.

> *"When people keep telling you that you can't do a thing, you kind of like to try it."*
>
> —Margaret Fuller

Feminist and Intellectual In 1836, Fuller first met Ralph Waldo Emerson (page 178) and stayed at his house in Concord while he was finishing his essay *Nature*. On first acquaintance he was uninterested in Fuller, put off by what he described as her "extreme plainness" and her "trick of opening and shutting her eyelids" and saying that the two would "never get far." Like many who knew her, however, he soon changed his opinion and developed great respect for Fuller. He wrote of Fuller, "she has noble traits and powers and cannot fail of a permanent success." They became close friends, and Fuller eventually joined his Transcendentalist Club.

In 1839 Fuller moved to Boston and began a series of language classes and formal conversations for women on topics such as literature, education, mythology, and philosophy. She was described as a dazzling discussion leader, and these meetings attracted many intellectuals and social activists. Though women were sometimes taught the same subjects as men, they had few opportunities to use their learning. Fuller's meetings provided an opportunity for women to discuss their ideas and speak their thoughts freely. These meetings gave her a formidable reputation, and in 1840 she was invited to edit *The Dial*, a transcendentalist magazine, in which she published her essay "The Great Lawsuit." She later expanded this essay into her groundbreaking feminist work, *Woman in the Nineteenth Century*. Her book reveals her extensive knowledge of literature and philosophy. It gained a wide audience and is an impressive argument for the equal status of women.

Activism Abroad In 1846 Fuller went to Europe as the first female foreign correspondent for the *New York Tribune*. While in Rome, she was involved with Italian aristocrat and revolutionary Giovanni Angelo Ossoli and eventually had a child with him. Ossoli was active in the Risorgimento, a movement to overthrow Rome's papal state and to unify Italy; Fuller vigorously supported the movement. She felt at home in Italy and saw the Risorgimento as an opportunity for women and the laboring class to gain freedom and human rights. When the 1848 revolution broke out, Fuller volunteered in a hospital and sent vivid reports home to the *Tribune* while Ossoli fought. The revolution failed, and in 1850 Fuller and Ossoli fled to the United States with their infant son, Angelo. Tragically, their ship sank off the coast of New York, and all three were killed.

Fuller's life is well summed up by her memorial in Cambridge: "in youth an insatiable student . . . in riper years teacher, writer, critic . . . in maturer age . . . earnest reformer in America and Europe."

Margaret Fuller was born in 1810 and died in 1850.

Connecting to the Essay

Would you challenge conventional wisdom to express an unpopular opinion that you held? Consider how Margaret Fuller challenges the accepted beliefs of her time.

Building Background

Fuller was one of the earliest and most vocal supporters of women's rights in the United States. She was writing at a time when laws were beginning to be changed in order to give women more of an equal status with men. Shortly before *Woman in the Nineteenth Century* was published, for example, laws were passed in some states allowing married women to own property separately from their husbands. Fuller's book laid the groundwork for the women's suffrage movement that in 1920 resulted in the Nineteenth Amendment to the Constitution, which guarantees women's right to vote. Horace Greeley, publisher of the *New York Tribune,* called her book "the ablest, bravest, broadest assertion yet made of what are termed Woman's Rights."

Setting Purposes for Reading

Big Idea Optimism and Individualism

As you read, notice how Fuller's feminism is an extension of Emerson's belief in the divinity of the individual.

Literary Element Thesis

A **thesis** is the main idea of a work of nonfiction. The thesis may be stated directly or implied. As you read this essay, look for the thesis of Fuller's essay.

• See Literary Terms Handbook, p. R19.

Literature Online Interactive Literary Elements Handbook To review or learn more about the literary elements, go to www.glencoe.com.

Reading Strategy Summarizing

Summarizing is briefly stating the main ideas of a selection in your own words and in a logical sequence. Summarizing what you have read is an excellent tool for understanding and remembering a passage. As you read, summarize Fuller's ideas to better understand this selection.

Vocabulary

ludicrous (loo′ də krəs) *adj.* deserving laughter; foolish; false; p. 196 *It would be ludicrous to go camping during this blizzard.*

commensurate (kə men′ sər it) *adj.* equal to; proportionate; p. 197 *Our participation in the development of this project was commensurate with your own.*

arbitrary (är′ bə trer′ ē) *adj.* of a random or unreasonable character; p. 197 *The organization of the police roadblocks appeared to be arbitrary.*

lot (lot) *n.* way of life or purpose as determined by fate; fortune; p. 198 *The lot of the poor family was full of hardship.*

reverence (rev′ ər əns) *n.* a feeling of respect or deep affection; p. 198 *The congregation had a great deal of reverence for their minister.*

INDIANA ACADEMIC STANDARDS (pages 194–199)
11.2.5 Analyze an author's implicit and explicit assumptions and beliefs about a subject.
11.2 Develop [reading] strategies...
11.5.9 Write...an analytical essay...
11.3.5 Analyze or evaluate works of literary or cultural significance in history...

WOMAN IN THE NINETEENTH CENTURY

Margaret Fuller

Mr. and Mrs. I. N. Phelps Stokes, 1897. John Singer Sargent. Oil on canvas, 84¼ x 39¾ in. The Metropolitan Museum of Art, New York.
Viewing the Art: What do you think of the different attitudes of the husband and wife portrayed in this painting? How does her attitude compare or contrast with Margaret Fuller's description of the role of women in marriage? Explain.

Knowing that there exists in the minds of men a tone of feeling toward women as toward slaves, such as is expressed in the common phrase, "Tell that to women and children"; that the infinite soul can only work through them in already ascertained limits; that the gift of reason, Man's highest prerogative,[1] is allotted to them in much lower degree; that they must be kept from mischief and melancholy by being constantly engaged in active labor, which is to be furnished and directed by those better able to think, etc., etc.,—we need not multiply instances, for who can review the experience of last week without recalling words which imply, whether in jest or earnest, these views, or views like these,—knowing this, can we wonder that many reformers think that measures are not likely to be taken in behalf of women, unless their wishes could be publicly represented by women?

"That can never be necessary," cry the other side. "All men are privately influenced by women; each has his wife, sister, or female friends, and is too much biased[2] by these relations to fail of representing their interests; and, if this is not enough, let them propose and enforce their wishes with the pen. The beauty of home would be destroyed, the delicacy of the sex be

---

1. *Prerogative* means "right."
2. Here, *biased* means "influenced."

The Morning Bell (a.k.a. The Old Mill), 1871. Winslow Homer. Oil on canvas,
24 x 38⅛ x 1 in. Yale University Art Gallery.
Viewing the Art: What mood does this painting by Winslow Homer evoke? How would you
describe this mood in comparison with the tone of Fuller's essay?

violated, the dignity of halls of legislation degraded, by an attempt to introduce them there. Such duties are inconsistent with those of a mother;" and then we have **ludicrous** pictures of ladies in hysterics at the polls, and senate-chambers filled with cradles.

But if, in reply, we admit as truth that Woman seems destined by nature rather for the inner circle, we must add that the arrangements of civilized life have not been, as yet, such as to secure it to her. Her circle, if the duller, is not the quieter. If kept from "excitement," she is not from drudgery. Not only the Indian squaw carries the burdens of the camp, but the favorites of Louis XIV[3] accompany him in his journeys, and the washerwoman stands at her tub, and carries home her work at all seasons, and in all states of health. Those who think the physical circumstances of Woman would make a part in the affairs of national government unsuitable, are by no means those who

think it impossible for negresses[4] to endure fieldwork, even during pregnancy, or for sempstresses[5] to go through their killing labors.

As to the use of the pen, there was quite as much opposition to Woman's possessing herself of that help to free agency as there is now to her seizing on the rostrum[6] or the desk; and she is likely to draw, from a permission to plead her cause that way, opposite inferences to what might be wished by those who now grant it.

As to the possibility of her filling with grace and dignity any such position, we should think those who had seen the great actresses, and heard the Quaker preachers of modern times, would not doubt that Woman can express publicly the fulness of thought and creation, without losing any of the peculiar beauty of her sex. What can pollute and tarnish is to act thus from any motive except that something needs to be said or done. Woman could take part in the processions, the songs, the dances

---

3. *Louis XIV* was the king of France from 1638–1715.

---

4. *Negresses* is an archaic term for women of black African descent.
5. *Sempstresses* are "seamstresses."
6. A *rostrum* is a platform for speakers.

of old religion; no one fancied her delicacy was impaired by appearing in public for such a cause.

As to her home, she is not likely to leave it more than she now does for balls, theatres, meetings for promoting missions, revival meetings, and others to which she flies,[7] in hope of an animation for her existence **commensurate** with what she sees enjoyed by men. Governors of ladies'-fairs are no less engrossed by such a charge, than the governor of a state by his; presidents of Washingtonian societies[8] no less away from home than presidents of conventions. If men look straitly to it, they will find that, unless their lives are domestic, those of the women will not be. A house is no home unless it contain food and fire for the mind as well as for the body. The female Greek, of our day, is as much in the street as the male to cry, "What news?" We doubt not it was the same in Athens of old. The women, shut out from the marketplace, made up for it at the religious festivals. For human beings are not so constituted that they can live without expansion. If they do not get it in one way, they must in another, or perish.[9]

As to men's representing women fairly at present, while we hear from men who owe to their wives not only all that is comfortable or graceful, but all that is wise, in the arrangement of their lives, the frequent remark, "You cannot reason with a woman,"—when from those of delicacy, nobleness, and poetic culture, falls the contemptuous[10] phrase "women and children," and that in no light sally[11] of the hour, but in works intended to give a permanent statement of the best experiences,—when not one man, in the million, shall I say? no, not in the hundred million, can rise above the belief that Woman was made *for Man*,—when such traits as these are daily forced upon the attention, can we feel that Man will always do justice to the interests of Woman? Can we think that he takes a sufficiently discerning and religious view of her office and destiny ever to do her justice, except when prompted by sentiment,—accidentally or transiently, that is, for the sentiment will vary according to the relations in which he is placed? The lover, the poet, the artist, are likely to view her nobly. The father and the philosopher have some chance of liberality; the man of the world, the legislator for expediency, none.

Under these circumstances, without attaching importance, in themselves, to the changes demanded by the champions of Woman, we hail them as signs of the times. We would have every **arbitrary** barrier thrown down. We would have every path laid open to Woman as freely as to Man. Were this done, and a slight temporary fermentation[12] allowed to subside, we should see crystallizations more pure and of more various beauty. We believe the divine energy would pervade nature to a degree unknown in the history of former ages, and that no discordant collision, but a ravishing harmony of the spheres,[13] would ensue.

Yet, then and only then will mankind be ripe for this, when inward and outward freedom for Woman as much as for Man shall be acknowledged as a right, not yielded as a concession. As the friend of the Negro assumes that one man cannot by right hold another in bondage, so should the friend of Woman assume that Man cannot by right lay even well-meant restrictions on Woman. If the Negro be a soul, if the woman be a soul, apparelled in flesh, to one Master only are they accountable. There is but one law for souls, and, if there is to be an

---

7. Here, *flies* means "rushing toward."
8. *Washingtonian societies* were patriotic groups similar to today's Daughters of the American Revolution.
9. Fuller is suggesting here that the women of ancient Greece, although excluded from male society, were able to find alternative modes of expression.
10. *Contemptuous* means "scornful."
11. Here, *sally* means "witty remark."

commensurate (kə men′ sər it) *adj.* equal to; proportionate

12. Here, *fermentation* means "unrest."
13. Fuller is referring to the ancient belief that the movement of the stars and planets created a perfect music, known as "the music of the spheres."

Big Idea Optimism and Individualism *How does this statement relate to transcendentalism?*

Literary Element Thesis *What details from the essay support this statement?*

Vocabulary

arbitrary (är′ bə trer′ ē) *adj.* of a random or unreasonable character interpreter of it, he must come not as man, or son of man, but as son of God.

Were thought and feeling once so far elevated that Man should esteem himself the brother and friend, but nowise[14] the lord and tutor, of Woman,—were he really bound with her in equal worship,—arrangements as to function and employment would be of no consequence. What Woman needs is not as a woman to act or rule, but as a nature to grow, as an intellect to discern, as a soul to live freely and unimpeded, to unfold such powers as were given her when we left our common home. If fewer talents were given her, yet if allowed the free and full employment of these, so that she may render back to the giver his own with usury,[15] she will not complain; nay, I dare to say she will bless and rejoice in her earthly birthplace, her earthly **lot.** Let us consider what obstructions impede this good era, and what signs give reason to hope that it draws near.

I was talking on this subject with Miranda,[16] a woman, who, if any in the world could, might speak without heat and bitterness of the position of her sex. Her father was a man who cherished no sentimental reverence for Woman, but a firm belief in the equality of the sexes. She was his eldest child, and came to him at an age when he needed a companion. From the time she could speak and go alone, he addressed her not as a plaything, but as a living mind. Among the few verses he ever wrote was a copy addressed to this child, when the first locks were cut from her head; and the **reverence** expressed on this occasion for that cherished head, he never belied.[17] It was to him the temple of immortal intellect. He respected his child, however, too much to be an indulgent parent. He called on her for clear judgment, for courage, for honor and fidelity; in short, for such virtues as he knew. In so far as he possessed the keys to the wonders of this universe, he allowed free use of them to her, and, by the incentive of a high expectation, he forbade, so far as possible, that she should let the privilege lie idle.

Thus this child was early led to feel herself a child of the spirit. She took her place easily, not only in the world of organized being, but in the world of mind. A dignified sense of self-dependence was given as all her portion, and she found it a sure anchor. Herself securely anchored, her relations with others were established with equal security. She was fortunate in a total absence of those charms which might have drawn to her bewildering flatteries, and in a strong electric[18] nature, which repelled those who did not belong to her, and attracted those who did. With men and women her relations were noble,—affectionate without passion, intellectual without coldness. The world was free to her, and she lived freely in it. Outward adversity came, and inward conflict; but that faith and self-respect had early been awakened which must always lead, at last, to an outward serenity and an inward peace.

Of Miranda I had always thought as an example, that the restraints upon the sex were insuperable[19] only to those who think them so, or who noisily strive to break them. She had taken a course of her own, and no man stood in her way. Many of her acts had been unusual, but excited no uproar. Few helped, but none checked her; and the many men who knew her mind and her life, showed to her confidence as to a brother, gentleness as to a sister. And not only refined, but very coarse men approved and aided one in whom they saw resolution and clearness of design. Her mind was often the leading one, always effective. ∽

---

14. *Nowise* means "not at all."
15. Here, *usury* means "interest."
16. *Miranda* is a fictional character based on Fuller's own experiences.
17. *Belied* means "betrayed" or "misrepresented."

---

18. Here, *electric* means "exciting."
19. *Insuperable* means "insurmountable."

RESPONDING AND THINKING CRITICALLY

Respond

1. Which of Fuller's arguments do you find most convincing? Explain.

Recall and Interpret

2. (a)Fuller says that women are kept from excitement. In her judgment, what are they not kept from? (b)Based on this judgment, what can you infer about the true motives of those opposed to women's rights?

3. (a)What are two examples that Fuller gives of women who fill public positions with "grace and dignity"? (b)How do these examples strengthen Fuller's argument?

4. (a)How do men respond to Miranda? (b)What is the reason for their response, and what does it suggest about women's education?

Analyze and Evaluate

5. (a)Why do you think Fuller presents opposing viewpoints throughout the essay? (b)How effective is her use of this rhetorical device?

6. Fuller makes an analogy between the plight of women and that of enslaved African Americans. Is this a valid analogy? Why or why not?

7. (a)Why do you think Fuller introduces Miranda into this essay? (b)Does Miranda help advance Fuller's arguments? Explain.

Connect

8. **Big Idea** **Optimism and Individualism** How does Fuller's feminism draw on the transcendentalist belief in optimism and individualism?

LITERARY ANALYSIS

Literary Element **Thesis**

The **thesis** statement in a nonfiction piece may be stated directly, or it may be implied. Writers often state the thesis in the opening paragraph. However, if the thesis is implied, the reader must closely examine the facts, details, and rhetorical devices used by the author to determine the thesis statement.

1. What is the thesis of this essay?

2. Is Fuller's thesis stated directly or implied?

Writing About Literature

Evaluate Contemporary Relevance Fuller says, "We would have every arbitrary barrier thrown down. We would have every path laid open to Woman as freely as to Man." Is this goal still relevant today? Write a brief essay in which you assess Fuller's goal in light of contemporary relationships between men and women.

Literature Online **Web Activities** For eFlashcards, Selection Quick Checks, and other Web activities, go to www.glencoe.com.

READING AND VOCABULARY

Reading Strategy **Summarizing**

Summarizing can help you come to a conclusion about an author's beliefs. Briefly summarize the main ideas of this essay. On the basis on your summary, state two of Fuller's beliefs.

Vocabulary **Practice**

Practice with Analogies Choose the word pair that best completes the analogy.

1. arbitrary : logical ::
   a. practical : instructions   **d.** perfect : flawed
   b. anxious : nervous   **e.** cautious : timid
   c. cancer : disease

2. ludicrous : buffoon ::
   a. word : language   **d.** canoe : boat
   b. festive : celebration   **e.** captive : free
   c. odd : strange

3. reverence : minister ::
   a. fairness : injustice   **d.** despair : comedian
   b. scorn : fool   **e.** schedule : agenda
   c. page : book

The Fireside Poets

IN THE MID-1800s, A GROUP OF HIGHLY popular American writers became known as the "Fireside Poets" because it was thought that families often sat by the fire and read or recited their poems aloud. Eager to help establish a truly national literature, these poets frequently created vivid pictures of the New England countryside in their lyrics or of famous events from American history in their narrative poems.

William Cullen Bryant (1794–1878) was the oldest of the Fireside Poets. Though his background was Puritan, Bryant was influenced by the English Romantic poets, such as William Wordsworth. He was the first to portray the American landscape in words. In such famous poems as "To a Waterfowl" and "To the Fringed Gentian," Bryant wrote of the wildlife he encountered while he was hiking through the Berkshire Mountains in western Massachusetts.

Henry Wadsworth Longfellow (1807–1882) entered Bowdoin College at the age of fifteen and graduated in the same class as Nathaniel Hawthorne. In his poetry, such as the narrative poems *Evangeline* and *The Song of Hiawatha*, he mythologized the American past by using rhyme and simple verse. *Tales of a Wayside Inn* (1863), a collection of stories in verse supposedly told by various people at an inn, includes one of Longfellow's best known poems, "Paul Revere's Ride." He was the first American to have a bust placed in the Poet's Corner of England's Westminster Abbey.

John Greenleaf Whittier (1807–1892) came from a poor Quaker farm family. His first book, *Legends of New England*, was published in 1831, but he became nationally famous with the work *Snow-Bound*, published in 1866. "Storytelling was a necessary resource in the long winter evenings," Whittier wrote, and *Snow-Bound* tells of a family isolated and telling stories during a storm. Whittier was devoted to the abolitionist movement, and much of his poetry, including "The Hunters of Men" and "Massachusetts to Virginia," reflects his stance against racism and slavery.

Oliver Wendell Holmes (1809–1894) studied both law and medicine but opted for a medical career.

USS Constitution vs. HMS Guerriere, c. 1813. Attributed to Thomas Birch. Oil on canvas. US Naval Academy Museum, Annapolis, MD.

Among his best-known poems are "The Chambered Nautilus" and "Old Ironsides," the nickname for the famous American warship, the USS *Constitution*. Rumors that the ship was about to be scrapped inspired Holmes's poem, which roused public sentiment in support of saving it.

James Russell Lowell (1819–1891) objected to slavery and the war with Mexico. In 1846 the first of *The Biglow Papers*, his antislavery and antiwar poetry series, was published to great acclaim. Lowell created the voice of a rural Yankee, Hosea Biglow, who expressed Lowell's views with wit and humor. Lowell became the first editor of the *Atlantic Monthly* in 1857.

Americans responded enthusiastically to the Fireside Poets, in part because their works celebrated the values of ordinary people—regard for hard work, respect for family, courage in the face of danger, love of one's country, and love of nature. Because Americans also believed that these writers were the equals of the British poets of the time, they became more confident about the future of their country's culture.

To the Fringed Gentian

William Cullen Bryant

Thou blossom bright with autumn dew,
And colored with the heaven's own blue,
That openest when the quiet light
Succeeds the keen and frosty night—

5   Thou comest not when violets lean
O'er wandering brooks and springs unseen,
Or columbines, in purple dressed,
Nod o'er the ground-bird's hidden nest.

Thou waitest late and com'st alone,
10   When woods are bare and birds are flown,
And frosts and shortening days portend
The aged year is near his end.

Then doth thy sweet and quiet eye
Look through its fringes to the sky,
15   Blue—blue—as if that sky let fall
A flower from its cerulean wall.

I would that thus, when I shall see
The hour of death draw near to me,
Hope, blossoming within my heart,
20   May look to heaven as I depart.

Old Ironsides

Oliver Wendell Holmes

Ay, tear her tattered ensign down!
Long has it waved on high,
And many an eye has danced to see
That banner in the sky;
5   Beneath it rung the battle shout,
And burst the cannon's roar; —
The meteor of the ocean air
Shall sweep the clouds no more.

Her deck, once red with heroes' blood,
10   Where knelt the vanquished foe,
When winds were hurrying o'er the flood,
And waves were white below,
No more shall feel the victor's tread,
Or know the conquered knee; —
15   The harpies of the shore shall pluck
The eagle of the sea!

Oh, better that her shattered hulk
Should sink beneath the wave;
Her thunders shook the mighty deep,
20   And there should be her grave;
Nail to the mast her holy flag,
Set every threadbare sail,
And give her to the god of storms,
The lightning and the gale!

Literature Online **Literary History** For more about the Fireside Poets, go to www.glencoe.com.

RESPONDING AND THINKING CRITICALLY

1. What does the speaker in "To the Fringed Gentian" describe in lines 9–12? What do these lines add to your understanding of the speaker's attitude towards the gentian?

2. How does Bryant use personification in lines 13 and 14? How do these lines relate to the end of the poem?

3. According to the speaker in "Old Ironsides," what events have taken place on the ship? What does his description of these events suggest about his attitude towards Old Ironsides?

4. In "Old Ironsides," explain the terms of the metaphor in lines 15–16.

INDIANA ACADEMIC STANDARDS (pages 200–201)

11.3.5 Analyze or evaluate works...that...were written by important authors in the respective major historical periods...

11.3.4 Analyze ways in which poetry...uses imagery, personification, figures of speech, and sounds...

from *Walden*

MEET HENRY DAVID THOREAU

Although he is best known for his simple lifestyle at Walden Pond, Henry David Thoreau was a complex man: opinionated, cranky, nonconformist, compassionate, and subtly humorous. He was an unconventional thinker who expressed his ideas about major issues such as war, slavery, wealth, taxes, friendship, vegetarianism, and the lessons that nature can teach, yet he also wrote about topics as simple as hoeing his garden and walking in the woods. Much of what Thoreau did, thought about, or saw—and he was a keen observer—later took the form of a journal entry, an essay, or part of a book.

Thoreau was born in Concord, Massachusetts, and lived there most of his life. He graduated from Harvard University in 1837 and took a teaching job at his old grammar school. However, he refused to physically discipline his students and quickly resigned. Thoreau founded a progressive school with his brother John in Concord the next year. Although the school was successful, it had to close in 1841 because of his brother's poor health.

> "In Wildness is the preservation of the world."
>
> —Thoreau, *Walking*

Life in the Woods While at Harvard, Thoreau was influenced by the works of Ralph Waldo Emerson, and the two men became friends. From 1841 to 1843, Thoreau lived with the Emerson family, assisting as a handyman. During this time he contributed a variety of works to *The Dial*, a Transcendentalist magazine, including poetry, literary essays, and the first of his nature essays. The act that probably most changed Thoreau's

life occurred in 1845, when he built a cabin on land that Emerson owned at Walden Pond near Concord. Thoreau lived there for more than two years spending most of his time reading, writing (including his most famous book, *Walden*), observing nature, and meditating.

Thoreau was deeply affected by his brother's death in 1842, and three years later decided to write an account of a camping and canoeing trip they had taken, referring to notes he had made along the way. The account became his first book, *A Week on the Concord and Merrimack Rivers,* written during his time at Walden Pond and published in 1849. The publisher returned the unsold copies, prompting Thoreau to later observe, "I now have a library of nearly nine hundred volumes, over seven hundred of which I wrote myself."

Thoreau's most famous book, *Walden, or, Life in the Woods,* was first published in 1854 and over time has become a classic. In *Walden* we learn what Thoreau considered most important in life. For example, he thought that most people spend too much time working to afford luxuries and do not take time to truly experience life. *Walden* also reflects a changing New England and Thoreau's response to industrialization. Most importantly, through *Walden* and his other works, Thoreau helped inspire a long tradition of nature writing in the United States. He remains an inspiration for environmentalists everywhere.

Henry David Thoreau was born in 1817 and died in 1862.

Literature Online Author Search For more about Henry David Thoreau, go to www.glencoe.com.

Connecting to the Essay

Do you ever wish for a life with fewer distractions and complications? In these excerpts from *Walden,* Thoreau discusses his reasons for leaving the city to live in the woods. Think about the following questions:

- What are the unimportant details in your life?
- What is really important to you?

Building Background

Thoreau lived in a rugged cabin that measured ten feet by fifteen feet at Walden Pond for two years, two months, and two days. The cabin, which he built himself, was simple and sturdy, with plastered walls and a shingled roof. His equipment consisted of an ax, two knives and a fork, three plates, one cup, one spoon, a jug for oil, a jug for molasses, and one lamp. He made his own furniture, including a bed, table, desk, and three chairs. At Walden, Thoreau devoted himself to observing the seasons, the animals, the plants and to writing his journals; however, he was not a hermit. Thoreau was able to visit his relatives and friends nearly every day, since the pond was only a mile from Concord.

Setting Purposes for Reading

Big Idea Kinship with Nature

As you read, look for the ways in which Thoreau stresses the importance of a close relationship with nature.

Literary Element Metaphor

A **metaphor** is a figure of speech that compares or equates two seemingly unlike things. In contrast to a **simile,** a metaphor implies the comparison instead of stating it directly, and does not use the connectives *like* or *as.* For example, Thoreau uses the metaphor "this chopping sea of civilized life" to suggest the perils and difficulties of modern living. As you read, identify other metaphors that Thoreau uses to convey his ideas.

- See Literary Terms Handbook, p. R11.

Reading Strategy Connecting

Connecting to personal experience means relating what you read to your own life. As you read, look for connections between Thoreau's observations and your own experiences and list ones that you find.

Vocabulary

deliberately (di lib′ ər it lē) *adv.* in a careful, thoughtful way; p. 204 *Thoreau deliberately nailed in place the roof to his cabin.*

resignation (rez′ ig nā′ shən) *n.* unresisting acceptance; submission; p. 204 *He practiced calm resignation to life's troubles.*

sublime (səb līm′) *adj.* of great spiritual or intellectual value; noble; p. 204 *To Emerson, intuition was a sublime power.*

rudiment (roo′ də mənt) *n.* an imperfect or undeveloped part; p. 205 *Though the rudiments of the plan look interesting, it needs more elaboration and detail.*

myriad (mir′ ē əd) *adj.* countless, innumerable; p. 205 *There were myriad efforts to improve society during the Age of Reform.*

Vocabulary Tip: Context Clues When you come across an unfamiliar word, examine its **context**—the surrounding words and sentences—for clues to its meaning. One familiar type of context clue, known as **contrast,** provides a word or phrase that is opposite in meaning to the unfamiliar word, as in the following example: "One is enough . . . what do you care for a *myriad*" (p. 205).

Literature Online **Interactive Literary Elements Handbook** To review or learn more about the literary elements, go to www.glencoe.com.

INDIANA ACADEMIC STANDARDS (pages 203–209)
11.3.4 Analyze ways in which...prose uses...figures of speech...
11.2 Develop [reading] strategies...
11.5.2 Write responses to literature...
11.7.18 Deliver oral responses to literature...

from WALDEN

Henry David Thoreau

from
Where I Lived and What I Lived For

I went to the woods because I wished to live **deliberately,** to front only the essential facts of life, and see if I could not learn what it had to teach, and not, when I came to die, discover that I had not lived. I did not wish to live what was not life, living is so dear; nor did I wish to practice **resignation,** unless it was quite necessary. I wanted to live deep and suck out all the marrow[1] of life, to live so sturdily and Spartanlike[2] as to put to rout all that was not life, to cut a broad swath and shave close,[3] to drive life into a corner, and reduce it to its lowest terms, and, if it proved to be mean,[4] why then to get the whole and genuine meanness of it, and publish its meanness to the world; or if it were **sublime,** to know it by experience, and be able to give a true account of it in my next excursion. For most men, it appears to me, are in a strange uncertainty about it, whether it is of the devil or of God, and have *somewhat hastily* concluded that it is the chief end of man here to "glorify God and enjoy him forever."

Still we live meanly, like ants; though the fable tells us that we were long ago changed into men;[5] like pygmies we fight with cranes;[6] it is error upon error, and clout upon clout, and our best virtue has for its occasion a superfluous and evitable[7] wretchedness. Our life is frittered away by detail. An honest man has hardly need to count more than his ten fingers, or in extreme

1. *Marrow* is the soft tissue inside bones. It also means "the best or most essential part."
2. Spartans were inhabitants of the ancient Greek city-state of Sparta. *Spartanlike* means simple, economical, and disciplined.
3. *[to cut . . . close]* means "to gather as much of the essence of life as possible."
4. Here, *mean* means "of little importance, worth, or consequence" or "ignoble."
5. The *fable* referred to is a Greek myth in which Zeus changes ants into men.
6. In Homer's *Iliad*, the Trojans are compared to cranes battling pygmies.
7. *Evitable* means "avoidable."

Reading Strategy Connecting *In what ways might people today "live what [is] not life"?*

Vocabulary

deliberately (di lib′ ər it lē) *adj.* in a careful, thoughtful way
resignation (rez′ ig nā′ shən) *n.* unresisting acceptance; submission

Vocabulary

sublime (səb līm′) *adj.* of great spiritual or intellectual value; noble cases he may add his ten toes, and lump the rest. Simplicity, simplicity, simplicity! I say, let your affairs be as two or three, and not a hundred or a thousand; instead of a million count half a dozen, and keep your accounts on your thumb nail. In the midst of this chopping sea of civilized life, such are the clouds and storms and quicksands and thousand-and-one items to be allowed for, that a man has to live, if he would not founder[8] and go to the bottom and not make his port at all, by dead reckoning,[9] and he must be a great calculator indeed who succeeds. Simplify, simplify. Instead of three meals a day, if it be necessary eat but one; instead of a hundred dishes, five; and reduce other things in proportion. . . .

Why should we live with such hurry and waste of life? We are determined to be starved before we are hungry. Men say that a stitch in time saves nine, and so they take a thousand stitches today to save nine tomorrow. As for *work*, we haven't any of any consequence. We have the Saint Vitus' dance,[10] and cannot possibly keep our heads still. If I should only give a few pulls at the parish bell-rope, as for a fire, that is, without setting the bell, there is hardly a man on his farm in the outskirts of Concord, notwithstanding that press of engagements which was his excuse so many times this morning, nor a boy, nor a woman, I might almost say, but would forsake all and follow that sound, not mainly to save property from the flames, but, if we will confess the truth, much more to see it burn, since burn it must, and we, be it known, did not set it on fire,—or to see it put out, and have a hand in it, if that is done as handsomely; yes, even if it were the parish church itself. Hardly a man takes a half hour's nap after dinner, but when he wakes he holds up his head and asks, "What's the news?" as if the rest of mankind had stood his sentinels. Some give directions to be waked every half hour, doubtless for no other purpose; and then, to pay for it, they tell what they have dreamed. After a night's sleep the news is as indispensable as the breakfast. "Pray tell me any

thing new that has happened to a man any where on this globe,"—and he reads it over his coffee and rolls, that a man has had his eyes gouged out this morning on the Wachito River;[11] never dreaming the while that he lives in the dark unfathomed mammoth cave of this world, and has but the **rudiment** of an eye himself.

For my part, I could easily do without the post-office. I think that there are very few important communications made through it. To speak critically, I never received more than one or two letters in my life—I wrote this some years ago—that were worth the postage. The penny-post is, commonly, an institution through which you seriously offer a man that penny for his thoughts which is so often safely offered in jest. And I am sure that I never read any memorable news in a newspaper. If we read of one man robbed, or murdered, or killed by accident, or one house burned, or one vessel wrecked, or one steamboat blown up, or one cow run over on the Western Railroad, or one mad dog killed, or one lot of grasshoppers in the winter,—we never need read of another. One is enough. If you are acquainted with the principle, what do you care for a **myriad** instances and applications? . . .

Time is but the stream I go a-fishing in. I drink at it; but while I drink I see the sandy bottom and detect how shallow it is. Its thin current slides away, but eternity remains. I would drink deeper; fish in the sky, whose bottom is pebbly with stars. I cannot count one. I know not the first letter of the alphabet. I have always been regretting that I was not as wise as the day I was born. The intellect is a cleaver; it discerns and rifts its way into the secret of things. I do not wish to be any more busy with my hands than is necessary. My head is hands and feet. I feel

---

8. *Founder* means "to sink, as a boat."
9. *Dead reckoning* is a method of navigation used by sailors when the stars cannot be seen.
10. *Saint Vitus'* dance is a nervous disorder characterized by involuntary twitching of the muscles in the face, arms, and legs.

11. The *Wachito River* (now called the Ouachita) flows from southern Arkansas into northern Louisiana. People in Thoreau's time thought that criminals went to that region to escape from the law.

Vocabulary

rudiment (rōō′ də mənt) *n.* an imperfect or undeveloped part
myriad (mir′ ē əd) *adj.* countless; innumerable

all my best faculties concentrated in it. My instinct tells me that my head is an organ for burrowing, as some creatures use their snout and fore-paws, and with it I would mine and burrow my way through these hills. I think that the richest vein is somewhere hereabouts; so by the divining rod[12] and thin rising vapors I judge; and here I will begin to mine.

from
Brute Neighbors

It is remarkable how many creatures live wild and free though secret in the woods, and still sustain themselves in the neighborhood of towns, suspected by hunters only. How retired the otter manages to live here! He grows to be four feet long, as big as a small boy, perhaps without any human being getting a glimpse of him. I formerly saw the raccoon in the woods behind where my house is built, and probably still heard their whinnering at night. Commonly I rested an hour or two in the shade at noon, after planting, and ate my lunch, and read a little by a spring which was the source of a swamp and of a brook, oozing from under Brister's Hill, half a mile from my field. The approach to this was through a succession of descending grassy hollows, full of young pitch pines, into a larger wood about the swamp. There, in a very secluded and shaded spot, under a spreading white pine, there was yet a clean firm sward[13] to sit on. I had dug out the spring and made a well of clear gray water, where I could dip up a pailful without roiling it, and thither I went for this purpose almost every day in mid-summer, when the pond was warmest. Thither too the woodcock led her brood, to probe the mud for worms, flying but a foot above them down the bank, while they ran in a troop beneath; but at last, spying me, she would leave her young and circle round and round me, nearer and nearer till within four or five feet, pretending broken wings and legs, to attract my attention, and get off her young, who would already have taken up their march, with faint wiry peep, single file through the swamp, as she directed. Or I heard the peep of the young when I could not see the parent bird. There too the turtle-doves sat over the spring, or fluttered from bough to bough of the soft white pines over my head; or the red squirrel, coursing down the nearest bough, was particularly familiar and inquisitive. You only need sit still long enough in some attractive spot in the woods that all its inhabitants may exhibit themselves to you by turns.

I was witness to events of a less peaceful character. One day when I went out to my wood pile, or rather my pile of stumps, I observed two large ants, the one red, the other much larger, nearly half an inch long, and black, fiercely contending with one another. Having once got hold they never let go, but struggled and wrestled and rolled on the chips incessantly. Looking farther, I was surprised

---

12. A *divining rod* is a forked stick believed to indicate the presence of underground minerals or water.

Big Idea Kinship with Nature *Why does Thoreau make this comment about the relationship between people and nature?*

---

13. *Sward* means a grassy piece of land.

Big Idea Kinship with Nature *How would you compare this suggestion with Thoreau's comments in the chapter "Where I Lived and What I Lived For"?*

to find that the chips were covered with such combatants, that it was not a *duellum*, but a *bellum*, a war between two races of ants, the red always pitted against the black, and frequently two red ones to one black. The legions of these Myrmidons[14] covered all the hills and vales in my wood-yard, and the ground was already strewn with the dead and dying, both red and black. It was the only battle which I have ever witnessed, the only battlefield I ever trod while the battle was raging; internecine[15] war; the red republicans on the one hand, and the black imperialists on the other. On every side they were engaged in deadly combat, yet without any noise that I could hear, and human soldiers never fought so resolutely. I watched a couple that were fast locked in each other's embraces, in a little sunny valley amid the chips, now at noonday prepared to fight till the sun went down, or life went out. The smaller red champion had fastened himself like a vice to his adversary's front, and through all the tumblings on that field never for an instant ceased to gnaw at one of his feelers near the root, having already caused the other to go by the board; while the stronger black one dashed him from side to side, and, as I saw on looking nearer, had already divested him of several of his members. They fought with more pertinacity than bulldogs. Neither manifested the least disposition to retreat. It was evident that their battle-cry was Conquer or die. In the meanwhile there came along a single red ant on the hillside of this valley, evidently full of excitement, who either had despatched his foe, or had not yet taken part in the battle; probably the latter, for he had lost none of his limbs; whose mother had charged him to return with his shield or upon it. Or perchance he was some Achilles,[16] who had

nourished his wrath apart, and had now come to avenge or rescue his Patroclus.[17] He saw this unequal combat from afar—for the blacks were nearly twice the size of the red—he drew near with rapid pace till he stood on his guard within half an inch of the combatants; then, watching his opportunity, he sprang upon the black warrior, and commenced his operations near the root of his right foreleg, leaving the foe to select among his own members; and so there were three united for life, as if a new kind of attraction had been invented which put all other locks and cements to shame. I should not have wondered by this time to find that they had their respective musical bands stationed on some eminent chip, and playing their national airs the while, to excite the slow and cheer the dying combatants. I was myself excited somewhat even as if they had been men. The more you think of it, the less the difference. And certainly there is not the fight recorded in Concord history, at least, if in the history of America, that will bear a moment's comparison with this, whether for the numbers engaged in it, or for the patriotism and heroism displayed. For numbers and for carnage it was an Austerlitz or Dresden.[18] Concord Fight! Two killed on the patriots' side, and Luther Blanchard wounded! Why here every ant was a Buttrick—"Fire! for God's sake fire!"—and thousands shared the fate of Davis and Hosmer.[19] There was not one hireling there. I have no doubt that it was a principle they fought for, as much as our ancestors, and not to avoid a three-penny tax

---

14. The *Myrmidons* were a legendary group of Thessalians who followed their king, Achilles, in the Trojan War. In modern English, *Myrmidon* can refer to any devoted, unquestioning follower.
15. *Internecine* means "deadly" or "marked by destruction."
16. In Greek mythology, *Achilles* was king of the Myrmidons. A handsome warrior reknowned for his bravery and greatness, he died in battle during the Trojan War.

17. *Patroclus* was Achilles' cousin and constant companion.
18. *Austerlitz* refers to the Battle of Austerlitz, which occurred on December 2, 1805 and was one of Napoleon's greatest victories. *Dresden* refers to the Battle of Dresden, Napoleon's last big victory over Germany. It was fought on August 26 and 27, 1813. *Concord* refers to the Battle of Concord, April 19, 1775, which was one of the opening battles of the American Revolutionary War.
19. *Luther Blanchard* was a fifer who was killed at the Battle of Concord. *Buttrick* refers to Major John Buttrick, an American commander at Concord. *Davis* and *Hosmer* refer to Captain Isaac Davis and Abner Hosmer, two American soldiers who died at the Battle of Concord.

Reading Strategy Connecting *What other events among animals might you compare to events among people?*

Literary Element Metaphor *How effective is this extended metaphor comparing the battling ants to human warfare?*

on their tea;[20] and the results of this battle will be as important and memorable to those whom it concerns as those of the battle of Bunker Hill,[21] at least.

I took up the chip on which the three I have particularly described were struggling, carried it into my house, and placed it under a tumbler on my window sill, in order to see the issue. Holding a microscope to the first-mentioned red ant, I saw that, though he was assiduously gnawing at the near foreleg of his enemy, having severed his remaining feeler, his own breast was all torn away, exposing what vitals he had there to the jaws of the black warrior, whose breastplate was apparently too thick for him to pierce; and the dark carbuncles[22] of the sufferer's eyes shone with ferocity such as war only could excite. They struggled half an hour longer under the tumbler, and when I looked again the black soldier had severed the heads of his foes from their bodies, and the still living heads were hanging on either side of him like ghastly trophies at his saddle-bow, still apparently as firmly fastened as ever, and he was endeavoring with feeble struggles, being without feelers and with only the remnant of a leg, and I know not how many other wounds, to divest himself of them; which at length, after half an hour more, he accomplished. I raised the glass, and he went off over the window sill in that crippled state. Whether he finally survived that combat, and spent the remainder of his days in some Hôtel des Invalides,[23] I do not know; but I thought that his industry would not be worth much thereafter. I never learned which party was victorious, nor the cause of the war; but I felt for the rest of that day as if I had had my feelings excited and harrowed by witnessing the struggle, the ferocity and carnage, of a human battle before my door.

---

20. *Three-penny tax on their tea* refers to the tea tax portion of the Townshend Acts, passed by the English Parliament in 1767 and designed to collect revenue from the American colonies. After protest from the colonists, the Townshend Acts were repealed in 1770, but the tea tax remained in place. That tax required a payment of three pennies per pound of imported tea.
21. *Bunker Hill* was the first major battle of the American Revolutionary War. It was fought in Charlestown (now Boston, Massachusetts) on June 17, 1775.
22. Here, *carbuncle* means a type of red precious stone.
23. The *Hôtel des Invalides* is a famous complex in Paris, France. Louis XIV founded the hospital to accommodate 7,000 elderly or injured veterans. Today, it houses several museums and a church.

from
Conclusion

. . . I left the woods for as good a reason as I went there. Perhaps it seemed to me that I had several more lives to live, and could not spare any more time for that one. It is remarkable how easily and insensibly we fall into a particular route, and make a beaten track for ourselves. I had not lived there a week before my feet wore a path from my door to the pond-side; and though it is five or six years since I trod it, it is still quite distinct. It is true, I fear that others may have fallen into it, and so helped to keep it open. The surface of the earth is soft and impressible by the feet of men; and so with the paths which the mind travels. How worn and dusty, then, must be the highways of the world, how deep the ruts of tradition and conformity! I did not wish to take a cabin passage,[24] but rather to go before the mast and on the deck of the world, for there I could best see the moonlight amid the mountains. I do not wish to go below now.

I learned this, at least, by my experiment; that if one advances confidently in the direction of his dreams, and endeavors to live the life which he has imagined, he will meet with a success unexpected in common hours. He will put some things behind, will pass an invisible boundary; new, universal, and more liberal laws will begin to establish themselves around and within him; or the old laws be expanded, and interpreted in his favor in a more liberal sense, and he will live with the license of a higher order of beings. In proportion as he simplifies his life, the laws of the universe will appear less complex, and solitude will not be solitude, nor poverty poverty, nor weakness weakness. If you have built castles in the air, your work need not be lost; that is where they should be. Now put the foundations under them. . . . ❧

---

24. A person who took a *cabin passage* on a sailing ship would travel in a private compartment, sheltered from the weather.

Literary Element Metaphor *Why might Thoreau have chosen to use this metaphor?*

Reading Strategy Connecting *How might you apply Thoreau's advice in your own life?*

RESPONDING AND THINKING CRITICALLY

Respond

1. With which of Thoreau's ideas do you strongly agree? With which ideas do you strongly disagree?

Recall and Interpret

2. (a)What did Thoreau hope to do at Walden? (b)How could being at Walden help him achieve his goal?

3. (a) What are Thoreau's views of the news and the mail? (b)What do these views tell you about his values?

4. (a)Summarize the battle between the ants that Thoreau describes. (b)Why do you think he becomes so fascinated with this battle?

Analyze and Evaluate

5. (a)How does Thoreau characterize the animals he observes? (b)Do you agree with his observations?

6. (a)Why does Thoreau insist that people need to simplify their lives? (b)Is he a credible speaker on this topic? Explain.

7. (a)What is Thoreau's central message in *Walden*? (b)Does Thoreau's decision to leave Walden affect your evaluation of his message?

Connect

8. Big Idea **Kinship with Nature** (a)What does Thoreau learn at Walden? (b)What role does nature play in what he learns?

LITERARY ANALYSIS

Literary Element Metaphor

Thoreau frequently uses **metaphor** and other types of figurative language to help convey his ideas. For example, the metaphor "Time is but the stream I go a-fishing in" (p. 205) compares time to a stream, suggesting that one moment follows another in an uninterrupted flow. Sometimes, Thoreau develops a metaphor throughout an entire paragraph—a technique called **extended metaphor.**

1. Why does Thoreau say he goes "a-fishing" in time?

2. Give an example of another metaphor from the reading.

Listening and Speaking

Guest Speaker Thoreau earned money and spread his ideas by giving lectures to local groups. Write and deliver a lecture that Thoreau might have given to high school students in which he explains his ideas about nature, materialism, and progress. Include examples from *Walden*.

Literature Online **Web Activities** For eFlashcards, Selection Quick Checks, and other Web activities, go to www.glencoe.com.

READING AND VOCABULARY

Reading Strategy Connecting

Connecting to Personal Experience Although Thoreau lived in the 1800s, his message remains relevant. What are some of the things that surround us in the United States today about which Thoreau might cry, "Simplify, simplify"?

Vocabulary Practice

Practice with Context Clues Choose the best meaning for each vocabulary word from *Walden*.

1. Trying not to jostle the ants, Thoreau **deliberately** picked up the chip on which they were fighting.
  a. carelessly   **c.** carefully
  b. forcefully   **d.** contemplatively

2. Realizing his own guilt, the prisoner bowed his head and listened with **resignation** as the verdict was read.
  a. anger   **c.** disbelief
  b. acceptance   **d.** amazement

3. Mozart's music seems **sublime,** as if created by a higher power.
  a. heavenly   **c.** quiet
  b. loud   **d.** bizarre

Comparing Literature *Across Time and Place*

Connecting to the Reading Selections

How far would you go to carry out your principles, beliefs, or values? The three writers compared here—Henry David Thoreau, Mohandas K. Gandhi, and Nelson Mandela—took a stand against injustice. In the following selections, they speak out against the oppression they witnessed during their lifetimes.

COMPARING THE `Big Idea` Optimism and Individualism

Some of the major American Romantic writers celebrated the spirit of individualism and optimism. Thoreau, for instance, believed that ordinary citizens can better themselves, their political system, and their society. Gandhi and Mandela, reformers from other cultures and eras, shared Thoreau's belief in the power of the individual to bring about change peacefully.

COMPARING Persuasive Messages

To bring about reform, Thoreau, Gandhi, and Mandela swayed audiences to share their views, gain their support, or rally them to take action. Each of these leaders used nonviolent methods to convey his message with clarity and force.

COMPARING Cultures

Thoreau, Gandhi, and Mandela belonged to different cultures and fought injustices that were unique to their surroundings. Social and historical circumstances presented each of them with distinct challenges. In meeting those challenges, they left their mark on their particular cultures—and changed the course of history.

LITERATURE PREVIEW

Connecting to the Essay

Would you risk being put in jail to stand up for something you believe in? In his essay, Thoreau reflects on his choice to disobey the law. As you read the essay, think about the following questions:

- What is the basic purpose of government?
- How much power should government have over citizens' lives?

Building Background

Thoreau's refusal to pay a tax led to his arrest—and interrupted his stay at Walden Pond. Thoreau's action was a protest against the U.S. war with Mexico, which took place between 1846 and 1848. He believed the government was fighting the war solely to expand territory and that it would lead to the expansion of slavery. In "Civil Disobedience" he reflects on the night he spent in jail for refusing to pay the tax and criticizes the government for straying from its true purpose—to serve the people.

Setting Purposes for Reading

Big Idea Optimism and Individualism

Thoreau's outlook reflected the Romantic spirit of optimism and individualism—the belief that ordinary citizens could better themselves, their political system, and their society. As you read, notice how Thoreau opposed limitations on personal freedom.

Literary Element Argument

An **argument** is a form of persuasion that uses logic, reasons, and evidence to influence an audience's ideas or actions. For example, in "Civil Disobedience," Thoreau argues for limiting the power of government. As you read Thoreau's essay, analyze how he develops his argument through various persuasive techniques.

- See Literary Terms Handbook, p. R2.

Literature Online **Interactive Literary Elements Handbook** To review or learn more about the literary elements, go to www.glencoe.com.

READING PREVIEW

Reading Strategy Evaluating Evidence

One way of evaluating the **evidence** presented in an argument is to distinguish between facts and opinions. Facts are statements that can be proved true, while opinions are statements that are based on personal beliefs. As you read "Civil Disobedience," ask yourself these questions:

- Do the facts seem relevant, reliable, and accurate?
- Do the opinions seem based on facts and thoughtful observations?

Reading Tip: Taking Notes Use a chart to list key facts and opinions in Thoreau's essay.

Facts	Opinions
"I have paid no poll-tax for six years." (relevant information)	"That government is best which governs least." (unsupported judgment)

Vocabulary

din (din) *n.* loud, continuous noise; p. 212 *The din of construction work kept me from concentrating.*

alacrity (ə lak´ rə tē) *n.* speed; swiftness; p. 212 *The soccer player's alacrity surprised the defense.*

expedient (ek spē´ dē ənt) *adj.* convenient or efficient for a certain purpose; p. 213 *In Thoreau's era, the railroad was the most expedient means of traveling from Boston to New York.*

blunder (blun´ dər) *n.* a serious error or mistake resulting from carelessness or confusion; p. 214 *The police's blunder allowed the criminal to escape through the back door.*

sanction (sangk´ shən) *n.* approval or support; p. 216 *The troops awaited sanction from their commanding officer before continuing their mission.*

from

Civil Disobedience

Henry David Thoreau

I heartily accept the motto, "That government is best which governs least"; and I should like to see it acted up to more rapidly and systematically. Carried out, it finally amounts to this, which also I believe—"That government is best which governs not at all"; and when men are prepared for it, that will be the kind of government which they will have. Government is at best but an expedient;[1] but most governments are usually, and all governments are sometimes, inexpedient. The objections which have been brought against a standing army, and they are many and weighty, and deserve to prevail, may also at last be brought against a standing government. The standing army is only an arm of the standing government. The government itself, which is only the mode which the people have chosen to execute their will, is equally liable to be abused and perverted before the people can act through it. Witness the present Mexican war, the work of comparatively a few individuals using the standing government as their tool; for, in the outset, the people would not have consented to this measure.

This American government—what is it but a tradition, though a recent one, endeavoring to transmit itself unimpaired to posterity,[2] but each instant losing some of its integrity? It has not the vitality and force of a single living man; for a single man can bend it to his will. It is a sort of wooden gun to the people themselves. But it is not the less necessary for this; for the people must have some complicated machinery or other, and hear its **din,** to satisfy that idea of government which they have. Governments show thus how successfully men can be imposed on, even impose on themselves, for their own advantage. It is excellent, we must all allow. Yet this government never of itself furthered any enterprise, but by the **alacrity** with which it got out of its way. *It* does not keep the country free. *It* does not settle the West. *It* does not educate. The character inherent in the American people has done all that has been accomplished; and it would have done somewhat more, if the government had not sometimes got in its way. For government is an expedient by which men would fain[3] succeed in letting one another alone; and, as has been said, when it is

---

2. *Posterity* means "future generations."
3. *Fain* means "gladly" or "willingly."

---

1. *Expedient* means "something employed to bring about a desired result; a means to an end."

Literary Element Argument *How does Thoreau support his argument?*

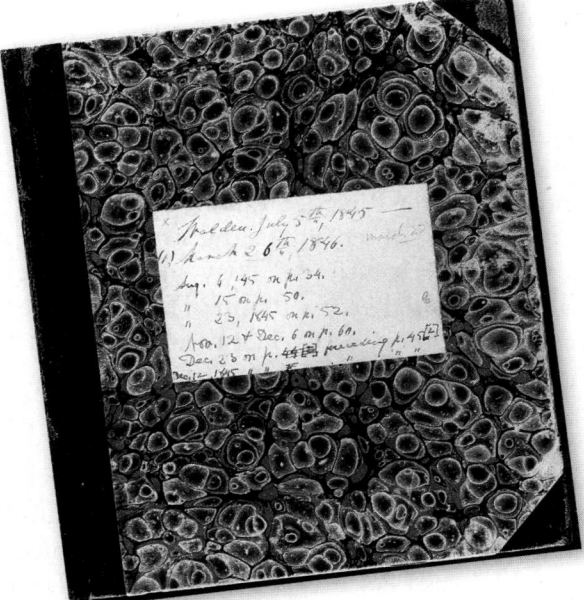

One of the notebooks in which Thoreau kept his journal

most **expedient,** the governed are most let alone by it. Trade and commerce, if they were not made of india-rubber, would never manage to bounce over the obstacles which legislators are continually putting in their way; and if one were to judge these men wholly by the effects of their actions and not partly by their intentions, they would deserve to be classed and punished with those mischievous persons who put obstructions on the railroads.

But, to speak practically and as a citizen, unlike those who call themselves no-government men, I ask for, not *at once* no government, but at once a better government. Let every man make known what kind of government would command his respect, and that will be one step toward obtaining it.

After all, the practical reason why, when the power is once in the hands of the people, a majority are permitted, and for a long period continue, to rule, is not because they are most likely to be in the right, nor because this seems fairest to the minority, but because they are physically the strongest. But a government in which the majority rule in all cases cannot be based on justice, even as far as men understand it. Can

there not be a government in which majorities do not virtually decide right and wrong, but conscience?—in which majorities decide only those questions to which the rule of expediency is applicable? Must the citizen ever for a moment, or in the least degree, resign his conscience to the legislator? Why has every man a conscience then? I think that we should be men first, and subjects afterward. It is not desirable to cultivate a respect for the law, so much as for the right. The only obligation which I have a right to assume is to do at any time what I think right. It is truly enough said that a corporation has no conscience; but a corporation of conscientious men is a corporation *with* a conscience. Law never made men a whit[4] more just; and, by means of their respect for it, even the well-disposed are daily made the agents of injustice. . . .

Some years ago, the State met me in behalf of the Church, and commanded me to pay a certain sum toward the support of a clergyman whose preaching my father attended, but never I myself. "Pay," it said, "or be locked up in the jail." I declined to pay. But, unfortunately, another man saw fit to pay it. I did not see why the schoolmaster should be taxed to support the priest, and not the priest the schoolmaster: for I was not the State's schoolmaster, but I supported myself by voluntary subscription. I did not see why the lyceum[5] should not present its tax-bill, and have the State to back its demand, as well as the Church. However, at the request of the selectmen,[6] I condescended to make some such statement as this in writing: "Know all men by these presents, that I, Henry Thoreau, do not wish to be regarded as a member of any incorporated society which I have not joined." This I gave to the town clerk; and he has it. The State, having thus learned that I did not wish to be regarded as a member of that church, has never made a like demand on me since; though it said that it must adhere to its original presumption that time. If I had known how to name them, I should then have signed off in detail from all the societies which I never signed on to; but I did not know where to find a complete list.

---

4. *Whit* means "a tiny amount" or "a bit."
5. A *lyceum* is an organization that sponsers educational programs, such as concerts and lectures.
6. *Selectmen* refers to a group of elected local officials.

I have paid no poll-tax[7] for six years. I was put into a jail once on this account, for one night; and, as I stood considering the walls of solid stone, two or three feet thick, the door of wood and iron, a foot thick, and the iron grating which strained the light, I could not help being struck with the foolishness of that institution which treated me as if I were mere flesh and blood and bones, to be locked up. I wondered that it should have concluded at length that this was the best use it could put me to, and had never thought to avail itself of my services in some way. I saw that, if there was a wall of stone between me and my townsmen, there was a still more difficult one to climb or break through, before they could get to be as free as I was. I did not for a moment feel confined, and the walls seemed a great waste of stone and mortar. I felt as if I alone of all my townsmen had paid my tax. They plainly did not know how to treat me, but behaved like persons who are underbred. In every threat and in every compliment there was a **blunder;** for they thought that my chief desire was to stand the other side of that stone wall. I could not but smile to see how industriously they locked the door on my meditations, which followed them out again without let[8] or hindrance, and they were really all that was dangerous. As they could not reach me, they had resolved to punish my body; just as boys, if they cannot come at some person against whom they have a spite, will abuse his dog. I saw that the State was half-witted, that it was timid as a lone woman with her silver spoons, and that it did not know its friends from its foes, and I lost all my remaining respect for it, and pitied it.

Thus the State never intentionally confronts a man's sense, intellectual or moral, but only his body, his senses. It is not armed with superior wit or honesty, but with superior physical strength. I was not born to be forced. I will breathe after my own fashion. Let us see who is the strongest. What force has a multitude? They only can force me who obey a higher law than I. They force me to become like themselves. I do not hear of *men* being *forced* to live this way or that by masses of men. What sort of life were that to live? When I meet a government which says to me, "Your money or your life," why should I be in haste to give it my money? It may be in a great strait, and not know what to do: I cannot help that. It must help itself; do as I do. It is not worth the while to snivel about it. I am not responsible for the successful working of the machinery of society. I am not the son of the engineer. I perceive that,

> ## They only can force me who obey a higher law than I.

when an acorn and a chestnut fall side by side, the one does not remain inert to make way for the other, but both obey their own laws, and spring and grow and flourish as best they can, till one, perchance, overshadows and destroys the other. If a plant cannot live according to its nature, it dies; and so a man.

The night in prison was novel and interesting enough. The prisoners in their shirt-sleeves were enjoying a chat and the evening air in the doorway, when I entered. But the jailer said, "Come, boys, it is time to lock up"; and so they dispersed, and I heard the sound of their steps returning into the hollow apartments. My room-mate was introduced to me by the jailer as "a first-rate fellow and a clever man." When the door was locked, he showed me where to hang my hat, and how he managed matters there. The rooms were whitewashed once a month; and this one, at least, was the whitest, most simply furnished, and probably the neatest apartment in the town. He naturally wanted to know where I came from, and what brought me there; and, when I had told him, I asked him in my turn how he came there, presuming him to be an honest man, of course; and, as the world goes, I believe he

---

7. A *poll tax,* now illegal, was a tax on people (not property). Payment was often required in order to vote.
8. Here, *let* means "an obstruction" or "an obstacle."

Big Idea Optimism and Individualism *Why does Thoreau believe he is freer than his "townsmen"?*

Vocabulary

blunder (blun´ dər) *n.* a serious error or mistake resulting from carelessness or confusion

Stump Speaking, 1853–54, George Caleb Bingham. Oil on canvas. Private collection.
Viewing the Art: What does the scene in the painting suggest about the relationship between citizens and the government in Thoreau's era?

was. "Why," said he, "they accuse me of burning a barn; but I never did it." As near as I could discover, he had probably gone to bed in a barn when drunk, and smoked his pipe there; and so a barn was burnt. He had the reputation of being a clever man, had been there some three months waiting for his trial to come on, and would have to wait as much longer; but he was quite domesticated and contented, since he got his board for nothing, and thought that he was well treated.

He occupied one window, and I the other; and I saw that if one stayed there long, his principal business would be to look out the window. I had soon read all the tracts[9] that were left

there, and examined where former prisoners had broken out, and where a grate had been sawed off, and heard the history of the various occupants of that room; for I found that even here there was a history and a gossip which never circulated beyond the walls of the jail. Probably this is the only house in the town where verses are composed, which are afterward printed in a circular form, but not published. I was shown quite a long list of verses which were composed by some young men who had been detected in an attempt to escape, who avenged themselves by singing them.

I pumped my fellow-prisoner as dry as I could, for fear I should never see him again; but at length he showed me which was my bed, and left me to blow out the lamp. It was like traveling into a far

---

9. *Tracts* are leaflets or pamphlets, especially those on religious or political topics.

HENRY DAVID THOREAU **215**

country, such as I had never expected to behold, to lie there for one night. It seemed to me that I never had heard the town-clock strike before, nor the evening sounds of the village; for we slept with the windows open, which were inside the grating. It was to see my native village in the light of the Middle Ages, and our Concord was turned

> ## I saw yet more distinctly the State in which I lived.

into a Rhine[10] stream, and visions of knights and castles passed before me. They were the voices of old burghers[11] that I heard in the streets. I was an involuntary spectator and auditor[12] of whatever was done and said in the kitchen of the adjacent village-inn—a wholly new and rare experience to me. It was a closer view of my native town. I was fairly inside of it. I never had seen its institutions before. This is one of its peculiar institutions; for it is a shire town.[13] I began to comprehend what its inhabitants were about.

In the morning, our breakfasts were put through the hole in the door, in small oblong-square tin pans, made to fit, and holding a pint of chocolate, with brown bread, and an iron spoon. When they called for the vessels again, I was green enough to return what bread I had left; but my comrade seized it, and said that I should lay that up for lunch or dinner. Soon after he was let out to work at haying in a neighboring field, whither he went every day, and would not be back till noon; so he bade me good-day, saying that he doubted if he should see me again.

When I came out of prison—for some one interfered, and paid that tax—I did not perceive that great changes had taken place on the common, such as he observed who went in a youth

and emerged a tottering and gray-headed man; and yet a change had to my eyes come over the scene—the town, and State, and country—greater than any that mere time could effect. I saw yet more distinctly the State in which I lived. . . .

The authority of government, even such as I am willing to submit to—for I will cheerfully obey those who know and can do better than I, and in many things even those who neither know nor can do so well—is still an impure one: to be strictly just, it must have the **sanction** and consent of the governed. It can have no pure right over my person and property but what I concede to it. The progress from an absolute to a limited monarchy, from a limited monarchy to a democracy, is a progress toward a true respect for the individual. Even the Chinese philosopher[14] was wise enough to regard the individual as the basis of the empire. Is a democracy, such as we know it, the last improvement possible in government? Is it not possible to take a step further towards recognizing and organizing the rights of man? There will never be a really free and enlightened State until the State comes to recognize the individual as a higher and independent power, from which all its own power and authority are derived, and treats him accordingly. I please myself with imagining a State at least which can afford to be just to all men, and to treat the individual with respect as a neighbor; which even would not think it inconsistent with its own repose[15] if a few were to live aloof from it, not meddling with it, nor embraced by it, who fulfilled all the duties of neighbors and fellow-men. A State which bore this kind of fruit, and suffered it to drop off as fast as it ripened, would prepare the way for a still more perfect and glorious State, which also I have imagined, but not yet anywhere seen. ∾

---

10. *Concord* refers to the Concord River. The *Rhine* River flows through Germany and the Netherlands.
11. *Burghers* is a term for inhabitants of a city.
12. Here, *auditor* means "someone who hears," or "a listener."
13. A *shire town*, or county town, is similar to a county seat.

---

14. The *Chinese philosopher* is Confucius (c. 551–479 B.C.)
15. Here, *repose* refers to the state's "peace of mind."

Big Idea Optimism and Individualism *What type of freedom does Thoreau desire?*

Vocabulary

sanction (sangk′ shən) n. approval or support

AFTER YOU READ

RESPONDING AND THINKING CRITICALLY

Respond

1. What was your reaction to Thoreau's opinion on disobeying the government?

Recall and Interpret

2. (a)Why was Thoreau jailed? (b)What does this tell you about Thoreau's beliefs?

3. (a)Why is Thoreau's cellmate in prison? (b)What does Thoreau presume about his cellmate's conviction?

4. (a)How does Thoreau react to his night in jail? (b)What does this say about his personality?

Analyze and Evaluate

5. How does Thoreau's perspective change when he is released from prison?

6. How does the fact that Thoreau spent only one night in jail affect your evaluation of his opinions?

7. (a)How do you evaluate Thoreau's criticism of democracy? (b)Is it accurate; is it fair? (c)Cite evidence from the story to support your opinion.

Connect

8. **Big Idea** **Optimism and Individualism** (a)What do you think are some essential qualities for an individual who wishes to reform society or the government? (b)Which of these qualities does Thoreau possess?

LITERARY ANALYSIS

Literary Element **Argument**

A valid **argument** relies on logic—the process of clear, well-organized thinking that leads to a reasonable conclusion.

Partner Activity What does Thoreau conclude about freedom and the role of government? Meet with another classmate to discuss whether Thoreau's conclusions are logical.

Writing About Literature

Evaluate Contemporary Relevance Based on the ideas in "Civil Disobedience" consider how Thoreau might encourage young people to become involved in their government. Write a brief essay in which you give examples of the political roles that young people might play.

Literature Online **Web Activities** For eFlashcards, Selection Quick Checks, and other Web activities, go to www.glencoe.com.

READING AND VOCABULARY

Reading Strategy **Evaluating Evidence**

A successful persuasive essay relies on various kinds of supporting evidence, such as facts and opinions.

1. What kind of evidence does Thoreau rely on more—facts or opinions?

2. Was the evidence presented in the essay strong enough to persuade you to agree with Thoreau's viewpoints? Why or why not?

Vocabulary **Practice**

Practice with Antonyms Choose the best antonym for each vocabulary word from "Civil Disobedience."

1. alacrity
   a. simplicity   **c.** wiliness
   b. slowness   **d.** custom

2. expedient
   a. dated   **c.** useless
   b. careful   **d.** creative

3. sanction
   a. ban   **c.** approval
   b. increase   **d.** innovation

On the Eve of Historic DANDI MARCH

Mohandas K. Gandhi

Building Background

Known as Mahatma, or "Great-Souled," Mohandas K. Gandhi led the movement against British rule in early twentieth-century India. From his devout mother he learned the Hindu principle of *ahimsa,* or noninjury to all life. Like his father he prepared for a government post. After law school in England, he moved to South Africa, where he helped lead the struggle against Indian discrimination. After returning to India in 1914, Gandhi led the opposition to British control. His method was based on *satyagraha*—"truth persistence"—non-violent resistance to injustice.

Gandhi's "salt march" in 1930 protested the salt monopoly, which required Indians to buy taxed salt from the British government. To demonstrate opposition to British economic control, marchers to the Arabian Sea defied British law by extracting salt from seawater.

Literature Online **Author Search** For more about Mohandas K. Gandhi, go to www.glencoe.com.

In all probability this will be my last speech to you. Even if the Government allow me to march tomorrow morning, this will be my last speech on the sacred banks of the Sabarmati.[1] Possibly these may be the last words of my life here.

I have already told you yesterday what I had to say. Today I shall confine myself to what you should do after my companions and I are arrested. The program[2] of the march to Jalalpur[3] must be fulfilled as originally settled. The enlistment of the volunteers for this purpose should be confined to Gujarat[4] only. From what I have seen and heard during the last fortnight, I am inclined to believe that the stream of civil resisters will flow unbroken.

But let there be not a semblance of breach of peace even after all of us have been arrested. We have resolved to utilize all our resources in the pursuit of an exclusively nonviolent struggle. Let no one commit a wrong in anger. This is my hope and prayer. I wish these words of mine reached every nook and corner of the land. My task shall be done if I perish and so do my comrades. It will then be for the Working Committee of the Congress[5] to show you the way and it will be up to you to follow its lead. So long as I have not reached Jalalpur, let nothing be done in contravention to the authority vested in me by the Congress. But once I am arrested, the whole responsibility shifts to the Congress. No one who believes in nonviolence, as

---

1. The *Sabarmati* is a river in western India.
2. Here, *program* means "mission."
3. *Jalalpur,* a city in India, was the last stop on Gandhi's march to Dandi.
4. *Gujarat* is a state in western India.

5. By *Congress,* Gandhi is referring to the Indian National Congress, a political party led by Gandhi in the 1920s and 1930s.

a creed, need, therefore, sit still. My compact with the Congress ends as soon as I am arrested. In that case there should be no slackness in the enrolment of volunteers. Wherever possible, civil disobedience of salt laws should be started. These laws can be violated in three ways. It is an offense to manufacture salt wherever there are facilities for doing so. The possession and sale of contraband salt, which includes natural salt or salt earth, is also an offense. The purchasers of such salt will be equally guilty. To carry away the natural salt deposits on the seashore is likewise violation of law. So is the hawking of such salt. In short, you may choose any one or all of these devices to break the salt monopoly.

We are, however, not to be content with this alone. There is no ban by the Congress and wherever the local workers have self-confidence other suitable measures may be adopted. I stress only one condition, namely, let our pledge of truth and non violence as the only means for the attainment of Swaraj[6] be faithfully kept. For the rest, every one has a free hand. But, that does not give a license to all and sundry to carry on on their own responsibility. Wherever there are local leaders, their orders should be obeyed by the people. Where there are no leaders and only a handful of men have faith in the program, they may do what they can, if they have enough self-confidence. They have a right, nay it is their duty, to do so. The history of the world is full of instances of men who rose to leadership, by sheer force of self-confidence, bravery and tenacity. We too, if we sincerely aspire to Swaraj and are impatient to attain it, should have similar self-confidence. Our ranks will swell and our hearts strengthen, as the number of our arrests by the Government increases.

Much can be done in many other ways besides these. The liquor and foreign cloth shops can be picketed. We can refuse to pay taxes if we have the requisite strength. The lawyers can give up practice. The public can boycott the law courts by refraining from litigation. Government servants can resign their posts. In the midst of the despair reigning all round people quake with fear of losing employment. Such men are unfit for Swaraj. But why this despair?

The number of Government servants in the country does not exceed a few hundred thousand. What about the rest? Where are they to go? Even free India will not be able to accommodate a greater number of public servants. A Collector then will not need the number of servants he has got today. He will be his own servant. Our starving millions can by no means afford this enormous expenditure. If, therefore, we are sensible enough, let us bid good-bye to Government employment, no matter if it is the post of a judge or a peon. Let all who are cooperating with the Government in one way or another, be it by paying taxes, keeping titles, or sending children to official schools, etc. withdraw their cooperation in all or as many ways as possible. Then there are women who can stand shoulder to shoulder with men in this struggle.

You may take it as my will. It was the message that I desired to impart to you before starting on the march or for the jail. I wish that there should be no suspension or abandonment of the war that commences tomorrow morning or earlier, if I am arrested before that time. I shall eagerly await the news that ten batches are ready as soon as my batch is arrested. I believe there are men in India to complete the work begun by me. I have faith in the righteousness of our cause and the purity of our weapons. And where the means are clean, there God is undoubtedly present with His blessings. And where these three combine, there defeat is an impossibility. A Satyagrahi,[7] whether free or incarcerated, is ever victorious. He is vanquished only when he forsakes truth and nonviolence and turns a deaf ear to the inner voice. If, therefore, there is such a thing as defeat for even a Satyagrahi, he alone is the cause of it. God bless you all and keep off all obstacles from the path in the struggle that begins tomorrow. ◦◦

---

7. *Satyagrahi* means someone who embodies Gandhi's ideal of satyagraha and practices nonviolent resistance.

Quickwrite

Gandhi insists that his followers must have self-confidence to succeed in their struggle against the British. Why is self-confidence important for someone using nonviolence as a tool for social justice? Write a paragraph explaining your views.

---

6. *Swaraj* means "home rule." It refers to Indians' desire to rule themselves, rather than be ruled by the British.

from
Long Walk to Freedom

Nelson Mandela

BEFORE YOU READ

Building Background

From prisoner to president of South Africa, Nelson Mandela was one of the political miracles of the twentieth century. Born the son of an African tribal chief in 1918, Mandela passed up his right to chieftainship to study law, starting a firm with fellow reformer Oliver Tambo. In 1944 he became a leader in the African National Congress (ANC), a political party that opposed apartheid, South Africa's policy of racial segregation.

After a massacre of unarmed Africans in 1960, Mandela dropped his nonviolent reform method in favor of supporting acts of sabotage against the government. In 1962 he was jailed and, after a widely publicized trial, was sentenced to life in prison in 1964. Over the years, Mandela became the world's best-known political prisoner, gaining international support in his fight against apartheid.

Literature Online Author Search For more about Nelson Mandela, go to www.glencoe.com.

May 10 dawned bright and clear. For the past few days, I had been pleasantly besieged by arriving dignitaries[1] and world leaders who were coming to pay their respects before the inauguration.[2] The inauguration would be the largest gathering ever of international leaders on South African soil.

The ceremonies took place in the lovely sandstone amphitheater formed by the Union Buildings in Pretoria.[3] For decades, this had been the seat of white supremacy, and now it was the site of a rainbow gathering of different colors and nations for the installation of South Africa's first democratic, nonracial government.

On that lovely autumn day I was accompanied by my daughter Zenani. On the podium, Mr. de Klerk[4] was first sworn in as second deputy president. Then Thabo Mbeki[5] was sworn in as first deputy president. When it was my turn, I pledged to obey and uphold the constitution and

---

1. *Dignitaries* are people who hold a rank of dignity, or honor.
2. An *inauguration* is a ceremonial induction into office, or a formal beginning.
3. *Pretoria* is the administrative capital of South Africa.

4. *F. W. de Klerk* served as president of South Africa from 1989 to 1994.
5. *Thabo Mbeki* is a politician who became the president of South Africa in 1999.

to devote myself to the well-being of the republic and its people. To the assembled guests and the watching world, I said:

Today, all of us do, by our presence here . . . confer[6] glory and hope to newborn liberty. Out of the experience of an extraordinary human disaster that lasted too long, must be born a society of which all humanity will be proud.

. . . We, who were outlaws not so long ago, have today been given the rare privilege to be host to the nations of the world on our own soil. We thank all of our distinguished international guests for having come to take possession with the people of our country of what is, after all, a common victory for justice, for peace, for human dignity.

We have, at last, achieved our political emancipation.[7] We pledge ourselves to liberate all our people from the continuing bondage of poverty, deprivation, suffering, gender, and other discrimination.

Never, never, and never again shall it be that this beautiful land will again experience the oppression of one by another. . . . The sun shall never set on so glorious a human achievement.

Let freedom reign. God bless Africa!

A few moments later we all lifted our eyes in awe as a spectacular array of South African jets, helicopters, and troop carriers roared in perfect formation over the Union Buildings. It was not only a display of pinpoint precision and military force, but a demonstration of the military's loyalty to democracy, to a new government that had been freely and fairly elected. Only moments before, the highest generals of the South African Defense Force and police, their chests bedecked[8] with ribbons and medals from days gone by, saluted me and pledged their loyalty. I was not unmindful of the fact that not so many years before they would not have saluted but arrested me. Finally a chevron of Impala jets[9] left a smoke trail of the black, red, green, blue, white, and gold of the new South African flag.

The day was symbolized for me by the playing of our two national anthems, and the vision of whites singing *"Nkosi Sikelel' iAfrika"* and blacks singing *"Die Stem,"* the old anthem of the republic. Although that day, neither group knew the lyrics of the anthem they once despised, they would soon know the words by heart.

On the day of the inauguration, I was overwhelmed with a sense of history. In the first decade of the twentieth century, a few years after the bitter Anglo-Boer War[10] and before my own birth, the white-skinned peoples of South Africa patched up their differences and erected a system of racial domination against the dark-skinned peoples of their own land. The structure they created formed the basis of one of the harshest, most inhumane societies the world has ever known. Now, in the last decade of the twentieth

Nelson Mandela visits schoolchildren in South Africa.

century, and my own eighth decade as a man, that system had been overturned forever and replaced by one that recognized the rights and freedoms of all peoples regardless of the color of their skin.

That day had come about through the unimaginable sacrifices of thousands of my people, people whose suffering and courage can never be counted or repaid. I felt that day, as I have on so many

6. *Confer* means "to bestow, or give, an honor."
7. *Emancipation* means "the process of becoming free from restraint or control."
8. *Bedecked* means "adorned or clothed."
9. Here, *chevron* is a V-shaped pattern; an *Impala jet* is a military fighter plane.

10. The *Anglo-Boer War* (1899–1902) was fought between Great Britain and the Boers, who are South Africans of Dutch decent.

other days, that I was simply the sum of all those African patriots who had gone before me. That long and noble line ended and now began again with me. I was pained that I was not able to thank them and that they were not able to see what their sacrifices had wrought.[11]

The policy of apartheid created a deep and lasting wound in my country and my people. All of us will spend many years, if not generations, recovering from that profound hurt. But the decades of oppression and brutality had another, unintended effect, and that was that it produced the Oliver Tambos, the Walter Sisulus, the Chief Luthulis, the Yusuf Dadoos, the Bram Fischers, the Robert Sobukwes[12] of our time—men of such extraordinary courage, wisdom, and generosity that their like may never be known again. Perhaps it requires such depth of oppression to create such heights of character. My country is rich in the minerals and gems that lie beneath its soil, but I have always known that its greatest wealth is its people, finer and truer than the purest diamonds.

It is from these comrades in the struggle that I learned the meaning of courage. Time and again, I have seen men and women risk and give their lives for an idea. I have seen men stand up to attacks and torture without breaking, showing a strength and resiliency that defies the imagination. I learned that courage was not the absence of fear, but the triumph over it. I felt fear myself more times than I can remember, but I hid it behind a mask of boldness. The brave man is not he who does not feel afraid, but he who conquers that fear.

I never lost hope that this great transformation would occur. Not only because of the great heroes I have already cited, but because of the courage of the ordinary men and women of my country. I always knew that deep down in every human heart, there is mercy and generosity. No one is born hating another person because of the color of his skin, or his background, or his religion. People must learn to hate, and if they can learn to hate, they can be taught to love, for love comes more naturally to the human heart than its opposite. Even in the grimmest times in prison, when my comrades and I were pushed to our limits, I would see a glimmer of humanity in one of the guards, perhaps just for a second, but it was enough to reassure me and keep me going. Man's goodness is a flame that can be hidden but never extinguished.

We took up the struggle with our eyes wide open, under no illusion that the path would be an easy one. As a young man, when I joined the African National Congress,[13] I saw the price my comrades paid for their beliefs, and it was high. For myself, I have never regretted my commitment to the struggle, and I was always prepared to face the hardships that affected me personally. But my family paid a terrible price, perhaps too dear a price for my commitment.

In life, every man has twin obligations—obligations to his family, to his parents, to his wife and children; and he has an obligation to his people, his community, his country. In a civil and humane society, each man is able to fulfill those obligations according to his own inclinations and abilities. But in a country like South Africa, it was almost impossible for a man of my birth and color to fulfill both of those obligations. In South Africa, a man of color who attempted to live as a human being was punished and isolated. In South Africa, a man who tried to fulfill his duty to his people was inevitably ripped from his family and home and was forced to live a life apart, a twilight existence of secrecy and rebellion. I did not in the beginning choose to place my people above my family, but in attempting to serve my people, I found that I was prevented from fulfilling my obligations as a son, a brother, a father, and a husband.

In that way, my commitment to my people, to the millions of South Africans I would never know or meet, was at the expense of the people I knew best and loved most. It was as simple and yet as incomprehensible as the moment a small child asks her father, "Why can you not be with us?" And the father must utter the terrible words: "There are other children like you, a great many of them . . ." and then one's voice trails off.

---

11. Here, *wrought* means "made."
12. The people Mandela refers to—*Tambo, Sisulu, Luthuli, Dadoo, Fischer,* and *Sobukwe*—are fellow South African reformers and opponents of apartheid.

---

13. The *African National Congress* (ANC) is a South African political party founded by blacks in 1912.

I was not born with a hunger to be free. I was born free—free in every way that I could know. Free to run in the fields near my mother's hut, free to swim in the clear stream that ran through my village, free to roast mealies[14] under the stars and ride the broad backs of slow-moving bulls. As long as I obeyed my father and abided by the customs of my tribe, I was not troubled by the laws of man or God.

It was only when I began to learn that my boyhood freedom was an illusion, when I discovered as a young man that my freedom had already been

The oppressed and the oppressor alike are robbed of their humanity.

taken from me, that I began to hunger for it. At first, as a student, I wanted freedom only for myself, the transitory freedoms of being able to stay out at night, read what I pleased, and go where I chose. Later, as a young man in Johannesburg, I yearned for the basic and honorable freedoms of achieving my potential, of earning my keep, of marrying and having a family —the freedom not to be obstructed in a lawful life.

But then I slowly saw that not only was I not free, but my brothers and sisters were not free. I saw that it was not just my freedom that was curtailed, but the freedom of everyone who looked like I did. That is when I joined the African National Congress, and that is when the hunger for my own freedom became the greater hunger for the freedom of my people. It was this desire for the freedom of my people to live their lives with dignity and self-respect that animated my life, that transformed a frightened young man into a bold one, that drove a law-abiding attorney to become a criminal, that turned a family-loving husband into a man without a home, that forced a life-loving man to live like a monk. I am not more virtuous or self-sacrificing than the next man, but I found that I could not even enjoy the poor and limited freedoms I was allowed when I knew my

people were not free. Freedom is indivisible; the chains on any one of my people were the chains on all of them, the chains on all of my people were the chains on me.

It was during those long and lonely years that my hunger for the freedom of my own people became a hunger for the freedom of all people, white and black. I knew as well as I knew anything that the oppressor must be liberated just as surely as the oppressed. A man who takes away another man's freedom is a prisoner of hatred, he is locked behind the bars of prejudice and narrow-mindedness. I am not truly free if I am taking away someone else's freedom, just as surely as I am not free when my freedom is taken from me. The oppressed and the oppressor alike are robbed of their humanity.

When I walked out of prison, that was my mission, to liberate the oppressed and the oppressor both. Some say that has now been achieved. But I know that is not the case. The truth is that we are not yet free; we have merely achieved the freedom to be free, the right not to be oppressed. We have not taken the final step of our journey, but the first step on a longer and even more difficult road. For to be free is not merely to cast off one's chains, but to live in a way that respects and enhances the freedom of others. The true test of our devotion to freedom is just beginning.

I walked that long road to freedom. I have tried not to falter; I have made missteps along the way. But I have discovered the secret that after climbing a great hill, one only finds that there are many more hills to climb. I have taken a moment here to rest, to steal a view of the glorious vista[15] that surrounds me, to look back on the distance I have come. But I can rest only for a moment, for with freedom come responsibilities, and I dare not linger, for my long walk is not yet ended. ◌

---

15. Here, *vista* means a "wide viewpoint of history."

Quickwrite ....

What qualities and values distinguish Nelson Mandela as a leader of the people? Write a paragraph describing these qualities and values. Use evidence from his autobiography to support your position.

---

14. A *mealie* is an ear of Indian corn.

Wrap-up: Comparing Literature Across Time and Place

- **from *Civil Disobedience***
  Henry David Thoreau
- **On the Eve of Historic Dandi March**
  Mohandas K. Gandhi
- **from *Long Walk to Freedom***
  Nelson Mandela

COMPARING THE Big Idea Optimism and Individualism

Partner Activity With a partner, read each of the following quotations. Then discuss how each quotation reflects the writer's optimism and individualism. Cite evidence from the selections.

> *"The only obligation which I have a right to assume is to do at any time what I think is right."*
>
> —Henry David Thoreau, *Civil Disobedience*

> *"A Satyagrahi, whether free or incarcerated, is ever victorious."*
>
> —Mohandas K. Gandhi, *On the Eve of Historic Dandi March*

> *"My country is rich in the minerals and gems that lie beneath its soil, but I have always known that its greatest wealth is its people, finer and truer than the purest diamonds."*
>
> —Nelson Mandela, *Long Walk to Freedom*

Former South African President Nelson Mandela gazes through the bars of the jail cell he spent more than two decades in as a political prisoner.

COMPARING Persuasive Messages

Group Activity Thoreau, Gandhi, and Mandela craft different arguments for social reform. With a small group discuss the following questions.

1. What is each writer's main message or philosophical assumption? What objections might some readers raise to the viewpoints presented?
2. What is the historical context that shapes each writer's message?
3. Evaluate the effectiveness of each writer's argument for both friendly and hostile audiences. Which writer best succeeds at stating his case? Why?
4. Which of the reading selections challenged you to think in a new way? Explain.

COMPARING Cultures

Visual Display Cultural, historical, and political forces influenced these writers. Thoreau was influenced by American Romanticism; Gandhi, by British colonialism; Mandela, by African culture and apartheid. Create a three-panel collage of images—one panel for each writer—illustrating these cultural, historical, and political forces.

INDIANA ACADEMIC STANDARDS (page 224)
11.3.8 Analyze the philosophical arguments presented in literary works...

PART 2

The Dark Side of Romanticism

The Fog Warning, 1885. Winslow Homer. Oil on canvas. Museum of Fine Arts, Boston.

"*All that we see or seem*
Is but a dream within a dream."

—Edgar Allan Poe

The First American Short Stories

AS THE AMERICAN NOVELIST and critic Henry James observed, "It takes a great deal of history to produce a little literature." At the beginning of the 1800s, the United States was still a very young country. American writers of the time were painfully conscious of the lack of a native literary tradition. This was particularly true in the area of fiction.

Dominated by Puritanism, early American culture had no place for made-up stories created largely for entertainment. This attitude toward fiction lingered for a long time. It was not until the period of American Romanticism that Washington Irving, Nathaniel Hawthorne, and Edgar Allan Poe laid the foundations of the American short story. In the process, they created literary forms and ideas about how to write short stories that remain important today.

The Headless Horseman Pursuing Ichabod Crane, 1858. John Quidor. Oil on canvas. Smithsonian American Art Museum, Washington, DC.

> *"It has been a matter of marvel, to my European readers, that a man from the wilds of America should express himself in tolerable English."*
>
> —Washington Irving

Literary Pioneers

Irving, the first American writer to become famous outside his own country, transplanted traditional European narratives and gave them American settings. For example, he based his story "Rip Van Winkle" on old legends about people captured by fairies. Hawthorne used both European material and the histories and legends of Puritan New England as the basis for his fiction. Poe helped develop the new American literary magazines (to which he contributed as both writer and editor) into mass-circulation marketplaces for short stories. More importantly, he was a true innovator who pioneered new literary forms—detective stories and science fiction.

Detective Stories and Science Fiction

Tales of robbery and murder had always existed. Poe's brilliant innovation was to combine such stories with the use of reason in the investigation of crime. This new investigative approach had not existed until the appearance of the first professional police forces in the early 1800s. In "The Murders in the Rue Morgue," Poe established many of the basic conventions that mystery writers have followed ever since:

- the brilliant, eccentric detective
- his less-gifted partner, who is an admiring foil
- the blundering official police force
- the "impossible crime" taking place in a locked room

Poe also has a claim to be the "father of science fiction." In some of his stories, such as "A Descent into the Maelstrom," he created Romantic tales of terror with an emphasis on factual detail that anticipated later science fiction. Poe so convincingy presented a hoax about a transatlantic balloon flight in one of his short stories that it was widely believed to have actually taken place.

Theory and Practice

Poe believed that the most effective short stories are those that can be read in a single sitting. He theorized that every detail in a well-constructed story should contribute to the creation of a certain unique and single effect. By effect, Poe meant the overall impact that the story makes upon the reader. Some favorite effects that Poe tried to achieve in his stories were feelings of dread, horror, and suspense. Poe's theory of a unique single effect remains a fundamental principle of short-story writing today.

Although Hawthorne's stories were finely crafted, he showed little interest in constructing literary theories. Hawthorne chose to focus on moral and psychological themes, such as the struggle between good and evil and the isolation of people from their fellow human beings. Unlike his friend Emerson, Hawthorne saw life as essentially tragic. His pessimistic view of human nature gave his stories a dark, shadowy quality that Poe criticized as "a somewhat too general or prevalent tone—a tone of melancholy and mysticism." Hawthorne's mystical outlook led him to rely heavily on symbolism and allegory to convey his meaning, often at the expense of a realistic rendering of everyday life. His distinguishing feature is his probing exploration of the role of guilt in the inner lives of human beings—an obsession that he inherited from his Puritan ancestors.

Literature Online Literary History For more about the first American short stories, go to www.glencoe.com.

Short Story Elements

The short story generally includes these elements.
Setting: the time and place in which the events occur
Characters: the participants in the story. The main character is the **protagonist.** There may be an **antagonist,** a character in conflict with the protagonist.
Point of view: the perspective of the storyteller, or narrator
Theme: the central message of the story that readers can apply to life. A theme may be stated clearly or implied.
Plot: the sequence of related events in a story. Most plots deal with a problem and develop around a conflict, a struggle between opposing forces.

Poster for Universal film *Murders in the Rue Morgue*, unknown artist, 1932. Everett Collection.

RESPONDING AND THINKING CRITICALLY

1. What was the attitude of readers in early American culture toward fiction? Why do you think early American readers had this attitude?

2. What materials did Irving use as the basis of his fiction? How did he use these materials?

3. What were Poe's important innovations in literary form? Explain how these innovations can be seen in literature today.

4. Compare and contrast Poe's and Hawthorne's attitudes toward literary theory and practice. Name one literary achievement that each author is famous for today.

INDIANA ACADEMIC STANDARDS (pages 226–227)
11.3.5 Analyze or evaluate works of literary...significance...that...reveal contrasts in major themes, styles, and trends.

The Devil and Tom Walker

MEET WASHINGTON IRVING

Named after his country's first president, Washington Irving won the battle for America's literary independence. He was the first American storyteller to be internationally recognized as a man of letters. The English novelist William Makepeace Thackeray summed up this accomplishment when he called Irving "the first Ambassador from the New World of Letters to the Old."

Lawyer and Writer The youngest of eleven children, Irving was born in New York City to a wealthy family with strict moral values. Though Irving had little formal education, he took an early interest in the study of law, later working in the law office of Josiah Ogden Hoffman. He soon fell in love with Hoffman's daughter Matilda, and the couple were engaged.

But his interest in law began to dwindle, and in 1802 he started to write, publishing a series of satirical essays in a New York newspaper. He soon began to publish a series of periodical essays called *Salmagundi*. The essays were witty sketches that poked fun at everything from Thomas Jefferson's politics to the latest fashions. The success of *Salmagundi* steered Irving away from law and toward writing.

Success and Heartbreak In 1809, under the pseudonym Diedrich Knickerbocker, he published his most popular work, Knickerbocker's *A History of New York from the Beginning of the World to the End of the Dutch Dynasty*. *A History* was a humorous, tongue-in-cheek combination of history, folklore, and opinion that delighted readers with hilarious sketches of the customs, manners, and families of old New York. That same year, however, Irving's fiancée, Matilda Hoffman, died suddenly of tuberculosis. Overwhelmed by grief, Irving put his writing career on hold. He later reflected that he considered this period the darkest of his life. Haunted perpetually by the memory of his lost fiancée, Irving was never to marry.

During his time away from writing, Irving held a variety of jobs. He traveled often, eventually moving to Europe to manage his brother's business interests. In 1818, after the family business went bankrupt, Irving resumed writing.

International Acclaim *The Sketch Book of Geoffrey Crayon, Gent* (1819–1820) established his literary reputation in Europe. The book included two stories that were to become classics, "The Legend of Sleepy Hollow" and "Rip Van Winkle." Irving borrowed the plots of these stories from two traditional German folktales before placing them in the Hudson Valley setting. Irving's ability to blend European sophistication with American flavor is the most distinctive characteristic of his writing.

After several years in London, Paris, and Madrid, Irving returned to the United States. There, he continued writing—travel books, histories, biographies of Columbus and Washington, and more tales and sketches.

Irving's enormous popularity at home and abroad earned him recognition as the father of American letters. His stories featured distinctively American settings and character types. He influenced a broad range of authors—from Romantics, such as Nathaniel Hawthorne and Edgar Allan Poe, to regionalist writers, such as Mark Twain and William Faulkner.

Washington Irving was born in 1783 and died in 1859.

Literature Online Author Search For more about Washington Irving, go to www.glencoe.com.

Connecting to the Story

In Irving's short story, the main character makes a fateful decision he later regrets. As you read the story, think about the following questions:

- Have you ever made a decision that you later regretted?
- Have you ever committed to do something and then changed your mind?

Building Background

"The Devil and Tom Walker" is one of the stories in Irving's popular collection, *Tales of a Traveler* (1824). The story takes place in New England in the 1720s—when Puritanism was fading and commercialism was on the rise. The story is an adaptation of the old German legend of Faust, a sixteenth-century astronomer who sold his soul to the devil. The most famous retelling of the Faust legend is a play written in the early 1800s by the German Romantic writer Johann Wolfgang von Goethe (yō′ hän vôlf′ gäng′ fôn gur′ tə).

Setting Purposes for Reading

Big Idea The Power of Darkness

As you read "The Devil and Tom Walker," notice how it reflects Romanticism's interest in exotic settings and supernatural events.

Literary Element Characterization

Characterization refers to the methods a writer uses to reveal the personality of a character. In **direct characterization** the writer makes explicit statements about a character. In **indirect characterization** the writer reveals a character through the character's words and actions and through what other characters think and say about that character. As you read, record details from the story about Tom Walker.

- See Literary Terms Handbook, p. R3.

Literature Online Interactive Literary Elements Handbook To review or learn more about the literary elements, go to www.glencoe.com.

Reading Strategy Making and Verifying Predictions

Predicting is making an educated guess about what will happen in a story. Predicting helps you anticipate events and appreciate less obvious parts of a story. To make predictions, combine clues the author provides with your own understanding of characters and events. Adjust or change your predictions as you continue to read and discover more clues.

··

Reading Tip: Predicting Ask yourself, "How do I think this situation will be resolved based on the clues I have discovered so far?" Write down your ideas. After reading, review your work to see whether your predictions were correct.

Vocabulary

prevalent (prev′ ə lent) *adj.* widespread; p. 230 *The flu was so prevalent that nearly everyone at school was sick.*

discord (dis′ kôrd) *n.* lack of agreement or harmony; conflict; p. 230 *There was noisy discord in the courtroom when the verdict was announced.*

melancholy (mel′ ən kol′ ē) *adj.* depressing; dismal; gloomy; p. 231 *The dark clouds put us in a melancholy mood.*

surmise (sər mīz′) *v.* to infer from little evidence; to guess; p. 233 *She surmised that the roses, which arrived unexpectedly, came from a secret admirer.*

speculate (spek′ yə lāt′) *v.* to engage in risky business ventures, hoping to make quick profits; p. 236 *He speculated by purchasing older houses for little money and then reselling them at high prices.*

··

Vocabulary Tip: Analogies Comparisons based on relationships between words are known as analogies. For example, in the analogy *weak : strong :: dark : light,* each pair of words is opposite in meaning. To complete an analogy, decide on the relationship represented by the first pair of words. Then apply that relationship to the second set of words.

INDIANA ACADEMIC STANDARDS (pages 229–241)

11.3 [Identify] story elements such as character...
11.2 Develop strategies such as...making predictions...

11.5.9 Write...an analytical essay...that...supports judgments with...well-chosen details...

The Devil and Tom Walker

Washington Irving

A few miles from Boston, in Massachusetts, there is a deep inlet, winding several miles into the interior of the country from Charles Bay, and terminating in a thickly wooded swamp or morass. On one side of this inlet is a beautiful dark grove; on the opposite side the land rises abruptly from the water's edge into a high ridge, on which grow a few scattered oaks of great age and immense size.

Under one of these gigantic trees, according to old stories, there was a great amount of treasure buried by Kidd the pirate. The inlet allowed a facility to bring the money in a boat, secretly and at night, to the very foot of the hill; the elevation of the place permitted a good lookout to be kept that no one was at hand; while the remarkable trees formed good landmarks by which the place might easily be found again. The old stories add, moreover, that the devil presided at the hiding of the money, and took it under his guardianship; but this, it is well known, he always does with buried treasure, particularly when it has been ill gotten. Be that as it may, Kidd never returned to recover his wealth, being shortly after seized at Boston, sent out to England, and there hanged for a pirate.

About the year 1727, just at the time that earthquakes were **prevalent** in New England and shook many tall sinners down upon their knees, there lived near this place a meager, miserly fellow, of the name of Tom Walker. He had a wife as miserly as himself; they were so miserly that they even conspired to cheat each other. Whatever the woman could lay hands on she hid away; a hen could not cackle but she was on the alert to secure the new laid egg. Her husband was continually prying about to detect her secret hoards, and many and fierce were the conflicts that took place about what ought to have been common property. They lived in a forlorn-looking house that stood alone and had an air of starvation. A few straggling savin trees, emblems of sterility, grew near it; no smoke ever curled from its chimney, no traveler stopped at its door. A miserable horse, whose ribs were as articulate as the bars of a gridiron, stalked about a field where a thin carpet of moss, scarcely covering the ragged beds of pudding stone,[1] tantalized and balked his hunger; and sometimes he would lean his head over the fence, look piteously at the passer-by, and seem to petition deliverance from this land of famine.

The house and its inmates had altogether a bad name. Tom's wife was a tall termagant,[2] fierce of temper, loud of tongue, and strong of arm. Her voice was often heard in wordy warfare with her husband, and his face sometimes showed signs that their conflicts were not confined to words. No one ventured, however, to interfere between them. The lonely wayfarer shrunk within himself at the horrid clamor and clapperclawing,[3] eyed the den of **discord** askance, and hurried on his way, rejoicing, if a bachelor, in his celibacy.

---

1. *Pudding stone* is a rock consisting of pebbles and gravel embedded in cement, like plums in a pudding.
2. A *termagant* is a quarrelsome, scolding woman.
3. *Clapperclawing* is scratching or clawing with the fingernails.

Literary Element Characterization *What does this detail tell you about Tom Walker and his wife?*

Vocabulary

prevalent (prev′ ə lent) *adj.* widespread

Vocabulary

discord (dis′ kôrd) *n.* lack of agreement or harmony; conflict

One day that Tom Walker had been to a distant part of the neighborhood, he took what he considered a short cut homeward, through the swamp. Like most short cuts it was an ill-chosen route. The swamp was thickly grown with great gloomy pines and hemlocks, some of them ninety feet high, which made it dark at noonday, and a retreat for all the owls of the neighborhood. It was full of pits and quagmires, partly covered with weeds and mosses, where the green surface often betrayed the traveler into a gulf of black, smothering mud; there were also dark and stagnant pools, the abodes of the tadpole, the bullfrog, and the water snake, where the trunks of pines and hemlocks lay half drowned, half rotting, looking like alligators sleeping in the mire.

Visual Vocabulary
A *bittern* is a marsh-dwelling wading bird with mottled brownish plumage and a deep, booming cry.

Tom had long been picking his way cautiously through this treacherous forest, stepping from tuft to tuft of rushes and roots, which afforded precarious footholds among deep sloughs, or pacing carefully, like a cat, along the prostrate[4] trunks of trees, startled now and then by the sudden screaming of the bittern or the quacking of a wild duck rising on the wing from some solitary pool. At length he arrived at a firm piece of ground, which ran out like a peninsula into the deep bosom of the swamp. It had been one of the strongholds of the Indians during their wars with the first colonists. Here they had thrown up a kind of fort, which they had looked upon as almost impregnable, and had used as a place of refuge for their squaws and children. Nothing remained of the old Indian fort but a few embankments, gradually sinking to the level of the surrounding earth, and already overgrown in part by oaks and other forest trees, the foliage of which formed a contrast to the dark pines and hemlocks of the swamp.

It was late in the dusk of evening when Tom Walker reached the old fort, and he paused there awhile to rest himself. Any one but he would have felt unwilling to linger in this lonely, **melancholy** place, for the common people had a bad opinion of it, from the stories handed down from the time of the Indian wars, when it was asserted that the savages held incantations[5] here, and made sacrifices to the evil spirit.

Tom Walker, however, was not a man to be troubled with any fears of the kind. He reposed himself for some time on the trunk of a fallen hemlock, listening to the boding cry of the tree toad, and delving with his walking staff into a mound of black mold at his feet. As he turned up the soil unconsciously, his staff struck against something hard. He raked it out of the vegetable mold, and lo! a cloven[6] skull, with an Indian tomahawk buried deep in it, lay before him. The rust on the weapon showed the time that had elapsed since this death blow had been given. It was a dreary memento of the fierce struggle that had taken place in this last foothold of the Indian warriors.

"Humph!" said Tom Walker, as he gave it a kick to shake the dirt from it.

"Let that skull alone!" said a gruff voice. Tom lifted up his eyes, and beheld a great black man seated directly opposite him on the stump of a tree. He was exceedingly surprised, having neither heard nor seen any one approach, and he was still more perplexed on observing, as well as the gathering gloom would permit, that the stranger was neither negro nor Indian. It is true he was dressed in a rude, half Indian garb,[7] and had a red belt or sash swathed round his body,

---

4. *Prostrate* means "lying down."

Reading Strategy Making and Verifying Predictions
How does this detail of the setting help you predict what might happen

Reading Strategy Making and Verifying Predictions
What purpose might this fort serve in the story? What clues lead you to this prediction?

5. *Incantations* are the recitations of verbal charms or spells to produce a magical effect.
6. *Cloven* means "split" or "divided."
7. *Garb* means "clothing" or "attire."

Big Idea The Power of Darkness *How does Irving's description reflect Romanticism's interest in exotic settings?*

Vocabulary

melancholy (mel´ ən kol´ē) *adj.* depressing; dismal; gloomy but his face was neither black nor copper color, but swarthy and dingy, and begrimed with soot, as if he had been accustomed to toil among fires and forges. He had a shock of coarse black hair, that stood out from his head in all directions, and bore an ax on his shoulder.

He scowled for a moment at Tom with a pair of great red eyes.

"What are you doing on my grounds?" said the black man, with a hoarse, growling voice.

"Your grounds!" said Tom with a sneer, "no more your grounds than mine; they belong to Deacon Peabody."

"Deacon Peabody be d——d," said the stranger, "as I flatter myself he will be if he does not look more to his own sins and less to those of his neighbors. Look yonder, and see how Deacon Peabody is faring."

Tom looked in the direction that the stranger pointed, and beheld one of the great trees, fair and flourishing without, but rotten at the core, and saw that it had been nearly hewn through, so that the first high wind was likely to blow it down. On the bark of the tree was scored the name of Deacon Peabody, an eminent man who had waxed[8] wealthy by driving shrewd bargains with the Indians. He now looked around, and found most of the tall trees marked with the name of some great man of the colony, and all more or less scored by the ax. The one on which he had been seated, and which had evidently just been hewn down, bore the name of Crowninshield, and he recollected a mighty rich man of that name, who made a vulgar display of wealth which it was whispered he had acquired by buccaneering.[9]

"He's just ready for burning!" said the black man, with a growl of triumph. "You see I am likely to have a good stock of firewood for winter."

"But what right have you," said Tom, "to cut down Deacon Peabody's timber?"

"The right of a prior claim," said the other. "This woodland belonged to me long before one of your white-faced race put foot upon the soil."

"And pray, who are you, if I may be so bold?" said Tom.

"Oh, I go by various names. I am the wild 'huntsman' in some countries, the 'black miner' in others. In this neighborhood I am known by the name of the 'black woodsman.' I am he to whom the red men consecrated this spot, and in honor of whom they now and then roasted a white man, by way of sweet-smelling sacrifice. Since the red men have been exterminated by you white savages, I amuse myself by presiding at the persecutions of Quakers and Anabaptists;[10] I am the great patron and prompter of slave dealers, and the grand master of the Salem witches."

"The upshot of all which is that, if I mistake not," said Tom sturdily, "you are he commonly called 'Old Scratch.'"[11]

"The same, at your service!" replied the black man, with a half civil nod.

Such was the opening of this interview, according to the old story, though it has almost too familiar an air to be credited. One would think that to meet with such a singular personage, in this wild, lonely place, would have shaken any man's nerves; but Tom was a hard-minded fellow, not easily daunted, and he had lived so long with a termagant wife that he did not even fear the devil.

It is said that after this commencement they had a long and earnest conversation together, as Tom returned homeward. The black man told him of great sums of money buried by Kidd the pirate under the oak trees on the high ridge, not far from the morass. All these were under his command, and protected by his power, so that none could find them but such as propitiated[12] his favor. These he offered to place within Tom Walker's reach, having conceived an especial kindness for him; but they were to be had only on certain conditions. What these conditions were may be easily **surmised,** though Tom never disclosed them publicly. They must have been very hard, for he required time to think of them, and he was not a man to stick at trifles when money was in view. When they had reached the edge of the swamp the stranger paused. "What proof have I that all you have been telling me is true?" said Tom. "There's my signature," said the black man, pressing his finger on Tom's forehead. So saying, he turned off among the thickets of the

---

8. Here, *waxed* means "grown" or "become."
9. *Buccaneering* is robbing ships at sea (piracy).
10. The *Quakers* and the *Anabaptists* were two religious groups in Massachusetts that were persecuted for their beliefs.
11. *Old Scratch* is a nickname for the devil.
12. *Propitiated* means "won over" or "gained by pleasing acts."

The Devil and Tom Walker, 1856. John Quidor. Oil on canvas. The Cleveland Museum of Art. Cleveland, OH.
Viewing the Art: Is this a faithful depiction of Tom Walker's encounter with the devil?

swamp, and seemed, as Tom said, to go down, down, down into the earth, until nothing but his head and shoulders could be seen, and so on, until he totally disappeared.

When Tom reached home he found the black print of a finger burned, as it were, into his forehead, which nothing could obliterate.

The first news his wife had to tell him was the sudden death of Absalom Crowninshield, the rich buccaneer. It was announced in the papers with the usual flourish, that a great man had fallen in Israel.[13]

Tom recollected the tree which his black friend had just hewn down, and which was ready for burning. "Let the freebooter[14] roast," said Tom; "who

cares!" He now felt convinced that all he had heard and seen was no illusion.

He was not prone to let his wife into his confidence, but as this was an uneasy secret he willingly shared it with her. All her avarice was awakened at the mention of hidden gold, and she urged her husband to comply with the black man's terms, and secure what would make them wealthy for life. However Tom might have felt disposed to sell himself to the devil, he was determined not to do so to oblige his wife, so he flatly refused, out of the mere spirit of contradiction. Many and bitter were the quarrels they had on the subject, but the more she

---

13. Here, *Israel* is a biblical reference to 2 Samuel 3:38: "Know ye not that there is a prince and a great man fallen this day in Israel?" The Puritans referred to New England as "Israel," their Promised Land.

14. A *freebooter* is a pirate.

Literary Element Characterization *What does the manner in which Tom speaks to Old Scratch reveal about Tom's character?*

Literary Element Characterization *How does Irving use the attitudes of Tom and his wife toward the devil to develop their characters? Is this direct or indirect characterization?*

Vocabulary

surmise (sər mīz′) *v.* to infer from little evidence; to guess

Swamp Sunset, c. 1850–1884. Harold Rudolph. Oil on canvas. The Ogden Museum of Southern Art, University of New Orleans.

Viewing the Art: What mood does this painting evoke? How would the mood be different if the scene had been depicted in broad daylight? How is the swamp scene in the painting similar to or different from the one where Tom Walker first met the devil?

---

talked the more resolute was Tom not to be damned to please her.

At length she determined to drive the bargain on her own account, and, if she succeeded, to keep all the gain to herself. Being of the same fearless temper as her husband, she set off for the old Indian fort towards the close of a summer's day. She was many hours absent. When she came back she was reserved and sullen in her replies. She spoke something of a black man whom she had met about twilight hewing at the root of a tall tree. He was sulky, however, and would not come to terms; she was to go again with a propitiatory offering, but what it was she forbore to say.

The next evening she set off again for the swamp, with her apron heavily laden. Tom waited and waited for her, but in vain; midnight came, but she did not make her appearance; morning, noon, night returned, but still she did not come. Tom now grew uneasy for her safety, especially as he found she had carried off in her apron the silver teapot and spoons and every portable article of value. Another

night elapsed, another morning came, but no wife. In a word, she was never heard of more.

What was her real fate nobody knows, in consequence of so many pretending to know. It is one of those facts which have become confounded by a variety of historians. Some asserted that she lost her way among the tangled mazes of the swamp, and sank into some pit or slough; others, more uncharitable, hinted that she had eloped with the household booty,[15] and made off to some other province; while others surmised that the tempter had decoyed her into a dismal quagmire, on the top of which her hat was found lying. In confirmation of this it was said a great black man, with an ax on his shoulder, was seen late that very evening coming out of the swamp, carrying a bundle tied in a check apron, with an air of surly triumph.

The most current and probable story, however, observes that Tom Walker grew so anxious about the fate of his wife and his property that he set out at length to seek them both at the Indian fort. During a long summer's afternoon

---

Reading Strategy Making and Verifying Predictions
What do you think has happened to Tom's wife?

---

15. *Booty* is stolen goods.

he searched about the gloomy place, but no wife was to be seen. He called her name repeatedly, but she was nowhere to be heard. The bittern alone responded to his voice, as he flew screaming by, or the bullfrog croaked dolefully from a neighboring pool. At length, it is said, just in the brown hour of twilight, when the owls began to hoot and the bats to flit about, his attention was attracted by the clamor of carrion crows[16] hovering about a cypress tree. He looked up, and beheld a bundle tied in a check apron and hanging in the branches of the tree, with a great vulture perched hard by, as if keeping watch upon it. He leaped with joy, for he recognized his wife's apron and supposed it to contain the household valuables.

"Let us get hold of the property," said he consolingly to himself, "and we will endeavor to do without the woman."

As he scrambled up the tree the vulture spread its wide wings and sailed off, screaming, into the deep shadows of the forest. Tom seized the check apron, but, woeful sight! found nothing but a heart and liver tied up in it!

Such, according to this most authentic old story, was all that was to be found of Tom's wife. She had probably attempted to deal with the black man as she had been accustomed to deal with her husband; but though a female scold is generally considered a match for the devil, yet in this instance she appears to have had the worst of it. She must have died game, however, for it is said Tom noticed many prints of cloven feet deeply stamped about the tree, and found handfuls of hair that looked as if they had been plucked from the coarse black shock of the woodman. Tom knew his wife's prowess by experience. He shrugged his shoulders as he looked at the signs of a fierce clapperclawing. "Egad," said he to himself, "Old Scratch must have had a tough time of it!"

Tom consoled himself for the loss of his property with the loss of his wife, for he was a man of fortitude. He even felt something like gratitude towards the black woodman, who, he considered, had done him a kindness. He sought, therefore, to cultivate a further acquaintance with him, but for some time without success; the old blacklegs played shy, for whatever people may think, he is not always to be had for calling for; he knows how to play his cards when pretty sure of his game.

At length, it is said, when delay had whetted Tom's eagerness to the quick, and prepared him to agree to anything rather than not gain the promised treasure, he met the black man one evening in his usual woodman's dress, with his ax on his shoulder, sauntering along the swamp, and humming a tune. He affected to receive Tom's advances with great indifference, made brief replies, and went on humming his tune.

By degrees, however, Tom brought him to business, and they began to haggle about the terms on which the former was to have the pirate's treasure. There was one condition which need not be mentioned, being generally understood in all cases where the devil grants favors; but there were others about which, though of less importance, he was inflexibly obstinate. He insisted that the money found through his means should be employed in his service. He proposed, therefore, that Tom should employ it in the black traffic,—that is to say, that he should fit out a slave ship. This, however, Tom resolutely refused; he was bad enough, in all conscience, but the devil himself could not tempt him to turn slave trader.

Finding Tom so squeamish on this point, he did not insist upon it, but proposed, instead, that he should turn usurer,[17] the devil being extremely anxious for the increase of usurers, looking upon them as his peculiar[18] people.

To this no objections were made, for it was just to Tom's taste.

"You shall open a broker's shop in Boston next month," said the black man.

---

16. *Carrion crows* are crows that feed on dead or decaying flesh.

Literary Element Characterization *Why does Irving use humor to describe the disappearance of Tom's wife? How does this reflect on Tom?*

17. A *usurer* is a person who lends money, especially at an excessive or unlawfully high rate of interest.
18. Here, *peculiar* means "special."

Reading Strategy Making and Verifying Predictions *What will be the outcome of this relationship?*

"I'll do it tomorrow, if you wish," said Tom Walker.

"You shall lend money at two percent a month."

"Egad, I'll charge four!" replied Tom Walker.

"You shall extort[19] bonds, foreclose mortgages, drive the merchants to bankruptcy—"

"I'll drive them to the d—l!" cried Tom Walker.

"You are the usurer for my money!" said blacklegs with delight. "When will you want the rhino?"[20]

"This very night."

"Done!" said the devil.

"Done!" said Tom Walker. So they shook hands and struck a bargain.

A few days' time saw Tom Walker seated behind his desk in a countinghouse in Boston.

His reputation for a ready-moneyed man, who would lend money out for a good consideration, soon spread abroad. Everybody remembers the time of Governor Belcher,[21] when money was particularly scarce. It was a time of paper credit. The country had been deluged with government bills; the famous Land Bank[22] had been established; there had been a rage for **speculating**; the people had run mad with schemes for new settlements, for building cities in the wilderness; land jobbers[23] went about with maps of grants and townships and Eldorados,[24] lying nobody knew where, but which everybody was ready to purchase. In a word, the great speculating fever which breaks out every now and then in the country had raged to an alarming degree, and everybody was dreaming of making sudden fortunes from nothing. As usual the fever had subsided, the dream had gone off, and the imaginary fortunes with it; the patients were left in doleful plight, and the whole country resounded with the consequent cry of "hard times."

> His reputation for a ready-moneyed man, who would lend money out for a good consideration, soon spread abroad.

At this propitious time of public distress did Tom Walker set up as usurer in Boston. His door was soon thronged by customers. The needy and adventurous, the gambling speculator, the dreaming land jobber, the thriftless tradesman, the merchant with cracked credit,— in short, everyone driven to raise money by desperate means and desperate sacrifices hurried to Tom Walker.

Thus Tom was the universal friend of the needy, and acted like a "friend in need"; that is to say, he always exacted good pay and good security. In proportion to the distress of the applicant was the hardness of his terms. He accumulated bonds and mortgages, gradually squeezed his customers closer and closer, and sent them at length, dry as a sponge, from his door.

In this way he made money hand over hand, became a rich and mighty man, and exalted his cocked hat upon 'Change.[25] He built himself, as usual, a vast house, out of ostentation,[26] but left the greater part of it unfinished and unfurnished, out of parsimony. He even set up a carriage in the fullness of his vainglory,[27] though he nearly starved the horses which drew it; and as the ungreased wheels

---

19. *Extort* means "to obtain by threats, force, or other types of oppression."
20. *Rhino* is a slang term for money.
21. Jonathan *Belcher* was governor of Massachusetts and New Hampshire from 1730 to 1741.
22. Boston merchants organized the *Land Bank* in 1739. Landowners could borrow money in the form of mortgages on their property and then repay the loans with cash or manufactured goods. When the bank was outlawed in 1741, many colonists lost money.
23. *Land jobbers* are people who buy and sell land for profit.
24. *Eldorados* are places of great wealth or opportunity. The term comes from the name El Dorado, a legendary region of South America sought by Spanish explorers for its gold and jewels.

---

25. The *'Change*, or Exchange, was a financial center where merchants, bankers, and brokers met to do business.
26. *Ostentation* means "a display meant to impress others."
27. *Vainglory* is boastful, undeserved pride in one's accomplishments or qualities.

Tom Walker's Flight, 1856. John Quidor. Oil on canvas. The Fine Arts Museum of San Francisco.
Viewing the Art: In what ways does this painting reflect the fantastic nature of Irving's story?

groaned and screeched on the axletrees you would have thought you heard the souls of the poor debtors he was squeezing.

As Tom waxed old, however, he grew thoughtful. Having secured the good things of this world, he began to feel anxious about those of the next. He thought with regret on the bargain he had made with his black friend, and set his wits to work to cheat him out of the conditions. He became, therefore, all of a sudden, a violent churchgoer. He prayed loudly and strenuously, as if heaven were to be taken by force of lungs. Indeed, one might always tell when he had sinned most during the week by the clamor of his Sunday devotion. The quiet Christians who had been modestly and steadfastly

traveling Zionward,[28] were struck with self-reproach at seeing themselves so suddenly outstripped in their career by this new-made convert. Tom was as rigid in religious, as in money, matters; he was a stern supervisor and censurer of his neighbors, and seemed to think every sin entered up to their account became a credit on his own side of the page. He even talked of the expediency of reviving the persecution of Quakers and Anabaptists. In a word, Tom's zeal became as notorious as his riches.

Still, in spite of all this strenuous attention to forms, Tom had a lurking dread that the devil, after all, would have his due. That he might not be taken unawares, therefore, it is said he always carried a small Bible in his coat pocket. He had also a great folio Bible on his countinghouse desk, and would frequently be found reading it when people called

Reading Strategy Making and Verifying Predictions
Do you think Tom will succeed in cheating the devil?

Literary Element Characterization *How does this statement develop Tom's character?*

28. *Zionward* means "toward heaven."

Big Idea The Power of Darkness *What is the effect of including details of the thunderstorm?*

on business. On such occasions he would lay his green spectacles in the book, to mark the place, while he turned round to drive some usurious bargain.

Some say that Tom grew a little crack-brained in his old days, and that, fancying his end approaching, he had his horse new shod, saddled, and bridled, and buried with his feet uppermost, because he supposed that at the last day the world would be turned upside down, in which case he should find his horse standing ready for mounting, and he was determined at the worst to give his old friend a run for it. This, however, is probably a mere old wives' fable. If he really did take such a precaution it was totally superfluous; at least, so says the authentic old legend, which closes his story in the following manner.

One hot summer afternoon in the dog days,[29] just as a terrible, black thunder gust was coming up, Tom sat in his counting-house, in his white linen cap and India silk morning gown. He was on the point of foreclosing a mortgage, by which he would complete the ruin of an unlucky land speculator for whom he had professed the greatest friendship. The poor land jobber begged him to grant a few months' indulgence. Tom had grown testy and irritated, and refused another day.

"My family will be ruined and brought upon the parish," said the land jobber.

"Charity begins at home," replied Tom; "I must take care of myself in these hard times."

"You have made so much money out of me," said the speculator.

Tom lost his patience and his piety. "The devil take me," said he, "if I have made a farthing."[30]

Just then there were three loud knocks at the street door. He stepped out to see who was there. A black man was holding a black horse, which neighed and stamped with impatience.

"Tom, you're come for," said the black fellow gruffly. Tom shrank back, but too late. He had left his little Bible at the bottom of his coat pocket, and his big Bible on the desk buried under the mortgage he was about to foreclose; never was sinner taken more unawares. The black man whisked him like a child into the saddle, gave the horse a lash, and away he galloped, with Tom on his back, in the midst of the thunderstorm. The clerks stuck their pens behind their ears, and stared after him from the windows. Away went Tom Walker, dashing down the streets, his white cap bobbing up and down, his morning gown fluttering in the wind, and his steed striking fire out of the pavement at every bound. When the clerks turned to look for the black man he had disappeared.

Tom Walker never returned to foreclose the mortgage. A countryman, who lived on the border of the swamp, reported that in the height of the thunder gust he had heard a great clattering of hoofs and a howling along the road, and running to the window caught sight of a figure such as I have described, on a horse that galloped like mad across the fields, over the hills, and down into the black hemlock swamp towards the old Indian fort, and that shortly after, a thunderbolt falling in that direction seemed to set the whole forest in a blaze.

The good people of Boston shook their heads and shrugged their shoulders, but had been so much accustomed to witches and goblins, and tricks of the devil, in all kinds of shapes, from the first settlement of the colony, that they were not so much horror-struck as might have been expected. Trustees were appointed to take charge of Tom's effects. There was nothing, however, to administer upon. On searching his coffers,[31] all his bonds and mortgages were found reduced to cinders. In place of gold and silver his iron chest was filled with chips and shavings; two skeletons lay in his stable instead of his half starved horses; and the very next day his great house took fire and was burned to the ground.

Such was the end of Tom Walker and his ill-gotten wealth. Let all griping money brokers lay this story to heart. The truth of it is not to be doubted. The very hole under the oak trees, whence he dug Kidd's money, is to be seen to this day, and the neighboring swamp and old Indian fort are often haunted in stormy nights by a figure on horseback, in morning gown and white cap, which is doubtless the troubled spirit of the usurer. In fact, the story has resolved itself into a proverb, and is the origin of that popular saying, so prevalent throughout New England, of "the devil and Tom Walker." ∽

---

31. *Coffers* are strongboxes used to hold money or other valuables.

Big Idea The Power of Darkness *Why do you think Irving adds this detail?*

---

29. *Dog days* are the hot, sultry days of summer.
30. A *farthing* was a British coin worth one-fourth of a penny.

RESPONDING AND THINKING CRITICALLY

Respond

1. (a)What was your reaction to Tom Walker at the beginning of the story? (b)Did your opinion of him change by the end?

Recall and Interpret

2. (a)How does Tom react to the devil and his offer? (b)What does this tell you about Tom?

3. (a)What kind of person is Tom's wife? (b)How does she contribute to Tom's agreement with the devil?

4. (a)What eventually happens to Tom's wife? (b)Which version of what happened to her does the narrator want the readers to believe? Explain.

5. (a)What finally happens to Tom Walker? (b)How do you interpret what happens to his possessions?

Analyze and Evaluate

6. (a)The narrator often uses disclaimers by saying "people said" or "it is said." Why might Irving have used this tactic? (b)How trustworthy does the narrator appear to be?

7. What can you infer about the narrator's attitude toward money and human greed?

8. **Satire** is a form of writing that uses humor as a way of criticizing someone or something. (a)In what ways is this story a satire? (b)Do you agree with Irving's implied criticisms?

Connect

9. **Big Idea** **The Power of Darkness** Irving wrote "The Devil and Tom Walker" when Puritanism was fading and the urge to acquire wealth was growing. How does Irving portray the dark side of both religion and wealth in his story?

YOU'RE THE CRITIC: Different Viewpoints

HOW CREATIVE WAS IRVING?

Some of Washington Irving's most famous stories, such as "Rip Van Winkle" and "The Devil and Tom Walker," are adaptations of European folktales. As a result, some critics have faulted Irving for a lack of originality, creativity, and imagination.

Read the two excerpts of literary criticism on Irving from novelist and essayist Charles Dudley Warner and critic and biographer Edward Wagenknecht. As you read the two excerpts, ask yourself how you would define creativity and whether Irving displayed creativity in "The Devil and Tom Walker."

"It has been said that Irving lacked imagination. . . . Now, it seems to me that the transmutation of the crude and heretofore unpoetical materials which he found in the New World into what is as absolute a creation as exists in literature, was a distinct work of the imagination."
—Charles Dudley Warner

"[In 'The Devil and Tom Walker,'] Irving began with the legends of Captain Kidd and his buried treasure and . . . he grafted upon this material a much wider variety of motifs drawn from German folklore. . . . The devil himself, for example, is a compound of German, American Indian, and Puritan elements."
—Edward Wagenknecht

Group Activity

Discuss the following questions with your classmates. Refer to the two passages above and cite evidence from "The Devil and Tom Walker" to support your answers.

1. How does Washington Irving show imagination in "The Devil and Tom Walker"?

2. How important do you think it is for a writer to be completely original in creating a literary work? How can a writer be creative in using existing sources?

Literary Element Characterization

In "The Devil and Tom Walker," Irving uses either direct or indirect characterization at different points in the story. Through these methods of characterization, he creates dramatic effects, generates humor, and foreshadows future events.

1. Identify examples of both indirect and direct characterization used in "The Devil and Tom Walker." Record these details in a chart like the one shown below. Why do you think Irving chose each method in each instance?

Tom Walker	
Direct Characterization	Indirect Characterization
p. 230 "...a meager, miserly fellow"	p. 235 "He leaped with joy, for he recognized his wife's apron and supposed it to contain the household valuables."

2. If characters are tools used by the author to develop a story, in what ways did Irving use the narrator? Tom's wife? Tom?

Review: Archetype

As you learned in Unit One, an **archetype** is a character type, a setting, an image, or a story pattern that occurs frequently in literature across many cultures and evokes strong emotional responses. For example, heroes like Luke Skywalker are archetypal figures, as are evil-hearted villains like Darth Vader. What archetypes does Irving use in "The Devil and Tom Walker"? Why do you think he chose to use them?

Reading Strategy Making and Verifying Predictions

Making Predictions About Plot An inference involves using reasoning and experience to come up with an idea based on what a writer implies or suggests but does not directly state. A **prediction** is a type of inference, one that involves making an educated guess about what will happen in a story.

1. How did you use your own experiences and reasoning to predict the outcome of the story? Was the outcome of the story different from your original prediction? Explain.

2. List details in "The Devil and Tom Walker" that Irving uses to **foreshadow** later events in the story.

Vocabulary Practice

Practice with Analogies Choose the word that best completes each analogy.

1. prevalent : common :: continual :
   a. low   **b.** nonstop   **c.** fast

2. war : discord :: famine :
   a. abundance   **b.** scarcity   **c.** happiness

3. surmise : evidence :: prove :
   a. facts   **b.** ideas   **c.** questions

4. preserve : save :: speculate :
   a. predict   **b.** rebuild   **c.** gamble

Academic Vocabulary

Here are two vocabulary words from the vocabulary list on page R86. These words will help you think, write, and talk about the selection.

commission (kə mish′ ən) *n.* an authorization or command to act in a certain manner or to perform certain acts

benefit (ben′ ə fit) *n.* a positive gain resulting from some other action

Practice and Apply
1. What **commission** does the devil give Tom Walker when he receives Kidd's treasure?
2. What **benefit** does the devil gain from his pact with Tom Walker?

Writing About Literature

Analyze Character A character sketch is a profile that reveals personality and physical appearance. Write a brief character sketch of Tom Walker, using details from the story to support your depiction of him.

To create a vivid character sketch, you should

- decide on the overall impression you want to convey

- include details showing the person's behavior, appearance, and personality—for these details, review the chart you completed for the Literary Element activity on page 240

- describe possessions or other objects that reveal character

As you draft, follow the writing model shown here to help you organize your character sketch.

START

Introduction ···▶ State your impression of Tom Walker.

Body Paragraph(s) ···▶ Write several paragraphs that provide details to support your impression.

Conclusion ···▶ Provide a final insight about the character.

FINISH

After you complete your draft, meet with a peer reviewer to evaluate each other's work and to suggest revisions. Then proofread and edit your draft for errors in spelling, grammar, and punctuation.

Literature Online Web Activities For eFlashcards, Selection Quick Checks, and other Web activities, go to www.glencoe.com.

Irving's Language and Style

Choosing the Right Word In "The Devil and Tom Walker," Irving creates an eerie atmosphere by using precise nouns that require no modifiers and nouns that are modified by colorful adjectives. Consider, for example, how much less effective his description of the swamp might be without these descriptive details:

> "It was full of pits and quagmires, partly covered with weeds and mosses, where the green surface often betrayed the traveler into a gulf of black, smothering mud; there were also dark and stagnant pools, the abodes of the tadpole, the bullfrog, and the water snake, where the trunks of pines and hemlocks lay half drowned, half rotting, looking like alligators sleeping in the mire."

Notice some of Irving's most effective word choices:

Descriptive Word	Part of Speech
quagmires	noun
smothering	adjective
stagnant	adjective
rotting	adjective
mire	noun

Activity Create a chart of your own, listing more descriptive details from the passage above. For each of Irving's strong nouns, try to substitute a noun modified by an adjective. For each modified noun, try to substitute a noun specific enough not to need a modifier.

Revising Check

The Right Word Diction, or word choice, is important to consider when revising your own writing. With a partner, go through your character sketch of Tom Walker and note places where more precise nouns and adjectives would make your sketch clearer and more vivid. Revise your draft to improve diction. Use a thesaurus if you need to.

The Raven and The Pit and the Pendulum

MEET EDGAR ALLAN POE

Today's authors might well envy Edgar Allan Poe. More than 150 years after his death, he is still one of the world's most popular writers and continues to captivate a wide audience. Known primarily as a master of horror and suspense tales, he is also credited with inventing the detective story and contributing to the development of science fiction. Despite his talent, Poe led a troubled life marked by poverty, restlessness, and loneliness.

"They who dream by day are cognizant of many things which escape those who dream only by night."

—Edgar Allan Poe, from "Eleonora"

Poe's Early Life Poe was born in Boston, the son of traveling actors. His father abandoned the family when Poe was an infant, and his mother died a year later. John and Frances Allan, a wealthy couple from Richmond, Virginia, became his foster parents. Though Poe got along well with his foster mother, he and John Allan frequently quarreled. Allan refused to pay for Poe's education at the University of Virginia because of his heavy gambling debts and wild life. Later, when Poe was expelled from West Point for deliberately breaking rules, his relationship with his foster father abruptly ended.

Penniless, Poe moved to Baltimore, where he lived with his aunt and her daughter, Virginia Clemm. He had already published three volumes of poems and now began to write short stories. In 1835 he returned to Richmond, where he edited the *Southern Literary Messenger* and married his cousin Virginia.

Poe's World During Poe's lifetime, the literary world in the United States was centered in Boston, New York, and Philadelphia. Poe contributed stories and poems to an assortment of journals in these cities.

Still, he spent much of his life struggling—moving from city to city, from job to job. He was unable to escape his spirit-breaking poverty.

In 1847, just as Poe seemed to be gaining recognition for his writing, his world collapsed. His wife died at the age of twenty-four, and Poe plunged into a sorrow too deep to bear. Two years after his wife's death, Poe was found delirious on the streets of Baltimore and died shortly thereafter, completely alone.

Poe's Influence Nineteenth-century French poets such as Charles Baudelaire greatly admired Poe for his use of symbolism in his poetry. To the Irish poet W. B. Yeats, Poe was "certainly the greatest of American poets." Poe's story "The Unparalleled Adventures of One Hans Pfaal" influenced Jules Verne and other science-fiction writers. Fictional detectives such as Sherlock Holmes, Hercule Poirot, and many others are modeled after C. Auguste Dupin, the detective Poe introduced in "The Murders in the Rue Morgue." Modern writers of horror influenced by Poe include Richard Matheson, Anne Rice, and Stephen King.

The Mystery Writers of America (MWA) annually confers the Edgar Allan Poe Awards® to recognize outstanding achievement in the mystery genre. The award is a statuette of Poe. But perhaps the strongest proof of Poe's enduring popularity is the name of the National Football League team in Baltimore—the Ravens.

Edgar Allan Poe was born in 1809 and died in 1849.

Literature Online Author Search For more about Edgar Allan Poe, go to www.glencoe.com.

Connecting to the Poem

Have you ever enjoyed a song, movie, or story that dealt with extremes of emotion? Perhaps it was a sad song about lost love, a suspenseful film of high adventure, or a chilling tale that riveted you to the edge of your seat.

- Why do you think stories involving extremes of emotion are popular?
- What types of settings in stories or movies can produce extremes of emotion?

Building Background

"The Raven" was first published in 1845 in the *Evening Mirror,* a New York newspaper. In commenting on this work, Poe wrote that he set out to create a poem with a melancholy effect and that *nevermore* was the first word that came into his mind, both for its sound and for its meaning. The subject of the poem, he decided, would be the death of a beautiful woman, "unquestionably, the most poetical topic in the world." His first thought was to have *nevermore* repeated by a parrot, but he decided that a raven was "equally capable of speech, and infinitely more in keeping with the intended tone."

Setting Purposes for Reading

Big Idea The Power of Darkness

As you read, notice how the Romantics' fascination with madness and death is displayed in "The Raven."

Literary Element Narrative Poem

A **narrative poem** is a poem that tells a story. Although the story is told in lines and stanzas—and may include figurative language, imagery, rhythm, and rhyme—narrative poetry also includes elements of storytelling such as setting, characters, and plot. As you read "The Raven," notice these elements of fiction.

- See Literary Terms Handbook, p. R12.

Literature Online Interactive Literary Elements Handbook To review or learn more about the literary elements, go to www.glencoe.com.

Reading Strategy Analyzing Sound Devices

Poets take advantage of words' sounds as well as their meanings. Two common sound devices are the repetition of words and **alliteration,** the repetition of consonant sounds at the beginnings of words. For example, Poe uses alliteration to create an almost hypnotic effect in phrases like "weak and weary." As you read, look for examples of these sound devices.

Reading Tip: Taking Notes On a chart, list examples of repetition and alliteration and describe their effects.

Sound Devices	Examples	Effects
alliteration	"nodded, nearly napping"	

Vocabulary

lattice (laʹtəs) *n.* a structure of crisscrossed strips, commonly wood or metal, that forms a pattern of openings; p. 246 *The neighbor's dog tried to push its nose through the fence lattice between our yards.*

beguile (bi gīlʹ) *v.* to influence by deceit; to trick; p. 246 *The amateur magician's tricks beguiled only the children in the audience.*

placid (plaʹsəd) *adj.* calm; peaceful; undisturbed; p. 247 *The surface of the placid lake reflected the few clouds in the sky.*

respite (resʹpət) *n.* a period of rest or relief, as from work or sorrow; p. 247 *The students all looked forward to the respite of summer vacation.*

balm (bäm) *n.* something that heals or soothes, as an ointment; p. 248 *The aloe gel worked as a balm, cooling my painful sunburn.*

INDIANA ACADEMIC STANDARDS (pages 243–249)
11.2 Develop strategies such as...analyzing structure...
11.3.3 Analyze the ways in which...the "sound" of language achieve[s] specific...aesthetic (artistic) purposes...
11.7.20 Recite poems...with attention to performance details...to demonstrate an understanding of the meaning...

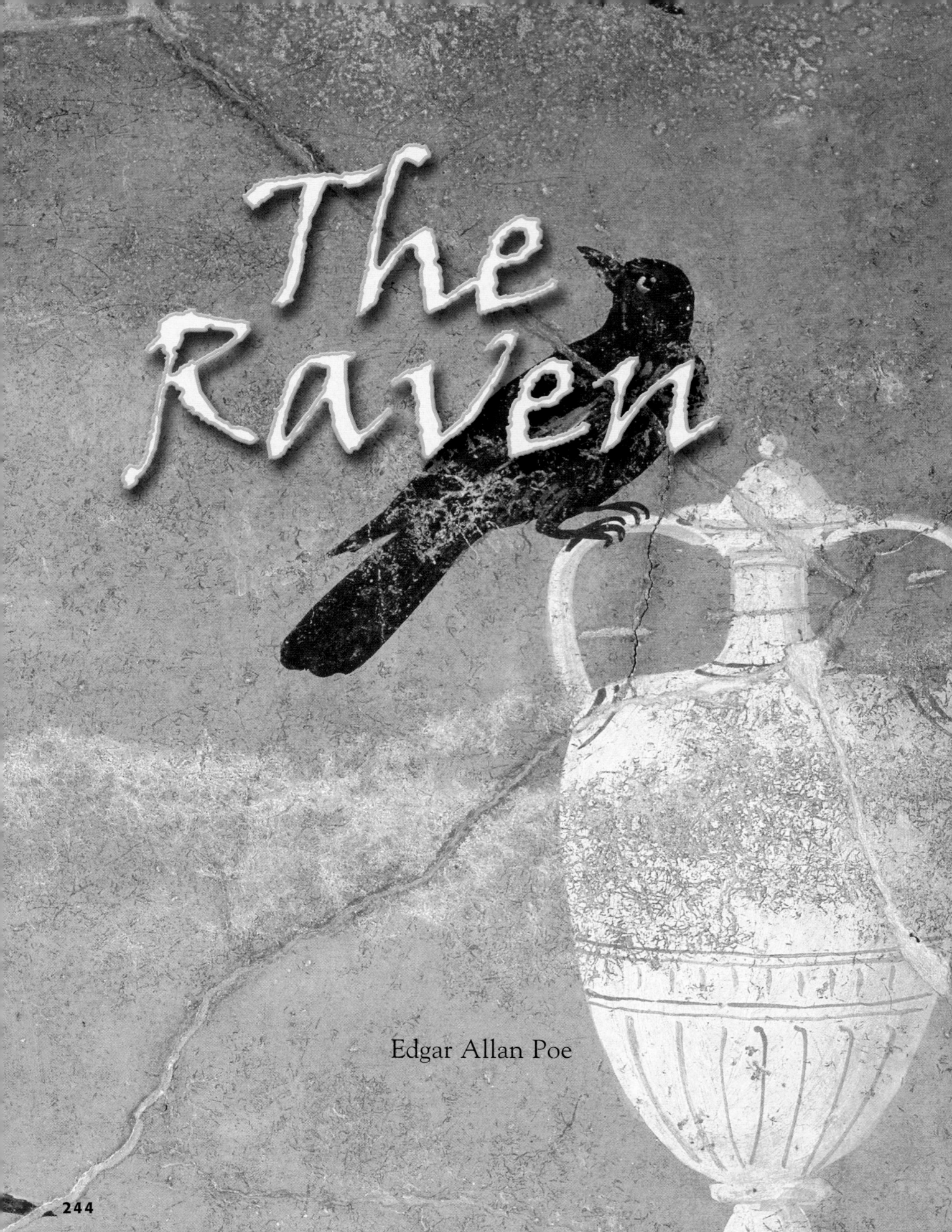

The Raven

Edgar Allan Poe

Once upon a midnight dreary, while I pondered, weak and weary,
Over many a quaint and curious volume of forgotten lore—
While I nodded, nearly napping, suddenly there came a tapping,
As of someone gently rapping, rapping at my chamber[1] door.
5   "'Tis some visitor," I muttered, "tapping at my chamber door—
        Only this and nothing more."

Ah, distinctly I remember it was in the bleak December;
And each separate dying ember wrought its ghost upon the floor.
Eagerly I wished the morrow;—vainly I had sought to borrow
10 From my books surcease[2] of sorrow—sorrow for the lost Lenore—
For the rare and radiant maiden whom the angels name Lenore—
        Nameless *here* for evermore.

And the silken, sad, uncertain rustling of each purple curtain
Thrilled me—filled me with fantastic terrors never felt before;
15 So that now, to still the beating of my heart, I stood repeating
"'Tis some visitor entreating entrance at my chamber door—
Some late visitor entreating entrance at my chamber door;—
        This it is and nothing more."

Presently my soul grew stronger; hesitating then no longer,
20 "Sir," said I, "or Madam, truly your forgiveness I implore;
But the fact is I was napping, and so gently you came rapping,
And so faintly you came tapping, tapping at my chamber door,
That I scarce was sure I heard you"—here I opened wide the door;—
        Darkness there and nothing more.

25 Deep into that darkness peering, long I stood there wondering, fearing,
Doubting, dreaming dreams no mortal ever dared to dream before;
But the silence was unbroken, and the stillness gave no token,
And the only word there spoken was the whispered word, "Lenore!"
This I whispered, and an echo murmured back the word, "Lenore!"
30   Merely this and nothing more.

---

1. A *chamber* is a room.
2. *Surcease* means "an end."

Literary Element   Narrative Poem *What element of storytelling is established in these lines?*

Reading Strategy   Analyzing Sound Devices *Why might Poe have used alliteration in this line?*

Back into the chamber turning, all my soul within me burning,
Soon again I heard a tapping somewhat louder than before.
"Surely," said I, "surely that is something at my window **lattice;**
Let me see, then, what thereat is, and this mystery explore—
35   Let my heart be still a moment and this mystery explore;—
        'Tis the wind and nothing more!"

Open here I flung the shutter, when, with many a flirt and flutter
In there stepped a stately Raven of the saintly days of yore.[3]
Not the least obeisance[4] made he; not a minute stopped or stayed he;
40   But, with mien of lord or lady, perched above my chamber door—
Perched upon a bust of Pallas[5] just above my chamber door—
        Perched, and sat, and nothing more.

Then this ebony bird **beguiling** my sad fancy into smiling,
By the grave and stern decorum of the countenance[6] it wore,
45   "Though thy crest be shorn and shaven, thou," I said, "art sure no craven,
Ghastly grim and ancient Raven wandering from the Nightly shore—
Tell me what thy lordly name is on the Night's Plutonian[7] shore!"
        Quoth the Raven "Nevermore."

Much I marveled this ungainly fowl to hear discourse so plainly,
50   Though its answer little meaning—little relevancy bore;
For we cannot help agreeing that no living human being
Ever yet was blessed with seeing bird above his chamber door—
Bird or beast upon the sculptured bust above his chamber door,
        With such name as "Nevermore."

---

3. *Days of yore* means "days of long ago." Here Poe is referring to a Bible story in
    which ravens feed the Hebrew prophet Elijah during a sojourn in the wilderness.
    (1 Kings 17:1–7)
4. *Obeisance* means "a movement or gesture, such as a bow, that expresses respect."
5. A *bust* is a statue of someone's head and shoulders. *Pallas* refers to Pallas Athena,
    the Greek goddess of wisdom.
6. Here, *countenance* means "facial expression."
7. *Plutonian* refers to Pluto, the Roman god of the dead and ruler of the underworld.

Reading Strategy Analyzing Sound Devices *What effect does Poe create by
repeating the description "above my chamber door"?*

Big Idea The Power of Darkness *How does this bit of dialogue reflect the
dark side of Romanticism?*

Vocabulary

lattice (laʹtəs) *n.* a structure of crisscrossed strips, commonly wood or metal,
that forms a pattern of openings
beguile (bi gīlʹ) *v.* to influence by deceit; to trick

55　But the Raven, sitting lonely on the **placid** bust, spoke only
　　That one word, as if his soul in that one word he did outpour.
　　Nothing farther then he uttered—not a feather then he fluttered—
　　Till I scarcely more than muttered "Other friends have flown before—
　　On the morrow *he* will leave me, as my Hopes have flown before."
60　　　　　Then the bird said "Nevermore."

　　Startled at the stillness broken by reply so aptly spoken,
　　"Doubtless," said I, "what it utters is its only stock and store
　　Caught from some unhappy master whom unmerciful Disaster
　　Followed fast and followed faster till his songs one burden bore—
65　Till the dirges[8] of his Hope that melancholy burden bore
　　　　　Of 'Never—nevermore.'"

　　But the Raven still beguiling all my fancy into smiling,
　　Straight I wheeled a cushioned seat in front of bird, and bust and door;
　　Then, upon the velvet sinking, I betook myself to linking
70　Fancy unto fancy, thinking what this ominous bird of yore—
　　What this grim, ungainly, ghastly, gaunt, and ominous bird of yore
　　　　　Meant in croaking "Nevermore."

　　This I sat engaged in guessing, but no syllable expressing
　　To the fowl whose fiery eyes now burned into my bosom's core;
75　This and more I sat divining,[9] with my head at ease reclining
　　On the cushion's velvet lining that the lamplight gloated o'er,
　　But whose velvet violet lining with the lamplight gloating o'er,
　　　　　She shall press, ah, nevermore!

　　Then, methought, the air grew denser, perfumed from an unseen censer[10]
80　Swung by Seraphim[11] whose foot-falls tinkled on the tufted floor.
　　"Wretch," I cried, "thy God hath lent thee—by these angels he hath sent thee
　　Respite—**respite** and nepenthe[12] from thy memories of Lenore;
　　Quaff,[13] oh quaff this kind nepenthe and forget this lost Lenore!"
　　　　　Quoth the Raven "Nevermore."

---

8. *Dirges* are slow, mournful pieces of music, such as funeral hymns.
9. *Divining* means "knowing through insight or intuition" or "guessing."
10. A *censer* is a container in which incense is burned.
11. *Seraphim* are angels of the highest rank.
12. The ancient Greeks believed the drug *nepenthe* (ni pen′ thē) would ease pain and grief by causing forgetfulness.
13. *Quaff* means "to drink heartily and deeply."

Reading Strategy　Analyzing Sound Devices　*How is this repetition of the word* nevermore *different than others in the poem, and what is the significance of that difference?*

Vocabulary

placid (pla′ səd) *adj.* calm; peaceful; undisturbed
respite (res′ pət) *n.* a period of rest or relief, as from work or sorrow

85 "Prophet!" said I, "thing of evil!—prophet still, if bird or devil!—
    Whether Tempter[14] sent, or whether tempest tossed thee here ashore,
    Desolate yet all undaunted, on this desert land enchanted—
    On this home by Horror haunted—tell me truly, I implore—
    Is there—*is* there **balm** in Gilead?[15]—tell me—tell me, I implore!"
90   Quoth the Raven "Nevermore."

    "Prophet!" said I, "thing of evil!—prophet still, if bird or devil!
    By that Heaven that bends above us—by that God we both adore—
    Tell this soul with sorrow laden if, within the distant Aidenn,[16]
    It shall clasp a sainted maiden whom the angels name Lenore—
95 Clasp a rare and radiant maiden whom the angels name Lenore."
          Quoth the Raven "Nevermore."

    "Be that word our sign of parting, bird or fiend!" I shrieked, upstarting—
    "Get thee back into the tempest and the Night's Plutonian shore!
    Leave no black plume as a token of that lie thy soul hath spoken!
100 Leave my loneliness unbroken!—quit the bust above my door!
    Take thy beak from out my heart, and take thy form from off my door!"
          Quoth the Raven "Nevermore."

    And the Raven, never flitting, still is sitting, *still* is sitting
    On the pallid[17] bust of Pallas just above my chamber door;
105 And his eyes have all the seeming of a demon's that is dreaming,
    And the lamp-light o'er him streaming throws his shadow on the floor;
    And my soul from out that shadow that lies floating on the floor
          Shall be lifted—nevermore!

---

14. *Tempter* refers to the devil.
15. *Gilead* was a region in ancient Palestine. Here Poe uses a phrase from the Bible (Jeremiah 8:22):
    "Is there no balm in Gilead?" By this he means, "Is there no relief from my suffering?"
16. *Aidenn* means "Eden."
17. *Pallid* means "lacking in color" or "pale."

Reading Strategy Analyzing Sound Devices *What is the effect of the repetition in this line?*

Literary Element Narrative Poem *How is the end of this poem similar to the end of a short story?*

Vocabulary

balm (bäm) *n.* something that heals or soothes, as an ointment

RESPONDING AND THINKING CRITICALLY

Respond

1. In your opinion, what is the most haunting image in this poem?

Recall and Interpret

2. (a)Why is the speaker reading at the beginning of the poem? (b)How would you describe his emotional state in the first six stanzas?

3. (a)What is the speaker's first reaction to the raven's entrance? (b)Why does he react this way?

4. (a)What will never be lifted from the raven's shadow? (b)What does the future probably hold for the speaker?

Analyze and Evaluate

5. (a)What is the effect of the repetition of the raven's single word, *nevermore*? (b)Is the word appropriate in the context of the poem, or would some other word have been as effective?

6. (a)How would you describe Poe's purpose in writing this poem? (b)Did he achieve his purpose? Explain.

Connect

7. **Big Idea** **The Power of Darkness** Which details contribute to the mood of this poem, and how do they illustrate the dark side of Romanticism?

LITERARY ANALYSIS

Literary Element Narrative Poem

Like short stories, narrative poems include a narrator, or speaker. The speaker may take part in the story or retell a tale that he or she has heard.

1. Who is the "I" in "The Raven"?

2. What words would you use to describe this speaker?

Performing

Dramatic Reading Work with a classmate to deliver a dramatic reading of "The Raven." One reader should deliver the narrator's words that are set off in quotation marks; the other should read all the other lines.

- Vary your facial expressions, the pace of your reading, and the tone and volume of your voice to reflect the narrator's mounting anxiety.
- One reader might provide background sounds, such as an intermittent tapping during the first six stanzas.

Literature Online **Web Activities** For eFlashcards, Selection Quick Checks, and other Web activities, go to www.glencoe.com.

READING AND VOCABULARY

Reading Strategy Analyzing Sound Devices

The music of Poe's verses derives from his use of sound devices, most of which are kinds of repetition.

1. What is the effect of the repetition of the word *tapping*?

2. The words *grim, ungainly, ghastly,* and *gaunt* describe the raven. How do these words contribute to the meaning of the poem?

Vocabulary Practice

Practice with Synonyms Choose the best synonym for each vocabulary word.

1. lattice
  a. border   **c.** mesh
  b. barrier   **d.** block

2. beguile
  a. charm   **c.** candor
  b. repel   **d.** evade

3. placid
  a. tempestuous **c.** chaotic
  b. blustery   **d.** serene

4. respite
  a. persistence **c.** hesitation
  b. lull   **d.** turmoil

LITERATURE PREVIEW

Connecting to the Story

Think about a moment when you felt terrified. What thoughts crossed your mind? How did you feel? In "The Pit and the Pendulum," you will read about a prisoner's terrifying experience inside an underground dungeon. Consider the following questions:

- What sorts of things scare people the most?
- What happens when someone is overcome by fear?

Building Background

This story is set during the last years of the Spanish Inquisition (1478–1834). Established in 1231 by the Roman Catholic Church, the Inquisition was a court that arrested and tried suspected heretics, or those who opposed Church teaching. Those convicted of heresy were imprisoned for life or sentenced to death. Pope Innocent IV authorized the use of torture to obtain confessions to heresy in 1252, and Pope Sixtus IV authorized the Spanish Inquisition in 1478. Spanish inquisitors, or judges, were especially harsh. None was more feared than Tomás de Torquemada, named the grand inquisitor for Castile in 1483. He was responsible for approximately two thousand burnings at the stake. Today, the Inquisition is remembered as a period of mercilessness and brutality.

Setting Purposes for Reading

Big Idea The Power of Darkness

As you read, note how darkness and terror, both aspects of Romanticism, are portrayed in "The Pit and the Pendulum."

Literary Element Suspense

Suspense is a feeling of curiosity, uncertainty, or even dread about what is going to happen next. Writers heighten the suspense in a story by creating a threat to the central character, or protagonist, and giving readers clues about what might happen. As you read this story, examine how Poe creates suspense.

- See Literary Terms Handbook, p. R18.

Literature Online **Interactive Literary Elements Handbook** To review or learn more about the literary elements, go to www.glencoe.com.

READING PREVIEW

Reading Strategy Identifying Sequence

Sequence is the logical order of ideas or events. To indicate time order, writers often use signal words or phrases, such as *before, earlier that morning,* or *after that.* As you read Poe's story, look for signal words that indicate the sequence of events.

Reading Tip: Taking Notes Use a chart to record the sequence of events.

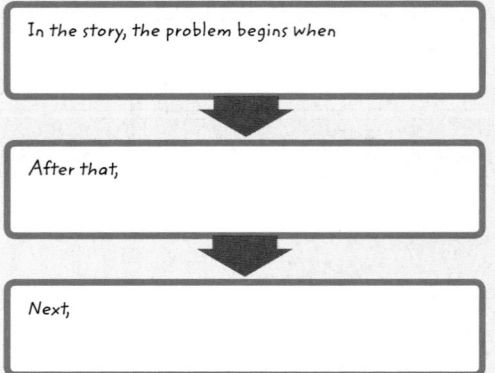

SEQUENCE OF EVENTS

In the story, the problem begins when

After that,

Next,

Vocabulary

deduce (di dōōs′, -dūs′) *v.* to draw a conclusion from something known or assumed; p. 253 *Several clues helped us deduce the location of the runaways.*

impede (im pēd′) *v.* to slow or block progress or action; obstruct; p. 253 *Road construction will impede travel this summer.*

lethargy (leth′ ər jē) *n.* sluggish inactivity or drowsiness; p. 255 *Dad told Bill to be active and get over his lethargy.*

proximity (prok sim′ə tē) *n.* closeness in space, time, sequence, or degree; nearness; p. 258 *The proximity of the cobra made us nervous.*

diffuse (di fuz′) *v.* to spread widely; to scatter in all directions; p. 260 *Green dye was diffused into the river on St. Patrick's Day.*

 INDIANA ACADEMIC STANDARDS (pages 250–263)
11.3.3 Analyze...mood...
11.5.9 Write...a literary analysis...

11.2 Develop strategies such as...identifying and analyzing structure [and] organization...

The Pit and the Pendulum

Edgar Allan Poe

I was sick—sick unto death with that long agony; and when they at length unbound me, and I was permitted to sit, I felt that my senses were leaving me. The sentence—the dread sentence of death—was the last of distinct accentuation which reached my ears.

After that, the sound of the inquisitorial voices seemed merged in one dreamy indeterminate hum. It conveyed to my soul the idea of *revolution*—perhaps from its association in fancy with the burr of a millwheel. This only for a brief period; for presently I heard no more. Yet, for a while, I saw; but with how terrible an exaggeration! I saw the lips of the black-robed judges. They appeared to me white—whiter than the sheet upon which I trace these words—and thin even to grotesqueness;[1] thin with the intensity of their expression of firmness—of immovable resolution—of stern contempt of human torture. I saw that the decrees of what to me was Fate, were still issuing from those lips. I saw them writhe with a deadly locution.[2] I saw them fashion the syllables of my name; and I shuddered because no sound succeeded. I saw, too, for a few moments of delirious horror, the soft and nearly imperceptible waving of the sable draperies which enwrapped the walls of the apartment. And then my vision fell upon the seven tall candles upon the table. At first they wore the aspect of charity, and seemed white slender angels who would save me; but then, all at once, there came a most deadly nausea over my spirit, and I felt every fiber in my frame thrill as if I had touched the wire of a galvanic battery,[3] while the angel forms became meaningless specters,[4] with heads of flame, and I saw that from them there would be no help. And then there stole into my fancy, like a rich musical note, the thought of what sweet rest there must be in the grave. The thought came gently and

---

1. *Grotesqueness* is the state of being distorted or unnatural in shape or appearance.

Literary Element Suspense *The narrator obviously lives to tell his story despite his death sentence. How do you think the author will maintain interest in his tale?*

Big Idea The Power of Darkness *What is the effect of Poe's description of extreme whiteness here?*

---

2. *Locution* is a form or style of verbal expression.
3. In a *galvanic battery,* direct electric current is produced by means of chemical action.
4. *Specters* are ghosts or ghostly visions.

stealthily, and it seemed long before it attained full appreciation; but just as my spirit came at length properly to feel and entertain it, the figures of the judges vanished, as if magically, from before me; the tall candles sank into nothingness; their flames went out utterly; the blackness of darkness supervened; all sensations appeared swallowed up in a mad rushing descent as of the soul into Hades.[5] Then silence, and stillness, and night were the universe.

I had swooned; but still will not say that all of consciousness was lost. What of it there remained I will not attempt to define, or even to describe; yet all was not lost. In the deepest slumber—no! In delirium—no! In a swoon—no! In death—no! even in the grave all *is not* lost. Else there is no immortality[6] for man. Arousing from the most profound[7] of slumbers, we break the gossamer web of *some* dream. Yet in a second afterward, (so frail may that web have been) we remember not that we have dreamed. In the return to life from the swoon there are two stages; first, that of the sense of mental or spiritual; secondly, that of the sense of physical, existence. It seems probable that if, upon reaching the second stage, we could recall the impressions of the first, we should find these impressions eloquent in memories of the gulf beyond. And that gulf is—what? How at least shall we distinguish its shadows from those of the tomb? But if the impressions of what I have termed the first stage, are not, at will, recalled, yet, after long interval, do they not come unbidden, while we marvel whence they come? He who has never swooned, is not he who finds strange palaces and wildly familiar faces in coals that glow; is not he who beholds floating in midair the sad visions that the many may not view; is not he who ponders over the perfume of some novel[8] flower—is not he whose brain grows bewildered with the

> Very suddenly there came back to my soul motion and sound . . . .

meaning of some musical cadence which has never before arrested his attention.

Amid frequent and thoughtful endeavors to remember; amid earnest struggles to regather some token of the state of seeming nothingness into which my soul had lapsed, there have been moments when I have dreamed of success; there have been brief, very brief periods when I have conjured up remembrances which the lucid reason of a later epoch assures me could have had reference only to that condition of seeming unconsciousness. These shadows of memory tell, indistinctly, of tall figures that lifted and bore me in silence down—down—still down—till a hideous dizziness oppressed me at the mere idea of the interminableness[9] of the descent. They tell also of a vague horror at my heart, on account of that heart's unnatural stillness. Then comes a sense of sudden motionlessness throughout all things; as if those who bore me (a ghastly train!) had outrun, in their descent, the limits of the limitless, and paused from the wearisomeness of their toil. After this I call to mind flatness and dampness; and that all is *madness*—the madness of a memory which busies itself among forbidden things.

Very suddenly there came back to my soul motion and sound—the tumultuous motion of the heart, and, in my ears, the sound of its beating. Then a pause in which all is blank. Then again sound, and motion, and touch—a tingling sensation pervading my frame. Then the mere consciousness of existence, without thought—a condition which lasted long. Then, very suddenly, *thought*, and shuddering terror, and earnest endeavor to comprehend my true state. Then a strong desire to lapse into insensibility.[10] Then a rushing revival of soul and a successful

---

9. *Interminableness* means "endlessness."
10. The narrator is describing his wish to return to unconsciousness (*insensibility*).

Reading Strategy Identifying Sequence *Note the number of times the narrator repeats the word* then *in this paragraph. What does this repetition tell you about the stages the narrator goes through as he gradually regains consciousness?*

---

5. In Greek myth, *Hades* is the underground place of the dead.
6. Here, *immortality* means "eternal life."
7. Here, *profound* means "complete" or "deep."
8. A *novel* flower is new and unusual.

effort to move. And now a full memory of the trial, of the judges, of the sable draperies, of the sentence, of the sickness, of the swoon. Then entire forgetfulness of all that followed; of all that a later day and much earnestness of endeavor have enabled me vaguely to recall.

So far, I had not opened my eyes. I felt that I lay upon my back, unbound. I reached out my hand, and it fell heavily upon something damp and hard. There I suffered[11] it to remain for many minutes, while I strove to imagine where and *what* I could be. I longed, yet dared not to employ my vision. I dreaded the first glance at objects around me. It was not that I feared to look upon things horrible, but that I grew aghast lest there should be *nothing* to see. At length, with a wild desperation at heart, I quickly unclosed my eyes. My worst thoughts, then, were confirmed. The blackness of eternal night encompassed me. I struggled for breath. The intensity of the darkness seemed to oppress and stifle me. The atmosphere was intolerably close. I still lay quietly, and made effort to exercise my reason. I brought to mind the inquisitorial proceedings,[12] and attempted from that point to **deduce** my real condition. The sentence had passed; and it appeared to me that a very long interval of time had since elapsed. Yet not for a moment did I suppose myself actually dead. Such a supposition, notwithstanding what we read in fiction, is altogether inconsistent with real existence;—but where and in what state was I? The condemned to death, I knew, perished usually at the *autos-da-fé*,[13] and one of these had been held on the very night of the day of my trial. Had I been remanded to my dungeon, to await the next sacrifice which would not take place for many months? This I at once saw could not be. Victims had been in immediate demand. Moreover, my dungeon, as well as all the condemned cells at Toledo,[14] had stone floors, and light was not altogether excluded.

A fearful idea now suddenly drove the blood in torrents upon my heart, and for a brief period, I once more relapsed into insensibility. Upon recovering, I at once started to my feet, trembling convulsively in every fiber. I thrust my arms wildly above and around me in all directions. I felt nothing; yet dreaded to move a step, lest I should be **impeded** by the walls of the *tomb*. Perspiration burst from every pore and stood in cold big beads on my forehead. The agony of suspense grew at length intolerable, and I cautiously moved forward, with my arms extended, and my eyes straining from their sockets, in the hope of catching some faint ray of light. I proceeded for many paces; but still all was blackness and vacancy. I breathed more freely. It seemed evident that mine was not, at least, the most hideous of fates.

And now, as I still continued to step cautiously onward, there came thronging upon my recollection a thousand vague rumors of the horrors of Toledo. Of the dungeons there had been strange things narrated—fables I had always deemed them—but yet strange, and too ghastly to repeat, save in a whisper. Was I left to perish of starvation in the subterranean[15] world of darkness; or what fate, perhaps even more fearful, awaited me? That the result would be death, and a death of more than customary bitterness, I knew too well the character of my

---

11. Here, *suffered* means "allowed."
12. During the Inquisition, a person's refusal to confess was taken as evidence of guilt.
13. Often, the sentence was to be burned alive in public ceremonies called *autos-da-fé* (ô′ tōz də fā′). The phrase is Portuguese for "acts of faith," referring to the Inquisitors' faith that the condemned persons were guilty as charged.

Big Idea The Power of Darkness *How does the narrator's description of his surroundings reflect the Gothic tradition?*

Vocabulary

deduce (di doos′) *v.* to draw a conclusion from something known or assumed

---

14. The Spanish city of *Toledo* was important during the Inquisition.
15. *Subterranean* describes things that exist or occur below the earth's surface.

Literary Element Suspense *How do the narrator's physical and psychological torments add to the suspense?*

Vocabulary

impede (im pēd′) *v.* to slow or block progress or action; obstruct judges to doubt. The mode and the hour were all that occupied or distracted me.

My outstretched hands at length encountered some solid obstruction. It was a wall, seemingly of stone masonry—very smooth, slimy, and cold. I followed it up; stepping with all the careful distrust with which certain antique narratives had inspired me. This process, however, afforded me no means of ascertaining the dimensions of my dungeon; as I might make its circuit, and return to the point whence I set out, without being aware of the fact; so perfectly uniform seemed the wall. I therefore sought the knife which had been in my pocket, when led into the inquisitorial chamber; but it was gone; my clothes had been exchanged for a wrapper of coarse serge. I had thought of forcing the blade in some minute crevice of the masonry, so as to identify my point of departure. The difficulty, nevertheless, was but trivial; although, in the disorder of my fancy, it seemed at first insuperable.[16] I tore a part of the hem from the robe and placed the fragment at full length, and at right angles to the wall. In groping my way around the prison I could not fail to encounter this rag upon completing the circuit. So, at least I thought: but I had not counted upon the extent of the dungeon, or upon my own weakness. The ground was moist and slippery. I staggered onward for some time, when I stumbled and fell. My excessive fatigue induced me to remain prostrate; and sleep soon overtook me as I lay.

Upon awakening, and stretching forth an arm, I found beside me a loaf and a pitcher with water. I was too much exhausted to reflect upon this circumstance, but ate and drank with avidity.[17] Shortly afterward, I resumed my tour around the prison, and with much toil, came at last upon the fragment of the serge. Up to the period when I fell I had counted fifty-two paces, and upon resuming my walk, I counted forty-eight more;—when I arrived at the rag. There were in all, then, a hundred paces; and admitting two paces to the yard, I presumed the dungeon to be fifty yards in circuit.

Half length portrait of a man bending over, 18th c. Giovanni Battista Piranesi. Pen and ink on paper, 15.8 x 21.6 cm. Hamburger Kunsthalle, Hamburg, Germany. **Viewing the Art:** How might this drawing reflect the emotional state of the narrator?

I had met, however, with many angles in the wall, and thus I could form no guess at the shape of the vault; for vault I could not help supposing it to be.

I had little object—certainly no hope—in these researches; but a vague curiosity prompted me to continue them. Quitting the wall, I resolved to cross the area of the enclosure. At first I proceeded with extreme caution, for the floor, although seemingly of solid material, was treacherous with slime. At length, however, I took courage, and did not hesitate to step firmly; endeavoring to cross in as direct a line as possible. I had advanced some ten or twelve paces in this manner, when the remnant of the torn hem of my robe became entangled between my legs. I stepped on it, and fell violently on my face.

In the confusion attending my fall, I did not immediately apprehend a somewhat startling circumstance, which yet, in a few seconds afterward, and while I still lay prostrate, arrested my attention. It was this—my chin rested upon the floor of the prison, but my lips and the upper portion of my head, although seemingly at a less elevation than the chin, touched nothing. At the same time my forehead seemed bathed in a clammy vapor, and the peculiar smell of decayed fungus arose to my nostrils. I put forward my

---

16. Something that's *insuperable* cannot be overcome.
17. *Avidity* is eagerness and enthusiasm.

Literary Element Suspense *How does this sentence build tension?*

Reading Strategy Identifying Sequence *What signal words indicate the sequence of events in this paragraph?*

arm, and shuddered to find that I had fallen at the very brink of a circular pit, whose extent, of course, I had no means of ascertaining at the moment. Groping about the masonry just below the margin, I succeeded in dislodging a small fragment, and let it fall into the abyss.[18] For many seconds I hearkened to its reverberations as it dashed against the sides of the chasm in its descent; at length there was a sullen plunge into water, succeeded by loud echoes. At the same moment there came a sound resembling the quick opening, and a rapid closing of a door overhead, while a faint gleam of light flashed suddenly through the gloom, and as suddenly faded away.

I saw clearly the doom which had been prepared for me, and congratulated myself upon the timely accident by which I had escaped. Another step before my fall, and the world had seen me no more. And the death just avoided, was of that very character which I had regarded as fabulous and frivolous[19] in the tales respecting the Inquisition. To the victims of its tyranny, there was the choice of death with its direst physical agonies, or death with its most hideous moral horrors. I had been reserved for the latter. By long suffering my nerves had been unstrung, until I trembled at the sound of my own voice, and had become in every respect a fitting subject for the species of torture which awaited me.

Shaking in every limb, I groped my way back to the wall; resolving there to perish rather than risk the terrors of the wells, of which my imagination now pictured many in various positions about the dungeon. In other conditions of mind I might have had courage to end my misery at once by a plunge into one of these abysses; but now I was the veriest of cowards. Neither could I forget what I had read of these pits—that the *sudden* extinction of life formed no part of their most horrible plan.

Agitation of spirit kept me awake for many long hours; but at length I again slumbered. Upon arousing, I found by my side as before, a loaf and a pitcher of water. A burning thirst consumed me, and I emptied the vessel at a draught. It must have been drugged; for scarcely had I drunk, before I became irresistibly drowsy. A deep sleep fell upon me—a sleep like that of death. How long it lasted of course, I know not; but when, once again, I unclosed my eyes, the objects around me were visible. By a wild sulphurous luster, the origin of which I could not at first determine, I was enabled to see the extent and aspect of the prison.

In its size I had been greatly mistaken. The whole circuit of its walls did not exceed twenty-five yards. For some minutes this fact occasioned me a world of vain trouble; vain indeed! for what could be of less importance, under the terrible circumstances which environed[20] me, than the mere dimensions of my dungeon? But my soul took a wild interest in trifles, and I busied myself in endeavors to account for the error I had committed in my measurement. The truth at length flashed upon me. In my first attempt at exploration I had counted fifty-two paces, up to the period when I fell; I must then have been within a pace or two of the fragments of serge; in fact, I had nearly performed the circuit of the vault. I then slept, and upon awaking, I must have returned upon my steps—thus supposing the circuit nearly double what it actually was. My confusion of mind prevented me from observing that I began my tour with the wall to the left, and ended it with the wall to the right.

I had been deceived, too, in respect to the shape of the enclosure. In feeling my way around I had found many angles, and thus deduced an idea of great irregularity; so potent is the effect of total darkness upon one arousing from **lethargy** or sleep! The angles were simply those of a few slight depressions, or niches, at odd intervals. The general shape

---

18. Here, *abyss* (ə bis′) refers to "an extremely deep hole."
19. Here, *fabulous* means "fictional," and *frivolous* means "silly" or "unimportant."

Literary Element Suspense *How do the opening and closing of a door overhead help create suspense?*

Big Idea The Power of Darkness *How does this sentence reflect Romanticism's fascination with disease and madness?*

---

20. To *environ* is to encircle or surround.

Reading Strategy Identifying Sequence *Why does the author alternate periods of activity with periods of inaction?*

Vocabulary

lethargy (leth′ ər jē) *n.* sluggish inactivity or drowsiness of the prison was square. What I had taken for masonry seemed now to be iron, or some other metal, in huge plates, whose sutures or joints occasioned the depression. The entire surface of this metallic enclosure was rudely daubed in all the hideous and repulsive devices[21] to which the charnel[22] superstitions of the monks has given rise. The figures of fiends in aspects of menace, with skeleton forms, and other more really fearful images, overspread and disfigured the walls. I observed that the outlines of these monstrosities were sufficiently distinct, but that the colors seemed faded and blurred, as if from the effects of a damp atmosphere. I now noticed the floor, too, which was of stone. In the center yawned the circular pit from whose jaws I had escaped; but it was the only one in the dungeon.

All this I saw distinctly and by much effort: for my personal condition had been greatly changed during slumber. I now lay upon my back, and at full length, on a species of low framework of wood. To this I was securely bound by a long strap resembling a surcingle.[23] It passed in many convolutions about my limbs and body, leaving at liberty only my head, and my left arm to such extent that I could, by dint of much exertion, supply myself with food from an earthen dish which lay by my side on the floor. I saw, to my horror, that the pitcher had been removed. I say to my horror; for I was consumed with intolerable thirst. This thirst it appeared to be the design of my persecutors to stimulate: for the food in the dish was meat pungently seasoned.

Looking upward I surveyed the ceiling of my prison. It was some thirty or forty feet overhead, and constructed much as the side walls. In one of its panels a very singular figure riveted my whole attention. It was the painted figure of Time as he is commonly represented, save that, in lieu of[24] a scythe, he held what, at a casual glance, I supposed to be the pictured image of a huge pendulum such as we see on antique clocks. There was something, however, in the appearance of this machine which caused me to regard it more attentively. While I gazed directly upward at it (for its position was immediately over my own) I fancied that I saw it in motion. In an instant afterward the fancy was confirmed. Its sweep was brief, and of course slow. I watched it for some minutes, somewhat in fear, but more in wonder. Wearied at length with observing its dull movement, I turned my eyes upon the other subjects in the cell.

A slight noise attracted my notice, and, looking to the floor, I saw several enormous rats traversing it. They had issued from the well, which lay just within view to my right. Even then, while I gazed, they came up in troops, hurriedly, with ravenous eyes, allured by the scent of the meat. From this it required much effort and attention to scare them away.

It might have been half an hour, perhaps even an hour, (for I could take but imperfect note of time) before I again cast my eyes upward. What I then saw confounded and amazed me. The sweep of the pendulum had increased in extent by nearly a yard. As a natural consequence, its velocity was also much greater. But what mainly disturbed me was the idea that it had perceptibly *descended*. I now observed—with what horror it is needless to say—that its nether extremity[25] was formed of a crescent of glittering steel, about a foot in length from horn to horn; the horns upward, and the under edge evidently as keen as that of a razor. Like a razor also, it seemed massy and heavy, tapering from the edge into a solid and broad structure above. It was appended to a weighty rod of brass, and the whole *hissed* as it swung through the air.

I could no longer doubt the doom prepared for me by monkish ingenuity[26] in torture. My cognizance of the pit had become known to the inquisitorial agents—*the pit* whose horrors had been destined for so bold a recusant[27] as myself—*the pit*, typical of hell, and regarded by

21. Here, the *devices* are ornamental designs.
22. Here, *charnel* means "gruesome" or "deathlike." As a noun, it refers to a vault where bones or bodies are placed.
23. A *surcingle* is a belt or band used to hold a saddle or pack on a horse or pack animal.
24. *In lieu* (in lo͞o) *of* means "in place of" or "instead of."

25. The pendulum's *nether extremity* is its lower end.
26. *Ingenuity* (in´ jə no͞o´ ə tē)—the noun form of *ingenious*—is creative ability or inventiveness.
27. A *recusant* (re´ kyə zənt) is one who refuses to accept or obey established authorities.

Reading Strategy Identifying Sequence *How does this reference to the passage of time contribute to the suspense of the following sentence?*

Carceri d'Invenzione, Plate XIII, 1780. Giovanni Battista Piranesi. Etching, 16 x 22 in. Private collection.
Viewing the Art: What in this illustration suggests a setting similar to the one described by the narrator?

rumor as the Ultima Thule[28] of all their punishments. The plunge into this pit I had avoided by the merest of accidents, and I knew that surprise, or entrapment into torment, formed an important portion of all the grotesquerie of these dungeon deaths. Having failed to fall, it was no part of the demon plan to hurl me into the abyss; and thus (there being no alternative) a different and a milder destruction awaited me. Milder! I half smiled in my agony as I thought of such application of such a term.

What boots it[29] to tell of the long, long hours of horror more than mortal, during which I counted the rushing vibrations of the steel! Inch by inch— line by line—with a descent only appreciable at intervals that seemed ages—down and still down it came! Days passed—it might have been that many days passed—ere it swept so closely over me as to fan me with its acrid breath. The odor of the sharp steel forced itself into my nostrils. I prayed—I wearied heaven with my prayer for its more speedy descent. I grew frantically mad, and struggled to force myself upward against the sweep of the fearful scimitar.[30] And then I fell suddenly calm, and lay smiling at the glittering death, as a child at some rare bauble.[31]

There was another interval of utter insensibility; it was brief; for, upon again lapsing into life there had been no perceptible descent in the pendulum. But it might have been long; for I knew there were demons who took note of my swoon, and who could have arrested the vibration at pleasure. Upon my recovery, too, I felt very—oh, inexpressibly sick and weak, as if through long inanition.[32] Even amid the agonies of that period, the human nature craved food. With painful effort I outstretched my left arm as

---

28. Here, *Ultima Thule* (ul′ tə mə thōō lē) means "extreme limit" or "greatest degree." In ancient times, this was the name of the northernmost part of the known world.
29. *What boots it?* is an expression meaning "What good is it?"

Literary Element Suspense *What is to be his fate? Why is the destruction "milder?"*

30. A *scimitar* is a curved, single-edged sword of Asian origin.
31. A *bauble* is any showy but worthless trinket.
32. The exhaustion caused by a lack of food or water is called *inanition.*

far as my bonds permitted, and took possession of the small remnant which had been spared me by the rats. As I put a portion of it within my lips, there rushed to my mind a half formed thought of joy—of hope. Yet what business had I with hope? It was, as I say, a half formed thought— man has many such which are never completed. I felt that it was of joy—of hope; but I felt also that it had perished in its formation. In vain I struggled to perfect—to regain it. Long suffering had nearly annihilated all my ordinary powers of mind. I was an imbecile—an idiot.

The vibration of the pendulum was at right angles to my length. I saw that the crescent was designed to cross the region of the heart. It would fray the serge of my robe—it would return and repeat its operations—again—and again. Notwithstanding its terrifically wide sweep (some thirty feet or more) and the hissing vigor of its descent, sufficient to sunder these very walls of iron, still the fraying of my robe would be all that, for several minutes, it would accomplish. And at this thought I paused. I dared not go farther than this reflection. I dwelt upon it with a pertinacity[33] of attention—as if, in so dwelling, I could arrest *here* the descent of the steel. I forced myself to ponder upon the sound of the crescent as it should pass across the garment—upon the peculiar thrilling sensation which the friction of cloth produces on the nerves. I pondered upon all this frivolity until my teeth were on edge.

Down—steadily down it crept. I took a frenzied pleasure in contrasting its downward with its lateral velocity. To the right—to the left—far and wide—with the shriek of a damned spirit; to my heart with the stealthy pace of the tiger! I alternately laughed and howled as the one or the other idea grew prominent.

Down—certainly, relentlessly down! It vibrated within three inches of my bosom! I struggled violently, furiously, to free my left arm. This was free only from the elbow to the hand. I could reach the latter, from the platter beside me, to my mouth, with great effort, but no farther. Could I have broken the

fastenings above the elbow, I would have seized and attempted to arrest the pendulum. I might as well have attempted to arrest an avalanche!

Down—still unceasingly—still inevitably down! I gasped and struggled at each vibration. I shrunk convulsively at its every sweep. My eyes followed its outward or upward whirls with the eagerness of the most unmeaning despair; they closed themselves spasmodically at the descent, although death would have been a relief, oh! how unspeakable! Still I quivered in every nerve to think how slight a sinking of the machinery would precipitate that keen, glistening axe upon my bosom. It was *hope* that prompted the nerve to quiver—the frame to shrink. It was *hope*—the hope that triumphs on the rack[34]—that whispers to the death-condemned even in the dungeons of the Inquisition.

I saw that some ten or twelve vibrations would bring the steel in actual contact with my robe, and with this observation there suddenly came over my spirit all the keen, collected calmness of despair. For the first time during many hours—or perhaps days—I *thought*. It now occurred to me that the bandage, or surcingle, which enveloped me, was *unique*. I was tied by no separate cord. The first stroke of the razor-like crescent athwart any portion of the band, would so detach it that it might be unwound from my person by means of my left hand. But how fearful, in that case, the **proximity** of the steel! The result of the slightest struggle how deadly! Was it likely, moreover, that the minions of the torturer had not foreseen and provided for this possibility! Was it probable that the bandage crossed my bosom in the track of the pendulum? Dreading to find my faint, and, as it seemed, my last hope frustrated, I so far elevated my head as to obtain a distinct view of my breast. The surcingle enveloped my limbs and body close in all directions—*save in the path of the destroying crescent*.

---

34. The *rack* was an instrument of torture used to stretch or pull a victim's body in different directions.

Reading Strategy Identifying Sequence *How does the repetition of the word* down *at the beginning of each of three paragraphs indicate the passing of time?*

Vocabulary

proximity (prok sim′ ə tē) *n.* closeness in space, time, sequence, or degree; nearness

---

33. *Pertinacity* is stubborn persistence.

Reading Strategy Identifying Sequence *How does the repetition of the signal word* again *heighten the feeling of terror?*

Scarcely had I dropped my head back into its original position, when there flashed upon my mind what I cannot better describe than as the unformed half of that idea of deliverance to which I have previously alluded, and of which a moiety[35] only floated indeterminately through my brain when I raised food to my burning lips. The whole thought was now present—feeble, scarcely sane, scarcely definite,—but still entire. I proceeded at once, with the nervous energy of despair, to attempt its execution.

For many hours the immediate vicinity of the low framework upon which I lay, had been literally swarming with rats. They were wild, bold, ravenous; their red eyes glaring upon me as if they waited but for motionlessness on my part to make me their prey. "To what food," I thought, "have they been accustomed in the well?"

They had devoured, in spite of all my efforts to prevent them, all but a small remnant of the contents of the dish. I had fallen into an habitual seesaw, or wave of the hand about the platter: and, at length, the unconscious uniformity of the movement deprived it of effect. In their voracity the vermin frequently fastened their sharp fangs into my fingers. With the particles of the oily and spicy viand which now remained, I thoroughly rubbed the bandage wherever I could reach it; then, raising my hand from the floor, I lay breathlessly still.

They were wild, bold, ravenous . . . .

At first the ravenous animals were startled and terrified at the change—at the cessation of movement. They shrank alarmedly back; many sought the well. But this was only for a moment. I had not counted in vain upon their voracity. Observing that I remained without motion, one or two of the boldest leaped upon the frame-work, and smelt at the surcingle. This seemed the signal for a general rush. Forth from the well they hurried in fresh troops. They clung to the wood—they overran it, and leaped in hundreds upon my person. The measured movement of the pendulum disturbed them not at all. Avoiding its strokes they busied themselves with the anointed bandage. They pressed—they swarmed upon me in ever accumulating heaps. They writhed upon my throat; their cold lips sought my own; I was half stifled by their thronging pressure; disgust, for which the world has no name, swelled my bosom, and chilled, with a heavy clamminess, my heart. Yet one minute, and I felt that the struggle would be over. Plainly I perceived the loosening of the bandage. I knew that in more than one place it must be already severed. With a more than human resolution I lay *still*.

Nor had I erred in my calculations—nor had I endured in vain. I at length felt that I was *free*. The surcingle hung in ribands from my body. But the stroke of the pendulum already pressed upon my bosom. It had divided the serge of the robe. It had cut through the linen beneath. Twice again it swung, and a sharp sense of pain shot through every nerve. But the moment of escape had arrived. At a wave of my hand my deliverers hurried tumultuously away. With a steady movement—cautious, sidelong, shrinking, and slow—I slid from the embrace of the bandage and beyond the reach of the scimitar. For the moment, at least, *I was free*.

Free!—and in the grasp of the Inquisition! I had scarcely stepped from my wooden bed of horror upon the stone floor of the prison, when the motion of the hellish machine ceased and I beheld it drawn up, by some invisible force through the ceiling. This was a lesson which I took desperately to heart. My every motion was undoubtedly watched. Free!—I had but escaped death in one form of agony, to be delivered unto worse than death in some other. With that thought I rolled my eyes nervously around the barriers of iron that hemmed me in. Something unusual—some change which at first I could not appreciate distinctly—it was obvious, had taken place in the apartment. For many minutes in a dreamy and trembling abstraction,[36] I busied myself in vain, unconnected conjecture.[37] During this period, I became aware, for the first time, of the origin of the sulphurous light which illuminated the cell. It proceeded from a fissure, about half an inch

---

36. *Abstraction* is the state of being lost in thought.
37. *Conjecture* is the forming of an opinion without definite or sufficient evidence.

Big Idea The Power of Darkness *What view of nature is presented here?*

---

35. A *moiety* of something is a portion of it.

in width, extending entirely around the prison at the base of the walls, which thus appeared, and were completely separated from the floor. I endeavored, but of course in vain, to look through the aperture.

As I arose from the attempt, the mystery of the alteration in the chamber broke at once upon my understanding. I have observed that, although the outlines of the figures upon the walls were sufficiently distinct, yet the colors seemed blurred and indefinite. These colors had now assumed, and were momentarily assuming, a startling and most intense brilliancy, that gave to the spectral and fiendish portraitures an aspect that might have thrilled even firmer nerves than my own. Demon eyes, of a wild and ghastly vivacity, glared upon me in a thousand directions, where none had been visible before, and gleamed with the lurid luster[38] of a fire that I could not force my imagination to regard as unreal.

Unreal!—Even while I breathed there came to my nostrils the breath of the vapor of heated iron! A suffocating odor pervaded the prison! A deeper glow settled each moment in the eyes that glared at my agonies! A richer tint of crimson **diffused** itself over the pictured horrors of blood. I panted! I gasped for breath! There could be no doubt of the design of my tormentors—oh! most unrelenting! oh! most demoniac of men! I shrank from the glowing metal to the center of the cell. Amid the thought of the fiery destruction that impended, the idea of the coolness of the well came over my soul like balm.[39] I rushed to its deadly brink. I threw my straining vision below. The glare from the enkindled roof illumined its inmost recesses. Yet, for a wild moment, did my spirit refuse to comprehend the meaning of what I saw. At length it forced—it wrestled its way into my soul—it burned itself in upon my shuddering reason.—Oh! for a voice to speak! oh! horror!—oh! any horror but this! With a shriek, I rushed from the margin, and buried my face in my hands—weeping bitterly.

The heat rapidly increased, and once again I looked up, shuddering as with a fit of the

ague.[40] There had been a second change in the cell—and now the change was obviously in the *form*. As before, it was in vain that I, at first, endeavoured to appreciate or understand what was taking place. But not long was I left in doubt. The Inquisitorial vengeance had been hurried by my two-fold escape, and there was to be no more dallying with the King of Terrors.[41] The room had been square. I saw that two of its iron angles were now acute—two, consequently, obtuse. The fearful difference quickly increased with a low rumbling or moaning sound. In an instant the apartment had shifted its form into that of a lozenge. But the alteration stopped not here—I neither hoped nor desired it to stop. I could have clasped the red walls to my bosom as a garment of eternal peace. "Death," I said, "any death but that of the pit!" Fool! might I have not known that *into the pit* it was the object of the burning iron to urge me? Could I resist its glow? or, if even that, could I withstand its pressure? And now, flatter and flatter grew the lozenge, with a rapidity that left me no time for contemplation. Its center, and of course, its greatest width, came just over the yawning gulf. I shrank back—but the closing walls pressed me resistlessly onward. At length for my seared and writhing body there was no longer an inch of foothold on the firm floor of the prison. I struggled no more, but the agony of my soul found vent in one loud, long, and final scream of despair. I felt that I tottered upon the brink—I averted my eyes—

There was a discordant hum of human voices! There was a loud blast of many trumpets! There was a harsh grating as of a thousand thunders! The fiery walls rushed back! An outstretched arm caught my own as I fell, fainting, into the abyss. It was that of General Lasalle.[42] The French army had entered Toledo. The Inquisition was in the hands of its enemies. ∾

---

38. The eyes are full of life (*vivacity*), with a fiery, reddish glare, (a *lurid* luster).
39. Although destruction was about to occur (*impended*), the idea of coolness seemed to be something calming or soothing (a *balm*).

Vocabulary

diffuse (di fūz´) *v.* to spread widely; to scatter in all directions

40. *Ague* (ā´ gū) is a fever accompanied by chills and shivering.
41. The *King of Terrors* could be either the "Inquisitorial vengeance" or death.
42. *Lasalle* was an officer of the French emperor Napoleon Bonaparte, whose army invaded Spain in 1808.

Literary Element   Suspense *How has the mystery of the pit heightened the suspense throughout the story?*

Big Idea   The Power of Darkness *An atmosphere of horror is essential to Gothic fiction. How does this passage create a sense of horror?*

RESPONDING AND THINKING CRITICALLY

Respond

1. (a)What emotions did you experience while reading this story? (b)Were you surprised by the ending? Why or why not?

Recall and Interpret

2. (a)To what fate has the narrator been sentenced? (b)What does his immediate reaction tell you about his state of mind?

3. (a)How does the narrator determine the size of his prison? (b)Why might he feel that he must find out about his surroundings?

4. (a)What kind of death does he associate with the pit? (b)Why might the pit put him in such a state of terror?

5. (a)What horror does the narrator face after avoiding the pit? (b)Why do you think the narrator makes the efforts he does in response to the second horror?

Analyze and Evaluate

6. (a)Why is the third method of torture especially frightening for the narrator? (b)Is Poe's portrayal of the third method as the most horrible convincing?

7. (a)What do the narrator's struggles and thoughts throughout his ordeal tell you about Poe's view of human nature? (b)Do you think the narrator's actions are realistic given his situation? Explain.

Connect

8. **Big Idea** **The Power of Darkness** How would you describe the overall mood or atmosphere of this story? How does Poe achieve this mood?

ATTACKING THE INQUISITION

One of the fiercest critics of the Spanish Inquisition was the painter and graphic artist Francisco de Goya (1746–1828). Many of his works deal with the suffering experienced by those judged to be heretics. Among these works is the series of prints known as *Los caprichos (The Caprices)*, published in 1799. In number 23 of the series, titled *Aquellos polbos (Those Specks of Dust)*, Goya presents a disabled woman arrested for selling love potions. Dressed in the typical robe and conical hat worn by condemned heretics, she slumps in front of the officers of the Inquisition.

Group Activity Discuss the following questions with your classmates.

1. Why do you think Goya might have chosen to depict the trial of this woman?

2. How are Poe's story and Goya's image alike and different as depictions of the Inquisition?

After your discussion, create your own illustration for Poe's story.

Aquellos polbos.

Literary Element Suspense

Suspense generally increases as the plot of a story moves toward its climax. In "The Pit and the Pendulum," Poe generates tension and uncertainty by pitting the narrator against one horror after another. The reader becomes more and more involved in the story, concerned about what will happen to the narrator.

1. The narrator undergoes moments of both physical and psychological torment. Give two examples of each. Describe the event, and tell how each event heightens the story's suspense.

2. In your opinion, what is the most suspenseful moment in the story? Explain your choice.

Review: Point of View

As you learned in Unit One, point of view refers to the perspective from which a story is told. Poe's story is told in the first-person point of view. The narrator is a character in the story who uses the pronouns *I, me,* and *my.* Everything that the reader learns is filtered through the eyes, ears, and thoughts of the narrator.

Partner Activity With another classmate discuss how the story's point of view helps create suspense. With your partner, design a web diagram. List examples in which the first-person point of view limits your knowledge of events, characters, and setting.

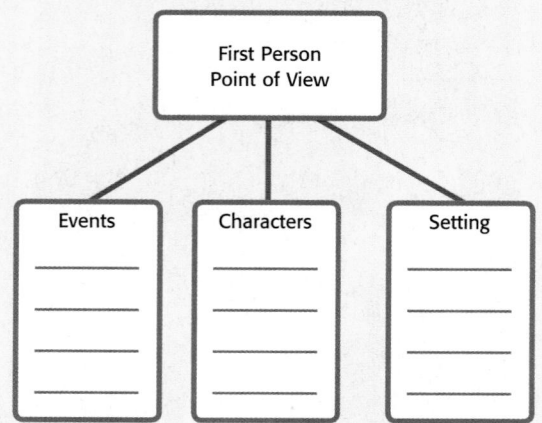

Reading Strategy Identifying Sequence

In their stories, writers need not always present the **sequence,** or the logical order of ideas or events, in the same way. In addition to using chronological, or time, order to retell events, authors can also use flashbacks or flash-forwards to show events that happened earlier or later in the sequence.

1. What method does the narrator use to retell the events of his tale in "The Pit and the Pendulum"?

2. The term *deus ex machina* originally meant a god that suddenly appeared in a Greek tragedy—sometimes lowered from a crane—to resolve a situation too complex for humans. Today, the term refers to an improbable, contrived, or artificial solution to a problem in a piece of fiction. Do you think that the ending of "The Pit and the Pendulum" is a *deus ex machina* or a part of the story's logical sequence? Explain.

Vocabulary Practice

Practice with Word Origins Match each vocabulary word from "The Pit and the Pendulum" with the word that has the same origin. Use a dictionary if necessary.

1. deduce
2. impede
3. lethargy
4. proximity
5. diffuse

a. pedometer
b. approximate
c. introduce
d. effusive
e. lethe

Academic Vocabulary

Here are two vocabulary words from the vocabulary list on page R86.

environment (en vī′ rən mənt, -vī′ ərn-) *n.* surroundings; the cultural and social conditions affecting an individual or community

maximize (mak′sə mīz′) *v.* to make as great as possible; increase to the maximum

Practice and Apply
1. Which details in the narrator's **environment** are Gothic?
2. How does Poe **maximize** suspense?

Writing About Literature

Analyze Mood is the emotional quality or atmosphere of a literary work. Write a brief essay explaining how Poe's language, subject matter, setting, and tone contribute to the mood of "The Pit and the Pendulum."

To generate ideas for your essay, use a cluster diagram. Write a word or phrase describing the mood of the story in the middle of a sheet of paper. Then, under each category, write related words. For example, write *torture* under Subject Matter. Under the related words, jot down evidence from the story. The finished cluster will list the main points of your essay and the supporting details.

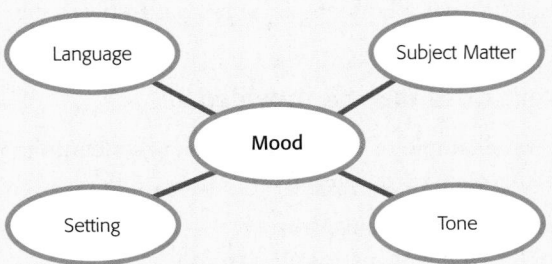

After you complete your draft, meet with a peer reviewer to evaluate each other's work and to suggest revisions. Then proofread and edit your draft for errors in spelling, grammar, and punctuation.

Internet Connection

Would you like to take a tour of the Poe museum in Richmond, Virginia? Do you want to learn more about Poe's life? Would you like to hear "The Raven" read aloud? You can do all this and more online. Use any major search engine and enter key words and phrases such as *Edgar Allan Poe, The Raven,* or other titles.

Black bird perched on a vase. Imperial Period (27 BCE–396 CE). Roman wall painting. Pompeii, Italy.

Poe's Language and Style

Using Abstract and Concrete Language In "The Pit and the Pendulum," Poe uses concrete words, or words that appeal to the reader's senses—sight, hearing, touch, taste, and smell—to help readers imagine the narrator's ordeal. For example, Poe describes the candles as "white slender angels," the narrator's last pleasant sight before being thrown into the dungeon. The description of the dungeon walls as "smooth, slimy, and cold" allows readers to imagine the dank chill that the narrator feels when his hand touches the stone.

Poe also uses abstract words in the story, or words that express ideas or qualities—such as order, hope, and despair—to describe what the senses cannot reveal. For example, the speaker refers to his "charity," "thought," and "immortality." Concrete nouns and adjectives can be forceful, but abstract words are essential in writing about ideas.

Abstract	Concrete
terrors	rustling
horror	tapping
dreamy	oily

Activity Scan "The Pit and the Pendulum" for other examples of concrete and abstract words that effectively convey the narrator's ordeal. Add these words to your Mood cluster diagram.

Revising Check

The Right Word Concrete and abstract words—which appeal to the reader's senses and convey ideas, concepts, or qualities—can increase the effectiveness of your writing. With a partner, review your essay on "The Pit and the Pendulum." Revise your writing by including effective concrete and abstract words to establish a mood or tone. If you wish, consult a thesaurus, to help you.

Literature Online **Web Activities** For eFlashcards, Selection Quick Checks, and other Web activities, go to www.glencoe.com.

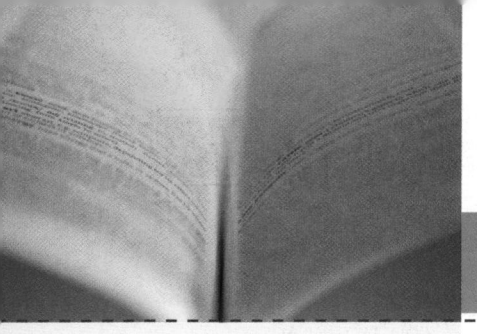

Vocabulary Workshop

Context Clues

▶ **Vocabulary Terms**

The **context** of a word refers to the *other* words and sentences surrounding that word. **Synonyms** are words that have similar meanings.

▶ **Test-Taking Tip**

When you are asked for the meaning of a word that appears in a reading passage, you will usually find one or more context clues near the word.

▶ **Reading Handbook**

For more about using context clues, see Reading Handbook, p. R20.

eFlashcards For eFlashcards and other vocabulary activities, go to www.glencoe.com.

ACADEMIC STANDARDS (page 264)

11.1.1 Understand unfamiliar words that refer to...themes in literature...

Determining the Meaning of Unfamiliar Words

"I had swooned; but still will not say that all of consciousness was lost."

—Edgar Allan Poe, from "The Pit and the Pendulum"

Connecting to Literature What does *swooned* mean in the quotation above? Sometimes the context, or placement, in which an unfamiliar word appears provides clues to the meaning of the word. If you are not familiar with the word *swooned*, you can get an idea of its meaning from the way it is used in the sentence. That the narrator "will not say that all of consciousness was lost" is a clue that *swooned* means "to fall in a faint."

One or more kinds of context clues may be provided.

- Context sometimes provides an **example** or examples of a word's meaning. *Falling into a dark pit would certainly be a calamity.*

- Context may provide a **definition** of a difficult word. *Tom Walker was gullible, and his wife was just as easy to fool.*

- Context sometimes supplies a word or phrase with an opposite meaning to **contrast** with the unfamiliar word. *Most people would be fearful of a talking raven, but not the dauntless narrator of "The Raven."*

- Context may provide a **synonym** for the unfamiliar word. *The devil provided sufficient, or enough, treasure to tempt the Walkers.*

Exercise

For each item below, use *context* clues to figure out the **meaning** of the underlined word. Identify the type of context clue used to uncover its meaning.

1. Edgar Allan Poe is credited with writing the first crime stories that use <u>ratiocination</u>, or logical thinking, to solve a mystery.
   a. reasoning   **b.** characters   **c.** mathematics   **d.** footprints

2. In one of Poe's stories, "The <u>Purloined</u> Letter," a detective is asked to get the stolen document back.
   a. ancient   **b.** personal   **c.** damaged   **d.** taken without consent

3. Other characters may think that a problem is <u>inexplicable</u>, but Poe's detective, C. Auguste Dupin, finds it easy to understand.
   a. mysterious   **b.** boring   **c.** simple   **d.** dangerous

4. Many modern <u>sleuths</u>, from Encyclopedia Brown and Nancy Drew to the police investigators on TV crime shows, owe their methods to Dupin.
   a. criminals   **b.** readers   **c.** detectives   **d.** authors

The Minister's Black Veil

MEET NATHANIEL HAWTHORNE

What do you think it would be like to spend a dozen years in self-imposed solitude? Nathaniel Hawthorne did just that, reading widely in New England history and perfecting his skills as a writer. The dark Puritan past haunted Hawthorne's imagination. His ancestors included one judge who had prosecuted Quakers in the 1650s and another who had served in the notorious witchcraft trials at Salem, Massachusetts, in 1692. No churchgoer, Hawthorne was still as keenly aware of problems of sin and guilt as any early Puritan. He explored complex questions of right and wrong in tales he called "allegories of the heart"—stories that teach a moral principle.

"What other dungeon is so dark as one's own heart! What jailer so inexorable as one's self!"

—Nathaniel Hawthorne
from *The House of the Seven Gables*

Habits of Solitude Born in Salem, young Hawthorne was an avid reader of poetry and stories of adventure. He also spent long periods alone in the remote Maine woods, where "I first got my cursed habits of solitude." After attending college in Maine, Hawthorne returned to Salem, where he secluded himself at home for the "twelve lonely years" of his apprenticeship as a writer. He produced two books, first a novel titled *Fanshawe* and later a collection of short stories, *Twice-Told Tales*. The novel was a failure, but reviewers praised *Twice-Told Tales*, and the book sold well. In the late 1830s, as Hawthorne was beginning to establish his reputation as a writer, he met and fell in love with Sophia Peabody, whom he married in 1842. The couple moved to Concord, where Hawthorne socialized with Ralph Waldo Emerson and Henry David Thoreau. However, Hawthorne was not in sympathy with Emerson's optimistic outlook and goals of reforming society.

Literary Success Unable to support his growing family as a writer, Hawthorne returned to Salem and took a government job that he disliked. When he lost the job, he turned again to writing, completing his masterpiece, *The Scarlet Letter*, in early 1850. Although he feared it would be a failure, the book was a sensation, and Hawthorne soon followed it with another successful novel, *The House of the Seven Gables*. During this period, he moved his family from Salem to the countryside, where a close neighbor was the writer Herman Melville. The two writers, who shared a dark view of human life, spent a great deal of time together.

Hawthorne's final years were shadowed by the coming of the Civil War. Not motivated by antislavery zeal, he saw the conflict as a collapse of the social order, not a sacred cause. In ill health, struggling to continue writing, and depressed, Hawthorne died while on a journey.

In his novels and stories, Hawthorne set himself the challenge of creating "a neutral ground where the Actual and the Imaginary might meet." When he succeeds, his fiction has, as the literary critic Alfred Kazin observes, "the mysterious authenticity and the self-sufficient form of a dream."

Nathaniel Hawthorne was born in 1804 and died in 1864.

Literature Online Author Search For more about Nathaniel Hawthorne, go to www.glencoe.com.

Connecting to the Story

Does everyone wear a "mask" of some kind? In Hawthorne's short story, a New England minister conceals his face literally with a black veil. As you read the story, think about the following questions:

- Under what circumstances might you want to distance yourself from those around you?
- How much does a person's appearance affect how people feel about him or her?

Building Background

"The Minister's Black Veil" is set in a small town in Puritan New England in the early 1700s. Puritanism was a sect that broke away from the Church of England in the 1500s. In the 1600s, Puritans came to New England and founded a community based on biblical laws. Puritans believed that human beings were sinful by nature and deserved eternal punishment but that God had "elected" some people to be saved. Puritans fought the "natural" tendency to sin and felt responsible for the moral welfare of others. Keeping a close eye on the behavior of others was elevated to a religious duty—"holy watching," or "doing the Lord's work." The subtitle of "The Minister's Black Veil" is "A Parable." A parable is a story with a moral lesson that teaches forgiveness of sinners.

Setting Purposes for Reading

Big Idea The Power of Darkness

As you read, notice how the Romantics' dark fascination with the strange and sinister is displayed in "The Minister's Black Veil."

Literary Element Symbol

A **symbol** is a person, place, or thing that has meaning in itself and also stands for something other than itself. A crossroads, for example, may symbolize choices in life. A symbol in a literary work may have many meanings and feelings associated with it, or it may point to something that cannot be precisely defined. As you read the story, examine how Hawthorne develops the symbolic meaning of the minister's decision to veil his face.

- See Literary Terms Handbook, p. R18.

Reading Strategy Making Inferences

To **infer** is to make a reasonable guess about the meaning of a literary work from what a writer implies. In a symbolic story such as "The Minister's Black Veil," we must observe details to infer the writer's meaning.

....

Reading Tip: Taking Notes Use a chart to record the inferences you draw from the details presented.

Detail	Inference
p. 269 "Many spread their clasped hands on their bosoms."	The members of the congregation seem to feel the minister can see into their hearts.

Vocabulary

venerable (ven′ ər ə bəl) *adj.* deserving respect because of age, character, or position; p. 268 *The people relied on the venerable judge's wisdom.*

iniquity (in ik′ wə tē) *n.* sin; p. 269 *He was too steeped in iniquity to tell right from wrong.*

sagacious (sə gā′ shəs) *adj.* having or showing wisdom and keen perception; p. 269 *Careful planning is typical of a sagacious person.*

irreproachable (ir′ i prō′ chə bəl) *adj.* free from blame; faultless; p. 274 *The lawyer's handling of the case was irreproachable, but her client still lost.*

zealous (zel′ əs) *adj.* filled with enthusiastic devotion; passionate; p. 274 *Overly zealous, the waiter kept asking if we needed anything.*

....

Vocabulary Tip: Synonyms Synonyms are words that have the same or similar meanings. Note that synonyms are always the same part of speech.

Literature Online **Interactive Literary Elements Handbook** To review or learn more about the literary elements, go to www.glencoe.com.

INDIANA ACADEMIC STANDARDS (pages 266–278)

11.3.4 Analyze ways in which...prose uses imagery...to evoke readers' emotions.

11.2 Develop [reading] strategies...

11.5.2 Write responses to literature that demonstrate... understanding of the significant ideas in works...

11.3.2 Analyze...theme...

A PARABLE

The Minister's Black Veil

Nathaniel Hawthorne

The sexton[1] stood in the porch of Milford meeting-house, pulling busily at the bell-rope. The old people of the village came stooping along the street. Children, with bright faces, tripped merrily beside their parents, or mimicked a graver gait, in the conscious dignity of their Sunday clothes. Spruce[2] bachelors looked sidelong at the pretty maidens, and fancied that the Sabbath sunshine made them prettier than on week days. When the throng had mostly streamed into the porch, the sexton began to toll the bell, keeping his eye on the Reverend Mr. Hooper's door. The first glimpse of the clergyman's figure was the signal for the bell to cease its summons.

"But what has good Parson Hooper got upon his face?" cried the sexton in astonishment.

All within hearing immediately turned about, and beheld the semblance of Mr. Hooper, pacing slowly his meditative way towards the meetinghouse. With one accord[3] they started,[4] expressing more wonder than if some strange minister were coming to dust the cushions of Mr. Hooper's pulpit.[5]

"Are you sure it is our parson?" inquired Goodman[6] Gray of the sexton.

"Of a certainty it is good Mr. Hooper," replied the sexton. "He was to have exchanged pulpits with Parson Shute, of Westbury; but Parson Shute sent to excuse himself yesterday, being to preach a funeral sermon."

The cause of so much amazement may appear sufficiently slight. Mr. Hooper, a gentlemanly person, of about thirty, though still a bachelor, was dressed with due clerical neatness, as if a careful wife had starched his band, and brushed

---

1. A *sexton* is a church employee who cares for church property and who may also ring the bells and dig graves.
2. *Spruce* means "neat and trim in appearance" or "dapper."
3. *With one accord* means "with complete agreement" or "with unity."
4. Here, *started* means "made a sudden involuntary movement, as from fear or surprise."
5. A *pulpit* is a raised structure from which a minister delivers a sermon or conducts a worship service.
6. *Goodman* is a title of polite address similar to "Mister."

the weekly dust from his Sunday's garb. There was but one thing remarkable in his appearance. Swathed about his forehead, and hanging down over his face, so low as to be shaken by his breath, Mr. Hooper had on a black veil. On a nearer view it seemed to consist of two folds of crepe,[7] which entirely concealed his features, except the mouth and chin, but probably did not intercept his sight, further than to give a darkened aspect to all living and inanimate things. With this gloomy shade before him, good Mr. Hooper walked onward, at a slow and quiet pace, stooping somewhat, and looking on the ground, as is customary with abstracted[8] men, yet nodding kindly to those of his parishioners who still waited on the meeting-house steps. But so wonder-struck were they that his greeting hardly met with a return.

"I can't really feel as if good Mr. Hooper's face was behind that piece of crepe," said the sexton.

"I don't like it," muttered an old woman, as she hobbled into the meeting-house. "He has changed himself into something awful, only by hiding his face."

"Our parson has gone mad!" cried Goodman Gray, following him across the threshold.

A rumor of some unaccountable phenomenon had preceded Mr. Hooper into the meeting-house, and set all the congregation astir. Few could refrain from twisting their heads towards the door; many stood upright, and turned directly about; while several little boys clambered upon the seats, and came down again with a terrible racket. There was a general bustle, a rustling of the women's gowns and shuffling of the men's feet, greatly at variance with that hushed repose which should attend the entrance of the minister. But Mr. Hooper appeared not to notice the perturbation[9] of his

> He has changed himself into something awful, only by hiding his face.

people. He entered with an almost noiseless step, bent his head mildly to the pews on each side, and bowed as he passed his oldest parishioner, a white-haired great grandsire, who occupied an arm-chair in the center of the aisle. It was strange to observe how slowly this venerable man became conscious of something singular in the appearance of his pastor. He seemed not fully to partake of the prevailing wonder, till Mr. Hooper had ascended the stairs, and showed himself in the pulpit, face to face with his congregation, except for the black veil. That mysterious emblem was never once withdrawn. It shook with his measured breath, as he gave out the psalm; it threw its obscurity between him and the holy page, as he read the Scriptures; and while he prayed, the veil lay heavily on his uplifted countenance.[10] Did he seek to hide it from the dread Being whom he was addressing?

Such was the effect of this simple piece of crepe, that more than one woman of delicate nerves was forced to leave the meeting-house. Yet perhaps the pale-faced congregation was almost as fearful a sight to the minister, as his black veil to them.

Mr. Hooper had the reputation of a good preacher, but not an energetic one: he strove to win his people heavenward by mild, persuasive influences, rather than to drive them thither by the thunders of the Word. The sermon which he now delivered was marked by the same characteristics of style and manner as the general series of his pulpit oratory. But there was something, either in the sentiment of the discourse itself, or in the imagination of the auditors,[11] which made it greatly the most powerful effort that they had

---

7. *Crepe* is a light, soft fabric with a crinkled surface.
8. Here, *abstracted* means "lost in thought" or "preoccupied."
9. *Perturbation* (pur´ tər bā´ shən) means "agitation" or "uneasiness."

10. *Countenance* means "face."
11. *Auditors* are "those who hear" or "listeners."

ever heard from their pastor's lips. It was tinged, rather more darkly than usual, with the gentle gloom of Mr. Hooper's temperament. The subject had reference to secret sin, and those sad mysteries which we hide from our nearest and dearest, and would fain[12] conceal from our own consciousness, even forgetting that the Omniscient[13] can detect them. A subtle power was breathed into his words. Each member of the congregation, the most innocent girl, and the man of hardened breast, felt as if the preacher had crept upon them, behind his awful veil, and discovered their hoarded **iniquity** of deed or thought. Many spread their clasped hands on their bosoms. There was nothing terrible in what Mr. Hooper said, at least, no violence; and yet, with every tremor of his melancholy voice, the hearers quaked. An unsought pathos[14] came hand in hand with awe. So sensible were the audience of some unwonted[15] attribute in their minister, that they longed for a breath of wind to blow aside the veil, almost believing that a stranger's visage[16] would be discovered, though the form, gesture, and voice were those of Mr. Hooper.

At the close of the services, the people hurried out with indecorous confusion, eager to communicate their pent-up amazement, and conscious of lighter spirits the moment they lost sight of the black veil. Some gathered in little circles, huddled closely together, with their mouths all whispering in the center; some went homeward alone, wrapt in silent meditation; some talked loudly, and profaned the Sabbath day with ostentatious laughter. A few shook their **sagacious** heads, intimating that they could penetrate the mystery; while one or two affirmed that there was no mystery at all, but only that Mr. Hooper's eyes were so weakened by the midnight lamp, as to require a shade. After a brief interval, forth came good Mr. Hooper also, in the rear of his flock. Turning his veiled face from one group to another, he paid due reverence to the hoary heads,[17] saluted the middle aged with kind dignity as their friend and spiritual guide, greeted the young with mingled authority and love, and laid his hands on the little children's heads to bless them. Such was always his custom on the Sabbath day. Strange and bewildered looks repaid him for his courtesy. None, as on former occasions, aspired to the honor of walking by their pastor's side. Old Squire Saunders, doubtless by an accidental lapse of memory, neglected to invite Mr. Hooper to his table, where the good clergyman had been wont[18] to bless the food, almost every Sunday since his settlement. He returned, therefore, to the parsonage, and, at the moment of closing the door, was observed to look back upon the people, all of whom had their eyes fixed upon the minister. A sad smile gleamed faintly from beneath the black veil, and flickered about his mouth, glimmering as he disappeared.

"How strange," said a lady, "that a simple black veil, such as any woman might wear on her bonnet, should become such a terrible thing on Mr. Hooper's face!"

"Something must surely be amiss with Mr. Hooper's intellects," observed her husband, the physician of the village. "But the strangest part of the affair is the effect of this vagary,[19] even on a sober-minded man like myself. The black veil, though it covers only our pastor's face, throws its influence over his whole person, and makes him ghostlike from head to foot. Do you not feel it so?"

"Truly do I," replied the lady; "and I would not be alone with him for the world. I wonder he is not afraid to be alone with himself!"

"Men sometimes are so," said her husband.

The afternoon service was attended with similar circumstances. At its conclusion, the bell tolled for the funeral of a young lady. The relatives and friends were assembled in the house, and the more distant acquaintances stood about the door, speaking of the good qualities of the deceased, when their talk was interrupted by the appearance of Mr. Hooper, still covered with his

---

12. *Fain* means "gladly" or "willingly."
13. *The Omniscient* is "the all-knowing," or God.
14. *Pathos* is a feeling of pity, compassion, or sorrow.
15. *Unwonted* means "not customary" or "unusual."
16. *Visage* means "face."

17. *Hoary heads* are white-haired heads.
18. *Wont* means "accustomed."
19. A *vagary* is an odd or erratic action or idea.

Literary Element Symbol *What meaning does this comment give to the symbolism of the veil?*

The Sermon, 1886. Julius Gari Melchers. Oil on canvas. Smithsonian American Art Museum, Washington, DC.
Viewing the Art: How does this artist show different responses to the minister's preaching?

black veil. It was now an appropriate emblem. The clergyman stepped into the room where the corpse was laid, and bent over the coffin, to take a last farewell of his deceased parishioner. As he stooped, the veil hung straight down from his forehead, so that, if her eyelids had not been closed forever, the dead maiden might have seen his face. Could Mr. Hooper be fearful of her glance, that he so hastily caught back the black veil? A person who watched the interview between the dead and living, scrupled[20] not to affirm, that, at the instant when the clergyman's features were disclosed, the corpse had slightly shuddered, rustling the shroud[21] and muslin cap, though the countenance retained the composure of death. A superstitious old woman was the only witness of this prodigy.[22] From the coffin Mr. Hooper passed into the chamber of the mourners, and thence to the head of the staircase, to make the funeral prayer. It was a tender and heart-dissolving prayer, full of sorrow, yet so imbued with celestial hopes, that the music of a heavenly harp, swept by the fingers of the dead, seemed faintly to be heard among the saddest accents of the minister. The people trembled, though they but darkly understood him when he prayed that they, and himself, and all of mortal race, might be ready, as he trusted this young maiden had been, for the dreadful hour that should snatch the veil from their faces. The bearers went heavily forth, and the mourners followed, saddening all the street, with

the dead before them, and Mr. Hooper in his black veil behind.

"Why do you look back?" said one in the procession to his partner.

"I had a fancy," replied she, "that the minister and the maiden's spirit were walking hand in hand."

"And so had I, at the same moment," said the other.

That night, the handsomest couple in Milford village were to be joined in wedlock. Though reckoned a melancholy man, Mr. Hooper had a placid cheerfulness for such occasions, which often excited a sympathetic smile where livelier merriment would have been thrown away. There was no quality of his disposition which made him more beloved than this. The company at the wedding awaited his arrival with impatience, trusting that the strange awe, which had gathered over him throughout the day, would now be dispelled. But such was not the result. When Mr. Hooper came, the first thing that their eyes rested on was the same horrible black veil, which had added deeper gloom to the funeral, and could portend[23] nothing but evil to the wedding. Such was its immediate effect on the guests that a cloud seemed to have rolled duskily from beneath the black crepe, and dimmed the light of the candles. The bridal pair stood up before the minister. But the bride's cold fingers quivered in the tremulous hand[24] of the bridegroom, and her deathlike paleness caused a whisper that the maiden who had been buried a few hours before was come from her grave to be married. If ever another wedding were so dismal, it was that famous one where they tolled the wedding knell.[25] After performing the ceremony, Mr. Hooper raised a glass of wine to

---

20. *Scrupled* means "hesitated."
21. A *shroud* is a cloth used to wrap a dead body for burial.
22. Here, *prodigy* means "an extraordinary event that causes amazement."

23. *Portend* means "to be a warning or an indication of."
24. A *tremulous hand* is one that is trembling or shaking.
25. Hawthorne is referring to his own short story "The Wedding Knell." A *knell* is the solemn sound of a bell ringing, as at a funeral.

Big Idea Power of Darkness *How does Hawthorne's description of the imaginings of those at the funeral service link his story to Gothic literature?*

his lips, wishing happiness to the newmarried couple in a strain of mild pleasantry that ought to have brightened the features of the guests, like a cheerful gleam from the hearth. At that instant, catching a glimpse of his figure in the looking-glass, the black veil involved his own spirit in the horror with which it overwhelmed all others. His frame shuddered, his lips grew white, he spilt the untasted wine upon the carpet, and rushed forth into the darkness. For the Earth, too, had on her Black Veil.

The next day, the whole village of Milford talked of little else than Parson Hooper's black veil. That, and the mystery concealed behind it, supplied a topic for discussion between acquaintances meeting in the street, and good women gossiping at their open windows. It was the first item of news that the tavern-keeper told to his guests. The children babbled of it on their way to school. One imitative little imp covered his face with an old black handkerchief, thereby so affrighting his playmates that the panic seized himself, and he well-nigh lost his wits by his own waggery.[26]

It was remarkable that of all the busybodies and impertinent people in the parish, not one ventured to put the plain question to Mr. Hooper, wherefore he did this thing. Hitherto, whenever there appeared the slightest call for such interference, he had never lacked advisers, nor shown himself averse to be guided by their judgment. If he erred at all, it was by so painful a degree of self-distrust, that even the mildest censure would lead him to consider an indifferent action as a crime. Yet, though so well acquainted with this amiable weakness, no individual among his parishioners chose to make the black veil a subject of friendly remonstrance. There was a feeling of dread, neither plainly confessed nor carefully

For the Earth, too, had on her Black Veil.

concealed, which caused each to shift the responsibility upon another, till at length it was found expedient to send a deputation[27] of the church, in order to deal with Mr. Hooper about the mystery, before it should grow into a scandal. Never did an embassy so ill discharge its duties. The minister received then with friendly courtesy, but became silent, after they were seated, leaving to his visitors the whole burden of introducing their important business. The topic, it might be supposed, was obvious enough. There was the black veil swathed round Mr. Hooper's forehead, and concealing every feature above his placid mouth, on which, at times, they could perceive the glimmering of a melancholy smile. But that piece of crepe, to their imagination, seemed to hang down before his heart, the symbol of a fearful secret between him and them. Were the veil but cast aside, they might speak freely of it, but not till then. Thus they sat a considerable time, speechless, confused, and shrinking uneasily from Mr. Hooper's eye, which they felt to be fixed upon them with an invisible glance. Finally, the deputies returned abashed[28] to their constituents, pronouncing the matter too weighty to be handled, except by a council of the churches, if, indeed, it might not require a general synod.[29]

But there was one person in the village unappalled by the awe with which the black veil had impressed all beside herself. When the deputies returned without an explanation, or even venturing to demand one, she, with the calm energy of her character, determined to chase away the strange cloud that appeared to be settling round Mr. Hooper, every moment more darkly than before. As his plighted wife,[30] it should be her privilege to

---

26. *Waggery* is mischievous or joking behavior.

Literary Element Symbol *What is Earth's "Black Veil"?*

Reading Strategy Making Inferences *How might the minister's self-distrust have led him to conceal his face?*

---

27. A *deputation* is a delegation.
28. *Abashed* means "ashamed" or "embarrassed."
29. A *synod* is a council of church officials or a governing body of all churches.
30. *Plighted wife* means "intended wife," or "fiancée."

know what the black veil concealed. At the minister's first visit, therefore, she entered upon the subject with a direct simplicity, which made the task easier both for him and her. After he had seated himself, she fixed her eyes steadfastly upon the veil, but could discern nothing of the dreadful gloom that had so overawed the multitude: it was but a double fold of crepe, hanging down from his forehead to his mouth, and slightly stirring with his breath.

"No," said she aloud, and smiling, "there is nothing terrible in this piece of crepe, except that it hides a face which I am always glad to look upon. Come, good sir, let the sun shine from behind the cloud. First lay aside your black veil: then tell me why you put it on."

Mr. Hooper's smile glimmered faintly.

"There is an hour to come," said he, "when all of us shall cast aside our veils. Take it not amiss, beloved friend, if I wear this piece of crepe till then."

"Your words are a mystery, too," returned the young lady. "Take away the veil from them, at least."

"Elizabeth, I will," said he, "so far as my vow may suffer me. Know, then, this veil is a type and a symbol, and I am bound to wear it ever, both in light and darkness, in solitude and before the gaze of multitudes, and as with strangers, so with my familiar friends. No mortal eye will see it withdrawn. This dismal shade must separate me from the world: even you, Elizabeth, can never come behind it!"

"What grievous affliction hath befallen you," she earnestly inquired, "that you should thus darken your eyes forever?"

"If it be a sign of mourning," replied Mr. Hooper, "I, perhaps, like most other mortals, have sorrows dark enough to be typified by a black veil."

"But what if the world will not believe that it is the type of an innocent sorrow?" urged Elizabeth. "Beloved and respected as you are, there may be whispers that you hide your face under the consciousness of secret sin. For the sake of your holy office, do away this scandal!"

The color rose into her cheeks as she intimated the nature of the rumors that were already abroad in the village. But Mr. Hooper's mildness did not forsake him. He even smiled again—that same sad smile, which always appeared like a faint glimmering of light, proceeding from the obscurity beneath the veil.

"If I hide my face for sorrow, there is cause enough," he merely replied; "and if I cover it for secret sin, what mortal might not do the same?"

And with this gentle, but unconquerable obstinacy did he resist all her entreaties.[31] At length Elizabeth sat silent. For a few moments she appeared lost in thought, considering, probably, what new methods might be tried to withdraw her lover from so dark a fantasy, which, if it had no other meaning, was perhaps a symptom of mental disease. Though of a firmer character than his own, the tears rolled down her cheeks. But, in an instant, as it were, a new feeling took the place of sorrow: her eyes were fixed insensibly on the black veil, when, like a sudden twilight in the air, its terrors fell around her. She arose, and stood trembling before him.

"And do you feel it then, at last?" said he mournfully.

She made no reply, but covered her eyes with her hand, and turned to leave the room. He rushed forward and caught her arm.

"Have patience with me, Elizabeth!" cried he, passionately. "Do not desert me, though this veil must be between us here on earth. Be mine, and hereafter there shall be no veil over my face, no darkness between our souls! It is but a mortal veil—it is not for eternity! O! you know not how lonely I am, and how frightened, to be alone behind my black veil. Do not leave me in this miserable obscurity forever!"

"Lift the veil but once, and look me in the face," said she.

"Never! It cannot be!" replied Mr. Hooper.

"Then farewell!" said Elizabeth.

She withdrew her arm from his grasp, and slowly departed, pausing at the door, to give

---

31. *Entreaties* are pleas.

Literary Element Symbol *Hawthorne closely links the minister's black veil with his "sad smile." How does this affect the meaning of the symbol?*

Reading Strategy Making Inferences *Why do you think Elizabeth decides to break off her engagement with Mr. Hooper?*

Literary Element Symbol *How does Mr. Hooper's reply to Elizabeth indicate another view of the veil's meaning?*

one long shuddering gaze, that seemed almost to penetrate the mystery of the black veil. But, even amid his grief, Mr. Hooper smiled to think that only a material emblem had separated him from happiness, though the horrors, which it shadowed forth, must be drawn darkly between the fondest of lovers.

From that time no attempts were made to remove Mr. Hooper's black veil, or, by a direct appeal, to discover the secret which it was supposed to hide. By persons who claimed a superiority to popular prejudice, it was reckoned merely an eccentric whim, such as often mingles with the sober actions of men otherwise rational, and tinges them all with its own semblance of insanity. But with the multitude, good Mr. Hooper was irreparably a bugbear.[32] He could not walk the street with any peace of mind, so conscious was he that the gentle and timid would turn aside to avoid him, and that others would make it a point of hardihood[33] to throw themselves in his way. The impertinence of the latter class compelled him to give up his customary walk at sunset to the burial ground; for when he leaned pensively over the gate, there would always be faces behind the gravestones, peeping at his black veil. A fable went the rounds that the stare of the dead people drove him thence. It grieved him, to the very depth of his kind heart, to observe how the children fled from his approach, breaking up their merriest sports, while his melancholy figure was yet afar off. Their instinctive dread caused him to feel more strongly than aught else, that a preternatural[34] horror was interwoven with the threads of the black crepe.

In truth, his own antipathy[35] to the veil was known to be so great, that he never willingly passed before a mirror, nor stooped to drink at a still fountain, lest, in its peaceful bosom, he should be affrighted by himself. This was what gave plausibility to the whispers, that Mr. Hooper's conscience tortured him for some great crime too horrible to be entirely concealed, or otherwise than so obscurely intimated. Thus, from beneath the black veil, there rolled a cloud into the sunshine, an ambiguity of sin or sorrow, which enveloped the poor minister, so that love or sympathy could never reach him. It was said that ghost and fiend consorted with him there. With self-shudderings and outward terrors, he walked continually in its shadow, groping darkly within his own soul, or gazing through a medium that saddened the whole world. Even the lawless wind, it was believed, respected his dreadful secret, and never blew aside the veil. But still good Mr. Hooper sadly smiled at the pale visages of the worldly throng as he passed by.

Among all its bad influences, the black veil had the one desirable effect, of making its wearer a very efficient clergyman. By the aid of his mysterious emblem—for there was no other apparent cause—he became a man of awful power over souls that were in agony for sin. His converts always regarded him with a dread peculiar to themselves, affirming, though but figuratively, that, before he brought them to celestial light, they had been with him behind the black veil. Its gloom, indeed, enabled him to sympathize with all dark affections. Dying sinners cried aloud for Mr. Hooper, and would not yield their breath till he appeared; though ever, as he stooped to whisper consolation, they shuddered at the veiled face so near their own. Such were the terrors of the black veil, even when Death had bared his visage! Strangers came long distances to attend service at his church, with the mere idle purpose of gazing at his figure, because it was forbidden them to behold his face. But many were made to quake ere they departed! Once, during Governor Belcher's[36] administration, Mr. Hooper was appointed to preach the election sermon.[37] Covered with his black veil, he stood before the chief magistrate, the council, and the representatives, and wrought[38] so deep an impression, that the legislative measures of that year were characterized by all the gloom and piety of our earliest ancestral sway.[39]

---

32. A *bugbear* is a real or imaginary object of fear.
33. *Hardihood* is offensive boldness or daring.
34. *Preternatural* means "supernatural."
35. *Antipathy* is a feeling of intense dislike.

36. Jonathan *Belcher* was a governor of Massachusetts and New Hampshire from 1730 to 1741.
37. Mr. Hooper was given the honor of preaching at the governor's inaugural ceremony.
38. Here, *wrought* means "made."
39. Here, *sway* means "influence."

Reading Strategy Making Inferences *What does Hawthorne mean by "dark affections"? Why has Mr. Hooper come to understand or share these emotions?*

In this manner Mr. Hooper spent a long life, **irreproachable** in outward act, yet shrouded in dismal suspicions; kind and loving, though unloved, and dimly feared; a man apart from men, shunned in their health and joy, but ever summoned to their aid in mortal anguish. As years wore on, shedding their snows above his sable veil,[40] he acquired a name throughout the New England churches, and they called him Father Hooper. Nearly all his parishioners, who were of mature age when he was settled, had been borne away by many a funeral: he had one congregation in the church, and a more crowded one in the churchyard; and having wrought[41] so late into the evening, and done his work so well, it was now good Father Hooper's turn to rest.

Several persons were visible by the shaded candlelight, in the death chamber of the old clergyman. Natural connections[42] he had none. But there was the decorously grave, though unmoved physician, seeking only to mitigate[43] the last pangs of the patient whom he could not save. There were the deacons, and other eminently pious members of his church. There, also, was the Reverend Mr. Clark, of Westbury, a young and **zealous** divine, who had ridden in haste to pray by the bedside of the expiring minister. There was the nurse, no hired handmaiden of death, but one whose calm affection had endured thus long in secrecy, in solitude, amid the chill of age, and would not perish, even at the dying hour. Who, but Elizabeth! And there lay the hoary head of good Father Hooper upon the death pillow, with the

> ## Are you ready for the lifting of the veil that shuts in time from eternity?

black veil still swathed about his brow, and reaching down over his face, so that each more difficult gasp of his faint breath caused it to stir. All through life that piece of crepe had hung between him and the world: it had separated him from cheerful brotherhood and woman's love, and kept him in that saddest of all prisons, his own heart; and still it lay upon his face, as if to deepen the gloom of his darksome chamber, and shade him from the sunshine of eternity.

For some time previous, his mind had been confused, wavering doubtfully between the past and the present, and hovering forward, as it were, at intervals, into the indistinctness of the world to come. There had been feverish turns, which tossed him from side to side, and wore away what little strength he had. But in his most convulsive struggles, and in the wildest vagaries of his intellect, when no other thought retained its sober influence, he still showed an awful solicitude[44] lest the black veil should slip aside. Even if his bewildered soul could have forgotten, there was a faithful woman at this pillow, who, with averted eyes, would have covered that aged face, which she had last beheld in the comeliness of manhood. At length the death-stricken old man lay quietly in the torpor[45] of mental and bodily exhaustion, with an imperceptible pulse, and breath that grew fainter and fainter, except when a long, deep, and irregular inspiration seemed to prelude the flight of his spirit.

The minister of Westbury approached the bedside. "Venerable Father Hooper," said he, "the moment of your release is at hand. Are you ready for the lifting of the veil that shuts in time from eternity?"

Father Hooper at first replied merely by a feeble motion of his head; then, apprehensive,

---

40. *[As years ... veil]* This phrase refers to the fact that his hair was turning white with time.
41. Here, *wrought* means "worked."
42. *Natural connections* are relatives.
43. *Mitigate* means "to make less intense, severe, or painful."

44. *Solicitude* means "concern" or "anxiety."
45. *Torpor* is a state of being unable to move or feel.

Literary Element Symbol *Several times the narrator describes the movement of the veil caused by Mr. Hooper's breath. What quality does this give to the symbol?*

One of the most representative examples of American colonial craft is the tombstone, which typically displays the sense of the nearness of death that was so deeply a part of this culture.

perhaps, that his meaning might be doubted, he exerted himself to speak.

"Yea," said he, in faint accents, "my soul hath a patient weariness until that veil be lifted."

"And is it fitting," resumed the Reverend Mr. Clark, "that a man so given to prayer, of such a blameless example, holy in deed and thought, so far as mortal judgment may pronounce; is it fitting that a father in the church should leave a shadow on his memory, that may seem to blacken a life so pure? I pray you, my venerable brother, let not this thing be! Suffer us to be gladdened by your triumphant aspect as you go to your reward. Before the veil of eternity be lifted, let me cast aside this black veil from your face!"

And thus speaking, the Reverend Mr. Clark bent forward to reveal the mystery of so many years. But, exerting a sudden energy, that made all the beholders stand aghast, Father Hooper snatched both his hands from beneath the bedclothes, and pressed them strongly on the black veil, resolute to struggle, if the minister of Westbury would contend with a dying man.

"Never!" cried the veiled clergyman. "On earth, never!"

"Dark old man!" exclaimed the affrighted minister, "with what horrible crime upon your soul are you now passing to the judgment?"

Father Hooper's breath heaved; it rattled in his throat; but, with a mighty effort, grasping forward with his hands, he caught hold of life, and held it back till he should speak. He even raised himself in bed; and there he sat, shivering with the arms of death around him, while the black veil hung down, awful, at that last moment, in the gathered terrors of a lifetime. And yet the faint, sad smile, so often there, now seemed to glimmer from its obscurity, and linger on Father Hooper's lips.

"Why do you tremble at me alone?" cried he, turning his veiled face round the circle of pale spectators. "Tremble also at each other! Have men avoided me, and women shown no pity, and children screamed and fled, only for my black veil? What, but the mystery which it obscurely typifies, has made this piece of crepe so awful? When the friend shows his inmost heart to his friend; the lover to his best beloved; when man does not vainly shrink from the eye of his Creator, loathsomely treasuring up the secret of his sin; then deem me a monster, for the symbol beneath which I have lived, and die! I look around me, and, lo! on every visage a Black Veil!"

While his auditors shrank from one another, in mutual affright, Father Hooper fell back upon his pillow, a veiled corpse, with a faint smile lingering on the lips. Still veiled, they laid him in his coffin, and a veiled corpse they bore him to the grave. The grass of many years has sprung up and withered on that grave, the burial stone is moss-grown, and good Mr. Hooper's face is dust; but awful is still the thought that it moldered[46] beneath the Black Veil! ❧

---

46. *Moldered* means "turned to dust" or "crumbled."

Literary Element   Symbol *To what "mystery" do you think the minister is referring?*

Big Idea   The Power of Darkness *How does this final detail reflect the dark side of Romanticism?*

RESPONDING AND THINKING CRITICALLY

Respond

1. (a)What was your first reaction to the minister's black veil? (b)Did your reaction change as the story developed?

Recall and Interpret

2. (a)How do the townspeople react when they first see Mr. Hooper wearing the black veil? (b)Why might the veil affect them as it does?

3. (a)What is the subject of Mr. Hooper's sermon on the first day he wears the black veil? (b)What do you think is the association between the veil and congregation's interpretation of the sermon?

4. (a)Briefly retell in your own words the main events of the story. (b)Which of these events was most surprising?

Analyze and Evaluate

5. (a)What is "the one desirable effect" that the veil has on Mr. Hooper? (b)What are the negative effects?

6. (a)What does Elizabeth's changing relationship with Mr. Hooper reveal about her personality? (b)Do you find her a sympathetic character? Explain.

7. (a)What do you think was most puzzling about the story? (b)Write your thoughts down in the form of question.

Connect

8. Do you think that the veil eventually causes Mr. Hooper to become a better minister? Why or why not?

9. **Big Idea** **The Power of Darkness** The Puritan view of sin and human nature is a basic element of this story. How is the Romantic view of human nature also shown?

YOU'RE THE CRITIC: Different Viewpoints

HOW PESSIMISTIC WAS HAWTHORNE?

Read the two excerpts of literary criticism below. Both critics agree that Hawthorne's writing has a light and a dark side. As you read the excerpts, notice the difference in emphasis between the two critics.

> *"What pleased [Hawthorne in gloomy subjects] was their picturesqueness, their rich duskiness of color, their chiaroscuro; but they were not the expression of a hopeless, or even of a predominantly melancholy, feeling about the human soul."*
> —Henry James

> *"Perhaps no writer has ever wielded this terrific thought [Original Sin] with greater terror than this same harmless Hawthorne. Still more: this black conceit pervades him through and through. You may be witched by his sunlight,—transported by the bright gildings in the skies he builds over you; but . . . even his bright gildings but fringe and play upon the edges of thunder-clouds."*
> —Herman Melville

Group Activity Discuss the following questions with classmates. Refer to the excerpts and cite evidence from "The Minister's Black Veil" for support.

1. (a)What is the difference in emphasis between James and Melville? (b)Which critic do you think comes closer to an accurate assessment of Hawthorne's pessimism? Explain.

2. Chiaroscuro is a technique used by visual artists to balance light and shadow. How might this technique apply to Hawthorne's outlook on the human condition?

Literary Element Symbol

There are two basic types of symbols—traditional and original. Traditional symbols usually have a single meaning. For example, the theater masks shown here are traditional symbols representing the two sides of drama—comedy and tragedy.

In contrast, writers often create original symbols that have no familiar meanings to readers. This allows writers more freedom to develop what the symbols represent.

1. What kind of symbol—traditional or original—does Hawthorne use in "The Minister's Black Veil"? Explain.

2. What different meanings do you think the black veil represents for Mr. Hooper, Elizabeth, and the townspeople?

3. Why do you think Hawthorne chose not to explain why Mr. Hooper wears the veil? How does this choice contribute to the power of the veil as a symbol?

Review: Characterization

Characterization refers to the various methods that a writer uses to develop the personality of a character.

Partner Activity Meet with a classmate and talk about how you got to know Mr. Hooper better as you read the story. Working with your partner, create a web diagram like the one below. Then fill it in with a striking example for each method of characterization that Hawthorne uses to portray Mr. Hooper.

Reading Strategy Making Inferences

Inferences About Theme The subtitle of "The Minister's Black Veil" is "A Parable." A parable is a story that teaches a moral lesson. By calling his story a parable, Hawthorne implies that it has a central message, or theme, but this theme is never directly stated. Review the inference chart you created for clues about the theme of this story.

1. What do you think is the theme of "The Minister's Black Veil"?

2. In support of your opinion, list three important details from the story and the inferences you drew from them.

Vocabulary Practice

Practice with Synonyms Find the synonym for each vocabulary word from "The Minister's Black Veil" listed in the first column. Use a dictionary or a thesaurus if you need help.

1. venerable   **a.** esteemed   **b.** famous

2. iniquity   **a.** guilt   **b.** wickedness

3. sagacious   **a.** wise   **b.** foolish

4. irreproachable   **a.** reckless   **b.** faultless

5. zealous   **a.** uncaring   **b.** enthusiastic

Academic Vocabulary

Here are two vocabulary words from the vocabulary list on page R86.

culture (kul' chər) *n.* a people's unique way of life—customs, art, rituals, and beliefs

ideology (ə' dē ŏl' ə jē) *n.* a set of principles and thoughts that guides an individual or a group

Practice and Apply

1. What did you learn about Puritan **culture** from reading "The Minister's Black Veil"?

2. How would you describe the **ideology** that guides Mr. Hooper's role as minister?

Writing About Literature

Respond to Theme The narrator of "The Minister's Black Veil" states that one's own heart is "the saddest of all prisons" (page 274). Write a brief essay explaining why you agree or disagree with this assertion. Use evidence from the story and examples from your own experience to defend your position.

As you draft, write from start to finish. Follow the writing path shown here to help you organize your essay and keep you on track.

START

Introduction ····▶ Present your interpretation of the quotation and the position you plan to defend.

Body Paragraph(s) ····▶ Add supporting evidence.

Conclusion ····▶ Briefly summarize your position and consider offering a related insight.

FINISH

After you complete your draft, meet with a peer reviewer to evaluate each other's work and to suggest revisions. Then proofread and edit your draft for errors in spelling, grammar, and punctuation.

Literary Criticism

Group Activity In his review of *Twice-Told Tales,* a collection of Hawthorne's short stories, Poe called "The Minister's Black Veil" a "masterly composition." Meet with a few of your classmates to collaborate on writing five blurbs—short descriptions from reviews that might appear on a book jacket for "The Minister's Black Veil." As you write the blurbs, praise the story for its greatest merits.

Literature Online **Web Activities** For eFlashcards, Selection Quick Checks, and other Web activities, go to www.glencoe.com.

Hawthorne's Language and Style

Choosing Precise Words In "The Minister's Black Veil," Hawthorne chooses adjectives that evoke a gloomy mood, or atmosphere:

> "*horrible* black veil"
> "*dreadful* secret"
> "*deathlike* paleness"

To help your readers better picture your ideas, use words with specific meanings. For example, in "The Minister's Black Veil," the noun *bonnet* is clearer than *hat,* the verb *strove* is clearer than *tried,* and the adjective *impertinent* is clearer than *impolite.*

- Make sure that the word's **denotation,** or literal definition, expresses the meaning you have in mind. Be especially careful to differentiate between words whose meanings are often confused, such as the examples below.

imply	infer
disinterested	uninterested
respectfully	respectively

- Be sensitive to a word's **connotation**—the positive or negative association that the word can evoke. Make sure that the connotation of the words you choose supports the meaning and tone you intend. The words below have similar meanings but very different connotations.

Positive	Negative
curious	nosy
thin	skinny
thrifty	cheap

Activity Scan Hawthorne's story for other examples of adjectives with positive or negative connotations suggesting gloom. Make a list of them to read aloud and explain to the class.

Revising Check

Precise Words Work with a partner to improve word choices in your essay for "The Minister's Black Veil."

Grammar Workshop

Sentence Structure

Correcting Dangling Modifiers

"Children, with bright faces, tripped merrily beside their parents, or mimicked a graver gait, in the conscious dignity of their Sunday clothes."

—Nathaniel Hawthorne, from *The Minister's Black Veil*

Connecting to Literature Notice how Hawthorne places the phrase "with bright faces" directly after the noun it modifies, *children*. If he had placed that modifier later in the sentence, its meaning may not have been clear. For example, if Hawthorne had written "Children tripped merrily beside their parents with bright faces . . . ," one could interpret that "with bright faces" modifies *parents*.

A modifier *changes* the meaning of a word. Although modifiers can help readers clarify meaning, a dangling modifier creates confusion. A dangling modifier is a phrase that does not clearly or logically modify any word in a sentence. Very often, a dangling modifier is a participle or participial phrase.

The dangling modifier is circled in the first sentence of each pair below. As written, these sentences seem to mean that a fire worked all night and that a door ran across a room. To correct a sentence that has a dangling modifier, make sure that the participial phrase, or modifier, clearly and sensibly modifies a word.

Below, an arrow points from the modifier to the word it modifies.

Dangling: Working all night long, the blaze was finally extinguished.

Corrected: Working all night long, the firefighters finally extinguished the blaze.

Dangling: Sprinting across the room, the heavy door slammed in my face.

Corrected: Sprinting across the room, I saw the heavy door slam in my face.

Exercise

Revise for Clarity Rewrite these sentences, correcting the dangling modifiers.

1. Looking for movie ideas, Poe's stories were discovered.
2. Working feverishly, the script was finally finished.
3. Watching the 1926 film *The Scarlet Letter*, the theater was filled.
4. Gesturing wildly, the audience smiled at the silent film actress.
5. Admitted to the theater late, the lights were out.

▶ **Participial Phrases**

A **participle** is a verb form that ends in *–ed* or *–ing*. **Participial phrases** always act as adjectives. A participial phrase at the beginning of a sentence is usually followed by a comma.

▶ **Test-Taking Tip**

Read grammar questions carefully on standardized tests, such as the SAT. It is easy to miss dangling modifiers. You may understand the writer's intention while missing the grammatical error.

▶ **Language Handbook**

For more on modifiers, see Language Handbook p. R46–R47.

eWorkbooks To link to the Grammar and Language eWorkbook, go to www.glencoe.com.

 ACADEMIC STANDARDS (page 279)
11.6.1 Demonstrate control of... sentence structure...

11.6.4 Identify and correctly use... phrases, including... participial...

from *Moby-Dick*

MEET HERMAN MELVILLE

NO! in thunder." This, according to Herman Melville, is what the true writer says. With his own great "NO!" Melville set himself against the optimism of Emerson and the Transcendentalists, challenged conformity, and rejected the idea of progress and prosperity that dominated the American mind in the 1800s.

Adventure and Fame Born in New York City, Melville faced many misfortunes in his youth despite being the son of a wealthy merchant. He was forced to leave school at twelve and instead of studying, he focused on finding a profession. Unable to do so, in 1841 he became a sailor aboard the whale ship *Acushnet,* bound for the South Pacific.

During his time as a sailor, Melville jumped ship and lived for a month with the Typee, a supposedly cannibalistic tribe that nevertheless treated him graciously, took part in a mutiny, and spent time in jail on the island of Tahiti. These sailing years gave him the background knowledge of ships and exotic islands that served him well in his first two novels, *Typee* (1846) and *Omoo* (1847), both popular tales of adventure.

The success of these novels brought temporary stability into Melville's life. In 1847, he married Elizabeth Shaw, the daughter of the chief justice of Massachusetts. He became a literary celebrity in both England and America. His sudden success, however, was short-lived because he refused to continue writing the sort of adventure books the public craved. His third novel, *Mardi* (1849), written in a new allegorical style, was not what readers of that era expected from an author of adventures, and as a result it was poorly received.

Critical Neglect In 1850, Melville purchased a farm near Pittsfield, Massachusetts, and befriended the writer Nathaniel Hawthorne, who lived just six miles away. The two writers had much in common: they shared the Puritan view of humanity as inherently evil, and they wrote fiction that explored the dark side of life.

Hawthorne's influence can be seen in Melville's later work, beginning with his masterpiece, *Moby-Dick,* a whaling story of great complexity and power, meant to rival the work of Shakespeare. Published in 1851, this tale of the obsessed hero-villain Captain Ahab and his doomed search for the white whale is now regarded as one of the greatest American novels. When the novel first appeared, however, it met with neither critical nor popular acclaim.

The commercial failure of his next two works convinced Melville that he could not support his family by writing. He was forced to sell his farm and spend nearly twenty years at a routine job, a customs inspector in New York City. Literary circles lost track of Melville. In his later years, he published some poems, which were overlooked by the public, and at his death he left behind the manuscript of his last work, the novel *Billy Budd.* It was published posthumously in 1924.

During his life, Herman Melville achieved fame and then watched it fade to nothing. His most important achievements were ridiculed by critics and ignored by the public. Nathaniel Hawthorne, however, asserted that no "writer ever put . . . reality before his reader more unflinchingly" than did Herman Melville. Generations later, readers began to discover the depth and power of his writing and to accept his bold rendering of reality.

Herman Melville was born in 1819 and died in 1891.

Literature Online **Author Search** For more about Herman Melville, go to www.glencoe.com.

Connecting to the Story

Have you ever met someone with a magnetic personality, perhaps a teacher, a coach, or a political speaker? In the following selection, Melville presents such a character in Captain Ahab. As you read, think about the following questions:

- What makes a personality magnetic?
- How do others usually respond to such an individual's message?

Building Background

Melville's novel is set in the early 1800s. It describes the voyage of the *Pequod,* a whale ship, which hunts and kills sperm whales for their oil. Ishmael, the young sailor who narrates the book, signs on because he is penniless but curious to find out what life aboard a whale ship is like. Such reasons for joining a whaling crew were common during the height of the whaling industry. Despite dangerous work, fierce weather, low pay, bad food, and harsh treatment, both Americans and foreigners alike were drawn to the adventure. Of course, the possibility of conquering "the mightiest creature on earth"—and living to tell about it—also provided an incentive.

Setting Purposes for Reading

Big Idea The Power of Darkness

As you read, consider why Captain Ahab regards the white whale Moby Dick as evil.

Literary Element Motivation

Motivation refers to the stated or implied reason or cause for a character's actions. A character's motivation helps the reader understand why he or she behaves in a certain way. In a great literary work such as *Moby-Dick,* the main character's motivation is complex, but comprehensible. As you read, consider why Captain Ahab acts as he does.

- See Literary Terms Handbook, p. R11.

Literature Online **Interactive Literary Elements Handbook** To review or learn more about the literary elements, go to www.glencoe.com.

Reading Strategy Monitoring Comprehension

Monitoring comprehension is a helpful way to make sure that you understand what you are reading. Melville's style is highly ornate, with long, complicated passages and sentences rich in descriptive detail. To get the most from this selection, reread challenging passages and break down difficult sentences.

Reading Tip: Breaking Down Difficult Sentences
Use the following tips to break down difficult sentences:

1. Identify the subject.
2. Isolate the verb or verb phrase.
3. Rephrase the sentence in your own words.

Vocabulary

fortitude (fôr′ tə tōōd′) *n.* strength, particularly strength of mind that enables one to encounter danger or bear adversity with courage; p. 284 *The soldier showed fortitude in facing the enemy.*

genial (jēn′ yəl) *adj.* mild or friendly; p. 284 *Despite her severe illness, my grandmother remained genial.*

recluse (rek′ lōōs) *n.* someone who leads a secluded or solitary life; p. 284 *The author was considered a recluse because he granted no interviews and never spoke in public.*

misanthropic (mis′ ən throp′ ik) *adj.* having hatred for humankind; p. 284 *Lack of compassion may be a sign of a misanthropic cast of mind.*

inscrutable (in skrōō′ tə bəl) *adj.* mysterious, or not able to be interpreted or understood; p. 287 *Her actions may be clear, but her intentions are inscrutable.*

Vocabulary Tip: Antonyms Words that have opposite meanings and are the same part of speech are called antonyms. For instance, *incense* and *pacify* are antonyms.

INDIANA ACADEMIC STANDARDS (pages 281–291)
11.3 [Identify] story elements such as character...
11.2 Develop [reading] strategies...

11.5.9 Write...a literary analysis that...supports judgments with relevant...evidence and well-chosen details...

from
Moby-Dick

Herman Melville

Ahab

For several days after leaving Nantucket, nothing above hatches[1] was seen of Captain Ahab. The mates regularly relieved each other at the watches, and for aught[2] that could be seen to the contrary, they seemed to be the only commanders of the ship; only they sometimes issued from the cabin with orders so sudden and peremptory, that after all it was plain they but commanded vicariously. Yes, their supreme lord and dictator was there, though hitherto unseen by any eyes not permitted to penetrate into the now sacred retreat of the cabin.

Every time I ascended to the deck from my watches below, I instantly gazed aft[3] to mark if any strange face were visible; for my first vague disquietude touching the unknown captain, now in the seclusion of the sea, became almost a perturbation. This was strangely heightened at times by the ragged Elijah's diabolical incoherences uninvitedly recurring to me, with a subtle energy I could not have before conceived of. But poorly could I withstand them, much as in other moods I was almost ready to smile at the solemn whimsicalities of that outlandish prophet of the wharves.[4] But whatever it was of apprehensiveness or uneasiness—to call it so—which I felt, yet whenever I came to look about me in the ship, it seemed against all warranty to cherish such emotions. For though the harpooneers, with the great body of the crew, were a far more barbaric, heathenish, and motley set than any of the tame merchant-ship companies which my previous experiences had made me acquainted with, still I ascribed this—and rightly ascribed it—to

---

1. *Above hatches* means "on deck."
2. Here, *aught* means "anything" or "all."
3. *Aft* means "the rear section of a ship."

Literary Element Motivation *Why does Ahab isolate himself from his crew?*

---

4. Before the *Pequod* set sail, an odd sailor, Elijah, warned Ishmael about Captain Ahab.

Reading Strategy Monitoring Comprehension *Whom does Ishmael describe in this passage?*

the fierce uniqueness of the very nature of that wild Scandinavian vocation in which I had so abandonedly embarked. But it was especially the aspect of the three chief officers of the ship, the mates, which was most forcibly calculated to allay these colorless misgivings, and induce confidence and cheerfulness in every presentment of the voyage. Three better, more likely sea-officers and men, each in his own different way, could not readily be found, and they were every one of the Americans; a Nantucketer, a Vineyarder, a Cape man. Now, it being Christmas when the ship shot from out her harbor, for a space we had biting Polar weather, though all the time running away from it to the southward; and by every degree and minute of latitude which we sailed, gradually leaving that merciless winter, and all its intolerable weather behind us. It was one of those less lowering, but still grey and gloomy enough mornings of the transition, when with a fair wind the ship was rushing through the water with a vindictive sort of leaping and melancholy rapidity, that as I mounted to the deck at the call of the forenoon watch, so soon as I levelled my glance towards the taffrail, foreboding shivers ran over me. Reality outran apprehension; Captain Ahab stood upon his quarter-deck.[5]

There seemed no sign of common bodily illness about him, nor of the recovery from any. He looked like a man cut away from the stake, when the fire has overrunningly wasted all the limbs without consuming them, or taking away one particle from their compacted aged robustness. His whole high, broad form, seemed made of solid bronze, and shaped in an unalterable mould, like Cellini's cast Perseus.[6] Threading its way out from among his grey hairs, and continuing right down one side of his tawny scorched face and neck, till it disappeared in his clothing, you saw a slender rod-like mark, lividly whitish. It resembled that perpendicular seam sometimes made in the straight, lofty trunk of a great tree, when the upper lightning tearingly darts down it, and without wrenching a single twig, peels and grooves out the bark from top to bottom, ere running off into the soil, leaving the tree still greenly alive, but branded. Whether that mark was born with him, or whether it was the scar left by some desperate wound, no one could certainly say. By some tacit consent, throughout the voyage little or no allusion was made to it, especially by the mates. But once Tashtego's senior, an old Gayhead Indian[7] among the crew, superstitiously asserted that not till he was full forty years old did Ahab become that way branded, and then it came upon him, not in the fury of any mortal fray, but in an elemental strife at sea. Yet, this wild hint seemed inferentially negatived, by what a grey Manxman[8] insinuated, an old sepulchral man, who, having never before sailed out of Nantucket, had never ere this laid eye upon wild Ahab. Nevertheless, the old sea-traditions, the immemorial credulities, popularly invested this old Manxman with preternatural powers of discernment. So that no white sailor seriously contradicted him when he said that if ever Captain Ahab should be tranquilly laid out—which might hardly come to pass, so he muttered—then, whoever should do that last office for the dead, would find a birthmark on him from crown to sole.

So powerfully did the whole grim aspect of Ahab affect me, and the livid[9] brand which streaked it, that for the first few moments I hardly noted that not a little of this overbearing grimness was owing to the barbaric white leg upon which he partly stood. It had previously come to me that this ivory leg had at sea been fashioned from the polished bone of the sperm whale's jaw. "Aye, he was dismasted[10] off Japan," said the old Gayhead Indian once; "but like his dismasted craft, he shipped another mast without coming home for it. He has a quiver of 'em."

I was struck with the singular posture he maintained. Upon each side of the Pequod's quarter deck, and pretty close to the mizen

---

5. The *quarter-deck* is the part of a ship set aside by the captain for official use.
6. *Cellini's cast Perseus* refers to Benvenuto Cellini's bronze statue that shows Perseus, a Greek mythological hero, holding Medusa's severed head.

Big Idea **The Power of Darkness** *How does this detail suggest that Ahab is strange, perhaps even unnatural?*

7. *Gayhead Indian* refers to a Native American from Gayhead, a town in Martha's Vineyard, Massachusetts.
8. A *Manxman* is someone from the Isle of Man, an island in the Irish Sea.
9. Here, *livid* means "pale."
10. Literally, *dismasted* means "with the mast removed or broken off." This term is used figuratively to describe Ahab's loss of his leg.

shrouds,[11] there was an auger hole, bored about half an inch or so, into the plank. His bone leg steadied in that hole; one arm elevated, and holding by a shroud; Captain Ahab stood erect, looking straight out beyond the ship's ever-pitching prow. There was an infinity of firmest **fortitude,** a determinate, unsurrenderable wilfulness, in the fixed and fearless, forward dedication of that glance. Not a word he spoke; nor did his officers say aught to him; though by all their minutest gestures and expressions, they plainly showed the uneasy, if not painful, consciousness of being under a troubled master-eye. And not only that, but moody stricken Ahab stood before them with a crucifixion in his face; in all the nameless regal overbearing dignity of some mighty woe.

Ere long, from his first visit in the air, he withdrew into his cabin. But after that morning, he was every day visible to the crew; either standing in his pivot-hole, or seated upon an ivory stool he had; or heavily walking the deck. As the sky grew less gloomy; indeed, began to grow a little **genial,** he became still less and less a **recluse;** as if, when the ship had sailed from home, nothing but the dead wintry bleakness of the sea had then kept him so secluded. And, by and by, it came to pass, that he was almost continually in the air; but, as yet, for all that he said, or perceptibly did, on the at last sunny deck, he seemed as unnecessary there as another mast. But the Pequod was only making a passage now; not regularly cruising; nearly all whaling preparatives needing supervision the mates were fully competent to, so that there was

Breaching Sperm Whale's tail fin.
New Zealand Photographer: Flip Nicklin.

little or nothing, out of himself to employ or excite Ahab, now; and thus chase away, for that one interval, the clouds that layer upon layer were piled upon his brow, as ever all clouds choose the loftiest peaks to pile themselves upon.

Nevertheless, ere long, the warm, warbling persuasiveness of the pleasant, holiday weather we came to, seemed gradually to charm him from his mood. For, as when the red-cheeked, dancing girls, April and May, trip home to the wintry, **misanthropic** woods; even the barest, ruggedest, most thunder-cloven old oak will at least send forth some few green sprouts, to welcome such glad-hearted visitants; so Ahab did, in the end, a little respond to the playful allurings of that girlish air. More than once did he put forth the faint blossom of a look, which, in any other man, would have soon flowered out in a smile.

As the Pequod sails farther south, Ahab grows increasingly restless. He paces the deck even in the dead of night when most of the crew are asleep. No longer able to relax and enjoy simple pleasures, he tosses his pipe into the sea.

---

11. *Shrouds* means "sails."

The Quarter-Deck

(Enter Ahab: Then, all.)

It was not a great while after the affair of the pipe, that one morning shortly after breakfast, Ahab, as was his wont, ascended the cabin-gangway to the deck. There most sea-captains usually walk at that hour, as country gentlemen, after the same meal, take a few turns in the garden.

Soon his steady, ivory stride[12] was heard, as to and fro he paced his old rounds, upon planks so familiar to his tread, that they were all over dented, like geological stones, with the peculiar mark of his walk. Did you fixedly gaze, too, upon that ribbed and dented brow; there also, you would see still stranger foot-prints—the foot-prints of his one unsleeping, ever-pacing thought.

But on the occasion in question, those dents looked deeper, even as his nervous step that morning left a deeper mark. And, so full of his thought was Ahab, that at every uniform turn that he made, now at the main-mast and now at the binnacle,[13] you could almost see that thought turn in him as he turned, and pace in him as he paced; so completely possessing him, indeed, that it all but seemed the inward mould of every outer movement.

"D'ye mark him, Flask?" whispered Stubb; "the chick that's in him pecks the shell. 'Twill soon be out."

The hours wore on;—Ahab now shut up within his cabin; anon, pacing the deck, with the same intense bigotry of purpose[14] in his aspect.

It drew near the close of day. Suddenly he came to a halt by the bulwarks,[15] and inserting his bone leg into the auger-hole there, and with one hand grasping a shroud, he ordered Starbuck to send everybody aft.

"Sir!" said the mate, astonished at an order seldom or never given on shipboard except in some extraordinary case.

"Send everybody aft," repeated Ahab. "Mast-heads, there! come down!"

When the entire ship's company were assembled, and with curious and not wholly unapprehensive faces, were eyeing him, for he looked not unlike the weather horizon when a storm is coming up, Ahab, after rapidly glancing over the bulwarks, and then darting his eyes among the crew, started from his stand-point; and as though not a soul were nigh[16] him resumed his heavy turns upon the deck. With bent head and half-slouched hat he continued to pace, unmindful of the wondering whispering among the men; till Stubb cautiously whispered to Flask, that Ahab must have summoned them there for the purpose of witnessing a pedestrian feat. But this did not last long. Vehemently pausing, he cried:—

"What do ye do when ye see a whale, men?"

"Sing out for him!" was the impulsive rejoinder[17] from a score of clubbed voices.

"Good!" cried Ahab, with a wild approval in his tones; observing the hearty animation into which his unexpected question had so magnetically thrown them.

"And what do ye next, men?"

"Lower away, and after him!"

"And what tune is it ye pull to, men?"

"A dead whale or a stove boat!"[18]

More and more strangely and fiercely glad and approving grew the countenance[19] of the old man at every shout; while the mariners began to gaze curiously at each other, as if marvelling how it was that they themselves became so excited at such seemingly purposeless questions.

But, they were all eagerness again, as Ahab, now half-revolving in his pivot-hole, with one hand reaching high up a shroud, and tightly, almost convulsively grasping it, addressed them thus:—

"All ye mast-headers have before now heard me give orders about a white whale. Look ye! d'ye see this Spanish ounce of gold?"—holding

---

12. *Ivory stride* refers to Ahab's walking with an artificial leg made from a whale's jawbone.
13. A *binnacle* is a compartment on a ship for the ship's lamp and compass.
14. *Bigotry of purpose* refers to Ahab's fierce single-mindedness.
15. The sides of a ship above the upper deck are known as the *bulwarks.*

Big Idea The Power of Darkness *What effect does Melville create by describing the routine walks of other sea captains and country gentlemen before describing Ahab's pacing?*

Literary Element Motivation *Why does Ahab pace the deck so resolutely?*

---

16. Here, *nigh* means "close" or "near."
17. An *impulsive rejoinder* is a spontaneous response or reply.
18. *A dead whale or a stove boat!* is a whaler's motto meaning, "We kill a whale or wreck our boat in the attempt!"
19. *Countenance* refers to the appearance or expression of the face that reveals mood or emotion.

Man in Boat Looking at White Whale. Christopher Zacharow.
Viewing the Art: Does this painting match your view of Ahab's character? Explain.

up a broad bright coin to the sun—"it is a six-teen dollar piece, men,—a doubloon. D'ye see it? Mr. Starbuck, hand me yon topmaul."

While the mate was getting the hammer, Ahab, without speaking, was slowly rubbing the gold piece against the skirts of his jacket, as if to heighten its lustre, and without using any words was meanwhile lowly humming to himself, producing a sound so strangely muffled and inarticulate that it seemed the mechanical humming of the wheels of his vitality in him.

Receiving the topmaul from Starbuck, he advanced towards the main-mast with the hammer uplifted in one hand, exhibiting the gold with the other, and with a high raised voice exclaiming: "Whosoever of ye raises[20] me a white-headed whale with a wrinkled brow and a crooked jaw; whosoever of ye raises me that white-headed whale, with three holes punctured in his starboard fluke[21]—look ye, whosoever of ye raises me that same white whale, he shall have this gold ounce, my boys!"

"Huzza! huzza!" cried the seamen, as with swinging tarpaulins they hailed the act of nailing the gold to the mast.

"It's a white whale, I say," resumed Ahab, as he threw down the topmaul; "a white whale. Skin your eyes for him, men; look sharp for white water; if ye see but a bubble, sing out."

All this while Tashtego, Daggoo, and Queequeg[22] had looked on with even more intense interest and surprise than the rest, and at the mention of the wrinkled brow and crooked jaw they had started as if each was separately touched by some specific recollection.

"Captain Ahab," said Tashtego, "that white whale must be the same that some call Moby Dick."

"Moby Dick?" shouted Ahab. "Do ye know the white whale then, Tash?"

"Does he fan-tail a little curious, sir, before he goes down?" said the Gayheader deliberately.

"And has he a curious spout, too," said Daggoo, "very bushy, even for a parmacetty,[23] and mighty quick, Captain Ahab?"

"And he have one, two, tree—oh! good many iron in him hide, too, Captain," cried Queequeg disjointedly, "all twiske-tee betwisk,

---

20. To *raise* a whale is to spot or identify it in the sea.
21. *Starboard fluke* means "the right half of a whale's tail."

---

22. *Tashtego, Daggoo, and Queequeg* are the harpooneers on the *Pequod;* Ishmael befriended Queequeg in Nantucket before signing up for the voyage.
23. *Parmacetty* (or spermaceti) is a white, waxy solid found in the oil of whales. Here, it refers to the whale itself.

like him—him—" faltering hard for a word, and screwing his hand round and round as though uncorking a bottle—"like him—him—"

"Corkscrew!" cried Ahab, "aye, Queequeg, the harpoons lie all twisted and wrenched in him;[24] aye, Daggoo, his spout is a big one, like a whole shock of wheat, and white as a pile of our Nantucket wool after the great annual sheep-shearing; aye, Tashtego, and he fan-tails like a split jib in a squall.[25] Death and devils! men, it is Moby Dick ye have seen—Moby Dick— Moby Dick!"

"Captain Ahab," said Starbuck, who, with Stubb and Flask, had thus far been eyeing his superior with increasing surprise, but at last seemed struck with a thought which somewhat explained all the wonder. "Captain Ahab, I have heard of Moby Dick—but it was not Moby Dick that took off thy leg?"

"Who told thee that?" cried Ahab; then pausing, "Aye, Starbuck; aye, my hearties all round; it was Moby Dick that dismasted me; Moby Dick that brought me to this dead stump I stand on now. Aye, aye," he shouted with a terrific, loud, animal sob, like that of a heart-stricken moose; "Aye, aye! it was that accursed white whale that razeed[26] me; made a poor pegging lubber of me for ever and a day!" Then tossing both arms, with measureless imprecations he shouted out: "Aye, aye! and I'll chase him round Good Hope, and round the Horn, and round the Norway Maelstrom, and round perdition's[27] flames before I give him up. And this is what ye have shipped for, men! to chase that white whale on both sides of land, and over all sides of earth, till he spouts black blood and rolls fin out. What say ye, men, will ye splice hands on it, now? I think ye do look brave."

"Aye, aye!" shouted the harpooneers and seamen, running closer to the excited old man: "A sharp eye for the White Whale; a sharp lance for Moby Dick!"

"God bless ye," he seemed to half sob and half shout. "God bless ye, men. Steward! go draw the great measure of grog.[28] But what's this long face about, Mr. Starbuck; wilt thou not chase the white whale? art not game for Moby Dick?"

"I am game for his crooked jaw, and for the jaws of Death too, Captain Ahab, if it fairly comes in the way of the business we follow; but I came here to hunt whales, not my commander's vengeance. How many barrels will thy vengeance yield thee even if thou gettest it, Captain Ahab? it will not fetch thee much in our Nantucket market."

"Nantucket market! Hoot! But come closer, Starbuck; thou requirest a little lower layer. If money's to be the measurer, man, and the accountants have computed their great counting-house the globe, by girdling it with guineas, one to every three parts of an inch; then, let me tell thee, that my vengeance will fetch a great premium *here*!"

"He smites[29] his chest," whispered Stubb, "what's that for? methinks it rings most vast, but hollow."

"Vengeance on a dumb brute!" cried Starbuck, "that simply smote thee from blindest instinct! Madness! To be enraged with a dumb thing, Captain Ahab, seems blasphemous."

"Hark ye yet again,—the little lower layer. All visible objects, man, are but as pasteboard masks. But in each event—in the living act, the undoubted deed—there, some unknown but still reasoning thing puts forth the mouldings of its features from behind the unreasoning mask. If man will strike, strike through the mask! How can the prisoner reach outside except by thrusting through the wall? To me, the white whale is that wall, shoved near to me. Sometimes I think there's naught beyond. But 'tis enough. He tasks me; he heaps me; I see in him outrageous strength, with an inscrutable malice sinewing it. That **inscrutable** thing is chiefly what I hate; and be the white whale agent, or be the white whale principal, I

---

24. Moby Dick has survived many attacks and bears the wounds (and mangled harpoons) inflicted by those who failed to kill him.
25. *Like a split jib in a squall* means "like a torn sail in a storm."
26. A *razee* is a "cut-off" ship, or a ship with its upper decks removed. Ahab, too, has had a part of himself removed, namely, his leg.
27. Here, *perdition* is hell.

28. *Grog* is alcoholic liquor, such as rum, often diluted with water.
29. To *smite* is to strike sharply.

Reading Strategy Monitoring Comprehension *Whom does Ahab describe in this passage?*

Vocabulary

inscrutable (in skrōō′ tə bəl) *adj.* mysterious, or not able to be interpreted or understood will wreak that hate upon him. Talk not to me of blasphemy, man; I'd strike the sun if it insulted me. For could the sun do that, then could I do the other; since there is ever a sort of fair play herein, jealousy presiding over all creations. But not my master, man, is even that fair play. Who's over me? Truth hath no confines. Take off thine eye! more intolerable than fiends' glarings is a doltish stare! So, so; thou reddenest and palest; my heat has melted thee to anger-glow. But look ye, Starbuck, what is said in heat, that thing unsays itself. There are men from whom warm words are small indignity.[30] I meant not to incense[31] thee. Let it go. Look! see yonder Turkish cheeks of spotted tawn—living, breathing pictures painted by the sun. The Pagan[32] leopards—the unrecking and unworshipping things, that live; and seek, and give no reasons for the torrid life they feel! The crew, man, the crew! Are they not one and all with Ahab, in this matter of the whale? See Stubb! he laughs! See yonder Chilean! he snorts to think of it. Stand up amid the general hurricane, thy one tost sapling cannot, Starbuck! And what is it? Reckon it. 'Tis but to help strike a fin; no wondrous feat for Starbuck. What is it more? From this one poor hunt, then, the best lance out of all Nantucket, surely he will not hang back, when every foremast-hand has clutched a whetstone? Ah! constrainings seize thee; I see! the billow lifts thee! Speak, but speak!—Aye, aye! thy silence, then, *that* voices thee. (*Aside*) Something shot from my dilated nostrils, he has inhaled it in his lungs. Starbuck now is mine; cannot oppose me now, without rebellion."

"God keep me!—keep us all!" murmured Starbuck, lowly.

But in his joy at the enchanted, tacit acquiescence of the mate, Ahab did not hear his foreboding invocation;[33] nor yet the low laugh from the hold; nor yet the presaging vibrations of the winds in the cordage;[34] nor yet the hollow flap of the sails against the masts, as for a moment their hearts sank in. For again Starbuck's downcast eyes lighted up with the stubbornness of life; the subterranean[35] laugh died away; the winds blew on; the sails filled out; the ship heaved and rolled as before. Ah, ye admonitions and warnings! why stay ye not when ye come? But rather are ye predictions than warnings, ye shadows! Yet not so much predictions from without, as verifications of the foregoing things within. For with little external to constrain us, the innermost necessities in our being, these still drive us on.

"The measure! the measure!" cried Ahab.

Receiving the brimming pewter, and turning to the harpooneers, he ordered them to produce their weapons. Then ranging them before him near the capstan, with their harpoons in their hands, while his three mates stood at his side with their lances, and the rest of the ship's company formed a circle round the group; he stood for an instant searchingly eyeing every man of his crew. But those wild eyes met his, as the bloodshot eyes of the prairie wolves meet the eye of their leader, ere he rushes on at their head in the trail of the bison; but, alas! only to fall into the hidden snare of the Indian.

"Drink and pass!" he cried, handing the heavy charged flagon to the nearest seaman. "The crew alone now drink. Round with it, round! Short draughts—long swallows, men; 'tis hot as Satan's hoof. So, so; it goes round excellently. It spiralizes in ye; forks out at the serpent-snapping eye. Well done; almost drained. That way it went, this way it comes. Hand it me—here's a hollow! Men, ye seem the years; so brimming life is gulped and gone. Steward, refill!

"Attend now, my braves. I have mustered ye all round this capstan;[36] and ye mates, flank me

---

30. An *indignity* is an insult.
31. *Incense* means "to cause extreme anger."
32. *Pagan* describes someone with little or no religion.
33. An *invocation* is the act of calling on an authority for help or support.

---

34. *Cordage* is the rope used in a ship's rigging.
35. Here, *subterranean* refers to something below the deck of the ship.
36. A *capstan* is a vertical drum around which a cable is turned to move or raise weights.

Scrimshaw on Whalebone. New Bedford Whaling Museum, New Bedford, MA.

with your lances; and ye harpooneers, stand there with your irons; and ye, stout mariners, ring me in, that I may in some sort revive a noble custom of my fisherman fathers before me. O men, you will yet see that—Ha! boy, come back? bad pennies come not sooner. Hand it me. Why, now, this pewter had run brimming again, wert not thou St. Vitus'[37] imp—away, thou ague!

"Advance, ye mates! Cross your lances full before me. Well done! Let me touch the axis." So saying, with extended arm, he grasped the three level, radiating lances at their crossed centre; while so doing, suddenly and nervously twitched them; meanwhile, glancing intently from Starbuck to Stubb; from Stubb to Flask. It seemed as though, by some nameless, interior volition,[38] he would fain[39] have shocked into them the same fiery emotion accumulated within the Leyden jar[40] of his own magnetic life. The three mates quailed before his strong, sustained, and mystic aspect. Stubb and Flask looked sideways from him; the honest eye of Starbuck fell downright.

"In vain!" cried Ahab; "but, maybe, 'tis well. For did ye three but once take the full-forced shock, then mine own electric thing, *that* had perhaps expired from out me. Perchance, too, it would have dropped ye dead. Perchance ye need it not. Down lances! And now, ye mates, I do appoint ye three cup-bearers to my three

pagan kinsmen there—yon three most honorable gentlemen and noblemen, my valiant harpooneers. Disdain the task? What, when the great Pope washes the feet of beggars, using his tiara for ewer? Oh, my sweet cardinals![41] your own condescension, *that* shall bend ye to it. I do not order ye; ye will it. Cut your seizings and draw the poles, ye harpooneers!"

Silently obeying the order, the three harpooneers now stood with the detached iron part of their harpoons so me three feet long, held, barbs up, before him.

"Stab me not with that keen steel! Cant them; cant them over! know ye not the goblet end? Turn up the socket! So, so; now, ye cup-bearers, advance. The irons! take them; hold them while I fill!" Forthwith, slowly going from one officer to the other, he brimmed the harpoon sockets with the fiery waters from the pewter.

"Now, three to three, ye stand. Commend the murderous chalices! Bestow them, ye who are now made parties to this indissoluble league. Ha! Starbuck! but the deed is done! Yon ratifying sun now waits to sit upon it. Drink, ye harpooneers! drink and swear, ye men that man the deathful whaleboat's bow—Death to Moby Dick! God hunt us all, if we do not hunt Moby Dick to his death!" The long, barbed steel goblets were lifted; and to cries and maledictions[42] against the white whale, the spirits were simultaneously quaffed down with a hiss. Starbuck paled, and turned, and shivered. Once more, and finally, the replenished pewter went the rounds among the frantic crew; when, waving his free hand to them, they all dispersed; and Ahab retired within his cabin. ❧

---

37. *St. Vitus'* or *St. Vitus' Dance* is a nervous disorder that causes shaking of the limbs. Ahab mocks the steward for having a shaky hand and spilling some of the liquor. An *ague* is a fever.
38. *Volition* is an act of choosing or willing something.
39. Here, *fain* means "rather."
40. A *Leyden jar* is a form of capacitor, or "electrical circuit element that can store an electrical charge temporarily."

41. *Cardinals* are high officials of the Roman Catholic Church; Ahab addresses his three mates as cardinals.
42. A *malediction* is a curse.

Big Idea The Power of Darkness *How does Ahab's use of religious language and ritual reveal the darker side of his intention?*

RESPONDING AND THINKING CRITICALLY

Respond

1. Would you want to sail with a captain like Ahab? Explain.

Recall and Interpret

2. (a)What does Ishmael notice about Ahab's appearance? (b)How does Ahab's appearance influence Ishmael's impression of him?

3. (a)Describe Ahab's posture as he stands on the quarter-deck. (b)How does his stance affirm his position as captain?

4. (a)What is Starbuck's reaction to Ahab's intention to hunt Moby Dick? (b)Why does he react this way?

Analyze and Evaluate

5. (a)What does Moby Dick represent to Ahab, Starbuck, and the crew of the *Pequod*? (b)Why does Melville present different perceptions of the whale?

6. (a)Why does Starbuck accuse Ahab of blasphemy? (b)Is Ahab guilty of blasphemy or not? Explain.

7. (a)Why does the crew choose to follow Ahab in his mission to kill Moby Dick? (b)How do you account for the "magnetism" between Ahab and his crew?

8. Is Ahab justified in not revealing the *Pequod's* true mission until the voyage is well underway? Support your answer with evidence from the story.

Connect

9. Big Idea **The Power of Darkness** How does Melville use Ahab and his mission as a means of exploring the mystery of evil in the world?

LITERARY ANALYSIS

Literary Element Motivation

Motivation is a central feature of psychological realism, the attempt to portray characters in a plausible, objective manner. Above all else, psychological realism insists that characters be clearly motivated; they should not act without apparent reason.

In *Moby-Dick,* Ahab's words and actions as well as the words and thoughts of the other characters, particularly Ishmael, provide clues to Ahab's motivation.

1. Are Ahab's motivations clearly depicted? Support your answer.

2. Is Ahab's motivation in hunting Moby Dick purely revenge? Explain.

Review: Metaphor

Metaphor refers to a figure of speech that equates two seemingly unlike things. In a metaphor the comparison is implied, rather than stated directly.

Partner Activity With a partner, discuss the implied comparison in Ahab's statement "it was Moby Dick that dismasted me." Then review the story to identify at least two other metaphors and explain what is being compared in them.

Metaphor	What Is Compared	Why It Is Appropriate
p. 287 "it was Moby Dick that dismasted me"		

Literature Online **Web Activities** For eFlashcards, Selection Quick Checks, and other Web activities, go to www.glencoe.com.

Reading Strategy Monitoring Comprehension

Reread this passage from page 288. Then break it down and answer the questions below.

"And what is it? Reckon it. 'Tis but to help strike a fin; no wondrous feat for Starbuck. What is it more? From this one poor hunt, then, the best lance out of all Nantucket, surely he will not hang back, when every foremast-hand has clutched a whetstone?"

1. To whom is Ahab speaking?

2. What is Ahab trying to do?

3. How would you summarize what happens in the passage?

Vocabulary

Practice with Antonyms Find the antonym for each vocabulary word from *Moby-Dick* listed in the first column. Use a dictionary or a thesaurus if you need help.

1. fortitude   morose

2. recluse   clear

3. misanthropic   cowardice

4. inscrutable   charitable

5. genial   socialite

Academic Vocabulary

Here are two words from the vocabulary list on page R86.

authority (ə thôr′ə tē) *n.* the ability to influence others' actions, thoughts, and behavior

goal (gōl) *n.* the desired result; aim

Practice and Apply

1. How would you describe Ahab's **authority** over his crew?

2. What is Ahab's **goal** in hunting down Moby Dick?

Writing About Literature

Analyze Character Ishmael describes Ahab as seemingly "made of solid bronze, and shaped in an unalterable mould, like Cellini's cast Perseus" (page 283). The statue to which Ishmael alludes shows Perseus holding Medusa's head after he has decapitated her. In the Greek myth, Medusa is a *gorgon,* or monster, that turns to stone anyone who looks at her. Using a mirrored shield for protection, Perseus is able to kill Medusa.

Analyze the importance of this allusion as a tool for understanding Ahab's character. Identify and list details in the story that reinforce the connection between Ahab and Perseus as monster-killers. Beside each detail, write a brief explanation of the connection.

After you complete your draft, meet with a peer reviewer to evaluate each other's work and to suggest revisions. Then edit and proofread your draft for errors in spelling, grammar, and punctuation.

Literary Criticism

Reviews of *Moby-Dick* consisted of both the congratulatory and the condemnatory. Despite the lack of critical consensus on the book, the *London Leader* proclaimed in its 1851 review that "Criticism may pick many holes in this work; but no criticism will thwart its fascination. . . ." Do you agree with this statement? Write a short literary review of the excerpts from *Moby-Dick* that you read in this selection. Then explain how the characteristics you identified in your review affected your overall experience of the work.

from # IN THE HEART OF THE SEA

Nathaniel Philbrick

National Book Award Winner

Building Background

In 1820 a sperm whale sank the Nantucket whaling ship *Essex*. The crew was lost at sea for four months; eight survived. This event inspired Herman Melville's *Moby-Dick*. In the chapters "Ahab" and "The Quarter-Deck" (see pages 282–289), Melville models his portrayal of Captain Ahab on first mate Owen Chase's account of the tragedy. The following selection, from historian Nathaniel Philbrick's nonfiction book, describes the *Essex* crew's first days stranded at sea.

Set a Purpose for Reading

Read to discover the historical basis for Melville's novel *Moby-Dick*.

Reading Strategy

Analyzing Historical Context

Analyzing **historical context** involves gathering background information and exploring social forces that influenced the writing of a literary work. As you read, take notes on the historical context for Melville's tale. Use a two-column chart like the one below.

World of Ahab	World of Owen Chase

AS DARKNESS APPROACHED AT THE END OF the first day, the wind built steadily, kicking up a steep, irregular chop.[1] The *Essex* whaleboats were hybrids—built for rowing but now adapted to sail—and the men were still learning how they handled. Instead of a rudder, each boat was equipped with a steering oar. This eighteen-foot lever enabled a rowed whaleboat to spin around in its own length, but it was not so effective in guiding a sailboat, and required the helmsman to stand at the cumbersome oar. At this early stage in the voyage, the whaleboats were dangerously overloaded. Instead of five hundred pounds of whaling equipment, each boat contained close to a thousand pounds of bread, water, and tortoises,[2] and waves broke over the built-up gunnels[3] and soaked the men. The boats were also without centerboards or skegs[4] to help them track through the water, forcing the helmsmen to tug and push their

---

1. Here, *chop* means "waves."
2. Tortoises were commonly kept aboard whaleships to be used as food for the crew.
3. A *gunnel* is the upper edge of a boat's side.
4. A *skeg* is the rear, or stern of a ship's keel, or main timber. A *centerboard* is a retractable keel.

steering oars as their little, deeply laden boats corkscrewed in the turbulent seas.

Each boat-crew was divided into two watches. While half the men attempted to rest—curling up with the Galapagos tortoises in the bilge[5] or leaning uncomfortably against the seats—the others steered, tended the sails, and bailed. They also attempted to keep an eye on the other boats, which would sometimes disappear entirely from view when they dipped down into the trough of a wave.

At the start it had been decided that every effort would be made to keep the three boats together. Together they could help if one of them ran into trouble; together they could keep one anothers' spirits up. "[U]naided, and unencouraged by each other," Chase[6] observed, "there were with us many whose weak minds, I am confident, would have sunk under the dismal retrospections of the past catastrophe, and who did not possess either sense or firmness enough to contemplate our approaching destiny, without the cheering of some more determined countenance than their own."

There was also a more practical reason for staying together: there was not enough navigational equipment to go around. Pollard[7] and Chase each had a compass, a quadrant, and a copy of *Bowditch's Navigator,* but Joy[8] had nothing. If his boat-crew should become separated from the other two, they would be unable to find their way across the ocean.

Night came on. Although moon and starlight still made it possible to detect the ghostly paleness of the whaleboats' sails, the men's field of vision shrank dramatically in the darkness even as their perception of sounds was heightened. The whaleboats' clinker, or lapstrake, construction (with planks overlapping, resembling the clapboards of a house) made them much noisier than a smooth-bottomed boat, and the fussy, fluted sound of water licking up against their

First Mate Owen Chase

boats' lapped sides would accompany them for the duration of the voyage.

Even at night the crews were able to maintain a lively three-way conversation among the boats. The subject on everyone's mind was of course the "means and prospects of our deliverance." It was agreed that their best chance of survival lay in happening upon a whaleship. The *Essex* had sunk about three hundred miles north of the Offshore Ground.[9] They still had about five days of sailing before they entered the Ground, where, they desperately hoped, they would come across a whaler.

A circumstance in their favor was that, unlike merchant vessels, whaleships almost always had a lookout posted at the masthead, so in whaling territory they had a better chance of being seen. Against them was the immensity of the Offshore Ground. It encompassed an enormous amount of ocean—more than twice the area of the state of Texas, a rectangle about three hundred miles north to south and almost two thousand miles from east to west. There were at least seven whaleships on the Offshore Ground at this time. But even if there were double that number, the odds were poor that three whaleboats sailing along a straight line through the Ground (which might take only four or five days to cross) would be spotted by a ship.

One possibility was to extend their time in the Offshore Ground and actively search for whalers. But that was a gamble. If they searched the region and didn't find a ship, they would jeopardize their chances of reaching South America before their food supplies ran out. As it was, they would be entering the western extreme of the Ground and would have a difficult time heading east against the southeasterly trades.[10]

There was another factor influencing their decision to continue on with the original plan. After having fallen victim to such a seemingly random and inexplicable attack, the men felt an

5. In this context *bilge* means "the lowest part of a ship's hull."
6. Owen *Chase* was the first mate aboard the *Essex.*
7. George *Pollard* was the captain of the *Essex.*
8. Matthew *Joy* was second mate aboard the *Essex.*

9. The *Offshore Ground* was a heavily whaled expanse of ocean off the coast of Peru.
10. The *trades* are trade winds, or winds that always move in the same direction.

The sea chest of
Captain George Pollard

overpowering need to reclaim at least some control of their own destiny. Being sighted by a whaleship would, according to Chase, not "depend on our own exertions, but on chance alone." Reaching South America, on the other hand, depended "on our own labors." From Chase's perspective, this made all the difference and demanded that they not "lose sight, for one moment, of the strong probabilities which, under Divine Providence, there were of our reaching land by the route we had prescribed to ourselves."

The plan had one iron requirement: they had to make their provisions last two months. Each man would get six ounces of hardtack and half a pint of water a day. Hardtack was a simple dried bread made out of flour and water. Baked into a moisture-free rock to prevent spoilage, hardtack had to be broken into small pieces or soaked in water before it was eaten, if a sailor didn't want to crack a tooth.

The daily ration was equivalent to six slices of bread, and it provided about five hundred calories. Chase estimated that this amounted to less than a third of the nourishment required by "an ordinary man." Modern dietary analysis indicates that for a five-foot, eight-inch person weighing 145 pounds, these provisions met about a quarter of his daily energy needs. True, the men of the Essex had more than just bread; they had tortoises. Each tortoise was a pod of fresh meat, fat, and blood that was capable of providing as many as 4,500 calories per man—the equivalent of nine days of hardtack. Yet, even augmented by the tortoises, their daily rations amounted to a starvation diet. If they did succeed in reaching South America in sixty days, each man knew he would be little more than a breathing skeleton.

But as they would soon discover, their greatest concern was not food but rather water. The human body, which is 70 percent water, requires a bare minimum of a pint a day to remove its waste products. The men of the Essex would have to make do with half that daily amount. If they experienced any hot weather, the deficit would only increase.

That first night of their journey, Chase, Pollard, and Joy distributed the rations of bread and water to their boat-crews. It was two days after the sinking now, and the men's interest in food had finally returned; the bread was quickly eaten. There was something else they craved: tobacco. A whaleman almost always had a quid[11] of tobacco in his mouth, going through more than seventy pounds of it in a single voyage. In addition to all their other woes, the crew of the Essex had to contend with the jittery withdrawal symptoms associated with nicotine addiction.

After the meager meal, the men not on watch went to sleep. "Nature became at last worn out with the watchings and anxieties of the two preceding nights," Chase recalled, "and sleep came insensibly upon us." But as his men fell into what he judged to be a dreamless stupor, Chase found himself in the middle of a waking nightmare.

Unable to sleep for the third night in a row, he continued to dwell obsessively on the circumstances of the ship's sinking. He could not get the creature out of his mind: "[T]he horrid aspect and revenge of the whale, wholly engrossed my reflections." In his desperate attempts to find some explanation for how a normally passive creature could suddenly become a predator, Chase was plagued by what psychologists call a "tormenting memory"—a common response to disasters. Forced to relive the trauma over and over again, the survivor finds larger, hidden forces operating through the incident. The philosopher William James felt this compulsion firsthand some years later. After the San Francisco earthquake of 1906, he wrote: "I realize now how inevitable were men's earlier mythological versions [of disaster] and how artificial and against the grain of our spontaneous perceiving are the later habits which science educates us."

For most disaster victims, the repeated flashbacks of a tormenting memory have a therapeutic value, gradually weaning the sufferer from anxieties that

---

11. A *quid* means "a cut of something chewable."

Ship Essex as she appeared On the morning of Nov 20 at 8 A.M. 1820

might otherwise interfere with his ability to survive. There are some, however, who cannot rid themselves of the memory. Melville, building upon Chase's account, would make his Captain Ahab a man who never emerged from the psychic depths in which Chase had writhed these three nights. Just as Chase was convinced that the whale that attacked the Essex exhibited "decided, calculating mischief," so was Ahab haunted by a sense of the white whale's "outrageous strength, with an inscrutable malice sinewing[12] it."

Locked in his own private chamber of horrors, Ahab resolved that his only escape was through hunting down and killing Moby Dick: "How can the prisoner reach outside except by thrusting through the wall? To me, the white whale is that wall, shoved near to me." Chase, on a tiny boat a thousand miles from land, did not have the possibility of revenge. Ahab was fighting a symbol; Chase and his shipmates were fighting for their lives. ∾

---

12. *Sinewing* means "supporting."

RESPONDING AND THINKING CRITICALLY

Respond

1. Are you surprised that the whale's attack on the *Essex* haunted Chase? Why or why not?

Recall and Interpret

2. Philbrick writes that "there was another factor influencing [the crew's] decision to continue on with the original plan." (a)What was that factor? (b)Do you think the crew was right to consider this factor?

3. (a)According to Philbrick, how did Chase's account influence Melville's portrayal of Ahab? (b)Why did Chase fascinate Melville?

Analyze and Evaluate

4. Both Chase and Ahab believe that the whales that attacked them had evil intentions. Do you think this is a reasonable conclusion? Why or why not?

5. After being attacked by a whale, the *Essex* crew "felt an overpowering need to reclaim at least some control of their own destiny". Do you think that this need for control drove Ahab's obsessive quest to hunt Moby Dick? Why or why not?

Connect

6. In an interview, Philbrick states, "I think all of us wonder while reading a survival tale, what would I have done in this situation? Would I have made it?" What questions did you think about as you read the story? Explain.

INDIANA ACADEMIC STANDARDS
(pages 292–295)
11.3.5 Analyze or evaluate works of literary or cultural significance...that were written by important authors...
11.2 Develop strategies such as asking questions...

Writing Workshop

Reflective Essay

 Reflecting on Nature

"Crossing a bare common, in snow puddles, at twilight, under a clouded sky, without having in my thoughts any occurrence of special good fortune, I have enjoyed a perfect exhilaration. I am glad to the brink of fear."

—Ralph Waldo Emerson, from "Nature"

Connecting to Literature In his writing Emerson often looks back, or reflects, on his experiences and uses them as jumping-off places for exploring his thoughts on a subject. This type of writing is usually referred to as the reflective essay. In a reflective essay, you narrate and describe a personal experience to show both what the experience taught you and what it might teach others. To write a successful essay you will need to learn the goals of reflective writing and the strategies to achieve those goals. These goals and strategies form the defining features of a reflective essay.

Rubric: Features of Reflective Essays

Goals	Strategies
To share a life lesson or fresh insight	☑ Explore the meaning of a personal experience or observation
To present events or actions in a clear order	☑ Use narrative details to tell a story with a clear beginning, middle, and end
To make vivid observations	☑ Use descriptive details to create a picture for your reader
	☑ Use active verbs and striking adjectives
To connect with an audience	☑ Use first-person point of view
	☑ Use a thoughtful but conversational style to help develop your personal writing voice

The Writing Process

In this workshop, you will follow the stages of the writing process. At any stage, you may think of new ideas to include and better ways to express them. Feel free to return to earlier stages as you write.

Prewriting

Drafting

Revising

➡ Focus Lesson: Elaborating Ideas

Editing & Proofreading

➡ Focus Lesson: Correcting Comma Splices

Presenting

Writing Models For models and other writing activities, go to www.glencoe.com.

ACADEMIC STANDARDS (pages 296–303)

11.5.3 Write reflective compositions that explore the significance of personal experiences...

11.4.1 Discuss ideas for writing with classmates...

Real-World Connection

For college applications, you might be asked to write an essay about a personal experience. Think about some ideas you might like to explore in a college application essay. As you will see in this Writing Workshop assignment, the key to success is to clearly show the significance of your experience.

> **Assignment**
>
> Write a reflective essay that describes one of your experiences with the natural world and expresses the insight you gained. As you move through the stages of the writing process, keep your audience and purpose in mind.
>
> **Audience:** peers and classmates
>
> **Purpose:** to explore the significance of a personal experience

Analyzing a Professional Model

In her autobiography, Pulitzer Prize-winning author Annie Dillard reflects on the significance of a childhood encounter with a moth. As you read the following passage, note how Dillard uses both narrative and descriptive details to convey her unique voice. Pay close attention to the comments in the margin. They point out features that you might want to include in your own reflective essay.

From *An American Childhood* by Annie Dillard

At school I saw a searing sight. It turned me to books; it turned me to jelly; it turned me much later, I suppose, into an early version of a runaway, a scapegrace. It was only a freshly hatched Polyphemus moth crippled because its mason jar was too small.

The mason jar sat on the teacher's desk; the big moth emerged inside it. The moth had clawed a hole in its hot cocoon and crawled out, as if agonizingly, over the course of an hour, one leg at a time; we children watched around the desk, transfixed. After it emerged, the wet, mashed thing turned around walking on the green jar's bottom, then painstakingly climbed the twig with which the jar was furnished.

There, at the twig's top, the moth shook its sodden clumps of wings. When it spread those wings—those beautiful wings—blood would fill their veins, and the birth fluids on the wings' frail sheets would harden to make them tough as sails. But the moth could not spread its wide wings at all; the jar was too small. The wings could not fill, so they hardened while they were still crumpled from the cocoon. A smaller moth could have spread its

First-Person Point of View

Use the pronoun *I* to speak directly to your reader

Introduction

Connect with your reader by starting your reflective essay in the middle of the action.

Narrative Details/ Chronological Order

Guide your reader from one event to the next by using transitional words and phrases such as *when, while,* and *at the top.*

Show, don't tell. Use vivid details to create a clear picture.

Narrative Details

Give precise details that tell your audience what happened or what you observed and when.

wings to their utmost in that mason jar, but the Polyphemus moth was big. Its gold furred body was almost as big as a mouse. Its brown, yellow, pink, and blue wings would have extended six inches from tip to tip, if there had been no mason jar. It would have been as big as a wren.

The teacher let the deformed creature go. We all left the classroom and paraded outside behind the teacher with pomp and circumstance. She bounced the moth from its jar and set it on the school's asphalt driveway. The moth set out walking. It could only heave the golden wrinkly clumps where its wings should have been; it could only crawl down the school driveway on its six frail legs. The moth crawled down the driveway toward the rest of Shadyside, an area of fine houses, expensive apartments, and fashionable shops. It crawled down the driveway because its shriveled wings were glued shut. It crawled down the driveway toward Shadyside, one of several sections of town where people like me were expected to settle after college, renting an apartment until they married one of the boys and bought a house. I watched it go.

Conversational Tone

Share your personal observations and thoughts by using an open and conversational tone.

I knew that this particular moth, the big walking moth, could not travel more than a few yards before a bird or cat began to eat it, or a car ran over it. Nevertheless, it was crawling with what seemed wonderful vigor, as if, I thought at the time, it was still excited from being born. I watched it go till the bell rang and I had to go in. I have told this story before, and may yet tell it again, to lay the moth's ghost, for I still see it crawl down the broad black driveway, and I still see its golden wing clumps heave.

Conclusion

Discuss the impact your experience had on your life. Explain any insights or lessons you might have learned and want to share.

Reading-Writing Connection Think about the writing techniques that you just encountered and try them out in the reflective essay that you write.

Prewriting

Gather Ideas Prewriting is the stage of the writing process during which you generate ideas. You can use many different strategies:

▶ Approach the idea of the natural world from different angles. Keep in mind that the natural world doesn't just mean a wilderness or the countryside. Weather is a part of nature. Nature is also present in cities and suburbs, as well as in parks, gardens, zoos, museums, and many other places.

▶ If you keep a journal, you might review it for entries dealing with nature. Thoreau referred to his journal as he wrote Walden.

▶ Look at family videos or photograph albums to recall events that relate to the natural world, such as a trip to a national park, a zoo, or a natural history museum.

▶ Use a cluster diagram. Start by putting the idea "nature" in the center and jot down general areas that you associate with nature. Then move outward to more specific associations until you think of an experience you want to write about. Using the diagram below, one student focused on a meeting with an animal rescuer.

Top Ten

Create a personal "Nature's Best" list: best landscape, body of water, season, time of day, weather, cloud formation, tree, flower, mammal, bird, fish, insect, and so on. What experiences do you associate with these choices?

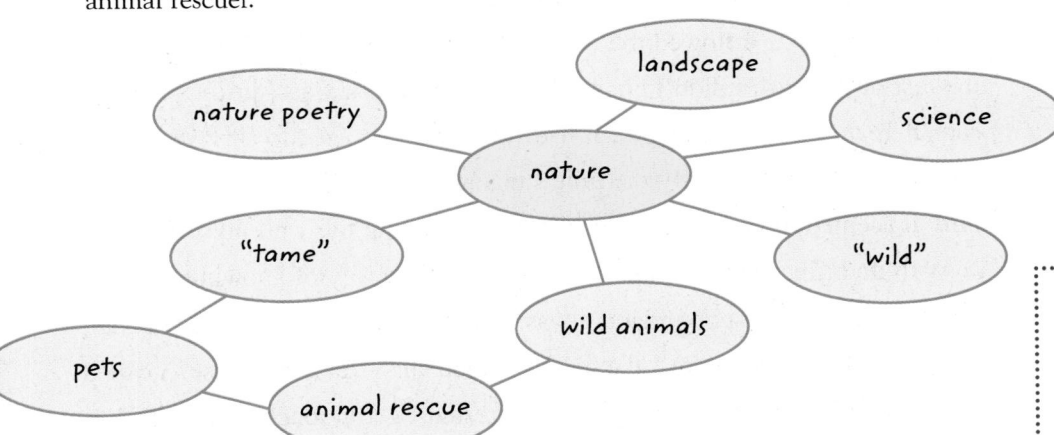

Choose a Subject After reviewing some of your experiences with nature, choose one of them as a subject for your reflective essay.

Talk About Your Ideas Meet with a partner to help focus on what you will say to your readers and how you will say it. Think about your essay as a conversation on the page in which you, the writer, do all the talking. To help develop your writing voice, take turns telling each other the most vivid details of your experience. As you and your partner speak, listen to the style of your language and your original approach to ideas. Jot down notes and refer to them when you are developing your essay.

Next, explore the significance of your experience.

▶ How did you feel about your experience at the time?

▶ Looking back, do you feel different about your experience now?

Test Prep

If you were writing this essay as part of an examination, how would you work differently? Time management is crucial to success in an essay test, especially in the prewriting stage.

Drafting

Just Jump In When you begin writing, don't get bogged down trying to find the perfect word or to make your sentences flow smoothly. You can polish your essay later. Do take the time to stop occasionally and reflect on your unfinished draft. If your writing is leading you in an unexpected direction, you may want to follow it. You could gain new insights about your experience—and yourself.

Analyzing a Workshop Model

Here is a final draft of a reflective essay. Read the essay and answer the questions in the margin. Use the answers to these questions to guide you as you write.

Animal 911

Introduction

Do the opening sentences introduce the essay topic in an exciting and suspenseful way? Why or why not?

First-Person Point of View

What are the advantages of using the first-person point of view? What effect would these sentences have if they were written in the third-person?

Conversational Tone

How does asking a question create a conversational tone?

Narrative Details/ Chronological Order

How do transitional phrases help your readers follow your ideas?

I generally like nature to keep its distance—wild things belong outside. So when I saw a white-flecked feather on the third step of the stairs leading up to the second floor, I knew it was a bad sign. There were two more feathers on the fifth step. I followed the trail of fluff to the kitchen, where I found the rest of the bird. I didn't know what kind of bird it was—just a small round creature with a long bill. It had somehow managed to survive a meeting with our family cat. By the time I managed to corner and capture the bird, it seemed to be in deep shock. I wasn't feeling too well myself.

With no bird experts around to consult, I had no way of knowing how seriously injured the poor creature was. Should I simply put the bird outside on the porch and let nature—the neighborhood cats—take its course? I called the vet who looked after our cat. He suggested I get in touch with a Mrs. Roberts, who lived not too far away. This woman took in injured animals that people brought her and cared for them until they were well enough to return to the wild. She sounded like just the person I needed. I put my injured bird into a shoe box lined with tissue and took the bus to see Mrs. Roberts.

Along the way, I began to think about the person I was about to meet. To start with, what would Mrs. Roberts look like? Since she was in the business of looking after hurt animals, I began to picture her as a very sweet and gentle sort of person—sort of cuddly. I was wrong.

When I got to her house, I rang the bell. Nobody responded, so I walked around to the back yard. I knew immediately I had come to the right place.

There were some large screened-in areas, where I could see a several different animals, including a deer. There were also two or three upright posts. A large, fierce-looking bird—some kind of hawk, I guess— gripped the top of one of these. It glared at me as if I were a mouse. As I stood there, I was startled by a clear, low voice behind me.

"May I help you?" she asked. I spun around, nearly dropping my shoe box.

"Mrs. Roberts?" I responded. She simply nodded in reply. My cuddly fantasy of an animal rescuer was immediately replaced by a far tougher reality. She was an old woman but clearly still very strong and sturdy, with dark eyes and sharp features. She looked a bit like a hawk herself.

"I have an injured bird here," I began, offering her my shoe box.

As she took the box and removed the lid, I noticed she seemed to smile. It may have been the sight of the tissue paper in which I had put the injured bird. She probably thought it looked like a doll bed created by a little kid. She picked up the bird in one strong, brown hand and studied it for a time before returning it to the box and replacing the cover.

"It's a starling," Mrs. Roberts said, as if she understood I wouldn't know. "I'm afraid there's nothing I can do for it."

"Really?" I asked, feeling a sharp stab of disappointment. "I thought you took care of—are you sure there's nothing?"

"It's a very old bird," she explained.

This comment was also a bit of shock. During my bus ride, I had decided—based on no knowledge at all—that the bird was young. Part of my fantasy had been visiting the bird as it got better.

"People bring me so many animals that I have to limit myself to aiding those that are worth saving," Mrs. Roberts explained. "This starling just isn't. Sorry. I'll dispose of the bird for you."

I was grateful she had relieved me of responsibility for the injured bird, but I still felt that somehow Mrs. Roberts didn't "care" for nature in the way I had expected. She wasn't cuddly. Thinking about her later, however, it was clear that she cared very much; but she only applied her concern to creatures that could benefit from it. My meeting with Mrs. Roberts taught me that to love nature does not mean to be sentimental about wild creatures. You can be both realistic and caring.

Descriptive Details

How do these details help your readers visualize the scene? How do they create tension?

Descriptive Details

How do these details help the readers visualize Mrs. Roberts? What do they tell about her character?

Narrative Details/Dialogue

How does the use of dialogue show your readers what is happening? Does it place the readers in the middle of the action?

Conclusion

Why is it important that you express how you felt at the time of your experience and how you feel now?

Revising

Peer Review Ask a peer reviewer to help you assess your essay. Talk over your ideas and ask your partner for feedback. Identify any strengths and weaknesses you find. Remember to refer to the traits of strong writing.

Use the rubric below to evaluate your writing.

► **Focus Lesson**

Elaborating Ideas

Give your readers a detailed picture of what is happening and when. Elaboration is a technique you can use to include details that develop, support, or explain the ideas presented in your essay. Here is a sentence from the Workshop Model followed by three kinds of elaboration—reasons, descriptions, and dialogue—you might want to try.

Draft:

As she took the box and removed the lid, I noticed she seemed to smile.

Revision:

As she took the box and removed the lid, I noticed she seemed to smile. It might have been the sight of the tissue paper in which I had put the injured bird.[1] She probably thought it looked like a doll bed created by a little kid.[2] "It's a starling," Mrs. Roberts said.[3]

1: Reasons   **2: Descriptions**   **3: Dialogue**

Traits of Strong Writing

Ideas message or theme and the details that develop it

Organization arrangement of main ideas and supporting details

Voice writer's unique way of using tone and style

Word Choice vocabulary a writer uses to convey meaning

Sentence Fluency rhythm and flow of sentences

Conventions correct spelling, grammar, usage, and mechanics

Presentation the way words and design elements look on a page

For more information on using the Traits of Strong Writing, see pages R33–R34 of the Writing Handbook.

Editing and Proofreading

Get It Right When you have completed the final draft of your essay, proofread for errors in grammar, usage, mechanics, and spelling. Refer to the Language Handbook, pages R45–R59, as a guide.

▶ **Focus Lesson**

Corrrecting Comma Splices

A comma splice is a type of run-on sentence that occurs when two main clauses are joined only by a comma. Below is an example of a run-on sentence from the Workshop Model. Note the three ways to correct this problem.

Comma Splice:

I was grateful she had relieved me of responsibility for the injured bird, I still felt that somehow Mrs. Roberts didn't "care" for nature in the way I had expected.

Solution A: Replace the comma with an end mark of punctuation, such as a period or a question mark, and begin the new sentence with a capital letter.

I was grateful she had relieved me of responsibility for the injured bird. I still felt that somehow Mrs. Roberts didn't "care" for nature in the way I had expected.

Solution B: Place a semicolon between the two main clauses.

I was grateful she had relieved me of responsibility for the injured bird; I still felt that somehow Mrs. Roberts didn't "care" for nature in the way I had expected.

Solution C: Add a coordinating conjunction after the comma.

I was grateful she had relieved me of responsibility for the injured bird, but I still felt that somehow Mrs. Roberts didn't "care" for nature in the way I had expected.

Give It a Rest

Try putting your essay aside for a day or two. When you return to it after a time, you may catch errors you missed earlier.

How Was That?

Try reading your essay aloud. Often you will be able to "hear" a mistake that you might not "see."

Writer's Portfolio

Place a copy of your reflective essay in your portfolio to review later.

Literature Online
Writing Models For models and other writing activities, go to www.glencoe.com.

Presenting

Appearance Matters Make your essay inviting to read. Handwritten papers should be neat and legible. If you are working on a word processor, double-space the lines of text and use a readable font, or typeface. Other design elements— such as boldfaced headings or pictures—can help you present information effectively as well as make your essay look more appealing. Be sure to check with your teacher about presentation guidelines.

Speaking, Listening, and Viewing Workshop

Delivering a Reflective Presentation

Connecting to Literature During Ralph Waldo Emerson's lifetime, more Americans probably became acquainted with his ideas from hearing him lecture than from reading his essays. After he spoke in Cincinnati, a newspaper there observed that "without his own language, his manner, his delivery," no report could really convey the effect he created. Emerson's speaking style was very much a part of the appeal of his thoughts. In this workshop, you will deliver an oral presentation of your reflective essay on nature.

> **Assignment** Create an oral presentation of your reflective essay on nature and perform it for an audience.

Planning Your Presentation

When you wrote your reflective essay, you were addressing an audience of readers. When you deliver your reflective presentation, you will be addressing an audience of listeners. Use your essay as a starting point.

- Read your essay aloud to a peer. Discuss which ideas you should keep or delete and how your might adjust the language to fit the purpose. For example, you might add informal expressions or vary sentence structure to make your essay sound even more conversational.
- Jot down vivid details, striking dialogue, and key ideas on note cards. Arrange the note cards in the same order as the elements appear in your essay. Use your note cards as a speaking prompt.
- Make sure that you note the significance of the personal experience you explored in your essay.

—to me, wild animals belong outside

—not happy when I found an injured bird in the kitchen

Creating Your Visual Media

As you work though the organization of your essay, think about how visual media, such as a photograph, collage, drawing, or computer presentation can make your ideas clearer to your audience. Reflect on how symbols, colors, and organization may work within your visual to effectively convey your point. Use the chart below to brainstorm ideas with a partner.

| What parts of my essay best reflect who I am? | What images can I create of my essay to illustrate these parts? | How will I use my choice of media to express myself? |

Rehearsing

Rehearsing your speech will strengthen your presentation. You will become familiar with the language and organization of your speech, and you will be able to identify any delivery flaws or grammar errors that you missed earlier. Rehearsing will also help you know when best to utilize visual aids and how to present them skillfully. It is helpful to rehearse in front of a family member or friend—you can practice eye contact and get feedback on details such as your pronunciation and pacing. Speak loudly, even when practicing, so you are familiar with volume, or how loudly you need to speak so that the whole class can hear you.

Use some of the verbal and nonverbal techniques listed below to ensure that your audience clearly understands you and is engaged in what you have to say.

Rubric: Techniques for Delivering a Presentation

Verbal Techniques	Nonverbal Techniques
☑ **Volume** Speak loudly enough so that everyone can hear you.	☑ **Posture** Stand up tall with your head straight.
☑ **Pronunciation** Speak clearly, pronouncing all the words.	☑ **Eye Contact** Make eye contact with people throughout your audience.
☑ **Pace** Speak at a moderate speed, but vary the rate and use pauses to convey your meaning.	☑ **Facial Expressions** Vary your facial expressions to reflect what you are saying.
☑ **Tone** Speak in an animated voice.	☑ **Gestures** Use natural gestures to reinforce your ideas.
☑ **Emphasis** Stress important words and ideas.	☑ **Visual Aids** Use a photograph, collage, drawing, or computer presentation to enhance your presentation.

Use a Mirror

Practice your gestures in front of a mirror until your body language looks natural.

Sound Check

Record your presentation and play it back to check on whether your voice expresses the right mood and your words are understandable.

Videotape

Videotape your performance and provide your own critique.

ACADEMIC STANDARDS (pages 304–305)

11.7.16 Deliver reflective presentations...

11.7.5 Use appropriate rehearsal strategies...

11.7.8 Evaluate when to use... visuals...to create effective productions.

For Independent Reading

IN THE LATE 1700s, READERS AND CRITICS BEGAN, FOR THE FIRST TIME, to accept the novel as a legitimate literary form. This shift can be partly attributed to the novels of English author Samuel Richardson. Specifically, his massive multi-volume novels *Pamela* and *Clarissa,* which were touted as books that "cultivate the principles of virtue and religion in the minds of the youth," received overwhelming popular acclaim in the mid-1700s. The first American novel, *The Power of Sympathy,* by William Hill Brown, mimicked Richardson's sentimental works and helped to inspire the rush of American imitators that followed until the end of the century.

By the 1820s, however, the first truly American novels emerged. Romanticism started to take hold in Europe and American writers embraced the movement's celebration of the individual, freedom from old forms, and love of nature.

The Last of the Mohicans

James Fenimore Cooper (1826)

James Fenimore Cooper's five-part series *The Leatherstocking Tales,* about a wilderness scout named Natty Bumppo, contains the first novels to depict realistic American frontier scenes and characters. *The Last of the Mohicans,* the second installment in the series, is set during the French and Indian War and portrays a group of Native Americans whose way of life is quickly disappearing. The novel presents a thrilling chase, punctuated by captures, escapes, unexpected attacks, and heroic rescues. Two ways of life are contrasted in the novel: the Native Americans' freedom and reverence for nature, and the settlers' drive to build farms and towns.

Two Years Before the Mast

Richard Henry Dana (1840)

Dana's novel is based on his own experiences as a sailor for two years aboard the merchant ship *Pilgrim.* Americans were fascinated by the day-to-day duties of a Yankee captain and crew. Dana's vivid descriptions of the captain's cruelty toward the crew led to public outcry and legal action against such treatment aboard ship. The novel's factual details influenced Herman Melville's writing of his sea adventures, including *Typee, Omoo,* and his masterpiece, *Moby-Dick.*

"[The Scarlet Letter] *is so terrible in its pictures of diseased human nature as to produce most questionable delight. The reader's interest never flags for a moment. There is nothing of episode or digression. The author is always telling his one story with a concentration of energy which, as we can understand, must have made it impossible for him to deviate. The reader will certainly go on with it to the end very quickly, entranced, excited, shuddering, and at times almost wretched. His consolation will be that he too has been able to see into these black deeps of the human heart."*

—Anthony Trollope, *The North American Review*
September 1879

The Scarlet Letter

Nathaniel Hawthorne (1850)

Rooted in American Puritanism, this tragic tale of colonial New England examines three complex characters—a woman who follows her heart rather than Puritan standards of behavior, a minister torn by guilt, and a husband consumed by hatred and revenge. Hawthorne, who called this a novel of "frailty and human sorrow," peers deeply into the mind and heart of each character to reveal tortuous moral dilemmas.

From the Glencoe Literature Library

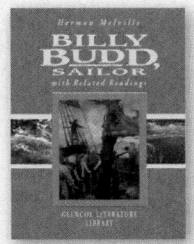

Billy Budd

Herman Melville

An industrious young sailor accidentally kills the tyrannical master-at-arms who victimized him.

The House of the Seven Gables

Nathaniel Hawthorne

For two centuries, the inhabitants of a New England mansion experience mysterious misfortunes that stem from the moral corruption of its first owner.

Walden

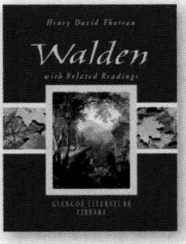

Henry David Thoreau

Thoreau abandons society and its comforts to pursue a solitary and independent life in the woods.

English Language Arts

Indiana Test Practice

Reading: Vocabulary, Comprehension, and Analysis

Carefully read the following passage. Use context clues to help you define any words with which you are unfamiliar. Pay close attention to the author's main idea and use of rhetorical devices. Then, on a separate sheet of paper, answer the questions on pages 309–310.

from *Self-Reliance* by Ralph Waldo Emerson

line

Society is a wave. The wave moves onward, but the water of which it is composed does not. The same particle does not rise from the valley to the ridge. Its unity is only phenomenal. The persons who make up a nation to-day, next year die, and their experience with them.

5
And so the reliance on Property, including the reliance on governments which protect it, is the want of self-reliance. Men have looked away from themselves and at things so long, that they have come to esteem the religious, learned, and civil institutions as guards of property, and they deprecate assaults on these, because they feel them to be assaults on property. They measure their esteem of each other by what each has, and not by what each is. But a cultivated man becomes ashamed of his property, out of new respect for his nature. Especially he hates what he has, if he see that it is

10
accidental,—came to him by inheritance, or gift, or crime; then he feels that it is not having; it does not belong to him, has no root in him, and merely lies there, because no revolution or no robber takes it away. But that which a man is does always by necessity acquire, and what the man acquires is living property, which does not wait the beck of rulers, or mobs, or revolutions, or fire, or storm, or bankruptcies, but perpetually renews itself wherever the man breathes. . . . It is only as a man puts off

15
all foreign support, and stands alone, that I see him to be strong and to prevail. He is weaker by every recruit to his banner. Is not a man better than a town? Ask nothing of men, and, in the endless mutation, thou only firm column must presently appear the upholder of all that surrounds thee. He who knows that power is inborn, that he is weak because he has looked for good out of him and elsewhere, and so perceiving, throws himself unhesitatingly on his thought, instantly rights himself,

20
stands in the erect position, commands his limbs, works miracles; just as a man who stands on his feet is stronger than a man who stands on his head.

So use all that is called Fortune. Most men gamble with her, and gain all, and lose all, as her wheel rolls. But do thou leave as unlawful these winnings, and deal with Cause and Effect, the chancellors of God. In the Will work and acquire, and thou hast chained the wheel of Chance, and

25
shalt sit hereafter out of fear from her rotations. A political victory, a rise of rents, the recovery of your sick, or the return of your absent friend, or some other favorable event, raises your spirits, and you think good days are preparing for you. Do not believe it. Nothing can bring you peace but yourself. Nothing can bring you peace but the triumph of principles.

1 In the first sentence, the author uses the literary or rhetorical device of
(A) parallelism
(B) connotative language
(C) hyperbole
(D) metaphor
(E) rhetorical question

2 In the first paragraph, the author appeals to the reader's
(A) ethics
(B) reason
(C) emotions
(D) emotions and ethics
(E) emotions and reason

3 The author suggests that that people deprecate assaults on religious, learned, and civil institutions because people
(A) hate property
(B) believe that these assaults are on property
(C) believe in self-reliance
(D) believe in relying solely on the government
(E) are afraid of all criticism

4 According to the author, a cultivated man becomes ashamed of his property because
(A) no robber or revolution has taken it away
(B) he has stolen it
(C) it came to him as an inheritance
(D) he realizes that it is alien to his true nature
(E) he has allowed it to deteriorate

5 The word "beck" (line 13) most nearly means
(A) command
(B) failure
(C) creation
(D) loss
(E) help

6 From the sentence "He is weaker by every recruit to his banner" (lines 15–16), it can be inferred that
(A) the individual should seek the support of others
(B) the individual cannot avoid receiving the support of others
(C) the individual becomes weak from relying on the support of others
(D) every cause is weakened by the individual
(E) only the individual can prevail

7 The literary or rhetorical device exemplified by the sentence "Is not a man better than a town?" (line 16) is
(A) parallelism
(B) connotative language
(C) metaphor
(D) rhetorical question
(E) allusion

8 The author uses the words "endless mutation" (lines 16–17) to refer to a quality of
(A) the physical world
(B) a firm column
(C) humanity
(D) foreign support
(E) inborn power

9 In line 19, the word "rights" probably means
(A) justifies
(B) subjects
(C) corrects
(D) claims as true
(E) liberates

10 In referring to the wheel of fortune (lines 22–23), the author is making use of the literary device of
(A) foreshadowing
(B) irony
(C) allusion
(D) motif
(E) analogy

11 Which characteristic of effective writing does the author display by the inclusion of the sentence "Do not believe it" (line 27)?
(A) Organization
(B) Presentation
(C) Word choice
(D) Sentence variety
(E) Voice

12 On the basis of this passage, it can be inferred that "Self-Reliance" is an example of
(A) informal essay
(B) persuasive essay
(C) expository essay
(D) narrative essay
(E) personal essay

13 With which of the following statements would the author of this passage be most likely to agree?
(A) People are generally solitary.
(B) Individuals are stronger than communities.
(C) There is no such thing as community.
(D) Only governments can protect private property.
(E) Private property must be outlawed.

14 The overall tone of this passage is
(A) despairing
(B) ironic
(C) authoritative
(D) angry
(E) sarcastic

15 The main idea expressed in this passage is that
(A) the individual is greedy and corrupt
(B) individuals should reject society
(C) there is no such thing as chance
(D) people must reject governments and property
(E) individuals must look to themselves to be free

Reading: Word Recognition

For each item in this section, choose the word or words that best complete the sentence.
Write your answers on a separate sheet of paper.

1 For the writers of the era, Romanticism was both a political _____ and a literary movement.
(A) prejudice
(B) ideology
(C) din
(D) issue
(E) debate

2 The agrarian South had few cities, whereas the _____ cities in the North were heavily industrialized.
(A) manifest
(B) inherent
(C) myriad
(D) blithe
(E) latent

3 The Age of Reform was marked by the rise of many _____ religious organizations that hoped to increase the overall _____ of America.
(A) melancholy . . . lethargy
(B) perennial . . . cognizance
(C) expedient . . . alacrity
(D) deliberately . . . resignation
(E) zealous . . . integrity

4 The _____ and clamor of the cities drove Thoreau into nature and a quiet life of seclusion.
(A) wealth
(B) size
(C) greed
(D) din
(E) pollution

5 Thoreau's life at Walden Pond was a response to his own _____ to live simply and deliberately.
(A) iniquity
(B) cognizance
(C) decorum
(D) admonition
(E) discord

6 In their writings, Poe and Hawthorne often deal with evil, or _____.
(A) expedient
(B) admonition
(C) iniquity
(D) lethargy
(E) torpor

7 Individualism, the _____ concern of the Transcendentalists, remains an important issue to this day.
(A) diffuse
(B) occult
(C) impregnable
(D) perennial
(E) melancholy

8 Poe crafted his _____ stories of the _____ in order to convey a sense of horror to the reader.
(A) melancholy . . . occult
(B) irreproachable . . . culture
(C) sublime . . . sage
(D) sagacious . . . culture
(E) prevalent . . . sublime

9 Ralph Waldo Emerson was a _____ writer and philosopher, known as the Sage of Concord.
(A) pessimistic
(B) venerable
(C) popular
(D) sinister
(E) superficial

10 Hawthorne was drawn to the stark Puritan _____ of the past.
(A) morality
(B) behavior
(C) culture
(D) landscape
(E) sermons

Writing: Process and Language Conventions

As you read the following paragraphs from the first draft of a reflective essay, pay close attention to the writer's use of **grammar, parallel construction, modifiers,** and **adjectives.** Then answer the questions. Write your answers on a separate sheet of paper.

(1) *I've always thought of myself as an optimistic person.* (2) *When troubles emerge.* (3) *I try my hardest to make those troubles work to my advantage.* (4) *I can remember plenty of times throughout my life when things seem particularly gloomy.* (5) *However, I improved the situation by looking at it in another way.*

(6) *I was on summer break.* (7) *Just before my sophomore year.* (8) *My mom, dad, and sister have gone to visit my grandmother, who had recently moved to Alaska.* (9) *Stuck having rehearsal for jazz band, Alaska was so far away.* (10) *It was horrible!* (11) *Even my mom's most trustworthy promise—to take us to visit grandma that following Christmas—was not enough to get rid of my deep disappointment.*

(12) *They were going to be gone for two whole weeks, to go fishing, hike, and white-water rafting, while I stayed at home, practicing my drums.* (13) *If things weren't bad enough, all of my friends were either on vacation with their families, or too busy with summer jobs, to notice that I was all by myself.*

1. Which of the following is the best way to write sentences 2 and 3?
   (A) When troubles emerge; I try my hardest to make those troubles work to my advantage.
   (B) When troubles emerge, I try my hardest to make them work to my advantage.
   (C) I try my hardest to make those troubles work to my advantage—when troubles emerge.
   (D) I try my hardest to make troubles work to my advantage—when those troubles emerge.
   (E) Emerging troubles, I try my hardest to turn to my advantage.

2. Which of the following is the best revision of sentence 4?
   (A) I can remember plenty of times during my life when things seem particularly gloomy.
   (B) There have been plenty of times during my life, when thing seemed particularly gloomy.
   (C) I can remember plenty of times throughout my life when things seemed particularly gloomy.
   (D) Plenty of times throughout my life, that I can remember, seem gloomy.
   (E) There are many times that seem gloomy.

3. Which of the following is the best way to improve sentence 5?
   (A) Change *improved* to *improve.*
   (B) Change *However* to *Although.*
   (C) Change *I improved* to *I was usually able to improve.*
   (D) Change *improved* to *seldom improved.*
   (E) Change *I improved* to *couldn't possibly improve.*

4. Which of the following sentences could the writer insert at the start of the second paragraph to improve the essay's organization?
   (A) Lots of bad things have happened to me.
   (B) In general I've been pretty lucky in the past.
   (C) Sometimes bad things happen to good people.
   (D) A different perspective can be a really good thing.
   (E) One occasion in particular springs to mind.

5. Which of the following is the best way to write sentences 6 and 7?
(A) I was on summer break, just before my sophomore year.
(B) Around the start of my sophomore year—I was on summer break.
(C) Just as my sophomore year was getting ready to start, I had summer break.
(D) In August, before the start of my sophomore year in high school, I had summer break.
(E) Just before the start of my sophomore year—I had summer break.

6. Which of the following errors appears in sentence 8?
(A) run-on sentence
(B) incorrect parallelism
(C) sentence fragment
(D) incorrect verb tense
(E) misplaced modifier

7. Which of the following is the best revision of sentence 9?
(A) Stuck having rehearsal for jazz band, Alaska stays far away.
(B) Because I was stuck with rehearsal for jazz band, I couldn't go to Alaska.
(C) Because there was rehearsal for jazz band, Alaska was far away from me.
(D) I have rehearsal for jazz band, so Alaska was far away.
(E) Jazz band rehearsal had me stuck, so Alaska was so far away.

8. Which of the following sentences could replace sentence 10 to illustrate better the reason for the writer's feelings?
(A) Alaska was so far away!
(B) I'd never been outside of my home state, and Alaska sure seemed exciting.
(C) I was pretty sure that Alaska wasn't horrible.
(D) Going to Alaska is about as exciting as going to jazz band.
(E) It is really unfair—my family should never have gone to Alaska.

9. Which of the following errors appears in sentence 12?
(A) run-on sentence
(B) misplaced modifier
(C) sentence fragment
(D) incorrect verb tense
(E) incorrect parallelism

10. While writing the concluding paragraphs of this draft, what information should the writer include to illustrate the essay's general idea?
(A) examples of other people wasting their free time
(B) how to get a summer job
(C) how the writer's optimism improved the situation
(D) details about band rehearsal
(E) details about his family's trip to Alaska

Writing: Applications

Ralph Waldo Emerson claimed that "nothing can bring you peace but yourself." Do you agree with this statement? Write a short reflective essay that expresses your ideas about individualism and Emerson's claim. As you write, keep in mind that your essay will be checked for **ideas, organization, voice, word choice, sentence fluency, conventions,** and **presentation.**

Literature Online **Unit Assessment** To prepare for the unit test, go to www.glencoe.com.

Lincoln's Drive Through Richmond, 1866. Dennis Malone Carter. Oil on canvas, 77.5 x 19.9 cm. Chicago Historical Society.

The Civil War Era

1850-1880

Looking Ahead

By the 1850s, the Southern states had become increasingly isolated from the rest of the country because of their support of slavery and their exclusion from the industrial boom in the North. Tensions between the North and South grew, and the end of the Union—or a war to preserve it—hovered on the horizon. Writers responded to the issues of slavery, regional conflict, and eventually the Civil War. Many moved from Romanticism to a realistic portrayal of the problems confronting the nation. Two major poets of the period also found inspiration in personal feelings and ordinary events.

Keep the following questions in mind as you read:

◇ How did the slavery question lead to the Civil War?

◇ How was the Civil War reflected in the writing of the period?

◇ What made the poetry of Whitman and Dickinson revolutionary?

INDIANA ACADEMIC STANDARDS (pages 315–327)

11.3.5 Analyze or evaluate works of literary or cultural significance in history (American…) that reflect a variety of genres in each of the respective historical periods; were written by important authors in the respective major historical periods; reveal contrasts in major themes, styles, and trends; reflect or shed light on the seminal philosophical, religious, social, political, or ethical ideas of their time.

Timeline 1850–1880

135,000 SETS, 270,000 VOLUMES SOLD.

UNCLE TOM'S CABIN

FOR SALE HERE.

The Greatest Book of the Age.

◀ Uncle Tom's Cabin

AMERICAN LITERATURE

1850

1852
Harriet Beecher Stowe's *Uncle Tom's Cabin* is published

1855
Walt Whitman's *Leaves of Grass* is published

1855
Frederick Douglass's autobiography, *My Bondage and My Freedom,* is published

1858
Abraham Lincoln gives A House Divided speech

1860

1859–1865
Emily Dickinson writes more than eight hundred poems

1861
Harriet Jacobs's *Incidents in the Life of a Slave Girl* is published under the pseudonym Linda Brent

1862
Julia Ward Howe's "Battle Hymn of the Republic" is published

1863
Abraham Lincoln delivers the Gettysburg Address

1865
Walt Whitman's *Drum-Taps* is published

UNITED STATES EVENTS

1850

1850
Compromise of 1850 strengthens Fugitive Slave Act

1854
Congress passes Kansas-Nebraska Act

1856
Proslavery forces sack Lawrence, Kansas, and antislavery forces retaliate with Pottawatomie Massacre in "Bleeding Kansas" conflict

1857
Dred Scott decision makes slavery legal in all territories

1859
John Brown raids federal arsenal at Harpers Ferry, VA.

1860

◀ **1860–1861**
Pony Express runs from Missouri to California

1860
Abraham Lincoln wins presidential election

1860
South Carolina secedes from the Union

1861
Jefferson Davis becomes the Confederate president

1861
Confederate forces fire on Fort Sumter in South Carolina, starting the Civil War

1861
First Battle of Bull Run is fought

1862
Richard Gatling patents the first practical machine gun

1863
Union collects income tax to fund the Civil War

WORLD EVENTS

1850

1850
Taiping Rebellion begins in China

1850
Elizabeth Barrett Browning's *Sonnets from the Portuguese* is published

1853
Commodore Perry opens Japan to world trade

1855
David Livingstone names Victoria Falls in Africa

1856
Crimean War ends

1857
Gustave Flaubert's *Madame Bovary* is published

1857–1858
Indian soldiers revolt in Sepoy Mutiny (known in India as First War of Independence)

1858
Benito Juárez becomes president of Mexico ▶

1860

1861
Alexander II, czar of Russia, frees serfs

1861
Burke and Wills expedition reaches Australia

1865
Lewis Carroll's *Alice's Adventures in Wonderland* is published

1867
Alfred Nobel receives British patent on dynamite

1868
Meiji Restoration reforms Japan's government

1868
Louisa May Alcott's *Little Women* is published

◀ Medal of Honor

1870

1873
Henry Timrod's "Cotton Boll" is published

1875
Mary Baker Eddy's *Science and Health with Key to the Scriptures* is published

1876
Mark Twain's *Adventures of Tom Sawyer* is published

1878
Henry James's *Daisy Miller* and *The Europeans* are published

1879
George W. Cable's *Old Creole Days* is published

SURRAT.   BOOTH.   HAROLD.

War Department, Washington, April 20, 1865,

$100,000 REWARD!

THE MURDERER

Of our late beloved President, Abraham Lincoln,

IS STILL AT LARGE.

$50,000   REWARD

Will be paid by this Department for his apprehension, in addition to any reward offered by Municipal Authorities or State Executives.

$25,000   REWARD

Will be paid for the apprehension of JOHN H SURRATT, one of Booth's Accomplices.

$25,000   REWARD

Will be paid for the apprehension of David C. Harold, another of Booth's accomplices.

EDWIN M. STANTON, Secretary of War.

1870

1863
Emancipation Proclamation declares freedom for enslaved persons in the Confederate states

1863
Battle of Gettysburg is fought

1864
Abraham Lincoln is reelected president

1865
Abraham Lincoln is assassinated by John Wilkes Booth

1865
Civil War ends

1866
Ku Klux Klan organizes in Tennessee

1868
Ulysses S. Grant is elected president; he holds office until 1877

1870
Hiram Revels becomes the first African American elected to the U.S. Senate

1876
Battle of the Little Bighorn (Custer's Last Stand) is fought

1877
Reconstruction ends

Ferdinand de Lesseps, engineer for Suez Canal

1869
Suez Canal opens in Egypt

1869
Mohandas K. Gandhi is born

1870

1870
Franco-German War begins

1872
Claude Monet completes *Impression: Sunrise*

1874
The Three-Cornered Hat by Pedro Antonio de Alarcón y Ariza is published

1876
First full production of Richard Wagner's *Ring of the Nibelung* is performed at Bayreuth

1879
Henrik Ibsen's *A Doll's House* is published

Literature Online Timeline Visit www.glencoe.com for an interactive timeline.

Reading Check

Analyzing Graphic Information:

1. How long did the Civil War last?

2. Which occurred first, the issuing of the Emancipation Proclamation or the freeing of the serfs in Russia?

By the Numbers

DIVISION OF RESOURCES BETWEEN THE UNION AND THE CONFEDERACY

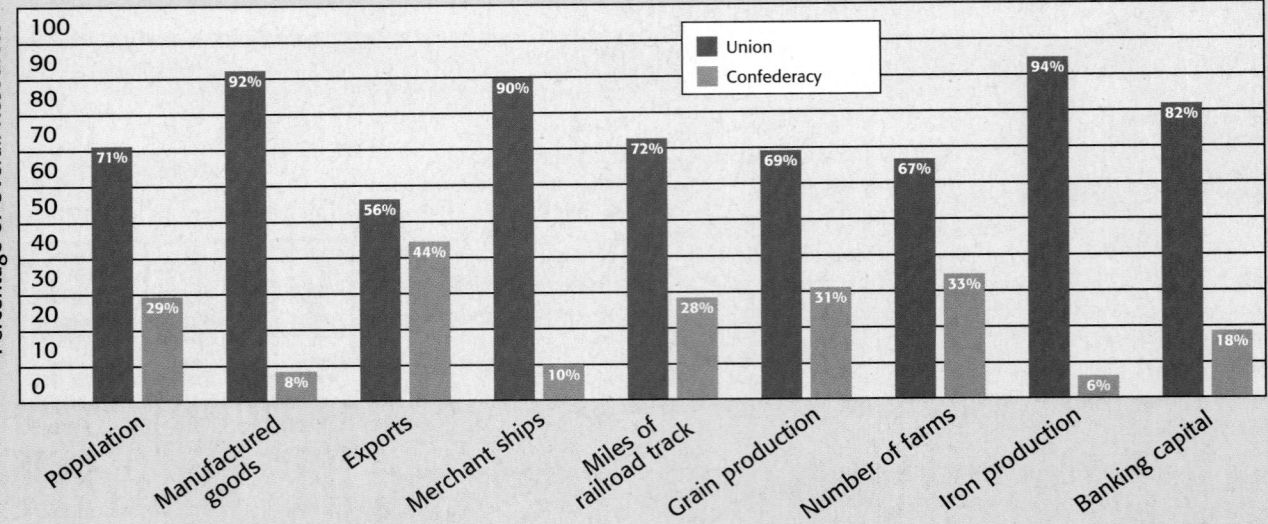

Source: *Historical Statistics of the United States*

How the War Was Won

To win the Civil War, the North took advantage of its resources: soldiers, supplies, and the industrial capacity to finance war efforts. The South had fewer soldiers and faced shortages of food, clothing, medicine, shelter, and money—both for troops and civilians.

Inflation in the South

Limited resources caused severe inflation in the South during the war. Compare the income of a Confederate soldier with the prices for these goods:

Monthly income: $18.00

Pound of coffee:	$12.00
Quart of milk:	$10.00
Pound of butter:	$6.25
Dozen eggs:	$6.00

SLAVERY

- At the start of the 1800s, there were 700,000 enslaved persons in the South. By 1860, there were four million.

CIVIL WAR FORCES

Union

Troops:	2,100,000
Casualties:	634,703
Military Deaths:	360,222

Confederate

Troops:	800,000
Casualties:	483,000
Military Deaths:	260,000

POPULATION

Most populous states in 1880:

State	Population
New York	5,082,871
Pennsylvania	4,282,891
Ohio	3,198,062
Illinois	3,077,871
Missouri	2,168,380

AFRICAN AMERICAN SOLDIERS

- Some 180,000 African Americans served in the Union army.

- There were 66 all-black regiments in the Union forces.

- Twenty-three African Americans won the Medal of Honor.

CIVIL WAR CASUALTIES

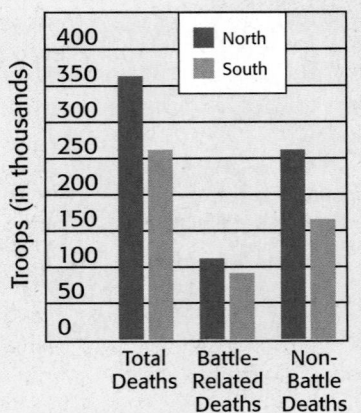

Source: *For the Common Defense*

A *Plantation on the Mississippi,* nineteenth century. Currier & Ives. Color lithograph. Museum of the City of New York.

B Wounded Union soldiers being cared for by nurse Anne Bell, 1861–1865. Photograph.

Being There

Before South Carolina seceded in December 1860, the nation stood on the brink of destruction. After secession began, the tensions between the industrial North and the agricultural South came to a violent head.

C *The Battle of Antietam,* 1862. Captain James Hope. Oil on canvas. U.S. Department of the Interior, Washington, DC.

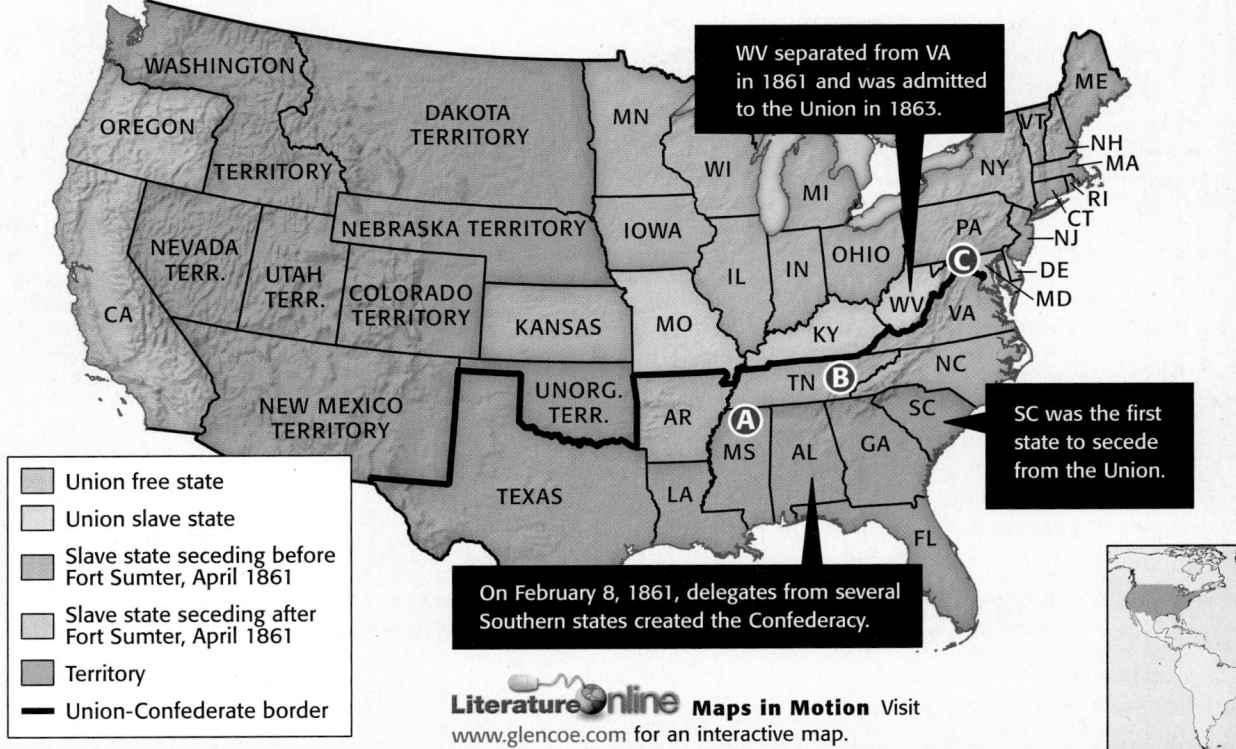

WV separated from VA in 1861 and was admitted to the Union in 1863.

SC was the first state to secede from the Union.

On February 8, 1861, delegates from several Southern states created the Confederacy.

- Union free state
- Union slave state
- Slave state seceding before Fort Sumter, April 1861
- Slave state seceding after Fort Sumter, April 1861
- Territory
- Union-Confederate border

Literature Online Maps in Motion Visit www.glencoe.com for an interactive map.

Reading Check

Analyzing Graphic Information:

1. In which category in the first bar graph is the difference between the resources of the Union and the Confederacy greatest?

2. How many slave states seceded, as shown on the map, before the firing on Fort Sumter?

3. How do the political boundaries west of the Mississippi River during the Civil War compare with those in the present-day United States?

The Civil War Era
1850–1880

Historical, Social, and Cultural Forces

The Path to War

As the nation expanded westward, it became evident that the legality of slavery in the new territories would have to be determined. Northerners in Congress pushed to prohibit slavery in new territories, while Southern senators argued that such a move would deny slaveholders their constitutional rights. In 1850, Senator Henry Clay, in an effort to save the Union, proposed several compromise measures. For the North, Congress admitted California as a free state. To appease the South, Congress passed the Fugitive Slave Act. This law mandated the return of enslaved Africans who had fled to the North and penalized individuals who helped them escape. The Compromise of 1850 averted immediate disaster for the Union, but it proved to be only a temporary solution.

Antislavery Movement

Most Northerners opposed the Fugitive Slave Act, and most free-state legislatures passed laws in an attempt to block it. The Underground Railroad, a secret network that aided enslaved fugitives escaping to the North, became more active than ever. The fugitives were known as "freight" or "packages," the homes where they were sheltered were "stations," and those who guided them were "conductors."

In 1852, Harriet Beecher Stowe's best-selling novel *Uncle Tom's Cabin* depicted the cruelty of slavery and the fight for freedom. Abolitionists hailed the book; one review proclaimed, "A slaveholder might read it without anger, but not easily without a secret abhorrence of the system which he himself upholds."

Abraham Lincoln with General George Brinton McClellan talking in a tent at the Antietam battlefield. Undated photo by Mathew Brady.

Secession

As the 1860 presidential election approached, the Republican Party nominated Abraham Lincoln. Lincoln was not an outright abolitionist; he simply believed that slavery should be excluded from the new territories. With Lincoln's victory, many

Southern states, anticipating that the new president would abolish slavery, felt that they had no choice but to leave the Union. On December 20, 1860, South Carolina seceded. Six more states soon followed. These states formed the Confederate States of America, or the Confederacy, which included eleven states by the start of the war. In Lincoln's inaugural address, he pleaded for the North and South to avoid bloodshed and violence. His plea was not heeded, and on April 12, 1861, Confederate troops attacked Fort Sumter, a federal fort in the harbor of Charleston, South Carolina. The Civil War had begun.

> *"We failed, but in the good providence of God apparent failure often proves a blessing."*
>
> —Confederate General Robert E. Lee

War

The South's long tradition of military service gave the Confederate army an early advantage over the Union. As the war continued, however, the Union grew stronger, while Confederate losses weakened the South. To win the war, Union General Ulysses S. Grant finally began to attack Southern resources as well as Confederate forces.

President Lincoln, assassinated on April 14, 1865, did not witness the end to the struggle that had divided the nation. After more than 600,000 deaths on both sides, the last Confederate soldiers surrendered in May 1865. The Thirteenth Amendment became law in December 1865, officially ending slavery in the entire nation. The North's victory in the Civil War destroyed the South's slave economy. Seceded states eventually returned to the Union, but a legacy of bitterness lingered long after the last Yankee soldier had marched home.

Reconstruction

Although the fighting had ended, the period of Reconstruction involved more than rebuilding and repairing the South. It would take years to restructure Southern society, grant rights to those who had been enslaved, and readmit the Southern states to the Union. Congress passed the Civil Rights Act in 1866 and then the Fourteenth Amendment—redefining citizenship to include African Americans and requiring their equal protection under the law—but the nation did little to help those who had been freed. After Reconstruction, the new South was in many ways similar to the pre-Civil War South: White Southern Democrats returned to power, and African Americans lost many of their civil rights.

PREVIEW   Big Ideas **of the Civil War Era**

1 Resistance to Slavery

The culture of African Americans was shaped by their struggle against slavery. Spirituals and slave narratives testified to the harshness of slavery and African Americans' fierce resistance to it.

See pages 322–323.

2 A Nation Divided

During the Civil War, Americans created a literary record that ranged from vivid accounts of wartime life to profound expressions of faith in American ideals.

See pages 324–325.

3 A Poetic Revolution

Poets Walt Whitman and Emily Dickinson experimented with new verse forms during this period. In divergent ways, they explored the self and its relation to the world.

See pages 326–327.

Resistance to Slavery

Suppose that you were not allowed to read or write or own anything. Picture yourself being whipped for disobeying orders or hunted after trying to escape. Imagine that you could be sold away from your family. That was life in slavery.

"There is no Negro problem. The problem is whether the American people have loyalty enough, honor enough, patriotism enough, to live up to their own Constitution."

—Frederick Douglass

The Realities of Slavery

Southern plantation owners purchased Africans for cultivating cotton, rice, or other crops. Southern laws made enslaved people property for life; even their children could be sold. It was illegal to teach enslaved people to read or write, for owners feared that knowledge would bring revolt and the ruin of their economic system. Escape was difficult; night patrols whipped or killed the slaves they caught.

Slavery was legal in the North, too; however, conditions there were different. Some enslaved persons were allowed to work in the industrial trades, and certain states allowed them to marry and acquire property. An enslaved person could be punished, but an owner who killed one could be charged with murder. Religious groups had always opposed slavery, and most Northerners came to believe that slavery was wrong. The argument over expanding slavery into new territories began to tear the nation apart.

Strength in Religion

Enslaved Africans combined traditional African music with Christian hymns to create spirituals, or songs of salvation and religious beliefs (see pages 330–335). Much of the imagery in spirituals was drawn from the Bible, as slaves likened their situation to that of the Jews held captive in Egypt.

Many songs had a dual meaning, expressing both religious faith and a hunger for freedom. Some also served as encoded messages. The first line of "Follow the Drinking Gourd"—"When the sun comes back and the first quail calls"—refers to late winter. "Conductors" on the Underground Railroad found that it took about a year for escapees to journey from the South to the Ohio River and that crossing the river was easiest during winter, when the river was frozen. Thus, the song suggests that enslaved Africans make their escape during winter and follow the "Drinking Gourd"—the Big Dipper constellation, whose cup points to the North Star.

Frederick Douglass

Frederick Douglass (see pages 337–344) was born on a Maryland plantation and was separated from his mother soon after birth. Early on Douglass realized that education was the path to freedom. As he taught himself to read and write, he grew determined to gain that freedom. After Douglass escaped at age twenty, he spoke at an antislavery meeting, launching his career as a powerful orator and an influential member of the abolitionist movement. In 1845, he authenticated his life story and the brutality he had endured by writing *Narrative of the Life of Frederick Douglass, an American Slave*, later expanded into *My Bondage and My Freedom* and *Life and Times of Frederick Douglass*.

Slave Narratives

Slave narratives became increasingly popular in the decades before the Civil War. In addition to Frederick Douglass, writers William Wells Brown, Solomon Northup, and Sojourner Truth sold tens of thousands of copies of their life stories. They not only provided Northerners and abolitionists with glimpses of the horrors of slavery but also contradicted the claims of slave owners. Through these narratives, slaves could be seen as people rather than property. For many people who knew no African Americans, these accounts revealed a culture and community that were founded on tradition, family, love, and respect.

The Hour of Emancipation, 1863. William Tolman Carlton. Oil on canvas. Private collection.

Frederick Douglass gave a speech to a white audience in Rochester, New York, on July 5, 1852.
The following paragraphs are taken from that speech.

from *The Meaning of July Fourth for the Negro* by Frederick Douglass

The blessings in which you, this day, rejoice, are not enjoyed in common. The rich inheritance of justice, liberty, prosperity and independence, bequeathed by your fathers, is shared by you, not by me. The sunlight that brought light and healing to you has brought stripes and death to me. This Fourth July is *yours,* not *mine. You* may rejoice, *I* must mourn. . . .

What, to the American slave, is your fourth of July? I answer, a day that reveals to him, more than all other days in the year, the gross injustice and cruelty to which he is the constant victim. To him, your celebration is a sham; your boasted liberty, an unholy license; your national greatness, swelling vanity; your sounds of rejoicing are empty and heartless; your denunciation of tyrants, brass fronted impudence; your shouts of liberty and equality, hollow mockery; your prayers and hymns, your sermons and thanksgivings, with all your religious parade and solemnity, are, to him mere bombast, fraud, deception, impiety, and hypocrisy—a thin veil to cover up crimes which would disgrace a nation of savages. There is not a nation on earth guilty of practices more shocking and bloody than are the people of the United States, at this very hour.

Reading Check

Analyzing Author's Purpose How did Douglass try to persuade his white readers and listeners to fight against slavery?

Big Idea 2
A Nation Divided

Fighting any war brings fear, loss, suffering, and death, but a war that turns the people of a country against each other is doubly bitter. In the American Civil War, communities and sometimes even families became divided by the conflict. Letters home were written from places most people had never heard of—Shiloh, Antietam, Gettysburg, and Chickamauga—all sites of major battles where thousands of soldiers were wounded or killed.

> *"Many are the hearts that are weary tonight, Wishing for the war to cease,"*
>
> —from the Civil War song "Tenting on the Old Campground" by Walter C. Kittredge

Revolution or Treason?

When Abraham Lincoln (see pages 386–392) was elected to the U.S. Congress in 1846, he voted against abolishing slavery, because he thought it would tear the Union apart. Although his goal was not to end slavery, he opposed its spreading to new territories. He believed that the territories should remain "places for poor people to go and better their condition." As antislavery sentiment grew in the North, it became clear that the United States was in danger of becoming divided.

In his speech A House Divided in 1858, Lincoln warned of the possible end of the Republic:

> "We are now far into the fifth year, since a policy was initiated with the avowed object and confident promise of putting an end to slavery agitation. . . . In my opinion, it will not cease until a crisis shall have been reached, and passed—'A house divided against itself cannot stand.'"

When Lincoln was elected president in 1860, his words proved true. The North saw secession as an act of treason. The South believed that it had launched a second American revolution, and the Civil War began soon after Lincoln took office.

Mary Chesnut's World

Mary Boykin Miller Chesnut (see pages 360–366) grew up in luxury on a large South Carolina plantation. Although she personally hated slavery, her family owned hundreds of slaves, and both her father and husband served as proslavery senators. Chesnut had little choice but to remain loyal to the South, but she documented the brutal cost of the war in her journal:

> July 1st [1862] . . . Edward Cheves, only son of John Cheves, killed. His sister kept crying, 'Oh, mother, what shall we do; Edward is killed,' but the mother sat dead still, white as a sheet, never uttering a word or shedding a tear. Are our women losing the capacity to weep?

Chesnut visited hospitals, rejoiced with friends at Confederate victories, and cried over Confederate losses. Through it all, she detailed the cruelties and evils of war in her journal. Her story told of her own fears and reactions, the devaluation of Confederate currency, and the inflation that forced families into starvation.

Lincoln's Vision and Words

Abraham Lincoln initially wished only to limit slavery and to preserve the Union, but he came under increasing pressure to turn the war into a campaign against slavery. He cautiously committed himself to eliminating slavery throughout the country, beginning with the Emancipation Proclamation, which announced that he would free the enslaved people in the South on January 1, 1863. The proclamation turned the war into a moral battle that aroused not only the spirit of the North but also the spirits of those who were enslaved. Lincoln's speeches reflected his dedication to the preservation of the Union and his desire to heal the nation. When Lincoln delivered the Gettysburg Address in 1863, he expressed a new vision of the United States.

The language of the Bible and of William Shakespeare inspired Lincoln's words. Lincoln's speeches were eloquent and moving, effectively combining simplicity with grandeur, emotion with power, and respect for human government with divine ideals.

from *Second Inaugural Address, March 4, 1865* by Abraham Lincoln

The Almighty has his own purposes. "Woe unto the world because of offenses! for it must needs be that offenses come; but woe to that man by whom the offense cometh!" If we shall suppose that American slavery is one of those offenses which, in the providence of God, must needs come, but which, having continued through His appointed time, He now wills to remove, and that He gives to both North and South, this terrible war, as the woe due to those by whom the offense came, shall we discern therein any departure from those divine attributes which the believers in a Living God always ascribe to Him? Fondly do we hope—fervently do we pray—that this mighty scourge of war may speedily pass away. Yet, if God wills that it continue, until all the wealth piled by the bond-man's two hundred and fifty years of unrequited toil shall be sunk, and until every drop of blood drawn with the lash, shall be paid by another drawn with the sword, as was said three thousand years ago, so still it must be said, "the judgments of the Lord, are true and righteous altogether."

With malice toward none; with charity for all; with firmness in the right, as God gives us to see the right, let us strive on to finish the work we are in; to bind up the nation's wounds; to care for him who shall have borne the battle, and for his widow, and his orphan—to do all which may achieve and cherish a just and lasting peace, among ourselves, and with all nations.

Reading Check

Summarizing Main Ideas What are the main ideas of each of the two paragraphs from Lincoln's Second Inaugural Address?

Big Idea 3
A Poetic Revolution

In the middle of the 1800s, two poets with dramatically contrasting lives and writing styles altered the course of American poetry. Walt Whitman and Emily Dickinson explored their emotions through poetry that broke with traditional themes and forms. Their work created two diverse inspirations for poets to this day.

> *"The genius of the United States is not best or most in its executives or legislatures, nor in its ambassadors or authors or colleges . . . but always most in the common people."*
>
> —Walt Whitman

Whitman's World

Walt Whitman (see pages 394–422) found poetry in the lives of everyday Americans. He took daily walks to absorb the sights and sounds of Brooklyn and its people, especially blue-collar workers. Whitman used his experiences as a reporter, teacher, laborer, and Civil War nurse to create his poetry. His distinctive style is marked by long, rollicking lines written in free verse—poetry based on the irregular rhythms of speech, rather than on traditional poetic meter. Whitman imagined his work as one long, boundless poem that expressed his all-embracing view of the world. *Leaves of Grass* captured the colorful speech and brash, optimistic spirit of a vital young nation. In an essay on the ideal poet, Ralph Waldo Emerson had observed: "The poet has a new thought; he has a whole new experience to unfold; he will tell us how it was with him, and all men will be the richer in his fortune." Inspired by Emerson's vision, Whitman saw himself as this poet.

Whitman on the War

When the Civil War came, Whitman's work reflected his sympathies for the struggles of the Union. The poems in *Drum-Taps* reflect his changing attitudes and experiences as a nurse.

Whitman cared for both Union and Confederate soldiers in war hospitals. Being on the scene was essential to him, whether he was sharing the energy of city life or the grief of battle casualties. In President Abraham Lincoln, Whitman found an American hero. He celebrated the "Rail-Splitter" who had emerged from humble origins to unify the nation and felt profound grief when Lincoln was assassinated. In the elegy "When Lilacs Last in the Dooryard Bloom'd," Whitman reflects on Lincoln—"the great star early droop'd in the western sky." The elegy addresses the nature of grief and embraces a theme of renewal in spite of the tragic assassination:

> "From deep secluded recesses,
> From the fragrant cedars and the ghostly pines so still, Came the carol of the bird."

Critic Alfred Kazin wrote that Whitman's elegy "is as much a monument as the Lincoln Memorial."

Dickinson's Introspection

While Whitman experienced America and its people, Emily Dickinson (see pages 423–443) observed the life of Amherst, Massachusetts, from her second-story bedroom window, composing poetry that could turn the ordinary into the deeply meaningful. Dickinson wrote approximately 1,775 poems, though less than a dozen were published in her lifetime. She suggested that her work had to make its points subtly: "The Truth must dazzle gradually / Or every man be blind." Although Dickinson created poetry during the Civil War, her poems do not place the reader on the battlefield and in the action as Whitman's do. Instead, her themes connect the reader to moments and feelings.

A *presentiment* is a premonition, or a feeling that something is about to happen. In her poem on the following page, Dickinson describes the time before darkness envelops the day. Her metaphor relates sunset and darkness to death. Though this poem is not about the Civil War, it conveys a fear of dying, appropriate to a period of war. Dickinson's poems could be categorized in conventional terms—love, nature,

Central Park, 20th century. George Luks. Oil on canvas, 31.5 x 34.4 in. Private collection.

eternity, loneliness, and death—but she brought irony and keen observation to these common topics. Her poetry included unconventional use of punctuation, especially dashes, and short, clipped lines that took rhythmic influence from the hymns that she had heard as a child. Dickinson has been described as an expert miniaturist because of the depth of expression contained in this tightly constructed poems.

"The Lightning is a yellow Fork"
by Emily Dickinson

The Lightning is a yellow Fork
From Tables in the sky
By inadvertent fingers dropt
The awful Cutlery

5 Of mansions never quite disclosed
And never quite concealed
The Apparatus of the Dark
To ignorance revealed.

"Cavalry Crossing a Ford"
by Walt Whitman

A line in long array where they wind betwixt
    green islands,
They take a serpentine course, their arms flash
    in the sun—hark to the musical clank,
Behold the silvery river, in it the splashing
    horses loitering stop to drink,
Behold the brown-faced men, each group, each
    person a picture, the negligent rest on the
    saddles,
5 Some emerge on the opposite bank, others are
    just entering the ford—while,
Scarlet and blue and snowy white,
The guidon flags flutter gayly in the wind.

Reading Check

Analyzing Imagery How does Whitman convey a sense of motion in his poem? To how many senses does this poem appeal and in what lines?

Analyzing Metaphor What two things does Dickinson compare in her poem?

Wrap-Up

Why It Matters

Up to and during the Civil War, writers shifted from Romanticism to Realism in response to the cultural and social forces affecting the nation. Depictions of slavery, and of fugitives from slavery, by Frederick Douglass and others stirred the Northern conscience and infuriated Southern planters.

But the North's resistance to slavery and the South's insistence on states' rights resulted in a bloody conflict that tore the nation apart. Civil War cemeteries and battlefields throughout Eastern and Southern states today are grim reminders of lives shattered or ended.

Walt Whitman claimed that "the United States themselves are essentially the greatest poem." Poets continue to emulate the free verse of Whitman and his exploration of the self in relationship to the world. Emily Dickinson is now recognized as one of the greatest American poets. Her work—with its concise style, experimental grammar and punctuation, and everyday subjects transformed into the meaningful and universal—has influenced poets worldwide.

Cultural Links

◇ Whitman has influenced scores of poets, including Allen Ginsberg, who called him "dear father, gray-beard, lonely old courage-teacher."

◇ One of the most famous movies ever made, *Gone with the Wind*, was based on a 1936 novel about the Civil War and Reconstruction by Southerner Margaret Mitchell.

You might try using this study organizer to take notes on the people, settings, and events you read about in this unit.

FOLDABLES Study Organizer   **THREE-TAB BOOK**

People   Places   Events

The Civil War Era

Literature Online **Big Ideas** Link to Web resources to further explore the Big Ideas at www.glencoe.com.

Connect to Today Use what you have learned about the period to do one of these activities.

1. Speaking/Listening Research a slave narrative and give an oral interpretation of part of it to the class.

2. Visual Literacy Create a timeline that represents the American people and the struggles they faced during the Civil War. Use works of art, photographs, advertisements, book covers, and posters in your timeline. Include brief descriptions of how these works reflect the period.

3. Writing Poet James Russell Lowell read his poem "Commemoration Ode" at Harvard College shortly after Lincoln's death. In the poem, he called Lincoln "the first American." Write a short essay explaining what you think he meant by this. Consider Lincoln's life, his writings, and his place in the American consciousness.

■ **INDIANA ACADEMIC STANDARDS (page 328)**
11.7.20 Recite...dramatic soliloquies with attention to performance details to achieve...aesthetic effect...

11.5.3 Write reflective compositions that draw comparisons between specific incidents and broader themes that illustrate the writer's...beliefs...

Literature Online **Study Central** Visit www.glencoe.com and click on Study Central to review The Civil War Era.

Resistance to Slavery

A Ride for Liberty, or The Fugitive Slaves, 1862. J. Eastman Johnson. 55.9 x 66.7 cm. Brooklyn Museum of Art, New York.

> "You have seen how a man was made a slave;
> you shall see how a slave was made a man."
>
> —Frederick Douglass
> *Narrative of the Life of Frederick Douglass, an American slave*

329

Three Spirituals

WHO WROTE THE SPIRITUALS?

The spirituals featured here came out of the oral tradition of African Americans enslaved in the South before the outbreak of the Civil War. These "sorrow songs," as they were called, were created by anonymous artists and transmitted by word of mouth. As a result, several versions of the same spiritual may exist. According to the Library of Congress, more than six thousand spirituals have been documented, though some are not known in their entirety.

African American spirituals combined the tunes and texts of Christian hymns with the rhythms, finger-snapping, clapping, and stamping of traditional African music. The spirituals allowed enslaved Africans to retain some of the culture of their homelands and forge a new culture while facing the hardships of captive life in the United States. Many spirituals followed a call-and-response pattern in which a leader sang the verses and was answered by a group of singers. The singers often improvised the songs by changing words or adding new verses.

> *"Every tone [in the spirituals] was a testimony against slavery, and a prayer to God for deliverance from chains."*
>
> —Frederick Douglass

Enslaved African Americans sang spirituals both in worship and while laboring in the field. Many of the songs have a dual meaning, expressing both religious faith and a hunger for freedom. The *New York Tribune* published "Go Down, Moses" after Reverend Lewis Lockwood heard African Americans singing it on September 3, 1861, and submitted the lyrics.

Some spirituals served as encoded messages by which enslaved field workers, forbidden to speak to each other, could communicate practical information about escape plans. Some typical code words included *Egypt,* referring to the South or the state of bondage, and the *promised land* or *heaven,* referring to the North or freedom. To communicate a message of hope, spirituals frequently recounted Bible stories about people liberated from oppression through divine intervention. The spiritual "Keep Your Hand on the Plow," for example, tells the story of Paul and Silas, who were released from prison after God sent an earthquake to free them.

The spirituals were saved from obscurity after the Civil War by the Jubilee Singers of Fisk University in Nashville, Tennessee. To raise money for the school during a time of financial hardship, the small university choir sang spirituals to church groups around the country. The Jubilee Singers were soon in demand and eventually performed the spirituals for President Ulysses S. Grant and England's Queen Victoria.

The spirituals became a part of American pop culture, paving the way for other musical forms including blues and jazz and influencing poets such as James Weldon Johnson. When Martin Luther King Jr. led the march in Washington, D.C., for civil rights in March 1963, he quoted from the spiritual "Free at Last": "You can hinder me here, but you can't hinder me there."

Connecting to the Spirituals

Many people find listening to, singing, playing, or even composing music to be a comfort in times of stress or loss. As you read, think about these questions:

- Why was it important for oppressed people to create these songs?
- What music do you turn to for inspiration or comfort?

Building Background

For many enslaved African Americans, the situation of the Jews in the Bible was especially poignant. According to the Bible, the Jews were forced into slavery by a pharaoh, or ruler, of Egypt. Moses, a leader of the Jews, asked the pharaoh to free his people, warning that otherwise God would send ten plagues upon the Egyptians. The plagues came, and the pharaoh released the Jews. After Egyptian soldiers chased the Jews to the shores of the Red Sea, Moses called upon God to part the waters so his people could cross. The sea rolled back for the Jews to pass but closed in on the Egyptian soldiers. When the Jews "reached the other shore," they were free people once again.

Setting Purposes for Reading

Big Idea Resistance to Slavery

As you read, consider the role spirituals played in the African American struggle for freedom.

Literary Element Refrain

A **refrain** is a line or lines repeated in a poem or song. For example, the line "Let my people go" is repeated in every stanza of the spiritual "Go Down, Moses." As you read, think about how the refrains in each spiritual help to emphasize a central idea.

- See Literary Terms Handbook, p. R15.

Reading Strategy Analyzing Historical Context

Understanding the context in which the spirituals were created can help you better appreciate them. The era that gave birth to the spirituals was an intensely difficult one for enslaved African Americans. They toiled long hours, were barred from communicating with each other, and were frequently threatened with violence. They were also subjected to damaging stereotypes about their supposed lack of intelligence and responsibility. Spirituals gave African Americans much-needed encouragement, information about escape, and a chance to define themselves. In spirituals, African Americans were depicted as the beloved children of a just and mighty God, destined for freedom.

According to travelers in the South and the slaves themselves, spirituals were a fundamental part of slave life. They were sung during worship, rest, work, and play. As you read the spirituals, jot down your thoughts about how they reflect the hopes and beliefs of slaves.

Reading Tip: Taking Notes Use a chart to record your thoughts about the spirituals.

Example from text	How it reflects hope
But still my soul feels heavenly bound	Even though life can be very difficult, the speaker believes his or her soul will find joy.

INDIANA ACADEMIC STANDARDS (pages 331–335)

11.2 Develop strategies such as...analyzing structure...

11.3.5 Analyze...works of...significance in history...

11.4.7 Develop presentations using...Internet sources.

Swing Low, Sweet Chariot

Swing Low, Sweet Chariot, 1944. William H. Johnson. Oil on board,
28½ x 26½ in. National Museum of American Art, Washington, DC.

Swing low, sweet chariot,
Coming for to carry me home,
Swing low, sweet chariot,
Coming for to carry me home.

5 I looked over Jordan[1] and what did I see,
Coming for to carry me home?
A band of angels coming after me,
Coming for to carry me home.

If you get there before I do,
10 Coming for to carry me home,
Tell all my friends I'm coming too;
Coming for to carry me home.

I'm sometimes up, I'm sometimes down,
Coming for to carry me home,
15 But still my soul feels heavenly bound;
Coming for to carry me home.

Swing low, sweet chariot,
Coming for to carry me home,
Swing low, sweet chariot,
20 Coming for to carry me home.

---

1. *Jordan* refers to the Jordan River. In the Book of Exodus
   in the Bible, when the Jews were fleeing from slavery in
   Egypt, they had to cross the Jordan to reach their
   Promised Land.

Literary Element Refrain *How does the refrain function in the spiritual?*

Harriet Tubman Series No. 11, 1939-40. Jacob Lawrence. Casein tempera on gessoed hardboard, 12 x 17⅞ in. Hampton University Museum, Hampton, VA.

Go Down, Moses

Go down, Moses,
'Way down in Egypt's land;
Tell ole Pharaoh
Let my people go.

5 When Israel was in Egypt's land,
Let my people go;
Oppressed so hard they could not stand,
Let my people go.

Thus saith the Lord, bold Moses said,
10 Let my people go;
Let them come out with Egypt's spoil,
Let my people go.

The Lord told Moses what to do,
Let my people go;
15 To lead the children of Israel thro',
Let my people go.

When they had reached the other shore,
Let my people go;
They sang a song of triumph o'er.
20 Let my people go.

Go down, Moses,
'Way down in Egypt's land;
Tell ole Pharaoh
Let my people go.

Big Idea Resistance to Slavery *How does this biblical allusion reflect the enslaved people's desire to escape slavery?*

Going to Church, 1940–1941. William H. Johnson. Oil on burlap, 38⅛ x 45½ in. Smithsonian American Art Museum, Washington, DC, U.S.A.

Keep your Hand on the Plow

Mary wo' three links of chain,
Ev'ry link was Jesus' name.
Keep your hand on the plow,
Hold on.

CHORUS
5   Hold on, hold on,
Keep your hand on the plow,
Hold on.

Paul and Silas bound in jail,[1]
Had nobody for to go their bail,
10 Keep your hand on the plow,
Hold on.

Paul and Silas began to shout,
Jail doors opened and they walked out . . .

Peter was so nice and neat,[2]
15 Wouldn't let Jesus wash his feet . . .

Jesus said, "If I wash them not,
You'll have no father in this lot" . . .

Peter got anxious and he said,
"Wash my feet, my hands and head," . . .

20 Got my hand on the gospel plow,
Wouldn't take nothin' for my journey now, . . .

---

1. In the Bible (Acts 16:16–40) the Apostle *Paul* and his companion *Silas* are imprisoned, but an earthquake shakes the prison and releases them.
2. In the Bible (John 13:4–20) the Apostle *Peter* objects at first when Jesus wants to wash his feet.

Big Idea Resistance to Slavery *How might these lines have helped singers and listeners endure slavery?*

Reading Strategy Analyzing Historical Context *Why might enslaved people have connected with these lines in the spiritual?*

RESPONDING AND THINKING CRITICALLY

Respond

1. Which phrases or lines from these spirituals did you find most comforting or inspiring?

Recall and Interpret

2. (a)What might the chariot in "Swing Low, Sweet Chariot" represent? (b)Who or what might be the "band of angels" in line 7?

3. (a)What feelings does the speaker express in lines 13–16? (b)Why do you think the speaker's "soul feels heavenly bound"?

4. (a)In lines 1–8 of "Go Down, Moses," what is the speaker asking Moses to do? (b)What might these lines say about the experiences and hopes of enslaved African Americans?

5. (a)Summarize the two Bible stories retold in "Keep Your Hand on the Plow." (b)Why do you think these particular stories were included in a spiritual? Explain.

Analyze and Evaluate

6. Enslaved African Americans highly valued, and frequently retold, stories from the Gospels. (a)In light of this, what do you think is the meaning of lines 1–3 of "Keep Your Hand on the Plow"? (b)In what way do these lines illuminate the **theme,** or overall message, of the song? Give details from the song to support your answer.

7. Describe the **mood,** or overall feeling or emotion, created by each of the spirituals. Use specific examples from each song to support your response.

Connect

8. **Big Idea** **Resistance to Slavery** What elements of the spirituals helped singers and listeners endure and overcome slavery? Include details from the spirituals in your answer.

LITERARY ANALYSIS

Literary Element **Refrain**

Spirituals usually contain at least one refrain that emphasizes the central idea, or **theme,** and that also helps establish the **mood.** In addition, refrains help create **rhythm.**

1. What mood is created by the refrain in "Swing Low, Sweet Chariot"?

2. The words "Let my people go" are repeated in every stanza of "Go Down, Moses." What impact does this repetition create?

Interdisciplinary Activity

Music Trying to imagine how a song sounds based on reading it is a little like trying to explain the taste of a strawberry to someone who's never eaten one. Working with a group, locate and listen to recordings of all three spirituals. Then work together to prepare a performance of one of the spirituals for the class.

Literature Online **Web Activities** For eFlashcards, Selection Quick Checks, and other Web activities, go to www.glencoe.com.

READING AND VOCABULARY

Reading Strategy **Analyzing Historical Context**

Spirituals often combined phrases from English hymns with harmonies and rhythms found in African music.

1. How do spirituals reflect the history of African Americans?

2. Why do you think people still sing spirituals today?

Academic Vocabulary

Here are two words from the vocabulary list on page R86. These words will help you think, write, and talk about the selections.

specific (spi sif′ ik) *adj.* definite; particular

rely (ri lī′) *v.* to be dependent

Practice and Apply
1. What is a **specific** example of farm imagery in the spirituals?
2. Which code words did runaway slaves **rely** on to communicate secret messages?

Comparing Literature Across Time and Place

Connecting to the Reading Selections

What characteristics are vital in someone who battles oppression? The three authors compared here—Frederick Douglass, Robert Hayden, and Quincy Troupe—portray people struggling against limitations placed on them by society. The works of these writers show both the stubbornness of racial oppression and the potential for individuals to overcome oppressive traditions.

COMPARING THE `Big Idea` Resistance to Slavery

The struggle against slavery has shaped African American culture. Literature about slavery and its legacy illustrates the resilient spirit that has helped African Americans endure hard times with dignity, overcome slavery, and resist the lingering effects of racism and discrimination.

COMPARING Portrayals of People

A portrayal reveals the essential qualities of an individual or group. By taking an individual as the subject, the writer of a literary portrayal explores that individual's character and personality, in addition to the social and cultural forces that shaped his or her life. A group portrayal reveals the traits that members of the group have in common. Douglass, Hayden, and Troupe create vivid portrayals of individuals and groups in the selections you are about to read.

COMPARING Historical Context

Works of literature often reflect the historical events that shape the way people see the world and live their lives. Recognizing the historical backdrop of a selection can increase your understanding of its themes and messages, as well as the author's purpose. Douglas, Hayden, and Troupe write within the historical context of slavery and its legacy of racism and discrimination.

from *My Bondage and My Freedom*

MEET FREDERICK DOUGLASS

Of all of the voices raised against slavery, few were as powerful as that of Frederick Douglass's. He was, as women's rights activist Elizabeth Cady Stanton wrote, "conscious of his dignity and power, grand in his proportions, majestic in his wrath."

"Where justice is denied, where poverty is enforced, where ignorance prevails, and where any one class is made to feel that society is in an organized conspiracy to oppress, rob, and degrade them, neither persons nor property will be safe."

—Frederick Douglass

From Bondage to Freedom Douglass was born on a Maryland plantation and given the name Frederick Bailey. When Frederick was eight years old, he went to work as a house servant for the Auld family in Baltimore. Mrs. Auld decided to teach Frederick how to read, which violated a Maryland state law. When her husband discovered what was happening, he forbade any further reading lessons. Frederick then secretly continued his education on his own. At the age of twenty, Frederick Bailey finally escaped to freedom. Soon after, Frederick changed his last name from Bailey to Douglass to avoid capture and a forced return to slavery.

In 1841 Douglass's life took a remarkable turn. He was asked to speak at an antislavery convention in Nantucket, Massachusetts. Although he was nervous about speaking, Douglass's speech about his experiences as a slave was so eloquent that it prompted abolitionist leaders to ask him to work as an agent for the Massachusetts Anti-Slavery Society. While Douglass toured for the society, his reputation quickly grew.

Public Life In 1845 Douglass wrote his autobiography, *Narrative of the Life of Frederick Douglass, an American Slave.* Because Douglass identified his former owner in the book, he sailed to Great Britain to avoid capture. Abolitionists welcomed Douglass and raised money to enable him to buy his freedom and return home in 1847. That same year he started publishing a newspaper, *The North Star.* The paper's masthead read: "Right is of no Sex—Truth is of no Color," proclaiming both Douglass's abolitionism and his support for women's rights.

At the outbreak of the Civil War in 1861, President Lincoln appointed Douglass one of his advisers. After the war, he remained a staunch supporter of civil rights for formerly enslaved people. Before his death in 1895, Douglass served as the marshal and recorder of deeds in Washington, D.C., and as consul general to Haiti. He also revised and republished his autobiography as *My Bondage and My Freedom* in 1855, and then again as *Life and Times of Frederick Douglass* in 1882. Douglass's autobiography remains one of the most important chronicles of the enslaved person's experience and displays the brilliance of Douglass's literary mind.

Frederick Douglass was born around 1818 and died in 1895.

Literature Online **Author Search** For more about Frederick Douglass, go to www.glencoe.com.

Connecting to the Autobiography

Do you agree with the saying "knowledge is power"? In Douglass's autobiography, he reflects on his struggle to learn to read and write in a society that made it a crime for enslaved persons to attain knowledge through literacy. As you read the autobiography, think about the following questions:

- How can newfound knowledge make it necessary to change one's life?
- Is knowledge gained through reading essential to personal freedom? Why or why not?

Building Background

As a result of slave codes, or restrictive laws against enslaved people, Douglass had to improvise to find ways of improving his reading and writing skills. For example, while running errands for workers in the Baltimore shipyards, he observed carpenters who were painting signs on boards.

The original version of Douglass's life story became a best seller when published in 1845. One reviewer called it "a specimen of powers of the black race, which prejudice persists in disputing." Douglass spent time with many other abolitionists during the 1850s, including Harriet Beecher Stowe, author of *Uncle Tom's Cabin.* His revised autobiography *My Bondage and My Freedom* includes more of his philosophy and personal feelings toward the essential problems of slavery.

Setting Purposes for Reading

Big Idea Resistance to Slavery

In this excerpt, Douglass reveals his inner, day-to-day thoughts about his life as an enslaved African American. As you read, notice how Douglass asserts his belief that education can fight slavery.

Literary Element Autobiography

An **autobiography** is a narrative that a person writes about his or her life. Douglass wrote about his own life in the wider historical context of slavery. As you read, determine Douglass's purposes in writing an account of his experiences in the form of an autobiography.

- See Literary Terms Handbook, p. R2.

Literature Online Interactive Literary Elements Handbook To review or learn more about the literary elements, go to www.glencoe.com.

Reading Strategy Analyzing Cause and Effect

When you analyze a literary work, you use your knowledge of separate parts to form an overall judgment. **Analyzing cause-and-effect relationships** means figuring out how a writer arranges details to show that certain events and ideas can *cause,* or bring about, certain results or *effects.* As you read, ask yourself the following questions:

- What are the major events that Douglass writes about in this excerpt?
- What effects were caused by these major events?

Reading Tip: Taking Notes Use a chart to record the cause-and-effect relationships you find in the selection.

Cause	Effect
Mrs. Auld introduces Douglass to reading.	Douglass determines to attain knowledge at any cost.

Vocabulary

benevolent (bə nev′ ə lent) *adj.* doing or desiring to do good; kind; p. 339 *The benevolent girl helped the woman who was struggling to carry bags of groceries.*

depravity (di′ prav′ ə tē) *n.* the state of being morally bad or corrupt; p. 339 *The brutal tactics of slave traders showed a depravity that has shocked modern audiences.*

induce (in do͞os′) *v.* to lead by persuasion or influence; p. 340 *The powerful speaker tried to induce the members of his audience to change their minds on the issue.*

vanquish (vang′ kwish) *v.* to defeat; p. 342 *President Lincoln decided that military force would be the only way to vanquish slavery in the South.*

censure (sen′ shər) *v.* to express disapproval of; to find fault with; to blame; p. 343 *The writer decided to censure the government policy in her report.*

Frederick Douglass

from

MY BONDAGE
and
MY FREEDOM

Series No. 8. Jacob Lawrence (1917–2000). Casein tempera on gessoed hardboard, 12 x 17 ⅞ in. Hampton University Museum, VA.

I lived in the family of master Hugh, at Baltimore, seven years, during which time—as the almanac[1] makers say of the weather—my condition was variable. The most interesting feature of my history here, was my learning to read and write, under somewhat marked disadvantages. In attaining this knowledge, I was compelled to resort to indirections by no means congenial to my nature, and which were really humiliating to me. My mistress—who, as the reader has already seen, had begun to teach

---

1. An *almanac* is a reference book that is published yearly. It includes calendars with weather forecasts and astronomical information.

me—was suddenly checked in her **benevolent** design, by the strong advice of her husband. In faithful compliance with this advice, the good lady had not only ceased to instruct me, herself, but had set her face as a flint against my learning to read by any means. It is due, however, to my mistress to say, that she did not adopt this course in all its stringency at the first. She either thought it unnecessary, or she lacked the **depravity** indispensable to shutting me up in mental darkness. It was, at least, necessary for her to have some training, and some hardening, in the exercise of the slaveholder's prerogative, to make her equal to forgetting my human nature and character, and to treating me as a thing destitute of a moral or an intellectual nature. Mrs. Auld—my mistress—was,

Reading Strategy Analyzing Cause and Effect *What is the cause of the change in Mrs. Auld's attitude toward Douglass's reading instruction?*

as I have said, a most kind and tender-hearted woman; and, in the humanity of her heart, and the simplicity of her mind, she set out, when I first went to live with her, to treat me as she supposed one human being ought to treat another.

It is easy to see, that, in entering upon the duties of a slaveholder, some little experience is needed. Nature has done almost nothing to prepare men and women to be either slaves or slaveholders. Nothing but rigid training, long persisted in, can perfect the character of the one or the other. One cannot easily forget to love freedom; and it is as hard to cease to respect that natural love in our fellow creatures. On entering upon the career of a slaveholding mistress, Mrs. Auld was singularly deficient; nature, which fits nobody for such an office, had done less for her than any lady I had known. It was no easy matter to **induce** her to think and to feel that the curly-headed boy, who stood by her side, and even leaned on her lap; who was loved by little Tommy, and who loved little Tommy in turn; sustained to her only the relation of a chattel.[2] I was *more* than that, and she felt me to be more than that. I could talk and sing; I could laugh and weep; I could reason and remember; I could love and hate. I was human, and she, dear lady, knew and felt me to be so. How could she, then, treat me as a brute, without a mighty struggle with all the noble powers of her own soul. That struggle came, and the will and power of the husband was victorious. Her noble soul was overthrown; but, he that overthrew it did not, himself, escape the consequences. He, not less than the other parties, was injured in his domestic peace by the fall.

When I went into their family, it was the abode of happiness and contentment. The mistress of the house was a model of affection and tenderness. Her fervent piety and watchful uprightness made it impossible to see her without thinking

and feeling—"*that woman is a Christian.*" There was no sorrow nor suffering for which she had not a tear, and there was no innocent joy for which she had not a smile. She had bread for the hungry, clothes for the naked, and comfort for every mourner that came within her reach. Slavery soon proved its ability to divest her of these excellent qualities, and her home of its early happiness. Conscience cannot stand much violence. Once thoroughly broken down, *who* is he that can repair the damage? It may be broken toward the slave, on Sunday, and toward the master on Monday. It cannot endure such shocks. It must stand entire, or it does not stand at all. If my condition waxed bad, that of the family waxed not better. The first step, in the wrong direction, was the violence done to nature and to conscience, in arresting the benevolence that would have enlightened my young mind. In ceasing to instruct me, she must begin to justify herself *to* herself; and, once consenting to take sides in such a debate, she was riveted to her position. One needs very little knowledge of moral philosophy, to see *where* my mistress now landed. She finally became even more violent in her opposition to my learning to read, than was her husband himself. She was not satisfied with simply doing as *well* as her husband had commanded her, but seemed resolved to better his instruction. Nothing appeared to make my poor mistress—after her turning toward the downward path—more angry, than seeing me, seated in some nook or corner, quietly reading a book or a newspaper. I have had her rush at me, with the utmost fury, and snatch from my hand such newspaper or book, with something of the wrath and consternation which a traitor might be supposed to feel on being discovered in a plot by some dangerous spy.

Mrs. Auld was an apt woman, and the advice of her husband, and her own experience, soon demonstrated, to her entire satisfaction, that education and slavery are incompatible with each other. When this conviction was thoroughly established,

---

2. An article of movable, personal property, such as furniture or livestock, is *chattel.* Enslaved people were sometimes referred to as *chattel.*

Big Idea　Resistance to Slavery *What does this statement say about the institution of slavery?*

Vocabulary

induce　(in doos') *v.* to lead by persuasion or influence

Literary Element　Autobiography *What is Douglass saying here about the effects of slavery on his own life?*

Big Idea　Resistance to Slavery *How does this incompatibility motivate Douglass to resist the institution of slavery?*

The Life of Frederick Douglass #29: The war was over. The slaves were literally turned out by their masters into a world unknown to them. They had ceased to be slaves of man and became slaves of nature, 1939. Jacob Lawrence. Casein tempera on hardboard, 17 x 12. Hampton University Museum, Hampton, VA.

I was most narrowly watched in all my movements. If I remained in a separate room from the family for any considerable length of time, I was sure to be suspected of having a book, and was at once called upon to give an account of myself. All this, however, was entirely *too late*. The first, and never to be retraced, step had been taken. In teaching me the alphabet, in the days of her simplicity and kindness, my mistress had given me the *"inch,"* and now, no ordinary precaution could prevent me from taking the *"ell."*[3]

Seized with a determination to learn to read, at any cost, I hit upon many expedients to accomplish the desired end. The plea which I mainly adopted, and the one by which I was most suc-

cessful, was that of using my young white playmates, with whom I met in the street, as teachers. I used to carry, almost constantly, a copy of Webster's spelling book in my pocket; and, when sent of errands, or when play time was allowed me, I would step, with my young friends, aside, and take a lesson in spelling. I generally paid my *tuition fee* to the boys, with bread, which I also carried in my pocket. For a single biscuit, any of my hungry little comrades would give me a lesson more valuable to me than bread. Not every one, however, demanded this consideration, for there were those who took pleasure in teaching me, whenever I had a chance to be taught by them. I am strongly tempted to give the names of two or three of those little boys, as a slight testimonial of the gratitude and affection I bear them, but prudence forbids; not that it would injure me, but it might, possibly, embarrass them; for it is almost an unpardonable offense to do any thing, directly or indirectly, to promote a slave's freedom, in a slave state. It is enough to say, of my warm-hearted little play fellows, that they lived on Philpot street, very near Durgin & Bailey's shipyard.

Although slavery was a delicate subject, and very cautiously talked about among grown up people in Maryland, I frequently talked about it—and that very freely—with the white boys. I would, sometimes, say to them, while seated on a curb stone or a cellar door, "I wish I could be free, as you will be when you get to be men." "You will be free, you know, as soon as you are twenty-one, and can go where you like, but I am a slave for life. Have I not as good a right to be free as you have?" Words like these, I observed, always troubled them; and I had no small satisfaction in wringing from the boys, occasionally, that fresh and bitter condemnation of slavery, that springs from nature, unseared and unperverted. Of all consciences, let me have those to deal with which have not been bewildered by the cares of life. I do not remember ever to have met with a *boy*, while I was in slavery, who defended the slave system; but I have often had boys to console me, with the hope that something would yet occur, by which I might be

---

3. An *ell* is an old English measure of length used mainly for cloth. It is equal to forty-five inches. Douglass is referring to the adage "give him an inch, and he'll take an ell."

Literary Element Autobiography *How does Douglass's choice of the genre of autobiography enhance the impact of this statement?*

made free. Over and over again, they have told me, that "they believed *I* had as good a right to be free as *they* had"; and that "they did not believe God ever made any one to be a slave." The reader will easily see, that such little conversations with my play fellows, had no tendency to weaken my love of liberty, nor to render me contented with my condition as a slave.

When I was about thirteen years old, and had succeeded in learning to read, every increase of knowledge, especially respecting the FREE STATES, added something to the almost intolerable burden of the thought—"I AM A SLAVE FOR LIFE." To my bondage I saw no end. It was a terrible reality, and I shall never be able to tell how sadly that thought chafed my young spirit. Fortunately, or unfortunately, about this time in my life, I had made enough money to buy what was then a very popular school book, viz:[4] the "Columbian Orator." I bought this addition to my library, of Mr. Knight, on Thames street, Fell's Point, Baltimore, and paid him fifty cents for it. I was first led to buy this book, by hearing some little boys say that they were going to learn some little pieces out of it for the Exhibition. This volume was, indeed, a rich treasure, and every opportunity afforded me, for a time, was spent in diligently perusing it. Among much other interesting matter, that which I had perused and reperused with unflagging satisfaction, was a short dialogue between a master and his slave. The slave is represented as having been recaptured, in a second attempt to run away; and the master opens the dialogue with an upbraiding speech, charging the slave with ingratitude, and demanding to know what he has to say in his own defense. Thus upbraided, and thus called upon to reply, the slave rejoins, that he knows how little anything that he can say will avail, seeing that he is completely in the hands of his owner; and with noble resolution, calmly says, "I submit to my fate." Touched by the slave's answer, the master insists upon his further speaking, and recapitulates the many acts of kindness

which he has performed toward the slave, and tells him he is permitted to speak for himself. Thus invited to the debate, the quondam[5] slave made a spirited defense of himself, and thereafter the whole argument, for and against slavery, was brought out. The master was **vanquished** at every turn in the argument; and seeing himself to be thus vanquished, he generously and meekly emancipates the slave, with his best wishes for his prosperity. It is scarcely necessary to say, that a dialogue, with such an origin, and such an ending—read when the fact of my being a slave was a constant burden of grief—powerfully affected me; and I could not help feeling that the day might come, when the well-directed answers made by the slave to the master, in this instance, would find their counterpart in myself. . . .

I had now penetrated the secret of all slavery and oppression, and had ascertained their true foundation to be in the pride, the power and the avarice of man. The dialogue and the speeches were all redolent of the principles of liberty, and poured floods of light on the nature and character of slavery. . . . Nevertheless, the increase of knowledge was attended with bitter, as well as sweet results. The more I read, the more I was led to abhor and detest slavery, and my enslavers. "Slaveholders," thought I, "are only a band of successful robbers, who left their homes and went into Africa for the purpose of stealing and reducing my people to slavery." I loathed them as the meanest and the most wicked of men. As I read, behold! the very discontent so graphically predicted by Master Hugh, had already come upon me. I was no longer the light-hearted, gleesome boy, full of mirth and play, as when I landed first at Baltimore. Knowledge had come; light had penetrated the moral dungeon where I dwelt; and, behold! there lay the bloody whip, for my back, and here was the iron chain; and my good,

---

4. *Viz* is an abbreviation for the Latin word *videlicet,* meaning "namely" or "that is."

Reading Strategy Analyzing Cause and Effect *What was the ironic effect of Douglass's learning to read?*

---

5. *Quondam* means "that once was" or "former."

Reading Strategy Analyzing Cause and Effect *What effect did reading this anecdote about the slave and his master have on Douglass?*

Vocabulary

vanquish (vang′ kwish) *v.* to defeat

kind master, he was the author of my situation. The revelation haunted me, stung me, and made me gloomy and miserable. As I writhed under the sting and torment of this knowledge, I almost envied my fellow slaves their stupid contentment. This knowledge opened my eyes to the horrible pit, and revealed the teeth of the frightful dragon that was ready to pounce upon me, but it opened no way for my escape. I have often wished myself a beast, or a bird—anything, rather than a slave. I was wretched and gloomy, beyond my ability to describe. I was too thoughtful to be happy. It was this everlasting thinking which distressed and tormented me; and yet there was no getting rid of the subject of my thoughts. All nature was redolent of it. Once awakened by the silver trump[6] of knowledge, my spirit was roused to eternal wakefulness. Liberty! the inestimable birthright of every man, had, for me, converted every object into an asserter of this great right. It was heard in every sound, and beheld in every object. It was ever present, to torment me with a sense of my wretched condition. The more beautiful and charming were the smiles of nature, the more horrible and desolate was my condition. I saw nothing without seeing it, and I heard nothing without hearing it. I do not exaggerate, when I say, that it looked from every star, smiled in every calm, breathed in every wind, and moved in every storm.

I have no doubt that my state of mind had something to do with the change in the treatment adopted, by my once kind mistress toward me. I can easily believe, that my leaden, downcast, and discontented look, was very offensive to her. Poor lady! She did not know my trouble, and I dared not tell her. Could I have freely made her acquainted with the real state of my mind, and given her the reasons therefor, it might have been well for both of us. Her abuse of me fell upon me like the blows of the false prophet upon his ass; she did not know that an

angel stood in the way;[7] and—such is the relation of master and slave—I could not tell her. Nature had made us *friends*; slavery made us *enemies*. My interests were in a direction opposite to hers, and we both had our private thoughts and plans. She aimed to keep me ignorant; and I resolved to know, although knowledge only increased my discontent. My feelings were not the result of any marked cruelty in the treatment I received; they sprung from the consideration of my being a slave at all. It was *slavery*—not its mere *incidents*—that I hated. I had been cheated. I saw through the attempt to keep me in ignorance; I saw that slaveholders would have gladly made me believe that they were merely acting under the authority of God, in making a slave of me, and in making slaves of others; and I treated them as robbers and deceivers. The feeding and clothing me well, could not atone for taking my liberty from me. The smiles of my mistress could not remove the deep sorrow that dwelt in my young bosom. Indeed, these, in time, came only to deepen my sorrow. She had changed; and the reader will see that I had changed, too. We were both victims to the same overshadowing evil—*she*, as mistress, *I*, as slave. I will not **censure** her harshly; she cannot censure me, for she knows I speak but the truth, and have acted in my opposition to slavery, just as she herself would have acted, in a reverse of circumstances.

---

6. *Trump* is a trumpet.

7. Douglass is referring to a biblical tale (Numbers 22:21–35) in which an ass (donkey), despite being beaten by its master, Balaam, cannot obey and move on because its way is blocked by an angel whom Balaam cannot see.

Literary Element Autobiography *What does this statement tell the reader about Douglass's priorities in life?*

Big Idea Resistance to Slavery *What does this statement say about the institution of slavery?*

Vocabulary

censure (sen´ shər) *v.* to express disapproval of; to find fault with; to blame

RESPONDING AND THINKING CRITICALLY

Respond

1. How did this narrative affect your appreciation of your personal freedom?

Recall and Interpret

2. (a)How does Mrs. Auld treat Douglass when he first arrives? (b)What does Douglass infer from her initial attitude toward him?

3. (a)How does Mrs. Auld's behavior toward Douglass change? (b)What does Douglass infer from these changes?

4. (a)Who later helps Douglass learn to read? (b)Compare these teachers' attitudes toward slavery with Mrs. Auld's attitude.

Analyze and Evaluate

5. (a)From his reading, what conclusion does Douglass draw about the foundation of slavery? (b)Do you agree with his analysis? Explain.

6. In your opinion, who is hurt more by the system of slavery—Douglass or the Auld family? Explain.

Connect

7. Douglass shows in his autobiography that his mind and spirit still remained free while he was physically held captive. In what ways might a person held in captivity keep his or her mind free? Explain.

8. **Big Idea** **Resistance to Slavery** Why do you think that slave narratives such as Douglass's were an important part of the antislavery effort?

LITERARY ANALYSIS

Literary Element **Autobiography**

Douglass's **autobiography** recounts his experiences both during his enslavement and as a free man, but it has another purpose—to provide a persuasive argument against slavery.

1. What do you think is Douglass's main idea or purpose in this excerpt from his autobiography?

2. Do you think Douglass presents himself as he really was, or might he be presenting a biased, or one-sided, view? Explain.

Listening and Speaking

Role Play Imagine Frederick Douglass meeting Mrs. Auld again later in life, when he is a famous writer and a free man. In a group, discuss what they might talk about. Then write a dialogue between these two characters and have two members of your group perform the dialogue for the class.

Literature Online **Web Activities** For eFlashcards, Selection Quick Checks, and other Web activities, go to www.glencoe.com.

READING AND VOCABULARY

Reading Strategy **Analyzing Cause and Effect**

Sometimes a cause can have more than one effect. Also, an effect can have multiple causes.

1. What effects did gaining knowledge through reading have on Douglass's ideas and behavior? What effect did his learning have on U.S. society?

2. What were the causes of the alienation between Mrs. Auld and Douglass?

Vocabulary **Practice**

Practice with Word Parts The words on the right share a word part with the vocabulary words on the left. Use a dictionary to do the following: (a)name the part of the word that is shared in each example; (b)identify the type of word part and its meaning; and (c)define each word on the right.

1. benevolent   malevolent
2. depravity   demote
3. induce   produce

BEFORE YOU READ

Building Background

Born in Detroit, Michigan, in 1913, Robert Hayden later worked as a researcher for the Federal Writers' Project in Michigan, one of the government's many New Deal programs intended to provide a livelihood for victims of the Great Depression. Hayden viewed history "as a long, tortuous, and often bloody process of becoming, of psychic evolution." He created elegant, well-crafted poetry, much of it concerned with African American history.

Hayden wanted to be known as a poet rather than as a black poet. He believed that racial labeling restricted African American poets, placing them "in a kind of literary ghetto," where the standards of other writers were not applied to them. Many African American writers disagreed with Hayden's position, especially during the height of the civil rights movement in the 1960s when political poetry was in vogue. However, Hayden's poetry does confront racial issues and features prominent African American historical figures such as Nat Turner, Frederick Douglass, and Malcolm X. Hayden taught at the university level for more than thirty years, although he said that he considered himself to be "a poet who teaches in order to earn a living so that he can write a poem or two now and then." In 1976 he was the first African American poet to be appointed poetry consultant to the Library of Congress. Hayden died in 1980.

Literature Online **Author Search** For more about Robert Hayden, go to www.glencoe.com.

Frederick Douglass

Robert Hayden

When it is finally ours, this freedom, this liberty, this beautiful
and terrible thing, needful to man as air,
usable as earth; when it belongs at last to all,
when it is truly instinct, brain matter, diastole,[1] systole,[2]
5 reflex action; when it is finally won; when it is more
than the gaudy mumbo jumbo of politicians:
this man, this Douglass, this former slave, this Negro
beaten to his knees, exiled, visioning a world
where none is lonely, none hunted, alien,
10 this man, superb in love and logic, this man
shall be remembered. Oh, not with statues' rhetoric,
not with legends and poems and wreaths of bronze alone,
but with the lives grown out of his life, the lives
fleshing his dream of the beautiful, needful thing.

Quickwrite

From reading this poetic portrayal, what did you learn about Frederick Douglass? Write a paragraph explaining what you learned about Douglass, using examples from the text to support your points.

---

1. *Diastole* (dī as′ tə lē′) is the period of normal relaxation of the heart between beats.
2. *Systole* (sis′ tə lē) is the period of normal contraction between diastoles.

Building Background

Poet Quincy Troupe, born in St. Louis, Missouri, in 1939, experienced firsthand the limitations that racial discrimination placed on generations of African Americans. Speaking of the inability of African Americans to achieve their potential, Troupe said, "When I would look into my grandmother's eyes, and my uncle's eyes, and my dad's eyes, I would see these holes full of loss and sadness." Thus, the subject matter of Troupe's award-winning poetry, in addition to celebrating the elation of seeing Magic Johnson play basketball or John Coltrane play the saxophone, also explores darker subject matter, such as the brutality of a slaughterhouse or the rage against racism.

In the following poem, "In Texas Grass," Troupe alludes to a "promise of forty acres & a mule." At the end of the Civil War, General William T. Sherman promised that freed African Americans would receive forty acres of land and a mule. However, few formerly enslaved African Americans ever received land, or even a mule, from the government. As a result, that phrase came to represent the failure of Reconstruction to assist African Americans emerging from slavery.

Literature Online **Author Search** For more about Quincy Troupe, go to www.glencoe.com.

In Texas Grass

Quincy Troupe

all along the railroad
tracks of texas
old train cars lay
rusted & overturned
5   like new african governments
long forgotten by the people
who built & rode them
till they couldn't run no more
10   & they remind me of old race horses
who've been put out to pasture
amongst the weeds
rain, sleet & snow
till they die & rot away
15   like photos fading
in grandma's picture book
of old black men & women, in mississippi
texas, who sit on dilapidated porches
that fall away
20   like dead man's skin
like white people's eyes
& inside the peeling photos
old men sit, sad eyed
& waiting, waiting for worm dust

25   thinking of the master & his long forgotten
promise of forty acres & a mule
& even now, if you pass across
this bleeding flesh
ever changing landscape
30   you will see the fruited
countryside, stretching, stretching
& old black men & young black
men, sitting on porches, waiting
waiting for rusted trains
35   silent in texas grass

Discussion Starter

Although this poem is set after the end of slavery in the United States, it describes in vivid and poignant detail slavery's legacy. With a small group, discuss the literal and figurative examples the poem gives of the conditions African Americans experienced after slavery. What conclusions about the journey from slavery to equality can you draw from these examples? Share your group's conclusions with the rest of the class.

Wrap-Up: Comparing Literature *Across Time and Place*

- from *My Bondage and My Freedom*
- *Frederick Douglass*
- *In Texas Grass*

COMPARING THE Big Idea Resistance to Slavery

Writing About Literature In the three selections you have read, each writer uses a different **tone**, or attitude toward his subject. How would you describe the tone used by each writer? Whose tone is most optimistic? Whose is most bitter? Write a brief essay in which you compare the tone used by each writer. Cite evidence from the selections to support your conclusions.

COMPARING Portrayals of People

Partner Activity With a partner, read each of the following quotations aloud. Then discuss how each quotation reflects people's struggling against slavery and its legacy of racial discrimination. How are the three quotations related to one another? Cite evidence from the selections.

> "How could she, then, treat me as a brute, without a mighty struggle with all the noble powers of her own soul."
>
> —Frederick Douglass, *My Bondage and My Freedom*

> ". . . this Douglass, this former slave, this Negro beaten to his knees, exiled, visioning a world where none is lonely, none is hunted, alien, . . ."
>
> —Robert Hayden, *"Frederick Douglass"*

> ". . . old black men, & young black men, sitting on porches, waiting waiting for rusted trains silent in texas grass"
>
> —Quincy Troupe, *"In Texas Grass"*

Be Free Three, 21st c. Kaaria Mucherera. Oil and acrylic on canvas, 30 x 40 in. Private collection.
Viewing the Art: How does this painting reflect the themes addressed by the three selections?

COMPARING Historical Context

Group Activity These selections treat both the progress and the setbacks in the journey of African Americans toward liberty and equality. With a small group, discuss the following questions.

1. What is the historical context that shapes each selection?
2. How effective is each writer's use of historical background? Which author presents the most compelling rendition of historical events?
3. Which of the selections most sparked your interest in the historical context? Explain.

Slave Narratives and Civil War Memoirs, Letters, and Diaries

IN THE NINETEENTH CENTURY, MANY writers shared their personal accounts of the two major issues of the day—slavery and the Civil War. These writings, which recount the emotions their authors felt, the details they saw, and the battles they fought, contribute much to the understanding of this tumultuous time in the United States.

Accounts of Slavery

Nineteenth-century African American writers, such as Frederick Douglass (pp. 337–344) and Sojourner Truth (pp. 354–357), told variations of one compelling story—the story of life in slavery, escape from bondage, and life as a free person. These accounts, called **slave narratives,** were written as early as 1760 and continued to be written after the Civil War. The pre-war narratives were in part intended to recruit Northerners to the abolitionist cause, especially after the Fugitive Slave Act was passed in 1850. **BI**

> *"Reader, be assured this narrative is no fiction. I am aware some of my adventures may seem incredible; but they are, nevertheless, strictly true."*
>
> —Harriet Jacobs
> from Preface to *Incidents in the Life of a Slave Girl,* 1861

After the Civil War, emancipated slaves, such as Elizabeth Keckley, who had worked for Mary Todd Lincoln as a dressmaker, continued to write autobiographies. Many writers hoped to show how well they had succeeded in a free society after the war. Others, especially those later in the century, expressed disappointment with the restrictions they still encountered.

Sarah Gudger age 121. North Carolina. Library of Congress photo.

From 1936 to 1938, during the Depression, writers and journalists from the Works Progress Administration (WPA) interviewed more than 2,300 former slaves and recorded their memories of the past. These narratives are a rich source of details about life on plantations and in cities.

Slave narratives have had an influence on modern literature as well, in the works of such writers as Richard Wright (pp. 900–908), Ernest J. Gaines, Alice Walker (pp. 1153–1157), and Toni Morrison (pp. 1302–1308).

Civil War Memoirs, Letters, and Diaries

Many people who lived through the Civil War felt that it was the central event of their lives. Writers on both sides of the conflict composed memoirs, letters, and diaries. These accounts ranged from those of generals recollecting great battles, to soldiers commenting on life on the battlefields, to civilians recounting details from the home front, especially in the South, where the battlefield and the home front were side-by-side.

Mark Twain persuaded his friend Ulysses S. Grant to write his acclaimed *Personal Memoirs of U. S. Grant*. He completed the memoirs a week before he died in 1885. Union Generals William T. Sherman, Philip H. Sheridan, and George B. McClellan also published memoirs of the war, but Grant's are considered some of the best military memoirs in history.

The letters of Confederate General Robert E. Lee were saved and published after his death. Some letters, such as his letter to Grant agreeing to release prisoners of war on both sides, give details of the war and its aftermath. Others, such as his letters to his family, including the letter to his son (pp. 370–371), express concern and describe the hardships of his troops, many of whom had no shoes.

> "I hope both you and Johnston will write the history of your campaigns. Every one should do all in his power to collect and disseminate the truth, in the hope that it may find a place in history and descend to posterity."
>
> —Robert E. Lee
> letter to Confederate General P. G. T. Beauregard, 1865

Soldiers—often farm boys who had never been away from home—also wrote letters to their families describing the excitement, horrors, and hardships of war as well as their longing for home. These letters were often written from prisons or hospitals. Nurse Clara Barton, in a letter to a cousin, wrote the night before a battle in Virginia: "The camp fires blaze with unwanted brightness, the sentry's tread is still but quick—the acres of little shelter tents are dark and still as death…"

Diarists such as Mary Chesnut (pp. 360–366) and Rachel Cormany documented everyday occurrences along with the worries, loneliness, and difficulties caused by the war. Chesnut's diary recounts her fear as the Union army swept through the South. These diaries provide unique details about day-to-day life on the home front.

These first-person accounts of slavery and the Civil War provide insight into what it was like to be enslaved, to face an enemy who was also a countryman, and to remain on the home front as family and friends left for war. Nineteenth-century writers documented their tumultuous lives and times to understand and preserve their stories. Today, their narratives, memoirs, letters, and diaries offer us great historical insights.

Ulysses S. Grant, American Civil War general, and later president, writing his memoirs at Mount McGregor, New York, 1885.

RESPONDING AND THINKING CRITICALLY

1. How might slave narratives have influenced the abolitionist cause?

2. A memoir, unlike an autobiography, focuses on only part of the writer's life, often a significant part. What are some reasons a person might choose to write a memoir? Explain.

3. Why are personal diaries and letters often of interest to general readers in later times?

Literature Online **Literary History** For more about slave narratives and civil war memoirs, letters and diaries, go to www.glencoe.com.

Media Link to Resistance to Slavery

Preview the Article

"Slavery Under Glass" examines how newly built African American museums educate the public on a dark period of U.S. history.

1. Examine the photographs on pages 351–353. What clues to the content of the article do these images give the reader?

2. Skim the first paragraph. From it, what do you think that this article might teach you about slavery?

Set a Purpose for Reading

Read to learn about new museums built to educate the public about slavery and the struggle for freedom.

Reading Strategy

Questioning

Questioning is asking yourself how information in a selection is important and whether you have understood what you have read. Have a running conversation with yourself as you read "Slavery Under Glass." Try to answer these questions:

- How is this idea important? Why?
- Do I understand this passage?
- How does this information relate to what I already know?

Create a graphic organizer to help you keep track of your answers.

Question	Answer
How is this idea important?	

ACADEMIC STANDARDS (pages 350–353)
11.2 Develop strategies such as asking questions...
11.2.5 Analyze an author's... assumptions and beliefs about a subject.

TIME

Slavery Under
GLASS

New African American–history museums try to balance authenticity and to uplift.

By RICHARD LACAYO

THE GLASS-WALLED MAIN ENTRY OF THE UNDERGROUND Railroad Freedom Center in Cincinnati, Ohio, faces south across the banks of the Ohio River. The center faces that direction for good reason—the river is at the heart of the story of the Underground Railroad. Separating free-soil Ohio from slave-holding Kentucky, the Ohio River was a desperate crossing point for runaway slaves. The river's north banks were the site of persistent low-intensity warfare between abolitionists and armed slave owners, who were permitted by law to pursue their human "property" into free states. In that era of escalating confrontation, Cincinnati and nearby towns became important way stations in the Underground Railroad. This informal network of safe houses, sympathetic whites, and free African Americans helped conduct escaped slaves to safety.

African American Life in Focus
The Freedom Center is part of a wave of more than 20 new museums dedicated to African American history that are in development around the country. They include the U.S. National Slavery Museum in Fredericksburg, Virginia, the International African American Museum in Charleston, South Carolina, the National Museum of African American History and Culture in Washington, D.C., and the Reginald F. Lewis Museum of Maryland African American History and Culture in Baltimore, Maryland. In addition, numerous locales from the 20th century civil rights movement, like the Montgomery, Alabama, bus stop where Rosa Parks was arrested, are being turned into monuments and pilgrimage points. Clearly, the story of African American life, for so long passed over in near silence, is finally being set down in stone.

The Delicate Subject of Slavery
All the same, telling the part of that story concerning slavery can be tricky. Any museum needs to inspire and instruct. It also needs to bring in paying customers.

Slavery is one of the most shameful chapters of American history, but shameful stories are not the kind that everybody wants to pay money to hear.

"There is a reluctance on the part of African Americans and whites to deal with slavery," says former Virginia Governor Doug Wilder. He conceived the National Slavery Museum, scheduled to open in 2007. "People don't want to discuss it. 'Let's get past it,' they say. Well, I say that attitude is insulting to our history. We need to develop a conscious awareness of how far we've come and who we are."

The museum envisioned by Wilder, a descendant of enslaved persons, will unabashedly be a museum about the brutal merchandising of human beings. The Freedom Center in Cincinnati, which cost $110 million to build and hopes to attract 250,000 visitors each year, is more cautious about its approach to a difficult subject. Even the center's name sidesteps the loaded word slavery. By taking the Underground Railroad as its focus, the center gets to emphasize biracial resistance, not racial victimization. The Underground Railroad was a rare triumph of African American and white cooperation in those days, not the far more usual story of white oppression. "The story of the Underground Railroad allows you to talk about slavery in a way that's productive, positive, and uplifting," says Ed Rigaud, the center's president.

Using the Past to Heal the Present

The project was first conceived 11 years ago by Robert C. Harrod. He is the executive director of the regional chapter of what was then called the National Conference of Christians and Jews, now the National Conference of Community and Justice. His hope was that it could help improve race relations in Cincinnati—it was only in 2002 that the Ku Klux Klan stopped its annual mounting of a Christmas tree in the city's main square. The desire for reconciliation is built into the center's mission. Its focus, says Spencer Crew, its executive director, "is not about finger pointing."

More than that, it also aims to be America's first museum intended not just to arouse feelings but also to resolve them safely. Concerned that people might exit the exhibition galleries with feelings of guilt (whites), anger (African Americans), and resentment (both), the center offers a final room that is not a gallery of any kind but a space for discussion. Trained facilitators will encourage visitors to examine their feelings and share them.

"Productive, positive, uplifting"— is this any way to tell a story so full of suffering? Well, maybe it is. For one thing, the Freedom Center is in many respects still the thing it claims not to be: a museum of

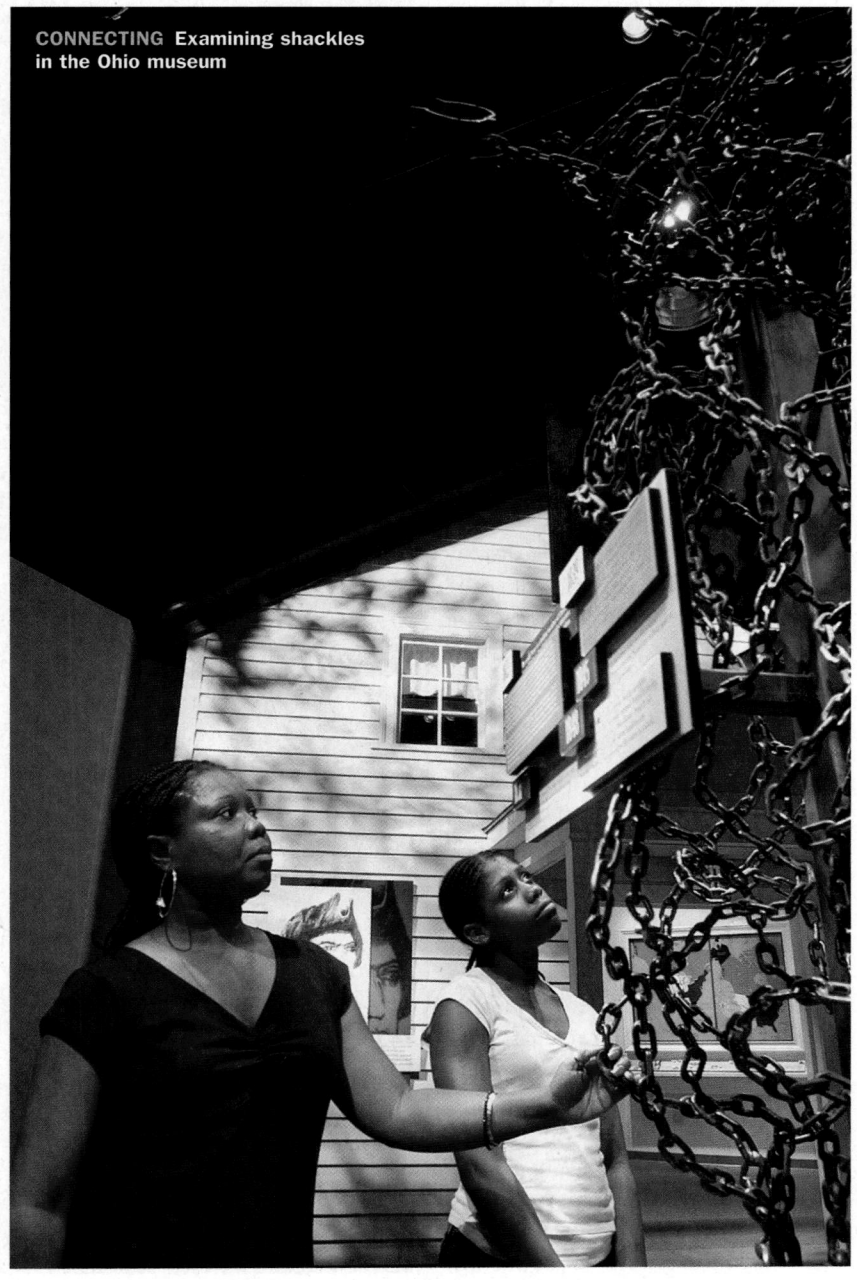

CONNECTING Examining shackles in the Ohio museum

A STARRY OPENING GALA

Joining in the center's festivities were Courtney Vance (left), Angela Bassett, and Oprah Winfrey, who said the Freedom Center honors those who "paid the price for me to be who I am."

slavery. Its largest feature is a two-story, rough-hewn log cabin rescued from a Kentucky farm. Built by slave trader Captain John W. Anderson, the structure held dozens of men and women waiting to be sold, shackled in pairs to a central chain and confined to sitting or lying. It lets visitors imagine themselves in the cramped space where enslaved persons were crammed. Carl Westmoreland, a historian and preservationist, was responsible for rescuing the cabin. The great-grandson of an enslaved blacksmith, Westmoreland says, "It's a place that's ugly and dark. But you've got to look at the ugly side of the journey to see the glory of our emergence."

Eyes Still on the Prize

The longest of the center's display areas is a series of galleries devoted to the history of slave labor, the miseries of the Middle Passage across the Atlantic from Africa, and the resistance struggles that eventually led to emancipation. Visitors can see an image of the scarred back of a whipped enslaved person and hear actors reading the testimonies of enslaved people who described the suffering they endured.

By placing so much stress on the system of escape routes for runaways, the center takes the risk of inflating the real importance of the Underground Railroad. By some estimates, of the 4 million enslaved persons in the United States when the Civil War began, no more than 100,000 benefited from the system. But that emphasis is essential for the center to sustain

AS IT STOOD It took six years to dismantle and reassemble the pen.

RELOCATED A curator calls the structure "a place of pain and awe."

CINCINNATI **A gallery at the Underground Railroad Freedom Center**

its uplifting message. Its next significant section of exhibits is the "Hall of Everyday Freedom Heroes." It offers portraits and touch-screen information about a whole spectrum of figures from throughout the world who fought for the rights of religious and racial minorities, women, and just about anyone who ever stood up against an oppressive system. That leads in turn to a final area, called "The Struggle Continues." Here interactive computer displays allow you to learn about ongoing efforts against oppression, hunger, illiteracy, bigotry, and modern-day slavery.

So you may well leave the last galleries with your mind far from the horrors of the slave experience or even the struggles against it. But the center will also have temporary exhibitions that will expand on both themes. "We will prove ourselves to be the museum of the future," promises Naomi Nelson, the center's director of education. She may be right about that. If it also always manages to do justice to the past, the future looks O.K.

— **UPDATED 2006, from TIME, August 30, 2004, and People, September 6, 2004**

RESPONDING AND THINKING CRITICALLY

Respond

1. What was your initial reaction to the idea of creating museums dedicated to the experience of slavery? How did your reaction change after reading the article?

Recall and Interpret

2. Return to the list of questions you created on page 350. What do you think are the most important ideas of the article?

3. (a)What is the emphasis of the Freedom Center? (b)Why do you think that this approach is favored in the center?

4. (a)What role did Cincinnati play in the antislavery movement? (b)Explain how the struggle for freedom is a contemporary issue, as well as a historical one.

Analyze and Evaluate

5. (a)According to the article, why is it difficult to create a successful museum dedicated to the subject of slavery? (b)What evidence does the author present to support this claim?

6. (a)How do you think the author feels that the goals of the Freedom Center compare with those of other slavery museums? (b)What evidence from the text supports your answer?

Connect

7. How do you think Frederick Douglass, Sojourner Truth, and other abolitionists would want the subject of slavery to be taught? How do you think it should be taught?

And Ain't I a Woman?

MEET SOJOURNER TRUTH

Armed with common sense and sharp wit, Sojourner Truth spent her long life battling slavery and demanding voting rights for women. Nearly six feet tall, Truth had a deep, smooth voice that quieted rowdy crowds and won devoted supporters. Resisting injustice, Truth believed, was her divinely ordained duty.

Sojourner Truth, whose given name was Isabella, was born into slavery in Ulster County, New York, a Dutch-speaking region. She endured cruel slave owners, backbreaking work, and harsh beatings until, at age twenty-nine, she escaped. Given refuge by Isaac and Maria Van Wagener, she took the name Isabella Van Wagener. Since childhood,

> *"There is no use in one man, or one nation, to try to do or be everything. It is a good thing to be dependent on each other for something, it makes us civil and peaceable."*
>
> —Sojourner Truth

Isabella had believed she saw visions and heard messages sent from God. In about 1843, she changed her name to Sojourner Truth—meaning that she would become a sojourner, or visiting traveler, spreading the truth of God—and started to preach throughout the northeastern United States. Before long, she began to weave antislavery messages into her preaching.

Truth also became an ardent champion of women's rights, especially the right to vote. In 1850 she began traveling the Midwest, attracting large crowds wherever she spoke. On this tour, in Akron, Ohio, she delivered what would become her most famous address, "And Ain't I a Woman?" Truth then moved to Battle Creek, Michigan, where she continued to agitate for women's rights and abolition. After the start of the Civil War in 1861, Truth worked to gather supplies and funds for black volunteer regiments. Toward the end of the war, Truth moved to Washington, D.C. where she accepted a job with the National Freedmen's Relief Association, counseling former slaves. At the age of seventy-eight, Truth returned to Battle Creek, where she remained until her death. A monument in downtown Battle Creek commemorates this remarkable woman.

Sojourner Truth was born in 1797 and died in 1883.

Literature Online Author Search For more about Sojourner Truth, go to www.glencoe.com.

Connecting to the Speech

Think of a time in your life when you felt you were treated unfairly. What was the situation, and how did you handle it? As you read, compare your experience with Truth's.

Building Background

On the second day of the 1851 Women's Rights Convention where Truth gave her speech, a number of male ministers spoke, insisting that women were too weak and intellectually inferior to vote. One man gave religious reasons against women's suffrage, or right to vote. Truth's speech is her answer to these critics. Her speech was not written or rehearsed, so many versions have survived—some in what might be interpreted as the dialect of an enslaved person from the South. In reality, Truth spoke Standard English and was originally from New York. So whose exact words are these? We may never know, but the spirit is certainly that of Sojourner Truth.

Setting Purposes for Reading

Big Idea   Resistance to Slavery

Read Sojourner Truth's speech to find out how one former enslaved woman spoke out against injustice ten years before the start of the Civil War and many years before women could vote.

Literary Element   Oratory

Oratory is the art of effective public speaking, or the use of persuasive skills when speaking. Oratory is common in politics, law, and religion. As you read the speech, notice how Truth uses persuasive devices, such as providing evidence from her personal experience, to achieve her purpose.

• See Literary Terms Handbook, p. R12.

Literature Online Interactive Literary Elements Handbook To review or learn more about the literary elements, go to www.glencoe.com.

Reading Strategy   Evaluating Argument

To **evaluate** is to make a judgment or form an opinion about something you read. In a persuasive speech such as "And Ain't I a Woman?," we must evaluate the argument to determine whether Truth has persuaded us. Think about how effective Truth is in convincing you to adopt her positions.

Reading Tip: Taking Notes Use a chart to record Sojourner Truth's major assertions, her reasons for those assertions, and whether you think her arguments are effective.

Assertion	Reason	Effective?
I have ploughed and planted, and gathered into barns, and no man could head me.	To prove that she is as physically strong as a man	

Vocabulary

racket (rak′ it) *n.* loud noise; clamor; din; p. 356 *The twins made such a racket that we couldn't hear the speaker.*

borne (bôrn) *v. past participle of* bear; given birth to; produced; p. 356 *The peach trees have not borne any fruit yet.*

oblige (ə blīj′) *v.* to make grateful or indebted; to do a favor or service for; p. 356 *I would be obliged if you would remove your hat.*

Vocabulary Tip: Context Clues Context clues are the words and sentences around an unfamiliar word that help you figure out the word's meaning. For example, when reading the phrase "I have borne thirteen children," you might guess that borne means "given birth to" or "produced" because of the word *children*.

INDIANA ACADEMIC STANDARDS (pages 355–357)
11.2.1 Analyze both the features and the rhetorical (persuasive) devices of...speeches...

11.2.6 Critique...arguments...in...speeches...
11.5.9 Write...analytical essays...

Anna Washington Derry, 1927. Laura Wheeler Waring (1887–1948). Oil on canvas, 20 x 16 in. Gift of the Harmon Foundation. Smithsonian American Art Museum, Washington, DC.

And Ain't I a Woman?

Address to the Ohio Women's Rights Convention, 1851

Sojourner Truth

Big Idea Resistance to Slavery *How does Truth connect slavery and women's rights?*

Vocabulary

racket (rak′ it) *n.* loud noise; clamor; din

borne (bôrn) *v.* past *participle of* bear; given birth to; produced

oblige (ə blīj′) *v.* to make grateful or indebted; to do a favor or service for

---

Well, children, where there is so much **racket** there must be something out of kilter.[1] I think that 'twixt[2] the Negroes of the South and the women at the North, all talking about rights, the white men will be in a fix pretty soon. But what's all this here talking about? That man over there says that women need to be helped into carriages, and lifted over ditches, and to have the best place everywhere. Nobody ever helps me into carriages, or over mud-puddles, or gives me any best place! And ain't I a woman? Look at me! Look at my arm. I have ploughed and planted, and gathered into barns, and no man could head[3] me! And ain't I a woman? I could work as much and eat as much as a man—when I could get it—and bear the lash as well! And ain't I a woman? I have **borne** thirteen children, and seen them most all sold off to slavery, and when I cried out with my mother's grief, none but Jesus heard me! And ain't I a woman?

Then they talk about this thing in the head; what's this they call it? [Intellect, someone whispers.] That's it, honey. What's that got to do with women's rights or Negroes rights? If my cup won't hold but a pint, and yours holds a quart, wouldn't you be mean not to let me have my little half-measure full?

Then that little man in black there, he says women can't have as much rights as men, 'cause Christ wasn't a woman! Where did your Christ come from? Where did your Christ come from? From God and a woman! Man had nothing to do with Him.

If the first woman God ever made was strong enough to turn the world upside down all alone, these women together ought to be able to turn it back, and get it right side up again! And now they is asking to do it, the men better let them.

Obliged to you for hearing me, and now old Sojourner ain't got nothing more to say. ❧

---

1. The phrase *out of kilter* means "out of order" or "mixed up."
2. *'Twixt* is the shortened form of *betwixt,* an Old English word meaning "between."
3. Here, Truth uses *head* to mean "to do better than" or "to get ahead of."

Reading Strategy Evaluating Argument *Who is the "little man in black"? Why is it appropriate that she addresses him during her speech?*

RESPONDING AND THINKING CRITICALLY

Respond

1. Imagine you are attending the Women's Rights Convention in 1851. How might you respond to Sojourner Truth's speech?

Recall and Interpret

2. (a)How does Truth refute the first three reasons given against women's suffrage? (b)What does Truth's response tell you about her character?

3. (a)What **repetition** does Truth use in the first part of her argument? (b)What is the effect of this repetition?

4. (a)How does Truth answer the religious argument against letting women vote? (b)What does her argument tell you about her religious beliefs?

Analyze and Evaluate

5. An **allusion** is a reference to a well-known character, place, or situation from history or from music, art, or another work of literature. (a)What allusion to the Bible does Truth make in the paragraph just before her closing statement? (b)Evaluate the impact of that allusion on her message.

Connect

6. **Big Idea** **Resistance to Slavery** (a)How does Truth introduce the antislavery message into her speech? (b)How appropriate is this message, given the purpose of the convention?

LITERARY ANALYSIS

Literary Element Oratory

Oratory is the art of effective public speaking, or the use of persuasive skills when speaking.

1. What is the purpose of Truth's speech?

2. Identify the qualities that you think make this speech effective and help Truth achieve her purpose. In your opinion, would these qualities appeal to contemporary audiences? Use details from the speech to support your answer.

Writing About Literature

Evaluate Rhetorical Devices Write a brief essay identifying and analyzing the rhetorical strategy that Truth employs in her argument. Explain how successful you think this strategy is.

Literature Online **Web Activities** For eFlashcards, Selection Quick Checks, and other Web activities, go to www.glencoe.com.

READING AND VOCABULARY

Reading Strategy Evaluating Argument

Evaluate one of Truth's arguments by analyzing her reasoning. Do you agree with her reasoning? Why or why not?

Vocabulary Practice

Practice with Context Clues Read the paragraph below. Use context clues to recall the meaning of each boldfaced vocabulary word.

*My mother says that being a parent is a difficult job, and I agree with her. She insists that pregnancy, while strenuous, is not the hardest part of motherhood: it is after a mother has **borne** her children that the real work starts. Instead of entering a tranquil and noiseless home after work, she is usually greeted by the **racket** of my younger brothers' playing basketball. However, despite the trials of being a parent, my mother also insists that it is the best job that she could ever have. For that sentiment and all of her hard work, I am **obliged**.*

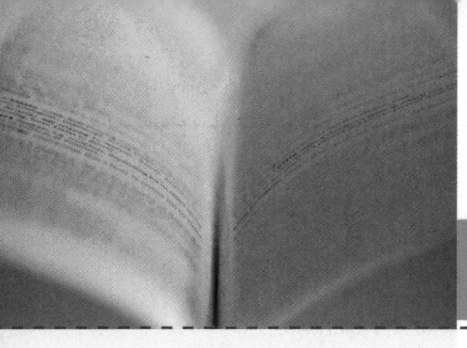

Vocabulary Workshop

Denotation and Connotation

▶ **Vocabulary Terms**

The **denotation** of a word is its literal meaning; the **connotation** of a word is its implied meaning.

▶ **Test-Taking Tip**

If, during a test, you are asked what the denotation of a word is, think about how you would define the word for someone else. To describe the word's connotations, think about the images and ideas the word brings to mind.

▶ **Reading Handbook**

For more about denotation and connotation, see Reading Handbook, R20.

Literature Online
eFlashcards For eFlashcards and other vocabulary activities, go to www.glencoe.com.

Using Semantic Charts

Connecting to Literature During the famous speech "And Ain't I a Woman," Sojourner Truth recounts the experience of watching helplessly as her children are sold into slavery. She says, "And when I cried out with my mother's grief, none but Jesus heard me!" Truth could have used words other than *grief*. For instance, she could have spoken of *sorrow* or *regret*—after all, those words have a similar meaning to *grief*. But they also have subtle differences. Words can have similar **denotations** (dictionary definitions) but different **connotations** (ideas, images, or feelings suggested by the word). The power of a word to suggest an array of connotations enables precision in speaking and in writing.

A chart like the one below can help you look more closely at the words *grief*, *sorrow*, and *regret*—at their similarities, their differences, and their shades of meaning. Follow these instructions to create the chart:

- Place the words to be analyzed in the left-hand column of the chart.
- Check a dictionary to gather different definitions for each word. These definitions are the words' denotations.
- In the second column of the chart, enter the definition for each term.
- In the third column of the chart, record ideas, images, or feelings that you associate with each word. For example, you may associate *grief* with disasters or funerals. Such associations are a word's connotations.

A semantic features chart has been started below.

	Denotation	Connotation
Grief		
Sorrow		
Regret		

Exercise

1. Complete the chart. With your classmates, discuss the denotations and connotations of the three words. Why do you think Truth chose to describe her feeling as *grief* and not as *sorrow* or *regret*? Explain.

2. Find three or four words that have denotations that are similar to each other in other selections in Unit 3, Part 1. Create and fill in the meanings for a semantic features chart with these words. Explain what particular shades of meaning the connotations of the words help the authors to suggest.

■ **ACADEMIC STANDARDS (page 358)**
11.4.8 Use systematic strategies to organize and record information...

PART 2

The Civil War: A Nation Divided

The Old Flag Never Touched The Ground. Rick Reeves.

"Many are the hearts that are weary tonight,
Wishing for the war to cease . . ."

— Walter C. Kittredge, "Tenting on the Old Campground"

from *Mary Chesnut's Civil War*

MEET MARY CHESNUT

Mary Boykin Chesnut's life was one of opposites. Before the Civil War, she was the privileged daughter of Stephen Miller, a wealthy plantation owner in South Carolina. When the war ended, however, she and her husband were financially ruined. Although she abhorred slavery, her family owned hundreds of slaves, and her father was a pro-slavery congressman, senator, and governor. Chesnut's observant nature, education, and social position made her an excellent chronicler of the South during the Civil War.

Education Unlike many women of her era, Chesnut received a formal education. She attended Madame Talvande's French School for Young Ladies in Charleston, South Carolina, where she was an excellent student. During her time at Madame Talvande's, she met James Chesnut Jr., a lawyer from a neighboring plantation. The couple married just after Chesnut turned seventeen years old. When James was elected to the Senate in 1858, the Chesnuts moved to Washington, D.C., where they entertained politicians who would become the leading figures of the Confederacy, such as Jefferson Davis, the future president of the Confederacy. When she was not charming her friends with her sharp wit, Chesnut immersed herself in reading history books and English and French novels.

When the war broke out, Chesnut remained loyal to the South despite her opposition to slavery. Her husband had relinquished his seat in the U.S. Senate in 1860 after the ideological differences between the North and South became too extreme. Afterward, he was a prominent figure in the Confederacy, and as a result the Chesnuts traveled throughout the South. Throughout the Civil War, Chesnut lamented the cruelties and evils of war in detailed journals that reflected what people of the time believed, thought, and said.

Publication After the war ended, Chesnut and her family came upon difficult times. They lost their plantation due to debt, and James died in 1884. After his death, Chesnut was left alone to oversee their struggling dairy farm. Despite these hardships, she still worked to publish her memoirs. Similar to many other works of the Civil War era, Chesnut's "diary" is actually a compilation of journal entries recorded during the war and recollections written after it ended. Chesnut wrote her memoirs between 1881 and 1884. Unfortunately, she died of a heart attack before it could reach publication. The first public version of her journals, *A Diary from Dixie*, was published almost twenty years later. Today it is lauded for its vivid descriptions and details of a life in the Confederacy.

Mary Chesnut was born in 1823 and died in 1886.

Literature Online **Author Search** For more about Mary Chesnut, go to www.glencoe.com.

Connecting to the Journal

Have you ever kept a journal or a diary? If so, what kinds of events and opinions did you document? If not, what might you choose to write about? As you read the journal entries, ask yourself the following questions:

- Why might someone choose to write a journal?
- What might you choose to write about in a journal?

Building Background

The passage you are about to read from Chesnut's journal describes the outbreak of the Civil War. By early 1861, South Carolina had seceded from the Union and claimed ownership of all federal property within the state. Only Fort Sumter, located in Charleston Harbor, remained under federal control. Confederate authorities demanded the removal of U.S. troops from the fort. President Lincoln refused their request, and on April 12, 1861, Confederate cannons opened fire on the fort. The Civil War had begun.

Setting Purposes for Reading

Big Idea A Nation Divided

As you read Chesnut's journal entries, think about the conflicting feelings she and other Southerners may have had about supporting the rebellion.

Literary Element Journal

A **journal** is a daily record of events by a participant in those events or a witness to them. Journals are subjective, which means that they reflect the writer's personal perspective. As you read these entries, think about what Chesnut's journal reveals about her personality and character.

- See Literary Terms Handbook, p. R10.

Literature Online Interactive Literary Elements Handbook To review or learn more about the literary elements, go to www.glencoe.com.

Reading Strategy Distinguishing Fact and Opinion

A **fact** is a statement that can be validated with proof, while an **opinion** offers a personal point of view or feeling. As you read Chesnut's journal, note where she offers an opinion rather than presenting the facts.

Reading Tip: Identifying Opinion Statements
Adverbs and adjectives, such as *delightfully, silly,* and *horrible,* are often indicators of opinion statements.

Vocabulary

allusion (ə lōō′ zhən) *n.* an indirect or casual reference; an incidental mention; p. 363 *To avoid trouble, he only made a brief allusion to his overdue assignment.*

audaciously (ô dā′ shəs lē) *adv.* boldly; arrogantly; p. 363 *The bold woman stepped audaciously to the front of the line.*

prostrate (pros′ trāt) *adj.* stretched out with face to the ground in humility, adoration, or submission; p. 363 *The priest was prostrate before the altar.*

delusion (di lōō′ zhen) *n.* a false impression or belief; p. 364 *Behind in the polls, the candidate still had the delusion that he could win.*

pervade (pər vād′) *v.* to spread through every part; p. 364 *After a week of rain, dampness pervaded the house.*

Vocabulary Tip: Context Clues You can often determine the meaning of an unfamiliar word by examining the sentence in which the word appears. Often, the tone of the sentence and the words preceding or following the unfamiliar word—called context clues—will help you define that word. For example, in the passage "Sound and fury, signifying nothing. A *delusion* and a snare . . . ," the phrase "signifying nothing" and the word *snare* can help you define *delusion* as "a false impression or belief."

INDIANA ACADEMIC STANDARDS (pages 361–366)
11.2.1 Analyze both...the features...of different types of public documents...and the way in which the authors use [them].

11.2 Develop [reading] strategies...
11.3.5 Analyze...works of...significance in history...

from

Mary Chesnut's Civil War

Mary Chesnut

April 7, 1861. . . . Today things seem to have settled down a little. One can but hope still. Lincoln or Seward[1] have made such silly advances and then far sillier drawings back. There may be a chance for peace, after all.

Things are happening so fast.

My husband has been made an aide-de-camp[2] of General Beauregard.[3] Three hours ago we were quietly packing to go home. The convention has adjourned.

Now he tells me the attack upon Fort Sumter may begin tonight. Depends upon Anderson and the fleet outside. The Herald says that this show of war outside of the bar[4] is intended for Texas.[5]

John Manning came in with his sword and red sash. Pleased as a boy to be on Beauregard's staff while the row goes on. He has gone with Wigfall to Captain Hartstene with instructions.

Mr. Chesnut[6] is finishing a report he had to make to the convention.

Mrs. Hayne called. She had, she said, "but one feeling, pity for those who are not here."

Jack Preston, Willie Alston—"the take-life-easys," as they are called—with John Green, "the

---

1. *William Henry Seward* was U.S. Secretary of State from 1861 to 1869.
2. An officer who serves as an assistant to a superior officer is an *aide-de-camp*.
3. *General Beauregard* commanded the Confederate forces surrounding Fort Sumter.

Big Idea A Nation Divided *How does this statement show the conflicting feelings of Southerners during the Civil War?*

---

4. *Bar* refers to a sand bar.
5. Texas, a pro-slavery state, had recently voted to secede from the Union.
6. *Mr. Chesnut* (also called Colonel Chesnut) refers to Mary's husband James, who served as the liaison between Confederate President Jefferson Davis and Colonel Anderson.

big brave," have gone down to the island—volunteered as privates.

Seven hundred men were sent over. Ammunition wagons rumbling along the streets all night. Anderson burning blue lights—signs and signals for the fleet outside, I suppose.

Today at dinner there was no **allusion** to things as they stand in Charleston Harbor. There was an undercurrent of intense excitement. There could not have been a more brilliant circle. In addition to our usual quartet (Judge Withers, Langdon Cheves, and Trescot) our two governors dined with us, Means and Manning.

These men all talked so delightfully. For once in my life I listened.

That over, business began. In earnest, Governor Means rummaged a sword and red sash from somewhere and brought it for Colonel Chesnut, who has gone to demand the surrender of Fort Sumter.

— ★ —

And now, patience—we must wait.

— ★ —

Why did that green goose Anderson go into Fort Sumter? Then everything began to go wrong.

Now they have intercepted a letter from him, urging them to let him surrender. He paints the horrors likely to ensue if they will not.

He ought to have thought of all that before he put his head in the hole.

April 12, 1861 . . . Anderson will not capitulate.

— ★ —

Yesterday was the merriest, maddest dinner we have had yet. Men were more **audaciously** wise and witty. We had an unspoken foreboding it was to be our last pleasant meeting. Mr. Miles dined with us today. Mrs. Henry King rushed in:

"The news, I come for the latest news—all of the men of the King family are on the island"—of which fact she seemed proud.

While she was here, our peace negotiator—or envoy—came in. That is, Mr. Chesnut returned—his interview with Colonel Anderson had been deeply interesting—but was not inclined to be communicative, wanted his dinner. Felt for Anderson. Had telegraphed to President Davis for instructions.

What answer to give Anderson, &c&c.[7] He has gone back to Fort Sumter, with additional instructions.

When they were about to leave the wharf, A. H. Boykin sprang into the boat, in great excitement; thought himself ill-used. A likelihood of fighting—and he to be left behind!

— ★ —

I do not pretend to go to sleep. How can I? If Anderson does not accept terms—at four—the orders are—he shall be fired upon.

I count four—St. Michael chimes. I begin to hope. At half-past four, the heavy booming of a cannon.

I sprang out of bed. And on my knees—**prostrate**—I prayed as I never prayed before.

There was a sound of stir all over the house—pattering of feet in the corridor—all seemed hurrying one way. I put on my double gown and a shawl and went, too. It was to the housetop.

The shells were bursting. In the dark I heard a man say "waste of ammunition."

I knew my husband was rowing about in a boat somewhere in that dark bay. And that the shells were roofing it over—bursting toward the fort. If Anderson was obstinate—he was to order the forts on our side to open fire. Certainly fire had begun. The regular roar of the cannon—there it was. And who could tell what each volley accomplished of death and destruction.

---

7. &c&c means "et cetera" or "and others."

Vocabulary

prostrate (pros´trāt) *adj.* stretched out with face to the ground in humility, adoration, or submission

Vocabulary

allusion (ə lo͞o´zhən) *n.* an indirect or casual reference; an incidental mention

audaciously (ô dā´shəs lē) *adv.* boldly; arrogantly

The women were wild, there on the housetop. Prayers from the women and imprecations[8] from the men, and then a shell would light up the scene. Tonight, they say, the forces are to attempt to land.

The Harriet Lane[9] had her wheelhouse smashed and put back to sea.

Visual Vocabulary
The *wheelhouse* is the enclosed area on the deck of a ship that shelters the steering equipment and the pilot.

— ★ —

We watched up there—everybody wondered. Fort Sumter did not fire a shot.

— ★ —

Today Miles and Manning, colonels now—aides to Beauregard—dined with us. The latter hoped I would keep the peace. I give him only good words, for he was to be under fire all day and night, in the bay carrying orders, &c.

— ★ —

Last night—or this morning truly—up on the housetop I was so weak and weary I sat down on something that looked like a black stool.

"Get up, you foolish woman—your dress is on fire," cried a man. And he put me out. It was a chimney, and the sparks caught my clothes. Susan Preston and Mr. Venable then came up. But my fire had been extinguished before it broke out into a regular blaze.

— ★ —

Do you know, after all that noise and our tears and prayers, nobody has been hurt. Sound and fury, signifying nothing.[10] A **delusion** and a snare....

---

8. *Imprecations* are curses.
9. The *Harriet Lane* was a federal ship that brought provisions to the troops at Fort Sumter.
10. "Sound and fury, signifying nothing" is taken from *Macbeth* (act 5, scene 5, lines 27–28), a play by Shakespeare.

Reading Strategy Distinguishing Fact and Opinion
Do you think that this statement is based on factual information, or is it Chesnut's opinion?

Vocabulary

delusion (di lōō′zhen) *n.* a false impression or belief

— ★ —

Somebody came in just now and reported Colonel Chesnut asleep on the sofa in General Beauregard's room. After two such nights he must be so tired as to be able to sleep anywhere. . . .
APRIL 13, 1861. . . . Nobody hurt, after all. How gay we were last night.

Reaction after the dread of all the slaughter we thought those dreadful cannons were making such a noise in doing.

Not even a battery[11] the worse for wear.

Fort Sumter has been on fire. He has not yet silenced any of our guns. So the aides—still with swords and red sashes by way of uniform—tell us.

But the sound of those guns makes regular meals impossible. None of us go to table. But tea trays **pervade** the corridors, going everywhere.

Some of the anxious hearts lie on their beds and moan in solitary misery. Mrs. Wigfall and I solace ourselves with tea in my room.

These women have all a satisfying faith. . . .

APRIL 15, 1861. . . . I did not know that one could live such days of excitement.

They called, "Come out—there is a crowd coming."

A mob indeed, but it was headed by Colonels Chesnut and Manning.

The crowd was shouting and showing these two as messengers of good news. They were escorted to Beauregard's headquarters. Fort Sumter had surrendered.

Those up on the housetop shouted to us, "The fort is on fire." That had been the story once or twice before.

— ★ —

When we had calmed down, Colonel Chesnut, who had taken it all quietly enough—if anything, more unruffled than usual in his serenity—told us how the surrender came about.

Wigfall was with them on Morris Island when he saw the fire in the fort, jumped in a little boat

---

11. A *battery* is an artillery unit.

Vocabulary

pervade (pər vād′) *v.* to spread through every part

Sunset at Fort Sumter, 1863. Conrad Wise Chapman.
Viewing the Art: What do the details of this painting reveal about the situation at Fort Sumter at this time?

and, with his handkerchief as a white flag, rowed over to Fort Sumter. Wigfall went in through a porthole.

When Colonel Chesnut arrived shortly after and was received by the regular entrance, Colonel Anderson told him he had need to pick his way warily, for it was all mined.

As far as I can make out, the fort surrendered to Wigfall.

But it is all confusion. Our flag is flying there. Fire engines have been sent to put out the fire.

Everybody tells you half of something and then rushes off to tell something else or to hear the last news. . . . ❧

Literary Element   Journal *Would a member of the Confederate army or a Confederate official agree that "it is all confusion"?*

RESPONDING AND THINKING CRITICALLY

Respond

1. What insights about the Civil War did these journal entries give you?

Recall and Interpret

2. (a)What activities in Chesnut's entry for April 7 suggest that war is about to begin? (b)What attitude does Chesnut express toward these activities?

3. (a)What major event takes place on April 12? (b)What hopes and fears does Chesnut convey in the entry for that day?

4. (a)What bit of good news does Chesnut report in her entry for April 13? (b)What does this entry reveal about her attitude toward the war?

Analyze and Evaluate

5. (a)Describe the **tone**, the writer's feelings about the topic and characters, in the first journal entry. (b)Is this what you might expect under the circumstances? Explain your response.

6. Many of Chesnut's entries document meals and the people who were present at them. (a)Why might she have documented these meals? (b)In what ways do they contribute to the impact of her journal?

7. (a)How would you describe Chesnut's state of mind at the end of this excerpt? (b)Given what you know about the Civil War, in what ways do her feelings foreshadow the events to come?

Connect

8. Although Chesnut did not approve of slavery, she believed in the Confederate cause. What factors might have motivated her to support the Confederacy?

9. **Big Idea** **A Nation Divided** Chesnut writes, "There may be a chance for peace, after all." From your reading here, do you think the events that took place at Fort Sumter could have been avoided? Explain your response.

LITERARY ANALYSIS

Literary Element **Journal**

Along with recording daily events, a **journal** writer includes thoughts, observations, and personal feelings. Chesnut captures the impact of the war on the everyday lives of Southerners and shares her reflections on what is happening around her.

1. How is Chesnut's journal different from a history or memoir that a politician or military officer of the time might have written?

2. How would you describe Chesnut's writing style?

Literature Groups

Understanding the Past What can Chesnut's journal entries teach you about this time period? What are the strengths and limitations of these entries? Discuss these questions in your group, using details from the selection to support your opinions.

Literature Online **Web Activities** For eFlashcards, Selection Quick Checks, and other Web activities, go to www.glencoe.com.

READING AND VOCABULARY

Reading Strategy **Distinguishing Fact and Opinion**

A personal diary account of a historic event, such as this one by Mary Chesnut, is likely to contain both **fact** and **opinion**. Review the excerpt and identify at least three statements of fact and three opinions.

Vocabulary **Practice**

Practice with Context Clues You can often determine the meaning of an unfamiliar word by examining the sentence in which the word appears. Often, the tone of the sentence and the words preceding or following the unfamiliar word—called context clues—will help you to define that word. Locate the context clues for the italicized words in these sentences.

1. "And on my knees—*prostrate*—I prayed as I had never prayed before."
2. "But tea trays *pervade* the corridors, going everywhere."

Grammar Workshop

Coherence

Using Transitional Expressions

"My husband has been made an aide-de-camp of General Beauregard. Three hours ago we were quietly packing to go home. The convention has adjourned. "Now he tells me the attack upon Fort Sumter may begin tonight."

> —Mary Chesnut, from "Mary Chesnut's Civil War"

Connecting to Literature In the quotation above there are **transitions**— words and phrases that help show the relationships between ideas—to show time relationships. The transitional phrase *three hours ago* tells when Mrs. Chesnut and her husband were packing. The transitional word *now* tells when she hears that the attack may begin soon.

Transitional words and phrases can clarify not only time order but other relationships as well. Each of those relationships uses particular transitions.

Relationship	Transitional Words and Phrases
Time	*first, next, now, today, yesterday, meanwhile*
Importance	*especially, above all, in fact, primarily, more importantly*
Cause and Effect	*because, as a result, consequently*
Contrast	*but, yet, now, on the other hand, however, nevertheless*
Example	*namely, for instance, that is, for example*

Examples

- *Because Anderson refused to surrender Fort Sumter, the battle began.*
  [*Because* shows a cause/effect relationship.]

- *The cannon fire was intense; however, no one was hurt.*
  [*However* shows a contrast relationship.]

Exercise

Revise for Clarity Add a transitional word or phrase to show a relationship between each pair of sentences. Underline the transition and tell what relationship it shows.

1. Many Charleston men were exhausted during the battle. Colonel Chesnut fell asleep on a sofa in the commanding general's quarters.
2. Mrs. Auld began to teach Frederick Douglass to read. She became angry when she saw him reading.
3. "Swing Low, Sweet Chariot" was sung in worship. It carried a coded meaning.

▶ **Test-Taking Tip**

To identify transitions in a test-taking situation, skim the text for key terms shown in the chart.

▶ **Language Handbook**

For more about transitions, see Writing Handbook, p. R34.

Literature Online
eWorkbooks To link to the Grammar and Language eWorkbook, go to www.glencoe.com.

ACADEMIC STANDARDS (page 367)
11.6.1 Demonstrate control of... sentence structure...

11.4.10 Revise...writing for meaning [and] clarity...

Letter to His Son

MEET ROBERT E. LEE

Adored by his troops and respected by his enemies, Robert E. Lee remains a symbol of Southern and American dignity. He was born into the famous Lee family of Virginia, who, according to President John Adams, had "more men of merit in it than any other family." His father was a cavalry commander during the Revolutionary War, a governor of Virginia, and a friend to George Washington. As a student at West Point, Lee earned many honors, including a commission to the elite Army Corps of Engineers. During the Mexican War (1846–1848), he rose to the rank of captain. General Winfield Scott said that Lee was "the very best soldier I ever saw in the field."

A Difficult Decision In 1861 Lee faced an agonizing decision. President Lincoln asked him to command the Union forces in the Civil War. Unwilling to fight against his state, Lee declined and resigned his position in the United States Army. He had been in the army for thirty-six years. Lee then joined the Confederate forces and took command of the Army of Northern Virginia in 1862.

Within three weeks of taking command, Lee had organized his troops, improved discipline and morale, and convinced his soldiers of his authority. Nevertheless, he knew that the powerful Union forces far outnumbered his own and had no doubt that his regiment would be crushed in the open battlefield.

> *"There was not a man in the Confederacy whose influence with the whole people was as great as his."*
>
> —Ulysses S. Grant

Victory and Defeat Lee achieved brilliant victories at the battles of Second Manassas, Fredericksburg, and Chancellorsville. Then, in order to keep fighting off of Virginia soil, Lee pushed north into Maryland and Pennsylvania, engaging the U.S. Army at Antietam and Gettysburg in June and July of 1863. However, after Gettysburg, the Union forces began to prevail. Lee's forces were malnourished and undersupplied, while those of Union General Grant had a fresh batch of recruits, superior armaments, and an impressive cavalry. Grant's troops progressed farther and farther into Virginia. On April 9, 1865, seeing that the end had come, Lee surrendered to General Grant at Appomattox. After the war Lee urged his fellow Southerners to put their bitterness behind them. An enduring U.S. hero, Lee was a brilliant soldier with a noble spirit and a chivalric manner.

Robert E. Lee was born in 1807 and died in 1870.

Literature Online Author Search For more about Robert E. Lee, go to www.glencoe.com.

Connecting to the Letter

What do you do when you are caught in a dilemma and are forced to make a painful choice? In this letter, Robert E. Lee tells his son of the inner conflict that arises when his dedication to the United States is pitted against his loyalty to and love for his home state of Virginia. As you read the letter, think about the following questions:

- Whom would you contact if you needed to talk about two conflicting loyalties or a tough decision? How would you expect this person to respond?
- Imagine that you are Robert E. Lee's son or daughter. How would you respond to this letter?

Building Background

In the days before telephones and e-mail, letters were the most common way to communicate at a distance. Robert E. Lee's letters are of interest because they throw light on historic events and reveal the mind and heart of a great leader. Lee wrote this letter on January 23, 1861. South Carolina had seceded from the Union in December 1860, followed quickly by Mississippi, Florida, and Alabama. Lee's home state of Virginia would secede approximately three months later, on April 17, 1861.

Setting Purposes for Reading

Big Idea A Nation Divided

As you read, consider how Lee's personal conflict reflects the sharp divide between the North and South.

Literary Element Diction

Diction is a writer's choice of words, an important element in the writer's "voice" or style. As you read, consider how Lee's choice of words expresses his concerns shortly before the outbreak of the Civil War.

- See Literary Terms Handbook, p. R5.

Literature Online Interactive Literary Elements Handbook To review or learn more about the literary elements, go to www.glencoe.com.

Reading Strategy Determining Main Idea and Supporting Details

The **main idea** in a paragraph is the guiding thought that all of the sentences in the paragraph support. As you read, identify Lee's main ideas and the **details** that **support** them.

Reading Tip: Taking Notes Use a chart to record Lee's main ideas and the details that support them.

Main Idea	Supporting Details

Vocabulary

perusal (pə rōō′ zəl) *n.* the process of examining carefully; p. 371 *Her perusal of the latest Harry Potter book totally engrossed her.*

anarchy (an′ ər kē) *n.* the absence of government; p. 371 *Lawmen were few in the frontier communities, and anarchy was frequently the rule.*

array (ə rā′) *v.* to place in proper or methodical order; p. 371 *The chess pieces were arrayed against each other.*

redress (rē′ dress′) *n.* compensation, as for wrong done; p. 371 *Our neighbor demanded redress for the damage to his house caused by a broken water main.*

contend (kən tend′) *v.* to argue; dispute; p. 371 *I contend that every citizen should be informed about current issues.*

Vocabulary Tip: Antonyms Antonyms are words that have opposite or nearly opposite meanings. Antonyms are always the same part of speech.

INDIANA ACADEMIC STANDARDS (pages 369–372)
11.2.2 Analyze the way in which clarity of meaning is affected by...word choice in the text.

11.2 Develop [reading] strategies...
11.5.2 Write responses to literature...

Letter to His Son

Robert E. Lee

I received Everett's[1] *Life of Washington* which you sent me, and enjoyed its **perusal**. How his spirit would be grieved could he see the wreck of his mighty labors! I will not, however, permit myself to believe, until all ground of hope is gone, that the fruit of his noble deeds will be destroyed, and that his precious advice and virtuous example will so soon be forgotten by his countrymen. As far as I can judge by the papers, we are between a state of **anarchy** and civil war. May God avert[2] both of these evils from us! I fear that mankind will not for years be sufficiently Christianized to bear the absence of restraint and force. I see that four states[3] have declared themselves out of the Union; four more will apparently follow their example.

Then, if the border states are brought into the gulf of revolution, one half of the country will be **arrayed** against the other. I must try and be patient and await the end, for I can do nothing to hasten or retard it.

The South, in my opinion, has been aggrieved by the acts of the North, as you say. I feel the aggression and am willing to take every proper step for **redress**. It is the principle I **contend** for, not individual or private benefit. As an American citizen, I take great pride in my country, her prosperity and institutions, and would defend any state if her rights were invaded. But I can anticipate no greater calamity for the country than a dissolution of the Union. It would be an accumulation of all the evils we complain of, and I am willing to sacrifice everything but honor for its preservation. I hope, therefore, that all constitutional means will be exhausted before there is a resort to force. Secession is nothing but revolution. The framers of our Constitution never exhausted so much labor, wisdom, and forbearance in its formation, and surrounded it with so many guards and securities, if it was intended to be broken by every member of the Confederacy at will. It was intended for "perpetual union," so expressed in the preamble, and for the establishment of a government, not a compact, which can only be dissolved by revolution or the consent of all the people in convention assembled. It is idle to talk of secession. Anarchy would have been established, and not a government, by Washington, Hamilton, Jefferson, Madison, and the other patriots of the Revolution. . . . Still, a Union that can only be maintained by swords and bayonets,[4] and in which strife and civil war are to take the place of brotherly love and kindness, has no charm for me. I shall mourn for my country and for the welfare and progress of mankind. If the Union is dissolved, and the government disrupted, I shall return to my native state and share the miseries of my people; and, save in defense, will draw my sword on none. ◡

---

1. Edward *Everett* was a noted American politician and orator.
2. Here, *avert* means "to ward off."
3. The first *four states* to secede from the Union were South Carolina, Mississippi, Florida, and Alabama. With Georgia, Louisiana, Texas, Virginia, Arkansas, Tennessee, and North Carolina, these states would make up the Confederate States of America.

Literary Element Diction *What does Lee's choice of adjectives indicate about his feelings toward George Washington?*

Vocabulary

perusal (pə rōō′ zəl) *n.* the process of examining carefully
anarchy (an′ ər kē) *n.* the absence of government
array (ə rā′) *v.* to place in proper or methodical order
redress (rē′ dress′) *n.* compensation, as for wrong done
contend (kən tend′) *v.* to argue; dispute

---

4. A *bayonet* is a large knife or dagger that can be attached to the muzzle of a rifle.

Big Idea A Nation Divided *What does this statement reveal about Lee's personal response to the imminent war?*

RESPONDING AND THINKING CRITICALLY

Respond

1. What questions would you like to ask Robert E. Lee after reading his letter?

Recall and Interpret

2. (a)How does Lee describe George Washington? (b)What do you learn about Lee's character from his description of Washington?

3. (a)What two evils does Lee say the country is between? (b)What do you think Lee means when he says, "I fear that mankind will not for years be sufficiently Christianized to bear the absence of restraint and force"?

4. (a)What decision does Lee announce at the end of the letter? (b)What kind of person does this letter reveal Lee to be?

Analyze and Evaluate

5. (a)How does Lee support his opinions about secession? (b)What can you infer from this about Lee's attitude toward his country?

6. (a)Why does Lee say that he will mourn for his country and "for the welfare and progress of mankind"? (b)How do you think Lee might react to events taking place today? Explain.

Connect

7. **Big Idea** **A Nation Divided** Mary Custis Lee wrote to a friend, "My husband has wept tears of blood over this terrible war, but as a man of honor and a Virginian, he must follow the destiny of his state." How was Lee's dilemma comparable to the one facing the country as a whole?

LITERARY ANALYSIS

Literary Element Diction

Diction is a writer's choice of words, one of the tools used to convey the desired **tone** and meaning. Lee's diction, which reflects the language that was used in the nineteenth-century, may seem formal and stilted to us. For example, Lee wrote, "But I can anticipate no greater calamity for the country than a dissolution of the Union."

1. Restate the above sentence using contemporary, informal diction.

2. What does Lee's diction contribute to the impact of his letter?

Writing About Literature

Respond to Theme Write a letter to Robert E. Lee in which you agree or disagree with his opinions about secession. Give reasons to support your position. If you wish, you may write as if you were his son or another member of his family.

Literature Online **Web Activities** For eFlashcards, Selection Quick Checks, and other Web activities, go to www.glencoe.com.

READING AND VOCABULARY

Reading Strategy Determining Main Idea and Supporting Details

Determining the main idea helps you discover an author's purpose for writing. Sometimes, the main idea is stated in a topic sentence; often, it is implied, rather than stated. To find the main idea, look for the one idea that the sentences in the paragraph or paragraphs in the selection seem to support.

1. What is Lee's main idea in the passage beginning "But I can anticipate. . . " and concluding ". . . and the other patriots of the Revolution"?

2. What details support the main idea?

Vocabulary Practice

Practice with Antonyms Antonyms are words that are opposite in meaning. For example, the words *virtue* and *vice* are antonyms. For each of the following words, choose the vocabulary word that is an antonym.

Practice and Apply
1. agree
2. order
3. scatter
4. skimming

An Occurrence at Owl Creek Bridge

MEET AMBROSE BIERCE

Ambrose Bierce did not trust people. Nor did he trust governments, businesses, or churches. Most of all, "Bitter Bierce," as he was known, did not trust easy answers or sentimentality. As his biographer Carey McWilliams wrote, Bierce was "idealistic, cynical, morose . . . a realist who wrote romances, a fine satirist and something of a charlatan."

"Nothing is so improbable as what is true. It is the unexpected that occurs; but that is not saying enough; it is also the unlikely—one might almost say the impossible."

—Ambrose Bierce, "The Short Story"

Soldier and Civilian Ambrose Bierce was born into an impoverished Ohio farm family. He was the tenth of thirteen children. After one year of high school at the Kentucky Military Institute, Bierce became a printer's apprentice for a newspaper in Indiana.

At the outbreak of the Civil War, Bierce enlisted in the Ninth Indiana Volunteers. He fought in several important battles, including Shiloh and Chickamauga. At the battle of Kennesaw Mountain in 1864, Bierce suffered a severe head wound. He would later say that the bullet "crushed my skull like a broken walnut." Bierce recovered and continued to serve in the army, eventually being promoted to major.

After the war, Bierce settled in San Francisco, California. For the next two years, he worked as a guard at the mint and studied for long periods of time at the public library. In 1868 Bierce landed a position at the *San Francisco News Letter and*

Commercial Advertiser, a financial weekly. He was put in charge of the paper's humor section, "The Town Crier." Bierce's columns often consisted of satirical attacks against politicians and business leaders, attracting great notoriety for himself and the *News Letter*.

Nuggets and Dust In 1872 Bierce and his wife Mary Ellen traveled to England. While overseas, he published three books of fiction, *The Fiend's Delight, Nuggets and Dust Panned Out in California,* and *Cobwebs from an Empty Skull*. In 1875 Bierce returned to San Francisco, but his life continued to be marked by a pattern of restlessness and dissatisfaction. He quit his job as an editor for the *Argonaut* and traveled to the Dakota Territory, hoping to leave journalism behind. There Bierce worked as a manager for a mining firm that was losing money. The firm collapsed and he returned to San Francisco. From 1881 to 1886, Bierce wrote for *Wasp*, a humor magazine. From 1887 to 1908, Bierce worked as a columnist for the *San Francisco Examiner*.

In 1914 Bierce disappeared in Mexico, which was then in the midst of a revolution. In a letter to a friend, he wrote, "Goodbye, if you hear of my being stood up against a Mexican stone wall and shot to rags please know that I think it a pretty good way to depart this life. It beats old age, disease, or falling down the cellar stairs." His disappearance and death remain a mystery.

Ambrose Bierce was born in 1842 and disappeared in 1914.

Literature Online **Author Search** For more about Ambrose Bierce, go to www.glencoe.com.

Connecting to the Story

How much of reality is constructed by our own minds? As you read Bierce's short story, think about the following questions:

- Have you ever used your imagination to protect yourself in an unpleasant situation?
- What thoughts flash through your mind during periods of heightened awareness, such as a crisis or an intense emotional experience?

Building Background

"An Occurrence at Owl Creek Bridge," set during the Civil War in rural Alabama, was inspired by events that Bierce witnessed at the Battle of Shiloh in 1862. Union troops, encamped at Pittsburg Landing in southwestern Tennessee, were planning a southward offensive, when Confederate troops unexpectedly attacked. In two days, 20,000 Union and Confederate soldiers were killed. This battle shocked both sides and was an indication of the enormous loss of life that was still to come. Bierce's grim depiction of war in his fiction was a direct result of the bloodshed he witnessed.

Setting Purposes for Reading

Big Idea A Nation Divided

As you read, notice how Bierce's attitudes toward the Civil War are reflected in this story.

Literary Element Point of View

Point of view is the relationship of the narrator, or story-teller, to the story. In a story with a **first-person point of view,** the story is told by one of the characters in the story. In a story with **third-person limited point of view,** the narrator is outside the story and reveals the thoughts, feelings, and observations of only one character in the story. In a story with an **omniscient,** or all-knowing, point of view, the narrator is outside the story and knows everything about all of the characters and events in the story. As you read the story, examine Bierce's use of point of view.

- See Literary Terms Handbook, p. R14.

Literature Online Interactive Literary Elements Handbook To review or learn more about the literary elements, go to www.glencoe.com.

Reading Strategy Making and Verifying Predictions

To **predict** means to make an educated guess about what will happen based on the clues that a writer provides. As you read, verify, adjust, or change your predictions as you get new information.

Reading Tip: Taking Notes Use a chart to record your predictions and the evidence on which you base those predictions.

Prediction	Evidence
Things are not what they seem. Something is wrong with the character's perceptions.	"great golden stars looking unfamiliar and grouped in strange constellations"

Vocabulary

protrude (prō trōōd′) v. to stick out; to project; p. 376 *After the accident, the victim had a large bump protruding from his forehead.*

adorn (ə dôrn′) v. to make beautiful; to decorate; p. 376 *The vain man adorned himself with jewelry and expensive clothes.*

ardently (ärd′ent lē) adv. passionately; enthusiastically; p. 377 *The man ardently pursued the woman he loved.*

assent (ə sent′) v. to express agreement; p. 378 *After meeting for three hours, the committee finally assented to the chairman's proposal.*

poignant (poin′ yənt) adj. sharp; severe; causing emotional or physical anguish; p. 378 *Dan experienced a poignant loss when his grandmother died.*

INDIANA ACADEMIC STANDARDS (pages 374–385)

11.4.3 Use point of view...for specific...purposes.

11.2 Develop reading strategies such as...making predictions...

11.5.9 Write...a literary analysis that develops a thesis [and] supports judgments with relevant and substantial evidence and well-chosen details...

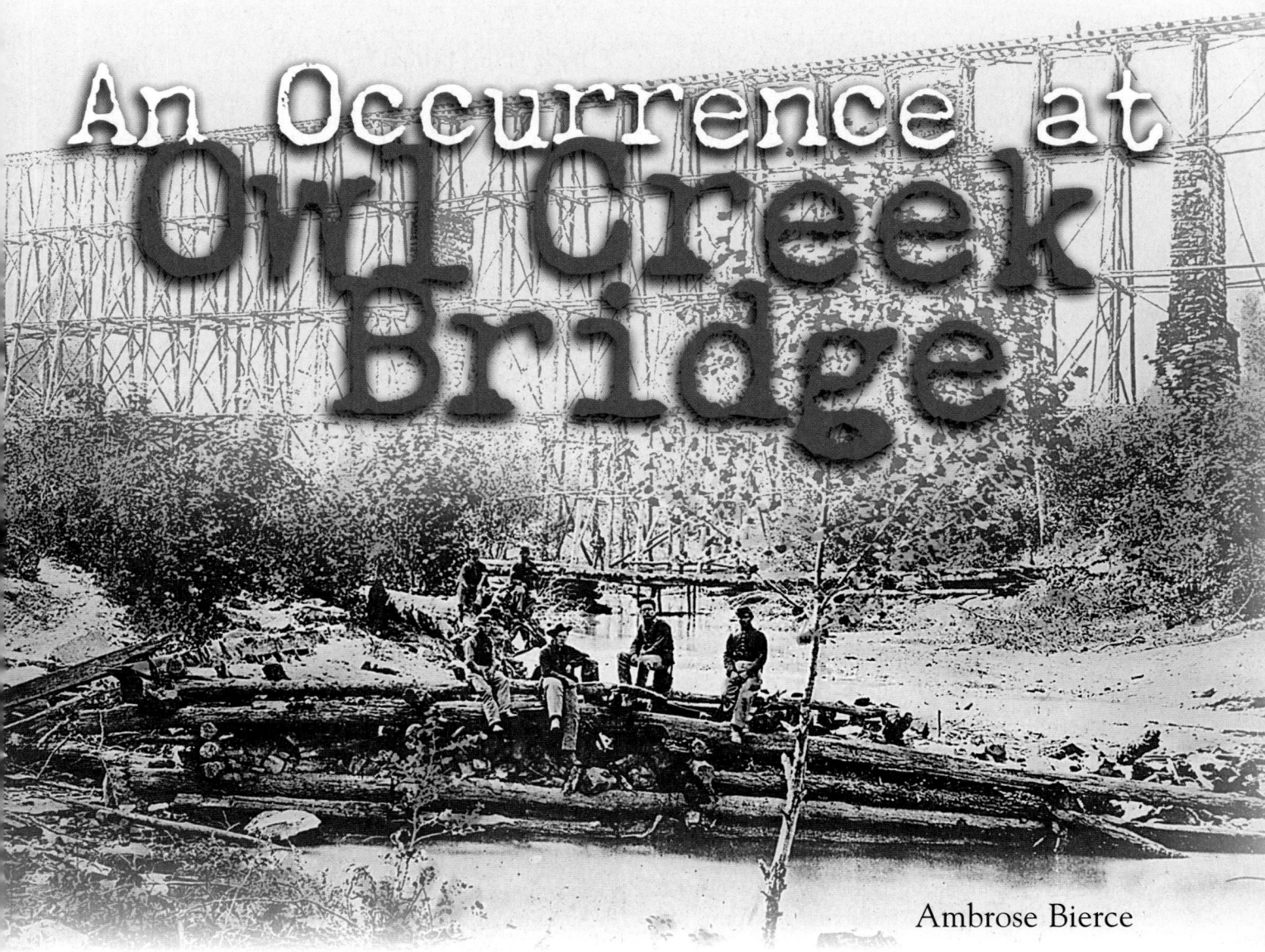

An Occurrence at Owl Creek Bridge

Ambrose Bierce

I

A man stood upon a railroad bridge in northern Alabama, looking down into the swift water twenty feet below. The man's hands were behind his back, the wrists bound with a cord. A rope closely encircled his neck. It was attached to a stout cross-timber above his head and the slack fell to the level of his knees. Some loose boards laid upon the sleepers supporting the metals of the railway supplied a footing for him and his executioners—two private soldiers of the Federal army, directed by a sergeant who in civil life may have been a deputy sheriff. At a short remove upon the same temporary platform was an officer in the uniform of his rank, armed. He was a cap-tain. A sentinel[1] at each end of the bridge stood with his rifle in the position known as "support," that is to say, vertical in front of the left shoulder, the hammer[2] resting on the forearm thrown straight across the chest—a formal and unnatural position, enforcing an erect carriage of the body. It did not appear to be the duty of these two men to know what was occurring at the center of the

---

1. A *sentinel* is a soldier who guards a point of passage.
2. A *hammer* is the part of a gun that helps to ignite the cartridge.

Literary Element Point of View *What does this detail tell the reader about the narrative point of view at this point in the story?*

bridge; they merely blockaded the two ends of the foot planking that traversed it.

Beyond one of the sentinels nobody was in sight; the railroad ran straight away into a forest for a hundred yards, then, curving, was lost to view. Doubtless there was an outpost farther along. The other bank of the stream was open ground—a gentle acclivity[3] topped with a stockade of vertical tree trunks, loop-holed for rifles, with a single embrasure through which **protruded** the muzzle of a brass cannon commanding the bridge. Midway of the slope between bridge and fort were the spectators—a single company of infantry in line, at "parade rest," the butts of the rifles on the ground, the barrels inclining slightly backward against the right shoulder, the hands crossed upon the stock. A lieutenant stood at the right of the line, the point of his sword upon the ground, his left hand resting upon his right. Excepting the group of four at the center of the bridge, not a man moved. The company faced the bridge, staring stonily, motionless. The sentinels, facing the banks of the stream, might have been statues to **adorn** the bridge. The captain stood with folded arms, silent, observing the work of his subordinates, but making no sign. Death is a dignitary who when he comes announced is to be received with formal manifestations of respect, even by those most familiar with him. In the code of military etiquette silence and fixity[4] are forms of deference.

The man who was engaged in being hanged was apparently about thirty-five years of age. He was a civilian, if one might judge from his habit,[5] which was that of a planter. His features were good—a straight nose, firm mouth, broad forehead, from which his long, dark hair was combed straight back, falling behind his ears to the collar of his well-fitting frock-coat. He wore a mustache and pointed beard, but no whiskers; his eyes were large and dark gray, and had a kindly expression which one would hardly have expected in one whose neck was in the hemp. Evidently this was no vulgar assassin. The liberal military code makes provision for hanging many kinds of persons, and gentlemen are not excluded.

The preparations being complete, the two private soldiers stepped aside and each drew away the plank upon which he had been standing. The sergeant turned to the captain, saluted and placed himself immediately behind that officer, who in turn moved apart one pace. These movements left the condemned man and the sergeant standing on the two ends of the same plank, which spanned three of the cross-ties[6] of the bridge. The end upon which the civilian stood almost, but not quite, reached a fourth. This plank had been held in place by the weight of the captain; it was now held by that of the sergeant. At a signal from the former the latter would step aside, the plank would tilt and the condemned man go down between two ties. The arrangement commended itself to his judgment as simple and effective. His face had not been covered nor his eyes bandaged. He looked a moment at his "unsteadfast footing," then let his gaze wander to the swirling water of the stream racing madly beneath his feet. A piece of dancing driftwood caught his attention and his eyes followed it down the current. How slowly it appeared to move! What a sluggish stream!

He closed his eyes in order to fix his last thoughts upon his wife and children. The water, touched to gold by the early sun, the brooding mists under the banks at some distance down the stream, the fort, the soldiers, the piece of drift—all had distracted him. And now he

Visual Vocabulary
A *frock-coat* is a man's coat that reaches to the knees. Popular in the nineteenth century, it is usually double-breasted and fitted at the waist.

---

3. An *acclivity* is an upward slope.
4. *Fixity* refers to a steady and unmoving stance.
5. *Habit* refers to a distinctive manner of dress or type of clothing.

Big Idea A Nation Divided *What does the condemned man's position in life suggest about the possible causes for his execution?*

Vocabulary

protrude (prō trōōd′) *v.* to stick out; to project
adorn (ə dôrn′) *v.* to make beautiful; to decorate

---

6. *Cross-ties* are the wooden pieces to which railroad rails are secured.

The Red Bridge, 1896. Julian Alden Weir. Oil on canvas, 24¼ x 33¾ in. The Metropolitan Museum of Art, New York.

became conscious of a new disturbance. Striking through the thought of his dear ones was a sound which he could neither ignore nor understand, a sharp, distinct, metallic percussion like the stroke of a blacksmith's hammer upon the anvil; it had the same ringing quality. He wondered what it was, and whether immeasurably distant or near by—it seemed both. Its recurrence was regular, but as slow as the tolling of a death knell.[7] He awaited each stroke with impatience and—he knew not why—apprehension. The intervals of silence grew progressively longer; the delays became maddening. With their greater infrequency the sounds increased in strength and sharpness. They hurt his ear like the thrust of a knife; he feared he would shriek. What he heard was the ticking of his watch.

He unclosed his eyes and saw again the water below him. "If I could free my hands," he thought, "I might throw off the noose and spring into the stream. By diving I could evade the bullets and, swimming vigorously, reach the bank, take to the woods and get away home. My home,

thank God, is as yet outside their lines; my wife and little ones are still beyond the invader's farthest advance."

As these thoughts, which have here to be set down in words, were flashed into the doomed man's brain rather than evolved from it the captain nodded to the sergeant. The sergeant stepped aside.

II

Peyton Farquhar was a well-to-do planter, of an old and highly respected Alabama family. Being a slave owner and like other slave owners a politician he was naturally an original secessionist[8] and **ardently** devoted to the Southern cause.

8. A *secessionist* was one in favor of breaking away from the Union.

Reading Strategy Making and Verifying Predictions
What can the reader predict about the condemned man from this statement?

Vocabulary

ardently (ärd′ent lē) *adv.* passionately; enthusiastically

7. A *knell* is the solemn sound of a bell ringing.

Circumstances of an imperious nature, which it is unnecessary to relate here, had prevented him from taking service with the gallant army that had fought the disastrous campaigns ending with the fall of Corinth, and he chafed[9] under the inglorious restraint, longing for the release of his energies, the larger life of the soldier, the opportunity for distinction. That opportunity, he felt, would come, as it comes to all in war time. Meanwhile he did what he could. No service was too humble for him to perform in aid of the South, no adventure too perilous for him to undertake if consistent with the character of a civilian who was at heart a soldier, and who in good faith and without too much qualification **assented** to at least a part of the frankly villainous dictum[10] that all is fair in love and war.

One evening while Farquhar and his wife were sitting on a rustic bench near the entrance to his grounds, a gray-clad[11] soldier rode up to the gate and asked for a drink of water. Mrs. Farquhar was only too happy to serve him with her own white hands.[12] While she was fetching the water her husband approached the dusty horseman and inquired eagerly for news from the front.

"The Yanks are repairing the railroads," said the man, "and are getting ready for another advance. They have reached the Owl Creek bridge, put it in order and built a stockade[13] on the north bank. The commandant has issued an order, which is posted everywhere, declaring that any civilian caught interfering with the railroad, its bridges, tunnels or trains will be summarily[14] hanged. I saw the order."

"How far is it to the Owl Creek bridge?" Farquhar asked.

"About thirty miles."

"Is there no force on this side the creek?"

"Only a picket post[15] half a mile out, on the railroad, and a single sentinel at this end of the bridge."

"Suppose a man—a civilian and student of hanging—should elude the picket post and perhaps get the better of the sentinel," said Farquhar, smiling, "what could he accomplish?"

The soldier reflected. "I was there a month ago," he replied. "I observed that the flood of last winter had lodged a great quantity of driftwood against the wooden pier at this end of the bridge. It is now dry and would burn like tow."[16]

The lady had now brought the water, which the soldier drank. He thanked her ceremoniously, bowed to her husband and rode away. An hour later, after nightfall, he repassed the plantation, going northward in the direction from which he had come. He was a Federal scout.[17]

As Peyton Farquhar fell straight downward through the bridge he lost consciousness . . .

III

As Peyton Farquhar fell straight downward through the bridge he lost consciousness and was as one already dead. From this state he was awakened—ages later, it seemed to him—by the pain of a sharp pressure upon his throat, followed by a sense of suffocation. Keen, **poignant**

---

9. *Chafe* means "to fret; to feel irritation."
10. A *dictum* is a formal, authoritative pronouncement.
11. Confederate soldiers wore *gray* uniforms.
12. [Mrs. Farquhar . . . hands] Ordinarily, a servant or slave would have served the guest. In this case, Mrs. Farquhar brought the soldier a drink of water.
13. A *stockade* is an enclosure made of posts in which prisoners may be kept.

Big Idea A Nation Divided *What does this statement imply about civilians during the Civil War?*

Vocabulary

assent (ə sent′) *v.* to express agreement
poignant (poin′ yənt) *adj.* sharp; severe; causing emotional or physical anguish

---

14. *Summarily* means "without delay; arbitrarily."
15. A *picket post* is a group of soldiers sent ahead to watch for and to warn of a surprise attack.
16. *Tow* (tō) is the coarse fibers of flax or hemp used to make yarn and twine.
17. Here, a *Federal scout* is a Union spy.

Reading Strategy Making and Verifying Predictions
What does this sentence enable the reader to predict about the outcome of Farquhar's mission to burn the bridge?

agonies seemed to shoot from his neck downward through every fiber of his body and limbs. These pains appeared to flash along well-defined lines of ramification[18] and to beat with an inconceivably rapid periodicity.[19] They seemed like streams of pulsating fire heating him to an intolerable temperature. As to his head, he was conscious of nothing but a feeling of fullness—of congestion. These sensations were unaccompanied by thought. The intellectual part of his nature was already effaced; he had power only to feel, and feeling was torment. He was conscious of motion. Encompassed in a luminous cloud, of which he was now merely the fiery heart, without material substance, he swung through unthinkable arcs of oscillation,[20] like a vast pendulum. Then all at once, with terrible suddenness, the light about him shot upward with the noise of a loud plash;[21] a frightful roaring was in his ears, and all was cold and dark. The power of thought was restored; he knew that the rope had broken and he had fallen into the stream. There was no additional strangulation; the noose about his neck was already suffocating him and kept the water from his lungs. To die of hanging at the bottom of a river!—the idea seemed to him ludicrous. He opened his eyes in the darkness and saw above him a gleam of light, but how distant, how inaccessible! He was still sinking, for the light became fainter and fainter until it was a mere glimmer. Then it began to grow and brighten, and he knew that he was rising toward the surface—knew it with reluctance, for he was now very comfortable. "To be hanged and drowned," he thought, "that is not so bad; but I do not wish to be shot. No; I will not be shot; that is not fair."

He was not conscious of an effort, but a sharp pain in his wrist apprised him that he was trying to free his hands. He gave the struggle his attention, as an idler[22] might observe the feat of a juggler, without interest in the outcome. What splendid effort!—what magnificent, what

superhuman strength! Ah, that was a fine endeavor! Bravo! The cord fell away; his arms parted and floated upward, the hands dimly seen on each side in the growing light. He watched them with a new interest as first one and then the other pounced upon the noose at his neck. They tore it away and thrust it fiercely aside, its undulations[23] resembling those of a water-snake. "Put it back, put it back!" He thought he shouted these words to his hands, for the undoing of the noose had been succeeded by the direst pang that he had yet experienced. His neck ached horribly; his brain was on fire; his heart, which had been fluttering faintly, gave a great leap, trying to force itself out at his mouth. His whole body was racked and wrenched with an insupportable anguish! But his disobedient hands gave no heed to the command. They beat the water vigorously with quick, downward strokes, forcing him to the surface. He felt his head emerge; his eyes were blinded by the sunlight; his chest expanded convulsively, and with a supreme and crowning agony his lungs engulfed a great draft of air, which instantly he expelled in a shriek!

He was now in full possession of his physical senses. They were, indeed, preternaturally[24] keen and alert. Something in the awful disturbance of his organic system had so exalted and refined them that they made record of things never before perceived. He felt the ripples upon his face and heard their separate sounds as they struck. He looked at the forest on the bank of the stream, saw the individual trees, the leaves and the veining of each leaf—saw the very insects upon them: the locusts, the brilliant-bodied flies, the gray spiders stretching their webs from twig to twig. He noted the prismatic colors in all the dewdrops upon a million blades of grass. The humming of the gnats that danced above the eddies[25] of the stream, the beating of the dragonflies' wings, the strokes of the water-spiders' legs,

---

18. Here, *ramification* means "the act of branching out."
19. *Periodicity* means "recurrence at regular intervals."
20. *Oscillation* is swinging back and forth with regular rhythm.
21. *Plash* is a splash or the sound of a splash.
22. An *idler* is a person who is lazy or not employed.

Literary Element   Point of View *What does this statement tell the reader about the narrator's point of view?*

23. *Undulations* are regular movements that come in waves.
24. *Preternaturally* (prē′ tər nach′ ər əl ē) means "going beyond what is normal" or "extraordinarily."
25. *Eddies* are currents that move contrary to the main current in a river or stream, usually in a circular motion.

Reading Strategy   Making and Verifying Predictions *What does this statement suggest about Farquhar's attempt to escape?*

Sugar Bridge Over Coulee, 1973. George Rodrigue. Oil on canvas, 48 x 75 in.
Private collection.
Viewing the Art: Does this painting look as if it could depict a scene from
"An Occurrence at Owl Creek Bridge"? Explain.

like oars which had lifted their boat—all these made audible music. A fish slid along beneath his eyes and he heard the rush of its body parting the water.

He had come to the surface facing down the stream; in a moment the visible world seemed to wheel slowly round, himself the pivotal point, and he saw the bridge, the fort, the soldiers upon the bridge, the captain, the sergeant, the two privates, his executioners. They were in silhouette against the blue sky. They shouted and gesticulated, pointing at him. The captain had drawn his pistol, but did not fire; the others were unarmed. Their movements were grotesque and horrible, their forms gigantic.

Suddenly he heard a sharp report[26] and something struck the water smartly within a few inches of his head, spattering his face with spray. He heard a second report, and saw one of the sentinels with his rifle at his shoulder, a light cloud of blue smoke rising from the muzzle. The man in the water saw the eye of the man on the bridge gazing into his own through the sights of the rifle. He observed that it was a gray eye and remembered having read that gray eyes were keenest, and that all famous marksmen had them. Nevertheless, this one had missed.

A counter-swirl had caught Farquhar and turned him half round; he was again looking into the forest on the bank opposite the fort. The sound of a clear, high voice in a monotonous singsong now rang out behind him and came across the water with a distinctness that pierced and subdued all other sounds, even the beating of the ripples in his ears. Although no soldier, he had frequented camps enough to know the dread significance of that deliberate, drawling, aspirated[27] chant; the lieutenant on shore was taking a part in the morning's work. How coldly and pitilessly—with what an even, calm intonation, presaging,[28] and enforcing tranquillity in the men—with what accurately measured intervals fell those cruel words:

---

26. Here, a *report* is an explosive sound or noise, especially from a rifle or a pistol when fired.

27. Here, *aspirated* refers to a breathy sort of speech.
28. *Presaging* means "acting as a sign or a warning of."

"Attention, company! . . . Shoulder arms! . . . Ready! . . . Aim! . . . Fire!"

Farquhar dived—dived as deeply as he could. The water roared in his ears like the voice of Niagara, yet he heard the dulled thunder of the volley[29] and, rising again toward the surface, met shining bits of metal, singularly flattened, oscillating slowly downward. Some of them touched him on the face and hands, then fell away, continuing their descent. One lodged between his collar and neck; it was uncomfortably warm and he snatched it out.

As he rose to the surface, gasping for breath, he saw that he had been a long time under water; he was perceptibly farther down stream—nearer to safety. The soldiers had almost finished reloading; the metal ramrods[30] flashed all at once in the sunshine as they were drawn from the barrels, turned in the air, and thrust into their sockets. The two sentinels fired again, independently and ineffectually.

The hunted man saw all this over his shoulder; he was now swimming vigorously with the current. His brain was as energetic as his arms and legs; he thought with the rapidity of lightning.

"The officer," he reasoned, "will not make that martinet's[31] error a second time. It is as easy to dodge a volley as a single shot. He has probably already given the command to fire at will. God help me, I cannot dodge them all!"

An appalling plash within two yards of him was followed by a loud, rushing sound diminuendo,[32] which seemed to travel back through the air to the fort and died in an explosion which stirred the very river to its deeps! A rising sheet of water curved over him, fell down upon him, blinded him, strangled him! The cannon had taken a hand in the game. As he shook his head free from the commotion of the smitten[33] water he heard the deflected shot humming through the air ahead, and in an instant it was cracking and smashing the branches in the forest beyond.

"They will not do that again," he thought; "the next time they will use a charge of grape.[34] I must keep my eye upon the gun; the smoke will apprise me—the report arrives too late; it lags behind the missile. That is a good gun."

Suddenly he felt himself whirled round and round—spinning like a top. The water, the banks, the forests, the now distant bridge, fort and men—all were commingled and blurred. Objects were represented by their colors only; circular horizontal streaks of color—that was all he saw. He had been caught in a vortex[35] and was being whirled on with a velocity of advance and gyration that made him giddy and sick. In a few moments he was flung upon the gravel at the foot of the left bank of the stream—the southern bank—and behind a projecting point which concealed him from his enemies. The sudden arrest of his motion, the abrasion of one of his hands on the gravel, restored him, and he wept with delight. He dug his fingers into the sand, threw it over himself in handfuls and audibly blessed it. It looked like diamonds, rubies, emeralds; he could think of nothing beautiful which it did not resemble. The trees upon the bank were giant garden plants; he noted a definite order in their arrangement, inhaled the fragrance of their blooms. A strange, roseate[36] light shone through the spaces among their trunks and the wind made in their branches the music of æolian harps.[37] He had no wish to perfect his escape—was content to remain in that enchanting spot until retaken.

A whiz and rattle of grapeshot among the branches high above his head roused him from his dream. The baffled cannoneer had fired him a random farewell. He sprang to his feet, rushed up the sloping bank, and plunged into the forest.

All that day he traveled, laying his course by

---

29. Here, a *volley* is a discharge of bullets in rapid succession.
30. *Ramrods* are rods used for stuffing the charge down the barrel of a rifle that is loaded from the muzzle.
31. A *martinet* is one who stresses strict attention to forms and rules.
32. *Diminuendo* (di min′ ū en′ dō) is a musical term that describes a gradual decrease in volume.

Big Idea A Nation Divided *How do you think Bierce's actual experiences in the war affected his descriptions of combat?*

---

33. Here, *smitten* means that the water has been bombarded with ammunition from the cannon.
34. *Grape* refers to grapeshot, a cluster of small iron balls that disperse when shot from a cannon.
35. Here, a *vortex* is a whirling mass of water that pulls everything to its center.
36. *Roseate* means "rose-colored."
37. *Æolian harps* produce musical sounds when air passes through the strings.

the rounding sun. The forest seemed intermible; nowhere did he discover a break in it, not even a woodman's road. He had not known that he lived in so wild a region. There was something uncanny[38] in the revelation.

By nightfall he was fatigued, footsore, famishing. The thought of his wife and children urged him on. At last he found a road which led him in what he knew to be the right direction. It was as wide and straight as a city street, yet it seemed untraveled. No fields bordered it, no dwelling anywhere. Not so much as the barking of a dog suggested human habitation. The black bodies of the trees formed a straight wall on both sides, terminating on the horizon in a point, like a diagram in a lesson in perspective. Overhead, as he looked up through this rift in the wood, shone great golden stars looking unfamiliar and grouped in strange constellations. He was sure they were arranged in some order which had a secret and malign[39] significance. The wood on either side was full of singular noises, among which—once, twice, and again—he distinctly heard whispers in an unknown tongue.

His neck was in pain and lifting his hand to it he found it horribly swollen. He knew that it had a circle of black where the rope had bruised it. His eyes felt congested; he could no longer close them. His tongue was swollen with thirst; he relieved its fever by thrusting it forward from between his teeth into the cold air. How softly the turf had carpeted the untraveled avenue— he could no longer feel the roadway beneath his feet!

Doubtless, despite his suffering, he had fallen asleep while walking, for now he sees another scene—perhaps he has merely recovered from a delirium. He stands at the gate of his own home. All is as he left it, and all bright and beautiful in the morning sunshine. He must have traveled the entire night. As he pushes open the gate and passes up the wide white walk, he sees a flutter of female garments; his wife, looking fresh and cool and sweet, steps down from the veranda to meet him. At the bottom of the steps she stands waiting, with a smile of ineffable[40] joy, an attitude of matchless grace and dignity. Ah, how beautiful she is! He springs forward with extended arms. As he is about to clasp her he feels a stunning blow upon the back of the neck; a blinding white light blazes all about him with a sound like the shock of a cannon—then all is darkness and silence!

Peyton Farquhar was dead; his body, with a broken neck, swung gently from side to side beneath the timbers of the Owl Creek bridge. ∾

Somerset Place at Creswell, North Carolina.

---

38. *Uncanny* means "eerie" or "weird."
39. *Malign* (mə līn´) means "evil or harmful in nature or effect."

Reading Strategy Making and Verifying Predictions
What do the uncanny quality of the woods and Peyton Farquhar's confusion suggest about the nature of his perceptions?

40. *Ineffable* means "indescribable" or "unspeakable."

Literary Element Point of View *What does this statement suggest to the reader about the reliability of the narrator in Part III of the story?*

Reading Strategy Making and Verifying Predictions
Does this statement verify your predictions? Explain.

RESPONDING AND THINKING CRITICALLY

Respond

1. What was your reaction to the end of the story?

Recall and Interpret

2. (a)Summarize the scene in the story's first two paragraphs. Who is involved? What reactions does the narrator describe? (b)Why do the observers of the event respond to it in the way they do?

3. (a)In sections I and II, what do you learn about Farquhar's appearance, personality, and background? (b)What can you infer about the narrator's attitude toward Farquhar from these descriptions?

4. (a)Describe the specific physical sensations that Farquhar experiences in section III. (b)How do his sensations change during the course of this section? (c)What do these changes suggest?

Analyze and Evaluate

5. (a)What literary device does Bierce use in section II of the story? (b)Did you find this literary device to be effective? Explain.

6. Do you think that the description of Farquhar's final thoughts is realistic? Explain.

Connect

7. **Big Idea** **A Nation Divided** How do you think Bierce's war experiences affected his attitude toward the events in this story? What view of people's desire to fight wars do you think Bierce expresses in this selection?

YOU'RE THE CRITIC: Point/Counterpoint

BIERCE'S OBSESSION WITH DEATH

Read the following two excerpts of literary criticism. The first is by Edmund Wilson, an American literary critic of the mid-twentieth century. The second is by Bierce's biographer and Civil War historian Roy Morris Jr. As you read, consider how these critics share similar assumptions but differ in their conclusions.

"But eventually, in his horror stories, the obsession with death becomes tiresome. If we try to read these stories in bulk, they get to seem not merely disgusting but dull . . . the trick repeated again and again. The executioner Death comes to us from outside our human world and, capriciously, gratuitously, cruelly, slices away our lives. It is an unpleasant limitation of Bierce's treatment of violent death that it should seem to him never a tragedy, but merely a bitter jest."
—Edmund Wilson

"One might quibble with the charge that Bierce's stories lack sympathy; they are, in their way enormously sympathetic, but it is the understated and unspoken sympathy of the modern stylist, not the breathy sentimentality of the Victorian. Besides, Bierce might have answered, such sentimental bosh is what got the soldiers in his stories into their deadly predicaments in the first place. It is not sympathy that Bierce is after, but clarity."
—Roy Morris Jr.

Group Activity

Discuss the following questions. Refer to the excerpts above and cite evidence from "An Occurrence at Owl Creek Bridge" to support your opinions.

1. (a)How do these two critics differ in their conclusions about Bierce? What assumptions do they share? (b)Which critic do you think comes closer to accurately assessing Bierce's attitude? Explain.

2. How does the "clarity" that Morris sees in Bierce's writings differ from the Transcendentalist clarity as described by Emerson in essays such as "Nature"?

Literary Element Point of View

Authors will sometimes shift the narrative **point of view** during a story. The shift might be dramatic, such as a change from the first- to the third-person point of view, or it might be a subtle shift from the third-person omniscient to the third-person limited point of view.

1. How does Bierce shift the point of view in this story? Explain.

2. What does Bierce achieve by using the third-person limited point of view for most of the story?

3. How do you think the effect on the reader would have been different had Bierce decided to use the omniscient narrator throughout the story?

Review: Description

As you learned in Unit One, **description** is the use of details to give the reader a vivid picture of a person, place, thing, or event.

Partner Activity Meet with a classmate and discuss the descriptions used in section III of the story. Pay attention to the author's use of precise and vivid adjectives, nouns, and verbs and sensory details, such as color, texture, or smell. Working with your partner, create a list of those descriptions that you found most compelling. Be sure to take note of what the author is describing and what kind of details he uses to describe it. Use a simple table, such as the one shown below.

What Is Described	Details
the lieutenant's order to fire	vivid adjectives: "deliberate" "drawling" "aspirated"

Reading Strategy Making and Verifying Predictions

Predictions can be made about various aspects of a text. For example, as you read you might make predictions about a character's motives, the theme of the story, or the outcome of a specific conflict. Inevitably, the predictions you make will sometimes be wrong. In "An Occurrence at Owl Creek Bridge," Bierce intentionally misleads the reader to make the ending a surprise. However, Bierce does provide clues to help the reader predict the plot's outcome.

1. What images, details, or descriptions do you notice that foreshadow the story's conclusion?

2. List any clues that you did not notice initially that now can be seen to foreshadow the conclusion.

Vocabulary Practice

Practice with Synonyms Find the synonym for each vocabulary word from "An Occurrence at Owl Creek Bridge" listed in the first column.

1. protrude   **a.** jut   **b.** impede

2. adorn   **a.** ornament   **b.** cover

3. ardently   **a.** greedily   **b.** fervently

4. assent   **a.** consent   **b.** believe

5. poignant   **a.** silly   **b.** emotional

Academic Vocabulary

Here are two words from the vocabulary list on page R86. These words will help you think, write, and talk about the selection.

physical (fiz´ i kəl) *adj.* having material existence

sequence (sē´ kwəns) *n.* a continuous or connected series

Practice and Apply

1. Describe some of Farquhar's **physical** characteristics.

2. What was the **sequence** of events that led Farquhar to his fate?

Writing About Literature

Analyze Flashback A flashback is a scene that interrupts the chronological flow of narrative to describe events that occurred earlier. What is the function of the flashback in section II? Write a short expository analysis that explains Bierce's use of this flashback. Use evidence from the story and examples from your own experience to support your main points.

Before you begin your draft, create a brief outline similar to the one shown below. Include all of the main points you plan to cover and the evidence you plan to use to support your main points.

I. Introductory Paragraph
- A. Context of Question
- B. Thesis Statement

II. Body Paragraph
- A. Supporting Evidence
- B. Supporting Evidence
- C. Supporting Evidence

III. Concluding Paragraph
- A. Summary of Key Points
- B. Restatement of Thesis

After completing your draft, exchange essays with a peer reviewer to evaluate each other's work and to suggest revisions. Then proofread and edit your draft for errors in spelling, grammar, and punctuation.

Literary Criticism

Group Discussion Critic Cathy N. Davidson identifies three main types of language that Bierce uses to narrate "An Occurrence at Owl Creek Bridge." In section I, according to Davidson, the narrator speaks in "military terminology, objective and distant." In section II, the narrator uses "jingoistic cant, deceiving and self-deceiving." In section III, Davidson describes the narrator's language as "lush and sensuous." Do you agree with Davidson's opinion? Meet with a group of classmates and discuss Bierce's use of language in the story. Present your conclusions to the class.

Bierce's Language and Style

Using Participial Phrases A participle is a verb form that can function as an adjective. For example:

*The **married** couple loved to travel.*

Here, the verb *married* acts as an adjective that modifies the noun *couple.*

A **participial phrase** contains a participle plus any complements or modifiers. These phrases can be used in various positions in a sentence and always function as adjectives. For example, in "An Occurrence at Owl Creek Bridge," Bierce writes, "The sentinels, facing the banks of the stream, might have been statues to adorn the bridge." Here, *facing the banks of the stream* is a participial phrase that modifies *sentinels.*

Participial phrases are useful for combining separate but related sentences, varying sentence type, and increasing general readability. It is important to keep in mind, however, that participial phrases must be closely attached to the nouns that they modify to avoid confusion. Consider the following examples.

1. *Badly needing sleep,* Tim's bed looked very inviting.

2. *Badly needing sleep,* Tim thought his bed looked very inviting.

In the first sentence, the participial phrase *badly needing sleep* modifies *bed,* which confuses the writer's intended meaning. In the second sentence, *badly needing sleep* modifies *Tim,* which eliminates the confusion.

Activity Scan "An Occurrence at Owl Creek Bridge" for other examples of participial phrases. Write down three sentences from the story that include participial phrases and underline the phrases. Then write three sentences imitating Bierce's style that use participial phrases.

Revising Check

Participial Phrases Work with a partner to review and revise your use of participial phrases in the essay you wrote for the Writing About Literature feature on this page.

Literature Online Web Activities For eFlashcards, Selection Quick Checks, and other Web activities, go to www.glencoe.com.

The Gettysburg Address

MEET ABRAHAM LINCOLN

Abraham Lincoln's impact on the history and culture of the United States has been immeasurable. He is a familiar figure to all Americans—even small children recognize his trademark hat. One of the United States' greatest presidents, Lincoln led the country through the Civil War, helping to preserve the Union and to end slavery. Lincoln and the United States showed the world that democracy can be a durable form of government.

> "A new nation, conceived in liberty, and dedicated to the proposition that all men are created equal."
>
> —Abraham Lincoln
> The Gettysburg Address

Politician Born in Hardin County, Kentucky, Lincoln grew up mainly on frontier farms in Indiana, where he worked as a rail-splitter, flatboatman, storekeeper, surveyor, and postmaster. Lincoln's parents were nearly illiterate and Lincoln received no formal education. Nevertheless, he developed a hunger for learning and read every book he could find. Following a move to New Salem, Illinois, Lincoln began to study law. At twenty-five, he was elected to the Illinois state legislature, marking the beginning of an astounding political career. In 1836, the self-taught Lincoln passed the bar examination and began to practice law. Twenty-four years later, after gaining national political prominence, he was nominated as the Republican presidential candidate. Lincoln won the election on November 6, 1860.

President and Commander in Chief Because Lincoln believed that Congress should prevent the spread of slavery, his victory prompted seven Southern states to secede from the Union. As a result the nation plunged into the Civil War. A man who had once described military glory as "that attractive rainbow that rises in showers of blood— that serpent's eye that charms to destroy" became a great war leader only because it was necessary to preserve the Union. Lincoln believed quite strongly that a Confederate victory would most likely have resulted in at least two separate nations. That, he felt, would have marked the failure of our nation's democracy. His policies as president proved shrewd, and the war ended on April 9, 1865, with victory for the North.

Public Speaker Lincoln's tragic and dramatic assassination cemented his place as a U.S. legend. His fame stems largely from the enduring power of his words, and the Gettysburg Address and his Second Inaugural Address are perhaps the most notable examples of Lincoln's mastery of public speaking. These speeches forcefully convey Lincoln's deepest convictions in spare, highly evocative language. Both speeches have had a vast influence on the language of U.S. politics.

Abraham Lincoln was born in 1809 and died in 1865.

Literature Online Author Search For more about Abraham Lincoln, go to www.glencoe.com.

Connecting to the Speech

In the Gettysburg Address, President Lincoln honors the Union soldiers killed in battle. Imagine yourself in the position of someone who has just lost a loved one in a war and is attending a memorial service for that person. Ask yourself the following questions:

- What words of comfort would you expect to hear?
- What rhetorical skills would you find appropriate for the speaker to use on such an occasion?

Building Background

Lincoln delivered the Gettysburg Address on November 19, 1863, at the dedication of a military cemetery in Gettysburg, Pennsylvania. A solemn group of people gathered on the battlefield to honor the Union soldiers killed there in early July. The main speaker at the ceremony was Edward Everett, one of the most famous orators of the time. The president was scheduled to deliver "remarks" following Everett's speech. Everett spoke first—for two hours. Lincoln spoke for approximately two minutes. Everett wrote to Lincoln afterward, "I should be glad if I could flatter myself that I came as near to the central idea of the occasion in two hours as you did in two minutes."

Setting Purposes for Reading

Big Idea **A Nation Divided**

As you read, notice how Lincoln stresses that the Civil War is a test of the United States' democracy.

Literary Element **Parallelism**

Parallelism is the use of a series of words, phrases, or sentences that have similar grammatical form. As you read the Gettysburg Address, notice how Lincoln uses this device as a rhetorical technique.

- See Literary Terms Handbook, p. R13.

Literature Online **Interactive Literary Elements Handbook** To review or learn more about the literary elements, go to www.glencoe.com.

Reading Strategy Analyzing Style

Style is a term that denotes the expressive qualities that distinguish an author's work. As you analyze Lincoln's style in this speech, note his word choice, the structure and length of his sentences, and his figurative language.

Reading Tip: Taking Notes Use a chart to record examples of Lincoln's style.

Style Element	Example
word choice	dedicate
repetition	consecrate

Vocabulary

score (skôr) *n.* a group of twenty items; p. 388 *Ben ordered ten tablecloths and six score of napkins.*

consecrate (kon´ sə krāt´) *v.* to set apart as sacred; to make or declare holy; p. 388 *A ceremony was held to consecrate the young couple's marriage.*

hallow (hal´ ō) *v.* to make or select as holy; to regard or honor as sacred; p. 388 *The church stands on hallowed ground.*

perish (per´ ish) *v.* to pass from existence; to disappear; p. 388 *Thousands of animals perish in forest fires.*

Vocabulary Tip: Analogies Analogies are comparisons based on relationships between words and ideas. For example, the relationship between *scissors* and *cloth* is the same as the relationship between *saw* and *wood*.

INDIANA ACADEMIC STANDARDS (pages 387–389)

11.2.1 Analyze both the features and the rhetorical (persuasive) devices of...speeches...

11.2.2 Analyze the way in which clarity of meaning is affected by...organization of language, and word choice in the text.

11.7.12 Critique a speaker's use of words and language in relation to the purpose of an oral communication...

THE GETTYSBURG ADDRESS

Abraham Lincoln

FOUR **SCORE** AND SEVEN YEARS AGO OUR FATHERS brought forth on this continent, a new nation, conceived in liberty, and dedicated to the proposition that all men are created equal.

Now we are engaged in a great civil war, testing whether that nation or any nation so conceived and so dedicated, can long endure. We are met on a great battle-field of that war. We have come to dedicate a portion of that field, as a final resting place for those who here gave their lives that that nation might live. It is altogether fitting and proper that we should do this.

But, in a larger sense, we can not dedicate—we can not **consecrate**—we can not **hallow**—this ground. The brave men, living and dead, who struggled here, have consecrated it, far above our poor power to add or detract. The world will little note, nor long remember what we say here, but it can never forget what they did here. It is for us the living, rather, to be dedicated here to the unfinished work which they who fought here have thus far so nobly advanced. It is rather for us to be here dedicated to the great task remaining before us—that from these honored dead we take increased devotion to that cause for which they gave the last full measure of devotion—that we here highly resolve that these dead shall not have died in vain—that this nation, under God, shall have a new birth of freedom—and that government of the people, by the people, for the people, shall not **perish** from the earth. ❧

Big Idea **A Nation Divided** *How do you think someone living in a Confederate state might have perceived this statement? Explain.*

Vocabulary

score (skôr) *n.* a group of twenty items

consecrate (kon′ sə krāt′) *v.* to set apart as sacred; to make or declare holy

hallow (hal′ ō) *v.* to make or select as holy; to regard or honor as sacred

perish (per′ish) *v.* to pass from existence; to disappear

Literary Element Parallelism *How is this sentence an example of parallelism?*

RESPONDING AND THINKING CRITICALLY

Respond

1. Which part of this speech made the greatest impression on you? Why?

Recall and Interpret

2. (a)In the opening sentence, what words does Lincoln use to describe the United States? (b)What does this sentence tell you about Lincoln's concept of government?

3. (a)According to Lincoln, why are he and those in the audience gathered together? (b)In what way does Lincoln believe that the battlefield has already been consecrated?

4. (a)To what does Lincoln say "the living" should dedicate themselves? (b)What does Lincoln mean by the "unfinished work" and the "great task remaining before us"?

Analyze and Evaluate

5. (a)How does Lincoln's speech affect your impressions of Lincoln? (b)What can you infer from this speech about Lincoln's character?

6. This speech is often quoted. What, in your opinion, makes it so memorable and inspiring?

7. What is unintentionally ironic about Lincoln's statement that "The world will little note, nor long remember what we say here, but it can never forget what they did here"?

Connect

8. **Big Idea** **A Nation Divided** Why did Lincoln consider the Civil War a test of U.S. democracy?

LITERARY ANALYSIS

Literary Element **Parallelism**

The Gettysburg Address contains one of the most famous examples of parallelism in American history: "of the people, by the people, for the people." The grammatical structure that is repeated here is the prepositional phrase.

1. Find another example of parallelism in this speech. Identify the grammatical structure that is repeated.

2. Explain how parallelism ties ideas together in this speech.

Writing About Literature

Evaluate Author's Craft Writers sometimes position opposite ideas next to each other to emphasize a point. This technique is called **antithesis.** Identify at least two uses of antithesis in Lincoln's speech and describe their roles in conveying Lincoln's message.

Literature Online **Web Activities** For eFlashcards, Selection Quick Checks, and other Web activities, go to www.glencoe.com.

READING AND VOCABULARY

Reading Strategy **Analyzing Style**

The style of the Gettysburg Address has been praised, particularly its word choice and sentence structure.

1. Some critics have pointed out that Lincoln's speeches possess a poetic quality. What elements of poetry can you detect in Lincoln's word choice? Explain.

2. Look at the final sentence of Lincoln's speech. (a)How does its structure differ from the sentence structure employed earlier? (b)Do you think this final sentence is an effective conclusion to the speech?

Vocabulary **Practice**

Practice with Analogies Choose the words that best complete each analogy.

1. twenty : score ::
   a. four : quarter   **d.** thrice : three
   b. twelve : dozen   **e.** ten : twenty
   c. hundred : millennium

2. consecrate : church ::
   a. sterilize : hospital   **d.** work : office
   b. sport : stadium   **e.** audience : theater
   c. learn : school

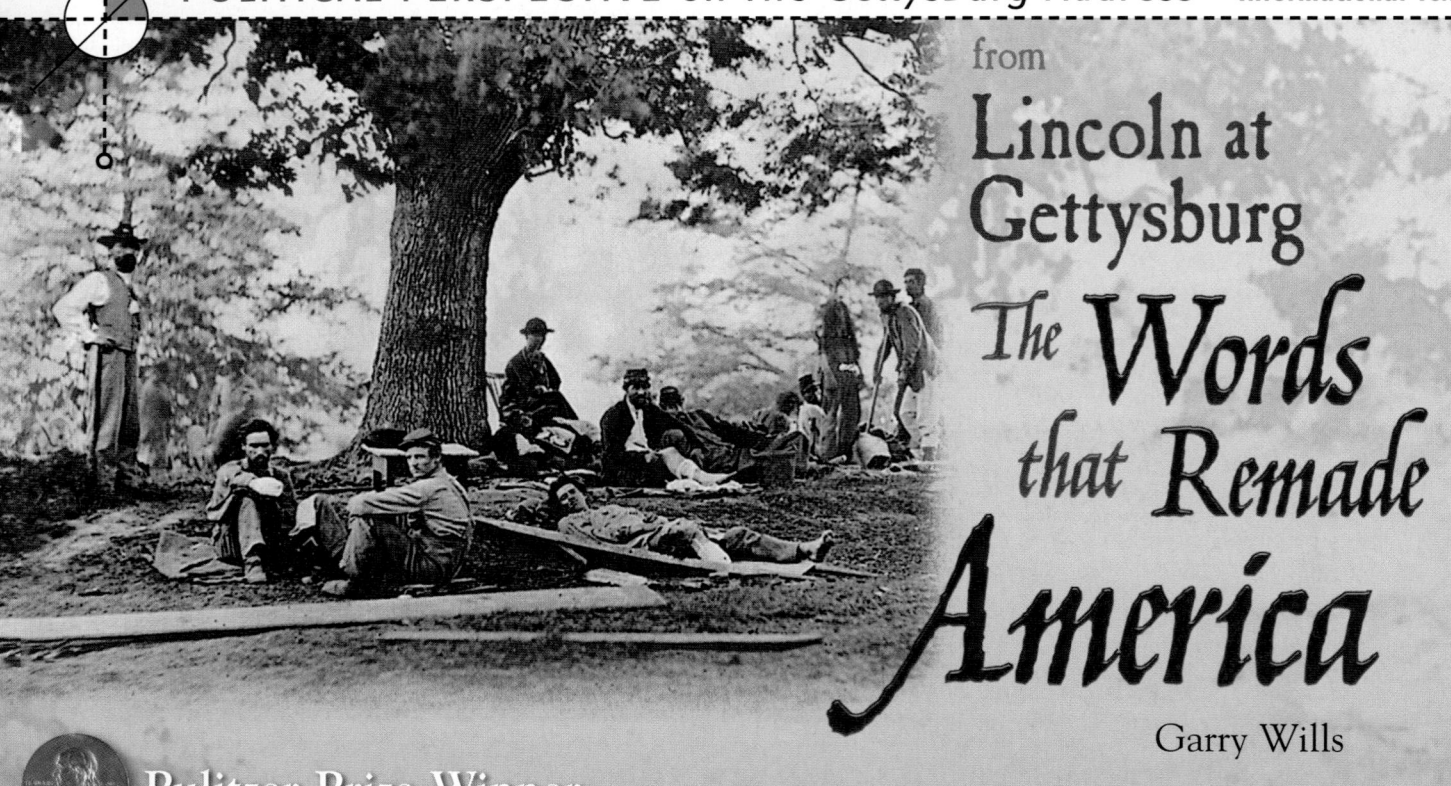

from

Lincoln at Gettysburg

The *Words that Remade America*

Garry Wills

Pulitzer Prize Winner

Building Background

In the following passage, historian Garry Wills closely examines the continuing significance of Lincoln's Gettysburg Address, which is considered one of the greatest speeches ever given by an American president. In Wills's Pulitzer Prize–winning book, he discusses the meaning of Lincoln's words, their long-term effect, and the historical environment in which Lincoln delivered the address. Wills maintains that the importance of Lincoln's brief 272-word speech is nearly unparalleled.

Set a Purpose for Reading

Read to discover the significance of the Gettysburg Address and why it remains important today.

Reading Strategy

Connecting to Political Context

Connecting to political context involves an examination of the political assumptions that influenced the writing of a literary work. As you read this selection, look for the answer to this question: What is the basic political assumption that Wills attributes to Lincoln in the Gettysburg Address? Cite evidence from the text to support your answer.

W hen Lincoln rose, it was with a sheet or two, from which he read—as had the minister who offered the invocation. Lincoln's three minutes would, ever after, be obsessively contrasted with Everett's[1] two hours in accounts of this day. It is even claimed that Lincoln disconcerted the crowd with his abrupt performance, so that people did not know how to respond ("Was that all?"). Myth tells of a poor photographer making leisurely arrangements to take Lincoln's picture, expecting him to be there for some time. But it is useful to look at the relevant part of the program as Wills's[2] committee printed it:

> *Music*, by BIRGFIELD'S Band.
> *Prayer*, by REV. T. H. STOCKTON, D.D.
> *Music*, by the Marine Band.
> *Oration*, by Hon. EDWARD EVERETT.

---

1. Edward *Everett,* who delivered the previous oration, had been president of Harvard University, a member of Congress, and the governor of Massachusetts. He was one of the most well-known speakers of his day.
2. David *Wills* was a prominent citizen of Gettysburg, Pennsylvania, and responsible for organizing the interstate commission that created the Gettysburg National Cemetery.

Music, Hymn composed by B. B. FRENCH, Esq.
Dedicatory Remarks, by the PRESIDENT OF THE UNITED STATES.
Dirge, sung by Choir selected for the occasion.
Benediction, by REV. H. L. BAUGHER, D.D.

There was only one "oration" announced or desired here. Though we call Lincoln's text *the* Gettysburg Address, that title clearly belongs to Everett. Lincoln's contribution, labeled "remarks," was intended to make the dedication formal (somewhat like ribbon-cutting at modern "openings"). Lincoln was not expected to speak at length, any more than Reverend Stockton was (though Stockton's prayer *is* four times the length of the President's remarks). In fact, Lincoln's contribution was as ancillary to Everett's as were those of Reverend Baugher and B. B. French (Lamon's friend, who rushed in where Longfellow, Bryant, and Whittier feared to tread[3]). Lincoln's text had about the same number of words as French's, and twice the number of Dr. Baugher's. It is instructive to look at *The New York Times'* coverage of the events in Gettysburg. It ranked Lincoln's talk, about which it had good things to say, with two given the night before in response to roving serenaders,[4] rather than with Everett's, which was kept in a category of its own. The headline reads:

IMMENSE NUMBERS OF VISITORS

ORATION BY HON. EDWARD EVERETT—SPEECHES OF PRESIDENT LINCOLN, MR. SEWARD AND GOVERNOR SEYMOUR

Lincoln was briefer, even, than New York's Governor Seymour had been the night before; but comparison with him was more natural at the time than with the designated orator of the day. A contrast of length with Everett's talk raises a false issue. Lincoln's text *is* startlingly brief for what it accomplished, but that would be equally true if Everett had spoken for a shorter time or had not spoken at all.

The contrast in other ways was strong. Everett's voice was sweet and expertly modulated; Lincoln's was high to the point of shrillness, and his Kentucky accent offended some Eastern sensibilities. But Lincoln derived an advantage from his high tenor voice—carrying power. If there is agreement on any one aspect of Lincoln's delivery, at Gettysburg and elsewhere, it is his audibility. Modern impersonators of Lincoln, like Walter Huston, Raymond Massey, Henry Fonda, and the various actors who give voice to Disneyland animations of the President, bring him before us as a baritone, which is considered a more manly or heroic voice—though both the Roosevelt presidents of our century were tenors. What should not be forgotten is that Lincoln was himself an actor, an expert raconteur[5] and mimic, and one who spent hours reading speeches out of Shakespeare to any willing (and some unwilling) audiences. He knew a good deal about rhythmic delivery and meaningful inflections. John Hay,[6] who had submitted to many of those Shakespeare readings, gave high marks to his boss's performance at Gettysburg. He put in his diary at the time that "the President, in a fine, free way, with more grace than is his wont, said his half dozen words of consecration." Lincoln's text was polished, his delivery emphatic, he was interrupted by applause five times. Read in a slow, clear way to the farthest listeners, the speech would take about three minutes. It is quite true that the audience did not take in all that happened in that short time—we are still trying to weigh the consequences of that amazing performance. But the myth that Lincoln was disappointed in the result—that he told the unreliable Lamon that his speech, like a bad plow, "won't scour"—has no basis. He had done what he wanted to do, and Hay shared the pride his superior took in an important occasion put to good use.

At the least, Lincoln had far surpassed David Wills's hope for words to disinfect the

---

3. Ward *Lamon* was Lincoln's friend and bodyguard; Henry Wadsworth *Longfellow* (1807–1882), William Cullen *Bryant* (1794–1878), and John Greenleaf *Whittier* (1807–1892) were all famous poets (see pages 196–197).
4. The night before the address, serenaders wandered through Gettysburg's crowded town square. The crowds prompted speeches from Lincoln's secretary of state, William Seward, and New York's governor, Horatio Seymour.
5. A *raconteur* is a storyteller.
6. John *Hay* was President Lincoln's personal secretary.

air of Gettysburg. The tragedy of macerated[7] bodies, the many bloody and ignoble aspects of this inconclusive encounter, are transfigured in Lincoln's rhetoric, where the physical residue of battle is volatilized as the product of an experiment *testing* whether a government can maintain the *proposition* of equality. The stakes of the three days' butchery are made intellectual, with abstract truths being vindicated. Despite verbal gestures to "that" battle and the men who died "here," there are no particulars mentioned by Lincoln—no names of men or sites or units, or even of sides (the Southerners are part of the "experiment," not foes mentioned in anger or rebuke). Everett succeeded with his audience by being thoroughly immersed in the details of the event he was celebrating. Lincoln eschews[8] all local emphasis. His speech hovers far above the carnage. He lifts the battle to a level of abstraction that purges it of grosser matter—even "earth" is mentioned as the thing from which the tested form of government shall not perish. More than William

Saunders[9] himself, Lincoln has aligned the dead in ranks of an ideal order. The nightmare realities have been etherealized[10] in the crucible of his language.

But that was just the beginning of this complex transformation. Lincoln did for the whole Civil War what he accomplished for the single battlefield. He has prescinded[11] from messy squabbles over constitutionality, sectionalism, property, states. Slavery is not mentioned, any more than Gettysburg is. The discussion is driven back and back, beyond the historical particulars, to great ideals that are made to grapple naked in an airy battle of the mind. Lincoln derives a new, a transcendental, significance from this bloody episode. Both North and South strove to win the battle for *interpreting* Gettysburg as soon as the physical battle had ended. Lincoln is after even larger game—he means to "win" the whole Civil War in ideological terms as well as military ones. And he will succeed: the Civil War *is*, to most Americans, what Lincoln wanted it to *mean*. Words had to complete the work of the guns.

---

7. *Macerated* means "wasted away."
8. *Eschew* means "to avoid."

9. *William Saunders* designed the Gettysburg National Cemetery.
10. *Etherealize* means "to eliminate physical properties."
11. *Prescinded* means "removed from thought."

RESPONDING AND THINKING CRITICALLY

Respond

1. What did you find most interesting in this essay?

Recall and Interpret

2. (a)Why does Wills say that comparing the lengths of Lincoln's address and Everett's oration "raises a false issue"? (b)How important to Wills is the length of the Gettysburg Address?

3. (a)What does Wills tell us about Lincoln's voice and delivery? (b)To what personal fact about Lincoln does Wills attribute the effectiveness of his performance?

Analyze and Evaluate

4. (a)To what plane does Wills claim that Lincoln elevated the discussion of the Civil War? (b)What evidence does he present to support this contention? (c)What effect do you think the Gettysburg Address has had on historians' interpretation of the war?

5. (a)Why do you think that Wills mentions several "myths" related to the address? (b)Do you find his points about these myths convincing? Explain.

Connect

6. Wills says that, because of the Gettysburg Address, "the Civil War *is*, to most Americans, what Lincoln wanted it to *mean*." What does the Civil War mean to you? How has the Gettysburg Address influenced your interpretation?

> **INDIANA ACADEMIC STANDARDS**
> **(pages 390–392)**
> 11.3.7 Analyze the clarity and consistency of political assumptions...

PART 3

A Poetic Revolution

The Girl I Left Behind Me, 1870–75. Eastman Johnson. Oil on canvas,
42 x 34⁷⁄₈ in. Smithsonian American Art Museum, Washington DC.

"*A child said What is the grass? fetching it to me with full hands;
How could I answer the child? I do not know what it is any more than he.*"

—Walt Whitman, "Song of Myself"

Whitman's Poetry

MEET WALT WHITMAN

When Walt Whitman first published *Leaves of Grass* in 1855, it marked the beginning of a revolution in poetry. At the time, however, few people noticed the young poet's radical work—and most of those who did were either dismayed or offended. Whitman's poetry was realistic, free flowing, and shockingly candid. No subject was too commonplace for his attention: not the mechanic nor the prisoner nor the lowly blade of grass. He was the first poet in English to write extensively in free verse, an open, unregulated form that reflected the cadences of everyday speech. Although it took decades for his poetry to be broadly accepted, *Leaves of Grass* eventually became an enduring symbol of the democratic spirit it celebrated.

"The United States themselves are essentially the greatest poem."

—Walt Whitman

An American Voice As a young man, Whitman loved to wander through the streets of Manhattan, a section of New York City. As he walked, he jotted down his impressions of the city's sights, sounds, and array of characters. A great reader, Whitman was nurtured by the transcendentalists, yet he was no country dweller delighting in the quiet joys of nature. Instead, he believed in gathering a wide range of experiences, so he held numerous jobs: office boy, doctor's helper, printer's assistant, journalist, typesetter, and printer. He also traveled down the Mississippi River, listening to the talk of working people, farmers, and soldiers. Whitman used his experiences to create a new kind of poetry that celebrated the multifaceted spirit of his country.

The first edition of *Leaves of Grass* contained just twelve poems, but they were enough to convince Ralph Waldo Emerson, the most famous literary figure of his day, of the unknown poet's genius. Here was the new American voice Emerson had been calling for. In a letter to Whitman, Emerson said the collection was "the most extraordinary piece of wit and wisdom that America has yet contributed." With the encouragement of a small group of admirers, Whitman pressed on with his life's work: revising, rearranging, and adding to *Leaves of Grass*, envisioning all of his work as one vast poem.

Witness to War Like all Americans, Whitman was deeply distressed by the Civil War. In 1862, he traveled to the Virginia battlefront to care for his brother George, who had been wounded in the first battle of Fredericksburg. Deeply moved by the suffering he encountered and finding his brother's condition stable, Whitman went on to Washington, D.C. to work as a volunteer nurse in army hospitals. His experiences during the Civil War inspired some of his greatest works, including "When Lilacs Last in the Dooryard Bloom'd," his elegy to President Lincoln.

Even in old age, Whitman kept writing, attempting to put "a Person, a human being (myself, in the latter half of the Nineteenth Century, in America) freely, fully, and truly on record." The final, "deathbed" edition of *Leaves of Grass* (1891), which contained 383 titled poems, put on record the man who had become America's national poet.

Walt Whitman was born in 1819 and died in 1892.

Literature Online Author Search For more about Walt Whitman, go to www.glencoe.com.

Connecting to the Poems

To Whitman, working people were the essence of America. As you read, think about the following questions:

- What kinds of jobs do people in your community have?
- How do these workers seem to feel about their jobs?

Building Background

For the first edition of *Leaves of Grass*, Whitman had to set the type himself and pay for the book's publication. Throughout his life, he continued to write poetry based on his experiences and to add poems to his groundbreaking collection. The shorter poems "I Hear America Singing," "When I Heard the Learn'd Astronomer," "A Sight in Camp in the Daybreak Gray and Dim," and "Beat! Beat! Drums!" reflect themes he explored during the Civil War.

Whitman wrote "I Hear America Singing" just before the war and "When I Heard the Learn'd Astronomer" at its end. "A Sight in Camp in the Daybreak Gray and Dim" captures one of the poet's experiences in army hospitals. "Beat! Beat! Drums!" is Whitman's response to the defeat of the Union army by the Confederate forces in the first battle of Bull Run.

Setting Purposes for Reading

Big Idea A Poetic Revolution

As you read, notice how Whitman uses ordinary details and sprawling lines to create a new kind of poetry.

Literary Element Free Verse

Whitman is famous for using **free verse**—a type of poetry that does not have a regular pattern of rhythm or rhyme. As you read, consider the effects Whitman creates by using free verse.

- See Literary Terms Handbook, p. R8.

Literature Online **Interactive Literary Elements Handbook** To review or learn more about the literary elements, go to www.glencoe.com.

Reading Strategy Paraphrasing

When you **paraphrase**, you put something you have read into your own words. As you read the poems, break down long sentences and restate them in your own words.

Reading Tip: Taking Notes Use a chart to record your paraphrases.

Original
"How soon unaccountable I became tired and sick..."

Paraphrase

Vocabulary

impromptu (im promp′ tōō, -tū) *adv.* done on the spur of the moment; p. 402 *The committee held an impromptu meeting to discuss some last-minute changes.*

incredulity (in′ krə dōō′ lə tē) *n.* disbelief; p. 403 *The football fans expressed incredulity when their losing team defeated their greatest rival.*

subsequently (sub′ sə kwent′ lē) *adv.* at a later time; p. 403 *She was given a gift of twenty dollars and subsequently donated it to a charity.*

susceptible (sə sep′ tə bəl) *adj.* easily influenced or affected; p. 403 *Because dogs do not sweat, they are more susceptible to overheating.*

convalescent (kon′ və le′ sənt) *n.* a person who is recovering from an illness, an injury, or a surgical operation; p. 404 *The hospital candy stripers brought a little cheer to the convalescent.*

INDIANA ACADEMIC STANDARDS (pages 395–398)
11.3.1 Analyze characteristics of...poetry...
11.2 Develop [reading] strategies...

11.7.20 Recite poems...

Cradling Wheat, 1938. Thomas Hart Benton. tempera and oil on board, 31 x 38 in.
T.H. Benton and R.P. Benton Testamentary Trusts/Licensed by VAGA,
New York, NY/The St. Louis Art Museum.

I Hear America Singing

Walt Whitman

   I hear America singing, the varied carols I hear,
   Those of mechanics, each one singing his as it should be blithe[1] and strong,
   The carpenter singing his as he measures his plank or beam,
   The mason singing his as he makes ready for work, or leaves off work,
5 The boatman singing what belongs to him in his boat,
     the deckhand singing on the steamboat deck,
   The shoemaker singing as he sits on his bench, the hatter singing as he stands,
   The wood-cutter's song, the ploughboy's on his way in the morning,
     or at noon intermission or at sundown,
   The delicious singing of the mother, or of the young wife at work,
     or of the girl sewing or washing,
   Each singing what belongs to him or her and to none else,
10 The day what belongs to the day—at night the party of young fellows,
     robust, friendly,
   Singing with open mouths their strong melodious songs.

---

1 *Blithe* means "lighthearted" or "cheerful."

Literary Element Free Verse *Why is free verse appropriate for the descriptions in this poem?*

When I Heard the Learn'd Astronomer

The Life of Harriet Tubman, #31, 1940.
Jacob Lawrence. Casein tempera
on hardboard, 17 7/8 x 12 in.
Hampton University Museum.

Walt Whitman

When I heard the learn'd astronomer,
When the proofs, the figures, were ranged in columns before me,
When I was shown the charts and diagrams, to add, divide, and measure them,
When I sitting heard the astronomer where he lectured with much applause
    in the lecture-room,
5 How soon unaccountable I became tired and sick,
Till rising and gliding out I wander'd off by myself,
In the mystical moist night-air, and from time to time,
Look'd up in perfect silence at the stars.

Reading Strategy   Paraphrasing *How would you rephrase these lines in your own words?*

RESPONDING AND THINKING CRITICALLY

Respond

1. Which of these poems do you prefer, and why?

I Hear America Singing
Recall and Interpret

2. (a)What occupations does the speaker say repre-sent America? (b)What do these occupations sug-gest about Whitman's view of his country?

3. (a)According to line 9, what does each laborer sing about? (b)What do the laborers' songs suggest about the work they do?

4. (a)What happens at night? (b)Why do you think the poem ends the way it does?

Analyze and Evaluate

5. (a)What **catalog,** or list of images and details, is included in this poem? (b)What effect does the catalog have on your reading of the poem?

6. (a)What about America does Whitman seem to be celebrating in this poem? (b)How does he achieve this focus?

When I Heard the Learn'd Astronomer
Recall and Interpret

7. (a)What techniques does the astronomer use to present information? (b)What does this suggest about the astronomer's approach to his subject?

8. (a)What does the speaker do in lines 6–8? (b)What conclusions can you draw about the speaker based on these actions?

Analyze and Evaluate

9. (a)How does the speaker's method for "studying" the stars differ from the astronomer's method? (b)What does this difference imply about the speaker's values?

10. (a)Why is the night air "mystical"? (b)What is implied by this word?

LITERARY ANALYSIS

Literary Element Free Verse

Free verse lacks a regular pattern of stressed and unstressed syllables. The lengths of the lines usually differ, and the lines may not be grouped together in stanzas. Instead, the way words and phrases are arranged and repeated creates a natural, conversa-tional rhythm in the poem. Free verse often sounds like spoken language.

1. With a partner, read one of Whitman's poems aloud. Do you find the rhythm of the poem similar to that of everyday speech? Explain.

2. In what ways might "I Hear America Singing" have a different effect if it were written in a regular pattern?

READING AND VOCABULARY

Reading Strategy Paraphrasing

Paraphrasing can help you judge whether you under-stand what you have read. This strategy also helps you appreciate particular words or phrases in the poem. Reread the following lines:

Till rising and gliding out I wander'd off by myself,
In the mystical moist night-air, and from time to time,
Look'd up in perfect silence at the stars.

1. How would you paraphrase these lines?

2. What is lost in your paraphrase?

Literature Online Web Activities For eFlashcards, Selection Quick Checks, and other Web activities, go to www.glencoe.com.

Encampment of Duryea's Zouaves, Virginia. 1862. William MacIlvaine the younger. Watercolor and gouache on paper, 18.1 x 27.3 in. New York Historical Society, NY.

A Sight in Camp in the Daybreak Gray and Dim

Walt Whitman

A sight in camp in the daybreak gray and dim,
As from my tent I emerge so early sleepless,
As slow I walk in the cool fresh air the path near by the hospital tent,
Three forms I see on stretchers lying, brought out there untended lying,
5   Over each the blanket spread, ample brownish woolen blanket,
Gray and heavy blanket, folding, covering all.

Curious I halt and silent stand,
Then with light fingers I from the face of the nearest the first just lift the blanket;
Who are you elderly man so gaunt and grim, with well-gray'd hair, and flesh all sunken
    about the eyes?
10 Who are you my dear comrade?

Then to the second I step—and who are you my child and darling?
Who are you sweet boy with cheeks yet blooming?

Then to the third—a face nor child nor old, very calm, as of beautiful yellow-white ivory;
Young man I think I know you—I think this face is the face of the Christ himself,
15 Dead and divine and brother of all, and here again he lies.

Big Idea   **A Poetic Revolution** *How is this description different from what you might read in poems from an earlier era?*

Beat! Beat! Drums!

Walt Whitman

The Wounded Drummer Boy, 1871.
Eastman Johnson. Oil on canvas, 40 x 36 in.
The Brooklyn Museum of Art, New York.

Beat! beat! drums!—blow! bugles! blow!
Through the windows—through doors—burst like a ruthless force,
Into the solemn church, and scatter the congregation,
Into the school where the scholar is studying;
5 Leave not the bridegroom quiet—no happiness must he have now with his bride,
Nor the peaceful farmer any peace, ploughing his field or gathering his grain,
So fierce you whirr and pound you drums—so shrill you bugles blow.

Beat! beat! drums!—blow! bugles! blow!
Over the traffic of cities—over the rumble of wheels in the streets;
10 Are beds prepared for sleepers at night in the houses? no sleepers must sleep in those beds,
No bargainers' bargains by day—no brokers or speculators[1]—would they continue?
Would the talkers be talking? would the singer attempt to sing?
Would the lawyer rise in the court to state his case before the judge?
Then rattle quicker, heavier drums—you bugles wilder blow.

15 Beat! beat! drums!—blow! bugles! blow!
Make no parley—stop for no expostulation,[2]
Mind not the timid—mind not the weeper or prayer,
Mind not the old man beseeching the young man,
Let not the child's voice be heard, nor the mother's entreaties,
20 Make even the trestles[3] to shake the dead where they lie awaiting the hearses,
So strong you thump O terrible drums—so loud you bugles blow.

---

1. *Speculators* are people who engage in risky business ventures hoping to make quick or large profits.
2. A *parley* is a conference between enemies to discuss terms of a truce or an agreement. *Expostulation* is the act of reasoning with a person to correct or dissuade him or her.
3. *Trestles* are structures in which a beam is supported by four diverging legs.

Reading Strategy Paraphrasing *Would your paraphrase of this line work with the rest of the poem?*

RESPONDING AND THINKING CRITICALLY

Respond

1. Which image or idea from these two poems stands out in your mind? Why?

A Sight in Camp in the Daybreak Gray and Dim
Recall and Interpret

2. (a)What item does the speaker describe in lines 5–6? (b)Why might the speaker have focused on this item?

3. (a)Describe the first two soldiers. (b)What do the speaker's questions imply about his feelings toward the soldiers?

Analyze and Evaluate

4. Why do you think Whitman presents the three soldiers in this order?

5. (a)What comparison does Whitman make in the last stanza? (b)What is the effect of comparing the third soldier to Christ?

Beat! Beat! Drums!
Recall and Interpret

6. (a)What instruments are mentioned in this poem? (b)What might they represent?

7. (a)What kinds of activities do the instruments interrupt? (b)What does the variety of activities suggest to you about the speaker's message?

Analyze and Evaluate

8. (a)Why might the people in stanza 3 be praying, beseeching, and so on? (b)What message does this stanza convey? Explain your answer.

9. (a)What attitude toward war does this poem express? (b)How well does it express that attitude? Support your answer.

LITERARY ANALYSIS

Literary Element Free Verse

Whitman's poetry is an example of **free verse** at its most impressive. Free verse is poetry that has an irregular rhythm and line length and attempts to avoid any predetermined verse structure. Despite this lack of regularity, free verse does have a structure, which seems to "grow" organically to fit its subject matter. Whitman pioneered this form and made it important in American poetry.

1. Find examples of rhythm and repetition in "Beat! Beat! Drums!" In particular, consider the effect of lines 1, 8, and 15.

2. How do these examples reinforce the meaning of the poem?

READING AND VOCABULARY

Reading Strategy Paraphrasing

In "Beat! Beat! Drums!" the sound effects reinforce the meaning of the poem. One way to appreciate these effects is to **paraphrase** selected lines and then compare your paraphrases with Whitman's original lines.

1. How would you paraphrase the last line of the first stanza?

2. How do the verbs and adjectives that describe the drums and bugles suggest that their sound is a "ruthless force"?

Literature Online **Web Activities** For eFlashcards, Selection Quick Checks, and other Web activities, go to www.glencoe.com.

from
Specimen Days

Walt Whitman

Building Background

While serving as a volunteer nurse during the Civil War, Whitman recorded his experiences in the form of journal entries. He comforted and cared for both Union and Confederate soldiers, dressing their wounds, writing letters for them, and bringing them items they needed, such as apples, oranges, and books. Writing about this experience, Whitman noted, "I supply often to some of these dear suffering boys . . . that which doctors nor medicines nor skill nor any routine assistance can give. . . . There is something in . . . the magnetic flood of sympathy that does, in its way, more good than all the medicine in the world."

Literary Element Historical Narrative

A **historical narrative** is a nonfiction work that tells the story of important historical events or developments. Often told from an individual's point of view, historical narratives provide a "you-are-there" perspective, allowing readers to experience history deeply and personally. As you read these excerpts from *Specimen Days,* consider how Whitman brings the Civil War home to his readers.

Literature Online **Interactive Literary Elements Handbook** To review or learn more about the literary elements, go to www.glencoe.com.

Opening of the Secession War

News of the attack on fort Sumter and *the flag* at Charleston harbor, S. C., was receiv'd in New York city late at night (13th April, 1861,) and was immediately sent out in extras of the newspapers. I had been to the opera in Fourteenth street that night, and after the performance was walking down Broadway toward twelve o'clock, on my way to Brooklyn, when I heard in the distance the loud cries of the newsboys, who came presently tearing and yelling up the street, rushing from side to side even more furiously than usual. I bought an extra and cross'd to the Metropolitan hotel (Niblo's) where the great lamps were still brightly blazing, and, with a crowd of others, who gather'd **impromptu**, read the news, which was evidently authentic. For the benefit of some who had no papers, one of us read the telegram aloud, while all listen'd silently and attentively. No remark was made by any of the crowd, which had increas'd to thirty or forty, but all stood a minute or two, I remember, before they dispers'd.

Literary Element Historical Narrative *How does this description set the tone for this entry?*

Vocabulary

impromptu (im promp′ tŏŏ, -tū) *adv.* done on the spur of the moment

I can almost see them there now, under the lamps at midnight again.

Contemptuous Feeling

Even after the bombardment of Sumter, however, the gravity of the revolt, and the power and will of the slave States for a strong and continued military resistance to national authority, were not at all realized at the North, except by a few. Nine-tenths of the people of the free States look'd upon the rebellion, as started in South Carolina, from a feeling one-half of contempt, and the other half composed of anger and **incredulity**. It was not thought it would be join'd in by Virginia, North Carolina, or Georgia. A great and cautious national official predicted that it would blow over "in sixty days," and folks generally believ'd the prediction. I remember talking about it on a Fulton ferry-boat with the Brooklyn mayor, who said he only "hoped the Southern fire-eaters would commit some overt act of resistance, as they would then be at once so effectually squelch'd, we would never hear of secession again—but he was afraid they never would have the pluck to really do anything." I remember, too, that a couple of companies of the Thirteenth Brooklyn, who rendezvou'd at the city armory, and started thence as thirty days' men, were all provided with pieces of rope, conspicuously tied to their musket-barrels, with which to bring back each man a prisoner from the audacious South, to be led in a noose, on our men's early and triumphant return!

Down at the Front

Falmouth, Va., opposite Fredericksburgh, December 21, 1862.—Begin my visits among the camp hospitals in the army of the Potomac. Spend a good part of the day in a large brick mansion on the banks of the Rappahannock, used as a hospital since the battle—seems to have receiv'd only the worst cases. Out doors, at the foot of a tree, within ten yards of the front of the house, I notice a heap of amputated feet, legs, arms, hands, &c., a full load for a one-horse cart. Several dead bodies lie near, each cover'd with its brown woolen blanket. In the door-yard, towards the river, are fresh graves, mostly of officers, their names on pieces of barrel-staves or broken boards, stuck in the dirt. (Most of these bodies were **subsequently** taken up and transported north to their friends.) The large mansion is quite crowded upstairs and down, everything impromptu, no system, all bad enough, but I have no doubt the best that can be done; all the wounds pretty bad, some frightful, the men in their old clothes, unclean and bloody. Some of the wounded are rebel soldiers and officers, prisoners. One, a Mississippian, a captain, hit badly in leg, I talk'd with some time; he ask'd me for papers, which I gave him. (I saw him three months afterward in Washington, with his leg amputated, doing well.) I went through the rooms, downstairs and up. Some of the men were dying. I had nothing to give at that visit, but wrote a few letters to folks home, mothers, &c. Also talk'd to three or four, who seem'd most **susceptible** to it, and needing it.

After First Fredericksburg

December 23 to 31.—The results of the late battle are exhibited everywhere about here in thousands of cases, (hundreds die every day,) in the camp, brigade, and division hospitals. These are merely tents, and sometimes very poor ones, the wounded lying on the ground, lucky, if their blankets are spread on layers of pine or hemlock twigs, or small leaves. No cots; seldom even a mattress. It is pretty cold. The ground is frozen hard, and there is occasional snow. I go around from one case to another. I do not see that I do much good to these wounded and dying; but I cannot leave them. Once in a while some youngster holds on to me convulsively, and I do what I can for him; at any rate, stop with him and sit near him for hours, if he wishes it.

Literary Element Historical Narrative *How would this information be presented in a textbook?*

Vocabulary

incredulity (in′ krə d$\overline{oo}$′ lə tē, -dū′-) *n.* disbelief

---

Literary Element Historical Narrative *What two different effects might this passage have had on readers during the Civil War?*

Vocabulary

subsequently (sub′ sə kwent′ lē) *adv.* at a later time
susceptible (sə sep′ tə bəl) *adj.* easily influenced or affected

Howard's Grove Hospital Near Richmond, Virginia, artist unknown, c. 19th century. Oil on canvas. The Chicago Historical Society.

Besides the hospitals, I also go occasionally on long tours through the camps, talking with the men, &c. Sometimes at night among the groups around the fires, in their shebang enclosures of bushes. These are curious shows, full of characters and groups. I soon get acquainted anywhere in camp, with officers or men, and am always well used. Sometimes I go down on picket with the regiment I know best. As to rations, the army here at present seems to be tolerably well supplied, and the men have enough, such as it is, mainly salt pork and hard tack. Most of the regiments lodge in the flimsy little shelter-tents. A few have built themselves huts of logs and mud, with fire-places.

No Good Portrait of Lincoln

Probably the reader has seen physiognomies (often old farmers, sea-captains, and such) that, behind their homeliness, or even ugliness, held superior points so subtle, yet so palpable, making the real life of their faces almost as impossible to depict as a wild perfume or fruit-taste, or a passionate tone of the living voice—and such was Lincoln's face, the peculiar color, the lines of it, the eyes, mouth, expression. Of technical beauty it had nothing—but to the eye of a great artist it furnished a rare study, a feast and fascination.

The current portraits are all failures—most of them caricatures.

A Soldier on Lincoln

May 28.—As I sat by the bedside of a sick Michigan soldier in hospital to-day, a **convalescent** from the adjoining bed rose and came to me, and presently we began talking. He was a middle-aged man, belonged to the 2d Virginia regiment, but lived in Racine, Ohio, and had a family there. He spoke of President Lincoln, and said: "The war is over, and many are lost. And now we have lost the best, the fairest, the truest man in America. Take him altogether, he was the best man this country ever produced. It was quite a while I thought very different; but some time before the murder, that's the way I have seen it." There was deep earnestness in the soldier. (I found upon further talk he had known Mr. Lincoln personally, and quite closely, years before.) He was a veteran; was now in the fifth year of his service; was a cavalry man, and had been in a good deal of hard fighting.

Vocabulary

convalescent (kon və leʹ sənt) *n.* a person who is recovering from an illness, an injury, or a surgical operation

RESPONDING AND THINKING CRITICALLY

Respond

1. What is your impression of the Civil War after reading these excerpts?

Recall and Interpret

2. (a)How has the soldier from the Virginia regiment changed his mind about Lincoln? (b)Why is Whitman fascinated by this soldier's story?

3. (a)Describe the attitude of many people in the North toward the South at the start of the war. (b)How would you account for this attitude?

4. (a)In "After First Fredericksburg," where does Whitman find the wounded soldiers lying? (b)Why do you think he includes this detail?

Analyze and Evaluate

5. (a)In "Down at the Front," what is Whitman's main theme? (b)How does he convey this theme?

6. (a)How would you describe the **tone** of "After First Fredericksburg"? (b)Do you think the tone is appropriate to the subject matter?

LITERARY ANALYSIS

Literary Element **Historical Narrative**

Historical narratives can provide compelling and intense portrayals of historical developments. One reason why these accounts can be so compelling is that they show large events from a human perspective. Seeing events through one person's eyes helps the reader experience what happened at a particular moment in history.

1. Why do you think Whitman chose to publish his journal notes?

2. How does reading Whitman's historical narrative compare with reading an account of the Civil War in a history book?

Writing About Literature

Apply Form: Historical Narrative In *Specimen Days,* Whitman describes his experiences during and personal feelings about an important historic event, the Civil War. Think about an influential or historic event that has happened in your lifetime. What was your experience during that occurrence, and how did it affect you emotionally? Write a few paragraphs describing your experience of that event and your reactions to it. If you wish, you might try writing your account in journal form, as Whitman did.

Literature Online **Web Activities** For eFlashcards, Selection Quick Checks, and other Web activities, go to www.glencoe.com.

READING AND VOCABULARY

Vocabulary **Practice**

Practice with Context Clues Choose the best meaning for each vocabulary word.

1. Walking slowly and in noticeable pain, the **convalescent** returned to his hospital room.
(a) surgeon (b) nurse (c) patient (d) technician

2. The exaggerated and bizarre account filled me with **incredulity**.
(a) belief (b) doubt (c) amazement (d) joy

3. The years **subsequent** to her recovery were filled with purpose and energy.
(a) later (b) earlier (c) disastrous (d) unpleasant

Academic Vocabulary

Here are two words from the vocabulary list on page R86. These words will help you think, write, and talk about the selection.

attitude (a′ tə to͞od′, -tūd′) *n.* an opinion or general feeling about something

individual (in′ də vi′ jo͞o əl) *adj.* existing as a distinct entity; separate

Practice and Apply

1. How would you describe Whitman's **attitude** toward the Civil War?

2. According to Whitman on page 404, what **individual** elements of Lincoln's face made it impossible to depict?

from Song of Myself

LITERATURE PREVIEW	READING PREVIEW

Connecting to the Poem

One of the poems that most fully captures the essence of Whitman is *Song of Myself*. In it he celebrates his individuality and his oneness with the world. Consider these questions:

- What might it mean to feel "connected" to nature and to all of humankind?
- If you were to write a poem that celebrates life itself, what images would you choose?

Building Background

When Whitman was young, he read Homer's classic epic poem the *Iliad* while "in a shelter'd hollow of rocks and sand, with the sea on each side." He felt that only the "presence of Nature" prevented him from being completely overwhelmed by the experience.

Several years later Whitman would create his own epic poem—*Song of Myself*. Like the *Iliad*, this poem describes the journey of a hero. The hero in this poem, however, is the poet himself, and his journey is in part a spiritual one. As the poem progresses, the poet attempts to connect with the spirit of the reader, of the American landscape, of the American people, and, finally, of the universe itself. *Song of Myself* encourages each reader to share the poet's journey and to celebrate his or her own heroic spirit.

Setting Purposes for Reading

Big Idea **A Poetic Revolution**

As you read, notice how Whitman uses sprawling lines and irregular rhythms to give form to his poem.

Literary Element **Voice**

Voice is the distinctive use of language that conveys the author's or speaker's personality to the reader. Voice is determined by several elements, including word choice and tone. In *Song of Myself*, Whitman set out to create a unique poetic voice—one that would reflect the nation as a whole and the language of the common people in particular. As you read this poem, think about how you would describe Whitman's voice.

- See Literary Terms Handbook, p. R19.

Reading Strategy Drawing Conclusions

Drawing conclusions about a text involves using pieces of given information to make a general statement about the meaning of a line, passage, or section. Many elements in a literary work—including word choice, voice, imagery, and figurative language—contribute to the meaning. In a long poem such as *Song of Myself*, it is important to identify these elements from time to time and to use them to draw conclusions about the poet's meaning.

....

Reading Tip: Taking Notes Use a chart to record the conclusions you draw as you read the poem.

Lines	Conclusions
"And what I assume you shall assume,/For every atom belonging to me as good belongs to you." (lines 2–3)	The speaker wants to make a connection to the reader as an equal.

Literature Online **Interactive Literary Elements Handbook** To review or learn more about the literary elements, go to www.glencoe.com.

INDIANA ACADEMIC STANDARDS (pages 406–415)
11.3.3 Analyze the ways in which...the "sound" of language achieve[s] specific...aesthetic (artistic) purposes...

11.2 Develop [reading] strategies...
11.5.9 Write expository essays...

from Song of Myself

Walt Whitman

1

I celebrate myself, and sing myself,
And what I assume you shall assume,
For every atom belonging to me as good belongs to you.

I loafe and invite my soul,
5   I lean and loafe at my ease observing a spear of summer grass.

My tongue, every atom of my blood, form'd from this soil, this air,
Born here of parents born here from parents the same, and their parents the same,
I, now thirty-seven years old in perfect health begin,
Hoping to cease not till death.

10 Creeds and schools in abeyance,[1]
Retiring back a while sufficed at what they are, but never forgotten,
I harbor for good or bad, I permit to speak at every hazard,
Nature without check with original energy.

6

A child said What is the grass? fetching it to me with full hands;
15 How could I answer the child? I do not know what it is any more than he.

I guess it must be the flag of my disposition, out of hopeful green stuff woven.

Or I guess it is the handkerchief of the Lord,
A scented gift and remembrancer[2] designedly dropt,
Bearing the owner's name someway in the corners, that we may see and remark,
    and say *Whose?*

---

1. *In abeyance* means "suspended" or "in a state of being undetermined."
2. A *remembrancer* is a reminder.

Big Idea   **A Poetic Revolution** *In line 14 the rhythmic pattern creates a rising and falling effect, ending in a stop. What pattern does Whitman use in line 15?*

Haymaking, Winslow Homer, 1864. Oil on canvas. The Columbus Museum of Art, Columbus, OH.

Viewing the Art: In what ways does this painting capture the mood of the poem? Explain, using details from both the painting and the poem.

20   What do you think has become of the young and old men?
     And what do you think has become of the women and children?

     They are alive and well somewhere,
     The smallest sprout shows there is really no death,
     And if ever there was it led forward life, and does not wait at the end to arrest it,
25   And ceas'd the moment life appear'd.

     All goes onward and outward, nothing collapses,
     And to die is different from what any one supposed, and luckier.

Reading Strategy   Drawing Conclusions   *Why is the speaker convinced that death does not exist?*

16

I am of old and young, of the foolish as much as the wise,
Regardless of others, ever regardful of others,
30   Maternal as well as paternal, a child as well as a man,
Stuff'd with the stuff that is coarse and stuff'd with the stuff that is fine,
One of the Nation of many nations, the smallest the same and the largest the same,
A Southerner soon as a Northerner, a planter nonchalant[3] and hospitable down by the
    Oconee[4] I live,
A Yankee bound my own way ready for trade, my joints the limberest joints on earth and
    the sternest joints on earth,
35   A Kentuckian walking the vale of the Elkhorn in my deer-skin leggings, a Louisianian
    or Georgian,
A boatman over lakes or bays or along coasts, a Hoosier,[5] Badger,[5] Buckeye;[5]
At home on Kanadian snow-shoes or up in the bush, or with fishermen off Newfoundland,
At home in the fleet of ice-boats, sailing with the rest and tacking,
At home on the hills of Vermont or in the woods of Maine, or the Texan ranch,
40   Comrade of Californians, comrade of free North-Westerners, (loving their big proportions,)
Comrade of raftsmen and coalmen, comrade of all who shake hands and welcome
    to drink and meat,
A learner with the simplest, a teacher of the thoughtfullest,
A novice beginning yet experient of myriads of seasons,
Of every hue and caste am I, of every rank and religion,
45   A farmer, mechanic, artist, gentleman, sailor, quaker,
Prisoner, fancy-man, rowdy,[6] lawyer, physician, priest.

I resist any thing better than my own diversity,
Breathe the air but leave plenty after me,
And am not stuck up, and am in my place.

50   (The moth and the fish-eggs are in their place,
The bright suns I see and the dark suns I cannot see are in their place,

The palpable[7] is in its place and the impalpable is in its place.)

17

These are really the thoughts of all men in all ages and lands, they
  are not original with me,
If they are not yours as much as mine they are nothing, or next to nothing,

---

3. *Nonchalant* means "showing a lack of interest or enthusiasm."
4. The *Oconee* is a river in Georgia.
5. *Hoosier, Badger,* and *Buckeye* are nicknames for natives or residents of Indiana, Wisconsin, and Ohio, respectively.
6. A *rowdy* is a rough, disorderly person.
7. *Palpable* means "able to be touched or felt."

Literary Element   Voice *What do these lines convey about the speaker's personality?*

55 If they are not the riddle and the untying of the riddle they are nothing,
If they are not just as close as they are distant they are nothing.

This is the grass that grows wherever the land is and the water is,
This is the common air that bathes the globe.

46

I know I have the best of time and space, and was never measured and
    never will be measured.

60 I tramp a perpetual journey, (come listen all!)
My signs are a rain-proof coat, good shoes, and a staff cut from the woods,
No friend of mine takes his ease in my chair,
I have no chair, no church, no philosophy,
I lead no man to a dinner-table, library, exchange,
65 But each man and each woman of you I lead upon a knoll,[8]
My left hand hooking you round the waist,
My right hand pointing to landscapes of continents and the public road.

Not I, not any one else can travel that road for you,
You must travel it for yourself.

70 It is not far, it is within reach,
Perhaps you have been on it since you were born and did not know,
Perhaps it is everywhere on water and on land.

Shoulder your duds[9] dear son, and I will mine, and let us hasten forth,
Wonderful cities and free nations we shall fetch as we go.

75 If you tire, give me both burdens, and rest the chuff of your hand[10] on my hip,

And in due time you shall repay the same service to me,
For after we start we never lie by again.

This day before dawn I ascended a hill and look'd at the crowded heaven,
And I said to my spirit *When we become the enfolders of those orbs, and the pleasure and
    knowledge of every thing in them, shall we be fill'd and satisfied then?*
80 And my spirit said *No, we but level that lift to pass and continue beyond.*
You are also asking me questions and I hear you,
I answer that I cannot answer, you must find out for yourself.

---

8. A *knoll* is a small, rounded hill.
9. *Duds* are personal belongings.
10. *Chuff of your hand* refers to the fat part of the palm.

Reading Strategy   Drawing Conclusions   *What message does the speaker convey about the reader's path in life?*

Sit a while dear son,
Here are biscuits to eat and here is milk to drink,
85 But as soon as you sleep and renew yourself in sweet clothes, I kiss you with a good-by kiss and open the gate for your egress hence.[11]

Long enough have you dream'd contemptible dreams,
Now I wash the gum from your eyes,
You must habit yourself to the dazzle of the light and of every moment of your life.

Long have you timidly waded holding a plank by the shore,
90 Now I will you to be a bold swimmer,
To jump off in the midst of the sea, rise again, nod to me, shout, and laughingly dash with your hair.

51

The past and present wilt—I have fill'd them, emptied them,
And proceed to fill my next fold of the future.

Listener up there! what have you to confide to me?
95 Look in my face while I snuff the sidle of evening,[12]
(Talk honestly, no one else hears you, and I stay only a minute longer.)

Do I contradict myself?
Very well then I contradict myself,
(I am large, I contain multitudes.)

100 I concentrate toward them that are nigh,[13] I wait on the door-slab.

Who has done his day's work? who will soonest be through with his supper?
Who wishes to walk with me?

Will you speak before I am gone? will you prove already too late?

52

The spotted hawk swoops by and accuses me, he complains of my gab and my loitering.

105 I too am not a bit tamed, I too am untranslatable,
I sound my barbaric yawp[14] over the roofs of the world.

---

11. *Egress hence* means "departure from this place."
12. *Snuff the sidle of evening* means "to put out the last light of the day, which is moving sideways across the sky."
13. *Nigh* means "near."
14. A *yawp* is a loud, sharp cry.

Literary Element Voice *How would you describe the intended relationship between the speaker and the reader of this poem?*

The Sand Team, George Bellows, 1917. Oil on canvas. The Brooklyn Museum of Art, New York.
Viewing the Art: In your opinion, what spirit of America does this painting convey? How is it similar to or different from Whitman's view of the American spirit?

The last scud[15] of day holds back for me,
It flings my likeness after the rest and true as any on the shadow'd wilds,
It coaxes me to the vapor and the dusk.

110 I depart as air, I shake my white locks at the runaway sun,
I effuse[16] my flesh in eddies, and drift it in lacy jags.

I bequeath myself to the dirt to grow from the grass I love,
If you want me again look for me under your boot-soles.

You will hardly know who I am or what I mean,
115 But I shall be good health to you nevertheless,
And filter and fibre your blood.

Failing to fetch me at first keep encouraged,
Missing me one place search another,
I stop somewhere waiting for you.

---

15. *Scud* refers to wind-driven clouds or rain.
16. *Effuse* means "to pour out or forth."

Reading Strategy Drawing Conclusions *What stage of his journey has the speaker reached?*

Literary Element Voice *How would you describe the poet's voice in the closing lines of the poem?*

RESPONDING AND THINKING CRITICALLY

Respond

1. How did you react to the speaker in the poem? Explain your answer.

Recall and Interpret

2. (a)What is the main topic of section 1? (b)What is the speaker saying in lines 10–13 about his past learning and his future?

3. (a)What does the speaker say about death in lines 20–27? (b)What do these lines suggest about the speaker's view of life and death?

4. (a)A **paradox** is a statement that seems to contradict itself but may actually be true. What paradoxes does Whitman list in section 16? (b)What do these lines suggest about Whitman's attitude toward himself?

Analyze and Evaluate

5. (a)How does the speaker seem to view himself in relation to nature and to the rest of the world? (b)In your opinion, is the speaker a hero? Explain.

6. (a)Summarize the speaker's advice to his "son" in lines 73–91. (b)In your opinion, why does he give this advice? Support your answer with details from the poem.

7. (a)Consider the image of the grass in sections 6 and 52. What does the grass have to do with life and death? (b)Why might Whitman have called his volume of poetry *Leaves of Grass*?

Connect

8. **Big Idea** **A Poetic Revolution** (a)Why is free verse particularly suited to Whitman's ideas? (b)How do you think the use of this form relates to Whitman's democratic principles?

YOU'RE THE CRITIC: Point/Counterpoint

RESPONSES TO WHITMAN

It took several years for the American public to embrace Whitman's poetry. At first, most readers—and there were few of them—were shocked by the unconventional subject matter, the unusual forms, and the break with standard rhyme and meter. A famous poet of that time, John Greenleaf Whittier, threw his copy of *Leaves of Grass* into his fireplace in disgust.

Whitman, however, did have some early supporters besides Ralph Waldo Emerson. They included Horace Traubel, an American, and John Addington Symonds, an Englishman. Each expressed a different view about what is most important in Whitman's work. As you read the two excerpts, notice their different perspectives.

> *"That's what Leaves of Grass all comes to. The declaration that the people are first. Not a portion of the people. Not the saving remnant. But the everyday people. The vast overflowing populations."*
>
> —Horace Traubel, 1912

> *"We can trace an order in [Whitman's] ideas. First comes religion or the concept of the universe; then personality, or the sense of self . . .; then love . . . and comradely emotions; then democracy, or the theory of human equality and brotherhood."*
>
> —John Addington Symonds, 1893

1. Find passages in *Song of Myself* that support the views of these critics.

2. Which of the two views do you think is more accurate? Explain.

Literary Element Voice

Voice is the writer's or speaker's personality that comes across in a piece of writing. Conveyed through elements such as sentence structure, word choice, and tone, voice can have a powerful impact on how readers react to the content of a poem. To detect voice, you must read actively and imaginatively. In your mind's "ear," listen to the rise and fall of a human voice, pausing, emphasizing, shifting tone. For example, consider Whitman's voice in lines 97–99:

> *"Do I contradict myself?*
> *Very well then I contradict myself,*
> *(I am large, I contain multitudes.)"*

You might describe this voice as rough, bold, and assertive. It is impatient of criticism and utterly self-confident.

1. How would you describe Whitman's voice in the opening lines of the poem? Support your answer with examples from the text.

2. How does Whitman's voice affect the impact of his message?

Review: Author's Purpose

As you learned in Unit One, **author's purpose** refers to an author's intent in writing a piece of literature. Once you understand the author's purpose, you can better evaluate what you are reading and respond appropriately.

Partner Activity With another classmate, identify and discuss the different themes, or messages, in *Song of Myself*. With your partner, create a web diagram. In the outer boxes, list the themes you discussed. Then, in the center, write down an overarching theme, or Whitman's main message in the poem.

Reading Strategy Drawing Conclusions

Skillful readers are always **drawing conclusions** and, in doing so, understand much more than an author says directly. This process is similar to that used by a detective solving a mystery. You examine evidence that the author provides—for example, word choice or imagery—and then combine it with your own experiences to reach a conclusion. Since poets imply more than they state directly, drawing conclusions is an especially useful tool for interpreting poetry. When you come upon difficult lines or passages in a poem, examine the surrounding lines to see if they provide any clues to help you figure out the meaning.

1. How does line 26 of *Song of Myself* help you interpret line 27?

2. How do the previous lines in Section 16 help you draw conclusions about the meaning of lines 47–49?

Academic Vocabulary

Here are two words from the vocabulary list on page R86. These words will help you think, talk, and write about the selection.

transform (trans fôrm´) *n.* to change in form, appearance, or structure

guideline (gīd´līn) *n.* any guide or indication of a future course of action

Practice and Apply

1. How does the speaker **transform** traditional ways of thinking about death in section 6 of *Song of Myself*?

2. How might the end of section 46 of *Song of Myself* serve as a **guideline** for living one's life?

Writing About Literature

Evaluate Author's Craft In *Song of Myself* and other poems, Whitman uses specific details to enrich his poetry. Choose one of Whitman's poems and list the details in that poem that you find most powerful. Then write a brief essay explaining the effect those details have on the poem. For example: Do they clarify the meaning? Do they make the images more memorable? Be specific in supporting your explanations.

Before you start writing, create a chart like the one below, listing key details on the left and describing their effect on the right. Use this chart as a source for examples when creating a draft. Write your draft from

Details	Effects
"observing a spear of summer grass"	Brings out the meaning more clearly: The speaker finds it worthwhile to examine the most ordinary things.

start to finish.

After you complete your draft, meet with a peer reviewer to evaluate each other's work and to suggest revisions. Then proofread and edit your draft for errors in spelling, grammar, and punctuation.

Performing

Group Activity With a group of classmates, prepare a reading of a section of *Song of Myself*. First decide on a portion of the poem to read. Then decide who will read each line or stanza: an individual, a pair of students, or the entire group. Also decide when a line should be read loudly or softly, quickly or slowly. Practice your lines on your own and rehearse as a group until your reading sounds fluid and natural. Perform the reading for your classmates or at a school assembly.

Literature Online Web Activities For eFlashcards, Selection Quick Checks, and other Web activities, go to www.glencoe.com.

Whitman's Language and Style

Using Specific Action Verbs Specific action verbs give the reader a clear sense of what the writer is describing. For example, consider line 73 of *Song of Myself*:

"Shoulder your duds dear son, and I will mine, and let us hasten forth."

In this line, Whitman uses the specific action verb *shoulder* to create a vivid image. A less specific verb such as *pick up* or *lift* would not have described the action as distinctly.

1. Review the chart you made for your essay on *Song of Myself*. Highlight action verbs in those details. Then replace some of the specific action verbs with more general ones. Compare the changes and note how the specific action verbs heighten the impact of the details.

2. Frequently used verbs can often be replaced by stronger, more specific ones. Write the verbs *run*, *fall*, and *see* in one column of a chart. In the other column, list two or more specific action verbs that could be used instead.

General Verbs	Specific Action Verbs
run	sprint
fall	tumble
see	notice

Activity Briefly explain how the verbs below help make the action clear and vivid.

"The spotted hawk swoops by..." (line 104)
"It flings my likeness after the rest..." (line 108)
"It coaxes me to the vapor..." (line 109)

Revising Check

Specific Action Verbs Work with a partner to review and revise the verbs in your essay on *Song of Myself*.

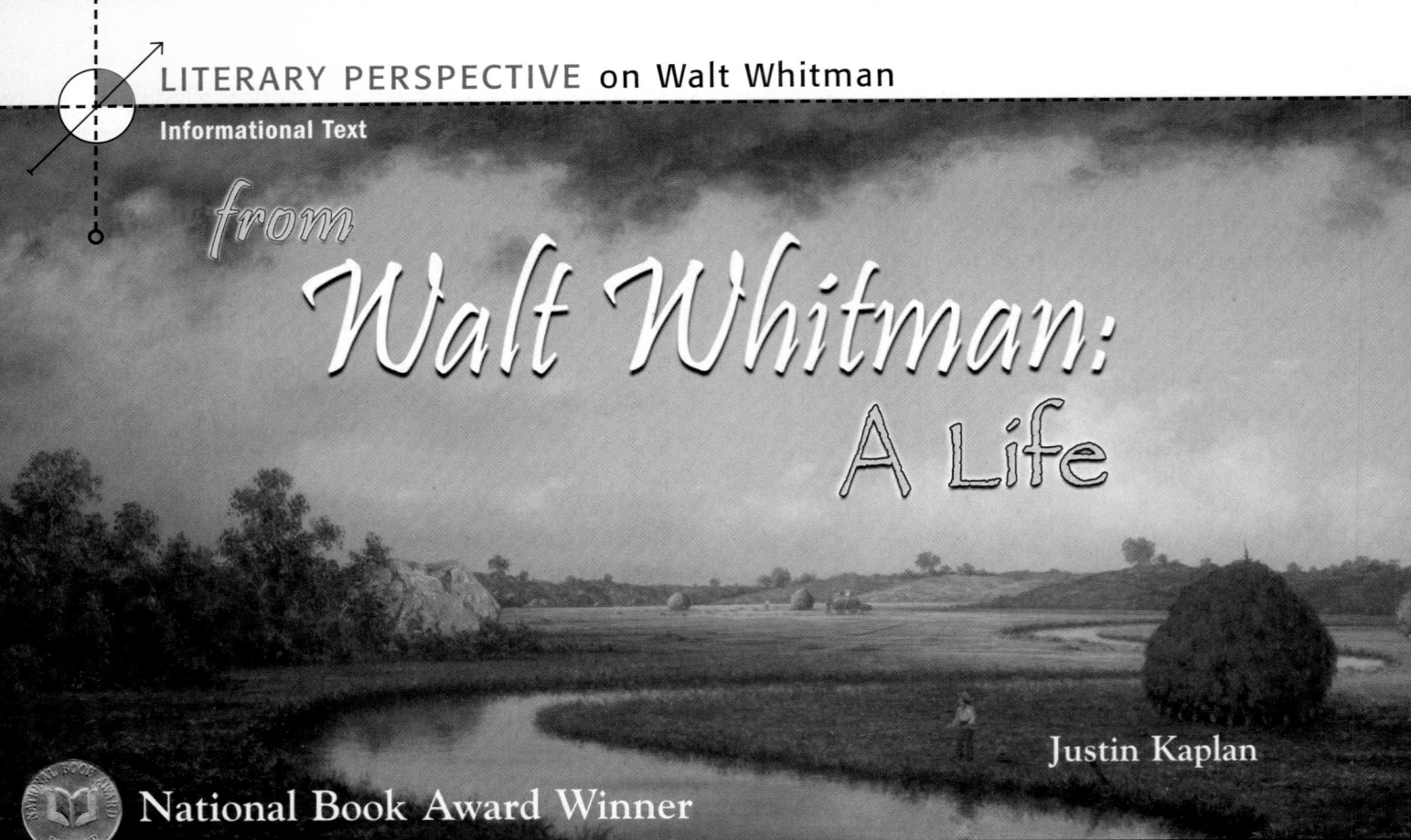

from Walt Whitman: A Life

Justin Kaplan

National Book Award Winner

Building Background

Today Walt Whitman is celebrated as one of the most original poets of the nineteenth century. When *Leaves of Grass* was first published in 1855, however, it received mixed reviews and little fanfare. Undaunted, Whitman set out to convince the public that his work was a literary sensation. In the following selection, historian and biographer Justin Kaplan describes how Whitman promoted his work and launched his career.

Set a Purpose for Reading

Read to learn about the early reviews of *Leaves of Grass* and Whitman's efforts to publicize his book.

Reading Strategy Synthesizing Information

Synthesizing is combining ideas to create something new. To synthesize information from varied sources, follow these steps:

- interpret the information
- identify similarities and differences between ideas
- combine ideas to create new knowledge

As you read this selection, take notes about Walt Whitman. Then generate new ideas about this poet by relating your notes to the information you derived from other sources in this unit.

"The beginning of a great career"

I

Do you take it I would astonish?
Does the daylight astonish? or the early red-
     start twittering through the woods?
Do I astonish more than they?

Reading these lines at his desk in Concord, in a complimentary copy sent him by an anonymous author, Emerson almost believed he had seen salvation and could depart in peace. "In raptures," as a visitor noted, Emerson pointed to a certain "oriental largeness of generalization" as evidence that an American Buddha, the long-awaited national poet, had spoken at last. "So extraordinary," he told a Boston friend, Samuel Gray Ward, "I must send it to you, & pray you to look it over." He wondered whether the author had not been "hurt by hard life & too animal experience," but still praised *Leaves of Grass* as "wonderful," "the American poem," "a nondescript monster," as he wrote to Carlyle,[1] "which yet had

---

1. Thomas *Carlyle* (1795–1881) was a British historian and
   essayist.

terrible eyes and buffalo strength." After some puzzlement over the identity and whereabouts of the new poet, Emerson composed a letter to Walter Whitman, Esq., in care of Fowler and Wells[2] in New York.

Concord Massachusetts 11 July 1855

DEAR SIR,

I am not blind to the worth of the wonderful gift of "Leaves of Grass." I find it the most extraordinary piece of wit & wisdom that America has yet contributed. I am very happy in reading it, as great power makes us happy. It meets the demand I am always making of what seemed the sterile & stingy Nature, as if too much handi-work or too much lymph[3] in the temperament were making our western wits fat & mean.

I give you joy of your free & brave thought. I have great joy in it. I find incomparable things said incompara-bly well, as they must be. I find the courage of *treatment*, which so delights us, & which large perception only can inspire.

I greet you at the beginning of a great career, which yet must have had a long foreground somewhere, for such a start. I rubbed my eyes a little to see if this sunbeam were no illusion; but the solid sense of the book is a sober certainty. It has the best merits, namely, of fortifying & encouraging.

I did not know until I, last night, saw the book advertised in a newspaper, that I could trust the name as real & available for a Post-office. I wish to see my benefactor, & have felt much like striking my tasks, & visiting New York to pay you my respects.

R. W. EMERSON

MR. WALTER WHITMAN.

> I find it the most extraordinary piece of wit & wisdom that America has yet contributed.

This five-page salute, Whitman later said, was the charter of "an emperor"—"I supposed the let-ter was meant to be blazoned." In the annals of literary partisanship and the laying-on of hands, Emerson's words are unmatched for their gener-osity and force, their shrewdness and simple jus-tice. Another insurgent scripture, *Walden*, published the summer before, had drawn only qualified praise from Emerson. Now he proclaimed the great-ness of *Leaves of Grass* to friends, casual visitors, and far-flung acquaintances. "Toward no other American, toward no contemporary excepting Carlyle, had Emerson used such strong expressions," said Moncure Conway, the young Harvard Divinity School grad-uate who was to be Emerson's first legate[4] to the new poet. "Emerson had been for many years our literary banker; paper that he had inspected, coin that had been rung on his counter, would pass safely anywhere." Stripped of its marketplace metaphors the same idea was echoed on the other side of the Atlantic by William Howitt, reviewer for the *London Weekly Dispatch*—"What Emerson has pronounced to be good must not be lightly treated." Even the *Criterion*, a high-toned New York weekly that dismissed Whitman's book as "a mass of stupid filth," had to acknowledge, apologetically, the quality of its credentials—"an unconsidered let-ter of introduction has oftentimes procured the admittance of a scurvy fellow into good society."

Emerson's letter admitted *Leaves of Grass* to a meeting of Philadelphia abolitionists where Lucretia Mott, the Quaker preacher, heard it discussed and praised. "R. W. Emerson calls it 'the book of the age,'" she wrote to her sister. "It is something Emersonian in style—a kind of unmeasured poetry in praise of America & tell-ing what true poetry is." She had no objection to the purchase of a copy for her seventeen-year-old granddaughter. The patrician[5] critic and scholar Charles Eliot Norton told his friend

---

2. *Fowler and Wells* was the publishing firm that printed the second edition of *Leaves of Grass*.
3. *Lymph* is a clear liquid that travels through the human lymphatic system, removing fat from the intestines.
4. A *legate* is an official representative.
5. Here, *patrician* means "aristocratic."

James Russell Lowell[6] that he had been alerted to the existence of this "literary curiosity" by the revered Emerson, who had apparently written a letter to the author "expressing the warmest admiration and encouragement." In his unsigned review in the September *Putnam's Monthly* Norton described *Leaves of Grass* as "preposterous yet somehow fascinating," a surprisingly harmonious fusion of "Yankee transcendentalism and New York rowdyism" that at times exhibited, in the "rough and ragged thicket of its pages," undeniable boldness and originality. Norton confessed that he had had to overcome his distaste for the book's "disgusting" and "intolerable" coarseness. "One cannot leave it about for chance readers," he told Lowell, "and would be sorry to know that any woman had looked into it past the title-page. I have got a copy for you, for there are things in it you will admire." ("No, no," Lowell replied, "the kind of thing you describe won't do.") Another member of Emerson's circle, the clergyman Edward Everett Hale, future author of *The Man Without a Country*, praised Whitman (in the January 1856 *North American Review*) for his "remarkable power," his "freshness, simplicity, and reality," and for living up to the claims made in the preface. Half a century later Hale was still congratulating himself for having written this review, the first that, in Whitman's recollection, had done his book anything close to justice.

In the summer of 1855, when he returned from his vacation on eastern Long Island, he had been greeted by a review of a different sort, prominent but grudging and even mischievous, by Charles A. Dana of the Tribune, Horace Greeley's[7] managing editor. A one-time member of the Brook Farm commune[8] who had lived on admiring terms with its founder, George Ripley, and with Margaret Fuller and Nathaniel Hawthorne, Dana had retrieved some remnants of idealism from the ruins of that experiment in plain living and high thinking. In the "nameless bard" of *Leaves of Grass* he recognized an oafish descendant of Emerson, Bronson Alcott[9], and other "prophets of the soul." He too praised Whitman's "bold, stirring thoughts," "genuine intimacy with nature," and "keen appreciation of beauty." But he argued that "the essential spirit of poetry" had found "an uncouth and grotesque embodiment." "His independence often becomes coarse and defiant. His language is too frequently reckless and indecent," Dana said, sounding the cry that Whitman was to hear to the end of his days, "and will justly prevent his volume from free circulation in scrupulous circles."

Because of such objections William Swayne, the Fulton Street bookseller listed in the original announcements in the *Tribune*, had withdrawn *Leaves of Grass* from his stock and his name from Fowler and Wells's advertisements. Even *Life Illustrated*, the firm's own "Family Newspaper," said the book was "perfect nonsense," "a series of *utterances*" that the public was advised to take or leave, "just as they prefer." Soon Samuel Wells, more of a businessman and less of a crusader than his partner Orson Fowler, suggested that Whitman omit "certain objectionable passages" or look for another publisher.

At Mickle Street[10] Whitman made an almost casual thing of it when he explained how Emerson's letter, a private and privileged

> Norton confessed that he had had to overcome his distaste for the book's "disgusting" and "intolerable" coarseness.

---

6. *James Russell Lowell* (1819–1891) was a famed American Fireside poet.
7. *Horace Greeley* (1811–1872) was an abolitionist and the founder of the *New York Tribune*.
8. The *Brook Farm commune* was an experimental utopian community in West Roxbury, Massachusetts, from 1841 to 1847.
9. *Bronson Alcott* (1799–1888) was a transcendentalist, a radical educator, and the father of novelist Louisa May Alcott.
10. *Mickle Street* in Camden, New Jersey, was the location of Whitman's house, which he purchased in 1884.

W W from life
one hot July forenoon 1855
Brooklyn N.Y.

source, views the matter from a more positive and less critical standpoint.

At first cautious and reluctant, just as his phrenological chart[11] had said, Whitman could justifiably claim to have been, up to this point, the unoffending victim of Dana's good intentions and unreliable assurances.* But once the letter was released he fell on it like a hawk—"I too am not a bit tamed." The life of his sacred book was in the balance. He sent the *Tribune* clipping to Longfellow and other celebrities, arranged to have the letter printed in *Life Illustrated,* and eventually distributed it to editors and critics in the form of a small broadside he printed up. It was headed "Copy for the convenience of private reading only" and changed Emerson's formal "Mr. Walter Whitman" to "Walt Whitman."

The letter became part of the fabric of his plans as he prepared the second edition of his book during 1855 and 1856. "Make no puns / funny remarks / Double entendres / 'witty' remarks / ironies / Sarcasms," he instructed himself in his notebook. "Only that which / is simply earnest, / meant,—harmless / to any one's feelings / —unadorned / unvarnished / nothing to / excite a / laugh / silence / silence / silence / silence / laconic[12] / taciturn,"[13] He vows to "Avoid all the 'intellectual / subtleties,' and 'withering doubts' and 'blasted hopes' and 'unrequited / loves,' and 'ennui'[14] and 'wretchedness' and the whole of the lurid and artistical and melo-dramatic / effects.—Preserve perfect calmness and sanity." He lists some of his casual acquaintances in New York—

communication, came to be published in the New York Tribune without the writer's permission or foreknowledge. He said that when he was walking down the street in New York he happened to run into Dana, who had heard about the letter along the transcendental grapevine, was eager to print it in his newspaper, and wanted Whitman to release the text to him. Whitman refused, but a week or so later changed his mind, with some justification, as "a friend of Mr. Emerson" and therefore in a responsible position to decide what was legitimate and proper for everyone concerned. He printed the letter in the *Tribune* on October 10 and prefaced it with a brief paragraph that suggested a turning-point in the public fortunes of *Leaves of Grass:*

We sometime since had occasion to call the attention of our readers to this original and striking collection of poems, by Mr. Whitman of Brooklyn. In so doing we could not avoid noticing certain faults which seemed to us to be prominent in the work. The following opinion, from a distinguished

---

11. A *phrenological chart* describes an individual's personality on the basis of the shape of his or her skull. Whitman believed in phrenology.
  * The official version of the episode, laid out by Bucke in 1883 with Whitman's approval, even denied there had been any evidence "that the letter was meant to be private." Whitman became more circumspect about such matters. In 1871, after he received a flattering letter from Tennyson, he cautioned a newspaper friend, "I rely on your promise not to publish the letter, nor any thing equivalent to it." But he had no objection to printing the news that he had received such a letter. (Richard Maurice Bucke, M.D., *Walt Whitman* [Philadelphia, 1883], p. 139.)
12. *Laconic* means "using few words."
13. *Taciturn* means "quiet."
14. *Ennui* means "weariness."

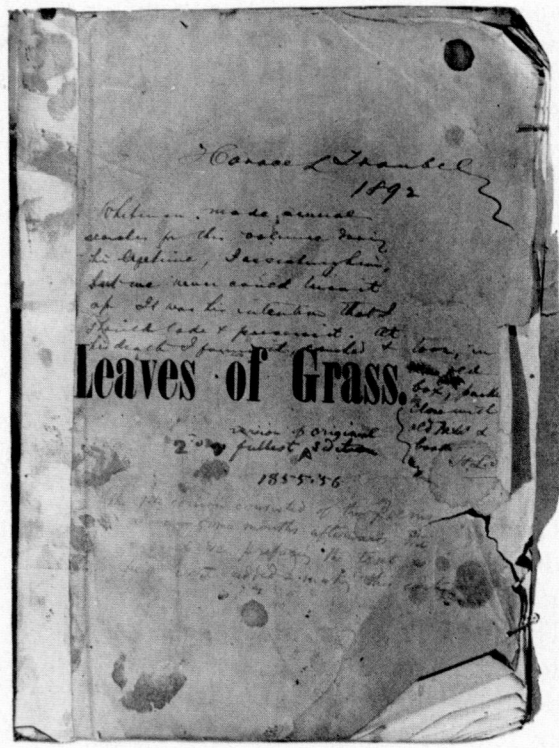

Sam (with black eyes & cap)
Nick (black eyes 40th st—small)
Joe (Canadian-Montreal)
Bill Young (milkman & driver)
George Applegate (tallest)
English Johnny (49th st Jockey cap)
Sam (49th st round shoulders light clothes)

—and also sketches out, in the pride of creation and mastery, his "Sun-Down Poem" ("Crossing Brooklyn Ferry") of 1856:

Poem of passage / the scenes on the river /
as I cross the / Fulton ferry / Others will see
the flow / of the river, also, / Others will see
on both / sides the city of / New York and
the city / of Brooklyn / a hundred years
hence others / will see them . . . The continual and hurried crowd of / men and
women crossing / The reflection of the sky /
in the water—the blinding / dazzle in a
track from / the most declined sun, / The
lighters—the sailors / in their picturesque
costumes / the nimbus[15] of light / around
the shadow of my / head in the sunset

---

15. A *nimbus* is a cloud or an atmosphere.

Further on, along with trial passages for another major new poem of 1856, "Song of the Broad-Axe," is an entry of a different sort. Enclosed within a large bracket, it occupies a page to itself:

"I greet you at the beginning of a great career"

R. W. EMERSON

Whitman made several layouts of these words on binder's paper left over from the first edition before he had them stamped in gold on the spine of the second edition around August 1856. Torn out of context, gaudily displayed, this Ali Baba[16] formula appeared to be an endorsement even of new poems Emerson could not possibly have seen. And further compounding what a Boston paper had called "the grossest violation of literary comity[17] and courtesy that ever passed under our notice," at the end of the book Whitman once again printed the entire letter along with a vaunt-ing[18] essay in the form of a public thank-you:

Brooklyn *August 1856.*

Here are thirty-two poems, which I send you, dear Friend and Master, not having found how I could satisfy myself with send-ing any usual acknowledgement of your let-ter. The first edition, on which you mailed me that till now unanswered letter, was twelve poems—I printed a thousand copies, and they readily sold; these thirty-two Poems I stereotype, to print several thousand copies of. I much enjoy making poems. Other work I have set for myself to do, to meet people and The States face to face, to confront them with an American rude tongue; but the work of my life is making poems. I keep on till I make a hundred, and then several hundred—perhaps a thousand. A few years, and the average annual call for my Poems is ten or twenty thousand—more, quite likely. Why should I hurry or compromise? . . . Master, I am a man of perfect faith.

---

16. *Ali Baba* is a woodcutter in *The Arabian Nights' Entertainments, or The Thousand and One Nights,* a collection of Asian stories. He gains access to the cave of the Forty Thieves by saying the magic phrase "open sesame."
17. *Comity* means "courteousness."
18. *Vaunting* means "boasting."

Even the loyal and resourceful Bucke,[19] utterly flummoxed[20] for once, had to admit that Whitman's "they readily sold" was "a plain lie." According to Bucke's information, the first edition had "no sale" and the second "little or no sale." "If the reader goes to a bookstore," Hale had pointed out in his review, "he may expect to be told, at first, as we were, that there is no such book, and has not been." Whitman himself said he doubted "if even ten were sold" and that he ended up giving away almost all of his first edition to "friends and relatives"—"Oh, as a money matter, the book was a dreadful failure." It was a "failure" despite the vigorous deployment of his talents as an impresario[21] with one lifelong act to manage. The lessons of P. T. Barnum's American

Museum, General Tom Thumb and the Swedish Nightingale had not been wasted on him.[22]

Whitman supplied friendly journals with the information that *Leaves of Grass* created "an extraordinary sensation in the literary world on both sides of the Atlantic"—"the emphatic commendation of America's greatest critic has been ratified by the public." And it was Whitman who wrote three anonymous reviews of *Leaves of Grass* that appeared around the end of 1855. "An American bard at last!" he announced in the *United States Review*. "Politeness this man has none, and regulation he has none. A rude child of the people!—No imitation—No foreigner—but a growth and idiom of America," he wrote in the Brooklyn *Daily Times*, and in sup-

---

19. Richard Maurice *Bucke* was a longtime friend and the first biographer of Whitman.
20. *Flummoxed* means "confused."
21. An *impresario* is a theatrical manager or producer.

22. *P. T. Barnum* (1810–1891) was an American showman who helped popularize the three-ring circus. His *American Museum* in New York City displayed curiosities. Charles S. Stratton, named *General Tom Thumb* by Barnum, was a 25-inch-tall performer. Jenny Lind, a Swedish soprano, was promoted by Barnum as the *Swedish Nightingale*.

port of these and similar claims he subjoined Lorenzo Fowler's[23] reading of the bard's skull and personality. In the *American Phrenological Journal*, a Fowler and Wells enterprise, he cited Tennyson's poetry with admiring tolerance but predicted his own, riding the wave of the future, might yet prove "the most glorious of triumphs, in the known history of literature."

Skillfully managed, Whitman's homemade appreciations made news in their own right. A friendly journalist, William Swinton, praised him in the New York *Times* for the "manly vigor" and "brawny health" of *Leaves of Grass*. "This man has brave stuff in him. He is truly astonishing." In the course of several thousand words of careful and sensitive discussion, Swinton reported that "proof slips of certain articles written about *Leaves of Grass*" had been delivered to the *Times* office together with a copy of the first edition

bound in green and gold and the printed text of a letter in which Ralph Waldo Emerson complimented the author "on the benefaction conferred on society":

> On subsequently comparing the critiques from the *United States Review* and the *Phrenological Journal* with the Preface of *Leaves of Grass* we discovered unmistakable evidence that Mr. Walt Whitman, true to the character of a Kosmos, was not content with writing a book, but was also determined to review it, so Mr. Walt Whitman has concocted both those criticisms of his own work, treating it we need not say how favorably.

Sensation generated sensation, Whitman had learned. So did neglect, if it was conspicuous enough. Later he tended to favor a history in which *Leaves of Grass*, far from "an extraordinary sensation," had been greeted in total silence or with howls of derision. ❧

---

23. **Lorenzo Fowler** was a phrenologist and the founder of Fowler and Wells, a publishing house.

RESPONDING AND THINKING CRITICALLY

Respond

1. How did you react to Kaplan's perspective on Walt Whitman?

Recall and Interpret

2. (a)How did Emerson respond to Whitman's *Leaves of Grass?* (b)Why do you think Emerson responded this way?

3. (a)What did Whitman do with the letter that Emerson had sent him? (b)What do Whitman's actions reveal about his motives?

Analyze and Evaluate

4. Did Whitman do the right thing in writing his own reviews of *Leaves of Grass?* Explain.

5. Which of the early comments on *Leaves of Grass* do you think sheds the most light on Whitman's work?

6. (a)Why does Kaplan compare Whitman to the showman P. T. Barnum? (b)Is Kaplan's comparison fair or not? Support your answer.

Connect

7. How would you compare the speaker in *Leaves of Grass* with Whitman himself, as depicted in Kaplan's perspective?

INDIANA ACADEMIC STANDARDS (pages 416–422)
11.3 [Make] connections across texts...

11.2.4 Make reasonable assertions about an author's arguments by using elements of the text to defend and clarify interpretations.

Dickinson's Poetry

MEET EMILY DICKINSON

Virtually unknown during her lifetime, Emily Dickinson now stands as a giant of American literature. Her stark, concise poems speak in an instantly recognizable voice, reflecting a sense of style as individual as a fingerprint. In spare, chiseled verses, Dickinson upended convention, posing the great questions of life in the form of riddles for the reader.

"I conclude that space and time are things of the body and have little or nothing to do with ourselves. My Country is Truth . . . I like Truth—it is a free Democracy."

—*Emily Dickinson*

Formative Years Dickinson was born into a distinguished and prosperous family in Amherst, Massachusetts. Her father was a lawyer who served in Congress. Though stern, he was a kind man whose integrity deeply influenced Dickinson.

At Amherst Academy and Mount Holyoke Female Seminary, Dickinson was a serious student with a mischievous streak. As the daughter of an intensely religious family, she was pressured to become an outspoken Christian. Despite her reverence for the Bible, she refused. She entertained strong religious feelings and equally strong doubts all her life, sharing her thoughts on the matter only with a few close friends.

In her late teens and twenties, Dickinson read authors considered by her parents to be shockingly secular: William Shakespeare, Ralph Waldo Emerson, George Eliot, and Charlotte and Emily Brontë. She also formed friendships with lawyers and ministers whose intelligence attracted her. In

her late twenties or early thirties, Dickinson seems to have experienced a devastating emotional setback, related perhaps to a disappointment in love. She began to spend a great deal of time in solitude in her family's Amherst home. Dickinson seemed fully absorbed in this solitary existence, remarking to a friend, "I find ecstasy in living—the mere sense of living is joy enough."

Greatness Achieved Dickinson seems to have dreamed of public acclaim, but she gave up these dreams when her friend Thomas Wentworth Higginson, editor of the *Atlantic Monthly,* urged her not to publish. Dickinson, while ceasing attempts to publish, continued to write as she pleased. She preferred obscurity to the sacrifice of originality.

After Dickinson's death from kidney failure, her sister Lavinia published the poems, but in altered form. Dashes were eliminated, capitalizations were undone, and some words were completely changed. In 1955, scholar Thomas H. Johnson began to publish the poems as Dickinson had written them. Dickinson has come to be recognized for what she was: a great American nonconformist and poet of rare purity.

Emily Dickinson was born in 1830 and died in 1886.

Literature Online **Author Search** For more about Emily Dickinson, go to www.glencoe.com.

Connecting to the Poems

Dickinson's poetry explores the complexity of the human soul. As you read, think about the following questions:

- What does it feel like to experience loss and longing?
- What is success? What is wisdom?

Building Background

Much of Dickinson's poetry features the use of dashes. They serve as interrupters and signal pauses while also calling attention to the words they enclose. Dashes may break off a line or thought suddenly; they may call attention to a shift in meaning or action; they may interrupt the rhythm; or they may draw attention to the moment of silence they create in oral readings of the poems.

Dickinson was also innovative in her use of capitalization. Throughout her poetry she capitalized many common nouns, thereby calling attention to them and emphasizing their importance.

In a further innovation, Dickinson rejected the then-dominant iambic pentameter, choosing instead to write in the meter of Protestant hymns. The alternating six- and eight-syllable lines in many of her poems echo the rhythm found in the songs of the great hymn composer Isaac Watts.

Setting Purposes for Reading

Big Idea A Poetic Revolution

As you read, notice the way Dickinson experiments with rhyme, rhythm, and punctuation to create a new poetic style.

Literary Element Rhyme

A **full rhyme** is the repetition of the same stressed vowel sounds and any succeeding sounds in two or more words. For example, *notation* rhymes with *vacation*. **Slant rhyme** occurs when the rhyme of two words depends on sounds that are similar but not identical. For instance, Dickinson rhymes *today* with *victory*. As you read, notice how the use of slant rhymes helps add tension and interest to the poems.

- See Literary Terms Handbook, p. R15.

Reading Strategy Analyzing Sound Devices

Sound devices are techniques that appeal to the ear. Poets use sound devices to create a sense of rhythm, emphasize particular sounds, or add to the musical quality of writing. Rhyme is one sound device. Others include **alliteration** (repeated consonant sounds at the beginnings of words), **assonance** (repeated vowel sounds), and **consonance** (repeated consonant sounds in the middle or at the ends of words). As you read, notice the rhythms and changes in emphasis that sound devices create.

Reading Tip: Close Reading To analyze sound devices, first read closely for specific examples.

Vocabulary

heave (hēv) *n.* an upward motion, or an effort to raise; p. 431 *The heave of the waves caused our boat to tip over.*

interpose (in´ tər pōz´) *v.* to intrude, intervene, or to put oneself between; p. 431 *My three-year-old brother tries to interpose himself between us when we talk.*

cathedral (kə thē´ drəl) *n.* a church that is the official seat of a bishop; p. 436 *We viewed photographs of the lovely cathedral of Notre Dame.*

imperial (im pēr´ ē əl) *adj.* of or relating to an empire or emperor; p. 436 *In A.D. 200, imperial Rome stretched across several continents.*

affliction (ə flik´ shən) *n.* great suffering, distress, or its cause; p. 436 *Reeling from the epidemic of tuberculosis, the country took years to recover from the affliction.*

Literature Online Interactive Literary Elements Handbook To review or learn more about the literary elements, go to www.glencoe.com.

INDIANA ACADEMIC STANDARDS (pages 424–427)
11.3.4 Analyze ways in which poetry...uses...sounds...
11.3.3 Analyze the ways in which...the "sound" of language achieve[s] specific...aesthetic (artistic) purposes...

11.5.2 Write responses to literature...

424 UNIT 3 THE CIVIL WAR ERA

If you were coming in the Fall

Emily Dickinson

If you were coming in the Fall,
I'd brush the Summer by
With half a smile, and half a spurn,
As Housewives do, a Fly.

5   If I could see you in a year,
I'd wind the months in balls—
And put them each in separate Drawers,
For fear the numbers fuse—

If only Centuries, delayed,
10 I'd count them on my Hand,
Subtracting, till my fingers dropped
Into Van Dieman's Land.[1]

If certain, when this life was out—
That yours and mine, should be
15 I'd toss it yonder, like a Rind,
And take Eternity—

But, now, uncertain of the length
Of this, that is between,
It goads me, like the Goblin Bee—
20 That will not state—its sting.

---

1. *Van Dieman's Land* is the former name for Tasmania, an
island that is part of Australia.

Literary Element   Rhyme *What is the rhyme scheme of
this stanza?*

My life closed twice before its close

Emily Dickinson

My life closed twice before its close—
It yet remains to see
If Immortality unveil
A third event to me

5 So huge, so hopeless to conceive
As these that twice befell.
Parting is all we know of heaven,
And all we need of hell.

Big Idea A Poetic Revolution *Why did events not described in the poem prompt the speaker to express these feelings in lines 7 and 8?*

The Soul selects her own Society

Emily Dickinson

The Soul selects her own Society—
Then—shuts the Door—
To her divine Majority—
Present no more—

5 Unmoved—she notes the Chariots—pausing—
At her low Gate—
Unmoved—an Emperor be kneeling
Upon her Mat—

I've known her—from an ample nation—
10 Choose One—
Then—close the Valves of her attention—
Like Stone—

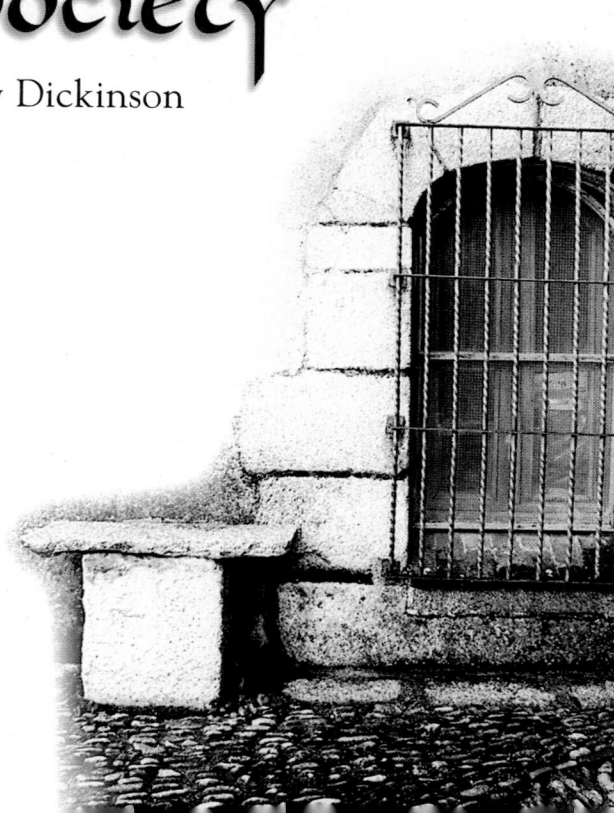

Reading Strategy Analyzing Sound Devices *How does the length of lines 10 and 12 reinforce the meaning of the stanza?*

RESPONDING AND THINKING CRITICALLY

Respond

1. Which of these poems most closely reflects your own experiences or feelings? Explain.

If you were coming in the Fall
Recall and Interpret

2. (a)What periods of time does the speaker describe in each of the first four stanzas? (b)Describe the actions the speaker imagines taking in each of these stanzas.

Analyze and Evaluate

3. How effective is the simile in the last verse of the poem at conveying suspense? Explain.

My life closed twice before its close
Recall and Interpret

4. (a)How does the speaker define parting? (b)How, in your opinion, do partings affect the speaker?

Analyze and Evaluate

5. How do the dash and the capitalization of "Immortality" affect the meaning of the poem? Explain.

The Soul selects her own Society
Recall and Interpret

6. (a)In your own words, explain what the soul selects. (b)From how many does the soul choose just one? Tell what you think this suggests about the soul.

Analyze and Evaluate

7. The last verse includes a **metaphor** describing the soul closing "the Valves of her attention." In your opinion, is this verse a fitting end given the content of the previous stanzas? Explain why or why not.

LITERARY ANALYSIS

Literary Element Rhyme

Slant rhyme refers to the words at the ends of lines of poetry that almost—but don't quite—rhyme. Dickinson makes repeated use of slant rhymes in her poems. The words rhymed can be connected by as little as two letters that sometimes rhyme, as in the rhyme of "be" and "fly." When you come across slant rhyme, you may notice that it heightens tension or the element of surprise.

1. Review "The Soul selects her own Society" and identify the example of slant rhyme in the second stanza.

2. In the last stanza, notice the contrast between the soft *o* sound of "One" and the longer, heavier *o* sound of "Stone." How does this final slant rhyme help reinforce the meaning of the poem?

Literature Online **Web Activities** For eFlashcards, Selection Quick Checks, and other Web activities, go to www.glencoe.com.

READING AND VOCABULARY

Reading Strategy Analyzing Sound Devices

In a poem, **sound devices** create rhythm, highlight particular words and sounds, and add to the musical quality of writing. The sound of a poem and the poem's meaning are closely linked, even inseparable. A poem's rhyming quality may help to make it memorable, while **alliteration** (repeated consonant sounds at the beginnings of words) may heighten the mood, or feeling, of a poem.

1. Look for and record examples of **internal rhyme** (rhyme that occurs within a single line of poetry) and **assonance** (repeated vowel sounds) in the last stanza of "If you were coming in the Fall." How do these techniques contribute to the poem's meaning?

2. (a)What words does the use of alliteration draw attention to in "My life closed twice before its close"? (b)Why are these words emphasized?

Much Madness is divinest Sense

Emily Dickinson

Woman Sitting in Darkness, Kari Van Tine.

Much Madness is divinest Sense—
To a discerning Eye—
Much Sense—the starkest Madness—
'Tis the Majority
5 In this, as All, prevail—
Assent—and you are sane—
Demur[1]—you're straightway dangerous—
And handled with a Chain—

---

1. *Demur* means "to hesitate" or "to protest."

Reading Strategy   Analyzing Sound Devices *What is the effect of the repeated consonant sounds in* assent *and* sane? *In* demur *and* dangerous?

Success is counted sweetest

Emily Dickinson

Success is counted sweetest
By those who ne'er succeed.
To comprehend a nectar[1]
Requires sorest need.

5 Not one of all the purple Host[2]
Who took the Flag today
Can tell the definition
So clear of Victory

As he defeated—dying—
10 On whose forbidden ear
The distant strains of triumph
Burst agonized and clear!

---

1. *Nectar* is a sweet liquid secreted by plants and used by bees in the making of honey. In Greek mythology, nectar is the drink of the gods that makes all who drink it immortal.
2. *Purple Host* means "winning army."

Big Idea A Poetic Revolution *Why does the poet enclose the word* dying *in dashes in line 9?*

Taps, c. 1907–1909. William Gilbert Gaul. Oil on canvas, 32¾ x 43 in. The Birmingham Museum of Art, Birmingham, AL.
Viewing the Painting How does this painting enhance your understanding of Dickinson's message in this poem?

RESPONDING AND THINKING CRITICALLY

Respond

1. Were you surprised by Dickinson's ideas about madness and success? Explain why or why not.

Much Madness is divinest Sense
Recall and Interpret

2. (a)According to the speaker, in lines 1–3, with what is sense often confused? (b)Who does the speaker say knows the difference?

3. (a)How is a person who disagrees with accepted ideas regarded? (b)What does the last word of the poem suggest about what happens to such a person?

Analyze and Evaluate

4. How would you describe the poet's attitude toward the popular concept of sanity?

Success is counted sweetest
Recall and Interpret

5. (a)What example of success is given in the second stanza? (b)In the third stanza, why do you think the poem calls the "defeated" one's perception of victory "agonized" and "clear"?

Analyze and Evaluate

6. (a)How is the observation about soldiers and armies in stanzas two and three related to lines 1–2? (b)Why, in your opinion, did Dickinson choose to use war **imagery** in a poem about success? Explain what this choice might suggest about Dickinson's views of the world or of personal fulfillment.

7. (a)What paradox lies at the heart of this poem? (b)Do you agree with the observation about success and human nature in the poem?

LITERARY ANALYSIS

Literary Element Rhyme

Dickinson tended to write in **axioms,** or sayings meant to express a truth. Her use of rhythm and rhyme makes these axioms easy to remember.

(a)In your opinion, which lines or verses in these poems are made especially memorable by rhyme? (b)Explain the importance of these lines and verses for the poem in which they are included.

Writing About Literature

Evaluate Contemporary Relevance Choose one of the poems and write a brief essay discussing whether the message it expresses is relevant to people today. Begin by putting the **theme** into your own words and telling what details in the poem support the theme. Then explain why the message she expresses had special relevance for her or people in her time. Finally, evaluate whether you think the message is true for your own day and time.

Literature Online **Web Activities** For eFlashcards, Selection Quick Checks, and other Web activities, go to www.glencoe.com.

READING AND VOCABULARY

Reading Strategy Analyzing Sound Devices

Meter is the pattern of stressed (´) and unstressed (˘) syllables that gives a line of poetry a more or less predictable **rhythm.** The basic unit of meter is a group of syllables known as the **foot.** In most of Dickinson's poems, every line is iambic (beginning with an unstressed syllable followed by a stressed one) and contains either three or four feet. Lines of four feet generally alternate with lines of three feet, as in the example below:

Much Mádness is divínest Sénse—

To a discérning Éye—

Write "Much Madness is divinest Sense" and mark the pattern of stressed and unstressed syllables for the whole poem. Is the pattern that Dickinson follows regular, that is, always predictable, or does the pattern occasionally deviate to become irregular? Explain how you think the rhythm affects the meaning of the poem. Does it lend a musical quality? Does it help to emphasize certain words or ideas?

I heard a Fly buzz when I died

Emily Dickinson

Caroline Auf Der Treppe. Caroline On the Stairs, 1825.
Caspar David Friedrich. Oil on canvas, 29 x 20.3 in.
Private collection.

I heard a Fly buzz—when I died—
The Stillness in the Room
Was like the Stillness in the Air—
Between the **Heaves** of Storm—

5   The Eyes around—had wrung them dry—
And Breaths were gathering firm
For that last Onset—when the King
Be witnessed—in the Room—

I willed my Keepsakes—Signed away
10   What portion of me be
Assignable—and then it was
There **interposed** a Fly—

With Blue—uncertain stumbling Buzz—
Between the light—and me—
15   And then the Windows failed—and then
I could not see to see—

Literary Element   Rhyme *How is the rhyme scheme in the final stanza different from the rhyme scheme of earlier stanzas?*

Vocabulary

heave (hēv) *n.* an upward motion, or an effort to raise
interpose (in´tər pōz´) *v.* to intrude, intervene, or to put oneself between

The Bustle in a House

Emily Dickinson

Interior, Morning. Patrick William Adam. Oldham Art Gallery, Lancashire, UK.

The Bustle in a House
The Morning after Death
Is solemnest of industries
Enacted upon Earth—

5   The Sweeping up the Heart
And putting Love away
We shall not want to use again
Until Eternity.

Reading Strategy Analyzing Sound Devices *How does line length function in this poem?*

RESPONDING AND THINKING CRITICALLY

Respond

1. Which images in these poems did you find especially striking? Why?

I heard a Fly buzz when I died
Recall and Interpret

2. In the first stanza of "I heard a Fly buzz when I died," to what is the atmosphere in the room compared?

3. (a)In lines 5 and 6, what are the "Eyes" and "Breaths" doing? (b)What do they await? Explain.

4. Summarize the last two stanzas. Explain what impression of death you received from these lines.

Analyze and Evaluate

5. (a)Why do you think the speaker calls his or her belongings "Keepsakes"? (b)What other words or phrases in the poem seem to indicate an implied truth about life, death, or the human soul?

6. How does Dickinson's account of someone dying compare with other representations of death?

The Bustle in a House
Recall and Interpret

7. (a)What words does the speaker use that suggest everyday household chores? (b)To what type of chores is Dickinson really referring?

8. (a)According to the second stanza, when will we again "use" the love we put aside on the morning after death? (b)What might this suggest about Dickinson's religious faith? Explain.

Analyze and Evaluate

9. (a)What **analogy** does the speaker make in this poem? (b)What does this analogy suggest about human reactions and needs after a death? Explain whether you found this analogy effective.

LITERARY ANALYSIS

Literary Element Rhyme

The sounds and images of a poem work together to create meaning. The jarring effect of a slant **rhyme** can underscore a word's importance.

1. In "The Bustle in a House," which words does Dickinson draw attention to through slant rhyme?

2. The poem contrasts the mundane with the elevated and abstract. Explain why Dickinson's use of slant rhyme reinforces this dual aspect of the poem.

Listening and Speaking

With a partner, take turns reading aloud this pair of poems. Vary the rhythm by emphasizing different words or pauses. Then discuss how hearing the poems read in different rhythms might affect your interpretations of them.

READING AND VOCABULARY

Reading Strategy Analyzing Sound Devices

Assonance is the repetition of similar vowel sounds, as in this example:

The Soul selects her own Society—

Consonance is the repetition of similar consonant sounds, typically within or at the ends of words.

Much Madness is divinest Sense—
To a discerning Eye—

Find examples of assonance and consonance in "The Bustle in a House." To do this, you may wish to copy the poem, using different colored pens to mark examples of the two devices. In your opinion, what does the poem gain from the use of consonance and assonance?

Literature Online **Web Activities** For eFlashcards, Selection Quick Checks, and other Web activities, go to www.glencoe.com.

Literary Element Personification

Personification is a figure of speech in which an animal, an object, a force of nature, or an idea is given human characteristics. The following poem personifies death to memorable—and creepy—effect. As you read, notice specific ways in which Death resembles a person.

Reading Strategy Clarifying Meaning

When you **clarify meaning,** you reread difficult sections of a text in order to clear up what is confusing. As you read the poem, go back and reread confusing sections more slowly. This will help you notice ideas you may have previously missed.

Because I could not stop for Death

Emily Dickinson

Because I could not stop for Death—
He kindly stopped for me—
The Carriage held but just Ourselves—
And Immortality.

5   We slowly drove—He knew no haste
And I had put away
My labor and my leisure too,
For His Civility[1]—

We passed the School, where Children strove
10   At Recess—in the Ring—
We passed the Fields of Gazing Grain—
We passed the Setting Sun—

Or rather—He passed Us—
The Dews drew quivering and chill—
15   For only Gossamer,[2] my Gown—
My Tippet[3]—only Tulle[4]—

We paused before a House that seemed
A Swelling of the Ground—
The Roof was scarcely visible—
20   The Cornice[5]—in the Ground—

Since then—'tis Centuries—and yet
Feels shorter than the Day
I first surmised the Horses' Heads
Were toward Eternity—

---

1. An old meaning of *civility* is "a community of citizens." Among the more modern meanings is "courtesy." Dickinson could have had either or both meanings in mind.
2. *Gossamer* is a light gauzelike fabric.
3. A *tippet* is a scarf for the neck and shoulders with loose ends that hang down in front.
4. *Tulle* is fine netting used in making scarves and veils.
5. A *cornice* is the projecting, decorative molding along the top of a building.

Literary Element Personification *How does the personification of the sun (he) introduce a shift in the poem?*

RESPONDING AND THINKING CRITICALLY

Respond

1. What were your first reactions upon reading this poem? Explain.

Recall and Interpret

2. (a)According to lines 1–2, why does "Death" stop for the speaker? Explain what these lines suggest about human behavior. (b)According to lines 3–4, what does "Death's" carriage hold?

3. (a)What places and things does the speaker pass in the third stanza? (b)What might these places and things represent?

4. What is the "House" in the ground described in the fifth stanza? Explain how you know.

5. (a)According to the sixth stanza, how much time has passed since the day of "Death's" visit? (b)Why did that day seem so long to the speaker? Support your answer with details from the poem.

Analyze and Evaluate

6. Reread lines 9–16. (a)How does the poem shift at line 13? (b)What effect is created by this? Explain your answer.

7. (a)How would you describe the **mood**, or emotional quality and atmosphere, of this poem? (b)Which **images** or details help to create this mood? Explain.

8. One critic says that in this poem, the question of death is presented "without making any final statement about it. There is no solution to the problem . . . the idea of immortality is confronted with the fact of physical disintegration. We are not told what to think; we are told to look at the situation." Do you agree? Explain why or why not.

9. This poem is one of Dickinson's most famous. Describe the elements of the poem that you think contribute the most to its effectiveness. Explain.

LITERARY ANALYSIS

Literary Element Personification

Dickinson uses **personification** when she portrays death as a gentlemanly carriage driver with human characteristics.

1. (a)What other object or idea is personified? (b)What is the effect of this personification? Explain.

2. Why do you think Dickinson chooses to portray death as she does? Use details from the poem to support your answer.

Literature Groups

Analyze Images Dickinson uses images of everyday objects and events to evoke the experience of dying. With your group, evaluate these images. Which images do you consider especially creative or striking? What is their overall effect in the poem? Support your opinions.

READING AND VOCABULARY

Reading Strategy Clarifying Meaning

When you **clarify meaning**, you take another look at difficult sections of a text in order to figure out the meaning of anything you do not understand. Rereading can help you notice important ideas you may have missed.

1. What is the relationship between the "Horses" in the last stanza and "Death"? To clarify, reread the poem.

2. What other points in the poem were clarified for you by rereading? Explain.

Literature Online **Web Activities** For eFlashcards, Selection Quick Checks, and other Web activities, go to www.glencoe.com.

There's a certain Slant of light

Emily Dickinson

There's a certain Slant of light,
Winter Afternoons—
That oppresses, like the Heft[1]
Of **Cathedral** Tunes—

5   Heavenly Hurt, it gives us—
We can find no scar,
But internal difference,
Where the Meanings, are—

None may teach it—Any—
10   'Tis the Seal[2] Despair—
An **imperial affliction**
Sent us of the Air—

When it comes, the Landscape listens—
Shadows—hold their breath—
15   When it goes, 'tis like the Distance
On the look of Death—

---

1. Here, *heft* means "heaviness."
2. Here, *seal* means "emblem."

Literary Element   Rhyme *Where are the slant rhymes in the last stanza?*

Vocabulary

cathedral (ke thē′drəl) *n.* a church that is the official seat of a bishop

imperial (im pēr′ ē əl) *adj.* of or relating to an empire or emperor

affliction (ə flik′shən) *n.* great suffering, distress, or its cause

A Woman Sewing in an Interior, 1901. Vihelm Hammershoi. Oil on canvas, 28 ¹⁵/₁₆ x 27 ¹⁵/₁₆ in. Detroit Institute of Arts. Founders Society Purchase, Robert H. Tannahill Foundation Fund.

This is my letter to the World

Emily Dickinson

At The Window, 1870. Karl Harald Alfred Broge. Oil on canvas, 21 x 17¼ in. Private Collection.

This is my letter to the World
That never wrote to Me—
The simple News that Nature told—
With tender Majesty

5   Her Message is committed[1]
To Hands I cannot see—
For love of Her—Sweet—countrymen—
Judge tenderly—of Me

---

1. *Committed* means "entrusted."

Big Idea   A Poetic Revolution   *Why does the poet capitalize majesty in line 4?*

RESPONDING AND THINKING CRITICALLY

Respond

1. What did you most like about these poems? Explain.

There's a certain Slant of light
Recall and Interpret

2. (a)What does the slant of light give us, according to the speaker? (b)Describe the **mood**, or feeling, that the slant of light brings.

3. (a)When does the speaker observe the slant of light? (b)Why is this significant? Explain.

4. What does the light seem to represent to the speaker? Explain how lines 15–16 reinforce this.

Analyze and Evaluate

5. (a)What feelings does Dickinson evoke with her descriptions of a "Heavenly Hurt" and "the Seal Despair"? (b)Does Dickinson bring out these feelings effectively?

This is my letter to the World
Recall and Interpret

6. (a)To whom is the letter addressed? (b)What might the speaker be referring to with the words "my letter"?

7. (a)What "News" does the letter contain? (b)What is the speaker's relationship to nature?

8. What plea does the speaker make in the second stanza?

Analyze and Evaluate

9. What does the fact that the world never wrote back suggest about the speaker?

Connect

10. **Big Idea** **A Poetic Revolution** Dickinson's poems transform simple, everyday experiences into the meaningful and universal. How do the poems you read accomplish this?

YOU'RE THE CRITIC: Point/Counterpoint

WHAT IS DICKINSON'S TRUE WORTH?

Along with Walt Whitman, Emily Dickinson is praised for her revolutionary effect on American poetry. Using the themes and language closest to her, she invented a style that reflects both uniquely American attitudes and her own inner nature.

Read the following two excerpts of literary criticism. Poet William Carlos Williams thought of Dickinson as his "patron saint." Critic Helen Vendler found both strengths and shortcomings in her poetry. As you read the two quotes, notice that they emphasize different qualities of Dickinson's work.

"She was an independent spirit. She did her best to get away from too strict an interpretation. . . . And she followed the American idiom . . . .She speaks the spoken language, the idiom, which would be deformed by Oxford English. . . . She was a real good guy."

—William Carlos Williams

"Emily Dickinson cuts things off very short, and that always seems to me rather shocking. She ends poems too soon for me."

—Helen Vendler

Group Activity

Discuss the following questions with your classmates. Refer to the two quotes and cite evidence from Dickinson's poems for support.

- Which aspects of Dickinson's poetry are praised by Williams? Which aspects are criticized by Vendler?

- Which of the critical assessments do you agree with more? Explain.

Literary Element Rhyme

Through the skillful manipulation of **rhyme**, poets can achieve subtle emotional effects. Aware that readers have a tendency to expect perfect, or full, rhymes as they read, poets may decide to delay the expression of a full rhyme in order to create tension. When the full rhyme arrives later than expected, the overall effect may be to provide satisfaction and to emphasize a certain meaning.

1. How is the strategy described above illustrated in "This is my letter to the World"?

2. What effect does **internal rhyme**, or rhyme that occurs within a line of poetry, have on the poem?

Review: Personification

Personification is a figure of speech in which an animal, an object, a force of nature, or an idea is given human characteristics.

Partner Activity With a partner, examine "There's a certain Slant of light" and "This is my letter to the World." Working with your partner, create two web diagrams like the one below, and fill them in with examples of personification from each poem. Then discuss which examples you found most memorable or effective. Also discuss why Dickinson uses personification as she does.

Reading Strategy Analyzing Sound Devices

Alliteration refers to the repetition of similar consonant sounds at the beginnings of words. For example, in "There's a certain Slant of light," alliteration occurs in the first line with the repetition of the *s* sound in "certain" and "Slant." Alliteration can heighten the musicality of a poem. It can also be used to emphasize certain words or ideas.

1. List three other instances of alliteration in "There's a certain Slant of light." What, in your opinion, is the effect of each of these instances on the sound and meaning of the poem? Explain your answer.

2. Notice the repetition of the *m* sound in "This is my letter to the World." List the words that begin with *m*. What effect might Dickinson have intended to create with this repetition? Support your answer.

Vocabulary Practice

Practice with Context Clues Tell what each boldfaced word means based on its context.

1. She had never been to a large city church until she visited St. Patrick's **Cathedral** in New York.
2. Ben always claimed to be suffering from some grave **affliction** or incurable disease.
3. The officer had an almost **imperial** authority; his orders were obeyed without question.

Academic Vocabulary

Here are two words from the vocabulary list on page R86. These words will help you think, write, and talk about the selection.

stress (stres) *v.* to accent or emphasize

contrast (kən trast′) *v.* to compare in respect to differences

Practice and Apply

1. What role does the **stress** of a syllable play in creating meter in a stanza of poetry?
2. In her poems, how does Dickinson **contrast** her inner world with the world outside?

Writing About Literature

Compare and Contrast Theme In her poetry, Dickinson presents various ideas about human nature. Choose two poems that convey a similar **theme,** or message. Write down details in each poem that give you insights into the message about human nature that the poem seeks to convey. Then write a brief essay comparing and contrasting each poem's **theme.** Answer these questions: What message about human nature does each poem convey? How are the two messages similar and different? Which details in the poems help to convey these messages? End with a general conclusion about Dickinson's portrayal of human nature. Be specific in supporting your ideas.

Before you start writing, create a chart like the one below for each poem. List key details on the left. On the right, tell what the details help you infer about the poem's message. At the bottom of your chart, summarize the poem's overall message. Use this chart to help you create your first draft.

Details	Poem's Message

The poem's theme is _____.

After you complete your draft, meet with a peer reviewer to evaluate each other's work and to suggest revisions. Then proofread and edit your draft for errors in spelling, grammar, and punctuation.

Internet Connection

Visit Emily Dickinson Online The life of this very private poet has become very public on the Internet. Conduct a search to find Web sites devoted to Dickinson's life and poetry. Visit one site and present a short review of it to your classmates. Include the address, the options at the site, and aspects of the site that make visiting it either a worthwhile or a time-wasting experience.

Dickinson's Language and Style

Examining Pronouns Emily Dickinson uses pronouns to achieve a concise style. A **pronoun** is a word that takes the place of a noun, a group of words acting as a noun, or another pronoun. The word or group of words that a pronoun refers to is called its **antecedent.** Using pronouns in place of nouns allows you to avoid repetition in your writing.

Personal pronouns are pronouns that refer to a specific person or thing. Personal pronouns have three cases: nominative, possessive, and objective. The case depends on the function of the pronoun. See the chart below for the case forms of personal pronouns.

Case	Singular Pronouns	Plural Pronouns
Nominative	I, you, she, he, it	we, you, they
Objective	me, you, her, him, it	us, you, them
Possessive	my, mine, your, his, yours, her, hers, its	our, ours, your, yours, their, theirs

Activity Briefly explain how the use of pronouns in the examples below helps make the writing concise.

If I could see you in a year,
I'd wind the months in balls—
And put them each in separate Drawers,
For fear the numbers fuse—

from "If you were coming in the Fall"

Revising Check

Pronouns Pronouns and personal pronouns are important to consider when revising your own writing. With a partner, read through your essay or theme and review the pronouns and personal pronouns to make sure they correspond with the proper antecedents.

Literature Online **Web Activities** For eFlashcards, Selection Quick Checks, and other Web activities, go to www.glencoe.com.

Emily Dickinson: An Introduction

Billy Collins

Poet Laureate 2001–2003

Building Background

Known for his witty, accessible poetry, Billy Collins served as the nation's poet laureate from 2001 to 2003. In the following passage from his introduction to *The Selected Poems of Emily Dickinson,* Collins discusses the myth that surrounds Emily Dickinson's life, the enduring power of her work, and the tools that she used in crafting her poems.

Set a Purpose for Reading

Read to learn more about Dickinson's life, her poems, and a critic's interpretation of each.

Reading Strategy

Analyzing Literary Criticism

Analyzing literary criticism involves recognizing the main ideas and supporting details in a piece of criticism in order to compare the critic's response to a piece of literature with your response. As you read, take notes on Collins's literary criticism. Use a two-column chart like the one below.

Critic's Response	My Response
zigzag logic in poems	

Today Emily Dickinson is recognized not only as a major poet of the American nineteenth century but also as one of the most intriguing poets of any place or time, in both her art and her life. The outline of her biography is well known. She was born in Amherst, Massachusetts, in 1830 and, except for a few excursions to Philadelphia, Washington, and Boston, spent her entire life there, increasingly limiting her activities to her father's house. "I do not cross my Father's ground to any House or Town," she wrote, referring to a personal reclusiveness that was noticeable even to her contemporaries. In the front corner bedroom of that house on Main Street, Dickinson wrote over 1,700 poems, often on scraps of paper and on the backs of grocery lists, only a handful of which were published in her lifetime and then anonymously. She was known to give poems to friends and neighbors, often as an accompaniment to the cakes and cookies she baked, sometimes lowering them from an upstairs window in a basket. Her habit of binding groups of poems together into little booklets called fascicles might indicate she felt her poems were presentable, but most of her poems never went farther than her desk drawer where they were discovered by her sister after Dickinson's death in 1886 of kidney failure. In her lifetime, her poetry remained unknown, and although a few small editions of her poems were published in the 1890s, it was not until 1955 that a reliable scholarly edition appeared, transcribing the poems precisely from the original manuscripts and preserving all of Dickinson's typographical eccentricities. Convincingly or not, she called publication "the auction of the mind" and compared the public figure to a frog croaking to the admiring audience of a bog.

It is fascinating to consider the case of a person who led such a private existence and whose poems remained unrecognized for so long after her death, as if she had lain asleep only to be awakened by the kiss of the twentieth century. The quirky circumstances of her life have received as much if not more commentary than the poems themselves. Some critics valorize[1] her seclusion as a form of female self-sufficiency; others make her out to be a victim of her culture. Still others believe that her solitariness has been exaggerated. She did attend school, after all, and she maintained many intimate relationships by letter. Moreover, it was less eccentric in her day than in ours for one daughter—she had a brother who was a lawyer and a sister who married—to remain home to run the household and assist her parents. Further, all writers need privacy; all must close the door on the world to think and compose. But Dickinson's separateness—which has caused her to be labeled a homebody, a spinster, and a feminist icon among other things—took extreme forms. She was so shy that her sister Lavinia would be fitted for her clothes; she wore only white for many years ("Wear nothing commoner than snow"); and she rarely would address an envelope, afraid that her handwriting would be seen by the eyes of strangers. When asked of her companions, she replied in a letter to Thomas Wentworth Higginson[2], "Hills, sir, and the sundown, and a dog large as myself that my father bought me."

However tempting it is to search through the biographical evidence for a solution to the enigma[3] of Emily Dickinson's life, we must remember that no such curiosity would exist

were it not for the poems themselves. Her style is so distinctive that anyone even slightly acquainted with her poems would recognize a poem on the page as an Emily Dickinson poem, if only for its shape. Here is a typical example:

> 'Tis little I could care for pearls
> Who own the ample sea;
> Or brooches[4] when the Emperor
> With rubies pelteth me;
>
> Or gold, who am the Prince of Mines;
> Or diamonds, when I see
> A diadem[5] to fit a dome
> Continual crowning me.

Such a short form leads to concision and quick-wittedness, her poems standing as dramatic examples of poetry's ability to compress wide meaning into small spaces. She was also fond of the riddle. The diadem that crowns her always is the sky. With the dome of earth overhead, the little poem wants to ask, who needs the grosser[6] riches of pearls, rubies, gold, or diamonds? The modest size of her poems (most are shorter than a sonnet) matches the modest space of house and garden in which she chose to live. The poems are also short because she does not waste time introducing the poem. She neither provides the details of a physical setting, as a conventional nature poem might do, nor does she explain the poem's occasion. The poems begin suddenly, often with a declaration ("Superiority to fate / Is difficult to learn") or a definition ("Hope is a subtle glutton"). Dickinson does not knock before entering, so the reader may feel swept up into the center of the poet's thought process without warning. To open a poem by saying "I felt a cleavage in my mind / As if my brain had split" is to thrust the reader into a psychic intimacy with the fractured speaker. Also, her poems tend to end abruptly and decisively, often with epigrammatic[7] authority ("The only secret people keep / Is Immortality").

Her tiny, untitled poems may fit her sensibility and provide the verbal equivalent of a home's safe enclosure—a room within a room—but the

---

1. *Valorize* means to "attach value or worth to something."
2. *Thomas Wentworth Higginson* was a noted abolitionist, ordained minister, and editor for the *Atlantic Monthly*.
3. An *enigma* is something puzzling or mysterious.
4. A *brooch* is a piece of jewelry that is fastened by a pin.
5. *Diadem* means "crown."
6. Here, *grosser* mean "less fine."
7. *Epigrammatic* means "in the manner of a pithy, wise saying."

shortness of her lines is due to something else: her preference for common meter, the meter of ballads and Protestant hymns, and even of nursery rhymes. In common meter, a line of four beats is followed by a line of three beats.

> Amazing grace, how sweet the sound
> That saved a wretch like me.

Or, more speedily,

> Old King Cole was a merry old soul
> And a merry old soul was he.

Or, with Dickinson,

> A thought went up my Mind to-day
> That I have had before, . . .

Rhythmically, the three-beat line sounds like an answer to the four-beat line, and it also provides a one-beat pause at the end, a space to breathe. Dickinson used other kinds of cadences, but common meter is the usual gait[8] of her poetry. Almost every Dickinson poem can be sung—like it or not—to the tune of "The Yellow Rose of Texas," a song in common meter. But unlike that song, her poems also include a counter-rhythm she created by interrupting the regular beat with dashes—her obsessive type of punctuation—and by her sudden jumps of thought. Instead of a steady run of meaning, the Dickinson poem hops from one figure to another in a kind of zigzag logic that requires not just our concentration but our own agility in making imaginative and grammatical leaps. Even her obituary in the *Springfield Republican* noted that she was "quick as the electric spark in her intuitions." ❧

---

8. Here, *gait* means "rhythm."

RESPONDING AND THINKING CRITICALLY

Respond

1. How did you respond to Emily Dickinson's seclusion?

Recall and Interpret

2. (a)To what does Dickinson compare the public figure? (b)How would you explain her disdain for public opinion?

3. Collins asserts that the meter of Dickinson's poems creates "the verbal equivalent of a home's safe enclosure." Why else do you think Dickinson may have used this meter?

Analyze and Evaluate

4. What does Collins suggest about the "commentary" related to Dickinson's seclusion?

5. Collins states that in her poetry Dickinson "compress[es] wide meaning into small spaces" and that Dickinson's poems require an agile reader who can make "imaginative and grammatical leaps"? Do you agree with his statement?

Connect

6. **Big Idea** **A Poetic Revolution** In what ways do you think Dickinson's poetic innovations are related to her separation from the world?

INDIANA ACADEMIC STANDARDS
(pages 441–443)
11.2.6 Critique the...validity, and truthfulness of arguments set forth in...essays...

Writing Workshop

Historical Research Paper

 Investigating the Civil War Era

> *"Prayers from the women and imprecations from the men, and then a shell would light up the scene. Tonight, they say, the forces are to attempt to land."*
>
> —Mary Chesnut, from "Mary Chesnut's Civil War"

Connecting to Literature Chesnut's diary is an example of a primary source, or a source that provides a firsthand account of events. A secondary source is a source created after an event and is often based upon primary sources. In a historical **research paper,** a writer presents facts and ideas gathered from various primary and secondary sources about a specific topic or issue.

Rubric: Features of Historical Research Papers

Goals	Strategies
To present a strong, focused thesis statement	☑ Make an arguable assertion that can be supported with research
	☑ Revise thesis statement to reflect insights gained from research and writing
To develop main ideas that support the thesis statement	☑ Gather information from a variety of primary and secondary sources
	☑ Brainstorm for ideas; reorganize notes
To organize main ideas in an effective, logical order	☑ Use an outline or some other method of organization to plan a coherent argument
	☑ Include a main idea and relevant details in each paragraph
To support and explain ideas, using well-documented facts and details	☑ Quote, paraphrase, and summarize relevant information; credit sources
	☑ Synthesize, analyze, and evaluate information to draw conclusions

---

The Writing Process

In this workshop, you will follow the stages of the writing process. At any stage, you may think of new ideas to include and better ways to express them. Feel free to return to earlier stages as you write.

Prewriting

Drafting

Revising

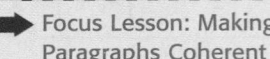 Focus Lesson: Making Paragraphs Coherent

Editing & Proofreading

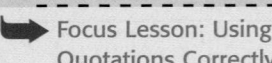 Focus Lesson: Using Quotations Correctly

Presenting

Writing Models For models and other writing activities, go to www.glencoe.com.

 ACADEMIC STANDARDS (pages 444–453)

11.5.10 Write...a research report...

11.5.4 Write historical investigation reports that...include a formal bibliography.

> ### Assignment
>
> Write a historical research paper in which you synthesize information from a variety of documented sources, draw conclusions, and discuss related insights. As you write, keep your audience and purpose in mind.
>
> **Audience:** classmates and teacher
>
> **Purpose:** to investigate a historical topic and report your conclusions

Prewriting

Investigate and Narrow a Topic Think about a perspective or a controversial event that sheds light on the Civil War era. Then narrow or expand your topic as needed.

▶ **Ask Questions** Think of a research report as a well-documented response to a significant question. List several research questions. As you learn more, refine your research questions and focus on a central idea.

▶ **Focus Your Topic** Once you have a general topic that interests you, use your research questions to help determine the scope of your topic. The topic should not be so broad that you will be writing in generalities nor so narrow that you cannot find adequate sources.

Compare the topics in the chart below to see the differences between topics that are too broad, too narrow, and appropriately limited.

Narrowing a Topic		
Too Broad	**Appropriately Limited**	**Too Narrow**
Civil War photography	Civil War photography of Mathew Brady	Mathew Brady's photographs of the battles of Bull Run
Women during the Civil War	Women soldiers during the Civil War	Women soldiers of the 95th Illinois Infantry Regiment

Gather Evidence After you narrow your topic, try to answer your research questions. Familiarize yourself with your topic's larger context and background. Then think about the historical situation or events that influenced your topic.

▶ **Find Reliable Sources** Use bibliography cards to keep track of all your sources. As you research, evaluate the credibility of your sources and make sure that they are not outdated, biased, or based on faulty data. For example, personal Web sites may promote personal agendas and not facts. However, books published by well-known publishers or universities are generally reliable.

▶ **Consider Different Perspectives** Keep in mind that people can have different perspectives on historical events. Consider perspectives that are often overlooked in the study of the Civil War.

Real-World Connection

You do research all the time, often without even realizing it. If you are going to buy a car, for example, you may test-drive several cars, find out which models are the safest or most fuel-efficient, and narrow your search to those that fit your budget. The information gained from research enables you to make informed decisions.

The Right Tone

Consider the purpose of your paper and how best to address your audience. Use a formal and objective tone to show that your research is serious and unbiased. Avoid slang and contractions. Use the third-person point of view.

Take Notes As you read through various sources, note important ideas, facts, and quotations. Record this information on note cards, in a notebook, or on separate computer files. Make sure to keep your information organized. For each source, record full publishing information (see the guidelines on pages R39–R41) and assign it a number or the author's last name. Then use this number or name as you label any notes taken from the source. This will save time and help you compile your Works Cited page(s) later. As you find information you want to include, decide how to best incorporate it into your paper.

▶ **Quote** Record direct quotations exactly as they appear, including punctuation. Use quotations sparingly.

▶ **Paraphrase** Restate someone else's original idea in your own words, giving credit to the author whose idea it is.

▶ **Summarize** Condense information to its key points and details.

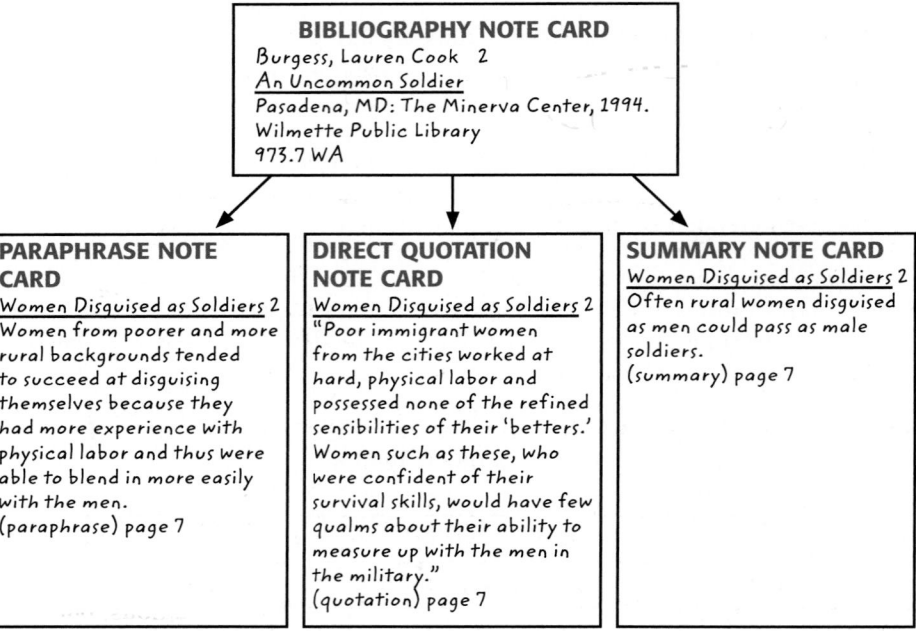

Analyze Information Once you have gathered a number of primary and secondary sources, look for patterns and similarities as well as contradictions. Organize your information around main ideas. For instance, a student writing about women soldiers during the Civil War divided her information into these categories: history of women in combat, Civil War era attitudes toward women, how the war influenced women, and how women helped the war effort. Remember that a successful research paper synthesizes ideas and presents new conclusions rather than simply stringing quotations together.

Make a Plan Once you are familiar with several expert perspectives on your topic, write a **thesis statement.** Keep in mind that you will probably revise your thesis as you gain insight and draw conclusions while writing. Use your notes to help you make an outline. Include only information that is relevant to your thesis. Choose an effective way to order the main ideas and keep related ideas together.

Drafting

Make Connections Start writing by following your outline and note cards. If you find it easier, write the body paragraphs before you write the introduction. Consider how each point in your outline relates to other points and to your thesis statement. Remember to explain those relationships to your reader.

Analyzing a Workshop Model

Here is a final draft of a historical research paper. Read the research paper and pay close attention to the comments in the margin. They point out features that you might want to include in your own paper. Answer the questions in the margin, and use the answers to guide you as you write your own draft.

On the Front Lines: Women Soldiers in the Civil War

Often disguised as men, women who fought on the front lines in the Civil War defied feminine stereotypes and nineteenth-century expectations. Unfortunately, these stereotypes labeled women who fought or attempted to fight in the Civil War as scandalous and criminal, yet their reasons for fighting were often not much different from those of male soldiers. Despite discrimination, women fought in the Civil War out of patriotism, love, and a desire for independence, adventure, and better status and pay.

Women had been fighting in wars and battles long before the Civil War. Joan of Arc's fifteenth-century battles may be the most famous, but other women warriors fought throughout history. Matilda of Tuscany fought for Pope Gregory VII in the eleventh and twelfth centuries, and Lakshmi Bai led the Bengal army against the British in India just before the American Civil War (Hall xi–xii). American women also took part in earlier wars. For example, Pennsylvanian Margaret Cochran Corbin joined the Continental army with her husband in 1776, and Mary Hays took over her husband's duties as gunner when he was injured in 1778 (Leonard 102–104). Therefore, by the opening salvos of the Civil War, women had been fighting in armies for centuries.

The Civil War, however, was different. Neither the Union army nor the Confederate army allowed women to enlist (Blanton, Part 1, 2). Those women who did enlist—and were later discovered to be female—were

Thesis Statement

State your topic and your perspective on it in the thesis statement. What information do you expect to see in this paper?

Main Ideas

Develop main ideas and organize them effectively to support your thesis successfully. Why does the writer begin the paper with this main idea?

Paraphrase

Paraphrase information rather than quote from an unremarkable passage. Do not use quotation marks. Why might the writer avoid a direct quotation here?

considered to be "of very bad character, indeed" (Burgess 6). When sisters Mary and Mollie Bell were discovered in 1864, they were accused of being prostitutes, arrested, and described as "manifestly crazy" (Burgess 6). Despite the restrictions and the threat of personal attacks, many women still enlisted. According to Mary Livermore, a women's rights activist of the time, there were about four hundred female soldiers during the Civil War (Hattaway 135). The more modern estimate is that between four hundred and six hundred women campaigned during the Civil War (Wagner 445).

Although enlistment was technically forbidden, there were many other legitimate ways for women to involve themselves in the war and support the army. Many Union women were considered *vivandières* or *cantinières*, women who assisted the troops by providing water and aid and carrying messages between commanders and soldiers (Varhola 120). Other women—more than three thousand in the Northern states—served as nurses and helped ill or injured soldiers. These nurses had to endure low pay and abysmal working conditions. Southern women also supported the troops by working as nurses, although they faced criticism for attending to "ruffians" (Ward 149). Still, women did not allow their roles as nurses to inhibit their involvement in combat.

However, for some women, working as a nurse or helping as a vivandière did not satisfy their motivations, so they turned toward disguise. In the Victorian age, gender was closely linked to exterior characteristics, such as clothing and hair. For example, if a person was seen wearing pants, "most people of the period would naturally have assumed that the person was a man" (Burgess 3). Such attitudes made it easy for women to disguise themselves as men. In addition, women cut their hair, wore fake mustaches, and, to create the illusion of muscles, padded their uniforms. Those who did not sport false facial hair found it easy to blend in among the boys and young men who were also fighting in the war. Women also created male pseudonyms—and army officials never asked for official identification (Blanton, Part 1, 2–3). Women from poorer and more rural backgrounds tended to succeed at disguise because they had more experience with physical labor and thus were able to blend in more easily with the men (Burgess 7). Yet some of the women, despite their best attempts at disguise, were discovered. Most were found out when they visited a hospital after becoming sick or wounded (Commager 241). For example, one woman was discovered only

Direct Quotations

Use direct quotations to retain the author's exact wording and to highlight particularly striking or meaningful phrases. What effect do these direct quotations have?

Supporting Details

Support your main ideas with relevant details. How do these details support the main idea of the paragraph?

Transitions

Shift gears by using transitional phrases or sentences that explain your thought process. Is this transition effective?

when she fainted after an injury (Hall 158). Many—both successfully and unsuccessfully—tried to reenlist in different regiments after their discovery.

There were many reasons for women to get involved in the Civil War, either in legitimate ways or by sneaking their way into battle, and many of these reasons did not differ from the motivations for men. Elizabeth D. Leonard, a prominent scholar, explains that, as with their male counterparts, "the traditional explanation has centered on pure, unadulterated patriotism" (227). The Civil War was a philosophical conflict as well as a military one. Many abolitionists were women. They identified with the fight for equality. For many women in the North, this was the first time that they had ever felt such intense loyalty to their country.

In addition, as Frank Moore noted in 1866, some women went to war because they could not bear separation from loved ones, while others went out of "a pure love of romance and adventure" (17). For instance, when her husband became a private, Bridget Divers joined the First Michigan Cavalry as a nurse. Her efforts extended into direct combat. She was known for helping move wounded men off the battlefield, rallying soldiers to retreat, and even occasionally fighting with the troops (Faust 221). As Leonard explains:

> Bridget Divers became widely known for her valiant efforts
> on behalf of the wounded, for her courage under fire in battle,
> and . . . for her willingness to position herself in such a way as
> to generate among the men in the ranks the greatest enthusiasm
> that they could muster for the fight (123).

Interestingly, in the heat of battle it did not matter to the other combatants that Bridget Divers was a woman. She still had the ability to inspire and help her fellow Americans.

Patriotism, love, and adventure were not the only reasons women became soldiers, however, and historians have only recently addressed the more practical reasons women risked their lives and reputations to fight. Another major reason that women—and men—joined the army was for the money. As Leonard asserts, a woman's service in the Civil War, "however patriotic in its essential motivation, however exciting in comparison with what most mid-century American women could expect from their normal daily lives, was compensated by wages" (230).

Supporting Facts

Include facts to support your main ideas. What do the facts about failed disguises contribute to the paper?

Secondary Sources

Use a combination of primary and secondary sources. Why might the writer have chosen to use a secondary source?

Long Quotations

For quotations four lines or longer, start a new line and indent the entire quotation ten spaces. Do not use quotation marks. What is the effect of the long quotation used here?

Coherent Paragraphs

Use transitions and repeat key words and phrases to help make your paragraphs coherent. How does the author connect this paragraph to the one before it?

Sarah Rosetta Wakeman, for example, disguised herself and joined the army to help her family pay off debts. In an 1862 letter home, she wrote:

> I enlisted for 3 years or soon [as] discharged. All the money I send you i want you should spend it for the family in clothing or something to eat. Don't save it for me for i can get all the money i want. If i ever return i shall have money enough for my self and to divide with you (Burgess 18).

A military salary was particularly attractive to women, who typically earned far less than men. Higher wages offered women independence that would have been otherwise unheard of in the 1860s. Implicitly, then, women were fighting to complete the promise of equality put forth during the American Revolution.

Several women became well known for their roles as soldiers in the war. Jennie Hodgers, under the pseudonym "Albert Cashier," served longer than any other woman on record. Hodgers completed a three-year enlistment with the Ninety-Fifth Illinois Infantry Regiment (Hall 20). This is the only documented case of a female soldier's fully completing an enlistment during the Civil War. After Hodgers enlisted in 1862, her regiment fought in the Vicksburg and Red River campaigns (Faust 119). Nearly fifty years after the war, when she was accidentally struck by a car and broke her hip, doctors discovered that she was a woman. She convinced the physicians to keep her secret, and they allowed her to live in the Soldiers' and Sailors' Home in Quincy, Illinois (Hall 21). After her death in 1915 (four years after she was discovered to be a woman), she "was buried in uniform with full military honors" (Hattaway 137).

The women who fought in the Civil War, often in disguise, exhibited courage and persistence and had to overcome substantial obstacles as a result of their gender. Their reasons for fighting included love and adventure but also more practical reasons. Today, U.S. women soldiers serve bravely alongside men in the armed forces. However, official rules still bar women from positions that involve direct combat. Although nearly 150 years have passed since the Civil War, women still face discrimination; yet female soldiers of today share many qualities—integrity, bravery, and determination—with those who fought in the Civil War. In essence, one of the lessons we can learn from the Civil War is that there are few differences in motivation and abilities between men and women in battle.

Primary Sources

Use a primary source to show an original, first-hand view of a historical event or situation. What does this primary source contribute to the paper?

Draw Conclusions

Synthesize the information from your sources and draw your own conclusions about what it means. How do the sentences after the long quotation strengthen the writer's point?

Summarize

Summarize when you want to condense information to its key points and details. What is the benefit of summarizing here?

Restate Thesis

In your conclusion, restate your thesis and summarize your main points. Why would the writer want to restate the thesis at the end of the paper?

Adding Insight

In your conclusion, draw inferences and add relevant insight. Leave the reader with something to think about. Is adding insight especially effective in a historical paper?

Works Cited

Blanton, DeAnne. "Women Soldiers of the Civil War." <u>Prologue Magazine</u> 25.1 Spring 1993 <http://www.archives.gov/publications/prologue/1993/spring/women-in-the-civil-war-1.html>.

Burgess, Lauren Cook, ed. <u>An Uncommon Soldier: The Civil War Letters of Sarah Rosetta Wakeman, alias Private Lyons Wakeman, 153rd Regiment, New York State Volunteers</u>. Pasadena, MD: The Minerva Center, 1994.

Commager, Henry Steele, ed. <u>The Civil War Archive: The History of the Civil War in Documents</u>. New York: Black Dog & Leventhal Publishers, 2000.

Faust, Patricia L., ed. "Divers, Bridget." <u>Historical Times Illustrated Encyclopedia of the Civil War</u>. New York: Harper & Row Publishers, 1986.

Hall, Richard. <u>Patriots in Disguise: Women Warriors of the Civil War</u>. New York: Paragon House, 1993.

Hattaway, Herman. <u>Shades of Blue and Gray: An Introductory Military History of the Civil War</u>. Columbia, MO: University of Missouri Press, 1997.

Leonard, Elizabeth D. <u>All the Daring of the Soldier: Women of the Civil War Armies</u>. New York: W. W. Norton & Company, 1999.

Moore, Frank. <u>Women of the War: Their Heroism and Self-Sacrifice</u>. 1866. Reprint. Alexander, NC: Blue/Gray Books, 1997.

Varhola, Michael J. <u>Everyday Life During the Civil War</u>. Cincinnati: Writer's Digest Books, 1999.

Wagner, Margaret E., Gary W. Gallagher, and Paul Finkelman, eds. <u>Civil War Desk Reference</u>. New York: Grand Central Press, 2002.

Ward, Geoffrey C. <u>The Civil War: An Illustrated History</u>. New York: Alfred A. Knopf, 1990.

Research

Reliable Sources

Internet sources may be less reliable than published sources. What indicates that this source should be reliable?

Primary Sources

Use primary sources to give original accounts of events, but check that they are reliable. How can you tell whether a primary source is reliable?

Encyclopedia Sources

Use encyclopedias and similar reference materials for general background and research. When would you use an encyclopedia as a source? When would you not?

Variety of Sources

Use a variety of sources from all perspectives in your research. How might an outdated source contribute to your paper if used correctly?

Revising

Peer Review After drafting, exchange papers with a partner. Note passages that seem unclear, irrelevant, incomplete, or out of place.

Use the rubric below to evaluate your writing.

Rubric: Writing an Effective Historical Research Paper
☑ Do you begin with a strong, clear thesis statement that guides your paper?
☑ Do you include a main idea in each paragraph?
☑ Do you support your main ideas with information from a variety of sources?
☑ Do you organize your paragraphs coherently?
☑ Do you quote, paraphrase, summarize information, and cite sources correctly?
☑ Do you synthesize information and draw your own conclusions?

▶ **Focus Lesson**

Making Paragraphs Coherent

To make your writing coherent, choose an organizational scheme, eliminate unrelated information, and use transitional words and phrases.

Draft: Incoherent paragraph

Sarah Rosetta Wakeman disguised herself and joined the army to help her family pay off debts (Burgess 18). As a child, Wakeman hunted squirrels. A military salary was particularly attractive to women, who typically earned far less than men.

Revision: Revise and reorganize the paragraph to make it coherent.

Another major reason that women—and men—joined the army was for the money.[1] Sarah Rosetta Wakeman, for example,[2] disguised herself and joined the army to help her family pay off debts (Burgess 18). ~~As a child, Wakeman hunted squirrels.~~[3] A military salary was particularly attractive to women, who typically earned far less than men. Higher wages offered women independence that would have been otherwise unheard of in the 1860s.[4]

1: **Begin with a topic sentence**

2: **Give an example**

3: **Eliminate unrelated information**

4: **Analyze details**

Traits of Strong Writing

Follow these traits of strong writing to express your ideas effectively.

Ideas message or theme and the details that develop it

Organization arrangement of main ideas and supporting details

Voice writer's unique way of using tone and style

Word Choice vocabulary a writer uses to convey meaning

Sentence Fluency rhythm and flow of sentences

Conventions correct spelling, grammar, usage, and mechanics

Presentation the way words and design elements look on a page

For more information on using the traits of strong writing, see pages R33–R34 of the Writing Handbook.

Editing and Proofreading

Get It Right When you have completed the final draft of your research paper, proofread it for errors in grammar, usage, mechanics, and spelling. Focus specifically on your citations and your Works Cited page. Refer to the Language Handbook, pages R46–R60, as a guide.

▶ **Focus Lesson**

Using Quotations Correctly

As you edit your draft, check to make sure that your quotations are cited correctly. Integrate quotations into your own writing to keep them from sounding choppy. In addition, always analyze the quotation in your own words so that its significance is made clear.

Problem: Too many direct quotations break up the flow of the paper.

"Although most accounts were neutral or complementary, some newspaper reports about women discovered in the ranks implied that they were of very bad character, indeed" (Burgess 6).

Solution A: Include part of the quotation in a sentence of your own.

Those women who did enlist—and were later discovered to be female—were considered to be "of very bad character, indeed" (Burgess 6).

Solution B: Quote a complete sentence but introduce it in your own words.

Historian Lauren Cook Burgess notes, "Although most accounts were neutral or complementary, some newspaper reports about women discovered in the ranks implied that they were of very bad character, indeed" (6).

Solution C: Omit words or sentences from a quotation and use ellipses in place of the omitted parts. Place brackets around any words you insert in place of omitted words or sentences. Be careful not to change the meaning of the quotation.

As historian Lauren Cook Burgess notes, "some newspaper reports about [disguised] women . . . implied that they were of very bad character, indeed" (6).

Quotations Within Quotations

Use single quotation marks for quoted material inside a direct quotation. Use double quotation marks for the main quotation.

Long Quotations

To use a long quotation (four or more lines), start a new line and indent the quotation. Do not use quotation marks, but be sure to introduce the quotation sufficiently and to analyze it in your own words.

Writer's Portfolio

Place a clean copy of your historical research paper in your portfolio to review later.

Literature Online
Writing Models For models and other writing activities, go to www.glencoe.com.

Presenting

Preparing Your Historical Research Paper Before you turn in your final paper, make sure that it is formatted correctly and that you are handing in a clean copy, including the Works Cited page. Check the indentation of long quotations. Ask your teacher about any additional presentation guidelines.

Speaking, Listening, and Viewing Workshop

Oral Report on a Historical Investigation

Connecting to Literature Daniel Mark Epstein is an award-winning poet and author of *Lincoln and Whitman: Parallel Lives in Civil War Washington.* According to Epstein, "Before the war Whitman believed he was the greatest poet since Shakespeare," but after visiting wounded soldiers in Washington hospitals, "he began to gain a certain amount of humility seeing these men struggle and seeing so many people give their lives to the ideal of liberty and union." This is an example of the type of interesting and insightful information that can be offered in an oral report about a historical investigation of the Civil War era. In this workshop, you will learn how to deliver an oral report based on the research you did for your historical research paper.

> **Assignment** Plan an oral report of your historical research paper and deliver it to an audience.

Planning Your Presentation

Your oral report should present the major findings of your research paper in a way that is interesting and informative to an audience of listeners. Follow these guidelines when planning your report:

- Decide on a logical organization for your report. Your thesis, or central idea, should be introduced near the beginning of the report.
- Choose several main ideas from your research paper that clearly support your thesis. Record them on note cards, which can be used as speaking prompts. Arrange the main-idea cards to follow your report's organization.
- Support each main idea with one or two interesting, significant, and relevant facts or details from your research. Record this support information on note cards to include with your main-idea cards.
- Frame your report with an engaging introduction and a logical conclusion. Open with an intriguing fact, quote, or description. Conclude by restating your thesis, summarizing your main ideas, or posing a new question your report raises.

Organization

Your presentation does not have to be organized like your research paper. It can be presented as cause and effect, comparison and contrast, problem and solution, topic by topic, or in time order—chronologically. Choose the organization that works best for your report.

Plagiarism

To avoid plagiarism when giving an oral report, provide the source of any direct quotes or statistics. For statistics, you may say, "according to [source]," before giving the statistics, or "from [source]" after giving them.

Creating Your Visual Media

As you plan your report, consider how charts, graphs, maps, and diagrams can clarify statistical or technical information and how photographs, paintings, and artifacts can allow the audience a glimpse into the time period. Use the chart below to brainstorm ideas for visual media with a partner.

| What is the best way to visually present statistics and technical data in my report? | What images can I find or create to illustrate the main ideas of my report? | What artifacts can I display to bring the history in my report to life? |

Rehearsing

Rehearse your oral report in front of an audience. Practice speaking naturally. If you use note cards, do not read directly from them. Refer to them only for guidance or for specific statistics. Make sure you are able to pronounce difficult names clearly and cite sources smoothly without fumbling for your cards. Practice putting each card out of the way after you have used it. Finally, be prepared for any questions your audience might ask. As you rehearse, have a friend ask impromptu questions so you can practice answering them.

Use some of the verbal and nonverbal techniques below to ensure that your audience clearly understands you and is engaged in what you have to say.

Use a Mirror

Practice your gestures in front of a mirror until your body language looks natural.

Sound Check

Record your presentation and play it back to check on whether your voice expresses the right mood and your words are understandable.

Videotape

Videotape your performance and provide your own critique.

Rubric: Techniques for Delivering a Presentation

Verbal Techniques	Nonverbal Techniques
☑ **Volume** Speak loudly enough so that everyone can hear you.	☑ **Posture** Stand up tall with your head straight.
☑ **Pronunciation** Speak clearly, pronouncing all the words.	☑ **Eye Contact** Make eye contact with your audience.
☑ **Pace** Speak at a moderate speed but vary the rate and use pauses.	☑ **Facial Expressions** Vary your facial expressions to reflect what you are saying.
☑ **Tone** Speak in an animated voice.	☑ **Gestures** Use natural gestures to reinforce your ideas.
☑ **Emphasis** Stress important words and ideas.	☑ **Visual Aids** Use photographs or other visual aids to enhance your presentation.

ACADEMIC STANDARDS (pages 454–455)
11.7.17 Deliver oral reports on historical investigations...
11.7.19 Deliver multimedia presentations that...select an appropriate medium for each element of the presentation...

For Independent Reading

THE CIVIL WAR'S BRUTALITY SHOCKED THE NATION. IN ITS WAKE, writers lost interest in Romantic depictions of exotic or idealized situations. They turned instead to Realism, a type of writing that portrayed everyday situations and people, as well as the imperfections of life.

Many of the great Realist novels analyze economic conditions and conflicts between people from different social classes. Conflicts are presented in an accurate and plausible way. Realist writers frequently focused on middle- and working-class settings and characters, often with the intent to spur reform.

Uncle Tom's Cabin

by Harriet Beecher Stowe (1852)

One early example of Realism predates the Civil War. Authored by an abolitionist, *Uncle Tom's Cabin* was the first work of American fiction to depict what life was like for slaves in the South. When Kentucky farmer Arthur Shelby decides to sell the slaves Uncle Tom and Harry, Harry's mother, Eliza, runs away with Harry in her arms, making her way to the free state of Ohio. Tom is put on a riverboat to be sold farther south. Stowe's graphic depiction of slaves' suffering made *Uncle Tom's Cabin* highly influential in stirring abolitionist sentiment.

Little Women

by Louisa May Alcott (1868–1869)

This tale of four sisters growing up in Concord, Massachusetts, during the Civil War era has become one of the best-loved American novels about the transition from adolescence to adulthood. Each sister in the March family has a distinctive personality. Meg, the oldest, is the most refined. Jo, fiery and independent, wants to be a writer. Beth is shy and musical. Amy, the youngest and most sensible, is the most beautiful. Alcott modeled the sisters, their levelheaded mother, and their idealistic father on her own family.

"In the execution of her very difficult task, Mrs. Stowe has displayed rare descriptive powers, a familiar acquaintance with slavery under its best and worst phases, uncommon moral and philosophical acumen, great facility of thought and expression, feelings and emotions of the strongest character. Intimate as we have been, for a score of years, with the features and operations of the slave system, and often as we have listened to the recitals of its horrors from the lips of the poor hunted fugitives, we confess to the frequent moistening of our eyes, and the making of our heart grow liquid as water, and the trembling of every nerve within us, in the perusal of the incidents and scenes so vividly depicted in her pages."

—*Liberator Review*, March 26, 1852

The American

by Henry James (1877)

In his novels, Henry James created acute portrayals of human psychology and of social and cultural mores. *The American* tells the story of Christopher Newman, a wealthy American businessman who travels to Europe. He there falls in love with beautiful Claire de Cintre. Though Christopher is friendly and intelligent as well as successful, Claire's relatives are unimpressed by him. They consider him to lack cultivation and propriety. James vividly dramatizes the clash of European and American sensibilities.

From the Glencoe Literature Library

Narrative of the Life of Frederick Douglass

by Frederick Douglass

The acclaimed autobiography of Frederick Douglass, a formerly enslaved man who escaped to freedom and became a renowned orator and abolitionist

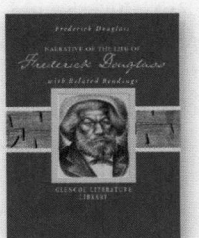

Great Expectations

by Charles Dickens

The orphaned Pip falls in love with the wealthy Estella and struggles to attain status in nineteenth-century England.

The Brothers Karamazov

by Fyodor Dostoevsky

The tragic and dramatic story of the murdered Fyodor Karamazov and his culpable sons

Indiana Test Practice

Reading: Vocabulary, Comprehension, and Analysis

Carefully read the following passage. Use context clues to help define any words with which you are unfamiliar. Pay close attention to the author's main idea and use of literary devices. Then answer the questions on pages 459–460.

from *My Bondage and My Freedom*
by Frederick Douglass

line

If at any one time of my life, more than another, I was made to drink the bitterest dregs of slavery, that time was during the first six months of my stay with Mr. Covey. We were worked all weathers.
5   It was never too hot or too cold; it could never rain, blow, snow, or hail too hard for us to work in the field. Work, work, work, was scarcely more the order of the day than the night. The longest days were too short for him, and the shortest
10 nights were too long for him. I was somewhat unmanageable when I first went there; but a few months of this discipline tamed me. Mr. Covey succeeded in breaking me. I was broken in body, soul and spirit. My natural elasticity was crushed;
15 my intellect languished; the disposition to read departed; the cheerful spark that lingered about my eye died; the dark night of slavery closed in upon me; and behold a man transformed into a brute!

Sunday was my only leisure time. I spent
20 this in a sort of beast-like stupor, between sleep and wake, under some large tree. At times, I would rise up, a flash of energetic freedom would dart through my soul, accompanied with a faint beam of hope, that flickered for a moment, and then vanished. I sank
25 down again, mourning over my wretched condition. I was sometimes prompted to take my life, and that of Covey, but was prevented by a combination of hope and fear. My sufferings on this plantation seem now like a dream rather than a stern reality.

30 Our house stood within a few rods of the Chesapeake bay, whose broad bosom was ever white with sails from every quarter of the habitable globe. Those beautiful vessels, robed in purest white, so delightful to the eye of freemen, were to
35 me so many shrouded ghosts, to terrify and torment me with thoughts of my wretched condition. I have often, in the deep stillness of a summer's Sabbath, stood all alone upon the banks of that noble bay, and traced, with saddened heart and tearful eye, the
40 countless number of sails moving off to the mighty ocean. The sight of these always affected me powerfully . . . .

I shall never be able to narrate the mental experience through which it was my lot to pass
45 during my stay at Covey's. I was completely wrecked, changed and bewildered; goaded almost to madness at one time, and at another reconciling myself to my wretched condition. Everything in the way of kindness, which I had experienced at
50 Baltimore; all my former hopes and aspirations for usefulness in the world, and the happy moments spent in the exercises of religion, contrasted with my then present lot, but increased my anguish.

I suffered bodily as well as mentally. I had
55 neither sufficient time in which to eat or to sleep, except on Sundays. The overwork, and the brutal chastisements of which I was the victim, combined with that ever-gnawing and soul-devouring thought—*"I am a slave—a slave for life—a slave*
60 *with no rational ground to hope for freedom"*—rendered me a living embodiment of mental and physical wretchedness.

1 Frederick Douglass says that, to Mr. Covey, the longest days were
  A like Sunday.
  B like nights.
  C too long.
  D too short.

2 From the context, it can be inferred that the word *discipline* in line 12 means
  A specialty.
  B affliction.
  C punishment.
  D training.

3 According to the passage, Douglass's transformation into a "brute" was caused by
  A Mr. Covey's success in breaking him.
  B the death of the spark in his eye.
  C the crushing of his elasticity.
  D his loss of the inclination to read.

4 In the passage, Douglass says that he spent his Sundays
  A at work.
  B in a stupor.
  C reading.
  D exercising his religious beliefs.

5 When Douglass writes that his sufferings seem "like a dream," he is using the literary device of
  A allusion.
  B personification.
  C simile.
  D irony.

6 When Douglass writes that that the Chesapeake Bay has a "broad bosom," he is using words that
  A imitate sounds.
  B refer to a nonhuman thing as if it were human.
  C refer indirectly to another work of literature.
  D make a comparison between unlike things.

7 From the passage, what can you infer about the source of Douglass's feelings about the ships in the Chesapeake Bay?
  A The ships reminded Douglass of the freedom that he did not have.
  B To Douglass, the ships represented Mr. Covey's cruelty.
  C The ships carried enslaved people and thus reminded Douglass of his own condition.
  D The ships reminded Douglass of ghosts.

8 From the context, it can be inferred that the word *present* in line 53 means
  A exhibited.
  B previous.
  C granted.
  D current.

9 What effect did Douglass's memories of Baltimore have on him?
  A They drove him to the brink of madness.
  B They increased his anguish.
  C They gave him hope.
  D They made him exercise his religion.

10 From the context, it can be inferred that the word *ground* in line 60 means
A land.
B position.
C floor.
D reason.

11 In this passage, Douglass reveals the personality of Mr. Covey mainly through
A direct characterization.
B indirect characterization.
C metaphor.
D symbols.

12 The author's tone in this passage is BEST described as
A authoritative.
B ironic.
C despairing.
D sarcastic.

13 The author's purpose for writing this passage was most likely
A to entertain.
B to persuade.
C to describe.
D to explain.

14 The point of view from which this passage is written is
A first person.
B second person.
C third-person omniscient.
D third-person limited.

15 In a few sentences, explain what main ideas about slavery Douglass conveys in this passage.

Reading: Word Recognition

For each question in this section, choose the best word to complete the sentence.

1 Robert E. Lee feared that the secession of the Southern states would result in lawlessness and _____ throughout the country.
  A depravity
  B anarchy
  C perusal
  D rackets
  E delusion

2 A series of misjudgments and military failures _____ the Confederacy to surrender in 1865.
  A consecrated
  B arrayed
  C induced
  D censured
  E hallowed

3 Frederick Douglass and Sojourner Truth both fought to _____ slavery.
  A vanquish
  B consecrate
  C pervade
  D adorn
  E induce

4 Because he had witnessed the horrors of combat, Ambrose Bierce rejected the idea that there could be a/an _____ war.
  A imperial
  B prostrate
  C poignant
  D benevolent
  E specific

5 In the nineteenth century, many people believed that Walt Whitman's poems were filled with _____ and that his books should be banned.
  A scores
  B redress
  C racket
  D allusions
  E depravity

6 Many soldiers _____ at the Battle of Gettysburg, which was one of the war's bloodiest.
  A hallowed
  B perished
  C assented
  D censured
  E obliged

7 Robert E. Lee was responsible for some of the Civil War's most brilliant and _____ military maneuvers.
  A audacious
  B imperial
  C prostrate
  D poignant
  E susceptible

8 A common _____ of slave owners was that they were "civilizing" the people they held in bondage.
  A cathedral
  B perusal
  C allusion
  D delusion
  E guideline

9 In the end, the South could not _____ with the North's overwhelming force.
  A protrude
  B pervade
  C induce
  D contend
  E assent

10 There was little actual _____ for those who had suffered so severely under slavery.
  A heave
  B redress
  C affliction
  D score
  E incredulity

Writing: Process and Language Conventions

For each question in this section, choose the best answer.

1 **What additional word in the sentence should be capitalized?**
The federal cemetery at Gettysburg was the site of president Lincoln's famous address.
A federal
B cemetery
C president
D address

2 **Which punctuation mark is needed in the sentence?**
Walt Whitman because he felt that he was receptive to the experiences of all people, wrote that he contained "multitudes."
A :
B ;
C .
D ,

3 **Which is the correct spelling of the word needed to complete the sentence?**
The small band of soldiers _____ attacked the artillery position.
A audaciously
B audacously
C audaicously
D audaciusly

4 **What type of error has the writer of this sentence made?**
Some people think Emily Dickinson to be the most significant poet of her time and that she is a giant of American literature.
A spelling
B capitalization
C run-on sentence
D parallelism

5 **Which punctuation mark is needed in this sentence?**
In the years before the Civil War, a number of slave narratives were published these provided people with insight into the realities of slavery.
A ,
B ;
C . . .
D !

6 **What additional word in the sentence should be capitalized?**
African American spirituals represent a fusion of features of christian hymns and features of traditional African music.
A spirituals
B christian
C traditional
D music

7 **What type of error has the writer of this sentence made?**
The Civil Rights Act of 1866 and the Fourteenth Amendment, established African Americans' status as U.S. citizens entitled to equal protection under the law.
A punctuation
B sentence fragment
C capitalization
D parallelism

8 **Which is the correct spelling of the word needed to complete the sentence?**
"An Occurrence at Owl Creek Bridge" is perhaps Ambrose Bierce's most _____ short story.
A poinyant
B poinyent
C poignant
D poignent

Writing: Applications

Complete the writing activity below. Do your planning and writing on separate sheets of paper.

Essay

> "Why should there not be a patient confidence in the ultimate justice of the people? Is there any better or equal hope in the world?"
> —Abraham Lincoln

Do you agree or disagree with this quotation? Write an essay in which you state and explain your opinion about the quotation. Support your opinion with examples and reasons drawn from your own experiences, observations, and/or reading.

Be sure to include
- at least five paragraphs, containing an introduction, a body, and a conclusion
- an opinion that reflects the assigned task
- examples and reasons to support your opinion

Use a separate sheet of paper to plan your writing. As you write, keep in mind that your essay will be evaluated for **ideas and content, organization, style, voice,** and **language conventions.**

Writing Checklist

Before you begin writing, be sure to
- ❏ brainstorm for ideas
- ❏ organize your ideas into a logical pattern
- ❏ develop a plan for an introduction, a body, and a conclusion

As you write your essay, be sure to
- ❏ refer to the quotation and clearly state you opinion about it
- ❏ provide reasons for your opinion
- ❏ use language that will convey a clear message and create interest
- ❏ maintain a tone that is appropriate for your intended audience
- ❏ use correct sentence structure, grammar, and punctuation

Literature Online **Unit Assessment** To prepare for the unit test, go to www.glencoe.com.

TEST PREPARATION AND PRACTICE **463**

Breezing Up (A Fair Wind), 1873–1876. Winslow Homer. Oil on canvas, 24⅛ x 38⅛ in. National Gallery of Art, Washington, DC. Gift of the W. L. and May T. Mellon Foundation.

Regionalism and Realism

1880–1910

Looking Ahead

The United States changed rapidly after the Civil War. American writers reacted to these changes by turning away from Romanticism toward Realism, a literary movement whose writers depicted life as they saw it, not as they imagined it to be. A literary movement that was akin to Realism was Regionalism, sometimes known as the local color movement, whose writers portrayed the distinctive traits of particular areas of the United States. A later, more extreme movement was Naturalism, whose writers sought to describe with scientific objectivity the effects of environment and heredity on character.

Keep the following questions in mind as you read:

⟹ How was the United States changing between 1880 and 1910?

⟹ What are the basic characteristics of Realism, Regionalism, and Naturalism?

⟹ How do you think the historical and cultural trends of this period continue to affect the United States today?

INDIANA ACADEMIC STANDARDS (pages 464–477)

11.3.5 Analyze or evaluate works of literary or cultural significance in history (American...) that reflect a variety of genres in each of the respective historical periods; were written by important authors in the respective major historical periods; reveal contrasts in major themes, styles, and trends; reflect or shed light on the seminal philosophical, religious, social, political, or ethical ideas of their time.

Timeline ❧ *1880–1910* ❧

AMERICAN LITERATURE

1880

1880
Joel Chandler Harris's *Uncle Remus, His Songs and His Sayings* is published

1881
Henry James's *The Portrait of a Lady* is published

1884
Helen Hunt Jackson's *Ramona* is published

1884
Mark Twain's *The Adventures of Huckleberry Finn* is published

1885
W. D. Howells's *The Rise of Silas Lapham* is published

1886
Sarah Orne Jewett's "A White Heron" is published

1890

1896
Paul Laurence Dunbar's *Lyrics of a Lowly Life* is published

1898
Stephen Crane's "The Open Boat" is published

1899
Kate Chopin's *The Awakening* is published

1899
Charles Waddell Chesnutt's *The Conjure Woman* is published

Queen Liliuokalani ▲

UNITED STATES EVENTS

1880

1881
Clara Barton founds American Association of the Red Cross

1881
Booker T. Washington founds Tuskegee Institute

1882
Renegade Jesse James is killed by one of his own gang

1884
George Eastman designs roll film for cameras

1885
William Le Baron Jenney builds the first skyscraper in Chicago

1886
President Grover Cleveland dedicates the Statue of Liberty in New York

1890

1890
Wounded Knee Massacre takes place

1891
James A. Naismith invents basketball

1892
Immigration center opens on Ellis Island

1893
Americans overthrow Queen Liliuokalani of Hawaii

1896
Plessy v. Ferguson case is tried

1896
Klondike gold rush begins

1898
Spanish-American War is fought

WORLD EVENTS

1880

1883
Krakatoa volcano erupts; ensuing tsunami kills over 36,000 people

1883
Standard time divides Earth into 24 time zones

1885
Indian National Congress is founded

1889
Eiffel Tower is completed in Paris

1889
Brazil becomes a republic

1890

1890
German chancellor Otto von Bismarck resigns, due to conflicts with Kaiser Wilhelm II

1892
Gerhart Hauptmann's *The Weavers* is published

1894
War begins between China and Japan

◀ 1896 Olympics

1895
Lumière Brothers introduce motion pictures

1896
First modern Olympic Games are held in Athens

1896
Famine that will kill millions of people begins in India

1898
Marie and Pierre Curie discover radium

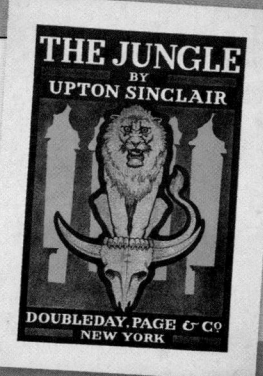
THE JUNGLE
BY
UPTON SINCLAIR

DOUBLEDAY. PAGE & Co
NEW YORK

1900

1900
L. Frank Baum's *The Wonderful Wizard of Oz* is published

1900
Theodore Dreiser's *Sister Carrie* is published

1900
Zitkala-Sa's (Gertrude Bonnin) *Impressions of an Indian Childhood* is published ▶

1901
Frank Norris's *The Octopus* is published

1901
Booker T. Washington's *Up from Slavery* is published

1903
W. E. B. Du Bois's *The Souls of Black Folk* is published

1903
Jack London's *The Call of the Wild* is published

1904
Henry James's *The Golden Bowl* is published

1906 ▲
Upton Sinclair's *The Jungle* is published

1907
Henry Adams's *The Education of Henry Adams* is completed

1908
Israel Zangwill's play *The Melting Pot* opens

1909
Gertrude Stein's *Three Lives* is published

1900

1900
Hawaii becomes a territory of the United States

1901
President McKinley is assassinated; Theodore Roosevelt becomes president

1903
Wright Brothers make first airplane flight ▶

1903
The Great Train Robbery, first narrative film, is shown

1904
The United States begins construction of the Panama Canal

1906
San Francisco earthquake takes place

1908
Ford Motor Company produces the Model T Ford

1908
Electric washing machine is invented

1909
National Association for the Advancement of Colored People (NAACP) is founded

1910
Angel Island facility for Asian immigrants is opened

1900

Pierre and Marie Curie

1900
Boxer Rebellion against European influence begins in China

1904
Russo-Japanese War begins

1905
Strikes and mass protests begin reform in Russia

1906
Finland is first European country to grant woman suffrage

1908
Oil is discovered in the Middle East

1910
Mexican Revolution begins

Literature Online **Timeline** Visit www.glencoe.com for an interactive timeline.

Reading Check

Analyzing Graphic Information Which events on the timeline continue to shape the daily life of people in the United States today?

By the Numbers

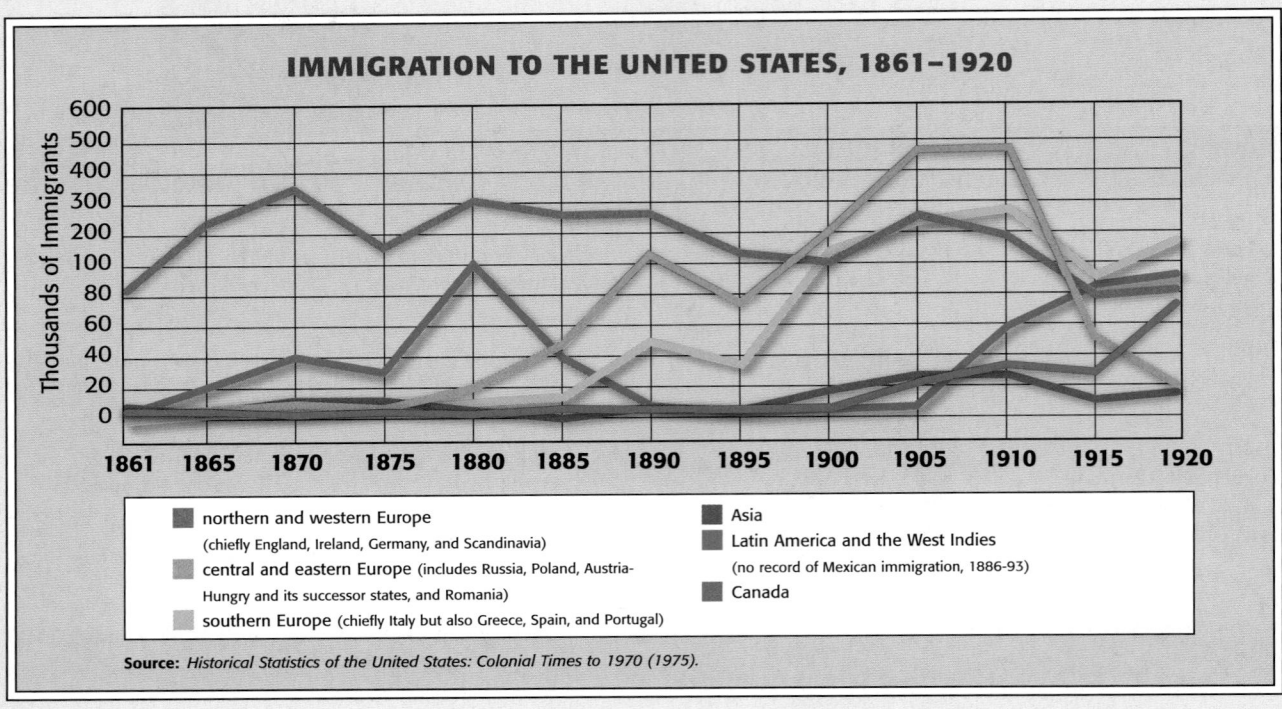

IMMIGRATION TO THE UNITED STATES, 1861–1920

(y-axis) Thousands of Immigrants — 600, 500, 400, 300, 200, 100, 80, 60, 40, 20, 0

(x-axis) 1861 1865 1870 1875 1880 1885 1890 1895 1900 1905 1910 1915 1920

- northern and western Europe (chiefly England, Ireland, Germany, and Scandinavia)
- central and eastern Europe (includes Russia, Poland, Austria-Hungry and its successor states, and Romania)
- southern Europe (chiefly Italy but also Greece, Spain, and Portugal)
- Asia
- Latin America and the West Indies (no record of Mexican immigration, 1886-93)
- Canada

Source: *Historical Statistics of the United States: Colonial Times to 1970 (1975).*

Railroad Time

Before the 1880s, each community set its clocks by the sun's position at high noon. At noon in Chicago, for example, it was 12:50 P.M. in Washington, D.C., 12:09 P.M. in Louisville, Kentucky, and 11:41 A.M. in St. Paul, Minnesota. Local time interfered with train scheduling and at times even threatened passenger safety: when two trains traveled on the same track, collisions could result from scheduling errors caused by regional variations in time. In 1883, to make rail service safer and more reliable, the American Railway Association divided the country into four time zones, each with its own standard time. The federal government ratified the change in 1918.

LIFE AND DEATH

- In 1900 the average life expectancy for an American was 47.3 years. Today it is more than 77 years.

STEEL PRODUCTION, 1865–1900

(y-axis) Millions of Tons — 12, 10, 8, 6, 4, 2, 0

(x-axis) 1870 1880 1890 1900

Source: *Historical Statistics of the United States: Colonial Times to 1970.*

EDUCATION

The number of public schools multiplied after the Civil War.

- In 1870 around 6,500,000 children attended school.

- By 1900 the number of children attending school had risen to over 17,300,000.

INEQUALITY OF WAGES

In the late 1890s, women were paid much less than men for the same type of work and the same hours. In the woolen industry, for example, male spinners made $7.50 per week in 1890; by 1900 this wage had risen to $9.50. By contrast, female spinners made only $5.50 a week in 1890; by 1900 this wage had only risen to $6.00.

MILES OF TRACK, 1870–1900

(y-axis) Total Miles of Railroad Operating (in thousands) — 175, 150, 125, 100, 75, 50, 25, 0

(x-axis / bars) 1870, 1875, 1880, 1885, 1890

Source: *Historical Statistics of the United States: Colonial Times to 1970.*

Being There

Between the Civil War and World War I, the growth of mining, ranching, and farming brought settlement to the West. At the same time, populations of cities in the East swelled as immigrants poured into the United States and job seekers from rural areas sought employment in industry.

A Immigrants in line leaving Ellis Island, waiting for ferry to New York. ca. 1900. Undated photograph.

B A group of cowboys sit on the grass beside their horses and a chuck wagon to eat. Western United States.

C Ranch located in Nebraska, 1887. Photograph. Library of Congress, Washington, DC.

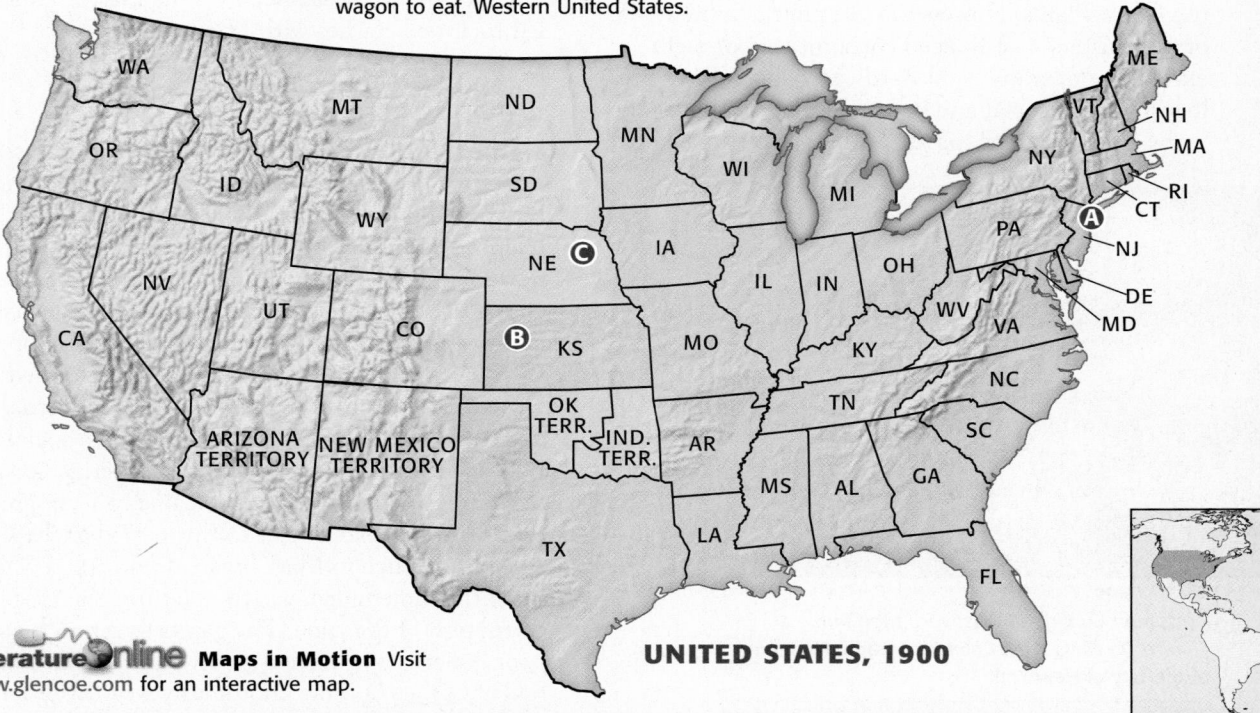

UNITED STATES, 1900

Literature Online **Maps in Motion** Visit www.glencoe.com for an interactive map.

Reading Check

Analyzing Graphic Information

1. Between what years did immigration from central and eastern Europe reach its peak?

2. In 1900, roughly how many times greater was school attendance than it had been in 1870?

3. What change did the western and eastern parts of the U.S. have in common during this time?

Regionalism and Realism

1880–1910

Historical, Social, and Cultural Forces

Westward Expansion

For a time during the early nineteenth century, American settlement paused at the edge of the Great Plains. Settlers felt challenged by these vast, treeless grasslands, which had little rainfall, a fierce climate, and soil that was very fertile but difficult to plow. But beginning in the 1860s, improvements in farming equipment, the expansion of the railroads, and the Homestead Act, which enabled settlers to claim public land, made more Americans willing to move to the Great Plains. However, these prairie farmers—or "sodbusters"—still faced constant toil, drought, extreme temperatures, blizzards, tornadoes, grass fires, locusts, and a social and cultural isolation that broke many homesteaders' spirits.

Across the Continent, Westward the Course of Empire Takes Its Way. Color lithograph. Museum of the City of New York.

The West's rich deposits of gold, silver, and copper served the needs of growing industries in the East. The lure of these precious metals brought the first wave of settlers that populated what would become the mountain states of the West.

Westward expansion was a disaster for the Native Americans of the region. Each new group of settlers further encroached on Native Americans' traditional ways of life. The Native Americans of the Great Plains had long depended on the herds of buffalo for food, clothing, and shelter. By the 1880s, the destruction of these herds by white hunters had doomed this way of life. After the Civil War, the policy of the U.S. government was to move Native Americans onto reservations, which were large tracts of land set aside for them. Resistance by some Native Americans led to armed clashes with U.S. troops.

The Gilded Age

As the Great Plains and the West were being settled, cities in the East and Midwest were also growing. New inventions, such as the electric light and the telephone, improved economic efficiency and created new jobs. Thousands of Americans moved to cities in search of work, and millions of immigrants arrived, many of them from southern and eastern Europe. By the early 1900s, Americans had transformed the United States into the world's leading industrial nation. However, this rapid growth had a social cost. Beneath the glittering surface of prosperity, corruption in business and politics became so widespread that historians often refer to this period as the Gilded Age, a reference to Mark Twain's scathing social satire of the same name, which described the greed and corruption of the time. The gap between rich and poor Americans widened greatly, and a few so-called robber barons became enormously wealthy as a result of the labors of their employees. Cities were overpopulated, and the poor were forced to live in tenement houses that were crowded, dirty, and unsafe.

Reformers and writers tried to improve working and housing conditions. Jane Addams founded Hull House, a settlement house to serve immigrants and poor working people in Chicago. Hull House offered hot lunches for factory workers and classes in English for foreign-language speakers. Some journalists—later called muckrakers—exposed the social problems brought on by industrialization and urbanization. Ida Tarbell analyzed the way in which the Standard Oil Company had come to control 95 percent of the country's oil-refining capacity. In his novel *The Jungle*, Upton Sinclair shocked and sickened readers with a graphic account of the filthy and unsafe conditions in Chicago's stockyards and meatpacking plants.

> *"I aimed at the public's heart, and by accident I hit it in the stomach."*
>
> —Upton Sinclair

Women's Rights

The fight to achieve women's right to vote began before the Civil War but slowed while many women focused on ending slavery. After the Civil War, reformers such as Susan B. Anthony realized that women would remain powerless until they could own property and vote. Anthony was devoted to securing equal rights for women and, with Elizabeth Cady Stanton, formed the National Woman Suffrage Association in 1869. Although the federal government balked at giving women the right to vote and own property, individual states in the West were more progressive. When Wyoming joined the union in 1890, it became the first state to give women the right to vote. By 1914, women had voting rights in fifteen states. It was not until 1920 that the Nineteenth Amendment guaranteed voting rights for all American women.

Regionalism, Realism, and Naturalism

Some American writers, known as Regionalists or local color writers, created vivid portrayals of their own regions and satisfied a curiosity many Americans of the time felt about the distinctive landscapes, speech, and customs of other parts of the country. In the mid-1800s, some artists and writers began to turn away from Romanticism. Realism, a new direction in art and literature, consisted of writers who attempted to portray people as they actually were, rather than idealizing them as Romanticists had often done. As the American novelist and critic William Dean Howells observed, "Realism is nothing more and nothing less than the truthful treatment of material." Other writers, known as Naturalists, were influenced by the theories of scientists such as Charles Darwin.

PREVIEW **Big Ideas** # Regionalism, Realism, and Naturalism

1 Regionalism

Following the Civil War, some American writers concentrated on the unique characteristics, or local color, of a particular region of the country. They attempted to portray the landscape, speech, customs, and other cultural details of their chosen region.

See pages 472–473

2 Realism

Writers of this period turned away from Romanticism and attempted to create the appearance of ordinary life. Known as Realists, these writers aimed not to transcend reality but to render the truth of everyday experience as they saw, heard, and felt it.

See pages 474–475

3 Naturalism

Naturalism, a more extreme movement, grew out of Realism. Naturalist writers, influenced by scientists such as Charles Darwin, believed that human beings are shaped by heredity and environment and dominated by economic, social, or natural forces.

See pages 476–477

Influenced by such factors as public education and mass media, culture in the United States today is probably more uniform than at any other time in our history. In the past, cultural differences among people from various parts of the United States were more marked. After the Civil War, a new group of American writers, known as Regionalists or local colorists, emphasized local cultures. Not all of these Regionalist writers were born and educated in the East, as most previous American writers had been. Many came from the South, Midwest, or West. Under the influence of the new emphasis on Realism in art and literature, they did not present the unusual characters and exotic settings familiar in Romanticist writing. Instead, local colorists depicted the ordinary people and everyday places around them.

In their writing, the local colorists emphasized setting, and their characters tended to be typical of a particular region, which was clear from their speech and beliefs. Often the narrator was an outsider who observed a world filled with unfamiliar or outdated characteristics and customs. This outsider frequently revealed the tension between the new and old, the modern and the old-fashioned. The mood of local color writing was sometimes nostalgic, serving as a reminder of a time before mass production and noisy urban life. At other times, the mood was more somber, presenting a criticism of habits and ideas considered long outmoded.

Mark Twain's Mississippi River

Born in a small Missouri town on the Mississippi River, Mark Twain vividly evoked the world of that river in a series of works, including his masterpiece *The Adventures of Huckleberry Finn*. In this novel, an orphaned boy and a runaway slave flee down the Mississippi in a raft. Through their innocent eyes, Twain presented a piercing view of American society in the pre-Civil War era and revealed the injustices of slavery and the culture that enforced it. He also employed a lively sense of humor and a fine ear for American dialect. His editor and friend William Dean Howells was the first to realize that Twain was more than a humorist or local colorist. In *The Adventures of Huckleberry Finn*, Twain had transformed our literature by writing a true American novel, in which the setting, subject matter, characters, and style were unmistakably American. Howells claimed Twain to be an American genius, hailing him as "incomparable, the Lincoln of our literature."

Bret Harte's Far West

Bret Harte told stories of the rude, lawless life of the California gold-mining country while describing places few people had ever seen. One of his earliest stories, "The Luck of Roaring Camp," made Harte famous. Readers in both the United States and Britain enthusiastically read about the gamblers, thieves, and social misfits that populate his work. Harte distinguished himself from other writers of the West by his ironic tone. His unsavory characters frequently undergo an unexpected reformation, which provides the narrator with an opportunity to make wry comments on their sudden changes of heart.

> *"Consciously, I was always, as I still am, trying to fashion a piece of literature out of the life next at hand."*
>
> —William Dean Howells

Willa Cather's Great Plains

When she was nine years old, Willa Cather's family left Virginia and moved to the open prairie of Nebraska—a move that would change her life dramatically. Cather's writing reflects her memories of prairie life, and many of her early works focus on the harshness and isolation of pioneers' lives. In her novel *O Pioneers!* she depicted immigrant farmers in Nebraska, whose tough yet sensitive natures and determination made their survival possible. In other works, such as *My Ántonia*, she celebrated the pioneer lifestyle for its freedom and simplicity.

Old Kentucky Home Life in the South, 1859. J. Eastman Johnson. Oil on canvas. Brooklyn Museum of Art, New York.

from *O Pioneers!* by Willa Cather

For the first three years after John Bergson's death, the affairs of his family prospered. Then came the hard times that brought every one on the Divide to the brink of despair; three years of drought and failure, the last struggle of a wild soil against the encroaching plowshare. The first of these fruitless summers the Bergson boys bore courageously. The failure of the corn crop made labor cheap. Lou and Oscar hired two men and put in bigger crops than ever before. They lost everything they spent. The whole country was discouraged. Farmers who were already in debt had to give up their land. A few foreclosures demoralized the county. The settlers sat about on the wooden sidewalks in the little town and told each other that the country was never meant for men to live in; the thing to do was to get back to Iowa, to Illinois, to any place that had been proved habitable. The Bergson boys, certainly, would have been happier with their uncle Otto, in the bakery shop in Chicago. Like most of their neighbors, they were meant to follow in paths already marked out for them, not to break trails in a new country. A steady job, a few holidays, nothing to think about, and they would have been very happy. It was no fault of theirs that they had been dragged into the wilderness when they were little boys. A pioneer should have imagination, should be able to enjoy the idea of things more than the things themselves.

Reading Check

Generalizing How would you describe the overall goals of the local color movement?

Big Idea 2
Realism

The emergence of American Realism in the second half of the 1800s was in part a reaction to the Romanticism of the previous era. Romanticism's glorification of the imagination became unappealing to Realists, who wanted to explore the motivations, behaviors, and actions of real people. Some of the most important writers of the time were considered Realists, including fiction writers Henry James, O. Henry, and William Dean Howells.

The Birth of Realism

Before Realism appeared in America, it was already flourishing in Europe. French novelist Honoré de Balzac is commonly considered the father of Realism. His masterpiece *The Human Comedy* is a massive collection of ninety novels and novellas that detail the panorama of French society. Balzac did not limit the scope of his masterpiece to an examination of one class of people or cultural environment. Instead he invented a complex and textured fictional world based on all levels of society.

Advanced by such authors as Gustave Flaubert, Leo Tolstoy, George Eliot, and Charles Dickens, Realism soon became the most prominent literary movement in Europe. These novelists examined the psychology of human behavior and created characters who struggle with problems that nineteenth-century readers would have recognized in their own lives or in the lives of their contemporaries.

The rise of Realism in the United States can be traced to disillusionment following the Civil War. For many, the war had destroyed the Romantic view of humanity. Like Mathew Brady in his famous photographs of the Civil War dead or Jacob Riis in his portraits of New York slum children, the Realists wanted to present life as it actually was—often cruel and never embellished. In fact, the rise of photography in general, and Brady's images in particular, fundamentally altered the ways in which Americans perceived reality. Photography enabled artists to capture and convey, with stark objectivity, the world as it appeared through the camera's lens. As a reporter observed upon seeing an exhibit of Brady's photographs, "If he has not brought bodies and laid them in our dooryards and along [our] streets, he has done something very like it." Many Realist writers aspired to adapt this kind of photographic realism to their literary works.

Kate Chopin and Women

During her lifetime, Kate Chopin was widely criticized for her realistic portrayal of women. She was the first American woman to write frankly about the suppressed passion and discontentment of women who were confined to the traditional roles of wives and mothers. She believed that the role of an artist was to rebel. As a character in her novel *The Awakening* observes, an artist must have "a soul that dares and defies." Chopin wrote of women "awakening" to their confined state and challenging the social values and patriarchal rules that defined and limited them. Chopin is sometimes considered to be a Regionalist writer, because in some of her stories she depicted the customs of Creoles and Cajuns in Louisiana, using their language and describing their lifestyles. She made their world real and confirmed their humanity by refusing to judge their lives or their struggles.

Paul Laurence Dunbar and African Americans

Paul Laurence Dunbar was one of the earliest African American poets to gain widespread recognition. William Dean Howells's favorable review of Dunbar's book *Majors and Minors* in *Harper's Weekly* helped to establish Dunbar as an international literary figure. While Dunbar wrote the bulk of his verse in the lofty poetic diction of his day, he is best known for his use of rural African American dialect. Dunbar's dialect poems depict the post-war lives of African Americans and reflect their frustrated aspirations in an era of white dominance. Throughout his life, Dunbar tried to strike a balance between the conventions of the European literary tradition and those of African American folk culture.

The City of Ambition, 1910. Alfred Stieglitz. Photogravure, 13⅜ x 10¼ in. Reunion des Musées Nationaux, France.

Edith Wharton and the Upper Classes

The characters in Edith Wharton's fiction, like Wharton herself, inhabited the upper crust of New York society. Crafted with penetrating psychological insight, her stories and novels depict the desires, prejudices, and foibles of her privileged and affluent characters. In two of her most famous novels, *The Age of Innocence* and *The House of Mirth,* Wharton presents a culture that devalues the individual in favor of class divisions, social status, and the pursuit and enjoyment of wealth. Her best fiction satirizes the hypocrisy of the American aristocracy of which she was a member.

from *The Awakening* by Kate Chopin

It was then past midnight. The cottages were all dark. A single faint light gleamed out from the hallway of the house. There was no sound abroad except the hooting of an old owl in the top of a water-oak, and the everlasting voice of the sea, that was not uplifted at that soft hour. It broke like a mournful lullaby upon the night.

The tears came so fast to Mrs. Pontellier's eyes that the damp sleeve of her *peignoir* no longer served to dry them. She was holding the back of her chair with one hand; her loose sleeve had slipped almost to the shoulder of her uplifted arm. Turning, she thrust her face, steaming and wet, into the bend of her arm, and she went on crying there, not caring any longer to dry her face, her eyes, her arms. She could not have told why she was crying. Such experiences as the foregoing were not uncommon in her married life. They seemed never before to have weighed much against the abundance of her husband's kindness and a uniform devotion which had come to be tacit and self-understood.

An indescribable oppression, which seemed to generate in some unfamiliar part of her consciousness, filled her whole being with a vague anguish. It was like a shadow, like a mist passing across her soul's summer day. It was strange and unfamiliar; it was a mood. She did not sit there inwardly upbraiding her husband, lamenting at Fate, which had directed her footsteps to the path which they had taken. She was just having a good cry all to herself. The mosquitoes made merry over her, biting her firm, round arms and nipping at her bare insteps.

Reading Check

Analyzing Cause and Effect What cultural shifts and historical events contributed to the rise of American Realism?

Big Idea 3
Naturalism

What do you think contributes most to shaping a person's life? Is it the biological factor of heredity? Is it the social and economic factor of environment? Or is it the result of other factors, such as an individual's own will? Realistic writers, for the most part, did not concern themselves with these philosophical questions. Toward the end of the 1800s, however, a group of writers known as Naturalists, who were strongly influenced by Charles Darwin's scientific theory of evolution by natural selection, adopted the view that people had little control over their own lives. They believed that human destiny was shaped by powerful forces, including heredity, social and economic pressures, and the natural environment. Like the Realist writers, Naturalists wrote about ordinary people, but they often focused on the working class and the poor, presenting the futile battles of individuals against a brutal society or an indifferent universe.

Edwin Arlington Robinson and Fate

Edwin Arlington Robinson said he felt "doomed, or elected, or sentenced for life, to the writing of poetry." His most famous poems are set in fictional Tilbury Town, which was modeled on his childhood hometown of Gardiner, Maine. The characters in his poems, like Robinson himself, are often loners or misfits. They live in communities where people feel pressure to conform and where creativity is misunderstood or simply ignored. Robinson's poems focus almost exclusively on an individual or on individual relationships. His tone is a blend of irony and compassion toward his characters, many of whose lives end in personal failure and despair.

Jack London and Nature

From the age of nine, Jack London was helping to support his family through hard physical labor. His early experiences made him sympathetic toward the working class and convinced him that capitalist society was brutal and repressive. London was also drawn to Social Darwinism, a movement that—unlike Darwin himself—attempted to apply Darwin's biological theories to human behavior. These ideas are important in several of London's works, including his most popular novels, *The Call of the Wild* and *The Sea-Wolf*. London spent time in the Alaskan wilderness and the South Seas, and many of his stories demonstrate the power of nature over civilization: "Nature has many tricks wherewith she convinces man of his finity—the ceaseless flow of the tides, the fury of the storm, the shock of the earthquake, the long roll of heaven's artillery."

> A man said to the universe:
> "Sir, I exist!"
> "However," replied the universe,
> "The fact has not created in me
> A sense of obligation."
>
> —Stephen Crane

Stephen Crane and War

In his writing, Stephen Crane was attracted to war and other forms of violent struggle. Though the Civil War had ended six years before Crane was born, he used it as the subject of his best-known book, *The Red Badge of Courage*. Later short stories express Crane's belief in the necessity of courage, honesty, and poise in the face of an indifferent universe. In "The Blue Hotel," Crane described humans as so many lice clinging "to a whirling, fire-smote, ice-locked, disease-stricken, space-lost bulb." The pathos of human helplessness in the face of brute fact closes the story "An Episode of War" as a young officer reacts to the loss of his arm: "'Oh, well,' he said, standing shamefaced amid these tears. 'I don't suppose it matters so much as all that.'" In The *Red Badge of Courage*, Crane presents his hero, a young recruit named Henry Fleming, who responds to his first experience of a new, violent environment—battle.

Newspaper boys, one missing a leg, stand on the steps of a bank near a busy trolley junction in Jersey City, New Jersey. 1912. Lewis Wickes Hine.

from *The Red Badge of Courage* by Stephen Crane

He was at a task. He was like a carpenter who has made many boxes, making still another box, only there was furious haste in his movements. He, in his thoughts, was careering off in other places, even as the carpenter who as he works whistles and thinks of his friend or his enemy, his home or a saloon. And these jolted dreams were never perfect to him afterward, but remained a mass of blurred shapes.

Presently he began to feel the effects of the war atmosphere—a blistering sweat, a sensation that his eyeballs were about to crack like hot stones. A burning roar filled his ears.

Following this came a red rage. He developed the acute exasperation of a pestered animal, a well-meaning cow worried by dogs. He had a mad feeling against his rifle, which could only be used against one life at a time.

He wished to rush forward and strangle with his fingers. He craved a power that would enable him to make a world-sweeping gesture and brush all back. His impotency appeared to him, and made his rage into that of a driven beast.

Buried in the smoke of many rifles his anger was directed not so much against the men whom he knew were rushing toward him as against the swirling battle phantoms which were choking him, stuffing their smoke robes down his parched throat. He fought frantically for respite for his senses, for air, as a babe being smothered attacks the deadly blankets.

Reading Check

Comparing and Contrasting How did the attitude of the Naturalists toward the place of humanity in the universe differ from that of the Transcendentalists?

Wrap-Up

Why It Matters

Between 1880 and 1910, a new type of writer appeared in the United States. New England writers no longer dominated American literature. Writers from the Midwest, the Great Plains, and the West expanded our country's literary frontiers, presenting exciting, unfamiliar worlds to readers at home and abroad. Known as Regionalists or local colorists, these writers enriched our literature with new kinds of American landscapes, characters, and styles of speech.

The effects of Realism are widespread and can be seen in journalism, film, the novel, and painting. By challenging the conventions of Romanticism, writers like Wharton, Chopin, and Dunbar redefined the boundaries of acceptable content in literature and paved the way for future workers.

Beginning in the 1890s, literary Naturalism shone a bright but harsh light on the human condition. Naturalist writers presented life as a brutal, losing battle between individuals and the forces of their environments, which could be as diverse as an Alaskan wilderness or a Chicago factory.

 Big Ideas Link to Web resources to further explore the Big Ideas at www.glencoe.com.

Cultural Links

⇒ The influence of the American Regionalist writers on subsequent American literature has been enormous. Ernest Hemingway once said, "All modern American literature comes from one book by Mark Twain called *Huckleberry Finn*."

⇒ Combining vivid, realistic descriptions of California frontier life with sentimental plots, Bret Harte largely invented the genre of the Western.

⇒ Kate Chopin's work is valued for its portrayals of attitudes toward race, class, ethnicity, and gender relations.

⇒ Stephen Crane was neglected for a time after his death in 1900 until writers began to recognize his experiments with subject, theme, and form.

Try using this organizer to explore your personal responses to the poetry, short stories, and nonfiction in this unit.

FOLDABLES Study Organizer **BOUND BOOK**

Connect to Today ⇒ Use what you have learned about the period to do one of these activities.

1. Speaking/Listening Work with other students to research art and music from the late 1800s to the early 1900s. Choose a piece of art or a song and find a connection to the social and economic situation of the United States during this time. Present your findings to the class.

2. Visual Literacy Create a map showing the regions of the country that were represented by Mark Twain, Willa Cather, Kate Chopin, and Bret Harte. For each area, create an icon to represent the author and the region.

3. Writing How would the muckraking social reformers of this period—such as Jane Addams and Upton Sinclair—view city life in the United States today? Write a brief essay that explores this question.

INDIANA ACADEMIC STANDARDS (page 478)
11.7.11 Evaluate the various ways in which events are presented…by visual image-makers…
11.5.3 Write reflective compositions that…draw comparisons between specific incidents and broader themes…

 Study Central Visit www.glencoe.com and click on Study Central to review Regionalism and Realism.

Regionalism and Local Color

Red Pepper Time, c. 1930. Oscar Edmund Berninghaus. Oil on canvas, 25 x 30¹⁄₁₆ in. Gift of Arvin Gottlieb. Smithsonian American Art Museum, Washington, DC.

"*Elsewhere the sky is the roof of the world; but here the earth is the floor of the sky.*"

—Willa Cather, *Death Comes for the Archbishop*

The Rise of Local Color Fiction

IN 1871, BRET HARTE SIGNED A $10,000 contract with *The Atlantic Monthly* magazine, the highest sum ever paid to an author at the time. The impressive sale of Harte's stories marked the beginning of the local color fiction boom. Still recovering from the devastation of the Civil War, readers welcomed the relief that Harte's light-hearted tales of the California Gold Rush provided.

Writers culturally reunited the country by crafting stories about real people, small towns, and regional lifestyles.

After the political reunification of the North and South, the focus on national issues gave way to smaller, regional concerns. Writers culturally reunited the country by crafting stories about real people, small towns, and regional lifestyles. In many cases, local color fiction reflected old-fashioned values, as if authors were writing to remember the country before it had been ravaged by war.

The Importance of Setting

Setting was the most distinct feature of local color stories, which most often took place in rural towns. Authors depicted in meticulous detail the time, place, and historical background in which events in their fiction occurred. The setting of local color fiction spanned the continent, from Harte's tales of California miners to Sarah Orne Jewett's stories of country dwellers in New England. Jewett, a prominent local colorist, wrote about common people living in coastal towns: doctors, sailors, mothers, and wives. Her most famous book, *The Country of the Pointed Firs*, was well received all over the nation. Local color writing appealed to a wide audience, regardless of its setting.

The Role of Character

While Harte and Jewett may have been among the first local colorists, the best known is Mark Twain. Twain's "The Celebrated Jumping Frog of Calaveras County" (page 484) continues to be one of the most popular works of local color fiction. Smiley, the story's protagonist, is typical of characters portrayed in local color writing. Characters are usually small-town residents, shown in their everyday lives performing everyday tasks.

The Landing, Bailey Island, Maine, c. 1907. Alfred Thompson Bricher. Oil on canvas, 38 x 81 in. Butler Institute of American Art, Youngstown, OH.

Smiley speaks with a regional dialect, another important trait of local color fiction. Twain, like many local colorists, peppered Smiley's dialogue with words and abbreviations unique to the area where the story takes place. For example, near the end of the story, Smiley exclaims, "Why, blame my cats, if he don't weigh five pound!" The realistic dialogue helps shape the reader's impression of both the character and what the town might be like.

The Lives of Women

Women writers had a strong presence in the local color movement. Willa Cather's "A Wagner Matinée" (page 520) relates the experience of a woman who gives up her passion for music in order to raise a family. Much local color fiction, especially from women authors, deals with the contrast between traditional values and changing perspectives. One of Cather's contemporaries, Mary E. Wilkins Freeman, wrote about women's social roles in her short story "A Church Mouse." Freeman's characters struggle with the desire for independence as opposed to the safety of marriage. Her work was widely published in women's magazines, which flourished in the late 1800s. The emergence of women's local color

Sod house and well in Custer County, Nebraska, c. 1890. Photograph.

fiction was also influenced by the woman suffrage movement, which had become active again after being halted by the Civil War.

Literature Online **Literary History** For more about local color fiction, go to www.glencoe.com.

RESPONDING AND THINKING CRITICALLY

1. Explain why you think local color fiction became so popular in the United States in the late nineteenth century.

2. Why did women writers have a strong presence in the local color movement?

3. How would you compare and contrast local color fiction with its predecessor, Romantic literature?

4. What are some examples of local color fiction that you know from books, movies, or television?

 INDIANA ACADEMIC STANDARDS (pages 480–481)
11.3 [Identify] story elements such as character [and] setting...

11.7.9 Analyze strategies used by the media to...transmit culture...

The Celebrated Jumping Frog of Calaveras County

MEET MARK TWAIN

"When I was born I was a member of a firm of twins," Twain told an audience in 1901. "And one of them disappeared." Although he was not actually a twin, Twain did have two sides to his personality. Born Samuel Langhorne Clemens, he took as his pen name a term used by riverboat pilots in navigation: *Mark Twain.*

Missouri Boyhood Samuel Clemens spent his early life in Missouri, chiefly in Hannibal, a city on the west bank of the Mississippi River. Life in this river town was full of adventure, but the death of Clemens's father when the boy was just eleven forced him to curtail his childhood escapades and his schooling in order to work as a printer's apprentice. At twenty-one, Clemens fulfilled his lifelong dream of becoming a riverboat pilot on the Mississippi River. He loved this profession better than any other because, as he declared, "a pilot was the only unfettered and entirely independent being that lived on the earth."

> "My books are water; those of the great geniuses are wine. Everybody drinks water."
>
> —Mark Twain

Travels When the Civil War closed the Mississippi River to commercial traffic, Samuel Clemens headed for Nevada in hopes of striking it rich. He prospected unsuccessfully there and in California, and eventually settled in San Francisco, where he met author Bret Harte. There he lectured and worked as a journalist, specializing in humorous feature stories. During this time, Twain wrote the story that brought him his first taste of fame: "The Celebrated Jumping Frog of Calaveras County." In 1867, as a traveling correspondent for the *Alta California,* Twain set out for Europe and the Middle East. This journey provided the material for *The Innocents Abroad; or, The New Pilgrim's Progress* (1869), which poked fun at inexperienced American travelers and quickly became a best seller.

Literary Success In 1870 Twain married Olivia Langdon, a wealthy easterner. They settled in Hartford, Connecticut, where Twain met William Dean Howells, the most influential literary critic of the day. In Howells's *Atlantic Monthly,* Twain recounted his experiences as a riverboat pilot in a series called "Old Times on the Mississippi," which he embellished and published eight years later as *Life on the Mississippi* (1883). *The Adventures of Tom Sawyer* (1876) established Twain as a master of fiction, and its sequel, *The Adventures of Huckleberry Finn* (1884), cemented Twain's place as one of the greatest novelists the United States has ever produced. His use of realism and detail influenced many later writers of American fiction, including Ernest Hemingway, who stated that "all modern American literature comes from one book by Mark Twain called *Huckleberry Finn.*"

Plagued by financial misfortunes and the deaths of loved ones, Twain's later years found him frequently embittered. In some of his later works, such as "The Man That Corrupted Hadleyburg," Twain brooded over the dark side of human nature. He is chiefly remembered today, however, for capturing the brash, optimistic spirit and youthful vitality of his fellow Americans.

Mark Twain was born in 1835 and died in 1910.

Literature Online **Author Search** For more about Mark Twain, go to www.glencoe.com.

Connecting to the Story

Mark Twain did not write a story; he told it. His mastery of American speech—the native vernacular—and his ability to "spin a yarn" are unrivaled. As you read, think about the following questions:

- Why do people love to spin yarns or tell tall tales—and to listen to them?
- What is the best way to tell a tall tale?

Building Background

This story takes place in the early 1860s in a small mining town called Angel's Camp, which still exists today in California. In 1848 James W. Marshall discovered rich deposits of gold at Sutter's Mill, near the Calaveras County town of Coloma. This discovery led to the California Gold Rush, during which many adventurous people thronged to California to prospect for gold, hoping to "strike it rich." In the remote mining camps and frontier towns, life was hard and entertainment was scarce. To create some fun, people invented tall tales—stories filled with humorous exaggerations. At Angel's Camp, Twain first heard someone tell the story that he later developed into "The Celebrated Jumping Frog of Calaveras County," his most famous western tale.

Setting Purposes for Reading

Big Idea Regionalism

As you read, notice the techniques Twain uses to give you the flavor of the Old West during the Gold Rush.

Literary Element Dialect

Dialect is a variation of a language spoken by a particular group, often within a specific region and time. Dialects may differ from the standard form of a language in vocabulary, pronunciation, or grammatical form. As you read, look for examples of dialect in this story.

- See Literary Terms Handbook, pp. R4–R5.

Literature Online **Interactive Literary Elements Handbook** To review or learn more about the literary elements, go to www.glencoe.com.

Reading Strategy Analyzing Comic Devices

In addition to dialect, Twain uses several other devices to create humor, including absurd situations, comic characters, and exaggerations.

Reading Tip: Taking Notes Use a web diagram to help you record details about each comic device listed.

Vocabulary

garrulous (gar′ ə ləs) *adj.* talkative; p. 484 *Our garrulous neighbor went on with his story, never pausing for breath.*

conjecture (kən jek′ chər) *v.* to form an opinion without definite evidence; to guess; p. 484 *Not really sure, I conjectured that she meant more than she said.*

dilapidated (di lap′ ə dā′ tid) *adj.* fallen into ruin or decay; shabby; p. 484 *Pigeons flew through the holes in the dilapidated roof.*

interminable (in tur′ mi nə bəl) *adj.* seemingly endless; p. 485 *Though the dull speech lasted only fifteen minutes, it seemed interminable.*

enterprising (en′ tər prī′ zing) *adj.* showing energy and initiative, especially in beginning new projects; p. 488 *The enterprising class planned to raise money in a new way—by having a silent auction.*

Vocabulary Tip: Word Roots When you are trying to figure out the meaning of an unfamiliar word, think of words that share a root with it. The words *interminable* and *terminal* share a root: the Latin word *terminus,* meaning "end" or "boundary."

INDIANA ACADEMIC STANDARDS (pages 483–489)
11.3.3 Analyze the ways in which...the author's style... achieve[s] specific...aesthetic (artistic) purposes...

11.2 Develop [reading] strategies...
11.5.9 Write...a literary analysis...

The Celebrated Jumping Frog of Calaveras County

Mark Twain

In compliance with the request of a friend of mine, who wrote me from the East, I called on good-natured, **garrulous** old Simon Wheeler, and inquired after my friend's friend, *Leonidas W. Smiley*, as requested to do, and I hereunto append[1] the result. I have a lurking suspicion that *Leonidas W.* Smiley is a myth; that my friend never knew such a personage; and that he only **conjectured** that, if I asked old Wheeler about him, it would remind him of his infamous *Jim* Smiley, and he would go to work and bore me nearly to death with some infernal[2] reminiscence of him as long and tedious as it should be useless to me. If that was the design, it certainly succeeded.

I found Simon Wheeler dozing comfortably by the bar-room stove of the old **dilapidated** tavern in the ancient mining camp of Angel's,[3] and I noticed that he was fat and bald-headed, and

---

1. *Append* means "to add as a supplement" or "to attach."

2. *Infernal* means "awful" or "thoroughly unpleasant."
3. *Angel's* refers to Angel's Camp.

Big Idea Regionalism *What sort of atmosphere would you expect to find in a mining camp?*

Vocabulary

garrulous (gar′ə ləs) *adj.* talkative
conjecture (kən jek′ chər) *v.* to form an opinion without definite evidence; to guess

Vocabulary

dilapidated (di lap′ə dā′tid) *adj.* fallen into ruin or decay; shabby had an expression of winning gentleness and simplicity upon his tranquil countenance.[4] He roused up and gave me good-day. I told him a friend of mine had commissioned me to make some inquiries about a cherished companion of his boyhood named *Leonidas W. Smiley—Rev. Leonidas W. Smiley*—a young minister of the Gospel, who he had heard was at one time a resident of Angel's Camp. I added that, if Mr. Wheeler could tell me any thing about this Rev. Leonidas W. Smiley, I would feel under many obligations to him.

Simon Wheeler backed me into a corner and blockaded me there with his chair, and then sat me down and reeled off the monotonous narrative which follows this paragraph. He never smiled, he never frowned, he never changed his voice from the gentle-flowing key to which he tuned the initial sentence, he never betrayed the slightest suspicion of enthusiasm; but all through the **interminable** narrative there ran a vein of impressive earnestness and sincerity, which showed me plainly that, so far from his imagining that there was any thing ridiculous or funny about his story, he regarded it as a really important matter, and admired its two heroes as men of transcendent[5] genius in finesse.[6]

To me, the spectacle of a man drifting serenely along through such a queer yarn without ever smiling, was exquisitely absurd. As I said before, I asked him to tell me what he knew of Rev. Leonidas W. Smiley, and he replied as follows. I let him go on in his own way, and never interrupted him once:

Visual Vocabulary
A *flume* is a trough or chute, often inclined, that carries water.

There was a feller here once by the name of *Jim* Smiley, in the winter of '49— or may be it was the spring of '50—I don't recollect exactly, somehow, though what makes me think it was one or the other is because I remember the big flume wasn't finished when he first came to the camp; but any way, he was the curiosest man about always betting on any thing that turned up you ever see, if he could get any body to bet on the other side; and if he couldn't he'd change sides. Any way that suited the other man would suit him—any way just so's he got a bet, *he* was satisfied. But still he was lucky, uncommon lucky; he most always come out winner. He was always ready and laying for a chance; there couldn't be no solitry thing mentioned but that feller'd offer to bet on it, and take any side you please, as I was just telling you. If there was a horse race, you'd find him flush,[7] or you'd find him busted at the end of it; if there was a dog-fight, he'd bet on it; if there was a cat-fight, he'd bet on it; if there was a chicken-fight, he'd bet on it; why, if there was two birds setting on a fence, he would bet you which one would fly first; or if there was a camp-meeting,[8] he would be there reg'lar, to bet on Parson Walker, which he judged to be the best exhorter[9] about here, and so he was, too, and a good man. If he even seen a straddle-bug[10] start to go anywheres, he would bet you how long it would take him to get wherever he was going to, and if you took him up, he would foller that straddle-bug to Mexico but what he would find out where he was bound for and how long he was on the road. Lots of the boys here has seen that Smiley, and can tell you about him. Why, it never made no difference to *him*—he would bet on *any* thing—the dangdest feller. Parson Walker's wife laid very sick once, for a good while, and it seemed as if they warn't going to save her; but one morning he come in, and Smiley asked how she was, and he said she was considerable better—thank the Lord for his inf'nit mercy—and coming on so smart that, with the blessing of Prov'dence,[11] she'd get well

---

4. A *tranquil countenance* is a calm face.
5. *Transcendent* means "surpassing others" or "superior."
6. *Finesse* is the smooth or artful handling of a situation.

7. Here, *flush* means "having a large amount of money" or "rich."
8. A *camp-meeting* is an outdoor religious gathering, sometimes held in a tent.
9. An *exhorter* is someone who urges by giving strong advice or warnings; here, a preacher.
10. A *straddle-bug* is a long-legged beetle.
11. *Prov'dence* (Providence) is God.

Vocabulary

interminable (in tur′mi nə bəl) *adj.* seemingly endless

Literary Element Dialect *How would you characterize Wheeler's use of language?*

Big Idea Regionalism *How does Twain evoke the region in this passage?*

yet; and Smiley, before he thought, says, "Well, I'll risk two-and-a-half[12] that she don't, any way."

Thish-yer[13] Smiley had a mare—the boys called her the fifteen-minute nag, but that was only in fun, you know, because, of course, she was faster than that—and he used to win money on that horse, for all she was so slow and always had the asthma, or the distemper, or the consumption,[14] or something of that kind. They used to give her two or three hundred yards start, and then pass her under way; but always at the fag-end[15] of the race she'd get excited and desperate-like, and come cavorting[16] and straddling up, and scattering her legs around limber, sometimes in the air, and sometimes out to one side amongst the fences, and kicking up m-o-r-e dust, and raising m-o-r-e racket with her coughing and sneezing and blowing her nose—and always fetch up at the stand[17] just about a neck ahead, as near as you could cipher it down.[18]

And he had a little small bull pup, that to look at him you'd think he wan't worth a cent,

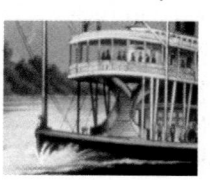

Visual Vocabulary
The *fo'castle*, or forecastle (fōkʹ səl), of a steamboat is a raised deck at the front of the boat.

but to set around and look ornery, and lay for a chance to steal something. But as soon as money was up on him, he was a different dog; his under-jaw'd begin to stick out like the fo'castle of a steamboat, and his teeth would uncover, and shine savage like the furnaces. And a dog might tackle him, and bully-rag[19] him, and bite him, and throw him over his shoulder two or three times, and Andrew Jackson—which was the name of the pup—Andrew Jackson would never let on but what *he* was satisfied, and hadn't expected nothing else—and the bets being doubled and doubled on the other side all the time, till the money was all up; and then all of a sudden he would grab that other dog jest by the

j'int of his hind leg and freeze to it—not chaw, you understand, but only jest grip and hang on till they throwed up the sponge,[20] if it was a year. Smiley always come out winner on that pup, till he harnessed[21] a dog once that didn't have no hind legs, because they'd been sawed off by a circular saw, and when the thing had gone along far enough, and the money was all up, and he come to make a snatch for his pet holt,[22] he saw in a minute how he'd been imposed on, and how the other dog had him in the door,[23] so to speak, and he 'peared surprised, and then he looked sorter discouraged-like, and didn't try no more to win the fight, and so he got shucked out[24] bad. He give Smiley a look, as much as to say his heart was broke, and it was *his* fault, for putting up a dog that hadn't no hind legs for him to take holt of, which was his main dependence in a fight, and then he limped off a piece and laid down and died. It was a good pup, was that Andrew Jackson, and would have made a name for hisself if he'd lived, for the stuff was in him, and he had genius—I know it, because he hadn't had no opportunities to speak of, and it don't stand to reason that a dog could make such a fight as he could under them circumstances, if he hadn't no talent. It always makes me feel sorry when I think of that last fight of his'n, and the way it turned out.

Well, thish-yer Smiley had rat-tarriers,[25] and chicken cocks,[26] and tom-cats, and all them kind of things, till you couldn't rest, and you couldn't fetch nothing for him to bet on but he'd match you. He ketched a frog one day, and took him home, and said he cal'klated[27] to edercate him; and so he never done nothing for three months but set in his back yard and learn[28] that frog to jump. And you bet you he

---

12. *Risk two-and-a-half* means "risk, or bet, $2.50."
13. *Thish-yer* is dialect for "this here."
14. *Consumption* is another name for tuberculosis.
15. The *fag-end* is the last part.
16. *Cavorting* means "running and jumping around playfully."
17. *Fetch up at the stand* means "arrive at the grandstand," which was placed at the finish line.
18. *Cipher it down* means "calculate it."
19. *Bully-rag* means "to intimidate" or "to abuse."

20. *Throwed up the sponge* means "gave up the contest."
21. Here, *harnessed* means "set up a fight with."
22. A *pet holt* is a favorite hold.
23. *Had him in the door* means "had him at a disadvantage or in a tight place."
24. *Shucked out* means "beaten" or "defeated."
25. *Rat-tarriers* are dogs (terriers) once used for catching rats.
26. *Chicken cocks* are adult male chickens (roosters) that are trained to fight.
27. *Cal'klated* is dialect for calculated, meaning "planned."
28. Here, *learn* means "teach."

Reading Strategy Analyzing Comic Devices *What makes this situation humorous?*

Viewing the Photograph: What aspects of life in a mining camp are captured in the photograph?

did learn him, too. He'd give him a little punch behind, and the next minute you'd see that frog whirling in the air like a doughnut—see him turn one summerset, or may be a couple, if he got a good start, and come down flat-footed and all right, like a cat. He got him up so in the matter of catching flies, and kept him in practice so constant, that he'd nail a fly every time as far as he could see him. Smiley said all a frog wanted was education, and he could do most any thing—and I believe him. Why, I've seen him set Dan'l Webster[29] down here on this floor—Dan'l Webster was the name of the frog—and sing out, "Flies, Dan'l, flies!" and quicker'n you could wink, he'd spring straight up, and snake a fly off'n the counter there, and flop down on the floor again as solid as a gob of mud, and fall to scratching the side of his head with his hind foot as indifferent as if he hadn't no idea he'd been doin' any more'n any frog might do. You never see a frog so modest and straightfor'ard as he was, for all he was so gifted. And when it come to fair and square jumping on a dead level, he could get over more ground at one straddle[30] than any animal of his breed you ever see. Jumping on a dead level was his strong suit, you understand; and when it come to that, Smiley would ante up[31] money on him as long as he had a red.[32] Smiley was monstrous proud of his frog, and well he might be, for fellers that had traveled and been everywheres, all said he laid over any frog that ever *they* see.

Well, Smiley kept the beast in a little lattice box, and he used to fetch him down town sometimes and lay for a bet. One day a feller—a stranger in the camp, he was—come across him with his box, and says:

"What might it be that you've got in the box?"

And Smiley says, sorter indifferent like, "It might be a parrot, or it might be a canary, may be, but it an't—it's only just a frog."

And the feller took it, and looked at it careful, and turned it round this way and that, and says, "H'm—so 'tis. Well, what's *he* good for?"

"Well," Smiley says, easy and careless, "He's good enough for *one* thing, I should judge—he can outjump any frog in Calaveras county."

The feller took the box again, and took another long, particular look, and give it back to

---

29. *Dan'l Webster* refers to Daniel Webster (1782–1852), a famous orator who served as a U.S. senator and a U.S. secretary of state.

Reading Strategy Analyzing Comic Devices *How does Twain create humor in this passage?*

---

30. Here, *straddle* means "to jump."
31. *Ante up* means "to put into the pool" or "to bet."
32. *A red* refers to a red cent, meaning "any money at all."

Smiley, and says, very deliberate, "Well, I don't see no p'ints[33] about that frog that's any better'n any other frog."

"May be you don't," Smiley says, "May be you understand frogs, and may be you don't understand 'em; may be you've had experience, and may be you an't only a amature, as it were. Anyways, I've got *my* opinion, and I'll risk forty dollars that he can outjump any frog in Calaveras county."

And the feller studied a minute, and then says, kinder sad like, "Well, I'm only a stranger here, and I an't got no frog; but if I had a frog, I'd bet you."

And then Smiley says, "That's all right—that's all right—if you'll hold my box a minute, I'll go and get you a frog." And so the feller took the box, and put up his forty dollars along with Smiley's, and set down to wait.

So he set there a good while thinking and thinking to hisself, and then he got the frog out and prized his mouth open and took a teaspoon and filled him full of quail shot[34]—filled him pretty near up to his chin—and set him on the floor. Smiley he went to the swamp and slopped around in the mud for a long time, and finally he ketched a frog, and fetched him in, and give him to this feller, and says:

"Now, if you're ready, set him alongside of Dan'l, with his fore-paws just even with Dan'l, and I'll give the word." Then he says, "One—two—three—jump!" and him and the feller touched up the frogs from behind, and the new frog hopped off, but Dan'l give a heave, and hysted up his shoulders—so—like a Frenchman, but it wan't no use—he couldn't budge; he was planted as solid as an anvil, and he couldn't no more stir than if he was anchored out. Smiley was a good deal surprised, and he was disgusted too, but he didn't have no idea what the matter was, of course.

The feller took the money and started away; and when he was going out at the door, he sorter

jerked his thumb over his shoulders—this way—at Dan'l, and says again, very deliberate, "Well, *I* don't see no p'ints about that frog that's any better'n any other frog."

Smiley he stood scratching his head and looking down at Dan'l a long time, and at last he says, "I do wonder what in the nation that frog throw'd off for—I wonder if there an't something the matter with him—he 'pears to look mighty baggy, somehow." And he ketched Dan'l by the nap of the neck, and lifted him up and says, "Why, blame my cats, if he don't weigh five pound!" and turned him upside down, and he belched out a double handful of shot. And then he see how it was, and he was the maddest man—he set the frog down and took out after that feller, but he never ketched him. And—

[Here Simon Wheeler heard his name called from the front yard, and got up to see what was wanted.] And turning to me as he moved away, he said: "Just set where you are, stranger, and rest easy—I an't going to be gone a second."

But, by your leave, I did not think that a continuation of the history of the **enterprising** vagabond *Jim* Smiley would be likely to afford[35] me much information concerning the Rev. *Leonidas W.* Smiley, and so I started away.

At the door I met the sociable Wheeler returning, and he buttonholed[36] me and recommenced:

"Well, thish-yer Smiley had a yaller one-eyed cow that didn't have no tail, only jest a short stump like a bannanner, and——"

"Oh! hang Smiley and his afflicted cow!" I muttered, good-naturedly, and bidding the old gentleman good-day, I departed. ✷

---

33. *P'ints* is dialect for points, meaning "qualities" or "characteristics."
34. *Quail shot* is ammunition made up of small lead pellets.

Reading Strategy Analyzing Comic Devices *How might the stranger's action bring about an absurd situation?*

35. *Afford* means "to give" or "to provide."
36. *Buttonholed* means "detained in conversation."

Literary Element Dialect *How would you express Wheeler's statement in Standard English?*

Vocabulary

enterprising (en′tər prī′zing) *adj.* showing energy and initiative, especially in beginning new projects

RESPONDING AND THINKING CRITICALLY

Respond

1. What questions would you like to ask Simon Wheeler?

Recall and Interpret

2. (a)How does the narrator come to meet Simon Wheeler and to hear his story? (b)What can you infer about the narrator's attitude toward Wheeler?

3. (a)Why does Wheeler call Smiley "the curiosest man"? (b)What conclusions can you draw about Smiley's character, based on the tale Wheeler tells?

4. (a)What does Smiley entice the stranger to do? (b)What event or events determine the outcome of the encounter with the stranger? Explain your answer.

Analyze and Evaluate

5. Why do you think Wheeler tells his listener about the mare and bull pup first, before focusing on the frog?

6. Who is the main character in this story? Explain.

7. (a)In this selection, one story serves as a frame for another story. Which story is the frame? (b)Why might Twain have chosen this structure?

Connect

8. **Big Idea** **Regionalism** How does Twain capture the flavor of the Old West in this story?

LITERARY ANALYSIS

Literary Element **Dialect**

Twain uses **dialect** to evoke the region and the people he is writing about, as in this example: "He ketched a frog one day, and took him home, and said he cal'klated to edercate him. . . ."

1. What words in the example above does Wheeler pronounce differently from Standard English?

2. What is the difference between Wheeler's language and the narrator's? What does this difference suggest about them?

Writing About Literature

Analyze Setting Write a brief essay to analyze the **setting** of this story. In your essay, explore the following questions:

- Why might Twain have selected this setting?

- How would the story have been different if the narrator had met Wheeler in a city?

Support your position with details from the story.

READING AND VOCABULARY

Reading Strategy **Analyzing Comic Devices**

Mark Twain first achieved fame as a western humorist, and his humor is irresistible. He once wrote, "The humorous story may be spun out to great length and may wander around as much as it pleases, and arrive nowhere in particular."

1. Does this story fit Twain's description of a comic story?

2. What elements of humor in this story do you find most effective?

Vocabulary Practice

Practice with Word Roots Match each of the root words listed below to a vocabulary word from the selection. Use a dictionary if you need help.

1. *dilapidare,* meaning "to pelt with stones" in Latin
2. *garrire,* meaning "to chatter" in Latin
3. *conjectura,* meaning "guess" in Latin
    a. garrulous **b.** conjecture **c.** dilapidated

Literature Online **Web Activities** For eFlashcards, Selection Quick Checks, and other Web activities, go to www.glencoe.com.

from

Two Views of the River

Mark Twain

BEFORE YOU READ

Literary Element **Analogy**

An **analogy** is a comparison made between two things to show the similarities between them. Writers use analogies in order to make experiences more vivid for the reader or to explain unfamiliar things by comparing them to familiar things. As you read, notice the analogy Twain uses in this memoir about his experiences as a riverboat pilot.

• See Literary Terms Handbook, p. R1.

Literature Online **Interactive Literary Elements Handbook** To review or learn more about the literary elements, go to www.glencoe.com.

Reading Strategy **Comparing and Contrasting Language**

Twain's first two sentences in this part of *Life on the Mississippi* suggest a contrast: ". . . I had made a valuable acquisition. But I had lost something, too." Twain develops this contrast by describing two different perspectives of the river. As you read, consider how the diction, or choice of words, reflects this contrast. Use a chart to record your notes and observations.

Now when I had mastered the language of this water and had come to know every trifling feature that bordered the great river as familiarly as I knew the letters of the alphabet, I had made a valuable acquisition. But I had lost something, too. I had lost something which could never be restored to me while I lived. All the grace, the beauty, the poetry had gone out of the majestic river! I still keep in mind a certain wonderful sunset which I witnessed when steamboating was new to me. A broad expanse of the river was turned to blood; in the middle distance the red hue brightened into gold, through which a solitary log came floating, black and conspicuous; in one place a long, slanting mark lay sparkling upon the water; in another the surface was broken by boiling, tumbling rings, that were as many-tinted as an opal; where the ruddy flush was faintest, was a smooth spot that was covered with graceful circles and radiating lines, ever so delicately traced; the shore on our left was densely wooded, and the somber shadow that fell from this forest was broken in one place by a long, ruffled trail that shone like silver; and high above the forest wall a clean-stemmed dead tree waved a single leafy bough that glowed like a flame in the unobstructed splendor that was flowing from the sun. There were graceful curves, reflected images, woody heights, soft distances; and over the whole scene, far and near, the dissolving lights drifted steadily, enriching it, every passing moment, with new marvels of coloring.

I stood like one bewitched.[1] I drank it in, in a speechless rapture. The world was new to me, and I had never seen anything like this at home. But as I have said, a day came when I began to cease from noting the glories and the charms which the moon and the sun and the twilight wrought[2] upon the river's face; another day came when I ceased altogether to note them. Then, if that sunset scene had been repeated, I should have looked upon it without rapture, and should have commented upon it, inwardly, after this fashion: This sun means that we are going to have wind tomorrow; that floating log means that the river is rising, small thanks to it; that slanting mark on the water refers to a bluff reef which is going to kill somebody's steamboat one of these nights, if it keeps on stretching out like that; those tumbling "boils" show a dissolving bar and a changing channel there; the lines and circles in the slick water over yonder are a warning that that troublesome place is shoaling up[3] dangerously; that silver streak in the shadow of the forest is the "break" from a new snag, and he has located himself in the very best place he could have found to fish for steamboats; that tall dead tree, with a single living branch, is not going to last long, and then how is a body ever going to get through this blind place at night without the friendly old landmark?

No, the romance and the beauty were all gone from the river. All the value any feature of it had for me now was the amount of usefulness it could furnish toward compassing the safe piloting of a

Mark Twain on Ship Deck, March 15, 1901.

Viewing the Photograph: How do you think Twain might have been feeling at the moment this photo was taken?

steamboat. Since those days, I have pitied doctors from my heart. What does the lovely flush in a beauty's cheek mean to a doctor but a "break" that ripples above some deadly disease? Are not all her visible charms sown thick with what are to him the signs and symbols of hidden decay? Does he ever see her beauty at all, or doesn't he simply view her professionally, and comment upon her unwholesome condition all to himself? And doesn't he sometimes wonder whether he has gained most or lost most by learning his trade? ꙮ

---

1. *Bewitched* means "captivated" or "entranced."
2. *Wrought* means "created."
3. A *shoal* is a shallow place in the water. To *shoal up* means "to become shallow."

Reading Strategy Comparing and Contrasting Language *How has Twain's perspective of the tree changed?*

Literary Element Analogy *What do doctors and riverboat pilots have in common?*

RESPONDING AND THINKING CRITICALLY

Respond

1. What are your impressions of Mark Twain's personality?

Recall and Interpret

2. (a)What is "the language of this water" that Twain masters? (b)Why does he suggest that learning how to navigate the river is like mastering a foreign language?

3. (a)What does Twain mean by "the romance and the beauty" of the river? (b)Why does he lose the ability to see these special qualities forever?

4. (a)What terms does Twain use that would be familiar mainly to riverboat pilots or people living along the river? (b)Why does Twain include these terms in this memoir?

Analyze and Evaluate

5. Do you think that Twain gained more or lost more by learning the trade of a riverboat pilot?

6. What do you think was Twain's main purpose for writing this memoir?

7. Does Twain make the job of riverboat pilot sound appealing?

Connect

8. **Big Idea** Regionalism Regionalist writers portrayed the distinctive traits of particular areas of the United States. From reading Twain's memoir, what did you learn about the challenges of life on the Mississippi River?

LITERARY ANALYSIS

Literary Element Analogy

In this memoir, Twain draws an **analogy** between a riverboat pilot and a medical doctor. Twain's audience knew much about doctors but knew little about riverboat pilots.

1. What does Twain achieve by concluding this section with an analogy?

2. Which of the following trades or professions might have been the best substitute for the profession of doctor in Twain's analogy?

- stagecoach driver
- train engineer
- factory worker
- musician
- farmer

3. Rewrite the end of the selection using the new analogy you chose.

Review: Tone

As you learned in Unit One, **tone** is the attitude that a writer expresses toward his or her subject matter. Tone is conveyed through elements such as word choice, punctuation, sentence structure, and figures of speech. A writer's tone may convey a variety of attitudes, such as sympathy, objectivity, or humor.

Partner Activity Meet with a classmate and discuss the tone of Twain's memoir. Fill in a chart like the one below with elements from the story that convey tone. Based on these elements, list the tone of the memoir at the top.

Tone:		
word choice	sentence structure	figures of speech

Reading Strategy Comparing and Contrasting Language

In this section of *Life on the Mississippi*, Twain describes how his perspective of the river shifted from the poetic to the practical as he learned the trade of a riverboat pilot.

1. What words in the first paragraph capture "the romance and the beauty" of the river?

2. What words in the second paragraph convey a practical view of the river?

Vocabulary Practice

The word *conjecture* is made up of the Latin prefix *con-*, meaning "together," and the root *-ject*, meaning "to throw." When you conjecture, you do not have enough evidence to draw a logical conclusion, so you throw thoughts together; you guess.

Practice Use your knowledge of the root *-ject* and familiar prefixes to answer the following questions.

1. Does a person with *dejected* spirits feel hopeful, sad, or outraged?

2. What might a person giving a speech do to *inject* some humor?

3. Which of the following is used as a *projectile*— a cannonball, a life raft, or a rocking chair?

Academic Vocabulary

Here are two words from the vocabulary list on page R86. These words will help you think, write, and talk about the selection.

region (rē′ jən) a broad geographic area distinguished by similar features

impact (im′ pakt) a significant or major effect

Practice and Apply
1. Which **regions** of the United States do Twain's writings depict?

2. What **impact** did Twain's training as a riverboat pilot have on his descriptions of the Mississippi

Writing About Literature

Evaluate Contemporary Relevance Mark Twain expresses two views of the Mississippi River—one poetic and one technical. Write an essay in which you use the same technique. Start by choosing an aspect of nature, such as a storm, as a writing topic. You might begin with your admiration for the storm, followed by the technical details about the storm's effects that influence your perspective. Follow the steps shown below.

Paragraph one	Introduce your topic.
Paragraph two	Tell what you admired or enjoyed about this topic.
Paragraph three	Describe some technical aspects of this topic.
Paragraph four	Tell what caused the difference between your two views.
Paragraph five	Draw conclusions about the tendency of people to be fooled by nature.

After you complete your draft, meet with a peer reviewer to evaluate each other's work and to suggest revisions. Then proofread and edit your draft for errors.

Interdisciplinary Activity: Science

Investigating a Local River With a group of classmates, create a report on an important river or other body of water in the region in which you live. Use a double entry journal to record your data.

Questions	Answers
1. What is the name of the river, and what is the origin of that name?	
2.	
3.	

Literature Online **Web Activities** For eFlashcards, Selection Quick Checks, and other Web activities, go to www.glencoe.com.

Preview the Article

"Life Along the Mississippi" documents the Mississippi River region's current struggle to prosper in a changing economy.

1. What have you already learned about life on the Mississippi from reading Twain's work? What else would you like to know?

2. Read the section headings throughout the article. What clues do these provide about the article's content?

Set a Purpose for Reading

Read to learn about the communities along the Mississippi, depicted in literature by Mark Twain, and how this region has changed over time.

Reading Strategy

Clarifying Meaning
When you **clarify the meaning** of a text, you work to unlock the meaning of each section or paragraph. Create a chart similar to the one below and answer the questions to help you clarify meaning as you read.

Questions	Answers
What does this section mean?	
How does this relate to the main idea?	

ACADEMIC STANDARDS (pages 494–498)
11.2.2 Analyze the way in which clarity of meaning is affected by the patterns of organization…

11.2 Develop strategies such as… asking questions…

TIME

Life Along the Mississippi

By NANCY GIBBS

UNLESS YOU ARE DRIVING ACROSS IT OR FLYING OVER it or floating down it, it is hard to see the actual Mississippi. Anyone who had anything to do with the river discovered long ago that this huge continental drainpipe was too powerful to leave alone. So the great engineers designed the levees and locks and dams that reduced the number of ships that sank and towns that vanished. But their work also hid the river behind its walls and left the rest to the imagination.

Aside from Mark Twain's *Huckleberry Finn*, the imagination may be the best guide for exploring the Mississippi River. Otherwise you need both a boat and a car, maybe a canoe and a bicycle too, for the skinny inlets and alleys along the way, and a lot of time and patience. We could at best splash in it a little, to see what it felt like and what we might learn—and unlearn—by stopping along the way. It was worth remembering Huck Finn's lesson: The river is the sanctuary; the shore is where you get into trouble.

In a country where travelers lament that every town looks the same—Where's Taco Bell? Where's Home Depot?—it's easy to assume that no region is really distinct anymore. We're all online now, and even in Baton Rouge, Louisiana, a local observes, the kids don't say "y'all" anymore. They say, "you guys," just like on TV.

Heading South

So we were surprised, everywhere we went. The more you explore the communities along the river, and the farther south you travel down into the Mississippi Delta, more than one thing becomes clear: This is still a land unto itself, defined by its colorful, bloody past. It is a land

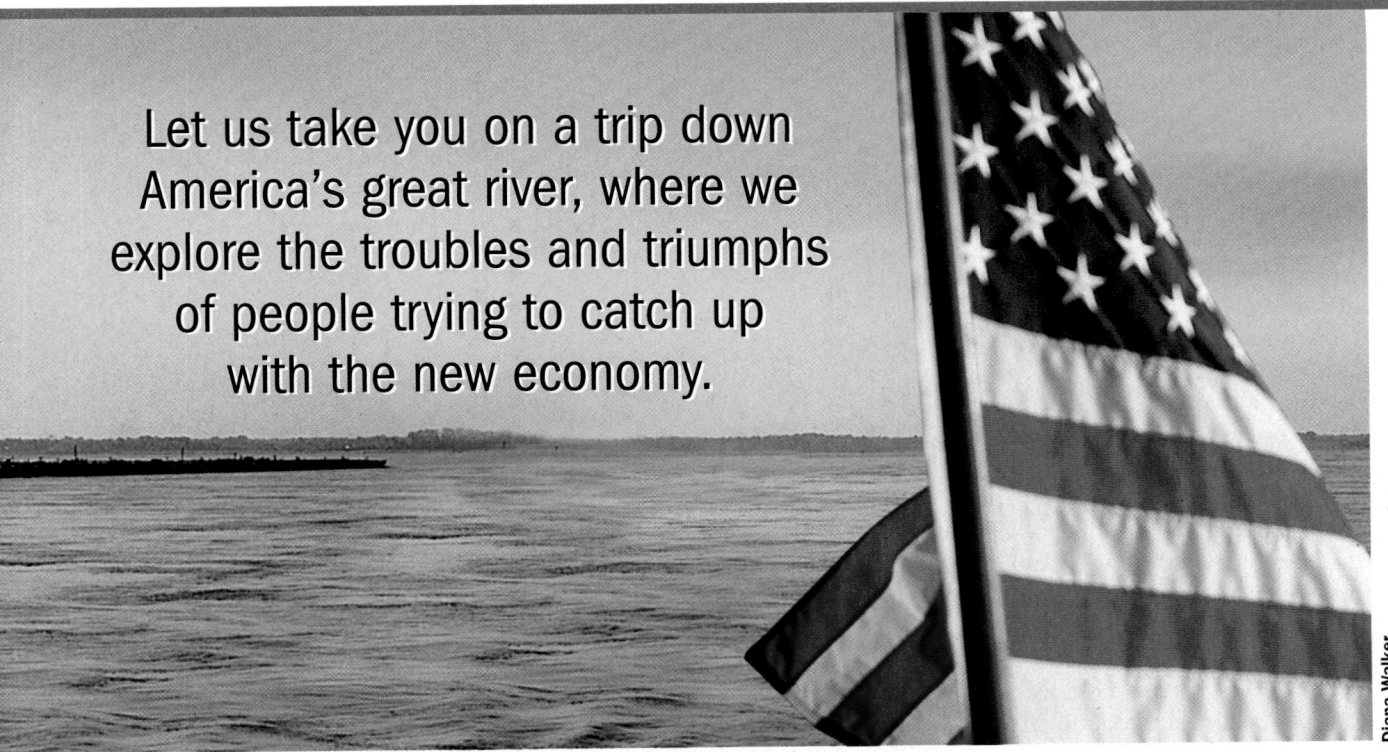

Let us take you on a trip down America's great river, where we explore the troubles and triumphs of people trying to catch up with the new economy.

Diana Walker

apart from the region that cradles the early stretches of the river itself, the Midwestern states of Minnesota, Wisconsin, and Iowa. While these states have reinvented themselves three times in a half century, moving from agriculture to industry to high technology, many communities in the Mississippi Delta have wrestled with the explosion of progress and prosperity.

The South is where the country's two wars were fought: the Civil War and, a century later, the battle for civil rights. "Of course the war is not over," says our 87-year-old guide in Vicksburg, Mississippi. Now there is a quieter conflict raging, not on the broad political stage but in the particulars of individual lives. Along the river, people hear about the new economy, but they don't have a ticket to get there. Information superhighway? Progress here is a back road, winding, scenic, and personal, but slow by the standards of a country that hurries into the future.

Even progress on race comes in the most intimate gestures: Last December, as Elnora Littleton in Rosedale, Mississippi, tells it, she became the first African American woman in those parts ever to preach at a white man's funeral. In this part of the country, she says, it is a milestone worth noting. "I made history," she says.

Diana Walker (4)

A Terrible Beauty

In the South, the river is the color of *café au lait* (coffee with milk). Down toward the mouth of the Mississippi, the land was formed of sedimentary deposits from farther upriver, including the rich topsoil blown from the hills of Wyoming into the Missouri and acres of Kansas prairie swallowed by flooding and swept downstream. Mark Twain's characters claimed that a man who drank the water could grow corn in his stomach. You know all this, and yet you are unprepared for the Delta, otherworldly and flat, the best place to grow cotton on this earth. It was once a hellish jungle, cleared by the backbreaking labor of enslaved persons and sharecroppers. It's like a wet western Kansas—beautiful, flat, and fertile.

The difference, of course, is that when faced with the shrinking labor needs of modern farming, the good people of western Kansas simply moved away in search of better lives elsewhere. While this happened in the Delta as well, a large number of people chose to stay in one of the poorest regions in the U.S. The average family of four here has an income of $16,538, slightly more than half the national average. In Mississippi County, Arkansas, 35% of kids live in poverty, and 40% of adults don't have a high school diploma.

If the new economy has not yet flowed downstream, there are lots of people who will tell you no one is even looking for it here. Whether or not a town stays afloat has a lot to do with whether the local factory is still open—the fate of the town rests in the hands of Continental Concrete, Sparta Printing, the Mississippi Lime Co., Tower Rock Quarry, Ralston Purina, and Pillsbury. When one of these leaves, and the farms start to fail, an entire town can shrivel and die. Laid-off workers lose their livelihood. Retired workers lose their health insurance.

Riverfront architecture in the Mississippi River town of Alton, Illinois, reflects the river's colorful past.

Town and Out?

We were left asking the same question all these towns face as the ground shifts beneath their feet: What's it going to be? Change? Or die? Is there maybe another choice? The towns individually try to reinvent themselves, and the region as a whole tries to reinvent itself. As you move farther south, many towns don't have the roads or infrastructure to recruit some big new car plant or distribution center.

The idea of luring a nice little software company is years away.

Suppose you have lost your brickyard, and the tugs no longer stop at your town, and the interstate has drawn the megastores, and even the schools and churches move away, and the young people leave, and Main Street is on life support. The Chamber of Commerce gets together and daydreams: What would it take to bring life back to

Diana Walker

this town? Or do we just roll up the streets and move on?

For many towns, the answer is to attract tourists. They say, if we can't find some big new employer to bring the new economy to town, how about reverting to the old economy—the very old one? In this polished and pasteurized vision, Main Street becomes a theme park of 19th–century life, with women wearing petticoats and shops selling candlesticks and

lemon drops. Kimmswick, Missouri, was almost dead after the lumberyard and the brickyard closed—until 7-Up heiress Luci Anna Ross began buying up collapsing buildings and renting them out as gift shops and bed-and-breakfasts. Now there is the Kimmswick Korner gift shop and lots of places to buy apple butter or have your horse reshod. The annual Apple Butter Festival gets 40,000 people. More than 100,000 come to Hannibal, Missouri, for Tom Sawyer Days on the Fourth of July weekend. Disney even sent a representative to Hannibal to learn how to re-create Tom Sawyer for its theme parks. Having developed everyplace else, Americans are homesteading the past.

Inventing History/Prettifying the Past

But because this re-creation of the past is for tourists, it's an airbrushed souvenir postcard. You see only the good side of a town's history—or a distorted version of that history. In Nauvoo, Illinois, the Mormons celebrate their 19th–century village life as they rebuild the town and its temple as a pilgrimage spot. Glossed over are the bloody religious battles that led to their being pillaged and expelled in the first place. The hotel owner in Kimmswick says the town's latest scheme is reenactments of the Civil War battle there. Was there ever really a Battle of Kimmswick? He concedes that it was, in his words, "just a skirmish that involved three Confederate soldiers hiding in a cave." Whatever.

This sort of thing is what social critics denounce as the strip-mining of history to market a version of the past that has a special appeal. This is not re-creating the past, they say, so much as distorting it. Back when life in these towns was real, it wasn't always quaint—yet

quaint is what sells now. Create a time that feels sweet and simple, and you don't have to smell the horses or die of cholera.

Cairo's "Main" Dilemma

If you want to visit the most unusual theme park in America, try the Main Street in Cairo, Illinois. It is a water slide of desolation, one abandoned building after another, with 90% of the storefronts dark and boarded over.

If Cairo is a ghost town, it was the fight for justice that killed it. "It used to be called Little Chicago," says Deputy Mayor Judson Childs, walking a couple of visitors to the town center, where civil rights battles flared in the 1960s. African Americans boycotted stores that discriminated; whites retaliated with violence; federal authorities intervened. But most whites chose to shut down their stores and leave Cairo rather than integrate. Over time the streets of Cairo became empty. Now if you want gas, you have to get it before 8 at night. To shop or go to a movie means driving 30 or 40 miles into Kentucky or Missouri. A woman in her late 20s sadly remarks, "This town is trapped in the past."

Maybe it's natural to try to market Cairo. Just turn the 1872 customhouse into a museum, get a big grant to repave the center of town with cobblestones and fake streetcar lines, peddle the old glory days of the big river town, and hope no one asks how it died. There is lots of history here, all fascinating but not pretty. So some residents aren't sure that the buses will ever come rolling in or the hotels ever reopen. "You ask the average person on the street what Cairo needs," says Mayor James Wilson, "and they'll say a McDonald's and a Wal-Mart."

Home of the Blues

The future of Clarksdale, Mississippi, is also tied to its past. This Delta town is trying to find its way by reengineering its cash crop, the blues.

IN FORT MADISON, IOWA, a town that has found a way to revive downtown, residents gather for a band concert.

Steve Liss

There is the newly reopened Delta Blues Museum, which honors such hometown heroes as Charley Patton, Son House, Robert Johnson, Muddy Waters, and John Lee Hooker. The history of the music is the story of the people who invented it and the suffering that created it. Without African American workers to clear the thickly wooded Delta plain and sharecroppers to pick the cotton, there would have been no plantation economy; without African Americans to sing the work songs and field chants and play diddley bows and mail-order guitars, there would be no Delta blues. Without the blues, there would be no rock 'n' roll to conquer the world and help sell all those burgers and jeans. The poorest, most oppressed people in America created its richest cultural legacy, and that, of course, yields all kinds of lessons for anyone willing to listen closely.

"Are you going to find anything good to write about?" people ask again and again. They are aware of how things must look to a bunch of outsiders. The natives know that much of what is great and sweet and honorable in these places never makes headlines. The Cairo deputy fire chief will tell you how many people appear in an instant when a windstorm sweeps through town and smashes a block of homes. Anyplace you have good friends is a place worth staying. Here and elsewhere, there are big groups of people—ministers and teachers and store owners and bureaucrats—who are prepared to give all their time and muscle to putting things right, making a place better. To the outsider, it would seem so much easier just to pick up and move on. Trying to stay, and to change, is an act of faith.

**–Updated 2005,
from TIME, July 10, 2000**

RESPONDING AND THINKING CRITICALLY

Respond

1. How did this article make you feel about the situation that many of the small towns along the Mississippi face?

Recall and Interpret

2. (a)What is the "new economy" the author refers to? (b)Why are the communities along the Mississippi not yet a part of this?

3. (a)What kinds of businesses have found success in many of the small towns along the Mississippi River? (b)Why might the towns want to "prettify" their past?

Analyze and Evaluate

4. (a)Return to the graphic organizer you created to clarify meaning. What ideas does the author express in the subsection "Home of the Blues"? (b)Why does the author claim that the past is connected to the future of the Mississippi Delta?

5. (a)How would you describe Gibbs's tone, or attitude toward her subject, in this article? Support your response with details from the text. (b)How might this **tone** contribute to an overall **bias**, or inclination toward a certain opinion?

Connect

6. Compare and contrast Mark Twain's and Nancy Gibbs's portrayals of the Mississippi Delta region. What are their similarities and differences?

Lucinda Matlock and
Fiddler Jones

MEET EDGAR LEE MASTERS

Edgar Lee Masters's *Spoon River Anthology* took early twentieth-century readers by surprise. Published in 1915, the anthology is a collection of free-verse first-person monologues spoken by the people of a small Midwestern town, who are now "sleeping on the hill." Masters called the poems epitaphs.

The realism and irony expressed in *Spoon River Anthology* were at odds with the romantic and sentimental poetry popular at the time. Though some critics questioned this new type of poetry, the book sold thousands of copies, is still in print, and has even been adapted for the stage. After the anthology's publication, Ezra Pound wrote of Masters, "At last! America has discovered a poet."

> *"It is all very well, but for
> myself I know
> I stirred certain vibrations in
> Spoon River
> Which are my true epitaph,
> more lasting than stone."*
>
> —Edgar Lee Masters
> "Percival Sharp"

From Small Town to Supreme Court Born in Kansas, Masters grew up in the small Illinois towns of Petersburg and Lewistown. As a boy, he spent long periods of time at his grandfather's farm, where he fished, rode horses, and read Charles Dickens and Ralph Waldo Emerson. After graduating high school, he worked as an apprentice for a local printer and attended Knox College for one year.

Although Masters wanted to study literature and be a writer, his father pushed him toward a career

in law. Masters eventually took up both pursuits and established his first law office in Chicago in 1893. He married Helen M. Jenkins, the daughter of another Chicago lawyer, in 1898, and they had three children. Masters was a successful attorney and argued some cases before the U.S. Supreme Court.

Literary Success Masters's first book, *A Book of Verses*, was published in 1898, and he published a number of other poetry books, a collection of essays, and several plays over the next sixteen years. Through his writing, he became friends with Carl Sandburg and Harriet Monroe, the editor of *Poetry* magazine. Despite Masters's ties to the Chicago community, he later separated from his family and moved to New York City. He married Elaine Coyne, a teacher, in 1926.

Spoon River Anthology was well received both critically and commercially. Masters was later awarded the Poetry Society of America Award, the Mark Twain silver medal, and the Shelley Memorial Award. By the end of his life, Masters had published more than fifty volumes, including poetry collections, plays, novels and biographies. *Spoon River*, however, remained his only literary success.

Edgar Lee Masters was born in 1868 and died in 1950.

Literature Online Author Search For more about Edgar Lee Masters, go to www.glencoe.com.

Connecting to the Poems

As you read "Lucinda Matlock" and "Fiddler Jones," note what experiences matter to the speakers of the poems. Think about these questions:

- If you were to sum up your life so far, what experiences would you focus on?
- What meaning would you find in those experiences?

Building Background

When Edgar Lee Masters read the epigrams from the *Greek Anthology*—an ancient collection of about 3,700 short poems—he was struck by their brevity, wit, and irony. He decided to write a similar collection comprising free-verse epitaphs in the form of monologues. The result was *Spoon River Anthology.* Masters's characters were inspired by people he knew; Lucinda Matlock, for example, is based on his grandmother, Lucinda Masters. Many of the monologues in *Spoon River Anthology* are related, so a complex history of numerous families unfolds.

Setting Purposes for Reading

Big Idea Regionalism

As you read these two poems, consider what they reveal about the customs and lifestyle of the people of Masters's fictional Midwestern town.

Literary Element Dramatic Monologue

Each of these poems is a **dramatic monologue,** a form of dramatic poetry in which the speaker addresses a silent listener. The speaker in these poems is not Masters but a character he created. As you read the poems, think about the philosophy of life each character expresses.

- See Literary Terms Handbook, p. R5.

Literature Online Interactive Literary Elements Handbook To review or learn more about the literary elements, go to www.glencoe.com.

Reading Strategy Drawing Conclusions About Characters

When you **draw a conclusion,** you use various pieces of information to make a general statement about people, places, events, and ideas. As you read the poems, look for specific details about each speaker. These details can be the basis for a general statement about each speaker. You can use a chart like the one below to keep track of these details.

Vocabulary

repose (ri pōz′) *n.* relaxation; tranquility; eternal rest; p. 501 *The elderly woman was not afraid of death; instead, she welcomed the idea of her repose.*

degenerate (di jen′ ər it) *adj.* having declined in condition or character; deteriorated; p. 501 *Despite spending time in jail, the thief continued to live a degenerate lifestyle.*

ruinous (rōō′ i nəs) *adj.* causing ruin; destructive; p. 502 *The extreme weather in Alaska can have a ruinous effect on highways there.*

Vocabulary Tip: Antonyms Words that have opposite or nearly opposite meanings are called antonyms. For instance, *ruinous* and *beneficial* are antonyms. Note that antonyms are always the same part of speech.

INDIANA ACADEMIC STANDARDS (pages 500–503)
11.3.8 Analyze the philosophical arguments presented in literary works...

11.3 [Identify] story elements such as character...
11.5.9 Write...an analytical essay...

Comtemplating Life, 1903. Richard Pfeiffer.

Lucinda Matlock

Edgar Lee Masters

I went to the dances at Chandlerville,
And played snap-out¹ at Winchester.
One time we changed partners,
Driving home in the moonlight of middle June,
5   And then I found Davis.
We were married and lived together for
   seventy years,
Enjoying, working, raising the twelve
   children,
Eight of whom we lost
Ere I had reached the age of sixty.
10   I spun, I wove, I kept the house, I nursed
   the sick,
I made the garden, and for holiday
Rambled over the fields where sang the larks,
And by Spoon River gathering many a shell,
And many a flower and medicinal weed—
15   Shouting to the wooded hills, singing to the
   green valleys.
At ninety-six I had lived enough, that is all,
And passed to a sweet **repose.**
What is this I hear of sorrow and weariness,
Anger, discontent and drooping hopes?
20   **Degenerate** sons and daughters,
Life is too strong for you—
It takes life to love Life.

Literary Element   Dramatic Monologue *What does this line tell you about the speaker's philosophy of life?*

Vocabulary

repose (ri pōz′) *n.* relaxation; tranquility; eternal rest
degenerate (di jen′ ər it) *adj.* having declined in condition or character; deteriorated

---

1. *Snap-out* (also known as crack-the-whip) is a game in which players link hands in a line and then run or skate so as to shake off those at the end of the line.

Fiddler Jones

Edgar Lee Masters

Pop and the Boys, 1963. Thomas Hart Benton. Oil on canvas, 67.7 x 47.7 cm. Fundación Colección Thyssen-Bornemisza, Madrid, Spain.

The earth keeps some vibration going
There in your heart, and that is you.
And if the people find you can fiddle,
Why, fiddle you must, for all your life.
5   What do you see, a harvest of clover?
Or a meadow to walk through to the river?
The wind's in the corn; you rub your hands
For beeves[1] hereafter ready for market;
Or else you hear the rustle of skirts
10 Like the girls when dancing at Little Grove.
To Cooney Potter a pillar of dust
Or whirling leaves meant **ruinous** drouth;[2]
They looked to me like Red-Head Sammy
Stepping it off, to "Toor-a-Loor."[3]
15 How could I till my forty acres
Not to speak of getting more,
With a medley of horns, bassoons and piccolos
Stirred in my brain by crows and robins
And the creak of a wind-mill—only these?
20 And I never started to plow in my life
That some one did not stop in the road
And take me away to a dance or picnic.
I ended up with forty acres;
I ended up with a broken fiddle—
25 And a broken laugh, and a thousand memories,
And not a single regret.

---

1. *Beeves* is the plural form of *beef;* here, it refers to beef cattle.
2. A *drouth* (also *drought*) is a long period of dry weather.
3. *Toor-a-Loor* refers to a phrase in an Irish folk song.

Reading Strategy Drawing Conclusions About Characters *What do these details suggest about the speaker's character?*

Vocabulary

ruinous (rōō´ i nəs) *adj.* causing ruin; destructive

RESPONDING AND THINKING CRITICALLY

Respond

1. Have you ever known anyone whose outlook on life resembles that of Lucinda Matlock or Fiddler Jones? Explain.

Recall and Interpret

2. (a)Describe how Lucinda Matlock spent her life. (b)What were her joys and her sorrows?

3. (a)Describe Lucinda's **tone**, or attitude toward her subject and audience, in lines 1–17. (b)How does her tone change in lines 18–22? What might you infer about her character from this change?

4. In lines 5–14 of "Fiddler Jones," Fiddler describes different ways of perceiving the same things. (a)Summarize these descriptions. (b)What point do you think he is trying to make?

5. (a)What reasons does Fiddler give for having neglected his farm? (b)How does he seem to feel about his work habits?

Analyze and Evaluate

6. (a)If you were to interview Lucinda Matlock, what questions might you ask her about facing life's ups and downs? (b)From your reading of the poem, what do you think her answers would be?

7. (a)What is Fiddler's philosophy of life? (b)What do you think of Fiddler's philosophy? Explain.

Connect

8. **Big Idea** **Regionalism** Both Lucinda Matlock and Fiddler Jones are from the same small Midwestern farming community. In your opinion, how might their philosophies be different if they had spent their lives in a busy city instead?

LITERARY ANALYSIS

Literary Element Dramatic Monologue

"Lucinda Matlock" and "Fiddler Jones" appear among a group of related **dramatic monologues** in *Spoon River Anthology.* The speakers all have something to say about their lives, and they want their audience—the living—to heed the lessons they have learned.

1. What general statement sums up the philosophy of life these two monologues share?

2. Paraphrase one of the dramatic monologues you have just read. Do you think this work would be as effective in prose as it is in poetry? Explain your response.

Writing About Literature

Compare and Contrast Characters Write a brief essay in which you compare and contrast Lucinda Matlock and Fiddler Jones. How did they spend their lives, and what was important to them? Do you think they would agree about what constitutes a good life? Use evidence from the poems to support your points.

READING AND VOCABULARY

Reading Strategy Drawing Conclusions About Characters

As you answer the following questions, review the details about the speakers in "Lucinda Matlock" and "Fiddler Jones" that you noted in your charts.

1. Why does Lucinda Matlock disapprove of the younger generation?

2. What do you think was Fiddler Jones's greatest joy?

Vocabulary Practice

Practice with Antonyms Find the antonym for each vocabulary word listed in the first column.

1. repose   **a.** shift   **b.** agitation
2. degenerate   **a.** improved   **b.** fabricated
3. ruinous   **a.** redeeming   **b.** advantage

Literature Online **Web Activities** For eFlashcards, Selection Quick Checks, and other Web activities, go to www.glencoe.com.

The Outcasts of Poker Flat

MEET BRET HARTE

If U.S. newspapers of the early 1870s had featured bestseller lists, one name would have appeared regularly at the top: Bret Harte. Not only was he one of the most widely read writers in the United States at the time, but he was also the best paid. The $10,000 the *Atlantic Monthly* awarded him in 1871 for 12 stories per year was the highest figure ever paid to an American writer at that time. Harte wrote colorful, romantic stories about the American West. In many of his stories, he conjured the flavor and characters of the California Gold Rush long after it had ended.

Born in Albany, New York, Harte ventured west when he was eighteen years old. He worked as a drugstore clerk and a Wells Fargo guard, and, according to some accounts, he may have also tried teaching school and prospecting before he found lasting work in journalism. However, when he wrote an editorial condemning the massacre of sixty Native Americans by local white men, he so outraged readers that he had to quit his job as editor of the *Northern Californian* and leave town.

> "The secret of the American short story was the treatment of characteristic American life, with absolute knowledge of its peculiarities."
>
> —Bret Harte
> "The Rise of the Short Story"

Literary Success While serving as editor of the *Overland Monthly*, a literary magazine, Harte wrote the story that made him famous, "The Luck of Roaring Camp." He followed that success with "The Outcasts of Poker Flat." Readers in the United States and England were eager for descriptions of California and the Wild West, and Harte gave them

the stories they wanted. However, when the prestigious Boston literary magazine the *Atlantic Monthly* offered Harte a contract, the writer accepted the offer and left California for the East. He never returned west.

Personal and family problems prevented Harte from maintaining his early literary success. He served as a diplomat in Prussia and Scotland before returning to writing as his sole profession. In England, Harte found an enthusiastic audience for his work long after readers in the United States had grown tired of his literary formula. However, his health failed rapidly, and he died in 1902 of throat cancer.

Harte and the Wild West Harte was one of the principal shapers of the fictional Wild West that has had a wide influence in U.S. popular culture. In the 20th century, the makers of film and television "Westerns" found in Harte's stories the prototypes for many of their familiar stock characters. Such stereotypes as the grizzled prospector, the dance-hall girl with a heart of gold, and the smooth gambler all originated in Harte's fiction. Because these characters have become a fundamental part of U.S. popular culture, Harte's portrait of the West has endured.

Bret Harte was born in 1836 and died in 1902.

Literature Online **Author Search** For more about Bret Harte, go to www.glencoe.com.

Connecting to the Story

To be *outcast* is to be driven out or rejected. In this story, the outcast characters are forced out of town with the threat of death should they return. As you read, think about the following questions:

- Why might a person be outcast from society?
- Can a person be an outcast without physically going somewhere else? Explain.

Building Background

Bret Harte's "The Outcasts of Poker Flat" is set in frontier California during the Gold Rush. The transformation of the West during the Gold Rush was rapid and spectacular. By the end of 1849, over 80,000 gold-seekers had come to California. Mining towns sprang up almost overnight. Drawn from all walks of life, the "Forty-Niners" created a rough, lawless, and sometimes violent world. Justice was spotty at best in these communities; the inhabitants themselves might take on the roles of judge, jury, and occasionally, executioner. Harte saw for himself the many types of people who were drawn to these communities. In his writing, he tried to look at these people with unblinking realism and to capture their peculiarities of speech and behavior.

Setting Purposes for Reading

Big Idea Regionalism

As you read "The Outcasts of Poker Flat," notice how Harte introduces regional details into the setting.

Literary Element Characterization

The methods a writer uses to reveal the personality of a character are called **characterization**. The writer may describe a character directly, or reveal a character's personality through his or her words, thoughts, and actions, and through the actions and reactions of other characters. As you read, look for direct statements about each character as well as action and dialogue that broaden your understanding of the characters' personalities.

- See Literary Terms Handbook, p. R3.

Literature Online **Interactive Literary Elements Handbook** To review or learn more about the literary elements, go to www.glencoe.com.

Reading Strategy Making Generalizations

A **generalization** is a broad statement based on a few facts, descriptions, or examples. Readers can use the details in a literary work to make generalizations about story elements such as plot, character, setting, or theme.

Reading Tip: Taking Notes As you read, use a chart like the one below to record details that you might use to make generalizations about the characters and setting.

Details of Setting or Character	Generalization
Uncle Billy: sluice-robber, confirmed drunkard	

Vocabulary

impropriety (im′ prə prī′ ə tē) *n.* the quality of being improper; inappropriate behavior; p. 507 *Newspapers accused the mayor of impropriety when he hired his relatives for city jobs.*

malevolence (mə lev′ə ləns) *n.* a disposition to wish harm to others; ill will; p. 508 *The bully's malevolence caused the other children to fear him.*

equanimity (ēk′ wə nim′ə te, ek′-) *n.* evenness of temper; calmness; p. 508 *The teacher became known for her equanimity during disruptions.*

hypothesis (hī poth′ə sis) *n.* an unproved explanation or assumption; p. 511 *Sharon's hypothesis was that a tree branch was causing the strange tapping sounds.*

seclusion (si kloo′zhən) *n.* separation from others; isolation; p. 511 *Seeking seclusion, the famous movie star shunned fans and reporters.*

Vocabulary Tip: Denotation and Connotation
A word's **denotation** is its literal, or dictionary, meaning. A word's **connotation**, however, is the feeling or association the word suggests.

INDIANA ACADEMIC STANDARDS (pages pages 505–516)
11.3 [Identify] story elements such as character...
11.2 Develop [reading] strategies...

11.5.9 Write...a summary...that...creates an organizing structure appropriate to purpose, audience, and context...

The Outcasts of Poker Flat

Bret Harte

As Mr. John Oakhurst, gambler, stepped into the main street of Poker Flat on the morning of the 23d of November, 1850, he was conscious of a change in its moral atmosphere since the preceding night. Two or three men, conversing earnestly together, ceased as he approached, and exchanged significant glances. There was a Sabbath lull in the air, which, in a settlement unused to Sabbath influences, looked ominous.

Mr. Oakhurst's calm, handsome face betrayed small concern in these indications. Whether he was conscious of any predisposing cause was another question. "I reckon they're after somebody," he reflected; "likely it's me." He returned to his pocket the handkerchief with which he had been whipping away the red dust of Poker Flat from his neat boots, and quietly discharged his mind of any further conjecture.

In point of fact, Poker Flat was "after somebody." It had lately suffered the loss of several thousand dollars, two valuable horses, and a prominent citizen. It was experiencing a spasm of virtuous reaction, quite as lawless and ungovernable as any of the acts that had provoked it. A secret committee had determined to rid the town of all improper persons. This was done permanently in regard of two men who were then hanging from the boughs of a sycamore in the gulch,[1] and temporarily in the banishment of certain other objectionable characters. I regret to say that some of these were ladies. It is but due to the sex, however, to state that their **impropriety** was professional, and it was only in such easily established standards of evil that Poker Flat ventured to sit in judgment.

Mr. Oakhurst was right in supposing that he was included in this category. A few of the committee had urged hanging him as a possible example and a sure method of reimbursing themselves from his pockets of the sums he had won from them. "It's

agin[2] justice," said Jim Wheeler, "to let this yer young man from Roaring Camp—an entire stranger—carry away our money." But a crude sentiment of equity residing in the breasts of those who had been fortunate enough to win from Mr. Oakhurst overruled this narrower local prejudice.

Mr. Oakhurst received his sentence with philosophic calmness, none the less coolly that he was aware of the hesitation of his judges. He was too much of a gambler not to accept fate. With him life was at best an uncertain game, and he recognized the usual percentage in favor of the dealer.

A body of armed men accompanied the deported wickedness of Poker Flat to the outskirts of the settlement. Besides Mr. Oakhurst, who was known to be a coolly desperate man, and for whose intimidation the armed escort was intended, the expatriated[3] party consisted of a young woman familiarly known as "The Duchess;" another who had won the title of "Mother Shipton;"[4] and "Uncle Billy," a suspected sluice-robber[5] and confirmed drunkard. The cavalcade[6] provoked no comments from the spectators, nor was any word uttered by the escort. Only when the gulch which marked the uttermost limit of Poker Flat was reached, the leader spoke briefly and to the point. The exiles were forbidden to return at the peril of their lives.

As the escort disappeared, their pent-up feelings found vent in a few hysterical tears from the Duchess, some bad language from Mother Shipton, and a Parthian[7] volley of expletives from Uncle Billy. The philosophic Oakhurst alone remained silent. He listened calmly to Mother Shipton's desire to cut somebody's heart out, to the repeated statements of the

---

1. A *gulch* is a small, narrow valley, especially one eroded by running water.

Reading Strategy Making Generalizations *Is Poker Flat ordinarily a very religious town? How can you tell?*

Vocabulary

impropriety (im′ prə prī′ə tē) *n.* the quality of being improper; inappropriate behavior

2. *Agin* is dialect for *against.*
3. *Expatriated* means "banished" or "exiled."
4. The original *Mother Shipton* (1488–1560) was an English woman accused of witchcraft.
5. A *sluice-robber* is someone who steals gold from sluices, long water troughs used by miners to separate gold ore from other materials.
6. A *cavalcade* (kav′ əl kād′) is a procession, especially of people on horseback.
7. Here, *Parthian* means "delivered when parting or retreating." The cavalry of the ancient country of Parthia (now part of Iran) was known for shooting arrows while retreating or pretending to retreat.

Literary Element Characterization *Based on this description, how would you describe Oakhurst's view of life?*

Duchess that she would die in the road, and to the alarming oaths that seemed to be bumped out of Uncle Billy as he rode forward. With the easy good humor characteristic of his class, he insisted upon exchanging his own riding-horse, "Five-Spot," for the sorry mule which the Duchess rode. But even this act did not draw the party into any closer sympathy. The young woman readjusted her somewhat draggled plumes with a feeble, faded coquetry;[8] Mother Shipton eyed the possessor of "Five-Spot" with **malevolence,** and Uncle Billy included the whole party in one sweeping anathema.[9]

The road to Sandy Bar—a camp that, not having as yet experienced the regenerating influences of Poker Flat, consequently seemed to offer some invitation to the emigrants—lay over a steep mountain range. It was distant a day's severe travel. In that advanced season the party soon passed out of the moist, temperate regions of the foothills into the dry, cold bracing air of the Sierras. The trail was narrow and difficult. At noon the Duchess, rolling out of her saddle upon the ground, declared her intention of going no farther, and the party halted.

The spot was singularly wild and impressive. A wooded amphitheatre, surrounded on three sides by precipitous cliffs of naked granite, sloped gently toward the crest of another precipice that overlooked the valley. It was,

Visual Vocabulary
Sierras refers to the Sierra Nevada, a mountain range in Eastern California.

undoubtedly, the most suitable spot for a camp, had camping been advisable. But Mr. Oakhurst knew that scarcely half the journey to Sandy Bar was accomplished, and the party were not equipped or provisioned for delay. This fact he pointed out to his companions curtly, with a philosophic commentary on the folly of "throwing up their hand before the game was played out." But they were furnished with liquor, which in this emergency stood them in place of food, fuel, rest, and prescience.[10] In spite of his remonstrances, it was not long before they were more or less under its influence. Uncle Billy passed rapidly from a bellicose[11] state into one of stupor, the Duchess became maudlin,[12] and Mother Shipton snored. Mr. Oakhurst alone remained erect, leaning against a rock, calmly surveying them.

Mr. Oakhurst did not drink. It interfered with a profession which required coolness, impassiveness, and presence of mind, and, in his own language, he "couldn't afford it." As he gazed at his recumbent[13] fellow exiles, the loneliness begotten of his pariah trade,[14] his habits of life, his very vices, for the first time seriously oppressed him. He bestirred himself in dusting his black clothes, washing his hands and face, and other acts characteristic of his studiously neat habits, and for a moment forgot his annoyance. The thought of deserting his weaker and more pitiable companions never perhaps occurred to him. Yet he could not help feeling the want of that excitement which, singularly enough, was most conducive to that calm **equanimity** for which he was notorious. He looked at the gloomy walls that rose a thousand feet sheer above the circling pines around him, at the sky ominously clouded, at the valley below, already deepening into shadow; and, doing so, suddenly he heard his own name called.

8. *Coquetry* (kō′ kə trē) means "flirtation."
9. An *anathema* (a nath′ ə mə) is a strong denunciation or a curse.

Literary Element Characterization *Note the different reactions of the four travelers. What do you learn about each character from his or her behavior?*

Big Idea Regionalism *How do the descriptions of the "wild and impressive" scenery contribute to your understanding of the region and its influence upon the people?*

Vocabulary
malevolence (mə lev′ ə ləns) *n.* a disposition to wish harm to others; ill will

10. *Prescience* (prē′ shē əns) is foresight.
11. *Bellicose* (bel′ ə kōs) means "showing an eagerness to fight" or "quarrelsome."
12. *Maudlin* (môd′ lin) means "excessively sentimental."
13. *Recumbent* (ri kum′ bənt) means "lying down" or "resting."
14. A *pariah* (pə rī′ ə) is an outcast, someone who is despised by others. A *pariah trade* is an occupation that is socially unacceptable.

Vocabulary
equanimity (ek′ wə nim′ ə tē) *n.* evenness of temper; calmness

A horseman slowly ascended the trail. In the fresh, open face of the newcomer Mr. Oakhurst recognized Tom Simson, otherwise known as "The Innocent," of Sandy Bar. He had met him some months before over a "little game," and had, with perfect equanimity, won the entire fortune—amounting to some forty dollars—of that guileless youth. After the game was finished, Mr. Oakhurst drew the youthful speculator behind the door and thus addressed him: "Tommy, you're a good little man, but you can't gamble worth a cent. Don't try it over again." He then handed him his money back, pushed him gently from the room, and so made a devoted slave of Tom Simson.

There was a remembrance of this in his boyish and enthusiastic greeting of Mr. Oakhurst. He had started, he said, to go to Poker Flat to seek his fortune. "Alone?" No, not exactly alone; in fact (a giggle), he had run away with Piney Woods. Didn't Mr. Oakhurst remember Piney? She that used to wait on the table at the Temperance House? They had been engaged a long time, but old Jake Woods had objected, and so they had run away, and were going to Poker Flat to be married, and here they were. And they were tired out, and how lucky it was they had found a place to camp, and company. All this the Innocent delivered rapidly, while Piney, a stout, comely damsel of fifteen, emerged from behind the pine-tree, where she had been blushing unseen, and rode to the side of her lover.

Mr. Oakhurst seldom troubled himself with sentiment, still less with propriety; but he had a vague idea that the situation was not fortunate. He retained, however, his presence of mind sufficiently to kick Uncle Billy, who was about to say something, and Uncle Billy was

Study of a Head (Portrait of Algernon Graves), c. 1881–1885. James A. McNeill Whistler. Oil on canvas, 22⅝ x 14½ in. The Columbus Museum of Art, OH. Bequest of Frederick W. Schumacher. **Viewing the Art:** What characteristics does this man appear to have that Mr. Oakhurst might also have?

sober enough to recognize in Mr. Oakhurst's kick a superior power that would not bear trifling.[15] He then endeavored to dissuade Tom Simson from delaying further, but in vain. He even pointed out the fact that there was no provision, nor means of making a camp. But, unluckily, the Innocent met this objection by assuring the party that he was provided with an extra mule loaded with provisions, and by the discovery of a rude attempt at a log house near the trail. "Piney can stay with Mrs. Oakhurst," said the Innocent, pointing to the Duchess, "and I can shift for myself."

Nothing but Mr. Oakhurst's admonishing foot saved Uncle Billy from bursting into a roar of laughter. As it was, he felt compelled

Literary Element Characterization *What does this sentence reveal about Oakhurst's character? What does it reveal about Tom's character?*

15. Here, *trifling* means "joking" or "mocking."

to retire up the cañon[16] until he could recover his gravity. There he confided the joke to the tall pine-trees, with many slaps of his leg, contortions of his face, and the usual profanity. But when he returned to the party, he found them seated by a fire—for the air had grown strangely chill and the sky overcast—in apparently amicable conversation. Piney was actually talking in an impulsive girlish fashion to the Duchess, who was listening with an interest and animation she had not shown for many days. The Innocent was holding forth, apparently with equal effect, to Mr. Oakhurst and Mother Shipton, who was actually relaxing into amiability. "Is this yer a d—d picnic?" said Uncle Billy, with inward scorn, as he surveyed the sylvan[17] group, the glancing fire-light, and the tethered animals in the foreground. Suddenly an idea mingled with the alcoholic fumes that disturbed his brain. It was apparently of a jocular[18] nature, for he felt impelled to slap his leg again and cram his fist into his mouth.

> "He looked over the valley, and summed up the present and future in two words, 'Snowed in!'"

As the shadows crept slowly up the mountain, a slight breeze rocked the tops of the pine-trees and moaned through their long and gloomy aisles. The ruined cabin, patched and covered with pine boughs, was set apart for the ladies. As the lovers parted, they unaffectedly exchanged a kiss, so honest and sincere that it might have been heard above the swaying pines. The frail Duchess and the malevolent Mother Shipton were probably too stunned to remark upon this last evidence of simplicity, and so turned without a word to the hut. The fire was replenished, the men lay down before the door, and in a few minutes were asleep.

Mr. Oakhurst was a light sleeper. Toward morning he awoke benumbed and cold. As he stirred the dying fire, the wind, which was now blowing strongly, brought to his cheek that which caused the blood to leave it,—snow!

He started to his feet with the intention of awakening the sleepers, for there was no time to lose. But turning to where Uncle Billy had been lying, he found him gone. A suspicion leaped to his brain, and a curse to his lips. He ran to the spot where the mules had been tethered—they were no longer there. The tracks were already rapidly disappearing in the snow.

The momentary excitement brought Mr. Oakhurst back to the fire with his usual calm. He did not waken the sleepers. The Innocent slumbered peacefully, with a smile on his good-humored, freckled face; the virgin Piney slept beside her frailer sisters as sweetly as though attended by celestial guardians; and Mr. Oakhurst, drawing his blanket over his shoulders, stroked his mustaches and waited for the dawn. It came slowly in a whirling mist of snowflakes that dazzled and confused the eye. What could be seen of the landscape appeared magically changed. He looked over the valley, and summed up the present and future in two words, "Snowed in!"

A careful inventory of the provisions, which, fortunately for the party, had been stored within the hut, and so escaped the felonious[19] fingers of Uncle Billy, disclosed the fact that with care and prudence they might last ten days longer. "That is," said Mr. Oakhurst *sotto voce*[20] to the Innocent, "if you're willing to board us. If you ain't—and perhaps you'd better not—you can wait till Uncle Billy gets back with provisions."

---

16. *Cañon* (kä nyōn´) is Spanish for *canyon*.
17. *Sylvan* means "situated in the woods."
18. *Jocular* means "humorous."

---

19. *Felonious* means "evil" or "villainous."
20. *Sotto voce* (sot´ ō vō´ chē) means "in a low tone of voice." The Italian words literally mean "under the voice."

Big Idea Regionalism *In Uncle Billy's behavior, what might Harte be suggesting about the regional characteristics of the West?*

Three Giants, Davos, 1879. Harry Goodwin. Oil on canvas. Private collection.

For some occult[21] reason, Mr. Oakhurst could not bring himself to disclose Uncle Billy's rascality, and so offered the **hypothesis** that he had wandered from the camp and had accidentally stampeded the animals. He dropped a warning to the Duchess and Mother Shipton, who of course knew the facts of their associate's defection. "They'll find out the truth about us *all* when they find out anything," he added significantly, "and there's no good frightening them now."

Tom Simson not only put all his worldly store at the disposal of Mr. Oakhurst, but seemed to enjoy the prospect of their enforced **seclusion.** "We'll have a good camp for a week, and then the snow'll melt, and we'll all go back together." The cheerful gayety of the young man and Mr. Oakhurst's calm infected the others. The Innocent, with the aid of pine boughs, extemporized[22] a thatch for the roofless cabin, and the Duchess directed Piney in the rearrangement of the interior with a taste and tact that opened the blue eyes of that provincial maiden to their fullest extent. "I reckon now you're used to fine things at Poker Flat," said Piney. The Duchess turned away sharply to conceal something that reddened her cheeks through their professional tint, and Mother Shipton requested Piney not to "chatter." But when Mr. Oakhurst returned from a weary search for the trail, he heard the sound of happy laughter echoed from the rocks. He

---

21. *Occult* means "mysterious."

Vocabulary

hypothesis (hī poth′ə sis) *n.* an unproved explanation or assumption

seclusion (si klōō′zhən) *n.* separation from others; isolation

22. *Extemporized* means "made without preparation" or "improvised."

Literary Element Characterization *On what evidence does Piney likely base this statement? What does it reveal about her character?*

stopped in some alarm, and his thoughts first naturally reverted to the whiskey, which he had prudently cachéd.[23] "And yet it don't somehow sound like whiskey," said the gambler. It was not until he caught sight of the blazing fire through the still blinding storm, and the group around it, that he settled to the conviction that it was "square fun."

Whether Mr. Oakhurst had cachéd his cards with the whiskey as something debarred the free access of the community, I cannot say. It was certain that, in Mother Shipton's words, he "didn't say 'cards' once" during that evening. Haply the time was beguiled by an accordion, pro-

Visual Vocabulary
Castanets are pairs of concave shells, often made of ivory or wood. The shells are held in the hand and played by clicking them together.

duced somewhat ostentatiously by Tom Simson from his pack. Notwithstanding some difficulties attending the manipulation of this instrument, Piney Woods managed to pluck several reluctant melodies from its keys, to an accompaniment by the Innocent on a pair of bone castanets. But the crowning festivity of the evening was reached in a rude[24] camp-meeting[25] hymn, which the lovers, joining hands, sang with great earnestness and vociferation. I fear that a certain defiant tone and Covenanter's swing[26] to its chorus, rather than any devotional quality, caused it speedily to infect the others, who at last joined in the refrain:—

"I'm proud to live in the service of the Lord,
    And I'm bound to die in His army."

The pines rocked, the storm eddied and whirled above the miserable group, and the flames of their altar leaped heavenward, as if in token of the vow.

---

23. *Cachéd* (kasht) means "hidden."
24. Here, *rude* means "vigorous" or "robust."
25. A *camp-meeting* is an outdoor religious gathering.
26. *Covenanter's swing* implies a lively rhythm. The Covenanters were Scottish Presbyterians who made covenants, or agreements, to resist rule by the Church of England.

Reading Strategy Making Generalizations *What generalization can you make about all of the characters based on this passage?*

At midnight the storm abated, the rolling clouds parted, and the stars glittered keenly above the sleeping camp. Mr. Oakhurst, whose professional habits had enabled him to live on the smallest possible amount of sleep, in dividing the watch with Tom Simson somehow managed to take upon himself the greater part of that duty. He excused himself to the Innocent by saying that he had "often been a week without sleep." "Doing what?" asked Tom. "Poker!" replied Oakhurst sententiously.[27] "When a man gets a streak of luck, he don't get tired. The luck gives in first. Luck," continued the gambler reflectively, "is a mighty queer thing. All you know about it for certain is that it's bound to change. And it's finding out when it's going to change that makes you. We've had a streak of bad luck since we left Poker Flat,—you came along, and slap you get into it, too. If you can hold your cards right along you're all right. For," added the gambler, with cheerful irrelevance—

" 'I'm proud to live in the service of the Lord,
    And I'm bound to die in His army.' "

The third day came, and the sun, looking through the white-curtained valley, saw the outcasts divide their slowly decreasing store of provisions for the morning meal. It was one of the peculiarities of that mountain climate that its rays diffused a kindly warmth over the wintry landscape, as if in regretful commiseration of the past. But it revealed drift on drift of snow piled high around the hut,—a hopeless, uncharted, trackless sea of white lying below the rocky shores to which the castaways still clung. Through the marvelously clear air the smoke of the pastoral[28] village of Poker Flat rose miles away. Mother Shipton saw it, and from a remote pinnacle of her rocky fastness hurled in that direction a final malediction.[29] It was her last vituperative[30] attempt, and perhaps for that reason was invested with a certain degree

---

27. *Sententiously* (sen ten′ shəs lē) means "in a concise, energetic manner."
28. *Pastoral* means "of, or relating to, rural life."
29. A *malediction* (mal′ ə dik′ shən) is a curse.
30. *Vituperative* (vi tōō′ pə rā′ tiv) means "characterized by abusive language and harsh criticism."

Big Idea Regionalism *Does this paragraph describe a region that is truly "kindly" toward the outcasts? Explain.*

of sublimity. It did her good, she privately informed the Duchess. "Just you go out there and cuss, and see." She then set herself to the task of amusing "the child," as she and the Duchess were pleased to call Piney. Piney was no chicken, but it was a soothing and original theory of the pair thus to account for the fact that she didn't swear and wasn't improper.

When night crept up again through the gorges, the reedy notes of the accordion rose and fell in fitful spasms and long-drawn gasps by the flickering campfire. But music failed to fill entirely the aching void left by insufficient food, and a new diversion was proposed by Piney,—story-telling. Neither Mr. Oakhurst nor his female companions caring to relate their personal experiences, this plan would have failed too, but for the Innocent. Some months before he had chanced upon a stray copy of Mr. Pope's[31] ingenious translation of the *Iliad*.[32] He now proposed to narrate the principal incidents of that poem—having thoroughly mastered the argument and fairly forgotten the words—in the current vernacular of Sandy Bar. And so for the rest of that night the Homeric demi-gods again walked the earth. Trojan bully and wily Greek wrestled in the winds, and the great pines in the cañon seemed to bow to the wrath of the son of Peleus.[33] Mr. Oakhurst listened with quiet satisfaction. Most especially was he interested in the fate of "Ashheels," as the Innocent persisted in denominating the "swift-footed Achilles."

So, with small food and much of Homer and the accordion, a week passed over the heads of the outcasts. The sun again forsook them, and again from leaden skies the snowflakes were sifted over the land. Day by day closer around them drew the snowy circle, until at last they looked from their prison over drifted walls of dazzling white, that towered twenty feet above their heads. It became more and more difficult to replenish their fires, even from the fallen trees beside them, now half hidden in the drifts. And yet no one complained. The lovers turned from the dreary prospect and looked into each other's eyes, and were happy. Mr. Oakhurst settled himself coolly to the losing game before him. The Duchess, more cheerful than she had been, assumed the care of Piney. Only Mother Shipton—once the strongest of the party— seemed to sicken and fade. At midnight on the tenth day she called Oakhurst to her side. "I'm going," she said, in a voice of querulous[34] weakness, "but don't say anything about it. Don't waken the kids. Take the bundle from under my head, and open it." Mr. Oakhurst did so. It contained Mother Shipton's rations for the last week, untouched. "Give 'em to the child," she said, pointing to the sleeping Piney. "You've starved yourself," said the gambler. "That's what they call it," said the woman querulously, as she lay down again, and turning her face to the wall, passed quietly away.

The accordion and the bones were put aside that day, and Homer was forgotten. When the body of Mother Shipton had been committed to the snow, Mr. Oakhurst took the Innocent aside, and showed him a pair of snowshoes, which he had fashioned from the old pack-saddle. "There's one chance in a hundred to save her yet," he said, pointing to Piney; "but it's there," he added, pointing toward Poker Flat. "If you can reach there in two days she's safe." "And you?" asked Tom Simson. "I'll stay here," was the curt reply.

The lovers parted with a long embrace. "You are not going, too?" said the Duchess, as she saw Mr. Oakhurst apparently waiting to accompany him. "As far as the cañon," he replied. He turned suddenly and kissed the Duchess, leaving her pallid[35] face aflame, and her trembling limbs rigid with amazement.

Night came, but not Mr. Oakhurst. It brought the storm again and the whirling snow. Then the Duchess, feeding the fire,

---

31. *Mr. Pope's* refers to the English poet Alexander Pope (1688–1744).
32. Homer's Greek epic poem the *Iliad* (ĭ′ lē əd) describes the war between the Trojans, natives of ancient Troy, and the Greeks.
33. The *son of Peleus* (pēl′ yüs′) is Achilles, Greek warrior and a hero in the *Iliad*.

34. *Querulous* means "whining" or "complaining."
35. *Pallid* means "pale."

Reading Strategy Making Generalizations *Earlier in the story, several characters made complaints. Why do you think none of the characters complain at this point in the story?*

found that some one had quietly piled beside the hut enough fuel to last a few days longer. The tears rose to her eyes, but she hid them from Piney.

The women slept but little. In the morning, looking into each other's faces, they read their fate. Neither spoke, but Piney, accepting the position of the stronger, drew near and placed her arm around the Duchess's waist. They kept this attitude for the rest of the day. That night the storm reached its greatest fury, and, rendering asunder the protecting vines, invaded the very hut.

Toward morning they found themselves unable to feed the fire, which gradually died away. As the embers slowly blackened, the Duchess crept closer to Piney, and broke the silence of many hours: "Piney, can you pray?" "No, dear," said Piney simply. The Duchess, without knowing exactly why, felt relieved, and, putting her head upon Piney's shoulder, spoke no more. And so reclining, the younger and purer pillowing the head of her soiled sister upon her virgin breast, they fell asleep.

The wind lulled as if it feared to waken them. Feathery drifts of snow, shaken from the long pine boughs, flew like white winged birds, and settled about them as they slept. The moon through the rifted clouds looked down upon what had been the camp. But all human stain, all trace of earthly travail, was hidden beneath the spotless mantle mercifully flung from above.

They slept all that day and the next, nor did they waken when voices and footsteps broke the silence of the camp. And when pitying fingers brushed the snow from their wan faces, you could scarcely have told from the equal peace that dwelt upon them which was she that had sinned. Even the law of Poker Flat recognized this, and turned away, leaving them still locked in each other's arms.

But at the head of the gulch, on one of the largest pine-trees, they found the deuce of clubs[36] pinned to the bark with a bowie-knife. It bore the following, written in pencil in a firm hand:

†

BENEATH THIS TREE
LIES THE BODY
OF
JOHN OAKHURST,
WHO STRUCK A STREAK OF BAD LUCK
ON THE 23RD OF NOVEMBER 1850,
AND
HANDED IN HIS CHECKS
ON THE 7TH DECEMBER, 1850.

†

And pulseless and cold, with a derringer by his side and a bullet in his heart, though still calm as in life, beneath the snow lay he who was at once the strongest and yet the weakest of the outcasts of Poker Flat. ❧

> **Toward morning they found themselves unable to feed the fire, which gradually died away.**

---

36. The *deuce of clubs* is the two of clubs. In a deck of cards, it has the lowest value.

Literary Element Characterization *Why does the narrator describe Oakhurst as "at once the strongest and yet the weakest of the outcasts of Poker Flat"?*

RESPONDING AND THINKING CRITICALLY

Respond

1. (a)Did the ending of the story surprise you? Why or why not? (b)Did the ending seem appropriate? Support your answer.

Recall and Interpret

2. (a)What has the secret committee of Poker Flat decided to do? Why? (b)What can you infer about the outcasts based on the committee's decision?

3. (a)Summarize what happens during the outcasts' second day in camp. (b)What do you learn about each of the characters, based on their behavior?

4. (a)When the searchers from Poker Flat arrive at the camp, what do you find? (b)How would you compare their treatment of the outcasts at the end of the story to their treatment at the beginning?

Analyze and Evaluate

5. (a)What is the narrator's tone, or attitude, toward the outcasts? (b)What words or phrases convey this tone?

6. (a)Which character from the story do you admire the most? Support your answer with examples from the text. (b)Which do you admire the least? Why?

7. (a)In your opinion, what message, or lesson, does this story convey? (b)How effectively does Harte convey this message?

Connect

8. **Big Idea** Regionalism Setting is considered integral when a story could not take place in another time and place. How does the setting—both time and place—influence the actions of the characters in this story?

LITERARY ANALYSIS

Literary Element Characterization

A character's personality can be revealed in many ways. The simplest method is **direct characterization.** Using this method, the writer makes explicit statements about a character. "Mr. Oakhurst was a coolly desperate man" is an example of direct characterization. The writer may prefer, however, for the reader to infer certain aspects of a character's personality. This method is called **indirect characterization.** There are many ways a writer can use indirect characterization. Physical descriptions, the character's words and actions, reactions from other characters, and even a character's name can reveal something about his or her personality.

1. How would you describe Tom Simson's character? Give two examples from the story of how his character is revealed.

2. Give an example of Mother Shipton's character from the beginning of the story. How does her final action reveal a change in her character? Explain.

Review: Motivation

Motivation is the stated or implied reason or cause for a character's actions.

Partner Activity Meet with another classmate and discuss John Oakhurst's motivations throughout the story. Working with your partner, create a chart listing Oakhurst's most important actions in the left column. In the right column, fill in what you think his motivations are for these actions. When you have completed this chart, examine it to see whether you can make a generalization about the motivations for his actions.

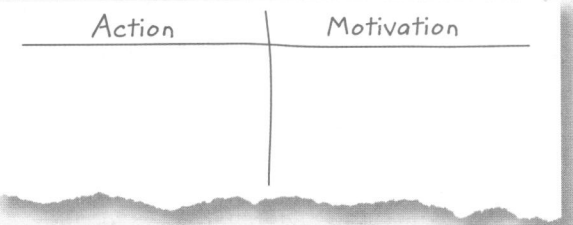

Action	Motivation

Reading Strategy Making Generalizations

Readers make **generalizations** by looking at details and noticing what they have in common. Review the chart you created on page 505 for details and generalizations about characters and setting.

1. Based on this story, what overall generalization can you make about Harte's characters?

2. What overall generalization can you make about Harte's use of setting?

Vocabulary Practice

Practice with Denotation and Connotation
Mr. Oakhurst, one of the "outcasts," is also described as a member of a "pariah trade." The words *outcast* and *pariah* have similar denotations, or literal meanings. However, *pariah* has much stronger negative connotations than *outcast*, suggesting a person who is not only rejected but despised. Each of the following pairs of words has similar denotations. In each pair, decide which word has stronger negative connotations.

1. **a.** impropriety   **b.** misstep
2. **a.** malevolence   **b.** grudge
3. **a.** equanimity   **b.** callousness
4. **a.** hypothesis   **b.** guess
5. **a.** seclusion   **b.** isolation

Academic Vocabulary

Here are two words from the vocabulary list on page R86. These words will help you think, write, and talk about the selection.

aggregate (ag′rə gāt) *n.* a whole composed of individual parts; sum total

external (iks turn′əl) *adj.* related to, of, or situated on the outside; superficial

Practice and Apply

1. What circumstance had been experienced by each individual in the **aggregate** of outcasts?

2. What **external** causes contributed to the outcasts' demise?

Writing About Literature

Apply Form In the story, Poker Flat does not have a town sheriff. If it did, however, imagine what the sheriff would have thought when Tom Simson, looking half-frozen and utterly exhausted, stumbled into town on a December afternoon in 1850 and asked for help.

Write an incident report based on the information Tom would have given the sheriff. To get started, remember that an incident report is a type of summary. When you summarize, you state the main ideas or events in your own words. To summarize an incident, you need to answer the questions *who, what, when, where, why,* and *how.* In answering the question *why,* include what is known about the outcasts' departure from Poker Flat.

Use a chart to jot down your responses:

Who was involved?	
What happened?	
When did it happen?	
Where did it happen?	
Why did it happen?	
How did it happen?	

As you revise your report, make sure it starts with a strong introductory sentence that presents the most important information. Organize the details in decreasing order of importance. And remember to present only the facts and to avoid expressing personal opinions.

Literary Criticism

Group Discussion Critic Arthur Inkersley noted in his 1897 article "Californian Literature" that Bret Harte "grew too big for his environment, and left California. . . . Though his present address is . . . London, his inspiration is still drawn from the . . . Pacific Coast." With a small group, discuss whether you think that an author needs to be in a specific setting in order to portray it. What benefits are there to writing about the place you are physically in? What are some benefits of writing about a place in your memory?

Literature Online Web Activities For eFlashcards, Selection Quick Checks, and other Web activities, go to www.glencoe.com.

Grammar Workshop

Mechanics

Punctuating Appositives

"As Mr. John Oakhurst, gambler, stepped into the main street of Poker Flat on the morning of the 23d of November, 1850, he was conscious of a change in its moral atmosphere since the preceding night."

—Bret Harte, from "The Outcasts of Poker Flat"

Connecting to Literature In the quotation, *gambler* is an **appositive**—a noun or a pronoun that further identifies another noun or pronoun. The appositive is set off with commas because it is not essential to the meaning of a sentence. The reader knows that Oakhurst is a particular person; the **nonessential** (or nonrestrictive) appositive tells something more about him. If Harte had begun the sentence "As the gambler John Oakhurst stepped into the main street," *John Oakhurst* would be an **essential** (or restrictive) appositive—it would give necessary information about the noun by telling which gambler.

Examples

- Tom Simson told stories from the <u>Iliad</u> by the poet ⟨Homer.⟩

  "The poet" could be any writer of verse. The appositive, *Homer*, tells which poet—it is essential to the meaning of the sentence.

- ⟨Uncle Billy,⟩ a suspected thief, was one of the outcasts.

  The **appositive phrase** *a suspected thief* gives extra information about Uncle Billy, so it is a nonessential appositive. An appositive phrase is an appositive and all its modifiers.

- The snow, beautiful and deadly, fell all night.

  There is no appositive in this sentence. *Beautiful* and *deadly* are adjectives that modify *snow*. Only a noun or a pronoun can be an appositive.

Exercise

Revise for Clarity Rewrite five of the sentences below, adding commas as necessary. One sentence needs no commas.

1. Bret Harte the most famous Western writer in the 1860s wrote about small mining towns.
2. "The Outcasts of Poker Flat" a well-known story contains a colorful cast of characters.
3. The town Poker Flat decides to get rid of its undesirables.
4. Oakhurst, the Duchess, Mother Shipton, and Uncle Billy a confirmed drunkard are escorted out of town.
5. Tom Simson a guileless youth was seen ascending the trail.
6. Oakhurst was found with a pistol a derringer by his side.

► **Appositives**

An **appositive** is a single noun, pronoun, or phrase that further identifies another noun or pronoun.

Restrictive (essential) appositives are not set off with commas. (My brother *Alfred* is a poet.)

Nonrestrictive (nonessential) appositives are set off with commas. (Alfred, *our family poet,* has never been published.)

► **Test-Taking Tip**

To determine whether to put commas around an appositive, try reading the sentence without it. If the appositive is not needed to identify a noun, add commas.

► **Language Handbook**

For more on Appositives, see Language Handbook, p. R46.

Literature Online
eWorkbooks To link to the Grammar and Language eWorkbook, go to www.glencoe.com.

 ACADEMIC STANDARDS (page 517)

11.6.4 Correctly use...the mechanics of punctuation...

11.4.10 Revise writing for...clarity [and] mechanics.

A Wagner Matinée

MEET WILLA CATHER

Although she spent fewer than thirteen years living on the Nebraskan prairie, readers best remember Willa Cather for her portrayal of the pioneer life and landscape. During the mid-twentieth century, the connection between Cather's writing and the prairie that inspired her began to undermine her literary status. Critics labeled her a regional writer, criticizing her for "escapism" and for romanticizing the American past. Nonetheless, Cather's books have never gone out of print, and there has been a renewed interest in her work over the past two decades. Cather is now recognized as a writer who explored the complexities of American life and showed how the tendency to link one's life to the past adds meaning—though not always happiness—to life in the present.

> "So the country and I had it out together and by the end of the first autumn the shaggy grass country had gripped me with a passion that I have never been able to shake. It has been the happiness and curse of my life."
>
> —Willa Cather

The Vast Frontier Cather's family moved from the Shenandoah Valley of Virginia to rural Red Cloud, Nebraska, when she was nine years old. Cather remarked that she felt "a kind of erasure of personality" as she first encountered the Nebraskan prairie, a feeling that would later permeate the characters in her fiction. In Red Cloud, Cather's initial homesickness gave way to curiosity about the ethnically diverse frontier town. She gained insight into the hardships of pioneer life and the intricate histories of her European immigrant neighbors. She learned French, German, Latin, and Greek, participated in plays, and attended local opera performances. In high school, Cather gained a reputation as both a remarkable student and a nonconformist. She enrolled at the University of Nebraska in 1891 and supported herself by writing bold literary reviews that earned her statewide recognition.

Returning East After graduating in 1895, Cather moved to Pittsburgh to begin editing for a woman's magazine, *Home Monthly*. She published her first poetry collection, *April Twilights*, in 1903 and a collection of stories, *The Troll Garden*, which includes "A Wagner Matinée," in 1905. The head of the progressive magazine *McClure's* was so impressed by *The Troll Garden* that he offered Cather a job in New York City. She became the magazine's managing editor by 1908 but felt unfulfilled because her position left little time to work on her own writing. In 1911, at the urging of her friend and mentor Sarah Orne Jewett, Cather left journalism to write fiction exclusively.

Although she never moved back to the prairie, Cather's memories of that vast landscape and the endurance of its people inspired several works, including *O Pioneers!* (1913), *Song of the Lark* (1915), and *My Ántonia* (1918). In her earlier stories, Cather focused on the desolation of pioneer life, including the lack of access to art and music. In later works, however, she celebrated the prairie landscape and the powerful dreams and illusions of those who attempted to cultivate it. Cather is recognized for her complex treatment of human emotion, her understanding of darker American themes, and her carefully crafted writing style.

Willa Cather was born in 1873 and died in 1947.

Literature Online **Author Search** For more about Willa Cather, go to www.glencoe.com.

Connecting to the Story

Have you ever moved away from or left a place and returned to it much later? How can music affect memory? As you read, think about the following questions:

- Why might revisiting a place one has chosen to leave be painful?
- How might hearing music affect memory in unique ways?

Building Background

The title "A Wagner Matinée" refers to the German composer Wilhelm Richard Wagner (1813–1883). A brilliant composer, Wagner revolutionized opera by creating works with uninterrupted musical scores and passionate, crashing sounds. Willa Cather based "A Wagner Matinée" on her Aunt Franc's and Uncle George's experience of moving to Nebraska after the passage of the Homestead Act in 1862. The act allowed settlers and immigrants who were at least twenty-one years old to claim 160 acres of public land. They would fully own the land once they farmed it and lived there for five years.

Setting Purposes for Reading

Big Idea Regionalism

As you read "A Wagner Matinée," note how the story's conflict centers on where the characters live and the opportunities opened or closed to them as a result.

Literary Element Point of View

Point of view refers to the relationship of the narrator to the story. In **first-person point of view,** the story is told by one of the characters, referred to as "I," and the reader sees everything through that character's eyes. In **third-person limited point of view,** the narrator reveals the thoughts and feelings of only one character, referred to as "he" or "she." In an **omniscient point of view,** the narrator knows everything about the characters and events. As you read the story, examine how point of view influences your understanding.

- See Literary Terms Handbook, p. R14.

Literature Online Interactive Literary Elements Handbook To review or learn more about the literary elements, go to www.glencoe.com.

Reading Strategy Identifying Sequence

To **identify sequence** means to find the logical order of ideas or events. Main events are often told in chronological order, but authors sometimes reveal important events and details through flashbacks. Be sure to identify the chronological order of events to better understand the themes, relationships, and events crucial to the story.

Reading Tip: Charting Story Sequence Make a diagram like the one shown to organize the events of the story into chronological order.

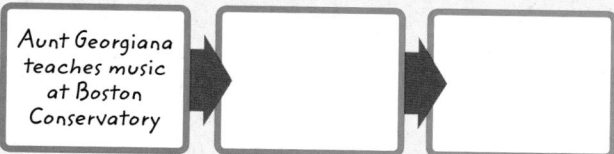

Aunt Georgiana teaches music at Boston Conservatory →

Vocabulary

legacy (leg′ə sē) *n.* an inheritance; p. 520 *Paul's generous grandfather left him a legacy when he died.*

reproach (ri prōch′) *n.* an expression of disapproval; a reprimand; p. 521 *Kim missed curfew and suffered her mother's reproach.*

doggedly (dô′gid lē) *adv.* in a stubbornly persistent manner; obstinately; p. 521 *The salesman doggedly pursued customers, even when they rebuffed him.*

trepidation (trep′ə dā′shən) *n.* nervous anticipation; anxiety; p. 522 *Dana could not shake her feeling of trepidation about the next day's exam.*

obliquely (ō blēk′lē) *adv.* in a slanting or sloping direction; p. 523 *Her hair hung obliquely across her face, hiding her left eye.*

Vocabulary Tip: Analogies An analogy is a comparison to show similarities between things that are otherwise dissimilar.

INDIANA ACADEMIC STANDARDS (pages 519–526)
11.3.2 Analyze the way in which the...meaning of a selection represents a view or comment on life...

11.2.2 Analyze...patterns of organization...

11.5.9 Write...an analytical essay...

A Wagner Matinée

Willa Cather

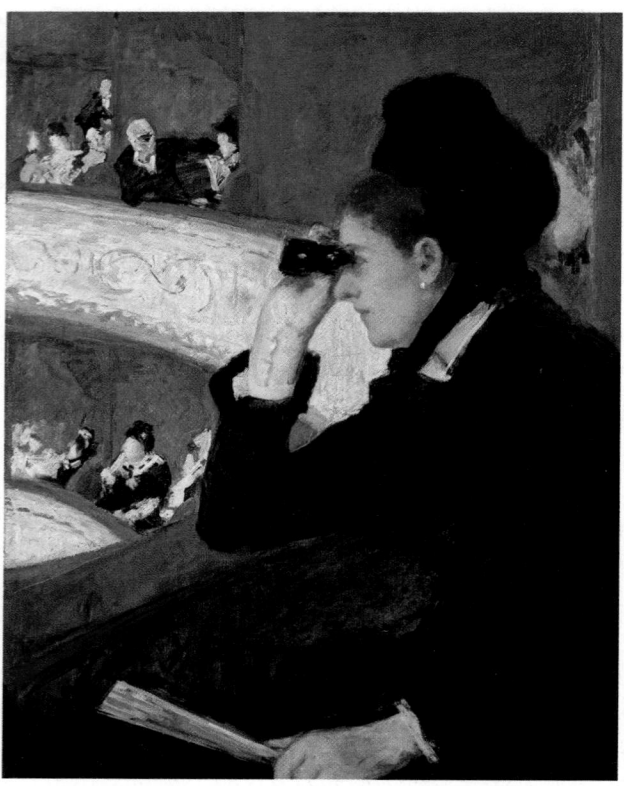

I received one morning a letter, written in pale ink on glassy, blue-lined note-paper, and bearing the postmark of a little Nebraska village. This communication, worn and rubbed, looking as if it has been carried for some days in a coat pocket that was none too clean, was from my uncle Howard, and informed me that his wife had been left a small **legacy** by a bachelor relative, and that it would be necessary for her to go to Boston to attend to the settling of the estate. He requested me to meet her at the station and render[1] her whatever services might be necessary. On examining the date indicated as that of her arrival, I found it to be no later than tomorrow. He had characteristically delayed writing until, had I been away from home for a day, I must have missed my aunt altogether.

The name of my Aunt Georgiana opened before me a gulf of recollection so wide and deep that, as the letter dropped from my hand, I felt suddenly a stranger to all the present conditions of my existence, wholly ill at ease and out of place amid the familiar surroundings of my study. I became, in short, the gangling farmer-boy my aunt had known, scourged[2] with chilblains[3] and bashfulness, my hands cracked and sore from the corn husking. I sat again before her parlour organ, fumbling the scales with my stiff, red fingers, while she, beside me, made canvas mittens for the huskers.

The next morning, after preparing my landlady for a visitor, I set out for the station. When the train arrived I had some difficulty in finding my aunt. She was the last of the passengers to alight, and it was not until I got her into the carriage that she seemed really to recognize me. She had come all the way in a day coach; her linen duster[4] had become black with soot and her black bonnet grey with dust during the journey. When we arrived at my boarding-house the landlady put her to bed at once and I did not see her again until the next morning.

---

2. *Scourged* means "afflicted."
3. *Chilblains* are red, swollen sores on the skin caused by exposure to the cold.
4. A *duster* is a long, lightweight coat worn to protect one's clothing from dust.

Reading Strategy Identifying Sequence *How does the narration shift after Clark sees Aunt Georgiana's name in the letter?*

---

1. *Render* means "to make available" or "to provide."

Vocabulary

legacy (leg′ ə sē) *n.* an inheritance

Whatever shock Mrs. Springer experienced at my aunt's appearance, she considerately concealed. As for myself, I saw my aunt's battered figure with that feeling of awe and respect with which we behold explorers who have left their ears and fingers north of Franz-Joseph-Land,[5] or their health somewhere along the Upper Congo.[6] My Aunt Georgiana had been a music teacher at the Boston Conservatory, somewhere back in the latter sixties. One summer, while visiting in the little village among the Green Mountains[7] where her ancestors had dwelt for generations, she had kindled the callow[8] fancy of my uncle, Howard Carpenter, then an idle, shiftless boy of twenty-one. When she returned to her duties in Boston, Howard followed her, and the upshot of this infatuation was that she eloped with him, eluding the **reproaches** of her family and the criticism of her friends by going with him to the Nebraska frontier. Carpenter, who, of course, had no money, took up a homestead in Red Willow County, fifty miles from the railroad. There they had measured off their land themselves, driving across the prairie in a wagon, to the wheel of which they had tied a red cotton handkerchief, and counting its revolutions. They built a dug-out in the red hillside, one of those cave dwellings whose inmates so often reverted to primitive conditions. Their water they got from the lagoons where the buffalo drank, and their slender stock of provisions was always at the mercy of bands of roving Indians. For thirty years my aunt had not been farther than fifty miles from the homestead.

I owed to this woman most of the good that ever came my way in my boyhood, and had a reverential[9] affection for her. During the years when I was riding herd for my uncle, my aunt, after cooking the three meals—the first of which was ready at six o'clock in the morning—and putting the six children to bed, would often stand until midnight at her ironing-board, with me at the kitchen table beside her, hearing me recite Latin declensions and conjugations,[10] gently shaking me when my drowsy head sank down over a page of irregular verbs. It was to her, at her ironing or mending, that I read my first Shakspere, and her old text-book on mythology was the first that ever came into my empty hands. She taught me my scales and exercises on the little parlor organ which her husband had bought her after fifteen years, during which she had not so much as seen a musical instrument. She would sit beside me by the hour, darning and counting, while I struggled with the "Joyous Farmer."[11] She seldom talked to me about music, and I understood why. Once when I had been **doggedly** beating out some easy passages from an old score of *Euryanthe*[12] I had found among her music books, she came up to me and, putting her hands over my eyes, gently drew my head back upon her shoulder, saying tremulously,[13] "Don't love it so well, Clark, or it may be taken from you."

When my aunt appeared on the morning after her arrival in Boston, she was still in a semi-somnambulant[14] state. She seemed not to realize that she was in the city where she had spent her youth, the place longed for hungrily half a lifetime. She had been so wretchedly train-sick throughout the journey that she had no recollection of anything but her discomfort, and, to all intents and purposes, there were but a few hours of nightmare between the farm in Red Willow County and my study on Newbury Street. I had planned a little pleasure for her that afternoon, to repay her for some of the glorious moments she had given me when we used to milk together in the straw-thatched cowshed and she, because I was more than usually tired, or

---

5. *Franz-Joseph-Land* is a group of islands in the Arctic Ocean.
6. The *Congo* River in central Africa is also called the Zaire River.
7. The *Green Mountains* extend from western Massachusetts through Vermont and into Canada.
8. *Callow* means "inexperienced" or "immature."
9. *Reverential* means "with a feeling of deep respect and awe."

Vocabulary

reproach (ri prōch´) *n.* an expression of disapproval; a reprimand

---

10. *Declensions* are different forms of nouns, pronouns, and adjectives. *Conjugations* are different forms of verbs. Students often memorize these forms when learning a new language.
11. *Joyous Farmer* is one of a series of compositions for children by Robert Shumann (1810–1856).
12. *Euryanthe* (ā ûr i än tā) is an opera by the German composer Carl Maria von Weber (1786–1826).
13. *Tremulously* means "in a trembling or shaking manner."
14. *Semi-somnambulant* (sem´ ē som nam´ byə lənt) means "bewildered or dazed, as if sleepwalking."

Literary Element Point of View *How is your understanding of this passage affected by the point of view of the story?*

Vocabulary

doggedly (dô´ gid lē) *adv.* in a stubbornly persistent manner; obstinately

Boston Common, 1901. Childe Hassam. Oil on canvas, 16 x 20 in.
David David Gallery, Philadelphia.

Viewing the Art: Look closely at the painting. Suppose Aunt
Georgiana saw this scene as soon as she arrived in Boston. How
might she have reacted? Explain.

because her husband had spoken sharply to me,
would tell me of the splendid performance of the
Huguenots[15] she had seen in Paris, in her youth.

At two o'clock the Symphony Orchestra was to
give a Wagner program, and I intended to take my
aunt; though, as I conversed with her, I grew doubtful about her enjoyment of it. I suggested our visiting the Conservatory and the Common[16] before
lunch, but she seemed altogether too timid to wish
to venture out. She questioned me absently about
various changes in the city, but she was chiefly concerned that she had forgotten to leave instructions
about feeding half-skimmed milk to a certain weakling calf, "old Maggie's calf, you know, Clark," she
explained, evidently having forgotten how long I
had been away. She was further troubled because
she had neglected to tell her daughter about the
freshly-opened kit of mackerel in the cellar, which
would spoil if it were not used directly.

I asked her whether she had ever heard any of
the Wagnerian operas, and found that she had not,
though she was perfectly familiar with their respec-

---

15. *Huguenots* (hū′ gə nots′) is a French opera by the German
    composer Giacomo Meyerbeer (1791–1864).
16. *Common* refers to Boston Common, a public park.

tive situations, and had once possessed the piano
score of *The Flying Dutchman*. I began to think it
would be best to get her back to Red Willow
County without waking her, and regretted having
suggested the concert.

From the time we entered the concert hall, however, she was a trifle less passive and inert, and for
the first time seemed to perceive her surroundings.
I had felt some **trepidation** lest she might become
aware of her queer, country clothes, or might experience some painful embarrassment at stepping suddenly into the world to which she had been dead
for a quarter of a century. But, again, I found how
superficially I had judged her. She sat looking about
her with eyes as impersonal, almost as stony, as
those with which the granite Rameses[17] in a
museum watches the froth and fret that ebbs and
flows[18] about his pedestal. I have seen this same
aloofness in old miners who drift into the Brown
hotel at Denver, their pockets full of bullion,[19] their
linen soiled, their haggard faces unshaven; standing
in the thronged corridors as solitary as though they
were still in a frozen camp on the Yukon.[20]

The matinée audience was made up chiefly of
women. One lost the contour of faces and figures,
indeed any effect of line whatever, and there was
only the color of bodices past counting, the shim-
mer of fabrics soft and firm, silky and sheer; red,
mauve, pink, blue, lilac, purple, écru,[21] rose, yellow,
cream, and white, all the colors that an impressionist[22] finds in a sunlit landscape, with here and
there the dead shadow of a frock coat. My Aunt

---

17. *Rameses* (ram′ ə sēz) is the name shared by several kings
    of ancient Egypt.
18. *[froth and fret . . . flows]* This phrase refers to the general
    busy activity that would come and go past a museum statue.
19. Here, *bullion* (bool′ yən) is gold.
20. *Yukon* refers to the Yukon River, a major route to the
    Klondike gold fields in Canada.
21. *Écru* (ā′ krōō) is beige.
22. An *impressionist* is a member of a movement in French
    painting that emphasized the play of light and color.

Big Idea **Regionalism** *How does the concert hall draw
Georgiana's attention away from the farm in a way the
city could not?*

Vocabulary

trepidation (trep′ ə dā′ shən) *n.* nervous anticipation;
anxiety

Georgiana regarded them as though they had been so many daubs of tube-paint on a palette.

When the musicians came out and took their places, she gave a little stir of anticipation, and looked with quickening interest down over the rail at that invariable grouping, perhaps the first wholly familiar thing that had greeted her eye since she had left old Maggie and her weakling calf. I could feel how all those details sank into her soul, for I had not forgotten how they had sunk into mine when I came fresh from ploughing forever and forever between green aisles of corn, where, as in a treadmill, one might walk from daybreak to dusk without perceiving a shadow of change. The clean profiles of the musicians, the gloss of their linen, the dull black of their coats, the beloved shapes of the instruments, the patches of yellow light on the smooth, varnished bellies of the 'cellos and the bass viols in the rear, the restless, wind-tossed forest of fiddle necks and bows—I recalled how, in the first orchestra I ever heard, those long bow-strokes seemed to draw the heart out of me, as a conjurer's stick reels out yards of paper ribbon from a hat.

The first number was the *Tannhauser* overture. When the horns drew out the first strain of the Pilgrim's chorus, Aunt Georgiana clutched my coat sleeve. Then it was I first realized that for her this broke a silence of thirty years. I saw again the tall, naked house on the prairie, black and grim as a wooden fortress; the black pond where I had learned to swim, its margin pitted with sun-dried cattle tracks; the rain gullied clay banks about the naked house, the four dwarf ash seedlings where the dish-cloths were always hung to dry before the kitchen door. The world there was the flat world of the ancients;[23] to the east, a cornfield that stretched to daybreak; to the west, a corral that reached to sunset; between, the conquests of peace, dearer-bought than those of war.

The overture closed, my aunt released my coat sleeve, but she said nothing. She sat staring dully at the orchestra. What, I wondered, did she get from it? She had been a good pianist in her day, I knew,

and her musical education had been broader than that of most music teachers of a quarter of a century ago. She had often told me of Mozart's operas and Meyerbeer's, and I could remember hearing her sing, years ago, certain melodies of Verdi.[24] When I had fallen ill with a fever in her house she used to sit by my cot in the evening—when the cool, night wind blew in through the faded mosquito netting tacked over the window and I lay watching a certain bright star that burned red above the cornfield—and sing "Home to our mountains, O, let us return!" in a way fit to break the heart of a Vermont boy near dead of homesickness already.

I watched her closely through the prelude to *Tristan and Isolde*, trying vainly to conjecture what that seething turmoil of strings and winds might mean to her, but she sat mutely staring at the violin bows that drove **obliquely** downward, like the pelting streaks of rain in a summer shower. Had this music any message for her? Had she enough left to at all comprehend this power which had kindled the world since she had left it? I was in a fever of curiosity, but Aunt Georgiana sat silent upon her peak in Darien.[25] She preserved this utter immobility throughout the number from *The Flying Dutchman*, though her fingers worked mechanically upon her black dress, as if, of themselves, they were recalling the piano score they had once played. Poor hands! They had been stretched and twisted into mere tentacles to hold and lift and knead with; on one of them a thin, worn band that had once been a wedding ring.

---

23. *The ancients* refers to those who lived in classical Greece and Rome.

24. Wolfgang Amadeus *Mozart* (woolf′ gang′ ä′ mə dā′ əs mōt′ särt) (1756–1791) was an Austrian composer. Giuseppe *Verdi* (jōō zep′ pe ver′ dē) (1813–1901) was an Italian composer of opera.

25. The phrase *"peak in Darien"* (dār′ ē en′) alludes to the poem "On First Looking into Chapman's Homer" by John Keats. The poem describes Spanish explorers on a mountain in Darien, now Panama, who stand silently and in awe, as the first Europeans to view the Pacific Ocean.

Literary Element Point of View *What effect does the first-person point of view have on the depiction of the concert?*

Big Idea Regionalism *What does the description of Georgiana's hands reveal about the difference between Boston and the Nebraska farm, according to Clark?*

Reading Strategy Identifying Sequence *How do the flashbacks contribute to the effect of Clark's realizations about his aunt?*

Vocabulary

obliquely (ō blēk′ lē) *adv.* in a slanting or sloping direction

As I pressed and gently quieted one of those groping hands, I remembered with quivering eyelids their services for me in other days.

Soon after the tenor began the "Prize Song," I heard a quick drawn breath and turned to my aunt. Her eyes were closed, but the tears were glistening on her cheeks, and I think, in a moment more, they were in my eyes as well. It never really died, then—the soul which can suffer so excruciatingly and so interminably; it withers to the outward eye only; like that strange moss which can lie on a dusty shelf half a century and yet, if placed in water, grows green again. She wept so throughout the development and elaboration of the melody.

During the intermission before the second half, I questioned my aunt and found that the "Prize Song" was not new to her. Some years before there had drifted to the farm in Red Willow County a young German, a tramp cowpuncher,[26] who had sung in the chorus at Bayreuth[27] when he was a boy, along with the other peasant boys and girls. Of a Sunday morning he used to sit on his gingham-sheeted bed in the hands' bedroom which opened off the kitchen, cleaning the leather of his boots and saddle, singing the "Prize Song," while my aunt went about her work in the kitchen. She had hovered over him until she had prevailed upon him to join the country church, though his sole fitness for this step, in so far as I could gather, lay in his boyish face and his possession of this divine melody. Shortly afterward, he had gone to town on the Fourth of July, been drunk for several days, lost his money at a faro[28] table, ridden a saddled Texas steer on a bet, and disappeared with a fractured collar-bone. All this my aunt told me huskily, wanderingly, as though she were talking in the weak lapses of illness.

"Well, we have come to better things than the old *Trovatore*[29] at any rate, Aunt Georgie?" I queried, with a well meant effort at jocularity.[30]

Her lip quivered and she hastily put her handkerchief up to her mouth. From behind it she murmured, "And you have been hearing this ever since you left me, Clark?" Her question was the gentlest and saddest of reproaches.

The second half of the program consisted of four numbers from the *Ring*, and closed with Siegfried's funeral march. My aunt wept quietly, but almost continuously, as a shallow vessel overflows in a rain-storm. From time to time her dim eyes looked up at the lights, burning softly under their dull glass globes.

The deluge of sound poured on and on; I never knew what she found in the shining current of it; I never knew how far it bore her, or past what happy islands. From the trembling of her face I could well believe that before the last number she had been carried out where the myriad[31] graves are, into the grey, nameless burying grounds of the sea; or into some world of death vaster yet, where, from the beginning of the world, hope has lain down with hope and dream with dream and, renouncing,[32] slept.

The concert was over; the people filed out of the hall chattering and laughing, glad to relax and find the living level again, but my kinswoman made no effort to rise. The harpist slipped the green felt cover over his instrument; the flute-players shook the water from their mouthpieces; the men of the orchestra went out one by one, leaving the stage to the chairs and music stands, empty as a winter cornfield.

I spoke to my aunt. She burst into tears and sobbed pleadingly. "I don't want to go, Clark, I don't want to go!"

I understood. For her, just outside the concert hall, lay the black pond with the cattle-tracked bluffs; the tall, unpainted house, with weather-curled boards, naked as a tower; the crook-backed ash seedlings where the dish-cloths hung to dry; the gaunt,[33] moulting turkeys picking up refuse about the kitchen door. ❧

---

26. *Cowpuncher* means "cowboy."
27. *Bayreuth* (bī roit') is a German city famous for its annual Wagnerian music festival.
28. *Faro* (fār' ō) is a gambling game played with a deck of cards.
29. *Trovatore* (tro və tōr'e) refers to *Il Trovatore,* an opera by Giuseppe Verdi.
30. *Jocularity* means "joking" or "humor."

31. *Myriad* means "countless" or "innumerable."
32. *Renouncing* means "giving up."
33. *Gaunt* means "extremely thin."

Literary Element Point of View *How does Clark know what his aunt is feeling?*

AFTER YOU READ

RESPONDING AND THINKING CRITICALLY

Respond

1. How did the story affect your impressions of nineteenth-century frontier life?

Recall and Interpret

2. (a)How does Clark react to the letter from his uncle? (b)Why does he react so strongly to the letter?

3. The narrator says that he owed to his aunt "most of the good that ever came my way in my boyhood." How is her influence apparent in his adult life?

4. (a)How does Georgiana behave after the concert ends? (b)What might the concert hall symbolize for her?

Analyze and Evaluate

5. (a)Georgiana seldom talks to Clark about music. Why then does she tell Clark about the *Huguenots* performance she saw in Paris? (b)Given Georgiana's reaction to the Wagner concert, how do concerts probably affect her in general?

6. Clark says of scenery on the farm: "one might walk from daybreak to dusk without perceiving a shadow of change." To whom might this statement be considered false and why?

7. After his experience with Georgiana, how might Clark perceive his access to concerts in Boston differently?

Connect

8. **Big Idea** **Regionalism** The story contrasts the limits of one region with the opportunities of another. What might these two "regions" be in Georgiana's view, specifically? Support your claim with evidence from the story.

LITERARY ANALYSIS

Literary Element Point of View

It is clear that "A Wagner Matinée" is written with a **first-person point of view** because the story is filtered through the sensations, thoughts, and memories of Clark, the narrator. The use of pronouns such as *I, you,* and *me* also indicates first-person point of view.

In stories told in first-person point of view, the narrator is always a character in the story. As you read stories told in first person, note that any story told from one perspective is limited to that character's knowledge, experience, and biases. The narrator may not be reliable, so judge whether you can trust that his or her interpretation of events is accurate. Pay attention to details in the story to help evaluate narrator reliability and to figure out parts of the story the narrator may not know or share.

1. Why might the reader trust Clark's interpretation of Georgiana?

2. Although Georgiana rarely speaks directly in the story, what details about her confirm Clark's interpretations?

Review: Voice

Voice refers to the distinctive language that conveys the author or narrator's personality to the reader. Voice is determined by elements of style such as word choice, sentence structure, and tone.

Partner Activity Meet with a partner to discuss how Clark's voice is revealed in the following passage. Then answer the questions that follow.

> "Had this music any message for her? Had she enough left to at all comprehend this power which had kindled the world since she had left it? I was in a fever of curiosity, but Aunt Georgiana sat silent upon her peak in Darien."

1. What does Clark's use of questions reveal?

2. What do words such as *power, kindled,* and *fever* and the Darien allusion reveal about Clark?

3. How does Clark's voice convey his personality?

WILLA CATHER **525**

Reading Strategy Identifying Sequence

A **flashback** is an interruption in the chronological order of a story that depicts an earlier event. Flashback can be used to give readers background about the main events of the story.

1. How does the flashback about Clark as a boy playing "Joyous Farmer" help the reader?

2. What provokes most of the flashbacks in the story?

3. Why might Cather have chosen to use flashback instead of organizing the events chronologically?

Vocabulary Practice

Practice with Analogies Choose the word that best completes the analogy.

1. grandparent : legacy :: groom :
   a. house   **c.** bride
   b. ring   **d.** husband

2. quickly : fast :: doggedly :
   a. stubborn   **c.** obediently
   b. proud   **d.** docile

3. reproach : disapproval :: compliment :
   a. criticism   **c.** affection
   b. approval   **d.** attention

4. sweat : trepidation :: wink :
   a. anxiety   **c.** mischief
   b. blink   **d.** eye

5. obliquely : direction :: passionately :
   a. reason   **c.** spontaneous
   b. instinct   **d.** feeling

Writing About Literature

Evaluate Author's Craft In fiction, **author's craft** refers to how an author uses various techniques, including word choice, sensory details, figurative language, and dialogue, to tell a story. In "A Wagner Matinée," Willa Cather uses comparisons as a technique to explore the relationship between Clark and Aunt Georgiana and the effects of the concert on both characters.

> *"As for myself, I saw my aunt's battered figure with that feeling of awe and respect..."*

Comparison Aunt Georgiana's aged figure is compared to Clark's memory of her.

Evaluation Clark's comment on his aunt's figure allows the reader to see that she has changed much since he last saw her and that she looks different from the women in Boston. The comparison alludes to the amount of time they have spent apart and to the differences between frontier and city life.

Write an essay evaluating how the use of comparisons in "A Wagner Matinée" contributes to the meaning of the story. As you draft, follow the plan below to help organize your essay.

Introduction	Present your evaluation.
First Comparison	
Second Comparison	Cite the comparisons and evaluate how they contribute to the story.
Third Comparison	
Conclusion	Summarize your evaluation and add insight.

When you are done writing, proofread and edit your draft for errors in spelling, grammar, and punctuation. Then meet with a partner and exchange drafts. Check to make sure your partner's evaluation is clear and well supported with examples from the story.

I Will Fight No More Forever

MEET CHIEF JOSEPH

Chief Joseph—whose given name was Hinmaton Yalaktit (hin mə tō′ yä läkh′ tet) or "Thunder Rolling Down the Mountain"—was born in the Wallowa Valley in what is now northeastern Oregon. When his father died in 1871, Joseph was elected to succeed him as a chief of the Nez Percé (nez′ purs′), the largest and most powerful of the Sahaptin-speaking tribes that lived in present-day central Idaho and contiguous areas in Oregon and Washington. Other Sahaptin-speaking tribes include the Cayuse, Tenino, Wallawalla, and Yakima.

The Nez Percé were more warlike than neighboring tribes, especially after acquiring the horse from the Plains Indians in the early eighteenth century. However, they had maintained peace with the whites for decades, ever since the Lewis and Clark expedition in 1805, which was their first significant contact with whites. Nevertheless, Joseph inherited a volatile situation. In 1863, following a gold rush into Nez Percé territory, the U.S. government had reclaimed three quarters of the land it had ceded to the tribe in an 1855 treaty. Chief Joseph successfully resisted efforts to remove his band from the Wallowa Valley until 1877, when the government threatened removal by force.

"Hear me, my chiefs. I am tired; my heart is sick and sad."

—Chief Joseph

Cooperator and Leader To avoid bloodshed, Chief Joseph decided to cooperate, but as he led his band toward a reservation in Idaho, he learned that three of his braves, enraged at the government's action, had killed a group of white settlers and prospectors. To escape retaliation by the U.S. Army, Chief Joseph led his people—some 200 to 300 warriors and their families—on a long, grueling march toward the Canadian border. They trekked through Oregon, Washington, Idaho, and Montana for nearly three months, covering 1,000 miles as the warriors successfully fought off U.S. troops. Within forty miles of their destination, in the Bear Paw mountains of Montana, the Nez Percé were surrounded and forced to surrender. The chase and intermittent skirmishes had claimed the lives of 239 Nez Percé, many of them women and children, as well as the lives of 266 U.S. Army personnel.

Lasting Legacy Although Chief Joseph had thought his people would be able to return home, they were removed to Indian Territory, or present-day Oklahoma, where many fell ill and died. In 1885 some of the survivors were returned to the Pacific Northwest, but about half, including Chief Joseph, were taken to Colville reservation, a non-Nez Percé reservation in Washington State. There Chief Joseph died, according to his doctor, "of a broken heart." At a ceremony honoring him, a Nez Percé chief named Yellow Bull said, "Joseph is dead, but his words will live forever."

Chief Joseph was born around 1840 and died in 1904.

Literature Online Author Search For more about Chief Joseph, go to www.glencoe.com.

Connecting to the Speech

What does it mean to lose with dignity? In this speech, Joseph explains the decision he has made to surrender. As you read, think about the following questions:

- What was Joseph's primary reason for surrendering?
- Have you ever been in a situation where surrender was the best or most noble option?

Building Background

The Nez Percé was the southeasternmost tribe in the Plateau culture, which developed on the high plateaus between the coastal mountain ranges and the Rocky Mountains. Each Plateau tribe spoke a language from one of three linguistic groups: Sahaptin, Salish, or Kutenai. Plateau tribes shared many cultural components. In the winter, they lived by rivers where fish were abundant. In the summer, they moved to mountain valleys to hunt and gather roots. By the time Chief Joseph came to power, the Nez Percé had strayed away from the Plateau culture and adopted many cultural components of the Plains Indians, including the war bonnet, the horse, and the teepee.

Setting Purposes for Reading

Big Idea Regionalism

As you read Chief Joseph's speech, consider the tragic consequences for Native Americans brought about by the westward expansion.

Literary Element Tone

Tone is the writer's attitude toward the subject of a work. Writers create the tone of a work primarily through diction, or word choice. As you read, notice Chief Joseph's diction and the tone it creates.

- See Literary Terms Handbook, p. R19.

Literature Online **Interactive Literary Elements Handbook** To review or learn more about the literary elements, go to www.glencoe.com.

Reading Strategy Evaluating Style

Tone is just one element of **style**, or the way that a writer or an orator uses language. Some other elements are diction, syntax, sentence length, and use of figurative language. When you evaluate style, you make a judgment about it based on the application of appropriate criteria, or standards. As you read Chief Joseph's speech, evaluate how the individual elements such as tone contribute to his style.

....

Reading Tip: Taking Notes Use a chart to record examples of different elements of Chief Joseph's style. In the right-hand column, explain briefly how the elements work.

Element	Example	Effect
Tone	"Maybe I shall find [the children] among the dead."	
Diction		
Syntax		
Sentence Length		
Figurative Language		

INDIANA ACADEMIC STANDARDS (pages 528–530)
11.3.3 Analyze the ways in which...tone...achieve[s] specific rhetorical...purposes...

11.2.6 Critique the power, validity, and truthfulness of arguments set forth in...speeches...

Chief Joseph Rides to Surrender, 1979. Howard Terpning. Oil on canvas. ©1979 Howard Terpning. ©1979 The Greenwich Workshop® Inc. Courtesy of The Greenwich Workshop Inc., Shelton, CT.

I Will Fight No More Forever

Chief Joseph

"Tell General Howard[1] I know his heart. What he told me before, I have in my heart. I am tired of fighting. Our chiefs are killed. Looking Glass[2] is dead. Too Hul Hul Suit[3] is dead. The old men are all dead. It is the young men who say yes and no. He who led on the young men is dead.[4] It is cold and we have no blankets. The little children are freezing to death. My people, some of them, have run away to the hills and have no blankets, no food; no one knows where they are—perhaps freezing to death. I want to have time to look for my children and see how many I can find. Maybe I shall find them among the dead. Hear me, my chiefs. I am tired; my heart is sick and sad. From where the sun now stands I will fight no more forever." ∾

---

1. *General* (Oliver Otis) *Howard* (1830–1909) had been a Union general in the Civil War. He sent troops to fight the Nez Percé in the Battle of White Bird Canyon.
2. *Looking Glass* was a respected leader of the Nez Percé. He took part in the 1877 retreat.
3. *Too Hul Hul Suit,* or Tu Ku Lxu C'uut (tœ kœl´ hu sœt´), leader of the White Bird tribe, was a member of the negotiating team that met with General Howard. He favored fighting for the Nez Percé land rather than moving to a reservation.
4. *[He who led . . . dead.]* refers to Chief Joseph's younger brother, Ollikut (ōl okh´ ut).

Reading Strategy Evaluating Style *What do the form and content of these two sentences emphasize? How do you think they affect the listener or reader?*

RESPONDING AND THINKING CRITICALLY

Respond

1. If you could speak to Chief Joseph, what would you say?

Recall and Interpret

2. (a)What has happened to the chiefs and the old men of the tribe? (b)How might these developments have affected Chief Joseph's decision to surrender?

3. (a)What words does Chief Joseph use to describe his heart? (b)How do the feelings he describes help you better understand the decision he has made?

Analyze and Evaluate

4. (a)What does Chief Joseph say about his children? (b)Why does he want to look for them?

5. (a)What words or phrases does Chief Joseph repeat? (b)What effect does this repetition create?

6. In this short speech, Chief Joseph explains a decision that will have an enormous impact on the lives of his people. Would a longer, more detailed speech have been more effective? Explain.

Connect

7. **Big Idea** **Regionalism** According to one critic, "'I Will Fight No More Forever' . . . is a classic statement of Native American pride and resolve in the midst of terrible suffering." (a)How does Chief Joseph display pride and resolve in this speech? (b)Which values of the Nez Percé does this speech reveal?

LITERARY ANALYSIS

Literary Element Tone

The **tone** of a piece of writing conveys the author's attitude toward the subject matter. In "I Will Fight No More Forever," the tone conveys feelings of weariness, resignation, sadness, and dignity. Chief Joseph's use of simple, direct language and brief sentences reinforces this sense of overwhelming loss.

1. What phrases help create a tone that is weary, resigned, and sad, yet dignified?

2. Find examples of simple, direct language and brief sentences. How do they affect the tone of the speech?

Interdisciplinary Activity

American History: Great Speeches Research speeches by other Native American orators such as Chief Tecumseh and Chief Red Eagle.

1. How are the other Native American speeches you found similar to and different from Chief Joseph's speech?

2. What is the style of each speech?

Literature Online **Web Activities** For eFlashcards, Selection Quick Checks, and other Web activities, go to www.glencoe.com.

READING AND VOCABULARY

Reading Strategy Evaluating Style

Style refers to a writer's individual, characteristic way of using language. Elements such as diction, phrasing, sentence length, tone, imagery, and figurative language contribute to style. Because writers use these elements in personal, distinctive ways, no two styles are exactly alike. To evaluate Chief Joseph's style, answer these questions:

1. Is the style appropriate for the message?

2. Does the style reveal the writer's personality?

Academic Vocabulary

Here are two words from the vocabulary list on page R86.

principle (prin′ sə pəl) *n.* a law or rule, usually regarding morals

impose (im pōz′) *v.* to force upon

Practice and Apply
1. What **principles** did Chief Joseph value?
2. How did the U.S. Army **impose** the government's policies on Native Americans?

Realism
and Naturalism

Mrs. Charles Thursby, 1897–1898. John Singer Sargent.
Oil on canvas, 78 x 39 ¾ in. Collection of The Newark Museum.

*"There are two ways of spreading light: to be
The candle or the mirror that reflects it."*

—Edith Wharton, "Vesalius in Zante"

The Two Faces of Urban America

IN THE LATE NINETEENTH AND EARLY twentieth centuries, despite the emergence of a growing middle class, rapid industrialization created two sharply contrasting urban classes: wealthy entrepreneurs and poor immigrants from Europe and Asia who provided them with cheap labor. Although dependent upon each other, these two groups seldom met, as they lived in starkly different neighborhoods. The wealthiest families established fashionable districts in the hearts of cities, where they built fabulous mansions.

By contrast, the majority of factory workers squeezed into dark, overcrowded tenements where crime, violence, fire, and disease were constant threats. U.S. writers of the time responded to and reflected these urban conditions in their novels, stories, essays, and articles.

Picnicking in Central Park, 1885. Robert L. Bracklow. Black and white photograph.

> "*The entire metropolitan center possessed a high and mighty air calculated to overawe and abash the common applicant, and to make the gulf between poverty and success seem both wide and deep.*"
>
> —Theodore Dreiser
> *Sister Carrie*

The Face of the Urban Rich

Two major Realist writers from the upper class who reflected and criticized its values, and who formed a famous literary friendship, were Edith Wharton and Henry James.

Edith Wharton was born in 1862 into one of New York's most prominent families. Her interest in architecture prompted her to criticize and satirize the "conspicuous consumption" (a term coined by social critic Thorstein Veblen) that led to the fashionable, cluttered interior decoration favored by the members of her social class. Wharton's early novel *The House of Mirth* (1905) uses architecture metaphorically, as her heroine Lily Bart's descent from wealth into poverty is mirrored by a decline in the houses she is forced to inhabit.

Wharton's older contemporary and friend Henry James was born into a distinguished Boston family in 1843. James became the master chronicler of the inner lives of his characters, and his subtle innovations in narrative point of view contributed to the literary technique that his brother William, the famous psychologist, called "the stream of consciousness." James used this technique to probe the complex relationship between wealth and culture. One of his favorite themes was the confrontation between naïve, wealthy, uncultured Americans and highly cultivated and sophisticated Europeans, whose aristocratic civilization was in decline. James's treatment of this theme reached its zenith in his late novel *The Ambassadors* (1903), in which the elderly, respectable American Lambert Strether is charmed by the pleasures of European civilization and learns too late that there is more to life than making money.

The Face of the Urban Poor

The plight of the urban poor was a favorite subject of the new group of Naturalist writers. Stephen Crane's *Maggie: A Girl of the Streets* is a bleak study of life in the slums of New York City. Although Crane later turned to other subjects, he retained his sympathy for urban characters such as Maggie.

Some writers focused their attention on the hardships of immigrants and ethnic groups who faced bigotry and discrimination as well as poverty in U.S. cities. Anzia Yezierska and Abraham Cahan wrote about the social, cultural, and political tensions experienced by Eastern European Jews living in New York's Lower East Side.

Perhaps the most famous writer to address the socioeconomic plight of the urban poor was Theodore Dreiser. Despite a mediocre education, his writing propelled him to the pinnacle of American Naturalism. In his first and perhaps greatest novel, *Sister Carrie* (1900), Dreiser tells the story of Carrie Meeber, a naïve country girl who comes to Chicago looking for work. While there, she endures the impersonal cruelty and loneliness of life in a large U.S. city at the turn of the century.

Reformers and Muckrakers

A social reform movement arose in the late nineteenth century that was dedicated to providing better conditions for the urban working class. Perhaps the most prominent of these reformers was Jane Addams. In *Twenty Years at Hull-House* (1910), she tells how she turned an old home in an immigrant neighborhood in Chicago into a settlement house where neighborhood residents could learn to speak English, discuss political events, and hold celebrations.

A group of journalists and novelists known as "muckrakers," a term coined by Theodore Roosevelt,

began to critically examine the social, economic, and political system that created the huge gulf between the rich and the poor. In his book *How the Other Half Lives* (1890), Jacob Riis attracted the attention of President Roosevelt to the squalor of life in New York City slum tenements. The result was an improved water supply, child labor laws, and other improvements. *The Jungle* (1906), Upton Sinclair's exposé of the brutal and degrading working conditions in the meatpacking industry, led to the Meat Inspection Act and the Pure Food and Drug Act of 1906.

Men gather in an alley called "Bandit's Roost" in Manhattan's Little Italy. Around the turn of the century, this part of Mulberry Bend was a notoriously dilapidated and dangerous section of New York City. ca. 1890s. Jacob August Riis.
Viewing the Photograph: How do the people in this scene compare with those of the previous page?

Literature Online **Literary History** For more about the literature of urban America, go to www.glencoe.com.

RESPONDING AND THINKING CRITICALLY

1. In Dreiser's *Sister Carrie,* the protagonist believes that the city will provide her with new opportunities and a new life. Would you have wanted to live in a large city at the turn of the twentieth century? Why or why not?

2. What were Edith Wharton's and Henry James's main criticisms of the wealthy upper class in the United States?

3. What was the chief aim of the muckrakers? Do you think that they were successful? Explain.

INDIANA ACADEMIC STANDARDS (pages 532–533)
11.3.5 Analyze or evaluate works of literary...significance in history...

April Showers

MEET EDITH WHARTON

Edith Wharton is best known for her novels depicting the intricate codes of conduct that ruled the lives of New York City's aristocracy at the end of the 1800s. Wharton felt that upper-class society discouraged both art and the artist.

> "Mrs. Ballinger is one of the ladies who pursue Culture in Bands, as though it were dangerous to meet it alone."
>
> —Edith Wharton
> *Xingu and Other Stories*, 1916

A Privileged Youth Edith Newbold Jones was born into one of New York City's wealthiest and most distinguished families. Taught by private tutors, she received an excellent education both in the United States and abroad. When she was sixteen, Edith privately published her first book. Her mother may have arranged the publication, hoping that Edith would feel fulfilled, stop writing, and take up interests considered more suited to her social position.

In 1885 Edith married Edward Wharton, a wealthy Boston banker. Shortly after, he began to suffer from both mental and physical illnesses. It was during this time that Wharton began seriously writing fiction with the intention of publishing. She modeled her work mostly after novelist Henry James—combining complicated psychological portraits with critiques of social convention. Throughout the 1890s, she contributed to various magazines and produced two collections of short stories.

A Novelist Abroad Wharton's first novel, *The Valley of Decision*, was published in 1902. Three

years later, *The House of Mirth*, which was both popular and praised by critics, appeared.

In 1907, after selling her home and separating from her husband, Wharton permanently settled in Paris, where she felt female artists were more accepted.

As World War I raged in Europe, Wharton worked in support of the French cause—aiding Belgian refugees and raising money from Americans. For this she was given the Cross of the Legion of Honor, the highest honor awarded to a foreigner in France.

This was perhaps the most productive time in Wharton's life, during which she published some of her greatest novels, including *Ethan Frome, The Reef, The Custom of the Country,* and *Summer. The Age of Innocence,* probably Wharton's best-known work, appeared in 1920. For this she became the first woman to be awarded a Pulitzer Prize for fiction.

Edith Wharton's greatness came from her ability to depict the interplay between the life of the mind and of society. Alternately tragic and satiric, Wharton's incisive fiction helped to establish Realism as the most important movement of her day.

Edith Wharton was born in 1862 and died in 1937.

Literature Online **Author Search** For more about Edith Wharton, go to www.glencoe.com.

Connecting to the Story

Have you ever neglected your responsibilities in order to devote yourself to a project you felt passionately about? In Wharton's story, the main character is so preoccupied with her novel that she forgets her household responsibilities. Think about the following questions:

- Under what circumstances might it be acceptable to neglect daily chores?
- How important is it to receive widespread recognition for the work that you do?

Building Background

"April Showers" is set in Massachusetts in the early 1900s. At the time, novels were often printed in magazines in serial form, appearing in weekly or monthly installments. The proliferation of magazines in the United States and Britain began in the 1800s, partly in response to the rise of the middle class and to the spread of public education. Publications aimed at the general public were inexpensive, had little literary content, and included a great deal of light entertainment. However, the more expensive magazines, such as *Atlantic Monthly* or *Harper's,* had more substantive content and a greater impact on the tastes and ideas of the day.

Setting Purposes for Reading

Big Idea Realism

As you read, notice how Realism's focus on psychology and human behavior is displayed in "April Showers."

Literary Element Flashback

A **flashback** is an interruption in the chronological order of a narrative to show an event that happened earlier. A flashback gives readers information that may help explain the main events of a story. As you read "April Showers," examine how Wharton incorporates a brief flashback near the start of the story and also near the end to help the reader better understand Theodora's character and the story's events.

- See Literary Terms Handbook, p. R7.

Literature Online **Interactive Literary Elements Handbook** To review or learn more about the literary elements, go to www.glencoe.com.

Reading Strategy Making and Verifying Predictions

To **predict** means to make an educated guess about what will happen in a text, using the clues that a writer provides. Predicting will help you stay engaged in the plot of a story as it evolves. While you read "April Showers," verify, adjust, or change your predictions as new information emerges in the text.

Reading Tip: Taking Notes Use a chart to record your predictions and the evidence on which you base those predictions.

Prediction	Evidence
Theodora's obsession with her novel will come back to haunt her.	Theodora is neglecting her family obligations.

Vocabulary

prosperous (pros′ pər əs) *adj.* wealthy or successful; p. 536 *The Smith family, who owned the area's largest factory, was the most prosperous family in town.*

obscure (əb skyoor′) *adj.* little known or having an insignificant reputation; p. 537 *The contributions of more obscure American painters were overlooked in the student's research paper.*

stupor (stoo′ pər) *n.* a confused or dazed state of mind; p. 538 *Jack had been in a stupor since his tonsils were removed the previous day.*

calamity (kə lam′ə tē) *n.* an unfortunate event or disaster; p. 539 *The hurricane's fierceness, combined with the lack of warning, resulted in a terrible calamity on the island.*

Vocabulary Tip: Synonyms Words that have the same or nearly the same meaning are called synonyms. The words *mirth* and *delight,* for example, are synonyms. Note that synonyms are always the same part of speech.

INDIANA ACADEMIC STANDARDS (pages 535–543)
11.2.2 Analyze the way in which clarity of meaning is affected by the patterns of organization...

11.2 Develop strategies such as...making predictions...
11.5.2 Write responses to literature...

April Showers

Edith Wharton

"But Guy's heart slept under the violets on Muriel's grave."

It was a beautiful ending; Theodora had seen girls cry over last chapters that weren't half as pathetic. She laid her pen aside and read the words over, letting her voice linger on the fall of the sentence; then, drawing a deep breath, she wrote across the foot of the page the name by which she had decided to become known in literature—Gladys Glyn.

Downstairs the library clock struck two. Its muffled thump sounded like an admonitory knock against her bedroom floor. Two o'clock! and she had promised her mother to be up early enough to see that the buttons were sewn on Johnny's reefer,[1] and that Kate had her cod-liver oil[2] before starting for school!

Lingeringly, tenderly she gathered up the pages of her novel—there were five hundred of them—and tied them with the blue satin ribbon that her Aunt Julia had given her. She had meant to wear the ribbon with her new dotted muslin on Sundays, but this was putting it to a nobler use. She bound it round her manuscript, tying the ends in a pretty bow. Theodora was clever at making bows, and could have trimmed hats beautifully, had not all her spare moments been given to literature. Then, with a last look at the precious pages, she sealed and addressed the package. She meant to send it off next morning to the *Home Circle*. She knew it would be hard to obtain access to a paper which numbered so many popular authors among its contributors, but she had been encouraged to make the venture by something her Uncle James had said the last time he had come down from Boston.

He had been telling his brother, Doctor Dace, about his new house out at Brookline. Uncle James was **prosperous,** and was always moving into new houses with more "modern improvements." Hygiene was his passion, and he migrated in the wake of sanitary plumbing.

"The bathrooms alone are worth the money," he was saying, cheerfully, "although it *is* a big rent. But then, when a man's got no children to save up for—" he glanced compassionately round Doctor Dace's crowded table "—and it *is* something to be in a neighborhood where the drainage is A-one. That's what I was telling our neighbor. Who do you suppose she is, by the way?" He smiled at Theodora. "I rather think that young lady knows all about her. Ever hear of Kathleen Kyd?"

---

1. A *reefer* is a short, heavy jacket.
2. *Cod-liver oil* is an unpleasant-tasting liquid rich in vitamins A and D.

Big Idea   Realism *What can you infer about Theodora's view of herself from this comment?*

Literary Element   Flashback *What does this sentence indicate about the paragraphs following it?*

Vocabulary

prosperous (pros′ pər əs) *adj.* wealthy or successful

Kathleen Kyd! The famous "society novelist," the creator of more "favorite heroines" than all her predecessors put together had ever turned out, the author of *Fashion and Passion, An American Duchess, Rhona's Revolt*. Was there any intelligent girl from Maine to California whose heart would not have beat faster at the mention of that name?

"Why, yes," Uncle James was saying, "Kathleen Kyd lives next door. Frances G. Wollop is her real name, and her husband's a dentist. She's a very pleasant, sociable kind of woman; you'd never think she was a writer. Ever hear how she began to write? She told me the whole story. It seems she was a saleswoman in a store, working on starvation wages, with a mother and a consumptive sister to support. Well, she wrote a story one day, just for fun, and sent it to the *Home Circle*. They'd never heard of her, of course, and she never expected to hear from them. She did, though. They took the story and passed their plate for more. She became a regular contributor and eventually was known all over the country. Now she tells me her books bring her in about ten thousand a year. Rather more than you and I can boast of, eh, John? Well, I hope *this* household doesn't contribute to her support." He glanced sharply at Theodora. "I don't believe in feeding youngsters on sentimental trash; it's like sewer gas—doesn't smell bad, and infects the system without your knowing it."

Theodora listened breathlessly. Kathleen Kyd's first story had been accepted by the *Home Circle*, and they had asked for more! Why should Gladys Glyn be less fortunate? Theodora had done a great deal of novel reading—far more than her parents were aware of—and felt herself competent to pronounce upon the quality of her own work. She was almost sure that "April Showers" was a remarkable book. If it lacked Kathleen Kyd's lightness of touch, it had an emotional intensity never achieved by that brilliant writer. Theodora did not care to amuse her readers; she left that to more frivolous talents. Her aim was to stir the depths of human nature, and she felt she had succeeded. It was a great thing for a girl to be able to feel that about her first novel. Theodora was only seventeen; and

she remembered, with a touch of retrospective compassion, that George Eliot[3] had not become famous till she was nearly forty.

No, there was no doubt about the merit of "April Showers." But would not an inferior work have had a better chance of success? Theodora recalled the early struggles of famous authors, the notorious antagonism[4] of publishers and editors to any new writer of exceptional promise. Would it not be wiser to write the book down to the average reader's level, reserving for some later work the great "effects" into which she had thrown all the fever of her imagination? The thought was sacrilege! Never would she lay hands on the sacred structure she had reared; never would she resort to the inartistic expedient of modifying her work to suit the popular taste. Better **obscure** failure than a vulgar triumph. The great authors never stooped to such concessions, and Theodora felt herself included in their ranks by the firmness with which she rejected all thought of conciliating[5] an unappreciative public. The manuscript should be sent as it was.

She woke with a start and a heavy sense of apprehension. The *Home Circle* had refused "April Showers"! No, that couldn't be it; there lay the precious manuscript, waiting to be posted. What was it, then? Ah, that ominous thump below stairs—nine o'clock striking! It was Johnny's buttons!

She sprang out of bed in dismay. She had been so determined not to disappoint her mother about Johnny's buttons! Mrs. Dace, helpless from chronic rheumatism,[6] had to entrust the care of the household to her eldest daughter; and Theodora honestly meant to see that Johnny had his full complement of buttons, and that Kate and Bertha went to school tidy. Unfortunately, the writing of a great novel leaves little time or memory for the lesser obligations of life, and Theodora usually found that her good intentions matured too late for practical results.

3. *George Eliot* (1819–1880) was the pen name of famed British novelist Mary Ann Cross.
4. *Antagonism* means "hostility."
5. *Conciliating* means "appeasing."
6. *Rheumatism* is an illness that causes discomfort in the joints or muscles.

Reading Strategy Making and Verifying Predictions
What is your prediction of Gladys Glyn's success?

Vocabulary

obscure (əb skyoor´) *adj.* little known or having an insignificant reputation

Her contrition[7] was softened by the thought that literary success would enable her to make up for all the little negligences of which she was guilty. She meant to spend all her money on her family; and already she had visions of a wheeled chair for her mother, a fresh wallpaper for the doctor's shabby office, bicycles for the girls, and Johnny's establishment at a boarding school where sewing on his buttons would be included in the curriculum. If her parents could have guessed her intentions, they would not have found fault with her as they did; and Doctor Dace, on this particular morning, would not have looked up to say, with his fagged,[8] ironical air:

"I suppose you didn't get home from the ball till morning?"

Theodora's sense of being in the right enabled her to take the thrust with a dignity that would have awed the unfeeling parent to fiction.

"I'm sorry to be late, father," she said.

Doctor Dace, who could never be counted on to behave like a father in a book, shrugged his shoulders impatiently.

"Your sentiments do you credit, but they haven't kept your mother's breakfast warm."

"Hasn't mother's tray gone up yet?"

"Who was to take it, I should like to know? The girls came down so late that I had to hustle them off before they'd finished breakfast, and Johnny's hands were so dirty that I sent him back to his room to make himself decent. It's a pretty thing for the doctor's children to be the dirtiest little savages in Norton!"

Theodora had hastily prepared her mother's tray, leaving her own breakfast untouched. As she entered the room upstairs, Mrs. Dace's patient face turned to her with a smile much harder to bear than her father's reproaches.

"Mother, I'm *so* sorry—"

> "I suppose you didn't get home from the ball till morning?"

"No matter, dear. I suppose Johnny's buttons kept you. I can't think what that boy does to his clothes!"

Theodora sat the tray down without speaking. It was impossible to own to having forgotten Johnny's buttons without revealing the cause of her forgetfulness. For a few weeks longer she must bear to be misunderstood; then—ah, then if her novel were accepted, how gladly would she forget and forgive! But what if it were refused? She turned aside to hide the dismay that flushed her face. Well, then she would admit the truth—she would ask her parents' pardon, and settle down without a murmur to an obscure existence of mending and combing.

She had said to herself that after the manuscript had been sent, she would have time to look after the children and catch up with the mending; but she had reckoned without the postman. He came three times a day; for an hour before each ring she was too excited to do anything but wonder if he would bring an answer this time, and for an hour afterward she moved about in a leaden **stupor** of disappointment. The children had never been so trying. They seemed to be always coming to pieces, like cheap furniture; one would have supposed they had been put together with bad glue. Mrs. Dace worried herself ill over Johnny's tatters, Bertha's bad marks at school, and Kate's open abstention[9] from cod-liver oil; and Doctor Dace, coming back late from a long round of visits to a fireless office with a smoky lamp, called out furiously to know if Theodora would kindly come down and remove the "East, West, home's best" that hung above the empty grate.

In the midst of it all, Miss Sophy Brill called. It was very kind of her to come, for she was the busiest woman in Norton. She made it her duty to look after other people's affairs, and there was not a house in town but had the benefit of her

---

7. *Contrition* means "remorse."
8. *Fagged* means "tired" or "weary."

---

9. *Abstention* means "the act of refraining from something."

Vocabulary

stupor (stoo′ pər) *n.* a confused or dazed state of mind personal supervision. She generally came when things were going wrong, and the sight of her bonnet on the doorstep was a surer sign of **calamity** than a crepe bow[10] on the bell. After she left, Mrs. Dace looked very sad, and the doctor punished Johnny for warbling down the entry:

> "Miss Sophy Brill
> Is a bitter pill!"

while Theodora, locking herself in her room, resolved with tears that she would never write another novel.

The week was a long nightmare. Theodora could neither eat nor sleep. She was up early enough, but instead of looking after the children and seeing that breakfast was ready, she wandered down the road to meet the postman, and came back wan and empty-handed, oblivious of her morning duties. She had no idea how long the suspense would last; but she didn't see how authors could live if they were kept waiting more than a week.

Then suddenly, one afternoon—she never quite knew how or when it happened—she found herself with a *Home Circle* envelope in her hands, and her dazzled eyes flashing over a wild dance of words that wouldn't settle down and make sense.

"Dear Madam:" (They called her *Madam!* And then; yes, the words were beginning to fall into line now.) "Your novel, 'April Showers,' has been received, and we are glad to accept it on the usual terms. A serial on which we were counting for immediate publication has been delayed by the author's illness, and the first chapters of 'April Showers' will therefore appear in our midsummer number. Thanking you for favoring us with your manuscript, we remain," and so forth.

Theodora found herself in the wood beyond the schoolhouse. She was kneeling on the ground, brushing aside the dead leaves and pressing her lips to the little bursting green things that pushed up eager tips through last year's decay. It was spring—spring! Everything was crowding toward the light and in her own heart hundreds of germinating hopes had burst into sudden leaf. She wondered if the thrust of those little green fingers hurt the surface of the earth as her springing raptures hurt—yes, actually hurt!—her hot, constricted breast! She looked up through interlacing boughs at a tender, opaque blue sky full of the coming of a milky moon. She seemed enveloped in an atmosphere of loving comprehension. The brown earth throbbed with her joy, the treetops trembled with it, and a sudden star broke through the branches like an audible "I know!"

Theodora, on the whole, behaved very well. Her mother cried, her father whistled and said he supposed he must put up with grounds in his coffee now, and be thankful if he ever got a hot meal again; while the children took the most deafening and harassing advantage of what seemed a sudden suspension of the laws of nature.

Within a week everybody in Norton knew that Theodora had written a novel, and that it was coming out in the *Home Circle*. On Sundays, when she walked up the aisle, her friends dropped their prayer books and the soprano sang false in her excitement. Girls with more pin money than Theodora had ever dreamed of copied her hats and imitated her way of speaking. The local paper asked her for a poem; her old school teachers stopped to shake hands and grew shy over their congratulations; and Miss Sophy Brill came to call. She had put on her Sunday bonnet and her manner was almost abject.[11] She ventured, very timidly, to ask her young friend how she wrote, whether it "just came to her," and if she had found that the kind of pen she used made any difference; and wound up by begging Theodora to write a sentiment in her album.

Even Uncle James came down from Boston to talk the wonder over. He called Theodora a "sly baggage," and proposed that she should give him her earnings to invest in a new patent greasetrap company. From what Kathleen Kyd had told him, he thought Theodora would probably get a thousand dollars for her story. He concluded by

---

10. A *crepe bow* is a piece of black fabric displayed as a sign of mourning.

Reading Strategy   Making and Verifying Predictions
What news do you think the envelope will contain?

Vocabulary

calamity (kə lam′ ə tē) *n.* an unfortunate event or disaster

---

11. *Abject* means "miserable."

Big Idea   Realism *What do these descriptions of people's reactions to Theodora's success suggest about human behavior?*

Trains at Paddington Station, London. 1910 .

suggesting that she should base her next romance on the subject of sanitation, making the heroine nearly die of sewer gas poisoning because her parents won't listen to the handsome young doctor next door, when he warns them that their plumbing is out of order. That was a subject that would interest everybody, and do a lot more good than the sentimental trash most women wrote.

At last the great day came. Theodora had left an order with the bookseller for the midsummer number of the *Home Circle* and before the shop was open she was waiting on the sidewalk. She clutched her precious paper and ran home without opening it. Her excitement was almost more than she could bear. Not heeding her father's call to breakfast, she rushed upstairs and locked herself in her room. Her hands trembled so that she could hardly turn the pages. At last—yes, there it was: "April Showers."

The paper dropped from her hands. What name had she read beneath the title? Had her emotion blinded her?

"April Showers, by *Kathleen Kyd*."

Kathleen Kyd! Oh, cruel misprint! Oh, dastardly typographer! Through tears of rage and disappointment Theodora looked again; yes, there was no mistaking the hateful name. Her glance ran on. She found herself reading a first paragraph that she had never seen before. She read farther. All was strange. The horrible truth burst upon her: *It was not her story!*

She never knew how she got back to the station. She struggled through the crowd on the platform, and a gold-banded arm pushed her into the train just starting for Norton. It would be dark

when she reached home; but that didn't matter—nothing mattered now. She sank into her seat, closing her eyes in the vain attempt to shut out the vision of the last few hours; but minute by minute memory forced her to relive it; she felt like a rebellious schoolchild dragged forth to repeat the same detested "piece."

Although she did not know Boston well, she had made her way easily enough to the *Home Circle* building; at least, she supposed she had, since she remembered nothing till she found herself ascending the editorial stairs as easily as one does incredible things in dreams. She must have walked very fast, for her heart was beating furiously, and she had barely breath to whisper the editor's name to a young man who looked out at her from a glass case, like a zoological specimen. The young man led her past other glass cases containing similar specimens to an inner enclosure which seemed filled by an enormous presence. Theodora felt herself enveloped in the presence, submerged by it, gasping for air as she sank under its rising surges.

Gradually fragments of speech floated to the surface. "'April Showers?' Mrs. Kyd's new serial? *Your* manuscript, you say? You have a letter from me? The name, please? Evidently some unfortunate misunderstanding. One moment." And then a bell ringing, a zoological specimen ordered to unlock a safe, her name asked for again, the manuscript, her own precious manuscript, tied with Aunt Julia's ribbon, laid on the table before her, and her outcries, her protests, her interrogations, drowned in a flood of bland apology: "An unfortunate accident—Mrs. Kyd's manuscript received the same day—extraordinary coincidence in the choice of a title—duplicate answers sent by mistake—Miss Dace's novel hardly suited to their purpose—should of course have been

Reading Strategy Making and Verifying Predictions
How does this turn of events compare with your predictions about Theodora's success?

returned—regrettable oversight—accidents would happen—sure she understood."

The voice went on, like the steady pressure of a surgeon's hand on a shrieking nerve. When it stopped she was in the street. A cab nearly ran her down, and a car bell jangled furiously in her ears. She clutched her manuscript, carrying it tenderly through the crowd, like a live thing that had been hurt. She could not bear to look at its soiled edges and the ink stain on Aunt Julia's ribbon.

The train stopped with a jerk and she opened her eyes. It was dark, and by the windy flare of gas on the platform she saw the Norton passengers getting out. She stood up stiffly and followed them. A warm wind blew into her face the fragrance of the summer woods, and she remembered how, two months earlier, she had knelt among the dead leaves, pressing her lips to the first shoots of green. Then for the first time she thought of home. She had fled away in the morning without a word, and her heart sank at the thought of her mother's fears. And her father—how angry he would be! She bent her head under the coming storm of his derision.

The night was cloudy, and as she stepped into the darkness beyond the station a hand was slipped in hers. She stood still, too weary to feel frightened, and a voice said, quietly:

"Don't walk so fast, child. You look tired."

"Father!" Her hand dropped from his, but he recaptured it, and drew it through his arm. When she found voice, it was to whisper, "You were at the station?"

"It's such a good night I thought I'd stroll down and meet you."

Her arm trembled against his. She could not see his face in the dimness, but the light of his cigar looked down on her like a friendly eye, and she took courage to falter out: "Then you knew—"

"That you'd gone to Boston? Well, I rather thought you had."

> "The voice went on, like the steady pressure of a surgeon's hand on a shrieking nerve."

They walked on slowly, and presently he added, "You see, you left the *Home Circle* lying in your room."

How she blessed the darkness and the muffled sky! She could not have borne the scrutiny of the tiniest star.

"Then mother wasn't very much frightened?"

"Why, no, she didn't appear to be. She's been busy all day over some toggery[12] of Bertha's."

Theodora choked. "Father, I'll—" She groped for words, but they eluded her. "I'll do things—differently; I haven't meant—" Suddenly she heard herself bursting out: "It was all a mistake, you know—about my story. They didn't want it; they won't have it!" and she shrank back involuntarily from his impending mirth.

She felt the pressure of his arm, but he didn't speak, and she figured his mute hilarity. They moved on in silence. Presently he said:

"It hurts a bit just at first, doesn't it?"

"O Father!"

He stood still, and the gleam of his cigar showed a face of unexpected participation.

"You see I've been through it myself."

"You, Father? You?"

"Why, yes. Didn't I ever tell you? I wrote a novel once. I was just out of college, and didn't want to be a doctor. No; I wanted to be a genius, so I wrote a novel."

The doctor paused, and Theodora clung to him in a mute passion of commiseration.[13] It was as if a drowning creature caught a live hand through the murderous fury of the waves.

"Father—O Father!"

"It took me a year—a whole year's hard work; and when I'd finished it the public wouldn't have it, either; not at any price and that's why I came down to meet you, because I remembered my walk home." ∾

---

12. *Toggery* means "clothes."
13. *Commiseration* means "sympathy."

Literary Element Flashback *What clues does this give you about the chronology of the story?*

Reading Strategy Making and Verifying Predictions *Is this a comment you would have expected from Doctor Dace? Why or why not?*

RESPONDING AND THINKING CRITICALLY

Respond

1. (a)How do you feel about Theodora? (b)Do you think she is a sympathetic character? Explain.

Recall and Interpret

2. (a)At the start of "April Showers," how does Theodora feel about her novel? (b)How do you think the narrator feels about it? Explain.

3. (a)Describe Theodora's reaction to both the letter she receives from *Home Circle* and to the midsummer issue of the magazine. (b)In what ways are these reactions similar? What does this tell you about Theodora's character?

4. (a)When Theodora goes to Boston, what explanation does the editor at *Home Circle* give her for the confusion over the novel? (b)What does this suggest to you about the quality of Theodora's novel?

Analyze and Evaluate

5. (a)What tone does the narrator take toward Theodora, her novel, and her goals? (b)Do you think the tone is appropriate? Why or why not?

6. (a)How does Theodora feel about neglecting her responsibilities at home? (b)Is she right to feel this way? Explain.

7. (a)**Irony** occurs when what happens is the opposite of what is expected. What is ironic about the fact that Theodora's father meets her at the train station? (b)How does your perception of his character change at the end of the story?

Connect

8. Would you advise Theodora to continue writing? Why or why not?

9. **Big Idea** Realism In what ways does this story demonstrate the techniques of Realism?

LITERARY ANALYSIS

Literary Element Flashback

In narrative writing, the author usually relates events in chronological order, or the order in which they occur. Sometimes, however, a writer disrupts a story's time sequence with a **flashback** to a scene that occurred before the narrative's plot began. The writer may prepare you for the flashback with a phrase such as *earlier that day* or *the previous week,* but many writers prefer to let readers figure it out themselves.

1. What clues in "April Showers" signal the two flashbacks?

2. What purpose do these flashbacks serve in the story?

3. Is Wharton's use of flashback effective in the story? Why or why not?

Review: Theme

The **theme** of a piece of literature is a dominant idea, often a universal message about life, that the writer communicates to the reader. Most short stories have one main, or central, theme. They may also have secondary themes.

Partner Activity Meet with a classmate to identify the central theme of "April Showers." Working with your partner, create a web diagram like the one below. First, write the theme in the center oval. Then fill in the outer ovals with evidence that supports the theme.

Reading Strategy Making and Verifying Predictions

Predictions About Plot Predictions can be made about various aspects of a text. For example, as you read, you might make predictions about a character's motives, the theme, or the outcome of a specific conflict. Inevitably, the predictions you make will sometimes be wrong. In "April Showers," Wharton intentionally withholds information in order to increase the dramatic tension. However, Wharton does provide clues throughout the text that make it possible to predict the plot's outcome.

1. What images, details, or descriptions did you notice that seemed to hint at the story's conclusion?

2. List any details you did not notice while reading that may seem relevant now.

Vocabulary Practice

Practice with Synonyms Find the synonym for each vocabulary word listed in the first column. Use a dictionary or a thesaurus if you need help.

1. prosperous   **a.** affluent   **b.** wild

2. obscure   **a.** unknown   **b.** furious

3. stupor   **a.** muddle   **b.** noise

4. calamity   **a.** hero   **b.** catastrophe

Academic Vocabulary

Here are two words from the vocabulary list on page R86. These words will help you think, write, and talk about the selection.

notion (nō´shən) *n.* a person's ideas or impression about something

controversy (kon´trə ver´sē) *n.* a disagreement or dispute

Practice and Apply

1. How does Theodora's **notion** of her father change at the end of "April Showers"?

2. Why does Theodora's writing cause **controversy** within her family?

Writing About Literature

Respond to Theme Theodora says that it is better to be an "obscure failure than a vulgar triumph" (page 537). Write a brief response explaining why you agree or disagree with this statement. Use evidence from the story and examples from your own experience to defend your position.

As you draft your essay, remember that in most paragraphs, the main idea is stated in a topic sentence, and all the details in the paragraph develop that idea.

The topic sentence is often at the beginning of each paragraph, but it can also be at the end or in the middle. Regardless of its location, the topic sentence should convey two things: what your topic is and what your paragraph will say about it. As you write your essay, check to make sure that each paragraph includes a topic sentence and adequate support.

After completing your draft, meet with a peer reviewer to evaluate each other's work and to suggest revisions. Then proofread and edit your draft for errors in spelling, grammar, and punctuation.

Literary Criticism

Group Activity In her discussion of Edith Wharton, Claire Preston states that her "novels remain a rich source of period understanding of manners, dress, cultural and social mores, architecture and interiors." As a group, discuss what you learned about these aspects of Wharton's era from reading "April Showers."

Time of Roses, ca. 1900. George Dunlop Leslie. Oil on canvas, 24 x 18¼ in. Hamburger Kunsthalle, Hamburg, Germany.

Literature Online Web Activities For eFlashcards, Selection Quick Checks, and other Web activities, go to www.glencoe.com.

Vocabulary Workshop

Language Resources

► **Technology Tip**

Many Internet and CD-ROM thesauruses have extra features such as audio pronunciation and the ability to define a word within an entry.

► **Test-Taking Tip**

To decide whether two words are synonyms, first determine what part of speech each word is. Synonyms must always be the same part of speech.

► **Reading Handbook**

For more about using a thesaurus, see Reading Handbook, p. R20.

Literature Online

eFlashcards For eFlashcards and other vocabulary activities, go to www.glencoe.com.

ACADEMIC STANDARDS (page 544)

11.4.7 [Use] creative and critical research strategies, such as... using Internet sources.

Using a Thesaurus

Connecting to Literature In "April Showers," one character describes the author Kathleen Kyd as a "pleasant, sociable kind of woman." *Pleasant* and *sociable* are **synonyms,** or words with similar meanings. Although some synonyms are practically interchangeable, many have subtle differences in meaning or connotation. For example, *pleasant* is a general word that means agreeable or enjoyable, whereas *sociable* suggests agreeable or pleasing as a social companion. Recognizing such differences in synonyms can improve your abilities in reading, writing, listening, and speaking.

Most dictionaries list and explain the differences between synonyms, but for many words you will need to search in a thesaurus. A **thesaurus** is a specialized dictionary of synonyms and **antonyms,** words with opposite meanings. There are a variety of formats for a thesaurus: CD-ROMs, word-processing software, the Internet, and print. Thesauruses (or thesauri) are organized in two different ways—the traditional-style thesaurus and the dictionary-style thesaurus.

Traditional Style Probably the best-known thesaurus is the traditional *Roget's Thesaurus*, which organizes large categories of words related to a basic concept. To find a synonym for the verb *taste*, for example, browse through the index of categories until you find the category *senses*, which includes the subentry *taste*. The index will refer you to the page for the subentry, where you will find a list of synonyms for *taste*.

Dictionary Style This type of thesaurus presents words in alphabetical order, exactly as a dictionary does. Each word is followed by several synonyms, which are grouped by part of speech. The entry also directs the reader to cross-referenced entries. In this type of thesaurus, you must look up a specific word, such as *taste* or *sweet*, to find its synonyms. When you find a synonym, look for it in the alphabetical listing to find additional synonyms. J. I. Rodale's *The Synonym Finder* is an example of a dictionary-style thesaurus.

Exercise

1. Using a thesaurus, find two synonyms for each word below. Then look up the definitions of those synonyms in a dictionary to identify the precise meaning for each one.

   a. pathetic **c.** muffled **e.** prosperous

   b. linger **d.** precious

2. Using the above list of words and the synonyms you have found, use each word in a sentence. Be sure that your sentences reflect the slight differences in meaning between each group of synonyms.

Comparing Literature *Across Time and Place*

Connecting to the Reading Selections

Have you ever had a relationship too complex to describe? Perhaps you have had a friendship that ended in a way you did not expect. The three works compared here—by Kate Chopin, Anton Chekhov, and Gabriela Mistral—attempt to re-create the eccentric behaviors and passionate reactions of people in pivotal moments of a relationship. The fictional worlds in these selections analyze how human interactions continue to surprise us.

COMPARING THE [Big Idea] Realism

The writers associated with Realism chose to depict life as they saw it rather than in a romanticized or idealized way. The characters in Realistic literature are often ordinary people who encounter struggles that are familiar to many people. Kate Chopin, Anton Chekhov, and Gabriela Mistral portray characters in ways that reveal insights into them that often contrast with their outward appearances.

COMPARING Narratives About Relationships

Relationships are complex; two people can view the same relationship in vastly different ways. These selections explore the interactions between people and the way these interactions connect to larger themes about individuality and society.

COMPARING Social Context

In these selections, the social context—the common values, habits, and beliefs of a certain society—provides a way of understanding characters' actions. In some cases, society creates roles that limit the potential of the individual. At other times, social interaction is the saving grace in a character's existence.

The Story of an Hour

MEET KATE CHOPIN

Kate Chopin (shō′ pan) was the first female writer in the United States to portray frankly the passions and discontents of women confined to traditional roles as wives and mothers. For this she was roundly condemned in her time. Critics focused their wrath on the publication of her novel *The Awakening*, the story of a woman who abandons her husband and children to search for her true identity. Reviewers characterized the novel as shocking, morbid, coarse, and vulgar.

Strong, Independent Women Chopin was born Katherine O'Flaherty in St. Louis, Missouri. She grew up in the late Victorian period, a time when the ideal woman gave up her independence and devoted herself to the will of her husband and to the welfare of her children. When Chopin was five, her father died in a railroad accident—an event that is echoed in "The Story of an Hour." She left school, and for the next two years she studied at home with her mother, grandmother, and great-grandmother. Growing up in a household of strong, independent women did much to shape Chopin as a person and a writer.

> *"The artist must possess the courageous soul that dares and defies."*
>
> —Kate Chopin, *The Awakening*

At age twenty, Kate married Oscar Chopin and moved with him to New Orleans. Business problems, however, soon forced them to move to Oscar's rural hometown of Cloutierville, Louisiana, an area that would later inspire many of Chopin's stories. When her husband died in 1882, Chopin was left with children to raise and support. She soon moved back to St. Louis to be near her family. When her mother died a year later, Chopin was overwhelmed with grief. At her doctor's advice, she turned to writing and published her first work in 1889.

Daring Pieces
During the next ten years, Chopin published more than 100 short stories, two story collections, and two novels. She earned praise for early stories that captured the local color of Louisiana. In later stories, Chopin explored women's issues considered controversial in her time. She modeled these stories on the work of Guy de Maupassant, the French master of the Realist short story. Not surprisingly, she had difficulty finding magazines willing to publish her most daring pieces, including "The Story of an Hour."

Though acutely aware of the criticisms many of her stories received, Chopin was not prepared for the reaction to *The Awakening* in 1899. The deluge of negative reviews destroyed her spirit. Chopin continued to write, but by 1903 her health was failing. After spending an entire day at the 1904 St. Louis World's Fair, Chopin came home complaining of a severe pain in her head. Two days later she died of a cerebral hemorrhage.

Lonely Pioneer For more than fifty years after her death, Chopin's works were ignored. Then, in 1969, at a time when the women's movement in the United States was gaining momentum, Per Seyersted published a biography of Chopin and her complete works. His efforts galvanized modern readers hungry to learn more about the woman who, according to Chopin scholar Emily Toth, had written "the most radical novel of the 1890s." Today *The Awakening* is one of the most read novels in colleges and universities across the United States. Kate Chopin is celebrated as the lonely pioneer who dared to write realistic portraits of women trapped and stifled by the social conventions of their time.

Kate Chopin was born in 1850 and died in 1904.

Literature Online **Author Search** For more about Kate Chopin, go to www.glencoe.com.

Connecting to the Story

In Kate Chopin's story, a woman learns that her husband has died. Think about the following questions:

- How would you feel if you learned that something you valued in life was taken from you?
- Under what circumstances might you sacrifice your own happiness for that of another person?

Building Background

Social tension marked the 1890s. While some women attended college and entered professions previously open only to men, many others were told that "the woman's place" was in the home. Although society glorified the roles of wives and mothers, women had few legal rights. For example, when Chopin's husband died, she had to petition the court to be appointed the legal guardian of her own children. This male-dominated society was the world that Chopin knew and wrote about. In much of her fiction, she criticized the institution of marriage and wrote about women who struggled against social convention in expressing their individuality.

Setting Purposes for Reading

Big Idea Realism

As you read, look for details that reveal Chopin's realistic description of Mrs. Mallard's thoughts and emotions when she learns of her husband's death.

Literary Element Conflict

Conflict is the central struggle between two opposing forces in a story or a drama. An **external conflict** exists when a character struggles against some outside force, such as another person, nature, society, or fate. An **internal conflict** is a struggle that takes place within the mind of a character who is torn between opposing feelings, desires, or goals. As you read this story, determine the types of conflict that are presented.

- See Literary Terms Handbook, p. R4.

Literature Online **Interactive Literary Elements Handbook** To review or learn more about the literary elements, go to www.glencoe.com.

Reading Strategy Applying Background Knowledge

Knowing the historical, social, and cultural forces that influenced an author can help you understand his or her writing. As you read "The Story of an Hour," ask yourself these questions:

- How does the information you have read about Kate Chopin affect your understanding of the story?
- If you knew nothing about when or by whom the story was written, how might your opinion of the characters be different?

Vocabulary

elusive (i $\text{l}\overline{\text{oo}}'$ siv) *adj.* difficult to explain or grasp; p. 549 *The speaker's elusive argument left the audience scratching their heads.*

tumultuously ($\text{t}\overline{\text{oo}}$ mul' $\text{ch}\overline{\text{oo}}$ əs lē) *adv.* in an agitated manner; violently; p. 549 *The wind blew across the plains, swirling tumultuously in every direction.*

exalted (ig zôl' təd) *adj.* elevated; p. 549 *The film star enjoyed the exalted status that fame afforded him.*

perception (pər sep' shən) *n.* an awareness; an insight; p. 549 *The music student acted modestly when she accepted the award in order to avoid the perception that she had worked hard for it.*

persistence (pər sis' təns) *n.* stubborn or determined continuance; p. 550 *The reporter pursued the politician with a persistence that frustrated the campaign workers who tried to block his way.*

Vocabulary Tip: Antonyms Words that have opposite or nearly opposite meanings are called **antonyms.** The words *uplifting* and *degrading,* for example, are antonyms. Note that antonyms are always the same part of speech.

▌**INDIANA ACADEMIC STANDARDS (pages 547–551)**
▌11.3 [Identify] story elements…
11.2 Develop [reading] strategies…

11.5.9 Write…an analytical essay…that…makes valid inferences…

The Story of an Hour

Kate Chopin

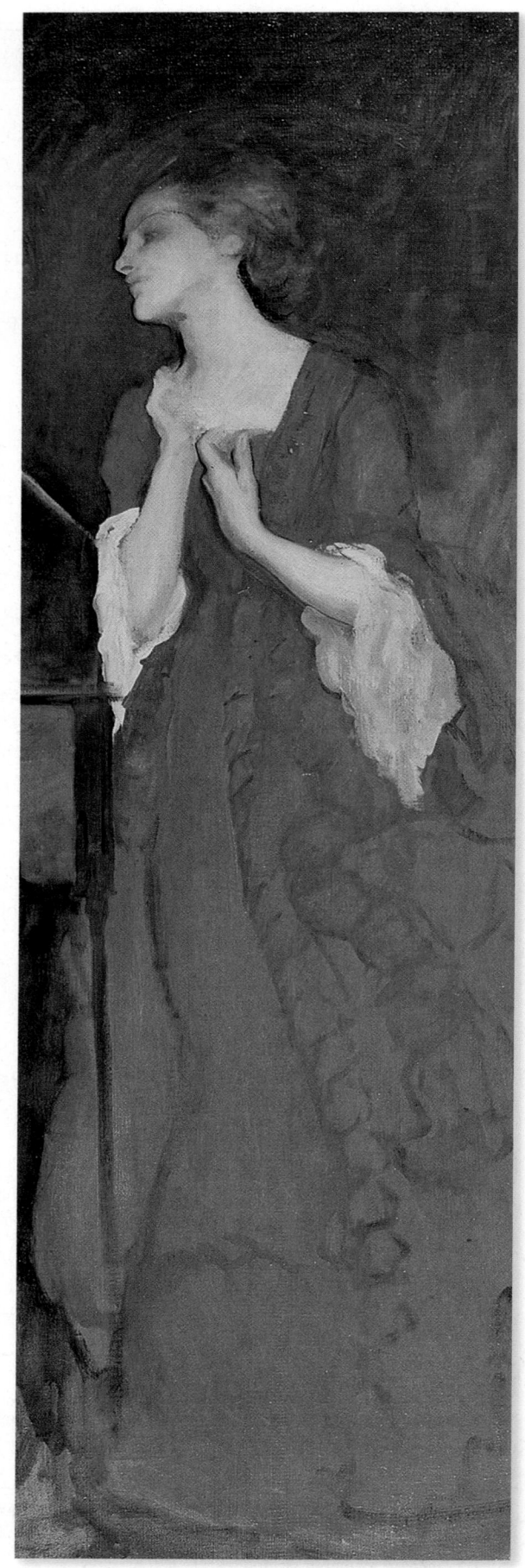

The Lady Anne, 1899. Edwin Austin Abbey.
Oil on canvas, 48 x 24 in. The Butler Institute
of American Art, Youngstown, OH.

Knowing that Mrs. Mallard was afflicted with a heart trouble, great care was taken to break to her as gently as possible the news of her husband's death. It was her sister Josephine who told her, in broken sentences; veiled[1] hints that revealed in half concealing. Her husband's friend Richards was there, too, near her. It was he who had been in the newspaper office when intelligence of the railroad disaster was received, with Brently Mallard's name leading the list of "killed." He had only taken the time to assure himself of its truth by a second telegram, and had hastened to forestall[2] any less careful, less tender friend in bearing the sad message.

She did not hear the story as many women have heard the same, with a paralyzed inability to accept its significance. She wept at once, with sudden, wild abandonment, in her sister's arms. When the storm of grief had spent[3] itself she went to her room alone. She would have no one follow her.

There stood, facing the open window, a comfortable, roomy armchair. Into this she sank, pressed down by a physical exhaustion that haunted her body and seemed to reach into her soul.

She could see in the open square before her house the tops of trees that were all aquiver with the new spring life. The delicious breath of rain was in the air. In the street below a peddler was crying his wares. The notes of a distant song which some one was singing reached her faintly, and countless sparrows were twittering in the eaves.

There were patches of blue sky showing here and there through the clouds that had met and piled one above the other in the west facing her window.

She sat with her head thrown back upon the cushion of the chair, quite motionless, except when a sob came up into her throat and shook her, as a child who has cried itself to sleep continues to sob in its dreams.

She was young, with a fair, calm face, whose lines bespoke repression and even a certain strength. But now there was a dull stare in her eyes, whose gaze was fixed away off yonder on one of those patches of blue sky. It was not a glance of reflection, but rather indicated a suspension of intelligent thought.

There was something coming to her and she was waiting for it, fearfully. What was it? She did not know; it was too subtle and **elusive** to name. But she felt it, creeping out of the sky, reaching toward her through the sounds, the scents, the color that filled the air.

Now her bosom rose and fell **tumultuously.** She was beginning to recognize this thing that was approaching to possess her, and she was striving to beat it back with her will—as powerless as her two white slender hands would have been.

When she abandoned herself a little whispered word escaped her slightly parted lips. She said it over and over under her breath: "free, free, free!" The vacant stare and the look of terror that had followed it went from her eyes. They stayed keen and bright. Her pulses beat fast, and the coursing[4] blood warmed and relaxed every inch of her body.

She did not stop to ask if it were or were not a monstrous joy that held her. A clear and **exalted perception** enabled her to dismiss the suggestion as trivial.

---

4. *Coursing* means "swiftly moving."

Literary Element Conflict *How does this passage complicate the conflict?*

Reading Strategy Applying Background Knowledge *How does your knowledge of the Victorian era affect your understanding of this passage?*

---

1. *Veiled* means "disguised" or "obscure."
2. *Forestall* means "to hinder or prevent by action taken in advance."
3. Here, *spent* means "exhausted."

Literary Element Conflict *Based on this passage, what do you think the main conflict will be?*

Vocabulary

elusive (i lōō′ siv) *adj.* difficult to explain or grasp
tumultuously (tōō mul′ chōō əs lē) *adv.* in an agitated manner; violently
exalted (ig zôl′ təd) *adj.* elevated
perception (pər sep′ shən) *n.* an awareness; an insight

She knew that she would weep again when she saw the kind, tender hands folded in death; the face that had never looked save[5] with love upon her, fixed and gray and dead. But she saw beyond that bitter moment a long procession of years to come that would belong to her absolutely. And she opened and spread her arms out to them in welcome.

There would be no one to live for her during those coming years; she would live for herself. There would be no powerful will bending hers in that blind **persistence** with which men and women believe they have a right to impose a private will upon a fellow-creature. A kind intention or a cruel intention made the act seem no less a crime as she looked upon it in that brief moment of illumination.

And yet she had loved him—sometimes. Often she had not. What did it matter! What could love, the unsolved mystery, count for in face of this possession of self-assertion which she suddenly recognized as the strongest impulse of her being!

"Free! Body and soul free!" she kept whispering.

Josephine was kneeling before the closed door with her lips to the keyhole, imploring for admission. "Louise, open the door! I beg; open the door—you will make yourself ill. What are you doing, Louise? For heaven's sake open the door."

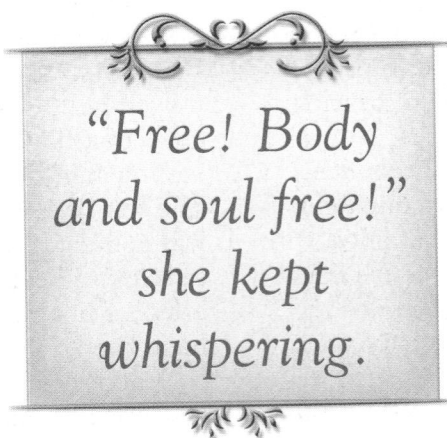

"Free! Body and soul free!" she kept whispering.

"Go away. I am not making myself ill." No; she was drinking in a very elixir of life[6] through that open window.

Her fancy was running riot along those days ahead of her. Spring days, and summer days, and all sorts of days that would be her own. She breathed a quick prayer that life might be long. It was only yesterday she had thought with a shudder that life might be long.

She arose at length and opened the door to her sister's importunities.[7] There was a feverish triumph in her eyes, and she carried herself unwittingly like a goddess of Victory. She clasped her sister's waist, and together they descended the stairs. Richards stood waiting for them at the bottom.

Some one was opening the front door with a latch-key. It was Brently Mallard who entered, a little travel-stained, composedly carrying his grip-sack[8] and umbrella. He had been far from the scene of accident, and did not even know there had been one. He stood amazed at Josephine's piercing cry; at Richards' quick motion to screen him from the view of his wife.

But Richards was too late.

When the doctors came they said she had died of heart disease—of joy that kills. ∾

---

5. Here, *save* means "except."

Big Idea Realism *Why does Chopin include this information about Mrs. Mallard's relationship with her husband?*

Vocabulary

persistence (pər sis′ təns) *n.* stubborn or determined continuance

---

6. An *elixir* (i lik′ sər) *of life* is a substance thought to prolong life indefinitely.
7. *Importunities* are persistent requests or demands.
8. A *grip-sack* is a small traveling bag.

Reading Strategy Applying Background Knowledge *How does this passage reflect what you know about Chopin's writing?*

RESPONDING AND THINKING CRITICALLY

Respond

1. At what points in the story did you feel sorry for Mrs. Mallard? Explain. How did the end of the story affect you?

Recall and Interpret

2. (a)How does Mrs. Mallard first react to the news about her husband? (b)What does her reaction indicate about her feelings toward him?

3. (a)How do Mrs. Mallard's feelings change while she is in her room? (b)Why might she fear this change at first but later welcome it?

4. (a)What words does the narrator use to describe Mrs. Mallard as she leaves her room? (b)How might the others interpret her appearance?

Analyze and Evaluate

5. What is your opinion of Mrs. Mallard? Support your evaluation with details from the story.

6. How does Mrs. Mallard's admission that often she had not loved her husband affect your evaluation of her character?

7. How would this story be different if it were set in the present rather than at the end of the nineteenth century? Explain.

Connect

8. **Big Idea** **Realism** How does the central conflict of this story illustrate the idea that Chopin wrote realistic portraits of women's lives? Support your answer with details from the story.

LITERARY ANALYSIS

Literary Element Conflict

The events of a story develop its **conflict**. The conflict builds until the story reaches a **climax**, which is the point of greatest emotional intensity. The story then concludes with the **resolution**, or the final outcome of the conflict.

1. Identify the conflict in Chopin's story. Is this conflict external or internal? Explain why.

2. How does Chopin develop this conflict? At what point does the conflict reach its climax?

3. What is the resolution of the conflict?

Writing About Literature

Evaluate Author's Craft The original title of "The Story of an Hour" was "The Dream of an Hour." How are the titles similar? Different? Why might Chopin have chosen to change the title? Which title do you think is more appropriate? Why? Write a paragraph or two in which you answer these questions.

Literature Online **Web Activities** For eFlashcards, Selection Quick Checks, and other Web activities, go to www.glencoe.com.

READING AND VOCABULARY

Reading Strategy Applying Background Knowledge

An author's message becomes more apparent when you apply background knowledge to your reading. This reading strategy can help you infer the commentary that Chopin's story makes about the institution of marriage in Victorian America.

Partner Activity Review your answers to the Reading Strategy questions on page 547. Meet with another classmate to compare how you each applied background information to the selection.

Vocabulary Practice

Practice with Antonyms Find the antonym for each boldfaced word.

1. elusive
 a. knowable **b.** vague
2. tumultuously
 a. simply **b.** peacefully
3. exalted
 a. lowered **b.** enchanted
4. perception
 a. incomprehension **b.** awareness
5. persistence
 a. insistence **b.** reluctance

The Darling

Anton Chekhov

BEFORE YOU READ

Building Background

Anton Chekhov studied both medicine and literature. He eventually focused on his literary pursuits, becoming a master of the short story as well as Russia's most revered playwright. His realistic stories, which focus on atmosphere and character rather than plot and action, became an essential influence on modern literature. Chekhov's substantial place in literature comes in part from his ability to reveal how ordinary events can have a huge impact on people's lives.

Born in southern Russia, Chekhov grew up apart from his parents. He rejoined them in Moscow after receiving a medical scholarship and supported his family by writing comic articles for newspapers and magazines. In medicine, his role models were doctors who worked for rural governments. He saw their work as altruistic. Later, Chekhov served as a doctor himself, providing medical support during a cholera epidemic in 1892. He died of tuberculosis.

Anton Chekhov was born in 1860 and died in 1904.

Literature Online **Author Search** For more about Anton Chekhov, go to www.glencoe.com.

Olenka,[1] the daughter of retired collegiate assessor Plemyannikov, sat on the porch in her yard, lost in thought. It was hot, the flies wouldn't leave her alone, and it was bliss to think it would soon be evening. Dark rain-clouds were moving up from the east, preceded by occasional wafts of humid air.

In the middle of the yard Snookin, manager-proprietor of the Tivoli Pleasure Gardens, who lodged across the yard in Olenka's fliegel,[2] stood gazing at the sky.

---

1. *Olenka* is a nickname for *Olga.* In Russia, people are often informally referred to by their given name and then a patronymic, which is a variation of their father's given name. If the father's name were Ivan, the son's patronymic name would be Ivanovich, and the daughter's would be Ivanovna. *Semyonovna* is Olga's patronymic.

2. A *fliegel* is a small house on the property of a larger house that might be rented out.

"Not again!" he was saying in despair. "Not rain again! Day after day, day after day, rain, rain, rain! Just my luck! What I have to put up with! I'm ruined! I'm losing huge sums every day!"

Throwing up his hands, he turned to Olenka and said:

"You see what our life's like, Olga Semyonovna. Enough to make you weep! You work hard and do your best, you worry and have sleepless nights, you're always thinking of improvements—and what's the result? Take audiences for a start. They're nothing but ignorant savages. I give them the best operetta and pantomime, top-quality burlesque,[3] but is that what they want? Do they appreciate it? No, they want some vulgar little peepshow. Then take the weather. Rain almost every evening. May 10th it started, and it's been at it right through May and June. Appalling! The public stays away, but who has to pay the rent, I ask you? Who has to pay the performers?"

Clouds began gathering at the same time next day.

"Oh yes, let it all come!" Snookin said, laughing hysterically. "Let it flood the whole Gardens and take me with it! I don't deserve any happiness in this world or the next! Let the performers take me to court! Why stop at that? Make it penal servitude in Siberia! The scaffold![4] Ha-ha-ha!"

It was the same next day. . . .

Olenka said nothing but listened to Snookin gravely, and sometimes tears came to her eyes. In the end his misfortunes moved her and she fell in love with him. He was short and skinny, with a sallow complexion and hair combed back off the temples, he spoke in a high-pitched tenor, twisting his mouth as he did so, and his face wore an expression of permanent despair—yet he aroused in her deep and genuine emotion. She was constantly in love with someone and could not live otherwise. Previously she had loved her Papa, now an invalid sitting in his armchair in a darkened room and breathing with difficulty; then she had loved her aunt, who came to visit them every other year from Bryansk;[5] and earlier still she had loved the French master at her school. She was a quiet, good-natured, tender-hearted girl, with soft gentle eyes, and in the best of health. Looking at her plump rosy cheeks and soft white neck with its dark birthmark, at the innocent, kindly smile on her face whenever she was listening to something pleasant, men said to themselves, "yes, not a bad one, that," and smiled, too, while her female visitors could not refrain from seizing her by the hand in the middle of a conversation and exclaiming with delight:

"You're such a darling!"

The house she had lived in all her life and was due to inherit stood on the edge of town in Gypsy Lane, not far from the Tivoli, so that in the evenings and at night, hearing the band playing and the rockets going off with a bang, she imagined this was Snookin challenging his fate and taking his chief enemy, the indifferent public, by storm; her heart would melt, she didn't feel a bit sleepy, and when he returned home in the early hours, she would knock softly on her bedroom window and, letting him see through the curtains only her face and one shoulder, smile affectionately. . . .

He proposed and they were married. Now that he could see her neck and both her plump healthy shoulders properly, he threw up his hands and said:

"You darling, you!"

He was happy, but since it rained on the wedding day *and* on the wedding night, the look of despair never left his face.

Life went well after the marriage. She sat in his box office, supervised the Gardens, wrote down expenses and paid out salaries, and you'd catch a glimpse of her rosy cheeks and sweetly innocent, radiant smile at the box office window one moment, behind stage the next, and now in the refreshment bar. Already she was telling her friends that nothing in the world was so remarkable, so important and necessary as the theatre, and only in the theatre could you experience real enjoyment and become an educated, civilized human being.

"But does the public appreciate that?" she would say. "What they want is a peepshow. Yesterday we did *Faust Inside Out* and almost all

---

3. An *operetta* is a form of opera that includes elaborate dancing and music, as well as a romantic, usually comic plot. A *pantomime* relies on body movement to tell a story. A *burlesque,* usually a series of comic short skits, uses exaggeration to ridicule.

4. The governments of Imperial Russia and the Soviet Union sent criminals to *Siberia,* an area known for being remote and having a harsh climate. Here, *scaffold* refers to the platform on which a criminal is executed.

5. *Bryansk* is a Russian city southwest of Moscow.

the boxes were empty, but if we'd put on something vulgar, me and Vanya,[6] we'd have been packed out, I can tell you. Tomorrow we're doing *Orpheus in the Underworld*, me and Vanya, why don't you come?"

Whatever Snookin said about the theatre and the actors, she repeated. Like him, she despised the public for its indifference to art and its ignorance, interfered in rehearsals, corrected the actors and made sure the musicians behaved, and whenever there was a bad notice in the local press, she would cry and then go round to the editorial office to have it out with them.

The actors were fond of her and called her "Me and Vanya" and "The Darling." She felt sorry for them and gave them small loans, and if they let her down, she just had a quiet cry and said nothing to her husband.

Life went well that winter, too. They hired the town theatre for the whole season and rented it out for short periods to a Ukrainian troupe, a conjuror, and the local amateur dramatic company. Olenka put on weight and positively radiated well-being, but Snookin looked thin and sallow, and complained of huge losses, even though business was quite good all winter. At night he coughed and she gave him raspberry or lime-blossom tea to drink, rubbed him with eau-de-Cologne and wrapped him in her soft shawls.

"My wonderful little man!" she would say with complete sincerity, as she stroked his hair. "My handsome little man!"

During Lent[7] he went off to Moscow to engage a new company, and in his absence she couldn't sleep, but sat by the window looking at the stars. She was like the hens, she thought, which stay awake all night and are restive when the cock isn't in the henhouse. Snookin was

Russian Woman at the Window, 1923. Boris Kustodiev. Watercolor over pencil on paper, 24.3 x 21.5 cm. Museum of Fine Arts, Kostroma, Russia.

delayed in Moscow but said he'd be back by Easter, and his letters were already giving her instructions about the Tivoli. But on the Sunday before Easter, late at night, there was a sudden ominous knocking outside. Someone was banging on the gate until it started booming like a barrel. The sleepy cook ran to answer, her bare feet splashing in the puddles.

"Open up, please!" someone outside was saying in a deep bass. "Telegram for you!"

Olenka had received telegrams from her husband before, but now for some reason she felt petrified. She opened it with trembling hands and read as follows:

"Ivan Petrovich[8] died suddenly today suchly await instructions funreal Tuesday."

That was what the telegram said, "funreal" and the other meaningless word "suchly"; it was signed by the producer of the operetta company.

"My darling!" Olenka sobbed. "My sweet darling little Vanya! Why did I ever meet you? Why did I come to know you and love you? Who's

6. *Vanya* is a nickname for Ivan, which is Snookin's given name.
7. *Lent* is a period of fasting and self-denial prior to the celebration of Easter that is observed by some Christian denominations.
8. *Ivan Petrovich* is Snookin's name.

going to look after your poor wretched Olenka now you've abandoned her?"

Snookin was buried on the Tuesday at the Vagankovo Cemetery in Moscow. Olenka returned home on Wednesday and as soon as she entered her room, flung herself down on the bed and sobbed so loudly she could be heard in the street and the neighboring yards.

"Poor darling!" the women neighbors said, crossing themselves. "She *is* taking it badly, poor darling Olga Semyonovna!"

Three months later Olenka, in full mourning, was returning home sadly one day from church. It so happened that a neighbor of hers, Vasily Andreich Pustovalov, manager of the merchant Babakayev's timber yard, was also returning from church and walking alongside her. He was wearing a straw hat and a white waistcoat[9] with a gold watch-chain, and looked more like a landowner than a tradesman.

"Everything has to take its proper course, Olga Semyonovna," he was saying soberly, with a sympathetic note in his voice, "and if someone dear to us dies, that means it is God's wish, so we must contain ourselves and bear it with resignation."

After seeing Olenka to her gate, he said goodbye and walked on. For the rest of the day she kept hearing that sober voice, and she had only to close her eyes to picture his dark beard to herself. She liked him very much. Evidently she had made an impression on him, too, for not long afterwards an elderly lady, whom she scarcely knew, came to drink coffee with her, and had no sooner sat down at the table than she started talking about Pustovalov, what a good, reliable man he was and how any young lady would be delighted to have him for a husband. Three days later Pustovalov himself paid her a visit, stayed no more than about ten minutes and said little, but Olenka fell for him so completely that she lay awake all night feeling hot and feverish, and next morning sent for the elderly lady. The match was quickly arranged, then came the wedding.

Life went well for Pustovalov and Olenka after their marriage. He would usually stay at the timber yard until lunch and then go out on business, whereupon Olenka would take his place and stay in the office until evening, doing the accounts and dispatching orders.

"Timber's going up by twenty percent a year now," she would tell customers and friends. "In the past we used to get our timber locally, but now, imagine, my Vasya[10] has to fetch it every year from Mogilyov Province. And the freight charges!" she would say, covering both cheeks with her hands in horror. "The freight charges!"

She felt that she had been dealing in timber for ages and ages, and it was the most vitally important thing in life, and the words joist, batten, offcut, purlin,[11] round beam, short beam, frame and slab, were like dear old friends to her. At night she dreamed of whole mountains of boards and battens, of never-ending convoys of carts carrying timber somewhere far beyond the town; she dreamed of a whole regiment of beams, thirty feet by nine inches, marching upright into battle against the timber yard, and how beams, joists and slabs banged together with the resounding thud of dry wood, falling over and then righting themselves, piling up on top of each other. Olenka would cry out in her sleep and Pustovalov would say to her tenderly:

"What's the matter, Olenka dear? Better cross yourself!"[12]

Whatever thoughts her husband had, she had also. If he thought the room was too hot or business had become quiet, she thought the same. Her husband did not like any entertainments and on holidays stayed at home; so did she.

"You're always at home or in the office," friends said to her. "You should go to the theatre, darling, or the circus."

"Me and Vasya have no time for theatres," she replied soberly. "We're working folk, we can't be bothered with trifles. What do people see in those theatres, anyway?"

On Saturdays she and Pustovalov attended the all-night vigil, and on feast days early-morning service. Afterwards, walking home side by side, they

---

9. A *waistcoat* is an ornamental vest worn under a jacket.

10. *Vasya* is a nickname for Vasily.

11. A *joist* is a type of wood beam; a *batten* is a piece of wood used on a boat or in a floor; an *offcut* is a small piece of wood; a *purlin* is a piece of wood used in a roof.

12. Pustovalov is suggesting that Olenka make the sign of a cross to help keep away her nightmare.

both looked deeply moved, they smelt fragrant, and her silk dress rustled agreeably. At home they drank tea, with rich white bread and various jams, then they had pie. Every day at noon the yard and the street outside the gates were filled with the appetizing smell of borsch[13] and roast lamb or duck, or fish on fast days, and no one could walk past without beginning to feel hungry. In the office the samovar[14] was always on the boil, and customers were treated to tea and buns. Once a week the couple went to the baths and walked home side by side, both red in the face.

"We're not complaining," Olenka told her friends. "Life's going well, praise be to God. May God grant everyone as good a life as me and Vasya."

When Pustovalov went off to Mogilyov Province for timber, she missed him terribly and could not sleep at night for crying. Sometimes she had an evening visit from the young man renting her fliegel, a regimental vet[15] called Smirnin. He would tell her about something or they'd play cards, and this cheered her up. She was particularly interested to hear about his own family life: he was married with a son, but had separated from his wife because she'd been unfaithful, and now he hated her and sent her forty roubles[16] a month for the boy's maintenance. As she listened, Olenka sighed and shook her head, and felt sorry for him.

"The Lord be with you," she would say, bidding him good night and lighting him to the top of the stairs with a candle. "It was kind of you to while away your time with me, may God and the Holy Mother watch over you. . . ."

She always expressed herself in the same sober, judicious tones, imitating her husband. The vet was already disappearing behind the downstairs door when she would call him back and say:

"Vladimir Platonych,[17] don't you think you should make it up with your wife? Forgive her, if only for your son's sake! That little chap knows just what's going on, be sure of that."

When Pustovalov returned, she would tell him in a hushed voice about the vet and his unhappy family situation, and both would sigh, shake their heads and talk of how the boy must be missing his father; then, by some strange association of ideas they would both kneel before the icons,[18] prostrate themselves and pray that God might send them children.

Thus did the Pustovalovs live for six years, quietly and peacefully, in love and complete harmony. But one winter's day at the yard Vasily Andreich went out bare-headed to dispatch some timber after drinking hot tea, caught cold and fell ill. He was treated by the best doctors, but the illness took its course and he died four months later.

Olenka had become a widow again.

"Who will look after me now, my darling?" she sobbed, after burying her husband. "How can I possibly live without you? I'm so wretched and unhappy! Pity me, good people, I'm all alone now. . . ."

She wore a black dress with weepers,[19] having vowed never to wear a hat or gloves again, went out seldom and then only to church or to her husband's grave, and lived at home like a nun. Six months passed before she discarded the weepers and began opening her shutters. Some mornings she was to be seen shopping for food in the market with her cook, but people could only surmise how she was living now and what her domestic arrangements were. They surmised when they saw her, for example, sitting in her little garden drinking tea with the vet while he read the newspaper out to her, and also when she bumped into a female friend at the post office and was heard to say:

"Our town has no proper veterinary inspection and that gives rise to many illnesses. You're always hearing of people being infected by milk or catching diseases from horses and cows. We really ought to treat the health of domestic animals as seriously as we do that of human beings."

She repeated the vet's thoughts and now shared his opinions on everything. It was clear

---

13. *Borsch* is beet soup.
14. A *samovar* is a type of urn used to make tea in Russia.
15. Here, *vet* is short for veterinarian.
16. *Roubles* is an alternate spelling of *rubles*, Russian currency.
17. *Vladimir Platonych* is Smirnin's formal name.
18. Here, *icons* refers to religious images, often painted on wood and used in religious practices.
19. Here, *weepers* means "a veil worn as a symbol of mourning."

Portrait of Vasily Mathé, 1902. Boris Kustodiev. Oil on canvas, 125 x 151 cm. The Russian Museum, St. Petersburg, Russia.

that she could not survive even for a year without an attachment and had found her new happiness in the fliegel next door. Anyone else would have been condemned for this, but no one could think ill of Olenka, her whole life was so transparent. She and the vet did not tell anyone about the change that had taken place in their relationship and tried to conceal it, but without success, because Olenka could not keep a secret. When regimental colleagues came to visit him and she was pouring out their tea or serving supper, she would start talking about cattle plague, pearl disease,[20] and the municipal slaughterhouses. This made him terribly embarrassed, and as they were leaving, he would seize her by the arm and hiss angrily:

"Haven't I told you before not to talk about things you don't understand? When we vets are talking shop, please don't butt in. It's extremely tedious."

She would look at him in alarm and astonishment, and say:

"But Volodya[21] dear, what *am* I to talk about?!"

With tears in her eyes she embraced him and begged him not to be angry, and they were both happy.

But this happiness did not last long. The vet departed with his regiment, and since they had been transferred somewhere very distant, practically to Siberia, his departure was permanent.

Olenka was left on her own.

This time she was completely on her own. Her father had long since died, and his armchair, with one leg missing, was gathering dust in the attic. She became plain and thin, and people meeting her in the street no longer looked at her and smiled as they used to; her best years were evidently gone for good, now a new, unknown life was beginning that did not bear thinking about. In the evenings Olenka sat on her porch and could hear the band playing and the rockets going off at the Tivoli, but this no longer made her think of anything. She gazed apathetically at her empty yard, had no thoughts or desires, and when night fell, went to bed and dreamed of her empty yard. She seemed reluctant even to eat or drink.

But the worst thing of all was no longer having any opinions. She saw objects round her and understood everything that was going on, but she could not form opinions about anything and did not know what to talk about. How awful it is not to have an opinion! You see a bottle, for example, standing there, or the rain falling, or a peasant going along in his cart, but what the bottle or rain or peasant are for, what sense they make, you can't say and couldn't say, even if they offered you a thousand roubles. In Snookin's and Pustovalov's time, and then with the vet, Olenka could explain everything and give her opinion on any subject you liked, whereas now her mind and heart were as empty as the yard outside. It was a horrible, bitter sensation, like a mouthful of wormwood.[22]

20. *Pearl disease* is a blood disease in cattle.
21. *Volodya* is Smirnin's nickname (his first name is Vladimir).
22. *Wormwood* is a plant that produces a bitter oil.

The town has gradually expanded in all directions. Gypsy Lane is now called a street, and where the Tivoli and the timber yards once stood, houses have sprung up and there are a number of side streets. How time flies! Olenka's house looks dingy, the roof has rusted, the shed is leaning to one side, and the yard is completely overgrown with weeds and stinging nettles.[23] Olenka herself has grown older and plainer. In summer she sits on her porch, with the same feeling of emptiness, boredom, and bitterness in her soul as before, in winter she sits by her window gazing at the snow. If she feels the breath of spring, or hears the sound of cathedral bells carried on the wind, memories suddenly flood in, tugging at her heart-strings, and copious tears stream down her face; but this lasts only a minute, then the same emptiness and sense of futility returns. Her black cat Bryska snuggles up to her, purring softly, but Olenka is unmoved by these feline caresses. Is that what she needs? No, she needs the kind of love that will possess her completely, mind and soul, that will provide her with thoughts and a direction in life, and warm her aging blood. She bundles black Bryska off her lap and says irritably:

"Go away . . . I don't want you here!"

It's the same day after day, year after year—she doesn't have a single joy in life or a single opinion. Whatever Mavra the cook says is good enough.

One hot July day, towards evening, when the town cattle were being driven past and clouds of dust had filled the yard, all of a sudden someone knocked at the gate. Olenka went to open it herself, took one look and was completely dumbfounded: Smirnin the vet was standing there, grey-haired and in civilian clothes. Suddenly everything came back to her, she broke down and burst into tears, laid her head on his chest without saying a word, and was so overcome that afterwards she had no recollection of how they went into the house together and sat down to drink tea.

"Vladimir Platonych," she murmured, trembling with joy, "dearest! Whatever brings you here?"

"I'd like to settle down here permanently," he told her. "I've resigned my commission and come to try my luck as a civilian, leading a settled life. Then there's my son, he's growing up and it's

time he went to grammar school. I've made it up with my wife, you know."

"And where is she now?" Olenka asked.

"At the hotel with the boy while I go round looking for lodgings."

"But good heavens, have *my* house, dear! Far better than lodgings. Oh heavens above, I don't want any rent," Olenka went on, becoming agitated and bursting into tears again. "You live here and the fliegel will do for me. Wonderful!"

Next day they were already painting the roof and whitewashing the walls, and Olenka was walking about the yard, arms on hips, giving orders. Her face shone with its old smile, and everything about her was fresh and lively, as if she had just woken from a long sleep. The vet's wife arrived, a thin, unattractive woman with short hair and a peevish expression. With her came the boy, Sasha, who was small for his age (he was over nine) and chubby, with bright blue eyes and dimpled cheeks. He had no sooner set foot in the yard than he began chasing the cat, and his merry, joyful laughter rang out.

"Is that your cat, Auntie?" he asked Olenka. "When it has babies, will you give us one, please? Mamma's scared stiff of mice."

Olenka chatted to him and gave him tea, and suddenly felt a warm glow and pleasurable tightening in her heart, as if this boy were her own son. And when he was sitting in the dining-room repeating his lessons in the evenings, she would look at him with tenderness and pity, and whisper:

"My darling, my pretty little child. . . . You're so clever and your skin is so fair."

"An island," he read out, "is an area of dry land surrounded on all sides by water."

"An island is an area of dry land . . ." she repeated, and this was the first opinion she had expressed with confidence after all those years of silence and emptiness of mind.

Now she had her own opinions and talked to Sasha's parents over supper about how hard children had to work at grammar school these days, but all the same a classical education was better than a modern one, because every career was open to you afterwards—doctor, engineer, whatever you wished.

---

23. *Stinging nettles* are a perennial herb with sharp leaves and white flowers.

Sasha had begun attending the grammar school. His mother went away to her sister's in Kharkov and did not come back, his father went off somewhere every day to inspect herds and might be away for three days at a time, and Olenka felt that Sasha was being completely neglected, his parents didn't want him and he must be starving to death; so she transferred him to her fliegel and fixed him up in a little room there.

Six months have now passed since Sasha began living in her fliegel. Every morning Olenka goes into his room: he is fast asleep with his hand under his cheek, breathing imperceptibly. She is sorry to have to wake him.

"Sashenka," she says sadly, "get up, dear! Time for school."

He gets up, dresses, says his prayers, and then sits down to drink tea; he drinks three glasses and consumes two large rolls and half a French loaf with butter. Still not fully awake, he is in a bad mood.

"You didn't learn your fable properly, you know, Sashenka," Olenka says, looking at him as if about to see him off on a long journey. "What a worry you are to me. You *must* make an effort to learn, dear, and do as the teachers say."

"Oh, stop nagging!" says Sasha.

Then he walks along the street to school, a small boy in a big cap, with a satchel on his back. Olenka follows silently behind.

"Sashenka-a!" she calls.

He looks round, and she pops a date or a caramel into his hand. When they turn into the school street, he feels ashamed at being followed by this tall, stout woman, looks round and says:

"You go home now, Auntie, I'll do the last bit on my own."

She stops and keeps her eyes fixed on him until he disappears through the school entrance. Oh, how she loves him! Not one of her previous attachments has been so deep, never before has she surrendered herself so wholeheartedly, unselfishly and joyfully as now, when her maternal feelings are being kindled more and more. For this boy, who is not hers, for his cap and his dimpled cheeks, she would give away her whole life, and do so with gladness and tears of emotion. Why? Who can possibly say why?

After seeing Sasha off, she returns home quietly, feeling so calm and contented, and overflowing with love. In these last six months her face has become younger, she is smiling and radiant, and people meeting her in the street feel pleasure as they look at her, and say:

"Olga Semyonovna darling, good morning! How are you, darling?"

"They have to work so hard at grammar school these days," she tells them in the market. "It's no laughing matter. Yesterday the first year had a fable to learn by heart *and* a Latin translation *and* a math problem. . . . How can a small boy cope?"

She goes on to talk about teachers and lessons and textbooks—repeating exactly what Sasha tells her.

Between two and three they have their meal together, and in the evening they do Sasha's homework together and cry. Putting him to bed, she spends a long time making the sign of the cross over him and whispering a prayer, then, on going to bed herself, she pictures that distant hazy future when Sasha has finished his degree and become a doctor or an engineer, has his own large house with horses and a carriage, marries and has children. . . . She falls asleep still thinking about it all, and tears run down her cheeks from her closed eyes. The black cat lies purring by her side: mrr, mrr, mrr. . . .

Suddenly there's a loud knock at the gate. Olenka wakes up, too terrified to breathe. Her heart is thumping. Half a minute passes, then there's another knock.

"It's a telegram from Kharkov," she thinks, beginning to tremble all over. "Sasha's mother wants him to live with her in Kharkov. . . . Oh heavens!"

She is in despair. Her head, arms and legs turn cold, she feels the unhappiest person in the world. But another minute passes and she hears voices. It's the vet, he's come back from his club.

"Oh, thank God," she thinks.

Gradually the pressure on her heart eases and she feels relaxed again. She lies down and thinks of Sasha, who is sleeping soundly in the room next door. From time to time he starts talking in his sleep:

"I'll show you! Get out! Stop fighting!" ❧

Quickwrite

Olenka is described as being "constantly in love" and unable to live without love. How does love affect Olenka? In what ways is her need for love both beneficial and detrimental to her? Write a short response explaining your views.

Richness

Gabriela Mistral
Translated by Doris Dana

I have a faithful joy
and a joy that is lost.
One is like a rose,
the other, a thorn.
5   The one that was stolen
I have not lost.
I have a faithful joy
and a joy that is lost.
I am as rich with purple
10   as with sorrow.
Ay! How loved is the rose,
how loving the thorn!
Paired as twin fruit,
I have a faithful joy
15   and a joy that is lost.

Wrap-Up: Comparing Literature *Across Time and Place*

- **The Story of an Hour**
  Kate Chopin

- **The Darling**
  Anton Chekhov

- **Richness**
  Gabriela Mistral

COMPARING THE `Big Idea` Realism

Group Activity In creating **verisimilitude,** or the illusion of reality in a literary work, Realist writers tend to focus more on the motivations of characters than on advancing a plot. These writers strive to portray the confusion and contradiction of their characters. Discuss how Mrs. Mallard in "The Story of an Hour," Olenka in "The Darling," and the speaker in "Richness" each respond to their problems.

1. Do you find their circumstances and their responses realistic?
2. What contradictions do you find in their thoughts and behaviors?
3. What misconceptions might other characters have about the main character or speaker?

COMPARING Narratives About Relationships

Writing Write a short-response essay comparing and contrasting how each quotation below represents the benefits and difficulties each character finds in relationships.

"She said it over and over under her breath: 'free, free, free!'"

—Kate Chopin, "The Story of an Hour"

"No, she needs the kind of love that will possess her completely, mind and soul, that will provide her with thoughts and a direction in life, and warm her aging blood."

—Anton Chekhov, "The Darling"

"One is like a rose, the other, a thorn."

—Gabriela Mistral, "Richness"

A Friendly Call, 1895. William Merritt Chase. Oil on canvas. National Gallery of Art, Washington, DC.

COMPARING Social Context

Partner Activity Social context, or the values and morals of society, plays a role in each of these selections. Chopin and Chekhov both use the actions and dialogue of various characters to reveal social context. However, Mistral renders the feelings of the poem's speaker in isolation from social context. With a partner, discuss the following questions.

1. Compare and contrast the use of social context in the stories by Chopin and Chekhov.
2. How does the lack of social context affect the reader's understanding of Mistral's poem?

INDIANA ACADEMIC STANDARDS (page 561)
11.3.7 Analyze the...beliefs...in a selection of literary works...

11.3.5 Analyze...works of literary significance...that reflect a variety of genres...

Douglass and We Wear the Mask

MEET PAUL LAURENCE DUNBAR

"I know why the caged bird sings, ah me, . . . When he beats his bars and he would be free. . . ."

—Paul Laurence Dunbar, "Sympathy"

These words aptly describe the complex plight of Paul Laurence Dunbar. To reach an audience for his poetry, he often felt he had to "sing" within the constraints of the taste and prejudice that dominated his times.

A Midwestern Childhood One of the first African American writers to attain national recognition, Dunbar was the son of formerly enslaved people. He grew up hearing their stories of pre-Emancipation days, which would later provide a wealth of material for his work. Dunbar had a close relationship with his mother throughout his life, but his father died when Dunbar was only twelve years old.

Dunbar was the only African American student at his Dayton, Ohio, high school. He excelled at his studies, edited the school paper, wrote plays for the drama club, and became class president. Despite his success in school, he could not afford college and had trouble finding a job in a newspaper or a legal office. He worked instead as an elevator operator and spent time writing between calls for the elevator. With help from the Wright Brothers—who owned a printing business in addition to pioneering aviation—he published the *Dayton Tattler*, an African American newsletter.

Dunbar the Poet Dunbar took out a loan in 1893 to publish his first volume of poetry, *Oak and Ivy*, which he sold to elevator passengers and at recitals. After it was published, he joined Frederick Douglass at the Chicago World's Fair, where he gave recitations of his poetry. His second volume, *Majors and Minors*, came out in 1895 and was followed by *Lyrics of a Lonely Life* in 1896. He married Alice Ruth Moore, an African American poet, in 1898. When the influential writer and critic William Dean Howells favorably reviewed *Majors and Minors*, Dunbar found himself famous and in great demand across the United States and in England as a reader.

Much to Dunbar's despair, the poems he wrote in black dialect—he called them "jingles in a broken tongue"—were his best-received works. He also wrote novels, librettos, short stories, and Standard English poems, but these received little attention from critics and readers. His poetry eventually garnered him a clerkship at the Library of Congress. Toward the end of his life, he told James Weldon Johnson, "I have never really gotten to the things I really wanted to do." Despite this sentiment, he was the first African American who was able to live solely on the profits of his writing, and his home became the first state memorial to an African American.

Paul Laurence Dunbar was born in 1872 and died in 1906.

Literature Online Author Search For more about Paul Laurence Dunbar, go to www.glencoe.com.

Connecting to the Poems

Sometimes it is difficult to express one's feelings. As a result, one might try to conceal them from others. For example, one might be afraid but hide behind a "mask" of confidence. As you read Dunbar's poems, ask yourself these questions:

- What kinds of "masks" do people wear and why?
- What are the advantages and disadvantages of masks?

Building Background

Dunbar wrote two kinds of poetry. He was known and loved for his sentimental verse, written in dialect, about an idyllic, pastoral, pre-Civil War plantation life. However, this portion of his work has led some to criticize him for failing to confront the issues of racial stereotypes and discrimination. Yet, Dunbar also produced less popular poems in Standard English that meditate on love, nature, or death; express pride in African Americans; or lament thwarted efforts to live and create freely. "Douglass" and "We Wear the Mask" are examples of his Standard English poems.

Setting Purposes for Reading

Big Idea Naturalism

Naturalism held that people often faced challenges beyond their control. As you read, consider how much control Dunbar seems to have felt he had over his own life and the challenges he faced.

Literary Element Rhyme Scheme

The pattern formed by end rhymes in a stanza or poem is called a **rhyme scheme.** If you assign a different letter to each ending *sound* in "Douglass," you can chart the rhyme scheme like this: *abba, abba, cdcdcd.* As you read, chart the rhyme scheme of "We Wear the Mask."

- See Literary Terms Handbook, p. R15.

Literature Online Interactive Literary Elements Handbook To review or learn more about the literary elements, go to www.glencoe.com.

Reading Strategy Clarifying Meaning

If you have trouble understanding a passage, you may need to carefully reread the section that confuses you to better comprehend its meaning. Be sure to read any footnotes and definitions that accompany the text and look for **context clues** to define unfamiliar words.

Reading Tip: Paraphrasing One way to clarify meaning is to **paraphrase,** or state a passage in your own words. When paraphrasing a poem, look for natural breaks in thoughts—at the ends of lines or stanzas and at end punctuation. Paraphrase each section, then add them together to form complete thoughts. For example, here is one way to paraphrase lines 11–14 of "Douglass": *Today, when there is so much disagreement, and we have no leaders whom we can trust, we need your clear voice, guiding arm, and inspiring presence to comfort us in difficult times.*

Vocabulary

salient (sāl′ yənt) *adj.* prominent or conspicuously noticeable; p. 564 *Arrogance was a salient aspect of his personality.*

tempest (tem′pist) *n.* a violent storm; p. 564 *The trees shook wildly in the tempest.*

dissension (di sen′shən) *n.* disagreement or discord; p. 564 *There was dissension in the drama club over which play to perform.*

guile (gīl) *n.* deceit or slyness; p. 565 *She swayed the jury with her guile.*

vile (vīl) *adj.* repulsive or digusting; p. 565 *The smell of the rotten fish was vile.*

Vocabulary Tip: Denotation and Connotation A word's **denotation** is its literal, or dictionary, meaning. A word's **connotation,** however, is the feeling or association the word suggests.

INDIANA ACADEMIC STANDARDS (pages 563–566)
11.2.2 Analyze...organization of language...
11.2 Develop [reading] strategies...

11.2.4 [Use] elements of the text to defend and clarify interpretations.

Douglass

Paul Laurence Dunbar

The Life of Frederick Douglass #30,1939. Jacob Lawrence.
Casein tempera on hardboard, 12 x 17⅞ in.

Ah, Douglass,[1] we have fall'n on evil days,
    Such days as thou, not even thou didst know,
    When thee, the eyes of that harsh long ago
Saw, **salient,** at the cross of devious ways,
5 And all the country heard thee with amaze.
    Not ended then, the passionate ebb and flow,[2]
    The awful tide that battled to and fro;
We ride amid a **tempest** of dispraise.

Now, when the waves of swift **dissension** swarm,
10 And Honor, the strong pilot, lieth stark,[3]
Oh, for thy voice high-sounding o'er the storm,
    For thy strong arm to guide the shivering bark,[4]
The blast-defying power of thy form,
    To give us comfort through the lonely dark.

---

1. Frederick *Douglass* escaped from slavery and became
   a great speaker and leader in the abolition movement.
2. *Ebb and flow* means "fall and rise."
3. *Stark* means "stiffly" or "rigidly."
4. A *bark* is a type of boat.

Reading Strategy   Clarifying Meaning *What does the speaker tell Douglass in the first two lines?*

Big Idea   Naturalism *From this statement, do you think that the speaker feels like he has control over his circumstances?*

Vocabulary

salient (sāl′yənt) *adj.* prominent or conspicuously noticeable

tempest (tem′pist) *n.* a violent storm

dissension (di sen′shən) *n.* disagreement or discord

We Wear the Mask

Paul Laurence Dunbar

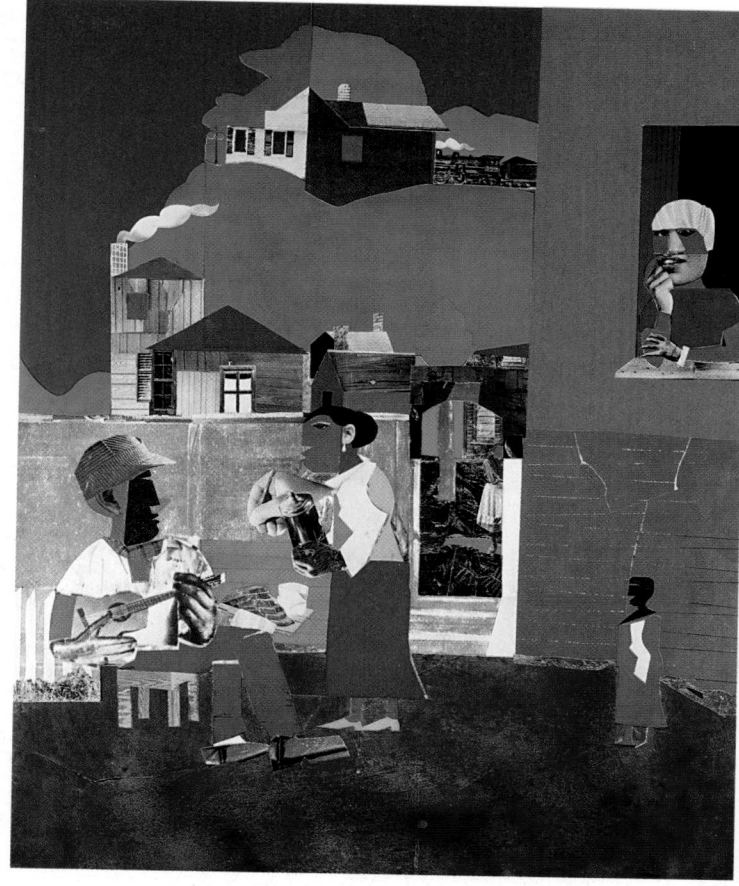

Back Home from Up the Country. Romare Bearden.
Romare Bearden Foundation/VAGA, New York.

We wear the mask that grins and lies,
It hides our cheeks and shades our eyes,—
This debt we pay to human **guile;**
With torn and bleeding hearts we smile,
5   And mouth with myriad[1] subtleties.[2]

Why should the world be overwise,
In counting all our tears and sighs?
Nay, let them only see us, while
    We wear the mask.

10   We smile, but, O great Christ, our cries
To thee from tortured souls arise.
We sing, but oh the clay is **vile**
Beneath our feet, and long the mile;
But let the world dream otherwise,
15   We wear the mask!

---

1. *Myriad* means "countless" or "innumerable."
2. *Subtleties* are things so slight that they are barely perceptible.

Vocabulary

guile (gīl) *n.* deceit or slyness
vile (vīl) *adj.* repulsive or disgusting

RESPONDING AND THINKING CRITICALLY

Respond

1. Which lines in these poems had the greatest emotional impact on you? Explain your choices.

Recall and Interpret

2. (a)According to the speaker in "Douglass," how does the present time compare to Douglass's time? (b)What does the speaker wish that Douglass could do?

3. (a)What words does the speaker in "We Wear the Mask" use to describe the mask? (b)Who wears the mask, and why must it be worn?

4. (a)What reality is hidden behind the mask? (b)What words and images describe this reality?

Analyze and Evaluate

5. The speaker in "Douglass" addresses his words directly to Frederick Douglass, even though Douglass had died by the time the poem was written. What is the purpose of this **apostrophe,** or direct address to an absent person?

6. Evaluate how well the extended metaphor used by the speaker in "Douglass" represents the struggle the speaker is describing.

7. Do you think the **theme,** or central message, of "We Wear the Mask" is relevant today? Explain.

Connect

8. **Big Idea** **Naturalism** Naturalist writers believed social pressures shaped human destiny. Do you see evidence of this belief in Dunbar's poems? Explain.

LITERARY ANALYSIS

Literary Element Rhyme Scheme

A **rhyme scheme** is the pattern formed by end rhymes in a stanza or a poem.

1. Compare the rhyme scheme of "We Wear the Mask" with that of "Douglass." How do the rhyme schemes in the poems differ?

2. What letter in "We Wear the Mask" represents an entire repeated line, or **refrain**?

Literary Criticism

Partner Activity Editor Dennis Poupard wrote of Dunbar's Standard English poems, "These poems consistently examine the nature and possibility of personal freedom." Discuss with a partner whether this statement applies to "Douglass" and "We Wear the Mask." Support your points with evidence from the poems.

READING AND VOCABULARY

Reading Strategy Clarifying Meaning

Paraphrase the lines below. It will be easier to paraphrase if you refer to the poems to **clarify** the context.

> This debt we pay to human guile;
> With torn and bleeding hearts we smile,
> And mouth with myriad subtleties.

Vocabulary Practice

Practice with Denotation and Connotation
Each of the following pairs of words have similar denotations. In each pair, decide which word has stronger negative connotations.

1. a. tempest   **b.** thunderstorm

2. a. slyness   **b.** guile

3. a. disgusting   **b.** vile

Literature Online **Web Activities** For eFlashcards, Selection Quick Checks, and other Web activities, go to www.glencoe.com.

Richard Cory and Miniver Cheevy

MEET EDWIN ARLINGTON ROBINSON

Edwin Arlington Robinson devoted his life almost exclusively to writing poetry, but recognition and success did not come easily. Describing his childhood in Gardiner, Maine, as stark and unhappy, he once wrote to a friend that by the time he was six years old he wondered why he had been born. He began writing at an early age because he felt "doomed, or elected, or sentenced for life, to the writing of poetry." As a high school student, he practiced writing in intricate verse forms under the guidance of a local poet. He continued to write during the two years he attended Harvard University until family financial problems forced him to leave and return to a troubled home. Robinson's father died in 1892, and his mother died of diphtheria in 1896. One of Robinson's brothers became a drug addict, and the other became an alcoholic; both died early.

> "I used to read about clearness, force, and elegance in the rhetoric books, but I'm afraid I go in chiefly for force. . . . There are too many elegant men in the world just now and they seem to be increasing."
>
> —Edwin Arlington Robinson

Hope and Despair The subjects of Robinson's character studies are often people who feel defeated or frustrated by life and who lack a sense of direction. Most of his poems are written with an ironic tone, contain philosophical themes, and end tragically. However, Robinson was not a true pessimist. He believed that life has meaning despite its hardships and that there is hope beyond what he described as "the black and awful chaos of the night." Most of Robinson's early poems are dramatic lyrics, and he became well known for his poetic structure based on natural diction and skillful rhyming patterns within stanzas. His later works include several long narrative poems in blank verse, which were often expanded versions of the psychological portraits he wrote during his earlier period. Robinson was not an experimental poet, yet his poems do break with the traditions of nineteenth-century romantic verse in their use of precise, conversational language and irregular lines.

Struggle for Recognition Robinson's first two books of poems, *The Torrent and the Night Before* and *The Children of the Night*, were published in 1896 and 1897 at his friends' expense. Robinson moved to New York City in 1897 when he was twenty-eight and poverty-stricken. He held a variety of jobs there but made little money and was unable to get more of his poems published. He was rescued from his desperate state by President Theodore Roosevelt, who had read and admired some of his work. Roosevelt arranged a position for Robinson at the U.S. Customs House in New York, an easy job that enabled him to write without worrying about money. Robinson dedicated his third collection, *The Town Down by the River*, to the president. He left his position at the Customs House in 1909 to devote himself entirely to his writing. Robinson was generally ignored by both critics and the public until relatively late in his career. The first collection that brought him critical acclaim was *The Man Against the Sky*, published in 1916. His later works include a trilogy based on Arthurian legend, *Merlin*, *Lancelot*, and *Tristram*, which was his biggest critical and popular success at the time. Eventually, Robinson won three Pulitzer Prizes and became one of America's favorite poets.

Edwin Arlington Robinson was born in 1869 and died in 1935.

Literature Online Author Search For more about Edwin Arlington Robinson, go to www.glencoe.com.

Connecting to the Poems

Have you ever been extremely sad or felt that you were isolated and misunderstood? As you read Robinson's poems, think about these questions:

- How does sorrow affect the title characters?
- What do you think is a good way to deal with unhappiness?

Building Background

More than sixty of Robinson's earliest and best-known poems are set in Tilbury Town, a fictional setting modeled on the poet's hometown, Gardiner, Maine. Robinson is daringly realistic in his portrayal of the town and its inhabitants. The people that he writes about tend to be loners and misfits, as Robinson often felt himself to be. The characters in Tilbury Town feel pressured to conform, and their creativity is wasted through their own despair or because of the neglect and misunderstanding of others.

Setting Purposes for Reading

Big Idea Naturalism

Robinson's poetry often focuses on characters who seem to have little control over their lives or who are unable to cope with the scientific, social, and environmental forces that affect them. As you read, notice how Richard Cory and Miniver Cheevy react to these forces.

Literary Element Irony

Irony is a contrast or discrepancy between appearance and reality. In literature it is often accompanied by grim humor. Be aware of what appears to be true and what is actually true as you read these poems.

- See Literary Terms Handbook, p. R10.

Literature Online Interactive Literary Elements Handbook To review or learn more about the literary elements, go to www.glencoe.com.

Reading Strategy Making Inferences About Characters

You **make inferences** when you use reason and your experience to understand meaning that is implied but not stated directly. As you read Robinson's portraits of Richard Cory and Miniver Cheevy, look for the clues that the poet offers about each man's public and private "faces"—how they appear to the world around them and how they appear to themselves.

Reading Tip: Taking Notes Use a chart to record the inferences you draw from the details presented.

Detail	Inference
p. 569 "He was a gentleman from sole to crown"	Richard Cory takes care of his appearance and dresses appropriately.

Vocabulary

imperially (im pēr′ ē əl ē) *adv.* majestically; magnificently; p. 569 *The queen walked imperially into the palace.*

assail (ə sāl′) *v.* to attack violently; p. 570 *The ship was assailed by the heavy storm.*

fragrant (frā′grənt) *adj.* having a strong, pleasant smell; p. 570 *The fragrant roses made the apartment look and smell lovely.*

incessantly (in ses′ənt lē) *adv.* continually; happening over and over without interruption; p. 570 *Alison's brother incessantly asked for a cookie.*

scorned (skôrnd) *v.* treated with open contempt; rejected something as worthless; p. 570 *The angry citizens scorned the mayor's proposal.*

Vocabulary Tip: Denotation and Connotation
A word's **denotation** is its literal, or dictionary, meaning. A word's **connotation,** however, is the feeling or association the word suggests.

INDIANA ACADEMIC STANDARDS (pages 568–571)
11.3.3 Analyze the ways in which irony...achieve[s] specific... aesthetic (artistic) purposes...

11.2 Develop [reading] strategies...

Richard Cory

Man with the Cat (Henry Sturgis Drinker), 1898. Cecilia Beaux. Oil on canvas, 48 x 34⅝ in. Bequest of Henry Ward Ranger through the National Academy of Design. Smithsonian American Art Museum, Washington, DC.

Edwin Arlington Robinson

Whenever Richard Cory went down town,
We people on the pavement looked at him:
He was a gentleman from sole to crown,
Clean favored,[1] and **imperially** slim.

5　And he was always quietly arrayed,[2]
And he was always human when he talked;
But still he fluttered pulses when he said,
"Good-morning," and he glittered when he walked.

And he was rich—yes, richer than a king—
10　And admirably schooled in every grace:
In fine,[3] we thought that he was everything
To make us wish that we were in his place.

So on we worked, and waited for the light,
And went without the meat, and cursed the bread;
15　And Richard Cory, one calm summer night,
Went home and put a bullet through his head.

---

1. *Clean favored* means "having a tidy appearance."
2. *Arrayed* means "dressed."
3. *In fine* means "in short."

Reading Strategy　Making Inferences About Characters
What can you infer about Richard Cory's relationship with the people based on the speaker's description?

Vocabulary

imperially (im pēr′ē əl ē) *adv.* majestically; magnificently

Miniver Cheevy

Edwin Arlington Robinson

Miniver Cheevy, child of scorn,
   Grew lean while he **assailed** the seasons;
He wept that he was ever born,
   And he had reasons.

5 Miniver loved the days of old
   When swords were bright and steeds were prancing;
The vision of a warrior bold
   Would set him dancing.

Miniver sighed for what was not,
10   And dreamed, and rested from his labors;
He dreamed of Thebes[1] and Camelot,[2]
   And Priam's[3] neighbors.

Miniver mourned the ripe renown
   That made so many a name so **fragrant**;
15 He mourned Romance, now on the town,[4]
   And Art, a vagrant.

Miniver loved the Medici,[5]
   Albeit he had never seen one;
He would have sinned **incessantly**
20   Could he have been one.

Miniver cursed the commonplace
   And eyed a khaki suit with loathing;
He missed the mediæval grace
   Of iron clothing.

25 Miniver **scorned** the gold he sought,
   But sore annoyed was he without it;
Miniver thought, and thought, and thought,
   And thought about it.

Miniver Cheevy, born too late,
30   Scratched his head and kept on thinking;
Miniver coughed, and called it fate,
   And kept on drinking.

1. *Thebes* (thēbz) was a city-state in ancient Greece.
2. *Camelot* is the legendary site of King Arthur's court.
3. In Homer's *Iliad*, *Priam* was the king of Troy.
4. *On the town* means "on welfare."
5. *Medici* (med' i chē) refers to a noble, rich, and powerful family in Florence, Italy (1300–1500).

Literary Element   Irony *What is the verbal irony in these lines?*

Vocabulary

assail (ə sāl´) *v.* to attack violently
fragrant (frā´grənt) *adj.* having a strong, pleasant smell
incessantly (in ses´ənt lē´) *adv.* continually; happening over and over without interruption
scorned (skôrnd) *v.* treated with open contempt; rejected something as worthless

RESPONDING AND THINKING CRITICALLY

Respond

1. What was your reaction to the last line in each poem? Give reasons for your answer.

Recall and Interpret

2. (a)Summarize the speaker's description of Richard Cory. (b)In what ways does Cory's life differ from the lives of the "people on the pavement"?

3. (a)What does Richard Cory do "one calm summer night"? (b)What does this action suggest about Cory's quality of life?

4. (a)What does Miniver Cheevy blame for his unhappiness? (b)What do you think is the real reason he is unhappy? Explain.

Analyze and Evaluate

5. (a)What is ironic about Richard Cory's life and death? (b)Do you find Cory a sympathetic figure? Explain.

6. (a)What is the speaker's **tone,** or attitude, toward the title character in "Miniver Cheevy"? (b)How does the speaker's tone affect your own attitude toward Cheevy?

Connect

7. Big Idea **Naturalism** Richard Cory has wealth; Miniver Cheevy is obsessed with the art and culture of the past. According to Robinson, why do money and art not necessarily make people happy or help them overcome their limitations?

LITERARY ANALYSIS

Literary Element Irony

Situational irony occurs when the actual outcome of a situation is the opposite of what is expected. **Verbal irony** occurs when the meaning of a statement is the opposite of what is said.

Partner Activity How does Robinson use situational and verbal irony to reveal details about the various characters—including the townspeople—in these poems? Discuss this question with one or more classmates.

Reading Further

For more of Edwin Arlington Robinson's poetry, see these books:

Collected Poems (1921) and *The Man Who Died Twice* (1924) were awarded the Pulitzer Prize.

Merlin (1917), *Lancelot* (1920), and *Tristram* (1928) are long narrative poems based on the legends of King Arthur. Robinson received his third Pulitzer Prize for *Tristram.*

Literature Online **Web Activities** For eFlashcards, Selection Quick Checks, and other Web activities, go to www.glencoe.com.

READING AND VOCABULARY

Reading Strategy Making Inferences About Characters

When you make inferences about characters, you use clues in the text to find information stated indirectly.

1. What clues indicate that the townspeople regard Richard Cory as many people regard royalty?

2. What details lead you to understand that Miniver Cheevy is an unhappy person who is unable or unwilling to improve his quality of life?

Vocabulary Practice

Practice with Denotation and Connotation
For each of the vocabulary words listed below, tell which word in parentheses is the word's denotation and which is its connotation.

1. fragrant (scented, perfumed)
2. incessantly (relentlessly, repeatedly)
3. scorned (rejected, disdained)

The Open Boat

MEET STEPHEN CRANE

By the time he reached college, Stephen Crane was better known for his baseball-playing skills than for his scholarly achievements. Within a decade, however, Crane's rebelliousness toward his schooling, his upbringing, and society at large would help shape a short but prolific literary career. In his work, Crane embraced a pessimistic realism that undermined earlier, romanticized visions of human experiences. In fiction, as in journalism, Crane portrayed life as it was, not as one wished it were.

"A man said to the universe:
'Sir, I exist!'
'However,' replied the universe,
'The fact has not created in me
A sense of obligation.'"

—Stephen Crane, "War Is Kind"

Bowery Life The fourteenth child of a Methodist minister and his devout wife, Crane chafed against the constraints of structured family life. University life left him with much the same feeling, and he attended classes sporadically before leaving college entirely to work as a newspaper writer. As a free-lance reporter, Crane lived in the Bowery district of Manhattan, reporting on the poverty of the district's slums through firsthand experience. His observations of Bowery life eventually became the basis for his controversial first novel, *Maggie: A Girl of the Streets* (1893). Crane's sympathetic but starkly realistic portrayal of New York slum life repelled publishers; he finally published the novel at his own expense under the pseudonym Johnston Smith. Crane's harsh story did not sell well. However, critics Hamlin Garland and William Dean Howells noticed Crane's talent and became his mentors.

Live Quick; Write Fast

Crane's second novel, *The Red Badge of Courage: An Episode of the American Civil War*, appeared first as a syndicated newspaper feature in 1894 and became a bestseller in 1895. At age twenty-four, the struggling journalist had reached international fame with the novel's success. In *The Red Badge of Courage*, Crane turned his power for acute observation inward, exploring the psychology of a Civil War soldier who grapples with his fear, cowardice, and pride in battle. Ironically, Crane became famous for his realistic portrayal of a soldier during battle even though he had not yet experienced war firsthand and was born six years after the Civil War ended. Nonetheless, many veterans applauded his ability to re-create the internal tension experienced during combat. In late 1895, Crane published a book of poems, *The Black Riders and Other Lines*, to less favorable reviews.

Fascinated with danger and war, Crane covered the Greco-Turkish War in Greece and the Spanish-American War in Cuba. He then settled in Sussex, England, in 1899, heavily in debt and ill with tuberculosis and recurrent malarial fever. Years of exposure, poor food, and lack of treatment ended Crane's life at twenty-eight.

Crane is known as a man who "lived quickly and wrote fast." Despite a brief literary career, his studies of characters overwhelmed by uncontrollable circumstances still resonate today. As Sherwood Anderson noted, "Stephen Crane was a craftsman. The stones he put in the wall are still there."

Literature Online **Author Search** For more about Stephen Crane, go to www.glencoe.com.

Connecting to the Story

What do you think it might be like to fight for your life? In "The Open Boat," four men struggle to survive in the Atlantic Ocean. As you read the story, think about the following questions:

- How do one's priorities change in times of great danger?
- How much of survival depends on personal will, and how much depends on outside circumstances?

Building Background

As a war correspondent, Stephen Crane traveled from Jacksonville, Florida, to Cuba aboard the steamship *Commodore* in January 1897. The ship sank, and Crane and three others faced the raging Atlantic in a ten-foot dinghy until they managed to reach the Florida coast. Afterward, Crane published a fictionalized account in *Scribner's Magazine*. The tale then became the title story in his book *The Open Boat and Other Tales of Adventure*. Throughout the story, Crane maintains suspense by pulling the characters between illusion and reality, hope and despair.

Setting Purposes for Reading

Big Idea Naturalism

Like other Naturalists, Crane does not soften his depiction of the struggle his characters face. As you read, notice how the characters in "The Open Boat" are continually at the mercy of environmental forces.

Literary Element Author's Purpose

An **author's purpose** is his or her intent in writing a literary work. For example, an author may want to inform, entertain, persuade, or express an opinion. An author's purpose may be expressed through direct commentary, through the dialogue, actions, and thoughts of the characters, or through tone, word choice, and narrative point of view. As you read, look for places in the story where Crane reveals his purpose.

- See Literary Terms Handbook, p. R2.

Literature Online **Interactive Literary Elements Handbook** To review or learn more about the literary elements, go to www.glencoe.com.

Reading Strategy Summarizing

Summarizing means stating the main ideas of a selection or passage in your own words and in a logical sequence. Summarizing will help you understand and think about what you have read.

Reading Tip: Answering the 5 Ws Use a chart to help you answer the who, what, where, when, and why questions about the passage you're summarizing.

Quotation: "After a search, somebody produced three dry matches, and thereupon the four waifs rode impudently in their little boat, and with an assurance of an impending rescue shining in their eyes, puffed at the big cigars and judged well and ill of all men."

Who The four members of the crew in the dinghy	What	Where	When	Why

Vocabulary

uncanny (un ka′ nē) *adj.* strangely unsettling; eerie; p. 576 *Yoshi found the presence of two dead birds on the path uncanny.*

emphatic (em fa′ tik) *adj.* forceful; p. 576 *Jon gave one last emphatic push, and the door opened.*

ingenuously (in jen′ ū əs lē) *adv.* honestly; frankly; p. 578 *The child talked ingenuously to the doctor about his broken arm.*

impudently (im′ pyə dənt lē) *adv.* in an offensively bold manner; p. 579 *The politician spoke so impudently that few voters trusted him.*

coerce (kō urs′) *v.* to force; p. 587 *The boy coerced his sister into giving him all her candy.*

Vocabulary Tip: Context Clues Context clues are the words and sentences around an unfamiliar word that help you figure out the word's meaning.

INDIANA ACADEMIC STANDARDS (pages 573–592)
11.2 Develop strategies such as…identifying and analyzing…purpose…

11.3.2 Analyze…theme
11.5.9 Write…an analytical essay…

the Open Boat

Stephen Crane

A tale intended to be after the fact. Being the experience of four men from the sunk steamer Commodore . . .

I

None of them knew the color of the sky. Their eyes glanced level, and were fastened upon the waves that swept toward them. These waves were of the hue of slate, save for the tops, which were of foaming white, and all of the men knew the colors of the sea. The horizon narrowed and widened, and dipped and rose, and at all times its edge was jagged with waves that seemed thrust up in points like rocks.

Many a man ought to have a bathtub larger than the boat which here rode upon the sea. These waves were most wrongfully and barbarously abrupt and tall, and each froth-top was a problem in small boat navigation.

The cook squatted in the bottom and looked with both eyes at the six inches of gunwale[1] which separated him from the ocean. His sleeves were rolled over his fat forearms, and the two flaps of his unbuttoned vest dangled as he bent to bail out the boat. Often he said: "Gawd! That was a narrow clip." As he remarked it he invariably gazed eastward over the broken sea.

The oiler,[2] steering with one of the two oars in the boat, sometimes raised himself suddenly to keep clear of water that swirled in over the stern.[3] It was a thin little oar and it seemed often ready to snap.

The correspondent, pulling at the other oar, watched the waves and wondered why he was there.

The injured captain, lying in the bow, was at this time buried in that profound dejection and indifference which comes, temporarily at least, to even the bravest and most enduring when, willy nilly,[4] the firm fails, the army loses, the ship goes down. The mind of the master of a vessel is rooted deep in the timbers of her, though he command for a day or a decade, and this captain had on him the stern impression of a scene in the grays of dawn of seven turned faces, and later a stump of a top-mast with a white ball on it that slashed to and fro at the waves, went low and lower, and down. Thereafter there was something

---

1. A *gunwale* is the upper edge of the side of a boat.

2. The *oiler* is the person responsible for oiling machinery in the engine room on a ship.
3. The *stern* is the rear part of a boat or ship.
4. *Willy nilly* means "whether one wishes it or not."

Big Idea Naturalism *How does this passage reflect characteristics of Naturalism?*

strange in his voice. Although steady, it was deep with mourning, and of a quality beyond oration[5] or tears.

"Keep'er a little more south, Billie," said he.

"'A little more south,' sir," said the oiler in the stern.

A seat in this boat was not unlike a seat upon a bucking bronco, and, by the same token, a bronco is not much smaller. The craft pranced and reared, and plunged like an animal. As each wave came, and she rose for it, she seemed like a horse making at a fence outrageously high. The manner of her scramble over these walls of water is a mystic thing, and, moreover, at the top of them were ordinarily these problems in white water, the foam racing down from the summit of each wave, requiring a new leap, and a leap from the air. Then, after scornfully bumping a crest, she would slide, and race, and splash down a long incline and arrive bobbing and nodding in front of the next menace.

A singular disadvantage of the sea lies in the fact that after successfully surmounting one wave you discover that there is another behind it just as important and just as nervously anxious to do something effective in the way of swamping boats. In a ten-foot dinghy one can get an idea of the resources of the sea in the line of waves that is not probable to the average experience, which is never at sea in a dinghy. As each slaty[6] wall of water approached, it shut all else from the view of the men in the boat, and it was not difficult to imagine that this particular wave was the final outburst of the ocean, the last effort of the grim water. There was a terrible grace in the move of the waves, and they came in silence, save for the snarling of the crests.

In the wan[7] light, the faces of the men must have been gray. Their eyes must have glinted in strange ways as they gazed steadily astern. Viewed from a balcony, the whole thing would doubtlessly have been weirdly picturesque. But the men in the boat had no time to see it, and if they had had leisure there were other things to occupy their minds. The sun swung steadily up the sky, and they knew it was broad day because the color of the sea changed from slate to emerald green, streaked with amber lights, and the foam was like tumbling snow. The process of the breaking day was unknown to them. They were aware only of this effect upon the color of the waves that rolled toward them.

In disjointed sentences the cook and the correspondent argued as to the difference between a lifesaving station and a house of refuge. The cook had said: "There's a house of refuge just north of the Mosquito Inlet Light, and as soon as they see us, they'll come off in their boat and pick us up."

"As soon as who see us?" said the correspondent.

"The crew," said the cook.

"Houses of refuge don't have crews," said the correspondent. "As I understand them, they are only places where clothes and grub are stored for the benefit of shipwrecked people. They don't carry crews."

"Oh, yes, they do," said the cook.

"No, they don't," said the correspondent.

"Well, we're not there yet, anyhow," said the oiler, in the stern.

"Well," said the cook, "perhaps it's not a house of refuge that I'm thinking of as being near Mosquito Inlet Light. Perhaps it's a lifesaving station."

"We're not there yet," said the oiler, in the stern.

II

As the boat bounced from the top of each wave, the wind tore through the hair of the hatless men, and as the craft plopped her stern down again the spray slashed past them. The crest of each of these waves was a hill, from the top of which the men surveyed, for a moment, a broad tumultuous[8] expanse, shining and wind-riven. It was probably splendid. It was probably glorious, this play of the free sea, wild with lights of emerald and white and amber.

"Bully good thing it's an onshore wind,"[9] said the cook. "If not, where would we be? Wouldn't have a show."

---

5. An *oration* is a formal speech.
6. *Slaty* means "having the bluish gray color of slate."
7. *Wan* means "pale."

Literary Element Author's Purpose *Why does Crane have the narrator address the reader in this paragraph?*

---

8. *Tumultuous* means "agitated" or "turbulent."
9. An *onshore wind* is one that blows toward the shore.

"That's right," said the correspondent.

The busy oiler nodded his assent.

Then the captain, in the bow, chuckled in a way that expressed humor, contempt, tragedy, all in one. "Do you think we've got much of a show, now, boys?" said he.

Whereupon the three were silent, save for a trifle of hemming and hawing. To express any particular optimism at this time they felt to be childish and stupid, but they all doubtless possessed this sense of the situation in their mind. A young man thinks doggedly[10] at such times. On the other hand, the ethics of their condition was decidedly against any open suggestion of hopelessness. So they were silent.

"Oh, well," said the captain, soothing his children, "we'll get ashore all right."

But there was that in his tone which made them think, so the oiler quoth: "Yes! If this wind holds!"

The cook was bailing. "Yes! If we don't catch hell in the surf."

Canton flannel gulls[11] flew near and far. Sometimes they sat down on the sea, near patches of brown seaweed that rolled over the waves with a movement like carpets on a line in a gale. The birds sat comfortably in groups, and they were envied by some in the dinghy, for the wrath of the sea was no more to them than it was to a covey of prairie chickens a thousand miles inland. Often they came very close and stared at the men with black bead-like eyes. At these times they were **uncanny** and sinister[12] in their unblinking scrutiny, and the men hooted angrily at them, telling them to be gone. One came, and evidently decided to alight on the top of the captain's head. The bird flew parallel to the boat and did not circle, but made short sidelong jumps in the air in chicken-fashion. His black eyes were wistfully fixed upon the captain's head. "Ugly brute," said the oiler to the bird. "You look as if you were made with a jackknife." The cook and the correspondent swore darkly at the creature. The captain naturally wished to knock it away with the end of the heavy painter,[13] but he did not dare do it, because anything resembling an **emphatic** gesture would have capsized this freighted boat, and so with his open hand, the captain gently and carefully waved the gull away. After it had been discouraged from the pursuit the captain breathed easier on account of his hair, and others breathed easier because the bird struck their minds at this time as being somehow gruesome and ominous.

In the meantime the oiler and the correspondent rowed. And also they rowed.

They sat together in the same seat, and each rowed an oar. Then the oiler took both oars; then the correspondent took both oars; then the oiler; then the correspondent. They rowed and they rowed. The very ticklish part of the business was when the time came for the reclining one in the stern to take his turn at the oars. By the very last star of truth, it is easier to steal eggs from under a hen than it was to change seats in the dinghy. First the man in the stern slid his hand along the thwart[14] and moved with care, as if he were of Sèvres.[15] Then the man in the rowing seat slid his hand along the other thwart. It was all done with the most extraordinary care. As the two sidled past each other, the whole party kept watchful eyes on the coming wave, and the captain cried: "Look out now! Steady there!"

The brown mats of seaweed that appeared from time to time were like islands, bits of earth. They were traveling, apparently, neither one way nor the other. They were, to all intents, stationary.

---

10. *Doggedly* means "in a stubbornly persistent manner."
11. *Canton flannel gulls* are gulls whose feathers resemble Canton flannel, a strong cotton fabric that is soft on one side and ribbed on the other.
12. *Sinister* means "evil" or "ominous."

Reading Strategy Summarizing *How would you summarize the thoughts of the four men at this point?*

Big Idea Naturalism *How is the influence of Naturalism reflected in this passage?*

Vocabulary

uncanny (un ka′nē) *adj.* strangely unsettling; eerie

---

13. A *painter* is a rope attached to the front of a boat, used for tying up to a dock.
14. A *thwart* is a seat going across a boat, on which a rower or passenger sits.
15. *Sèvres* (sev′ rə) refers to fine porcelain made in Sèvres, France.

Vocabulary

emphatic (em fa′tik) *adj.* forceful

Moonlit Shipwreck at Sea, 1901. Thomas Moran. Oil on canvas, 30 x 40¼ in. Private collection.

They informed the men in the boat that it was making progress slowly toward the land.

The captain, rearing cautiously in the bow, after the dinghy soared on a great swell, said that he had seen the lighthouse at Mosquito Inlet. Presently the cook remarked that he had seen it. The correspondent was at the oars, then, and for some reason he too wished to look at the lighthouse, but his back was toward the far shore and the waves were important, and for some time he could not seize an opportunity to turn his head. But at last there came a wave more gentle than the others, and when at the crest of it he swiftly scoured the western horizon.

"See it?" said the captain.

"No," said the correspondent, slowly, "I didn't see anything."

"Look again," said the captain. He pointed. "It's exactly in that direction."

At the top of another wave, the correspondent did as he was bid, and this time his eyes chanced on a small still thing on the edge of the swaying horizon. It was precisely like the point of a pin. It took an anxious eye to find a lighthouse so tiny.

"Think we'll make it, Captain?"

"If this wind holds and the boat don't swamp, we can't do much else," said the captain.

The little boat, lifted by each towering sea, and splashed viciously by the crests, made progress that in the absence of seaweed was not apparent to those in her. She seemed just a wee thing wallowing, miraculously, top up, at the mercy of five oceans. Occasionally, a great spread of water, like white flames, swarmed into her.

"Bail her, cook," said the captain, serenely.

"All right, Captain," said the cheerful cook.

III

It would be difficult to describe the subtle brotherhood of men that was here established on the seas. No one said that it was so. No one mentioned it. But it dwelt in the boat, and each man felt it warm him. They were a captain, an oiler, a

Literary Element   Author's Purpose *What is the function of the captain's optimistic reply to the correspondent?*

Reading Strategy   Summarizing *What is the main idea expressed in this paragraph?*

cook, and a correspondent, and they were friends, friends in a more curiously iron-bound degree than may be common. The hurt captain, lying against the water jar in the bow, spoke always in a low voice and calmly, but he could never command a more ready and swiftly obedient crew than the motley three of the dinghy. It was more than a mere recognition of what was best for the common safety. There was surely in it a quality that was personal and heartfelt. And after this devotion to the commander of the boat there was this comradeship that the correspondent, for instance, who had been taught to be cynical of men, knew even at the time was the best experience of his life. But no one said that it was so. No one mentioned it.

"I wish we had a sail," remarked the captain. "We might try my overcoat on the end of an oar and give you two boys a chance to rest." So the cook and the correspondent held the mast and spread wide the overcoat. The oiler steered, and the little boat made good way with her new rig. Sometimes the oiler had to scull[16] sharply to keep a sea from breaking into the boat, but otherwise sailing was a success.

Meanwhile the lighthouse had been growing slowly larger. It had now almost assumed color, and appeared like a little gray shadow on the sky. The man at the oars could not be prevented from turning his head rather often to try for a glimpse of this little gray shadow.

At last, from the top of each wave the men in the tossing boat could see land. Even as the lighthouse was an upright shadow on the sky, this land seemed but a long black shadow on the sea. It certainly was thinner than paper. "We must be about opposite New Smyrna,"[17] said the cook, who had coasted this shore often in schooners. "Captain, by the way, I believe they abandoned that lifesaving station there about a year ago."

"Did they?" said the captain.

The wind slowly died away. The cook and the correspondent were not now obliged to slave in order to hold high the oar. But the waves continued their old impetuous swooping at the dinghy, and the little craft, no longer under way, struggled woundily over them. The oiler or the correspondent took the oars again.

Shipwrecks are *apropos*[18] of nothing. If men could only train for them and have them occur when the men had reached pink condition, there would be less drowning at sea. Of the four in the dinghy none had slept any time worth mentioning for two days and two nights previous to embarking in the dinghy, and in the excitement of clambering about the deck of a foundering[19] ship they had also forgotten to eat heartily.

For these reasons, and for others, neither the oiler nor the correspondent was fond of rowing at this time. The correspondent wondered **ingenuously** how in the name of all that was sane could there be people who thought it amusing to row a boat. It was not an amusement; it was a diabolical punishment, and even a genius of mental aberrations could never conclude that it was anything but a horror to the muscles and a crime against the back. He mentioned to the boat in general how the amusement of rowing struck him, and the weary-faced oiler smiled in full sympathy. Previously to the foundering, by the way, the oiler had worked doublewatch in the engineroom of the ship.

"Take her easy, now, boys," said the captain. "Don't spend yourselves. If we have to run a surf you'll need all your strength, because we'll sure have to swim for it. Take your time."

Slowly the land arose from the sea. From a black line it became a line of black and a line of white—trees and sand. Finally, the captain said that he could make out a house on the shore. "That's the house of refuge, sure," said the cook. "They'll see us before long, and come out after us."

The distant lighthouse reared high. "The keeper ought to be able to make us out now, if he's looking through a glass," said the captain. "He'll notify the lifesaving people."

---

16. *Scull* means "to propel a boat forward by moving a single oar from side to side over the stern of a boat."
17. *New Smyrna* refers to the town of New Smyrna Beach, on the east coast of Florida.

18. *Apropos* means "relevant" or "pertinent."
19. *Foundering* means "sinking."

Big Idea Naturalism *From your understanding of Naturalism, why is this passage important to the story?*

Vocabulary

ingenuously (in jen′ ū əs lē) *adv.* honestly; frankly

"None of those other boats could have got ashore to give word of the wreck," said the oiler, in a low voice. "Else the lifeboat would be out hunting us."

Slowly and beautifully the land loomed out of the sea. The wind came again. It had veered from the northeast to the southeast. Finally, a new sound struck the ears of the men in the boat. It was the low thunder of the surf on the shore. "We'll never be able to make the lighthouse now," said the captain. "Swing her head a little more north, Billie."

"'A little more north,' sir," said the oiler.

Whereupon the little boat turned her nose once more down the wind, and all but the oarsman watched the shore grow. Under the influence of this expansion doubt and direful apprehension was leaving the minds of the men. The management of the boat was still most absorbing, but it could not prevent a quiet cheerfulness. In an hour, perhaps, they would be ashore.

Their backbones had become thoroughly used to balancing in the boat and they now rode this wild colt of a dinghy like circus men. The correspondent thought that he had been drenched to the skin, but happening to feel in the top pocket of his coat, he found therein eight cigars. Four of them were soaked with seawater; four were perfectly scatheless. After a search, somebody produced three dry matches, and thereupon the four waifs[20] rode **impudently** in their little boat, and with an assurance of an impending rescue shining in their eyes, puffed at the big cigars and judged well and ill of all men. Everybody took a drink of water.

IV

"Cook," remarked the captain, "there don't seem to be any signs of life about your house of refuge."

> "Funny they don't see us," said the men.

"No," replied the cook. "Funny they don't see us!"

A broad stretch of lowly coast lay before the eyes of the men. It was of dunes topped with dark vegetation. The roar of the surf was plain, and sometimes they could see the white lip of a wave as it spun up the beach. A tiny house was blocked out black upon the sky. Southward, the slim lighthouse lifted its little gray length.

Tide, wind, and waves were swinging the dinghy northward. "Funny they don't see us," said the men.

The surf's roar was here dulled, but its tone was, nevertheless, thunderous and mighty. As the boat swam over the great rollers, the men sat listening to this roar. "We'll swamp sure," said everybody.

It is fair to say here that there was not a lifesaving station within twenty miles in either direction, but the men did not know this fact and in consequence they made dark and opprobrious[21] remarks concerning the eyesight of the nation's lifesavers. Four scowling men sat in the dinghy and surpassed records in the invention of epithets.[22]

"Funny they don't see us."

The light-heartedness of a former time had completely faded. To their sharpened minds it was easy to conjure pictures of all kinds of incompetency and blindness and, indeed, cowardice. There was the shore of the populous land, and it was bitter and bitter to them that from it came no sign.

"Well," said the captain, ultimately, "I suppose we'll have to make a try for ourselves. If we stay out here too long, we'll none of us have strength left to swim after the boat swamps."

And so the oiler, who was at the oars, turned the boat straight for the shore. There was a sudden tightening of muscles. There was some thinking.

---

20. *Waifs* are persons having no apparent home.

Vocabulary

impudently (im′ pyə dənt lē) *adv.* in an offensively bold manner

21. *Opprobrious* (ə prō′ brē əs) means "derogatory."
22. *Epithets* are descriptive, sometimes abusive, words or phrases used with or in place of a name.

Reading Strategy Summarizing *In your own words, summarize what is happening in this paragraph.*

"If we don't all get ashore—" said the captain. "If we don't all get ashore, I suppose you fellows know where to send news of my finish?"

They then briefly exchanged some addresses and admonitions.[23] As for the reflections of the men, there was a great deal of rage in them. Perchance they might be formulated thus: "If I am going to be drowned—if I am going to be drowned—if I am going to be drowned, why, in the name of the seven mad gods who rule the sea,[24] was I allowed to come thus far and contemplate sand and trees? Was I brought here merely to have my nose dragged away as I was about to nibble the sacred cheese of life? It is preposterous. If this old ninny-woman, Fate,[25] cannot do better than this, she should be deprived of the management of men's fortunes. She is an old hen who knows not her intention. If she has decided to drown me, why did she not do it in the beginning and save me all this trouble. The whole affair is absurd. . . . But, no, she cannot mean to drown me. She dare not drown me. She cannot drown me. Not after all this work." Afterward the man might have had an impulse to shake his fist at the clouds. "Just you drown me, now, and then hear what I call you!"

The billows that came at this time were more formidable. They seemed always just about to break and roll over the little boat in a turmoil of foam. There was a preparatory and long growl in the speech of them. No mind unused to the sea would have concluded that the dinghy could ascend these sheer heights in time. The shore was still afar. The oiler was a wily[26] surfman. "Boys," he said, swiftly, "she won't live three minutes more and we're too far out to swim. Shall I take her to sea again, Captain?"

"Yes! Go ahead!" said the captain.

This oiler, by a series of quick miracles, and fast and steady oarsmanship, turned the boat in the middle of the surf and took her safely to sea again.

There was a considerable silence as the boat bumped over the furrowed sea to deeper water. Then somebody in gloom spoke. "Well, anyhow, they must have seen us from the shore by now."

The gulls went in slanting flight up the wind toward the gray desolate east. A squall,[27] marked by dingy clouds, and clouds brick-red, like smoke from a burning building, appeared from the southeast.

"What do you think of those lifesaving people? Ain't they peaches?"

"Funny they haven't seen us."

"Maybe they think we're out here for sport? Maybe they think we're fishin'. Maybe they think we're damned fools."

It was a long afternoon. A changed tide tried to force them southward, but wind and wave said northward. Far ahead, where coastline, sea, and sky formed their mighty angle, there were little dots which seemed to indicate a city on the shore.

"St. Augustine?"

The captain shook his head. "Too near Mosquito Inlet."

And the oiler rowed, and then the correspondent rowed. Then the oiler rowed. It was a weary business. The human back can become the seat of more aches and pains than are registered in books for the composite anatomy of a regiment. It is a limited area, but it can become the theater of innumerable muscular conflicts, tangles, wrenches, knots, and other comforts.

"Did you ever like to row, Billie?" asked the correspondent.

"No," said the oiler. "Hang it."

When one exchanged the rowing-seat for a place in the bottom of the boat, he suffered a bodily depression that caused him to be careless of everything save an obligation to wiggle one finger. There was cold seawater swashing to and fro in the boat, and he lay in it. His head, pillowed on a thwart, was within an inch of the swirl of a wave crest, and sometimes a

---

23. *Admonitions* are warnings or advice.
24. *[seven . . . the sea]* This description probably refers to the seven major seas, each at the mercy of a deity.
25. *Fate* implies a supernatural power guiding one to an inevitable end. In classical mythology, the three Fates were portrayed as old women.
26. *Wily* means "cunning" or "sly."

27. A *squall* is a short, sudden, strong windstorm, often accompanied by rain or snow.

Lord Ullin's Daughter, before 1907. Albert Pinkham Ryder. Oil on canvas, 20½ x 18⅜ in. Smithsonian American Art Museum, Gift of John Gellatly.
Viewing the Art: How does the painting convey a sense of the power of the sea?

particularly obstreperous[28] sea came inboard and drenched him once more. But these matters did not annoy him. It is almost certain that if the boat had capsized he would have tumbled comfortably out upon the ocean as if he felt sure that it was a great soft mattress.

"Look! There's a man on the shore!"

"Where?"

"There! See 'im? See 'im?"

"Yes, sure! He's walking along."

"Now he's stopped. Look! He's facing us!"

"He's waving at us!"

"So he is! By thunder!"

"Ah, now, we're all right! Now we're all right! There'll be a boat out here for us in half an hour."

"He's going on. He's running. He's going up to that house there."

The remote beach seemed lower than the sea, and it required a searching glance to dis-

cern the little black figure. The captain saw a floating stick and they rowed to it. A bath-towel was by some weird chance in the boat, and, tying this on the stick, the captain waved it. The oarsman did not dare turn his head, so he was obliged to ask questions.

"What's he doing now?"

"He's standing still again. He's looking, I think. . . . There he goes again. Toward the house. . . . Now he's stopped again."

"Is he waving at us?"

"No, not now! he was, though."

"Look! There comes another man!"

"He's running."

"Look at him go, would you."

"Why, he's on a bicycle. Now he's met the other man. They're both waving at us. Look!"

"There comes something up the beach."

"What the devil is that thing?"

"Why, it looks like a boat."

"Why, certainly it's a boat."

"No, it's on wheels."

"Yes, so it is. Well, that must be the lifeboat. They drag them along shore on a wagon."

"That's the lifeboat, sure."

"No, by——, it's—it's an omnibus."[29]

"I tell you it's a lifeboat."

"It is not! It's an omnibus. I can see it plain. See? One of those big hotel omnibuses."

"By thunder, you're right. It's an omnibus, sure as fate. What do you suppose they are doing with an omnibus? Maybe they are going around collecting the lifecrew, hey?"

"That's it, likely. Look! There's a fellow waving a little black flag. He's standing on the steps of the omnibus. There come those other two fellows. Now they're all talking together. Look at the fellow with the flag. Maybe he ain't waving it!"

"That ain't a flag, is it? That's his coat. Why, certainly, that's his coat."

---

28. *Obstreperous* (əb strep′ ər əs) means "unruly."

Reading Strategy Summarizing *Summarize this paragraph in your own words.*

---

29. An *omnibus,* or bus, would have been pulled by horses during this time period.

"So it is. It's his coat. He's taken it off and is waving it around his head. But would you look at him swing it!"

"Oh, say, there isn't any lifesaving station there. That's just a winter resort hotel omnibus that has brought over some of the boarders to see us drown."

"What's that idiot with the coat mean? What's he signaling, anyhow?"

"It looks as if he were trying to tell us to go north. There must be a lifesaving station up there."

"No! He thinks we're fishing. Just giving us a merry hand. See? Ah, there, Willie."

"Well, I wish I could make something out of those signals. What do you suppose he means?"

"He don't mean anything. He's just playing."

"Well, if he'd just signal us to try the surf again, or to go to sea and wait, or go north, or go south, or go to hell—there would be some reason in it. But look at him. He just stands there and keeps his coat revolving like a wheel. The ass!"

"There come more people."

"Now there's quite a mob. Look! Isn't that a boat?"

"Where? Oh, I see where you mean. No, that's no boat."

"That fellow is still waving his coat."

"He must think we like to see him do that. Why don't he quit it. It don't mean anything."

"I don't know. I think he is trying to make us go north. It must be that there's a lifesaving station there somewhere."

"Say, he ain't tired yet. Look at 'im wave."

"Wonder how long he can keep that up. He's been revolving his coat ever since he caught sight of us. He's an idiot. Why aren't they getting men to bring a boat out. A fishing boat—one of those big yawls[30]—could come out here all right. Why don't he do something?"

"Oh, it's all right, now."

"They'll have a boat out here for us in less than no time, now that they've seen us."

A faint yellow tone came into the sky over the low land. The shadows on the sea slowly deepened. The wind bore coldness with it, and the men began to shiver.

"Holy smoke!" said one, allowing his voice to express his impious mood, "if we keep on monkeying out here! If we've got to flounder out here all night!"

"Oh, we'll never have to stay here all night! Don't you worry. They've seen us now, and it won't be long before they'll come chasing out after us."

The shore grew dusky. The man waving a coat blended gradually into this gloom, and it swallowed in the same manner the omnibus and the group of people. The spray, when it dashed uproariously over the side, made the voyagers shrink and swear like men who were being branded.

"I'd like to catch the chump who waved the coat. I feel like soaking him one, just for luck."

"Why? What did he do?"

"Oh, nothing, but then he seemed so damned cheerful."

In the meantime the oiler rowed, and then the correspondent rowed, and then the oiler rowed. Gray-faced and bowed forward, they mechanically, turn by turn, plied the leaden oars. The form of the lighthouse had vanished from the southern horizon, but finally a pale star appeared, just lifting from the sea. The streaked saffron[31] in the west passed before the all-merging darkness, and the sea to the east was black. The land had vanished, and was expressed only by the low and drear thunder of the surf.

"If I am going to be drowned—if I am going to be drowned—if I am going to be drowned, why, in the name of the seven mad gods who rule the sea, was I allowed to come thus far and contemplate sand and trees? Was I brought here merely to have my nose dragged away as I was about to nibble the sacred cheese of life?"

The patient captain, drooped over the water jar, was sometimes obliged to speak to the oarsman.

"Keep her head up! Keep her head up!"

"'Keep her head up,' sir." The voices were weary and low.

---

30. A *yawl* is a sailboat with two masts, the large mast near the front of the boat and the smaller one near the back.

---

31. Here, *saffron* means "yellow-orange in color."

This was surely a quiet evening. All save the oarsman lay heavily and listlessly in the boat's bottom. As for him, his eyes were just capable of noting the tall black waves that swept forward in a most sinister silence, save for an occasional subdued growl of a crest.

The cook's head was on a thwart, and he looked without interest at the water under his nose. He was deep in other scenes. Finally he spoke. "Billie," he murmured, dreamfully, "what kind of pie do you like best?"

V

"Pie," said the oiler and the correspondent, agitatedly. "Don't talk about those things, blast you!"

"Well," said the cook, "I was just thinking about ham sandwiches, and—"

A night on the sea in an open boat is a long night. As darkness settled finally, the shine of the light, lifting from the sea in the south, changed to full gold. On the northern horizon a new light appeared, a small bluish gleam on the edge of the waters. These two lights were the furniture of the world. Otherwise there was nothing but waves.

Two men huddled in the stern, and distances were so magnificent in the dinghy that the rower was enabled to keep his feet partly warmed by thrusting them under his companions. Their legs indeed extended far under the rowing seat until they touched the feet of the captain forward. Sometimes, despite the efforts of the tired oarsman, a wave came piling into the boat, an icy wave of the night, and the chilling water soaked them anew. They would twist their bodies for a moment and groan, and sleep the dead sleep once more, while the water in the boat gurgled about them as the craft rocked.

The plan of the oiler and the correspondent was for one to row until he lost the ability, and then arouse the other from his seawater couch in the bottom of the boat.

The oiler plied the oars until his head drooped forward, and the overpowering sleep blinded him. And he rowed yet afterward. Then he touched a man in the bottom of the boat, and called his name. "Will you spell me for a little while?" he said, meekly.

"Sure, Billie," said the correspondent, awakening and dragging himself to a sitting position. They exchanged places carefully, and the oiler, cuddling down in the seawater at the cook's side, seemed to go to sleep instantly.

The particular violence of the sea had ceased. The waves came without snarling. The obligation of the man at the oars was to keep the boat headed so that the tilt of the rollers would not capsize her, and to preserve her from filling when the crests rushed past. The black waves were silent and hard to be seen in the darkness. Often one was almost upon the boat before the oarsman was aware.

In a low voice the correspondent addressed the captain. He was not sure that the captain was awake, although this iron man seemed to be always awake. "Captain, shall I keep her making for that light north, sir?"

The same steady voice answered him. "Yes. Keep it about two points off the port bow."[32]

The cook had tied a life belt around himself in order to get even the warmth which this clumsy cork contrivance could donate, and he seemed almost stove-like when a rower, whose teeth invariably chattered wildly as soon as he ceased his labor, dropped down to sleep.

The correspondent, as he rowed, looked down at the two men sleeping under foot. The cook's arm was around the oiler's shoulders, and, with their fragmentary clothing and haggard faces, they were the babes of the sea, a grotesque rendering of the old babes in the wood.[33]

Later he must have grown stupid at his work, for suddenly there was a growling of water, and a crest came with a roar and a swash into the boat, and it was a wonder that it did not set the cook afloat in his life belt. The cook continued to sleep, but the oiler sat up, blinking his eyes and shaking with the new cold.

---

32. The *bow* is the forward part of a boat or ship. The port bow, then, would be the left side of the forward part.
33. In the fairytale "Babes in the Wood," two children are left after their parents die. An uncle tries to have them killed, but the children are spared. Alone in the woods, the children are lulled to sleep by birds.

Big Idea Naturalism *From your understanding of Naturalism, why might discussion of food be dangerous, rather than pleasantly distracting, given the circumstances?*

Reading Strategy Summarizing *Summarize this paragraph. How have the crew's challenges changed?*

Moonlight, 1885. Albert Pinkham Ryder. Oil on canvas, 16 x 17¾ in. Smithsonian American Art Museum, Washington, DC.

"Oh, I'm awful sorry, Billie," said the correspondent, contritely.

"That's all right, old boy," said the oiler, and lay down again and was asleep.

Presently it seemed that even the captain dozed, and the correspondent thought that he was the one man afloat on all the oceans. The wind had a voice as it came over the waves, and it was sadder than the end.

There was a long, loud swishing astern of the boat, and a gleaming trail of phosphorescence, like blue flame, was furrowed on the black waters. It might have been made by a monstrous knife.

Then there came a stillness, while the correspondent breathed with the open mouth and looked at the sea.

Suddenly there was another swish and another long flash of bluish light, and this time it was alongside the boat, and might almost have been reached with an oar. The correspondent saw an enormous fin speed like a shadow through the water, hurling the crystalline spray and leaving the long glowing trail.

The correspondent looked over his shoulder at the captain. His face was hidden, and he seemed to be asleep. He looked at the babes of the sea. They certainly were asleep. So, being bereft[34] of sympathy, he leaned a little way to one side and swore softly into the sea.

But the thing did not then leave the vicinity of the boat. Ahead or astern, on one side or the other, at intervals long or short, fled the long sparkling streak, and there was to be heard the whiroo of the dark fin. The speed and power of the thing was greatly to be admired. It cut the water like a gigantic and keen projectile. The presence of this biding thing did not affect the man with the same horror that it would if he had been a picnicker. He simply looked at the sea dully and swore in an undertone.

Nevertheless, it is true that he did not wish to be alone with the thing. He wished one of his companions to awaken by chance and keep him company with it. But the captain hung motionless over the water jar and the oiler and the cook in the bottom of the boat were plunged in slumber.

VI

"If I am going to be drowned—if I am going to be drowned—if I am going to be drowned, why, in the name of the seven mad gods who rule the sea, was I allowed to come thus far and contemplate sand and trees?"

During this dismal night, it may be remarked that a man would conclude that it was really the intention of the seven mad gods to drown him, despite the abominable injustice of it. For it was certainly an abominable injustice to drown a man who had worked so hard, so hard. The man felt it would be a crime most unnatural. Other

---

34. *Bereft* means "lacking something needed."

Literary Element Author's Purpose *Why does Crane have the correspondent react this way to the shark?*

people had drowned at sea since galleys[35] swarmed with painted sails, but still—

When it occurs to a man that nature does not regard him as important, and that she feels she would not maim the universe by disposing of him, he at first wishes to throw bricks at the temple, and he hates deeply the fact that there are no bricks and no temples. Any visible expression of nature would surely be pelted with his jeers.

Then, if there be no tangible thing to hoot he feels, perhaps, the desire to confront a personification and indulge in pleas, bowed to one knee, and with hands supplicant, saying: "Yes, but I love myself."

A high cold star on a winter's night is the word he feels that she says to him. Thereafter he knows the pathos[36] of his situation.

The men in the dinghy had not discussed these matters, but each had, no doubt, reflected upon them in silence and according to his mind. There was seldom any expression upon their faces save the general one of complete weariness. Speech was devoted to the business of the boat.

To chime the notes of his emotion, a verse mysteriously entered the correspondent's head. He had even forgotten that he had forgotten this verse, but it suddenly was in his mind.

> A soldier of the Legion[37] lay dying in
>   Algiers,[38]
> There was lack of woman's nursing,
>   there was dearth of woman's tears;
> But a comrade stood beside him, and he
>   took that comrade's hand,
> And he said: "I never more shall see my
>   own, my native land."[39]

In his childhood, the correspondent had been made acquainted with the fact that a soldier of the Legion lay dying in Algiers, but he had never regarded it as important. Myriads of his schoolfellows had informed him of the soldier's plight, but the dinning[40] had naturally ended by making him perfectly indifferent. He had never considered it his affair that a soldier of the Legion lay dying in Algiers, nor had it appeared to him as a matter for sorrow. It was less to him than the breaking of a pencil's point.

Now, however, it quaintly came to him as a human, living thing. It was no longer merely a picture of a few throes[41] in the breast of a poet, meanwhile drinking tea and warming his feet at the grate; it was an actuality—stern, mournful, and fine.

The correspondent plainly saw the soldier. He lay on the sand with his feet out straight and still. While his pale left hand was upon his chest in an attempt to thwart the going of his life, the blood came between his fingers. In the far Algerian distance, a city of low square forms was set against a sky that was faint with the last sunset hues. The correspondent, plying the oars and dreaming of the slow and slower movements of the lips of the soldier, was moved by a profound and perfectly impersonal comprehension. He was sorry for the soldier of the Legion who lay dying in Algiers.

The thing which had followed the boat and waited had evidently grown bored at the delay. There was no longer to be heard the slash of the cut water, and there was no longer the flame of the long trail. The light in the north still glimmered, but it was apparently no nearer to the boat. Sometimes the boom of the surf rang in the correspondent's ears, and he turned the craft seaward then and rowed harder. Southward, some one had evidently built a watch fire on the beach. It was too low and too far to be seen, but it made a shimmering, roseate reflection upon the bluff back of it, and this could be discerned from the boat. The wind came stronger, and sometimes a wave suddenly raged out like a mountain cat and there was to be seen the sheen and sparkle of a broken crest.

The captain, in the bow, moved on his water jar and sat erect. "Pretty long night," he observed

---

35. A *galley* is a medieval ship propelled by sails and a row (or rows) of oars on either side.
36. *Pathos* means "deep sadness."
37. *Legion* refers to the French Foreign Legion, an army composed mainly of foreign volunteers.
38. *Algiers* (al jērz') is the capital of Algeria, a country in northern Africa that was once ruled by France.
39. This verse compresses the first stanza of "Bingen on the Rhine" by English poet Caroline E. S. Norton (1808–1877).

40. *Dinning* means "insistent repetition."
41. *Throes* are pains.

Reading Strategy   Summarizing *Summarize this passage. Why has the correspondent's reaction to the poem changed since he was a child?*

to the correspondent. He looked at the shore. "Those lifesaving people take their time."

"Did you see that shark playing around?"

"Yes, I saw him. He was a big fellow, all right."

"Wish I had known you were awake."

Later the correspondent spoke into the bottom of the boat.

"Billie!" There was a slow and gradual disentanglement. "Billie, will you spell me?"

"Sure," said the oiler.

As soon as the correspondent touched the cold comfortable seawater in the bottom of the boat, and had huddled close to the cook's life belt he was deep in sleep, despite the fact that his teeth played all the popular airs. This sleep was so good to him that it was but a moment before he heard a voice call his name in a tone that demonstrated the last stages of exhaustion. "Will you spell me?"

"Sure, Billie."

The light in the north had mysteriously vanished, but the correspondent took his course from the wide-awake captain.

Later in the night they took the boat farther out to sea, and the captain directed the cook to take one oar at the stern and keep the boat facing the seas. He was to call out if he should hear the thunder of the surf. This plan enabled the oiler and the correspondent to get respite together. "We'll give those boys a chance to get into shape again," said the captain. They curled down and, after a few preliminary chatterings and trembles, slept once more the dead sleep. Neither knew they had bequeathed to the cook the company of another shark, or perhaps the same shark.

As the boat caroused on the waves, spray occasionally bumped over the side and gave them a fresh soaking, but this had no power to break their repose. The ominous slash of the wind and the water affected them as it would have affected mummies.

"Boys," said the cook, with the notes of every reluctance in his voice, "she's drifted in pretty close. I guess one of you had better take her to sea again." The correspondent, aroused, heard the crash of the toppled crests.

As he was rowing, the captain gave him some whiskey and water, and this steadied the chills out of him. "If I ever get ashore and anybody shows me even a photograph of an oar—"

At last there was a short conversation.

"Billie . . . Billie, will you spell me?"

"Sure," said the oiler.

VII

When the correspondent again opened his eyes, the sea and the sky were each of the gray hue of the dawning. Later, carmine and gold was painted upon the waters. The morning appeared finally, in its splendor, with a sky of pure blue, and the sunlight flamed on the tips of the waves.

On the distant dunes were set many little black cottages, and a tall white windmill reared above them. No man, nor dog, nor bicycle appeared on the beach. The cottages might have formed a deserted village.

The voyagers scanned the shore. A conference was held in the boat. "Well," said the captain, "if no help is coming, we might better try a run through the surf right away. If we stay out here much longer we will be too weak to do anything for ourselves at all." The others silently acquiesced in this reasoning. The boat was headed for the beach. The correspondent wondered if none ever ascended the tall wind-tower, and if then they never looked seaward. This tower was a giant, standing with its back to the plight of the ants. It represented in a degree, to the correspondent, the serenity of nature amid the struggles of the individual—nature in the wind, and nature in the vision of men. She did not seem cruel to him then, nor beneficent, nor treacherous, nor wise. But she was indifferent, flatly indifferent. It is, perhaps, plausible that a man in this situation, impressed with the unconcern of the universe, should see the innumerable flaws of his life and have them taste wickedly in his mind and wish for another chance. A distinction between right and wrong seems absurdly clear to him, then, in this new ignorance of the grave-edge, and he understands that if he were given another opportunity he would mend his

Reading Strategy Summarizing *What is the main idea expressed in this paragraph?*

Big Idea Naturalism *How is Naturalism apparent in the correspondent's attitude in this paragraph?*

conduct and his words, and be better and brighter during an introduction, or at a tea.

"Now, boys," said the captain, "she is going to swamp sure. All we can do is to work her in as far as possible, and then when she swamps, pile out and scramble for the beach. Keep cool now, and don't jump until she swamps sure."

The oiler took the oars. Over his shoulders he scanned the surf. "Captain," he said, "I think I'd better bring her about, and keep her head-on to the seas and back her in."

"All right, Billie," said the captain. "Back her in." The oiler swung the boat then and, seated in the stern, the cook and the correspondent were obliged to look over their shoulders to contemplate the lonely and indifferent shore.

The monstrous inshore rollers heaved the boat high until the men were again enabled to see the white sheets of water scudding[42] up the slanted beach. "We won't get in very close," said the captain. Each time a man could wrest his attention from the rollers, he turned his glance toward the shore, and in the expression of the eyes during this contemplation there was a singular quality. The correspondent, observing the others, knew that they were not afraid, but the full meaning of their glances was shrouded.

As for himself, he was too tired to grapple fundamentally with the fact. He tried to coerce his mind into thinking of it, but the mind was dominated at this time by the muscles, and the muscles said they did not care. It merely occurred to him that if he should drown it would be a shame.

There were no hurried words, no pallor,[43] no plain agitation. The men simply looked at the shore. "Now, remember to get well clear of the boat when you jump," said the captain.

Seaward the crest of a roller suddenly fell with a thunderous crash, and the long white comber[44] came roaring down upon the boat.

Veiled Moon, 1995. Jane Wilson. Oil on linen, 18 x 18 in. Fischbach Gallery, NY.
Viewing the Art: How is nature portrayed in the painting?

"Steady now," said the captain. The men were silent. They turned their eyes from the shore to the comber and waited. The boat slid up the incline, leaped at the furious top, bounced over it, and swung down the long back of the wave. Some water had been shipped and the cook bailed it out.

But the next crest crashed also. The tumbling boiling flood of white water caught the boat and whirled it almost perpendicular. Water swarmed in from all sides. The correspondent had his hands on the gunwale at this time, and when the water entered at that place he swiftly withdrew his fingers, as if he objected to wetting them.

The little boat, drunken with this weight of water, reeled and snuggled deeper into the sea.

"Bail her out, cook! Bail her out," said the captain.

"All right, Captain," said the cook.

"Now, boys, the next one will do for us, sure," said the oiler. "Mind to jump clear of the boat."

---

42. *Scudding* means "moving swiftly."
43. Pallor is paleness or the lack of natural or healthy color.
44. A comber is a long, rolling wave that curls over and breaks.

Vocabulary

coerce (kō urs′) *v.* to force

The third wave moved forward, huge, furious, implacable.[45] It fairly swallowed the dinghy, and almost simultaneously the men tumbled into the sea. A piece of lifebelt had lain in the bottom of the boat, and as the correspondent went overboard he held this to his chest with his left hand.

The January water was icy, and he reflected immediately that it was colder than he had expected to find it off the coast of Florida. This appeared to his dazed mind as a fact important enough to be noted at the time. The coldness of the water was sad; it was tragic. This fact was somehow so mixed and confused with his opinion of his own situation that it seemed almost a proper reason for tears. The water was cold.

When he came to the surface he was conscious of little but the noisy water. Afterward he saw his companions in the sea. The oiler was ahead in the race. He was swimming strongly and rapidly. Off to the correspondent's left, the cook's great white and corked back bulged out of the water, and in the rear the captain was hanging with his one good hand to the keel[46] of the overturned dinghy.

There is a certain immovable quality to a shore, and the correspondent wondered at it amid the confusion of the sea.

It seemed also very attractive, but the correspondent knew that it was a long journey, and he paddled leisurely. The piece of life preserver lay under him, and sometimes he whirled down the incline of a wave as if he were on a hand-sled.

But finally he arrived at a place in the sea where travel was beset with difficulty. He did not pause swimming to inquire what manner of current had caught him, but there his progress ceased. The shore was set before him like a bit of scenery on a stage, and he looked at it and understood with his eyes each detail of it.

As the cook passed, much farther to the left, the captain was calling to him, "Turn over on your back, cook! Turn over on your back and use the oar."

"All right, sir." The cook turned on his back, and, paddling with an oar, went ahead as if he were a canoe.

Presently the boat also passed to the left of the correspondent with the captain clinging with one hand to the keel. He would have appeared like a man raising himself to look over a board fence, if it were not for the extraordinary gymnastics of the boat. The correspondent marvelled that the captain could still hold to it.

They passed on, nearer to shore—the oiler, the cook, the captain—and following them went the water jar, bouncing gayly over the seas.

The correspondent remained in the grip of this strange new enemy—a current. The shore, with its white slope of sand and its green bluff, topped with little silent cottages, was spread like a picture before him. It was very near to him then, but he was impressed as one who in a gallery looks at a scene from Brittany[47] or Holland.

He thought: "I am going to drown? Can it be possible? Can it be possible? Can it be possible?" Perhaps an individual must consider his own death to be the final phenomenon of nature.

But later a wave perhaps whirled him out of this small deadly current, for he found suddenly that he could again make progress toward the shore. Later still, he was aware that the captain, clinging with one hand to the keel of the dinghy, had his face turned away from the shore and toward him, and was calling his name. "Come to the boat! Come to the boat!"

> *Perhaps an individual must consider his own death to be the final phenomenon of nature.*

---

45. *Implacable* means "unrelenting" or "unyielding."
46. The *keel* runs along the center of the bottom of a boat. It supports the boat's frame and gives the boat stability.

Literary Element Author's Purpose *Why do you think Crane chose to narrate this part of the story from the correspondent's point of view?*

47. *Brittany* is a region in northwestern France.

In his struggle to reach the captain and the boat, he reflected that when one gets properly wearied, drowning must really be a comfortable arrangement, a cessation of hostilities accompanied by a large degree of relief, and he was glad of it, for the main thing in his mind for some moments had been horror of the temporary agony. He did not wish to be hurt.

Presently he saw a man running along the shore. He was undressing with most remarkable speed. Coat, trousers, shirt, everything flew magically off him.

"Come to the boat," called the captain.

"All right, Captain." As the correspondent paddled, he saw the captain let himself down to bottom and leave the boat. Then the correspondent performed his one little marvel of the voyage. A large wave caught him and flung him with ease and supreme speed completely over the boat and far beyond it. It struck him even then as an event in gymnastics, and a true miracle of the sea. An overturned boat in the surf is not a plaything to a swimming man.

The correspondent arrived in water that reached only to his waist, but his condition did not enable him to stand for more than a moment. Each wave knocked him into a heap, and the undertow pulled at him.

Then he saw the man who had been running and undressing, and undressing and running, come bounding into the water. He dragged ashore the cook, and then waded toward the captain, but the captain waved him away, and sent him to the correspondent. He was naked, naked as a tree in winter, but a halo was about his head, and he shone like a saint. He gave a strong pull, and a long drag, and a bully heave at the correspondent's hand. The correspondent, schooled in the minor formulæ, said: "Thanks, old man." But suddenly the man cried: "What's that?" He pointed a swift finger. The correspondent said: "Go."

In the shallows, face downward, lay the oiler. His forehead touched sand that was periodically, between each wave, clear of the sea.

The correspondent did not know all that transpired afterward. When he achieved safe ground he fell, striking the sand with each particular part of his body. It was as if he had dropped from a roof, but the thud was grateful to him.

It seems that instantly the beach was populated with men with blankets, clothes, and flasks, and women with coffeepots and all the remedies sacred to their minds. The welcome of the land to the men from the sea was warm and generous, but a still and dripping shape was carried slowly up the beach, and the land's welcome for it could only be the different and sinister hospitality of the grave.

When it came night, the white waves paced to and fro in the moonlight, and the wind brought the sound of the great sea's voice to the men on shore, and they felt that they could then be interpreters. ∾

Moonrise on the Seashore, 1821. Caspar David Friedrich. Oil on canvas, 22½ x 28½ in. Hermitage, St. Petersburg, Russia

Reading Strategy Summarizing *Summarize this paragraph and explain how the correspondent's goals have changed.*

Big Idea Naturalism *What ironic prophecy is fulfilled by the oiler's death?*

RESPONDING AND THINKING CRITICALLY

Respond

1. How did you react when you realized the correspondent survives but the oiler does not?

Recall and Interpret

2. (a)Summarize the situation in which the four men find themselves in part I. (b)From the discussion that three of the men have at the end of part I, what might you infer about each man's character?

3. (a)How does each man behave during the night at sea (parts V and VI)? (b)What can you infer about their characters from their actions?

4. (a)What is the outcome of the story? (b)How is the outcome ironic, and what might this imply about nature?

Analyze and Evaluate

5. (a)List several similes and metaphors Crane uses in the story. (b)What effect do these comparisons have on the reader?

6. How does Crane use foreshadowing to help prepare the reader for future events? Give specific examples.

7. Could the emotional effect of this story be conveyed just as well in the form of a newspaper article about the shipwreck and the men's struggle to survive? Explain.

Connect

8. Describe a time when you were part of a group in a difficult or dangerous situation. How did you feel about the others in the group as a result of your shared experience?

9. **Big Idea** **Naturalism** How might being lost at sea influence the crew's view of nature in a way that a less dangerous accident might not?

The Untouched Landscape

Moonlit Shipwreck at Sea was painted in 1901 by Thomas Moran, one of several American landscape painters known collectively as the Hudson River school. The Hudson River school artists were known for their use of light and shadow and their highly Romantic style. Their paintings attempted to evoke a specific mood and emotional state, often in order to express the sublime in nature. Rarely were the paintings simple observations.

Look at Moran's painting and answer these questions:

1. (a)What is the subject of the painting? (b)How is the human element treated? (c)How does this compare to Crane's story?

2. (a)What is the effect of the light and shadow in the painting? (b)How is this effect comparable to Crane's literary effects in "The Open Boat"?

3. (a)From what perspective is the viewer watching this scene? (b)How does this perspective contribute to the mood of the painting?

Literary Element **Author's Purpose**

An author can have more than one purpose in writing a literary work. For example, a short story writer's main purpose might be to convey an idea or present a philosophical view of life. In addition, the writer might have several other purposes, such as to construct a suspenseful plot, to create sympathetic characters, or to entertain the reader through humor, irony, or figurative language.

1. (a)What do you think was Crane's main purpose in writing "The Open Boat"? (b)Identify at least one of Crane's other purposes.

2. On page 578, the narrator says of the crew, ". . . there was this comradeship that the correspondent, for instance, who had been taught to be cynical of men, knew even at the time was the best experience of his life." What might Crane's purpose have been in having the narrator make this statement?

Review: Conflict

As you learned on page 547, **conflict** refers to the central struggle between two opposing forces in a story. External conflict exists when a character struggles against an outside force, such as another person, nature, society, or fate. Internal conflict is a struggle between two opposing thoughts or desires within the mind of a character.

Partner Activity With a partner, discuss the conflicts that the correspondent faces in "The Open Boat." Which type of conflict—internal or external—is more prevalent? Create a chart like the one below, filled in with textual evidence. With your partner, discuss whether one type of conflict is more prevalent or if they are equal.

External Conflict	Internal Conflict

Reading Strategy **Summarizing**

Summarizing Theme As the men become more resigned to the reality of their circumstances on the boat, the theme, or central message, of the story becomes clear. By analyzing the thoughts and dialogue of the crew and the description and events in the story, you can piece together the author's message about life.

1. Summarize the theme you feel is most important in the story.

2. What details from the story support your summary of the theme?

Vocabulary **Practice**

Practice with Context Clues Read the paragraph below. Use context clues around the boldfaced vocabulary words to make an informed guess as to what each word means.

An **emphatic** crash in the alley jolted Miranda awake. She was usually fearless, but the noise gave her an eerie, **uncanny** feeling. Miranda had to **coerce** herself to take a look. *It's nothing,* she thought frankly, growing less afraid. *I know it's nothing,* she repeated **ingenuously.** Outside, she shined a flashlight into the alley. A portly raccoon glanced at Miranda from a trashcan and then **impudently** went back to work, boldly clanking about as if he were all by himself.

Academic Vocabulary

Here are two words from the vocabulary list on page R86. These words will help you think, write, and talk about the selection.

technique (tek nēk′) *n.* the method or manner in which something is treated

create (krē āt′) *v.* to bring into existence or being

Practice and Apply
1. Give an example of a **technique** Crane uses to show internal conflict.
2. What mood does he **create** by describing the birds on page 576?

Writing About Literature

Evaluate Author's Craft Throughout "The Open Boat," Crane uses figures of speech—such as metaphors, similes, personification, and symbols—to help readers visualize and gain a deeper understanding of what he describes. Choose examples of figurative language from the text and determine what overall effect is created by Crane's use of these devices. Then write a short essay in which you evaluate the author's craft, analyzing how he uses figurative language to enhance the story and evaluating how successful he is. Use a graphic organizer like the one below to help you organize your thoughts.

After you complete your draft, exchange it with a partner to evaluate each other's work and suggest revisions. Make sure the examples of figurative language support the writer's evaluation of the author's craft. Then proofread and edit your draft for errors in spelling, grammar, and punctuation.

Interdisciplinary Activity: Film

Outlining a Screenplay "The Open Boat" is separated into seven parts. Create an outline for a screenplay by dividing the parts of the story into scenes of the movie, noting which parts you might cut and which you might focus on. The middle of the story has little action; think about how you might use other techniques, such as narration, to evoke the changing feelings of the characters. Compare your outline with a classmate's to see whether you focused on similar aspects of the story.

Crane's Language and Style

Varying Sentence Length Note the effect of Crane's varied sentence lengths in the passage below:

The January water was icy, and he reflected immediately that it was colder than he had expected to find it off the coast of Florida. This appeared to his dazed mind as a fact important enough to be noted at the time. The coldness of the water was sad; it was tragic. This fact was somehow so mixed and confused with his opinion of his own situation that it seemed almost a proper reason for tears. The water was cold.

—from "The Open Boat," page 588

Note how Crane uses short, direct sentences within the lengthier description of the correspondent's reaction to the water. These short, abrupt sentences evoke the shock of the cold water.

To make your writing interesting, vary sentence length. Too many short sentences can make your writing choppy, whereas too many long, complicated sentences may be confusing. Think about the effect you are trying to create with your writing and how the flow or rhythm of your sentences can enhance that effect.

- Shorter, simple sentences can have a fast-paced, abrupt effect.
- Compound and compound-complex sentences are usually longer than simple sentences and have a slow, meandering quality.

Activity With a partner, scan the story for other examples of varied sentence length and determine how they contribute to the story's tone and mood.

Revising Check

Sentence Length Work with a partner to review and revise the variety of sentence length in your essay for "The Open Boat."

Literature Online Web Activities For eFlashcards, Selection Quick Checks, and other Web activities, go to www.glencoe.com.

To Build a Fire

MEET JACK LONDON

In 1897 Jack London left college and went to the Yukon to join the Klondike gold rush. He never found gold, but he did find something that proved more precious to him: a wealth of raw material for the stories that eventually made him famous.

"I would rather be ashes than dust!"

—Jack London

An Adventurous Life Born in 1876 in San Francisco to an unstable mother and a father who refused to claim him, London was raised mainly by a family friend and a stepsister. From the age of eleven, he worked to earn money to help put food on his family's table. London loved the sea, so he hung around the harbor, doing odd jobs and learning to be an expert sailor. While still in his teens, he signed on to a schooner sailing to Siberia. From that adventure came his first published story.

At eighteen, London set off to ride the rails, living the life of a drifter as he traveled across the country on freight trains. This journey became a turning point in his life as he saw up close the raw, painful lives of men and women who did not seem to belong anywhere in society. As a result of the conditions he saw, London vowed to educate himself so he could survive by his mental powers rather than by his physical strength.

After completing high school in just one year, London attended the University of California at Berkeley for a semester before rushing off to the Klondike. He failed to strike it rich, however, so he came home and turned to writing for his

livelihood. In 1903, London published *The Call of the Wild*, the novel that firmly established his reputation. Before long, he became the country's highest-paid author—a stunning reversal of fortune for the once-impoverished writer.

Struggle to Make Ends Meet Throughout his life, London worked under pressure to support not only himself but also numerous family members and friends. He set himself the task of writing at least a thousand publishable words every day, and he rarely deviated from that schedule. But despite publishing more than fifty books and becoming the country's first millionaire author, London habitually spent more money than he earned, and he often wrote stories in order to pay off urgent debts.

In the last years of his life, London bought a ranch in northern California and began building his dream house, Wolf House, on it. In 1913, shortly before he was to move into the newly completed house, it burned down. The fire devastated London both emotionally and financially. He continued to live on the ranch but never rebuilt the house. Three years later, plagued by severe health problems and financial difficulties, London died. He was only forty years old.

Jack London was born in 1876 and died in 1916.

Literature Online **Author Search** For more about Jack London, go to www.glencoe.com.

Connecting to the Story

In "To Build a Fire," a lone man is pitted against a relentless Yukon winter. As you read the story, think about the following questions:

• When have you experienced extreme weather?
• How did it affect you physically and mentally?

Building Background

On July 17, 1897, sixty-eight miners arrived in Seattle on the steamship *Portland,* carrying boxes, suitcases, and gunnysacks filled with more than two tons of gold. Thousands of prospectors soon poured into the Klondike region of Canada, where gold had been discovered in the sands of Bonanza Creek, a tributary of the Klondike River. Many of the prospectors were unprepared for the brutal conditions in the north, where temperatures could sink below minus fifty degrees Fahrenheit.

The Klondike River is a tributary of the Yukon River, which is about 1,875 miles long and has a drainage basin of 330,000 square miles in the Yukon Territory in Canada and in the eastern and central parts of Alaska. The Yukon and its tributaries flow across Alaska's interior plateau, which comprises millions of acres of subarctic forest.

Setting Purposes for Reading

Big Idea Naturalism

A battle with nature is a common conflict in literature, particularly in Naturalist literature. As you read "To Build a Fire," consider whether humans ever win such a battle.

Literary Element Setting

The **setting** is the time and place in which the events of a literary work occur. Naturalist writers generally emphasize the setting, focusing on the importance of the environment in defining human character. As you read, note how London uses the setting to develop plot and character.

• See Literary Terms Handbook, p. R16.

Literature Online Interactive Literary Elements Handbook To review or learn more about the literary elements, go to www.glencoe.com.

Reading Strategy Analyzing Cause-and-Effect Relationships

Cause and effect refers to a relationship in which one event brings about a second event. The second event occurs not only after the first event but as a consequence of it. A cause may have several effects, and an effect may, in turn, cause other events to happen. In "To Build a Fire," cause-and-effect relationships are essential to the plot.

Reading Tip: Taking Notes Use a map to record cause-and-effect relationships in the story.

Cause	Effect
The temperature is colder than fifty below zero.	The man's spittle crackles in the air before falling to the snow.

Vocabulary

intangible (in tan´ jə bəl) *adj.* not easily defined or evaluated by the mind; p. 595 *Volunteer work brings not money but intangible benefits.*

immortality (im ôr tal´ ə tē) *n.* the condition of having eternal life; p. 596 *Unlike mortals, who live and then die, the gods in Greek myths enjoyed immortality.*

compel (kəm pel´) *n.* to force; p. 598 *His tardiness and lack of hustle compelled the coach to bench him.*

intervene (in´ tər vēn´) *v.* to come or lie between; p. 598 *He decided to intervene to prevent the quarrel between the angry motorists from escalating.*

apathetically (ap´ə thet´ i kal ē) *adv.* in a manner showing little interest or concern; p. 603 *Apathetically, she cast her vote, not really caring who would win or lose.*

■ **INDIANA ACADEMIC STANDARDS (pages 594–607)**
11.3 [Identify] story elements such as...setting...
11.2 Develop [reading] strategies...
11.5.9 Write...a literary analysis that develops a thesis...

to Build a Fire

Jack London

D ay had broken cold and gray, exceedingly cold and gray, when the man turned aside from the main Yukon[1] trail and climbed the high earth-bank, where a dim and little-traveled trail led eastward through the fat spruce timberland. It was a steep bank, and he paused for breath at the top, excusing the act to himself by looking at his watch. It was nine o'clock. There was no sun nor hint of sun, though there was not a cloud in the sky. It was a clear day, and yet there seemed an **intangible** pall over the face of things, a subtle gloom that made the day dark, and that was due to the absence of sun.

This fact did not worry the man. He was used to the lack of sun. It had been days since he had seen the sun, and he knew that a few more days must pass before that cheerful orb, due south, would just peep above the skyline and dip immediately from view.

---

1. Here, *Yukon* refers to the Yukon River. The river was a major route to the Klondike gold fields.

Literary Element Setting *What mood do these details create?*

Vocabulary

intangible (in tan´ jə bəl) *adj.* not easily defined or evaluated by the mind

The man flung a look back along the way he had come. The Yukon lay a mile wide and hidden under three feet of ice. On top of this ice were as many feet of snow. It was all pure white, rolling in gentle undulations[2] where the ice jams of the freeze up had formed. North and south, as far as his eye could see, it was unbroken white save for a dark hairline that curved and twisted from around the spruce-covered island to the south, and that curved and twisted away into the north, where it disappeared behind another spruce-covered island. This dark hairline was the trail—the main trail—that led south five hundred miles to the Chilkoot Pass, Dyea, and saltwater; and that led north seventy miles to Dawson, and still on to the north a thousand miles to Nulato,[3] and finally to St. Michael on Bering Sea, a thousand miles and half a thousand more.

But all this—the mysterious, far-reaching hairline trail, the absence of sun from the sky, the tremendous cold, and the strangeness and weirdness of it all—made no impression on the man. It was not because he was long used to it. He was a newcomer in the land, a *chechaquo*,[4] and this was his first winter. The trouble with him was that he was without imagination. He was quick and alert in the things of life, but only in the things, and not in the significances. Fifty degrees below zero meant eighty-odd degrees of frost. Such fact impressed him as being cold and uncomfortable, and that was all. It did not lead him to meditate upon his frailty in general, able only to live within certain narrow limits of heat and cold; and from there on it did not lead him to the conjectural[5] field of **immortality** and man's

---

2. *Undulations* are rippling or wavelike forms or outlines.
3. *Dyea* (dī′ ā) was a mining village in Alaska at the beginning of the route to the gold fields. The trail led through the *Chilkoot Pass* and to northern gold-mining centers in the Yukon such as *Dawson* and *Nulato* (nōō lä′ tō).
4. In the language of the Chinook, Native Americans of the Pacific Northwest, a *chechaquo* (chē chä′ kō) is a "newcomer" or a "tenderfoot."
5. *Conjectural* means "based on guesswork or indefinite evidence."

Literary Element Setting *Why does the author include these details?*

Reading Strategy Cause and Effect *Why is a good imagination especially important in this environment?*

Vocabulary

immortality (im′ ôr tal′ ə tē) *n.* the condition of having eternal life

place in the universe. Fifty degrees below zero stood for a bite of frost that hurt and that must be guarded against by the use of mittens, earflaps, warm moccasins, and thick socks. Fifty degrees below zero was to him just precisely fifty degrees below zero. That there should be anything more to it than that was a thought that never entered his head.

As he turned to go on, he spat speculatively. There was a sharp, explosive crackle that startled him. He spat again. And again, in the air, before it could fall to the snow, the spittle crackled. He knew that at fifty below spittle crackled on the snow, but this spittle had crackled in the air. Undoubtedly it was colder than fifty below—how much colder he did not know. But the temperature did not matter. He was bound for the old claim[6] on the left fork of Henderson Creek, where the boys were already. They had come over across the divide[7] from the Indian Creek country, while he had come the roundabout way to take a look at the possibilities of getting out logs in the spring from the islands in the Yukon. He would be in to camp by six o'clock; a bit after dark, it was true, but the boys would be there, a fire would be going, and a hot supper would be ready. As for lunch, he pressed his hand against the protruding bundle under his jacket. It was also under his shirt, wrapped up in a handkerchief and lying against the naked skin. It was the only way to keep the biscuits from freezing. He smiled agreeably to himself as he thought of those biscuits, each cut open and sopped in bacon grease, and each enclosing a generous slice of fried bacon.

He plunged in among the big spruce trees. The trail was faint. A foot of snow had fallen since the last sled had passed over, and he was glad he was without sled, traveling light. In fact, he carried nothing but the lunch wrapped in the handkerchief. He was surprised, however, at the cold. It certainly was cold, he concluded, as he rubbed his numb nose and cheekbones with his mittened hand. He was a warm-whiskered man, but the hair on his face did not protect the high cheekbones and the eager nose that thrust itself aggressively into the frosty air.

At the man's heel trotted a dog, a big native husky, the proper wolf dog, gray-coated and without

---

6. A *claim* is a piece of land registered for mining rights.
7. A *divide* is a ridge of land that separates two river drainage systems.

any visible or temperamental difference from its brother, the wild wolf. The animal was depressed by the tremendous cold. It knew that it was no time for traveling. Its instinct told a truer tale than was told to the man by the man's judgment. In reality, it was not merely colder than fifty below zero; it was colder than sixty below, than seventy below. It was seventy-five below zero. Since the freezing point is thirty-two above zero, it meant that one hundred and seven degrees of frost obtained. The dog did not know anything about thermometers. Possibly in its brain there was no sharp consciousness of a condition of very cold such as was in the man's brain. But the brute had its instinct. It experienced a vague but menacing apprehension that subdued it and made it slink along at the man's heels, and that made it question eagerly every unwonted[8] movement of the man as if expecting him to go into camp or to seek shelter somewhere and build a fire. The dog had learned fire, and it wanted fire, or else to burrow under the snow and cuddle its warmth away from the air.

> The dog had learned fire, and it wanted fire, or else to burrow under the snow and cuddle its warmth away from the air.

The frozen moisture of its breathing had settled on its fur in a fine powder of frost, and especially were its jowls, muzzle, and eyelashes whitened by its crystalled breath. The man's red beard and mustache were likewise frosted, but more solidly, the deposit taking the form of ice and increasing with every warm, moist breath he exhaled. Also, the man was chewing tobacco, and the muzzle of ice held his lips so rigidly that he was unable to clear his chin when he expelled the juice. The result was that a crystal beard of the color and solidity of amber was increasing its length on his chin. If he fell down it would shatter itself, like glass, into brittle fragments. But he did not mind the appendage.[9] It was the penalty all tobacco-chewers paid in that

country, and he had been out before in two cold snaps. They had not been so cold as this, he knew, but by the spirit thermometer[10] at Sixty Mile he knew they had been registered at fifty below and at fifty-five.

He held on through the level stretch of woods for several miles and dropped down a bank to the frozen bed of a small stream. This was Henderson Creek, and he knew he was ten miles from the forks. He looked at his watch. It was ten o'clock. He was making four miles an hour, and he calculated that he would arrive at the forks at half-past twelve. He decided to celebrate that event by eating his lunch there.

The dog dropped in again at his heels, with a tail drooping discouragement, as the man swung along the creek bed. The furrow[11] of the old sled trail was plainly visible, but a dozen inches of snow covered the marks of the last runners. In a month no man had come up or down that silent creek. The man held steadily on. He was not much given to thinking, and just then particularly he had nothing to think about save that he would eat lunch at the forks and that at six o'clock he would be in camp with the boys. There was nobody to talk to; and, had there been, speech would have been impossible because of the ice muzzle on his mouth. So he continued monotonously to chew tobacco and to increase the length of his amber beard.

Once in a while the thought reiterated[12] itself that it was very cold and that he had never experienced such cold. As he walked along he rubbed his cheekbones and nose with the back of his mittened hand. He did this automatically, now and again changing hands. But rub as he would, the instant he

---

8. *Unwonted* means "unusual."
9. An *appendage* is something that is added on or attached.

10. A *spirit thermometer* is an alcohol thermometer. It is used in areas of extreme cold, where the more common mercury thermometer would freeze.
11. A *furrow* is a long, narrow groove or depression.
12. *Reiterated* means "repeated."

Big Idea Naturalism *Why does the man still chew tobacco even after ice forms on his chin?*

Reading Strategy Cause and Effect *Why doesn't the man seek shelter and build a fire?*

stopped his cheekbones went numb, and the following instant the end of his nose went numb. He was sure to frost his cheeks; he knew that, and experienced a pang of regret that he had not devised a nose strap of the sort Bud wore in cold snaps. Such a strap passed across the cheeks, as well, and saved them. But it didn't matter much, after all. What were frosted cheeks? A bit painful, that was all; they were never serious.

Empty as the man's mind was of thoughts, he was keenly observant, and he noticed the changes in the creek, the curves and bends and timber jams, and always he sharply noted where he placed his feet. Once, coming around the bend, he shied[13] abruptly, like a startled horse, curved away from the place where he had been walking, and retreated several paces back along the trail. The creek he knew was frozen clear to the bottom—no creek could contain water in that arctic winter—but he knew also that there were springs that bubbled out from the hillsides and ran along under the snow and on top the ice of the creek. He knew that the coldest snaps never froze these springs, and he knew likewise their danger. They were traps. They hid pools of water under the snow that might be three inches deep, or three feet. Sometimes a skin of ice half an inch thick covered them, and in turn was covered by the snow. Sometimes they were alternate layers of water and ice skin, so that when one broke through he kept on breaking through for a while, sometimes wetting himself to the waist.

That was why he had shied in such panic. He had felt the give under his feet and heard the crackle of a snow-hidden ice skin. And to get his feet wet in such a temperature meant trouble and danger. At the very least it meant delay, for he would be forced to stop and build a fire, and under its protection to bare his feet while he dried his socks and moccasins. He stood and studied the creek bed and its banks, and decided that the flow of water came from the right. He reflected awhile, rubbing his nose and cheeks, then skirted to the left, stepping gingerly and testing the footing for each step. Once clear of the danger, he took a fresh chew of tobacco and swung along at his four-mile gait.

In the course of the next two hours he came upon similar traps. Usually the snow above the hidden pools had a sunken, candied appearance that advertised the danger. Once again, however,

he had a close call; and once, suspecting danger, he **compelled** the dog to go on in front. The dog did not want to go. It hung back until the man shoved it forward, and then it went quickly across the white, unbroken surface. Suddenly it broke through, floundered to one side, and got away to firmer footing. It had wet its forefeet and legs, and almost immediately the water that clung to it turned to ice. It made quick efforts to lick the ice off its legs, then dropped down in the snow and began to bite out the ice that had formed between the toes. This was a matter of instinct. To permit the ice to remain would mean sore feet. It did not know this. It merely obeyed the mysterious prompting that arose from the deep crypts[14] of its being. But the man knew, having achieved a judgment on the subject, and he removed the mitten from his right hand and helped tear out the ice particles. He did not expose his fingers more than a minute, and was astonished at the swift numbness that smote[15] them. It certainly was cold. He pulled on the mitten hastily, and beat the hand savagely across his chest.

At twelve o'clock the day was at its brightest. Yet the sun was too far south on its winter journey to clear the horizon. The bulge of the earth **intervened** between it and Henderson Creek, where the man walked under a clear sky at noon and cast no shadow. At half-past twelve, to the minute, he arrived at the forks of the creek. He was pleased at the speed he had made. If he kept it up, he would certainly be with the boys by six. He unbuttoned his jacket and shirt and drew forth his lunch. The action consumed no more than a quarter of a minute, yet in that brief moment the numbness laid hold of the exposed fingers. He did not put the mitten on, but, instead, struck the fingers a dozen sharp smashes against his leg. Then he sat down on a snow-covered log to eat. The sting that followed upon the striking of his fingers against his leg

---

14. Here, *crypts* means "hidden recesses."
15. *Smote* (past tense of smite) means "afflicted" or "attacked."

Literary Element Setting *What do these details suggest about the relationship of the man and the environment?*

Vocabulary

compel (kəm pel´) *v.* to force
intervene (in´ tər vēn´) *v.* to come or lie between

---

13. *Shied* means "moved suddenly, as in fear."

Viewing the Photograph: As you look at this photograph, jot down the first five words that come to mind. Which of these words seems most applicable to the story? Explain.

ceased so quickly that he was startled. He had had no chance to take a bite of biscuit. He struck the fingers repeatedly and returned them to the mitten, baring the other hand for the purpose of eating. He tried to take a mouthful, but the ice muzzle prevented. He had forgotten to build a fire and thaw out. He chuckled at his foolishness, and as he chuckled he noted the numbness creeping into his exposed fingers. Also, he noted that the stinging which had first come to his toes when he sat down was already passing away. He wondered whether the toes were warm or numb. He moved them inside the moccasins and decided that they were numb.

He pulled the mitten on hurriedly and stood up. He was a bit frightened. He stamped up and down until the sting returned into the feet. It certainly was cold, was his thought. That man from Sulphur Creek had spoken the truth when telling how cold it sometimes got in the country. And he had laughed at him at the time! That showed one must not be too sure of things. There was no mistake about it, it *was* cold. He strode up and down,

Reading Strategy Cause and Effect *Why does the man suddenly recall the man from Sulphur Creek?*

stamping his feet and threshing his arms, until reassured by the returning warmth. Then he got out matches and proceeded to make a fire. From the undergrowth, where high water of the previous spring had lodged a supply of seasoned twigs, he got his firewood. Working carefully from a small beginning, he soon had a roaring fire, over which he thawed the ice from his face and in the protection of which he ate his biscuits. For the moment the cold of space was outwitted. The dog took satisfaction in the fire, stretching out close enough for warmth and far enough away to escape being singed.

When the man had finished, he filled his pipe and took his comfortable time over a smoke. Then he pulled on his mittens, settled the earflaps of his cap firmly about his ears, and took the creek trail up the left fork. The dog was disappointed and yearned back toward the fire. This man did not know cold. Possibly all the generations of his ancestry had been ignorant of cold, of real cold, of cold one hundred and seven degrees below freezing point. But the dog knew; all its ancestry knew, and it had inherited the knowledge. And it knew that it was not good to walk abroad in such fearful cold. It was the time to lie snug in a hole in the snow and wait for a curtain of cloud to be drawn across the face of outer space whence this cold came. On the other hand, there was no keen intimacy between the dog and the man. The one was the toil slave of the other, and the only caresses it had ever received were the caresses of the whiplash and of harsh and menacing throat sounds that threatened the whiplash. So the dog made no effort to communicate its apprehension to the man. It was not concerned in the welfare of the man; it was for its own sake that it yearned back toward the fire. But the man whistled, and spoke to it with the sound of whiplashes, and the dog swung in at the man's heels and followed after.

The man took a chew of tobacco and proceeded to start a new amber beard. Also, his moist breath quickly powdered with white his mustache, eyebrows, and lashes. There did not seem to be so many springs on the left fork of the Henderson, and for half an hour the man saw no signs of any. And then it happened. At a place where there were no signs, where the soft, unbroken snow seemed to advertise solidity beneath, the man broke through. It was not deep. He wet himself to the knees before he floundered out to the firm crust.

He was angry, and cursed his luck aloud. He had hoped to get into camp with the boys at six o'clock, and this would delay him an hour, for he would have to build a fire and dry out his foot gear. This was imperative[16] at that low temperature—he knew that much; and he turned aside to the bank, which he climbed. On top, tangled in the underbrush about the trunks of several small spruce trees, was a high-water deposit of dry firewood—sticks and twigs, principally, but also larger portions of seasoned branches and fine, dry, last-year's grasses. He threw down several large pieces on top of the snow. This served for a foundation and prevented the young flame from drowning itself in the snow it otherwise would melt. The flame he got by touching a match to a small shred of birch bark that he took from his pocket. This burned even more readily than paper. Placing it on the foundation, he fed the young flame with wisps of dry grass and with the tiniest dry twigs.

He worked slowly and carefully, keenly aware of his danger. Gradually, as the flame grew stronger, he increased the size of the twigs with which he fed it. He squatted in the snow, pulling the twigs out from their entanglement in the brush and feeding directly to the flame. He knew there must be no failure. When it is seventy-five below zero, a man must not fail in his first attempt to build a fire—that is, if his feet are wet. If his feet are dry, and he fails, he can run along the trail for half a mile and restore his circulation. But the circulation of wet and freezing feet cannot be restored by running when it is seventy-five below. No matter how fast he runs, the wet feet will freeze the harder.

All this the man knew. The old-timer on Sulphur Creek had told him about it the previous fall, and now he was appreciating the advice. Already all sensation had gone out of his feet. To build the fire he had been forced to remove his mittens, and the fingers had quickly gone numb. His pace of four miles an hour had kept his heart pumping blood to the surface of his body and to all the extremities. But the instant he stopped, the action of the pump eased down. The cold of space smote the unprotected tip of the planet, and he, being on that unprotected tip, received the full force of the blow. The blood of his body recoiled before it. The blood was alive, like the dog, and like the dog it wanted to hide away and cover itself up from the fearful cold. So long as he walked four miles an hour, he pumped that blood, willy-nilly,[17] to the surface; but now it ebbed[18] away and sank down into the recesses of his body. The extremities were the first to feel its absence. His wet feet froze the faster, and his exposed fingers numbed the faster, though they had not yet begun to freeze. Nose and cheeks were already freezing, while the skin of all his body chilled as it lost its blood.

But he was safe. Toes and nose and cheeks would be only touched by the frost, for the fire was beginning to burn with strength. He was feeding it with twigs the size of his finger. In another minute he would be able to feed it with branches the size of his wrist, and then he could remove his wet foot gear, and, while it dried, he could keep his naked feet warm by the fire, rubbing them at first, of course, with snow. The fire was a success.

---

16. *Imperative* means "absolutely necessary."

Big Idea Naturalism *What view of nature is suggested by this passage?*

---

17. *Willy-nilly* means "without choice."
18. *Ebbed* means "flowed back" or "receded."

He was safe. He remembered the advice of the old-timer on Sulphur Creek, and smiled. The old-timer had been very serious in laying down the law that no man must travel alone in the Klondike after fifty below. Well, here he was; he had had the accident; he was alone; and he had saved himself. Those old-timers were rather womanish, some of them, he thought. All a man had to do was to keep his head, and he was all right. Any man who was a man could travel alone. But it was surprising, the rapidity with which his cheeks and nose were freezing. And he had not thought his fingers could go lifeless in so short a time. Lifeless they were, for he could scarcely make them move together to grip a twig, and they seemed remote from his body and from him. When he touched a twig, he had to look and see whether or not he had hold of it. The wires were pretty well down between him and his finger-ends.

All of which counted for little. There was the fire, snapping and crackling and promising life with every dancing flame. He started to untie his moccasins. They were coated with ice; the thick German socks were like sheaths of iron halfway to the knees; and the moccasin strings were like rods of steel all twisted and knotted as by some conflagration. For a moment he tugged with his numb fingers, then, realizing the folly of it, he drew his sheath-knife.

But before he could cut the strings, it happened. It was his own fault or, rather, his mistake. He should not have built the fire under the spruce tree. He should have built it in the open. But it had been easier to pull twigs from the brush and drop them directly on the fire. Now the tree under which he had done this carried a weight of snow on its boughs. No wind had blown for weeks, and each bough was fully freighted. Each time he had pulled a twig he had communicated a slight agitation to the tree—an imperceptible agitation, so far as he was concerned, but an agitation sufficient to bring about the disaster. High up in the tree one bough capsized its load of snow. This fell on the boughs beneath, capsizing them. This process continued, spreading

> There was the fire, snapping and crackling and promising life with every dancing flame.

out and involving the whole tree. It grew like an avalanche, and it descended without warning upon the man and the fire, and the fire was blotted out! Where it had burned was a mantle of fresh and disordered snow.

The man was shocked. It was as though he had just heard his own sentence of death. For a moment he sat and stared at the spot where the fire had been. Then he grew very calm. Perhaps the old-timer on Sulphur Creek was right. If he had only had a trail mate he would have been in no danger now. The trail mate could have built the fire. Well, it was up to him to build the fire over again, and this second time there must be no failure. Even if he succeeded, he would most likely lose some toes. His feet must be badly frozen by now, and there would be some time before the second fire was ready.

Such were his thoughts, but he did not sit and think them. He was busy all the time they were passing through his mind. He made a new foundation for a fire, this time in the open, where no treacherous tree could blot it out. Next, he gathered dry grasses and tiny twigs from the high-water flotsam.[19] He could not bring his fingers together to pull them out, but he was able to gather them by the handful. In this way he got many rotten twigs and bits of green moss that were undesirable, but it was the best he could do. He worked methodically, even collecting an armful of the larger branches to be used later when the fire gathered strength. And all the while the dog sat and watched him, a certain yearning wistfulness[20] in its eyes, for it looked upon him as the fire provider, and the fire was slow in coming.

---

19. *Flotsam* (flot′ səm) is floating debris, here left behind by a river or stream in the spring when the water rises with the runoff from melting snow and ice.
20. *Wistfulness* means "thoughtful sadness."

Reading Strategy Cause and Effect *Why does the man make a crucial mistake when his life is on the line?*

When all was ready, the man reached in his pocket for a second piece of birch bark. He knew the bark was there, and, though he could not feel it with his fingers, he could hear its crisp rustling as he fumbled for it. Try as he would, he could not clutch hold of it. And all the time, in his consciousness, was the knowledge that each instant his feet were freezing. This thought tended to put him in a panic, but he fought against it and kept calm. He pulled on his mittens with his teeth, and threshed his arms back and forth, beating his hands with all his might against his sides. He did this sitting down, and he stood up to do it; and all the while the dog sat in the snow, its wolf brush of a tail curled around warmly over its forefeet, its sharp wolf ears pricked forward intently as it watched the man. And the man, as he beat and threshed with his arms and hands, felt a great surge of envy as he regarded the creature that was warm and secure in its natural covering.

After a time he was aware of the first faraway signals of sensation in his beaten fingers. The faint tingling grew stronger till it evolved into a stinging ache that was excruciating, but which the man hailed with satisfaction. He stripped the mitten from his right hand and fetched forth the birch bark. The exposed fingers were quickly going numb again. Next he brought out his bunch of sulphur matches. But the tremendous cold had already driven the life out of his fingers. In his effort to separate one match from the others, the whole bunch fell in the snow. He tried to pick it out of the snow, but failed. The dead fingers could neither touch nor clutch. He was very careful. He drove the thought of his freezing feet, and nose, and cheeks, out of his mind, devoting his whole soul to the matches. He watched, using the sense of vision in place of that of touch, and when he saw his fingers on each side of the bunch, he closed them—that is, he willed to close them, for the wires were down, and the fingers did not obey. He pulled the mitten on the right hand, and beat it fiercely against his knee. Then, with both mittened hands, he scooped the bunch of matches, along with much snow, into his lap. Yet he was no better off.

After some manipulation he managed to get the bunch between the heels of his mittened hands. In this fashion he carried it to his mouth. The ice crackled and snapped when by a violent effort he opened his mouth. He drew the lower jaw in, curled the upper lip out of the way, and scraped the bunch with his upper teeth in order to separate a match. He succeeded in getting one, which he dropped on his lap. He was no better off. He could not pick it up. Then he devised a way. He picked it up in his teeth and scratched it on his leg. Twenty times he scratched before he succeeded in lighting it. As it flamed he held it with his teeth to the birch bark. But the burning brimstone[21] went up his nostrils and into his lungs, causing him to cough spasmodically.[22] The match fell into the snow and went out.

The old-timer on Sulphur Creek was right, he thought in the moment of controlled despair that ensued;[23] after fifty below, a man should travel with a partner. He beat his hands, but failed in exciting any sensation. Suddenly he bared both hands, removing his mittens with his teeth. He caught the whole bunch between the heels of his hands. His arm muscles not being frozen enabled him to press the hand heels tightly against the matches. Then he scratched the bunch along his leg. It flared into flame, seventy sulphur matches at once! There was no wind to blow them out. He kept his head to one side to escape the strangling fumes, and held the blazing bunch to the birch bark. As he so held it, he became aware of sensation in his hand. His flesh was burning. He could smell it. Deep down below the surface he could feel it. The sensation developed into pain that grew acute. And still he endured it, holding the flame of the matches clumsily to the bark that would not light readily because his own

21. *Brimstone* is sulfur.
22. *Spasmodically* means "in a sudden, violent manner" or "convulsively."
23. *Ensued* means "happened afterward" or "followed."

Big Idea Naturalism *Why is the dog better adapted to survive in this environment? Explain.*

Big Idea Naturalism *Why does the author use the phrase* the wires were down?

Reading Strategy Cause and Effect *What will be the likely consequences of the man's failure to build a fire a second time?*

burning hands were in the way, absorbing most of the flame.

At last, when he could endure no more, he jerked his hands apart. The blazing matches fell sizzling into the snow, but the birch bark was alight. He began laying dry grasses and the tiniest twigs on the flame. He could not pick and choose, for he had to lift the fuel between the heels of his hands. Small pieces of rotten wood and green moss clung to the twigs, and he bit them off as well as he could with his teeth. He cherished the flame carefully and awkwardly. It meant life, and it must not perish. The withdrawal of blood from the surface of his body now made him begin to shiver, and he grew more awkward. A large piece of green moss fell squarely on the little fire. He tried to poke it out with his fingers, but his shivering frame made him poke too far, and he disrupted the nucleus of the little fire, the burning grasses and tiny twigs separating and scattering. He tried to poke them together again, but in spite of the tenseness of the effort, his shivering got away with him, and the twigs were hopelessly scattered. Each twig gushed a puff of smoke and went out. The fire provider had failed. As he looked **apathetically** about him, his eyes chanced on the dog, sitting across the ruins of the fire from him, in the snow, making restless, hunching movements, slightly lifting one forefoot and then the other, shifting its weight back and forth on them with wistful eagerness.

Timber wolf in snowstorm.

The sight of the dog put a wild idea into his head. He remembered the tale of the man, caught in a blizzard, who killed a steer and crawled inside the carcass, and so was saved. He would kill the dog and bury his hands in the warm body until the numbness went out of them. Then he could build another fire. He spoke to the dog, calling it to him; but in his voice was a strange note of fear that frightened the animal, who had never known the man to speak in such way before. Something was the matter, and its suspicious nature sensed danger—it knew not what danger, but somewhere, somehow, in its brain arose an apprehension of the man. It flattened its ears down at the sound of the man's voice, and its restless, hunching movements and the liftings and shiftings of its forefeet became more pronounced; but it would not come to the man. He got on his hands and knees and crawled toward the dog. This unusual posture again excited suspicion, and the animal sidled mincingly[24] away.

The man sat up in the snow for a moment and struggled for calmness. Then he pulled on

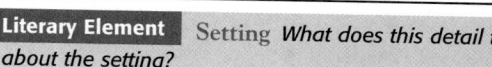
Literary Element Setting *What does this detail tell you about the setting?*

Vocabulary

apathetically (ap´ ə thet´i kal ē) *adv.* in a manner showing little interest or concern

24. *Sidled mincingly* means "moved sideways in a careful manner."

his mittens, by means of his teeth, and got upon his feet. He glanced down at first in order to assure himself that he was really standing up, for the absence of sensation in his feet left him unrelated to the earth. His erect position in itself started to drive the webs of suspicion from the dog's mind; and when he spoke peremptorily,[25] with the sound of whiplashes in his voice, the dog rendered its customary allegiance and came to him. As it came within reaching distance, the man lost his control. His arms flashed out to the dog, and he experienced genuine surprise when he discovered that his hands could not clutch, that there was neither bend nor feeling in the fingers. He had forgotten for the moment that they were frozen and that they were freezing more and more. All this happened quickly, and before the animal could get away, he encircled its body with his arms. He sat down in the snow, and in this fashion held the dog, while it snarled and whined and struggled.

But it was all he could do, hold its body encircled in his arms and sit there. He realized that he could not kill the dog. There was no way to do it. With his helpless hands he could neither draw nor hold his sheath knife nor throttle the animal. He released it, and it plunged wildly away, with tail between its legs, and still snarling. It halted forty feet away and surveyed him cautiously, with ears sharply pricked forward. The man looked down at his hands in order to locate them, and found them hanging on the ends of his arms. It struck him as curious that one should have to use his eyes in order to find out where his hands were. He began threshing his arms back and forth, beating the mittened hands against his sides. He did this for five minutes, violently, and his heart pumped enough blood up to the surface to put a stop to his shivering. But no sensation was aroused in the hands. He had an impression that they hung like weights on the ends of his arms, but when he tried to run the impression down, he could not find it.

A certain fear of death, dull and oppressive, came to him. This fear quickly became poignant[26] as he realized that it was no longer a mere matter of freezing his fingers and toes, or of losing his hands and feet, but that it was a matter of life and death with the chances against him. This threw him into a panic, and he turned and ran up the creek bed along the old, dim trail. The dog joined in behind and kept up with him. He ran blindly, without intention, in fear such as he had never known in his life. Slowly, as he ploughed and floundered through the snow, he began to see things again—the banks of the creek, the old timber jams, the leafless aspens, and the sky. The running made him feel better. He did not shiver. Maybe, if he ran on, his feet would thaw out; and, anyway, if he ran far enough, he would reach camp and the boys. Without doubt he would lose some fingers and toes and some of his face; but the boys would take care of him, and save the rest of him when he got there. And at the same time there was another thought in his mind that said he would never get to the camp and the boys; that it was too many miles away, that the freezing had too great a start on him, and that he would soon be stiff and dead. This thought he kept in the background and refused to consider. Sometimes it pushed itself forward and demanded to be heard, but he thrust it back and strove to think of other things.

It struck him as curious that he could run at all on feet so frozen that he could not feel them when they struck the earth and took the weight of his body. He seemed to himself to skim along above the surface, and to have no connection with the earth. Somewhere he had once seen a winged Mercury,

Visual Vocabulary
In Roman mythology, *Mercury* is the messenger of the gods. He is portrayed wearing a winged hat and winged sandals.

---

25. *Peremptorily* (pə remp′ tə rə lē) means "authoritatively" or "dictatorially."

Reading Strategy Cause and Effect *Why does the man forget that his hands are frozen?*

26. *Poignant* (poin′ yənt) means "sharply felt" or "intensely distressing."

Reading Strategy Cause and Effect *Why does the man try to repress thoughts of his impending death?*

and he wondered if Mercury felt as he felt when skimming over the earth.

His theory of running until he reached camp and the boys had one flaw in it: he lacked the endurance. Several times he stumbled, and finally he tottered, crumpled up, and fell. When he tried to rise, he failed. He must sit and rest, he decided, and next time he would merely walk and keep on going. As he sat and regained his breath, he noted that he was feeling quite warm and comfortable. He was not shivering, and it even seemed that a warm glow had come to his chest and trunk. And yet, when he touched his nose or cheeks, there was no sensation. Running would not thaw them out. Nor would it thaw out his hands and feet. Then the thought came to him that the frozen portions of his body must be extending. He tried to keep this thought down, to forget it, to think of something else; he was aware of the panicky feeling that it caused, and he was afraid of the panic. But the thought asserted itself, and persisted, until it produced a vision of his body totally frozen. This was too much, and he made another wild run along the trail. Once he slowed down to a walk, but the thought of the freezing extending itself made him run again.

And all the time the dog ran with him, at his heels. When he fell down a second time, it curled its tail over its forefeet and sat in front of him, facing him, curiously eager and intent. The warmth and security of the animal angered him, and he cursed it till it flattened down its ears appeasingly. This time the shivering came more quickly upon the man. He was losing in his battle with the frost. It was creeping into his body from all sides. The thought of it drove him on, but he ran no more than a hundred feet, when he staggered and pitched headlong. It was his last panic. When he had recovered his breath and control, he sat up and entertained in his mind the conception of meeting death with dignity. However, the conception did not come to him in such terms. His idea of it was that he had been making a fool of himself, running around like a chicken with its head cut off—such was the simile that occurred to him. Well, he was

bound to freeze anyway, and he might as well take it decently. With this newfound peace of mind came the first glimmerings of drowsiness. A good idea, he thought, to sleep off to death. It was like taking an anaesthetic.[27] Freezing was not so bad as people thought. There were lots worse ways to die.

He pictured the boys finding his body next day. Suddenly he found himself with them, coming along the trail and looking for himself. And, still with them, he came around a turn in the trail and found himself lying in the snow. He did not belong with himself any more, for even then he was out of himself, standing with the boys and looking at himself in the snow. It certainly was cold, was his thought. When he got back to the States he could tell the folks what real cold was. He drifted on from this to a vision of the old-timer on Sulphur Creek. He could see him quite clearly, warm and comfortable, and smoking a pipe.

"You were right, old hoss; you were right," the man mumbled to the old-timer on Sulphur Creek.

Then the man drowsed off into what seemed to him the most comfortable and satisfying sleep he had ever known. The dog sat facing him and waiting. The brief day drew to a close in a long, slow twilight. There were no signs of a fire to be made, and, besides, never in the dog's experience had it known a man to sit like that in the snow and make no fire. As the twilight drew on, its eager yearning for the fire mastered it, and with a great lifting and shifting of its forefeet, it whined softly, then flattened its ears down in anticipation of being chidden[28] by the man. But the man remained silent. Later, the dog whined loudly. And still later it crept close to the man and caught the scent of death. This made the animal bristle and back away. A little longer it delayed, howling under the stars that leaped and danced and shone brightly in the cold sky. Then it turned and trotted up the trail in the direction of the camp it knew, where were the other food providers and fire providers. ❧

---

27. An *anaesthetic* is something that produces a loss of sensation.
28. *Chidden* (past participle of *chide*) means "scolded."

Big Idea Naturalism *What do these thoughts tell us about the man as he faces this hostile environment?*

Literary Element Setting *Why does the author describe the stars as leaping and dancing?*

RESPONDING AND THINKING CRITICALLY

Respond

1. Which images from the story do you find the most vivid and memorable?

Recall and Interpret

2. (a)Where is the man going and what is his attitude toward his journey? (b)What can you infer about the man's personality and character based on the first five paragraphs?

3. (a)Describe how the man's dog behaves. (b)What event does the dog's behavior foreshadow?

4. (a)What mishap occurs shortly after the man eats lunch and resumes his journey? (b)What external and internal forces must the man struggle against?

5. (a)What happens to the man at the end of the story? What happens to his dog? (b)What lesson or lessons might be learned from reading this story?

Analyze and Evaluate

6. (a)Explain how the **mood,** or atmosphere, changes as the story develops. (b)How are the events of the story reflected in the change of mood?

7. (a)What are two contrasting qualities of the dog and of the man? (b)What does the ending suggest about London's view of these qualities and their relationship to survival in the natural world?

8. Is the dog merely a **foil,** or a character used to contrast with another character, or is it an important character in its own right? Support your answer.

Connect

9. **Big Idea** Naturalism (a)What elements of Naturalism does the story contain? (b)How might the story have been different if it had been written by a Romantic writer?

Literary Element Setting

"To Build a Fire" is set in a specific historical time and place. The setting of London's story is well-defined and essential; without the **setting,** this particular story could not have been written.

1. (a)How does the setting of the story establish the central conflict? (b)How does it influence the resolution, or final outcome, of this conflict?

2. How does London reveal the man's character through his interactions with the physical environment? Give specific examples.

3. How would you describe the relationship between humans and the environment in this story?

Review: Suspense

Suspense is a feeling of curiosity, anticipation, or even dread about what is going to happen next. Writers can increase the level of suspense in a story by creating a threat to the central character, or **protagonist,** and by giving readers clues as to what might happen.

Group Activity With a small group of classmates, discuss how London builds suspense in "To Build a Fire." Fill in a flow chart like the one below, showing how each event builds suspense, ultimately leading to the final scene.

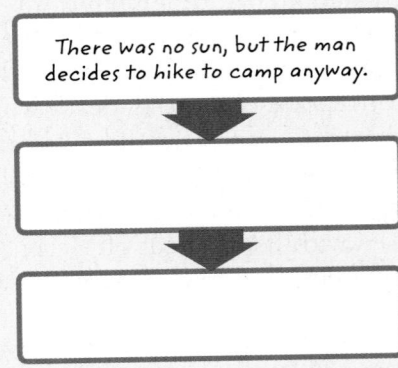

There was no sun, but the man decides to hike to camp anyway.

Reading Strategy Analyzing Cause-and-Effect Relationships

In "To Build a Fire," each event moves the plot forward, setting up a chain reaction of events. Review the cause-and-effect map you created on page 594 and then consider the following questions:

1. What events do you feel had the greatest effect on the outcome of the story?

2. What different decisions do you think the man could have made in order to survive?

Vocabulary Practice

Practice with Word Origins Dictionary entries often include the **etymology,** which tells the origin of the word. For example:

im·mor·tal·ity Latin *immortalis,* deathless, *mors,* death

This entry shows that the word *immortality* derives from the Latin word *mors,* which means "death."

Match each vocabulary word with its corresponding Latin source. Use a dictionary for assistance.

1. intangible
2. compel
3. intervene
4. apathetically

a. *pellere,* meaning "to drive"
b. *pathein,* meaning "to suffer"
c. *tangere,* meaning "to touch"
d. *venire,* meaning "to come"

Academic Vocabulary

Here are two words from the vocabulary list on page R86.

interval (in′tər vəl) *n.* intervening time and space; a temporary stop or break in an action

sole (sōl) *adj.* being the only one; single; individual

Practice and Apply

1. In what **interval** of time did the man expect to return to his camp?
2. What does the **sole** survivor of the expedition suggest about the value of instincts?

Writing About Literature

Evaluate Author's Craft At crucial points in "To Build a Fire," the traveler recalls the old-timer from Sulphur Creek. Though this character appears only in the traveler's thoughts, he is still important. Write a brief essay exploring why London includes this character in the story. Use evidence from the story to support your views.

As you draft, follow the plan shown here to develop your ideas.

START

Beginning — Introduce the topic and state your thesis, the opinion you intend to defend.

Middle — Support your opinion with evidence.

End — Close your essay with a parting thought about this character's function and importance.

FINISH

When you have finished, exchange your draft with a peer reviewer to evaluate each other's work and to suggest revisions. Then proofread and edit your draft for errors in spelling, grammar, and punctuation.

Literature Online Web Activities For eFlashcards, Selection Quick Checks, and other Web activities, go to www.glencoe.com.

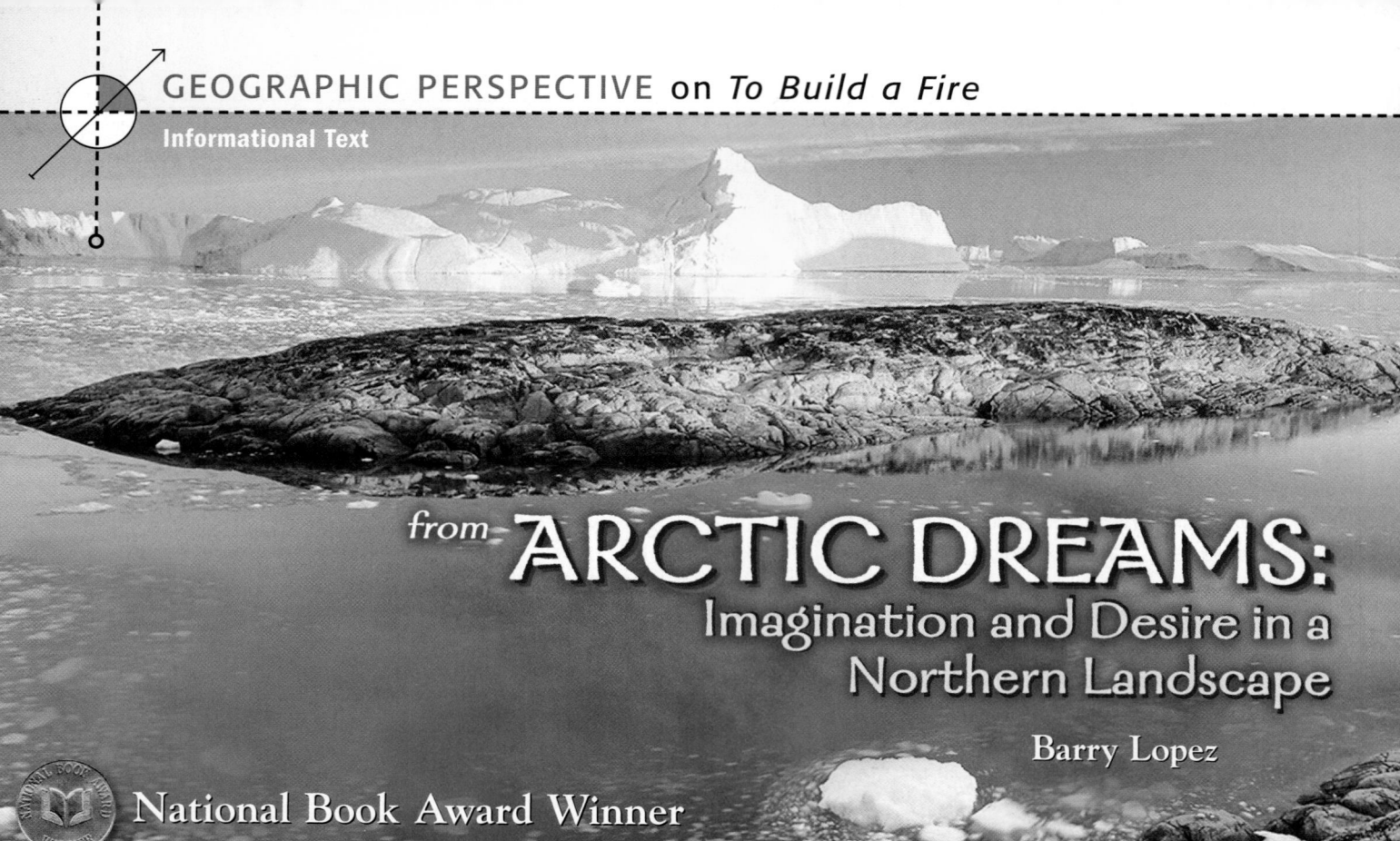

from ARCTIC DREAMS:
Imagination and Desire in a
Northern Landscape

Barry Lopez

National Book Award Winner

Building Background

Writer and photographer Barry Lopez finds many of the subjects for his writing in nature and the environment. He is often drawn to extreme locales, describing his own experiences in those harsh regions. In the following passage from *Arctic Dreams,* Lopez describes his experiences working with scientists in the Arctic Ocean.

Set a Purpose for Reading

Read to learn about survival in the Arctic and what may compel a person to take on such an adventure.

Reading Strategy

Analyzing Relevance of Setting

Analyzing the **relevance of setting** involves gathering information about the importance of time and place in a literary work. Remember that setting is not limited to the characters' physical surroundings. As you read, take notes about the setting of both *Arctic Dreams* and "To Build a Fire." Use a two-column chart like the one below.

Setting of "To Build a Fire"	Setting of *Arctic Dreams*

We left our camp on Pingok Island[1] one morning knowing a storm was moving in from the southwest, but we were not worried. We were planning to work in open water between the beach and the edge of the pack ice,[2] only a few miles out, making bottom trawls[3] from an open 20-foot boat. The four of us were dressed, as usual, in heavy clothes and foul-weather gear.

You accept the possibility of death in such situations, prepare for it, and then forget about it. We carried emergency and survival equipment in addition to all our scientific gear—signal flares, survival suits, a tent, and each of us had a pack with extra clothing, a sleeping bag, and a week's worth of food. Each morning we completed a checklist of the boat and radioed a distant base camp with our day plan. When we departed, we left a handwritten note on the table in our cabin, saying what time we left, the compass bearing we were taking, and when we expected to return.

---

1. *Pingok Island* lies in the Beaufort Sea, which is a part of the Arctic Ocean.
2. *Pack ice* is ice formed in the sea from the crashing together of floes and other ice masses.
3. *Trawls* are large nets that are dragged along the bottom of a body of water to gather marine life.

My companions, all scientists, were serious about this, but not solemn or tedious. They forestalled trouble by preparing for it, and were guided, not deterred, by the danger inherent in their work. It is a pleasure to travel with such people. As in other walks of life, the person who feels compelled to dramatize the risks or is either smugly complacent or eager to demonstrate his survival skills is someone you hope not to meet.

Our camaraderie came from our enthusiasm for the work and from exhilaration with the landscape, the daily contact with seabirds, seals, and fish. We rarely voiced these things to each other; they surfaced in a word of encouragement or understanding around rough work done in unending dampness and cold. Our mutual regard was founded in the accomplishment of our tasks and was as important to our survival as the emergency gear stowed in a blue box forward of the steering console.

We worked through the morning, sorting the contents of bottom trawls and vertical plankton tows.[4] Around noon we shut the engines off and drifted under overcast skies, eating our lunch. The seas were beginning to slap at the hull, but we had another couple of hours before they built up to three or four feet—our match, comfortably. We decided, then, to search for seals in the ice front before heading in. An hour later, by a movement of the ice so imperceptible it was finished before we realized it, we were cut off from the sea. The wind, compacting the ice, was closing off the channels of calm water where we had been cruising. We were suddenly 200 yards from open water, and a large floe, turning off the wind and folding in from the west, threatened to close us off even deeper in the pack. Already we had lost steerageway[5]—the boat was pinned at that moment on all four sides.

In those first hours we worked wordlessly and diligently. We all knew what we faced. Even if someone heard our distress call over the radio, we could not tell him precisely where we were, and we were in pack ice moving east. A three-day storm was coming on. The floes might crush the boat and drive it

under, or they could force it out of the water where we would have it for shelter.

We took advantage of any momentary opening in the ice to move toward open water, widening the channels with ice chisels, pushing with the twin 90-horsepower engines, the four of us heaving at the stern and gunnels.[6] We were angling for a small patch of water within the pack. From there, it seemed, after a quick reconnoiter[7] ahead on foot, we might be able to get out to the open sea. Thirty feet shy of our patch of water, we doubted the wisdom of taking ice chisels to one particular chunk of weathered pressure ice that blocked our path. Fractured the wrong way, its center of gravity would shift and the roll could take the boat under. The only way around it was to pull the boat, which weighed 3000 pounds, completely out of the water. With an improvised system of ice anchors, lines, and block and tackle,[8] and out of the terrific desire to get free, we set to. We got the boat up on the floe, across it, and back into the water.

Had that been open water, we would have cheered. As it was, we exchanged quick glances of justifiable but not foolish hope. While we had been winching the boat over the ice toward it, this patch of water had been closing up. And another large floe still separated us from the ocean. Where the surf broke against it, it fell a sheer four feet to the sea. Even if we got the boat over that ice, we could never launch it from such a precipice.

Two stayed in the boat. I and one other went in opposite directions along the floe. Several hundred yards to the east I found a channel. I looked it over quickly and then signaled with the upraised shaft of my ice chisel for the others. It was barely negotiable to begin with, and in the few minutes it took to get the boat there, the channel closed. We put the prow[9] of the boat against the seaward floe and brought both engines up to full power, trying to hold it against the wind. The ice beside it continued to move east. The channel started to open. With the engines roaring, the gap opened to six feet. With a silent, implicit understanding each of us acted

---

4. *Vertical plankton tows* are funnel-shaped nets that are dropped into the water and lifted straight up to collect samples, such as plankton, from the water.
5. *Steerageway* is the minimum rate of movement needed to make a boat respond to its rudder.

6. The *stern* is the rear of a boat. The *gunnel*, or gunwale, is the upper edge of the side of a ship.
7. *Reconnoiter* means "to survey."
8. A *block and tackle* is a series of pulleys used to pull or lift a heavy object.
9. The *prow*, or bow, is the front of a boat.

decisively. The man at the helm reversed the engines, heeled the boat around, and burst up the channel. We made 20 quick feet, careened the boat over on its port[10] gunnel, and pivoted through a 120° turn. One ran ahead, chopping swift and hard at the closing ice with a chisel. Two of us heaved, jumping in and out of the boat, stabbing at chunks of ice closing on the props.[11] One man remained at the throttles. Suddenly he lunged away, yanking the starboard[12] engine clear of fouling ice. The man ahead threw his ice chisel into the boat and jumped across to help lift at the port gunnel. We could *feel* how close. The starboard side of the boat slid off the ice, into the water. The bow lifted on the open sea. There was nothing more for our legs to strain against. We pulled ourselves over the gunnel and fell into the boat, limp as feed sacks. Exhausted. We were out.

We were out, and the seas were running six feet. And we were miles now from a shore that we could not see. In the hours we had been in the ice, the storm had built considerably, and we had been carried we did not know how far east. The seas were as much as the boat could handle, and too big to quarter[13]—we had to take them nearly bow-on. The brief views from wave crests showed us nothing. We could not see far enough through the driving sleet and spray, and the arctic coast here lies too low, anyway. We could only hope we were east of Pingok, the westernmost of the barrier islands, and not to the west, headed down into Harrison Bay,[14] where the wind has a greater fetch[15] and the shore is much farther on.

We took water over the bow and shouted strategy to each other over the wind and the sound of engines screaming as the props came out of the water. We erected a canvas shelter forward to break the force of the sea and shed water. We got all the weight we could out of the bow. A resolute steadiness came over us. We were making headway. We were secure. If we did not broach[16] and if we were far enough to the

east, we would be able to run up on a leeward[17] shore somewhere and wait out the storm.

We plowed ahead. Three of us stood hunched backward to the weather.

I began to recognize in the enduring steadiness another kind of calmness, or relief. The distance between my body and my thoughts slowly became elongated, and muffled like a dark, carpeted corridor. I realized I was cold, that I was shivering. I sensed the dry pits of warmth under my clothes and, against this, an opening and closing over my chest, like cold breath. I realized with dreamlike stillness that the whole upper right side of my body was soaked. The shoulder seams of my foul-weather gear were torn open.

I knew I had to get to dry clothes, to get them on. But desire could not move my legs or arms. They were too far away. I was staring at someone, then moving; the soaked clothes were coming off. I could not make a word in my mouth. I felt suspended in a shaft in the earth, and then imagined I was sitting on a bare earthen floor somewhere within myself. The knowledge that I was being slammed around like a wooden box in the bottom of the boat was like something I had walked away from.

In dry wool and protected by a tarp from the seas, I understood that I was safe; but I could not understand the duration of time. I could not locate any visual image outside myself. I concentrated on trying to gain a sense of the boat; and then on a rhythmic tensing and loosening of my muscles. I kept at it and at it; then I knew time was passing. There was a flow of time again. I heard a shout. I tried to

---

10. *Port* is a ship's left side.
11. Here, *props* means "propellers."
12. *Starboard* is a ship's right side.
13. Here, *quarter* means "to travel in a crisscross manner."
14. *Harrison Bay* is a shallow inlet of the Beaufort Sea.
15. Here, *fetch* means "intensity."
16. Here, *broach* means "to be turned broadside into the wind."

17. *Leeward,* or the lee side, means "facing the same direction toward which the wind is blowing."

Small boat by iceberg in Disko Bay, Greenland.

shout myself, and when I heard an answer I knew that I was at the edge of time again, and could just step into it. I realized I was sitting up, that I was bracing myself against heavy seas.

The shouts were for the coast. We had found Pingok.

We anchored the boat under the lee shore and went into the cabin and changed clothes and fixed dinner. Our sense of relief came out in a patter of jokes at each other's expense. We ate quietly and went to bed and slept like bears in winter.

The storm blew for two days. We nearly lost the boat when an anchor line parted, and got wet and cold again trying to secure it; but that seemed no more than what we had chosen by coming here. I went for a long walk on the afternoon of the second day, after the storm had become only fretful gusts and sunlight threatened to break through the low clouds.

I still felt a twinge of embarrassment at having been reduced from a state of strength to such an impassive weight, to a state of disassociation, so quickly. But I did not dwell on it long. And we would go out again, when the seas dropped. We would go into the ice again. We would watch more closely; but nothing, really, had changed.

With the experience so fresh in my mind, I began thinking of frail and exposed craft as I walked down the beach, of the Irish carraughs and Norse knarrs[18] that brought people across the Atlantic, bucking pack ice streaming southward on the East Greenland Current.

My God, what had driven them? All we know is what we have deduced from the records of early historians. And the deference those men showed to their classical predecessors, to Ptolemy, Solinus, and Isidore,[19] their own nationalism and religious convictions, their vanity, and the shape of the ideas of their age—all this affected what they expressed. And when it was translated, or when they themselves translated from others, interpolations, adaptation, and plain error colored the historical record further. So the early record of arctic exploration is open to interpretation. And this refined history is less real, less harrowing than what had happened to us in the boat. It is events mulled and adjudicated.[20]

I wanted to walk the length of the seaside beach on Pingok, knowing the storm was dying away. I brooded over the fates of those early immigrants, people whose names no one knows, who sailed in ships of which there are neither descriptions nor drawings, through ice and storms like this one—but so much farther from a shore, with intentions and dreams I could only imagine.

The earliest arctic voyages are recorded in the Icelandic sagas and Irish imramha. But they were written down hundreds of years after the fact by people who did not make the journeys, who only heard about them. The Norse Eddas[21] and Icelandic sagas, wrote the arctic explorer and historian Fridtjof Nansen, are "narratives somewhat in the light of historical romances, founded upon legend and more or less uncertain traditions." The same can be said of the imramha and the records of Saint Brendan's voyage,[22] though in tone and incident these latter are different from the sagas.

In the following ages, beginning in a time before the sagas, the notion of a road to Cathay, a

---

18. *Carraughs* and *knarrs* are both types of ships.

19. *Ptolemy* (c. 85–c. 165 B.C.) was an Egyptian geographer and astronomer; Gaius Julius *Solinus* (third century A.D.) was a Latin grammarian who wrote a book titled *The Wonders of the World;* Saint *Isidore* of Seville (560–636 A.D.) was a Spanish theologian and historian.
20. *Adjudicated* means "settled" or "judged."
21. The *sagas, imramha,* and *Eddas* are all tales of sea voyages.
22. *Saint Brendan* (c. 484–c. 578 A.D.) was an Irish monk who is said to have gone on a seven-year sea voyage in search of the Garden of Eden. Some believe he found North America during this voyage.

Tourist on Ellesmere Island.

Visions of achievement drove them on. In the worst moments they were held together by regard for each other, by invincible bearing, or by stern naval discipline. Whether one finds such resourceful courage among a group of young monks on a spiritual voyage in a carraugh, or among worldly sailors with John Davis in the sixteenth century, or in William Parry's[25] snug winter quarters on Melville Island in 1819–20, it is a sterling human quality.

In the journals and histories I read of these journeys I was drawn on by a sharp leaning in the human spirit: pure desire—the complexities of human passion and cupidity. Someone, for example, had to pay for these trips; and whoever paid was looking for a way to be paid back. Rarely was the goal anything as selfless as an increase in mankind's geographical knowledge. An arctic voyage in quest of unknown riches, or of a new passage to known riches, could mean tangible wealth for investors, and it could mean fame and social position for a captain or pilot. For a common seaman the reward might only mean some slip of the exotic, or a chance at the riches himself—at the very least a good story, probably something astounding. Enough, certainly, to sign on.

As I read, I tried to imagine the singular hunger for such things, how desire alone might convey a group of people into those fearsome seas. The achievement of one's desires may reveal what one considers moral; but it also reveals the aspiration and tack of an individual life, and the tenor of an age. In this light, one can better understand failures of nerve in the Arctic, such as Bering's in the Chukchi Sea in 1728—he simply did not have Peter the Great's[26] burning desire to define eastern Russia. And one can better understand figures in arctic exploration so obsessed with their own

Northwest Passage,[23] emerges. The quest for such a corridor, a path to wealth that had to be followed through a perilous landscape, gathers the dreams of several ages. Rooted in this search is one of the oldest of all human yearnings—finding the material fortune that lies beyond human struggle, and the peace that lies on the other side of hope.

I should emphasize two points. Few original documents point up the unadorned character, the undisguised sensibilities, of the participants in these dramas. And the most common simile of comparison for these journeys—the exploits of astronauts—falls short. The astronaut is suitably dressed for his work, professionally trained, assiduously looked after en route, and nationally regarded. He possesses superb tools of navigation and observation. The people who first came into the Arctic had no photograph of the far shore before they left. They sailed in crude ships with cruder tools of navigation, and with maps that had no foundation or geographic authority. They shipwrecked so often that it is difficult to find records of their deaths, because shipwreck and death were unremarkable at the time. They received, for the most part, no support—popular or financial. They suffered brutally and fatally from the weather and from scurvy,[24] starvation, Eskimo hostility, and thirst. Their courage and determination in some instances were so extreme as to seem eerie and peculiar rather than heroic.

---

25. Sir *William Parry* (1790–1855), a British explorer, discovered and named several islands in the Arctic, including the inhospitable Melville Island, where he and his group were forced to spend a winter because of sea ice.
26. Vitus *Bering* (1681–1741) was a Danish-born Russian explorer. The Russian tsar *Peter the Great* chose Bering to discover whether Asia and North America were connected. Heavy fog caused Bering to return to Russia, where he was criticized for not actually seeing the American coast.

---

23. *Cathay* is an old name for China; the *Northwest Passage* is a route through the Arctic that passes from the Atlantic Ocean to the Pacific Ocean.
24. *Scurvy* is a disease brought on by lack of vitamin C.

achievement that they found it irksome to acknowledge the Eskimos, unnamed companions, and indefatigable dogs who helped them.

Arctic history became for me, then, a legacy of desire—the desire of individual men to achieve their goals. But it was also the legacy of a kind of desire that transcends heroics and which was privately known to many—the desire for a safe and honorable passage through the world.

As I walked the beach I stopped now and then to pick over something on the storm-hardened shore—bits of whale vertebrae, waterlogged feathers, the odd but ubiquitous piece of plastic, a strict reminder against romance.

The narratives I carried in my head that afternoon fascinated me, but not for what they recorded of geographic accomplishment or for how they might be used in support of one side or another of a controversy, such as whether Frederick Cook or Robert Peary[27] got to the Pole first. They held the mind because of what they said about human endeavor. Behind the polite and abstemious journal entries of British naval officers, behind the self-conscious prose of dashing explorers, were the lives of courageous, bewildered, and dreaming people. Some reports suggest that heroic passage took place for many just offstage. They make clear that others struggled mightily to find some meaning in what they were doing in those regions, for the very act of exploration seemed to them at times completely mad. They wanted to feel that what they were doing was necessary, if not for themselves then for the nation, for mankind.

The literature of arctic exploration is frequently offered as a record of resolute will before the menacing fortifications of the landscape. It is more profitable I think to disregard this notion—that the land is an adversary bent on human defeat, that the people who came and went were heroes or failures in this. It is better to contemplate the record of human longing to achieve something significant, to be free of some of the grim weight of life. That weight was ignorance, poverty of spirit, indolence, and the threat of anonymity and destitution. This harsh landscape became the focus of a desire to separate oneself from those things and to overcome them. In these arctic narratives, then, are the threads of dreams that serve us all. ❧

---

27. *Frederick Cook* (1865–1940) and *Robert Peary* (1856–1920) were both American explorers. While Peary is usually listed as the first person to reach the North Pole (in April 1909), Cook claimed to have reached it in 1908.

RESPONDING AND THINKING CRITICALLY

Respond

1. What part of this narrative did you find the most engaging? Explain.

Recall and Interpret

2. (a)How does Lopez feel about the scientists with whom he worked? (b)Why is the quality of their relationships important?

3. (a)How does the boat become stuck in the ice? (b)What does this incident suggest about the arctic environment? (c)What does it suggest about the expedition?

Analyze and Evaluate

4. How do Lopez's descriptions at the end of this excerpt compare with Jack London's descriptions at the end of "To Build a Fire"?

5. Lopez recounts the stories of earlier arctic explorers. Do you agree that in these stories are "the threads of dreams that serve us all"? Why or why not?

Connect

6. Briefly describe some of the differences and similarities in the settings of *Arctic Dreams* and "To Build a Fire." How do these settings affect the events of each?

■ **INDIANA ACADEMIC STANDARDS (pages 608–613)**
11.3 [Identify] story elements such as...setting, and [make] connections and comparisons across texts...

Writing Workshop

Literary Analysis

 Analyzing a Short Story

> *"The difference between the almost right word and the right word is the difference between the lightning-bug and the lightning."*
>
> —Mark Twain, from "William Dean Howells"

Connecting to Literature Mark Twain's quotation analyzes the importance of precise word choice in writing. This comment is a kind of **literary analysis**—a close-up view of a literary work. When writing a literary analysis of a short story, first consider your immediate impression of the story. Then as you reread the story, you can look for themes and techniques that contributed to your impression. By analyzing these elements, you will clarify the deeper meanings and understand how they are revealed in the story. Study the rubric below to learn the goals and strategies for writing a successful literary analysis.

Rubric: Features of Literary Analysis Essays

Goals	Strategies
Analyze important and original aspects of the story	☑ Show how language, imagery, themes, and original aspects of the text contribute to the story's meaning as a whole
Write a concise thesis statement	☑ Begin with your thesis, or your interpretation of the story you will analyze
	☑ In the conclusion, restate your thesis and summarize your analysis
Support your analysis with evidence	☑ Use evidence from the story to support and develop your analysis
	☑ Use secondary sources such as dictionaries and literary criticism, if applicable, as further support
Organize your main points in a logical, effective order	☑ Organize your major points in chronological order or in order of importance

The Writing Process

In this workshop, you will follow the stages of the writing process. At any stage, you may think of new ideas to include and better ways to express them. Feel free to return to earlier stages as you write.

Prewriting

- - - - - - - - - - - - - - -

Drafting

- - - - - - - - - - - - - - -

Revising

 Focus Lesson: Improving Sentence Variety and Style

Editing & Proofreading

- - - - - - - - - - - - - - -

Focus Lesson: Subject-Verb Agreement

Presenting

- - - - - - - - - - - - - - -

Writing Models For models and other writing activities, go to www.glencoe.com.

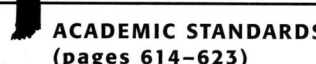

ACADEMIC STANDARDS (pages 614–623)

11.5.9 Write…a literary analysis…

11.4.11 Edit and proofread… writing…using an editing checklist.

11.4.12 Revise text to…improve sentence variety and style…

> ▶ **Assignment**
>
> Write a literary analysis essay about a story from the unit that shows how the author's language, characters, plot, setting, themes, and other elements of the text contribute to the story's meaning. As you move through the stages of the writing process, keep your audience and purpose in mind.
>
> ---
>
> **Audience:** peers, classmates, and teachers who are familiar with the story
>
> **Purpose:** to demonstrate an understanding of the author's style and appreciation of the effects created

Analyzing a Professional Model

In her literary analysis essay, Bettina L. Knapp analyzes the effects of terror on the crew in Stephen Crane's "The Open Boat." As you read the following passage, note how Knapp uses direct evidence from the story and explains the significance of that evidence. Pay close attention to the comments in the margin. They point out features that you may want to include in your own literary analysis.

From *Stephen Crane: Tales of Adventure*
by Bettina L. Knapp

"None of them knew the color of the sky," is perhaps one of the most celebrated opening lines of any short story. The opening line conveys the fierce struggle between finite man and the infinitude that engulfs him—as in Melville's *Moby-Dick*. The sea for Crane, as it is for Melville, is "the image of the ungraspable phantom of life."

The men's agony at not knowing their fate is underscored by the power of those surging waters—waves that could sweep the men under at any moment. "The horizon narrowed and widened, and dipped and rose, at all times its edge was jagged with waves that seemed thrust up in points like rocks."

Man, like the helpless survivors in the boat, is thrust here and there and floats about in utter helplessness. No matter how hard people try to fix and direct themselves, they are castaways. Salvation—if there is one—lies in the bonds between men that assuage their implacable solitude.

The craft pranced and reared, and plunged like an animal. As each wave came, and she rose for it, she seemed like a horse making at a fence outrageously high. The manner of her scramble over these walls of water is a mystic thing, and moreover, at the top of them were ordinarily these

Thesis

Make a concise judgment that analyzes a literary element, such as theme, throughout the story.

Major Points

Make sure that your major points support your thesis.

problems in white water, the foam racing down from the summit of each wave, requiring a new leap, and a leap from the air.

Crane's use of changing rhythms throughout the tale points up the terror of the dinghy's passengers and exemplifies the utter senselessness of existence itself.

Crane suggests that if an observer were to look upon the events objectively, viewing them "from a balcony, the whole thing would doubtless have been weirdly picturesque. But the men in the boat had no time to see it, and even if they had had leisure, there were other things to occupy their minds." Values of virtue, bravery, integrity were once of importance, but now are meaningless in a godless universe where nature observes impassively human despair and frustration. Yet, the harrowing sea journey creates a new morality, which gives fresh meaning to life: "the brotherhood of men . . . was established on the seas. No one said that it was so. No one mentioned it. But it dwelt in the boat, and each man felt it warm him." Comfort and feelings of well-being emerge as each helps the other assuage his growing terror.

In the midst of fear and harrowing terror, there is also irony and humor:

> If I am going to be drowned—if I am going to be drowned—if I am going to be drowned, why, in the name of the seven mad gods who rule the sea, was I allowed to come thus far and contemplate sand and trees? Was I brought here merely to have my nose dragged away as I was about to nibble the sacred cheese of life? It is preposterous. If this old ninny-woman, Fate, cannot do better than this, she should be deprived of the management of men's fortunes. She is an old hen who knows not her intention. If she has decided to drown me, why did she not do it in the beginning and save me all this trouble. The whole affair is absurd. . . . But, no, she cannot mean to drown me. Not after all this work.

A mystical relationship exists between the men in the dinghy—and the sea and heavens. Crane feels compelled to point out man's smallness, to set him back into nature and reduce him to size.

Conversations between the oiler and the cook, seemingly trivial, since they revolve around food—"What kind of pie do you like best?"—serve in reality to point out the absurdity of humankind's preoccupations. They also act as a way of dispelling progressive terror. As for the captain, he is ridiculed; the men laugh at him, again distracting themselves from their great fear of death.

The sight of a shark heightens the men's dreadful tension. Crane does not mention the shark by name, but the reader can almost hear the shark's fin cut

---

Analysis of Literary Element

Analyze language, setting, character, and unique aspects of the text to show how these elements contribute to the story's meaning as a whole.

Primary Source

Support your analysis with direct evidence from the story.

Explanation of Evidence

Draw connections between your evidence and your thesis, and explain the significance to your reader.

Explanation of Ambiguities

Identify and explain ambiguities, complexities, and nuances in the text to reveal additional layers of meaning.

the water's surface and see its phosphorescent gleaming body. Like the survivors of "Raft of the Medusa," whose harrowing episode is famous in French maritime history, the men in the dinghy do not know there is a lifesaving station twenty miles away.

When the ordeal is over, the men, safely on land, look back at the water: "white waves paced to and fro in the moonlight, and the wind brought the sound of the great sea's voice to the men on shore, and they felt that they could then be interpreters." The narrator's voice withdraws, as it were, from the chaotic drama, introducing a sense of spatial and temporal distance. Comfortable on land, the narrator can indulge in the luxury of waxing poetic and thus transform subjective emotions into a work of art.

Its poetry and rhythmic schemes make "The Open Boat" the match of Melville's "White Jacket" and the best of Jack London and Joseph Conrad. This tale's unusually punctuated sentences of contrasting length simulate the heart beat of a man under extreme stress, producing an incantatory quality. Crane's sensual images of man struggling against the sea remain vivid long after the reading of "The Open Boat." The salt spray and deafening roar of the waves pounding against the dinghy can almost be tasted and heard.

Organization

Order your analysis in a logical, effective way, such as by chronological order.

Explanation of Evidence

Draw your own conclusions about your evidence, making sure to connect it to your thesis.

Conclusion

Summarize your thesis and major points, and leave your reader with something to think about.

Reading-Writing Connection Think about the writing techniques that you just encountered and try them out in your own expository literary analysis.

Prewriting

Choose a Story to Analyze First decide which story in the unit to analyze. It need not be the story you liked best or the one you understood the best. In fact, the best essays often analyze challenging stories that initially leave the reader with mixed feelings or unanswered questions. Choose a story that left you with a strong impression and will give you enough to talk about in your analysis.

Explore Your Story Once you select your story, review it to gain a comprehensive understanding of the text. Remember that *analyzing* a text means looking at its separate parts individually and then determining how the parts work together as a whole. Focus on a literary element—such as character, setting, plot, theme, point of view, or style—to examine significant ideas apparent throughout the text. For example, think about how a character changes or how the setting or point of view influences the meaning of the story. As you explore your story, look for patterns and recurring themes that contribute to its overall meaning.

The Duchess: Her selflessness and concern for Piney are revealed.

Mother Shipton: Her compassion and sacrifice for others are revealed.

Uncle Billy: He remains a thief.

Piney Woods: She remains innocent, optimistic, and obedient.

Mr. Oakhurst: His ability to lead, honor, and respect others, as well as a possible cowardice, are revealed.

Tom Simson: He remains innocent, cheerful, and obedient.

Analysis: The devastating storm reveals the true nature of each character.

Clarify Your Thesis In a literary analysis essay, your thesis should be a concise judgment that interprets, analyzes, and evaluates a specific element throughout the entire story. Your one- to two-sentence thesis statement should include the element you will analyze and the conclusion you reached about the story.

Gather Evidence As you develop your major points, remember to support your ideas and viewpoints with evidence—accurate, detailed references to the story. The story will be your primary source, but you can use secondary sources such as dictionaries and literary criticism to reinforce your claims. A strong argument depends on the ability to make clear to the reader connections between such evidence and the thesis. After giving evidence, explain its significance to your argument, noting other possible interpretations.

Organize Your Major Points In the body of your essay, organize your major points in an effective, logical order. If you are analyzing a change that occurs in the story, use chronological order. In other analyses, you may prefer to use order of importance. Adjust the order to maximize the impact of your points.

Drafting

Present and Expand Your Points Present your major points in a straightforward, logical way and back them up with direct evidence from the story. Maintain the present tense throughout your literary analysis. Use direct quotations where appropriate, especially to emphasize a point. As you discuss more complex interpretations and connections, explain the significance of your evidence to the reader and clarify how it supports your thesis. Using your thesis as a guide, revise your writing as necessary.

Analyzing a Workshop Model

Here is a final draft of a literary analysis essay. Read the essay and answer the questions in the margin. Use the answers to these questions to guide you as you write your own essay.

In Search of Character: Defying Reputation in "The Outcasts of Poker Flat"

In many works of literature, an outside event affects the lives of characters and the community in which they live. Often this outside event functions as a turning point, after which characters reveal their true natures and behave accordingly. Ultimately, their actions change not only the way others think, but also the course of events. In Bret Harte's story "The Outcasts of Poker Flat," a group of "improper persons" is banished from Poker Flat and becomes trapped in a mountain cabin during a snowstorm. The behavior resulting from the storm and subsequent entrapment reveals the true character of these outcasts, often belying or complicating their earlier reputations.

The outcasts include Mr. Oakhurst, a gambler; Mother Shipton, a vulgar, malevolent woman; the Duchess, a self-absorbed, wanton woman; and Uncle Billy, a thief—all of whom have questionable backgrounds and reputations. Had the outcasts left Poker Flat and crossed over the mountains, they would most likely have reached Sand Bar and continued to live as they had previously in Poker Flat. However, Mother Shipton, the Duchess, and Billy become intoxicated along the way, and the group is forced to stop for the night.

While the other members of the group act as might be expected of outcasts, Mr. Oakhurst shows signs of good judgment and concern for others. He does not drink, and he remains cool and impassive during the journey. While the others are forced to rest because of their drunken stupor, Mr. Oakhurst contemplates "the loneliness begotten of his pariah trade, his habits of life, his very vices," and for the first time in his life, his behavior bothers him (508). Although he yearns for excitement, he does not desert "his weaker and more pitiable companions" (508). The diction suggests that Mr. Oakhurst sympathizes with the group, even as their irresponsibility puts his own life at risk. Later, the narrator suggests that the gambler has "cachéd" his cards, and

Author and Title
Why is this information necessary?

Element to Analyze
How does stating this information strengthen the analysis?

Thesis
What is the author's conclusion about the story?

Background
Why is this information important to the analysis?

Major Point
How does this point help develop the analysis?

Primary Source
How do these quotations contribute to the analysis?

Mother Shipton notes that he "didn't say 'cards' once" (512). Despite his own yearnings, Mr. Oakhurst focuses on others instead of himself.

With the arrival of Tom Simson and Piney Wood, a young couple eloping to Poker Flat, the group's fate is sealed. The snowstorm that traps them in the cabin reveals their true characters. At the first sign of snow, Uncle Billy reveals his cowardice and selfishness. During the night, he runs away with the group's mules, suggesting that in his case, his reputation is accurate. Billy is the same selfish thief on the inside that everyone saw on the outside. Conversely, Mr. Oakhurst takes charge of the group and establishes a tone that the others adopt. Unable to "bring himself to disclose Uncle Billy's rascality," Mr. Oakhurst implies that Billy left to get provisions for the group, and that letting the animals escape was accidental (511). Mr. Oakhurst's concerns are mostly for Piney, and he tries not to let anyone frighten her. He warns the older women, "They'll find out the truth about us *all* when they find out anything . . . and there's no good frightening them now" (511). The two older women follow his understated yet commanding lead, and eventually their concern for Piney overshadows their concern for themselves.

Tom, nicknamed "The Innocent," encourages an atmosphere of gaiety during the snowstorm. Singing and laughing, he and Piney remain unaware of the impending danger. Mr. Oakhurst does nothing to diminish their enjoyment, even as he fears what may lie ahead, and Mother Shipton and the Duchess follow his example.

The characters most fully reveal their true selves as the gravity of the situation becomes apparent. The storm stops, but it is still too cold for the group to risk leaving the cabin. The music and storytelling can no longer substitute for physical necessities, as food and fuel supplies run dangerously low by the end of the week. Despite the gravity of the situation, the Duchess is "more cheerful than she had been" and assumes the care of Piney (513). Mother Shipton, once the strongest of the group, grows noticeably ill. Her true character is revealed when she shows Mr. Oakhurst the reason for her failing health: she has been setting aside her food rations for Piney instead of eating them herself. She asks Mr. Oakhurst not to "say anything about it. Don't waken the kids" (513). Beneath her hard exterior is compassion that induces Mother Shipton, without fanfare, to sacrifice her life for another. After Mr. Oakhurst sends Tom to Poker Flat for supplies, Mr. Oakhurst decides to leave the cabin as well. Gradually the Duchess realizes that he will not make it back. She shields Piney from the sad news, and continues to protect Piney as best as she can. When the two die together peacefully in each other's arms, the Duchess's nobility in the final days of her life becomes apparent. The narrator notes the townspeople's reaction to the women's embrace: "you could scarcely have told from the equal peace that dwelt upon them which was she that had sinned" (514). This suggests that in the eyes of the now "pitying" townspeople, the Duchess's reputation has been restored. They leave the women's bodies untouched.

Although the character of Mr. Oakhurst changes during the event, his is the most ambiguous characterization of the group. Although Uncle Billy, Piney, and Tom remain unchanged throughout the event, and Mother Shipton and the Duchess reveal a strength of character diametrically opposed to what is expected, Mr. Oakhurst is "at once the strongest and yet the weakest of the outcasts" (514). Some may interpret his suicide as cowardice, as he chooses to kill himself, ending his own suffering and shielding himself from the agony of others' suffering. This final unspoken sacrifice, however, has much in common with Mother Shipton's sacrifice. Mr. Oakhurst leaves extra fuel for the others and spares the women from perceiving the grim reality of his mission. Assuming death to be inevitable, he confronts it calmly and directly, on his own terms. The tone of Mr. Oakhurst's suicide note reflects the attitude he adheres to before and throughout the snowstorm—namely, that he is "too much of a gambler not to accept fate. With him life was at best an uncertain game, and he recognized the usual percentage in favor of the dealer" (507). The fact that Mr. Oakhurst recognized his "streak of bad luck" and was able to accept his fate and "[hand] in his checks" suggests that suicide, for him, was the most honest and honorable option (514).

Thus, the snowstorm and its aftermath, in "The Outcasts of Poker Flat," reveal the true depth and complexity of the characters. The fatal event shows that Billy's weak character confirms his bad reputation, whereas the stronger characters of Mother Shipton and the Duchess belie their reputations. Although he gives up playing cards and shows concern for others over himself, Mr. Oakhurst retains the discretion, calm, and acceptance of a gambler until his death. His reputation as a gambler is not so much contradicted as it is redefined.

Explanation of Evidence

How does this sentence strengthen the analysis?

Explanation of Ambiguity

What does identifying and explaining ambiguities add to the analysis?

Counterargument

Why might the author include a point that undermines his or her thesis?

Restatement of Thesis

Why might the author restate the thesis in the conclusion of the analysis?

Final Insight

How can adding a final insight make an analysis more compelling?

Revising

Peer Review After you complete your literary analysis, exchange drafts with a partner to help you identify areas of your essay that can be improved. Check to confirm that the organization is logical and that the ideas are clear and support the thesis. Remember to refer to the traits of strong writing.

Use the rubric below to evaluate your writing.

Rubric: Writing an Effective Literary Analysis
☑ Do you examine important aspects of the text separately to determine how they contribute to the story's meaning as a whole?
☑ Do you state your conclusions about the story in a concise thesis in your introduction?
☑ Do you use direct evidence from the story to support and develop your analysis?
☑ Do you identify and explain complexities, ambiguities, and nuances?
☑ Do you organize your main points in a logical, effective order?

> **Focus Lesson**

Improving Sentence Variety and Style

As you revise, note the style and variety of your sentences. Do your sentences flow smoothly from one idea to the next, or do they sound choppy? Combine sentences and vary sentence structure to achieve more fluid, rhythmic sentences.

Draft:

Billy is the same selfish thief that everyone thought he was. Mr. Oakhurst is different. He takes charge of the group. He sets a tone that the others follow. He does not even "disclose Uncle Billy's rascality" (511). Mr. Oakhurst implies that Billy left to get provisions for the group. Letting the animals escape was accidental.

Revision:

Billy is the same selfish thief <u>on the inside</u> that everyone saw <u>on the outside.</u>[1] <u>Conversely,</u>[2] Mr. Oakhurst takes charge of the group and sets a tone that the others adopt. <u>Unable to "bring himself to disclose Uncle Billy's rascality,"</u> Mr. Oakhurst implies that Billy left to get provisions for the group and that letting the animals escape was accidental (511).[3]

1: <u>Use parallelism to emphasize the relationship between ideas.</u>

2: <u>Use sentence openers on occasion to add stylistic interest.</u>

3: <u>Vary the length and structure of sentences by combining related sentences.</u>

Traits of Strong Writing

Ideas message or theme and the details that develop it

Organization arrangement of main ideas and supporting details

Voice writer's unique way of using tone and style

Word Choice vocabulary a writer uses to convey meaning

Sentence Fluency rhythm and flow of sentences

Conventions correct spelling, grammar, usage, and mechanics

Presentation the way words and design elements look on a page

For more information on using the Traits of Strong Writing, see pages R33-R34 of the Writing Handbook.

Editing and Proofreading

Get It Right When you have completed the final draft of your essay, proofread for errors in grammar, usage, mechanics, and spelling. Refer to the Language Handbook, pages R53–R60, as a guide.

▶ **Focus Lesson**

Subject-Verb Agreement

The form of a verb must agree in person and number with its subject. It can be difficult to identify the subject, however, when the subject is a collective noun (a noun that names a group as a whole). A collective noun is usually considered singular. Note the examples.

Problem: Incorrect identification of a collective noun as subject

While some of the group acts as might be expected of outcasts, Mr. Oakhurst shows signs of good judgment and concern for others.

Solution: The plural indefinite pronoun *some*, not the singular collective noun *group*, is the subject here and therefore requires a plural verb.

While some of the group act as might be expected of outcasts, Mr. Oakhurst shows signs of good judgment and concern for others.

Problem: Incorrect identification of a collective noun as plural

However, Mother Shipton, the Duchess, and Billy become intoxicated along the way, and the group are forced to stop for the night.

Solution: When a collective noun refers to a group as a whole, it is considered singular and therefore requires a singular verb.

However, Mother Shipton, the Duchess, and Billy become intoxicated along the way, and the group is forced to stop for the night.

E-mail Exchange

Create an electronic word document of your essay and e-mail it to a peer reviewer. Ask him or her to edit and proofread the essay and return the corrected version to you.

Presenting

The Right Look Before you turn in your paper, make sure that it is neat and presentable. Papers should be typed (double-spaced) and should have appropriate margins. Be sure to include an interesting title that catches your reader's attention from the start. Check with your teacher for additional presentation guidelines.

Writer's Portfolio

Place a copy of your literary analysis in your portfolio to review later.

Speaking, Listening, and Viewing Workshop

Delivering an Oral Response to Literature

Connecting to Literature After reading thought-provoking literature such as "To Build a Fire," readers often enjoy expressing their opinions and interpretations. Participating in group discussion is a useful way for people to express their responses to literature and enhance their understanding of a piece of writing. Discussion helps people solve problems, explore ideas, and exchange information.

> **Assignment** Working in groups, discuss and respond to the major themes in "To Build a Fire" or another literary work.

Setting Time Limits

Set time limits for your group to ensure that enough time is allowed for discussion of each idea or topic.

Organizing a Discussion Group

When you wrote your expository literary analysis, you were addressing an audience of readers. When you participate in a group discussion, each member contributes ideas. Assign roles, such as facilitator and recorder, to members of your group. Each group member is to be equally responsible for discussion.

This chart will help you understand these roles.

Facilitator	
☑ Introduces the discussion topic	☑ Keeps track of the time
☑ Invites each participant to speak	☑ Helps participants arrive at a consensus
☑ Keeps the discussion focused and interactive	

Group Participants (All)	
☑ Form ideas and questions about the literature before discussion	☑ Support any opinions with facts
☑ Contribute throughout the discussion	☑ Listen carefully to other group members
☑ Avoid repeating what has been said earlier	☑ Evaluate and respect the opinions of others

Recorder	
☑ Helps the group leader form conclusions based on the discussion	☑ Keeps track of the most important points
	☑ Helps summarize the discussion

Thinking About Your Topic

Let your mind play with the images of the story. What impressions do the images spark in you? Begin with one particular event or image and let your responses branch out from it. Use these responses to help you brainstorm about ideas for discussion.

Making a web diagram can be helpful in preparing your oral response to literature. Below is the beginning of a web diagram for a scene from Jack London's "To Build a Fire."

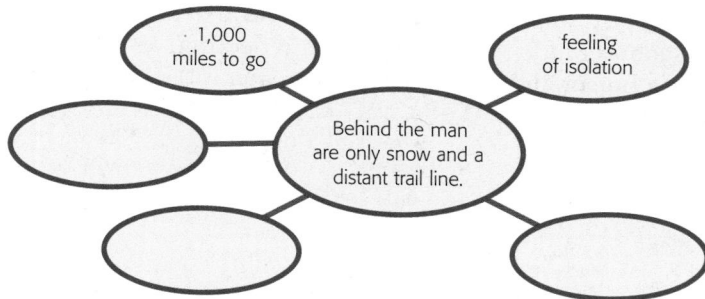

Preparing for Discussion

Think about some ideas and responses you would like to share with your group. Use the following questions to guide you as you prepare and deliver your oral response to the literature:

- Have I thought about questions and ideas for discussion?
- Am I prepared to contribute throughout the entire discussion?
- Am I clearly stating my views when responding?
- Am I supporting my views with text evidence and background information?
- Are my ideas presented in a logical order?

Rubric: Techniques for Delivering an Oral Response to Literature	
☑ **Pacing** Allow each group member time to voice his or her opinion.	☑ **Listening** Remain quiet until it is your turn to speak.
☑ **Discussion** Ask open-ended questions to promote discussion.	☑ **Focus** Direct your attention on the group member who is speaking.
☑ **Delivery** Encourage more reserved group members to voice their opinions.	☑ **Poise** Use nonverbal communication to show you understand what the speaker is saying.
☑ **Evaluation** Set aside some time after discussion to evaluate the group's ability to work together.	☑ **Gestures** Avoid nervous habits and other movements that may distract the speaker.

For Independent Reading

THE LATE 1800s AND EARLY 1900s SAW GREAT DEVELOPMENTS IN technology, industry, and science. As the world changed, novelists found inspiration in various places. Some, like Henry James, turned inward. These writers used insights from the developing field of psychology and focused on the thoughts and perceptions of their characters. Other writers, like Frank Norris, were struck by the turmoil of rapid industrialization and portrayed the vast, impersonal economic forces that were overwhelming individuals. Still others, such as Mark Twain, focused on reflecting the regional lifestyles in the United States, using humor and satire to portray greater truths about human nature and U.S. culture.

The Octopus

Frank Norris (1901)

Frank Norris was the first notable Naturalist writer in the United States. *The Octopus* was the opening novel in an unfinished trilogy—he died before the final book was written—that examines the social forces that drive agriculture and industry. In *The Octopus*, Norris describes the struggle between the railroad companies and California wheat farmers, exposing the dangers of concentrated economic power. The railroads have become a multi-tentacled monster, dominating every aspect of life, from the state legislature to the very land the farmers work. Farmers fight back, only to learn that the railroads have become the masters of those they were intended to serve.

The Ambassadors

Henry James (1903)

In *The Ambassadors*, James explores the collision of American and European culture through the story of Louis Lambert Strether, a middle-aged American sent to Paris to coerce a young American, Chadwick Newsome, to return home. However, the task proves harder than expected for Strether, especially as he finds himself becoming increasingly enamored with Europe. Notably, James considered this novel to be his best work.

"The Concord, Mass. Public Library committee has decided to exclude Mark Twain's latest book from the library. One member of the committee says that, while he does not wish to call it immoral, he thinks [it] contains but little humor, and that of a very coarse type. He regards it as the veriest trash. The librarian and the other members of the committee entertain similar views, characterizing it as rough, coarse and inelegant, dealing with a series of experiences not elevating, the whole book being more suited to the slums than to intelligent, respectable people."

—*The Boston Transcript*, March 17, 1885

The Adventures of Huckleberry Finn

Mark Twain (1885)

In his novel *The Adventures of Huckleberry Finn*, Mark Twain describes the travels of the runaway orphan Huck and his new friend Jim, an African American fleeing slavery and the South. Huck's reflections on various aspects of life in the prewar South are delivered in a slangy, colloquial voice that will serve as a model for later writers. The episodic story moves between satire, slapstick, and touching portrayals of the relationship between Huck and Jim.

From the Glencoe Literature Library

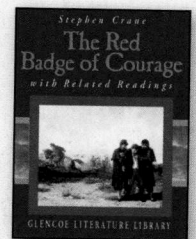

The Red Badge of Courage

Stephen Crane

A young Civil War recruit contemplates the meaning of courage as he faces battle.

The Jungle

Upton Sinclair

This shocking story of an immigrant family working in Chicago's meatpacking industry led to the establishment of the Food and Drug Administration.

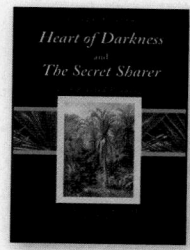

Heart of Darkness

Joseph Conrad

In this symbolic tale, a man describes a dark and dangerous trip he took to investigate a Belgian trader in the Congo.

◆ Indiana Test Practice

Reading: Vocabulary, Comprehension, and Analysis

Carefully read the following two passages. Use context clues to help you define any words with which you are unfamiliar. In each selection, pay close attention to the author's purpose, main idea, and use of literary and rhetorical devices. Then, on a separate sheet of paper, answer the questions on pages 631–632.

from *The Jungle* by Upton Sinclair

line

When he opened his eyes again it was to the clanging of the bell of an ambulance. He was lying in it, covered by a blanket, and it was threading its way slowly through the holiday-shopping crowds. They took
5 him to the county hospital, where a young surgeon set his arm; then he was washed and laid upon a bed in a ward with a score or two more of maimed and mangled men.

Jurgis spent his Christmas in this hospital,
10 and it was the pleasantest Christmas he had had in America. Every year there were scandals and investigations in this institution, the newspapers charging that doctors were allowed to try fantastic experiments upon the patients; but Jurgis knew
15 nothing of this—his only complaint was that they used to feed him upon tinned meat, which no man who had ever worked in Packingtown would feed to his dog. Jurgis had often wondered just who ate the canned corned beef and "roast beef" of the
20 stockyards; now he began to understand—that it was what you might call "graft meat," put up to be sold to public officials and contractors, and eaten by soldiers and sailors, prisoners and inmates of institutions, "shantymen" and gangs of railroad laborers.
25   Jurgis was ready to leave the hospital at the end of two weeks. This did not mean that his arm was strong and that he was able to go back to work, but simply that he could get along without further

from *The Jungle* by Upton Sinclair *(continued)*

attention, and that his place was needed for some
30   one worse off than he. That he was utterly helpless,
and had no means of keeping himself alive in the
meantime, was something which did not concern
the hospital authorities, nor any one else in the city.

As it chanced, he had been hurt on a
35   Monday, and had just paid for his last week's board
and his room rent, and spent nearly all the balance
of his Saturday's pay. He had less than seventy-five
cents in his pockets, and a dollar and a half due him
for the day's work he had done before he was hurt.
40   He might possibly have sued the company, and got
some damages for his injuries, but he did not know
this, and it was not the company's business to tell
him. He went and got his pay and his tools, which
he left in a pawnshop for fifty cents. Then he went
45   to his landlady, who had rented his place and had no
other for him; and then to his boardinghouse keeper,
who looked him over and questioned him. As he
must certainly be helpless for a couple of months,
and had boarded there only six weeks, she decided
50   very quickly that it would not be worth the risk to
keep him on trust.

So Jurgis went out into the streets, in a most
dreadful plight. It was bitterly cold, and a heavy
snow was falling, beating into his face. He had no
55   overcoat, and no place to go, and two dollars and
sixty-five cents in his pocket, with the certainty that
he could not earn another cent for months.

from *How the Other Half Lives* by Jacob Riis

line

The twenty-five cent lodging-house keeps
up the pretence of a bedroom, though the head-high
partition enclosing a space just large enough to hold
a cot and a chair and allow the man room to pull off
5   his clothes is the shallowest of all pretences. The
fifteen-cent bed stands boldly forth without screen
in a room full of bunks with sheets as yellow and
blankets as foul. At the ten-cent level the locker for
the sleeper's clothes disappears. There is no longer
10   need of it. The tramp limit is reached, and there is
nothing to lock up save, on general principles, the
lodger. Usually the ten- and seven-cent lodgings are

from *How the Other Half Lives* by Jacob Riis (continued)

different grades of the same abomination. Some sort
of an apology for a bed, with mattress and blanket,
15 represents the aristocratic purchase of the tramp
who, by a lucky stroke of beggary, has exchanged
the chance of an empty box or ash-barrel for shelter
on the quality floor of one of these "hotels." A strip
of canvas, strung between rough timbers, without
20 covering of any kind, does for the couch of the seven-
cent lodger who prefers the questionable comfort of a
red-hot stove close to his elbow. . . . On cold winter
nights, when every bunk had its tenant, I have stood in
such a lodging-room more than once, and listening to
25 the snoring of the sleepers like the regular strokes of
an engine, and the slow creaking of the beams under
their restless weight, imagined myself on shipboard
and experienced the very real nausea of sea-sickness.
The one thing that did not favor the deception was
30 the air; its character could not be mistaken.

The proprietor of one of these seven-cent
houses was known to me as a man of reputed wealth
and respectability. He "ran" three such establishments
and made, it was said, $8,000 a year clear profit on
35 his investment. He lived in a handsome house quite
near to the stylish precincts of Murray Hill, where the
nature of his occupation was not suspected. A notice
that was posted on the wall of the lodgers' room
suggested at least an effort to maintain his up-town
40 standing in the slums. It read: "No swearing or loud
talking after nine o'clock." Before nine no exceptions
were taken to the natural vulgarity of the place; but
that was the limit.

There are no licensed lodging-houses known to
45 me which charge less than seven cents for even such
a bed as this canvas strip, though there are unlicensed
ones enough where one may sleep on the floor for
five cents a spot, or squat in a sheltered hallway for
three. The police station lodging-house, where the soft
50 side of a plank is the regulation couch, is next in order.
The manner in which this police bed is "made up" is
interesting in its simplicity. The loose planks that make
the platform are simply turned over, and the job is done,
with an occasional coat of whitewash thrown in to
55 sweeten things.

Questions 1–10 are based on the passage from *The Jungle* (pages 628–629).

1 In the context of line 3, what does the word *threading* mean?
   A sewing
   B winding
   C whirling
   D racing

2 What can you infer about Jurgis from the sentence that begins the second paragraph?
   A He does not enjoy Christmas.
   B He is a new arrival to the United States.
   C He has never celebrated Christmas.
   D He is surprised to learn that Christmas is celebrated in the United States.

3 In the context of line 13, what does the word *fantastic* mean?
   A wonderful
   B amazing
   C zealous
   D strange

4 What is Jurgis's only complaint about the hospital?
   A The quality of the tinned meat is poor.
   B The doctors perform experiments.
   C Scandals are reported.
   D The young doctor is a poor surgeon.

5 Why does Jurgis leave the hospital after two weeks?
   A He is completely healed.
   B He is eager to return to his work.
   C He can get along without further attention.
   D He needs to speak with the boardinghouse keeper.

6 Which of the following is an effect of Jurgis's injury?
   A He loses his ability to work.
   B He is released too soon from the hospital.
   C He sues the company.
   D He spends all his Saturday pay.

7 What is the central conflict presented in this passage?
   A man versus nature
   B man versus man
   C man versus fate
   D man versus society

8 In this passage, how does Sinclair reveal the personality of Jurgis?
   A direct characterization
   B indirect characterization
   C metaphor
   D symbol

9 From what point of view is this passage written?
   A first person
   B second person
   C third-person omniscient
   D third-person limited

10 In this passage from *The Jungle*, how does the setting influence the characters and the plot? Support your answer with evidence from the selection. Write your answer on your paper and use no more than five lines.

Questions 11–20 are based on the passage from *How the Other Half Lives* (pages 629–630).

11 According to Riis, why does the locker disappear at the ten-cent level?
  A There is no room for it.
  B There is no desire for it.
  C There is no need for it.
  D It is what the proprietor wants.

12 From the context, what do you conclude that the word *save* in line 11 means?
  A rescue
  B protect
  C collect
  D except

13 Where does Riis say the seven-cent lodger sleeps?
  A in an empty box
  B on a strip of canvas
  C. on a mattress
  D. behind a partition

14 What literary device is Riis using when he compares the snoring to the "strokes of an engine" in lines 25–26?
  A simile
  B metaphor
  C allusion
  D personification

15 In the context of line 30, what does the word *character* mean?
  A personality
  B person
  C quality
  D reputation

16 What can you infer about Riis's feelings toward the wealthy proprietor?
  A He finds him humorous.
  B He thinks that the proprietor is a swindler.
  C He respects his position of authority.
  D He is envious of his wealth.

17 What is the tone of the sentence "Before nine no exceptions were taken to the natural vulgarity of the place; but that was the limit" in lines 41–43?
  A reportorial
  B comic
  C ironic
  D angry

18 What is the overall tone of this passage?
  A reportorial
  B comic
  C ironic
  D angry

19 On the basis of this passage, which of the following do you think best describes the author's purpose in *How the Other Half Lives*?
  A to entertain
  B to persuade
  C to describe
  D to explain

20 In this passage from *How the Other Half Lives*, in what ways does Riis use figurative and connotative language to support his argument? Do you find his argument convincing? Explain. Write your answer on your paper and use no more than five lines.

Writing: Process and Language Conventions

Each of the following sentences contains either one error or no errors. If the sentence contains an error, write the letter of the underlined word or words that need to be corrected. If the sentence is correct, write *E*.

1 Mark Twain <u>loved</u> being a riverboat pilot
           A
<u>because of</u> the freedom <u>and</u> independence
  B   C
that the job <u>offered</u>. <u>No Error</u>
         D   E

2 Life on the Great Plains <u>were</u> difficult, <u>for</u>
                A   B
settlers <u>there</u> had to endure both isolation
     C
and harsh <u>weather</u> conditions. <u>No Error</u>
       D   E

3 The monologues <u>in</u> *Spoon River Anthology*,
            A
<u>spoken</u> by the dead of a <u>Midwestern</u> town,
  B   C
reveal the <u>essance</u> of small-town life. <u>No Error</u>
      D   E

4 <u>When</u> it is used in moderation, direct
   A
characterization can be an <u>effective</u> means
                  B
of <u>conveying</u> a <u>characters'</u> qualities. <u>No Error</u>
   C   D   E

5 <u>Through</u> his focus <u>on evoking</u> atmosphere and
   A   B
character, Anton Chekhov <u>is influencing</u>
                 C
many later <u>short story</u> writers. <u>No Error</u>
      D   E

6 Do you think that the <u>19th century</u> West was
              A
really <u>populated</u> mainly by gamblers, thieves,
      B
and social misfits, <u>like</u> <u>those</u> in Harte's stories?
          C   D
<u>No Error</u>
 E

Writing: Applications

Write an essay explaining what it means to struggle against injustice. As you write, keep in mind that your essay will be checked for **ideas, organization, voice, word choice, sentence fluency, conventions,** and **presentation.**

Literature Online Unit Assessment To prepare for the unit test, go to www.glencoe.com.

TEST PREPARATION AND PRACTICE **633**

The Great White Way, Times Square, c. 1925. Howard A. Thain. Oil on canvas, New York Historical Society.

BEGINNINGS
OF THE
MODERN AGE
1910–1930s

Looking Ahead

Modern American literature developed in a turbulent era characterized by extremes—both despair and exuberance. The violence of World War I caused many people to lose faith in traditional values. Following the war, an economic boom ushered in an age of prosperity and confidence. Writers of the time created new literary works that mirrored this period of rapid change and clashing values.

Keep the following questions in mind as you read:

- How did World War I change Americans' view of the world?

- How was Modernism a departure from the American literary tradition?

- What social and cultural forces shaped the Harlem Renaissance?

INDIANA ACADEMIC STANDARDS (pages 634–647)

11.3.5 Analyze or evaluate works of literary or cultural significance in history (American…) that reflect a variety of genres in each of the respective historical periods; were written by important authors in the respective major historical periods; reveal contrasts in major themes, styles, and trends; reflect or shed light on the seminal philosophical, religious, social, political, or ethical ideas of their time.

TIMELINE
1910–1930s

Hemingway passport

No. 359666

AMERICAN LITERATURE

1910

1910
Twenty Years at Hull-House by Jane Addams

1912
Harriet Monroe founds *Poetry: A Magazine of Verse*

1913
A Boy's Will poetry collection by Robert Frost

1914
Tender Buttons by Gertrude Stein

1916
Chicago Poems by Carl Sandburg

1919
Winesburg, Ohio by Sherwood Anderson

1920

1920
The Age of Innocence by Edith Wharton

1920
Main Street by Sinclair Lewis

1921
American Indian Stories by Zitkala-Sa

UNITED STATES EVENTS

1910

1910
W. E. B. Du Bois founds the *Crisis* magazine

1911
National Urban League formed to assist African Americans moving into cities

1911
The Nestor Company builds the first Hollywood film studio

1913
Henry Ford introduces assembly-line productivity

1913
U.S. mint issues first "buffalo," or "Indian head," nickel

1914
Marcus Garvey founds Universal Negro Improvement Association

1916
Great Migration begins

1917
United States declares war on Germany

1919
Black Sox Scandal rocks American baseball

1920

1920
Prohibition Amendment outlaws the sale of alcohol

1920
Nineteenth Amendment gives women the right to vote

1920
The nation's first commercial radio station, KDKA, begins broadcasting in Pittsburgh

WORLD EVENTS

1910

1910
Mexican Revolution begins

1910
Japan takes over Korea

1911
Manchu Dynasty overthrown in China

1912
Native American Jim Thorpe stars at the Olympic Games

1912
Titanic sinks after striking an iceberg near Newfoundland

1913
The Rite of Spring by Russian composer Igor Stravinsky marks the beginning of Modernism in music

1913
Marcel Proust publishes the first volume of *Remembrance of Things Past*

Souvenir of **PANAMA AND THE CANAL**

1914 ▲
Panama Canal opens

1914
World War I begins

1918
Armistice signed November 11 in France, ending World War I

1920

1920
First meeting of the League of Nations in Geneva, Switzerland

1921
Diego Rivera begins work on his first mural in Mexico

1921
Mongolia gains independence from China

Langston Hughes

1930

1921
All–African American musical *Shuffle Along* opens on Broadway

1922
The Waste Land by T. S. Eliot

1922
The Enormous Room by E. E. Cummings

1923
Edna St. Vincent Millay wins Pulitzer Prize in poetry

1925
The *New Yorker* magazine established

1925
The Great Gatsby by F. Scott Fitzgerald

1926
The Weary Blues by Langston Hughes ▲

1926
The Sun Also Rises by Ernest Hemingway

1928
Home to Harlem by Claude McKay

1930
Flowering Judas by Katherine Anne Porter

1936
Eugene O'Neill wins Nobel Prize in Literature

1930

1924
Immigration Act bars nearly all Asians

1925
Schoolteacher John Scopes goes on trial for teaching evolution in Tennessee

1926
Jelly Roll Morton and his Red Hot Peppers begin a series of jazz recordings

1927
Conclusion of Sacco-Vanzetti murder trial draws world attention

1927 ▲
Charles Lindbergh flies the first nonstop solo flight across the Atlantic Ocean

1927
Babe Ruth hits 60 home runs, a record until 1961

1927
First feature-length "talkie," or talking motion picture, *The Jazz Singer*, is released

1929
League of United Latin American Citizens founded

1929
The stock market crashes; Great Depression begins

1931
"The Star-Spangled Banner" becomes national anthem

1935
George H. Gallup begins the Gallup Poll

1938
Minimum wage is established in the Fair Labor Standards Act

1930

1922
Irish writer James Joyce publishes *Ulysses*

1926
Economic turmoil leads to a general strike in Britain

1928
Fifteen countries sign the Kellogg-Briand Pact, condemning war

1928
Joseph Stalin starts eliminating private businesses in Soviet Union

▲ Mohandas K. Gandhi

1930
Mohandas K. Gandhi leads protest against British salt monopoly in India

Reading Check

Analyzing Graphic Information How many changes of government throughout the world are shown on this timeline?

Literature Online **Timeline** Visit www.glencoe.com for an interactive timeline.

BY THE NUMBERS

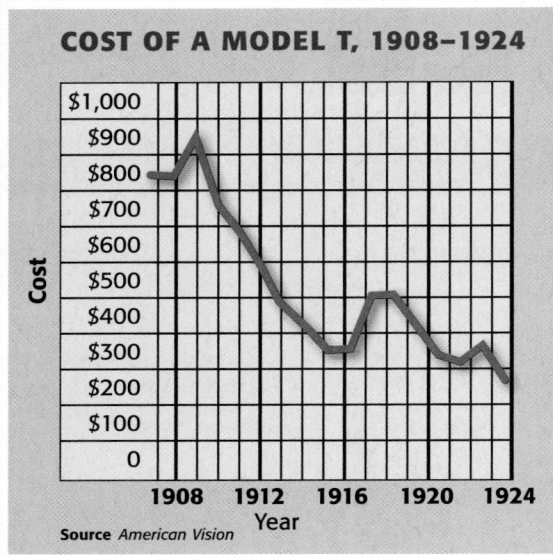

COST OF A MODEL T, 1908–1924

Cost

$1,000
$900
$800
$700
$600
$500
$400
$300
$200
$100
0

1908   1912   1916   1920   1924

Year

Source *American Vision*

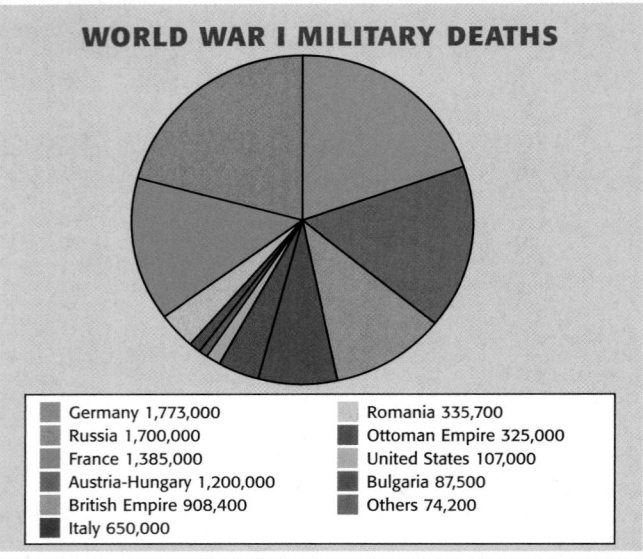

WORLD WAR I MILITARY DEATHS

- Germany 1,773,000
- Russia 1,700,000
- France 1,385,000
- Austria-Hungary 1,200,000
- British Empire 908,400
- Italy 650,000
- Romania 335,700
- Ottoman Empire 325,000
- United States 107,000
- Bulgaria 87,500
- Others 74,200

Back in My Day

The value of a dollar and the cost of goods changed dramatically during the course of the twentieth century. Here are some economic numbers from 1915:

Average Yearly Income

- Workers in finance, insurance, and real estate $1,040
- Industrial workers $687
- Retail trade workers $510
- Farm laborers $355
- Domestic servants $342
- Public school teachers $328

Price of Goods

- Bicycle $11.95
- Baseball $1.15
- Hotel room $1.00
- Dozen eggs   .39
- Glass of cola   .50
- Large roll of toilet paper   .70

HERO'S WELCOME

Charles Lindbergh thrilled people in the United States and abroad in 1927 with his nonstop, 33½-hour flight from New York to Paris. Upon returning he received:

- ticker-tape parade in New York City that used 1,800 pounds of shredded paper
- 7,000 job offers
- 3.5 million letters

GREAT MIGRATION

- In 1910, 75 percent of African Americans lived on farms, and 90 percent lived in the South.
- In the late 1910s and the 1920s, 1.5 million Southern blacks moved to cities—a movement called the "Great Migration."
- During this period, Chicago's black population increased by 148%, Cleveland's by 307%, and Detroit's by 611%.

IMMIGRATION

- More than 17 million immigrants entered the United States in the first quarter of the twentieth century.
- In 1921 Congress passed the Emergency Quota Act, restricting newcomers from Europe to 3 percent of a nationality's U.S. population in the 1910 census. In 1924 this was cut down to 2 percent and was changed to reflect the 1890 census population numbers to further limit immigration.

THE SHORTENING SKIRT

- In 1919, the average distance of a skirt hem above the ground in proportion to a woman's height was 10 percent.
- In 1924, it was 15 percent.
- In 1925, it was 20 percent.
- In 1927, it surpassed 25 percent, reaching the knee.

BEING THERE

A A 1910s farmhouse in rural New England, similar to the one in Derry, New Hampshire, in which Robert Frost lived and wrote.

At the beginnings of the modern era there was war, economic boom and collapse, and the rise of an international culture. These images show the East Coast of the United States, an area strongly affected by these developments.

MAINE

B Women Walking with Girls in Harlem, ca. 1920. Underwood & Underwood. Black and white photograph.

VERMONT

NEW HAMPSHIRE

A

Lake Ontario

NEW YORK

Rochester

Boston

MASSACHUSETTS

Buffalo

RHODE ISLAND

CONNECTICUT

PENNSYLVANIA

B

C New York City

NEW

Philadelphia JERSEY

Baltimore

MARYLAND DELAWARE

C Fifth Avenue at 42nd Street in New York City, photograph 1924. In 1920, for the first time in the country's history, a majority of people lived in cities instead of in rural areas.

Reading Check

Analyzing Graphic Information

1. Which nation had the greatest number of military deaths during World War I?

2. How much less did a Model T cost in 1920 than in 1910?

3. What can you infer about the literature in this unit from the images of Harlem and a rural farmhouse in New Hampshire?

Literature Online **Maps in Motion** Visit www.glencoe.com for an interactive map.

BEGINNINGS OF THE MODERN AGE

1910–1930s

Historical, Social, and Cultural Forces

World War I

Europe exploded into war following the assassination of Austria-Hungary's Archduke Franz Ferdinand in 1914. Complex military alliances and national rivalries quickly divided European countries into two opposing forces. They became known as the Allies (Britain, France, Russia, and Italy) and the Central Powers (Germany, Austria-Hungary, and the Turkish Ottoman Empire). Before the onset of war, Colonel E. M. House, chief adviser to President Woodrow Wilson, said, "The situation is extraordinary. It is militarism run stark mad. . . . There is too much hatred, too many jealousies." For three years, massive armies fought each other all over Europe. The United States joined the war in 1917, in part because a German submarine had sunk an unarmed British ship, the *Lusitania,* in the Atlantic in 1915. Of the 1,198 people lost in the *Lusitania* incident, 128 were U.S. citizens. On November 11, 1918, the Allies emerged victorious. Ten million soldiers died in the war; more lives were lost in World War I than in all wars during the century preceding it. The staggering rate of casualties is attributed to the introduction of tanks, warplanes, machine guns, and poison gas.

The Roaring Twenties

As the world emerged from war, and U.S. soldiers, known as doughboys, returned home, people in the United States longed for a good time. The result was the decade called the Roaring Twenties. The Twenties were marked by a booming economy, jazz, and late-night parties where people danced the Charleston. Young women, nicknamed flappers, wore short skirts, short hair, and lipstick. Some even drove automobiles. Many authorities were unsettled by what they saw as society's loosening morals. Congress had attempted to

set enforcement guidelines for alcohol with the National Prohibition Act of 1919. The law did little to limit drinking. Instead, it contributed to the rise of gangsters such as Al Capone, who secretly transported liquor and ran "speakeasies," nightclubs where people could drink illegally.

Women's Rights

The push for women's right to vote, or suffrage, grew stronger in the early twentieth century. The work of reformer Carrie Chapman Catt led to some states in the Midwest and West granting women the right to vote. However, the move toward a nationwide amendment to the Constitution stalled. In 1917, suffragist leaders such as Alice Paul picketed the White House and went on hunger strikes when they were jailed for their protests. Women finally got the vote when the Nineteenth Amendment became law in 1920. Women also gained a greater place in the workforce and legally enlisted in the military for the first time during this period.

The Great Migration

African Americans left the rural South for northern cities in huge numbers during the 1910s and 1920s. A labor shortage caused by men's leaving to fight in World War I and new limits on immigration from Europe opened up many well-paying jobs for African Americans in cities and industrial areas. Brutal southern segregation policies and widespread crop failure also drove blacks north. With its affordable housing and thriving cultural life, New York City's Harlem was an especially good place to relocate. This largely African American neighborhood was the center of an explosion of creativity in the 1920s, which became a cultural movement known as the Harlem Renaissance.

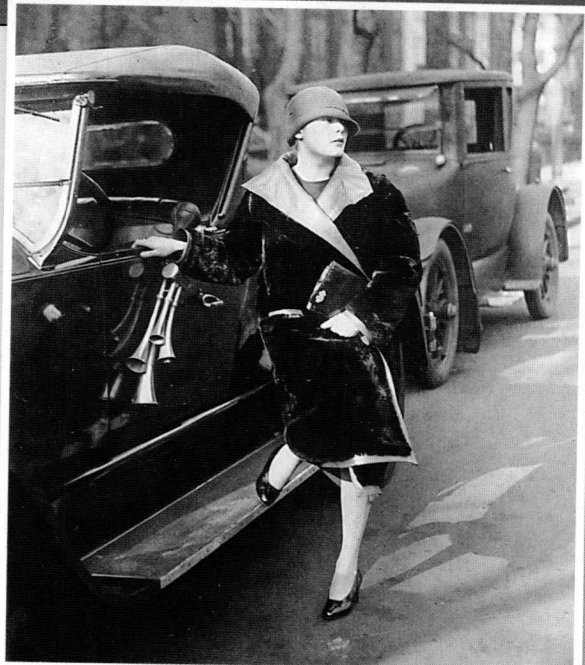

Suzette Dewey, daughter of Charles Dewey, posed beside roadster, c. 1926. Herbert E. French. Photographic print, Library of Congress.

Popular Culture

In the 1920s, U.S. popular culture was transformed by the automobile, radio, movies, advertising, and other innovations. Henry Ford's introduction of the assembly line in 1913 enabled factories to produce cars at prices the average person could afford. During the 1920s, radios became a fixture in U.S. homes, allowing people from across the country to tune in to soap operas, comedy shows, sports, and music. People in the United States became fascinated with the exploits of popular heroes such as baseball star Babe Ruth, tennis champion Bill Tilden, and aviator Charles Lindbergh—who electrified the nation in 1927 by flying the first solo, nonstop transatlantic flight from New York to Paris. Even before the release of the first feature-length "talking" picture in 1927, movies were already an essential part of U.S. life. Attendance continued to rise throughout the 1930s, as movies provided a temporary escape from the hard times of the Depression.

The Great Depression

The stock market crash on October 29, 1929, known as "Black Tuesday," ended the prosperity of the Roaring Twenties. Market conditions were ripe for a collapse, as investors bought stock on credit, and banks did not have enough money in reserve to cover all their customers' deposits. In 1929, investors became worried that their stocks were overvalued and began selling at a frantic pace. Disastrously, no one was buying. By 1933, about a quarter of the population was unemployed, and many families became homeless, depending on soup kitchens and migrant camps for food and shelter.

PREVIEW Big Ideas of the Modern Age

1 New Poetics

In the first part of the twentieth century, American poetry pushed the boundaries of subject matter, form, and style. Poets in this era found inspiration in a wide range of sources and created new ways to capture individual experience.

See pages 642–643.

2 Modern Fiction

World War I created a generation of writers who questioned traditional values. As a result, many of them focused on social problems, a loss of belief in the old truths, and human despair.

See pages 644–645.

3 The Harlem Renaissance

African Americans who flocked to New York City's Harlem turned it into a center of creativity. Out of this cultural whirlwind came literature that both celebrated African American culture and emphasized the struggle against racial prejudice.

See pages 646–647.

Big Idea 1
New Poetics

Have you ever had a feeling that is both unusually strong and remarkably inexpressible? Shortly before the turn of the twentieth century, many U.S. poets tried new ways to express their feelings and observations. Their new, experimental ways of writing became known as Modernism. Some people thought the new poetics, or methods for writing poetry, were an assault on literature. To others, modern poetry spoke eloquently about the mind and the heart of the individual, doing so in new ways linked to the groundbreaking work of earlier poets Walt Whitman and Emily Dickinson (see pages 394–440).

New Directions

Writers in this period believed that American poetry had become stagnant. As Ezra Pound (see pages 652–655) said, the modern poets sought to "Make it new!" Modern poets found inspiration in a wide range of sources beyond the traditional lyric and Romantic poetry of England. The French Symbolist poets, avant-garde, or experimental, painters such as Pablo Picasso, traditional Chinese and Japanese poetry, and everyday life all influenced the new poets.

> "A classic is classic not because it conforms to certain structural rules, or fits certain definitions (of which its author had quite probably never heard). It is classic because of a certain external and irrepressible freshness.
>
> —Ezra Pound
> from *ABC of Reading*

The Imagists

The Imagist movement (see pages 650–651), largely founded by Ezra Pound, flourished after 1910. Imagist poets believed that traditional poetry wasted energy by describing, generalizing, and rhyming. To reform poetry, they insisted on direct presentation of images. "An 'Image' is that which presents an intellectual and emotional complex in an instant of time," Pound wrote. He and other Imagist poets, such as Amy Lowell and H.D. (Hilda Doolittle), also wrote manifestos, statements explaining their artistic philosophy. Imagism strongly influenced William Carlos Williams (see pages 666–670), among others, to expand the subject matter of poetry to include visual impressions that capture the mysterious power of ordinary experience.

Eliot's Perspective

Modernism took a different form in the poetry of T. S. Eliot (see pages 656–665). Wide-ranging allusions—references to history, art, and literature—are a fundamental part of his poetic method. Eliot said: "The poet must become more and more comprehensive, more allusive, more indirect, in order to force, to dislocate if necessary, language into its meaning." Eliot believed that the effects of war and industry had shattered the human spirit. His 1922 poem *The Waste Land*, which takes a pessimistic view of civilization, is considered the most influential poem of this period.

Breaking the Rules

E. E. Cummings (see pages 694–698) didn't care for the literary conventions that govern the arrangement of words, punctuation, and capitalization—or the increasing conformity of individuals in U.S. society either. He insisted on an irregular use of capital and lowercase letters, creating poems that looked ungrammatical, and celebrating the individual—especially the artist. Also a painter, Cummings drew inspiration from the visual arts, using typography and layout in new ways—both playful and serious.

Telegraph Poles with Buildings, 1917. Joseph Stella. Oil on canvas, 36¼ x 30¼ in. Daniel J. Terra Collection, Terra Foundation for American Art, Chicago.

Frost's New England

One major poet of this period, Robert Frost (see pages 704–724), did not follow Modernist poetics. He held firm to traditional New England settings for inspiration, and his lyric poetry is often traditional in form as well. Frost relied largely on rhyme and regular meter, and his language is frequently colloquial. Several of his poems are written as dialogue between two people. Frost often wrote of the loneliness and isolation of the individual, a typical theme in modern poetry.

from I: Six Nonlectures
by E. E. Cummings

Poetry is being, not doing. If you wish to follow, even at a distance, the poet's calling (and here, as always, I speak from my own totally biased and entirely personal point of view) you've got to come out of the measurable doing universe into the immeasurable house of being. I am quite aware that, wherever our socalled civilization has slithered, there's every reward and no punishment for unbeing. But if poetry is your goal, you've got to forget all about punishments and all about rewards and all about selfstyled obligations and duties and responsibilities etcetera ad infinitum and remember one thing only: that it's you—nobody else—who determine your destiny and decide your fate. Nobody else can be alive for you; nor can you be alive for anybody else. Toms can be Dicks and Dicks can be Harrys, but none of them can ever be you. There's the artist's responsibility; and the most awful responsibility on earth. If you can take it, take it—and be.

Reading Check

Summarizing How were the goals of the Modernist poets different from those of more traditional American poetry?

Big Idea 2
Modern Fiction

What is the best way to tell a story? How many ways are there to tell the same story? Modernist fiction writers broke from tradition, as they omitted standard beginnings, transitions, and endings in order to tell stories that reproduced the complex ways in which people think.

The Shadow of War

War often leads to dramatic developments in art and literature. World War I prompted many writers to question cultural traditions and the meaning of life, turning quite a few youthful optimists into premature cynics. One of them, John F. Carter, wrote in an issue of the *Atlantic Monthly*, "The older generation had certainly pretty well ruined this world before passing it on to us. They give us this thing, knocked to pieces, leaky, red-hot, threatening to blow up; and then they are surprised that we don't accept it with the same attitude of pretty, decorous enthusiasm with which they received it." With this shattered world in view, modern fiction writers probed the complex inner workings of the mind and the breakdown of traditional values in the modern age.

The Lost Generation

Many writers left the United States during this period and established new lives in Europe. This led to a more international perspective that contrasted with the regionalism that had dominated American literature after the Civil War. American poet Gertrude Stein, a longtime resident of Paris, remarked to a new American expatriate, the writer Ernest Hemingway (see pages 732–740), that the young people of the time were a "lost generation." This description became a famous label for those who had lost faith in U.S. society and were unsure where to turn. The protagonist, or main character, in Hemingway's novel *The Sun Also Rises* comments on this dilemma when he says, "You can't get away from yourself by moving from one place to another. There's nothing to that." In modern fiction, themes of change, indecision, and broken attachments often replace those of stability, heroism, and love.

The Jazz Age

F. Scott Fitzgerald (pages 742–761) gave the label "the Jazz Age" to the period between the end of World War I and the beginning of the Great Depression. To him, this time was both exuberant and mournful. In his short life, Fitzgerald embodied the frantic pace and social ambitions typical of the Jazz Age. Yet, beneath the surface, he believed that the United States was fundamentally in disarray. He said there was a new "generation grown up to find all Gods dead, all wars fought, all faiths in man shaken." In the United States, desire for consumer goods soared after the war, and symbols of success, such as cars, were everywhere. But many writers were disgusted by what they viewed as shallow materialism. In his novel *The Great Gatsby*, Fitzgerald memorably created glamorous and wealthy characters who dash from one party to the next, yet cannot find happiness.

> "It seemed only a question of a few years before the older people would step aside and let the world be run by those who saw things as they were."
>
> —F. Scott Fitzgerald
> from *Echoes of the Jazz Age*

Hemingway's Prose

Ernest Hemingway wrote in a concise style influenced by his background as a newspaper reporter. His spare style was markedly different from the elaborate prose that short-story writers and novelists had often used in the 1800s. Through understatement and irony, Hemingway's fiction suggests connections that the reader is left to infer. "I always try to write on the principle of the iceberg," he said. "There is seven-eighths of it underwater for every part that shows." Hemingway's first novel, *The Sun Also Rises,* is about members of the lost generation. It is told by Jake Barnes, an American newspaperman who has been wounded in World War I.

New York, 1911. George Bellows. Oil on canvas, 42 x 60 in. National Gallery of Art, Washington, DC.
Collection of Mr. and Mrs. Paul Mellon.

from *The Sun Also Rises* by Ernest Hemingway

You paid some way for everything that was any good. I paid my way into enough things that I liked, so that I had a good time. Either you paid by learning about them, or by experience, or by taking chances, or by money. Enjoying living was learning to get your money's worth and knowing when you had it. You could get your money's worth. The world was a good place to buy in. It seemed like a fine philosophy. In five years, I thought, it will seem just as silly as all the other fine philosophies I've had.

Perhaps that wasn't true, though. Perhaps as you went along you did learn something. I did not care what it was all about. All I wanted to know was how to live in it. Maybe if you found out how to live in it you learned from that what it was all about.

Reading Check

Analyzing Cause and Effect How did World War I affect fiction writing?

Music inspires many of today's writers and artists, just as it did during the Harlem Renaissance. Artists fed off the energy of jazz and their community and changed American art. As Countee Cullen stated in his poem "I Have a Rendezvous With Life," it was time to "face the road, the wind and rain, / To heed the calling deep." The Harlem Renaissance represented the coming-of-age of African American culture and the flowering of the community's creative impulses, especially for southern blacks, who had been exploited for generations in the United States.

Good morning, daddy!
Ain't you heard
The boogie-woogie rumble
Of a dream deferred?

—Langston Hughes
from *Montage of a Dream Deferred*

Blues to Jazz

Out of the African American tradition of spirituals and work songs came blues music. Influenced by blues, jazz developed later in New Orleans as a type of music that combined West African rhythms, ragtime, and some European instruments, such as the string bass. Jazz was largely improvisational, or spontaneous, within a rhythmic framework. Langston Hughes (see pages 809–821) transposed themes and rhythms from blues and jazz into poems that celebrated the everyday life of African Americans and their strength in the face of oppression. Hughes said, "I tried to write poems like the songs they sang on Seventh Street … [these songs] had the pulse beat of the people who keep on going." Jazz inspired an energetic social life and filled clubs. Hughes reported that at one Harlem party thrown by black socialite A'Lelia Walker, it was so crowded that even a Scandinavian prince couldn't get in; he could only have a beverage delivered to his car idling outside the apartment building.

The Neighborhood

Harlem became a main destination during the Great Migration. Word about the vibrant community life and affordable rents in this New York neighborhood quickly spread, attracting writers, artists, and musicians. It was a haven where African Americans could escape the restrictions they faced in the rest of society. In 1929, when the whole country felt the economic shock of the stock market crash, there was less money available to spend on the arts—and as a result, the Harlem Renaissance was over. However, writers in the 1930s and 1940s such as Richard Wright (see pages 900–908) and Ralph Ellison continued the artistic coming-of-age that this movement had begun.

The Deferred Dream

W. E. B. Du Bois's magazine of the NAACP, the *Crisis*, brought racial issues to the forefront of U.S. culture. He wrote that the "problem of the twentieth century is the problem of the color-line." Racial segregation was widespread, and Du Bois said this created a veil of perception that forced African Americans to see themselves through the eyes of whites. The African American "simply wishes to make it possible for a man to be both a Negro and an American, . . . without having the doors of Opportunity closed roughly in his face," Du Bois said. Racial identity became a pivotal issue for writers in this period. For example, Countee Cullen (see pages 830–833) believed that race was a huge issue, but that a poet's race should not determine how he or she writes or how readers and critics understand him or her. Other writers, such as Arna Bontemps (see pages 826–829), believed that a writer's work could not be separated from his or her racial identity.

"The thing to do is to grab the broom of anger and drive off the beast of fear."

—Zora Neale Hurston

The Janitor Who Paints, ca. 1937. Palmer Hayden. Oil on canvas, 39⅛ x 32⅞ in. Smithsonian American Art Museum, Washington, DC.

Hurston's Folklore

Zora Neale Hurston (see pages 790–798) explored the folklore of African Americans, and the building of community in the South during Reconstruction. A student of anthropology, she applied her training to record her own experiences growing up in southern African American communities in works such as *Dust Tracks on a Road.* Hurston first went to Harlem at sixteen when she was traveling as a member of a theater group. Although her work became associated with the Harlem Renaissance, she resisted being classified by any artistic movement. "All clumps of people turn out to be individuals on close inspection," she said.

from *"The Negro Artist and the Racial Mountain"* by Langston Hughes

Most of my own poems are racial in theme and treatment, derived from the life I know. In many of them I try to grasp and hold some of the meanings and rhythms of jazz. I am as sincere as I know how to be in these poems and yet after every reading I answer questions like these from my own people: Do you think Negroes should always write about Negroes? I wish you wouldn't read some of your poems to white folks. How do you find anything interesting in a place like a cabaret? Why do you write about black people? You aren't black. What makes you do so many jazz poems?

But jazz to me is one of the inherent expressions of Negro life in America; the eternal tom-tom beating in the Negro soul—the tom-tom of revolt against weariness in a white world, a world of subway trains, and work, work, work; the tom-tom of joy and laughter, and pain swallowed in a smile. . . .

We younger Negro artists who create now intend to express our individual dark-skinned selves without fear or shame. If white people are pleased we are glad. If they are not, it doesn't matter. We know we are beautiful. And ugly too. The tom-tom cries and the tom-tom laughs. If colored people are pleased we are glad. If they are not, their displeasure doesn't matter either. We build our temples for tomorrow, strong as we know how, and we stand on top of the mountain, free within ourselves.

Reading Check

Analyzing Cause and Effect How did the Harlem Renaissance contribute to the beginnings of the modern age in literature?

WRAP-UP

Why It Matters

The writers who created Modernism challenged the traditional values of society and forms of literature. They believed their innovations brought literature closer to capturing human experience. Today, writers such as Dave Eggers, Jhumpa Lahiri, and Sherman Alexie take on the challenge of portraying reality in the twenty-first century.

Modern poets' use of imagery and everyday speech further convinced people that a poem could be about any subject. The poetry and manifestos of the Imagist movement provided inspiration for many groundbreaking poems of the 1950s and 1960s, such as those of Anne Sexton and Sylvia Plath (see pages 1220–1225).

The Harlem Renaissance was an influential time in African American and United States history. The leading figures in the movement blazed a trail for later African American writers, such as James Baldwin and Ralph Ellison, and helped to push forward the battle for civil rights in the 1960s.

 Literature Online Big Ideas Link to Web resources to further explore the Big Ideas at www.glencoe.com.

Cultural Links

≈ The "little magazines" such as *Poetry* that sprouted up during the period championed modern Imagism and other Modernist experimentation. *Poetry*'s founder, Harriet Monroe, wrote, "The Open Door will be the policy of this magazine—may the great poet we are looking for never find it shut, or half-shut, against his ample genius!" Today, *Poetry* receives about 90,000 submissions per year.

≈ William Carlos Williams influenced the Beat Generation writers of the 1950s with his accessible language and experimentation with form.

≈ The Harlem Renaissance has influenced modern African American poets and hip-hop artists who strive to be leaders for the black community.

You might try using this study organizer to keep track of the big ideas in this unit.

FOLDABLES Study Organizer **THREE-TAB BOOK**

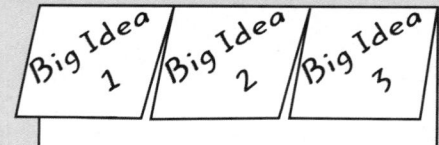

Connect to Today

Use what you have learned about the period to do one of these activities.

Speaking/Listening Working with several other students, create a brief presentation for your class about how Modernism's portrayals of life differ from traditional portrayals of the past. You can use examples from literature, fine art, music, movies, or other kinds of expression.

Visual Literacy Create an illustrated graphic organizer that shows the various influences of World War I on American literature and culture. You might show how writers responded to the effects of war, as well as to the postwar economic boom.

Writing Review the political, social, cultural, and economic aspects of the modern period. How many of these aspects are still a part of United States culture and literature today? Write a brief essay exploring this question.

INDIANA ACADEMIC STANDARDS (page 648)
11.7.19 Deliver multimedia presentations that combine text, images, and sound...

11.4.8 Use systematic strategies to organize...information...

11.5.4 Write historical investigation reports...

 Literature Online Study Central Visit www.glencoe.com and click on Study Central to review the Beginnings of the Modern Age.

PART 1

MODERN POETRY

American Landscape, c. 1930. Charles Sheeler. Oil on canvas, 24 x 31 in. The Museum of Modern Art, New York.

*"Poetry is the opening and closing of a door,
leaving those who look through to guess about
what is seen during a moment."*

—Carl Sandburg, "Poetry Considered"

Symbolist and Imagist Poetry

PHOTOGRAPHERS CAPTURE MOMENTS in time. Painters depict visual ideas through arrangements of colors and shapes. What methods allow writers to use words as someone else might use a camera or a paintbrush? In the beginning of the modern age, a group of poets called the Imagists developed new, influential techniques for presenting visual impressions. Much of their inspiration came from the Symbolists, across the Atlantic Ocean, in France.

The Symbolist Foundation

The avant-garde, or experimental, Symbolist movement in Paris dominated French poetry and art in the late 1800s and inspired the Imagists. Symbolist poets such as Charles Baudelaire, Stéphane Mallarmé, Arthur Rimbaud, and Paul Verlaine reacted against Realism by focusing their attention inward on moods and sensations. These poets believed that direct explanation could not capture emotion. They sought access to the inner workings of the mind through suggestion, metaphor, and symbols. The Symbolists took inspiration from Edgar Allan Poe, whose work is rich in symbolism.

> "No good poetry is ever written in a manner twenty years old, for to write in such a manner shows conclusively that the writer thinks from books, convention and cliché, and not from life."
>
> —Ezra Pound
> "A Retrospect"

The American Imagists

Contrasting with the Symbolists' abstract, atmospheric poetry, the Imagists presented a concrete, tangible image that appeared frozen in time. "Essentially, it is a moment of revealed truth," wrote critic William Pratt on Imagism. In that sense, the

The Flatiron Building, Evening, from *Camera Work*, April, 1906. Edward Steichen.

Imagist method is similar to photography. Beyond that, however, Imagist poetry explores the effect of the image on an observer at a precise moment.

"In a Station of the Metro" by Ezra Pound (see page 654) is a classic example of an Imagist poem. Pound responded to the sight of faces in a train station. Pound deleted words to condense a first draft of thirty lines into two lines of fourteen words and two striking images. He believed that the poet should "use no superfluous word, no adjective which does not reveal something." He found a model for this intense compression in Asian poetry, such as in this haiku (three lines, seventeen syllables, in the original) by Japanese poet Matsuo Basho:

> On a dead limb
> squats a crow—
> Autumn night.
> *(Lucien Stryk translation)*

Sudden Rain Shower on Ohashi Bridge, from *One Hundred Views of Famous Places in Edo,* 1850. Ando Hiroshige. Woodblock print. Musée des Arts Asiatiques-Guimet, Paris. **Viewing the Art:** This wood-block print recalls the style of Japanese haiku masters such as Basho. What does this print have in common with Imagism?

In 1912 Pound submitted three poems by H.D. (Hilda Doolittle) to *Poetry: A Magazine of Verse*. One of the published poems was "Oread" (following). In Greek mythology, the Oreads were nymphs, minor female divinities of nature, from the mountains. Notice the irregular, jagged look of the lines and how the line breaks are determined by the poet's sense of imagery.

Whirl up, sea—
Whirl your pointed pines,
Splash your great pines
On our rocks.
Hurl your green over us—
Cover us with your pools of fir.

H.D. and Amy Lowell were central figures in the Imagist movement. At a poetry reading, Lowell reportedly said to her audience, "Well, clap or hiss, I don't care which, but . . . do something!" Such bold statements energized American poetry, which often displays the Imagist method of compressing an emotion or idea into a sharply observed image.

Imagist Principles

The Imagists issued manifestos, or public declarations on their poetic principles. The following are sample manifestos in the style of those issued:

- The image is the essence, the raw material, of poetry.
- Poetry should be expressed in brief, clear, concrete language that forms precise images.
- These images should instantly convey to the reader the poem's meaning and emotion.
- The language of these poetic images should sound like simple speech—not be made up of predictable rhythms and rhymes but of freer, more-modern verse forms.
- Topics for poems need not be high-minded or "poetic." No topic is unsuitable for a poem.

RESPONDING AND THINKING CRITICALLY

1. Why did the Symbolist poets refrain from directly explaining their themes?

2. What did the Imagists want to eliminate from poetry? Why?

3. What type of images does H.D. create in "Oread"? What impressions and associations do they evoke?

4. Compare and contrast the ways in which the poems on these two pages reflect the themes of Imagist poets. Which do you find most interesting?

INDIANA ACADEMIC STANDARDS
(pages 650–651)
11.3.5 Analyze...works of literary or cultural significance... that...shed light on the...philosophical ideas of their time.

Literature Online Literary History For more about Symbolist and Imagist poetry, go to www.glencoe.com.

In a Station of the Metro and A Pact

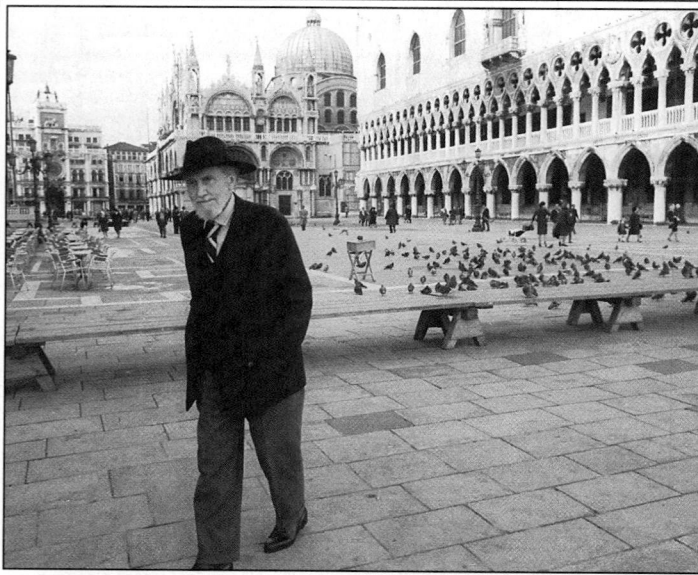

MEET EZRA POUND

Though Ezra Pound's literary accomplishments were immense, many hated him. As his friend and protégé William Carlos Williams wrote, "Pound is a fine fellow, but not one person in a thousand likes him, and a great many people detest him." Nevertheless, T. S. Eliot claimed that Pound was "more responsible for the twentieth-century revolution in poetry than [was] any other individual."

Imagism Pound was born in a small town in Idaho, but two years later his family moved east. When he was still young, he determined that "at thirty [he] would know more about poetry than any living man." Pound entered the University of Pennsylvania at age fifteen but completed his undergraduate education at Hamilton College. As a student, he immersed himself in the Latin, Greek, and French classics.

> "I have weathered the storm,
> I have beaten out my exile."
>
> —Ezra Pound, "The Rest"

After receiving his master's degree in 1906, Pound briefly taught languages at a small Presbyterian college in Indiana. His eccentric manner did not fit well with the school's character, and, at the age of 23, Pound left for Europe. He settled first in London, then Paris, and finally in Italy. There he wrote poetry and criticism and translated verse from nine languages. He also served as an overseas editor for *Poetry* magazine—a position he used to nurture the careers of Robert Frost and T. S. Eliot, among others. In 1912, Pound helped establish Imagism's manifesto. It called for "direct treatment of the 'thing'" and the use of "the language of common speech, but . . . always the exact word."

A Complex Writer Though Pound declared that writers should "Make it new!" he did not believe in newness for its own sake and relied heavily on the literature of the past. In *The Cantos*, his longest and best-known work, Pound combined materials from different cultures and languages, historical texts, and newspaper articles. *The Cantos* is an extremely complex work, notorious for its difficulty and uneven quality.

Politics, Prison, and Exile During World War II, Pound supported Fascist Italian dictator Benito Mussolini and made radio broadcasts openly criticizing the United States and the efforts of the Allies in the war. After Italy fell, Pound spent six months as a prisoner of war near Pisa. Here he wrote *The Pisan Cantos*, generally considered the greatest section of his long work.

After being declared mentally unfit to stand trial for treason, Pound was sent to St. Elizabeth's Hospital for the criminally insane in Washington, D.C. He spent the next twelve years at the hospital, after which the charges against him were dropped. Pound then left the United States, returning to Italy, where he stayed until his death in Venice in 1972.

Ezra Pound was born in 1885 and died in 1972.

Literature Online **Author Search** For more about Ezra Pound, go to www.glencoe.com.

Connecting to the Poems

Have you ever experienced a moment in which an image, a sound, or an idea grabbed your attention and changed how you saw the world? This is what the speaker in each of the following poems experiences. Think about the following questions:

- Have you ever looked at something that you see every day as if for the first time? Explain.
- How can striking images change the way we think about mundane aspects of the world?

Building Background

"In a Station of the Metro" and "A Pact" were originally published together in *Poetry* in 1916. Pound was impressed with the brief but evocative Japanese haiku form (see Literary Terms Handbook, p. R1). After experiencing the moment that inspired "In a Station of the Metro," Pound composed a thirty-line poem. He destroyed this first attempt, calling it a work "of second intensity." After two other tries, he created a short, haiku-like poem with a single powerful image.

Setting Purposes for Reading

Big Idea New Poetics

As you read, notice how Pound employs free verse and the rules of Imagism in his work.

Literary Element Imagery

Imagery is the "word pictures" that writers create to make their subject more vivid or to evoke an emotional response in the reader. In creating effective images, writers use sensory details, or descriptions that appeal to one or more of the five sense: sight, hearing, touch, taste, and smell. As you read the poems, examine how Pound uses imagery to heighten the effect of his words.

- See Literary Terms Handbook, p. R9.

Literature Online Interactive Literary Elements Handbook To review or learn more about the literary elements, go to www.glencoe.com.

Reading Strategy Questioning

Questioning is asking yourself regularly whether you've understood what you have read. In an Imagist poem such as "In a Station of the Metro," it is important to use questioning to slow down your reading in order to fully understand the poet's meaning.

Reading Tip: Taking Notes As you read "In a Station of the Metro" and "A Pact," note in a double-entry journal any questions that occur to you.

Questions	Answers
How does Pound feel about Walt Whitman?	

Vocabulary

apparition (ap′ ə rish′ ən) *n.* a ghostlike or nearly invisible appearance; p. 654 *Those who saw the shadowy apparition in the cemetery believed it was a ghost.*

bough (bou) *n.* tree branch; p. 654 *The baby bird clung to the bough as it waited for food.*

detest (di test′) *v.* to greatly dislike or loathe; p. 654 *I have detested television ever since my favorite show was canceled.*

sap (sap) *n.* a watery source of nutrients that flows through a plant's circulatory system; p. 654 *I decided never to park under a tree again after finding my car covered in sap.*

commerce (kom′ ərs) *n.* exchange of ideas and opinions; p. 654 *Through lively debate and commerce, the two opposing political sides were able to reach an agreement.*

Vocabulary Tip: Context Clues When you look at the words and sentences surrounding a new or unfamiliar word to define it, you are using context clues.

INDIANA ACADEMIC STANDARDS (pages 653–655)
11.3.4 Analyze ways in which poetry...uses imagery...
11.2 Develop strategies such as asking questions...

11.5.2 Write responses to literature that...analyze the use of...language...

A Pact

Ezra Pound

I make a pact with you, Walt Whitman—
I have **detested** you long enough.
I come to you as a grown child
Who has had a pig-headed father;
5 I am old enough now to make friends.
It was you that broke the new wood,
Now is a time for carving.
We have one **sap** and one root—
Let there be **commerce** between us.

Vocabulary

detest (di test′) v. to greatly dislike or loathe
sap (sap) n. a watery source of nutrients that flows through a plant's circulatory system
commerce (kom′ ərs) n. exchange of ideas and opinions

Big Idea New Poetics *What does line 6 suggest about Pound's understanding of Walt Whitman's relationship to modern poetry?*

In a Station of the Metro [1]

Ezra Pound

The **apparition** of these faces in the crowd;
Petals on a wet, black **bough.**

---

1 The *Metro* refers to the Paris subway.

Vocabulary

apparition (ap′ ə rish′ ən) n. a ghostlike or nearly invisible appearance
bough (bou) n. tree branch

RESPONDING AND THINKING CRITICALLY

Respond

1. Which of these poems do you think reveals more about the poet? Explain.

Recall and Interpret

2. (a)In the first line of "In a Station of the Metro," what word does the speaker use to describe how the faces look to him? (b)What might that word suggest about the faces?

3. (a)In the second line, to what image does the speaker compare the faces? (b)From this image, what can you infer about the speaker's feelings?

4. (a)In "A Pact," to whom is the poem addressed? In what way have the speaker's feelings changed about that person? (b)What might be the reason?

5. (a)What is the **extended metaphor** used in the last four lines of "A Pact"? (b)What idea do you think the speaker expresses in these lines?

Analyze and Evaluate

6. Pound once wrote, "The image is the poet's pigment." How is "In a Station of the Metro" like a painting? Explain.

7. (a)Briefly describe the most important differences in tone, form, and content of these two poems. (b)Which poem seems more compelling? Explain.

Connect

8. [Big Idea] **New Poetics** How do these poems embody the values and stylistic goals of Modernism and Imagism?

LITERARY ANALYSIS

[Literary Element] Imagery

While most of the **imagery** in literature appeals to the sense of sight, imagery can appeal to all five senses. Sometimes the same image will involve more than a single sense. For example, Edgar Allan Poe's "The Raven" (page 244) includes the following line: "And the silken, sad, uncertain rustling of each purple curtain." In this line, Poe appeals to the senses of touch, hearing, and sight.

1. Which senses does Pound appeal to in "In a Station of the Metro"?

2. Identify one image from "A Pact" that appeals to the sense of sight.

Writing About Literature

Compare and Contrast Tone Write a brief essay in which you compare and contrast the tones of "In a Station of the Metro" and "A Pact." Consider how word choice and imagery work together to create a specific tone for each poem. You might want to organize your ideas in a Venn diagram before you begin.

READING AND VOCABULARY

[Reading Strategy] Questioning

Questioning can help you determine an author's purpose and the parts of a selection that are the most important. As you read a text, be sure to continually ask yourself whether you understand the ideas the author is trying to convey.

1. What do you think was Pound's purpose for writing "A Pact"?

2. Write and answer two questions you might ask about the poem that could help you determine Pound's purpose. Give evidence for your answers.

[Vocabulary] Practice

Practice with Context Clues For each blank identify the appropriate vocabulary word.

1. Anger never solved anything; we need healthy dialogue and ____ to solve the problem.

2. I highly doubt that some ghostly ____ stole your homework.

3. The heavy storm caused the ____ of a tree to fall and crash into my windshield.

4. I have never enjoyed travel in an airplane; in fact, I have always ____ it.

The Love Song of J. Alfred Prufrock

MEET T. S. ELIOT

T. S. Eliot revolutionized poetry more than any other twentieth-century writer. His experiments in language and form and his introduction of the scenes and concerns of everyday life into poetry changed literary tastes and influenced future poets.

Eliot was born in St. Louis, Missouri, into a distinguished family that provided him with the best education available. In 1906 he matriculated at Harvard, where he steeped himself in literature and published his first poems. At Harvard, he studied under Irving Babbitt, the New Humanist critic of Romanticism, who helped Eliot develop his taste for classicism in literature. Eliot then studied philosophy at the Sorbonne in Paris, at Harvard, and at Oxford. He eventually settled in England.

The First Modernist Poet In his youth, Eliot was influenced by the French Symbolist poets. In England, Eliot met the Imagist poet Ezra Pound, another American expatriate. Pound had an even stronger influence on Eliot. He championed Eliot's writing and served as his editor. In 1915 Pound persuaded *Poetry* magazine to publish "The Love Song of J. Alfred Prufrock." Often called the first Modernist poem, "Prufrock" captures the emptiness and alienation many people experienced while living in impersonal modern cities. The poem baffled and angered many readers. They found its subject matter "unpoetic," its fragmented structure off-putting, and its allusions, difficult to understand.

The outbreak of World War I prevented Eliot's return to Harvard for his final doctoral examinations. He remained in England, where he married Vivien Haigh-Wood, taught school, and worked for Lloyds Bank. He also continued to write poetry and literary essays. His best-known work, *The Waste Land*, was published in 1922; in it he expresses the disillusionment that many people felt after World War I and decries the inability to find meaning and purpose in life. The work brought him international acclaim, but not happiness. Eliot was facing great strain in his marriage and in his job.

> "Genuine poetry can communicate before it is understood."
>
> —T. S. Eliot

Finding a Purpose Eventually, Eliot began a new, more satisfying career as a book editor and joined the Church of England. In Christianity he found a purpose in life, and in his poems, such as "The Hollow Men," "Ash Wednesday," and *Four Quartets*, he described the importance and difficulty of belief in a spiritually impoverished world.

In his later years, Eliot wrote several plays, attempting to adapt verse drama to the modern stage. *Murder in the Cathedral* (1935), about the martyrdom of Saint Thomas à Becket, was a great success in both England and the United States. He also wrote literary criticism. In recognition of his achievements, he received the Nobel Prize in Literature in 1948. Eliot's poetry has been praised for the power of its symbolism, its precise, often ironic language, and its mastery of form. At the time of his death in 1965, Eliot was considered by many to be the most important and influential poet and critic writing in the English language.

T. S. Eliot was born in 1888 and died in 1965.

Literature Online **Author Search** For more about T. S. Eliot, go to www.glencoe.com.

Connecting to the Poem

In Eliot's poem, the speaker asks himself, "Do I dare?" about several things. As you read, think about the following questions:

- What makes the speaker afraid to dare?
- Do you find the questions that the speaker asks himself to be important or trivial? What would you choose to do if you were in the speaker's situation?

Building Background

When Eliot wrote "The Love Song of J. Alfred Prufrock," cities were growing at a rapid rate. In many countries, city dwellers outnumbered those inhabiting rural areas. Factories overran residential neighborhoods, and people crowded into huge tenement buildings. Factory owners amassed great wealth at the expense of workers who toiled under miserable conditions. In his poems, Eliot expressed the feelings of loneliness, alienation, and frustration that came with these changes.

Setting Purposes for Reading

Big Idea New Poetics

As you read, notice how Eliot deliberately rejects some of the conventions of traditional poetry.

Literary Element Allusion

An **allusion** is an indirect reference to a character, a place, or a situation from history, art, music, or literature. For example, "The Love Song of J. Alfred Prufrock" can be seen as an extended allusion to Dante's *Inferno*. By quoting Dante in the epigraph, Eliot suggests that Prufrock's journey with a companion through the streets of London to "the room" is similar to the journey that Dante and Virgil make through the underworld to the center of hell.

- See Literary Terms Handbook, p. R1.

 Literature Online Interactive Literary Elements Handbook To review or learn more about the literary elements, go to www.glencoe.com.

INDIANA ACADEMIC STANDARDS (pages 657–665)
11.3 [Identify] connections and comparisons across texts…
11.3.5 Analyze…works…that…reflect or shed light on…social…ideas of their time.

11.5.2 Write responses to literature that…assess the impact of perceived ambiguities…within the text.

Reading Strategy Connecting to Cultural Context

A piece of writing is more meaningful to you when you place it in its cultural context. Think about the society in which the writer lived, the technologies that surrounded the writer, and the historical forces that influenced the writer's choice of subject matter, point of view, and tone. "Prufrock," like much of Eliot's work, is set in the cultural context of England's upper-middle-class society in London before, during, and after World War I.

Vocabulary

insidious (in si′dē əs) *adj.* slyly dangerous; deceitful; p. 658 *The insidious criminal gained the confidence of his victims.*

presume (pri zōōm′) *v.* to expect something without justification; to take for granted; p. 660; *The employee presumed she would be promoted because her boss liked her.*

digress (dī gres′) *v.* to depart from the main subject; to ramble; p. 660 *The history teacher liked to digress by telling the class amusing personal anecdotes.*

malinger (mə ling′gər) *v.* to pretend incapacity or illness to avoid work; p. 660 *In order to avoid the big math test, John decided to malinger and stayed home.*

deferential (def′ə ren′shəl) *adj.* yielding to someone else's opinions or wishes; p. 662 *The devoted son was always deferential toward his father.*

Vocabulary Tip: Antonyms Antonyms are words that have opposite or nearly opposite meanings. Antonyms are always the same part of speech.

The Love Song of J. Alfred Prufrock

T. S. Eliot

Winter Night, 1928. Stefan Hirsch. Oil on panel, 22½ x 19¾ in.
Collection of the Newark Museum.

S'io credessi che mia resposta fosse
a persona che mai tornasse al mondo,
questa fiamma staria senza più scosse.
Ma per ciò che giammai di questo fondo
non tornò vivo alcun, s'i'odo il vero,
senza tema d'infamia ti respondo.[1]

Let us go then, you and I,
When the evening is spread out against the sky
Like a patient etherised[2] upon a table;
Let us go, through certain half-deserted streets,
5   The muttering retreats
Of restless nights in one-night cheap hotels
And sawdust restaurants with oyster-shells:
Streets that follow like a tedious[3] argument
Of **insidious** intent
10   To lead you to an overwhelming question . . .
Oh, do not ask, 'What is it?'
Let us go and make our visit.

1. The epigraph is from Dante's *Inferno,* Canto XXVII, in which a condemned spirit in hell confesses his sins. He says, "If I thought that I was speaking / to someone who would go back to the world, / this flame would shake no more. / But since nobody has ever / gone back alive from this place, if what I hear is true, / I answer you without fear of infamy."
2. *Etherised (etherized)* (ē′ thə rīzd′) means "anesthetized with ether, as before an operation"; in other words, "made insensitive to pain."
3. *Tedious* means "tiresome because of length" or "boring."

Big Idea New Poetics *How is this simile an example of Modernism in poetry?*

Vocabulary

insidious (in si′ dē əs) *adj.* slyly dangerous; deceitful

In the room the women come and go
Talking of Michelangelo.[4]

15 The yellow fog that rubs its back upon the window-panes,
The yellow smoke that rubs its muzzle on the window-panes,
Licked its tongue into the corners of the evening,
Lingered upon the pools that stand in drains,
Let fall upon its back the soot that falls from chimneys,
20 Slipped by the terrace, made a sudden leap,
And seeing that it was a soft October night,
Curled once about the house, and fell asleep.
And indeed there will be time
For the yellow smoke that slides along the street
25 Rubbing its back upon the window-panes;
There will be time, there will be time
To prepare a face to meet the faces that you meet;
There will be time to murder and create,
And time for all the works and days of hands
30 That lift and drop a question on your plate;
Time for you and time for me,
And time yet for a hundred indecisions,
And for a hundred visions and revisions,
Before the taking of a toast and tea.

35 In the room the women come and go
Talking of Michelangelo.

And indeed there will be time
To wonder, 'Do I dare?' and, 'Do I dare?'
Time to turn back and descend the stair,
40 With a bald spot in the middle of my hair—
(They will say: 'How his hair is growing thin!')
My morning coat,[5] my collar mounting firmly to the chin,
My necktie rich and modest, but asserted[6] by a simple pin—
(They will say: 'But how his arms and legs are thin!')
45 Do I dare
Disturb the universe?
In a minute there is time
For decisions and revisions which a minute will reverse.

For I have known them all already, known them all—
50 Have known the evenings, mornings, afternoons,

4. *Michelangelo* Buonarroti (mī′ kəl an′ jə lō bwô nä rô′ tē) (1475–1564) was a gifted Italian sculptor and painter.

5. A *morning coat* is a man's jacket that slopes away from a front button at the waist to tails at the back. It was worn for formal daytime dress.

6. Here, *asserted* means "made more bold" or "enhanced."

Reading Strategy Connecting to Cultural Context *What is the cultural difference between this room and the streets through which Prufrock has traveled?*

Big Idea New Poetics *How does Eliot disregard traditional poetic elements in these lines? What traditional element does he keep?*

I have measured out my life with coffee spoons;
I know the voices dying with a dying fall
Beneath the music from a farther room.
   So how should I **presume?**

55 And I have known the eyes already, known them all—
The eyes that fix you in a formulated[7] phrase,
And when I am formulated, sprawling on a pin,
When I am pinned and wriggling on the wall,
Then how should I begin
60 To spit out all the butt-ends of my days and ways?
   And how should I presume?
And I have known the arms already, known them all—
Arms that are braceleted and white and bare
(But in the lamplight, downed with light brown hair!)?
65 Is it perfume from a dress
That makes me so **digress?**
Arms that lie along a table, or wrap about a shawl.
   And should I then presume?
   And how should I begin?
70 Shall I say, I have gone at dusk through narrow streets
And watched the smoke that rises from the pipes
Of lonely men in shirt-sleeves, leaning out of windows? . . .
I should have been a pair of ragged claws
Scuttling across the floors of silent seas.
75 And the afternoon, the evening, sleeps so peacefully!
Smoothed by long fingers,
Asleep . . . tired . . . or it **malingers,**
Stretched on the floor, here beside you and me.
Should I, after tea and cakes and ices,
80 Have the strength to force the moment to its crisis?
But though I have wept and fasted, wept and prayed,
Though I have seen my head (grown slightly bald) brought in
   upon a platter[8]
I am no prophet[9]—and here's no great matter;
I have seen the moment of my greatness flicker,

7. *Formulated* means "reduced to or expressed as a formula," thereby losing individuality.

8. [*head . . . platter*] This biblical reference is to the beheading of the prophet John the Baptist (Matthew 14:1–11). King Herod was so pleased with the dancing of Salome, his stepdaughter, that he promised her anything she desired. Prompted by her mother, Salome asked for the head of John on a platter. Herod granted her request.

9. A *prophet* is a person who predicts the future or who speaks by divine inspiration.

Reading Strategy Connecting to Cultural Context *What does this metaphor tell the reader about the society that Prufrock inhabits?*

Literary Element Allusion *Although he claims not to be a prophet, Prufrock compares himself to John the Baptist. In what sense does Prufrock envision his head "brought in upon a platter"?*

Vocabulary

presume (pri zoom′) *v.* to expect something without justification; to take for granted
digress (dī gres′) *v.* to depart from the main subject; to ramble
malinger (mə ling′gər) *v.* to pretend incapacity or illness to avoid work

Rainy Night, 1930. Charles Burchfield. Watercolor, 30 x 42 in. San Diego Museum of Art.

85   And I have seen the eternal Footman[10] hold my coat, and
     snicker,
     And in short, I was afraid.

     And would it have been worth it, after all,
     After the cups, the marmalade, the tea,
     Among the porcelain, among some talk of you and me,
90   Would it have been worth while,
     To have bitten off the matter with a smile,
     To have squeezed the universe into a ball

     To roll it towards some overwhelming question,
     To say: 'I am Lazarus, come from the dead,[11]
95   Come back to tell you all, I shall tell you all'—
     If one, settling a pillow by her head,
         Should say: 'That is not what I meant at all.
         That is not it, at all.'
     And would it have been worth it, after all,
100 Would it have been worth while,

10. The *eternal Footman* is Death.

11. [*I am Lazarus . . . dead*] This
     biblical reference is to John
     11:1–44 in which Jesus restores
     his friend Lazarus to life after he
     has been dead for four days.

Reading Strategy   Connecting to Cultural Context *How does this
symbol characterize the cultural context of the poem?*

Literary Element   Allusion *How is Prufrock's allusion to Lazarus ironic?*

After the sunsets and the dooryards and the sprinkled streets,
After the novels, after the teacups, after the skirts that trail
along the floor—
And this, and so much more?—
It is impossible to say just what I mean!

105 But as if a magic lantern[12] threw the nerves in patterns on a
screen:
Would it have been worth while
If one, settling a pillow or throwing off a shawl,
And turning toward the window, should say:
    'That is not it at all,
110   That is not what I meant, at all.'

No! I am not Prince Hamlet,[13] nor was meant to be;
Am an attendant lord, one that will do
To swell a progress,[14] start a scene or two,
Advise the prince; no doubt, an easy tool,
115 **Deferential,** glad to be of use,
Politic,[15] cautious, and meticulous;
Full of high sentence, but a bit obtuse;[16]
At times, indeed, almost ridiculous—
Almost, at times, the Fool.

120 I grow old . . . I grow old . . .
I shall wear the bottoms of my trousers rolled.

Shall I part my hair behind? Do I dare to eat a peach?
I shall wear white flannel trousers, and walk upon the beach.
I have heard the mermaids singing, each to each.

125 I do not think that they will sing to me.

I have seen them riding seaward on the waves
Combing the white hair of the waves blown back
When the wind blows the water white and black.

We have lingered in the chambers of the sea
130 By sea-girls wreathed with seaweed red and brown
Till human voices wake us, and we drown.

12. The *magic lantern*, a forerunner of the modern slide projector, was a device for projecting enlarged images.

13. *Prince Hamlet* is the Prince of Denmark, the tragic hero of Shakespeare's play *Hamlet*.
14. *To swell a progress* is to participate in, and thereby increase (swell) the number of people in a royal procession or a play.
15. *Politic* (po′ lə tik) means "characterized by prudence or shrewdness in managing, dealing, or promoting a policy."
16. *High sentence* is fancy, pompous speech full of advice, like that of the old counselor Polonius in *Hamlet*. *Obtuse* (əb to͞os) means "slow in understanding" or "dull."

Literary Element Allusion *What does this allusion tell the reader about how Prufrock sees himself?*

Big Idea New Poetics *How is this line an example of the new poetics of Modernism?*

Vocabulary

deferential (def′ ə ren′shəl) *adj.* yielding to someone else's opinions or wishes

662 UNIT 5 BEGINNINGS OF THE MODERN AGE

RESPONDING AND THINKING CRITICALLY

Respond

1. What image does the name *J. Alfred Prufrock* conjure up for you? How does Prufrock, as his character and personality are expressed throughout the poem, illustrate this image?

Recall and Interpret

2. (a)In lines 1–9, what do the images that Prufrock uses to describe the evening and the places he will travel through evoke? (b)What do these descriptions suggest about his state of mind?

3. (a)What kinds of activities does Prufrock say he will have time for in lines 26–48? (b)What does he mean by "Do I dare/Disturb the universe"?

4. (a)How does Prufrock describe himself and his life in lines 49–74? (b)What does Prufrock's description of his life suggest about his personal self-assessment?

Analyze and Evaluate

5. (a)What are being compared in the extended metaphor in lines 15–22? (b)How does this metaphor contribute to the meaning of the poem?

6. (a)In lines 26–27, Prufrock says that there will be time "To prepare a face to meet the faces that you meet." For what occasions does one "prepare a face"? Explain. (b)What is the difference between meeting a "face" and meeting a person?

7. (a)What, in your opinion, is Prufrock's "overwhelming question" (lines 10 and 93)? (b)Why does Prufrock never ask the question?

8. (a)What does the allusion to mermaids (lines 124–130) suggest about Prufrock's state of mind? (b)What is the function of the final line of the poem?

Connect

9. **Big Idea** New Poetics (a)How does this "love song" differ from traditional love poetry? (b)How is the title of the poem ironic?

VISUAL LITERACY: Fine Art

Study the painting *Rainy Night* below. The painter, Charles Burchfield (1893–1967), is known for his watercolors. This work was painted in 1930 and is representative of the second phase of the artist's career, when he painted scenes depicting the bleakness of city life.

1. What is your overall impression of the painting? Cite details in the painting that contribute to your impression.

2. Which images or lines from "The Love Song of J. Alfred Prufrock" might you use to describe this painting? Explain.

Rainy Night, 1930. Charles Burchfield. Watercolor, 30 x 42 in. San Diego Museum of Art.

Literary Element | Allusion

When an author uses an **allusion,** he or she appeals to the reader to appreciate and enjoy a shared artistic experience. An allusion can add richness and depth to a work of literature through its association of ideas. For example, lines 92–93 contain an allusion to Andrew Marvell's poem "To His Coy Mistress," in which the speaker says, "Let us roll all our strength and all / Our sweetness into one ball, / And tear our pleasures with rough strife / Through the iron gates of life." This allusion is ironic because Prufrock, after squeezing "the universe into a ball," is unable to "roll it towards some overwhelming question."

1. In the allusion to Shakespeare in lines 111–119, why does Prufrock claim he is *not* Prince Hamlet?

2. In the poem, Prufrock makes allusions to John the Baptist, Lazarus, and Hamlet. What do these characters have in common? How do they relate to Prufrock?

3. In your opinion, what is the overall effect of Eliot's use of allusions in this poem?

Review: Dramatic Monologue

As you learned on page 500, a **dramatic monologue** is an extended speech by a literary character to a silent listener. When that silent listener is the reader, the speech takes the form of an interior monologue, also known as **stream of consciousness,** a term first used by the psychologist William James to describe the spontaneous flow of a person's random thoughts and feelings. Some readers have interpreted "Prufrock" as a stream-of-consciousness monologue in which Prufrock addresses his *alter ego,* or the opposite side of his personality.

Partner Activity Meet with a classmate and talk about the function of the dramatic monologue in "The Love Song of J. Alfred Prufrock." Address these questions during your discussion:

1. Who is the "you" in line 1?

2. What is the relationship between the "you" in the poem and the "you" in the epigraph from Dante's *Inferno?*

3. Does Prufrock maintain the same tone throughout the poem? Explain.

Reading Strategy | Connecting to Cultural Context

You can use what you know about the **cultural context** of the poem to enhance its meaning. For example, the allusion "In the room the women come and go / Talking of Michelangelo" (lines 13–14, 35–36) refers to the great Italian Renaissance painter.

1. What sort of room do you imagine the women are in? Describe it.

2. What can you infer about these women?

3. Why do you think that the lines are repeated? What can you infer from this repetition about the nature of the women's conversations?

Vocabulary | Practice

Practice with Antonyms Find the antonym for each vocabulary word from "The Love Song of J. Alfred Prufrock" listed in the first column. Use a dictionary if you need help.

1. insidious	a. candid	b. honest
2. presume	a. demur	b. defer
3. digress	a. stray	b. focus
4. malinger	a. persevere	b. pretend
5. deferential	a. rude	b. arrogant

Academic Vocabulary

Here are two words from the vocabulary list on page R86. These words will help you think, write, and talk about the selection.

comment (ko´ment) *v.* to make an observation or criticism; to express an opinion

seek (sēk) *v.* to go in search of; to look for

Practice and Apply

1. **Comment** on how successful you think Eliot was in finding new forms and new poetics to express his ideas in "The Love Song of J. Alfred Prufrock."

2. What does the speaker seem to **seek** throughout the poem? Does he find it?

Writing About Literature

Analyze Character Is Prufrock a tragic character—is the reader supposed to feel sorrow and pity about his situation? Or is he a comic character—is the reader supposed to laugh at him or think he is foolish? Write a brief essay in which you express and support your opinion. Begin by formulating a main idea in which you state that Prufrock is essentially tragic or comic—or a combination of both. Then review the poem to find lines and images that support your position. Organize your thoughts in a graphic organizer, such as the one below.

Main Idea

Supporting Detail

Supporting Detail

Supporting Detail

Conclusion

Then write a draft, making sure to include all your supporting details. Make smooth transitions between your ideas.

After you complete your draft, meet with a peer reviewer. Evaluate each other's work and suggest revisions. Then proofread and edit your draft for errors in spelling, grammar, and punctuation. Submit the final copy to your teacher.

Performing

Put Yourself in Prufrock's Shoes Choose a section (at least 15–20 lines) of "Prufrock" to perform. In planning your performance, you can create a costume or use props if you wish, but it is more important to choose a physical posture and vocal quality appropriate to the character. Plan your facial expressions, gestures, and movements. Also, practice speaking the lines aloud to determine the appropriate volume, intonation, and timing—and to determine which words and phrases you should emphasize. Finally, perform your piece for the class.

Literature Online **Web Activities** For eFlashcards, Selection Quick Checks, and other Web activities, go to www.glencoe.com.

Eliot's Language and Style

Using Infinitives An **infinitive** is a verb form that is usually preceded by the word *to* and is used as a noun, an adjective, or an adverb. In "The Love Song of J. Alfred Prufrock," Eliot uses infinitives to achieve emphasis through repetition and grammatical parallelism. Consider the following stanzas:

"And would it have been worth it, after all,
After the cups, the marmalade, the tea,
Among the porcelain, among some talk of you
    and me,
Would it have been worth while,
To have bitten off the matter with a smile,
To have squeezed the universe into a ball

To roll it towards some overwhelming question,
To say: 'I am Lazarus, come from the dead,
Come back to tell you all, I shall tell you all'—
If one, settling a pillow by her head,
    Should say: 'That is not what I meant at all.
    That is not it, at all.'"

Notice the grammatical parallelism in this stanza. All but one infinitive serve as appositives to "it."

Infinitive	Part of Speech	Function
To have bitten	noun	appositive
To have squeezed	noun	appositive
To roll	noun	appositive
To say	noun	appositive
To tell	adverb	modifies "come back"

Activity Create a chart similar to the one above in which you list other infinitives in the poem, their parts of speech, and their functions.

Revising Check

Using Infinitives With a partner, go through the character analysis essay you wrote earlier. Look for places where you could improve clarity by using infinitives. Revise your essay accordingly.

The Red Wheelbarrow and This Is Just to Say

MEET WILLIAM CARLOS WILLIAMS

William Carlos Williams led a double life as a doctor and an award-winning poet. Often he would write between seeing patients, sometimes even jotting down poems on prescription pads. Despite the fact that his attention was divided, Williams managed to write some of the most memorable poems of the Imagist movement. In his poetry, he captured America's colloquial speech and presented everyday events in powerful, compact lines.

> "Eyes stand first in the poet's equipment."
>
> —William Carlos Williams

Doctor and Poet Williams was born in Rutherford, New Jersey, and came from a diverse background: his mother was born in Puerto Rico, and his father was British. Williams began writing poetry in high school and soon settled on the goal of becoming both a doctor and a writer.

While attending the University of Pennsylvania Medical School, Williams wrote many of the poems that would appear in his first book, *Poems*, published in 1909. At school he also met and befriended the poet Ezra Pound. Pound would become a great influence on the young Williams, even arranging for the publication of his second collection, *The Tempers*, in 1913.

After completing his internship in New York and further study in advanced pediatrics in Leipzig, Germany, Williams returned to Rutherford, where he began his medical practice and continued to write. In his next book, *Al Que Quiere! (To Him Who Wants It!)*, published in 1917, Williams drew upon his Spanish and Puerto Rican heritage and established himself as a major voice in modern poetry. However, Williams soon began to drift away from Pound and mainstream Imagism. He felt that Pound's ideas were too rooted in the cultural values of Europe, and not those of the United States, which Williams so adored.

During the 1920s and 1930s, Williams published several books, including two collections of poetry, *Kora in Hell* and *Spring and All*; a book of essays, *In the American Grain*; and a novel, *White Mule*, which was the first in a trilogy telling the story of an American family. From 1946 through 1958, Williams worked on his masterpiece, *Paterson*. This epic poem, which spans five volumes, mythologizes the world of northern New Jersey. In 1963 Williams was awarded a posthumous Pulitzer Prize for his collection *Pictures from Brueghel and Other Poems*.

Visionary and Legacy Believing that poetry should be grounded in everyday things and scenes, Williams was famous for saying, "No ideas but in things." He explored the world around him, writing of New Jersey's gritty, industrial landscape and of his patients and neighbors, many of whom were impoverished immigrants struggling to succeed in the United States. Williams left an impressive legacy of work that had an enormous influence on the writers of the 1950s and 1960s and continues to be very important to poets today. Somehow, while accomplishing so much as a writer, he also managed to deliver more than two thousand babies.

William Carlos Williams was born in 1883 and died in 1963.

Literature Online **Author Search** For more about William Carlos Williams, go to www.glencoe.com.

Connecting to the Poems

How do the things we see, hear, feel, smell, and taste affect how we interact with the world? In Williams's poems, the speaker expresses awe and delight with ordinary aspects of the physical world. Think about the following questions:

- Have you ever found beauty in an ordinary thing or sound?
- How does beauty reveal itself in everyday life?

Building Background

Imagism's influence is obvious in "The Red Wheelbarrow" and "This Is Just to Say." Of the experience that inspired "The Red Wheelbarrow," Williams wrote, "The sight impressed me somehow as about the most important, the most integral that it had ever been my pleasure to gaze upon." About writing in this style, Williams wrote: "Cut and cut again whatever you write—while you leave by your art no trace of your cutting—and the final utterance will remain packed with what you have to say."

Big Idea New Poetics

As you read, notice how Williams's spare style exemplifies Imagism and evokes the American landscape.

Literary Element Form

Form is the structure of a poem. Many contemporary writers use loosely structured poetic forms instead of following stricter, more traditional patterns. These poets vary the length of the lines and stanzas, relying on emphasis, rhythm, and the placement of words and phrases to convey meaning. As you read these poems, examine how Williams uses and breaks with traditional forms as a means of adding depth and complexity to his poems.

- See Literary Terms Handbook, p. R7.

Literature Online **Interactive Literary Elements Handbook** To review or learn more about the literary elements, go to www.glencoe.com.

Reading Strategy Recognizing Author's Purpose

An **author's purpose** is the author's intent in writing a piece of literature. Authors typically write in order to persuade, inform, explain, entertain, or describe. While reading these poems, try to determine Williams's purpose for writing them.

Reading Tip: Taking Notes Make a list of questions to ask yourself as you read "The Red Wheelbarrow" and "This Is Just to Say." As you think about your answers, decide what the author's purpose might be.

Question	Answer	Evidence
What did I learn that I didn't already know?	I learned that simple things can leave a lasting impression.	The poem is about a simple red wheelbarrow sitting in the rain.

Vocabulary

depend (di pend´) v. to rely on; p. 668 *In football, the whole team depends on the quarterback to get the ball to the end zone.*

glazed (glāzd) adj. covered with a smooth, glossy coating; p. 668 *The cinnamon rolls were glazed with icing.*

delicious (di lish´ əs) adj. having a very pleasing taste; p. 669 *I love all kinds of ice cream flavors but I find chocolate to be the most delicious.*

Vocabulary Tip: Antonyms When two words have opposite or nearly opposite meanings, they are called antonyms. Note that antonyms are always the same part of speech.

INDIANA ACADEMIC STANDARDS (pages 667–670)
11.2 Develop strategies such as...identifying and analyzing structure [and] purpose...

11.5.2 Write responses to literature that...analyze...unique aspects of the text...

The Red Wheelbarrow

William Carlos Williams

so much depends
upon

a red wheel
barrow

5   glazed with rain
water

beside the white
chickens.

Literary Element   Form   *What effect does the break
between the words* wheel *and* barrow *have?*

Vocabulary

depend (di pend´) *v.* to rely on
glazed (glāzd) *adj.* covered with a smooth, glossy coating

Plums and Pears. Paul Cezanne. Oil on canvas, 7¾ x 14 in.
The Barnes Foundation Collection, Merion Station, PA.

This Is Just to Say

William Carlos Williams

I have eaten
the plums
that were in
the icebox

5   and which
you were probably
saving
for breakfast

Forgive me
10 they were **delicious**
so sweet
and so cold

Reading Strategy   Recognizing Author's
Purpose *What does line 9 suggest about the
author's purpose?*

Vocabulary

delicious (di lish′ əs) *adj.* having a very
pleasing taste

RESPONDING AND THINKING CRITICALLY

Respond

1. What feelings do the images, tones, and word choice in these poems evoke?

Recall and Interpret

2. What do the first two lines of "The Red Wheelbarrow" suggest about the speaker's response to the scene?

3. (a)What does Williams describe in stanzas 3 and 4? (b)What do you think Williams is saying by introducing these elements into his poem?

4. (a)In "This Is Just to Say," what does the speaker admit to in the first two lines of the poem? (b)What does this admission suggest about the speaker's relationship with the person being addressed?

5. (a)What does the speaker want from the person being addressed? (b)What is described in the final lines of the poem? Why do you think these things are described?

Analyze and Evaluate

6. (a)Williams carefully arranges his words, including breaking up the words *rainwater* and *wheelbarrow*. How, in your opinion, does the breaking of these words across lines affect their meaning? (b)What do you think of this technique? Explain.

7. (a)What is the tone of "This Is Just to Say"? (b)Why is this tone appropriate?

Connect

8. **Big Idea** **New Poetics** How are these poems innovative in their subject matter and style?

LITERARY ANALYSIS

Literary Element **Form**

No poem is ever entirely without **form**. Even free-verse poems contain some formal elements. Because poetic forms vary greatly from period to period, and from poet to poet, it can occasionally be difficult to identify the forms being used. For example, Williams's poems appear, at first glance, to be written in free verse—lacking any formal structure. However, these poems have consistent stanza and line lengths, and though not technically metered, they have strong rhythmic qualities.

1. Briefly describe the forms used in "The Red Wheelbarrow" and "This Is Just to Say."

2. Why do you think Williams used these forms?

Writing About Literature

Compare and Contrast Form Write a brief essay in which you compare and contrast the form in "The Red Wheelbarrow" with that of another poem you have previously read. Make sure to include in your essay a discussion of how form affects the meaning in each poem.

READING AND VOCABULARY

Reading Strategy **Recognizing Author's Purpose**

Writers of fiction or nonfiction generally have purposes that can be easily identified. This is not always true of poets. In Williams's "This Is Just to Say," the purpose at first seems to be to apologize to an unnamed listener, but it goes beyond that.

1. What do you think is the author's purpose in "The Red Wheelbarrow"? What evidence do you find for this purpose in the poem?

2. What do you think is the author's purpose in "This Is Just to Say"? What evidence do you find for this purpose in the poem?

Literature Online **Web Activities** For eFlashcards, Selection Quick Checks, and other Web activities, go to www.glencoe.com.

Vocabulary Workshop

Word Meanings

Defining Compound Words

so much depends
upon

a red wheel
barrow

— William Carlos Williams, from "The Red Wheelbarrow"

Connecting to Literature *Wheelbarrow* is a **compound word**; that is, a word made up of two words that together have a meaning different from each word's meaning. Compound words may be spelled open (*magic lantern*), closed (*sawdust*), or hyphenated (*half-deserted*). You can check a dictionary to find out whether a compound word is closed, open, or hyphenated. Notice that Williams turns *wheelbarrow*, which is normally closed, into an open compound word and puts *barrow* on a new line for poetic effect.

Examples

The meanings of many compound words are obvious from the parts that make up the word. For example:

- What is *sawdust*?
  It is the dust created by sawing wood.

- What is a *look-alike*?
  It's someone or something that looks just like someone or something else.

- What is a *natural resource*?
  It is a naturally occurring material that is useful to humans, such as mineral deposits, forests, or water.

The meanings of other compound words, however, may be less obvious. To learn the meaning of less familiar compound words, you should consult a dictionary.

Exercise

A. Use your understanding of the following compound words to match each word with its definition.

1. elbow room
2. seaweed
3. grillwork
4. swaybacked
5. ill-used

a. underwater plant
b. metal screen or grating
c. mistreated
d. adequate space
e. having a sagging spine

B. Define the following compound words based on their word parts. Discuss your definitions with a partner. Then check your definitions.

1. ivory tower
2. dark horse
3. icebox
4. green revolution

▶ **Vocabulary Tip**

A **compound word** is made of two separate words that each have a different meaning standing alone.

▶ **Test-Taking Tip**

If a compound word does not appear in a dictionary, it is most likely spelled open.

▶ **Reading Handbook**

For more about compound words, see Reading Handbook, p. R20.

LiteratureOnline
eFlashcards For eFlashcards and other vocabulary activities, go to www.glencoe.com.

ACADEMIC STANDARDS (page 671)
11.1.2 Draw inferences about the meaning of vocabulary in literature or other subject areas.

Summer Rain and Fireworks

MEET AMY LOWELL

Amy Lowell was a brash, controversial, uncompromising woman, and one of the most important poets of the Imagist movement. Her promotion of Imagism in the United States, along with her irreverent personality, turned Lowell into one of the most well-known poets of her generation.

Amy Lowell was born in Brookline, Massachusetts. Her family was wealthy and socially prominent: Lowell was related to Fireside poet James Russell Lowell (see pages 200–201), her brother Abbott served as the president of Harvard University from 1909 to 1933, and her brother Percival was a famed astronomer. Lowell spent her first twenty-eight years like most women in her social set. She traveled, was educated in private schools in Boston, and considered prospects for marriage. However, in 1902, Lowell chose a new path and dedicated her life to poetry.

An Imagist Poet In 1913 Lowell read several poems by Imagist poet H.D. (Hilda Doolittle) in *Poetry* magazine. Lowell connected immediately to the Imagist style. She traveled to England that same year, met Ezra Pound (page 652), and joined his Imagist circle. The first anthology of Imagist poetry, *Des Imagistes*, edited by Pound, appeared the next year and included a poem by Lowell. Also in 1914, Lowell published her book *Sword Blades and Poppy Seed.*

Lowell also began to make friends with many literary figures, including Robert Frost (page 704) and D. H. Lawrence. In 1915 she helped launch Frost's career with a favorable review of his collection *North of Boston* in the *New Republic.*

Poetic Influence Lowell's growing influence within the Imagist movement caused Pound to remove himself from it. He would later sarcastically refer to the group as "Amygism" after it had fully come under Lowell's influence. Over the next several years, she edited three volumes of the annual anthology *Some Imagist Poets.* Before 1920 she published many more books of poetry and prose, including *Can Grande's Castle, Tendencies in Modern American Poetry,* and *Men, Women, and Ghosts.*

> "Why should one read Poetry? That seems to me a good deal like asking: Why should one eat?"
>
> —Amy Lowell

Inspired by a lecture she gave about John Keats in 1921 and by a lifelong fascination with the English Romantic poet, Lowell published a biography of Keats. This, unfortunately, would be her last publication during her life. In 1925 Lowell died of a cerebral hemorrhage. One volume of her poetry, *What's O'Clock,* appeared after her death and was awarded the Pulitzer Prize.

Lowell is important not just for her literary contributions, but also for her promotion of the poetic innovation of Imagism. Fellow Modernist T. S. Eliot called her "the demon saleswoman of poetry." Through her tenacity, her brilliant mind, and her poems, Lowell helped to define the texture of twentieth-century verse.

Amy Lowell was born in 1874 and died in 1925.

Literature Online **Author Search** For more about Amy Lowell, go to www.glencoe.com.

Connecting to the Poems

Can you ever "see" your feelings? Do your feelings ever seem to have weight, shape, or color? In "Summer Rain" and "Fireworks," Lowell describes emotions that are so powerful that they take on vibrant colors and swift action. As you read the poems, think about the following questions:

- How do your feelings about others change your reaction to your environment?
- What do you think hate looks like? What might love look like?

Building Background

Both "Summer Rain" and "Fireworks" appeared in Lowell's collection *Pictures of the Floating World*. This book contains nearly 200 Imagistic free-verse poems and is broken into multiple parts. The poems from the first section, "Lacquer Prints," are based on a set of Japanese prints and very closely resemble haiku, a Japanese poetic form. The section from which "Summer Rain" and "Fireworks" are drawn is titled "Planes of Personality." This section lyrically celebrates intense emotions such as love, hate, and longing.

Setting Purposes for Reading

Big Idea Modern Poetry

As you read, notice how Lowell uses imagery to convey emotions and ideas.

Literary Element Enjambment

Enjambment is the continuation of a sentence across a line break without a punctuated pause between lines. A poet may choose to use enjambment for a number of reasons: to maintain a rhyme scheme or a rhythm, to increase readability, or to create exciting juxtapositions of language or ideas. As you read, pay attention to Lowell's use of enjambment and how it affects the poems.

- See Literary Terms Handbook, p. R5.

 Literature Online **Interactive Literary Elements Handbook** To review or learn more about the literary elements, go to www.glencoe.com.

Reading Strategy Interpreting Imagery

Imagery is the "word pictures" authors use to evoke an emotional response in the reader. Poets may use figures of speech, including metaphors, similes, and personification, to create images. Often it is possible to explicitly determine the meaning of imagery. Other times different readers will have different interpretations of the same image.

Reading Tip: Taking Notes Use a chart like the one below to record your interpretations of Lowell's imagery.

Imagery	Interpretation
p. 675 "It spits and sparkles in stars and balls, Buds into roses—and flares, and falls."	The speaker is filled with intense emotion upon seeing this hated person.

Vocabulary

pepper (pe′pər) *v.* to shower with small objects; p. 675 *The crowd was peppered with candy from the passing parade floats.*

crimson (krim′zən) *adj.* a bright purplish red; p. 675 *The girl's crimson coat caught the eye of many people.*

azure (ā′zhər) *adj.* a light purplish blue; p. 675 *The azure sky was a beautiful sight.*

mount (mount) *v.* to ascend or to soar; p. 675 *As the rocket mounted, the crowd began to cheer.*

Vocabulary Tip: Synonyms

When two words have nearly the same meaning, they are called **synonyms**. Note that synonyms always have the same part of speech.

INDIANA ACADEMIC STANDARDS (pages 673–676)

11.3 Develop strategies such as...identifying and analyzing structure...

11.3.4 Analyze ways in which poetry...uses imagery...

11.5.2 Write responses to literature that...analyze...unique aspects of the text...

Summer Rain

Amy Lowell

*A*ll night our room was outer-walled with rain.
Drops fell and flattened on the tin roof,
And rang like little disks of metal.
Ping!—Ping!—and there was not a pinpoint of silence between them.
5 The rain rattled and clashed,
And the slats of the shutters danced and glittered.
But to me the darkness was red-gold and crocus-coloured
With your brightness,
And the words you whispered to me
10 Sprang up and flamed—orange torches against the rain.
Torches against the wall of cool, silver rain!

Literary Element Enjambment *Why do you think Lowell chose to use enjambment in lines 9–10?*

Fireworks

Amy Lowell

You hate me and I hate you,
And we are so polite, we two!

But whenever I see you, I burst apart
And scatter the sky with my blazing heart.
5   It spits and sparkles in stars and balls,
Buds into roses—and flares, and falls.

Scarlet buttons, and pale green disks,
Silver spirals and asterisks,
Shoot and tremble in a mist
10 **Peppered** with mauve and amethyst.

I shine in the windows and light up the trees,
And all because I hate you, if you please.

And when you meet me, you rend asunder[1]
And go up in a flaming wonder
15 Of saffron[2] cubes, and **crimson** moons,
And wheels all amaranths[3] and maroons.

Golden lozenges and spades,
Arrows of malachites[4] and jades,
Patens[5] of copper, **azure** sheaves.
20 As you **mount**, you flash in the glossy leaves.

Such fireworks as we make, we two!
Because you hate me and I hate you.

---

1. *Rend asunder* means "to tear apart."
2. Here, *saffron* refers to an orange-yellow color.
3. Here, *amaranth* refers to a reddish purple color.
4. *Malachite* is a deep green stone.
5. *Patens* are small metal plates.

Reading Strategy   Interpreting Imagery *What do you think the imagery in these lines means?*

Vocabulary

pepper (pe′pər) *v.* to shower with small objects
crimson (krim′zən) *adj.* a bright purplish red
azure (ā′zhər) *adj.* a light purplish blue
mount (mount) *v.* to ascend or to soar

RESPONDING AND THINKING CRITICALLY

Respond

1. In your opinion, which poem expresses the speaker's emotion most effectively? Explain.

Recall and Interpret

2. (a)In "Summer Rain," in what ways does the speaker describe the sound of the rain? (b)What do these descriptions suggest about the speaker's feelings for the rain?

3. (a)How does the speaker see "the darkness"? (b)What does this suggest about the speaker's feelings for the person addressed?

4. (a)In the first couplet of "Fireworks," besides hate, how does the speaker characterize the relationship described in the poem? (b)What does this description suggest about the poem's "fireworks"?

5. (a)What does the speaker claim to do in the window and to the trees? (b)In your opinion, how does this image affect the following line?

Analyze and Evaluate

6. (a)How does the rhyme scheme in "Fireworks" differ from that in "Summer Rain"? (b)Which poem's rhyme scheme do you prefer? Explain.

7. (a)In what way does the content of the couplets in "Fireworks" differ from that in the quatrains? (b)Is the variation in stanza length effective?

Connect

8. **Big Idea** New Poetics In your opinion, how are the ideals of Modernism reflected in these poems? How are the more classical ideas and techniques reflected?

LITERARY ANALYSIS

Literary Element Enjambment

Enjambed lines contrast with end-stopped lines, in which both meaning and grammatical structure come to an end or a definitive pause. In both "Fireworks" and "Summer Rain," **enjambment** serves to emphasize certain words or to expand their meanings by placing them in different contexts. This technique also serves to express the flow of the speaker's thoughts and to establish rhythm.

Partner Activity Meet with a classmate to discuss the effect Lowell creates with each example of enjambment in "Fireworks."

Writing About Literature

Compare and Contrast Form In what ways are the structures of "Summer Rain" and "Fireworks" different? How are they the same? Write a brief essay in which you compare and contrast the forms and structures of these poems.

Literature Online Web Activities For eFlashcards, Selection Quick Checks, and other Web activities, go to www.glencoe.com.

READING AND VOCABULARY

Reading Strategy Interpreting Imagery

The **imagery** in a poem can contribute to its tone. Use the imagery chart you created on page 673 to determine the tone of each poem based on the imagery. How would you describe the tone of each of these poems? Support your opinion with examples from the poems.

Vocabulary Practice

Practice with Synonyms Read the following sentences. Choose the best synonym for the underlined word. Use a dictionary if you need help.

1. Mark Twain's literature was often <u>peppered</u> with regional dialect.
   a. dotted   **b.** flashed   **c.** pestered

2. All that remained of the sunset was a splash of <u>crimson</u> fading into the horizon.
   a. violet   **b.** scarlet   **c.** black

3. The morning sky was a beautiful <u>azure</u> color until the black storm clouds rolled in.
   a. blue   **b.** pastel   **c.** dark

4. The movie ended when the cowboy <u>mounted</u> his horse and rode off into the sunset.
   a. brushed   **b.** galloped   **c.** ascended

Comparing Literature *Across Time and Place*

Connecting to the Reading Selections

How does one distinguish between what is ordinary and what is exhilarating? In asking such questions, poets trace the development of their work from an initial feeling or idea to a condensed and captivating piece of writing. The four writers compared here—Archibald MacLeish, Rainer Maria Rilke, Mark Strand, and Ishmael Reed—explore their enthusiasms for both reading and writing poetry in the following selections.

COMPARING THE `Big Idea` New Poetics

During the twentieth century, the boundaries of subject matter, form, and style were extended. Poets from the United States and elsewhere—such as MacLeish, Rilke, Strand, and Reed—sought to capture individual experience by bending the traditional rules and conventions of poetic form.

COMPARING Imagist Poetry

Modernist poets let content dictate form. In the early 1900s, the Imagists employed clear, concrete language to convey precise images. In abandoning traditional language, the Imagists' poetry and their principles are reflected in the poetry of the later twentieth century.

COMPARING Literary Trends

Like other aspects of culture, literature has trends. However, sometimes a literary trend is not identified until years after it has passed. Distinct styles become apparent when one compares literary movements, such as local-color writing and Modernism.

Ars Poetica

MEET ARCHIBALD MACLEISH

Archibald MacLeish was a poet with a purpose. He believed that, through love and awareness, U.S. citizens could achieve the goals of freedom and equality set down in the Declaration of Independence. MacLeish's idealism is evident both in his poetry and in his public life.

> "But what, then, is the business of poetry? Precisely to make sense of the chaos of our lives."
>
> —Archibald MacLeish

Creative Echoes Born in the late 1800s in Glencoe, Illinois, MacLeish was keenly aware of both the traditional world and the constantly evolving cultural landscape of the early twentieth century. After attending Yale University, where he played football, MacLeish entered Harvard Law School at the age of twenty-three. Being at Harvard further enlivened his interest in, as MacLeish put it, "the vision of mental time, of the interminable journey of the human mind, the great tradition of the intellectual past which knows the bearings of the future." Within the next two years, he married singer Ada Hitchcock and enlisted in the army. After World War I, he became a successful lawyer, but he soon quit his job to move with his wife and

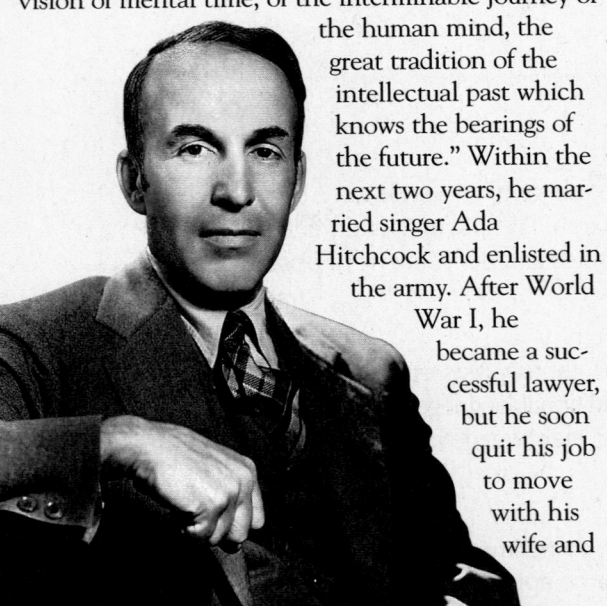

two small children to Paris. MacLeish pursued his writing there and published four poetry collections in five years. In 1928 MacLeish returned with his family to the United States, where he continued writing poetry. In 1933 he won his first Pulitzer Prize for *Conquistador*, an epic poem about the conquest of Mexico by the Spanish.

Public Interests Concerned about the nation's social problems, MacLeish also wrote journalistic articles and supported President Franklin D. Roosevelt's New Deal economic reforms and anti-Hitler stance. Critic David Luytens called MacLeish "the poet laureate of the New Deal." In the 1940s, MacLeish served as director of a wartime office of propaganda, as assistant secretary of state, and as a librarian of Congress. He was also chairman of the U.S. delegation for the founding conference of UNESCO (the United Nations Educational, Scientific, and Cultural Organization) in 1945. Through all these diplomatic commitments, MacLeish continued to write poetry as well as drama. His first play to be produced—*Panic: A Play in Verse*—was based on the biblical story of Cain but was set in the Great Depression. MacLeish, who was also on the editorial board of the business magazine *Fortune*, lamented the economic hardship and growing despair brought on by the Depression.

In the 1950s, MacLeish won two more Pulitzer Prizes: one for poetry and one for drama. Between 1944 and 1954—during what has been called his "second renaissance" as a poet—he published more than eighty poems. MacLeish's later works continued to explore both the poetic expression of the mysteries and feelings of the poet's inner world, and of the core meaning of U.S. citizenship as passed down through the founders of the nation. Critic Hayden Carruth said, "MacLeish wrote not as a personal crusader, never as a political crank or lonely visionary, but instead as the spokesman of the people."

Archibald MacLeish was born in 1892 and died in 1982.

Literature Online **Author Search** For more about Archibald MacLeish, go to www.glencoe.com.

Connecting to the Poem

How do you judge an experience or a piece of art? Are there clear criteria that help you form an evaluation, or do more subjective factors inform your response, transcending mere positive or negative impressions? In "Ars Poetica," MacLeish expresses what he believes a poem should be. As you read this poem, think about the following questions:

- How do you judge a poem?
- What qualities should a good poem have?

Building Background

Ars poetica, a Latin phrase meaning "the art of poetry," is the title of a work written around 13 B.C. by the Roman poet Horace. In this text, Horace laid down his own rules for writing poetry. In 1926 MacLeish published his poem "Ars Poetica" in a collection titled *Streets in the Moon*. When he wrote it, MacLeish was living in Paris and was part of a circle of innovative writers—among them Ernest Hemingway, F. Scott Fitzgerald, and E. E. Cummings—who were working to perfect their own creative skills.

Setting Purposes for Reading

Big Idea New Poetics

Although the concept for this poem has deep historical roots, MacLeish's style is innovative and modern. As you read, note how the unique pattern of lines and creative, startling imagery add to his purpose.

Literary Element Theme

A **theme** is a central idea presented in a literary work. In some works the theme is stated directly, but in most works the theme is implied and revealed gradually. A literary work may have more than one theme. As you read "Ars Poetica," look for events, dialogue, and description that help develop the theme of the poem.

- See Literary Terms Handbook, p. R18.

Literature Online **Interactive Literary Elements Handbook** To review or learn more about the literary elements, go to www.glencoe.com.

Reading Strategy Analyzing Style

Combining knowledge about the separate parts of something to form an overall judgment of it is **analyzing**. Writers' **style** includes the expressive qualities that distinguish their work, such as word choice, the length and arrangement of sentences, and the use of figurative language and imagery. As you read "Ars Poetica," analyze MacLeish's style. Consider why he chose to break the lines the way he did and how the imagery and word choice contribute to the overall effect of the poem.

Reading Tip: Taking Notes Record the effects of MacLeish's style in a chart like the one below.

Author's Style	Overall Effect
Irregular line length	Helps emphasize certain words

Vocabulary

palpable (pal′pə bəl) *adj.* tangible; able to be touched or felt; p. 680 *The tension was palpable in the team's locker room before the big game.*

mute (mūt) *adj.* silent; p. 680 *James hit the mute button on the television and decided to focus on his homework.*

entangled (en tan′gəld) *adj.* twisted together; caught p. 680 *The fish was entangled in the fisherman's net.*

Vocabulary Tip: Analogies An analogy is a type of comparison that is based on the relationships between things or ideas. To solve an analogy question, identify the relationship in the first pair of words. These five types of relationships are a good place to start:

- Association or Usage
- Example/Class
- Object/Characteristic
- Part/Whole
- Synonym or Antonym

INDIANA ACADEMIC STANDARDS (pages 679–681)
11.3.2 Analyze...theme...
11.3.3 Analyze...author's style...

11.5.2 Write responses to literature that...analyze...unique aspects of the text...

Ars Poetica

Archibald MacLeish

A poem should be **palpable** and **mute**
As a globed fruit

Dumb[1]
As old medallions to the thumb

5   Silent as the sleeve-worn stone
Of casement[2] ledges where the moss has grown—

A poem should be wordless
As the flight of birds

A poem should be motionless in time
10 As the moon climbs

Leaving, as the moon releases
Twig by twig the night-**entangled** trees,

Leaving, as the moon behind the winter leaves,
Memory by memory the mind—

15 A poem should be motionless in time
As the moon climbs

A poem should be equal to:
Not true

For all the history of grief
20 An empty doorway and a maple leaf

For love
The leaning grasses and two lights above the sea—

A poem should not mean
But be

1. *Dumb*: here, unable to speak.

2. *casement*: a window that opens on hinges.

Literary Element   Theme *How does MacLeish develop the idea that a poem can be "wordless"?*

Vocabulary

palpable (pal′pə bəl) *adj.* tangible; able to be touched or felt
mute (mūt) *adj.* silent
entangled (en tan′gəld) *adj.* twisted together; caught

RESPONDING AND THINKING CRITICALLY

Respond

1. Which image in the poem could you see, feel, or hear most vividly in your imagination? Why?

Recall and Interpret

2. (a)What five adjectives in lines 1–8 describe what a poem should be? (b)What is ironic about the use of these words to describe a poem?

3. (a)To what does the speaker compare poetry in lines 9–16? (b)What does this image suggest about the function of poetry?

4. (a)How does the speaker suggest that grief and love should be represented in poetry? (b)What can you infer from this suggestion about the way poems should express emotions?

Analyze and Evaluate

5. In your opinion, how effective are the images in this poem in appealing to the senses? Explain.

6. How does the repetition in lines 9–10 and lines 15–16 contribute to the poem?

7. In your opinion, do lines 20 and 22 adequately capture the emotions of grief and love? Why or why not?

8. A simile is a figure of speech in which things are compared through the use of words such as *like* or *as*. How do the similes in "Ars Poetica" contribute to the effectiveness of the poem?

Connect

9. **Big Idea** **New Poetics** MacLeish was a believer in both tradition and innovation. What traits of Modernism do you see in "Ars Poetica"?

LITERARY ANALYSIS

Literary Element Theme

The **themes** of a literary work are different from its topics. In MacLeish's poem, the topic is poetry itself, but the theme is a statement about poetry that suggests its relation to life in general.

1. What themes do you find in the poem?

2. Are the themes stated directly or implied? Explain.

Writing About Literature

Analyze Genre Elements Where do you draw the line between poetry and prose? Many writers of the modern era wrote works that blur the traditional distinctions between the two. Although MacLeish's poem is written in rhymed couplets, the lines in the poem are of irregular length and meter. How do you think MacLeish decided where to break the lines? Write a brief essay in which you analyze the features that make this selection poetry rather than prose. Be sure to show how these features contribute to the author's purpose.

Literature Online **Web Activities** For eFlashcards, Selection Quick Checks, and other Web activities, go to www.glencoe.com.

READING AND VOCABULARY

Reading Strategy Analyzing Style

Style is made up of the expressive qualities that distinguish an author's work. It can reveal an author's personality as well as his or her purpose in writing.

Group Activity Meet with a group of classmates to discuss how each of the following elements contributes to MacLeish's poem as a whole.

- figurative language
- diction
- sentence length and structure

Vocabulary Practice

Practice with Analogies Choose the pair of words below that best completes each analogy.

1. palpable : real ::
   a. durable : strong
   b. malleable : heat
2. mute : noisy ::
   a. smart : curiously
   b. slowly : quickly

Building Background

Rainer Maria Rilke was born in 1875 in Prague, which was then part of Austria-Hungary and is now the capital of the Czech Republic. He spoke and usually wrote in German. In 1902 Rilke went to Paris to write a book about Auguste Rodin, the great French sculptor. Rodin quickly became Rilke's friend and mentor, sharing with the young poet a creative methodology based on an ethic of hard work and dedication to minute detail. Rodin's theories about the creative process ran counter to the popular idea that art is an inspiration that comes from a muse, or an outside force or spirit long depicted in female form.

The following selection is from a collection of letters

Rilke wrote to Franz Xaver Kappus, an aspiring poet. The letters were written during a five-year period that started in 1903, when Rilke was in Paris. In these letters, Rilke passed on to Kappus the bravado and confidence that he had learned from Rodin. Rilke said, "Love consists in this, that two solitudes protect and touch and greet each other." Rilke died in Switzerland in 1926, but his letters and poetry continue to influence many writers here and abroad.

Rainer Maria Rilke was born in 1875 and died in 1926.

Literature Online **Author Search** For more about Rainer Maria Rilke, go to www.glencoe.com.

from Letters to a Young Poet

Rainer Maria Rilke

The Heart Called "Rancho Pastel", Jim Dine. Private collection.

You ask whether your poems are good. You send them to publishers; you compare them with other poems; you are disturbed when certain publishers reject your attempts. Well now, since you have given me permission to advise you, I suggest that you give all that up. You are looking outward and, above all else, that you must not do now. No one can advise and help you, no one.

There is only one way: Go within. Search for the cause, find the impetus[1] that bids you write. Put it to this test: Does it stretch out its roots in the deepest place of your heart? Can you avow[2] that you would die if you were forbidden to write? Above all, in the most silent hour of your night, ask yourself this: *Must* I write? Dig deep into yourself for a true answer. And if it should ring its assent, if you can confidently meet this serious question with a simple, "I must," then build your life upon it. It has become your necessity. Your life, in even the most mundane and least significant hour, must become a sign, a testimony to this urge.

---

1. An *impetus* is a something that encourages or stimulates activity.

2. To *avow* is to declare openly.

Then draw near to nature. Pretend you are the very first man and then write what you see and experience, what you love and lose. Do not write love poems, at least at first; they present the greatest challenge. It requires great, fully ripened power to produce something personal, something unique, when there are so many good and sometimes even brilliant renditions[3] in great numbers. Beware of general themes. Cling to those that your everyday life offers you. Write about your sorrows, your wishes, your passing thoughts, your belief in anything beautiful. Describe all that with fervent,[4] quiet, and humble sincerity. In order to express yourself, use things in your surroundings, the scenes of your dreams, and the subjects of your memory.

If your everyday life appears to be unworthy subject matter, do not complain to life. Complain to yourself. Lament that you are not poet enough to call up its wealth. For the creative artist there is no poverty—nothing is insignificant or unimportant. Even if you were in a prison whose walls would shut out from your senses the sounds of the outer world, would you not then still have your childhood, this precious wealth, this treasure house of memories? Direct your attention to that. Attempt to resurrect these sunken sensations of a distant past. You will gain assuredness. Your aloneness will expand and will become your home, greeting you like the quiet dawn. Outer tumult will pass it by from afar.

If, as a result of this turning inward, of this sinking into your own world, *poetry* should emerge, you will not think to ask someone whether it is good poetry. And you will not try to interest publishers of magazines in these works. For you will hear in them your own voice; you will see in them a piece of your life, a natural possession of yours. A piece of art is good if it is born of necessity. This, its source, is its criterion; there is no other.

Therefore, my dear friend, I know of no other advice than this: Go within and scale the depths of your being from which your very life springs forth. At its source you will find the answer to the question, whether you *must* write. Accept it, however it sounds to you, without analyzing. Perhaps it will become apparent to you that you are indeed called to be a writer. Then accept that fate; bear its burden, and its grandeur, without asking for the reward, which might possibly come from without. For the creative artist must be a world of his own and must find everything within himself and in nature, to which he has betrothed[5] himself.

It is possible that, even after your descent into your inner self and into your secret place of solitude, you might find that you must give up becoming a poet. As I have said, to feel that one could live without writing is enough indication that, in fact, one should not. Even then this process of turning inward, upon which I beg you to embark, will not have been in vain. Your life will no doubt from then on find its own paths. That they will be good ones and rich and expansive— that I wish for you more than I can say.

What else shall I tell you? It seems to me everything has been said, with just the right emphasis. I wanted only to advise you to progress quietly and seriously in your evolvement.[6] You could greatly interfere with that process if you look outward and expect to obtain answers from the outside— answers which only your innermost feeling in your quietest hour can perhaps give you. ❧

---

3. *Renditions* are versions.
4. *Fervent* means "with intense feeling."

5. *Betrothed* means "engaged."
6. *Evolvement* is growth.

Discussion Starter ....

In this letter, Rilke insists that the individual finds the most powerful means of expression by looking inward. He also says that a writer *must* write in order to express himself or herself, just as one must breathe in order to live. In what ways does Rilke's advice to the young poet apply to other aspirations people have in life?

Building Background

Mark Strand developed as a writer during the 1960s—a period when, he later noted, "Poets were underground pop stars." Strand was born on Canada's Prince Edward Island in 1934 and grew up in various cities in the United States. Strand is a noted poet, public reader, and translator who has taught at numerous universities—including Harvard, the University of Utah, and the University of Iowa (where he also received a master's degree in creative writing). He was named U.S. Poet Laureate in 1990 and won a Pulitzer Prize for his collection of poetry *Blizzard of One* in 1999.

Influenced by the work of Archibald MacLeish, Strand's poetry is noted for its surreal imagery and exploration of the power of presence and absence in life. Critic Jane Candia Coleman commented that although Strand's poetry can be abstract and difficult, "the reader who delves, who meets the poet halfway, will be rewarded by glimpses of a different world, that changeable one of dreams and the elusive beauty that haunts us all."

Mark Strand was born in 1934.

Literature Online **Author Search** For more about Mark Strand, go to www.glencoe.com.

Eating Poetry

Mark Strand

House on Fire with People Inside. John Ritter

Small Ferocious Dog. John Ritter.

Ink runs from the corners of my mouth.
There is no happiness like mine.
I have been eating poetry.

The librarian does not believe what she sees.
5   Her eyes are sad
and she walks with her hands in her dress.

The poems are gone.
The light is dim.
The dogs are on the basement stairs and coming up.

10   Their eyeballs roll,
their blond legs burn like brush.
The poor librarian begins to stamp her feet and weep.

She does not understand.
When I get on my knees and lick her hand,
15   she screams.

I am a new man.
I snarl at her and bark.
I romp with joy in the bookish dark.

Quickwrite ....

Strand has said, "A poem may be the residue of an inner urgency, one through which the self wishes to register itself, write itself into being, and, finally, to charm another self, the reader, into belief." Strand's description of the speaker in "Eating Poetry" is purposefully ambiguous. Write a paragraph in which you interpret the character of the speaker in this poem. Identify the poet's purpose and cite evidence from the text to support your view.

Building Background

Ishmael Reed has described his eclectic writing style as "Neoamerican hoodooism," an expression that implies a melding of the magic healing in African folk culture and many other U.S. cultural elements. Reed was born in 1938 in Chattanooga, Tennessee, but he grew up in Buffalo, New York, where he studied at the University of Buffalo. He later moved to New York City. Throughout his career, Reed has shown a razor-edged satirical wit, often addressing the failures he sees in the cultural and political institutions of his country. Reed's style blends European and African traditions and showcases his broad-ranging cultural and historical knowledge.

In his poems, Reed's innovative approach is obvious. He purposely omits vowels, uses ampersands instead of the word *and,* and inserts punctuation at unexpected places. One effect of his techniques is to quicken and vary the pace of his poetry. The following selection is included in Reed's second book of poetry, *Conjure.* The book, published in 1972, was nominated for a National Book Award.

Ishmael Reed was born in 1938.

Literature Online **Author Search** For more about Ishmael Reed, go to www.glencoe.com.

beware: do not read this poem

Ishmael Reed

Hallway, 1995. Mary Iverson.

tonite ,   thriller[1] was
abt an ol woman   ,so vain she
surrounded herself w/
          many mirrors

5   it got so bad that finally she
locked herself indoors & her
whole life became the
          mirrors

one day the villagers broke
10 into her house ,   but she was too
swift for them .   she disappeared
          into a mirror

---

1. *Thriller* was a television show hosted by horror-film actor Boris Karloff that ran from 1960 to 1962. The hour-long episodes were divided between mystery and horror genres.

each tenant who bought the house
after that   ,   lost a loved one to
15   the ol woman in the mirror :
            first a little girl
            then a young woman
            then the young woman/s husband

            the hunger of this poem is legendary
20   it has taken in many victims
     back off from this poem
     it has drawn in yr feet
     back off from this poem
     it has drawn in yr legs

25   back off from this poem
     it is a greedy mirror
     you are into this poem .   from
                the waist down
     nobody can hear you can they ?
30   this poem has had you up to here
                belch
     this poem aint got no manners
     you cant call out frm this poem
     relax now & go w/ this poem
35   move & roll on to this poem
     do not resist this poem
     this poem has yr eyes
     this poem has his head
     this poem has his arms
40   this poem has his fingers
     this poem has his fingertips
     this poem is the reader & the
     reader this poem

     statistic :   the us bureau of missing persons reports
45   that in 1968 over 100,000 people disappeared
     leaving no solid clues
               nor trace   only
     a space   in the lives of their friends

Quickwrite

The title of this selection naturally attracts the reader's interest. Despite the fact that the title warns the reader not to continue reading, the poem focuses on the relationship that exists in poetry between the reader and the writer. Write a paragraph in which you discuss how this selection develops the idea that "this poem is the reader & the / reader this poem."

Wrap-up: Comparing Literature Across Time and Place

- ## Ars Poetica
  Archibald MacLeish

- ## from Letters to a Young Poet
  Rainer Maria Rilke

- ## Eating Poetry
  Mark Strand

- ## beware: do not read this poem
  Ishmael Reed

COMPARING THE `Big Idea` New Poetics

Group Activity Each of the writers compared here explains what he believes poetry should be. Read the four quotations below from the selections and discuss the following questions with a group of classmates.

1. Which writer's statement about what poetry should be appeals to you most? Explain why.
2. In what ways does each selection break the traditional rules of poetry?
3. How does each writer demonstrate what the experience of poetry should be for both reader and writer, and how does each provide criteria for evaluating poetry?

> "A poem should not mean
> But be"
>
> —MacLeish, "Ars Poetica"

> "Put it to this test: Does it stretch out its roots in the deepest place of your heart?"
>
> —Rilke, *Letters to a Young Poet*

> "There is no happiness like mine.
> I have been eating poetry."
>
> —Strand, "Eating Poetry"

> "do not resist this poem
> this poem has yr eyes"
>
> —Reed, "beware: do not read this poem"

Full Moon at Takanawa, from *Celebrated places in the Eastern Capital of Edo,* 1832. Ando or Utagawa Hiroshige. Woodblock color print, 10 x 15 in. Brooklyn Museum of Art, NY.

"A poem should be wordless
As the flight of birds"

—MacLeish, "Ars Poetica"

COMPARING Imagist Poetry

Visual Display What images struck you most as you read the poems by MacLeish, Strand, and Reed, and the letter by Rilke? Create a visual display that represents the imagery you saw in your mind as you read these selections.

COMPARING Literary Trends

Writing Research the literary trends associated with MacLeish, Rilke, Strand, and Reed. Write a short essay in which you discuss how each writer is a part of a literary trend.

 INDIANA ACADEMIC STANDARDS (page 688)
11.3.7 Analyze...intentions in a selection of literary works...
11.3.4 Analyze ways in which poetry...uses imagery...

11.4.7 Develop presentations using...Internet sources.

Study of Two Pears and from *The Man with the Blue Guitar*

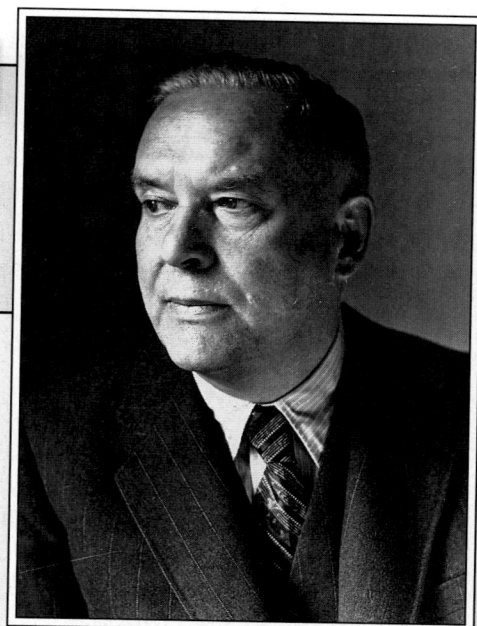

MEET WALLACE STEVENS

For a poet with such a powerful imagination, Wallace Stevens led an outwardly quiet and uneventful life. His entire professional career was spent as an employee of an insurance company. In his journals he expressed embarrassment about writing poems: "Keep all this a great secret. There is something absurd about all this writing of verses; but the truth is, it elates and satisfies me to do it."

> *"How full of trifles everything is! It is only one's thoughts that fill a room with something more than furniture."*
>
> —Wallace Stevens

Youth Stevens was born in Reading, Pennsylvania. His father was a country lawyer, and his mother was a teacher. Stevens enrolled at Harvard College in 1897, where he became friends with the philosopher George Santayana, who encouraged Stevens to publish his early poems in the *Harvard Advocate*. Stevens left school abruptly after only three years, failing to complete his degree. He moved to New York City and worked briefly as a reporter for the *Herald Tribune*. Then, after enrolling at the New York Law School, he acquired his degree and was admitted to the bar in 1904. For the next several years, Stevens worked for various law firms throughout the city before moving to Connecticut where he worked for the Hartford Accident and Indemnity Company until his death.

In 1914 *Poetry* magazine published four of Stevens's poems. These poems were eventually included in his first book, *Harmonium*, which appeared in 1923. It was well received by critics but sold only one hundred copies. However, *Harmonium* contains some of Stevens's most recognizable and important work. It shows the influence of both the French Symbolists and the English Romantics, particularly Wordsworth and Coleridge. The volume was reissued in 1931 and then again in 1947. In this book, Stevens illustrates his belief that "the imagination is man's power over nature."

Maturity and Acceptance During the 1930s, Stevens published three more books, *Ideas and Order, Owl's Clover*, and *The Man with the Blue Guitar*, which reveal the progressive development of his poetic style. By the 1940s, Stevens had entered the most creatively fertile time in his life. He gradually abandoned the intricate forms and lavish imagery of his early work in favor of a more concise, abstract style. In 1954 Stevens's *Collected Poems* appeared. With this publication, shortly before his death, Stevens attracted widespread attention for the first time. The *Collected Poems* was awarded the Pulitzer Prize for Poetry in 1955.

Poet of the Imagination Central to all of Stevens's poetry is the primacy of the creative imagination. According to Stevens, the role of the poet is to use the imagination to "become the light in the minds of others" by helping people to discover new ways of viewing reality and to experience a sense of order in a chaotic world devoid of a clear spiritual definition. His best work explored the complex relationship between the shaping power of the imagination and the physical world.

Wallace Stevens was born in 1879 and died in 1955.

Literature Online **Author Search** For more about Wallace Stevens, go to www.glencoe.com.

Connecting to the Poems

How do artists approach the natural world? What is the best way for artists to represent the things they observe in a way that is true to reality, creative, and meaningful? As you read the poems, think about the following questions:

- When you view a physical object, how can you distinguish its appearance from its reality?
- How might a writer imaginatively transform his or her perceptions of the physical world?

Building Background

This excerpt from "The Man with the Blue Guitar" is the first stanza of a much longer poem that appeared in 1937. Although it is tempting to connect the title of this poem to Pablo Picasso's famous painting *The Old Guitarist*, a product of Picasso's so-called "blue period," Stevens asserted that he had no particular painting of Picasso's in mind when he wrote the poem. Stevens was deeply affected by the artistic experiments of Cubist painters, like the later Picasso, who were attempting to subvert painters' traditional use of perspective. Stevens's poetry, like Cubist painting, often mixes multiple points of view that culminate in interesting variations on the perspectives of observed objects.

Setting Purposes For Reading

Big Idea **New Poetics**

As you read, notice how Stevens's poems lead the reader to explore the way in which imagination can transform and deepen our perceptions of everyday experience.

Literary Element **Motif**

A **motif** is a significant image, description, idea, or other element repeated throughout a literary work to help convey its theme. As you read Stevens's poems, try to identify the motifs that he uses.

- See Literary Terms Handbook, p. R11.

Literature Online **Interactive Literary Elements Handbook** To review or learn more about the literary elements, go to www.glencoe.com.

Reading Strategy Recognizing Author's Purpose

An **author's purpose** is the author's intent in writing a piece of literature. Authors typically write to accomplish one or more of the following goals: to persuade, to inform, to explain, to explore, to entertain, or to describe. While reading these poems, try to determine Stevens's purpose for writing.

Reading Tip: Double-Entry Journal Use a double-entry journal to determine an author's purpose. Ask yourself questions like the ones below.

Questions to Ask	Answers
What is the tone?	Serious, instructive, and musical
What kinds of details are there?	
What are some descriptive words?	

Vocabulary

bulge (bulj) *v.* to swell or curve outward; p. 691 *The shoplifter's shirt was bulging with the goods he had taken.*

taper (tā′ pər) *v.* to become progressively thinner or smaller; p. 691 *The river slowly tapered out as it entered the dry gorge.*

glisten (gli′ sən) *v.* to shine or to reflect light; p. 691 *All morning the dew was glistening on the grass.*

Vocabulary Tip: Synonyms Synonyms are words that have the same or similar meanings. Synonyms are always the same part of speech.

INDIANA ACADEMIC STANDARDS (pages 690–693)
11.3.4 Analyze ways in which poetry...uses imagery...
11.2 Develop strategies such as...identifying...purpose...

11.3.2 Analyze the way in which the theme...of a selection represents a view or comment on life...

690 UNIT 5 BEGINNINGS OF THE MODERN AGE

Study of Two Pears

Wallace Stevens

I

Opusculum paedagogum.[1]
The pears are not viols,[2]
Nudes or bottles.
They resemble nothing else.

II

The are yellow forms
Composed of curves
Bulging toward the base.
They are touched red.

III

They are not flat surfaces
Having curved outlines.
They are round
Tapering toward the top.

IV

In the way they are modelled
There are bits of blue.
A hard dry leaf hangs
From the stem.

V

The yellow glistens.
It **glistens** with various yellows,
Citrons,[3] oranges and greens
Flowering over the skin.

VI

The shadows of the pears
Are blobs on the green cloth.
The pears are not seen
As the observer wills.

Two Pears from the Jardinage, 2003. Simon Fletcher.
Watercolor on paper. Private collection.

1. *Opusculum paedagogum* is Latin for "a small instructional text."
2. A *viol* is a bowed stringed instrument used chiefly in music of the sixteenth and seventeenth centuries.
3. *Citron* is a shade of yellowish green.

Big Idea New Poetics *What is the speaker saying in this stanza about the difference between art and physical reality?*

Reading Strategy Recognizing Author's Purpose *What do these lines suggest about Stevens's purpose for composing this poem?*

Vocabulary

bulge (bulj) *v.* to swell or curve outward
taper (tā′ pər) *v.* to become progressively thinner or smaller
glisten (glis′ ən) *v.* to shine or to reflect light

from *The Man with the Blue Guitar*

Wallace Stevens

I

The man bent over his guitar,
A shearsman[1] of sorts. The day was green.

They said, "You have a blue guitar,
You do not play things as they are."

The man replied, "Things as they are
Are changed upon the blue guitar."

And they said then, "But play, you must,
A tune beyond us, yet ourselves,

A tune upon the blue guitar
Of things exactly as they are."

---

1. *Shearsman* refers to the posture of the guitarist, squatting like a tailor working on cloth.

Literary Element Motif *How does the motif "things as they are" help to convey the theme of the poem?*

The Old Guitarist, 1903–04. Pablo Picasso. Oil on panel, (48¾ x 32½). The Art Institute of Chicago.
Viewing the Art: How does the guitarist in the painting compare with your picture of the one described in the poem?

RESPONDING AND THINKING CRITICALLY

Respond

1. Which of these poems do you prefer? Explain.

Recall and Interpret

2. (a)In the final stanza of "Study of Two Pears," what does the speaker mean by saying that the pears are not seen as the observer wills? (b)How does this statement relate to the speaker's assertion in the first stanza?

3. (a)In "The Man with the Blue Guitar," what do the listeners accuse the guitarist of doing? How does the guitarist respond? (b)What does this exchange tell you about the guitar and the guitarist?

4. (a)What do the listeners tell the guitarist to do in the last two stanzas? (b)The guitarist does not reply. If he did reply, what do you think he would say?

Analyze and Evaluate

5. (a)Why do you think Stevens chose to divide "Study of Two Pears" into multiple sections? How does this structure affect the poem's meaning? (b)Do you think that dividing the poem into sections strengthens or weakens the poem? Explain.

6. (a)How does Stevens use rhyme in "The Man with the Blue Guitar"? Why do you think that Stevens chose to employ this rhyme scheme? (b)Do you find the rhyme scheme effective? Explain.

7. (a)In "The Man with the Blue Guitar," the listeners demand that the guitarist play "a tune beyond us, yet ourselves." What do you think this demand means? (b)In your opinion, what kinds of art may fulfill this dual function?

Connect

8. **Big Idea** **New Poetics** How do these two poems illustrate various aspects of Modernism?

LITERARY ANALYSIS

Literary Element Motif

A **motif** is the repetition of an image, description, idea, or other element that helps to convey the theme. In the poems of a Modernist like Stevens, the motifs are often symbols or image clusters.

1. Identify a motif in "Study of Two Pears." Explain how this motif relates to the poem's theme.

2. Identify the main motifs in "The Man with the Blue Guitar." How do they convey the poem's theme?

Reading Further

Look for these works by or about Wallace Stevens:

Poetry Collections *Wallace Stevens: Collected Poetry and Prose*, published by the Library of America.

Biographies *Souvenirs and Prophecies: The Young Wallace Stevens* by Holly Bright Stevens (1977)

Wallace Stevens by Joan Richardson (1986)

READING AND VOCABULARY

Reading Strategy Recognizing Author's Purpose

An **author's purpose** and the theme of a literary work are often interrelated.

1. (a)What is the poem's theme? (b)What was Stevens's purpose in writing a "Study of Two Pears"?

2. What do you think was Stevens's purpose in writing "The Man with the Blue Guitar"?

Vocabulary Practice

Practice with Synonyms Find the synonym for each vocabulary word from "Study of Two Pears."

1. bulge	a. shrink	b. protrude
2. taper	a. narrow	b. race
3. glisten	a. shine	b. disappear

Literature Online Web Activities For eFlashcards, Selection Quick Checks, and other Web activities, go to www.glencoe.com.

somewhere i have never travelled, gladly beyond and anyone lived in a pretty how town

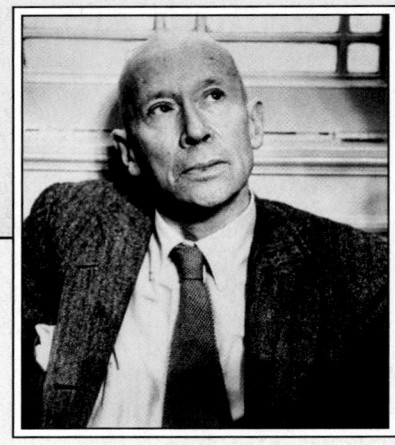

MEET E. E. CUMMINGS

Edward Estlin Cummings coined the term "mostpeople" to describe conformists. Throughout his life, Cummings rebelled against the authoritarian forces that tend to suppress uniqueness. Challenging the social norms of the day, he married three times and only briefly held a regular job. Friends and family came to his rescue when he needed money. "I'm living so far beyond my income," he once wrote, "that we may almost be said to be living apart." His rebellion against authority took radical form in his poetry. People often view language as a fixed system. Cummings did not see it that way; he saw language as a flexible tool. In his poems, he combined words, playing with punctuation and syntax to create unique forms of poetic expression.

"To be nobody-but-myself—in a world which is doing its best, night and day, to make me everybody else—means to fight the hardest battle which any human being can fight and never stop fighting."

—E. E. Cummings

Cummings was born in Cambridge, Massachusetts, the son of a Unitarian minister and a mother who encouraged him to write and keep a journal. A year after receiving a master's degree from Harvard University in 1916, Cummings volunteered to serve as an ambulance driver in World War I. He and a friend were wrongly arrested and imprisoned in France on charges of spying. A few months later, they were released, and Cummings wrote about his experiences there in *The Enormous Room* (1922).

Art and Poetry After the war, Cummings settled in New York City's Greenwich Village, studied art in Paris, and published his first book of poetry, *Tulips and Chimneys* (1923). In New York City, he continued his experiments with free verse and painted in the Cubist style, exhibiting his work regularly. He traveled in Europe in the 1920s and divided his time between New York City and a farm in New Hampshire owned by his family. In 1925, two more volumes of his verse were published, and Cummings received a $2,000 award from *Dial* magazine. In 1928 the Provincetown Playhouse produced a Cummings play called *Him*, which ran for 27 performances. Most critics hated it, but audience response was more favorable.

Applause at Last Cummings continued to publish his poetry throughout the 1930s and 1940s. His *Collected Poems* (1938) received generally good reviews but sold poorly. He had won a Guggenheim Fellowship in 1933, but it was not until the 1950s that he received more recognition, winning the Harriet Monroe Prize in 1950, another Guggenheim Fellowship in 1951, and the Bollingen Prize in Poetry in 1958. He also began to read his poetry to enthusiastic audiences, and in 1952–1953 he lectured at Harvard. Biographer Richard S. Kennedy summed up Cummings's work by writing "What he produced will long amuse, titillate, thrill, provoke, or enthrall his readers."

Edward Estlin Cummings was born in 1894 and died in 1962.

Literature Online **Author Search** For more about E. E. Cummings, go to www.glencoe.com.

Connecting to the Poems

Despite differences in fashion, lifestyle, and technology, are people pretty much the same? In these poems, Cummings attempts to convey the feelings of someone tentatively exploring a love relationship and to portray the experience of the average life of "anyone." As you read the poems, think about the following questions:

- Do you think it is possible to convey emotions accurately through language?
- Is there some common experience that binds us together as human beings?

Building Background

The first thing that readers often notice about Cummings's poems is the unusual arrangement of words, the varied use of punctuation, and the uncommon use of capitalization. These experiments in language and grammar, what former poet laureate Billy Collins called "typographical high jinks," were Cummings's way of expressing his individuality and encouraging readers to look at the world in a new way. Although Cummings's poems are innovative in style, they often explore traditional poetic subjects—such as love, death, and the natural world.

Setting Purposes for Reading

Big Idea New Poetics

Cummings was influenced by Imagist ideas, but he soon developed his own unique style, which to a great extent depended on visual images.

Literary Element Rhythm

Rhythm is the arrangement of stressed and unstressed syllables. Regular rhythm has a predictable pattern, whereas irregular rhythm has no definite pattern. Although both of these Cummings poems have irregular rhythm, the particular arrangement of stressed and unstressed syllables in the second poem plays an especially important role.

- See Literary Terms Handbook, p. R15.

Literature Online **Interactive Literary Elements Handbook** To review or learn more about the literary elements, go to www.glencoe.com.

Reading Strategy Analyzing Style

Style refers to the expressive qualities that distinguish an author's work. Such things as word choice, figurative language, and imagery all help determine an author's style. Cummings's style is in part determined by his arrangement of words on a page. His sentence patterns, use of parentheses, division of words, and capitalization or lack of capitalization all contribute to his instantly recognizable style.

Reading Tip: Asking Questions In your first encounter with a Cummings poem, you will probably have some questions about his style. Write them down in your notebook. You can discuss them later in class.

1. In the first poem, who is being addressed?
2.
3.
4.
5.

Vocabulary

render (ren′ dər) v. to reproduce or depict in verbal or artistic form; p. 696 *The painting was the artist's attempt to render her emotional response to the tragedy.*

reap (rēp) v. to gather, as in harvesting a crop; p. 697 *Tim hoped he would reap the results of his hard work with a good grade on the test.*

apt (apt) adj. likely; having a tendency; p. 697 *Peoples' minds are apt to wander from doing homework on sunny days.*

Vocabulary Tip: Analogies An analogy is a comparison to show similarities between things that are otherwise dissimilar. Writers often use an analogy to explain something unfamiliar by comparing it to something familiar.

INDIANA ACADEMIC STANDARDS (pages 695–698)

11.2 [Analyze] structure…

11.3.3 Analyze the ways in which…the author's style… achieve[s] specific…aesthetic (artistic) purposes…

11.4.7 [Use] Internet sources.

Open Door on the Beach. Konstantine Rodko.
Private collection, New York.

somewhere i have never travelled, gladly beyond

E. E. Cummings

somewhere i have never travelled,gladly beyond
any experience, your eyes have their silence:
in your most frail gesture are things which enclose me,
or which i cannot touch because they are too near

5   your slightest look easily will unclose me
though i have closed myself as fingers,
you open always petal by petal myself as Spring opens
(touching skilfully,mysteriously) her first rose

or if your wish be to close me,i and
10   my life will shut very beautifully,suddenly,
as when the heart of this flower imagines
the snow carefully everywhere descending;

nothing which we are to perceive in this world equals
the power of your intense fragility:whose texture
15   compels me with the colour of its countries,
rendering death and forever with each breathing

(i do not know what it is about you that closes
and opens;only something in me understands
the voice of your eyes is deeper than all roses)
20   nobody,not even the rain,has such small hands

Reading Strategy Analyzing Style *Cummings purposefully plays with sentence structure. How would you untangle the syntax in these lines?*

Big Idea New Poetics *What images recur in this poem? How are these images connected?*

Vocabulary

render (ren′ dər) *v.* to reproduce or depict in verbal or artistic form

anyone lived in a pretty how town

E. E. Cummings

Jealousy, 1892. Tihamer Margitay. National Gallery Budapest, Hungary.

anyone lived in a pretty how town
(with up so floating many bells down)
spring summer autumn winter
he sang his didn't he danced his did.

5   Women and men(both little and small)
cared for anyone not at all
they sowed their isn't they **reaped** their same
sun moon stars rain

children guessed(but only a few
10 and down they forgot as up they grew
autumn winter spring summer)
that noone loved him more by more

when by now and tree by leaf
she laughed his joy she cried his grief
15 bird by snow and stir by still
anyone's any was all to her

someones married their everyones
laughed their cryings and did their dance
(sleep wake hope and then)they
20 said their nevers they slept their dream
stars rain sun moon
(and only the snow can begin to explain

how children are **apt** to forget to remember
with up so floating many bells down)

25 one day anyone died i guess
(and noone stooped to kiss his face)
busy folk buried them side by side
little by little and was by was

all by all and deep by deep
30 and more by more they dream their sleep
noone and anyone earth by april
wish by spirit and if by yes.

Women and men(both dong and ding)
summer autumn winter spring
35 reaped their sowing and went their came
sun moon stars rain

Reading Strategy   Analyzing Style   *What features of Cummings's poetry stand out from the other poetry you have read?*

Reading Strategy   Analyzing Style   *Cummings uses familiar words in unfamiliar ways. What effect does this stylistic element have on your understanding of the poem?*

Literary Element   Rhythm   *What effect does the rhythm have on the overall tone of the poem?*

Vocabulary

reap (rēp) *v.* to gather, as in harvesting a crop

Vocabulary

apt (apt) *adj.* likely; having a tendency

RESPONDING AND THINKING CRITICALLY

Respond

1. What was your first reaction to the strange syntax and the other unusual features in Cummings's poems?

Recall and Interpret

2. In the first two stanzas of "somewhere i have never travelled,gladly beyond," how would you characterize the loved one's effect on the speaker?

3. (a)What metaphors are used throughout the poem, and what are they comparing? (b)Are the images presented in these metaphors typical for a love poem? Why or why not?

4. (a)In "anyone lived in a pretty how town," what is the name of the main character, and what is the name of his wife? (b)What do their names suggest to you?

5. (a)According to the speaker in lines 5–6, what do "women and men" do? (b)What seems to be the speaker's attitude toward these people?

6. (a)What happens to children as they grow up? (b)What is Cummings suggesting about the difference between children and adults?

Analyze and Evaluate

7. In "somewhere i have never travelled,gladly beyond," Cummings frequently appeals to two senses at the same time. Explain how eyes can be silent or have a voice.

8. (a)In "anyone lived in a pretty how town," what happens to the two main characters at the end of the poem, and how would you characterize the townspeople's reaction? (b)Do you think that this is an appropriate ending? Why or why not?

Connect

9. **Big Idea** **New Poetics** Painters known as Cubists painted objects that looked fragmented. How might these Cubist ideas in painting have influenced Cummings's ideas about poetry?

LITERARY ANALYSIS

Literary Element Rhythm

The **rhythm**, or the particular arrangement of stressed and unstressed syllables, plays an important role in "anyone lived in a pretty how town."

Women and men (both little and small)
cared for anyone not at all

1. Which lines in the poem have the same or nearly the same rhythm as the lines presented above? Which lines have a different rhythm?

2. What do you think the differences in rhythm emphasize?

Internet Connection

E. E. Cummings on the Web Look for Web sites devoted to Cummings. Print out or copy down two more of his poems. Compare your reactions to these poems with those you had to the poems in your textbook. Share your thoughts with a partner.

READING AND VOCABULARY

Reading Strategy Analyzing Style

Some words in "anyone lived in a pretty how town" can have more than one meaning. With a partner, examine the possible meanings and discuss how they affect your reading of the poem.

Vocabulary Practice

Practice with Analogies For each question, decide what the relationship is between the first pair of words. Then apply that relationship to the second pair.

1. artist : render :: forecaster :
   a. guess   **c.** weather
   b. tells   **d.** predict

2. reap : farmer :: run :
   a. marathon   **c.** athlete
   b. jog   **d.** coach

Literature Online **Web Activities** For eFlashcards, Selection Quick Checks, and other Web activities, go to www.glencoe.com.

Chicago and Grass

MEET CARL SANDBURG

Although influenced by Ezra Pound and the Imagists, Carl Sandburg broke away from them. He sought to reach a wider audience—and he did. From the 1916 publication of *Chicago Poems* until his death in 1967, Sandburg was one of America's most popular and successful poets.

Carl Sandburg collected material for his poetry from his broad and varied life experience. Besides being a poet and biographer, he worked as a milk-truck driver, bricklayer, and traveling salesman.

"Time is the coin of your life. It is the only coin you have, and only you can determine how it will be spent. Be careful lest you let other people spend it for you."

—Carl Sandburg

Sandburg grew up in Galesburg, Illinois, the son of Swedish immigrants. He quit school after eighth grade and took odd jobs to help support his family. When he was nineteen, he set out to explore the United States, joining the many hoboes of the period who hitched rides on freight trains. Later he fought in the Spanish-American War, attended college, and then moved to Chicago. There he became a journalist, learning to write clearly and protesting social and racial injustices. He also began to contribute poems to *Poetry* magazine.

Literary Giant In the early twentieth century, Chicago was a vibrant place for a poet to live. It was home not only to the influential *Poetry* magazine, founded in 1912 by Harriet Monroe, but also to notable writers such as Sherwood Anderson, Theodore Dreiser, Vachel Lindsay, and Edgar Lee Masters. In 1914 *Poetry* magazine published six of

Sandburg's poems, and with the publication of *Chicago Poems* two years later, Sandburg emerged as one of Chicago's literary giants. Dubbed "the Bard of the Midwest," he soon wrote three more volumes of poetry that established his national reputation as a poet: *Cornhuskers* (1918), *Smoke and Steel* (1920), and *Slabs of the Sunburnt West* (1922).

Critics, however, were divided over Sandburg's poetic merits. Supporters praised his original subject matter and voice, while detractors criticized his free-verse technique and focus on social issues. In response, Sandburg wrote that his goal in writing poetry was simply "to sing, blab, chortle, yodel, like people."

The People's Poet A great admirer of Walt Whitman, Sandburg might be considered Whitman's successor in his enthusiasm for the common people. Sandburg's poems, like Whitman's, are noted for their use of the rhythms of everyday speech and for their democratic subjects and themes. They also include colorful use of sayings and anecdotes.

An extremely popular performer, Sandburg frequently traveled throughout the United States, lecturing on the lives of Whitman and Abraham Lincoln, reading his poems aloud, and singing folk songs while playing the guitar. Sandburg won the Pulitzer Prize for his biography of Lincoln in 1940 and for his *Complete Poems* in 1951. He continued to write throughout his final years.

Carl Sandburg was born in 1878 and died in 1967.

Literature Online **Author Search** For more about Carl Sandburg, go to www.glencoe.com.

Connecting to the Poems

In "Chicago," Sandburg responds to criticisms leveled against his adopted city. As you read the poem, think about the following questions:

- How do you feel when someone criticizes the city or community in which you live?
- What is the best way to respond to such criticism?

Building Background

In the late nineteenth century, Chicago was an economic lifeline of the United States. Sandburg was excited and deeply impressed when, at age eighteen, he first saw the bustling city. In 1896 Chicago's waterways and web of railroads united the nation, linking the wealth of the East with the agriculture of the West, Midwest, and South. From Chicago, meat and grain flowed out to feed the nation.

The city had grown exponentially, from a small trading post in 1830 to an expanding metropolis at the turn of the century. Beginning in the 1840s, waves of immigrants from many different countries settled in Chicago. By the 1880s, the city was half a million strong; three-quarters were immigrants from northern and eastern Europe and their children. The city's rapid industrial growth brought many labor disputes, including riots and a strike by railroad workers. During his years as a Chicago journalist, Sandburg observed first-hand the struggles and triumphs of the growing city.

Setting Purposes for Reading

Big Idea New Poetics

In the first part of the twentieth century, American poetry pushed the boundaries of subject matter, form, and style. As you read, consider how Sandburg breaks new ground in these poems.

Literary Element Apostrophe

Apostrophe is a figure of speech in which a writer directly addresses an inanimate object, an idea, or an absent person. For example, in "Chicago," the speaker says to the city, "they tell me you are crooked." As you read, look for other examples of this technique.

- See Literary Terms Handbook, p. R2.

Reading Strategy Making Inferences About Theme

The **theme** is the central message of a work of literature that readers can apply to life. The theme of a poem is often implied rather than stated directly. You can infer the theme by analyzing elements such as diction, imagery, and figurative language. As you read, look for evidence in the poem that suggests the theme.

....

Reading Tip: Taking Notes Use a diagram to record direct statements, images, and examples of figurative language that support a theme in these poems.

Vocabulary

husky (hus′kē) *adj.* strong; burly; p. 701 *He has a short, husky build.*

wanton (wont′ən) *adj.* resulting from extreme cruelty or neglect; p. 701 *The house is in a state of wanton disrepair.*

sneer (snēr) *v.* to smile or laugh scornfully or critically; p. 701 *The bully did nothing but sneer at the other children.*

....

Vocabulary Tip: Synonyms Synonyms are words that have the same or similar meanings. Note that synonyms are always the same part of speech.

Literature Online Interactive Literary Elements Handbook To review or learn more about the literary elements, go to www.glencoe.com.

INDIANA ACADEMIC STANDARDS (pages 700–703)
11.3.4 Analyze ways in which poetry...uses...figures of speech...to evoke readers' emotions.

11.3.2 Analyze...theme...
11.5.2 Write responses to literature...

CHICAGO

Carl Sandburg

Hog Butcher for the World,
Tool Maker, Stacker of Wheat,
Player with Railroads and the Nation's Freight Handler;
Stormy, **husky**, brawling,
5   City of the Big Shoulders:
They tell me you are wicked and I believe them, for I have seen your painted
     women under the gas lamps luring the farm boys.
And they tell me you are crooked and I answer: Yes, it is true I have seen the
     gunman kill and go free to kill again.
And they tell me you are brutal and my reply is: On the faces of women and
     children I have seen the marks of **wanton** hunger.
And having answered so I turn once more to those who **sneer** at this my city,
     and I give them back the sneer and say to them:
10   Come and show me another city with lifted head singing so proud to be alive
     and coarse and strong and cunning.
Flinging magnetic curses amid the toil of piling job on job, here is a tall bold
     slugger set vivid against the little soft cities;
Fierce as a dog with tongue lapping for action, cunning as a savage pitted
     against the wilderness,
        Bareheaded,
        Shoveling,
15   Wrecking,
        Planning,
        Building, breaking, rebuilding,
Under the smoke, dust all over his mouth, laughing with white teeth,
Under the terrible burden of destiny laughing as a young man laughs,
20   Laughing even as an ignorant fighter laughs who has never lost a battle,
Bragging and laughing that under his wrist is the pulse, and under his ribs the
     heart of the people,
        Laughing!
Laughing the stormy, husky, brawling laughter of Youth, half-naked, sweating,
     proud to be Hog Butcher, Tool Maker, Stacker of Wheat, Player
     with Railroads and Freight Handler to the Nation.

Reading Strategy   Making Inferences About Theme   *What does this phrase suggest about Chicago?*

Vocabulary

husky (hus′kē) *adj.* strong; burly
wanton (wont′ən) *adj.* resulting from extreme cruelty or neglect
sneer (snēr) *v.* to smile or laugh scornfully or critically

The Sky Is Blue, the Grass Is Green, 1972. Joan Mitchell. Oil on canvas. Musee National d'Art Moderne, Centre Georges Pompidou, Paris, France.

Carl Sandburg

Pile the bodies high at Austerlitz and Waterloo.[1]
Shovel them under and let me work—
       I am the grass; I cover all.

And pile them high at Gettysburg[2]
5   And pile them high at Ypres and Verdun.[3]

Shovel them under and let me work.
Two years, ten years, and passengers ask the conductor:
       What place is this?
       Where are we now?

10   I am the grass.
       Let me work.

1. *Austerlitz and Waterloo* refer to battle sites in Moravia (the present-day Czech Republic) and Belgium during the Napoleonic Wars in the early 1800s.
2. *Gettysburg* refers to a battlefield in southern Pennsylvania where Union and Confederate forces fought a horrific battle in 1863 during the Civil War.
3. *Ypres and Verdun* refer to battle sites in Belgium and northern France where well over a million soldiers were slain in World War I.

Big Idea New Poetics *How would you describe the speaker's attitude toward the dead?*

RESPONDING AND THINKING CRITICALLY

Respond

1. Which images in these poems impress you the most? Explain.

Chicago
Recall and Interpret

2. (a)What names does the speaker give Chicago in the first five lines? (b)What do these names reveal?

3. (a)List some of the positive adjectives the speaker uses to describe Chicago. (b)What do these words reveal about the city's inhabitants and the speaker's attitude toward them?

Analyze and Evaluate

4. How well does Sandburg's diction, or word choice, help create a vivid image of the city? Explain.

Grass
Recall and Interpret

5. (a)Who is the speaker in this poem? (b)What does the speaker want to do?

6. (a)Why does the speaker mention famous battle sites from different wars? (b)What battle sites would you add to the speaker's list?

Analyze and Evaluate

7. (a)Why does the speaker describe passengers on a train in lines 7–9? (b)How well does this image support the view of war presented in the poem?

Connect

8. **Big Idea** **New Poetics** Ezra Pound stated that modern poets should "Make it new!" What do you find new about Sandburg's poems?

LITERARY ANALYSIS

Literary Element **Apostrophe**

Poets often use **apostrophe** either to achieve a formal tone or to convey a sense of emotional immediacy.

1. In which lines does the speaker address the city as "you" in "Chicago"?

2. What effects do you think Sandburg's overall use of apostrophe creates? Explain.

Writing About Literature

Explore Author's Purpose Does the speaker in "Chicago" exhibit pride for the city or defend its poor public image? Write a few paragraphs to explain and support your opinion.

Literature Online **Web Activities** For eFlashcards, Selection Quick Checks, and other Web activities, go to www.glencoe.com.

READING AND VOCABULARY

Reading Strategy **Making Inferences About Theme**

1. On the basis of the evidence you listed in your diagram on page 700, how would you state the theme of "Chicago"?

2. Notice two **similes,** or comparisons using the word *like* or *as,* that Sandburg uses in lines 19–20 of "Chicago." How effective are these similes in suggesting the theme?

Vocabulary **Practice**

Practice with Synonyms Choose the best synonym for each vocabulary word from "Chicago."

1. husky
  a. frail   **b.** stocky   **c.** huge

2. wanton
  a. cautious   **b.** sincere   **c.** inhumane

3. sneer
  a. scoff   **b.** grin   **c.** weep

Robert Frost's Poetry

MEET ROBERT FROST

Robert Frost—a poet of dignity, simplicity, and ambiguity—was one of the most honored poets of the twentieth century. A four-time winner of the Pulitzer Prize for Poetry, Frost received special recognition from Congress in 1960. The following January, at age eighty-six, he had the honor of reciting his poem "The Gift Outright" at President John F. Kennedy's inauguration.

Although closely associated with New England, Frost spent his first eleven years in San Francisco. After his father died in 1885, his mother moved Frost and his sister to the gritty industrial city of Lawrence, Massachusetts. She taught school and wrote poetry, introducing Frost to the work of the English Romantic writers, the New England Transcendentalists, and the poets of her native Scotland. Frost graduated from high school and went off to Dartmouth College, but he left the school after less than a year.

Farming and Teaching Frost married Elinor White in 1895. (They had been co-valedictorians of their high school class.) They had six children, two

of whom died young. Frost supported his growing family by farming and teaching school. At age twenty-six, Frost moved his family to a farm near Derry, New Hampshire, where he got to know the rugged landscape and inhabitants of rural New England. There, between farm chores, Frost wrote poems describing the region's often harsh conditions and the experiences of his fellow New Englanders. In 1912, unable to get his poems published in the United States, he sold his farm and moved his family to England.

Success and Enduring Acclaim In London Frost became acquainted with Ezra Pound and other Modernist poets. He was able to publish his first volume of poetry, *A Boy's Will*, in 1913, and *North of Boston* soon after. Praised by poet Amy Lowell in a review, *North of Boston* was soon published in the United States and sold well. By the time Frost returned to New England in 1915, at the start of the First World War, he was well on the road to fame. Prominent publishers backed his work, and prestigious universities sought him to teach.

> "[A poem] begins in delight and ends in wisdom . . . in a clarification of life—not necessarily a great clarification, . . . but in a momentary stay against confusion."
>
> —Robert Frost

Frost's later years were filled with accolades. He received more awards than any other twentieth-century poet and was chosen as poetry consultant to the Library of Congress. By the time of his death, his poetry had deeply embedded itself in the American imagination, and it continues to live there today.

Robert Frost was born in 1874 and died in 1963.

Literature Online **Author Search** For more about Robert Frost, go to www.glencoe.com.

Connecting to the Poems

Robert Frost's poems have a strong sense of place. Often set in the New England countryside, they describe the landscape and the people, capturing their speech patterns in a quiet, reflective voice. Think about the people who live near you and consider the following questions:

- What activities, if any, bring you and your neighbors together?
- What things keep you apart?

Building Background

From 1900 to 1909, Frost tried to earn a living on a small family farm he had bought in Derry, New Hampshire. Farming in New England was difficult because of the rocky soil, short growing season, and harsh climate.

Although Frost loved the outdoors, he was unsuited for farm life. He found working around livestock awkward, disliked regular chores and early rising, feared darkness and storms, and had a somewhat frail build. Three years before leaving for England, Frost abandoned farming and resumed his teaching career. Despite his lack of success as a farmer, Frost drew inspiration for many poems from his memories of New England farm life.

Setting Purposes for Reading

Big Idea New Poetics

Though Frost uses traditional forms for his poems, he often explores typical themes of modern poetry such as loneliness and isolation. As you read, notice how "Mending Wall" and "Birches" reflect these themes.

Literary Element Blank Verse

Blank verse is poetry written in unrhymed iambic pentameter. Each line has a basic pattern of five pairs of syllables, with each pair made up of an unstressed syllable followed by a stressed syllable. As you read, listen to the rhythms Frost creates by using blank verse.

- See Literary Terms Handbook, p. R3.

Literature Online **Interactive Literary Elements Handbook** To review or learn more about the literary elements, go to www.glencoe.com.

Reading Strategy Comparing and Contrasting Speakers

The **speaker** is the voice of a poem, similar to the narrator in a work of prose. Sometimes the speaker's voice is that of the poet, and sometimes it is that of a fictional person or even a thing. The speaker's words communicate a particular **tone**, or attitude, toward the subject of a poem. By comparing and contrasting the speakers of these poems, you can identify the qualities that distinguish each one.

Reading Tip: Using a Venn Diagram As you read, consider how the speakers of "Mending Wall" and "Birches" are similar and different. Use a Venn diagram to record your information.

Vocabulary

enamel (i nam′əl) *n.* a cosmetic or paint that gives a smooth, glossy appearance; p. 708 *The pot was covered in an enamel to make it waterproof.*

bracken (bra′kən) *n.* a type of fern that grows in humid, temperate areas; p. 708 *Bracken covered the forest floor in summer.*

poise (poiz′) *n.* a state of balance; p. 709 *Her grace and poise made us think she must be a dancer.*

coax (kōks′) *v.* to persuade gently; p. 716 *I tried to coax the cat out of the tree with a catnip toy.*

kin (kin) *n.* relatives, or a group of people with common ancestry; p. 720 *Sara had kin from four countries present at her wedding ceremony.*

Vocabulary Tip: Synonyms Synonyms are words that have the same or similar meanings. Note that synonyms are always the same part of speech.

INDIANA ACADEMIC STANDARDS (pages 705–710)
11.3.4 Analyze…poetry…

11.3.3 Analyze the ways in which…tone…achieve[s] specific… aesthetic (artistic) purposes…

The Last Stone Walls, Dogtown, 1936–37. Marsden Hartley. Oil on canvas, 17½ x 23½ in. Yale University Art Gallery, New Haven, CT. Gift of Walter Bareiss, B.A. 1940.
Viewing the Art: In what ways might this wall be like the one in "Mending Wall"? In what ways might it be different?

Mending Wall

Robert Frost

Something there is that doesn't love a wall,
That sends the frozen-ground-swell under it,
And spills the upper boulders in the sun;
And makes gaps even two can pass abreast.
5   The work of hunters is another thing:
I have come after them and made repair
Where they have left not one stone on a stone,
But they would have the rabbit out of hiding,
To please the yelping dogs. The gaps I mean,

10　No one has seen them made or heard them made,
　　But at spring mending-time we find them there.
　　I let my neighbour know beyond the hill;
　　And on a day we meet to walk the line
　　And set the wall between us once again.
15　We keep the wall between us as we go.
　　To each the boulders that have fallen to each.
　　And some are loaves and some so nearly balls
　　We have to use a spell to make them balance:
　　'Stay where you are until our backs are turned!'
20　We wear our fingers rough with handling them.
　　Oh, just another kind of out-door game,
　　One on a side. It comes to little more:
　　There where it is we do not need the wall:
　　He is all pine and I am apple orchard.
25　My apple trees will never get across
　　And eat the cones under his pines, I tell him.
　　He only says, 'Good fences make good neighbours.'
　　Spring is the mischief in me, and I wonder
　　If I could put a notion in his head:
30　'Why do they make good neighbours? Isn't it
　　Where there are cows? But here there are no cows.
　　Before I built a wall I'd ask to know
　　What I was walling in or walling out,
　　And to whom I was like to give offence.
35　Something there is that doesn't love a wall,
　　That wants it down.' I could say 'Elves' to him,
　　But it's not elves exactly, and I'd rather
　　He said it for himself. I see him there
　　Bringing a stone grasped firmly by the top
40　In each hand, like an old-stone savage armed.
　　He moves in darkness as it seems to me,
　　Not of woods only and the shade of trees.
　　He will not go behind his father's saying,
　　And he likes having thought of it so well
45　He says again, 'Good fences make good neighbours.'

Big Idea　New Poetics *What do these lines tell you about the relationship between the two neighbors?*

Reading Strategy　Comparing and Contrasting Speakers *What do these lines reveal about the speaker?*

Literary Element　Blank Verse *How does the rhythm of these lines help create a conversational tone?*

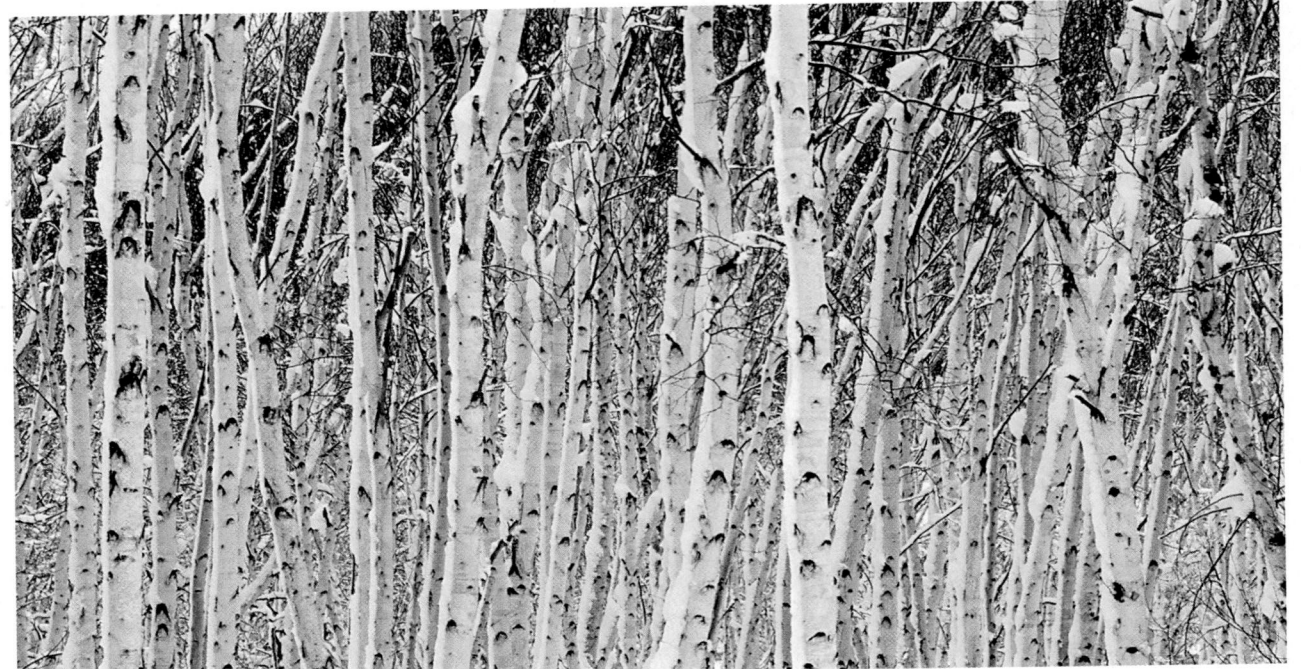

Birches

Robert Frost

When I see birches bend to left and right
Across the lines of straighter darker trees,
I like to think some boy's been swinging them.
But swinging doesn't bend them down to stay
5   As ice-storms do. Often you must have seen them
Loaded with ice a sunny winter morning
After a rain. They click upon themselves
As the breeze rises, and turn many-colored
As the stir cracks and crazes their **enamel.**
10 Soon the sun's warmth makes them shed crystal shells
Shattering and avalanching on the snow-crust—
Such heaps of broken glass to sweep away
You'd think the inner dome of heaven had fallen.
They are dragged to the withered **bracken** by the load,
15 And they seem not to break; though once they are bowed
So low for long, they never right themselves:

Literary Element   Blank Verse *Which syllables are
stressed in this sentence?*

You may see their trunks arching in the woods
Years afterwards, trailing their leaves on the ground
Like girls on hands and knees that throw their hair
20 Before them over their heads to dry in the sun.
But I was going to say when Truth broke in
With all her matter-of-fact about the ice-storm
I should prefer to have some boy bend them
As he went out and in to fetch the cows—
25 Some boy too far from town to learn baseball,
Whose only play was what he found himself,
Summer or winter, and could play alone.
One by one he subdued[1] his father's trees
By riding them down over and over again
30 Until he took the stiffness out of them,
And not one but hung limp, not one was left
For him to conquer. He learned all there was
To learn about not launching out too soon
And so not carrying the tree away
35 Clear to the ground. He always kept his **poise**
To the top branches, climbing carefully
With the same pains you use to fill a cup
Up to the brim, and even above the brim.
Then he flung outward, feet first, with a swish,
40 Kicking his way down through the air to the ground.
So was I once myself a swinger of birches.
And so I dream of going back to be.
It's when I'm weary of considerations,
And life is too much like a pathless wood
45 Where your face burns and tickles with the cobwebs
Broken across it, and one eye is weeping
From a twig's having lashed across it open.
I'd like to get away from earth awhile
And then come back to it and begin over.
50 May no fate willfully misunderstand me
And half grant what I wish and snatch me away
Not to return. Earth's the right place for love:
I don't know where it's likely to go better.
I'd like to go by climbing a birch tree,
55 And climb black branches up a snow-white trunk
Toward heaven, till the tree could bear no more,
But dipped its top and set me down again.
That would be good both going and coming back.
One could do worse than be a swinger of birches.

---

1. *Subdued* means "brought under control" or "conquered."

Big Idea New Poetics *Why does the poet include these details about the boy?*

Reading Strategy Comparing and Contrasting Speakers
What does the speaker admire about the boy who swings on birches?

Vocabulary

poise (poiz′) *n.* a state of balance

RESPONDING AND THINKING CRITICALLY

Respond

1. Which images from the poems do you find the most powerful? Explain.

Mending Wall
Recall and Interpret

2. (a)According to the speaker, what causes a wall to fall apart? (b)To what might the "something" that "doesn't love a wall" refer?

3. (a)Describe how the speaker and the neighbor fix the wall. (b)How do their opinions differ?

Analyze and Evaluate

4. (a)What does the speaker suggest by describing the neighbor as "an old-stone savage"? (b)How does dialogue help emphasize the differences between the speaker and the neighbor?

5. (a)Why does the speaker refer to this spring ritual as "another kind of out-door game" (line 21)? (b)What might walls and fences symbolize in this poem?

Birches
Recall and Interpret

6. (a)What does the speaker want to think has caused the birches to bend? What has really caused them to bend? (b)Why might the speaker want to believe in the imaginary cause?

7. (a)To what does the speaker compare the ice that falls from birches? To what does he compare their trunks and leaves? (b)What can you infer about the speaker's feelings regarding the birches?

Analyze and Evaluate

8. (a)In describing the boy who lives "too far from town to learn baseball," whom is the speaker really describing? (b)What kinds of activities might swinging on birches represent?

9. **Big Idea** **New Poetics** In "Birches," Frost compares life to a pathless wood. Do you think this is an appropriate simile? Why or why not?

LITERARY ANALYSIS

Literary Element **Blank Verse**

Both "Mending Wall" and "Birches" are written in **blank verse,** or unrhymed iambic pentameter. To determine the rhythm of any line, mark or scan its stressed and unstressed syllables. For example, the first line of "Birches" scans as follows:

When I see birches bend to left and right

Because Frost uses blank verse to imitate spoken English, every line in these poems is not perfectly regular.

1. Practice scanning several lines from each poem. What is unusual about the first line of "Mending Wall"?

2. Why are the rhythms of natural speech suitable for the subjects of these poems?

Literature Online **Web Activities** For eFlashcards, Selection Quick Checks, and other Web activities, go to www.glencoe.com.

READING AND VOCABULARY

Reading Strategy **Comparing and Contrasting Speakers**

Refer to the Venn diagram you created on page 705 to answer the following questions:

1. How are the speakers of the poems similar and different?

2. How would you contrast the tone of each poem?

Vocabulary **Practice**

Practice with Synonyms Synonyms are words that have the same or similar meanings. Choose the synonym for each vocabulary word listed from Frost's poems.

1. enamel
   a. glaze   b. rough   c. coat   d. pottery

2. kin
   a. children   b. strangers   c. relatives   d. oven

Winter Forest, 1991. Gerrit Greve.

Stopping by Woods on a Snowy Evening

Robert Frost

Whose woods these are I think I know.
His house is in the village though;
He will not see me stopping here
To watch his woods fill up with snow.

5 My little horse must think it queer
To stop without a farmhouse near
Between the woods and frozen lake
The darkest evening of the year.

He gives his harness bells a shake
10 To ask if there is some mistake.
The only other sound's the sweep
Of easy wind and downy flake.

The woods are lovely, dark and deep.
But I have promises to keep,
15 And miles to go before I sleep,
And miles to go before I sleep.

Reading Strategy Comparing and Contrasting
Speakers *What might "sleep" mean to the speaker?*

RESPONDING AND THINKING CRITICALLY

Respond

1. Which lines from the poem did you find most powerful or meaningful? Explain.

Recall and Interpret

2. (a)Where does the owner of the woods live, and what will he not see? (b)Why might the speaker care that the owner will not see this?

3. (a)According to the speaker, what must the horse think? (b)How might the horse's instincts differ from those of the speaker?

4. (a)What adjectives describe the woods in line 13? (b)What **mood** do these words create?

Analyze and Evaluate

5. (a)How does the **setting** of the poem contribute to its meaning? (b)What might the woods **symbolize**?

6. (a)Why does the speaker not embrace the peaceful escape offered by the woods? (b)How does the **repetition** in the final lines affect their meaning?

Connect

7. **Big Idea** **New Poetics** What themes of modern poetry does "Stopping by Woods on a Snowy Evening" reflect?

LITERARY ANALYSIS

Literary Element Rhyme Scheme

"Mending Wall" and "Birches" are written in blank verse, or unrhymed iambic pentameter. "Stopping by Woods on a Snowy Evening," on the other hand, contains end rhymes. A **rhyme scheme,** as you learned in Unit Four, is the pattern of end rhymes in a poem. For example, the rhyme scheme in the first stanza of the poem is *aaba*. Because the "b" sound is repeated in the second stanza, the rhyme scheme for that stanza is *bbcb.*

1. Determine the rhyme schemes for the final two stanzas.

2. What is the effect of repeating a sound from each stanza in the one that follows it?

3. How does the rhyme scheme in the last stanza reinforce the meaning of the poem?

Writing About Literature

Compare and Contrast Form In a brief essay, compare and contrast a Frost poem written in blank verse (such as "Mending Wall" or "Birches") with one that contains end rhyme (such as "Stopping by Woods on a Snowy Evening"). While writing, consider the following questions: How does rhyme affect the meaning in each poem? Which style do you prefer?

READING AND VOCABULARY

Reading Strategy Comparing and Contrasting Speakers

Unlike the speaker in "Mending Wall," the speaker in "Stopping by Woods on a Snowy Evening" is serious, not playful or mischievous. Even while pausing to absorb the beauty and tranquility of a winter scene, he never forgets his responsibilities, the promises he must keep.

1. How does the owner of the woods differ from the speaker?

2. How is the speaker similar to most people journeying through life?

Academic Vocabulary

Here is a word from the vocabulary list on page R86.

design (di zīn´) *n.* the arrangement of elements or details in a product or work of art

Practice and Apply

1. How does the **design** of "Stopping by Woods on a Snowy Evening" add to the poem's overall meaning?

Literature Online **Web Activities** For eFlashcards, Selection Quick Checks, and other Web activities, go to www.glencoe.com.

Acquainted with the Night

Robert Frost

Park Row, Leeds, England, 1882. John Atkinson Grimshaw. Oil on canvas.
Private Collection.

I have been one acquainted with the night.
I have walked out in rain—and back in rain.
I have outwalked the furthest city light.

I have looked down the saddest city lane.
5 I have passed by the watchman on his beat
And dropped my eyes, unwilling to explain.

I have stood still and stopped the sound of feet
When far away an interrupted cry
Came over houses from another street,

10 But not to call me back or say good-bye;
And further still at an unearthly height,
One luminary[1] clock against the sky

Proclaimed[2] the time was neither wrong nor right.
I have been one acquainted with the night.

---

1. *Luminary* means "giving light."
2. *Proclaimed* means "declared publicly."

Reading Strategy Comparing and Contrasting Speakers
What does this line tell you about the speaker's mood?

RESPONDING AND THINKING CRITICALLY

Respond

1. Which image from this poem is most memorable?

Recall and Interpret

2. (a)When and where has the speaker walked in lines 1–3? What has he seen in line 4? (b)Why might the speaker be out walking alone at night?

3. (a)What does the speaker do when passing the watchman? (b)Why does the speaker choose to do this?

4. (a)What does the clock proclaim? (b)Why does the speaker not reveal the exact time?

Analyze and Evaluate

5. (a)What is the night in this poem like? (b)What do you think "the night" **symbolizes**?

6. Why does Frost repeat line 1 in line 14?

7. How does Frost create a **mood** of loneliness or isolation in this poem?

Connect

8. **Big Idea** **New Poetics** What Modernist themes does Frost explore in this poem?

LITERARY ANALYSIS

Literary Element **Rhyme Scheme**

As in "Stopping by Woods on a Snowy Evening," rhyme supports the meaning in "Acquainted with the Night." In this poem Frost uses a traditional form, derived from Italian poetry, known as *terza rima*. It consists of three-line stanzas, or tercets, in which the first and third lines rhyme.

1. Identify the rhyme scheme of this poem.

2. How is one tercet connected to the next?

3. What effects does Frost create in the final stanza?

Performing

Choose a Robert Frost poem, or a section of a poem, that you like or feel particularly strongly about to read in front of your class or a small group. To prepare for your reading, identify the sound devices the poem uses, such as its rhyme scheme. Practice your reading in front of a mirror beforehand, paying attention to your pronunciation, speed, and gestures.

Literature Online Web Activities For eFlashcards, Selection Quick Checks, and other Web activities, go to www.glencoe.com.

READING AND VOCABULARY

Reading Strategy **Comparing and Contrasting Speakers**

In important ways, this poem is different from "Mending Wall," "Birches," and "Stopping by Woods on a Snowy Evening." For one thing, it is set in an urban area, not in the New England countryside. The speaker, moreover, is unlike those in the other three poems.

1. How would you characterize the speaker in this poem?

2. What sets this speaker apart from the other speakers created by Frost?

Academic Vocabulary

Here are two words from the vocabulary list on page R86.

feature (fē´chər) *n.* a quality or attribute of something

perceive (pər sēv´) *v.* to become aware of something by way of the senses, or in one's mind

Practice and Apply

1. Describe one **feature** of "Acquainted with the Night" that you felt added to the poem's mood.

2. How does the speaker **perceive** the city in the poem?

The Death of the Hired Man

Robert Frost

BEFORE YOU READ

Literary Element Dramatic Poetry

A **dramatic poem** reveals the personalities of one or more characters by using dialogue and monologue as well as description. While dramatic poetry may include narrative, the focus is on the characters, not the events. As you read "The Death of the Hired Man," consider what the dialogue reveals about the characters' personalities.

- See Literary Terms Handbook, p. R5.

Reading Strategy Evaluating Characterization

Characterization refers to the methods a writer uses to reveal the personality of a character. In **direct characterization,** the writer makes explicit statements about a character. In **indirect characterization,** the writer reveals a character through the character's words and actions and through what other characters think and say about that character. As you read, notice the details Frost uses to reveal the hired man's personality and consider how well they work.

> Mary sat musing[1] on the lamp-flame at the table
> Waiting for Warren. When she heard his step,
> She ran on tip-toe down the darkened passage
> To meet him in the doorway with the news
> 5   And put him on his guard. "Silas is back."
> She pushed him outward with her through the door
> And shut it after her. "Be kind," she said.
> She took the market things from Warren's arms
> And set them on the porch, then drew him down
> 10   To sit beside her on the wooden steps.

---

1. *Musing* means "meditating" or "pondering."

Literary Element Dramatic Poetry *What does this line of dialogue suggest about Mary's values?*

Meade Family (detail), 1941.
Jack Delano. Silver gelatin print.

"When was I ever anything but kind to him?
But I'll not have the fellow back," he said.
"I told him so last haying, didn't I?
If he left then, I said, that ended it.
15 What good is he? Who else will harbor[2] him
At his age for the little he can do?
What help he is there's no depending on.
Off he goes always when I need him most.
He thinks he ought to earn a little pay,
20 Enough at least to buy tobacco with,
So he won't have to beg and be beholden.[3]
'All right,' I say, 'I can't afford to pay
Any fixed wages, though I wish I could.'
'Someone else can.' 'Then someone else will have to.'
25 I shouldn't mind his bettering himself
If that was what it was. You can be certain,
When he begins like that, there's someone at him
Trying to **coax** him off with pocket-money,—
In haying time, when any help is scarce.
30 In winter he comes back to us. I'm done."

2. *Harbor* means "to give shelter or protection to."
3. *Beholden* means "obligated" or "indebted."

Reading Strategy Evaluating Characterization *What are Warren's reasons for not wanting Silas back?*

Vocabulary

coax (kōks′) *v.* to persuade gently

"Sh! not so loud: he'll hear you," Mary said.

"I want him to: he'll have to soon or late."

"He's worn out. He's asleep beside the stove.
When I came up from Rowe's I found him here,
35 Huddled against the barn-door fast asleep,
A miserable sight, and frightening, too—
You needn't smile—I didn't recognize him—
I wasn't looking for him—and he's changed.
Wait till you see."

40   "Where did you say he'd been?"

"He didn't say. I dragged him to the house,
And gave him tea and tried to make him smoke.
I tried to make him talk about his travels.
Nothing would do: he just kept nodding off."
45 "What did he say? Did he say anything?"

"But little."

                     "Anything? Mary, confess
He said he'd come to ditch[4] the meadow for me."

"Warren!"

50   "But did he? I just want to know."

"Of course he did. What would you have him say?
Surely you wouldn't grudge the poor old man
Some humble way to save his self-respect.
He added, if you really care to know,
55 He meant to clear the upper pasture, too.
That sounds like something you have heard before?
Warren, I wish you could have heard the way
He jumbled everything. I stopped to look
Two or three times—he made me feel so queer[5]—
60 To see if he was talking in his sleep.
He ran on[6] Harold Wilson—you remember—

---

4. Here, *ditch* means "to dig long, narrow channels." These channels, or ditches, are often used for drainage or irrigation.
5. *Queer* means "odd" or "strange."
6. *Ran on* means "talked continuously about."

Reading Strategy   Evaluating Characterization   *What is happening to Silas?*

The boy you had in haying four years since.
He's finished school, and teaching in his college.
Silas declares you'll have to get him back.
65 He says they two will make a team for work:
Between them they will lay this farm as smooth!
The way he mixed that in with other things.
He thinks young Wilson a likely lad, though daft[7]
On education—you know how they fought
70 All through July under the blazing sun,
Silas up on the cart to build the load,
Harold along beside to pitch it on."

"Yes, I took care to keep well out of earshot."

"Well, those days trouble Silas like a dream.
75 You wouldn't think they would. How some things linger![8]
Harold's young college boy's assurance piqued[9] him.
After so many years he still keeps finding
Good arguments he sees he might have used.
I sympathize.[10] I know just how it feels
80 To think of the right thing to say too late.
Harold's associated in his mind with Latin.
He asked me what I thought of Harold's saying
He studied Latin like the violin
Because he liked it—that an argument!
85 He said he couldn't make the boy believe
He could find water with a hazel prong[11]—
Which showed how much good school had ever done him.
He wanted to go over that. But most of all
He thinks if he could have another chance
90 To teach him how to build a load of hay—"

"I know, that's Silas' one accomplishment.
He bundles every forkful in its place,
And tags and numbers it for future reference,
So he can find and easily dislodge[12] it
95 In the unloading. Silas does that well.
He takes it out in bunches like big birds' nests.
You never see him standing on the hay
He's trying to lift, straining to lift himself."

---

7. *Daft* means "foolish."
8. *Linger* means "to continue to exist" or "to endure."
9. *Piqued* means "aroused a feeling of anger or resentment in."
10. *Sympathize* means "to share in or to agree with the feelings or ideas of another."
11. A *hazel prong* is a stick believed to indicate the presence of underground water.
12. *Dislodge* means "to move or to force from a position."

"He thinks if he could teach him that, he'd be
100 Some good perhaps to someone in the world.
He hates to see a boy the fool of books.
Poor Silas, so concerned for other folk,
And nothing to look backward to with pride,
And nothing to look forward to with hope,
105 So now and never any different."

Part of a moon was falling down the west,
Dragging the whole sky with it to the hills.
Its light poured softly in her lap. She saw it
And spread her apron to it. She put out her hand
110 Among the harp-like morning-glory[13] strings,
Taut[14] with the dew from garden bed to eaves,
As if she played unheard some tenderness
That wrought[15] on him beside her in the night.
"Warren," she said, "he has come home to die:
115 You needn't be afraid he'll leave you this time."

"Home," he mocked gently.

                              "Yes, what else but home?
It all depends on what you mean by home.
Of course he's nothing to us, any more
120 Than was the hound that came a stranger to us
Out of the woods, worn out upon the trail."

"Home is the place where, when you have to go there,
They have to take you in."

                              "I should have called it
125 Something you somehow haven't to deserve."

---

13. A *morning glory* is a vine that produces trumpet-shaped flowers.
    Gardeners often position a lattice or strings for a vine to grow along.
14. *Taut* means "stretched tight."
15. *Wrought* means "worked."

Big Idea New Poetics *How is Silas depicted in these lines?*

Literary Element Dramatic Poetry *What does the description in these lines reveal about Mary?*

Literary Element Dramatic Poetry *What is the difference between Mary's view of a person's home and Warren's?*

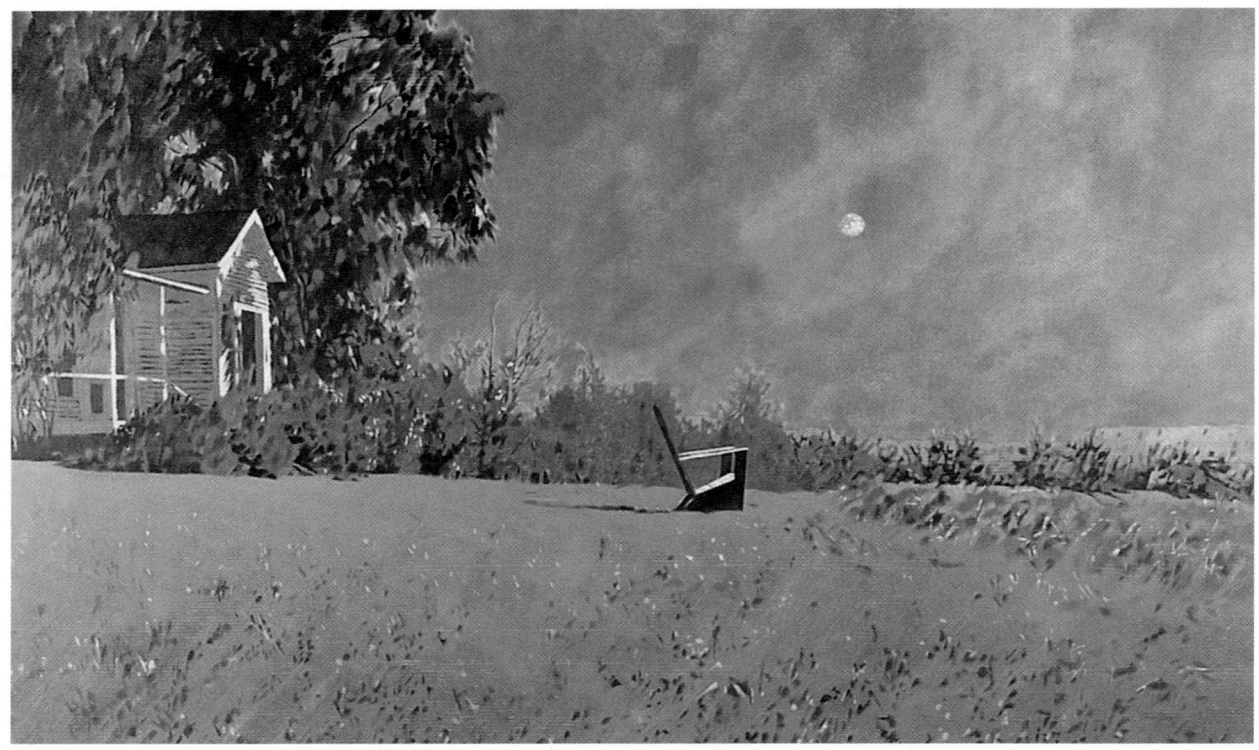

Moonlight in Vermont. 1982. Daniel Lang. Oil on canvas, 48 x 72 in. Collection of Harrison Young, Beijing, China. Reproduced in *Spirit of Place* by John Arthur.

Viewing the Art: How does the mood of this painting compare with Mary's in lines 170–171?

Warren leaned out and took a step or two,
Picked up a little stick, and brought it back
And broke it in his hand and tossed it by.
"Silas has better claim on us you think

130   Than on his brother? Thirteen little miles
As the road winds would bring him to his door.
Silas has walked that far no doubt to-day.
Why didn't he go there? His brother's rich,
A somebody—director in the bank."

135   "He never told us that."

                              "We know it though."

"I think his brother ought to help, of course.
I'll see to that if there is need. He ought of right
To take him in, and might be willing to—

140   He may be better than appearances.
But have some pity on Silas. Do you think
If he had any pride in claiming **kin**

Or anything he looked for from his brother,
He'd keep so still about him all this time?"

145   "I wonder what's between them."

                                        "I can tell you.
Silas is what he is—we wouldn't mind him—
But just the kind that kinsfolk can't abide.[16]
He never did a thing so very bad.
150   He don't know why he isn't quite as good
As anybody. Worthless though he is,
He won't be made ashamed to please his brother."

"*I* can't think Si ever hurt anyone."

"No, but he hurt my heart the way he lay
155   And rolled his old head on that sharp-edged chair-back.
He wouldn't let me put him on the lounge.
You must go in and see what you can do.
I made the bed up for him there to-night.
You'll be surprised at him—how much he's broken.
160   His working days are done; I'm sure of it."

"I'd not be in a hurry to say that."

"I haven't been. Go, look, see for yourself.
But, Warren, please remember how it is:
He's come to help you ditch the meadow.
165   He has a plan. You mustn't laugh at him.
He may not speak of it, and then he may.
I'll sit and see if that small sailing cloud
Will hit or miss the moon."

                                        It hit the moon.
170   Then there were three there, making a dim row,
The moon, the little silver cloud, and she.

Warren returned—too soon, it seemed to her,
Slipped to her side, caught up her hand and waited.

"Warren?" she questioned.

175   "Dead," was all he answered.

---

16. *Abide* means "to put up with" or "to tolerate."

Reading Strategy   Evaluating Characterization   *Is Mary a good judge of Silas's character? Explain.*

RESPONDING AND THINKING CRITICALLY

Respond

1. How do you feel about the characters in this poem?

Recall and Interpret

2. (a)Describe what Mary does and says upon Warren's return in lines 1–10. (b)Why does she feel the need to put Warren "on his guard"?

3. (a)How does Silas look when Mary first sees him? (b)Why does Warren refuse to believe that Silas will tackle the chores he says he will?

4. (a)Who is Harold Wilson, and what does Silas dislike about him? (b)What do Silas's thoughts and emotions regarding Harold reveal about Silas's personality?

5. (a)According to Mary, why has Silas come to the house? (b)Why does Silas avoid asking his brother for help?

Analyze and Evaluate

6. (a)From your reading of lines 1–30, how would you describe the differences between Mary and Warren? (b)Why does Frost associate Mary with moonlight in lines 108–109 and lines 170–171?

7. In this poem Frost presents two different definitions of home. Which definition do you prefer, and why?

8. (a)What does the end of the poem suggest about Warren's feelings toward Silas? (b)Could Frost have chosen a better ending for the poem? Support your evaluation.

9. How does Frost's use of dialogue affect the **tone** of the poem?

Connect

10. **Big Idea** New Poetics "The Death of the Hired Man," contends scholar C. M. Bowra, "is about the pathos of men who have no roots and no ties and no firm grip on life." Which of the themes of modern poetry does Bowra's reading illustrate? Do you agree with Bowra's comment? Explain why or why not.

DAILY LIFE AND CULTURE

Rural Life in the Early 1900s

"The Death of the Hired Man" is set on a farm in the early years of the twentieth century. At that time, life was vastly different from the way it is today, especially in rural areas. In the year 1900, when Robert Frost was twenty-six, most people had neither electricity nor indoor plumbing. They heated their homes with a stove, often set up in the living room.

Those fortunate enough to own a telephone shared a "party line" with several others. To make a call, a person first had to dial the operator and indicate the number he or she wished to reach. If there was someone else already on the line, the caller had to wait for that conversation to finish before placing the call.

At the beginning of the twentieth century, boys and girls in rural areas combined schooling with chores at home. After leaving school at about age fourteen, boys often worked as farm laborers. Some became apprentices and learned trades or worked in stores. When they were not in school, girls helped with household chores such as cooking, sewing, and making cheese or butter. Men and women usually married in their twenties. Most babies were born at home, and infant mortality rates were high.

Although a few people owned automobiles, horses were the usual method of transportation. They pulled wagons, carriages, and even fire engines and hearses. Of course, no one in 1900 had ever flown in an airplane, listened to a radio, played a video game, or visited a shopping mall.

Group Activity Discuss the following questions with your classmates.

1. How has life changed since 1900, and why?

2. Is today's society a better place to live compared with the early 1900s? Support your opinion.

LITERARY ANALYSIS

Literary Element Dramatic Poetry

In "The Death of the Hired Man," Frost reveals the personalities of Silas, Mary, and Warren through dialogue. He also includes purely narrative or descriptive passages.

1. How is this poem similar to a play?

2. Do you think this poem would have been as powerful if Frost had revealed Silas's personality through description only instead of dialogue and description together? Explain.

3. How does the language used in the dialogue between Mary and Warren differ from that used in the descriptive passages?

Review: Blank Verse

As you learned when studying the poems "Mending Wall" and "Birches," **blank verse** is unrhymed poetry that is written in a rhythmic pattern called **iambic pentameter.** In iambic pentameter, each line has five feet, or basic units of measurement of a line of metrical poetry; each foot contains an unstressed syllable followed by a stressed syllable. Pauses do not always come at the ends of lines but wherever they make sense.

Partner Activity With two classmates, read aloud the first fifty lines of "The Death of the Hired Man." One person should read the narrative or descriptive passages; the other two should read the lines of Mary and Warren. After your reading, discuss how iambic pentameter captures the cadences and rhythms of ordinary speech.

ROBERT FROST
—1874-1963—
Some of the best-loved poems in the English language are associated with this small farm owned by the poet from 1900 to 1911. Here Frost farmed, taught at nearby Pinkerton Academy, and developed the poetic voice which later won him the Pulitzer Prize for poetry four times and world fame as one of our foremost poets.

READING AND VOCABULARY

Reading Strategy Evaluating Characterization

In "The Death of the Hired Man," Frost uses indirect characterization. Simply put, he shows rather than tells, letting the reader draw his or her own inferences about the characters from the details provided in the poem. Remarkably, though Silas remains offstage, the reader learns much about this hired man. Seeing him through Warren's and Mary's eyes, the reader learns about Silas's physical condition, his work habits, his interaction with Harold Wilson, his estrangement from his brother, and his motivation for his final return to the farm. Through his choice of details, Frost attempts to bring Silas to life in the reader's imagination.

1. Is Silas a realistic, well-developed character? Support your answer.

2. What does Frost accomplish by keeping Silas offstage?

Vocabulary Practice

Practice with Synonyms Choose the synonym for each vocabulary word listed from Frost's poems. Use a dictionary or thesaurus if you need help.

1. poise
  a. elegant   **c.** dancer
  b. balance   **d.** clumsy

2. coax
  a. scam   **c.** prevent
  b. persuade   **d.** ask

3. bracken
  a. bramble   **c.** broken
  b. wire   **d.** fern

Academic Vocabulary

Here are two words from the vocabulary list on page R86.

task (task) *n.* an assigned piece of work

partner (pärt´nər) *n.* associate or colleague

Practice and Apply
1. What **task** did Silas do best on the farm?
2. What two skills did Silas want to teach Harold Wilson, his former working **partner**?

Writing About Literature

Compare and Contrast Characters How would you compare and contrast Silas and Harold Wilson? Write a brief essay to explore this question, using evidence from the poem to support your ideas. To help you get started, jot down notes about the characters using a Venn diagram.

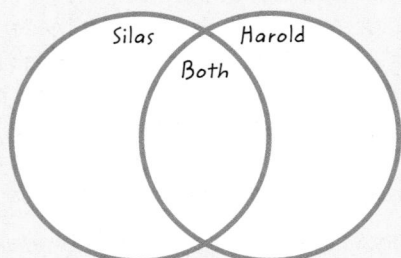

As you draft, introduce your topic in the first paragraph and develop the notes listed on your diagram in the middle paragraph(s). Conclude your essay with a parting thought about Silas and Harold as foil characters in the poem.

Exchange your draft with a peer reviewer; then revise if necessary. Proofread your paper for errors in usage and spelling.

Reading Further

If you are interested in reading more by or about Robert Frost, look for the following:

Poetry Collections: *Robert Frost: Collected Poems, Prose and Plays,* edited by Richard Poirier and Mark Richardson, is a comprehensive collection of Frost's work published by The Library of America.

Poems by Robert Frost: A Boy's Will and North of Boston (2001), introduction by William H. Pritchard, is a one-volume collection of Frost's early works.

Biographies: *Frost: A Literary Life Reconsidered* (1993), by William H. Pritchard, is a narrative exploring the interaction between Frost's life and work.

Robert Frost: A Life (1999), by Jay Parini, provides an analysis of Frost's poetry and a balanced look at his life.

Literature Online Web Activities For eFlashcards, Selection Quick Checks, and other Web activities, go to www.glencoe.com.

Frost's Language and Style

Using Prepositional Phrases A prepositional phrase consists of a preposition, its object, and any modifiers of the object. A prepositional phrase can function as an adjective, modifying a noun or a pronoun. (Mary noticed the light *from the moon.*) A prepositional phrase may also function as an adverb when it modifies a verb, an adverb, or an adjective. (Silas rolled his head *on the chair-back.*)

- Set off two or more introductory prepositional phrases or a single long one with a comma.

> *During the busiest part of the summer, Silas deserted the farm.*
>
> *In their conversation about Silas in the evening, Mary and Warren disagreed.*

- Do not use a comma if the introductory prepositional phrase is immediately followed by a verb.

> *In the heat of July worked Silas and Harold Wilson.*

Activity In "The Death of the Hired Man," Frost often uses prepositional phrases, sometimes to describe actions or reinforce the somber mood:

"She ran *on tip-toe down the darkened passage*"

"Its light poured softly *in her lap*"

Identify other examples of prepositional phrases in the poem and indicate whether each phrase functions as an adjective or an adverb. Read your list to the class.

Revising Check

Punctuation Work with a partner to review and revise the punctuation of commas after introductory prepositional phrases in your essay for "The Death of the Hired Man."

REMARKS AT AMHERST COLLEGE

President John F. Kennedy

Pulitzer Prize Winner

Building Background

In October 1963, President John F. Kennedy presented the following remarks at Amherst College, in Amherst, Massachusetts. The speech was given in honor of the groundbreaking of the Robert Frost Library, which was completed two years later. This would be one of Kennedy's last public appearances before his assassination less than a month later. Robert Frost, who died earlier in the year, had long been associated with Amherst College, having taught English there periodically throughout his career.

Setting Purposes for Reading

Read to discover the historical and social impacts of Robert Frost's poetry.

Reading Strategy

Analyzing Philosophical Assumptions

Analyzing philosophical assumptions involves gathering information to determine an author's implicit and explicit philosophical assumptions and beliefs about a subject. As you read, take notes about the assumptions you discover in President Kennedy's speech.

*Mr. McCloy, President Plimpton, Mr. MacLeish,[1]
distinguished guests, ladies and gentlemen:*

I am very honored to be here with you on this occasion which means so much to this college and also means so much to art and the progress of the United States. This college is part of the United States. It belongs to it. So did Mr. Frost, in a large sense. And, therefore, I was privileged to accept the invitation somewhat rendered to me in the same way that Franklin Roosevelt rendered his invitation to Mr. MacLeish, the invitation which I received from Mr. McCloy.[2] The powers of the Presidency are often described. Its limitations should occasionally be remembered. And therefore when the Chairman of our Disarmament Advisory Committee, who has

---

1. John Jay *McCloy* (1895–1989), a diplomat and lawyer, served as an adviser to every president from Franklin Delano Roosevelt to Ronald Reagan. Calvin Hastings *Plimpton* was the president of Amherst College from 1960 to 1971. Archibald *MacLeish* (1892–1982) was a famed poet and playwright. MacLeish also served as a librarian of Congress and briefly as an assistant secretary of state.
2. Kennedy is referring to President Franklin Roosevelt's invitation to MacLeish to become a librarian of Congress.

President John F. Kennedy delivers a speech in 1962.

labored so long and hard, Governor Stevenson's[3] assistant during the very difficult days at the United Nations during the Cuban crisis, a public servant for so many years, asks or invites the President of the United States, there is only one response. So I am glad to be here.

Amherst has had many soldiers of the king since its first one, and some of them are here today: Mr. McCloy, who has long been a public servant; Jim Reed who is the Assistant Secretary of the Treasury; President Cole, who is now our Ambassador to Chile; Mr. Ramey, who is a Commissioner of the Atomic Energy Commission; Dick Reuter, who is head of the Food for Peace. These and scores of others down through the years have recognized the obligations of the advantages which the graduation from a college such as this places upon them to serve not only their private interest but the public interest as well.

3. Adlai *Stevenson* (1900–1965) served as governor of Illinois from 1948 to 1952 and as the U.S. delegate to the United Nations during the Kennedy administration. John McCloy served as Stevenson's assistant during the Cuban missile crisis.

Many years ago, Woodrow Wilson said, what good is a political party unless it is serving a great national purpose? And what good is a private college or university unless it is serving a great national purpose? The Library being constructed today, this college, itself—all of this, of course, was not done merely to give this school's graduates an advantage, an economic advantage, in the life struggle. It does do that. But in return for that, in return for the great opportunity which society gives the graduates of this and related schools, it seems to me incumbent[4] upon this and other schools' graduates to recognize their responsibility to the public interest.

Privilege is here, and with privilege goes responsibility. And I think, as your president said, that it must be a source of satisfaction to you that this school's graduates have recognized it. I hope that the students who are here now will also recognize it in the future. Although Amherst has been in the forefront of extending aid to needy and talented students, private colleges, taken as a whole, draw 50 percent of their students from the wealthiest 10 percent of our Nation. And even State universities and other public institutions derive 25 percent of their students from this group. In March 1962, persons of 18 years or older who had not completed high school made up 46 percent of the total labor force, and such persons comprised 64 percent of those who were unemployed. And in 1958, the lowest fifth of the families in the United States had 4 1/2 percent of the total personal income, the highest fifth, 44 1/2 percent. There is inherited wealth in this country and also inherited poverty. And unless the graduates of this college and other colleges like it who are given a running start in life—unless they are willing to put back into our society, those talents, the broad sympathy, the understanding, the compassion—unless they are willing to put those qualities back into the service of the Great Republic, then obviously the presuppositions upon which our democracy are based are bound to be fallible.

The problems which this country now faces are staggering, both at home and abroad. We need the service, in the great sense, of every educated man or woman to find 10 million jobs in the next

4. Here, *incumbent* means "imposed."

2 1/2 years, to govern our relations—a country which lived in isolation for 150 years, and is now suddenly the leader of the free world—to govern our relations with over 100 countries, to govern those relations with success so that the balance of power remains strong on the side of freedom, to make it possible for Americans of all different races and creeds to live together in harmony, to make it possible for a world to exist in diversity and freedom. All this requires the best of all of us.

Therefore, I am proud to come to this college, whose graduates have recognized this obligation and to say to those who are now here that the need is endless, and I am confident that you will respond.

Robert Frost said:

> Two roads diverged in a wood, and I—
> I took the one less traveled by,
> And that has made all the difference.

I hope that road will not be the less traveled by, and I hope your commitment to the Great Republic's interest in the years to come will be worthy of your long inheritance since your beginning. This day devoted to the memory of Robert Frost offers an opportunity for reflection which is prized by politicians as well as by others, and even by poets, for Robert Frost was one of the granite figures of our time in America. He was supremely two things: an artist and an American. A nation reveals itself not only by the men it produces but also by the men it honors, the men it remembers.

In America, our heroes have customarily run to men of large accomplishments. But today this college and country honors a man whose contribution was not to our size but to our spirit, not to our political beliefs but to our insight, not to our self-esteem, but to our self-comprehension. In honoring Robert Frost, we therefore can pay honor to the deepest sources of our national strength. That strength takes many forms, and the most obvious forms are not always the most significant. The men who create power make an indispensable contribution to the Nation's greatness, but the men who question power make a contribution just as indispensable, especially when that questioning is disinterested, for they determine whether we use power or power uses us.

Our national strength matters, but the spirit which informs and controls our strength matters just as much. This was the special significance of Robert Frost. He brought an unsparing instinct for reality to bear on the platitudes[5] and pieties[6] of society. His sense of the human tragedy fortified him against self-deception and easy consolation. "I have been" he wrote, "one acquainted with the night." And because he knew the midnight as well as the high noon, because he understood the ordeal as well as the triumph of the human spirit, he gave his age strength with which to overcome despair. At bottom, he held a deep faith in the spirit of man, and it is hardly an accident that Robert Frost coupled poetry and power, for he saw poetry as the means of saving power from itself. When power leads man towards arrogance, poetry reminds him of his limitations. When power narrows the areas of man's concern, poetry reminds him of the richness and diversity of his existence. When power corrupts, poetry cleanses. For art establishes the basic human truth which must serve as the touchstone of our judgment.

The artist, however faithful to his personal vision of reality, becomes the last champion of the individual mind and sensibility against an intrusive society and an officious state. The great artist is thus a solitary figure. He has, as Frost said, a lover's quarrel with the world. In pursuing his perceptions of reality, he must often sail against the currents of his time. This is not a popular role. If Robert Frost was much honored in his lifetime, it was because a good many preferred to ignore his darker truths. Yet in retrospect, we see how the artist's fidelity has strengthened the fibre of our national life.

If sometimes our great artists have been the most critical of our society, it is because their sensitivity and their concern for justice, which must motivate any true artist, makes him aware that our Nation falls short of its highest potential. I see little of more importance to the future of our country and our civilization than full recognition of the place of the artist.

If art is to nourish the roots of our culture, society must set the artist free to follow his vision wherever it takes him. We must never forget that art is not a form of propaganda; it is a form of truth. And as Mr. MacLeish once remarked of poets, there is nothing worse for our trade than to be in style. In free society art is not

---

5. *Platitudes* are unoriginal statements.
6. *Pieties* are reverent statements.

a weapon and it does not belong to the spheres of polemic[7] and ideology. Artists are not engineers of the soul. It may be different elsewhere. But democratic society—in it, the highest duty of the writer, the composer, the artist is to remain true to himself and to let the chips fall where they may. In serving his vision of the truth, the artist best serves his nation. And the nation which disdains the mission of art invites the fate of Robert Frost's hired man, the fate of having "nothing to look backward to with pride, and nothing to look forward to with hope."

I look forward to a great future for America, a future in which our country will match its military strength with our moral restraint, its wealth with our wisdom, its power with our purpose. I look forward to an America which will not be afraid of grace and beauty, which will protect the beauty of our natural environment, which will preserve the great old American houses and squares and parks of our national past, and which will build handsome and balanced cities for our future.

I look forward to an America which will reward achievement in the arts as we reward

---

7. *Polemic* means "argumentation."

achievement in business or statecraft. I look forward to an America which will steadily raise the standards of artistic accomplishment and which will steadily enlarge cultural opportunities for all of our citizens. And I look forward to an America which commands respect throughout the world not only for its strength but for its civilization as well. And I look forward to a world which will be safe not only for democracy and diversity but also for personal distinction.

Robert Frost was often skeptical about projects for human improvement, yet I do not think he would disdain this hope. As he wrote during the uncertain days of the Second War:

> *Take human nature altogether since time began . . .*
> *And it must be a little more in favor of man,*
> *Say a fraction of one percent at the very least . . .*
> *Our hold on this planet wouldn't have so increased.*

Because of Mr. Frost's life and work, because of the life and work of this college, our hold on this planet has increased. ❧

RESPONDING AND THINKING CRITICALLY

Respond

1. What is your opinion of Kennedy's claim that "society must set the artist free to follow his vision wherever it takes him"? Are there limits to artistic expression? Explain.

Recall and Interpret

2. (a)According to Kennedy, the artist becomes the last champion of what? (b)How might this championing help to bring about Kennedy's vision of America in the future?

3. (a)In Kennedy's view, art is never a form of what type of information? (b)Why do you think he made this statement?

Analyze and Evaluate

4. (a)Why do you think Kennedy claimed that "a good many preferred to ignore [Frost's] darker truths"? (b)Do you agree with Kennedy that Frost's poems often hold "darker truths"? Why or why not?

5. (a)Why do you think Kennedy began his address by discussing economics and education? (b)What do you think of this portion of the address?

Connect

6. Briefly compare and contrast Kennedy's arguments about artists and society with the beliefs held by particular literary movements of other arguments you've read by literary figures.

▶ **INDIANA ACADEMIC STANDARDS (pages 725–728)**
11.2.5 Analyze an author's implicit and explicit assumptions and beliefs about a subject.

11.3.8 Analyze the philosophical arguments presented in literary works...

PART 2

MODERN FICTION

A Doughboy's Equipment, c. 1921. Charles A. Meurer. Oil on canvas, 68 x 40 in. Butler Institute of American Art, Youngstown, OH.

"The hardest thing to do is to write straight honest prose on human beings."

—Ernest Hemingway

The Modern American Short Story

SINCE THE ERA of Poe, Hawthorne, and Irving, the short story has been one of the most popular genres among American writers. The early stories of American Romanticism featured supernatural plots and clear moral themes adapted from well-known European myths and tales. As literary styles and themes shifted in the 1800s during the movements of Realism and Naturalism, however, short story writers in the United States began to portray plots and characters that mirrored real life. Modernist writers continued this progression by experimenting with new ways of capturing the rich complexity of human life and by responding to a world that was just beginning to rise from the ashes of World War I.

> *"There are no plot stories in life."*
> —Sherwood Anderson

Literary Mavericks

Writers such as Sherwood Anderson, Ernest Hemingway, F. Scott Fitzgerald, Henry James, and Katherine Anne Porter energized the short story in the early 1900s by peering into the private world of human thought. "The task of finding concrete ways to communicate emotional states becomes the central problem for most short story writers in the twentieth century," wrote critic Charles E. May. A representative example was Sherwood Anderson's *Winesburg, Ohio*, published in 1919. This groundbreaking collection of short stories explored the minds of characters that Anderson called "grotesque." Some of the stories, including "Hands," had previously appeared in a variety of journals that provided a forum for innovative stories. The characters in these stories are troubled by their difficult circumstances, yet endearing. Anderson's goal in portraying them was "to at last go out of myself, truly into others, the others I met constantly in the streets of the city, in the office where I then worked, and still others remembered out of my childhood in an American small town."

Stream of Consciousness

Many modernist short story writers in the early 1900s were influenced by the new psychological theories of the time, including the writings of Sigmund Freud, who believed in the presence of unconscious causes for people's behavior. This flurry of interest in the human mind spawned a new literary technique called **stream of consciousness.** American psychologist William James, the brother of writer Henry James, coined the phrase in 1890. He believed people have a constant stream of thoughts that flow through their minds without clear logic or order.

James Joyce, Virginia Woolf, William Faulkner, and Katherine Anne Porter (see page 774) are some of the notable practitioners of this method of narration. In stories that employ stream of consciousness, certain memories trigger seemingly random thoughts. Stream of consciousness stories include the following elements:

- first-person point of view
- a lack of conventional sentence structure or grammar
- "free associations" that flow through a character's mind and link distinctly separate events
- interior monologues

Room in New York, 1932. Edward Hopper. Oil on Canvas, 28½ x 35½ in. F.M. Hall Collection.

The Interior World

Modernist writers reacted against formulaic, plot-driven stories that dominated the early 1900s, including the surprise endings that made the fiction of O. Henry famous. Irish short-story writer Frank O'Connor explained that Modernists instead strove for the "artful approach to the significant moment." Another Irish writer, James Joyce, brought this idea of the moment charged with meaning to full effect in his 1914 short story collection *Dubliners*, in which he introduced the **epiphany,** or moment of revelation, and used it to redefine the short story.

Many writers of the period cited Russian writer Anton Chekhov (see page 552) as a key influence. Translations of his work into English between 1916 and 1923 brought his method of storytelling to the United States. Chekhov was a master at employing realistic detail and **understatement**—a de-emphasis on the importance of something or someone. He preferred to use "slice of life" anecdotes in his stories rather than traditional plots. Chekhov's stories, such as "Gooseberries," lack obvious external conflicts, action-packed events, and clear climaxes. Instead, the drama rages inside characters' minds. The protagonists in modern short stories, notably by Hemingway and Fitzgerald, are often **antiheroes,** or conflicted characters engulfed by indecision.

The language in modern short stories is often subtle and poetic, and requires the reader to infer what is left unsaid. British short-story writer and critic H. E. Bates said, "It is no longer necessary to describe; it is enough to suggest. The full-length portrait, in full dress, with scenic background, has become superfluous; now it is enough that we should know a woman by the shape of her hands."

Hemingway (see page 732), who was influenced by Chekhov's style, was also a master of understatement. Hemingway's terse, suggestive language, a staple of the modern short story, was frequently imitated. Hemingway used the metaphor of an iceberg to explain his view of the short story. "There is seven-eighths of it underwater for every part that shows."

Features of the Modern Short Story

Note the following features of modern short stories to help enrich your understanding of these works.

- understatement
- irony
- stream of consciousness
- antiheroes
- unspectacular, or everyday, settings
- themes of instability and loss
- plots without a clear climax or resolution

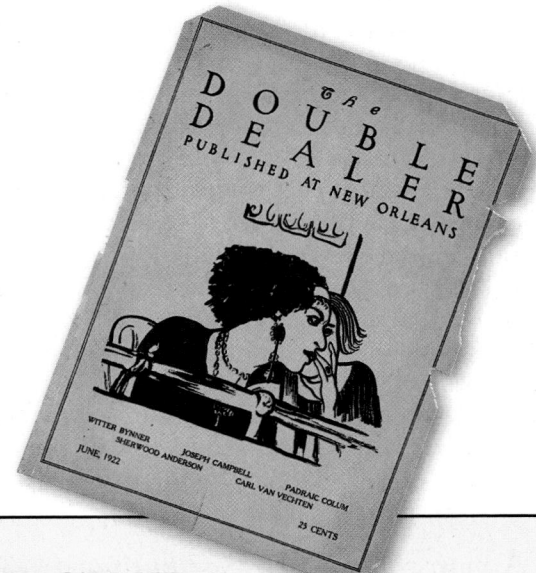

RESPONDING AND THINKING CRITICALLY

1. What factors inspired writers in the modern period to revamp the short story?

2. (a) What is stream of consciousness?
(b) What influenced its emergence in modern fiction?

3. Look back at one of the short stories in Unit Two: American Romanticism. How is it similar to and different from one of the modern short stories in Unit Five?

 Literary History For more about the modern short story, go to www.glencoe.com.

INDIANA ACADEMIC STANDARDS
(pages 730–731)
11.3.5 Analyze or evaluate works of literary or cultural significance in history…

In Another Country

MEET ERNEST HEMINGWAY

Big-game hunters, deep-sea fishermen, soldiers, boxers, bullfighters—these are the types of characters found in Ernest Hemingway's fiction. Yet the Hemingway hero is not the typical action-adventure daredevil. Strong but sensitive, brainy as well as brawny, he is usually someone who has been wounded by life, though he keeps his suffering to himself. Inextricably linked to Hemingway's own adventurous life and personality, the Hemingway hero captured the public's imagination and granted the author celebrity status that extended beyond the world of literature. His style and depiction of characters has been widely imitated by generations of writers.

Coming of Age Born in the Chicago suburb of Oak Park, Illinois, Ernest Hemingway spent large chunks of his childhood camping, hunting, and fishing with his father. He began writing in high school and upon graduating landed a job as a cub reporter for the *Kansas City Star*. Soon after, when the United States entered World War I, Hemingway was determined to be part of the action. Rejected by the U.S. military because of an eye defect, he volunteered to serve as a Red Cross ambulance driver near the battlefront in Italy, and was seriously wounded less than a month before his nineteenth birthday. The injury, said critic Alfred Kazin, "was a shock that went straight into Hemingway's early stories and fables of the war."

> "A man can be destroyed but not defeated."
> —Ernest Hemingway
> from *The Old Man and the Sea*

After medical treatment in Italy and recuperation back home, Hemingway accepted a job as foreign correspondent for the *Toronto Star*. Settling in Paris, he joined the colony of American writers and artists who, disillusioned by the war but reluctant to leave the continent where they had fought it, chose to live as expatriates. Many expatriates often gathered at the Paris home of American author Gertrude Stein, who coined the term *lost generation* to describe the alienated writers and artists of the post–World War I era.

A Celebrity Author In 1925, encouraged by Stein and others, Hemingway published *In Our Time*, a story collection that established his presence as an important new writer. He followed with *The Sun Also Rises* (1926), a novel of the lost generation in 1920s Paris and Spain, and *A Farewell to Arms* (1929), a tragic World War I love story.

Hemingway drew on his personal adventures as he wrote his fiction and won fame for his lifestyle as much as for his writing style. He wrote his bullfighting novel, *Death in the Afternoon* (1932), after attending bullfights in Spain, and his story "The Snows of Kilimanjaro" (1936) came after he went on safari in Africa. In 1952 Hemingway published *The Old Man and the Sea*, a short novel that drew on his own experiences as a deep-sea fisherman off the coast of Cuba. In 1954 Hemingway won the Nobel Prize for Literature "for his mastery of the art of narrative, most recently demonstrated in *The Old Man and the Sea*, and for the influence that he has exerted on contemporary style." He is one of fewer than ten U.S. writers to be presented with a Nobel Prize.

Ernest Hemingway was born in 1899 and died in 1961.

Literature Online **Author Search** For more about Ernest Hemingway, go to www.glencoe.com.

Connecting to the Story

Hemingway once defined "guts," or courage, as the ability to display "grace under pressure." In "In Another Country," several of the characters have been awarded medals for behaving courageously. As you read the story, think about the following questions:

- What are some different forms of courage?
- Can a person be courageous in a situation even after he or she becomes disillusioned by it?

Building Background

"In Another Country" takes place in the northern Italian city of Milan during World War I. The war, fought from 1914 to 1918, pitted the Allied Powers, which included England and France, against the Central Powers, which included Germany and Austria-Hungary. The United States joined the Allied Powers only a year before the war ended, but Italy joined the Allied Powers in 1915. The war exacted a high toll of casualties; in fact, of the 65 million people who fought in World War I, over 10 million were killed, and more than 20 million more were wounded.

Setting Purposes for Reading

Big Idea Modern Fiction

As you read, notice how Hemingway's story differs from earlier fiction you have read in terms of both subject matter and style.

Literary Element Style

Style is the writer's characteristic way of writing. It includes elements such as word choice, sentence structure, and tone. Hemingway, who was strongly influenced by his training as a journalist, pioneered a simple, unadorned style that has been frequently imitated. As you read the story, look for examples of Hemingway's simple, journalistic style.

- See Literary Terms Handbook, p. R18.

Literature Online **Interactive Literary Elements Handbook** To review or learn more about the literary elements, go to www.glencoe.com.

Reading Strategy Recognizing Author's Purpose

Writers have different **purposes,** or reasons, for writing. For some, the main purpose is to entertain. Others want to present stories with as much realism as possible. Some writers may also want to teach a lesson or present a set of values or an approach toward life. As you read Hemingway's story, think about what his purpose may have been.

Reading Tip: Tracking Ideas Use a chart to note your ideas about the author's purposes.

Detail	Purpose
p. 735: "It was cold in the fall in Milan. . . . Beyond the old hospital were the new brick pavilions."	to portray the setting realistically

Vocabulary

lurch (lurch) *v.* to move suddenly and unevenly; p. 735 *When I shoved the refrigerator, it lurched a few inches to the right.*

withered (wi′thərd) *adj.* shriveled; p. 735 *Fresh water did not revive the withered flowers.*

detached (di tacht′) *adj.* not involved emotionally; aloof; indifferent; p. 737 *Others tried to befriend him, but he remained detached.*

jostle (jo′səl) *v.* to bump, push, or shove while moving, as in a crowd; p. 737 *Did the crowd jostle you, or did you just trip and fall on your own?*

resign (ri zīn′) *v.* to make oneself accept something; p. 738 *I will have to resign myself to the situation, since I cannot change it.*

Vocabulary Tip: Antonyms Words that have opposite or nearly opposite meanings are called antonyms. Note that antonyms are always the same part of speech.

 INDIANA ACADEMIC STANDARDS (pages 733–740)
11.2.2 Analyze the way in which clarity of meaning is affected by...word choice in the text.
11.2 Develop strategies such as...identifying...purpose...
11.5.2 Write responses to literature...

In Another Country

Ernest Hemingway

The Invincible Soldier. B.V. Cerbakov. Tretyakov Gallery, Moscow, Russia.

In the fall the war[1] was always there, but we did not go to it any more. It was cold in the fall in Milan[2] and the dark came very early. Then the electric lights came on, and it was pleasant along the streets looking in the windows. There was much game[3] hanging outside the shops, and the snow powdered in the fur of the foxes and the wind blew their tails. The deer hung stiff and heavy and empty, and small birds blew in the wind and the wind turned their feathers. It was a cold fall and the wind came down from the mountains.

We were all at the hospital every afternoon, and there were different ways of walking across the town through the dusk to the hospital. Two of the ways were alongside canals, but they were long. Always, though, you crossed a bridge across a canal to enter the hospital. There was a choice of three bridges. On one of them a woman sold roasted chestnuts. It was warm, standing in front of her charcoal fire, and the chestnuts were warm afterward in your pocket. The hospital was very old and very beautiful, and you entered through a gate and walked across a courtyard and out a gate on the other side. There were usually funerals starting from the courtyard. Beyond the old hospital were the new brick pavilions, and there we met every afternoon and were all very polite and interested in what was the matter, and sat in the machines that were to make so much difference.

The doctor came up to the machine where I was sitting and said: "What did you like best to do before the war? Did you practice a sport?"

I said: "Yes, football."

"Good," he said. "You will be able to play football again better than ever."

My knee did not bend and the leg dropped straight from the knee to the ankle without a calf,

and the machine was to bend the knee and make it move as in riding a tricycle. But it did not bend yet, and instead the machine **lurched** when it came to the bending part. The doctor said: "That will all pass. You are a fortunate young man. You will play football again like a champion."

In the next machine was a major who had a little hand like a baby's. He winked at me when the doctor examined his hand, which was between two leather straps that bounced up and down and flapped the stiff fingers, and said: "And will I too play football, captain-doctor?" He had been a very great fencer, and before the war the greatest fencer in Italy.

The doctor went to his office in the back room and brought a photograph which showed a hand that had been **withered** almost as small as the major's, before it had taken a machine course, and after was a little larger. The major held the photograph with his good hand and looked at it very carefully. "A wound?" he asked.

"An industrial accident," the doctor said.

"Very interesting, very interesting," the major said, and handed it back to the doctor.

"You have confidence?"

"No," said the major.

There were three boys who came each day who were about the same age I was. They were all three from Milan, and one of them was to be a lawyer, and one was to be a painter, and one had intended to be a soldier, and after we were finished with the machines, sometimes we walked back together to the Café Cova, which was next door to the Scala.[4] We walked the short way through the communist quarter because we were four together. The people hated us because we were officers, and from a wine-shop some one would call out, "A basso

---

4. *The Scala* (skä′ lə) is Milan's world-famous opera house.

1. The *war* is World War I (1914–1918). The United States, Italy, and other countries fought Germany and its allies.
2. *Milan* is a city in northern Italy.
3. Here, *game* refers to wild animals that have been hunted and killed for food.

Piazza Corvetto in Genoa in 1918. Alessandro Milesi. Oil on canvas.
Galleria d'Arte Moderna di Nervi, Genoa, Italy.

Viewing the Art: In what ways does this painting reflect the sense of detachment that the characters feel in "In Another Country"?

gli ufficiali!"[5] as we passed. Another boy who walked with us sometimes and made us five wore a black silk handkerchief across his face because he had no nose then and his face was to be rebuilt. He had gone out to the front[6] from the military academy and been wounded within an hour after he had gone into the front line for the first time. They rebuilt his face, but he came from a very old family and they could never get the nose exactly right. He went to South America and worked in a bank. But this was a long time ago, and then we did not any of us know how it was going to be afterward. We only knew then that there was always the war, but that we were not going to it any more.

We all had the same medals, except the boy with the black silk bandage across his face, and he had not been at the front long enough to get any medals. The tall boy with a very pale face who was to be a lawyer had been a lieutenant of Arditi[7] and had three medals of the sort we each had only one of. He had lived a very long time with death and was a little

5. In Italian, *A basso gli ufficiali!* (a bä´ sō lyē ōō fē chä´ lē) means "Down with officers!"
6. The *front* is the line or area of conflict between opposing armies.

Literary Element Style *How would you describe the tone in which this gruesome information is relayed?*

7. The *Arditi* (ar dē´ tē) was a corps of soldiers specially selected for dangerous operations.

detached. We were all a little detached, and there was nothing that held us together except that we met every afternoon at the hospital. Although, as we walked to the Cova through the tough part of town, walking in the dark, with light and singing coming out of the wine-shops, and sometimes having to walk into the street when the men and women would crowd together on the sidewalk so that we would have had to **jostle** them to get by, we felt held together by there being something that had happened that they, the people who disliked us, did not understand.

We ourselves all understood the Cova, where it was rich and warm and not too brightly lighted, and noisy and smoky at certain hours, and there were always girls at the tables and the illustrated papers on a rack on the wall. The girls at the Cova were very patriotic, and I found that the most patriotic people in Italy were the café girls—and I believe they are still patriotic.

The boys at first were very polite about my medals and asked me what I had done to get them. I showed them the papers, which were written in very beautiful language and full of *fratellanza* and *abnegazione*,[8] but which really said, with the adjectives removed, that I had been given the medals because I was an American. After that their manner changed a little toward me, although I was their friend against outsiders. I was a friend, but I was never really one of them after they had read the citations,[9] because it had been different with them and they had done very different things to get their medals. I had been wounded, it was true; but we all knew that being wounded, after all, was really an accident. I was never ashamed of the ribbons, though, and

---

8. *Fratellanza* (fra tāl än′ za) and *abnegazione* (ab nā ga tzyo′ nā) are Italian for "brotherhood" and "self-denial."
9. *Citations* are specific references to military achievements worthy of reward or praise.

Big Idea Modern Fiction *How is the portrayal of these characters different from portrayals of war heroes in literature from earlier periods?*

Vocabulary

detached (di tacht′) *adj.* not involved emotionally; aloof; indifferent

jostle (jo′ səl) *v.* to bump, push, or shove while moving, as in a crowd

---

sometimes, after the cocktail hour, I would imagine myself having done all the things they had done to get their medals; but walking home at night through the empty streets with the cold wind and all the shops closed, trying to keep near the street lights, I knew that I would never have done such things, and I was very much afraid to die, and often lay in bed at night by myself, afraid to die and wondering how I would be when I went back to the front again.

The three with the medals were like hunting-hawks; and I was not a hawk, although I might seem a hawk to those who had never hunted; they, the three, knew better and so we drifted apart. But I stayed good friends with the boy who had been wounded his first day at the front, because he would never know now how he would have turned out; so he could never be accepted either, and I liked him because I thought perhaps he would not have turned out to be a hawk either.

The major, who had been the great fencer, did not believe in bravery, and spent much time while we sat in the machines correcting my grammar. He had complimented me on how I spoke Italian, and we talked together very easily. One day I had said that Italian seemed such an easy language to me that I could not take a great interest in it; everything was so easy to say. "Ah, yes," the major said. "Why, then, do you not take up the use of grammar?" So we took up the use of grammar, and soon Italian was such a difficult language that I was afraid to talk to him until I had the grammar straight in my mind.

The major came very regularly to the hospital. I do not think he ever missed a day, although I am sure he did not believe in the machines. There was a time when none of us believed in the machines, and one day the major said it was all nonsense. The machines were new then and it was we who were to prove them. It was an idiotic idea, he said, "a theory, like another." I had not learned my grammar, and he said I was a stupid impossible disgrace, and he was a fool to have bothered with me. He was a small man and he sat straight up in his chair with his right hand thrust

---

Big Idea Modern Fiction *How does the close proximity of these three unrelated statements reflect new ideas of Modernism?*

into the machine and looked straight ahead at the wall while the straps thumped up and down with his fingers in them.

"What will you do when the war is over if it is over?" he asked me. "Speak grammatically!"

"I will go to the States."

"Are you married?"

"No, but I hope to be."

"The more of a fool you are," he said. He seemed very angry. "A man must not marry."

"Why, Signor Maggiore?"[10]

"Don't call me 'Signor Maggiore.'"

"Why must not a man marry?"

"He cannot marry. He cannot marry," he said angrily. "If he is to lose everything, he should not place himself in a position to lose that. He should not place himself in a position to lose. He should find things he cannot lose."

He spoke very angrily and bitterly, and looked straight ahead while he talked.

"But why should he necessarily lose it?"

"He'll lose it," the major said. He was looking at the wall. Then he looked down at the machine and jerked his little hand out from between the straps and slapped it hard against his thigh. "He'll lose it," he almost shouted. "Don't argue with me!" Then he called to the attendant who ran the machines. "Come and turn this thing off."

He went back into the other room for the light treatment and the massage. Then I heard him ask the doctor if he might use his telephone and he shut the door. When he came back into the room, I was sitting in another machine. He was wearing his cape and had his cap on, and he came directly toward my machine and put his arm on my shoulder.

"I am so sorry," he said, and patted me on the shoulder with his good hand. "I would not be rude. My wife has just died. You must forgive me."

> And then crying, his head up looking at nothing, carrying himself straight and soldierly, with tears on both his cheeks and biting his lips, he walked past the machines and out the door.

"Oh—" I said, feeling sick for him. "I am *so* sorry."

He stood there biting his lower lip. "It is very difficult," he said. "I cannot **resign** myself."

He looked straight past me and out through the window. Then he began to cry. "I am utterly unable to resign myself," he said and choked. And then crying, his head up looking at nothing, carrying himself straight and soldierly, with tears on both his cheeks and biting his lips, he walked past the machines and out the door.

The doctor told me that the major's wife, who was very young and whom he had not married until he was definitely invalided[11] out of the war, had died of pneumonia. She had been sick only a few days. No one expected her to die. The major did not come to the hospital for three days. Then he came at the usual hour, wearing a black band on the sleeve of his uniform. When he came back, there were large framed photographs around the wall, of all sorts of wounds before and after they had been cured by the machines. In front of the machine the major used were three photographs of hands like his that were completely restored. I do not know where the doctor got them. I always understood we were the first to use the machines. The photographs did not make much difference to the major because he only looked out of the window. ∽

---

11. *Invalided* means "removed from active duty because of sickness or disability."

Reading Strategy Recognizing Author's Purpose *What might the unexpected death of the major's wife reveal about the author's purpose?*

Big Idea Modern Fiction *How is Hemingway's omission of facts about the machines, the photos, and the fate of the major characteristic of the Modernist approach to fiction?*

Vocabulary

resign (ri zīn´) *v.* to make oneself accept something

---

10. *Signor Maggiore* (sē nyor´ ma jō´ rā) means "Mr. Major." In Italy, one said *Signor* before an officer's rank as a sign of respect.

RESPONDING AND THINKING CRITICALLY

Respond

1. How did you react to the end of the story? Explain.

Recall and Interpret

2. (a)Why do the narrator and the others go to the hospital every afternoon? (b)What might the machines represent?

3. (a)What is the effect of the narrator's grammar lessons? (b)Based on this effect, what generalization can you make about the narrator's views on the world?

4. (a)What makes the narrator suspicious of the machines? (b)What do his suspicions show about his attitude toward authority and the likelihood of his recovery?

Analyze and Evaluate

5. (a)To what type of bird does the narrator compare the three young Italian men with medals? (b)How does this comparison affect your view of the three young men, and how does it stress the difference between them and the narrator?

6. (a)What is ironic about the bad news that the major receives? (b)How realistic do you find his reaction to this news?

7. (a)Besides their physical injuries, how might the narrator and the other soldiers be wounded? (b)How effectively does the story convey their attitudes?

Connect

8. **Big Idea** **Modern Fiction** How is the portrayal of war in this story different from heroic depictions in times past?

LITERARY ANALYSIS

Literary Element Style

When he began working for the *Kansas City Star*, Hemingway received a **style** sheet that instructed reporters to "avoid the use of adjectives, especially such extravagant ones as *splendid, gorgeous, grand, magnificent,* etc." Short sentences, brief opening paragraphs, and "vigorous English" were also required. Hemingway later called these "the best rules I ever learned for the business of writing."

1. What repeated words, images, and sentence rhythms appear in the opening paragraph? What effect do these elements have on the story's mood or tone?

2. How does Hemingway's style underscore the story's themes?

3. Do you think that Hemingway's journalistic tone, with its emphasis on reporting facts without emotion, robs the story of the emotion it otherwise would have? Why or why not? Support your opinion with examples.

Review: Setting

As you learned on page 594, **setting** is the time and place in which the events of a literary work occur.

Partner Activity Meet with another classmate to discuss the setting of "In Another Country." Consider the relevance of the story's title and how it highlights the situation of the narrator or the other characters. Also consider how the setting helps determine the story's plot events and themes. You might gather your ideas in a diagram like the one below.

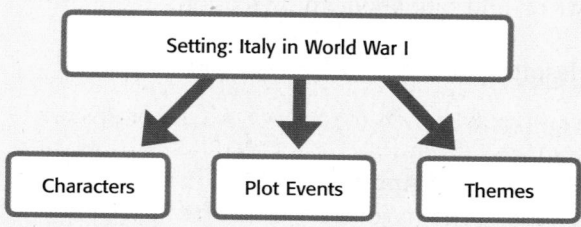

Reading Strategy Recognizing Author's Purpose

In traditional fiction, the **author's purpose** is often to entertain readers with an exciting story that builds to a climax and ends with a satisfying resolution. Most Modernist writers do not follow that formula. Instead their stories are more fragmentary, with seemingly unrelated events that may not build to a climax and often leave readers hanging at the end.

1. How do Hemingway's fragmentary presentation and lack of a clear resolution help convey his themes about modern life and modern warfare?

2. Would you say that the story is without a climax? Explain.

Vocabulary Practice

Practice with Antonyms Find the antonym for each vocabulary word from "In Another Country" listed in the first column below. Use a dictionary or a thesaurus if you need help.

1. lurched   **a.** twisted   **b.** glided

2. withered   **a.** shrunk   **b.** thickened

3. detached   **a.** concerned   **b.** separated

4. jostle   **a.** restrain   **b.** injure

5. resign   **a.** refuse   **b.** accept

Academic Vocabulary

Here are two words from the vocabulary list on page R86. These words will help you think, write, and talk about the selection.

despite (di spīt′) *prep.* in spite of; regardless

resolve (ri zolv′) *v.* to solve, settle, or answer

Practice and Apply

1. Why is the major skeptical of the machines' effectiveness **despite** the doctor's assurances?
2. How does the narrator **resolve** his feelings of boredom while in the hospital?

Writing About Literature

Respond to Theme The major says, "A man must not marry" (page 738). He goes on to explain that a man should not put himself in a position to lose something dear to him but should instead "find things he cannot lose." Do you agree or disagree with this theme—that people should distance themselves from others to avoid loss? Write a brief essay explaining your personal response.

Before you begin drafting, prewrite by jotting down your reasons for agreeing or disagreeing with the major's views. Then, to support your reasons, list examples from personal experience and analogies, or comparisons that clarify the main quality of one thing by comparing it to another.

Model Analogy

> *Not marrying because you fear loss of a loved one*

is like

> *Not using a new mug because you fear you might break it*

After you complete prewriting, use the details you've collected to draft your response. Meet with a peer reviewer to evaluate each other's work and suggest ways to improve it. Finally, proofread your draft for errors in spelling, grammar, and punctuation.

Literary Criticism

Group Activity "I always try to write on the principle of the iceberg," Hemingway once noted. "There is seven-eighths of it underwater for every part that shows." Meet with classmates and discuss how "In Another Country" illustrates Hemingway's iceberg principle. In your discussion, consider at least five details in the story and discuss the underlying meaning of each one.

Literature Online **Web Activities** For eFlashcards, Selection Quick Checks, and other Web activities, go to www.glencoe.com.

Grammar Workshop

Sentence Structure

Using Coordinating Conjunctions

"In the fall the war was always there, but we did not go to it any more."

—Ernest Hemingway, "In Another Country"

Connecting to Literature Before handing in written work, check to see that you have used coordinating conjunctions correctly. A **conjunction** is a word, like *but* in the quotation above, that joins single words or groups of words in a sentence. A **coordinating conjunction** joins words or groups of words that are of equal grammatical importance in a sentence.

Coordinating Conjunctions

| and | but | or | nor | for | yet | so |

Use coordinating conjunctions to join the parts of a sentence or to link short, choppy sentences.

He looked straight past me <u>and</u> out through the window.

Hemingway was rejected by the military, <u>so</u> he became an ambulance driver.

Try to use appropriate coordinating conjunctions. For example, use *but* and *yet* only when there is a contrast between the clauses in a sentence.

In the fall the war was always there, <u>but</u> we did not go to it any more.

Exercise

Inserting Conjunctions Rewrite the following sentences, combining the sentence parts by using one of the coordinating conjunctions in parentheses.

1. A woman sold chestnuts, (and, but) we didn't buy them often.
2. The doctor told the men to exercise (or, and) face the consequences.
3. The hospital was old, (so, and) it was beautiful.
4. The major had neither confidence (or, nor) the ability to fence again.
5. We were glad to be safe in the city, (so, for) there was still fighting elsewhere.
6. The people hated us, (yet, so) they were not violent.
7. I could speak Italian, (but, and) the major tried to correct my grammar.
8. The major's wife had died, (for, so) he cried and looked out the window.

▶ **Commas and Coordinate Conjunctions**

Use a comma before conjunctions when they join clauses that could stand on their own as complete sentences.

- He had complimented me on how I spoke Italian, and we talked together very easily.

A comma is generally used between clauses connected by the conjunction *for* to avoid confusion.

- We stopped the car, for we were lost.

▶ **Test-Taking Tip**

Before handing in a written test, check to see that you have used appropriate coordinating conjunctions.

▶ **Language Handbook**

For more on coordinating conjunctions, see Language Handbook, p. R47.

Literature Online
eWorkbooks To link to the Grammar and Language eWorkbook, go to www.glencoe.com.

ACADEMIC STANDARDS (page 741)

11.6.1 Demonstrate control of... sentence structure...

11.6.4 Correctly use...the mechanics of punctuation...

Winter Dreams

MEET F. SCOTT FITZGERALD

F Scott Fitzgerald once wrote that "all the stories that came into my head had a touch of disaster in them . . . I was pretty sure living wasn't the reckless, careless business these people thought." Many of Fitzgerald's stories and novels describe the reckless lifestyles of young, wealthy Americans in the 1920s.

> *"Show me a hero and I will write you a tragedy."*
>
> —F. Scott Fitzgerald, from *Notebooks*

Fitzgerald was born in St. Paul, Minnesota. He attended Princeton University, where he wrote for the newspaper and participated in the drama club. Fitzgerald joined the army before graduating, and while stationed in the South in 1918, he met Zelda Sayre at a country club dance. He fell in love, but Zelda was at first reluctant to marry him. That same summer, a New York publisher rejected the manuscript of his novel *The Romantic Egotist*.

Literary Success Following his stint in the army, Fitzgerald settled in New York City, where he worked for an advertising agency, but he eventually returned home to St. Paul to begin revising his novel. The publisher accepted the revision of his book, retitled *This Side of Paradise*, and Fitzgerald was ecstatic. He and Zelda were married in 1920, and in 1921 they made their first trip to Europe, returning to St. Paul for the birth of their only child, daughter Frances Scott (Scottie).

Fitzgerald's second novel, *The Beautiful and the Damned*, and "Winter Dreams" were published in 1922. While in France and Italy, he wrote and

revised his most successful novel, *The Great Gatsby* (1925). He and Zelda lived lavishly, both in the United States and abroad, and spent most of the money Fitzgerald earned from his writing. They regularly moved from Paris to various cities on the French Riviera and then back to Paris. But when the frantic decade ended with the stock market crash in 1929, Fitzgerald's private life and prosperous career also crashed. His lucrative writing career began to dry up with the onset of the Depression. In 1930 Zelda suffered a series of nervous breakdowns and was hospitalized in Europe and the United States.

Later Years Though Fitzgerald struggled in the 1930s with alcoholism and with his marriage, he continued to write stories and novels. *Tender Is the Night* was published in 1934, and under contract with MGM, Fitzgerald worked on several screenplays in Hollywood. He was working on his fifth novel, *The Last Tycoon*, when he died in Hollywood of a heart attack at the age of 44. Zelda died in a hospital fire in North Carolina in 1948.

Fitzgerald's works, and his life with Zelda, have inspired more than twenty films of varying success. There have been three film versions of *The Great Gatsby* alone. Reviews were mixed of all of the movie versions of the novel. There are few dissenters about the book itself, however. Tobias Wolff says that Fitzgerald "saw our American world . . . with clearer eyes than any of his contemporaries."

F. Scott Fitzgerald was born in 1896 and died in 1940.

Literature Online **Author Search** For more about F. Scott Fitzgerald, go to www.glencoe.com.

Connecting to the Story

Do you think most people have an unfulfilled dream? Have most people been misled by a dream? As you read, think about the following questions:

- Do you think it is possible to love someone your entire life even though you are not with that person?
- Can money provide true happiness?

Building Background

Many of Fitzgerald's stories, including "Winter Dreams," are somewhat autobiographical. In 1915 he met Ginevra King at a party in St. Paul. She lived in Lake Forest, Illinois, north of Chicago, and was attending school in Connecticut. She was sixteen and he was eighteen and in his sophomore year at Princeton. The attraction was instant. Fitzgerald and Ginevra corresponded regularly, and Ginevra kept a diary in which she recorded that she was "madly in love with him." Ginevra had other boyfriends, however, and Fitzgerald was jealous. The romance was doomed. Ginevra ended up marrying a wealthy Lake Forest stockbroker, and shortly after, Scott married Zelda. Critics see aspects of Ginevra in most of Fitzgerald's heroines, however, including Judy Jones in "Winter Dreams."

Setting Purposes for Reading

Big Idea Modern Fiction

As you read "Winter Dreams," notice what it reveals about romantic feelings and relationships during the Jazz Age.

Literary Element Motivation

Motivation refers to the stated or implied reason or cause for a character's actions. It is often revealed through a combination of the character's desires and morals and the circumstances in which the character finds himself or herself. As you read "Winter Dreams," think about what motivates the two main characters.

- See Literary Terms Handbook, p. R11.

Literature Online Interactive Literary Elements Handbook To review or learn more about the literary elements, go to www.glencoe.com.

Reading Strategy Evaluating Sensory Details

Sensory details are details that appeal to one or more of the five senses. Writers use these details to help the reader imagine or experience more deeply the content of their work. As you read Fitzgerald's story, evaluate the effectiveness of these details.

Reading Tip: Taking Notes Use a chart like the one below to record the sensory details you find as you read.

Detail	Sense It Appeals To
"desolate sand-boxes knee-deep in crusted ice"	sight

Vocabulary

grimace (grim´is) n. facial expression showing contempt, disgust, or pain; p. 745 *The doctor's needle made the child grimace.*

ominous (om´ə nəs) adj. threatening; p. 746 *Black clouds in the west looked ominous.*

perturbation (pur´tər bā´shən) n. state of being perturbed, anxious, or uneasy; p. 746 *The clerk showed perturbation when the police appeared.*

ingenuous (in jen´ū əs) adj. lacking in sophistication; naïve; p. 747 *Her argument with the judge was ingenuous, to say the least.*

mundane (mun dān´) adj. ordinary; p. 751 *The mundane details disappointed them.*

Vocabulary Tip: Word Parts If a word has a suffix, you can usually tell what part of speech that word is. For example, the suffix -ous forms adjectives (*ambitious*) and -ly forms adverbs (*merrily*). The suffixes -ion or -ian form nouns (*musician*). The suffix -er forms nouns (*driver*).

 INDIANA ACADEMIC STANDARDS (pages 743–761)
11.3 [Identify] story elements such as character...
11.2 Develop [reading] strategies...

11.5.9 Write...a literary analysis that...supports judgments with...substantial evidence and well-chosen details...

Winter Dreams

F. Scott Fitzgerald

Some of the caddies were poor as sin and lived in one-room houses with a neurasthenic[1] cow in the front yard, but Dexter Green's father owned the second best grocery-store in Black Bear—the best one was "The Hub," patronized by the wealthy people from Sherry Island—and Dexter caddied only for pocket-money.

In the fall when the days became crisp and gray, and the long Minnesota winter shut down like the white lid of a box, Dexter's skis moved over the snow that hid the fairways of the golf course. At these times the country gave him a feeling of profound melancholy—it offended him that the links should be in enforced fallowness, haunted by ragged sparrows for the long season. It was dreary, too, that on the tees where the gay colors fluttered in summer there were now only the desolate sand-boxes knee-deep in crusted ice. When he crossed the hills the wind blew cold as misery, and if the sun was out he tramped with his eyes squinted up against the hard dimensionless glare.

In April the winter ceased abruptly. The snow ran down into Black Bear Lake scarcely tarrying for the early golfers to brave the season with red and black balls. Without elation, without an interval of moist glory, the cold was gone.

Dexter knew that there was something dismal about this Northern spring, just as he knew there was something gorgeous about the fall. Fall made him clinch his hands and tremble and repeat idiotic sentences to himself, and make brisk abrupt gestures of command to imaginary audiences and armies. October filled him with hope which November raised to a sort of ecstatic triumph, and in this mood the fleeting brilliant impressions of the summer at Sherry Island were ready grist to his mill. He became a golf champion and defeated Mr. T. A. Hedrick in a marvellous match played a hundred times over the fairways of his imagination, a match each detail of which he changed

---

1. A *neurasthenic* cow is one that is thin and weak.

Reading Strategy Evaluating Sensory Details *What details in this paragraph help you visualize the gloomy setting?*

Literary Element Motivation *Why do you think Dexter has these particular daydreams?*

about untiringly—sometimes he won with almost laughable ease, sometimes he came up magnificently from behind. Again, stepping from a Pierce-Arrow automobile, like Mr. Mortimer Jones, he strolled frigidly into the lounge of the Sherry Island Golf Club—or perhaps, surrounded by an admiring crowd, he gave an exhibition of fancy diving from the spring-board of the club raft. . . . Among those who watched him in open-mouthed wonder was Mr. Mortimer Jones.

And one day it came to pass that Mr. Jones—himself and not his ghost—came up to Dexter with tears in his eyes and said that Dexter was the — — best caddy in the club, and wouldn't he decide not to quit if Mr. Jones made it worth his while, because every other — — caddy in the club lost one ball a hole for him—regularly——

"No, sir," said Dexter decisively, "I don't want to caddy any more." Then, after a pause: "I'm too old."

"You're not more than fourteen. Why the devil did you decide just this morning that you wanted to quit? You promised that next week you'd go over to the State tournament with me."

"I decided I was too old."

Dexter handed in his "A Class" badge, collected what money was due him from the caddy master, and walked home to Black Bear Village.

"The best — — caddy I ever saw," shouted Mr. Mortimer Jones over a drink that afternoon. "Never lost a ball! Willing! Intelligent! Quiet! Honest! Grateful!"

The little girl who had done this was eleven—beautifully ugly as little girls are apt to be who are destined after a few years to be inexpressibly lovely and bring no end of misery to a great number of men. The spark, however, was perceptible. There was a general ungodliness in the way her lips twisted down at the corners when she smiled, and in the—Heaven help us!—in the almost passionate quality of her eyes. Vitality is born in such women. It was utterly in evidence now, shining through her thin frame in a sort of glow.

She had come eagerly out on to the course at nine o'clock with a white linen nurse and five small new golf-clubs in a white canvas bag which the nurse was carrying. When Dexter first saw her she was standing by the caddy houses, rather ill at ease and trying to conceal the fact by engaging her nurse in an obviously unnatural conversation graced by startling and irrelevant **grimaces** from herself.

"Well, it's certainly a nice day, Hilda," Dexter heard her say. She drew down the corners of her mouth, smiled, and glanced furtively around, her eyes in transit falling for an instant on Dexter.

Then to the nurse:

"Well, I guess there aren't very many people out here this morning, are there?"

The smile again—radiant, blatantly artificial—convincing.

"I don't know what we're supposed to do now," said the nurse, looking nowhere in particular.

"Oh, that's all right. I'll fix it up."

Dexter stood perfectly still, his mouth slightly ajar. He knew that if he moved forward a step his state would be in her line of vision—if he moved backward he would lose his full view of her face. For a moment he had not realized how young she was. Now he remembered having seen her several times the year before—in bloomers.[2]

Suddenly, involuntarily, he laughed, a short abrupt laugh—then, startled by himself, he turned and began to walk quickly away.

"Boy!"

Dexter stopped.

"Boy—"

Beyond question he was addressed. Not only that, but he was treated to that absurd smile, that preposterous smile—the memory of which at least a dozen men were to carry into middle age.

"Boy, do you know where the golf teacher is?"

"He's giving a lesson."

"Well, do you know where the caddy-master is?"

"He isn't here yet this morning."

"Oh." For a moment this baffled her. She stood alternately on her right and left foot.

"We'd like to get a caddy," said the nurse. "Mr. Mortimer Jones sent us out to play golf, and we don't know how without we get a caddy."

---

2. *Bloomers* are baggy trousers gathered at the knee and once worn by girls and women as an athletic costume.

grimace (grim´is) n. facial expression showing contempt, disgust, or pain

Portrait of a Woman Golfer, 1922. Maude Martin Ellis. Private Collection.

Viewing the Art: How does the woman in this image compare with your picture of Miss Jones?

Here she was stopped by an **ominous** glance from Miss Jones, followed immediately by the smile.

"There aren't any caddies here except me," said Dexter to the nurse, "and I got to stay here in charge until the caddy-master gets here."

"Oh."

Miss Jones and her retinue[3] now withdrew, and at a proper distance from Dexter became involved in a heated conversation, which was concluded by Miss Jones taking one of the clubs and hitting it on the ground with violence. For further emphasis she raised it again and was about to bring it down smartly upon the nurse's bosom, when the nurse seized the club and twisted it from her hands.

---

3. A *retinue* is an attendant or a helper.

Literary Element Motivation *Do you think Miss Jones's anger is justified? Why or why not?*

Vocabulary

ominous (om´ə nəs) *adj.* threatening

"You damn little mean old *thing*!" cried Miss Jones wildly.

Another argument ensued. Realizing that the elements of comedy were implied in the scene, Dexter several times began to laugh, but each time restrained the laugh before it reached audibility. He could not resist the monstrous conviction that the little girl was justified in beating the nurse.

The situation was resolved by the fortuitous appearance of the caddy-master, who was appealed to immediately by the nurse.

"Miss Jones is to have a little caddy, and this one says he can't go."

"Mr. McKenna said I was to wait here till you came," said Dexter quickly.

"Well, he's here now." Miss Jones smiled cheerfully at the caddy-master. Then she dropped her bag and set off at a haughty mince[4] toward the first tee.

"Well?" The caddy-master turned to Dexter. "What you standing there like a dummy for? Go pick up the young lady's clubs."

"I don't think I'll go out to-day," said Dexter.

"You don't—"

"I think I'll quit."

The enormity of his decision frightened him. He was a favorite caddy, and the thirty dollars a month he earned through the summer were not to be made elsewhere around the lake. But he had received a strong emotional shock, and his **perturbation** required a violent and immediate outlet.

It was not so simple as that, either. As so frequently would be the case in the future, Dexter was unconsciously dictated to by his winter dreams.

II

Now, of course, the quality and the seasonability of these winter dreams varied, but the stuff of them remained. They persuaded Dexter several

---

4. A *mince* is a proper, affected walk.

Big Idea Modern Fiction *What is the "emotional shock" that has made Dexter quit caddying?*

Vocabulary

perturbation (pur´tər bā´shən) *n.* state of being perturbed, anxious, or uneasy years later to pass up a business course at the State university—his father, prospering now, would have paid his way—for the precarious advantage of attending an older and more famous university in the East, where he was bothered by his scanty funds. But do not get the impression, because his winter dreams happened to be concerned at first with musings on the rich, that there was anything merely snobbish in the boy. He wanted not association with glittering things and glittering people—he wanted the glittering things themselves. Often he reached out for the best without knowing why he wanted it—and sometimes he ran up against the mysterious denials and prohibitions in which life indulges. It is with one of those denials and not with his career as a whole that this story deals.

He made money. It was rather amazing. After college he went to the city from which Black Bear Lake draws its wealthy patrons. When he was only twenty-three and had been there not quite two years, there were already people who liked to say: "Now *there's* a boy—" All about him rich men's sons were peddling bonds precariously, or investing patrimonies[5] precariously, or plodding through the two dozen volumes of the "George Washington Commercial Course," but Dexter borrowed a thousand dollars on his college degree and his confident mouth, and bought a partnership in a laundry.

It was a small laundry when he went into it, but Dexter made a specialty of learning how the English washed fine woolen golf-stockings without shrinking them, and within a year he was catering to the trade that wore knickerbockers.[6] Men were insisting that their Shetland hose and sweaters go to his laundry, just as they had insisted on a caddy who could find golf-balls. A little later he was doing their wives' lingerie as well—and running five branches in different parts of the city. Before he was twenty-seven he owned the largest string of laundries in his section of the country. It was then that he sold out and went to New York. But the part of his story that concerns us goes back to the days when he was making his first big success.

When he was twenty-three Mr. Hart—one of the gray-haired men who liked to say "Now there's a boy"—gave him a guest card to the Sherry Island Golf Club for a week-end. So he signed his name one day on the register, and that afternoon played golf in a foursome with Mr. Hart and Mr. Sandwood and Mr. T. A. Hedrick. He did not consider it necessary to remark that he had once carried Mr. Hart's bag over this same links, and that he knew every trap and gully with his eyes shut—but he found himself glancing at the four caddies who trailed them, trying to catch a gleam or gesture that would remind him of himself, that would lessen the gap which lay between his present and his past.

It was a curious day, slashed abruptly with fleeting, familiar impressions. One minute he had the sense of being a trespasser—in the next he was impressed by the tremendous superiority he felt toward Mr. T. A. Hedrick, who was a bore and not even a good golfer any more.

Then, because of a ball Mr. Hart lost near the fifteenth green, an enormous thing happened. While they were searching the stiff grasses of the rough there was a clear call of "Fore!" from behind a hill in their rear. And as they all turned abruptly from their search a bright new ball sliced abruptly over the hill and caught Mr. T. A. Hedrick in the abdomen.

"By Gad!" cried Mr. T. A. Hedrick, "they ought to put some of these crazy women off the course. It's getting to be outrageous."

A head and a voice came up together over the hill:

"Do you mind if we go through?"

"You hit me in the stomach!" declared Mr. Hedrick wildly.

"Did I?" The girl approached the group of men. "I'm sorry. I yelled 'Fore!'"

Her glance fell casually on each of the men—then scanned the fairway for her ball.

"Did I bounce into the rough?"

It was impossible to determine whether this question was **ingenuous** or malicious. In a moment,

---

5. A *patrimony* is an inheritance from a father.
6. *Knickerbockers* are full pants gathered just below the knee.

Vocabulary

ingenuous (in jen′ū əs) *adj.* lacking in sophistication; naïve however, she left no doubt, for as her partner came up over the hill she called cheerfully:

"Here I am! I'd have gone on the green except that I hit something."

As she took her stance for a short mashie[7] shot, Dexter looked at her closely. She wore a blue gingham dress, rimmed at throat and shoulders with a white edging that accentuated her tan. The quality of exaggeration, of thinness, which had made her passionate eyes and down-turning mouth absurd at eleven, was gone now. She was arrestingly beautiful. The color in her cheeks was centered like the color in a picture—it was not a "high" color, but a sort of fluctuating and feverish warmth, so shaded that it seemed at any moment it would recede and disappear. This color and the mobility of her mouth gave a continual impression of flux, of intense life, of passionate vitality—balanced only partially by the sad luxury of her eyes.

She swung her mashie impatiently and without interest, pitching the ball into a sand-pit on the other side of the green. With a quick, insincere smile and a careless "Thank you!" she went on after it.

"That Judy Jones!" remarked Mr. Hedrick on the next tee, as they waited—some moments—for her to play on ahead. "All she needs is to be turned up and spanked for six months and then to be married off to an old-fashioned cavalry captain."

"My God, she's good-looking!" said Mr. Sandwood, who was just over thirty.

"Good-looking!" cried Mr. Hedrick contemptuously. "She always looks as if she wanted to be kissed! Turning those big cow-eyes on every calf in town!"

It was doubtful if Mr. Hedrick intended a reference to the maternal instinct.

"She'd play pretty good golf if she'd try," said Mr. Sandwood.

"She has no form," said Mr. Hedrick solemnly.

"She has a nice figure," said Mr. Sandwood.

"Better thank the Lord she doesn't drive a swifter ball," said Mr. Hart, winking at Dexter.

Later in the afternoon the sun went down with a riotous swirl of gold and varying blues and scarlets, and left the dry, rustling night of Western summer. Dexter watched from the veranda of the Golf Club, watched the even overlap of the waters in the little wind, silver molasses under the harvest-moon. Then the moon held a finger to her lips and the lake became a clear pool, pale and quiet. Dexter put on his bathing-suit and swam out to the farthest raft, where he stretched dripping on the wet canvas of the springboard.

There was a fish jumping and a star shining and the lights around the lake were gleaming. Over on a dark peninsula a piano was playing the songs of last summer and of summers before that—songs from "Chin-Chin" and "The Count of Luxemburg" and "The Chocolate Soldier"[8]—and because the sound of a piano over a stretch of water had always seemed beautiful to Dexter he lay perfectly quiet and listened.

The tune the piano was playing at that moment had been gay and new five years before when Dexter was a sophomore at college. They had played it at a prom once when he could not afford the luxury of proms, and he had stood outside the gymnasium and listened. The sound of the tune precipitated in him a sort of ecstasy and it was with that ecstasy he viewed what happened to him now. It was a mood of intense appreciation, a sense that, for once, he was magnificently attuned to life and that everything about him was radiating a brightness and a glamour he might never know again.

A low, pale oblong detached itself suddenly from the darkness of the Island, spitting forth the reverberated sound of a racing motor-boat. Two white streamers of cleft water rolled themselves out behind it and almost immediately the boat was beside him, drowning out the hot tinkle of the piano in the drone of its spray. Dexter raising himself on his arms was aware of a figure standing at the wheel, of two dark eyes regarding him over the lengthening space of water—then the boat had gone by

---

7. A *mashie* is a five iron used in playing golf.

---

8. *"Chin-Chin," "The Count of Luxemburg,"* and *"The Chocolate Soldier"* are all musicals or light operas popular at the time of the story.

The Music Pavilion. Henri Le Sidaner. Oil on canvas, 73 x 60.5 cm. Private collection.

and was sweeping in an immense and purpose-less circle of spray round and round in the middle of the lake. With equal eccentricity one of the circles flattened out and headed back toward the raft.

"Who's that?" she called, shutting off her motor. She was so near now that Dexter could see her bathing-suit, which consisted apparently of pink rompers.[9]

The nose of the boat bumped the raft, and as the latter tilted rakishly he was precipitated toward her. With different degrees of interest they recognized each other.

"Aren't you one of those men we played through this afternoon?" she demanded.

He was.

"Well, do you know how to drive a motor-boat? Because if you do I wish you'd drive this one so I can ride on the surf-board behind. My name is Judy Jones"—she favored him with an absurd smirk—rather, what tried to be a smirk, for, twist her mouth as she might, it was not grotesque, it was merely beautiful—"and I live in a house over there on the Island, and in that house there is a man waiting for me. When he drove up at the door I drove out of the dock because he says I'm his ideal."

There was a fish jumping and a star shining and the lights around the lake were gleaming. Dexter sat beside Judy Jones and she explained how her boat was driven. Then she was in the water, swimming to the floating surf-board with a sinuous crawl. Watching her was without effort to the eye, watching a branch waving or a sea-gull flying. Her arms, burned to butternut, moved sinuously among the dull platinum ripples, elbow appearing first, casting the forearm back with a cadence of falling water, then reaching out and down, stabbing a path ahead.

They moved out into the lake; turning, Dexter saw that she was kneeling on the low rear of the now uptilted surf-board.

"Go faster," she called, "fast as it'll go."

Obediently he jammed the lever forward and the white spray mounted at the bow. When he looked around again the girl was standing up on the rushing board, her arms spread wide, her eyes lifted toward the moon.

"It's awful cold," she shouted. "What's your name?"

He told her.

"Well, why don't you come to dinner to-morrow night?"

His heart turned over like the fly-wheel of the boat, and, for the second time, her casual whim gave a new direction to his life.

III

Next evening while he waited for her to come down-stairs, Dexter peopled the soft deep summer room and the sun-porch that opened from it with the men who had already loved Judy Jones. He knew the sort of men they were—the men who when he first went to college had entered from

---

9. *Rompers* are a one-piece outfit that includes loose pants gathered at the knee.

Victorian Ball. Vincent McIndoe.
Viewing the Art: What elements of high society depicted in this painting might Dexter find attractive?

the great prep schools with graceful clothes and the deep tan of healthy summers. He had seen that, in one sense, he was better than these men. He was newer and stronger. Yet in acknowledging to himself that he wished his children to be like them he was admitting that he was but the rough, strong stuff from which they eternally sprang.

When the time had come for him to wear good clothes, he had known who were the best tailors in America, and the best tailors in America had made him the suit he wore this evening. He had acquired that particular reserve peculiar to his university, that set it off from other universities. He recognized the value to him of such a mannerism and he had adopted it; he knew that to be careless in dress and manner required more confidence than to be careful. But carelessness was for

his children. His mother's name had been Krimplich. She was a Bohemian[10] of the peasant class and she had talked broken English to the end of her days. Her son must keep to the set patterns.

At a little after seven Judy Jones came down-stairs. She wore a blue silk afternoon dress, and he was disappointed at first that she had not put on something more elaborate. This feeling was accentuated when, after a brief greeting, she went to the door of a butler's pantry and pushing it open called: "You can serve dinner, Martha." He had rather expected that a butler would announce dinner, that there would be a cocktail. Then he put these thoughts behind him as they sat down side by side on a lounge and looked at each other.

"Father and mother won't be here," she said thoughtfully.

He remembered the last time he had seen her father, and he was glad the parents were not to be here to-night—they might wonder who he was. He had been born in Keeble, a Minnesota village fifty miles farther north, and he always gave Keeble as his home instead of Black Bear Village. Country towns were well enough to come from if they weren't inconveniently in sight and used as footstools by fashionable lakes.

They talked of his university, which she had visited frequently during the past two years, and of the near-by city which supplied Sherry Island with its patrons, and whither Dexter would return next day to his prospering laundries.

During dinner she slipped into a moody depression which gave Dexter a feeling of uneasiness. Whatever petulance[11] she uttered in her throaty voice worried him. Whatever she smiled at—at

---

10. A *Bohemian* is a native of Bohemia, now part of the Czech Republic.
11. *Petulance* is irritability or impatience.

Literary Element Motivation *What does Dexter's reason for giving Keeble as his home tell you about him?*

him, at a chicken liver, at nothing—it disturbed him that her smile could have no root in mirth, or even in amusement. When the scarlet corners of her lips curved down, it was less a smile than an invitation to a kiss.

Then, after dinner, she led him out on the dark sun-porch and deliberately changed the atmosphere.

"Do you mind if I weep a little?" she said.

"I'm afraid I'm boring you," he responded quickly.

"You're not. I like you. But I've just had a terrible afternoon. There was a man I cared about, and this afternoon he told me out of a clear sky that he was poor as a church-mouse. He'd never even hinted it before. Does this sound horribly **mundane**?"

"Perhaps he was afraid to tell you."

"Suppose he was," she answered. "He didn't start right. You see, if I'd thought of him as poor—well, I've been mad about loads of poor men, and fully intended to marry them all. But in this case, I hadn't thought of him that way, and my interest in him wasn't strong enough to survive the shock. As if a girl calmly informed her fiancé that she was a widow. He might not object to widows, but—

"Let's start right," she interrupted herself suddenly. "Who are you, anyhow?"

For a moment Dexter hesitated. Then:

"I'm nobody," he announced. "My career is largely a matter of futures."

"Are you poor?"

"No," he said frankly, "I'm probably making more money than any man my age in the Northwest. I know that's an obnoxious remark, but you advised me to start right."

There was a pause. Then she smiled and the corners of her mouth drooped and an almost imperceptible sway brought her closer to him, looking up into his eyes. A lump rose in Dexter's throat, and he waited breathless for the experiment, facing the unpredictable compound that

would form mysteriously from the elements of their lips. Then he saw—she communicated her excitement to him, lavishly, deeply, with kisses that were not a promise but a fulfilment. They aroused in him not hunger demanding renewal but surfeit that would demand more surfeit . . . kisses that were like charity, creating want by holding back nothing at all.

It did not take him many hours to decide that he had wanted Judy Jones ever since he was a proud, desirous little boy.

IV

It began like that—and continued, with varying shades of intensity, on such a note right up to the dénouement. Dexter surrendered a part of himself to the most direct and unprincipled personality with which he had ever come in contact. Whatever Judy wanted, she went after with the full pressure of her charm. There was no divergence of method, no jockeying for position or premeditation of effects—there was a very little mental side to any of her affairs. She simply made men conscious to the highest degree of her physical loveliness. Dexter had no desire to change her. Her deficiencies were knit up with a passionate energy that transcended and justified them.

When, as Judy's head lay against his shoulder that first night, she whispered, "I don't know what's the matter with me. Last night I thought I was in love with a man and to-night I think I'm in love with you——" —it seemed to him a beautiful and romantic thing to say. It was the exquisite excitability that for the moment he controlled and owned. But a week later he was compelled to view this same quality in a different light. She took him in her roadster to a picnic supper, and after supper she disappeared, likewise in her roadster, with another man. Dexter became enormously upset and was scarcely able to be decently civil to the other people present. When she assured him that she had not kissed the other man, he knew she was lying—yet he was glad that she had taken the trouble to lie to him.

He was, as he found before the summer ended, one of a varying dozen who circulated about her. Each of them had at one time been favored

Literary Element | Motivation *What prompts Judy to smile and look into Dexter's eyes, when she has been moodily depressed up until this point?*

Vocabulary

mundane (mun dān´) *adj.* ordinary

Big Idea | Modern Fiction *What does Dexter's discovery foreshadow about his relationship with Judy?*

above all others—about half of them still basked in the solace of occasional sentimental revivals. Whenever one showed signs of dropping out through long neglect, she granted him a brief honeyed hour, which encouraged him to tag along for a year or so longer. Judy made these forays upon the helpless and defeated without malice, indeed half unconscious that there was anything mischievous in what she did.

When a new man came to town every one dropped out—dates were automatically cancelled.

The helpless part of trying to do anything about it was that she did it all herself. She was not a girl who could be "won" in the kinetic sense—she was proof against cleverness, she was proof against charm; if any of these assailed her too strongly she would immediately resolve the affair to a physical basis, and under the magic of her physical splendor the strong as well as the brilliant played her game and not their own. She was entertained only by the gratification of her desires and by the direct exercise of her own charm. Perhaps from so much youthful love, so many youthful lovers, she had come, in self-defense, to nourish herself wholly from within.

Succeeding Dexter's first exhilaration came restlessness and dissatisfaction. The helpless ecstasy of losing himself in her was opiate rather than tonic.[12] It was fortunate for his work during the winter that those moments of ecstasy came infrequently. Early in their acquaintance it had seemed for a while that there was a deep and spontaneous mutual attraction—that first August, for example— three days of long evenings on her dusky veranda, of strange wan kisses through the late afternoon, in shadowy alcoves or behind the protecting trellises of the garden arbors, of mornings when she was fresh as a dream and almost shy at meeting him in the clarity of the rising day. There was all the ecstasy of an engagement about it, sharpened by his realization that there was no engagement. It was during those three days that, for the first time, he had asked her to marry him. She said "maybe some day," she said "kiss me," she said "I'd like to marry you," she said "I love you"— she said—nothing.

The three days were interrupted by the arrival of a New York man who visited at her house for half September. To Dexter's agony, rumor engaged them. The man was the son of the president of a great trust company. But at the end of a month it was reported that Judy was yawning. At a dance one night she sat all evening in a motor-boat with a local beau, while the New Yorker searched the club for her frantically. She told the local beau that she was bored with her visitor, and two days later he left. She was seen with him at the station, and it was reported that he looked very mournful indeed.

On this note the summer ended. Dexter was twenty-four, and he found himself increasingly in a position to do as he wished. He joined two clubs in the city and lived at one of them. Though he was by no means an integral part of the stag-lines[13] at these clubs, he managed to be on hand at dances where Judy Jones was likely to appear. He could have gone out socially as much as he liked—he was an eligible young man, now, and popular with down-town fathers. His confessed devotion to Judy Jones had rather solidified his position. But he had no social aspirations and rather despised the dancing men who were always on tap for the Thursday or Saturday parties and who filled in at dinners with the younger married set. Already he was playing with the idea of going East to New York. He wanted to take Judy Jones with him. No disillusion as to the world in which

---

12. *Opiate rather than tonic* means that Dexter's helpless ecstasy is numbing rather than stimulating.

Literary Element Motivation *Why do Dexter and the other men tolerate Judy's behavior?*

Reading Strategy Evaluating Sensory Details *What do the words* dusky, shadowy, *and* protecting trellises *imply about the nature of Dexter and Judy's relationship?*

---

13. *Stag-lines* are lines of single men waiting for dance partners at the clubs.

Le cercle - The Club, 1911. Jean Beraud. Oil on canvas, 61 x 73.5 cm. Musee d'Orsay, Paris, France.

Viewing the Art: What might Judy's suitors have in common with the two men in this painting?

she had grown up could cure his illusion as to her desirability.

Remember that—for only in the light of it can what he did for her be understood.

Eighteen months after he first met Judy Jones he became engaged to another girl. Her name was Irene Scheerer, and her father was one of the men who had always believed in Dexter. Irene was light-haired and sweet and honorable, and a little stout, and she had two suitors whom she pleasantly relinquished when Dexter formally asked her to marry him.

Summer, fall, winter, spring, another summer, another fall—so much he had given of his active life to the incorrigible lips of Judy Jones. She had treated him with interest, with encouragement, with malice, with indifference, with contempt. She had inflicted on him the innumerable little slights and indignities possible in such a case—as if in revenge for

Big Idea Modern Fiction *Why do you think this is the only description of Irene, despite the fact that Dexter becomes engaged to her?*

having ever cared for him at all. She had beckoned him and yawned at him and beckoned him again and he had responded often with bitterness and narrowed eyes. She had brought him ecstatic happiness and intolerable agony of spirit. She had caused him untold inconvenience and not a little trouble. She had insulted him, and she had ridden over him, and she had played his interest in her against his interest in his work—for fun. She had done everything to him except to criticise him—this she had not done—it seemed to him only because it might have sullied the utter indifference she manifested and sincerely felt toward him.

When autumn had come and gone again it occurred to him that he could not have Judy Jones. He had to beat this into his mind but he convinced himself at last. He lay awake at night for a while and argued it over. He told himself the trouble and the pain she had caused him, he enumerated her glaring deficiencies as a wife. Then he said to himself that he loved her, and after a while he fell asleep. For a week, lest he imagined her husky voice over the telephone or her eyes opposite him at lunch, he worked hard and late, and at night he went to his office and plotted out his years.

At the end of a week he went to a dance and cut in on her once. For almost the first time since they had met he did not ask her to sit out with him or tell her that she was lovely. It hurt him that she did not miss these things—that was all. He was not jealous when he saw that there was a new man to-night. He had been hardened against jealousy long before.

He stayed late at the dance. He sat for an hour with Irene Scheerer and talked about books and about music. He knew very little about either. But he was beginning to be master of his own time now, and he had a rather priggish notion that he—the young and already fabulously successful Dexter Green—should know more about such things.

That was in October, when he was twenty-five. In January, Dexter and Irene became engaged. It was to be announced in June, and they were to be married three months later.

The Minnesota winter prolonged itself interminably, and it was almost May when the winds came soft and the snow ran down into Black Bear Lake at last. For the first time in over a year Dexter was enjoying a certain tranquillity of spirit. Judy Jones had been in Florida, and afterward in Hot Springs, and somewhere she had been engaged, and somewhere she had broken it off. At first, when Dexter had definitely given her up, it had made him sad that people still linked them together and asked for news of her, but when he began to be placed at dinner next to Irene Scheerer people didn't ask him about her any more—they told him about her. He ceased to be an authority on her.

May at last. Dexter walked the streets at night when the darkness was damp as rain, wondering that so soon, with so little done, so much of ecstasy had gone from him. May one year back had been marked by Judy's poignant, unforgivable, yet forgiven turbulence—it had been one of those rare times when he fancied she had grown to care for him. That old penny's worth of happiness he had spent for this bushel of content. He knew that Irene would be no more than a curtain spread behind him, a hand moving among gleaming tea-cups, a voice calling to children . . . fire and loveliness were gone, the magic of nights and the wonder of the varying hours and seasons . . . slender lips, down-turning, dropping to his lips and bearing him up into a heaven of eyes. . . . The thing was deep in him. He was too strong and alive for it to die lightly.

In the middle of May when the weather balanced for a few days on the thin bridge that led to deep summer he turned in one night at Irene's house. Their engagement was to be announced in a week now—no one could be surprised at it. And to-night they would sit to-gether on the lounge at the University Club and look on for an hour at the dancers. It gave him a sense of solidity to go with her—she was so sturdily popular, so intensely "great."

He mounted the steps of the brownstone house and stepped inside.

"Irene," he called.

Mrs. Scheerer came out of the living-room to meet him.

"Dexter," she said, "Irene's gone up-stairs with a splitting head-ache. She wanted to go with you but I made her go to bed."

"Nothing serious, I—"

"Oh, no. She's going to play golf with you in the morning. You can spare her for just one night, can't you, Dexter?"

Her smile was kind. She and Dexter liked each other. In the living-room he talked for a moment before he said good-night.

Returning to the University Club, where he had rooms, he stood in the doorway for a moment and watched the dancers. He leaned against the door-post, nodded at a man or two—yawned.

"Hello, darling."

The familiar voice at his elbow startled him. Judy Jones had left a man and crossed the room to him—Judy Jones, a slender enamelled doll in cloth of gold: gold in a band at her head, gold in two slipper points at her dress's hem. The fragile glow of her face seemed to blossom as she smiled at him. A breeze of warmth and light blew through the room. His hands in the pockets of his dinner-jacket tightened spasmodically. He was filled with a sudden excitement.

"When did you get back?" he asked casually.

"Come here and I'll tell you about it."

She turned and he followed her. She had been away—he could have wept at the wonder of her return. She had passed through enchanted streets, doing things that were like provocative music. All mysterious happenings, all fresh and quickening hopes, had gone away with her, come back with her now.

She turned in the doorway.

"Have you a car here? If you haven't, I have."

"I have a coupé."[14]

In then, with a rustle of golden cloth. He slammed the door. Into so many cars she

---

14. A *coupé* is a small two-door car.

Reading Strategy Evaluating Sensory Details *What do these two images tell you about Dexter's attitude toward Irene?*

Reading Strategy Evaluating Sensory Details *What does this emphasis on gold seem to symbolize?*

had stepped—like this—like that—her back against the leather, so—her elbow resting on the door—waiting. She would have been soiled long since had there been anything to soil her—except herself—but this was her own self outpouring.

With an effort he forced himself to start the car and back into the street. This was nothing, he must remember. She had done this before, and he had put her behind him, as he would have crossed a bad account from his books.

He drove slowly down-town and, affecting abstraction, traversed the deserted streets of the business section, people here and there where a movie was giving out its crowd or where consumptive or pugilistic[15] youth lounged in front of pool halls. The clink of glasses and the slap of hands on the bars issued from saloons, cloisters of glazed glass and dirty yellow light.

She was watching him closely and the silence was embarrassing, yet in this crisis he could find no casual word with which to profane the hour. At a convenient turning he began to zigzag back toward the University Club.

"Have you missed me?" she asked suddenly.

"Everybody missed you."

He wondered if she knew of Irene Scheerer. She had been back only a day—her absence had been almost contemporaneous with his engagement.

"What a remark!" Judy laughed sadly—without sadness. She looked at him searchingly. He became absorbed in the dashboard.

"You're handsomer than you used to be," she said thoughtfully. "Dexter, you have the most rememberable eyes."

He could have laughed at this, but he did not laugh. It was the sort of thing that was said to sophomores. Yet it stabbed at him.

Winter Evening. Leon Dabo. Oil on canvas, 53.3 x 71.1 cm. Florence Griswold Museum, Old Lyme, Connecticut.
Viewing the Art: Do you think this painting might be a good representation of Dexter's winter dreams? Explain.

15. *Consumptive* means "wasteful," and *pugilistic* means "eager to fight."

"I'm awfully tired of everything, darling."
She called every one darling, endowing the
endearment with careless, individual camaraderie. "I wish you'd marry me."

The directness of this confused him. He should
have told her now that he was going to marry
another girl, but he could not tell her. He could as
easily have sworn that he had never loved her.

"I think we'd get along," she continued, on
the same note, "unless probably you've forgotten
me and fallen in love with another girl."

Her confidence was obviously enormous.
She had said, in effect, that she found such
a thing impossible to believe, that if it were
true he had merely committed a childish indis-
cretion—and probably to show off. She would
forgive him, because it was not a matter of
any moment but rather something to be
brushed aside lightly.

"Of course you could never love anybody but
me," she continued, "I like the way you love me.
Oh, Dexter, have you forgotten last year?"

"No, I haven't forgotten."

"Neither have I!"

Was she sincerely moved—or was she carried
along by the wave of her own acting?

"I wish we could be like that again," she said,
and he forced himself to answer:

"I don't think we can."

"I suppose not. . . . I hear you're giving Irene
Scheerer a violent rush."

There was not the faintest emphasis on the
name, yet Dexter was suddenly ashamed.

"Oh, take me home," cried Judy suddenly; "I
don't want to go back to that idiotic dance—
with those children."

Then, as he turned up the street that led to
the residence district, Judy began to cry quietly
to herself. He had never seen her cry before.

The dark street lightened, the dwellings of
the rich loomed up around them, he stopped
his coupé in front of the great white bulk of
the Mortimer Joneses' house, somnolent, gorgeous, drenched with the splendor of the damp
moonlight. Its solidity startled him. The strong
walls, the steel of the girders, the breadth and
beam and pomp of it were there only to bring

out the contrast with the young beauty beside
him. It was sturdy to accentuate her slight-
ness—as if to show what a breeze could be
generated by a butterfly's wing.

He sat perfectly quiet, his nerves in wild
clamor, afraid that if he moved he would find her
irresistibly in his arms. Two tears had rolled down
her wet face and trembled on her upper lip.

"I'm more beautiful than anybody else," she
said brokenly, "why can't I be happy?" Her
moist eyes tore at his stability—her mouth
turned slowly downward with an exquisite sadness: "I'd like to marry you if you'll have me,
Dexter. I suppose you think I'm not worth having, but I'll be so beautiful for you, Dexter."

A million phrases of anger, pride, passion,
hatred, tenderness fought on his lips. Then a perfect wave of emotion washed over him, carrying
off with it a sediment of wisdom, of convention,
of doubt, of honor. This was his girl who was
speaking, his own, his beautiful, his pride.

"Won't you come in?" He heard her draw in
her breath sharply.

Waiting.

"All right," his voice was trembling.
"I'll come in."

V

It was strange that neither when it was over
nor a long time afterward did he regret that
night. Looking at it from the perspective of ten
years, the fact that Judy's flare for him endured
just one month seemed of little importance. Nor
did it matter that by his yielding he subjected
himself to a deeper agony in the end and gave
serious hurt to Irene Scheerer and to Irene's parents, who had befriended him. There was nothing sufficiently pictorial about Irene's grief to
stamp itself on his mind.

Dexter was at bottom hard-minded. The attitude of the city on his action was of no importance to him, not because he was going to leave
the city, but because any outside attitude on the
situation seemed superficial. He was completely
indifferent to popular opinion. Nor, when he had
seen that it was no use, that he did not possess in

Literary Element Motivation *Why do you think Dexter decides not to tell Judy that he is engaged?*

Literary Element Motivation *Why does Dexter agree to go in after his earlier doubts?*

himself the power to move fundamentally or to hold Judy Jones, did he bear any malice toward her. He loved her, and he would love her until the day he was too old for loving—but he could not have her. So he tasted the deep pain that is reserved only for the strong, just as he had tasted for a little while the deep happiness.

Even the ultimate falsity of the grounds upon which Judy terminated the engagement that she did not want to "take him away" from Irene—Judy, who had wanted nothing else—did not revolt him. He was beyond any revulsion or any amusement.

He went East in February with the intention of selling out his laundries and settling in New York—but the war[16] came to America in March and changed his plans. He returned to the West, handed over the management of the business to his partner, and went into the first officers' training-camp in late April. He was one of those young thousands who greeted the war with a certain amount of relief, welcoming the liberation from webs of tangled emotion.

Even the ultimate falsity of the grounds upon which Judy terminated the engagement that she did not want to "take him away" from Irene—Judy, who had wanted nothing else—did not revolt him. He was beyond any revulsion or any amusement.

VI

This story is not his biography, although things creep into it which have nothing to do with those dreams he had when he was young. We are almost done with them and with him now. There is only one more incident to be related here, and it happens seven years farther on.

It took place in New York, where he had done well—so well that there were no barriers too high for him. He was thirty-two years old, and, except for one flying trip immediately after the war, he had not been West in seven years. A man named Devlin from Detroit came into his office to see him in a business way, and then and there this incident occurred, and closed out, so to speak, this particular side of his life.

"So you're from the Middle West," said the man Devlin with careless curiosity. "That's funny—I thought men like you were probably born and raised on Wall Street. You know—wife of one of my best friends in Detroit came from your city. I was an usher at the wedding."

Dexter waited with no apprehension of what was coming.

"Judy Simms," said Devlin with no particular interest; "Judy Jones she was once."

"Yes, I knew her." A dull impatience spread over him. He had heard, of course, that she was married—perhaps deliberately he had heard no more.

"Awfully nice girl," brooded Devlin meaninglessly, "I'm sort of sorry for her."

"Why?" Something in Dexter was alert, receptive, at once.

"Oh, Lud Simms has gone to pieces in a way. I don't mean he ill-uses her, but he drinks and runs around—"

"Doesn't she run around?"

"No. Stays at home with her kids."

"Oh."

"She's a little too old for him," said Devlin.

"Too old!" cried Dexter. "Why, man, she's only twenty-seven."

He was possessed with a wild notion of rushing out into the streets and taking a train to Detroit. He rose to his feet spasmodically.

"I guess you're busy," Devlin apologized quickly. "I didn't realize—"

"No, I'm not busy," said Dexter, steadying his voice. "I'm not busy at all. Not busy at all. Did you say she was—twenty-seven? No, I said she was twenty-seven."

"Yes, you did," agreed Devlin dryly.

"Go on, then, Go on."

---

16. *The war* refers to World War I, which the United States entered in 1917.

Big Idea Modern Fiction *Do you think Dexter really feels this way, or is he fooling himself?*

"What do you mean?"

"About Judy Jones."

Devlin looked at him helplessly.

"Well, that's—I told you all there is to it. He treats her like the devil. Oh, they're not going to get divorced or anything. When he's particularly outrageous she forgives him. In fact, I'm inclined to think she loves him. She was a pretty girl when she first came to Detroit."

A pretty girl! The phrase struck Dexter as ludicrous.

"Isn't she—a pretty girl, any more?"

"Oh, she's all right."

"Look here," said Dexter, sitting down suddenly. "I don't understand. You say she was a 'pretty girl' and now you say she's 'all right.' I don't understand what you mean—Judy Jones wasn't a pretty girl, at all. She was a great beauty. Why, I knew her, I knew her. She was—"

Devlin laughed pleasantly.

"I'm not trying to start a row," he said. "I think Judy's a nice girl and I like her. I can't understand how a man like Lud Simms could fall madly in love with her, but he did." Then he added: "Most of the women like her."

Dexter looked closely at Devlin, thinking wildly that there must be a reason for this, some insensitivity in the man or some private malice.

"Lots of women fade just like *that*," Devlin snapped his fingers. "You must have seen it happen. Perhaps I've forgotten how pretty she was at her wedding. I've seen her so much since then, you see. She has nice eyes."

A sort of dullness settled down upon Dexter. For the first time in his life he felt like getting very drunk. He knew that he was laughing loudly at something Devlin had said, but he did not know what it was or why it was funny. When, in a few minutes, Devlin went he lay down on his lounge and looked out the window at the New York sky-line into which

the sun was sinking in dull lovely shades of pink and gold.

He had thought that having nothing else to lose he was invulnerable at last—but he knew that he had just lost something more, as surely as if he had married Judy Jones and seen her fade away before his eyes.

The dream was gone. Something had been taken from him. In a sort of panic he pushed the palms of his hands into his eyes and tried to bring up a picture of the waters lapping on Sherry Island and the moonlit veranda, and gingham on the golf-links and the dry sun and the gold color of her neck's soft down. And her mouth damp to his kisses and her eyes plaintive with melancholy and her freshness like new fine linen in the morning. Why, these things were no longer in the world! They had existed and they existed no longer.

For the first time in years the tears were streaming down his face. But they were for himself now. He did not care about mouth and eyes and moving hands. He wanted to care, and he could not care. For he had gone away and he could never go back any more. The gates were closed, the sun was gone down, and there was no beauty but the gray beauty of steel that withstands all time. Even the grief he could have borne was left behind in the country of illusion, of youth, of the richness of life, where his winter dream had flourished.

"Long ago," he said, "long ago, there was something in me, but now that thing is gone. Now that thing is gone, that thing is gone. I cannot cry. I cannot care. That thing will come back no more." ✎

Big Idea Modern Fiction *What dream has gone, and why has it gone?*

RESPONDING AND THINKING CRITICALLY

Respond

1. At the end of the story, Dexter is obviously undergoing a significant life crisis. What would you tell him if you were with him?

Recall and Interpret

2. (a)What are Dexter's winter dreams? (b)What do these dreams tell you about him?

3. In giving up caddying, "Dexter was unconsciously dictated to by his winter dreams." Explain how these dreams affected his decision.

4. (a)What is the point of view of this story? (b)How does this point of view affect the plot?

Analyze and Evaluate

5. How do Dexter's laundry business and his round of golf in Part II tell you that he is still under the influence of his winter dreams?

6. (a)In Part III, is Dexter becoming a snob, with his emphasis on clothes and his hometown, or is he simply trying to fit in? Explain. (b)Why does he tell Judy that he is making "more money than any man his age in the Northwest"?

7. Why do you think Dexter becomes engaged to Irene?

8. In Part VI, after Dexter learns about Judy's marriage, why is he so disturbed?

9. (a)Do you think Dexter really loves Judy? Explain. (b)Do you think Dexter would have been happier if he had married Judy? Why or why not?

Connect

10. **Big Idea** Modern Fiction Is Judy's reckless disregard for the feelings of others a symptom of the Jazz Age, or could her character appear in a story from any period? Explain.

11. In what ways is this short story more modern than traditional short stories like those in Unit Four?

VISUAL LITERACY: Graphic Organizer

THEME CHART

The **theme** is the central message of a work of literature that readers can apply to life. Some works directly state the theme. More often, however, the theme is implied, and it is up to the reader to figure it out based on events, dialogue, or descriptions in the text. A literary work may have more than one theme.

You may find it helpful to isolate key passages from the text that can help you uncover the theme. Use a chart such as the one at right to list significant passages from "Winter Dreams." In the second column of the chart, identify how each passage is related to the theme of the story. Then fill in additional passages from the story that you find.

Group Activity

Discuss the following questions with classmates. Use your chart to support your views.

1. What do you think is the theme of "Winter Dreams"?

2. Do you think this theme is specific to the time and place of this story, or does it apply today?

Passage from the Story	Relationship to Theme
1. "and sometimes he ran up against the mysterious denials and prohibitions in which life indulges. It is with one of those denials and not with his career as a whole that this story deals." (page 747)	
2.	
3.	

Literary Element Motivation

In literature, **motivation** refers to the reasons or causes for a character's actions. Lack of clear motivation for actions is considered a weakness in a story or play. Sometimes motivation is subtle, however, and may not be immediately apparent.

1. What is the chief motivation for most of Dexter's actions?

2. What do you think motivates Judy to behave as she does in her relationships with Dexter and others before she is married?

3. What is Judy's motivation in mentioning Irene to Dexter after he becomes engaged?

4. What do you think motivated Judy to get married?

Review: Conflict

As you learned in Unit Four, Part 2, **conflict** is the main struggle between two opposing forces in a story or drama. An **external conflict** is a struggle between a character and an outside force, such as another character. An **internal conflict** is a struggle between opposing thoughts in a character's mind.

Group Activity In a small group, discuss the nature of the conflict in "Winter Dreams." Answer these questions.

1. What is the conflict in "Winter Dreams"?

2. Is this conflict internal or external?

3. How is the conflict resolved?

Reading Strategy Evaluating Sensory Details

Sensory details are details that appeal to the senses. Often, these details contribute to the meaning and mood, or atmosphere, of a story.

Partner Activity A passage in the last part of "Winter Dreams" reads: "the sun was sinking in dull lovely shades of pink and gold." How does this passage seem to sum up Dexter's feelings and his life? Meet with another classmate to discuss this question.

Vocabulary Practice

Practice with Word Parts Suffixes can often help you identify or change the part of speech of a word. Add one of the following suffixes to the word parts below to form the correct word in each sentence.

adjective suffix -ous
noun suffixes -ian, -ion, **or** -er
adverb suffix -ly

1. The prisoner in the courtroom was a grimac_____. He made faces all the time.

2. He seemed so omin_____ that we tried not to look at him.

3. At first he acted quite mundane_____.

4. We didn't know whether he was clever or ingenu_____.

5. Later, we were filled with perturbat_____.

Academic Vocabulary

Here are two words from the vocabulary list on page R86.

outcome *n.* (out′kum′) something that follows as a result; an effect; a consequence

affect *v.* (ə fekt′) to produce an influence on; to make a change in

Practice and Apply
1. What is the **outcome** of Dexter's romance?
2. How does news of Judy's married life **affect** Dexter?

Writing About Literature

Analyze Conflict Write a brief essay in which you analyze the main conflict in "Winter Dreams." Use evidence from the story to support your analysis.

To help you organize your essay, make a flowchart showing the major events from the beginning to the end of the story, the conflicts that arise from these events, and the resolutions, if any, of these conflicts. The first part is done for you as an example.

SEQUENCE OF EVENTS

> Dexter first sees Judy age 11

> emotional shock; begins yearning for a different life

> quits caddying

>

>

>

After you complete your draft, meet with a peer reviewer to evaluate each other's work and to suggest revisions. Then proofread and edit your draft for errors in spelling, grammar, and punctuation.

Literature Online **Web Activities** For eFlashcards, Selection Quick Checks, and other Web activities, go to www.glencoe.com.

Fitzgerald's Language and Style

Using Active and Passive Voice A verb is in the **active voice** if the subject of the sentence performs the action. A verb is in the **passive voice** if the subject of the sentence receives the verb's action. Different uses of a verb in a sentence allow a writer to emphasize what is most important and enhance a particular style. Notice the difference in emphasis in these two pairs of sentences that contain active and passive voice from "Winter Dreams."

"The nose of the boat bumped the raft." (p. 749)

The raft was bumped by the nose of the boat.

"Dexter walked the streets at night . . ." (p. 754)

The streets were walked by Dexter at night.

Although you should try to use the active voice whenever possible because it is stronger and more direct, sometimes the passive voice is preferred or necessary if the doer of the action is secret, unimportant, or unknown.

"Their engagement was to be announced in a week now—no one could be surprised at it." (p. 754)

In this example, the person who will announce the engagement is unimportant or unknown.

To form the passive voice, use a form of the auxiliary verb *be* with the past participle of the main verb. The tense of the auxiliary verb determines the tense of the passive verb.

Activity For each sentence below, identify the voice as passive or active.

1. A ball came bouncing onto the green.

2. Mr. Hedrick acted annoyed.

3. Mr. Hedrick was annoyed by the interruption.

4. The ball was bounced right onto the green.

Revising Check

Using Active and Passive Voice Work with a partner to review and revise passive sentences that would be more appropriate in active voice in your essay for "Winter Dreams."

from The

Perfect

Hour

James L. W. West III

Guggenheim Fellow

Building Background

F. Scott Fitzgerald met Ginevra King, a woman who would influence him for the rest of his life, in 1915, when he was only eighteen. King became the model for some of Fitzgerald's most memorable characters, including Judy Jones in "Winter Dreams," and, most famously, Daisy Buchanan in *The Great Gatsby*. Her recently discovered diary and letters to Fitzgerald shed light on their previously mysterious relationship. The following selection from *The Perfect Hour*, James L. W. West's discussion of their romance and its effect on Fitzgerald's fiction, describes their first meeting and the start of their correspondence.

Setting a Purpose for Reading

Read to find out more about the inspiration for Judy Jones in Fitzgerald's "Winter Dreams."

Reading Strategy

Evaluating Historical Influences

Evaluating historical influences involves examining how the social influences of a historical period affect the characters, plots, and settings of a literary work. As you read, take notes on how Ginevra King and her relationship with Fitzgerald influenced "Winter Dreams."

CHAPTER TWO
The Romance

Scott met Ginevra in St. Paul on the evening of Monday, January 4, 1915. She was in the city to visit Marie ("Bug") Hersey, a classmate at Westover[1] who had been one of Scott's childhood sweethearts. Ginevra was sixteen years old; Scott, then eighteen, was midway through his second year at Princeton. The two met at an informal party at Marie's house on Summit Avenue. Scott was scheduled to take the Pullman[2] east that night; his Christmas vacation was over, and he was due back at Princeton for classes. He was so smitten with Ginevra, however, that he decided to postpone the journey for twenty-four hours. He wanted to spend Tuesday afternoon with her and to attend a dance being

---

1. *Westover* was a boarding school founded in 1910, in Middlebury, Connecticut.
2. The *Pullman* is a train's sleeping car intended for overnight travel.

given in her honor Tuesday evening by Elizabeth ("Lib") McDavitt, another local girl. Ginevra was flattered: "Scott perfectly darling," she wrote in her diary that night. "Am dipped about."*

They spent the afternoon of January 5th crowded next to each other in the back seat of Reuben Warner's car. (Reuben, a rival for Ginevra's affections, was taking some teenagers for an auto ride across the river to see Minneapolis.) They were together again that evening at Lib McDavitt's dance: this time, however, Scott had to catch his train. He had hoped for time alone with Ginevra at the dance, but he was unable to pry her away from the other party

---

* The diaries are original documents in Ginevra's hand and are quoted verbatim. The letters are transcriptions by a typist: obvious errors have been corrected and a few marks of punctuation added for readability.

guests. At eleven o'clock he stood with her in the front hall of the McDavitt house. They squeezed hands and exchanged regretful glances; he promised to write, and she promised to answer. The next day she set down her impressions of the party in her diary. "Danced and sat with Scott most all evening," she wrote. "He left for Princeton at 11—oh—!"

. . . As soon as he was back at Princeton, he sent her a special-delivery letter. It was the custom then that if one met a young woman and meant to pursue her seriously, one sent her a "special-dellie" almost immediately after the first encounter. The letter reached Ginevra on Thursday, January 7th, while she was still visiting in St. Paul. She made a matter-of-fact note of its arrival in her diary: "Got a Special Delivery from *Scott* this morning."

Train in the Snow, 1875. Claude Monet. Oil on canvas, 59 x 78 cm.
Musée Marmottan-Claude Monet, Paris, France.

As a popular girl, pursued by many boys, Ginevra might have expected to receive Scott's special delivery as a matter of course, but she surely did not anticipate the deluge of mail that would follow. Letters began to arrive from her Princeton admirer frequently and in bulk, and her diary entries became more intense with each letter. She received "a *sweet* one from Scott" on January 14th. Another arrived on the fifteenth: "Wonderful letter from Scott again to-day!" she notes in surprise. On January 23rd: "*Wonderful one from Scott* (he is so darling)." And on January 28th: "*Long wonderful* letter from Scott this morn." On February 6th there arrived a "marvelous wonderful heavenly letter from *Scott*—24 pages— cheered me up immensely." And on February 12th, "24 pages from Scott. *Thrills.*" Her affections, she wrote him on February 7th, were "thriving under the stimulus of so much mail."

The dynamics of letter-writing for teenagers of Scott and Ginevra's time were elaborate. A girl's popularity was measured in part by which boys wrote to her and how many letters she received. There was much banter[3] about who was writing to whom and how often the letters were arriving. Many weekday evenings were taken up with letter-writing; popular girls learned to complain about how many boys they had to correspond with. Girls would wander in and out of one another's rooms during letter-writing sessions. One girl might look over another's shoulder as she wrote and, if she knew the boy, might pick up a pen and (with permission) add marginalia[4] or a postscript.

Girls would give readings to their friends from letters they had received; often the girl would supply running commentary on the boy who had written the letter. Certain parts of

---

3. *Banter* means "quick-witted conversation."
4. *Marginalia* are notes written in the margins of printed pages.

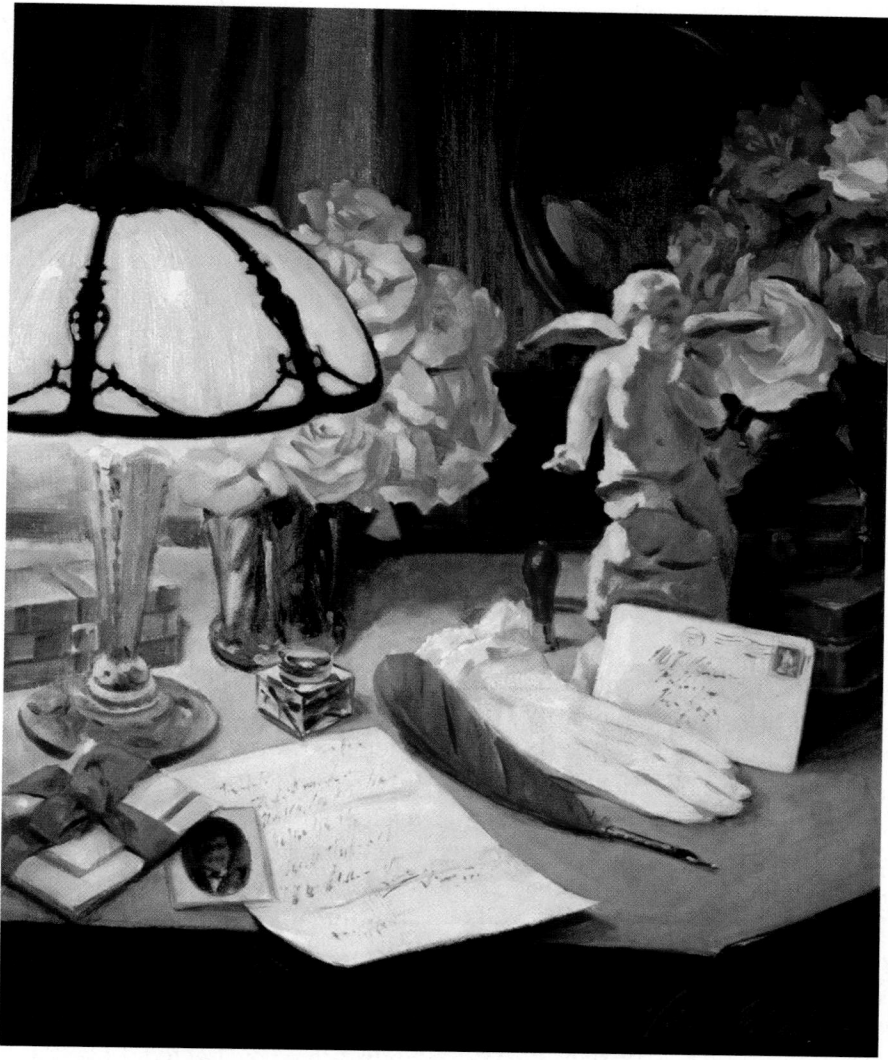

Victorian Writing Desk. Vincent McIndoe.

the letters (the affectionate or intimate bits) would be omitted, although if the boy had been fresh or the girl had a perverse streak, these passages might be read aloud and giggled over. The boys who wrote the letters were aware that this might happen, and they knew to be careful about what they put in their letters. Girls knew it too: boys would show letters to their friends as trophies or would read the sentimental passages aloud—to the accompaniment of eye-rolling and guffaws. No girl wanted to have her personal feelings exposed in this way. Thus there was wariness on both sides until a boy and a girl felt they could trust each other. Only then would they begin to include confidences or confessions of emotion in their letters.

Ginevra does not seem to have worried overly much about this sort of thing. Once she was sure of Scott's interest, she came to enjoy writing to him. "You know, it's queer, but I've always been able to write reams to you and never get bored or tired," she told him on October 13th. He might have said the same thing. So lengthy were his epistles to her that he sometimes had to send them in two envelopes, marked "Part I" and "Part II."

Letter-writing provided Ginevra with an escape. She was not happy about going back to Westover; she made this clear to Scott in her first letter, written on January 11th. "I dread school," she said. "I simply cant go back. I loathe the thought. I curse the fates that call for my education. I rebel at another

8 weeks of grind." Her days at Westover consisted mostly of classes, tests, gym period, glee club, and Bible study (which she began to skip in order to write letters to Scott). Nights were taken up with studying, card games, and chit-chat with girlfriends. Incoming letters were the most exciting events of the day.

Most of these missives[5], one imagines, were pedestrian; boys in their teens typically do not excel at the epistolary[6] arts. Scott Fitzgerald, however, quickly proved himself to be a wonderful correspondent. He was observant and witty, gossipy and funny, full of news and speculations and questions. In other letters of his that have survived from this period, he often included impromptu verse or humorous drawings, and sometimes he sent letter/collages, with cut-out images of swimsuit queens or of movie stars with bobbed hair. Best of all, he could strike a note of longing when he needed to, telling a girl that he was perishing to see her. He must have been a most satisfying young man with whom to trade mail. Ginevra told him so: "Your last letter was a marvel—" she wrote him on January 25th. "I howled over it and wept over it by turns!"

Scott's letters to Ginevra seem to have been playful at first. His opening letter to her (according to her January 11th reply) was signed "Temporarily Devotedly Yrs." She was amused and responded in kind, closing her first letter to him, "Yours *Fickely* sometimes but Devotedly at present. . . ." In the same letter she asked for a photograph of him, claiming to remember only his "yellow hair and big blue eyes." Photographs were an important part of this game and often became objects of near-fetishistic devotion. At one point Ginevra had five photos of Scott on her dresser and another on her desk.

Scott was undoubtedly fascinated with Ginevra, or at least with the image of her that he was carrying about in his head. He continued to write, and she referred to his letters in her replies, sometimes quoting snippets from them. He knew how to keep the correspondence going. He seems to have rationed the flattery, which Ginevra would have been accustomed to, and to have been irreverent instead. In one letter he asked her how much the Big Four[7] weighed (in toto).[8] In another he sent her a list of current undergraduate slang at Princeton. . . .

In more serious moments he began to urge Ginevra to reveal herself to him, frankly and honestly. This was a lifelong habit with him. He often questioned people about themselves and prodded them into confessing things that they might not ordinarily have admitted to. Later in his life he irritated some of his friends, including Sara Murphy[9] and Ernest Hemingway, with these interrogations. Ginevra did not reveal much to Scott at first; self-analysis did not come naturally to her. Scott, however, was persistent and pressed her to disclose her techniques. How did she charm so many boys and entice them into falling for her? Ginevra seems to have been puzzled by the question. Scott was assuming that her behavior, like his, was planned for effect. She could not really tell him why so many boys were drawn to her—only that they were, and that she liked the attention. Thus when he called her a vamp[10] in a letter written late in January, she took exception. "I want you to apologize for calling me a vampire," she admonished him on January 29th. "Très[11] rude I should say."

Ginevra did reveal a little about herself in her letters: "I *know* I am a flirt and I can't stop it," she admitted on January 20th. "A few years ago I took pleasure in being called 'fast,'" she confessed; "I didn't care *how* I acted, I liked it, and so I didn't care for what people said." But that attitude had not lasted: "About a year ago I began to see that there was something better in life than what I had been doing, and I honestly tried to act properly, but I am afraid I'll never be able to wholly reform." She understood the double standard of her time: "I am pretty good on the whole, but you know how much alike we are, and in a boy it doesn't matter, but a girl has to control her feelings, which is hard for me, as I am emotional." These confidences, she hoped, were what he was after. "This is the kind of letter you said you wanted," she told him, "and so this is what I wrote."

---

5. *Missives* are notes or letters.
6. *Epistolary* means of or relating to "letter writing."
7. The *Big Four* was a social group of four young, wealthy socialites in Chicago, of which Ginevra was a member.
8. *In toto* means "in total."
9. *Sara Murphy* was a wealthy American expatriate and a friend of Fitzgerald.
10. A *vamp* is a woman who seduces men.
11. *Très* is French for "very."

Scott soon learned that his romance with Ginevra was causing a stir at Westover. On February 6th he received a cryptic telegram telling him not to expect his usual letter from her the following day. "G.K.'S DAILY DELAYED. UNAVOIDABLE. REASON EXPLAINED LATER," read the wire. A special delivery from Ginevra arrived the next day to explain what had happened. One of her friends from down the hall had wandered into her room while she was composing a letter to him. The girl had wanted to read the letter, but Ginevra had refused to show it to her. The girl had tried to snatch it, precipitating[13] a playful tussle. "In the scramble I shut up the letter in the desk-drawer, and it went so tight that no amount of pulling would open it," she explained. "I only had 15 minutes to get it in the last mail . . . and we got started laughing and then of course lost all our strength—I was screaming—So Midge said—'Well, it's my fault, now I'll send a telegram and tell him he wont get his daily letter.' . . . I said all right, so she went and did it." This was heady stuff for an eighteen-year-old college boy. He was becoming, in absentia[14], a celebrity at Westover.

Ginevra knew how to provoke Scott. In a January 25th letter she recalled their farewell in St. Paul and his failure to kiss her. "I hear you had plans for kissing me goodbye publicly," she wrote him. "My goodness, I'm glad you didn't—I'd have had to be severe as anything with you!" Though perhaps not, to judge from her next sentence: "*Ans. this— Why didn't you?* (KISS ME)." ꙮ

---

13. *Precipitating* means "causing."

14. *In absentia* means "in absence."

RESPONDING AND THINKING CRITICALLY

Respond

1. What aspect of King and Fitzgerald's relationship interested you the most? Explain.

Recall and Interpret

2. (a)According to West, why did young people have to be careful about what they included in letters to members of the opposite sex? (b)What does this suggest about young people's motivation for writing these letters?

3. (a)How did students at Westover react to Ginevra and Fitzgerald's relationship? What does West think Fitzgerald's reaction to this was? (b)What does Fitzgerald's response suggest about his personality?

Analyze and Evaluate

4. (a)West states that "Scott was undoubtedly fascinated with Ginevra, or at least with the image of her that he was carrying about in his head." In what ways do you think this statement is relevant to the character of Dexter Green in "Winter Dreams"?

(b)Is West's characterization of Fitzgerald's "fascination" believable? Why or why not?

5. (a)Ginevra came from a far wealthier family than Fitzgerald's. How do you think this affected their relationship? (b)How do you think it affected his representation of her in his stories? (c)From what you learned about Ginevra in this excerpt from *The Perfect Hour*, do you think Fitzgerald's representation of her in "Winter Dreams" is accurate? Explain.

Connect

6. How does Fitzgerald's semiautobiographical style relate to developments in Modernist fiction?

INDIANA ACADEMIC STANDARDS (pages 762–767)
11.3.5 Evaluate works…that…reflect or shed light on the seminal…social…ideas of their time.

Soldiers of the Republic

MEET DOROTHY PARKER

As a writer, editor, and critic, Dorothy Parker was both famed and feared for her scathing commentary. She once infamously dismissed Katharine Hepburn's acting performance as running "the whole gamut of emotion from A to B." Withering comments such as this one were hallmarks of Parker's fiction, poetry, and especially her criticism.

"Wit has truth in it; wisecracking is simply calisthenics with words."

—Dorothy Parker

New York and Hollywood After an unhappy childhood marred by the deaths of several close family members, Parker left school and began working in New York City. Early on, she got a job as a drama critic for *Vanity Fair*, but was soon fired because of the harshness of her reviews. In 1919 Parker cofounded the influential Algonquin Round Table, an informal group of writers named for the New York hotel where they frequently met. Parker is the best-known female member of the group, which included literary celebrities such as humorist and drama critic Robert Benchley and playwrights Robert Sherwood and George S. Kaufman. In the mid-1920s, Parker published her first book of verse and became a frequent contributor to the fledgling magazine the *New Yorker*, writing reviews, stories, and poems. Throughout the twenties, Parker's writings, and her poems in particular, expertly captured the lenient, "anything goes" attitude of the time as well as the jaded cynicism that could result from too much freedom and recklessness.

In 1934 Parker married actor and writer Alan Campbell and the couple left New York City for Hollywood shortly thereafter. Despite the fact that Parker hated Hollywood, she and Campbell collaborated as screenwriters on a number of lucrative projects, including the hit 1937 film *A Star Is Born*.

Political Passions Parker's celebrated wit and famous pranks—she once hung a sign reading "MEN" on her office door to attract company—often drew public attention away from her serious involvement in social issues. She became active in left-wing politics while she was in Hollywood and chaired an antifascist committee during the Spanish Civil War of the late 1930s. In 1937 she traveled to Spain in support of the Popular Front and did a radio broadcast from Madrid. Parker's leftist sympathies were held against her years later during the surge of anticommunism that gripped Hollywood (and the nation) after World War II. In the mid-1950s, the House Un-American Activities Committee (HUAC) tried to force Parker to name people she believed to have communist sympathies, but Parker refused. She was blacklisted, and as a result she was unable to work in the film industry.

Today's readers enjoy Parker's work for its combination of wit and substance. As one critic said of Parker's play *The Ladies of the Corridor*, Parker was skilled not only at witty dialogue, but also at depicting "the acute understanding of human loneliness, cruelty, stupidity, and occasional glowing, unpredictable fortitude that gives the characters their intermittent flashes of absolute fidelity to life."

Dorothy Parker was born in 1893 and died in 1967.

Literature Online **Author Search** For more about Dorothy Parker, go to www.glencoe.com.

Connecting to the Story

Have you ever had a complete stranger share a personal story with you? What was your reaction? In "Soldiers of the Republic," Dorothy Parker listens to six Spanish soldiers reveal their concerns about the effect of war on their families. Think about the following questions:

- Why do you think a person might tell a stranger a personal story during wartime?
- Why might a person hold back a personal story from a close friend or family member during wartime?

Building Background

Parker's short story is set during the Spanish Civil War. In 1936, Spanish military forces, led by General Francisco Franco, revolted against Spain's democratically elected left-wing government. A brutal and bloody civil war began, and was soon complicated by foreign intervention. The governments of Nazi Germany and fascist Italy aided Franco's forces with arms, money, and troops. The Spanish Republican government was aided by forty thousand foreign volunteers (including many from the United States) and by trucks, planes, tanks, and military advisers from the Soviet Union. The Spanish Civil War came to an end when Franco's forces captured Madrid in 1939, and he established a dictatorship.

Setting Purposes for Reading

Big Idea **Modern Fiction**

As you read "Soldiers of the Republic," note how it reflects characteristics of modern fiction such as understatement and irony.

Literary Element **Setting**

Setting includes not only the time and place of a literary work, but also the ideas, customs, values, and beliefs of the people in that time and place. As you read this short story, pay attention to these aspects of setting.

- See Literary Terms Handbook, p. R16.

Literature Online **Interactive Literary Elements Handbook** To review or learn more about the literary elements, go to www.glencoe.com.

Reading Strategy Visualizing

Visualizing is picturing a writer's ideas or descriptions in your mind's eye. As you read the story, pay attention to how Parker describes people, places, and things. Ask yourself questions about what these things might look like.

Reading Tip: Taking Notes Use a chart like the one below to record what you visualize in each paragraph of the story.

Paragraph	What I See
1	The narrator and others sit in a café in Spain. An attentive waiter brings them drinks.

Vocabulary

dissembling (di sem′ bling) *n.* the act of concealing one's true character, feelings, or intentions; p. 771 *The salesman's dissembling didn't convince me the used car was a good buy.*

contrivance (kən trī′ vəns) *n.* a cleverly designed device; p. 771 *The inventor designed an interesting contrivance.*

vehemently (vē′ ə mənt lē) *adv.* in a strong or passionate manner; p. 771 *Eleanor yelled vehemently as the thief fled with her purse.*

whimsically (hwim′ zik lē) *adv.* in a quaintly humorous manner; p. 772 *The circus clowns paraded whimsically into the center ring.*

stoically (stō′ ik lē) *adv.* calmly and unemotionally, especially despite pain or suffering; p. 772 *Without hope of parole, the prisoner still faced his jail sentence stoically.*

Vocabulary Tip: Analogies An analogy is a type of comparison that is based on the relationships between things or ideas.

INDIANA ACADEMIC STANDARDS (pages 769–773)
11.3 [Identify] story elements such as...setting...
11.2 Develop [reading] strategies...

11.4.4 Structure ideas and arguments in a sustained and persuasive way and support them with...relevant examples.

DOROTHY PARKER **769**

Soldiers ≫≫ of the Republic

Dorothy Parker

That Sunday afternoon we sat with the Swedish girl in the big café in Valencia.[1] We had vermouth[2] in thick goblets, each with a cube of honey-combed gray ice in it. The waiter was so proud of that ice he could hardly bear to leave the glasses on the table, and thus part from it forever. He went to his duty—all over the room they were clapping their hands and hissing to draw his attention—but he looked back over his shoulder.

It was dark outside, the quick, new dark that leaps down without dusk on the day; but, because there were no lights in the streets, it seemed as set and as old as midnight. So you wondered that all the babies were still up. There were babies everywhere in the café, babies serious without solemnity[3] and interested in a tolerant way in their surroundings.

At the table next ours, there was a notably small one; maybe six months old. Its father, a little man in a big uniform that dragged his shoulders down, held it carefully on his knee. It was doing nothing whatever, yet he and his thin young wife, whose belly was already big again under her sleazy dress, sat watching it in a sort of ecstasy of admiration, while their coffee cooled in front of them. The baby was in Sunday white; its dress was patched so delicately that you would have thought the fabric whole had not the patches varied in their shades of whiteness. In its hair was a bow of new blue ribbon, tied with absolute balance of loops and ends. The ribbon was of no use; there was not enough hair to require restraint. The bow was sheerly an adornment, a calculated bit of dash.

"Oh, for God's sake, stop that!" I said to myself. "All right, so it's got a piece of blue ribbon on its hair. All right, so its mother went without eating so it could look pretty when its father came home on leave. All right, so it's her business, and none of yours. All right, so what have you got to cry about?"

The big, dim room was crowded and lively. That morning there had been a bombing from the air, the more horrible for broad daylight. But nobody in the café sat tense and strained, nobody desperately forced forgetfulness. They drank coffee or bottled lemonade, in the pleasant, earned ease of Sunday afternoon, chatting of small, gay matters, all talking at once, all hearing and answering.

There were many soldiers in the room, in what appeared to be the uniforms of twenty different armies until you saw that the variety lay in the differing ways the cloth had worn or faded. Only a few of them had been wounded; here and there you saw one stepping gingerly, leaning on a crutch or two canes, but so far on toward recovery that his face had color. There were many men, too, in civilian clothes—some of them soldiers home on leave, some of them governmental workers, some of them anybody's guess. There

---

1. *Valencia* (vä len´ sē´ ä) is a port city and tourist resort on the Mediterranean coast of Spain.
2. *Vermouth* (vər mōoth´) is a white wine used in cocktails.
3. *Solemnity* is deep seriousness.

Reading Strategy Visualizing *What does the description of the baby in this paragraph indicate about its parents?*

Literary Element Setting *In this paragraph, what do the details of the setting indicate about people's attitude toward the war?*

were plump, comfortable wives, active with paper fans, and old women as quiet as their grandchildren. There were many pretty girls and some beauties, of whom you did not remark, "There's a charming Spanish type," but said, "What a beautiful girl!" The women's clothes were not new, and their material was too humble ever to have warranted skillful cutting.

"It's funny," I said to the Swedish girl, "how when nobody in a place is best-dressed, you don't notice that everybody isn't."

"Please?" the Swedish girl said.

No one, save an occasional soldier, wore a hat. When we had first come to Valencia, I lived in a state of puzzled pain as to why everybody on the streets laughed at me. It was not because "West End Avenue" was writ across my face as if left there by a customs officer's chalked scrawl. They like Americans in Valencia, where they have seen good ones—the doctors who left their practices and came to help, the calm young nurses, the men of the International Brigade.[4] But when I walked forth, men and women courteously laid their hands across their splitting faces and little children, too innocent for **dissembling**, doubled with glee and pointed and cried, "*Olé!*"[5] Then, pretty late, I made my discovery, and left my hat off; and there was laughter no longer. It was not one of those comic hats, either; it was just a hat.

The café filled to overflow, and I left our table to speak to a friend across the room. When I came back to the table, six soldiers were sitting there. They were crowded in, and I scraped past them to my chair. They looked tired and dusty and little, the way that the newly dead look little, and the first things you saw about them were the tendons in their necks. I felt like a prize sow. They were all in conversation with the Swedish girl. She has Spanish, French, German, anything in Scandinavian,[6] Italian, and English. When she has a moment for regret, she sighs that her Dutch is so rusty she can no longer speak it, only read it, and the same is true of her Rumanian.

They had told her, she told us, that they were at the end of forty-eight hours' leave from the trenches, and, for their holiday, they had all pooled their money for cigarettes, and something had gone wrong, and the cigarettes had never come through to them. I had a pack of American cigarettes—in Spain rubies are as nothing to them—and I brought it out, and by nods and smiles and a sort of breast stroke, made it understood that I was offering it to those six men yearning for tobacco. When they saw what I meant, each one of them rose and shook my hand. Darling of me to share my cigarettes with the men on their way back to the trenches. Little Lady Bountiful. The prize sow.

Each one lit his cigarette with a **contrivance** of yellow rope that stank when afire and was also used, the Swedish girl translated, for igniting grenades. Each one received what he had ordered, a glass of coffee, and each one murmured appreciatively over the tiny cornucopia[7] of coarse sugar that accompanied it. Then they talked.

They talked through the Swedish girl, but they did to us that thing we all do when we speak our own language to one who has no knowledge of it. They looked us square in the face, and spoke slowly, and pronounced their words with elaborate movements of their lips. Then, as their stories came, they poured them at us so **vehemently**, so emphatically that they were sure we must understand. They were so convinced we would understand that we were ashamed for not understanding.

But the Swedish girl told us. They were all farmers and farmers' sons, from a district so poor that you try not to remember there is that kind

---

4. Allied with the Republicans, the *Brigade* was a military force.
5. *Olé!* (ō lā´) is a cheer used at bullfights.
6. *Scandinavian* refers to Danish, Norwegian, and Swedish.

Vocabulary

dissembling (di sem´ bling) *n.* the act of concealing one's true character, feelings, or intentions

---

7. Here, *cornucopia* means "abundance." A cornucopia is a curved horn overflowing with fruit and grain.

Vocabulary

contrivance (kən trī´ vəns) *n.* a cleverly designed device
vehemently (vē´ ə mənt lē) *adv.* in a strong or passionate manner

of poverty. Their village was next that one where the old men and the sick men and the women and children had gone, on a holiday, to the bullring; and the planes had come over and dropped bombs on the bullring, and the old men and the sick men and the women and the children were more than two hundred.

They had all, the six of them, been in the war for over a year, and most of that time they had been in the trenches. Four of them were married. One had one child, two had three children, one had five. They had not had word from their families since they had left for the front. There had been no communication; two of them had learned to write from men fighting next them in the trench, but they had not dared to write home. They belonged to a union,[8] and union men, of course, are put to death if taken. The village where their families lived had been captured, and if your wife gets a letter from a union man, who knows but they'll shoot her for the connection?

They told about how they had not heard from their families for more than a year. They did not tell it gallantly or **whimsically** or **stoically**. They told it as if—Well, look. You have been in the trenches, fighting, for a year. You have heard nothing of your wife and your children. They do not know if you are dead or alive or blinded. You do not know where they are, or if they are. You must talk to somebody. That is the way they told about it.

One of them, some six months before, had heard of his wife and his three children—they had such beautiful eyes, he said—from a brother-in-law in France. They were all alive then, he was told, and had a bowl of beans a day. But his wife had not complained of the food, he heard. What had troubled her was that she had no thread to mend the children's ragged clothes. So that troubled him, too.

"She has no thread," he kept telling us. "My wife has no thread to mend with. No thread."

"**S**he has no thread," he kept telling us. "My wife has no thread to mend with. No thread."

We sat there, and listened to what the Swedish girl told us they were saying. Suddenly one of them looked at the clock, and then there was excitement. They jumped up, as a man, and there were calls for the waiter and rapid talk with him, and each of them shook the hand of each of us. We went through more swimming motions to explain to them that they were to take the rest of the cigarettes—fourteen cigarettes for six soldiers to take to war—and then they shook our hands again. Then all of us said "*Salud!*"[9] as many times as could be for six of them and three of us, and then they filed out of the café, the six of them, tired and dusty and little, as men of a mighty horde are little.

Only the Swedish girl talked, after they had gone. The Swedish girl has been in Spain since the start of the war. She has nursed splintered men, and she has carried stretchers into the trenches and, heavier laden, back to the hospital. She has seen and heard too much to be knocked into silence.

Presently it was time to go, and the Swedish girl raised her hands above her head and clapped them twice together to summon the waiter. He came, but he only shook his head and his hand, and moved away.

The soldiers had paid for our drinks. ❧

---

8. The Republicans belonged to trade *unions*.

9. *Salud!* (sä lōōd′), meaning "Health!" is a toast, like *Cheers!*

RESPONDING AND THINKING CRITICALLY

Respond

1. What surprised you most about the story? Explain.

Recall and Interpret

2. (a)What difficult circumstances do the people of Valencia and the soldiers in the café face? (b)What attitude do they have toward these circumstances?

3. (a)How do the soldiers react to the gift of cigarettes? (b)How do you explain their reactions?

Analyze and Evaluate

4. (a)How do you think the author wants readers to feel about the people of Valencia and the soldiers? (b)Do you think the author was successful in making you feel a certain way? Use examples from the story to support your answer.

5. In your opinion, are the soldiers in this story like other people who face danger, or do they handle their situation differently? Explain.

6. (a)How does the narrator feel about herself in relation to the people of Valencia? (b)In your opinion, why does she feel this way?

7. What did you find most puzzling about the narrator? Put your thoughts in the form of a question.

Connect

8. This story shows the basic decency, almost nobility, of ordinary soldiers during wartime. How do you think the story would change had Parker decided to focus on a group of high-ranking military officers instead?

9. **Big Idea** **Modern Fiction** Irony, the contrast between appearance and reality, is a basic characteristic of modern fiction. How does this story display irony?

LITERARY ANALYSIS

Literary Element Setting

Setting often influences the mood, or atmosphere, of a literary work. For example, a story set in a dark and gloomy castle might have a forbidding or melancholy mood. "Soldiers of the Republic" is set in a café in Valencia, a large city in Spain, during the Spanish Civil War.

1. What mood is created by the story's setting?

2. How might the mood of the story be different if there were not a war going on?

Writing About Literature

Analyze Theme From what you have read, what conclusions can you draw about Parker's attitude toward ordinary people during wartime? Using details from the story, identify the author's position and write a few paragraphs to persuade your classmates to share your point of view.

Literature Online **Web Activities** For eFlashcards, Selection Quick Checks, and other Web activities, go to www.glencoe.com.

READING AND VOCABULARY

Reading Strategy Visualizing

Visualizing is one of the best ways to understand and remember information in fiction, nonfiction, and informational text.

1. What images came to mind as you visualized the café setting?

2. How did you imagine that the narrator and her companions look as compared with the soldiers?

Vocabulary Practice

Practice with Analogies Choose the word pair that best completes each analogy.

1. dissembling : concealment ::
   a. sympathy : compassion **b.** deceit : truth

2. vehemently : fanatic ::
   a. greedily : miser **b.** humbly : aristocrat

3. contrivance : clever ::
   a. toad : beautiful **b.** infant : helpless

4. stoically : unemotionally ::
   a. fearfully : bravely **b.** brashly : boldly

The Jilting of Granny Weatherall

MEET KATHERINE ANNE PORTER

Katherine Anne Porter, who published her first collection of short stories when she was forty, described herself as "a late starter." But "a late finisher" might be more accurate. During her long career, she tended to write and rewrite her stories, sometimes putting them aside for many years. Porter sought to tell each story "as clearly and purely and simply as I can."

Experiences of Death and Near-Death

Katherine Anne Porter was born in a small log house on a farm in central Texas. Her mother died before she was two, and Porter and her four siblings were raised by one of their grandmothers. The grandmother's death when Porter was eleven had a powerful emotional impact on the family. Afterward, Porter's family moved to San Antonio, Texas, where she studied acting.

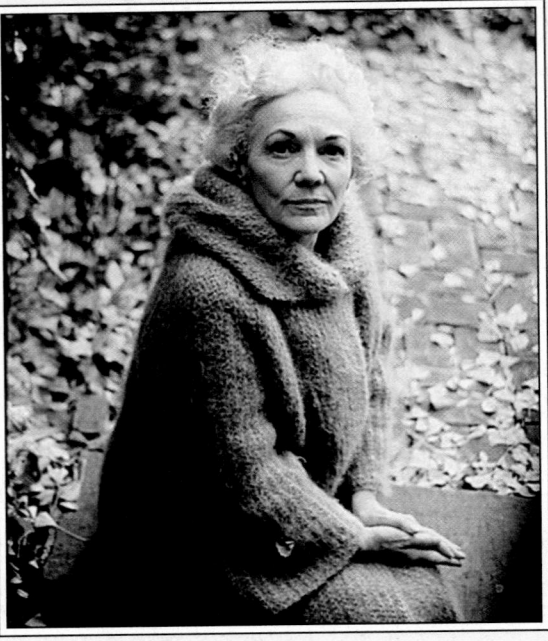

> "I knew what death was, and had almost experienced it. I had . . . the happy vision just before death. Now if you have had that, and survived it, come back from it, you are no longer like other people."
>
> —Katherine Anne Porter

Shortly after moving to Dallas, Texas, in 1915, Porter became ill with tuberculosis and believed she had only a few months to live. She recovered only to be hit by the World War I flu epidemic, and she came so close to death that her family finalized her burial arrangements. Porter's struggle to survive, the close friendships she formed with other young women in a sanatorium in Texas, and the opportunities she had to reflect on her life during this period were to have a profound effect on her creative activities. She emerged from several years of illness with a new career goal: to be a writer.

A Creative Restlessness Porter spent most of her thirties living abroad. She took on a range of writing projects and sought out the company of friends and circles of writers and artists who provided her with the intense interpersonal experiences that inspired her writing.

Porter published several collections of short stories, starting with *Flowering Judas* (1929). Although it was her novel, *Ship of Fools* (1962), that became a best seller, Porter was primarily a practitioner of the short story. Many of her stories, including "The Jilting of Granny Weatherall," are set in the South and feature women who have profound self-realizations at crucial moments in their lives. At age seventy-six, two years after the publication of twenty-seven of her stories in *The Collected Stories of Katherine Anne Porter*, Porter received a Pulitzer Prize and the National Book Award.

Katherine Anne Porter was born in 1890 and died in 1980.

Literature Online **Author Search** For more about Katherine Anne Porter, go to www.glencoe.com.

Connecting to the Story

Granny Weatherall was jilted on her wedding day, causing social humiliation and a painful loss of love. As you read the story, think about how people learn to live with—or never quite accept—a social disgrace. Consider the following questions:

- How would you feel if you were left waiting on your wedding day?
- What might be especially painful about losing a loved one in this way?

Building Background

This story is set in the South in the early twentieth century. Women of the time were often confined to the traditional roles of wife, mother, and homemaker. Roman Catholicism figures prominently in Porter's story. Granny Weatherall's religious beliefs and her ideas about guilt and forgiveness are important elements of the story.

Big Idea Modern Fiction

As you read "The Jilting of Granny Weatherall," notice the Modernist techniques that Porter uses. For example, she rearranges the chronology of events to provide insight into the inner and outer worlds of the protagonist.

Literary Element Stream of Consciousness

Stream of consciousness is a technique that a writer uses to imitate the flow of thoughts, feelings, images, and memories of a character in a literary work. Stream of consciousness replaces traditional chronological order with a seemingly random collection of impressions, forcing the reader to piece together the plot or theme of the work. Porter uses stream of consciousness to represent Granny's thoughts and memories as well as her overall state of mind. As you read, you might want to create a timeline to help you understand when the events in the story take place.

- See Literary Terms Handbook, p. R17.

Literature Online Interactive Literary Elements Handbook To review or learn more about the literary elements, go to www.glencoe.com.

Reading Strategy Drawing Conclusions About the Protagonist

To **draw conclusions** means to use different pieces of information to make a general statement. A **protagonist** is the central character in a literary work, around whom the main conflict revolves. As Granny's thoughts skip from one person or subject to another, and back and forth in time, various clues about her past emerge. To draw conclusions about Granny's character, read carefully and combine the clues in the story.

Reading Tip: Taking Notes Use a chart to record details and draw conclusions based on them.

Details	Conclusion
Granny calls the doctor a brat.	Granny thinks of the doctor as a kid.

Vocabulary

tactful (takt′ fəl) *adj.* able to speak or act without offending others; p. 777 *Southern women were expected to be tactful in their relations.*

dutiful (dōō′ ti fəl) *adj.* careful to fulfill obligations; p. 777 *Only a dutiful person could take care of a farm and raise several children.*

vanity (van′ i tē) *n.* excessive pride, as in one's looks; p. 779 *The man's vanity made it hard for him to see why he had not received the award.*

jilt (jilt) *v.* to drop or reject as a sweetheart; p. 779 *None of her children had been jilted; they had all married their first loves.*

piety (pī′ ə tē) *n.* religious devoutness; goodness; p. 781 *Piety was a common response to the moral issues raised by the war.*

Vocabulary Tip: Context Clues You often can determine the meaning of an unfamiliar word by looking at the words that surround it.

INDIANA ACADEMIC STANDARDS (pages 775–784)
11.3 [Identify] story elements…
11.2 Develop [reading] strategies…

11.5.1 Write fictional…narratives that narrate a sequence of events and communicate their significance to the audience…

The White Bed Jacket, c. 1905. Lilla Cabot Perry. Pastel on tan paper, 25½ x 31½ in. Hirschl & Adler Galleries Inc. New York.

The Jilting of Granny Weatherall

Katherine Anne Porter

She flicked her wrist neatly out of Doctor Harry's pudgy careful fingers and pulled the sheet up to her chin. The brat ought to be in knee-breeches. Doctoring around the country with spectacles on his nose. "Get along now, take your schoolbooks and go. There's nothing wrong with me."

Doctor Harry spread a warm paw like a cushion on her forehead where the forked green vein danced and made her eyelids twitch. "Now, now, be a good girl, and we'll have you up in no time."

"That's no way to speak to a woman nearly eighty years old just because she's down. I'd have you respect your elders, young man."

"Well, missy, excuse me." Doctor Harry patted her cheek. "But I've got to warn you, haven't I? You're a marvel,[1] but you must be careful or you're going to be good and sorry."

"Don't tell me what I'm going to be. I'm on my feet now, morally speaking. It's Cornelia. I had to go to bed to get rid of her."

Her bones felt loose, and floated around in her

---

1. A *marvel* is a wonderful or astonishing thing.

skin, and Doctor Harry floated like a balloon around the foot of the bed. He floated and pulled down his waistcoat[2] and swung his glasses on a cord. "Well, stay where you are, it certainly can't hurt you."

"Get along and doctor your sick," said Granny Weatherall. "Leave a well woman alone. I'll call for you when I want you . . . Where were you forty years ago when I pulled through milk-leg[3] and double pneumonia? You weren't even born. Don't let Cornelia lead you on," she shouted, because Doctor Harry appeared to float up to the ceiling and out. "I pay my own bills, and I don't throw my money away on nonsense!"

She meant to wave good-bye, but it was too much trouble. Her eyes closed of themselves, it was like a dark curtain drawn round the bed. The pillow rose and floated under her, pleasant as a hammock in a light wind. She listened to the leaves rustling outside the window. No, somebody was swishing newspapers: no, Cornelia and Doctor Harry were whispering together. She leaped broad awake, thinking they whispered in her ear.

"She was never like this, *never* like this!" "Well, what can we expect?" "Yes, eighty years old . . ."

Well, and what if she was? She still had ears. It was like Cornelia to whisper round doors. She always kept things secret in such a public way. She was always being **tactful** and kind. Cornelia was **dutiful**; that was the trouble with her. Dutiful and good: "So good and dutiful," said Granny, "that I'd like to spank her." She saw herself spanking Cornelia and making a fine job of it.

---

2. A *waistcoat* is a vest.
3. *Milk-leg* is a painful swelling of the leg that may occur after childbirth.

Literary Element Stream of Consciousness *How does this paragraph show that Granny's mind travels back and forth between the past and present?*

Reading Strategy Drawing Conclusions About the Protagonist *Do Granny's thoughts refer to the past or present? Explain.*

Vocabulary

tactful (takt´ fəl) *adj.* able to speak or act without offending others
dutiful (doo´ ti fəl) *adj.* careful to fulfill obligations

"What'd you say, Mother?"
Granny felt her face tying up in hard knots.
"Can't a body think, I'd like to know?"
"I thought you might want something."
"I do. I want a lot of things. First off, go away and don't whisper."

She lay and drowsed, hoping in her sleep that the children would keep out and let her rest a minute. It had been a long day. Not that she was tired. It was always pleasant to snatch a minute now and then. There was always so much to be done. Let me see: tomorrow.

Tomorrow was far away and there was nothing to trouble about. Things were finished somehow when the time came; thank God there was always a little margin over for peace: then a person could spread out the plan of life and tuck in the edges orderly. It was good to have everything clean and folded away, with the hairbrushes and tonic bottles sitting straight on the white embroidered linen; the day started without fuss and the pantry shelves laid out with rows of jelly glasses and brown jugs and white stone-china jars with blue whirligigs[4] and words painted on them: coffee, tea, sugar, ginger, cinnamon, all-spice; and the bronze clock with the lion on the top nicely dusted off. The dust that lion could collect in twenty-four hours! The box in the attic with all those letters tied up, well, she'd have to go through that tomorrow. All those letters—George's letters and John's letters and her letters to them both—lying around for the children to find afterwards made her uneasy. Yes, that would be tomorrow's business. No use to let them know how silly she had been once.

While she was rummaging round she found death in her mind and it felt clammy and unfamiliar. She had spent so much time preparing for

Visual Vocabulary
Allspice, a spice thought to combine the flavors of cloves, cinnamon, and nutmeg, comes from the dried berries of the pimento tree.

---

4. *Whirligigs* (hwur´ li gigz´) are circular patterns, or swirls.

Literary Element Stream of Consciousness *In what way is this paragraph an unpredictable flow of feelings, thoughts, memories, and images?*

death there was no need for bringing it up again. Let it take care of itself now. When she was sixty she had felt very old, finished, and went round making farewell trips to see her children and grandchildren, with a secret in her mind: This is the very last of your mother, children! Then she made her will and came down with a long fever. That was all just a notion like a lot of other things, but it was lucky too, for she had once for all got over the idea of dying for a long time. Now she couldn't be worried. She hoped she had better sense now. Her father had lived to be one hundred and two years old and had drunk a noggin[5] of strong hot toddy[6] on his last birthday. He told the reporters it was his daily habit, and he owed his long life to that. He had made quite a scandal and was very pleased about it. She believed she'd just plague Cornelia a little.

"Cornelia! Cornelia!" No footsteps, but a sudden hand on her cheek. "Bless you, where have you been?"

"Here, mother."

"Well, Cornelia, I want a noggin of hot toddy."

"Are you cold, darling?"

"I'm chilly, Cornelia. Lying in bed stops the circulation. I must have told you that a thousand times."

Well, she could just hear Cornelia telling her husband that Mother was getting a little childish and they'd have to humor her. The thing that most annoyed her was that Cornelia thought she was deaf, dumb, and blind. Little hasty glances and tiny gestures tossed around her and over her head, saying, "Don't cross her, let her have her way, she's eighty years old," and she sitting there as if she lived in a thin glass cage. Sometimes Granny almost made up her mind to pack up and move back to her own house where nobody could remind her every minute that she was old. Wait, wait,

Cornelia, till your own children whisper behind your back!

In her day she had kept a better house and had got more work done. She wasn't too old yet for Lydia to be driving eighty miles for advice when one of the children jumped the track, and Jimmy still dropped in and talked things over: "Now, Mammy, you've a good business head, I want to know what you think of this . . . ?" Old. Cornelia couldn't change the furniture round without asking. Little things, little things! They had been so sweet when they were little. Granny wished the old days were back again with the children young and everything to be done over. It had been a hard pull, but not too much for her. When she thought of all the food she had cooked, and all the clothes she had cut and sewed, and all the gardens she had made— well, the children showed it. There they were, made out of her, and they couldn't get away from that. Sometimes she wanted to see John again and point to them and say, "Well, I didn't do so badly, did I?" But that would have to wait. That was for tomorrow. She used to think of him as a man, but now all the children were older than their father, and he would be a child beside her if she saw him now. It seemed strange and there was something wrong in the idea. Why, he couldn't possibly recognize her. She had fenced in a hundred acres once, digging the post holes herself and clamping the wires with just a Negro boy to help. That changed a woman. John would be looking for a young woman with the peaked Spanish comb in her hair and the painted fan. Digging post holes changed a woman. Riding country roads in the winter when women had their babies was another thing: sitting up nights with sick horses and sick Negroes and sick children and hardly ever losing one. John, I hardly ever lost one of them! John would see that in a minute; that would be something he could understand, she wouldn't have to explain anything!

> *Lighting the lamps had been beautiful. The children huddled up to her and breathed like little calves waiting at the bars in the twilight.*

---

5. A *noggin* is a small mug or cup.
6. A *hot toddy* is a drink made with liquor, hot water, sugar, and spices.

Reading Strategy Drawing Conclusions About the Protagonist *How does Granny view herself as a mother?*

It made her feel like rolling up her sleeves and putting the whole place to rights again. No matter if Cornelia was determined to be everywhere at once, there were a great many things left undone on this place. She would start tomorrow and do them. It was good to be strong enough for everything, even if all you made melted and changed and slipped under your hands, so that by the time you finished you almost forgot what you were working for. What was it I set out to do? she asked herself intently, but she could not remember. A fog rose over the valley, she saw it marching across the creek swallowing the trees and moving up the hill like an army of ghosts. Soon it would be at the near edge of the orchard, and then it was time to go in and light the lamps. Come in, children, don't stay out in the night air.

Lighting the lamps had been beautiful. The children huddled up to her and breathed like little calves waiting at the bars in the twilight. Their eyes followed the match and watched the flame rise and settle in a blue curve, then they moved away from her. The lamp was lit, they didn't have to be scared and hang on to mother any more. Never, never, never more. God, for all my life I thank Thee. Without Thee, my God, I could never have done it. Hail, Mary, full of grace.[7]

I want you to pick all the fruit this year and see that nothing is wasted. There's always someone who can use it. Don't let good things rot for want of using. You waste life when you waste good food. Don't let things get lost. It's bitter to lose things. Now, don't let me get to thinking, not when I am tired and taking a little nap before supper . . .

The pillow rose about her shoulders and pressed against her heart and the memory was being squeezed out of it: oh, push down the pillow, somebody; it would smother her if she tried to hold it. Such a fresh breeze blowing and such a green day with no threats in it. But he had not come, just the same. What does a woman do when she has put on the white veil and set out the white cake for a man and he doesn't come? She tried to remember. No, I swear he never harmed me but in that. He never harmed me but in that . . . and what if he did? There was the day, the day, but a whirl of dark smoke rose and covered it, crept up and over into the bright field where everything was planted so carefully in orderly rows. That was hell, she knew hell when she saw it. For sixty years she had prayed against remembering him and against losing her soul in the deep pit of hell, and now the two things were mingled in one, and the thought of him was a smoky cloud from hell that moved and crept in her head when she had just got rid of Doctor Harry and was trying to rest a minute. Wounded **vanity,** Ellen, said a sharp voice in the top of her mind. Don't let your wounded vanity get the upper hand of you. Plenty of girls get **jilted.** You were jilted, weren't you? Then stand up to it. Her eyelids wavered and let in streamers of blue-gray light like tissue paper over her eyes. She must get up and pull the shades down or she'd never sleep. She was in bed again and the shades were not down. How could that happen? Better turn over, hide from the light; sleeping in the light gave you nightmares. "Mother, how do you feel now?" and a stinging wetness on her forehead. But I don't like having my face washed in cold water!

Hapsy? George? Lydia? Jimmy? No, Cornelia, and her features were swollen and full of little puddles. "They're coming, darling, they'll all be here soon." Go wash your face, child, you look funny.

Instead of obeying, Cornelia knelt down and put her head on the pillow. She seemed to be talking but there was no sound. "Well, are you tongue-tied? Whose birthday is it? Are you going to give a party?"

Cornelia's mouth moved urgently in strange shapes. "Don't do that, you bother me, daughter."

"Oh, no, Mother. Oh, no . . ."

Nonsense. It was strange about children. They disputed your every word. "No what, Cornelia?"

---

7. *Hail, Mary, full of grace* is the beginning of a Roman Catholic prayer to the Virgin Mary.

Big Idea Modern Fiction *How is this method of showing Granny's thoughts related to Modernism?*

Literary Element Stream of Consciousness *In writing that uses stream of consciousness, some information is often unclear. What is unclear here?*

Vocabulary

vanity (van′ i tē) *n.* excessive pride, as in one's looks
jilt (jilt) *v.* to drop or reject as a sweetheart

The Seamstress, 1914. Knud Larsen. Oil on canvas, 20 x 18½ in. Private collection.
Viewing the Art: How might the woman in the painting be like Cornelia at that age?

"Here's Doctor Harry."

"I won't see that boy again. He just left five minutes ago."

"That was this morning, Mother. It's night now. Here's the nurse."

"This is Doctor Harry, Mrs. Weatherall. I never saw you look so young and happy!"

"Ah, I'll never be young again—but I'd be happy if they'd let me lie in peace and get rested."

She thought she spoke up loudly, but no one answered. A warm weight on her forehead, a warm bracelet on her wrist and a breeze went on whispering, trying to tell her something. A shuffle of leaves in the everlasting hand of God, He blew on them and they danced and rattled. "Mother, don't mind, we're going to give you a little hypodermic." "Look here, daughter, how do ants get in this bed? I saw sugar ants yesterday." Did you send for Hapsy too?

It was Hapsy she really wanted. She had to go a long way back through a great many rooms to find Hapsy standing with a baby on her arm. She seemed to herself to be Hapsy also, and the baby on Hapsy's arm was Hapsy and himself and herself, all at once, and there was no surprise in the meeting. Then Hapsy melted from within and turned flimsy as gray gauze and the baby was a gauzy shadow, and Hapsy came up close and said, "I thought you'd never come," and looked at her very searchingly and said, "You haven't changed a bit!" They leaned forward to kiss, when Cornelia began whispering from a long way off, "Oh, is there anything you want to tell me? Is there anything I can do for you?"

Yes, she had changed her mind after sixty years and she would like to see George. I want you to find George. Find him and be sure to tell him I forgot him. I want him to know I had my husband just the same, and my children and my house, like any other woman. A good house too and a good husband that I loved and fine children out of him. Better than I hoped for, even.

Reading Strategy Drawing Conclusions About the Protagonist *In this paragraph, is Granny thinking about the past or present? How do you know?*

Tell him I was given back everything he took away, and more. Oh, no, O God, no, there was something else besides the house and the man and the children. Oh, surely they were not all? What was it? Something not given back . . . Her breath crowded down under her ribs and grew into a monstrous frightening shape with cutting edges; it bored[8] up into her head, and the agony was unbelievable. Yes, John, get the doctor now, no more talk, my time has come.

When this one was born it should be the last. The last. It should have been born first, for it was the one she had truly wanted. Everything came in good time. Nothing left out, left over. She was strong, in three days she would be as well as ever. Better. A woman needed milk in her to have her full health.

"Mother, do you hear me?"

"I've been telling you—"

"Mother, Father Connolly's here."

"I went to Holy Communion only last week. Tell him I'm not so sinful as all that."

"Father just wants to speak to you."

He could speak as much as he pleased. It was like him to drop in and inquire about her soul as if it were a teething baby, and then stay on for a cup of tea and a round of cards and gossip. He always had a funny story of some sort, usually about an Irishman who made his little mistakes and confessed them, and the point lay in some absurd thing he would blurt out in the confessional[9] showing his struggles between native **piety** and original sin. Granny felt easy about her soul. Cornelia, where are your manners? Give Father Connolly a chair. She had her secret comfortable understanding with a few favorite saints who cleared a straight road to God for her. All as surely signed and sealed as the papers for the new Forty Acres. For ever . . . heirs and assigns[10] forever.

---

8. Here, to *bore* means "to make a hole, as by drilling or pushing."
9. A *confessional* is a small booth in a Catholic church where a person confesses his or her sins to a priest and asks forgiveness from God through the priest.
10. *Assigns* are people to whom property is legally transferred.

Literary Element Stream of Consciousness *What causes this shift in Granny's thoughts?*

Vocabulary

piety (pī′ ə tē) *n.* religious devoutness; goodness

Since the day the wedding cake was not cut, but thrown out and wasted. The whole bottom dropped out of the world, and there she was, blind and sweating, with nothing under her feet and the walls falling away. His hand had caught her under the breast, she had not fallen; there was the freshly polished floor with the green rug on it, just as before. He had cursed like a sailor's parrot and said, "I'll kill him for you." "Don't lay a hand on him, for my sake leave something to God." "Now, Ellen, you must believe what I tell you . . ."

So there was nothing, nothing to worry about any more, except sometimes in the night one of the children screamed in a nightmare, and they both hustled out shaking and hunting for the matches and calling, "There, wait a minute, here we are!" John, get the doctor now, Hapsy's time has come. But there was Hapsy standing by the bed in a white cap. "Cornelia, tell Hapsy to take off her cap. I can't see her plain."

Her eyes opened very wide and the room stood out like a picture she had seen somewhere. Dark colors with the shadows rising towards the ceiling in long angles. The tall black dresser gleamed with nothing on it but John's picture, enlarged from a little one, with John's eyes very black when they should have been blue. You never saw him, so how do you know how he looked? But the man insisted the copy was perfect, it was very rich and handsome. For a picture, yes, but it's not my husband. The table by the bed had a linen cover and a candle and a crucifix. The light was blue from Cornelia's silk lampshades. No sort of light at all, just frippery.[11] You had to live forty years with kerosene lamps to appreciate honest electricity. She felt very strong and she saw Doctor Harry with a rosy nimbus[12] around him.

"You look like a saint, Doctor Harry, and I vow that's as near as you'll ever come to it."

"She's saying something."

"I heard you, Cornelia. What's all this carrying-on?"

"Father Connolly's saying—"

---

11. *Frippery* is a showy, useless display.
12. A *nimbus* is a disk or ring of light; a halo.

Reading Strategy Drawing Conclusions About the Protagonist *Besides the jilting, what events in Granny's life appear to have the most importance for her?*

Cornelia's voice staggered and bumped like a cart in a bad road. It rounded corners and turned back again and arrived nowhere. Granny stepped up in the cart very lightly and reached for the reins, but a man sat beside her, and she knew him by his hands, driving the cart. She did not look in his face, for she knew without seeing, but looked instead down the road where the trees leaned over and bowed to each other and a thousand birds were singing a Mass. She felt like singing too, but she put her hand in the bosom of her dress and pulled out a rosary, and Father Connolly murmured Latin in a very solemn voice and tickled her feet.[13] My God, will you stop that nonsense? I'm a married woman. What if he did run away and leave me to face the priest by myself? I found another a whole world better. I wouldn't have exchanged my husband for anybody except St. Michael[14] himself, and you may tell him that for me, with a thank you into the bargain.

Did You Know?
A *rosary* is a string of beads used to help count specific prayers as they are recited.

Light flashed on her closed eyelids, and a deep roaring shook her. Cornelia, is that lightning? I hear thunder. There's going to be a storm. Close all the windows. Call the children in . . . "Mother, here we are, all of us." "Is that you, Hapsy?" "Oh, no, I'm Lydia. We drove as fast as we could." Their faces drifted above her, drifted away. The rosary fell out of her hands and Lydia put it back. Jimmy tried to help, their hands fumbled together, and Granny closed two fingers round Jimmy's thumb. Beads wouldn't do, it must be something alive. She was so amazed her thoughts ran round and round. So, my dear Lord, this is my death and I wasn't even thinking about it. My children have come to see me die.

But I can't, it's not time. Oh, I always hated surprises. I wanted to give Cornelia the amethyst[15] set—Cornelia, you're to have the amethyst set, but Hapsy's to wear it when she wants, and, Doctor Harry, do shut up. Nobody sent for you. Oh, my dear Lord, do wait a minute. I meant to do something about the Forty Acres, Jimmy doesn't need it and Lydia will later on, with that worthless husband of hers. I meant to finish the altar cloth and send six bottles of wine to Sister Borgia for her dyspepsia.[16] I want to send six bottles of wine to Sister Borgia, Father Connolly, now don't let me forget.

Cornelia's voice made short turns and tilted over and crashed. "Oh, Mother, oh, Mother, oh, Mother . . ."

"I'm not going, Cornelia. I'm taken by surprise. I can't go."

You'll see Hapsy again. What about her? "I thought you'd never come." Granny made a long journey outward, looking for Hapsy. What if I don't find her? What then? Her heart sank down and down, there was no bottom to death, she couldn't come to the end of it. The blue light from Cornelia's lampshade drew into a tiny point in the center of her brain, it flickered and winked like an eye, quietly it fluttered and dwindled. Granny lay curled down within herself, amazed and watchful, staring at the point of light that was herself; her body was now only a deeper mass of shadow in an endless darkness and this darkness would curl round the light and swallow it up. God, give a sign!

For the second time there was no sign. Again no bridegroom and the priest in the house. She could not remember any other sorrow because this grief wiped them all away. Oh, no, there's nothing more cruel than this—I'll never forgive it. She stretched herself with a deep breath and blew out the light. ❧

---

13. The priest is administering the Sacrament of the Infirm, a Catholic ritual that includes saying prayers and applying oil to the many parts of a person's body.
14. *St. Michael* is an archangel, usually depicted as a handsome knight.

Big Idea Modern Fiction *How is the characterization in this story different from traditional characterization?*

---

15. *Amethyst* (am′ ə thist) is purple or violet quartz and is typically used in jewelry.
16. *Dyspepsia* is indigestion.

Literary Element Stream of Consciousness *What is unclear about this moment in the story?*

RESPONDING AND THINKING CRITICALLY

Respond

1. What was your reaction to Granny Weatherall's train of thought throughout the story?

Recall and Interpret

2. (a)At the beginning of the story, what attitudes does Granny have toward Dr. Harry, Cornelia, and her own illness? (b)What do Granny's attitudes reveal about her state of mind?

3. (a)Who is Hapsy, and where does Granny see her? (b)How does this experience relate to what occurs at the end of the story?

4. (a)Which event does Granny recall with particular anger and sadness? (b)What does her "message" for the person involved allow you to infer about her feelings toward him?

Analyze and Evaluate

5. (a)In your opinion, did Granny live a full life? Support your answer with details from the story. (b)What is symbolic about the name Weatherall?

6. (a)How do the present and past merge when the priest appears? (b)How does Porter use religion to add an extra layer of meaning to the story? Explain.

7. Evaluate whether Porter brings this story to an effective close. Explain your answer using details from the story.

Connect

8. Big Idea **Modern Fiction** How does the stream of consciousness technique that Porter uses to tell the story clarify the role that memories, experiences, and inner and outer worlds play in one's life?

LITERARY ANALYSIS

Literary Element **Stream of Consciousness**

By using **stream of consciousness,** Porter takes the reader deep into the mind of Granny Weatherall and presents a vivid picture of death. Look back at the time-line you created as you answer the following questions:

1. What kinds of clues help the reader distinguish the past from the present?

2. Is stream of consciousness a good technique for telling the story of the hours and minutes leading up to death? Why or why not?

Review: Characterization

Characterization refers to the various methods that a writer uses to develop the personality of a character. These include description, dialogue, the character's actions, and sometimes, as in this story, the character's thoughts.

Partner Activity Work with a classmate to review how you learned about Cornelia as you read the story. Create a web diagram like the one below, adding new circles with specific information from the story.

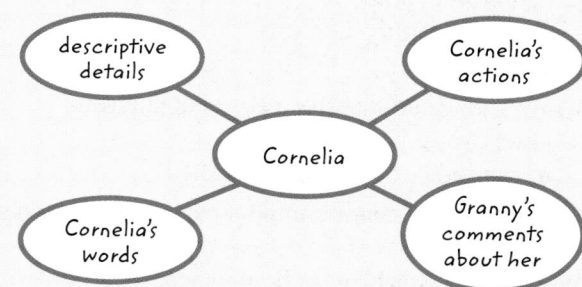

Reading Strategy Drawing Conclusions About the Protagonist

Compared with most of the women of her time and culture, Granny Weatherall was very independent, both financially and personally. Review the chart you filled in as you read to draw conclusions about her traits.

1. What are two important events in Granny's life that illustrate her independence?

2. Near the end of her life, how does Granny's desire to remain independent affect her attitudes toward Cornelia, Dr. Harry, and George?

Vocabulary Practice

Practice with Context Clues Read each of the following sentences and then decide which of the choices is closest in meaning to the boldfaced word.

1. Annette was very **tactful** and complimented each of her friends.
   a. blunt   **b.** polite

2. We wanted to leave a **dutiful** caretaker in charge of the animals so they would all remain healthy.
   a. conscientious   **b.** quick

3. My uncle's **vanity** was great enough that he felt sure he'd win the contest.
   a. enthusiasm   **b.** conceit

4. My sister cried for three days after she was **jilted** by her boyfriend.
   a. praised   **b.** rejected

5. Joseph, who always carried a rosary, was known for his **piety**.
   a. religious faith   **b.** personal style

Literature⌐nline Web Activities For eFlashcards, Selection Quick Checks, and other Web activities, go to www.glencoe.com.

Writing About Literature

Apply Point of View Choose any character in the story except Granny Weatherall, and write several paragraphs that present events from this person's point of view, using stream of consciousness. Incorporate events from the story but invent the character's response to them.

List the events, feelings, and memories that you wish to write about from your character's point of view. Then create a flow chart like the one below to show how you will connect them. Link the events with memories and feelings.

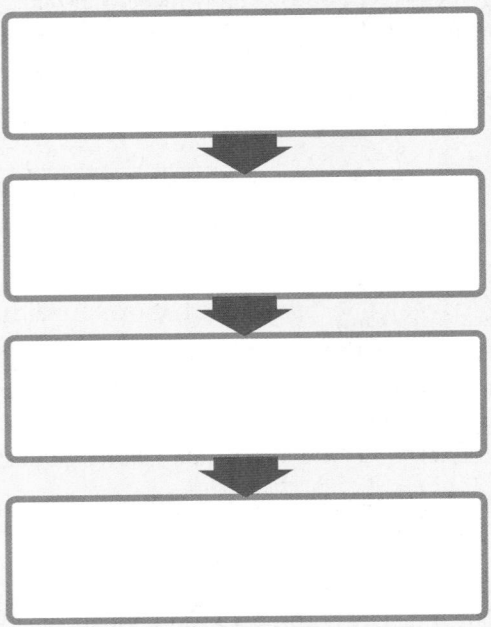

SEQUENCE OF EVENTS

After you complete your draft, have a peer read it and suggest revisions. Then proofread and edit your work for errors in spelling, grammar, and punctuation.

Listening and Speaking

Imagine that George arrives in Granny's room or calls her on the phone. Write and present a monologue in which Granny speaks to George. Keep Granny's character, condition, and situation in mind. As you prepare, ask yourself the following questions:

- What would Granny really want to say to George?
- What would she actually say to him?

THE HARLEM RENAISSANCE

The Bitter Nest, Part II: The Harlem Renaissance Party, c. 1988. Faith Ringgold. Acrylic on canvas with printed, dyed, and pieced fabric, 94 x 83 in. Smithsonian American Art Museum, Washington, DC.

"I, too, am America."

—Langston Hughes, "I, Too"

My City

MEET JAMES WELDON JOHNSON

Both as an artist and an activist, James Weldon Johnson spent his life introducing the United States to the creative voice of African Americans while fighting the racism and the social injustices he believed hindered their progress. For Johnson, writing poetry and fighting for equality served the same goal: winning a respected place in society for African Americans.

Born in Jacksonville, Florida, Johnson grew up in a stable middle-class home and was raised to have an appreciation of the arts and a love of learning. Later, as a student at Atlanta University, he embraced the school's philosophy that educated African Americans should devote their lives to public service—and he did just that.

> "I believe that the richest contributions the Negro poet can make to the American literature of the future will be the fusion into it of his own individual artistic gifts."
>
> —James Weldon Johnson
> "Preface," *The Book of American Negro Poetry*

Born to be a New Yorker In 1900, he and his brother Rosamond composed the spiritual-influenced song "Lift Every Voice and Sing," which would later be referred to as "the Negro National Anthem." Shortly after that, the brothers began writing hit songs for Broadway musicals and the stage. They quickly realized that living in Florida was a disadvantage for that profession, and by 1902 Johnson resigned his post as principal of Stanton School and the brothers relocated to New York City. For Johnson, New York City proved "an alluring world, a tempting world, a world of greatly lessened restraints . . . but, above all, a world of tremendous artistic potentialities."

During the 1920s, Harlem became "the recognized Negro capital," and the passionate innovations in African American music, art, and literature that developed there became known as the Harlem Renaissance. Johnson was involved in the movement not only as an author but also as a mentor of young writers, such as Claude McKay and Langston Hughes. He urged artists to find their inspiration in real-life African American communities. In these artists he saw "a group whose ideals are becoming increasingly more vital than those of the traditionally artistic group, even if its members are less picturesque." In 1922, Johnson published his widely acclaimed anthology, *The Book of American Negro Poetry*.

Devoted to Public Service Though most famous for his literary contributions, Johnson's work outside the creative sphere was equally impressive and, in some ways, groundbreaking. Johnson was the first African American lawyer to be admitted to the bar in Florida, and as a leader in the National Association for the Advancement of Colored People (NAACP), he was instrumental in helping the organization become a national force capable of lobbying in Washington. He played an integral role in bringing attention to the issues of social desegregation and the abolishment of discrimination in housing, education, employment, and voting. Johnson's contributions as a Civil Rights activist, poet, and novelist continue to impact modern society.

James Weldon Johnson was born in 1871 and died in 1938.

Literature Online Author Search For more about James Weldon Johnson, go to www.glencoe.com.

Connecting to the Poem

Do you love the city or town you live in? What would you miss most if you had to leave? In Johnson's poem, he celebrates New York City and what the city means to him. Think about the following questions:

- What is your favorite place? Why?
- How would you feel if you could never visit it again?

Building Background

At the beginning of his literary career, Johnson often modeled his writing after classic poets of the English language—writing in a formal style and using rhymed verse in traditional forms such as the sonnet. "My City" is an example of a Petrarchan sonnet, named for Francesco Petrarca (or Francis Petrarch), the Italian poet who developed the form in the 1300s. During the Harlem Renaissance, Johnson began experimenting with free verse. Inspired by the powerful rhythms of African American preachers, he wrote a collection of poems styled after folk sermons, called *God's Trombones*.

Setting Purposes for Reading

Big Idea The Harlem Renaissance

In "My City," Johnson celebrates Manhattan, the most well-known borough (or administrative unit) of New York City. Harlem is a neighborhood in Manhattan. As you read, note what Johnson's poem suggests about the vitality of the city during the Harlem Renaissance.

Literary Element Sonnet

A **sonnet** is a lyric poem of fourteen lines, typically written in iambic pentameter and usually following strict patterns of stanza division and rhyme. "My City" is a Petrarchan (or Italian) sonnet, which has fourteen lines divided into two stanzas, an eight-line *octave* and a six-line *sestet*. The octave typically sets up a situation or poses a question that is developed or responded to in the sestet. Notice this structure as you read.

- See Literary Terms Handbook, p. R17.

Literature Online Interactive Literary Elements **Handbook** To review or learn more about the literary elements, go to www.glencoe.com.

Reading Strategy Interpreting Imagery

Imagery is the "word pictures" that a writer creates to make the text more vivid or evoke an emotional response. Writers often use sensory details—or descriptions that appeal to the five senses—to create effective images. As you read "My City," note how Johnson's imagery differs in each stanza.

....

Reading Tip: Taking Notes Use a chart like the one below to understand the pattern of imagery in "My City." Record the images in the poem and give your interpretation of how they contribute to the poem's impact.

Image	Impact

Vocabulary

subtle (sə´ təl) *adj.* faint; barely noticeable; not obvious; p. 788 *Although her smirk was subtle, I saw it.*

stark (stärk) *adj.* absolute; complete; p. 788 *Pablo's opinion was in stark contrast to mine.*

unutterable (un ə´ tə rə bəl) *adj.* too deep or great to be put into words; p. 788 *The apprehended thief experienced unutterable regret.*

Vocabulary Tip: Antonyms Antonyms are words that have opposite or nearly opposite meanings. Note that antonyms are always the same part of speech.

INDIANA ACADEMIC STANDARDS (pages 787–789)
11.2 Develop strategies such as...identifying and analyzing structure...

11.3.4 Analyze ways in which poetry...uses imagery...to evoke readers' emotions.

My City

James Weldon Johnson

Fulton and Nostrand, 1958. Jacob Lawrence. Tempera on masonite, 24 x 30 in. Private collection. Courtesy Terry Dintenfass Gallery, New York.

When I come down to sleep death's endless night,
The threshold of the unknown dark to cross,
What to me then will be the keenest loss,
When this bright world blurs on my fading sight?
5 Will it be that no more I shall see the trees
Or smell the flowers or hear the singing birds
Or watch the flashing streams or patient herds?
No. I am sure it will be none of these.

But, ah! Manhattan's sights and sounds, her smells,
10 Her crowds, her throbbing force, the thrill that comes
From being of her a part, her **subtle** spells,
Her shining towers, her avenues, her slums—
O God! the **stark**, **unutterable** pity,
To be dead, and never again behold my city.

Big Idea The Harlem Renaissance *How do you think the speaker feels toward Manhattan's "shining towers" and "slums"?*

Vocabulary

subtle (sə′ təl) *adj.* faint; barely noticeable; not obvious
stark (stärk) *adj.* absolute; complete
unutterable (un ə′ tə rə bəl) *adj.* too deep or great to be put into words

RESPONDING AND THINKING CRITICALLY

Respond

1. How did "My City" make you feel about New York City as it was during the Harlem Renaissance?

Recall and Interpret

2. (a)What question does the speaker pose for himself at the beginning of the poem? (b)Is the speaker's age implied in this question? If so, how?

3. (a)What possible answers to his question does the speaker first explore? (b)Why might he propose these answers?

4. (a)What answer does the speaker finally provide? (b)What reasons does he give? (c)What does this answer tell you about the speaker's personality?

Analyze and Evaluate

5. (a)What, according to the speaker, is "the stark, unutterable pity" (line 13)? (b)Why might the speaker feel this way about the city?

6. (a)How does the rhyme scheme connect to what the poem says? (b)Would the poem have the same effect if it didn't have a rhyme scheme? Explain.

7. (a)A caesura is a pronounced pause in the middle of a line of poetry that is often indicated by punctuation. Where does Johnson use caesuras in the poem? (b)What is the effect of these pauses?

Connect

8. **Big Idea** **The Harlem Renaissance** (a)How does Johnson's poem reflect the general mood of the Harlem Renaissance? (b)Why do you think he titled the poem "My City"?

LITERARY ANALYSIS

Literary Element **Sonnet**

Petrarchan **sonnets** always have two stanzas: an octave and a sestet. The relationship between these two stanzas can vary, however. After the octave establishes the main idea of the poem, the sestet can either further develop that idea or offer a new, even contradictory idea.

1. What relationship do the octave and sestet have in "My City"? Explain.

2. How does the division of this poem into an octave and a sestet contribute to its effectiveness?

Learning for Life

A Brochure of Poetic Places Using a map and tourist information about Manhattan, locate places that match Johnson's descriptions. Then create an illustrated tourism guide for "My City." Before you turn in your guide, share it with another student and ask for feedback on how well it expresses Johnson's love of Manhattan.

Literature Online **Web Activities** For eFlashcards, Selection Quick Checks, and other Web activities, go to www.glencoe.com.

READING AND VOCABULARY

Reading Strategy **Interpreting Imagery**

Johnson uses **imagery** in "My City" not only to evoke the reader's emotions, but also to help the reader understand what the speaker is seeing and feeling. Look at the chart you made as you read.

1. How does the imagery change from the octave to the sestet?

2. How does this change reinforce the meaning of the poem?

Vocabulary Practice

Practice with Antonyms Find the antonym for each vocabulary word from "My City" listed in the first column. Use a dictionary or a thesaurus if you need help.

1. subtle   **a.** obvious   **b.** detailed

2. stark   **a.** incomplete   **b.** plain

3. unutterable   **a.** massive   **b.** explainable

from *Dust Tracks on a Road*

MEET ZORA NEALE HURSTON

In 1973, writer Alice Walker traveled to Fort Pierce, Florida, to visit Zora Neale Hurston's grave. According to Walker, what she found looked "more like an abandoned field" than a cemetery. Walker ordered a headstone to mark Hurston's grave. "I wanted to mark Zora's grave so that one day all our daughters and sons would be able to locate the remains of a human mountain in Florida's and America's so frequently flat terrain," Walker explains.

Introduction to Folklore Zora Neale Hurston grew up in Eatonville, Florida, one of the first incorporated black towns in the United States, where her father was the mayor. Only thirteen years old when her mother died, Hurston spent the next two decades working as a waitress, a manicurist, and a maid, while trying to complete a high school education. Finally she enrolled in Howard University, and later Barnard College. There, she came to the attention of celebrated anthropologist Franz Boas, who invited Hurston to become formally trained as an anthropologist and a folklorist.

After completing her studies, Hurston used her training to collect the folklore of Eatonville and other southern African American communities. She later used this material as a source for much of the fiction writing she pursued when not documenting folklore.

"There is no agony like bearing an untold story inside you."

—Zora Neale Hurston

Literary Success and Obscurity Although considered an important figure in the Harlem Renaissance, Hurston was a fierce individualist who resisted membership in any one school of thought.

She once remarked, "I am so put together that I do not have much of a herd instinct. Or if I must be connected with the flock, let *me* be the shepherd my ownself. That is just the way I am made." Her ideas sometimes got her into trouble with her fellow writers, some of whom felt that documenting the speech and folkways of small-town African Americans could expose the community to ridicule. Over the years Hurston's popularity declined. By the time of her death in a Florida retirement home, she was penniless.

Today, thanks to Walker and other admirers, Hurston's books are widely read. She is remembered for her ability to capture the rich traditions and poetic speech of southern African American culture. Her book *Mules and Men* is recognized as the first history of African American folklore written by an African American, and her most admired novel, *Their Eyes Were Watching God,* has sold more than a million copies since its republication in 1969. Hurston's work is rich in human insights about both community and the individual, and frequently portrays characters with complex longings for a free and wide-ranging way of life. In her autobiography, Hurston recalled, "I used to climb to the top of one of the huge chinaberry trees which guarded our front gate and look out over the world. The most interesting thing I saw was the horizon. . . . It grew upon me that I ought to walk out to the horizon and see what the end of the world was like."

Zora Neale Hurston was born in 1891 and died in 1960.

Literature Online **Author Search** For more about Zora Neale Hurston, go to www.glencoe.com.

Connecting to the Story

Have you ever received a gift that changed your perceptions of another person? As you read this excerpt, think about the following questions:

- What gifts tend to be the most meaningful?
- What can you learn about someone from his or her reactions to a gift?

Building Background

This excerpt takes place about 1900 in Eatonville, Florida. Zora Neale Hurston frequently celebrated the customs and speech of her hometown in her writing. Although the autobiography *Dust Tracks on a Road* is fascinating for what it reveals about Hurston and her background, it conceals much about her life at the same time. Hurston never tells when she was born, never mentions her second marriage, and contradicts details about her life that she wrote about in private letters to friends.

Setting Purposes for Reading

Big Idea The Harlem Renaissance

Although Hurston resisted being defined by any particular literary movement, she participated in New York musical and literary scenes and, with other Harlem intellectuals, helped to create a vibrant culture. Her works were among the first to celebrate Southern African American life. As you read, notice details of Southern life that Hurston considered worthy of recording and celebrating.

Literary Element Voice

The **voice** of a literary work is the distinctive use of language that conveys the author's or narrator's personality to the reader. Voice is determined by elements of style such as word choice and tone. As you read, pay attention to what the narrator's voice reveals about her personality and background.

- See Literary Terms Handbook, p. R19.

Literature Online Interactive Literary Elements Handbook To review or learn more about the literary elements, go to www.glencoe.com.

Reading Strategy Analyzing Language

When you **analyze** a selection, you look at separate parts to see how they work together to produce an underlying meaning. As you read, examine the ways Hurston uses precise, vivid words, dialect (local speech patterns), and regional expressions to create a rich portrait of childhood in Eatonville.

Reading Tip: Reading Slowly When you read material that contains unfamiliar words, phrases, or concepts, slow down your reading rate to aid comprehension.

Vocabulary

brazenness (brā′zən nəs) *n.* defiant behavior; boldness; p. 792 *We laughed at the comic's brazenness when he ridiculed the mayor.*

exalt (ig zôlt′) *v.* to lift up; to put in high spirits; p. 793 *I always exalt the influence of my mother.*

snicker (sni′kər) *n.* a snide, partly suppressed laugh, often expressing disrespect; p. 794 *When the actor forgot his lines, a man in the audience let out a snicker.*

indifferent (in dif′ər ənt) *adj.* lacking feeling or concern; p. 796 *Jim played for the joy of it; he was completely indifferent to whether he won or lost.*

Vocabulary Tip: Analogies Analogies are comparisons that show similarities between two things that are otherwise dissimilar. An analogy can help explain something unfamiliar by comparing it to something familiar.

INDIANA ACADEMIC STANDARDS (pages 791–798)
11.3.3 Analyze...tone...

11.2.2 Analyze the way in which clarity of meaning is affected by...language, and word choice in the text.

ZORA NEALE HURSTON **791**

Harlem Series, no. 28: The Libraries Are Appreciated, 1943. Jacob Lawrence.
Gouache on paper, 14½ x 21¼ in. Philadelphia Museum of Art, PA.

from Dust Tracks on a Road

Zora Neale Hurston

I used to take a seat on top of the gate-post and watch the world go by. One way to Orlando ran past my house, so the carriages and cars would pass before me. The movement made me glad to see it. Often the white travelers would hail[1] me, but more often I hailed them, and asked, "Don't you want me to go a piece of the way with you?" They always did. I know now that I must have caused a great deal of amusement among them, but my self-assurance must have carried the point, for I was always invited to come along. I'd ride up the road for perhaps a half-mile, then walk back. I did not do this with the permission of my parents, nor with their foreknowledge.

When they found out about it later, I usually got a whipping. My grandmother worried about my forward ways a great deal. She had known slavery and to her my **brazenness** was unthinkable.

"Git down offa dat gate-post! You li'l sow, you! Git down! Setting up dere looking dem white folks right in de face! They's gowine[2] to lynch you, yet. And don't stand in dat doorway gazing out at 'em neither. Youse too brazen to live long."

---

1. *Hail* means "to greet."

2. *Gowine* is dialect for "going."

Literary Element   Voice *What does this passage suggest about the young Hurston's personality?*

Vocabulary

brazenness (brā′ zən nəs) *n.* defiant behavior; boldness

Nevertheless, I kept right on gazing at them, and "going a piece of the way" whenever I could make it. The village seemed dull to me most of the time. If the village was singing a chorus, I must have missed the tune.

Perhaps a year before the old man[3] died, I came to know two other white people for myself. They were women.

It came about this way. The whites who came down from the North were often brought by their friends to visit the village school. A Negro school was something strange to them, and while they were always sympathetic and kind, curiosity must have been present, also. They came and went, came and went. Always, the room was hurriedly put in order, and we were threatened with a prompt and bloody death if we cut one caper[4] while the visitors were present. We always sang a spiritual, led by Mr. Calhoun himself. Mrs. Calhoun always stood in the back, with a palmetto switch[5] in her hand as a squelcher. We were all little angels for the duration, because we'd better be. She would cut her eyes[6] and give us a glare that meant trouble, then turn her face towards the visitors and beam as much as to say it was a great privilege and pleasure to teach lovely children like us. They couldn't see that palmetto hickory in her hand behind all those benches, but we knew where our angelic behavior was coming from.

Usually, the visitors gave warning a day ahead and we would be cautioned to put on shoes, comb our heads, and see to ears and fingernails. There was a close inspection of every one of us before we marched in that morning. Knotty heads, dirty ears and fingernails got hauled out of line, strapped and sent home to lick the calf[7] over again.

This particular afternoon, the two young ladies just popped in. Mr. Calhoun was flustered,[8] but he put on the best show he could. He dismissed the class that he was teaching up at the front of the room, then called the fifth grade in reading. That was my class.

So we took our readers and went up front. We stood up in the usual line, and opened to the lesson. It was the story of Pluto and Persephone.[9] It was new and hard to the class in general, and Mr. Calhoun was very uncomfortable as the readers stumbled along, spelling out words with their lips, and in mumbling undertones before they exposed them experimentally to the teacher's ears.

Then it came to me. I was fifth or sixth down the line. The story was not new to me, because I had read my reader through from lid to lid, the first week that Papa had bought it for me.

That is how it was that my eyes were not in the book, working out the paragraph which I knew would be mine by counting the children ahead of me. I was observing our visitors, who held a book between them, following the lesson. They had shiny hair, mostly brownish. One had a looping gold chain around her neck. The other one was dressed all over in black and white with a pretty finger ring on her left hand. But the thing that held my eyes were their fingers. They were long and thin, and very white, except up near the tips. There they were baby pink. I had never seen such hands. It was a fascinating discovery for me. I wondered how they felt. I would have given those hands more attention, but the child before me was almost through. My turn next, so I got on my mark, bringing my eyes back to the book and made sure of my place. Some of the stories I had re-read several times, and this Greco-Roman myth was one of my favorites. I was **exalted** by it, and that is the way I read my paragraph.

---

3. The *old man*, a white farmer who was a friend of Hurston's family, took Zora Neale fishing and gave her advice.
4. *Cut one caper* is slang for "play a trick or prank" or "behave extravagantly or noisily."
5. A *palmetto switch*, a whip used for discipline, was made from the flexible stem of a leaf from a palmetto palm.
6. *Cut her eyes* is slang for "look at with scorn or contempt."
7. *Lick the calf* is slang for "get cleaned up."

Big Idea The Harlem Renaissance *What do these details reveal about the United States at the time?*

Reading Strategy Analyzing Language *Why does the author include phrases such as "lick the calf"?*

8. *Flustered* means "nervous" or "agitated."
9. The myth of *Pluto and Persephone* (pər sefʹə nē) explains the origin of the seasons. Pluto is god of the underworld, and Persephone is his wife.

Literary Element Voice *What does the use of the word "exalted" convey about the feelings the myth stirs in the young Hurston?*

Vocabulary

exalt (ig zôltʹ) *v.* to lift up; to put in high spirits

"Yes, Jupiter[10] had seen her (Persephone). He had seen the maiden picking flowers in the field. He had seen the chariot of the dark monarch pause by the maiden's side. He had seen him when he seized Persephone. He had seen the black horses leap down Mount Aetna's[11] fiery throat. Persephone was now in Pluto's dark realm and he had made her his wife."

The two women looked at each other and then back to me. Mr. Calhoun broke out with a proud smile beneath his bristly moustache, and instead of the next child taking up where I had ended, he nodded to me to go on. So I read the story to the end, where flying Mercury, the messenger of the Gods, brought Persephone back to the sunlit earth and restored her to the arms of Dame Ceres, her mother, that the world might have springtime and summer flowers, autumn and harvest. But because she had bitten the pomegranate while in Pluto's kingdom, she must return to him for three months of each year, and be his queen. Then the world had winter, until she returned to earth.

The class was dismissed and the visitors smiled us away and went into a low-voiced conversation with Mr. Calhoun for a few minutes. They glanced my way once or twice and I began to worry. Not only was I barefooted, but my feet and legs were dusty. My hair was more uncombed than usual, and my nails were not shiny clean. Oh, I'm going to catch it now. Those ladies saw me, too. Mr. Calhoun is promising to 'tend to me. So I thought.

Then Mr. Calhoun called me. I went up thinking how awful it was to get a whipping before company. Furthermore, I heard a **snicker** run over the room. Hennie Clark and Stell Brazzle did it out loud, so I would be sure to hear them. The smart-aleck was going to get it. I slipped one hand behind me and switched my dress tail at them, indicating scorn.

"Come here, Zora Neale," Mr. Calhoun cooed as I reached the desk. He put his hand on my shoulder and gave me little pats. The ladies smiled and held out those flower-looking fingers towards me. I seized the opportunity for a good look.

"Shake hands with the ladies, Zora Neale," Mr. Calhoun prompted and they took my hand one after the other and smiled. They asked me if I loved school, and I lied that I did. There was *some* truth in it, because I liked geography and reading, and I liked to play at recess time. Whoever it was invented writing and arithmetic got no thanks from me. Neither did I like the arrangement where the teacher could sit up there with a palmetto stem and lick me whenever he saw fit. I hated things I couldn't do anything about. But I knew better than to bring that up right there, so I said yes, I *loved* school.

"I can tell you do," Brown Taffeta gleamed. She patted my head, and was lucky enough not to get sandspurs[12] in her hand. Children who roll and tumble in the grass in Florida are apt to get sandspurs in their hair. They shook hands with me again and I went back to my seat.

When school let out at three o'clock, Mr. Calhoun told me to wait. When everybody had gone, he told me I was to go to the Park House, that was the hotel in Maitland, the next afternoon to call upon Mrs. Johnstone and Miss Hurd. I must tell Mama to see that I was clean and brushed from head to feet, and I must wear shoes and stockings. The ladies liked me, he said, and I must be on my best behavior.

The next day I was let out of school an hour early, and went home to be stood up in a tub of suds and be scrubbed and have my ears dug into. My sandy hair sported a red ribbon to match my red and white checked gingham dress, starched until it could stand alone. Mama saw to it that my shoes were on the right feet, since I was careless about left and right. Last thing, I was given a handkerchief to carry, warned again about my behavior, and sent off, with my big brother John to go as far as the hotel gate with me.

---

10. In Roman mythology, *Jupiter* is king of the gods and Pluto's brother.
11. *Mount Aetna* (et′nə) (also spelled *Etna*) is a volcano in eastern Sicily, Italy.

Vocabulary

snicker (sni′kər) *n.* a snide, partly suppressed laugh, often expressing disrespect

---

12. *Sandspurs* (also called *sandburs*) are spiny burs that grow on a grass of the same name.

Big Idea The Harlem Renaissance *What kinds of details about the old southern way of life does the author celebrate?*

Gwendolyn, 1918. John Sloan. Oil on canvas, 24 x 20 in. Smithsonian American Art Museum, Washington, DC.

Viewing the Art: How does the girl in the painting compare with your picture of the girl in the story? Support your response.

First thing, the ladies gave me strange things, like stuffed dates and preserved ginger, and encouraged me to eat all that I wanted. Then they showed me their Japanese dolls and just talked. I was then handed a copy of *Scribner's Magazine*, and asked to read a place that was pointed out to me. After a paragraph or two, I was told with smiles, that that would do.

I was led out on the grounds and they took my picture under a palm tree. They handed me what was to me then a heavy cylinder done up in fancy paper, tied with a ribbon, and they told me good-bye, asking me not to open it until I got home.

My brother was waiting for me down by the lake, and we hurried home, eager to see what was in the thing. It was too heavy to be candy or anything like that. John insisted on toting it for me.

My mother made John give it back to me and let me open it. Perhaps, I shall never experience such joy again. The nearest thing to that moment was the telegram accepting my first book. One hundred goldy-new pennies rolled out of the cylinder. Their gleam lit up the world. It was not avarice[13] that moved me. It was the beauty of the thing. I stood on the mountain. Mama let me play with my pennies for a while, then put them away for me to keep.

That was only the beginning. The next day I received an Episcopal hymn-book bound in white leather with a golden cross stamped into the front cover, a copy of The Swiss Family Robinson, and a book of fairy tales.

I set about to commit the song words to memory. There was no music written there, just the words. But there was to my consciousness music in between them just the same. "When I survey the Wondrous Cross" seemed the most beautiful to me, so I committed that to memory first of all. Some of them seemed dull and without life, and I pretended they were not there. If white people liked trashy singing like that, there must be something funny about them that I had not noticed before. I stuck to the pretty ones where the words marched to a throb I could feel.

A month or so after the two young ladies returned to Minnesota, they sent me a huge box packed with clothes and books. The red coat with a wide circular collar and the red tam pleased me more than any of the other things. My chums pretended not to like anything that I had, but even then I knew that they were jealous. Old Smarty had gotten by them again. The clothes were not new, but they were very good. I shone like the morning sun.

---

13. *Avarice* is greed, or excessive desire for wealth.

Reading Strategy Analyzing Language *How would you characterize the language in this passage?*

Literary Element Voice *What does Hurston's choice of words suggest about her faith in her own sense of judgment?*

But the books gave me more pleasure than the clothes. I had never been too keen on dressing up. It called for hard scrubbings with Octagon soap suds getting in my eyes, and none too gentle fingers scrubbing my neck and gouging in my ears.

In that box were Gulliver's Travels, Grimm's Fairy Tales, Dick Whittington, Greek and Roman Myths, and best of all, Norse Tales. Why did the Norse tales strike so deeply into my soul? I do not know, but they did. I seemed to remember seeing Thor[14] swing his mighty short-handled hammer as he sped across the sky in rumbling thunder, lightning flashing from the tread of his steeds and the wheels of his chariot. The great and good Odin,[15] who went down to the well of knowledge to drink, and was told that the price of a drink from that fountain was an eye. Odin drank deeply, then plucked out one eye without a murmur and handed it to the grizzly keeper, and walked away. That held majesty for me.

Of the Greeks, Hercules moved me most. I followed him eagerly on his tasks. The story of the choice of Hercules as a boy when he met Pleasure and Duty, and put his hand in that of Duty and followed her steep way to the blue hills of fame and glory, which she pointed out at the end, moved me profoundly. I resolved[16] to be like him. The tricks and turns of the other Gods and Goddesses left me cold. There were other thin books about this and that sweet and gentle little girl who gave up her heart to Christ and good works. Almost always they died from it, preaching as they passed.[17] I was utterly **indifferent** to their deaths. In the first place I could not conceive of death, and in the next place they never had any funerals that amounted to a hill of beans, so I didn't care how soon they rolled up their big, soulful, blue eyes and kicked the bucket. They had no meat on their bones.

But I also met Hans Andersen and Robert Louis Stevenson. They seemed to know what I wanted to hear and said it in a way that tingled me. Just a little below these friends was Rudyard Kipling in his Jungle Books. I loved his talking snakes as much as I did the hero.

I came to start reading the Bible through my mother. She gave me a licking one afternoon for repeating something I had overheard a neighbor telling her. She locked me in her room after the whipping, and the Bible was the only thing in there for me to read. I happened to open to the place where David[18] was doing some mighty smiting,[19] and I got interested. David went here and he went there, and no matter where he went, he smote 'em hip and thigh. Then he sung songs to his harp awhile, and went out and smote some more. Not one time did David stop and preach about sins and things. All David wanted to know from God was who to kill and when. He took care of the other details himself. Never a quiet moment. I liked him a lot. So I read a great deal more in the Bible, hunting for some more active people like David. Except for the beautiful language of Luke and Paul,[20] the New Testament still plays a poor second to the Old Testament for me. The Jews had a God who laid about[21] Him when they needed Him. I could see no use waiting till Judgment Day to see a man who was just crying for a good killing, to be told to go and roast.[22] My idea was to give him a good killing first, and then if he got roasted later on, so much the better. ❧

---

14. In Norse mythology, *Thor* is the god of thunder. His magical hammer returns to him like a boomerang after being thrown.
15. *Odin* (ō´din), the father of Thor, is the supreme god in Norse mythology and the creator of the first man and woman. Odin traded an eye for a drink from the well of wisdom, which was guarded by a giant.
16. *Resolved* means "decided."
17. *Passed* is short for "passed on" or "passed away" and means "died."

18. *David* was the second king of Judah and Israel. He killed the giant Goliath.
19. *Smiting* means "striking hard, as with a hand or a weapon, so as to cause serious injury or death."
20. *Luke* and *Paul* were authors of much of the New Testament of the Christian Bible.
21. *Laid about* means "hit out in all directions."
22. *Roast* is slang for "burn in hell."

Reading Strategy Analyzing Language *Why is the language in this passage humorous?*

Literary Element Voice *What do you infer about Hurston from the language in this passage?*

RESPONDING AND THINKING CRITICALLY

Respond

1. How did you react to the narrator? Cite passages to support your response.

Recall and Interpret

2. (a)What does the young Hurston do at the beginning of the selection? (b)What does this action tell you about her character?

3. (a)How do the teachers and students react to the white visitors? (b)Why do you think they behave this way?

4. (a)Which gifts from the white women does Hurston enjoy most? (b)What do those gifts provide for her that the other gifts do not?

Analyze and Evaluate

5. In your opinion, does Hurston do a good job of portraying the setting (the time and place) in which she grew up? Explain.

6. Think back to what you were like in the fifth grade. Do you think Hurston accurately recreates the thoughts of a fifth grader? Support your answer with examples.

7. (a)When Hurston reads aloud from the story of Persephone, what does she reveal about her personality and abilities? (b)Where else in the selection does she reveal these traits? Explain the overall impression of Hurston that you received.

Connect

8. Big Idea **The Harlem Renaissance**
The Harlem Renaissance emphasized the value of African Americans' contributions to the country as a whole. How is this emphasis reflected in the selection? Explain.

LITERARY ANALYSIS

Literary Element Voice

In *Dust Tracks on a Road,* key information about the author is conveyed through the narrator's **voice.** For instance, when Hurston writes, "If the village was singing a chorus, I must have missed the tune," the wit and informality of the language suggest an opinionated girl with common sense. Hurston's distinctive voice also affects the work's tone, plot, and setting.

1. How would you describe Hurston's voice in this selection? Explain.

2. What tone, or attitude toward her subject matter, did the voice allow Hurston to convey? Explain.

Review: Allusion

An **allusion** is a reference in a work of literature to a character, place, or situation from history or from music, art, or another work of literature.

Partner Activity Hurston makes an allusion to a figure in the Bible named David, a shepherd boy who grows up to become the king of Israel. In one of his many exploits, David kills the giant Goliath with a single stone fired from a sling. With a partner, reread the final paragraph of the selection. Make a web like the one below to show the character traits young Hurston may have felt she had in common with David.

Reading Strategy Analyzing Language

Hurston specialized in using colloquial, or everyday, language to bring to life the customs, geography, feelings, and way of speaking of the people she was writing about. In *Dust Tracks on a Road*, the inclusion of colorful regional expressions and local dialect lends the narration a powerful authenticity.

1. List examples of dialect or regional expressions that Hurston uses to evoke the people of Eatonville.

2. What ideas about or impressions of Eatonville do you glean from these examples? Explain.

Vocabulary Practice

Practice with Analogies Complete each analogy below using vocabulary words from *Dust Tracks on a Road*. Use a dictionary if you need help.

1. shyness : brazenness :: calmness :
   a. timidness **b.** serenity **c.** turbulence

2. snicker : laugh :: smirk :
   a. giggle **b.** grin **c.** frown

3. exalt : celebration :: weep :
   a. contest **b.** trial **c.** funeral

4. indifferent : fascinated :: ignorant :
   a. enlightened **b.** aggravated **c.** inundated

Academic Vocabulary

Here are two words from the vocabulary list on page R86. These words will help you think, write, and talk about the selection.

range (rānj) *n.* extent to which or limits between which something varies

complex (com´pleks) *adj.* difficult to understand, analyze, or execute

Practice and Apply

1. In *Dust Tracks on a Road*, what was the **range** of the narrator's reading by the time she had finished her first week in fifth grade?

2. What **complex** story did the young speaker read several paragraphs of aloud for the white visitors?

Writing About Literature

Analyze Cultural Context The **context** of a work is the overall environment that surrounds it. In this selection, the context is the United States in the early years of the last century, when Hurston was growing up. What do you learn about Eatonville within this larger context? Discuss your answer in a brief essay, explaining how Hurston's language, characters, and the events she describes contribute to your ideas about Eatonville.

Before you draft, use a graphic like the one below to organize your analysis. Include any additional elements that you feel are significant. Refer to the organizer as you draft to keep on track.

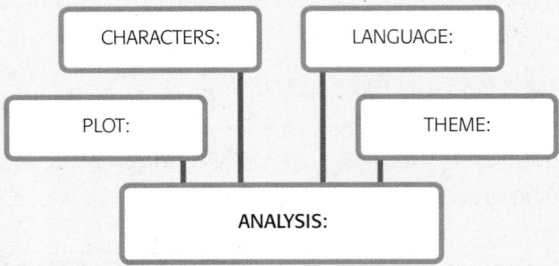

After you complete your draft, meet with a partner. Exchange drafts and suggest revisions. Then proofread and edit your draft for errors in spelling, grammar, and punctuation.

Literature Groups

Evaluating an Autobiography Critics have complained that Hurston's autobiography is not always factual. In a small group, discuss the following: Does it matter to you if Hurston's autobiography is absolutely true or not? What reasons might a writer have for distorting the facts in his or her autobiography? Do you think these are valid reasons? Why or why not? Share your conclusions with the class.

Literature Online **Web Activities** For eFlashcards, Selection Quick Checks, and other Web activities, go to www.glencoe.com.

Vocabulary Workshop

Word Meanings

Understanding Homonyms

"Often the white travelers would hail me, but more often I hailed them, and asked, 'Don't you want me to go a piece of the way with you?'"

Connecting to Literature Homonyms are words that sound alike but have different meanings and sometimes different spellings. They can also be different parts of speech. For example, the words *hail* and *hale* are homonyms. Consider Zora Neale Hurston's use of the word *hail* in the quote from *Dust Tracks on a Road* above. We know from the context that here *hail* is a verb and means "to greet someone." The word *hail* as a noun means "pellets of ice."

The English language is full of homonyms. Here is a sample list.

Word	Meaning	Example
bear bear	an animal to endure	The brown *bear* came dangerously close to our campsite. The entire team must *bear* the burden of defeat
bank bank	a mound or border a place where money is kept	We stood on the river's *bank* and watched the swift current. My *bank* informed me that my account was overdrawn.
break brake	to crack, split, or smash to stop a movement	Enslaved people endeavored to *break* their bonds. The negligent driver failed to *brake* for the pedestrian.
hear here	to listen in this place	In the village, we could *hear* the pealing of church bells. I am resolved to remain *here* until I am evicted.
piece peace	a part of something tranquility	I completed the last *piece* of the puzzle. In the midst of war, people long for *peace*.
holy wholly holey	sacred completely full of holes	The pilgrims consider the shrine to be *holy*. I am not *wholly* convinced of your arguments. My *holey* socks are in need of repair.

Exercise

Choose the correct homonym to fit each sentence. Consult a dictionary if you need help.

1. The angler tried to (real, reel) in the fish.
2. The lion is the (main, mane) attraction at the zoo.
3. Most graduates considered the commencement speaker to be a (boar, bore).
4. This is a perfect (sight, site, cite) for the new museum.
5. The (scent, cent, sent) of exotic spices emanated from the Indian restaurant.
6. Upon his release, the prisoner told a (tail, tale) of woe.
7. Coffee is one of the (principle, principal) exports of Colombia.
8. On a dark (knight, night), I lost my way.
9. The new student was intimidated by the hostile (stares, stairs) of the class.
10. The teacher could not be heard in the back of the room because he was a little (horse, hoarse).

▶ **Test-Taking Tip**

To determine the meaning of a homonym, use context clues. The part of speech can sometimes help you understand the intended meaning.

▶ **Reading Handbook**

For more about homonyms, see Reading Handbook, p. R20.

Literature Online
eFlashcards For eFlashcards and other vocabulary activities, go to www.glencoe.com.

ACADEMIC STANDARDS (page 799)
11.1.2 Draw inferences about the meaning of vocabulary in literature or other subject areas.

799

If We Must Die and The Tropics in New York

MEET CLAUDE MCKAY

Some critics have identified the publication of "If We Must Die" in 1919 as the spark that ignited the Harlem Renaissance. Though he was not an innovator in modern verse—his sonnets were strongly influenced by British literary traditions—McKay's focus on the African American experience distinguished him as a new, outspoken voice in American literature. The poets of the Harlem Renaissance, such as Langston Hughes and Countee Cullen, hailed McKay as a leader because of his frank approach to racial and social issues in his work.

McKay was born and educated in rural Jamaica. His brother Uriah Theophilus, a schoolteacher, and Englishman Walter Jekyll, a British scholar collecting Jamaican folklore, encouraged McKay's creativity. With access to their books, McKay read Victorian authors, as well as the medieval Italian writer Dante and the French poet Baudelaire.

Culture Shock After winning an award for his poetry in 1912, McKay used the money to come to the United States. McKay was drawn to this country, seeing it as "a new land to which all people who had youth and a youthful mind turned," and believing that "surely there would be opportunity in this land, even for a Negro." However, when McKay arrived, he was shocked by the blatant racism and violence he found, and he spent much of his life looking for ways to counter the "ignoble cruelty" of racism through his poetry and his actions.

McKay admired poets who wrote about their own struggles in society, and he strove to do the same in his own writing: "In their poetry I could feel their race, their class, their roots in the soil . . . I could not feel the reality of them without that. So likewise I could not realize myself writing without conviction." A later work, *Home to Harlem*, follows a protagonist, Jake, through Jazz-Age Harlem, as he explores its seedy cabarets, poolrooms, and dining cars. With its focus on the racial and social realities of the United States, *Home to Harlem* reached the best seller list— the first novel by an African American to do so.

> "All my life I have been a troubadour wanderer, nourishing myself mainly on the poetry of existence. And all I offer here is the distilled poetry of my experience."
>
> —Claude McKay

Lost and Then Found McKay truly represented the spirit of the "New Negro." Through his poem "If We Must Die," he captured a universal sentiment of resistance in the face of injustice. So universal was this theme that Winston Churchill quoted the poem to rally the British people during World War II.

By the time of his death, McKay had become virtually unknown. It was only years later that he was rediscovered and fully recognized for his achievements. In 1973 author Jean Wagner concluded that "McKay remains beyond a doubt the immediate forerunner and one of the leading forces of the Renaissance, the man without whom it could never have achieved what it did."

Claude McKay was born in 1890 and died in 1948.

Literature Online Author Search For more about Claude McKay, go to www.glencoe.com.

Connecting to the Poems

Have you or has someone you know ever faced prejudice? In "If We Must Die," Claude McKay advocates facing hatred with courage. As you read, consider the following questions:

- What is the best response to prejudice?
- What different purposes can heroism serve?

Building Background

"If We Must Die" reflects the atmosphere of racial strife in the United States just after World War I. During the summer of 1919, McKay worked as a waiter in a railroad dining car, and he and his coworkers feared being attacked. As McKay later wrote, "We were less light-hearted. We did not separate from one another gaily to spend ourselves in speakeasies or gambling joints. . . . We stayed in our quarters all through the dreary ominous nights, for we never knew what was going to happen. It was during those days that the sonnet, 'If We Must Die,' exploded out of me. And for it the Negro people unanimously hailed me as a poet."

Setting Purposes for Reading

Big Idea The Harlem Renaissance

As you read McKay's poems, pay attention to the different ways in which the two poems address the social and cultural challenges faced by African Americans at the time of the Harlem Renaissance.

Literary Element Meter

Meter is the regular pattern of stressed (´) and unstressed (˘) syllables that gives a line of poetry a predictable rhythm. The basic unit of meter is the foot, and the length of a metrical line can be expressed in terms of the number of feet it contains. Notice how McKay uses meter in both "If We Must Die" and "The Tropics in New York."

- See Literary Terms Handbook, p. R11.

Literature Online Interactive Literary Elements **Handbook** To review or learn more about the literary elements, go to www.glencoe.com.

Reading Strategy Analyzing Tone

Tone is an author's attitude toward his or her subject matter. Authors convey tone through word choice, punctuation, sentence structure, and figures of speech. The poems "If We Must Die" and "The Tropics in New York" have extremely different tones.

Reading Tip: Comparing and Contrasting
Use a chart to note the elements in each poem that contribute to the tone.

	"If We Must Die"	"The Tropics in New York"
Elements	• simile—"like hogs hunted and penned" • •	• • •
Tone		

Vocabulary

nobly (nō´ blē) adv. with superior morals or character; p. 802 *The businessman nobly gave his fortune to the poor.*

constrained (kən strānd´) v. forced or limited; p. 802 *In the 1800s strict laws constrained African Americans and women from voting.*

kinsmen (kinz´ men) n. those who share the same racial or cultural background as another; p. 802 *Although not brothers by birth, the two friends were kinsmen by culture.*

benediction (ben´ ə dik´ shən) n. a blessing or something that fosters goodness; p. 803 *The homeless shelter was a benediction for the men and women who needed it.*

INDIANA ACADEMIC STANDARDS (pages 801–804)
11.2 Develop strategies such as...analyzing structure...
11.3.3 Analyze the ways in which...tone...achieve[s] specific... aesthetic (artistic) purposes...
11.5.2 Write responses to literature...

Two Heads, 1946. Charles White. Watercolor, 16¾ x 24¼ in. Collection of Martin & Sondra Sperber, New York. Courtesy Heritage Gallery, Los Angeles, CA.

If We Must Die

Claude McKay

If we must die, let it not be like hogs
Hunted and penned in an inglorious[1] spot,
While round us bark the mad and hungry dogs,
Making their mock at our accursed[2] lot.
5   If we must die, O let us **nobly** die,
So that our precious blood may not be shed
In vain; then even the monsters we defy
Shall be **constrained** to honor us though dead!
O **kinsmen**! we must meet the common foe!
10 Though far outnumbered let us show us brave,
And for their thousand blows deal one deathblow!
What though before us lies the open grave?
Like men we'll face the murderous, cowardly pack,
Pressed to the wall, dying, but fighting back!

---

1. *Inglorious* means "shameful" or "disgraceful."
2. *Accursed* (ə kur´ sid) means "being under a curse" or "doomed."

Reading Strategy   Analyzing Tone   *What tone does McKay establish here? What type of words does he use to achieve this?*

Vocabulary

nobly (nō´ blē) *adv.* with superior morals or character
constrained (kən strānd´) *v.* forced or limited
kinsmen (kinz´ men) *n.* those who share the same racial or cultural background as another

The Tropics in New York

Claude McKay

Bananas ripe and green, and ginger-root,
  Cocoa in pods and alligator pears,
And tangerines and mangoes and grape fruit,
  Fit for the highest prize at parish fairs,

5 Set in the window, bringing memories
  Of fruit-trees laden by low-singing rills,
And dewy dawns, and mystical blue skies
  In **benediction** over nun-like hills.

My eyes grew dim, and I could no more gaze;
10 A wave of longing through my body swept,
And, hungry for the old, familiar ways,
  I turned aside and bowed my head and wept.

Big Idea The Harlem Renaissance *How does this detail reflect the African American experience during the Harlem Renaissance?*

Vocabulary

benediction (ben′ ə dik′ shən) *n.* a blessing or something that fosters goodness

RESPONDING AND THINKING CRITICALLY

Respond

1. (a)Which images from the poems stand out in your mind? (b)What effects do these images have on you?

Recall and Interpret

2. (a)In "If We Must Die," what two animals does the speaker name? Which animals are the hunters, and which are the hunted? (b)With which animals does the speaker identify? Explain.

3. (a)How does the speaker want his kinsmen to behave? (b)Why is this important to him?

4. (a)In "The Tropics in New York," what does the speaker see in the window? (b)What memories does that sight bring?

5. (a)How does the speaker react when he recalls his homeland? (b)Why might he have this reaction?

Analyze and Evaluate

6. Some critics believe the publication of "If We Must Die" marked the beginning of the Harlem Renaissance. Why might this poem have led to such a creative outpouring?

7. In "The Tropics in New York," how does McKay use sensory details to convey his meaning? Explain.

8. "The Tropics in New York" is broken into three stanzas. What does each of the stanzas present? Why do you think McKay chose to organize the poem in this way?

Connect

9. **Big Idea** **The Harlem Renaissance** The thinkers, writers, and artists of the Harlem Renaissance struggled with problems of racism and identity. (a)What lesson about racism does McKay present in "If We Must Die"? (b)What message about identity is implied in "The Tropics in New York"?

LITERARY ANALYSIS

Literary Element **Meter**

The metrical foot that McKay uses in both poems is the iamb, consisting of one unstressed syllable followed by one stressed syllable, as in the word *divide*. Most lines have five iambic feet, or beats, forming the meter known as **iambic pentameter.**

1. How regular is McKay's use of iambic pentameter in these two poems?

2. How does the meter's effect differ in these poems?

Writing About Literature

Evaluate Sound Devices Writers use sound devices to enhance the sense of rhythm, to emphasize particular sounds, or to add a musical quality to their writing. Examples of sound devices are alliteration, assonance, consonance, onomatopoeia, and rhyme. Write a brief essay comparing the sound devices used in these two poems.

Literature Online **Web Activities** For eFlashcards, Selection Quick Checks, and other Web activities, go to www.glencoe.com.

READING AND VOCABULARY

Reading Strategy **Tone**

The subject matter of these two poems is extremely different, and McKay uses a different **tone** in each to convey that subject matter.

1. Look at the chart you created as you read the poems. What words or images helped you understand the tone of each poem?

2. How would you describe the tone in each poem?

Vocabulary **Practice**

Practice with Word Origins Match each word with the meaning of its root. Use a dictionary for assistance.

1. nobly   a. "to constrict"

2. kinsmen   b. "notable"

3. constrained   c. "to speak well"

4. benediction   d. "birth or race"

Media Link to African American Culture

Preview the Article

In "Stanzas from a Black Epic," the author describes how Harlem artist Jacob Lawrence depicted the Great Migration, the mass movement of African Americans from the South to the North during the early 1900s.

1. Examine the title. What might the author mean by a "black epic"?

2. Look at the paintings on pages 806–808. What can you predict about the content of the article from these images?

Set a Purpose for Reading

Read to learn how a Harlem artist viewed the African American experience.

Reading Strategy

Scanning Text to Find Specific Information Scanning is the process of searching quickly through text for a particular fact. When you scan text, your eyes sweep across a page in search of key words and specific information.

Scan the article for the key words *Harlem* and *painting*. What do you learn about these topics? Use a graphic organizer to record information.

Word	Information
Harlem	Lawrence—younger than and different from Harlem Renaissance artists

ACADEMIC STANDARDS (pages 805–808)
11.2.1 Analyze...the features...of different types of public documents...

TIME

STANZAS FROM A BLACK EPIC

The 60 paintings in Jacob Lawrence's great *Migration* series present piercing images of the African American experience

By ROBERT HUGHES

THE SIXTY PAINTINGS THAT MAKE UP JACOB LAWRENCE'S *Migration* series are works that anyone interested in African American cultural history—or, in a wider way, the story of American painting as a whole—should see.

More than 60 years have passed since Lawrence made these little pictures, on store-bought panels in his Harlem studio; and they are of far greater power than almost all the acreage of Works Progress Administration (WPA) murals that preceded them in the 1930s. They were almost immediately bought, half by the Phillips Collection in Washington, D.C., and half by the Museum of Modern Art (MOMA) in New York City, and were in fact the first paintings by a black artist to enter MOMA's collection. It seemed to the directors of both museums that Lawrence's series represented a unique combination of African American experience, history painting, and a modernist style. They were right. From Benjamin West to Robert Rauschenberg, American art is sown with attempts, varying between saccharine sentimentality and stunning success, to image forth the American story. And for reasons that are sadly obvious, few of these were created by African Americans, until Lawrence appeared.

Younger than the painters and writers who took part in the Harlem Renaissance of the 1920s, Lawrence was also at an angle to them: He was not interested in the kind of idealized portrayals of African Americans that others tended to produce. These fake-primitive images were being created as an antidote to the vile stereotypes with which white popular art had flooded the culture since Reconstruction. Nevertheless, Lawrence gained self-confidence from the cultural climate of

Harlem—in particular, from Alain Locke, a Harvard-trained art critic. Locke believed strongly that art created by African Americans could speak explicitly to their community and still embody the values of modernism. Or, in Locke's words: "There is in truly great art no essential conflict between racial or national traits and universal human values."

The Great Migration

What are the paintings about? A huge subject, which no artist could touch and only an African American one could have handled with the depth of feeling it required. The migration of African Americans from the rural South to the industrial North, as it unfolded in the first decades of the 20th century, had an epic character. It was a collective Odyssey to match the Iliad of the Civil War. This migration was forced by the merciless Southern white reaction that came in the wake of Reconstruction. The African American population—all poor, nearly all rural—of the Southern states was plunged into a hell where their rights were abolished.

In the South, 1900 to 1925 brought the high tide of Jim Crow laws, lynchings, and the terrorism of the Ku Klux Klan. Unable to vote, powerless to change their political status, Southern blacks voted with their feet. By the end of the 1930s more than a million of them (the exact figures will probably never be known) had flocked to mid-Atlantic, Northeastern, and Midwestern cities, looking for a better America than the one they had known. Some of them no doubt imagined they were going to a promised land; and in this they were sharply disappointed, especially after 1929, when they arrived in a North economically devastated by the Depression. But there was no way back. The South was drained of its black workforce, while the North acquired a new one. From these

The Female Workers Were the Last to Arrive North Pane #57 from the *Migration* series by Jacob Lawrence. The Phillips Collection, Washington, DC.

migrants grew a radically altered conception of African American culture: distinctively urban but still Southern in its origins and collective memory. This was the culture that produced the Harlem Renaissance. In it, African Americans reinvented themselves.

A Harlem Education

Born in Atlantic City, New Jersey, in 1917, Lawrence was schooled in Harlem and grew up among migrants and their children. When, years later, he told an interviewer that "I am the black community," he was neither bragging nor kidding. He trained as a painter at the Harlem Art Workshop, inside the public library's 135th Street branch. Indeed the library itself, with its Schomburg Collection, Manhattan's chief archive on African American life and history, was to shape his series. Lawrence did months of painstaking research there to get the historical background right, even though the final paintings rarely allude to specific events. He took on the task with a youthful earnestness (he was in his early 20s) that remains one of the most touching aspects of the final work and goes far beyond self-expressiveness. You sense that something is speaking through Lawrence.

One of the remarkable things about the *Migration* series is the language it does not use. Lawrence was not a propagandist. He avoided the caricatures used in Popular Front, Social Realist art, then at its peak in America. Considering the violence and suffering of so much of his subject matter—prisons, deserted communities, city slums, race riots, labor camps—his images are restrained, and all the more piercing. When he painted a lynching, for instance (No. 15), he left out the dangling body and the jeering crowd: there is only bare earth, a branch, an empty noose, and the huddled lump of a grieving woman. He set aside the muralist influence that lay so heavily on other artists—he wasn't painting murals but images closer in size to single pages, no more than 18 inches by 12 inches.

Painting an Epic

Nevertheless, Lawrence imagined the paintings as integrally connected—a single work of art, no less united than a mural is, but portable. The *Migration* series has the effect of a visual ballad, with each painting a stanza: taut, compressed, pared down to the barest requirements of narration. Number 10, *They Were Very Poor*, takes the elements of a Southern sharecropper's life down to the static minimum. It shows a man and a woman staring at empty bowls on a bare brown plane and an empty basket hung on the wall by an enormous nail—the sort of nail you imagine in a crucifixion. There is no trace of sentimentality. Lawrence called his style "dynamic Cubism," and its debt to late Cubism is obvious—the flat, sharp overlaps of form, legible silhouettes, and generally high degree of abstraction in the color. Yet, his style also tends to an Egyptian stillness, friezelike even when you know the subject was in motion, like the crowd surging into the narrow slot between two railroad cars in Number 23, "And the Migration Spread."

They Were Very Poor Panel 10 from the *Migration* series by Jacob Lawrence. The Museum of Modern Art/Licensed by SCALA/Art Resource, New York.

And the Migration Spread Panel 23 from the *Migration* series by Jacob Lawrence. The Phillips Collection, Washington, DC.

Lawrence's style gives his pictures a solid gravity. His dense and well-locked compositions are prime illustrations of the permanence and resistance that are his key themes. These themes are integral to the African Americans depicted throughout Lawrence's *Migration* series—the first, and arguably still the best, treatment of the African American historical experience by an African American artist.

**—Updated 2006,
from TIME, December 6, 1993**

RESPONDING AND THINKING CRITICALLY

Respond

1. How do you react to the paintings of Jacob Lawrence?

Recall and Interpret

2. (a)What was the Great Migration? (b)How do Lawrence's paintings show this event?

3. (a)Name four or more subjects of the paintings in the *Migration* series. (b)How did Lawrence treat these subjects differently than others before him did?

4. (a)What is the artistic style of the paintings in the *Migration* series? (b)What is the effect of the style on the subject matter?

Analyze and Evaluate

5. (a)According to Hughes, why is the *Migration* series so important? (b)How well does Hughes back up his claim?

6. (a)What does Hughes mean by "stanzas from a black epic"? (b)How well does his title fit his essay? Explain.

7. The art critic Alain Locke said, "There is in truly great art no essential conflict between racial or national traits and universal human values." How is this idea evident in Lawrence's work?

Connect

8. How does this selection relate to the Harlem Renaissance? How does it go beyond it to tell more about African American history and culture?

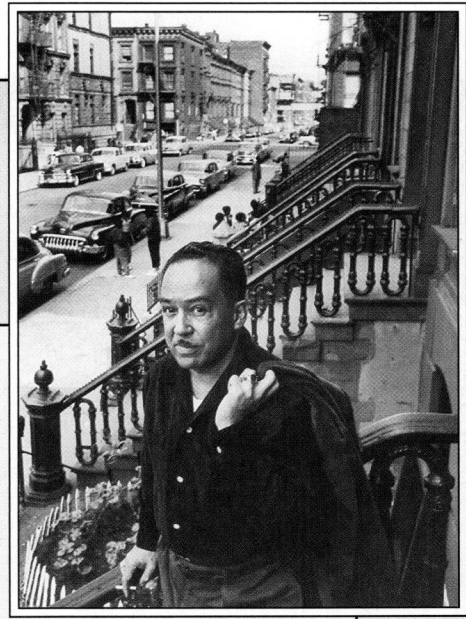

Langston Hughes's Poetry and Prose

MEET LANGSTON HUGHES

In 1921 Langston Hughes moved to New York City and enrolled at Columbia University to learn more about poetry—in the nightclubs and streets of Harlem. "To see *Shuffle Along* was the main reason I wanted to go to Columbia," Hughes said. "When I saw it, I was thrilled and delighted." The first musical written and performed by African Americans, *Shuffle Along* became a Broadway sensation and launched several careers. Many African Americans were moving north for good-paying jobs and vibrant city life, yet Hughes knew their life was bittersweet. The remnants of slavery and the struggle with segregation held back African Americans from the American dream that was readily available to many whites during the Roaring Twenties.

Hughes's writing celebrated the dignity of ordinary, working-class African Americans, helping many realize that black was beautiful. "They seemed to me like the gayest and the bravest people possible—these Negroes from the Southern ghettos—facing tremendous odds, working and laughing and trying to get somewhere in the world," Hughes said. This sentiment fit into the Modernist notion that everyday images, speech, and events belong in the highest forms of literature.

Many Homes Born in Joplin, Missouri, Hughes lived in six different cities by the time he was twelve. It was a childhood of books, music, and poverty. His father moved to Mexico, and his mother moved frequently in search of employment. When his mother sought work, Hughes stayed in Lawrence, Kansas, with his grandmother.

After finishing high school, he visited his father, by then a prosperous lawyer in Mexico. Crossing the Mississippi River on the train gave Hughes the inspiration for his poem "The Negro Speaks of Rivers." "I put it down on the back of an envelope I had in my pocket, and within the space of ten or fifteen minutes, as the train gathered speed in the dusk, I had written this poem." His father offered

to pay his college tuition if Hughes left the United States. He refused, wanting to try life in New York City. The city captivated him, but he was unhappy at school. He dropped out—later he would finish his degree elsewhere—and worked odd jobs while traveling to Africa and France.

Harlem's Bard Returning to the United States, Hughes worked as a hotel busboy in Washington, D.C. In 1925 he left three poems by the plate of well-known poet Vachel Lindsay, who was astounded by Hughes's work. Newspapers reported the next day that Lindsay had discovered an astonishing poet, who happened to be an African American busboy. Hughes soon moved back to Harlem, able to support himself through his writing. His career began in 1926 with the publication of a book of his poetry, *The Weary Blues*. Hughes, considered the poet laureate of Harlem, also wrote novels, nonfiction, plays, and children's books. Even death could not dampen his sense of humor. Hughes arranged for a jazz trio to play the Duke Ellington tune "Do Nothing Till You Hear from Me" at his funeral in New York City.

His legacy as a spokesperson of the Harlem Renaissance lives on in contemporary culture. Critic Kevin Powell writes, "The very people that he documented so well . . . were the people who created hip-hop. . . . We're still asking the same questions that Langston Hughes was asking."

Langston Hughes was born in 1902 and died in 1967.

Literature Online Author Search For more about Langston Hughes, go to www.glencoe.com.

Connecting to the Poems

With what group of people do you feel most closely associated? Are you a part of the computer culture? Sports culture? Hip-hop culture? Langston Hughes decided to align himself with his fellow African Americans. As you read the poems, ask yourself the following questions:

- In what ways does Hughes assert that he is as American as anyone else?
- In what ways does Hughes claim a share in the history of the world?

Building Background

When Hughes began writing in the 1920s, little progress had been made in securing basic rights for African Americans. In the South, laws legalized segregation. In the North, African American workers were generally hired only for low-wage jobs. Hughes's father had left for Mexico because he was fed up with discrimination in the United States. Hughes's college-educated mother moved from city to city looking for work but found only menial jobs. In Harlem, many artists, writers, and intellectuals hoped their artistic movement would help bring about an end to such discrimination.

Setting Purposes for Reading

Big Idea **The Harlem Renaissance**

As you read, notice how Hughes insists not only on the place of African Americans in American culture but insists as well on the beauty and dignity of African American people.

Literary Element **Repetition**

Repetition is the recurrence of sounds, words, phrases, lines, and other elements in a literary work. Repetition increases the sense of unity in a work and can call attention to particular ideas. As you read, notice how Hughes uses repetition to create refrains.

- See Literary Terms Handbook, p. R15.

Reading Strategy **Making Predictions About Theme**

Making predictions about the theme of a literary work can help give you a purpose for reading. Verifying predictions can help you understand a work. Read the titles of the poems. What do you predict these poems will be about?

....

Reading Tip: Use Titles to Make Predictions A title like "I, Too" implies a connection. Ask yourself, "a connection to what?" Start with the phrase *I, too* and mentally extend it into a sentence.

| I, too, (am) _____. |

| I, too, (can) _____. |

Now complete the sentence to make predictions about the theme of the poem.

Use a similar approach for the second poem. What does the title imply? What might an African American want to say about rivers?

Vocabulary

lull (lul) *v.* to soothe or cause to sleep; p. 812 *The mother rocked her baby to lull him to sleep.*

bosom (booz′ əm) *n.* the chest or heart; p. 812 *The frantic woman pressed her child to her bosom once she found him again.*

dusky (dus′ kē) *adj.* murky or dark in color; p. 812 *The sailors could not see the bottom of the muddy, dusky water.*

....

Vocabulary Tip: Denotation and Connotation The denotation is the literal definition of a word. The connotation is its implied meaning. For example, *dark* can have a negative connotation suggesting mysteriousness or wickedness.

INDIANA ACADEMIC STANDARDS (pages 810–813)

11.2.2 Analyze...repetition...in the text.

11.2 Develop strategies such as...making predictions...

11.4.7 Develop presentations using...Internet sources.

Literature Online **Interactive Literary Elements Handbook** To review or learn more about the literary elements, go to www.glencoe.com.

Against All Odds, 2003. Colin Bootman.
Oil on board. Private Collection.

I, Too

Langston Hughes

I, too, sing America.

I am the darker brother.
They send me to eat in the kitchen
When company comes,
5 But I laugh,
And eat well,
And grow strong.

Tomorrow,
I'll be at the table
10 When company comes.
Nobody'll dare
Say to me,
"Eat in the kitchen,"
Then.

15 Besides,
They'll see how beautiful I am
And be ashamed—

I, too, am America.

Big Idea   The Harlem Renaissance   *What do lines 8–10 imply about the future of African Americans?*

The Negro Speaks of Rivers

Langston Hughes

I've known rivers:
I've known rivers ancient as the world and older than the
     flow of human blood in human veins.

My soul has grown deep like the rivers.

I bathed in the Euphrates[1] when dawns were young.
5   I built my hut near the Congo[2] and it lulled me to sleep.
I looked upon the Nile[3] and raised the pyramids above it.
I heard the singing of the Mississippi when Abe Lincoln
     went down to New Orleans,[4] and I've seen its muddy
     bosom turn all golden in the sunset.

I've known rivers:
Ancient, dusky rivers.

10 My soul has grown deep like the rivers.

---

1. The *Euphrates* (yoō frā′ tēz) River flows from Turkey through Syria and Iraq. Many ancient civilizations flourished in the area between the Euphrates and Tigris rivers.
2. The *Congo,* also called the Zaire, is a river in central Africa.
3. The *Nile,* which runs through northeast Africa, is the longest river in the world.
4. According to legend, Abraham Lincoln decided that slavery should be abolished after witnessing his first slave auction in *New Orleans,* Louisiana, along the Mississippi River.

Reading Strategy Making Predictions About Theme *What do you expect this poem to be about, after reading the title and the first line?*

Literary Element Repetition *What idea does the repetition in line 10 emphasize?*

Vocabulary

lull (lul) *v.* to soothe or cause to sleep
bosom (booz′əm) *n.* the chest or heart
dusky (dus′ kē) *adj.* murky or dark in color

RESPONDING AND THINKING CRITICALLY

Respond

1. Which lines from the poems would you most like to have Langston Hughes explain? Put your response in the form of a question.

Recall and Interpret

2. (a)What is the identity of the speaker and of the other people in "I, Too"? (b)Does the speaker feel at one with these people or separate from them?

3. (a)How is the speaker treated? (b)How does the speaker respond to this treatment?

4. (a)How does the speaker in "The Negro Speaks of Rivers" describe the rivers he has known? (b)For what reason might he emphasize their age?

5. (a)What do the activities associated with these rivers communicate about the history of African Americans? (b)In your opinion, what do the rivers **symbolize**, or stand for?

Analyze and Evaluate

6. (a)How would you describe the **mood** of "I, Too"? (b)What elements of the poem contribute to this mood?

7. (a)What historical realities does the poem "I, Too" reflect? (b)In what ways has the speaker in "The Negro Speaks of Rivers" been affected by the history of his people?

8. (a)One of these poems looks toward the future, and one looks toward the past. Which of these positions do you find more persuasive? Why? (b)Which of these poems do you think might have found more acceptance among the white Americans of the 1920s? Why?

Connect

9. **Big Idea** **The Harlem Renaissance** How do these poems affirm the place of African Americans in the cultural history of this country?

LITERARY ANALYSIS

Literary Element **Repetition**

Repetition is the recurrence of sounds, words, phrases, lines, or other elements. Repetition can call attention to particular ideas.

1. What words are repeated in two lines of "I, Too"? How does the difference between these lines develop the theme of the poem?

2. What does the **refrain** in "The Negro Speaks of Rivers" contribute to the theme of the poem?

Learning for Life

Evaluate Reviews Use your library or the Internet to research reviews of and commentaries on Langston Hughes's poetry. Choose two of the reviews and write an evaluation of them. From your reading of the poems, do the reviews seem accurate?

Literature Online **Web Activities** For eFlashcards, Selection Quick Checks, and other Web activities, go to www.glencoe.com.

READING AND VOCABULARY

Reading Strategy **Making Predictions About Theme**

Recall your **predictions** about the poems. How accurate were they?

Academic Vocabulary

Here are two words from the vocabulary list on page R86.

distribute (dis trib′ ūt) *v.* to share among many; to scatter over an area

emerge (i murj′) *v.* to come into view; to rise from an inferior position

Practice and Apply

1. Was opportunity **distributed** equally among races in this country during Hughes's time?
2. How did Vachel Lindsay help Langston Hughes **emerge** as an important poet?

Connecting to the Autobiography

Are you a "with it" kind of person? Are you constantly where the action is? By moving to Harlem, Langston Hughes put himself in the right place at the right time, in the burgeoning art movement. As you read, think about the following questions:

- Who determines what is the right place and the right time?
- Do people and places of importance usually last a long time? Why or why not?

Building Background

Langston Hughes was nineteen years old when he moved to New York City. His first book of poetry, *The Weary Blues,* was published in 1926. To help his mentor, Carl Van Vechten, with his introduction to that book, Hughes wrote a brief essay, "L'histoire de ma vie" ("History of My Life") that so dazzled Van Vechten and publisher Alfred A. Knopf that they urged Hughes to write an autobiography. But Hughes replied, "I am still too much enmeshed in the effects of my young life to write about it." It was not until he was thirty-eight that he would write his autobiography, *The Big Sea.*

Setting Purposes for Reading

Big Idea The Harlem Renaissance

As you read, think about why Harlem was thought of as the center of the renaissance of African American arts in the 1920s and 1930s.

Literary Element Juxtaposition

The placing of two or more distinct things side by side is called **juxtaposition.** This is commonly done to contrast or compare the things and may evoke an emotional response in the reader. As you read, notice how Hughes juxtaposes the Harlem natives with the "Nordics," or white tourists. Does either group appear in a more favorable light from being juxtaposed?

- See Literary Terms Handbook, p. R10.

Literature Online **Interactive Literary Elements Handbook** To review or learn more about the literary elements, go to www.glencoe.com.

Reading Strategy Analyzing Concrete Details

Good writers use **concrete,** or specific, **details** to help readers visualize scenes that they describe. For example, when Hughes describes Gladys Bentley as "a large, dark, masculine lady, whose feet pounded the floor while her fingers pounded the keyboard—a perfect piece of African sculpture," you can visualize her.

Reading Tip: Mapping Details Create a web like the one shown to note the concrete details you encounter as you read.

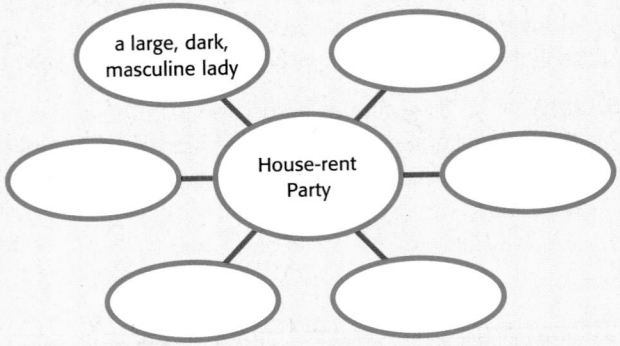

Vocabulary

scintillating (sin′ tə lā′ ting) *adj.* brilliant; sparkling; p. 815 *Her scintillating conversation drew a large number of partygoers to her side.*

vogue (vōg) *n.* fashion; style; p. 815 *It seems to be the vogue today to wear sunglasses indoors.*

patronage (pā′ trə nij) *n.* business; trade; custom; p. 816 *A large part of the restaurant's patronage comes from local people.*

millennium (mi le′ nē əm) *n.* a period of great happiness, peace, or prosperity; p. 818 *For Roger, being a movie critic was like the millennium.*

impromptu (im promp′ tōō) *adj.* offhand; without preparation; p. 818 *The comic had developed quite a reputation for impromptu characterizations.*

INDIANA ACADEMIC STANDARDS (pages 814–821)
11.2.2 Analyze the way in which clarity of meaning is affected by the patterns of organization…

11.2 Develop [reading] strategies…
11.5.9 Write…a literary analysis…

When the Negro Was in Vogue

Langston Hughes

Aspects of Negro Life: Song of the Towers, 1934. Aaron Douglas. Oil on canvas, 9 x 9 ft. Photo: Manu Sassoonian. Schomburg Center for Research in Black Culture, The New York Public Library, New York.

The 1920's were the years of Manhattan's black Renaissance. It began with *Shuffle Along, Running Wild,* and the Charleston.[1] Perhaps some people would say even with *The Emperor Jones,* Charles Gilpin, and the tom-toms at the Provincetown. But certainly it was the musical revue, *Shuffle Along,* that gave a **scintillating** send-off to that Negro **vogue** in Manhattan, which reached its peak just before the crash of 1929, the crash that sent Negroes, white folks, and all rolling down the hill toward the Works Progress Administration.[2]

Shuffle Along was a honey of a show. Swift, bright, funny, rollicking, and gay, with a dozen danceable, singable tunes. Besides, look who were in it: The now famous choir director, Hall Johnson, and the composer, William Grant Still, were a part of the orchestra. Eubie Blake and Noble Sissle wrote the music and played and acted in the show. Miller and Lyles were the comics. Florence Mills skyrocketed to fame in the second act. Trixie Smith sang "He May Be Your Man But He Comes to See Me Sometimes." And Caterina Jarboro, now a European prima donna,[3] and the internationally celebrated Josephine Baker were merely in the chorus. Everybody was in the audience—including me. People came back to see it innumerable times. It was always packed.

To see *Shuffle Along* was the main reason I wanted to go to Columbia. When I saw it, I was thrilled and delighted. From then on I was in the gallery of the Cort Theatre every time I got a chance. That year, too, I saw Katharine Cornell in *A Bill of Divorcement,* Margaret Wycherly in *The Verge,* Maugham's *The Circle* with Mrs. Leslie Carter, and the Theatre Guild production of Kaiser's *From Morn Till Midnight.* But I remember *Shuffle Along* best of all. It gave just the proper push—a pre-Charleston kick—to that Negro vogue of the 20's, that spread to books, African sculpture, music, and dancing.

Put down the 1920's for the rise of Roland Hayes, who packed Carnegie Hall, the rise of Paul Robeson in New York and London, of Florence

---

1. The *Charleston* is an energetic dance to jazz music. The Lindy Hop and the black-bottom, mentioned later, are similar dances.
2. The *Works Progress Administration* was a government agency established in 1935 to give employment to out-of-work people.

3. A *prima donna* (prē′ mə don′ ə) is a principal or featured woman singer.

Big Idea **The Harlem Renaissance** *What factors helped make New York the center of African American culture?*

Mills over two continents, of Rose McClendon in Broadway parts that never measured up to her, the booming voice of Bessie Smith and the low moan of Clara on thousands of records, and the rise of that grand comedienne of song, Ethel Waters, singing: "Charlie's elected now! He's in right for sure!" Put down the 1920's for Louis Armstrong and Gladys Bentley and Josephine Baker.

White people began to come to Harlem in droves.[4] For several years they packed the expensive Cotton Club on Lenox Avenue. But I was never there, because the Cotton Club was a Jim Crow[5] club for gangsters and monied whites. They were not cordial[6] to Negro **patronage**, unless you were a celebrity like Bojangles. So Harlem Negroes did not like the Cotton Club and never appreciated its Jim Crow policy in the very heart of their dark community. Nor did ordinary Negroes like the growing influx[7] of whites toward Harlem after sundown, flooding the little cabarets and bars where formerly only colored people laughed and sang, and where now the strangers were given the best ringside tables to sit and stare at the Negro customers—like amusing animals in a zoo.

The Negroes said: "We can't go downtown and sit and stare at you in your clubs. You won't even let us in your clubs." But they didn't say it out loud—for Negroes are practically never rude to white people. So thousands of whites came to Harlem night after night, thinking the Negroes loved to have them there, and firmly believing that all Harlemites left their houses at sundown to sing and dance in cabarets, because most of the whites saw nothing but the cabarets, not the houses.

Some of the owners of Harlem clubs, delighted at the flood of white patronage, made the grievous error of barring their own race, after the manner of the famous Cotton Club. But most of these quickly lost business and folded up, because they failed to realize that a large part of the Harlem attraction for downtown New Yorkers lay in simply watching the colored customers amuse themselves. And the smaller clubs, of course, had no big floor shows or a name band like the Cotton Club, where Duke Ellington usually held forth, so, without black patronage, they were not amusing at all.

Some of the small clubs, however, had people like Gladys Bentley, who was something worth discovering in those days, before she got famous, acquired an accompanist, specially written material, and conscious vulgarity. But for two or three amazing years, Miss Bentley sat, and played a big piano all night long, literally all night, without stopping—singing songs like "The St. James Infirmary," from ten in the evening until dawn, with scarcely a break between the notes, sliding from one song to another, with a powerful and continuous underbeat of jungle rhythm. Miss Bentley was an amazing exhibition of musical energy—a large, dark, masculine lady, whose feet pounded the floor while her fingers pounded the keyboard—a perfect piece of African sculpture, animated by her own rhythm.

But when the place where she played became too well known, she began to sing with an accompanist, became a star, moved to a larger place, then downtown, and is now in Hollywood. The old magic of the woman and the piano and the night and the rhythm being one is gone. But everything goes, one way or another. The '20's are gone and lots of fine things in Harlem night life have disappeared like snow in the sun—since it became utterly commercial, planned for the downtown tourist trade, and therefore dull.

The lindy-hoppers at the Savoy even began to practise acrobatic routines, and to do absurd things for the entertainment of the whites, that probably never would have entered their heads to attempt merely for their own effortless amusement. Some of the lindy-hoppers had cards printed with their names on them and became dance professors teaching the tourists. Then Harlem nights became show nights for the Nordics.[8]

---

4. *Droves* are large crowds.
5. *Jim Crow* refers to segregation or discrimination against African Americans.
6. *Cordial* (kôr′ jəl) means "warm and friendly."
7. An *influx* is a continual coming in of people or things.

8. *Nordics* usually refers to people of Scandinavia; here, the word means white people in general.

Some critics say that that is what happened to certain Negro writers, too—that they ceased to write to amuse themselves and began to write to amuse and entertain white people, and in so doing distorted and over-colored their material, and left out a great many things they thought would offend their American brothers of a lighter complexion. Maybe—since Negroes have writer-racketeers, as has any other race. But I have known almost all of them, and most of the good ones have tried to be honest, write honestly, and express their world as they saw it.

All of us know that the gay and sparkling life of the so-called Negro Renaissance of the '20's was not so gay and sparkling beneath the surface as it looked. Carl Van Vechten, in the character of Byron in *Nigger Heaven,* captured some of the bitterness and frustration of literary Harlem that Wallace Thurman later so effectively poured into his *Infants of the Spring*—the only novel by a Negro about that fantastic period when Harlem was in vogue.

It was a period when, at almost every Harlem upper-crust dance or party, one would be introduced to various distinguished white celebrities there as guests. It was a period when almost any Harlem Negro of any social importance at all would be likely to say casually: "As I was remarking the other day to Heywood—," meaning Heywood Broun. Or: "As I said to George—," referring to George Gershwin. It was a period when local and visiting royalty were not at all uncommon in Harlem. And when the parties of A'Lelia Walker, the Negro heiress, were filled with guests whose names would turn any Nordic social climber green with envy. It was a period when Harold Jackman, a handsome young Harlem school teacher of modest means, calmly announced one day that he was sailing for the Riviera for a fortnight, to attend Princess Murat's yachting party. It was a period when Charleston preachers opened up shouting churches as sideshows for white tourists. It was a period when at least one charming colored chorus girl, amber enough to

Literary Element Juxtaposition *Hughes often juxtaposes two distinct people or situations. What is he saying about the situation in Harlem with this juxtaposition?*

pass for a Latin American, was living in a pent house, with all her bills paid by a gentleman whose name was banker's magic on Wall Street. It was a period when every season there was at least one hit play on Broadway acted by a Negro cast. And when books by Negro authors were being published with much greater frequency and much more publicity than ever before or since in history. It was a period when white writers wrote about Negroes more successfully (commercially speaking) than Negroes did about themselves. It was the period (God help us!) when Ethel Barrymore appeared in blackface in *Scarlet Sister Mary!* It was the period when the Negro was in vogue.

I was there. I had a swell time while it lasted. But I thought it wouldn't last long. (I remember the vogue for things Russian, the season the Chauve-Souris first came to town.) For how could a large and enthusiastic number of people be crazy about Negroes forever? But some Harlemites thought the **millennium** had come. They thought the race problem had at last been solved through Art plus Gladys Bentley. They were sure the New Negro would lead a new life from then on in green pastures of tolerance created by Countee Cullen, Ethel Waters, Claude McKay, Duke Ellington, Bojangles, and Alain Locke.

I don't know what made any Negroes think that—except that they were mostly intellectuals doing the thinking. The ordinary Negroes hadn't heard of the Negro Renaissance. And if they had, it hadn't raised their wages any. As for all those white folks in the speakeasies[9] and night clubs of Harlem—well, maybe a colored man could find *some* place to have a drink that the tourists hadn't yet discovered.

Then it was that house-rent parties began to flourish—and not always to raise the rent either. But, as often as not, to have a get-together of one's own, where you could do the black-bottom with no stranger behind you trying to do it, too. Non-theatrical, non-intellectual Harlem was an unwilling victim of its own vogue. It didn't like to be stared at by white folks. But perhaps the downtowners never knew this—for the cabaret owners, the entertainers, and the speakeasy proprietors treated them fine—as long as they paid.

The Saturday night rent parties that I attended were often more amusing than any night club, in small apartments where God knows who lived—because the guests seldom did—but where the piano would often be augmented[10] by a guitar, or an odd cornet, or somebody with a pair of drums walking in off the street. And where awful bootleg[11] whiskey and good fried fish or steaming chitterling were sold at very low prices. And the dancing and singing and **impromptu** entertaining went on until dawn came in at the windows.

These parties, often termed whist[12] parties or dances, were usually announced by brightly colored cards stuck in the grille of apartment house elevators. Some of the cards were highly entertaining in themselves.

Almost every Saturday night when I was in Harlem I went to a house-rent party. I wrote lots of poems about house-rent parties, and ate thereat many a fried fish and pig's foot—with liquid refreshments on the side. I met ladies' maids and truck drivers, laundry workers and shoe shine boys, seamstresses and porters. I can still hear their laughter in my ears, hear the soft slow music, and feel the floor shaking as the dancers danced. ∾

---

10. *Augmented* (ôg ment′ əd) means "accompanied; enlarged."
11. *Bootleg* means "made, transported, or sold illegally."
12. *Whist* is a card game similar to bridge.

---

9. During Prohibition, *speakeasies* were secret clubs where alcoholic drinks were sold illegally.

RESPONDING AND THINKING CRITICALLY

Respond

1. If you had lived in Harlem in the 1920s, what aspect of its culture do you think you would have enjoyed most? Explain.

Recall and Interpret

2. (a)How was the musical *Shuffle Along* instrumental in Hughes's move to Harlem? (b)According to Hughes, what was the musical's importance to the African American community?

3. How did the Jim Crow policy operate in the Cotton Club? (b)How did the residents of Harlem respond to the Jim Crow policy?

4. (a)What were house-rent parties? (b)How does Hughes compare them to other forms of entertainment?

Analyze and Evaluate

5. (a)How did the coming of white spectators to Harlem affect business there? (b)How did the regular club patrons respond to the coming of the whites?

6. (a)What did the "ordinary Negroes" who lived in Harlem think about the Renaissance? (b)Why did they think that way?

7. (a)What happened to the career of Gladys Bentley? (b)How does Hughes respond to the change in Gladys Bentley's fortune?

8. (a)What did it mean for "the Negro" to be "in vogue"? (b)Put together what Hughes has to say about this vogue with what you know about vogues to write a **generalization** about why the Harlem Renaissance did not last.

Connect

9. Think about how Langston Hughes might respond to certain African American artists today. Put your response in the form of a question to Hughes.

10. **Big Idea** **The Harlem Renaissance** What expectations did some Harlemites have about how the Renaissance would affect race relations? Were they realistic?

DAILY LIFE AND CULTURE

HARLEM

By the middle of the 1920s, Harlem had become the largest community of people of African ancestry in the world. The 1920 census reported that over 150,000 African Americans lived in New York City.

Even though laws were less oppressive in the North than in the South, African Americans still faced prejudice. Hughes mentions the whites-only policy of the Cotton Club; some other theaters and nightclubs excluded Harlemites as well. In addition, Harlem was overcrowded, since its population kept growing rapidly and surrounding neighborhoods did not welcome African Americans.

Employment opportunities also were limited. Nearly half of African American men held service jobs as messengers, janitors, or waiters. Another sizeable number labored on the docks, loading and unloading ships. Few African Americans found work in the skilled trades, and many unions were closed to them.

Over 60 percent of African American women were employed—far more than for any other group of women at the time. More than half of them did laundry or worked as maids, both low-paying jobs.

Group Activity

Discuss the following questions with classmates.

1. What opportunities and difficulties might a person from the rural South have faced in Harlem?

2. What problems might a young family have faced if both parents held jobs?

Literary Element Juxtaposition

Juxtaposition is the placing together of two or more distinct things for the purpose of comparing or contrasting them. In "When the Negro Was in Vogue," Langston Hughes juxtaposes people, places, and activities.

1. Why do you think Hughes juxtaposes "ladies' maids and truck drivers, laundry workers and shoe shine boys, seamstresses and porters" in his description of the house-rent parties?

2. The white tourists are juxtaposed to the regular customers in the cabarets and bars. What is the effect?

3. What is Hughes's conclusion from his juxtaposition of the "intellectual" African Americans and the "ordinary" Harlem African Americans?

Review: Historical Narrative

As you learned on page 402, a **historical narrative** is a work of nonfiction that tells the story of important historical events or developments.

Partner Activity Meet with another classmate and talk about the many people that Hughes mentions in this historical narrative. Sort them out, as best you can, using the context in which Hughes mentions them. Use a chart like this one to take notes.

African Americans in Harlem			
Writers & Poets	Singers & Actors	Musicians & Composers	Not Sure

When you have listed all the names, go back and highlight any that you have heard of before. Why do you suppose Hughes does not identify each of the people he mentions, such as George Gershwin, the songwriter and jazz composer?

Reading Strategy Analyzing Concrete Details

Concrete details help readers visualize a scene. Writers who want to create a vivid picture include specific details relating to the senses of sight, sound, smell, taste, and touch.

1. List some of the concrete details Hughes mentions in his description of the rent parties.

2. Can you picture the scene? Contribute three more concrete details Hughes does not mention but that you think you might find if you went to one of these parties.

Vocabulary Practice

Practice with Synonyms For each numbered vocabulary word from "When the Negro Was in Vogue," find the lettered synonym. You will not use all the lettered words. Use a dictionary or thesaurus if you need help.

1. impromptu
2. millennium
3. patronage
4. scintillating
5. vogue

a. business
b. not legal
c. fashion
d. unknown thing
e. young people
f. brilliant
g. time of happiness
h. tragic
i. unclear
j. without preparation

Academic Vocabulary

Here are two words from the vocabulary list on p. R86.

label (lā′ bəl) *v.* to name; identify

dimension (dĭ men′ shən) *n.* scope or importance

Practice and Apply

1. How does Hughes **label** the white tourists who flocked to Harlem for entertainment?

2. Did the **dimension** of the Harlem Renaissance extend throughout the country? Explain.

Writing About Literature

Explore Author's Purpose An author's purpose for writing may be to entertain, to inform, to express, or to persuade—or a combination of these. Write a brief essay explaining what you think was Langston Hughes's purpose in writing "When the Negro Was in Vogue." (It is an excerpt from his autobiography, *The Big Sea.*) In your essay, explore how Hughes's purpose for writing may have influenced the choices he made about things such as form, voice, diction, and use of personal references and opinions.

As you draft, write from start to finish. Follow the writing path shown here to help you organize your essay.

After you complete your draft, meet with a peer reviewer to evaluate each other's work and to suggest revisions. Then proofread and edit your draft for errors in spelling, grammar, and punctuation.

Interdisciplinary Activity: Art

Work with a small group of classmates to research a Harlem Renaissance artist, such as Jacob Lawrence, Aaron Douglas, Palmer Hayden, Malvin Gray Johnson, Hale Woodruff, or Augusta Savage. Plan a brief presentation that includes music from the time or a dramatic reading about the artist.

Literature Online **Web Activities** For eFlashcards, Selection Quick Checks, and other Web activities, go to www.glencoe.com.

Hughes's Language and Style

Using Rhythmic Language Many critics praise Hughes's poetry for its use of the strong, shifting rhythms of jazz and blues music. You know that **rhythm** in literature is the pattern of beats created by the arrangement of stressed and unstressed syllables, especially in poetry. Notice how the rhythm shifts in this line from "The Negro Speaks of Rivers."

> I've known rivers ancient as the world and older
> than the flow of human blood in human veins.

The line begins with three stresses, continues with a flow of mainly unstressed syllables, and ends with a regular alternation of unstressed and stressed syllables.

Patterns of rhythm can also add emphasis to particular words. In these lines from "I, Too," the repeated stresses emphasize "eat well" and "grow strong."

> They send me to eat in the kitchen
> When company comes,
> But I laugh,
> And eat well,
> And grow strong.

Activity Copy a few lines of one of the poems and mark the pattern of stressed and unstressed syllables. Does the pattern create a rhythm? Emphasize particular words? Now experiment with rephrasing the lines you copied to keep the meaning but change the rhythm. How does the rephrased version compare with the original?

Revising Check

Rhythm in Prose Reread the essay you wrote about author's purpose. Do you see any opportunities for adding rhythmic language by repeating similar sentence structures? Decide whether such rhythm would enhance the effect of your writing or would interfere with what you have to say. Revise your essay accordingly.

Your World

MEET GEORGIA DOUGLAS JOHNSON

Georgia Douglas Johnson was a generous and prolific writer, whose true contributions to the Harlem Renaissance may never be fully known. Much of her writing was thrown out on the day of her funeral by workers clearing out her house. In addition, Johnson used numerous pseudonyms during her lifetime.

Nevertheless, her known efforts form an impressive body of work. Johnson wrote hundreds of poems, numerous plays, and columns for twenty weekly newspapers. In addition, she edited almost one hundred books and hosted weekly literary gatherings that historian David Levering Lewis described as a "freewheeling jumble of the gifted, famous, and odd." For ten years, she hosted lively salons, where African American writers met and supported each other.

Education and Family Life Georgia Douglas Camp was born in Atlanta, Georgia. Her background was racially mixed: one grandparent was English, one was Native American, and one was African American. She was well educated and attended college and two music schools. Although Johnson first dreamed of becoming a musician, she eventually decided against it. Instead she taught school, became an assistant principal, and then married Henry Lincoln Johnson, a lawyer. While teaching, Johnson began to publish stories and poems in newspapers and magazines.

Writer and Publisher In 1910 the family moved to Washington, D.C., where Johnson spent the rest of her life. While her husband disapproved of her writing, he did support her financially. Johnson's famous Saturday-night literary gatherings were attended by many other Harlem Renaissance poets, including Countee Cullen, Langston Hughes, and Zora Neale Hurston.

In 1918 Johnson published her first book of poetry, *The Heart of a Woman*. Within ten years she published two more: *Bronze* and *An Autumn Love Cycle*. In 1925 Johnson's husband died, and she had to return to work. She worked full-time at various jobs, and managed to put both her sons through college and graduate school.

> *It seems to me an art to forget those things that make the heart heavy. If one can soar, he should soar, leaving his chains behind.*
>
> —Georgia Douglas Johnson

Despite her heavy work schedule, Johnson continued to write. The year after her husband died, she started writing plays that address serious racial issues such as lynching. Many were not published, and only three of her more than two dozen plays were produced.

Johnson wrote well into old age. In 1962 she published her last book of poetry, *Share My World*, which contained the poem "Your World." One Johnson biographer, Valerie Jean, wrote, "I think this poem shows how this creative, giving soul would wish to be remembered."

Georgia Douglas Johnson was born around 1880 and died in 1966.

Literature Online Author Search For more about Georgia Douglas Johnson, go to www.glencoe.com.

Connecting to the Poem

The following poem is one writer's view of how life should be lived. As you read the poem, think about the following questions:

- What do you think is the best way to live life?
- How much of life is determined by attitude?

Building Background

Although Harlem is in New York City, the writers, artists, and composers who took part in the Harlem Renaissance lived in other places too. This poem was written toward the end of Johnson's life, after she had overcome numerous challenges. The images in the poem directly relate to those used in the title poem of her first book, *The Heart of a Woman.* In that poem, she compares the heart of a woman to a lone bird that "tries to forget it has dreamed of the stars."

Setting Purposes for Reading

Big Idea The Harlem Renaissance

Johnson not only wrote but also provided a haven for other African American artists. She said that she called her home "Half-Way House" because "I'm halfway between everybody and everything, and I bring them together." As you read, notice how "Your World" captures some of the ideals of the Harlem Renaissance.

Literary Element Mood

The **mood** of a literary work is its emotional quality or general feeling. A writer creates mood through figurative language, diction, subject matter, tone, and sound devices such as rhythm. Mood is not the same as *atmosphere,* which refers more to the physical details—location and weather, for instance—in a poem or piece of fiction. As you read the poem, notice the different aspects that create the mood.

- See Literary Terms Handbook, p. R1

Literature Online Interactive Literary Elements Handbook To review or learn more about the literary elements, go to www.glencoe.com.

Reading Strategy Visualizing

To **visualize** means to use your imagination to form pictures of the setting, characters, and action in a literary work. As you read, pay close attention to sensory details and descriptions in the poem.

Reading Tip: Noting Sensory Details Use a web diagram like the one below to record sensory details and to show how they are connected in the poem.

Vocabulary

encircled (en sur´kəld) *v.* to create a circle around; p. 824 *A silver bracelet encircled her wrist.*

immensity (i men´sə tē) *n.* greatness in size and degree; p. 824 *Alone in a small boat, I was always aware of the immensity of the ocean.*

battered (bat´ərd) *v.* to beat with blows; to attack fiercely and repeatedly; p. 824 *The soldiers battered the locked castle gates.*

Vocabulary Tip: Word Roots If you do not know the meaning of a new word, look at the root word by eliminating any prefixes or suffixes. The root word may help you determine the word's meaning.

INDIANA ACADEMIC STANDARDS (pages 823–825)
11.3.3 Analyze the ways in which…mood…achieve[s] specific… aesthetic (artistic) purposes…
11.2 Develop [reading] strategies…

11.7.20 Recite poems…

Your World

Abstract Female Figure. Riva Brown.

Georgia Douglas Johnson

1. Here, *abide* may mean either "dwell" or "remain."

2. *Cordons* are barriers.

3. *Rapture* is the condition of being carried away by strong emotions such as joy or love.

Your world is as big as you make it.
I know, for I used to abide[1]
In the narrowest nest in a corner,
My wings pressing close to my side.

5   But I sighted the distant horizon
Where the sky line **encircled** the sea
And I throbbed with a burning desire
To travel this **immensity**.

     I **battered** the cordons[2] around me
10   And cradled my wings on the breeze
Then soared to the uttermost reaches
With rapture[3], with power, with ease!

Literary Element Mood *How does the contrast between these words and lines 2–4 help you identify the mood of this poem?*

Vocabulary

encircle (en sur´kəl) *v.* to create a circle around
immensity (i men´sə tē) *n.* greatness in size and degree
batter (bat´ər) *v.* to beat with blows; to attack fiercely and repeatedly

RESPONDING AND THINKING CRITICALLY

Respond

1. Which images in the poem remind you most of feelings that you have had in your own life? Explain.

Recall and Interpret

2. (a)To what does the speaker compare herself or himself? (b)How does the metaphor in the poem match the speaker's message?

3. (a)**Alliteration** is the repetition of the consonant sounds at the beginnings of words. Find an example of alliteration in the first stanza of "Your World." (b)How does it contribute to the poem's effect?

4. (a)What does the speaker see in the second stanza? (b)How does the mood change in this stanza?

Analyze and Evaluate

5. How well does the speaker support the belief that "Your world is as big as you make it"? Use details from the poem in your response.

6. (a)How do you visualize the speaker at the end of the poem? (b)Compare that image with the way in which you visualized the speaker in the first stanza and explain why the images might be different.

7. Read aloud the last two lines of the poem and assess how the rhythm contributes to the poem's emotional effect. Summarize your ideas.

Connect

8. **Big Idea** **The Harlem Renaissance** In what ways might historical events have influenced the author's attitudes?

Literary Element Mood

The **mood** of a literary work is the overall emotion created by that work. Usually mood can be described with one or two words, such as *melancholy* or *optimistic*. Note that the mood of a work can shift.

1. What words or images contribute to the mood in the first and last stanzas?

2. What words suggest struggle? Success?

Performing

Dramatic Reading With a group, prepare a dramatic reading of "Your World." Decide who will read each line or stanza: an individual, a pair, or the whole group. Discuss how each line should be read, then practice your lines individually and as a group. Finally, perform your dramatic reading for your classmates.

Literature Online **Web Activities** For eFlashcards, Selection Quick Checks, and other Web activities, go to www.glencoe.com.

Reading Strategy Visualizing

Visualizing is an effective method of comprehending a literary work and remembering details. If you are having trouble visualizing a particular image, reread that section of the text. Look for patterns in the images and try to determine their meanings from the context.

1. Read the details used to describe the speaker and the place the speaker "used to abide." What do these images make you visualize?

2. What are three actions you can picture in the last stanza? How do these actions differ from one another?

Vocabulary Practice

Practice with Word Roots Look at each vocabulary word. Find the other word with the same root below it. Use a dictionary to identify the meaning of the root.

1. encircled
   battering
   circular

2. immensity
   circles
   immensely

3. battered
   immense
   battery

A black man talks of reaping

MEET ARNA BONTEMPS

As a historian, an educator, and an author of poems, plays, and novels, Arna Bontemps helped draw attention to the misleading education he felt many U.S. citizens had received about the heritage and accomplishments of African Americans. He has been credited with helping to create the "trickle of interest in Negro American literature—that trickle which is now a torrent." Bontemps wrote, "Had I not gone home summers and hobnobbed with Negroes, . . . I would have come out [of college] imagining that the story of the Negro could be told in two short paragraphs: a statement about jungle people in Africa and an equally brief account of the slavery issue in American history."

"In the Harlem Renaissance poetry led the way for the other arts. It touched off the awakening that brought novelists, painters, sculptors, dancers, dramatists, and scholars of many kinds to the notice of a nation that had nearly forgotten about the gifts of its Negro people."

—Arna Bontemps

A Childhood Teacher Bontemps was born in Alexandria, Louisiana, but racism there led his father to take the family to Los Angeles, California, when Bontemps was three years old. During Bontemps's childhood, his great-uncle Buddy shared with Bontemps his love of variety shows, folk stories, and dialect, all of which were staples of African American culture at the time. Bontemps would go on to incorporate the rich cultural achievements of African Americans in his work.

When Bontemps was a student at UCLA, he discovered a book by Claude McKay, a poet whose work eventually helped to spark the Harlem Renaissance. Bontemps read McKay's book twice in one day and then "began telling everybody I knew about it." In 1923, when he moved to New York, he became friends with Langston Hughes, Countee Cullen, and other Harlem Renaissance artists.

Adult Achievements Bontemps's father wished his son would become a mason, but Bontemps preferred to try his luck as a writer. He believed that literature could both educate and empower. Soon after his arrival in Harlem, he won recognition for his poetry and for his first novel, *God Sends Sunday*. He also began writing literature for children.

In 1943 Bontemps became the librarian at Fisk University in Nashville, Tennessee, where he devoted himself to recording the history of African Americans. He said that his book *The Story of the Negro* "consists mainly of things I learned after I left school that I wish I had known much earlier." Bontemps went on to write more than twenty-five books, including *The Harlem Renaissance Remembered* and *Golden Slippers*, the first children's anthology of African American poetry.

Arna Bontemps was born in 1902 and died in 1973.

Literature Online Author Search For more about Arna Bontemps, go to www.glencoe.com.

Connecting to the Poem

In "A black man talks of reaping," Bontemps evokes the feelings of people who have been deprived of the fruits of their labor. As you read the poem, ask yourself the following questions:

- How you would feel if others benefited from your work but you did not?
- How would you feel if you unfairly benefited from someone else's work?

Building Background

Langston Hughes's vision of the role of African American artists greatly influenced Bontemps. Hughes wrote, "We younger Negro artists who create now intend to express our individual dark-skinned selves without fear or shame. If white people are pleased we are glad. If they are not, it doesn't matter. We know we are beautiful. And ugly too. The tom-tom cries and the tom-tom laughs. If colored people are pleased we are glad. If they are not, their displeasure doesn't matter either." Bontemps admired Hughes' unapologetic embrace of the African American experience.

Setting Purposes for Reading

Big Idea　The Harlem Renaissance

As you read, notice the way that Bontemps' poem addresses injustices stemming from racial inequality.

Literary Element　Metaphor

A **metaphor** is a figure of speech that compares two seemingly unlike things. In contrast to a simile, a metaphor does not use the words *like* or *as* in making a comparison. For example, the phrase "the car was lightning and thunder" compares a noisy and speedy car to lightning and thunder. "A black man talks of reaping" includes an implied **extended metaphor**—a metaphor that is developed over more than one line.

- See Literary Terms Handbook, p. R11.

Literature Online **Interactive Literary Elements Handbook** To review or learn more about the literary elements, go to www.glencoe.com.

Reading Strategy　Connecting to Personal Experience

To gain a deeper understanding of what you read, try **connecting** the events and ideas of a literary work to your own life or to other works you've read. As you read, try asking yourself: Do I know someone like this? Have I ever felt this way? What else have I read that reminds me of this poem?

Reading Tip: Taking Notes Use a chart like the one below to record the connections you find between the events, ideas, and feelings of "A black man talks of reaping" and your own experiences or beliefs.

Events, ideas, or feelings in the poem	My connections

Vocabulary

sown (sōn) *v.* planted; p. 828 *Two weeks after the seeds were sown, the plants sprouted.*

lean (lēn) *adj.* unproductive; lacking; p. 828 *The farmers fear that this year will be a lean one.*

reap (rēp) *v.* to gather or to harvest; p. 828 *Each fall, the farmers reap the grain in the fields.*

Vocabulary Tip: Using Context Clues Context clues are the words and sentences around an unfamiliar word that can help you figure out the word's meaning. When you come across an unfamiliar word, consider its most likely meaning given the details that surround it.

INDIANA ACADEMIC STANDARDS (pages 827–829)
11.3.4 Analyze...figures of speech...
11.2 Develop [reading] strategies...

11.7.1 Summarize a speaker's...point of view and ask questions to draw interpretations of the speaker's...attitude...

ARNA BONTEMPS　**827**

Share Croppers, c. 1941. Robert Gwathmey. Watercolor, 45 x 32.4 cm. ©Estate of Robert Gwathmey/Licensed by VAGA, New York/San Diego Museum of Art. Museum purchase with funds provided by Mrs. Leon D. Bonnet.

A black man talks of reaping

Arna Bontemps

I have sown beside all waters in my day.
I planted deep, within my heart the fear
that wind or fowl would take the grain away.
I planted safe against this stark, lean year.

5　I scattered seed enough to plant the land
in rows from Canada to Mexico
but for my reaping only what the hand
can hold at once is all that I can show.

Yet what I sowed and what the orchard yields
10　my brother's sons are gathering stalk and root;
small wonder then my children glean[1] in fields
they have not sown, and feed on bitter fruit.

---

1. *Glean* means "to gather grain left on a field after reaping."

Literary Element　Metaphor *What might be the underlying reason that the speaker has profited little from the hard work of sowing (lines 7–8)?*

Vocabulary

sown (sōn) *v.* planted
lean (lēn) *adj.* unproductive; lacking
reap (rēp) *v.* to gather or to harvest

RESPONDING AND THINKING CRITICALLY

Respond

1. How did this poem affect you? Explain.

Recall and Interpret

2. (a)What is the work done by the speaker in the poem? (b)How would you explain the fears and concerns expressed in the first stanza?

3. (a)Who are "my brother's sons," and what are they doing? (b)Why do you think they are able to act in such a way?

4. (a)What does the speaker mean by "my children glean in fields they have not sown"? (b)What might be the "bitter fruit" the children feed on? Explain.

Analyze and Evaluate

5. In this poem, Bontemps uses **end rhyme,** or words that rhyme at the end of each line of poetry. What

ideas might Bontemps be trying to emphasize through his use of rhyme?

6. African American author James Baldwin wrote, "Color is not a human or a personal reality; it is a political reality." How well does this poem illustrate Baldwin's point? Explain.

7. How well does the title of the poem help you understand the poem's overall meaning? Explain. Cite details from the poem in your answer.

Connect

8. **Big Idea** **The Harlem Renaissance** The Harlem Renaissance encouraged authors to make the experiences and concerns of African Americans central to their writing. In what ways does this poem reflect both the history of African Americans and the goals of the Harlem Renaissance?

LITERARY ANALYSIS

Literary Element **Metaphor**

An **extended metaphor** is a metaphor that is developed over more than one line. In "A black man talks of reaping," the metaphor is implied rather than directly stated.

1. What comparison is Bontemps making?

2. What details in the poem convey the metaphor?

3. How does the metaphor help support the **theme,** or underlying message, of the poem?

Learning for Life

Interview an Activist Locate an educator or activist in your community who is working to improve what he or she feels is an unjust situation. Conduct an interview with the person and ask him or her to explain the unjust situation and how he or she is working to change it. Share the results of your interview with the class.

Literature Online **Web Activities** For eFlashcards, Selection Quick Checks, and other Web activities, go to www.glencoe.com.

READING AND VOCABULARY

Reading Strategy **Connecting to Personal Experience**

Arna Bontemps hoped to bring his experiences and those of other African Americans to the attention of others. Look at the chart you made noting the links between the situation and feelings described in the poem and your own feelings, ideas, and experiences.

1. How do your ideas and experiences compare with the ideas and experiences Bontemps wrote about?

2. Think of a time you were treated unfairly. How did you respond? Explain what you learned from this.

Vocabulary **Practice**

Practice with Context Clues For each of the following sentences, use context clues to write a definition of the boldfaced word.

1. I plan to **reap** the benefits of my studying once exam time comes.

2. Our tomato plants produced far fewer tomatoes than they did last season; it was a **lean** crop.

Any Human to Another

MEET COUNTEE CULLEN

Probably more than any other writer during the Harlem Renaissance, Countee Cullen embodied the ideal of the "New Negro" and fulfilled the goals of African American leaders W. E. B. DuBois and James Weldon Johnson. He successfully reached both African American and white audiences and eloquently addressed the issues of racism and injustice in the United States. Though some argued that Cullen spurned his African American heritage because he considered himself simply a *poet* and not an *African American poet,* he never denied his African American culture. His verse—even as it showed the influence of English Romantic poetry—echoed the struggle and violence of the times.

Cullen was born Countee Porter. His birthplace remains a mystery, but most scholars believe it was Louisville, Kentucky. Cullen was raised by a woman who was thought to be his grandmother, and when she died in 1917, he went to live with Reverend Frederick A. Cullen, pastor of the Salem Methodist Episcopal Church in Harlem, and his wife, Carolyn. Although not legally adopted by the Cullens, he eventually took their last name.

Cullen excelled in school and won several poetry awards, including a citywide contest. Before he graduated from New York University, his first book of poems, *Color,* was published to good

Countee Porter Cullen, 1925. Winold Reiss. Pastel on artist board. National Portrait Gallery, Smithsonian Institution, Washington, DC.

reviews. By the time he received his master's degree from Harvard, Cullen had become the most esteemed African American poet of his time.

> "I shall not write of Negro subjects for the purpose of propaganda. That is not what a poet is concerned with. Of course, when the emotion rising out of the fact that I am a Negro is strong, I express it."
>
> —Countee Cullen

Contradictions Unlike some of his contemporaries, Cullen wrote his poems in highly structured and traditional European forms. He wanted to prove that African Americans could write poetry as well as whites could. His belief in art's ability to unite people of all races often prompted him to caution other African American poets, such as Langston Hughes, against becoming "racial poets."

Although James Weldon Johnson understood Cullen's desire to avoid the "Negro poet" label, he also noted the paradox between Cullen's beliefs and his work, observing, "Strangely, it is because Cullen revolts against . . . racial limitations—technical and spiritual—that the best of his poetry is motivated by race."

Legacy Cullen published several collections of poetry after *Color.* Although critical acclaim for his works waned in later years, Cullen's popularity never suffered, and today his literary legacy remains due to the eloquent, artfully crafted poems that he wrote during the Harlem Renaissance.

Countee Cullen was born in 1903 and died in 1946.

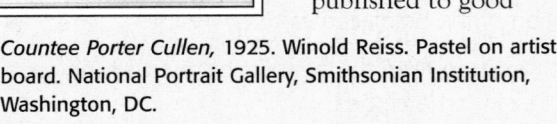 **Author Search** For more about Countee Cullen, go to www.glencoe.com.

Connecting to the Poem

In "Any Human to Another," Countee Cullen reflects on how sorrow unites all human beings. As you read the poem, think about the following questions:

- How much can we empathize with—very deeply feel—another human being's troubles?
- Which do you think unites us more with other people: sharing our joys or sharing our sorrows?

Building Background

Growing up in Harlem, Cullen was part of an expanding African American cultural awareness and learned about African American pride, unity, and art. Yet Cullen was also immersed in white U.S. culture: he was formally educated in primarily white upper-class schools, he read the works of European writers, and he modeled his writing after that of John Keats and other English Romantic poets. This combination of influences—white and African American, formal and informal—is reflected in his work.

Setting Purposes for Reading

Big Idea The Harlem Renaissance

Although Cullen did not want to be known as a "racial poet," much of his work addresses the issue of racism in the United States. As you read "Any Human to Another," be aware of how he envisioned the world and the role of art as a means of breaking down racial barriers.

Literary Element Stanza

A **stanza** is a group of lines forming a unit in a poem or song. A stanza tends to focus on a certain topic or feeling. Typically, stanzas are separated by a line space and often have the same number of lines, the same meter, and the same rhyme scheme. As you read "Any Human to Another," notice the focus of each stanza and how the stanzas are arranged.

- See Literary Terms Handbook, p. R17.

Literature Online **Interactive Literary Elements Handbook** To review or learn more about the literary elements, go to www.glencoe.com.

Reading Strategy Connecting to Contemporary Issues

Cullen's poem reflects his desire to see people as individuals rather than as representatives of a group by focusing on what unites human beings. As you read, think about his outlook on life in the context of the contemporary world.

Reading Tip: Record Your Observations To assess the values you identify in Cullen's poem in the context of contemporary issues, you might record your observations in a chart like the one below:

Cullen's Beliefs	Contemporary Issues	Observations
Sorrow unites people	Terrorist attacks	Cullen would understand why people unite after terrorist attacks.

Vocabulary

fused (fūzd) *adj.* blended; p. 832 *The jeweler crafted a bracelet made of fused metals.*

diverse (di vurs´) *adj.* composed of different elements; p. 832 *Because of newcomers from Asia and Latin America, the town had become more ethnically diverse.*

unique (ū nēk´) *adj.* unusual; p. 832. *The artist generally paints religious paintings, so this landscape painting is unique.*

unsheathed (un shēthd´) *adj.* removed from a protective case; p. 832 *The unsheathed sword appeared both menacing and beautiful.*

Vocabulary Tip: Antonyms Antonyms are words that have opposite meanings, such as *gloomy* and *cheerful*. Note that antonyms are always the same part of speech.

INDIANA ACADEMIC STANDARDS (pages 831–833)
11.2 Develop strategies such as...analyzing structure...
11.2.5 Analyze an author's...beliefs about a subject.

11.5.2 Write responses to literature...
11.2.4 Make...assertions about an author's arguments...

COUNTEE CULLEN **831**

Civilization is a method of living, an attitude of equal respect for all men, from the series *Great Ideas of Western Man,* 1955. George Giusti. India ink and gouache on paper sheet, 24⁷/₈ x 18⁵/₁₆ in. National Museum of American Art, Smithsonian Institution, Washington, DC.

Any Human to Another

Countee Cullen

The ills I sorrow at
Not me alone
Like an arrow,
Pierce to the marrow,
5 Through the fat
And past the bone.

Your grief and mine
Must intertwine
Like sea and river,
10 Be **fused** and mingle,
Diverse yet single,
Forever and forever.

Let no man be so proud
And confident,
15 To think he is allowed
A little tent
Pitched in a meadow
Of sun and shadow
All his little own.

20 Joy may be shy, **unique**,
Friendly to a few,
Sorrow never scorned to speak
To any who
Were false or true.

25 Your every grief
Like a blade
Shining and **unsheathed**
Must strike me down.
Of bitter aloes[1] wreathed,
30 My sorrow must be laid
On your head like a crown.

1. *Aloes* refers to the spiny leaves of the aloe plant, whose juices are used to make a bitter medicine.

Big Idea Harlem Renaissance *What types of people might the speaker be referring to here?*

Vocabulary

fused (fūzd) *adj.* blended
diverse (di vurs′) *adj.* composed of different elements
unique (ū nēk′) *adj.* unusual
unsheathed (un shēthd′) *adj.* removed from a protective case

RESPONDING AND THINKING CRITICALLY

Respond

1. (a)What did you first think of when you read the poem's title? (b)How did your response change after you read the poem?

Recall and Interpret

2. (a)Who is the speaker in this poem? (b)Whom does the speaker address?

3. A **simile** is a comparison that uses words such as *like* or *as.* What similes does Cullen use in the first and second stanzas?

4. What image of human isolation and self-sufficiency does the speaker introduce in the third stanza, and what is his view of it?

5. (a)What point does the speaker make about joy in the fourth stanza? (b)How does the speaker contrast this point to the effect of sorrow?

Analyze and Evaluate

6. (a)What comparisons are introduced in the last stanza? (b)Why might Cullen have selected those particular comparisons?

7. In this poem, Cullen **personifies,** or gives human attributes to, the emotions of joy and sorrow. (a)What might be the purpose of this personification? (b)Is it effective? Explain.

Connect

8. **Big Idea** **The Harlem Renaissance** Racism is not specifically mentioned anywhere in "Any Human to Another." What attitude toward racism can be inferred from this poem?

LITERARY ANALYSIS

Literary Element Stanza

Stanzas of a poem are often similar in structure and have the same rhyme scheme, number of lines, and meter. However, some poems have stanzas with different numbers of lines or different rhyme schemes.

1. (a)How many stanzas does "Any Human to Another" have? (b)How many lines are in each stanza? (c)How do Cullen's stanzas reflect the definition of a stanza?

2. What idea is presented in each stanza?

3. What effect does Cullen create through his choice of stanza form?

Writing About Literature

Respond to Theme Do you agree with the argument Cullen makes? Write a short essay stating why you do or do not agree with Cullen. Use examples from the poem to support your points.

Literature Online Web Activities For eFlashcards, Selection Quick Checks, and other Web activities, go to www.glencoe.com.

READING AND VOCABULARY

Reading Strategy Connecting to Contemporary Issues

Look back over the chart you made on page 831 in which you recorded your observations about the values expressed in "Any Human to Another."

1. What beliefs did you identify?

2. What contemporary issues did you identify?

3. How relevant do you think Cullen's poem is today?

Vocabulary Practice

Practice with Antonyms Choose the best antonym for each vocabulary word.

1. diverse
    a. rare   **b.** uniform   **c.** varied

2. fused
    a. separated   **b.** joined   **c.** stuck

3. unique
    a. distinctive   **b.** terrible   **c.** common

Writing Workshop

Literary Analysis

 Analyzing a Poem

The Writing Process

In this workshop, you will follow the stages of the writing process. At any stage, you may think of new ideas to include and better ways to express them. Feel free to return to and revise earlier stages as you write.

Prewriting

Drafting

Revising

Focus Lesson: Sharpening the Precision of Word Choice

Editing & Proofreading

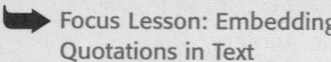
Focus Lesson: Embedding Quotations in Text

Presenting

"[Robert Frost's] sense of the human tragedy fortified him against self-deception and easy consolation. 'I have been' he wrote, 'one acquainted with the night.' And because he knew the midnight as well as the high noon, because he understood the ordeal as well as the triumph of the human spirit, he gave his age strength with which to overcome despair."

—John F. Kennedy, from *"Remarks at Amherst College"*

Connecting to Literature In the passage above, John F. Kennedy examines the aspects of Frost's character revealed through his poetry in order to honor Frost's achievement as a whole. Similarly, in a literary analysis, you examine the parts of a text to understand better the meaning of the text as a whole. The rubric below will help you learn the goals and strategies for writing a successful expository literary analysis of a poem.

Writing Models For models and other writing activities, go to www.glencoe.com.

ACADEMIC STANDARDS (pages 834–841)

11.5.9 Write…a literary analysis…

11.4.13 Integrate quotations… into a written text while maintaining the flow of ideas.

11.4.12 Revise text to…enhance subtlety of meaning…

Features of Literary Analysis Writing

Goals	Strategies
To analyze the meaning and techniques used in a poem	☑ Show how form, meter, language, and speaker contribute to meaning
To write a concise interpretation of the poem	☑ In your introduction, state your interpretation of the poem's meaning ☑ In the conclusion, summarize your interpretation and major points
To support your analysis with evidence	☑ Use direct quotations and concrete examples from the poem for support
To organize your analysis logically	☑ Organize your discussion of elements in a logical, coherent way

Real-World Connection

When you analyze a poem, think of yourself as a detective trying to solve a mystery. Before you talk about the solution, you must examine each clue separately to determine what it may reveal about the case as a whole. Some clues may not seem to lead anywhere, and some may have a meaning that is not immediately obvious. As a detective draws connections between clues to solve a mystery, try to draw connections between literary elements to investigate the meaning of your poem.

> ### Assignment
>
> Analyze a poem by identifying its meaning and then write an expository literary essay that explains how various techniques help create that meaning. As you move through the stages of the writing process, keep your audience and purpose in mind.
>
> ---
>
> **Audience:** peers, classmates, and teachers who are familiar with the poem
>
> **Purpose:** to demonstrate an understanding of the poem's meaning and an appreciation of the effects that create that meaning

Analyzing a Professional Model

In his expository literary analysis, Lawrence Raab argues that Robert Frost's "Mending Wall" is less about revealing a particular meaning than showing the reader *how* to find meaning. As you read the analysis, pay attention to the comments in the margin. They point out features that you might want to include in your own literary analysis.

From "Robert Frost's 'Mending Wall'" by Lawrence Raab

"Mending Wall" opens with a riddle: "Something there is . . ." And a riddle, after all, is a series of hints calculated to make us imagine and then name its hidden subject. The poem doesn't begin, "I hate walls," or even, "Something dislikes a wall." Its first gesture is one of elaborate and playful concealment, a calculated withholding of meaning. Notice also that it is the speaker himself who repairs the wall after the hunters have broken it. And it is the speaker each year who notifies his neighbor when the time has come to meet and mend the wall. Then can we safely claim that the speaker views the wall simply as a barrier between human contact and understanding?

Speaker and neighbor work together and equally. Although the job is tedious and hard, the speaker considers it "just another kind of outdoor game / One on a side." He acknowledges that his whimsical spell—"'Stay where you are until our backs are turned!'"—is useless, and that the result is impermanent and perhaps less important than something else. For all practical purposes this particular wall is not needed. But the project of mending it has taken on significance: "Spring is the mischief in me, and I wonder / If I could put a notion in his head . . ."

Introduction

Engage your reader with an interesting introduction. Show how your analysis is a new way of interpreting the poem.

Supporting Evidence

Use direct quotations from the poem to support your analysis.

Major Point

Clearly state your major points to guide your reader.

The speaker's mischievous impulse is to plant an idea. He does not say that he wants to change his neighbor's mind, to make him believe what he himself believes. He wants to nudge the neighbor's imagination, just as a teacher might wish to challenge a student. So he asks questions: "'*Why* do they make good neighbors? Isn't it / Where there are cows? But here there are no cows.'" But the neighbor is unwilling to play this game of teacher and student. He won't answer the questions, or consider the riddle. . . .

Supporting Evidence

Use concrete examples to support your analysis.

This is the poem's essential challenge, which the neighbor will not accept. But the challenge is ours as well—our work, our play. The relationship between speaker and neighbor is like the relationship between poem and reader, another kind of indoor game, one on a side.

Literary Element

In your analysis, focus on specific literary elements—such as the speaker's point of view—to show how these contribute to the poem's meaning.

But this is a relationship between poem and reader, not poet and reader. Frost, I want to believe, is not the speaker *exactly*. He is behind the whole poem, rather than narrowly inside it. We need to be at least a little skeptical of the speaker and not associate him automatically with the side of upholding freedom, reason, and tolerance. At the end, because the neighbor won't play his game, the speaker imagines him as "an old-stone savage," a harsh judgment to apply even to the most recalcitrant student. Because the neighbor will only repeat what he remembers his father having said, he seems to "move in darkness . . . Not of woods only and the shade of trees." . . . It's his refusal to be playful and imaginative that irks the speaker, and his unwillingness to consider work as anything more than a job to be accomplished. The speaker, after all, does not ask the neighbor to give up his father's notion. He wants him to "go behind" it. If, as I want to suggest, the poem is about education, this

Literary Analysis

Explain how quotations and examples support your major points.

distinction is important. The poem does not merely advocate one position over another. It asks neither for advocacy nor for application, but for investigation. It is not a statement but a performance. It enacts its meanings. . . .

"Mending Wall" is a poem that lures the unwary reader into believing that thinking is merely voting, choosing up sides, taking out of the poem what most fits our own preconceived ideas. It adopts this subversive tactic because its ultimate purpose is to challenge us to go behind what we might

Conclusion

Summarize your thesis in the conclusion and leave the reader with something to ponder.

find initially appealing in the formulas that lie on its surface. "We ask people to think," Frost says, "and we don't show them what thinking is." "Mending Wall" is less a poem about what to think than it is a poem about what thinking is, and where it might lead.

Reading-Writing Connection Think about the writing techniques that you just encountered and try them out in the expository literary analysis essay you write.

Prewriting

Choose a Poem to Analyze When choosing a poem to write about, think about a poem in this unit you find provocative or challenging, one that you would like to understand better. Make sure that the poem you choose is substantive enough to discuss in your essay.

Explore Your Poem After you select a poem, explore its meaning and the techniques the poet uses to convey that meaning. You may find it helpful to make a copy of the poem to mark up as you analyze. Try these strategies:

▶ Paraphrase the poem's general meaning in your own words. Then focus on specific words, punctuation, sounds, and figures of speech. Analyze the ways these elements contribute to the meaning of the poem.

▶ Reread the poem. You probably will not notice everything at once.

▶ Focus on smaller sections of the poem in detail. Explore the images in each section and think about how they bring out the poet's message.

Analyze the Elements Remember that when you analyze something, you break it into parts and examine each part, determining how the parts work together as a whole. A chart like the one below can help you work out your analysis of a poem and can serve as evidence to support your thesis in your draft.

Poem	"I, Too" by Langston Hughes
Form	5 stanzas; 18 lines
Rhyme Scheme	unrhymed
Repetition	Lines nearly repeat: "When company comes" (lines 4 and 10) and "eat in the kitchen" (lines 3 and 13).
Imagery	image of eating in kitchen repeated in stanzas 2 and 3
Figurative Language	"I, too, sing America" (line 1); "I, too, am America" (line 18)
Speaker/ Characters	African American speaker; "They" (Americans excluding African Americans)
Tone	Confident and proud in stanzas 1, 2, 3, and 5; uncertain and doubting in stanza 4
Theme	The speaker wants not only to be able to participate in what "America" is but also to be admired and seen as an individual.

Clarify Your Thesis Look at your analysis chart and decide which elements are most important in the poem you chose. You need not discuss every element in your analysis, only the most important ones. Then examine your paraphrase and the notes in your chart to sum up your interpretation of the meaning of the poem in a thesis statement. Your thesis should explain how particular literary elements illustrate or contribute to the theme of the poem.

Make a Plan As you write, use the elements in your chart to support your thesis. Organize your major points so that your analysis follows a logical, effective order.

Every Word Counts

Poets choose each word in a poem specifically to give the poem meaning and impact. Always look for multiple meanings of a word and note how different meanings may enhance or complicate the meaning of the poem.

Test Prep

When you analyze a poem for a timed test, examine the literary elements first. This analysis will form the support for your thesis.

Use a graphic organizer
to help you organize
your body paragraphs.

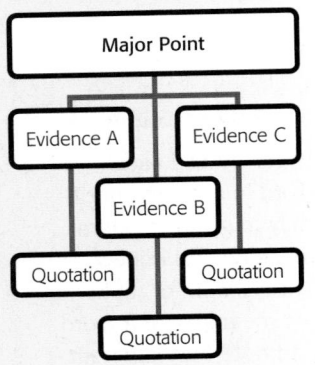

Drafting

Use Your Plan as a Guide You may begin drafting by incorporating your thesis into an introduction, or you may choose to focus on the body of the essay first. Organize your main points in a straightforward way in the body of your essay, supporting each point with direct evidence from the poem. Explain the significance of quotations and examples and make clear how they support your thesis.

Analyzing a Workshop Model

Here is the final draft of a literary analysis essay. Read the essay and answer the questions in the margin. Use the answers to these questions to guide you as you write your own essay.

Part of America: Langston Hughes's "I, Too"

Langston Hughes's poem "I, Too" comments on the past, present, and possible future treatment of African Americans in the United States. Strong imagery, repetition, changing tone, and a varying formal arrangement in Hughes's poem are employed as the speaker questions the limited definition of *America*. The poem reflects the speaker's desire not only to be able to participate in what America is but also to be recognized as an individual, as part of the very definition of America.

Hughes's poem can be interpreted as a direct response to Walt Whitman's poem "I Hear America Singing." Whitman writes about America's diversity by describing how each individual sings a unique song. In "I, Too" the speaker's response is a wish to be recognized as one of those individual voices. The opening line of the poem, set apart for emphasis, suggests a direct reply to Whitman. "I, too, sing America," proclaims the speaker, pleading for attention and recognition and wondering why he was excluded from Whitman's poetic list of Americans (line 1).

The second stanza of the poem describes the speaker's current situation. The line "I am the darker brother" implies that there is a relation to the rest of America, but by describing the speaker as "darker," Hughes identifies the speaker as an African American (line 2). Hughes describes an ambiguous "they" who send the speaker away "when company comes," segregating and hiding him from other people (lines 3, 4). Although he is shoved aside, he attempts to make the best of his situation by laughing, eating, and getting stronger (lines 5–7). Hughes illustrates how, even when they are being discounted, African Americans remain optimistic, knowing that a better future lies ahead.

Thesis

What makes this thesis effective?

Major Point

Why might the writer decide to include a major point here?

Supporting Evidence

What is the effect of directly quoting the words from the poem here?

The third stanza shifts from present to future tense and point of view, as the speaker speculates on how the treatment of African Americans will change "Tomorrow." To highlight this shift, the speaker repeats the main image of the second stanza and follows a similar structure in both stanzas. The turning point, "When company comes," from line 4 is repeated exactly in line 10 but to a different effect. In the third stanza, the speaker looks forward to the day when he will sit at the table with everybody else, in a time when nobody will even consider telling him to "'Eat in the kitchen'" (line 13). In this stanza, Hughes cements the symbolism of "the table," which represents the basic rights and freedoms of a participating American. The speaker describes a time when he will be allowed to join in with the rest of Americans without being told that he cannot or should not.

The fourth stanza continues in the present tense as the speaker further speculates on the changes the future will bring for African Americans. The three-line structure of this stanza sharply diverges from the structure of other stanzas, and the "Besides" introduces this stanza as an aside that similarly diverges from the main text of the poem (lines 15–17). In this stanza, the speaker shifts from affirming that "they" will allow him (and all African Americans) to participate, or "eat at the table," to affirming that "they" will eventually recognize him as *beautiful* and be ashamed of their past treatment of him (line 16–17). Therefore, the speaker wants—and expects—not only to be allowed to share the same freedoms and liberties as other American citizens, to participate in what "America" is, but also to be admired and seen as an individual. Line 17 ends abruptly with a dash, however, suggesting that the speaker suddenly doubts his own statement. This dash serves to undercut the proud, confident, determined tone of the speaker in the first three stanzas, each of which ends with a period. The speaker seems to acknowledge that the future he described may not happen.

With the final line, Hughes brings the poem full circle, concluding with "I, too, am America" (line 18). This line, in effect, repeats the opening of the poem, lending a sense of symmetry and closure to the whole. The speaker is not just participating in ("singing") America; he is also a part of it—he *is* America. Yet even this confident closing line cannot erase the hint of doubt from the preceding line. The speaker expresses his feeling that the exclusion and degradation must stop, although he does not seem convinced that it will happen in the near future. Placing the final line in the present tense, as if it were already true, emphasizes the pain behind the statement, as well as the insistence on strength and hope, even as "Tomorrow" seems further and further away.

Exposition

Organization

How is this essay organized, and why is this method effective?

Embedded Quotation

How are embedded quotations cited?

Literary Element

Why might the writer address the form of the poem here?

Literary Analysis

How does this statement contribute to the reader's understanding of the poem?

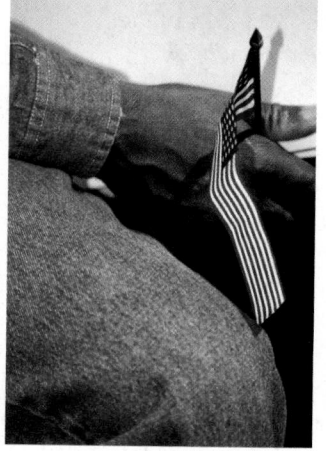

Conclusion

How might this conclusion give the reader something to ponder further?

Revising

Peer Review Exchange your finished draft with that of a partner to identify the strengths and weaknesses of each draft. Partners should make sure that each analysis is logically organized and should comment on the tone of the essay. Analyses should be interesting but formal in tone.

Use the rubric below to evaluate your writing.

Rubric: Writing an Effective Literary Analysis of a Poem
☑ Do you analyze the techniques in the poem to show how they contribute to the poem's meaning?
☑ Do you state your interpretation in a concise thesis statement?
☑ Do you support your analysis with quotations and examples from the poem?
☑ Do you organize your analysis in a logical, coherent way?
☑ Do you restate your thesis and summarize your major points in your conclusion?

▶ **Focus Lesson**

Sharpening the Precision of Word Choice

Concrete, precise writing appeals to readers because it evokes feelings and images that help them personally relate to what is being discussed. In your essay, help your readers understand your ideas by replacing abstract statements with precise words and vivid examples. Review your thesis and major points in particular, making sure your ideas are as accurate and precise as possible.

Draft:

The poem, however, shifts toward a sense of doubt, suggesting that the speaker and his views have changed. The tone and the punctuation in the final stanza contribute to this effect.

Revision:

Line 17 ends abruptly with a dash,[1] however, suggesting that the speaker suddenly doubts his own statement.[2] This dash serves to undercut the proud, confident, determined tone of the speaker in the first three stanzas, each of which ends in a period.[3]

> **1:** Be concise and concrete.
> **2:** Give specific rather than general explanations.
> **3:** Replace vague examples with vivid, precise examples.

Editing and Proofreading

Get It Right When you have completed the final draft of your essay, proofread it for errors in grammar, usage, mechanics, and spelling. Refer to the Language Handbook, pages R46–R60, as a guide.

▶ **Focus Lesson**

Embedding Quotations in Text

In your essay, much of your direct evidence will be in the form of quotations embedded within your analysis. Remember to place quotation marks around only the quotation, excluding any introductory or explanatory remarks. In general separate such remarks from the actual quotation with a comma. When a quotation is interrupted by an explanatory remark, use two sets of quotation marks.

Problem: Direct evidence is not set off in quotation marks and is not set off with a comma from the introductory remarks.

The turning point when company comes from line 4 is repeated exactly in line 10, but to a different effect.

Solution: Place quotation marks around the quotation and set off with commas the introductory remark from the actual quotation.

The turning point, "When company comes," from line 4 is repeated exactly in line 10 but to a different effect.

Problem: Quotation marks include material not in the quotation.

Hughes describes an ambiguous "they who send the speaker away when company comes," segregating and hiding him from other people (lines 3, 4).

Solution: Place quotation marks around only quoted material, using two or more sets of quotation marks if necessary.

Hughes describes an ambiguous "they" who send the speaker away "when company comes," segregating and hiding him from other people (lines 3, 4).

Quoting Poetry

When you quote poetry, be sure to give the line numbers (rather than page numbers) in parentheses after each quotation. Use a slash (/) to indicate a line break. Example:

"Tomorrow, / I'll be at the table" (lines 8–9)

Presenting

The Final Touch After you finish editing and proofreading your analysis, and check that all quotations are cited correctly, focus on presentation. Make sure your analysis is typed in a legible font and type size, with reasonable margins and spacing. Give your analysis an interesting title that will make your essay stand out. Check with your teacher about any additional presentation guidelines.

Writer's Portfolio

Place a clean copy of your literary analysis in your portfolio to review later.

Speaking, Listening, and Viewing Workshop

Oral Interpretation of a Poem

Connecting to Literature What is "I, Too" by Langston Hughes about? One reader might say that it is about belonging; another might say that it is about rebelling. What image is strongest in Carl Sandburg's poem about Chicago? Is it the dusty city, "laughing with white teeth," or the faces of the women and children marked with "wanton hunger"? Think about these poems and others you have read and discussed in Unit 5. Have you noticed that there is no single "correct" way to interpret a particular poem? When you read a poem aloud and explain your understanding of it, you are presenting an oral interpretation of it.

> **Assignment**   Plan and deliver an oral interpretation of a poem.

Planning Your Presentation

To interpret a poem successfully, you should do the following:

- Understand the **literal** meaning. Read the poem several times to decide what the speaker is saying and why he or she is saying it. In other words, what is the meaning of the poem, and what action or image is being described?
- Understand the **implied** meaning. If the literal meaning is *what* the poet is saying, then the implied meaning is *why* the poet is saying it. How did you feel after reading the poem? Why might the poet want you to feel that way?

Creating Your Visual Media

Poetry is full of striking visual images, so it makes sense to include visual elements in your presentation. Possible visual aids include photographs of the poet or a painting or drawing representing the meaning of the poem. Use the chart below to help you brainstorm for other ideas about visual media.

What are some of the memorable images or ideas in the poem? | How can I find or create visual representations of those images or ideas? | What artifacts can I display to highlight those images or ideas?

Clarifying Meaning

One of the best ways to check your understanding of the literal meaning of a poem is to paraphrase it—or rephrase it in your own words. You may paraphrase it line by line, stanza by stanza, or any other way that makes sense to you.

Using Background Information

You can draw information from a poet's background into your interpretation. For example, many critics felt that T. S. Eliot's poem "The Love Song of J. Alfred Prufrock" reflected Eliot's sense of the growing alienation of modern industry. Elements such as economics, race, or politics can all influence a poet's work.

Rehearsing

To perfect your oral interpretation, rehearse before you present it to your audience. Ask a friend to listen and to offer helpful feedback as you practice.

- Practice your oral interpretation often, experimenting with different tones, volumes, speeds, and other vocal devices.
- When you present your interpretation, first read the poem you have chosen to your audience. Plan ahead to decide where you will pause for breath during the reading. Pause at the end of a line only if a punctuation mark appears there or if it seems like a natural place to pause.
- Look for imagery and figurative language. Think about ways to communicate these images and figures of speech in your interpretation.
- Consider how the poet has used sound devices, such as rhyme, rhythm, alliteration, assonance, and consonance. Decide how you will emphasize these elements in your oral presentation.
- Read the poem to yourself several times, focusing on your own reactions to it. Think of ways to use your voice to communicate your reactions.

Rubric: Techniques for Delivering an Oral Interpretation of Poem

Verbal Techniques	Nonverbal Techniques
☑ **Volume** Vary the volume of your voice as needed but speak loudly enough that everyone can hear you.	☑ **Posture** Stand up tall with your head straight.
☑ **Pronunciation** Speak clearly, enunciating all the words.	☑ **Eye Contact** Direct eye contact with members of the audience will convey that you are knowledgeable and confident in your interpretation.
☑ **Pace** Let the poem's punctuation guide your pacing—pause for spaces and line breaks and stop briefly for periods.	☑ **Facial Expressions** Vary your facial expressions to reflect what you are saying.
☑ **Tone** To set a strong, fierce tone, speak loudly; speaking softly will create a quieter, softer tone.	☑ **Gestures** Use gestures to emphasize important ideas in the poem.
☑ **Emphasis** Stress important words and ideas.	☑ **Visual Aids** Use photographs, drawings, or artifacts that express elements of the poem's imagery and ideas.

Listen to the Poet

If you have chosen a contemporary poet, visit the library to see if there are any recordings of the poet reading his or her work. This can guide you in your recitation and also make an interesting aid to your presentation.

Use a Mirror

Practice your gestures in front of a mirror until your body language looks natural.

Sound Check

Record your presentation and play it back to check on whether your voice expresses the right mood and your words are understandable.

ACADEMIC STANDARDS (pages 842–843)

11.7.20 Recite poems...with attention to performance details...

11.7.18 Deliver oral responses to literature...

11.7.19 Deliver multimedia presentations...

For Independent Reading

MANY POST–WORLD WAR I writers saw the war as an indication of the failure of the old ways and thus tried to explore new subject matter, styles, and themes. A common literary subject at the start of the Modern Age was the lifestyle of rich and fashionable members of society. Edith Wharton, who was a member of that society, and F. Scott Fitzgerald, who was not, brought different outlooks to this topic. Ernest Hemingway had a different attitude toward society: he turned his back on it and created characters who are outcasts rather than members of high society. With the publication of their influential works, Wharton, Fitzgerald, and Hemingway helped to create the modern novel.

The Age of Innocence

by Edith Wharton (1920)

Through the story of a doomed love, Edith Wharton presents an illuminating study of New York society in the 1870s. She describes the suffocating effects of living in the insulated world of the very rich, where deviation from accepted conventions resulted in unhappiness, scandal, and ruination. In an ideal match, worldly and wealthy Newland Archer is engaged to young and beautiful May Welland, a member of the same elite social circle. However, the presence of May's cousin, the exotic and aristocratic Ellen Olenska who is estranged from her husband, disrupts the couple's perfect union. Swept away by Olenska, Archer becomes torn between the two women. Wharton was awarded a Pulitzer Prize for this story of Archer's struggle between passion and society's conventions.

The Great Gatsby

by F. Scott Fitzgerald (1925)

Both the glamour and the dark side of the Roaring Twenties are reflected in Fitzgerald's story of Jay Gatsby, a man who possesses mysterious wealth, throws lavish parties, and lives for his idealistic but doomed pursuits of a woman, Daisy Buchanan, and the American dream. Told from the point of view of Gatsby's wide-eyed neighbor, Nick Carraway, the story captures the spirit of the Jazz Age, a period that Fitzgerald called "an age of miracles, . . . an age of art, . . . an age of excess."

"No amount of analysis can convey the quality of 'The Sun Also Rises.' It is a truly gripping story, told in a lean, hard, athletic narrative prose that puts more literary English to shame. Mr. Hemingway knows how not only to make words be specific but how to arrange a collection of words which shall betray a great deal more than is to be found in the individual parts. It is magnificent writing, filled with that organic action which gives a compelling picture of character."

—*The New York Times*, October 31, 1926

The Sun Also Rises

By Ernest Hemingway (1926)

World War I, though long over, casts a deep shadow over this story of young people physically and perhaps psychologically damaged by the war. Set in the cafés of Paris and the bullrings of Spain, Hemingway's novel paints in poignant detail the aimless lives of a group of disillusioned characters. The story focuses on narrator Jake Barnes, a wounded war veteran, and Lady Brett Ashley, the love of his life. Barnes's love for Lady Brett and resentment toward her fiancé, Mike Campbell, fuel this story of longing and loss.

From the Glencoe Literature Library

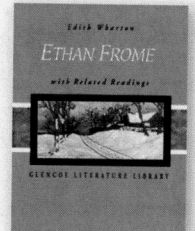

Ethan Frome

By Edith Wharton

A tragic love triangle between the title character, his ailing wife, and her young cousin.

My Ántonia

By Willa Cather

A young boy moves west from Virginia to the Nebraska plains and must adjust to life on the American frontier.

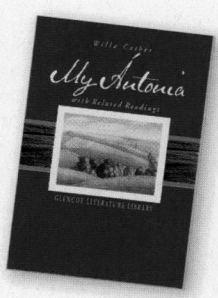

All Quiet on the Western Front

By Erich Maria Remarque

A German soldier experiences the horrors of battle during World War I and later struggles to adjust upon his return home.

Indiana Test Practice

Reading: Vocabulary, Comprehension, and Analysis

Carefully read the following passage. Use context clues to help you define any words with which you are unfamiliar. Pay close attention to the theme, use of literary devices, and tone. Then, on a separate sheet of paper, answer the questions on page 848.

Early Autumn by Langston Hughes

When Bill was very young, they had been in love. Many nights they had spent walking, talking together. Then something not very important had come between them, and they didn't speak.

5 Impulsively, she had married a man she thought she loved. Bill went away, bitter about women.

Yesterday, walking across Washington Square, she saw him for the first time in years.

"Bill Walker," she said.

10 He stopped. At first he did not recognize her, to him she looked so old.

"Mary! Where did you come from?"

Unconsciously, she lifted her face as though wanting a kiss, but he held out his hand. She took it.

15 "I live in New York now," she said.

"Oh"—smiling politely. Then a little frown came quickly between his eyes.

"Always wondered what happened to you, Bill."

20 "I'm a lawyer. Nice firm, way downtown."

"Married yet?"

"Sure. Two kids."

"Oh," she said.

A great many people went past them through

25 the park. People they didn't know. It was late afternoon. Nearly sunset. Cold.

"And your husband?" he asked her.

"We have three children. I work in the bursar's office at Columbia."

30   "You're looking very . . ." (he wanted to say *old*) ". . . well," he said.

    She understood. Under the trees in Washington Square, she found herself desperately reaching back into the past. She had been older than
35   he then in Ohio. Now she was not young at all. Bill was still young.

    "We live on Central Park West," she said. "Come and see us sometime."

    "Sure," he replied. "You and your husband
40   must have dinner with my family some night. Any night. Lucille and I'd love to have you."

    The leaves fell slowly from the trees in the Square. Fell without wind. Autumn dusk. She felt a little sick.

45   "We'd love it," she answered.

    "You ought to see my kids." He grinned.

    Suddenly the lights came on up the whole length of Fifth Avenue, chains of misty brilliance in the blue air.

50   "There's my bus," she said.

    He held out his hand, "Good-bye."

    "When . . . " she wanted to say, but the bus was ready to pull off. The lights on the avenue blurred, twinkled, blurred. And she was afraid to
55   open her mouth as she entered the bus. Afraid it would be impossible to utter a word.

    Suddenly she shrieked very loudly, "Good-bye!" But the bus door had closed.

    The bus started. People came between them
60   outside, people crossing the street, people they didn't know. Space and people. She lost sight of Bill. Then she remembered she had forgotten to give him her address—or to ask him for his—or tell him that her youngest boy was named Bill, too.

1 According to the passage, Bill and Mary ended their relationship because
   A Mary impulsively married another man.
   B they stopped speaking.
   C they both moved to New York.
   D something came between them.

2 Mary probably lifts her face as though wanting a kiss because
   A she is still in love with Bill.
   B she is unhappy to see Bill in New York.
   C she has momentarily forgotten the past.
   D she hopes to make Bill less bitter.

3 The title "Early Autumn" is BEST described as symbolizing
   A the changing weather in New York.
   B the changing of a relationship.
   C the ages of Bill and Mary.
   D the time of the meeting.

4 The paragraph beginning in line 24 mostly contributes to the story element of
   A character.
   B setting.
   C plot.
   D conflict.

5 What has Mary "understood" in line 32?
   A that Bill's life is better than hers
   B that Bill has noticed her age
   C that Bill is wealthy
   D that Bill is unhappy

6 Mary and Bill first met in
   A Ohio.
   B Washington Square.
   C New York City.
   D Central Park.

7 In the sentence beginning in line 47, the literary device that is most evident is
   A allusion.
   B imagery.
   C metaphor.
   D simile.

8 From the context, it can be inferred that the word *brilliance* in line 48 means
   A intelligence.
   B sharpness.
   C preciousness.
   D brightness.

9 Mary is most likely "afraid it would be impossible to utter a word" (lines 55–56) because
   A she is afraid of upsetting Bill.
   B she is aware that Bill sees her as old.
   C she senses that she and Bill can no longer communicate.
   D she thinks that Bill will ignore whatever she might say.

10 In the paragraph beginning in line 57, one example of connotative language is the word
   A very.
   B closed.
   C shrieked.
   D good-bye.

11 The "space and people" in line 61 are most likely symbolic of
   A the emotional distance between Bill and Mary.
   B Bill's and Mary's children and spouses.
   C Bill and Mary's youthful relationship.
   D the movement of the bus as it pulls away.

12 The main technique the author uses to reveal Mary's personality is
   A metaphor.
   B symbolism.
   C direct characterization.
   D indirect characterization.

13 The point of view from which this passage is written is
   A first person.
   B second person.
   C third-person omniscient.
   D third-person limited.

14 The author's tone in "Early Autumn" is BEST described as
   A serious.
   B humorous.
   C mischievous.
   D furious.

15 In a few sentences, describe the theme of this passage. Support your answer with two details from the passage.

Writing: Process and Language Conventions

Read carefully through the following passage from the first draft of an essay. Pay close attention to the **verb tenses, use of clauses,** and **commas.** Then, on a separate sheet of paper, answer the questions.

(1) The opening line immediately signals the reader that this poem will disclose something important. (2) That something—later revealed to be the wheelbarrow the white chickens, and rainwater—is supporting "so much." (3) The line stands out too, because it was the only line not dedicated to imagery. (4) Also, by never identifying what actually "depends," Williams creates a host of possible interpretations for his poem.

(5) Williams dedicates the next three stanzas almost entirely to the eye. (6) Each adds a detail to the poem's imagery, each drops another puzzle piece into place. (7) The wheelbarrow is presented first. (8) Williams described it outright, without embellishment. (9) However, he unexpectedly breaks the word wheelbarrow *between two lines. (10) By breaking this compound noun into its composite parts, the poet draws the reader's attention to the word itself, more than to the word's meaning. (11) The wheelbarrow is simultaneously an actual physical thing and the words that are used to describe it.*

(12) The next stanza, "which tells us that the wheelbarrow is glazed with rain / water," similarly breaks the word rainwater *between lines. (13) This, even more than the last, creates a situation in which things, and the language used to describe those things, become confused. (14) Williams is aided by the closeness in meaning of the words* rain *and* water. *(15) One is a component of the other, rain itself can never really be separated from the water that makes it up.*

(16) William Carlos Williams's "The Red Wheelbarrow" is a deceptively simple poem. (17) Deceptively simple in that, although it is succinct and its imagery plain and concrete, it expresses complex ideas. (18) Williams has written a very simple poem. (19) In eight lines Williams created a poem that shines a light on the underlying notions of language, literature, and representation.

1 Which of the following is the best revision of sentence 2?

A That something—later revealed to be the "wheelbarrow the white chickens and rainwater"—is supporting "so much."

B That something—later revealed to be the wheelbarrow the white chickens and rainwater—is supporting so much.

C That something—later revealed to be the wheelbarrow, the white chickens, and rainwater—is supporting "so much."

D That something later revealed to be the wheelbarrow the white chickens and rainwater is supporting "so much."

2 Which of the following is the best revision of sentence 3?

A The line stands out too, because it was not dedicated to imagery.

B The line stands out too, because it is the only line not dedicated to imagery.

C These lines were the only lines not dedicated to the creation of the poem's central image.

D This was the only line without imagery.

3 Which of the following errors appears in sentence 6?

A run-on sentence

B incorrect parallelism

C sentence fragment

D incorrect verb tense

4 Which of the following is the best revision of sentence 8?
  A Williams describes it outright, without embellishment.
  B Outright, Williams described it, without embellishment.
  C Williams, describing it outright, without embellishment.
  D Williams is without embellishment.

5 Which of the following is the best revision of sentence 12?
  A The next stanza, which tells us that the wheelbarrow is glazed with rain / water, similarly breaks the word *rainwater* between lines.
  B The next stanza, "which tells us that the wheelbarrow is glazed with rain / water," similarly breaks the word *rainwater* across lines.
  C The next stanza, which tells us that the wheelbarrow is glazed with rain / water, similarly breaks the word *rainwater* between lines.
  D The next stanza, which tells us that the wheelbarrow is "glazed with rain / water," similarly breaks the word *rainwater* between lines.

6 Which of the following errors appears in sentence 17?
  A run-on sentence
  B incorrect parallelism
  C sentence fragment
  D incorrect verb tense

7 What information would best fit in a new paragraph inserted between the third and fourth paragraphs?
  A biographical information about William Carlos Williams
  B a discussion of the poem's final stanza
  C a discussion of other poems by Williams
  D more background information concerning the writing of the poem

8 Which of the following sentences adds the least to the last paragraph?
  A 16   **C** 18
  B 17   **D** 19

9 Which of the following is the best revision of sentence 19?
  A Williams created a poem that shines a light on the underlying notions of language literature and representation.
  B In eight lines Williams created a poem that shines a light on the underlying notions of language, and literature, and representation.
  C Williams shines a light on the underlying notions of literature.
  D In eight lines, Williams created a poem that shines a light on the underlying notions of language, literature, and representation.

10 What is most noticeably missing from this essay?
  A a concluding paragraph
  B an opening paragraph
  C evidence
  D a visual aid

Writing: Applications

Complete the writing activity below. Do your planning and writing on separate sheets of paper.

Essay

"Poetry is news that STAYS news." —Ezra Pound

Respond to Pound's statement by writing an essay in which you interpret its meaning. Use examples and inferences from your own observations and reading to support your interpretation.

Be sure to include
- at least five paragraphs, containing an introduction, a body, and a conclusion
- an interpretation that reflects the assigned task
- examples and reasons to support your interpretation

Use a separate sheet of paper to plan your writing. As you write, keep in mind that your essay will be evaluated for **ideas and content, organization, style, voice,** and **language conventions.**

Writing Checklist

Before you begin writing, be sure to
- ❏ brainstorm for ideas
- ❏ organize your ideas into a logical pattern
- ❏ develop a plan for an introduction, a body, and a conclusion

As you write your essay, be sure to
- ❏ refer to the quotation and clearly state what you think it means
- ❏ provide reasons for your interpretation
- ❏ use language that will convey a clear message and create interest
- ❏ maintain a tone that is appropriate for your intended audience
- ❏ use correct sentence structure, grammar, and punctuation

Literature Online **Unit Assessment** To prepare for the unit test, go to www.glencoe.com.

Baseball at Night, 1934. Morris Kantor. Oil on linen, 37 x 47¼ in. Smithsonian American Art Museum, Washington DC.

FROM DEPRESSION TO COLD WAR

1930s–1960s

Looking Ahead

During this period, the United States faced extraordinary challenges. In the 1930s, people in the United States struggled with the effects of the Great Depression, the worst economic crisis in U.S. history. U.S. entry into World War II in 1941 signaled the beginning of global responsibilities for the United States. The postwar world brought the United States an uneasy peace marked by anxiety about nuclear conflict.

Keep the following questions in mind as you read:

>> How did the Depression encourage a revival of Regionalist literature?

>> In what different ways did the writers of this period present urban life?

>> How did the role of the United States in the world change as a result of World War II and the Cold War?

INDIANA ACADEMIC STANDARDS (pages 852–865)

11.3.5 Analyze or evaluate works of literary or cultural significance in history (American...) that reflect a variety of genres in each of the respective historical periods; were written by important authors in the respective major historical periods; reveal contrasts in major themes, styles, and trends; reflect or shed light on the seminal philosophical, religious, social, political, or ethical ideas of their time.

TIMELINE

1930s–1960s

THE GRAPES of WRATH
John Steinbeck

AMERICAN LITERATURE

1930

1930
Sinclair Lewis becomes first U.S. citizen to win Nobel Prize for Literature

1936
Absalom, Absalom! by William Faulkner

1937
Their Eyes Were Watching God by Zora Neale Hurston

1938
Thornton Wilder stages *Our Town*

1939
The Grapes of Wrath by John Steinbeck

1940

1940
Native Son by Richard Wright

1943
Oklahoma! opens on Broadway

1945
Tennessee Williams stages *The Glass Menagerie*

1945
Black Boy by Richard Wright

1945
A Street in Bronzeville by Gwendolyn Brooks

1947
Tennessee Williams stages *A Streetcar Named Desire*

UNITED STATES EVENTS

1930

1930
Depression deepens; bank failures increase

1932
Franklin D. Roosevelt is elected president

1933
New Deal is launched

1934
Dust Bowl begins in the southern Great Plains

1935
Social Security Act is passed

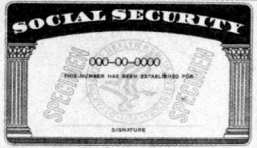

1940

1941
Japan attacks Pearl Harbor; United States enters World War II

1942
Internment of Americans of Japanese descent begins

1943
Race riots occur in Detroit; Zoot Suit Riots occur in Los Angeles

1944
D-Day invasion begins in northern France

1945
President Roosevelt dies; Vice President Harry S. Truman becomes president

1945
United States drops atomic bombs on Japan

WORLD EVENTS

1930

1930
Mohandas Gandhi leads Salt March in India

1933
Adolf Hitler and the Nazi party come to power in Germany

1935
Nazis deprive German Jews of citizenship with the Nürnberg Laws

1936
Spanish Civil War begins

1937
Pablo Picasso paints *Guernica*

1939
Germany invades Poland; World War II begins

Emblem required by Nazis to be worn by Jews

1940

1940
France surrenders to Germany

1940
Battle of Britain begins

1942
Nazi "final solution" establishes concentration and extermination camps for Jews

United Nations logo

1943
Soviets defeat Germans at Stalingrad

1945
Germany surrenders; Allied forces liberate Nazi death camps

Literature Online **Timeline** Visit www..glencoe.com for an interactive timeline.

Franklin D. Roosevelt button

Jackie Robinson button

1950   ## 1960

1949
Arthur Miller's *Death of a Salesman* is staged

1949 ▼
William Faulkner wins Nobel Prize in Literature

1952
Invisible Man by Ralph Ellison

1955
A Good Man Is Hard to Find by Flannery O'Connor

1955
Notes of a Native Son by James Baldwin

1957
On the Road by Jack Kerouac

1959
Lorraine Hansberry's *A Raisin in the Sun* is staged

1960
To Kill a Mockingbird by Harper Lee

1961
Catch-22 by Joseph Heller

1950   ## 1960

1946
First electronic digital computer begins operation

1947
Jackie Robinson is first African American to play Major League Baseball

1949
North Atlantic Treaty Organization (NATO) is founded

1950
Senator McCarthy charges that Communists staff the U.S. State Department

1954
Supreme Court rules school segregation unconstitutional in *Brown v. Board of Education of Topeka*

1955
Montgomery bus boycott begins

1962
Cuban Missile Crisis occurs

1963
President John F. Kennedy is assassinated; Vice President Lyndon Johnson becomes president

1950   ## 1960

1945
United Nations Charter signed

1945
Japan surrenders; World War II ends

1948
U.N. establishes State of Israel

1949
People's Republic of China established

1950
Korean War begins

1953 ▼
Watson and Crick crack DNA code

1957 ▲
Soviet Union launches *Sputnik 1* and *Sputnik 2*, which carried a dog named Laika

1959
Fidel Castro overthrows Batista government in Cuba

1961
Soviets erect Berlin Wall to separate East Germany from the West

Reading Check

Analyzing Graphic Information Which events on the timeline show the effects of Nazi racial policies?

BY THE NUMBERS

Stock Market Crash

On October 29, 1929, 16 million stock shares were sold. By mid-November, stock prices were cut in half, costing investors about $30 billion—a sum that was equal to the total wages of all Americans for 1929. Nearly 1.5 million investors had previously purchased stock, and many lost everything. By 1933, more than 12 million people were unemployed, and between 1929 and 1932 the average family income dropped from $2,300 to $1,600 a year.

CYCLICAL EFFECT OF THE GREAT DEPRESSION

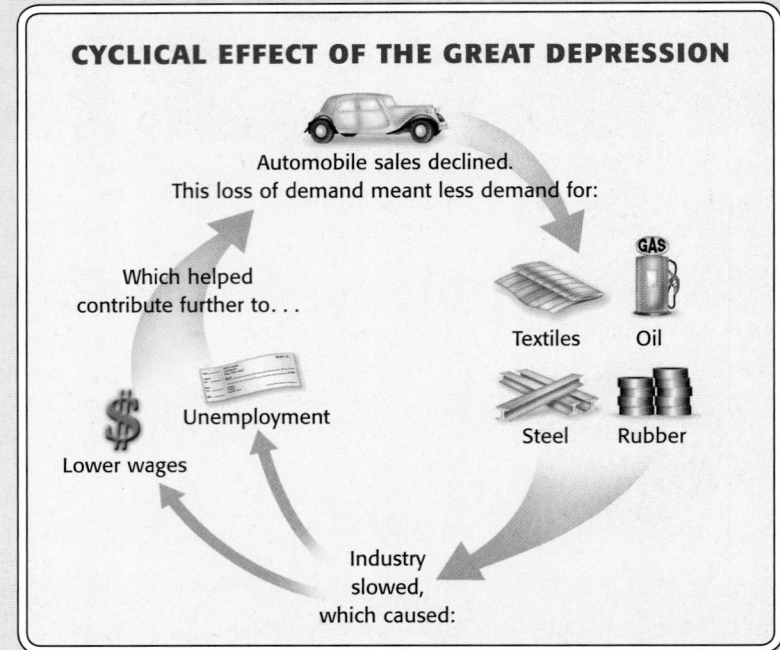

Automobile sales declined. This loss of demand meant less demand for:

GAS

Textiles   Oil

Steel   Rubber

Industry slowed, which caused:

Unemployment

Lower wages

Which helped contribute further to. . .

THE DUST BOWL

- During 1933 and 1935, unusually dry weather began to turn parts of the Great Plains into a desert.

- Between 1934 and 1939, nearly 350,000 farm families left the Dust Bowl; most of them migrated to California.

- In 1934 there were 22 dust storms; in 1937 there were 72.

- Throughout most of the 1930s, millions of tons of airborne topsoil buried crops and killed livestock.

- Westerly winds carried dust as far as the Atlantic Ocean.

THE SECOND GREAT MIGRATION

- The Depression slowed the Great Migration of rural African Americans from the South to the North that had begun during World War I.

- War production during World War II created new jobs, prompting a "Second Great Migration."

- Mechanization of southern farming in the 1950s forced more rural southern African Americans to move north seeking work.

- The African American populations of big cities in the North and West increased greatly. The black population of Chicago, for example, grew from 278,000 to 813,000 between 1940 and 1960.

AUTO PRODUCTION 1941–1945

Automobiles Produced (in millions)

Year	Value
1941	3,779,628 (4)
1942	222,862
1943	139
1944	610
1945	70,001

Source *Historical Statistics of the United States: Colonial Times to 1970*

TANK PRODUCTION 1941–1945

Tanks Produced (in thousands)

Year	Value
1941	4,203
1942	23,884
1943	29,497
1944	17,565
1945	11,184

Source *Historical Statistics of the United States: Colonial Times to 1970*

BEING THERE

In the 1930s, American artists, like American writers, were divided between Regionalists, who depicted rural life in the Midwest and West, and Social Realists, who focused on American cities, particularly New York.

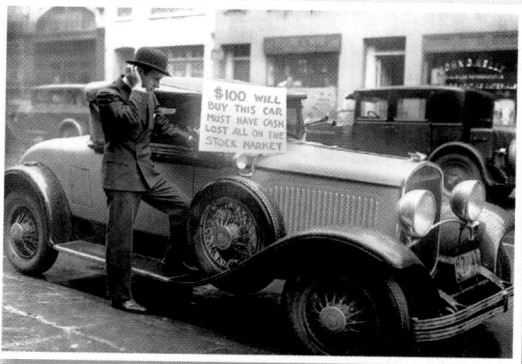

A *Against Barbwire Fence,* 1933. Arthur Rothstein. Black and white photograph.

B *Bankrupt Investor Walter Thornton Selling Roadster After Stock Market Crash,* 1929. Black and white photograph.

$100 WILL BUY THIS CAR MUST HAVE CASH LOST ALL ON THE STOCK MARKET

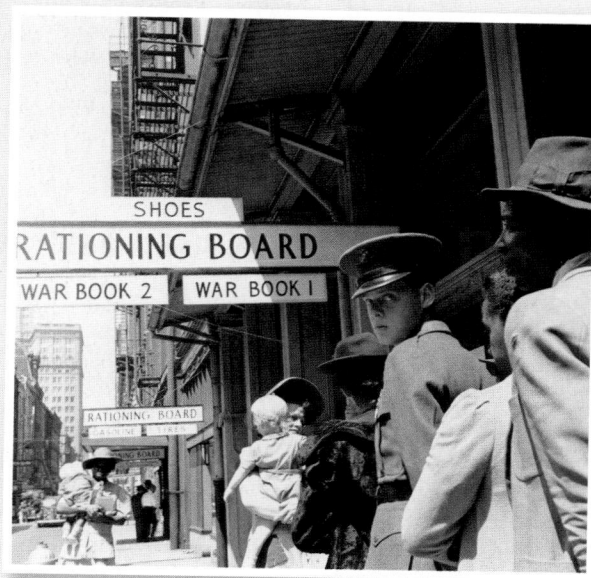

SHOES
RATIONING BOARD
WAR BOOK 2   WAR BOOK I
RATIONING BOARD

C *Line at Ration Board,* 1943. John Vachon. Black and white photograph.

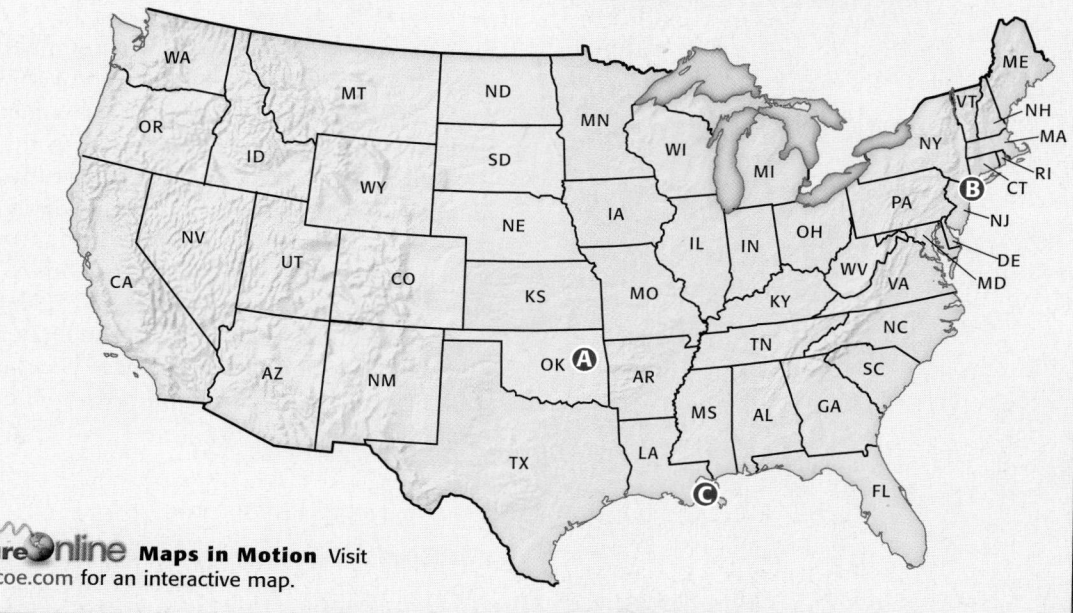

Literature Online **Maps in Motion** Visit www.glencoe.com for an interactive map.

Reading Check

Analyzing Graphic Information:

1. How many more dust storms were there in 1937 than in 1934?

2. In what year during World War II were the fewest automobiles and the most tanks produced?

3. What effect did unemployment and lower wages have on automobile sales? See diagram on p. 856.

FROM DEPRESSION TO COLD WAR

Historical, Social, and Cultural Forces

The Depression

The stock market crashed in 1929, taking with it the optimism and prosperity of the 1920s. The crash started a chain reaction that cost millions of people their jobs and homes. Banks failed when loans could not be repaid. People frantically removed their savings from banks, causing more banks to fail, which in turn caused factories and businesses to close. The popular song "Brother, Can You Spare a Dime?" captured the bleak spirit of the people of the United States, many of whom were now forced to sell their possessions, relinquish their homes, and stand in bread lines for food. When President Herbert Hoover ran for reelection in 1932, Franklin Delano Roosevelt defeated him soundly, carrying 42 of the 48 states. Soon programs and policies aimed at economic recovery and social reform, which Roosevelt called the New Deal, offered some relief to the beleaguered nation.

The New Deal

New Deal agencies employed people in public works programs, such as reforestation; improved the nation's roads and schools; and built sidewalks, dams, and bridges. The New Deal played a role in the arts as well, employing out-of-work artists, writers, actors, and musicians to decorate public buildings and produce plays and musicals. Even with the new agencies, some people—dependent mothers, children, and the elderly— were unemployable. In 1935, Congress passed the Social Security Act, which offered unemployment insurance and retirement benefits that were financed through payroll taxes paid by employers and workers.

Persistent Racism

Although decades removed from slavery, African Americans and other minority groups, such as Jews and Native Americans, continued to suffer prejudice and segregation. The New Deal failed to enact programs that challenged racism. For example, the Agricultural Adjustment Act (AAA) did not provide loans to African American sharecroppers in the

Man in a Dust Storm, c. 1930. Black and white photograph.

South because they were tenant farmers, not land-owners. Other agencies refused to hire African Americans, and some that did segregated blacks and paid them lower wages. Violence against African Americans, including lynching and race riots, remained widespread.

> "Dust storms are bringing distress and death to 300,000 square miles."
>
> —Margaret Bourke-White

The Dust Bowl

A combination of drought and poor farming methods during the 1920s turned a large area of the Great Plains into what became known as the Dust Bowl. Topsoil blew as far as the Atlantic coast. Many families left their farms and headed west in search of work. Not everyone found work, however, and the Farm Security Administration (FSA) built camps to house migrants. Those who stayed on their farms got help from the Soil Conservation Service (SCS), which advocated contour plowing to help keep the soil from blowing away.

World War II and the Cold War

By the 1930s, antidemocratic governments had seized power in Italy, Germany, and Japan. Italy's Fascists, Germany's Nazis, and Japan's military rulers formed an alliance known as the Axis Powers. Military aggression by these countries brought on World War II in 1939. During the early months of the war, the Axis forces overwhelmed their enemies, until only Britain still resisted. After a period of neutrality, the United States entered the war on Britain's side after the Japanese attack on Pearl Harbor in December 1941. Nearly four years of global warfare followed, ending with the final defeat of the Axis Powers in 1945. When World War II ended, it resulted in a world dominated by the United States and the Soviet Union. An intense political and economic rivalry developed between these two superpowers. The ensuing struggle, known as the Cold War, led to a massive buildup of armaments—including nuclear weapons—by both sides.

PREVIEW **Big Ideas** # of the Era of the Depression and the Cold War

1 Return to Regionalism

The crisis of the Depression encouraged a revival of Regionalism in literature. Some writers saw the values of ordinary people in the United States as a source of strength in hard times. Other writers examined how characters' lives were shaped—and sometimes distorted—by the history and culture of their regions.

See pages 860–861.

2 Life in the City

During the first half of the twentieth century, the big cities of the United States were magnets for foreign-born immigrants and rural U.S. citizens, who came seeking better lives for themselves and their families. Responding to modern urban life, American writers portrayed both its richness and its problems.

See pages 862–863.

3 The United States and the World

In 1941 aggression by the Axis Powers forced the United States to enter World War II. The end of the war saw the development of the Cold War between the United States and the Soviet Union. American writers examined both wartime struggles and postwar anxieties.

See pages 864–865.

Return to Regionalism

The word "America" means something different to each person in the United States. Among the many factors that shape its meaning are the communities that people come from—their histories, traditions, customs, and values. During the Great Depression, some American writers rediscovered Regionalism, the literary movement that places emphasis on the themes, characters, and settings of a particular geographical region. Unlike the local colorists of the late 1800s (see pages 480–481), the Regionalists of the mid-twentieth century were less concerned with peculiarities of local dialect or dress than with the deeper impact of setting on character.

John Steinbeck and Migrant Workers

During the Depression, the morale of people in the United States weakened and many lost faith in national institutions, such as the federal government and big business. As a result, some writers turned to regional traditions and the values of ordinary people as sources of continuity and strength. California writer John Steinbeck (see pages 868–874) found an enduring humanity in the struggles of Dust Bowl migrants. Steinbeck's most famous novel, *The Grapes of Wrath*, describes the effects of the Depression and Dust Bowl on farmers from the southern Great Plains (derisively called "Okies" since many of them were from Oklahoma), who traveled westward to seek work as migrant laborers in California. The toughness and optimism of these Okies in the face of hardship and discrimination reflects the spirit of the New Deal era and Steinbeck's belief in the ability of ordinary people to defeat despair and rebuild their lives by achieving a sense of community.

William Faulkner and Yoknapatawpha County

One part of the United States where Regionalism was particularly active was the South. The richness of modern Southern writing has caused some literary historians to speak of the Southern Literary Renaissance in the twentieth century. Many of these writers focused on the South's relationship to its complex, often bitter history and on the interaction between Southern whites and blacks. The most famous of these Southern writers, William Faulkner (see pages 876–889), used carefully detailed regional settings and situations to present universal themes, such as the burden of the past, the complexity of human relationships, the nature of time and history, and the loneliness and alienation of modern life. In order to analyze the effects that Southern history had on its people, Faulkner created a fictional Mississippi region he called Yoknapatawpha County. He populated it with former slaves, poor white families, wealthy businessmen, and plantation owners. As the county begins to change and slowly absorb Northern influences, its citizens struggle to either resist or keep up with the outside world. In his brilliant experimental novel *The Sound and the Fury*, Faulkner used a series of interior monologues to portray the psychological deterioration and moral decay of a once proud aristocratic family, the Compsons, whose members cannot face the changing realities of race, class, culture, and economics in the modern South.

Flannery O'Connor and Southern Gothic

One category of modern writing is sometimes referred to as Southern Gothic. Southern Gothic literature has some of the same elements as the Gothic literature of the Romantic period. The characters are similar to those in Edgar Allan Poe's stories: sometimes weird, alienated, and prone to strange actions and bizarre thoughts. Yet the reader is meant to feel sympathy for these characters and to understand what has blighted their lives. Another Southern writer, Flannery O'Connor (see pages 913–925), sought to shock her readers through "distortions of modern life." Her characters often encounter a force that threatens to change their lives and beliefs forever. When critics claimed that her stories were grotesque, O'Connor responded, "I have found that anything that comes out of the South is going to be called grotesque by the Northern reader, unless it is grotesque, in which case it is going to be called realistic."

Valley Farms, 1933–34. Ross Dickinson. Oil on canvas, 39½ x 49⅗ in. Smithsonian American Art Museum, Washington DC.

from *The Grapes of Wrath* by John Steinbeck

The cars of the migrant people crawled out of the side roads onto the great cross-country highway, and they took the migrant way to the West. In the daylight they scuttled like bugs to the westward; and as the dark caught them, they clustered like bugs near to shelter and to water. And they were lonely and perplexed, because they had all come from a place of sadness and worry and defeat, and because they were all going to a new mysterious place, they huddled together; they talked together, they shared their lives, their food, and the things they hoped for in the new country. Thus it might be that one family camped near a spring, and another camped for the spring and for company, and a third because two families had pioneered the place and found it good. And when the sun went down, perhaps twenty families and twenty cars were there.

In the evening a strange thing happened: the twenty families became one family, the children were the children of all. The loss of home became one loss, and the golden time in the West was one dream. And it might be that a sick child threw despair into the hearts of twenty families, of a hundred people; that a birth there in a tent kept a hundred people quiet and awestruck through the night and filled a hundred people with the birth-joy in the morning. A family which the night before has been lost and fearful might search its goods to find a present for the new baby. In the evening, sitting about the fires, the twenty were one.

Reading Check

Making Inferences Why do you think a preoccupation with the past was a major characteristic of Southern Regionalist writing?

A s the historian Richard Hofstadter famously observed in 1955, "The United States was born in the country and has moved to the city." Over the last hundred years, U.S. life has been shaped by cities, which have given direction to the economy, politics, and culture of the United States. The rapid urbanization of U.S. society had already begun in the late nineteenth century, as immigrants to the United States swelled urban populations and rural citizens also began migrating to the cities. By 1920, the urban population of the United States exceeded the rural population.

Modern U.S. cities became busy, exciting places, but were also crowded, dirty, and often dangerous. Large urban populations encouraged the growth of a varied, dynamic cultural life that ranged from museums and opera houses to movie theaters and nightclubs. However, the same rapid growth also produced slums and crime. In the twentieth century, many writers explored both the vitality and the malaise of U.S. cities.

> *"The city is like poetry: it compresses all life, all races and breeds, into a small island and adds music and the accompaniment of internal engines."*
>
> —E. B. White, "Here Is New York"

E. B. White and New York City

New York City was the center of modern U.S. culture, and the *New Yorker* magazine helped to set urban trends and styles for the rest of the country. While writing for the *New Yorker*, E. B. White (see pages 927–934) captivated the U.S. public with his sophisticated essays and sketches. White's essays covered a range of topics, including personal experiences, the problems of urban living, and current events.

Ralph Ellison's Invisible Man

Decades after the Civil War, African Americans still suffered from prejudice and segregation. To Ralph Ellison, the African American man remained an "invisible man," marginalized by mainstream white society and uncertain of his own role and identity. The nameless narrator and protagonist of Ellison's award-winning novel *Invisible Man* struggles vainly to overcome racial and social stereotypes and to be perceived as an individual. Finally, he comes to realize the absurdity of his situation and goes underground, living in an abandoned basement that he symbolically fills with lightbulbs. "In my novel," Ellison wrote, "the narrator's development is one through blackness to light; that is, from ignorance to enlightenment: invisibility to visibility."

Bernard Malamud and Brooklyn

The parents of Bernard Malamud (see pages 940–956) were Russian Jews who had emigrated to the United States and settled in the New York City borough of Brooklyn. Malamud's fiction has typically focused on the experience of urban Jews in the United States. His work often combines sharply contrasting elements—humor and pain, fantasy and realism—as he explores a character's ability to overcome isolation and suffering. His family's difficult experiences in Brooklyn are clearly evident in his stories. "People say I write so much about misery, but . . . no matter how much happiness or success you collect, you cannot obliterate your early experience."

Gwendolyn Brooks and Bronzeville

Between World War I and the 1960s, more than 6 million African Americans migrated from the rural South to northern cities. Many of them settled on the south side of Chicago, forming the large African American community later known as Bronzeville. African American writer Gwendolyn Brooks grew up in Bronzeville, which became the setting for much of her work. Her poetry and fiction are distinguished by a compassionate understanding of the lives of America's black urban poor, who struggle to survive both poverty and racism.

Subway, c. 1934. Lily Furedi. Oil on canvas, 39 x 48½ in. Smithsonian American Art Musuem, Washington DC.

Suburbia

Despite the importance of cities in the development of the United States, a deep distrust of urban life also has been a part of the U.S. character. By 1900 U.S. cities were already ringed with suburbs. The growth of suburbia continued to accelerate throughout the twentieth century. For millions of people in the United States, a home in the suburbs came to symbolize the American dream. Nevertheless, some writers have depicted suburbia as a cultural wasteland inhabited by conformists. John Cheever and John Updike are two writers who have explored the culture of suburbs in the United States.

from *A Street in Bronzeville*
by Gwendolyn Brooks

kitchenette building

We are things of dry hours and the involuntary plan,
Grayed in, and gray. "Dream" makes a giddy sound, not strong
Like "rent," "feeding a wife," "satisfying a man."

But could a dream send up through onion fumes
Its white and violet, fight with fried potatoes
And yesterday's garbage ripening in the hall,
Flutter, or sing an aria down these rooms

Even if we were willing to let it in,
Had time to warm it, keep it very clean,
Anticipate a message, let it begin?

We wonder. But not well! not for a minute!
Since Number Five is out of the bathroom now,
We think of lukewarm water, hope to get in it.

Reading Check

Analyzing Cause and Effect How did cities affect the development of American literature in the mid-twentieth century?

Big Idea 3

The United States and the World

Can you remember where you were when you first learned of the 9/11 terrorist attacks? Psychologists describe how the experience of a deeply felt or traumatic event can produce an intense "flashbulb memory." For millions of U.S. citizens who were alive on December 7, 1941, the Japanese attack on Pearl Harbor produced such a memory.

The Good War

World War II has become enshrined in American public memory as the "good war"—a heroic crusade against an evil enemy. However, most people in the United States were strongly opposed to U.S. military involvement following the outbreak of war in Europe in September 1939. This attitude changed abruptly after Japan attacked Pearl Harbor and the United States mobilized for war against the Axis powers, which included Japan, Germany, and Italy. On the battlefront, U.S. forces turned the tide in both Europe and the Pacific and played a crucial role in the victory of the Allies. On the home front, U.S. workers quickly transformed the U.S. economy into the most productive and efficient war machine in the world.

> "We are now in this war. We are all in it—all the way. Every single man, woman, and child is a partner in the most tremendous undertaking of our American history."
>
> —Franklin D. Roosevelt, wartime radio broadcast December 9, 1941

Tension on the Home Front

Wartime production helped restore prosperity to the United States after the long years of the Depression. Although minorities shared in this wartime prosperity, racism and ethnic animosities persisted. Following the Japanese attack on Pearl Harbor, the U.S. govern-ment gathered 120,000 people of Japanese ancestry—77,000 of whom were United States citizens—and forced them into internment camps in early 1942. The renewed migration of African Americans from the South to big cities in the North and West some-times resulted in racial violence, as in Detroit, Michigan, where 25 African Americans and 9 whites were killed during riots in June of 1943. During that same month, riots in Los Angeles occurred after hun-dreds of U.S. soldiers and sailors attacked a group of young Mexican American men.

The Holocaust

Shortly after seizing power in the 1930s, the Nazis began a brutal campaign of violence against Jews and other groups that they considered subhuman. During the early years of World War II, the Nazis rounded up and shot large numbers of Jews, Communists, Unitarians, Gypsies, and Slavs in conquered areas. Later, they expanded this program of genocide into the "final solution," a huge project of "ethnic cleans-ing" that involved a network of death camps in which millions of disabled persons, Jews, Poles, Russians, Gypsies, and other non-Aryans were sys-tematically killed. In only a few years, the Jewish communities of Europe, which had existed for more than 1,000 years, were largely obliterated in what has become known as the Holocaust.

The Cold War

The years after World War II brought changes to the United States. Many U.S. citizens began to chal-lenge racial discrimination at home. The devastation in Europe allowed U.S. industries to dominate world markets, and the wartime economic boom continued through the 1950s. However, the United States and the Soviet Union—wartime allies in the struggle against the Axis Powers—became tense Cold War rivals in a worldwide struggle for power between cap-italism and communism. The two world superpowers never went to war, but they continued to develop and stockpile nuclear weapons. An anxious world now lived under a new cloud—the mushroom cloud of the atomic age.

Family in Bomb Shelter, 1955. Black and white photograph.

Father and Daughter Entering Bomb Shelter, 1955. Black and white photograph.

from *"The Four Freedoms"* by Franklin D. Roosevelt

In the future days, which we seek to make secure, we look forward to a world founded upon four essential human freedoms.

The first is freedom of speech and expression—everywhere in the world.

The second is freedom of every person to worship God in his own way everywhere in the world.

The third is freedom from want, which, translated into world terms, means economic understandings which will secure to every nation a healthy peacetime life for its inhabitants everywhere in the world.

The fourth is freedom from fear—which, translated into world terms, means a worldwide reduction of armaments to such a point and in such a thorough fashion that no nation will be in a position to commit an act of physical aggression against any neighbor—anywhere in the world.

That is no vision of a distant millennium. It is a definite basis for a kind of world attainable in our own time and generation. That kind of world is the very antithesis of the so-called new order of tyranny which the dictators seek to create with the crash of a bomb.

Reading Check

Analyzing Cause and Effect How did World War II lead to the development of the United States as a superpower?

Why It Matters

Beginning in the 1930s, Regionalism reasserted itself in the face of economic difficulties. Distrustful of big business and modern culture, some Regionalist writers found moral strength and universal significance in the lives and values of ordinary people in the United States. Other writers, particularly in the South, explored how their region's history and culture defined and distorted people's lives. Their focus on the macabre, which is often called Southern Gothic, had a significant influence on subsequent American literature.

The major global struggles of the period from the 1930s to the 1960s—World War II and the Cold War—shaped the contemporary world. The position of the United States as an economic and military superpower was established during this period and the nuclear arms race began. The Holocaust led to the founding of the State of Israel, which continues to be a source of tension and hostility in the Middle East.

Literature Online **Big Ideas** Link to Web resources to further explore the Big Ideas at www.glencoe.com.

Cultural Links

>> John Steinbeck's Tom Joad, the main character of *The Grapes of Wrath*, was celebrated as a folk hero by American progressives such as Woody Guthrie, who wrote a ballad about him.

>> The influence of William Faulkner on both American and foreign writers has been enormous. Among the most prominent world writers who have acknowledged his influence are the Colombian writer Gabriel García Márquez and the Indian writer R. K. Narayan.

You might try using this study organizer to explore the different literary genres in this unit.

 FOUR-TAB BOOK

Poetry   Fiction   Nonfiction   Drama

Connect to Today >>

Use what you have learned about the period to do one of these activities.

1. Speaking/Listening Work with a small group to research music from one of the decades from the 1930s to 1960s. Find connections among the social, cultural, and musical styles of the decade that you choose. For example, you might research the songs of Woody Guthrie about the Dust Bowl period. Present your findings to the class, and, if possible, play recordings of some of the music.

2. Visual Literacy One of the New Deal's enduring cultural programs was the decoration of public buildings (often post offices) throughout the United States with murals and sculptures. View and take photographs of examples in your area of the art produced by the Works Progress Administration (WPA). Assemble a photo album to present to the class.

3. Writing Research the conditions of homeless people and migrant workers in the United States today and any state or federal programs designed to help them. Write an editorial for your school or local newspaper in which you assess these programs.

 INDIANA ACADEMIC STANDARDS (page 866)

11.7.19 Deliver multimedia presentations...

11.7.11 Interpret and evaluate the various ways in which events are presented...by visual image-makers...

11.5.4 Write historical investigation reports...

Literature Online **Study Central** Visit www.glencoe.com and click on Study Central to review the era from the Depression to the Cold War.

PART 1

The New Regionalism and the City

American Gothic, 1930. Grant Wood. Oil on beaverboard, 29 x 25 in. Art Institute of Chicago.

"Not everything that is faced can be changed,
but nothing can be changed until it is faced."

—James Baldwin

Breakfast

MEET JOHN STEINBECK

On October 25, 1962, during the Cuban missile crisis, John Steinbeck turned on his television set to see "if the world was still turning." He was greeted by a news flash announcing that he had just been awarded the Nobel Prize in Literature. Often during his long career, Steinbeck enjoyed both critical acclaim and enormous popularity. His greatest work, *The Grapes of Wrath* (1939), was among the most widely read novels of the twentieth century.

> *"The writer is delegated to declare and to celebrate man's proven capacity for greatness of heart and spirit—for gallantry in defeat, for courage, compassion, and love."*
>
> —John Steinbeck
> from his Nobel Prize banquet speech

Crusader for Social Justice John Steinbeck was born and raised in Salinas, California, a small town nestled in a sprawling valley of lettuce farms. Bright and popular in high school, Steinbeck was accepted to Stanford University but yearned for more life experiences. He drifted in and out of college, never earning a degree. Instead he wrote and worked, taking an assortment of jobs that included ranch hand, fruit picker, factory worker, salesclerk, freelance newspaper writer, construction worker, and farm laborer.

These life experiences furnished Steinbeck with material for his novels and stories. His fourth work, the novel *Tortilla Flat* (1935), was his first to receive public acclaim. Set in his familiar Salinas Valley, it vividly and humorously depicted the joys and sorrows of a group of unemployed men. Several literary successes followed it: *In Dubious Battle* (1936), which included realistic and violent scenes based on labor strikes in California; *Of Mice and Men* (1937), which described the tragic friendship of two migrant workers; and *Travels with Charley* (1962), a nonfiction work that recounted the author's journey across the United States in a pickup truck with his poodle, Charley.

Steinbeck's fiction offers a strong sense of social justice, a heightened sensitivity to the colors and textures of the U.S. landscape, and compelling plots. His characters often are society's forgotten people, struggling to survive and to preserve their humanity amid harrowing social and environmental conditions. Memorable and authentic, Steinbeck's characters seem to step right off the page.

Literary Distinction Steinbeck wrote his masterpiece, *The Grapes of Wrath* (1939), when the United States was recovering from the Great Depression of the 1930s. This 1940 Pulitzer Prize winner traces a dispossessed Oklahoma family's migration to California in search of a better life. There the family and others like it suffer tragically from injustice meted out by powerful landowners and corrupt officials. Today *The Grapes of Wrath* is universally respected for its depiction of the individual's quest for justice and dignity.

A little more than two decades after publishing *The Grapes of Wrath*, Steinbeck was awarded the Nobel Prize in Literature. Six years after receiving this award, Steinbeck died in New York City. He remains one of the most popular and respected authors of the twentieth century.

John Steinbeck was born in 1902 and died in 1968.

Literature Online **Author Search** For more about John Steinbeck, go to www.glencoe.com.

Connecting to the Story

The main character in Tennessee Williams's famous play *A Streetcar Named Desire* exclaims: "I have always depended on the kindness of strangers." In "Breakfast," the narrator recalls an encounter with strangers and the kindness they show him. As you read this story, think about these questions:

- When have you benefited from the kindness of strangers?
- Why is it important to be kind to people?

Building Background

This story is set in northern California in the 1930s. The idea for this story came to Steinbeck while he was interviewing migrant workers for his novel *In Dubious Battle*. "Breakfast" was originally published in 1938 in a short-story collection called *The Long Valley* and later adapted and included as part of a chapter in *The Grapes of Wrath*. Steinbeck's odd jobs during the early 1920s gave him a firsthand look at the desperate working and living conditions forced upon most farm laborers. These observations helped Steinbeck develop the themes and plots of many of his major works. He wrote about the working person's quest for dignity and about the stark challenges presented by nature, society, and fate.

Setting Purposes for Reading

Big Idea Return to Regionalism

As you read this story, consider what Steinbeck reveals about the values of ordinary working people.

Literary Element Implied Theme

The theme of a piece of literature is a dominant idea—often a universal message about life—that the writer communicates to the reader. Authors rarely state a theme outright. Instead they use an **implied theme,** letting the main idea or message reveal itself through events, dialogue, or descriptions. As you read, look for details that suggest the author's message about life.

- See Literary Terms Handbook, p. R18.

Reading Strategy Connecting to Personal Experience

Connecting to personal experience means linking what you read to events in your own life or to other selections you've read. By connecting events, emotions, and characters to your own life, you create meaning in a selection and recall information and ideas better. To apply this strategy, ask yourself these questions: Do I know someone like this? Have I ever felt this way? What else have I read that is like this selection?

Reading Tip: Noting Familiar Details Use a chart like the one below to record connections between your experiences and details in the story.

Story Details	My Experiences
encounter with a family camping out	Last summer I met other campers at a state park.

Vocabulary

scuffle (skuf′əl) *v.* to move with a slow, heavy, shuffling gait; p. 870 *The losing players lowered their eyes and scuffled down the ramp to the locker room.*

dissipate (dis′ə pāt′) *v.* to cause to scatter and gradually vanish; to break up and drive off; p. 870 *As the fog slowly dissipated, more and more of the road ahead became visible.*

avert (ə vurt′) *v.* to turn away or aside; p. 871 *Terribly upset, the bystander averted her eyes from the car wreck.*

Literature Online **Interactive Literary Elements Handbook** To review or learn more about the literary elements, go to www.glencoe.com.

INDIANA ACADEMIC STANDARDS (pages 869–874)

11.3.2 Analyze the way in which the theme...of a selection represents a view or comment on life...

11.2 Develop [reading] strategies...

11.5.2 Write responses to literature...

Breakfast

John Steinbeck

This thing fills me with pleasure. I don't know why, I can see it in the smallest detail. I find myself recalling it again and again, each time bringing more detail out of a sunken memory, remembering brings the curious warm pleasure.

It was very early in the morning. The eastern mountains were black-blue, but behind them the light stood up faintly colored at the mountain rims with a washed red, growing colder, grayer and darker as it went up and overhead until, at a place near the west, it merged with pure night.

And it was cold, not painfully so, but cold enough so that I rubbed my hands and shoved them deep into my pockets, and I hunched my shoulders up and **scuffled** my feet on the ground. Down in the valley where I was, the earth was that lavender gray of dawn. I walked along a country road and ahead of me I saw a tent that was only a little lighter gray than the ground. Beside the tent there was a flash of orange fire seeping out of the cracks of an old rusty iron stove. Gray smoke spurted up out of the stubby stovepipe, spurted up a long way before it spread out and **dissipated.**

I saw a young woman beside the stove, really a girl. She was dressed in a faded cotton skirt

Vocabulary

scuffle (skuf′əl) *v.* to move with a slow, heavy, shuffling gait

dissipate (dis′ə pāt′) *v.* to cause to scatter and gradually vanish; to break up and drive off and waist.[1] As I came close I saw that she carried a baby in a crooked arm and the baby was nursing, its head under her waist out of the cold. The mother moved about, poking the fire, shifting the rusty lids of the stove to make a greater draft, opening the oven door; and all the time the baby was nursing, but that didn't interfere with the mother's work, nor with the light quick gracefulness of her movements. There was something very precise and practiced in her movements. The orange fire flicked out of the cracks in the stove and threw dancing reflections on the tent.

I was close now and I could smell frying bacon and baking bread, the warmest, pleasantest odors I know. From the east the light grew swiftly. I came near to the stove and stretched my hands out to it and shivered all over when the warmth struck me. Then the tent flap jerked up and a young man came out and an older man followed him. They were dressed in new blue dungarees[2] and in new dungaree coats with the brass buttons shining. They were sharp-faced men, and they looked much alike.

The younger had a dark stubble beard and the older had a gray stubble beard. Their heads and faces were wet, their hair dripped with water, and water stood out on their stiff beards and their cheeks shone with water. Together they stood looking quietly at the lightening east; they yawned together and looked at the light on the hill rims. They turned and saw me.

"Morning," said the older man. His face was neither friendly nor unfriendly.

"Morning, sir," I said.

"Morning," said the young man.

> The orange fire flicked out of the cracks in the stove and threw dancing reflections on the tent.

The water was slowly drying on their faces. They came to the stove and warmed their hands at it.

The girl kept to her work, her face **averted** and her eyes on what she was doing. Her hair was tied back out of her eyes with a string and it hung down her back and swayed as she worked. She set tin cups on a big packing box, set tin plates and knives and forks out too. Then she scooped fried bacon out of the deep grease and laid it on a big tin platter, and the bacon cricked[3] and rustled as it grew crisp. She opened the rusty oven door and took out a square pan full of high big biscuits.

When the smell of that hot bread came out, both of the men inhaled deeply.

The elder man turned to me, "Had your breakfast?"

"No."

"Well, sit down with us, then."

That was the signal. We went to the packing case and squatted on the ground about it. The young man asked, "Picking cotton?"

"No."

"We had twelve days' work so far," the young man said.

The girl spoke from the stove. "They even got new clothes."

The two men looked down at their new dungarees and they both smiled a little.

The girl set out the platter of bacon, the brown high biscuits, a bowl of bacon gravy and a pot of coffee, and then she squatted down by the box too. The baby was still nursing, its head up under her waist out of the cold. I could hear the sucking noises it made.

---

3. Here, *cricked* means "turned or twisted."

Big Idea Return to Regionalism *What does the young man's comment reveal about economic conditions for ordinary workers during the Great Depression?*

Vocabulary

avert (ə vurt′) *v.* to turn away or aside

---

1. Here, a *waist* is a blouse.
2. *Dungarees* are blue denim pants.

Reading Strategy Connecting to Personal Experience
Why do odors leave a lasting impression in one's memory?

We filled our plates, poured bacon gravy over our biscuits and sugared our coffee. The older man filled his mouth full and he chewed and chewed and swallowed. Then he said, "God Almighty, it's good," and he filled his mouth again.

The young man said, "We been eating good for twelve days."

We all ate quickly, frantically, and refilled our plates and ate quickly again until we were full and warm. The hot bitter coffee scalded our throats. We threw the last little bit with the grounds in it on the earth and refilled our cups.

There was color in the light now, a reddish gleam that made the air seem colder. The two men faced the east and their faces were lighted by the dawn, and I looked up for a moment and saw the image of the mountain and the light coming over it reflected in the older man's eyes.

Then the two men threw the grounds from their cups on the earth and they stood up together. "Got to get going," the older man said.

The younger turned to me. "'Fyou want to pick cotton, we could maybe get you on."

"No. I got to go along. Thanks for breakfast."

The older man waved his hand in a negative. "O.K. Glad to have you." They walked away together. The air was blazing with light at the eastern skyline. And I walked away down the country road.

That's all. I know, of course, some of the reasons why it was pleasant. But there was some element of great beauty there that makes the rush of warmth when I think of it. ∽

Big Idea Return to Regionalism *What can you infer about the family's experiences until recently?*

Literary Element Implied Theme *How does this detail provide a clue to the theme of the story?*

RESPONDING AND THINKING CRITICALLY

Respond

1. How did you react to the characters in this story? Explain.

Recall and Interpret

2. (a)What are the first things the narrator describes? (b)What do these descriptions tell you about the narrator?

3. (a)What observations does the narrator make about the family of migrant workers? (b)What seems to be important to the family? Explain.

4. (a)What does the narrator say about his memory at the end of the story? (b)What might his attachment to this memory suggest about his life? What deeper understanding or awareness of life does he seem to gain?

Analyze and Evaluate

5. Steinbeck wrote about migrant workers who lived in small, supportive communities. In what ways does he portray the narrator as part of such a supportive community?

6. The reader never learns why the narrator is walking on a country road or where he is going. Why do you think Steinbeck chose not to reveal much about the narrator?

7. (a)What are some of your favorite sensory details in this story? (b)How did these sensory details affect your reading of the story?

Connect

8. **Big Idea** **Return to Regionalism** Which values of migrant people does Steinbeck highlight in this story?

Literary Element **Implied Theme**

In "Breakfast," the **implied theme** is built around the narrator's warm recollection of an encounter with a family of migrant workers.

1. What is the implied theme, or message about life, in this selection?

2. What details and descriptions support this theme?

Review: Tone

Tone is a reflection of a writer's or a speaker's attitude toward the subject matter, as conveyed through elements such as word choice, punctuation, sentence structure, and figures of speech. A writer's tone might convey a variety of attitudes, such as sympathy, objectivity, or humor.

Partner Activity With a partner, examine the word choice and the dialogue in "Breakfast." Create a chart like the one started below, and fill it in with examples of effective word choice and dialogue. Then answer the following question: What tone is conveyed by the family's words and actions?

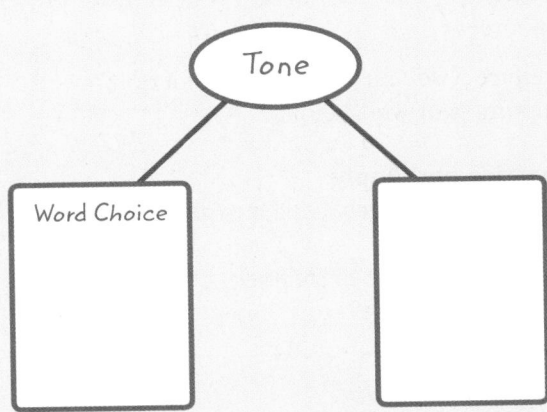

Reading Strategy — Connecting to Personal Experience

Connecting to personal experience involves drawing parallels between the people, places, and events in the story and the people, places, and events in your own life. Review the chart you filled in as you read "Breakfast."

1. To which details in the story did you relate most strongly?

2. What new insights about your experiences did you discover by connecting them to people and events in this story?

Vocabulary Practice

Practice with Antonyms Find the antonym for each vocabulary word from "Breakfast" listed in the first column below. Use a dictionary or a thesaurus if you need help.

1. scuffle **a.** shuffle **b.** glide

2. dissipate **a.** unite **b.** scatter

3. avert **a.** confront **b.** avoid

Academic Vocabulary

Here are two words from the vocabulary list on page R86. These words will help you think, write, and talk about the selection.

challenge (chal′inj) *n.* a test of abilities or resources

welfare (wel′fār′) *n.* the state of doing well; happiness or well-being

Practice and Apply

1. What **challenges** test the migrant family's spirit in "Breakfast"?

2. What values does Steinbeck believe promote human **welfare**?

Literature Online Web Activities For eFlashcards, Selection Quick Checks, and other Web activities, go to www.glencoe.com.

Writing About Literature

Respond to Setting Steinbeck creates vivid pictures of the setting by using concrete nouns and specific adjectives, adverbs, and verbs. Consider the following example: "there was a flash of orange fire seeping out of the cracks of an old rusty iron stove." The vivid language helps the reader imagine and relive the narrator's experience.

Write a short essay about Steinbeck's use of vivid language in "Breakfast." Include examples of descriptions that come alive for you and explain why they are effective. Before drafting your essay, list your examples in a chart like the one below.

Description	Evaluation
"cold enough so that I rubbed my hands and shoved them deep into my pockets"	

As you draft, write from start to finish. Begin by stating your purpose. In the body of the essay, present your examples of vivid language and explain why each is effective. Conclude with an assessment of how Steinbeck's vivid descriptions enhance your understanding and appreciation of the story.

After you finish your draft, meet with a classmate to evaluate each other's work and to suggest revisions. Then proofread and edit your draft for errors in spelling, grammar, and punctuation.

Literary Criticism

Group Activity According to critic Daniel Aaron, Steinbeck portrays migrant workers as the "preservers of the old American verities, innocent of bourgeois properties, perhaps, but courteous, trusting, friendly, and generous. . . . What preserved them in the end . . . was a recovery of a neighborly interdependence that an acquisitive society had almost destroyed." Using details from "Breakfast," discuss Aaron's position with a small group of classmates.

Vocabulary Workshop

Word Parts

Understanding Roots, Prefixes, and Suffixes

"The girl kept to her work, her face averted and her eyes on what she was doing."

—John Steinbeck, from "Breakfast"

Connecting to Literature One way to determine the meaning of an unfamiliar word is to analyze its parts. The Latin **root** *vert* means "turn." It is a common root, found in the words *averse, aversion, reverse, subvert, divert,* and others. The **prefix** *a-* can mean "in the state or condition of"; and, of course, the **suffix** *-ed* shows past tense. So an *averted* face is turned away, not directly facing someone.

If you recognize the word root or the base word, you are well on your way to understanding the word's meaning. Knowing some common Greek and Latin roots can improve your understanding of what you read.

Prefixes	Roots	Suffixes
geo- Earth	*graph* writing of	*-ical* having the nature of
dis- the reverse of	*place* position	*-ment* the condition of being
contra- against	*dic(t)* speak	*-tion* action or process of
in- within, into	*spir* breathe	*-ed* the past tense of a verb

Exercise

For each item below, refer to the prefixes, roots, and suffixes in the chart to help you select the best answer.

1. During the Great Depression, some authors wrote of particular **geographical** regions. Geographical regions are

a. particular times.
b. beside the ocean.
c. in the mountains.
d. particular places on Earth.

2. John Steinbeck writes about the human cost of the Dust Bowl migrants' **displacement** from their homes. *Displacement* means

a. being moved away.
b. being put in prison.
c. being confused.
d. being invited to stay.

3. Flannery O'Connor **contradicted** Northern critics who called her stories grotesque. O'Connor

a. agreed with her critics.
b. disagreed with them.
c. ignored them.
d. complimented them.

4. Steinbeck drew **inspiration** from the migrants who shared their breakfast with him. The migrants

a. gave him more spirit.
b. discouraged him.
c. frightened him.
d. did not impress him.

▶ **Vocabulary Terms**

A **prefix** is a word part that is inserted at the beginning of a word root or base word to create a new meaning. A **suffix** is a combination of letters or a single letter added at the end of a base word or word part. Prefixes and suffixes together are called **affixes**.

▶ **Test-Taking Tip**

When you are asked for the meaning of a word that appears in a reading passage, check the root, prefix, and suffix of the word. If you recognize the root, you can probably figure out what the word means.

▶ **Reading Handbook**

For more about roots, prefixes, and suffixes, see Reading Handbook, p. R20.

eFlashcards For eFlashcards and other vocabulary activities, go to www.glencoe.com.

ACADEMIC STANDARDS (page 875)

11.1.2 Apply knowledge of roots and word parts from Greek and Latin to draw inferences about the meaning of vocabulary in literature or other subject areas.

A Rose for Emily and Address upon Receiving the Nobel Prize in Literature

MEET WILLIAM FAULKNER

As a young man, William Faulkner did not seem destined for literary renown. He was both a high school and college dropout. His neighbors nicknamed him "Count No'count," and few guessed that this seemingly lazy youth was a literary genius who would one day write fiction that captured the struggles of the human heart and immortalized a region of rural America.

Art Imitates Life Born in Albany, Mississippi, Faulkner was a true "son of the South." When he was five, his family moved to Oxford, Mississippi, where his grandfather's connections secured various positions for Faulkner's father.

Faulkner himself held various jobs because he did not have the patience to deal with the daily monotonies of steady work. One of his longest employments, almost three years, was as postmaster at the university in Oxford.

Although Faulkner read extensively, none of his reading concerned the history of the area where he lived. The flavor and settings of his stories were gleaned through word of mouth from the people around him.

Yoknapatawpha As a young man, Faulkner traveled abroad for some time and eventually landed in New Orleans, Louisiana, where he became acquainted with Sherwood Anderson and other writers. It was here that he began to write seriously. His first book, a poetry collection entitled *The Marble Faun*, was less than successful. Anderson advised him to attempt fiction. Faulkner published his first novel, *Soldier's Pay*, in 1926, and his second novel, *Mosquitoes*, the following year.

> "I never read any history. I talked to people around who had lived through it, and I would pick it up—I was just saturated with it but never read about it."
>
> —William Faulkner

With his third novel, *Sartoris*, Faulkner found the formula that would place him among the greatest of American writers. In this book he created the fictional world of Yoknapatawpha County, which was based on the region of northern Mississippi where he lived. Over the next thirty years, he continued to explore the "history" of this county and its fictional inhabitants.

Faulkner's style often makes his writing difficult to follow. He experimented with repetition, multiple points of view, and stream of consciousness. Because of the difficulty of his writing style, Faulkner was not widely read until *The Portable Faulkner* was published in 1946 and catapulted him to world fame. Three years later he won the Nobel Prize in Literature. Faulkner kept writing until his death.

William Faulkner was born in 1897 and died in 1962.

Literature Online **Author Search** For more about William Faulkner, go to www.glencoe.com.

Connecting to the Story

Most people harbor two identities. One is the public face that we show to our friends and families, while the other is the private self. As you read, think about the following questions:

- How different can a person's public identity be from his or her private identity?
- At what point might the secrets that divide a person's public and private lives cross the line into insanity?

Building Background

Faulkner's writings draw upon his knowledge of genteel aristocrats, unsophisticated sharecroppers, and Native Americans, as well as African Americans who had endured first the dehumanization of slavery and then the discrimination of Jim Crow.

The language in Faulkner's work reflects the vernacular and dialect of the South in his era. Modern readers may be shocked or offended by his use of racial slurs in this selection. Faulkner, like Mark Twain, does not use this language to offend or shock. He uses it merely to reflect the language of the time and place he describes.

Setting Purposes for Reading

Big Idea Return to Regionalism

As you read, imagine the people and the circumstances that Faulkner presents. Do they mesh with what you think a small southern town would have been like one hundred years ago?

Literary Element Foreshadowing

Foreshadowing is the use of clues by the author to prepare readers for events that will happen later in the story. In "A Rose for Emily," for example, the bad smell coming from Miss Emily's house foreshadows death and decay. As you read, consider which events might foreshadow important plot developments.

- See Literary Terms Handbook, p. R7.

Literature Online Interactive Literary Elements Handbook To review or learn more about the literary elements, go to www.glencoe.com.

Reading Strategy Identifying Sequence

Faulkner shifts time frames so often in "A Rose for Emily" that it can be difficult for readers to understand exactly when the events in the story take place. To keep track of what happens, list the events as they occur in the narrative and then number them in the sequence they occur in Emily's life.

Reading Tip: Making a Sequence Chart Use a sequence chart to help you keep track of events. Order the events as they occur in Emily's life. Use the list you wrote above to guide you.

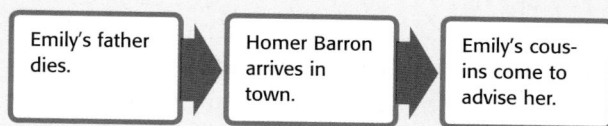

| Emily's father dies. | Homer Barron arrives in town. | Emily's cousins come to advise her. |

Vocabulary

sluggishly (slug′ ish lē) *adv.* slowly; without strength or energy; p. 879 *The exhausted hikers crawled sluggishly into their tents.*

vindicate (vin′ də kāt′) *v.* to justify; to prove correct in light of later circumstances; p. 881 *Winning the competition vindicated her efforts.*

haughty (hô′ tē) *adj.* conceited; arrogant; p. 882 *The haughty old woman would never admit a mistake.*

circumvent (sur′ kəm vent′) *v.* to get around or to avoid by clever maneuvering; p. 883 *We had to circumvent the usual procedure in order to finish the job quickly.*

virulent (vir′ yə lənt) *adj.* extremely poisonous or harmful; p. 883 *After World War I, a virulent strain of influenza killed more than 20 million people.*

Vocabulary Tip: Connotation and Denotation The **connotation** of a word is its suggested or implied meaning. The **denotation** is its literal definition.

INDIANA ACADEMIC STANDARDS (pages 877–889)
11.2.2 Analyze...patterns of organization...in the text.
11.2 Develop strategies such as...analyzing structure...
11.5.2 Write responses to literature that demonstrate a comprehensive understanding of...ideas in works...

A Rose for Emily

William Faulkner

When Miss Emily Grierson died, our whole town went to her funeral: the men through a sort of respectful affection for a fallen monument, the women mostly out of curiosity to see the inside of her house, which no one save an old man-servant—a combined gardener and cook—had seen in at least ten years. It was a big, squarish frame house that had once been white, decorated with cupolas[1] and spires and scrolled balconies in the heavily lightsome style of the seventies,[2] set on what had once been our most select street. But garages and cotton gins had encroached and obliterated even the august[3] names of that neighborhood; only Miss Emily's house was left, lifting its stubborn and coquettish[4] decay above the cotton wagons and the gasoline pumps—an eyesore among eyesores. And now Miss Emily had gone to join the representatives of those august names where they lay in the cedar-bemused[5] cemetery among the ranked and anonymous graves of Union and Confederate soldiers who fell at the battle of Jefferson.

Alive, Miss Emily had been a tradition, a duty, and a care; a sort of hereditary obligation upon the town, dating from that day in 1894 when Colonel Sartoris, the mayor—he who fathered the edict that no Negro woman should appear on the streets without an apron—remitted her taxes, the dispensation dating from the death of her father on into perpetuity.[6] Not that Miss Emily would have accepted charity. Colonel Sartoris invented an involved tale to the effect that Miss Emily's father had loaned money to the town, which the town, as a matter of business, preferred this way of repaying. Only a man of Colonel Sartoris' generation and thought could have invented it, and only a woman could have believed it.

When the next generation, with its more modern ideas, became mayors and aldermen, this arrangement created some little dissatisfaction. On the first of the year they mailed her a tax notice. February came, and there was no reply. They wrote her a formal letter, asking her to call at the sheriff's office at her convenience. A week later the mayor wrote her himself, offering to call or to send his car for her, and received in reply a note on paper of an archaic[7] shape, in a thin, flowing

---

1. *Cupolas* are small, domed structures rising above a roof.
2. *Lightsome* means "light and graceful." *Seventies* refers to the 1870s.
3. *August* (ô gust´) means "distinguished" or "prominent."
4. *Coquettish* (kō ket´ ish) means "flirtatious."
5. *Cedar-bemused* means "lost among the cedar trees" (literally, "confused by cedars").

Big Idea **Return to Regionalism** *What does the opening of "A Rose for Emily" tell you about the town and the type of people who live there?*

---

6. *[remitted . . . perpetuity]* This phrase means that Miss Emily was excused from paying taxes forever after her father's death.
7. Here, *archaic* means "old-fashioned."

Reading Strategy Identifying Sequence *Which clues reveal that the narrator is moving into a flashback?*

calligraphy[8] in faded ink, to the effect that she no longer went out at all. The tax notice was also enclosed, without comment.

They called a special meeting of the Board of Aldermen.[9] A deputation[10] waited upon her, knocked at the door through which no visitor had passed since she ceased giving china-painting lessons eight or ten years earlier. They were admitted by the old Negro into a dim hall from which a stairway mounted into still more shadow. It smelled of dust and disuse—a close, dank smell. The Negro led them into the parlor. It was furnished in heavy, leather-covered furniture. When the Negro opened the blinds of one window, they could see that the leather was cracked; and when they sat down, a faint dust rose **sluggishly** about their thighs, spinning with slow motes[11] in the single sun-ray. On a tarnished gilt[12] easel before the fireplace stood a crayon portrait of Miss Emily's father.

They rose when she entered—a small, fat woman in black, with a thin gold chain descending to her waist and vanishing into her belt, leaning on an ebony cane with a tarnished gold head. Her skeleton was small and spare; perhaps that was why what would have been merely plumpness in another was obesity in her. She looked bloated, like a body long submerged in motionless water, and of that pallid[13] hue. Her eyes, lost in the fatty ridges of her face, looked like two small pieces of coal pressed into a lump of dough as they moved from one face to another while the visitors stated their errand.

She did not ask them to sit. She just stood in the door and listened quietly until the spokesman came to a stumbling halt. Then they could hear the invisible watch ticking at the end of the gold chain.

Her voice was dry and cold. "I have no taxes in Jefferson. Colonel Sartoris explained it to me. Perhaps one of you can gain access to the city records and satisfy yourselves."

"But we have. We are the city authorities, Miss Emily. Didn't you get a notice from the sheriff, signed by him?"

"I received a paper, yes," Miss Emily said. "Perhaps he considers himself the sheriff . . . I have no taxes in Jefferson."

"But there is nothing on the books to show that, you see. We must go by the—"

"See Colonel Sartoris. I have no taxes in Jefferson."

"But, Miss Emily—"

"See Colonel Sartoris." (Colonel Sartoris had been dead almost ten years.) "I have no taxes in Jefferson. Tobe!" The Negro appeared. "Show these gentlemen out."

II

So she vanquished them, horse and foot, just as she had vanquished their fathers thirty years before about the smell. That was two years after her father's death and a short time after her sweetheart—the one we believed would marry her—had deserted her. After her father's death she went out very little; after her sweetheart went away, people hardly saw her at all. A few of the ladies had the temerity[14] to call, but were not received, and the only sign of life about the place was the Negro man—a young man then—going in and out with a market basket.

"Just as if a man—any man—could keep a kitchen properly," the ladies said; so they were not surprised when the smell developed. It was another link between the gross, teeming world and the high and mighty Griersons.

---

8. *Calligraphy* is an elegant type of handwriting.
9. The *Board of Aldermen* is the group formed by members of a city or town council.
10. A *deputation* is a "a small group that represents a larger one."
11. *Motes* are particles or specks, as of dust.
12. *Gilt* means "covered with gold."
13. *Pallid* means "lacking healthy color" or "pale."

14. *Temerity* (tə mer′ ə tē) is excessive boldness.

Literary Element Foreshadowing *What might the painting foreshadow?*

Vocabulary

sluggishly (slug′ ish lē) *adv.* slowly; without strength or energy

Reading Strategy Identifying Sequence *By the time Emily had "vanquished" the town officials about the "smell," what significant events had already occurred in Emily's life? List them in order.*

Literary Element Foreshadowing *What might this statement about the "smell" and Emily foreshadow?*

Autumn Glory: The Old Mill, 1869. John Atkinson Grimshaw. Oil on canvas, 62.2 x 87.6 cm.
Leeds Museums and Galleries, City Art Gallery, U.K.

A neighbor, a woman, complained to the mayor, Judge Stevens, eighty years old.

"But what will you have me do about it, madam?" he said.

"Why, send her word to stop it," the woman said. "Isn't there a law?"

"I'm sure that won't be necessary," Judge Stevens said. "It's probably just a snake or a rat that nigger of hers killed in the yard. I'll speak to him about it."

The next day he received two more complaints, one from a man who came in diffident deprecation.[15] "We really must do something about it, Judge. I'd be the last one in the world to bother Miss Emily, but we've got to do something." That night the Board of Aldermen met—three graybeards and one younger man, a member of the rising generation.

"It's simple enough," he said. "Send her word to have her place cleaned up. Give her a certain time to do it in, and if she don't . . ."

"Dammit, sir," Judge Stevens said, "will you accuse a lady to her face of smelling bad?"

So the next night, after midnight, four men crossed Miss Emily's lawn and slunk about the house like burglars, sniffing along the base of the brickwork and at the cellar openings while one of them performed a regular sowing motion with his hand out of a sack slung from his shoulder. They broke open the cellar door and sprinkled lime there, and in all the outbuildings.[16] As they recrossed the lawn, a window that had been dark was lighted and Miss Emily sat in it, the light behind her, and her upright torso motionless as that of an idol. They crept quietly across the lawn and into the shadow of the locusts[17] that lined the street. After a week or two the smell went away.

---

15. *Diffident deprecation* means "timid disapproval."

16. *Outbuildings* are separate buildings, such as a woodshed or barn, associated with a main building.

17. *Locusts* are deciduous trees. Several varieties have thorns and fragrant flowers that hang down in clusters.

That was when people had begun to feel really sorry for her. People in our town, remembering how old lady Wyatt, her great-aunt, had gone completely crazy at last, believed that the Griersons held themselves a little too high for what they really were. None of the young men were quite good enough for Miss Emily and such. We had long thought of them as a tableau,[18] Miss Emily a slender figure in white in the background, her father a spraddled[19] silhouette in the foreground, his back to her and clutching a horsewhip, the two of them framed by the back-flung front door. So when she got to be thirty and was still single, we were not pleased exactly, but **vindicated**; even with insanity in the family she wouldn't have turned down all of her chances if they had really materialized.

When her father died, it got about that the house was all that was left to her; and in a way, people were glad. At last they could pity Miss Emily. Being left alone, and a pauper,[20] she had become humanized. Now she too would know the old thrill and the old despair of a penny more or less.

The day after his death all the ladies prepared to call at the house and offer condolence and aid, as is our custom. Miss Emily met them at the door, dressed as usual and with no trace of grief on her face. She told them that her father was not dead. She did that for three days, with the ministers calling on her, and the doctors, trying to persuade her to let them dispose of the body. Just as they were about to resort to law and force, she broke down, and they buried her father quickly.

We did not say she was crazy then. We believed she had to do that. We remembered all the young men her father had driven away, and we knew that with nothing left, she would have to cling to that which had robbed her, as people will.

---

18. A *tableau* (tab lō′) is a striking or artistic grouping of people or objects.
19. *Spraddled* means "sprawled" or "spread wide apart."
20. A *pauper* is a very poor person.

III

She was sick for a long time. When we saw her again her hair was cut short, making her look like a girl, with a vague resemblance to those angels in colored church windows—sort of tragic and serene.

The town had just let the contracts for paving the sidewalks, and in the summer after her father's death they began the work. The construction company came with niggers and mules and machinery, and a foreman named Homer Barron, a Yankee—a big, dark, ready man, with a big voice and eyes lighter than his face. The little boys would follow in groups to hear him cuss the niggers, and the niggers singing in time to the rise and fall of picks. Pretty soon he knew everybody in town. Whenever you heard a lot of laughing anywhere about the square, Homer Barron would be in the center of the group. Presently we began to see him and Miss Emily on Sunday afternoons driving in the yellow-wheeled buggy and the matched team of bays from the livery stable.

At first we were glad that Miss Emily would have an interest, because the ladies all said, "Of course a Grierson would not think seriously of a Northerner, a day laborer." But there were still others, older people, who said that even grief could not cause a real lady to forget *noblesse oblige*[21]—without calling it *noblesse oblige*. They just said, "Poor Emily. Her kinsfolk should come to her." She had some kin in Alabama; but years ago her father had fallen out with them over the estate of old lady Wyatt, the crazy woman, and there was no communication between the two families. They had not even been represented at the funeral.

And as soon as the old people said, "Poor Emily," the whispering began. "Do you suppose it's really so?" they said to one another. "Of course it is. What else could . . ." This

---

21. The French expression *noblesse oblige* (nō bles′ ō blēzh′) suggests that those of high birth or rank have a responsibility to act kindly and honorably toward others.

Visual Vocabulary
Jalousies (jal′ ə sēz) are overlapping, adjustable slats that cover a door or window.

behind their hands; rustling of craned[22] silk and satin behind jalousies closed upon the sun of Sunday afternoon as the thin, swift clop-clop-clop of the matched team passed: "Poor Emily."

She carried her head high enough—even when we believed that she was fallen. It was as if she demanded more than ever the recognition of her dignity as the last Grierson; as if it had wanted that touch of earthiness to reaffirm her imperviousness. Like when she bought the rat poison, the arsenic. That was over a year after they had begun to say "Poor Emily," and while the two female cousins were visiting her.

"I want some poison," she said to the druggist. She was over thirty then, still a slight woman, though thinner than usual, with cold, **haughty** black eyes in a face the flesh of which was strained across the temples and about the eye-sockets as you imagine a lighthousekeeper's face ought to look. "I want some poison," she said.

"Yes, Miss Emily. What kind? For rats and such? I'd recom—"

"I want the best you have. I don't care what kind."

The druggist named several. "They'll kill anything up to an elephant. But what you want is—"

"Arsenic," Miss Emily said. "Is that a good one?"

"Is . . . arsenic? Yes, ma'am. But what you want—"

"I want arsenic."

The druggist looked down at her. She looked back at him, erect, her face like a strained flag. "Why, of course," the druggist said. "If that's what you want. But the law requires you to tell what you are going to use it for."

Miss Emily just stared at him, her head tilted back in order to look him eye for eye, until he looked away and went and got the arsenic and wrapped it up. The Negro delivery boy brought her the package; the druggist didn't come back. When she opened the package at home there was written on the box, under the skull and bones: "For rats."

IV

So the next day we all said, "She will kill herself"; and we said it would be the best thing. When she had first begun to be seen with Homer Barron, we had said, "She will marry him." Then we said, "She will persuade him yet," because Homer himself had remarked—he liked men, and it was known that he drank with the younger men in the Elks' Club—that he was not a marrying man. Later we said, "Poor Emily" behind the jalousies as they passed on Sunday afternoon in the glittering buggy, Miss Emily with her head high and Homer Barron with his hat cocked and a cigar in his teeth, reins and whip in a yellow glove.

Then some of the ladies began to say that it was a disgrace to the town and a bad example to the young people. The men did not want to interfere, but at last the ladies forced the Baptist minister—Miss Emily's people were Episcopal—to call upon her. He would never divulge what happened during that interview, but he refused to go back again. The next Sunday they again drove about the streets, and the following day the minister's wife wrote to Miss Emily's relations in Alabama.

So she had blood-kin under her roof again and we sat back to watch developments. At first nothing happened. Then we were sure that they were to be married. We learned that Miss Emily had been to the jeweler's and ordered a man's toilet set[23] in silver, with the letters H. B. on

---

22. *Craned* means "stretched."

Vocabulary

haughty (hô′ tē) *adj.* conceited; arrogant

---

23. A *toilet set* is a set of articles used for personal grooming (hairbrush, comb, etc.).

Literary Element Foreshadowing *What might Emily's purchase at the drugstore foreshadow? What makes her purchase seem particularly suspicious?*

Big Idea Return to Regionalism *What does the town's involvement in Emily's affairs suggest about its morals and values? Why is Emily a threat?*

Day After the Funeral, 1925. Edward Hopper. Watercolor on paper. Private collection.
James Goodman Gallery, New York.

each piece. Two days later we learned that she had bought a complete outfit of men's clothing, including a nightshirt, and we said, "They are married." We were really glad. We were glad because the two female cousins were even more Grierson than Miss Emily had ever been.

So we were not surprised when Homer Barron—the streets had been finished some time since—was gone. We were a little disappointed that there was not a public blowing-off,[24] but we believed that he had gone on to prepare for Miss Emily's coming, or to give her a chance to get rid of the cousins. (By that time it was a cabal,[25] and we were all Miss Emily's allies to help **circumvent** the cousins.) Sure enough, after another week they departed. And, as we had expected all along, within three days

Homer Barron was back in town. A neighbor saw the Negro man admit him at the kitchen door at dusk one evening.

And that was the last we saw of Homer Barron. And of Miss Emily for some time. The Negro man went in and out with the market basket, but the front door remained closed. Now and then we would see her at a window for a moment, as the men did that night when they sprinkled the lime, but for almost six months she did not appear on the streets. Then we knew that this was to be expected too; as if that quality of her father which had thwarted her woman's life so many times had been too **virulent** and too furious to die.

---

24. A *blowing-off* is a celebration.
25. A *cabal* (kə bäl´) is a group united in a secret plot.

Vocabulary

circumvent (sur´ kəm vent´) *v.* to get around or to avoid by clever maneuvering

---

Literary Element   Foreshadowing *What might the juxta-position of these two sentences foreshadow about Emily and Homer Barron?*

Vocabulary

virulent (vir´ yə lənt) *adj.* extremely poisonous or harmful

When we next saw Miss Emily, she had grown fat and her hair was turning gray. During the next few years it grew grayer and grayer until it attained an even pepper-and-salt iron-gray, when it ceased turning. Up to the day of her death at seventy-four it was still that vigorous iron-gray, like the hair of an active man.

From that time on her front door remained closed, save for a period of six or seven years, when she was about forty, during which she gave lessons in china-painting. She fitted up a studio in one of the downstairs rooms, where the daughters and granddaughters of Colonel Sartoris' contemporaries were sent to her with the same regularity and in the same spirit that they were sent to church on Sundays with a twenty-five-cent piece for the collection plate. Meanwhile her taxes had been remitted.

Then the newer generation became the backbone and the spirit of the town, and the painting pupils grew up and fell away and did not send their children to her with boxes of color and tedious brushes and pictures cut from the ladies' magazines. The front door closed upon the last one and remained closed for good. When the town got free postal delivery, Miss Emily alone refused to let them fasten the metal numbers above her door and attach a mailbox to it. She would not listen to them.

Daily, monthly, yearly we watched the Negro grow grayer and more stooped, going in and out with the market basket. Each December we sent her a tax notice, which would be returned by the post office a week later, unclaimed. Now and then we would see her in one of the downstairs windows—she had evidently shut up the top floor of the house—like the carven torso of an idol in a niche,[26] looking or not looking at us, we could never tell which. Thus she passed from generation to generation—dear, inescapable, impervious, tranquil, and perverse.

And so she died. Fell ill in the house filled with dust and shadows, with only a doddering Negro man to wait on her. We did not even know she was sick; we had long since given up trying to get any information from the Negro. He talked to no one, probably not even to her, for his voice had grown harsh and rusty, as if from disuse.

She died in one of the downstairs rooms, in a heavy walnut bed with a curtain, her gray head propped on a pillow yellow and moldy with age and lack of sunlight.

V

The Negro met the first of the ladies at the front door and let them in, with their hushed, sibilant[27] voices and their quick, curious glances, and then he disappeared. He walked right through the house and out the back and was not seen again.

The two female cousins came at once. They held the funeral on the second day, with the town coming to look at Miss Emily beneath a mass of bought flowers, with the crayon face of her father musing profoundly above the bier[28] and the ladies sibilant and macabre;[29] and the very old men—some in their brushed Confederate uniforms—on the porch and the lawn, talking of Miss Emily as if she had been a contemporary of theirs, believing that they had danced with her and courted her perhaps, confusing time with its mathematical progression, as the old do, to whom all the past is not a diminishing road but, instead, a huge meadow which no winter ever quite touches, divided from them now by the narrow bottle-neck of the most recent decade of years.

Already we knew that there was one room in that region above stairs which no one had seen in forty years, and which would have to be forced. They waited until Miss Emily was decently in the ground before they opened it.

The violence of breaking down the door seemed to fill this room with pervading dust. A thin, acrid pall[30] as of the tomb seemed to lie

---

27. *Sibilant* (sĭ′ bə lənt) means "making a hissing sound."
28. A *bier* is a stand for a coffin.
29. *Macabre* (mə kä′ brə) means "gruesome" or "suggesting the horror of death."
30. An *acrid pall* is a bitter-smelling covering.

Big Idea Return to Regionalism *How do Emily's servant's actions before and after her death reflect the general change in the town and in the South overall during this period?*

Reading Strategy Identifying Sequence *How do you think Faulkner's nonlinear sequence of events enhances the story about Emily?*

---

26. A *niche* (nĭch) is a recessed area in a wall, sometimes used for displaying a statue.

The Sunny Parlor, c. 1901. Wilhelm Hammershoi. Oil on canvas, 49.7 x 40 cm. Nationalgalerie, Staatliche Museen zu Berlin, Germany.

everywhere upon this room decked and furnished as for a bridal:[31] upon the valance curtains of faded rose color, upon the rose-shaded lights, upon the dressing table, upon the delicate array of crystal and the man's toilet things backed with tarnished silver, silver so tarnished that the monogram was obscured. Among them lay a collar and tie, as if they had just been removed, which, lifted, left upon the surface a pale crescent in the dust. Upon a chair hung the suit, carefully folded; beneath it the two mute shoes and the discarded socks.

The man himself lay in the bed.

For a long while we just stood there, looking down at the profound and fleshless grin. The body had apparently once lain in the attitude of an embrace, but now the long sleep that outlasts love, that conquers even the grimace of love, had cuckolded[32] him. What was left of him, rotted beneath what was left of the nightshirt, had become inextricable from the bed in which he lay; and upon him and upon the pillow beside him lay that even coating of the patient and biding dust.

Then we noticed that in the second pillow was the indentation of a head. One of us lifted something from it, and leaning forward, that faint and invisible dust dry and acrid in the nostrils, we saw a long strand of iron-gray hair. ∾

---

31. Here, *bridal* means "wedding."

32. *Cuckolded* means "betrayed," in the sense of a husband deceived by an unfaithful wife.

Address upon Receiving the Nobel Prize in Literature

Stockholm, December 10, 1950

William Faulkner

I feel that this award was not made to me as a man, but to my work—a life's work in the agony and sweat of the human spirit, not for glory and least of all for profit, but to create out of the materials of the human spirit something which did not exist before. So this award is only mine in trust. It will not be difficult to find a dedication for the money part of it commensurate[1] with the purpose and significance of its origin. But I would like to do the same with the acclaim too, by using this moment as a pinnacle[2] from which I might be listened to by the young men and women already dedicated to the same anguish and travail,[3] among whom is already that one who will some day stand here where I am standing.

Our tragedy today is a general and universal physical fear so long sustained by now that we can even bear it. There are no longer problems of the spirit. There is only the question: When will I be blown up? Because of this, the young man or woman writing today has forgotten the problems of the human heart in conflict with itself which alone can make good writing because only that is worth writing about, worth the agony and the sweat.

He must learn them again. He must teach himself that the basest of all things is to be afraid; and, teaching himself that, forget it forever, leaving no room in his workshop for anything but the old verities and truths of the heart, the old universal truths lacking which any story is ephemeral[4] and doomed—love and honor and pity and pride and compassion and sacrifice. Until he does so, he labors under a curse. He writes not of love but of lust, of defeats in which nobody loses anything of value, of victories without hope and, worst of all, without pity or compassion. His griefs grieve on no universal bones, leaving no scars. He writes not of the heart but of the glands.

Until he relearns these things, he will write as though he stood among and watched the end of man. I decline to accept the end of man. It is easy enough to say that man is immortal simply because he will endure: that when the last ding-dong of doom has clanged and faded from the last worthless rock hanging tideless in the last red and dying evening, that even then there will still be one more sound: that of his puny inexhaustible voice, still talking. I refuse to accept this. I believe that man will not merely endure: he will prevail. He is immortal, not because he alone among creatures has an inexhaustible voice, but because he has a soul, a spirit capable of compassion and sacrifice and endurance. The poet's, the writer's, duty is to write about these things. It is his privilege to help man endure by lifting his heart, by reminding him of the courage and honor and hope and pride and compassion and pity and sacrifice which have been the glory of his past. The poet's voice need not merely be the record of man, it can be one of the props, the pillars to help him endure and prevail. ❧

---

1. *Commensurate* (kə men′ sər it) means "of equal measure."
2. *Pinnacle* (pin′ ə kəl) means "highest point" or "peak."
3. *Travail* (trə vāl′) is exhausting mental or physical work.
4. *Ephemeral* (i fem′ ər əl) means "lasting a very brief time" or "short-lived."

Big Idea Return to Regionalism *How might stories such as "A Rose for Emily" reflect Faulkner's desire to write about "the human heart in conflict with itself"?*

Reading Strategy Identifying Sequence *Why might Faulkner have chosen to place this statement at the end and not the beginning of his speech?*

RESPONDING AND THINKING CRITICALLY

Respond

1. Were you surprised by the ending of the story? Why or why not?

Recall and Interpret

2. (a)How did Miss Emily receive the delegation that came to explain that she must pay taxes? (b)What does her behavior demonstrate about her character?

3. (a)What happens when Miss Emily's house begins to smell and when her father dies? (b)How does the community interpret her response to these incidents?

4. (a)In Faulkner's "Address upon Receiving the Nobel Prize in Literature," what are modern writers concerned with, according to Faulkner? (b)Why is this problematic?

5. In the speech, what does Faulkner say is the only thing worth writing about? Why?

Analyze and Evaluate

6. (a)In "A Rose for Emily," what was the effect of Emily's father on her relationships with men? (b)What clues does Faulkner use to reveal this effect?

7. (a)How would you characterize the narrator of "A Rose for Emily"? (b)What can you infer about the narrator's attitude toward Miss Emily? Explain.

8. (a)In Faulkner's speech, what is his view of our future and of the writer's role in that future? (b)Do you agree with this view? Explain.

Connect

9. (a)How do you think the events of Faulkner's time influenced this speech? (b)How are his views still relevant today?

10. **Big Idea** **Return to Regionalism** In "A Rose for Emily," how do the southern traditions and attitudes of her neighbors affect Miss Emily?

YOU'RE THE CRITIC: Similar Viewpoints

WORK OR PLEASURE?

William Faulkner has a reputation for prose that is difficult to follow. First, he does not unfold his plots in a linear fashion. As Dean Morgan Schmitter explains in his essay "The Faulkner Legend":

"Another feature of Faulkner's style is the manner in which he releases information, sometimes preventing the reader from having full perspective on what is happening. Although the reader accumulates information as he goes along, often he must wait pages to find the facts he needs . . . "

The second reason that Faulkner's writing is hard to follow is that his sentences are often long and rambling, as though he wants to present entire human experiences within a single written breath. As Conrad Aiken writes,

"And at once, if one considers these queer sentences not simply by themselves, as monsters of grammar or awkwardness, but in their relation to the book as a whole, one sees a functional reason and necessity for their being as they are. They parallel in a curious and perhaps inevitable way, and not without aesthetic justification, the whole elaborate method of deliberately withheld meaning, of progressive and partial and delayed disclosure, which so often gives the characteristic shape of the novels themselves."

Group Activity

Discuss the following questions with your classmates.

1. What examples can you find of confusing sequences of events and rambling sentences in "A Rose for Emily"?

2. (a)Do you find the story difficult to follow? (b)Is it worth the effort? Explain.

Literary Element Foreshadowing

Faulkner's style, which pulls his readers back and forth through time to reveal the events in his plots, can make it difficult to recognize **foreshadowing**. Because there is no single time frame in which a reader can comfortably base his or her perspective, it is important to pay special attention to details to see how they affect future outcomes or how they relate to events that occurred previously. In fact, some details foreshadow events that occur earlier in Emily's life, even though they are revealed later in the narration.

1. Which event in the narration is the earliest foreshadowing of Homer Barron's fate?

2. What is the next event that foreshadows Barron's fate?

3. As you read the story, were you able to recognize any examples of foreshadowing even though Faulkner jumbled events in his story? If you did, explain how you recognized them. If you did not, explain why you were fooled.

Review: Flashback

A **flashback** is an interruption in a plot to portray an incident that happened in the past. Writers use flashbacks to explain why characters behave as they do or how the plot has developed as it has.

Partner Activity Meet with another classmate to discuss Faulkner's use of flashback in "A Rose for Emily." Use the five sections as numbered by the author to determine where the flashbacks are and at what point in Emily's life each one occurs.

Section	Flashback
1	
2	
3	

Reading Strategy Identifying Sequence

As you have seen, Faulkner does not often take his readers on a chronological journey through his stories. "A Rose for Emily" is no exception.

1. Use the list and the sequence chart that you made as you read the story to write one or two paragraphs describing the important events in Emily's life. Use sequencing words, such as *first, next, then,* and *finally,* and specific times and dates to put the events in proper chronological order.

2. Explain how the convoluted sequence adds to or detracts from the story's meaning.

Vocabulary Practice

Practice with Denotation and Connotation
For each of the vocabulary words listed below, circle the word in parentheses that is the word's denotation and underline the word that is its connotation.

1. sluggishly   (inactively, lazily)

2. circumvent   (avoid, evade)

3. virulent   (poisonous, harmful)

4. vindicate   (avenge, justify)

5. haughty   (proud, snobby)

Academic Vocabulary

Here are two words from the vocabulary list on page R86. These words will help you think, write, and talk about the selection.

justify (jəs′ tə fī) *v.* to give good reason for a specific action to be taken

prior (prī′ər) *adj.* occurring before a given time or event

Practice and Apply
1. How did Colonel Sartoris **justify** Miss Emily's not having to pay taxes to the town?
2. **Prior** to her relationship with Homer Barron, what was Miss Emily's experience with young men?

Writing About Literature

Respond to Conflict Faulkner once described "A Rose for Emily" as a "manifestation of man's injustice to man, of the poor tragic human being struggling with its own heart, with others, with its environment, for the simple things which all human beings want." Write a brief essay in which you explain why one of the four conflicts Faulkner mentions above is central to the story.

The introduction of your essay should state which conflict you feel is central to the story and why. The conclusion should summarize your thoughts and perhaps offer a related insight. Each body paragraph should include a major point and evidence from the story to support your viewpoint. Use a graphic organizer like the one below to organize your body paragraphs:

After you complete your draft, meet with a partner to offer suggestions on how to improve each other's work. Then edit and proofread your essay for errors in spelling, grammar, and punctuation.

Learning for Life

Write a radio or television news story about the discovery of Homer Barron's body in Miss Emily's bedroom. Use details from "A Rose for Emily" as the basis for your story. Then choose several characters from the story and invent quotes from each one that reveal that character's involvement with and impact on Miss Emily's life.

Faulkner's Language and Style

Choosing Fresh Adjectives Faulkner is a master of description. He chooses adjectives that are precise and unusual:

> "*coquettish* decay"
> "*cedar-bemused* cemetery"
> "*profound and fleshless* grin"
> "Thus she passed from generation to generation— *dear, inescapable, impervious, tranquil, and perverse.*"

Imagine how spare these nouns would sound without such colorful adjectives.

When describing people, things, or places in your writing, avoid adjectives that are so overused that they convey little meaning to readers. For example, the adjective *bad* is so unoriginal that it connotes no specific image for a reader. Words like *sinister* or *hostile* suggest menace, while *brutal* and *vicious* show a more violent type of evil.

Before you write a description, think carefully about what you are describing. Picture it in your mind and choose adjectives that will stick with your reader. If you have difficulty, consult an indexed thesaurus. A good thesaurus will suggest various nuances and connotations for the overused adjectives that often crowd more exact and descriptive words from a writer's mind.

Activity Scan "A Rose for Emily" for other examples of fresh, precise adjectives. Make a list of them to read aloud to the class.

Revising Check

Fresh Adjectives Work with a partner to review and revise any overused or imprecise adjectives that you used in your essay on "A Rose for Emily."

Literature Online **Web Activities** For eFlashcards, Selection Quick Checks, and other Web activities, go to www.glencoe.com.

A Worn Path

MEET EUDORA WELTY

Eudora Welty admitted to living a sheltered life. Born and raised in Jackson, Mississippi, she lived in her family's house there until her death at age ninety-two. Welty maintained, though, that "a sheltered life can be a daring life as well. For all serious daring starts from within."

Pleasant Childhood Welty's parents filled their house with books and loved to read on their own and to their children. Once she learned to read herself, Welty read everything she could get her hands on. Her mother, however, put one restriction on her reading. She told the town librarian that Eudora could read anything in the library except the then-popular novel *Elsie Dinsmore*. When Eudora asked why, her mother explained that the main character fainted and fell off her piano stool after being made to practice for a long time. Her mother told Eudora that she was too impressionable: "You'd read that and the very first thing you'd do, you'd fall off the piano stool." Thereafter, Welty could never hear the word *impressionable* without calling up the image of falling off a piano stool.

> "Writing a story is one way of discovering sequence in experience, of stumbling upon cause and effect in the happenings of a writer's own life. This has been the case with me. Connections slowly emerge."
>
> —Eudora Welty

Work with the WPA Welty's love of reading and her lively imagination inspired her decision to become a writer for the Works Progress Administration (WPA). This government agency, founded during the Great Depression, gave people work on public projects, such as constructing roads and buildings, clearing trails in parks, and painting murals. Welty traveled around Mississippi and wrote articles about WPA projects in the state. Welty later said that, through her travels, she gained her first glimpses of the very different ways in which people live. Her musings and imaginings about the people she saw, talked to, and photographed inspired her writing throughout her life.

Successful Writing Career Welty had her first short story published when she was twenty-seven. Five years later, she published *A Curtain of Green*, a collection of short stories in which "A Worn Path" first appeared. In her thirties, she published her first novels, *The Robber Bridegroom* (1942) and *Delta Wedding* (1946). Welty went on to write award-winning fiction for many years, until severe arthritis forced her to give up writing at age eighty-five.

Southern Charm At Welty's funeral, her agent, Timothy Seldes, told a revealing story about Welty's last words. He said that when her doctor leaned over her bed and asked if there was anything he could do for her, she replied, "No, but thank you for inviting me to the party." This polite response illustrates Welty's southern charm and gracious warmth—qualities that Welty brought to her writing. Her compassionate portrayals of people living in the deep South powerfully illuminate their shared values and complicated history.

Eudora Welty was born in 1909 and died in 2001.

Literature Online Author Search For more about Eudora Welty, go to www.glencoe.com.

Connecting to the Story

Think about elderly people whom you respect and admire—people you know personally or people you know about. What is it that you admire about them? As you read the story, reflect on the following questions:

- What problems do older people face?
- What qualities of character do elderly people demonstrate as they deal with the difficulties of their lives?

Building Background

"A Worn Path" is set near the city of Natchez (nach′ iz), Mississippi, around 1930. The Natchez Trace was an old trail that led from the Native American villages along the banks of the lower Mississippi River northeastward six hundred miles to settlements along the Cumberland River, in what is now Tennessee. Travelers who boated down the Mississippi had to walk or ride the Natchez Trace to return to locations upstream. Around the turn of the nineteenth century, the Natchez Trace was one of the most well-traveled trails in the United States. However, new, powerful steamships that could travel against the Mississippi's strong current were introduced and allowed river travelers to make their way upstream by boat. As a result, the Natchez Trace fell into disuse around 1820.

Setting Purposes for Reading

Big Idea **Return to Regionalism**

As you read, think about how the lives of the characters have been shaped by the history and culture of the South.

Literary Element **Description**

Description is writing that captures the physical sensations of a place or of an experience. As you read, notice the details Welty includes to help readers imagine that they can see, hear, smell, taste, and feel what she is describing.

- See Literary Terms Handbook, p. R4.

Literature Online **Interactive Literary Elements Handbook** To review or learn more about the literary elements, go to www.glencoe.com.

Reading Strategy Visualizing

Visualizing is picturing a writer's ideas or descriptions in the mind's eye. Visualizing is one of the best ways to help you understand and remember information in a story.

....

Reading Tip: Sketch On a separate sheet of paper, make quick sketches showing how you visualize each important scene that you read.

Vocabulary

grave (grāv) *adj.* dignified and gloomy; somber; p. 892 *Mark wore a grave look as he delivered the eulogy.*

vigorously (vig′ər əs lē) *adv.* with power, energy, and strength; p. 894 *Katie vigorously shook the rug to get the dust out.*

ceremonial (ser′ə mo′nē əl) *adj.* formal; p. 896 *The graduates wore ceremonial robes.*

solemn (sol′əm) *adj.* serious; somber; p. 896 *With a solemn expression, the child tended to her sick puppy.*

comprehension (kom′pri hen′shən) *n.* the act of grasping mentally; understanding; p. 896 *Mia's comprehension of math is excellent.*

....

Vocabulary Tip: Analogies Comparisons that reveal the relationship between two words or ideas are called **analogies.** In analogies exercises, you are frequently presented with a pair of words that demonstrates a relationship and then are asked to combine two other words to indicate a similar relationship. To complete such an exercise, decide on the relationship represented by the first two words. Then apply that relationship to the second set of words.

INDIANA ACADEMIC STANDARDS (pages 891–899)

11.3 [Identify] story elements such as character [and] setting...

11.2 Develop [reading] strategies...

11.5.9 Write...an analytical essay...that...creates an organizing structure appropriate to purpose, audience, and context...

A Worn Path

Eudora Welty

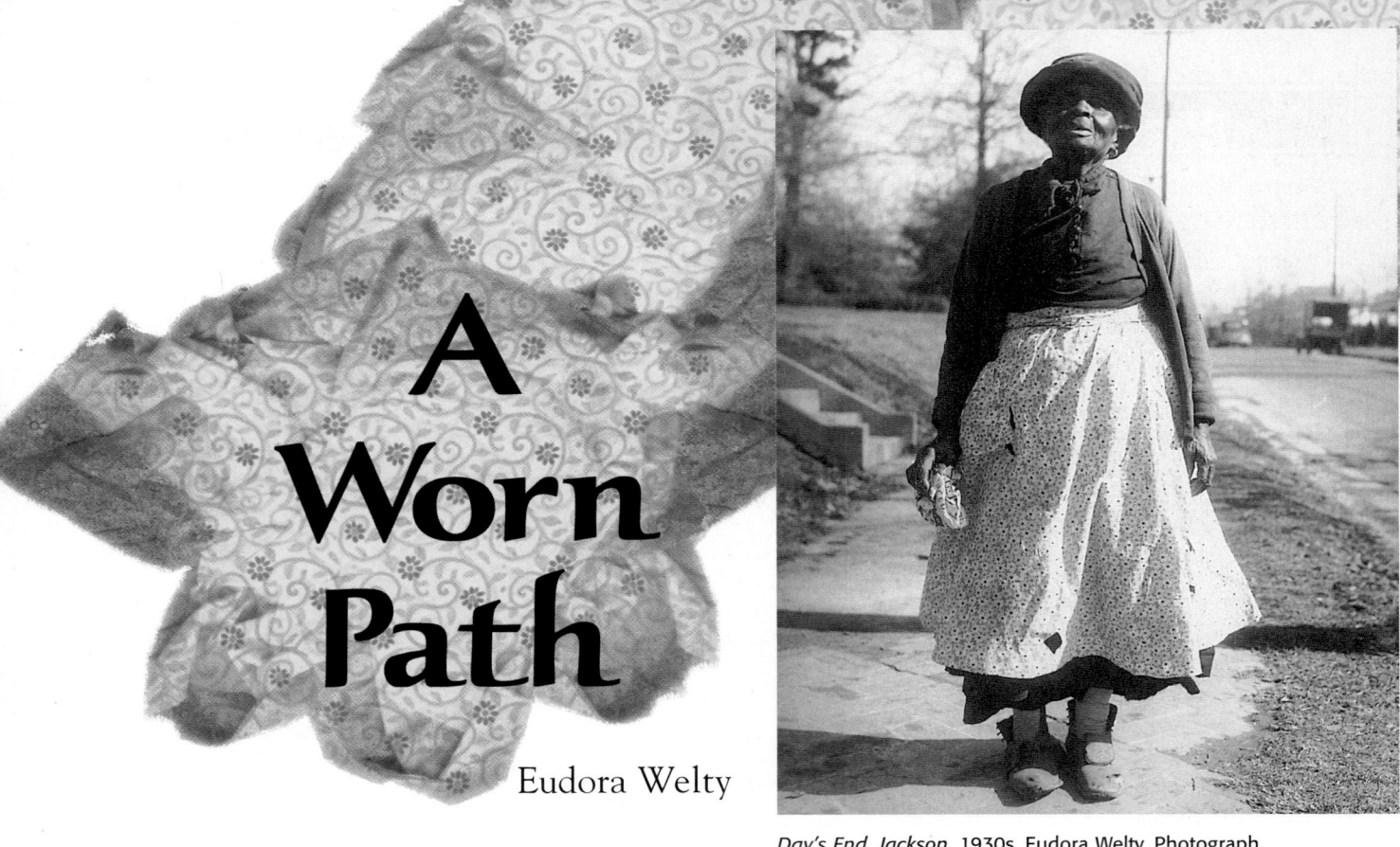

Day's End, Jackson, 1930s. Eudora Welty. Photograph. Mississippi Department of Archives and History, Jackson, MS. Eudora Welty Collection.

It was December—a bright frozen day in the early morning. Far out in the country there was an old Negro woman with her head tied in a red rag, coming along a path through the pinewoods. Her name was Phoenix Jackson. She was very old and small and she walked slowly in the dark pine shadows, moving a little from side to side in her steps, with the balanced heaviness and lightness of a pendulum in a grandfather clock. She carried a thin, small cane made from an umbrella, and with this she kept tapping the frozen earth in front of her. This made a **grave** and persistent noise in the still air, that seemed meditative like the chirping of a solitary little bird.

She wore a dark striped dress reaching down to her shoe tops, and an equally long apron of bleached sugar sacks, with a full pocket: all neat and tidy, but every time she took a step she might have fallen over her shoelaces, which dragged from her unlaced shoes. She looked straight ahead. Her eyes were blue with age.

Her skin had a pattern all its own of numberless branching wrinkles and as though a whole little tree stood in the middle of her forehead, but a golden color ran underneath, and the two knobs of her cheeks were illumined by a yellow burning under the dark. Under the red rag her hair came down on her neck in the frailest of ringlets, still black, and with an odor like copper.

Now and then there was a quivering in the thicket. Old Phoenix said, "Out of my way, all you foxes, owls, beetles, jack rabbits, coons and wild animals! . . . Keep out from under these feet, little bob-whites[1]. . . . Keep the big wild hogs out of my path. Don't let none of those come running my direction. I got a long way." Under her small black-freckled hand her cane, limber as a buggy whip, would switch at the brush as if to rouse up any hiding things.

---

1. *Bob-whites,* also called quails or partridges, are birds with mottled brown plumage and white markings.

Vocabulary

grave (grāv) *adj.* dignified and gloomy; somber

On she went. The woods were deep and still. The sun made the pine needles almost too bright to look at, up where the wind rocked. The cones dropped as light as feathers. Down in the hollow[2] was the mourning dove—it was not too late for him.

The path ran up a hill. "Seem like there is chains about my feet, time I get this far," she said, in the voice of argument old people keep to use with themselves. "Something always take a hold of me on this hill—pleads I should stay."

After she got to the top she turned and gave a full, severe look behind her where she had come. "Up through pines," she said at length. "Now down through oaks."

Her eyes opened their widest, and she started down gently. But before she got to the bottom of the hill a bush caught her dress.

Her fingers were busy and intent, but her skirts were full and long, so that before she could pull them free in one place they were caught in another. It was not possible to allow the dress to tear. "I in the thorny bush," she said. "Thorns, you doing your appointed[3] work. Never want to let folks pass, no sir. Old eyes thought you was a pretty little *green* bush."

Finally, trembling all over, she stood free, and after a moment dared to stoop for her cane.

"Sun so high!" she cried, leaning back and looking, while the thick tears went over her eyes. "The time getting all gone here."

At the foot of this hill was a place where a log was laid across the creek.

"Now comes the trial," said Phoenix.

Putting her right foot out, she mounted the log and shut her eyes. Lifting her skirt, leveling her cane fiercely before her, like a festival figure in some parade, she began to march across. Then she opened her eyes and she was safe on the other side.

"I wasn't as old as I thought," she said.

But she sat down to rest. She spread her skirts on the bank around her and folded her hands over her knees. Up above her was a tree in a pearly cloud of mistletoe. She did not dare to close her eyes, and when a little boy brought her a plate with a slice of marble-cake on it she spoke to him. "That would be acceptable," she said. But when she went to take it there was just her own hand in the air.

So she left that tree, and had to go through a barbed-wire fence. There she had to creep and crawl, spreading her knees and stretching her fingers like a baby trying to climb the steps. But she talked loudly to herself: she could not let her dress be torn now, so late in the day, and she could not pay for having her arm or her leg sawed off if she got caught fast where she was.

At last she was safe through the fence and risen up out in the clearing. Big dead trees, like black men with one arm, were standing in the purple stalks of the withered cotton field. There sat a buzzard.

"Who you watching?"

In the furrow[4] she made her way along.

"Glad this not the season for bulls," she said, looking sideways, "and the good Lord made his snakes to curl up and sleep in the winter. A pleasure I don't see no two-headed snake coming around that tree, where it come once. It took a while to get by him, back in the summer."

She passed through the old cotton and went into a field of dead corn. It whispered and shook and was taller than her head. "Through the maze now," she said, for there was no path.

Then there was something tall, black, and skinny there, moving before her.

At first she took it for a man. It could have been a man dancing in the field. But she stood still and listened, and it did not make a sound. It was as silent as a ghost.

"Ghost," she said sharply, "who be you the ghost of? For I have heard of nary[5] death close by."

---

2. A *hollow* is a small valley.
3. *Appointed* means "assigned" or "designated."

Literary Element   Description *Why does the author include details about the animals in the woods as well as about the silence and sunlight there?*

Big Idea   Return to Regionalism *From what you have read so far, what do you infer about Phoenix Jackson's background as well as about her present life?*

---

4. A *furrow* is a long, narrow channel in the ground made by a plow.
5. *Nary* means "not one."

Reading Strategy   Visualizing *How do you imagine Phoenix Jackson looks and sounds as she goes through the fence?*

Road Between High Banks, Hinds County, 1940s. Eudora Welty. Photograph. Mississippi Department of Archives and History, Jackson, MS. Eudora Welty Collection.

Viewing the Photograph: In what ways is the path in the photograph similar to or different from the path in the story?

But there was no answer—only the ragged dancing in the wind.

She shut her eyes, reached out her hand, and touched a sleeve. She found a coat and inside that an emptiness, cold as ice.

"You scarecrow," she said. Her face lighted. "I ought to be shut up for good," she said with laughter. "My senses is gone. I too old. I the oldest people I ever know. Dance, old scarecrow," she said, "while I dancing with you."

She kicked her foot over the furrow, and with mouth drawn down, shook her head once or twice in a little strutting way. Some husks blew down and whirled in streamers about her skirts.

Then she went on, parting her way from side to side with the cane, through the whispering field.

At last she came to the end, to a wagon track where the silver grass blew between the red ruts. The quail were walking around like pullets,[6] seeming all dainty and unseen.

"Walk pretty," she said. "This the easy place. This the easy going."

She followed the track, swaying through the quiet bare fields, through the little strings of trees silver in their dead leaves, past cabins silver from weather, with the doors and windows boarded shut, all like old women under a spell sitting there. "I walking in their sleep," she said, nodding her head **vigorously.**

In a ravine[7] she went where a spring was silently flowing through a hollow log. Old Phoenix bent and drank. "Sweet-gum[8] makes the water sweet," she said, and drank more. "Nobody know who made this well, for it was here when I was born."

The track crossed a swampy part where the moss hung as white as lace from every limb. "Sleep on, alligators, and blow your bubbles." Then the track went into the road.

Deep, deep the road went down between the high green-colored banks. Overhead the live-oaks met, and it was as dark as a cave.

A black dog with a lolling tongue came up out of the weeds by the ditch. She was meditating, and not ready, and when he came at her she only hit him a little with her cane. Over she went in the ditch, like a little puff of milkweed.[9]

Down there, her senses drifted away. A dream visited her, and she reached her hand up, but nothing reached down and gave her a pull. So she lay there and presently went to talking. "Old woman," she said to herself, "that black dog come up out of the weeds to stall you off, and now there he sitting on his fine tail, smiling at you."

A white man finally came along and found her— a hunter, a young man, with his dog on a chain.

---

6. *Pullets* are young hens.
7. A *ravine* is a deep, narrow valley, especially one eroded by running water.
8. The *sweet-gum* tree discharges a fragrant gum through cracks and crevices in its trunk.
9. The pods of a *milkweed* plant split open and release seeds with puffs of white, silky down.

Vocabulary

vigorously (vig′ ər əs lē) *adv.* with power, energy, and strength

"Well, Granny!" he laughed. "What are you doing there?"

"Lying on my back like a June-bug waiting to be turned over, mister," she said, reaching up her hand.

He lifted her up, gave her a swing in the air, and set her down. "Anything broken, Granny?"

"No sir, them old dead weeds is springy enough," said Phoenix, when she had got her breath. "I thank you for your trouble."

"Where do you live, Granny?" he asked, while the two dogs were growling at each other.

"Away back yonder, sir, behind the ridge. You can't even see it from here."

"On your way home?"

"No sir, I going to town."

"Why, that's too far! That's as far as I walk when I come out myself, and I get something for my trouble." He patted the stuffed bag he carried, and there hung down a little closed claw. It was one of the bob-whites, with its beak hooked bitterly to show it was dead. "Now you go on home, Granny!"

"I bound to go to town, mister," said Phoenix. "The time come around."

He gave another laugh, filling the whole landscape. "I know you old colored people! Wouldn't miss going to town to see Santa Claus!"

But something held old Phoenix very still. The deep lines in her face went into a fierce and different radiation.[10] Without warning, she had seen with her own eyes a flashing nickel fall out of the man's pocket onto the ground.

"How old are you, Granny?" he was saying.

"There is no telling, mister," she said, "no telling."

Then she gave a little cry and clapped her hands and said, "Git on away from here, dog! Look! Look at that dog!" She laughed as if in admiration. "He ain't scared of nobody. He a big black dog." She whispered, "Sic him!"

"Watch me get rid of that cur," said the man. "Sic him, Pete! Sic him!"

Phoenix heard the dogs fighting, and heard the man running and throwing sticks. She even heard a gunshot. But she was slowly bending forward by that time, further and further forward, the lids stretched down over her eyes, as if she were doing this in her sleep. Her chin was lowered almost to her knees. The yellow palm of her hand came out from the fold of her apron. Her fingers slid down and along the ground under the piece of money with the grace and care they would have in lifting an egg from under a setting hen. Then she slowly straightened up, she stood erect, and the nickel was in her apron pocket. A bird flew by. Her lips moved. "God watching me the whole time. I come to stealing."

The man came back, and his own dog panted about them. "Well, I scared him off that time," he said, and then he laughed and lifted his gun and pointed it at Phoenix.

She stood straight and faced him.

"Doesn't the gun scare you?" he said, still pointing it.

"No, sir, I seen plenty go off closer by, in my day, and for less than what I done," she said, holding utterly still.

He smiled, and shouldered the gun. "Well, Granny," he said, "you must be a hundred years old, and scared of nothing. I'd give you a dime if I had any money with me. But you take my advice and stay home, and nothing will happen to you."

"I bound to go on my way, mister," said Phoenix. She inclined her head in the red rag. Then they went in different directions, but she could hear the gun shooting again and again over the hill.

She walked on. The shadows hung from the oak trees to the road like curtains. Then she smelled wood-smoke, and smelled the river, and she saw a steeple and the cabins on their steep steps. Dozens of little black children whirled around her. There ahead was Natchez shining. Bells were ringing. She walked on.

In the paved city it was Christmas time. There were red and green electric lights strung and crisscrossed everywhere, and all turned on in the

---

10. Here, *radiation* means "a pattern of rays or waves."

Reading Strategy Visualizing *Picture the scene as the man helps Phoenix.*

Literary Element Description *What does the description of Phoenix suggest about her thoughts as she spies the nickel?*

Big Idea Return to Regionalism *What does this exchange suggest about the way whites and African Americans in the town behaved toward each other?*

daytime. Old Phoenix would have been lost if she had not distrusted her eyesight and depended on her feet to know where to take her.

She paused quietly on the sidewalk where people were passing by. A lady came along in the crowd, carrying an armful of red-, green- and silver-wrapped presents; she gave off perfume like the red roses in hot summer, and Phoenix stopped her.

"Please, missy, will you lace up my shoe?" She held up her foot.

"What do you want, Grandma?"

"See my shoe," said Phoenix. "Do all right for out in the country, but wouldn't look right to go in a big building."

"Stand still then, Grandma," said the lady. She put her packages down on the sidewalk beside her and laced and tied both shoes tightly.

"Can't lace 'em with a cane," said Phoenix. "Thank you, missy. I doesn't mind asking a nice lady to tie up my shoe, when I gets out on the street."

Moving slowly and from side to side, she went into the big building, and into a tower of steps, where she walked up and around and around until her feet knew to stop.

She entered a door, and there she saw nailed up on the wall the document that had been stamped with the gold seal and framed in the gold frame, which matched the dream that was hung up in her head.

"Here I be," she said. There was a fixed and **ceremonial** stiffness over her body.

"A charity case, I suppose," said an attendant who sat at the desk before her.

But Phoenix only looked above her head. There was sweat on her face, the wrinkles in her skin shone like a bright net.

"Speak up, Grandma," the woman said. "What's your name? We must have your history, you know. Have you been here before? What seems to be the trouble with you?"

Old Phoenix only gave a twitch to her face as if a fly were bothering her.

"Are you deaf?" cried the attendant.

But then the nurse came in.

"Oh, that's just old Aunt Phoenix," she said. "She doesn't come for herself—she has a little grandson. She makes these trips just as regular as clockwork. She lives away back off the Old Natchez Trace." She bent down. "Well, Aunt Phoenix, why don't you just take a seat? We won't keep you standing after your long trip." She pointed.

The old woman sat down, bolt upright in the chair.

"Now, how is the boy?" asked the nurse.

Old Phoenix did not speak.

"I said, how is the boy?"

But Phoenix only waited and stared straight ahead, her face very **solemn** and withdrawn into rigidity.

"Is his throat any better?" asked the nurse. "Aunt Phoenix, don't you hear me? Is your grandson's throat any better since the last time you came for the medicine?"

With her hands on her knees, the old woman waited, silent, erect and motionless, just as if she were in armor.

"You mustn't take up our time this way, Aunt Phoenix," the nurse said. "Tell us quickly about your grandson, and get it over. He isn't dead, is he?"

At last there came a flicker and then a flame of **comprehension** across her face, and she spoke.

"My grandson. It was my memory had left me. There I sat and forgot why I made my long trip."

"Forgot?" The nurse frowned. "After you came so far?"

Then Phoenix was like an old woman begging a dignified forgiveness for waking up frightened in the night. "I never did go to school, I was too old at the Surrender,"[11] she said in a soft voice. "I'm an old woman without an education. It was my memory fail me. My little grandson, he is just the same, and I forgot it in the coming."

---

11. The *Surrender* of Robert E. Lee to Ulysses S. Grant in 1865 ended the Civil War.

School Children, Jackson, 1930s. Eudora Welty. Photograph. Mississippi Department of Archives and History, Jackson, MS. Eudora Welty Collection.

Viewing the Photograph: Do you think Eudora Welty might have had her story "A Worn Path" in mind when she took this photograph? Why or why not?

"Throat never heals, does it?" said the nurse, speaking in a loud, sure voice to old Phoenix. By now she had a card with something written on it, a little list. "Yes. Swallowed lye. When was it?—January—two-three years ago—"

Phoenix spoke unasked now. "No, missy, he not dead, he just the same. Every little while his throat begin to close up again, and he not able to swallow. He not get his breath. He not able to help himself. So the time come around, and I go on another trip for the soothing medicine."

"All right. The doctor said as long as you came to get it, you could have it," said the nurse. "But it's an obstinate case."

"My little grandson, he sit up there in the house all wrapped up, waiting by himself," Phoenix went on. "We is the only two left in the world. He suffer and it don't seem to put him back at all. He got a sweet look. He going to last. He wear a little patch quilt and peep out holding his mouth open like a little bird. I remembers so plain now. I not going to forget him again, no, the whole enduring time. I could tell him from all the others in creation."

Big Idea Return to Regionalism *What do you infer about the situation of Phoenix and her grandson?*

Reading Strategy Visualizing *After rereading the details of the grandson's appearance, picture him in your mind. What impressions do you have of the boy and of Phoenix's feelings about him?*

"All right." The nurse was trying to hush her now. She brought her a bottle of medicine. "Charity," she said, making a check mark in a book.

Old Phoenix held the bottle close to her eyes, and then carefully put it into her pocket.

"I thank you," she said.

"It's Christmas time, Grandma," said the attendant. "Could I give you a few pennies out of my purse?"

"Five pennies is a nickel," said Phoenix stiffly.

"Here's a nickel," said the attendant.

Phoenix rose carefully and held out her hand. She received the nickel and then fished the other nickel out of her pocket and laid it beside the new one. She stared at her palm closely, with her head on one side.

Then she gave a tap with her cane on the floor.

"This is what come to me to do," she said. "I going to the store and buy my child a little windmill they sells, made out of paper. He going to find it hard to believe there such a thing in the world. I'll march myself back where he waiting, holding it straight up in this hand."

She lifted her free hand, gave a little nod, turned around, and walked out of the doctor's office. Then her slow step began on the stairs, going down. ❧

Literary Element Description *Notice the descriptions of Phoenix Jackson's manners, bearing, and plans she has for her money. What do these details suggest about her character?*

RESPONDING AND THINKING CRITICALLY

Respond

1. What is your favorite incident or image from "A Worn Path"? What is it about the image or incident that especially appeals to you?

Recall and Interpret

2. (a)What does Phoenix Jackson look like? (b)What does Phoenix Jackson's appearance tell you about her?

3. (a)Describe in detail the path Phoenix is taking. (b)From its description, what can you infer about the path? Explain what the path may symbolize, or represent. Support your answer.

4. (a)What is Phoenix's destination and purpose? (b)At what point in the story do you learn this?

5. What does the purpose of Phoenix's trip tell you about her character?

Analyze and Evaluate

6. (a)Do you feel empathy toward Phoenix? (b)Why or why not? Relate your answer to events in the story as well as to your own experiences.

7. In Greek mythology, the phoenix is a bird that, at the end of its life, burns itself to death; from its ashes, a new phoenix rises. Why may Welty have named her main character Phoenix?

8. (a)An author uses description to create a picture of a person, place, or thing. In your opinion, how effective are Welty's descriptions in creating a believable portrait of Phoenix Jackson? (b)How effective is Welty's writing in creating a vivid picture of the "worn path"?

Connect

9. Refer to your response to the Connecting to the Story activity on page 891. Would you add Phoenix Jackson to your list? Why or why not?

10. **Big Idea** **Return to Regionalism** What does "A Worn Path" reveal about the way conditions in the South during the 1930s affected the lives of people there?

LITERARY ANALYSIS

Literary Element Description

A **description** is a detailed portrayal of a person, place, or thing. When authors write descriptions, they include vivid and precise adjectives, nouns, and verbs. Authors may use details to describe tangible things, such as the appearance of a character. Or they may use details to describe intangible things, such as a character's personality traits.

1. Identify details in the story that describe the countryside around the Natchez Trace. Which details do you consider most vivid or striking? Explain.

2. In the city, Phoenix Jackson speaks first to a woman carrying presents and later to an attendant and a nurse. How do the descriptions in these scenes help to suggest that Jackson has a certain amount of pride despite her humble situation?

Review: Archetype

An **archetype** is an image, a character type, or a plot pattern that occurs frequently in literature, mythology, folklore, and religion. Archetypes call up strong—and sometimes illogical—emotions in the reader.

Group Activity Meet with a small group and discuss Eudora Welty's use of archetypes in "A Worn Path." Possible archetypes to discuss include the strong grandmother, the kind stranger, the poor but determined woman, and the sick child. Share your thoughts on Welty's use of these archetypes with the class.

Reading Strategy Visualizing

Read the passage below from page 897. Try to **visualize** the facial expressions and body language of the two characters.

> "Here's a nickel," said the attendant.
> Phoenix rose carefully and held out her hand. She received the nickel and then fished the other nickel out of her pocket and laid it beside the new one. She stared at her palm closely, with her head on one side.

1. Describe the probable facial expression and body language of the attendant.

2. Why do you suppose Phoenix holds her head to one side as she looks at the nickels? Support your answer.

Vocabulary Practice

Practice with Analogies Choose the word that best completes each analogy.

1. practice : competence :: study :
   a. books
   b. comprehension
   c. mathematics

2. party : festive :: funeral :
   a. solemn
   b. sermon
   c. ceremony

3. serious : trivial :: informal :
   a. tuxedo
   b. gathering
   c. ceremonial

4. weakly : feebly :: forcefully :
   a. vigorously
   b. eagerly
   c. reluctantly

5. lighthearted : cheerful :: somber :
   a. brokenhearted
   b. expressionless
   c. grave

Writing About Literature

Compare and Contrast Character In "A Worn Path," Phoenix Jackson encounters several secondary **characters** on her journey. The character portrayed in most detail is the hunter. Write a brief essay in which you compare Phoenix with the hunter. Include your thoughts about the way in which the social makeup of the South during the 1930s is reflected in these characters. Use evidence from the story to support your points.

Before you write your first draft, complete a chart like the one below to compare Phoenix with the hunter in terms of age, appearance, activities, attitudes, dialect, and any other elements that you think are important.

Characteristics	Phoenix	Hunter

Then follow the writing path shown here as you write your first draft.

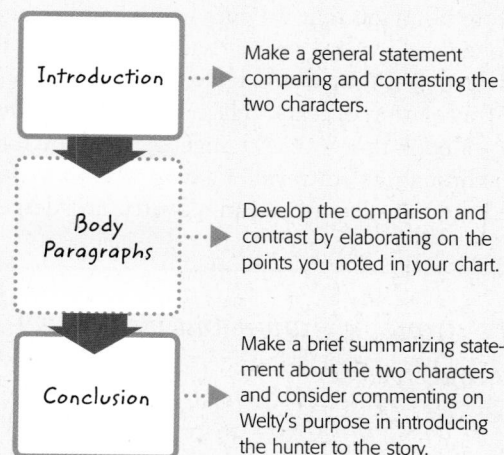

Introduction ····▶ Make a general statement comparing and contrasting the two characters.

Body Paragraphs ····▶ Develop the comparison and contrast by elaborating on the points you noted in your chart.

Conclusion ····▶ Make a brief summarizing statement about the two characters and consider commenting on Welty's purpose in introducing the hunter to the story.

Before writing your final version, meet with a peer reviewer to evaluate each other's first drafts and to offer suggestions about areas that can be improved. Then proofread and edit your work for errors in spelling, grammar, and punctuation.

Literature Online Web Activities For eFlashcards, Selection Quick Checks, and other Web activities, go to www.glencoe.com.

EUDORA WELTY 899

from *Black Boy*

MEET RICHARD WRIGHT

As a writer, Richard Wright wanted to "wage a war with words," and he succeeded, becoming one of the first major African American literary figures. His books are raw and forceful—whether they are portraying life in the urban ghettos of the North or the oppression of African Americans in the South.

Wright's first book, *Uncle Tom's Children*, was praised by critics, and Malcolm Cowley of the *New Republic* claimed it was "heartening, as evidence of a vigorous new talent, and terrifying as the expression of a racial hatred that has never ceased to grow and gets no chance to die." However, Wright was dissatisfied with the book, because he felt that it did not adequately portray the reality of racism and violence in the United States. "I had written a book [*Uncle Tom's Children*] which even banker's daughters could read and weep over and feel good. I swore to myself that if I ever wrote another book, no one would weep over it; that it would be so hard and deep that they would have to face it without the consolation of tears." His next work was *Native Son*—a book that would change U.S. culture forever through its portrayal of a man who has suffered the injustices of racism, poverty, and despair.

> *"It's strong, it's raw—but it's life as I see and lived it."*
>
> —Richard Wright

Literature from Life In the opinion of many, *Black Boy* is Wright's most important work because it was not only his autobiography but a social documentary of the hardships caused by racism. Ralph Ellison, who was strongly influenced by Wright,

Literature Online **Author Search** For more about Richard Wright, go to www.glencoe.com.

claimed that "In *Black Boy* Wright has used his own life to probe what qualities of will, imagination, and intellect are required of a Southern Negro in order to possess the meaning of his life in the United States."

Born in 1908 in Mississippi, Wright experienced fear and oppression early. He first witnessed racial violence at the age of eight when his uncle was lynched by a group of white men. Throughout his life, Wright repeatedly saw members of his race degraded by whites, yet he refused to believe that African Americans were inferior. He began reading and educating himself, and at nineteen he left for the North, mistakenly believing that he could live a life without discrimination there.

Outspoken Expatriate Realizing that social conditions for African Americans were not changing for the better, Wright moved his family to Paris, France, in 1947. He published no books for seven years but instead wrote articles on politics. While in France, he became friends with the writers Jean Paul Sartre, Albert Camus, and André Gide. Their existential views influenced his later work.

Wright's reputation and literary influence declined during the 1950s, as young African American writers such as James Baldwin and Ralph Ellison emerged. Amid the Black Arts movement of the 1960s, however, Wright's work was rediscovered, inspiring and influencing a new generation of African Americans. Unfortunately, Wright died before he could take part in this emerging black unity and pride and the fight for equality that he yearned for.

Richard Wright was born in 1908 and died in 1960.

Connecting to the Story

What experiences have helped form your values and beliefs? In *Black Boy*, Wright recalls his childhood and the fear and oppression he lived with every day. His experiences shaped his beliefs and actions for the rest of his life. As you read, think about the following questions:

- What events have influenced your beliefs?
- How do you think your childhood will affect what you do later in life?

Building Background

Richard Wright's father was a sharecropper near Natchez, Mississippi. Although he received a small cabin and some income from the cotton crop, he had a difficult time making ends meet. Eventually Wright's family was forced to give up sharecropping and moved within the city limits. However, their luck was not much better inside Natchez, and Wright's father abandoned them when Wright was six. Wright, his mother, and his brother were left with little income and a life marked by hunger and fear. Their struggles and the events that followed their abandonment are detailed in this selection from *Black Boy*.

Setting Purposes for Reading

Big Idea Life in the City

As you read, notice how Wright examines the impact of segregation and racism on his life.

Literary Element Flash-forward

A **flash-forward** is an interruption in the chronological sequence of a narrative to leap forward in time. A writer may signal a flash-forward with a new paragraph or with a description of a new setting. As you read *Black Boy*, notice how Wright uses flash-forward to signal events that take place in the future.

- See Literary Terms Handbook, p. R7.

Literature Online **Interactive Literary Elements Handbook** To review or learn more about the literary elements, go to www.glencoe.com.

Reading Strategy Comparing and Contrasting Characters

When you **compare and contrast characters,** you note the similarities and differences between them. Comparing and contrasting can help you to better understand who the characters are and why they act in certain ways.

....

Reading Tip: Venn Diagrams As you read, use Venn diagrams to compare and contrast characters.

1. Physical Appearance

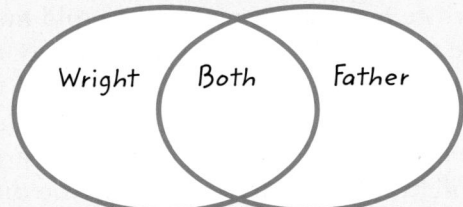

Wright | Both | Father

Vocabulary

futile (fū′til) *adj.* serving no practical purpose; useless; worthless; p. 903 *Trying to lift the chair was futile because it was nailed to the floor.*

hostile (host′əl) *adj.* feeling or showing hatred; antagonistic; p. 903 *The woman became hostile when the salesclerk refused to answer her questions.*

vindictive (vin dik′tiv) *adj.* desiring revenge; p. 903 *He was known for displaying vindictive behavior when he felt betrayed.*

poised (poizd) *adj.* having a calm, controlled, and dignified manner; composed; p. 906 *Though angry, she remained poised when her boss questioned her about her work.*

alien (ā′lē ən) *adj.* strange; unfamiliar; foreign; p. 906 *The alien surroundings of her new town made her uncomfortable.*

....

Vocabulary Tip: Context Clues When you see an unfamiliar word, pay attention to its context, or the words around it. The context provides clues to the meaning of the word.

INDIANA ACADEMIC STANDARDS (pages 901–908)
11.2.2 Analyze...patterns or organization...
11.3 [Identify] story elements such as character...

11.5.9 Write...a literary analysis that...provides a coherent conclusion.

from Black Boy

Richard Wright

When I awakened one morning my mother told me that we were going to see a judge who would make my father support me and my brother. An hour later all three of us were sitting in a huge crowded room. I was overwhelmed by the many faces and the voices which I could not understand. High above me was a white face which my mother told me was the face of the judge. Across the huge room sat my father, smiling confidently, looking at us. My mother warned me not to be fooled by my father's friendly manner; she told me that the judge might ask me questions, and if he did I must tell him the truth. I agreed, yet I hoped that the judge would not ask me anything.

For some reason the entire thing struck me as being useless; I felt that if my father were going to feed me, then he would have done so regardless of what a judge said to him. And I did not want my father to feed me; I was hungry, but my thoughts of food did not now center about him. I waited, growing restless, hungry. My mother gave me a dry sandwich and I munched and stared, longing to go home. Finally I heard my mother's name called; she rose and began weeping so copiously[1] that she could not talk for a few moments; at last she managed to say that her husband had deserted her and her two children, that her children were hungry, that they stayed hungry, that she worked, that she was trying to raise them alone. Then my father was called; he came forward jauntily, smiling. He tried to kiss my mother, but she turned away from him. I only heard one sentence of what he said.

"I'm doing all I can, Your Honor," he mumbled, grinning.

It had been painful to sit and watch my mother crying and my father laughing and I was glad when we were outside in the sunny streets. Back at home my mother wept again and talked complainingly about the unfairness of the judge who had accepted my father's word. After the court scene, I tried to forget my father; I did not hate him; I simply did not want to think of him. Often when we were hungry my mother would beg me to go to my father's job and ask him for a dollar, a dime, a nickel . . . But I would never consent to go. I did not want to see him.

My mother fell ill and the problem of food became an acute, daily agony. Hunger was with us always. Sometimes the neighbors would feed us or a dollar bill would come in the mail from my grandmother. It was winter and I would buy a dime's worth of coal each morning from the corner coalyard and lug it home in paper bags. For a time I remained out of school to wait upon my mother, then Granny came to visit us and I returned to school.

At night there were long, halting discussions about our going to live with Granny, but nothing came of it. Perhaps there was not enough money for railroad fare. Angered by having been hauled into court, my father now spurned us completely. I heard long, angrily whispered conversations between my mother and grandmother to the effect that "that woman ought to be killed for breaking up a home." What irked me was the ceaseless talk and no action. If someone had suggested that my father be killed, I would perhaps have become interested; if someone had suggested that his name never be mentioned, I would no doubt have agreed; if someone had suggested that we move to another city, I would have been glad. But there was only endless talk that led nowhere and I began to keep away from home as much as possible,

---

1. *Copiously* means "in great quantity."

preferring the simplicity of the streets to the worried, **futile** talk at home.

Finally we could no longer pay the rent for our dingy flat;[2] the few dollars that Granny had left us before she went home were gone. Half sick and in despair, my mother made the rounds of the charitable institutions, seeking help. She found an orphan home that agreed to assume the guidance of me and my brother provided my mother worked and made small payments. My mother hated to be separated from us, but she had no choice.

The orphan home was a two-story frame building set amid trees in a wide, green field. My mother ushered me and my brother one morning into the building and into the presence of a tall, gaunt, mulatto[3] woman who called herself Miss Simon. At once she took a fancy to me and I was frightened speechless; I was afraid of her the moment I saw her and my fear lasted during my entire stay in the home.

The house was crowded with children and there was always a storm of noise. The daily routine was blurred to me and I never quite grasped it. The most abiding feeling I had each day was hunger and fear. The meals were skimpy and there were only two of them. Just before we went to bed each night we were given a slice of bread smeared with molasses. The children were silent, **hostile, vindictive,** continuously complaining of hunger. There was an overall atmosphere of nervousness and intrigue, of children telling tales upon others, of children being deprived of food to punish them.

The home did not have the money to check the growth of the wide stretches of grass by having it mown, so it had to be pulled by hand. Each morning after we had eaten a breakfast that seemed like no breakfast at all, an older child would lead a herd of us to the vast lawn and we would get to our knees and wrench the grass loose from the dirt with our fingers. At intervals Miss Simon would make a tour of inspection, examining the pile of pulled grass beside each child, scolding or praising according to the size of the pile. Many mornings I was too weak from hunger to pull the grass; I would grow dizzy and my mind would become blank and I would find myself, after an interval of unconsciousness, upon my hands and knees, my head whirling, my eyes staring in bleak astonishment at the green grass, wondering where I was, feeling that I was emerging from a dream…

During the first days my mother came each night to visit me and my brother, then her visits stopped. I began to wonder if she, too, like my father, had disappeared into the unknown. I was rapidly learning to distrust everything and everybody. When my mother did come, I asked her why had she remained away so long and she told me that Miss Simon had forbidden her to visit us, that Miss Simon had said that she was spoiling us with too much attention. I begged my mother to take me away; she wept and told me to wait, that soon she would take us to Arkansas. She left and my heart sank.

Miss Simon tried to win my confidence; she asked me if I would like to be adopted by her if my mother consented and I said no. She would take me into her apartment and talk to me, but her words had no effect. Dread and distrust had already become a daily part of my being and my memory grew sharp, my senses more impressionable; I began to be aware of myself as a distinct personality striving against others. I held myself in, afraid to act or speak until I was sure of my surroundings, feeling most of the time that I was suspended over a void. My imagination soared; I dreamed of running away. Each morning I vowed that I would leave the next morning, but the next morning always found me afraid.

One day Miss Simon told me that thereafter I was to help her in the office. I ate lunch with her and, strangely, when I sat facing her at the table, my hunger vanished. The woman killed

---

2. A *flat* is an apartment.
3. *Mulatto*, a word seldom used today, describes a biracial person, one of mixed African American and white ancestry.

Reading Strategy Comparing and Contrasting Characters *How do Wright's feelings in the house compare with the feelings of the other children there?*

Vocabulary

futile (fū′til) *adj.* serving no practical purpose; useless; worthless
hostile (host′əl) *adj.* feeling or showing hatred; antagonistic
vindictive (vin dik′tiv) *adj.* desiring revenge

Reading Strategy Comparing and Contrasting Characters *Why does Wright immediately compare his mother's actions to those of his father?*

Big Idea Life in the City *Why might Wright be afraid to run away from the orphan home?*

something in me. Next she called me to her desk where she sat addressing envelopes.

"Step up close to the desk," she said. "Don't be afraid."

I went and stood at her elbow. There was a wart on her chin and I stared at it.

"Now, take a blotter from over there and blot each envelope after I'm through writing on it," she instructed me, pointing to a blotter that stood about a foot from my hand.

I stared and did not move or answer.

"Take the blotter," she said.

I wanted to reach for the blotter and succeeded only in twitching my arm.

"Here," she said sharply, reaching for the blotter and shoving it into my fingers.

She wrote in ink on an envelope and pushed it toward me. Holding the blotter in my hand, I stared at the envelope and could not move.

"Blot it," she said.

I could not lift my hand. I knew what she had said; I knew what she wanted me to do; and I had heard her correctly. I wanted to look at her and say something, tell her why I could not move; but my eyes were fixed upon the floor. I could not summon enough courage while she sat there looking at me to reach over the yawning space of twelve inches and blot the wet ink on the envelope.

"Blot it!" she spoke sharply.

Still I could not move or answer.

"Look at me!"

I could not lift my eyes. She reached her hand to my face and I twisted away.

"What's wrong with you?" she demanded.

I began to cry and she drove me from the room. I decided that as soon as night came I would run away. The dinner bell rang and I did not go to the table, but hid in a corner of the hallway. When I heard the dishes rattling at the table, I opened the door and ran down the walk to the street. Dusk was falling. Doubt made me stop. Ought I go back? No; hunger was back there, and fear. I went on, coming to concrete sidewalks. People passed me. Where was I going? I did not know. The farther I walked the more frantic I became. In a confused and vague way I knew that I was doing more running *away* from than running *toward* something. I stopped. The streets seemed dangerous. The buildings were massive and dark. The moon shone and the trees loomed frighteningly. No, I could not go on. I would go back. But I had walked so far and had

Jim, 1930. William H. Johnson. Oil on canvas, 21⅝ x 18¼ in. Smithsonian American Art Museum, Washington, DC.

turned too many corners and had not kept track of the direction. Which way led back to the orphan home? I did not know. I was lost.

I stood in the middle of the sidewalk and cried. A "white" policeman came to me and I wondered if he was going to beat me. He asked me what was the matter and I told him that I was trying to find my mother. His "white" face created a new fear in me. I was remembering the tale of the "white" man who had beaten the "black" boy. A crowd gathered and I was urged to tell where I lived. Curiously, I was too full of fear to cry now. I wanted to tell the "white" face that I had run off from an orphan home and that Miss Simon ran it, but I was afraid. Finally I was taken to the police station where I was fed. I felt better. I sat in a big chair where I was surrounded by "white" policemen, but they seemed to ignore me. Through the window I could see that night had completely fallen and that lights now gleamed in the streets. I grew sleepy and dozed. My shoulder was shaken gently and I opened my eyes and looked into a "white" face of another policeman who was sitting beside me. He asked me questions in a quiet, confidential tone, and quite before I knew it he was not "white" any more. I told him

Big Idea Life in the City *Why might Wright think of this tale when he is lost?*

that I had run away from an orphan home and that Miss Simon ran it.

It was but a matter of minutes before I was walking alongside a policeman, heading toward the home. The policeman led me to the front gate and I saw Miss Simon waiting for me on the steps. She identified me and I was left in her charge. I begged her not to beat me, but she yanked me upstairs into an empty room and lashed me thoroughly. Sobbing, I slunk off to bed, resolved to run away again. But I was watched closely after that.

My mother was informed upon her next visit that I had tried to run away and she was terribly upset.

"Why did you do it?" she asked.

"I don't want to stay here," I told her.

"But you must," she said. "How can I work if I'm to worry about you? You must remember that you have no father. I'm doing all I can."

"I don't want to stay here," I repeated.

"Then, if I take you to your father…"

"I don't want to stay with him either," I said.

"But I want you to ask him for enough money for us to go to my sister's in Arkansas," she said.

Again I was faced with choices I did not like, but I finally agreed. After all, my hate for my father was not so great and urgent as my hate for the orphan home. My mother held to her idea and one night a week or so later I found myself standing in a room in a frame house. My father and a strange woman were sitting before a bright fire that blazed in a grate. My mother and I were standing about six feet away, as though we were afraid to approach them any closer.

"It's not for me," my mother was saying. "It's for your children that I'm asking you for money."

"I ain't got nothing," my father said, laughing.

"Come here, boy," the strange woman called to me.

I looked at her and did not move.

"Give him a nickel," the woman said. "He's cute."

"Come here, Richard," my father said, stretching out his hand.

I backed away, shaking my head, keeping my eyes on the fire.

"He is a cute child," the strange woman said.

"You ought to be ashamed," my mother said to the strange woman. "You're starving my children."

"Now, don't you-all fight," my father said, laughing.

"I'll take that poker and hit you!" I blurted at my father.

He looked at my mother and laughed louder.

"You told him to say that," he said.

"Don't say such things, Richard," my mother said.

"You ought to be dead," I said to the strange woman.

The woman laughed and threw her arms about my father's neck. I grew ashamed and wanted to leave.

"How can you starve your children?" my mother asked.

"Let Richard stay with me," my father said.

"Do you want to stay with your father, Richard?" my mother asked.

"No," I said.

"You'll get plenty to eat," he said.

"I'm hungry now," I told him. "But I won't stay with you."

"Aw, give the boy a nickel," the woman said.

My father ran his hand into his pocket and pulled out a nickel.

"Here, Richard," he said.

"Don't take it," my mother said.

"Don't teach him to be a fool," my father said. "Here, Richard, take it."

I looked at my mother, at the strange woman, at my father, then into the fire. I wanted to take the nickel, but I did not want to take it from my father.

"You ought to be ashamed," my mother said, weeping. "Giving your son a nickel when he's hungry. If there's a God, He'll pay you back."

"That's all I got," my father said, laughing again and returning the nickel to his pocket.

We left. I had the feeling that I had had to do with something unclean. Many times in the years after that the image of my father and the strange woman, their faces lit by the dancing flames, would surge up in my imagination so vivid and strong that I felt I could reach out and touch it; I would stare at it, feeling that it possessed some vital meaning which always eluded me.

Reading Strategy Comparing and Contrasting Characters *How does Wright compare his father's girlfriend with his mother?*

Literary Element Flash-forward *Why does Wright tell the reader that he continued to think about his father and that night for years?*

RICHARD WRIGHT **905**

Negro Cabin, Sedalia, North Carolina (No. 1), 1930. Loïs Mailou Jones. Watercolor on paper, 14⅛ x 19⅛ in. Collection of the artist.
Viewing the Art: Does this painting capture the aspects of the father's shack that cause Wright to pity him? Explain.

A quarter of a century was to elapse between the time when I saw my father sitting with the strange woman and the time when I was to see him again, standing alone upon the red clay of a Mississippi plantation, a sharecropper, clad in ragged overalls, holding a muddy hoe in his gnarled, veined hands—a quarter of a century during which my mind and consciousness had become so greatly and violently altered that when I tried to talk to him I realized that, though ties of blood made us kin, though I could see a shadow of my face in his face, though there was an echo of my voice in his voice, we were forever strangers, speaking a different language, living on vastly distant planes of reality. That day a quarter of a century later when I visited him on the plantation—he was standing against the sky, smiling toothlessly, his hair whitened, his body bent, his eyes glazed with dim recollection, his fearsome aspect of twenty-five years ago gone forever from him—I was overwhelmed to realize that he could

never understand me or the scalding experiences that had swept me beyond his life and into an area of living that he could never know. I stood before him, **poised,** my mind aching as it embraced the simple nakedness of his life, feeling how completely his soul was imprisoned by the slow flow of the seasons, by wind and rain and sun, how fastened were his memories to a crude and raw past, how chained were his actions and emotions to the direct, animalistic impulses of his withering body . . .

From the white landowners above him there had not been handed to him a chance to learn the meaning of loyalty, of sentiment, of tradition. Joy was as unknown to him as was despair. As a creature of the earth, he endured, hearty, whole, seemingly indestructible, with no regrets and no hope. He asked easy, drawling questions about me, his other son, his wife, and he laughed, amused, when I informed him of their destinies. I forgave him and pitied him as my eyes looked past him to the unpainted wooden shack. From far beyond the horizons that bound this bleak plantation there had come to me through my living the knowledge that my father was a black peasant who had gone to the city seeking life, but who had failed in the city; a black peasant whose life had been hopelessly snarled in the city, and who had at last fled the city—that same city which had lifted me in its burning arms and borne me toward **alien** and undreamed-of shores of knowing. ∾

Big Idea Life in the City *How did life in the South affect the choices of Wright's father and Wright's future?*

Vocabulary

poised (poizd) *adj.* having a calm, controlled, and dignified manner; composed
alien (āʹ lē ən) *adj.* strange; unfamiliar; foreign

RESPONDING AND THINKING CRITICALLY

Respond

1. What was your reaction to the events of Wright's life? Explain.

Recall and Interpret

2. (a)Why do Wright and his brother go to the orphan home? (b)How is the orphan home different from and similar to his old home?

3. (a)Why does Wright run away? (b)What do you learn about Wright's attitudes and perceptions about race from this incident?

4. (a)What deal does Wright's mother make with him as she takes him out of the orphan home? (b)What do you learn about Wright's character from his interactions with his father just after leaving the home?

5. (a)What ultimately happens to Wright's father? (b)What does Wright's visit with his elderly father reveal about Wright and what he values in life? Explain, using details from the selection.

Analyze and Evaluate

6. Does Wright's father become more or less sympathetic as the story progresses? Explain.

7. (a)What is the tone of the selection? (b)How effective is the tone in expressing the author's main point?

Connect

8. (a)How does knowing that this selection is from an autobiography affect your reaction to it? (b)Would you react differently if it were fiction? Explain.

9. **Big Idea** **Life in the City** How are Wright's attitudes and perceptions about race shaped by the time and the place he lives in?

LITERARY ANALYSIS

Literary Element Flash-forward

Although most stories are told in the order in which the events occur, sometimes writers interrupt the chronological flow. An author can use a technique called a **flashback** to explain an event that happened before the action in the story. This technique provides essential information about the character or prior events so that the reader can better understand the character's motivations. An interruption in events to leap forward in time is a **flash-forward.** Wright uses this device to show how his views had changed since the events in the excerpt had taken place.

1. Where is the flash-forward in this selection?

2. How does Wright signal that he is skipping ahead of the main narrative?

3. (a)What effect does this flash-forward create in Wright's narrative? (b)Does it strengthen or weaken the narrative? Explain.

Review: Autobiography

An **autobiography** is the story of a person's life written by that person. Unlike a memoir, which tends to focus on specific events or parts of the author's life, an autobiography usually encompasses most of the author's life.

Activity Complete the chart below by finding descriptions from the story about Wright's life, his parents, and the South during his childhood. Determine how each of these affected him and his choices.

	Description	Effects on Wright
His life		
Mother		
Father		
The South		

Reading Strategy Comparing and Contrasting Characters

Authors **compare and contrast settings and characters** to help the reader understand them better. Noticing these comparisons will help you understand the characters' motivations and relationships with one another and with their environments. Use your Venn diagrams to answer the following questions.

1. What does Wright find that he has in common with his father?

2. How has the city affected him and his father differently?

Vocabulary Practice

Practice with Context Clues Choose the best meaning for each vocabulary word below. Use the context clues in each sentence to help you.

1. Going to court was **futile** because my father was never going to help feed us.
   - **a.** helpful
   - **b.** pointless
   - **c.** scary
   - **d.** interesting

2. After seeing my father with that woman, I became **hostile** and threatened to hit him with a poker.
   - **a.** aggressive
   - **b.** friendly
   - **c.** annoyed
   - **d.** sad

3. Many of the children in the orphan home were **vindictive,** and sought revenge against those they didn't like.
   - **a.** sentimental
   - **b.** cooperative
   - **c.** friendly
   - **d.** vengeful

4. I spoke with him in a **poised** and controlled voice, even though the sight of him filled me with anger and hatred.
   - **a.** delighted
   - **b.** self-assured
   - **c.** reckless
   - **d.** hateful

5. My **alien** surroundings scared me, and I wanted to run to the safety of my home.
   - **a.** normal
   - **b.** comfortable
   - **c.** dirty
   - **d.** unfamiliar

Literature Online **Web Activities** For eFlashcards, Selection Quick Checks, and other Web activities, go to www.glencoe.com.

Writing About Literature

Compare and Contrast Setting When Wright's mother drops off him and his brother at the orphan home, Wright is immediately terrified. He describes the unhappiness of the home in a matter-of-fact way. The orphanage was both different from and similar to his home.

Write a brief essay comparing and contrasting the orphan home with the home of Wright's mother and his feelings about both places. When writing your essay, be sure to use quotations from the story to support your point. It may help you to compare and contrast the actions of Miss Simon and Wright's mother and the way Wright feels about both women. As you draft your essay, use a graphic organizer like the one below to help you structure your essay.

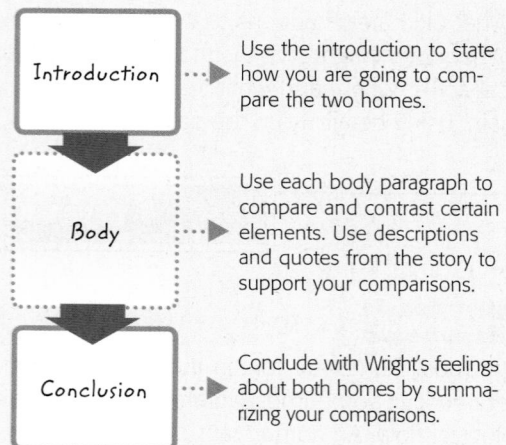

Introduction · · ▶ Use the introduction to state how you are going to compare the two homes.

Body · · ▶ Use each body paragraph to compare and contrast certain elements. Use descriptions and quotes from the story to support your comparisons.

Conclusion ▶ Conclude with Wright's feelings about both homes by summarizing your comparisons.

After completing your draft, meet with a peer reviewer to evaluate each other's work and to suggest revisions. Then proofread and edit your draft for errors in spelling, grammar, and punctuation.

Reading Further

If you enjoyed this excerpt from *Black Boy,* you may enjoy these other works by Richard Wright.

Novel *Native Son,* by Richard Wright, tells the story of a man who is driven to desperate acts after being subjected to a life of racism and poverty.

Short Stories *Eight Men: Short Stories,* by Richard Wright, includes "The Man Who Lived Underground"— the story of a man on the run after he is accused of a murder he did not commit.

Erskine Caldwell and
Margaret Bourke-White

from

You Have Seen Their Faces

O. Henry Prize Winner

Iron Mountain, Tennessee, 1937. Margaret Bourke-White. Silver gelatin print. Time & Life Pictures.

Building Background

Photojournalist Margaret Bourke-White documented some of the most important events of the twentieth century, including the liberation of Nazi concentration camps and the Korean War. In 1937 Bourke-White and her future husband, novelist Erskine Caldwell, collaborated on *You Have Seen Their Faces.* This book powerfully depicts the plight that southern sharecroppers faced.

Set a Purpose for Reading

Read to learn about the sharecropping system.

Reading Strategy

Analyzing the Purpose of Historical Texts and Photographs

Analyzing the purpose of historical texts and photographs involves examining the ideas and culture presented by texts and images. As you read, use a chart to take notes about the selection and the photographs in order to determine their purpose.

Text Passage and Purpose	Photograph and Purpose

THE MISSISSIPPI VALLEY DELTA and the Black Belt[1] of Alabama are two sections of the South that still produce cotton in abundance. It grows, matures, and yields without fertilizer and without effort. The soil there will be deep, fertile, and productive for a long time to come. Elsewhere the sub-soil, both sand and clay, is being plowed up to be mixed with the little top-soil that remains in an effort to make plants grow. There is no fertility in sub-soil, but when brought to the surface it gives the appearance of fertility and, when mixed with fertilizer, will produce enough cotton, providing that the rains and sun are not extreme, to pay for the fertilizer in normal times. Farming in sand or clay is a back-breaking, spirit-crushing existence.

There are reasons for this impoverishment[2] of the soil that go deep into the economic life of the South. The successful cotton-raisers have always been plantation-owners. The plantations were large, generally from five hundred to five

---

1. *The Black Belt* is a strip of land with black, fertile soil across central Alabama and Mississippi.
2. *Impoverishment* means "the state of being drained of essential nutrients."

thousand acres of land in size. The owners for the most part had one main concern, and that was to make as much money as they could as quickly as they could.

Nothing made money like cotton. Nothing else grew like cotton. Cotton was king.

Now the day of the plantation is over, except in the Delta country and in the Black Belt, and cotton is not king any longer.

The plantation system pauperized[3] the soil to such a great degree that raising cotton became a means of making a living rather than a method of making a fortune. The plantation-owner, when he became aware of what had happened to the soil, withdrew to the nearest city to live the remainder of his life on his accumulated wealth.

What he left behind was eroded, depleted, unprofitable land. His tenants still had to work for a living, even if he did not, and out of their desperation grew a new system. The owner became an absentee-landlord. The plantation was divided into one-man farms and rented to the tenants. The rent was paid either in half of the cotton produced or in an agreed upon number of bales, or on a basis combining the two methods. The plantation system was traded for the sharecropping system, and the South to its sorrow was the victim of the deal.

Before he knew it, the landlord had a new source of income that was larger than his previous one had been. And, besides, in the old days he had had to take his own chances with his crop of cotton, losing money when it rained too much or too little, dipping into profits from preceding years when expenditures were larger than income. In the new era he had a source of income and profit that was as certain and secure as the seasons themselves.

Rent was paid to him for the use of the land on a sharing basis, and he saw to it that the tenant raised a maximum number of bales. When a hundred tenants produced six bales each, the landlord received three hundred bales, the individual tenant three bales. Cotton was not king any longer, but the institution of sharecropping was making a few men richer than kings, and much better enthroned.[4] They did not have to concern themselves about the welfare of their subjects.

The tenant who set out to farm his portion of the plantation discovered that the land required fertilizer. Without fertilizer he could not grow enough cotton to provide himself with a living, and to pay rent. The rent came first. The landlord generally saw to it that the tenant paid his three or four bales for rent before the sharing began. If there was nothing left to share after the rent had been paid, there was nothing the tenant could do about it. He could only look forward to the coming year, hoping he would be able to make more than the minimum number of bales the rent required. If the following year was a good one for him, he paid off the chattel mortgage[5] he had given in payment for fertilizer he had bought in an effort to produce the rent-cotton.

It is difficult to find a good word to say about such an agricultural system. The sharecropping system was born of the plantation system, and the new was anything but an improvement over the old. The old produced numerous families of wealth who developed a culture that was questionable. The new has concentrated wealth in the hands of a few families who are determined that no culture shall exist.

Much can be said about the detrimental effects of such an agricultural system, more especially when there are ten million persons now living under its yoke.[6] They live in this cotton country on tenant farms which, in many cases, are little more than sand dunes and clay stacks. They are either already worn out physically and spiritually, or are in the act of wearing themselves out. They are grouped in families of man and wife and from one to sixteen children. They are farming, for the most part, soil that has been yielding diminishing returns for fifty and a hundred years. No matter if they get up an hour earlier to work by lantern light, no matter if half a dozen more children are begotten[7] to supply additional hands in the field, they will continue to fall steadily behind as long as they live on land that produces less and less each time a new crop of cotton is planted.

---

3. *Pauperized* means "depleted or drained."
4. *Enthroned* means "installed as king" and implies that the landlords were distanced from the sharecroppers just as a king might be removed from his subjects.

5. A *chattel mortgage* is a mortgage on personal property that is used as a guarantee for a debt.
6. Here, *yoke* refers to "something that causes servitude or bondage."
7. *Begotten* means "conceived."

This is nothing new. It is not a situation that has suddenly come about overnight. But it is a circumstance that becomes more acute day by day as the exhaustion and erosion of cotton land progresses. Fertilizer will increase the yield of cotton, but fertilizer costs money and requires credit that the tenant farmer does not have. A larger farm will produce more cotton, but there is a physical limit to the number of acres a man and his family can cultivate.

The sharecropping system has in recent years branched out into several forms, none of them any more economically sound than the source from which they sprang, and most of them working greater hardships on human lives than the plantation system ever did. Sharecropping has deprived millions of persons of what the rest of America considers the necessities of life.

It deprives children of adequate education because many of them have to work either part of the school year or all of it on their fathers' farms so that enough cotton can be raised to pay rent and buy fertilizer and to get food and clothing. It forces families to live in buildings that are detrimental to health, and it forces them to exist on food that is insufficient. Worse still, it continues in operation year after year, wringing dry the bodies and souls of men, women, and children; dragging down to its own level from higher economic planes new numbers to take the places of those crushed and thrown aside; breeding families of eight, ten, twelve, fourteen, sixteen, and more, in order to furnish an ever-increasing number of persons necessary to supply the rent-cotton for the landlord.

It is foolish to ask a tenant farmer why he remains where he is. He does move from farm to farm from time to time, but only rarely can he improve his status. Such a question is usually asked with the purpose of covering up an inability to suggest what the farmer could do to lift

Child of sharecropper family, Louisiana, 1936. Margaret Bourke-White. Silver gelatin print. Time & Life Pictures.

himself from the hole he stands in. There is cotton to be raised, and he has trained himself to raise it. That is his specialty. It is his life and, if sharecropping continues as an institution, it will become his death.

The tenant farmer in the South is trying to hold onto a spinning world until by some means he is enabled to get a grip on a better way of life. He knows he cannot buy land of his own from the profits of sharecropping. He knows just as well that he cannot save until he earns, and that he cannot earn much more than a bare living from sterile, barren land. He does well, under the circumstances, to hold on at all.

ERSKINE CALDWELL AND MARGARET BOURKE-WHITE **911**

Now that his condition has sunk to depths that stop just short of peonage,[8] there has appeared the first sign of hope. What there is in store for him in the future remains to be seen, but now for the first time there is hope. There has been talk, from one end of the South to the other, of joining with other tenant farmers to take collective action against the institution of sharecropping. The day when it was a sacred bull has passed. The sign of its passing was when the landlords began putting into force other forms of farm tenancy. Farms were leased to tenants, but sharing of the cotton continued; tenants were paid to work by the day, but their pay was received in a share of the cotton. No one was fooled, least of all tenant farmers themselves.

The farmer has little, if anything, to show for his years of labor in the past. But the hardships he has experienced will stand him in

good stead when the time comes for him to begin thinking about taking over the job of raising cotton—the job in which the landlord failed to treat him fairly and squarely. ∿

---

8. *Peonage* is the use of workers who are forced to labor for someone to work off a debt.

RESPONDING AND THINKING CRITICALLY

Respond

1. In your opinion, do the photographs or the text better convey the hardships experienced by sharecroppers? Explain.

Recall and Interpret

2. (a)According to Caldwell and Bourke-White, what caused the soil's impoverishment? (b)What does this suggest to you about the rise of the sharecropping system?

3. (a)What effect did sharecropping have on the size of families? Of what did sharecropping deprive children? (b)What might be the outcome of these two effects?

Analyze and Evaluate

4. (a)In a short paragraph, describe how the images add to your understanding of sharecropping. (b)Which image most enhances your understanding of the institution? Explain.

5. (a)What is the main idea of this selection? (b)Do you think that Caldwell and Bourke-White are successful in conveying this idea? Why or why not?

Connect

6. Based on this selection and its images, in what ways has your opinion of Richard Wright's father—as he is depicted in *Black Boy*—changed? Explain.

■ **INDIANA ACADEMIC STANDARDS (pages 909–912)**
11.7.11 Interpret and evaluate the various ways in which events are presented and information is communicated by visual image-makers (such as...photographers).

11.3.5 Analyze...works of literary or cultural significance in history...

The Life You Save May Be Your Own

MEET FLANNERY O'CONNOR

Award-winning author Flannery O'Connor often delighted in telling friends and interviewers that the highlight of her life occurred when, as a five-year-old, she taught a chicken to walk backwards. It was on such odd yet ordinary experiences that O'Connor later based her work.

"Highly Unladylike" Mary Flannery O'Connor was born in Savannah, Georgia. Soon after, her family moved to Milledgeville, a small city in central Georgia. After graduating from college in 1945, she attended the prestigious Iowa Writers' Workshop at the University of Iowa, earning an MFA degree. While at Iowa, O'Connor had her first short story, "The Geranium," published in the summer of 1946.

> *"The truth does not change according to our ability to stomach it."*
>
> —Flannery O'Connor

More short stories followed, including "The Life You Save May Be Your Own" (1953), "A Good Man Is Hard to Find" (1955), and "Everything That Rises Must Converge" (published posthumously in 1965). In these stories and in her first novel, *Wise Blood* (1952), O'Connor often drew upon her experiences as a devout Roman Catholic to explore harsh and disturbing realities: hard luck, hypocrisy, and failed expectations. Her work was widely read by the public and highly praised by critics. A review appearing in *Time* magazine hailed O'Connor as "highly unladylike [with] a brutal irony, a slam-bang humor, and a style of writing as balefully direct as a death sentence."

Along with William Faulkner, Carson McCullers, and Tennessee Williams, O'Connor is sometimes classified as a Southern Gothic writer because of her detailed renderings of small town Southern life and her flair for creating eccentric—even grotesque—characters. Commenting on these characters, Alice Walker, an African American writer, observed, "O'Connor's characters—whose humanity if not their sanity is taken for granted, and who are miserable, ugly, narrow-minded, . . . with not a graceful, pretty one anywhere who is not, at the same time, a joke—shocked and delighted me."

Return to Georgia In 1952, at the age of 27, O'Connor was stricken with a near fatal attack of lupus, the incurable disease from which her father had died. She was forced to move back to her mother's dairy farm outside Milledgeville, where she remained for the rest of her life. Despite her illness, she managed to correspond with friends, lecture on writing, raise her prized peacocks—and continue to write.

Although O'Connor died from lupus at the age of 39, her fiction has inspired generations of writers. She is a major literary voice of the American South.

Flannery O'Connor was born in 1925 and died in 1964.

Literature Online Author Search For more about Flannery O'Connor, go to www.glencoe.com.

Connecting to the Story

Have you ever judged someone on the basis of your first impressions? In "The Life You Save May Be Your Own," two characters, an old woman and a tramp, do exactly that. As you read the story, think about the following questions:

- What do you look for when you meet someone for the first time?
- Are your first impressions usually accurate or off the mark?

Building Background

Widespread unemployment during the Great Depression brought hard times to many. Unemployed men, and occasionally women, often became wanderers, referred to as "tramps" or "hoboes." They went from city to city and house to house, particularly in rural areas, seeking odd jobs in return for food, clothes, or shelter. When World War II began, many regularly employed workers joined the armed forces. As a result, the previously unemployed, and men wounded and sent home from the war, frequently filled in at temporary jobs.

Setting Purposes for Reading

Big Idea Return to Regionalism

As you read, consider how this story reflects life in the rural South during the later years of the Great Depression.

Literary Element Dialogue

Dialogue is the conversation between characters in a literary work. Through dialogue, an author reveals the feelings, thoughts, and intentions of characters; develops conflicts; and moves the plot forward. As you read, notice what the dialogue reveals about the characters in this story.

- See Literary Terms Handbook, p. R5.

Literature Online **Interactive Literary Elements Handbook** To review or learn more about the literary elements, go to www.glencoe.com.

Reading Strategy Applying Background Knowledge

Background knowledge refers to what you already know about the setting, characters, and situations in a literary work. You can add to your background knowledge by reading carefully the information included under the Building Background section preceding the selections in this book. By relating what you know to what you are reading, you create meaning and enrich your understanding of the text.

Reading Tip: Using a Preview Chart Skim the story for information about the setting, characters, and possible conflicts in the story. Use a preview chart like the one below to record details from the story and from your background knowledge.

Details	What I Know
rural setting	fewer people, less technology
Great Depression	people needed money and work

Vocabulary

gaunt (gônt) *adj.* thin, bony, and hollow-eyed, as from hunger or illness; p. 915 *Her face looked long and gaunt, as though she suffered from poor health.*

ravenous (rav′ə nəs) *adj.* extremely hungry; p. 918 *After fasting for a long time, the prisoner was ravenous for food.*

stately (stāt′lē) *adj.* noble; dignified; majestic; p. 919 *The mansion, elegant and stately, seemed like a palace for a king or queen.*

morose (mə rōs′) *adj.* bad-tempered, gloomy, and withdrawn; p. 920 *His morose disposition led him to keep to himself and brood over his troubles.*

rue (rōō) *v.* to regret; to be sorry for; p. 922 *When the car did not start, I rued the day I had bought it.*

INDIANA ACADEMIC STANDARDS (pages 914–925)

11.3 [Identify] story elements such as character...

11.3.3 Analyze the ways in which...the author's style...achieve[s] specific...aesthetic (artistic) purposes...

11.2 Develop [reading] strategies...

11.5.2 Write responses to literature that...identify and assess the impact of perceived ambiguities...within the text.

The Life You Save May Be Your Own

Flannery O'Connor

The old woman and her daughter were sitting on their porch when Mr. Shiftlet came up their road for the first time. The old woman slid to the edge of her chair and leaned forward, shading her eyes from the piercing sunset with her hand. The daughter could not see far in front of her and continued to play with her fingers. Although the old woman lived in this desolate[1] spot with only her daughter and she had never seen Mr. Shiftlet before, she could tell, even from a distance, that he was a tramp and no one to be afraid of.

His left coat sleeve was folded up to show there was only half an arm in it and his **gaunt** figure

---

1. A *desolate* spot is miserable, lonely, and cheerless.

listed slightly to the side as if the breeze were pushing him. He had on a black town suit and a brown felt hat that was turned up in the front and down in the back and he carried a tin tool box by a handle. He came on, at an amble, up her road, his face turned toward the sun which appeared to be balancing itself on the peak of a small mountain.

The old woman didn't change her position until he was almost into her yard; then she rose with one hand fisted on her hip. The daughter, a large girl in a short blue organdy dress, saw him all at once and jumped up and began to stamp and point and make excited speechless sounds.

Mr. Shiftlet stopped just inside the yard and set his box on the ground and tipped his hat at her as if she were not in the least afflicted; then he turned toward the old woman and swung the hat all the way off. He had long black slick hair that hung flat from a part in the middle to beyond the tips of his ears on either side. His face descended in forehead for more than half its length and ended suddenly with his features just balanced over a jutting steel-trap jaw. He seemed to be a young man but he had a look of composed dissatisfaction as if he understood life thoroughly.

"Good evening," the old woman said. She was about the size of a cedar fence post and she had a man's gray hat pulled down low over her head.

The tramp stood looking at her and didn't answer. He turned his back and faced the sunset. He swung both his whole and his short arm up slowly so that they indicated an expanse of sky and his figure formed a crooked cross. The old woman watched him with her arms folded across her chest as if she were the owner of the sun, and the daughter watched, her head thrust forward and her fat helpless hands hanging at the wrists. She had long pink-gold hair and eyes as blue as a peacock's neck.

He held the pose for almost fifty seconds and then he picked up his box and came on to the porch and dropped down on the bottom step. "Lady," he said in a firm nasal voice, "I'd give a fortune to live where I could see me a sun do that every evening."

"Does it every evening," the old woman said and sat back down. The daughter sat down too and watched him with a cautious sly look as if he were a bird that had come up very close. He leaned to one side, rooting in his pants pocket, and in a second he brought out a package of chewing gum and offered her a piece. She took it and unpeeled it and began to chew without taking her eyes off him. He offered the old woman a piece but she only raised her upper lip to indicate she had no teeth.

Mr. Shiftlet's pale sharp glance had already passed over everything in the yard—the pump near the corner of the house and the big fig tree that three or four chickens were preparing to roost in—and had moved to a shed where he saw the square rusted back of an automobile. "You ladies drive?" he asked.

"That car ain't run in fifteen year," the old woman said. "The day my husband died, it quit running."

"Nothing is like it used to be, lady," he said. "The world is almost rotten."

Reading Strategy Applying Background Knowledge
Why does Mr. Shiftlet focus his attention on the automobile?

Literary Element Dialogue *What does this exchange reveal about Mr. Shiftlet?*

"That's right," the old woman said. "You from around here?"

"Name Tom T. Shiftlet," he murmured, looking at the tires.

"I'm pleased to meet you," the old woman said. "Name Lucynell Crater and daughter Lucynell Crater. What you doing around here, Mr. Shiftlet?"

He judged the car to be about a 1928 or '29 Ford. "Lady," he said, and turned and gave her his full attention, "lemme tell you something. There's one of these doctors in Atlanta that's taken a knife and cut the human heart—the human heart," he repeated, leaning forward, "out of a man's chest and held it in his hand," and he held his hand out, palm up, as if it were slightly weighted with the human heart, "and studied it like it was a day-old chicken, and lady," he said, allowing a long significant pause in which his head slid forward and his clay-colored eyes brightened, "he don't know no more about it than you or me."

"That's right," the old woman said.

"Why, if he was to take that knife and cut into every corner of it, he still wouldn't know no more than you or me. What you want to bet?"

"Nothing," the old woman said wisely. "Where you come from, Mr. Shiftlet?"

He didn't answer. He reached into his pocket and brought out a sack of tobacco and a package of cigarette papers and rolled himself a cigarette, expertly with one hand, and attached it in a hanging position to his upper lip. Then he took a box of wooden matches from his pocket and struck one on his shoe. He held the burning match as if he were studying the mystery of flame while it traveled dangerously toward his skin. The daughter began to make loud noises and to point to his hand and shake her finger at him, but when the flame was just before touching him, he leaned down with his hand cupped over it as if he were going to set fire to his nose and lit the cigarette.

He flipped away the dead match and blew a stream of gray into the evening. A sly look came over his face. "Lady," he said, "nowadays, people'll do anything anyways. I can tell you my name is Tom T. Shiftlet and I came from Tarwater, Tennessee, but you never have seen me before: how you know I ain't lying? How you know my name ain't Aaron Sparks, lady, and I come from

---

Literary Element Dialogue *How does this statement make you feel about Mr. Shiftlet?*

neck. He told the old woman then that all most people were interested in was money, but he asked what a man was made for. He asked her if a man was made for money, or what. He asked her what she thought she was made for but she didn't answer, she only sat rocking and wondered if a one-armed man could put a new roof on her garden house. He asked a lot of questions that she didn't answer. He told her that he was twenty-eight years old and had lived a varied life. He had been a gospel singer, a foreman on the railroad, an assistant in an undertaking parlor, and he had come over the radio for three months with Uncle Roy and his Red Creek Wranglers. He said he had fought and bled in the Arm Service of his country and visited every foreign land and that everywhere he had seen people that didn't care if they did a thing one way or another. He said he hadn't been raised thataway.

A fat yellow moon appeared in the branches of the fig tree as if it were going to roost there with the chickens. He said that a man had to escape to the country to see the world whole and that he wished he lived in a desolate place like this where he could see the sun go down every evening like God made it to do.

"Are you married or are you single?" the old woman asked.

There was a long silence. "Lady," he asked finally, "where would you find you an innocent woman today? I wouldn't have any of this trash I could just pick up."

The daughter was leaning very far down, hanging her head almost between her knees, watching him through a triangular door she had made in her overturned hair; and she suddenly fell in a heap on the floor and began to whimper. Mr. Shiftlet straightened her out and helped her get back in the chair.

Singleberry, Georgia, or how you know it's not George Speeds and I come from Lucy, Alabama, or how you know I ain't Thompson Bright from Toolafalls, Mississippi?"

"I don't know nothing about you," the old woman muttered, irked.[2]

"Lady," he said, "people don't care how they lie. Maybe the best I can tell you is, I'm a man; but listen lady," he said and paused and made his tone more ominous[3] still, "what is a man?"

The old woman began to gum a seed. "What you carry in that tin box, Mr. Shiftlet?" she asked.

"Tools," he said, put back. "I'm a carpenter."

"Well, if you come out here to work, I'll be able to feed you and give you a place to sleep but I can't pay. I'll tell you that before you begin," she said.

There was no answer at once and no particular expression on his face. He leaned back against the two-by-four that helped support the porch roof. "Lady," he said slowly, "there's some men that some things mean more to them than money." The old woman rocked without comment and the daughter watched the trigger that moved up and down in his

---

2. To be *irked* is to be annoyed or bothered.
3. Something *ominous* is, or seems to be, threatening.

Reading Strategy Applying Background Knowledge
Should the old woman trust Mr. Shiftlet or not? Explain.

Big Idea Return to Regionalism *Why does the author include these details?*

FLANNERY O'CONNOR **917**

"Is she your baby girl?" he asked.

"My only," the old woman said, "and she's the sweetest girl in the world. I wouldn't give her up for nothing on earth. She's smart too. She can sweep the floor, cook, wash, feed the chickens, and hoe. I wouldn't give her up for a casket of jewels."

"No," he said kindly, "don't ever let any man take her away from you."

"Any man come after her," the old woman said, " 'll have to stay around the place."

Mr. Shiftlet's eye in the darkness was focused on a part of the automobile bumper that glittered in the distance. "Lady," he said, jerking his short arm up as if he could point with it to her house and yard and pump, "there ain't a broken thing on this plantation that I couldn't fix for you, one-arm jackleg⁴ or not. I'm a man," he said with a sullen dignity, "even if I ain't a whole one. I got," he said, tapping his knuckles on the floor to emphasize the immensity of what he was going to say, "a moral intelligence!" and his face pierced out of the darkness into a shaft of doorlight and he stared at her as if he were astonished himself at this impossible truth.

The old woman was not impressed with the phrase. "I told you you could hang around and work for food," she said, "if you don't mind sleeping in that car yonder."

"Why listen, Lady," he said with a grin of delight, "the monks of old slept in their coffins!"

"They wasn't as advanced as we are," the old woman said.

The next morning he began on the roof of the garden house while Lucynell, the daughter, sat on a rock and watched him work. He had not been around a week before the change he had made in the place was apparent. He had patched the front and back steps, built a new hog pen, restored a fence, and taught Lucynell, who was completely deaf and had never said a word in her life, to say the word "bird." The big rosy-faced girl followed him

everywhere, saying "Burrttddt ddbirrrttdt," and clapping her hands. The old woman watched from a distance, secretly pleased. She was **ravenous** for a son-in-law.

Mr. Shiftlet slept on the hard narrow back seat of the car with his feet out the side window. He had his razor and a can of water on a crate that served him as a bedside table and he put up a piece of mirror against the back glass and kept his coat neatly on a hanger that he hung over one of the windows.

In the evenings he sat on the steps and talked while the old woman and Lucynell rocked violently in their chairs on either side of him. The old woman's three mountains were black against the dark blue sky and were visited off and on by various planets and by the moon after it had left the chickens. Mr. Shiftlet pointed out that the reason he had improved this plantation was because he had taken a personal interest in it. He said he was even going to make the automobile run.

He had raised the hood and studied the mechanism and he said he could tell that the car had been built in the days when cars were really built. You take now, he said, one man puts in one bolt and another man puts in another bolt and another man puts in another bolt so that it's a man for a bolt. That's why you have to pay so much for a car: you're paying all those men. Now if you didn't have to pay but one man, you could get you a cheaper car and one that had had a personal interest taken in it, and it would be a better car. The old woman agreed with him that this was so.

Mr. Shiftlet said that the trouble with the world was that nobody cared, or stopped and took any trouble. He said he never would have been able to teach Lucynell to say a word if he hadn't cared and stopped long enough.

"Teach her to say something else," the old woman said.

"What you want her to say next?" Mr. Shiftlet asked.

The old woman's smile was broad and toothless and suggestive. "Teach her to say 'sugarpie,'" she said.

---

4. A *jackleg*, like a jack-of-all-trades, can do many different kinds of work for which he or she has not been trained.

Literary Element Dialogue *Why might Mrs. Crater say this to Mr. Shiftlet?*

Vocabulary

ravenous (rav′ə nəs) *adj.* extremely hungry

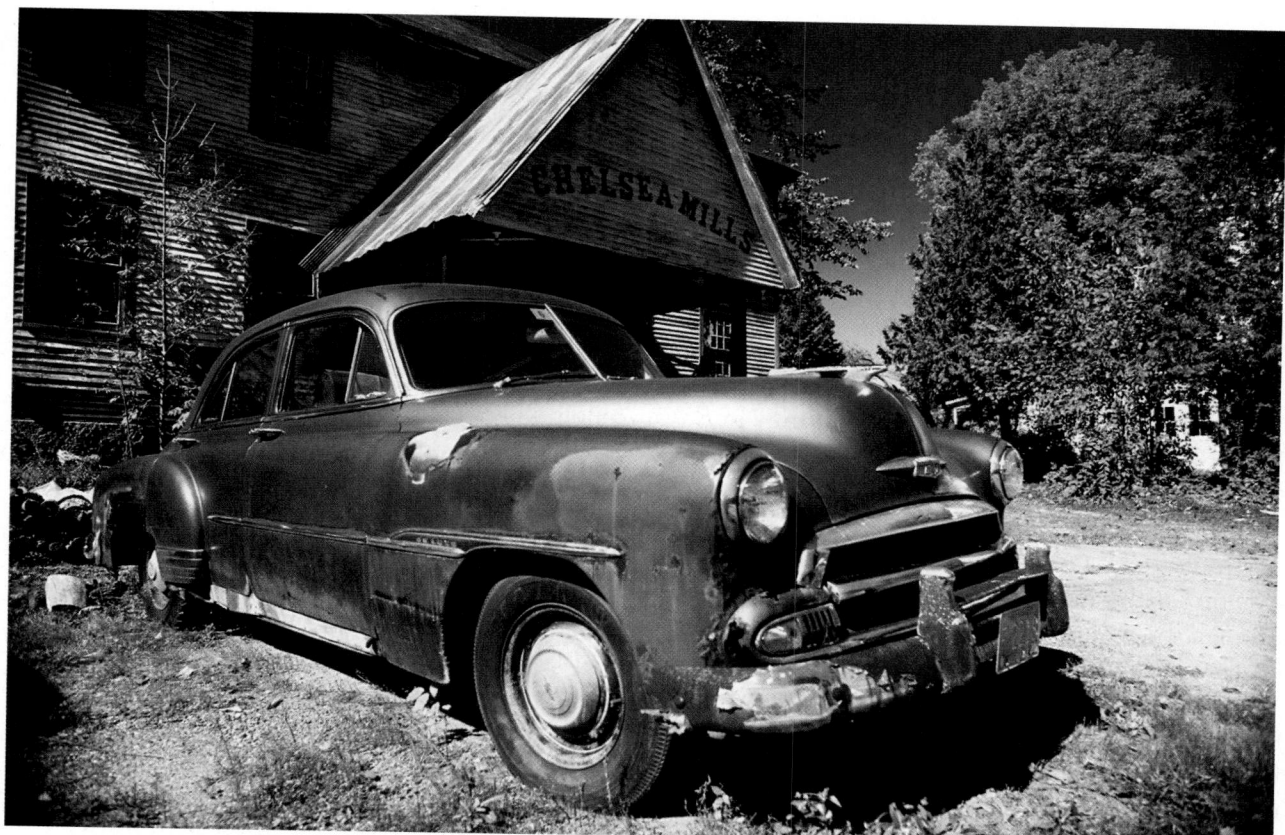

Mr. Shiftlet already knew what was on her mind.

The next day he began to tinker with the automobile and that evening he told her that if she would buy a fan belt, he would be able to make the car run.

The old woman said she would give him the money. "You see that girl yonder?" she asked, pointing to Lucynell who was sitting on the floor a foot away, watching him, her eyes blue even in the dark. "If it was ever a man wanted to take her away, I would say, 'No man on earth is going to take that sweet girl of mine away from me!' but if he was to say, 'Lady, I don't want to take her away, I want her right here,' I would say, 'Mister, I don't blame you none. I wouldn't pass up a chance to live in a permanent place and get the sweetest girl in the world myself. You ain't no fool,' I would say."

"How old is she?" Mr. Shiftlet asked casually.

"Fifteen, sixteen," the old woman said. The girl was nearly thirty but because of her innocence it was impossible to guess.

"It would be a good idea to paint it too," Mr. Shiftlet remarked. "You don't want it to rust out."

"We'll see about that later," the old woman said.

The next day he walked into town and returned with the parts he needed and a can of gasoline. Late in the afternoon, terrible noises issued from the shed and the old woman rushed out of the house, thinking Lucynell was somewhere having a fit. Lucynell was sitting on a chicken crate, stamping her feet and screaming, "Burrddttt! bddurrd-dtttt!" but her fuss was drowned out by the car. With a volley of blasts it emerged from the shed, moving in a fierce and **stately** way. Mr. Shiftlet was in the driver's seat, sitting very erect. He had an expression of serious modesty on his face as if he had just raised the dead.

That night, rocking on the porch, the old woman began her business at once. "You want you an innocent woman, don't you?" she asked sympathetically. "You don't want none of this trash."

"No'm, I don't," Mr. Shiftlet said.

"One that can't talk," she continued, "can't sass you back or use foul language. That's the kind for you to have. Right there," and she pointed to Lucynell sitting cross-legged in her chair, holding both feet in her hands.

"That's right," he admitted. "She wouldn't give me any trouble."

"Saturday," the old woman said, "you and her and me can drive into town and get married."

Mr. Shiftlet eased his position on the steps.

"I can't get married right now," he said. "Everything you want to do takes money and I ain't got any."

"What you need with money?" she asked.

"It takes money," he said. "Some people'll do anything anyhow these days, but the way I think, I wouldn't marry no woman that I couldn't take on a trip like she was somebody. I mean take her to a hotel and treat her. I wouldn't marry the Duchesser Windsor,"[5] he said firmly, "unless I could take her to a hotel and give her something good to eat.

"I was raised thataway and there ain't a thing I can do about it. My old mother taught me how to do."

"Lucynell don't even know what a hotel is," the old woman muttered. "Listen here, Mr. Shiftlet," she said, sliding forward in her chair, "you'd be getting a permanent house and a deep well and the most innocent girl in the world. You don't need no money. Lemme tell you something: there ain't any place in the world for a poor disabled friendless drifting man."

The ugly words settled in Mr. Shiftlet's head like a group of buzzards in the top of a tree. He didn't answer at once. He rolled himself a cigarette and lit it and then he said in an even voice, "Lady, a man is divided into two parts, body and spirit."

The old woman clamped her gums together.

"A body and a spirit," he repeated. "The body, lady, is like a house: it don't go anywhere; but the spirit, lady, is like a automobile: always on the move, always . . ."

"Listen, Mr. Shiftlet," she said, "my well never goes dry and my house is always warm in the winter and there's no mortgage on a thing about this place. You can go to the courthouse and see for yourself. And yonder under that shed is a fine automobile." She laid the bait carefully. "You can have it painted by Saturday. I'll pay for the paint."

In the darkness, Mr. Shiftlet's smile stretched like a weary snake waking up by a fire. After a second he recalled himself and said, "I'm only saying a man's spirit means more to him than anything else. I would have to take my wife off for the weekend without no regards at all for cost. I got to follow where my spirit say to go."

"I'll give you fifteen dollars for a weekend trip," the old woman said in a crabbed voice. "That's the best I can do."

"That wouldn't hardly pay for more than the gas and the hotel," he said. "It wouldn't feed her."

"Seventeen-fifty," the old woman said. "That's all I got so it isn't any use you trying to milk me. You can take a lunch."

Mr. Shiftlet was deeply hurt by the word "milk." He didn't doubt that she had more money sewed up in her mattress but he had already told her he was not interested in her money. "I'll make that do," he said and rose and walked off without treating[6] with her further.

On Saturday the three of them drove into town in the car that the paint had barely dried on and Mr. Shiftlet and Lucynell were married in the Ordinary's[7] office while the old woman witnessed. As they came out of the courthouse, Mr. Shiftlet began twisting his neck in his collar. He looked **morose** and bitter as if he had been insulted while someone held him. "That didn't satisfy me none," he said. "That was just something a woman in an office did, nothing but paper work and blood tests. What do they know about my blood? If they was to take my heart and cut it out," he said, "they wouldn't know a thing about me. It didn't satisfy me at all."

"It satisfied the law," the old woman said sharply.

---

6. Here, *treating* means "negotiating or discussing terms."

7. An *Ordinary* is a local judge who, in many states, is called the "justice of the peace."

Reading Strategy Applying Background Knowledge
Why does the author compare Mr. Shiftlet's smile to a snake?

Vocabulary

morose (mə rōs′) *adj.* bad-tempered, gloomy, and withdrawn

---

5. Shiftlet is referring to the American woman for whom Britain's King Edward VIII gave up the throne in 1936. The new king gave them the titles Duke and Duchess of *Windsor*.

Literary Element Dialogue *Why does Mrs. Crater insult Mr. Shiftlet?*

"The law," Mr. Shiftlet said and spit. "It's the law that don't satisfy me."

He had painted the car dark green with a yellow band around it just under the windows. The three of them climbed in the front seat and the old woman said, "Don't Lucynell look pretty? Looks like a baby doll." Lucynell was dressed up in a white dress that her mother had uprooted from a trunk and there was a Panama hat on her head with a bunch of red wooden cherries on the brim. Every now and then her placid[8] expression was changed by a sly isolated little thought like a shoot of green in the desert. "You got a prize!" the old woman said.

Mr. Shiftlet didn't even look at her.

They drove back to the house to let the old woman off and pick up the lunch. When they were ready to leave, she stood staring in the window of the car, with her fingers clenched around the glass. Tears began to seep sideways out of her eyes and run along the dirty creases in her face. "I ain't ever been parted with her for two days before," she said.

Mr. Shiftlet started the motor.

"And I wouldn't let no man have her but you because I seen you would do right. Good-bye, Sugarbaby," she said, clutching at the sleeve of the white dress. Lucynell looked straight at her and didn't seem to see her there at all. Mr. Shiftlet eased the car forward so that she had to move her hands.

The early afternoon was clear and open and surrounded by pale blue sky. Although the car would go only thirty miles an hour, Mr. Shiftlet imagined a terrific climb and dip and swerve that went entirely to his head so that he forgot his morning bitterness. He had always wanted an automobile but he had never been able to afford one before. He drove very fast because he wanted to make Mobile[9] by nightfall.

Occasionally he stopped his thoughts long enough to look at Lucynell in the seat beside him. She had eaten the lunch as soon as they were out of the yard and now she was pulling the cherries off the hat one by one and throwing them out the window. He became depressed in spite of the car. He had driven about a hundred miles when he decided that she must be hungry again and at the next small town they came to, he stopped in front of an aluminum-painted eating place called The Hot Spot and took her in and ordered her a plate of ham and grits. The ride had made her sleepy and as soon as she got up on the stool, she rested her head on the counter and shut her eyes. There was no one in The Hot Spot but Mr. Shiftlet and the boy behind the counter, a pale youth with a greasy rag hung over his shoulder. Before he could dish up the food, she was snoring gently.

"Give it to her when she wakes up," Mr. Shiftlet said. "I'll pay for it now."

---

8. *Placid* means "calm" or "peaceful."

Literary Element Dialogue *Why does Mrs. Crater think Mr. Shiftlet will "do right" by her daughter?*

9. *Mobile* (mō′bēl) is a port city in southwestern Alabama.

Big Idea Return to Regionalism *How do these details contribute to the setting?*

The boy bent over her and stared at the long pink-gold hair and the half-shut sleeping eyes. Then he looked up and stared at Mr. Shiftlet. "She looks like an angel of Gawd," he murmured.

"Hitchhiker," Mr. Shiftlet explained. "I can't wait. I got to make Tuscaloosa."[10]

The boy bent over again and very carefully touched his finger to a strand of the golden hair and Mr. Shiftlet left.

He was more depressed than ever as he drove on by himself. The late afternoon had grown hot and sultry and the country had flattened out. Deep in the sky a storm was preparing very slowly and without thunder as if it meant to drain every drop of air from the earth before it broke. There were times when Mr. Shiftlet preferred not to be alone. He felt too that a man with a car had a responsibility to others and he kept his eye out for a hitchhiker. Occasionally he saw a sign that warned: "Drive carefully. The life you save may be your own."

The narrow road dropped off on either side into dry fields and here and there a shack or a filling station stood in a clearing. The sun began to set directly in front of the automobile. It was a reddening ball that through his windshield was slightly flat on the bottom and top. He saw a boy in overalls and a gray hat standing on the edge of the road and he slowed the car down and stopped in front of him. The boy didn't have his hand raised to thumb the ride, he was only standing there, but he had a small cardboard suitcase and his hat was set on his head in a way to indicate that he had left somewhere for good. "Son," Mr. Shiftlet said, "I see you want a ride."

The boy didn't say he did or he didn't but he opened the door of the car and got in, and Mr. Shiftlet started driving again. The child held the suitcase on his lap and folded his arms on top of it. He turned his head and looked out the window away from Mr. Shiftlet. Mr. Shiftlet felt oppressed.[11] "Son," he said after a minute, "I got

the best old mother in the world so I reckon you only got the second best."

The boy gave him a quick dark glance and then turned his face back out the window.

"It's nothing so sweet," Mr. Shiftlet continued, "as a boy's mother. She taught him his first prayers at her knee, she give him love when no other would, she told him what was right and what wasn't, and she seen that he done the right thing. Son," he said, "I never **rued** a day in my life like the one I rued when I left that old mother of mine."

The boy shifted in his seat but he didn't look at Mr. Shiftlet. He unfolded his arms and put one hand on the door handle.

"My mother was an angel of Gawd," Mr. Shiftlet said in a very strained voice. "He took her from heaven and giver to me and I left her." His eyes were instantly clouded over with a mist of tears. The car was barely moving.

The boy turned angrily in the seat. "You go to the devil!" he cried. "My old woman is a flea bag and yours is a stinking pole cat!" and with that he flung the door open and jumped out with his suitcase into the ditch.

Mr. Shiftlet was so shocked that for about a hundred feet he drove along slowly with the door still open. A cloud, the exact color of the boy's hat and shaped like a turnip, had descended over the sun, and another, worse looking, crouched behind the car. Mr. Shiftlet felt that the rottenness of the world was about to engulf him. He raised his arm and let it fall again to his breast. "Oh Lord!" he prayed. "Break forth and wash the slime from this earth!"

The turnip continued slowly to descend. After a few minutes there was a guffawing peal of thunder from behind and fantastic raindrops, like tin-can tops, crashed over the rear of Mr. Shiftlet's car. Very quickly he stepped on the gas and with his stump sticking out the window he raced the galloping shower into Mobile. ❧

---

10. *Tuscaloosa*, in west central Alabama, is nearly 200 miles north of Mobile.

Literary Element Dialogue *Why does Mr. Shiftlet lie to the boy behind the counter?*

Reading Strategy Applying Background Knowledge *What does the road sign mean to motorists?*

11. Here, *oppressed* means "distressed" or "burdened."

Literary Element Dialogue *What is ironic about Mr. Shiftlet's prayer?*

Vocabulary

rue (r$\overline{oo}$) *v.* to regret; to be sorry for

RESPONDING AND THINKING CRITICALLY

Respond

1. What was your reaction to the outcome of the story? Explain.

Recall and Interpret

2. (a)How does Mr. Shiftlet present himself to Mrs. Crater? (b)What clues to his true character does she fail to notice?

3. (a)What does Mr. Shiftlet accomplish during his week on the Crater farm? (b)What does Mr. Shiftlet want from Mrs. Crater, and how do you know?

4. (a)What is Lucynell's disability, and how does it affect her? (b)Why does Mrs. Crater consider Mr. Shiftlet a good match for her daughter?

5. (a)What two agreements do Mr. Shiftlet and Mrs. Crater make? (b)What factors might motivate Mr. Shiftlet to make each agreement?

Analyze and Evaluate

6. Whom do you think O'Connor intended to be the protagonist of the story? Support your interpretation.

7. (a)What happens to each of the characters at the end of the story? (b)Whose life—if anyone's—do you think may have been saved at the end of the story?

8. (a)Situational irony occurs when the outcome of a situation is different from the expectations of a character or the reader. Explain the situational irony in this story. (b)Why do you think O'Connor uses this technique?

Connect

9. **Big Idea** **Return to Regionalism** How would this story have been different if it were set in a modern-day city instead of on a rural plantation in the South in the 1940s?

VISUAL LITERACY: Graphic Organizers

Creating a Story Map

A story map is a visual diagram of the events in a story. This graphic organizer can help you identify and relate key details in the story. Fill in a story map similar to the one shown with details from "The Life You Save May Be Your Own."

Group Activity Discuss the following questions with a small group of classmates. Refer to the story map you created and cite other details from "The Life You Save May Be Your Own" to support your answers.

1. What might Mrs. Crater have done to bring about a different outcome?

2. How might the conflict or resolution have changed if other characters were involved in the story, such as Mrs. Crater's husband or other children besides Lucynell?

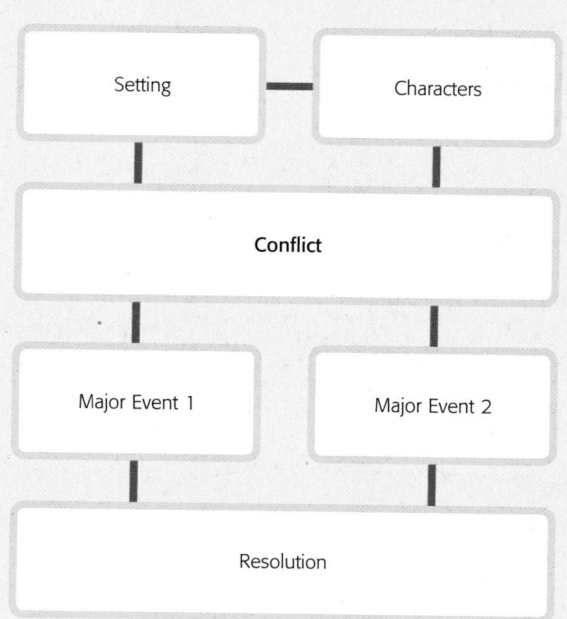

Literary Element Dialogue

In this story O'Connor uses **dialogue** not only to provide local color but also to reveal characters' personalities and traits. Dialogue brings characters to life by showing what they are thinking and feeling as they react to other characters. Think about the dialogue in "The Life You Save May Be Your Own" as you answer the questions below.

1. How does the dialogue between Mrs. Crater and Mr. Shiftlet reveal their true characters? Give specific examples.

2. What impact does Lucynell's lack of dialogue have on the story?

Review: Foreshadowing

Foreshadowing, as you learned in examining "A Rose for Emily," is the use of clues by the author to prepare readers for later events in a story.

Group Activity Meet with a small group to discuss O'Connor's use of foreshadowing in "The Life You Save May Be Your Own." Use a chart like the one below to record examples of foreshadowing throughout the story.

Event	Foreshadowing
Mr. Shiftlet steals Mrs. Crater's car.	

Reading Strategy Applying Background Knowledge

To understand the interactions between Mrs. Crater and Mr. Shiflet, you must apply what you know about the Great Depression and the rural South. Review the preview chart you created on page 914, and then answer the following questions.

1. Why does Mr. Shiflet agree to work for Mrs. Crater?

2. How important is money to both Mr. Shiflet and Mrs. Crater?

Vocabulary Practice

Practice with Synonyms Think about the meanings of the underlined words in the sentences below. Then, from the vocabulary words, choose a synonym that better fits the context.

1. Too sick from the flu to eat, he appeared quite <u>thin</u>.
2. Liza's <u>gloomy</u> attitude made it difficult for her to make friends.
3. I did <u>regret</u> not buying the dress, as it sold out quickly.
4. The castle belonging to the royal family had a <u>splendid</u> appearance.
5. Having eaten neither breakfast nor lunch, I was <u>hungry</u> by dinnertime.

Academic Vocabulary

Here are two words from the vocabulary list on page R86.

orient (ôr´ ē ent´) *v.* to acquaint with the existing situation or environment

generation (jen´ ə rā´ shən) *n.* a group of people born around the same time period

Practice and Apply
1. How does O'Connor **orient** the reader in the story's setting?
2. What does Mr. Shiftlet think about the values of the younger **generation**?

Writing About Literature

Evaluate Title The title, or name, of a work of literature is sometimes linked to the work's central theme or to the traits of a major character. The link may be subtle or obvious. Is the title of this story effective or not? Write a brief essay explaining your position and supporting it with evidence from the story.

As you draft, use the following writing plan to organize your essay.

START

Introduction ▸ Introduce your topic and then state your position or thesis.

Middle ▸ Present one or more reasons and support them with evidence from the story.

Conclusion ▸ Restate your position and give the reader a parting thought about O'Connor's title.

FINISH

After you complete your draft, meet with a peer reviewer to evaluate each other's work and to suggest revisions. Then proofread and edit your draft for errors in spelling, grammar, and punctuation.

Interdisciplinary Activity: Theater

Imagine that you are to stage a production of "The Life You Save May Be Your Own." With a partner or a small group, write a proposal stating your plans. Create a proposal portfolio that contains the following:

- a statement about the story and why you think it could be successfully adapted into a drama

- a cast list, including a brief description of each character in the play

- a scene-by-scene description of the settings, with a list of the materials and props you will need (including sketches of each set)

- a description of the costumes needed for each cast member (including sketches if possible)

O'Connor's Language and Style

Avoiding Double Negatives In "The Life You Save May Be Your Own," O'Connor's characters speak in a regional dialect that includes the use of the double negative—that is, two or more negative words in the same clause to express the same idea.

"I *don't* know *nothing* about you . . . "
"And I *wouldn't* let *no* man have her but you . . . "

Notice that O'Connor also uses Standard English—only one negative word in a clause—to express a negative idea.

Mr. Shiflet said that the trouble with the world was that *nobody* cared.
"*Nothing* is like it used to be, lady."

Double negatives are effective for O'Connor's purpose, but they should be avoided in standard writing and speech because one negative word "cancels out" another.

Dialect	"I wouldn't give her up for nothing on earth."
Standard English	"I wouldn't give her up for anything on earth."
Standard English	"I would give her up for nothing on earth."

Activity Find three other examples of double negatives in "The Life You Save May Be Your Own." Revise them to change each into Standard English.

Revising Check

Avoiding Double Negatives In most cases, writers use Standard English in their work, except in direct quotations that provide local color. With a partner, review your essay on "The Life You Save May Be Your Own" to identify any double negatives that you may have overlooked earlier. Revise your draft to correct these errors in one of the two ways provided in the examples above.

Literature Online **Web Activities** For eFlashcards, Selection Quick Checks, and other Web activities, go to www.glencoe.com.

Grammar Workshop

Sentence Structure

▶ **Vocabulary Terms**

An **introductory phrase** or an **introductory clause** begins a sentence and provides additional information about the main clause.

▶ **Test-Taking Tip**

To decide whether an introductory phrase needs a comma, decide whether the sentence makes sense without the phrase. If so, the introductory phrase probably needs a comma after it.

▶ **Reading Handbook**

For more about phrases and clauses, see Reading Handbook, p. R20.

eWorkbooks To link to the Grammar and Language eWorkbook, go to www.glencoe.com.

ACADEMIC STANDARDS (page 926)

11.6.4 Identify and correctly use... phrases...and the mechanics of punctuation...

Using Introductory Phrases and Clauses

"As they came out of the courthouse, Mr. Shiftlet began twisting his neck in his collar."
— Flannery O'Connor, from "The Life You Save May Be Your Own"

Connecting to Literature Introductory phrases and clauses add information about the main clause. *As they came out of the courthouse* is an **introductory clause**—a dependent clause that begins a sentence. Like other dependent clauses, an introductory clause has a subject and predicate, but it does not express a complete thought. Use a comma after an introductory clause.

"In the darkness, Mr. Shiftlet's smile stretched like a weary snake waking up by a fire."

In the darkness is an **introductory phrase** that tells where the action happens. Like other phrases, an introductory phrase lacks a subject and predicate. You must use a comma after an introductory phrase if it contains a verb form (participle, gerund, or infinitive). In addition, use a comma after a long introductory prepositional phrase or a series of prepositional phrases. A comma after a short introductory prepositional phrase is usually not necessary.

Examples

To fix the car, Mr. Shiftlet raised the hood and studied the engine.
To fix the car is an introductory infinitive phrase that tells why Mr. Shiftlet raised the hood. Because it is an infinitive phrase, it needs a comma after it.

In the evenings Mr. Shiftlet sat on the porch steps and talked.
The introductory prepositional phrase *in the evenings* is short, so it needs no comma.

In the afternoon of the next day, Mr. Shiftlet got the car to start.
A comma is necessary after the two introductory prepositional phrases.

"If you come out here to work, I'll be able to feed you and give you a place to sleep."
If you come out here to work is an introductory clause, so it needs a comma after it.

Exercise

Combine each pair of sentences by changing one of them into an introductory phrase or clause.

1. O'Connor was disabled by lupus in 1952. She spent the remainder of her life on her mother's farm.
2. Mr. Shiftlet came up the road for the first time. The old woman and her daughter were sitting on their porch.
3. Eudora Welty was raised in the South. Much of her work was inspired by Southern settings.

The Second Tree from the Corner

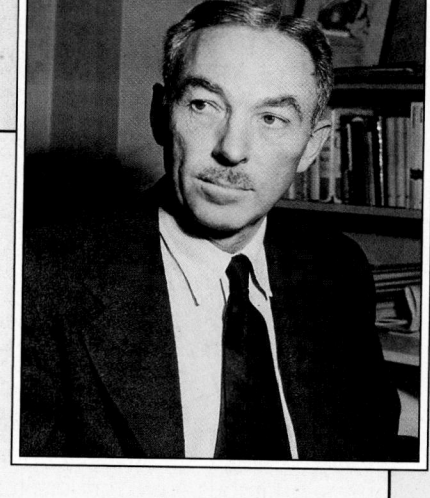

MEET E. B. WHITE

Although the beloved children's classics *Charlotte's Web* and *Stuart Little* remain two of Elwyn Brooks (E. B.) White's best-known works, he is also highly acclaimed for his essays and short stories. In fact, it was while working for *The New Yorker* magazine in his late twenties that White first captivated the American public. There, he worked with other legendary writers such as James Thurber, Dorothy Parker, and Robert Benchley to create a sophisticated and clever "New York" voice for the new magazine.

The Road to *The New Yorker* The youngest child in a large, affectionate family, White was born in rural Mount Vernon, a suburb of New York City. In 1921 he graduated from Cornell University. At Cornell he received the nickname Andy, by which he was known for the rest of his life. (All Cornell students named White were dubbed "Andy," after the university's co-founder, Andrew Dickson White.)

After college, Andy White traveled and worked at a series of miscellaneous jobs for about five years. Returning to New York, he worked in an ad agency and began sending manuscripts to *The New Yorker*. The editor of the magazine, Harold Ross, recognized talent when he saw it, and he soon hired White as a staff writer. White married Katherine Sergeant Angell, the magazine's literary editor, in 1929. According to Brendan Gill, a fellow *New Yorker* staff member, Andy and Katherine worked so closely together over the years that most people thought of them as one person, referred to as "the Whites."

On the Farm In 1938 the Whites decided to leave the city and return to a simple rural life, this time in North Brooklin, Maine. Andy kept animals on their farm there, some of which made their way into his stories and books. He remained on the staff of *The New Yorker*, continuing to produce essays and his unsigned column "Notes and Comments."

He also contributed to *Harper's Magazine* from 1938 to 1943, writing the column "One Man's Meat."

On the farm, he penned his famed children's stories. The first one, *Stuart Little*, features an adventurous mouse-child, born into a human family. The second, *Charlotte's Web*, is about the friendship between Wilbur, a young pig, and Charlotte, a spider who saves his life through her clever web weavings. The third, *The Trumpet of the Swan*, tells the story of a mute swan who becomes a celebrity after learning to trumpet. The themes of friendship, tolerance, loyalty, and rural living are common threads in these books.

> "I arise in the morning torn between a desire to improve (or save) the world and a desire to enjoy (or savor) the world. This makes it hard to plan the day."
>
> —E. B. White

White was awarded the Presidential Medal of Freedom in 1963 and the Laura Ingalls Wilder Award from the American Library Association in 1970. In 1973 he was elected to the American Academy of Arts and Letters.

E. B. White was born in 1899 and died in 1985.

Literature Online **Author Search** For more about E. B. White, go to www.glencoe.com.

Connecting to the Story

Imagine that someone asks you, "What do you want out of life?" How would you answer? What are your goals and desires? As you read, think about these questions:

- What is most important in life?
- What do your dreams and goals reveal about you?

Building Background

"The Second Tree from the Corner" takes place in Manhattan, a part of New York City, probably in the late 1940s. One clue to the story's time frame comes from a reference to Ethel Merman, a popular Broadway singer and actress of the time. Other references to famous New York institutions and places appear in the story as well. The narrator mentions the *Times,* which is *The New York Times* newspaper; the "Park," which is Central Park; the "East Seventies," a section of Manhattan known for its wealthy residents; and Madison Avenue, a famous luxury shopping district.

Setting Purposes for Reading

Big Idea Life in the City

As you read, notice how White weaves in references to city life, transportation, scenery, and culture in "The Second Tree from the Corner." Ask yourself which of these scenes, situations, and attitudes could happen only in a city and not in the country.

Literary Element Plot

A **plot** is the sequence of events that constitutes a narrative, usually involving characters in conflict. A plot includes **rising action** (development of the conflict), **climax** (sometimes called the crisis or turning point), and **falling action** (sometimes called the resolution of the conflict). As you read the story, be aware of how White develops these elements of the plot.

- See Literary Terms Handbook, p. R13.

Literature Online Interactive Literary Elements Handbook To review or learn more about the literary elements, go to www.glencoe.com.

Reading Strategy Analyzing Text Structure

Analyzing text structure means taking a close look at the organizational pattern of a piece of writing. A writer might use chronological order (order of time), comparison and contrast, cause and effect, or order of importance as a frame on which to hang the text. Most fiction, including this story, is organized primarily in chronological order.

Reading Tip: Finding Time References Use a graphic organizer like the one below to keep track of the time references in the story.

| Trexler felt the time passing. | He had already used up pretty nearly four seconds. | |

Vocabulary

amorphous (ə môr′ fəs) *adj.* without definite form; p. 929 *Amorphous clouds filled the sky.*

retractable (ri trak′ tə bəl) *adj.* capable of being drawn back or in; p. 930 *Cats have retractable claws.*

hemorrhage (he′ mə rij) *n.* a severe discharge of blood; p. 930 *The doctor was able to stop the hemorrhage.*

inquisitor (in kwi′ zə tər) *n.* one who asks questions; p. 931 *Jennifer refused to answer the rude inquisitor.*

intimation (in′ tə mā′ shən) *n.* a hint; a suggestion; p. 932 *Mike's reputation was hurt by the intimation of scandal.*

Vocabulary Tip: Word Parts Root words can be combined with prefixes and suffixes to form new words. The word *unattainable,* for example, is formed from the root word *attain* (meaning "to get"), the prefix *un-* (meaning "not"), and the suffix *-able* (meaning "capable of").

INDIANA ACADEMIC STANDARDS (pages 928–934)
11.3 [Identify] story elements such as...plot...
11.2 Develop strategies such as...analyzing structure...
11.5.2 Write responses to literature that...analyze the use of imagery...

928 UNIT 6 FROM DEPRESSION TO COLD WAR

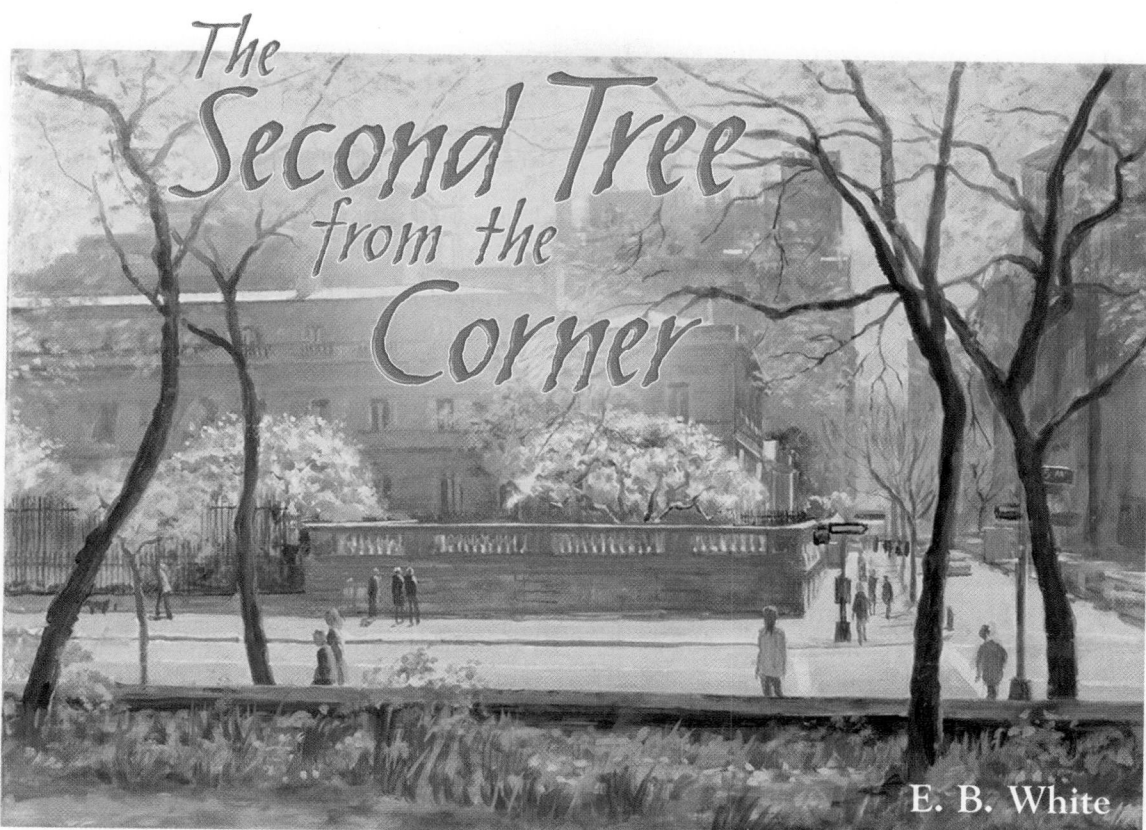

The Second Tree from the Corner

E. B. White

The Frick Gallery, 1997. Julian Barrow. Oil on canvas, 18 x 24 in. Private Collection.

"Ever have any bizarre thoughts?" asked the doctor.

Mr. Trexler failed to catch the word. "What kind?" he said.

"Bizarre," repeated the doctor, his voice steady. He watched his patient for any slight change of expression, any wince. It seemed to Trexler that the doctor was not only watching him closely but was creeping slowly toward him, like a lizard toward a bug. Trexler shoved his chair back an inch and gathered himself for a reply. He was about to say "Yes" when he realized that if he said yes the next question would be unanswerable. Bizarre thoughts, bizarre thoughts? Ever have any bizarre thoughts? What kind of thoughts *except* bizarre had he had since the age of two?

Trexler felt the time passing, the necessity for an answer. These psychiatrists were busy men, overloaded, not to be kept waiting. The next patient was probably already perched out there in the waiting room, lonely, worried, shifting around on the sofa, his mind stuffed with bizarre thoughts and **amorphous** fears. Poor fellow, thought Trexler. Out there all alone in that misshapen antechamber,[1] staring at the filing cabinet and wondering whether to tell the doctor about that day on the Madison Avenue bus.

Let's see, bizarre thoughts. Trexler dodged back along the dreadful corridor of the years to see what he could find. He felt the doctor's eyes upon him and knew that time was running out. Don't be so conscientious, he said to himself. If a bizarre thought is indicated here, just reach into the bag and pick anything at all. A man as well supplied with bizarre thoughts as you are should have no difficulty producing one for the record. Trexler darted into the bag, hung for a moment before one of his thoughts, as a hummingbird pauses in the delphinium. No, he said, not that one. He darted to another (the one about the rhesus monkey), paused, considered. No, he said, not that.

---

1. An *antechamber,* or waiting room, is a smaller room serving as an entrance to a larger or main room.

Literary Element   Plot *How would you describe Mr. Trexler's internal conflict at this point?*

Vocabulary

amorphous (ə môr′ fəs) *adj.* without definite form

Trexler knew he must hurry. He had already used up pretty nearly four seconds since the question had been put. But it was an impossible situation—just one more lousy, impossible situation such as he was always getting himself into. When, he asked himself, are you going to quit maneuvering yourself into a pocket? He made one more effort. This time he stopped at the asylum, only the bars were lucite[2]—fluted, **retractable**. Not here, he said. Not this one.

He looked straight at the doctor. "No," he said quietly. "I never have any bizarre thoughts."

The doctor sucked in on his pipe, blew a plume of smoke toward the rows of medical books. Trexler's gaze followed the smoke. He managed to make out one of the titles, *The Genito-Urinary System*. A bright wave of fear swept cleanly over him and he winced under the first pain of kidney stones.[3] He remembered when he was a child, the first time he ever entered a doctor's office, sneaking a look at the titles of the books—and the flush of fear, the shirt wet under the arms, the book on t.b.,[4] the sudden knowledge that he was in the advanced stages of consumption,[5] the quick vision of the **hemorrhage**. Trexler sighed wearily. Forty years, he thought, and I still get thrown by the title of a medical book. Forty years and I still can't stay on life's little bucky horse. No wonder I'm sitting here in this dreary joint at the end of this woebegone[6] afternoon, lying about my bizarre thoughts to a doctor who looks, come to think of it, rather tired.

The session dragged on. After about twenty minutes, the doctor rose and knocked his pipe

2. *Lucite* is the trademark name of a transparent plastic.
3. *Kidney stones* are small, hard calcium deposits that sometimes form in the kidneys and cause pain.
4. Tuberculosis, a disease that often affects the lungs, is sometimes referred to as *t.b.*
5. *Consumption* is another name for tuberculosis.
6. *Woebegone* means "sorrowful" or "filled with grief"; it can also suggest "dreary and miserable."

Reading Strategy Analyzing Text Structure *How do you know the author is using chronological order to organize the story?*

Literary Element Plot *In what way is Mr. Trexler trying to resolve his internal conflict?*

Vocabulary

retractable (ri trak′ tə bəl) *adj.* capable of being drawn back or in

hemorrhage (he′ mə rij) *n.* a severe discharge of blood

out. Trexler got up, knocked the ashes out of his brain, and waited. The doctor smiled warmly and stuck out his hand. "There's nothing the matter with you—you're just scared. Want to know how I know you're scared?"

"How?" asked Trexler.

"Look at the chair you've been sitting in! See how it has moved back away from my desk? You kept inching away from me while I asked you questions. That means you're scared."

"Does it?" said Trexler, faking a grin. "Yeah, I suppose it does."

They finished shaking hands. Trexler turned and walked out uncertainly along the passage, then into the waiting room and out past the next patient, a ruddy pin-striped man who was seated on the sofa twirling his hat nervously and staring straight ahead at the files. Poor, frightened guy, thought Trexler, he's probably read in the *Times* that one American male out of every two is going to die of heart disease by twelve o'clock next Thursday. It says that in the paper almost every morning. And he's also probably thinking about that day on the Madison Avenue bus.

A week later, Trexler was back in the patient's chair. And for several weeks thereafter he continued to visit the doctor, always toward the end of the afternoon, when the vapors hung thick above the pool of the mind and darkened the whole region of the East Seventies.[7] He felt no better as time went on, and he found it impossible to work. He discovered that the visits were becoming routine and that although the routine was one to which he certainly did not look forward, at least he could accept it with cool resignation, as once, years ago, he had accepted a long spell with a dentist who had settled down to a steady fooling with a couple of dead teeth. The visits, moreover, were now assuming a pattern recognizable to the patient.

Each session would begin with a resumé of symptoms—the dizziness in the streets, the constricting

7. Most of the streets that run east to west in Manhattan are identified by numbers rather than names. *East Seventies* refers to the section of streets from 70–79 that are on the east side of Manhattan.

Reading Strategy Analyzing Text Structure *About how much time has passed since the opening scene of the story? How do you know?*

pain in the back of the neck, the apprehensions, the tightness of the scalp, the inability to concentrate, the despondency[8] and the melancholy times, the feeling of pressure and tension, the anger at not being able to work, the anxiety over work not done, the gas on the stomach. Dullest set of neurotic symptoms in the world, Trexler would think, as he obediently trudged back over them for the doctor's benefit.

As he became familiar with the pattern Trexler found that he increasingly tended to identify himself with the doctor, transferring himself into the doctor's seat—probably (he thought) some rather slick form of escapism. At any rate, it was nothing new for Trexler to identify himself with other people. Whenever he got into a cab, he instantly became the driver, saw everything from the hackman's angle (and the reaching over with the right hand, the nudging of the flag, the pushing it down, all the way down along the side of the meter), saw everything—traffic, fare, everything—through the eyes of Anthony Rocco, or Isidore Freedman, or Matthew Scott. In a barbershop, Trexler was the barber, his fingers curled around the comb, his hand on the tonic. Perfectly natural, then, that Trexler should soon be occupying the doctor's chair, asking the questions, waiting for the answers. He got quite interested in the doctor, in this way. He liked him, and he found him a not too difficult patient.

It was on the fifth visit, about halfway through, that the doctor turned to Trexler and said, suddenly, "What do you want?" He gave the word "want" special emphasis.

"I d'know," replied Trexler uneasily. "I guess nobody knows the answer to that one."

Gridlock NYC, 1998. Bill Jacklin. Oil on canvas, 152.4 x 152.4 cm. Private collection.

"Sure they do," replied the doctor.

"Do *you* know what *you* want?" asked Trexler narrowly.

"Certainly," said the doctor. Trexler noticed that at this point the doctor's chair slid slightly backward, away from him. Trexler stifled a small, internal smile. Scared as a rabbit, he said to himself. Look at him scoot!

"What *do* you want?" continued Trexler, pressing his advantage, pressing it hard.

The doctor glided back another inch away from his **inquisitor.** "I want a wing on the small house I own in Westport.[9] I want more money, and more leisure to do the things I want to do."

Trexler was just about to say, "And what are those things you want to do, Doctor?" when he caught himself. Better not go too far, he mused.

---

9. *Westport* is a residential community and summer resort on the coast of Connecticut.

Literary Element Plot *In what way does the doctor's original question help Mr. Trexler begin to solve his own problems?*

Vocabulary

inquisitor (in kwi′ zə tər) *n.* one who asks questions

---

8. *Despondency* means "hopelessness" or "depression."

Big Idea Life in the City *How does this paragraph give the reader an idea of what it would be like to live in a big city such as New York?*

Better not lose possession of the ball. And besides, he thought, what the hell goes on here, anyway—me paying fifteen bucks a throw for these séances[10] and then doing the work myself, asking the questions, weighing the answers. So he wants a new wing! There's a fine piece of theatrical gauze for you! A new wing.

Trexler settled down again and resumed the role of patient for the rest of the visit. It ended on a kindly, friendly note. The doctor reassured him that his fears were the cause of his sickness, and that his fears were unsubstantial. They shook hands, smiling.

Trexler walked dizzily through the empty waiting room and the doctor followed along to let him out. It was late; the secretary had shut up shop and gone home. Another day over the dam. "Goodbye," said Trexler. He stepped into the street, turned west toward Madison, and thought of the doctor all alone there, after hours, in that desolate hole—a man who worked longer hours than his secretary. Poor, scared, over-worked guy, thought Trexler. And that new wing!

It was an evening of clearing weather, the Park showing green and desirable in the distance, the last daylight applying a high lacquer to the brick and brownstone walls and giving the street scene a luminous and intoxicating splendor. Trexler meditated, as he walked, on what he wanted. "What do you want?" he heard again. Trexler knew what he wanted, and what, in general, all men wanted; and he was glad in a way, that it was both inexpressible and unattainable, and that it wasn't a wing. He was satisfied to remember that it was deep, formless, enduring, and impossible of fulfillment, and that it made men sick, and that when you sauntered along Third Avenue and looked through the doorways into the dim saloons, you could sometimes pick out from the unregenerate ranks the ones who had not forgotten, gazing steadily into the bottoms of the glasses on the long chance that they could get another little peek at it. Trexler found himself renewed by the remembrance that what he wanted was at once great and microscopic, and that although it borrowed from the nature of large deeds and of youthful love and of old songs and early **intimations,** it was not any one of these things, and that it had not been isolated or pinned down, and that a man who attempted to define it in the privacy of a doctor's office would fall flat on his face.

Trexler felt invigorated. Suddenly his sickness seemed health, his dizziness stability. A small tree, rising between him and the light, stood there saturated with the evening, each gilt-edged leaf perfectly drunk with excellence and delicacy. Trexler's spine registered an ever so slight tremor as it picked up this natural disturbance in the lovely scene. "I want the second tree from the corner, just as it stands," he said, answering an imaginary question from an imaginary physician. And he felt a slow pride in realizing that what he wanted none could bestow, and that what he had none could take away. He felt content to be sick, unembarrassed at being afraid; and in the jungle of his fear he glimpsed (as he had so often glimpsed them before) the flashy tail feathers of the bird courage.

Then he thought once again of the doctor, and of his being left there all alone, tired, frightened. (The poor, scared guy, thought Trexler.) Trexler began humming "Moonshine Lullaby," his spirit reacting instantly to the hypodermic of Merman's[11] healthy voice. He crossed Madison, boarded a downtown bus, and rode all the way to Fifty-second Street before he had a thought that could rightly have been called bizarre. ❧

Visual Vocabulary
Brownstone is the name of a reddish-brown sandstone as well as a type of house made with it.

---

10. A *séance* is a meeting in which people attempt to communicate with the spirits of the dead. Here, Trexler is questioning the scientific validity of his psychiatric sessions.

Big Idea Life in the City *What elements in this paragraph are unique to the city and would not be found in the country?*

11. Ethel *Merman* (1909–1984) was an American actress and singer known for her powerful voice.

Literary Element Plot *How has Mr. Trexler resolved his internal conflict?*

Vocabulary

intimation (in′ tə mā′ shən) *n.* a hint; a suggestion

RESPONDING AND THINKING CRITICALLY

Respond

1. What questions would you like to ask Mr. Trexler? Explain.

Recall and Interpret

2. (a)What question does the doctor ask Mr. Trexler at the beginning of the story? What is Trexler's answer? (b)In your opinion, what does Trexler's reaction to the doctor's first question reveal about Trexler's state of mind?

3. (a)What, according to the doctor, is wrong with Trexler? (b)Do you agree with the doctor's early diagnosis of Trexler? Explain.

4. (a)How does Trexler respond to the question "What do you want?" (b)What does the question make him think about after his visit to the doctor? (c)In your opinion, what does Trexler want?

Analyze and Evaluate

5. Is Trexler's reaction to his discovery of what he wants in life realistic? Why or why not?

6. (a)Why do you think Trexler pities others? (b)Do you think his observations are accurate? Explain.

7. (a)What personality traits—both positive and negative—does Trexler exhibit? (b)On the basis of these traits, do you find Trexler to be a sympathetic character? Explain.

Connect

8. Do you think "the second tree from the corner" is an effective **symbol,** or representation, of what Trexler wants from life? Explain.

9. **Big Idea** **Life in the City** What does "The Second Tree from the Corner" reveal about city life? Explain using details from the story.

LITERARY ANALYSIS

Literary Element **Plot**

At the center of a story's **plot,** there is usually a struggle, or **conflict,** between two opposing forces. The conflict might be **external**—between the main character and another person or an outside force—or it may be **internal**—between opposing thoughts or desires within the character's mind.

1. Identify and discuss Trexler's internal conflicts after the psychiatrist asks him if he has ever had any bizarre thoughts.

2. Consider Trexler's comment that his identification with other people is "some rather slick form of escapism." Is it possible that Trexler's ability to look through others' eyes leads to a resolution of his conflict? Explain.

3. Discuss how the psychiatrist's question "What do you want?" helps Trexler to resolve his inner conflict.

Review: Irony

As you learned on page 568, **irony** is a contrast or discrepancy between appearance and reality. **Verbal irony** occurs when someone says one thing but means another. **Situational irony** exists when the outcome of a situation is the opposite of someone's expectations.

Group Activity Meet with a small group to discuss E. B. White's use of irony in "The Second Tree from the Corner." Together, create a web diagram like the one below, filling in the circles with examples of irony in the story.

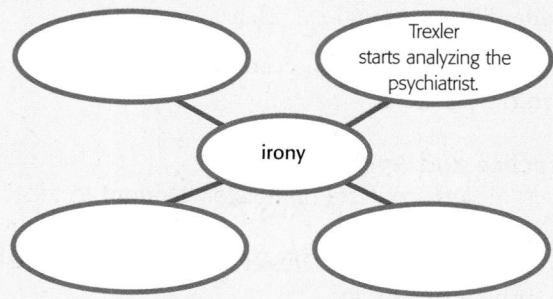

Reading Strategy Analyzing Text Structure

Authors often embed several organizational methods within the same text. For example, a story might proceed mainly in chronological order but show cause-and-effect relationships or comparison and contrast at the same time.

1. (a)Identify an instance in which White uses cause and effect as an organizational method. (b)In what way does this example advance the plot?

2. (a)Find an example of comparison and contrast in the story. (b)What does this example reveal about Trexler's character?

Vocabulary Practice

Practice with Word Parts Identify the meaning of the underlined part of each vocabulary word below. Consult a dictionary if you need help.

1. **amorphous**
   a. without   **b.** form
2. **retractable**
   a. back   **b.** capable of
3. **hemorrhage**
   a. blood   **b.** severe
4. **inquisitor**
   a. question   **b.** one who
5. **intimation**
   a. the act of   **b.** suggest

Academic Vocabulary

Here are two words from the vocabulary list on page R86.

evident (e′və dənt) *adj.* clear; apparent

normal (nôr′ məl) *adj.* conforming to a set pattern or standard

Practice and Apply

1. Is Trexler's conflict immediately **evident** to the doctor? Explain.
2. Would you describe Trexler's thoughts as **normal** or bizarre? Explain.

Writing About Literature

Evaluate Author's Craft E. B. White uses many visual images to describe Trexler's thoughts and feelings. For example, Trexler thinks the doctor "was creeping slowly toward him, like a lizard toward a bug." Write a brief essay in which you address the following questions. Support your answers with evidence from the story.

- How would you describe the images used in the beginning of the story? What do these images suggest about Trexler?

- In what way do the images toward the end of the story differ from the earlier ones? What does this difference suggest about the changes that have occurred in Trexler?

Before you begin your first draft, complete a chart like the one below, listing visual images in the story. Comment on how each image helps the reader gain a better understanding of Trexler's character.

Image	What It Reveals About Trexler
"The doctor was not only watching him closely but was creeping slowly toward him, like a lizard toward a bug."	Trexler views himself as small and vulnerable.
"Trexler dodged back along the dreadful corridor of the years."	

After you complete your first draft, meet with a peer reviewer to evaluate each other's work and to suggest ways to improve it. Then proofread and edit your draft for errors in spelling, grammar, and punctuation.

Literature Online Web Activities For eFlashcards, Selection Quick Checks, and other Web activities, go to www.glencoe.com.

To Don at Salaam and The Bean Eaters

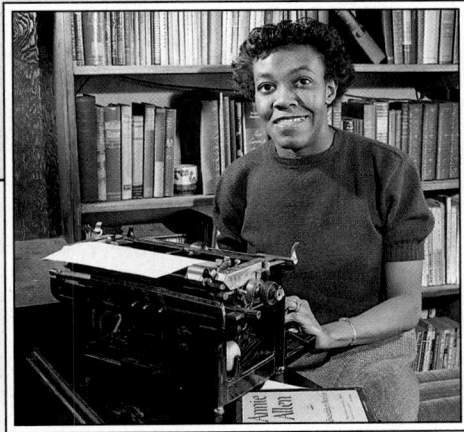

MEET GWENDOLYN BROOKS

The sounds, sights, and rhythm of urban life pour out of the poetry of Gwendolyn Brooks. As Brooks once said, "I wanted to write poems that I could take into the streets." With an ear for the beat of the city and the hum of everyday life, Brooks re-created the lives of African Americans in the city and elsewhere.

Although she was born in Topeka, Kansas, Brooks grew up in Chicago. A shy girl, Gwendolyn Brooks spent much of her childhood alone reading books and writing poetry. "My mother says I began rhyming at seven. . . . *Of course* I would be a poet! *Was* a poet! Didn't I write a poem every day? Sometimes *two* poems?" Her mother's belief in her talent gave her the confidence she needed to keep writing, and Brooks published her first poem, "Eventide," when she was thirteen. By the late 1930s, she had published seventy-five poems in the *Chicago Defender*.

> "*I want to write poems that will be meaningful . . . things that will touch* [readers]."
>
> —Gwendolyn Brooks

Literary Influences Brooks's mother took her to see poets read whenever they came to Chicago. Two of these poets—James Weldon Johnson and Langston Hughes—became important influences on her career and writing. Johnson played the role of advisor, urging her to read modern poets such as T. S. Eliot and E. E. Cummings—poets whose styles would be reflected in her later work. When Brooks was sixteen, she went to see Langston Hughes read. After the reading, she gave him some of her poems, which he read immediately. He encouraged her to continue writing and would later become her close friend and inspiration. As a poet, Brooks shared Hughes's ability to respond to the struggles of the black community and express the black experience in a time of rapid change.

Poetic Transformation In 1945 Brooks's first book, *A Street in Bronzeville*, was published to rave reviews. In her early work, Brooks wrote poetic narratives, using traditional verse forms—such as the sonnet and ballad. In the 1960s, however, her voice and style changed, and she brought a new consciousness of her racial identity to her work. Inspired by black activism, Brooks began to overtly address political issues, especially the need for racial unity. As she became more involved with the Black Arts movement in Chicago, Brooks moved from major publishing houses to smaller ones run by African Americans. Although her commitment to racial unity was evident and her verse powerful, her poetry was never bitter.

Role of the Poet Success and recognition didn't change Brooks's outlook. In fact, it made her more committed to art and to helping young artists. With the publication of her second book, *Annie Allen*, she became the first African American to win the Pulitzer Prize. She would later be named Poet Laureate of Illinois, poetry consultant to the Library of Congress, and a member of the National Women's Hall of Fame. Most important to Brooks were her visits to local schools and the classes and contests she sponsored to help urban children "see" the poetry in the world around them. Today, Brooks remains one of America's most beloved and inspirational poets.

Gwendolyn Brooks was born in 1917 and died in 2000.

Literature Online Author Search For more about Gwendolyn Brooks, go to www.glencoe.com.

Connecting to the Poems

Gwendolyn Brooks was a keen observer of people, writing in particular about the lives and struggles of the people in her Chicago neighborhood. What are the people in your neighborhood like? As you read "The Bean Eaters" and "To Don at Salaam," think about the following questions:

- What is unique about your neighborhood and the people who live there?
- What have you learned about life from the people in your community?

Building Background

Many of Brooks's characters, such as the old couple in "The Bean Eaters," were inspired by people who lived in her neighborhood on Chicago's South Side. Through such characters, Brooks chronicled the dreams and disappointments of the African American urban poor. Other characters, like the man in "To Don at Salaam," were inspired by the young black artists and activists of the 1960s and onward, who possessed what Brooks called "a general energy, an electricity, in look, walk, speech, [and] *gesture. . . ."* Through such characters, Brooks expresses a "black is beautiful" theme.

Setting Purposes for Reading

Big Idea Life in the City

As you read "The Bean Eaters," notice how the characters are influenced by their urban setting.

Literary Element Rhyme Scheme

Rhyme scheme is the pattern that end rhymes form in a stanza or a poem. Rhyme schemes are designated by assigning a different letter of the alphabet to each new rhyme. For example, the rhyme scheme of a poem that repeats the same rhyme in every other line is *abab*. Notice how Brooks uses rhyme scheme in "The Bean Eaters" and the effect it creates.

- See Literary Terms Handbook, p. R1

Literature Online **Interactive Literary Elements Handbook** To review or learn more about the literary elements, go to www.glencoe.com.

Reading Strategy Evaluating Language

An important element of a writer's voice and style is word choice, or **diction.** As you read these poems, note how Brooks's individual word choices help create the tone and convey meaning.

Reading Tip: Taking Notes Use a chart like the one below to write down important words and their effect on each poem's meaning.

Word or Words	Effect on Meaning
beans	suggest ordinariness or poverty

Vocabulary

impudent (im′ pyə dənt) *adj.* cocky, bold; p. 937 *In the army, Sean stopped his impudent behavior only after being punished by an officer.*

tribute (tri′ byüt) *n.* something given to show affection, gratitude, or respect; p. 937 *Marco gave a speech in tribute to his son on his wedding day.*

consolidation (kən sä lə da′ shən) *n.* the process of uniting or merging; p. 937 *The consolidation of the two companies led to greater efficiency but fewer jobs.*

twinge (twinj) *n.* a sudden, sharp physical or emotional pain; p. 938 *She felt a twinge of sadness at the sight of her dead grandmother's photograph.*

Vocabulary Tip: Connotation Connotation refers to the suggested or implied meanings associated with a word beyond its dictionary definition. A word can have a positive or negative connotation.

INDIANA ACADEMIC STANDARDS (pages 936–939)
11.2.2 Analyze the way in which clarity of meaning is affected by the patterns of organization...

11.3.3 Analyze the ways in which...language achieve[s] specific... aesthetic (artistic) purposes...

To Don at Salaam

Gwendolyn Brooks

I like to see you lean back in your chair
so far you have to fall but do not—
your arms back, your fine hands
in your print pockets.

5   Beautiful. **Impudent.**
Ready for life.
A tied storm.

I like to see you wearing your boy smile
whose **tribute** is for two of us or three.

10   Sometimes in life
things seem to be moving
and they are not
and they are not
there.
15   You are there.

Your voice is the listened-for music.
Your act is the **consolidation.**

I like to see you living in the world.

Hombre ante el infinito (Man before the infinite). Rufino Tamayo.
Musée d'Art Moderne, Brussels, Belgium.

Salaam is an Arabic word that means "peace."

The Bean Eaters

Gwendolyn Brooks

Onion Tears, 1929. Cagnaccio di San Pietro. Camera di Lavoro, Trieste, Italy.

They eat beans mostly, this old yellow pair.
Dinner is a casual affair.
Plain chipware on a plain and creaking wood,
Tin flatware.

5   Two who are Mostly Good.
Two who have lived their day,
But keep on putting on their clothes
And putting things away.

And remembering . . .
10   Remembering, with twinklings and **twinges,**
As they lean over the beans in their rented back room that
      is full of beads and receipts and dolls and cloths,
      tobacco crumbs, vases and fringes.

Big Idea City Life *What is city life like for the bean eaters?*

Vocabulary

twinge (twinj) *n.* a sudden, sharp physical or emotional pain

RESPONDING AND THINKING CRITICALLY

Respond

1. Would you like to meet the man described in "To Don at Salaam"? Explain.

Recall and Interpret

2. (a)What is the setting in "The Bean Eaters"? (b)What do the details of the setting show?

3. (a)How does Brooks describe the characters in "The Bean Eaters"? (b)What do the couple's actions suggest about them?

4. (a)In "To Don at Salaam," what adjectives or adjective phrases does the speaker use to describe the man? (b)What do these modifiers suggest about the man? (c)What do they suggest about the speaker?

Analyze and Evaluate

5. A word's **connotation** is its suggested or implied meanings. (a)Name four or more words in "The Bean Eaters" that have meanings beyond their dictionary definitions. (b)Explain how the connotations of the word *yellow* help to describe the couple.

6. (a)How would you describe the tone of "The Bean Eaters"? (b)How does the tone help you understand the meaning of the poem?

7. (a)How does Brooks use imagery to describe the man in "To Don at Salaam"? (b)How well do these images tell you what the speaker sees in the man?

Connect

8. **Big Idea** **Life in the City** What aspects of life in a big city does "The Bean Eaters" show?

LITERARY ANALYSIS

Literary Element Rhyme Scheme

Rhyme schemes are often predictable, which often reinforces meaning and aids the reader by providing a flowing, logical structure. In contrast, some poets employ rhyme without using a rigid rhyme scheme.

1. (a)What is the rhyme scheme of "The Bean Eaters"? (b)Is the rhyme scheme predictable? Explain.

2. Explain how the rhyme scheme affects the poem's tone and meaning.

Internet Connection

Poet Laureates are given the responsibility of raising the status of poetry and helping individuals see poetry in their everyday lives. Brooks was named Poet Laureate of Illinois in 1968. Use the Internet to research Brooks's role as Poet Laureate and what she accomplished during that time. Use your research to write a short essay about Brooks as a Poet Laureate, and share your findings with the class.

Literature Online **Web Activities** For eFlashcards, Selection Quick Checks, and other Web activities, go to www.glencoe.com.

READING AND VOCABULARY

Reading Strategy Evaluating Language

Because poems are so compact, each word can carry a great deal of meaning. Look at the chart you created to **evaluate the language** of the poems. It may help you answer the following questions.

1. In "The Bean Eaters," what does Brooks mean by "twinklings and twinges"? How do these words communicate both meaning and attitude?

2. In "To Don at Salaam," the speaker says, "Your act is the consolidation." What does the speaker mean? Why does the poet choose the word *consolidation*?

Vocabulary Practice

Practice with Connotation Decide whether each vocabulary word and its synonym below has a positive or negative connotation. Use a dictionary or thesaurus if necessary.

1. twinge   pang
2. tribute   repayment
3. impudent   bold
4. consolidation merger

The Magic Barrel

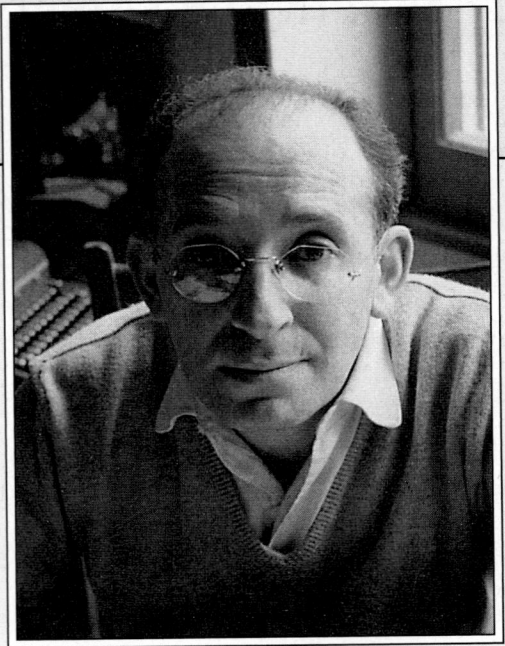

MEET BERNARD MALAMUD

Bernard Malamud was born to Russian Jewish immigrants who worked sixteen hours a day in their small grocery store on New York City's Lower East Side. Reflecting on his childhood, he would recall that there were no books in his home, no records or musical instruments, and no pictures on the walls. He would, however, recall the generosity of his father, who bought him the twenty-volume *Book of Knowledge* in 1923, when he was a nine-year-old recovering from pneumonia.

Inspired by his father's stories of life in czarist Russia, Malamud began creating stories of his own for his boyhood friends. He graduated from City College of New York and Columbia University, and while teaching evening classes he wrote short stories that appeared in *Harper's Bazaar* and other magazines. His first novel, written in 1952 when he was in his late thirties, was *The Natural,* the story of the rise and fall of a baseball player. The novel was later made into a popular movie starring Robert Redford. His second novel, *The Assistant,* written in 1957, brought him fame as a major Jewish American writer. His novel of injustice in czarist Russia, *The Fixer* (1966), won both the National Book Award and the Pulitzer Prize.

> "*People say I write so much about misery, but you write about what you know best.*"
>
> —Bernard Malamud

Master of Characterization Though most of the characters in his stories and novels are Jewish, Malamud thought of Jewishness as a spiritual condition rather than as a cultural heritage or religious creed. To be Jewish, he felt, was to struggle with life's limitations and responsibilities. Malamud said that he wrote about Jews "because they set my imagination going. I know something about their history, the quality of experience and belief, and of their literature, though not as much as I would like."

He saw himself as a storyteller whose fictions were about "simple people struggling to make their lives better in a world of bad luck." His characters are often pursued by a sense of injustice, burdened with grief, and strengthened by their own persistence. They are intensely aware of the past as they try to make a life for themselves in the modern world. The mixture of victory and defeat in their lives endows Malamud's work with a tragicomic character.

Malamud won highest acclaim as a writer of short stories, and "The Magic Barrel" is considered one of his best. His stories contain a robust humor, striking contrasts, a strong sense of compassion, and a complete understanding of his characters and their way of life.

Bernard Malamud was born in 1914 and died in 1986.

Literature Online Author Search For more about Bernard Malamud, go to www.glencoe.com.

Connecting to the Story

In Malamud's short story, a young rabbinical student decides it is time to get married and sets out to find a suitable spouse. If you were in a similar situation, what steps would you take to choose a spouse? As you read the story, think about the following questions:

- Would you list the qualities you wanted in a spouse, or would you simply rely on your gut feelings?
- Would you ask someone to help you meet the right person?

Building Background

"The Magic Barrel" takes place in New York City, probably during the 1950s. Between 1880 and 1914, about two million Jews from Eastern Europe immigrated to the United States. The largest concentration of Jewish immigrants settled on the Lower East Side of Manhattan. They brought with them their culture and traditions, which included the use of matchmakers—people paid to bring young men and women together for the purpose of marriage.

Setting Purposes for Reading

Big Idea Life in the City

Malamud mentions various locations, newspapers, customs, and sights that are unique to New York City. As you read, ask yourself what the story reveals about life in that city.

Literary Element Dialect

Dialect is a way of speaking and writing that is characteristic of a particular group, often within a particular region and time. Dialects may differ from the standard form of a language in vocabulary, pronunciation, or grammatical form. As you read, notice how Malamud uses dialect in the story.

- See Literary Terms Handbook, p. R4.

Literature⌐Online Interactive Literary Elements Handbook To review or learn more about the literary elements, go to www.glencoe.com.

Reading Strategy Analyzing Characterization

Analyzing characterization means examining the methods an author uses to reveal a character's personality. In direct characterization the writer makes explicit statements about a character. In indirect characterization the writer reveals a character through the character's thoughts, words, actions, or appearance or through what other characters think and say about that character. The reader must then use these details to make inferences about the character.

Reading Tip: Taking Notes on Characters There are two main characters in "The Magic Barrel": Leo Finkle and Pinye Salzman. For each character, list the details that the writer provides and the inferences you make from them.

Character	Details	Inferences
Pinye Salzman	dresses shabbily	not wealthy

Vocabulary

meager (mē′gər) *adj.* deficient in quantity or completeness; p. 943 *The orphans were fed a meager breakfast of oatmeal and water.*

amiable (ā′mē ə bəl) *adj.* friendly; p. 943 *Marla's amiable smile put her guests at ease.*

animated (an′ə mā′tid) *adj.* full of life; active; lively; p. 943 *The zoo visitors enjoyed the monkeys' animated antics.*

enamored (en am′ərd) *adj.* inspired with love; charmed; captivated; p. 949 *Ben was completely enamored with Julie.*

abjectly (ab′jekt lē) *adv.* in a humiliating, mean, or degrading manner; p. 950 *Disappointed with his performance, Carl abjectly accepted his third-place medal.*

▸ **INDIANA ACADEMIC STANDARDS (pages 941–956)**
11.3.3 Analyze the ways in which...language achieve[s] specific... aesthetic (artistic) purposes...

11.3 [Identify] story elements such as character...
11.5.9 Write...a literary analysis...

THE MAGIC BARREL

Bernard Malamud

Intensive study, 1910. Unknown. Oil on canvas, 32¼ x 29 in. Judaica Coll. Max Berger, Vienna, Austria.

Not long ago there lived in uptown New York in a small, almost **meager** room, though crowded with books, Leo Finkle, a rabbinical student in the Yeshivah University.[1] Finkle, after six years of study, was to be ordained in June and had been advised by an acquaintance that he might find it easier to win himself a congregation if he were married. Since he had no present prospects of marriage, after two tormented days of turning it over in his mind, he called in Pinye Salzman, a marriage broker whose two-line advertisement he had read in the *Forward*.[2]

The matchmaker appeared one night out of the dark fourth-floor hallway of the graystone rooming house where Finkle lived, grasping a black, strapped portfolio that had been worn thin with use. Salzman, who had been long in the business, was of slight but dignified build, wearing an old hat, and an overcoat too short and tight for him. He smelled frankly of fish, which he loved to eat, and although he was missing a few teeth, his presence was not displeasing, because of an **amiable** manner curiously contrasted with mournful eyes. His voice, his lips, his wisp of beard, his bony fingers were **animated,** but give him a moment of repose and his mild blue eyes revealed a depth of sadness, a characteristic that put Leo a little at ease although the situation, for him, was inherently tense.

He at once informed Salzman why he had asked him to come, explaining that his home was in Cleveland, and that but for his parents, who had married comparatively late in life, he was alone in the world. He had for six years devoted himself almost entirely to his studies, as a result of which, understandably, he had found himself without time for a social life and the company of young women. Therefore he thought it the better part of trial and error—of embarrassing fumbling—to call in an experienced person to advise him on these matters. He remarked in passing that the function of the marriage broker was ancient and honorable, highly approved in the Jewish community, because it made practical the necessary without hindering joy. Moreover, his own parents had been brought together by a matchmaker. They had made, if not a financially profitable marriage—since neither had possessed any worldly goods to speak of—at least a successful one in the sense of their everlasting devotion to each other. Salzman listened in embarrassed surprise, sensing a sort of apology. Later, however, he experienced a glow of pride in his work, an emotion that had left him years ago, and he heartily approved of Finkle.

The two went to their business. Leo had led Salzman to the only clear place in the room, a table near a window that overlooked the lamp-lit city. He seated himself at the matchmaker's side but facing him, attempting by an act of will to suppress the unpleasant tickle in his throat. Salzman eagerly unstrapped his portfolio and removed a loose rubber band from a thin packet of much-handled cards. As he flipped through them, a gesture and sound that physically hurt Leo, the student pretended not to see and gazed steadfastly out the window. Although it was still February, winter was on its last legs, signs of which he had for the first time in years begun to notice. He now observed the round white moon, moving high in the sky through a cloud menagerie,[3] and watched with half-open mouth as it penetrated a huge hen, and dropped out of her like an egg laying itself. Salzman, though pretending

---

1. *Yeshivah* (yə shē′ və) *University* in New York City, originally a seminary for rabbis, today offers both theological and secular courses.

2. The Yiddish-language newspaper the *Jewish Daily Forward* was published daily in New York.

Big Idea Life in the City *Which details in the first paragraph tell you something about Jewish life in New York City?*

Reading Strategy Analyzing Characterization *Why does the author include these details about Salzman?*

Vocabulary

meager (mē′ gər) *adj.* deficient in quantity or completeness

amiable (ā′ mē ə bəl) *adj.* friendly

animated (an′ ə mā′ tid) *adj.* full of life; active; lively

---

3. A *menagerie* (mi naj′ ər ē) is a collection of wild or unusual animals.

Torah Binder, 1848. Shimshon Kurzman. Ink and watercolor on cotton. The Jewish Museum, New York.

through eyeglasses he had just slipped on, to be engaged in scanning the writing on the cards, stole occasional glances at the young man's distinguished face, noting with pleasure the long, severe scholar's nose, brown eyes heavy with learning, sensitive yet ascetic[4] lips, and a certain, almost hollow quality of the dark cheeks. He gazed around at shelves upon shelves of books and let out a soft, contented sigh.

When Leo's eyes fell upon the cards, he counted six spread out in Salzman's hand.

"So few?" he asked in disappointment.

"You wouldn't believe me how much cards I got in my office," Salzman replied. "The drawers are already filled to the top, so I keep them now in a barrel, but is every girl good for a new rabbi?"

Leo blushed at this, regretting all he had revealed of himself in a curriculum vitae[5] he had sent to Salzman. He had thought it best to acquaint him with his strict standards and specifications, but in having done so,

felt he had told the marriage broker more than was absolutely necessary.

He hesitantly inquired, "Do you keep photographs of your clients on file?"

"First comes family, amount of dowry,[6] also what kind promises," Salzman replied, unbuttoning his tight coat and settling himself in the chair. "After comes pictures, rabbi."

"Call me Mr. Finkle. I'm not yet a rabbi."

Salzman said he would, but instead called him doctor, which he changed to rabbi when Leo was not listening too attentively.

Salzman adjusted his horn-rimmed spectacles, gently cleared his throat and read in an eager voice the contents of the top card:

"Sophie P. Twenty-four years. Widow one year. No children. Educated high school and two years college. Father promises eight thousand dollars. Has wonderful wholesale business. Also real estate. On the mother's side comes teachers, also one actor. Well known on Second Avenue."

Leo gazed up in surprise. "Did you say a widow?"

---

4. Here, *ascetic* means "severe" or "stern."
5. A *curriculum vitae* (kə riˊ kyə ləm vēˊ tī) is a summary of a person's education and work experience, usually given to a prospective employer. Finkle has provided Salzman with a summary of the "highlights" of his life.

6. A *dowry* is money or property a woman brings to her husband at the time of marriage.

Reading Strategy Analyzing Characterization *What do these details reveal about Finkle and Salzman?*

Big Idea Life in the City *What information about New York City can you infer from this passage?*

"A widow don't mean spoiled, rabbi. She lived with her husband maybe four months. He was a sick boy she made a mistake to marry him."

"Marrying a widow has never entered my mind."

"This is because you have no experience. A widow, especially if she is young and healthy like this girl, is a wonderful person to marry. She will be thankful to you the rest of her life. Believe me, if I was looking now for a bride, I would marry a widow."

Leo reflected, then shook his head.

Salzman hunched his shoulders in an almost imperceptible gesture of disappointment. He placed the card down on the wooden table and began to read another:

"Lily H. High school teacher. Regular. Not a substitute. Has savings and new Dodge car. Lived in Paris one year. Father is successful dentist thirty-five years. Interested in professional man. Well Americanized family. Wonderful opportunity."

"I knew her personally," said Salzman. "I wish you could see this girl. She is a doll. Also very intelligent. All day you could talk to her about books and theyater[7] and what not. She also knows current events."

"I don't believe you mentioned her age?"

"Her age?" Salzman said, raising his brows. "Her age is thirty-two years."

Leo said after a while, "I'm afraid that seems a little too old."

Salzman let out a laugh. "So how old are you, rabbi?"

"Twenty-seven."

"So what is the difference, tell me, between twenty-seven and thirty-two? My own wife is seven years older than me. So what did I suffer?—Nothing. If Rothschild's[8] a daughter wants to marry you, would you say on account her age, no?"

"Yes," Leo said dryly.

Salzman shook off the no in the yes. "Five years don't mean a thing. I give you my word that when you will live with her for one week you will forget her age. What does it mean five years—that she lived more and knows more than somebody who is younger? On this girl, God bless her, years are not wasted. Each one that it comes makes better the bargain."

"What subject does she teach in high school?"

"Languages. If you heard the way she speaks French, you will think it is music. I am in the business twenty-five years, and I recommend her with my whole heart. Believe me, I know what I'm talking, rabbi."

"What's on the next card?" Leo said abruptly.

Salzman reluctantly turned up the third card:

"Ruth K. Nineteen years. Honor student. Father offers thirteen thousand cash to the right bridegroom. He is a medical doctor. Stomach specialist with marvelous practice. Brother-in-law owns own garment business. Particular people."

Salzman looked as if he had read his trump card.

"Did you say nineteen?" Leo asked with interest.

"On the dot."

"Is she attractive?" He blushed. "Pretty?"

Salzman kissed his finger tips. "A little doll. On this I give you my word. Let me call the father tonight and you will see what means pretty."

But Leo was troubled. "You're sure she's that young?"

"This I am positive. The father will show you the birth certificate."

> "If you heard the way she speaks French, you will think it is music."

---

7. *Theyater* is the way Salzman is pronouncing the word theater.

Reading Strategy Analyzing Characterization *What qualities does Salzman consider important in a wife?*

Literary Element Dialect *How does the use of dialect in this passage contribute to the characterization of Salzman?*

---

8. The *Rothschilds* were a prominent, wealthy Jewish family.

"Are you positive there isn't something wrong with her?" Leo insisted.

"Who says there is wrong?"

"I don't understand why an American girl her age should go to a marriage broker."

A smile spread over Salzman's face.

"So for the same reason you went, she comes."

Leo flushed. "I am pressed for time."

Salzman, realizing he had been tactless, quickly explained. "The father came, not her. He wants she should have the best, so he looks around himself. When we will locate the right boy he will introduce him and encourage. This makes a better marriage than if a young girl without experience takes for herself. I don't have to tell you this."

"But don't you think this young girl believes in love?" Leo spoke uneasily.

Salzman was about to guffaw but caught himself and said soberly, "Love comes with the right person, not before."

Leo parted dry lips but did not speak. Noticing that Salzman had snatched a glance at the next card, he cleverly asked, "How is her health?"

"Perfect," Salzman said, breathing with difficulty. "Of course, she is a little lame on her right foot from an auto accident that it happened to her when she was twelve years, but nobody notices on account she is so brilliant and also beautiful."

Leo got up heavily and went to the window. He felt curiously bitter and upbraided himself for having called in the marriage broker. Finally, he shook his head.

"Why not?" Salzman persisted, the pitch of his voice rising.

"Because I detest stomach specialists."

"So what do you care what is his business? After you marry her do you need him? Who says he must come every Friday night in your house?"

Ashamed of the way the talk was going, Leo dismissed Salzman, who went home with heavy, melancholy eyes.

Though he had felt only relief at the marriage broker's departure, Leo was in low spirits the next day. He explained it as arising from Salzman's failure to produce a suitable bride for him. He did not care for his type of clientele. But when Leo found himself hesitating whether to seek out another matchmaker, one more polished than Pinye, he wondered if it could be—his protestations to the contrary, and although he honored his father and mother—that he did not, in essence, care for the match making institution? This thought he quickly put out of mind yet found himself still upset. All day he ran around in the woods[9]—missed an important appointment, forgot to give out his laundry, walked out of a Broadway cafeteria without paying and had to run back with the ticket in his hand; had even not recognized his landlady in the street when she passed with a friend and courteously called out, "A good evening to you, Doctor Finkle." By nightfall, however, he had regained sufficient calm to sink his nose into a book and there found peace from his thoughts.

Almost at once there came a knock on the door. Before Leo could say enter, Salzman, commercial cupid, was standing in the room. His face was gray and meager, his expression hungry, and he looked as if he would expire on his feet. Yet the marriage broker managed, by some trick of the muscles, to display a broad smile.

"So good evening. I am invited?"

Leo nodded, disturbed to see him again, yet unwilling to ask the man to leave.

Beaming still, Salzman laid his portfolio on the table. "Rabbi, I got for you tonight good news."

"I've asked you not to call me rabbi. I'm still a student."

"Your worries are finished. I have for you a first-class bride."

"Leave me in peace concerning this subject." Leo pretended lack of interest.

"The world will dance at your wedding."

"Please, Mr. Salzman, no more."

"But first must come back my strength," Salzman said weakly. He fumbled with the portfolio straps and took out of the leather case an oily paper bag, from which he extracted a hard,

---

9. [*ran . . . woods*] Here, this phrase means that Finkle was nervous and distracted.

Reading Strategy Analyzing Characterization *How does this description of Salzman differ from the description of him when he first entered Finkle's home?*

Literary Element Dialect *How would this passage be written in Standard English?*

Literary Element Dialect *What inversion does Salzman make?*

seeded roll and a small, smoked white fish. With a quick motion of his hand he stripped the fish out of its skin and began ravenously to chew. "All day in a rush," he muttered.

Leo watched him eat.

"A sliced tomato you have maybe?" Salzman hesitantly inquired.

"No."

The marriage broker shut his eyes and ate. When he had finished he carefully cleaned up the crumbs and rolled up the remains of the fish, in the paper bag. His spectacled eyes roamed the room until he discovered, amid some piles of books, a one-burner gas stove. Lifting his hat he humbly asked, "A glass tea you got, rabbi?"

Conscience-stricken, Leo rose and brewed the tea. He served it with a chunk of lemon and two cubes of lump sugar, delighting Salzman.

After he had drunk his tea, Salzman's strength and good spirits were restored.

"So tell me, rabbi," he said amiably, "you considered some more the three clients I mentioned yesterday?"

"There was no need to consider."

"Why not?"

"None of them suits me."

"What then suits you?"

Leo let it pass because he could give only a confused answer.

Without waiting for a reply, Salzman asked, "You remember this girl I talked to you—the high school teacher?"

"Age thirty-two?"

But, surprisingly, Salzman's face lit in a smile. "Age twenty-nine."

Leo shot him a look. "Reduced from thirty-two?"

"A mistake," Salzman avowed. "I talked today with the dentist. He took me to his safety deposit box and showed me the birth certificate. She was twenty-nine years last August. They made her a party in the moun-

Portrait of Miss Stryker (Portrait of an Aristocrat). Ella Condie Lamb. Pastels on paper, 26½ x 22⅝ in. Collection of The Newark Museum, NJ.

tains where she went for her vacation. When her father spoke to me the first time I forgot to write the age and I told you thirty-two, but now I remember this was a different client, a widow."

"The same one you told me about? I thought she was twenty-four?"

"A different. Am I responsible that the world is filled with widows?"

"No, but I'm not interested in them, nor for that matter, in school teachers."

Salzman pulled his clasped hands to his breast. Looking at the ceiling he devoutly exclaimed, "Yiddishe kinder,[10] what can I say

10. *Yiddishe kinder* (yid′ ish ə kint′ ər) means "Jewish children" or "Jewish young people."

to somebody that he is not interested in high school teachers? So what then you are interested?"

Leo flushed but controlled himself.

"In what else will you be interested," Salzman went on, "if you not interested in this fine girl that she speaks four languages and has personally in the bank ten thousand dollars? Also her father guarantees further twelve thousand. Also she has new car, wonderful clothes, talks on all subjects, and she will give you a first-class home and children. How near do we come in our life to paradise?"

"If she's so wonderful, why wasn't she married ten years ago?"

"Why?" said Salzman with a heavy laugh. "—Why? Because she is *partikiler*.[11] This is why. She wants the *best*."

Leo went silent, amused at how he had entangled himself. But Salzman had aroused his interest in Lily H., and he began seriously to consider calling on her. When the marriage broker observed how intently Leo's mind was at work on the facts he had supplied, he felt certain they would soon come to an agreement.

Late Saturday afternoon, conscious of Salzman, Leo Finkle walked with Lily Hirschorn along Riverside Drive.[12] He walked briskly and erectly, wearing with distinction the black fedora[13] he had that morning taken with trepidation out of the dusty hat box on his closet shelf, and the heavy black Saturday coat he had thoroughly whisked clean. Leo also owned a walking stick, a present from a distant relative, but quickly put temptation aside and did not use it. Lily, petite and not unpretty, had on something signifying the approach of spring. She was au courant[14] animatedly, with all sorts of subjects, and he weighed her words and found her surprisingly sound—score another for Salzman, who he uneasily sensed to be somewhere around, hiding perhaps high in a tree along the street, flashing the lady signals with a pocket mirror; or perhaps a cloven-hoofed Pan, piping nuptial ditties as he danced his invisible way before them, strewing wild buds on the walk and purple grapes in their path, symbolizing fruit of a union, though there was of course still none.

Lily startled Leo by remarking, "I was thinking of Mr. Salzman, a curious figure, wouldn't you say?"

Not certain what to answer, he nodded.

She bravely went on, blushing, "I for one am grateful for his introducing us. Aren't you?"

He courteously replied, "I am."

"I mean," she said with a little laugh—and it was all in good taste, or at least gave the effect of being not in bad—"do you mind that we came together so?"

He was not displeased with her honesty, recognizing that she meant to set the relationship aright, and understanding that it took a certain amount of experience in life, and courage, to want to do it quite that way. One had to have some sort of past to make that kind of beginning.

He said that he did not mind. Salzman's function was traditional and honorable—valuable for what it might achieve, which, he pointed out, was frequently nothing.

Lily agreed with a sigh. They walked on for a while and she said after a long silence, again with a nervous laugh, "Would you mind if I asked you something a little bit personal? Frankly, I find the subject fascinating." Although Leo shrugged, she went on half embarrassedly, "How was it that you came to your calling? I mean was it a sudden passionate inspiration?"

Visual Vocabulary
In Greek mythology, *Pan* was a god of pastures, flocks, and shepherds who was believed to foster reproduction and growth. He was traditionally depicted as a musician who was part man and part goat.

---

11. *Partikiler* is the way Salzman is pronouncing the word *particular*.
12. *Riverside Drive*, a major road on the west side of Manhattan, runs beside the Hudson River.
13. A *fedora* (fi dôr′ ə) is a soft felt hat with a curved brim and a lengthwise crease in the crown.
14. The French words *au courant* (ō koo rän′) literally mean "in the current" but are most often used to mean "fully informed" or "up-to-date."

Big Idea Life in the City *Which details depict a stroll in New York City rather than in the country?*

Reading Strategy Analyzing Characterization *What does this passage reveal about Finkle's state of mind?*

Leo, after a time, slowly replied, "I was always interested in the Law."

"You saw revealed in it the presence of the Highest?"

He nodded and changed the subject. "I understand that you spent a little time in Paris, Miss Hirschorn?"

"Oh, did Mr. Salzman tell you, Rabbi Finkle?" Leo winced but she went on, "It was ages ago and almost forgotten. I remember I had to return for my sister's wedding."

And Lily would not be put off. "When," she asked in a trembly voice, "did you become **enamored** of God?"

He stared at her. Then it came to him that she was talking not about Leo Finkle, but of a total stranger, some mystical figure, perhaps even passionate prophet that Salzman had dreamed up for her—no relation to the living or dead. Leo trembled with rage and weakness. The trickster had obviously sold her a bill of goods, just as he had him, who'd expected to become acquainted with a young lady of twenty-nine, only to behold, the moment he laid eyes upon her strained and anxious face, a woman past thirty-five and aging rapidly. Only his self control had kept him this long in her presence.

"I am not," he said gravely, "a talented religious person," and in seeking words to go on, found himself possessed by shame and fear. "I think," he said in a strained manner, "that I came to God not because I loved Him, but because I did not."

This confession he spoke harshly because its unexpectedness shook him.

Lily wilted. Leo saw a profusion of loaves of bread go flying like ducks high over his head, not unlike the winged loaves by which he had counted himself to sleep last night. Mercifully, then, it snowed, which he would not put past Salzman's machinations.

He was infuriated with the marriage broker and swore he would throw him out of the room the minute he reappeared. But Salzman did not come that night, and when Leo's anger had subsided,[15] an unaccountable despair grew in its place. At first he thought this was caused by his disappointment in Lily, but before long it became evident that he had involved himself with Salzman without a true knowledge of his own intent. He gradually realized—with an emptiness that seized him with six hands—that he had called in the broker to find him a bride because he was incapable of doing it himself. This terrifying insight he had derived as a result of his meeting and conversation with Lily Hirschorn. Her probing questions had somehow irritated him into revealing—to himself more than her—the true nature of his relationship to God, and from that it had come upon him, with shocking force, that apart from his parents, he had never loved anyone. Or perhaps it went the other way, that he did not love God so well as he might, because he had not loved man. It seemed to Leo that his whole life stood starkly revealed and he saw himself for the first time as he truly was—unloved and loveless. This bitter but somehow not fully unexpected revelation brought him to a point of panic, controlled only by extraordinary effort. He covered his face with his hands and cried.

The week that followed was the worst of his life. He did not eat and lost weight. His beard darkened and grew ragged. He stopped attending seminars and almost never opened a book. He seriously considered leaving the Yeshivah, although he was deeply troubled at the thought of the loss of all his years of study—saw them like pages torn from a book, strewn over the city—and at the devastating effect of this decision upon his parents. But he had lived without knowledge of himself, and never in the Five Books and all the Commentaries[16]— mea culpa[17]—had the truth been revealed to him. He did not know where to turn, and in all this desolating loneliness there was no *to whom*, although he often thought of Lily but not once could bring himself to go downstairs

---

Literary Element Dialect *How could you rephrase this sentence using a standard grammatical form?*

Reading Strategy Analyzing Characterization *What does this confession reveal about Finkle?*

Vocabulary

enamored (en am′ ərd) *adj.* inspired with love; charmed; captivated

15. *Subsided* means "decreased in intensity."
16. *The Pentateuch* (pen′ tə took′), or first *Five Books* of the Hebrew Bible (Genesis, Exodus, Leviticus, Numbers, and Deuteronomy), are known collectively in Judaism as the Torah, or the Law. *Commentaries* provide explanatory and scholarly information about the biblical texts.
17. *Mea culpa* (mā′ ə kool′ pə) means "my own fault" in Latin.

and make the call. He became touchy and irritable, especially with his landlady, who asked him all manner of personal questions; on the other hand, sensing his own disagreeableness, he waylaid her on the stairs and apologized **abjectly,** until mortified, she ran from him. Out of this, however, he drew the consolation that he was a Jew and that a Jew suffered. But gradually, as the long and terrible week drew to a close, he regained his composure and some idea of purpose in life: to go on as planned. Although he was imperfect, the ideal was not. As for his quest of a bride, the thought of continuing afflicted him with anxiety and heartburn, yet perhaps with this new knowledge of himself he would be more successful than in the past. Perhaps love would now come to him and a bride to that love. And for this sanctified seeking who needed a Salzman?

The marriage broker, a skeleton with haunted eyes, returned that very night. He looked, withal, the picture of frustrated expectancy—as if he had steadfastly waited the week at Miss Lily Hirschorn's side for a telephone call that never came.

Casually coughing, Salzman came immediately to the point: "So how did you like her?"

Leo's anger rose and he could not refrain from chiding the matchmaker: "Why did you lie to me, Salzman?"

Salzman's pale face went dead white, the world had snowed on him.

"Did you not state that she was twenty-nine?" Leo insisted.

"I give you my word—"

"She was thirty-five, if a day. *At least* thirty-five."

> *Perhaps love would now come to him and a bride to that love.*

"Of this don't be too sure. Her father told me—"

"Never mind. The worst of it was that you lied to her."

"How did I lie to her, tell me?"

"You told her things about me that weren't true. You made me out to be more, consequently less than I am. She had in mind a totally different person, a sort of semi-mystical Wonder Rabbi."

"All I said, you was a religious man."

"I can imagine."

Salzman sighed. "This is my weakness that I have," he confessed. "My wife says to me I shouldn't be a salesman, but when I have two fine people that they would be wonderful to be married, I am so happy that I talk too much." He smiled wanly.[18] "This is why Salzman is a poor man."

Leo's anger left him. "Well, Salzman, I'm afraid that's all."

The marriage broker fastened hungry eyes on him.

"You don't want any more a bride?"

"I do," said Leo, "but I have decided to seek her in a different way. I am no longer interested in an arranged marriage. To be frank, I now admit the necessity of premarital love. That is, I want to be in love with the one I marry."

"Love?" said Salzman, astounded. After a moment he remarked, "For us, our love is our life, not for the ladies. In the ghetto they—"

"I know, I know," said Leo. "I've thought of it often. Love, I have said to myself, should be a by-product of living and worship rather than its own end. Yet for myself I find it necessary to establish the level of my need and fulfill it."

Salzman shrugged but answered, "Listen, rabbi, if you want love, this I can find for you also. I have such beautiful clients that you will love them the minute your eyes will see them."

Leo smiled unhappily. "I'm afraid you don't understand."

Reading Strategy Analyzing Characterization *What does this third description of Salzman suggest about him?*

Vocabulary

abjectly (ab′ jekt lē) *adv.* in a humiliating, mean, or degrading manner

---

18. Here, *wanly* means "sadly" or "in a dejected way."

Reading Strategy Analyzing Characterization *Why does Finkle reach this conclusion?*

But Salzman hastily unstrapped his portfolio and withdrew a manila packet from it.

"Pictures," he said, quickly laying the envelope on the table.

Leo called after him to take the pictures away, but as if on the wings of the wind, Salzman had disappeared.

March came. Leo had returned to his regular routine. Although he felt not quite himself yet—lacked energy—he was making plans for a more active social life. Of course it would cost something, but he was an expert in cutting corners; and when there were no corners left he would make circles rounder. All the while Salzman's pictures had lain on the table, gathering dust. Occasionally as Leo sat studying, or enjoying a cup of tea, his eyes fell on the manila envelope, but he never opened it.

> Her face deeply moved him. Why, he could at first not say.

The days went by and no social life to speak of developed with a member of the opposite sex—it was difficult, given the circumstances of his situation. One morning Leo toiled up the stairs to his room and stared out the window at the city. Although the day was bright his view of it was dark. For some time he watched the people in the street below hurrying along and then turned with a heavy heart to his little room. On the table was the packet. With a sudden relentless gesture he tore it open. For a half-hour he stood by the table in a state of excitement, examining the photographs of the ladies Salzman had included. Finally, with a deep sigh he put them down. There were six, of varying degrees of attractiveness, but look at them long enough and they all became Lily Hirschorn: all past their prime, all starved behind bright smiles, not a true personality in the lot. Life, despite their frantic yoohooings, had passed them by; they were pictures in a brief case that stank of fish. After a while, however, as Leo attempted to return the photographs into the envelope, he found in it another, a snapshot of the type taken by a machine for a quarter. He gazed at it a moment and let out a cry.

Her face deeply moved him. Why, he could at first not say. It gave him the impression of youth—spring flowers, yet age—a sense of having been used to the bone, wasted; this came from the eyes, which were hauntingly familiar, yet absolutely strange. He had a vivid impression that he had met her before, but try as he might he could not place her although he could almost recall her name, as if he had read it in her own handwriting. No, this couldn't be; he would have remembered her. It was not, he affirmed, that she had an extraordinary beauty—no, though her face was attractive enough; it was that *something* about her moved him. Feature for feature, even some of the ladies of the photographs could do better; but she leaped forth to his heart—had *lived*, or wanted to—more than just wanted, perhaps regretted how she had lived—had somehow deeply suffered: it could be seen in the depths of those reluctant eyes, and from the way the light enclosed and shone from her, and within her, opening realms of possibility: this was her own. Her he desired. His head ached and eyes narrowed with the intensity of his gazing, then as if an obscure fog had blown up in the mind, he experienced fear of her and was aware that he had received an impression, somehow, of evil. He shuddered, saying softly, it is thus with us all. Leo brewed some tea in a small pot and sat sipping it without sugar, to calm himself. But before he had finished drinking, again with excitement he examined the face and found it good: good for Leo Finkle. Only such a one could understand him and help him seek whatever he was seeking. She might, perhaps, love him. How she had happened to be among the discards in Salzman's barrel he could never guess, but he knew he must urgently go find her.

Leo rushed downstairs, grabbed up the Bronx[19] telephone book, and searched for Salzman's home

---

19. *The Bronx* is one of five boroughs, or divisions, that make up New York City. Manhattan is another.

Big Idea Life in the City *How do the descriptions of city life here enhance the tone?*

Reading Strategy Analyzing Characterization *Why is Finkle experiencing fear here?*

address. He was not listed, nor was his office. Neither was he in the Manhattan book. But Leo remembered having written down the address on a slip of paper after he had read Salzman's advertisement in the "personals" column of the *Forward*. He ran up to his room and tore through his papers, without luck. It was exasperating. Just when he needed the matchmaker he was nowhere to be found.

Visual Vocabulary
A *skullcap*, or yarmulke (yä′ mə kə), is a brimless cap worn by many Jewish men and boys, especially during religious services.

Fortunately Leo remembered to look in his wallet. There on a card he found his name written and a Bronx address. No phone number was listed, the reason—Leo now recalled—he had originally communicated with Salzman by letter. He got on his coat, put a hat on over his skullcap and hurried to the subway station. All the way to the far end of the Bronx he sat on the edge of his seat. He was more than once tempted to take out the picture and see if the girl's face was as he remembered it, but he refrained, allowing the snapshot to remain in his inside coat pocket, content to have her so close. When the train pulled into the station he was waiting at the door and bolted out. He quickly located the street Salzman had advertised.

The building he sought was less than a block from the subway, but it was not an office building, nor even a loft, nor a store in which one could rent office space. It was a very old tenement[20] house. Leo found Salzman's name in pencil on a soiled tag under the bell and climbed three dark flights to his apartment. When he knocked, the door was opened by a thin, asthmatic, gray-haired woman in felt slippers.

"Yes?" she said, expecting nothing. She listened without listening. He could have sworn he had seen her, too, before but knew it was an illusion.

"Salzman—does he live here? Pinye Salzman," he said, "the matchmaker?"

She stared at him a long minute. "Of course."

He felt embarrassed. "Is he in?"

"No." Her mouth, though left open, offered nothing more.

"The matter is urgent. Can you tell me where his office is?"

"In the air." She pointed upward.

"You mean he has no office?" Leo asked.

"In his socks."

He peered into the apartment. It was sunless and dingy, one large room divided by a half-open curtain, beyond which he could see a sagging metal bed. The near side of a room was crowded with rickety chairs, old bureaus, a three-legged table, racks of cooking utensils, and all the apparatus of a kitchen. But there was no sign of Salzman or his magic barrel, probably also a figment of the imagination. An odor of frying fish made Leo weak to the knees.

"Where is he?" he insisted. "I've got to see your husband."

At length she answered, "So who knows where he is? Every time he thinks a new thought he runs to a different place. Go home, he will find you."

"Tell him Leo Finkle."

She gave no sign she had heard.

He walked downstairs, depressed.

But Salzman, breathless, stood waiting at his door.

Leo was astounded and overjoyed. "How did you get here before me?"

"I rushed."

"Come inside."

They entered. Leo fixed tea, and a sardine sandwich for Salzman. As they were drinking he reached behind him for the packet of pictures and handed them to the marriage broker.

Salzman put down his glass and said expectantly, "You found somebody you like?"

"Not among these."

The marriage broker turned away.

"Here is the one I want." Leo held forth the snapshot.

Salzman slipped on his glasses and took the picture into his trembling hand. He turned ghastly and let out a groan.

"What's the matter?" cried Leo.

"Excuse me. Was an accident this picture. She isn't for you."

---

20. A *tenement* is an apartment building or rooming house that is built or maintained poorly and is often overcrowded.

Big Idea Life in the City *What details set the scene in New York City?*

Salzman frantically shoved the manila packet into his portfolio. He thrust the snapshot into his pocket and fled down the stairs.

Leo, after momentary paralysis, gave chase and cornered the marriage broker in the vestibule.[21] The landlady made hysterical outcries but neither of them listened.

"Give me back the picture, Salzman."

"No." The pain in his eyes was terrible.

"Tell me who she is then."

"This I can't tell you. Excuse me."

He made to depart, but Leo, forgetting himself, seized the matchmaker by his tight coat and shook him frenziedly.

"Please," sighed Salzman. *"Please."*

Leo ashamedly let him go. "Tell me who she is," he begged. "It's very important for me to know."

"She is not for you. She is a wild one—wild, without shame. This is not a bride for a rabbi."

"What do you mean wild?"

"Like an animal. Like a dog. For her to be poor was a sin. This is why to me she is dead now."

"In God's name, what do you mean?"

"Her I can't introduce to you," Salzman cried.

"Why are you so excited?"

"Why, he asks," Salzman said, bursting into tears. "This is my baby, my Stella, she should burn in hell."

Leo hurried up to bed and hid under the covers. Under the covers

The Lover of Books, 1934. Moses Soyer. Oil on canvas, 42 x 23½ in. The Jewish Museum, New York.

he thought his life through. Although he soon fell asleep he could not sleep her out of his mind. He woke, beating his breast. Though he prayed to be rid of her, his prayers went unanswered. Through days of torment he endlessly struggled not to love her; fearing success, he escaped it. He then concluded

21. A *vestibule* (ves′ tə būl′) is an entrance hall or lobby.

Reading Strategy Analyzing Characterization *Why does his daughter's wildness cause Salzman to reject her?*

to convert her to goodness, himself to God. The idea alternately nauseated and exalted him.

He perhaps did not know that he had come to a final decision until he encountered Salzman in a Broadway cafeteria. He was sitting alone at a rear table, sucking the bony remains of a fish. The marriage broker appeared haggard, and transparent to the point of vanishing.

Salzman looked up at first without recognizing him. Leo had grown a pointed beard and his eyes were weighted with wisdom.

"Salzman," he said, "love has at last come to my heart."

"Who can love from a picture?" mocked the marriage broker.

"It is not impossible."

"If you can love her, then you can love anybody. Let me show you some new clients that they just sent me their photographs. One is a little doll."

"Just her I want," Leo murmured.

"Don't be a fool, doctor. Don't bother with her."

"Put me in touch with her, Salzman," Leo said humbly. "Perhaps I can be of service."

Salzman had stopped eating and Leo understood with emotion that it was now arranged.

Leaving the cafeteria, he was, however, afflicted by a tormenting suspicion that Salzman had planned it all to happen this way.

Leo was informed by letter that she would meet him on a certain corner, and she was there one spring night, waiting under a street lamp. He appeared, carrying a small bouquet of violets and rosebuds. Stella stood by the lamp post, smoking. She wore white with red shoes, which fitted his expectations, although in a troubled moment he had imagined the dress red, and only the shoes white. She waited uneasily and shyly. From afar he saw that her eyes—clearly her father's—were filled with desperate innocence. He pictured, in her, his own redemption. Violins and lit candles revolved in the sky. Leo ran forward with flowers outthrust.

Around the corner, Salzman, leaning against a wall, chanted prayers for the dead. ∾

Reading Strategy Analyzing Characterization *How is Finkle's date with Stella different from his previous date with Lily Hirschorn?*

RESPONDING AND THINKING CRITICALLY

Respond

1. Were you surprised by the outcome of the story? Explain why or why not.

Recall and Interpret

2. (a)Why does Leo Finkle decide to consult a marriage broker, or matchmaker? (b)What do you think consulting a marriage broker represents for Finkle?

3. (a)Who are the first three women Salzman describes? (b)How does Finkle react to the description of each? (c)What does Finkle's attitude toward the women reveal about his personality?

4. (a)How does Finkle feel about Salzman at the end of the story? (b)Do you think Finkle's suspicion about Salzman at the end of the story is correct? Support your answer with evidence from the story.

Analyze and Evaluate

5. Why might Finkle have responded so strongly to the snapshot of Stella?

6. How does the setting of Salzman's apartment add to the author's characterization of the matchmaker? Explain with details from the selection.

7. Imagine that you are buying something and the salesperson uses methods like Salzman's. How would you respond? Explain your answer.

8. How does Malamud use suspense to draw the reader into the story? Support your response.

Connect

9. **Big Idea** **Life in the City** In what ways does the city environment shape and influence Finkle's life?

LITERARY ANALYSIS

Literary Element Dialect

In "The Magic Barrel," Salzman speaks in a **dialect** of English influenced by Yiddish grammar and syntax. For example, he says "She lived with her husband maybe four months. He was a sick boy she made a mistake to marry him." In Standard English, this passage might read, "She lived with her husband for perhaps four months. He was a sick boy; it was a mistake for her to marry him."

1. Find three more examples of dialect in Salzman's speech in the story.

2. Notice that Salzman speaks in dialect but Finkle does not. What do these differences in speech tell you about these characters?

Review: Motivation

Motivation is the reason or cause for a character's actions. The cause may be internal (for example, a character's ambition, fear, or love) or external (for example, societal pressure or danger). Most characters are motivated by both internal and external factors.

Group Activity Meet with a small group to discuss the motivations of Leo Finkle in "The Magic Barrel." Create a chart like the one shown, and fill it in by identifying the motivation for each action listed.

LEO FINKLE

Motivation	Actions
	1. calls in Salzman
	2. rejects Salzman's three candidates
	3. agrees to meet Lily Hirschorn
	4. stops eating and attending seminars
	5. falls in love with Stella's snapshot

Reading Strategy Analyzing
Characterization

In "The Magic Barrel," Malamud primarily uses indirect **characterization** to reveal the personalities of his two main characters. Indirect characterization requires readers to interpret details and events—to reach conclusions on the basis of the clues provided by the author.

1. Find three instances in which Malamud portrays Salzman's character.

2. Identify the method used to reveal character in each instance: for example, through the character's thoughts, words, actions, or appearance or through what other characters think and say about that character.

3. Write a brief sketch of Salzman's character based on these passages.

Vocabulary Practice

Practice with Word Origins You know that Latin roots form the basis of many English words and that the meaning of an English word is related to the meaning of its root. Study the meanings of these Latin roots:

ami(c)—"friend" *anim*—"mind; soul" *amat* or *amor*—"to love"

Now notice how the roots affect the meanings of three vocabulary words from the selection:

*ami*able—"friendly"

*anim*ated—"full of life, or soul"

en*amor*ed—"filled with love"

Write each word below and underline its Latin root. Then tell how the root contributes to the meaning of the word.

1. amateur
2. amicable
3. amity
4. magnanimous
5. amorous

Writing About Literature

Analyze Cultural Context "The Magic Barrel" is set primarily in a Jewish community in New York City. Write a brief essay analyzing this cultural context. Discuss the following questions and use evidence from the story to support your ideas.

1. What is the general attitude of the Jewish population toward rabbis? What does this suggest about the importance of religion in the lives of the people?

2. Marriage brokers play an important role in the social life of the community. What does this tell you about the community's attitude toward marriage and the family?

3. What qualities does Salzman esteem in a wife? What does this suggest about the community's values?

Before you begin your first draft, complete a chart like the one started below. List the qualities valued by Finkle and Salzman, the representatives of the culture.

	Rabbis and Religion	Marriage and Family	Qualities Desirable in a Wife
Finkle's Attitude	wants to be a rabbi but has conflicted feelings about God		
Salzman's Attitude	respects rabbis		

After you complete your first draft, get together with a classmate to evaluate each other's work and to suggest revisions. Then proofread and edit your draft for errors in spelling, grammar, and punctuation.

Learning for Life

Group Activity For many people who are busy or shy, or who have trouble meeting romantic partners for other reasons, dating services have taken the place of matchmakers. Imagine yourself as the owner of a dating service. Write the text for a brochure to persuade people like Leo Finkle and Lily Hirschorn to use your service. Keep in mind that such a brochure would be a form of persuasive writing.

Literature Online **Web Activities** For eFlashcards, Selection Quick Checks, and other Web activities, go to www.glencoe.com.

The Rockpile

MEET JAMES BALDWIN

James Baldwin wrote constantly about controversial topics, such as race, politics, love, and religion. In the course of his career, Baldwin produced a formidable body of work, which holds a place of honor in American literature. To achieve that eminence, he had to overcome many obstacles.

The grandson of slaves, Baldwin grew up in a large, impoverished family in the Harlem neighborhood of New York during the economic hard times of the Great Depression. He once said that he wanted to be rich and famous simply so no one could evict his family again. Alhough he wrote plays, short stories, and novels, Baldwin is perhaps most highly regarded as an essayist. Among his most famous essay collections are *Notes of a Native Son*, *Nobody Knows My Name*, and *The Fire Next Time*. In both his fiction and his nonfiction, he examined issues of African American identity and the sources of racial bigotry in the twentieth-century United States.

> "I love America more than any other country in the world, and exactly for this reason, I insist on the right to criticize her perpetually."
>
> —James Baldwin

Confronting the Past Baldwin's work first became known to a wide audience when he published his novel *Go Tell It on the Mountain* in 1953, a work that reflects the author's search for his roots. Baldwin had struggled with the novel for ten years, noting that, "In a sense, I wrote to redeem my father. I had to understand the forces, the experience, the life that shaped him before I could grow up myself, before I could become a writer." Baldwin's ability to accept and use the pain of the past—while not being consumed by it—became the basis for much of his work, both fiction and nonfiction.

Changing Perspectives Baldwin's later work focused primarily on protesting racial inequality. He said, "It is a terrible, an inexorable, law that one cannot deny the humanity of another without diminishing one's own: in the face of one's victim, one sees himself." Besides achieving fame as a writer, Baldwin was also a popular speaker during the civil rights movement of the 1950s and 1960s. His uncompromising honesty and realism, his ear for language, and his early experience as a minister combined to make him a powerful force at the podium.

In 1969 Baldwin moved to France, where he lived for the majority of the rest of his life. In the United States, Baldwin had never won a major literary prize. In France, he was honored with one of the literary world's most prestigious awards: Commander of the Legion of Honor. When James Baldwin died, his body was sent back to Harlem and buried only a few blocks from the house where he was born. More than 5,000 mourners gathered to pay their respects to the man who once said, "An artist is here not to give you answers, but to ask you questions."

James Baldwin was born in 1924 and died in 1987.

Literature Online **Author Search** For more about James Baldwin, go to www.glencoe.com.

Connecting to the Story

Have you ever known someone who chose to side with a brother, sister, or friend even though it meant breaking the rules? In "The Rockpile," a boy gives his word to his brother and honors it even though he could end up hurting them both. As you read the story, think about the following questions:

- When is it justified to break the rules?
- What would you risk to keep your word to someone?

Building Background

This story is set in the New York City neighborhood of Harlem. Although no precise time is given, it appears to be the 1930s—the time of Baldwin's youth. "The Rockpile" may well be set near the first home Baldwin remembered living in, at Park Avenue and 131st Street. Like John in the story, Baldwin was the oldest child in a large family. His mother married David Baldwin three years after James's birth, so, like John, young Baldwin was a stepson. Like the father in the story, David Baldwin was a Protestant minister and a stern man who did not like his children playing in the streets. In fact, he believed that going outside, except to go to church or to the store, was certain to lead to sin.

Setting Purposes for Reading

Big Idea Life in the City

As you read the story, look for details about the setting and characters that provide information about urban life in the Depression-era United States.

Literary Element Foil

A **foil** is a minor character whose contrast with a main character highlights particular traits of that main character. As you read "The Rockpile," examine how your understanding of the main character is expanded as a result of the presence of the foil.

- See Literary Terms Handbook, p. R7.

Literature Online Interactive Literary Elements Handbook To review or learn more about the literary elements, go to www.glencoe.com.

Reading Strategy Making Generalizations About Characters

A **generalization** is a broad conclusion drawn from specific details. As you read, use details to make generalizations about the family members in "The Rockpile."

Reading Tip: Taking Notes In a chart, record details and generalizations about the main characters.

Details	Generalizations
Roy gazed at the street, wishing he had wings; John was afraid of the rockpile.	Roy and John have different personalities.

Vocabulary

grapple (grap′əl) v. to struggle in hand-to-hand combat; to wrestle; p. 959 *The man grappled with his attacker.*

loiter (loi′tər) v. to stand or linger idly or aimlessly about a place; p. 960 *We thought it best not to loiter in the empty street.*

intimidated (in tim′ə dāt′əd) adj. made timid or fearful; frightened into submission or inaction; p. 960 *When the large man pushed me, I was so intimidated that I was speechless.*

engrossed (en grōst′) adj. fully attentive to; completely engaged in; absorbed; p. 961 *I spoke to my mother, but she was engrossed in the newspaper and did not look up.*

jubilant (jōō′bə lənt) adj. extremely happy; triumphantly joyful; p. 961 *The people were jubilant when they heard that the war had ended.*

Vocabulary Tip: Analogies An **analogy** is a comparison that shows similarities between two things that are otherwise dissimilar.

INDIANA ACADEMIC STANDARDS (pages 958–966)
11.3 [Identify] story elements such as character...
11.5.2 Write responses to literature that...analyze the use of imagery [and] language...

11.2 Develop [reading] strategies...
11.3.4 Analyze ways in which...prose uses imagery...to evoke readers' emotions.

The Rockpile

James Baldwin

Across the street from their house, in an empty lot between two houses, stood the rockpile. It was a strange place to find a mass of natural rock jutting out of the ground; and someone, probably Aunt Florence, had once told them that the rock was there and could not be taken away because without it the subway cars underground would fly apart, killing all the people. This, touching on some natural mystery concerning the surface and the center of the earth, was far too intriguing an explanation to be challenged, and it invested the rockpile, moreover, with such mysterious importance that Roy felt it to be his right, not to say his duty, to play there.

Other boys were to be seen there each afternoon after school and all day Saturday and Sunday. They fought on the rockpile. Surefooted, dangerous, and reckless, they rushed each other and **grappled** on the heights, sometimes disappearing down the other side in a confusion of dust and screams and upended, flying feet. "It's a wonder they don't kill themselves," their mother said, watching sometimes from the fire escape. "You children stay away from there, you hear me?" Though she said "children," she was looking at Roy, where he sat beside John on the fire escape. "The good Lord knows," she continued, "I don't want you to come home bleeding like a hog every day the Lord sends." Roy shifted impatiently, and continued to stare at the street, as though in this gazing he might somehow acquire wings. John said nothing. He had not really been spoken to: he was afraid of the rockpile and of the boys who played there.

Big Idea **Life in the City** *What does this superstition reveal about how the residents view their neighborhood?*

Reading Strategy Making Generalizations About Characters *From this detail, what generalizations might you make about Roy?*

Literary Element Foil *What does this detail suggest about the difference between the two brothers?*

Vocabulary

grapple (grap′əl) *v.* to struggle in hand-to-hand combat; to wrestle

Each Saturday morning John and Roy sat on the fire escape and watched the forbidden street below. Sometimes their mother sat in the room behind them, sewing, or dressing their younger sister, or nursing the baby, Paul. The sun fell across them and across the fire escape with a high, benevolent indifference; below them, men and women, and boys and girls, sinners all, **loitered**; sometimes one of the church-members passed and saw them and waved. Then, for the moment that they waved decorously back, they were **intimidated.** They watched the saint, man or woman, until he or she had disappeared from sight. The passage of one of the redeemed made them consider, however vacantly, the wickedness of the street, their own latent wickedness in sitting where they sat; and made them think of their father, who came home early on Saturdays and who would soon be turning this corner and entering the dark hall below them.

But until he came to end their freedom, they sat, watching and longing above the street. At the end of the street nearest their house was the bridge which spanned the Harlem River[1] and led to a city called the Bronx;[2] which was where Aunt Florence lived. Nevertheless, when they saw her coming, she did not come from the bridge, but from the opposite end of the street. This, weakly, to their minds, she explained by saying that she had taken the subway, not wishing to walk, and that, besides, she did not live in *that* section of the Bronx. Knowing that the Bronx was across the river, they did not believe this story ever, but, adopting toward her their father's attitude, assumed that she had just left some sinful place which she dared not name, as, for example, a movie palace.

In the summertime boys swam in the river, diving off the wooden dock, or wading in from the garbage-heavy bank. Once a boy, whose name was Richard, drowned in the river. His mother had not known where he was; she had even come to their house, to ask if he was there. Then, in the evening, at six o'clock, they had heard from the street a woman screaming and wailing; and they ran to the windows and looked out. Down the street came the woman, Richard's mother, screaming, her face raised to the sky and tears running down her face. A woman walked beside her, trying to make her quiet and trying to hold her up. Behind them walked a man, Richard's father, with Richard's body in his arms. There were two white policemen walking in the gutter, who did not seem to know what should be done. Richard's father and Richard were wet, and Richard's body lay across his father's arms like a cotton baby. The woman's screaming filled all the street; cars slowed down and the people in the cars stared; people opened their windows and looked out and came rushing out of doors to stand in the gutter, watching. Then the small procession disappeared within the house which stood beside the rockpile. Then, *"Lord, Lord, Lord!"* cried Elizabeth, their mother, and slammed the window down.

One Saturday, an hour before his father would be coming home, Roy was wounded on the rockpile and brought screaming upstairs. He and John had been sitting on the fire escape and their mother had gone into the kitchen to sip tea with Sister McCandless. By and by Roy became bored and sat beside John in restless silence; and John began drawing into his schoolbook a newspaper advertisement which featured a new electric locomotive. Some friends of Roy passed beneath the fire escape and called him. Roy began to fidget, yelling down to them through the bars. Then a silence fell. John looked up. Roy stood looking at him.

"I'm going downstairs," he said.

"You better stay where you is, boy. You know Mama don't want you going downstairs."

---

1. The *Harlem River* separates the Bronx and Manhattan, two boroughs of New York City.
2. *The Bronx* is actually one of five boroughs, or divisions, that make up New York City. It is not a separate city.

Reading Strategy Making Generalizations About Characters *From this detail, what generalizations might you make about how the brothers view their father?*

Vocabulary

loiter (loi′tər) *v.* to stand or linger idly or aimlessly about a place

intimidated (in tim′ə dāt′əd) *adj.* made timid or fearful; frightened into submission or inaction

Woman in Calico, 1944. William H. Johnson. Oil on paperboard, 26½ x 20½ in. Smithsonian American Art Museum. Gift of the Harmon Foundation.

"I be right *back.* She won't even know I'm gone, less you run and tell her."

"I ain't *got* to tell her. What's going to stop her from coming in here and looking out the window?"

"She's talking," Roy said. He started into the house.

"But Daddy's going to be home soon!"

"I be back before *that.* What you all the time got to be so *scared* for?" He was already in the house and he now turned, leaning on the windowsill, to swear impatiently, "I be back in *five* minutes."

John watched him sourly as he carefully unlocked the door and disappeared. In a moment he saw him on the sidewalk with his friends. He did not dare to go and tell his mother that Roy had left the fire escape because he had practically promised not to. He started to shout, *Remember, you said five minutes!* but one of Roy's friends was looking up at the fire escape. John looked down at his schoolbook: he became **engrossed** again in the problem of the locomotive.

When he looked up again he did not know how much time had passed, but now there was a gang fight on the rockpile. Dozens of boys fought each other in the harsh sun: clambering up the rocks and battling hand to hand, scuffed shoes sliding on the slippery rock; filling the bright air with curses and **jubilant** cries. They filled the air, too, with flying weapons: stones, sticks, tin cans, garbage, whatever could be picked up and thrown. John watched in a kind of absent amazement—until he remembered that Roy was still downstairs, and that he was one of the boys on the rockpile. Then he was afraid; he could not see his brother among the figures in the sun; and he stood up, leaning over the fire-escape railing. Then Roy appeared from the other side of the rocks; John saw that his shirt was torn; he was laughing. He moved until he stood at the very top of the rockpile. Then, something, an empty tin can, flew out of the air and hit him on the forehead, just above the eye. Immediately, one side of Roy's face ran with blood, he fell and rolled on his face down the rocks. Then for a moment there was no movement at all, no sound, the sun, arrested, lay on the street and the sidewalk and the arrested boys. Then someone screamed or shouted; boys began to run away, down the street, toward the bridge. The figure on the ground, having caught its breath and felt its own blood, began to shout. John cried, "Mama! Mama!" and ran inside.

"Don't fret, don't fret," panted Sister McCandless as they rushed down the dark, narrow, swaying stairs, "don't fret. Ain't a boy been born don't get his knocks every now and again.

Literary Element Foil *What does Roy's statement to his brother suggest about the nature of their relationship?*

Reading Strategy Making Generalizations About Characters *From this detail, what generalizations can you make about John?*

Vocabulary

engrossed (en grōst′) *adj.* fully attentive to; completely engaged in; absorbed

jubilant (jōō′bə lənt) *adj.* extremely happy; triumphantly joyful

Lord!" They hurried into the sun. A man had picked Roy up and now walked slowly toward them. One or two boys sat silent on their stoops; at either end of the street there was a group of boys watching. "He ain't hurt bad," the man said, "Wouldn't be making this kind of noise if he was hurt real bad."

Elizabeth, trembling, reached out to take Roy, but Sister McCandless, bigger, calmer, took him from the man and threw him over her shoulder as she once might have handled a sack of cotton. "God bless you," she said to the man, "God bless you, son." Roy was still screaming. Elizabeth stood behind Sister McCandless to stare at his bloody face.

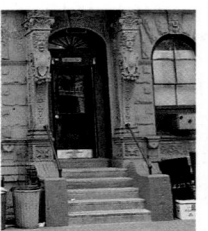

Visual Vocabulary
A *stoop* is a structure at the entrance of a building or house, consisting of stairs and a raised platform.

"It's just a flesh wound," the man kept saying, "just broke the skin, that's all." They were moving across the sidewalk, toward the house. John, not now afraid of the staring boys, looked toward the corner to see if his father was yet in sight.

Upstairs, they hushed Roy's crying. They bathed the blood away, to find, just above the left eyebrow, the jagged, superficial scar. "Lord, have mercy," murmured Elizabeth, "another inch and it would've been his eye." And she looked with apprehension toward the clock. "Ain't it the truth," said Sister McCandless, busy with bandages and iodine.

"When did he go downstairs?" his mother asked at last.

Sister McCandless now sat fanning herself in the easy chair, at the head of the sofa where Roy lay, bound and silent. She paused for a moment to look sharply at John. John stood near the window, holding the newspaper advertisement and the drawing he had done.

"We was sitting on the fire escape," he said. "Some boys he knew called him."

"When?"

"He said he'd be back in five minutes."

"Why didn't you tell me he was downstairs?"

He looked at his hands, clasping his notebook, and did not answer.

"Boy," said Sister McCandless, "you hear your mother a-talking to you?"

He looked at his mother. He repeated:

"He said he'd be back in five minutes."

"He said he'd be back in five minutes," said Sister McCandless with scorn, "don't look to me like that's no right answer. You's the man of the house, you supposed to look after your baby brothers and sisters—you ain't supposed to let them run off and get half-killed. But I expect," she added, rising from the chair, dropping the cardboard fan, "your Daddy'll make you tell the truth. Your Ma's way too soft with you."

He did not look at her, but at the fan where it lay in the dark red, depressed seat where she had been. The fan advertised a pomade[3] for the hair and showed a brown woman and her baby, both with glistening hair, smiling happily at each other.

"Honey," said Sister McCandless, "I got to be moving along. Maybe I drop in later tonight. I don't reckon you going to be at Tarry Service tonight?"

Tarry Service was the prayer meeting held every Saturday night at church to strengthen believers and prepare the church for the coming of the Holy Ghost on Sunday.

"I don't reckon," said Elizabeth. She stood up; she and Sister McCandless kissed each other on the cheek. "But you be sure to remember me in your prayers."

"I surely will do that." She paused, with her hand on the door knob, and looked down at Roy and laughed. "Poor little man," she said, "reckon he'll be content to sit on the fire escape *now*."

Elizabeth laughed with her. "It sure ought to be a lesson to him. You don't reckon," she asked nervously, still smiling, "he going to keep that scar, do you?"

---

3. *Pomade* is a perfumed ointment, especially one used as a hair dressing.

"Lord, no," said Sister McCandless, "ain't nothing but a scratch. I declare, Sister Grimes, you worse than a child. Another couple of weeks and you won't be able to *see* no scar. No, you go on about your housework, honey, and thank the Lord it weren't no worse." She opened the door; they heard the sound of feet on the stairs. "I expect that's the Reverend," said Sister McCandless, placidly, "I *bet* he going to raise cain."[4]

"Maybe it's Florence," Elizabeth said. "Sometimes she get here about this time." They stood in the doorway, staring, while the steps reached the landing below and began again climbing to their floor. "No," said Elizabeth then, "that ain't her walk. That's Gabriel."

"Well, I'll just go on," said Sister McCandless, "and kind of prepare his mind." She pressed Elizabeth's hand as she spoke and started into the hall, leaving the door behind her slightly ajar. Elizabeth turned slowly back into the room. Roy did not open his eyes, or move; but she knew that he was not sleeping; he wished to delay until the last possible moment any contact with his father. John put his newspaper and his notebook on the table and stood, leaning on the table, staring at her.

"It wasn't my fault," he said. "I couldn't stop him from going downstairs."

"No," she said, "you ain't got nothing to worry about. You just tell your Daddy the truth."

He looked directly at her, and she turned to the window, staring into the street. What was Sister McCandless saying? Then from her bedroom she heard Delilah's thin wail and she turned, frowning, looking toward the bedroom and toward the still open door. She knew that John was watching her. Delilah continued to wail, she thought, angrily, *Now that girl's getting too big for that*, but she feared

Funky Soho, 2002. Patti Mollica. Oil on canvas. Private collection.

that Delilah would awaken Paul and she hurried into the bedroom. She tried to soothe Delilah back to sleep. Then she heard the front door open and close—too loud, Delilah raised her voice, with an exasperated sigh Elizabeth picked the child up. Her child and Gabriel's, her children and Gabriel's: Roy, Delilah, Paul. Only John was nameless and a stranger, living, unalterable testimony to his mother's days in sin.

"What happened?" Gabriel demanded. He stood, enormous, in the center of the room, his black lunchbox dangling from his hand, staring at the sofa

4. *To raise cain* is an idiom meaning "to make a great disturbance" or "to lose one's temper."

Reading Strategy | Making Generalizations About Characters *What generalizations can you make about Sister McCandless from this comment?*

Reading Strategy | Making Generalizations About Characters *From these details, what generalizations can you make about John's status in the family?*

Church on Lenox Avenue, 1939–1940. William H. Johnson. Tempera on paper, 24 x 18⅛ in. Smithsonian American Art Museum. Gift of the Harmon Foundation.

Viewing the Art: What connections can you find between this image and the story?

dropped his lunchbox with a clatter and knelt by the sofa.

"How you feel, son? Tell your Daddy what happened?"

Roy opened his mouth to speak and then, relapsing into panic, began to cry. His father held him by the shoulder.

"You don't want to cry. You's Daddy's little man. Tell your Daddy what happened."

"He went downstairs," said Elizabeth, "where he didn't have no business to be, and got to fighting with them bad boys playing on that rockpile. That's what happened and it's a mercy it weren't nothing worse."

He looked up at her. "Can't you let this boy answer me for hisself?"

Ignoring this, she went on, more gently: "He got cut on the forehead, but it ain't nothing to worry about."

"You call a doctor? How you know it ain't nothing to worry about?"

"Is you got money to be throwing away on doctors? No, I ain't called no doctor. Ain't nothing wrong with my eyes that I can't tell whether he's hurt bad or not. He got a fright more'n anything else, and you ought to pray God it teaches him a lesson."

"You got a lot to say *now,*" he said, "but I'll have *me* something to say in a minute. I'll be wanting to know when all this happened, what you was doing with your eyes *then.*" He turned back to Roy, who had lain quietly sobbing eyes wide open and body held rigid: and who now, at his father's touch, remembered the height, the sharp, sliding rock beneath his feet, the sun, the explosion of the sun, his plunge into darkness and his salty blood; and recoiled, beginning to scream, as his father touched his forehead. "Hold still, hold still," crooned his father, shaking, "hold still. Don't cry. Daddy ain't going to hurt you, he just wants to see this bandage, see what they've done to his little man." But Roy continued to scream and would not be still and Gabriel dared not lift the bandage for fear of hurting him more. And he looked at Elizabeth in fury: "Can't you put that child down and help me with this boy?"

where Roy lay. John stood just before him, it seemed to her astonished vision just below him, beneath his fist, his heavy shoe. The child stared at the man in fascination and terror—when a girl down home she had seen rabbits stand so paralyzed before the barking dog. She hurried past Gabriel to the sofa, feeling the weight of Delilah in her arms like the weight of a shield, and stood over Roy, saying:

"Now, ain't a thing to get upset about, Gabriel. This boy sneaked downstairs while I had my back turned and got hisself hurt a little. He's alright now."

Roy, as though in confirmation, now opened his eyes and looked gravely at his father. Gabriel

---

Literary Element Foil *How might Elizabeth be said to act as Gabriel's foil at this point in the story?*

John, take your baby sister from your mother—don't look like neither of you got good sense."

John took Delilah and sat down with her in the easy chair. His mother bent over Roy, and held him still, while his father, carefully—but still Roy screamed—lifted the bandage and stared at the wound. Roy's sobs began to lessen. Gabriel readjusted the bandage. "You see," said Elizabeth, finally, "he ain't nowhere near dead."

"It sure ain't your fault that he ain't dead." He and Elizabeth considered each other for a moment in silence. "He came mightly close to losing an eye. Course, his eyes ain't as big as your'n, so I reckon you don't think it matters so much." At this her face hardened; he smiled. "Lord, have mercy," he said, "you think you ever going to learn to do right? Where was you when all this happened? Who let him go downstairs?"

"Ain't nobody let him go downstairs, he just went. He got a head just like his father, it got to be broken before it'll bow. I was in the kitchen."

"Where was Johnnie?"

"He was in here?"

"Where?"

"He was on the fire escape."

"Didn't he know Roy was downstairs?"

"I reckon."

"What you mean, you reckon? He ain't got your big eyes for nothing, does he?" He looked over at John. "Boy, you see your brother go downstairs?"

"Gabriel, ain't no sense in trying to blame Johnnie. You know right well if you have trouble making Roy behave, he ain't going to listen to his brother. He don't hardly listen to me."

"How come you didn't tell your mother Roy was downstairs?"

John said nothing, staring at the blanket which covered Delilah.

"Boy, you hear me? You want me to take a strap to you?"

"No, you ain't," she said. "You ain't going to take no strap to this boy, not today you ain't. Ain't a soul to blame for Roy's lying up there now but you—you because you done spoiled him so that he thinks he can do just anything and get away with it. I'm here to tell you that ain't no way to raise no child. You don't pray to the Lord to help you do better than you been doing, you going to live to shed bitter tears that the Lord didn't take his soul today." And she was trembling. She moved, unseeing, toward John and took Delilah from his arms. She looked back at Gabriel, who had risen, who stood near the sofa, staring at her. And she found in his face not fury alone, which would not have surprised her; but hatred so deep as to become insupportable in its lack of personality. His eyes were struck alive, unmoving, blind with malevolence—she felt, like the pull of the earth at her feet, his longing to witness her perdition.[5] Again, as though it might be propitiation,[6] she moved the child in her arms. And at this his eyes changed, he looked at Elizabeth, the mother of his children, the helpmeet given by the Lord. Then her eyes clouded; she moved to leave the room; her foot struck the lunchbox lying on the floor.

"John," she said, "pick up your father's lunchbox like a good boy."

She heard, behind her, his scrambling movement as he left the easy chair, the scrape and jangle of the lunchbox as he picked it up, bending his dark head near the toe of his father's heavy shoe. ❧

---

5. *Perdition* (pər dish′ ən) means "the loss of one's soul and of heavenly salvation" or "eternal damnation."

6. *Propitiation* is a pleasing act intended to soothe, pacify, or win favor.

Reading Strategy Making Generalizations About Characters *From this detail, what generalizations can you make about Gabriel's character?*

RESPONDING AND THINKING CRITICALLY

Respond

1. Describe your emotional response to this story.

Recall and Interpret

2. (a)Why is the rockpile so tempting for Roy? (b)Why do you think that John is not tempted by it?

3. (a)How do the adults in the story see themselves as different from other people in the neighborhood? (b)How is their self-image reflected in their actions?

4. (a)What important fact is revealed about Gabriel just before he arrives home? (b)How does this fact explain Gabriel's attitude toward his two sons?

Analyze and Evaluate

5. Using **foreshadowing**, a writer provides hints to events that will occur later in the story. (a)What event or events are foreshadowed in "The Rockpile"? (b)What effect does this foreshadowing have on the story?

6. (a)What do you think the rockpile symbolizes? (b)Do you find this symbol effective? Explain.

7. (a)What is the main source of conflict between Gabriel and Elizabeth in the story? (b)Is this conflict resolved at the end of the story? Explain.

Connect

8. **Big Idea** Life in the City How important is the setting to this story? What picture of city life does the author create with this setting?

LITERARY ANALYSIS

Literary Element Foil

The purpose of a **foil** is to highlight a particular quality of the main character in the story. Although "The Rockpile" may appear to be about Roy, it actually tells just as much or more about John. The reader gets a clearer understanding of both John and Roy through the many contrasts presented between them.

1. How do John and Roy differ in terms of their status within the family?

2. Who else might be a foil in this story? Support your response with evidence from the selection.

Writing About Literature

Evaluate Author's Craft In "The Rockpile," James Baldwin uses a number of **symbols,** or things that stand for something beyond themselves. Write a brief essay in which you evaluate Baldwin's use of symbolism throughout the story and how it contributes to the story's meaning. After you complete your draft, meet with a partner to revise each other's work.

Literature Online **Web Activities** For eFlashcards, Selection Quick Checks, and other Web activities, go to www.glencoe.com.

READING AND VOCABULARY

Reading Strategy Making Generalizations About Characters

Use the notes you made in your chart and other details from the story to make generalizations about the characters in "The Rockpile."

1. What generalizations can you make about the effect of the setting on the characters?

2. What generalization can you make about the attitudes of Roy and John toward Gabriel?

Vocabulary Practice

Practice with Analogies Choose the word that best completes the analogy.

1. engrossed : fascinated :: expedient :
   a. convenient   c. fortuitous
   b. coincidental

2. loiter : stand :: search :
   a. find   c. seek
   b. collect

3. jubilant : pleased :: terrified :
   a. anxious   c. sorrowful
   b. frozen

The United States and the World

Three Flags, 1958. Jasper Johns. Encaustic on canvas, 30⅞ x 45 x 5 in. Fiftieth Anniversary Gift of the Gilman Foundation, Inc., The Lauder Foundation, A. Alfred Taubman, an anonymous donor, and purchase 80.32

"We must be the great arsenal of democracy."

—Franklin D. Roosevelt, radio broadcast, 1940

War Message to Congress

MEET FRANKLIN DELANO ROOSEVELT

Franklin D. Roosevelt was an intensely competitive and social person. His charismatic demeanor, rich voice, and wide smile expressed confidence and optimism and gave him the power to be very persuasive. In the dark days of the Great Depression and World War II, his buoyant leadership was one of the United States' greatest assets.

"Let me assert my firm belief that the only thing we have to fear is fear itself—"

—Franklin D. Roosevelt
First Inaugural Address

Roosevelt was a distant cousin of Theodore Roosevelt, the twenty-sixth president of the United States. He was born into a wealthy New York family and educated at Harvard University and Columbia Law School. While at Harvard, he became acquainted with Theodore Roosevelt's niece, Eleanor. Soon afterward, Franklin and Eleanor were married.

Political Gains and Personal Setbacks Shortly after leaving law school, Roosevelt entered politics and won a seat in the New York State Senate. He earned a reputation as a progressive reformer willing to stand up to the party bosses. In 1921, he contracted a fever and soon felt numbness in his legs. He had contracted the disease known as polio. Although there was no cure, Roosevelt refused to give up and began a vigorous exercise program to restore some of his muscle control.

While recovering from polio, Roosevelt depended on his wife to keep his name prominent in the New York Democratic Party. Eleanor Roosevelt became an effective orator, and her efforts during this time kept her husband's political career alive. By the mid-1920s,

Franklin Roosevelt was again active in the Democratic Party and was elected governor of New York. While governor, he gained great popularity by cutting taxes for farmers, reducing the rates charged by public utilities, and giving aid to unemployed New Yorkers.

Roosevelt's popularity paved the way for his presidential win in 1932. Many people in the United States applauded Roosevelt's use of power to help people in economic distress. In the first three months of his presidency, Congress passed fifteen major acts to provide economic relief to the nation, later known as the First New Deal. Roosevelt's popular relief programs helped him win reelection three times. He has the remarkable legacy of being the only president to serve more than two terms.

Tension in Europe Meanwhile, World War II officially began when Germany invaded Poland on September 1, 1939. After the horrors of World War I, most U.S. citizens were in favor of remaining neutral during the war. On December 7, 1941, Japanese fighter pilots made a surprise attack on Pearl Harbor. The damage was severe and crippling. Roosevelt quickly changed his mind about the war. The following day, he delivered his famous "War Message to Congress." But President Roosevelt did not live to see victory; he died from a stroke just months before the war's end.

Franklin D. Roosevelt was born in 1882 and died in 1945.

Literature Online **Author Search** For more about Franklin D. Roosevelt, go to www.glencoe.com.

Connecting to the Speech

Can you imagine having to make a decision that would affect an entire country? In President Roosevelt's "War Message to Congress," he informs the nation of the attack on Pearl Harbor and requests permission from Congress to declare war. Think about the following questions:

- Have you ever had to make a difficult decision that affected other people such as friends or family?
- What possible consequences did you weigh as you made your decision?

Building Background

Prior to the attack on Pearl Harbor, U.S. intelligence had decoded Japanese communications that made it clear that Japan was preparing to attack the United States. However, no one knew when or where the attack would occur. Japan's surprise attack on December 7, 1941, sank or damaged 21 ships of the U.S. Pacific Fleet. The attack also destroyed 188 airplanes and killed 2,403 Americans. Another 1,178 were injured. Following the president's speech, the Senate voted 82 to 0 and the House voted 388 to 1 to declare war on Japan.

Setting Purposes for Reading

Big Idea The United States and the World

As you read, think about both the political and human consequences that President Roosevelt had to consider before asking Congress to declare war.

Literary Element Author's Purpose

An **author's purpose** is his or her intent in writing a piece of literature. Authors typically write to accomplish one or more of the following purposes: to persuade, to inform, to explain, to entertain, or to describe. You can begin to figure out an author's purpose by thinking critically about the form, the tone, and the content of the first few paragraphs. As you read, decide what Roosevelt's purpose is in his "War Message to Congress."

- See Literary Terms Handbook, p. R2.

Literature Online Interactive Literary Elements Handbook To review or learn more about the literary elements, go to www.glencoe.com.

Reading Strategy Distinguishing Fact and Opinion

A **fact** is a statement that can be verified or proved. An **opinion** is a personal judgment. Opinions cannot be verified or proved true, because they are expressions of a person's beliefs or feelings. Different people might have different opinions on the same issue.

Reading Tip: Taking Notes As you read, create a chart like the one below to record examples of facts and opinions you find throughout "War Message to Congress."

Detail	Fact or Opinion
"a date which will live in infamy"	opinion

Vocabulary

infamy (in'fə mē) *n.* a reputation as something evil or harmful; p. 970 *The Ku Klux Klan gained infamy for its racism.*

diplomatic (dip'lə mat'ik) *adj.* negotiating in a peaceful manner; p. 970 *Tyler and I tried to be diplomatic when we debated who could use the car Friday night.*

implication (im'plə kā'shən) *n.* an effect or consequence; p. 971 *Not brushing your teeth can have severe implications, such as cavities and tooth decay.*

premeditated (prē med'ə tāt'əd) *adj.* thought about beforehand; p. 971 *The bank robbery turned out to be premeditated, as the criminal had developed the plan weeks before.*

inevitable (i nev'ə tə bəl) *adj.* certain to happen; p. 971 *Once the black clouds appeared overhead, we feared rain was inevitable.*

 INDIANA ACADEMIC STANDARDS (pages 969–972)

11.2 Develop strategies such as...analyzing...purpose...
11.2.6 Critique the power, validity, and truthfulness of arguments set forth in...speeches...

11.7.4 Use logical...ethical, and emotional appeals that enhance a specific tone and purpose.

FRANKLIN D. ROOSEVELT
WAR MESSAGE TO CONGRESS,
December 8, 1941

Yesterday, December 7, 1941—a date which will live in **infamy**—the United States of America was suddenly and deliberately attacked by naval and air forces of the Empire of Japan.

The United States was at peace with that nation and, at the solicitation of Japan, was still in conversation with its Government and its Emperor looking toward the maintenance of peace in the Pacific. Indeed, one hour after Japanese air squadrons had commenced bombing in the American Island of Oahu, the Japanese Ambassador to the United States and his colleague delivered to our Secretary of State a formal reply to a recent American message. And, while this reply stated that it seemed useless to continue the existing **diplomatic** negotiations, it contained no threat or hint of war or of armed attack.

It will be recorded that the distance of Hawaii from Japan makes it obvious that the attack was deliberately planned many days or even weeks ago. During the intervening time the Japanese Government has deliberately sought to deceive the United States by false statements and expressions of hope for continued peace.

The attack yesterday on the Hawaiian Islands has caused severe damage to American naval and military forces. I regret to tell you that very many American lives have been lost. In addition American ships have been reported torpedoed on the high seas between San Francisco and Honolulu.

Vocabulary

infamy (in′ fə mē) *n.* a reputation as something evil or harmful

diplomatic (dip′ lə mat′ ik) *adj.* negotiating in a peaceful manner

---

Reading Strategy Distinguishing Fact and Opinion
Which parts of this statement are based on factual information? Which parts are formed by opinions?

President Franklin D. Roosevelt signs the declaration of war against Japan, December 8, 1941.

Yesterday the Japanese Government also launched an attack against Malaya.

Last night Japanese forces attacked Hong Kong.

Last night Japanese forces attacked Guam.

Last night Japanese forces attacked the Philippine Islands.

Last night the Japanese attacked Wake Island.

And this morning the Japanese attacked Midway Island.

Japan has, therefore, undertaken a surprise offensive extending throughout the Pacific area. The facts of yesterday and today speak for themselves. The people of the United States have already formed their opinions and well understand the **implications** to the very life and safety of our nation.

As Commander in Chief of the Army and Navy I have directed that all measures be taken for our defense.

Always will our whole nation remember the character of the onslaught against us.

No matter how long it may take us to overcome this **premeditated** invasion, the American people in their righteous might will win through to absolute victory. I believe that I interpret the will of the Congress and of the people when I assert that we will not only defend ourselves to the uttermost but will make it very certain that this form of treachery shall never again endanger us.

Hostilities exist. There is no blinking at the fact that our people, our territory, and our interests are in grave danger.

With confidence in our armed forces—with the unbounding determination of our people—we will gain the **inevitable** triumph. So help us God.

I ask that the Congress declare that since the unprovoked and dastardly attack by Japan on Sunday, December 7, 1941, a state of war has existed between the United States and the Japanese Empire. ❧

Big Idea The United States and the World *How does Roosevelt use rhetoric to make the nation feel confident of victory?*

Vocabulary

implication (im′ plə kā′ shən) *n.* an effect or consequence

premeditated (prē med′ ə tāt′ əd) *adj.* thought about beforehand

inevitable (i nev′ ə tə bəl) *adj.* certain to happen

RESPONDING AND THINKING CRITICALLY

Respond

1. What was your reaction to Roosevelt's speech?

Recall and Interpret

2. (a)Why, according to Roosevelt, was the United States unprepared for the attack on Pearl Harbor? (b)How do you think this information might have influenced Congress?

3. (a)Why does Roosevelt claim it was obvious that the attack on Pearl Harbor was planned "many days or weeks ago"? (b)How do you think this influenced the president's reaction to the attack?

4. (a)Which places does Roosevelt say Japan has attacked? (b)What effect does Roosevelt seem to want this information to have on his audience?

Analyze and Evaluate

5. (a)What does Roosevelt mean when he says, "The people of the United States have already formed their opinions"? (b)What do you think he is trying to accomplish with this statement?

6. (a)How does Roosevelt assure the public of a war victory? (b)Why do you think he does this?

Connect

7. **Big Idea** **The United States and the World** Explain whether you feel the president did an accurate job of addressing both the political and human consequences of declaring war on Japan in "War Message to Congress."

LITERARY ANALYSIS

Literary Element Author's Purpose

An effective speaker such as Franklin D. Roosevelt makes every word count by supporting his or her arguments and appealing to the hearts and minds of his or her audience.

1. What, in your opinion, is the purpose of Roosevelt's speech?

2. Roosevelt uses the rhetorical device of **repetition.** Find an example of this device and explain how it helps him influence and persuade his audience.

Interdisciplinary Activity: U.S. History

Debate When World War II began, many people in the United States favored neutrality because it would keep U.S. troops out of harm's way. Others believed that taking sides was a requisite step in protecting the United States. Form two small groups. Have one group take the pro-neutrality side. Have another group take the pro-involvement position. Stage a debate between the two groups and invite the rest of the class to decide which side presented the stronger case.

Literature Online **Web Activities** For eFlashcards, Selection Quick Checks, and other Web activities, go to www.glencoe.com.

READING AND VOCABULARY

Reading Strategy Distinguishing Fact and Opinion

Roosevelt includes both fact and opinion in his "War Message to Congress." Return to the chart you created on fact and opinion on page 969. Be aware that a writer shows **bias** when he or she demonstrates a strong, personal, or sometimes unreasonable opinion. Bias is most often present in editorials, documentaries, and advertisements.

1. How does Roosevelt use both fact and opinion in his speech?

2. How is bias present in Roosevelt's speech?

Vocabulary Practice

Practice with Connotation and Denotation
The words in each pair below have similar denotations, or literal meanings. Indicate which word in each pair has a more negative connotation, or implied meaning.

1. **a.** infamy   **b.** disgrace
2. **a.** diplomatic   **b.** smooth
3. **a.** inevitable   **b.** certain
4. **a.** implication   **b.** allegation

Vocabulary Workshop

Word Parts

Understanding Unfamiliar Math and Science Terms

"Indeed, one hour after Japanese air squadrons had commenced bombing… Oahu, the Japanese Ambassador to the United States and his colleague delivered to our Secretary of State a formal reply to a recent American message."

— Franklin Delano Roosevelt, from "War Message to Congress"

Connecting to Literature *Squadron* is related to the Latin word *quadrum*, meaning "square." Several math and science terms come from the Latin *quadrum*: *quadrangle*, *quadrant*, *quadruped*, and *quadratic*, for example. You have probably figured out that *quadru-* or *quadr-* means "four."

Examples

You can figure out many math and science terms if you know some common word parts such as those below. Study this group of word parts and their definitions.

astro- *astr-*	star; celestial body; outer space	*-pede*	foot
milli-	thousand	*-gon*	a figure having a specified kind or number of angles
hydro- *hydr-*	water; liquid	*-nomy*	body of knowledge about a specific field
poly-	more than one; many; much	*-sphere*	a celestial body, such as a planet or star
penta-	five		

Exercise

Answer the following questions by combining two word parts from the list above. Consult a dictionary to check your answers. Write the answers on a piece of paper.

1. What is the word for a small animal that has an external skeleton and numerous feet?
2. What is the word for the scientific study of the planets and stars in outer space?
3. What is the word for a closed plane figure bounded by straight lines?
4. What is the word for water vapor in Earth's atmosphere?
5. What is the word for a five-sided polygon?

▶ **Vocabulary Terms**

Many math and science terms come from the Latin language, as do many of the **word parts** at the left.

▶ **Test-Taking Tip**

When you are asked for the meaning of a word that appears in a reading passage, knowledge of some common word parts can help you. Use your prior knowledge to help you recall similar words.

▶ **Reading Handbook**

For more about interpreting unfamiliar math and science terms, see Reading Handbook, p. R20.

Literature Online
eFlashcards For eFlashcards and other vocabulary activities, go to www.glencoe.com.

 ACADEMIC STANDARDS (page 973)
11.1.2 Apply knowledge of roots and word parts from Greek and Latin to draw inferences about the meaning of vocabulary in literature or other subject areas.

The Death of the Ball Turret Gunner

MEET RANDALL JARRELL

Randall Jarrell's influence on other writers in the mid-twentieth century was enormous. His work as a critic, teacher, novelist, and poet helped define poetry's path during the 1950s and early 1960s. Jarrell's longtime friend and fellow poet Robert Lowell observed, "His gifts . . . were wit, pathos, and brilliance of intelligence."

Jarrell was born in Nashville, Tennessee, but spent most of his youth in Long Beach, California. Jarrell's interest in poetry began during his time at Vanderbilt University. There he studied under notable southern writers John Crowe Ransom and Robert Penn Warren, who nurtured Jarrell's skills as a poet and critic. After earning BA and MA degrees from Vanderbilt, Jarrell began a career as a professor of English literature, first at Kenyon College and then at the University of Texas.

"If I can think of it, it isn't what I want.
I want . . . I want a ship from some
near star
To land in the yard"

—Randall Jarrell, "A Sick Child"

Military Life In 1942, when Jarrell published his first book of poems, *Blood for a Stranger,* the United States had just entered World War II. That same year, he joined the war effort by enlisting in the Army Air Forces. He served as a control tower operator and trained B-29 bomber pilots. World War II had a profound effect on Jarrell, inspiring him to write with great rancor, pity, and drama about the evils of war. Many of his greatest poems appear in *Little Friend, Little Friend* (1945) and *Losses* (1948). Both books deal extensively with themes of dehumanization, war, and violence. Jarrell also displayed great compassion in his portraits of people trapped in meaningless lives.

He exhibited particular sensitivity to the victimization of women and children.

When the war ended, Jarrell taught for a year at Sarah Lawrence College. He later translated his teaching experiences at the women's academy into the satirical novel *Pictures from an Institution.* After a year at Sarah Lawrence, Jarrell took a professorship at the University of North Carolina in Greensboro. From 1956 until 1958, he served as poetry consultant to the Library of Congress.

Critical Acclaim In the two decades after World War II, Jarrell produced several collections of verse and commentary. His criticism was some of the most shrewd and acerbic of its day. Jarrell could be brutal, and he often lambasted mediocre poetry. As many have noted, however, the fierceness of Jarrell's reviews was not a display of aggression but, rather, a measure of his love for poetry. He was a passionate advocate for verse that met his high standards. Robert Frost, William Carlos Williams, and Walt Whitman all met these standards and therefore received revitalized acclaim as a result of Jarrell's critical attention.

In 1965, Jarrell was struck and killed by a car. It is unclear whether his death was accidental or whether Jarrell, like so many poets of his generation, chose suicide. Whatever the cause of his death, his importance is unquestionable. Jarrell's poetry captured what poet Karl Shapiro called "the common dialogue of Americans," a dialogue that modulates from weariness to terror, from hopefulness to ecstasy.

Randall Jarrell was born in 1914 and died in 1965.

Literature Online **Author Search** For more about Randall Jarrell, go to www.glencoe.com.

Connecting to the Poem

Can you imagine the horrors of war? What is it like to face death? In Jarrell's poem, a gunner aboard a U.S. bomber relates his own death in eerie, dreamlike terms. As you read the poem, think about the following questions:

- Do the circumstances of someone's death change the meaning of that person's death?
- What is your view of war? Can war be justified?

Building Background

The aircraft that Jarrell mentions in his note were long-range bombers that the U.S. Army used in bombing raids over Europe and the Pacific during World War II. The B-17 was called the *Flying Fortress,* because it could withstand severe damage and still remain aloft. The B-24, known as the *Liberator,* was developed a few years later. Its wing-span was slightly longer than that of the B-17, and it had a greater range. Both the B-17 and B-24 had Plexiglas ball turrets that housed machine gunners. Although both were powerful aircraft, these ball turrets made them vulnerable to attack. In his poem, Jarrell describes the life and death of a turret gunner aboard one of these aircraft. Although Jarrell himself was not a crew member of a U.S. bomber, he had a great sense of compassion and love for the men that he trained.

Setting Purposes for Reading

Big Idea The United States and the World

As you read, consider how Jarrell's "The Death of the Ball Turret Gunner" represents the human story of World War II.

Literary Element Imagery

Imagery is the "word pictures" that writers create to evoke an emotional response. In creating imagery, writers use sensory details, or descriptions that appeal to one or more of the five senses. Imagery is often an integral part of modern and contemporary poetry. As you read "The Death of the Ball Turret Gunner," examine how Jarrell uses imagery to establish his setting and generate emotion.

- See Literary Terms Handbook, p. R9.

Reading Strategy Visualizing

To **visualize** is to use the imagination to picture the setting, characters, and action in a work of literature. As you read, pay close attention to sensory details and descriptions.

Reading Tip: Taking Notes In a web diagram, record powerful images and other images connected to them.

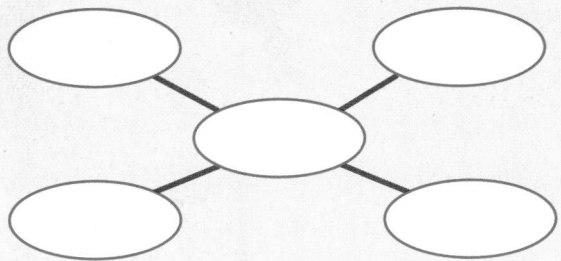

Vocabulary

turret (tur´it) *n.* a small, rotating domelike structure that is mounted with guns and attached to the body of an aircraft; p. 976 *The turret turned and the gunner began firing on the approaching enemy planes.*

Plexiglas (plek´si glas´) *n.* a light and very durable transparent plastic; p. 976 *Due to its low cost and light weight, Plexiglas is often used in manufacturing.*

gunner (gun´ər) *n.* an airman or a soldier who operates a gun; p. 976 *The gunner aimed at the enemy aircraft and fired, scoring a direct hit.*

fetus (fē´təs) *n.* an unborn child that has been in utero for at least eight weeks; p. 976 *The family breathed a collective sigh of relief after learning that the fetus was perfectly healthy.*

Literature Online **Interactive Literary Elements Handbook** To review or learn more about the literary elements, go to www.glencoe.com.

 INDIANA ACADEMIC STANDARDS (pages 975–977)

11.3.4 Analyze ways in which poetry...uses imagery...to evoke readers' emotions.

11.2 Develop [reading] strategies...

11.5.2 Write responses to literature that demonstrate a comprehensive understanding of the significant ideas in works...

The Death of the Ball Turret Gunner

Randall Jarrell

From my mother's sleep I fell into the State,
And I hunched in its belly till my wet fur froze.
Six miles from earth, loosed from its dream of life,
I woke to black flak[1] and the nightmare fighters.
When I died they washed me out of the **turret** with a hose.

---

1. *Flak* is the fire of antiaircraft guns.

Literary Element   Imagery *Which other images does this image align with to convey the overall meaning of the poem? What do these images suggest?*

Vocabulary

turret (tur´it) *n.* a small, rotating domelike structure that is mounted with guns and attached to the body of an aircraft

Plexiglas (spelling corrected; plek´si glas´) *n.* a light and very durable transparent plastic

gunner (gun´ər) *n.* an airman or a soldier who operates a gun

fetus (fē´təs) *n.* an unborn child that has been in utero for at least eight weeks

NOTE FROM THE AUTHOR:

A ball turret was a **plexiglass** sphere set into the belly of a B-17 or B-24, and inhabited by two .50 caliber machine guns and one man, a short small man. When this **gunner** tracked with his machine guns a fighter attacking his bomber from below, he revolved with the turret; hunched upside down in his little sphere, he looked like the **fetus** in the womb. The fighters which attacked him were armed with cannon firing explosive shells. The hose was a steam hose.

—Randall Jarrell

RESPONDING AND THINKING CRITICALLY

Respond

1. Which phrase or image was the most potent for you? Why?

Recall and Interpret

2. (a)What happens to the speaker in the first two lines? (b)What do these lines suggest about his attitude toward the situation? What do they suggest about the poet's view of the gunner?

3. (a)Where is the speaker in line 3? (b)What do you think he means by "loosed from its dream of life"?

4. (a)What happens to the speaker in line 4? (b)What does the dream of life entail? What realization does the gunner have in line 4?

Analyze and Evaluate

5. What is ironic about Jarrell's comparison of the ball turret gunner and a fetus in the womb?

6. Critics have characterized Jarrell as a master of plain speech and clear, stark language. Do these apply to this poem? Explain.

7. (a)How would you describe the personality of the gunner? (b)Do you think his personality is sufficiently well established? Explain.

Connect

8. **Big Idea** **The United States and the World** In what ways has this poem helped to develop your understanding of World War II?

LITERARY ANALYSIS

Literary Element **Imagery**

Imagery can have a profound impact on the mood of a literary work. The mood is the emotional quality or atmosphere of a piece. Each image in a poem or piece of fiction acts like a color in a painting—the darker the image, the darker the literary work will be. Sometimes when images with highly contrasting moods are juxtaposed, the results can be jarring, ironic, or even humorous.

1. What is the mood of "The Death of the Ball Turret Gunner"? What images in this poem contribute to its mood?

2. Identify imagery in this poem that causes contrasts in mood. How does this imagery alter the poem?

Writing About Literature

Analyze Tone Information can be conveyed in different ways, depending on the writer's attitude toward the subject and the audience. Gather into groups of four or five and read the poem and the note from the author, focusing on the tone. Then use the basic information from these texts to write an official report of the event. Then discuss your work with your classmates.

Literature Online **Web Activities** For eFlashcards, Selection Quick Checks, and other Web activities, go to www.glencoe.com.

READING AND VOCABULARY

Reading Strategy **Visualizing**

Visualizing is a useful method of comprehending a text. Try to visualize the actions, characters, and settings of each line in relation to the piece as a whole.

1. Briefly describe how the image in line 1 functions in the poem as a whole.

2. What other images are easier to understand once they are placed in context? Explain.

Academic Vocabulary

Here are two words from the vocabulary list on page R86. These words will help you think, write, and talk about the selection.

internal (in turn′əl) *adj.* existing or situated inside something else

invest (in vest′) *v.* to endow with certain predominant qualities

Practice and Apply

1. What does Jarrell compare the **internal** part of the turret to in "The Death of the Ball Turret Gunner"?

2. What characteristics does Jarrell **invest** the bomber with?

Comparing Literature Across Time and Place

Connecting to the Reading Selections

How do you respond to tragic events in life? Many people prefer to bury the memories of these types of events, rather than confront them. In the following selections, Elie Wiesel, Garrett Hongo, and Art Spiegelman show the value of confronting the horrors of the past—both to understand the present and to ensure that the disasters of history do not repeat themselves.

COMPARING THE [Big Idea] The United States and the World

World War I was supposed to be the "war to end all wars." In the 1930s, however, the Nazis began a brutal campaign of violence against Jews. Wiesel and Spiegelman show the horrible tragedy of the Holocaust and a world that could not find the resources to stop it. Hongo addresses a byproduct of World War II: the wartime paranoia that led to Japanese American internment in the United States.

COMPARING Reflections

Wiesel, Hongo, and Spiegelman reflect on the past in these selections. Wiesel looks back on his own experiences; Hongo and Spiegelman learn about history through the memories of their elders. The reflections presented in these selections show both the significance of personal experience and the importance of learning about history through firsthand accounts.

COMPARING Cultures

Cultures can be a source of pride as well as a target for hatred. The Jewish communities presented in Wiesel's memoir and Spiegelman's graphic novel must band together to survive the atrocities of the Nazis. Hongo expresses his hope that Japanese American culture can overcome its lingering discomfort from the legacy of internment and finally fully express itself.

from *All Rivers Run to the Sea*

MEET ELIE WIESEL

As a Holocaust survivor, Elie Wiesel has a vision of a future with deep ties to past generations. Called the "conscience of the Holocaust," Wiesel believes that memory can be a powerful foundation for unity. This notion echoes his personal struggle with the past and illustrates his attempt to transform his struggle into a universal fight against oppression and indifference. Wiesel gave a stirring speech at the U.S. Holocaust Memorial Museum dedication in 1993. His famous words are engraved in stone at the museum's entrance, encouraging future generations to recognize this collective duty:

"For the dead and the living, we must bear witness."

—Elie Wiesel

The Holocaust Wiesel spent his childhood in Sighet, Romania, where he gained a deep understanding of Jewish identity. Synagogues, day schools, and Jewish newspapers flourished in Sighet during Wiesel's youth, reflecting a vibrant Jewish community. Wiesel began attending *kheder* (religious elementary school) when he was three years old. He studied secular subjects, played the violin, and eventually found a local scholar with whom he could study Kabbalah, a mystical interpretation of Hebrew Scriptures.

In the spring of 1944, Wiesel's life changed forever. Fifteen-year-old Wiesel and his family were deported from Sighet to the death camp Auschwitz-Birkenau in Poland. Wiesel was separated from his mother and sisters—his mother and youngest sister were immediately gassed to death. Wiesel remained with his father at Auschwitz and later at Buchenwald, another concentration camp. Tragically, his father died just months before the liberation of the camp in 1945. Wiesel survived the horrors of the concentration camps and was later reunited with his older sisters.

Giving Voice to Memory After the liberation, Wiesel vowed to keep silent about the horrors he had witnessed. He evacuated to France, where he continued his education. While studying in Paris, he began work as a journalist, writing stories for the Yiddish newspaper *Zion in Kamf* and the Israeli newspaper *Yedi'ot Akharonot*. Journalism put him in contact with a crucial figure, French writer François Mauriac. In 1954, at Mauriac's behest, Wiesel broke his silence and finally gave voice to his memories. Wiesel wrote and published his Yiddish memoir, *Un Di Velt Hot Geshvign* ("And the World Kept Silent"), in 1956. Under Mauriac's guidance, Wiesel revised the text and translated it into French under the title *La Nuit* in 1958; in 1960 this seminal work was translated into English as *Night*.

Wiesel moved to the United States in 1956 and was naturalized as a citizen in 1963. As a result of his prolific writing and lecturing, Wiesel has become one of the most visible and renowned Holocaust survivors, eventually winning the Nobel Peace Prize in 1986. In his Nobel acceptance speech, Wiesel acknowledged the problem of oppression, but even more so, the danger of indifference: "we must always take sides. Neutrality helps the oppressor, never the victim. Silence encourages the tormentor, never the tormented. Sometimes we must interfere." By confronting and exploring his own horrific past, Wiesel has transformed his experiences into collective understanding, dialogue, and action.

Elie Wiesel was born in 1928.

Literature Online **Author Search** For more about Elie Wiesel, go to www.glencoe.com.

Connecting to the Memoir

What events have defined your life thus far? Perhaps an ancestor's immigration to the U.S., the neighborhood your parents chose to live in, or a tragedy changed your life. In his memoir, Wiesel reflects on the repercussions of the Holocaust on his life. As you read, think about the following questions:

- How do your memories impact your everyday life?
- Why do you think large-scale acts of evil still occur in today's world?

Building Background

All Rivers Run to the Sea is Wiesel's memoir of his years growing up, both directly before and after the Holocaust and World War II. In the following excerpt, from the chapter entitled "Darkness," he reflects on his experience of being torn from his home and taken to the most notorious Nazi concentration camp, Auschwitz-Birkenau. Nazi forces rounded up Jews in Poland and Germany and brought them by train to the camps. Most Jews did not realize what lay ahead at Auschwitz, though many suspected the worst. Many attempted to flee. In the camps, Nazis performed inhumane medical experiments on prisoners and executed millions of innocent Jews.

Setting Purposes for Reading

Big Idea The United States and the World

After World War I, many countries isolated themselves to avoid the kinds of complex military alliances that had spurred that war. As you read, consider how Wiesel explores the question of why the world neglected its responsibility to stop the Nazi campaign.

Literary Element Narrator

The **narrator** is the person who tells a story. The narrator may be a character in the story or someone from the outside looking in. As you read this excerpt from *All Rivers Run to the Sea,* note how the perspective of the narrator affects your understanding of the selection.

- See Literary Terms Handbook, p. R12.

Literature Online **Interactive Literary Elements Handbook** To review or learn more about the literary elements, go to www.glencoe.com.

Reading Strategy Activating Prior Knowledge

Reading is an interactive process. When you read, you bring your **prior knowledge** and past experiences to the task. For example, to fully understand Wiesel's memoir, you must attempt to draw on your knowledge of modern history and life in general.

Reading Tip: Taking Notes On a piece of paper, list the prior knowledge or personal experiences that help you to understand each event or statement in this selection.

Prior Knowledge	Event in Selection
Many people are prejudiced toward particular cultural or ethnic groups.	Nazis treat Jews as subhuman.

Vocabulary

ineffably (in ef′ə blē) *adv.* to a degree that is impossible to express; indescribably; p. 981 *James was ineffably sad when he said goodbye to his family and boarded the train for Chicago.*

succumb (sə kum′) *v.* to give in or submit to; p. 984 *The marathon runner insisted that she would finish the race and not succumb to fatigue.*

premonition (prē′mə nish′ ən) *n.* a warning, or foreboding about the future; p. 985 *Jane had a premonition that something bad would happen later that afternoon.*

trepidation (trep′ə dā′ shən) *n.* a feeling of alarm or apprehension; dread; p. 986 *Bill turned down the darkened alley with trepidation.*

curt (kurt) *adj.* rudely brief, or short; terse; p. 986 *The curt reply Mr. Jenkins gave to Lydia's question suggested he didn't want to be bothered.*

INDIANA ACADEMIC STANDARDS (pages 980–989)

11.2.5 Analyze an author's...beliefs about a subject.

11.2 Develop [reading] strategies...

11.5.2 Demonstrate a comprehensive understanding of the significant ideas in works or passages...

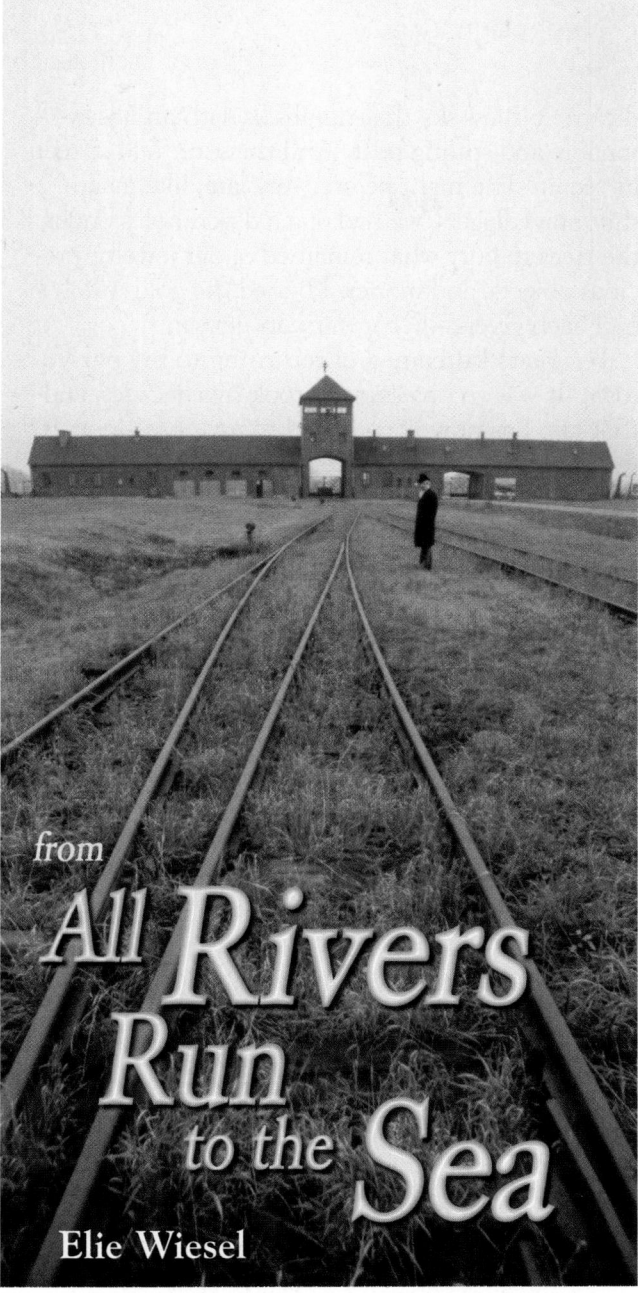

from

All Rivers Run to the Sea

Elie Wiesel

Our turn came on Tuesday, May 16. "All Jews out!" the gendarmes[1] screamed, and we found ourselves in the street. There was another heat wave. My little sister was thirsty, and my grandmother too. They didn't complain, but I did, not openly, but it amounted to the same thing. I felt queasy, ill. I was suffering, but didn't know from what. I was **ineffably** sad. As in the presence

---

1. *Gendarmes* are police officers.

Vocabulary

ineffably (in efʹə blē) *adv.* to a degree that is impossible to express; indescribably

of death, I didn't dare raise my voice. This was where my childhood and my adolescence, my prayers, studies, and fasting had led. These moments would remain forever etched within me. Wherever life took me, a part of me would always remain in that street, in front of my empty house, awaiting the order to depart.

I see my little sister, I see her with her rucksack, so cumbersome, so heavy. I see her and an immense tenderness sweeps over me. Never will her innocent smile fade from my soul. Never will her glance cease to sear me. I tried to help her; she protested. Never will the sound of her voice leave my heart. She was thirsty, my little sister was thirsty. Her lips were parched. Pearls of sweat formed on her clear forehead. I gave her a little water. "I can wait," she said, smiling. My little sister wanted to be brave. And I wanted to die in her place.

I seldom speak of her in my writing, for I dare not. My little sister with her sun-bathed golden hair is my secret. I never even talked to Marion[2] or to my son Elisha about her. It mortifies me to talk about her in the past tense, for she is present. Her presence is more real to me than my own. My little sister Tsiporah, my little angel scorched by a darkened sun, I cannot picture you as death's hostage. You will remain on our street, on the pavement in front of our house.

I gazed at the house—we all did—with anguish. Here we had lived a Jewish family life that was now gone forever. The laughter and laments, the peace of Shabbat, the prayer of the God of Abraham whispered by my mother and my grandmother, the festival of Sukkoth, the songs of Rosh Hashana, the Passover meals, the community gatherings, my grandfather's visits.[3] The stories of beggars and of refugees,

---

2. *Marion* is Wiesel's wife.
3. *Shabbat* refers to the "Sabbath" or holy day for Jews, which occurs each week from sunset on Friday to the following night. In the Bible, *Abraham* is considered a patriarch, or father figure, to the Hebrew people. *Sukkoth* is a Jewish harvest festival. *Rosh Hashana* is the Jewish new year.

Reading Strategy Activating Prior Knowledge *What memories are forever etched in your mind?*

the forbidden broadcasts of Radio London and Radio Moscow that we listened to at night, curtains drawn and shutters closed. I picture myself sitting under an acacia tree, a book in my hands, talking to the clouds. Tsipouka is playing with a hoop. "Come and play with me," she says, but I don't feel like it. And now, as I write these words, my heart is pounding. I should have closed my book and stopped my dream, dropped everything to play with my little sister. Other images rise up: the sleigh in winter, the horse and carriage in summer; a cousin's funeral (a fortune-teller is said to have foretold her death); Bea sick with typhus:[4] she lies in a room of her own, feverish and contagious, hovering between life and death. My grandmother asks me to go with her to the synagogue. It is night. She opens the Holy Ark[5] and sobs, "Holy Torah, intercede on behalf of Batya, daughter of Sarah. She is young and can still accomplish many good deeds for your glory. Tell the Lord, blessed be His name, to let her live. She will be more useful to Him than I." She closes the Ark and backs slowly to the door. There she stops and says, "If I have any years to live, Lord, give them to her. I exchange my future for hers. Let that be my gift." When Bea takes a few steps, I glance at my grandmother. She has offered her life. What will become of her now? I picture our house and see Hilda inside, Hilda the oldest of the children, whose radiant beauty drew all the matchmakers[6] of the region.

I see the people who came through that door day and night to consult with my father—my father who now, bent under the weight of his pack, knows not to whom he might turn for advice. And my mother, always gracious and brave, afraid to look at us, afraid to see the house, afraid to burst into tears only to find she can never stop. So she looks at the sky, the pitiless sky that numbs us with an unseasonable and stifling heat. And the sun? Will it keep its secret? The night before, very late, like makeshift gravediggers, we had dug a dozen holes under the trees to bury what remained of our jewelry, precious objects, and money. I buried the gold watch I had been given as a bar mitzvah[7] present.

For years I dreamed of returning to my native town. It was an obsession. It took two decades, and that trip has now been added to my obsessions. It was night. There was a sleeping town and a sleeping house which hadn't changed: the same gate, same garden, same well. Choked with fear, as though caught in a whirlwind of hallucinations, I wondered whether it had all been a dream, whether our Jewish neighbors were still there, and my parents and my sisters too. Terror swept me away and carried me back. I waited for a window to open and for a boy who looked like the child I had been to call out to me: Hey, mister, what are you doing in my dream?

But strangers were living in my house. They had never heard my name. Inside, nothing had changed: the same furniture, the same tile stove my father had borrowed money to buy; the beds, tables, and chairs were ours, still in the same places. My feverish eyes wandered left and right, up and down. Was it possible that not a single trace of us remained? But there was one, just one. On the wall above my bed had been a photograph of my beloved master, Rebbe Israel of Wizhnitz. I remember it well: I had hung it there the day he died, the second day of the month of Sivan.[8] I can see myself standing there, a heavy hammer in my hand, driving in the nail and hanging the frame. As I write these words, I suddenly realize that my mother died eight years later on exactly the same day, along with my little sister and Grandma Nissel. I cried for the Rebbe's death as I hung his photograph above my bed. The nail was still there. A huge cross was hanging from it.

"We must go now," my mother said. "We must stay together."

---

4. *Typhus* is a disease characterized by high fever and delirium.
5. The *Holy Ark* is a cabinet in a synagogue where the scrolls of the Torah, or the first five books of the Hebrew scriptures, are stored.
6. *Matchmakers* are people who set up marriages.

Big Idea The United States and the World *What effect do you think international news can have on acts of injustice carried out by a government?*

---

7. A *bar mitzvah* is a celebration of a Jewish boy's thirteenth birthday, marking the beginning of his adult and religious duties.
8. *Rebbe* means "Rabbi," a Jewish spiritual teacher. *Sivan* is the ninth month in the Jewish year.

Literary Element Narrator *What do you know about the narrator at this point? What type of perspective does he have?*

It was Tuesday afternoon. We were still in Sighet.[9] Our convoy would not leave for several days. We had been temporarily transferred to the smaller ghetto, whose inhabitants had just been driven out.

We moved into the home of Mendel, my father's brother. My mother cooked our favorite dish, latkes, potato pancakes. This time there was no rationing; we ate all we wanted.

Mendel was my silent uncle. He had married Golda, daughter of my maternal uncle Israel. He was pious[10] and shy. They had three children. Their photograph lies before me, saved by a relative.

Sacred books were scattered on the floor. Someone must have removed them from his bag at the last minute. The table was set, and there was food on the plates. They had been taken away in the middle of a meal. This was what remained of a family.

After the war I questioned every survivor of the second transport I could find, seeking news of Uncle Mendel and his family. I thought I found the answer in 1988, when an elderly man called out to me in the lobby of a Miami Beach hotel. He was, like me, of Romanian-Hungarian origin, from a small village near Sighet, and he told me he had stayed in the smaller ghetto until its evacuation. In fact, he had been in the same camp with my uncle. "Really?" I exclaimed. "You knew my uncle?" "Knew him!" he said. "For years I've seen him, even in my sleep." And then he told me. At first Mendel and his son had been spared, like my father and me, and had been sent to a camp where conditions were relatively tolerable. But they were in different barracks and saw each other only during the day, at work.

> The Germans, however, did not shrink from killing a father and son together, without a second thought, as one would step on two insects.

One night they could not bear to be separated. When the roll was called, the SS[11] Blockführer counted and recounted the prisoners and ordered: "Let the prisoner who does not belong in this barracks show himself." Mendel's son took a few steps forward. "Closer!" the officer shouted. My young cousin obeyed, halting when he reached the SS man. The officer slowly drew his revolver and shot my cousin in the head, point-blank. My uncle, that sweet and timid man, hurled himself onto his son's body, as if to protect him in death. The SS man stared at him for a long moment and then shot him in the head too. "Ever since then," my witness said, "I see Mendel and his son in my dreams."

And I, I think of the biblical law that, out of compassion for animals, forbids the slaughter of an ox and his calf on the same day. The Germans, however, did not shrink from killing a father and son together, without a second thought, as one would step on two insects.

Fishel and Voïcsi, my cousins from Antwerp,[12] later gave me a different version of their deaths. What is certain, though, is that the enemy annihilated my Uncle Mendel's family.

And what happened to my Aunt Zlati, my father's younger sister? I search my memories of the ghetto for her, but she is not there.

She was married to Nahman-Elye. I don't remember their two very young children, nor do I recall their presence during the weeks before the transport. Nahman-Elye, it seems, was among those the Hungarian army released from the labor battalions to be locked up in the ghetto. It seems he was deported with the first

---

9. *Sighet* is a town in Romania and the birthplace of Wiesel.
10. *Pious* means "seriously or devoutly religious."

Reading Strategy Activating Prior Knowledge *How does Wiesel's account of his family's experience add to your understanding of the Holocaust?*

---

11. *SS* refers to the Nazi paramilitary forces.
12. *Antwerp* is a city in Belgium.

Literary Element Narrator *How does Wiesel shape his account of the Holocaust?*

Survivors at Buchenwald concentration camp remain in their barracks after liberation by Allies on April 16, 1945. Elie Wiesel, the Nobel Prize-winning author, is on the second bunk from the bottom, sixth from the left.

transport and later **succumbed** to the pressures and temptations of the camp life and became a cruel and murderous kapo.[13] It seems he was tried, sentenced to death, and executed by former deportees. My uncle in the enemy's service? A kapo? My uncle a torturer of his brothers in misfortune? I don't want to believe it.

But yes, that's the way it was.

We arrived at the station, where the cattle cars were waiting. Ever since my book *Night* I have pursued those nocturnal trains that crossed the devastated continent. Their shadow haunts my writing. They symbolize solitude, distress, and the relentless march of Jewish multitudes toward agony and death. I freeze every time I hear a train whistle.

Why were those trains allowed to roll unhindered into Poland? Why were the tracks leading to Birkenau[14] never bombed? I have put these questions to American presidents and generals and to high-ranking Soviet officers. Since Moscow and Washington knew what the killers were doing in the death camps, why was nothing done at least to slow down their "production"? That not a single Allied military aircraft ever tried to destroy the rail lines converging on Auschwitz remains an outrageous enigma to me. Birkenau was "processing" ten thousand Jews a day. Stopping a single convoy for a single night—or even for just a few hours—would have prolonged so many lives. At the least it would have been a warning to the Germans: Jewish lives do matter. But the free world didn't care whether Jews lived or died, whether they were annihilated one day or the next. And so the sealed trains continued to shatter the silence of Europe's flowering landscapes.

Meanwhile, our world contracted[15] steadily. The country became a city, the city a street, the street a house, the house a room, the room a sealed cattle car, the cattle car a concrete cellar where . . .

No, let us go no further. Decency and custom forbid it. I said it earlier, when speaking of my grandfather: In Jewish tradition a man's death belongs to him alone. Let the gas chambers remain closed to prying eyes, and to the imagination. We will never know all that happened behind those doors of steel. They say the victims fought among themselves for a breath of air, for one more second of life, that they climbed on the shoulders of the weakest in the so-called *Todeskampf*, the final struggle among the dying. Much has been said when silence ought to have prevailed. Let the dead speak for themselves, if they so choose. If not, may they be left in peace.

---

13. *Kapo* refers to a prisoner who has been appointed by the enemy to police his or her own people.
14. *Birkenau* refers to Auschwitz-Birkenau, the most notorious of the Nazi concentration camps.

Vocabulary

succumb (sə kum´) *v.* to give in or submit to

---

15. Here, *contracted* means "shrunk, or made smaller."

Big Idea **The United States and the World** *How does Wiesel argue that international monitoring of human rights is necessary?*

Literary Element **Narrator** *What qualities make Wiesel an effective storyteller of the Holocaust?*

It is unbelievable how fast people adapt. It hurts to admit it, but within hours of first breathing the cattle car's nauseating air, we began to feel at home. "Home" was the edge of the wooden plank I sat on as I dreamed of the Jewish exiles of antiquity and the Middle Ages. More curious than afraid, I thought of myself as their brother. Mixed into my sadness there was undeniable excitement, for we were living a historic event, a historic adventure. The main thing was that we were still together. Had we been told that this journey would last for weeks or even years, we would have replied: May God grant that it be so, for nothing is worse than the unknown, and that was our destination—the unknown. I remember clinging to the thought that nothing is unknown to God, while nothing is truly known to man.

A rumor spread through the train. The Jewish doctors and their families, until recently allowed to live outside the ghetto, had been ordered to return to the ghetto the night before the transport and to join us that morning at the station. But we had seen no sign of them. It was now said that they had gathered at one of their homes the night before and decided to kill themselves. The rumor was apparently false, for in Birkenau I ran into our family doctor, Dr. Fisch, who had helped deliver Tsipouka. But thirty years later I found that the story was true after all. I was lecturing at a large university near Boston when a member of the physics department came up to me. "You're from Sighet, aren't you?" he asked. "So am I." He introduced himself, and the name gave me a start: he was the son of a famous surgeon. In Sighet we had evolved in different circles, but we had been brought to Auschwitz in the same convoy. We had a long talk about our town, and at one point I asked him about the rumor. He confirmed it. The doctors had indeed agreed on a collective suicide pact. "But why? Since at the time we didn't know where they were taking us." It turned out that his father did know. He had operated on a German officer who told him everything. Afterward he had summoned his colleagues to discuss what to do. The majority voted not to board the trains, deciding they might as well die at home. Some of the suicides did not succeed. They were carried to the cattle cars on stretchers.

My new friend the physics professor died one night in June 1991. A suicide, rumor had it. I was struck by the date. I realized that he too had died on the second day of the month of Sivan, exactly forty-seven years after his missed appointment with death in Birkenau.

Life in the cattle cars was the death of my adolescence. How quickly I aged. As a child I loved the unexpected: a visitor from afar, an unforeseen event, a marriage, a storm, even a disaster. Anything was preferable to routine. Now it was just the opposite. Anything was preferable to change. We clung to the present, we dreaded the future.

Hunger, thirst, and heat, the fetid[16] stench, the hysterical howling of a woman gone mad—we were ready to endure it all, to suffer it all. So much so that a "normal," structured social life soon took shape in the car. Families stayed together, sharing whatever came their way: hard-boiled eggs, dried cakes, or fruit, respecting strict rules about drinking water, allowing each member a turn near the barred openings or at the waste pail shielded by blankets. People adjusted with disconcerting rapidity. Morning and evening we said our prayers together. I had brought some precious books along in my pack: a commentary by Rabbi Haim David Azoulai (the Hida), the K'dushat Levi of the Berdichever Rebbe. I opened them and tried hard to concentrate. A phrase of the Zohar, a major work of the Kabala,[17] haunted me: When the people of Israel set out into exile, God went with them. And now? I wondered. How far would God follow us now?

On the last day, when the train stopped near the Auschwitz station, our **premonitions** resurfaced. A few "neighbors" devoured more than their rations, as though sensing that their

---

16. *Fetid* means "having a bad odor."
17. The *Kabala,* also spelled "Kabbalah," is a book of mystical teachings based on the Jewish faith.

Reading Strategy Activating Prior Knowledge *What do you know about the way people tend to react in a crisis? How does Wiesel's experience compare and contrast with your expectations?*

Vocabulary

premonition (prē´mə nish´ən) *n.* a warning, or foreboding about the future days were numbered. My mother kept entreating us: Stay together at all costs. Someone, I can't remember who, asked, "What if we can't? What if they separate us?" My mother's answer: "Then we'll meet again at home as soon as the war is over."

Certain images of the days and nights spent on that train invade my dreams even now: anticipation of danger, fear of the dark; the screams of poor Mrs. Schechter, who, in her delirium, saw flames in the distance; the efforts to make her stop; the terror in her little boy's eyes. I recall every hour, every second. How could I forget? They were the last hours I spent with my family: the murmured prayers of my grandmother, whose eyes saw beyond this world; my mother's gestures, which had never been more tender; the troubled face of my little sister, who refused to show her fear. Yes, my memory gathered it all in, retained it all.

There was sudden **trepidation** that gripped us when, toward midnight, the train lurched forward again after stopping for several hours. I can still hear the whistle. Elsewhere I have told of what happened next—or rather, I have tried to tell it. But it feels like yesterday. It feels like now. Through the cracks in the boards I see barbed wire stretching to infinity. A thought occurs to me: The Kabala is right, infinity exists.

I see myself sitting there, haggard and disoriented, a shadow among shadows. I hear my little sister's fitful breathing. I try to conjure up my mother's features, and my father's. I need someone to reassure me. My heart thunders in deafening beats. Then there is silence, heavy and complete. Something was about to happen, we could feel it. Fate would at last reveal a truth reserved exclusively for us, a primordial truth, an ultimate postulate[18] that would annihilate or

> I see myself sitting there, haggard and disoriented, a shadow among shadows.

overshadow all received ideas. There was a burst of noise and the night was shattered into a thousand pieces. I felt myself shaken, pulled to my feet, pushed toward the door, toward strange shouting beings and barking dogs, a swelling throng that would cover the earth.

In *Night* I tell of the wrath of the "veterans." They swore at us. "What the hell are you *Schweinehunde*[19] doing here?" I was puzzled. Did they think we had come to this hell voluntarily, out of curiosity? Only years later did I understand. Two of their former companions, Rudolf Vrba and Alfred Wetzler, had managed to escape from Birkenau in 1944 to warn Hungarian Jews of what was awaiting them. That's why they were so enraged. They thought we should have known. Some of them even hit us.

Where were we going? It mattered little, for it was the same everywhere. All roads led to the enemy; it was he who would throw open the invisible black door that awaited us. "Stay together," my mother said. For another minute we did, clinging to one another's arms. Nothing in the world could separate us. The entire German army could not take my little sister from me. Then a **curt** order was issued—men on one side, women on the other—and that was that. A single order, and we were separated. I stared intently, trying desperately not to lose sight of my mother, my little sister with her hair of gold and sun, my grandmother, my older sisters. I see them always, for I am still looking for them, trying to embrace them one last time. We were taken away before I could tell my mother goodbye, before I could kiss her hand and beg her forgiveness for the wrongs I must have done her, before I could squeeze

---

18. A *postulate* is a truth, or basic principle.

Vocabulary

trepidation (trep′ ə dā′ shən) *n.* a feeling of alarm or apprehension; dread

---

19. *Schweinehunde,* meaning "pig dogs," is a German word expressing a stereotypical insult.

Vocabulary

curt (kurt) *adj.* rudely brief, or short; terse

Tsipouka, my little sister, to my heart. What remains of that night like no other is an irremediable[20] sense of loss, of parting. My mother and my little sister left, and I never said goodbye. It all remains unreal. It's only a dream, I told myself as I walked, hanging on my father's arm. It's a nightmare that they have torn me from those I love, that they are beating people to death, that Birkenau exists and that it harbors a gigantic altar where demons of fire devour our people. It's in God's nightmare that human beings are hurling living Jewish children into the flames.

I reread what I have just written, and my hand trembles. I who barely weep am in tears. I see the flames again, and the children, and yet again I tell myself that it is not enough to weep.

It took me a long time to convince myself I was not somehow mistaken. I have checked with others who arrived that same night, consulted documents of the Sonderkommandos,[21] and yes, a thousand times yes: Unable to "handle" such a large number of Hungarian Jews in the crematoria, the killers were not content merely to incinerate children's dead bodies. In their barbarous madness they cast living Jewish children into specially tended furnaces.

And if I bear within me a nameless grief and disillusionment, a bottomless despair, it is because that night I saw good and thoughtful Jewish children, bearers of mute words and dreams, walking into darkness before being consumed by the flames. I see them now, and I still curse the killers, their accomplices, the indifferent spectators who knew and kept silent, and Creation itself, Creation and those who perverted and distorted it. I feel like screaming, howling like a madman so that that world, the world of the murderers, might know it will never be forgiven.

To this day I am shaken when I see a child, for behind him I glimpse other children. Starving, terrified, drained, they march without a backward glance toward truth and death—which are perhaps the same. Uncomplaining, unprotesting, asking no one's pity, it is as if they have had enough of living on a planet so cruel, so vile and so filled with hate that their very innocence has brought their death. Do not deny it, I forbid you to deny it. Know, then, that the world that let the killers annihilate a million and a half Jewish children bears its guilt within itself.

That night someone within me, my other self, told me it was impossible that these atrocities could be committed in the middle of the twentieth century while the world stayed silent. This was not the Middle Ages. My very last resistance broken, I let myself be pulled, pushed, and kicked, like a deaf and mute sleepwalker. I could see everything, grasp it and register it, but only later would I try to put in order all the sensations and all the memories. How stunned I was, for example, to discover another time outside time, a universe parallel to this one, a creation within Creation, with its own laws, customs, structures, and language. In this universe some men existed only to kill and others only to die. And the system functioned with exemplary efficiency: tormentors tormented and crushed their prey, torturers tortured human beings whom they met for the first time, slaughterers slaughtered their victims without so much as a glance, flames rose to heaven and nothing ever jammed the mechanism. It was as if it all unfolded according to a plan decreed from the beginning of time.

And what of human ideals, or of the beauty of innocence or the weight of justice? And what of God in all that?

I didn't understand, though I wanted to. Ask any survivor and you will hear the same thing: above all, we tried to understand. Why all these deaths? What was the point of this death factory? How to account for the demented mind that devised this black hole of history called Birkenau?

Perhaps there was nothing to understand. ❧

---

20. *Irremediable* means "impossible to correct."
21. *Sonderkommandos* refers to "special commandos," a group of Jewish prisoners whose job was to maintain and clean the crematoria, or gas chambers.

Big Idea The United States and the World *What do you think is Wiesel's purpose in spreading the blame for the atrocities of the Holocaust?*

AFTER YOU READ

RESPONDING AND THINKING CRITICALLY

Respond

1. How did you react to Wiesel's account of the Holocaust?

Recall and Interpret

2. (a)How does Wiesel's family handle the order to leave their home? (b)What do you think their response shows about them?

3. (a)How has Wiesel's home changed when he returns to it years later? (b)What does this suggest about the power of memory?

4. (a)When is Wiesel separated from his sister and his mother? (b)What does this say about the nature of life for Jewish people during this era?

Analyze and Evaluate

5. What does Wiesel's report of the differing accounts he has heard about the fate of his Uncle Mendel demonstrate?

6. Why do you think Wiesel decides not to describe the gas chambers?

7. How do the interludes in which Wiesel describes conversations with fellow Holocaust survivors add to his memoir?

8. How do you reconcile Wiesel's final statement in this selection, "Perhaps there was nothing to understand"?

Connect

9. **Big Idea** **The United States and the World** Wiesel describes the concentration camp as a world of its own, operating on a system of values totally foreign to the outside world. How does he respond to this environment?

LITERARY ANALYSIS

Literary Element Narrator

In a memoir such as Wiesel's, the writer is the **narrator.** This creates a first-person point of view that offers the reader a distinct insight into the narrator's experiences.

1. (a)How does Wiesel offer a unique perspective on the Holocaust? (b)What does he leave out of his account?

2. (a)What method of storytelling does Wiesel employ as a narrator? (b)How does this method contribute to the selection?

Review: Autobiography

As you learned in Unit One, an **autobiography** is the story an author writes about his or her own life. A **memoir** is a specific type of autobiography—an account of an event or a period in the author's life that emphasizes the author's personal experience. *All Rivers Run to the Sea* is a memoir in that it reexamines Wiesel's holocaust experience and its repercussions on his life and on the world.

1. How does Wiesel's memoir *All Rivers Run to the Sea* differ from a traditional autobiography? Think about Wiesel's use of flashback.

2. Do you think that Wiesel wrote this memoir for himself or for others? Explain.

Partner Activity *All Rivers Run to the Sea* hinges on Wiesel's skillful melding of childhood recollections with reflections as an adult on the past. Both contribute to a picture of Wiesel as a person. Meet with another classmate to discuss your impressions of Wiesel's character and personality. Then present your findings to the class.

Literary Criticism

Group Activity Brad Hopper of *Booklist* wrote in a review of *All Rivers Run to the Sea,* "[Wiesel] cease-lessly pricks the conscience of a world that thinks it is possible to have heard 'enough' about the Holocaust." Do you agree with this statement? Meet with a few of your classmates to write three blurbs—short descriptions from reviews that might appear on a book jacket for *All Rivers Run to the Sea.*

READING AND VOCABULARY

Reading Strategy Activating Prior Knowledge

You derive meaning from literature by **activating prior knowledge,** or combining what you already know with the information provided in the text. Even if you have not endured the same experiences as the writer or character, there are many experiences you have had that can help you understand the text.

1. Cite two examples of details in the text that you were instantly able to connect with given your prior knowledge or experience.

2. Memoirs are narrated from the first-person point of view and often include very personal details from the writer's life. Do you think that this makes it easier or more difficult to connect with the speaker? Explain.

Partner Activity What prior knowledge did you activate as you read Wiesel's memoir? Meet with another classmate to discuss your experience of reading about the atrocities of the Holocaust.

Vocabulary Practice

Practice with Word Parts Below are three groups of words. Each group consists of a vocabulary word from *All Rivers Run to the Sea,* followed by three other words that share a word part. For each group, explain the meaning of the shared part. Use a dictionary if you need to.

1. **ineffably**
   incapable   inability   inadequate
2. **premonition**
   preconceived   premature   preview
3. **trepidation**
   instigation   congratulation manifestation

Literature Online **Web Activities** For eFlashcards, Selection Quick Checks, and other Web activities, go to www.glencoe.com.

WRITING AND EXTENDING

Writing About Literature

Respond to Theme and Craft In *All Rivers Run to the Sea,* Wiesel writes, "This was where my childhood and my adolescence, my prayers, studies, and fasting had led. These moments would remain forever etched within me." Write a brief essay explaining how this statement informs and drives Wiesel's narrative. Use evidence from the memoir and examples from your own experience to explain your response. Pay particular attention to the way that Wiesel comes back to this moment during various parts of his life and how he weaves details from different times in his life into a cohesive narrative.

As you draft, write from start to finish. Follow the writing path shown here to help you organize your essay and keep on track.

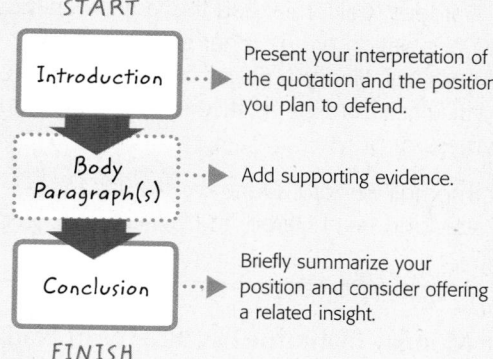

After you complete your draft, meet with a peer reviewer to evaluate each other's work and to suggest revisions. Then proofread and edit your work for errors in spelling, grammar, and punctuation.

Interdisciplinary Activity: Government

The Danger of Propaganda Hitler and the Third Reich used propaganda to gather support for their brutal campaign against the Jews. Their techniques included scapegoating and stereotyping. By blaming Jews for all the problems in Germany, the Nazis used them as scapegoats and rallied support. By stereotyping the Jews as "subhuman," the Nazis attempted to convince the public that the Jews did not deserve rights. Research Nazi propaganda, including the persuasive techniques that this propaganda employs.

from Kubota

Garrett Hongo

BEFORE YOU READ

Building Background

Although Garrett Hongo was born in Hawaii in 1951, his family moved to southern California when he was six. On the mainland, he interacted with many groups of immigrants, each with rich, diverse cultures. His town of Gardena, California, had the largest Japanese American population of any other city except for Honolulu, Hawaii. Hongo's poetry frequently touches on the difficulties immigrants face in U.S. society and the bitterness of prejudice.

Hongo's memoir *Kubota* addresses the Japanese military attack on Pearl Harbor in Hawaii that prompted the United States to enter World War II. Although Hongo was not alive during this attack, his family was deeply affected by it. During the war, more than 120,000 Japanese Americans were forced to live in internment camps set up by the U.S. government. Decades later the government apologized for this injustice and paid reparations.

Garrett Hongo was born in 1951.

Literature Online **Author Search** For more about Garrett Hongo, go to www.glencoe.com.

It was a Monday night, the day after Pearl Harbor, and there was a rattling knock at the front door. Two FBI agents presented themselves, showed identification, and took my grandfather in for questioning in Honolulu. He didn't return home for days. No one knew what had happened or what was wrong. But there was a roundup going on of all those in the Japanese-American community suspected of sympathizing with the enemy and worse.

My grandfather was suspected of espionage,[1] of communicating with offshore Japanese submarines launched from the attack fleet days before the war began. Torpedo planes and escort fighters, decorated with the insignia of the Rising Sun, had taken an approach route from northwest of Oahu directly across Kahuku Point and on toward Pearl. They had strafed[2] an auxiliary air station near the fishing grounds my grandfather loved and destroyed a small gun battery there, killing three men. Kubota[3] was known to have sponsored and harbored Japanese nationals in his own home. He had a radio. He had wholesale access to firearms. Circumstances and an undertone of racial resentment had combined with wartime hysteria in the aftermath of the tragic naval battle to cast suspicion on the loyalties of my grandfather and all other Japanese Americans. The FBI reached out and pulled hundreds of them in for questioning in dragnets cast throughout the West Coast and Hawaii.

My grandfather was lucky; he'd somehow been let go after only a few days. Others were not as fortunate. Hundreds, from small communities in Washington, California, Oregon, and Hawaii, were rounded up and, after what appeared to be routine questioning, shipped off under Justice

---

1. *Espionage* means spying.
2. *Strafed* means "attacked with machine guns from low-flying aircraft."

3. *Kubota* (ko͞o bō′tä)

Department orders to holding centers in Leuppe on the Navaho reservation in Arizona, in Fort Missoula in Montana, and on Sand Island in Honolulu Harbor. There were other special camps on Maui in Ha'iku and on Hawaii—the Big Island—in my own home village of Volcano.

Many of these men—it was exclusively the Japanese-American men suspected of ties to Japan who were initially rounded up—did not see their families again for more than four years. Under a suspension of due process[4] that was only after the fact ruled as warranted by military necessity, they were, if only temporarily, "disappeared" in Justice Department prison camps scattered in particularly desolate areas of the United States designated as militarily "safe." These were grim forerunners of the assembly centers and concentration camps for the 120,000 Japanese-American evacuees that were to come later.

I am Kubota's eldest grandchild, and I remember him as a lonely, habitually silent old man who lived with us in our home near Los Angeles for most of my childhood and adolescence. It was the fifties, and my parents had emigrated from Hawaii to the mainland in the hope of a better life away from the old sugar plantation. After some success, they had sent back for my grandparents and taken them in. And it was my grandparents who did the work of the household while my mother and father worked their salaried city jobs. My grandmother cooked and sewed, washed our clothes, and knitted in the front room under the light of a huge lamp with a bright three-way bulb. Kubota raised a flower garden, read up on soils and grasses in gardening books, and planted a zoysia lawn in front and a dichondra[5] one in back. He planted a small patch near the rear block wall with green onions, eggplant, white Japanese radishes, and cucumber. While he hoed and spaded the loamless, clayey earth of Los Angeles, he sang particularly plangent[6] songs in Japanese about plum blossoms and bamboo groves.

Once, in the mid-sixties, after a dinner during which, as always, he had been silent while he worked away at a meal of fish and rice spiced with dabs of Chinese mustard and catsup thinned with soy sauce, Kubota took his own dishes to the kitchen sink and washed them up. He took a clean jelly jar out of the cupboard—the glass was thick and its shape squatty like an old-fashioned. He reached around to the hutch below where he kept his bourbon. He made himself a drink and retired to the living room where I was expected to join him for "talk story," the Hawaiian idiom for chewing the fat.

I was a teenager and, though I was bored listening to stories I'd heard often enough before at holiday dinners, I was dutiful. I took my spot on the couch next to Kubota and heard him out. Usually, he'd tell me about his schooling in Japan where he learned judo along with mathematics and literature. He'd learned the *soroban* there— the abacus, which was the original pocket calculator of the Far East—and that, along with his strong, judo-trained back, got him his

Visual Vocabulary
On an abacus the positions of beads stand for numbers.

first job in Hawaii. This was the moral. "Study *ha-ahd*," he'd say with pidgin[7] emphasis. "Learn read good. Learn speak da kine *good* English." The message is the familiar one taught to any children of immigrants: succeed through education. And imitation. But this time, Kubota reached down into his past and told me a different story. I was thirteen by then, and I suppose he thought me ready for it. He told me about Pearl Harbor, how the planes flew in wing after wing of formations over his old house in La'ie in Hawaii, and how, the next day, after Roosevelt[8] had made his famous "Day of Infamy" speech about the treachery of the Japanese, the FBI agents had come to his door and taken him in,

---

4. *Due process* is the administration of the law according to prescribed procedures.
5. *Zoysia* (zoi ′ zhə) is a type of grass. *Dichondra* (dī kän′ drə) is a type of herb used for lawns.
6. *Plangent* (plan′ jənt) can mean either "mournful" or "loud and echoing."

7. *Pidgin* (pij′ ən) is a hybrid language that is a mixture of two or more languages and that has a simplified vocabulary and grammatical structure.
8. President Franklin D. *Roosevelt* (1882–1945) addressed Congress the day after the bombing of Pearl Harbor on December 7, 1941, saying it was "a date which will live in infamy."

Barracks, Tule Lake,
California, 1945. Taneyuki
Dan Harada. Oil on canvas,
27 x 31 in. Collection of
Michael D. Brown.

hauled him off to Honolulu for questioning, and held him without charge for several days. I thought he was lying. I thought he was making up a kind of horror story to shock me and give his moral that much more starch. But it was true. I asked around. I brought it up during history class in junior high school, and my teacher, after silencing me and stepping me off to the back of the room, told me that it was indeed so. I asked my mother and she said it was true. I asked my schoolmates, who laughed and ridiculed me for being so ignorant. We lived in a Japanese-American community, and the parents of most of my classmates were the *nisei*[9] who had been interned[10] as teenagers all through the war. But there was a strange silence around all of this. There was a hush, as if one were invoking the ill powers of the dead when one brought it up. No one cared to speak

about the evacuation and relocation for very long. It wasn't in our history books, though we were studying World War II at the time. It wasn't in the family albums of the people I knew and whom I'd visit staying over weekends with friends. And it wasn't anything that the family talked about or allowed me to keep bringing up either. I was given the facts, told sternly and pointedly that "it was war" and that "nothing could be done." *"Shikatta ga nai"*[11] is the phrase in Japanese, a kind of resolute and determinist pronouncement on how to deal with inexplicable tragedy. I was to know it but not to dwell on it. Japanese Americans were busy trying to forget it ever happened and were having a hard enough time building their new lives after "camp." It was as if we had no history for four years and the relocation was something unspeakable.

But Kubota would not let it go. In session after session, for months it seemed, he pounded away at his story. He wanted to tell me the

9. The Japanese word *nisei* (nē′ sā) refers to children of Japanese immigrants; that is, the first generation of Japanese Americans born in the United States.
10. *Interned* means "confined or restricted to a particular place, especially during war."

11. *"Shikatta ga nai"* is pronounced (shē kä′ tä gä nī).

names of the FBI agents. He went over their questions and his responses again and again. He'd tell me how one would try to act friendly toward him, offering him cigarettes while the other, who hounded him with accusations and threats, left the interrogation room. Good cop, bad cop, I thought to myself, already superficially streetwise from stories black classmates told of the Watts[12] riots and from my having watched too many episodes of *Dragnet* and *The Mod Squad*.[13] But Kubota was not interested in my experiences. I was not made yet, and he was determined that his stories be part of my making. He spoke quietly at first, mildly, but once into his narrative and after his drink was down, his voice would rise and quaver with resentment and he'd make his accusations. He gave his testimony to me and I held it at first cautiously in my conscience like it was an heirloom too delicate to expose to strangers and anyone outside of the world Kubota made with his words. "I give you story now," he once said, "and you learn speak good, eh?" It was my job, as the disciple of his preaching I had then become, Ananda to his Buddha,[14] to reassure him with a promise. "You learn speak good like the Dillingham," he'd say another time, referring to the wealthy scion of the grower family who had once run, unsuccessfully, for one of Hawaii's first senatorial seats. Or he'd then invoke a magical name, the name of one of his heroes, a man he thought particularly exemplary and righteous. "Learn speak dah good Ing-rish like *Mistah Inouye*," Kubota shouted. "He *lick* dah Dillingham even in debate. I saw on *terre-bision* myself." He

Visual Vocabulary
Daniel K. Inouye (in′ ō ye′) (born 1924), was the first Japanese American to serve in congress as a U.S. Senator from Hawaii.

was remembering the debates before the first senatorial election just before Hawaii was admitted to the Union as its fiftieth state. "You *tell* story," Kubota would end. And I had my injunction.[15]

The town we settled in after the move from Hawaii is called Gardena, the independently incorporated city south of Los Angeles and north of San Pedro harbor. At its northern limit, it borders on Watts and Compton, black towns. To the southwest are Torrance and Redondo Beach, white towns. To the rest of L.A., Gardena is primarily famous for having legalized five-card draw poker after the war. On Vermont Boulevard, its eastern border, there is a dingy little Vegas-like strip of card clubs with huge parking lots and flickering neon signs that spell out "The Rainbow" and "The Horseshoe" in timed sequences of varicolored lights. The town is only secondarily famous as the largest community of Japanese Americans in the United States outside of Honolulu, Hawaii. When I was in high school there, it seemed to me that every *sansei*[16] kid I knew wanted to be a doctor, an engineer, or a pharmacist. Our fathers were gardeners or electricians or nurserymen or ran small businesses catering to other Japanese Americans. Our mothers worked in civil service for the city or as cashiers for Thrifty Drug. What the kids wanted was a good job, good pay, a fine home, and no troubles. No one wanted to mess with the law—from either side—and no one wanted to mess with language or art. They all talked about getting into the right clubs so that they could go to the right schools. There was a certain kind of sameness, an intensely enforced system of conformity. Style was all. Boys wore moccasin-sewn shoes from Flagg Brothers, black A-1 slacks, and Kensington shirts with high collars. Girls wore

Visual Vocabulary
A *bouffant* (bo͞o fänt′) is a hairstyle in which the hair is puffed out.

their hair up in stiff bouffants solidified in hairspray and knew all the latest dances from the

---

12. *Watts,* a section of Los Angeles, was the site of severe racial violence in 1965.
13. *Dragnet* and *The Mod Squad* were popular television police shows.
14. *Buddha* (563?–483? B.C.) was the title given to Siddhartha Gautama (si där′ tə gou′ tə mə), the founder of Buddhism. *Ananda* (ä nän′ dä) was his cousin and "Beloved Disciple."

15. An *injunction* is a command or an order.
16. The *sansei* (sän′ sā′) are the children of the *nisei.*

Japanese Americans interned at Santa Anita.
Viewing the Photograph: What insights into the Japanese American internment do you get from this photograph?

slauson to the funky chicken. We did well in chemistry and in math, no one who was Japanese but me spoke in English class or in history unless called upon, and no one talked about World War II. The day after Robert Kennedy was assassinated, after winning the California Democratic primary, we worked on calculus and elected class coordinators for the prom, featuring the 5th Dimension.[17] We avoided grief. We avoided government. We avoided strong feelings and dangers of any kind. Once punished, we tried to maintain a concerted emotional and social discipline and would not willingly seek to fall out of the narrow margin of protective favor again.

But when I was thirteen, in junior high, I'd not understood why it was so difficult for my classmates, those who were themselves Japanese American, to talk about the relocation. They had cringed, too, when I tried to bring it up during our discussions of World War II. I was Hawaiian-born.

They were mainland-born. Their parents had been in camp, had been the ones to suffer the complicated experience of having to distance themselves from their own history and all things Japanese in order to make their way back and into the American social and economic mainstream. It was out of this sense of shame and a fear of stigma I was only beginning to understand that the *nisei* had silenced themselves. And, for their children, among whom I grew up, they wanted no heritage, no culture, no contact with a defiled history. I recall the silence very well. The Japanese-American children around me were burdened in a way I was not. Their injunction was silence. Mine was to speak. ༄

---

17. The 5th Dimension was a popular music group in the late 1960s.

Quickwrite

Is Kubota right to urge his grandson to discuss what happened to Japanese Americans during World War II? Why do you think some people seem to disagree with this stance? Write a short response in which you explain your position. Support your argument with details from the selection and historical information.

from

MAUS

A SURVIVOR'S TALE

MY FATHER BLEEDS HISTORY

Art Spiegelman

BEFORE YOU READ

Building Background

Art Spiegelman learned to read by reading comics and, in turn, has taught a generation of readers that the comic book, or graphic novel, format can be as powerful as any other form of literature. He observes, "There've been lots of rotten novels and paintings, and zillions of rotten comics. But in the hands of someone who knows how to use their medium, great things can happen." Born in Stockholm, Sweden, Spiegelman came to the U.S. as a child. In high school he studied cartooning. At sixteen, he started drawing professionally, and, after leaving college, he soon became an important figure in the underground comics movement of the late 1960s.

Born in Poland, Spiegelman's Jewish parents were both sent to Auschwitz by the Nazis. Though they survived, Spiegelman's mother, Anja (to whom *Maus* is dedicated), eventually committed suicide in 1968. During the 1970s, Spiegelman began to create comics based on his father's (Vladek's) memories of the Nazi occupation of Poland. Between 1980 and 1986, these efforts grew into *Maus: A Survivor's Tale*, a full-length graphic novel. He published a sequel, *Maus II,* in 1991.

Spiegelman portrays not only his father's experiences but also his relationship with his father, both when he was a child and when he was an adult. Throughout the books, Spiegelman represents the Jews as mice and the Nazis as cats. Other groups are represented by different animals. In 1992 Spiegelman was awarded a Pulitzer Prize for *Maus,* the first time a graphic-novel artist had received this award.

There are several unfamiliar terms and people mentioned in the excerpt that follows. The German word *gemeinde* refers to a Jewish committee within the community. Richieu is the first son of Vladek and Anja, Spiegelman's parents. Richieu was sent to live with relatives during the war, but he did not survive the Holocaust. Lolek and Lonia are cousins of the Spiegelmans. Tosha and Wolfe are Anja's older sister and her husband.

Art Spiegelman was born in 1948.

Literature Online **Author Search** For more about Art Spiegelman, go to www.glencoe.com.

Discussion Starter

Graphic novels combine words and pictures. In the work of some comic artists, graphic elements dominate; in the work of others, words have greater importance. Look over these panels from *Maus* to determine the balance between words and pictures in Art Spiegelman's work. With a group of classmates, discuss how the imagery and words work together and how one panel transitions into the next.

Wrap-Up: Comparing Literature *Across Time and Place*

- from *All Rivers Run to the Sea*
  Elie Wiesel

- from *Kubota*
  Garrett Hongo

- from *Maus: A Survivor's Tale*
  Art Spiegelman

COMPARING THE Big Idea The United States and the World

Group Activity Multiculturalism is an increasingly important and respected feature of U.S. society. With a group of classmates, discuss the following questions.

1. In what ways do Wiesel and Spiegelman address the need to tell the truth about the establishment of concentration camps by the Nazis in the 1930s and 1940s?
2. What does Kubota hope to accomplish by asking Hongo to tell his story about Japanese American internment?
3. Evaluate the statements about history and personal expression made in these selections. Which of them did you find most powerful? Explain.

COMPARING Reflections

Writing Activity The stories in these works explore the lives of people who have survived particularly difficult experiences. Read the following quotations from the selections. Then write a brief essay, evaluating how the quotes exemplify the way these selections explore the significance of personal experience.

> "I freeze every time I hear a train whistle."
>
> —Elie Wiesel, *All Rivers Run to the Sea*

> "I brought it up during history class in junior high school, and my teacher, after silencing me and stepping me off to the back of the room, told me that it was indeed so."
>
> —Garrett Hongo, *Kubota*

> "Well . . . It's enough for today. Yes, Artie?"
>
> —Art Spiegelman, *Maus*

Children liberated from a Nazi concentration camp show the numbers tattooed on their arms.

COMPARING Cultures

Visual Display The horrors of World War II had a great impact on various cultures in different ways. From the selections you have read, create a three-panel collage of images—one for each selection—that illustrates the experiences of these cultures during the war.

INDIANA ACADEMIC STANDARDS (page 998)
11.3.5 Analyze...works of literary or cultural significance...that...shed light on the seminal philosophical...social, political, or ethical ideas of their time.

from *Hiroshima*

MEET JOHN HERSEY

John Hersey spent his adult life bearing witness to some of the pivotal events of the twentieth century. Hersey was born in China to missionary parents, but he spent most of his life writing about the United States' military influence in other countries.

After Hersey's father died from an illness he contracted in China, the family settled in New York. Hersey attended Yale University, where he studied English literature and began his professional career working for the *Yale Daily News*. His first job after college was as private secretary to the Nobel Prize-winning writer Sinclair Lewis.

"Journalism allows its readers to witness history; fiction gives its readers an opportunity to live it."

—John Hersey

On the War Front Between 1937 and 1946, Hersey worked for *Time* and *Life* magazines as a foreign correspondent in the Pacific. To write his first book, *Men on Bataan*, he combined his own experience with other sources, including letters, speeches, and memos written by the soldiers stationed in the Pacific. One aspect of the book that captured the attention of critics was Hersey's ability to combine fictional techniques—such as characterization, description, and foreshadowing—with factual reporting. His later experiences in Italy were reshaped into his first novel, *A Bell for Adano*, for which Hersey was awarded the 1945 Pulitzer Prize for fiction.

Hiroshima In 1945, the nuclear age began when United States forces dropped atomic bombs on Hiroshima and Nagasaki, two Japanese cities.

Although much was written about the event at the time, most of those articles were recitations of facts and statistics. Hersey wanted to alert the public to the nightmarish aftermath of the bombing and its human and moral consequences.

Hersey spent several weeks interviewing people in Japan and writing about the devastation he witnessed in Hiroshima. A few months later, the *New Yorker*, a publication renowned for its literary quality, devoted all of its editorial space to Hersey's piece. The work created an unprecedented amount of interest in the publishing world. The book's publication not only established Hersey's literary reputation but also originated a new type of literary journalism that went beyond mere reporting of events to capture the human toll of a wartime incident. *Hiroshima's* focus on the human costs of war prompted years of discussion about nuclear weapons and their moral implications.

Truth as Fiction Hersey wrote that he believed that fiction better allowed him to depict reality. "It makes truth plausible," he wrote. Hersey continued to write books that dealt with important issues of his times: war, education, racism, and politics. Hersey was such an important literary figure that his death in 1993 was front-page news. *New York Times* writer Richard Severo described him "not only as a first-rate reporter but also as a storyteller who nurtured the idea that writers had to pursue a moral goal."

John Hersey was born in 1914 and died in 1993.

Literature Online **Author Search** For more about John Hersey, go to www.glencoe.com.

Connecting to the Story

Hersey wrote about ordinary people and war's effect on their lives. As you read the excerpt, think about the following questions:

- Under what circumstances, if any, do you think the dropping of an atomic bomb would be necessary?
- What does this selection show about the effects of war on ordinary civilians?

Building Background

In 1945, the United States and Japan were adversaries in World War II. As the war dragged on, casualties mounted on both sides. The Japanese had been warned that they would face "utter destruction" if they did not surrender, but many officials predicted that the island nation would continue to fight. On August 6, a B-29 aircraft named the *Enola Gay* dropped the first atomic bomb ever used in wartime.

Setting Purposes for Reading

Big Idea The United States and the World

As you read this selection, think about why the world came to see nuclear warfare as something to be avoided at all costs.

Literary Element Point of View

Point of view is the perspective from which the narrator tells the story. In **first-person point of view**, the narrator is a character in the story and uses "I" or "me" to tell the story. In **third-person point of view**, the narrator is not a character but describes the action and the characters from outside the story. In **third-person omniscient point of view**, the narrator is all-knowing. In **third-person limited**, the narrator describes only what one character could know. In **objective point of view**, the narrator knows only what can be heard and seen about the characters. As you read the excerpt, examine how point of view affects your understanding of the narrative.

- See Literary Terms Handbook, p. R14.

Literature Online **Interactive Literary Elements Handbook** To review or learn more about the literary elements, go to www.glencoe.com.

Reading Strategy Drawing Conclusions About Author's Beliefs

When you **draw conclusions,** you use a number of clues to make a general statement about something. Often, by looking at the types of details that an author includes and omits, you can draw some conclusions about that author's beliefs.

....

Reading Tip: Chart Clues Use a graphic organizer to record details that you will use to draw conclusions about the author's beliefs.

| Detail | Detail | Detail |

| Conclusion |

Vocabulary

evacuate (i vak′ū āt′) *v.* to vacate or leave a place; p. 1001 *Citizens were told to evacuate the city if they heard a siren.*

volition (vō lish′ən) *n.* act of choosing or deciding; p. 1001 *They were in the right place by accident rather than volition.*

debris (də brē′) *n.* large number of fragments or broken pieces; p. 1005 *The explosion filled the streets with debris.*

xenophobic (zen′ə fō′bik) *adj.* having an extreme fear of foreigners or strangers; p. 1007 *The people were xenophobic and trusted no newcomers.*

terminus (tur′mə nəs) *n.* one end of a travel route or the station placed there; p. 1008 *When the train entered the terminus, the passengers collected their belongings and prepared to disembark.*

INDIANA ACADEMIC STANDARDS (pages 1000–1012)

11.3.3 Analyze the ways in which...author's style...achieve[s] specific aesthetic (artistic) purposes...

11.2.5 Analyze an author's...beliefs about a subject.

11.5.4 Write historical investigation reports...

11.4.7 Develop presentations using clear research questions and...interviews...

from
Hiroshima

John Hersey

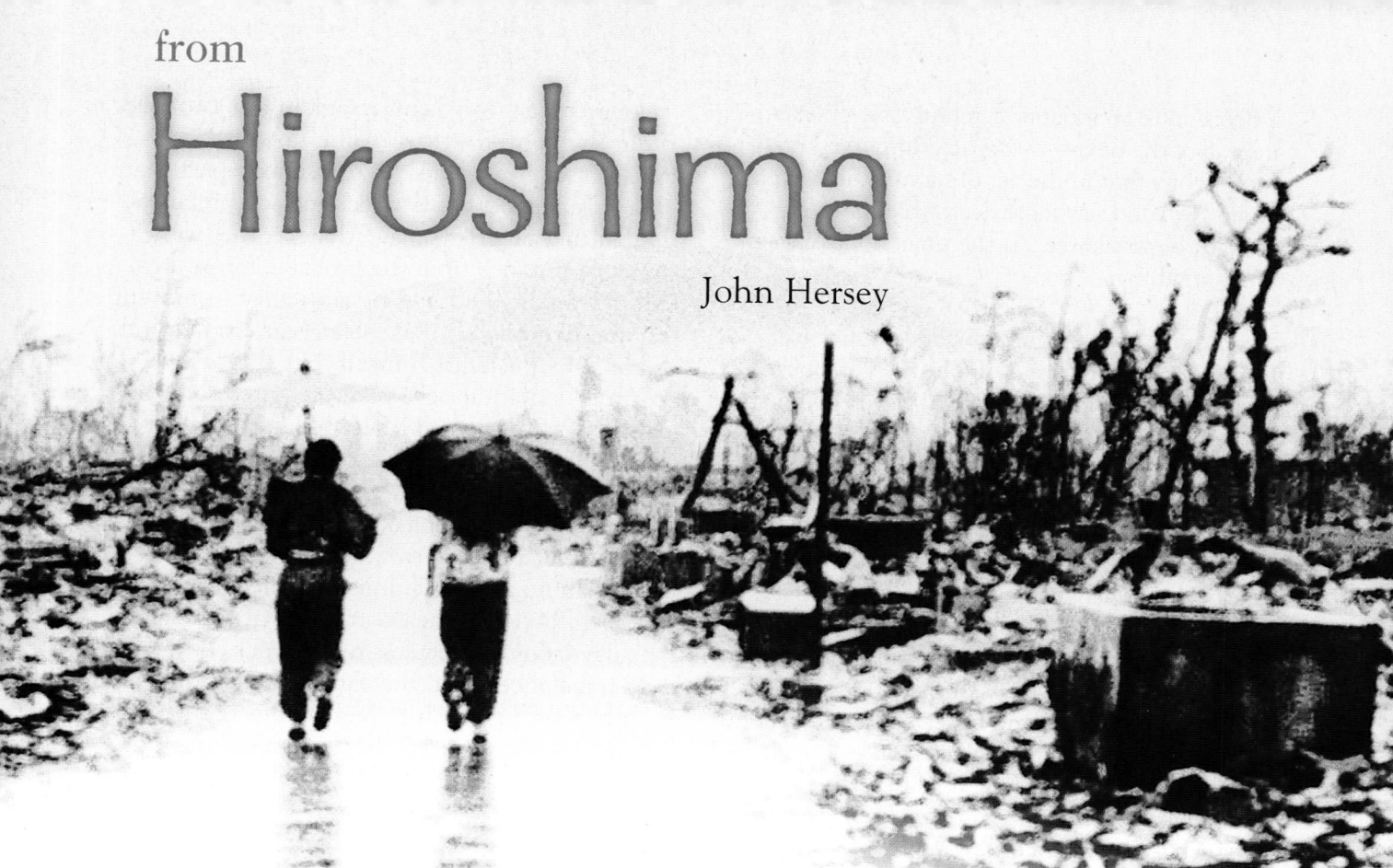

At exactly fifteen minutes past eight in the morning, on August 6, 1945, Japanese time, at the moment when the atomic bomb flashed above Hiroshima, Miss Toshiko Sasaki, a clerk in the personnel department of the East Asia Tin Works, had just sat down at her place in the plant office and was turning her head to speak to the girl at the next desk. At that same moment, Dr. Masakazu Fujii was settling down cross-legged to read the Osaka *Asahi* on the porch of his private hospital, overhanging one of the seven deltaic[1] rivers which divide Hiroshima; Mrs. Hatsuyo Nakamura, a tailor's widow, stood by the window of her kitchen, watching a neighbor tearing down his house because it lay in the path of an air-raid-defense fire lane; Father Wilhelm Kleinsorge, a German priest of the Society of Jesus, reclined in his underwear on a cot on the top floor of his order's three-story mission house, reading a Jesuit magazine, *Stimmen der Zeit*; Dr. Terufumi Sasaki, a young member of the surgical staff of the city's large, modern Red Cross Hospital, walked along one of the hospital corridors with a blood specimen for a Wassermann test[2] in his hand; and the Reverend Mr. Kiyoshi Tanimoto, pastor of the Hiroshima Methodist Church, paused at the door of a rich man's house in Koi, the city's western suburb, and prepared to unload a handcart full of things he had **evacuated** from town in fear of the massive B-29 raid which everyone expected Hiroshima to suffer. A hundred thousand people were killed by the atomic bomb, and these six were among the survivors. They still wonder why they lived when so many others died. Each of them counts many small items of chance or **volition**—a step taken in time,

---

1. *Deltaic* refers to a delta that forms at the mouth of a river. The city of Hiroshima straddles six channels and several islets that make up the delta at the mouth of the Ota River.

2. A *Wasserman test* is a blood test once widely used to diagnose syphilis.

Literary Element   Point of View *Based on your reading of the first paragraph, what kind of point of view does Hersey use?*

Vocabulary

evacuate (i vak′ū āt′) *v.* to vacate or leave a place
volition (vō lish′ ən) *n.* act of choosing or deciding

a decision to go indoors, catching one streetcar instead of the next—that spared him. And now each knows that in the act of survival he lived a dozen lives and saw more death than he ever thought he would see. At the time, none of them knew anything.

The Reverend Mr. Tanimoto got up at five o'clock that morning. He was alone in the parsonage, because for some time his wife had been commuting with their year-old baby to spend nights with a friend in Ushida, a suburb to the north. Of all the important cities of Japan, only two, Kyoto and Hiroshima, had not been visited in strength if *B-san*, or Mr. B, as the Japanese, with a mixture of respect and unhappy familiarity, called the B-29; and Mr. Tanimoto, like all his neighbors and friends, was almost sick with anxiety. He had heard uncomfortably detailed accounts of mass raids on Kure, Iwakuni, Tokuyama, and other nearby towns; he was sure Hiroshima's turn would come soon. He had slept badly the night before, because there had been several air-raid warnings. Hiroshima had been getting such warnings almost every night for weeks, for at that time the B-29s were using Lake Biwa, northeast of Hiroshima, as a rendezvous point, and no matter what city the Americans planned to hit, the Superfortresses streamed in over the coast near Hiroshima. The frequency of the warnings and the continued abstinence of Mr. B with respect to Hiroshima had made its citizens jittery; a rumor was going around that the Americans were saving something special for the city.

Mr. Tanimoto is a small man, quick to talk, laugh, and cry. He wears his black hair parted in the middle and rather long; the prominence of the frontal bones just above his eyebrows and the smallness of his moustache, mouth, and chin give him a strange, old-young look, boyish and yet wise, weak and yet fiery. He moves nervously and fast, but with a restraint which suggests that he is a cautious, thoughtful man. He showed, indeed, just those qualities in the uneasy days before the bomb fell. Besides having his wife spend the nights in Ushida, Mr. Tanimoto had been carrying all the portable things from his church, in the close-packed residential district called Nagaragawa, to a house that belonged to a rayon manufacturer in Koi, two miles from the center of town. The rayon man, a Mr. Matsui, had opened his then unoccupied estate to a large number of his friends and acquaintances, so that they might evacuate whatever they wished to a safe distance from the probable target area. Mr. Tanimoto had had no difficulty in moving chairs, hymnals, Bibles, altar gear, and church records by pushcart himself, but the organ console and an upright piano required some aid. A friend of his named Matsuo had, the day before, helped him get the piano out to Koi; in return, he had promised this day to assist Mr. Matsuo in hauling out a daughter's belongings. That is why he had risen so early.

Mr. Tanimoto cooked his own breakfast. He felt awfully tired. The effort of moving the piano the day before, a sleepless night, weeks of worry and unbalanced diet, the cares of his parish—all combined to make him feel hardly adequate to the new day's work. There was another thing, too: Mr. Tanimoto had studied theology at Emory College, in Atlanta, Georgia; he had graduated in 1940; he spoke excellent English; he dressed in American clothes; he had corresponded with many American friends right up to the time the war began; and among a people obsessed with a fear of being spied upon—perhaps almost obsessed himself—he found himself growing increasingly uneasy. The police had questioned him several times, and just a few days before, he had heard that an influential acquaintance, a Mr. Tanaka, a retired officer of the Toyo Kisen Kaisha steamship line, an anti-Christian, a man famous in Hiroshima for his showy philanthropies[3] and notorious for his personal tyrannies, had been telling people that Tanimoto should not be trusted. In compensation, to show himself publicly a good Japanese, Mr. Tanimoto had taken on the chairmanship of his local *tonarigumi*, or Neighborhood Association, and to his other duties and concerns this position

---

3. *Philanthropies* are good works designed to benefit people.

Literary Element Point of View *How does the point of view affect your understanding of Mr. Tanimoto?*

Reading Strategy Drawing Conclusions About Author's Beliefs *Which words and phrases show the author's disdain for certain personality traits?*

Big Idea The United States and the World *Why are the people of Hiroshima so worried about the Americans?*

had added the business of organizing air-raid defense for about twenty families.

Before six o'clock that morning, Mr. Tanimoto started for Mr. Matsuo's house. There he found that their burden was to be a *tansu*, a large Japanese cabinet, full of clothing and household goods. The two men set out. The morning was perfectly clear and so warm that the day promised to be uncomfortable. A few minutes after they started, the air-raid siren went off—a minute-long blast that warned of approaching planes but indicated to the people of Hiroshima only a slight degree of danger, since it sounded every morning at this time, when an American weather plane came over. The two men pulled and pushed the handcart through the city streets. Hiroshima was a fan-shaped city, lying mostly on the six islands formed by the seven estuarial rivers that branch out from the Ota River; its main commercial and residential districts, covering about four square miles in the center of the city, contained three-quarters of its population, which had been reduced by several evacuation programs from a wartime peak of 380,000 to about 245,000. Factories and other residential districts, or suburbs, lay compactly around the edges of the city. To the south were the docks, an airport, and the island-studded Inland Sea.[4] A rim of mountains runs around the other three sides of the delta. Mr. Tanimoto and Mr. Matsuo took their way through the shopping center, already full of people, and across two of the rivers to the sloping streets of Koi, and up them to the outskirts and foothills. As they started up a valley away from the tight-ranked houses, the all-clear sounded. (The Japanese radar operators, detecting only three planes, supposed that they comprised a reconnaissance.) Pushing the handcart up to the rayon man's house was tiring, and the men, after they had maneuvered their load into the driveway and to the front steps, paused to rest awhile. They stood with a wing of the house between them and the city. Like most homes in this part of Japan, the house consisted of a wooden frame and wooden walls supporting a heavy tile roof. Its front hall, packed with rolls of bedding and clothing, looked like a cool cave full of fat cushions. Opposite the house, to the right of the front door, there was a large, finicky rock garden. There was no sound of planes. The morning was still; the place was cool and pleasant.

Then a tremendous flash of light cut across the sky. Mr. Tanimoto has a distinct recollection that it traveled from east to west, from the city toward the hills. It seemed a sheet of sun. Both he and Mr. Matsuo reacted in terror—and both had time to react (for they were 3,500 yards, or two miles, from the center of the explosion).

Comparisons of Hiroshima Before and After Atomic Bomb. Hiroshima on April 13 and August 11, 1945.

Mr. Matsuo dashed up the front steps into the house and dived among the bedrolls and buried himself there. Mr. Tanimoto took four or five steps and threw himself between two big rocks in the garden. He bellied up very hard against one of them. As his face was against the stone, he did not see what happened. He felt a sudden pressure, and then splinters and pieces of board and fragments of tile fell on him. He heard no roar. (Almost no one in Hiroshima recalls hearing any noise of the bomb. But a fisherman in his sampan[5] on the Inland Sea near Tsuzu, the man with whom Mr. Tanimoto's mother-in-law and sister-in-law were living, saw the flash and heard a tremendous explosion; he was nearly twenty miles from Hiroshima, but the thunder was greater than when the B-29s hit Iwakuni, only five miles away.)

When he dared, Mr. Tanimoto raised his head and saw that the rayon man's house had collapsed. He thought a bomb had fallen directly on it. Such clouds of dust had risen that there was a sort of twilight around. In panic, not thinking for the moment of Mr. Matsuo under the ruins, he dashed out into the street. He noticed as he ran that the concrete wall of the estate had fallen over—toward the house rather than away from it. In the street, the first thing he saw was a squad of soldiers who had been burrowing into the hillside opposite, making one of the thousands of dugouts in which the Japanese apparently intended to resist invasion, hill by hill, life for life; the soldiers were coming out of the hole, where they should have been safe, and blood was running

---

4. The *Inland Sea* lies between the Japanese islands of Kyushu, Shikoku, and Honshu, where Hiroshima is located.

5. A *sampan* is a small boat.

People hurry past a fire burning in the wake of an atomic explosion.
Hiroshima, Japan. August 1945.

from their heads, chests, and backs. They were silent and dazed.

Under what seemed to be a local dust cloud, the day grew darker and darker.

At nearly midnight, the night before the bomb was dropped, an announcer on the city's radio station said that about two hundred B-29s were approaching southern Honshu and advised the population of Hiroshima to evacuate to their designated "safe areas." Mrs. Hatsuyo Nakamura, the tailor's widow, who lived in the section called Noboricho and who had long had a habit of doing as she was told, got her three children—a ten-year-old boy, Toshio, an eight-year-old girl, Yaeko, and a five-year-old girl, Myeko—out of bed and dressed them and walked with them to the military area known as the East Parade Ground, on the northeast edge of the city. There she unrolled some mats and the children lay down on them. They slept until about two, when they were awakened by the roar of the planes going over Hiroshima.

As soon as the planes had passed, Mrs. Nakamura started back with her children. They reached home a little after two-thirty and she immediately turned on the radio, which, to her distress, was just then broadcasting a fresh warning. When she looked at the children and saw how tired they were, and when she thought of the number of trips they had made in past weeks,

all to no purpose, to the East Parade Ground, she decided that in spite of the instructions on the radio, she simply could not face starting out all over again. She put the children in their bedrolls on the floor, lay down herself at three o'clock, and fell asleep at once, so soundly that when the planes passed over later, she did not waken to their sound.

The siren jarred her awake at about seven. She arose, dressed quickly, and hurried to the house of Mr. Nakamoto, the head of her Neighborhood Association, and asked him what she should do. He said that she should remain at home unless an urgent warning—a series of intermittent blasts of the siren—was sounded. She returned home, lit the stove in the kitchen, set some rice to cook, and sat down to read that morning's Hiroshima *Chugoku.* To her relief, the all-clear sounded at eight o'clock. She heard the children stirring, so she went and gave each of them a handful of peanuts and told them to stay on their bedrolls, because they were tired from the night's walk. She had hoped that they would go back to sleep, but the man in the house directly to the south began to make a terrible hullabaloo of hammering, wedging, ripping, and splitting. The prefectural government,[6] convinced, as everyone in Hiroshima was, that the city would be attacked soon, had begun to press with threats and warnings for the completion of wide fire lanes, which, it was hoped, might act in conjunction with the rivers to localize any fires started by an incendiary[7] raid; and the neighbor was reluctantly sacrificing his home to the city's safety. Just the day before, the prefecture had ordered all able-bodied girls from

6. *Prefectural* refers to the forty-seven geopolitical divisions within Japan known as *prefectures,* which are governed by governors and assemblies similar to state and local government in the United States.
7. Here *incendiary* means "designed to deliberately start fires."

the secondary schools to spend a few days helping to clear these lanes, and they started work soon after the all-clear sounded.

Mrs. Nakamura went back to the kitchen, looked at the rice, and began watching the man next door. At first, she was annoyed with him for making so much noise, but then she was moved almost to tears by pity. Her emotion was specifically directed toward her neighbor, tearing down his home, board by board, at a time when there was so much unavoidable destruction, but undoubtedly she also felt a generalized, community pity, to say nothing of self-pity. She had not had an easy time. Her husband, Isawa, had gone into the Army just after Myeko was born, and she had heard nothing from or of him for a long time, until, on March 5, 1942, she received a seven-word telegram: "Isawa died an honorable death at Singapore." She learned later that he had died on February 15th, the day Singapore fell, and that he had been a corporal. Isawa had been a not particularly prosperous tailor, and his only capital was a Sankoku sewing machine. After his death, when his allotments stopped coming, Mrs. Nakamura got out the machine and began to take in piecework herself, and since then had supported the children, but poorly, by sewing.

As Mrs. Nakamura stood watching her neighbor, everything flashed whiter than any white she had ever seen. She did not notice what happened to the man next door; the reflex of a mother set her in motion toward her children. She had taken a single step (the house was 1,350 yards, or three-quarters of a mile, from the center of the explosion) when something picked her up and she seemed to fly into the next room over the raised sleeping platform, pursued by parts of her house.

Timbers fell around her as she landed, and a shower of tiles pummeled her; everything became dark, for she was buried. The **debris** did not cover her deeply. She rose up and freed herself. She heard a child cry, "Mother, help me!," and saw her youngest—Myeko, the five-year-old—buried up to her breast and unable to move. As Mrs. Nakamura started frantically to claw her way toward the baby, she could see or hear nothing of her other children.

In the days right before the bombing, Dr. Masakazu Fujii, being prosperous, hedonistic, and at the time not too busy, had been allowing himself the luxury of sleeping until nine or nine-thirty, but fortunately he had to get up only the morning the bomb was dropped to see a house guest off on a train. He rose at six, and half an hour later walked with his friend to the station, not far away, across two of the rivers. He was back home by seven, just as the siren sounded its sustained warning. He ate breakfast and then, because the morning was already hot, undressed down to his underwear and went out on the porch to read the paper. This porch—in fact, the whole building—was curiously constructed. Dr. Fujii was the proprietor of a peculiarly Japanese institution: a private, single-doctor hospital. This building, perched beside and over the water of the Kyo River, and next to the bridge of the same name, contained thirty rooms for thirty patients and their kinfolk—for, according to Japanese custom, when a person falls sick and goes to a hospital, one or more members of his family go and live there with him, to cook for him, bathe, massage, and read to him, and to offer incessant familial sympathy, without which a Japanese patient would be miserable indeed. Dr. Fujii had no beds—only straw mats—for his patients. He did, however, have all sorts of modern equipment: an X-ray machine, diathermy apparatus, and a fine tiled laboratory. The structure rested two-thirds on the land, one-third on piles over the tidal waters of the Kyo. This overhang, the part of the building where Dr. Fujii lived, was queer-looking, but it was cool in summer and from the porch, which faced away from the center of the city, the prospect of the river, with pleasure boats drifting up and down it, was always refreshing. Dr. Fujii had occasionally had anxious moments when the Ota and its mouth

---

Big Idea The United States and the World *How do these details show the power of the bomb?*

Vocabulary

debris (də brē´) *n.* large number of fragments or broken pieces

Reading Strategy Drawing Conclusions About Author's Beliefs *Hersey includes many details about Japanese life and culture. Why do you think it is important to the author to include this information?*

branches rose to flood, but the piling[8] was apparently firm enough and the house had always held.

Dr. Fujii had been relatively idle for about a month because in July, as the number of untouched cities in Japan dwindled and as Hiroshima seemed more and more inevitably a target, he began turning patients away, on the ground that in case of a fire raid he would not be able to evacuate them. Now he had only two patients left—a woman from Yano, injured in the shoulder, and a young man of twenty-five recovering from burns he had suffered when the steel factory near Hiroshima in which he worked had been hit. Dr. Fujii had six nurses to tend his patients. His wife and children were safe; his wife and one son were living outside Osaka, and another son and two daughters were in the country on Kyushu. A niece was living with him, and a maid and a manservant. He had little to do and did not mind, for he had saved some money. At fifty,

he was healthy, convivial, and calm, and he was pleased to pass the evenings drinking whiskey with friends, always sensibly and for the sake of conversation. Before the war, he had affected brands imported from Scotland and America; now he was perfectly satisfied with the best Japanese brand, Suntory.

Dr. Fujii sat down cross-legged in his underwear on the spotless matting of the porch, put on his glasses, and started reading the Osaka *Asahi*. He liked to read the Osaka news because his wife was there. He saw the flash. To him—faced away from the center and looking at his paper—it seemed a brilliant yellow. Startled, he began to rise to his feet. In that moment (he was 1,500 yards from the center), the hospital leaned behind his rising and, with a terrible ripping noise, toppled into the river. The doctor, still in the act of getting to his feet, was thrown forward and around and over; he was buffeted and gripped; he lost track of everything, because things were so speeded up; he felt the water.

Dr. Fujii hardly had time to think that he was dying before he realized that he was alive, squeezed tightly by two long timbers in a V across his chest,

---

8. *Piles* are long, columnar timbers or poles that have one end anchored in the ground and are grouped into *pilings* to hold up buildings or other structures.

Rain falls on buildings reduced to rubble by an atomic bomb blast a few months after the U.S. attack that led to the end of World War II. October 1945.

like a morsel suspended between two huge chop-sticks—held upright, so that he could not move, with his head miraculously above water and his torso and legs in it. The remains of his hospital were all around him in a mad assortment of splintered lumber and materials for the relief of pain. His left shoulder hurt terribly. His glasses were gone.

Father Wilhelm Kleinsorge, of the Society of Jesus, was, on the morning of the explosion, in rather frail condition. The Japanese wartime diet had not sustained him, and he felt the strain of being a foreigner in an increasingly **xenophobic** Japan; even a German, since the defeat of the Fatherland,[9] was unpopular. Father Kleinsorge had, at thirty-eight, the look of a boy growing too fast— thin in the face, with a prominent Adam's apple, a hollow chest, dangling hands, big feet. He walked clumsily, leaning forward a little. He was tired all the time. To make matters worse, he had suffered for two days, along with Father Cieslik, a fellow-priest, from a rather painful and urgent diarrhea, which they blamed on the beans and black ration bread they were obliged to eat. Two other priests then liv-ing in the mission compound, which was in the Noboricho section—Father Superior LaSalle and Father Schiffer—had happily escaped this affliction.

Father Kleinsorge woke up about six the morning the bomb was dropped, and half an hour later—he was a bit tardy because of his sickness—he began to read Mass in the mission chapel, a small Japanese-style wooden building which was without pews, since its worshipers knelt on the usual Japanese matted floor, facing an altar graced with splendid silks, brass, silver, and heavy embroideries. This morning, a Monday, the only worshipers were Mr. Takemoto, a theological student living in the mis-sion house; Mr. Fukai, the secretary of the diocese;[10] Mrs. Murata, the mission's devoutly Christian house-keeper; and his fellow-priests. After Mass, while Father Kleinsorge was reading the Prayers of

---

9. *Fatherland* refers to Germany, which had surrendered to Allied forces a few months before the attack on Hiroshima.
10. A *diocese* is a district within the Roman Catholic church.

Big Idea The United States and the World *What do these details show about the horrors of nuclear war?*

Vocabulary

xenophobic (zenʹə fōʹ bik) *adj.* having an extreme fear of foreigners or strangers

Thanksgiving, the siren sounded. He stopped the service and the missionaries retired across the com-pound to the bigger building. There, in his room on the ground floor, to the right of the front door, Father Kleinsorge changed into a military uniform which he had acquired when he was teaching at the Rokko Middle School in Kobe and which he wore during air-raid alerts.

After an alarm, Father Kleinsorge always went out and scanned the sky, and in this instance, when he stepped outside, he was glad to see only the single weather plane that flew over Hiroshima each day about this time. Satisfied that nothing would happen, he went in and breakfasted with the other Fathers on substitute coffee and ration bread, which, under the circumstances, was espe-cially repugnant to him. The Fathers sat and talked awhile, until, at eight, they heard the all-clear. They went then to various parts of the building. Father Schiffer retired to his room to do some writing. Father Cieslik sat in his room in a straight chair with a pillow over his stomach to ease his pain, and read. Father Superior LaSalle stood at the window of his room, thinking. Father Kleinsorge went up to a room on the third floor, took off all his clothes except his underwear, and stretched out on his right side on a cot and began reading his *Stimmen der Zeit*.

After the terrible flash—which, Father Kleinsorge later realized, reminded him of something he had read as a boy about a large meteor colliding with the earth—he had time (since he was 1,400 yards from the center) for one thought: A bomb has fallen directly on us. Then, for a few seconds or minutes, he went out of his mind.

Father Kleinsorge never knew how he got out of the house. The next things he was conscious of were that he was wandering around in the mission's vegetable garden in his underwear, bleeding slightly from small cuts along his left flank; that all the building round about had fallen down except the Jesuits' mission house, which had long before been braced and double-braced by a priest named Gropper, who was terrified of earth-quakes; that the day had turned dark; and that Murata-san, the housekeeper, was nearby,

Literary Element Point of View *How would this passage read differently if it was in the first-person point of view?*

crying over and over, *"Shu Jesusu, awaremi tamai!* Our Lord Jesus, have pity on us!"

On the train on the way into Hiroshima from the country, where he lived with his mother, Dr. Terufumi Sasaki, the Red Cross Hospital surgeon, thought over an unpleasant nightmare he had had the night before. His mother's home was in Mukai-hara, thirty miles from the city, and it took him two hours by train and tram to reach the hospital. He had slept uneasily all night and had wakened an hour earlier than usual, and, feeling sluggish and slightly feverish, had debated whether to go to the hospital at all; his sense of duty finally forced him to go, and he had started out on an earlier train than he took most mornings. The dream had particularly frightened him because it was so closely associated, on the surface at least, with a disturbing actuality. He was only twenty-five years old and had just completed his training at the Eastern Medical University, in Tsingtao, China. He was something of an idealist and was much distressed by the inadequacy of medical facilities in the country town where his mother lived. Quite on his own, and without a permit, he had begun visiting a few sick people out there in the evenings, after his eight hours at the hospital and four hours' commuting. He had recently learned that the penalty for practicing without a permit was severe; a fellow-doctor whom he had asked about it had given him a serious scolding. Nevertheless, he had continued to practice. In his dream, he had been at the bedside of a country patient when the police and the doctor he had consulted burst into the room, seized him, dragged him outside, and beat him up cruelly. On the train, he just about decided to give up the work in Mukai-hara, since he felt it would be impossible to get a permit, because the authorities would hold that it would conflict with his duties at the Red Cross Hospital.

At the **terminus,** he caught a streetcar at once. (He later calculated that if he had taken

Atomic bomb damage to Nagasaki, Japan.

his customary train that morning, and if he had had to wait a few minutes for the streetcar, as often happened, he would have been close to the center at the time of the explosion and would surely have perished.) He arrived at the hospital at seven-forty and reported to the chief surgeon. A few minutes later, he went to a room on the first floor and drew blood from the arm of a man in order to perform a Wassermann test. The laboratory containing the incubators for the test was on the third floor. With the blood specimen in his left hand, walking in a kind of distraction he had felt all morning, probably because of the dream and his restless night, he started along the main corridor on his way toward the stairs. He was one step beyond an open window when the light of the bomb was reflected, like a gigantic photographic flash, in the corridor. He ducked down on one knee and said to himself, as only a Japanese would, "Sasaki, *gambare!* Be brave!" Just then (the

Reading Strategy   Drawing Conclusions About Author's Beliefs *Based on this detail, what aspect of Japanese culture made an impression on Hersey?*

Vocabulary

terminus (tur′ mə nəs) *n.* one end of a travel route or the station placed there building was 1,650 yards from the center), the blast ripped through the hospital. The glasses he was wearing flew off his face; the bottle of blood crashed against one wall; his Japanese slippers zipped out from under his feet—but otherwise, thanks to where he stood, he was untouched.

Dr. Sasaki shouted the name of the chief surgeon and rushed around to the man's office and found him terribly cut by glass. The hospital was in horrible confusion: Heavy partitions and ceilings had fallen on patients, beds had overturned, windows had blown in and cut people, blood was spattered on the walls and floors, instruments were everywhere, many of the patients were running about screaming, many more lay dead. (A colleague working in the laboratory to which Dr. Sasaki had been walking was dead; Dr. Sasaki's patient, whom he had just left and who a few moments before had been dreadfully afraid of syphilis, was also dead.) Dr. Sasaki found himself the only doctor in the hospital who was unhurt.

Dr. Sasaki, who believed that the enemy had hit only the building he was in, got bandages and began to bind the wounds of those inside the hospital; while outside, all over Hiroshima, maimed and dying citizens turned their unsteady steps toward the Red Cross Hospital to begin an invasion that was to make Dr. Sasaki forget his private nightmare for a long, long time.

Miss Toshiko Sasaki, the East Asia Tin Works clerk, who is not related to Dr. Sasaki, got up at three o'clock in the morning on the day the bomb fell. There was extra housework to do. Her eleven-month-old brother, Akio, had come down the day before with a serious stomach upset; her mother had taken him to the Tamura Pediatric Hospital and was staying there with him. Miss Sasaki, who was about twenty, had to cook breakfast for her father, a brother, a sister, and herself, and—since the hospital, because of the war, was unable to provide food—to prepare a whole day's meals for her mother and the baby, in time for her father, who worked in a factory making rubber earplugs for artillery crews, to take the food by on his way to the plant. When she had finished and had cleaned and put away the cooking things, it was nearly seven. The family lived in Koi, and she had a forty-five-minute trip to the tin works, in the section of town called Kannon-machi. She was in charge of the personnel records in the factory. She left Koi at seven, and as soon as she reached the plant, she went with some of the other girls from the personnel department to the factory auditorium. A prominent local Navy man, a former employee, had committed suicide the day before by throwing himself under a train—a death considered honorable enough to warrant a memorial service, which was to be held at the tin works at ten o'clock that morning. In the large hall, Miss Sasaki and the others made suitable preparations for the meeting. This work took about twenty minutes.

Miss Sasaki went back to her office and sat down at her desk. She was quite far from the windows, which were off to her left, and behind her were a couple of tall bookcases containing all the books of the factory library, which the personnel department had organized. She settled herself at her desk, put some things in a drawer, and shifted papers. She thought that before she began to make entries in her lists of new employees, discharges, and departures for the Army, she would chat for a moment with the girl at her right. Just as she turned her head away from the windows, the room was filled with a blinding light. She was paralyzed by fear, fixed still in her chair for a long moment (the plant was 1,600 yards from the center).

Everything fell, and Miss Sasaki lost consciousness. The ceiling dropped suddenly and the wooden floor above collapsed in splinters and the people up there came down and the roof above them gave way; but principally and first of all, the bookcases right behind her swooped forward and the contents threw her down, with her left leg horribly twisted and breaking underneath her. There, in the tin factory, in the first moment of the atomic age, a human being was crushed by books. ∾

Big Idea The United States and the World *How does this excerpt show that people were unprepared for the true extent of atomic warfare?*

Reading Strategy Drawing Conclusions About Author's Beliefs *How does this sentence help you understand how Hersey feels about the bombing?*

Big Idea The United States and the World *What does this suggest about Hersey's attitude toward the atomic age?*

RESPONDING AND THINKING CRITICALLY

Respond

1. (a)What was your initial reaction to Hersey's unemotional retelling of the events? (b)What was your response to the number of details that he included about the people who lived in Hiroshima and their culture?

Recall and Interpret

2. (a)What were the professions of the six people? (b)Why would Hersey choose to focus on these people?

3. (a)Does Hersey ever explain why the atomic bomb was dropped on Hiroshima? (b)How does this affect the narrative?

4. (a)Even before the bomb dropped, how had the war affected people? (b)Why do you think Hersey might have included this information?

Analyze and Evaluate

5. Which characters did you find most sympathetic and why?

6. Do you think that Hersey's detailed style was the best way to recount what happened, or would some other way have been more effective? Explain.

7. What are some details that show Hersey's interest in exploring morality as well as in traditional reporting?

Connect

8. Why do you think people still read *Hiroshima* six decades after it was first written?

9. **Big Idea** The United States and the World In what ways is *Hiroshima* written not only for the United States but also for the world?

PRIMARY SOURCE QUOTATION

On August 6, 1945, President Harry Truman announced that the United States had bombed the city of Hiroshima. Read the following excerpt from President Truman's speech, keeping in mind what you have already learned about the bombing of Hiroshima.

Group Activity Discuss the following questions with classmates. Refer back to the quotation and cite evidence from *Hiroshima* for support.

1. After reading the excerpt from *Hiroshima*, how would you respond to President Truman's statement?

2. How do you think President Truman would respond to Hersey's narrative? Explain.

"Sixteen hours ago an American airplane dropped one bomb on Hiroshima, an important Japanese army base. That bomb had more power than 20,000 tons of T.N.T. It had more than two thousand times the blast power of the British 'Grand Slam' which is the largest bomb ever yet used in the history of warfare.

"The Japanese began the war from the air at Pearl Harbor. They have been repaid many fold. And the end is not yet. With this bomb we have now added a new and revolutionary increase in destruction to supplement the growing power of our armed forces."

—President Harry Truman

The Enola Gay. The B-29 bomber, which dropped the first atomic bomb on Japan, stands on the runway at Tinian following the raid. August 1945.

Literary Element Point of View

The excerpt from *Hiroshima* is written with a third-person objective **point of view,** which reports on how people respond to a disastrous event. The use of pronouns such as *he, she,* and *they* also indicate third-person point of view.

While stories told in first-person point of view are limited to only one perspective, narratives told in third-person objective point of view can reveal many perspectives on one topic. Much nonfiction journalistic writing, like *Hiroshima,* is told in third-person objective point of view in order to give a more complete account of events.

1. Why do you think Hersey uses the third-person objective point of view to narrate *Hiroshima?*

2. Are there points where Hersey veers from a completely objective point of view? Explain.

Review: Author's Purpose

Author's purpose is an author's intent in writing a piece of literature. Authors often write to persuade, to inform, to explain, to describe, or to entertain.

Partner Activity Meet with another classmate and identify Hersey's purpose in writing *Hiroshima.* Find at least three details that support your response. Afterward, compare your conclusions with those of your classmates and discuss.

Reading Strategy Drawing Conclusions About Author's Beliefs

During wartime, many people, including writers, tend to view wartime opponents as "the enemy." Hersey does not do this; instead, each person is described as an ordinary human being, with hopes and fears. As a result, readers can draw certain conclusions about the author's beliefs.

1. How do you think Hersey felt about the citizens of Hiroshima? List details to support your answer.

2. Which character or characters do you think he felt special sympathy for? Give reasons for your answer.

Vocabulary Practice

Practice with Word Origins A word's origins, or history, often give clues to its meaning. For example, *xenophobic* comes from the Greek roots *xenos,* meaning "stranger," and *phobos,* meaning "fear." Thus, *xenophobic* means "fear of strangers."

Match each vocabulary word with its corresponding root word. Use a dictionary for assistance.

1. evacuate   **a.** *vol,* meaning "to wish"

2. volition   **b.** *term,* meaning "end," or "boundary"

3. terminus   **c.** *vacuus,* meaning "to empty"

Academic Vocabulary

Here are two words from the vocabulary list on page R86.

minimum (min′ə məm) *n.* smallest possible amount or degree

internal (in turn′əl) *adj.* interior; of or relating to the inside

Practice and Apply

1. What did Mrs. Nakamura, who had the bare **minimum** of time before the bomb's impact, do before it reached her?

2. By revealing the **internal** thoughts and feelings of his characters, what effect does Hersey create?

Writing About Literature

Apply Form *Hiroshima* originated as a feature article about an important event in the twentieth century. Hersey based his article on interviews, observation, and careful research. Write a feature article about a major event that has happened in your community. Like Hersey, base your article on interviews, observation, and research.

To organize the large number of details, create a timeline like the one shown here. Use it to make notes about when and to whom things happened.

SEQUENCE OF EVENTS

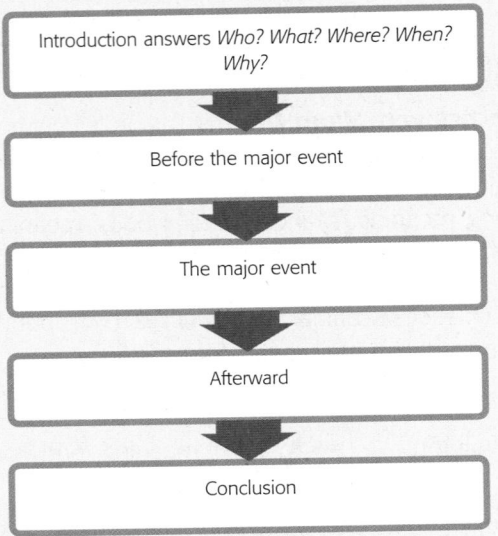

Introduction answers *Who? What? Where? When? Why?*

Before the major event

The major event

Afterward

Conclusion

As you draft your article, write with unemotional language and detailed descriptions. Use transitional words and phrases to clarify the sequence of events. After drafting, meet with a peer reviewer to evaluate each other's work and suggest revisions. Then edit and proofread your draft for errors in spelling, grammar, or punctuation.

Listening and Speaking

Group Activity More than half a century later, people are still debating whether it was necessary to drop an atomic bomb in order to end World War II. Hold a debate on this topic. Do research to learn why so many people at the time supported this decision and why so many now regret it. Then form two groups, each supporting a different point of view. With your team, develop strong arguments for your point of view and be ready to refute opposing arguments. Limit each speaker to two minutes.

Hersey's Language and Style

Using Reportorial Style When you write a news article, you are trying to provide readers with factual information, not an argument. To do so, you need to write like a reporter and use unbiased, unemotional language. You should include numerous facts and statistics that can be observed and verified. Within the first few paragraphs, you should answer the questions *who? what? where? when? why?* and *how?*

Choose **precise words** that create clear and accurate images in readers' minds. For example, in the excerpt from *Hiroshima*, Hersey uses the word *dashed* instead of *ran* and *hullabaloo* instead of *loud noise* because they are more precise and descriptive.

Imprecise	Precise
mad	furious, sullen, irritated
nice	friendly, amiable, affectionate

Activity Create a two-column chart of your own. List descriptive words from *Hiroshima* in the left column and synonyms that Hersey might have used for these words in the right column. Discuss with a partner whether Hersey's word or your word is the better fit.

Revising Check

Reportorial Style Read through your feature article with a partner and notice places where you have veered away from reportorial style. Did you answer *who, what, where, when, why,* and *how* questions? Replace any imprecise words with more precise language. Use a thesaurus if necessary.

Literature Online Web Activities For eFlashcards, Selection Quick Checks, and other Web activities, go to www.glencoe.com.

The Portrait

MEET TOMÁS RIVERA

The life of Tomás Rivera, the "Dean of Mexican American Literature," is a true rags-to-riches story. From modest beginnings, Rivera became a successful writer and educator—an inspiration to many. He was born in Crystal City, Texas, the son of two agricultural workers. After graduating from high school, Rivera, like his parents, began working as a migrant worker. Until he reached his early twenties, Rivera traveled with other migrant workers, picking fruit and vegetables across the United States from Texas to the Midwest.

Despite all his traveling, Rivera managed to earn a formal education by attending different schools. He received his bachelor's and master's degrees in English education from Southwest Texas State University. After a stint teaching in public schools and at Southwest Texas Junior College in Uvalde, he attended the University of Oklahoma, where he earned a master's degree in Spanish literature, and, in 1969, a doctorate in Romance languages and literature.

> "He searched for stories about his people and finally gave their words sound, wrote the books he didn't have, we didn't have . . ."
>
> —Pat Mora

In 1971 Rivera published his only novel, *y no se lo trago la tierra*, also known as *And the Earth Did Not Devour Him*. Originally written in Spanish, the book was published in both Spanish and English. It is an unconventional novel, made up of twenty-seven interrelated stories and sketches that describe, often grimly, the indomitable spirit of migrant farm workers. The novel was not meant to support any particular political point of view, but instead to reflect a world and experiences that Rivera knew well. *Y no se lo trago la tierra* won the prestigious Quinto Sol Award in 1971. The success of Rivera's novel inspired other Mexican Americans to add their voices to the literature of the United States.

Besides providing inspiration, Rivera also helped people in direct ways, serving on the boards of numerous Mexican American organizations. He also had a distinguished academic career, eventually becoming chancellor of the University of California at Riverside. He was one of the founders of the National Council of Chicanos in Higher Education. Both President Jimmy Carter and President Ronald Reagan appointed Rivera to commissions on higher education.

Rivera was working on a new book when he died in Fontana, California. After his death, the University of Texas at Austin inaugurated the Tomás Rivera Professorship in Spanish Language and Literature. It is a fitting tribute to a generous man who sought, according to one source, to develop "hospitable and fertile space for Hispanic Americans in America's institutions."

Tomás Rivera was born in 1935 and died in 1984.

Literature Online **Author Search** For more about Tomás Rivera, go to www.glencoe.com.

Connecting to the Story

In "The Portrait," the main character and his wife cherish a particular photograph of their deceased son. As you read the story, think about these questions:

- What are the most precious items you and your family own—the things you would least want to lose?
- Why are these items important to your family?
- To what extent would you go to preserve the memory of a loved one?

Building Background

This story takes place in Texas during the 1950s, when the United States was involved in the Korean War. More than 50,000 U.S. troops died in that war, and about twice that number were wounded or missing in action. At that time, salespeople traveling from house to house were a familiar sight in cities and towns, selling everything from encyclopedias to vacuum cleaners. In this story, the salespeople have timed their visits to coincide with the return of newly paid migrant workers— agricultural workers who follow the harvests around the United States.

Setting Purposes for Reading

Big Idea **The United States and the World**

"The Portrait" is set during the time of the Korean War. As you read, consider how the war affects the main character.

Literary Element **Idiom**

An **idiom** is a saying, or group of words, that takes on special meaning, usually one different from the literal meanings of the words it is composed of. For example, "over the hill" really means "being older or elderly." Phrases such as "catch his eye," "turn the tables," and "keep tabs on" are other examples of idioms. Note that this selection is a translation and the idioms have different meanings in the original Spanish. They have been translated into English idioms that have equivalent meanings, but the individual words may not correspond word-for-word with the Spanish versions. As you read "The Portrait," notice the idioms and consider what they mean.

- See Literary Terms Handbook, p. R9.

Reading Strategy Responding to Plot and Characters

A **static character** remains basically the same throughout the story. A **dynamic character,** on the other hand, grows and changes during the story. As you read "The Portrait," think about whether the main character, Don Mateo, is static or dynamic.

Reading Tip: Using a Response Chart To better understand Don Mateo, take notes about him. Write down quotations from the story and your responses.

Quotation	My Response
"But you take good care of that picture for us because it's the only one we have of our son grown up." p. 1016	Don Mateo is concerned about the only photo he has of his grown son, yet he wants to "fix up" the photo to better preserve it. He trusts the salesman.

Vocabulary

installment (in stôl′ mənt) n. one part of a payment that has been divided; p. 1015 *The bedroom set was expensive so we paid for it in monthly installments.*

swindle (swin′ dəl) v. to cheat someone out of money or property; p. 1017 *At the carnival a vendor swindled me out of twenty dollars, selling me jewels worth only a few cents.*

Vocabulary Tip: Context Clues When you come upon an unfamiliar word or idiom, search the context, or the surrounding words and sentences, for clues to its meaning.

Literature Online **Interactive Literary Elements Handbook** To review or learn more about the literary elements, go to www.glencoe.com.

INDIANA ACADEMIC STANDARDS (pages 1014–1019)
11.3.3 Analyze ways in which...language achieve[s] specific... aesthetic (artistic) purposes...

11.3 [Identify] story elements such as character...
11.5.2 Write responses to literature...

The Portrait

Tomás Rivera

As soon as the people returned from up north the portrait salesmen began arriving from San Antonio. They would come to rake in. They knew that the workers had money and that was why, as Dad used to say, they would flock in. They carried suitcases packed with samples and always wore white shirts and ties; that way they looked more important and the people believed everything they would tell them and invite them into their homes without giving it much thought. I think that down deep they even longed for their children to one day be like them. In any event, they would arrive and make their way down the dusty streets, going house to house carrying suitcases full of samples.

I remember once I was at the house of one of my father's friends when one of these salesmen arrived. I also remember that that particular one seemed a little frightened and timid. Don Mateo asked him to come in because he wanted to do business.

"Good afternoon, traveler. I would like to tell you about something new that we're offering this year."

"Well, let's see, let's see . . ."

"Well, sir, see, you give us a picture, any picture you may have, and we will not only enlarge it for you but we'll also set it in a wooden frame like this one and we'll shape the image a little, like this—three dimensional, as they say."

"And what for?"

"So that it will look real. That way . . . look, let me show you . . . see? Doesn't he look real, like he's alive?"

"Man, he sure does. Look, vieja.[1] This looks great. Well, you know, we wanted to send some pictures to be enlarged . . . but now, this must cost a lot, right?"

"No, I'll tell you, it costs about the same. Of course, it takes more time."

"Well, tell me, how much?"

"For as little as thirty dollars we'll deliver it to you done with inlays just like this, one this size."

"Boy, that's expensive! Didn't you say it didn't cost a lot more? Do you take **installments**?"

"Well, I'll tell you, we have a new manager and he wants everything in cash. It's very fine work. We'll make it look like real. Shaped like that, with inlays . . . take a look. What do you think? Some fine work, wouldn't you say? We can have it all finished for you in a

Visual Vocabulary
Inlays are pieces of material such as wood or ivory, set or embedded into the surface of something else to form a design.

---

1. Here, the Spanish word *vieja* (vē ā′ hä′) is used as a term of endearment; literally, it means "old" or "old woman."

Vocabulary

installment (in stôl′ mənt) *n.* one part of a payment that has been divided month. You just tell us what color you want the clothes to be and we'll come by with it all finished one day when you least expect, framed and all. Yes, sir, a month at the longest. But like I say, this man, who's the new manager, he wants the full payment in cash. He's very demanding, even with us."

"Yes, but it's much too expensive."

"Well, yes. But the thing is, this is very fine work. You can't say you've ever seen portraits done like this, with wood inlays."

"No, well, that's true. What do you think, vieja?"

"Well, I like it a lot. Why don't we order one? And if it turns out good . . . my Chuy . . . may he rest in peace. It's the only picture we have of him. We took it right before he left for Korea. Poor m'ijo,[2] we never saw him again. See . . . this is his picture. Do you think you can make it like that, make it look like he's alive?"

"Sure, we can. You know, we've done a lot of them in soldier's uniforms and shaped it, like you see in this sample, with inlays. Why, it's more than just a portrait. Sure. You just tell me what size you want and whether you want a round or square frame. What do you say? How should I write it down?"

"What do you say, vieja, should we have it done like this one?"

"Well, I've already told you what I think. I would like to have m'ijo's picture fixed up like that and in color."

"All right, go ahead and write it down. But you take good care of that picture for us because it's the only one we have of our son grown up. He was going to send us one all dressed up in uniform with the American and Mexican flags crossed over his head, but he no sooner got there when a letter arrived telling us that he was lost in action. So you take good care of it."

"Don't you worry. We're responsible people. And we understand the sacrifices that you people make. Don't worry. And you just wait and see, when we bring it, you'll see how pretty it's gonna look. What do you say,

2. In Spanish, *m'ijo* (mē' hō) is the colloquial form of *mi hijo*, meaning "my son."

Big Idea The United States and the World *What does "vieja" really want more than the portrait?*

Literary Element Idiom *What does "you just wait and see" mean here?*

Adolfo, Zapote de Peraita, Guanajuato, Mexico, from the series *Family and Photography, A Portrait of a Family in Two Cultures,* 1979. Robert C. Buitrón. Silver gelatin print, 20 x 16 in. Collection of the artist.

should we make the uniform navy blue?"

"But he's not wearing a uniform in that picture."

"No, but that's just a matter of fixing it up with some wood fiber overlays. Look at these. This one, he didn't have a uniform on but we put one on him. So what do you say? Should we make it navy blue?"

"All right."

"Don't you worry about the picture."

And that was how they spent the entire day, going house to house, street by street, their suitcases stuffed with pictures. As it turned out, a whole lot of people had ordered enlargements of that kind.

"They should be delivering those portraits soon, don't you think?"

"I think so, it's delicate work and takes more time. That's some fine work those people do. Did you see how real those pictures looked?"

Reading Strategy Responding to Plot and Characters *How much time has passed since the salesman visited Don Mateo?*

"Yeah, sure. They do some fine work. You can't deny that. But it's already been over a month since they passed by here."

"Yes, but from here they went on through all the towns picking up pictures . . . all the way to San Antonio for sure. So it'll probably take a little longer."

"That's true, that's true."

And two more weeks had passed by the time they made the discovery. Some very heavy rains had come and some children, who were playing in one of the tunnels leading to the dump, found a sack full of pictures, all worm-eaten and soaking wet. The only reason that they could tell that these were pictures was because there were a lot of them and most of them the same size and with faces that could just barely be made out. Everybody caught on right away. Don Mateo was so angry that he took off to San Antonio to find the so and so who had **swindled** them.

"Well, you know, I stayed at Esteban's house. And every day I went with him to the market to sell produce. I helped him with everything. I had faith that I would run into that son of a gun some day soon. Then, after I'd been there for a few days, I started going out to the different barrios[3] and I found out a lot that way. It wasn't so much the money that upset me. It was my poor vieja, crying and all because we'd lost the only picture we had of Chuy. We found it in the sack with all the other pictures but it was already ruined, you know."

"I see, but tell me, how did you find him?"

"Well, you see, to make a long story short, he came by the stand at the market one day. He stood right in front of us and bought some vegetables. It was like he was trying to remember who I was. Of course, I recognized him right off. Because when you're angry enough, you don't forget a face. I just grabbed him right then and there. Poor guy couldn't even talk. He was all scared. And I told him that I wanted that portrait of my son and that I wanted it three dimensional and that he'd best get it for me or I'd let him have it. And I went with him to where he lived. And I put him to work right then and there. The poor guy didn't know where to begin. He had to do it all from memory."

"And how did he do it?"

"I don't know. I suppose if you're scared enough, you're capable of doing anything. Three days later he brought me the portrait all finished, just like you see it there on that table by the Virgin. Now tell me, how do you like the way my boy looks?"

"Well, to be honest, I don't remember too well how Chuy looked. But he was beginning to look more and more like you, isn't that so?"

"Yes, I would say so. That's what everybody tells me now. That Chuy's a chip off the old block and that he was already looking like me. There's the portrait. Like they say, one and the same." ☙

---

3. *Barrios* (bär′ ē ōs) are neighborhoods.

Literary Element   Idiom *What does Don Mateo mean when he says "to make a long story short"?*

Reading Strategy   Responding to Plot and Characters *How likely is it that the salesman will be able to create a realistic portrait of Don Mateo's son?*

RESPONDING AND THINKING CRITICALLY

Respond

1. What would you say to Don Mateo about the portrait of his son? Why would you choose those words?

Recall and Interpret

2. (a)What do Don Mateo and "vieja" finally decide to do with the photograph of their son? (b)What deeper meaning might this offer have for them?

3. (a)What happens to the photographs the salesman collects? (b)How would you explain Don Mateo's strong feelings and his decisive action?

4. (a)What happens when Don Mateo finds the salesman? (b)Why do you think the salesman follows Don Mateo's orders?

Analyze and Evaluate

5. (a)How does Don Mateo feel about what he finally receives from the salesman? (b)What does this reaction tell you about Don Mateo?

6. (a)What does the dialogue reveal about Don Mateo and "vieja"? (b)How effective is the dialogue in conveying the message of this story?

7. (a)How would you describe the role and perspective of the narrator throughout this story? (b)In your opinion, how effective is this kind of narrator in telling the story?

Connect

8. **Big Idea** **The United States and the World** Is Don Mateo a casualty of the Korean War even though he never fought on the battlefield? Support your answer.

LITERARY ANALYSIS

Literary Element Idiom

Idioms add realism to dialogue and enhance characterization. Idioms may be difficult for non-native speakers to understand because their meanings differ from the meanings of the individual words that constitute them. Examining the context may provide clues to the meaning.

1. Don Mateo tells the salesman that he will "let him have it" if he doesn't get the portrait. What does this saying mean? Why might Don Mateo say it that way?

2. At the end of the story, Don Mateo describes Chuy as "a chip off the old block." What does that mean? What does it suggest about the portrait?

Review: Plot

Plot is the sequence of events in a drama or a narrative work of fiction. The plot begins with **exposition**, which introduces the story's characters, setting, and situation. The **rising action** adds complications to the conflicts, or problems, leading to the **climax**, or point of highest emotional pitch. The **falling action** is the logical result of the climax, and the **resolution**, or dénouement (dā´ noō män´), presents the final outcome.

Partner Activity Meet with another classmate to discuss the plot of "The Portrait." Then create a diagram like the one below and list the events that make up the stages of the plot.

READING AND VOCABULARY

Reading Strategy Responding to Plot and Characters

A writer can use several methods to reveal a character's personality. The writer can make direct statements about a character, or reveal the person's character indirectly through the character's words and actions and through what other characters think and say about that person. Use the notes on your response chart to help you answer the following questions.

1. What steps did Don Mateo take to obtain the portrait he had ordered?

2. What character traits did Don Mateo reveal during his search for the man who had cheated him?

3. Do you think that Don Mateo goes through a significant change because of the events in this story? Why or why not?

Vocabulary Practice

Practice with Context Clues Use context clues to figure out the meaning of each boldfaced vocabulary word in the sentences below.

1. He bought the car on an **installment** plan and will pay 300 dollars a month.
2. I felt **swindled** once I realized that the necklace was worth far less than what I paid for it.

Academic Vocabulary

Here are two words from the vocabulary list on page R86. These words will help you think, write, and talk about the selection.

dispose (di spōz′) *v.* to get rid of; to finish or settle

fee (fē) *n.* a charge for a service or privilege

Practice and Apply
1. How did the salesman **dispose** of the photographs he had been given?
2. Why do you think the salesman refused to accept his **fee** in installments?

WRITING AND EXTENDING

Writing About Literature

Respond to Conflict Conflict is the central struggle between two opposing forces in a story or drama. Write a brief essay analyzing the main conflict in "The Portrait." Use evidence from the story and from your own experiences to support your ideas.

As you draft, use the plan shown below to organize your essay.

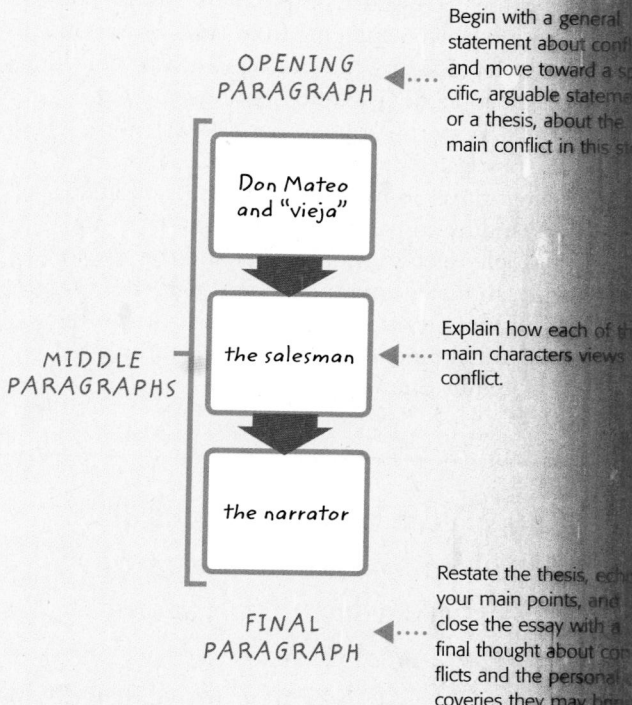

OPENING PARAGRAPH — Begin with a general statement about conflict and move toward a specific, arguable statement, or a thesis, about the main conflict in this story.

Don Mateo and "vieja"

MIDDLE PARAGRAPHS — the salesman — Explain how each of the main characters views the conflict.

the narrator

FINAL PARAGRAPH — Restate the thesis, echo your main points, and close the essay with a final thought about conflicts and the personal discoveries they may bring.

Literature Groups

With a small group of your classmates, debate this question: Does Don Mateo really get what he wants or does he remain the victim of a swindler? Support your opinion by citing evidence from the story. Summarize the results of your debate for the rest of your class.

Literature Online Web Activities For eFlashcards, Selection Quick Checks, and other Web activities, go to www.glencoe.com.

Cultural Rebels: Writers of the Beat Generation

IN THE LATE 1940s, WRITERS JACK KEROUAC and John Clellon Holmes were searching for a way to capture the essence of their generation. They saw a nation slowly emerging from years of war and economic depression, years during which it seemed that most people held similar opinions and led predictable, responsible lives. For Kerouac and Holmes, postwar society was epitomized by anonymous dress, as in the uniform suits of office workers, and by conventional taste. But they saw young people rejecting conformity and turning to creativity. In pursuit of unique identities, the young looked for more artistic and less money-driven lives. Kerouac and Holmes decided that this trend was encapsulated by one word: *Beat*.

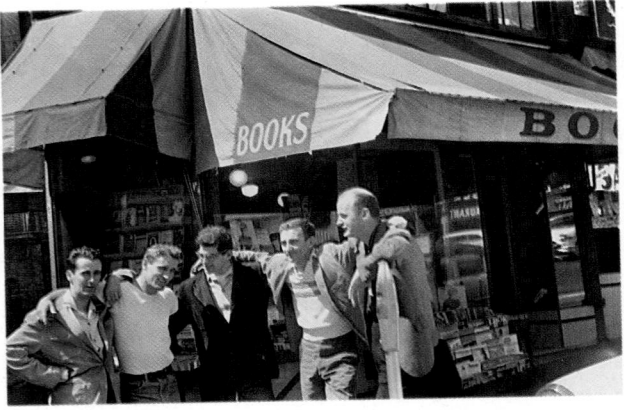

Legendary Beat writers stand outside Lawrence Ferlinghetti's City Lights bookstore in San Francisco in 1956. Pictured left to right: Bob Donlin, Neal Cassady, Allen Ginsberg, Robert LaVinge, Lawrence Ferlinghetti. Photograph by Allen Ginsberg.

> *"How to even begin to get it all down and without modified restraints and all hung-up on like literary inhibitions and grammatical fears . . ."*
>
> —Jack Kerouac, from *On the Road*

Beat had many connotations, ranging from the sordid to the sublime. Kerouac first heard the term from the street hustler Herbert Huncke, who used it as slang for "tired and beaten down." Kerouac saw in *Beat* a suggestion of *beatitude*, saintly or otherworldly beauty and happiness. Poet Allen Ginsberg said, "The point of Beat is that you get beat down to a certain nakedness where you actually are able to see the world in a visionary way."

The core group of Beat Generation writers—Kerouac, Ginsberg, and William S. Burroughs—met in New York City in the areas around Columbia University and in Greenwich Village. The movement soon attracted attention throughout the country, establishing hubs in both New York City and San Francisco. Other leading writers of the new movement were Gary Snyder, Gregory Corso, Lawrence

Ferlinghetti (founder of the innovative City Lights Press and bookstore in San Francisco), Diane Di Prima, and Anne Waldman. Rejecting the prevailing dictates of style and topic, these writers were unabashed experimenters who addressed issues previously considered taboo. Their fearlessness appealed to a newly arising community of bohemians, people who pursued artistic or literary interests and lived nonconformist lives.

Howl

A central work in the Beat Movement is Allen Ginsberg's book-length poem *Howl* (1956), which created a stir with critics, the public, and even law enforcement. (For selling the book, Lawrence Ferlinghetti was briefly held under arrest.) In a free verse style strongly influenced by Walt Whitman, *Howl* catalogs the wonders and horrors of U.S. society in dizzying abundance:

> *"I saw the best minds of my generation destroyed by*
> *   madness, starving hysterical naked, . . .*
> *angelheaded hipsters burning for the ancient heavenly*
> *   connection to the starry dynamo in the machinery*
> *   of night . . ."*

In her memoirs, Diane Di Prima recounts her reactions upon first reading *Howl*. She writes, "It followed that if there was one Allen there must be more, other people besides my few buddies writing what they spoke, what they heard, living, however obscurely and shamefully, what they knew, hiding out here and there as we were—and now, suddenly, about to speak out."

Wild Form

For many, the word *Beat* is synonymous with Jack Kerouac's novel *On the Road*. Kerouac published his novel in 1957, after years of rejections from publishers. While traveling and living in a variety of places, Kerouac wrote multiple drafts. He revised his drafts into their final form in one three-week sprint, during which he typed nearly nonstop on a continuous, 120-foot-long scroll of paper he fed through his typewriter.

On the Road is essentially a *roman à clef,* a novel about real events and people whose names have been changed. The long, rhythmic, bebop-jazz inflected sentences of *On the Road* capture a series of road trips Kerouac took with his friend and Beat Generation icon Neal Cassady (called Dean Moriarty in the novel). *On the Road* expresses Kerouac's openness to the nation's desolate places as well as its exciting cities and to its humble people as well as its mighty. Kerouac had a talent for communicating impulsive generosity and a spirit of fun. For readers who were exhausted by societal complacence and stodginess, Kerouac's adventures were revolutionary.

Kerouac's style was influenced by other writers, particularly the American novelist Thomas Wolfe. As did Wolfe, Kerouac insisted on pushing boundaries. If he wished to write long, breathless

City Lights Bookstore, 1969. Sal Veder. Black and white photograph.

sentences that owed more to vernacular and to the jazz spirit than they did to Establishment polish, he did. Kerouac wrote in a letter, "[W]hat I am beginning to discover now is something beyond the novel and beyond the arbitrary confines of the story . . . *wild form,* man, *wild form* . . ."

from *On the Road*

"[T]he only people for me are the mad ones, the ones who are mad to live, mad to talk, mad to be saved, desirous of everything at the same time, the ones who never yawn or say a commonplace thing, but burn, burn, burn like fabulous yellow roman candles exploding like spiders across the stars and in the middle you see the blue centerlight pop and everybody goes 'Awww!'"

RESPONDING AND THINKING CRITICALLY

1. Why were the members of the Beat Generation considered cultural rebels?

2. What significance did Allen Ginsberg's poetry have for his early readers?

3. What methods did Jack Kerouac employ in his writing?

Literature Online **Literary History** For more about the Beat Generation, go to www.glencoe.com.

INDIANA ACADEMIC STANDARDS (pages 1020–1021)
11.3.5 Analyze or evaluate works of literary or cultural significance in history...that...shed light on the seminal philosophical, religious, social, political, or ethical ideas of their time.

The Crucible, Act One

MEET ARTHUR MILLER

As a young boy, Arthur Miller sat in the Shubert Theater on Lennox Avenue in New York City, completely entranced. A new world had opened up before him. Years later, in his autobiography, Miller remarked, "And so I learned that there were two kinds of reality, but that of the stage was far more real."

Fame in a Dark Time Miller began writing plays during college. In 1947, at the age of thirty-two, he scored his first major theatrical success with the production of *All My Sons*, a dramatic work about a manufacturer of defective war supplies. The play received the New York Drama Critics' Circle Award and was released as a film in 1948. The following year, *Death of a Salesman*, a tragedy about the failure of the American dream, won a Pulitzer Prize and established Miller as one of the greatest playwrights in the United States.

> "One of the strongest urges in the writer's heart . . . is to reveal what has been hidden and denied."
>
> —Arthur Miller

By his late thirties, Miller was embroiled in a dark chapter of U.S. history as a result of his fame and outspoken opinions. Fear of Communism—the "Red Scare"—had taken hold of U.S. citizens, and Congress created the House Un-American Activities Committee (HUAC) to investigate an alleged Communist conspiracy. Among the main targets of the investigation were people in the entertainment industry. The HUAC demanded not only that individuals "confess" to earlier involvement in leftist organizations but that they name others who had held similar views. People who refused to cooperate were often blacklisted or denied employment. The ruthless tactics used by vigilantes such as Senator Joseph McCarthy reminded Miller of the witch trials in seventeenth-century colonial America.

McCarthyism and Witch Hunts Oppressed by the disturbing direction in which his country was moving, Miller immersed himself in the study of the Salem witch trials of 1692, which he described as "one of the strangest and most awful chapters in human history." From this research emerged *The Crucible*, which was first staged on Broadway in 1953. Its relevance to the political situation during the McCarthy era was clear, and the phrase "McCarthy witch hunts" became an enduring symbol of the perversion of power in U.S. history. Viewing the playwright as a potentially subversive figure, the U.S. State Department refused to renew Miller's passport. When Miller was called to testify before HUAC, he refused to implicate his friends and colleagues. He was charged with contempt, fined, and sentenced to jail. His sentence, however, was overturned on appeal in 1958, and he never served a jail term.

A tireless writer, Miller saw his last play produced just a year before his death at 89. On almost any given day, it is said, a theater somewhere in the world is producing *The Crucible*.

Arthur Miller was born in 1915 and died in 2005.

Literature Online Author Search For more about Arthur Miller, go to www.glencoe.com.

Connecting to the Play

A good reputation is a valuable and surprisingly fragile commodity. You have probably seen in your own experience, or in the news, how rumors and gossip can damage people. As you read *The Crucible*, think about the following questions:

- How do you respond when you hear negative comments about people you know?
- How do you think you would react if a rumor spread that you were behaving improperly?

Building Background

The Crucible takes place in 1692 in Salem, a small town in the Massachusetts Bay Colony that had been founded in the 1620s by a group of Puritans. The Puritans had fled England for North America to escape persecution and to establish a religious community. But independence did not ensure harmony. Under the rigid authority of the Reverend Samuel Parris, relations among the villagers of Salem became bitter. In the winter of 1691–1692, several teenage girls, including Parris's daughter and his niece, began behaving strangely. Many people in the community suspected that the girls were victims of witchcraft.

Setting Purposes for Reading

Big Idea The United States and the World

The struggle for power between the Soviet Union and the United States, known as the Cold War, aroused concern among many U.S. citizens about the threat of Communist subversion within their country.

Literary Element Dialogue

Dialogue is the conversation between characters in a literary work. In a play—which consists almost entirely of dialogue—the author must develop plot, theme, and characterization by means of direct speech. As you read, note how Miller expresses his ideas through dialogue.

- See Literary Terms Handbook, p. R5.

Literature Online Interactive Literary Elements Handbook To review or learn more about the literary elements, go to www.glencoe.com.

Reading Strategy Drawing Conclusions About Characters

How do you learn what someone is like? In literature, as in life, you observe what that person says and does. Then you piece together a portrait of him or her.

Reading Tip: Taking Notes Below is a web diagram with notes about one of the characters in the play. As you read, use similar diagrams to take notes on and draw conclusions about the other main characters.

ABIGAIL WILLIAMS—ACT ONE

Vocabulary

compromise (kom′ prə mīz′) *v.* to endanger the reputation or interests of; to expose to suspicion; p. 1027 *Doing business with a known criminal will certainly compromise the company's good name.*

contention (kən ten′ shən) *n.* a verbal argument or struggle; quarreling; p. 1028 *Contention broke out at the meeting over the length of the school day.*

subservient (səb sur′ vē ənt) *adj.* useful in an inferior capacity; submissive; p. 1030 *Jenna resented her subservient role in the family.*

pretense (prē′ tens) *n.* a false show or appearance, especially for the purpose of deceiving; falseness; p. 1033 *Whenever I drop by, he makes a pretense of being hard at work.*

evade (i vād′) *v.* to escape or avoid, as by cleverness; *The fugitive tried to evade capture.*

 INDIANA ACADEMIC STANDARDS (pages 1023–1045)
11.3 [Identify] story elements such as character...
11.2 Develop [reading] strategies...

11.5.2 Write responses to literature that...analyze the use of imagery, language, universal themes, and unique aspects of the text...

ARTHUR MILLER

The Crucible

Arthur Miller

CHARACTERS

(in order of appearance)

REVEREND PARRIS	MERCY LEWIS	FRANCIS NURSE
BETTY PARRIS	MARY WARREN	EZEKIEL CHEEVER
TITUBA	JOHN PROCTOR	MARSHAL HERRICK
ABIGAIL WILLIAMS	REBECCA NURSE	JUDGE HATHORNE
SUSANNA WALCOTT	GILES COREY	DEPUTY GOVERNOR DANFORTH
MRS. ANN PUTNAM	REVEREND JOHN HALE	SARAH GOOD
THOMAS PUTNAM	ELIZABETH PROCTOR	HOPKINS

Act One

(An Overture)

[*A small upper bedroom in the home of* REVEREND
SAMUEL PARRIS, *Salem, Massachusetts, in the
spring of the year 1692.*

*There is a narrow window at the left. Through
its leaded panes the morning sunlight streams. A
candle still burns near the bed, which is at the right.
A chest, a chair, and a small table are the other furnishings. At the back a door opens on the landing
of the stairway to the ground floor. The room
gives off an air of clean spareness. The roof rafters are exposed, and the wood colors are raw
and unmellowed.*

As the curtain rises, REVEREND PARRIS *is discovered
kneeling beside the bed, evidently in prayer. His
daughter,* BETTY PARRIS, *aged ten, is lying on the
bed, inert.*

REVEREND PARRIS *is praying now, and, though we
cannot hear his words, a sense of his confusion
hangs about him. He mumbles, then seems about
to weep; then he weeps, then prays again; but his
daughter does not stir on the bed.*

The door opens, and his Negro slave enters.
TITUBA[1] *is in her forties.* PARRIS *brought her with
him from Barbados,[2] where he spent some years
as a merchant before entering the ministry. She
enters as one does who can no longer bear to be
barred from the sight of her beloved, but she is
also very frightened because her slave sense has
warned her that, as always, trouble in this house
eventually lands on her back.*]

TITUBA. [*Already taking a step backward.*] My
Betty be hearty soon?

PARRIS. Out of here!

TITUBA. [*Backing to the door.*] My Betty not goin'
die . . .

PARRIS. [*Scrambling to his feet in a fury.*] Out of
my sight! [*She is gone.*] Out of my—[*He is overcome with sobs. He clamps his teeth against them
and closes the door and leans against it, exhausted.*]
Oh, my God! God help me! [*Quaking with fear,
mumbling to himself through his sobs, he goes to the
bed and gently takes* BETTY'*s hand.*] Betty. Child.
Dear child. Will you wake, will you open up your
eyes! Betty, little one . . .

[*He is bending to kneel again when his niece,* ABI-
GAIL WILLIAMS, *seventeen, enters—a strikingly
beautiful girl, an orphan, with an endless capacity
for dissembling.[3] Now she is all worry and apprehension and propriety.*]

ABIGAIL. Uncle? [*He looks to her.*] Susanna
Walcott's here from Doctor Griggs.

PARRIS. Oh? Let her come, let her come.

ABIGAIL. [*Leaning out the door to call to* SUSANNA,
who is down the hall a few steps.] Come in, Susanna.

---

3. *Dissembling* means "concealing one's true motives."

Literary Element Dialogue *Tituba's way of speaking
helps us understand something that Miller has already mentioned about her in the stage directions. What is it?*

Reading Strategy Drawing Conclusions About
Characters *What does this phrase tell us about Abigail?*

---

1. *Tituba* (ti tōō′ bə)
2. *Barbados* (bär bā′ dōz) is an island in the Caribbean that
was, at the time of the play, an English colony.

[SUSANNA WALCOTT, *a little younger than ABI-GAIL, a nervous, hurried girl, enters.*]

PARRIS. [*Eagerly.*] What does the doctor say, child?

SUSANNA. [*Craning around PARRIS to get a look at BETTY.*] He bid me come and tell you, reverend sir, that he cannot discover no medicine for it in his books.

PARRIS. Then he must search on.

SUSANNA. Aye, sir, he have been searchin' his books since he left you, sir. But he bid me tell you, that you might look to unnatural things for the cause of it.

PARRIS. [*His eyes going wide.*] No—no. There be no unnatural cause here. Tell him I have sent for Reverend Hale of Beverly, and Mr. Hale will surely confirm that. Let him look to medicine and put out all thought of unnatural causes here. There be none.

SUSANNA. Aye, sir. He bid me tell you. [*She turns to go.*]

ABIGAIL. Speak nothin' of it in the village, Susanna.

PARRIS. Go directly home and speak nothing of unnatural causes.

SUSANNA. Aye, sir. I pray for her. [*She goes out.*]

ABIGAIL. Uncle, the rumor of witchcraft is all about; I think you'd best go down and deny it yourself. The parlor's packed with people, sir. I'll sit with her.

PARRIS. [*Pressed, turns on her.*] And what shall I say to them? That my daughter and my niece I discovered dancing like heathen in the forest?

ABIGAIL. Uncle, we did dance; let you tell them I confessed it—and I'll be whipped if I must be. But they're speakin' of witchcraft. Betty's not witched.

PARRIS. Abigail, I cannot go before the congregation when I know you have not opened[4] with me. What did you do with her in the forest?

ABIGAIL. We did dance, uncle, and when you leaped out of the bush so suddenly, Betty was frightened and then she fainted. And there's the whole of it.

PARRIS. Child. Sit you down.

ABIGAIL. [*Quavering, as she sits.*] I would never hurt Betty. I love her dearly.

PARRIS. Now look you, child, your punishment will come in its time. But if you trafficked[5] with spirits in the forest I must know it now, for surely my enemies will, and they will ruin me with it.

ABIGAIL. But we never conjured[6] spirits.

PARRIS. Then why can she not move herself since midnight? This child is desperate! [*ABIGAIL lowers her eyes.*] It must come out—my enemies will bring it out. Let me know what you done there. Abigail, do you understand that I have many enemies?

ABIGAIL. I have heard of it, uncle.

PARRIS. There is a faction[7] that is sworn to drive me from my pulpit. Do you understand that?

ABIGAIL. I think so, sir.

PARRIS. Now then, in the midst of such disruption, my own household is discovered to be the very center of some obscene practice. Abominations[8] are done in the forest—

ABIGAIL. It were sport,[9] uncle!

PARRIS. [*Pointing at BETTY.*] You call this sport? [*She lowers her eyes. He pleads.*] Abigail, if you know something that may help the doctor, for God's sake tell it to me. [*She is silent.*] I saw Tituba waving her arms over the fire when I came on you. Why was she doing that? And I heard a screeching and gibberish coming from her mouth. She were swaying like a dumb beast over that fire!

---

4. Here, *have not opened* means "have not been completely honest."

5. *Trafficked* means "dealt or did business."
6. Here, *conjured* means "summoned by using magic words or spells."
7. A *faction* is a small segment of people who disagree with the larger group on an issue or set of issues.
8. *Abominations* are vile or shameful acts.
9. Here, *sport* means "innocent recreation."

Big Idea The United States and the World *What word might a U.S. citizen, watching this play in the 1950s, have substituted for "witchcraft?"*

Reading Strategy Drawing Conclusions About Characters *What can we learn about Reverend Parris from this remark?*

ABIGAIL. She always sings her Barbados songs, and we dance.

PARRIS. I cannot blink[10] what I saw, Abigail, for my enemies will not blink it. I saw a dress lying on the grass.

ABIGAIL. [*Innocently.*] A dress?

PARRIS. [*It is very hard to say.*] Aye, a dress. And I thought I saw—someone naked running through the trees!

ABIGAIL. [*In terror.*] No one was naked! You mistake yourself, uncle!

PARRIS. [*With anger.*] I saw it! [*He moves from her. Then, resolved.*] Now tell me true, Abigail. And I pray you feel the weight of truth upon you, for now my ministry's at stake, my ministry and perhaps your cousin's life. Whatever abomination you have done, give me all of it now, for I dare not be taken unaware when I go before them down there.

ABIGAIL. There is nothin' more. I swear it, uncle.

PARRIS. [*Studies her, then nods, half convinced.*] Abigail, I have fought here three long years to bend these stiff-necked people to me, and now, just now when some good respect is rising for me in the parish, you **compromise** my very character. I have given you a home, child, I have put clothes upon your back—now give me upright answer. Your name in the town—it is entirely white, is it not?

ABIGAIL. [*With an edge of resentment.*] Why, I am sure it is, sir. There be no blush about my name.

PARRIS. [*To the point.*] Abigail, is there any other cause than you have told me, for your being discharged from Goody[11] Proctor's service? I have heard it said, and I tell you as I heard it, that she comes so rarely to the church this year for she will not sit so close to something soiled. What signified that remark?

---

10. Here, *blink* means "to deliberately overlook or ignore."
11. *Goody* is short for *Goodwife,* a term of polite address for a married woman.

Literary Element Dialogue *Why might Miller have inserted a dash between "saw" and "someone naked?"*

Vocabulary

compromise (kom′ prə mīz′) *v.* to endanger the reputation or interests of; to expose to suspicion

ABIGAIL. She hates me, uncle, she must, for I would not be her slave. It's a bitter woman, a lying, cold, sniveling woman, and I will not work for such a woman!

PARRIS. She may be. And yet it has troubled me that you are now seven month out of their house, and in all this time no other family has ever called for your service.

ABIGAIL. They want slaves, not such as I. Let them send to Barbados for that. I will not black my face for any of them! [*With ill-concealed resentment at him.*] Do you begrudge my bed, uncle?

PARRIS. No—no.

ABIGAIL. [*In a temper.*] My name is good in the village! I will not have it said my name is soiled! Goody Proctor is a gossiping liar!

[*Enter* MRS. ANN PUTNAM. *She is a twisted soul of forty-five, a death-ridden woman, haunted by dreams.*]

PARRIS. [*As soon as the door begins to open.*] No—no, I cannot have anyone. [*He sees her, and a certain deference*[12] *springs into him, although his worry remains.*] Why, Goody Putnam, come in.

MRS. PUTNAM. [*Full of breath, shiny-eyed.*] It is a marvel. It is surely a stroke of hell upon you.

PARRIS. No, Goody Putnam, it is—

MRS. PUTNAM. [*Glancing at* BETTY.] How high did she fly, how high?

PARRIS. No, no, she never flew—

MRS. PUTNAM. [*Very pleased with it.*] Why, it's sure she did. Mr. Collins saw her goin' over Ingersoll's barn, and come down light as bird, he says!

PARRIS. Now, look you, Goody Putnam, she never—[*Enter* THOMAS PUTNAM, *a well-to-do, hard-handed landowner, near fifty.*] Oh, good morning, Mr. Putnam.

---

12. *Deference* is courteous respect or regard.

Big Idea The United States and the World *Why do you think that Abigail is so concerned about her good name?*

Reading Strategy Drawing Conclusions About Characters *Do you think that "hard-handed" is meant as a compliment? Explain your answer.*

PUTNAM. It is a providence[13] the thing is out now! It is a providence. [*He goes directly to the bed.*]

PARRIS. What's out, sir, what's—?

[*MRS. PUTNAM goes to the bed.*]

PUTNAM. [*Looking down at BETTY.*] Why, *her* eyes is closed! Look you, Ann.

MRS. PUTNAM. Why, that's strange. [*To PARRIS.*] Ours is open.

PARRIS. [*Shocked.*] Your Ruth is sick?

MRS. PUTNAM. [*With vicious certainty.*] I'd not call it sick; the Devil's touch is heavier than sick. It's death, y'know, it's death drivin' into them, forked and hoofed.

PARRIS. Oh, pray not! Why, how does Ruth ail?

MRS. PUTNAM. She ails as she must—she never waked this morning, but her eyes open and she walks, and hears naught,[14] sees naught, and cannot eat. Her soul is taken, surely.

[*PARRIS is struck.*]

PUTNAM. [*As though for further details.*] They say you've sent for Reverend Hale of Beverly?

PARRIS. [*With dwindling conviction[15] now.*] A precaution only. He has much experience in all demonic arts, and I—

MRS. PUTNAM. He has indeed; and found a witch in Beverly last year, and let you remember that.

PARRIS. Now, Goody Ann, they only thought that were a witch, and I am certain there be no element of witchcraft here.

PUTNAM. No witchcraft! Now look you, Mr. Parris—

PARRIS. Thomas, Thomas, I pray you, leap not to witchcraft. I know that you—you least of all, Thomas, would ever wish so disastrous a charge laid upon me. We cannot leap to witchcraft. They will howl me out of Salem for such corruption in my house.

PUTNAM. [*At the moment, he is intent upon getting PARRIS, for whom he has only contempt, to move toward the abyss.*] Mr. Parris, I have taken your part in all **contention** here, and I would continue; but I cannot if you hold back in this. There are hurtful, vengeful spirits layin' hands on these children.

PARRIS. But, Thomas, you cannot—

PUTNAM. Ann! Tell Mr. Parris what you have done.

MRS. PUTNAM. Reverend Parris, I have laid seven babies unbaptized in the earth. Believe me, sir, you never saw more hearty babies born. And yet, each would wither in my arms the very night of their birth. I have spoke nothin', but my heart has clamored intimations.[16] And now, this year, my Ruth, my only—I see her turning strange. A secret child she has become this year, and shrivels like a sucking mouth were pullin' on her life too. And so I thought to send her to your Tituba—

PARRIS. To Tituba! What may Tituba—?

MRS. PUTNAM. Tituba knows how to speak to the dead, Mr. Parris.

PARRIS. Goody Ann, it is a formidable sin to conjure up the dead!

MRS. PUTNAM. I take it on my soul, but who else may surely tell us what person murdered my babies?

PARRIS. [*Horrified.*] Woman!

MRS. PUTNAM. They were murdered, Mr. Parris! And mark this proof! Mark it! Last night my Ruth were ever so close to their little spirits; I know it, sir. For how else is she struck dumb now except some power of darkness would stop her mouth? It is a marvelous sign, Mr. Parris!

PUTNAM. Don't you understand it, sir? There is a murdering witch among us, bound to keep herself in the dark. [*PARRIS turns to BETTY, a frantic terror rising in him.*] Let your enemies make of it what they will, you cannot blink it more.

---

16. A heart that has *clamored intimations* has nagged its owner with suggestions (of possible witchcraft).

Big Idea **The United States and the World** *In making this statement, what chain of events is Mr. Putnam initiating?*

Vocabulary

contention (kən ten′ shən) *n.* verbal argument or struggle; quarreling

---

13. Here, *providence* means "a blessing" or "an act of divine care."
14. *Naught* means "nothing."
15. Here, *conviction* means "certainty."

PARRIS. [To ABIGAIL.] Then you were conjuring spirits last night.

ABIGAIL. [Whispering.] Not I, sir—Tituba and Ruth.

PARRIS. [Turns now, with new fear, and goes to BETTY, looks down at her, and then, gazing off.] Oh, Abigail, what proper payment for my charity! Now I am undone.

PUTNAM. You are not undone! Let you take hold here. Wait for no one to charge you—declare it yourself. You have discovered witchcraft—

PARRIS. In my house? In my house, Thomas? They will topple me with this! They will make of it a—

[Enter MERCY LEWIS, the PUTNAMS' servant, a fat, sly, merciless girl of eighteen.]

MERCY. Your pardons. I only thought to see how Betty is.

PUTNAM. Why aren't you home? Who's with Ruth?

MERCY. Her grandma come. She's improved a little, I think—she give a powerful sneeze before.

MRS. PUTNAM. Ah, there's a sign of life!

MERCY. I'd fear no more, Goody Putnam. It were a grand sneeze; another like it will shake her wits together, I'm sure. [She goes to the bed to look.]

PARRIS. Will you leave me now, Thomas? I would pray a while alone.

ABIGAIL. Uncle, you've prayed since midnight. Why do you not go down and—

PARRIS. No—no. [To PUTNAM.] I have no answer for that crowd. I'll wait till Mr. Hale arrives. [To get MRS. PUTNAM to leave.] If you will, Goody Ann . . .

PUTNAM. Now look you, sir. Let you strike out against the Devil, and the village will bless you for it! Come down, speak to them—pray with them. They're thirsting for your word, Mister! Surely you'll pray with them.

PARRIS. [Swayed.] I'll lead them in a psalm, but let you say nothing of witchcraft yet. I will not discuss it. The cause is yet unknown. I have had enough contention since I came; I want no more.

MRS. PUTNAM. Mercy, you go home to Ruth, d'y'hear?

MERCY. Aye, mum.

[MRS. PUTNAM goes out.]

PARRIS. [To ABIGAIL.] If she starts for the window, cry for me at once.

ABIGAIL. I will, uncle.

PARRIS. [To PUTNAM.] There is a terrible power in her arms today. [He goes out with PUTNAM.]

ABIGAIL. [With hushed trepidation.][17] How is Ruth sick?

MERCY. It's weirdish, I know not—she seems to walk like a dead one since last night.

ABIGAIL. [Turns at once and goes to BETTY, and now, with fear in her voice.] Betty? [BETTY doesn't move. She shakes her.] Now stop this! Betty! Sit up now!

[BETTY doesn't stir. MERCY comes over.]

MERCY. Have you tried beatin' her? I gave Ruth a good one and it waked her for a minute. Here, let me have her.

ABIGAIL. [Holding MERCY back.] No, he'll be comin' up. Listen, now; if they be questioning us, tell them we danced—I told him as much already.

MERCY. Aye. And what more?

ABIGAIL. He knows Tituba conjured Ruth's sisters to come out of the grave.

MERCY. And what more?

ABIGAIL. He saw you naked.

MERCY. [Clapping her hands together with a frightened laugh.] Oh, Jesus!

---

17. *Trepidation* means "fear" or "anxiety."

Reading Strategy Drawing Conclusions About Characters *What sort of a friend do you think Abigail would make? Explain.*

Reading Strategy Drawing Conclusions About Characters *How does this remark illustrate the irony in Miller's stage directions when Mercy first enters?*

[*Enter* MARY WARREN, *breathless. She is seventeen, a* **subservient**, *naive, lonely girl.*]

MARY WARREN. What'll we do? The village is out! I just come from the farm; the whole country's talkin' witchcraft! They'll be callin' us witches, Abby!

MERCY. [*Pointing and looking at* MARY WARREN.] She means to tell, I know it.

MARY WARREN. Abby, we've got to tell. Witchery's a hangin' error, a hangin' like they done in Boston two year ago! We must tell the truth, Abby! You'll only be whipped for dancin', and the other things!

ABIGAIL. Oh, *we'll* be whipped!

MARY WARREN. I never done none of it, Abby. I only looked!

MERCY. [*Moving menacingly toward* MARY.] Oh, you're a great one for lookin', aren't you, Mary Warren? What a grand peeping courage you have!

[BETTY, *on the bed, whimpers.* ABIGAIL *turns to her at once.*]

ABIGAIL. Betty? [*She goes to* BETTY.] Now, Betty, dear, wake up now. It's Abigail. [*She sits* BETTY *up and furiously shakes her.*] I'll beat you, Betty! [BETTY *whimpers.*] My, you seem improving. I talked to your papa and I told him everything. So there's nothing to—

BETTY. [*Darts off the bed, frightened of* ABIGAIL, *and flattens herself against the wall.*] I want my mama!

ABIGAIL. [*With alarm, as she cautiously approaches* BETTY.] What ails you, Betty? Your mama's dead and buried.

BETTY. I'll fly to Mama. Let me fly! [*She raises her arms as though to fly, and streaks for the window, gets one leg out.*]

ABIGAIL. [*Pulling her away from the window.*] I told him everything; he knows now, he knows everything we—

Literary Element Dialogue *How might the actress playing Abigail make these lines particularly effective?*

Vocabulary

subservient (səb sur´ vē ənt) *adj.* useful, in an inferior capacity, to promote an end; submissive

---

BETTY. You drank blood, Abby! You didn't tell him that!

ABIGAIL. Betty, you never say that again! You will never—

BETTY. You did, you did! You drank a charm to kill John Proctor's wife! You drank a charm to kill Goody Proctor!

ABIGAIL. [*Smashes her across the face.*] Shut it! Now shut it!

BETTY. [*Collapsing on the bed.*] Mama, Mama! [*She dissolves into sobs.*]

ABIGAIL. Now look you. All of you. We danced. And Tituba conjured Ruth Putnam's dead sisters. And that is all. And mark this. Let either of you breathe a word, or the edge of a word, about the other things, and I will come to you in the black of some terrible night and I will bring a pointy reckoning that will shudder you. And you know I can do it; I saw Indians smash my dear parents' heads on the pillow next to mine, and I have seen some reddish work[18] done at night, and I can make you wish you had never seen the sun go down! [*She goes to* BETTY *and roughly sits her up.*] Now, you—sit up and stop this!

[*But* BETTY *collapses in her hands and lies inert on the bed.*]

MARY WARREN. [*With hysterical fright.*] What's got her? [ABIGAIL *stares in fright at* BETTY.] Abby, she's going to die! It's a sin to conjure, and we—

ABIGAIL. [*Starting for* MARY.] I say shut it, Mary Warren!

[*Enter* JOHN PROCTOR. *On seeing him,* MARY WARREN *leaps in fright.*]

MARY WARREN. Oh! I'm just going home, Mr. Proctor.

PROCTOR. Be you foolish, Mary Warren? Be you deaf? I forbid you leave the house, did I not? Why shall I pay you? I am looking for you more often than my cows!

---

18. **Reddish work** means "bloody deeds."

Reading Strategy Drawing Conclusions About Characters *What new insight into Abigail's character do these remarks offer?*

MARY WARREN. I only come to see the great doings in the world.

PROCTOR. I'll show you a great doin' on your arse one of these days. Now get you home; my wife is waitin' with your work! [*Trying to retain a shred of dignity, she goes slowly out.*]

MERCY LEWIS. [*Both afraid of him and strangely titillated.*][19] I'd best be off. I have my Ruth to watch. Good morning, Mr. Proctor.

[*MERCY sidles out. Since PROCTOR's entrance, ABIGAIL has stood as though on tiptoe, absorbing his presence, wide-eyed. He glances at her, then goes to BETTY on the bed.*]

ABIGAIL. Gah! I'd almost forgot how strong you are, John Proctor!

PROCTOR. [*Looking at ABIGAIL now, the faintest suggestion of a knowing smile on his face.*] What's this mischief here?

ABIGAIL. [*With a nervous laugh.*] Oh, she's only gone silly somehow.

PROCTOR. The road past my house is a pilgrimage to Salem all morning. The town's mumbling witchcraft.

ABIGAIL. Oh, posh! [*Winningly she comes a little closer, with a confidential, wicked air.*] We were dancin' in the woods last night, and my uncle leaped in on us. She took fright, is all.

PROCTOR. [*His smile widening.*] Ah, you're wicked yet, aren't y'! [*A trill of expectant laughter escapes her, and she dares come closer, feverishly looking into his eyes.*] You'll be clapped in the stocks[20] before you're twenty.

[*He takes a step to go, and she springs into his path.*]

ABIGAIL. Give me a word, John. A soft word. [*Her concentrated desire destroys his smile.*]

PROCTOR. No, no, Abby. That's done with.

---

19. To be *titillated* is to be pleasantly excited or stimulated.
20. The word *stocks* refers to a heavy wooden frame with holes for confining the ankles and wrists of someone found guilty of a crime.

Literary Element Dialogue *What do the other girls call Proctor? How does Abigail's use of his first name help define their relationship?*

Big Idea The United States and the World *What does this menacing statement foreshadow?*

ABIGAIL. [*Tauntingly.*][21] You come five mile to see a silly girl fly? I know you better.

PROCTOR. [*Setting her firmly out of his path.*] I come to see what mischief your uncle's brewin' now. [*With final emphasis.*] Put it out of mind, Abby.

ABIGAIL. [*Grasping his hand before he can release her.*] John—I am waitin' for you every night.

PROCTOR. Abby, I never give you hope to wait for me.

ABIGAIL. [*Now beginning to anger—she can't believe it.*] I have something better than hope, I think!

PROCTOR. Abby, you'll put it out of mind. I'll not be comin' for you more.

ABIGAIL. You're surely sportin' with me.

PROCTOR. You know me better.

ABIGAIL. I know how you clutched my back behind your house and sweated like a stallion whenever I come near! Or did I dream that? It's she put me out, you cannot pretend it were you. I saw your face when she put me out, and you loved me then and you do now!

PROCTOR. Abby, that's a wild thing to say—

ABIGAIL. A wild thing may say wild things. But not so wild, I think. I have seen you since she put me out; I have seen you nights.

PROCTOR. I have hardly stepped off my farm this sevenmonth.

ABIGAIL. I have a sense for heat, John, and yours has drawn me to my window, and I have seen you looking up, burning in your loneliness. Do you tell me you've never looked up at my window?

PROCTOR. I may have looked up.

ABIGAIL. [*Now softening.*] And you must. You are no wintry man. I know you, John. I *know* you. [*She is weeping.*] I cannot sleep for dreamin'; I cannot dream but I wake and walk about the house as though I'd find you comin' through some door. [*She clutches him desperately.*]

PROCTOR. [*Gently pressing her from him, with great sympathy but firmly.*] Child—

ABIGAIL. [*With a flash of anger.*] How do you call me child!

---

21. *Tauntingly* means "in a scornful or mocking way."

PROCTOR. Abby, I may think of you softly from time to time. But I will cut off my hand before I'll ever reach for you again. Wipe it out of mind. We never touched, Abby.

ABIGAIL. Aye, but we did.

PROCTOR. Aye, but we did not.

ABIGAIL. [*With a bitter anger.*] Oh, I marvel how such a strong man may let such a sickly wife be—

PROCTOR. [*Angered—at himself as well.*] You'll speak nothin' of Elizabeth!

ABIGAIL. She is blackening my name in the village! She is telling lies about me! She is a cold, sniveling woman, and you bend to her! Let her turn you like a—

PROCTOR. [*Shaking her.*] Do you look for whippin'?

[*A psalm is heard being sung below.*]

ABIGAIL. [*In tears.*] I look for John Proctor that took me from my sleep and put knowledge in my heart! I never knew what **pretense** Salem was, I never knew the lying lessons I was taught by all these Christian women and their covenanted[22] men! And now you bid me tear the light out of my eyes? I will not, I cannot! You loved me, John Proctor, and whatever sin it is, you love me yet! [*He turns abruptly to go out. She rushes to him.*] John, pity me, pity me!

[*The words "going up to Jesus" are heard in the psalm, and BETTY claps her ears suddenly and whines loudly.*]

ABIGAIL. Betty? [*She hurries to BETTY, who is now sitting up and screaming. PROCTOR goes to BETTY as ABIGAIL is trying to pull her hands down, calling "Betty!"*]

---

22. A covenant is an agreement or promise. Among the Puritans, a *covenanted* person had made a commitment to the church and had signed an agreement testifying to his or her faith.

Reading Strategy Drawing Conclusions About Characters *In your opinion, does Proctor show strength or weakness in this denial?*

Literary Element Dialogue *In your opinion, is Abigail sincere in this speech? Explain.*

Vocabulary

pretense (prē′ tens) *n.* a false show or appearance, especially for the purpose of deceiving; falseness

---

PROCTOR. [*Growing unnerved.*] What's she doing? Girl, what ails you? Stop that wailing!

[*The singing has stopped in the midst of this, and now PARRIS rushes in.*]

PARRIS. What happened? What are you doing to her? Betty! [*He rushes to the bed, crying, "Betty, Betty!" MRS. PUTNAM enters, feverish with curiosity, and with her THOMAS PUTNAM and MERCY LEWIS. PARRIS, at the bed, keeps lightly slapping BETTY's face, while she moans and tries to get up.*]

ABIGAIL. She heard you singin' and suddenly she's up and screamin'.

MRS. PUTNAM. The psalm! The psalm! She cannot bear to hear the Lord's name!

PARRIS. No, God forbid. Mercy, run to the doctor! Tell him what's happened here! [*MERCY LEWIS rushes out.*]

MRS. PUTNAM. Mark it for a sign, mark it!

[*REBECCA NURSE, seventy-two, enters. She is white-haired, leaning upon her walking-stick.*]

PUTNAM. [*Pointing at the whimpering BETTY.*] That is a notorious sign of witchcraft afoot, Goody Nurse, a prodigious[23] sign!

MRS. PUTNAM. My mother told me that! When they cannot bear to hear the name of—

PARRIS. [*Trembling.*] Rebecca, Rebecca, go to her, we're lost. She suddenly cannot bear to hear the Lord's—

[*GILES COREY, eighty-three, enters. He is knotted with muscle, canny,[24] inquisitive, and still powerful.*]

REBECCA. There is hard sickness here, Giles Corey, so please to keep the quiet.

GILES. I've not said a word. No one here can testify I've said a word. Is she going to fly again? I hear she flies.

PUTNAM. Man, be quiet now!

[*Everything is quiet. REBECCA walks across the room to the bed. Gentleness exudes[25] from her. BETTY is quietly whimpering, eyes shut. REBECCA simply stands over the child, who gradually quiets.*]

MRS. PUTNAM. [*Astonished.*] What have you done?

---

23. *Prodigious* means "amazing."
24. *Canny* means "sharp, clever, and careful in one's dealings with others."
25. *Exudes* means "gives forth."

[REBECCA, *in thought, now leaves the bedside and sits.*]

PARRIS. [*Wondrous and relieved.*] What do you make of it, Rebecca?

PUTNAM. [*Eagerly.*] Goody Nurse, will you go to my Ruth and see if you can wake her?

REBECCA. [*Sitting.*] I think she'll wake in time. Pray calm yourselves. I have eleven children, and I am twenty-six times a grandma, and I have seen them all through their silly seasons, and when it come on them they will run the Devil bowlegged keeping up with their mischief. I think she'll wake when she tires of it. A child's spirit is like a child, you can never catch it by running after it; you must stand still, and, for love, it will soon itself come back.

PROCTOR. Aye, that's the truth of it, Rebecca.

MRS. PUTNAM. This is no silly season, Rebecca. My Ruth is bewildered, Rebecca; she cannot eat.

REBECCA. Perhaps she is not hungered yet. [*To PARRIS.*] I hope you are not decided to go in search of loose spirits, Mr. Parris. I've heard promise of that outside.

PARRIS. A wide opinion's running in the parish that the Devil may be among us, and I would satisfy them that they are wrong.

PROCTOR. Then let you come out and call them wrong. Did you consult the wardens[26] before you called this minister to look for devils?

PARRIS. He is not coming to look for devils!

PROCTOR. Then what's he coming for?

PUTNAM. There be children dyin' in the village, Mister!

PROCTOR. I seen none dyin'. This society will not be a bag to swing around your head, Mr. Putnam. [*To PARRIS.*] Did you call a meeting before you—?

PUTNAM. I am sick of meetings; cannot the man turn his head without he have a meeting?

PROCTOR. He may turn his head, but not to Hell!

---

26. The church *wardens* were members who managed the congregation's business affairs.

Reading Strategy Drawing Conclusions About Characters *How do the Putnams and Rebecca disagree on the subject of witchcraft?*

REBECCA. Pray, John, be calm. [*Pause. He defers to her.*] Mr. Parris, I think you'd best send Reverend Hale back as soon as he come. This will set us all to arguin' again in the society, and we thought to have peace this year. I think we ought rely on the doctor now, and good prayer.

MRS. PUTNAM. Rebecca, the doctor's baffled!

REBECCA. If so he is, then let us go to God for the cause of it. There is prodigious danger in the seeking of loose spirits. I fear it, I fear it. Let us rather blame ourselves and—

PUTNAM. How may we blame ourselves? I am one of nine sons; the Putnam seed have peopled this province. And yet I have but one child left of eight—and now she shrivels!

REBECCA. I cannot fathom that.

MRS. PUTNAM. [*With a growing edge of sarcasm.*] But I must! You think it God's work you should never lose a child, nor grandchild either, and I bury all but one? There are wheels within wheels in this village, and fires within fires![27]

PUTNAM. [*To PARRIS.*] When Reverend Hale comes, you will proceed to look for signs of witchcraft here.

PROCTOR. [*To PUTNAM.*] You cannot command Mr. Parris. We vote by name in this society, not by acreage.

PUTNAM. I never heard you worried so on this society, Mr. Proctor. I do not think I saw you at Sabbath meeting since snow flew.

PROCTOR. I have trouble enough without I come five mile to hear him preach only hellfire and bloody damnation. Take it to heart, Mr. Parris. There are many others who stay away from church these days because you hardly ever mention God any more.

---

27. The expression *wheels within . . . fires!* means "things are not so simple or innocent as they seem."

Reading Strategy Drawing Conclusions About Characters *Why does Proctor listen to Rebecca with respect?*

Big Idea The United States and the World *What danger might Rebecca be referring to? Why is it safer to "blame ourselves"?*

Reading Strategy Drawing Conclusions About Characters *What do we learn about Reverend Parris's priorities as a minister from Proctor's accusation?*

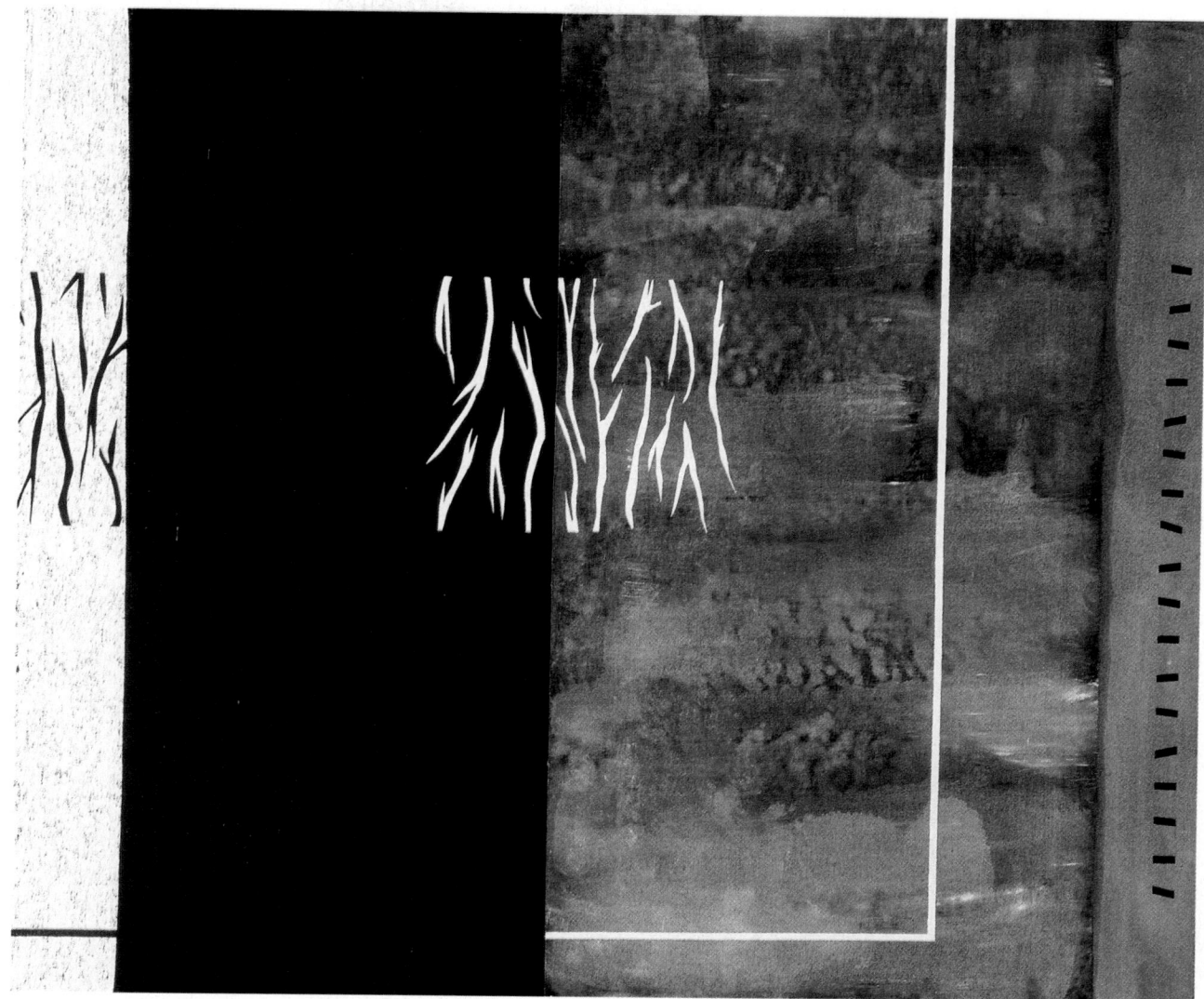

Window View—Scapeology #3, 1995. Nanette Carter. Oil on canvas, 40¾ x 45½ in. Sande Webster Gallery, Philadelphia, PA.

Viewing the Art: What contrasts and divisions do you see in this painting? How might they reflect the contrasts and divisions among the people gathered in Betty's room?

PARRIS. [*Now aroused.*] Why, that's a drastic charge!

REBECCA. It's somewhat true; there are many that quail[28] to bring their children—

PARRIS. I do not preach for children, Rebecca. It is not the children who are unmindful of their obligations toward this ministry.

REBECCA. Are there really those unmindful?

PARRIS. I should say the better half of Salem village—

PUTNAM. And more than that!

PARRIS. Where is my wood? My contract provides I be supplied with all my firewood. I am waiting since November for a stick, and even in November I had to show my frostbitten hands like some London beggar!

GILES. You are allowed six pound a year to buy your wood, Mr. Parris.

PARRIS. I regard that six pound as part of my salary. I am paid little enough without I spend six pound on firewood.

PROCTOR. Sixty, plus six for firewood—

PARRIS. The salary is sixty-six pound, Mr. Proctor! I am not some preaching farmer with a book under my arm; I am a graduate of Harvard College.

---

28. To *quail* is to hesitate, to lose heart, or to retreat in fear.

GILES. Aye, and well instructed in arithmetic!

PARRIS. Mr. Corey, you will look far for a man of my kind at sixty pound a year! I am not used to this poverty; I left a thrifty business in the Barbados to serve the Lord. I do not fathom it, why am I persecuted here? I cannot offer one proposition but there be a howling riot of argument. I have often wondered if the Devil be in it somewhere; I cannot understand you people otherwise.

PROCTOR. Mr. Parris, you are the first minister ever did demand the deed to this house—

PARRIS. Man! Don't a minister deserve a house to live in?

PROCTOR. To live in, yes. But to ask ownership is like you shall own the meeting house itself; the last meeting I were at you spoke so long on deeds and mortgages I thought it were an auction.

PARRIS. I want a mark of confidence, is all! I am your third preacher in seven years. I do not wish to be put out like the cat whenever some majority feels the whim. You people seem not to comprehend that a minister is the Lord's man in the parish; a minister is not to be so lightly crossed and contradicted—

PUTNAM. Aye!

PARRIS. There is either obedience or the church will burn like Hell is burning!

PROCTOR. Can you speak one minute without we land in Hell again? I am sick of Hell!

PARRIS. It is not for you to say what is good for you to hear!

PROCTOR. I may speak my heart, I think!

PARRIS. [*In a fury.*] What, are we Quakers?[29] We are not Quakers here yet, Mr. Proctor. And you may tell that to your followers!

PROCTOR. My followers!

PARRIS. [*Now he's out with it.*] There is a party in this church. I am not blind; there is a faction and a party.

PROCTOR. Against you?

PUTNAM. Against him and all authority!

PROCTOR. Why, then I must find it and join it.

[*There is shock among the others.*]

REBECCA. He does not mean that.

PUTNAM. He confessed it now!

PROCTOR. I mean it solemnly, Rebecca; I like not the smell of this "authority."

REBECCA. No, you cannot break charity[30] with your minister. You are another kind, John. Clasp his hand, make your peace.

PROCTOR. I have a crop to sow and lumber to drag home. [*He goes angrily to the door and turns to* COREY *with a smile.*] What say you, Giles, let's find the party. He says there's a party.

GILES. I've changed my opinion of this man, John. Mr. Parris, I beg your pardon. I never thought you had so much iron in you.

PARRIS. [*Surprised.*] Why, thank you, Giles!

GILES. It suggests to the mind what the trouble be among us all these years. [*To all.*] Think on it. Wherefore is everybody suing everybody else? Think on it now, it's a deep thing, and dark as a pit. I have been six time in court this year—

PROCTOR. [*Familiarly, with warmth, although he knows he is approaching the edge of* GILES' *tolerance with this.*] Is it the Devil's fault that a man cannot say you good morning without you clap him for defamation?[31] You're old, Giles, and you're not hearin' so well as you did.

GILES. [*He cannot be crossed.*] John Proctor, I have only last month collected four pound damages for you publicly sayin' I burned the roof off your house, and I—

---

30. For the Puritans, *charity* was Christian love, including mercy, forgiveness, kindness, and trust.
31. An attack on one's good name or reputation is an act of *defamation* (def′ ə mā′ shən).

Big Idea The United States and the World *What "authority" might a U.S. audience in 1953 have thought of on hearing this line?*

Literary Element Dialogue *How does Miller engage the audience's sympathy for Proctor in this line of dialogue?*

---

29. *Quakers* is the familiar name for members of the Society of Friends. They have no definite creed and are guided by their doctrine of "inner light."

Literary Element Dialogue *How does Miller use dialogue on this page to advance the plot?*

PROCTOR. [Laughing.] I never said no such thing, but I've paid you for it, so I hope I can call you deaf without charge. Now come along, Giles, and help me drag my lumber home.

PUTNAM. A moment, Mr. Proctor. What lumber is that you're draggin', if I may ask you?

PROCTOR. My lumber. From out my forest by the riverside.

PUTNAM. Why, we are surely gone wild this year. What anarchy[32] is this? That tract is in my bounds, it's in my bounds, Mr. Proctor.

PROCTOR. In your bounds! [Indicating REBECCA.] I bought that tract from Goody Nurse's husband five months ago.

PUTNAM. He had no right to sell it. It stands clear in my grandfather's will that all the land between the river and—

PROCTOR. Your grandfather had a habit of willing land that never belonged to him, if I may say it plain.

GILES. That's God's truth; he nearly willed away my north pasture but he knew I'd break his fingers before he'd set his name to it. Let's get your lumber home, John. I feel a sudden will to work coming on.

PUTNAM. You load one oak of mine and you'll fight to drag it home!

GILES. Aye, and we'll win too, Putnam—this fool and I. Come on! [He turns to PROCTOR and starts out.]

PUTNAM. I'll have my men on you, Corey! I'll clap a writ[33] on you!

[Enter REVEREND JOHN HALE of Beverly. He appears loaded down with half a dozen heavy books.]

HALE. Pray you, someone take these!

PARRIS. [Delighted.] Mr. Hale! Oh! it's good to see you again! [Taking some books.] My, they're heavy!

HALE. [Setting down his books.] They must be; they are weighted with authority.

PARRIS. [A little scared.] Well, you do come prepared!

HALE. We shall need hard study if it comes to tracking down the Old Boy.[34] [Noticing REBECCA.] You cannot be Rebecca Nurse?

REBECCA. I am, sir. Do you know me?

HALE. It's strange how I knew you, but I suppose you look as such a good soul should. We have all heard of your great charities in Beverly.

PARRIS. Do you know this gentleman? Mr. Thomas Putnam. And his good wife Ann.

HALE. Putnam! I had not expected such distinguished company, sir.

PUTNAM. [Pleased.] It does not seem to help us today, Mr. Hale. We look to you to come to our house and save our child.

HALE. Your child ails too?

MRS. PUTNAM. Her soul, her soul seems flown away. She sleeps and yet she walks . . .

PUTNAM. She cannot eat.

HALE. Cannot eat! [Thinks on it. Then, to PROCTOR and GILES COREY.] Do you men have afflicted children?

PARRIS. No, no, these are farmers. John Proctor—

GILES COREY. He don't believe in witches.

PROCTOR. [To HALE.] I never spoke on witches one way or the other. Will you come, Giles?

GILES. No—no, John, I think not. I have some few queer questions of my own to ask this fellow.

PROCTOR. I've heard you to be a sensible man, Mr. Hale. I hope you'll leave some of it in Salem.

[PROCTOR goes. HALE stands embarrassed for an instant.]

PARRIS. [Quickly.] Will you look at my daughter, sir? [Leads HALE to the bed.] She has tried to leap out the window; we discovered her this

---

32. *Anarchy* is lawless confusion and political disorder due to the absence of governmental authority. Here, Putnam uses the word to mean "lawlessness."
33. A *writ* is a judge's order.

34. *Old Boy* is another name for Satan.

Reading Strategy Drawing Conclusions About Characters *What do we learn about Proctor's character from this remark?*

The Crucible, 1996.

morning on the highroad, waving her arms as though she'd fly.

HALE. [*Narrowing his eyes.*] Tries to fly.

PUTNAM. She cannot bear to hear the Lord's name, Mr. Hale; that's a sure sign of witchcraft afloat.

HALE. [*Holding up his hands.*] No, no. Now let me instruct you. We cannot look to superstition in this. The Devil is precise; the marks of his presence are definite as stone, and I must tell you all that I shall not proceed unless you

are prepared to believe me if I should find no bruise of hell upon her.

PARRIS. It is agreed, sir—it is agreed—we will abide by your judgment.

HALE. Good then. [*He goes to the bed, looks down at* BETTY. *To* PARRIS.] Now, sir, what were your first warning of this strangeness?

PARRIS. Why, sir—I discovered her—[*Indicating* ABIGAIL.]—and my niece and ten or twelve of the other girls, dancing in the forest last night.

HALE. [*Surprised.*] You permit dancing?

PARRIS. No, no, it were secret—

MRS. PUTNAM. [*Unable to wait.*] Mr. Parris's slave has knowledge of conjurin', sir.

Big Idea The United States and the World *How might Miller's 1950s audiences have connected Reverend Hale's use of the word* superstition *to contemporary events?*

PARRIS. [*To MRS. PUTNAM.*] We cannot be sure of that, Goody Ann—

MRS. PUTNAM. [*Frightened, very softly.*] I know it, sir. I sent my child—she should learn from Tituba who murdered her sisters.

REBECCA. [*Horrified.*] Goody Ann! You sent a child to conjure up the dead?

MRS. PUTNAM. Let God blame me, not you, not you, Rebecca! I'll not have you judging me any more! [*To HALE.*] Is it a natural work to lose seven children before they live a day?

PARRIS. Sssh!

[*REBECCA, with great pain, turns her face away. There is a pause.*]

HALE. Seven dead in childbirth.

MRS. PUTNAM. [*Softly.*] Aye. [*Her voice breaks; she looks up at him. Silence. HALE is impressed. PARRIS looks to him. He goes to his books, opens one, turns pages, then reads. All wait, avidly.*][35]

PARRIS. [*Hushed.*] What book is that?

MRS. PUTNAM. What's there, sir?

HALE. [*With a tasty love of intellectual pursuit.*] Here is all the invisible world, caught, defined, and calculated. In these books the Devil stands stripped of all his brute disguises. Here are all your familiar spirits—your incubi and succubi;[36] your witches that go by land, by air, and by sea; your wizards of the night and of the day. Have no fear now—we shall find him out if he has come among us, and I mean to crush him utterly if he has shown his face! [*He starts for the bed.*]

REBECCA. Will it hurt the child, sir?

HALE. I cannot tell. If she is truly in the Devil's grip we may have to rip and tear to get her free.

REBECCA. I think I'll go, then. I am too old for this. [*She rises.*]

PARRIS. [*Striving for conviction.*] Why, Rebecca, we may open up the boil of all our troubles today!

REBECCA. Let us hope for that. I go to God for you, sir.

PARRIS. [*With trepidation—and resentment.*] I hope you do not mean we go to Satan here! [*Slight pause.*]

REBECCA. I wish I knew. [*She goes out; they feel resentful of her note of moral superiority.*]

PUTNAM. [*Abruptly.*] Come, Mr. Hale, let's get on. Sit you here.

GILES. Mr. Hale, I have always wanted to ask a learned man—what signifies the readin' of strange books?

HALE. What books?

GILES. I cannot tell; she hides them.

HALE. Who does this?

GILES. Martha, my wife. I have waked at night many a time and found her in a corner, readin' of a book. Now what do you make of that?

HALE. Why, that's not necessarily—

GILES. It discomfits[37] me! Last night—mark this—I tried and tried and could not say my prayers. And then she close her book and walks out of the house, and suddenly—mark this—I could pray again!

HALE. Ah! The stoppage of prayer—that is strange. I'll speak further on that with you.

GILES. I'm not sayin' she's touched the Devil, now, but I'd admire to know what books she reads and why she hides them. She'll not answer me, y' see.

HALE. Aye, we'll discuss it. [*To all.*] Now mark me, if the Devil is in her you will witness some frightful wonders in this room, so please to keep your wits about you. Mr. Putnam, stand close in case she flies. Now, Betty, dear, will you sit up? [*PUTNAM comes in closer, ready-handed. HALE sits BETTY up, but she hangs limp in his hands.*] Hmmm. [*He observes her carefully. The others watch breathlessly.*] Can you hear me? I am John Hale, minister of Beverly. I have come to help you, dear. Do you remember my two little girls in Beverly? [*She does not stir in his hands.*]

---

37. *Discomfits* means "confuses and frustrates."

Big Idea The United States and the World *What is Giles suspicious of? How are his suspicions similar to those of Senator McCarthy during the 1950s?* **B12**

---

35. *Avidly* means "with intense interest."
36. *Incubi* (ing′ kyə bī′) and *succubi* (suk′ yə bī′) are evil spirits or demons.

PARRIS. [*In fright.*] How can it be the Devil? Why would he choose my house to strike? We have all manner of licentious[38] people in the village!

HALE. What victory would the Devil have to win a soul already bad? It is the best the Devil wants, and who is better than the minister?

GILES. That's deep, Mr. Parris, deep, deep!

PARRIS. [*With resolution now.*] Betty! Answer Mr. Hale! Betty!

HALE. Does someone afflict you, child? It need not be a woman, mind you, or a man. Perhaps some bird invisible to others comes to you—perhaps a pig, a mouse, or any beast at all. Is there some figure bids you fly? [*The child remains limp in his hands. In silence he lays her back on the pillow. Now, holding out his hands toward her, he intones.*] In nomine Domini Sabaoth sui filiique ite ad infernos.[39] [*She does not stir. He turns to* ABIGAIL, *his eyes narrowing.*] Abigail, what sort of dancing were you doing with her in the forest?

ABIGAIL. Why—common dancing is all.

PARRIS. I think I ought to say that I—I saw a kettle in the grass where they were dancing.

ABIGAIL. That were only soup.

HALE. What sort of soup were in this kettle, Abigail?

ABIGAIL. Why, it were beans—and lentils, I think, and—

HALE. Mr. Parris, you did not notice, did you, any living thing in the kettle? A mouse, perhaps, a spider, a frog—?

PARRIS. [*Fearfully.*] I—do believe there were some movement—in the soup.

ABIGAIL. That jumped in, we never put it in!

HALE. [*Quickly.*] What jumped in?

ABIGAIL. Why, a very little frog jumped—

PARRIS. A frog, Abby!

HALE. [*Grasping* ABIGAIL.] Abigail, it may be your cousin is dying. Did you call the Devil last night?

ABIGAIL. I never called him! Tituba, Tituba . . .

PARRIS. [*Blanched.*] She called the Devil?

HALE. I should like to speak with Tituba.

PARRIS. Goody Ann, will you bring her up? [MRS. PUTNAM *exits.*]

HALE. How did she call him?

ABIGAIL. I know not—she spoke Barbados.

HALE. Did you feel any strangeness when she called him? A sudden cold wind, perhaps? A trembling below the ground?

ABIGAIL. I didn't see no Devil! [*Shaking* BETTY.] Betty, wake up. Betty! Betty!

HALE. You cannot **evade** me, Abigail. Did your cousin drink any of the brew in that kettle?

ABIGAIL. She never drank it!

HALE. Did you drink it?

ABIGAIL. No, sir!

HALE. Did Tituba ask you to drink it?

ABIGAIL. She tried, but I refused.

HALE. Why are you concealing? Have you sold yourself to Lucifer?

ABIGAIL. I never sold myself! I'm a good girl! I'm a proper girl!

[MRS. PUTNAM *enters with* TITUBA, *and instantly* ABIGAIL *points at* TITUBA.]

ABIGAIL. She made me do it! She made Betty do it!

TITUBA. [*Shocked and angry.*] Abby!

ABIGAIL. She makes me drink blood!

PARRIS. Blood!!

MRS. PUTNAM. My baby's blood?

TITUBA. No, no, chicken blood. I give she chicken blood!

---

38. *Licentious* people disregard commonly accepted standards of right and wrong or good and evil.

39. [*In nomine . . . infernos.*] "In the name of the God of the Heavenly Hosts and of His Son, go to hell." Hale is performing an exorcism, a ritual intended to drive out evil spirits.

Reading Strategy Drawing Conclusions About Characters *What aspect of her character does Abigail confirm with these remarks?*

Vocabulary

evade (i vād´) v. to escape or avoid, as by cleverness

HALE. Woman, have you enlisted these children for the Devil?

TITUBA. No, no, sir, I don't truck[40] with no Devil!

HALE. Why can she not wake? Are you silencing this child?

TITUBA. I love me Betty!

HALE. You have sent your spirit out upon this child, have you not? Are you gathering souls for the Devil?

ABIGAIL. She sends her spirit on me in church; she makes me laugh at prayer!

PARRIS. She have often laughed at prayer!

ABIGAIL. She comes to me every night to go and drink blood!

TITUBA. You beg *me* to conjure! She beg *me* make charm—

ABIGAIL. Don't lie! [*To* HALE.] She comes to me while I sleep; she's always making me dream corruptions!

TITUBA. Why you say that, Abby?

ABIGAIL. Sometimes I wake and find myself standing in the open doorway and not a stitch on my body! I always hear her laughing in my sleep. I hear her singing her Barbados songs and tempting me with—

TITUBA. Mister Reverend, I never—

HALE. [*Resolved now.*] Tituba, I want you to wake this child.

TITUBA. I have no power on this child, sir.

HALE. You most certainly do, and you will free her from it now! When did you compact with[41] the Devil?

TITUBA. I don't compact with no Devil!

PARRIS. You will confess yourself or I will take you out and whip you to your death, Tituba!

---

40. *Truck* is another way of saying "to have dealings."
41. To *compact with* is to make an agreement or contract with.

Literary Element Dialogue *How does Miller's use of dialogue ensure that Tituba is so quickly on the defensive?*

Literary Element Dialogue *What is Tituba accusing Abigail of in this dialogue? Do you think she will be believed? Explain.*

PUTNAM. This woman must be hanged! She must be taken and hanged!

TITUBA. [*Terrified, falls to her knees.*] No, no, don't hang Tituba! I tell him I don't desire to work for him, sir.

PARRIS. The Devil?

HALE. Then you saw him! [*TITUBA weeps.*] Now Tituba, I know that when we bind ourselves to Hell it is very hard to break with it. We are going to help you tear yourself free—

TITUBA. [*Frightened by the coming process.*] Mister Reverend, I do believe somebody else be witchin' these children.

HALE. Who?

TITUBA. I don't know, sir, but the Devil got him numerous witches.

HALE. Does he! [*It is a clue.*] Tituba, look into my eyes. Come, look into me. [*She raises her eyes to his fearfully.*] You would be a good Christian woman, would you not, Tituba?

TITUBA. Aye, sir, a good Christian woman.

HALE. And you love these little children?

TITUBA. Oh, yes, sir, I don't desire to hurt little children.

HALE. And you love God, Tituba?

TITUBA. I love God with all my bein'.

HALE. Now, in God's holy name—

TITUBA. Bless Him. Bless Him. [*She is rocking on her knees, sobbing in terror.*]

HALE. And to His glory—

TITUBA. Eternal glory. Bless Him—bless God . . .

HALE. Open yourself, Tituba—open yourself and let God's holy light shine on you.

TITUBA. Oh, bless the Lord.

HALE. When the Devil comes to you does he ever come—with another person? [*She stares up into his face.*] Perhaps another person in the village? Someone you know.

PARRIS. Who came with him?

Big Idea The United States and the World *How is the assumption that Tituba is guilty similar to assumptions made during the McCarthy "witch hunts"?*

Omen, 1993. Katherine Bowling. Oil and spackle on wood, 24 x 24 in. The SBC Collection of Twentieth Century American Art. Courtesy SBC Communications.

Viewing the Art: What connections might you make between this painting and the description of the night the girls went to the forest?

PUTNAM. Sarah Good? Did you ever see Sarah Good with him? Or Osburn?

PARRIS. Was it man or woman came with him?

TITUBA. Man or woman. Was—was woman.

PARRIS. What woman? A woman, you said. What woman?

TITUBA. It was black dark, and I—

PARRIS. You could see him, why could you not see her?

TITUBA. Well, they was always talking; they was always runnin' round and carryin' on—

PARRIS. You mean out of Salem? Salem witches?

TITUBA. I believe so, yes, sir.

[*Now* HALE *takes her hand. She is surprised.*]

HALE. Tituba. You must have no fear to tell us who they are, do you understand? We will protect you. The Devil can never overcome a minister. You know that, do you not?

TITUBA. [*Kisses* HALE's *hand.*] Aye, sir, I do.

HALE. You have confessed yourself to witchcraft, and that speaks a wish to come to Heaven's side. And we will bless you, Tituba.

TITUBA. [*Deeply relieved.*] Oh, God bless you, Mr. Hale!

HALE. [*With rising exaltation.*][42] You are God's instrument put in our hands to discover the Devil's agents among us. You are selected, Tituba, you are chosen to help us cleanse our village. So speak utterly, Tituba, turn your back on him and face God—face God, Tituba, and God will protect you.

TITUBA. [*Joining with him.*] Oh, God, protect Tituba!

HALE. [*Kindly.*] Who came to you with the Devil? Two? Three? Four? How many?

[*TITUBA pants, and begins rocking back and forth again, staring ahead.*]

TITUBA. There was four. There was four.

PARRIS. [*Pressing in on her.*] Who? Who? Their names, their names!

TITUBA. [*Suddenly bursting out.*] Oh, how many times he bid me kill you, Mr. Parris!

PARRIS. Kill me!

TITUBA. [*In a fury.*] He say Mr. Parris must be kill! Mr. Parris no goodly man, Mr. Parris mean man and no gentle man, and he bid me rise out of my bed and cut your throat! [*They gasp.*] But I tell him, "No! I don't hate that man. I don't want kill that man." But he say, "You work for me, Tituba, and I make you free! I give you pretty dress to wear, and put you way high up in the air, and you gone fly back to Barbados!" And I say, "You lie, Devil, you lie!" And then he come one stormy night to me, and he say, "Look! I have *white* people belong to me." And I look—and there was Goody Good.

PARRIS. Sarah Good!

TITUBA. [*Rocking and weeping.*] Aye, sir, and Goody Osburn.

MRS. PUTNAM. I knew it! Goody Osburn were midwife[43] to me three times. I begged you, Thomas, did I not? I begged him not to call Osburn because I feared her. My babies always shriveled in her hands!

HALE. Take courage, you must give us all their names. How can you bear to see this child suffering? Look at her, Tituba. [*He is indicating* BETTY *on the bed.*] Look at her God-given innocence; her soul is so tender; we must protect her, Tituba; the Devil is out and preying on her like a beast upon the flesh of the pure lamb. God will bless you for your help.

[*ABIGAIL rises, staring as though inspired, and cries out.*]

ABIGAIL. I want to open myself! [*They turn to her, startled. She is enraptured,*[44] *as though in a*

---

42. Here, *exaltation* means "great enthusiasm" or "joyful ecstasy."

Reading Strategy Drawing Conclusions About Characters *What does Putnam's eagerness to name specific people reveal about his character?*

Big Idea The United States and the World *How is this tactic similar to that used by the House Un-American Activities Committee?*

---

43. A *midwife* is a woman who assists other women in childbirth.
44. *Enraptured* means "filled with intense joy or delight."

Reading Strategy Drawing Conclusions About Characters *What is going on in Tituba's mind that she would make up information like this?*

Ocean Greyness, 1953. Jackson Pollock. Oil on canvas, 4 ft. 9¾ in. x 7 ft. 6⅛ in. Solomon R. Guggenheim Museum, New York.

Viewing the Art: Look at the interplay of colors in this painting. What characters or events in act 1 might these colors represent? Explain.

pearly light.] I want the light of God, I want the sweet love of Jesus! I danced for the Devil; I saw him; I wrote in his book; I go back to Jesus; I kiss His hand. I saw Sarah Good with the Devil! I saw Goody Osburn with the Devil! I saw Bridget Bishop with the Devil!

[*As she is speaking,* BETTY *is rising from the bed, a fever in her eyes, and picks up the chant.*]

BETTY. [*Staring too.*] I saw George Jacobs with the Devil! I saw Goody Howe with the Devil!

PARRIS. She speaks! [*He rushes to embrace* BETTY.] She speaks!

HALE. Glory to God! It is broken, they are free!

BETTY. [*Calling out hysterically and with great relief.*] I saw Martha Bellows with the Devil!

ABIGAIL. I saw Goody Sibber with the Devil! [*It is rising to a great glee.*]

PUTNAM. The marshal, I'll call the marshal!

[PARRIS *is shouting a prayer of thanksgiving.*]

BETTY. I saw Alice Barrow with the Devil!

[*The curtain begins to fall.*]

HALE. [*As* PUTNAM *goes out.*] Let the marshal bring irons!

ABIGAIL. I saw Goody Hawkins with the Devil!

BETTY. I saw Goody Bibber with the Devil!

ABIGAIL. I saw Goody Booth with the Devil!

[*On their ecstatic cries.*]

THE CURTAIN FALLS

Reading Strategy Drawing Conclusions About Characters *Why do you think that Abigail makes this confession?*

Literary Element Dialogue *How do these concluding lines make an effective ending to Act One of the play?*

RESPONDING AND THINKING CRITICALLY

Respond

1. Which characters or situations in Act One do you find it easiest to identify with? Explain.

Recall and Interpret

2. (a)What is Reverend Parris praying for at the beginning of Act One? (b)What else might explain why he is praying so desperately?

3. (a)What reasons does Abigail give Parris for her discharge as the Proctors' servant? (b)What might be another reason?

4. (a)How does Tituba first respond to Hale's accusation of witchcraft? How does she change her response? (b)Why might Tituba, as well as Abigail and Betty, make accusations at the end of Act One?

Analyze and Evaluate

5. (a)How would you classify the atmosphere, or mood, of Act One? (b)What techniques does Miller use to create this mood?

6. (a)How does Miller dramatize the behavior of the young girls in Act One? (b)Do you find their behavior believable? Explain.

7. Act One ends with Betty and Abigail as the center of interest. (a)How is their behavior the same? How is it different? (b)Do you find their behavior believable? Explain.

Connect

8. **Big Idea** **The United States and the World** Arthur Miller drew a connection between the Salem witch hunts of 1692 and the Communist "witch hunts" in the 1950s. Under what circumstances might a similar situation arise in the United States today?

LITERARY ANALYSIS

Literary Element Dialogue

Much of the **dialogue** in *The Crucible* centers on series of questions and answers bandied between the characters. In fact, the play opens with Tituba's question, "My Betty be hearty soon?"

1. Which characters do the main questioning in Act One? Which characters are the subjects of the questioning?

2. What do the characters hope to determine by asking their questions?

Writing About Literature

Analyze Plot Miller called Act One an overture—an introduction. In literary terms, it would be called an **exposition**. Write two or three paragraphs analyzing how Miller has "set the stage" for the rest of the play with the setting, characters, and plot of Act One. Describe what, for you, is the narrative hook.

Literature Online **Web Activities** For eFlashcards, Selection Quick Checks, and other Web activities, go to www.glencoe.com.

READING AND VOCABULARY

Reading Strategy Drawing Conclusions About Characters

The numbered items below include a phrase Miller uses in his stage directions to describe the character in question. Give an example of each character's behavior that matches the description.

1. Abigail: *an endless capacity for dissembling*

2. Rebecca Nurse: *Gentleness exudes from her.*

Vocabulary Practice

Practice with Word Parts Each of the vocabulary words selected from Act One begins with a familiar **prefix.** Use a dictionary or a thesaurus to find other words that use the same prefixes and match the definitions below. Each answer will have one of the following prefixes: *com-, con-, sub-, pre-.*

1. to stop something happening

2. a town lying outside a city

3. to throw someone out of a residence

LITERATURE PREVIEW

READING PREVIEW

Building Background

The Puritans believed that if one member of the community sinned, misfortune could befall the entire community. Blame, therefore, was a common way to deal with personal misfortune. The Puritans also believed that all aspects of life must be guided by the Bible. In fact, communities built schools so that all could learn to read it. These efforts were intended to counteract the work of Satan, who people believed tried to "keep men from the knowledge of the scriptures."

A Puritan doctrine held that the active instrument of salvation was the Holy Spirit. Puritans tended to discredit reason as irrelevant or even harmful. For most Puritans, witchcraft and black magic were real and present dangers. To defeat this enemy from within, books such as *The Discovery of Witches* (1647) informed readers how to identify and destroy demonic spirits.

Setting Purposes for Reading

Literary Element Stage Directions

Stage directions are the instructions written by the playwright that describe the sets, costumes, and lighting as well as the appearance, movements, and dramatic attitudes of the characters. Stage directions are commonly written in italics and placed in brackets or parentheses to set them off from the spoken lines of the script. Note the stage directions in the example below. The first describes how the actress playing Elizabeth should say her lines. The second is an instruction in bodily movement for the actor playing Mr. Hale.

ELIZABETH. [*Unable to restrain herself.*] Mr. Hale. [*He turns.*] I do think you are suspecting me somewhat? Are you not?

As you read Act Two, observe how Miller's stage directions influence your understanding of the play.

- See Literary Terms Handbook, p. R17.

Literature Online **Interactive Literary Elements Handbook** To review or learn more about the literary elements, go to www.glencoe.com.

Reading Strategy Recognizing Bias

Bias is the author's personal inclination toward a certain opinion or position on a topic. Bias is seldom overtly stated in a dramatic work, but it can be detected by close attention to the way the dramatist expresses ideas through the dialogue of the characters and the stage directions. As you read Act Two of *The Crucible*, look for evidence of Miller's bias.

Reading Tip: Personality Profile Take careful note of how the author presents the characters.

- Notice the stage directions. These may indicate the author's bias.
- Assess the characters. An author will often express his or her ideas through a sympathetic character's speech.

Vocabulary

reprimand (rep′ rə mand′) *v.* to reprove or correct sharply; p. 1047 *I'm afraid that the boss will reprimand me for arriving late.*

base (bās) *adj.* morally low; dishonorable; p. 1054 *We did not expect base behavior from such a respected member of the community.*

covet (kuv′ it) *v.* to desire, especially to an excessive degree, something belonging to another; p. 1057 *Judy coveted her sister's shoes.*

subtle (sut′ əl) *adj.* not open, direct, or obvious; crafty; sly; p. 1060 *Blowing that bugle was not a subtle way of waking us up!*

ineptly (i nept′ lē) *adv.* incompetently; awkwardly; clumsily; p. 1061 *Ralph drove so ineptly that Maria got out and took the bus.*

INDIANA ACADEMIC STANDARDS (pages 1046–1066)
11.2.2 Analyze the way in which clarity of meaning is affected by the patterns of organization...

11.2.5 Analyze an author's implicit and explicit assumptions and beliefs about a subject.

11.5.9 Write...a literary analysis that...supports judgments with relevant...evidence and well-chosen details.

Act Two

[*The common room of* PROCTOR'S *house, eight days later.*

At the right is a door opening on the fields outside. A fireplace is at the left, and behind it a stairway leading upstairs. It is the low, dark, and rather long living room of the time. As the curtain rises, the room is empty. From above, ELIZABETH *is heard softly singing to the children. Presently the door opens and* JOHN PROCTOR *enters, carrying his gun. He glances about the room as he comes toward the fireplace, then halts for an instant as he hears her singing. He continues on to the fireplace, leans the gun against the wall as he swings a pot out of the fire and smells it. Then he lifts out the ladle and tastes. He is not quite pleased. He reaches to a cupboard, takes a pinch of salt, and drops it into the pot. As he is tasting again, her footsteps are heard on the stair. He swings the pot into the fireplace and goes to a basin and washes his hands and face.* ELIZABETH *enters.*]

ELIZABETH. What keeps you so late? It's almost dark.

PROCTOR. I were planting far out to the forest edge.

ELIZABETH. Oh, you're done then.

PROCTOR. Aye, the farm is seeded. The boys asleep?

ELIZABETH. They will be soon. [*And she goes to the fireplace, proceeds to ladle up stew in a dish.*]

PROCTOR. Pray now for a fair summer.

ELIZABETH. Aye.

PROCTOR. Are you well today?

ELIZABETH. I am. [*She brings the plate to the table, and, indicating the food.*] It is a rabbit.

PROCTOR. [*Going to the table.*] Oh, is it! In Jonathan's trap?

ELIZABETH. No, she walked into the house this afternoon; I found her sittin' in the corner like she come to visit.

PROCTOR. Oh, that's a good sign walkin' in.

ELIZABETH. Pray God. It hurt my heart to strip her, poor rabbit. [*She sits and watches him taste it.*]

PROCTOR. It's well seasoned.

ELIZABETH. [*Blushing with pleasure.*] I took great care. She's tender?

PROCTOR. Aye. [*He eats. She watches him.*] I think we'll see green fields soon. It's warm as blood beneath the clods.

ELIZABETH. That's well.

[PROCTOR *eats, then looks up.*]

PROCTOR. If the crop is good I'll buy George Jacob's heifer. How would that please you?

ELIZABETH. Aye, it would.

PROCTOR. [*With a grin.*] I mean to please you, Elizabeth.

ELIZABETH. [*It is hard to say.*] I know it, John.

[*He gets up, goes to her, kisses her. She receives it. With a certain disappointment, he returns to the table.*]

PROCTOR. [*As gently as he can.*] Cider?

ELIZABETH. [*With a sense of **reprimanding** herself for having forgot.*] Aye! [*She gets up and goes and pours a glass for him. He now arches his back.*]

PROCTOR. This farm's a continent when you go foot by foot droppin' seeds in it.

ELIZABETH. [*Coming with the cider.*] It must be.

PROCTOR. [*Drinks a long draught, then, putting the glass down.*] You ought to bring some flowers in the house.

ELIZABETH. Oh! I forgot! I will tomorrow.

PROCTOR. It's winter in here yet. On Sunday let you come with me, and we'll walk the farm together; I never see such a load of flowers on the earth. [*With good feeling he goes and looks up at the sky through the open doorway.*] Lilacs have a purple smell. Lilac is the smell of nightfall, I think. Massachusetts is a beauty in the spring!

ELIZABETH. Aye, it is.

[*There is a pause. She is watching him from the table as he stands there absorbing the night. It is as though she would speak but cannot. Instead, now, she takes up his plate and glass and fork and goes with them to the basin. Her back is turned to him. He turns to her and watches her. A sense of their separation rises.*]

PROCTOR. I think you're sad again. Are you?

ELIZABETH. [*She doesn't want friction, and yet she must.*] You come so late I thought you'd gone to Salem this afternoon.

PROCTOR. Why? I have no business in Salem.

ELIZABETH. You did speak of going, earlier this week.

PROCTOR. [*He knows what she means.*] I thought better of it since.

ELIZABETH. Mary Warren's there today.

PROCTOR. Why'd you let her? You heard me forbid her go to Salem any more!

ELIZABETH. I couldn't stop her.

PROCTOR. [*Holding back a full condemnation of her.*] It is a fault, it is a fault, Elizabeth—you're the mistress here, not Mary Warren.

ELIZABETH. She frightened all my strength away.

PROCTOR. How may that mouse frighten you, Elizabeth? You—

ELIZABETH. It is a mouse no more. I forbid her go, and she raises up her chin like the daughter

Painting, 1948. Willem de Kooning. Enamel and oil on canvas, 42⅝ x 56⅛ in. ©2000 Willem de Kooning Revocable Trust/Artists Rights Society, NY, The Museum of Modern Art, New York.

Viewing the Art: What emotions does this painting evoke in you? How might it represent the emotions that John Proctor and Elizabeth are expressing at this point in the play?

of a prince and says to me, "I must go to Salem, Goody Proctor; I am an official of the court!"

PROCTOR. Court! What court?

ELIZABETH. Aye, it is a proper court they have now. They've sent four judges out of Boston, she says, weighty magistrates[1] of the General Court, and at the head sits the Deputy Governor of the Province.

PROCTOR. [*Astonished.*] Why, she's mad.

ELIZABETH. I would to God she were. There be fourteen people in the jail now, she says. [*PROCTOR simply looks at her, unable to grasp it.*] And they'll be tried, and the court have power to hang them too, she says.

PROCTOR. [*Scoffing, but without conviction.*] Ah, they'd never hang—

ELIZABETH. The Deputy Governor promise hangin' if they'll not confess, John. The town's gone wild, I think. She speak of Abigail, and I thought she were a saint, to hear her. Abigail brings the other girls into the court, and where she walks

---

Literary Element   **Stage Directions** *What does Elizabeth mean? How would this stage direction influence the way the actor playing Proctor said his lines?*

---

1. *Weighty* means "important." *Magistrates* are judges.

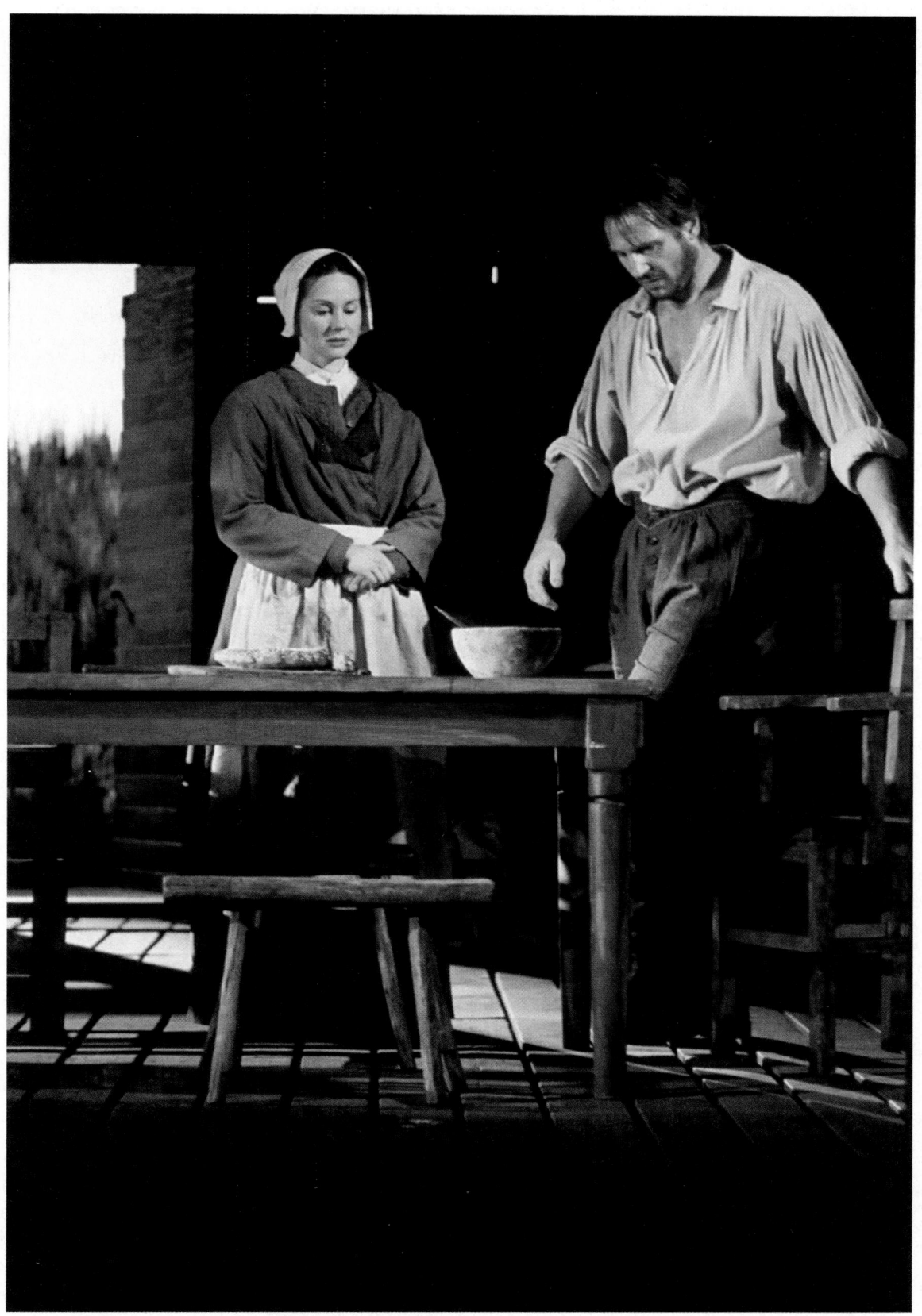

The Crucible on Stage in New York City, NY.

the crowd will part like the sea for Israel. And folks are brought before them, and if they scream and howl and fall to the floor—the person's clapped in the jail for bewitchin' them.

PROCTOR. [*Wide-eyed.*] Oh, it is a black mischief.

ELIZABETH. I think you must go to Salem, John. [*He turns to her.*] I think so. You must tell them it is a fraud.

PROCTOR. [*Thinking beyond this.*] Aye, it is, it is surely.

ELIZABETH. Let you go to Ezekiel Cheever—he knows you well. And tell him what she said to you last week in her uncle's house. She said it had naught to do with witchcraft, did she not?

PROCTOR. [*In thought.*] Aye, she did, she did. [*Now, a pause.*]

ELIZABETH. [*Quietly, fearing to anger him by prodding.*] God forbid you keep that from the court, John. I think they must be told.

PROCTOR. [*Quietly, struggling with his thought.*] Aye, they must, they must. It is a wonder they do believe her.

ELIZABETH. I would go to Salem now, John—let you go tonight.

PROCTOR. I'll think on it.

ELIZABETH. [*With her courage now.*] You cannot keep it, John.

PROCTOR. [*Angering.*] I know I cannot keep it. I say I will think on it!

ELIZABETH. [*Hurt, and very coldly.*] Good, then, let you think on it. [*She stands and starts to walk out of the room.*]

PROCTOR. I am only wondering how I may prove what she told me, Elizabeth. If the girl's a saint now, I think it is not easy to prove she's fraud, and the town gone so silly. She told it to me in a room alone—I have no proof for it.

ELIZABETH. You were alone with her?

Big Idea The United States and the World *What is wrong with this form of justice? What might Miller's audience have thought on hearing these lines?*

Reading Strategy Recognizing Bias *How does Miller's use of the words "quietly" and "thought" in the last three stage directions reveal his attitude toward John and Elizabeth?*

PROCTOR. [*Stubbornly.*] For a moment alone, aye.

ELIZABETH. Why, then, it is not as you told me.

PROCTOR. [*His anger rising.*] For a moment, I say. The others come in soon after.

ELIZABETH. [*Quietly—she has suddenly lost all faith in him.*] Do as you wish, then. [*She starts to turn.*]

PROCTOR. Woman. [*She turns to him.*] I'll not have your suspicion any more.

ELIZABETH. [*A little loftily.*] I have no—

PROCTOR. I'll not have it!

ELIZABETH. Then let you not earn it.

PROCTOR. [*With a violent undertone.*] You doubt me yet?

ELIZABETH. [*With a smile, to keep her dignity.*] John, if it were not Abigail that you must go to hurt, would you falter now? I think not.

PROCTOR. Now look you—

ELIZABETH. I see what I see, John.

PROCTOR. [*With solemn warning.*] You will not judge me more, Elizabeth. I have good reason to think before I charge fraud on Abigail, and I will think on it. Let you look to your own improvement before you go to judge your husband any more. I have forgot Abigail, and—

ELIZABETH. And I.

PROCTOR. Spare me! You forget nothin' and forgive nothin'. Learn charity, woman. I have gone tiptoe in this house all seven month since she is gone. I have not moved from there to there without I think to please you, and still an everlasting funeral marches round your heart. I cannot speak but I am doubted, every moment judged for lies, as though I come into a court when I come into this house!

ELIZABETH. John, you are not open with me. You saw her with a crowd, you said. Now you—

PROCTOR. I'll plead my honesty no more, Elizabeth.

ELIZABETH. [*Now she would justify herself.*] John, I am only—

PROCTOR. No more! I should have roared you down when first you told me your suspicion. But I wilted, and, like a Christian, I confessed.

Literary Element Stage Directions *What aspect of Elizabeth's character is stressed in this stage direction?*

Confessed! Some dream I had must have mistaken you for God that day. But you're not, you're not, and let you remember it! Let you look sometimes for the goodness in me, and judge me not.

ELIZABETH. I do not judge you. The magistrate sits in your heart that judges you. I never thought you but a good man, John—[*With a smile.*]—only somewhat bewildered.

PROCTOR. [*Laughing bitterly.*] Oh, Elizabeth, your justice would freeze beer! [*He turns suddenly toward a sound outside. He starts for the door as* MARY WARREN *enters. As soon as he sees her, he goes directly to her and grabs her by her cloak, furious.*] How do you go to Salem when I forbid it? Do you mock me? [*Shaking her.*] I'll whip you if you dare leave this house again!

[*Strangely, she doesn't resist him, but hangs limply by his grip.*]

MARY WARREN. I am sick, I am sick, Mr. Proctor. Pray, pray, hurt me not. [*Her strangeness throws him off, and her evident pallor[2] and weakness. He frees her.*] My insides are all shuddery; I am in the proceedings all day, sir.

PROCTOR. [*With draining anger—his curiosity is draining it.*] And what of these proceedings here? When will you proceed to keep this house, as you are paid nine pound a year to do—and my wife not wholly well?

[*As though to compensate,* MARY WARREN *goes to* ELIZABETH *with a small rag doll.*]

MARY WARREN. I made a gift for you today, Goody Proctor. I had to sit long hours in a chair, and passed the time with sewing.

ELIZABETH. [*Perplexed, looking at the doll.*] Why, thank you, it's a fair poppet.

MARY WARREN. [*With a trembling, decayed voice.*] We must all love each other now, Goody Proctor.

ELIZABETH. [*Amazed at her strangeness.*] Aye, indeed we must.

MARY WARREN. [*Glancing at the room.*] I'll get up early in the morning and clean the house. I must sleep now. [*She turns and starts off.*]

PROCTOR. Mary. [*She halts.*] Is it true? There be fourteen women arrested?

MARY WARREN. No, sir. There be thirty-nine now—[*She suddenly breaks off and sobs and sits down, exhausted.*]

ELIZABETH. Why, she's weepin'! What ails you, child?

MARY WARREN. Goody Osburn—will hang!

[*There is a shocked pause, while she sobs.*]

PROCTOR. Hang! [*He calls into her face.*] Hang, y'say?

MARY WARREN. [*Through her weeping.*] Aye.

PROCTOR. The Deputy Governor will permit it?

MARY WARREN. He sentenced her. He must. [*To ameliorate[3] it.*] But not Sarah Good. For Sarah Good confessed, y'see.

PROCTOR. Confessed! To what?

MARY WARREN. That she—[*In horror at the memory.*]—she sometimes made a compact with Lucifer, and wrote her name in his black book— with her blood—and bound herself to torment Christians till God's thrown down—and we all must worship Hell forevermore.

[*Pause.*]

PROCTOR. But—surely you know what a jabberer she is. Did you tell them that?

MARY WARREN. Mr. Proctor, in open court she near to choked us all to death.

PROCTOR. How, choked you?

MARY WARREN. She sent her spirit out.

ELIZABETH. Oh, Mary, Mary, surely you—

MARY WARREN. [*With an indignant[4] edge.*] She tried to kill me many times, Goody Proctor!

---

2. *Pallor* refers to a pale complexion.

---

3. To *ameliorate* is to improve a situation that was unpleasant or unbearable before.
4. *Indignant* means "expressing righteous anger."

Big Idea The United States and the World *How do you think that Miller wants his audience to respond to what is happening in Salem?*

ELIZABETH. Why, I never heard you mention that before.

MARY WARREN. I never knew it before. I never knew anything before. When she come into the court I say to myself, I must not accuse this woman, for she sleep in ditches, and so very old and poor. But then—then she sit there, denying and denying, and I feel a misty coldness climbin' up my back, and the skin on my skull begin to creep, and I feel a clamp around my neck and I cannot breathe air; and then—[*Entranced.*]—I hear a voice, a screamin' voice, and it were my voice—and all at once I remembered everything she done to me!

PROCTOR. Why? What did she do to you?

MARY WARREN. [*Like one awakened to a marvelous secret insight.*] So many time, Mr. Proctor, she come to this very door, beggin' bread and a cup of cider—and mark this: whenever I turned her away empty, she *mumbled.*

ELIZABETH. Mumbled! She may mumble if she's hungry.

MARY WARREN. But *what* does she mumble? You must remember, Goody Proctor. Last month—a Monday, I think—she walked away, and I thought my guts would burst for two days after. Do you remember it?

ELIZABETH. Why—I do, I think, but—

MARY WARREN. And so I told that to Judge Hathorne, and he asks her so. "Sarah Good," says he, "what curse do you mumble that this girl must fall sick after turning you away?" And then she replies—[*Mimicking an old crone.*][5] —"Why, your excellence, no curse at all. I only say my commandments; I hope I may say my commandments," says she!

ELIZABETH. And that's an upright answer.

MARY WARREN. Aye, but then Judge Hathorne say, "Recite for us your commandments!"—[*Leaning avidly toward them.*]—and of all the ten she could not say a single one. She never knew no commandments, and they had her in a flat lie!

---

5. A *crone* is a withered old woman.

Reading Strategy Recognizing Bias *What is Miller's opinion of Mary? How is it revealed in this passage?*

PROCTOR. And so condemned her?

MARY WARREN. [*Now a little strained, seeing his stubborn doubt.*] Why, they must when she condemned herself.

PROCTOR. But the proof, the proof!

MARY WARREN. [*With greater impatience with him.*] I told you the proof. It's hard proof, hard as rock, the judges said.

PROCTOR. [*Pauses an instant, then.*] You will not go to court again, Mary Warren.

MARY WARREN. I must tell you, sir, I will be gone every day now. I am amazed you do not see what weighty work we do.

PROCTOR. What work you do! It's strange work for a Christian girl to hang old women!

MARY WARREN. But, Mr. Proctor, they will not hang them if they confess. Sarah Good will only sit in jail some time—[*Recalling.*]—and here's a wonder for you; think on this. Goody Good is pregnant!

ELIZABETH. Pregnant! Are they mad? The woman's near to sixty!

MARY WARREN. They had Doctor Griggs examine her, and she's full to the brim. And smokin' a pipe all these years, and no husband either! But she's safe, thank God, for they'll not hurt the innocent child. But be that not a marvel? You must see it, sir, it's God's work we do. So I'll be gone every day for some time. I'm—I am an official of the court, they say, and I—[*She has been edging toward offstage.*]

PROCTOR. I'll official you! [*He strides to the mantel, takes down the whip hanging there.*]

MARY WARREN. [*Terrified, but coming erect, striving for her authority.*] I'll not stand whipping any more!

ELIZABETH. [*Hurriedly, as* PROCTOR *approaches.*] Mary, promise now you'll stay at home—

Reading Strategy Recognizing Bias *Do you think Proctor is speaking for Miller here? Explain.*

Big Idea The United States and the World *How did this distorted logic subvert justice in the Salem witch trials and in the McCarthy hearings?*

MARY WARREN. [*Backing from him, but keeping her erect posture, striving, striving for her way.*] The Devil's loose in Salem, Mr. Proctor; we must discover where he's hiding!

PROCTOR. I'll whip the Devil out of you! [*With whip raised he reaches out for her, and she streaks away and yells.*]

MARY WARREN. [*Pointing at ELIZABETH.*] I saved her life today!

[*Silence. His whip comes down.*]

ELIZABETH. [*Softly.*] I am accused?

MARY WARREN. [*Quaking.*] Somewhat mentioned. But I said I never see no sign you ever sent your spirit out to hurt no one, and seeing I do live so closely with you, they dismissed it.

ELIZABETH. Who accused me?

MARY WARREN. I am bound by law, I cannot tell it. [*To PROCTOR.*] I only hope you'll not be so sarcastical no more. Four judges and the King's deputy sat to dinner with us but an hour ago. I—I would have you speak civilly to me, from this out.

PROCTOR. [*In horror, muttering in disgust at her.*] Go to bed.

MARY WARREN. [*With a stamp of her foot.*] I'll not be ordered to bed no more, Mr. Proctor! I am eighteen and a woman, however single!

PROCTOR. Do you wish to sit up? Then sit up.

MARY WARREN. I wish to go to bed!

PROCTOR. [*In anger.*] Good night, then!

MARY WARREN. Good night. [*Dissatisfied, uncertain of herself, she goes out. Wide-eyed, both, PROCTOR and ELIZABETH stand staring.*]

ELIZABETH. [*Quietly.*] Oh, the noose, the noose is up!

PROCTOR. There'll be no noose.

ELIZABETH. She wants me dead. I knew all week it would come to this!

PROCTOR. [*Without conviction.*] They dismissed it. You heard her say—

ELIZABETH. And what of tomorrow? She will cry me out until they take me!

PROCTOR. Sit you down.

ELIZABETH. She wants me dead, John, you know it!

PROCTOR. I say sit down! [*She sits, trembling. He speaks quietly, trying to keep his wits.*] Now we must be wise, Elizabeth.

ELIZABETH. [*With sarcasm, and a sense of being lost.*] Oh, indeed, indeed!

PROCTOR. Fear nothing. I'll find Ezekiel Cheever. I'll tell him she said it were all sport.

ELIZABETH. John, with so many in the jail, more than Cheever's help is needed now, I think. Would you favor me with this? Go to Abigail.

PROCTOR. [*His soul hardening as he senses . . .*] What have I to say to Abigail?

ELIZABETH. [*Delicately.*] John—grant me this. You have a faulty understanding of young girls. There is a promise made in any bed—

PROCTOR. [*Striving against his anger.*] What promise!

ELIZABETH. Spoke or silent, a promise is surely made. And she may dote on[6] it now—I am sure she does—and thinks to kill me, then to take my place.

[*PROCTOR's anger is rising; he cannot speak.*]

ELIZABETH. It is her dearest hope, John, I know it. There be a thousand names; why does she call mine? There be a certain danger in calling such a name—I am no Goody Good that sleeps in ditches, nor Osburn, drunk and half-witted. She'd dare not call out such a farmer's wife but there be monstrous profit in it. She thinks to take my place, John.

PROCTOR. She cannot think it! [*He knows it is true.*]

ELIZABETH. ["*Reasonably.*"] John, have you ever shown her somewhat of contempt? She cannot pass you in the church but you will blush—

PROCTOR. I may blush for my sin.

---

6. To *dote on* is to show extreme affection for or to pay excessive attention to.

Big Idea **The United States and the World** *Many U.S. citizens opposed to Senator McCarthy accused him of promoting his own career in hunting for Communists. What is similar about the situation described here?*

Literary Element **Stage Directions** *What does this stage direction indicate?*

The Crucible, 1996.

ELIZABETH. I think she sees another meaning in that blush.

PROCTOR. And what see you? What see you, Elizabeth?

ELIZABETH. [*"Conceding."*] I think you be somewhat ashamed, for I am there, and she so close.

PROCTOR. When will you know me, woman? Were I stone I would have cracked for shame this seven month!

ELIZABETH. Then go and tell her she's a whore. Whatever promise she may sense—break it, John, break it.

PROCTOR. [*Between his teeth.*] Good, then. I'll go. [*He starts for his rifle.*]

ELIZABETH. [*Trembling, fearfully.*] Oh, how unwillingly!

PROCTOR. [*Turning on her, rifle in hand.*] I will curse her hotter than the oldest cinder in hell. But pray, begrudge me not my anger!

ELIZABETH. Your anger! I only ask you—

Literary Element Stage Directions *Why might Miller refer to the rifle in this stage direction?*

PROCTOR. Woman, am I so **base**? Do you truly think me base?

ELIZABETH. I never called you base.

PROCTOR. Then how do you charge me with such a promise? The promise that a stallion gives a mare I gave that girl!

ELIZABETH. Then why do you anger with me when I bid you break it?

PROCTOR. Because it speaks deceit, and I am honest! But I'll plead no more! I see now your spirit twists around the single error of my life, and I will never tear it free!

ELIZABETH. [*Crying out.*] You'll tear it free— when you come to know that I will be your only wife, or no wife at all! She has an arrow in you yet, John Proctor, and you know it well!

[*Quite suddenly, as though from the air, a figure appears in the doorway. They start slightly. It is*

Literary Element Stage Directions *How does this stage direction help to develop plot and atmosphere?*

Vocabulary

base (bās) *adj.* morally low; dishonorable

MR. HALE. *He is different now—drawn a little, and there is a quality of deference, even of guilt, about his manner now.*]

HALE. Good evening.

PROCTOR. [*Still in his shock.*] Why, Mr. Hale! Good evening to you, sir. Come in, come in.

HALE. [*To* ELIZABETH.] I hope I do not startle you.

ELIZABETH. No, no, it's only that I heard no horse—

HALE. You are Goodwife Proctor.

PROCTOR. Aye; Elizabeth.

HALE. [*Nods, then.*] I hope you're not off to bed yet.

PROCTOR. [*Setting down his gun.*] No, no. [HALE *comes further into the room. And* PROCTOR, *to explain his nervousness.*] We are not used to visitors after dark, but you're welcome here. Will you sit you down, sir?

HALE. I will. [*He sits.*] Let you sit, Goodwife Proctor.

[*She does, never letting him out of her sight. There is a pause as* HALE *looks about the room.*]

PROCTOR. [*To break the silence.*] Will you drink cider, Mr. Hale?

HALE. No, it rebels my stomach; I have some further traveling yet tonight. Sit you down, sir. [PROCTOR *sits.*] I will not keep you long, but I have some business with you.

PROCTOR. Business of the court?

HALE. No—no, I come of my own, without the court's authority. Hear me. [*He wets his lips.*] I know not if you are aware, but your wife's name is—mentioned in the court.

PROCTOR. We know it, sir. Our Mary Warren told us. We are entirely amazed.

HALE. I am a stranger here, as you know. And in my ignorance I find it hard to draw a clear opinion of them that come accused before the court. And so this afternoon, and now tonight, I go from house to house—I come now from Rebecca Nurse's house and—

ELIZABETH. [*Shocked.*] Rebecca's charged!

HALE. God forbid such a one be charged. She is, however—mentioned somewhat.

ELIZABETH. [*With an attempt at a laugh.*] You will never believe, I hope, that Rebecca trafficked with the Devil.

HALE. Woman, it is possible.

PROCTOR. [*Taken aback.*] Surely you cannot think so.

HALE. This is a strange time, Mister. No man may longer doubt the powers of the dark are gathered in monstrous attack upon this village. There is too much evidence now to deny it. You will agree, sir?

PROCTOR. [*Evading.*] I—have no knowledge in that line. But it's hard to think so pious[7] a woman be secretly a Devil's bitch after seventy year of such good prayer.

HALE. Aye. But the Devil is a wily[8] one, you cannot deny it. However, she is far from accused, and I know she will not be. [*Pause.*] I thought, sir, to put some questions as to the Christian character of this house, if you'll permit me.

PROCTOR. [*Coldly, resentful.*] Why, we—have no fear of questions, sir.

HALE. Good, then. [*He makes himself more comfortable.*] In the book of record that Mr. Parris keeps, I note that you are rarely in the church on Sabbath Day.

PROCTOR. No, sir, you are mistaken.

HALE. Twenty-six time in seventeen month, sir. I must call that rare. Will you tell me why you are so absent?

PROCTOR. Mr. Hale, I never knew I must account to that man for I come to church or stay at home. My wife were sick this winter.

HALE. So I am told. But you, Mister, why could you not come alone?

PROCTOR. I surely did come when I could, and when I could not I prayed in this house.

HALE. Mr. Proctor, your house is not a church; your theology[9] must tell you that.

---

7. *Pious* means "having a sincere reverence for God."
8. *Wily* means "crafty" or "sly and full of tricks."
9. Here, Hale uses the term *theology* to refer to Proctor's own religious beliefs.

Big Idea **The United States and the World** *Why do you think that Reverend Hale has come to believe that witchcraft is responsible for the girls' strange behavior? How does this kind of unsubstantiated belief relate to the McCarthy era?*

The Crucible, 1996.

PROCTOR. It does, sir, it does; and it tells me that a minister may pray to God without he have golden candlesticks upon the altar.

HALE. What golden candlesticks?

PROCTOR. Since we built the church there were pewter[10] candlesticks upon the altar; Francis Nurse made them, y'know, and a sweeter hand never touched the metal. But Parris came, and for twenty week he preach nothin' but golden candlesticks until he had them. I labor the earth from dawn of day to blink of night, and I tell you true, when I look to heaven and see my money glaring at his elbows—it hurt my prayer, sir, it hurt my prayer. I think, sometimes, the man dreams cathedrals, not clapboard meetin' houses.

HALE. [*Thinks, then.*] And yet, Mister, a Christian on Sabbath Day must be in church. [*Pause.*] Tell me—you have three children?

PROCTOR. Aye. Boys.

HALE. How comes it that only two are baptized?

PROCTOR. [*Starts to speak, then stops, then, as though unable to restrain this.*] I like it not that Mr. Parris should lay his hand upon my baby. I see no light of God in that man. I'll not conceal it.

HALE. I must say it, Mr. Proctor; that is not for you to decide. The man's ordained, therefore the light of God is in him.

PROCTOR. [*Flushed with resentment but trying to smile.*] What's your suspicion, Mr. Hale?

---

10. *Pewter* is an alloy, or a substance composed of two or more metals or of a metal and a nonmetal. Tin is the main metal in pewter, and it is often mixed with lead.

Reading Strategy Recognizing Bias *In a choice between authority and the individual conscience, which side do you think Arthur Miller would take? Explain.*

HALE. No, no, I have no—

PROCTOR. I nailed the roof upon the church, I hung the door—

HALE. Oh, did you! That's a good sign, then.

PROCTOR. It may be I have been too quick to bring the man to book, but you cannot think we ever desired the destruction of religion. I think that's in your mind, is it not?

HALE. [*Not altogether giving way.*] I—have—there is a softness in your record, sir, a softness.

ELIZABETH. I think, maybe, we have been too hard with Mr. Parris. I think so. But sure we never loved the Devil here.

HALE. [*Nods, deliberating this. Then, with the voice of one administering a secret test.*] Do you know your Commandments, Elizabeth?

ELIZABETH. [*Without hesitation, even eagerly.*] I surely do. There be no mark of blame upon my life, Mr. Hale. I am a covenanted Christian woman.

HALE. And you, Mister?

PROCTOR. [*A trifle unsteadily.*] I—am sure I do, sir.

HALE. [*Glances at her open face, then at JOHN, then.*] Let you repeat them, if you will.

PROCTOR. The Commandments.

HALE. Aye.

PROCTOR. [*Looking off, beginning to sweat.*] Thou shalt not kill.

HALE. Aye.

PROCTOR. [*Counting on his fingers.*] Thou shalt not steal. Thou shalt not **covet** thy neighbor's goods, nor make unto thee any graven image.[11] Thou shalt not take the name of the Lord in vain; thou shalt have no other gods before me. [*With some hesitation.*] Thou shalt remember the

---

11. Here, a *graven image* is an idol.

Vocabulary

covet (kuv´ it) *v.* to desire, especially to an excessive degree, something belonging to another

---

Sabbath Day and keep it holy. [*Pause. Then.*] Thou shalt honor thy father and mother. Thou shalt not bear false witness. [*He is stuck. He counts back on his fingers, knowing one is missing.*] Thou shalt not make unto thee any graven image.

HALE. You have said that twice, sir.

PROCTOR. [*Lost.*] Aye. [*He is flailing for it.*]

ELIZABETH. [*Delicately.*] Adultery, John.

PROCTOR. [*As though a secret arrow had pained his heart.*] Aye. [*Trying to grin it away—to HALE.*] You see, sir, between the two of us we do know them all. [*HALE only looks at PROCTOR, deep in his attempt to define this man. PROCTOR grows more uneasy.*] I think it be a small fault.

HALE. Theology, sir, is a fortress; no crack in a fortress may be accounted small. [*He rises; he seems worried now. He paces a little, in deep thought.*]

PROCTOR. There be no love for Satan in this house, Mister.

HALE. I pray it, I pray it dearly. [*He looks to both of them, an attempt at a smile on his face, but his misgivings are clear.*] Well, then—I'll bid you good night.

ELIZABETH. [*Unable to restrain herself.*] Mr. Hale. [*He turns.*] I do think you are suspecting me somewhat? Are you not?

HALE. [*Obviously disturbed—and evasive.*] Goody Proctor, I do not judge you. My duty is to add what I may to the godly wisdom of the court. I pray you both good health and good fortune. [*To JOHN.*] Good night, sir. [*He starts out.*]

ELIZABETH. [*With a note of desperation.*] I think you must tell him, John.

HALE. What's that?

ELIZABETH. [*Restraining a call.*] Will you tell him?

[*Slight pause. HALE looks questioningly at JOHN.*]

PROCTOR. [*With difficulty.*] I—I have no witness and cannot prove it, except my word be taken. But I know the children's sickness had naught to do with witchcraft.

Literary Element Stage Directions *What is the significance of this stage direction?*

HALE. [*Stopped, struck.*] Naught to do—?

PROCTOR. Mr. Parris discovered them sportin' in the woods. They were startled and took sick.

[*Pause.*]

HALE. Who told you this?

PROCTOR. [*Hesitates, then.*] Abigail Williams.

HALE. Abigail!

PROCTOR. Aye.

HALE. [*His eyes wide.*] Abigail Williams told you it had naught to do with witchcraft!

PROCTOR. She told me the day you came, sir.

HALE. [*Suspiciously.*] Why—why did you keep this?

PROCTOR. I never knew until tonight that the world is gone daft[12] with this nonsense.

HALE. Nonsense! Mister, I have myself examined Tituba, Sarah Good, and numerous others that have confessed to dealing with the Devil. They have *confessed* it.

PROCTOR. And why not, if they must hang for denyin' it? There are them that will swear to anything before they'll hang; have you never thought of that?

HALE. I have. I—I have indeed. [*It is his own suspicion, but he resists it. He glances at ELIZABETH, then at JOHN.*] And you—would you testify to this in court?

PROCTOR. I—had not reckoned with goin' into court. But if I must I will.

HALE. Do you falter here?

PROCTOR. I falter nothing, but I may wonder if my story will be credited in such a court. I do wonder on it, when such a steady-minded minister as you will suspicion such a woman that never lied, and cannot, and the world knows she cannot! I may falter somewhat, Mister; I am no fool.

HALE. [*Quietly—it has impressed him.*] Proctor, let you open with me now, for I have a rumor that troubles me. It's said you hold no belief that there may even be witches in the world. Is that true, sir?

PROCTOR. [*He knows this is critical, and is striving against his disgust with HALE and with himself for even answering.*] I know not what I have said, I may have said it. I have wondered if there be witches in the world—although I cannot believe they come among us now.

HALE. Then you do not believe—

PROCTOR. I have no knowledge of it; the Bible speaks of witches, and I will not deny them.

HALE. And you, woman?

ELIZABETH. I—I cannot believe it.

HALE. [*Shocked.*] You cannot!

PROCTOR. Elizabeth, you bewilder him!

ELIZABETH. [*To HALE.*] I cannot think the Devil may own a woman's soul, Mr. Hale, when she keeps an upright way, as I have. I am a good woman, I know it; and if you believe I may do only good work in the world, and yet be secretly bound to Satan, then I must tell you, sir, I do not believe it.

HALE. But, woman, you do believe there are witches in—

ELIZABETH. If you think that I am one, then I say there are none.

HALE. You surely do not fly against the Gospel, the Gospel—

PROCTOR. She believe in the Gospel, every word!

ELIZABETH. Question Abigail Williams about the Gospel, not myself!

[*HALE stares at her.*]

PROCTOR. She do not mean to doubt the Gospel, sir, you cannot think it. This be a Christian house, sir, a Christian house.

HALE. God keep you both; let the third child be quickly baptized, and go you without fail each Sunday in to Sabbath prayer; and keep a solemn, quiet way among you. I think—

[*GILES COREY appears in doorway.*]

---

12. *Daft* means "without sense or reason," "crazy," or "silly."

Literary Element Stage Directions *Why do you think that Miller included a pause here?*

Big Idea The United States and the World *What does Proctor mean by "such a court," and why would he hesitate to tell the truth?*

Reading Strategy Recognizing Bias *Judging from this remark and from Elizabeth's character, where do you think Miller would have stood on the issue of feminism and women's rights? Explain.*

Confrontation, 1964. Ben Shahn. Watercolor on rice paper mounted on artist's board, 24 x 32 in. ©Estate of Ben Shahn/Licensed by VAGA, New York, NY/The Lane Collection. Courtesy Museum of Fine Arts, Boston.
Viewing the Art: How might this painting convey the confrontation between John Proctor and Mr. Hale?

GILES. John!

PROCTOR. Giles! What's the matter?

GILES. They take my wife.

[*FRANCIS NURSE enters.*]

GILES. And his Rebecca!

PROCTOR. [*To FRANCIS.*] Rebecca's in the *jail!*

FRANCIS. Aye, Cheever come and take her in his wagon. We've only now come from the jail, and they'll not even let us in to see them.

ELIZABETH. They've surely gone wild now, Mr. Hale!

FRANCIS. [*Going to HALE.*] Reverend Hale! Can you not speak to the Deputy Governor? I'm sure he mistakes these people—

HALE. Pray calm yourself, Mr. Nurse.

FRANCIS. My wife is the very brick and mortar of the church, Mr. Hale—[*Indicating GILES.*]—and Martha Corey, there cannot be a woman closer yet to God than Martha.

HALE. How is Rebecca charged, Mr. Nurse?

FRANCIS. [*With a mocking, half-hearted laugh.*] For murder, she's charged! [*Mockingly quoting the warrant.*] "For the marvelous and supernatural murder of Goody Putnam's babies." What am I to do, Mr. Hale?

HALE. [*Turns from FRANCIS, deeply troubled, then.*] Believe me, Mr. Nurse, if Rebecca Nurse be

---

Reading Strategy Recognizing Bias *How do you think Miller wants his audience to react to Francis's mockery?*

Literary Element Stage Directions *How do these words in the stage direction affect Hale's speech?*

ARTHUR MILLER **1059**

tainted,[13] then nothing's left to stop the whole green world from burning. Let you rest upon the justice of the court; the court will send her home, I know it.

FRANCIS. You cannot mean she will be tried in court!

HALE. [*Pleading.*] Nurse, though our hearts break, we cannot flinch; these are new times, sir. There is a misty plot afoot so **subtle** we should be criminal to cling to old respects and ancient friendships. I have seen too many frightful proofs in court—the Devil is alive in Salem, and we dare not quail to follow wherever the accusing finger points!

PROCTOR. [*Angered.*] How may such a woman murder children?

HALE. [*In great pain.*] Man, remember, until an hour before the Devil fell, God thought him beautiful in Heaven.[14]

GILES. I never said my wife were a witch, Mr. Hale; I only said she were reading books!

HALE. Mr. Corey, exactly what complaint were made on your wife?

GILES. That bloody mongrel Walcott charge her. Y'see, he buy a pig of my wife four or five year ago, and the pig died soon after. So he come dancin' in for his money back. So my Martha, she says to him, "Walcott, if you haven't the wit to feed a pig properly, you'll not live to own many," she says. Now he goes to court and claims that from that day to this he cannot keep a pig alive for more than four weeks because my Martha bewitch them with her books!

[*Enter EZEKIEL CHEEVER. A shocked silence.*]

---

13. Something *tainted* is spoiled, inferior, or corrupted.
14. [*before the Devil fell . . . Heaven*] According to the Bible, the devil was heaven's highest angel before he was driven out because of his excessive pride.

Big Idea The United States and the World *How is Hale's attitude here similar to that of Senator McCarthy in the 1950s?*

Literary Element Stage Directions *Why is there a "shocked silence" when Ezekiel enters?*

Vocabulary

subtle (sut´ əl) *adj.* not open, direct, or obvious; crafty; sly

CHEEVER. Good evening to you, Proctor.

PROCTOR. Why, Mr. Cheever. Good evening.

CHEEVER. Good evening, all. Good evening, Mr. Hale.

PROCTOR. I hope you come not on business of the court.

CHEEVER. I do, Proctor, aye. I am clerk of the court now, y'know.

[*Enter MARSHAL HERRICK, a man in his early thirties, who is somewhat shamefaced at the moment.*]

GILES. It's a pity, Ezekiel, that an honest tailor might have gone to Heaven must burn in Hell. You'll burn for this, do you know it?

CHEEVER. You know yourself I must do as I'm told. You surely know that, Giles. And I'd as lief[15] you'd not be sending me to Hell. I like not the sound of it, I tell you; I like not the sound of it. [*He fears PROCTOR, but starts to reach inside his coat.*] Now believe me, Proctor, how heavy be the law, all its tonnage I do carry on my back tonight. [*He takes out a warrant.*] I have a warrant for your wife.

PROCTOR. [*To HALE.*] You said she were not charged!

HALE. I know nothin' of it. [*To CHEEVER.*] When were she charged?

CHEEVER. I am given sixteen warrant tonight, sir, and she is one.

PROCTOR. Who charged her?

CHEEVER. Why, Abigail Williams charge her.

PROCTOR. On what proof, what proof?

CHEEVER. [*Looking about the room.*] Mr. Proctor, I have little time. The court bid me search your house, but I like not to search a house. So will you hand me any poppets that your wife may keep here?

PROCTOR. Poppets?

---

15. *As lief* (lēv) means "prefer that."

Reading Strategy Recognizing Bias *Do you think that Giles is speaking for Miller here? Explain.*

Big Idea The United States and the World *Cheever excuses himself by explaining that he is only carrying out orders. What other historical events is Miller reminding his audience of here? Explain.*

ELIZABETH. I never kept no poppets, not since I were a girl.

CHEEVER. [*Embarrassed, glancing toward the mantel where sits MARY WARREN's poppet.*] I spy a poppet, Goody Proctor.

ELIZABETH. Oh! [*Going for it.*] Why, this is Mary's.

CHEEVER. [*Shyly.*] Would you please to give it to me?

ELIZABETH. [*Handing it to him, asks HALE.*] Has the court discovered a text in poppets now?

CHEEVER. [*Carefully holding the poppet.*] Do you keep any others in this house?

PROCTOR. No, nor this one either till tonight. What signifies a poppet?

CHEEVER. Why, a poppet—[*He gingerly turns the poppet over.*]—a poppet may signify—Now, woman, will you please to come with me?

PROCTOR. She will not! [*To ELIZABETH.*] Fetch Mary here.

CHEEVER. [*Ineptly reaching toward ELIZABETH.*] No, no, I am forbid to leave her from my sight.

PROCTOR. [*Pushing his arm away.*] You'll leave her out of sight and out of mind, Mister. Fetch Mary, Elizabeth. [*ELIZABETH goes upstairs.*]

HALE. What signifies a poppet, Mr. Cheever?

CHEEVER. [*Turning the poppet over in his hands.*] Why, they say it may signify that she—[*He has lifted the poppet's skirt, and his eyes widen in astonished fear.*] Why, this, this—

PROCTOR. [*Reaching for the poppet.*] What's there?

CHEEVER. Why—[*He draws out a long needle from the poppet.*]—it is a needle! Herrick, Herrick, it is a needle!

[*HERRICK comes toward him.*]

PROCTOR. [*Angrily, bewildered.*] And what signifies a needle!

CHEEVER. [*His hands shaking.*] Why, this go hard with her, Proctor, this—I had my doubts, Proctor, I had my doubts, but here's calamity. [*To HALE, showing the needle.*] You see it, sir, it is a needle!

Vocabulary

ineptly (i nept′ lē) *adv.* incompetently; awkwardly; clumsily

HALE. Why? What meanin' has it?

CHEEVER. [*Wide-eyed, trembling.*] The girl, the Williams girl, Abigail Williams, sir. She sat to dinner in Reverend Parris's house tonight, and without word nor warnin' she falls to the floor. Like a struck beast, he says, and screamed a scream that a bull would weep to hear. And he goes to save her, and, stuck two inches in the flesh of her belly, he draw a needle out. And demandin' of her how she come to be so stabbed, she—[*To PROCTOR now.*]—testify it were your wife's familiar spirit pushed it in.

PROCTOR. Why, she done it herself! [*To HALE.*] I hope you're not takin' this for proof, Mister!

[*HALE, struck by the proof, is silent.*]

CHEEVER. 'Tis hard proof! [*To HALE.*] I find here a poppet Goody Proctor keeps. I have found it, sir. And in the belly of the poppet a needle's stuck. I tell you true, Proctor, I never warranted to see such proof of Hell, and I bid you obstruct me not, for I—

[*Enter ELIZABETH with MARY WARREN. PROCTOR, seeing MARY WARREN, draws her by the arm to HALE.*]

PROCTOR. Here now! Mary, how did this poppet come into my house?

MARY WARREN. [*Frightened for herself, her voice very small.*] What poppet's that, sir?

PROCTOR. [*Impatiently, pointing at the doll in CHEEVER's hand.*] This poppet, this poppet.

MARY WARREN. [*Evasively, looking at it.*] Why, I—I think it is mine.

PROCTOR. It is your poppet, is it not?

MARY WARREN. [*Not understanding the direction of this.*] It—is, sir.

Literary Element Stage Directions *What does this stage direction suggest about Hale?*

Big Idea The United States and the World *Making the accused person prove a negative statement to establish innocence is typical of a miscarriage of justice. What is Elizabeth going to be asked to prove here?*

1954, 1954. Clyfford Still. Oil on canvas, 9 ft. 5½ in. x 13 ft. Albright-Knox Art Gallery, Buffalo, NY. Gift of Seymour H. Knox.

Viewing the Art: How, in your opinion, does this painting express the mood of Salem's community in act 2?

PROCTOR. And how did it come into this house?

MARY WARREN. [*Glancing about at the avid faces.*] Why—I made it in the court, sir, and—give it to Goody Proctor tonight.

PROCTOR. [*To HALE.*] Now, sir—do you have it?

HALE. Mary Warren, a needle have been found inside this poppet.

MARY WARREN. [*Bewildered.*] Why, I meant no harm by it, sir.

PROCTOR. [*Quickly.*] You stuck that needle in yourself?

MARY WARREN. I—I believe I did, sir, I—

PROCTOR. [*To HALE.*] What say you now?

HALE. [*Watching MARY WARREN closely.*] Child, you are certain this be your natural memory?

May it be, perhaps, that someone conjures you even now to say this?

MARY WARREN. Conjures me? Why, no, sir, I am entirely myself, I think. Let you ask Susanna Walcott—she saw me sewin' it in court. [*Or better still.*] Ask Abby, Abby sat beside me when I made it.

PROCTOR. [*To HALE, of CHEEVER.*] Bid him begone. Your mind is surely settled now. Bid him out, Mr. Hale.

ELIZABETH. What signifies a needle?

HALE. Mary—you charge a cold and cruel murder on Abigail.

MARY WARREN. Murder! I charge no—

HALE. Abigail were stabbed tonight; a needle were found stuck into her belly—

ELIZABETH. And she charges me?

HALE. Aye.

ELIZABETH. [*Her breath knocked out.*] Why—! The girl is murder! She must be ripped out of the world!

CHEEVER. [*Pointing at ELIZABETH.*] You've heard that, sir! Ripped out of the world! Herrick, you heard it!

PROCTOR. [*Suddenly snatching the warrant out of CHEEVER's hands.*] Out with you.

CHEEVER. Proctor, you dare not touch the warrant.

PROCTOR. [*Ripping the warrant.*] Out with you!

CHEEVER. You've ripped the Deputy Governor's warrant, man!

PROCTOR. Damn the Deputy Governor! Out of my house!

HALE. Now, Proctor, Proctor!

PROCTOR. Get y'gone with them! You are a broken minister.

HALE. Proctor, if she is innocent, the court—

PROCTOR. If *she* is innocent! Why do you never wonder if Parris be innocent, or Abigail? Is the accuser always holy now? Were they born this morning as clean as God's fingers? I'll tell you what's walking Salem—vengeance is walking Salem. We are what we always were in Salem, but now the little crazy children are jangling the keys of the kingdom, and common vengeance writes the law! This warrant's vengeance! I'll not give my wife to vengeance!

ELIZABETH. I'll go, John—

PROCTOR. You will not go!

HERRICK. I have nine men outside. You cannot keep her. The law binds me, John, I cannot budge.

PROCTOR. [*To HALE, ready to break him.*] Will you see her taken?

HALE. Proctor, the court is just—

PROCTOR. Pontius Pilate! God will not let you wash your hands of this!¹⁶

---

16. [*Pontius Pilate . . . this!*] According to the Christian Bible, the Roman official Pontius Pilate consented to the crucifixion of Jesus despite the lack of formal charges or evidence. Pilate then washed his hands and declared himself innocent of shedding Jesus' blood.

Literary Element Stage Directions *What does this stage direction mean?*

Reading Strategy Recognizing Bias *Do you think that Proctor is expressing Miller's views in this passage? Explain.*

ELIZABETH. John—I think I must go with them. [*He cannot bear to look at her.*] Mary, there is bread enough for the morning; you will bake, in the afternoon. Help Mr. Proctor as you were his daughter—you owe me that, and much more. [*She is fighting her weeping. To PROCTOR.*] When the children wake, speak nothing of witchcraft—it will frighten them. [*She cannot go on.*]

PROCTOR. I will bring you home. I will bring you soon.

ELIZABETH. Oh, John, bring me soon!

PROCTOR. I will fall like an ocean on that court! Fear nothing, Elizabeth.

ELIZABETH. [*With great fear.*] I will fear nothing. [*She looks about the room, as though to fix it in her mind.*] Tell the children I have gone to visit someone sick.

[*She walks out the door, HERRICK and CHEEVER behind her. For a moment, PROCTOR watches from the doorway. The clank of chain is heard.*]

PROCTOR. Herrick! Herrick, don't chain her! [*He rushes out the door. From outside.*] Damn you, man, you will not chain her! Off with them! I'll not have it! I will not have her chained!

[*There are other men's voices against his. HALE, in a fever of guilt and uncertainty, turns from the door to avoid the sight; MARY WARREN bursts into tears and sits weeping. GILES COREY calls to HALE.*]

GILES. And yet silent, minister? It is fraud, you know it is fraud! What keeps you, man?

[*PROCTOR is half braced, half pushed into the room by two deputies and HERRICK.*]

PROCTOR. I'll pay you, Herrick, I will surely pay you!

HERRICK. [*Panting.*] In God's name, John, I cannot help myself. I must chain them all. Now let you keep inside this house till I am gone! [*He goes out with his deputies.*]

[*PROCTOR stands there, gulping air. Horses and a wagon creaking are heard.*]

HALE. [*In great uncertainty.*] Mr. Proctor—

PROCTOR. Out of my sight!

Literary Element Stage Directions *How do the stage directions contradict Elizabeth's statement?*

Polar Stampede, 1960. Lee Krasner. Oil on cotton duck, 93⅝ x 159¾ in. Courtesy of The Robert Miller Gallery, NY/©2000 Pollock-Krasner Foundation/Artists Rights Society (ARS), New York.

Viewing the Art: In what ways might this painting echo John Proctor's words, "And the wind, God's icy wind, will blow!"?

HALE. Charity, Proctor, charity. What I have heard in her favor, I will not fear to testify in court. God help me, I cannot judge her guilty or innocent—I know not. Only this consider: the world goes mad, and it profit nothing you should lay the cause to the vengeance of a little girl.

PROCTOR. You are a coward! Though you be ordained in God's own tears, you are a coward now!

HALE. Proctor, I cannot think God be provoked so grandly by such a petty cause. The jails are packed—our greatest judges sit in Salem now—and hangin's promised. Man, we must look to cause proportionate. Were there murder done, perhaps, and never brought to light? Abomination? Some secret blasphemy[17] that stinks to Heaven? Think on cause, man, and let you help me to discover it. For there's your way, believe it, there is your only way, when such confusion strikes upon the world. [*He goes to* GILES *and* FRANCIS.] Let you counsel among yourselves; think on your village and what may have drawn from heaven such thundering wrath upon you all. I shall pray God open up our eyes.

[*HALE goes out.*]

FRANCIS. [*Struck by* HALE's *mood.*] I never heard no murder done in Salem.

PROCTOR. [*He has been reached by* HALE's *words.*] Leave me, Francis, leave me.

GILES. [*Shaken.*] John—tell me, are we lost?

PROCTOR. Go home now, Giles. We'll speak on it tomorrow.

GILES. Let you think on it. We'll come early, eh?

PROCTOR. Aye. Go now, Giles.

GILES. Good night, then.

---

17. *Blasphemy* is an act or expression showing contempt for God or anything sacred.

Literary Element Stage Directions *Why is Proctor "reached" by Hale's words?*

Man's Heart,
John Ritter.

[GILES COREY *goes out. After a moment.*]

MARY WARREN. [*In a fearful squeak of a voice.*] Mr. Proctor, very likely they'll let her come home once they're given proper evidence.

PROCTOR. You're coming to the court with me, Mary. You will tell it in the court.

MARY WARREN. I cannot charge murder on Abigail.

PROCTOR. [*Moving menacingly toward her.*] You will tell the court how that poppet come here and who stuck the needle in.

MARY WARREN. She'll kill me for sayin' that! [PROCTOR *continues toward her.*] Abby'll charge lechery[18] on you, Mr. Proctor!

PROCTOR. [*Halting.*] She's told you!

MARY WARREN. I have known it, sir. She'll ruin you with it, I know she will.

PROCTOR. [*Hesitating, and with deep hatred of himself.*] Good. Then her saintliness is done with. [MARY *backs from him.*] We will slide together into our pit; you will tell the court what you know.

---

18. *Lechery* means "excessive indulgence of sexual desire." In Salem, this was sinful and, therefore, illegal.

Reading Strategy Recognizing Bias *How does Miller gain the audience's sympathy and admiration for Proctor in this speech?*

MARY WARREN. [*In terror.*] I cannot, they'll turn on me—

[PROCTOR *strides and catches her, and she is repeating, "I cannot, I cannot!"*]

PROCTOR. My wife will never die for me! I will bring your guts into your mouth but that goodness will not die for me!

MARY WARREN. [*Struggling to escape him.*] I cannot do it, I cannot!

PROCTOR. [*Grasping her by the throat as though he would strangle her.*] Make your peace with it! Now Hell and Heaven grapple on our backs, and all our old pretense is ripped away—make your peace! [*He throws her to the floor, where she sobs, "I cannot, I cannot . . ." And now, half to himself, staring, and turning to the open door.*] Peace. It is a providence, and no great change; we are only what we always were, but naked now. [*He walks as though toward a great horror, facing the open sky.*] Aye, naked! And the wind, God's icy wind, will blow!

[*And she is over and over again sobbing, "I cannot, I cannot, I cannot . . ."*]

THE CURTAIN FALLS

RESPONDING AND THINKING CRITICALLY

Respond

1. What event in Act Two surprised you the most? Explain.

Recall and Interpret

2. (a)Why might Proctor have previously hesitated to tell the members of the court what Abigail told him about witchcraft? (b)What does this hesitation suggest about his character?

3. (a)What does the court accept as evidence that someone is a witch? (b)Which characters seem to consider this evidence valid, and which do not? (c)What do you think accounts for their differences of opinion?

4. (a)Why does Hale come to the Proctors' house? (b)How does Hale seem to feel about his own judgment and the court's? Explain.

Analyze and Evaluate

5. (a)Analyze how events in Salem have spiraled out of control between Acts One and Two. (b)Do you find what has happened believable? Explain.

6. (a)What questions does Hale ask the Proctors in order to test their virtue? (b)Do his methods strike you as reasonable and justified? Explain.

7. (a)How does John Proctor's behavior compare with that of his wife? (b)Which character do you think behaves more wisely? Explain.

Connect

8. **Big Idea** The United States and the World (a)How does fear influence the way people behave in Act Two of *The Crucible*? (b)Give an example from your own experience or from your knowledge of current events of how the power of fear can affect a person's ability to make sound decisions.

LITERARY ANALYSIS

Literary Element Stage Directions

The reader of a play must imagine what the audience in a theater can see. **Stage directions** can be particularly useful to the reader as well as to the actors. They help the reader visualize what is happening on stage by describing the actions, expressions, and even the tone of voice used by the actors.

1. What do you learn about the characters' actions from the stage directions at the start of Act Two?

2. How do the stage directions for Proctor's last speech in Act Two help you visualize the actor's delivery?

Writing About Literature

Analyze Internal Conflict Reverend Hale is a man in a state of internal conflict. Write four or five paragraphs describing why he is troubled and how the events of Act Two have affected him. Be sure to support your analysis with examples from the play.

Literature Online **Web Activities** For eFlashcards, Selection Quick Checks, and other Web activities, go to www.glencoe.com.

READING AND VOCABULARY

Reading Strategy Recognizing Bias

By the words and actions of their characters, playwrights can often express opinions as clearly as if they were lecturing in a classroom. Think of the action you have witnessed in Act Two of *The Crucible*. Which of his characters does Arthur Miller clearly want you to admire? Which are not so admirable in his eyes?

Vocabulary Practice

Practice with Analogies Find the vocabulary word that best completes each analogy.

1. reprimand : scold :: flee : _____
  a. approach **b.** escape **c.** lecture

2. base : noble :: polite : _____
  a. stupid **b.** mannerly **c.** rude

3. covet : possession :: celebrate : _____
  a. victory **b.** grief **c.** weekend

4. subtle : clever :: dull : _____
  a. miserable **b.** boring **c.** ingenious

5. ineptly : inexperience :: calmly : _____
  a. confidence **b.** intelligence **c.** age

LITERATURE PREVIEW

Building Background

Arthur Miller expressed pride in *The Crucible*, which deals with the tragic combination of mass hysteria and social and political repression. Deciding to produce the play is often a response to similar circumstances. "I can almost tell what the political situation in a country is when the play is suddenly a hit there," Miller wrote, "—it is either a warning of tyranny on the way or a reminder of tyranny just past." When *The Crucible* played in China, one Chinese writer told Miller that she was sure the play could have been written only by someone who had suffered persecution in China's Cultural Revolution.

Setting Purposes for Reading

Literary Element Plot

Plot refers to the sequence of events in a short story, novel, or drama. Most plots deal with a problem and develop around a conflict, or struggle between opposing forces. An external conflict is a struggle between a character and an outside force, such as another character, society, nature, or fate. An internal conflict takes place within the mind of a character who struggles with opposing feelings. The plot begins with exposition, or introduction to the story's characters, setting, and situation. The rising action adds complications to the conflicts, leading to the climax, or the point of highest emotional pitch. Falling action is the logical result of the climax, and the denouement, or resolution, presents the final outcome.

As you read Act Three, notice how Miller intensifies the conflicts he introduced in the previous two acts.

• See Literary Terms Handbook, p. R13.

Literature Online Interactive Literary Elements Handbook To review or learn more about the literary elements, go to www.glencoe.com.

READING PREVIEW

Reading Strategy Evaluating Argument

Argument is a form of persuasion. While some persuasive writing depends on emotional appeals, argument depends on logic, reasoning, and evidence. The authorities and individual characters in *The Crucible* often cite reasons for acting and thinking the way they do. It is up to you, the reader, to form an opinion about—or evaluate—these arguments.

Reading Tip: Taking Notes As you read, use a chart similar to the one below to record faulty logic, questionable arguments, or flawed evidence. Write your evaluations in the right-hand column.

Example	Evaluation
p. 1069 Giles thinks his wife is arrested for reading books.	Probably true. Puritans were suspicious of all reading material except the Bible.

Vocabulary

vile (vīl) *adj.* evil; foul; repulsive; degrading; p. 1071 *A vile crime must be punished.*

immaculate (i mak′ yə lit) *adj.* unblemished; flawless; pure; p. 1076 *Our tenants left the apartment in immaculate condition.*

guile (gīl) *n.* cunning; deceit; slyness; p. 1078 *Through a combination of charm and guile, he persuaded his grandmother to include him in her will.*

contemplation (kon′ təm plā′ shən) *n.* the act of thinking about something long and seriously; p. 1079 *Our summer cabin is the perfect place for reading and contemplation.*

unperturbed (un pər turbd′) *adj.* undisturbed; calm; p. 1084 *Unperturbed by his seemingly stressful day, John slept soundly.*

INDIANA ACADEMIC STANDARDS (pages 1067–1088)

11.3 [Identify] story elements such as...plot...

11.3.8 Analyze the philosophical arguments presented in literary works to determine...the credibility of the characters.

11.5.2 Write responses to literature...

11.5.1 Write fictional...narratives...

Act Three

[*The vestry room of the Salem meeting house, now serving as the anteroom*[1] *of the General Court. As the curtain rises, the room is empty, but for sunlight pouring through two high windows in the back wall. The room is solemn, even forbidding. Heavy beams jut out, boards of random widths make up the walls. At the right are two doors leading into the meeting house proper, where the court is being held. At the left another door leads outside.*

There is a plain bench at the left, and another at the right. In the center a rather long meeting table, with stools and a considerable armchair snugged up to it. Through the partitioning wall at the right we hear a prosecutor's voice, JUDGE HATHORNE's, asking a question; then a woman's voice, MARTHA COREY's, replying.]

HATHORNE'S VOICE. Now, Martha Corey, there is abundant evidence in our hands to show that you have given yourself to the reading of fortunes. Do you deny it?

MARTHA COREY'S VOICE. I am innocent to a witch. I know not what a witch is.

HATHORNE'S VOICE. How do you know, then, that you are not a witch?

MARTHA COREY'S VOICE. If I were, I would know it.

HATHORNE'S VOICE. Why do you hurt these children?

MARTHA COREY'S VOICE. I do not hurt them. I scorn it!

GILES' VOICE. [*Roaring.*] I have evidence for the court!

[*Voices of townspeople rise in excitement.*]

DANFORTH'S VOICE. You will keep your seat!

GILES' VOICE. Thomas Putnam is reaching out for land!

DANFORTH'S VOICE. Remove that man, Marshal!

GILES' VOICE. You're hearing lies, lies!

---

1. The *meeting house* was both a community hall and the house of worship. Its *vestry* was an *anteroom*, or small outer room, that served as a waiting area and entrance to the main room.

Reading Strategy Evaluating Argument *How is this question typical of the prosecution's faulty logic throughout the play?*

[*A roaring goes up from the people.*]

HATHORNE'S VOICE. Arrest him, excellency!

GILES' VOICE. I have evidence. Why will you not hear my evidence?

[*The door opens and GILES is half carried into the vestry room by HERRICK.*]

GILES. Hands off, damn you, let me go!

HERRICK. Giles, Giles!

GILES. Out of my way, Herrick! I bring evidence—

HERRICK. You cannot go in there, Giles; it's a court!

[*Enter HALE from the court.*]

HALE. Pray be calm a moment.

GILES. You, Mr. Hale, go in there and demand I speak.

HALE. A moment, sir, a moment.

GILES. They'll be hangin' my wife!

[*JUDGE HATHORNE enters. He is in his sixties, a bitter, remorseless Salem judge.*]

HATHORNE. How do you dare come roarin' into this court! Are you gone daft, Corey?

GILES. You're not a Boston judge yet, Hathorne. You'll not call me daft!

[*Enter DEPUTY GOVERNOR DANFORTH and, behind him, EZEKIEL CHEEVER and PARRIS. On his appearance, silence falls. DANFORTH is a grave man in his sixties, of some humor and sophistication that does not, however, interfere with an exact loyalty to his position and his cause. He comes down to GILES, who awaits his wrath.*]

DANFORTH. [*Looking directly at GILES.*] Who is this man?

PARRIS. Giles Corey, sir, and a more contentious—

GILES. [*To PARRIS.*] I am asked the question, and I am old enough to answer it! [*To DANFORTH, who impresses him and to whom he smiles through his strain.*] My name is Corey, sir, Giles Corey. I have six hundred acres, and timber in addition.

Literary Element Plot *Giles is in physical conflict here with Herrick. What is the larger conflict in which he is involved?*

It is my wife you be condemning now. [*He indicates the courtroom.*]

DANFORTH. And how do you imagine to help her cause with such contemptuous riot? Now be gone. Your old age alone keeps you out of jail for this.

GILES. [*Beginning to plead.*] They be tellin' lies about my wife, sir, I—

DANFORTH. Do you take it upon yourself to determine what this court shall believe and what it shall set aside?

GILES. Your Excellency, we mean no disrespect for—

DANFORTH. Disrespect indeed! It is disruption, Mister. This is the highest court of the supreme government of this province, do you know it?

GILES. [*Beginning to weep.*] Your Excellency, I only said she were readin' books, sir, and they come and take her out of my house for—

DANFORTH. [*Mystified.*] Books! What books?

GILES. [*Through helpless sobs.*] It is my third wife, sir; I never had no wife that be so taken with books, and I thought to find the cause of it, d'y'see, but it were no witch I blamed her for. [*He is openly weeping.*] I have broke charity with the woman, I have broke charity with her. [*He covers his face, ashamed. DANFORTH is respectfully silent.*]

HALE. Excellency, he claims hard evidence for his wife's defense. I think that in all justice you must—

DANFORTH. Then let him submit his evidence in proper affidavit.[2] You are certainly aware of our procedure here, Mr. Hale. [*To HERRICK.*] Clear this room.

HERRICK. Come now, Giles. [*He gently pushes COREY out.*]

FRANCIS. We are desperate, sir; we come here three days now and cannot be heard.

DANFORTH. Who is this man?

FRANCIS. Francis Nurse, Your Excellency.

HALE. His wife's Rebecca that were condemned this morning.

DANFORTH. Indeed! I am amazed to find you in such uproar. I have only good report of your character, Mr. Nurse.

HATHORNE. I think they must both be arrested in contempt, sir.

DANFORTH. [*To FRANCIS.*] Let you write your plea, and in due time I will—

FRANCIS. Excellency, we have proof for your eyes; God forbid you shut them to it. The girls, sir, the girls are frauds.

DANFORTH. What's that?

FRANCIS. We have proof of it, sir. They are all deceiving you.

[*DANFORTH is shocked, but studying FRANCIS.*]

HATHORNE. This is contempt, sir, contempt!

DANFORTH. Peace, Judge Hathorne. Do you know who I am, Mr. Nurse?

FRANCIS. I surely do, sir, and I think you must be a wise judge to be what you are.

DANFORTH. And do you know that near to four hundred are in the jails from Marblehead to Lynn, and upon my signature?

FRANCIS. I—

DANFORTH. And seventy-two condemned to hang by that signature?

FRANCIS. Excellency, I never thought to say it to such a weighty judge, but you are deceived.

[*Enter GILES COREY from left. All turn to see as he beckons in MARY WARREN with PROCTOR. MARY is keeping her eyes to the ground; PROCTOR has her elbow as though she were near collapse.*]

PARRIS. [*On seeing her, in shock.*] Mary Warren! [*He goes directly to bend close to her face.*] What are you about here?

PROCTOR. [*Pressing PARRIS away from her with a gentle but firm motion of protectiveness.*] She would speak with the Deputy Governor.

---

2. An *affidavit* is a written declaration sworn to be true, usually before a judge.

Big Idea The United States and the World *What connection might Miller's audiences have made between this statement and the McCarthy hearings?*

Reading Strategy Evaluating Argument *How would you evaluate this claim by Hathorne?*

Reading Strategy Evaluating Argument *The last time we saw Proctor he was violently attacking Mary. Do you think his change in attitude is inconsistent?*

The Crucible, 1996.

DANFORTH. [*Shocked by this, turns to* HERRICK.] Did you not tell me Mary Warren were sick in bed?

HERRICK. She were, Your Honor. When I go to fetch her to the court last week, she said she were sick.

GILES. She has been strivin' with her soul all week, Your Honor; she comes now to tell the truth of this to you.

DANFORTH. Who is this?

PROCTOR. John Proctor, sir. Elizabeth Proctor is my wife.

PARRIS. Beware this man, Your Excellency, this man is mischief.

HALE. [*Excitedly.*] I think you must hear the girl, sir, she—

DANFORTH. [*Who has become very interested in* MARY WARREN *and only raises a hand toward* HALE.] Peace. What would you tell us, Mary Warren?

[PROCTOR *looks at her, but she cannot speak.*]

PROCTOR. She never saw no spirits, sir.

DANFORTH. [*With great alarm and surprise, to* MARY.] Never saw no spirits!

GILES. [*Eagerly.*] Never.

PROCTOR. [*Reaching into his jacket.*] She has signed a deposition,[3] sir—

DANFORTH. [*Instantly.*] No, no, I accept no depositions. [*He is rapidly calculating this; he turns from her to* PROCTOR.] Tell me, Mr. Proctor, have you given out this story in the village?

PROCTOR. We have not.

PARRIS. They've come to overthrow the court, sir! This man is—

DANFORTH. I pray you, Mr. Parris. Do you know, Mr. Proctor, that the entire contention of the state in these trials is that the voice of Heaven is speaking through the children?

---

3. A *deposition* is a sworn, written statement given by a witness out of court and intended to be used as testimony in court.

Literary Element Plot *How does this open disagreement between Parris and Hale represent a new conflict in the play?*

Big Idea The United States and the World *How might this idea relate to the McCarthy "witch hunts" of the 1950s?*

PROCTOR. I know that, sir.

DANFORTH. [*Thinks, staring at* PROCTOR, *then turns to* MARY WARREN.] And you, Mary Warren, how came you to cry out people for sending their spirits against you?

MARY WARREN. It were pretense, sir.

DANFORTH. I cannot hear you.

PROCTOR. It were pretense, she says.

DANFORTH. Ah? And the other girls? Susanna Walcott, and—the others? They are also pretending?

MARY WARREN. Aye, sir.

DANFORTH. [*Wide-eyed.*] Indeed. [*Pause. He is baffled by this. He turns to study* PROCTOR's *face.*]

PARRIS. [*In a sweat.*] Excellency, you surely cannot think to let so **vile** a lie be spread in open court!

DANFORTH. Indeed not, but it strike hard upon me that she will dare come here with such a tale. Now, Mr. Proctor, before I decide whether I shall hear you or not, it is my duty to tell you this. We burn a hot fire here; it melts down all concealment.

PROCTOR. I know that, sir.

DANFORTH. Let me continue. I understand well, a husband's tenderness may drive him to extravagance in defense of a wife. Are you certain in your conscience, Mister, that your evidence is the truth?

PROCTOR. It is. And you will surely know it.

DANFORTH. And you thought to declare this revelation in the open court before the public?

PROCTOR. I thought I would, aye—with your permission.

DANFORTH. [*His eyes narrowing.*] Now, sir, what is your purpose in so doing?

PROCTOR. Why, I—I would free my wife, sir.

DANFORTH. There lurks nowhere in your heart, nor hidden in your spirit, any desire to undermine this court?

Reading Strategy Evaluating Argument *What assumption are Danforth and Parris both making? How would you assess it?*

Vocabulary

vile (vīl) *adj.* evil; foul; repulsive; degrading

PROCTOR. [*With the faintest faltering.*] Why, no, sir.

CHEEVER. [*Clears his throat, awakening.*] I—Your Excellency.

DANFORTH. Mr. Cheever.

CHEEVER. I think it be my duty, sir—[*Kindly, to* PROCTOR.] You'll not deny it, John. [*To* DANFORTH.] When we come to take his wife, he damned the court and ripped your warrant.

PARRIS. Now you have it!

DANFORTH. He did that, Mr. Hale?

HALE. [*Takes a breath.*] Aye, he did.

PROCTOR. It were a temper, sir. I knew not what I did.

DANFORTH. [*Studying him.*] Mr. Proctor.

PROCTOR. Aye, sir.

DANFORTH. [*Straight into his eyes.*] Have you ever seen the Devil?

PROCTOR. No, sir.

DANFORTH. You are in all respects a Gospel Christian?

PROCTOR. I am, sir.

PARRIS. Such a Christian that will not come to church but once in a month!

DANFORTH. [*Restrained—he is curious.*] Not come to church?

PROCTOR. I—I have no love for Mr. Parris. It is no secret. But God I surely love.

CHEEVER. He plow on Sunday, sir.

DANFORTH. Plow on Sunday!

CHEEVER. [*Apologetically.*] I think it be evidence, John. I am an official of the court, I cannot keep it.

PROCTOR. I—I have once or twice plowed on Sunday. I have three children, sir, and until last year my land give little.

GILES. You'll find other Christians that do plow on Sunday if the truth be known.

HALE. Your Honor, I cannot think you may judge the man on such evidence.

DANFORTH. I judge nothing. [*Pause. He keeps watching* PROCTOR, *who tries to meet his gaze.*]

Reading Strategy Evaluating Argument *How does the rest of Danforth's speech contradict this statement?*

I tell you straight, Mister—I have seen marvels in this court. I have seen people choked before my eyes by spirits; I have seen them stuck by pins and slashed by daggers. I have until this moment not the slightest reason to suspect that the children may be deceiving me. Do you understand my meaning?

PROCTOR. Excellency, does it not strike upon you that so many of these women have lived so long with such upright reputation, and—

PARRIS. Do you read the Gospel, Mr. Proctor?

PROCTOR. I read the Gospel.

PARRIS. I think not, or you should surely know that Cain were an upright man, and yet he did kill Abel.[4]

PROCTOR. Aye, God tells us that. [*To DAN-FORTH.*] But who tells us Rebecca Nurse murdered seven babies by sending out her spirit on them? It is the children only, and this one will swear she lied to you.

[*DANFORTH considers, then beckons HATHORNE to him. HATHORNE leans in, and he speaks in his ear. HATHORNE nods.*]

HATHORNE. Aye, she's the one.

DANFORTH. Mr. Proctor, this morning, your wife send me a claim in which she states that she is pregnant now.

PROCTOR. My wife pregnant!

DANFORTH. There be no sign of it—we have examined her body.

PROCTOR. But if she say she is pregnant, then she must be! That woman will never lie, Mr. Danforth.

DANFORTH. She will not?

PROCTOR. Never, sir, never.

DANFORTH. We have thought it too convenient to be credited. However, if I should tell you now that I will let her be kept another month; and if she begin to show her natural signs, you shall have her living yet another year until she is delivered—what say you to that? [*JOHN PROCTOR is struck silent.*] Come now.

You say your only purpose is to save your wife. Good, then, she is saved at least this year, and a year is long. What say you, sir? It is done now. [*In conflict, PROCTOR glances at FRANCIS and GILES.*] Will you drop this charge?

PROCTOR. I—I think I cannot.

DANFORTH. [*Now an almost imperceptible hardness in his voice.*] Then your purpose is somewhat larger.

PARRIS. He's come to overthrow this court, Your Honor!

PROCTOR. These are my friends. Their wives are also accused—

DANFORTH. [*With a sudden briskness of manner.*] I judge you not, sir. I am ready to hear your evidence.

PROCTOR. I come not to hurt the court; I only—

DANFORTH. [*Cutting him off.*] Marshal, go into the court and bid Judge Stoughton and Judge Sewall declare recess for one hour. And let them go to the tavern, if they will. All witnesses and prisoners are to be kept in the building.

HERRICK. Aye, sir. [*Very deferentially.*] If I may say it, sir, I know this man all my life. It is a good man, sir.

DANFORTH. [*It is the reflection on himself he resents.*] I am sure of it, Marshal. [*HERRICK nods, then goes out.*] Now, what deposition do you have for us, Mr. Proctor? And I beg you be clear, open as the sky, and honest.

PROCTOR. [*As he takes out several papers.*] I am no lawyer, so I'll—

DANFORTH. The pure in heart need no lawyers. Proceed as you will.

PROCTOR. [*Handing DANFORTH a paper.*] Will you read this first, sir? It's a sort of testament.[5] The people signing it declare their good opinion of Rebecca, and my wife, and Martha Corey. [*DANFORTH looks down at the paper.*]

---

5. Here, the *testament* is a statement of beliefs or opinions offered as evidence of the truth.

Literary Element   Plot *What conflict is referred to in this stage direction?*

Reading Strategy   Evaluating Argument *What rings false about Danforth's remark?*

---

4. According to the Bible, Adam and Eve's son Cain kills his brother Abel, becoming the first murderer.

Literary Element   Plot *How has the questioning of Proctor contributed to the rising action of the plot?*

Window View—Scapeology #9, 1995. Nanette Carter. Oil on canvas, 41 x 40 in. Sande Webster Gallery, Philadelphia, PA.

Viewing the Art: Look closely at the painting. In what ways might it mirror the events and feelings evident so far in act 3?

PARRIS. [*To enlist* DANFORTH'S *sarcasm.*] Their good opinion! [*But* DANFORTH *goes on reading, and* PROCTOR *is heartened.*]

PROCTOR. These are all landholding farmers, members of the church. [*Delicately, trying to point out a paragraph.*] If you'll notice, sir— they've known the women many years and never saw no sign they had dealings with the Devil.

[PARRIS *nervously moves over and reads over* DANFORTH's *shoulder.*]

DANFORTH. [*Glancing down a long list.*] How many names are here?

FRANCIS. Ninety-one, Your Excellency.

PARRIS. [*Sweating.*] These people should be summoned. [DANFORTH *looks up at him questioningly.*] For questioning.

FRANCIS. [*Trembling with anger.*] Mr. Danforth, I gave them all my word no harm would come to them for signing this.

PARRIS. This is a clear attack upon the court!

HALE. [*To PARRIS, trying to contain himself.*] Is every defense an attack upon the court? Can no one—?

PARRIS. All innocent and Christian people are happy for the courts in Salem! These people are gloomy for it. [*To DANFORTH directly.*] And I think you will want to know, from each and every one of them, what discontents them with you!

HATHORNE. I think they ought to be examined, sir.

DANFORTH. It is not necessarily an attack, I think. Yet—

FRANCIS. These are all covenanted Christians, sir.

DANFORTH. Then I am sure they may have nothing to fear. [*Hands CHEEVER the paper.*] Mr. Cheever, have warrants drawn for all of these—arrest for examination. [*To PROCTOR.*] Now, Mister, what other information do you have for us? [*FRANCIS is still standing, horrified.*] You may sit, Mr. Nurse.

FRANCIS. I have brought trouble on these people; I have—

DANFORTH. No, old man, you have not hurt these people if they are of good conscience. But you must understand, sir, that a person is either with this court or he must be counted against it, there be no road between. This is a sharp time, now, a precise time—we live no longer in the dusky afternoon when evil mixed itself with good and befuddled the world. Now, by God's grace, the shining sun is up, and them that fear not light will surely praise it. I hope you will be one of those. [*MARY WARREN suddenly sobs.*] She's not hearty, I see.

PROCTOR. No, she's not, sir. [*To MARY, bending to her, holding her hand, quietly.*] Now remember what the angel Raphael said to the boy Tobias. Remember it.

Reading Strategy Evaluating Argument *How is Parris twisting the argument in order to win Danforth to his side?*

Big Idea The United States and the World *What connection do you see between Danforth's tactics and the tactics of Senator McCarthy?*

Reading Strategy Evaluating Argument *What logical fallacy is Danforth guilty of here?*

MARY WARREN. [*Hardly audible.*] Aye.

PROCTOR. "Do that which is good, and no harm shall come to thee."

MARY WARREN. Aye.

DANFORTH. Come, man, we wait you.

[*MARSHAL HERRICK returns, and takes his post at the door.*]

GILES. John, my deposition, give him mine.

PROCTOR. Aye. [*He hands DANFORTH another paper.*] This is Mr. Corey's deposition.

DANFORTH. Oh? [*He looks down at it. Now HATHORNE comes behind him and reads with him.*]

HATHORNE. [*Suspiciously.*] What lawyer drew this, Corey?

GILES. You know I never hired a lawyer in my life, Hathorne.

DANFORTH. [*Finishing the reading.*] It is very well phrased. My compliments. Mr. Parris, if Mr. Putnam is in the court, will you bring him in? [*HATHORNE takes the deposition, and walks to the window with it. PARRIS goes into the court.*] You have no legal training, Mr. Corey?

GILES. [*Very pleased.*] I have the best, sir—I am thirty-three time in court in my life. And always plaintiff, too.

DANFORTH. Oh, then you're much put-upon.

GILES. I am never put-upon; I know my rights, sir, and I will have them. You know, your father tried a case of mine—might be thirty-five year ago, I think.

DANFORTH. Indeed.

GILES. He never spoke to you of it?

DANFORTH. No, I cannot recall it.

GILES. That's strange, he give me nine pound damages. He were a fair judge, your father. Y'see, I had a white mare that time, and this fellow come to borrow the mare—[*Enter PARRIS with THOMAS PUTNAM. When he sees PUTNAM, GILES' ease goes; he is hard.*] Aye, there he is.

DANFORTH. Mr. Putnam, I have here an accusation by Mr. Corey against you. He states that you coldly prompted your daughter to cry witchery upon George Jacobs that is now in jail.

PUTNAM. It is a lie.

DANFORTH. [*Turning to* GILES.] Mr. Putnam states your charge is a lie. What say you to that?

GILES. [*Furious, his fists clenched.*] A fart on Thomas Putnam, that is what I say to that!

DANFORTH. What proof do you submit for your charge, sir?

GILES. My proof is there! [*Pointing to the paper.*] If Jacobs hangs for a witch he forfeit up his property—that's law! And there is none but Putnam with the coin to buy so great a piece. This man is killing his neighbors for their land!

DANFORTH. But proof, sir, proof.

GILES. [*Pointing at his deposition.*] The proof is there! I have it from an honest man who heard Putnam say it! The day his daughter cried out on Jacobs, he said she'd given him a fair gift of land.

HATHORNE. And the name of this man?

GILES. [*Taken aback.*] What name?

HATHORNE. The man that give you this information.

GILES. [*Hesitates, then.*] Why, I—I cannot give you his name.

HATHORNE. And why not?

GILES. [*Hesitates, then bursts out.*] You know well why not! He'll lay in jail if I give his name!

HATHORNE. This is contempt of the court, Mr. Danforth!

DANFORTH. [*To avoid that.*] You will surely tell us the name.

GILES. I will not give you no name. I mentioned my wife's name once and I'll burn in hell long enough for that. I stand mute.

DANFORTH. In that case, I have no choice but to arrest you for contempt of this court, do you know that?

Reading Strategy Evaluating Argument *How is Danforth guilty of using a double standard in this demand?*

Big Idea The United States and the World *What resemblance can you see here between Giles Corey and Arthur Miller?* **BI₂**

GILES. This is a hearing; you cannot clap me for contempt of a hearing.

DANFORTH. Oh, it is a proper lawyer! Do you wish me to declare the court in full session here? Or will you give me good reply?

GILES. [*Faltering.*] I cannot give you no name, sir, I cannot.

DANFORTH. You are a foolish old man. Mr. Cheever, begin the record. The court is now in session. I ask you, Mr. Corey—

PROCTOR. [*Breaking in.*] Your Honor—he has the story in confidence, sir, and he—

PARRIS. The Devil lives on such confidences! [*To* DANFORTH.] Without confidences there could be no conspiracy, Your Honor!

HATHORNE. I think it must be broken, sir.

DANFORTH. [*To* GILES.] Old man, if your informant tells the truth let him come here openly like a decent man. But if he hide in anonymity I must know why. Now sir, the government and central church demand of you the name of him who reported Mr. Thomas Putnam a common murderer.

HALE. Excellency—

DANFORTH. Mr. Hale.

HALE. We cannot blink it more. There is a prodigious fear of this court in the country—

DANFORTH. Then there is a prodigious guilt in the country. Are you afraid to be questioned here?

HALE. I may only fear the Lord, sir, but there is fear in the country nevertheless.

DANFORTH. [*Angered now.*] Reproach[6] me not with the fear in the country; there is fear in the country because there is a moving plot to topple Christ in the country!

HALE. But it does not follow that everyone accused is part of it.

DANFORTH. No uncorrupted man may fear this court, Mr. Hale! None! [*To* GILES.] You are under arrest in contempt of this court. Now sit you down and take counsel with yourself, or

---

6. To *reproach* is to blame or to express disapproval of.

Reading Strategy Evaluating Argument *What has Danforth just concluded from Hale's comment? What fallacy do you detect in his reasoning?*

you will be set in the jail until you decide to answer all questions.

[*GILES COREY makes a rush for* PUTNAM. *PROCTOR lunges and holds him.*]

PROCTOR. No, Giles!

GILES. [*Over* PROCTOR'S *shoulder at* PUTNAM.] I'll cut your throat, Putnam, I'll kill you yet!

PROCTOR. [*Forcing him into a chair.*] Peace, Giles, peace. [*Releasing him.*] We'll prove ourselves. Now we will. [*He starts to turn to* DANFORTH.]

GILES. Say nothin' more, John. [*Pointing at* DANFORTH.] He's only playin' you! He means to hang us all!

[*MARY WARREN bursts into sobs.*]

DANFORTH. This is a court of law, Mister. I'll have no effrontery⁷ here!

PROCTOR. Forgive him, sir, for his old age. Peace, Giles, we'll prove it all now. [*He lifts up* MARY'S *chin.*] You cannot weep, Mary. Remember the angel, what he say to the boy. Hold to it, now; there is your rock. [MARY *quiets. He takes out a paper, and turns to* DANFORTH.] This is Mary Warren's deposition. I—I would ask you remember, sir, while you read it, that until two week ago she were no different than the other children are today. [*He is speaking reasonably, restraining all his fears, his anger, his anxiety.*] You saw her scream, she howled, she swore familiar spirits choked her; she even testified that Satan, in the form of women now in jail, tried to win her soul away, and then when she refused—

DANFORTH. We know all this.

PROCTOR. Aye, sir. She swears now that she never saw Satan; nor any spirit, vague or clear, that Satan may have sent to hurt her. And she declares her friends are lying now.

[PROCTOR *starts to hand* DANFORTH *the deposition, and* HALE *comes up to* DANFORTH *in a trembling state.*]

HALE. Excellency, a moment. I think this goes to the heart of the matter.

DANFORTH. [*With deep misgivings.*] It surely does.

---

7. *Effrontery* is boldness and disrespect.

Literary Element Plot *How is the rising action gradually propelling Proctor toward the center of attention and the climax of the act?*

HALE. I cannot say he is an honest man; I know him little. But in all justice, sir, a claim so weighty cannot be argued by a farmer. In God's name, sir, stop here; send him home and let him come again with a lawyer—

DANFORTH. [*Patiently.*] Now look you, Mr. Hale—

HALE. Excellency, I have signed seventy-two death warrants; I am a minister of the Lord, and I dare not take a life without there be a proof so **immaculate** no slightest qualm⁸ of conscience may doubt it.

DANFORTH. Mr. Hale, you surely do not doubt my justice.

HALE. I have this morning signed away the soul of Rebecca Nurse, Your Honor. I'll not conceal it, my hand shakes yet as with a wound! I pray you, sir, *this* argument let lawyers present to you.

DANFORTH. Mr. Hale, believe me; for a man of such terrible learning you are most bewildered—I hope you will forgive me. I have been thirty-two year at the bar, sir, and I should be confounded were I called upon to defend these people. Let you consider, now—[*To* PROCTOR *and the others.*] And I bid you all do likewise. In an ordinary crime, how does one defend the accused? One calls up witnesses to prove his innocence. But witchcraft is *ipso facto*,⁹ on its face and by its nature, an invisible crime, is it not? Therefore, who may possibly be witness to it? The witch and the victim. None other. Now we cannot hope the witch will accuse herself; granted? Therefore, we must rely upon her victims—and they do testify, the children certainly do testify. As for the witches, none will deny that we are most eager for all their confessions. Therefore, what is left for a lawyer to bring out? I think I have made my point. Have I not?

---

8. *Qualm* (kwäm) means "doubt."
9. The Latin legal term *ipso facto* means, literally, "by that very fact" or "by the fact itself."

Literary Element Plot *How has the development of Hale's character contributed to the conflict in the play?*

Reading Strategy Evaluating Argument *What hope does the logic of this argument give to people accused of witchcraft? Explain.*

Vocabulary

immaculate (i mak′ yə lit) *adj.* unblemished; flawless; pure

---

HALE. But this child claims the girls are not truthful, and if they are not—

DANFORTH. That is precisely what I am about to consider, sir. What more may you ask of me? Unless you doubt my probity?[10]

HALE. [*Defeated.*] I surely do not, sir. Let you consider it, then.

DANFORTH. And let you put your heart to rest. Her deposition, Mr. Proctor.

[PROCTOR *hands it to him.* HATHORNE *rises, goes beside* DANFORTH, *and starts reading.* PARRIS *comes to his other side.* DANFORTH *looks at* JOHN PROCTOR, *then proceeds to read.* HALE *gets up, finds position near the judge, reads too.* PROCTOR *glances at* GILES. FRANCIS *prays silently, hands pressed together.* CHEEVER *waits placidly, the sublime official, dutiful.* MARY WARREN *sobs once.* JOHN PROCTOR *touches her head reassuringly. Presently* DANFORTH *lifts his eyes, stands up, takes out a kerchief and blows his nose. The others stand aside as he moves in thought toward the window.*]

PARRIS. [*Hardly able to contain his anger and fear.*] I should like to question—

DANFORTH. [*His first real outburst, in which his contempt for* PARRIS *is clear.*] Mr. Parris, I bid you be silent! [*He stands in silence, looking out the window. Now, having established that he will set the gait.*][11] Mr. Cheever, will you go into the court and bring the children here? [CHEEVER *gets up and goes out upstage.* DANFORTH *now turns to* MARY.] Mary Warren, how came you to this turnabout? Has Mr. Proctor threatened you for this deposition?

MARY WARREN. No, sir.

DANFORTH. Has he ever threatened you?

MARY WARREN. [*Weaker.*] No, sir.

DANFORTH. [*Sensing a weakening.*] Has he threatened you?

MARY WARREN. No, sir.

10. *Probity* involves moral excellence, integrity, and honesty.
11. To *set the gait* is an expression that means "to determine how a matter will proceed."

Literary Element Plot *How does Danforth's aggressive questioning of Mary contribute to the rising action?*

DANFORTH. Then you tell me that you sat in my court, callously lying, when you knew that people would hang by your evidence? [*She does not answer.*] Answer me!

MARY WARREN. [*Almost inaudibly.*] I did, sir.

DANFORTH. How were you instructed in your life? Do you not know that God damns all liars? [*She cannot speak.*] Or is it now that you lie?

MARY WARREN. No, sir—I am with God now.

DANFORTH. You are with God now.

MARY WARREN. Aye, sir.

DANFORTH. [*Containing himself.*] I will tell you this—you are either lying now, or you were lying in the court, and in either case you have committed perjury[12] and you will go to jail for it. You cannot lightly say you lied, Mary. Do you know that?

MARY WARREN. I cannot lie no more. I am with God, I am with God.

[*But she breaks into sobs at the thought of it, and the right door opens, and enter* SUSANNA WALCOTT, MERCY LEWIS, BETTY PARRIS, *and finally* ABIGAIL. CHEEVER *comes to* DANFORTH.]

CHEEVER. Ruth Putnam's not in the court, sir, nor the other children.

DANFORTH. These will be sufficient. Sit you down, children. [*Silently they sit.*] Your friend, Mary Warren, has given us a deposition. In which she swears that she never saw familiar spirits, apparitions, nor any manifest of the Devil.[13] She claims as well that none of you have seen these things either. [*Slight pause.*] Now, children, this is a court of law. The law, based upon the Bible, and the Bible, writ by Almighty God, forbid the practice of witchcraft, and describe death as the penalty thereof. But likewise, children, the law and Bible damn all bearers of false witness. [*Slight pause.*]

12. *Perjury* is the act of swearing under oath to the truth of something that one knows to be untrue.
13. *Familiar spirits* are supernatural beings (not ghosts) believed to serve demons or humans; *apparitions* are ghosts of dead people; and a *manifest of the Devil* is a form in which the devil reveals himself.

Literary Element Plot *How does Abigail's delayed entry contribute to the tension in this scene?*

Now then. It does not escape me that this deposition may be devised to blind us; it may well be that Mary Warren has been conquered by Satan, who sends her here to distract our sacred purpose. If so, her neck will break for it. But if she speak true, I bid you now drop your **guile** and confess your pretense, for a quick confession will go easier with you. [*Pause.*] Abigail Williams, rise. [*ABIGAIL slowly rises.*] Is there any truth in this?

ABIGAIL. No, sir.

DANFORTH. [*Thinks, glances at* MARY, *then back to* ABIGAIL.] Children, a very augur bit[14] will now be turned into your souls until your honesty is proved. Will either of you change your positions now, or do you force me to hard questioning?

ABIGAIL. I have naught to change, sir. She lies.

DANFORTH. [*To* MARY.] You would still go on with this?

MARY WARREN. [*Faintly.*] Aye, sir.

DANFORTH. [*Turning to* ABIGAIL.] A poppet were discovered in Mr. Proctor's house, stabbed by a needle. Mary Warren claims that you sat beside her in the court when she made it, and that you saw her make it and witnessed how she herself stuck her needle into it for safe-keeping. What say you to that?

ABIGAIL. [*With a slight note of indignation.*] It is a lie, sir.

DANFORTH. [*After a slight pause.*] While you worked for Mr. Proctor, did you see poppets in that house?

ABIGAIL. Goody Proctor always kept poppets.

PROCTOR. Your Honor, my wife never kept no poppets. Mary Warren confesses it was her poppet.

CHEEVER. Your Excellency.

DANFORTH. Mr. Cheever.

CHEEVER. When I spoke with Goody Proctor in that house, she said she never kept no poppets. But she said she did keep poppets when she were a girl.

PROCTOR. She has not been a girl these fifteen years, Your Honor.

HATHORNE. But a poppet will keep fifteen years, will it not?

PROCTOR. It will keep if it is kept, but Mary Warren swears she never saw no poppets in my house, nor anyone else.

PARRIS. Why could there not have been poppets hid where no one ever saw them?

PROCTOR. [*Furious.*] There might also be a dragon with five legs in my house, but no one has ever seen it.

PARRIS. We are here, Your Honor, precisely to discover what no one has ever seen.

PROCTOR. Mr. Danforth, what profit this girl to turn herself about? What may Mary Warren gain but hard questioning and worse?

DANFORTH. You are charging Abigail Williams with a marvelous cool plot to murder, do you understand that?

PROCTOR. I do, sir. I believe she means to murder.

DANFORTH. [*Pointing at* ABIGAIL, *incredulously.*][15] This child would murder your wife?

PROCTOR. It is not a child. Now hear me, sir. In the sight of the congregation she were twice this year put out of this meetin' house for laughter during prayer.

DANFORTH. [*Shocked, turning to* ABIGAIL.] What's this? Laughter during—!

PARRIS. Excellency, she were under Tituba's power at that time, but she is solemn now.

---

14. Here, *augur bit* refers to an auger, a tool for boring holes.

Reading Strategy Evaluating Argument *Compare Danforth's treatment of Mary to his treatment of the other girls. How is this another example of Danforth's double standard in administering justice?*

Vocabulary

guile (gīl) *n.* cunning; deceit; slyness

---

15. *Incredulously* means "in a disbelieving manner."

Big Idea The United States and the World *Opponents of Senator McCarthy's investigations used to refer sarcastically to finding "Reds under the beds." What connection does this phrase have to Parris's observation?*

Literary Element Plot *What new development has occurred in the plot that brings the rising action nearer to the climax?*

GILES. Aye, now she is solemn and goes to hang people!

DANFORTH. Quiet, man.

HATHORNE. Surely it have no bearing on the question, sir. He charges **contemplation** of murder.

DANFORTH. Aye. [*He studies* ABIGAIL *for a moment, then.*] Continue, Mr. Proctor.

PROCTOR. Mary. Now tell the Governor how you danced in the woods.

PARRIS. [*Instantly.*] Excellency, since I come to Salem this man is blackening my name. He—

DANFORTH. In a moment, sir. [*To* MARY WAR-REN, *sternly, and surprised.*] What is this dancing?

MARY WARREN. I—[*She glances at* ABIGAIL, *who is staring down at her remorselessly. Then, appealing to* PROCTOR.] Mr. Proctor—

PROCTOR. [*Taking it right up.*] Abigail leads the girls to the woods, Your Honor, and they have danced there naked—

PARRIS. Your Honor, this—

PROCTOR. [*At once.*] Mr. Parris discovered them himself in the dead of night! There's the "child" she is!

DANFORTH. [*It is growing into a nightmare, and he turns, astonished, to* PARRIS.] Mr. Parris—

PARRIS. I can only say, sir, that I never found any of them naked, and this man is—

DANFORTH. But you discovered them dancing in the woods? [*Eyes on* PARRIS, *he points at* ABI-GAIL.] Abigail?

HALE. Excellency, when I first arrived from Beverly, Mr. Parris told me that.

DANFORTH. Do you deny it, Mr. Parris?

PARRIS. I do not, sir, but I never saw any of them naked.

DANFORTH. But she have *danced?*

PARRIS. [*Unwillingly.*] Aye, sir.

[DANFORTH, *as though with new eyes, looks at* ABIGAIL.]

HATHORNE. Excellency, will you permit me? [*He points at* MARY WARREN.]

DANFORTH. [*With great worry.*] Pray, proceed.

HATHORNE. You say you never saw no spirits, Mary, were never threatened or afflicted by any manifest of the Devil or the Devil's agents.

MARY WARREN. [*Very faintly.*] No, sir.

HATHORNE. [*With a gleam of victory.*] And yet, when people accused of witchery con-fronted you in court, you would faint, saying their spirits came out of their bodies and choked you—

MARY WARREN. That were pretense, sir.

DANFORTH. I cannot hear you.

MARY WARREN. Pretense, sir.

PARRIS. But you did turn cold, did you not? I myself picked you up many times, and your skin were icy. Mr. Danforth, you—

DANFORTH. I saw that many times.

PROCTOR. She only pretended to faint, Your Excellency. They're all marvelous pretenders.

HATHORNE. Then can she pretend to faint now?

PROCTOR. Now?

PARRIS. Why not? Now there are no spirits attacking her, for none in this room is accused of witchcraft. So let her turn herself cold now, let her pretend she is attacked now, let her faint. [*He turns to* MARY WARREN.] Faint!

MARY WARREN. Faint?

PARRIS. Aye, faint. Prove to us how you pre-tended in the court so many times.

MARY WARREN. [*Looking to* PROCTOR.] I— cannot faint now, sir.

PROCTOR. [*Alarmed, quietly.*] Can you not pre-tend it?

Vocabulary

contemplation (kon′ təm plā′ shən) *n.* the act of thinking about something long and seriously

Literary Element Plot *At this point in the proceedings, in which direction does Danforth appear to be leaning?*

Reading Strategy Evaluating Argument *Do you think that Parris's scheme for testing Mary's claim that she pretended to faint is a fair test? Explain.*

MARY WARREN. I—[*She looks about as though searching for the passion to faint.*] I—have no *sense* of it now, I—

DANFORTH. Why? What is lacking now?

MARY WARREN. I—cannot tell, sir, I—

DANFORTH. Might it be that here we have no afflicting spirit loose, but in the court there were some?

MARY WARREN. I never saw no spirits.

PARRIS. Then see no spirits now, and prove to us that you can faint by your own will, as you claim.

MARY WARREN. [*Stares, searching for the emotion of it, and then shakes her head.*] I—cannot do it.

PARRIS. Then you will confess, will you not? It were attacking spirits made you faint!

MARY WARREN. No, sir, I—

PARRIS. Your Excellency, this is a trick to blind the court!

MARY WARREN. It's not a trick! [*She stands.*] I—I used to faint because I—I thought I saw spirits.

DANFORTH. *Thought* you saw them!

MARY WARREN. But I did not, Your Honor.

HATHORNE. How could you think you saw them unless you saw them?

MARY WARREN. I—I cannot tell how, but I did. I—I heard the other girls screaming, and you, Your Honor, you seemed to believe them, and I—It were only sport in the beginning, sir, but then the whole world cried spirits, spirits, and I—I promise you, Mr. Danforth, I only thought I saw them but I did not.

[*DANFORTH peers at her.*]

PARRIS. [*Smiling, but nervous because DANFORTH seems to be struck by MARY WARREN's story.*] Surely Your Excellency is not taken by this simple lie.

DANFORTH. [*Turning worriedly to ABIGAIL.*] Abigail. I bid you now search your heart and tell me this—and beware of it, child, to God every soul is precious and His vengeance is terrible on them that take life without cause. Is it possible, child, that the spirits you have seen are illusion only, some deception that may cross your mind when—

ABIGAIL. Why, this—this—is a base question, sir.

DANFORTH. Child, I would have you consider it—

ABIGAIL. I have been hurt, Mr. Danforth; I have seen my blood runnin' out! I have been near to murdered every day because I done my duty pointing out the Devil's people—and this is my reward? To be mistrusted, denied, questioned like a—

DANFORTH. [*Weakening.*] Child, I do not mistrust you—

ABIGAIL. [*In an open threat.*] Let you beware, Mr. Danforth. Think you to be so mighty that the power of Hell may not turn your wits? Beware of it! There is—[*Suddenly, from an accusatory attitude, her face turns, looking into the air above—it is truly frightened.*]

DANFORTH. [*Apprehensively.*] What is it, child?

ABIGAIL. [*Looking about in the air, clasping her arms about her as though cold.*] I—I know not. A wind, a cold wind, has come. [*Her eyes fall on MARY WARREN.*]

MARY WARREN. [*Terrified, pleading.*] Abby!

MERCY LEWIS. [*Shivering.*] Your Honor, I freeze!

PROCTOR. They're pretending!

HATHORNE. [*Touching ABIGAIL's hand.*] She is cold, Your Honor, touch her!

MERCY LEWIS. [*Through chattering teeth.*] Mary, do you send this shadow on me?

MARY WARREN. Lord, save me!

SUSANNA WALCOTT. I freeze, I freeze!

ABIGAIL. [*Shivering visibly.*] It is a wind, a wind!

MARY WARREN. Abby, don't do that!

DANFORTH. [*Himself engaged and entered by ABIGAIL.*] Mary Warren, do you witch her? I say to you, do you send your spirit out?

[*With a hysterical cry MARY WARREN starts to run. PROCTOR catches her.*]

Literary Element Plot *How is Danforth instrumental in maintaining the tension during this scene?*

Reading Strategy Evaluating Argument *Is it wise for Abigail to confront the chief judge in this manner? Is her ploy successful? Explain.*

MARY WARREN. [Almost collapsing.] Let me go, Mr. Proctor, I cannot, I cannot—

ABIGAIL. [Crying to Heaven.] Oh, Heavenly Father, take away this shadow!

[Without warning or hesitation, PROCTOR leaps at ABIGAIL and, grabbing her by the hair, pulls her to her feet. She screams in pain. DANFORTH, astonished, cries, "What are you about?" and HATHORNE and PARRIS call, "Take your hands off her!" and out of it all comes PROCTOR's roaring voice.]

PROCTOR. How do you call Heaven! Whore![16] Whore!

[HERRICK breaks PROCTOR from her.]

HERRICK. John!

DANFORTH. Man! Man, what do you—

PROCTOR. [Breathless and in agony.] It is a whore!

DANFORTH. [Dumfounded.][17] You charge—?

ABIGAIL. Mr. Danforth, he is lying!

PROCTOR. Mark her! Now she'll suck a scream to stab me with, but—

DANFORTH. You will prove this! This will not pass!

PROCTOR. [Trembling, his life collapsing about him.] I have known her, sir. I have known her.

DANFORTH. You—you are a lecher?

FRANCIS. [Horrified.] John, you cannot say such a—

PROCTOR. Oh, Francis, I wish you had some evil in you that you might know me! [To DANFORTH.] A man will not cast away his good name. You surely know that.

DANFORTH. [Dumfounded.] In—in what time? In what place?

PROCTOR. [His voice about to break, and his shame great.] In the proper place—where my beasts are bedded. On the last night of my joy, some eight months past. She used to serve me in my house, sir. [He has to clamp his jaw to keep from weeping.]

A man may think God sleeps, but God sees everything, I know it now. I beg you, sir, I beg you—see her what she is. My wife, my dear good wife, took this girl soon after, sir, and put her out on the highroad. And being what she is, a lump of vanity, sir—[He is being overcome.] Excellency, forgive me, forgive me. [Angrily against himself, he turns away from the Governor for a moment. Then, as though to cry out is his only means of speech left.] She thinks to dance with me on my wife's grave! And well she might, for I thought of her softly. God help me, I lusted, and there is a promise in such sweat. But it is a whore's vengeance, and you must see it; I set myself entirely in your hands. I know you must see it now.

DANFORTH. [Blanched,[18] in horror, turning to ABIGAIL.] You deny every scrap and tittle of this?

ABIGAIL. If I must answer that, I will leave and I will not come back again!

[DANFORTH seems unsteady.]

PROCTOR. I have made a bell of my honor! I have rung the doom of my good name—you will believe me, Mr. Danforth! My wife is innocent, except she knew a whore when she saw one!

ABIGAIL. [Stepping up to DANFORTH.] What look do you give me? [DANFORTH cannot speak.] I'll not have such looks! [She turns and starts for the door.]

DANFORTH. You will remain where you are! [HERRICK steps into her path. She comes up short, fire in her eyes.] Mr. Parris, go into the court and bring Goodwife Proctor out.

PARRIS. [Objecting.] Your Honor, this is all a—

DANFORTH. [Sharply to PARRIS.] Bring her out! And tell her not one word of what's been spoken here. And let you knock before you enter. [PARRIS goes out.] Now we shall touch the bottom

18. Here, blanched means "drained of color."

Reading Strategy Evaluating Argument *What does Proctor hope to accomplish in this conclusion to his confession?*

Reading Strategy Evaluating Argument *How does Abigail choose to defend herself against Proctor's accusations? How effective do you think her method will be?*

16. Here, *whore* refers to a "loose" woman, not that she has taken money for sexual services.
17. *Dumfounded* means "speechless."

Literary Element Plot *How is this moment crucial to the development of the plot?*

of this swamp. [*To* PROCTOR.] Your wife, you say, is an honest woman.

PROCTOR. In her life, sir, she have never lied. There are them that cannot sing, and them that cannot weep—my wife cannot lie. I have paid much to learn it, sir.

DANFORTH. And when she put this girl out of your house, she put her out for a harlot?

PROCTOR. Aye, sir.

DANFORTH. And knew her for a harlot?

PROCTOR. Aye, sir, she knew her for a harlot.

DANFORTH. Good then. [*To* ABIGAIL.] And if she tell me, child, it were for harlotry, may God spread His mercy on you! [*There is a knock. He calls to the door.*] Hold! [*To* ABIGAIL.] Turn your back. Turn your back. [*To* PROCTOR.] Do likewise. [*Both turn their backs—* ABIGAIL *with indignant slowness.*] Now let neither of you turn to face Goody Proctor. No one in this room is to speak one word, or raise a gesture aye or nay. [*He turns toward the door, calls.*] Enter! [*The door opens.* ELIZABETH *enters with* PARRIS. PARRIS *leaves her. She stands alone, her eyes looking for* PROCTOR.] Mr. Cheever, report this testimony in all exactness. Are you ready?

CHEEVER. Ready, sir.

DANFORTH. Come here, woman. [ELIZABETH *comes to him, glancing at* PROCTOR'S *back.*] Look at me only, not at your husband. In my eyes only.

ELIZABETH. [*Faintly.*] Good, sir.

DANFORTH. We are given to understand that at one time you dismissed your servant, Abigail Williams.

ELIZABETH. That is true, sir.

DANFORTH. For what cause did you dismiss her? [*Slight pause. Then* ELIZABETH *tries to glance at* PROCTOR.] You will look in my eyes only and not at your husband. The answer is in your memory and you need no help to give it to me. Why did you dismiss Abigail Williams?

ELIZABETH. [*Not knowing what to say, sensing a situation, wetting her lips to stall for time.*] She—dissatisfied me. [*Pause.*] And my husband.

DANFORTH. In what way dissatisfied you?

ELIZABETH. She were—[*She glances at* PROCTOR *for a cue.*]

DANFORTH. Woman, look at me! [ELIZABETH *does.*] Were she slovenly?[19] Lazy? What disturbance did she cause?

ELIZABETH. Your Honor, I—in that time I were sick. And I—My husband is a good and righteous man. He is never drunk as some are, nor wastin' his time at the shovelboard,[20] but always at his work. But in my sickness—you see, sir, I were a long time sick after my last baby, and I thought I saw my husband somewhat turning from me. And this girl—[*She turns to* ABIGAIL.]

DANFORTH. Look at me.

ELIZABETH. Aye, sir. Abigail Williams—[*She breaks off.*]

DANFORTH. What of Abigail Williams?

ELIZABETH. I came to think he fancied her. And so one night I lost my wits, I think, and put her out on the highroad.

DANFORTH. Your husband—did he indeed turn from you?

ELIZABETH. [*In agony.*] My husband—is a goodly man, sir.

DANFORTH. Then he did not turn from you.

ELIZABETH. [*Starting to glance at* PROCTOR.] He—

DANFORTH. [*Reaches out and holds her face, then.*] Look at me! To your own knowledge, has John Proctor ever committed the crime of lechery? [*In a crisis of indecision she cannot speak.*] Answer my question! Is your husband a lecher!

ELIZABETH. [*Faintly.*] No, sir.

DANFORTH. Remove her, Marshal.

PROCTOR. Elizabeth, tell the truth!

---

19. To be *slovenly* is to be untidy or careless, especially in appearance.
20. *Shovelboard* is a tabletop version of shuffleboard.

Literary Element Plot *How might Proctor's comment foreshadow the ironic reversal that occurs later in this scene?*

Literary Element Plot *How do these two words alter the direction of the plot?*

The Crucible, 1996.

DANFORTH. She has spoken. Remove her!

PROCTOR. [*Crying out.*] Elizabeth, I have confessed it!

ELIZABETH. Oh, God! [*The door closes behind her.*]

PROCTOR. She only thought to save my name!

HALE. Excellency, it is a natural lie to tell; I beg you, stop now before another is condemned! I may shut my conscience to it no more—private vengeance is working through this testimony! From the beginning this man has struck me true. By my oath to Heaven, I believe him now, and I pray you call back his wife before we—

DANFORTH. She spoke nothing of lechery, and this man has lied!

HALE. I believe him! [*Pointing at* ABIGAIL.] This girl has always struck me false! She has—

Reading Strategy Evaluating Argument *Danforth and Hale draw different conclusions from the preceding scene. Which one has come closer to the truth? Explain.*

[ABIGAIL, *with a weird, wild, chilling cry, screams up to the ceiling.*]

ABIGAIL. You will not! Begone! Begone, I say!

DANFORTH. What is it, child? [*But* ABIGAIL, *pointing with fear, is now raising up her frightened eyes, her awed face, toward the ceiling—the girls are doing the same—and now* HATHORNE, HALE, PUTNAM, CHEEVER, HERRICK, *and* DANFORTH *do the same.*] What's there? [*He lowers his eyes from the ceiling, and now he is frightened; there is real tension in his voice.*] Child! [*She is transfixed—with all the girls, she is whimpering open-mouthed, agape at the ceiling.*] Girls! Why do you—?

MERCY LEWIS. [*Pointing.*] It's on the beam! Behind the rafter!

DANFORTH. [*Looking up.*] Where!

ABIGAIL. Why—? [*She gulps.*] Why do you come, yellow bird?

PROCTOR. Where's a bird? I see no bird!

ABIGAIL. [*To the ceiling.*] My face? My face?

PROCTOR. Mr. Hale—

DANFORTH. Be quiet!!

PROCTOR. [*To* HALE.] Do you see a bird?

DANFORTH. Be quiet!

ABIGAIL. [*To the ceiling, in a genuine conversation with the "bird," as though trying to talk it out of attacking her.*] But God made my face; you cannot want to tear my face. Envy is a deadly sin, Mary.

MARY WARREN. [*On her feet with a spring, and horrified, pleading.*] Abby!

ABIGAIL. [**Unperturbed,** *continuing to the "bird."*] Oh, Mary, this is a black art to change your shape. No, I cannot, I cannot stop my mouth; it's God's work I do.

MARY WARREN. Abby, I'm *here!*

PROCTOR. [*Frantically.*] They're pretending, Mr. Danforth!

ABIGAIL. [*Now she takes a backward step, as though in fear the bird will swoop down momentarily.*] Oh, please, Mary! Don't come down.

SUSANNA WALCOTT. Her claws, she's stretching her claws!

PROCTOR. Lies, lies.

ABIGAIL. [*Backing further, eyes still fixed above.*] Mary, please don't hurt me!

MARY WARREN. [*To* DANFORTH.] I'm not hurting her!

DANFORTH. [*To* MARY WARREN.] Why does she see this vision?

MARY WARREN. She sees nothin'!

ABIGAIL. [*Now staring full front as though hypnotized, and mimicking the exact tone of* MARY WARREN's *cry.*] She sees nothin'!

MARY WARREN. [*Pleading.*] Abby, you mustn't!

Reading Strategy Evaluating Argument *What is Abigail trying to accomplish in this scene? Is she successful? Explain.*

Big Idea The United States and the World *How does this stage direction help to explain why Mary betrays Proctor and why many witnesses at the McCarthy hearings betrayed their friends and colleagues?*

Vocabulary

unperturbed (un pər turbd´) *adj.* undisturbed; calm

ABIGAIL AND ALL THE GIRLS. [*All transfixed.*] Abby, you mustn't!

MARY WARREN. [*To all the girls.*] I'm here, I'm here!

GIRLS. I'm here, I'm here!

DANFORTH. [*Horrified.*] Mary Warren! Draw back your spirit out of them!

MARY WARREN. Mr. Danforth!

GIRLS. [*Cutting her off.*] Mr. Danforth!

DANFORTH. Have you compacted with the Devil? Have you?

MARY WARREN. Never, never!

GIRLS. Never, never!

DANFORTH. [*Growing hysterical.*] Why can they only repeat you?

PROCTOR. Give me a whip—I'll stop it!

MARY WARREN. They're sporting. They—!

GIRLS. They're sporting!

MARY WARREN. [*Turning on them all hysterically and stamping her feet.*] Abby, stop it!

GIRLS. [*Stamping their feet.*] Abby, stop it!

MARY WARREN. Stop it!

GIRLS. Stop it!

MARY WARREN. [*Screaming it out at the top of her lungs, and raising her fists.*] Stop it!!

GIRLS. [*Raising their fists.*] Stop it!!

[MARY WARREN, *utterly confounded, and becoming overwhelmed by* ABIGAIL's—*and the girls'—utter conviction, starts to whimper, hands half raised, powerless, and all the girls begin whimpering exactly as she does.*]

DANFORTH. A little while ago you were afflicted. Now it seems you afflict others; where did you find this power?

MARY WARREN. [*Staring at* ABIGAIL.] I—have no power.

GIRLS. I have no power.

PROCTOR. They're gulling[21] you, Mister!

DANFORTH. Why did you turn about this past two weeks? You have seen the Devil, have you not?

HALE. [*Indicating* ABIGAIL *and the girls.*] You cannot believe them!

---

21. *Gulling* means "deceiving."

Sympathizer, 1956. Elaine de Kooning. Oil on canvas, 40¼ x 31 in. Estate of Elaine de Kooning.

Viewing the Art: What are your reactions to this painting? Are they similar to or different from the reactions you have to Mary Warren in act 3? Explain.

MARY WARREN. I—

PROCTOR. [Sensing her weakening.] Mary, God damns all liars!

DANFORTH. [Pounding it into her.] You have seen the Devil, you have made compact with Lucifer, have you not?

PROCTOR. God damns liars, Mary!

[MARY utters something unintelligible, staring at ABIGAIL, who keeps watching the "bird" above.]

DANFORTH. I cannot hear you. What do you say? [MARY utters again unintelligibly.] You will confess yourself or you will hang! [He turns her roughly to face him.] Do you know who I am? I say you will hang if you do not open with me!

PROCTOR. Mary, remember the angel Raphael—do that which is good and—

ABIGAIL. [Pointing upward.] The wings! Her wings are spreading! Mary, please, don't, don't—!

HALE. I see nothing, Your Honor!

DANFORTH. Do you confess this power! [He is an inch from her face.] Speak!

ABIGAIL. She's going to come down! She's walking the beam!

DANFORTH. Will you speak!

MARY WARREN. [Staring in horror.] I cannot!

GIRLS. I cannot!

PARRIS. Cast the Devil out! Look him in the face! Trample him! We'll save you, Mary, only stand fast against him and—

ABIGAIL. [Looking up.] Look out! She's coming down!

[She and all the girls run to one wall, shielding their eyes. And now, as though cornered, they let out a gigantic scream, and MARY, as though infected, opens her mouth and screams with them. Gradually ABIGAIL and the girls leave off, until only MARY is left there, staring up at the "bird," screaming madly. All watch her, horrified by this evident fit. PROCTOR strides to her.]

Big Idea **The United States and the World** *What connection would Miller's 1950s audiences have made between Danforth's questions and the McCarthy hearings?*

Literary Element Plot *How does Arthur Miller create tension in this scene?*

PROCTOR. Mary, tell the Governor what they— [He has hardly got a word out, when, seeing him coming for her, she rushes out of his reach, screaming in horror.]

MARY WARREN. Don't touch me—don't touch me! [At which the girls halt at the door.]

PROCTOR. [Astonished.] Mary!

MARY WARREN. [Pointing at PROCTOR.] You're the Devil's man!

[He is stopped in his tracks.]

PARRIS. Praise God!

GIRLS. Praise God!

PROCTOR. [Numbed.] Mary, how—?

MARY WARREN. I'll not hang with you! I love God, I love God.

DANFORTH. [To MARY.] He bid you do the Devil's work?

MARY WARREN. [Hysterically, indicating PROCTOR.] He come at me by night and every day to sign, to sign, to—

DANFORTH. Sign what?

PARRIS. The Devil's book? He come with a book?

MARY WARREN. [Hysterically, pointing at PROCTOR, fearful of him.] My name, he want my name. "I'll murder you," he says, "if my wife hangs! We must go and overthrow the court," he says!

[DANFORTH's hand jerks toward PROCTOR, shock and horror in his face.]

PROCTOR. [Turning, appealing to HALE.] Mr. Hale!

MARY WARREN. [Her sobs beginning.] He wake me every night, his eyes were like coals and his fingers claw my neck, and I sign, I sign . . .

HALE. Excellency, this child's gone wild!

PROCTOR. [As DANFORTH's wide eyes pour on him.] Mary, Mary!

MARY WARREN. [Screaming at him.] No, I love God; I go your way no more. I love God, I bless God. [Sobbing, she rushes to ABIGAIL.]

Literary Element Plot *How might this be a turning point in the plot?*

Abby, Abby, I'll never hurt you more! [*They all watch, as* ABIGAIL, *out of her infinite charity, reaches out and draws the sobbing* MARY *to her, and then looks up to* DANFORTH.]

DANFORTH. [*To* PROCTOR.] What are you? [PROCTOR *is beyond speech in his anger.*] You are combined with anti-Christ, are you not? I have seen your power; you will not deny it! What say you, Mister?

HALE. Excellency—

DANFORTH. I will have nothing from you, Mr. Hale! [*To* PROCTOR.] Will you confess yourself befouled with Hell, or do you keep that black allegiance yet? What say you?

PROCTOR. [*His mind wild, breathless.*] I say—
I say—God is dead!

PARRIS. Hear it, hear it!

PROCTOR. [*Laughs insanely, then.*] A fire, a fire is burning! I hear the boot of Lucifer, I see his filthy face! And it is my face, and yours, Danforth! For them that quail to bring men out of ignorance, as I have quailed, and as you quail now when you know in all your black hearts that this be fraud—God damns our kind especially, and we will burn, we will burn together!

DANFORTH. Marshal! Take him and Corey with him to the jail!

HALE. [*Starting across to the door.*] I denounce[22] these proceedings!

Caged Man in Flames. John Ritter.

PROCTOR. You are pulling Heaven down and raising up a whore!

HALE. I denounce these proceedings, I quit this court! [*He slams the door to the outside behind him.*]

DANFORTH. [*Calling to him in a fury.*] Mr. Hale! Mr. Hale!

THE CURTAIN FALLS

---

22. Here, *denounce* means "to publicly pronounce something to be evil."

 The United States and the World Senator *McCarthy and his followers were convinced that undercover Communists were everywhere. How does Danforth's comment reveal a similar state of mind?*

Big Idea The United States and the World Senator *McCarthy's power began to decline when he launched an investigation into the United States Army. How is this a similar situation?*

RESPONDING AND THINKING CRITICALLY

Respond

1. Which of the characters did you like better after reading Act Three? Which did you like less? Explain your choices.

Recall and Interpret

2. (a)How and why does Giles Corey interrupt the court proceedings? (b)What does the response of the judges to him and Francis Nurse suggest about the way the trials are being conducted?

3. (a)Why does Proctor bring Mary Warren to court? (b)How does Mary Warren's confession threaten Danforth, Parris, and Hathorne?

4. (a)What does Abigail do when Hale gives his opinion of her? (b)What can you infer about the general emotional state surrounding these accusations and condemnations?

Analyze and Evaluate

5. (a)How do Hale's attitudes toward Elizabeth's lie and Abigail's deception differ? (b)Do you agree with his distinction?

6. (a)How does Abigail succeed in controlling the investigation. (b)Do you think it would have been possible for Proctor to have prevailed over Abigail? Explain.

7. Shortly before Proctor is arrested, he says, ". . . God is dead!" What do you think that Proctor means by this remark?

Connect

8. **Big Idea** **The United States and the World** Do you think that Miller successfully compared the HUAC hearings with the Salem witch trials? Explain.

LITERARY ANALYSIS

Literary Element Plot

When you read or see a play, the sequence of **plot** events builds to a point at which you feel the greatest emotional intensity, interest, or suspense. This point is called the climax. Usually the climax is a turning point after which the resolution of a conflict becomes clear.

1. Which event do you see as the climax of Act Three of *The Crucible*?

2. Which conflict or conflicts are now on the way to being resolved?

Writing About Literature

Respond to Character Imagine that you are Abigail Williams or Reverend Hale. Write a series of diary entries set during the time period covered in Act Three. Use your imagination to explain your diarist's innermost thoughts and motivations, but be sure to base these on actual events and characters in the play.

Literature Online **Web Activities** For eFlashcards, Selection Quick Checks, and other Web activities, go to www.glencoe.com.

READING AND VOCABULARY

Reading Strategy Evaluating Argument

When **evaluating an argument,** use reason and sound evidence to support your evaluation. Examine the following examples of how characters reason in Act Three. For each statement, give your evaluation and support it with a persuasive explanation.

1. Hathorne argues that a person may be a witch without knowing it.

2. Elizabeth Proctor reasons that it is better to protect her husband than to tell the truth.

Vocabulary Practice

Context Clues In the examples below, identify the context clue that helps the reader to identify the vocabulary word: *definition, example, comparison, contrast,* or *cause and effect.*

1. Old Mr. Alvarez was **unperturbed** by the noise <u>because he is completely deaf.</u>

2. My car is in **immaculate** condition. Yours, <u>on the other hand, is old and rusty.</u>

3. I was in no mood for **contemplation.** Bill was <u>similarly eager for action.</u>

LITERATURE PREVIEW

Building Background

The characters in Miller's play are based on historical persons, although in some cases Miller combined several people into one character, adjusted some of the characters' ages, and invented their motives. Nevertheless, Miller states, "The fate of each character is exactly that of the historical model, and there is no one in the drama who did not play a similar—and in some cases exactly the same—role in history." For example, shortly after the girls started acting strangely, three women, including one named Tituba, were accused of being witches and were arrested. In all, nineteen people were hanged as witches, and one was pressed to death for refusing to testify.

The nightmare ended when Massachusetts authorities realized the danger of accepting the "spectral evidence" of dreams or visions and put an end to the trials. To ensure that such a slaughter of the innocents could never happen again, the courts decreed that witchcraft was no longer punishable by death.

Literary Element Tragedy

A **tragedy** is a play in which a main character suffers a downfall. That character, the **tragic hero,** is typically a person of exalted status who possesses admirable qualities. The downfall may result from outside forces or from a weakness within the character, which is known as a tragic flaw. As you read Act Four of *The Crucible,* determine whether any of the characters fulfill the requirements of a tragic hero.

- See Literary Terms Handbook, p. R19.

READING PREVIEW

Reading Strategy Identifying Problem and Solution

As you read Act Four, consider the problems that the characters face. Whether insignificant or life-threatening, each of these problems requires a **solution** that will propel the action of the drama to its conclusion.

Reading Tip: Asking Questions Good readers are always asking *why* and *how* questions. These questions will help you identify problems and solutions. As you read Act Four, ask yourself questions such as the following: How will this character solve his or her problem? Why is he or she behaving this way?

Vocabulary

conciliatory (kən sil′ ē ə tôr′ ē) *adj.* trying to gain the good will of another by friendly acts; p. 1094 *The boys who broke the window mowed our lawn as a conciliatory gesture.*

reprieve (ri prēv′) *n.* official postponement of the carrying out of a sentence; p. 1095 *A last-minute reprieve from the governor saved him from hanging.*

retaliation (ri tal′ ē ā′ shən) *n.* the act of repaying an injury or a wrong by committing the same, or a similar, act; p. 1095 *In retaliation for the bombing, the rebels shot down a helicopter.*

adamant (ad′ ə mənt) *adj.* completely firm and unyielding; p. 1095 *Mom is adamant about my observing a midnight curfew.*

indictment (in dīt′ mənt) *n.* a formal legal accusation, charging the commission or omission of an act, which is punishable by law; p. 1098 *The indictment led to her trial and conviction.*

Literature Online Interactive Literary Elements Handbook To review or learn more about the literary elements, go to www.glencoe.com.

INDIANA ACADEMIC STANDARDS (pages 1089–1107)
11.3.6 Analyze the way in which authors have used archetypes...
11.2 Develop [reading] strategies...
11.5.9 Write...a literary analysis that...supports judgments with relevant and substantial evidence...

Act Four

[*A cell in Salem jail, that fall.*
At the back is a high barred window; near it,
a great, heavy door. Along the walls are two
benches.
The place is in darkness but for the moonlight seeping
through the bars. It appears empty. Presently foot-
steps are heard coming down a corridor beyond the
wall, keys rattle, and the door swings open. MARSHAL
HERRICK enters with a lantern.
He is nearly drunk, and heavy-footed. He goes to a
bench and nudges a bundle of rags lying on it.]

HERRICK. Sarah, wake up! Sarah Good! [*He then*
crosses to the other bench.]

SARAH GOOD. [*Rising in her rags.*] Oh, Majesty!
Comin', comin'! Tituba, he's here, His Majesty's
come!

HERRICK. Go to the north cell; this place is
wanted now. [*He hangs his lantern on the wall.*
TITUBA sits up.]

TITUBA. That don't look to me like His Majesty;
look to me like the marshal.

HERRICK. [*Taking out a flask.*] Get along with you
now, clear this place. [*He drinks, and SARAH*
GOOD comes and peers up into his face.]

SARAH GOOD. Oh, is it you, Marshal! I thought
sure you be the devil comin' for us. Could I have
a sip of cider for me goin'-away?

HERRICK. [*Handing her the flask.*] And where are
you off to, Sarah?

TITUBA. [*As SARAH drinks.*] We goin' to
Barbados, soon the Devil gits here with the
feathers and the wings.

HERRICK. Oh? A happy voyage to you.

SARAH GOOD. A pair of bluebirds wingin'
southerly, the two of us! Oh, it be a grand
transformation, Marshal! [*She raises the flask to*
drink again.]

HERRICK. [*Taking the flask from her lips.*] You'd
best give me that or you'll never rise off the
ground. Come along now.

TITUBA. I'll speak to him for you, if you desire to
come along, Marshal.

HERRICK. I'd not refuse it, Tituba; it's the proper
morning to fly into Hell.

TITUBA. Oh, it be no Hell in Barbados. Devil,
him be pleasureman in Barbados, him be
singin' and dancin' in Barbados. It's you
folks—you riles him up 'round here; it be too
cold 'round here for that Old Boy. He freeze his
soul in Massachusetts, but in Barbados he just
as sweet and—[*A bellowing cow is heard, and*
TITUBA leaps up and calls to the window.] Aye,
sir! That's him, Sarah!

SARAH GOOD. I'm here, Majesty! [*They hur-*
riedly pick up their rags as HOPKINS, a guard,
enters.]

HOPKINS. The Deputy Governor's arrived.

HERRICK. [*Grabbing TITUBA.*] Come along, come
along.

TITUBA. [*Resisting him.*] No, he comin' for me.
I goin' home!

HERRICK. [*Pulling her to the door.*] That's not
Satan, just a poor old cow with a hatful of milk.
Come along now, out with you!

TITUBA. [*Calling to the window.*] Take me home,
Devil! Take me home!

SARAH GOOD. [*Following the shouting TITUBA out.*]
Tell him I'm goin', Tituba! Now you tell him
Sarah Good is goin' too!

[*In the corridor outside TITUBA calls on—"Take*
me home, Devil; Devil take me home!" and HOP-
KINS' voice orders her to move on. HERRICK
returns and begins to push old rags and straw into
a corner. Hearing footsteps, he turns, and enter
DANFORTH and JUDGE HATHORNE. They are in
greatcoats and wear hats against the bitter cold.
They are followed in by CHEEVER, who carries a
dispatch case and a flat wooden box containing his
writing materials.]

HERRICK. Good morning, Excellency.

National Theater Production of *The Crucible* by Arthur Miller. National Theater, London, UK.

DANFORTH. Where is Mr. Parris?

HERRICK. I'll fetch him. [*He starts for the door.*]

DANFORTH. Marshal. [*HERRICK stops.*] When did Reverend Hale arrive?

HERRICK. It were toward midnight, I think.

DANFORTH. [*Suspiciously.*] What is he about here?

HERRICK. He goes among them that will hang, sir. And he prays with them. He sits with Goody Nurse now. And Mr. Parris with him.

Reading Strategy Identifying Problem and Solution
What problem might Hale be attempting to resolve with his visits to the condemned?

DANFORTH. Indeed. That man have no authority to enter here, Marshal. Why have you let him in?

HERRICK. Why, Mr. Parris command me, sir. I cannot deny him.

DANFORTH. Are you drunk, Marshal?

HERRICK. No, sir; it is a bitter night, and I have no fire here.

DANFORTH. [*Containing his anger.*] Fetch Mr. Parris.

HERRICK. Aye, sir.

DANFORTH. There is a prodigious stench in this place.

HERRICK. I have only now cleared the people out for you.

DANFORTH. Beware hard drink, Marshal.

HERRICK. Aye, sir. [*He waits an instant for further orders. But DANFORTH, in dissatisfaction, turns his back on him, and HERRICK goes out. There is a pause. DANFORTH stands in thought.*]

HATHORNE. Let you question Hale, Excellency; I should not be surprised he have been preaching in Andover lately.

DANFORTH. We'll come to that; speak nothing of Andover. Parris prays with him. That's strange. [*He blows on his hands, moves toward the window, and looks out.*]

HATHORNE. Excellency, I wonder if it be wise to let Mr. Parris so continuously with the prisoners. [*DANFORTH turns to him, interested.*] I think, sometimes, the man has a mad look these days.

DANFORTH. Mad?

HATHORNE. I met him yesterday coming out of his house, and I bid him good morning—and he wept and went his way. I think it is not well the village sees him so unsteady.

DANFORTH. Perhaps he have some sorrow.

CHEEVER. [*Stamping his feet against the cold.*] I think it be the cows, sir.

DANFORTH. Cows?

CHEEVER. There be so many cows wanderin' the highroads, now their masters are in the jails, and much disagreement who they will belong to now. I know Mr. Parris be arguin' with farmers all yesterday—there is great contention, sir, about the cows. Contention make him weep, sir; it were always a man that weep for contention. [*He turns, as do HATHORNE and DANFORTH, hearing someone coming up the corridor. DANFORTH raises his head as PARRIS enters. He is gaunt, frightened, and sweating in his greatcoat.*]

PARRIS. [*To DANFORTH, instantly.*] Oh, good morning, sir, thank you for coming, I beg your pardon wakin' you so early. Good morning, Judge Hathorne.

DANFORTH. Reverend Hale have no right to enter this—

PARRIS. Excellency, a moment. [*He hurries back and shuts the door.*]

HATHORNE. Do you leave him alone with the prisoners?

DANFORTH. What's his business here?

PARRIS. [*Prayerfully holding up his hands.*] Excellency, hear me. It is a providence. Reverend Hale has returned to bring Rebecca Nurse to God.

DANFORTH. [*Surprised.*] He bids her confess?

PARRIS. [*Sitting.*] Hear me. Rebecca have not given me a word this three month since she came. Now she sits with him, and her sister and Martha Corey and two or three others, and he pleads with them, confess their crimes and save their lives.

DANFORTH. Why—this is indeed a providence. And they soften, they soften?

PARRIS. Not yet, not yet. But I thought to summon you, sir, that we might think on whether it be not wise, to—[*He dares not say it.*] I had thought to put a question, sir, and I hope you will not—

DANFORTH. Mr. Parris, be plain, what troubles you?

PARRIS. There is news, sir, that the court— the court must reckon with. My niece, sir, my niece—I believe she has vanished.

DANFORTH. Vanished!

PARRIS. I had thought to advise you of it earlier in the week, but—

DANFORTH. Why? How long is she gone?

PARRIS. This be the third night. You see, sir, she told me she would stay a night with Mercy Lewis. And next day, when she does not return, I send to Mr. Lewis to inquire. Mercy told him she would sleep in *my* house for a night.

Literary Element Tragedy *What is it about Reverend Parris's actions and character that make him an unlikely tragic hero?*

Reading Strategy Identifying Problem and Solution *What is the real motive behind Reverend Hale's visits to Rebecca and the other condemned women?*

DANFORTH. They are both gone?!

PARRIS. [*In fear of him.*] They are, sir.

DANFORTH. [*Alarmed.*] I will send a party for them. Where may they be?

PARRIS. Excellency, I think they be aboard a ship. [DANFORTH *stands agape.*] My daughter tells me how she heard them speaking of ships last week, and tonight I discover my—my strongbox is broke into. [*He presses his fingers against his eyes to keep back tears.*]

HATHORNE. [*Astonished.*] She have robbed you?

PARRIS. Thirty-one pound is gone. I am penniless. [*He covers his face and sobs.*]

DANFORTH. Mr. Parris, you are a brainless man! [*He walks in thought, deeply worried.*]

PARRIS. Excellency, it profit nothing you should blame me. I cannot think they would run off except they fear to keep in Salem any more. [*He is pleading.*] Mark it, sir, Abigail had close knowledge of the town, and since the news of Andover has broken here—

DANFORTH. Andover is remedied. The court returns there on Friday, and will resume examinations.

PARRIS. I am sure of it, sir. But the rumor here speaks rebellion in Andover, and it—

DANFORTH. There is no rebellion in Andover!

PARRIS. I tell you what is said here, sir. Andover have thrown out the court, they say, and will have no part of witchcraft. There be a faction here, feeding on that news, and I tell you true, sir, I fear there will be riot here.

HATHORNE. Riot! Why at every execution I have seen naught but high satisfaction in the town.

PARRIS. Judge Hathorne—it were another sort that hanged till now. Rebecca Nurse is no Bridget that lived three year with Bishop

before she married him. John Proctor is not Isaac Ward that drank his family to ruin. [*To* DANFORTH.] I would to God it were not so, Excellency, but these people have great weight yet in the town. Let Rebecca stand upon the gibbet[1] and send up some righteous prayer, and I fear she'll wake a vengeance on you.

HATHORNE. Excellency, she is condemned a witch. The court have—

DANFORTH. [*In deep concern, raising a hand to* HATHORNE.] Pray you. [*To* PARRIS.] How do you propose, then?

PARRIS. Excellency, I would postpone these hangin's for a time.

DANFORTH. There will be no postponement.

PARRIS. Now Mr. Hale's returned, there is hope, I think—for if he bring even one of these to God, that confession surely damns the others in the public eye, and none may doubt more that they are all linked to Hell. This way, unconfessed and claiming innocence, doubts are multiplied, many honest people will weep for them, and our good purpose is lost in their tears.

DANFORTH. [*After thinking a moment, then going to* CHEEVER.] Give me the list.

[CHEEVER *opens the dispatch case, searches.*]

PARRIS. It cannot be forgot, sir, that when I summoned the congregation for John Proctor's excommunication[2] there were hardly thirty people come to hear it. That speak a discontent, I think, and—

DANFORTH. [*Studying the list.*] There will be no postponement.

PARRIS. Excellency—

DANFORTH. Now, sir—which of these in your opinion may be brought to God? I will myself strive with him till dawn. [*He hands the list to* PARRIS, *who merely glances at it.*]

PARRIS. There is not sufficient time till dawn.

Reading Strategy Identifying Problem and Solution
How is Abigail's disappearance a significant problem for Danforth?

Reading Strategy Identifying Problem and Solution
The audience learns here that Abigail turned to theft and escape as a solution to her problem. What problem was she trying to avoid?

1. The *gibbet* (jib′ it) is the gallows.
2. *Excommunication* is the act, by church authorities, of expelling a person from membership in a church.

Reading Strategy Identifying Problem and Solution
How does Parris misunderstand Hale's motives?

Through the Fire, 1992. Gayle Ray. Acrylic on canvas. Private collection.
Viewing the Art: How might this painting illustrate the struggles of the characters in *The Crucible?*

DANFORTH. I shall do my utmost. Which of them do you have hope for?

PARRIS. [*Not even glancing at the list now, and in a quavering voice, quietly.*] Excellency—a dagger— [*He chokes up.*]

DANFORTH. What do you say?

PARRIS. Tonight, when I open my door to leave my house—a dagger clattered to the ground. [*Silence. DANFORTH absorbs this. Now PARRIS cries out.*] You cannot hang this sort. There is danger for me. I dare not step outside at night!

[*REVEREND HALE enters. They look at him for an instant in silence. He is steeped in sorrow, exhausted, and more direct than he ever was.*]

DANFORTH. Accept my congratulations, Reverend Hale; we are gladdened to see you returned to your good work.

HALE. [*Coming to DANFORTH now.*] You must pardon them. They will not budge.

[*HERRICK enters, waits.*]

DANFORTH. [**Conciliatory.**] You misunderstand, sir; I cannot pardon these when twelve are already hanged for the same crime. It is not just.

PARRIS. [*With failing heart.*] Rebecca will not confess?

Big Idea The United States and the World *An ideologue is an official who systematically follows a particular set of beliefs. How were both Senator McCarthy and Judge Danforth ideologues?*

Vocabulary

conciliatory (kən sil′ ē ə tôr′ ē) *adj.* trying to gain the good will of another by friendly acts

HALE. The sun will rise in a few minutes. Excellency, I must have more time.

DANFORTH. Now hear me, and beguile yourselves no more. I will not receive a single plea for pardon or postponement. Them that will not confess will hang. Twelve are already executed; the names of these seven are given out, and the village expects to see them die this morning. Postponement now speaks a floundering on my part; **reprieve** or pardon must cast doubt upon the guilt of them that died till now. While I speak God's law, I will not crack its voice with whimpering. If **retaliation** is your fear, know this—I should hang ten thousand that dared to rise against the law, and an ocean of salt tears could not melt the resolution of the statutes. Now draw yourselves up like men and help me, as you are bound by Heaven to do. Have you spoken with them all, Mr. Hale?

HALE. All but Proctor. He is in the dungeon.

DANFORTH. [*To* HERRICK.] What's Proctor's way now?

HERRICK. He sits like some great bird; you'd not know he lived except he will take food from time to time.

DANFORTH. [*After thinking a moment.*] His wife—his wife must be well on with child now.

HERRICK. She is, sir.

DANFORTH. What think you, Mr. Parris? You have closer knowledge of this man; might her presence soften him?

PARRIS. It is possible, sir. He have not laid eyes on her these three months. I should summon her.

DANFORTH. [*To* HERRICK.] Is he yet **adamant**? Has he struck at you again?

HERRICK. He cannot, sir, he is chained to the wall now.

DANFORTH. [*After thinking on it.*] Fetch Goody Proctor to me. Then let you bring him up.

HERRICK. Aye, sir. [HERRICK *goes. There is silence.*]

HALE. Excellency, if you postpone a week and publish to the town that you are striving for their confessions, that speak mercy on your part, not faltering.

DANFORTH. Mr. Hale, as God have not empowered me like Joshua to stop this sun from rising, so I cannot withhold from them the perfection of their punishment.

HALE. [*Harder now.*] If you think God wills you to raise rebellion, Mr. Danforth, you are mistaken!

DANFORTH. [*Instantly.*] You have heard rebellion spoken in the town?

HALE. Excellency, there are orphans wandering from house to house; abandoned cattle bellow on the highroads, the stink of rotting crops hangs everywhere, and no man knows when the harlots' cry will end his life—and you wonder yet if rebellion's spoke? Better you should marvel how they do not burn your province!

DANFORTH. Mr. Hale, have you preached in Andover this month?

HALE. Thank God they have no need of me in Andover.

DANFORTH. You baffle me, sir. Why have you returned here?

HALE. Why, it is all simple. I come to do the Devil's work. I come to counsel Christians they should belie themselves. [*His sarcasm collapses.*] There is blood on my head! Can you not see the blood on my head!!

PARRIS. Hush! [*For he has heard footsteps. They all face the door.* HERRICK *enters with* ELIZABETH. *Her wrists are linked by heavy chain, which* HERRICK *now removes. Her clothes are dirty; her face is pale and gaunt.* HERRICK *goes out.*]

DANFORTH. [*Very politely.*] Goody Proctor. [*She is silent.*] I hope you are hearty?

ELIZABETH. [*As a warning reminder.*] I am yet six month before my time.

DANFORTH. Pray be at your ease, we come not for your life. We—[*Uncertain how to plead, for he*

The Last Judgement, 1955. Abraham Rattner. Watercolor on paper, 40 x 29½ in. The Lane Collection. Courtesy Museum of Fine Arts, Boston.

Viewing the Art: In what ways might this painting and its title reflect the events in act 4?

is not accustomed to it.] Mr. Hale, will you speak with the woman?

HALE. Goody Proctor, your husband is marked to hang this morning.

[*Pause.*]

ELIZABETH. [*Quietly.*] I have heard it.

HALE. You know, do you not, that I have no connection with the court? [*She seems to doubt it.*] I come of my own, Goody Proctor. I would save your husband's life, for if he is taken I count myself his murderer. Do you understand me?

ELIZABETH. What do you want of me?

HALE. Goody Proctor, I have gone this three month like our Lord into the wilderness. I have sought a Christian way, for damnation's doubled on a minister who counsels men to lie.

HATHORNE. It is no lie, you cannot speak of lies.

HALE. It is a lie! They are innocent!

DANFORTH. I'll hear no more of that!

HALE. [*Continuing to ELIZABETH.*] Let you not mistake your duty as I mistook my own. I came into this village like a bridegroom to his beloved, bearing gifts of high religion; the very crowns of holy law I brought, and what I touched with my bright confidence, it died; and where I turned the eye of my great faith, blood flowed up. Beware, Goody Proctor— cleave[3] to no faith when faith brings blood. It is mistaken law that leads you to sacrifice. Life, woman, life is God's most precious gift; no principle, however glorious, may justify the taking of it. I beg you, woman, prevail upon[4] your husband to confess. Let him give his lie. Quail not before God's judgment in this, for it may well be God damns a liar less than he that throws his life away for pride. Will you plead with him? I cannot think he will listen to another.

ELIZABETH. [*Quietly.*] I think that be the Devil's argument.

HALE. [*With a climactic desperation.*] Woman, before the laws of God we are as swine! We cannot read His will!

ELIZABETH. I cannot dispute with you, sir; I lack learning for it.

DANFORTH. [*Going to her.*] Goody Proctor, you are not summoned here for disputation. Be there no wifely tenderness within you? He will die with the sunrise. Your husband. Do you understand it? [*She only looks at him.*] What say you? Will you contend with him? [*She is silent.*] Are you stone? I tell you true, woman, had I no other proof of your unnatural life, your dry eyes now would be sufficient evidence that you delivered up your soul to Hell! A very ape would weep at such calamity! Have the devil dried up any tear of pity in you? [*She is silent.*] Take her out. It profit nothing she should speak to him!

ELIZABETH. [*Quietly.*] Let me speak with him, Excellency.

PARRIS. [*With hope.*] You'll strive with him? [*She hesitates.*]

DANFORTH. Will you plead for his confession or will you not?

ELIZABETH. I promise nothing. Let me speak with him.

[*A sound—the sibilance[5] of dragging feet on stone. They turn. A pause. HERRICK enters with JOHN PROCTOR. His wrists are chained. He is another man, bearded, filthy, his eyes misty as though webs had overgrown them. He halts inside the doorway, his eye caught by the sight of ELIZABETH. The emotion flowing between them prevents anyone from speaking for an instant. Now HALE, visibly affected, goes to DANFORTH and speaks quietly.*]

HALE. Pray, leave them, Excellency.

DANFORTH. [*Pressing HALE impatiently aside.*] Mr. Proctor, you have been notified, have you not? [*PROCTOR is silent, staring at ELIZABETH.*] I see light in the sky, Mister; let you counsel

---

3. Here, *cleave* means "to stick tight," or "to remain attached."
4. To *prevail upon* means "to persuade."

Literary Element Tragedy *How does Hale justify his advising Elizabeth to persuade Proctor to lie? What character flaw does he warn her against?*

---

5. A *sibilance* is a hissing sound.

Reading Strategy Identifying Problem and Solution *How would Elizabeth's convincing Proctor to confess represent a solution for Parris, Danforth, and Hale?*

with your wife, and may God help you turn your back on Hell. [PROCTOR *is silent, staring at* ELIZABETH.]

HALE. [*Quietly.*] Excellency, let—

[DANFORTH *brushes past* HALE *and walks out.* HALE *follows.* CHEEVER *stands and follows,* HATHORNE *behind.* HERRICK *goes.* PARRIS, *from a safe distance, offers.*]

PARRIS. If you desire a cup of cider, Mr. Proctor, I am sure I—[PROCTOR *turns an icy stare at him, and he breaks off.* PARRIS *raises his palms toward* PROCTOR.] God lead you now. [PARRIS *goes out.*]

[*Alone.* PROCTOR *walks to her, halts. It is as though they stood in a spinning world. It is beyond sorrow, above it. He reaches out his hand as though toward an embodiment*[6] *not quite real, and as he touches her, a strange soft sound, half laughter, half amazement, comes from his throat. He pats her hand. She covers his hand with hers. And then, weak, he sits. Then she sits, facing him.*]

PROCTOR. The child?

ELIZABETH. It grows.

PROCTOR. There is no word of the boys?

ELIZABETH. They're well. Rebecca's Samuel keeps them.

PROCTOR. You have not seen them?

ELIZABETH. I have not. [*She catches a weakening in herself and downs it.*]

PROCTOR. You are a—marvel, Elizabeth.

ELIZABETH. You—have been tortured?

PROCTOR. Aye. [*Pause. She will not let herself be drowned in the sea that threatens her.*] They come for my life now.

ELIZABETH. I know it.

[*Pause.*]

PROCTOR. None—have yet confessed?

ELIZABETH. There be many confessed.

PROCTOR. Who are they?

ELIZABETH. There be a hundred or more, they say. Goody Ballard is one; Isaiah Goodkind is one. There be many.

PROCTOR. Rebecca?

ELIZABETH. Not Rebecca. She is one foot in Heaven now; naught may hurt her more.

PROCTOR. And Giles?

ELIZABETH. You have not heard of it?

PROCTOR. I hear nothin', where I am kept.

ELIZABETH. Giles is dead.

[*He looks at her incredulously.*]

PROCTOR. When were he hanged?

ELIZABETH. [*Quietly, factually.*] He were not hanged. He would not answer aye or nay to his **indictment;** for if he denied the charge they'd hang him surely, and auction out his property. So he stand mute, and died Christian under the law. And so his sons will have his farm. It is the law, for he could not be condemned a wizard without he answer the indictment, aye or nay.

PROCTOR. Then how does he die?

ELIZABETH. [*Gently.*] They press him, John.

PROCTOR. Press?

ELIZABETH. Great stones they lay upon his chest until he plead aye or nay. [*With a tender smile for the old man.*] They say he give them but two words. "More weight," he says. And died.

PROCTOR. [*Numbed—a thread to weave into his agony.*] "More weight."

ELIZABETH. Aye. It were a fearsome man, Giles Corey.

[*Pause.*]

PROCTOR. [*With great force of will, but not quite looking at her.*] I have been thinking I would

---

6. *Embodiment,* here, suggests a vision or a spirit rather than a solid form.

Literary Element Tragedy *John and Elizabeth Proctor are ragged and dirty prisoners. How does Arthur Miller manage to elevate them to heroic stature?*

Big Idea The United States and the World *How might Miller be making a favorable comparison between himself and Giles Corey?*

Vocabulary

indictment (in dīt′ mənt) *n.* a formal legal accusation, charging the commission or omission of an act, which is punishable by law confess to them, Elizabeth. [*She shows nothing.*] What say you? If I give them that?

ELIZABETH. I cannot judge you, John.

[*Pause.*]

PROCTOR. [*Simply—a pure question.*] What would you have me do?

ELIZABETH. As you will, I would have it. [*Slight pause.*] I want you living, John. That's sure.

PROCTOR. [*Pauses, then with a flailing of hope.*] Giles' wife? Have she confessed?

ELIZABETH. She will not.

[*Pause.*]

PROCTOR. It is a pretense, Elizabeth.

ELIZABETH. What is?

PROCTOR. I cannot mount the gibbet like a saint. It is a fraud. I am not that man. [*She is silent.*] My honesty is broke, Elizabeth; I am no good man. Nothing's spoiled by giving them this lie that were not rotten long before.

ELIZABETH. And yet you've not confessed till now. That speak goodness in you.

PROCTOR. Spite only keeps me silent. It is hard to give a lie to dogs. [*Pause, for the first time he turns directly to her.*] I would have your forgiveness, Elizabeth.

ELIZABETH. It is not for me to give, John, I am—

PROCTOR. I'd have you see some honesty in it. Let them that never lied die now to keep their souls. It is pretense for me, a vanity that will not blind God nor keep my children out of the wind. [*Pause.*] What say you?

ELIZABETH. [*Upon a heaving sob that always threatens.*] John, it come to naught that I should forgive you, if you'll not forgive yourself. [*Now he turns away a little, in great agony.*] It is not my soul, John, it is yours. [*He stands, as though in physical pain, slowly rising to his feet with a great immortal longing to find his answer.*

Reading Strategy Identifying Problem and Solution
What are Proctor's two options? How does each cause a problem for him?

Literary Element Tragedy *For what flaw does Elizabeth urge Proctor to forgive himself?*

It is difficult to say, and she is on the verge of tears.] Only be sure of this, for I know it now: Whatever you will do, it is a good man does it. [*He turns his doubting, searching gaze upon her.*] I have read my heart this three month, John. [*Pause.*] I have sins of my own to count. It needs a cold wife to prompt lechery.

PROCTOR. [*In great pain.*] Enough, enough—

ELIZABETH. [*Now pouring out her heart.*] Better you should know me!

PROCTOR. I will not hear it! I know you!

ELIZABETH. You take my sins upon you, John—

PROCTOR. [*In agony.*] No, I take my own, my own!

ELIZABETH. John, I counted myself so plain, so poorly made, no honest love could come to me! Suspicion kissed you when I did; I never knew how I should say my love. It were a cold house I kept! [*In fright, she swerves, as HATHORNE enters.*]

HATHORNE. What say you, Proctor? The sun is soon up.

[*PROCTOR, his chest heaving, stares, turns to ELIZABETH. She comes to him as though to plead, her voice quaking.*]

ELIZABETH. Do what you will. But let none be your judge. There be no higher judge under Heaven than Proctor is! Forgive me, forgive me, John—I never knew such goodness in the world! [*She covers her face, weeping.*]

[*PROCTOR turns from her to HATHORNE; he is off the earth, his voice hollow.*]

PROCTOR. I want my life.

HATHORNE. [*Electrified, surprised.*] You'll confess yourself?

PROCTOR. I will have my life.

HATHORNE. [*With a mystical tone.*] God be praised! It is a providence! [*He rushes out the door, and his voice is heard calling down the corridor.*] He will confess! Proctor will confess!

PROCTOR. [*With a cry, as he strides to the door.*] Why do you cry it? [*In great pain he turns back to her.*] It is evil, is it not? It is evil.

ELIZABETH. [*In terror, weeping.*] I cannot judge you, John, I cannot!

Literary Element Tragedy *What flaw does Elizabeth see in herself?*

The Crucible, 1996.

PROCTOR. Then who will judge me? [*Suddenly clasping his hands.*] God in Heaven, what is John Proctor, what is John Proctor? [*He moves as an animal, and a fury is riding in him, a tantalized[7] search.*] I think it is honest, I think so; I am no saint. [*As though she had denied this he calls angrily at her.*] Let Rebecca go like a saint; for me it is fraud!

---

7. Here, *tantalized* means "tormented."

Literary Element   Tragedy   *What is the cause of the "fury . . . riding" in Proctor? What might this strong feeling foreshadow?*

[*Voices are heard in the hall, speaking together in suppressed excitement.*]

ELIZABETH. I am not your judge, I cannot be. [*As though giving him release.*] Do as you will, do as you will!

PROCTOR. Would you give them such a lie? Say it. Would you ever give them this? [*She cannot answer.*] You would not; if tongs of fire were singeing you you would not! It is evil. Good, then—it is evil, and I do it!

[*HATHORNE enters with DANFORTH, and, with them, CHEEVER, PARRIS, and HALE. It is a businesslike, rapid entrance, as though the ice had been broken.*]

DANFORTH. [*With great relief and gratitude.*] Praise to God, man, praise to God; you shall be blessed in Heaven for this. [*CHEEVER has hurried to the bench with pen, ink, and paper. PROCTOR watches him.*] Now then, let us have it. Are you ready, Mr. Cheever?

PROCTOR. [*With a cold, cold horror at their efficiency.*] Why must it be written?

DANFORTH. Why, for the good instruction of the village, Mister; this we shall post upon the church door! [*To PARRIS, urgently.*] Where is the marshal?

PARRIS. [*Runs to the door and calls down the corridor.*] Marshal! Hurry!

DANFORTH. Now, then, Mister, will you speak slowly, and directly to the point, for Mr. Cheever's sake. [*He is on record now, and is really dictating to CHEEVER, who writes.*] Mr. Proctor, have you seen the Devil in your life? [*PROCTOR's jaws lock.*] Come, man, there is light in the sky; the town waits at the scaffold; I would give out this news. Did you see the Devil?

PROCTOR. I did.

PARRIS. Praise God!

DANFORTH. And when he come to you, what were his demand? [*PROCTOR is silent. DANFORTH helps.*] Did he bid you to do his work upon the earth?

PROCTOR. He did.

DANFORTH. And you bound yourself to his service? [*DANFORTH turns, as REBECCA NURSE enters, with HERRICK helping to support her. She is barely able to walk.*] Come in, come in, woman!

REBECCA. [*Brightening as she sees PROCTOR.*] Ah, John! You are well, then, eh?

[*PROCTOR turns his face to the wall.*]

DANFORTH. Courage, man, courage—let her witness your good example that she may come to God herself. Now hear it, Goody Nurse! Say on, Mr. Proctor. Did you bind yourself to the Devil's service?

REBECCA. [*Astonished.*] Why, John!

PROCTOR. [*Through his teeth, his face turned from REBECCA.*] I did.

DANFORTH. Now, woman, you surely see it profit nothin' to keep this conspiracy any further. Will you confess yourself with him?

REBECCA. Oh, John—God send his mercy on you!

DANFORTH. I say, will you confess yourself, Goody Nurse?

REBECCA. Why, it is a lie, it is a lie; how may I damn myself? I cannot, I cannot.

DANFORTH. Mr. Proctor. When the Devil came to you did you see Rebecca Nurse in his company? [*PROCTOR is silent.*] Come, man, take courage—did you ever see her with the Devil?

PROCTOR. [*Almost inaudibly.*] No.

[*DANFORTH, now sensing trouble, glances at JOHN and goes to the table, and picks up a sheet—the list of condemned.*]

DANFORTH. Did you ever see her sister, Mary Easty, with the Devil?

PROCTOR. No, I did not.

DANFORTH. [*His eyes narrow on PROCTOR.*] Did you ever see Martha Corey with the Devil?

PROCTOR. I did not.

DANFORTH. [*Realizing, slowly putting the sheet down.*] Did you ever see anyone with the Devil?

PROCTOR. I did not.

DANFORTH. Proctor, you mistake me. I am not empowered to trade your life for a lie. You have most certainly seen some person with the Devil. [*PROCTOR is silent.*] Mr. Proctor, a score of people have already testified they saw this woman with the Devil.

PROCTOR. Then it is proved. Why must I say it?

DANFORTH. Why "must" you say it! Why, you should rejoice to say it if your soul is truly purged[8] of any love for Hell!

---

8. To be *purged* is to be cleansed of whatever is unclean or undesirable.

Big Idea **The United States and the World** *Many of the names given during the HUAC hearings had been revealed previously. Why might the investigators of witches in Salem and the investigators of Communists in Washington have wanted to hear the names repeated at the hearings?*

Reading Strategy Identifying Problem and Solution
Why is Rebecca astonished at Proctor's choice of the solution to his problem?

The Crucible, 1996.

PROCTOR. They think to go like saints. I like not to spoil their names.

DANFORTH. [*Inquiring, incredulous.*] Mr. Proctor, do you think they go like saints?

PROCTOR. [*Evading.*] This woman never thought she done the Devil's work.

DANFORTH. Look you, sir. I think you mistake your duty here. It matters nothing what she thought—she is convicted of the unnatural murder of children, and you for sending your spirit out upon Mary Warren. Your soul alone is the issue here, Mister, and you will prove its whiteness or you cannot live in a Christian country. Will you tell me now what persons conspired with you in the Devil's company? [*PROCTOR is silent.*] To your knowledge was Rebecca Nurse ever—

Reading Strategy Identifying Problem and Solution
How would Proctor's admission that he had seen Rebecca Nurse in the devil's company solve a problem for Danforth?

PROCTOR. I speak my own sins; I cannot judge another. [*Crying out, with hatred.*] I have no tongue for it.

HALE. [*Quickly to DANFORTH.*] Excellency, it is enough he confess himself. Let him sign it, let him sign it.

PARRIS. [*Feverishly.*] It is a great service, sir. It is a weighty name; it will strike the village that Proctor confess. I beg you, let him sign it. The sun is up, Excellency!

DANFORTH. [*Considers; then with dissatisfaction.*] Come, then, sign your testimony. [*To CHEEVER.*] Give it to him. [*CHEEVER goes to PROCTOR, the confession and a pen in hand. PROCTOR does not look at it.*] Come, man, sign it.

PROCTOR. [*After glancing at the confession.*] You have all witnessed it—it is enough.

DANFORTH. You will not sign it?

PROCTOR. You have all witnessed it; what more is needed?

DANFORTH. Do you sport with me? You will sign your name or it is no confession, Mister! [*His breast heaving with agonized breathing,* PROCTOR *now lays the paper down and signs his name.*]

PARRIS. Praise be to the Lord!

[PROCTOR *has just finished signing when DAN-FORTH reaches for the paper. But PROCTOR snatches it up, and now a wild terror is rising in him, and a boundless anger.*]

DANFORTH. [*Perplexed, but politely extending his hand.*] If you please, sir.

PROCTOR. No.

DANFORTH. [*As though* PROCTOR *did not under-stand.*] Mr. Proctor, I must have—

PROCTOR. No, no. I have signed it. You have seen me. It is done! You have no need for this.

PARRIS. Proctor, the village must have proof that—

PROCTOR. Damn the village! I confess to God, and God has seen my name on this! It is enough!

DANFORTH. No, sir, it is—

PROCTOR. You came to save my soul, did you not? Here! I have confessed myself; it is enough!

DANFORTH. You have not con—

PROCTOR. I have confessed myself! Is there no good penitence[9] but it be public? God does not need my name nailed upon the church! God sees my name; God knows how black my sins are! It is enough!

DANFORTH. Mr. Proctor—

PROCTOR. You will not use me! I am no Sarah Good or Tituba, I am John Proctor! You will not use me! It is no part of salvation that you should use me!

DANFORTH. I do not wish to—

PROCTOR. I have three children—how may I teach them to walk like men in the world, and I sold my friends?

DANFORTH. You have not sold your friends—

PROCTOR. Beguile me not! I blacken all of them when this is nailed to the church the very day they hang for silence!

---

9. *Penitence* is humble sorrow for one's wrongdoing.

Big Idea The United States and the World *People named as Communists before HUAC were often placed on a "black list" and denied the opportunity of making a living. How does this blacklisting compare to the situation Proctor describes?*

DANFORTH. Mr. Proctor, I must have good and legal proof that you—

PROCTOR. You are the high court, your word is good enough! Tell them I confessed myself; say Proctor broke his knees and wept like a woman; say what you will, but my name cannot—

DANFORTH. [*With suspicion.*] It is the same, is it not? If I report it or you sign to it?

PROCTOR. [*He knows it is insane.*] No, it is not the same! What others say and what I sign to is not the same!

DANFORTH. Why? Do you mean to deny this confession when you are free?

PROCTOR. I mean to deny nothing!

DANFORTH. Then explain to me, Mr. Proctor, why you will not let—

PROCTOR. [*With a cry of his whole soul.*] Because it is my name! Because I cannot have another in my life! Because I lie and sign myself to lies! Because I am not worth the dust on the feet of them that hang! How may I live without my name? I have given you my soul; leave me my name!

DANFORTH. [*Pointing at the confession in* PROC-TOR's *hand.*] Is that document a lie? If it is a lie I will not accept it! What say you? I will not deal in lies, Mister! [PROCTOR *is motionless.*] You will give me your honest confession in my hand, or I cannot keep you from the rope. [PROCTOR *does not reply.*] Which way do you go, Mister?

[*His breast heaving, his eyes staring,* PROCTOR *tears the paper and crumples it, and he is weeping in fury, but erect.*]

DANFORTH. Marshal!

PARRIS. [*Hysterically, as though the tearing paper were his life.*] Proctor, Proctor!

HALE. Man, you will hang! You cannot!

PROCTOR. [*His eyes full of tears.*] I can. And there's your first marvel, that I can. You have made your magic now, for now I do think I see some shred of goodness in John Proctor. Not

Literary Element Tragedy *Why would Miller portray Proctor as "weeping . . . but erect?"*

enough to weave a banner with, but white enough to keep it from such dogs. [*ELIZABETH, in a burst of terror, rushes to him and weeps against his hand.*] Give them no tear! Tears pleasure them! Show honor now, show a stony heart and sink them with it! [*He has lifted her, and kisses her now with great passion.*]

REBECCA. Let you fear nothing! Another judgment waits us all!

DANFORTH. Hang them high over the town! Who weeps for these, weeps for corruption!

[*He sweeps out past them. HERRICK starts to lead REBECCA, who almost collapses, but PROCTOR catches her, and she glances up at him apologetically.*]

REBECCA. I've had no breakfast.

HERRICK. Come, man.

[*HERRICK escorts them out, HATHORNE and CHEEVER behind them. ELIZABETH stands staring at the empty doorway.*]

PARRIS. [*In deadly fear, to ELIZABETH.*] Go to him, Goody Proctor! There is yet time!

[*From outside a drumroll strikes the air. PARRIS is startled. ELIZABETH jerks about toward the window.*]

PARRIS. Go to him! [*He rushes out the door, as though to hold back his fate.*] Proctor! Proctor!

[*Again, a short burst of drums.*]

HALE. Woman, plead with him! [*He starts to rush out the door, and then goes back to her.*] Woman! It is pride, it is vanity. [*She avoids his eyes, and moves to the window. He drops to his knees.*] Be his helper!—What profit him to bleed? Shall the dust praise him? Shall the worms declare his truth? Go to him, take his shame away!

Four People Behind Bars. Todd Davidson.

ELIZABETH. [*Supporting herself against collapse, grips the bars of the window, and with a cry.*] He have his goodness now. God forbid I take it from him!

[*The final drumroll crashes, then heightens violently. HALE weeps in frantic prayer, and the new sun is pouring in upon her face, and the drums rattle like bones in the morning air.*]

THE CURTAIN FALLS ❧

Literary Element Tragedy *Why doesn't Elizabeth save her husband, as Parris and Hale urge?*

RESPONDING AND THINKING CRITICALLY

Respond

1. (a)What were your thoughts at the end of the play? (b)Do you have any unanswered questions? Explain.

Recall and Interpret

2. (a)What news does Parris convey to Danforth about Abigail? (b)What is Danforth's reaction? Why might he react this way?

3. (a)What has Hale been trying to do with the condemned prisoners? (b)What do his words reveal about his values?

4. (a)What might Proctor's ultimate decision mean for him? For Salem? (b)What might Elizabeth mean when she says that John has "his goodness now"?

Analyze and Evaluate

5. (a)Analyze the mood of the Salem residents at the beginning of Act Four. (b)Given what has happened during the three months since the end of Act Three, do you think that this mood is to be expected? Explain.

6. (a)Contrast the characters of Danforth and Hathorne. (b)Which do you consider more dangerous? Explain.

7. (a)Choose a character in the play who is static, or unchanging, and another who is dynamic, or capable of growth. Explain your classification. (b)Which type of character do you think Miller intends us to prefer? Why?

Connect

8. **Big Idea** **The United States and the World** (a)What message do you think Miller was trying to convey about the emotional climate of the witch trials in his portrayal of Salem at the opening of Act Four? (b)How might this message also apply to the emotional climate of the HUAC hearings?

DAILY LIFE AND CULTURE

LIFE IN PURITAN NEW ENGLAND

Hard work was essential to the godly life in seventeenth-century Massachusetts. A Puritan who acquired personal wealth at his farm or business was seen as being favored by God. Idleness, on the other hand, was a snare laid by the devil to capture Christian souls. To protect their citizens from Satan, Puritan authorities banned many amusements that might tempt young men and women to idleness. These included playing cards, shuffleboard, and dice, dancing around a Maypole, attending plays, and even beachcombing. Showy clothing was frowned upon, as was hair long enough to cover a man's ears. The enjoyment of food and drink was not discouraged, but gluttony and intemperance were condemned as two of the "seven deadly sins."

Spying on one's neighbor was commonplace. Because a virtuous society depended upon everyone behaving according to God's law, Puritans were encouraged to report on each other for sinning. Missing church services or sleeping during the sermon, quarreling with one's husband or wife, swearing, or even playing certain musical instruments were punishable activities. In Puritan New England, privacy was a place where Satan lurked, and pleasure was considered a temptation. No Puritan could have conceived the phrase "the pursuit of happiness." Rather, the Puritan ideal was the pursuit of godliness.

1. Some of the aspects of Puritan society described above may seem strange and unattractive to modern readers. What advantages might there be to living in such a close-knit culture?

2. How does the information given here help explain the behavior of some of the characters in *The Crucible?* Give specific examples.

Literary Element Tragedy

In common usage, the word *hero* applies to almost anyone who acts bravely. In a literary **tragedy,** however, the term **tragic hero** has a specific meaning. It refers to the main character in a drama who suffers downfall and death because of a **tragic flaw** in his or her character. According to the Greek philosopher Aristotle, the tragic hero's fate is intended to inspire pity and terror. Tragic heroes may behave badly, but audiences are meant to respond sympathetically to them because of their noble and admirable qualities.

1. Who is the tragic hero of *The Crucible?* What noble or admirable qualities does this hero possess?

2. What is the tragic flaw that causes the hero's downfall and death?

Review: Conflict

Conflict is the struggle between two opposing forces in a story or drama. **External conflict** exists when a character struggles against some outside force, such as nature, society, or another character. An **internal conflict** is a struggle between two opposing thoughts or desires within the mind of a character.

Partner Activity Meet with a classmate and create a three-column chart similar to the one below. In the left column, list the names of the principal characters. In the other two columns describe the external and internal conflicts in which these characters are involved.

Character	External Conflict	Internal Conflict
Reverend Hale	Pleads with prisoners to confess	considers himself guilty of sending innocent people to their deaths

Reading Strategy Identifying Problem and Solution

Some problems—especially the physical ones—are easily resolved. If you are cold, you might put on a sweater; if you are thirsty, try drinking water! But what if you are depressed, torn by guilt, or unable to achieve a personal goal? The solutions to mental or spiritual problems are often difficult and elusive. One of the purposes of literature is to provide the reader with examples of characters who have problems and to show how they cope with them. *The Crucible* is a drama full of problems and solutions. For each of the problems listed below, identify its solution. For each solution, identify the problem from which it arose.

1. **Problem:** Reverend Hale feels guilty about having signed the death warrants of so many innocent people convicted of witchcraft.

   Solution: Abigail and her young friends pretend that they see Mary Warren's spirit in the form of a bird.

2. **Problem:** John Proctor is torn between wanting to live and wanting to be truthful.

   Solution: Mary Warren accuses John Proctor of witchcraft.

Vocabulary Practice

Practice with Synonyms In the paragraph below, replace each underlined word with a synonym taken from the list of vocabulary words from Act Four of *The Crucible: conciliatory, reprieve, retaliation, adamant, indictment.*

When Ms. Ortiz accused me of theft and gave me a failing grade, it was as if a jury had issued a criminal **1** <u>charge</u>. She claimed that I had stolen her grade book in **2** <u>revenge</u> for having done badly on my midterm exam. I tried to tell her what had really happened, but she was **3** <u>stubborn</u> and stuck to her story. After the facts came out, the principal gave me a **4** <u>pardon</u> and wrote an **5** <u>apologetic</u> letter to my parents.

Writing About Literature

Analyze Historical Context Not only the characters, but the entire community of Salem went through a severe test during the witch trials. Using evidence from the play, write an analysis of the impact the witch trials might have had on the community, the government, and the economy.

When planning your essay, keep track of your evidence and thoughts by using an organizer like the one below.

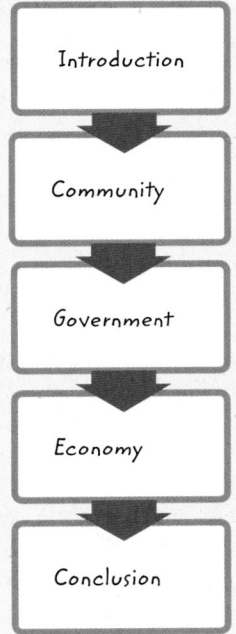

After you complete your draft, meet with a peer reviewer to evaluate each other's work and to suggest revisions. Then proofread and edit your draft for errors in spelling, grammar, and punctuation.

Performing

Act It Out Work with a group to dramatize part of *The Crucible*. If you prefer, assign cooperative roles: actors, director, and set and costume designers. Consider enhancing your production with the use of video clips, a sound track, or computer lighting. When your group is ready, perform your part of the play for the rest of the class.

Literature Online Web Activities For eFlashcards, Selection Quick Checks, and other Web activities, go to www.glencoe.com.

Miller's Language and Style

Using Dialect and Standard English Because Miller is writing a realistic drama about events that occurred over three hundred years ago, he has his characters speak in the dialect, or language variation, in use at the time and place in which the play is set. When he addresses the reader in his stage directions, however, Miller uses **Standard English** in order to make his ideas and instructions absolutely clear. Standard English is speech or writing that follows generally accepted rules of grammar, punctuation, and usage. It is the language of the business place, the political arena, the school, and the media.

Dialect is a way of speaking and writing that is characteristic of a particular group of people, often within a particular region and time. Dialect differs from Standard English in that it is not a universal way of communicating and may depart from the conventions of vocabulary, pronunciation, and grammar.

In *The Crucible*, Arthur Miller tries to create the impression of the language used in seventeenth-century New England. Note how Miller uses dialect in this exchange of dialogue from Act One.

> **MERCY.** Have you tried beatin' her? I gave Ruth a good one and it waked her for a minute. Here, let me have her.
>
> **ABIGAIL.** [*Holding* MERCY *back*.] No, he'll be comin' up. Listen, now; if they be questioning us, tell them we danced — I told him as much already.

Activity Create a chart similar to the one below to analyze the characters' use of dialect in *The Crucible*.

Character	Use of Dialogue	Analysis
Tituba	"That don't look to me like His Majesty; look to me like the marshal."	use of plural verb *don't*; singular subject *That* requires singular verb *doesn't*

Revising Check

Standard English Work with partners to check for the consistent use of Standard English in your essay about *The Crucible*.

Modern American Drama

THOUGH POETRY AND FICTION WERE well established as American literary genres by the middle of the nineteenth century, this was not the case with drama. Up until the early decades of the twentieth century, drama made little impact on American literature as a whole. Then, with Eugene O'Neill, American drama suddenly came of age.

O'Neill's Influence

A major event was the 1916 performance of Eugene O'Neill's *Bound East for Cardiff* by the Provincetown Players, a "little theater" company that produced original works by unknown talents. The first American dramatist to achieve an international reputation, O'Neill thrilled audiences and impressed critics as he explored the tragic relationship between fate and character and depicted the complex depths of the human mind.

A Streetcar Named Desire, 1947.

O'Neill's plays, including *Strange Interlude* (1928), *The Iceman Cometh* (1946), and *Long Day's Journey into Night* (1939–1941), reflect his New England background, his Irish American heritage, his reading of the Scandinavian playwrights Henrik Ibsen and August Strindberg, and his fascination with the theories and discoveries of modern psychology. Like the Modernists, he too blazed new trails, experimenting with form, style, and symbolism. His innovations intrigued audiences and greatly influenced subsequent playwrights.

> "*On the stage it is always now; the personages are standing on that razor edge, between the past and the future, which is the essential character of conscious being.*"
>
> —Thornton Wilder

Led by O'Neill, American drama flourished between the two world wars. Elmer Rice wrote a realistic portrait of tenement life called *Street Scene* (1929); Clifford Odets explored serious social problems in *Awake and Sing* (1935) and *Waiting for Lefty* (1935); and Lillian Hellman created a successful drama of social criticism in *The Little Foxes* (1939), a play about a predatory southern family. Thornton Wilder's *Our Town* (1938), a surrealistic play about everyday life in a New England town, enjoyed astonishing success. It has been said that not a day has passed since its original performance that *Our Town* has not been performed somewhere in the United States.

Postwar Playwrights

Tennessee Williams and Arthur Miller dominated the American theater in the decade after World War II. Williams was noted for his lyrical dialogue and wrote plays that explored some of the darker aspects of human psychology. He first achieved success with *The Glass Menagerie* (1945). In this play, as in *A Streetcar Named Desire* (1947) and other works, Williams sensitively portrayed fragile characters trapped in harsh and sometimes brutal circumstances. Continuing the tradition of strong realistic drama, Arthur Miller wrote *Death of a Salesman* (1949), which is about the fate of the "little man" in modern society. In *The Crucible* (1953), Miller used the Salem witch trials to comment on society's hysteria during the McCarthy era.

Recent History

In the 1960s and 1970s, Edward Albee experimented with a variety of styles, including the theater of the absurd and the theater of cruelty. The theater of cruelty,

Death of a Salesman, 2000.

which strives to produce a visceral reaction in the audience, influenced the scathing dialogue in Albee's acclaimed *Who's Afraid of Virginia Woolf?* (1962).

When it opened in 1959, *A Raisin in the Sun* by Lorraine Hansberry was the first drama by an African American woman to be produced on Broadway. Hansberry's realistic portrayal of black characters and her fearless depiction of social injustice marked a new era in African American drama. Beginning in 1982, August Wilson chronicled African American experience in a series of ten plays, each set in a different decade of the twentieth century. In *Fences* (1985), the second play in the series, the main character is a former baseball player, a victim of discrimination who was denied access to the major leagues. Wilson's play has already emerged as a classic.

Some of the most significant plays of the recent past are the work of women writers. These plays include *Crimes of the Heart* (1979) by Beth Henley and *'night, Mother* (1983) by Marsha Norman. In *The Heidi*

Chronicles (1989), Wendy Wasserstein explores the challenges faced by educated women competing in a male-dominated culture.

Musical Theater

A popular cousin to serious drama, the musical remains one of America's distinct contributions to the theater. The form ultimately derives from operettas, minstrel shows, and revues. During World War II, the watershed musical *Oklahoma!* (1943), by Richard Rodgers and Oscar Hammerstein II, brought the form to new heights, integrating music, story, and dance to develop plot and character.

The musical reached its peak after World War II in other works by Rodgers and Hammerstein and in those by Alan Jay Lerner and Frederick Loewe, Leonard Bernstein, and Stephen Sondheim. Later decades saw musicals break new ground. In 1968, *Hair* introduced rock music to theater audiences. *A Chorus Line* (1975) and *Chicago* (1976) brought dance-centered musicals to the fore. In 2001, Mel Brooks's musical comedy *The Producers* won a record twelve Tony Awards and once again made American musical theater popular with theatergoers.

Though drama developed much later than poetry and fiction in the United States, it flourished during the twentieth century and continues to do so. Some of the most gifted and creative writers—O'Neill, Williams, Miller, Albee, and Wilson—created masterpieces for the stage. Their techniques have influenced dramatists the world over. With a rich legacy of outstanding works, American drama is primed to reflect and respond to life in a new century.

Literature Online **Literary History** For more about modern American drama, go to www.glencoe.com.

RESPONDING AND THINKING CRITICALLY

1. What do you think live theater offers its audiences that movies and television programs do not?

2. How did Eugene O'Neill revolutionize American drama?

3. What innovations has Edward Albee made in the theater?

4. In what way did *Oklahoma!* differ from previous musicals?

INDIANA ACADEMIC STANDARDS (pages 1108–1109)
11.3.5 Analyze or evaluate works of literary or cultural significance...that...reveal contrasts in major themes, styles, and trends...

Writing Workshop

The Writing Process

In this workshop, you will follow the stages of the writing process. At any stage, you may think of new ideas to include and better ways to express them. Feel free to return to earlier stages as you write.

Prewriting

- - - - - - - - - - - - - - - -

Drafting

- - - - - - - - - - - - - - - -

Revising

- - - - - - - - - - - - - - - -

 Focus Lesson:
Avoiding Stilted Language

Editing & Proofreading

- - - - - - - - - - - - - - - -

 Focus Lesson:
Correcting Verb Tense

Presenting

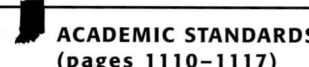
Writing Models For models and other writing activities, go to www.glencoe.com.

**ACADEMIC STANDARDS
(pages 1110–1117)**
11.5.1 Write...autobiographical ...narratives that narrate a sequence of events and communicate their significance to the audience...

Autobiographical Narrative

 Exploring Your Roots

"I see myself sitting there, haggard and disoriented, a shadow among shadows. . . . My heart thunders in deafening beats. Then there is silence, heavy and complete. Something was about to happen, we could feel it. Fate would at last reveal a truth reserved exclusively for us, a primordial truth, an ultimate postulate that would annihilate or overshadow all received ideas."

—Elie Wiesel, from *All Rivers Run to the Sea*

Connecting to Literature In much of his writing, Wiesel reveals his personal experiences during World War II. This type of writing is generally referred to as **autobiographical narrative,** in which a writer tells a sequence of past events from his or her life and reveals the personal significance of the experience. Although Wiesel's writing concerns a historical event with worldwide significance, an autobiographical narrative can be about any event, as long as it is personally meaningful. Study the rubric below to learn the goals and strategies for writing a successful autobiographical narrative.

Rubric: Features of Autobiographical Narrative Writing

Goals	Strategies
To relate a personally meaningful experience	☑ Narrate an autobiographical event and show its significance to the audience
To use specific details to describe the experience	☑ Describe sensory images, emotions, and shifts in perspective in concrete detail
	☑ Use dialogue and interior monologue
To narrate the experience in a logical order	☑ Use chronological order, adding flashbacks as necessary
	☑ Pace the action to match changes in time, space, or mood
To illustrate your beliefs and make generalizations about life	☑ Draw comparisons between specific experiences and broader themes about life

Real-World Connection

Many college applications require an autobiographical essay in which you reveal a significant experience from your life and tell how it affected you. Employers often ask similar questions of potential employees. Universities and employers alike want to see how you respond to life changes and how you learn from such experiences.

Assignment

Write an autobiographical narrative essay to describe a personal experience and to show how the experience was meaningful. As you move through the stages of the writing process, keep your audience and purpose in mind.

Audience: peers and classmates

Purpose: to relate a personal experience and to communicate its significance

Analyzing a Professional Model

In this excerpt from her autobiography, Pulitzer Prize-winning author Eudora Welty explores her discovery of the moon during childhood and how the experience became meaningful to her as a writer. As you read the following passage, note Welty's use of concrete details, sensory images, and interior monologue, all of which help her communicate a vivid, significant experience from her own life. As you read, pay attention to the comments in the margin. They point out features that you might want to include in your own autobiographical narrative.

From *One Writer's Beginnings* by Eudora Welty

Learning stamps you with its moments. Childhood's learning is made up of moments. It isn't steady. It's a pulse.

In a children's art class, we sat in a ring on kindergarten chairs and drew three daffodils that had just been picked out of the yard; and while I was drawing, my sharpened yellow pencil and the cup of the yellow daffodil gave off whiffs just alike. That the pencil doing the drawing should give off the same smell as the flower it drew seemed part of the art lesson—as shouldn't it be? Children, like animals, use all their senses to discover the world. Then artists come along and discover it the same way, all over again. Here and there, it's the same world. Or now and then we'll hear from an artist who's never lost it.

In my sensory education I include my physical awareness of the *word*. Of a certain word, that is; the connection it has with what it stands for. At around age six, perhaps, I was standing by myself in our front yard

Introduction

Hint at the significance of your experience in your introduction.

Effective Description

Use descriptive details to locate scenes in specific places.

waiting for supper, just at that hour in a late summer day when the sun is already below the horizon and the risen full moon in the visible sky stops being chalky and begins to take on light. There comes the moment, and I saw it then, when the moon goes from flat to round. For the first time it met my eyes as a globe. The word "moon" came into my mouth as though fed to me out of a silver spoon. Held in my mouth the moon became a word. It had the roundness of a Concord grape Grandpa took off his vine and gave me to suck out of its skin and swallow whole, in Ohio.

This love did not prevent me from living for years in foolish error about the moon. The new moon just appearing in the west was the rising moon to me. The new should be rising. And in early childhood the sun and moon, those opposite reigning powers, I just as easily assumed rose in east and west respectively in their opposite sides of the sky, and like partners in a reel they advanced, sun from the east, moon from the west, crossed over (when I wasn't looking) and went down on the other side. My father couldn't have known I believed that when, bending behind me and guiding my shoulder, he positioned me at our telescope in the front yard and, with careful adjustment of the focus, brought the moon close to me.

The night sky over my childhood Jackson was velvety black. I could see the full constellations in it and call their names; when I could read, I knew their myths. Though I was always waked for eclipses, and indeed carried to the window as an infant in arms and shown Halley's Comet in my sleep, and though I'd been taught at our diningroom table about the solar system and knew the earth revolved around the sun, and our moon around us, I never found out the moon didn't come up in the west until I was a writer and Herschel Brickell, the literary critic, told me after I misplaced it in a story. He said valuable words to me about my new profession: "Always be sure you get your moon in the right part of the sky."

Sensory Details

Describe sights, textures, sounds, and tastes with concrete sensory details.

Temporal Shift

Pace the action to reflect shifts in time and space.

Effective Description

Describe the specific actions, movements, and gestures of characters.

Sequence of Events

Narrate a sequence of events in a logical, effective order.

Communicate Significance

Communicate the meaning of your experience to your audience, showing how the incidents relate to more abstract beliefs.

Reading-Writing Connection
Think about the writing techniques that you just encountered and try them out in the autobiographical narrative you write.

Prewriting

Decide on an Experience As you decide on an experience to write about, think about events from your own life that were meaningful to you and that others might find interesting. The experience should be something that you remember well enough to explain in detail and that you feel comfortable sharing.

Gather Details As you gather details of your experience, keep in mind your audience and purpose to help you decide which details to include.

▶ **Recall the Experience** Make sure you clearly remember the important details and the order of events of your experience. Visualize the details by replaying the experience in your mind and discussing it with other people who were involved. Photos and journal entries might help jog your memory as well.

▶ **Connect to Your Audience** Think about what context or background information your audience will need to participate in your experience and to feel its full impact. As you narrate the experience, include your own thoughts to make the significance of the event clear.

▶ **Be Specific and Concrete** To help your readers feel like they are *there*, describe the details in concrete, precise language. Consider what sensory images, dialogue, and personal feelings stand out in your memory; you will want to further elaborate, or "flesh out," those details for your audience.

Make a Plan Telling your events in chronological order is often the most clear and logical way to narrate your experience. Consider organizing the narrative around the climax of the experience, and feel free to narrate some events in flashback or flash-forward to add background information or suspense.

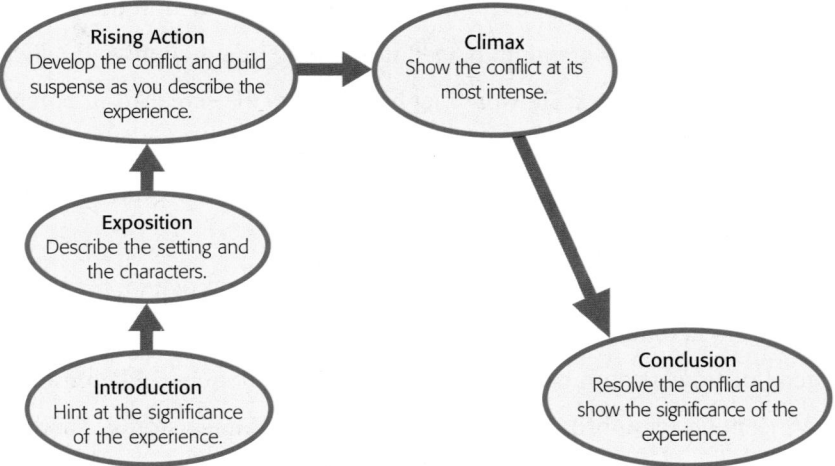

Talk About Your Ideas Meet with a partner to help develop your writing voice. Take turns telling each other the most vivid details of your experience. Jot down notes and refer to them as you develop your essay.

Explore Meaning When drafting, keep in mind that the details of your experience should help reveal its significance to your audience. Think about how the experience changed you or what it taught you. Hint at its significance in your introduction, but wait until the conclusion to reveal the experience's full meaning.

Build Suspense with Flashback

If telling the events of your experience in purely chronological order diminishes the suspense, add a flashback. A **flashback** is an interruption in the narrative to show an event that happened earlier. A flashback gives readers information that may help explain the main events of the narrative.

Test Prep

For essay tests, you will not be able to consult other people or photos to help you remember your experience. Before you begin writing, make sure you have chosen a meaningful, interesting experience that you remember well enough to explain in full detail.

Drafting

Go with the Flow When you begin your draft, do not get stuck trying to find the perfect word or detail. You will have time to do this when you revise your draft later. Instead, focus on relating the events of your experience in order and in a personal, natural voice. Try to build suspense and lead the reader to the climax before the conclusion of the narrative. Occasionally step back from your draft to assess your narrative and its overall direction. Remember that following an unexpected direction may lead to new insights about your experience.

Analyzing a Workshop Model

Here is a final draft of an autobiographical narrative. Read the narrative and answer the questions in the margin. Use the answers to these questions to guide you as you write your own autobiographical narrative.

Antique Jim

I had always expected that older generations had their problems mostly worked out. They were there to help the rest of us, to clean up children with scraped knees and bee stings, and to comfort worrying parents. They were supposed to know who they were. They weren't supposed to change.

Jim had always been there, tall and lank and cheerfully idle, dropping in at my grandmother's ranch house. I have never been quite sure where Jim came from, or how he ended up stuck with our family. He had been dating my grandmother for decades, ever since my grandfather died in the 1970s.

When we went to my grandmother's house on Saturdays, Jim would always show up just before dinner. He would let himself into the screened-in porch with a loud "Hullo!" for whoever was around to hear. Like Christopher and I, Jim always forgot and let the porch door slam. With him, however, my grandmother only sighed and pretended not to notice.

"Well, hullo, Mary!" Jim would say as he entered the kitchen, his blue eyes sparkling behind octagonal bifocals.

Instead of flowers, Jim brought my grandmother antiques gathered from Saint Vincent de Paul thrift shops, estate sales, and vintage stores. This particular time it was a crafty wooden structure that turned out to be a cuckoo clock. When Jim unveiled it, I could tell that my grandmother had no idea what to do with the thing. She appreciated antiques, but her house was only so big. Unlike Jim, she had young grandchildren who would hurt themselves on fancy things—or smash them to bits.

"Picked her up at Saint Vinny's this afternoon," Jim said, dusting off the

Introduction

How does the writer hint at the significance of the experience? What might the experience be about?

Effective Description

How does describing Jim's presents help reveal his personality ?

face and gently pulling the bird from behind its wooden door to show my brother and me. He worked on the clock at the dining room table while my grandmother set the plates and cutlery around him. Later, when Jim left, my grandmother always shook her head at these extravagances. I knew what she was thinking: our family needed groceries and haircuts, not one-of-a-kind German clocks.

"Well, maybe we should eat now, before this gets cold," she urged quietly. Christopher and I sat in our seats while Jim pried deeper into the mangled gears of the clock.

"All the way from the Black Forest!" Jim cried, shaking his head at the wooden marvel. "All the original parts." Finally, seeing us waiting, Jim said, "Well, hey now. C'mon kids, up to the table now. Looks like we're about ready to eat." Reluctantly, he placed the cuckoo clock on the counter, slapped the dust from his hands, and joined us.

Years later, I should not have been surprised, but I was. I was helping my grandmother prepare Thanksgiving dinner while the rest of the family passed a football back and forth in the yard. My grandmother told me the news nonchalantly, the way you talk about people you only know casually, or people you used to know, long ago. "Remember Jim?" She was whipping the mashed potatoes in steady, measured strokes. Of course I remembered Jim. I had been wondering when he'd turn up and what festive ensemble he would be wearing tonight. "Well, we don't see each other much anymore," she said calmly. "Things change, you know." She knocked the potato masher against the side of the bowl three times and tossed it in the sink. That was that. "Have you decided which college you want to go to?" she asked me then, as if nothing had, in fact, changed.

I was shocked. My grandmother brought stability to everyone else's life, and here she was, taking it away from her own. At her age, things weren't supposed to change anymore.

I did see Jim again, later, at—where else?—Saint Vinny's. Staring at him sifting through a brassy pile of pocket watches, I finally got it. Jim was funny and kind and one of the most interesting people I had ever met, but he wasn't like my grandmother at all. In the fifteen years I'd known him, Jim had resisted change, replaying his favorite parts over and over. My grandmother, on the other hand, had a bustling family that *counted on* her to change—to keep up—in good times and bad. While Jim rummaged leisurely through strangers' family histories, my grandmother was busy creating her own.

Effective Description

What is the writer describing in this scene? Why might this description be important?

Dialogue

Why might dialogue be more effective than description here?

Sequence of Events

How are the events of the narrative ordered? Why is this effective?

Sensory Details

How do the sensory details here enhance the characters' feelings and dialogue?

Communicate Significance

How does the writer communicate the meaning of the experience to the reader?

Revising

Peer Review After you complete your draft, read it out loud to your partner. Then have your partner discuss which parts were most vivid and interesting and which parts seemed vague or general. Partners should note places to add interior monologue, sensory details, and temporal or spatial changes and ways to add background or suspense. Refer to the traits of strong writing for reference.

Use the rubric below to evaluate your writing

Rubric: Writing an Effective Autobiographical Narrative
☑ Do you narrate a sequence of autobiographical events in an effective, logical order?
☑ Do you communicate the significance of the events to the audience?
☑ Do you describe specific details such as sensory images and the appearances, gestures, and feelings of the characters?
☑ Do you use dialogue and interior monologue to show characters' feelings?
☑ Do you draw comparisons between specific experiences and broader themes about life or your personal beliefs?

▶ **Focus Lesson**

Avoiding Stilted Language

When you are writing an autobiographical narrative, use natural, unaffected language. Readers respond to writing that they can connect with, and they will be turned off by pretentious or unnecessarily complicated language. As you revise your narrative, replace stilted language with precise words and clear, vivid expressions. Note the revised sentences from the Workshop Model below.

Draft:

During my formative years, Jim promenaded languidly through life as though the golden age would repeat itself without resistance. My grandmother, however, resigned herself to the duties of the family matriarch, following the ebb and flow of the lives of her progeny.

Revision:

In the fifteen years I'd known him,[1] Jim had resisted change,[2] replaying his favorite parts over and over. My grandmother, on the other hand, had a bustling family that counted on her to change—to keep up—in good times and bad.[3]

1: Precise details   **2:** Clear expression   **3:** Natural, unpretentious language

Editing and Proofreading

Get It Right When you have completed the final draft of your essay, proofread for errors in grammar, usage, mechanics, and spelling. Refer to the Language Handbook, pages R45–R59, as a guide.

> **Focus Lesson**

Correcting Verb Tense

As you edit your narrative, check that your verb tenses are formed correctly and that any shifts in tense are accurate and consistent. Below are some examples from the Workshop Model.

Problem: The verb ending is missing or incorrect.

He work on the clock at the dining room table while my grandmother set the plates and cutlery around him.

Solution: Add *-ed* to a regular verb to form the past tense.

He worked on the clock at the dining room table while my grandmother set the plates and cutlery around him.

Problem: There is an unnecessary shift in tense.

Christopher and I sat in our seats while Jim pries deeper into the mangled gears of the clock.

Solution: When two or more events occur at the same time, use the same verb tense to describe each event.

Christopher and I sat in our seats while Jim pried deeper into the mangled gears of the clock.

Problem: The lack of shift in verb tense does not show that the events occurred at different times.

He dated my grandmother for decades, ever since my grandfather died in the 1970s.

Solution: Shift from the past tense to the past perfect tense to show that the grandmother's actions began and ended before Jim's action began.

He had been dating my grandmother for decades, ever since my grandfather died in the 1970s.

Presenting

Check Your Appearance After you finish final editing and proofreading, look over your draft one last time. Make sure that the paper is typed and double-spaced with appropriate fonts and margins. Check with your teacher about any additional presentation guidelines.

Take Another Look

Put your paper away for a few days. Then, when you reread it, you will have a fresh perspective. Unnatural voice, stilted language, and mistakes in verb tense are often easier to spot after you get a fresh perspective.

Writer's Portfolio

Place a clean copy of your autobiographical narrative in your portfolio to review later.

Speaking, Listening, and Viewing Workshop

Art or Photo Essay

"She wore a dark striped dress reaching down to her shoe tops, and an equally long apron of bleached sugar sacks, with a full pocket: all neat and tidy, but every time she took a step she might have fallen over her shoelaces, which dragged from her unlaced shoes. She looked straight ahead. Her eyes were blue with age."

—Eudora Welty, "A Worn Path"

Do Your Research

Before creating a photo essay, research other art and photo exhibits. What is it about these pieces that speak to the audience and stand out above everyday images? You should incorporate these elements into your own presentation.

Connecting to Literature In her story "A Worn Path," Eudora Welty uses vivid description to give the reader a clear image of Phoenix Jackson. By using actual images, photographs, and art to represent people and ideas, you allow an audience to experience details and emotions that may not come across in writing alone. One way to accomplish this is by creating a photo or art essay. To create a photo or art essay, you combine photographs, artwork, drawings, or artifacts to represent an issue or event you feel strongly about.

During the Great Depression, government researcher Dorothea Lange used photography to document the hardships and struggles of the poor. Examine the images below. What do Lange's photographs reveal about life during the Great Depression? Think about what it is that you want to reveal about your subject.

A migratory family from Amarillo, Texas, lives in a trailer in an open field, with no sanitation or running water. November 1940.

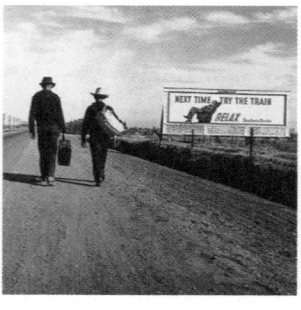

Unemployed men carrying suitcases to Los Angeles, California, during the Great Depression. March 1937.

The family of a Cordale, Alabama, turpentine worker earning one dollar per day. July 1936.

Planning Your Presentation

Just like written essays, your photo or art essay needs to have a main idea. Ask yourself, what idea or message would I like to convey? Then decide how to present that idea to your audience. For example, if you want to show the harmful effects of pollution, you might display photographs of litter on the beach or create a collage showing the effects of global warming. Your presentation should be compelling and interesting in order to gain and keep your audience's attention.

Follow these guidelines when presenting an art or photo essay:

- Research the topic well. You should be prepared to answer any questions the audience may have about your topic.
- Allow enough time to prepare. Think about how many pieces you would like to have in your essay, as well as what kind of images would best suit your purpose.
- Decide how you will showcase your work. Will you use an easel, poster board, a slide projector, or a computer presentation?

Creating Meaning in Visual Media

It's often been said that a picture is worth a thousand words. Your pictures need to be able to "speak" to the audience, or convey emotion and feeling. Most importantly, the art you create should be meaningful to you.

How do you think Lange felt about her subjects? What emotion is conveyed in her photograph "Mother with Children" (at right)?

Background Information

You may want to include captions or note cards to go with your photographs or art, giving information such as the date and location the picture was taken or what your art represents.

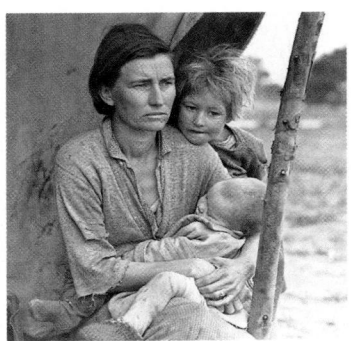

A migrant agricultural worker's wife and children in camp. Nimpo, California. March 1936.

Rubric: Techniques for Delivering an Art or Photo Essay

Verbal Techniques	Nonverbal Techniques
☑ **Volume** Speak loudly and clearly so that your audience can understand any background information you provide.	☑ **Eye Contact** Make frequent eye contact with the audience; however, you should also look at the photographs or art to draw attention to important details.
☑ **Pace** Allow the audience enough time to view and react to each piece of your essay before moving on to the next photograph or piece of art.	☑ **Gestures** Point out key details in your art; however, be careful not to block your essay when presenting.
☑ **Tone** The tone of your speech should match the tone of your photo or art essay. If your essay is of a serious nature, you should speak in a dignified, serious tone. More lighthearted essays can be presented with an informal tone and elements of comedy.	☑ **Display** Use an easel or poster board to display your images. The art and photographs should be presented prominently enough so that your entire audience can view them.

ACADEMIC STANDARDS
(pages 1118–1119)

11.7.19 Deliver multimedia presentations that...use the selected media skillfully...

11.4.9 Use a computer to integrate...pictures and graphics...

For Independent Reading

LITERATURE FROM THE 1930s THROUGH THE 1960s IS AS VARIED AS THE period that produced it. The writers John Steinbeck, Rachel Carson, and Ralph Ellison reacted directly to conditions in the world yet also explored private experiences and feelings. Steinbeck's works provide a window into the history of his time. In addition to *The Grapes of Wrath*, which remains the seminal expression of the hardships of the Great Depression era, Steinbeck's abundant output included *Cannery Row* (1945), a postwar novel set in Monterey, California; and *Travels with Charley* (1961), a work of nonfiction.

Rachel Carson was a marine biologist and writer whose second book, *The Sea Around Us*, sold more than a million copies. *Silent Spring* (1962), published two years before her death, is credited with signaling the beginning of the environmental movement in the United States.

Ralph Ellison began his career by studying at the Tuskegee Normal and Industrial Institute (now Tuskegee University) and later joining the Federal Writer's Project in New York City. After serving in the military during World War II, he spent seven years writing *Invisible Man*.

The Grapes of Wrath

John Steinbeck (1939)

Set during the Great Depression, this gripping novel tells the story of the Joads, an Oklahoma farm family driven to seek work in the natural paradise of California. Through the struggles of their journey and the disillusionment that awaits them, they learn how poor, exploited people can unite as a community to survive. The novel aroused widespread sympathy for the plight of migrant farmworkers. Steinbeck won a Pulitzer Prize for *The Grapes of Wrath* in 1940, and the story was made into a memorable movie starring Henry Fonda.

The Sea Around Us

Rachel Carson (1951)

Sometimes called a biography of the sea, this fascinating book opens with "The Gray Beginnings," a chapter that tells how the seas began. Subsequent chapters cover the formation of islands, plant and animal life, tides, wind, waves, and historic voyages. The book won the 1952 National Book Award and the John Burroughs Medal, named for the naturalist John Burroughs. It was translated into more than thirty languages and was a best seller. More than fifty years after its initial publication, it is still in print.

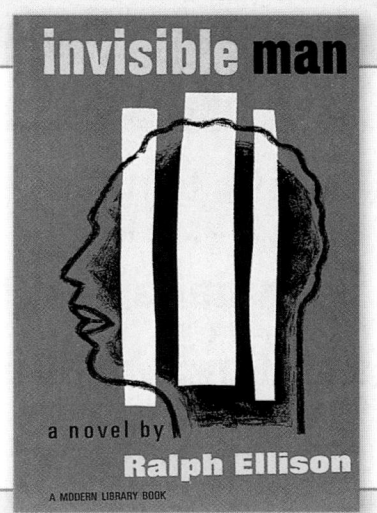

"Invisible Man is not a great Negro novel; it is a work of art any contemporary writer could point to with pride."

—Harvey Curtis Wester, *Saturday Review*, April 12, 1952

"Ellison has an abundance of that primary talent without which neither craft nor intelligence can save a novelist; he is richly, wildly inventive; his scenes rise and dip with tension; his people bleed; his language stings. No other writer has captured so much of the confusion and agony, the hidden gloom and surface gaiety of Negro life."

—Irving Howe, *Nation*, May 10, 1952

Invisible Man

Ralph Ellison (1952)

Invisible Man shocked readers when it first appeared but went on to win great acclaim, including the 1953 National Book Award for fiction. Ellison looked at the United States through the eyes of a nameless young African American man. Full of idealism when he first leaves the South for the streets of Harlem, he journeys through a variety of strange and disillusioning experiences. Along the way, he realizes that he has been made invisible—rejected and robbed of his identity by racism and by an impersonal society.

From the Glencoe Literature Library

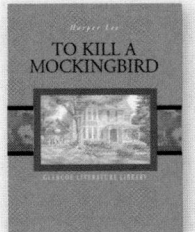

To Kill a Mockingbird

Harper Lee

A precocious, observant young girl and her brother watch as their father defends an African American man on trial in the South.

Our Town

Thornton Wilder

The Gibbs and Webb families of Grover's Corners, New Hampshire, experience the daily joys and tragedies of life in a small town.

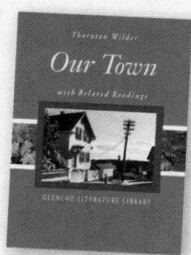

The Yearling

Marjorie Kinnan Rawlings

A young boy who longs for a pet adopts a fawn against his mother's wishes.

Indiana Test Practice

Reading: Vocabulary, Comprehension, and Analysis

Carefully read the following passage written by an observer of the Dust Bowl in the mid-1930s. Use context clues to help define any words with which you are unfamiliar. Pay close attention to the author's main idea and use of rhetorical devices. Then answer the questions on page 1123.

from *Dust Changes America* by Margaret Bourke-White

line

Vitamin K they call it—the dust which sifts under the door sills, and stings in the eyes, and seasons every spoonful of food. The dust storms have distinct personalities, rising in formation like rolling clouds, creeping up silently like formless fog, approaching violently like a tornado. Where has it come from? It provides topics of endless speculation. Red, it is the topsoil from Oklahoma; brown, it is the fertile earth

5 of western Kansas; the good grazing land of Texas and New Mexico sweeps by as a murky yellow haze. Or, tracing it locally, "My uncle will be along pretty soon," they say; "I just saw his farm go by."

The town dwellers stack their linen in trunks, stuff wet cloths along the window sills, estimate the tons of sand in the darkened air above them, paste cloth masks on their faces with adhesive tape, and try to joke about Vitamin K. But on the farms and ranches there is an attitude of despair.

10 By coincidence I was in the same parts of the country where last year I photographed the drought. As short a time as eight months ago there was an attitude of false optimism. "Things will get better," the farmers would say. "We're not as hard hit as other states. The government will help out. This can't go on." But this year there is an atmosphere of utter hopelessness. Nothing to do. No use digging out your chicken coops and pigpens after the last "duster" because the next one will be coming along soon. No use trying

15 to keep the house clean. No use fighting off that foreclosure any longer. No use even hoping to give your cattle anything to chew on when their food crops have literally blown out of the ground. . . .

The storm comes in a terrifying way. Yellow clouds roll. The wind blows such a gale that it is all my helper can do to hold my camera to the ground. The sand whips into my lens. I repeatedly wipe it away trying to snatch an exposure before it becomes completely coated again. The light becomes

20 yellower, the wind colder. Soon there is no photographic light, and we hurry for shelter to the nearest farmhouse. Three men and a woman are seated around a dust-caked lamp, on their faces grotesque masks of wet cloth. The children have been put to bed with towels tucked over their heads. My host greets us: "It takes grit to live in this country." They are telling stories: A bachelor harnessed the sandblast which ripped through the keyhole by holding his pots and pans in it until they were spick

25 and span. A pilot flying over Amarillo got caught in a sand storm. His motor clogged; he took to his parachute. It took him six hours to shovel his way back to earth. And when a man from the next county was struck by a drop of water, he fainted, and it took two buckets of sand to revive him. . . .

And this same dust that coats the lungs and threatens death to cattle and men alike, that ruins the stock of the storekeeper lying unsold on his shelves, that creeps into the gear shifts of automobiles,

30   that sifts through the refrigerator into the butter, that makes housekeeping, and gradually life itself, unbearable, this swirling drifting dust is changing the agricultural map of the United States. It piles ever higher on the floors and beds of a steadily increasing number of deserted farmhouses. A half-buried plowshare, a wheat binder ruffled over with sand, the skeleton of a horse near a dirt-filled water hole are stark evidence of the meager life, the wasted savings, the years of toil that the farmer is leaving behind him.

1. The sentence "Where has it come from?" in line 3 exemplifies the rhetorical device of:
   A. parallelism.
   B. connotative language.
   C. metaphor.
   D. rhetorical question.

2. What literary or rhetorical device is most evident in the first sentence in the second paragraph?
   F. Parallelism
   G. Connotative language
   H. Metaphor
   J. Rhetorical question

3. According to the passage, Bourke-White was in the Dust Bowl region:
   A. by coincidence.
   B. to photograph the poor.
   C. to photograph dust storms.
   D. to photograph the drought.

4. As it is used in line 13, the word *atmosphere* refers to:
   F. the physical environment.
   G. the mood of the environment.
   H. an exotic or romantic quality.
   J. the gaseous elements of the environment.

5. In the sentence beginning in line 21, an example of connotative language is the word:
   A. seated.
   B. grotesque.
   C. wet.
   D. lamp.

6. According to the passage, the children have been put to bed with towels over their heads to:
   F. block out the noise of the storm.
   G. prevent them from hearing the adult conversation.
   H. make them more comfortable.
   J. prevent their breathing in the dust.

7. In the sentence "It takes grit to live in this country" (line 23), the word *grit* is:
   A. a metaphor.
   B. a symbol.
   C. a simile.
   D. a motif.

8. According to the passage, the farmers tell humorous stories about dust storms because:
   F. they are insensitive.
   G. they want to distract the children.
   H. they want to lighten the mood.
   J. they want to relate local news.

9. The literary or rhetorical device most evident in the sentence that begins the last paragraph is:
   A. parallelism.
   B. connotative language.
   C. metaphor.
   D. rhetorical question.

10. Which statement best expresses the main idea of the passage?
   F. The farmers do not understand the seriousness of the situation.
   G. Nobody knows what causes dust storms.
   H. The farmers are optimistic that the storms will end soon.
   J. The region has become an agricultural and human disaster.

11. It can reasonably be inferred that the author's main purpose for writing this passage was:
   A. to entertain.
   B. to persuade.
   C. to describe.
   D. to analyze.

Carefully read this passage and answer the questions that follow it. Be sure to pay close attention to details and to any instructions that are provided.

Memo

To: *Committee Chairpersons*

From: *Lisa Hopkins, Dean of Student Activities*

Date: *February 8, 2006*

Re: *Committee Chairperson Meeting*

We need to schedule the quarterly meeting on facility distribution for all of the school's committee chairpersons. In light of this, I suggest that we hold our meeting in the school library at 3:00 on Thursday, February 16. If you are unable to make this date, for whatever reason, please let me know as soon as possible.

Subcommittee heads are not required to attend this meeting. However, because we will be discussing financing for the upcoming term, these representatives are encouraged to attend. There will also be a meeting expressly for subcommittee heads on Wednesday, February 22.

12. According to the memo, subcommittee heads will be required to attend a meeting on:
   F. Thursday, February 16.
   G. Wednesday, February 22.
   H. Monday, February 20.
   J. Monday, February 13

13. Certain subcommittee heads are advised to attend the meeting on Thursday, February 16, in order to:
   A. discuss facility distribution.
   B. gather in the school library.
   C. confer with committee chairpersons.
   D. discuss finances.

14. Committee chairpersons who are unable to attend the meeting should:
   F. attend the meeting scheduled for subcommittee heads.
   G. meet individually with the subcommittee heads.
   H. contact Lisa Hopkins as soon as possible.
   J. meet individually with the other committee chairpersons.

Writing: Process and Language Conventions

In the following excerpt from a student draft of an essay, you will find underlined phrases and sentences. The number beneath each underlined phrase or sentence corresponds to a numbered item on the next page. In each item, select the best choice to replace the underlined phrase or sentence. If you think the original should not be changed, choose "NO CHANGE."

The boxed numbers refer to questions about specific paragraphs.

My grandfather was an infantryman during World War II. He often tells me stories about his experiences overseas—describing the people that he met and the things that he did and saw. Grandpa Will is amazing for other things too. <u>He was one of the best woodworkers in East Texas.</u> The sculptures and vessels that

1
he carves on his lathe are beautiful. Grandpa Will's life, art, and the stories that he tells have had a great influence on me.

    <u>Joining at the age of sixteen, the army was a vastly different experience.</u> *It was five days after*

2
Pearl Harbor had been bombed. <u>Will, like the rest of the country, was in an uproar over the attack.</u> He

3
decided that he had to do something. <u>After saying goodbye to his parents, his friends, and relatives Will</u>

4
<u>*signed up and was shipped off to boot camp.*</u>

4

    Will saw a lot of combat during the war. He fought in some of the bloodiest battles in Europe, including the Battle of the Bulge. He also lost a lot of friends in the fighting and saw some terrible tragedies. <u>Grandpa Will believes that the war against fascism was worth it, but whenever he talks about it</u>

5
<u>*he always said: "War hurts a lot of people."*</u>

5

    <u>When he returned from Europe, Will started working for a paper mill.</u> He worked there until he

6
retired, just ten years ago. 7 *He started by taking some classes at the local community college, and then he joined a woodworkers' organization. After a couple of years, Grandpa Will started producing some really amazing pieces. <u>Yet,</u> Grandpa Will has won several prizes for his work, and some of his sculptures*

8
are even on display at a small Houston art gallery. <u>Striking angles and textured colors, Grandpa Will</u>

9
<u>*makes sculptures that always grab the eye.*</u> 10

9

Literature Online **Unit Assessment** To prepare for the unit test, go to www.glencoe.com.

TEST PREPARATION AND PRACTICE **1125**

1. A. NO CHANGE
   B. In East Texas, he was one of the best woodworkers.
   C. He is one of the best woodworkers in East Texas.
   D. Of the best woodworkers, he was one.

2. F. NO CHANGE
   G. Joining at the age of sixteen, Will found the army to be vastly different from any experience he had had before.
   H. The army was a vastly different experience for Will.
   J. Will joined at the age of sixteen.

3. A. NO CHANGE
   B. The rest of the country was in an uproar over the attack.
   C. Will, like the rest of the country, is in an uproar over the attack.
   D. Like the rest of the country, Will is in an uproar over the attack.

4. F. NO CHANGE
   G. After saying goodbye to his parents, friends, and relatives, Will signed up and was shipped off to boot camp.
   H. After saying goodbye to his parents his friends and relatives Will signed up and was shipped off to boot camp.
   J. After saying goodbye to his parents and relatives Will signed up and was shipped off to boot camp.

5. A. NO CHANGE
   B. Grandpa Will believes that the war against fascism was worth it.
   C. Whenever Grandpa Will talks about it he always said: "War hurts a lot of people."
   D. Grandpa Will believes that the war against fascism was worth it, but whenever he talks about it, he always says: "War hurts a lot of people."

6. F. NO CHANGE
   G. When he returned from Europe, he worked for a paper mill.
   H. When he returned from Europe Will started working for a paper mill.
   J. Returning from Europe, a paper mill company gave him a job.

7. Which of the following sentences, if inserted at this point, would provide the most effective transition in this paragraph?
   A. Grandpa Will actually never liked his job at the mill.
   B. The war had changed Grandpa Will's whole attitude about people, work, and school.
   C. Since then, Grandpa Will has been honing his skills as a craftsman.
   D. However, Grandpa Will wanted to keep working at the mill.

8. F. NO CHANGE
   G. However,
   H. In fact,
   J. Although,

9. A. NO CHANGE
   B. Grandpa Will makes sculptures that always grab the eye.
   C. Striking angles and textured colors Grandpa Will makes sculptures that always grab the eye.
   D. Grandpa Will makes sculptures with striking angles and textured colors that always grab the eye.

10. Which of the following should the writer include when writing a concluding paragraph?
   F. Information not included in previous paragraphs
   G. A summary of the key points
   H. Opposing viewpoints
   J. Further descriptions of the grandfather's war experiences

Writing: Applications

Complete the writing activity below. Do your planning and writing on separate sheets of paper.

Essay

> "Let me assert my firm belief that the only thing we have to fear is fear itself—nameless, unreasoning, unjustified terror which paralyzes needed efforts to convert retreat into advance."
> —President Franklin Delano Roosevelt

Write an essay describing an experience from your own life that exemplifies Roosevelt's contention that "the only thing we have to fear is fear itself." Be sure that you clearly relate the details of the experience to the quotation.

Be sure to include

- at least five paragraphs, containing an introduction, a body, and a conclusion
- a description of an experience that reflects the assigned task
- details that convey the relationship between the experience and the quotation

Use a separate sheet of paper to plan your writing. As you write, keep in mind that your essay will be evaluated for **ideas and content, organization, style, voice,** and **language conventions.**

Writing Checklist

Before you begin writing, be sure to

- ❏ brainstorm for ideas
- ❏ organize your ideas into a logical pattern
- ❏ develop a plan for an introduction, a body, and a conclusion

As you write your essay, be sure to

- ❏ refer to the quotation and clearly relate it to your experience
- ❏ use language that will convey a clear message and create interest
- ❏ maintain a tone that is appropriate for your intended audience
- ❏ use correct sentence structure, grammar, and punctuation

Pin Ball #12, 1984. Charles Bell. Oil on canvas. Louis K. Meisel Gallery.

Into the 21st Century

1960s–Present

Looking Ahead

The United States is being reshaped today by profound political and social changes, watershed technological innovation, increasing ethnic diversity, and a complex mixture of cultures. As in the past, contemporary American writers have responded to these historical and cultural forces, both by adapting traditional literary forms and by finding new ones.

Keep the following questions in mind as you read:

➤ What political, social, and cultural forces contributed to the rise of protest movements in the 1960s and 1970s?

➤ How has environmentalism affected contemporary American literature?

➤ How have today's writers reshaped the traditions of Modernism?

INDIANA ACADEMIC STANDARDS (pages 1128–1141)

11.3.5 Analyze or evaluate works of literary or cultural significance in history (American...) that reflect a variety of genres in each of the respective historical periods; were written by important authors in the respective major historical periods; reveal contrasts in major themes, styles, and trends; reflect or shed light on the seminal philosophical, religious, social, political, or ethical ideas of their time.

Timeline
1960s–Present

AMERICAN LITERATURE

1960

1960
To Kill a Mockingbird
by Harper Lee

1962
Silent Spring by Rachel Carson

1963
"I Have a Dream" speech by
Martin Luther King Jr.;
The Feminine Mystique by
Betty Friedan

1965
*The Autobiography of
Malcolm X*

1966
In Cold Blood by Truman
Capote

1969
Slaughterhouse Five by Kurt
Vonnegut

1970

1970
*I Know Why the Caged Bird
Sings* by Maya Angelou

1971
*Bury My Heart at Wounded
Knee* by Dee Brown

1975
Ragtime by E. L. Doctorow

1976
*Roots: The Saga of an American
Family* by Alex Haley

1982 ▲
The Color Purple by Alice
Walker

1984
Cathedral by Raymond
Carver

UNITED STATES EVENTS

1960

1960
First sit-in protests for civil
rights

1963
March on Washington;
President Kennedy
assassinated

1964
Civil Rights Act of 1964;
Gulf of Tonkin Resolution

1968
Martin Luther King Jr. and
Senator Robert Kennedy
assassinated

1969 ▲
Apollo 11 landing on the moon

1970

1970
First Earth Day observed;
students killed at Kent State
during antiwar protests

1972
DDT banned; President
Richard Nixon visits China

1973
U.S. signs cease-fire with
North Vietnam

▲ Cooling Towers at Three
Mile Island

1973
Last Americans withdrawn
from Vietnam

1974
President Nixon resigns

1979
Nuclear accident at Three
Mile Island

WORLD EVENTS

1960

1961
Cosmonaut Yury Gagarin
becomes first man in space

1966 ▼
China's Cultural Revolution
begins

1967
Six-Day War breaks out
between Israel and multiple
Arab nations

1968
Tet Offensive launched by
communist forces in
Vietnam; Soviets invade
Czechoslovakia

1970

1973
Paris Peace Accords signed,
ending the Vietnam War

1975
South Vietnam defeated by
North Vietnam

1979
Soviets invade Afghanistan

1981 ▶
AIDS identified

1985
Mikhail Gorbachev becomes
Soviet leader

1989
Tiananmen Square protests
in China; fall of Berlin Wall

Literature Online Timeline Visit www.glencoe
.com for an interactive timeline.

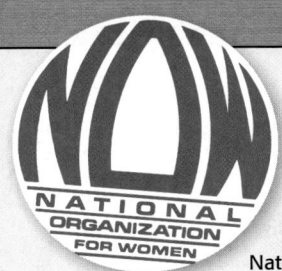

National Organization
for Women button

1990

1987
Beloved by Toni Morrison

1989 ▼
The Joy Luck Club by Amy Tan

1990
The Things They Carried by Tim O'Brien; "afternoon, a story" hypertext fiction by Michael Joyce

1992
Art Spiegelman awarded a Pulitzer Prize for his graphic novel *Maus*

1993
Toni Morrison wins Nobel Prize in Literature

1996
Infinite Jest by David Foster Wallace

1999
Michael Cunningham wins Pulitzer Prize for Fiction for *The Hours*

2000

2000
The Interpreter of Maladies by Jhumpa Lahiri

2004
Personal Weblogs, or *blogs*, affect traditional news coverage and public opinion

Towers of Light WTC Memorial, 2002.

1990

1981 ▶
Sandra Day O'Connor becomes first female Supreme Court justice

1982
Equal Rights Amendment fails; Vietnam Veterans Memorial dedicated in Washington, D.C.

1986
Space shuttle *Challenger* explodes

1992
United States, Mexico, and Canada inaugurate NAFTA trade pact

1993
Mosaic, the first popular Web browser, is introduced

1995
Terrorist bombing in Oklahoma City

1999
Columbine High School shootings in Littleton, Colorado

2001 ▲
Terrorist attacks destroy World Trade Center and damage Pentagon

2003
War in Iraq begins

2000

1991
Persian Gulf War; Soviet Union collapses, end of Cold War

1992
Ethnic cleansing kills 200,000 in former Yugoslavia

1993
European Union established

1994 ▲
Nelson Mandela elected president of South Africa; 800,000 killed in Rwanda

1997
Kyoto Protocol on global warming

Indonesian tsunami victim

2000
Second *intifada* uprising begins in West Bank and Gaza

◀ **2004**
Massive tsunami in Southeast Asia kills at least 225,000

Reading Check

Analyzing Graphic Information According to this timeline, when was the first popular Web browser introduced?

By the Numbers

U.S. Consumption

In May 2001, there were about 284 million people in the United States. India's population was about 1.03 billion. But Americans used 25 percent of the world's resources and produced 25 to 30 percent of the world's waste. Compared with the typical person in India, the average U.S. citizen used:

- 50 times more steel
- 56 times more energy
- 170 times more synthetic rubber
- 170 times more newsprint
- 250 times more motor fuel
- 300 times more plastic

United States in the Vietnam War

UNITED STATES IN THE VIETNAM WAR

Source *Statistical Abstract of the United States.*

OPPOSITION TO THE WAR

1965 U.S. escalates involvement

1973 Cease-fire signed

1969 First withdrawal of U.S. troops

1968 Tet offensive

Source: *The Gallup Poll: Public Opinion.*

ESTIMATED U.S. POPULATION GROWTH

Source *U.S. Census Bureau*

CELL PHONE USE, 2005

- There was almost one cell phone for every two Americans. (By comparison, it took landline phones nearly 100 years to reach this level.)
- About 7.5 million Americans abandoned landline phones and used cell phones exclusively.

U.S. HISPANIC POPULATION GROWTH, 1980–2000

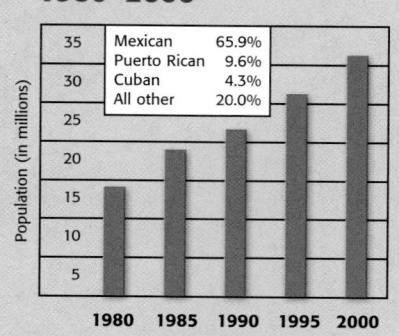

Mexican	65.9%
Puerto Rican	9.6%
Cuban	4.3%
All other	20.0%

Source *Statistical Abstract of the United States.*

COMPUTER USE

- 42,000 bachelor's degrees in computer and information sciences were awarded by U.S. colleges in 2001, up from 2,388 in 1971.
- 99 percent of U.S. schools had Internet access in 2002, up from 50 percent in 1995.

- Online retail sales in the United States for 2003 amounted to $156 billion.
- Projections indicate that 635,000 computer systems analysts will be employed in the United States by 2012, an increase of about 40 percent from 2002.

Being There

Since the 1960s, increased immigration has brought many newcomers to the United States from regions beyond Europe. These newcomers have changed the cultural life of many American communities.

A Muslim Fatina Abrabboh jogs on a bridge spanning the Charles River in Cambridge, Massachusetts, 2005. John Nordell. Color photograph.

B *Children Riding Bicycles Past Mural,* 1991. Ralf-Finn Hestoft. Color photograph.

C *Chinese New Year in Los Angeles.* Nik Wheeler. Color photograph.

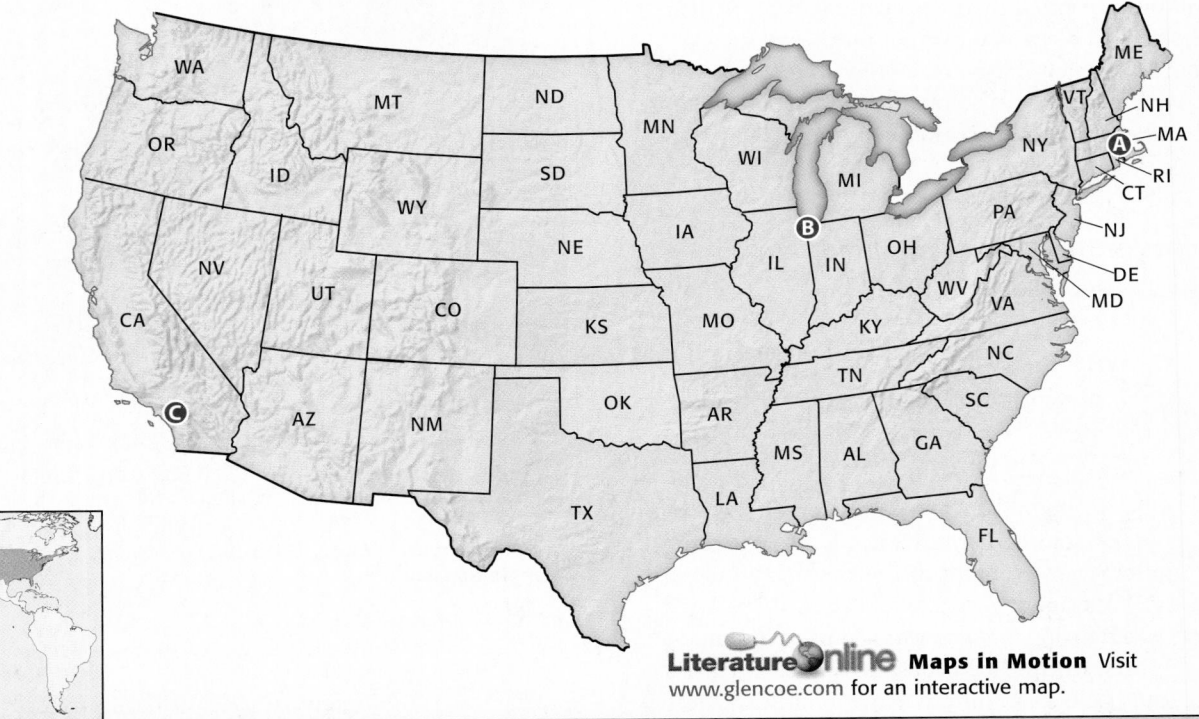

LiteratureOnline **Maps in Motion** Visit www.glencoe.com for an interactive map.

Reading Check

Analyzing Graphic Information:

1. In what year did U.S. troop strength in Vietnam peak? In what year did opposition to the Vietnam War peak?

2. How many more degrees in computer and information sciences were granted in 2001 than in 1971?

3. What is distinctive about each of the cultures represented in the photographs shown above?

Into the 21st Century

1960s–Present

Historical, Social, and Cultural Forces

The Civil Rights Movement

In the mid-1950s, under the inspiring leadership of Martin Luther King Jr., African Americans launched the modern Civil Rights Movement. This heroic, nonviolent campaign to end segregation and secure voting rights for African Americans in the South achieved many of its goals in the mid-1960s, when the federal government enacted landmark civil rights legislation. Inspired by the successes of the African American civil rights movement, other groups—including women, Hispanics, Asian Americans, and Native Americans—also organized to secure greater political equality and economic power.

"Injustice anywhere is a threat to justice everywhere."

—Martin Luther King Jr.

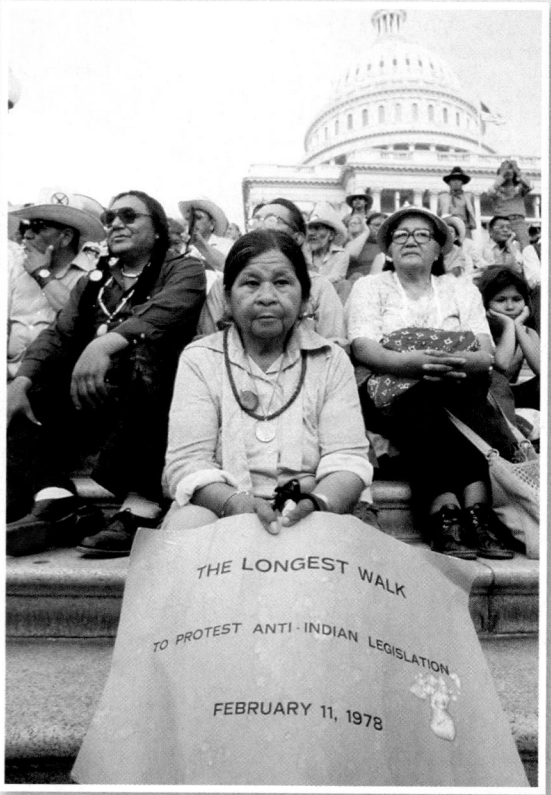

"The Longest Walk," protest, 1978. Wally McNamee. Color photograph.

The Vietnam War

Beginning in the mid-1950s, American efforts to stop the spread of communist influence led to growing U.S. military involvement in the Southeast Asian country of Vietnam. By the mid-1960s, the United States was fighting a major war against Vietnamese communists. In the late 1960s, heavy American casualties and the U.S. failure to achieve military victory in Southeast Asia led to growing opposition to the war at home. The United States signed a cease-fire agreement in 1973 with communist North Vietnam. By early 1975, the last Americans were withdrawn from South Vietnam, which promptly fell to communist North Vietnam.

Environmentalism

During the 1960s, many Americans began to feel that environmental problems plagued every region of their nation. In 1962 Rachel Carson's book *Silent Spring* first raised widespread concerns about the effects of pollution on the natural environment. By 1970, a grassroots environmental movement developed. In April of that year, the movement sponsored the first Earth Day. Once the environmental movement gained public support, the federal government also took action and established the Environmental Protection Agency (EPA) in 1970.

The Computer Revolution

The introduction of the first digital computer in 1946 launched a technological revolution. In the succeeding decades, advances such as the integrated circuit greatly reduced the size and increased the speed of computers. By the mid-1970s, the first practical and affordable home computers became available. In the late 1980s, the development of government-funded supercomputer centers paved the way for the Internet, a global information system that operates commercially.

Globalization

Since the 1990s, the Internet, portable communications equipment, and trade deregulation have spurred on the drive for companies to globalize. Often the component parts for consumer goods, like televisions or automobiles, are manufactured in various countries around the world. This trend has been criticized by those who believe that globalization exploits laborers in developing nations, where many of these goods are produced. Some argue that it has slowly siphoned away America's high-wage manufacturing jobs. However, others believe that globalization, in the long term, will benefit both established and developing nations.

Multiculturalism

In literature, writers of European descent have been historically privileged over other groups. Multiculturalism—a product of the 1960s Civil Rights Movement—attempts to correct this by exposing readers to unique voices from a variety of ethnic backgrounds. However, unlike most previous literary movements, there are few poets or novelists who would label themselves "multicultural." Instead, this is primarily a critical trend that endeavors to bring recognition to the unrecognized.

Postmodernism

The term *Postmodernism* is used to refer to trends in art, architecture, literature, and music created after World War II. Postmodernists favor unusual juxtapositions of styles, such as linking fine art and popular culture. Postmodern writing reflects an awareness of the growing influence of the media on modern sensibilities and an enthusiasm for this trend. Postmodernists also share a willingness to question traditional attitudes toward the central place of Western cultures in world civilization.

PREVIEW **Big Ideas** of the Twentieth Century

1 An Era of Protest

From the mid-1950s to the mid-1970s, U.S. society experienced political and social upheaval resulting from the Civil Rights Movement and opposition to the Vietnam War. U.S. writers responded to the powerful questions raised by these historical events.
See pages 1136–1137.

2 Nature and Technology

As U.S. citizens became aware of threats to the environment in recent decades, some writers reassessed the importance of the human relationship to nature. At the same time, watershed changes in technology provided new subject matter and new forms for American literature.
See pages 1138–1139.

3 Extending and Remaking Traditions

Increases in immigration and changing attitudes toward ethnic identity are helping to create a much more diverse U.S. society and literature. Innovative approaches to art, such as Postmodernism, are also building on past traditions to reshape contemporary American literature.
See pages 1140–1141.

An Era of Protest

Everyone is troubled by injustices—great and small. When injustice or unfairness is part of the basic fabric of a society, however, it may take a social revolution to change things.

Segregation

Throughout the first half of the twentieth century, segregation dominated the lives of African Americans, severely limiting their political freedom and economic opportunities. Segregation was enforced by laws throughout the South. As a result, African Americans were denied equal access to good schools and housing and were barred from public facilities such as hotels, theaters, buses, and trains.

Integration

In 1954 the U.S. Supreme Court ruled in its land-mark *Brown vs. Board of Education* decision that segregated education for whites and blacks was unconstitutional. However, progress in desegregating schools and other public facilities was very slow. Beginning in December 1955, African Americans in Montgomery, Alabama, organized a successful yearlong boycott of the city's segregated buses. The leader of this protest was an eloquent young minister named Martin Luther King Jr. In the years that followed, Dr. King inspired a nonviolent African American civil rights movement through his power-ful speeches and writing. This heroic campaign to end segregation and secure voting rights in the South had made huge strides by the mid-1960s, when the federal government enacted landmark civil rights legislation.

Black Power

While King advocated a nonviolent path to integra-tion, other African American civil rights leaders favored armed struggle and black separatism. In the early 1960s, militant leader Malcolm X rose to promi-nence by promoting race pride and black national-ism—the idea that African Americans should band together to gain economic independence and to cre-ate a sense of community. In 1966, Student Nonviolent Coordinating Committee chairman Stokely Carmichael took "Black Power"— a black nationalist motto— and created the "Black Power" movement, which championed self-defense, auton-omy, economic and political power, and black pride.

> *"Violence often brings about momentary results."*
>
> —Martin Luther King Jr.

Women and Hispanics

During the 1960s and 1970s, a large number of American women organized a push for greater rights and opportunities. The publication of Betty Friedan's *The Feminine Mystique* in 1963 gave steam to the bur-geoning women's movement. Friedan joined other activists in 1966 to form the National Organization for Women (NOW) which worked for legislation against gender discrimination in employment, hous-ing, and education. Around the same time that the women's movement began in the early 1960s, César Chavez and Dolores Huerta started organizations that fought for the rights of Hispanic farmworkers.

A Divisive War

The Vietnam War was one of the most divisive con-flicts in U.S. history. When large numbers of U.S. troops first went to Vietnam in the spring of 1965, a majority of Americans supported the military effort. As time passed, however, claims by U.S. military lead-ers that victory was near were contradicted by reports in the media, especially on television. Vietnam was the first "living room war"; people in the United States were deeply disturbed by nightly images of wounded and dead U.S. soldiers on television news programs. As casualties mounted in Vietnam, many people began to protest publicly against the war and demand that the United States pull out.

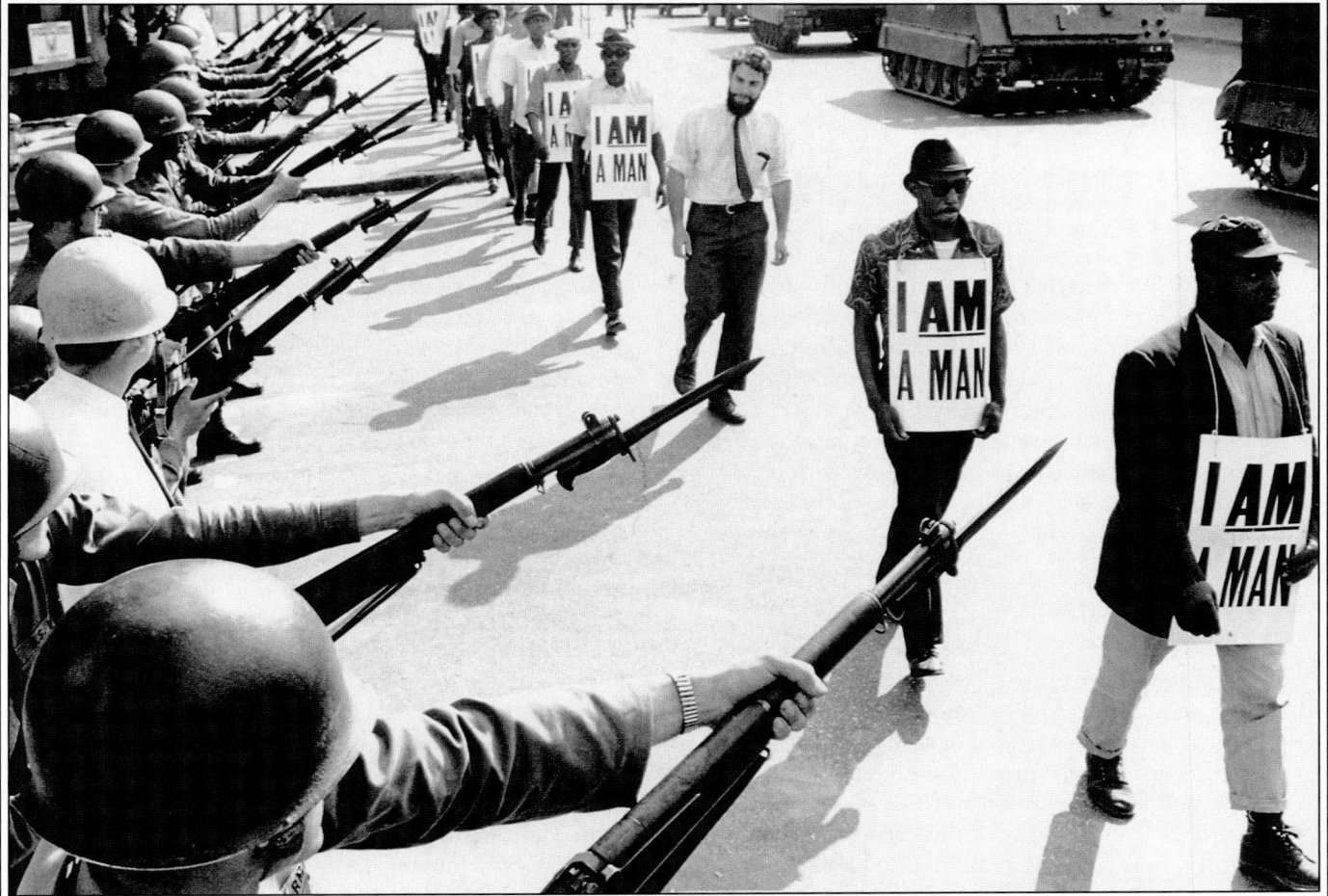

Civil rights marchers with "I Am A Man" signs, 1968. Black and white photograph.

from *Letter from a Birmingham Jail* by Martin Luther King Jr.

Oppressed people cannot remain oppressed forever. The yearning for freedom eventually manifests itself, and that is what has happened to the American Negro. Something within has reminded him of his birthright of freedom; something without has reminded him that he can gain it. Consciously or unconsciously, he has been swept in by what the Germans call the *Zeitgeist*, and with his black brothers of Africa, and his brown and yellow brothers of Asia, South America and the Caribbean, he is moving with a sense of cosmic urgency toward the promised land of racial justice. Recognizing this vital urge that has engulfed the Negro community, one should readily understand public demonstrations. The Negro has many pent-up resentments and latent frustrations. He has to get them out. So let him march sometime; let him have his prayer pilgrimages to the city hall; understand why he must have sit-ins and freedom rides. If his repressed emotions do not come out in these nonviolent ways, they will seek ominous expressions of violence. This is not a threat; it is a fact of history. So I have not said to my people "get rid of your discontent." But I have tried to say that this normal and healthy discontent can be channelized through the creative outlet of nonviolent direct action.

Reading Check

Analyzing Cause and Effect How did the rise of Black Power later confirm Dr. King's warning about violence in "Letter from a Birmingham Jail"?

Big Idea 2

Nature and Technology

Americans today are living through events that have the potential to fundamentally change the way we will live for years to come. Among the most basic of these are long-range changes to the natural environment as a result of industrialization and the revolution in communications created by modern technology, including computers.

The Environmental Movement

During the 1960s and 1970s, a growing number of U.S. citizens began to become alarmed at how their highly industrialized society was affecting the natural environment. Widespread use of pesticides had damaged many forms of wildlife. Rising levels of air and water pollution were seen as a threat to health. A leading cause of this change in public perception was the work of marine biologist Rachel Carson. Carson's 1962 book *Silent Spring* attacked the increasing use of pesticides, particularly DDT. She contended that in addition to controlling harmful insects, pesticides such as DDT also killed the birds, fish, and other creatures further up the food chain. Carson warned Americans of a "silent spring," in which few birds would remain to herald the season with their songs.

> *"There was a strange stillness. The birds, for example—where had they gone?"*
>
> —Rachel Carson, *Silent Spring*

By 1970, with the observance of the first Earth Day, a grassroots environmental movement began to take shape. Citizens formed local environmental groups, while long-established organizations, such as the Sierra Club and the Audubon Society, gained greater influence. All these groups worked to protect the environment and promote the conservation of natural resources. The federal government also became involved, establishing the Environmental Protection Agency and passing legislation aimed at curbing air and water pollution and protecting endangered wildlife.

Responding to Nature

Going back at least as far as Thoreau's *Walden*, nature writing has been a persistent strain in American literature. Heightened concern about the environment, coupled with the "back to nature" impulse that was a significant element of the counterculture of the 1960s, prompted a minor renaissance of American nature writing in the recent past. Edward Abbey, Annie Dillard, Edward Hoagland, Terry Tempest Williams, Barry Lopez, John McPhee, and many other writers have evoked a variety of wilderness landscapes, from the desert to the Arctic, and reflected on the lessons nature has to teach.

The Information Age

In the twentieth century, the world experienced a revolution in communications unmatched since the invention of the printing press in the fifteenth century. Modern Americans became enthusiastic users of a wide variety of new media, including telephones, radio, television, video games, cell phones, and the Internet. These new media have created a society in which one of the most valuable commodities is information.

One of the consequences of the Cold War rivalry between the United States and the Soviet Union was competition for dominance in space exploration. In addition to such achievements as the Moon landings and the shuttle missions, the U.S. space program has contributed to advances in a wide range of technologies, such as the satellites that are part of today's telecommunications networks.

Wind Farm at Sunset, David Seed. Color photograph.

A recent and revolutionary form of new media is the worldwide communications system of the Internet. With the development of the hypertext transport protocol (http) and new software known as Web browsers, Internet use began to expand rapidly. As early as 1988, it was growing at the rate of 100 percent a year. By the late 1990s, the number of Internet users exceeded 30 million. During its brief existence, the Internet has had a profound effect on many aspects of modern life, from the explosive development of online commerce to the creation of new computer-based literary forms such as hypertext fiction, which uses computer technology to expand the possible sequencings of a narrative.

from *Lost* by David Wagoner

Stand still. The trees ahead and bushes beside you
Are not lost. Wherever you are is called Here,
And you must treat it as a powerful stranger,
Must ask permission to know it and be known.
The forest breathes. Listen. It answers,
I have made this place around you.
If you leave it you may come back again, saying Here.
No two trees are the same to Raven.
No two branches are the same to Wren.
If what a tree or a bush does is lost on you,
You are surely lost. Stand still. The forest knows
Where you are. You must let it find you.

Reading Check

Interpreting What two different attitudes toward the natural environment are reflected in David Wagoner's poem "Lost"?

Extending and Remaking Traditions

In the past, newcomers to the United States were urged to "Americanize" themselves as soon and as fully as possible. The model was "the melting pot," meaning a place in which a complete blending of peoples and cultures takes place. Today, there is a new cultural model that stresses the value of maintaining ethnic diversity in American society.

The New Immigrants

The United States has always been a nation of immigrants. Restrictive immigration laws and economic depression kept immigrant levels low between World War I and World War II. However, since the end of World War II, immigration has been rising. The Immigration Reform Act of 1965 allowed more immigrants from countries outside of northern and western Europe. By the 1980s and 1990s, immigration had reached levels approaching the all-time highs of the early twentieth century. Most of these recent immigrants come from the western hemisphere (primarily Mexico) and from Asia. By 1995 almost 9 percent of Americans were foreign born. Consequently, the traditional canon of American literature is expanding greatly to include works by writers from many different backgrounds.

Cultural Diversity

Newcomers are helping to make U.S. society more culturally diverse. As a result, many communities in the United States have an increasingly multiethnic texture that incorporates language, food, family values, social life, and entertainment. With diversity increasing and opportunities for women expanding, American literature draws upon a wider range of experience than ever before. The literature published in the United States includes fiction, nonfiction, and poetry by African American writers such as Henry Louis Gates Jr. and Rita Dove; by Native American writers such as N. Scott Momaday and Louise Erdrich; by Hispanic writers such as Sandra Cisneros and Julia Alvarez; and by Asian American writers such as Amy Tan and Jhumpa Lahiri. The enthusiasm with which the works of these writers are received

shows that their own ethnic traditions are becoming an integral part of the American cultural experience.

Postmodernism

The Modernists of the early part of the twentieth century believed that as contemporary life became more complex and artificial it also became increasingly inhumane. Postmodernists, such as novelists John Barth and Thomas Pynchon, reject this conclusion. They argue that the modern world's complexities should be explored, even celebrated. Like pop artists, Postmodernists often investigate artifice, or the surfaces of things, to reveal some truth just underneath. These writers accomplish this through a variety of forms and strategies, such as creating literary collages or stories-within-stories, blending genres, introducing material from popular culture, and introducing themselves as characters into their own fiction.

> "Postmodernism is tying your necktie while simultaneously explaining the step-by-step procedure of necktie-tying and chatting about the history of male neckwear—and managing a perfect full windsor anyhow."
>
> —John Barth

New Literary Forms

The characteristic literary forms of Postmodernism emphasize the blending of genres, such as the "nonfiction novel," which uses the strategies of fiction to present actual events. One of the earliest and best-known literary works to adopt this strategy was *In Cold Blood*, Truman Capote's 1965 account of the brutal murder of a Kansas family. Another Postmodern literary form, the graphic novel, blends high and low culture by expanding one of the most familiar forms of twentieth century American popular

Technology, 1991. Nam June Paik.

culture, the comic book, to address serious literary subjects. Probably the best-known graphic novel is *Maus* by Art Spiegelman, which won a Pulitzer Prize in 1992. Spiegelman uses comic book panels and cat and mouse characters to tell a story about the Holocaust.

from *The Latin Deli: An Ars Poetica*
by Judith Ortiz Cofer

Presiding over a formica counter,
plastic Mother and Child magnetized
to the top of an ancient register,
the heady mix of smells from the open bins
of dried codfish, the green plantains
hanging in stalks like votive offerings,
she is the Patroness of Exiles,
a woman of no-age who was never pretty,
who spends her days selling canned memories
while listening to the Puerto Ricans complain
that it would be cheaper to fly to San Juan
than to buy a pound of Bustelo coffee here,
and to Cubans perfecting their speech
of a "glorious return" to Havana—where no one
has been allowed to die and nothing to change
   until then;
to Mexicans who pass through, talking lyrically
of *dolares* to be made in El Norte—
                all wanting the comfort
of spoken Spanish, to gaze upon the family portrait
of her plain wide face, her ample bosom
resting on her plump arms, her look of maternal interest
as they speak to her and each other
of their dreams and disillusions—
how she smiles understanding,
when they walk down the narrow aisles of her store
reading the labels of packages aloud, as if
they were the names of lost lovers: *Suspiros,
Merengues,* the stale candy of everyone's childhood.
           She spends her days
slicing *jamón y queso* and wrapping it in wax paper
tied with string: plain ham and cheese
that would cost less at the A&P, but it would not satisfy
the hunger of the fragile old man lost in the folds
of his winter coat, who brings her lists of items
that he reads to her like poetry, or the others,
whose needs she must divine, conjuring up products
from places that now exist only in their hearts—
closed ports she must trade with.

Reading Check

Evaluating What values of cultural diversity are expressed in Judith Ortiz Cofer's "The Latin Deli"?

Wrap-Up

Why It Matters

The African American civil rights movement, the women's movement, and the related political movements among Hispanics and other groups, transformed American society. Although important problems remain to be resolved, these movements achieved major advances in social justice and economic opportunity during the twentieth century. The legacy of the antiwar movement is far less clear. Americans remain deeply divided on the morality and practicality of military intervention in the affairs of other nations.

The environmental movement has heightened the awareness of U.S. citizens about a broad range of issues, including public health, consumer safety, and preservation of natural resources. It has made people realize that the United States is part of a world that is interdependent environmentally as well as economically.

The U.S. has never been more ethnically diverse or culturally complex. American literature has followed this national trend, growing ever more diverse as it has grown more unique, humorous, and self-aware.

Literature Online **Big Ideas** Link to Web resources to further explore the Big Ideas at www.glencoe.com.

Cultural Links

➤ In the 1970s, Alice Walker successfully revived interest in the Harlem Renaissance writer Zora Neale Hurston, who had been largely forgotten.

➤ The critical and popular success of the oral histories of Studs Terkel has helped to revitalize this literary form.

➤ The work of Theodore Roethke shows the influence of such Modernist poets as T. S. Eliot and Wallace Stevens.

You might try using this study organizer to jot down questions you have about the readings in this unit.

LAYERED-LOOK BOOK

Reader's Questions
Who?
What?
Where?
When?
Why?

Connect to Today

Use what you have learned about the period to do one of these activities.

1. Speaking/Listening Working with other students, research Postmodernist literature and create a brief presentation for your class, describing some of its typical forms, including the nonfiction novel, hypertext fiction, and the graphic novel.

2. Visual Literacy Create a visual timeline of the period from 1960 to the present, using images that have become iconic representations of the time (for example, Elizabeth Eckford walking past jeering white students during the desegregation of Central High School in Little Rock in September 1957). When you have completed your timeline, share it with the class.

INDIANA ACADEMIC STANDARDS (page 1142)
11.7.17 Deliver oral reports on historical investigations that ...describe similarities and differences between research sources...
11.7.19 Deliver multimedia presentations...

Literature Online **Study Central** Visit www.glencoe. com and click on Study Central to review the Contemporary Era.

An Era of Protest

Challenge America, 1964. Lois Mailou Jones. Photomechanical reproduction, acrylic and paper on canvas, 39⅛ x 30⅛ in. Hirshhorn Museum and Sculpture Garden, Smithsonian Institution, Washington DC.

"We know through painful experience that freedom is never voluntarily given by the oppressor; it must be demanded by the oppressed."

—Martin Luther King Jr., "Letter from a Birmingham Jail"

TIME

The Torchbearer

ROSA PARKS's simple act of protest galvanized America's civil rights revolution

By RITA DOVE

How she sat there,
the time right inside a place
so wrong it was ready.
—From "Rosa," in *On the Bus with Rosa Parks* by Rita Dove

We know the story. One December evening, a woman left work and boarded a bus for home. She was tired; her feet ached. But this was Montgomery, Alabama, in 1955, and as the bus became crowded, the woman, a black woman, was ordered to give up her seat to a white passenger. When she remained seated, that simple decision eventually led to the disintegration of institutionalized segregation in the South and ushered in a new era of the Civil Rights movement.

This, anyway, was the story I had heard from the time I was curious enough to eavesdrop on adult conversations. I was three years old when a white bus driver warned Rosa Parks, "Well, I'm going to have you arrested," and she replied, "You may go on and do so." As a child, I didn't understand how doing nothing had caused so much activity, but I recognized the template: David slaying the giant Goliath, or the boy who saved his village by sticking his finger in the dike. Perhaps it is precisely the lure of fairy-tale retribution that colors the lens we look back through. Parks was 42 years old when she refused to give up her seat. She has insisted that her feet were not aching; she was, by her own testimony, no more tired than usual. She did not plan her fateful act: "I did not get on the bus to get arrested," she has said. "I got on the bus to go home."

Montgomery's segregation laws were complex: Blacks were required to pay their fare to the driver and then get off and reboard through the back door. Sometimes the bus would drive off before the paid-up customers made it to the back entrance. If the white section was full and another white

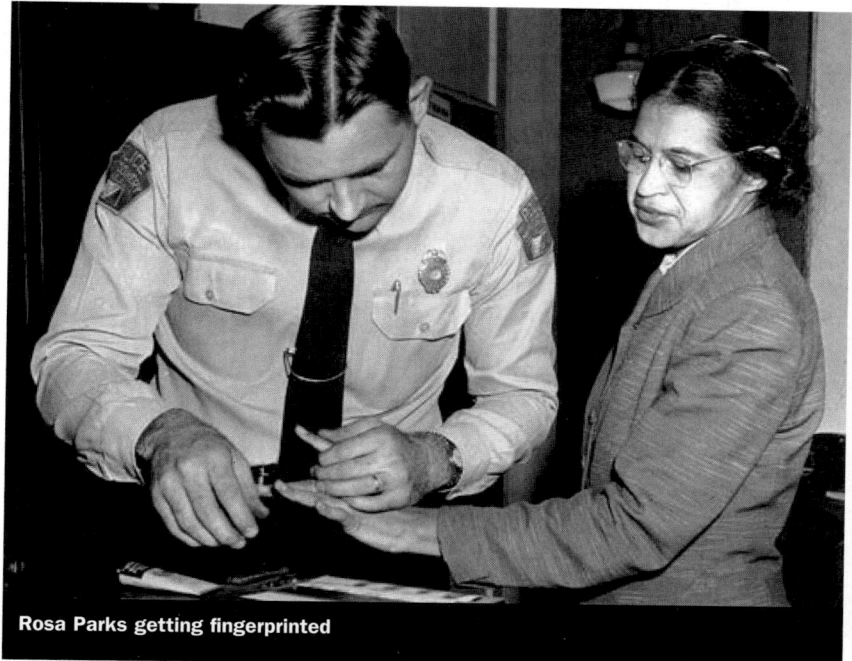

Rosa Parks getting fingerprinted

customer entered, blacks were required to give up their seats and move farther to the back; a black person was not even allowed to sit across the aisle from whites. These humiliations were compounded by the fact that two-thirds of the bus riders in Montgomery were black.

Parks was not the first to be detained for this offense. Eight months earlier, Claudette Colvin, 15, refused to give up her seat and was arrested. Black activists met with this girl to determine if she would make a good test case. As secretary of the local chapter of the National Association for the Advancement of Colored People (NAACP), Parks attended the meeting, where it was finally decided that a more "upstanding" candidate than Colvin was necessary to withstand the scrutiny of the courts and the press. Then, in October, a young woman named Mary Louise Smith was arrested; NAACP leaders rejected her, too, as their vehicle, looking for someone more able to withstand media scrutiny. Smith paid the fine and was released.

Six weeks later, the time was ripe. The facts, rubbed shiny for retelling, are these: On December 1, 1955, Mrs. Rosa Parks, seamstress for the Montgomery Fair department store, boarded the Cleveland Avenue bus. She took a seat in the fifth row—the first row of the "Colored Section." The driver was the same one who had put her off a bus 12 years earlier for refusing to get off and reboard through the back door. ("He was still mean-looking," she has said.) Did that make her stubborn? Or had her work in the NAACP sharpened her sensibilities so that she knew what to do—or more precisely, what not to do: Don't frown, don't struggle, don't shout, don't pay the fine?

At the news of the arrest, local civil rights leader E.D. Nixon exclaimed, "My God, look what segregation has put in my hands!" Parks was not only above moral reproach (securely married, reasonably employed), but she possessed a quiet fortitude as well as political savvy. In short, she was the ideal candidate for a test case.

She was arrested on a Thursday; bail was posted by Clifford Durr, the white lawyer whose wife had employed Parks as a seamstress. That evening, after talking it over with her mother and husband, Rosa Parks agreed to challenge the constitutionality of Montgomery's segregation laws. During a midnight meeting of the Women's Political Council, 35,000 handbills were printed for distribution to all black schools the next morning. The message was simple:

"We are . . . asking every Negro to stay off the buses Monday in protest of the arrest and trial . . . You can afford to stay out of school for one day. If you work, take a cab, or walk. But please, children and grown-ups, don't ride the bus at all on Monday. Please stay off the buses Monday."

Monday came. Rain threatened, yet the black population of Montgomery stayed off the buses, either walking or catching one of the black cabs stopping at every municipal bus stop for 10 cents per customer—the standard bus fare. Meanwhile, Parks was scheduled to appear in court. She made her way through the throngs at the courthouse, a demure figure in a long-sleeved black dress with white collar and cuffs, a trim black velvet hat, gray coat, and white gloves. A girl in the crowd caught sight of her and cried out, "Oh, she's so sweet. They've messed with the wrong one now!"

Yes, indeed. The trial lasted 30 minutes, with the expected conviction and penalty. That afternoon, the Montgomery Improvement Association was formed. So as not to ruffle any local activists' feathers, the members elected as their president a relative newcomer to Montgomery, the young minister of Dexter Avenue Baptist Church: the Rev. Martin Luther King Jr. That evening, addressing a crowd gathered at the Holt Street Baptist Church, King declared in that sonorous, ringing voice the world would soon thrill to: "There comes a time that people get tired." When he was finished, Parks stood up so the audience could see her. She did not speak; there was no need to.

Here I am, her silence said, *among you.* And she has been with us ever since—a persistent symbol of human

Rosa alone

dignity in the face of brutal authority. The famous UPI photo (actually taken more than a year later, on December 21, 1956, the day Montgomery's public transportation system was legally integrated) is a study of calm strength. She is looking out the bus window, her hands resting in the folds of her checked dress, while a white man sits, unperturbed, in the row *behind* her. That clear profile, the neat hat and eyeglasses and sensible coat—she could have been my mother or anybody's favorite aunt.

History is often portrayed as a grand opera, full of great intrigues and larger-than-life heroics. Some of the most tumultuous events, however, have been provoked by serendipity—the assassination of an unimportant archduke spawned World War I, a kicked-over lantern may have sparked the Great Chicago Fire. One cannot help wondering what role Martin Luther King Jr. would have played in the civil rights movement if the opportunity had not presented itself that first evening of the boycott. What if Rosa Parks had chosen a row farther back from the outset? Or what if she had missed the bus altogether?

At the beginning of this new millennium (and after a particularly noisy century), it is the modesty of Rosa Parks's example that sustains us. It is no less than the belief in the power of the individual, that cornerstone of the American Dream, that she inspires. Her life offers the hope that when crunch time comes, all of us—even the least of us—could be that brave, that serenely human.

— Updated 2005, from TIME, June 14, 1999

RESPONDING AND THINKING CRITICALLY

Respond

1. Using Rosa Parks's actions as an example, how would you define heroism?

Recall and Interpret

2. (a)What were the segregation laws for Montgomery's bus system? (b)Why were these laws especially humiliating to African American people?

3. (a)Why did the NAACP reject two other bus riders before meeting Parks? (b)What does this indicate about the organization?

4. (a)Who was elected president of the Montgomery Improvement Association? (b)Why is this important?

Analyze and Evaluate

5. (a)Why were Parks's appearance and social standing important? (b)How might you have reacted if you were at Parks's trial?

6. (a) How do you think the author feels about the Montgomery bus boycott? (b)What evidence supports your conclusion?

7. (a)Return to the graphic organizer you created. What is the chronological order of events presented in the article? (b)Why do you think Dove chose to organize the article in chronological order?

Connect

8. In "The Torchbearer" Dove writes "What if Rosa Parks had chosen a row farther back from the outset? Or what if she had missed the bus altogether?" In what ways do you think these changes would have affected the civil rights movement?

from *Stride Toward Freedom*

MEET MARTIN LUTHER KING JR.

Martin Luther King Jr. fundamentally altered the way people in the United States look at race. He showed that segregation and forced inequality could be successfully combated without recourse to violence. King's steady advocacy uplifted the despondent and challenged the complacent. Combining high ideals with practicality, King inspired people from all races and backgrounds to demand the best from themselves and their country.

> *"Do your work so well that no one could do it better. Do it so well that all the hosts of heaven and earth will have to say: Here lived a man who did his job as if God Almighty called him at this particular time in history to do it."*
>
> —Martin Luther King Jr.

Historic Struggles Born the son of a minister in Atlanta, Georgia, King distinguished himself at school and entered Morehouse College at fifteen. After receiving his PhD in theology, King became a minister in Montgomery, Alabama.

Shortly after King moved to Montgomery, the first major nonviolent protest of the civil rights movement took place: the Montgomery bus boycott. The boycott was an attempt to end the practice of segregation on public buses. For more than a year, Montgomery's fifty thousand black citizens stayed off the buses. The boycott was successful, and King's outstanding public speaking and leadership skills drew national attention. After the boycott, the Southern Christian Leadership Conference was founded to confront all forms of segregation, and King became its president.

Commitment and Dedication When the center of the civil rights struggle shifted to Birmingham, Alabama, in 1963, King was there. He and other demonstrators were jailed, and violence exploded in the streets, but King's stance on nonviolent resistance remained firm: "We will go on," he told his supporters, "because we have started a fire in Birmingham that water cannot put out. We are going on because we love Birmingham and we love democracy. And we are going to remain nonviolent."

One of the best-known triumphs of the civil rights movement was the March on Washington in 1963. There King delivered his famous "I Have a Dream" speech to an audience of approximately 250,000 people. One year later, he became the youngest person ever to win the Nobel Peace Prize.

Despite his commitment to nonviolence, King himself was the target of threats and violence. In 1968, at the age of thirty-nine, he fell victim to an assassin's bullet. King's funeral took place at the church where he had acted as pastor, Ebenezer Baptist Church in Atlanta, Georgia. Over a thousand people, including political leaders and foreign dignitaries, crowded into the church for the service. Outside, almost one hundred thousand more paid tribute.

Martin Luther King Jr. was born in 1929 and died in 1968.

Literature Online **Author Search** For more about Martin Luther King Jr., go to www.glencoe.com.

Connecting to the Selection

Unfair situations can be difficult to deal with, but Martin Luther King Jr. convinced many people that injustices can be remedied. He also argued that those who experience injustice have the responsibility to prevent themselves from feeling hatred and despair. As you read, think about the following questions:

- What is a situation in the United States today that you think is unjust and needs to be changed?
- What are your highest principles or ideals?

Building Background

King based his theory of nonviolent resistance on the ideas of Henry David Thoreau, Mohandas Gandhi, and others. The movement was supported by the Fellowship of Reconciliation, a group that promoted nonviolent direct action. James Lawson, a young African American pacifist who had learned about Gandhi's nonviolent strategies during travels in India, also helped by teaching workshops on nonviolence. In the end, nonviolence succeeded in the civil rights movement because of the courage of those who practiced it.

Setting Purposes for Reading

Big Idea An Era of Protest

As you read, think about the different groups of people that King sought to convince as he embarked upon his campaign of nonviolent resistance.

Literary Element Structure

Structure is the order or pattern a writer uses to present ideas in a logical way. By focusing his argument on three main points and giving evidence for each point before moving to the next, King is able to express his position clearly and methodically. As you read, carefully examine the reasons and evidence he gives as he seeks to persuade his audience that nonviolence is the best way to fight injustice.

- See Literary Terms Handbook, p. R17.

Literature Online Interactive Literary Elements Handbook To review or learn more about the literary elements, go to www.glencoe.com.

Reading Strategy Paraphrasing

When you state in your own words the main point of a piece of writing, you are **paraphrasing.** Paraphrasing helps you better remember and understand what you read. As you read this selection, pause from time to time and ask yourself questions to help you paraphrase King's arguments about nonviolence.

Reading Tip: Paraphrasing Use a chart to paraphrase important details.

Detail	Paraphrase
" . . . the oppressed resign themselves to their doom. They tacitly adjust themselves to oppression, and thereby become conditioned to it."	People who suffer from injustice believe there is no way out. They get so used to living with injustice that they come to accept it.

Vocabulary

ordeal (ôr dēl′) *n.* a circumstance or experience that is painful or difficult; a trial; p. 1149 *The storm was a physical ordeal for people on the ship.*

stature (stach′ ər) *n.* a level attained; standing; status; p. 1150 *Mayor Evans is a person of great stature in our community.*

imperative (im per′ ə tiv) *n.* something absolutely necessary; an essential; p. 1151 *When you write a business letter, correct spelling is an imperative.*

repudiate (ri pū′ dē āt′) *v.* to refuse to accept as valid; to reject; to renounce; p. 1151 *The mayor gave a speech to repudiate reports of a scandal.*

Vocabulary Tip: Analogies An **analogy** is a comparison made between two things to show how they relate to each other.

INDIANA ACADEMIC STANDARDS (pages 1148–1152)
11.2.2 Analyze the way in which clarity of meaning is affected by the patterns of organization [and] organization of language... in the text.

11.2 Develop [reading] strategies...

from Stride Toward Freedom

Martin Luther King Jr.

. . . Oppressed people deal with their oppression in three characteristic ways. One way is acquiescence:[1] the oppressed resign themselves to their doom. They tacitly[2] adjust themselves to oppression, and thereby become conditioned to it. In every movement toward freedom some of the oppressed prefer to remain oppressed. Almost 2,800 years ago Moses set out to lead the children of Israel from the slavery of Egypt[3] to the freedom of the promised land.[4] He soon discovered that slaves do not always welcome their deliverers. They become accustomed to being slaves. They would rather bear those ills they have, as Shakespeare pointed out, than flee to others

that they know not of.[5] They prefer the "fleshpots of Egypt" to the **ordeals** of emancipation.

There is such a thing as the freedom of exhaustion. Some people are so worn down by the yoke of oppression that they give up. A few years ago in the slum areas of Atlanta, a Negro guitarist used to sing almost daily: "Ben down so long that down don't bother me." This is the type of negative freedom and resignation that often engulfs the life of the oppressed.

But this is not the way out. To accept passively an unjust system is to cooperate with that system; thereby the oppressed become as evil as the oppressor. Noncooperation with evil is as much a moral obligation as is cooperation with good. The oppressed must never allow the conscience of the oppressor to slumber. Religion

---

1. *Acquiescence* means "the act of consenting or agreeing silently, without objections."
2. *Tacitly* means "silently."
3. *[Moses . . . of Egypt]* As Moses led the Israelites across the wilderness, supplies brought from Egypt ran out. The Bible (Exodus 16:2–3) tells how the people complained and began to regret having left Egypt where, although they were in bondage, they had sufficient food.
4. In the Bible, the *Promised Land* is the land of Canaan, promised by God to Abraham's descendants.

5. *[Shakespeare . . . know not of]* In Shakespeare's play *Hamlet,* the title character says (act 3, scene 1, lines 80–81): ". . . And makes us rather bear those ills we have, / Than fly to others that we know not of."

Reading Strategy Paraphrasing *Rephrase this passage in your own words.*

Literary Element Structure *What do the opening sentences suggest about the way King intends to organize his ideas?*

Vocabulary

ordeal (ôr dēl´) *n.* a circumstance or experience that is painful or difficult; a trial reminds every man that he is his brother's keeper. To accept injustice or segregation passively is to say to the oppressor that his actions are morally right. It is a way of allowing his conscience to fall asleep. At this moment the oppressed fails to be his brother's keeper. So acquiescence—while often the easier way—is not the moral way. It is the way of the coward. The Negro cannot win the respect of his oppressor by acquiescing; he merely increases the oppressor's arrogance and contempt. Acquiescence is interpreted as proof of the Negro's inferiority. The Negro cannot win the respect of the white people of the South or the peoples of the world if he is willing to sell the future of his children for his personal and immediate comfort and safety.

A second way that oppressed people sometimes deal with oppression is to resort to physical violence and corroding hatred. Violence often brings about momentary results. Nations have frequently won their independence in battle. But in spite of temporary victories, violence never brings permanent peace. It solves no social problem; it merely creates new and more complicated ones.

Violence as a way of achieving racial justice is both impractical and immoral. It is impractical because it is a descending spiral ending in destruction for all. The old law of an eye for an eye leaves everybody blind. It is immoral because it seeks to humiliate the opponent rather than win his understanding; it seeks to annihilate rather than to convert. Violence is immoral because it thrives on hatred rather than love. It destroys community and makes brotherhood impossible. It leaves society in monologue rather than dialogue. Violence ends by defeating itself. It creates bitterness in the survivors and brutality in the destroyers. A voice echoes through time saying to every potential Peter, "Put up your sword."[6] History is cluttered with the wreckage of nations that failed to follow this command.

If the American Negro and other victims of oppression succumb to the temptation of using violence in the struggle for freedom, future generations will be the recipients of a desolate night of bitterness, and our chief legacy to them will be an endless reign of meaningless chaos. Violence is not the way.

The third way open to oppressed people in their quest for freedom is the way of nonviolent resistance. Like the synthesis in **Hegelian** philosophy, the principle of nonviolent resistance seeks to reconcile the truths of two opposites—acquiescence and violence—while avoiding the extremes and immoralities of both. The nonviolent resister agrees with the person who acquiesces that one should not be physically aggressive toward his opponent; but he balances the equation by agreeing with the person of violence that evil must be resisted. He avoids the nonresistance of the former and the violent resistance of the latter. With nonviolent resistance, no individual or group need submit to any wrong, nor need anyone resort to violence in order to right a wrong.

It seems to me that this is the method that must guide the actions of the Negro in the present crisis in race relations. Through nonviolent resistance the Negro will be able to rise to the noble height of opposing the unjust system while loving the perpetrators of the system. The Negro must work passionately and unrelentingly for full **stature** as a citizen, but he must not use inferior methods to gain it. He must never come to terms with falsehood, malice, hate, or destruction.

Visual Vocabulary
German philosopher Georg *Hegel* (hā′ gəl) (1770–1831) proposed the theory that for each idea or concept (thesis) there is an opposite (antithesis), and that these two eventually merge to form a new, unified idea or concept (synthesis).

Reading Strategy Paraphrasing *How does nonviolent resistance reconcile those who abhor injustice and those who abhor violence?*

Literary Element Structure *Notice that King first addresses acquiescence to oppression, then violent resistance, and finally nonviolent resistance. Why does he choose this order for his argument?*

Vocabulary

stature (stach′ ər) n. a level attained; standing; status

---

6. *[Peter . . . sword]* In the New Testament (Matthew 26:52, John 18:11), when the soldiers and priests come to arrest Jesus, the disciple Peter cuts off the ear of the high priest's servant. Jesus condemns this use of violence.

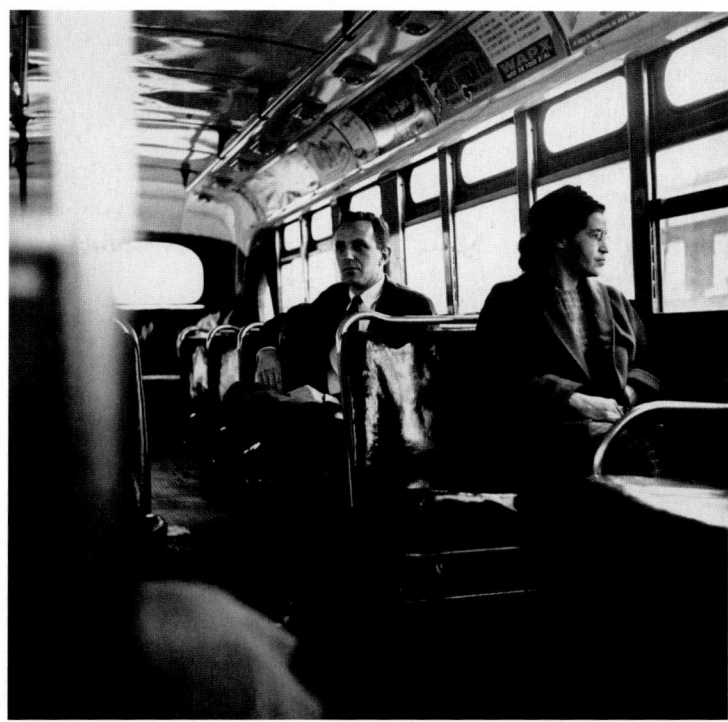

Nonviolent resistance makes it possible for the Negro to remain in the South and struggle for his rights. The Negro's problem will not be solved by running away. He cannot listen to the glib[8] suggestion of those who would urge him to migrate en masse[9] to other sections of the country. By grasping his great opportunity in the South he can make a lasting contribution to the moral strength of the nation and set a sublime example of courage for generations yet unborn.

By nonviolent resistance, the Negro can also enlist all men of good will in his struggle for equality. The problem is not a purely racial one, with Negroes set against whites. In the end, it is not a struggle between people at all, but a tension between justice and injustice. Nonviolent resistance is not aimed against oppressors but against oppression. Under its banner consciences, not racial groups, are enlisted.

If the Negro is to achieve the goal of integration, he must organize himself into a militant and nonviolent mass movement. All three elements are indispensable. The movement for equality and justice can only be a success if it has both a mass and militant character; the barriers to be overcome require both. Nonviolence is an **imperative** in order to bring about ultimate community.

A mass movement of a militant quality that is not at the same time committed to nonviolence tends to generate conflict, which in turn breeds anarchy. The support of the participants and the sympathy of the uncommitted are both inhibited by the threat that bloodshed will engulf the community. This reaction in turn encourages the opposition to threaten and resort to force. When, however, the mass movement **repudiates** violence while moving resolutely toward its goal, its opponents are revealed as the instigators and practitioners of violence if it occurs. Then public support is magnetically attracted to the advocates of nonviolence, while those who employ violence are literally disarmed by overwhelming sentiment against their stand. ⁘

---

8. *Glib* means "offhanded" or "showing little thought or concern."
9. The French expression *en masse* (än mas´) means "in a group" or "all together."

Big Idea An Era of Protest *Why should African Americans remain in the South and struggle for their rights, according to King?*

Literary Element Structure *According to King, how does their opponents' violence tend to ultimately advance the goals of nonviolent resisters?*

Vocabulary

imperative (im per´ ə tiv) *n.* something absolutely necessary; an essential

repudiate (ri pū´ dē āt´) *v.* to refuse to accept as valid; to reject; to renounce

RESPONDING AND THINKING CRITICALLY

Respond

1. What sudden insights did you gain as you read King's arguments? Explain.

Recall and Interpret

2. (a)What does King think about violence as a means for bringing about social change? (b)What does his opinion about violence tell you about King himself?

3. (a)What is nonviolent resistance? (b)How is it similar to and different from both passive acceptance and violent resistance?

4. (a)Against whom or what should nonviolence be aimed, according to King? (b)Why do you suppose King took pains to make this target clear?

Analyze and Evaluate

5. (a)What reasons and evidence does King give to support his claim that "to accept passively an unjust system is to cooperate with that system"? (b)Do you see any flaws with this claim? Explain why or why not.

6. (a)Booker T. Washington said, "I shall allow no man to belittle my soul by making me hate him." How might King respond to this quote? (b)Do you agree with the quote? Why or why not?

7. This selection was first published in 1958. Do you think King's ideas are still relevant today? Explain.

Connect

8. **Big Idea** **An Era of Protest** (a)Considering what you know about the era leading up to the civil rights movement, what would you say was distinctive about King's method of protesting injustice? (b)What qualities would a protestor need to possess in order to follow King's directions?

LITERARY ANALYSIS

Literary Element Structure

The **structure** of persuasive or expository writing may vary. Listing detailed information, using cause and effect, or describing a problem and its solution are some ways of presenting a topic. In this selection, King uses a list to present his points.

1. (a)What does King state in the first sentence? (b)Explain how this sentence helps set up the structure of the entire piece.

2. Would switching the order of King's three points affect his argument? Why or why not?

Review: Allusion

As you learned in Unit 1, an **allusion** is a reference in a work of literature to a character, a place, or a situation from history, music, art, or another work of literature.

Partner Activity With a partner, go back and identify three allusions in the selection. Together, decide which allusion most effectively illustrates King's points, supporting your responses with evidence from the selection. Share your thoughts with the class.

READING AND VOCABULARY

Reading Strategy Paraphrasing

When you **paraphrase**, you put details or ideas from a selection into your own words. Paraphrasing can help you better understand difficult passages.

1. What is the main point of this selection?

2. Which particular passages or details did paraphrasing help you to better understand? Explain.

Vocabulary Practice

Practice with Analogies Choose the word that best completes each analogy below.

1. stature : standing :: background : _____
   a. heritage   **b.** education   **c.** behavior

2. ordeal : survival :: epidemic : _____
   a. disease   **b.** celebration   **c.** health

Literature Online **Web Activities** For eFlashcards, Selection Quick Checks, and other Web activities, go to www.glencoe.com.

Choice: A Tribute to Dr. Martin Luther King Jr.

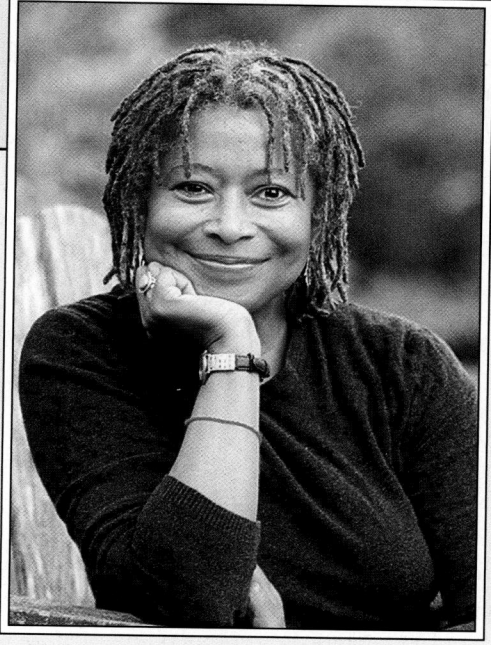

MEET ALICE WALKER

"**W**riting permits me to be more than I am," declares Alice Walker. Born into a poor, rural life in Eatonton, Georgia, Walker had experienced being made to feel less than she was. She knew how it felt to bear the legacy of slavery, racism, and segregation. Her parents and grandparents worked on what had been a plantation, she recalled decades later, toiling "all their lives for barely enough food and shelter to sustain them. They were sharecroppers—landless peasants—the product of whose labor was routinely stolen from them."

"We will be ourselves and free, or die in the attempt. Harriet Tubman was not our great-grandmother for nothing."

—Alice Walker

Early Struggles in the South Awarded a scholarship, Walker entered Spelman College in 1961, at the peak of the Civil Rights movement. There she first met Dr. Martin Luther King Jr. She continued her education at Sarah Lawrence College in New York, and after graduation she worked in the New York City Welfare Department. Returning to the South in 1966, Walker became a Head Start worker in Mississippi and helped organize voter registration in Georgia. Reflecting on the Civil Rights movement, she called it "a time of intense friendships, passions, and loves among the people who came south (or lived there), and who risked everything to change [the] system." She remembers the movement's many triumphs, but she also recalls that the cost "still bruises the heart." In 1967 Walker married a fellow Civil Rights worker. She had to do so in the North, however, for she married a white man and interracial marriage was still illegal in the South.

The Rights of Women Interestingly, the Civil Rights leader whom Walker calls her "spiritual ancestor" is not Dr. King or another figure from the Civil Rights movement, but Sojourner Truth—a former slave who became an abolitionist and advocate for women's rights in the nineteenth century. Walker says it gives her joy to realize she shares her name with Sojourner Truth. *Walker* and *sojourner* can have roughly the same meaning, and *Alice* means "truth" in ancient Greek. Aside from their names, their common bond, Walker says, is a concern not only for the rights of African Americans but also for the rights of women. In fact, much of Walker's writing can be called *womanist*, a term Walker coined to describe work appreciating women's culture, characters, and feelings.

Since the publication of her novel *The Color Purple*, which won both a Pulitzer Prize and an American Book Award and was adapted into a highly successful film, Walker has been a celebrity. Beside novels, she has written short stories, poems, essays, and children's books. She also has won acclaim for her nonfiction work, including *Anything We Love Can Be Saved: A Writer's Activism*.

Alice Walker was born in 1944.

Literature Online Author Search For more about Alice Walker, go to www.glencoe.com.

Connecting to the Speech

Imagine having to leave a place you love, a place where your family and friends have lived for generations. This was the lot of many poor African Americans who were forced from their land in the rural South in order to find enough work to lead decent lives. As you read Walker's speech, think about the following questions:

- What gives the places you love their special quality?
- Where are your family's roots, and how important are they to you?

Building Background

In her speech, Walker gives an abbreviated history of African Americans since the late nineteenth century. She refers to the period after the Civil War called Reconstruction (1865–1877), a time when African Americans enjoyed new rights. Reconstruction ended when Southern whites regained control of state government. In the climate of oppression that followed, millions of African Americans left the South. Walker then shifts her discussion to 1960, when a federal court ordered the University of Georgia to admit African American students. Her final reference is to the desegregation of a Mississippi restaurant. Beginning in 1960, protestors held sit-in demonstrations in restaurants, forcing them to comply with desegregation laws.

Setting Purposes for Reading

Big Idea An Era of Protest

As you read Walker's speech, try to understand the resentment that would naturally build up when a group of people are deprived of basic rights and the means of a decent livelihood over many generations.

Literary Element Anecdote

An **anecdote** is a brief account of an interesting event. As you read, note any anecdotes Walker tells and consider why she uses them.

- See Literary Terms Handbook, p. R1.

Literature Online Interactive Literary Elements Handbook To review or learn more about the literary elements, go to www.glencoe.com.

Reading Strategy Activating Prior Knowledge

As a reader, your **prior knowledge** and personal experiences help you understand a text. While reading Walker's speech, draw upon what you already know to understand the topics she discusses.

Reading Tip: Applying What You Know Use a chart like the one below to help you make connections between Walker's ideas and your prior knowledge.

from "Choice"	What I Know
Yet the history of my family, like that of all black Southerners, is a history of dispossession.	The ancestors of black Southerners were taken from their land in Africa and enslaved in America.

Vocabulary

ancestral (an ses′ trəl) *adj.* of or relating to those from whom one is descended; p. 1155 *My family's ancestral property was sold long ago.*

colossal (kə los′ əl) *adj.* extraordinary in size or degree; enormous; p. 1156 *A colossal wave overturned the ship.*

continuity (kon′ tə noo′ ə tē) *n.* the state or quality of going on without interruption; p. 1156 *If the President dies in office, the Vice President immediately takes over to ensure continuity.*

ephemeral (i fem′ rəl) *adj.* lasting for a very brief time; short-lived; p. 1156 *A rainbow is brilliant but ephemeral.*

Vocabulary Tip: Antonyms When two words have the opposite meaning, we say they are antonyms. The words *complex* and *uncomplicated*, for example, are antonyms. Note that antonyms are always the same part of speech.

INDIANA ACADEMIC STANDARDS (pages 1154–1157)

11.2.2 Analyze the way in which clarity of meaning is affected by the patterns of organization...in the text.

11.2 Develop [reading] strategies...

11.5.3 Write reflective compositions...

Stewart's Farm, 1995. Jonathan Green. Oil on canvas, 48 x 60 in. Collection of the artist.

Choice:
A Tribute to
Dr. Martin Luther King Jr.

Alice Walker

This address was made in 1972 at a Jackson, Mississippi, restaurant that refused to serve people of color until forced to do so by the Civil Rights movement a few years before.

My great-great-great-grandmother walked as a slave from Virginia to Eatonton, Georgia—which passes for the Walker **ancestral** home—with two babies on her hips. She lived to be a hundred and twenty-five years old and my own father knew her as a boy. (It is in memory of this walk that I choose to keep and to embrace my "maiden" name, Walker.)

There is a cemetery near our family church where she is buried; but because her marker was made of wood and rotted years ago, it is impossible to tell exactly where her body lies. In the same cemetery are most of my mother's people, who have lived in Georgia for so long nobody even remembers when they came. And all of my great-aunts and uncles are there, and my grandfather and grandmother, and, very recently, my own father.

If it is true that land does not belong to anyone until they have buried a body in it, then the land of my birthplace belongs to me, dozens of times over. Yet the history of my family, like that of all black Southerners, is a history of dispossession. We loved the land and worked the land, but we never owned it; and even if we bought land, as my great-grandfather did after the Civil War, it was always in danger of being taken away, as his was, during the period following Reconstruction.

My father inherited nothing of material value from his father, and when I came of age in the early sixties I awoke to the bitter knowledge that in order just to continue to love the land of my birth, I was expected to leave it. For black people —including my parents—had learned a long time ago that to stay willingly in a beloved but brutal place is to risk losing the love and being forced to acknowledge only the brutality.

It is a part of the black Southern sensibility that we treasure memories; for such a long time, that is all of our homeland those of us who at one time or another were forced away from it have been allowed to have.

I watched my brothers, one by one, leave our home and leave the South. I watched my sisters do the same. This was not unusual; abandonment, except for memories, was the common thing, except for those who "could not do any better," or those whose strength or stubbornness was so **colossal** they took the risk that others could not bear.

In 1960, my mother bought a television set, and each day after school I watched Hamilton Holmes and Charlayne Hunter as they struggled to integrate—fair-skinned as they were—the University of Georgia. And then, one day, there appeared the face of Dr. Martin Luther King Jr. What a funny name, I thought. At the moment I first saw him, he was being handcuffed and shoved into a police truck. He had dared to claim his rights as a native son, and had been arrested. He displayed no fear, but seemed calm and serene, unaware of his own extraordinary courage. His whole body, like his conscience, was at peace.

At the moment I saw his resistance I knew I would never be able to live in this country without resisting everything that sought to disinherit me, and I would never be forced away from the land of my birth without a fight.

He was The One, The Hero, The One Fearless Person for whom we had waited. I hadn't even realized before that we *had* been waiting for Martin Luther King Jr. but we had. And I knew it for sure when my mother added his name to the list of people she prayed for every night.

I sometimes think that it was literally the prayers of people like my mother and father, who had bowed down in the struggle for such a long time, that kept Dr. King alive until five years ago. For years we went to bed praying for his life, and awoke with the question "Is the 'Lord' still here?"

The public acts of Dr. King you know. They are visible all around you. His voice you would recognize sooner than any other voice you have heard in this century—this in spite of the fact that certain municipal libraries, like the one in downtown Jackson, do not carry recordings of his speeches, and the librarians chuckle cruelly when asked why they do not.

You know, if you have read his books, that his is a complex and revolutionary philosophy that few people are capable of understanding fully or have the patience to embody in themselves. Which is our weakness, which is our loss.

And if you know anything about good Baptist preaching, you can imagine what you missed if you never had a chance to hear Martin Luther King Jr. preach at Ebenezer Baptist Church.

You know of the prizes and awards that he tended to think very little of. And you know of his concern for the disinherited: the American Indian, the Mexican American, and the poor American white—for whom he cared much.

You know that this very room, in this very restaurant, was closed to people of color not more than five years ago. And that we eat here together tonight largely through his efforts and his blood. We accept the common pleasures of life, assuredly, in his name.

But add to all of these things the one thing that seems to me second to none in importance: He gave us back our heritage. He gave us back our homeland; the bones and dust of our ancestors, who may now sleep within our caring *and* our hearing. He gave us the blueness of the Georgia sky in autumn as in summer; the colors of the Southern winter as well as glimpses of the green of vacation-time spring. Those of our relatives we used to invite for a visit we now can ask to stay. . . . He gave us full-time use of our own woods, and restored our memories to those of us who were forced to run away, as realities we might each day enjoy and leave for our children.

He gave us **continuity** of place, without which community is **ephemeral.** He gave us home. ◞

Big Idea **An Era of Protest** *How might a person's concern for the disinherited help make that person a hero during this period?*

Literary Element Anecdote *How does this observation add to the interest of Walker's anecdote?*

Reading Strategy Activating Prior Knowledge *What "public acts" or other facts do you know about Dr. King, and how does that knowledge help you understand this speech better?*

Vocabulary

colossal (kə los′ əl) *adj.* extraordinary in size or degree; enormous

continuity (kon′ tə noo′ ə tē) *n.* the state or quality of going on without interruption

ephemeral (i fem′ rəl) *adj.* lasting for a very brief time; short-lived

RESPONDING AND THINKING CRITICALLY

Respond

1. What ideas in this speech will you remember? Why?

Recall and Interpret

2. (a)Why did the author choose "to keep and to embrace" the name Walker? (b)In what ways is this name more than just a name to her?

3. (a)What circumstances kept Walker's family from owning land? (b)How did the circumstances affect her family history?

4. (a)According to Walker, what was the most important thing Dr. King did for African Americans? (b)From her description of this contribution, what can you infer about Walker and what she values?

Analyze and Evaluate

5. (a)What is the connection between Walker's story about her brothers and sisters leaving the land and what she calls Dr. King's great achievement? (b)If you had been in the audience the day Walker delivered this speech, how do you think this argument would have affected you?

6. (a)How does Walker describe Dr. King to make him seem more than a human being? (b)In your opinion, does she prove that he lived up to this superhuman introduction? Explain.

Connect

7. **Big Idea** **An Era of Protest** On the basis of this speech, how important would you say individual leadership was to the Civil Rights movement? Explain.

LITERARY ANALYSIS

Literary Element Anecdote

Typically, writers use an **anecdote** to entertain, to explain an idea, or to reveal the personality of a character. In this speech, Walker tells an anecdote about seeing Dr. King for the first time.

1. What does this anecdote tell you about Walker as a child?

2. What does it tell you about why Dr. King became a hero to African Americans?

Writing About Literature

Analyze Genre Elements Many speeches reference or celebrate the lives of famous men and women. Compose a speech about a person who has influenced your life. Identify your audience. Then focus on the most important aspects of your subject and grab your listeners' attention with one or two interesting anecdotes.

Literature Online **Web Activities** For eFlashcards, Selection Quick Checks, and other Web activities, go to www.glencoe.com.

READING AND VOCABULARY

Reading Strategy Activating Prior Knowledge

A reader typically brings two types of knowledge to a piece of writing: hard facts and personal experiences.

1. Identify a passage from Walker's speech that interests you. What factual or personal knowledge can you bring to it?

2. Walker's anecdote begins with the purchase of a television set in 1960. List one factual and one personal piece of information that helped you understand this part of the anecdote.

Vocabulary Practice

Practice with Antonyms Identify the antonym for each vocabulary word.

1. ancestral   **a.** modern   **b.** intelligent

2. colossal   **a.** minuscule   **b.** statuary

3. continuity   **a.** lawlessness   **b.** impermanence

4. ephemeral   **a.** dull   **b.** permanent

Vocabulary Workshop

Denotation and Connotation

▶ **Vocabulary Terms**

Loaded words express strong opinions or emotions. Some reveal **bias,** or prejudice. **Hyperbole** is the use of exaggeration to make a point. **Propaganda** is language that may distort the truth to be persuasive.

▶ **Test-Taking Tip**

Ask yourself, "Why did the writer write this? What is his or her point of view?" Once you have established the author's purpose for writing, look for words or phrases that support this stance.

▶ **Reading Handbook**

For more about loaded words, see Reading Handbook, p. R20.

eFlashcards For eFlashcards and other vocabulary activities, go to www.glencoe.com.

ACADEMIC STANDARDS (page 1158)
11.1.2 Draw inferences about the meaning of vocabulary in literature or other subject areas...

Recognizing Loaded Words

"He displayed no fear, but seemed calm and serene, unaware of his own extraordinary courage. His whole body, like his conscience, was at peace."

　　　—Alice Walker, from "Choice: A Tribute to Dr. Martin Luther King Jr."

Connecting to Literature This passage describes Martin Luther King Jr. when Alice Walker first saw him. It leaves no doubt that she admires Dr. King. The words and phrases she has chosen—*calm, serene, "extraordinary courage"*—all help her sing his praises. "Loaded words" such as these can make speech and writing powerful and persuasive. We encounter them at political rallies, on TV commercials, in the editorial pages of our newspapers, and in our own everyday conversation. Loaded words are powerful weapons. It is important to know how to use them responsibly.

There are different kinds of loaded words.

- Language that expresses an author's prejudice demonstrates **bias.** Try substituting *bold* for *reckless* in the statement below. Note how *bold* produces a positive bias, while *reckless* suggests disapproval.
  One particularly <u>reckless</u> young protestor scaled the White House fence.

- Exaggerated language used to make a point is referred to as **hyperbole.**
  <u>All the police dogs in the world</u> could not have stopped this demonstration.

- Language that may distort the truth in order to influence the public is known as **propaganda.**
  <u>Communists</u> and other <u>anti-American elements</u> infiltrated the Civil Rights Movement in order to <u>betray</u> our nation's values.

Exercise

From the loaded words or phrases that follow the paragraph below, select those that best support the author's opposition to a war.

　　This was no one's idea of a just war. It was a war conceived by **1.** _____ politicians, who watched from their **2.** _____ as **3.** _____ of our finest young men marched to their deaths. It was a conflict that finally revealed the rulers of the "free world" to be little more than **4.** _____.

1. a. brilliant　　**b.** cynical　　**c.** elected

2. a. workplaces　　**b.** homes　　**c.** ivory towers

3. a. a generation　　**b.** many　　**c.** several

4. a. war criminals　　**b.** ordinary people　　**c.** heroes

from *Working*
Roberto Acuna, Farm Worker

MEET STUDS TERKEL

Would you report on the March on Washington and leave out Martin Luther King Jr.'s "I Have a Dream" speech? That's what Studs Terkel did. Rather than focus on the typical center of attention, he depicted a group of people from Chicago as they rode to and from the famous 1963 civil rights gathering. While other reporters and newscasters deluged the public with stories of heroes and big events, Terkel quietly explored the motivations, choices, dilemmas, and dreams of everyday people.

Born Louis Terkel in New York, Terkel spent most of his life in Chicago. He borrowed the nickname "Studs" from a fictional Chicago character, Studs Lonigan. Although he received a law degree, he took a job in radio. He moved from acting on radio soap operas to writing radio shows to eventually having his own show.

Interviews and Oral Histories As a talk show host on Chicago radio, Terkel brought a natural talent to the job of interviewing. His skill, which grew with practice, translated well to the work for which he has become most famous, collecting oral histories. His first book of oral histories, *Division Street: America,* was published in 1967. This collection of more than seventy interviews with Chicago residents focuses on the topic of the gap between rich and poor. As one critic noted, the experience of reading the book is a lot like "eavesdropping or reading people's diaries."

What Terkel did in *Division Street* was the same thing he would do again and again: interview "real people" about real-life events and lay the bits and pieces of their lives out before the American reading public. He reflected, through interviews, on the American dream. And, perhaps most famously of all, he collected a world of insight into how Americans felt about their working lives.

A Voice of Protest Terkel's work is both history and commentary. Terkel spoke out early in the struggle against Jim Crow laws, poll taxes, and economic inequality. His work also expresses great empathy for the "working man" and the working class.

> "I was constantly astonished by the extraordinary dreams of ordinary people. No matter how bewildering the times, . . . those we call ordinary are aware of a sense of personal worth—or more often a lack of it—in the work they do."
>
> —Studs Terkel

With his sympathetic ear for the voices of real people, Studs Terkel influenced a whole generation of radio talk show hosts and had a powerful effect on the interviewing style on popular public radio shows. In 1985, he won the Pulitzer Prize in nonfiction for *The Good War: An Oral History of World War II.* Terkel continues to work, interview, and listen.

Studs Terkel was born in 1912.

Literature Online Author Search For more about Studs Terkel, go to www.glencoe.com.

Connecting to the Interview

Almost everyone has to work, but not everyone feels good about his or her job. What factors can make a job satisfying or unbearable? As you read this account of life as a farm worker during the 1960s, think about the following questions:

- What do people hope to find in a job?
- What working conditions do you think should be guaranteed to all workers?

Building Background

This interview comes from a collection called *Working: People Talk About What They Do All Day and How They Feel About What They Do.* It comprises several dozen interviews with people from all walks of life. Because Terkel regarded his interactions with workers as "conversations," most selections, like the one you will read, do not have a traditional interview format. Rather they consist of excerpts and fragments. Changes in type (from roman, or "regular," type to italics) show where one train of thought or part of the conversation leaves off and another begins.

Setting Purposes for Reading

Big Idea An Era of Protest

As you read this excerpt from *Working,* focus on the aspects of life that Roberto Acuna found most difficult to accept and those that he found were most in need of change.

Literary Element Oral History

Oral History is history that passes by word of mouth and begins with those who actually lived it. As you read the interview with Roberto Acuna, think about how the thoughts of an ordinary farm worker help you understand the events, as well as the hopes and frustrations, of farm workers in the 1960s.

- See Literary Terms Handbook, p. R12.

Literature Online Interactive Literary Elements Handbook To review or learn more about the literary elements, go to www.glencoe.com.

Reading Strategy Analyzing Cause-and-Effect Relationships

When you **analyze cause-and-effect relationships,** you look for the causes or reasons why something happened and relate them to the effects or results. A single cause can have any number of effects. Sometimes, causes and effects are linked together in a chain: one effect causes the next, like a falling domino knocking over the next domino in a line.

Reading Tip: Taking Notes Use a chart to record cause-and-effect relationships as you read.

Cause	Effect
picking lettuce	swollen, callused hands
falling behind at work	foreman puts pressure on worker

Vocabulary

civic (siv′ik) *adj.* related to citizenship; p. 1162 *Voting is a civic responsibility.*

degrading (di grā′ding) *adj.* tending to drag down in character or social status; p. 1163 *Having to ride in the back of the bus was degrading.*

compensation (kom′pən sa′shən) *n.* payment; p. 1166 *The compensation for babysitting depends on how long you work.*

solidarity (sol′ə dar′ə tē) *n.* unity of a group that produces a sense of community; p. 1166 *Their sense of solidarity helped them work together for voting rights.*

stipulate (stip′yə lāt′) *v.* to require or demand as part of an agreement; p. 1167 *The negotiators stipulate four requirements for a successful treaty.*

INDIANA ACADEMIC STANDARDS (pages 1160–1169)

11.2.1 Analyze...the features...of public documents...

11.2 Develop [reading] strategies...

11.5.2 Write responses to literature that demonstrate a comprehensive understanding of the significant ideas...

from

Working

Roberto Acuna, Farm Worker

Studs Terkel

I walked out of the fields two years ago. I saw the need to change the California feudal system,[1] to change the lives of farm workers, to make these huge corporations feel they're not above anybody. I am thirty-four years old and I try to organize for the United Farm Workers of America.

His hands are calloused and each of his thumbnails is singularly[2] cut. "If you're picking lettuce, the thumbnails fall off 'cause they're banged on the box. Your hands get swollen. You can't slow down because the foreman[3] sees you're so many boxes behind and you'd better get on. But people would help each other. If you're feeling bad that day, somebody who's feeling pretty good would help. Any people that are

suffering have to stick together, whether they like it or not, whether they be black, brown, or pink."

According to Mom, I was born on a cotton sack out in the fields, 'cause she had no money to go to the hospital. When I was a child, we used to migrate from California to Arizona and back and forth. The things I saw shaped my life. I remember when we used to go out and pick carrots and onions, the whole family. We tried to scratch a livin' out of the ground. I saw my parents cry out in despair, even though we had the whole family working. At the time, they were paying sixty-two and a half cents an hour. The average income must have been fifteen hundred dollars, maybe two thousand.[4]

---

1. A *California feudal system* is a bitter metaphor comparing the use of serfs on feudal manors in the Middle Ages to the use of farm workers by growers in California.
2. *Singularly* means "oddly."
3. A *foreman* is any leader of a work crew.

4. Acuna adds: "Today, because of our struggles, the pay is up to two dollars an hour. Yet we know that is not enough."

Literary Element   Oral History *In what ways is the speaker an ordinary person or "common man"?*

This was supplemented[5] by child labor. During those years, the growers used to have a Pick-Your-Harvest Week. They would get all the migrant kids out of school and have 'em out there pickin' the crops at peak harvest time. A child was off that week and when he went back to school, he got a little gold star. They would make it seem like something **civic** to do.

We'd pick everything: lettuce, carrots, onions, cucumbers, cauliflower, broccoli, tomatoes—all the salads you could make out of vegetables, we picked 'em. Citrus fruits, watermelons—you name it. We'd be in Salinas about four months. From there we'd go down into the Imperial Valley. From there we'd go to picking citrus. It was like a cycle. We'd follow the seasons.

After my dad died, my mom would come home and she'd go into her tent and I would go into ours. We'd roughhouse and everything and then we'd go into the tent where Mom was sleeping and I'd see her crying. When I asked her why she was crying she never gave me an answer. All she said was things would get better. She retired a beaten old lady with a lot of dignity. That day she thought would be better never came for her.

"One time, my mom was in bad need of money, so she got a part-time evening job in a restaurant. I'd be helping her. All the growers would come in and they'd be laughing, making nasty remarks, and make passes at her. I used to go out there and kick 'em and my mom told me to leave 'em alone, she could handle 'em. But they would embarrass her and she would cry.

"My mom was a very proud woman. She brought us up without any help from nobody. She kept the family strong. They say that a family that prays together stays together. I say that a family that works together stays together—because of the suffering. My mom couldn't speak English too good. Or much Spanish, for that matter. She wasn't educated. But she knew some prayers and she used to make us say

them. That's another thing: when I see the many things in this world and this country, I could tear the churches apart. I never saw a priest out in the fields trying to help people. Maybe in these later years they're doing it. But it's always the church taking from the people.

"We were once asked by the church to bring vegetables to make it a successful bazaar. After we got the stuff there, the only people havin' a good time were the rich people because they were the only ones that were buyin' the stuff . . ."

I'd go barefoot to school. The bad thing was they used to laugh at us, the Anglo kids. They would laugh because we'd bring tortillas and frijoles[6] to lunch. They would have their nice little compact lunch boxes with cold milk in their thermos and they'd laugh at us because all we had was dried tortillas. Not only would they laugh at us, but the kids would pick fights. My older brother used to do most of the fighting for us and he'd come home with black eyes all the time.

What really hurt is when we had to go on welfare. Nobody knows the erosion of man's dignity. They used to have a label of canned goods that said, "U.S. Commodities.[7] Not to be sold or exchanged." Nobody knows how proud it is to feel when you bought canned goods with your own money.

"I wanted to be accepted. It must have been in sixth grade. It was just before the Fourth of July. They were trying out students for this patriotic play. I wanted to do Abe Lincoln, so I learned the Gettysburg Address inside and out. I'd be out in the fields pickin' the crops and I'd be memorizin'. I was the only one who didn't have to read the part, 'cause I learned it. The part was given to a girl who was a grower's daughter. She had to read it out of a book, but they said she had better diction.

---

5. *Supplemented* means "added to."

Reading Strategy Analyzing Cause-and-Effect Relationships *What kept migrant workers on the move?*

Vocabulary

civic (siv′ ik) *adj.* related to citizenship

---

6. *Tortillas* are thin, flat, unleavened bread. *Frijoles* is the Spanish word for beans.
7. *Commodities* are goods.

Big Idea An Era of Protest *In addition to the work, what else strikes Roberto Acuna as unfair?*

Literary Element Oral History *How do both the meaning and the language of this comment reveal what type of person Acuna is?*

I was very disappointed. I quit about eighth grade.

"Any time anybody'd talk to me about politics, about civil rights, I would ignore it. It's a very **degrading** thing because you can't express yourself. They wanted us to speak English in the school classes. We'd put out a real effort. I would get into a lot of fights because I spoke Spanish and they couldn't understand it. I was punished. I was kept after school for not speaking English."

We used to have our own tents on the truck. Most migrants would live in the tents that were already there in the fields, put up by the company. We got one for ourselves, secondhand, but it was ours. Anglos[8] used to laugh at us. "Here comes the carnival," they'd say. We couldn't keep our clothes clean, we couldn't keep nothing clean, because we'd go by the dirt roads and the dust. We'd stay outside the town.

I never did want to go to town because it was a very bad thing for me. We used to go to the small stores, even though we got clipped[9] more. If we went to the other stores, they would laugh at us. They would always point at us with a finger. We'd go to town maybe every two weeks to get what we needed. Everybody would walk in a bunch. We were afraid. (Laughs.) We sang to keep our spirits up. We joked about our poverty. This one guy would say, "When I get to be rich, I'm gonna marry an Anglo woman, so I can be accepted into society." The other guy would say, "When I get rich I'm gonna marry a Mexican woman, so I can go to that Anglo society of yours and see them hang you for marrying an Anglo." Our world was around the fields.

Filipino migrant workers cut lettuce in a field of the Imperial Valley of California, 1939. Dorothea Lange.

I started picking crops when I was eight. I couldn't do much, but every little bit counts. Every time I would get behind on my chores, I would get a carrot thrown at me by my parents. I would daydream: If I were a millionaire, I would buy all these ranches and give them back to the people. I would picture my mom living in one area all the time and being admired by all the people in the community. All of a sudden I'd be rudely awaken by a broken carrot in my back. That would bust your whole dream apart and you'd work for a while and come back to daydreaming.

We used to work early, about four o'clock in the morning. We'd pick the harvest until about six. Then we'd run home and get into our supposedly clean clothes and run all the way to school because we'd be late. By the time we got to school, we'd be all tuckered out.[10] Around maybe eleven o'clock, we'd be dozing off. Our teachers would send notes to the house telling Mom that we were inattentive. The only thing I'd make fairly good grades on was spelling. I couldn't do anything else. Many times we never did our homework, because we were out in the fields. The teachers couldn't understand that. I would get whacked there also.

School would end maybe four o'clock. We'd rush home again, change clothes, go back to work until seven, seven thirty at night. That's

---

8. *Anglos* refers to people who do not have a Hispanic or Latino heritage.
9. Here, *clipped* is an informal way of saying "cheated."

Reading Strategy Analyzing Cause-and-Effect Relationships *What was one reason why Anglos made fun of migrant workers?*

Vocabulary

degrading (di grā′ ding) *adj.* tending to drag down in character or social status

---

10. *Tuckered out* means "exhausted."

A migrant Mexican field worker's home on the edge of a frozen pea field in California's Imperial Valley, 1937. Dorothea Lange.

not counting the weekends. On Saturday and Sunday, we'd be there from four thirty in the morning until about seven thirty in the evening. This is where we made the money, those two days. We all worked.

I would carry boxes for my mom to pack the carrots in. I would pull the carrots out and she would sort them into different sizes. I would get water for her to drink. When you're picking tomatoes, the boxes are heavy. They weigh about thirty pounds. They're dropped very hard on the trucks so they have to be sturdy.

The hardest work would be thinning and hoeing with a short-handled hoe. The fields would be about a half a mile long. You would be bending and stooping all day. Sometimes you would have hard ground and by the time you got home, your hands would be full of calluses. And you'd have a backache. Sometimes I wouldn't have dinner or anything. I'd just go home and fall asleep and wake up just in time to go out to the fields again.

I remember when we just got into California from Arizona to pick up the carrot harvest. It was very cold and very windy out in the fields.

We just had a little old blanket for the four of us kids in the tent. We were freezin' our tail off. So I stole two brand-new blankets that belonged to a grower. When we got under those blankets it was nice and comfortable. Somebody saw me. The next morning the grower told my mom he'd turn us in unless we gave him back his blankets—sterilized.[11] So my mom and I and my kid brother went to the river and cut some wood and made a fire and boiled the water and she scrubbed the blankets. She hung them out to dry, ironed them, and sent them back to the grower. We got a spanking for that.

I remember this labor camp that was run by the city. It was a POW[12] camp for German soldiers. They put families in there and it would have barbed wire all around it. If you were out after ten o'clock at night, you couldn't get back in until the next day at four in the morning. We didn't know the rules. Nobody told us. We went to visit some relatives. We got back at about ten thirty and they wouldn't let us in. So we slept in the pickup outside the gate. In the morning, they let us in, we had a fast breakfast and went back to work in the fields.[13]

The grower would keep the families apart, hoping they'd fight against each other. He'd have three or four camps and he'd have the people over here pitted against the people over there. For jobs. He'd give the best crops to the people he thought were the fastest workers. This way he kept us going harder and harder, competing.

When I was sixteen, I had my first taste as a foreman. Handling braceros,[14] aliens, that came from Mexico to work. They'd bring these people

---

11. Here, *sterilized* means "free from germs."
12. *POW* stands for prisoner of war.
13. Acuna adds: "Since we started organizing, this camp has been destroyed. They started building housing on it."
14. A *bracero* is a Mexican citizen who comes to the U.S. temporarily to do agricultural labor.

Big Idea An Era of Protest *What reasons for protest are implied in these facts and other facts on this page?*

Literary Element Oral History *What does this oral history tell you that a history of U.S. agriculture might not tell?*

Literary Element Oral History *Why would it be unusual to hear this point of view in a traditional history?*

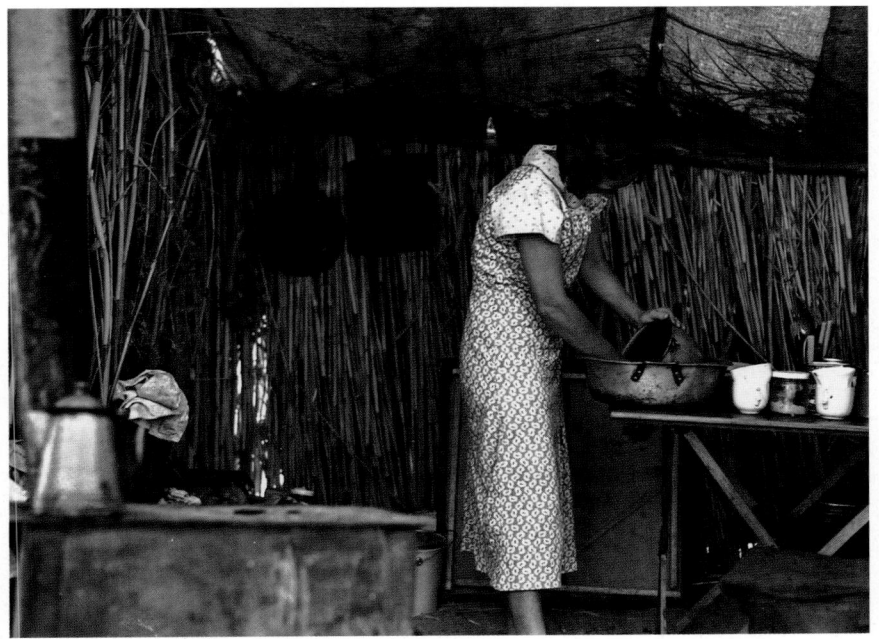

A woman cooking in a camp for migrant agricultural workers. Imperial Valley, California, February-March 1937. Dorothea Lange.

to work over here and then send them back to Mexico after the season was over. My job was to make sure they did a good job and pushin' 'em even harder. I was a company man, yes. My parents needed money and I wanted to make sure they were proud of me. A foreman is recognized. I was very naïve. Even though I was pushing the workers, I knew their problems. They didn't know how to write, so I would write letters home for them. I would take 'em to town, buy their clothes, outside of the company stores. They had paid me $1.10 an hour. The farm workers' wage was raised to eighty-two and a half cents. But even the braceros were making more money than me, because they were working piecework.[15] I asked for more money. The manager said, "If you don't like it you can quit." I quit and joined the Marine Corps.

"I joined the Marine Corps at seventeen. I was very mixed up. I wanted to become a first-class citizen. I wanted to be accepted and I was very proud of my uniform. My mom didn't want to sign the papers, but she knew I had to better myself and maybe I'd get an education in the services.

"I did many jobs. I took a civil service exam and was very proud when I passed. Most of the others were college kids. There were only three Chicanos in the group of sixty. I got a job as a correctional officer in a state prison. I quit after eight months because I couldn't take the misery I saw. They wanted me to use a rubber hose on some of the prisoners—mostly Chicanos and blacks. I couldn't do it. They called me chicken-livered because I didn't want to hit nobody. They constantly harassed me after that. I didn't quit because I was afraid of them but because they were trying to make me into a mean man. I couldn't see it. This was Soledad State Prison."

I began to see how everything was so wrong. When growers can have an intricate watering system to irrigate their crops but they can't have running water inside the houses of workers. Veterinarians tend to the needs of domestic animals but they can't have medical care for the workers. They can have land subsidies[16] for the growers but they can't have adequate unemployment compensation for the workers. They treat him like a farm implement. In fact, they treat their implements better and their domestic animals better. They have heat and insulated barns for the animals but the workers live in beat-up shacks with no heat at all.

Illness in the fields is 120 percent higher than the average rate for industry. It's mostly back trouble, rheumatism and arthritis, because the damp weather and the cold. Stoop labor is very hard on a person. Tuberculosis is high. And now because of the pesticides, we have many respiratory diseases.

The University of California at Davis has government experiments with pesticides and chemicals. To get a bigger crop each year. They haven't any regard as to what safety precautions are needed. In 1964 or '65, an airplane was spraying these chemicals on the fields. Spraying rigs

---

15. *Piecework* is work paid by the amount done, rather than by the hour.

Reading Strategy Analyzing Cause-and-Effect Relationships *Why do you think Acuna joined the Marine Corps?*

16. *Subsidies* are grants of money from the government to companies or private individuals for projects that serve the public interest.

Big Idea An Era of Protest *What does Acuna view as wrong?*

they're called. Flying low, the wheels got tangled on the fence wire. The pilot got up, dusted himself off, and got a drink of water. He died of convulsions. The ambulance attendants got violently sick because of the pesticides he had on his person. A little girl was playing around a sprayer. She stuck her tongue on it. She died instantly.

These pesticides affect the farm worker through the lungs. He breathes it in. He gets no **compensation**. All they do is say he's sick. They don't investigate the cause.

There were times when I felt I couldn't take it any more. It was 105 in the shade and I'd see endless rows of lettuce and I felt my back hurting . . . I felt the frustration of not being able to get out of the fields. I was getting ready to jump any foreman who looked at me cross-eyed. But until two years ago, my world was still very small.

I would read all these things in the papers about Cesar Chavez[17] and I would denounce[18] him because I still had that thing about becoming a first-class patriotic citizen. In Mexicali they would pass out leaflets and I would throw 'em away. I never participated. The grape boycott[19] didn't affect me much because I was in lettuce. It wasn't until Chavez came to Salinas, where I was working in the fields, that I saw what a beautiful man he was. I went to this rally,[20] I still intended to stay with the company. But something—I don't know—I was close to the workers. They couldn't speak English and wanted me to be their spokesman in favor of going on strike. I don't know—I

just got caught up with it all, the beautiful feeling of **solidarity**.

You'd see the people on the picket lines at four in the morning, at the camp fires, heating up beans and coffee and tortillas. It gave me a sense of belonging. These were my own people and they wanted change. I knew this is what I was looking for. I just didn't know it before.

My mom had always wanted me to better myself. I wanted to better myself because of her. Now when the strikes started, I told her I was going to join the union and the whole movement. I told her I was going to work without pay. She said she was proud of me. (His eyes glisten. A long, long pause.) See, I told her I wanted to be with my people. If I were a company man,[21] nobody would like me any more. I had to belong to somebody and this was it right here. She said,

---

17. *Cesar Chavez* (1927-1993) was an activist and community organizer who helped unionize farm workers.

18. Here, *denounce* means "criticize."

19. The *grape boycott* was a successful national effort to persuade citizens not to buy table grapes so that growers would give in to workers' demands for better wages and conditions.

20. Here, a *rally* is a large meeting for the purpose of creating enthusiasm.

---

21. A *company man* is a worker who unquestioningly carries out the policies of an employer.

"I pushed you in your early years to try to better yourself and get a social position. But I see that's not the answer. I know I'll be proud of you."

All kinds of people are farm workers, not just Chicanos. Filipinos started the strike. We have Puerto Ricans and Appalachians too, Arabs, some Japanese, some Chinese. At one time they used us against each other. But now they can't and they're scared, the growers. They can organize conglomerates.[22] Yet when we try organization to better our lives, they are afraid. Suffering people never dreamed it could be different. Cesar Chavez tells them this and they grasp the idea—and this is what scares the growers.

Now the machines are coming in. It takes skill to operate them. But anybody can be taught. We feel migrant workers should be given the chance. They got one for grapes. They got one for lettuce. They have cotton machines that took jobs away from thousands of farm workers. The people wind up in the ghettos of the city, their culture, their families, their unity destroyed.

We're trying to **stipulate** it in our contract that the company will not use any machinery without the consent of the farm workers. So we can make sure the people being replaced by the machines will know how to operate the machines.

Working in the fields is not in itself a degrading job. It's hard, but if you're given regular hours, better pay, decent housing, unemployment and medical compensation, pension plans[23]—we have a very relaxed way of living. But the growers don't recognize us as persons. That's the worst thing, the way they treat you. Like we have no

An unidentified Mexican shows his permit to cross the border and work in the fields of South Texas under the Brancero program. The federal government has now decided to keep the Mexican Brancero south of the border. August 1964.

brains. Now we see they have no brains. They have only a wallet in their head. The more you squeeze it, the more they cry out.

If we had proper compensation we wouldn't have to be working seventeen hours a day and following the crops. We could stay in one area and it would give us roots. Being a migrant, it tears the family apart. You get in debt. You leave the area penniless. The children are the ones hurt the most. They go to school three months in one place and then on to another. No sooner do they make friends, they are uprooted again. Right here, your childhood is taken away. So when they grow up, they're looking for this childhood they have lost.

If people could see—in the winter, ice on the fields. We'd be on our knees all day long. We'd build fires and warm up real fast and go back onto the ice. We'd be picking watermelons in 105 degrees all day long. When people have melons or cucumber or carrots or lettuce, they don't know how they got on their table and the consequences to the people who picked it. If I had enough money, I would take busloads of people out to the fields and into the labor camps. Then they'd know how that fine salad got on their table.

---

22. *Conglomerates* are large corporations made up of many different types of companies.
23. A *pension* is a fixed sum paid regularly to someone after retirement.

Vocabulary

stipulate (stip′ yə lāt′) *v.* to require or demand as part of an agreement

Literary Element Oral History *In what ways does this sound like the real voice of a real person?*

RESPONDING AND THINKING CRITICALLY

Respond

1. Is Roberto Acuna like anyone you know, or is he completely unlike anyone you've ever met? Explain.

Recall and Interpret

2. (a)How old was Acuna when he became a farm worker? (b)Why did he become a farm worker at such an early age?

3. (a)What did Acuna do as a foreman? (b)How did he feel about the work?

4. (a)How did Acuna react when people first talked to him about politics and civil rights? (b)Why didn't Acuna get involved at first?

Analyze and Evaluate

5. (a)In your opinion, what was the most difficult part of Acuna's life? Support your answer with details

from the story. (b)How does hearing about Acuna in his own voice help you understand the challenges he faced?

6. (a)What was Acuna's childhood like? (b)How well does the interview communicate the details and feelings of that time in his life? Use details from the selection in your answer.

7. Studs Terkel once said, "Poor people never lose hope. They can't afford to." How well does this opinion relate to the life of Roberto Acuna as recounted in *Working*?

Connect

8. **Big Idea** **An Era of Protest** Do you regard this selection more as a work of protest or as an ordinary narrative of a working life? Explain.

Literary Element Oral History

This **oral history** is brimming with details, large and small, told almost exclusively in the first person. The use of the pronouns *I, we, me, my,* and *mine* help create an intimate voice, a voice that may seem to be talking only to you, or from the pages of a diary.

1. How does the use of the first person help you hear Acuna's voice and understand his history? Cite at least one example.

2. Name one or more other places in the narrative where you feel as if you are listening to a real person. Explain why.

Review: Structure

Structure is the particular order or pattern a writer uses to present ideas. Fiction and nonfiction narratives are mainly chronological in structure. Other nonfiction works often use a combination of structures, including cause and effect, main idea and details, problem and solution, and other patterns.

1. In addition to cause-and-effect and chronological order, what other organizational methods do you find in this interview? Name one method and identify the page and paragraph where you find it.

2. This selection is presented as a series of recollections rather than one simple story told from beginning to end. What advantages and disadvantages do you see to this structure?

Partner Activity Choose one passage of three or more paragraphs and work with a classmate to analyze its structure.

Passage begins with . . .	Pattern or Order
One time, my mom . . .	chronological
My mom was a very . . .	
We were once asked . . .	

Reading Strategy Analyzing Cause-and-Effect Relationships

Sometimes, events are related in a chain. In some ways, Roberto Acuna's life is a **chain of events** rather than a series of unrelated causes and effects. Review the cause-and-effect chart you filled in as you read the selection and also reflect on the selection as a whole.

1. In the first paragraph, you learn that Acuna organizes for the United Farm Workers. Name at least three events in the chain of events that led to this work.

2. Write or sketch a cause-and-effect chain that shows how a person might make progress as a farm worker. Base your work on the text.

Vocabulary Practice

Practice with Context Clues Read the following sentences and then decide which of the choices is closest in meaning to the boldfaced word.

1. Many consider voting a **civic** duty.
   a. related to joy   **b.** related to citizenship
2. The company president faced the **degrading** prospect of going to prison.
   a. humiliating   **b.** unfair
3. The **compensation** for that job is too low.
   a. payment   **b.** entry level
4. All the marchers at the rally felt a sense of **solidarity.**
   a. fear   **b.** unity
5. The workers **stipulate** higher pay as a term of their contract.
   a. reject   **b.** require

Academic Vocabulary

Here are two words from the vocabulary list on page R86. These words will help you think, write, and talk about the selection.

recover (ri kuv′ ər) *v.* to get back

transport (trans pôrt′) *v.* to carry or transfer from one place to another

Practice and Apply
1. How does Acuna **recover** his pride?
2. Why was Acuna's mother not **transported** to a hospital when she was in labor with her son?

Writing About Literature

Explore Author's Purpose What was Studs Terkel's purpose in presenting this interview? Does his method of presenting a somewhat free-form oral history serve this purpose best? If so, why? Do you think another method might work better? Present your answer in a persuasive essay.

Begin by identifying and stating your opinion in a clear thesis statement. Then gather evidence from the essay that supports your point of view.

START

Introduction ····▸ Introduce the topic and present a thesis with your opinion.

Body ····▸ Present supporting evidence from the selection. Relate all your evidence to your thesis.

Conclusion ····▸ End by summarizing your position and adding a clincher statement or other insight.

FINISH

After you complete your draft, have a peer read it and suggest revisions. Then proofread and edit your work for errors in spelling, grammar, and punctuation.

Literary Criticism

The review of *Working* in *Business Week* magazine proclaimed that "the people we meet [in *Working*] are not digits in a poll but real people with real names who share their anecdotes, adventures, and aspirations with us." Why might portraying working people in an oral history be a better medium than a poll or survey? What advantages might a survey have over an oral history for presenting information on jobs in the United States? Write a paragraph describing the advantages and disadvantages of using oral histories to describe people's jobs.

Literature Online **Web Activities** For eFlashcards, Selection Quick Checks, and other Web activities, go to www.glencoe.com.

Grammar Workshop

Sentence Structure

▶ **Vocabulary Terms**

A **run-on sentence** occurs when two or more complete sentences are written as through they were one sentence.

▶ **Test-Taking Tip**

When writing in a test-taking situation, return to any sentences that present more than one thought. Check carefully to be sure that each clause has proper punctuation and any necessary conjunctions.

▶ **Language Handbook**

For more about run-on sentences, see the Language Handbook, p. R51.

eWorkbooks To link to the Grammar and Language eWorkbook, go to www.glencoe. com.

■ **ACADEMIC STANDARDS (page 1170)**

11.6.1 Demonstrate control of... sentence structure...

11.6.4 Correctly use clauses...and the mechanics of punctuation...

Avoiding Run-On Sentences

"They didn't know how to write, so I would write letters home for them."

—Studs Terkel, "Roberto Acuna, Farm Worker"

Connecting to Literature Connecting ideas are presented in a **compound sentence**—a sentence with two or more main clauses. Carelessness with compound sentences, however, can lead to **run-on sentences,** which are two or more complete sentences written as though they were one sentence.

Note the following run-on sentence problems and their solutions.

Problem 1 Two main clauses are separated by only a comma.

Everybody would walk in a bunch, we were afraid.

Problem 2 Two main clauses do not have punctuation between them.

I knew this was what I was looking for I just did not know it before.

Solution A Break the sentence into two short sentences.

Everybody would walk in a bunch. We were afraid.

I knew this was what I was looking for. I just did not know it before.

Solution B Separate the clauses with a semicolon.

Everybody would walk in a bunch; we were afraid.

I knew this was what I was looking for; I just did not know it before.

Solution C Add a coordinating conjunction after the comma.

Everybody would walk in a bunch, for we were afraid.

I knew this was what I was looking for, but I just did not know it before.

Problem 3 Two main clauses do not have a comma before the coordinating conjunction.

He gets no compensation and all they do is say that he is sick.

Solution Add a comma before the coordinating conjunction.

He gets no compensation, and all they do is say that he is sick.

Exercise

Rewrite these sentences, applying one of the solutions shown above.

1. When you are picking tomatoes, the boxes are heavy they weigh about thirty pounds.
2. I would pull the carrots out and she would sort them.
3. Sometimes you would have hard ground, by the time you got home, your hands would be full of calluses.

Comparing Literature *Across Time and Place*

Connecting to the Reading Selections

War has always been part of the human experience. What would your life be like if it were touched by war? The three writers compared here—Tim O'Brien, Tran Mong Tu, and Pin Yathay—explore how war affects individuals swept up in its complex events. In the following selections, they describe the horrors of war and its tragic consequences.

COMPARING THE `BIG IDEA` An Era of Protest

People protest, or voice objections, in different ways. Some hold vigils; others march together, waving banners or placards. Still others create literature to change minds and stir hearts. Tim O'Brien, Tran Mong Tu, and Pin Yathay protest war by showing their readers its human cost.

COMPARING Themes

The **theme** is the central message of a work of literature—an insight that readers can apply to their own lives. Each of these writers uses literary elements to convey a theme about war and its consequences.

COMPARING Cultures

Tim O'Brien, Tran Mong Tu, and Pin Yathay all belong to different cultures, each of which influences the writer's message significantly. Through their choice of words and details, the writers invite readers to enter their worlds, relive their experiences, and share their messages.

Ambush

MEET TIM O'BRIEN

Recognized as one of the major writers on the Vietnam War, Tim O'Brien has earned both critical and popular acclaim for his novels, short stories, and nonfiction works. His writing often describes the experiences of ordinary soldiers in Vietnam and explores philosophical issues, such as the meaning of courage, duty, and honor.

As a political science major at Macalester College in Minnesota, O'Brien protested the U.S. military involvement in Vietnam and supported a peace candidate, Senator Eugene McCarthy, for president. Then, shortly after his college graduation, O'Brien received a draft notice. For the rest of that summer, he struggled with his conscience trying to decide what to do. He considered escaping to Canada, where many other war protesters had fled. Finally, he decided to report for induction and enter the service, thereby honoring a family tradition.

"The object of storytelling, like the object of magic, is not to explain or to resolve, but rather to create and to perform miracles of the imagination."

—Tim O'Brien

Soldier and Writer Beginning in 1968, O'Brien spent just over a year in Quang Ngai Province, Vietnam, as an infantryman and as a clerk. He became a sergeant and earned several medals, including the Purple Heart, an award given to U.S. soldiers wounded or killed in battle. While stationed in Vietnam, O'Brien kept a journal, recording his observations and impressions. These journal entries later furnished material for his books. His first book, *If I Die in a Combat Zone, Box Me Up and Ship Me Home* (1973), is a memoir of his tour of duty in Vietnam.

Writer of War Stories In 1978, O'Brien wrote a novel called *Going After Cacciato* (kä chä′ tō), about a soldier who simply decides to walk away from the Vietnam War one day. O'Brien won the National Book Award for this novel in 1979. He was also nominated for a Pulitzer Prize for his short-story collection, *The Things They Carried* (1990).

O'Brien's fiction has been compared to that of Stephen Crane, Ernest Hemingway, Joseph Heller, and others who have written about war. Like those authors, he builds a picture of soldiers' daily lives by compiling masses of sensory details. Unlike Crane and Hemingway, he intertwines fantasy with reality in his war stories.

O'Brien has said that he probably will continue to write about the Vietnam War because he believes that the emotions in war and those in ordinary life are almost identical. Moreover, his own passions as a person and a writer intersect in Vietnam, which he envisions as a spiritual arena where values, or "the issues of Vietnam," stand in sharp relief: "courage, rectitude, enlightenment, holiness, trying to do the right thing in the world."

O'Brien has said that for him the source of a story is often an image, "a picture of a human being doing something." This image elicits feelings, memories, and questions that guide his work. His recent novels include *In the Lake of the Woods* (1994) and *Tomcat in Love* (1999). Each of these novels alludes to events that occurred in Vietnam.

Tim O'Brien was born in 1946.

Literature Online Author Search For more about Tim O'Brien, go to www.glencoe.com.

Connecting to the Story

In "Ambush," the narrator recalls a combat experience that he cannot put behind him. As you read the story, think about the following questions:

- What situations do people usually react to without thinking?
- Why do some experiences continue to haunt one's memory?

Building Background

The story takes place in Vietnam, near the village of My Khe (mē kā), around 1968. From 1965 to 1973, U.S. troops fought alongside the South Vietnamese in their struggle against a communist movement from the North. Human losses in the war were heavy; it is estimated that more than two million Vietnamese and 57,000 Americans died. The Vietcong were guerrilla forces who supported communist North Vietnam. They sometimes disguised themselves as innocent civilians before ambushing South Vietnamese and U.S. troops.

Setting Purposes for Reading

Big Idea An Era of Protest

During the Vietnam War, student protests were common in the United States; protests were also frequent in South Vietnam, especially among Buddhists and other religious groups. As you read, consider how this story expresses a protest against the Vietnam War.

Literary Element Mood

The **mood** of a story or poem is the feeling or atmosphere that a writer creates for the reader. Writers develop a mood with carefully chosen words and details that vividly describe the setting and the events of the story. As you read the story, look for words and details that help to create the mood.

- See Literary Terms Handbook, p. R11.

Literature Online **Interactive Literary Elements Handbook** To review or learn more about the literary elements, go to www.glencoe.com.

Reading Strategy Analyzing Concrete Details

Concrete details are vivid sensory details, or evocative words and phrases that appeal to one or more of the five senses. For example, to give the reader an experience of fear, a writer might include concrete details such as a clenched jaw, a dry mouth, or sweaty palms in his or her description. As you read this story, notice the concrete details and ask yourself these questions:

- What do the details emphasize?
- What does this emphasis imply?

Reading Tip: Noting Details Use a chart to record concrete details in the story and what they imply.

Details	Implications
"the dense brush along the trail"	The narrator's hiding place seems safe and well-hidden.

Vocabulary

grope (grōp) v. to feel about uncertainly with the hands; to search blindly; p. 1174 *I groped in the dark while searching for my keys.*

stooped (stoopt) adj. bent forward and downward; p. 1175 *Stooped with fatigue, he looked as though he carried a heavy load on his shoulders.*

ponder (pon' dər) v. to think about thoroughly and carefully; p. 1175 *In combat, soldiers have no time to reflect and ponder; instead, they must react quickly without thinking.*

gape (gāp) v. to stare with the mouth open, as in wonder or surprise; p. 1175 *Stunned and shaken, the soldier gaped at his fallen comrade.*

dwell (dwel) v. to think about at length; p. 1175 *Even if one tries not to dwell on painful memories, they sometimes refuse to go away.*

ACADEMIC STANDARDS (pages 1173–1176)

11.3.3 Analyze the ways in which...mood...achieve[s] specific... aesthetic (artistic) purposes...

11.2 Develop [reading] strategies...

11.5.2 Write responses to literature...

Indiana Rangers: The Army Guard in Vietnam, 1984. Mort Künstler. Oil on canvas, 24 x 32 in. Collection National Guard Bureau, Pentagon, Washington, DC.

AMBUSH

Tim O'Brien

When she was nine, my daughter Kathleen asked if I had ever killed anyone. She knew about the war; she knew I'd been a soldier. "You keep writing these war stories," she said, "so I guess you must've killed somebody." It was a difficult moment, but I did what seemed right, which was to say, "Of course not," and then to take her onto my lap and hold her for a while. Someday, I hope, she'll ask again. But here I want to pretend she's a grown-up. I want to tell her exactly what happened, or what I remember happening, and then I want to say to her that as a little girl she was absolutely right. This is why I keep writing war stories:

He was a short, slender young man of about twenty. I was afraid of him—afraid of something—and as he passed me on the trail I threw a grenade that exploded at his feet and killed him.

Or to go back:

Shortly after midnight we moved into the ambush site outside My Khe. The whole platoon[1] was there, spread out in the dense brush along the trail, and for five hours nothing at all happened. We were working in two-man teams—one man on guard while the other slept, switching off every two hours—and I remember it was still dark when Kiowa shook me awake for the final watch. The night was foggy and hot. For the first few moments I felt lost, not sure about directions, **groping** for my helmet and weapon. I reached out and found three grenades and lined them up in front of me; the pins had already been straightened for quick throwing. And then for maybe half an hour I kneeled there and waited. Very gradually, in tiny slivers, dawn began to break through the fog, and from my position in the brush I could see ten or fifteen meters up the trail. The mosquitoes were fierce.

Reading Strategy Analyzing Concrete Details *Why does the author include this detail?*

Vocabulary

grope (grōp) *v.* to feel about uncertainly with the hands; to search blindly

---

1. A *platoon* is a military unit, usually commanded by a lieutenant, that forms part of a company.

I remember slapping at them, wondering if I should wake up Kiowa and ask for some repellent, then thinking it was a bad idea, then looking up and seeing the young man come out of the fog. He wore black clothing and rubber sandals and a gray ammunition belt. His shoulders were slightly **stooped,** his head cocked to the side as if listening for something. He seemed at ease. He carried his weapon in one hand, muzzle down, moving without any hurry up the center of the trail. There was no sound at all—none that I can remember. In a way, it seemed, he was part of the morning fog, or my own imagination, but there was also the reality of what was happening in my stomach. I had already pulled the pin on a grenade. I had come up to a crouch. It was entirely automatic. I did not hate the young man; I did not see him as the enemy; I did not **ponder** issues of morality or politics or military duty. I crouched and kept my head low. I tried to swallow whatever was rising from my stomach, which tasted like lemonade, something fruity and sour. I was terrified. There were no thoughts about killing. The grenade was to make him go away—just evaporate—and I leaned back and felt my mind go empty and then felt it fill up again. I had already thrown the grenade before telling myself to throw it. The brush was thick and I had to lob it high, not aiming, and I remember the grenade seeming to freeze above me for an instant, as if a camera had clicked, and I remember ducking down and holding my breath and seeing little wisps of fog rise from the earth. The grenade bounced once and rolled across the trail. I did not hear it, but there must've been a sound, because the young man dropped his weapon and began to run, just two or three quick steps, then he hesitated, swiveling to his right, and he glanced down at the grenade and tried to cover his head but never did. It occurred to me then that he was about to die. I wanted to warn him. The grenade made a popping noise—not soft but not loud either—not what I'd expected—and there was a puff of dust and smoke—a small white puff—and the young man seemed to jerk upward as if pulled by invisible wires. He fell on his back. His rubber sandals had been blown off. There was no wind. He lay at the center of the trail, his right leg bent beneath him, his one eye shut, his other eye a huge star-shaped hole.

It was not a matter of live or die. There was no real peril. Almost certainly the young man would have passed by. And it will always be that way.

Later, I remember, Kiowa tried to tell me that the man would've died anyway. He told me that it was a good kill, that I was a soldier and this was a war, that I should shape up and stop staring and ask myself what the dead man would've done if things were reversed.

None of it mattered. The words seemed far too complicated. All I could do was **gape** at the fact of the young man's body.

Even now I haven't finished sorting it out. Sometimes I forgive myself, other times I don't. In the ordinary hours of life I try not to **dwell** on it, but now and then, when I'm reading a newspaper or just sitting alone in a room, I'll look up and see the young man coming out of the morning fog. I'll watch him walk toward me, his shoulders slightly stooped, his head cocked to the side, and he'll pass within a few yards of me and suddenly smile at some secret thought and then continue up the trail to where it bends back into the fog. ✌

Literary Element Mood *What feelings does this detail stir in you?*

Vocabulary

stooped (stoopt) *adj.* bent forward and downward
ponder (pon´ dər) *v.* to think about thoroughly and carefully

---

Big Idea An Era of Protest *What attitude toward war do these sentences reveal?*

Vocabulary

gape (gāp) *v.* to stare with the mouth open, as in wonder or surprise
dwell (dwel) *v.* to think about at length

AFTER YOU READ

RESPONDING AND THINKING CRITICALLY

Respond

1. If you could speak with the narrator about his experience in Vietnam, what would you talk about?

Recall and Interpret

2. (a)How does the narrator respond to his daughter's question? (b)In your opinion, why does he lie to her?

3. (a)What does the narrator do when he sees the young man? (b)What does this episode suggest about the role of a soldier in wartime?

4. (a)What does Kiowa tell the narrator, and how does the narrator feel about this advice? (b)What does this exchange suggest to you about the narrator's values?

Analyze and Evaluate

5. What do you think the story's title signifies? Who, besides the enemy soldier, might have been ambushed?

6. Do the narrator's reactions to the killing of an enemy soldier seem convincing to you? Explain.

7. A **frame story** is a story that either surrounds or introduces a more important story. What effect does O'Brien achieve by using a frame story?

Connect

8. **Big Idea** **An Era of Protest** In what ways does this story protest the Vietnam War?

LITERARY ANALYSIS

Literary Element Mood

To determine the **mood** of a literary work, look closely at scene-setting descriptions and the reactions of characters to events.

1. How would you describe the mood of "Ambush"? Give examples of details that contribute to the mood.

2. How does the mood of the story affect its overall impact on you? Explain.

Writing About Literature

Respond to Conflict In the story, the narrator cannot resolve his internal conflict over killing an enemy soldier. Write a brief essay in which you state and support your opinion about the narrator's actions in combat. Support your opinion with details from the story.

Literature Online **Web Activities** For eFlashcards, Selection Quick Checks, and other Web activities, go to www.glencoe.com.

READING AND VOCABULARY

Reading Strategy Analyzing Concrete Details

Review the **concrete details** that describe the young man's appearance in the story.

1. What is the effect of reading about what the young man wore, carried, and did immediately before and after the narrator tosses the grenade?

2. How do the concrete details in the final paragraph enhance your understanding of the narrator?

Vocabulary Practice

Practice with Context Clues Choose the vocabulary word from "Ambush" that fits the context of each sentence.

grope   stooped   ponder   gape   dwell

1. Sometimes it is better to forget unpleasant incidents than to _____ on them.

2. I had to _____ in the dark for my helmet.

3. Don't just stand there and _____—do something.

4. Her shoulders were bent, _____ with age.

5. I must _____ this question instead of giving it a quick answer.

The Gift in Wartime

Tran Mong Tu
Translated by Vann Phan

BEFORE YOU READ

Building Background

"War is a terrible thing," says Tran Mong Tu (trän mông tōō), who has had firsthand experience with the war in Vietnam. She was born in Hai Dong, North Vietnam. She and her family were forced to relocate to South Vietnam in 1954 during the French-Indochina War, in which communist forces battled and eventually drove out the French. Yet South Vietnam did not remain safe for long; a civil war soon raged between communist and non-communist sympathizers.

By the time the United States became heavily involved in the Vietnam War in the 1960s, Tran worked for the Associated Press (a large U.S. news service) in Saigon, the capital of South Vietnam. When the United States pulled its troops out of South Vietnam in 1975, the Associated Press evacuated its Vietnamese employees because it feared communist reprisal against those working for U.S. interests. Tran's immediate family and thousands of other Vietnamese also fled to the United States at that time.

Tran Mong Tu was born in 1943.

Literature Online **Author Search** For more about Tran Mong Tu, go to www.glencoe.com.

Quickwrite

Much of the power of this poem comes from the writer's use of contrasting images. In two or three paragraphs, discuss these contrasting images and comment on their overall impact.

I offer you roses
Buried in your new grave
I offer you my wedding gown
To cover your tomb still green with grass

5 You give me medals
Together with silver stars
And the yellow pips[1] on your badge
Unused and still shining

I offer you my youth
10 The days we were still in love
My youth died away
When they told me the bad news

You give me the smell of blood
From your war dress
15 Your blood and your enemy's
So that I may be moved

I offer you clouds
That linger on my eyes on summer days
I offer you cold winters
20 Amid my springtime of life

You give me your lips with no smile
You give me your arms without tenderness
You give me your eyes with no sight
And your motionless body

25 Seriously, I apologize to you
I promise to meet you in our next life
I will hold this shrapnel[2] as a token
By which we will recognize each other

---

1. *Pips* are military badges of rank worn on the shoulder.
2. *Shrapnel* are fragments scattered from an exploding shell or bomb.

Building Background

Pin Yathay (pin yä′ tī) was born in the village of Oudong, just north of Phnom Penh, Cambodia's capital and largest city. An excellent high school student, he won the Cambodian national prize for mathematics and earned a scholarship to study abroad in Montreal, Canada. There he learned French and studied engineering. After completing his studies, he returned to his homeland and started a family.

When the Khmer Rouge, a communist political organization, seized power in Cambodia in 1975, Pin Yathay knew he was in danger because of his position as an employee of the state. As the situation worsened, he and his family joined the refugees who clogged the roads, seeking safety away from the cities. Eventually, most of Pin Yathay's family died of malnutrition, disease, or murder. The Khmer Rouge, which controlled the government until 1979, executed an estimated one to three million citizens—anyone it felt was a threat. Pin Yathay survived this nightmare and lived to tell audiences throughout the world about his ordeal.

Pin Yathay was born in 1943.

Literature Online **Author Search** For more about Pin Yathay, go to www.glencoe.com.

from Stay Alive, My Son

Pin Yathay
with John Man

My first reaction was to give way to despair, to give up, to surrender to my fate. Everything was lost, I was going to die anyway, I knew that. There was no escape. We swelled up[1] and died. It was the law of nature, unalterable. We all died one after another. There was nothing to be done. What did it matter? I would die, and the sooner the better, there in the house with my wife and son.

Then the true **enormity** of my situation struck me. There would be no such choice. Even that tiny freedom would be taken from me. There would be no gentle, natural passing with my family beside me. They were going to slaughter me, like an animal, away in the forest.

At that thought, I felt another sensation, a surge of raw energy that drove out all other feelings. The instinct for self-preservation took over, and I suddenly, desperately, wanted to stay alive. I told myself: "Pull yourself together! Sharpen up! Get out of this! You've always succeeded before! This is your last chance! Do something!"

I began to think. What was to be done? Leave alone? But there was Nawath across the hut, lying prostrate,[2] his limbs swollen. I could hardly

---

1. Their bodies *swelled up,* or became bloated, from malnutrition and vitamin deficiencies.

Vocabulary

enormity (i nôr′ mə tē) *n.* outrageousness; state of being monstrous

---

2. *Prostrate* means "flat on the ground," in this case from exhaustion.

bear the thought of leaving him and Any. But neither could I imagine escaping with them. Better they should have a chance to live here than die with me. Better that I should get away, and give myself a chance to live, or at least die on my own terms.

It was all very simple. My mind was made up. I had to tell Any of my decision, that very evening.

After we had eaten, as we sat on the floor opposite each other, with Nawath sleeping behind his cloth partition across the hut, I prepared myself to speak. I was certain of my course, but that did not make me any less nervous. It was a terrible thing to do to us as a family, a terrible thing to impose on Any. But as I glanced up at her, and saw her sweet and wasted features lit dimly by the flickering flames of the cooking fire, I knew there was no other course. It was purposeless to stay on there merely to face death. They would be alone all too soon, anyway.

"Any, my dearest," I said, "I have something to tell you." She looked up, without surprise, and I realized she had been expecting a decision of some kind. She too must have known that I could not stay. Speaking softly in order not to wake Nawath—I could see his little bloated face round the edge of the partition—I began to explain. I was doomed, I said. All the former high officials had disappeared. I was trained in the West. I was irredeemable[3] in the eyes of the Khmer Rouge. They would come for me in a week, and that would be that. "But you're a woman, Any, if you were alone with Nawath I don't think they would harm you."

She said nothing, but I saw her gaze turn to one of horror.

"You can live on here with Nawath," I went on. "It's the only answer. I'll take my chances in the forest. If I succeed, we'll meet again. But I have to go soon. In one week, it'll be too late."

"You'll leave?" she said. "Leave me here with Nawath?" And suddenly she began to sob as if she were being torn apart.

"Yes, my dearest. It's the only way," I said, desperately. For the first time, I began to realize that she had not come to the same conclusion as me. "What did you think?"

"Not that. Not that."

I said nothing, for there was only one other course open, the one that was impossible to contemplate. She would see that in a few minutes, I thought, and accept my decision.

But no. With hesitations and bitter sobs, she went on, "It's impossible, my dearest Thay . . . I don't want to be separated from you . . . I prefer to die with you rather than to stay here . . ." As I listened to her in silence, unable to say anything to stem the slow, whispered outpouring of words and sobs and tears, I couldn't believe that she understood what she was saying. Soon, soon, she would see, and know why I had to go alone. "I cannot live without you!" she sobbed. "I prefer to die quickly and cleanly, with you."

She paused, wracked by sobs. I waited for her to say: But if you think it is for the best, of course that is how it must be.

Silence.

To my astonishment, I began to realize she meant what she said. For the first time in our lives, she was refusing to accept my judgment of what was best.

The silence dragged on, broken only by her gasps. She was looking at me. I could see the highlights cast by the fire on her cheeks and in her eyes. Still she said nothing further. I knew then she had understood all along what she was saying.

I felt the strength of her, as well. Once, she had asked my opinion even before buying a dress. Now she had been hardened by experience. She knew what she was doing, knew that in any event she and Nawath would die, knew that we were in the process not of choosing life over death, but of choosing different ways of dying.

And she knew that, having chosen, there was one more fearful choice still to make. There seemed nothing I could do or say to help her through it. It was too awful for me to put into words. If I spoke the words, it would turn something that was merely a nightmarish fear into dreadful reality. I could not say them.

"But," she said at last. "But what shall we do with Nawath?"

Yes: those were the words I had refused to utter.

"Tell me, Thay dearest. What shall we do with Nawath?" She broke down again as she struggled

---

3. *Irredeemable* here refers to being unable to be changed or reformed to accept the new government.

to express the thought. "He can't come with us. We can't carry him, and he can't walk far. They would catch us and kill us before . . ." She paused, her face working to control her emotion. "We . . . we have to leave him behind. But . . . what are we going to do with him if we leave him?" She broke off again, overcome by sobs.

Could she really contemplate leaving Nawath? It seemed an extraordinary thing for a mother to do. I realize now that she had made a mother's supreme sacrifice. People say that for a mother the supreme sacrifice is to die with her child. No—if death is **inevitable**, the mother's supreme sacrifice is to abandon her child, if thereby she can prolong her own life.

I did not understand all that right then and there. But I felt her resolve, and knew there was nothing I could say to make her change her mind. After what we had been through, after being made one body with her by what we had endured together, it never even occurred to me to argue her out of her decision. I don't think I could have done so. I simply had to accept that things were different now.

Any was still sobbing. "What do we do with Nawath?" she asked again, and fell silent. I knew from her tone of voice, and the silence, that she already knew the answer, for there was only one. Knowing it, again neither of us could bring ourselves to express it. Again, expressing it would make it **irrevocable**.

> *But I felt her resolve, and knew there was nothing I could say to make her change her mind.*

I glanced at Nawath, still asleep. I felt I wanted to go to him, stroke his head, provide some comfort for him, or myself. But I did not move. I couldn't risk waking him. I glanced back at Any. Her eyes were lowered, as if waiting for me to pronounce sentence.

After another eternal minute, the burden of silence became intolerable. I felt it as an accusation against me for evading responsibility.

"You know there is only one thing to do," I whispered. "We must take him to the hospital."

The hospital, where people went only to die.

I looked into the shadows of her eyes. "We must," I said.

She knew that this time I was right. Nawath's chances were better in that morgue of a place than in the forest, while ours were better in the forest than there in the village. We would all die anyway; but to **ensure** we all lived as long as possible we had to leave him. While we would at least die together, he would die alone, abandoned by the only ones who cared for him. ∽

Vocabulary

inevitable (i nev´ ə tə bəl) *adj.* incapable of being avoided or evaded

Vocabulary

irrevocable (i rev´ ə kə bəl) *adj.* not possible to undo
ensure (en shoor´) *v.* to make certain; guarantee

Discussion Starter

Meet with a small group to discuss whether Pin Yathay and Any made the only reasonable choice in their situation or not. Consider whether they acted according to their values or whether they were simply trying to save themselves. Summarize your discussion for the rest of your class.

Wrap-Up: Comparing Literature *Across Time and Place*

- ***Ambush***
  by Tim O'Brien
- ***The Gift in Wartime***
  by Tran Mong Tu
- **from *Stay Alive,***
  My Son
  by Pin Yathay

COMPARING THE [Big Idea] An Era of Protest

Partner Activity With a partner, read each of the following quotations. Then discuss how each quotation reveals the human cost of war. Cite additional evidence from each selection to support your interpretation.

> *"[H]e'll pass within a few yards of me and suddenly smile at some secret thought and then continue up the trail to where it bends back into the fog."*
>
> —Tim O'Brien, *Ambush*

> *"I will hold this shrapnel as a token By which we will recognize each other"*
>
> —Tran Mong Tu, *The Gift in Wartime*

> *"She knew what she was doing, . . . knew that we were in the process not of choosing life over death, but of choosing different ways of dying."*
>
> —Pin Yathay, from *Stay Alive, My Son*

Marker at the extermination camp of Choeung Ek.

COMPARING Themes

Group Activity Though Tim O'Brien, Tran Mong Tu, and Pin Yathay all write about the tragedy of war, each conveys a distinct theme, or message, about this subject. With a small group, discuss the following questions:

1. What message about war does each writer share with the reader?
2. What literary elements does each writer use to convey his or her message?
3. Which of the selections, in your opinion, makes the most effective protest against war? Support your answer.

COMPARING Cultures

Visual Display A writer's culture influences his or her ideas and choice of subject, words, and images. Tim O'Brien grew up in the United States; Tran Mong Tu, in Vietnam; and Pin Yathay, in Cambodia. Create a visual display to accompany one of the three selections. In your display, include images that reflect the writer's culture, such as a collage of photographs or works of art. Share your display with your classmates.

INDIANA ACADEMIC STANDARDS (page 1181)
11.3.7 Analyze the clarity and consistency of political assumptions...in a selection of literary works...on a topic.

11.3.8 Analyze the philosophical arguments presented in literary works to determine...the authors' positions...

The Asians Dying, Separation, and When You Go Away

MEET W. S. MERWIN

"It makes me angry to feel that the natural world is taken to have so little importance," American poet W. S. Merwin once said. It is no wonder then that the pervading themes of Merwin's poetry revolve around our self-imposed separation from nature and the terrible consequences that come from humanity's irresponsible treatment of the natural world.

"Poetry . . . tries to convey the sense of what one has seen to those to whom it may matter, including, if possible, one's self."

—W. S. Merwin

William Stanley Merwin was born in New York City, but grew up in Pennsylvania. His father was a Presbyterian minister, and at the age of five, Merwin was writing hymns for his father's church services. When Merwin was a teenager, he met Ezra Pound, who advised him to write seventy-five lines of poetry a day and to learn languages. He told Merwin that poetry "arises out of discipline and continual devotion." Merwin took this advice to heart. In 1947, at age twenty, Merwin graduated from Princeton University with a degree in English. In 1952, he published his first poetry collection, *A Mask for Janus*.

Style and Substance Merwin's early poetry was inspired by Biblical stories and classical myths. These early poems adhered to traditional narrative forms and regular meter patterns. By the 1960s, Merwin had become a pacifist, environmentalist, and an anti-Vietnam War activist. His poetry became more personal as he delved deeper into the failures of humanity. His language became more relaxed and colloquial. He abandoned punctuation and traditional narrative forms in favor of free verse. In 1967, the protest movement against the Vietnam War had grown in the United States as the war itself had escalated and the numbers of casualties had increased. That year, Merwin published *The Lice*, a collection of angry poems in which he lashed out against society's lack of moral responsibility. Included in this collection was "The Asians Dying," considered Merwin's most overt anti-Vietnam War poem. The poems in his next collection, *The Carrier of Ladders*, for which he won the Pulitzer Prize for poetry in 1971, begin to show signs of hope for the human condition.

Beyond Anger Merwin's later poetry moved beyond the angry, "searing, dumb vision" that guided him in *The Lice*. "One can't live only in despair and anger," he said, "without eventually destroying the thing one is angry in defense of."

In his long and illustrious career, Merwin has published more than 30 volumes of poetry, contributed to a variety of magazines and anthologies, written three plays, and translated the works of classical writers such as Dante and contemporary poets such as Pablo Neruda. In reviewing one of Merwin's recent poems, a critic commented that the poem "will not recompense the lives lost to history. It will not stop wars or stay death. Merwin, for all his acute awareness of loss, writes not to alter the world but to honor it."

W. S. Merwin was born in 1927.

Literature Online Author Search For more about W. S. Merwin, go to www.glencoe.com.

Connecting to the Poems

Love and war represent two extremes of human experience. As you read the poems, think about the following questions:

- How much responsibility do we as individuals bear for the effects of war?
- Why is it hard to bear the absence of someone we love?

Building Background

American poetry became more political and radical during the turbulent 1960s. It abandoned the formal tone and rigid meter of previous eras and became more open and free, reflecting the same desire for change and the same anger over repression that fueled the Civil Rights and anti-Vietnam War Movements. Many poets spoke out against social injustice. Merwin's poetry changed during this time period. He eliminated punctuation from his work in an attempt to "transmit [poetry] more directly in words and do it in a way that carried more of the cadences of pure language, of speech."

Setting Purposes for Reading

Big Idea An Era of Protest

As you read the poems, notice how Merwin protests the Vietnam War and the absence of a loved one.

Literary Element Figurative Language

Figurative language is descriptive language that goes beyond its literal meaning to convey ideas and emotions. For example, the phrase, "my words are the garment" is a metaphor that is not literally true. As you read, examine how Merwin uses figurative language to create vivid, haunting images of war and feelings of loss.

- See Literary Terms Handbook, p. R7.

Literature Online Interactive Literary Elements Handbook To review or learn more about the literary elements, go to www.glencoe.com.

Reading Strategy Clarifying Meaning

Free verse often does not always use conventional punctuation or sentence patterns. As a result, poems written in this form can be challenging. As you read Merwin's poems, take time to **reread** lines that are confusing to **clarify meaning**. Be sure to read the footnotes for further help. If you still cannot figure out what something means, ask questions to clarify.

Reading Tip: Ask Questions Use the chart to jot down questions that you have after rereading.

Poem	Questions	Answer
"The Asians Dying"	What does "Over the watercourses / Like ducks in the time of the ducks" mean?	

Vocabulary

possessor (pə zes′ ər) n. one who has or takes control of something; owner; p. 1184 *As the possessor of all the land in the region, she determined how the area was to be developed.*

pointless (point′ lis) n. making no sense; p. 1184 *They can't hear you; it's pointless to speak.*

garment (gär′ mənt) n. a piece of clothing; p. 1185 *The fabric of his outer garment had been worn thin.*

Vocabulary Tip: Analogies Analogies are comparisons that are based on the relationships between things or ideas. For example, the relationship between "movement" and "symphony" is the same as the relationship between "chapter" and "book": movements and chapters are both sections of symphonies and books, respectively.

INDIANA ACADEMIC STANDARDS (pages 1183–1187)

11.3.4 Analyze ways in which poetry...uses...figures of speech... to evoke readers' emotions.

11.2 Develop [reading] strategies...

11.5.2 Write responses to literature that...demonstrate an understanding of the author's style...

11.4.7 Develop presentations using...interviews...

THE ASIANS DYING

W. S. Merwin

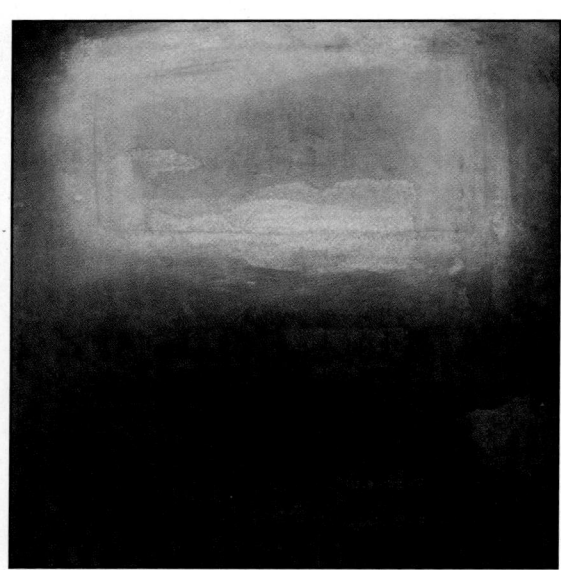

Untitled, 2000. Brenda Chrystie.

When the forests have been destroyed their darkness remains
The ash the great walker follows the **possessors**
Forever
Nothing they will come to is real
5   Nor for long
Over the watercourses[1]
Like ducks in the time of the ducks[2]
The ghosts of the villages trail in the sky
Making a new twilight

10   Rain falls into the open eyes of the dead
Again again with its **pointless** sound
When the moon finds them they are the color of everything

The nights disappear like bruises but nothing is healed
The dead go away like bruises
15   The blood vanishes into the poisoned farmlands
Pain the horizon
Remains
Overhead the seasons rock
They are paper bells
20   Calling to nothing living

The possessors move everywhere under Death their star
Like columns of smoke they advance into the shadows
Like thin flames with no light
They with no past
25   And fire their only future

---

1. *Watercourses* are streams of water, such as a river or a brook.
2. The phrase *ducks in the time of ducks* recalls the Asian belief that the year of one's birth is influenced by the traits of particular animals.

Big Idea An Era of Protest *Who are the possessors? What does Merwin think is going to happen to them?*

Literary Element Figurative Language *What are the similes in these lines comparing? What ideas about war do these comparisons suggest?*

Vocabulary

possessor (pə zes′ ər) *n.* one who has or takes control of something; owner
pointless (point′ lis) *n.* making no sense

Separation

W. S. Merwin

Your absence has gone through me
Like thread through a needle.
Everything I do is stitched with its color.

When You Go Away

W. S. Merwin

When you go away the wind clicks around to the north
The painters work all day but at sundown the paint falls
Showing the black walls
The clock goes back to striking the same hour
5   That has no place in the years

And at night wrapped in the bed of ashes
In one breath I wake
It is the time when the beards of the dead get their growth
I remember that I am falling
10 That I am the reason
And that my words are the **garment** of what I shall never be
Like the tucked sleeve of a one-armed boy

Reading Strategy   Clarifying Meaning *What does the simile in line 12 mean?*

Vocabulary

garment (gär′mənt) *n.* a piece of clothing

RESPONDING AND THINKING CRITICALLY

Respond

1. Which of these three poems did you like best? Why?

Recall and Interpret

2. (a)In "The Asians Dying," what happens to the forests, and, subsequently, what happens to the villages? (b)How does this connect to what happens to the farmlands?

3. (a)Summarize lines 10–12 of "The Asians Dying." (b)What do you think the speaker is trying to tell you about the dead in these lines?

4. (a)In "When You Go Away," what happens to the painters' work and to the clocks? (b)What do these events mean?

Analyze and Evaluate

5. In "The Asians Dying," Merwin employs a series of paradoxes—the forests have been destroyed, yet their darkness remains; bruises disappear, but nothing is healed; and there are flames, but no light. What do these paradoxes suggest about the effects of war?

6. (a)Both speakers in "The Asians Dying" and "When You Go Away" reflect on their feelings at "twilight" or "sundown." What might this time of day symbolize? (b)How does this setting reflect the meaning and tone of these poems?

7. (a)Whom is the speaker of "Separation" addressing? (b)Through the use of figurative language, what feeling is Merwin attempting to convey?

Connect

8. **Big Idea** **An Era of Protest** (a)What effect do you think the images in "The Asians Dying" would have had on those who were protesting the Vietnam War? (b)How could the poems be used to strengthen their protests?

Literary Element ### Figurative Language

Figurative language is often found in poetry, which relies on imagery to convey ideas. Figurative language includes similes, metaphors, personification, hyperbole, and symbolism. A poet can use each of these literary devices to emphasize an idea, create an effect, or establish a particular mood. For example, when the speaker of "The Asians Dying" says, "The ash the great walker follows the possessors," he is using personification to say that the ash, which is all that remains of the war-ravaged forests, has the human ability to follow around those who caused the destruction.

1. When the speaker of "Separation" says, "Everything I do is stitched with its color," what kind of figurative language is he using?

2. Find two other examples of figurative language in the poems and explain how each helps you to understand an idea.

Review: Free Verse

As you learned in Unit 3, **free verse** is poetry that has no fixed pattern of meter, rhyme, line length, or stanza arrangement. Poets who use free verse often do not follow the traditional rules of grammar and punctuation.

Partner Activity Pair up with a partner and discuss the use of free verse in "The Asians Dying," "Separation," and "When You Go Away." Working with your partner, create a chart like the one below. Then fill it with examples of the poetic techniques that Merwin uses in his free verse. Working with your partner, create a chart like the one shown below for each poem.

	"The Asians Dying"
Repetition	
Alliteration	
Assonance	
Consonance	

Reading Strategy Clarifying Meaning

The main concepts of Merwin's poems may be diffi-cult to understand because of the irregular sentence patterns and a lack of punctuation. Look back at the questions you wrote in your chart from page 1183. Reread the lines that caused you problems and try to put them in your own words.

1. What is the main message of "The Asians Dying"?

2. In "When You Go Away," how does the speaker feel about the absent person?

Vocabulary Practice

Practice with Analogies Choose the word pair that best completes the analogy.

1. possessor : owner ::
   a. army : soldier
   b. supplier : consumer
   c. manager : supervisor
2. pointless : significant ::
   a. remote : distant
   b. responsible : trustworthy
   c. meaningful : irrelevant
3. garment : shirt ::
   a. tool : pliers
   b. hat : head
   c. rain : snow

Academic Vocabulary

Here are two words from the vocabulary list on page R86.

target (tär′ gət) *n.* someone or something affected by an action

objective (əb jek′ tiv) *n.* end result; aim; goal

Practice and Apply
1. Who is the **target** of most political poetry?
2. (a)What do you think Merwin's **objective** is in "The Asians Dying"? (b)Do you think that he achieved this objective?

Writing About Literature

Respond to Theme and Craft If you could interview Merwin, what questions would you ask him? Think about the themes that he develops in his poetry and note the distinctive ways in which he chooses to express those themes. With a partner, create a list of questions for Merwin and then write answers from his point of view.

As you begin to brainstorm ideas with your partner, reread Merwin's poems and take notes on their themes and poetic techniques. These notes will help you write your questions and responses. Also, refer to your chart from page 1183 and see if it contains any unanswered questions that you would like to include in your interview. Keep in mind that good interview questions elicit thoughtful responses that lead to a meaningful dialogue between the interviewer and interviewee. Make sure to review your questions and reword any of them that can be answered with a simple "yes" or "no." These kinds of questions can discourage conversation. Proofread and edit your questions and answers for errors in spelling, grammar, and punctuation. You and your partner may wish to role-play your interview for your classmates.

Literature Groups

Poetry and Politics W. S. Merwin has suggested that the poet takes a tremendous chance when he writes political poetry; by doing so, the poet's voice, which is naturally private and integral to his own life, "may be deformed into a mere loudspeaker" in danger of losing its individuality and surprising nature. What other conse-quences might a successful poet face as the result of writing political poetry? Why would Merwin or any other poet take these risks? Share your ideas with the class.

Literature Online Web Activities For eFlashcards, Selection Quick Checks, and other Web activities, go to www.glencoe.com.

In Thai Binh (Peace) Province

MEET DENISE LEVERTOV

Denise Levertov was extraordinary for the depth of commitment she brought to every area of her life. In her work, she conducted a thorough exploration of both the intricacies of language and the responsibilities of the individual in a chaotic, sometimes violent world.

Born and raised in England, Levertov came from a family of Welsh intellectuals on her mother's side and Hasidic Jewish scholars on her father's side. She was homeschooled, and, as a child, spent free time taking lessons in ballet, French, music, and art. After World War II, Levertov married and immigrated to the United States. She embarked on a career as a university professor, became involved with the Black Mountain school of poets, and established herself as one of the most important writers of her generation. Colleagues from the Black Mountain school, such as Robert Creeley, Charles Olson, and Robert Duncan, helped shape Levertov's ideas about poetry and influenced her burgeoning American sensibility.

An Anti-War Voice Levertov's was an early and sustained voice in the protest against the war in Vietnam. She joined the War Resisters League and both lectured and wrote in protest of the war. In 1972, she traveled to North Vietnam with Muriel Rukeyser and Jane Hart (to whom the poem "In Thai Binh (Peace) Province" is dedicated). The experience of witnessing the suffering of war-torn Vietnam firsthand strengthened Levertov's conviction that U.S. policy in the region had been disastrous for the Vietnamese people. Levertov saw no other choice but to explore the issue in her poetry. She did so in ways that went beyond the ideological or doctrinaire. Levertov's poems probed her own culpability as well as the culpability of her government. Nevertheless, her choice of subject matter created controversy among the poets of the Black Mountain school.

Consummate Poet Levertov may have written about political themes, but she was also an artist who gave careful thought to the technical aspects of poetry. In lectures and interviews, Levertov praised precise line breaks, lambasted sentimentality, and expounded on the need for a "good ear"—an ear capable of distinguishing rough or thick sounds from light and airy ones.

Levertov explicitly rejected traditional forms of poetry, which, according to her, belonged to eras that were less chaotic and uncertain than the present. "I think that we should acknowledge the chaos we live in and deal with it; open forms can allow one to explore chaos and see what can be discovered there," she said. Her abandonment of traditional forms did not translate into indifference to standards or technique. She remarked, "For a poet, the thinking-feeling process is not merely immediately transposed into language. Rather, it takes place in language. For example, the way that a poem is written on the page is a score for the way it should be read aloud, and the way that it will be experienced . . . I believe strongly that the line itself is expressive of patterns of seeing."

As a working mother and wife, Levertov taught, wrote, and served as poetry editor for several magazines. She worked as a professor at the University of Washington and at Stanford University before retiring to live in Seattle. Though her last years were ailing ones, Levertov maintained a lively correspondence and engagement with the world until the end.

Denise Levertov was born in 1923 and died in 1997.

Literature Online Author Search For more about Denise Levertov, go to www.glencoe.com.

Connecting to the Poem

Why might someone support or protest a war? As you read the poem, think about the following questions:

- What most disturbs you about war?
- What circumstances or events would cause you to protest a war?

Building Background

Thai Binh is a province in Vietnam. It is located northeast of Hanoi in what was once North Vietnam. Bordered by the ocean and home to the Red River Delta, the province is a green place where rice grows in paddies and water buffalo graze. It is home both to pagodas, buildings which frequently house Buddhist temples, as well as churches. (The French and other missionaries brought Christianity to Vietnam.) Thousands of North Vietnamese soldiers from this peaceful-looking province died during the Vietnam War. Bombing of the province by the U.S. and South Vietnamese, along with the effects of the American-made chemical Agent Orange, affected the lives of thousands of others. Ironically, *su thai binh* means "peace" in Vietnamese.

Setting Purposes for Reading

Big Idea An Era of Protest

As you read "In Thai Binh (Peace) Province," think about what Levertov may be suggesting about the true cost of the Vietnam War, for the United States as well as for Vietnam.

Literary Element Setting

Setting is the time and place in which the events of a literary work occur. Setting includes not only the physical surroundings, but also the ideas, customs, values, and beliefs of a particular time and place. In a poem, the setting may play an important role, or it may be only incidental. As you read, determine the role of setting in "In Thai Binh."

- See Literary Terms Handbook, p. R16.

Reading Strategy Visualizing

When you **visualize,** you picture the writer's ideas or descriptions in your mind's eye. Visualizing as you read can help to strengthen your engagement with a poem.

Reading Tip: Taking Notes Use a chart to record what you picture as you read.

Detail	What I Picture
"quietly grazing buffalo"	buffalo in a large, empty, green field on a sunny day

Vocabulary

bewildered (bi wil′ dərd) *adj.* confused; p. 1190 *The bewildered man could not find the bus stop.*

fabled (fā′ bəld) *adj.* famous, well-known; told about in stories; p. 1190 *Many explorers had searched for the fabled city of gold.*

persistent (pər sis′ tənt) *adj.* continuing or going forward, despite problems or obstacles; p. 1190 *Although other students gave up, Derek was persistent.*

Vocabulary Tip: Synonyms Synonyms are words that have the same or similar meanings. Synonyms are always the same part of speech.

Literature Online Interactive Literary Elements Handbook To review or learn more about the literary elements, go to www.glencoe.com.

INDIANA ACADEMIC STANDARDS (pages 1189–1191)

11.3 [Identify] story elements such as...setting...

11.2 Develop [reading] strategies...

11.7.18 Deliver oral responses to literature that demonstrate a comprehensive understanding of the significant ideas...

DENISE LEVERTOV **1189**

In Thai Binh (Peace) Province

Denise Levertov

For Muriel and Jane

I've used up all my film on bombed hospitals,
bombed village schools, the scattered
lemon-yellow cocoons at the bombed silk-factory,

and for the moment all my tears too
are used up, having seen today
yet another child with its feet blown off,
        a girl, this one, eleven years old,
patient and **bewildered** in her home, a fragile
small house of mud bricks among rice fields.

So I'll use my dry burning eyes
to photograph within me
dark sails of the river boats,
warm slant of afternoon light
apricot on the brown, swift, wide river,
village towers—church and pagoda[1]—on the far shore,

and a boy and small bird both
perched, relaxed, on a quietly grazing
buffalo.   Peace within the
        long war.

It is that life, unhurried, sure, **persistent,**
I must bring home when I try to bring
the war home.
        Child, river, light.

Here the future, **fabled** bird
that has migrated away from America,
nests, and breeds, and sings,

common as any sparrow.

---

1. A *pagoda* is a building with an upward curved roof, or a series of
   upward carved roofs, built as a temple or memorial.

Reading Strategy Visualizing *What do you picture as you read
these lines?*

Literary Element Setting *Why does Levertov include these
details in a poem about war?*

Vocabulary

bewildered (bi wil′ dərd) *adj.* confused
persistent (pər sis′ tənt) *adj.* continuing or going forward,
despite problems or obstacles
fabled (fā′ bəld) *adj.* famous, well-known; told about in stories

RESPONDING AND THINKING CRITICALLY

Respond

1. What do you think is the most powerful image in this poem? Explain.

Recall and Interpret

2. (a)What does the speaker photograph with a camera? (b)What do these images reveal about Thai Binh?

3. (a)What does the speaker "photograph" with her eyes? (b)What do these images tell you about Thai Binh?

4. (a)What is the "fabled bird" doing in Thai Binh? (b)What does the speaker mean by "fabled bird"?

Analyze and Evaluate

5. (a)Why might this be called an antiwar poem? (b)How well does the poem demonstrate the negative consequences of war? Support your answers.

6. Explain the contrast Levertov develops between violent or disturbing occurrences and images that evoke peace, hope, or health. Why do you think Levertov suggests that it is the latter type of image she must "bring home" with her?

7. (a)What is the "future, fabled bird" mentioned in line 24? (b)Why does the poet suggest that the bird has "migrated away from America"?

Connect

8. **Big Idea** **An Era of Protest** (a)What exactly might reading the speaker's personal reactions have helped Americans to understand about the Vietnam War? (b)Do you think this poem is effective as a means of protest? Explain.

LITERARY ANALYSIS

Literary Element Setting

Details about **setting** can help to create a poem's atmosphere, or **mood**. A powerful visual detail can be disturbing or evoke feelings of joy.

1. How does the setting the speaker imagines differ from the one she sees?

2. What role does setting play in the development of the poem's theme?

Listening and Speaking

Levertov wrote many other poems about her experiences in Vietnam. With a group, locate and read three of these poems. Then write and deliver an informational speech about them. In your speech, summarize the poems and explain what themes you think are conveyed by them. Also discuss particularly striking examples of poetic technique. End with a conclusion about the purpose and meaning of Levertov's Vietnam poetry.

READING AND VOCABULARY

Reading Strategy Visualizing

In her poem, Levertov vividly contrasts war and peace.

1. What do war and peace look like to the speaker?

2. What images or details of the poem did visualizing best help you to appreciate? Explain.

Vocabulary Practice

Practice with Synonyms Find the synonym for each vocabulary word listed in the first column. Use a dictionary or thesaurus if you need help.

1. bewildered   **a.** confused   **b.** amused

2. fabled   **a.** famous   **b.** fake

3. persistent   **a.** unknown   **b.** continuous

Literature Online Web Activities For eFlashcards, Selection Quick Checks, and other Web activities, go to www.glencoe.com.

PROPOSAL FOR the Vietnam Veterans Memorial

Maya Lin

National Design Award Winner

Building Background

Architect Maya Lin was only twenty-one years old when she submitted this design proposal for the Vietnam Veterans Memorial. Unlike most prior war memorials, it features no statues of soldiers in heroic, determined stances. Instead, it is a seemingly endless black granite wall that first rises from and then falls to the earth. On its surface are the names of the American men and women who were killed during the Vietnam War. "I thought about what death is, what a loss is," Lin explains. "A sharp pain that lessens with time but can never quite heal over. A scar. The idea occurred to me there on the site. Take a knife and cut open the earth, and with time the grass will heal it."

Set a Purpose for Reading

Read to find out how Lin hopes that her memorial will inspire visitors.

Reading Strategy

Analyzing Political Assumptions

Analyzing political assumptions involves carefully examining political beliefs that have shaped an author's argument or proposal. An author may state each opinion or assumption directly or may merely imply it.

Walking through this park-like area, the memorial appears as a rift[1] in the earth—a long, polished black stone wall, emerging from and receding into the earth. Approaching the memorial, the ground slopes gently downward, and the low walls emerging on either side, growing out of the earth, extend and converge at a point below and ahead. Walking into the grassy site contained by the walls of this memorial we can barely make out the carved names upon the memorial's walls. These names, seemingly infinite in number, convey the sense of overwhelming numbers, while unifying those individuals into a whole. For this memorial is meant not as a monument to the individual, but rather as a memorial to the men and women who died during this war, as a whole.

The memorial is composed not as an unchanging monument, but as a moving composition, to be understood as we move into and out of it; the passage itself is gradual, the descent to the origin slow, but it is at the origin that the meaning of this memorial is to be

---

1. A *rift* is a deep crack or slash.

The two panels of Maya Lin's Competition architectural drawing, including her textual description.

The Vietnam Memorial at night, with the Washington Monument in the distance.
Viewing the Photograph What aspects of the Vietnam Memorial are captured in this photograph?

fully understood.[2] At the intersection of these walls, on the right side, at this wall's top is carved the date of the first death. It is followed by the names of those who have died in the war, in chronological order. These names continue on this wall, appearing to recede into the earth at the wall's end. The names resume on the left wall, as the wall emerges from the earth, continuing back to the origin, where the date of the last death is carved, at the bottom of this wall. Thus the war's beginning and end meet; the war is "complete," coming full circle, yet broken by

the earth that bounds the angle's open side, and contained within the earth itself. As we turn to leave, we see these walls stretching into the distance, directing us to the Washington Monument to the left and the Lincoln Memorial to the right, thus bringing the Vietnam Memorial into historical context. We, the living, are brought to a concrete realization of these deaths.

Brought to a sharp awareness of such a loss, it is up to each individual to resolve or come to terms with this loss. For death is in the end a personal and private matter, and the area contained within this memorial is a quiet place meant for personal reflection and private reckoning.[3] The black granite walls, each 200 feet long, and 10 feet

---

2. The monument stands in a long, grassy park in Washington, D.C. Visitors standing at the monument can look to the left and right and see the faraway ends of the park. At one end stands a tall white obelisk, the Washington Monument, and at the other end stands the Lincoln Memorial, with its famous statue of the seated Abraham Lincoln.

---

3. *Private reckoning* suggests deep, personal thoughts about the magnitude of the war dead.

below ground at their lowest point (gradually ascending towards ground level) effectively act as a sound barrier, yet are of such a height and length so as not to appear threatening or enclosing. The actual area is wide and shallow, allowing for a sense of privacy, and the sunlight from the memorial's southern exposure along with the grassy park surrounding and within its wall contribute to the serenity of the area. Thus this memorial is for those who have died, and for us to remember them.

The memorial's origin is located approximately at the center of this site; its legs each extending 200 feet towards the Washington Monument and the Lincoln Memorial. The walls, contained on one side by the earth, are 10 feet below ground at their point of origin,

gradually lessening in height, until they finally recede totally into the earth at their ends. The walls are to be made of a hard, polished black granite, with the names to be carved in a simple Trajan[4] letter, 3/4 inch high, allowing for nine inches in length for each name. The memorial's construction involves recontouring the area within the wall's boundaries so as to provide for an easily accessible descent, but as much of the site as possible should be left untouched (including trees).[5] The area should be made into a park for all the public to enjoy.

---

4. *Trajan* is the name of the font that Lin has chosen for the letters in the names.
5. Lin specifies here that some recontouring, or excavating, of the land will be necessary in order to accommodate the downward slope of the granite walls.

RESPONDING AND THINKING CRITICALLY

Respond

1. Imagine being a visitor at the Vietnam Veterans Memorial. How do you think you would respond to the memorial? Explain.

Recall and Interpret

2. (a)Describe the appearance of the memorial. (b)Why may Lin have wanted the names to convey "the sense of overwhelming numbers"?

3. (a)In what order are the names arranged on the monument? (b)Why may Lin have chosen this type of order instead of alphabetical order?

4. How does Lin conclude her proposal? Why do you think she ends with this idea?

Analyze and Evaluate

5. At first, many people were shocked and disappointed with Maya Lin's design. They expected a more traditional monument, such as a statue conveying the bravery of U.S. soldiers. Do you agree, with the critics, that such a monument would have been more appropriate than Lin's memorial, or do you favor Lin's design? Explain.

6. Lin envisioned the memorial "not as an unchanging monument, but as a moving composition, to be understood as we moved into and out of it." From her description of the memorial and the pictures accompanying the proposal, do you believe that she accomplished that vision? Explain.

Connect

7. **Big Idea** **An Era of Protest** Do you think that the Vietnam Veterans Memorial reflects an "era of protest"? Why or why not?

INDIANA ACADEMIC STANDARDS (pages 1192–1195)
11.3.7 Analyze the clarity and consistency of political assumptions...beliefs, or intentions in...literary works...

11.2.5 Analyze an author's implicit and explicit assumptions and beliefs about a subject.

A Hard Rain's A-Gonna Fall

MEET BOB DYLAN

Born Robert Zimmerman and raised in the small mining town of Hibbing, Minnesota, Bob Dylan received his first guitar at the age of fourteen. Throughout his teens, he listened to the music of Hank Williams, Elvis Presley, and Little Richard.

> *"I see my light come shining
> From the west unto the east.
> Any day now, any day now,
> I shall be released."*
>
> —Bob Dylan, "I Shall Be Released"

Protest Singer In 1959, the summer before Dylan enrolled at the University of Minnesota he first heard the records of Woody Guthrie, the folk singer who would become his idol. In Minneapolis, he first encountered the era's beatnik, folk-inflected counterculture. Dylan dropped out of college at the end of his freshman year and headed for New York City in search of Guthrie, who had vanished from the public eye due to illness.

When he arrived in New York City in 1961, Dylan had already changed his name and was developing his distinct musical sound. While playing in small clubs throughout Greenwich Village, the center of bohemian New York, he regularly visited Guthrie, who was suffering from Huntington's chorea, a nervous system disorder.

In September 1961, the *New York Times* gave one of Dylan's live performances a positive review, prompting John Hammond, Columbia Records' premier talent scout, to take notice. In less than a year, Dylan recorded and released his first album, which received mixed reviews. However, his next album, *The Freewheelin' Bob Dylan*, earned widespread acclaim.

In 1963, Dylan played at the Newport Folk Festival in Rhode Island. His performance at that festival firmly established Dylan as the new voice of folk music. This phase in Dylan's career crested with the release of his next album, *The Times They Are A-Changin'*. Dylan now personified the folk "protest song" movement, which influenced the Civil Rights, free speech, and anti-war movements of that period.

Going Electric Dylan, however, was on the cusp of a significant artistic change. The album *Bringing It All Back Home*, released in 1965, featured electric instruments, shocking his purist folk fans. *Highway 61 Revisited*, Dylan's next album, included surreal lyrics and a heavy electric sound—but no protest songs. *Blonde on Blonde*, the critically acclaimed following album, followed suit. The tours promoting these albums became legendary: feeling betrayed, angry fans booed and jeered Dylan to show their displeasure.

In 1966, Dylan was involved in a motorcycle accident, forcing him into a period of seclusion. When he emerged, his musical style changed again. His next two albums—*John Wesley Harding*, released in 1968, and the country infused *Nashville Skyline*, released in 1969—again defied expectations.

Throughout the 1980s and 1990s, Dylan toured and recorded with decidedly mixed results. Inducted into the Rock and Roll Hall of Fame, he earned multiple Grammies, including Album of the Year for *Time Out of Mind* in 1998. Recently, Dylan released *Chronicles*, the first volume of his memoirs, to overwhelmingly positive reviews.

Bob Dylan was born in 1941.

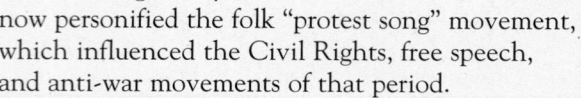 **Author Search** For more about Bob Dylan, go to www.glencoe.com.

Connecting to the Song

Have you ever felt frightened by what tomorrow might bring? In this protest song, Dylan voices a prophetic warning about the future. As you read the song, think about the following questions:

- Do you think life will be better or worse ten years from now?
- What alarming trends in today's world would you like to see changed?

Building Background

Dylan wrote "A Hard Rain's A-Gonna Fall" during the Cuban missile crisis in 1962, when the United States and the Soviet Union were on the brink of nuclear war. This crisis began when the United States discovered that the Soviet Union was installing ballistic missiles on the island of Cuba, approximately ninety miles from the U.S. mainland. These missiles were capable of destroying millions of lives within minutes. In response to this threat, President Kennedy set up a naval blockade around Cuba, thereby further escalating tensions between the United States and the Soviet Union. The world feared that nuclear war was imminent and unavoidable. The crisis ended when the Soviet Union agreed to remove the missiles in exchange for the United States' promise not to invade Cuba. Though nuclear war was averted, the crisis left a gnawing anxiety in the minds of most people. They were forced to recognize that the threat of nuclear disaster was a grim reality.

Setting Purposes for Reading

Big Idea An Era of Protest

As you read, consider how this song responds to issues raised by historical events.

Literary Element Rhythm

Rhythm refers to the pattern of beats created by the arrangement of stressed and unstressed syllables, especially in poetry. Rhythm gives poetry a musical quality, can add emphasis to certain words, and may help convey the poem's meaning. As you read the protest song aloud, listen to the rhythm and consider how it might support the meaning.

- See Literary Terms Handbook, p. R15.

Reading Strategy Analyzing Rhetorical Devices

In "A Hard Rain's A-Gonna Fall," Dylan uses several **rhetorical devices,** including juxtaposition, parallelism, and repetition. Juxtaposition refers to the placing of two or more distinct things next to each other in order to compare or contrast them. Parallelism is the use of a series of words, phrases, or sentences that have similar grammatical form. Repetition is the recurrence of sounds, words, phrases, or lines. These devices call attention to particular ideas and evoke emotional responses in the reader. As you read, notice these devices and consider their effects.

Reading Tip: Taking Notes Use a chart to record rhetorical devices and their effects.

Rhetorical Device	Effect
Juxtaposition: "I saw a newborn baby with wild wolves all around it" (line 13)	

 Literature Online **Interactive Literary Elements Handbook** To review or learn more about the literary elements, go to www.glencoe.com.

INDIANA ACADEMIC STANDARDS (pages 1197–1201)

11.2.2 Analyze the way in which clarity of meaning is affected by the patterns of organization...

11.2.1 Analyze...rhetorical persuasive devices...

11.5.9 Write academic essays...

Bob Dylan

A Hard Rain's A-Gonna Fall

Oh, where have you been, my blue-eyed son?
Oh, where have you been, my darling young one?
I've stumbled on the side of twelve misty mountains,
I've walked and I've crawled on six crooked highways,
5　I've stepped in the middle of seven sad forests,
I've been out in front of a dozen dead oceans,
I've been ten thousand miles in the mouth of a graveyard,
And it's a hard, and it's a hard, it's a hard, and it's a hard,
And it's a hard rain's a-gonna fall.

10　Oh, what did you see, my blue-eyed son?
Oh, what did you see, my darling young one?
I saw a newborn baby with wild wolves all around it
I saw a highway of diamonds with nobody on it,
I saw a black branch with blood that kept drippin',
15　I saw a room full of men with their hammers a-bleedin',
I saw a white ladder all covered with water,
I saw ten thousand talkers whose tongues were all broken,
I saw guns and sharp swords in the hands of young children,
And it's a hard, and it's a hard, it's a hard, it's a hard,
20　And it's a hard rain's a-gonna fall.

Big Idea　An Era of Protest　*Who do you think these men might represent?*

And what did you hear, my blue-eyed son?
And what did you hear, my darling young one?
I heard the sound of a thunder, it roared out a warnin',
Heard the roar of a wave that could drown the whole world,
25   Heard one hundred drummers whose hands were a-blazin',
Heard ten thousand whisperin' and nobody listenin',
Heard one person starve, I heard many people laughin',
Heard the song of a poet who died in the gutter,
Heard the sound of a clown who cried in the alley,
30   And it's a hard, and it's a hard, it's a hard, it's a hard,
And it's a hard rain's a-gonna fall.

Oh, who did you meet, my blue-eyed son?
Who did you meet, my darling young one?
I met a young child beside a dead pony,
35   I met a white man who walked a black dog,
I met a young woman whose body was burning,
I met a young girl, she gave me a rainbow,
I met one man who was wounded in love,
I met another man who was wounded with hatred,
40   And it's a hard, it's a hard, it's a hard, it's a hard,
It's a hard rain's a-gonna fall.

Oh, what'll you do now, my blue-eyed son?
Oh, what'll you do now, my darling young one?
I'm a-goin' back out 'fore the rain starts a-fallin',
45   I'll walk to the depths of the deepest black forest,
Where the people are many and their hands are all empty,
Where the pellets of poison are flooding their waters,
Where the home in the valley meets the damp dirty prison,
Where the executioner's face is always well hidden,
50   Where hunger is ugly, where souls are forgotten,
Where black is the color, where none is the number,
And I'll tell it and think it and speak it and breathe it,
And reflect it from the mountain so all souls can see it,
Then I'll stand on the ocean until I start sinkin',
55   But I'll know my song well before I start singin',
And it's a hard, it's a hard, it's a hard, it's a hard,
It's a hard rain's a-gonna fall.

Literary Element   Rhythm *How would you describe the rhythm of these lines?*

Reading Strategy   Analyzing Rhetorical Devices *What rhetorical device is found in this line? What effect does it create?*

RESPONDING AND THINKING CRITICALLY

Respond

1. What image did you find most powerful in this song? Explain.

Recall and Interpret

2. (a)Who are the speakers in this song? (b)What effect does the poet create by using questions and responses?

3. (a)Who is on the "highway of diamonds" in line 13? (b)What do you think this image represents in relation to the song's historical context?

4. (a)What is unusual about the "executioner's face" in line 52? (b)What might this detail suggest?

Analyze and Evaluate

5. This protest song mostly concerns the past but ends while describing the future. How does the shift in time affect the poet's message?

6. (a)Why did Dylan give his song the title "A Hard Rain's A-Gonna Fall"? (b)Do you think the title is effective? Explain.

Connect

7. **Big Idea** **An Era of Protest** What do you think Dylan hoped to accomplish with this protest song? Explain.

LITERARY ANALYSIS

Literary Element **Rhythm**

Rhythm can be regular or irregular. For example in Robert Frost's "Stopping by Woods on a Snowy Evening," the rhythm is regular:

Whose woods these are I think I know

His house is in the village though

Even if the rhythm is irregular, you can still get a sense of it by paying attention to the number and position of stressed syllables, or beats, in each line.

1. About how many beats does each line of "A Hard Rain's A-Gonna Fall" usually contain?

2. How does the rhythm of the song influence its meaning?

3. Why do you think Dylan chose irregular rhythm and rhyme? Explain.

Review: Mood

As you learned on page 823, **mood** is the feeling or atmosphere that an author creates in a literary work.

Partner Activity Meet with another classmate to determine the mood of this song and discuss the literary elements Dylan uses to create it. Working with your partner, create a web diagram like the one below. Then fill it in with examples of the elements that contribute to the mood of the song.

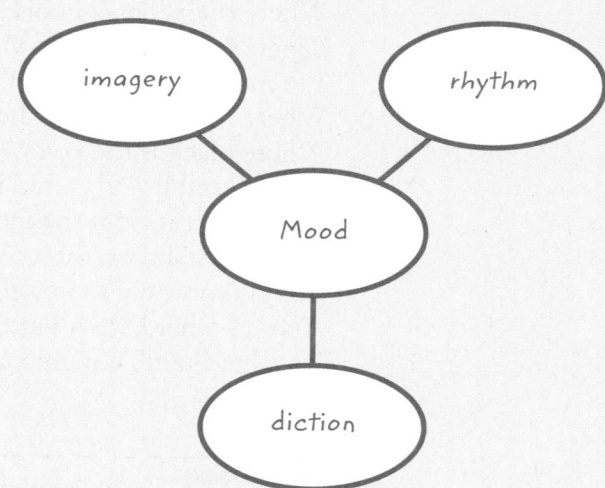

READING AND VOCABULARY

Reading Strategy Analyzing Rhetorical Devices

Though most often found in persuasive essays or speeches, **rhetorical devices** sometimes support an implied argument in poetry and fiction. Review the chart you created on page 1197 listing rhetorical devices in this protest song.

1. What argument is implied in "A Hard Rain's A-Gonna Fall"?

2. List three rhetorical devices and explain how each one helps advance that argument.

Academic Vocabulary

Here are two words from the vocabulary list on page R86.

specific (spi si′ fik) *v.* exact or definite

emphasis (em′ fə sis) *n.* a special stress, accent, or importance given to something

Practice and Apply
1. Identify a **specific** line in "A Hard Rain's A-Gonna Fall" that contains juxtaposition.
2. Which parts of each stanza receive greater **emphasis** because of the use of repetition?

Bob Dylan in 1968-1969.

WRITING AND EXTENDING

Writing About Literature

Evaluate Author's Craft How well do the images in "A Hard Rain's A-Gonna Fall" reinforce the mood and theme of this protest song? Write a brief essay in which you evaluate the author's craft. Use examples from the protest song to support your position.

As you draft, write from start to finish. Follow the writing plan shown here to keep on track.

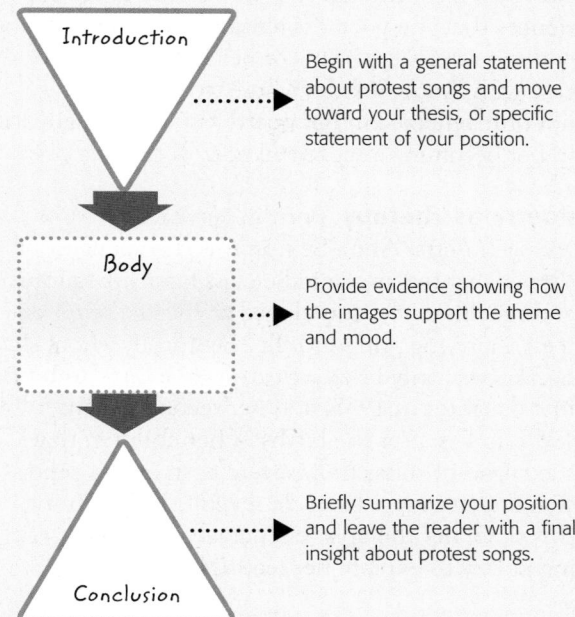

Introduction — Begin with a general statement about protest songs and move toward your thesis, or specific statement of your position.

Body — Provide evidence showing how the images support the theme and mood.

Conclusion — Briefly summarize your position and leave the reader with a final insight about protest songs.

After you complete your draft, meet with a peer reviewer to evaluate each other's work and to suggest revisions. Then proofread and edit your draft for errors in spelling, grammar, and punctuation.

Listening and Speaking

Partner Activity Listen to Bob Dylan's recording of this protest song. Then with a partner discuss how listening to the recording affects your response to the song and your interpretation of it. Be sure to pay close attention to the song's rhythm. How would you describe Dylan's delivery and singing style? Is the work more powerful when sung than when read silently?

Literature Online **Web Activities** For eFlashcards, Selection Quick Checks, and other Web activities, go to www.glencoe.com.

Courage

MEET ANNE SEXTON

Is it possible to understand poetry without understanding the poet? The work of some poets is so intimately bound to the poet's experiences that the poetry is almost never discussed without references to his or her life. Such is the case with Anne Sexton, whose troubled life was not only reflected in her poetry but also actually led to her becoming a successful poet in the first place.

Poetry as Therapy Born in Newton, Massachusetts, Anne Sexton was the youngest of three daughters in a middle class family. Beautiful and rebellious, Sexton eloped at the age of nineteen, marrying Alfred Muller Sexton II, whom she had known only briefly. Sexton gave birth to her first daughter in 1953, and her second daughter in 1955. It was after the births of her children that she began to suffer from severe postpartum depression and attempted suicide several times. During this time, her therapist encouraged her to try writing poetry to explore her feelings.

> "Poetry should be a shock to the senses. It should almost hurt."
>
> —Anne Sexton

Sexton approached writing poetry with fervor. In 1960, Sexton published her first collection of poems titled *To Bedlam and Part Way Back,* which chronicled her early struggles with mental illness. This was followed, in 1962, by the publication of *All My Pretty Ones.* These first collections received mixed reviews. Some critics praised Sexton's work as "remarkable," "full of the exact flavors of places and peoples remembered," and "an honest and impressive achievement." Others saw her work as flawed and nothing more than a "determinedly outspoken soap-opera."

Fame and Pain Sexton, meanwhile, was becoming firmly established as a member of the "Confessional School," a group of poets who wrote during the late 1950s and 1960s and were categorized by their intensely introspective writing styles. At first, Sexton railed against being labeled a "confessional." Later she said, "I decided I was the only confessional poet."

While much of her work over the following years remained "confessional" and decidedly feminist, Sexton did occasionally go outside of herself for material. *Transformations,* published in 1971, is a retelling of the popular fairy tales of the Brothers Grimm. Reviewers delighted in the "colorful imagery" and sharp wit that Sexton exhibited in this collection.

During her career, Anne Sexton published ten books of poetry, as well a play, essays, and several children's books. Sexton received the Pulitzer Prize in 1967 for her collection *Live or Die.* As her fame grew, Sexton took on other responsibilities. She taught poetry workshops and creative writing, and she became a popular figure at poetry readings on college campuses. All the while, Sexton continued to struggle with mental illness. On October 4, 1974, she met with close friend Maxine Kumin to review the page galleys for her latest collection, *The Awful Rowing Toward God.* Later that day, Anne Sexton took her own life.

Anne Sexton was born in 1928 and died in 1974.

Literature Online **Author Search** For more about Anne Sexton, go to www.glencoe.com.

Connecting to the Essay

We often associate courage with great acts of bravery. Sexton, however, sees courage in seemingly ordinary acts. As you read the poem, think about the following questions:

- Would you call yourself courageous?
- Do you think that people who express pain and show vulnerability lack courage?

Building Background

The Awful Rowing Toward God, in which "Courage" appears, was Sexton's last collection of poetry. When Sexton wrote these poems, she was battling severe mental illness and was frequently an inpatient at mental hospitals. Many reviewers, including some of her close friends, criticized the poems in this collection as being too personal, disjointed, and lacking the strength of her earlier and best poems. Sexton herself called the poems "raw" and "unworked." *The Awful Rowing Toward God* was published in 1975. By that time, Anne Sexton was dead, and the poems had become prophetic.

Setting Purposes for Reading

Big Idea An Era of Protest

As you read the poem, notice how the poet focuses on the individual's conflicts with society.

Literary Element Verse Paragraph

A **verse paragraph** is a group of lines in a poem that form a unit. While stanzas traditionally have a fixed number of lines and are typical of poems written before the twentieth century, verse paragraphs are not uniform in length and reflect the open, freer form of contemporary verse. As you read the poem, examine how Sexton has used each verse paragraph to organize her ideas about courage and life.

- See Literary Terms Handbook, p. R19.

Literature Online Interactive Literary Elements Handbook To review or learn more about the literary elements, go to www.glencoe.com.

Reading Strategy Examining Connotation and Denotation

The **denotation** of a word is its literal, or dictionary, meaning. The **connotation** of a word is the meaning or association that the word has beyond its literal meaning. As you read, consider the positive or negative feelings that the connotations of specific words evoke.

Reading Tip: List Words Use a chart to list words with positive and negative connotations in the poem.

Positive Connotation	Negative Connotation
awesome	fatty

Vocabulary

wallowing (wol′ ō ing) *v.* moving in a clumsy manner or with difficulty; p. 1204 *After the heavy rain, we found ourselves wallowing through muddy ditches to get home.*

fondle (fond′ əl) *v.* to handle gently; p. 1204 *The puppy squirmed as the children tried to pet and fondle it.*

transfusion (trans fū′ zhən) *n.* the act of passing life-saving fluids from one to another; p. 1205 *He received a blood transfusion during the operation.*

transformed (trans fôrmd′) *adj.* changed in a dramatic way; p. 1205 *The messy vacant lot had been transformed into a lush flower garden.*

Vocabulary Tip: Context Clues Context clues for unfamiliar words are often found in words and sentences surrounding the word. Look for a synonym or an antonym nearby to provide a clue to the word.

INDIANA ACADEMIC STANDARDS (pages 1203–1206)
11.2 Develop strategies such as...analyzing structure...
11.1.2 Draw inferences about the meaning of vocabulary...
11.5.8 Deliver multimedia presentations that combine text [and] images...

Courage

Anne Sexton

It is in the small things we see it.
The child's first step,
as awesome as an earthquake.
The first time you rode a bike,
wallowing up the sidewalk.
The first spanking when your heart
went on a journey all alone.
When they called you crybaby
or poor or fatty or crazy
and made you into an alien,[1]
you drank their acid
and concealed it.

Later,
if you faced the death of bombs and bullets
you did not do it with a banner,
you did it with only a hat to
cover your heart.
You did not **fondle** the weakness inside you
though it was there.
Your courage was a small coal
that you kept swallowing.
If your buddy saved you
and died himself in so doing,
then his courage was not courage,
it was love, love as simple as shaving soap.

The Deluge, 1920. Winifred Knights. Oil on canvas, 59⅓ x 71⅓ in. Tate Gallery, London, UK.

---

1. *Alien* here means "someone who feels like an outsider."

Literary Element   Verse Paragraph *How do the lines that follow develop this idea?*

Big Idea   An Era of Protest *According to the speaker, how does the person addressed in this verse paragraph face death?*

Vocabulary

wallowing (wol′ ō ing) *v.* moving in a clumsy manner or with difficulty
fondle (fond′ əl) *v.* to handle gently

Later,
if you have endured a great despair,
then you did it alone,
getting a **transfusion** from the fire,
picking the scabs off your heart,
then wringing it out like a sock.
Next, my kinsman,[2] you powdered your sorrow,
you gave it a back rub
and then you covered it with a blanket
and after it had slept a while
it woke to the wings of the roses
and was **transformed**.[3]

Later,
when you face old age and its natural conclusion[4]
your courage will still be shown in the little ways,
each spring will be a sword you'll sharpen,
those you love will live in a fever of love,
and you'll bargain with the calendar
and at the last moment
when death opens the back door
you'll put on your carpet slippers
and stride out.

---

2. *Kinsman* is a relative. Here the speaker aligns herself with those who suffer the pain of loneliness and despair.
3. The poet may be making an illusion to the Phoenix, a mythical bird that burns itself to ashes and then rises anew from the ashes to live again.
4. The *natural conclusion* of life is death.

Reading Strategy Examining Denotation and Connotation *Why do you think the poet chose to use the word* powdered *instead of some other phrase?*

Vocabulary

transfusion (trans fū′ zhən) *n.* the act of passing life-saving fluids from one to another
transformed (trans fôrməd′) *adj.* changed in a dramatic way

RESPONDING AND THINKING CRITICALLY

Respond

1. How do Sexton's ideas of courage compare with your own? Do you agree that it takes a certain amount of courage to experience life? Explain.

Recall and Interpret

2. (a)According to the speaker, how does the child respond when bullied or abused? (b)What does this suggest about the speaker's attitude towards childhood?

3. (a)What image is used in the second verse paragraph to suggest that a great act of courage can be very simple and even common? (b)How does this image relate to the main idea of the first verse paragraph?

4. (a)How does the speaker let the audience know that she shares their suffering and pain? (b)What does this suggest to you about the speaker's life?

Analyze and Evaluate

5. (a)What images does Sexton use to describe how people can recover from the emotional pain that life inflicts? (b)What role does Sexton see for other people in this process?

6. (a)What does the speaker envision in the last verse paragraph? (b)Why does Sexton, at the end of the poem, describe the encounter with death as she does?

Connect

7. **Big Idea** **An Era of Protest** The 1970s saw the emergence of the women's movement and the crisis of the Vietnam War. How might this poem be viewed as an expression of discontent and an argument for change?

LITERARY ANALYSIS

Literary Element **Verse Paragraph**

Poets use **verse paragraphs** to organize a poem into thoughts in much the same way that writers use paragraphs to organize ideas in prose. For example, in "Courage," Anne Sexton uses each verse paragraph to describe a different stage of a person's life.

1. How does Sexton show chronological order both between and within the verse paragraphs?

2. How does the poet view courage at each stage in a person's life?

Interdisciplinary Activity: Art

Create a Mural As a class, plan and create a four-section mural based on the four verse paragraphs in "Courage." Decide on the mediums you will use to create the mural. Then separate into groups and have each group choose a verse paragraph to discuss and design. Display your mural accompanied by a copy of the poem.

Literature Online **Web Activities** For eFlashcards, Selection Quick Checks, and other Web activities, go to www.glencoe.com.

READING AND VOCABULARY

Reading Strategy **Examining Connotation and Denotation**

Poets choose words for their sound and for their meaning. The **denotation** of a word is its literal meaning. Words that have different **connotations**, or shades of meaning, have an added impact on the meaning and effect of the poem. In "Courage," Sexton uses words that have very negative connotations, like "crybaby," "alien," and "acid." Identify words that have negative connotations in the third verse paragraph. Explain the connotation of each.

Vocabulary **Practice**

Practice with Context Clues For each of the following vocabulary words, construct a sentence that uses context clues to give the meaning of the word.

1. wallowing

2. fondle

3. transfusion

4. transformed

Nature and Technology

Moonwalk, 1987. Andy Warhol. Screenprint on lenox museum board, 38 x 38 in. The Andy Warhol Foundation for the Visual Arts.

"The 'control of nature' is a phrase conceived in arrogance, born of the Neanderthal age of biology and the convenience of man."

—Rachel Carson, *Silent Spring*

The Fish and *Filling Station*

MEET ELIZABETH BISHOP

The poet Elizabeth Bishop once told her writing class at Harvard University, "Use the dictionary. It's better than the critics." Bishop's wit and devotion to careful, precise language came through in her own writing, which earned her nearly every major poetry prize in the United States.

For Bishop, writing poetry was an act of "self-forgetfulness," in which she focused on shaping and sharing her impressions of the physical world rather than on giving the details of her personal life. Her childhood in Worcester, Massachusetts, was difficult. When she was very young, her father died and her mother was permanently hospitalized, so Bishop was raised by relatives, first in Canada and later in Worcester. After graduation from Vassar College in 1934, Bishop traveled frequently and lived in many places, including Florida, New York, and Europe. For sixteen years, she made her home in Brazil. She kept in touch with people she met in her travels through thousands of letters, some of which were collected and published in her book *One Art.*

> *"[It is] far more important to just keep writing poetry than to think of yourself as a poet whose job it is to write poetry all the time."*
>
> —Elizabeth Bishop

A formative experience for Bishop was her 1934 introduction to the poet Marianne Moore, who became Bishop's valued friend and mentor. Bishop also became close to poet Robert Lowell, who provided unstinting moral support and helped Bishop obtain grants, fellowships, and awards. Bishop and Lowell critiqued each other's poetry and remained staunch allies throughout their lives.

Described by many friends as generous and wise, Bishop was also complicated and intensely private. Though she suffered from bouts of depression, people who knew her were struck by her warmth and self-deprecating sense of humor. Bishop deeply appreciated friends and relatives who made her laugh. In a letter, she wrote, "I have been very lucky in having had, most of my life, some witty friends,—and I mean real wit, quickness, wild fancies, remarks that make one cry with laughing."

In her work, Bishop often captured subtle moments of engagement with nature. Her voice is one of the most distinctive in American poetry, conveying not only the sights and sounds of nature but also the thoughts and feelings of a speaker groping toward an understanding of nature. Bishop was preoccupied with questions of guilt, loss, and artistic vision, and these issues appear in her poetry.

Over her fifty-year writing career, Bishop published five slim volumes of poetry with a total of 101 poems. Of her final poetry collection, critic Alfred Corn wrote that Bishop achieved "a perfected transparence of expression, warmth of tone, and a singular blend of sadness and good humor, of pain and acceptance—a radiant patience few people ever achieve and few writers ever successfully render." Besides writing, Bishop taught at Harvard for seven years and served as a poetry consultant to the Library of Congress.

Elizabeth Bishop was born in 1911 and died in 1979.

Literature Online Author Search For more about Elizabeth Bishop, go to www.glencoe.com.

Connecting to the Poems

In these poems, the close examination of everyday objects leads to moments of intense clarity. As you read, think about these questions:

- When have you discovered something unexpected about a familiar person or place?
- How can appearances deceive us? How can they give us insight?

Building Background

A lover of animals and the physical world, Bishop wrote careful descriptions of scenes she witnessed or experienced outdoors. The following passage from a letter Bishop wrote to Marianne Moore may have developed into her poem "The Fish."

> The other day I caught a parrot fish, almost by accident. They are ravishing fish—all iridescent, with a silver edge to each scale, and a real bull-like mouth just like turquoise; the eye is very big and wild, and the eyeball is turquoise too—they are very humorous-looking fish. A man on the dock immediately scraped off three scales, then threw him back; he was sure it wouldn't hurt him. I'm enclosing one [scale], if I can find it.

Setting Purposes for Reading

Big Idea Nature and Technology

In these poems, carefully examine the observations about the fish and the filling (or gas) station. Think about what Bishop's patient reflections tell you about modern life and nature's role in it.

Literary Element Tone

Tone is the attitude that an author expresses toward his or her subject matter. When we speak, we choose a tone of voice to give clues to underlying attitudes such as humor, formality, anger, or sadness. Similarly, authors carefully choose words and sentence structure in order to set the tone.

- See Literary Terms Handbook, p. R19.

Reading Strategy Evaluating Sensory Details

Sensory details are evocative words or phrases that appeal to one or more of the five senses. Poets use sensory details to help the reader imagine or experience more deeply the content of poems. As you read, carefully examine the sensory details and think about what feeling or meaning they convey to you.

Reading Tip: Chart Sensory Details Record sensory details in a chart like the one shown. List the sense that the detail appeals to. Then jot down notes on what feeling or meaning the detail conveys to you.

Sensory detail	Sense appealed to	Feeling or meaning

Literature Online **Interactive Literary Elements Handbook** To review or learn more about the literary elements, go to www.glencoe.com.

Vocabulary

tarnish (tär′nish) v. to dull, soil, or stain; p. 1210 *The cabinet was tarnished by the fire.*

permeate (pur′mē āt′) v. to penetrate, spread through, or diffuse; p. 1212 *Water may permeate the bag if it is not sealed shut before the storm.*

extraneous (ek strā′nē əs) adj. not intrinsically belonging; not forming a vital part; coming from outside; p. 1213 *The music seemed extraneous to the scientific presentation.*

Vocabulary Tip: Context Clues If, during your reading, you come across a word with which you are unfamiliar, the words and sentences surrounding the word may provide clues to its meaning. Such clues are known as context clues.

INDIANA ACADEMIC STANDARDS (pages 1209–1215)
11.3.3 Analyze the ways in which...tone...achieve[s] specific... aesthetic (artistic) purposes...

11.2 Develop [reading] strategies...
11.5.2 Write responses to literature...

Returning Fishing Boats, 1883. Winslow Homer. Watercolor.
Fogg Museum of Art, Harvard University, Cambridge, MA.

The Fish

Elizabeth Bishop

I caught a tremendous fish
and held him beside the boat
half out of water, with my hook
fast in a corner of his mouth.
5   He didn't fight.
He hadn't fought at all.
He hung a grunting weight,
battered and venerable[1]
and homely. Here and there
10 his brown skin hung in strips
like ancient wall-paper,
and its pattern of darker brown
was like wall-paper:
shapes like full-blown roses
15 stained and lost through age.
He was speckled with barnacles,
fine rosettes of lime,
and infested
with tiny white sea-lice,
20 and underneath two or three
rags of green weed hung down.
While his gills were breathing in
the terrible oxygen
—the frightening gills,
25 fresh and crisp with blood,
that can cut so badly—
I thought of the coarse white flesh
packed in like feathers,
the big bones and the little bones,
30 the dramatic reds and blacks
of his shiny entrails,[2]
and the pink swim-bladder[3]
like a big peony.
I looked into his eyes
35 which were far larger than mine
but shallower, and yellowed,
the irises backed and packed
with **tarnished** tinfoil

---

1. Venerable means "deserving respect because of age."
2. *Entrails* are internal organs.
3. A *swim-bladder,* or air bladder, is an air sac that enables
   some fish to maintain buoyancy and equilibrium.

Big Idea Nature and Technology *What relationship between people and animals do these lines establish?*

Reading Strategy Evaluating Sensory Details *What ideas about the fish do these visual details convey?*

Vocabulary

tarnish (tär′nĭsh) *v.* to dull, soil, or stain

        seen through the lenses
40   of old scratched isinglass.[4]
        They shifted a little, but not
        to return my stare.
        —It was more like the tipping
        of an object toward the light.
45   I admired his sullen face,
        the mechanism of his jaw,
        and then I saw
        that from his lower lip
        —if you could call it a lip—
50   grim, wet, and weapon-like,
        hung five old pieces of fish-line,
        or four and a wire leader
        with the swivel still attached,
        with all their five big hooks
55   grown firmly in his mouth.
        A green line, frayed at the end
        where he broke it, two heavier lines,
        and a fine black thread
        still crimped from the strain and snap
60   when it broke and he got away.
        Like medals with their ribbons
        frayed and wavering,
        a five-haired beard of wisdom
        trailing from his aching jaw.
65   I stared and stared
        and victory filled up
        the little rented boat,
        from the pool of bilge[5]
        where oil had spread a rainbow
70   around the rusted engine
        to the bailer rusted orange,
        the sun-cracked thwarts,[6]
        the oarlocks on their strings,
        the gunnels[7]—until everything
75   was rainbow, rainbow, rainbow!
        And I let the fish go.

---

4. *Isinglass* (ī′ zin glas′) was used in windows before glass panes became common.
5. *Bilge* (bilj) is stagnant water in the bottom of a boat.
6. *Thwarts* (thwôrts) are seats going across a small boat.
7. *Gunnels* (gə′ nəlz) are the upper edges of the sides of a boat.

Reading Strategy Evaluating Sensory Details *What do these details reveal about the fish?*

Literary Element Tone *What do these lines reveal about the speaker's attitude toward the fish?*

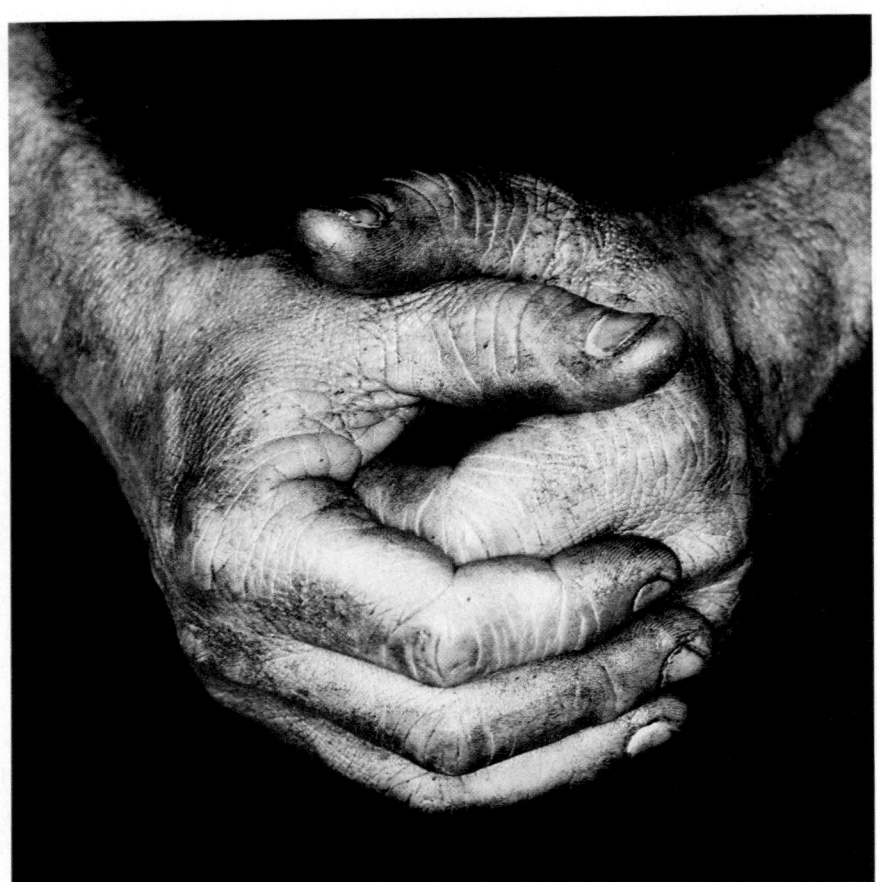

Filling Station

Elizabeth Bishop

Oh, but it is dirty!
—this little filling station,
oil-soaked, oil-**permeated**
to a disturbing, over-all
5   black translucency.
Be careful with that match!

Father wears a dirty,
oil-soaked monkey suit
that cuts him under the arms,
10   and several quick and saucy
and greasy sons assist him
(it's a family filling station),
all quite thoroughly dirty.

Literary Element Tone *What does this line suggest about the speaker's attitude toward the gas station?*

Vocabulary

permeate (pur´ mē āt´) *v.* to penetrate, spread through, or diffuse

Do they live in the station?
15 It has a cement porch
behind the pumps, and on it
a set of crushed and grease-
impregnated wickerwork;
on the wicker sofa
20 a dirty dog, quite comfy.

Some comic books provide
the only note of color—
of certain color. They lie
upon a big dim doily[1]
25 draping a taboret[2]
(part of the set), beside
a big hirsute[3] begonia.

Why the **extraneous** plant?
Why the taboret?
30 Why, oh why, the doily?
(Embroidered in daisy stitch
with marguerites, I think,
and heavy with gray crochet.)

Somebody embroidered the doily.
35 Somebody waters the plant,
or oils it, maybe. Somebody
arranges the rows of cans
so that they softly say:
esso—so—so—so
40 to high-strung automobiles.
Somebody loves us all.

---

1. A *doily* is a small, often decorative, napkin.
2. A *taboret* is a seat or stool without arms or back.
3. *Hirsute* means "hairy."

Reading Strategy Evaluating Sensory Details
What is significant about the doily's presence?

Vocabulary

extraneous (ek strā′ nē əs) *adj.* not intrinsically belonging; not forming a vital part; coming from outside

Respond

1. What was your initial reaction to the fish in the first poem and the filling station in the second? Did your reactions change as you read? Explain.

Recall and Interpret

2. (a)In "The Fish," what details about the fish are provided in lines 1–21? (b)How would you characterize the fish based on these details? Cite words and phrases from the poem to support your conclusion.

3. (a)To what does the speaker compare the fish-lines hanging from the fish's mouth? (b)What does this comparison tell you about how the speaker sees the fish? Explain.

4. (a)In line 66, what does the speaker say fills the boat? (b)What, in your opinion, motivates the speaker to let the fish go? Explain.

5. (a)In "Filling Station," who runs the filling station? (b)In what terms does the speaker describe the station and the people who run it?

6. (a)What details in the poem may provide clues about the lives of the people who run the station?

(b)To the speaker, what do these details suggest about people in general? Explain.

Analyze and Evaluate

7. One critic wrote that Bishop focused less on an event than on what she "saw and felt and shared with others." In what ways do these two poems support and contradict this statement? Explain your answer citing details from the poem.

8. (a)In "The Fish," how do the speaker's feelings and ideas about the fish develop over the course of the poem? (b)If you had been in the boat, would you have drawn the same conclusions about the fish that the speaker does? Explain.

9. Why do you think Bishop chose to end "Filling Station" with the sentence in line 41? Explain how this sentence influences the meaning of the poem as a whole.

Connect

10. **Big Idea** **Nature and Technology** On the basis of "The Fish," what attitude would you say that Bishop adopted toward the natural world? Explain your answer.

Literary Element **Tone**

Tone is the author's attitude toward his or her subject matter. Some tones are clearly defined. Other tones are more complicated, reflecting a combination of emotions in the author.

1. How would you describe the tone in the first half of "The Fish"? Cite examples of words or sentences that you feel indicate the tone.

2. How does the tone of "The Fish" change in the second half of the poem? What does the change in tone reveal about the speaker's perceptions of the fish? Give examples of words or sentences that demonstrate the changed tone. Then explain how the tone works with other elements of the poem to create an overall meaning, or **theme**. Include a summary of the theme in your answer.

Review: Setting

As you learned in unit 4, **setting** is the time and place in which the events of a literary work occur. Setting includes not only physical surroundings, but also the ideas and customs of a time and place. In "Filling Station," much energy is devoted to investigating and detailing the setting.

Partner Activity Meet with another classmate to discuss the setting of "Filling Station." Create a web like the one below and use it to list the different elements of the poem's setting. Then discuss what atmosphere, or mood, these details of setting help to create. Share your thoughts with the class.

READING AND VOCABULARY

Reading Strategy Evaluating Sensory Details

Sensory details are images that appeal to the reader's senses of hearing, sight, smell, taste, and touch. These images help readers to more closely experience the content of a poem.

1. Identify an image from each poem that appeals to your sense of sight. For each image, tell what you see in your mind's eye.

2. One critic says that "the more we examine the description of contrast, the more we understand the poetry of Elizabeth Bishop." How does this statement apply to "The Fish" and "Filling Station"? In your answer, include examples of sensory details.

Vocabulary Practice

Practice with Context Clues For each sentence, use context clues to determine the meaning of the word in boldface.

1. If you incorrectly apply the cleanser, you may **tarnish** the candlestick.
   a. illuminate   **b.** warm   **c.** stain

2. Acid is strong; it can **permeate** almost any container.
   a. penetrate   **b.** isolate   **c.** distill

3. If you add **extraneous** elements to the recipe, the food will taste wrong.
   a. excellent   **b.** outside   **c.** characteristic

Academic Vocabulary

Here are two words from the vocabulary list on page R86. These words will help you think, write, and talk about the selection.

energy (en′ ər jē) *n.* vigor; power; vitality or intensity of expression

pursue (pər sŏŏ′) *v.* to strive to gain or accomplish

Practice and Apply

1. In "The Fish," how does the fish's high level of **energy** save its life?

2. What elements did you examine to **pursue** your understanding of "Filling Station"?

WRITING AND EXTENDING

Writing About Literature

Evaluate Author's Craft Poetry often creates strong responses and opinions in its readers. According to critic Ronald E. McFarland,

> readers of Elizabeth Bishop's "The Fish" commonly pose objections which concern opposite ends of the critical spectrum. One objection is to the integrity of Bishop's fish: it does not seem realistic; it is too ugly; what kind of fish is it supposed to be anyway? Another is to the conceptual limitations of the poem: the imagery is admirable, but that is not enough . . . ; after close examination of [the] ugly old fish, [the] fisherman releases it—so what?

What is your opinion of the Bishop poems you have read? Do you agree with either of the opinions noted by McFarland? Write a review of either "The Fish" or "The Filling Station." Discuss what you liked or disliked about either of the poems in your review. You may choose to respond to critical reactions to the poems in your review. Support your opinions with examples from the text. In your review, you should also discuss the poem's theme as well as the tone, mood, and setting.

Performing

Create a Multimedia Presentation With a group, do research to create a multimedia presentation on "The Fish."

- Begin your presentation by giving a brief overview of Bishop's life and work. You may include photographs, slides, and/or recordings of Bishop reading her poems.

- Next, present an analysis of "The Fish." You may wish to begin your group's analysis by reading the poem out loud. During the reading, you may play music to help reinforce the mood of the poem.

- Accompany your discussion with photographs, works of fine art, or any other visual or auditory elements that you think will enhance your discussion.

- End the presentation by giving a conclusion about "The Fish" and presenting two or three questions for further research.

Literature Online **Web Activities** For eFlashcards, Selection Quick Checks, and other Web activities, go to www.glencoe.com.

Root Cellar

MEET THEODORE ROETHKE

A much loved and acclaimed poet during his lifetime, Theodore Roethke won many prestigious awards, including the Pulitzer Prize, the National Book Award, and the Bollingen Prize. However, many of his poems have received higher honors than official prizes can bestow: They have become personal favorites for many readers, touching their lives deeply.

Roethke fashioned many of his poems from intense memories of his childhood in Saginaw, Michigan. His father and grandfather were florists, and Roethke grew up in a world of flowers, plants, and large commercial greenhouses. From these early experiences, he acquired a passionate love for nature and a deep understanding of natural processes. Like Emerson and Whitman, he almost mystically identified with nature: "In my veins, in my bones I feel it." Images of growth and decay recur in all of his volumes of poetry, including *Open House* (1941), *The Lost Son and Other Poems* (1948), *The Waking* (1953), and *Words for the Wind* (1958).

> "For Roethke, boundaries between outer and inner dissolve; the natural world seems a vast landscape of the psyche, just as the voyage inward leads to natural things—roots, leaves, and flowers—as emblems of the recesses of the self."
>
> —Mark Doty, from *A Profile of Twentieth-Century American Poetry*

Finding His Calling During Roethke's sophomore year of high school, his father died from lung cancer. This loss devastated Roethke. At seventeen, he entered the University of Michigan, the first in his family to attend college. He graduated *magna cum laude* and after a semester in law school, enrolled as a graduate student in literature, first at the University of Michigan and one year later at Harvard University.

At Harvard, Roethke handed three of his poems to Robert Hillyer, a poet and professor. After reading them, Hillyer said, "Any editor who wouldn't buy these is a fool!" Encouraged by Hillyer, Roethke submitted the poems to different journals and dedicated his life to writing poetry.

Poet and Teacher Despite his success in getting his poems published, Roethke could not afford to continue graduate school in 1931, when the United States was mired in the Great Depression. He took a position teaching English at Lafayette College in Easton, Pennsylvania, and later taught at Michigan State College, Pennsylvania State University, Bennington College, and the University of Washington.

Roethke brought the same passion to teaching as he did to writing poetry. Throughout his adult life, however, he struggled with psychological problems. He died of a heart attack when he was only fifty-five.

Theodore Roethke was born in 1908 and died in 1963.

Literature Online Author Search For more about Theodore Roethke, go to www.glencoe.com.

Connecting to the Poem

In "Root Cellar," the speaker recalls a sensory-rich place in nature. As you read the poem, think about the following questions:

- Which places in nature can you recall in great detail?
- What did these places teach you about life?

Building Background

A root cellar is a dark, moist place where root vegetables, including carrots, beets, and potatoes, are stored for the winter along with potting soil and fertilizers. Root cellars are commonly built into the sides of hills, where the surrounding earth and the dirt floors help keep the temperature inside cool and the humidity high. Even in root cellars, however, produce can spoil. Sometimes, mold forms on the surfaces of plants, causing them to decay. Other times, vegetables stored too long begin to sprout, causing the roots or bulbs to rot.

Setting Purposes for Reading

Big Idea Nature and Technology

As you read "Root Cellar," consider what the speaker suggests about the relationship between humans and nature.

Literary Element Simile

A **simile** is a figure of speech using a word or phrase such as *like* or *as* to compare seemingly unlike things. As you read this poem, look for examples of similes and notice what is compared.

- See Literary Terms Handbook, p. R16.

Reading Strategy Interpreting Imagery

Interpreting imagery can help you better understand the meaning of a poem and the poet's intention. Imagery refers to any "word pictures" that writers create to evoke emotional responses. Imagery includes sensory details, or descriptions that appeal to one or more of the five senses: sight, hearing, touch, taste, and smell.

Reading Tip: Taking Notes Use a chart to record the images in this poem and their sensory appeal.

Details	Sensory appeal
Bulbs broke out of boxes	

Vocabulary

mildewed (mil´dyūd) *adj.* coated or partially coated with a fungus that causes spoilage; p. 1218 *We threw out the books stored in the basement because they were mildewed and damaged.*

congress (kong´gris) *n.* a formal meeting; p. 1218 *There was a congress of physicists at the convention center.*

rank (rangk) *adj.* having a strong, offensive odor; p. 1218 *The clothing left in the gym lockers was dirty and rank.*

Vocabulary Tip: Synonyms Words that have the same or nearly the same meaning are called synonyms. For example, the words *dank* and *moist* are synonyms. Synonyms are always the same part of speech.

Literature Online Interactive Literary Elements Handbook To review or learn more about the literary elements, go to www.glencoe.com.

INDIANA ACADEMIC STANDARDS (pages 1217–1219)
11.3.4 Analyze ways in which poetry...uses imagery [and] figures of speech...to evoke readers' emotions.
11.1.3 Analyze the meaning of analogies encountered...
11.5.3 Write reflective compositions...

ROOT CELLAR

Theodore Roethke

In the Beginning. Freyda Miller.

Nothing would sleep in that cellar, dank as a ditch,
Bulbs[1] broke out of boxes hunting for chinks[2] in the dark,
Shoots dangled and drooped,
Lolling obscenely from mildewed crates,
5   Hung down long yellow evil necks, like tropical snakes.
And what a congress of stinks!—
Roots ripe[3] as old bait,
Pulpy stems, rank, silo-rich,[4]
Leaf-mold, manure, lime,[5] piled against slippery planks.
10   Nothing would give up life:
Even the dirt kept breathing a small breath.

---

1. *Bulbs,* here, refer to modified, underground stems surrounded by fleshy leaves that serve as the food supply for the growing plant.
2. *Chinks* are narrow openings.
3. *Ripe,* here, means "giving off a very foul odor."
4. A *silo* is a tall, cylindrical structure in which plant materials are stored. The adjective *silo-rich* refers to an odor similar to that emitted by partially fermented plant materials stored in a silo.
5. *Lime,* here, refers to a chemical used as a fertilizer for plants.

Big Idea **Nature and Technology** *Why does the speaker describe the necks of the shoots as evil?*

Reading Strategy **Interpreting Imagery** *How do the sensory details change with line 6 of the poem?*

Vocabulary

mildewed (mil´ dyūd) *adj.* coated or partially coated with a fungus that causes spoilage
congress (kong´ gris) *n.* a formal meeting
rank (rangk) *adj.* having a strong, offensive odor

RESPONDING AND THINKING CRITICALLY

Respond

1. Which details from this poem surprised you the most? Explain.

Recall and Interpret

2. (a)Which word does the speaker use to describe the root cellar? (b)What does this word usually suggest?

3. (a)What does the speaker observe happening in the root cellar? (b)What do the last two lines of the poem suggest about the speaker's attitude toward what he observes? Explain.

4. What might the root cellar symbolize in this poem?

Analyze and Evaluate

5. (a)What examples of **alliteration,** or the repetition of initial consonant sounds, can you find in this poem? (b)What effects does this technique help to create?

6. In this poem Roethke uses **free verse,** with the line length and the meter expanding and contracting as needed. How is the form of the poem appropriate to the subject?

7. Roethke claimed that in some of his early poems, he began "with small things and had tried to make plain words do the trick." To what extent does Roethke's statement apply to the subject and the diction of this poem? Explain.

Connect

8. **Big Idea** **Nature and Technology** What does Roethke suggest about the relationship between humans and nature in this poem?

LITERARY ANALYSIS

Literary Element **Simile**

Writers use **similes** to make descriptions more vivid or to explain something unfamiliar by comparing it to something familiar.

1. Identify three similes in the poem.

2. Which simile did you find most vivid and original?

Writing About Literature

Respond to Theme Using the poem "Root Cellar" as a model, write your own poem about a sensory-rich place in nature. Include similes that are natural, yet original, and diction that is clear, direct, and striking.

Literature Online **Web Activities** For eFlashcards, Selection Quick Checks, and other Web activities, go to www.glencoe.com.

READING AND VOCABULARY

Reading Strategy **Interpreting Imagery**

"Root Cellar" is remarkable for the number and variety of its sensory details. Review the chart you made on page 1217 that lists examples of these details in the poem.

1. Which sensory details do you think create the most vivid images?

2. What do the sensory details suggest about the root cellar?

Vocabulary **Practice**

Practice with Synonyms Find the synonym for each vocabulary word from "Root Cellar" listed in the first column. Use a dictionary or a thesaurus if you need help.

1. congress   **a.** announcement   **b.** caucus

2. mildewed   **a.** parched   **b.** moldy

3. rank   **a.** fragrant   **b.** putrid

Sleep in the Mojave Desert and Crossing the Water

MEET SYLVIA PLATH

It seemed that Sylvia Plath was born to be a poet. She was only eight years old when a Boston newspaper published her first poem. In high school, Plath won numerous literary prizes and excelled academically, earning a scholarship to Smith College. During her time in college, her poetry and prose were published in prestigious national magazines, and she continued to win awards for her work. Sadly, however, her creative journey was shadowed by bouts of severe depression, during which she struggled with thoughts of death. These struggles ended when Plath took her own life at the age of thirty, a month after her critically acclaimed novel, *The Bell Jar*, was first published. Because much of her writing was so starkly personal, Plath's struggles and death have been closely tied to her image as a poet. However, Plath's dark, beautiful poems speak on their own, fulfilling her ambition to create profound and lasting works.

as valedictorian. Plath's father died when she was just eight, and the loss deeply affected her.

After graduating from Smith College, Plath was awarded a Fulbright Fellowship and went on to Cambridge, England, for her graduate studies in poetry. It was there, in February 1956, that she met an ambitious young British poet, the soon-to-be-famous Ted Hughes. By June they were married, beginning a passionate but turbulent relationship that heavily influenced the poetry of both Plath and Hughes. They were exploring an emerging type of literature—confessional poetry, which draws heavily on intimate details from the writer's life. After Cambridge, Plath returned to Massachusetts with Hughes and took a writing class with Robert Lowell, a highly regarded poet of the confessional school.

After a short time teaching and writing in the United States, Plath and Hughes moved back to England, where Plath published her first book of poems, *Colossus*, in 1960. During the last years of her life, she wrote at an often feverish pace. Many of these final poems were included in Plath's landmark collection *Ariel*, which was published two years after her death in February 1963. Over the next twenty years, more of Plath's poems would be collected and published by Hughes. Her final book, *The Collected Poems*, was awarded the Pulitzer Prize in 1982, the final step of her long journey into literary greatness.

Sylvia Plath was born in 1932 and died in 1963.

> *"I think my poems immediately come out of the sensuous and emotional experiences I have, but . . . I believe that one should be able to control and manipulate experiences, even the most terrific."*
>
> —Sylvia Plath
> from a 1962 interview with Peter Orr

Confessions of a Poet Plath was born in Jamaica Plain, Massachusetts. Her father, Otto Plath, was a German immigrant and respected college professor who wrote a renowned study on bees. Her mother, Aurelia, had been one of her father's students at Boston University, where she graduated

Literature Online Author Search For more about Sylvia Plath, go to www.glencoe.com.

Connecting to the Poem

In the poems you are about to read, the speaker is isolated in nature, and the landscapes take on the qualities of a dream. As you read the poems, think about these questions:

- Have you ever been in a place that you thought reflected how you felt?
- Do your dreams ever symbolize what is going on in your life?

Building Background

The poems "Crossing the Water" and "Sleep in the Mojave Desert," written in the early 1960s, appeared in collections that were published posthumously, or after her death. Her final years in England were the most productive period of her creative life. These poems were among the dozens that Plath wrote as she struggled with her deepening depression. Dark feelings pervade these startlingly original poems, which address loneliness, human suffering, and death. Although they do not include specific personal details, these are considered confessional poems because they explore Plath's emotions.

Setting Purposes for Reading

Big Idea Nature and Technology

As you read, notice how the speaker in these poems is an outsider within the natural setting.

Literary Element Mood

Mood refers to the emotional quality, or atmosphere, of a literary work. The language, pace, and imagery combine to convey the mood of a poem. The mood conveys the poet's view of the world and influences the expression of the poem itself. Particularly in writing that deals with intense emotion, mood can be a powerful element.

- See Literary Terms Handbook, p. R11.

Literature Online **Interactive Literary Elements Handbook** To review or learn more about the literary elements, go to www.glencoe.com.

Reading Strategy Analyzing Voice

Voice is the personality that a writer conveys in a piece of writing. The reader can **analyze** voice by examining a poet's choice of words and the **tone,** or attitude toward the subject matter, that a poem expresses. As you analyze voice, pay close attention to the kind of language the poet uses.

Reading Tip: Describing Voice Describe each element of voice in a chart like the one below. Consider what these elements contribute to the poem's overall voice and write a description of that voice.

Element	Description
Word choice	
Tone	
Voice	

Vocabulary

recede (ri sēd′) *v.* to move back or away from a limit, point, or mark; p. 1222 *After the storm passed, we could see the floodwater recede.*

swelter (swel′ tər) *v.* to suffer from oppressive heat; p. 1222 *The crowd will swelter under the sun.*

congregate (kong′ gri gāt′) *v.* to bring or come together in a group, a crowd, or an assembly; p. 1222 *The team will congregate in the dugout.*

valedictory (val′ ə dik′ tə′ rē) *adj.* of or relating to an occasion or expression of farewell; p. 1223 *In his valedictory address, he bade farewell.*

Vocabulary Tip: Synonyms Two words that have the same or nearly the same meaning are called **synonyms.** Note that synonyms are always the same part of speech.

 INDIANA ACADEMIC STANDARDS (pages 1221–1225)
11.3.3 Analyze...tone [and] mood...
11.2 Develop [reading] strategies...

11.5.9 Write...a literary analysis that...supports judgments with relevant...evidence and well-chosen details...

Sleep in the Mojave Desert

Sylvia Plath

Back of Marie's No. 4, 1931. Georgia O' Keeffe. Oil on canvas, 16 x 30 in. The Georgia O' Keeffe Museum, Santa Fe, NM.

Out here there are no hearthstones,[2]
Hot grains, simply. It is dry, dry.
And the air dangerous. Noonday acts queerly
On the mind's eye, erecting a line
5   Of poplars[3] in the middle distance, the only
Object beside the mad, straight road
One can remember men and houses by.
A cool wind should inhabit those leaves
And a dew collect on them, dearer than money,
10   In the blue hour before sunup.
Yet they **recede**, untouchable as tomorrow,
Or those glittery fictions of spilt water
That glide ahead of the very thirsty.

I think of the lizards airing their tongues
15   In the crevice of an extremely small shadow
And the toad guarding his heart's droplet.
The desert is white as a blind man's eye,
Comfortless as salt. Snake and bird
Doze behind the old masks of fury.
20   We **swelter** like firedogs[4] in the wind.
The sun puts its cinder out. Where we lie
The heat-cracked crickets **congregate**
In their black armorplate and cry.
The day-moon lights up like a sorry mother,
25   And the crickets come creeping into our hair
To fiddle the short night away.

1. The *Mojave Desert* is an arid region of southeastern California and parts of Arizona, Nevada, and Utah. Once part of an ancient inland sea, the desert was formed by volcanic action and materials deposited by the Colorado River.
2. *Hearthstones* are the stones used to create the floor of a fireplace; the word also conveys the sense of family life or home.
3. *Poplars* are fast-growing deciduous trees (trees that lose their leaves seasonally).
4. *Firedogs,* or *andirons,* are a pair of metal supports that hold logs in a fireplace.

Reading Strategy   Analyzing Voice   *How does this passage help define the author's voice?*

Big Idea   Nature and Technology   *How does this sentence reflect the role of nature in this poem?*

Vocabulary

recede (ri sēd´) *v.* to move back or away from a point, limit, or mark

swelter (swel´ tər) *v.* to suffer from oppressive heat

congregate (kong´ gri gāt´) *v.* to bring or come together in a group, crowd, or assembly

Crossing the Water

Sylvia Plath

Black lake, black boat, two black, cut-paper people.
Where do the black trees go that drink here?
Their shadows must cover Canada.

A little light is filtering from the water flowers.
Their leaves do not wish us to hurry:
They are round and flat and full of dark advice.

Cold worlds shake from the oar.
The spirit of blackness is in us, it is in the fishes.
A snag[1] is lifting a **valedictory**, pale hand;

Stars open among the lilies.
Are you not blinded by such expressionless sirens?[2]
This is the silence of astounded souls.

---

1. A *snag* is a tree or tree branch embedded in water that prevents navigation.
2. In Greek mythology, *Sirens* were half-bird, half-woman sea creatures whose sweet singing lured mariners to destruction on the rocks that surrounded their island.

Literary Element   Mood *What technique does Plath use in the opening lines to create mood?*

Vocabulary

valedictory (val′ ə dik′ tə′ rē) *adj.* of or relating to an occasion or expression of farewell

RESPONDING AND THINKING CRITICALLY

Respond

1. Which images did you find most interesting or intriguing?

Recall and Interpret

2. (a)In "Sleep in the Mojave Desert," to what common desert illusion do the lines "Or those glittery fictions of spilt water / That glide ahead of the very thirsty" refer? (b)What does the image represent in the poem?

3. (a)In "Crossing the Water," what does the speaker say the water flowers' leaves do not want her to do? (b)Why does she say this?

4. (a)In "Crossing the Water," what concrete image does the line "Cold worlds shake from the oar" conjure up? (b)What does the line convey about the speaker's emotions?

Analyze and Evaluate

5. In lines 14–16 of "Sleep in the Mojave Desert," the poem seems to "zoom in" to provide close-up views of images. How does the poet achieve this effect, and what images does she use to suggest it?

6. In the last six lines of "Sleep in the Mojave Desert," how does the poet create the effect of darkness that is closing in?

7. The first and last stanzas in "Crossing the Water" connect the beginning and the end of the poem by sharing the same structure. Why do you think the poet chose to do this?

Connect

8. **Big Idea** Nature and Technology The speaker relates to nature differently in each of these poems. Compare the relationship between the speaker and nature in these poems.

LITERARY ANALYSIS

Literary Element Mood

Mood is a broad term that encompasses the overall impression created by a poem. Specific elements—such as language, subject matter, tone, setting, rhyme and rhythm—can all contribute to the mood. Because mood influences the poem as a whole, it can affect the way that images and events are portrayed or perceived. Mood is like a filter through which the poem is seen.

1. Identify the language, in the first three lines of "Sleep in the Mojave Desert," that helps establish the mood. What mood does this language create?

2. How does the setting in "Sleep in the Mojave Desert" contribute to the mood of the poem?

3. What is the overall mood of "Crossing the Water"? How does it affect the way you interpret the last line?

Review: Figurative Language

Figurative Language is language used for descriptive effect, in order to convey ideas or emotions. Figurative expressions are not literally true but express some truth beyond the literal level.

Partner Activity With a partner, identify three or more examples of strong figurative language in the poems. Discuss how the language is used and analyze it together by determining (a)what it is describing within the poem and (b)what idea or emotion it is conveying. Record your analysis in a chart like the one below.

Figurative Language	What It Describes	Idea or Emotion That It Conveys

READING AND VOCABULARY

Reading Strategy Analyzing Voice

Poets create **voice** through the distinctive use of language. Voice in a poem is embodied by the speaker and defined by the speaker's attitude. In some poems, the voice is simply an extension of the writer as represented in the work. In other poems, the voice takes on its own character or **persona**—a mask or voice through which the writer speaks. **Analyzing voice** requires close examination of the speaker in the poem.

Although Plath's poems often explore her own life and emotions, the voice she creates is usually a persona represented by the speaker. Confessional poetry carefully uses voice to blur the distinction between personal truth and poetic fiction.

1. These poems share a similar voice. What do the voices have in common?

2. How does the voice in these poems contribute to the effect they have? Support your answer with an example from the text.

Vocabulary Practice

Practice with Synonyms Read the following sentences. Choose the best synonym for the underlined word. Consult a dictionary if you need help.

1. His underlined valedictory speech brought tears to the eyes of all who were present.
   (a) sad   **(b)** funeral   **(c)** farewell

2. The crowd underlined receded as the funeral procession approached.
   (a) cooled   **(b)** returned   **(c)** retreated

3. With no trees for shade, the horses underlined sweltered in the sun.
   (a) thirsted **(b)** overheated **(c)** died

4. The townspeople underlined congregated for the controversial town council meeting.
   (a) froze **(b)** contemplated **(c)** gathered

WRITING AND EXTENDING

Writing About Literature

Compare and Contrast Setting The **setting**, or the time and place in which a poem occurs, often helps create an atmosphere or mood. In both "Crossing the Water" and "Sleep in the Mojave Desert," the setting plays an important role. Write a brief essay comparing and contrasting the setting in these two poems. Discuss the various elements that make up the setting of each poem and cite examples from the text. In addition, make sure to compare and contrast the ways in which the setting is used. For example, you should show how the setting contributes to the atmosphere or mood of each poem.

Before you begin writing, you can organize your ideas by means of a Venn Diagram. In the overlapping area list elements that the two settings have in common. In the outer section of each circle, list elements that are unique to each setting.

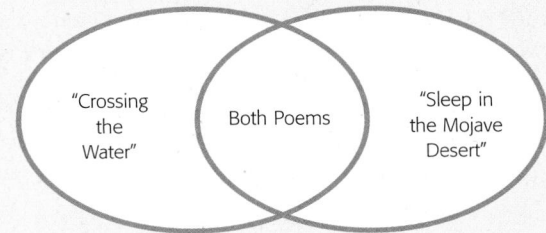

After you complete your draft, meet with a partner to review each other's work and to suggest revisions that might strengthen each essay. Then proofread your draft for errors in spelling, grammar, and punctuation.

Literary Criticism

Group Activity The critic M.D. Uroff asserts that Plath's confessional poems do not utter "uninformed cries from the heart . . ."; rather, she "deal[s] with her experience by creating characters who could not deal with theirs." In what ways do you think this claim is true or untrue for the two Plath poems you have just read? Discuss this question with a small group of classmates.

Literature Online Web Activities For eFlashcards, Selection Quick Checks, and other Web activities, go to www.glencoe.com.

The War Against the Trees

MEET STANLEY KUNITZ

Stanley Kunitz wrote many books of poetry and received numerous awards. His earlier work displays great wit and defiance; his later poems often express a passionate search for meaning and identity. One of the finest expressions of that quest is found in his poem "The Layers":

> I have walked through many lives,
> some of them my own,
> and I am not who I was,
> though some principle of being
> abides, from which I struggle
> not to stray.

Kunitz, who twice served as U.S. Poet Laureate, has won several literary awards, including a Pulitzer Prize for his *Selected Poems: 1928–1958* and a National Book Award for *Passing Through: The Later Poems, New and Selected*. In 1993, President Clinton awarded Kunitz the National Medal of the Arts.

Early Years Born in Worcester, Massachusetts, Stanley Kunitz studied at Harvard, where he graduated *summa cum laude* in 1926 and earned a master's degree in 1927. "I felt very isolated as a young person," he stated. "I didn't know another soul with whom I could share my interests. Eventually, after my Harvard years, I gravitated to New York, the magnet city of the arts, where I found an editorial job and began to send out my poems [for publication in literary magazines] . . . but I was too busy and too shy to make friends easily, so I still felt like an outsider." In poetry, Kunitz found an outlet for his loneliness and a vehicle for exploring his "hidden self."

Poet and Teacher *Intellectual Things,* his first volume of poetry, was published in 1930, when he was only twenty-five years old. Fourteen years later, *Passport to War* was published. Then, after serving in World War II, Kunitz accepted a teaching position at Bennington College, where he joined fellow poet Theodore Roethke. Eventually, Kunitz taught at several other esteemed colleges and universities, including Yale, Princeton, Rutgers, and the New School for Social Research. He also served as poet-in-residence at the University of Washington, Queens College, Brandeis University, and Princeton and for many years taught in the graduate writing program at Columbia University, which he helped found. To further encourage and develop young writers, Kunitz founded the Fine Arts Work Center in Provincetown, Massachusetts, and Poets House in New York City.

Kunitz, indeed, always enjoyed mentoring and encouraging young people interested in the arts. In 1984 the National Endowment for the Arts awarded him a Senior Fellowship "for his inordinate generosity in working with younger writers." Kunitz often responded to such accolades with characteristic wit. During an interview he said, "As for my companionship with younger poets, I feel that I'm the one who's blessed in that relationship."

In addition to his poetry and literary criticism, Kunitz translated Russian poems by Yevtushenko, Stolzenberg, Akhmatova, and others into English and edited volumes of poetry by the British poets William Blake and John Keats. Kunitz was considered one of the most gifted and influential writers of the modern era.

Stanley Kunitz was born in 1905 and died in 2006.

Literature Online **Author Search** For more about Stanley Kunitz, go to www.glencoe.com.

Connecting to the Poem

Like the Romantic poets, Stanley Kunitz cherishes his relationship with nature. "I've found that I am more at peace with myself when I'm in daily contact with the natural world," he has said. "The War Against the Trees" reflects his respect for nature and the value of unspoiled land. As you read, think about the following questions:

- Which is more important to you: natural landscape or new development?
- What happens when a natural landscape is destroyed?

Building Background

After World War II, the United States enjoyed a booming economy. Many soldiers and sailors returning home from the war attended college on the G.I. Bill, married, and started families. Cities spread out, and suburbs sprang up. In many parts of the country, land was cleared to make way for factories, housing developments, shopping malls, and schools. The national mood was optimistic, and growth and development were regarded as sure signs of the triumph of technology. Swept along in the march of progress, the public often condoned the destruction of natural landscapes.

Setting Purposes for Reading

Big Idea Nature and Technology

As you read this poem, notice how Kunitz depicts the conflict between nature and technology.

Literary Element Personification

Personification is a figure of speech in which an animal, an object, a force of nature, or an idea is given human characteristics. For example, in the poem "Because I could not stop for Death," Emily Dickinson personifies death as a courtly gentleman. As you read "The War Against the Trees," look for examples of personification.

- See Literary Terms Handbook, p. R13.

Literature Online **Interactive Literary Elements Handbook** To review or learn more about the literary elements, go to www.glencoe.com.

Reading Strategy Evaluating Figures of Speech

A **figure of speech** is a specific device or kind of figurative language. Poets use figures of speech to create descriptive effects and to convey ideas or emotions. In this poem, Kunitz often uses **metaphor**, a figure of speech that equates two unlike things. As you read, note and evaluate examples of metaphor.

Reading Tip: Charting Figurative Language Use a chart to list metaphors and the effect of the comparison.

Metaphor	Things Compared	Effect
"the bulldozers ... overthrowing first the privet-row."	the bulldozers and an attacking army	

Vocabulary

lopped (lopt) *v.* trimmed or chopped off, as the branches of a tree; p. 1228 *With its branches lopped off, the tree looked stubby and bare.*

subverting (səb vurt´ ing) *v.* overthrowing and destroying; p. 1228 *The people were intent on subverting the dictator and replacing him with a merciful ruler.*

rampages (ram´ pāj´ iz) *v.* rushes wildly about; scurries; p. 1228 *The hungry squirrel rampages from tree to tree, searching for acorns.*

grievous (grē´ vəs) *adj.* causing or characterized by grief; extremely sad; p. 1228 *The memorial service was a grievous occasion for both family and friends.*

INDIANA ACADEMIC STANDARDS (pages 1227–1229)

11.3.4 Analyze ways in which poetry...uses...personification [and] figures of speech...to evoke readers' emotions.

11.5.2 Write responses to literature...

11.5.3 Write reflective compositions that maintain a balance in describing individual events and relating those events to more general and abstract ideas.

The War Against the Trees

Stanley Kunitz

The man who sold his lawn to standard oil[1]
Joked with his neighbors come to watch the show
While the bulldozers, drunk with gasoline,
Tested the virtue of the soil
5   Under the branchy sky
By overthrowing first the privet-row.[2]

Forsythia-forays and hydrangea-raids
Were but preliminaries to a war
Against the great-grandfathers of the town,
10   So freshly **lopped** and maimed.
They struck and struck again,
And with each elm a century went down.[3]

All day the hireling engines charged the trees,
Subverting them by hacking underground
15   In grub-dominions, where dark summer's mole[4]
Rampages through his halls,
Till a northern seizure shook
Those crowns,[5] forcing the giants to their knees.

I saw the ghosts of children at their games
20   Racing beyond their childhood in the shade,
And while the green world turned its death-foxed page
And a red wagon wheeled,
I watched them disappear
Into the suburbs of their **grievous** age.

25   Ripped from the craters much too big for hearts
The club-roots bared their amputated coils,
Raw gorgons[6] matted blind, whose pocks and scars
Cried Moon! on a corner lot
One witness-moment, caught
30   In the rear-view mirrors of the passing cars.

---

1. An oil company has bought the land.
2. A *privet-row* is a row of bushes.
3. Elm trees grow very tall and, if they survive such onslaughts as Dutch Elm Disease, can live for more than a hundred years.
4. Both *grubs* and *moles* live underground. Grubs are the wormlike larvae of beetles, and moles are burrowing rodents.
5. *Crowns* refers to the top branches of the trees.
6. In Greek mythology, the *Gorgons* were three monstrous sisters with coiled snakes for hair.

Reading Strategy Evaluating Figures of Speech *Why does the poet include this metaphor?*

Literary Element Personification *What are "the hireling engines," and what human qualities does the poet give them?*

Big Idea Nature and Technology *What does this line suggest about the conflict between technology and nature?*

Vocabulary

lopped (lopt) *v.* trimmed or chopped off, as the branches of a tree
subverting (səb vurt´ ing) *v.* overthrowing and destroying
rampages (ram´ pāj´ iz) *v.* rushes wildly about; scurries
grievous (grē´ vəs) *adj.* causing or characterized by grief; extremely sad

RESPONDING AND THINKING CRITICALLY

Respond

1. What are your thoughts or feelings after reading this poem?

Recall and Interpret

2. (a)Why is the land being cleared of trees? (b)Why have the neighbors "come to watch the show"?

3. (a)What are the "preliminaries" to the "war against the trees"? (b)Why does the speaker describe the bulldozers as "drunk with gasoline"?

4. (a)How do the bulldozers attack the trees? (b)Why does this action eventually topple them?

5. (a)What scene does the speaker imagine as the trees are coming down? (b)What message does the speaker convey through this scene? Explain.

Analyze and Evaluate

6. (a)After the trees have fallen, why does the speaker compare the land to the moon's surface? (b)Is this comparison effective or not? Explain.

7. (a)In the last two lines of the poem, what does the speaker suggest about the motorists driving by? (b)Does this image provide an effective ending to the poem? Explain why or why not.

Connect

8. **Big Idea** **Nature and Technology** Which people might conclude that they have won this "war"? Which people might conclude that they have lost it?

LITERARY ANALYSIS

Literary Element **Personification**

Poets often use **personification** to give ordinary, life-less objects human characteristics such as personality, dignity, motive, and force.

1. How does the speaker personify the trees and the bulldozers? What do these personifications suggest?

2. With coiled snakes for hair, the gorgons of Greek mythology were hideous creatures. Anyone who had the misfortune to behold them was immediately turned into stone. In the final stanza, the speaker personifies the exposed roots of the trees as gor-gons. What physical characteristics of the roots might prompt the speaker to personify them in this way?

Writing About Literature

Evaluate Contemporary Relevance Is the **theme**, or message about life, that Kunitz conveys in "The War Against the Trees" still relevant today? Write a few paragraphs explaining your views. Support them with details from the poem and your personal experiences.

Literature Online **Web Activities** For eFlashcards, Selection Quick Checks, and other Web activities, go to www.glencoe.com.

READING AND VOCABULARY

Reading Strategy **Evaluating Figures of Speech**

Occasionally, writers use an **extended metaphor,** or one that develops beyond a single line. What extended metaphor is used in "The War Against the Trees"? How effective do you think it is?

Vocabulary Practice

Practice with Analogies Choose the word pair that best completes each analogy.

1. grievous : loss ::
   a. slight : prediction
   b. glorious : victory
   c. humble : award
   d. shameful : honor
2. lopped : cut ::
   a. ignite : extinguish
   b. gaze : look
   c. climb : descend
   d. succeed : fail

from Silent Spring

Rachel Carson

National Book Award Winner

Building Background

In 1962, scientist and author Rachel Carson published *Silent Spring* in an effort to warn the public about the serious environmental risks of such pesticides as DDT. Carson argued that chemicals, widely used to increase agricultural productivity, were polluting U.S. rivers and streams, killing birds and fish, and greatly increasing the risks for many forms of cancer. Immediately, the chemical industry, agricultural organizations, and many government officials questioned the validity of the book's findings. However, scientific studies ordered by President John F. Kennedy found evidence to support Carson's research. These studies led to new legislation that banned or limited pesticide use.

Set a Purpose for Reading

Read to discover Carson's persuasive dramatization of the dangers that chemicals pose to the environment.

Reading Strategy

Recognizing Author's Purpose

To determine an **author's purpose,** carefully analyze such elements as the tone, structure, and content. As you read, jot down clues that will help you identify Carson's purpose for beginning *Silent Spring* with a tale about a town destroyed by chemicals.

There was once a town in the heart of America where all life seemed to live in harmony with its surroundings. The town lay in the midst of a checkerboard[1] of prosperous farms, with fields of grain and hillsides of orchards where, in spring, white clouds of bloom drifted above the green fields. In autumn, oak and maple and birch set up a blaze of color that flamed and flickered across a backdrop of pines. Then foxes barked in the hills and deer silently crossed the fields, half hidden in the mists of the fall mornings.

Along the roads, laurel, viburnum and alder,[2] great ferns and wildflowers delighted the traveler's eye through much of the year. Even in winter the roadsides were places of beauty, where countless birds came to feed on the berries and on the seed heads of the dried weeds rising above the snow. The countryside was, in fact, famous for the abundance and variety of

---

1. The farmland looks somewhat like a *checkerboard* because each square field, planted with different crops, is slightly different in color and texture.
2. *Laurel* refers to the flowering shrub mountain laurel; *viburnum* is the scientific name for the fragrant honeysuckle bush; *alder* is the name of trees in the birch family.

First Public Test of Insecticide Machine. Beachgoers are sprayed with DDT as a new machine for distributing the insecticide is tested for the first time. 1945.

its bird life, and when the flood of migrants[3] was pouring through in spring and fall people traveled from great distances to observe them. Others came to fish the streams, which flowed clear and cold out of the hills and contained shady pools where trout lay. So it had been from the days many years ago when the first settlers raised their houses, sank their wells, and built their barns.

Then a strange blight[4] crept over the area and everything began to change. Some evil spell had settled on the community: mysterious maladies[5] swept the flocks of chickens; the cattle and sheep sickened and died. Everywhere was a shadow of death. The farmers spoke of much illness among their families. In the town the doctors had become more and more puzzled by new kinds of sickness appearing among their patients. There had been several sudden and unexplained deaths, not only among adults but even among children, who would be stricken suddenly while at play and die within a few hours.

There was a strange stillness. The birds, for example—where had they gone? Many people spoke of them, puzzled and disturbed. The feeding stations in the backyards were deserted. The few birds seen anywhere were moribund;[6] they trembled violently and could not fly. It was a spring without voices. On the mornings that had once throbbed with the dawn chorus of robins, catbirds, doves, jays, wrens, and scores of other bird voices there was now no sound; only silence lay over the fields and woods and marsh.

On the farms the hens brooded, but no chicks hatched. The farmers complained that they were unable to raise any pigs—the litters were small and the young survived only a few days. The apple trees were coming into bloom but no bees droned among the blossoms, so there was no pollination and there would be no fruit.

---

3. Here, *migrants* refers to migrating birds.
4. A *blight* is a widespread withering or illness caused by such negative forces as pollution, bacteria, insects, or parasites.
5. *Maladies* are illnesses.

6. *Moribund* means "having very little strength left." The remaining birds are weakening and dying.

The roadsides, once so attractive, were now lined with browned and withered vegetation as though swept by fire. These, too, were silent, deserted by all living things. Even the streams were now lifeless. Anglers[7] no longer visited them, for all the fish had died.

In the gutters under the eaves and between the shingles of the roofs, a white granular powder still showed a few patches; some weeks before it had fallen like snow upon the roofs and the lawns, the fields and streams.

No witchcraft, no enemy action had silenced the rebirth of new life in this stricken world.

> *On the mornings that had once throbbed with the dawn chorus of robins, catbirds, doves, jays, wrens, and scores of other bird voices there was now no sound . . .*

The people had done it themselves.

This town does not actually exist, but it might easily have a thousand counterparts in America or elsewhere in the world. I know of no community that has experienced all the misfortunes I describe. Yet every one of these disasters has actually happened somewhere, and many real communities have already suffered a substantial number of them. A grim specter has crept upon us almost unnoticed, and this imagined tragedy may easily become a stark reality we all shall know.

---

7. An *angler* is a person who fishes with a rod and reel.

RESPONDING AND THINKING CRITICALLY

Respond

1. What most shocked or surprised you about the possible effects of environmental pollution that Carson suggests? Explain.

Recall and Interpret

2. (a)Describe the change that occurs in the town. (b)What might the "white granular powder" have been? Explain your interpretation.

3. (a)What shift occurs in the final paragraph? (b)What effect do you think Carson is trying to achieve with this shift?

Analyze and Evaluate

4. Though Carson's book makes scientific claims about the power of pesticides, she chose to begin the work with a simple tale rather than with dramatic examples of the misuse of dangerous chemicals. Why do you think she made that choice? Explain whether you think it was a wise choice.

5. This fable is set in a perfect, rural setting. Do you think it would have been more effective if Carson had chosen some other setting, such as a large city or suburb? Explain.

Connect

6. What thoughts about the environmental health of your community did this selection inspire in you? Explain.

INDIANA ACADEMIC STANDARDS
(pages 1230–1232)
11.2 Develop strategies such as...identifying and analyzing... purpose...

SQ

MEET URSULA K. LE GUIN

Ursula Le Guin revolutionized science fiction writing. Before she began publishing her work in the 1960s, the genre of science fiction was dominated by male writers. Le Guin's stories, in which women and people from different cultures began to appear as main characters, broadened the genre.

A Rich Background Le Guin grew up in Berkeley, California, where her father, an internationally respected anthropology professor, taught at the university. Her mother, a writer with a background in psychology, wrote mainly children's books but was famous for her nonfiction work about the lone survivor of the Yahi tribe of California. This book, *Ishi in Two Worlds*, is still read and admired today.

Scholar, Writer, and Mother Le Guin always considered herself to be a writer. She wrote her first fantasy story at age nine. By age twelve, she had submitted a science fiction story for publication in a magazine. Although the story was not accepted, Le Guin took pride in receiving a "real rejection slip." Unfazed, she continued writing. Her father, however, encouraged Le Guin to be practical when it was time to choose a career. A talented scholar of languages, Le Guin graduated from Radcliffe College (the women's college associated with Harvard) in 1951 with a degree in French. By the next year, she had completed her master's degree in the same subject. She planned to write a dissertation, receive her doctorate, and make a career of teaching at the university level.

That plan soon changed. In 1953 Le Guin was on her way to Europe on a Fulbright scholarship to study Italian and French Renaissance literature. Traveling on the ocean liner the *Queen Mary*, Le Guin met another Fulbright scholar, Charles Le Guin, who was also going to study in Europe. The two fell in love and were married by the end of the year.

> "My father studied real cultures and I make them up—in a way, it's the same thing."
>
> —Ursula K. Le Guin

When the Le Guins returned to the United States, Ursula decided to stop her program of study to pursue writing and to raise a family. She sold her first science fiction story in 1962. Four years later, her first novel was published.

A Prolific Career Le Guin has published more than thirty novels, including numerous works for children and young adult readers. Her short stories number over one hundred. Le Guin has received dozens of awards for her work, among them the prestigious Hugo and Nebula awards for her science fiction and the National Book Award. She has written poetry, essays, and literary criticism; collaborated on screenplays and an opera; and taught classes and workshops for many aspiring science fiction and fantasy writers. Le Guin believes strongly in the importance of the imagination, asserting that "It is above all by the imagination that we achieve perception, compassion, and hope."

Ursula K. Le Guin was born in 1929.

Literature Online Author Search For more about Ursula K. Le Guin, go to www.glencoe.com.

Connecting to the Story

Everyone has moments in which they act "crazy," meaning that they do things that they know they should not do, or that are extravagant, unwise, or simply silly. But what does it mean to label people as "crazy" or "insane"? "SQ" explores this question. As you read the story, think about the following questions:

- Is there an objective way to define insanity? Can a test measure someone's mental health?
- What would be the benefits and drawbacks of checking mental health on a regular basis?

Building Background

"SQ" is set in an unspecified time in the future when one government rules the entire world. Over time, one department of the government gains more and more power. The head of this department, Dr. Speakie, advocates regular and frequent testing of the mental health of everyone in the world. Dr. Speakie uses a standardized test for this purpose.

Standardized tests are often used to test people's mastery of academic subjects or their aptitude for different professions. In addition, standardized tests have been devised to measure intelligence. Such tests are called *intelligence quotient,* or *IQ,* tests. Although widely used, these tests remain controversial in terms of what exactly they can measure.

Setting Purposes for Reading

Big Idea Nature and Technology

As you read, assess the importance of technology in Dr. Speakie's plan.

Literary Element Satire

Satire is writing that uses humor to comment on philosophical ideas, social customs, political institutions, and even general human tendencies. As you read "SQ," identify the different things that Le Guin satirizes.

- See Literary Terms Handbook, p. R16.

Literature Online **Interactive Literary Elements Handbook** To review or learn more about the literary elements, go to www.glencoe.com.

Reading Strategy Identifying Genre

A **short story** is a brief fictional narrative in prose that generally includes setting, characters, plot, and theme. **Science fiction** is a type of fiction that deals with the impact of science, technology, or both on individuals and society. Science fiction is often set in the future.

Reading Tip: Taking Notes Use a chart like the one below to record details that indicate this work is a science fiction story.

Science Fiction Characteristics	
Setting	
Impact of Science	
Impact of Technology	

Vocabulary

implementation (im′ plə mən tā′ shən) *n.* putting into effect; putting into use; p. 1236 *The implementation of a test involves several steps.*

infrastructure (in′frə struk′chər) *n.* the underlying base for an organization or a system; p. 1237 *Without the infrastructure of teachers, administrators, and building support staff, it would be difficult to educate the youth of our nation.*

stigma (stig′ mə) *n.* mark or characteristic of disgrace; p. 1239 *Ripped jeans have changed from stigma to fashion statement.*

hysterical (his ter′ i kəl) *adj.* characterized by panic or other uncontrolled emotion; p. 1241 *A person who is hysterical might not make sense.*

uncanny (un kan′ ē) *adj.* peculiarly unsettling in an eerie way; p. 1243 *Bob's knowledge of my unspoken thoughts was uncanny.*

Vocabulary Tip: Word Analogies An analogy is a way of showing that two relationships are the same.

INDIANA ACADEMIC STANDARDS (pages 1234–1245)

11.3.1 Analyze characteristics of...satire...

11.3.2 Analyze the way in which...a selection represents a view or comment on life...

11.5.1 Write fictional...narratives...

SQ

Ursula K. Le Guin

Man Disappearing through Closed Door. Janusz Kapusta.

I think what Dr. Speakie has done is wonderful. He is a wonderful man. I believe that. I believe that people need beliefs. If I didn't have my belief, I really don't know what would happen.

And if Dr. Speakie hadn't truly believed in his work, he couldn't possibly have done what he did Where would he have found the courage? What he did proves his genuine sincerity.

There was a time when a lot of people tried to cast doubts on him. They said he was seeking power. That was never true. From the very beginning all he wanted was to help people and make a better world. The people who called him a power seeker and a dictator were just the same ones who used to say that Hitler was insane and

Nixon[1] was insane and all the world leaders were insane and the arms race was insane and our misuse of natural resources was insane and the whole world civilization was insane and suicidal. They were always saying that. And they said it about Dr. Speakie. But he stopped all that insanity, didn't he? So he was right all along, and he was right to believe in his beliefs.

Literary Element Satire *What form of humor is Le Guin using here?*

---

1. *Nixon* refers to Richard M. Nixon, who was U.S. president from 1969 to 1974. As president, Nixon was involved in a political scandal known as Watergate. In 1974 he opted to resign from office rather than face an impeachment trial.

I came to work for him when he was named the Chief of the Psychometric[2] Bureau. I used to work at the U.N.,[3] and when the World Government took over the New York U.N. Building, they transferred me up to the thirty-fifth floor to be the head secretary in Dr. Speakie's office. I knew already that it was a position of great responsibility, and I was quite excited the whole week before my new job began. I was so curious to meet Dr. Speakie, because of course he was already famous. I was there right at the dot of nine on Monday morning, and when he came in, it was so wonderful. He looked so kind. You could tell that the weight of his responsibilities was always on his mind, but he looked so healthy and positive, and there was a bounce in his step—I used to think it was as if he had rubber balls in the toes of his shoes. He smiled and shook my hand and said in such a friendly, confident voice, "And you must be Mrs. Smith! I've heard wonderful things about you. We're going to have a wonderful team here, Mrs. Smith!"

Later on he called me by my first name, of course.

That first year we were mostly busy with Information. The World Government Presidium and all the Member States had to be fully informed about the nature and purpose of the SQ Test, before the actual **implementation** of its application could be eventualized. That was good for me too, because in preparing all that information I learned all about it myself. Often, taking

dictation,[4] I learned about it from Dr. Speakie's very lips. By May I was enough of an "expert" that I was able to prepare the Basic SQ Information Pamphlet for publication just from Dr. Speakie's notes. It was such fascinating work. As soon as I began to understand the SQ Test Plan, I began to believe in it. That was true of everybody else in the office and in the Bureau. Dr. Speakie's sincerity and scientific enthusiasm were infectious. Right from the beginning we had to take the Test every quarter, of course, and some of the secretaries used to be nervous before they took it, but I never was. It was so obvious that the Test was *right*. If you scored under 50 it was nice to know that you were sane, but even if you scored over 50 that was fine too, because then you could be *helped*. And anyway it is always best to know the truth about yourself.

As soon as the Information service was functioning smoothly, Dr. Speakie transferred the main thrust of his attention to the implementation of Evaluator training, and planning for the structurization of the Cure Centers, only he changed the name to SQ Achievement Centers. It seemed a very big job even then. We certainly had no idea how big the job would finally turn out to be!

As he said at the beginning, we were a very good team. We all worked hard, but there were always rewards.

I remember one wonderful day. I had accompanied Dr. Speakie to the Meeting of the Board of the Psychometric Bureau. The emissary[5] from the State of Brazil announced that his State had adopted the Bureau Recommendations for Universal Testing—we had known that that was going to be announced. But then the delegate from Libya and the delegate from China announced that their States had adopted the Test too! Oh, Dr. Speakie's face was just like the sun for a minute,

---

2. *Psychometric* (sī′ kə met′ rik) relates to a branch of psychology that deals with tests designed to measure any psychological variable, such as intelligence, aptitude, or personality type.
3. *U.N.* is an abbreviation that stands for the United Nations.

Reading Strategy Identifying Genre *What detail of the setting helps you identify this story as science fiction?*

Big Idea Nature and Technology *What does this sentence suggest about the author's attitude toward technology?*

Vocabulary

implementation (im′ plə mən tā′ shən) *n.* putting into effect; putting into use

---

4. *Taking dictation* is the act of writing down what someone else is saying. It used to be common for secretaries to take dictation from their bosses. They would type up the information as a letter, a memo, or in another written format.
5. An *emissary* is a person sent on a mission to represent or advance the interests of another person, especially those of a leader of a nation.

Reading Strategy Identifying Genre *What aspect of the story's subject helps you identify the story as science fiction?*

Fearful Man Turned Away From Crowd. John Ritter.
Viewing the Art What aspects of Dr. Speakie's personality does the man in this image capture?

just *shining.* I wish I could remember exactly what he said, especially to the Chinese delegate, because of course China was a very big State and its decision was very influential. Unfortunately I do not have his exact words because I was changing the tape in the recorder. He said something like, "Gentlemen, this is a historic day for humanity." Then he began to talk at once about the effective implementation of the Application Centers, where people would take the Test, and the Achievement Centers, where they would go if they scored over 50, and how to establish the Test Administrations and Evaluations **infrastructure** on such a large

Big Idea Nature and Technology *Does this technology seem advanced? Why or why not?*

Vocabulary

infrastructure (in´ frə struk´ chər) *n* the underlying base for an organization or a system

scale, and so on. He was always modest and practical. He would rather talk about doing the job than talk about what an important job it was. He used to say, "Once you know what you're doing, the only thing you need to think about is how to do it." I believed that that is deeply true.

From then on, we could hand over the Information program to a subdepartment and concentrate on How to Do It. Those were exciting times! So many States joined the Plan, one after another. When I think of all we had to do, I wonder that we didn't all go crazy! Some of the office staff did fail their quarterly Test, in fact. But most of us working in the Executive Office with Dr. Speakie remained quite stable, even when we were on the job all day and half the night. I think his presence was an inspiration. He was always calm and positive, even when we had to arrange things like training 113,000 Chinese Evaluators in three months. "You can

Literary Element Satire *The narrator considers Dr. Speakie's statement to be wise and profound. How does it strike you?*

Man Entering Room of Men. John Ritter.

Viewing the Art How does the man in this image appear different from the one on the previous page?

always find out 'how' if you just know the 'why'!" he would say. And we always did.

When you think back over it, it really is quite amazing what a big job it was—so much bigger than anybody, even Dr. Speakie, had realized it would be. It just changed everything. You only realize that when you think back to what things used to be like. Can you imagine when we began planning Universal Testing for the State of China, we only allowed for eleven hundred Achievement Centers, with sixty-eight hundred Staff? It really seems like a joke. But it is not. I was going through some of the old files yesterday, making sure everything is in order, and I found the first China Implementation Plan, with those figures written down in black and white.

I believe the reason why even Dr. Speakie was slow to realize the magnitude of the operation was

that even though he was a great scientist, he was also an optimist. He just kept hoping against hope that the average scores would begin to go down, and this prevented him from seeing that universal application of the SQ Test was eventually going to involve everybody either as Inmates or Staff.

When most of the Russias and all the African States had adopted the Recommendations and were busy implementing them, the debates in the General Assembly of the World Government got very excited. That was the period when so many bad things were said about the Test and about Dr. Speakie. I used to get quite angry, reading the *World Times* reports of debates. When I went as his secretary with Dr. Speakie to General Assembly meetings, I had to sit and listen in person to people insulting him personally, casting aspersions[6] on his motives, and questioning his scientific integrity and even his sincerity. Many of those people were very disagreeable and obviously

---

Reading Strategy Identifying Genre *What do you think ends up happening with the testing plan in China?*

6. *Casting aspersions* on something means saying uncomplimentary things about it.

unbalanced. But he never lost his temper. He would just stand up and prove to them, again, that the SQ Test did actually literally scientifically show whether the testee was sane or insane, and the results could be proved, and all psychometrists accepted them. So the Test Ban[7] people couldn't do anything but shout about freedom and accuse Dr. Speakie and the Psychometric Bureau of trying to "turn the world into a huge insane asylum." He would always answer quietly and firmly, asking them how they thought a person could be "free" if they lacked mental health. What they called freedom might well be a delusional system with no contact with reality. In order to find out, all they had to do was to become testees. "Mental health *is* freedom," he said. "'Eternal vigilance is the price of liberty,' they say,[8] and now we have an eternally vigilant watchdog: the SQ Test. *Only the testees can be truly free!*"

There really was no answer they could make to that. Sooner or later the delegates even from Member States where the Test Ban movement was strong would volunteer to take the SQ Test to prove that their mental health was adequate to their responsibilities. Then the ones that passed the test and remained in office would begin working for Universal Application in their home State. The riots and demonstrations, and things like the burning of the Houses of Parliament in London in the State of England (where the Nor-Eurp SQ Center was housed), and the Vatican Rebellion, and the Chilean H-Bomb,[9] were the work of

insane fanatics appealing to the most unstable elements of the populace. Such fanatics, as Dr. Speakie and Dr. Waltraute pointed out in their Memorandum to the Presidium, deliberately aroused and used the proven instability of the crowd, "mob psychosis." The only response to mass delusion of that kind was immediate implementation of the Testing Program in the disturbed States, and immediate amplification[10] of the Asylum Program.

That was Dr. Speakie's own decision, by the way, to rename the SQ Achievement Centers "Asylums." He took the word right out of his enemies' mouths. He said: "An asylum means a place of *shelter*, a place of *cure*. Let there be no **stigma** attached to the word 'insane,' to the word 'asylum,' to the words 'insane asylum'! No! For the asylum is the haven of mental health— the place of cure, where the anxious gain peace, where the weak gain strength, where the prisoners of inadequate reality assessment win their way to freedom! Proudly let us use the word 'asylum.' Proudly let us go to the asylum, to work to regain our own God-given mental health, or to work with others less fortunate to help them win back their own inalienable right to mental health. And let one word be written large over the door of every asylum in the world—'WELCOME!'"

Those words are from his great speech at the General Assembly on the day World Universal Application was decreed by the Presidium. Once or twice a year I listen to my tape of that speech. Although I am too busy ever to get really depressed, now and then I feel the need of a tiny "pick-me-up," and so I play that tape. It never fails to send me back to my duties inspired and refreshed.

---

7. The use of the term *Test Ban* alludes to nuclear weapons and the popular movements in the 1960s and 1970s to try to limit them. The Nuclear Test-Ban Treaty was signed in 1963 between the United States, the Soviet Union, and more than one hundred other nations to ban the testing of nuclear weapons anywhere on or near Earth except underground.
8. The quote *"Eternal vigilance is the price of liberty"* means that people must always be aware if they want to hold on to their freedoms. This quote is based on a sentence in a speech made by Irish statesman John Philpot Curran in 1790.
9. An *H-bomb* is an abbreviation for a hydrogen bomb, a powerful nuclear weapon.

Reading Strategy Identifying Genre *What specific issue related to science and society is raised here?*

Big Idea Nature and Technology *What does this reference indicate about the level of resistance to the testing plan in some parts of the world?*

---

10. Here, *amplification* means "enlargement."

Literary Element Satire *Do you agree with the narrator's assessment of the protesters? Why or why not?*

Literary Element Satire *Do you think Le Guin wants you to believe what Dr. Speakie says in this speech? Why or why not?*

Vocabulary

stigma (stig′ mə) *n.* mark or characteristic of disgrace

Man with Giant Pencil and Paper. John Ritter.

Considering all the work there was to do, as the Test scores continued to come in always a little higher than the Psychometric Bureau analysts estimated, the World Government Presidium did a wonderful job for the two years that it administered Universal Testing. There was a long period, six months, when the scores seemed to have stabilized, with just about half of the testees scoring over 50 and half under 50. At that time it was thought that if 40 percent of the mentally healthy were assigned to Asylum Staff work, the other 60 percent could keep up routine basic world functions such as farming, power supply, transportation, etc. This proportion had to be reversed when they found that over 60 percent of the mentally healthy were volunteering for Staff work, in order to be with their loved ones in the Asylums. There was some trouble then with the routine basic world functions functioning. However, even then contingency plans were being made for

---

Big Idea Nature and Technology *What types of technology do you think a government would need to successfully carry out periodic standardized testing of every single person in the world?*

the inclusion of farmlands, factories, power plants, etc., in the Asylum Territories, and the assignment of routine basic world functions work as Rehabilitation Therapy, so that the Asylums could become totally self-supporting if it became advisable. This was President Kim's special care, and he worked for it all through his term of office. Events proved the wisdom of his planning. He seemed such a nice, wise little man. I still remember the day when Dr. Speakie came into the office and I knew at once that something was wrong. Not that he ever got really depressed or reacted with inopportune emotion,[11] but it was as if the rubber balls in his shoes had gone just a little bit flat. There was the slightest tremor of true sorrow in his voice when he said, "Mary Ann, we've had a bit of bad news I'm afraid." Then he smiled to reassure me, because he knew what a strain we were all working under, and certainly didn't want to give anybody a shock that might push their score up higher on the next quarterly Test! "It's President Kim," he said, and I knew at once—I knew he didn't mean the President was ill or dead.

"Over 50?" I asked, and he just said quietly and sadly, "55."

Poor little President Kim, working so efficiently all that three months while mental ill health was growing in him! It was very sad and also a useful warning. High-level consultations were begun at once, as soon as President Kim was committed;[12] and the decision was made to administer the Test monthly, instead of quarterly, to anyone in an executive position.

Even before this decision, the Universal scores had begun rising again. Dr. Speakie was not distressed. He had already predicted that this rise was highly probable during the transition period to World Sanity. As the number of

---

11. *Inopportune emotion* is inappropriate feeling.
12. *Committed,* here, means "to put into a place for confinement or for preservation."

Reading Strategy Identifying Genre *What effect does learning the narrator's name this late in the story have on your impression of the character?*

Literary Element Satire *What hint do you have that Le Guin is poking fun at the ideas that the narrator expresses here?*

the mentally healthy living outside the Asylums grew fewer, the strain on them kept growing greater, and they became more liable to break down under it—just as poor President Kim had done. Later, he predicted, when the Rehabs began coming out of the Asylums in ever increasing numbers, this stress would decrease. Also, the crowding in the Asylums would decrease, so that the Staff would have more time to work on individually orientated therapy, and this would lead to a still more dramatic increase in the number of Rehabs released. Finally, when the therapy process was completely perfected, there would be no Asylums left in the world at all. Everybody would be either mentally healthy or a Rehab, or "neonormal," as Dr. Speakie liked to call it.

It was the trouble in the State of Australia that precipitated[13] the Government crisis. Some Psychometric Bureau officials accused the Australian Evaluators of actually falsifying Test returns, but that is impossible since all the computers are linked to the World Government Central Computer Bank in Keokuk.[14] Dr. Speakie suspected the Australian Evaluators had been falsifying *the Test itself*, and insisted that they themselves all be tested immediately. Of course he was right. It had been a conspiracy, and the suspiciously low Australian Test scores had resulted from the use of a false Test. Many of the conspirators tested higher than 80 when forced to take the genuine Test! The State Government in Canberra[15] had been unforgivably lax. If they had just admitted it, everything would have been all right. But they got **hysterical,** and moved the State Government to a sheep station in Queensland,[16] and tried to

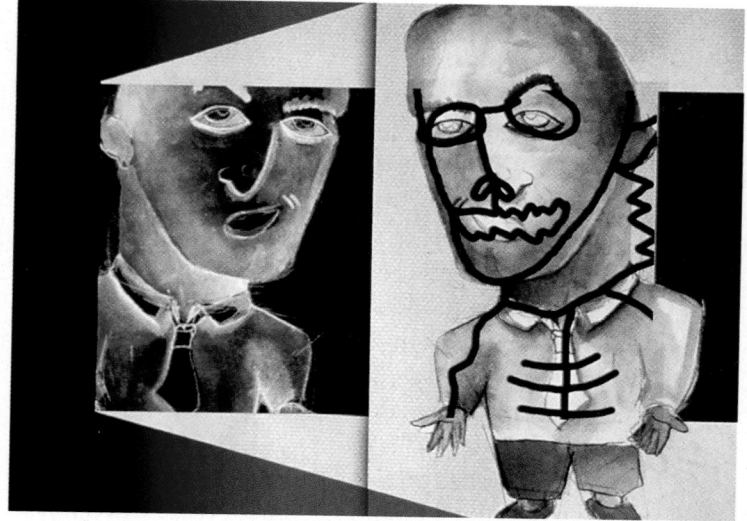

Painting Of Man with Negative. John Ritter.

withdraw from the World Government. (Dr. Speakie said that was a typical mass psychosis: reality evasion, followed by fugue[17] and autistic withdrawal.[18]) Unfortunately, the Presidium seemed to be paralyzed. Australia seceded[19] on the day before the President and Presidium were due to take their monthly Test, and probably they were afraid of overstraining their SQ with agonizing decisions. So the Psychometric Bureau volunteered to handle the episode. Dr. Speakie himself flew on the plane with the H-bombs, and helped to drop the information leaflets. He never lacked personal courage.

When the Australian incident was over, it turned out that most of the Presidium, including President Singh, had scored over 50. So the Psychometric Bureau took over their functions temporarily. Even on a long-term basis this made good sense, since all the problems now facing the World Government had to do with administering and evaluating the Test, training the Staff, and providing full self-sufficiency structuration to all Asylums.

13. Here, *precipitated* means "brought about suddenly."
14. *Keokuk* is a small town in Iowa on the western banks of the Mississippi River.
15. *Canberra* is the capital of Australia.
16. *Queensland* is one of the states that make up Australia; raising sheep is an important industry there.

Reading Strategy Identifying Genre *How do you think the idea that people can manipulate the Test relates to the theme of the story?*

Vocabulary

hysterical (his ter´ i kəl) *adj.* characterized by panic or other uncontrolled emotion

17. In psychology, a *fugue* is a state in which a person seems to be conscious of his or her actions but later has no recollection of these actions; a fugue may last for months and is a sign of severe mental stress.
18. *Autistic withdrawal* is a form of mental illness that involves extreme withdrawal from reality.
19. *Seceded* means "to formally withdraw from an alliance."

Big Idea Nature and Technology *What does this use of technology tell you about Dr. Speakie and the government he is a part of?*

Literary Element Satire *Why is this statement funny? What point is Le Guin making here?*

What this meant in personal terms was that Dr. Speakie, as Chief of the Psychometric Bureau, was now Interim President of the United States of the World. As his personal secretary, I was, I will admit it, just terribly proud of him. But he never let it go to his head.

He was so modest. Sometimes he used to say to people, when he introduced me, "This is Mary Ann, my secretary," he'd say with a little twinkle, "and if it wasn't for her I'd have been scoring over 50 long ago!"

There were times, as the World SQ scores rose and rose, that I would become a little discouraged. Once the week's Test figures came in on the readout, and the *average* score was 71. I said, "Doctor, there are moments I believe the whole world is going insane!"

But he said, "Look at it this way, Mary Ann. Look at those people in the Asylums—3.1 billion inmates now, and 1.8 billion staff—but look at them. What are they doing? They're pursuing their therapy, doing rehabilitation work on the farms and in the factories, and striving all the time, too, to *help* each other toward mental health. The preponderant inverse sanity quotient is certainly very high at the moment; they're mostly insane, yes. But you have to admire them. They are fighting for mental health. They will—they *will* win through!" And then he dropped his voice and said as if to himself, gazing out the window and bouncing just a little on the balls of his feet, "If I didn't believe that, I couldn't go on."

And I knew he was thinking of his wife.

Mrs. Speakie had scored 88 on the very first American Universal Test. She had been in the Greater Los Angeles Territory Asylum for years now.

Anybody who still thinks Dr. Speakie wasn't sincere should think about that for a minute! He gave up everything for his belief.

And even when the Asylums were all running quite well, and the epidemics in South Africa

Looking For the Ideal Candidate. Janusz Kapusta.

and the famines in Texas and the Ukraine were under control, still the workload on Dr. Speakie never got any lighter, because every month the personnel of the Psychometric Bureau got smaller, since some of them always flunked their monthly Test and were committed to Bethesda.[20] I never could keep any of my secretarial staff any more for longer than a month or two. It was harder and harder to find replacements, too, because most sane young people volunteered for Staff work in the Asylums, since life was much easier and more sociable inside the Asylums than outside. Everything so convenient, and lots of friends and acquaintances! I used to positively envy those girls! But I knew where my job was.

At least it was much less hectic here in the U.N. Building, or the Psychometry Tower as it had been renamed a long time ago. Often there wouldn't be anybody around the whole

20. *Bethesda* is a suburban community near Washington, D.C.

Literary Element Satire *What is Le Guin making fun of with Dr. Speakie's answer to Mary Ann?*

Reading Strategy Identifying Genre *Based on how the plot has progressed, does this information surprise you? How does it relate to Le Guin's theme?*

building all day long but Dr. Speakie and myself, and maybe Bill the janitor (Bill scored 32 regular as clockwork every quarter). All the restaurants were closed, in fact most of Manhattan was closed, but we had fun picnicking in the old General Assembly Hall. And there was always the odd call from Buenos Aires[21] or Reykjavik[22], asking Dr. Speakie's advice as Interim President about some problem, to break the silence.

But last November 8, I will never forget the date, when Dr. Speakie was dictating the Referendum for World Economic Growth for the next five-year period, he suddenly interrupted himself. "By the way, Mary Ann," he said, "how was your last score?"

We had taken the Test two days before, on the sixth. We always took the Test every first Monday. Dr. Speakie never would have dreamed of excepting himself from Universal Testing regulations.

"I scored 12," I said, before I thought how strange it was of him to ask. Or, not just to ask, because we often mentioned our scores to each other; but to ask then, in the middle of executing important world government business.

"Wonderful," he said, shaking his head. "You're wonderful, Mary Ann! Down two from last month's Test, aren't you?"

"I'm always between 10 and 14," I said. "Nothing new about that, Doctor."

"Some day," he said, and his face took on the expression it had when he gave his great speech about the Asylums, "some day, this world of ours will be governed by men fit to govern it. Men whose SQ score is Zero. Zero, Mary Ann!"

"Well, my goodness, Doctor," I said jokingly—his intensity almost alarmed me a little—"even *you* never scored lower than 3, and you haven't done that for a year or more now!"

He stared at me almost as if he didn't see me. It was quite **uncanny.** "Some day," he said in just the same way, "nobody in the world will have a Quotient higher than 50. Some day, nobody in the world will have a Quotient higher than 30! Higher than 10! The therapy will be perfected. I was only the diagnostician.[23] But the Therapy will be perfected! The cure will be found! Some day!" And he went on staring at me, and then he said, "Do you know what my score was on Monday?"

"7," I guessed promptly. The last time he had told me his score it had been 7.

"92," he said.

I laughed, because he seemed to be laughing. He had always had a puckish[24] sense of humor. But I thought we really should get back to the World Economic Growth Plan, so I said laughingly, "That really is a very bad joke, Doctor!"

"92," he said, "and you don't believe me, Mary Ann, but that's because of the cantaloupe."

I said, "What cantaloupe, Doctor?" and that was when he jumped across his desk and began to try to bite through my jugular vein.

I used a judo hold and shouted to Bill the janitor, and when he came, I called a robo-ambulance to take Dr. Speakie to Bethesda Asylum.

That was six months ago. I visit Dr. Speakie every Saturday. It is very sad. He is in the McLean area, which is the Violent Ward, and every time he sees me he screams and foams. But I do not take it personally. One should never take mental ill health personally. When the Therapy is perfected, he will be completely rehabilitated. Meanwhile, I just hold on here. Bill keeps the floors clean, and I run the World Government. It really isn't as difficult as you might think. ❧

---

23. A *diagnostician* is someone who figures out the nature of a problem, especially by identifying an illness.
24. *Puckish* means "mischievous."

Reading Strategy Identifying Genre *How have things changed since the beginning of the story? What is the cause of this breakdown in society?*

Literary Element Satire *Do you think that this scene is supposed to be funny? Explain.*

Big Idea Nature and Technology *What does the existence of this technology imply about the way the world runs by the end of the story?*

Vocabulary

uncanny (un kan´ ē) *adj.* peculiarly unsettling in an eerie way

RESPONDING AND THINKING CRITICALLY

Respond

1. Were you surprised by what happened to Dr. Speakie at the end of the story? Why or why not?

Recall and Interpret

2. (a)What does the SQ Test measure? (b)How does the story present the use of such a test?

3. (a)How does SQ testing come to be universal? (b)What does this imply about the government that controls the world in this story?

4. (a)What happens when the testing program is applied to everyone in the world? (b)Given this information, what is Le Guin's attitude toward the test?

Analyze and Evaluate

5. (a)What point of view does the writer use in this story? (b)How does this point of view help reinforce the story's irony?

6. **Jargon** is specialized language used by a particular group of people, such as government bureaucracies. Bureaucratic jargon can include complex wording and specialized titles for things. (a)What are some examples of jargon in this story? (b)How does Le Guin's use of jargon strengthen the story's satire?

7. **Irony** involves a deliberate contrast, in which what is written is the opposite of what is really meant. In this story, Le Guin sometimes uses irony to highlight her main message. Identify one or more such examples of irony, and explain how each relates to the story's main message.

Connect

8. How do you think this story comments on or relates to contemporary society?

9. **Big Idea** **Nature and Technology** (a)How important is technology in this story? (b)Why do you think Le Guin avoids giving explicit details about the technology involved in SQ testing?

Literary Element **Satire**

The story "SQ" is a **satire** because Le Guin uses humor to comment on society and its foibles. In the questions above, you explored how Le Guin uses jargon and irony for comic effect. She also uses parody and understatement as part of her satire. **Parody** is humorous imitation. **Understatement** is language that makes something seem less important than it really is.

1. How is the title of this short story a parody? If necessary, reread the Building Background information on page 1234 and then think about what the initials in the title most likely stand for.

2. Find an example of understatement in this short story. How does the understatement contribute to the humor of the story?

Review: Narrator

As you learned in Unit Six, a **narrator** is the person telling a story in a work of fiction. In a story with a first-person point of view, the narrator is a character in the story. In "SQ," the narrator is a woman named Mary Ann Smith.

Group Activity A first-person narrator tends to have a limited perspective that presents a particular viewpoint. In a small group, discuss the narrator's perspective and opinions in "SQ." What makes the narrator a good source of information for this story? What makes her an unreliable source of information? Use the scale below to rate the narrator's reliability. Discuss your rating with the class.

Narrator's Reliability

```
1   2   3   4   5   6   7   8   9   10
|___|___|___|___|___|___|___|___|___|
Very                              Very
Reliable                     Unreliable
```

Reliability Rating _____

Reasons

1.
2.
3.

Reading Strategy Identifying Genre

Science fiction uses an imaginary setting to explore the impact of science and technology on society. Although the setting may be futuristic or otherwise different from the world we know, it has to be believable, or readers are unlikely to take seriously the issues raised by the writer.

1. What makes "SQ" seem realistic? What elements of the story are not true to life?

2. On the whole, do you think this science fiction story is believable? Why or why not?

Vocabulary Practice

Practice with Analogies To solve a word analogy, identify the relationship between the first pair of words. As you read the answer choices, look for a pair of words that has the same relationship as the first pair. Choose the word pair that best completes each analogy below.

1. hysterical : calm ::
   a. reluctant : forgiving
   b. exemplary : outstanding
   c. miserable : happy
2. shame : stigma ::
   a. erasure : marking
   b. recreation : work
   c. pride : badge
3. power supply : infrastructure ::
   a. doctor : health care system
   b. bridge : river
   c. teacher : student
4. implementation : application ::
   a. wheel : axle
   b. flower : petal
   c. agenda : schedule
5. eerie : uncanny ::
   a. probable : unlikely
   b. durable : long-lasting
   c. realistic : imaginary

Writing About Literature

Apply Craft Until the very end of "SQ", the narrator's perspective and Dr. Speakie's perspective are very similar. However, their perspectives at the end of the story most likely diverge. Rewrite the ending of "SQ," making Dr. Speakie the narrator. Start from Dr. Speakie's question on page 1243, "By the way, Mary Ann, how was your last score?" Write a new, five-paragraph ending to the story. Incorporate the answers to these questions in your new ending:

- How does Dr. Speakie feel about Mary Ann's test score?

- How does Dr. Speakie feel about his own test score?

- How does Dr. Speakie feel about what has happened to the world as a result of universal SQ testing?

- How does Dr. Speakie feel about being committed to Bethesda Asylum?

As you work on your draft, try to indicate the answers to these questions through the characters' actions and thoughts rather than by stating them outright.

After you complete your draft, exchange story endings with a peer reviewer. Suggest ways to emphasize the perspective of Dr. Speakie. When you have revised your story, proofread and edit it to correct any errors in grammar, spelling, and punctuation.

Learning for Life

Interviewing Mary Ann Smith Working with a partner, create a mock interview with Mary Ann Smith. One person should take the role of Mrs. Smith; the other person should take the role of a television news reporter doing a story on the state of the world. The reporter should compose a list of eight to twelve questions on this topic to ask Mrs. Smith. After Mrs. Smith has had a chance to formulate her answers, rehearse the interview, changing or rephrasing questions to improve the interview. Then conduct the interview in front of the class.

Literature Online Web Activities For eFlashcards, Selection Quick Checks, and other Web activities, go to www.glencoe.com.

Grammar Workshop

Sentence Structure

Avoiding Misplaced Modifiers

> "Often, taking dictation, I learned about it from Dr. Speakie's very lips."
> —Ursula Le Guin, "SQ"

Connecting to Literature By putting the words "taking dictation" just before "I," Ursula Le Guin makes sure we understand that the words refer to the narrator—that it was Mary Ann Smith who was taking dictation. Imagine, however, that the sentence had been written like this:

> "Often I learned about it from Dr. Speakie's very lips, taking dictation."

The result would be the amusing but incorrect picture of Dr. Speakie's lips writing notes on a notepad. In this case, the phrase "taking dictation" would be a **misplaced modifier**. A misplaced modifier seems to modify the wrong word or more than one word in a sentence.

To correct misplaced modifiers, think about what you want to say.

Problem 1 A misplaced modifier
Growing from his experience, the writer created stories.

Solution Move the misplaced word or phrase as close as possible to the word it modifies. This may require creating a subordinate clause and changing the form of some words, as in this example.
The writer created stories that grew from his experience.

Problem 2 The adverb *only* is misplaced.
Molly only buys groceries at Cost-Cutters.

Solution Place *only* immediately before the word or group of words it modifies. The sentence above indicates that buying groceries is the only thing that Molly does. Options for revising are below; the correct choice is the one that reflects the writer's intended meaning.
Molly buys only groceries at Cost-Cutters. (Molly does not buy hardware or any other products at this store.)
Molly buys groceries only at Cost-Cutters. (Molly does not buy groceries at any other store.)

Exercise

Rewrite the following sentences, correcting any misplaced modifiers. If the sentence is already correct, write *Correct*.

1. I have nearly read every story ever written by Tomás Rivera.
2. We read a novel called *The Grapes of Wrath* in Mr. Hooper's class that was very enjoyable.
3. A copy of "The Rockpile" lay on the table that Colin had read.
4. *And the Earth Did Not Devour Him* tells about poor migrant farm workers who struggle to make a living.
5. I have only read the first chapter of Rivera's novel and not any further.

▶ **Vocabulary Terms**

A **misplaced modifier** is one that modifies the wrong word or seems to modify more than one word.

▶ **Test-Taking Tip**

To find misplaced modifiers during a test, reread the given sentence. If you can clearly identify the subject and action, the modifier is probably in the correct position. If the sentence seems unclear or confusing, the modifier may be misplaced.

▶ **Language Handbook**

For more about positioning modifiers, see *Adjective* and *Adverb* in the Language Handbook, p. R46.

eWorkbooks To link to the Grammar and Language eWorkbook, go to www.glencoe.com.

ACADEMIC STANDARDS (page 1246)
11.6.1 Demonstrate control of... sentence structure, and an understanding of English usage.

Snow

MEET JULIA ALVAREZ

At the age of ten, Julia Alvarez found herself thrust into a culture that was unfamiliar to her. Although she was born in New York City, she had grown up in the Dominican Republic during the brutal regime of General Rafael Trujillo, a military dictator who terrorized the nation for thirty-one years. Fleeing their country in the last few months of Trujillo's rule, Alvarez and her family settled in New York City.

Culture Shock Moving from her mother's family compound in the Dominican Republic to the Bronx was not easy for Alvarez. Unable to feel at home in cold and crowded New York City, she turned to the world of books and took comfort in reading and writing. "I consider this radical uprooting from my culture, my native language, my country, the reason I began writing," the award-winning poet and novelist has stated. "English, not the United States, was where I landed and sank deep roots."

Alvarez learned her new language quickly. During high school, she enjoyed writing and even began to think of it as a possible career. By the time she entered college, Alvarez was devoting serious attention to her writing. "I was raised in a very traditional, Old World family," she said, "so I never had thoughts about having a career. Moving to a new country, having to learn a new language, I got interested in words, and suddenly being in a world where there were books and encouragement of women to discover their talents contributed to my becoming a writer."

A Migrant Poet Alvarez graduated from Middlebury College and later received a graduate degree from Syracuse University. Then she began her career as what she calls "a migrant poet," in which she taught writing in prisons and senior-citizen centers as well as in several schools and colleges. "I would go anywhere," she told one interviewer. Finally she returned to Middlebury College, where she earned tenure as a member of the English Department. She has won several awards for her poetry and prose.

> "I feel like one of the blessings in life is to be doing the work you think you were put here to do. You have to keep writing and achieving it day by day. The one thing I would want for myself is to keep writing and growing."
>
> —Julia Alvarez

Her first novel, *How the García Girls Lost Their Accents*, was an immediate success. Published in 1991, it tells the story of four Dominican sisters and their struggle to make a new home in the United States. Alvarez's own three sisters saw many similarities between their experiences and those of the young women in the novel. "My sisters were a little taken aback," Alvarez admitted, "but they're also very proud of me."

Alvarez's other novels include *In the Time of the Butterflies* and *¡Yo!* (or, in the English translation, *I!*), which describes the García girls as adults. Her poetry collections include *Homecoming* and *The Other Side/El Otro Lado*.

Julia Alvarez was born in 1950.

Literature Online Author Search For more about Julia Alvarez, go to www.glencoe.com.

Connecting to the Story

Reading about something, or watching it on television, is never the same as experiencing it for oneself. In "Snow" a little girl from the Dominican Republic is astonished by something that many people in the United States take for granted. As you read Alvarez's story, think about the following questions:

- What amazed you as a child when you experienced it for the first time?
- Did you react more strongly to new sights and sounds when you were younger?

Building Background

This selection is set about the time of the 1962 Cuban missile crisis, when President John F. Kennedy ordered a naval blockade to prevent shipment of missiles from the Soviet Union to Cuba. The world waited for the Soviets to respond, deeply fearful of a nuclear war.

All over the United States, schools established air-raid drills in an attempt to prepare and protect the nation's children against injury from nuclear attack. At the sound of a siren, students were to file quickly to a hallway away from windows or doors or to crouch under their desks. They were to remain in this position until an all-clear signal sounded. Fortunately, the crisis ended peacefully, and these inadequate safety measures were never taken.

Big Idea Nature and Technology

As you read the story, notice how nature and technology become confused in the mind of a young girl.

Literary Element Indirect Characterization

A writer uses **indirect characterization** to reveal the personality of a character through that character's words and actions or through what others think and say about that character.

- See Literary Terms Handbook, p. R3.

Literature Online Interactive Literary Elements Handbook To review or learn more about the literary elements, go to www.glencoe.com.

Reading Strategy Connecting to Contemporary Issues

Connecting to contemporary issues enriches our appreciation of what we read. As you read the story, consider how recent events in cities around the world have made people fearful about security measures that seem inadequate.

Reading Tip: Keeping Informed Learn something about the context of the works you are reading to help you understand them better.

- Keep up with current affairs by means of the newspaper, Internet, radio, or television.
- Ask yourself, "What was happening in the world when this literary work was written?"

Vocabulary

enunciate (i nun′ sē āt′) v. to pronounce distinctly; p. 1249 *Unless you enunciate clearly, we will be unable to understand you.*

holocaust (hol′ ə kôst′) n. great or complete destruction, especially by fire; p. 1249 *The Cuban missile crisis brought the world to the brink of a nuclear holocaust.*

ominous (om′ ə nəs) adj. like an evil omen; threatening; p. 1249 *An ominous bank of clouds caused us to change our outdoor barbecue plans.*

random (ran′ dəm) adj. lacking a definite pattern; haphazard; p. 1249 *Up close the painting looked like a random collection of brush strokes.*

warily (wār′ ə lē) adv. in a watchful or alert manner; cautiously; p. 1249 *From high on its branch, the bird warily watched the cat.*

Vocabulary Tip: Word Parts Many English words consist of parts that occur in various combinations. The word *enunciate* has as its root the Latin word *nuntiare*, meaning "to report." Another word that stems from *nuntiare* is the verb *announce*.

INDIANA ACADEMIC STANDARDS (pages 1248–1250)
11.3 [Identify] story elements such as...character...
11.2 Develop [reading] strategies...
11.5.8 Deliver multimedia presentations that...select an appropriate medium for each element...

Snow

Julia Alvarez

Our first year in New York we rented a small apartment with a Catholic school nearby, taught by the Sisters of Charity, hefty women in long black gowns and bonnets that made them look peculiar, like dolls in mourning. I liked them a lot, especially my grandmotherly fourth grade teacher, Sister Zoe. I had a lovely name, she said, and she had me teach the whole class how to pronounce it. Yo-lan-da. As the only immigrant in my class, I was put in a special seat in the first row by the window, apart from the other children so that Sister Zoe could tutor me without disturbing them. Slowly, she **enunciated** the new words I was to repeat: *laundromat, cornflakes, subway, snow.*

Soon I picked up enough English to understand **holocaust** was in the air. Sister Zoe explained to a wide-eyed classroom what was happening in Cuba. Russian missiles were being assembled, trained supposedly on New York City. President Kennedy, looking worried too, was on the television at home, explaining we might have to go to war against the Communists. At school, we had air-raid drills: an **ominous** bell would go off and we'd file into the hall, fall to the floor, cover our heads with our coats, and imagine our hair falling out, the bones in our arms going soft. At home, Mami and my sisters and I said a rosary[1] for world peace. I heard new vocabulary: nuclear bomb, radioactive fallout,[2] bomb shelter. Sister Zoe explained how it would happen. She drew a picture of a mushroom on the blackboard and dotted a flurry of chalkmarks for the dusty fallout that would kill us all.

The months grew cold, November, December. It was dark when I got up in the morning, frosty when I followed my breath to school. One morning as I sat at my desk daydreaming out the window, I saw dots in the air like the ones Sister Zoe had drawn—**random** at first, then lots and lots. I shrieked, "Bomb! Bomb!" Sister Zoe jerked around, her full black skirt ballooning as she hurried to my side. A few girls began to cry.

But then Sister Zoe's shocked look faded. "Why, Yolanda dear, that's snow!" She laughed. "Snow."

"Snow," I repeated. I looked out the window **warily.** All my life I had heard about the white crystals that fell out of American skies in the winter. From my desk I watched the fine powder dust the sidewalk and parked cars below. Each flake was different, Sister Zoe said, like a person, irreplaceable and beautiful. ～

---

1. For Roman Catholics, a *rosary* is a circle of beads and also the prayers said as one holds these beads.
2. *Fallout,* made of tiny radioactive particles, is released into the atmosphere after a nuclear explosion.

Reading Strategy Connecting to Contemporary Issues
What are some examples of new vocabulary that current events have introduced into the lexicon today?

Big Idea Nature and Technology *Why does the narrator contrast the comparison of snowflakes to bombs with the comparison of snowflakes to people?*

Vocabulary

ominous (om′ ə nəs) *adj.* like an evil omen; threatening

random (ran′ dəm) *adj.* lacking a definite pattern; haphazard

warily (wār′ ə lē) *adv.* in a watchful or alert manner; cautiously

Literary Element Indirect Characterization *What do these details reveal about Sister Zoe's character?*

Vocabulary

enunciate (i nun′ sē āt′) *v.* to pronounce distinctly

holocaust (hol′ ə kôst′) *n.* great or complete destruction, especially by fire

RESPONDING AND THINKING CRITICALLY

Respond

1. Which of Yolanda's thoughts or experiences do you find most memorable?

Recall and Interpret

2. (a)What words does Sister Zoe teach Yolanda? (b)Why might those words have been particularly useful for her to understand?

3. (a)What causes Yolanda to shriek suddenly? (b)Why does she react in this way?

4. (a)At the end of the selection, how does Sister Zoe describe snow? (b)Why does she say the same applies to people?

Analyze and Evaluate

5. (a)How does Alvarez convey the tense mood—or emotional atmosphere—of the 1950s and 1960s in U.S. history? (b)What detail do you find most effective?

6. How might the fact that Yolanda is an immigrant affect her state of mind?

7. If you were Sister Zoe, what might you write in an assessment of Yolanda?

Connect

8. **Big Idea** Nature and Technology (a)What is ironic about the ending of this story? (b)Does Alvarez see nature and technology as working with or against each other? Explain your answer.

LITERARY ANALYSIS

Literary Element Indirect Characterization

Alvarez uses **indirect characterization** to develop the character of Sister Zoe. That is, she reveals Sister Zoe's personality through her words and actions and through what the narrator, a character in the story, says about her.

1. Give two examples of Sister Zoe's actions or words that reveal a particular character trait. Then name and explain that trait.

2. Describe the age and physical appearance of Sister Zoe according to details supplied by the narrator.

Interdisciplinary Activity: Art

Good writers often describe a scene so vividly that readers can picture it clearly in their minds. Imagine that you are an artist who has been commissioned to draw pictures for Julia Alvarez's story "Snow." Choose at least two incidents from the story and illustrate them. You might even consider creating a whole comic strip with a series of pictures.

Literature Online **Web Activities** For eFlashcards, Selection Quick Checks, and other Web activities, go to www.glencoe.com.

READING AND VOCABULARY

Reading Strategy Connecting to Contemporary Issues

Understanding how the world in which a novel or story takes place resembles the world of today will support your appreciation of why characters behave as they do.

1. What similarities between the world in which Yolanda was living and your world add to your appreciation of the story?

2. If this story were set in today's world, what issues might affect Yolanda?

Vocabulary Practice

Practice with Word Parts Use a dictionary or a thesaurus to help you match the words in the second column of the two columns below with their meanings.

1. a type of medicine that treats the whole body

2. a three-dimensional image created by lasers

3. capable of burning away flesh

a. caustic

b. hologram

c. holistic

Cottonmouth Country and *Daisies*

MEET LOUISE GLÜCK

When Louise Glück was a young girl, she had an experience that helped define her feelings about poetry. While driving Glück and her classmates to school, a classmate's mother asked Glück to recite the poem that she had written for a school assignment. The burgeoning poet was happy to share her work and was particularly excited about the experimental ending of her new poem. For effect, she had purposefully omitted the rhyme in the final line. To her developing ear, Glück says the result "was exhilarating, a kind of explosion of form." After she recited the poem, her classmate's mother said it was very good, but then corrected the final line, explaining that all it was missing was the last rhyme. The young poet was furious. She hadn't even reached middle school yet, but Glück had already developed a passion to write and be heard in her own precise, original voice. Fifty years after her back-seat recital, the talented Glück was named Poet Laureate of the United States.

"*It seems to me that the desire to make art produces an ongoing experience of longing. . . . It's like a lighthouse, except that, as one swims toward it, it backs away.*"

—Louise Glück

Born Poet Glück was born in New York City and raised on Long Island. Her father ran a successful business with her uncle, but while growing up, he had wanted to be a writer. He shared with his daughter a love of stories. However, it was Glück's mother—a well-educated woman who had fought to go to college and revered creative gifts—who became the first reader of her poems and who gave the young writer her earliest critiques. Glück began devouring poetry and stories at an early age, and her reading of Greek myths provided figures and images that she frequently references in her own poems.

Poetic Influence While studying at Columbia University, Glück met her greatest influence, poet Stanley Kunitz. Glück began to blossom as a writer. She published her first collection of poems, *Firstborn*, when she was twenty-five. Since that debut, Glück's work has been recognized with a National Book Critics Circle Award and a Pulitzer Prize. Glück's poems express mythical, mystic perceptions of everyday objects and experiences. Her exacting language and unexpected line breaks create distinct, often haunting, verses.

In addition to writing poetry, Glück frequently teaches and provides young poets with the kind of support and encouragement that Kunitz offered her.

Louise Glück was born in 1943.

Literature Online **Author Search** For more about Louise Glück, go to www.glencoe.com.

Connecting to the Poems

The poems you're about to read invite the reader into a personal, private encounter with the natural world. As you read the poems, think about these questions:

- Where do you go to think or to be alone?
- Have you ever felt as though you could communicate with nature?

Building Background

The poem "Cottonmouth Country" was first published in 1968, in Glück's book *Firstborn*. "Daisies" appeared in her 1992 book *The Wild Iris*. Despite the twenty-four-year gap between these poems, both works demonstrate the important role of setting, or time and place, in Glück's work. In some of Glück's poems, setting is so important that it becomes a distinct character.

Setting Purposes for Reading

Big Idea Nature and Technology

As you read, pay attention to the way the poems juxtapose elements from the natural world with man-made elements. Think about what Glück suggests about humanity's relationship with nature.

Literary Element Free Verse

Many contemporary poems are written in –**free verse**, which means that they do not adhere to a fixed rhyme, meter, line, or stanza structure. Working in free verse allows poets to create their own patterns and to depart from those patterns. Some works of free verse contain lines that flow in the same unfettered way that conversation or private thoughts might flow. Unusual changes in rhythm or startling **line breaks** (the endings of lines) may be used to create drama or tension. As you read these poems, notice what words or ideas the line breaks help to emphasize. Also notice how they contribute to the ebb and flow of the rhythm.

- See Literary Terms Handbook, p. R8.

 Literature Online Interactive Literary Elements Handbook To review or learn more about the literary elements, go to www.glencoe.com.

Reading Strategy Making Inferences About Theme

In poetry, images, events, and observations frequently convey an underlying message, or **theme**. In the poems you're about to read, nature imagery and other details help to express one or more themes about nature, life, and humanity. By considering each poem's imagery and language, you can make **inferences**, or conclusions based on reason and evidence, about the themes in the poems.

Reading Tip: Making Inferences As you read, note your reactions to specific images or ideas in a chart like the one below. Then note your inferences about the poem's themes.

Images or Ideas	Inference about Theme

Vocabulary

woo (wo͞o) *v.* to tempt or invite; p. 1253 *The candidate tried to woo voters with big promises.*

rear (rir) *v.* to lift upright; raise; p. 1253 *The bull reared his head before he charged.*

nostalgia (nə stal′ jə) *n.* a bittersweet longing for things, persons, or situations of the past; p. 1254 *As she grew older, she felt nostalgia for her youth.*

scorn (skorn) *n.* contempt or disdain felt toward a person or object considered despicable or unworthy; p. 1254 *She felt scorn for the thief.*

Vocabulary Tip: Analogies In analogy exercises on a test, you will frequently be asked to determine the relationship between one pair of words and then demonstrate that relationship in a second pair of words.

INDIANA ACADEMIC STANDARDS (pages 1252–1256)

11.2 Develop strategies such as...analyzing structure...

11.3.2 Analyze the way in which the theme or meaning of a selection represents a view or comment on life, using textual

evidence to support the claim.

11.4.8 Use systematic strategies to organize and record information...

Fish. Tadek Beutlich. Color woodcut/linocut. Victoria and Albert Museum, London, UK.

Cottonmouth Country

Louise Glück

1   Fish bones walked the wave off Hatteras.
     And there were other signs
     That Death **wooed** us, by water, wooed us
     By land: among the pines
5   An uncurled cottonmouth[1] that rolled on moss
     Reared in the polluted air.
     Birth, not death, is the hard loss.
     I know. I also left a skin there.

---

1. Also known as a *water moccasin,* this snake is a semiaquatic pit viper of lowlands and swampy regions of the southern United States.

Reading Strategy   Making Inferences About Theme *Why does the image of "polluted air" reinforce Death's presence?*

Vocabulary

woo (wo͞o) *v.* to tempt or invite
rear (rir) *v.* to lift upright; raise

Daisies

Louise Glück

1　Go ahead: say what you're thinking. The garden
　is not the real world. Machines
　are the real world. Say frankly what any fool
　could read in your face: it makes sense
5　to avoid us, to resist
　nostalgia. It is
　not modern enough, the sound the wind makes
　stirring a meadow of daisies: the mind
　cannot shine following it. And the mind
10　wants to shine, plainly, as
　machines shine, and not
　grow deep, as, for example, roots. It is very touching,
　all the same, to see you cautiously
　approaching the meadow's border in early morning,
15　when no one could possibly
　be watching you. The longer you stand at the edge,
　the more nervous you seem. No one wants to hear
　impressions of the natural world: you will be
　laughed at again; **scorn** will be piled on you.
20　As for what you're actually
　hearing this morning: think twice
　before you tell anyone what was said in this field
　and by whom.

Big Idea　Nature and Technology *Why does the speaker say that it makes sense to avoid the daisies (lines 4–5)?*

Literary Element　Free Verse *What dramatic effect is created by the varying line lengths in the last four lines?*

Vocabulary

nostalgia (nə stal′ jə) *n.* a bittersweet longing for things, persons, or situations of the past

scorn (skorn) *n.* contempt or disdain felt toward a person or object considered despicable or unworthy

RESPONDING AND THINKING CRITICALLY

Respond

1. Which one of these poems did you connect with more? Explain.

Recall and Interpret

2. (a)What words and images in "Cottonmouth Country" suggest death? (b)Why do you think the speaker says that "birth, not death, is the hard loss"?

3. (a)Who or what are the speakers in "Daisies"? (b)What do the speakers say is not "modern enough" for the listener? (c)Explain who you think the listener, or person the poem is addressed to, might be.

4. (a)What do lines 6–12 of "Daisies" suggest about human habits or inclinations? (b)What attitude do you think the poem expresses toward these inclinations? Explain.

5. (a)Why do you think the listener in "Daisies" "cautiously" approaches the meadow's border, when no one could possibly be watching? (b)Why does gazing at the meadow make the listener nervous?

Analyze and Evaluate

6. (a)In "Cottonmouth Country," how does the image in the last line of the poem echo the images in the first and fifth lines? (b)Given what comes before, was the image in the last line an effective way to end the poem? Explain.

7. Why do the daisies in "Daisies" seem to be all-knowing about the listener's thoughts? Explain what this might suggest about nature.

8. (a)Which lines in "Daisies" suggest that people are reluctant to engage with nature? (b)Did the perceptions expressed in these lines ring true to you? Explain your answer.

Connect

9. **Big Idea** **Nature and Technology** (a)In these poems, how does the modern world intrude on nature? (b)Explain the conflict that you think Glück's poems may be intended to illuminate. Tell who or what the conflict is between and what opinion of this conflict the poems convey.

Literary Element Free Verse

On the first reading, a **free verse** poem may appear to have no regular form at all. However, analysis usually reveals one or more poetic techniques that help to make the poem memorable and give it meaning. One verse may follow a strict form, while the next verse may depart completely from that form.

Neither of these poems contains fixed meter, fixed line lengths, or formal stanza structures. "Daisies" makes use of rhyme, and "Cottonmouth Country" employs techniques such as slant rhyme and **repetition,** the use of recurring sounds, words, or phrases.

1. (a)List one or two examples of slant rhyme or repetition in "Cottonmouth Country." (b)What is the effect of these techniques on the poem's meaning, musicality, or overall unity?

2. Do you think free verse is an especially good way to convey the words of the speaker in "Daisies"? Support your answer with details from the poem.

Review: Voice

As you learned in Unit 3, **voice** is the personality that a writer conveys in a piece of writing. By examining a poet's choice of words and the **tone,** or attitude toward the subject matter, that a poem expresses, you can arrive at a clearer understanding of the poet's voice.

Partner Activity With a partner, discuss the voice in each of the poems. How would you describe the voice? Which words or phrases in each poem are especially good examples of the distinctive use of voice? For each poem, use a graphic organizer like the one shown to record your examples, give your characterization of the voice, and tell what the voice adds to the poem.

Examples of distinctive use of voice → My description of the voice → What the voice adds to the poem

Reading Strategy Making Inferences About Theme

The **theme** of a poem is its underlying message about life. In some works, the theme is stated directly. In other works, the theme is implied, or stated indirectly, through imagery, events, or observations. One must read carefully to **infer** the theme from the details in the work.

1. What is the theme of "Cottonmouth Country"? Is there a line that best embodies that theme?

2. What is the poem "Daisies" saying about the relationship between people and nature? Support your answer with details from the poem.

3. What is the theme of "Daisies"? Is this theme stated or implied? Explain.

Vocabulary Practice

Practice with Analogies Choose the word that best completes each analogy below.

1. woo : courtship :: study :
   a. hardship **b.** apprenticeship **c.** relationship

2. rear : raise :: ascend :
   a. descend **b.** envelop **c.** climb

3. nostalgia : reminisce :: grief :
   a. mourn **b.** celebrate **c.** withdraw

4. scorn : admire :: praise :
   a. explore **b.** debate **c.** criticize

Academic Vocabulary

Here are two words from the vocabulary list on page R86.

reject (ri jekt´) *v.* to refuse to accept, submit to, believe, or make use of

image (i´mij) *n.* a vivid description or representation

Practice and Apply

1. Near the end of "Cottonmouth Country," what idea does the speaker **reject**?

2. In "Daisies," what **image** does the speaker use to evoke the "real world"?

Writing About Literature

Evaluate Author's Craft The role of the Poet Laureate of the United States is to help foster a greater appreciation for reading and writing poetry. Louise Glück was U.S. Poet Laureate from 2003 to 2004. Consider how the craft displayed in these two poems proves that Glück was a good choice for poet laureate. Then use what you know about Glück to write a brief essay evaluating the selection of Glück as poet laureate. Discuss specific examples of Glück's artistry, such as her poetic language, imagery, and choice of subject matter.

Use a flow chart like the one below to begin organizing your essay. In the three boxes, jot down notes as you construct the essay's introduction, body, and conclusion.

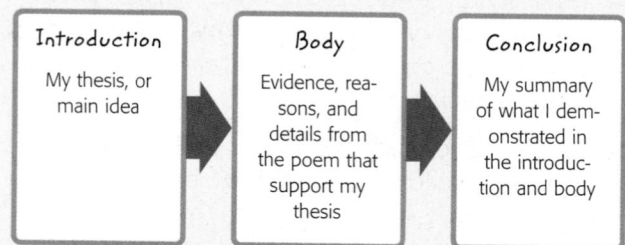

Introduction	Body	Conclusion
My thesis, or main idea	Evidence, reasons, and details from the poem that support my thesis	My summary of what I demonstrated in the introduction and body

After you complete your draft, meet with a partner to review each other's work and to suggest revisions that might strengthen each essay. Then proofread your draft for errors in spelling, grammar, and punctuation.

Reading Further

If you enjoyed these poems, you may enjoy these other works by Louise Glück.

Poetry

Ararat, Glück's sixth book of poetry, deals primarily with her relationship with her parents.

The Wild Iris is Glück's Pulitzer Prize-winning book of poems that portrays the poet's attempt to make sense of her role in the universe.

Essays

Proofs & Theories: Essays on Poetry is Glück's book of sixteen essays in which she comments on topics such as the future, education, and the work of other poets.

Literature Online **Web Activities** For eFlashcards, Selection Quick Checks, and other Web activities, go to www.glencoe.com.

Extending and Remaking Traditions

The Museum of Modern Art, 1973. Malcah Zeldis.

"We became filled with a hunger—I call it now, sometimes, Latino Hunger. A hunger to see ourselves, our families and friends, our values and lives and realities reflected in something other than our own minds."

—Carmen Tafolla, "Mi Familia"

from *The Woman Warrior*

MEET MAXINE HONG KINGSTON

Finding meaning was Maxine Hong Kingston's primary mission when she began to write *The Woman Warrior: Memories of a Girlhood among Ghosts*. The American daughter of Chinese immigrants, Kingston had long been fascinated by the differing ways in which women were viewed by her parents and by other Chinese immigrants of their generation. In talking to her parents, Kingston discovered that cherished myths about powerful warrior women existed side by side with what Kingston perceived as sexist ideas. Kingston's mother often sang the *Ballad of Mu Lan*, about a young woman who took her father's place in battle. She also talked about her own experiences training and working as a doctor in China at a time when few women could gain an education, take on a profession, or work outside the home. Nevertheless, Kingston's mother would often say, "It's better to raise geese than girls."

A Life of Her Own Kingston began writing poetry when she was nine years old. A talented student, she attended the University of California at Berkeley before marrying Earll Kingston, an actor. She taught English and creative writing for almost a decade before submitting her writing for publication.

Writing as a Way of Life Kingston's first book, *The Woman Warrior*, won the National Book Critics' Circle Award and was named one of the ten best nonfiction books of the 1970s by *Time* magazine. In the *New York Times*, John Leonard wrote, "As an account of

growing up female and Chinese American in California . . . it is antinostalgic; it burns the fat right out of the mind. As a dream—of the 'female avenger'—it is dizzying, elemental, a poem turned into a sword."

> *"I have no idea how people who don't write endure their lives . . . words and stories create order. And some of the things that happen to us in life seem to have no meaning, but when you write them down you find the meanings for them . . ."*
>
> —Maxine Hong Kingston

While she was still writing *The Woman Warrior*, Kingston began another work, *China Men*, which later won the American Book Award. She considers the two books one big book. The first is the story of the women in her family, the second, the story of the men.

In recent years, Kingston has written articles, novels, nonfiction, and many short stories. In addition to her writing, Kingston teaches English and math. She has said, "I get a recurring dream in which my mother appears and she says to me: 'What have you done to educate America? Have you educated America yet? And what about the rest of the world? Have you gotten them educated yet?' . . . Those are my orders!"

Maxine Hong Kingston was born in 1940.

Literature Online **Author Search** For more about Maxine Hong Kingston, go to www.glencoe.com.

Connecting to the Story

The following story describes the thoughts and attitudes of family members on the day of a long-awaited reunion. As you read the story, think about the following questions:

- How does a person change over time?
- When family members have been raised in different cultures, how does it affect their relationships with one another?

Building Background

The main character in this selection is Kingston's mother, Brave Orchid. When Brave Orchid came to the United States, she left her younger sister, Moon Orchid, behind in China. Moon Orchid later joined her sister in 1969. During that time, the Vietnam War was under way, and the U.S. military had drafted hundreds of thousands of young men to fight in it. The war was becoming increasingly unpopular, and many draft-age men went to Canada to avoid going to Vietnam. The war was on Brave Orchid's mind as she waited at the airport to welcome her sister to a new country.

Setting Purposes for Reading

Big Idea **Extending and Remaking Traditions**

As you read, notice that Kingston's subject matter, the lives of immigrants and their families, allows her to present a fresh take on U.S. culture and history.

Literary Element **Exposition**

Exposition in nonfiction presents information that readers will need to understand the characters, the setting, and the situation discussed in a narrative. As you read, identify sections where Kingston uses exposition and sections where she requires you to make inferences to understand the story.

- See Literary Terms Handbook, p. R6.

Literature Online **Interactive Literary Elements Handbook** To review or learn more about the literary elements, go to www.glencoe.com.

Reading Strategy **Making Inferences About Characters**

When you **make inferences,** you use your reason and experience to understand what an author does not say directly. Inferring helps you look more deeply at characters and points you toward the **theme,** or overall message, of a selection.

Reading Tip: Character Web Use a web like the one below to record details about the main character in the selection, Brave Orchid. Then record the inferences you make based on these details.

Vocabulary

downy (dou′nē) *adj.* soft and fluffy, like the feathers of young birds; p. 1261 *With their downy feathers, baby birds look innocent and cute.*

inaudibly (in ô′ də blē) *adv.* in a manner not able to be heard; p. 1263 *We could see her mouth moving, but she was speaking inaudibly.*

gravity (grav′ə tē) *n.* seriousness; importance p. 1263 *He wanted to laugh but didn't because he recognized the gravity of the graduation ceremony.*

oblivious (ə bliv′ē əs) *adj.* without conscious awareness; p. 1263 *We jumped up and down in joy, oblivious to the stares of the people around us.*

dusk (dusk) *n.* the time of day just before nightfall; p. 1264 *We returned home before dusk.*

Vocabulary Tip: Synonyms Words that have the same or similar meanings are called **synonyms.** Knowing synonyms for a word can help you add interest and variety to your writing.

 INDIANA ACADEMIC STANDARDS (pages 1259–1267)

11.2.1 Analyze...the features...of...public documents...

11.5.1 Write fictional...narratives...

11.3.8 Determine whether the authors' positions have contributed to...the credibility of the characters.

from The Woman Warrior

Maxine Hong Kingston

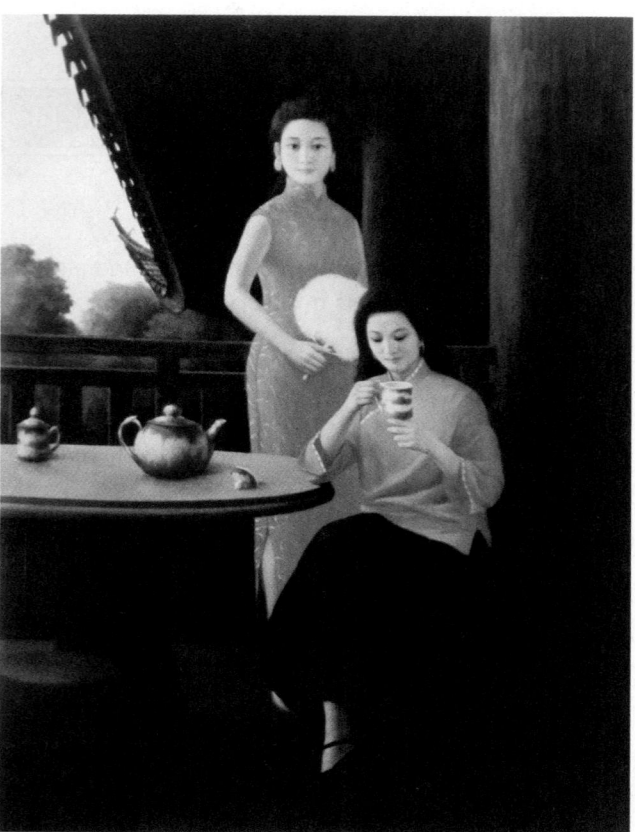

A Sunny Day with Gentle Breeze, 1993. Zifen Qian. Oil on canvas, 42 x 56 in. Private collection.

When she was about sixty-eight years old, Brave Orchid took a day off to wait at San Francisco International Airport for the plane that was bringing her sister to the United States. She had not seen Moon Orchid for thirty years. She had begun this waiting at home, getting up a half-hour before Moon Orchid's plane took off in Hong Kong. Brave Orchid would add her will power to the forces that keep an airplane up. Her head hurt with the concentration. The plane had to be light, so no matter how tired she felt, she dared not rest her spirit on a wing but continuously and gently pushed up on the plane's belly. She had already been waiting at the airport for nine hours. She was wakeful.

Next to Brave Orchid sat Moon Orchid's only daughter, who was helping her aunt wait. Brave Orchid had made two of her own children come too because they could drive, but they had been lured away by the magazine racks and the gift shops and coffee shops. Her American children could not sit for very long. They did not understand sitting; they had wandering feet. She hoped they would get back from the pay T.V.'s or the pay toilets or wherever they were spending their money before the plane arrived. If they did not come back soon, she would go look for them.

Literary Element Exposition *What details help you understand the situation of Brave Orchid and her family?*

If her son thought he could hide in the men's room, he was wrong.

"Are you all right, Aunt?" asked her niece.

"No, this chair hurts me. Help me pull some chairs together so I can put my feet up."

She unbundled a blanket and spread it out to make a bed for herself. On the floor she had two shopping bags full of canned peaches, real peaches, beans wrapped in taro[1] leaves, cookies, Thermos bottles, enough food for everybody, though only her niece would eat with her. Her bad boy and bad girl were probably sneaking hamburgers, wasting their money. She would scold them.

---

1. *Taro* (tär′ ō) is a tropical Asian plant with broad leaves. It is customary in Chinese cooking to wrap rice, vegetables, or fish in the leaves for steaming.

Reading Strategy Making Inferences About Characters *What does this detail tell you about Brave Orchid's character?*

Big Idea Extending and Remaking Traditions *From Brave Orchid's thoughts here, what can you infer about differences between Brave Orchid and her children?*

Many soldiers and sailors sat about, oddly calm, like little boys in cowboy uniforms. (She thought "cowboy" was what you would call a Boy Scout.) They should have been crying hysterically on their way to Vietnam. "If I see one that looks Chinese," she thought, "I'll go over and give him some advice." She sat up suddenly; she had forgotten about her own son, who was even now in Vietnam. Carefully she split her attention, beaming half of it to the ocean, into the water to keep him afloat. He was on a ship. He was in Vietnamese waters. She was sure of it. He and the other children were lying to her. They had said he was in Japan, and then they said he was in the Philippines. But when she sent him her help, she could feel that he was on a ship in Da Nang.[2] Also she had seen the children hide the envelopes that his letters came in.

"Do you think my son is in Vietnam?" she asked her niece, who was dutifully eating.

"No. Didn't your children say he was in the Philippines?"

"Have you ever seen any of his letters with Philippine stamps on them?"

"Oh, yes. Your children showed me one."

"I wouldn't put it past them to send the letters to some Filipino they know. He puts Manila[3] postmarks on them to fool me."

"Yes, I can imagine them doing that. But don't worry. Your son can take care of himself. All your children can take care of themselves."

"Not him. He's not like other people. Not normal at all. He sticks erasers in his ears, and the erasers are still attached to the pencil stubs. The captain will say, 'Abandon ship,' or, 'Watch out for bombs,' and he won't hear. He doesn't listen to orders. I told him to flee to Canada, but he wouldn't go."

She closed her eyes. After a short while, plane and ship under control, she looked again at the children in uniforms. Some of the blond ones looked like baby chicks, their crew cuts like the downy yellow on baby chicks. You had to feel sorry for them even though they were Army and Navy Ghosts.[4]

Suddenly her son and daughter came running. "Come, Mother. The plane's landed early. She's here already." They hurried, folding up their mother's encampment. She was glad her children were not useless. They must have known what this trip to San Francisco was about then. "It's a good thing I made you come early," she said.

Brave Orchid pushed to the front of the crowd. She had to be in front. The passengers were separated from the people waiting for them by glass doors and walls. Immigration Ghosts were stamping papers. The travelers crowded along some conveyor belts to have their luggage searched. Brave Orchid did not see her sister anywhere. She stood watching for four hours. Her children left and came back. "Why don't you sit down?" they asked.

"The chairs are too far away," she said.

"Why don't you sit on the floor then?"

No, she would stand, as her sister was probably standing in a line she could not see from here. Her American children had no feelings and no memory.

To while away time, she and her niece talked about the Chinese passengers. These new immigrants had it easy. On Ellis Island[5] the people were thin after forty days at sea and had no fancy luggage.

"That one looks like her," Brave Orchid would say.

---

2. *Da Nang* (dä näng), a port city in South Vietnam, was the site of a major U.S. military base during the Vietnam War.
3. *Manila* (mə nil′ ə) is the capital of the Philippines and its largest city.

Big Idea Extending and Remaking Traditions *Why do you think Brave Orchid is mistrustful of her children? Why does she have more trust in her niece?*

---

4. Here, *ghosts* refers to white people.
5. From 1892 to 1943, *Ellis Island,* in upper New York Bay, was the chief U.S. immigration station.

Reading Strategy Making Inferences About Characters *What do the children's actions tell you about the children? What does Brave Orchid's remark reveal about her?*

Literary Element Exposition *Why are these details about the setting important to the story?*

Reading Strategy Making Inferences About Characters *What can you infer about Brave Orchid's background from her thoughts here?*

Vocabulary

downy (dou′ nē) *adj.* soft and fluffy, like the feathers of young birds

"No, that's not her."

Ellis Island had been made out of wood and iron. Here everything was new plastic, a ghost trick to lure immigrants into feeling safe and spilling their secrets. Then the Alien Office could send them right back. Other-wise, why did they lock her out, not letting her help her sister answer questions and spell her name? At Ellis Island when the ghost asked Brave Orchid what year her husband had cut off his pigtail, a Chinese who was crouching on the floor motioned her not to talk. "I don't know," she had said. If it weren't for that Chinese man, she might not be here today, or her husband either. She hoped some Chinese, a janitor or a clerk, would look out for Moon Orchid. Luggage conveyors fooled immigrants into thinking the Gold Mountain was going to be easy.

Brave Orchid felt her heart jump—Moon Orchid. "There she is," she shouted. But her niece saw it was not her mother at all. And it shocked her to discover the woman her aunt was pointing out. This was a young woman, younger than herself, no older than Moon Orchid the day the sisters parted. "Moon Orchid will have changed a little, of course," Brave Orchid was saying. "She will have learned to wear western clothes." The woman wore a navy blue suit with a bunch of dark cherries at the shoulder.

"No, Aunt," said the niece. "That's not my mother."

"Perhaps not. It's been so many years. Yes, it is your mother. It must be. Let her come closer, and we can tell. Do you think she's too far away for me to tell, or is it my eyes getting bad?"

"It's too many years gone by," said the niece.

Brave Orchid turned suddenly—another Moon Orchid, this one a neat little woman with a bun. She was laughing at something the person ahead of her in line said. Moon Orchid was just like that, laughing at nothing. "I would be able

> *Brave Orchid momentarily saw, like a larger, younger outline around this old woman, the sister she had been waiting for.*

to tell the difference if one of them would only come closer," Brave Orchid said with tears, which she did not wipe. Two children met the woman with the cherries, and she shook their hands. The other woman was met by a young man. They looked at each other gladly, then walked away side by side.

Up close neither one of those women looked like Moon Orchid at all. "Don't worry, Aunt," said the niece. "I'll know her."

"I'll know her too. I knew her before you did."

The niece said nothing, although she had seen her mother only five years ago. Her aunt liked having the last word.

Finally Brave Orchid's children quit wandering and drooped on a railing. Who knew what they were thinking? At last the niece called out, "I see her! I see her! Mother! Mother!" Whenever the doors parted, she shouted, probably embarrassing the American cousins, but she didn't care. She called out, "Mama! Mama!" until the crack in the sliding doors became too small to let in her voice. "Mama!" What a strange word in an adult voice. Many people turned to see what adult was calling, "Mama!" like a child. Brave Orchid saw an old, old woman jerk her head up, her little eyes blinking confusedly, a woman whose nerves leapt toward the sound anytime she heard "Mama!" Then she relaxed to her own business again. She was a tiny, tiny lady, very thin, with little fluttering hands, and her hair was in a gray knot. She was dressed in a gray wool suit; she wore pearls around her neck and in her earlobes. Moon Orchid *would* travel with her jewels showing. The familiar dim halo faded, leaving the woman so old, so gray. So old. Brave Orchid pressed against the glass. *That* old lady? Yes, that old lady facing the ghost who stamped her papers without questioning her was her sister. Then, without noticing her family, Moon Orchid walked smiling over to the Suitcase Inspector Ghost, who took her boxes apart, pulling out puffs of tissue. From where she

---

Reading Strategy Making Inferences About Characters
What do Brave Orchid's unrealistic ideas about her sister tell you about Brave Orchid?

Reading Strategy Making Inferences About Characters
What trait, or personal characteristic, of Brave Orchid is suggested by this remark?

was, Brave Orchid could not see what her sister had chosen to carry across the ocean. She wished her sister would look her way. Brave Orchid thought that if *she* were entering a new country, she would be at the windows. Instead Moon Orchid hovered over the unwrapping, surprised at each reappearance as if she were opening presents after a birthday party.

"Mama!" Moon Orchid's daughter kept calling. Brave Orchid said to her children, "Why don't you call your aunt too? Maybe she'll hear us if all of you call out together." But her children slunk away. Maybe that shame-face they so often wore was American politeness.

"Mama!" Moon Orchid's daughter called again, and this time her mother looked right at her. She left her bundles in a heap and came running. "Hey!" the Customs Ghost yelled at her. She went back to clear up her mess, talking **inaudibly** to her daughter all the while. Her daughter pointed toward Brave Orchid. And at

last Moon Orchid looked at her—two old women with faces like mirrors.

Their hands reached out as if to touch the other's face, then returned to their own, the fingers checking the grooves in the forehead and along the side of the mouth. Moon Orchid, who never understood the **gravity** of things, started smiling and laughing, pointing at Brave Orchid. Finally Moon Orchid gathered up her stuff, strings hanging and papers loose, and met her sister at the door, where they shook hands, **oblivious** to blocking the way.

"You're an old woman," said Brave Orchid.

"Aiaa. *You're* an old woman."

"But you are really old. Surely, you can't say that about me. I'm not old the way you're old."

"But *you* really are old. You're one year older than I am."

"Your hair is white and your face all wrinkled."

Big Idea Extending and Remaking Traditions *How does this sentence help explain why there is tension between Brave Orchid and her children?*

MAXINE HONG KINGSTON **1263**

Hong Kong city skyline from Victoria harbor.
Viewing the Photograph: Moon Orchid travels to San Francisco from Hong Kong. Does this photograph change the way you imagine her? Explain.

"You're so skinny."

"You're so fat."

"Fat women are more beautiful than skinny women."

The children pulled them out of the doorway. One of Brave Orchid's children brought the car from the parking lot, and the other heaved the luggage into the trunk. They put the two old ladies and the niece in the back seat. All the way home—across the Bay Bridge, over the Diablo hills,[6] across the San Joaquin River to the valley, the valley moon so white at **dusk**—all the way home, the two sisters exclaimed every time they turned to look at each other, "Aiaa! How old!"

Brave Orchid forgot that she got sick in cars, that all vehicles but palanquins made her dizzy. "You're so old," she kept saying. "How did you get so old?"

Brave Orchid had tears in her eyes. But Moon Orchid said, "You look older than I. You are older than I," and again she'd laugh. "You're wearing an old mask to tease me." It surprised Brave Orchid that after thirty years she could still get annoyed at her sister's silliness.

Visual Vocabulary
A **palanquin** (pal′ ən kēn′) is a covered or enclosed couch, carried on the shoulders of two or more men by means of poles.

---

6. The *Bay Bridge* crosses the San Francisco Bay, connecting the cities of San Francisco and Oakland. The *Diablo* (dē ä′ blō) *hills* are at the base of Mount Diablo, a peak located about twenty miles east of Oakland.

Literary Element Exposition *How does the author develop the details about character and plot that were introduced in the first part of the story?*

Vocabulary

dusk (dusk) n. the time of day just before nightfall

Reading Strategy Making Inferences About Characters *Why is Brave Orchid annoyed by her sister's remarks?*

RESPONDING AND THINKING CRITICALLY

Respond

1. Did you find this selection serious, humorous, or both? Describe your impressions.

Recall and Interpret

2. (a)How long before her sister's plane is scheduled to land does Brave Orchid arrive at the airport? (b)Why do you think Brave Orchid does this?

3. (a)Who else goes to the airport with Brave Orchid? (b)Why do you think Kingston chose not to refer to these people by name?

4. (a)How do Brave Orchid and Moon Orchid react when they see each other? (b)Why do the sisters respond to each other as they do?

Analyze and Evaluate

5. Since this narrative is from Kingston's memoir, a reader might expect a **first-person point of view.** Why might Kingston have chosen to use the **third person point of view** here? (See Literary Terms Handbook, page R14.)

6. Kingston's memoir uses different methods of **characterization** (see page R1) to convey Brave Orchid's personality. In what ways do these methods—such as details about Brave Orchid's thoughts, words, and actions—help you understand the selection? Support your response with examples.

7. Brave Orchid finds her children to be a mystery. Why might she feel this way? Explain.

8. (a)Write a phrase or sentence summarizing the **theme,** or message about life or human nature, conveyed by this selection. Explain which aspects of the selection helped you to arrive at the theme. (b)Did you find Kingston's rendering of the family convincing and true-to-life? Why or why not?

Connect

9. **Big Idea** **Extending and Remaking Traditions** In recent years, many writers have written about the experiences of immigrants in the United States. How does this excerpt from *The Woman Warrior* portray the immigrant experience?

VISUAL LITERACY: Graphic Organizer

COMPARING AND CONTRASTING CHARACTERS

As you did for Brave Orchid, make a web diagram to record details and inferences about Moon Orchid's character. After you have completed the web about Moon Orchid, examine both webs to see how Brave Orchid's and Moon Orchid's characters are similar and different. You may want to use a Venn diagram to record which traits, actions, thoughts and other details the two characters share and which they possess independently.

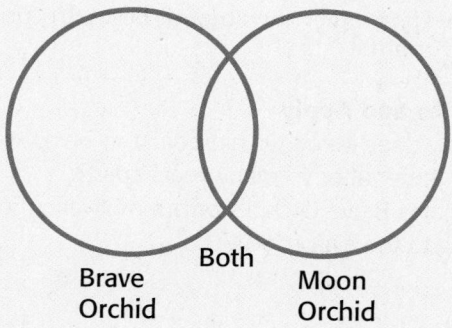

Group Activity

Share the graphic organizers you made with one or more classmates.

1. Work with a partner or group to discuss how Brave Orchid and Moon Orchid are similar and different.

2. At what points in the selection do you receive critical information about each of the two characters? For each character, explain how thoughts, words, actions, or some combination of the three provided the information.

Literary Element Exposition

Exposition in a nonfiction narrative provides information that is crucial to an understanding of the work's characters, setting, and plot. In this selection, Kingston provides exposition in the first two paragraphs. As the selection progresses, Kingston expands on this information.

1. What aspect of the story's setting is introduced in the exposition and developed further in the pages that follow?

2. Select one character and a trait of that character as introduced in the exposition. Explain briefly how that trait becomes important as the story unfolds.

Review: Dialogue

As you learned in Unit Six, **dialogue** is conversation between characters in a literary work. Through dialogue, an author reveals the feelings, thoughts, and intentions of characters; establishes conflicts; and advances the plot.

1. Examine the dialogue between Brave Orchid and her niece. (a)How do you think the niece views Brave Orchid? (b)Explain what impression you receive of the relationship between Brave Orchid and her niece from these dialogues.

2. (a)Reread the final conversation between Brave Orchid and Moon Orchid. Why do you think that the sisters say the things they say? (b)Explain whether you found their exchange moving, humorous, or both. Support your answer.

Hong Kong, city skyline and Victoria Harbor.

Reading Strategy Making Inferences About Characters

The characters of Brave Orchid and Moon Orchid are central to this selection, but other characters, such as Brave Orchid's children, also appear.

1. What inferences can you make about how Brave Orchid's children feel about their day at the airport? List the details that support your inferences.

2. (a)In what ways are Brave Orchid's children important to the story? (b)How do they deepen your understanding of Brave Orchid and of the family situation in general?

Vocabulary Practice

Practice with Synonyms Find the synonym for each vocabulary word listed in the first column.

1. downy
   a. hardy   **c.** straight
   b. fluffy   **d.** innocuous

2. inaudibly
   a. indistinctly   **c.** vigorously
   b. raucously   **d.** indelibly

3. gravity
   a. density   **c.** velocity
   b. importance   **d.** sensitivity

4. oblivious
   a. memorable   **c.** obligatory
   b. unaware   **d.** obvious

5. dusk
   a. twilight   **c.** noon
   b. sunrise   **d.** midnight

Academic Vocabulary

Here are two words from the vocabulary list on page R86. These words will help you think, write, and talk about the selection.

adjust (ə just′) *v.* to bring to a more effective or satisfactory state; to make conform; to adapt

prime (prīm) *adj.* the chief or best part; principal or original

Practice and Apply

1. How does Moon Orchid **adjust** to being with her sister after so many years apart?

2. What is Brave Orchid's **prime** motivation for getting to the airport early?

Writing About Literature

Apply Mood Imagine that you are a newspaper reporter who comes across Brave Orchid and her family at the airport. You sense a story and stop to interview Brave Orchid and Moon Orchid. Write a feature story about their reunion. Base the action and dialogue in your story on what you know about each character. In your article, convey the **mood,** or emotional quality or atmosphere, of the scene at the airport.

First, use a chart like the one shown below to figure out the essential details of the story.

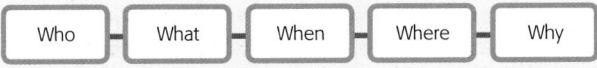

Who — What — When — Where — Why

Refer to your chart as you write your story. Begin your story by setting the scene for your readers. Explain who the characters are, where they are, and why they are there. Discuss the characters' background and the various emotions and expectations they have as they await Moon Orchid's arrival. To make your readers feel like they are at the scene, include details that convey the airport's atmosphere. As you retell the story of what happens as Moon Orchid arrives, include description and quoted dialogue in the style of newspaper reporting.

After you have completed your article, exchange your work with a fellow student. Critique each other's articles for their effectiveness at conveying the mood and the important details of the story. On the basis of the critique you receive, revise your article. Proofread and edit it to correct any errors in spelling, grammar, and punctuation.

Internet Connection

Chinese American Communities Today To learn more about the Chinese American community today, do research on the Internet. Try to find the answers to these questions: How many Chinese Americans currently reside in the United States? Which aspects of their community and culture are Chinese Americans proud? What issues are of special concern for them? Work with a small group to make a poster showing what you learn from your research.

Literature Online Web Activities For eFlashcards, Selection Quick Checks, and other Web activities, go to www.glencoe.com.

Kingston's Language and Style

Correcting Sentence Fragments In this selection from *The Woman Warrior,* Maxine Hong Kingston sometimes uses sentence fragments to show how a character talks: "Not him. He's not like other people. Not normal at all." The narrator, however, uses clear, complete sentences to tell her story. Kingston avoids **sentence fragments**—sentences that are missing an essential part, such as the subject, the predicate, or both. Sentence fragments are incomplete thoughts. They confuse readers by failing to adequately indicate who is acting or what the action is. Consider, for example, how confusing the following sentences would be if the subject—the word "she"—had been omitted:

> She had already been waiting at the airport for nine hours. She was wakeful.

Notice what the effect would have been if, throughout the story, Kingston had omitted the subjects, the predicates, or both from her sentences. Examine the examples below. (Note that Kingston does occasionally include a sentence fragment to create a special effect or to create dialogues that reproduce the sound of actual speech.)

Missing Sentence Part	Solution
Pushed to the front of the crowd (missing subject)	Brave Orchid pushed to the front of the crowd.
If her son thought he could hide in the men's room. Wrong. (missing subject and predicate)	If her son thought he could hide in the men's room, he was wrong.

Revising Check

Complete Sentences Complete sentences make your writing easier to understand and more effective. With a partner, review your feature story about Brave Orchid's and Moon Orchid's reunion. Revise your writing by completing sentence fragments.

Everything Stuck to Him

MEET RAYMOND CARVER

In the summer of 1958, Raymond Carver borrowed $125 from the pharmacist for whom he delivered prescriptions. With that money, he moved his young family to the outskirts of Chico, California, where he would attend college. Although he and his wife were already working hard to support their two children, the twenty-year-old Carver knew that he wanted to be a writer and felt that this move would help him pursue his dream. That fall at Chico State College, he met writer John Gardner, who became his mentor. Gardner paid special attention to Carver's work and offered him the key to his office, a gesture Carver called "a turning point" in his life. Every weekend, Carver spent part of the day in Gardner's office, typing page after page, developing his craft. With the gift of that key, Carver began his journey toward becoming an important twentieth-century writer.

> "Every great, or even every very good writer, makes the world over according to his own specifications."
>
> —Raymond Carver
> from "A Storyteller's Shoptalk"

Working-Class Perspective Raymond Carver was born in Clatskanie, Oregon. By the time he was three, his family had moved to Yakima, Washington, where his father worked at a sawmill. Carver's childhood in Yakima was beset with troubles. His father was an alcoholic, the family was dreadfully poor, and survival was a daily challenge.

Throughout his twenties and thirties, the young writer struggled financially and battled with alcoholism. Still, during these years of hardship, Carver kept his eye trained on the world around him, gathering material for his fiction and poetry from his observations and experiences. By the time he reached forty, Carver had quit drinking and had established himself as an emerging master of the short story.

Literary Acclaim One of the lessons Carver learned from Gardner was that revision, revision, and *more* revision were essential to good writing. By following this process, Carver gradually began to pare down the language in his stories, creating spare, realistic fiction. Carver told stories about everyday people in a singular voice that added tension and depth to his narration.

Carver won numerous awards for his writing, and received a National Book Award nomination for fiction in 1977. His short stories appear in several collections, including *Will You Be Quiet, Please?* (1976), *Furious Seasons* (1977), and *Where I'm Calling From* (1988). He published three collections of poetry during his lifetime, and another collection was published posthumously. Though Carver died at the age of fifty from lung cancer, his reputation continues to grow. A source of inspiration for writers today, Carver provided some of the most enduring human portraits of the twentieth century.

Raymond Carver was born in 1938 and died in 1988.

Literature Online Author Search For more about Raymond Carver, go to www.glencoe.com.

Connecting to the Story

In "Everything Stuck to Him," a teenage father must choose between his own pleasures and his responsibilities to his family. Most people have faced a similar choice between fun and responsibility at some time in their lives. As you read the story, think about the following questions.

- When might you choose pleasure over responsibility?
- When might you choose responsibility over pleasure?

Building Background

"Everything Stuck to Him" was included in Carver's collection of short stories *What We Talk About When We Talk About Love*. Published in 1981, the collection represents Carver at the peak of his early period, when he perfected a spare, succinct style of storytelling. Carver used direct, everyday language, which was perfectly suited to the content and characters in his stories. He is also known for his innovative techniques, such as blending dialogue and narration. Though simply told, Carver's stories are usually tense and gripping.

Setting Purposes for Reading

Big Idea Extending and Remaking Traditions

As you read, notice the innovative techniques Carver uses in this story.

Literary Element Frame Story

A **frame story** is a plot structure that includes the telling of one story within another story. The frame is the outer story, which precedes and usually follows the inner, more important story. In this way, the outer story "frames" the inner one. For example, Mark Twain uses a frame in "The Celebrated Jumping Frog of Calaveras County" (see page 480). As you read "Everything Stuck to Him," notice the frame story and the inner story.

- See Literary Terms Handbook, p. R8.

Literature Online Interactive Literary Elements Handbook To review or learn more about the literary elements, go to www.glencoe.com.

Reading Strategy Questioning

Questioning involves asking yourself whether you understand what you are reading. To use this strategy, ask yourself questions such as the following: Do I understand what I've just read? How does this action fit into the overall conflict? As you read "Everything Stuck to Him," have a running conversation with yourself by asking questions about the plot and the characters.

Reading Tip: Taking Notes Use a chart to record your questions while reading the story. You can fill in the answers to these questions after you finish reading.

Questions	Answers
Why does the father tell his daughter about the dentist's letterhead?	

Vocabulary

coincide (kō´ in sīd´) *v.* to occur at the same time; p. 1270 *His birthday coincided with the exam.*

ambition (am bish´ ən) *n.* a desire to achieve a particular end; p. 1270 *Driven by ambition, she worked tirelessly to become a champion gymnast.*

striking (strī´ king) *adj.* impressive; attractive; p. 1271 *The model was even more striking in person than in her magazine photographs.*

marvel (mär´ vəl) *v.* to be filled with wonder; p. 1271 *The diver marveled at the coral reef.*

fitfully (fit´ fəl lē) *adv.* irregularly; in stops and starts; p. 1271 *The sick child coughed fitfully at night.*

Vocabulary Tip: Word Parts When taking a word apart to determine meaning, consider these basic elements: **root,** or the main part of a word; **prefix,** or a word part added to the beginning of a word; and **suffix,** or a word part added to the end of a word.

INDIANA ACADEMIC STANDARDS (pages 1269–1275)
11.2 Develop strategies such as asking questions [and] identifying and analyzing structure...

11.5.9 Write...a literary analysis that...supports judgments with relevant and substantial evidence...

Everything Stuck to Him

Raymond Carver

Mother and Child. Ditz. Private collection.

She's in Milan for Christmas and wants to know what it was like when she was a kid.

Tell me, she says. Tell me what it was like when I was a kid. She sips Strega, waits, eyes him closely.

She is a cool, slim, attractive girl, a survivor from top to bottom.

That was a long time ago. That was twenty years ago, he says.

You can remember, she says. Go on.

What do you want to hear? he says. What else can I tell you? I could tell you about something that happened when you were a baby. It involves you, he says. But only in a minor way.

Tell me, she says. But first fix us another so you won't have to stop in the middle.

He comes back from the kitchen with drinks, settles into his chair, begins.

They were kids themselves, but they were crazy in love, this eighteen-year-old boy and this seventeen-year-old girl when they married. Not all that long afterwards they had a daughter.

The baby came along in late November during a cold spell that just happened to **coincide** with the peak of the waterfowl season. The boy loved to hunt, you see. That's part of it.

The boy and girl, husband and wife, father and mother, they lived in a little apartment under a dentist's office. Each night they cleaned the dentist's place upstairs in exchange for rent and utilities. In summer they were expected to maintain the lawn and the flowers. In winter the boy shoveled snow and spread rock salt on the walks. Are you still with me? Are you getting the picture?

I am, she says.

That's good, he says. So one day the dentist finds out they were using his letterhead for their personal correspondence. But that's another story.

He gets up from his chair and looks out the window. He sees the tile rooftops and the snow that is falling steadily on them.

Tell the story, she says.

The two kids were very much in love. On top of this they had great **ambitions**. They were always talking about the things they were going to do and the places they were going to go.

Now the boy and girl slept in the bedroom, and the baby slept in the living room. Let's say

---

Big Idea Extending and Remaking Traditions *Why do you think the author does not use quotation marks to indicate dialogue?*

Literary Element Frame Story *How does the reader know that the narrator is beginning to tell a story about himself?*

Vocabulary

coincide (kō′ in sīd′) *v.* to occur at the same time

Big Idea Extending and Remaking Traditions *Why does the author identify the couple by the roles they play?*

Vocabulary

ambition (am bish′ ən) *n.* a desire to achieve a particular end the baby was about three months old and had only just begun to sleep through the night.

On this one Saturday night after finishing his work upstairs, the boy stayed in the dentist's office and called an old hunting friend of his father's.

Carl, he said when the man picked up the receiver, believe it or not, I'm a father.

Congratulations, Carl said. How is the wife?

She's fine, Carl. Everybody's fine.

That's good, Carl said, I'm glad to hear it. But if you called about going hunting, I'll tell you something. The geese are flying to beat the band. I don't think I've ever seen so many. Got five today. Going back in the morning, so come along if you want to.

I want to, the boy said.

The boy hung up the telephone and went downstairs to tell the girl. She watched while he laid out his things. Hunting coat, shell bag, boots, socks, hunting cap, long underwear, pump gun.

What time will you be back? the girl said.

Probably around noon, the boy said. But maybe as late as six o'clock. Would that be too late?

It's fine, she said. The baby and I will get along fine. You go and have some fun. When you get back, we'll dress the baby up and go visit Sally.

The boy said, Sounds like a good idea.

Sally was the girl's sister. She was **striking**. I don't know if you've seen pictures of her. The boy was a little in love with Sally, just as he was a little in love with Betsy, who was another sister the girl had. The boy used to say to the girl, If we weren't married, I could go for Sally.

What about Betsy? the girl used to say. I hate to admit it, but I truly feel she's better looking than Sally and me. What about Betsy?

Betsy too, the boy used to say.

After dinner he turned up the furnace and helped her bathe the baby. He **marveled** again at

the infant who had half his features and half the girl's. He powdered the tiny body. He powdered between fingers and toes.

He emptied the bath into the sink and went upstairs to check the air. It was overcast and cold. The grass, what there was of it, looked like canvas, stiff and gray under the street light.

Snow lay in piles beside the walk. A car went by. He heard sand under the tires. He let himself imagine what it might be like tomorrow, geese beating the air over his head, shotgun plunging against his shoulder.

Then he locked the door and went downstairs.

In bed they tried to read. But both of them fell asleep, she first, letting the magazine sink to the quilt.

It was the baby's cries that woke him up.

The light was on out there, and the girl was standing next to the crib rocking the baby in her arms. She put the baby down, turned out the light, and came back to the bed.

He heard the baby cry. This time the girl stayed where she was. The baby cried **fitfully** and stopped. The boy listened, then dozed. But the baby's cries woke him again. The living-room light was burning. He sat up and turned on the lamp.

I don't know what's wrong, the girl said, walking back and forth with the baby. I've changed her and fed her, but she keeps on crying. I'm so tired I'm afraid I might drop her.

You come back to bed, the boy said. I'll hold her for a while.

He got up and took the baby, and the girl went to lie down again.

Just rock her for a few minutes, the girl said from the bedroom. Maybe she'll go back to sleep.

The boy sat on the sofa and held the baby. He jiggled it in his lap until he got its eyes to close, his own eyes closing right along. He rose carefully and put the baby back in the crib.

It was a quarter to four, which gave him forty-five minutes. He crawled into bed and dropped

Reading Strategy Questioning *Though Carl, Sally, and Betsy do not actually appear in the story, they are the only characters who are named in it. Why does Carver name them?*

Vocabulary

striking (strī´king) *adj.* impressive; attractive
marvel (mär´vəl) *v.* to be filled with wonder

Reading Strategy Questioning *Why does the boy have this vision of himself hunting geese?*

Vocabulary

fitfully (fit´fəl lē) *adv.* irregularly; in stops and starts off. But a few minutes later the baby was crying again, and this time they both got up.

The boy did a terrible thing. He swore.

For God's sake, what's the matter with you? the girl said to the boy. Maybe she's sick or something. Maybe we shouldn't have given her the bath.

The boy picked up the baby. The baby kicked its feet and smiled.

Look, the boy said, I really don't think there's anything wrong with her.

How do you know that? the girl said. Here, let me have her. I know I ought to give her something, but I don't know what it's supposed to be.

The girl put the baby down again. The boy and the girl looked at the baby, and the baby began to cry.

The girl took the baby. Baby, baby, the girl said with tears in her eyes.

Probably it's something on her stomach, the boy said.

The girl didn't answer. She went on rocking the baby, paying no attention to the boy.

The boy waited. He went to the kitchen and put on water for coffee. He drew his woolen underwear on over his shorts and T-shirt, buttoned up, then got into his clothes.

What are you doing? the girl said.

Going hunting, the boy said.

I don't think you should, she said. I don't want to be left alone with her like this.

Carl's planning on me going, the boy said. We've planned it.

I don't care about what you and Carl planned, she said. And I don't care about Carl, either. I don't even know Carl.

You've met Carl before. You know him, the boy said. What do you mean you don't know him?

That's not the point and you know it, the girl said.

What is the point? the boy said. The point is we planned it.

The girl said, I'm your wife. This is your baby. She's sick or something. Look at her. Why else is she crying?

Portrait of Denis Lucas. Paul Bullard. Oil on canvas, 59 x 48 in. Private collection.

I know you're my wife, the boy said.

The girl began to cry. She put the baby back in the crib. But the baby started up again. The girl dried her eyes on the sleeve of her nightgown and picked the baby up.

The boy laced up his boots. He put on his shirt, his sweater, his coat. The kettle whistled on the stove in the kitchen.

You're going to have to choose, the girl said. Carl or us. I mean it.

What do you mean? the boy said.

You heard what I said, the girl said. If you want a family, you're going to have to choose.

They stared at each other. Then the boy took up his hunting gear and went outside. He started the car. He went around to the car windows and, making a job of it, scraped away the ice.

Reading Strategy   Questioning *Why does the girl ignore the boy?*

He turned off the motor and sat awhile. And then he got out and went back inside.

The living-room light was on. The girl was asleep on the bed. The baby was asleep beside her.

The boy took off his boots. Then he took off everything else. In his socks and his long underwear, he sat on the sofa and read the Sunday paper.

The girl and the baby slept on. After a while, the boy went to the kitchen and started frying bacon.

The girl came out in her robe and put her arms around the boy.

Hey, the boy said.

I'm sorry, the girl said.

It's all right, the boy said.

I didn't mean to snap like that.

It was my fault, he said.

You sit down, the girl said. How does a waffle sound with bacon?

Sounds great, the boy said.

She took the bacon out of the pan and made waffle batter. He sat at the table and watched her move around the kitchen.

She put a plate in front of him with bacon, a waffle. He spread butter and poured syrup. But when he started to cut, he turned the plate into his lap.

I don't believe it, he said, jumping up from the table.

If you could see yourself, the girl said.

The boy looked down at himself, at everything stuck to his underwear.

Reading Strategy   Questioning *When the girl first gives the boy an ultimatum, he leaves. Why does he now go back inside?*

I was starved, he said, shaking his head.

You were starved, she said, laughing.

He peeled off the woolen underwear and threw it at the bathroom door. Then he opened his arms and the girl moved into them.

We won't fight anymore, she said.

The boy said, We won't.

He gets up from his chair and refills their glasses.

That's it, he says. End of story. I admit it's not much of a story.

I was interested, she says.

He shrugs and carries his drink over to the window. It's dark now but still snowing.

Things change, he says. I don't know how they do. But they do without your realizing it or wanting them to.

Yes, that's true, only—But she does not finish what she started.

She drops the subject. In the window's reflection he sees her study her nails. Then she raises her head. Speaking brightly, she asks if he is going to show her the city, after all.

He says, Put your boots on and let's go.

But he stays by the window, remembering. They had laughed. They had leaned on each other and laughed until the tears had come, while everything else—the cold, and where he'd go in it—was outside, for a while anyway. ❧

Literary Element   Frame Story *What questions do you have about the time between the inner story and the frame story?*

Reading Strategy   Questioning *What does the cold represent in the story?*

RESPONDING AND THINKING CRITICALLY

Respond

1. How did you react to the end of this story?

Recall and Interpret

2. (a)Where did the couple live? (b)What does this tell you about them at the time?

3. (a)What was the boy planning to do in the morning? (b)Why is this activity so important to him?

4. (a)What is it that sticks to the boy? (b)What might this image **symbolize** in the story?

Analyze and Evaluate

5. (a)What does the narrator choose not to confirm about the baby? (b)How does this affect the reader's view of the argument between the boy and girl?

6. What does the father mean at the end of the story when he says "Things change"?

7. (a)After hearing her father's story, why does the daughter stop speaking in mid-sentence? (b)What do you think she was about to say?

8. (a)Why do you think the father chooses to keep the last part of his story to himself? (b)How does placing this memory at the end increase the power of the story's conclusion?

Connect

9. **Big Idea** **Extending and Remaking Traditions** What do you find most intriguing about Carver's style? Support your opinion.

LITERARY ANALYSIS

Literary Element **Frame Story**

In some cases, a **frame story** provides a stark contrast to the inner story. In other cases, a frame story is closely related to the inner story, providing greater context to deepen its meaning, as in "Everything Stuck to Him." By examining the relationship between a frame story and its inner story, you can explore the meaning of a literary work and the author's intent.

1. In "Everything Stuck to Him," what do the frame story and the inner story have in common?

2. How does framing the inner story in the present affect how you view it?

3. Why do you think Carver chose not to mention the mother in the frame story?

Review: Style

As you learned from reading "In Another Country" in Unit Five, style refers to the expressive qualities that distinguish an author's work, including word choice and the length and arrangement of sentences, as well as the use of figurative language and imagery. Carver's style resembles Ernest Hemingway's in its terse, spare language.

Partner Activity Meet with another classmate and find examples of Carver's style in "Everything Stuck to Him." Then compare those examples with the opening or closing paragraphs from Nathaniel Hawthorne's "The Minister's Black Veil" (p. 265). Working with your partner, fill in a chart like the one below to record what you learn.

	Carver's style	Hawthorne's style
word choice		
sentence length		
use of imagery		

Reading Strategy Questioning

Asking questions while you read is the first step in the process of generating meaning. The next step—answering those questions—usually requires more time and analysis. Sometimes, you may need to speculate about a character's motive or the author's intent.

1. What does Carver achieve by identifying the characters in the man's story merely as "the boy" and "the girl"?

2. Why do you think the girl and the boy eventually break up?

Vocabulary Practice

Practice with Word Parts The word *coincide* is made up of the Latin prefix *co-*, meaning "with" or "together," and the verb *incidere*, meaning "to fall on." *Incidere*, in turn, is made up of the Latin prefix *in-*, meaning "in" or "within," and the root *cad or cid*, meaning "to fall." When two events coincide, they "fall together," or they happen at the same time.

Use your knowledge of the root *cad/cid* and familiar prefixes to answer the following questions. Refer to a dictionary if you need help.

1. What happens to *deciduous* leaves in the autumn?
2. If someone exclaims, "What a *coincidence!*" what does he or she mean?
3. If a nation is in a state of *decadence*, is it thriving or losing its moral fiber?
4. Is a *cascade* a small waterfall or a steep ascent?

Writing About Literature

Analyze Conflict In "Everything Stuck to Him," Carver develops both external and internal conflicts. Write a brief essay analyzing these conflicts and explaining how they are reflected in elements of the story (such as plot, dialogue, setting, and imagery). Support your analysis with evidence from the story.

Before writing your essay, organize your ideas by filling in a chart like the one below. In the first column, identify the main conflicts in the story; in the second column, note whether each conflict is internal or external; and in the third column, list examples of story elements that reflect each conflict. As you draft, use the chart to help keep your writing on track.

Conflicts	Internal / External	Story Elements

After you complete your draft, meet with a peer reviewer to evaluate each other's work and to suggest revisions. Then proofread your draft for errors in spelling, grammar, and punctuation.

Literary Criticism

Minimalist fiction refers to fiction that is written in a flat tone and in a simple style. In minimalist fiction, scene and dialogue are more prominent than complex narration. Though many critics still consider Carver's fiction minimalist, others challenge that assessment. For example, critic David Lipsky contends, "Carver has not been a minimalist but a precisionist." Which view best describes Carver's story "Everything Stuck to Him"? Explain your answer in a brief paragraph analyzing the story.

Literature Online **Web Activities** For eFlashcards, Selection Quick Checks, and other Web activities, go to www.glencoe.com.

RAYMOND CARVER **1275**

El Olvido

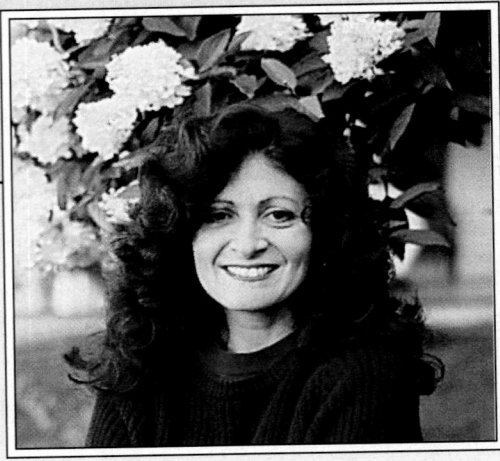

MEET JUDITH ORTIZ COFER

Culture clash is a familiar theme in the work of Judith Ortiz Cofer (ôr tēz′ kō′ fer). Many of her poems, novels, and autobiographical essays dramatize the differences between the values of her Puerto Rican relatives and the values of people in the United States.

Born in Puerto Rico, she moved to the United States at the age of three. Until she was sixteen, however, her childhood was split almost evenly between the two places. Ortiz Cofer usually spent about six months of each year in Paterson, New Jersey where she lived the urban life of a Puerto Rican immigrant, speaking Spanish at home, experiencing discrimination, and struggling to fit in at school. Ortiz Cofer often spent the remaining part of each year in Puerto Rico, where her mother took her every time her father, a career navy man, shipped out. There she lived a more relaxed, rural life and was embraced by a large extended family.

Split in Half Yet Doubled The effects of frequent relocation were challenging to Ortiz Cofer's friendships and education. All in all, the geographical fragmentation left Ortiz Cofer with two indelible marks on her soul: the feeling of never really belonging in either place and the curious gift of possessing, fully and deeply, two cultures and languages simultaneously.

When Ortiz Cofer was sixteen, her family's United States home shifted to Augusta, Georgia, presenting yet another cultural and social adjustment for her. However, some things remained constant. Her parents still spoke Spanish at home, and Catholicism remained a major force in her family life and her education.

A Late Start As a Writer Ortiz Cofer did not begin to write poetry until she was studying for her master's degree. It was then that she began to recognize the literary and narrative influences that had been part of her makeup all along. These included a grandmother who was a storyteller and a grandfather who was a reader and writer of poetry. When Ortiz Cofer's writing began to flow, it was perhaps no surprise to those who knew her best that her imagination readily drew on both of her cultural identities. She did not choose to identify as either American or Puerto Rican but rather showed how new cultural identities simultaneously seem to spring from, move away from, and reclaim the old.

> *"The assimilation of a new culture is the coming into maturity by accepting the terms necessary for survival."*
>
> —Judith Ortiz Cofer

Much of Ortiz Cofer's work is autobiographical or uses the facts of her childhood as a springboard. One of her most successful books, *Silent Dancing: A Partial Remembrance of a Puerto Rican Childhood*, is made up of thirteen essays about her experiences growing up. Memories of her parents, she says, are always finding their way into her poetry and stories as well. "My family is one of the main topics of my poetry," Cofer has said. "In tracing their lives, I discover more about mine."

Judith Ortiz Cofer was born in 1952.

Literature Online Author Search For more about Judith Ortiz Cofer, go to www.glencoe.com.

Connecting to the Poem

Does everyone forget at least some of what their mothers tell them? In "El Olvido," the speaker calls such forgetting dangerous. As you read the poem, think about the following questions:

- What are some things you once learned from a parent or other older adult that you have "forgotten"?
- Why do you think you forget or ignore at least some of what you learn from older people?

Building Background

Many people experience a cultural shift when they move from Puerto Rico to the United States, especially in terms of religion. For example, unlike the average person in the United States, Ortiz Cofer's Puerto Rican ancestors would have often seen statues of saints in shops, in backyards, and on city streets. They would also have commonly repeated or invoked the names of the holy family, *Jesús, María, y José* (Jesus, the son; Mary, his mother; and Joseph, Mary's husband) as part of daily conversation.

Setting Purposes for Reading

Big Idea **Extending and Remaking Traditions**

As you read, pay attention to the old ways, or traditions, that are being forgotten and the new ways that are taking their place.

Literary Element **Point of View**

Point of view is the relationship of the narrator to a story or the speaker to a poem. Point of view in poetry is determined, in part, by how close or removed the speaker is from the events or ideas of the poem. As you read, identify where the speaker in this poem stands in relation to the ideas and events in the poem.

- See Literary Terms Handbook, p. R14.

Reading Strategy **Examining Connotations**

Examining connotations is identifying the feelings, attitudes, and suggestions that go beyond the dictionary definition of a word. In a poem such as "El Olvido," word choice helps show the attitudes and feelings of the speaker.

Reading Tip: Taking Notes Use a chart like the one below to record the connotations of some of the words Ortiz Cofer uses.

Word or Phrase	Connotation
choke out	violent, strangling

Vocabulary

spurn (spurn) *v.* to reject with contempt; to scorn; p. 1278 *Poor but proud, the family spurned all offers of charity.*

disdain (dis dān′) *v.* to look down on, to despise; p. 1278 *The classical violinist disdains popular music.*

Vocabulary Tip: Synonyms Words that have the same or almost the same meaning are called synonyms. The words *spurn* and *reject*, for example, are synonyms—both involve refusing to accept something—but *spurn* is a more forceful, emotional rejection. Note that synonyms are always the same part of speech.

 Literature Online **Interactive Literary Elements Handbook** To review or learn more about the literary elements, go to www.glencoe.com.

INDIANA ACADEMIC STANDARDS (pages 1277–1279)
11.3.4 Analyze...poetry...
11.1.2 Draw inferences about the meaning of vocabulary...
11.5.3 Write reflective compositions that explore the significance of personal experiences...

Ancestral Dream I, 1996. Maria Eugenia Terrazas.
Watercolor, 70 x 60 cm. Private collection.

El Olvido[1]
(Según las Madres)[2]

Judith Ortiz Cofer

It is a dangerous thing
to forget the climate of
your birthplace; to choke out
the voices of the dead relatives when
5   in dreams they call you by
your secret name; dangerous
to **spurn** the clothes you were
born to wear for the sake of fashion;
to use weapons and sharp instruments you
10   are not familiar with; dangerous
to **disdain** the plaster saints before
which your mother kneels praying for you with
embarassing fervor that you survive in
the place you have chosen to live; a costly,
15   bare and elegant room with no pictures
on the walls: a forgetting place where
she fears you might die of exposure.
Jesús, María y José.
El olvido is a dangerous thing.

---

1. *El Olvido* (el ōl vē′dō) is Spanish for "the forgetting" or
   "heedlessness" or "the end of memory."
2. *Según las Madres* (sə gōōn′ läs mä′dräs) means "according
   to mothers."

Big Idea Extending and Remaking Traditions *Why might
the speaker consider such a room dangerous?*

Vocabulary

spurn (spurn) *v.* to reject with contempt; to scorn
disdain (dis dān′) *v.* to look down on, to despise

RESPONDING AND THINKING CRITICALLY

Respond

1. In what way is the mother in this poem like or unlike mothers you know?

Recall and Interpret

2. (a)According to lines 1–12, what kinds of things are dangerous? (b)Why do you think the speaker calls them dangerous?

3. (a)What fear does the mother have? (b)Why might she have this fear?

4. (a)What words does the poet write in Spanish in the poem? (b)How are these words linked?

Analyze and Evaluate

5. (a)Look at line 17 and think about the phrase "die of exposure." Do these words have literal meanings in the poem, or are they a figure of speech?

Explain. (b)What do these words contribute to the tone of the poem?

6. (a)What mothers does the subtitle "según las madres" refer to? (b)How well does the subtitle match the content of the poem?

7. (a)What seems to be the relationship between the speaker, the mother, and the person or people called "you"? (b)Is this poem about just one mother and child or is it about mothers and children generally? Explain.

Connect

8. **Big Idea** **Extending and Remaking Traditions** Has this poem convinced you that forgetting one's roots "is a dangerous thing" or even a possible thing? Why or why not?

Literary Element Point of View

Point of view can be first-, second-, or third-person. In first-person point of view, the speaker is a character in the poem and uses *I*. In second-person point of view, the speaker uses *you*. In third-person point of view, the speaker is not a character in the poem and refers to others as *he, she,* or *they.*

1. (a)Is this poem written in the first-, second-, or third-person point of view? How do you know? (b)Why does the speaker use this point of view?

2. How does the point of view affect the tone and message of the poem?

Writing About Literature

Respond to Theme Write a free verse poem on the topic of forgetting one's culture, one's roots, or one's past. Think about what has been lost or changed in your own family over time, in the family of someone you know, or in general as people move away from parents and guardians and reject traditions.

Reading Strategy Examining Connotations

"El Olvido" is full of words with powerful connotations. Review the chart you made on page 1277 listing words and their connotations in this poem.

1. Find a word you recorded whose connotative meaning is different from its denotative meaning, or dictionary definition. Write the word and both meanings.

2. Write a word you recorded that you think has powerful connotations and explain why.

Vocabulary Practice

Practice with Synonyms Some thesauruses list *spurn* and *disdain* as synonyms. Find two other synonyms for these words and explain the slight differences in meaning or connotation among the four words. When you finish, you will know a variety of ways to express a negative attitude toward something.

Literature Online **Web Activities** For eFlashcards, Selection Quick Checks, and other Web activities, go to www.glencoe.com.

My Father and the Figtree

MEET NAOMI SHIHAB NYE

In the introduction to her collection *Words Under the Words*, poet Naomi Shihab Nye shares a simple story about looking through a childhood photo album. The album was barely intact—its pages in a stack and no longer bound. Some of the black and white photos were as many as forty years old. The pages were not in chronological order, so as she looked through the pictures, her impressions and memories fluctuated in time. Nye saw herself, "Preparing to blow out two candles on a cake . . . With neighbors who disappeared into the world . . . With baby brother freshly home from the hospital. With grandparents who died." She continued paging through the album and recalled stories about when the photos were taken. While she looked, however, Nye began to wonder about the moments not captured in the photos. It struck her that it is the hidden details of life—the forgotten memories—that make all of us who we are and in some way put us all on common ground. Nye's poems in some ways resemble timeless family portraits in which we recognize ourselves. Her writing draws not only from her own memories and heritage but also from a variety of cultural traditions. Nye is committed to revealing what people have in common and to exploring the themes of acceptance and conciliation.

> "The mystery of remembering has added its own light to the garden. Whatever existed then has deepened, been forgotten or restored in some other form. We planted our voices."
>
> —Naomi Shihab Nye

Connecting to the World Nye grew up in a nurturing, creative home in St. Louis. Her Palestinian father and American mother encouraged her to express herself. Nye has said that even as a child she was "fascinated by the power of words on the page to make us look differently at our lives, to help us see and connect." She was first published at the age of seven, when a children's magazine accepted one of her poems. She has been publishing steadily ever since.

At the age of fourteen, Nye spent a year in Jerusalem, where she was able to meet the Palestinian side of her family. She grew especially close to her grandmother, who appears in many of her poems and a children's book called *Sitte's Secrets*. Working as a journalist, teacher, poet, and children's author, Nye has spent her adult life in San Antonio. She won a National Poetry Series prize for *Hugging the Box* and was a National Book Award finalist for *19 Varieties of Gazelle*.

Reaching Out to the Reader Nye's open and straightforward style appeals to a diverse audience and to readers of all ages. "Ultimately, I look at writing as a form of discovery," she told an interviewer. "I hope my words reach out to the reader and they can say yes to them." She often writes about connections between people separated by time or distance, and her poems emphasize our shared humanity. Nye uses the ordinary, familiar settings of everyday life and the power of memory to create poetry that is rich with "the gleam of particulars."

Naomi Shihab Nye was born in 1952.

Literature Online Author Search For more about Naomi Shihab Nye, go to www.glencoe.com.

Connecting to the Poem

"My Father and the Figtree" is about Nye's relationship with her father. In the poem, father and daughter engage in an ongoing dialogue about her father's passion for figs. This recurring conversation forges a connection between them. As you read the poem, consider the following questions:

- What do you think you will continue to be passionate about as you grow older?
- Is there anything unique that you share with a family member or friend that connects the two of you?

Building Background

Like much of Nye's writing, "My Father and the Figtree" reflects the cultural heritage that she began to absorb when her father told her folktales at bedtime. Understanding the poem's use of Arab folklore and symbolism is key to determining its meaning. Figs have been a popular fruit since ancient times. The fig tree is common in the Middle East and can grow in rocky, arid climates, producing fruit and providing shade. Another cultural reference in the poem is a character named Joha. In Arab folklore, Joha is a wise fool or trickster, and he plays that role in a variety of traditional tales.

Setting Purposes for Reading

Big Idea Extending and Remaking Traditions

As you read, notice how Nye has taken elements of traditional tales and placed them in a contemporary context, creating her own modern folktale.

Literary Element Symbol

A **symbol** is any object, person, place, or experience that represents something beyond the literal meaning. As you read the poem, identify and interpret Nye's symbols.

- See Literary Terms Handbook, p. R18.

Reading Strategy Summarizing

Summarizing is briefly restating the events or ideas in a literary work in your own words. After reading a poem, you can summarize what happened by determining the main ideas and events and placing them in a logical order.

Reading Tip: Making a Chronological List List the main ideas and events in the poem in the order in which they occur. Look for time clues, such as "At age six," or "Years passed."

Vocabulary

indifferent (in dif′ ər ənt) *adj.* having no marked feeling for or against; p. 1282 *Most of the audience was indifferent toward the mediocre performance.*

vivid (viv′ id) *adj.* perceived as bright and distinct; brilliant; p. 1282 *The vivid tropical fish swam in the clear blue water.*

token (tō′ ken) *n.* something serving as an indication, proof, or expression of something else; a sign; p. 1283 *The gift was a token of his appreciation.*

emblem (em′ bləm) *n.* an object or a representation that functions as a symbol; p. 1283 *The keys were an emblem of his new independence.*

Vocabulary Tip: Synonyms Synonyms are words that have the same or similar meanings. As you read, look for synonyms for unfamiliar words that you come across.

Literature Online **Interactive Literary Elements Handbook** To review or learn more about the literary elements, go to www.glencoe.com.

INDIANA ACADEMIC STANDARDS (pages 1281–1284)

11.3.4 Analyze the ways in which poetry...uses imagery...to evoke readers' emotions.

11.2 Develop [reading] strategies...

11.5.3 Write reflective compositions...

11.5.1 Write...autobiographical...narratives that...describe with specific details...characters...

My Father and the Figtree

NAOMI SHIHAB NYE

For other fruits my father was **indifferent**.
He'd point at the cherry trees and say,
"See those? I wish they were figs."
In the evenings he sat by my bed
5   weaving folktales like **vivid** little scarves.
They always involved a figtree.
Even when it didn't fit, he'd stick it in.
Once Joha was walking down the road and he saw a figtree.
Or, he tied his camel to a figtree and went to sleep.
10   Or, later when they caught and arrested him,
his pockets were full of figs.

At age six I ate a dried fig and shrugged.
"That's not what I'm talking about!" he said,
"I'm talking about a fig straight from the earth—
15   gift of Allah![1]—on a branch so heavy it touches the ground.
I'm talking about picking the largest fattest sweetest fig
in the world and putting it in my mouth."
(Here he'd stop and close his eyes.)

---

1. *Allah* is the Arabic word for God.

Vocabulary

indifferent (in dif′ ər ənt) *adj.* having no marked feeling for or against
vivid (viv′ id) *adj.* perceived as bright and distinct; brilliant

Years passed, we lived in many houses, none had figtrees.
20   We had lima beans, zucchini, parsley, beets.
"Plant one!" my mother said, but my father never did.
He tended garden half-heartedly, forgot to water,
let the okra[2] get too big.
"What a dreamer he is. Look how many things he starts
25   and doesn't finish."

The last time he moved, I got a phone call.
My father, in Arabic, chanting a song I'd never heard.
"What's that?"
"Wait till you see!"
30   He took me out to the new yard.
There, in the middle of Dallas, Texas,
a tree with the largest, fattest, sweetest figs in the world.
"It's a figtree song!" he said,
plucking his fruits like ripe **tokens**,
35   **emblems**, assurance
of a world that was always his own.

---

2. *Okra* is a plant with pods that are eaten as vegetables.

| Reading Strategy | Summarizing *Summarize the main event that occurs in this stanza.* |

Big Idea   Extending and Remaking Traditions *How does Nye place a traditional element in a modern context in these lines?*

Literary Element   Symbol *What does the fig tree symbolize for the speaker's father?*

Vocabulary

token (tō′ ken) *n.* something serving as an indication, proof, or expression of something else; a sign

emblem (em′ bləm) *n.* an object or a representation that functions as a symbol

RESPONDING AND THINKING CRITICALLY

Respond

1. Were you surprised that the speaker's father finally plants a fig tree at the end? Why or why not?

Recall and Interpret

2. (a)What does the speaker compare her father's folktales to? (b)What does this image suggest?

3. (a)How does the speaker's father react when she eats a dried fig? (b)Why do you think he responds in this way?

4. (a)Where does the speaker's father finally plant the fig tree? (b)What is the significance of this location?

Analyze and Evaluate

5. Why do you think Nye includes the references to Joha in the poem?

6. (a)What images seem especially significant in the poem? (b)How would the poem be affected if these images were removed?

7. How effective is the fig tree as a symbol in the poem? Explain.

Connect

8. **Big Idea** **Extending and Remaking Traditions** Do you think the poem seems more like a traditional folktale or a modern one? Explain.

LITERARY ANALYSIS

Literary Element Symbol

The simplest type of **symbol** is a single object, such as a fruit or a plant, that represents an abstract idea, such as love or hope. Poets can expand on that symbolism by using the same object in different settings and events in the poem, so that the meaning of the symbol might change or grow throughout the work.

1. What is the symbolism of the speaker eating the dried fig when she is young?

2. What do the father's gardening skills and the okra symbolize?

3. Why do you think Nye uses the fig tree and figs as the main symbols in the poem?

Writing About Literature

Respond to Character In "My Father and the Figtree," Nye uses the fig as a symbol to help describe her father. Write your own poem about someone you know well using a concrete object as a symbol.

Literature Online **Web Activities** For eFlashcards, Selection Quick Checks, and other Web activities, go to www.glencoe.com.

READING AND VOCABULARY

Reading Strategy Summarizing

Summarizing the sequence of events in a poem is one way to analyze it. But when you get deeper into a poem, it is helpful to summarize some of its other elements.

1. Briefly summarize the changes in the speaker's age throughout "My Father and the Figtree."

2. Summarize how the meaning of the fig tree to the father changes from the beginning to the end of the poem.

Vocabulary Practice

Practice with Synonyms Choose the best synonym for each vocabulary word.

1. indifferent
   a. neutral   **b.** fearful   **c.** shy

2. vivid
   a. hazy   **b.** clear   **c.** stark

3. token
   a. demerit   **b.** ticket   **c.** sign

4. emblem
   a. symbol   **b.** delegate   **c.** relative

I Chop Some Parsley While Listening to Art Blakey's Version of "Three Blind Mice"

MEET BILLY COLLINS

Before he became Poet Laureate of the United States in 2001, Billy Collins found himself on a whirlwind poetry tour of the Midwest. At a large high school, Billy Collins stood at a gymnasium podium and read to an enthusiastic crowd of students as part of their "Poetry Day." Collins thought poetry had an important part to play in modern society, but also realized that many people—especially young readers—are intimidated by contemporary poetry. This experience helped to inspire one of his signature endeavors. As Poet Laureate, Collins founded the program "Poetry 180: A Poem a Day for American High Schools." This program works to bring poetry to high school students by having a new poem read aloud every day. Collins wanted to create an environment where students could hear and enjoy poetry, but did not have to officially respond. The project is a prime example of one of Collins's missions as a writer—to make poetry a part of people's daily lives. His dedication to expanding poetry's audience and deepening its connection with people has helped to make Collins one of the most popular poets in the United States.

> "Clarity is the real risk in poetry. To be clear means opening yourself up to judgment."
>
> —Billy Collins
> from the introduction to *Poetry 180*

Student, Teacher, Poet Collins was born in the same New York hospital where pioneering poet William Carlos Williams worked as a pediatrician. Collins grew up in New York City and attended parochial school there. He went on to Holy Cross College and eventually earned a Ph.D. in Romantic Poetry at the University of California, Riverside in 1971. After finishing his graduate work, Collins began teaching at Lehman College, City University of New York, and continued teaching there for over thirty years. He published his first collection of poems, *Pokerface*, in 1977, and has since received numerous fellowships and awards for his work. From 2001 to 2003, Collins was Poet Laureate of the United States.

Celebration of Daily Life Collins's poetry illuminates the ordinary aspects of daily life by revealing the universal themes that those scenes can hide. He uses a conversational tone, the cadences of everyday speech, and familiar settings to engage readers. His poems are full of imaginative leaps; a dog's constant barking connects to Beethoven's musical genius, and a day at the beach ends with the speaker walking across the Atlantic toward Spain. However, in order for readers to connect with these ideas, Collins believes it is vital to provide them with an easy entrance: "Usually I try to create a hospitable tone at the beginning of a poem. Stepping from the title to the first lines is like stepping into a canoe. A lot of things can go wrong."

Billy Collins was born in 1941.

Literature Online Author Search For more about Billy Collins, go to www.glencoe.com.

Connecting to the Poem

As suggested in the title, "I Chop Some Parsley While Listening to Art Blakey's Version of 'Three Blind Mice,'" the speaker of the poem is cooking while listening to jazz. Listening to music while we go about our daily routine is a common element of modern life, and we are often influenced by the music we hear. Before you read the poem, consider these questions:

- Do you recall a time when a routine part of your day was changed by music?
- Can you think of a time when listening to music sparked an unusual train of thought?

Building Background

The poem begins and ends with musical references, and both men mentioned—Blakey and Freddie Hubbard—are famous U.S. jazz musicians. Blakey was a pioneering drummer and bandleader in the 1950s and '60s. Hubbard, who was born a few years before Collins, is a jazz trumpeter from the generation after Blakey's. The song "Three Blind Mice" is a jazz standard inspired by the well-known nursery rhyme. "Blue Moon" is a popular jazz ballad characterized by its moody tone.

Setting Purposes for Reading

Big Idea Extending and Remaking Traditions

As you read, note how the poem's tone and structure differ from more traditional poetry you have read.

Literary Element Personification

Personification is a figure of speech in which an animal, an object, a force of nature, an idea, or an emotion is given human characteristics. For example, the phrase, "the city never sleeps" is a personification because it endows the city with the ability to sleep, which is a human quality.

- See Literary Terms Handbook, p. R13.

Literature Online Interactive Literary Elements Handbook To review or learn more about the literary elements, go to www.glencoe.com.

Reading Strategy — Connecting to Personal Experience

One of the best ways to examine a poem is to identify ideas or facets that **connect to your experience**. Ask yourself, have I ever felt his way? What else have I read that is like this selection? Do I know someone like this?

Reading Tip: Finding Common Ground Choose a personal experience that you can link to the poem and create a Venn Diagram. Use one circle for your experience and one circle for the poem. In the overlapping area, list what your experience and the poem have in common.

Vocabulary

congenital (kən je′ nə təl) *adj.* of or relating to a condition that is present at birth, as a result of either heredity or environmental influences; p. 1287 *The baby had a congenital heart defect.*

brood (brood) *v.* to focus the attention on a subject persistently and moodily; worry; p. 1287 *The whole team sat brooding over the last-second loss.*

sear (sēr) *v.* to char, scorch, or burn the surface with or as if with a sudden application of intense heat; p. 1287 *The lava seared the earth as it poured down the mountainside.*

cynic (si′ nik) *n.* a person whose outlook is scornfully and often habitually negative; p. 1288 *He never donated to charity because he was a cynic and was convinced that they would waste his money.*

Vocabulary Tip: Synonyms When two words have the same or nearly the same meaning, they are called synonyms. For example, *brood* and *fret* have nearly the same meaning. Note that synonyms are always the same part of speech. In that example, *brood* is being used in its verb, not noun, form, and thus *family* would not be its synonym.

INDIANA ACADEMIC STANDARDS (pages 1286–1289)

11.3.4 Analyze ways in which poetry...uses... personification...to evoke readers' emotions.

11.2 Develop [reading] strategies...

11.4.7 Develop presentations using...Internet sources.

I Chop Some Parsley While Listening to Art Blakey's Version of "Three Blind Mice"

Billy Collins

Soulful Solace, 1997. Gil Mayers.

And I start wondering how they came to be blind.
If it was **congenital**, they could be brothers and sisters,
and I think of the poor mother
brooding over her sightless young triplets.

5   Or was it a common accident, all three caught
in a **searing** explosion, a firework perhaps?
If not,
if each came to his or her blindness separately,

how did they ever manage to find one another?
10   Would it not be difficult for a blind mouse
to locate even one fellow mouse with vision
let alone two other blind ones?

Reading Strategy   Connecting to Personal Experience
Why might someone try to unravel a mystery or figure out a silly riddle that other people take for granted?

Vocabulary

congenital (kən je′ nə təl) *adj.* of or relating to a condition that is present at birth, as a result of either heredity or environmental influences

brood (brood) *v.* to focus the attention on a subject persistently and moodily; worry

sear (sēr) *v.* to char, scorch, or burn the surface with or as if with a sudden application of intense heat

And how, in their tiny darkness,
could they possibly have run after a farmer's wife
15 or anyone else's wife for that matter?
Not to mention why.

Just so she could cut off their tails
with a carving knife, is the **cynic's** answer,
but the thought of them without eyes
20 and now without tails to trail through the moist grass

or slip around the corner of a baseboard
has the cynic who always lounges within me
up off his couch and at the window
trying to hide the rising softness that he feels.

25 By now I am on to dicing an onion
which might account for the wet stinging
in my own eyes, though Freddie Hubbard's
mournful trumpet on "Blue Moon,"

which happens to be the next cut,
30 cannot be said to be making matters any better.

Reading Strategy   Connecting to Personal Experience
This image has a strong effect on the speaker of the poem. Can you think of a time where you experienced similar feelings?

Literary Element   Personification *What is being personified here?*

Vocabulary

cynic (si′ nik) *n.* a person whose outlook is scornfully and often habitually negative

RESPONDING AND THINKING CRITICALLY

Respond

1. What was your first reaction to the title of this poem?

Recall and Interpret

2. (a)In the first line of the poem, what is the speaker wondering about? (b)What causes the speaker to think about this topic?

3. The speaker of the poem gives several reasons why the mice might be blind. What are those reasons?

4. (a)After they chase the farmer's wife, what happens to the mice? (b)How does the speaker of the poem react to this?

5. (a)At the end of the poem, what vegetable does the speaker begin to cut and what song is playing? (b)What is the connection between the vegetable and the song?

Analyze and Evaluate

6. (a)Throughout the poem, the speaker poses a series of questions. Which questions would you call silly or humorous, and which questions seem to have larger, more serious implications? (b)How does posing unanswered questions affect the tone and meaning of the poem?

7. Identify the musical references Collins employs and explain how these references work in the poem.

8. At the end of the poem, what might the pun on "cut" suggest?

Connect

9. **Big Idea** **Extending and Remaking Traditions** Did the poem's conversational tone make it easier or harder for you to connect with the poem? Why or why not?

LITERARY ANALYSIS

Literary Element Personification

Personification is a device that writers use to imbue the world with life and motion by assigning familiar human emotions and traits to ideas, animals, and inanimate objects. In our daily lives, we use personification all the time to help us understand the world we live in.

1. How does the personification in this poem dramatize the speaker's inner conflict?

2. (a)Does this help you to better understand the speaker's emotions? (b)Why or why not?

Internet Connection

When he was Poet Laureate, Billy Collins founded the Web site project *Poetry 180* to showcase accessible contemporary poetry. Use the Internet to research how your class or your school can participate in the project.

Literature Online **Web Activities** For eFlashcards, Selection Quick Checks, and other Web activities, go to www.glencoe.com.

READING AND VOCABULARY

Reading Strategy Connecting to Personal Experience

Sometimes you may not connect with any of the specific events or experiences in a poem, particularly when reading work from different cultures or a different time period. In these cases it helps to broaden your strategy and seek out more general connections.

1. What element or part of the poem did you feel most strongly connected to? Explain your answer.

2. What did you gain by attempting to connect?

Vocabulary Practice

Practice with Synonyms Choose the best synonym for the underlined word.

1. Hamlet is characterized by his tendency to *brood* instead of act.
   a. abuse   **b.** loaf   **c.** agonize

2. My aunt is the epitome of a *cynic*: she criticizes everything.
   a. optimist   **b.** pragmatist   **c.** pessimist

The Names of Women

MEET LOUISE ERDRICH

Louise Erdrich (âr´ drik) grew up in a Native American culture of storytelling that encouraged her to tell stories of her own. Her parents also actively supported her desire to write. Erdrich recalled, "My father used to give me a nickel for every story I wrote, and my mother wove strips of construction paper and stapled them into book covers. So at an early age I felt myself to be a published author, earning substantial royalties."

Erdrich is the daughter of a German American father and an Ojibway (ō jib´ wā) mother who was born on the Turtle Mountain Reservation in North Dakota. The oldest of seven children, Erdrich grew up in Wahpeton, North Dakota, where her parents worked for a boarding school run by the Bureau of Indian Affairs. Erdrich entered Dartmouth College in 1972, the first year that the college admitted women. She enrolled in the new Native American studies department. From Dartmouth, Erdrich went on to Johns Hopkins University, where she wrote poems and stories and earned a master's degree.

> "When you grow up constantly hearing stories rise, break, and fall, it gets into you somehow."
>
> —Louise Erdrich

Popular and Critical Success Before she turned thirty, Erdrich published her first novel, *Love Medicine*. It was acclaimed by both readers and critics, and won the National Book Critics Circle Award in 1984. The novels *Beet Queen* and *Tracks*, which also had wide popular and literary appeal, followed soon after.

In the late 1980s and early 1990s, Erdrich became well-known as an accomplished novelist and a voice of Native American culture. Her marriage to Michael Dorris, a writer, anthropologist, and spokesperson for Native American ways of life, intensified her reputation and literary output. Together, the couple embarked on a series of literary projects while raising several children.

Sources from Life Many of Erdrich's life experiences appear in her work. On her way to success as a writer, Erdrich held many different jobs, working as a beet weeder, a lifeguard, a waitress, and a construction flag signaler. She notes that these experiences have lent authenticity to her work by enabling her to realistically portray characters in her novels. Not all of her ideas come from her own experience, or even her own imagination, however. She admits that some of her plots are culled from old Native American stories, though her own characters usually take over. Erdrich has described herself as "an emissary of the between-world, that increasingly common margin where cultures mix and collide." "The Names of Women," originally a piece of nonfiction, was eventually incorporated into a novel.

Erdrich continues to write both nonfiction and fiction, including stories for children. Her life's work also includes learning the language of the Ojibway and studying the culture and traditions of her great-grandmothers. In 2001 she opened a bookstore in Minneapolis, Minnesota that specializes in books by and about Native Americans.

Louise Erdrich was born in 1954.

Literature Online **Author Search** For more about Louise Erdrich, go to www.glencoe.com.

Connecting to the Essay

"Who am I?" is one of the questions that Louise Erdrich asks and partially answers in this brief exploration of her own Native American and family history. As you read, think about the following questions:

- Which family members, past or present, have helped to shape your personality and values?
- What past events, places, or cultural or other groups have helped form your identity?

Building Background

The Anishinabe (a nish′ i nä′ bā)—also known as the Ojibway, Ojibwe, or Chippewa—are one of the largest groups of Native Americans in North America. After the mid-1600s, they migrated west from the Great Lakes region to areas such as Wisconsin, North Dakota, and Montana. Many Anishinabe families still live on the Turtle Mountain Reservation in North Dakota today.

Setting Purposes for Reading

Big Idea Extending and Remaking Traditions

As you read this essay, think about how Erdrich reveals the present by focusing on and cataloging details from the past.

Literary Element Catalog

A **catalog** is a list of images, details, people, or events in a piece of writing. The items in a catalog are related and are of relatively equal importance. As you read, identify what Erdrich lists and think about her reasons for doing so.

- See Literary Terms Handbook, p. R3.

 Literature Online Interactive Literary Elements Handbook To review or learn more about the literary elements, go to www.glencoe.com.

INDIANA ACADEMIC STANDARDS
(pages 1291–1297)
11.2.2 Analyze the way in which clarity of meaning is affected by patterns of organization...
11.2 Develop [reading] strategies...
11.5.9 Write...a literary analysis that...makes valid inferences...

Reading Strategy Distinguishing Fact and Opinion

A fact is a statement that can be verified, or proved true, either through direct experience or by consulting an authoritative source. An opinion is a personal judgment that, unlike a fact, cannot be verified because it expresses a person's beliefs or feelings. When you **distinguish fact and opinion,** you consider each claim the writer makes and determine whether it is a verifiable statement or a personal belief.

Reading Tip: Taking Notes As you read Erdrich's essay, use a chart like the one below to record the facts and opinions you find.

Example	Fact or Opinion	How I Know
Names of Erdrich's ancestors	Fact	Names can be verified in historical records.

Vocabulary

decimated (des′ ə māt əd) *adj.* destroyed or killed in large numbers; p. 1292 *The battle left the village decimated.*

presumptuous (pri zump′ ch$\overline{oo}$ əs) *adj.* going beyond what is proper; excessively bold; p. 1292 *It was presumptuous of us to ask for so much money.*

ecclesiastical (i klē′ zē as′ ti kəl) *adj.* of or relating to the church; p. 1293 *The woman felt comfortable in the ecclesiastical setting.*

undeviating (un dē′ vē āt′ ing) *adj.* not turning away from; p. 1293 *The commander showed undeviating concern for the troops.*

wane (wān) *v.* to decrease gradually; to decline; p. 1294 *All fads wane in popularity over time.*

Vocabulary Tip: Word Origins The origin, or history, of most words can be found in a dictionary. Usually, the language and root from which the word originated reveal the word's history.

The Names of Women

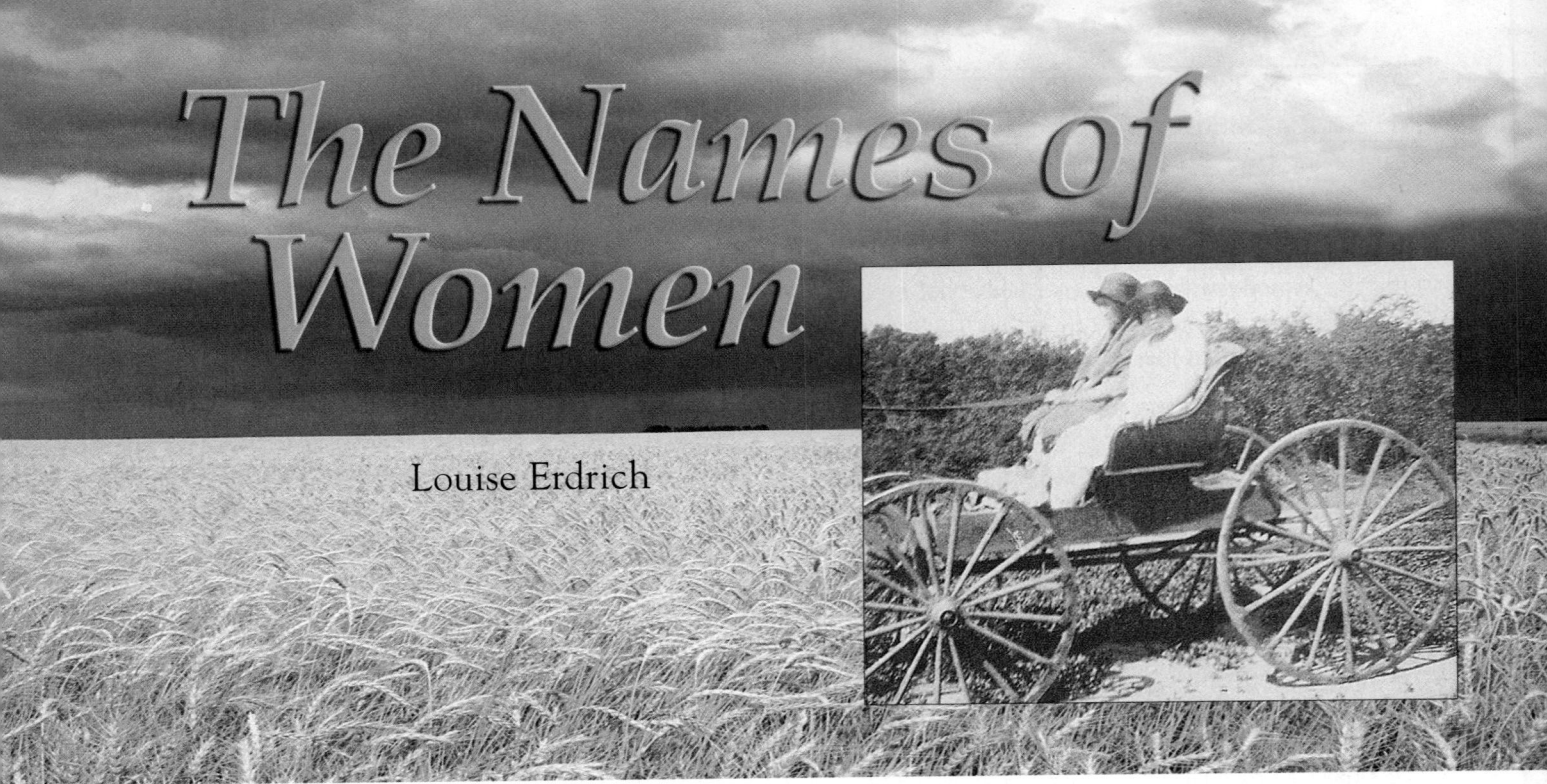

Louise Erdrich

Ikwe[1] is the word for woman in the language of the Anishinabe, my mother's people, whose descendants, mixed with and married to French trappers and farmers, are the Michifs[2] of the Turtle Mountain reservation in North Dakota. Every Anishinabe *Ikwe*, every mixed-blood descendant like me, who can trace her way back a generation or two, is the daughter of a mystery. The history of the woodland Anishinabe—**decimated** by disease, fighting Plains Indians tribes to the west and squeezed by European settlers to the east—is much like most other Native American stories, a confusion of loss, a tale of absences, of a culture that was blown apart and changed so radically in such a short time that only the names survive.

And yet, those names.

The names of the first women whose existence is recorded on the rolls of the Turtle Mountain Reservation, in 1892, reveal as much as we can ever recapture of their personalities, complex natures and relationships. These names tell stories, or half stories, if only we listen closely.

There once were women named *Standing Strong, Fish Bones, Different Thunder.* There once was a girl called *Yellow Straps.* Imagine what it was like to pick berries with *Sky Coming Down,* to walk through a storm with *Lightning Proof.* Surely, she was struck and lived, but what about the person next to her? People always avoided *Steps Over Truth,* when they wanted a straight answer, and *I Hear,* when they wanted to keep a secret. *Glittering* put coal on her face and watched for enemies at night. The woman named *Standing Across* could see things moving far across the lake. The old ladies gossiped about *Playing Around,* but no one dared say anything to her face. *Ice* was good at gambling. *Shining One Side* loved to sit and talk to *Opposite the Sky.* They both knew *Sounding Feather, Exhausted Wind* and *Green Cloud,* daughter of *Seeing Iron.* *Center of the Sky* was a widow. *Rabbit, Prairie Chicken* and *Daylight* were all little girls. *She Tramp* could make great distance in a day of walking.

---

1. *Ikwe* (ik′ wā)
2. *Michifs* (mi′ chifz)

Vocabulary

decimated (des′ ə māt′ əd) *adj.* destroyed or killed in large numbers

Reading Strategy Distinguishing Fact and Opinion
In this paragraph, which statement is a fact and which is an opinion?

Cross Lightning had a powerful smile. When *Setting Wind* and *Gentle Woman Standing* sang together the whole tribe listened. *Stop the Day* got her name when at her shout the afternoon went still. *Log* was strong, *Cloud Touching Bottom* weak and consumptive.[3] *Mirage* married *Wind*. Everyone loved *Musical Cloud*, but children hid from *Dressed in Stone*. *Lying Down Grass* had such a gentle voice and touch, but no one dared to cross *She Black of Heart*.

We can imagine something of these women from their names. Anishinabe historian Basil Johnston notes that 'such was the mystique and force of a name that it was considered **presumptuous** and unbecoming, even vain, for a person to utter his own name. It was the custom for a third person, if present, to utter the name of the person to be identified. Seldom, if ever, did either husband or wife speak the name of the other in public.'

Shortly after the first tribal roll, the practice of renaming became an **ecclesiastical** exercise, and, as a result, most women in the next two generations bear the names of saints particularly beloved by the French. *She Knows the Bear* became Marie. *Sloping Cloud* was christened Jeanne. *Taking Care of the Day* and *Yellow Day Woman* turned into Catherines. Identities are altogether lost. The daughters of my own ancestors, *Kwayzancheewin*[4]—*Acts Like a Boy* and *Striped Earth Woman*—go unrecorded, and no hint or reflection of their individual natures comes to light through the scattershot records of those times, although they must have been genetically tough in order to survive: there were epidemics of typhoid, flu, measles and other diseases that winnowed the tribe each winter. They had to have grown up sensible, hard-working, **undeviating** in their attention to their tasks. They had to have been lucky. And if very lucky, they acquired carts.

It is no small thing that both of my great-grandmothers were known as women with carts.

The first was Elise Eliza McCloud, the great-granddaughter of *Striped Earth Woman*. The buggy she owned was somewhat grander than a cart. In her photograph [page 1292], Elise Eliza gazes straight ahead, intent, elevated in her pride. Perhaps she and her daughter Justine, both wearing reshaped felt fedoras,[5] were on their way to the train that would take them from Rugby, North Dakota, to Grand Forks, and back again. Back and forth across the upper tier of the plains, they peddled their hand-worked tourist items—dangling moccasin brooches and little beaded hats, or, in the summer, the wild berries, plums and nuts that they had gathered from the wooded hills. Of Elise Eliza's industry there remains in the family only an intricately beaded pair of buffalo horns and a piece of real furniture, a 'Highboy', an object once regarded with some awe, a prize she won for selling the most merchandise from a manufacturer's catalogue.

Visual Vocabulary
A *highboy* is a tall chest of drawers having two sections and four legs.

The owner of the other cart, Virginia Grandbois [page 1295], died when I was nine years old: she was a fearsome and fascinating presence, an old woman seated like an icon behind the door of my grandparents' house. Forty years before I was born, she was photographed on her way to fetch drinking water at the reservation well. In the picture she is seated high, the reins in her fingers

---

3. Someone who is *consumptive* suffers from a disease (especially tuberculosis) in which body tissue wastes away.
4. *Kwayzancheewin* (kwā′ zän chē′ win)

---

5. *Fedoras* (fi dôr′ əz) are soft felt hats with curved brims and lengthwise creases in the crown.

LOUISE ERDRICH　**1293**

connected to a couple of shaggy fetlocked draft ponies. The barrel she will fill stands behind her. She wears a man's sweater and an expression of vast self-pleasure. She might have been saying *Kaygoh*,[6] a warning, to calm the horses. She might have been speaking to whomever it was who held the camera, still a novel luxury.

Virginia Grandbois was known to smell of flowers. In spite of the potato picking, water hauling, field and housework, she found the time and will to dust her face with pale powder, in order to look more French. She was the great-great-granddaughter of the daughter of the principal leader of the *A-waus-e*,[7] the Bullhead clan, a woman whose real name was never recorded but who, on marrying a Frenchman, was 'recreated' as Madame Cadotte. It was Madame Cadotte who acted as a liaison[8] between her Ojibway relatives and her husband so that, even when French influence **waned** in the region, Jean-Baptiste Cadotte stayed on as the only trader of importance, the last governor of the fort at Sault St. Marie.[9]

By the time I knew Virginia Grandbois, however, her mind had darkened, and her body deepened, shrunk, turned to bones and leather. She did not live in the present or in any known time at all. Periodically, she would awaken from dim and unknown dreams to find herself seated behind the door in her daughter's house. She then cried out for her cart and her horses. When they did not materialize, Virginia Grandbois rose with great energy and purpose. Then she walked towards her house, taking the straightest line.

That house, long sold and gone, lay over one hundred miles due east and still Virginia Grandbois charged ahead, no matter what lay in her path—fences, sloughs,[10] woods, the yards of other families. She wanted home, to get home, to be home. She wanted her own place back, the place she had made, not her daughter's, not anyone else's. Hers. There was no substitute, no kindness, no reality that would change her mind. She had to be tied to the chair, and the chair to the wall, and still there was no reasoning with Virginia Grandbois. Her entire life, her hard-won personality, boiled down in the end to one stubborn, fixed, desperate idea.

I started with the same idea—this urge to get home, even if I must walk straight across the world. Only, for me, the urge to walk is the urge to write. Like my great-grandmother's house, there is no home for me to get to. A mixed-blood, raised in the Sugarbeet Capital, educated on the Eastern seaboard, married in a tiny New England village, living now on a ridge directly across from the Swan Range in the Rocky Mountains, my home is a collection of homes, of wells in which the quiet of experience shales away into sweet bedrock.

Elise Eliza pieced the quilt my mother slept under, a patchwork of shirts, pants, other worn-out scraps, bordered with small rinsed and pressed Bull Durham[11] sacks. As if in another time and place, although it is only the dim barrel of a four-year-old's memory, I see myself lying wrapped under smoky quilts and dank green army blankets in the house in which my mother was born. In the fragrance of tobacco, some smoked in home-rolled cigarettes, some offered to the Manitous[12] whose presence still was honored, I dream myself home. Beneath the rafters, shadowed with bunches of plants and torn calendars, in the nest of a sagging bed, I listen to mice

6. *Kaygoh* (kā gō´)
7. *A-waus-e* (ä´ wôs ē)
8. Here, a *liaison* (lē ā´ zon) is a person who maintains or improves communications between two parties.
9. *Sault St.* (or *Ste.*, meaning *Sainte*) *Marie* (sōō´ sānt mə rē´), Michigan, and its sister city, Sault Ste. Marie, Ontario, lie along the St. Mary's River between Lake Huron and Lake Superior.

10. *Sloughs* (slōōz) are marshes, swamps, or bogs.
11. *Bull Durham* was a brand of tobacco.
12. *Manitous* (man´ ə tōōz´) are spirits worshiped as governing forces of life and nature.

Vocabulary

wane (wān) *v.* to decrease gradually; to decline

Big Idea Extending and Remaking Traditions *How does this passage serve as a metaphor for Erdrich's life?*

rustle and the scratch of an owl's claws as it paces the shingles.

Elise Eliza's daughter-in-law, my grandmother Mary LeFavor, kept that house of hand-hewed and stacked beams, mudded between. She managed to shore it up and keep it standing by stuffing every new crack with disposable diapers. Having used and reused cloth to diaper her own children, my grandmother washed and hung to dry the paper and plastic diapers that her granddaughters bought for her great-grandchildren. When their plastic-paper shredded, she gathered them carefully together and one day, on a summer visit, I woke early to find her tamping[13] the rolled stuff carefully into the cracked walls of that old house.

It is autumn in the Plains, and in the little sloughs ducks land, and mudhens, whose flesh always tastes greasy and charred. Snow is coming soon, and after its first fall there will be a short, false warmth that brings out the sweet-sour odor of highbush cranberries. As a descendant of the women who skinned buffalo and tanned and smoked the hides, of women who pounded berries with the dried meat to make winter food, who made tea from willow bark and rosehips, who gathered snakeroot, I am affected by the change of seasons. Here is a time when plants consolidate[14] their tonic and drop seed, when animals store energy and grow thick fur. As for me, I start keeping longer hours, writing more, working harder, though I am obviously not a creature of a traditional Anishinabe culture. I was not raised speaking the old language, or adhering to the cycle of religious ceremonies that

govern the Anishinabe spiritual relationship to the land and the moral order within human configurations. As the wedding of many backgrounds, I am free to do what simply feels right.

My mother knits, sews, cans, dries food and preserves it. She knows how to gather tea, berries, snare rabbits, milk cows and churn butter. She can grow squash and melons from seeds she gathered the fall before. She is, as were the women who came before me, a repository[15] of all of the homely virtues, and I am the first in a long line who has not saved the autumn's harvest in birch bark makuks[16] and skin bags and in a cellar dry and cold with dust. I am the first who scratches the ground for pleasure, not survival, and grows flowers instead of potatoes. I record rather than practise the arts that filled the hands and days of my mother and her mother, and all the mothers going back into the shadows, when women wore names that told us who they were. ∾

---

15. Here, a *repository* (ri poz′ ə tōr′ ē) is a person who stores something.
16. *makuks* (mä′ kuks)

Big Idea Extending and Remaking Traditions *Why is this idea important?*

Big Idea Extending and Remaking Traditions *How is Erdrich extending and remaking her cultural inheritance?*

---

13. *Tamping* means "forcing or packing in with a series of light taps."
14. To *consolidate* (kən sol′ ə dāt′) means "to combine."

Literary Element Catalog *What is the purpose of this catalog?*

RESPONDING AND THINKING CRITICALLY

Respond

1. If you wrote about your family's or culture's history, whom or what would you focus on? Why?

Recall and Interpret

2. (a)What does Erdrich reveal in the first paragraph about her ethnic heritage and the history of her ancestors? (b)What is Erdrich's attitude toward her ancestors' history?

3. (a)What words does Erdrich use to describe her great-grandmothers? (b)How do you think Erdrich feels about her great-grandmothers? Use specific details from the selection to explain your answers.

4. (a)What do Erdrich's great-grandmother Virginia Grandbois and Erdrich have in common? (b)What do you think Erdrich is saying about her own character when she explains what she has in common with Virginia Grandbois? Use details from the selection to support your answer.

Analyze and Evaluate

5. In your opinion, what is the **theme,** or message about life, of this selection? Support your response with evidence from the text.

6. (a)Why does Erdrich title this essay "The Names of Women"? (b)Do you think this title is appropriate? Why or why not?

Connect

7. Do you think that writing about what people have done in the past is important? Why or why not?

8. **Big Idea** **Extending and Remaking Traditions** Do you think that Erdrich is extending or remaking the traditions of her past? Explain why or why not.

LITERARY ANALYSIS

Literary Element Catalog

Many forms of literature include **catalogs.** For example, some epic poems list the names of heroes or weapons. The poets Walt Whitman and Carl Sandburg often included catalogs in their poems as Erdrich does in "The Names of Women."

1. Describe two catalogs that appear in this selection.

2. Why might Erdrich present this information in the form of catalogs?

Review: Symbol

As you learned in Unit 2, a **symbol** is any object, person, place, or experience that represents itself on a literal level but also stands for something else, usually something abstract. For example, a dove is often used to symbolize peace. In some cases, names can also be symbolic.

Partner Activity Pair up with a classmate to identify symbols in "The Names of Women." Working with your partner, create a two-column chart similar to the one below. Fill in the left-hand column with examples of symbols or symbolic content from the text. In the right-hand column, explain what the name, object, or other symbol represents.

Symbol	What It Represents
The name Standing Strong	
The great-grandmother's carts	

READING AND VOCABULARY

Reading Strategy Distinguishing Fact and Opinion

Although opinions cannot be proved true, they may be supported by evidence. These are called **valid opinions.** Keep in mind that opinions are sometimes presented as if they are facts. For example, the statement "Life was better in the past because people had a greater appreciation for nature than people do today" might seem like a fact at first but is actually an expression of one person's beliefs. Another person might argue that life is better today because of technological advances. You must analyze a text very carefully in order to distinguish valid opinions from facts.

1. Find two valid opinions in "The Names of Women."

2. What details make these opinions valid?

Vocabulary Practice

Word Origins Choose the language from which each term originated. Use a dictionary to find word histories.

1. decimated
   a. Latin   **b.** Algonquian

2. presumptuous
   a. Sanskrit   **b.** Latin

3. ecclesiastical
   a. Norse   **b.** Greek

4. undeviating
   a. Latin   **b.** Greek

5. wane
   a. Algonquian **b.** Old English

Academic Vocabulary

Here are two words from the vocabulary list on page R86.

assign (ə sīn′) *v.* to distribute or allot; to designate

ambiguous (am big′ ū əs) *adj.* open to multiple interpretations; unclear

Practice and Apply

1. What special significance does Erdrich say is **assigned** to the names of women?

2. Do you think names have definite or **ambiguous** meanings?

WRITING AND EXTENDING

Writing About Literature

Analyze Cultural Context To understand fully a work of literature, you may need to evaluate how the cultural context in which the work was written helped to shape it. Write a brief essay analyzing the ways that Native American culture influenced Erdrich's essay. Consider Erdrich's connection to her past and her ancestors. How would the essay be different if it were removed from this cultural context and focused only on women's names?

Before you begin writing, you may want to organize your thoughts in a web like the one below.

How cultural context affects essay

After you complete your draft, meet with a peer reviewer to evaluate each other's work and to suggest revisions. Then proofread and edit your draft for errors in spelling, grammar, and punctuation.

Listening and Speaking

With a group, plan and hold a panel discussion on the importance of preserving historical and cultural documents and other items, including photographs and handmade artifacts. Make sure you address the following questions in your discussion.

- In what ways do people preserve historical items from their families or cultures?

- Why is it important to preserve these types of historical items?

- How might historical and cultural artifacts help us understand past cultures and time periods?

- How might historical and cultural artifacts provide insight into the present?

Literature Online **Web Activities** For eFlashcards, Selection Quick Checks, and other Web activities, go to www.glencoe.com.

Salvador Late or Early

MEET SANDRA CISNEROS

As the only girl in a family with six sons, Sandra Cisneros always felt a bit like an outsider. She was also frequently the new kid on the block. Cisneros was born in Chicago. Her mother was Mexican American and her father was Mexican. Her father was devoted to his mother in Mexico, so he was often homesick. As a result, Cisneros said, the family "returned like the tides, back and forth to Mexico City."

The Outsider One result of this continual migration was that Cisneros retreated into books, becoming an avid, if isolated, reader. This habit was encouraged by her mother, who made sure that her daughter had a library card even before the child was able to read.

During her sophomore year of high school, Cisneros had an English teacher whom she described as "bright and vivacious." This teacher encouraged Cisneros to write. After college she applied to and was accepted by the University of Iowa Writers' Workshop.

Success In Iowa Cisneros felt isolated and out of place. "My classmates were from the best schools in the country," she wrote later. "They had been bred as fine hot-house flowers. I was a yellow weed among the city's cracks." Suddenly, though, she realized what made her special and therefore what she would write about—her own experiences. The result was *The House on Mango Street*, published when Cisneros was twenty-nine. In a series of interlocking stories, the book tells the tale of a young Chicana girl growing up in a Chicago barrio, much like the neighborhoods where Cisneros once lived. The book received high praise and was awarded the Before Columbus American Book Award in 1985. It has sold over two million copies, making Cisneros one of the best-known Latina authors in the United States.

Cisneros next published *My Wicked Wicked Ways*, a collection of poetry, in 1987, and *Woman*

Hollering Creek and Other Stories in 1991. Critics disagreed about whether to call the latter book prose or poetry, as the author included elements of both genres.

> "To me, the definition of a story is something that someone wants to listen to. If someone doesn't want to listen to you, then it's not a story."
>
> —Sandra Cisneros

Cisneros began writing a story about her father. However, she kept traveling different paths until her story had mushroomed into a 450-page book, *Caramelo*, that took almost ten years to complete. "You start a story," said Cisneros, "—oh, but you have to explain something first. So you take a detour, but that leads to something else. Then you get back to your story."

Today Cisneros teaches, gives readings, and writes. She still remains somewhat on the outside of society, but this is by choice. "I really like my solitude," she said to an interviewer. "I don't like being lonely, but I'm not lonely. I need to be alone to work."

Sandra Cisneros was born in 1954.

Literature Online Author Search For more about Sandra Cisneros, go to www.glencoe.com.

Connecting to the Story

The following story is a description of a boy named Salvador. As you read the story, think about the following questions:

- What factors influence a person's childhood?
- Whose job is it to protect children from being prematurely thrust into the adult world?

Building Background

A child's family, culture, and economic level all affect the type of childhood that individual will have. While some children have school as their only responsibility, other children have numerous family obligations that shape their lives. These children may work alongside their parents in fields, in shops, or in the home. They may spend hours caring for younger or older relatives. Although laws require children to go to school, not all children are able to do so regularly. In some cultures, family obligations are primary, and a child's individual needs may give way to other family pressures.

Setting Purposes for Reading

Big Idea **Extending and Remaking Traditions**

As you read this selection, notice how the language comprises elements of both prose and poetry, reshaping them into a new form.

Literary Element **Imagery**

Imagery is made up of the "word pictures" a writer uses to evoke an emotional response. To create effective images, a writer uses sensory details, or descriptions that appeal to one of the five senses: sight, hearing, touch, taste, and smell. As you read the selection, pay attention to words and phrases that create images.

- See Literary Terms Handbook, p. R9.

 Literature Online **Interactive Literary Elements Handbook** To review or learn more about the literary elements, go to www.glencoe.com.

Reading Strategy Analyzing Sound Devices

Sound devices are techniques designed to appeal to the ear. Writers use sound devices to emphasize particular words or sounds, to create or enhance rhythm, or to add to the musical quality of their writing. Sound devices include alliteration, assonance, repetition, rhyme, and rhythm.

Reading Tip: Keep Track As you read the selection, use the web to record sound devices that catch your ear. Add to the web as needed.

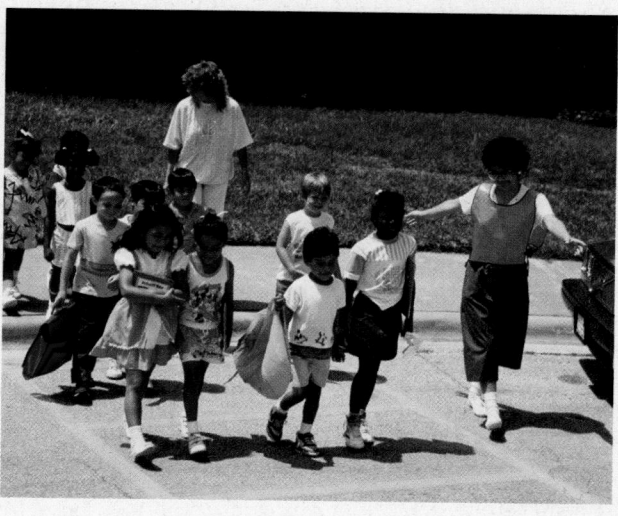

INDIANA ACADEMIC STANDARDS (pages 1299–1301)
11.3.4 Analyze ways in which...prose uses imagery...to evoke readers' emotions.

11.4.7 Develop presentations using...Internet sources.

11.3.3 Analyze the ways in which...the "sound" of language achieve[s] specific...aesthetic (artistic) purposes...

SANDRA CISNEROS **1299**

Salvador Late or Early

Sandra Cisneros

Salvador with eyes the color of caterpillar, Salvador of the crooked hair and crooked teeth, Salvador whose name the teacher cannot remember, is a boy who is no one's friend, runs along somewhere in that vague direction where homes are the color of bad weather, lives behind a raw wood doorway, shakes the sleepy brothers awake, ties their shoes, combs their hair with water, feeds them milk and corn flakes from a tin cup in the dim dark of the morning.

Salvador, late or early, sooner or later arrives with the string of younger brothers ready. Helps his mama, who is busy with the business of the baby. Tugs the arms of Cecilio, Arturito, makes them hurry, because today, like yesterday, Arturito has dropped the cigar box of crayons, has let go the hundred little fingers of red, green, yellow, blue, and nub of black sticks that tumble and spill over and beyond the asphalt puddles until the crossing-guard lady holds back the blur of traffic for Salvador to collect them again.

Salvador inside that wrinkled shirt, inside the throat that must clear itself and apologize each time it speaks, inside that forty-pound body of boy with its geography of scars, its history of hurt, limbs stuffed with feathers and rags, in what part of the eyes, in what part of the heart, in that cage of the chest where something throbs with both fists and knows only what Salvador knows, inside that body too small to contain the hundred balloons of happiness, the single guitar of grief, is a boy like any other disappearing out the door, beside the schoolyard gate, where he has told his brothers they must wait. Collects the hands of Cecilio and Arturito, scuttles off dodging the many schoolyard colors, the elbows and wrists crisscrossing, the several shoes running. Grows small and smaller to the eye, dissolves into the bright horizon, flutters in the air before disappearing like a memory of kites.

Literary Element   Imagery *What do these images suggest about Salvador and his life?*

Big Idea   Extending and Remaking Traditions *What elements of both prose and poetry do you see in these lines?*

Literary Element   Imagery *How could the writer have said the same thing without imagery?*

Reading Strategy   Analyzing Sound Devices *What sounds are repeated, and what is the effect of such repetition?*

RESPONDING AND THINKING CRITICALLY

Respond

1. (a)What was your reaction to learning about Salvador's life? (b)What would you say to Salvador if you could speak to him?

Recall and Interpret

2. (a)What colors are mentioned in the first sentence of "Salvador Late or Early"? (b)What do these colors suggest about the boy's life?

3. (a)Describe Salvador's role in his family. What are his jobs? (b)What does his role reveal about how the boy is viewed by his family?

4. (a)What images describe Salvador in the third paragraph? (b)What do these details show about his history?

Analyze and Evaluate

5. A major part of Cisneros's style in "Salvador Late or Early" is her use of unusually long sentences. In your opinion, do these long sentences add to or detract from the effectiveness of her writing? Explain.

6. What are some of the details that help you infer that Salvador lives in poverty?

7. The narrator describes Salvador as "a boy who is no one's friend." Who or what is responsible for the boy's situation, do you think? Explain your answer.

Connect

8. **Big Idea** **Extending and Remaking Traditions** Speculate why Cisneros might have written in a literary form that lies partway between poetry and prose. Use examples from the selection to support your response.

LITERARY ANALYSIS

Literary Element **Imagery**

Imagery often suggests feelings or ideas that are not stated. For example, Cisneros writes that Salvador "arrives with the string of younger brothers ready." These words create an image of a line of boys following Salvador. The image also conveys the idea that people see Salvador as attached to his brothers more than they see him as a separate person.

1. What image do the words "in that cage of the chest where something throbs with both fists" create?

2. What image in the story do you find most striking?

Internet Connection

Leading Figures Sandra Cisneros is one of the leading figures in Hispanic literature today. Search the Internet for information about other Hispanics who are leaders in their fields. Choose from any area you like, such as art, science, or politics. Present your findings to the class.

Literature Online **Web Activities** For eFlashcards, Selection Quick Checks, and other Web activities, go to www.glencoe.com.

READING AND VOCABULARY

Reading Strategy **Analyzing Sound Devices**

Many sound devices, such as **alliteration**, **assonance**, **repetition**, **rhyme**, and **rhythm**, are more closely associated with poetry than with prose. Yet Cisneros uses all of these in this story.

1. Give an example of each sound device from the story.

2. What effect do these have on your reading of it?

Academic Vocabulary

Here are two words from the vocabulary list on page R86.

acknowledge (ak nol′ ij) *v.* to recognize or admit

distinct (dis tingkt′) *adj.* separate or different from

Practice and Apply

1. How does the crossing-guard lady **acknowledge** that Salvador has a problem?

2. What is one detail that makes Arturito **distinct** from his brother Cecilio?

Thoughts on the African-American Novel

MEET TONI MORRISON

Highly acclaimed as a novelist, essayist, and literary critic, Toni Morrison won the Nobel Prize in Literature in 1993, the first African American to do so. Reflecting on this honor, she stated that to become a writer she had to defy stereotypes and value her own potential. "Had I lived the life that the state planned for me from the beginning," she said, "I would have lived and died in somebody else's kitchen, on somebody else's land, and never written a word."

Instead of working as a maid or a sharecropper, Morrison became a writer and expressed her emotions and perceptions as an African American and a woman in award-winning novels and other creative works. When asked whether she considered herself a black writer or a female writer, Morrison responded, "I've just insisted—insisted!—upon being called a black woman novelist."

Early Years Born Chloe Anthony Wofford, Morrison grew up in Lorain, Ohio, a setting that figures prominently in many of her novels. Her family had moved there from the South, looking for better opportunities. With her family's help, she attended Howard University in Washington, D.C., where she studied English and the classics. There she adopted the name Toni, because people had trouble pronouncing her first name.

Morrison graduated from Howard and later earned an M.A. degree from Cornell University. She married, had two sons, and began a long and distinguished career as a teacher and editor. In 1964 Morrison and her husband separated. Eventually they divorced, and for years Morrison brought up her family as a single mother, working by day and writing late at night after her sons were asleep.

> "Writing . . . became the one thing I was doing that I had absolutely no intention of living without."
>
> —Toni Morrison

An African American Writer Morrison's first novel, *The Bluest Eye*, was published in 1970. In this novel and others that followed—including *Sula* (1973), *Song of Solomon* (1977), and *Tar Baby* (1981)—Morrison grappled with some of the themes that pervade her fiction: racism, family, identity, and loss. She also created fiction that spoke directly to African Americans, using poetic and precise language to capture the "music of black talk."

In 1987, Morrison's novel *Beloved* became a financial blockbuster. An exploration of boundless love and institutionalized evil, this novel won the Pulitzer Prize for Fiction and later was adapted into a successful film, starring Oprah Winfrey.

Despite her prominence and influence as a writer and Nobel laureate, Morrison does not rest on her laurels. She continues to write, to lecture, and to teach. Today her work includes several acclaimed novels, an impressive body of nonfiction, and a play about the murder of Emmett Till, *Dreaming Emmett*.

Toni Morrison was born in 1931.

Literature Online **Author Search** For more about Toni Morrison, go to www.glencoe.com.

Connecting to the Essay

In this essay, Toni Morrison explains how novels work and why a society needs them. As you read this essay, think about the following questions:

- What novels have you particularly enjoyed reading?
- Why do people read novels?

Building Background

In "Thoughts on the African-American Novel," Toni Morrison explores some of the characteristics of "Black art." Even as a young woman, Morrison was deeply influenced by the music, legends, and oral traditions of her African American heritage. When she began writing, the civil rights movement was becoming a force for social change. Morrison, then a teacher, knew several people, both poets and political leaders, who were active in that struggle. Today, Morrison is recognized as one of the pioneers in the field of African American literature. A gifted and inspiring storyteller, Morrison also has worked tirelessly to promote other African American writers.

Setting Purposes for Reading

Big Idea Extending and Remaking Traditions

As you read this essay, consider the connections Morrison makes between her novels and the traditions of "Black art."

Literary Element Essay

An **essay** is a type of nonfiction that conveys a writer's ideas and opinions on a specific topic. Essays may be formal or informal. An **informal essay** has a lighter tone and a more fluid structure than a **formal essay**, which features a carefully structured progression of opinions and supporting information. As you read, consider whether Morrison's essay is formal or informal.

- See Literary Terms Handbook, p. R6.

Literature Online Interactive Literary Elements Handbook To review or learn more about the literary elements, go to www.glencoe.com.

Reading Strategy Determining Main Idea and Supporting Details

Determining an author's **main idea** is finding the most important thought in a paragraph or in a selection. Look for the one idea that all of the sentences in a paragraph, or all of the paragraphs in a selection, are about. **Supporting details,** which may include facts, examples, reasons, and anecdotes, provide additional information about the main idea.

Reading Tip: Taking Notes To map out the main idea and details of a selection, write the main idea in the middle circle and list supporting details around it.

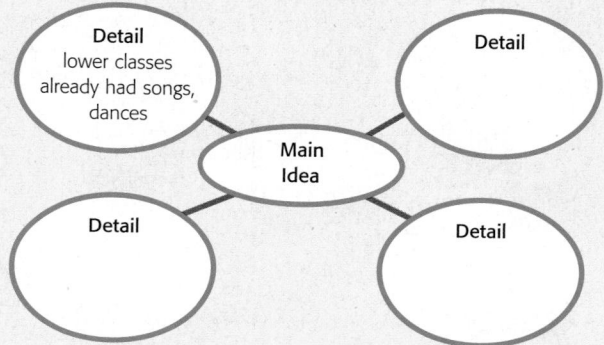

Vocabulary

aristocracy (a´ rə sto´ krə sē) *n.* people with high social status due to birth or title; p. 1305 *The peasant envied the aristocracy.*

exclusively (iks´ kloo´ siv lē) *adv.* without the inclusion or involvement of any others; p. 1305 *This room is used exclusively by club members.*

enlighten (en līt´ ən) *v.* to give knowledge or wisdom to; p. 1305 *A classic novel can enlighten readers, showing them how to meet life's challenges.*

meandering (mē an´ dər ing) *adj.* following a winding course; p. 1306 *We took a meandering, not a direct, route home.*

unorthodox (un ôr´ thə doks´) *adj.* not customary or traditional; p. 1306 *Although the mathematician's methods were unorthodox, she was right.*

INDIANA ACADEMIC STANDARDS (pages 1303–1308)
11.2.6 Critique the...arguments set forth in...essays...
11.2 Develop [reading] strategies...
11.5.2 Write responses to literature...
11.7.18 Deliver oral responses to literature...

The Library, 1960. Jacob Lawrence. Tempera on fiberboard, 24 x 29 ⅞ in. Smithsonian American Art Museum, Washington, D.C.

Thoughts on the African-American Novel

Toni Morrison

The label "novel" is useful in technical terms because I write prose that is longer than a short story. My sense of the novel is that it has always functioned for the class or the group that wrote it. The history of the novel as a form began when there was a new class, a middle class, to read it; it was an art form that they needed. The lower classes didn't need novels at that time because they had an art form already: they had songs, and dances, and ceremony, and gossip, and celebrations. The **aristocracy** didn't need it because they had the art that they had patronized,[1] they had their own pictures painted, their own houses built, and they made sure their art separated them from the rest of the world. But when the industrial revolution[2] began, there emerged a new class of people who were neither peasants nor aristocrats. In large measure they had no art form to tell them how to behave in this new situation. So they produced an art form: we call it the novel of manners, an art form designed to tell people something they didn't know. That is, how to behave in this new world, how to distinguish between the good guys and the bad guys. How to get married. What a good living was. What would happen if you strayed from the fold. So that early works such as *Pamela,* by Samuel Richardson, and the Jane Austen material provided social rules and explained behavior, identified outlaws, identified the people, habits, and customs that one should approve of. They were didactic in that sense. That, I think, is probably why the novel was not missed among the so-called peasant cultures. They didn't need it, because they were clear about what their responsibilities were and who and where was evil, and where was good.

But when the peasant class, or lower class, or what have you, confronts the middle class, the city, or the upper classes, they are thrown a little bit into disarray. For a long time, the art form that was healing for Black people was music. That music is no longer *exclusively* ours, we don't have exclusive rights to it. Other people sing it and play it; it is the mode[3] of contemporary music everywhere. So another form has to take that place, and it seems to me that the novel is needed by African Americans now in a way that it was not needed before—and it is following along the lines of the function of novels everywhere. We don't live in places where we can hear those stories anymore; parents don't sit around and tell their children those classical, mythological archetypal stories[4] that we heard years ago. But new information has got to get out, and there are several ways to do it. One is in the novel. I regard it as a way to accomplish certain very strong functions—one being the one I just described.

It should be beautiful, and powerful, but it should also *work*. It should have something in it that **enlightens;** something in it that opens the door and points the way. Something in it that suggests what the conflicts are, what the problems are. But it need not solve those problems because it is not a case study, it is not a recipe. There are things that I try to incorporate into my fiction that are directly and deliberately related to what I regard as the major characteristics of Black art, wherever it is. One of which is the ability to be

---

1. Here, *patronize* (pā′ trə nīz′) means "to give financial support or encouragement to."
2. The *industrial revolution* helped develop a middle class of workers who began to gain some control over where, for whom, and for what wages they would work.

Reading Strategy Main Idea and Supporting Details *What main idea do these details support?*

Vocabulary

aristocracy (a′ rə sto′ krə sē) *n.* people with high social status due to birth or title

---

3. Here, *mode* means "a manner of expression." The type of music once considered an art form belonging to African Americans is now the preferred form of contemporary music for many modern listeners.
4. *Archetypal* (är′ kə tī′ pəl) *stories* come from ideas inherited through the ages.

Literary Element Essay *How does this sentence function in the essay?*

Reading Strategy Main Idea and Supporting Details *What details support this main idea?*

Vocabulary

exclusively (iks′ klōō siv lē) *adv.* without the inclusion or involvement of any others
enlighten (en līt′ ən) *v.* to give knowledge or wisdom to

both print and oral literature: to combine those two aspects so that the stories can be read in silence, of course, but one should be able to hear them as well. It should try deliberately to make you stand up and make you feel something profoundly in the same way that a Black preacher requires his congregation to speak, to join him in the sermon, to behave in a certain way, to stand up and to weep and to cry and to accede or to change and to modify—to expand on the sermon that is being delivered. In the same way that a musician's music is enhanced when there is a response from the audience. Now in a book, which closes, after all—it's of some importance to me to try to make that connection—to try to make that happen also. And, having at my disposal only the letters of the alphabet and some punctuation, I have to provide the places and spaces so that the reader can participate. Because it is the affective and participatory relationship[5] between the artist or the speaker and the audience that is of primary importance, as it is in these other art forms that I have described.

To make the story appear oral, **meandering,** effortless, spoken—to have the reader *feel* the narrator without *identifying* that narrator, or hearing him or her knock about, and to have the reader work *with* the author in the construction of the book—is what's important. What is left out is as important as what is there. To describe sexual scenes in such a way that they are not clinical, not even explicit—so that the reader brings his own sexuality to the scene and thereby participates in it in a very personal way. And owns it. To construct the dialogue so that it is heard. So that there are no adverbs attached to them: "loudly," "softly," "he said menacingly." The menace should be in the sentence. To use, even formally, a chorus. The real presence of a chorus. Meaning the community or the reader at large, commenting on the action as it goes ahead.

In the books that I have written, the chorus has changed but there has always been a choral note, whether it is the "I" narrator of *Bluest Eye,* or the town functioning as a character in *Sula,* or the neighborhood and the community that responds in the two parts of town in *Solomon.* Or, as extreme as I've gotten, all of nature thinking and feeling and watching and responding to the action going on in *Tar Baby,* so that they are in the story: the trees hurt, fish are afraid, clouds report, and the bees are alarmed. Those are the ways in which I try to incorporate, into that traditional genre the novel, **unorthodox** novelistic characteristics—so that it is, in my view, Black, because it uses the characteristics of Black art. I am not suggesting that some of these devices have not been used before and elsewhere—only the reason why I do. I employ them as well as I can. And those are just some; I wish there were ways in which such things could be talked about in the criticism. My general disappointment in some of the criticism that my work has received has nothing to do with approval. It has something to do with the vocabulary used in order to describe these things. I don't like to find my books condemned as bad or praised as good, when that condemnation or that praise is based on criteria from other paradigms. I would much prefer that they were dismissed or embraced based on the success of their accomplishment within the culture out of which I write.

I don't regard Black literature as simply books written *by* Black people, or simply as literature written *about* Black people, or simply as literature that uses a certain mode of language in which you just sort of drop g's. There is something very special and very identifiable about it and it is my struggle to *find* that elusive but identifiable style in the books. My joy is when I think that I have approached it; my misery is when I think I can't get there. ❧

---

5. An *affective and participatory relationship* influences one's emotions and encourages one to take an active part in the relationship.

Big Idea Extending and Remaking Traditions *What does Morrison do to give a story an oral quality?*

Vocabulary

meandering (mē an′ dər ing) *adj.* following a winding course

Big Idea Extending and Remaking Traditions *What connections does Morrison see between her novels and "Black art"?*

Vocabulary

unorthodox (un ôr′ thə doks′) *adj.* not customary or traditional

RESPONDING AND THINKING CRITICALLY

Respond

1. Which of Morrison's ideas about novels did you find most interesting? Explain.

Recall and Interpret

2. (a)According to Morrison, what event and what class of people caused the birth of the novel as a literary form? (b)Why was the novel of manners important to that class at that time?

3. (a)What did music provide for African Americans in times past? (b)Why do African Americans need novels at the present time?

4. (a)According to Morrison, what specific qualities should an African American novel have? (b)Explain Morrison's comparison between the novel and an African American preacher.

Analyze and Evaluate

5. How well do novels help readers "distinguish between the good guys and the bad guys"?

6. Why does Morrison include a chorus in her novels?

7. Morrison says that a novel should present problems but need not solve them. Do you agree or disagree with this statement? Why?

Connect

8. **Big Idea** Extending and Remaking Traditions In what ways does Morrison extend the traditions of "Black art" in her novels?

LITERARY ANALYSIS

Literary Element Essay

A **formal essay** may sound like a dignified speech. An **informal essay,** however, has a lighter tone and often sounds like a conversation. Moreover, an informal essay may even contain sentence fragments and informal language.

1. Find examples of sentence fragments and informal language in Morrison's essay.

2. What does the use of sentence fragments and informal language contribute to the overall **tone** of this essay?

Review: Parallelism

As you learned in reading "The Gettysburg Address" in Unit Three, **parallelism** is the use of a series of words, phrases, or sentences that have a similar grammatical form. In "Thoughts on the African-American Novel," Morrison often uses this technique, as in the following example: "*to stand up* and *to weep* and *to cry* and *to accede* or *to change* and *to modify* . . . "

Partner Activity With a classmate, look for additional examples of parallelism in Morrison's essay. List them on a chart and discuss how they reinforce Morrison's central message. Share your list with the rest of your class.

Example of Parallelism	Effect
"it is not a case study, it is not a recipe"	

Reading Strategy Determining Main Ideas and Supporting Details

As you read, it is important to identify the **main idea** of a paragraph or passage. Overall, works of fiction and nonfiction can contain several main ideas. Some writers directly state main ideas in topic sentences, while others imply a main idea with examples and other clues. Determining the main ideas prepares you to summarize a selection and discover the author's purpose for writing.

1. Morrison mentions that she strives to help readers create their own experiences while reading her novels. What details does she provide to explain how she does this?

2. What does Morrison find disappointing in some of the criticisms of her work?

Vocabulary Practice

Practice with Context Clues To figure out the meaning of an unfamiliar word, look for clues in the context, or the surrounding words. For example, in the phrase "those classical, mythological, archetypal stories that we heard years ago," you can use the clues "mythological" and "years ago" to infer that the word *archetypal* means "passed down through the ages."

Identify the type of context clue that is found in each of the following sentences. Types of context clues include *example, definition, contrast,* or *synonym*.

1. A straight path is shorter than one that meanders.
2. Enlighten me; in other words, explain it to me.
3. The list named dukes, earls, and other members of the aristocracy.
4. His clothing is unorthodox; and his ideas, too, are nontraditional.
5. Is this pool exclusively for residents, or can nonresidents swim in it too?

Writing About Literature

Explore the Author's Purpose With a small group, hold a panel discussion about Toni Morrison's purpose for writing "Thoughts on the African-American Novel." Envision your discussion as a radio broadcast honoring Morrison as a writer and then write a brief essay presenting the ideas and evidence you discussed. Use the following plan to organize your writing.

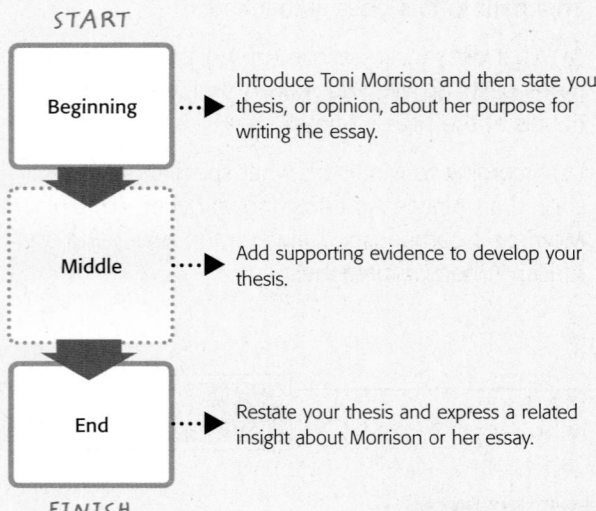

START

Beginning ····▶ Introduce Toni Morrison and then state your thesis, or opinion, about her purpose for writing the essay.

Middle ····▶ Add supporting evidence to develop your thesis.

End ····▶ Restate your thesis and express a related insight about Morrison or her essay.

FINISH

With other group members, take turns reading your work aloud. Keep revising your draft until it sounds like natural speech. Then proofread and edit your draft for errors in spelling, grammar, and punctuation.

Literature Groups

Toni Morrison's work is often the subject of critical reviews. With your group, begin a critical discussion about her essay. Which ideas did you particularly like or agree with? Which did you dislike or disagree with? Why? Be specific and support your opinions with facts, examples, and sound reasoning. Then summarize the group's views and share them with your class.

Literature Online **Web Activities** For eFlashcards, Selection Quick Checks, and other Web activities, go to www.glencoe.com.

Vocabulary Workshop

Word Parts

Using Suffixes To Form Nouns

"But new information has got to get out, and there are several ways to do it."
—Toni Morrison, from "Thoughts on the African-American Novel"

Connecting to Literature You may recognize the word *information* without realizing that it is a noun formed from a verb. The suffix *-ation* turns the verb to *inform* into a noun. This suffix and others are called **noun suffixes**, because they change other parts of speech into nouns. Knowledge of noun suffixes can often help you determine the meaning of unfamiliar words.

Common Noun Suffixes

Suffix	Meaning	Base word or word root	Example
-ee	receiver of action	train	trainee
-ance, -ence	state, quality	relevant persist	relevance persistence
-ant, -eer	agent, doer	contest puppet	contestant puppeteer
-ist	one who does, makes, or studies	cycle drama geology	cyclist dramatist geologist
-ment	result, condition	accomplish	accomplishment
-ness	action, state	bright	brightness
-tion, -ion	the act of	prosecute	prosecution

- When you see a word that acts as a noun, determine whether it has a noun suffix.
  Morrison feels <u>disappointment</u> about the way some critics describe her work.
  Novels should allow readers to become part of the <u>narration.</u>

- When you see a word with a noun suffix, try to identify the root or the base word.
  Morrison wants her readers to participate in her novels.
  The <u>participation</u> of readers adds a new dimension to the books.

Exercise

From the table above, choose a suffix that changes each word below to a noun. Write each complete word. (Sometimes a final letter in a base word is dropped before a suffix is added. A *y* at the end of a word is usually changed to *i*.)

1. disappoint   **4.** punctuate   **7.** descend   **10.** kind

2. celebrate   **5.** novel   **8.** fragrant

3. accomplish   **6.** congregate   **9.** construct

▶ **Vocabulary Terms**

Suffixes are word parts that are added to the ends of words to create new words.

▶ **Test-Taking Tip**

When you are asked for the meaning of a word that contains a suffix, think about the meaning of the root or base word. If you are unsure of the meaning of that word, try to think of other words that contain the same root or base word.

▶ **Reading Handbook**

For more about suffixes, see Reading Handbook, p. R20.

eFlashcards For eFlashcards and other vocabulary activities, go to www.glencoe.com.

ACADEMIC STANDARDS (page 1309)
11.1.2 Apply knowledge of...word parts...to draw inferences about the meaning of vocabulary...

From Comic Strips to Graphic Novels

> *"A comic artist begins with a white sheet of paper and dreams up his whole business—he is playwright, director, editor, and artist at once."*
>
> —Alex Raymond, creator of *Flash Gordon*

ONE OF THE UNITED STATES' most popular and influential contributions to world culture has been the comic strip and its later development, the comic book. Among the many forerunners of the comic form was the dime novel, cheaply-made tabloids which usually featured rugged frontiersmen, romantic heroines, or hardened detectives. Often displaying lurid covers that anticipated comic books and pulp fiction, these pocket-sized publications sold by the millions in the years after the Civil War. Newspaper comic strips first appeared in the mid-1890s, largely as a result of fierce competition for readers between big New York City dailies. From the very beginning, comic strips reflected a wide variety of approaches to subject matter and graphic style, ranging from the rough urban slapstick of *The Yellow Kid* to the elaborate graphic fancies of *Little Nemo in Slumberland*. Immediately popular, comic strips were soon being syndicated in newspapers across the United States. Comic strips and comic books continue to shape U.S. popular culture, as seen by the success of movies like *X-Men* and *Sin City,* based on comic books, and the devoted reader base of comics ranging from *The Avengers* to *Astro Girl*.

The Golden Age of Comics

During the Great Depression of the 1930s, comic strips evolved into a new form, the comic book. The first comic books were simply reprints of popular newspaper comic strips. However, growing demand prompted comic book publishers to employ writers and artists to create original stories. The comic book business received a boost in June of 1938 with the arrival of Superman in *Action Comics #1*, published by DC Comics. The first of a long line of superheroes, the

Man of Steel was soon followed by Batman, Wonder Woman, Captain America, Plastic Man, and a host of others. During World War II, these costumed fighters battled the enemies of the United States, and they have remained a basic element of U.S. popular culture ever since. The period from 1938 to the early 1950s is often referred to as the Golden Age of Comics because of the surge in comics production and sales. Toward the end of this period, the dominance of superheroes was challenged by the increasing popularity of violent crime and horror comics.

Backlash and Recovery

In the conservative climate of the early 1950s, comic books came under serious attack. Critics, such as psychiatrist Fredric Wertham, author of *Seduction of the Innocent*, claimed that comics were far too sexual

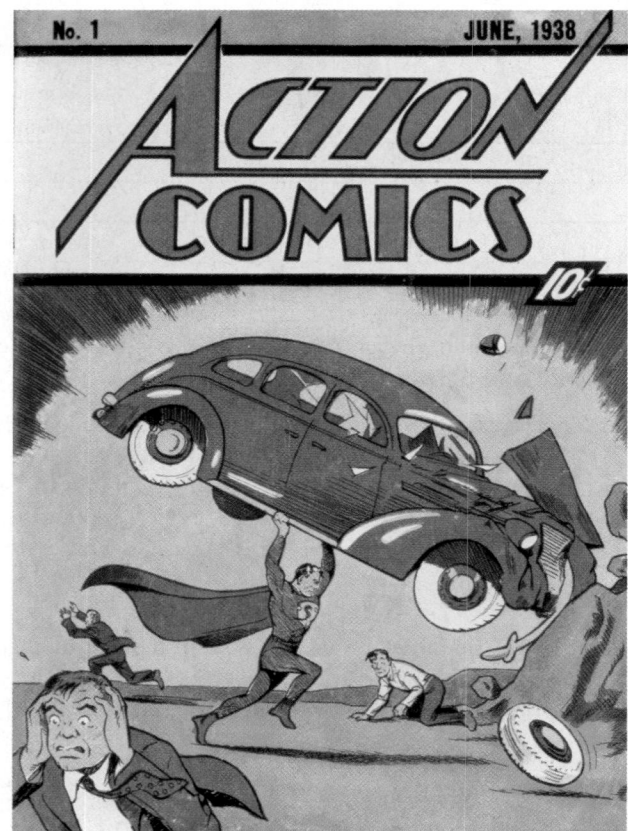

Action Comics No. 1, Joe Shuster, 1938. Comic book.

and violent, attacked authority, and destroyed a young person's taste for literature. The comic book industry responded by instituting self-censorship in the form of a set of guidelines known as the Comic Code. The result was bland comic books. During the later 1950s, a new generation of thoughtful, yet flawed superheroes, such as Spider-Man, helped restore the vigor and popularity of comic books. The period from the 1950s to the early 1970s is often called the Silver Age of Comics, marked by a rise in more complicated plots made popular by Marvel Comics. The "underground" comics movement also originated as a subversive alternative to the main-stream comic industry. Reflecting the spirit of the 1960s, underground comics scorned traditional values and celebrated artistic experimentation.

Graphic Novels

Another major development in the evolution of the comics form was the appearance of what are now generally referred to as **graphic novels**. This term is loosely applied to any lengthy story in comic book form. Comic book pioneer Will Eisner popularized the term in the late 1970s in connection with his work *A Contract with God, and Other Tenement Stories*. Since then it has been applied to an extraordinarily broad range of comic book stories. The most widely acclaimed graphic novel is Art Spiegelman's *Maus* (see page 995), in which he uses a comic book format and animal characters to present his father's experiences during the Holocaust. Spiegelman received a Pulitzer Prize for *Maus* in 1992. Other well known graphic novels include Daniel Clowes's *Ghost World*, Frank Miller's *Sin City*, and Chris Ware's *Jimmy Corrigan: The Smartest Kid on Earth*. Some comic book creators object to the distinction between "comic books" and "graphic novels," viewing it as largely

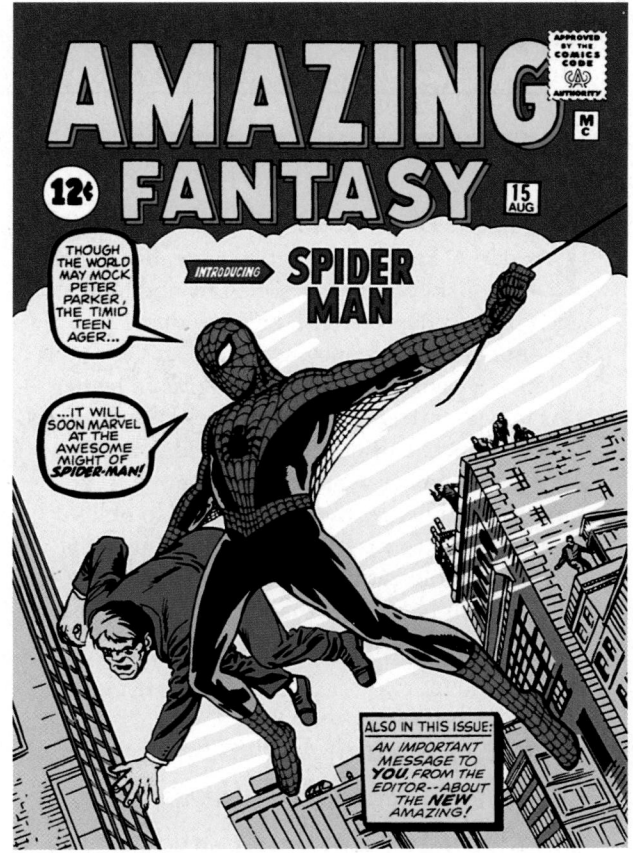

Amazing Fantasy, No. 15, Jack Kirby and Steve Ditko, 1962. Comic book.

artificial. However, others see the graphic novel as representing a new direction for the visual artform. Comic book artist Eddie Campbell, who collaborated with writer Alan Moore on the graphic novel *From Hell*, says the goal is "to take the form of the comic book, which has become an embarrassment, and raise it to a more ambitious and meaningful level."

RESPONDING AND THINKING CRITICALLY

1. Why do you think superheroes became so popular during the 1930s and 1940s?

2. How does a graphic novel differ from a comic book?

3. Do you think that comic books and graphic novels are a true art form? Explain.

INDIANA ACADEMIC STANDARDS
(pages 1310–1311)
11.7.11 Evaluate the various ways in which events are presented...by...graphic artists...

Literature **Online** **Literary History** For more about comic strips and graphic novels, go to www.glencoe.com.

Nineteen Thirty-Seven

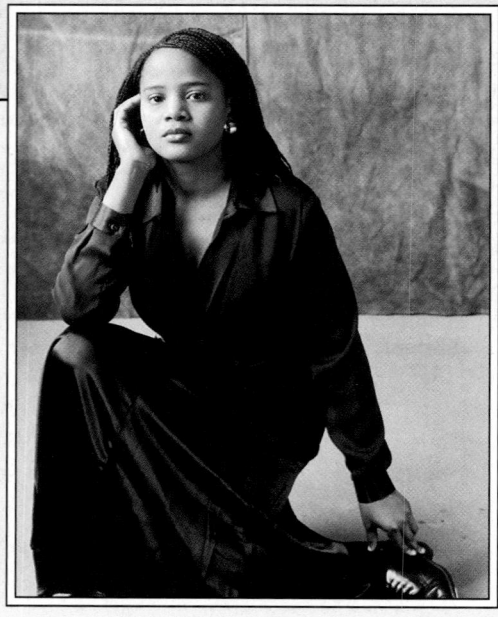

MEET EDWIDGE DANTICAT

Born in Haiti, Edwidge Danticat (ed wēj´ dän tē kä´) was only two when her father immigrated to New York City and four when her mother followed. Her parents planned to work hard, save money, and then send for their children. Meanwhile, Danticat was raised by her aunt in a poor neighborhood of the Haitian capital, Port-au-Prince. During her childhood, Danticat asked for a number of gifts from her mother in America, and her mother did her best to oblige. Many of the presents never arrived, including a Barbie doll, gold earrings, and a gold chain. But one gift did reach her—a manual typewriter with black and red ribbons. A writer's career was underway.

"I write to unearth all those things that scare me, to reach those places in my soul that may seem remote and dark to others."

—Edwidge Danticat

Haitian Roots "While I was growing up, most of the writers I knew were either in hiding, missing, or dead," Danticat says. "We were living under the brutal Duvalier dictatorship in Haiti, and silence was the law of the land." Furthermore, writing was not considered a useful or proper career for a young woman. "Writing was as forbidden as dark rouge on the cheeks or a first date before eighteen," she once wrote. But Danticat, who had written her first story when she was nine, put her typewriter to good use. She typed letters for relatives and neighbors—and learned a lot about life in the process. "They would dictate their most intimate thoughts, forgetting that I was only ten years old."

Danticat was happily reunited with her parents in New York when she was twelve. At first, however, her new life in Brooklyn was an ordeal. Classmates teased her because of her clothing and called her a "boat person." Fluent only in Haitian Creole (based on French), she had to learn English as a second language. "It was like being a baby—learning everything for the first time," Danticat recalls.

Eight Million Stories Danticat excelled in high school and went on to major in French literature at Barnard College. She briefly considered a career in business but returned instead to her first love: the telling of stories. In 1993, when she was twenty-four, she received a master of fine arts degree from Brown University. Her first novel, *Breath, Eyes, Memory*, was published the following year. The story of a young Haitian girl who joins her mother in New York City, it echoes Danticat's own life story. The short-story collection *Krik? Krak!* followed the year after and was nominated for a National Book Award. Then, in 1998, Oprah Winfrey announced that she had selected *Breath, Eyes, Memory* for her book club. The novel became a number-one best seller, and its author became an instant celebrity.

Edwidge Danticat was born in 1969.

Literature Online Author Search For more about Edwidge Danticat, go to www.glencoe.com.

Connecting to the Story

In today's media-saturated world, you do not have to look very far to find news of people undergoing terrible hardship and suffering. Some pull through their ordeals; others are crushed by their experiences. As you read Danticat's story, think about the following questions:

- How do you deal with difficult or unpleasant memories?
- Why do bad experiences sometimes make a person stronger?

Building Background

"Nineteen Thirty-Seven" is set in Haiti in the 1950s or 1960s. Haiti is an impoverished Caribbean nation occupying the western third of the island of Hispaniola. The eastern part of the island makes up the Spanish-speaking Dominican Republic. The title of the story refers to a historical event that occurred in 1937. In that year, the Dominican dictator Rafael Trujillo authorized the massacre of thousands of Haitian immigrants, who had come across the border to work. Many of the victims fell on the banks of the Río Masacre (Massacre River), which separates the two countries.

Setting Purposes for Reading

Big Idea Extending and Remaking Traditions

In recent years, American authors from diverse backgrounds have infused literature with fresh subject matter and new approaches. As you read, notice what Danticat chooses to write about and how she approaches her subject.

Literary Element Magical Realism

Magical realism is a literary style in which the writer combines realistic settings, characters, dialogue, and other details with elements that are magical, supernatural, or fantastic. As you read, note how Danticat's narrative blends together the believable with the impossible.

- See Literary Terms Handbook, p. R10.

Reading Strategy Visualizing

"Nineteen Thirty-Seven" describes many extraordinary images and events. Using your imagination to picture these descriptions—a process known as **visualizing**—will help you better understand and remember the story. As you read, pause to visualize especially striking images or scenes that are difficult to figure out.

Reading Tip: "Watch" the Action Reading a story can be like watching a movie when you visualize the action.

- Notice the details: Authors often include precise physical information about people and places. Picture these as you read.
- Imagine the scene: How many characters are present? Where are they? What are they doing?

Vocabulary

grimace (gri′məs) v. to contort the face, especially to express pain or displeasure; p. 1315 *I saw him grimace after his poor performance.*

delirium (di lēr′ē əm) n. a temporary state of mental disturbance characterized by confusion and disorientation; p. 1319 *In her delirium, the old lady believed that she was a little girl again.*

console (kən sōl′) v. to comfort; to cheer; p. 1319 *Nothing could console Hong when her puppy died.*

rejuvenated (ri jōō′ və nāt′ əd) adj. restored to youthful vigor or appearance; renewed; p. 1320 *She appeared rejuvenated after her summer vacation.*

balmy (bä′ mē) adj. soothing; p. 1321 *A balmy spring breeze made us forget the long winter.*

Vocabulary Tip: Antonyms An antonym is a word that has the opposite meaning of another word. Note that antonyms are always the same part of speech.

Literature Online Interactive Literary Elements Handbook To review or learn more about the literary elements, go to www.glencoe.com.

INDIANA ACADEMIC STANDARDS (pages 1313–1323)

11.3.3 Analyze the ways in which...the author's style...achieve[s] ...aesthetic (artistic) purposes...

11.2 Develop [reading] strategies...

11.5.2 Write responses to literature that...support statements with evidence from the text...

NINETEEN THIRTY-SEVEN

Edwidge Danticat

My Madonna[1] cried. A miniature teardrop traveled down her white porcelain face, like dew on the tip of early morning grass. When I saw the tear I thought, surely, that my mother had died. I sat motionless observing the Madonna the whole day. It did not shed another tear. I remained in the rocking chair until it was nightfall, my bones aching from the thought of another trip to the prison in Port-au-Prince.[2] But, of course, I had to go.

The roads to the city were covered with sharp pebbles only half buried in the thick dust. I chose to go barefoot, as my mother had always done on her visits to the Massacre River, the river separating Haiti from the Spanish-speaking country that she had never allowed me to name because I had been born on the night that El Generalissimo, Dios Trujillo,[3] the honorable chief of state, had ordered the massacre of all Haitians living there.

The sun was just rising when I got to the capital. The first city person I saw was an old woman carrying a jar full of leeches.[4] Her gaze was glued to the Madonna tucked under my arm.

"May I see it?" she asked.

I held out the small statue that had been owned by my family ever since it was given to my great-great-great-grandmother Défilé by a French man who had kept her as a slave.

The old woman's index finger trembled as it moved toward the Madonna's head. She closed her eyes at the moment of contact, her wrists shaking.

"Where are you from?" she asked. She had layers of 'respectable' wrinkles on her face, the kind my mother might also have one day, if she has a chance to survive.

"I am from Ville Rose," I said, "the city of painters and poets, the coffee city, with beaches where the sand is either black or white, but never mixed together, where the fields are endless and sometimes the cows are yellow like cornmeal."

The woman put the jar of leeches under her arm to keep them out of the sun.

"You're here to see a prisoner?" she asked.

"Yes."

"I know where you can buy some very good food for this person."

---

1. A *Madonna* is a representation of the Virgin Mary, the mother of Jesus Christ.
2. The capital city and main port in Haiti is *Port-au-Prince* (port´ ō prins´).
3. General Rafael Leónidas *Trujillo* Molina (rä fä´ el lā ō´ nē däs trōō hē´ yō mō lē´ nä), the tyrannical dictator of the Dominican Republic from 1930 until his assassination in 1961, was responsible for the deaths of thousands of Haitians living in the Dominican Republic in 1937.

Literary Element Magical Realism *How do you react to the narrator's statement that the Madonna cried?*

---

4. *Leeches* are bloodsucking worms once thought to cure illness by sucking out "bad" blood.

She led me by the hand to a small alley where a girl was selling fried pork and plantains wrapped in brown paper. I bought some meat for my mother after asking the cook to fry it once more and then sprinkle it with spiced cabbage.

The yellow prison building was like a fort, as large and strong as in the days when it was used by the American marines[5] who had built it. The Americans taught us how to build prisons. By the end of the 1915 occupation, the police in the city really knew how to hold human beings trapped in cages, even women like Manman[6] who was accused of having wings of flame.

The prison yard was quiet as a cave when a young Haitian guard escorted me there to wait. The smell of the fried pork mixed with that of urine and excrement was almost unbearable. I sat on a pile of bricks, trying to keep the Madonna from sliding through my fingers. I dug my buttocks farther into the bricks, hoping perhaps that my body might sink down to the ground and disappear before my mother emerged as a ghost to greet me.

The other prisoners had not yet woken up. All the better, for I did not want to see them, these bone-thin women with shorn[7] heads, carrying clumps of their hair in their bare hands, as they sought the few rays of sunshine that they were allowed each day.

My mother had grown even thinner since the last time I had seen her. Her face looked like the gray of a late evening sky. These days, her skin barely clung to her bones, falling in layers, flaps, on her face and neck. The prison guards watched her more closely because they thought that the wrinkles resulted from her taking off her skin at night and then putting it back on in a hurry, before sunrise. This was why Manman's sentence had been extended to life. And when she died, her remains were to be burnt in the prison yard, to prevent her spirit from wandering into any young innocent bodies.

I held out the fried pork and plantains to her. She uncovered the food and took a peek before **grimacing,** as though the sight of the meat nauseated her. Still she took it and put it in a deep pocket in a very loose fitting white dress that she had made herself from the cloth that I had brought her on my last visit.

I said nothing. Ever since the morning of her arrest, I had not been able to say anything to her. It was as though I became mute the moment I stepped into the prison yard. Sometimes I wanted to speak, yet I was not able to open my mouth or raise my tongue. I wondered if she saw my struggle in my eyes.

Visual Vocabulary
A *plantain* (plan′ tən) is a starchy tropical fruit that resembles a banana.

She pointed at the Madonna in my hands, opening her arms to receive it. I quickly handed her the statue. She smiled. Her teeth were a dark red, as though caked with blood from the initial beating during her arrest. At times, she seemed happier to see the Madonna than she was to see me.

She rubbed the space under the Madonna's eyes, then tasted her fingertips, the way a person tests for salt in salt water.

"Has she cried?" Her voice was hoarse from lack of use. With every visit, it seemed to get worse and worse. I was afraid that one day, like me, she would not be able to say anything at all.

I nodded, raising my index finger to show that the Madonna had cried a single tear. She pressed the statue against her chest as if to reward the Madonna and then, suddenly, broke down and began sobbing herself.

I reached over and patted her back, the way one burps a baby. She continued to sob until a

---

5. Following years of political instability in Haiti, the United States *Marines* occupied the country from 1915 to 1934.
6. *Manman* (mä män′) is a Creole word meaning "mother."
7. *Shorn,* the past participle of *shear,* means "clipped" or "shaved."

Big Idea Extending and Remaking Traditions *What does this paragraph suggest about the Haitian government?*

Reading Strategy Visualizing *How are these wrinkles different from the "respectable" wrinkles that the old woman with the leeches had?*

Vocabulary

grimace (gri′məs) *v.* to contort the face, especially to express pain or displeasure guard came and nudged her, poking the barrel of his rifle into her side. She raised her head, keeping the Madonna lodged against her chest as she forced a brave smile.

"They have not treated me badly," she said. She smoothed her hands over her bald head, from her forehead to the back of her neck. The guards shaved her head every week. And before the women went to sleep, the guards made them throw tin cups of cold water at one another so that their bodies would not be able to muster up enough heat to grow those wings made of flames, fly away in the middle of the night, slip into the slumber of innocent children and steal their breath.

Manman pulled the meat and plantains out of her pocket and started eating a piece to fill the silence. Her normal ration of food in the prison was bread and water, which is why she was losing weight so rapidly.

"Sometimes the food you bring me, it lasts for months at a time," she said. "I chew it and swallow my saliva, then I put it away and then chew it again. It lasts a very long time this way."

A few of the other women prisoners walked out into the yard, their chins nearly touching their chests, their shaved heads sunk low on bowed necks. Some had large boils on their heads. One, drawn by the fresh smell of fried pork, came to sit near us and began pulling the scabs from the bruises on her scalp, a line of blood dripping down her back.

All of these women were here for the same reason. They were said to have been seen at night rising from the ground like birds on fire. A loved one, a friend, or a neighbor had accused them of causing the death of a child. A few other people agreeing with these stories was all that was needed to have them arrested. And sometimes even killed.

I remembered so clearly the day Manman was arrested. We were new to the city and had been

> *"Lougarou, witch, criminal!" they shouted.*

sleeping on a cot at a friend's house. The friend had a sick baby who was suffering with colic. Every once in a while, Manman would wake up to look after the child when the mother was so tired that she no longer heard her son's cries.

One morning when I woke up, Manman was gone. There was the sound of a crowd outside. When I rushed out I saw a group of people taking my mother away. Her face was bleeding from the pounding blows of rocks and sticks and the fists of strangers. She was being pulled along by two policemen, each tugging at one of her arms as she dragged her feet. The woman we had been staying with carried her dead son by the legs. The policemen made no efforts to stop the mob that was beating my mother.

"*Lougarou*,[8] witch, criminal!" they shouted.

I dashed into the street, trying to free Manman from the crowd. I wasn't even able to get near her.

I followed her cries to the prison. Her face was swollen to three times the size that it had been. She had to drag herself across the clay floor on her belly when I saw her in the prison cell. She was like a snake, someone with no bones left in her body. I was there watching when they shaved her head for the first time. At first I thought they were doing it so that the open gashes on her scalp could heal. Later, when I saw all the other women in the yard, I realized that they wanted to make them look like crows, like men.

Now, Manman sat with the Madonna pressed against her chest, her eyes staring ahead, as though she was looking into the future. She had never talked very much about the future. She had always believed more in the past.

When I was five years old, we went on a pilgrimage to the Massacre River, which I had

---

8. The Creole word *lougarou* (lo͞o ′ gä ro͞o ′) means "witch" or "a follower of evil."

Reading Strategy   Visualizing *Visualize the events described in this paragraph. Why is the mob beating the mother?*

Big Idea   Extending and Remaking Traditions *Why does the author include these details?*

Reading Strategy   Visualizing *How do you visualize the scene as the narrator and her mother are reunited?*

1937: Grandmother Told Me That the Massacre River Was Bloody, c. 1975.
Ernst Prophete. Oil on masonite, 20 x 24 in. Collection of Jonathan Demme.

expected to be still crimson with blood, but which was as clear as any water that I had ever seen. Manman had taken my hand and pushed it into the river, no farther than my wrist. When we dipped our hands, I thought that the dead would reach out and haul us in, but only our own faces stared back at us, one indistinguishable from the other.

With our hands in the water, Manman spoke to the sun. "Here is my child, Josephine. We were saved from the tomb of this river when she was still in my womb. You spared us both, her and me, from this river where I lost my mother."

My mother had escaped El Generalissimo's soldiers, leaving her own mother behind. From the Haitian side of the river, she could still see the soldiers chopping up *her* mother's body and throwing it into the river along with many others.

We went to the river many times as I was growing up. Every year my mother would invite a few more women who had also lost their mothers there.

Until we moved to the city, we went to the river every year on the first of November.[9] The women would all dress in white. My mother would hold my hand tightly as we walked toward the water. We were all daughters of that river,

9. On November 1, Haitians celebrate La Toussaint (lä tōō´ sän), or All Saints' Day, as a national holiday. The day is also a Roman Catholic holy day commemorating all Catholic saints.

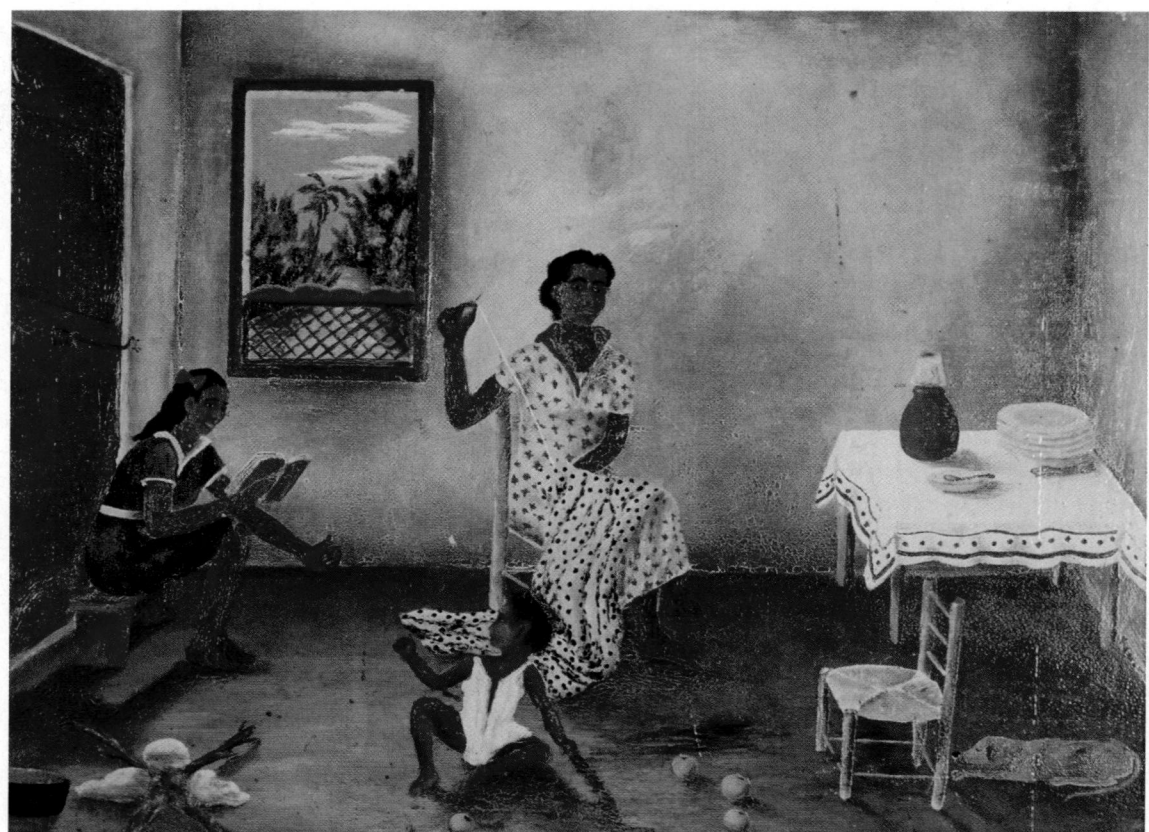

Family in Interior, date unknown. Poisson. Haitian Folk Art

which had taken our mothers from us. Our mothers were the ashes and we were the light. Our mothers were the embers and we were the sparks. Our mothers were the flames and we were the blaze. We came from the bottom of that river where the blood never stops flowing, where my mother's dive toward life—her swim among all those bodies slaughtered in flight—gave her those wings of flames. The river was the place where it had all begun.

"At least I gave birth to my daughter on the night that my mother was taken from me," she would say. "At least you came out at the right moment to take my mother's place."

Now in the prison yard, my mother was trying to avoid the eyes of the guard peering down at her.

"One day I will tell you the secret of how the Madonna cries," she said.

I reached over and touched the scabs on her fingers. She handed me back the Madonna.

I know how the Madonna cries. I have watched from hiding how my mother plans weeks in advance for it to happen. She would put a thin layer of wax and oil in the hollow space of the Madonna's eyes and when the wax melted, the oil would roll down the little face shedding a more perfect tear than either she and I could ever cry.

"You go. Let me watch you leave," she said, sitting stiffly.

I kissed her on the cheek and tried to embrace her, but she quickly pushed me away.

"You will please visit me again soon," she said.

I nodded my head yes.

"Let your flight be joyful," she said, "and mine too."

I nodded and then ran out of the yard, fleeing before I could flood the front of my dress with my tears. There had been too much crying already.

Big Idea Extending and Remaking Traditions *In making so many references to light and fire, what is the narrator suggesting about these women?*

Literary Element Magical Realism *If Josephine knows that the tears are not real, why does she still think that they are important?*

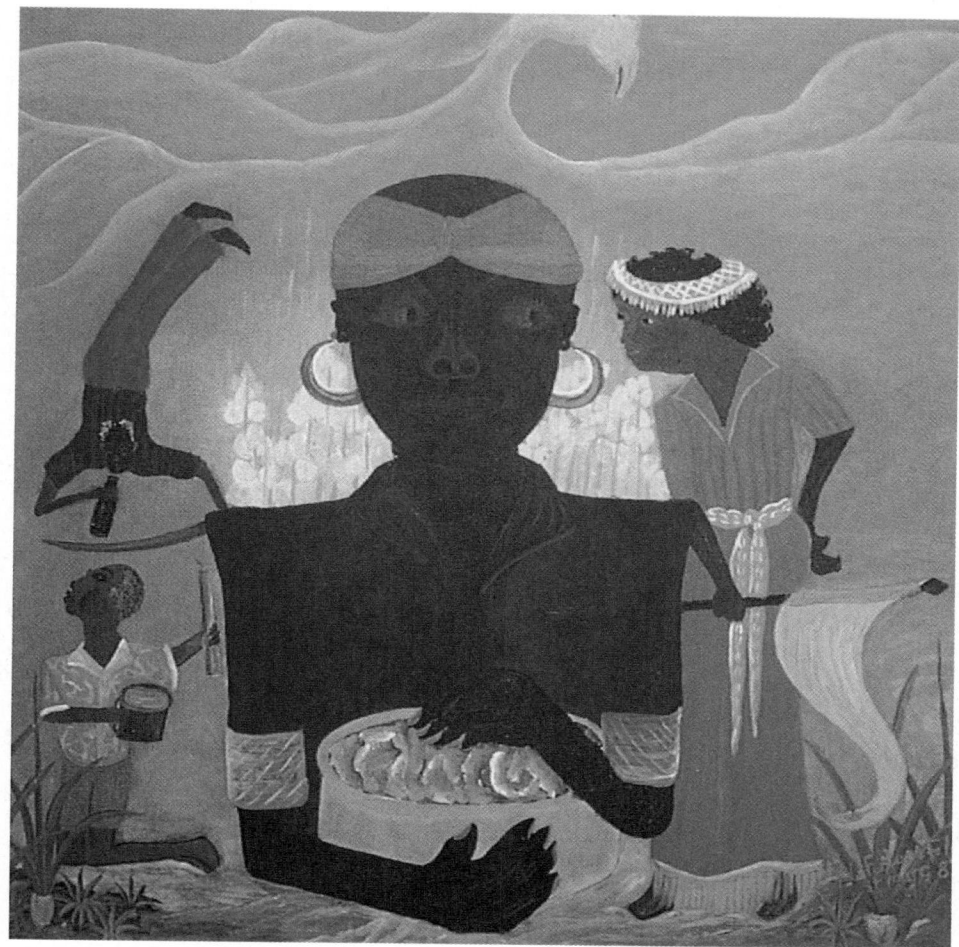

The Phoenix, 1985. Lafortune Félix. Yale University Art Gallery, New Haven, CT. Gift of Selden Rodman.

Viewing the Art: What connections can you make between the images in this painting and the images evoked by the river scenes in "Nineteen Thirty-Seven"?

The guard was looking directly at us. Manman still had a fever that made her body tremble. Her eyes had the look of **delirium.**

"Keep the Madonna when I am gone," she said. "When I am completely gone, maybe you will have someone to take my place. Maybe you will have a person. Maybe you will have some *flesh* to **console** you. But if you don't, you will always have the Madonna."

"Manman, did you fly?" I asked her.

She did not even blink at my implied accusation.

"Oh, now you talk," she said, "when I am nearly gone. Perhaps you don't remember. All the women who came with us to the river, they could go to the moon and back if that is what they wanted."

⎯

A week later, almost to the same day, an old woman stopped by my house in Ville Rose on her way to Port-au-Prince. She came in the middle of the night, wearing the same white dress that the women usually wore on their trips to dip their hands in the river.

Reading Strategy Visualizing *What does the image of a white-clad woman in the night suggest?*

⎯

Manman had a cough the next time I visited her. She sat in a corner of the yard, and as she trembled in the sun, she clung to the Madonna.

"The sun can no longer warm God's creatures," she said. "What has this world come to when the sun can no longer warm God's creatures?"

I wanted to wrap my body around hers, but I knew she would not let me.

"God only knows what I have got under my skin from being here. I may die of tuberculosis, or perhaps there are worms right now eating me inside."

⎯

When I went again, I decided that I would talk. Even if the words made no sense, I would try to say something to her. But before I could even say hello, she was crying. When I handed her the Madonna, she did not want to take it.

Vocabulary

delirium (di lēr′ ē əm) *n.* a temporary state of mental disturbance characterized by confusion and disorientation
console (kən sōl′) *v.* to comfort; to cheer

"Sister," the old woman said from the doorway. "I have come for you."

"I don't know you," I said.

"You *do* know me," she said. "My name is Jacqueline. I have been to the river with you."

I had been by the river with many people. I remembered a Jacqueline who went on the trips with us, but I was not sure this was the same woman. If she were really from the river, she would know. She would know all the things that my mother had said to the sun as we sat with our hands dipped in the water, questioning each other, making up codes and disciplines by which we could always know who the other daughters of the river were.

"Who are you?" I asked her.

"I am a child of that place," she answered. "I come from that long trail of blood."

"Where are you going?"

"I am walking into the dawn."

"Who are you?"

"I am the first daughter of the first star."

"Where do you drink when you're thirsty?"

"I drink the tears from the Madonna's eyes."

"And if not there?"

"I drink the dew."

"And if you can't find dew?"

"I drink from the rain before it falls."

"If you can't drink there?"

"I drink from the turtle's hide."

"How did you find your way to me?"

"By the light of the mermaid's comb."

"Where does your mother come from?"

"Thunderbolts, lightning, and all things that soar."

"Who are you?"

"I am the flame, and the spark by which my mother lived."

"Where do you come from?"

"I come from the puddle of that river."

"Speak to me."

"You hear my mother who speaks through me. She is the shadow that follows my shadow. The flame at the tip of my candle. The ripple in the stream where I wash my face. Yes. I will eat my tongue if ever I whisper that name, the name of that place across the river that took my mother from me."

I knew then that she had been with us, for she knew all the answers to the questions I asked.

"I think you do know who I am," she said, staring deeply into the pupils of my eyes. "I know who *you* are. You are Josephine. And your mother knew how to make the Madonna cry."

I let Jacqueline into the house. I offered her a seat in the rocking chair, gave her a piece of hard bread and a cup of cold coffee.

"Sister, I do not want to be the one to tell you," she said, "but your mother is dead. If she is not dead now, then she will be when we get to Port-au-Prince. Her blood calls to me from the ground. Will you go with me to see her? Let us go to see her."

We took a mule for most of the trip. Jacqueline was not strong enough to make the whole journey on foot. I brought the Madonna with me, and Jacqueline took a small bundle with some black rags in it.

When we got to the city, we went directly to the prison gates. Jacqueline whispered Manman's name to a guard and waited for a response.

"She will be ready for burning this afternoon," the guard said.

My blood froze inside me. I lowered my head as the news sank in.

"Surely, it is not that much a surprise," Jacqueline said, stroking my shoulder. She had become **rejuvenated,** as though strengthened by the correctness of her prediction.

"We only want to visit her cell," Jacqueline said to the guard. "We hope to take her personal things away."

The guard seemed too tired to argue, or perhaps he saw in Jacqueline's face traces of some long-dead female relative whom he had not done enough to please while she was still alive.

He took us to the cell where my mother had spent the last year. Jacqueline entered first, and then I followed. The room felt damp, the clay breaking into small muddy chunks under our feet.

I inhaled deeply to keep my lungs from aching. Jacqueline said nothing as she carefully walked

---

Literary Element Magical Realism *What elements of magical realism does this paragraph contain?*

Vocabulary

rejuvenated (ri jōō′ və nāt′ əd) *adj.* restored to youthful vigor or appearance; renewed around the women who sat like statues in different corners of the cell. There were six of them. They kept their arms close to their bodies, like angels hiding their wings. In the middle of the cell was an arrangement of sand and pebbles in the shape of a cross for my mother. Each woman was either wearing or holding something that had belonged to her.

One of them clutched a pillow as she stared at the Madonna. The woman was wearing my mother's dress, the large white dress that had become like a tent on Manman.

I walked over to her and asked, "What happened?"

"Beaten down in the middle of the yard," she whispered.

"Like a dog," said another woman.

"Her skin, it was too loose," said the woman wearing my mother's dress. "They said prison could not cure her."

The woman reached inside my mother's dress pocket and pulled out a handful of chewed pork and handed it to me. I motioned her hand away.

"No no, I would rather not."

She then gave me the pillow, my mother's pillow. It was open, half filled with my mother's hair. Each time they shaved her head, my mother had kept the hair for her pillow. I hugged the pillow against my chest, feeling some of the hair rising in clouds of dark dust into my nostrils.

Jacqueline took a long piece of black cloth[10] out of her bundle and wrapped it around her belly.

"Sister," she said, "life is never lost, another one always comes up to replace the last. Will you come watch when they burn the body?"

"What would be the use?" I said.

"They will make these women watch, and we can keep them company."

When Jacqueline took my hand, her fingers felt **balmy** and warm against the lifelines in my palm. For a brief second, I saw nothing but black. And then I *saw* the crystal glow of the river as we had seen it every year when my mother dipped my hand in it.

"I would go," I said, "if I knew the truth, whether a woman can fly."

"Why did you not ever ask your mother," Jacqueline said, "if she knew how to fly?"

Then the story came back to me as my mother had often told it. On that day so long ago, in the year nineteen hundred and thirty-seven, in the Massacre River, my mother did fly. Weighted down by my body inside hers, she leaped from Dominican soil into the water, and out again on the Haitian side of the river. She glowed red when she came out, blood clinging to her skin, which at that moment looked as though it were in flames.

In the prison yard, I held the Madonna tightly against my chest, so close that I could smell my mother's scent on the statue. When Jacqueline and I stepped out into the yard to wait for the burning, I raised my head toward the sun thinking, One day I may just see my mother there.

"Let her flight be joyful," I said to Jacqueline. "And mine and yours too." ❧

---

10. The tying of a *black cloth* in this manner is a sign of mourning that precedes weeping for the deceased.

RESPONDING AND THINKING CRITICALLY

Respond

1. Which part of the story elicited the strongest reaction from you? Explain.

Recall and Interpret

2. (a)Why are Josephine's mother and the other women in prison? (b)What do the charges against them, and the treatment they receive, tell you about the society in which they live?

3. (a)What happened at the Massacre River the year Josephine was born? (b)What meaning do you think the river holds for the women? Explain your answer by using details from the story.

4. (a)Why does the Madonna cry, according to Josephine? (b)Given Josephine's explanation, how would you explain the event described in the first paragraph of the story? Explain what these details contribute to the **mood,** or atmosphere, of the story.

5. Describe Josephine's last visit with her mother. In your opinion, what does the mother mean when she says that the women who went to the river

"could go to the moon and back if that is what they wanted"? Explain.

Analyze and Evaluate

6. How would you define the relationship between Josephine and her mother? Describe a detail or incident from the story that reveals this relationship.

7. (a)How does Danticat prepare the reader for the mother's death? (b)Do you think the story would have been as effective if the mother had remained alive? Support your answer.

8. Why do you think Danticat entitled the story "Nineteen Thirty-Seven"? Explain what the title may suggest about the significance of the events described in the story.

9. Does this story seem tragic or uplifting to you? Explain your answer.

Connect

10. **Big Idea** Extending and Remaking Traditions What innovations in subject matter and literary technique does Danticat bring to this story? Explain.

LITERARY ANALYSIS

Literary Element Magical Realism

Throughout her story, Danticat refers to supernatural events in an otherwise painfully realistic narrative. For example, the narrator's suggestion that certain women could fly with "wings of flame" implies a magical quality about characters whose lives have otherwise been filled with horrible realities.

1. What are other references to magical, supernatural, or bizarre events in "Nineteen Thirty-Seven"?

2. Which events does the narrator find ordinary explanations for? Which does she present as magical?

Review: Style

As you learned in Unit 5, word choice, the length and arrangement of sentences, and the use of figurative language and imagery all contribute to an author's individual **style.**

Partner Activity With a partner, choose a passage from "Nineteen Thirty-Seven" that you think is a good example of the author's style. Using a chart like the one shown, analyze the textual elements that contribute to the style. In a paragraph, describe the style. Compare your analysis with that of another pair.

Text Elements	Contribution to Style
sentence length	

Reading Strategy Visualizing

Many successful movies have been based upon works of fiction, in part because the original story or novel provided precise visual descriptions of characters and settings. For scenes and people not fully described, the film's director and director of photography use their imaginations to fill in the missing details.

1. If you were directing a film of "Nineteen Thirty-Seven," how would Josephine's mother appear?

2. Imagine that you are creating a poster for a movie of "Nineteen Thirty-Seven." What striking scene, character, or image would your poster feature? Describe your poster in detail.

Vocabulary Practice

Practice with Antonyms Choose the best antonym for each vocabulary word.

1. **grimace**
   a. sad
   b. happy
   c. smile
   d. scowl

2. **delirium**
   a. sanity
   b. crazy
   c. intelligence
   d. clever

3. **console**
   a. refresh
   b. gloomy
   c. sorrow
   d. depress

Academic Vocabulary

Here are two words from the vocabulary list on page R86.

interact (in´tər akt´) *v.i.* to act upon one another

process (pro´ses) *n.* a series of actions

Practice and Apply

1. From the way in which they **interact,** what do you infer about the relationship between Josephine and the old woman?

2. What **process** must Josephine follow to see her mother?

Writing About Literature

Respond to Style How did you respond to the powerful style of Edwidge Danticat, which is characterized by sometimes gruesome imagery and a mixture of magic and reality? Would you like to read other works by Danticat? Write a brief essay giving your answers to these questions. Support your opinions with specific examples and quotes from the story.

It may be that your opinion does not rest firmly on one side or the other. In that case, assess your ideas with a seesaw organizer like the one below. Use the notes from your organizer to help you construct your argument when you begin to write.

After completing your draft, work with a partner to evaluate each other's work. Suggest revisions. Finally, proofread and edit your draft for errors in spelling, grammar, and punctuation.

READING FURTHER

If you would like to read more by Edwidge Danticat, you may enjoy these works:

Novels: *Breath, Eyes, Memory*, the account of a young Haitian woman caught between two cultures. *The Farming of Bones*, a story set during the 1937 massacre of Haitian workers in the Dominican Republic and its long, bitter aftermath. *Behind the Mountains*, in which a Haitian family struggles to adjust to life in the United States.

Short Stories: *Krik? Krak!*, a collection of engaging scenes from Haitian life.

Nonfiction: *After the Dance: A Walk Through Carnival in Jacmel, Haiti*, Danticat's first-hand account of Haiti's boisterous carnival celebrations.

Literature Online **Web Activities** For eFlashcards, Selection Quick Checks, and other Web activities, go to www.glencoe.com.

The Man with the Saxophone

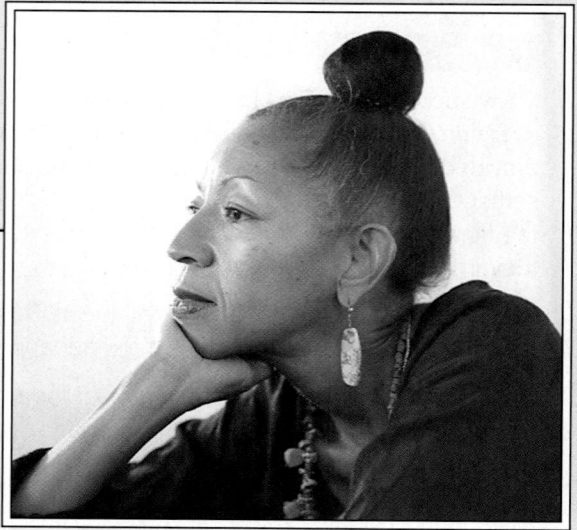

MEET AI

Ai uses her given middle name as her pen name. She also fiercely claims that it is the only name by which she should be known. She grew up as Florence Anthony; her last name, she learned as an adult, was that of her stepfather and not of her father by blood. Her genetic father was Japanese, and the name *Ai* means "love" in that language.

A Young Poet Ai was born in Albany, Texas. Her family was very poor and moved often. As a child, Ai lived not only in Texas, but also in Tucson, Arizona; San Francisco and Los Angeles, California; and Las Vegas, Nevada. When she was fourteen, she lived in Los Angeles. At school she saw an ad for a local poetry contest. She composed a poem, but before she could enter the contest, her family moved to Tucson. In spite of that disappointment, Ai found that writing poetry suited her. She continued composing poems, and later said, "As I grew older I realized that poetry offered a way to express things that I couldn't do otherwise."

Ai went to college at the University of Arizona. There she majored in Japanese and was also a very serious student of Buddhism. Then she went on to get a master's degree in fine arts from the University of California. Ai had her first book of poetry published two years later, in 1973. She's been writing and teaching writing ever since.

A Distinctive Style Almost all of Ai's poems are dramatic monologues—writing told from the first-person point of view. Most of her poems feature the voices of unnamed, imaginary characters. However, some of her poems use the voices of famous historical figures or celebrities, including President John F. Kennedy, movie star Marilyn Monroe, rock star Elvis Presley, and movie director Alfred Hitchcock.

Ai relies on biographies for information when she wants to write in the voice of a real person.

However, fictional speakers take even more work. Ai fleshes out all of her characters fully in her head before beginning to write. For each individual character she says, "I've got to know what kind of person he or she is. What are they doing? What would they wear? What colors do they like?" Once she has a clear picture of a character, she can start crafting a poem in that voice. About this process, Ai has said, "Every time I write a poem, I'm someone else without actually being that person. . . . It's really great."

> *"I'm irrevocably tied to the lives of all people, both in and out of time."*
>
> —Ai

Readers and critics have sometimes tried to peg Ai as an African American poet. However, Ai refuses to be labeled. She points out that she's part African American, part Japanese, part Choctaw, part Cheyenne, part Irish, and part Dutch. She says that she lets any and all of her characters speak, "regardless of sex, race, creed, or color." In summary, she says, "I'm simply a writer. I don't want to be catalogued and my characters don't want to be catalogued and my poems don't want to be catalogued. If a poet's work isn't universal, then what good is it?"

Ai was born in 1947.

Literature Online **Author Search** For more about Ai, go to www.glencoe.com.

Connecting to the Poem

Some people, like the speaker in the poem "The Man with the Saxophone," like to be out and about in the quiet of the early morning. In addition to liking early morning, the speaker also likes being alone. As you read the poem, think about the following questions:

- What associations do you have with early morning?
- What does it feel like to be alone?
- What can make a chance meeting with a stranger a pleasant experience? An unpleasant experience?

Building Background

"The Man with the Saxophone" is set in New York City on the streets of Manhattan. Most Manhattan streets are laid out in a grid pattern; the north-south streets are numbered avenues. First Avenue is to the east and Tenth Avenue is to the west. The east-west streets are numbered streets. The higher the number, the farther north the street. The speaker in "The Man with the Saxophone" is walking south on Fifth Avenue.

Setting Purposes for Reading

Big Idea Extending and Remaking Traditions

Poems that present dramatic monologues have long been part of the American literary tradition. The speaker in Edgar Allan Poe's "The Raven" narrates an encounter with an eerie bird. In Edgar Lee Masters's "Lucinda Matlock," the speaker relates the experiences of her long happy life. The speaker in Robert Frost's "Acquainted with the Night" tells of late-night isolation. As you read, consider how "The Man with the Saxophone" extends or remakes that tradition.

Literary Element Narrative Poetry

A **narrative poem** is a poem that tells a story. Like other stories, narrative poems have a plot, a setting, and characters. As you read "The Man with the Saxophone," take note of the exposition, the rising action, the climax, and the falling action of the plot.

- See Literary Terms Handbook, p. R12.

Reading Strategy Connecting to Cultural Context

The setting of "The Man with the Saxophone" is Manhattan, and the characters are musicians. Both elements help provide a cultural context for this poem. As you read the poem, note other aspects of culture that may relate to the poet's message.

Reading Tip: Asking Questions To connect with some of the cultural aspects of the poem, ask yourself questions such as the following:

- Have you ever been in a large city like the one described in the poem?
- Do you know anyone who is like the speaker? Like the man with the saxophone?

Vocabulary

amble (am′ bəl) v. to walk at a leisurely pace; to stroll; p. 1326 *On window-shopping trips, my friends amble from one downtown store to the next, looking for unusual gifts.*

solitude (sol′ e tōōd′) n. the state of being alone; p. 1326 *After attending meetings all day, a quiet walk brought me much-needed solitude.*

unencumbered (ən in kəm′ bərd) adj. unhindered; unburdened; p. 1327 *I took off my heavy backpack and, unencumbered, danced down the empty hallway.*

Vocabulary Tip: Word Parts Understanding word parts can help you decipher the meaning of unfamiliar words. Identify the different word parts in the vocabulary terms, and use a dictionary to find their meanings.

Literature Online Interactive Literary Elements Handbook To review or learn more about the literary elements, go to www.glencoe.com.

INDIANA ACADEMIC STANDARDS (pages 1325–1328)

11.3.4 Analyze...poetry...

11.7.20 Recite poems...with attention to performance details to achieve clarity, force, and aesthetic effect...

11.3.5 Analyze or evaluate works of literary or cultural significance...that...shed light on the seminal...social, political, or ethical ideas of their time.

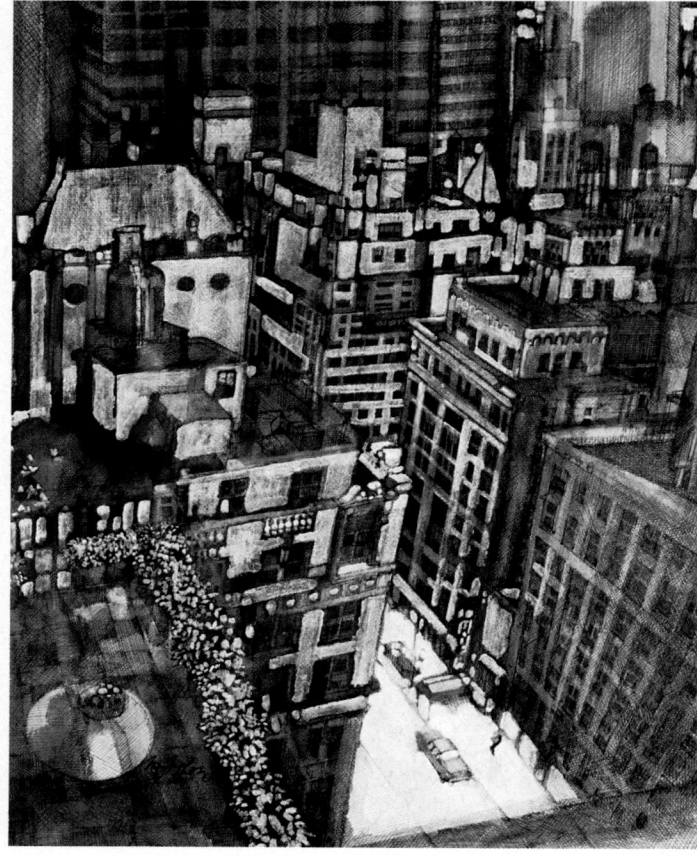

New York Buildings at Night. Franklin McMahon.

New York. Five A.M.
The sidewalks empty.
Only the steam
pouring from the manhole covers[1] seems alive,
5   as I **amble** from shop window to shop window,
sometimes stopping to stare, sometimes not.
Last week's snow is brittle now
and unrecognizable as the soft, white hair
that bearded the face of the city.
10   I head farther down Fifth Avenue
toward the thirties,[2]
my mind empty[3]
like the Buddhists tell you is possible
if only you don't try.
15   If only I could
turn myself into a bird
like the shaman[4] I was meant to be,
but I can't,
I'm earthbound
20   and **solitude** is my companion,
the only one you can count on.
Don't, don't try to tell me otherwise.
I've had it all and lost it
and I never want it back,
25   only give me this morning to keep,
the city asleep

1. You might observe *steam pouring from manhole covers* on a cold day. Water vapor in the warm air rising from the sewer condenses as steam.
2. The phrase *toward the thirties* refers to the east-west streets in Manhattan, from 30th Street to 39th Street.
3. In line 12, *my mind empty* refers to a goal of Buddhism—to empty the mind through meditation.
4. A *shaman* is a priest in some tribal societies.

Literary Element Narrative Poetry *Does the speaker seem to have a definite destination? Explain.*

Reading Strategy Connecting to Cultural Context *What does the speaker's statement here tell you about his or her culture and goals? Name two or more things.*

Vocabulary

amble (am′ bəl) *v.* to walk at a leisurely pace; to stroll
solitude (sol′ e tood′) *n.* the state of being alone

The Man with the Saxophone

Ai

and there on the corner of Thirty-fourth and Fifth,
the man with the saxophone,
his fingerless gloves caked with grime,
30 his face also,
the layers of clothes welded to his skin.
I set down my case,
he steps backward
to let me know I'm welcome,
35 and we stand a few minutes
in the silence so complete
I think I must be somewhere else, not here,
not in this city, this heartland of pure noise.
Then he puts the sax to his lips again
40 and I raise mine.
I suck the air up from my diaphragm
and bend over into the cold, golden reed,[5]
waiting for the notes to come,
and when they do,
45 for that one moment,
I'm the **unencumbered** bird of my imagination,
rising only to fall back
toward concrete,
each note a black flower,
50 opening, mercifully opening
into the unforgiving new day.

---

5. The *reed* in the mouthpiece of a saxophone makes the vibrations
   that produce sound.

Literary Element   Narrative Poetry *If you had a graph showing
plot development, including exposition, rising action, climax, and falling action, where would you place these lines?*

Reading Strategy   Connecting to Cultural Context *Why do you
think the poet includes this explanation? In a different cultural context
what might stepping backward mean?*

Big Idea   Extending and Remaking Traditions *How does the
speaker's attitude seem new or surprising?*

Vocabulary

unencumbered (ən in kəm′ bərd) *adj.* unhindered; unburdened

RESPONDING AND THINKING CRITICALLY

Respond

1. Which aspects of this poem were easy for you to connect to? Which were harder to connect to?

Recall and Interpret

2. The poem is set in New York City. (a)What is the exact time? What time of year do you think it is? (b)Why do you think the speaker is out and about at this time?

3. (a)How does the speaker characterize the sound of the city, both normally and during the events of the poem? (b)How does this difference seem to affect the speaker?

4. (a)Summarize what happens in the poem. (b)Is this poem hopeful or despairing? Explain, referring to specific lines of the poem.

Analyze and Evaluate

5. Ai says that she aims for her poetry to illustrate transcendence, no matter what the characters in her poems go through. Do you think Ai met this goal with "The Man with the Saxophone"? Explain.

6. Ai uses many different images in this poem. (a)Which image do you think is the strongest? (b)What do you think makes this image strong?

7. The speaker of the poem says that "solitude is my companion, / the only one you can count on." What do you think he or she means by this statement? Do you agree?

Connect

8. **Big Idea** **Extending and Remaking Traditions** How does "The Man with the Saxophone" seem different from other narrative poems you have read?

Literary Element **Narrative Poetry**

Narrative poetry has all of the elements of other narrative fiction. This includes characters as well as plot. Both can be extremely important to the meaning and message of a narrative poem.

1. What problem does the speaker of the poem face that is key to the plot of the poem? How is the problem resolved?

2. How does Ai make Manhattan a character in the poem? Cite specific images or lines of the poem in your answer.

Performing

Dramatic Reading Poetry is meant to be heard. Read "The Man with the Saxophone" aloud to yourself several times. Figure out how you can use your voice, gestures, and props to make the poem come alive. Practice your dramatic reading of the poem and then perform it for the class.

Reading Strategy **Connecting to Cultural Context**

The urban setting of "The Man with the Saxophone" and the focus on music and musicians give this poem two very obvious contexts for culture. However, the poem also hints at other more subtle cultural contexts. Reread the poem, looking for other important aspects of culture. What other cultural connections does the poem make?

Vocabulary **Practice**

Practice with Word Parts Match each word part to its meaning or definition.

1. un-		**a.** alone
2. en-		**b.** hindrance or burden
3. -tude-		**c.** to cause to be
4. -cumber-		**d.** state or quality of
5. soli-		**e.** not

Literature Online **Web Activities** For eFlashcards, Selection Quick Checks, and other Web activities, go to www.glencoe.com.

Ending Poem

MEET ROSARIO MORALES AND AURORA LEVINS MORALES

Sometimes two or more writers collaborate on a single piece of literature. Rosario Morales and her daughter Aurora Levins Morales have created several works of literature together.

Early Family Life Rosario Morales was born in New York in 1930. After getting married, she and her husband, Ricardo Levins, moved to Puerto Rico, where Aurora was born in 1954. It was there that Rosario instilled in Aurora a love of reading and writing. Aurora gives her mother credit for teaching her to appreciate female writers, such as Virginia Woolf and Toni Morrison.

The family returned to the United States, where Richard worked at different universities, Rosario continued to write, and Aurora studied and wrote. This professional Jewish Puerto Rican family did not fit into most people's conceptions of what it meant to be Puerto Rican. Both mother and daughter shared a keen awareness of that fact.

Aurora once wrote, "I am new. History made me. My first language was spanglish." She did not see her own cultural heritage reflected in what she read. As a result, she often addresses issues of identity, culture, and racism.

> "Writers have to be leaders in their communities."
> —Aurora Levins Morales

Education While in college, Aurora moved to California to finish her education. There, she began to publish her work. During the 1990s, she received recognition and awards for her writing, including the Ardella Mills Prize for journalistic prose. Her writing has appeared in journals, magazines, and books.

In addition to her academic and writing work, Aurora speaks throughout the United States on social issues, such as the treatment of Puerto Ricans by other U.S. citizens. "The vast majority of the popular culture's portrayal of Puerto Ricans is extremely stereotyped and oppressive," she says.

A Family Matter Her work is her response to this problem. Her literary writing includes essays, poems, short stories, and multi-media plays, some of which have been published in anthologies, including *Cuentos: Stories by Latinas*.

When Aurora was a child, she and her mother shared their writing with each other, each providing feedback and encouragement. Later, this sharing took a more concrete form. A series of long-distance telephone conversations between mother and daughter developed into *Getting Home Alive*, which was published in 1986. This collection of fiction, poetry, diary entries, and essays explores the lives of two Puerto Rican women living separate lives in different cultures.

Rosario Morales was born in 1930.
Aurora Levins Morales was born in 1954.

Literature Online **Author Search** For more about Rosario Morales and Aurora Levins Morales, go to www.glencoe.com.

Connecting to the Poem

The following poem is a statement of identity created by two people. As you read the poem, think about the following questions:

- What determines who a person is?
- Can a person's identity be summed up in a single word or phrase?

Building Background

The speakers in "Ending Poem" celebrate a multicultural identity. They mention the Tainos, the indigenous people of Puerto Rico, or Boriquen, as it was called when Christopher Columbus arrived in 1493. The Spanish intermarried with the Tainos, as they did with the enslaved African people whom they brought to the island in the 1500s. As a result, most Puerto Ricans are *mestizos*—a blend of Taino, African, and Spanish. The speakers also mention *jibaros*, rural farmers of Puerto Rico. These rugged people appear often in Puerto Rican folklore, where they are portrayed as generous, loving, hardworking, and courageous.

Setting Purposes for Reading

Big Idea **Extending and Remaking Traditions**

As you read this poem, notice how the speakers refer to the traditions of the past.

Literary Element Motif

A **motif** is a significant word, phrase, description, idea, or other element that is repeated throughout a work and is related to the theme. As you read this poem, look for motifs and consider what they add to the meaning of the poem.

- See Literary Terms Handbook, p. R11.

Literature Online Interactive Literary Elements Handbook To review or learn more about the literary elements, go to www.glencoe.com.

Reading Strategy Making Generalizations

A **generalization** is a statement that may be true for a group, but there are always exceptions. To make a generalization, readers must look at details to find relationships that the writer suggests but does not state directly.

....

Reading Tip: Group Ideas Use a graphic organizer to record details you used to make generalizations.

Detail	Generalization
"My people didn't go to dinner parties."	

Vocabulary

diaspora (dī as′pər ə) *n.* the scattering of a people; p. 1331 *The war-torn country saw a diaspora of its artists and writers.*

shtetl (shte′təl) *n.* small Jewish town or community; p. 1331 *Jewish folktales often take place in a shtetl.*

ghetto (get′ō) *n.* neighborhood where a particular group of people are forced to live either by law, poverty, or social exclusion; p. 1331 *During World War II, Jews were forced to live in ghettos.*

....

Vocabulary Tip: Context Clues A word's context—the other words around it—often offer clues about its meaning.

INDIANA ACADEMIC STANDARDS (pages 1330–1333)
11.3.2 Analyze the way in which the...meaning of a selection represents a view or comment on life...
11.2 Develop [reading] strategies...

11.3.3 Analyze the ways in which...tone...achieve[s] specific... aesthetic (artistic) purposes...

Ending Poem

Kitchen with View of Viaduct, 1995. Elena Climent. Oil on canvas. Phoenix Art Museum, Arizona. Mr. and Mrs. Gene Lemon in honor of Clayton Kirking.

Rosario Morales and Aurora Levins Morales

I am what I am.
A child of the Americas.
A light-skinned mestiza of the Caribbean.
A child of many **diaspora,** *born into this continent at a crossroads.*
5   I am Puerto Rican. I am U.S. American.
I am New York Manhattan and the Bronx.
A mountain-born, country-bred, homegrown jíbara[1] child,
up from the **shtetl,** *a California Puerto Rican Jew*
A product of the New York **ghettos** I have never known.
10 *I am an immigrant*
and the daughter and granddaughter of immigrants.
We didn't know our forbears' names with a certainty.
They aren't written anywhere.
First names only or mija, negra, ne, honey, sugar, dear

15 I come from the dirt where the cane was grown.
My people didn't go to dinner parties. They weren't invited.
I am caribeña, island grown.
Spanish is in my flesh, ripples from my tongue, lodges in my hips,
the language of garlic and mangoes.

---

1. *jíbara:* peasant

Reading Strategy   Making Generalizations *What do these lines suggest about the way the speaker's forebears were treated?*

Vocabulary

diaspora (dī as′pər ə) *n.* the scattering of a people
shtetl (shte′təl) *n.* small Jewish town or community
ghetto (get′ō) *n.* neighborhood where a particular group of people are forced to live either by law, poverty, or social exclusion

20   *Boricua.²* As *Boricuas come from the isle of Manhattan.*
        I am of latinoamerica, rooted in the history of my continent.
        I speak from that body. Just brown and pink and full of drums inside.
        I am not African.
        Africa waters the roots of my tree, but I cannot return.
25   I am not Taína.
        I am a late leaf of that ancient tree,
        and my roots reach into the soil of two Americas.
        Taíno is in me, but there is no way back.

        I am not European, though I have dreamt of those cities.
30   *Each plate is different.*
        wood, clay, papier mâché, metals, basketry, a leaf, a coconut shell.
        Europe lives in me but I have no home there.

        The table has a cloth woven by one, dyed by another,
        embroidered by another still.
35   I am a child of many mothers.
        They have kept it all going

        All the civilizations erected on their backs.
        All the dinner parties given with their labor.

        We are new.
40   *They gave us life, kept us going,*
        brought us to where we are.
        Born at a crossroads.
        Come, lay that dishcloth down. Eat, dear, eat.
        History made us.
45   We will not eat ourselves up inside anymore.

        And we are whole.

---

2. *Boricua*: Puerto Rican

Literary Element   Motif *What underlying idea shown here is repeated several times during the poem?*

Big Idea   Extending and Remaking Traditions *How do these lines refer to the traditions of the past?*

RESPONDING AND THINKING CRITICALLY

Respond

1. (a)Which lines in the poem spoke most directly to you? (b)In what ways are the speakers' identities similar to your own? How are they different?

Recall and Interpret

2. (a)In the opening stanza, what does the speaker first say she is? (b)What attitude does the speaker seem to have toward her?

3. (a)What does the speaker say she is not? (b)What motive might she have for saying this?

4. (a)What does the speaker say her female ancestors did for her? (b)What examples illustrate this?

Analyze and Evaluate

5. How would you categorize the qualities that the speaker says that she has?

6. What is the speaker trying to express when she says "I am the child of many mothers"?

7. How do you interpret the final four lines of the poem?

Connect

8. Which traditions does the speaker view positively?

9. **Big Idea** **Extending and Remaking Traditions** What kinds of traditions does the speaker expect to remake?

LITERARY ANALYSIS

Literary Element **Motif**

Motifs appear in both literature and other art forms. A motif can emphasize important ideas and show the connections between different parts of a work.

1. What motifs appear in this poem?

2. What motif do you notice in the appearance of the poem, and why do you think the poets use it?

Review: Tone

Tone is the author's attitude toward the subject matter or the audience. Tone is conveyed through many elements, such as word choice, figures of speech, and imagery.

Partner Activity Meet with a classmate to discuss the authors' attitudes about their mixed heritage. How would you describe this tone? Working with your partner, create a web diagram. Fill it with details that you think create the tone of the poem.

READING AND VOCABULARY

Reading Strategy **Making Generalizations**

A large number of details may make it difficult to get an overall perspective. **Generalizations** help you see the larger picture.

1. According to this poem, what are some of the issues related to racial identity that immigrants face in the United States?

2. What other issues are identified in this poem?

Vocabulary **Practice**

Practice with Context Clues For each item below, identify which type of context clue helps you know the meaning of the underlined word: contrast, definition, or example.

1. Artists were able to move into *ghettos*, such as New York's Harlem and New Orleans's French Quarter.

2. Many connections were lost after the *diaspora*, or scattering, of families that emigrated.

3. Most families come from large cities, but my family came from a Polish *shtetl*.

Literature Online **Web Activities** For eFlashcards, Selection Quick Checks, and other Web activities, go to www.glencoe.com.

Writing Workshop

In this workshop, you will follow the stages of the writing process. At any stage, you may think of new ideas to include and better ways to express them. Feel free to return to earlier stages as you write.

Prewriting

- - - - - - - - - - - - - - -

Drafting

- - - - - - - - - - - - - - -

Revising

- - - - - - - - - - - - - - -

 Focus Lesson: Tone and Voice

Editing & Proofreading

 Focus Lesson: Pronoun-Antecedent Agreement

Presenting

- - - - - - - - - - - - - - -

Writing Models For models and other writing activities, go to www.glencoe.com.

ACADEMIC STANDARDS (pages 1334–1341)

11.5.9 Write...a persuasive essay...

11.5.6 Use varied and extended vocabulary, appropriate for specific forms and topics.

11.4.4 Structure ideas and arguments in a sustained and persuasive way...

Editorial

 Persuading Your Readers

"No witchcraft, no enemy action, had silenced the rebirth of new life in this stricken world. The people had done it themselves. This town does not actually exist, but it might easily have a thousand counterparts in America and elsewhere in the world. . . . A grim specter has crept upon us almost unnoticed, and this imagined tragedy may easily become a stark reality we all shall know."

—Rachel Carson, from *Silent Spring*

Connecting to Literature Persuasive writing urges the reader to accept an opinion or to take action. For example, in *Silent Spring*, Carson sounded an alarm about the use of deadly pesticides in our environment. To support her viewpoint, she gathered facts, told anecdotes, and employed a compelling tone. (For a review of persuasive strategies, see "The Rhetoric of Revolution" on pages 104–105.) To write a strong editorial, follow the goals and strategies featured below.

Rubric: Features of Editorial Writing

Goals	Strategies
To present a clearly stated opinion	☑ Present a well-focused thesis statement.
To engage the intended audience from start to finish	☑ Employ a logical tone and a consistent voice.
To provide a well-supported opinion	☑ Support opinions with reasons, facts, anecdotes, examples, and other evidence. Provide sound counterarguments.
To convince an audience that your viewpoint is correct	☑ Use rhetorical devices—appeals to logic, ethics, and emotion. Also use connotative language effectively.

> **Assignment**
>
> Write an editorial for your school newspaper that explains your opinion about an issue related to technology. As you move through the stages of the writing process, keep your audience and purpose in mind.
>
> ---
>
> **Audience:** classmates, teachers, and other readers of the school newspaper
>
> **Purpose:** to persuade readers that your opinion about technology is valid

Analyzing a Professional Model

In this newspaper editorial, Jeremy Blachman, a blogger, presents his outlook on Weblogs. *Blogs* are a shortened word for *Weblogs*—Web pages or online journals that often include personal viewpoints about a certain issue. As you read the editorial, notice how Blachman targets his likely readers—people who like to blog. Pay close attention to the comments in the margin. They point out features that you may want to include in your own editorial.

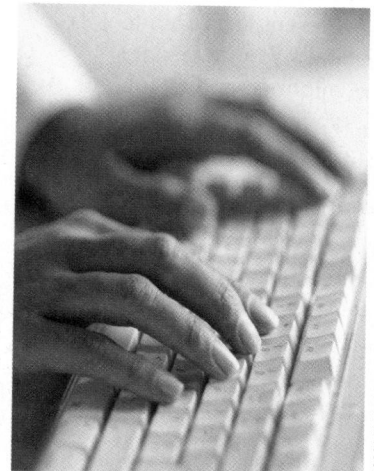

Job Posting: *The New York Times* by Jeremy Blachman

Last month, an associate beauty editor at a women's magazine was about to resign and take a job at a teen magazine, where she had been offered a similar position. Then the two magazines discovered she was blogging about work, and she lost both jobs. The women's magazine asked her to leave immediately; the teen magazine rescinded its offer.

It's understandable that the magazines would be angry about confidential information being posted on the Internet—internal financial reports, insider stock tips, studies disproving the women's magazine's recent claim that stress makes people fat.

Except the associate beauty editor wasn't posting anything like that. No, she wrote about the "magic little bags" she received at the office "stuffed with conditioner and moisturizer and lip gloss," and her addiction to perfume. But even these innocent revelations were apparently too much for the magazines to handle.

It's likely that I narrowly escaped the same fate as the associate beauty editor. This past December, I was publicly outed as the author of a Weblog called Anonymous Lawyer, where I post about life inside a corporate law firm. It's fiction, but many of the stories are inspired by events from the

Introduction

Engage your reader by using a hook, or strong opener. A hook can be a story, a quotation, a startling fact, or another attention grabber.

Counterarguments

Address opposing viewpoints and present counterarguments.

Voice

Use your own personal voice to connect with your readers and appeal to their emotions.

Thesis Statement

Lead up smoothly and logically to your thesis and state it clearly.

Facts and Examples

Present facts both to keep your audience informed and to support your argument.

Counterarguments

Point out the weaknesses or drawbacks of an opposing viewpoint and present a counterargument.

Connotations

Consider the connotations of the words you choose. For example, the word *honest* appeals to the reader's sense of ethics.

summer I spent at a law firm between my second and third years of law school. Had the firm discovered the blog while I was there, I'm guessing they would have fired me. And under current law, they would have had every right to, no matter that I wasn't writing about real people, real cases or anything that would expose the firm to liability.

Given my own blogging experience, I feel that the natural argument for me to make would be that employers shouldn't be able to fire bloggers simply for having a blog, and that the law should protect us.

But when it comes to keeping your job—at least in the private sector—the law hardly protects anyone. You can be fired for being ugly, you can be fired for being left-handed, you can be fired for something you say to your secretary. And if you can be fired for something you say to your own secretary, it seems silly to say you shouldn't be able to be fired for something you post on the Internet for everyone else's secretary to read.

Besides, there are good reasons employers might want to fire people with Weblogs. Surely it's not great for the work environment if your boss finds out that you are telling the world what a jerk he is. If you're revealing trade secrets or confidential information, clearly your employer has a right to be upset. Even if you are writing innocent content, the mere fact that there's an employee in the ranks who is communicating something to a larger audience can be legitimately scary to companies that are used to controlling the information that gets out.

But here's the problem: Weblogs are worth protecting. It used to be that if you wanted to know what it was like to work for a law firm or a beauty magazine, you had to have a friend on the inside. But now that everyone can publish online, we can get these incredible glimpses into worlds we might otherwise never get to see. People across the world can share stories, commiserate and connect with each other. Potential employees can see beyond the marketing pitches.

If no one was reading, employers wouldn't be concerned. There's a demand for the first-person narratives people are writing about their jobs. There's nowhere else to go to create honest conversation about the working world.

So maybe it does make sense that the law should provide special protection for bloggers, because of the social benefits Weblogs provide. The simplest place to start would be to put the burden on employers to show actual harm, if they are firing someone because of her Weblog.

This would protect the kind of innocent revelations that bloggers like the associate beauty editor make on their sites, while still giving employers rights if their employees are revealing secrets, disclosing client and customer information or otherwise driving business away. In addition, companies should create Weblog policies that let employees know what management feels is off limits for public consumption.

In any case, blogs may not hurt companies as much as they fear. On Anonymous Lawyer, I paint a frightening picture of life at a law firm. People trip each other in the halls for fun, lawyers work from the hospital while giving birth and no one ever gets a weekend off. Yet a number of law students, not realizing that my blog is fiction, have assumed that the law firm I write about actually exists and have sent me résumés, wanting to work there. Maybe the truth wouldn't be as harmful as some of these employers think. Maybe it's O.K. to let people write about their jobs.

Or maybe it's just too risky for us to know that beauty editors get free nail polish.

Persuasion

Tone

Convey a thoughtful, logical tone throughout the editorial.

Conclusion

End your editorial memorably. Restate your thesis; write a clincher statement; or make a final logical, emotional, or ethical appeal.

Reading-Writing Connection Think about the writing techniques that you have just encountered and try them out in the editorial you write.

Prewriting

Choose an Issue and Gather Ideas Think of a technological issue that concerns you. Take a stand on the issue and consider opposing arguments that others might make against your position. Then work with a small group to develop a pro-and-con chart like the one shown:

Cell Phones in School

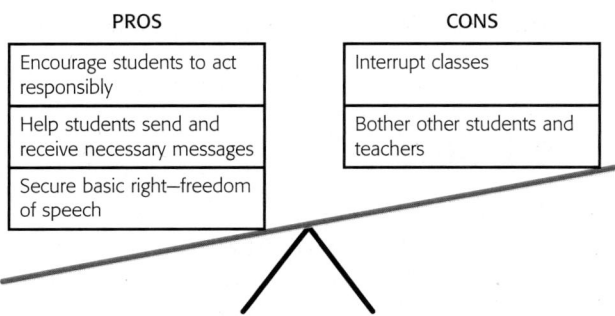

PROS

| Encourage students to act responsibly |
| Help students send and receive necessary messages |
| Secure basic right—freedom of speech |

CONS

| Interrupt classes |
| Bother other students and teachers |

What's the Scoop?

To explore topics, list current technology, such as the latest fads in cars, food manufacturing, or communications. For each topic, jot down any controversies you've heard, such as those related to energy, health, or privacy issues.

Map Out Your Editorial

Introduction
- Create interest.
- Introduce the topic.
- Narrow the topic.
- State the thesis.

Body Paragraph(s)
- Support your opinion.
- Respond to counterarguments.

Conclusion
- End memorably.

State Your Opinion Study your graphic organizer. Decide what you want to say about the issue. In most persuasive writing, a good way to organize an opinion statement or thesis is by using a sentence structure like this one:

_____ *should* _____
because _____.

However your thesis is structured, it should clearly state your opinion and concisely sum up the basic reasons for that opinion.

Talk About Your Ideas Meet with a partner. Read your opinion statement aloud. Then, briefly discuss the reasons for your opinion. As you do so, listen to your own voice. How do you sound as you discuss this topic? What makes you most excited or passionate as you explain your ideas? What specific words, what tone, and what kinds of sentences do you use to convey your opinion and feelings? To develop your writing voice, listen to your own speaking voice so that you can remember what you said and how you said it.

Make an Organizational Plan Outline your editorial by writing how you might begin, what main points you might address, where you might state your opinion, and how you might conclude.

▶ Focus on getting the reader's attention and state your thesis in the first paragraph. You might experiment with placing your thesis in another paragraph, but make sure the thesis does not disrupt the logical flow of ideas.

▶ Win your readers over by sounding logical. Contest opposing arguments as you build support for your own opinion. Present reasons, examples, anecdotes, facts, statistics, and other relevant details.

▶ Wrap up your editorial with a compelling conclusion.

Drafting

Let Your Ideas Flow Drafting is the time for transferring your ideas to sentences and paragraphs. As you write, don't get distracted by spelling, grammar, and punctuation errors you might make. Instead, focus on the single task of getting your words on the page in an order that makes sense.

Analyzing a Workshop Model

Here is a final draft of an editorial. Read the editorial and answer the questions in the margin. Use the answers to these questions to guide you as you write.

Introduction

How does this opening sentence create interest?

Appeals to Logic and Emotion

How does this anecdote, or little story, appeal to both logic and emotion?

Cell Phone Logic

Last week, Lauren Eckler at Madison High was suspended for breaking a rule—sneaking her cell phone into school. After her phone rang during Mr. Palmerino's seventh-period biology class, he sent her to the office. There Mrs. Wu promptly suspended Lauren for two days because it was her third offense.

Who was on the phone when Lauren's phone rang? It was her mother, asking Lauren to pick up her little brother after school. Mrs. Eckler was frantic. She had had an unexpected meeting and had been unable able to reach Lauren all day. Lauren's mother was worried that Lauren's little brother would be stranded after band practice.

It's understandable that Mr. Palmerino, or any other teacher, would not want his or her class interrupted. No one is arguing that students *shouldn't* turn their cell phones off during class. After all, a ringing phone doesn't bother just the teacher. Plenty of students at this school groan when somebody's phone rings at the wrong time. Just about everyone agrees that a phone shouldn't ring in class.

Nevertheless, the cell phone rule instituted at Madison High last fall should be changed. The current policy of asking students to "bank" their cell phones at the office before first period and to return them at the end of each day is an unfair rule and a huge waste of time for the office staff. This policy keeps students from getting important information during the day and robs them of their basic right to freedom of speech.

Students have a right to have cell phones. Like everyone else, students need to keep in touch with their families. They need to make plans with friends. Many also need to get or send messages to employers during the school day. If students had access to their phones, all of their calls could be made or received during many parts of the day, when students are not in class. For example, students could use their phones while changing class, eating lunch, and taking free periods. There might also be times when using a cell phone would be acceptable in the homeroom. Using the phone at these times would probably not bother anyone else. Students could get and receive messages without disturbing a class.

For this plan to work, students would need to learn to act responsibly. They would have to turn off their cell phones each time they entered a class. Teachers could help them develop this habit by reminding students at the beginning of each class—just as people say at plays, concerts, and other gatherings—"Please turn off your cell phones." Students at Madison High are mature enough to understand and follow that request.

Instead, under the current rules, students are being treated like children or prisoners. Students don't have the right to their own property during the day. They are not trusted to store their phones in their lockers or shut them off during class. They are denied the chance to send and receive important and necessary messages during the day. In a place where students are supposed to be learning how to act as mature adults, it is ironic that they are not even given the chance to learn how to use their cell phones responsibly.

For all these reasons, it's time to change the cell phone policy at Madison High. Students should be able to carry their own cell phones. They should be trusted to become responsible for using their phones, including shutting them off during classes. Most of all, students should be able to talk to their parents, to get messages for picking up their younger brothers or sisters, and to practice being reliable citizens.

Counterargument

How does the writer address the opposing viewpoint?

Thesis

What is the writer's opinion? How clearly is it stated?

Reasons, Facts, and Examples

What reasons, facts, and examples does the writer offer?

Tone

What is the writer's tone?

Connotations

Which words in this sentence pack an emotional punch?

Ethical and Emotional Appeals

What ethical and emotional appeals does the writer make?

Conclusion

How does the writer conclude? What makes the final paragraph effective?

Revising

Peer Review Ask a peer reviewer to read your editorial and to identify the opinion statement. Then ask your reviewer to comment on parts that seem most persuasive or effective and parts that seem least convincing. Have your reviewer explain comments by referring to the traits of strong writing.

Use the rubric below to evaluate your writing.

Rubric: Writing an Effective Editorial
☑ Do you state your opinion clearly in a thesis statement?
☑ Do you keep your audience interested from beginning to end?
☑ Do you use reasons, facts, examples and other evidence to support your opinion?
☑ Do you use a logical, thoughtful tone and a consistent voice?
☑ Do you use connotative language effectively?
☑ Do you give sound counterarguments?
☑ Do you include appeals to logic, ethics, or emotion?

▶ **Focus Lesson**

Tone and Voice

Tone refers to the emotions or attitude an author expresses in a piece of writing. For your own editorial writing, you probably want the tone to sound logical, respectful, and thoughtful. Tone contributes to your overall voice and style. **Voice** includes the unique way you use language that helps your readers sense the "real person" behind the words. Notice how the writer of "Cell Phone Logic" revised the tone and style.

Draft:

It's totally ridiculous for students not to have their cell phones. Like everyone else, they need to call home. They need to call their friends!!! The need to contact their place of employment also necessitates the use of a phone.

Revision:

Students have a right to have cell phones.[1] Like everyone else, students need to keep in touch with their families. They need to make plans with friends. Many also need to get or send messages to employers during the school day.[2]

    1: <u>Appropriate Tone</u>   **2:** <u>Consistent Tone and Voice</u>

Editing and Proofreading

Get It Right When you have completed the final draft of your essay, proofread for errors in grammar, usage, mechanics, and spelling. Refer to the Language Handbook, pages R46–R60, as a guide.

► **Focus Lesson**

Pronoun-Antecedent Agreement

A pronoun must agree in number and gender with its antecedent. If the **antecedent,** or word the pronoun refers to, is singular and masculine, (for example, *he*), the pronoun that refers to it must be singular and masculine, too (*his*).

Original:

Most of all, any student should be able to talk to their parents, to get messages for picking up their younger brothers or sisters, and to practice being reliable citizens.

Improved: Edit the sentence so that the pronoun (*their*) agrees with its antecedent.

Most of all, students should be able to talk to their parents, to get messages for picking up their younger brothers or sisters, and to practice being reliable citizens.

In the following sentence, the plural pronoun *their* does not agree with its singular antecedent *Everyone*.

Original:

Everyone would have to turn off their cell phones each time they entered a class.

Improved: Make both the pronoun and its antecedent plural.

They would have to turn off their cell phones each time they entered a class.

Presenting

Follow Models and Guidelines Newspapers usually have guidelines for the content of an editorial, including the writer's full name, address, and telephone number. Glance at the published letters in your school or local newspaper, check the format, and follow the guidelines for submitting letters. As always, neatly word-processed work, double-spaced and carefully proofread, is a plus.

E-mail Exchange

If possible, create a word-processing document of your editorial and e-mail it to a peer reviewer. Ask him or her to edit and proofread your document and then e-mail the corrected version to you.

Writer's Portfolio

Place a copy of your editorial in your portfolio to review later.

Speaking, Listening, and Viewing Workshop

Conducting a Debate

Types of Propositions

A **proposition of fact** states that something is or is not true, such as "Fast foods contribute to obesity."

A **proposition of value** expresses a judgment of a person, place, thing, idea, or event, such as, "Fast food presents a danger to the people of Madison."

A **proposition of policy** suggests a course of action, set of rules, or a law, such as, "The town of Madison should not allow any new fast-food restaurants."

A **proposition of problem** asks a question, such as, "What should public officials in Madison do about the problem of obesity?"

Connecting to Literature The accuracy and scientific validity of Rachel Carson's *Silent Spring* has stirred debate since it was first published in 1962. Nevertheless, the book caused a dramatic change in the way people think about the environment. One reason for this effect was Carson's persuasive skill. In this workshop, you will learn to how to present and defend your own opinions—as well as how to anticipate and respond to counterarguments—in a formal debate.

> **Assignment** Conduct a formal debate on the topic you presented in your editorial on technology.

Planning Your Presentation

When you wrote your editorial, you were persuading an audience of readers. When you debate, your goal is to persuade an audience of listeners.

A **debate** is a formal persuasive-speaking competition. To debate, you use some of the same skills that you have already developed to write persuasively. In addition, you must learn new skills, rules, and vocabulary specific to debating.

- Form a group of two, four, or six students. Read your editorials aloud. Choose one with particularly strong positive arguments (pros) and counterarguments (cons) to re-create as a debate.
- Develop a proposition based on the editorial. A **proposition** is a formal statement of an issue. A proposition is usually phrased like this: *Resolved: That the policy of confiscating cell phones at Madison High School should be stopped immediately.*
- Form two teams: **affirmative,** or those in favor of the proposition; and **negative,** or those against it.
- As separate teams, prepare your brief. A **brief** is a complete outline of the debate. It includes the following:
  - the proposition
  - the key ideas of the debate, in order of importance
  - arguments for and against each key idea
  - evidence (with sources cited) that supports each of your arguments and counters each of your opponent's arguments

Having a thorough brief will help prepare you for a successful debate. To win a debate, however, you must provide enough proof to establish your position and **refute,** or prove wrong, your opponent's position. When you refute, you do the following:

- challenge the quality or credibility of your opponent's evidence
- note where your opponent's evidence is insufficient, or lacking in quantity
- challenge the logic of your opponent's reasoning

Debate formats vary. In a typical, traditional formal debate, both sides make opening and closing **constructive speeches** of ten minutes each, in this order: first affirmative, first negative, second affirmative, second negative. After a short intermission, **rebuttal speeches** of five minutes each begin in the opposite order. The rebuttal gives you a chance to rebuild your case. Although you cannot introduce a new argument during the rebuttal, you can do the following:

- restate and expand your previous arguments
- offer more evidence and reasoning to counter objections your opponent has raised
- point out weaknesses in your opponent's arguments

Rehearsing

Review and rehearse the format (but not the specific content) of your debate as a group. Establish when each person will speak and how much time he or she will have.

As separate affirmative and negative teams, rehearse your opening and closing speeches and rebuttal speeches. As you rehearse, revise answers for wording that sounds most reasonable, and coach one another to speak in a tone appropriate to a formal debate. Avoid exaggerated emotion, sarcasm, or ridicule, and refrain from making personal attacks.

Techniques for Listening to a Debate

☑ **Keep an Open Mind** Try not to prejudge the speaker or the argument. Give all speakers and both sides of the argument equal and unbiased attention.

☑ **Listen Purposefully** In a debate, your purpose for listening is to identify the arguments and counterarguments and to judge their worth.

☑ **Take Notes** Note what the arguments are and how well you think that each was delivered, proved, or disproved.

☑ **Listen for Persuasive Devices** Separate logical, reasoned arguments from illogical arguments. Listen for and dismiss arguments that attack the person, arguments that reduce the topic to a case of false either-or reasoning, present false cause-and-effect relationships, and make false generalizations or overgeneralizations.

Go Online

Read, listen to, or view a real debate. Note that most debaters treat each other with respect. While viewing a debate, you might also note that debaters use good posture, listen thoughtfully, and speak carefully.

Record and Revise

Record your practice session. Are your words effective? Is your tone reasonable? Are your answers relevant, persuasive, and complete? Identify what you can improve.

Get the Ratings

Prepare a rating sheet for listeners to rate both your content and your delivery. See how you can improve in future debates.

ACADEMIC STANDARDS (pages 1342–1343)
11.7.1 Summarize a speaker's purpose and point of view and ask questions to draw interpretations of the speaker's content and attitude toward the subject.

11.7.3 Use various forms of logical arguments...

For Independent Reading

AS OPPORTUNITIES FOR WOMEN AND MINORITIES EXPANDED, AMERICAN literature from the 1950s on drew upon a wider range of experience than ever before. In their works, writers Harper Lee, Annie Dillard, and Amy Tan deal with topics such as racism, personal and generational change, and relationships with the natural world. Lee's only novel, *To Kill a Mockingbird*, was published during the Civil Rights Movement, and it brought to the forefront the racial inequalities and intolerance of the 1930s South. Amy Tan's novel *The Joy Luck Club* explores the differing values of two generations of Chinese women. The older generation, born in China and now living in the United States, clings to tradition. The younger generation, in a dilemma faced by many sons and daughters of immigrants, finds the old ways embarrassing. Both *To Kill a Mockingbird* and *The Joy Luck Club* were made into acclaimed films. Annie Dillard's *Pilgrim at Tinker Creek* is an introspective account of a year the author spent observing the life in and around a creek in the Blue Ridge Mountains of Virginia. In addition to its meticulous natural observations, *Pilgrim at Tinker Creek* also ruminates on the wonders of the natural world.

To Kill a Mockingbird

by Harper Lee (1960)

To Kill a Mockingbird weaves together the stories of Boo Radley, a misunderstood recluse, and Tom Robinson, an African American man arrested for rape. Atticus Finch defends Robinson, exposing in court the lies of his accusers, but an all-white jury convicts Robinson. Robinson tries to escape from jail and is killed. Later, one of the accusers, feeling he has been humiliated, attacks Finch's children. Boo Radley saves the pair. The book won a Pulitzer Prize in 1961.

Pilgrim at Tinker Creek

by Annie Dillard (1974)

Dillard's book is as much a meditation on spirituality as it is a piece of American nature writing. The nonfiction work details Dillard's explorations in her neighborhood near Roanoke, Virginia, over the course of a year, and her reflections about her findings. In chapter one, she writes: "I propose to keep here what Thoreau called 'a meteorological journal of the mind.'" As Dillard observes the birds, trees, frogs, flowers, and insects which inhabit the seasons on Tinker Creek, she ponders both nature's and God's purposes. The widely acclaimed book won a Pulitzer Prize for Nonfiction in 1975.

"*While we as readers grope to know whose mother or grandmother is getting married in an unfamiliar ceremony, or why a concubine is committing suicide, we are ironically being reminded not just of the nightmarishness of being a woman in traditional China, but of the enormity of the confusing mental journey Chinese emigrants had to make. And, most ironic, we are also reminded by these literary disjunctions that it is precisely this mental chasm that members of the younger generation must now recross in reverse in order to resolve themselves as whole Chinese-Americans; in "The Joy Luck Club" we get a suggestion of the attendant confusion they must expect to endure in order to get to the other side. . . . [Amy Tan] has written a jewel of a book.*"

—Orville Schell, *The New York Times*, 1989

The Joy Luck Club

by Amy Tan (1989)

This novel by first-generation Chinese American Amy Tan draws on her family history. In the novel, four female Chinese immigrants meet regularly to play mahjong, eat, gossip, raise money, and support one another. Skillfully interweaving the voices of the immigrant mothers and their Chinese American daughters, Tan confronts issues of gender, generation, culture, and family in this powerful and touching narrative.

From the Glencoe Literature Library

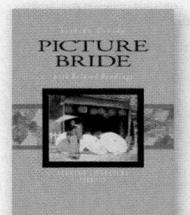

Picture Bride

by Yoshiko Uchida

A young woman leaves Japan for an arranged marriage in the United States, where she faces hard work, prejudice, and difficult circumstances with courage and dignity.

A Raisin in the Sun

by Lorraine Hansberry

The members of a poor African American family have conflicting ideas about how to spend a $10,000 insurance check.

Barrio Boy

by Ernesto Galarza

This autobiography tells the story of Galarza's youth in a Sacramento barrio, where his family moved to avoid the upheaval of the Mexican Revolution of 1910.

◼ Indiana Test Practice
Reading: Vocabulary, Comprehension, and Analysis

Carefully read the following two passages. Use context clues to help define any words with which you are unfamiliar. In each selection, pay close attention to the author's purpose, main idea, and uses of literary and rhetorical devices. Then, on a separate sheet of paper, answer the questions on page 1348.

from "Transfiguration" by Annie Dillard

line

One night a moth flew into the candle, was caught, burnt dry, and held. I must have been staring at the candle, or maybe I looked up when a shadow crossed my page; at any rate, I saw it all. A golden female moth, a biggish one with a two-inch wingspan, flapped into the fire, dropped her
5 abdomen into the wet wax, stuck, flamed, frazzled and fried in a second. Her moving wings ignited like tissue paper, enlarging the circle of light in the clearing and creating out of the darkness the sudden blue sleeves of my sweater, the green leaves of jewelweed by my side, the ragged red trunk of a pine. At once the light contracted again and the moth's wings vanished in
10 a fine, foul smoke. At the same time her six legs clawed, curled, blackened, and ceased, disappearing utterly. And her head jerked in spasms, making a spattering noise; her antennae crisped and burned away and her heaving mouth parts crackled like pistol fire. When it was all over, her head was, so far as I could determine, gone, gone the long way of her wings and legs.
15 Had she been new, or old? Had she mated and laid her eggs, had she done her work? All that was left was the glowing horn shell of her abdomen and thorax—a fraying, partially collapsed gold tube jammed upright in the candle's round pool.
   And then this moth-essence, this spectacular skeleton, began to act as
20 a wick. She kept burning. The wax rose in the moth's body from her soaking abdomen to her thorax to the jagged hole where her head should be, and widened into flame, a saffron-yellow flame that robed her to the ground like any immolating monk. That candle had two wicks, two flames of identical height, side by side. The moth's head was fire. She burned for two hours,
25 until I blew her out . . . .
   And that is why I believe those hollow crisps on the bathroom floor are moths. I think I know moths, and fragments of moths, and chips and tatters

of utterly empty moths, in any state. How many of you, I asked the people
in my class, which of you want to give your lives and be writers? I was
30 trembling from coffee, or cigarettes, or the closeness of faces all around me.
(Is this what we live for? I thought; is this the only final beauty: the color of
any skin in any light, and living, human eyes?) All hands rose to the
question. (You, Nick? Will you? Margaret? Randy? Why do I want them to
mean it?) And then I tried to tell them what the choice must mean: you
35 can't be anything else. You must go at your life with a broadax. . . . They
had no idea what I was saying. (I have two hands, don't I? And all this
energy, for as long as I can remember. I'll do it in the evenings, after skiing,
or on the way home from the bank, or after the children are asleep. . . .)
They thought I was raving again. It's just as well.

"Traveling Through the Dark" by William Stafford

line

Traveling through the dark I found a deer
dead on the edge of the Wilson River road.
It is usually best to roll them into the canyon:
that road is narrow; to swerve might make more dead.

5 By glow of the tail-light I stumbled back of the car
and stood by the heap, a doe, a recent killing;
she had stiffened already, almost cold.
I dragged her off; she was large in the belly.

My fingers touching her side brought me the reason—
10 her side was warm; her fawn lay there waiting,
alive, still, never to be born.
Beside that mountain road I hesitated.

The car aimed ahead its lowered parking lights;
under the hood purred the steady engine.
15 I stood in the glare of the warm exhaust turning red;
around our group I could hear the wilderness listen.

I thought hard for us all—my only swerving—,
then pushed her over the edge into the river.

Questions 1–8 are based on the passage from "Transfiguration" (pages 1346–1347).

1 From the first four sentences of this passage, it can reasonably be inferred that
  A Dillard is a keen observer of nature.
  B Dillard uses candles to get rid of insects.
  C moths are one of Dillard's special interests.
  D large golden moths are especially drawn to flames.

2 The phrase "wet wax, stuck, flamed, frazzled and fried in a second" exemplifies the sound device of
  A rhyme.
  B consonance.
  C alliteration.
  D assonance.

3 The moth most likely ignited so quickly because
  A its wings were very flammable.
  B the flapping of its wings fanned the flame.
  C pines emit substances that are flammable.
  D female moths burn more quickly than male moths.

4 According to the passage, the moth "kept burning" because
  A its horn shell had a wick inside it.
  B its head was jerking in spasms.
  C its force of will sustained it.
  D its thorax became saturated with wax.

5 The author's tone in the first paragraph is BEST described as
  A ironic.
  B upbeat.
  C solemn.
  D analytical.

6 From the context, it can be inferred that the word *saffron* in line 22 refers to
  A a material used to make candle wicks.
  B a monk's robe.
  C a type of prayer book.
  D a yellow substance used as a dye.

7 Which of the following statements BEST expresses the main idea of the extended analogy in the last paragraph?
  A A moth is like a candle wick.
  B A teacher is like an observant scientist.
  C A writer is like a moth drawn irresistibly to a flame.
  D A moth is like an attentive student who is eager to write.

8 In a brief paragraph, describe the author's tone in the last paragraph, citing two details from the passage that support your idea.

Questions 9–12 are based on the poem "Traveling Through the Dark" (page 1347).

9 One literary device that Stafford uses in the first two lines of the poem is
  A metaphor.
  B enjambment.
  C personification.
  D end rhyme.

10 According to the speaker, "it is usually best to roll them into the canyon" because, by doing so, one can
  A avoid laboring in the dark.
  B avoid dealing with an animal's death.
  C prevent the spread of disease.
  D prevent accidents.

11 The speaker's statement "I could hear the wilderness listen" contains an example of
  A metaphor.
  B enjambment.
  C personification.
  D alliteration.

12 In a brief paragraph, describe the overall mood of the poem, citing two details from it that support your idea.

Reading: Word Recognition

Choose the option that best completes each sentence.

1 Although many in the civil rights movement faced the threat of violence, they did not _____ to intimidation.
A repudiate
B rear
C succumb
D console
E grope

2 The _____ impact of the Vietnam War can still be felt today.
A meandering
B oblivious
C ancestral
D colossal
E imperative

3 Many claim that the Internet has made information more _____ and less concrete.
A striking
B ephemeral
C didactic
D grievous
E indifferent

4 Those who supported the Vietnam War believed that those who opposed it were _____ the national interest.
A rearing
B groping
C wallowing
D pondering
E subverting

5 The _____ of the events on September 11, 2001, made many _____ the place of the United States in the world.
A continuity . . . enlighten
B imperative . . . enunciate
C aristocracy . . . woo
D gravity . . . ponder
E ordeal . . . woo

6 The effects of the global economy are too _____ to be determined with certainty.
A complex
B balmy
C stooped
D downy
E fabled

7 Many older people were shocked by the _____ attitudes, dress, and lifestyles adopted by the baby boomer generation.
A ominous
B unorthodox
C ecclesiastical
D decimated
E indifferent

8 The nation, _____ by the economic boom after World War II, attained new _____ in the world.
A rejuvenated . . . stature
B presumptuous . . . scorn
C random . . . delirium
D inaudible . . . paradigm
E decimated . . . ambition

9 Many social, economic, and political changes caused the Soviet Union's power to _____ and eventually to fail.
A coincide
B rampage
C wane
D dwell
E marvel

10 The daily _____ faced by minorities before the civil rights movement was profound.
A nostalgia
B transfusion
C preliminaries
D dusk
E ordeal

Writing: Process and Language Conventions

Choose the option that is the best way of rewriting the underlined portion of each sentence. If you think the original wording is best, choose that option.

1 <u>Casualties mounting in Vietnam</u>, many Americans began to engage in public protests against the war, demanding that the United States pull out.
- **A** Casualties mounting in Vietnam
- **B** After casualties began to be mounting in Vietnam
- **C** As casualties mounted in Vietnam
- **D** Despite the mounting casualties in Vietnam
- **E** Having the mounted casualties in Vietnam

2 After graduating from college, Sandra Cisneros attended the University of Iowa Writers' Workshop, <u>she</u> felt out of place there.
- **A** she
- **B** but she
- **C** because she
- **D** where she
- **E** while she

3 The use of a number of chemical pesticides has been banned, <u>having been shown to kill wildlife and increase the risk of cancer</u>.
- **A** having been shown to kill wildlife and increase the risk of cancer
- **B** while chemicals are shown to kill wildlife and increase the risk of cancer
- **C** having been shown to kill wildlife, increasing the risk of cancer
- **D** since these chemicals have been shown to kill wildlife and increase the risk of cancer
- **E** chemicals having been killing wildlife and increasing the risk of cancer

4 American writers have responded to contemporary historical and cultural forces both by adapting traditional literary forms <u>and by devising new forms</u>.
- **A** and by devising new forms
- **B** and devising new forms
- **C** and have devised new forms
- **D** and new forms
- **E** or by devising new forms

5 Although many modern poets have employed free verse <u>to create striking poetic effects, and some critics</u> have likened writing free verse to playing tennis without a net.
- **A** to create striking poetic effects, and some critics
- **B** by creating striking poetic effects, some critics
- **C** and created striking poetic effects, and some critics
- **D** to create striking poetic effects, whereas some critics
- **E** to create striking poetic effects, some critics

6 Studs Terkel found the chronicling of oral histories <u>to be very successfully conveying</u> the problems, aspirations, and concerns of average Americans.
- **A** to be very successfully conveying
- **B** to be a very successful way of conveying
- **C** very successful to be conveying
- **D** very successfully conveying
- **E** to be a more successful conveying of

7 <u>By refusing to give up</u> her seat on a Montgomery bus, Rosa Parks helped to ignite a movement for racial justice in this country.
- **A** By refusing to give up
- **B** Although she refused to give up
- **C** By having refused giving up
- **D** She was refusing to give up
- **E** Not giving up

8 The widespread appreciation of graphic novels by <u>critics have done much to remove</u> the stigma that formerly attached to comic books.
- **A** critics have done much to remove
- **B** critics have done much removing of
- **C** critics, it has done much to remove
- **D** critics has done much to remove
- **E** critics doing much to remove

Writing: Applications

Complete the writing activity below. Do your planning and writing on separate sheets of paper.

Essay

> "The ability of writers to imagine what is not the self, to familiarize the strange and mystify the familiar, is the test of their power." —Toni Morrison

Write an essay in which you explain how a story you have read provides evidence for or against Morrison's statement. Indicate whether you agree or disagree with the statement, and cite specific aspects of the story to support your opinion.

Be sure to include

- at least five paragraphs, containing an introduction, a body, and a conclusion
- an opinion that reflects the assigned task
- examples that support your opinion

Use a separate sheet of paper to plan your writing. As you write, keep in mind that your essay will be evaluated for **ideas and content, organization, style, voice,** and **language conventions.**

Writing Checklist

Before you begin writing, be sure to

- ❏ brainstorm for ideas
- ❏ organize your ideas into a logical pattern
- ❏ develop a plan for an introduction, a body, and a conclusion

As you write your essay, be sure to

- ❏ refer to the quotation and clearly state your opinion about it
- ❏ support your opinion with specific references to a story
- ❏ use language that will convey a clear message and create interest
- ❏ maintain a tone that is appropriate for your intended audience
- ❏ use correct sentence structure, grammar, and punctuation

Literature Online **Unit Assessment** To prepare
for the unit test, go to www.glencoe.com.

REFERENCE SECTION

A

Abstract language Language that expresses an idea or intangible reality, as opposed to a specific object or occurrence or a concrete reality. The *Declaration of Independence*, page 114, includes abstract language such as *safety, happiness, prudence,* and *laws of nature*.

See also CONCRETE LANGUAGE.

Absurd, Theater of the Drama, primarily of the 1950s and 1960s, that does not tell a story but instead presents a series of scenes in which the characters, confused and anxious, seem to exist in a meaningless world. Edward Albee is a leading American playwright of absurdist and other plays.

See also SURREALISM.

Act A major unit of a drama, or play. Modern drama has one, two, or three acts. Older drama may have five acts. Acts may be divided into one or more scenes.

See also DRAMA, SCENE.

Allegory A literary work in which all or most of the characters, settings, and events stand for ideas, qualities, or figures beyond themselves. The overall purpose of an allegory is to teach a moral lesson. Nathaniel Hawthorne sometimes used allegorical techniques. "The Minister's Black Veil," page 267, can be read as an allegory dealing with sin and admission of sin.

See also SYMBOL.

Alliteration The repetition of consonant sounds at the beginnings of words. It can be used to reinforce meaning or create a musical effect. James Weldon Johnson uses alliteration in the following line from "My City," page 788:

> But, ah! Manhattan's sights and sounds,
> her smells, . . .

See also SOUND DEVICES.

Allusion A reference to a well-known character, place, or situation from history or from music, art, or another work of literature. In "The Love Song of J. Alfred Prufrock," page 658, T. S. Eliot alludes to the Italian artist Michelangelo, to Lazarus, who was restored to life by Jesus, and to Hamlet, the tragic hero of Shakespeare's play of the same name.

See pages 75, 657, 797, and 1152.

Ambiguity The state of having more than one meaning. The richness of literary language lies in its ability to evoke multiple layers of meaning.

Analogy A comparison that shows similarities between two things that are otherwise dissimilar. Writers often use an analogy to explain something unfamiliar by comparing it to something familiar.

See page 490.

See also METAPHOR, SIMILE.

Anapest A metrical foot of three syllables; two unaccented syllables are followed by an accented one (˘˘´). In the following line from Edgar Allan Poe's poem "Annabel Lee," the feet are divided by slashes.

> And the stars / never rise, / but I feel / the
> bright eyes . . .

See also FOOT, METER, SCANSION.

Anecdote A brief account of an interesting event. Essayists often use anecdotes to support their opinions, clarify their ideas, get a reader's attention, or entertain. Biographers often include one or more anecdotes in a biography to illustrate a point about their subject.

See page 1154.

Antagonist A person or a force that opposes the protagonist, or central character, in a story or drama. The reader is generally meant not to sympathize with the antagonist. In Stephen Crane's "The Open Boat," page 574, many critics argue that the sea is the antagonist.

See also CONFLICT, PROTAGONIST.

Anthropomorphism The assignment of human characteristics to gods, animals, or inanimate objects. In the myth "The Sky Tree," page 35, all the water animals—turtle, beaver, mink, muskrat, and otter—behave like human beings.

Aphorism A short, pointed statement that expresses a wise or clever observation about human experience. "Poor

Richard's Almanack" by Benjamin Franklin, page 102, contains many aphorisms, such as "What you would seem to be, be really."

See page 102.

See also MAXIM.

Apostrophe A figure of speech in which a speaker addresses an inanimate object, an idea, or an absent person. Ezra Pound addresses the long-dead Walt Whitman in "A Pact," page 654, an example of apostrophe.

See page 700.

See also PERSONIFICATION.

Archetype A character type, descriptive detail, image, or story pattern that recurs frequently in the literature of a culture. It derives from a Greek word meaning "the original example."

See pages 23, 240, and 898.

Argument A type of persuasive writing in which logic or reason is used to try to influence a reader's ideas or actions. "Civil Disobedience," page 212, is Henry David Thoreau's argument for disobeying a government's laws or protesting its policies.

See page 211.

See also PERSUASION.

Aside In a play, a character's comment that is directed to the audience or another character but is not heard by any other characters on the stage. Asides, which are rare in modern drama, reveal what a character is thinking or feeling.

Assonance The repetition of the same or similar vowel sounds, especially in a line of poetry. The repeated *o* sound in this line from an Emily Dickinson poem is an example of assonance:

> The S_ou_l selects her _ow_n S_o_ciety . . .

See also SOUND DEVICES.

Atmosphere The physical qualities that contribute to the mood of a literary work, such as time, place, and weather. The dominant atmosphere of Edgar Allan Poe's "The Pit and the Pendulum," page 251, is one of wretched darkness.

Author The original writer of a work. The word *author* comes from a Latin word meaning "to create."

Author's note A note accompanying a literary work and containing explanatory information. Author's notes usually include helpful but nonessential information. Randall Jarrell provides an author's note along with his poem "The Death of the Ball Turret Gunner," page 976.

Author's purpose An author's intent in writing a literary work. Authors typically write for one or more of the following purposes: to persuade, to inform, to explain, to entertain, or to describe.

See pages 48, 86, 414, 969, and 1011.

See also DICTION, STYLE, THEME, TONE.

Autobiography The story of a person's life written by that person. Autobiographies can give insights into the author's view of himself or herself and of the society in which he or she lived. *The Autobiography of Benjamin Franklin* is a famous example of the genre.

See pages 97, 338, 907, and 988.

See also BIOGRAPHY, MEMOIR, NONFICTION.

B

Ballad A narrative song or poem. Folk ballads, which usually recount an exciting or dramatic episode, were passed down by word of mouth for generations before being written down. Literary ballads are written in imitation of folk ballads but have a known author.

See also FOLKLORE, NARRATIVE POETRY, ORAL TRADITION.

Ballad stanza A quatrain, or four-line stanza, in which the first and third lines have four stressed syllables, and the second and fourth lines have three stressed syllables. Only the second and fourth lines rhyme.

> Cólder and lóuder bléw the wínd,
>> A gále from the Nórtheast,
> The snów féll híssing in the bríne,
>> And the bíllows fróthed like yéast.
> Henry Wadsworth Longfellow, "The Wreck of the Hesperus"

See also METER, QUATRAIN, SCANSION, STANZA.

Bias An inclination toward a certain opinion or position on a topic.

See also NONFICTION.

Biography An account of a person's life written by someone other than the subject. Biographies have been written about many of the writers in this text.

See also AUTOBIOGRAPHY, MEMOIR, NONFICTION.

Blank verse Poetry or lines of dramatic verse written in unrhymed iambic pentameter. Each line has five feet, with each foot made up of an unstressed syllable followed by a stressed syllable. Because it may attempt to imitate spoken English, every line need not be perfectly regular. Robert Frost wrote "Birches" in blank verse:

 When I see birches bend to left and right . . .

See pages 705 and 723.

See also FOOT, IAMBIC PENTAMETER, SCANSION.

Blues A melancholy style of music that originated among African Americans in the South. The blues stanza has three lines, and the first two lines are usually identical. Many writers have incorporated the idea of the blues into their work, among them Langston Hughes in his poem "The Weary Blues" and James Baldwin in his story "Sonny's Blues."

See also STANZA.

C

Cadence The rhythmic rise and fall of language when it is spoken or read aloud.

See also FREE VERSE, METER.

Caesura A pause in a line of poetry, usually near the middle of a line, with two stressed syllables before and two after, creating a strong rhythm. A caesura is used to produce variations in meter and to draw attention to certain words. Some pauses are indicated by punctuation, others by phrasing or meaning. In the lines below, the caesuras are marked by double vertical lines. The pauses are indicated by punctuation.

 The tide rises, || the tide falls,

 The twilight darkens, || the curlew calls;

 Henry Wadsworth Longfellow, "The Tide Rises, the Tide Falls"

See also RHYTHM.

Catalog The listing of images, details, people, or events in a literary work. In *Song of Myself*, page 407, Walt Whitman catalogs different kinds of workers from all over the United States.

See page 1291.

Character A person portrayed in a literary work. A *main character* is central to the story and is typically fully characterized. A *minor character* displays few personality traits and is used to help develop the story. Characters who show varied and sometimes contradictory traits, such as Dexter in F. Scott Fitzgerald's "Winter Dreams," page 744, are called *round*. Characters who reveal only one personality trait are called *flat*. A stereotype, or stock character, is typically flat. A *dynamic character* grows and changes during the story, as does the captain in Stephen Crane's "The Open Boat," page 574. A *static character* remains basically the same throughout the story.

See also CHARACTERIZATION, STEREOTYPE.

Characterization The methods a writer uses to reveal the personality of a character. In *direct characterization,* the writer makes explicit statements about a character, as William Faulkner does in "A Rose for Emily," page 878. In *indirect characterization*, the writer reveals a character through his or her words, thoughts, and actions and through what other characters think and say about that character, as in Kate Chopin's "The Story of an Hour," page 548.

See pages 229, 277, 505, 783, and 1248.

See also CHARACTER.

Classicism A style that reflects the principles and concerns of the art and literature of ancient Greece and Rome. Typically, a classical style displays simple, harmonious form.

Cliché A word or phrase that is so overused that it is virtually meaningless. "Dead as a doornail," "piece of cake," and "last but not least" are all clichés.

Climax The point of greatest emotional intensity, interest, or suspense in a literary work. Usually the climax comes at the turning point in a story or drama, the point just before the resolution of the conflict, as in Ernest Hemingway's "In Another Country," page 734, when the major loses his temper with the narrator.

See also page 1067.

See also CONFLICT, DÉNOUEMENT, PLOT, RESOLUTION.

Colloquial language Informal language used in everyday conversation but not in formal writing or speech. Simon Wheeler's language throughout "The Celebrated Jumping Frog of Calaveras County, " page 484, is full of colloquialisms such as "Why, it never made no difference to *him*—he would bet on *any* thing—the dangdest feller."

See also DIALECT, VERNACULAR.

Comedy A type of drama that is humorous and often has a happy ending.

See also DRAMA, FARCE, HUMOR, PARODY, SATIRE, WIT.

Comic relief A humorous scene, event, or speech in a serious drama. It provides relief from emotional intensity, while at the same time highlighting the seriousness of the story.

Conceit An elaborate figure of speech that makes a comparison between two significantly different things. The conceit draws an analogy between some object from nature or everyday life and the subject or theme of a poem.

See also ANALOGY, EXTENDED METAPHOR, IMAGERY.

Concrete language Specific language about actual things or occurrences. Words like *dog* and *sky* are concrete, while words like *truth* and *evil* are abstract.

See also ABSTRACT LANGUAGE.

Confessional poetry A movement in poetry begun in the 1950s in which the poet writes about his or her own personal experiences. Confessional poets described their problems with mental illness, alcohol abuse, and troubled relationships in an open and direct style. Robert Lowell, Anne Sexton, and Sylvia Plath were known as members of the Confessional school of poets.

Conflict The central struggle between two opposing forces in a story or drama. An *external conflict* exists when a character struggles against some outside force, such as another person, nature, society, or fate. An *internal conflict* is a struggle that takes place within the mind of a character who is torn between opposing feelings, desires, or goals. In "The Second Tree from the Corner," page 929, the conflict is largely internal. In "The Open Boat," page 574, the conflict is mostly external.

See pages 547, 591, 760, and 1106.

See also ANTAGONIST, PLOT, PROTAGONIST.

Connotation The suggested or implied meanings associated with a word beyond its dictionary definition, or denotation. A word can have a positive, negative, or neutral connotation.

See also AMBIGUITY, DENOTATION, FIGURATIVE LANGUAGE.

Consonance The repetition of consonant sounds, typically at the end of nonrhyming words and preceded by different vowel sounds, as "met-cat" or "morn-barn."

See also SOUND DEVICES.

Couplet Two consecutive, paired lines of rhymed verse usually forming a stanza. The last two lines of Phillis Wheatley's "To His Excellency, General Washington," page 131, are a couplet.

See page 130.

See also HEROIC COUPLET, RHYME, SONNET, STANZA.

Crisis In a narrative, a moment of high tension that requires a decision. In Bret Harte's "The Outcasts of Poker Flat," page 506, the crisis comes when the "outcasts" are stranded in a cabin during a blizzard and begin to run out of food.

See also CLIMAX, DRAMATIC STRUCTURE, RISING ACTION.

D

Dactyl A three-syllable metrical foot in which the first syllable is stressed and the following two are unstressed. The first line of the song "America" is dactylic.

My country 'tis of thee, . . .

Deism The belief that God created the world but no longer has influence or control over life or nature. Many of America's founders were deists.

Denotation The literal, or dictionary, meaning of a word.

See also CONNOTATION, LITERAL LANGUAGE.

Dénouement The outcome, or resolution, of the plot. The climax and dénouement may come close together as in Edgar Allan Poe's "The Pit and the Pendulum," page 251.

See also CLIMAX, CONFLICT, PLOT, RESOLUTION.

Description A detailed portrayal of a person, a place, an object, or an event. Good descriptive writing appeals to the senses through imagery. Eudora Welty's description of Phoenix Jackson in the first two paragraphs of "A Worn Path," page 892, is an example of detailed description.

See pages 135, 384, and 891.

See also FIGURATIVE LANGUAGE, IMAGERY.

Dialect A variation of a language spoken within a particular region or class. Dialects may differ from the standard form of a language in vocabulary, pronunciation, or grammatical form. Mark Twain's story "The Celebrated Jumping Frog of Calaveras County," page 484, contains the following example of dialect:

Well, thish-yer Smiley had a yaller one-eyed cow that didn't have no tail, only jest a short stump like a bannanner . . .

See pages 483 and 941.

See also COLLOQUIAL LANGUAGE, LOCAL COLOR, REGIONALISM, VERNACULAR.

Dialogue Conversation between characters in a literary work. Dialogue can contribute to characterization, create mood, advance the plot, and develop theme.

See pages 914, 1023, and 1266.

Diary An individual's daily record of impressions, events, or thoughts, written for personal use rather than for publication.

See also JOURNAL.

Diction A writer's choice of words. Diction is an important element in the writer's "voice" or style. Skilled writers choose their words carefully to convey a particular tone and meaning. Ernest Hemingway was known for his spare, simple diction, as in these lines from "In Another Country," page 734:

In the fall the war was always there, but we did not go to it any more. It was cold in the fall in Milan and the dark came very early.

See pages 61, 127, and 369.

See also AUTHOR'S PURPOSE, STYLE, VOICE.

Dimeter A line of verse consisting of two feet.

See also FOOT, METER.

Drama A story intended to be performed before an audience by actors on a stage. The script of a dramatic work may include stage directions that explain how characters should look, speak, move, and behave. The script might also specify details of the setting and scenery, such as lighting, props, and sound effects. A drama may be divided into *acts*, which may also be broken up into *scenes*, indicating changes in location or the passage of time.

See also COMEDY, PLAY, STAGE DIRECTIONS, TRAGEDY.

Dramatic convention Any of several devices that a theater audience accepts as a substitute for reality. For example, an audience accepts that a wood floor is a beach or a meadow, that a recording of birdsong is the real thing, or that the fifteen-minute interval between acts is a substitute for a longer passage of time.

Dramatic irony *See IRONY.*

Dramatic monologue A form of dramatic poetry in which a speaker addresses a silent listener. Edgar Allan Poe's poem "To Helen," in which the speaker passionately addresses his beloved, is an example of dramatic monologue.

See pages 500 AND 664.

See also DRAMATIC POETRY, MONOLOGUE.

Dramatic poetry Poetry in which characters are revealed through dialogue and monologue, as well as through description. Robert Frost's "The Death of the Hired Man," page 715, is an example of dramatic poetry.

See also DIALOGUE, DRAMATIC MONOLOGUE.

Dramatic structure The structure of a serious play. Common elements are exposition, rising action, climax, falling action, and resolution.

See also PLOT.

Dynamic character *See CHARACTER.*

E

Elegy A poem mourning a death or another great loss. Walt Whitman's "Sight in Camp in the Daybreak Gray and Dim," page 399, is an elegy for soldiers killed in the Civil War.

Empathy Close identification with a person, a place, or an event, as when audience members experience the same emotions as a character in a play.

End rhyme The rhyming of words at the ends of lines as in Edwin Arlington Robinson's "Richard Cory," page 569.

Enjambment *See RUN-ON LINE.*

End-stopped line A line of poetry that contains a complete thought, thus requiring a semicolon or period at the end.

If ever two were one, then surely we.

Anne Bradstreet, "To My Dear and Loving Husband"

See also RUN-ON LINE.

Epic A long narrative poem that traces the adventures of a hero. Epics intertwine myths, legends, and history, reflecting the values of the societies in which they originate. Homer's *Iliad* and *Odyssey* are two famous epics.

See also LEGEND, MYTH, ORAL TRADITION.

Epigram A short, witty verse or saying.

> Classic. A book which people praise and don't read.
>
> Mark Twain, *Following the Equator*

See also APHORISM, MAXIM.

Epigraph A quotation from another work that suggests the theme, or main idea, of the work at hand. It is often up to the reader to determine how the quoted work relates to the literature it introduces. T. S. Eliot's "The Love Song of J. Alfred Prufrock," page 658, contains a six-line epigraph in Italian from Dante's *Inferno.*

Epiphany A sudden intuitive recognition of the meaning or essence of something. At the end of E. B. White's "The Second Tree from the Corner," page 929, the main character has an epiphany when he finally realizes what he wants from life.

Epistle Any letter, such as Abigail Adams's letter to her daughter or Robert E. Lee's letter to his son, pages 138 and 370. Often the term is applied to a more literary work than the informal communication written by most people. Travel letters are common and usually intended for publication.

Epitaph A brief statement commemorating a dead person, often inscribed on a gravestone. Edgar Lee Masters's poems in *Spoon River Anthology*, pages 501 and 502, are epitaphs in the form of monologues about imaginary people.

Epithet A brief phrase used to characterize a person, place, or thing. Both "Honest Abe" and "The Great Emancipator" are epithets for Abraham Lincoln. Stephen A. Douglas, who debated Lincoln, was known as "The Little Giant."

Essay A short piece of nonfiction writing on any topic. The purpose of the essay is to communicate an idea or opinion. A *formal essay* is serious and impersonal, often with the purpose of instructing or persuading. Typically, the author strikes a serious tone and develops a main idea, or thesis, in a logical, highly organized way. An *informal*, or *personal, essay* entertains while it informs, usually in light, conversational style. Ralph Waldo Emerson's "Nature," page 180, is an example of a formal essay.

See page 1303.

See also NONFICTION.

Exaggeration *See HYPERBOLE.*

Exposition *See PLOT.*

Extended metaphor A metaphor that compares two unlike things in various ways throughout a paragraph, a stanza, or a literary work. In *Song of Myself*, page 407, Walt Whitman answers the question "What is the grass?" with an extended metaphor:

> I guess it must be the flag of my disposition, out
>   of a hopeful green stuff woven.
> Or I guess it is the handkerchief of the Lord,
> A scented gift and remembrancer designedly dropt,
> Bearing the owner's name someway in the corners,
>   that we may see and remark, and say *Whose?*

See pages 83 and 827.

See also METAPHOR.

F

Fable A short, often humorous, tale intended to teach a lesson about human behavior or to give advice about how to behave. Many fables end by stating the moral or lesson to be learned, while others leave it up to the reader to infer the moral. In a beast fable, animals talk and act like humans.

See also LEGEND, PARABLE, THEME.

Fairy tale A type of folktale that features supernatural elements, such as spirits, talking animals, and magic.

See also FOLKTALE.

Falling action *See PLOT.*

Fantasy A literary work that is set in an unfamiliar world and that often features unbelievable characters and events. Washington Irving wrote the earliest American fantasies with his stories "Rip Van Winkle" and "The Legend of Sleepy Hollow."

See also SCIENCE FICTION.

Farce A type of comedy with ridiculous situations, characters, or events.

See also COMEDY, HUMOR, PARODY, SATIRE.

Fiction A narrative in which situations and characters are invented by the writer. Some aspects of a fictional work may be based on fact or experience, however.

Fictional works include short stories, novels, and plays. Washington Irving's "The Devil and Tom Walker," page 230, and Nathaniel Hawthorne's *The Scarlet Letter* are examples of fiction.

See also DRAMA, NONFICTION, NOVEL, SHORT STORY.

Figurative language Language used for descriptive effect in order to convey ideas or emotions. Figurative expressions are not literally true but express some truth beyond the literal level. Figurative language is especially common in poetry. The following line contains personification, a kind of figurative language, in which the sea is treated as a person.

> The sea awoke at midnight from its sleep, . . .
>
> Henry Wadsworth Longfellow, "The Sound of the Sea"

See pages 183, 1183, and 1224.

Figure of speech A specific kind of figurative language such as metaphor, personification, or simile.

Flashback An interruption in the chronological order of a narrative to show an event that happened earlier. A flashback gives readers information that may help explain the main events of a story. Ambrose Bierce's "An Occurrence at Owl Creek Bridge," page 375, features a flashback in the middle of the story.

See pages 535 and 888.

See also FLASH-FORWARD.

Flash-forward An interruption in the chronological sequence of a narrative to leap forward in time. Richard Wright uses this device in his autobiography, *Black Boy*, page 902, when he describes a visit to his father that occurs many years after the time of the story.

See page 901.

See also FLASHBACK.

Flat character *See CHARACTER.*

Foil A minor character whose contrast with a main character highlights particular characteristics, often flaws, of the main character. The dog in Jack London's "To Build a Fire," page 595, exhibits a caution and respect for the cold of the Yukon that the man obviously lacks.

See page 958.

See also ANTAGONIST, CHARACTER, CHARACTERIZATION, PROTAGONIST.

Folklore Traditional beliefs, customs, stories, songs, and dances of a culture. Folklore is passed down through oral tradition and is based on the concerns of ordinary people. Washington Irving used elements of folklore in "The Devil and Tom Walker," page 230, when he wrote of a pact with the devil, who appears in human form.

See also BALLAD, EPIC, FOLKTALE, LEGEND, MYTH, ORAL TRADITION, TALL TALE.

Folktale An anonymous traditional story passed down orally long before being written down. Folktales include animal stories, trickster stories, fairy tales, myths, legends, and tall tales.

See also EPIC, FAIRY TALE, FOLKLORE, LEGEND, MYTH, ORAL TRADITION, TALL TALE.

Foot The basic unit in the measurement of a line of metrical poetry. A foot usually contains one stressed syllable (′) and one or more unstressed syllables (˘). The basic metrical feet are the anapest (˘ ˘ ′), the dactyl (′ ˘˘), the iamb (˘ ′), the spondee (′ ′), and the trochee (′ ˘).

See also METER, RHYTHM, SCANSION, STANZA.

Foreshadowing An author's use of clues to prepare readers for events that will happen later in a story. In Tomás Rivera's "The Portrait," page 1015, the salesman's demand for full cash payment foreshadows the fact that the transaction is a swindle.

See pages 877 and 924.

See also PLOT, SUSPENSE.

Form The structure of a poem. Many modern writers use loosely structured poetic forms instead of following traditional or formal patterns. These poets vary the lengths of lines and stanzas, relying on emphasis, rhythm, pattern, or the placement of words and phrases to convey meaning.

See page 667.

See also RHYTHM, STANZA, STRUCTURE.

Formal essay *See ESSAY.*

Formal speech A speech whose main purpose is to persuade, although it may also inform and entertain. Patrick Henry's "Speech to the Second Virginia Convention," page 108, is a formal speech to persuade. The four main types of formal speech are legal, political, ceremonial, and religious.

Fourth wall The imaginary wall that separates the performers onstage in a play from the audience watching the performance.

Frame story A story that surrounds another story or that serves to link several stories together. The frame is the outer story, which usually precedes and follows the inner, more important story. Mark Twain uses a frame in "The Celebrated Jumping Frog of Calaveras County," page 484. Some literary works have frames that bind together many different stories.

See page 1269.

Free verse Poetry that has no fixed pattern of meter, rhyme, line length, or stanza arrangement. Leslie Marmon Silko's "Prayer to the Pacific," page 42, is an example of free verse. Although poets who write free verse ignore traditional rules, they use techniques such as repetition and alliteration to create musical patterns in their poems.

See pages 395, 1186, and 1252.

See also RHYTHM, RHYME, METER.

G–H

Genre A category or type of literature. Examples of genres are poetry, drama, fiction, and nonfiction.

Gothic novel A novel that has a gloomy, ominous setting and contains strong elements of horror, mystery, and the supernatural. Edgar Allan Poe included some gothic features in his story "The Fall of the House of Usher."

Haiku A traditional Japanese form of poetry that has three lines and seventeen syllables. The first and third lines have five syllables each; the middle line has seven syllables. Usually about nature, a haiku presents striking imagery to evoke a variety of feelings and associations.

Harlem Renaissance A cultural and literary movement among African Americans during the 1920s. The center of the movement was the Harlem section of Manhattan, in New York City, which attracted artists, musicians, and writers such as Langston Hughes, Countee Cullen, Zora Neale Hurston, and others.

See page 785.

Heptameter A metrical line of seven feet.

See also FOOT, METER.

Hero The chief character in a literary work, typically one whose admirable qualities or noble deeds arouse admiration. Although the word *hero* is applied only to males in traditional usage—*heroine* being the term used for females—contemporary usage applies the term to either gender.

See also EPIC, LEGEND, MYTH, PROTAGONIST, TALL TALE, TRAGEDY.

Heroic couplet A pair of rhymed lines in iambic pentameter that work together to express an idea or make a point. A heroic couplet is based on the poetic form used by ancient Greek and Roman poets in their heroic epics. Anne Bradstreet uses the heroic couplet in "To My Dear and Loving Husband," page 85:

I prize / thy love / more than / whole mines / of gold

Or all / the rich / es that / the East / doth hold.

See page 130.

See also IAMBIC PENTAMETER, METER, RHYTHM.

Hexameter A line of verse consisting of six feet.

See also FOOT, METER.

Historical fiction Fiction that sets characters against the backdrop of a period other than the author's own. Some works of historical fiction include actual historical people along with fictitious characters.

See also FICTION.

Historical narrative A work of nonfiction that tells the story of important historical events or developments. In *La Relación*, page 56, Álvar Núñez Cabeza de Vaca provides a historical narrative of the experiences of a group of Spanish explorers.

See pages 402 and 820.

History A factual account of real events that occurred in the past. Typically, a history is arranged chronologically and seeks to provide an objective description of what happened.

Humor The quality of a literary work that makes the characters and their situations seem funny, amusing, or ludicrous. Humor often points out human failings and the irony found in many situations. Humorous language includes sarcasm, exaggeration, puns, and verbal irony. Mark Twain's story "The Celebrated Jumping Frog of Calaveras County," page 484, is told with humor, as is E. B. White's "The Second Tree from the Corner" on page 929.

See also COMEDY, FARCE, PARODY, PUN, SATIRE, WIT.

Hymn A lyric poem or song addressed to a divine being or expressing religious sentiments.

See also LYRIC.

Hyperbole A figure of speech that uses exaggeration to express strong emotion, to make a point, or to evoke humor. American folklore is full of hyperbole, particularly in the stories of Paul Bunyan, who was said to have created the Grand Canyon, Puget Sound, and the Black Hills. Thomas Paine's *The Crisis, No. 1*, page 124, contains hyperbolic language.

See also FIGURATIVE LANGUAGE, UNDERSTATEMENT.

I

Iamb A two-syllable metrical foot consisting of one unaccented syllable and one accented syllable, as in the word *divide*.

Iambic pentameter A poetic meter in which each line is composed of five feet (pentameter), most of which are iambs.

> Tall, som / ber, grim, / a gainst / the morn / ing sky . . .
> **Paul Hamilton Hayne, "Aspects of the Pines"**

See also BLANK VERSE, FOOT, HEROIC COUPLET, METER, RHYTHM, SCANSION.

Idiom An expression whose meaning is different from the literal meaning of the words that make it up. Phrases such as "catch his eye," "turn the tables," "over the hill," and "keep tabs on" are idiomatic expressions understood by native speakers but often puzzling to non-native speakers. Idioms can add realism to dialogue in a story and contribute to characterization.

See page 1014.

See also DIALECT.

Imagery The "word pictures" that writers create to evoke an emotional response. In creating effective images, writers use sensory details, or descriptions that appeal to one or more of the five senses. In the following lines from "Snow," page 1249, Julia Alvarez uses visual imagery to make a scene vivid to the reader:

> All my life I had heard about the white crystals
> that fell out of American skies in the winter.
> From my desk I watched the fine powder dust
> the sidewalk and parked cars below.

See pages 89, 653, 975, and 1299.

See also FIGURATIVE LANGUAGE, SENSORY DETAILS.

Imagism A movement among early twentieth-century poets, including Ezra Pound and Amy Lowell, who believed that the image was the essence of poetry, conveying a poem's meaning and emotion. The language of poetry, they believed, should be brief, clear, concrete, and similar to spoken language. A classic Imagist poem is Pound's "In a Station of the Metro," page 654.

See also MODERNISM.

Impressionism A nineteenth-century movement in art and literature. In literature, characters and scenes are presented as the author's or a particular character's impressions rather than as they actually are. The passage below is impressionistic:

> From beyond a curtain of green woods there
> came the sound of some stupendous scuffle, as
> if two animals of the size of islands were fighting.
> At a distance there were occasional appearances
> of swift-moving men, horses, batteries, flags,
> and with the crashing of infantry volleys were
> heard, often, wild and frenzied cheers.
>
> **Stephen Crane, "A Mystery of Heroism"**

See also POINT OF VIEW.

Informal essay *See ESSAY.*

Interior monologue A technique that records a character's emotions, memories, and opinions. A brief bit of interior monologue is present in Kate Chopin's "The Story of an Hour," page 548. Interior monologue is a characteristic of the stream-of-consciousness style of writing.

See also STREAM OF CONSCIOUSNESS.

Internal conflict *See CONFLICT.*

Internal rhyme Rhyme that occurs within a single line of poetry. Poets use internal rhyme to convey meaning, to evoke mood, or simply to create a musical effect. Edgar Allan Poe uses internal rhyme in his poem "The Raven," page 244:

> Once upon a midnight <u>dreary</u>, while I pondered,
> weak and <u>weary</u>

See also RHYME.

Inversion Reversal of the usual word order for emphasis or variety. Writers use inversion to maintain rhyme scheme or meter, or to emphasize certain words. In the third line below, the verb comes before the subject, a reversal of the usual order of subject plus verb.

Between the dark and the daylight,
When the night is beginning to lower,
Comes a pause in the day's occupations,
That is known as the Children's Hour.
Longfellow, "The Children's Hour"

Irony A contrast or discrepancy between appearance and reality. *Situational irony* exists when an occurrence is the opposite of someone's expectations, as at the end of Kate Chopin's "The Story of an Hour," page 548, when the main character's husband, thought to be dead, arrives at the front door. *Verbal irony* occurs when the meaning of a statement is the reverse of what is meant, as when someone says of a mean person, "Nice guy!" *Dramatic irony* occurs when playgoers have information unknown to characters onstage. In Shakespeare's *Romeo and Juliet*, the audience knows Juliet is dead before Romeo knows.

See pages 568 and 933.

J–L

Journal A daily record of events kept by a participant in those events or a witness to them. Mary Chesnut's journal about life in the South during the Civil War, page 362, became well-known.

See page 361.

Juxtaposition The placing of two or more distinct things side by side in order to contrast or compare them. It is commonly used to evoke an emotional response in the reader. For example, in her poem "Richness," page 560, Gabriela Mistral juxtaposes the images of a rose and a thorn.

See page 814.

Legend A traditional story handed down from the past, based on actual people and events, and tending to become more exaggerated and fantastical over time. "The Sky Tree," page 35, as retold by Joseph Bruchac, is a legend about how Earth came to be.

See also FABLE, FOLKLORE, FOLKTALE, HERO, MYTH, ORAL TRADITION, TALL TALE.

Legendary Heroes Idealized figures, sometimes based on real people, who embody qualities admired by the cultural group to which they belong. The adventures and accomplishments of these heroes are preserved in legends or tales that are handed down from generation to generation.

See also FOLKTALE.

Literal language Language that is simple, straightforward, and free of embellishment. It is the opposite of figurative language, which conveys ideas indirectly.

See also DENOTATION.

Literary criticism A type of writing in which the writer analyzes and evaluates a literary work.

Local color The evocative portrayal of a region's distinctive ways of talking and behaving. Bret Harte's "The Outcasts of Poker Flat," page 506, is a classic story for its use of local color.

See page 480.

See also DIALECT, REGIONALISM, VERNACULAR.

Lost Generation A term attributed to writer Gertrude Stein describing a group of American writers, many of whom lived abroad, who became disillusioned at the end of World War I. Included in this "generation" were Ernest Hemingway and F. Scott Fitzgerald.

Lyric A poem that expresses a speaker's personal thoughts and feelings. Lyrics are usually short and musical. Emily Dickinson's "This is my letter to the World," page 437, is an example of a lyric.

See also POETRY.

M

Magical realism A literary style in which the writer combines realistic events, settings, characters, dialogue, and other details with elements that are magical, supernatural, fantastic, or bizarre. In Edwidge Danticat's "Nineteen Thirty-Seven," page 1314, the suggestion that certain women could fly with "wings of flames" implies a magical or supernatural quality about these women.

See page 1313.

Maxim A short saying that contains a general truth or gives practical advice, particularly about morality and behavior. Also known as an adage or aphorism.

Memoir A type of narrative nonfiction that presents the story of a period in the writer's life. It is usually written from the first-person point of view and emphasizes the narrator's own experience of this period. It may also reveal the impact of significant historical events on his or her life. "All Rivers Run to the Sea," by Elie Wiesel, page 981, is an example of a memoir.

See also AUTOBIOGRAPHY, BIOGRAPHY.

Metaphor A figure of speech that compares or equates two seemingly unlike things. In contrast to a simile, a metaphor implies the comparison instead of stating it directly; hence there is no use of connectives such as *like* or *as*. "The past is a bucket of ashes" is a metaphor by Carl Sandburg.

See pages 83, 203, and 290.

See also EXTENDED METAPHOR, FIGURATIVE LANGUAGE.

Meter A regular pattern of stressed (´) and unstressed (�‌) syllables that gives a line of poetry a more or less predictable rhythm. The basic unit of meter is the foot. The length of a metrical line can be expressed in terms of the number of feet it contains:
dimeter, two feet; trimeter, three feet;
tetrameter, four feet; pentameter, five feet;
hexameter, six feet; heptameter, seven feet.
The following lines from "Old Ironsides," by Oliver Wendell Holmes, show one line of iambic tetrameter and one line of iambic trimeter:

Ăy, teár hĕr táttĕréd eńsiǵn doẃn!

Lŏng hás ĭt wáveḋ oṅ hiǵh

See page 801.

See also FOOT, IAMBIC PENTAMETER, SCANSION.

Metonymy A figure of speech in which a word or phrase is substituted for another that is related. For example, the executive branch of the U.S. government is often referred to as the White House.

See page 187.

See also FIGURATIVE LANGUAGE.

Minimalism A movement in visual arts, music, architecture, and literature. Minimalist writers include the fewest words possible in their works and depict ordinary people. Sandra Cisneros, page 1298, is often considered a minimalist writer.

Modernism A term applied to a variety of twentieth-century artistic movements that shared a desire to break with the past. In addition to technical experimentation, modern playwrights, writers, and artists in the first half of the twentieth century were interested in the irrational or inexplicable, as well as in the workings of the unconscious mind. The poetry of T. S. Eliot and Ezra Pound, with its new subject matter, diction, and metrical patterns, came to define Modernism. One example is Eliot's "The Love Song of J. Alfred Prufrock," page 658.

See also IMAGISM, STREAM OF CONSCIOUSNESS, SYMBOLIST POETRY.

Monologue A long speech by a character in a literary work.

See also DRAMATIC MONOLOGUE, SOLILOQUY.

Mood The emotional quality of a literary work. A writer's choice of language, subject matter, setting, and tone, as well as sound devices such as rhyme and rhythm, contribute to creating mood. Mood is a broader term than *tone*, which refers to the attitude of a speaker or narrator toward the reader. It also differs from *atmosphere*, which is concerned mainly with the physical qualities that contribute to a mood, such as time, place, and weather.

See pages 823, 1173, 1200, and 1221.

See also ATMOSPHERE, SETTING, TONE.

Moral A practical lesson about right and wrong conduct, often taught in a fable or parable.

Motif A significant word, phrase, image, description, idea, or other element repeated throughout a literary work and related to the theme.

See pages 690 and 1330.

Motivation The stated or implied reason or cause for a character's actions.

See pages 281, 515, 743, and 955.

See also PSYCHOLOGICAL REALISM.

Muckrakers American writers who searched for and exposed dishonesty in American government and business in the early 1900s. Ida Tarbell, Upton Sinclair, and Lincoln Steffens were leading muckrakers.

See page 533.

Myth A traditional story that deals with goddesses, gods, heroes, and supernatural forces. A myth may explain a belief, a custom, or a force of nature. "How the World Was Made," page 24, is an origin myth.

See also EPIC, FOLKLORE, FOLKTALE, LEGEND, ORAL TRADITION.

N

Narrative Writing or speech that tells a story. Narratives may be fiction or nonfiction, prose or poetry.

See also NARRATIVE POEM.

Narrative poetry Verse that tells a story. Narrative poetry includes ballads and epics as well as shorter forms that are usually more selective and concentrated than are prose stories. Edgar Allan Poe's "The Raven," page 244, is a narrative poem.

See pages 243 and 1325.

See also BALLAD, EPIC, NARRATIVE.

Narrator The person who tells a story. The narrator may be a character in the story, as in John Steinbeck's "Breakfast," page 870, or outside the story, as in Bernard Malamud's "The Magic Barrel," page 942.

See also NARRATIVE, POINT OF VIEW.

Naturalism The literary movement characterized by a belief that people have little control over their own lives. Naturalist writers such as Frank Norris and Stephen Crane focused on the powerful economic, social, and environmental forces that shape the lives of individuals. In Stephen Crane's "The Open Boat," page 574, four men face the power of the relentless sea.

See pages 476 and 573.

See also PSYCHOLOGICAL REALISM.

Nobel Prize A very prestigious award established in 1901 by Alfred Bernhard Nobel, a Swedish chemist and inventor, to honor individuals' achievements in many fields, including medicine, physics, and literature.

Nonfiction Literature that deals with real people, places, and events. Written from either the first- or third-person point of view, works of narrative nonfiction tell a story and commonly have characteristics of fiction, such as setting, characters, theme, and plot. Biographies, autobiographies, memoirs, and essays are types of narrative nonfiction. *The Life of Olaudah Equiano,* page 68, is narrative nonfiction. Works of informative nonfiction include essays, speeches, and articles that explain a topic or promote an opinion.

See also AUTOBIOGRAPHY, BIOGRAPHY, ESSAY, FICTION.

Novel A book-length fictional prose narrative, typically having a plot, character, setting, and theme. A short novel is called a novelette or novella.

See also FICTION, SHORT STORY.

O

Octave The first eight lines of a Petrarchan, or Italian, sonnet. The octave usually presents a situation, an idea, or a question.

See also SONNET.

Octet A group of eight lines in a poem.

Ode An elaborate lyric poem expressed in a dignified and sincere way. Some odes celebrate a person or an event; others are more private meditations.

See also LYRIC.

Onomatopoeia The use of a word or phrase that imitates or suggests the sound of what it describes. The words *mew, hiss, caw,* and *buzz* are onomatopoetic words. In the following example, the writer has tried to convey the sound of a character's movements:

> She heard, behind her, his scrambling movement as he left the easy chair, the scrape and jangle of the lunchbox as he picked it up…
>
> James Baldwin, "The Rockpile"

See also SOUND DEVICES.

Oral history The recording of people's memories and feelings. Oral history creates a more vivid and personal picture of the past and gives a voice to people who might have been hidden from ordinary historical records. It is the oldest form of historical inquiry, preceding the written word, and has become a crucial tool, following the invention of tape recorders in the 1940s.

Oral tradition Literature that passes by word of mouth from one generation to the next. Oral literature was a way of recording the past, glorifying leaders, and teaching morals and traditions to young people.

See page 34.

See also BALLAD, EPIC, FOLKLORE, FOLKTALE, LEGEND, MYTH, TALL TALE.

Oratory The art of effective public speaking, or the use of persuasive skills when speaking. Oratory is common in politics, law, and religion. Today, oratory is usually called "public speaking."

See page 355.

Oxymoron A figure of speech in which opposite ideas are combined. Examples are "bright darkness," "wise fool," and "hateful love."

See also FIGURATIVE LANGUAGE, PARADOX.

P–Q

Parable A simple story pointing to a moral or religious lesson. It differs from a fable in that the characters are people instead of animals. Nathaniel Hawthorne's short story "The Minister's Black Veil," page 267, is a parable.

See also FABLE.

Paradox A situation or statement that seems to be impossible or contradictory but is nevertheless true, literally or figuratively.

> When my love swears that she is made of truth,
> I do believe her, though I know she lies.
> > William Shakespeare, Sonnet 138

See also OXYMORON.

Parallelism The use of a series of words, phrases, or sentences that have similar grammatical structure. Parallelism emphasizes relationships between ideas. For example, Walt Whitman uses parallelism in *Song of Myself,* page 407:

> What do you think has become of the young
> > and old men?
> And what do you think has become of the
> > women and children?

See pages 113, 387, and 1307.

See also REPETITION.

Parody A humorous imitation of a literary work that aims to point out the work's shortcomings. A parody may imitate the plot, characters, or style of another work, usually through exaggeration.

See also COMEDY, FARCE, HUMOR, SATIRE.

Pastoral Poetry that idealizes the simple lives of shepherds in a rural setting. Pastoral poems often exaggerate the rural pleasures and the innocence of country people living in harmony with nature.

Pentameter A metrical line of five feet.

See also FOOT.

Persona The mask or voice through which an author speaks. Willa Cather's "A Wagner Matinée," page 520, is told from the first person; however, the narrator is not Cather but the voice in which she chose to tell her story.

Personification A figure of speech in which an animal, an object, a force of nature, or an idea is given human characteristics. In Emily Dickinson's "Because I could not stop for Death," page 434, death is personified.

See pages 434, 439, 1227, and 1286.

See also APOSTROPHE, FIGURATIVE LANGUAGE.

Persuasion Writing, usually nonfiction, that attempts to move readers to a particular viewpoint. Writers of persuasive works use appeals to logic or emotion, and other techniques to sway their readers. Thomas Paine's "The Crisis, No. 1" page 124, is an excellent example of persuasive writing.

See also ARGUMENT.

Petrarchan sonnet *See SONNET.*

Plain style A style of writing common among the Puritan settlers that focused on communicating ideas as clearly as possible. This marked a change from the ornate style used by European writers of that time. Colonial writers such as William Bradford thought of writing as a practical tool for spiritual self-examination and religious instruction, not as an opportunity to demonstrate cleverness.

Play A literary work of any length intended for performance on a stage with actors assuming the roles of the characters and speaking from a playwright's script.

See also DRAMA.

Plot The sequence of events in a short story, novel, or drama. Most plots deal with a problem and develop around a *conflict*, a struggle between opposing forces. An *external conflict* is a struggle between a character and an outside force, such as another character, society, nature, or fate. An *internal conflict* takes place within the mind of a character who struggles with opposing feelings. The plot begins with *exposition*, which introduces the story's characters, setting, and situation. The *rising action* adds complications to the conflicts, or problems, leading to the *climax*, or the point of highest emotional pitch. *Falling action* is the logical result of the climax, and the *resolution*, or dénouement, presents the final outcome.

See pages 928, 1018, and 1067.

See also CLIMAX, CONFLICT, DÉNOUEMENT, EXPOSITION, FALLING ACTION, RESOLUTION, RISING ACTION.

Poetic license The freedom given to poets to ignore standard rules of grammar or proper diction in order to create a desired artistic effect.

Poetry A form of literary expression that differs from prose in emphasizing the line, rather than the sentence, as the unit of composition. Many other traditional characteristics of poetry apply to some poems but not to others. Some of these characteristics are emotional, imaginative language; use of figures of speech; division into stanzas; and the use of rhyme and regular patterns of meter.

Point of view The standpoint from which a story is told. In a story with *first-person* point of view, the narrator is a character in the story and uses the words *I* and *me* as in "In Another Country," page 734. In a story told from *third-person* point of view, the narrator is someone who stands outside the story and describes the characters and action as in "The Story of an Hour," page 548. *Third-person omniscient*, or all-knowing point of view, means that the narrator knows everything about the characters and events and may reveal details that the characters themselves could not reveal. If the narrator describes events as only one character perceives them, as in "The Jilting of Granny Weatherall," page 776, the point of view is called *third-person limited*.

See pages 55, 262, 374, 519, 1000, and 1277.

See also NARRATOR, SPEAKER.

Postmodernism A movement in art, music, film, literature, and other disciplines in the late twentieth century. Unreliable narration, the blending of multiple styles and genres within a single work, and magical realism are all features of postmodern literature.

See also MODERNISM.

Propaganda Written or spoken material designed to bring about a change or to damage a cause through use of emotionally charged words, name-calling, or other techniques.

Props A theater term (a shortened form of *properties*) for objects and elements of the scenery of a stage play or movie or television set.

See also DRAMA.

Prologue An introductory section of a play, speech, or other literary work.

Prose Written language that is not versified. Novels, short stories, and essays are usually written in prose.

Prose poem A short prose composition that uses rhythm, imagery, and other poetic devices to express an idea or emotion. Prose poetry does not have line breaks; instead, the sentences appear in standard paragraph form.

Protagonist The central character in a literary work, around whom the main conflict revolves. Generally the audience is meant to sympathize with the protagonist.

See also ANTAGONIST, CONFLICT, HERO.

Proverb A saying that expresses some truth about life or contains some bit of popular wisdom such as "faint heart never won fair lady," "marry in haste, repent at leisure," or "out of sight, out of mind."

Psalm A song of praise most commonly found in the biblical book of Psalms. David, king of Israel around 1000 B.C., wrote many of these psalms. Occasionally a modern poet will title his or her poem a psalm.

Psychological realism An attempt to portray characters in an objective, plausible manner. Above all else, psychological realism insists that characters be clearly motivated; they should not act without apparent reason.

See also MOTIVATION, NATURALISM, REALISM.

Pun A humorous use of words that are similar in sound (*merry* and *marry*) or of a word with several meanings. In Shakespeare's *Romeo and Juliet*, when Mercutio is fatally wounded, he says, "Ask for me tomorrow and you shall find me a *grave* man," meaning both "serious" and "dead."

Punctuation mark Any standard mark, such as a period, semicolon, hyphen, or comma, inserted to clarify meaning.

Quatrain A stanza of four lines. Edwin Arlington Robinson's poems "Richard Cory" and "Miniver Cheevy," pages 569 and 570, are written in four-line stanzas.

See also COUPLET, OCTAVE, SESTET, STANZA.

R

Rationalism A philosophy that values reason over feeling or imagination.

See also ROMANTICISM.

Realism A literary movement first prominent in the late nineteenth and early twentieth centuries. Realism seeks to portray life as it is really lived. Realistic fiction often focuses on middle- or working-class settings and characters, often with reformist intent. Mark Twain was a realist writer, as were Stephen Crane and Theodore Dreiser.

See page 474.

See also NATURALISM, PSYCHOLOGICAL REALISM.

Refrain A line or lines repeated regularly, usually in a poem or song. "Let my people go" is a refrain in the spiritual "Go Down, Moses" on page 333.

See page 331.

See also REPETITION.

Regionalism An emphasis on themes, characters, customs, and settings of a particular geographical region. Much of Mark Twain's work deals with life in Missouri and along the Mississippi River, where he spent his boyhood and youth. Early twentieth-century regionalists include Sarah Orne Jewett and Mary E. Wilkins Freeman in New England and Booth Tarkington and Hamlin Garland in the Midwest. Later Southern regionalists include William Faulkner and Robert Penn Warren.

See page 472.

See also DIALECT, LOCAL COLOR, VERNACULAR.

Repetition The recurrence of sounds, words, phrases, lines, or stanzas in a speech or literary work. Repetition increases the sense of unity in a work and can call attention to particular ideas. Walt Whitman's "Beat! Beat! Drums!" on page 400 makes use of repetition.

See page 810.

See also PARALLELISM, REFRAIN.

Resolution *See PLOT.*

Rhetorical question A question to which no answer is expected or the answer is obvious. In his autobiography, page 68, Olaudah Equiano uses rhetorical questions to argue against slavery: "Why are parents to lose their children, brothers their sisters, or husbands their wives?" he asks.

See page 107.

Rhyme The repetition of the same stressed vowel sounds and any succeeding sounds in two or more words. *End rhyme* occurs at the ends of lines of poetry. *Internal rhyme* occurs within a single line. *Slant rhyme* occurs when words include sounds that are similar but not identical (*jackal* and *buckle*). Slant rhyme typically involves some variation of consonance (the repetition of similar consonant sounds) or assonance (the repetition of similar vowel sounds).

See page 424.

See also ASSONANCE, CONSONANCE, INTERNAL RHYME, RHYME SCHEME, SOUND DEVICES.

Rhyme scheme The pattern that end rhymes form in a stanza or a poem. Rhyme scheme is designated by the assignment of a different letter of the alphabet to each new rhyme. The rhyme scheme of Edgar Allan Poe's "To Helen" follows:

Helen, thy beauty is to me	*a*
Like those Nicéan barks of yore,	*b*
That gently, o'er a perfumed sea,	*a*
The weary, way-worn wanderer bore	*b*
To his own native shore.	*b*

See pages 563 and 936.

See also RHYME.

Rhythm The pattern of beats created by the arrangement of stressed and unstressed syllables, especially in poetry. Rhythm gives poetry a musical quality, can add emphasis to certain words, and may help convey the poem's meaning. Rhythm can be *regular*, with a predictable pattern or meter, or *irregular*. Notice how the rhythm of the first two lines of E. E. Cummings's "anyone lived in a pretty how town," page 697, gives a lilting quality to the poem.

See pages 695 and 1197.

See also IAMBIC PENTAMETER, METER.

Rising action *See PLOT.*

Romanticism An artistic movement that began in Europe and valued imagination and feeling over intellect and reason. Nineteenth-century American writers Ralph Waldo Emerson, Henry David Thoreau, Edgar Allan Poe, Walt Whitman, and Emily Dickinson were heavily influenced by Romanticism.

See page 162.

See also TRANSCENDENTALISM.

Round character *See CHARACTER.*

Run-on line Also called enjambment, the continuation of a sentence from one line of a poem to another.

To him who in the love of Nature holds
Communion with her visible forms, she speaks
A various language;

William Cullen Bryant, "Thanatopsis"

Run-on lines enable poets to create a conversational tone, breaking lines at a point where people would normally pause in conversation, yet still maintaining the unit of thought.

See page 673.

See also END-STOPPED LINE.

S

Sarcasm The use of bitter or caustic language to point out shortcomings or flaws.

See also IRONY, SATIRE.

Satire Writing that comments, sometimes humorously, on human flaws, ideas, social customs, or institutions. The purpose of satire may be to reform or to entertain.

See page 1234.

See also COMEDY, FARCE, HUMOR, PARODY, SARCASM, WIT.

Scansion The analysis of the meter of a line of verse. To scan a line of poetry means to note the stressed and unstressed syllables and to divide the line into its feet, or rhythmical units. Stressed syllables (´) and unstressed syllables (˘) are marked. Note the scansion of these lines from Paul Laurence Dunbar's "We Wear the Mask," page 565.

We wear/ the mask /that grins/ and lies,

It hides /our cheeks /and shades/ our eyes, . . .

Since each line has four feet and the rhythm is an iamb, we can describe the lines as iambic tetrameter.

See also FOOT, METER, RHYTHM.

Scene A subdivision of an act in a play. A scene is shorter than an act.

See also ACT, DRAMA.

Science fiction Fiction that deals with the impact of science and technology—real or imagined—on society and on individuals. Sometimes occurring in the future, science fiction commonly portrays space travel, exploration of other planets, and possible future societies.

See also FANTASY.

Screenplay The script of a film, which, in addition to dialogue and stage directions, usually contains detailed instructions about camera shots and angles.

See also STAGE DIRECTIONS.

Sensory details Evocative words or phrases that appeal to one or more of the five senses. Elizabeth Bishop's "The Fish," page 1210, uses sensory details that appeal to the sense of sight.

See page 89.

See also IMAGERY.

Septet A stanza of seven lines.

Sestet A six-line stanza.

See also SONNET.

Setting The time and place in which the events of a literary work occur. Setting includes not only the physical surroundings, but also the ideas, customs, values, and beliefs of a particular time and place. Setting often helps create an atmosphere or a mood. Setting plays an important part in William Faulkner's "A Rose for Emily," page 878.

See pages 594, 739, 769, 1189, and 1214.

See also ATMOSPHERE, MOOD.

Shakespearean sonnet *See SONNET.*

Short story A brief fictional narrative that generally includes the following major elements: setting, characters, plot, point of view, and theme.

See also FICTION, NOVEL.

Simile A figure of speech that uses *like* or *as* to compare seemingly unlike things. A famous simile appears at the opening of T. S. Eliot's "The Love Song of J. Alfred Prufrock," page 658.

Let us go then, you and I,
When the evening is spread out against the sky
Like a patient etherised upon a table. . . .

See page 1217.

See also ANALOGY, FIGURATIVE LANGUAGE, METAPHOR.

Slant rhyme *See RHYME.*

Slave narrative Autobiographical account of the life of a former enslaved person. These documents helped expose the cruelty and inhumanity of slavery. The excerpt from Frederick Douglass's *My Bondage and My Freedom*, page 339, is a slave narrative.

See page 67.

See also AUTOBIOGRAPHY, MEMOIR.

Soliloquy In a drama, a long speech by a character who is alone on stage. A soliloquy reveals the private thoughts and emotions of that character.

See also DRAMATIC MONOLOGUE, MONOLOGUE.

Sonnet A lyric poem of fourteen lines, typically written in iambic pentameter and usually following strict patterns of stanza divisions and rhymes.

The *Shakespearean*, or *English*, sonnet consists of three quatrains, or four-line stanzas, followed by a couplet, or pair of rhyming lines. The rhyme scheme is typically *abab, cdcd, efef, gg*. The rhyming couplet often presents a conclusion to the issues or questions presented in the three quatrains.

In the *Petrarchan*, or *Italian*, sonnet, fourteen lines are divided into two stanzas, the eight-line octave and the six-line sestet. The sestet usually responds to a question or situation posed by the octave. The rhyme scheme for the octave is typically *abbaabba*; for the sestet the rhyme scheme is typically *cdecde*. "Douglass" by Paul Laurence Dunbar, page 564, is a Petrarchan sonnet.

See page 787.

See also COUPLET, RHYME SCHEME, STANZA.

Sound devices Techniques used, especially in poetry, to appeal to the ear. Writers use sound devices to enhance the sense of rhythm, to emphasize particular sounds, or to add to the musical quality of their writing and rhyme.

See also ALLITERATION, ASSONANCE, CONSONANCE, ONOMATOPOEIA, RHYME.

Speaker The voice speaking in a poem, similar to a narrator in a work of prose. Sometimes the speaker's voice is that of the poet, sometimes that of a fictional person or even a thing. The speaker's words communicate a particular tone, or attitude, toward the subject of the poem. In Anne Bradstreet's "To My Dear and Loving Husband," page 85, the speaker is the poet, who addresses her husband in a tone of passionate devotion. One should never assume that the speaker and the writer are identical, however. The speaker in "The Raven," page 244, is not Edgar Allan Poe, the poet.

See also TONE.

Spondee A metrical foot of two accented syllables.

See also FOOT, METER.

Stage directions Instructions written by a playwright to describe the appearance and actions of characters, as well as the sets, costumes, and lighting. Arthur Miller's play *The Crucible*, page 1024, and Tennessee Williams's play *The Glass Menagerie* contain numerous stage directions.

See page 1046.

See also DRAMA.

Stanza A group of lines forming a unit in a poem or song. A stanza in a poem is similar to a paragraph in prose. Typically, stanzas in a poem are separated by a line of space.

See page 831.

See also SONNET.

Stereotype A character who is not developed as an individual, but instead represents a collection of traits and mannerisms supposedly shared by all members of a group.

See also CHARACTER.

Stream of consciousness The literary representation of a character's free-flowing thoughts, feelings, and memories. Stream-of-consciousness writing does not always employ conventional sentence structure or other rules of grammar and usage. Parts of T. S. Eliot's poem "The Love Song of J. Alfred Prufrock," page 658, exemplify stream of consciousness; Katherine Anne Porter's "The Jilting of Granny Weatherall," page 776, does as well.

See pages 658, 775, and 776.

See also SURREALISM.

Structure The particular order or pattern a writer uses to present ideas. Narratives commonly follow a chronological order, while the structure of persuasive or expository writing may vary. Listing detailed information, using cause and effect, or describing a problem and then offering a solution are some other ways a writer can present a topic.

See pages 1148 and 1168.

Style The expressive qualities that distinguish an author's work, including word choice and the length and arrangement of sentences, as well as the use of figurative language and imagery. Style can reveal an author's attitude and purpose in writing.

See pages 733, 1274, and 1322.

See also AUTHOR'S PURPOSE, DICTION, FIGURATIVE LANGUAGE, IMAGERY, TONE.

Subject The topic of a literary work.

Surprise ending An unexpected plot twist at the end of a story. The ending might surprise readers because the author provides misleading clues or withholds important information.

Surrealism A literary and artistic style that originated in Europe in the 1920s. Surrealist works feature bizarre and impossible events treated as if they were normal. Surrealist poetry expresses the workings of the unconscious mind and how these workings interact with outer reality. This poetry is characterized by the use of images from dreams and stream-of-consciousness associations.

See also STREAM OF CONSCIOUSNESS.

Suspense A feeling of curiosity, uncertainty, or even dread about what is going to happen next in a story. Writers increase the level of suspense by creating a threat to the central character and raising questions in a reader's mind about the outcome of a conflict. Suspense is especially important in the plot of an adventure or mystery story.

See pages 250 and 606.

See also PROTAGONIST.

Symbol Any object, person, place, or experience that exists on a literal level but also represents, or stands for, something else, usually something abstract. In Carl Sandburg's "Chicago," page 701, the hog butcher, tool maker, and stacker of wheat symbolize the city of Chicago.

See pages 266, 1281, and 1296.

See also ALLEGORY, FIGURATIVE LANGUAGE.

Symbolist poetry A kind of poetry that emphasizes suggestion and inward experience instead of explicit description. The symbolist poets influenced twentieth-century writers such as T. S. Eliot and Ezra Pound.

See page 650.

See also IMAGISM, MODERNISM.

Synecdoche A figure of speech in which a part is used for the whole or a whole is used for a part. In "All nations, and kindreds, and people, and tongues," *tongues* (a part) is used for the whole (languages).

T

Tall tale A type of folklore associated with the American frontier. Tall tales are humorous stories that contain wild exaggerations and inventions. Typically, their heroes are bold but sometimes foolish characters who may have superhuman abilities or who may act as if they do. Tall tales are not intended to be believable; their exaggerations are used for comic effect, as in Mark Twain's "The Celebrated Jumping Frog of Calaveras County," when Simon Wheeler describes the frog on page 487: "[Y]ou'd see that frog whirling in the air like a doughnut—see him turn one summerset, or may be a couple, if he got a good start, and come down flat-footed and all right, like a cat."

See also FOLKLORE, FOLKTALE.

Tercet A stanza of three rhyming lines.

Terza rima A verse form with a sequence of three-line stanzas rhyming *aba, bcb, cdc,* and so on. Robert Frost's poem "Acquainted with the Night," page 713, is written in terza rima.

Tetrameter A metrical line of four feet.

> Listen, / my children, / and you / shall hear
> Of the mid / night ride / of Paul / Revere, . . .
>   Henry Wadsworth Longfellow, "Paul Revere's Ride"

See also FOOT, METER.

Theater of the absurd *See ABSURD, THEATER OF THE*

Theme The central message of a work of literature, often expressed as a general statement about life. Some works have a *stated* theme, which is expressed directly. More works have an *implied* theme, which is revealed gradually through events, dialogue, or description. A literary work may have more than one theme. Some themes are universal, meaning that they are widely held ideas about life. Themes and topics are different. The *topic* of a work might be love; the *theme* would be what the writer says about love, that it is painful or wonderful or both, for example.

See pages 179, 542, 679, and 869.

See also AUTHOR'S PURPOSE, FABLE, MORAL.

Thesis The main idea of a work of nonfiction. The thesis may be stated directly or implied.

See page 194.

See also NONFICTION.

Tone An author's attitude toward his or her subject matter or the audience. Tone is conveyed through elements such as word choice, punctuation, sentence structure, and figures of speech. A writer's tone might convey a variety of attitudes such as sympathy, objectivity, or humor.

See pages 123, 185, 492, 528, 873, 1209, and 1333.

See also AUTHOR'S PURPOSE, DICTION, FIGURATIVE LANGUAGE, MOOD, STYLE, VOICE.

Tragedy A play in which a main character suffers a downfall. That character, the *tragic hero*, is typically a person of dignified or heroic stature. The downfall may result from outside forces or from a weakness within the character, which is known as a *tragic flaw*.

See page 1089.

See also DRAMA, HERO.

Transcendentalism A philosophical and literary movement whose followers believed that basic truths could be reached only by "going beyond," or transcending, reason and reflecting on the world of the spirit and on one's own deep and free intuition. Transcendentalists believed that the individual could transform the world—not only through writing, but also through utopian communities, antislavery activity, and other social action.

See page 170.

See also RATIONALISM, ROMANTICISM.

Trimeter A metrical line of three feet.

See also FOOT, METER

Triplet *See TERCET.*

Trochee A metrical foot made up of one accented and one unaccen ted syllable. The lines below, each of which have four feet, can be described as trochaic tetrameter.

Filled with / awe was / Hia / watha

At the / aspect / of his / father.
Henry Wadsworth Longfellow, *The Song of Hiawatha*

See also FOOT.

U–W

Understatement Language that makes something seem less important than it really is.

See also HYPERBOLE.

Unreliable narrator A narrator whose account of events is faulty or distorted in some way. Some unreliable narrators intentionally mislead readers. Others fail to understand the true meaning of the events they describe. For example, if a story is narrated by a small child, he or she might misinterpret the behavior of adult characters. Most stories with unreliable narrators are written in the first person.

See also POSTMODERNISM.

Verisimilitude The illusion of reality, often achieved by presenting concrete, detailed descriptions.

Vernacular Ordinary speech of a particular country or region. Vernacular language is more casual than cultivated, formal speech. Slang and dialect are commonly described as vernacular language. Regional writers sometimes employ vernacular language for enhanced realism. Use of vernacular is common in the works of Mark Twain, Zora Neale Hurston, and Alice Walker.

See also COLLOQUIAL LANGUAGE, DIALECT, LOCAL COLOR, REGIONALISM.

Verse paragraph A group of lines in a poem that form a unit. Unlike a stanza, a verse paragraph does not have a fixed number of lines. While poems written before the twentieth century usually contain stanzas, many contemporary poems are made up of verse paragraphs. Verse paragraphs help to organize a poem into thoughts, as paragraphs help to organize prose.

See page 1203.

See also STANZA.

Voice The distinctive use of language that conveys the author's or narrator's personality to the reader. Voice is determined by elements of style such as word choice and tone.

See pages 406, 525, 791, and 1255.

See also AUTHOR'S PURPOSE, DICTION, NARRATOR, STYLE, TONE.

Wit An exhibition of cleverness and humor. The works of Dorothy Parker, Mark Twain, and Donald Barthelme are known for their wit.

See also COMEDY, HUMOR, SARCASM, SATIRE.

Word choice *See DICTION.*

The Reading Process

Being an active reader is a crucial part of being a lifelong learner. It is also an ongoing task. Good reading skills are recursive; that is, they build on each other, providing the tools you'll need to understand text, to connect selections to your own life, to interpret ideas and themes, and to read critically.

Vocabulary Development

To develop a rich vocabulary, consider these four important steps:

- **Read** a wide variety of texts.
- **Enjoy** and engage in word play and word investigation.
- **Listen** carefully to how others use words.
- **Participate** regularly in good classroom discussions.

Using context to discover meaning

When you look at the words and sentences surrounding a new word, you are using context. **Look** before, at, and after a new word or phrase. **Connect** what you know with what an author has written. Then **guess** at a possible meaning. **Try again** if your guess does not make sense. Consider these strategies for using context:

- Look for a synonym or antonym nearby to provide a clue to the word's meaning.
- Notice if the text relates the word's meaning to another word.
- Check for a description of an action associated with the word.
- Try to find a general topic or idea related to the word.

Using word parts and word origins

Consider these basic elements when taking a word apart to determine meaning:

- **Base words** Locate the most basic part of a word to predict a core meaning.
- **Prefixes** Look at syllables attached before a base that add to or change a meaning.
- **Suffixes** Look at syllables added to the ends of base words that create new meanings.

Also consider **word origins**—Latin, Greek, and Anglo-Saxon roots—that are the basis for much of English vocabulary. Knowing these roots can help you determine derivations and spellings, as well as meanings in English.

Using reference materials

When using context and analyzing word parts do not help to unlock the meaning of a word, go to a reference source like a dictionary, glossary, thesaurus, or even the Internet. Use these tips:

- **Locate** a word by using the guide words at the top of the pages.
- **Look** at the parts of the reference entry, like part of speech, definition, or synonym.
- **Choose** between multiple meanings by thinking about what makes sense.
- **Apply** the meaning to what you're reading.

Distinguishing between meanings

Determining subtle differences between word meanings also aids comprehension. **Denotation** refers to the dictionary meaning or meanings of a word. **Connotation** refers to an emotion or underlying value that accompanies a word's dictionary meaning. The word *fragrance* has a different connotation than the word *odor,* even though the denotation of both words is "smell."

Comprehension Strategies

Because understanding is the most critical reading task, lifelong learners use a variety of reading strategies before, during, and after reading to ensure their comprehension.

Establishing and adjusting purposes for reading

To establish a purpose for reading, preview or **skim** a selection by glancing quickly over the entire piece, reading headings and subheadings, and noticing the organizational pattern of the text.

If you are reading to learn, solve a problem, or perform a task involving complex directions, consider these tips:

- Read slowly and carefully.
- Reread difficult passages.
- Take careful notes or construct a graphic.

Adjust your strategies as your purpose changes. To locate specific information in a longer selection, or to enjoy an entertaining plot, you might allow yourself a faster pace. Know when to speed up or slow down to maintain your understanding.

Drawing on personal background

When you recall information and personal experiences that are uniquely your own, you **draw on your personal background.** By thus **activating prior knowledge,** and combining it with the words on a page, you create meaning in a selection. To expand and extend your prior knowledge, share it interactively in classroom discussions.

Monitoring and modifying reading strategies

Check or **monitor your understanding** as you read, using the following strategies:

- Summarize
- Clarify
- Question
- Predict what will come next

You can use these four important steps once or twice in an easy, entertaining passage, or after every paragraph in a conceptually dense nonfiction selection. As you read, think about asking interesting questions, rather than passively waiting to answer questions your teacher may ask later on.

All readers find that understanding sometimes breaks down when material is difficult. Consider these steps to modify or change your reading strategies when you don't understand what you've read:

- Reread the passage.
- Consult other sources, including text resources, teachers, and other students.
- Write comments or questions on another piece of paper for later review or discussion.

Constructing graphic organizers

Graphic organizers, such as charts, maps, and diagrams, help you construct ideas in a visual way so you can remember them later on. Look at the following model. Like a Venn diagram, which compares and contrasts two ideas or characters, a **semantic features analysis** focuses on the discriminating features of ideas or words. The items or ideas you want to compare are listed down the side, and the discriminating features are listed across the top. In each box use a + if the feature or characteristic applies to the item, or use a − if the feature or characteristic does not apply.

People in Goverment	Elected	Appointed	Passes Laws	Vetoes Laws
President	+	−	−	+
State Governor	+	−	−	+
Supreme Court Justice	−	+	−	−
Secretary of Defense	−	+	−	−

A **flow chart** helps you keep track of the sequence of events. Arrange ideas or events in a logical, sequential order. Then draw arrows between your ideas to indicate how one idea or event flows into another. Look at the following flow chart to see how you might show the chronological sequence of a story. Use a flow chart to make a **change frame,** recording causes and effects in sequence to illustrate how something changed.

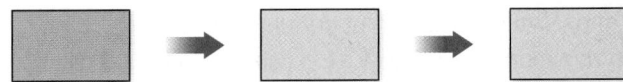

A **web** can be used for a variety of purposes as you read a selection.

- To **map out the main idea and details** of a selection, put the main idea in the middle circle, and, as you read, add supporting details around the main thought.

- To **analyze a character in a story,** put the character's name in the middle, and add that character's actions, thoughts, reputation, plot involvement, and personal development in the surrounding circles.

- To **define a concept,** put a word or an idea in the middle circle, and then add a more general category, descriptions, examples, and non-examples in the surrounding circles.

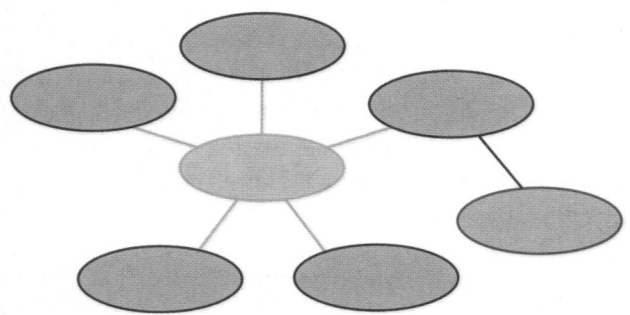

Analyzing text structures

To follow the logic and message of a selection and to remember it, analyze the **text structure,** or organization of ideas, within a writer's work. In narrative as well as in informational text, writers may embed one structure within another, but it is usually possible to identify one main pattern of organization. Recognizing the pattern of organization can help you discover the writer's purpose and will focus your attention on the important ideas in the selection. **Look for signal words** to point you to the structure.

- **Chronological order** often uses words like *first, then, after, later*, and *finally*.

- **Cause-and-effect order** can include words like *therefore, because, subsequently,* or *as a result of*.

- **Comparison-contrast order** may use words like *similarly, in contrast, likewise,* or *on the other hand*.

Interpreting graphic aids

Graphic aids provide an opportunity to see and analyze information at a glance. Charts, tables, maps, and diagrams allow you to analyze and compare information. Maps include a compass rose and legend to help you interpret direction and symbols. Charts and graphs compare information in categories running horizontally and vertically.

Tips for Reading Graphic Aids

- Examine the title, labels, and other explanatory features.
- Apply the labels to the graphic aid.
- Interpret the information.

Look carefully at the models below.

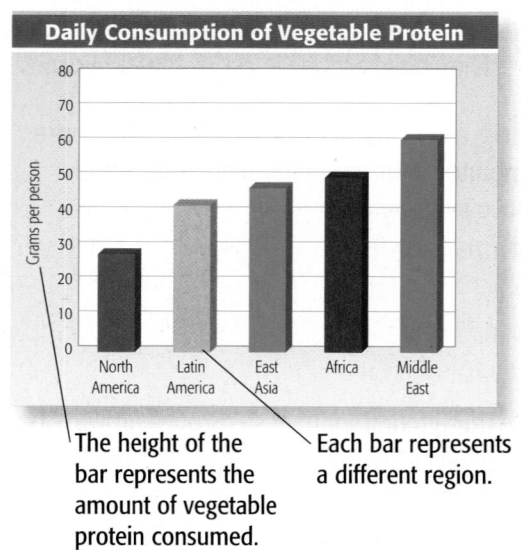

The height of the bar represents the amount of vegetable protein consumed.

Each bar represents a different region.

Sequencing

The order in which thoughts are arranged is called a **sequence**. A good sequence is one that is logical, given the ideas in a selection. **Chronological order, spatial order,** and **order of importance** are common forms of sequencing. Think about the order of a writer's thoughts as you read and pay particular attention to sequence when **following complex written directions**.

Summarizing

A summary is a short restatement of the main ideas and important details of a selection. Summarizing what you have read is an excellent tool for understanding and remembering a passage.

Tips for Summarizing

- Identify the **main ideas** or most important thoughts within a selection.
- Determine the essential **supporting details**.
- Relate all the main ideas and the essential details in a **logical sequence**.
- **Paraphrase**, that is, use your own words.
- Answer **who, what, why, where,** and **when** questions when you summarize.

The best summaries can easily be understood by someone who has not read the selection. If you're not sure whether an idea is a main idea or a detail, try taking it out of your summary. Does your summary still sound complete?

Drawing inferences and supporting them

An **inference** involves using your reason and experience to come up with an idea based on what a writer implies or suggests, but does not directly state. The following strategic reading behaviors are examples of inference:

- **Making a prediction** is taking an educated guess about what a text will be about based on initial clues a writer provides.
- **Drawing a conclusion** is making a general statement you can explain with reason or with supporting details from a text.
- **Making a generalization** is generating a statement that can apply to more than one item or group.

What is most important when inferring is to be sure that you have accurately based your thoughts on supporting details from the text as well as on your own knowledge.

Reading silently for sustained periods

When you read for long periods of time, your task is to avoid distractions. Check your comprehension regularly by summarizing what you've read so far. Using study guides or graphic organizers can help get you through difficult passages. Take regular breaks when you need them and vary your reading rate with the demands of the task.

Synthesizing information

You will often need to read across texts; that is, in different sources, combining or **synthesizing** what you've learned from varied sources to suit your purposes. Follow these suggestions:

- Understand the information you've read in each source.
- Interpret the information.
- Identify similarities and differences in ideas or logic.
- Combine like thoughts in a logical sequence.
- Add to the information or change the form to suit your purposes.

Literary Response

Whenever you share your thoughts and feelings about something you've read, you are responding to text. While the way you respond may vary with the type of text you read and with your individual learning style, as a strategic reader you will always need to adequately support your responses with proof from the text.

Responding to informational and aesthetic elements

When you respond both intellectually *and* emotionally, you connect yourself with a writer and with other people. To respond in an intellectual way, ask yourself if the ideas you have read are logical and well supported. To respond emotionally, ask yourself how you feel about those ideas and events. Choose a way to respond that fits your learning style. Class discussions, journal entries, oral interpretations, enactments, and graphic displays are some of the many ways to share your thoughts and emotions about a writer's work.

Comparing responses with authoritative views

Critics' reviews may encourage you to read a book, see a movie, or attend an event. They may also warn you that whatever is reviewed is not acceptable entertainment or is not valued by the reviewer. Deciding whether or not to value a review depends on the credibility of the reviewer and also on your own personal views and feelings. Ask yourself the following questions:

- What is the reviewer's background?
- What qualifies the reviewer to write this evaluation?
- Is the review balanced? Does it include both positive and negative responses?
- Are arguments presented logically?
- Are opinions supported with facts?
- What bias does this reviewer show?
- Do I agree? Why or why not?

Analysis and Evaluation

Good readers want to do more than recall information or interpret thoughts and ideas. When you read, read critically, forming opinions about characters and ideas, and making judgments using your own prior knowledge and information from the text.

Analyzing characteristics of texts

To be a critical reader and thinker, start by analyzing the characteristics of the text. Think about what specific characteristics make a particular selection clear, concise, and complete. Ask yourself these questions:

- What **pattern of organization** has this writer used to present his or her thoughts? Cause/effect? Comparison/contrast? Problem/solution? Does this organization make the main ideas clear or vague? Why?
- What word order, or **syntax,** gives force and emphasis to this writer's ideas? Does the grammatical order of the words make ideas sound complete, or is the sentence structure confusing?
- What **word choices** reveal this writer's tone, or attitude about the topic? Is the language precise or too general? Is it economical and yet descriptive?

Evaluating the credibility of sources

Evaluating the credibility of a source involves making a judgment about whether a writer is knowledgeable and truthful. Consider the following steps:

- **Decide on the writer's purpose or motive.** What will the writer gain if you accept his or her ideas or if you act on his or her suggestions?
- **Investigate the writer's background.** How has the writer become an authority in his or her field? Do others value what he or she says?
- **Evaluate the writer's statements.** Is the writer's information factual? Can it be proved? Are opinions clearly stated as such? Are they adequately supported with details so that they are valid? Are any statements nonfactual? Check to be sure.

Analyzing logical arguments and modes of reasoning

When you analyze works you've read, ask yourself whether the reasoning behind a writer's works is logical. Two kinds of logical reasoning are

Inductive Reasoning By observing a limited number of particular cases, a reader arrives at a general or universal statement. This logic moves from the specific to the general.

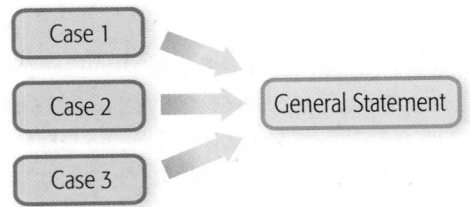

Deductive Reasoning This logic moves from the general to the specific. The reader takes a general statement and, through reasoning, applies it to specific situations.

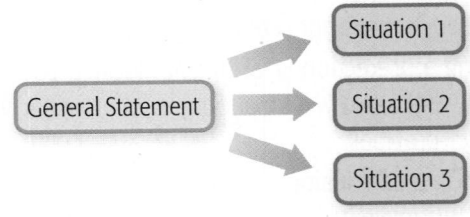

Faulty reasoning, on the other hand, is vague and illogical. Look for either/or reasoning or oversimplified statements when analyzing faulty reasoning. Failure to understand a writer's work may be the result of poorly presented, unsupported arguments, sequenced in a haphazard way.

A writer shows **bias** when he or she demonstrates a strong personal, and sometimes unreasonable, opinion. Look for bias when evaluating editorials, documentaries, and advertisements.

Writers use **persuasive techniques** when they try to get readers to believe a certain thing or act in a particular way. A writer may have a strong personal bias and still compose a persuasive essay that is logical and well supported. On the other hand, deceptive arguments can be less than accurate in order to be persuasive. Read carefully to judge whether a writer's bias influences his or her writing in negative or positive ways.

Reading and Thinking with Foldables™

by Dinah Zike, M.Ed., Creator of Foldables™

Using Foldables™ Makes Learning Easy and Enjoyable

Anyone who has paper, scissors, and maybe a stapler or some glue can use Foldables in the classroom. Just follow the illustrated step-by-step directions. Check out the following sample:

 Reading Objective: to understand how one character's actions affect other characters in a short story

Use this Foldable to keep track of what the main character does and how his or her actions affect the other characters.

1. Place a sheet of paper in front of you so that the short side is at the top. Fold the paper in half from top to bottom.

2. Fold in half again, from side to side, to divide the paper into two columns. Unfold the paper so that the two columns show.

3. Draw a line along the column crease. Then, through the top layer of paper, cut along the line you drew, forming two tabs.

4. Label the tabs *Main character's actions* and *Effects on others.*

5. As you read, record the main character's actions under the first tab. Record how each of those actions affects other characters under the second tab.

> Practice reading and following step-by-step directions.

> Illustrations make directions easier to follow.

> Become an active reader, tracking and reorganizing information so that you can better comprehend the selection.

Short Story

 Reading Objective: to analyze a short story on the basis of its literary elements

As you read, use the following Foldable to keep track of five literary elements in the short story.

1. Stack three sheets of paper with their top edges about a half-inch apart. Be sure to keep the side edges straight.

2. Fold up the bottom edges of the paper to form six tabs, five of which will be the same size.

3. Crease the paper to hold the tabs in place and staple the sheets together along the crease.

4. Turn the sheets so that the stapled side is at the top. Write the title of the story on the top tab. Label the five remaining tabs *Setting, Characters, Plot, Point of View,* and *Theme.*

5. Use your Foldable as you read the short story. Under each labeled tab, jot down notes about the story in terms of that element.

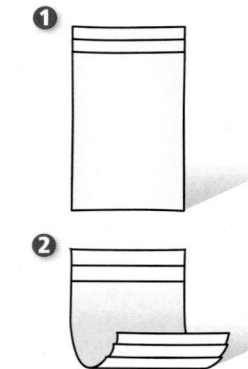

You may adapt this simple Foldable in several ways.

- ◼ Use it with dramas, longer works of fiction, and some narrative poems—wherever five literary elements are present in the story.

- ◼ Change the labels to focus on something different. For example, if a story or a play has several settings, characters, acts, or scenes, you could devote a tab to each one.

Drama

 Reading Objective: to understand conflict and plot in a drama

As you read the drama, use the following Foldable to keep track of conflicts that arise and ways that those conflicts are resolved.

1. Place a sheet of paper in front of you so that the short side is at the top. Fold the paper in half from side to side.

2. Fold the paper again, one inch from the top as shown here.

3. Unfold the paper and draw lines along all of the folds. This will be your chart.

4. At the top, label the left column *Conflicts* and the right column *Resolutions.*

5. As you read, record in the left column the various conflicts that arise in the drama. In the right column, explain how each conflict is resolved by the end of the drama.

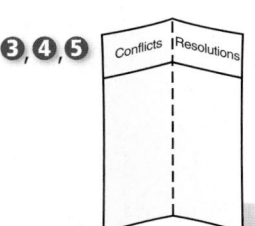

You may adapt this simple Foldable in several ways.

- ◼ Use it with short stories, longer works of fiction, and many poems—wherever conflicts and their resolutions are important.

- ◼ Change the labels to focus on something different. For example, you could record the actions of two characters, or you could record the thoughts and feelings of a character before and after the story's climax.

Lyric Poem

Reading Objective: to interpret the poet's message by understanding the speaker's thoughts and feelings

As you read the poem, use the following Foldable to help you distinguish between what the speaker *says* and what the poet *means*.

1. Place a sheet of paper in front of you so that the short side is at the top. Fold the paper in half from top to bottom.

2. Fold the paper in half again from left to right.

3. Unfold and cut through the top layer of paper along the fold lines. This will make two tabs.

4. Label the left tab *Speaker's Words.* Label the right tab *Poet's Meaning.*

5. Use your Foldable to jot down notes on as you read the poem. Under the left tab, write down key things the speaker says. Under the right tab, write down what you think the poet means by having the speaker say those things.

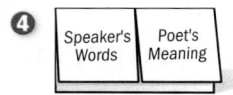

You may adapt this simple Foldable in several ways.

- Use it to help you visualize the images in a poem. Just replace *Speaker's Words* with *Imagery* and replace *Poet's Meaning* with *What I See.*

- Replace the label *Speaker's Words* with *Speaker's Tone* and write adjectives under the tab that describe the tone of the speaker's words.

- If the poem you are reading has two stanzas, you might devote each tab to notes about one stanza.

Informational Text

Study Organizer

Reading Objective: to understand and remember ideas in informational text

As you read a nonfiction selection, use this Foldable to help you identify what you already know about the topic, what you might want to know about it, and what you learn about it from the selection.

1. Hold a sheet of paper in front of you so that the short side is at the top. Fold the bottom of the paper up and the top down to divide the paper into thirds.

2. Unfold the paper and turn it so that the long side is at the top. Draw lines along the folds and label the three columns *Know, Want to Know,* and *Learned.*

3. Before you read the selection, write what you already know about the topic under the left heading and what you want to know about it under the middle heading. As you read, jot down what you learn about the topic under the last heading.

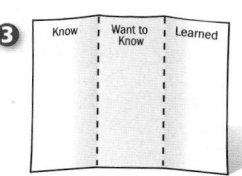

You may adapt this simple Foldable in several ways.

- Use it with magazine and newspaper articles, textbook chapters, reference articles, and informational Web sites—anything you might read to look for information.

- Use this three-part Foldable to record information from three sources. Label each column with the name of one source and write notes from that source under its heading.

- For a two-column Foldable, just fold the sheet of paper in half. For four columns, fold it in half and then in half again.

The Writing Process

Writing is a process with five stages: *prewriting, drafting, revising, editing/ proofreading*, and *publishing/presenting*. These stages often overlap, and their importance, weight, and even their order vary according to your needs and goals. Because writing is recursive, you almost always have to double back somewhere in this process, perhaps to gather more information or to reevaluate your ideas.

The Writing Process

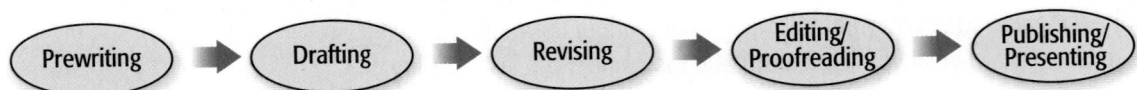

Prewriting → Drafting → Revising → Editing/ Proofreading → Publishing/ Presenting

Prewriting

The prewriting stage includes coming up with ideas, making connections, gathering information, defining and refining the topic, and making a plan for a piece of writing.

Tips for prewriting

- Begin with an interesting idea (*what* you will write about).
- Decide the purpose of the writing (*why* you are writing).
- Identify the audience (for *whom* you are writing).
- Explore your idea through a technique such as freewriting, clustering, making diagrams, or brainstorming.

   Freewriting is writing nonstop for a set time, usually only five or ten minutes. The idea is to keep pace with your thoughts, getting them on paper before they vanish. Freewriting can start anywhere and go anywhere.

   Clustering begins with writing a word or phrase in the middle of a sheet of paper. Circle the word or phrase; then think of related words and ideas. Write them in bubbles connected to the central bubble. As you cluster, connect related ideas. The finished cluster will be a diagram of how your ideas can be organized.

   Brainstorming is creating a free flow of ideas with a group of people—it's like freewriting with others. Start with a topic or question; encourage everyone to join in freely. Accept all ideas without

judgment, and follow each idea as far as it goes. You can evaluate the ideas later.

- Search for information in print and nonprint sources.
- If you are writing a personal essay, all of the information may come from your own experiences and feelings. If you are writing a report or a persuasive essay, you will probably need to locate pertinent factual information and take notes on it. Besides library materials, such as books, magazines, and newspapers, you will want to use the Internet and other on-line resources. You may also want to interview people with experience or specialized knowledge related to your topic.
- As you gather ideas and information, jot them down on note cards to use as you draft.
- Evaluate all ideas and information to determine or fine-tune the topic.
- Organize information and ideas into a plan that serves as the basis for writing.
- Develop a rough outline reflecting the method of organization you have chosen. Include your main points and supporting details.
- Find and include missing information or ideas that might add interest or help accomplish the purpose of the writing.

Drafting

In this stage you translate into writing the ideas and information you gathered during prewriting. Drafting is an opportunity to explore and develop your ideas.

Tips for drafting

- Follow the plan made during prewriting, but be flexible. New and better ideas may come to you as you develop your ideas; be open to them.
- Transform notes and ideas into related sentences and paragraphs, but don't worry about grammar or mechanics. At this point, it is usually better to concentrate on getting your ideas on paper. You might want to circle or annotate ideas or sections that need more work.
- Determine the tone or attitude of the writing.
- Try to formulate an introduction that will catch the interest of your intended audience.

Revising

In this stage, review and evaluate your draft to make sure it accomplishes its purpose and speaks to its intended audience. When revising, interacting with a peer reviewer can be especially helpful.

Using peer review

Ask one or more of your classmates to read your draft. Here are some specific ways in which you can direct their responses.

- Have readers tell you in their own words what they have read. If you do not hear your ideas restated, you will want to revise for clarity.
- Ask readers to tell you what parts of your writing they liked best and why.
- Discuss the ideas in your writing with your readers. Include in your revision any new insights you gain.
- Ask readers for suggestions about things such as organization and word choice.

You may want to take notes on your readers' suggestions so you will have a handy reference as you revise.

Tips for the peer reviewer

When you are asked to act as a reviewer for a classmate's writing, the following tips will help you do the most effective job:

- Read the piece all the way through—without commenting—to judge its overall effect.
- Tell the writer how you responded to the piece. For example, did you find it informative? interesting? amusing?
- Ask the writer about parts you don't understand.
- Think of questions to ask that will help the writer improve the piece.
- Be sure that your suggestions are constructive.
- Help the writer make improvements.
- Answer the writer's questions honestly. Think about how you would like someone to respond to you.

Tips for revising

- Be sure you have said everything you wanted to say. If not, *add.*
- If you find a section that does not relate to your topic, *cut it.*
- If your ideas are not in a logical order, *rearrange* sentences and paragraphs.
- *Rewrite* any unclear sentences.
- Evaluate your introduction to be sure it creates interest, leads the reader smoothly into your topic, and states your main idea. Also evaluate your conclusion to be sure it either summarizes your writing or effectively brings it to an end.
- Evaluate your word choices. Choose vivid verbs and precise nouns. Use a thesaurus to help you.
- Consider the comments of your peer reviewer. Evaluate them carefully and apply those that will help you create a more effective piece of writing.

Editing/Proofreading

In the editing stage, you polish your revised draft and proofread it for errors in grammar and spelling. Use this proofreading checklist to help you check for errors, and use the proofreading symbols in the chart below to mark places that need corrections.

- ☑ Have I avoided run-on sentences and sentence fragments and punctuated sentences correctly?
- ☑ Have I used every word correctly, including plurals, possessives, and frequently confused words?
- ☑ Do verbs and subjects agree? Are verb tenses correct?
- ☑ Do pronouns refer clearly to their antecedents and agree with them in person, number, and gender?
- ☑ Have I used adverb and adjective forms and modifying phrases correctly?
- ☑ Have I spelled every word correctly and checked the unfamiliar ones in a dictionary?

Publishing/Presenting

There are a number of ways you can share your work. You could publish it in a magazine, a class anthology, or another publication, or read your writing aloud to a group. You could also join a writer's group and read one another's works.

Proofreading Symbols

⊙	Lieut Brown	Insert a period.
∧	No one came_to the party.	Insert a letter or a word.
=	I enjoyed paris.	Capitalize a letter.
/	The Class ran a bake sale.	Make a capital letter lowercase.
⌢	The campers are home sick.	Close up a space.
⟨sp⟩	They visited N.Y. ⟨sp⟩	Spell out.
∧ ⌃	Sue please come I need your help.	Insert a comma or a semicolon.
∩	He enjoyed feild day.	Transpose the position of letters or words.
#	alltogether	Insert a space.
ℰ	We went to to Boston.	Delete letters or words.
�v v v	She asked, Whos coming?	Insert quotation marks or an apostrophe.
/ = /	mid January	Insert a hyphen.
¶	"Where?" asked Karl. "Over there," said Ray.	Begin a new paragraph.

Using the Traits of Strong Writing

What are some basic terms you can use to discuss your writing with your teacher or classmates? What should you focus on as you revise and edit your compositions? Check out the following seven terms, or traits, that describe the qualities of strong writing. Learn the meaning of each trait and find out how using the traits can improve your writing.

Ideas   The message or the theme and the details that develop it

Writing is clear when readers can grasp the meaning of your ideas right away. Check to see whether you're getting your message across.

- ☑ Does the title suggest the theme of the composition?
- ☑ Does the composition focus on a single narrow topic?
- ☑ Is the thesis—the main point or central idea—clearly stated?
- ☑ Do well-chosen details elaborate your main point?

Organization   The arrangement of main ideas and supporting details

An effective plan of organization points your readers in the right direction and guides them easily through your composition from start to finish. Find a structure, or order, that best suits your topic and writing purpose. Check to see whether you've ordered your key ideas and details in a way that keeps your readers on track.

- ☑ Are the beginning, middle, and end clearly linked?
- ☑ Is the internal order of ideas easy to follow?
- ☑ Does the introduction capture your readers' attention?
- ☑ Do sentences and paragraphs flow from one to the next in a way that makes sense?
- ☑ Does the conclusion wrap up the composition?

Voice   A writer's unique way of using tone and style

Your writing voice comes through when your readers sense that a real person is communicating with them. Readers will respond to the **tone** (or attitude) that you express toward a topic and to the **style** (the way that you use language and shape your sentences). Read your work aloud to see whether your writing voice comes through.

- ☑ Does your writing sound interesting?
- ☑ Does your writing reveal your attitude toward your topic?
- ☑ Does your writing sound like you—or does it sound like you're imitating someone else?

Word Choice   The vocabulary a writer uses to convey meaning

Words work hard. They carry the weight of your meaning, so make sure you choose them carefully. Check to see whether the words you choose are doing their jobs well.

- ☑ Do you use lively verbs to show action?
- ☑ Do you use vivid words to create word pictures in your readers' minds?
- ☑ Do you use precise words to explain your ideas simply and clearly?

Sentence Fluency The smooth rhythm and flow of sentences that vary in length and style

The best writing is made up of sentences that flow smoothly from one sentence to the next. Writing that is graceful also sounds musical–rhythmical rather than choppy. Check for sentence fluency by reading your writing aloud.

☑ Do your sentences vary in length and structure?

☑ Do transition words and phrases show connections between ideas and sentences?

☑ Does parallelism help balance and unify related ideas?

Conventions Correct spelling, grammar, usage, and mechanics

A composition free of errors makes a good impression on your readers. Mistakes can be distracting, and they can blur your message. Try working with a partner to spot errors and correct them. Use this checklist to help you.

☑ Are all words spelled correctly?

☑ Are all proper nouns—as well as the first word of every sentence—capitalized?

☑ Is your composition free of sentence fragments?

☑ Is your composition free of run-on sentences?

☑ Are punctuation marks—such as apostrophes, commas, and end marks—inserted in the right places?

Presentation The way words and design elements look on a page

Appearance matters, so make your compositions inviting to read. Handwritten papers should be neat and legible. If you're using a word processor, double-space the lines of text and choose a readable font. Other design elements– such as boldfaced headings, bulleted lists, pictures, and charts–can help you present information effectively as well as make your papers look good.

Preparing a manuscript

Follow the guidelines of the Modern Language Association when you prepare the final copy of your research paper.

- **Heading** On separate lines in the upper left-hand corner of the first page, include your name, your teacher's name, the course name, and the date.
- **Title** Center the title on the line below the heading.
- **Numbering** Number the pages one-half inch from the top of the page in the right-hand corner. Write your last name before each page number after the first page.
- **Spacing** Use double spacing throughout.
- **Margins** Leave one-inch margins on all sides of every page.

Writing Modes

Writing may be classified as expository, descriptive, narrative, or persuasive. Each of these classifications, or modes, has its own purpose.

Expository Writing

Expository writing gives instructions, defines or explains new terms or ideas, explains relationships, compares one thing or opinion to another, or explains how to do something. Expository essays usually include a thesis statement in the introduction.

☑ Does the opening contain attention-grabbing details or intriguing questions to hook the reader?

☑ Have I provided sufficient information to my audience in a clear and interesting way?

☑ Have I checked the accuracy of the information I have provided?

☑ Are my comparisons and contrasts clear and logical?

Descriptive Writing

Description re-creates an experience primarily through the use of sensory details. A writer should strive to create a single impression that all the details support. To do so requires careful planning as well as choices about order of information, topic sentences, and figurative language.

☑ Did I create interest in my introduction?

☑ Are my perspective and my subject clearly stated in my topic sentence?

☑ Did I organize details carefully and consistently?

☑ Did I order information effectively?

☑ Have I chosen precise, vivid words?

☑ Do transitions clearly and logically connect the ideas?

☑ Have I created a strong, unified impression?

Narrative Writing

Narrative writing, whether factual or fictional, tells a story and has these elements: characters, plot, point of view, theme, and setting. The plot usually involves a conflict between a character and an opposing character or force.

☑ Did I introduce characters and a setting?

☑ Did I develop a plot that begins with an interesting problem or conflict?

☑ Did I build suspense, lead the reader to a climax, and end with a resolution?

☑ Did I use dialogue to move the story along?

Persuasive Writing

Persuasive writing expresses a writer's opinion. The goal of persuasion is to make an audience change its opinion and, perhaps, take action. Effective persuasive writing uses strong, relative evidence to support its claims. This kind of writing often requires careful research, organization, and attention to language.

☑ Did I keep my audience's knowledge and attitudes in mind from start to finish?

☑ Did I state my position in a clear thesis statement?

☑ Have I included ample supporting evidence?

☑ Have I addressed opposing viewpoints?

☑ Have I avoided errors in logic?

Research Paper Writing

More than any other type of paper, research papers are the product of a search—a search for data, for facts, for informed opinions, for insights, and for new information.

Selecting a topic

- If a specific topic is not assigned, choose a topic. Begin with the assigned subject or a subject that interests you. Read general sources of information about that subject and narrow your focus to some aspect of it that interests you. Good places to start are encyclopedia articles and the tables of contents of books on the subject. A computerized library catalog will also display many subheads related to general topics. Find out if sufficient information about your topic is available.

- As you read about the topic, develop your paper's central idea, which is the purpose of your research. Even though this idea might change as you do more research, it can begin to guide your efforts. For example, if you were assigned the subject of the Civil War, you might find that you're interested in women's roles during that war. As you read, you might narrow your topic down to women who went to war, women who served as nurses for the Union, or women who took over farms and plantations in the South.

Conducting a broad search for information

- Generate a series of researchable questions about your chosen topic. Then research to find answers to your questions.

- Among the many sources you might use are the card catalog, the computer catalog, the *Reader's Guide to Periodical Literature* (or an electronic equivalent), newspaper indexes, and specialized references such as biographical encyclopedias.

- If possible, use primary sources as well as secondary sources. A **primary source** is a firsthand account of an event–for example, the diary of a woman who served in the army in the Civil War is a primary source. **Secondary sources** are sources written by people who did not experience or influence the event. Locate specific information efficiently by using the table of contents, indexes, chapter headings, and graphic aids.

Developing a working bibliography

If a work seems useful, write a **bibliography card** for it. On an index card, write down the author, title, city of publication, publisher, and date of publication, and any other information you will need to identify the source. Number your cards in the upper right-hand corner so you can keep them in order.

Following are model bibliography, or source, cards.

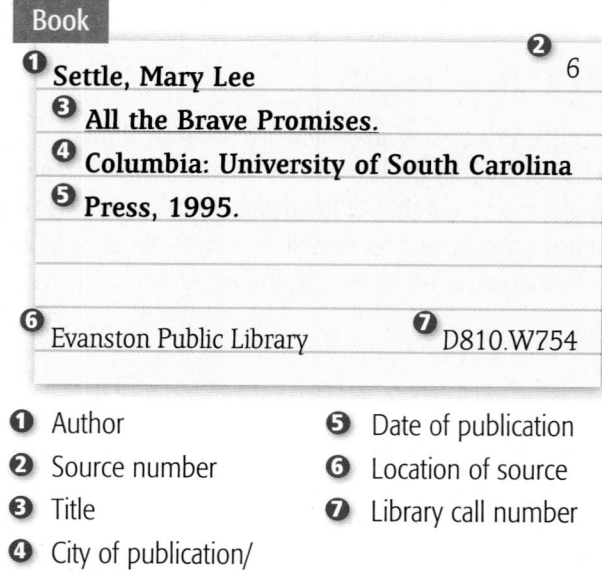

Book

❶ Settle, Mary Lee ❷ 6
❸ All the Brave Promises.
❹ Columbia: University of South Carolina
❺ Press, 1995.

❻ Evanston Public Library ❼ D810.W754

❶ Author
❷ Source number
❸ Title
❹ City of publication/ Publisher
❺ Date of publication
❻ Location of source
❼ Library call number

Periodical

❶ Chelminski. R. ❷ 2
❸ "The Maginot Line"
❹ *Smithsonian*, June 1997: 90-99

❶ Author
❷ Source number
❸ Title
❹ Title of magazine/date/page number(s)

Online source

❶ "Job Hunting Resources"　　❷ 6
❸ The Career Building Network
❹ CareerBuilder
❺ 14 Feb. 2002
❻ http://www.careerbuilder.com

❶ Title　　　　　　　❹ Sponsoring organization
❷ Source number　　　❺ Date of access
❸ Title of database　　❻ URL

Evaluating your sources

Your sources should be **a**uthoritative, **r**eliable, **t**imely, and **s**uitable. **(arts)**

- The source should be **authoritative.** The author should be well-known in the field. An author who has written several books or articles about a subject or who is frequently quoted may be considered an authority. You might also consult *Book Review Index* and *Book Review Digest* to find out how other experts in the field have evaluated a book or an article.

- The source should be **reliable.** If possible, avoid material from popular magazines in favor of that from more scholarly journals. Be especially careful to evaluate material from online sources. For example, the Web site of a well-known university is more reliable than that of an individual. (You might also consult a librarian or your instructor for guidance in selecting reliable online sources.)

- The source should be **timely.** Use the most recent material available, particularly for subjects of current importance. Check the publication date of books as well as the month and year of periodicals.

- The source should be **suitable,** or **appropriate.** Consider only material that is relevant to the purpose of your paper. Do not waste time on books or articles that have little bearing on your topic. If you are writing on a controversial topic, you should include material that represents more than one point of view.

Compiling and organizing note cards

Careful notes will help you to organize the material for your paper.

- As you reread and study sources, write useful information on index cards. Be sure that each note card

identifies the source (use the number of the bibliography card that corresponds to each source).

- In the lower right-hand corner of the card write the page number on which you found the information. If one card contains several notes, write the page number in parentheses after the relevant material.

- Three helpful ways to take notes are paraphrasing, summarizing, and quoting directly.

  1. **Paraphrase** important details that you want to remember; that is, use your own words to restate specific information.

  2. **Summarize** main ideas that an author presents. When you summarize several pages, be sure to note the page on which the material begins and the page on which it ends—for example, 213–221.

  3. **Quote** the exact words of an author only when the actual wording is important. Be careful about placing the author's words in quotation marks.

- Identify the subject of each note card with a short phrase written in the upper left.

Avoid **plagiarism**—presenting an author's words or ideas as if they were your own. Remember that you must credit the source not only for material directly quoted but also for any facts or ideas obtained from the source.

See the sample note card below, which includes information about careers and goals from three pages.

Careers and goals　　　　　　　　　12
Many people "crave work that will
spark... excitement and energy."
(5) Sher recognizes that a career does
not necessarily satisfy a person's aim
in life. (24) She also offers advice on
how to overcome obstacles that people
experience in defining their goals. (101)

- Organize your note cards to develop a **working outline.** Begin by sorting them into piles of related cards. Try putting the piles together in different ways that suggest an organizational pattern. (If, at this point, you discover that you do not have enough information, go back and do further research.) Many methods of organization are possible. You might also combine methods of organization.

Developing a thesis statement

A thesis statement tells what your topic is and what you intend to say about it—for example, "World War II changed the lives of African Americans and contributed to the rise of the Civil Rights movement."

- Start by examining your central idea.
- Refine it to reflect the information that you gathered in your research.
- Next, consider your approach to the topic. What is the purpose of your research? Are you proving or disproving something? illustrating a cause-and-effect relationship? offering a solution to a problem? examining one aspect of the topic thoroughly? predicting an outcome?
- Revise your central idea to reflect your approach.
- Be prepared to revise your thesis statement if necessary.

Drafting your paper

Consult your working outline and your notes as you start to draft your paper.

- Concentrate on getting your ideas down in a complete and logical order.
- Write an introduction and a conclusion. An effective introduction creates interest, perhaps by beginning with a question or a controversial quotation; it should also contain your thesis statement. An effective conclusion will summarize main points, restate your thesis, explain how the research points to important new questions to explore, and bring closure to the paper.

Documenting sources

Since a research paper, by its nature, is built on the work of others, you must carefully document all the sources you have used.

- Name the sources of words, ideas, and facts that you borrow.
- In addition to citing books and periodicals from which you take information, cite song lyrics, letters, and excerpts from literature.
- Also credit original ideas that are expressed graphically in tables, charts, and diagrams, as well as the sources of other visual aids you may include, such as photographs.
- You need not cite the source of any information that is common knowledge, such as "John F. Kennedy was assassinated in 1963 in Dallas, Texas."

In-text citations The most common method of crediting sources is with parenthetical documentation within the text. Generally a reference to the source and page number is included in parentheses at the end of each quotation, paraphrase, or summary of information borrowed from a source. An in-text citation points readers to a corresponding entry in your **works-cited list**—a list of all your sources, complete with publication information, that will appear as the final page of your paper. The Modern Language Association (MLA) recommends the following guidelines for crediting sources in text. You may wish to refer to the *MLA Handbook for Writers of Research Papers* by Joseph Gibaldi for more information and examples.

- **Put in parentheses the author's last name and the page number where you found the information.**

  An art historian has noted, "In Woods's idyllic farmscapes, man lives in complete harmony with Nature; he is the earth's caretaker" (Corn 90).

- **If the author's name is mentioned in the sentence, put only the page number in parentheses.**

  Art historian Wanda Corn has noted, "In Woods's idyllic farmscapes, man lives in complete harmony with Nature; he is the earth's caretaker" (90).

- **If no author is listed, put the title or a shortened version of the title in parentheses. Include a page number if you have one.**

  Some critics believe that Grant Wood's famous painting *American Gothic* pokes fun at small-town life and traditional American values ("Gothic").

Compiling a list of works cited

At the end of your text, provide an alphabetized list of published works or other sources cited.

- Include complete publishing information for each source.
- For magazine and newspaper articles, include the page numbers. If an article is continued on a different page, use + after the first page number.
- For online sources, include the date accessed.
- Cite only those sources from which you actually use information.
- Arrange entries in alphabetical order according to the author's last name. Write the last name first. If no author is given, alphabetize by title.
- For long entries, indent five spaces every line after the first.

How to cite sources

On the next three pages, you'll find sample style sheets that can help you prepare your list of sources—the final page of the research paper. Use the one your teacher prefers.

MLA Style

MLA style is most often used in English and social studies classes. Center the title *Works Cited* at the top of your list.

Source	Style
Book with one author	Witham, Barry B. *The Federal Theatre Project: A Case Study.* New York: Cambridge UP, 2003. ["UP" is an abbreviation for "University Press."].
Book with two or three authors	Hoy, Pat C., II, Esther H. Schor, and Robert DiYanni. *Women's Voices: Visions and Perspectives.* New York: McGraw-Hill, 1990. [If a book has more than three authors, name only the first author and then write "et al." (Latin abbreviation for "and others").]
Book with editor(s)	Komunyakaa, Yusef, and David Lehman, eds. *The Best American Poetry 2003.* New York: Scribners, 2003.
Book with an organization or a group as author or editor	Smithsonian Institution. *Aircraft of the National Air and Space Museum.* Washington: Smithsonian Institution Press, 1998.
Work from an anthology	Cofer, Judith Ortiz. "Tales Told Under the Mango Tree." *Hispanic American Literature.* Ed. Nicolas Kanellos. New York: HarperCollins, 1995. 34–44.
Introduction in a published book	Weintraub, Stanley. Introduction. *Great Expectations.* By Charles Dickens. New York: Signet, 1998. v–xii.
Encyclopedia article	"Jazz." *Encyclopaedia Britannica.* 15th ed. 1998.
Weekly magazine article	Franzen, Jonathan. "The Listener." *New Yorker* 6 Oct. 2003: 85–99.
Monthly magazine article	Quammen, David. "Saving Africa's Eden." *National Geographic* Sept. 2003: 50–77.
Newspaper article	Dionne, E. J., Jr. "California's Great Debate." *Washington Post* 26 Sept. 2003: A27. [If no author is named, begin the entry with the title of the article.]
Internet	"Visit Your Parks." *National Park Service.* 1 Oct. 2003. National Park Service, U.S. Dept. of the Interior. 3 Nov. 2003 <http://www.nps.gov/parks.html>.
Online magazine article	Martin, Richard. "How Ravenous Soviet Viruses Will Save the World." *Wired Magazine* 11.10 (October 2003). 17 Oct. 2003 <http://www.wired.com/wired/archive/11.10/phages.html>.
Radio or TV program	"Orcas." *Champions of the Wild.* Animal Planet. Discovery Channel. 21 Oct. 2003.
Videotape or DVD	Hafner, Craig, dir. *The True Story of Seabiscuit.* DVD. A & E Home Video, 2003. [For a videotape (VHS) version, replace "DVD" with "Videocassette."]
Interview	Campeche, Tanya. E-mail interview. 25 Feb. 2004. [If an interview takes place in person, replace "E-mail" with "Personal"; if it takes place on the telephone, use "Telephone."]

CMS Style

CMS style was created by the University of Chicago Press to meet its publishing needs. This style, which is detailed in *The Chicago Manual of Style* (CMS), is used in a number of subject areas. Center the title *Bibliography* at the top of your list.

Source	Style
Book with one author	Witham, Barry B. *The Federal Theatre Project: A Case Study.* New York: Cambridge University Press, 2003.
Book with multiple authors	Hoy, Pat C., II, Esther H. Schor, and Robert DiYanni. *Women's Voices: Visions and Perspectives.* New York: McGraw-Hill, 1990. [If a book has more than ten authors, name only the first seven and then write "et al." (Latin abbreviation for "and others").]
Book with editor(s)	Komunyakaa, Yusef, and David Lehman, eds. *The Best American Poetry 2003.* New York: Scribners, 2003.
Book with an organization or a group as author or editor	Smithsonian Institution. *Aircraft of the National Air and Space Museum.* Washington, DC: Smithsonian Institution Press, 1998.
Work from an anthology	Cofer, Judith Ortiz. "Tales Told Under the Mango Tree." *Hispanic American Literature,* edited by Nicolas Kanellos, 34–44. New York: HarperCollins, 1995.
Introduction in a published book	Dickens, Charles. *Great Expectations.* New introduction by Stanley Weintraub. New York: Signet, 1998.
Encyclopedia article	[Credit for encyclopedia articles goes in your text, not in your bibliography.]
Weekly magazine article	Franzen, Jonathan. "The Listener." *New Yorker,* October 6, 2003, 85–99.
Monthly magazine article	Quammen, David. "Saving Africa's Eden." *National Geographic,* September 2003, 50–77.
Newspaper article	Dionne, E. J., Jr. "California's Great Debate." *Washington Post,* September 26, 2003, A27. [Credit for unsigned newspaper articles goes in your text, not in your bibliography.]
Internet	U.S. Dept. of the Interior. "Visit Your Parks." *National Park Service.* http://www.nps.gov/parks.html.
Online magazine article	Martin, Richard. "How Ravenous Soviet Viruses Will Save the World." *Wired Magazine* 11.10 (October 2003). http://www.wired.com/wired/archive/11.10/phages.html.
Radio or TV program	[Credit for radio and TV programs goes in your text, not in your bibliography.]
Videotape or DVD	Hafner, Craig, dir. *The True Story of Seabiscuit.* A & E Home Video, 2003. DVD. [For a videotape (VHS) version, replace "DVD" with "Videocassette."]
Interview	[Credit for interviews goes in your text, not in your bibliography.]

APA Style

The American Psychological Association (APA) style is commonly used in the sciences. Center the title *References* at the top of your list.

Source	Style
Book with one author	Witham, B. B. (2003). *The federal theatre project: A case study.* New York: Cambridge University Press.
Book with multiple authors	Hoy, P. C., II, Schor, E. H., & DiYanni, R. (1990). *Women's voices: Visions and perspectives.* New York: McGraw-Hill. [If a book has more than six authors, list the first six authors and then write "et al." (Latin abbreviation for "and others").]
Book with editor(s)	Komunyakaa, Y., & Lehman, D. (Eds.). (2003). *The best American poetry 2003.* New York: Scribners.
Book with an organization or a group as author or editor	Smithsonian Institution. (1998). *Aircraft of the National Air and Space Museum.* Washington, DC: Smithsonian Institution Press.
Work from an anthology	Cofer, J. O. (1995). Tales told under the mango tree. In N. Kanellos (Ed.), *Hispanic American Literature* (pp. 34–44). New York: HarperCollins.
Introduction in a published book	[Credit for introductions goes in your text, not in your references.]
Encyclopedia article	Jazz. (1998). In *Encyclopaedia Britannica.* (Vol. 6, pp. 519–520). Chicago: Encyclopaedia Britannica.
Weekly magazine article	Franzen, J. (2003, October 6). The listener. *The New Yorker,* 85–99.
Monthly magazine article	Quammen, D. (2003, September). Saving Africa's Eden. *National Geographic,* 204, 50–77.
Newspaper article	Dionne, E. J., Jr. (2003, September 26). California's great debate. *The Washington Post,* p. A27. [If no author is named, begin the entry with the title of the article.]
Internet	U.S. Dept. of Interior, National Park Service. (2003, October 1). *National Park Service.* Visit your parks. Retrieved October 17, 2003, from http://www.nps.gov/parks.html
Online magazine article	Martin, R. (2003, October). How ravenous Soviet viruses will save the world. *Wired Magazine,* 11.10. Retrieved October 17, 2003, from http://www.wired.com/wired/archive/11.10/phages.html
Radio or TV program	Orcas. (2003, October 21). *Champions of the wild* [Television series episode]. Animal Planet. Silver Spring, MD: Discovery Channel.
Videotape or DVD	Hafner, C. (Director). (2003). *The true story of Seabiscuit* [DVD]. A & E Home Video. [For a videotape (VHS) version, replace "DVD" with "Videocassette."]
Interview	[Credit for interviews goes in your text, not in your references.]

BUSINESS WRITING

Business writing and technical writing are specialized forms of expository writing. Business writing might include documents such as letters, memorandums, reports, briefs, proposals, and articles for business publications. Business writing must be clear, concise, accurate, and correct in style and usage.

Letter of Application

One form of business writing that follows a conventional format is a letter of application. A letter of application can be used when applying for a job, an internship, or a scholarship. In most cases, the letter is intended to accompany a résumé or an application. Because detailed information is usually included in the accompanying form, a letter of application should provide a general overview of your qualifications and the reasons you are submitting an application. A letter of application should be concise. You should clearly state which position you are applying for and then explain why you are interested and what makes you qualified. The accompanying material should speak for itself.

---

32 South Street
Austin, Texas 78746
May 6, 20__

Melissa Reyes
City Life magazine
2301 Davis Avenue
Austin, Texas 78764

❶ Re: Internship

Dear Ms. Reyes:

   I am a junior at City High School and editor of the City High Herald. I ❷ am writing to apply for your summer internship at City Life magazine. As a journalism student and a longtime fan of your magazine, I feel that an internship with your magazine would provide me with valuable experience in the field of journalism. I believe that my role with the City High Herald ❸ has given me the skills necessary to be a useful contributor to your magazine this summer. In addition, my enclosed application shows that I ❹ am also a diligent worker.

   I thank you for considering my application for your summer internship, and I hope to be working with you in the coming months.

Sincerely,

Anne Moris

Anne Moris

---

❶ The optional subject line indicates the topic of the letter.

❷ The writer states her purpose directly and immediately.

❸ The writer comments briefly on her qualifications.

❹ The writer makes reference to the accompanying material.

Activity: Choose a local business where you might like to work. Write a letter of application for an internship at that business. Assume that you will be submitting this letter along with a résumé or an internship application that details your experience and qualifications.

Résumé

The purpose of a résumé is to provide the employer with a comprehensive record of your background information, related experience, and qualifications. Although a résumé is intended to provide a great deal of information, the format is designed to provide this information in the most efficient way possible.

All résumés should include the following information: a heading that provides your name and contact information; a job goal or a career objective; your education information; your work experience; other related experience; relevant activities, associations, organizations, or projects in which you have participated. You may also want to include honors that you have received and list individuals whom the employer can contact for a reference. When listing work experience, be sure to give the employer's name, your job title, and a few brief bulleted points describing your responsibilities. The format may vary from résumé to résumé, but it should always be consistent within each résumé.

---

❶ Jane Wiley
909 West Main Street, Apt. #1
Urbana, Illinois 61802
(217) 555-0489 • jane@internet.edu

Goal
Seeking position in television news production

❷ Education
Junior standing in the College of Communications at the University of Illinois, Urbana-Champaign
2000 graduate of City High School

Honors
Member of National Honor Society

Activities
❸ Member, Asian American Association: 2001–Present
Environmental Committee Chairperson, Asian American Association: August 2002–May 2003

Work Experience
❹ Radio Reporter, WPGU, 107.1 FM, Champaign, Illinois: May 2002–Present
❺ • Rewrote and read stories for afternoon newscasts
• Served as field reporter for general assignments

Cashier, Del's Restaurant, Champaign, Illinois: May 2002–August 2002
• Responsible for taking phone orders
• Cashier for pickup orders

Assistant Secretary, Office of Dr. George Wright, Woodstock, Illinois: May 2001–August 2001
• Answered phones
• Made appointments

---

❶ Header includes all important contact information.

❷ All important education background is included.

❸ Related dates are included for all listed activities.

❹ Job title is included along with the place of employment.

❺ Job responsibilities are briefly listed.

Activity: Create an outline that lists the information that you would want to include in a résumé. Use a word processor if possible.

Job Application

When applying for a job, you usually need to fill out a job application. When you fill out the application, read the instructions carefully. Examine the entire form before beginning to fill it out. Write neatly and fill out the form completely, providing all information directly and honestly.

If a question does not apply to you, indicate that by writing *n/a,* short for "not applicable." Keep in mind that you will have the opportunity to provide additional information in your résumé, in your letter of application, or during the interview process.

❶ Please type or print neatly in blue or black ink.

❷ Name: _____ **Today's date:** _____

Address: _____

Phone: _____ **Birth date:** _____ **Sex:** _____ **Soc. Sec. #:** _____
___

****

❸ Job History (List each job held, starting with the most recent job.)

1. Employer: _____ Phone #: _____
Dates of employment: _____
Position held: _____
❹ Duties: _____

2. Employer: _____ Phone #: _____
Dates of employment: _____
Position held: _____
Duties: _____

****

Education (List the most recent level of education completed.)
_____
_____

****

Personal References:

1. Name: _____ Phone #: _____
Relationship: _____

2. Name: _____ Phone #: _____
Relationship: _____

❶ The application provides specific instructions.

❷ All of the information requested should be provided in its entirety.

❸ The information should be provided neatly and succinctly.

❹ Experience should be stated accurately and without embellishment.

Activity: Pick up a job application from a local business or use the sample application above. Complete the application thoroughly. Fill out the application as if you were actually applying for the job. Be sure to pay close attention to the guidelines mentioned above.

Memos

A memorandum (memo) conveys precise information to another person or a group of people. A memo begins with a leading block. It is followed by the text of the message. A memo does not have a formal closing.

TO: All Employees
FROM: Jordan Tyne, Human Resources Manager
❶ SUBJECT: New Human Resources Assistant Director
DATE: November 3, 20___

❷ Please join me in congratulating Leslie Daly on her appointment as assistant director in the Human Resources Department. Leslie comes to our company with five years of experience in the field. Leslie begins work on Monday, ❸ November 10. All future general human resource inquiries should be directed to Leslie.

Please welcome Leslie when she arrives next week.

❶ The topic of the memo is stated clearly in the subject line.

❷ The announcement is made in the first sentence.

❸ All of the important information is included briefly in the memo.

Business E-mail

E-mail is quickly becoming the most common form of business communication. While e-mail may be the least formal and most conversational method of business writing, it shouldn't be written carelessly or too casually. The conventions of business writing—clarity, attention to your audience, proper grammar, and the inclusion of relevant information—apply to e-mail.

An accurate subject line should state your purpose briefly and directly. Use concise language and avoid rambling sentences.

To: LiamS@internet.com
From: LisaB@internet.com
CC: EricC@internet.com
Date: January 7, 8:13 A.M.
❶ Subject: New Product Conference Call

Liam,

❷ I just wanted to make sure that arrangements have been made for next week's conference call to discuss our new product. The East Coast sales team has already scheduled three sales meetings at the end of the month with potential buyers, so it's important that our sales team is prepared to talk about the ❸ product. Please schedule the call when the manufacturing director is available, since he will have important information for the sales team.

Lisa

❶ Subject line clearly states the topic.

❷ The purpose is stated immediately and in a conversational tone.

❸ Important details are included in a brief, direct fashion.

Activity: Write an e-mail to your coworkers. Inform them of a change in company procedure that will affect them. State the specific information that they need to know. Indicate to your coworkers whether action needs to be taken on their part.

Grammar Glossary

This glossary will help you quickly locate information on parts of speech and sentence structure.

A

Absolute phrase. *See* Phrase.

Abstract noun. *See* Noun chart.

Action verb. *See* Verb.

Active voice. *See* Voice.

Adjective A word that modifies a noun or pronoun by limiting its meaning. Adjectives appear in various positions in a sentence. (The *gray* cat purred. The cat is *gray*.)

Many adjectives have different forms to indicate **degree of comparison**. *(short, shorter, shortest)*

The **positive degree** is the simple form of the adjective. *(easy, interesting, good)*

The **comparative degree** compares two persons, places, things, or ideas. *(easier, more interesting, better)*

The **superlative degree** compares more than two persons, places, things, or ideas. *(easiest, most interesting, best)*

A **predicate adjective** follows a linking verb and further identifies or describes the subject. (The child is *happy*.)

A **proper adjective** is formed from a proper noun and begins with a capital letter. Many proper adjectives are created by adding these suffixes: *-an, -ian, -n, -ese,* and *-ish. (Chinese, African)*

Adjective clause. *See* Clause chart.

Adverb A word that modifies a verb, an adjective, or another adverb by making its meaning more specific. When modifying a verb, an adverb may appear in various positions in a sentence. (Cats *generally* eat less than dogs. *Generally,* cats eat less than dogs.) When modifying an adjective or another adverb, an adverb appears directly before the modified word. (I was *quite* pleased that they got along *so* well.) The word *not* and the contraction *-n't* are adverbs. (Mike *wasn't* ready for the test today.) Certain adverbs of time, place, and degree also have a negative meaning. (He's *never* ready.)

Some adverbs have different forms to indicate degree of comparison. *(soon, sooner, soonest)*

The **comparative** degree compares two actions. *(better, more quickly)*

The **superlative** degree compares three or more actions. *(fastest, most patiently, least rapidly)*

Adverb clause. *See* Clause chart.

Antecedent. *See* Pronoun.

Appositive A noun or a pronoun that further identifies another noun or pronoun. (My friend *Julie* lives next door.)

Appositive phrase. *See* Phrase.

Article The adjective *a, an,* or *the.*

Indefinite articles (*a* and *an*) refer to one of a general group of persons, places, or things. (I eat *an* apple *a* day.)

The **definite article** (*the*) indicates that the noun is a specific person, place, or thing. (*The* alarm woke me up.)

Auxiliary verb. *See* Verb.

B

Base form. *See* Verb tense.

C

Clause A group of words that has a subject and a predicate and that is used as part of a sentence. Clauses fall into two categories: *main clauses,* which are also called *independent clauses,* and *subordinate clauses,* which are also called *dependent clauses.*

A **main clause** can stand alone as a sentence. There must be at least one main clause in every sentence. (*The rooster crowed,* and *the dog barked.*)

A **subordinate clause** cannot stand alone as a sentence. A subordinate clause needs a main clause to complete its meaning. Many subordinate clauses begin with subordinating conjunctions or relative pronouns. (*When Geri sang her solo,* the audience became quiet.) The chart on the next page shows the main types of subordinate clauses.

TYPES OF SUBORDINATE CLAUSES

Clause	Function	Example	Begins with . . .
Adjective clause	Modifies a noun or pronoun	Songs *that have a strong beat* make me want to dance.	A relative pronoun such as *which, who, whom, whose,* or *that*
Adverb clause	Modifies a verb, an adjective, or an adverb	*Whenever Al calls me,* he asks to borrow my bike.	A subordinating conjunction such as *after, although, because, if, since, when,* or *where*
Noun clause	Serves as a subject, an object, or a predicate nominative	*What Philip did* surprised us.	Words such as *how, that, what, whatever, when, where, which, who, whom, whoever, whose,* or *why*

Collective noun. *See* Noun chart.

Common noun. *See* Noun chart.

Comparative degree. *See* Adjective; Adverb.

Complement A word or phrase that completes the meaning of a verb. The four basic kinds of complements are *direct objects, indirect objects, object complements,* and *subject complements.*

A **direct object** answers the question *What?* or *Whom?* after an action verb. (Kari found a *dollar.* Larry saw *Denise.*)

An **indirect object** answers the question *To whom? For whom? To what?* or *For what?* after an action verb. (Do *me* a favor. She gave the *child* a toy.)

An **object complement** answers the question *What?* after a direct object. An object complement is a noun, a pronoun, or an adjective that completes the meaning of a direct object by identifying or describing it. (The director made me the *understudy* for the role. The little girl called the puppy *hers.*)

A **subject complement** follows a subject and a linking verb. It identifies or describes a subject. The two kinds of subject complements are *predicate nominatives* and *predicate adjectives.*

A **predicate nominative** is a noun or pronoun that follows a linking verb and tells more about the subject. (The author of "The Raven" is *Poe.*)

A **predicate adjective** is an adjective that follows a linking verb and gives more information about the subject. (Ian became *angry* at the bully.)

Complex sentence. *See* Sentence.

Compound preposition. *See* Preposition.

Compound sentence. *See* Sentence.

Compound-complex sentence. *See* Sentence.

Conjunction A word that joins single words or groups of words.

A **coordinating conjunction** *(and, but, or, nor, for, yet, so)* joins words or groups of words that are equal in grammatical importance. (David *and* Ruth are twins. I was bored, *so* I left.)

Correlative conjunctions *(both . . . and, just as . . . so, not only . . . but also, either . . . or, neither . . . nor, whether . . . or)* work in pairs to join words and groups of words

of equal importance. (Choose *either* the muffin *or* the bagel.)

A **subordinating conjunction** *(after, although, as if, because, before, if, since, so that, than, though, until, when, while)* joins a dependent idea or clause to a main clause. (Beth acted *as if* she felt ill.)

Conjunctive adverb An adverb used to clarify the relationship between clauses of equal weight in a sentence. Conjunctive adverbs are used to replace *and (also, besides, furthermore, moreover)*; to replace *but (however, nevertheless, still)*; to state a result *(consequently, therefore, so, thus)*; to state equality *(equally, likewise, similarly)*. (Ana was determined to get an A; *therefore,* she studied often.)

Coordinating conjunction. *See* Conjunction.

Correlative conjunction. *See* Conjunction.

D

Declarative sentence. *See* Sentence.

Definite article. *See* Article.

Demonstrative pronoun. *See* Pronoun.

Direct object. *See* Complement.

E

Emphatic form. *See* Verb tense.

F

Future tense. *See* Verb tense.

G

Gerund A verb form that ends in *-ing* and is used as a noun. A gerund may function as a subject, the object of a verb, or the object of a preposition. (*Smiling* uses fewer muscles than *frowning.* Marie enjoys *walking.*)

Gerund phrase. *See* Phrase.

I

Imperative mood. *See* Mood of verb.

Imperative sentence. *See* Sentence chart.

Indicative mood. *See* Mood of verb.

Indirect object. *See* Complement.

Infinitive A verb form that begins with the word *to* and functions as a noun, an adjective, or an adverb. (No one wanted *to answer.*) Note: When *to* precedes a verb, it is not a preposition but instead signals an infinitive.

Infinitive phrase. *See* Phrase.

Intensive pronoun. *See* Pronoun.

Interjection A word or phrase that expresses emotion or exclamation. An interjection has no grammatical connection to other words. Commas follow mild ones; exclamation points follow stronger ones. (*Well,* have a good day. *Wow!*)

Interrogative pronoun. *See* Pronoun.

Intransitive verb. *See* Verb.

Inverted order In a sentence written in *inverted order,* the predicate comes before the subject. Some sentences are written in inverted order for variety or special emphasis. (Up the beanstalk *scampered Jack.*) The subject also generally follows the predicate in a sentence that begins with *here* or *there.* (*Here was* the solution to his problem.) Questions, or interrogative sentences, are generally written in inverted order. In many questions, an auxiliary verb precedes the subject and the main verb follows it. (*Has* anyone *seen* Susan?) Questions that begin with *who* or *what* follow normal word order.

Irregular verb. *See* Verb tense.

L

Linking verb. *See* Verb.

M

Main clause. *See* Clause.

Mood of verb A verb expresses one of three moods: indicative, imperative, or subjunctive.

The **indicative mood** is the most common. It makes a statement or asks a question. (We *are* out of bread. *Will* you *buy* it?)

The **imperative mood** expresses a command or makes a request. (*Stop* acting like a child! Please *return* my sweater.)

The **subjunctive mood** is used to express, indirectly, a demand, suggestion, or statement of necessity (I demand that he *stop* acting like a child. It's necessary that she *buy* more bread.) The subjunctive is also used to state a condition or wish that is contrary to fact. This use of the subjunctive requires the past tense. (If you *were* a nice person, you *would return* my sweater.)

N

Nominative pronoun. *See* Pronoun.

Noun A word that names a person, a place, a thing, or an idea. The chart on this page shows the main types of nouns.

TYPES OF NOUNS		
Noun	**Function**	**Examples**
Abstract noun	Names an idea, a quality, or a characteristic	capitalism, terror
Collective noun	Names a group of things or people	herd, troop
Common noun	Names a general type of person, place, thing, or idea	city, building
Compound noun	Is made up of two or more words	checkerboard, globe-trotter
Noun of direct address	Identifies the person or persons being spoken to	*Maria,* please stand.
Possessive noun	Shows possession, ownership, or the relationship between two nouns	my *sister's* room
Proper noun	Names a particular person, place, thing, or idea	Cleopatra, Italy, Christianity

Noun clause. *See* Clause chart.

Noun of direct address. *See* Noun chart.

Number A noun, pronoun, or verb is *singular* in number if it refers to one; *plural* if it refers to more than one.

O

Object. *See* Complement.

P

Participle A verb form that can function as an adjective. Present participles always end in *-ing.* (The woman comforted the *crying* child.) Many past participles end in *-ed.* (We bought the beautifully *painted* chair.) However, irregular verbs form their past participles in some other way. (Cato was Caesar's *sworn* enemy.)

Passive voice. *See* Voice.

Past tense. *See* Verb tense.

Perfect tense. *See* Verb tense.

Personal pronoun. *See* Pronoun, Pronoun chart.

Phrase A group of words that acts in a sentence as a single part of speech.

An **absolute phrase** consists of a noun or pronoun that is modified by a participle or participial phrase but has no grammatical relation to the complete subject or predicate. (*The vegetables being done,* we finally sat down to eat dinner.)

An **appositive phrase** is an appositive along with any modifiers. If not essential to the meaning of the sentence, an appositive phrase is set off by commas. (Jack plans to go to the jazz concert, *an important musical event.*)

A **gerund phrase** includes a gerund plus its complements and modifiers. (*Playing the flute* is her hobby.)

An **infinitive phrase** contains the infinitive plus its complements and modifiers. (It is time *to leave for school.*)

A **participial phrase** contains a participle and any modifiers necessary to complete its meaning. (The woman *sitting over there* is my grandmother.)

A **prepositional phrase** consists of a preposition, its object, and any modifiers of the object. A prepositional phrase can function as an adjective, modifying a noun or a pronoun. (The dog *in the yard* is very gentle.) A prepositional phrase may also function as an adverb when it modifies a verb, an adverb, or an adjective. (The baby slept *on my lap.*)

A **verb phrase** consists of one or more auxiliary verbs followed by a main verb. (The job *will have been completed* by noon tomorrow.)

Positive degree. *See* Adjective.

Possessive noun. *See* Noun chart.

Predicate The verb or verb phrase and any objects, complements, or modifiers that express the essential thought about the subject of a sentence.

A **simple predicate** is a verb or verb phrase that tells something about the subject. (We *ran.*)

A **complete predicate** includes the simple predicate and any words that modify or complete it. (We *solved the problem in a short time.*)

A **compound predicate** has two or more verbs or verb phrases that are joined by a conjunction and share the same subject. (We *ran to the park and began to play baseball.*)

Predicate adjective. *See* Adjective; Complement.

Predicate nominative. *See* Complement.

Preposition A word that shows the relationship of a noun or pronoun to some other word in the sentence. Prepositions include *about, above, across, among, as, behind, below, beyond, but, by, down, during, except, for, from, into, like, near, of, on, outside, over, since, through, to, under, until, with.* (I usually eat breakfast *before* school.)

A **compound preposition** is made up of more than one word. *(according to, ahead of, as to, because of, by means of, in addition to, in spite of, on account of)* (We played the game *in spite of* the snow.)

Prepositional phrase. *See* Phrase.

Present tense. *See* Verb tense.

Progressive form. *See* Verb tense.

Pronoun A word that takes the place of a noun, a group of words acting as a noun, or another pronoun. The word or group of words that a pronoun refers to is called its antecedent. (In the following sentence, *Mari* is the antecedent of *she. Mari likes Mexican food, but she doesn't like Italian food.*)

A **demonstrative pronoun** points out specific persons, places, things, or ideas. *(this, that, these, those)*

An **indefinite pronoun** refers to persons, places, or things in a more general way than a noun does. *(all, another, any, both, each, either, enough, everything, few, many, most, much, neither, nobody, none, one, other, others, plenty, several, some)*

An intensive pronoun adds emphasis to another noun or pronoun. If an intensive pronoun is omitted, the meaning of the sentence will be the same. (Rebecca *herself* decided to look for a part-time job.)

An interrogative pronoun is used to form questions. *(who? whom? whose? what? which?)*

A personal pronoun refers to a specific person or thing. Personal pronouns have three cases: nominative, possessive, and objective. The case depends upon the function of the pronoun in a sentence. The chart on this page shows the case forms of personal pronouns.

A reflexive pronoun reflects back to a noun or pronoun used earlier in the sentence, indicating that the same person or thing is involved.

(We told *ourselves* to be patient.)

A relative pronoun is used to begin a subordinate clause. *(who, whose, that, what, whom, whoever, whomever, whichever, whatever)*

Proper adjective. *See* Adjective.

Proper noun. *See* Noun chart.

R

Reflexive pronoun. *See* Pronoun.

Relative pronoun. *See* Pronoun.

S

Sentence A group of words expressing a complete thought. Every sentence has a subject and a predicate. Sentences can be classified by function or by structure. The chart on this page shows the categories by function; the following subentries describe the categories by structure. *See also* Subject; Predicate; Clause.

A simple sentence has only one main clause and no subordinate clauses. *(Alan found an old violin.)*

A simple sentence may contain a compound subject or a compound predicate or both. *(Alan and Teri found an old violin. Alan found an old violin and tried to play it. Alan and Teri found an old violin and tried to play it.)* The subject and the predicate can be expanded with adjectives, adverbs, prepositional phrases, appositives, and verbal phrases. As long as the sentence has only one main clause, however, it remains a simple sentence. *(Alan, rummaging in the attic, found an old violin.)*

A compound sentence has two or more main clauses. Each main clause has its own subject and predicate, and these main clauses are usually joined by a comma and a coordinating conjunction. *(Cats meow, and dogs bark, but ducks quack.)* Semicolons may also be used to join the main clauses in a compound sentence. *(The helicopter landed; the pilot had saved four passengers.)*

A complex sentence has one main clause and one or more

PERSONAL PRONOUNS

Case	Singular Pronouns	Plural Pronouns	Function in Sentence
Nominative	I, you, she, he, it	we, you, they	subject or predicate nominative
Objective	me, you, her, him, it	us, you, them	direct object, indirect object, or object of a preposition
Possessive	my, mine, your, yours, her, hers, his, its	our, ours, your, yours, their, theirs	replacement for the possessive form of a noun

TYPES OF SENTENCES

Sentence Type	Function	Ends with . . .	Examples
Declarative sentence	Makes a statement	A period	I did not enjoy the movie.
Exclamatory sentence	Expresses strong emotion	An exclamation point	What a good writer Consuela is!
Imperative sentence	Makes a request or gives a command	A period or an exclamation point	Please come to the party. Stop!
Interrogative sentence	Asks a question	A question mark	Is the composition due today?

subordinate clauses. *(Since the movie starts at eight, we should leave here by seven-thirty.)*

A **compound-complex sentence** has two or more main clauses and at least one subordinate clause. *(If we leave any later, we may miss the previews, and I want to see them.)*

A **run-on sentence** is two or more complete sentences written as though they were one sentence. There are two types of run-on sentences. The first occurs when two main clauses are joined by just a comma. This is called a comma splice. The second type of run-on sentence occurs when two main clauses have no punctuation separating them. This can occur with or without a conjunction.

Simple predicate. *See* Predicate.

Simple subject. *See* Subject.

Subject The part of a sentence that tells what the sentence is about.

A **simple subject** is the main noun or pronoun in the subject. *(Babies* crawl.*)*

A **complete subject** includes the simple subject and any words that modify it. *(The man from New Jersey* won the race.) In some sentences, the simple subject and the complete subject are the same. *(Birds* fly.*)*

A **compound subject** has two or more simple subjects joined by a conjunction. The subjects share the same verb. *(Firefighters* and *police officers* protect the community.*)*

Subjunctive mood. *See* Mood of verb.

Subordinate clause. *See* Clause.

Subordinating conjunction. *See* Conjunction.

Superlative degree. *See* Adjective; Adverb.

T

Tense. *See* Verb tense.

Transitive verb. *See* Verb.

V

Verb A word that expresses action or a state of being. *(cooks, seem, laughed)*

An **action verb** tells what someone or something does. Action verbs can express either physical or mental action. (Crystal *decided* to *change* the tire herself.)

A **transitive verb** is an action verb that is followed by a word or words that answer the question *What?* or *Whom?* (I *held* the baby.)

An **intransitive verb** is an action verb that is not followed by a word that answers the question *What?* or *Whom?* (The baby *laughed.*)

A **linking verb** expresses a state of being by linking the subject of a sentence with a word or an expression that identifies or describes the subject. (The lemonade *tastes* sweet. He *is* our new principal.) The most commonly used linking verb is *be* in all its forms *(am, is, are, was, were, will be, been, being)*. Other linking verbs include *appear, become, feel, grow, look, remain, seem, sound, smell, stay, taste.*

An **auxiliary verb**, or helping verb, is a verb that accompanies the main verb to form a verb phrase. (I *have been* swimming.) The forms of *be* and *have* are the most common auxiliary verbs:

(am, is, are, was, were, being, been; has, have, had, having). Other auxiliaries include *can, could, do, does, did, may, might, must, shall, should, will, would.*

Verb tense The tense of a verb indicates when the action or state of being occurs. All the verb tenses are formed from the four principal parts of a verb: a base form *(talk)*, a present participle *(talking)*, a simple past form *(talked)*, and a past participle *(talked)*. A **regular verb** forms its simple past and past participle by adding *-ed* to the base form. *(climb, climbed)* An **irregular verb** forms its past and past participle in some other way. *(get, got, gotten)*

In addition to present, past, and future tense, there are three perfect tenses.

The **present perfect tense** expresses an action or a condition that occurred at some indefinite time in the past. This tense also shows an action or a condition that began in the past and continues into the present. (She *has played* the piano for four years.)

The **past perfect tense** indicates that one past action or condition began *and* ended before another past action started. (Andy *had finished* his homework before I even began mine.)

The **future perfect tense** indicates that one future action or condition will begin *and* end before another future event starts. Use *will have* or *shall have* with the past participle of a verb. (By tomorrow, I *will have finished* my homework, too.)

The **progressive form** of a verb expresses a continuing action with any of the six tenses. To make the progressive forms, use the appropriate tense of the verb *be* with the present participle of the main verb. (She *is swimming*. She *has been swimming*.)

The **emphatic form** adds special force, or emphasis, to the present and past tense of a verb. For the emphatic form, use *do, does,* or *did* with the base form. (Toshi *did want* that camera.)

Verbal A verb form that functions in a sentence as a noun, an adjective, or an adverb. The three kinds of verbals are gerunds, infinitives, and participles. *See* Gerund; Infinitive; Participle.

Voice The **voice** of a verb shows whether the subject performs the action or receives the action of the verb.

A verb is in the **active voice** if the subject of the sentence performs the action. (The referee *blew* the whistle.)

A verb is in the **passive voice** if the subject of the sentence receives the action of the verb. (The whistle *was blown* by the referee.)

Mechanics

This section will help you use correct capitalization, punctuation, and abbreviations in your writing.

Capitalization

This section will help you recognize and use correct capitalization in sentences.

Rule: Capitalize the first word in any sentence, including direct quotations and sentences in parentheses unless they are included in another sentence.

Example: She said, "Come back soon."

Emily Dickinson became famous only after her death. (She published only six poems during her lifetime.)

Rule: Always capitalize the pronoun *I* no matter where it appears in the sentence.

Example: Some of my relatives think that I should become a doctor.

Rule: Capitalize proper nouns, including

a. names of individuals and titles used in direct address preceding a name or describing a relationship.

Example: George Washington; Dr. Morgan; Aunt Margaret

b. names of ethnic groups, national groups, political parties and their members, and languages.

Example: Italian Americans; Aztec; the Republican Party; a Democrat; Spanish

c. names of organizations, institutions, firms, monuments, bridges, buildings, and other structures.

Example: Red Cross; Stanford University; General Electric; Lincoln Memorial; Tappan Zee Bridge; Chrysler Building; Museum of Natural History

d. trade names and names of documents, awards, and laws.

Example: Microsoft; Declaration of Independence; Pulitzer Prize; Sixteenth Amendment

e. geographical terms and regions or localities.

Example: Hudson River; Pennsylvania Avenue; Grand Canyon; Texas; the Midwest

f. names of planets and other heavenly bodies.

Example: Venus; Earth; the Milky Way

g. names of ships, planes, trains, and spacecraft.

Example: USS *Constitution; Spirit of St. Louis; Apollo 11*

h. names of most historical events, eras, calendar items, and religious names and items.

Example: World War II; Age of Enlightenment; June; Christianity; Buddhists; Bible; Easter; God

i. titles of literary works, works of art, and musical compositions.

Example: "Why I Live at the P.O."; *The Starry Night; Rhapsody in Blue*

j. names of specific school courses.

Example: Advanced Physics; American History

Rule: Capitalize proper adjectives (adjectives formed from proper nouns).

Example: Christmas tree; Hanukkah candles; Freudian psychology; American flag

Punctuation

This section will help you use these elements of punctuation correctly.

Rule: Use a **period** at the end of a declarative sentence or a polite command.

Example: I'm thirsty.

Example: Please bring me a glass of water.

Rule: Use an **exclamation point** to show strong feeling or after a forceful command.

Example: I can't believe my eyes!

Example: Watch your step!

Rule: Use a **question mark** to indicate a direct question.

Example: Who is in charge here?

Rule: Use a **colon**

a. to introduce a list (especially after words such as *these, the following,* or *as follows*) and to introduce material that explains, restates, or illustrates previous material.

Example: The following states voted for the amendment: Texas, California, Georgia, and Florida.

Example: The sunset was colorful: purple, orange, and red lit up the sky.

b. to introduce a long or formal quotation.

Example: It was Mark Twain who stated the following proverb: "Man is the only animal that blushes. Or needs to."

c. in precise time measurements, biblical chapter and verse references, and business letter salutations.

Example: 3:35 P.M.   7:50 A.M.
Gen. 1:10–11   Matt. 2:23
Dear Ms. Samuels: Dear Sir:

Rule: Use a **semicolon**

a. to separate main clauses that are not joined by a coordinating conjunction.

Example: There were two speakers at Gettysburg that day; only Lincoln's speech is remembered.

b. to separate main clauses joined by a conjunctive adverb or by *for example* or *that is*.

Example: Because of the ice storm, most students could not get to school; consequently, the principal canceled all classes for the day.

c. to separate the items in a series when these items contain commas.

Example: The students at the rally came from Senn High School, in Chicago, Illinois; Niles Township High School, in Skokie, Illinois; and Evanston Township High School, in Evanston, Illinois.

d. to separate two main clauses joined by a coordinating conjunction when such clauses already contain several commas.

Example: The designer combined the blue silk, brown linen, and beige cotton into a suit; but she decided to use the yellow chiffon, yellow silk, and white lace for an evening gown.

Rule: Use a **comma**

a. between the main clauses of a compound sentence.

Example: Ryan was late getting to study hall, and his footsteps echoed in the empty corridor.

b. to separate three or more words, phrases, or clauses in a series.

Example: Mel bought carrots, beans, pears, and onions.

c. between coordinate modifiers.

Example: That is a lyrical, moving poem.

d. to set off parenthetical expressions, interjections, and conjunctive adverbs.

Example: Well, we missed the bus again.

Example: The weather is beautiful today; however, it is supposed to rain this weekend.

e. to set off nonessential words, clauses, and phrases, such as:
—adverbial clauses

Example: Since Ellen is so tall, the coach assumed she would be a good basketball player.

—adjective clauses

Example: Scott, who had been sleeping, finally woke up.

—participles and participial phrases

Example: Having found what he was looking for, he left.

—prepositional phrases

Example: On Saturdays during the fall, I rake leaves.

—infinitive phrases

Example: To be honest, I'd like to stay awhile longer.

—appositives and appositive phrases

Example: Ms. Kwan, a soft-spoken woman, ran into the street to hail a cab.

f. to set off direct quotations.

Example: "My concert," Molly replied, "is tonight."

g. to set off an antithetical phrase.

Example: Unlike Tom, Rob enjoys skiing.

h. to set a title after a person's name.

Example: Margaret Thomas, Ph.D., was the guest speaker.

i. to separate the various parts of an address, a geographical term, or a date.

Example: My new address is 324 Indian School Road, Albuquerque, New Mexico 85350.

I moved on March 13, 1998.

j. after the salutation of an informal letter and after the closing of all letters.

Example: Dear Helen,   Sincerely,

k. to set off parts of a reference that direct the reader to the exact source.

Example: You can find the article in the *Washington Post*, April 4, 1997, pages 33–34.

l. to set off words or names used in direct address and in tag questions.

Example: Yuri, will you bring me my calculator?

Lottie became a lawyer, didn't she?

Rule: Use a **dash** to signal a change in thought or to emphasize parenthetical material.

Example: During the play, Maureen—and she'd be the first to admit it—forgot her lines.

Example: There are only two juniors attending— Mike Ramos and Ron Kim.

Rule: Use **parentheses** to set off supplemental material. Punctuate within the parentheses only if the punctuation is part of the parenthetical expression.

Example: If you like jazz (and I assume you do), you will like this CD. (The soloist is Miles Davis.)

Example: The upper Midwest (which states does that include?) was hit by terrible floods last year.

Rule: Use **brackets** to enclose information that you insert into a quotation for clarity or to enclose a parenthetical phrase that already appears within parentheses.

Example: "He serves his [political] party best who serves the country best." —*Rutherford B. Hayes*

Example: The staircase (which was designed by a famous architect [Frank Lloyd Wright]) was inlaid with ceramic tile.

Rule: Use **ellipsis points** to indicate the omission of material from a quotation.

Example: ". . . Neither an individual nor a nation can commit the least act of injustice against the obscurest individual. . . ."
—*Henry David Thoreau*

Rule: Use **quotation marks**

a. to enclose a direct quotation, as follows:

Example: "Hurry up!" shouted Lisa.

When a quotation is interrupted, use two sets of quotation marks.

Example: "A cynic," wrote Oscar Wilde, "is someone who knows the price of everything and the value of nothing."

Use single quotation marks for a quotation within a quotation.

Example: "Did you say 'turn left' or 'turn right'?" asked Leon.

In writing dialogue, begin a new paragraph and use a new set of quotation marks every time the speaker changes.

Example: "Do you really think the spaceship can take off?" asked the first officer. "Our engineer assures me that we have enough power," the captain replied.

b. to enclose titles of short works, such as stories, poems, essays, articles, chapters, and songs.

Example: "The Lottery" [short story]
"Provide, Provide" [poem]
"Civil Disobedience" [essay]

c. to enclose unfamiliar slang terms and unusual expressions.

Example: The man called his grandson a "rapscallion."

d. to enclose a definition that is stated directly.

Example: *Gauche* is a French word meaning "left."

Rule: Use **italics**

a. for titles of books, lengthy poems, plays, films, television series, paintings and sculptures, long musical compositions, court cases, names of newspapers and magazines, ships, trains, airplanes, and spacecraft. Italicize and capitalize articles *(a, an, the)* at the beginning of a title only when they are part of the title.

Example: *E.T.* [film]; *The Piano Lesson* [play];
The Starry Night [painting];
the *New Yorker* [magazine];
Challenger [spacecraft];
The Great Gatsby [book];
the *Chicago Tribune* [newspaper]

b. for foreign words and expressions that are not used frequently in English.

Example: Luciano waved good-bye, saying, *"Arrivederci."*

c. for words, letters, and numerals used to represent themselves.

Example: There is no *Q* on the telephone keypad.

Example: Number your paper from *1* through *10*.

Rule: Use an **apostrophe**

a. for a possessive form, as follows:

Add an apostrophe and *s* to all singular nouns, plural nouns not ending in *s*, singular indefinite pronouns, and compound nouns. Add only an apostrophe to a plural noun that ends in *s*.

Example: the tree's leaves
the man's belt
the bus's tires
the children's pets
everyone's favorite
my mother-in-law's job
the attorney general's decision
the baseball player's error
the cats' bowls

If two or more persons possess something jointly, use the possessive form for the last person named. If they possess it individually, use the possessive form for each one's name.

Example: Ted and Harriet's family
Ted's and Harriet's bosses
Lewis and Clark's expedition
Lewis's and Clark's clothes

b. to express amounts of money or time that modify a noun.

Example: two cents' worth

Example: three days' drive (You can use a hyphenated adjective instead: a three-day drive.)

c. in place of omitted letters or numerals.

Example: haven't [have not]   the winter of '95

d. to form the plural of letters, numerals, symbols, and words used to represent themselves. Use an apostrophe and *s*.

Example: You wrote two 5's instead of one.

Example: How many *s*'s are there in Mississippi?

Example: Why did he use three *!*'s at the end of the sentence?

Rule: Use a **hyphen**

a. after any prefix joined to a proper noun or proper adjective.

Example: all-American   pre-Columbian

b. after the prefixes *all-, ex-,* and *self-* joined to any noun or adjective, after the prefix *anti-* when it joins a word beginning with *i,* after the prefix *vice-* (except in *vice president*), and to avoid confusion between words that begin with *re-* and look like another word.

Example: ex-president
self-important
anti-inflammatory
vice-principal
re-creation of the event
recreation time
re-pair the socks
repair the computer

c. in a compound adjective that precedes a noun.

Example: a bitter-tasting liquid

d. in any spelled-out cardinal or ordinal numbers up to *ninety-nine* or *ninety-ninth,* and with a fraction used as an adjective.

Example: twenty-three   eighty-fifth
one-half cup

e. to divide a word at the end of a line between syllables.

Example: air-port   scis-sors
fill-ing   fin-est

Abbreviations

Abbreviations are shortened forms of words.

Rule: Use only one period if an abbreviation occurs at the end of a sentence. If the sentence ends with a question mark or exclamation point, use the period and the second mark of punctuation.

Example: We didn't get home until 3:30 A.M.

Example: Did you get home before 4:00 A.M.?

Example: I can't believe you didn't get home until 3:30 A.M.!

Rule: Capitalize abbreviations of proper nouns and abbreviations related to historical dates.

Example: John Kennedy Jr.   P.O. Box 333
800 B.C.   A.D. 456   1066 C.E.

Use all capital letters and no periods for most abbreviations of organizations and government agencies.

Example: CBS   CIA   PIN
CPA   IBM   NFL
MADD   GE   FBI

Spelling

The following basic rules, examples, and exceptions will help you master the spellings of many words.

Forming plurals

English words form plurals in many ways. Most nouns simply add *s*. The following chart shows other ways of forming plural nouns and some common exceptions to the pattern.

General Rules for Forming Plurals		
If the word ends in	**Rule**	**Example**
ch, s, sh, x, z	add *es*	glass, glasses
a consonant + *y*	change *y* to *i* and add *es*	caddy, caddies
a vowel + *y* or *o*	add only *s*	cameo, cameos monkey, monkeys
a consonant + *o* common exceptions	generally add *es* but sometimes add only *s*	potato, potatoes cello, cellos
f or *ff* common exceptions	add *s* change *f* to *v* and add *es*	cliff, cliffs hoof, hooves
lf	change *f* to *v* and add *es*	half, halves

A few plurals are exceptions to the rules in the previous chart, but they are easy to remember. The following chart lists these plurals and some examples.

Special Rules for Forming Plurals	
Rule	**Example**
To form the plural of most proper names and one-word compound nouns, follow the general rules for plurals.	Cruz, Cruzes Mancuso, Mancusos crossroad, crossroads
To form the plural of hyphenated compound nouns or compound nouns of more than one word, make the most important word plural.	sister-in-law, sisters-in-law motion picture, motion pictures
Some nouns have unusual plural forms.	goose, geese child, children
Some nouns have the same singular and plural forms.	moose scissors pants

Adding prefixes

When adding a prefix to a word, keep the original spelling of the word. Use a hyphen only when the original word is capitalized or with prefixes such as *all-, ex-,* and *self-* joined to a noun or adjective.

co + operative = cooperative
inter + change = interchange
pro + African = pro-African
ex + partner = ex-partner

Suffixes and the silent *e*

Many English words end in a silent letter *e*. Sometimes the *e* is dropped when a suffix is added. When adding a suffix that begins with a consonant to a word that ends in silent *e*, keep the *e*.

like + ness = likeness sure + ly = surely
COMMON EXCEPTIONS awe + ful = awful;
judge + ment = judgment

When adding a suffix that begins with a vowel to a word that ends in silent *e*, usually drop the *e*.

believe + able = believable
expense + ive = expensive
COMMON EXCEPTION mile + age = mileage

When adding a suffix that begins with *a* or *o* to a word that ends in *ce* or *ge*, keep the *e* so the word will retain the soft *c* or *g* sound.

notice + able = noticeable
courage + ous = courageous

When adding a suffix that begins with a vowel to a word that ends in *ee* or *oe*, keep the final *e*.

see + ing = seeing   toe + ing = toeing

Drop the final silent *e* after the letters *u* or *w*.

argue + ment = argument
owe + ing = owing

Keep the final silent *e* before the suffix *-ing* when necessary to avoid ambiguity.

singe + ing = singeing

Suffixes and the final *y*

When adding a suffix to a word that ends in a consonant + *y*, change the *y* to *i* unless the suffix begins with *i*. Keep the *y* in a word that ends in a vowel + *y*.

try + ed = tried   fry + ed = fried
stay + ing = staying   display + ed = displayed
copy + ing = copying   joy + ous = joyous

Adding *ly* and *ness*

When adding *ly* to a word that ends in a single *l*, keep the *l*, but when the word ends in a double *l*, drop one *l*. When the word ends in a consonant + *le*, drop the *le*. When adding *-ness* to a word that ends in *n*, keep the *n*.

casual + ly = casually
practical + ly = practically
dull + ly = dully
probable + ly = probably
open + ness = openness
mean + ness = meanness

Doubling the final consonant

Double the final consonant in words that end in a consonant preceded by a single vowel if the word is one syllable, if it has an accent on the last syllable that remains there even after the suffix is added, or if it is a word made up of a prefix and a one-syllable word.

stop + ing = stopping
admit + ed = admitted
replan + ed = replanned

Do not double the final consonant if the accent is not on the last syllable, or if the accent shifts when the suffix is added. Also do not double the final consonant if the final consonant is *x* or *w*. If the word ends in a consonant and the suffix begins with a consonant, do not double the final consonant.

benefit + ed = benefited
similar + ly = similarly
raw + er = rawer
box + like = boxlike
friend + less = friendless
rest + ful = restful

Forming compound words

When joining a word that ends in a consonant to a word that begins with a consonant, keep both consonants.

out + line = outline
after + noon = afternoon
post + card = postcard
pepper + mint = peppermint

ie and *ei*

Learning this rhyme can save you many misspellings: "Write *i* before *e* except after *c*, or when sounded like *a* as in *neighbor* and *weigh*." There are many exceptions to this rule, including *seize, seizure, leisure, weird, height, either, neither, forfeit.*

cede, ceed, and *sede*

Because of the relatively few words with *sēd* sounds, these words are worth memorizing.

These words use *-cede:* **accede, precede, secede.**
One word uses *-sede:* **supersede.**
Three words use *-ceed:* **exceed, proceed, succeed.**

Succeeding on Tests

This section is designed to help you prepare for both classroom and standardized tests. You will become familiar with the various formats of tests and the types of questions you will be required to answer.

Preparing for Classroom Tests

This section will help you learn how to prepare for classroom tests.

Thinking ahead

- Write down information about an upcoming test— when it will be given, what it will cover, and so on—so you can plan your study time effectively.
- Review your textbook, quizzes, homework assignments, class notes, and handouts. End-of-chapter review questions often highlight key points from your textbook.
- Develop your own questions about main ideas and important details, and practice answering them. Writing your own practice tests is an excellent way to get ready for a real test.
- Make studying into an active process. Rather than simply rereading your notes or a chapter in your textbook, try to create a summary of the material. This can be an outline, a list of characters, or a timeline. Try to include details from both your lecture notes and your textbook reading so you will be able to see connections between the two.
- Form study groups. Explaining information to a peer is one of the best ways to learn the material.
- Sleep well the night before a test. Spreading your study time over several days should have given you enough confidence to go to bed at your regular time the night before a test.
- Remember that eating well helps you remain alert. Students who eat a regular meal on the morning of a test generally score higher than those who do not.

Taking objective tests

Many of the tests you take in your high school classes will be objective tests, meaning that they ask questions that have specific, correct answers. Time is often limited for these tests, so be sure to use your time efficiently.

- First, read the directions carefully. If anything is unclear, ask questions.
- Try to respond to each item on the test, starting with the easier ones.
- Skip difficult questions rather than dwelling on them. You can always come back to them at the end of the test.
- Try to include some time to review your test before turning it in.

Below are tips for answering specific kinds of objective test items:

Kind of item	Tips
Multiple-choice	Read all the answer choices provided before choosing one; even if the first one seems nearly correct, a later choice may be a better answer. Be cautious when choosing responses that contain absolute words such as *always, never, all,* or *none*. Since most generalizations have exceptions, absolute statements are often incorrect.
True/False	If *any* part of the item is false, the correct answer must be "false."
Short-answer	Use complete sentences to help you write a clear response.
Fill-in	Restate fill-ins as regular questions if you are not sure what is being asked.
Matching	Note in the directions whether some responses can be used more than once, or not used at all.

Taking subjective (essay) tests

You will also take subjective tests during high school. Typically, these tests ask questions that require you to write an essay. Your grade is based more on how well you are able to make your point than on whether you choose a correct answer.

- When you receive the test, first read it through. If there are several questions, determine how much time to spend on each question.
- Begin your answer by jotting down ideas on scratch paper for several minutes. Read the test question again to make sure you are answering it. Then create a rough outline from which you can create your essay.
- Start your essay with a thesis statement in the first paragraph, and follow with paragraphs that provide supporting evidence. Give as much information as possible, including examples and illustrations where appropriate.
- Finish your essay with a conclusion, highlighting the evidence you have provided and restating your thesis.
- You will probably not have time to revise and recopy your essay. After you are finished writing, spend any remaining time proofreading your answer and neatly making any necessary corrections.

Preparing for Standardized Tests

Standardized tests are designed to be administered to very large groups of students, not just those in a particular class. Three of the most widely known standardized tests, all part of the college application process, are the ACT (American College Testing), the PSAT (Preliminary Scholastic Assessment Test), and the SAT (Scholastic Assessment Test). The strategies in this handbook refer specifically to the PSAT and SAT tests, but they also can apply to preparing for the ACT and other standardized tests.

The PSAT is generally administered to students in the 11th grade, though some schools offer it to students in the 10th grade as well. This test is designed to predict how well you will do on the SAT. For most students, the PSAT is simply a practice test. Those who perform exceptionally well on the 11th grade PSAT, however, will qualify for National Merit Scholarship competition.

The Scholastic Assessment Tests consist of the SAT-I: Reasoning Test and a variety of SAT-II: Subject Tests. The SAT-I is a three-hour test that evaluates your general verbal and mathematics skills. The SAT-II: Subject Tests are hour-long tests given in specific subjects and are designed to show specifically how much you have learned in a particular subject area.

Tips for taking standardized tests

Standardized tests are often administered outside of regular class time and require registration. Ask your teacher or guidance counselor how you can register early to ensure that you can take the test at a time and location most convenient for you. In addition, follow these tips:

- Skip difficult questions at first. Standardized tests are usually timed, so first answer items you know. You can return later to those you skipped.
- Mark only your answers on the answer sheet. Most standardized tests are scored by a computer, so stray marks can be read as incorrect answers.
- Frequently compare the question numbers on your test with those on your answer sheet to avoid putting answers in the wrong spaces.
- If time permits, check your answers. If you are not penalized for guessing, fill in answers for any items you might have skipped.

Preparing for the PSAT and the SAT-I

The verbal sections of the PSAT and SAT-I contain sentence completion items and reading comprehension questions.

Sentence completion

Sentence completion items provide a sentence with one or two blanks and ask you to select the word or pair of words that best fits in the blank(s). Here is some general information to help you with these questions on the PSAT and SAT-I.

- Start by reading the sentence and filling in your own word to replace the blank. Look for words that show how the word in the blank is related to the rest of the sentence–*and, but, since, therefore, although.*
- Do not read the sentence with the words from each answer choice inserted. This may leave you with several choices that "sound good."
- Once you have chosen your own word to fill in the blank, pick the word from the answer choices that is closest in meaning to your word.

- If you have trouble coming up with a specific word to fill in the blank, try to determine whether the word should be positive or negative. Even this bit of information can help you eliminate some answer choices. If you can eliminate even one answer choice, take a guess at the correct answer.

Reading comprehension

Reading Comprehension questions on the PSAT and SAT-I measure your ability to understand and interpret what you read. Each reading passage is followed by a series of questions. Here are some points to keep in mind when working with these questions:

- You get points for answering questions correctly, not for reading passages thoroughly. Therefore, it is to your advantage to read the passages quickly and spend your time working on the questions.

- After quickly reading the passage, briefly summarize it. This will help you answer general questions, which are based on the passage as a whole.

- To answer specific questions based on details included in the passage, return to the passage to find the correct answers. Reading Comprehension is like an open-book test; you are expected to look at the passage while answering the questions.

- Reading Comprehension passages almost never include controversial opinions. Therefore, an answer choice like "advocated the overthrow of the government" is very likely to be incorrect.

- If you can eliminate even one answer choice, take a guess at the correct answer.

Taking Essay Tests

Writing prompts, or long essay questions, include key words that signal the strategy you will use to bring your ideas into sharp focus. Similarly, these key words also appear in a constructed responses, or short essay questions.

Key Word	Strategy
Analyze	To **analyze** means to systematically and critically examine all parts of an issue or event.
Classify or categorize	To **classify** or **categorize** means to put people, things, or ideas into groups, based on a common set of characteristics.
Compare and contrast	To **compare** is to show how things are similar or alike. To **contrast** is to show how things are different.
Describe	To **describe** means to present a sketch or an impression. Rich details, especially details that appeal to the senses, flesh out a description.
Discuss	To **discuss** means to systematically write about all sides of an issue or event.
Evaluate	To **evaluate** means to make a judgment and support it with evidence.
Explain	To **explain** means to clarify or make plain.
Illustrate	To **illustrate** means to provide examples or to show with a picture or other graphic.
Infer	To **infer** means to read between the lines or to use knowledge or experience to draw conclusions, make generalizations, or form a prediction.
Justify	To **justify** means to prove or to support a position with specific facts and reasons.
Predict	To **predict** means to tell what will happen in the future based on an understanding of prior events and behaviors.
State	To **state** means to briefly and concisely present information.
Summarize	To **summarize** means to give a brief overview of the main points of an event or issue.
Trace	To **trace** means to present the steps or stages in a process or an event in sequential or chronological order.

GLOSSARY/GLOSARIO

Pronunciation Key

This glossary lists the vocabulary words found in the selections in this book. The definition given is for the word as it is used in the selection; you may wish to consult a dictionary for other meanings of these words. The key below is a guide to the pronunciation symbols used in each entry.

a	at	ō	hope	ng	sing
ā	ape	ô	fork, all	th	thin
ä	father	oo	wood, put	th	this
e	end	ōō	fool	zh	treasure
ē	me	oi	oil	ə	ago, taken, pencil,
i	it	ou	out		lemon, circus
ī	ice	u	up	′	indicates primary stress
o	hot	ū	use	′	indicates secondary

| ENGLISH | ESPAÑOL |

A

abate (ə bāt′) *v.* to lessen or reduce in force or intensity; **p. 90**

abhor (ab hoî′) *v.* to regard with disgust; **p. 91**

abjectly (ab′ jekt lē) *adv.* in a humiliating, mean, or degrading manner; **p. 950**

abominable (ə bom′ə nə bəl) *adj.* disgusting; detestable; **p. 91**

accommodate (ə kom′ə dāt′) *v.* to provide room or facilities for; **p. 138**

acquiesce (ak′ wē es′) *v.* to consent or agree silently, without objections; to comply passively; **p. 116**

adamant (ad′ ə mənt) *adj.* completely firm and unyielding; **p. 1095**

admonition (ad′ mə nish′ ən) *n.* a warning; cautionary advice; **p. 183**

adorn (ə dôrn′) *v.* to make beautiful; to decorate; **p. 376**

A

abate/aminorar *v.* disminuir o reducir en fuerza o intensidad; **p. 90**

abhor/aborrecer *v.* despreciar; odiar algo en particular; **p. 91**

abjectly/abyectamente *adv.* de modo humillante, infame o indecente; **p. 947**

abominable/abominable *adj.* espantoso; detestable; **p. 91**

accommodate/alojar *v.* proporcionar hospedaje o habitación; **p. 138**

acquiesce/acatar *v.* aceptar o consentir sin protestar; acceder pasivamente; **p. 116**

adamant/obstinado *adj.* empeñado en un fin; terco; **p. 1095**

admonition/amonestación *s.* advertencia; consejo severo; **p. 183**

adorn/adornar *v.* embellecer; decorar; **p. 376**

affliction (ə flik′shən) *n.* great suffering, distress, or its cause; **p. 436**

alacrity (ə lak′rə tē) *n.* speed; swiftness; **p. 212**

alien (ā′lē ən) *adj.* strange; unfamiliar; foreign; **p. 906**

alight (ə līt′) *v.* to descend and come to rest; **p. 24**

allusion (ə lōō′ zhən) *n.* an indirect or casual reference; an incidental mention; **p. 363**

ambition (am bish′ən) *n.* a desire to achieve a particular end; **p. 1270**

amble (am′ bəl) *v.* to walk at a leisurely pace; to stroll; **p. 1326**

ambulatory (am′ byə lə tôr′ē) *adj.* moving from place to place; **p. 98**

amiable (ā′ mē ə bəl) *adj.* friendly; **p. 943**

amorphous (ə môr′ fəs) *adj.* without definite form; **p. 929**

anarchy (an′ ər kē) *n.* the absence of government; **p. 371**

ancestral (an ses′ trəl) *adj.* of or relating to those from whom one is descended; **p. 1155**

animated (an′ ə mā′ tid) *adj.* full of life; active; lively; **p. 943**

apathetically (ap′ ə thet′i kal ē) *adv.* in a manner showing little interest or concern; **p. 603**

apparition (ap′ ə rish′ ən) *n.* a ghostlike or nearly invisible appearance; **p. 654**

appease (ə pēz′) *v.* to bring to a state of peace or quiet; soothe; **p. 90**

apprehension (ap′ ri hen′ shən) *n.* fear of what may happen in the future; anxiety; **p. 70**

apt (apt) *adj.* likely; having a tendency; **p. 697**

arbitrary (är′ bə trer′ ē) *adj.* of a random or unreasonable character; **p. 197**

ardently (ärd′ent lē) *adv.* passionately; enthusiastically; **p. 377**

arduous (är′jōō əs) *adj.* requiring great exertion or endurance; difficult; **p. 109**

aristocracy (a′ rə sto′ krə sē) *n.* people with high social status due to birth or title; **p. 1305**

array (ə rā′) *v.* to place in proper or methodical order; **p. 371**

assail (ə sāl′) *v.* to attack violently; **p. 570**

affliction/aflicción *s.* gran sufrimiento, angustia, o su causa; **p. 436**

alacrity/alacridad *s.* prontitud; presteza; **p. 212**

alien/ajeno *adj.* extraño; foráneo; extranjero; **p. 906**

alight/apearse *v.* descender; bajar; **p. 24**

allusion/alusión *s.* referencia indirecta o casual; mención casual; **p. 363**

ambition/ambición *s.* deseo de conseguir algo, esp. poder o riquezas; **p. 1270**

amble/pasear *v.* andar por distracción y sin prisa; deambular; **p. 1326**

ambulatory/ambulante *adj.* que va de un lugar a otro; **p. 98**

amiable/amigable *adj.* amistoso; **p. 943**

amorphous/amorfo *adj.* sin forma definida; **p. 929**

anarchy/anarquía *s.* ausencia de gobierno; **p. 371**

ancestral/ancestral *adj.* relativo o perteneciente a los antepasados; **p. 1155**

animated/animado *adj.* lleno de vida; activo; vivaz; **p. 943**

apathetically/apáticamente *adv.* con una actitud que muestra poco interés o preocupación; **p. 603**

apparition/aparición *s.* apariencia de un fantasma o algo casi invisible; **p. 654**

appease/apaciguar *v.* calmar o aquietar; tranquilizar; **p. 90**

apprehension/aprensión *s.* temor vago de lo que pueda pasar; ansiedad; **p. 70**

apt/propenso(a) *adj.* que tiende (a); que tiene la tendencia (a); **p. 697**

arbitrary/arbitrario(a) *adj.* que actúa por capricho o de forma ilógica; **p. 197**

ardently/ardientemente *adv.* apasionadamente; con mucho entusiasmo; **p. 377**

arduous/arduo *adj.* que requiere gran esfuerzo o trabajo; difícil; **p. 109**

aristocracy/aristocracia *s.* personas de un nivel social alto por razón de nacimiento o título; **p. 1305**

array/disponer *v.* colocar en el orden adecuado; arreglar; **p. 371**

assail/embestir *v.* atacar con violencia; **p. 570**

assent (ə sent′) v. to express agreement; **p. 378**

audaciously (ô dā′shəs lē) adv. boldly; arrogantly; **p. 363**

avert (ə vurt′) v. to turn away or aside; **p. 871**

azure (ā′zhər) adj. a light purplish blue; **p. 675**

B

balm (bäm) n. something that heals or soothes, as an ointment; **p. 248**

balmy (bä′ mē) adj. soothing; **p. 1321**

base (bās) adj. morally low; dishonorable; **p. 1054**

battered (bat′ərd) v. to beat with blows; to attack fiercely and repeatedly; **p. 824**

beguile (bi gīl′) v. to influence by deceit; to trick; **p. 246**

benediction (ben′ ə dik′ shən) n. a blessing or something that fosters goodness; **p. 803**

benefactor (ben′ ə fak′ tər) n. one who gives help or financial aid; **p. 184**

benevolent (bə nev′ ə lent) adj. doing or desiring to do good; kind; **p. 339**

bereft (bi reft′) adj. deprived of the possession or use of something; **p. 84**

bewildered (bi wil′ dərd) adj. confused; **p. 1190**

blithe (blīth) adj. lighthearted and carefree; cheerful; **p. 181**

blunder (blun′ dər) n. a serious error or mistake resulting from carelessness or confusion; **p. 214**

borne (bôrn) v. past *participle* of bear; given birth to; produced; **p. 356**

bosom (bo͞oz′ əm) n. the chest or heart; **p. 812**

bough (bou) n. tree branch; **p. 654**

bracken (bra′ kən) n. a type of fern that grows in humid, temperate areas; **p. 708**

brazenness (brā′ zən nəs) n. defiant behavior; boldness; **p. 792**

brood (brood) v. to focus the attention on a subject persistently and moodily; worry; **p. 1287**

bulge (bulj) v. to swell or curve outward; **p. 691**

assent/asentir v. afirmar; expresar acuerdo; **p. 378**

audaciously/audazmente adv. atrevidamente; de manera osada; **p. 363**

avert/desviar v. apartar; evitar; **p. 871**

azure/azul celeste adj. azul claro como el cielo; **p. 675**

B

balm/bálsamo s. sustancia medicinal que cura o alivia, por ejemplo: un ungüento; **p. 248**

balmy/calmante adj. confortable; agradable; **p. 1321**

base/vil adj. de baja condición moral; deshonesto; **p. 1054**

battered/estropeado(a) pp. maltratar con golpes; golpear repetida y violentamente; **p. 824**

beguile/engañar v. influenciar con mentiras; engatusar; **p. 246**

benediction/bendición s. con morales superiores o un carácter superior; **p. 799**

benefactor/benefactor s. que respalda una causa o ayuda con dinero; **p. 184**

benevolent/benevolente adj. que hace el bien; amable; **p. 339**

bereft/despojado adj. privado de algo; **p. 84**

bewildered/desconcertado(a) adj. confundido; **p. 1190**

blithe/alegre adj. despreocupado; animado; **p. 181**

blunder/error craso s. equivocación o desacierto grave; **p. 214**

borne/nacido(a) pp. Que se le dio a luz; que dio fruto; **p. 356**

bosom/pecho s. (lit.) seno, tórax o corazón; **p. 812**

bough/rama s. parte que nace del tronco de una planta o árbol; **p. 654**

bracken/helecho s. tipo de planta criptógama que crece en áreas húmedas y templadas; **p. 708**

brazenness/descaro s. actitud desafiante; atrevimiento; **p. 792**

brood/cavilar v. entregarse del todo a la contemplación, al dolor; preocupar; **p. 1287**

bulge/sobresalir v. hincharse o aumentar de tamaño; **p. 691**

C

calamity (kə lam′ ə tē) *n.* an unfortunate event or disaster; **p. 539**

cathedral (ke thē′drəl) *n.* a church that is the official seat of a bishop; **p. 436**

censure (sen′ shər) *v.* to express disapproval of; to find fault with; to blame; **p. 343**

ceremonial (ser′ ə mō′ nē əl) *adj.* formal; **p. 896**

chide (chīd) *v.* to find fault with or to blame; **p. 84**

circumvent (sur′ kəm vent′) *v.* to get around or to avoid by clever maneuvering; **p. 883**

civic (siv′ ik) *adj.* related to citizenship; **p. 1162**

clamor (klam′ ər) *n.* confused, insistent shouting; **p. 72**

coax (kōks′) *v.* to persuade gently; **p. 716**

coerce (kō urs′) *v.* to force; **p. 587**

coincide (kō′ in sīd′) *v.* to occur at the same time; **p. 1270**

colossal (kə los′ əl) *adj.* extraordinary in size or degree; enormous; **p. 1156**

commensurate (kə men′ sər it) *adj.* equal to; proportionate; **p. 197**

commerce (kom′ ərs) *n.* exchange of ideas and opinions; **p. 654**

commodity (kə mod′ə′ tē) *n.* a product or economic good; an article of trade; **p. 64**

compassion (kəm pash′ ən) *n.* deep awareness of another's suffering with a desire to help; **p. 76**

compel (kəm pel′) *v.* to force; **p. 598**

compensation (kom′ pən sa′ shən) *n.* payment; **p. 1166**

comprehension (kom′ pri hen′ shən) *n.* the act of grasping mentally; understanding; **p. 896**

compromise (kom′ prə mīz′) *v.* to endanger the reputation or interests of; to expose to suspicion ; **p. 1027**

conciliatory (kən sil′ ē ə tôr′ ē) *adj.* trying to gain the goodwill of another by friendly acts; **p. 1094**

congenital (kən je′ nə təl) *adj.* of or relating to a condition that is present at birth, as a result of either heredity or environmental influences; **p. 1287**

C

calamity/calamidad *s.* desgracia o infortunio; un disastre; **p. 539**

cathedral/catedral *s.* iglesia principal donde el obispo tiene su sede; **p. 436**

censure/censurar *v.* expresar desacuerdo; criticar algo; reprobar; **p. 343**

ceremonial/ceremonial *adj.* formal; relativo a las ceremonias; **p. 896**

chide/reprender *v.* hallar defectos con algo o reprobar; **p. 84**

circumvent/circunvenir *v.* rodear o evitar mediante una acción astuta; **p. 883**

civic/cívico(a) *adj.* relatado a las instituciones e intereses de la patria; **p. 1162**

clamor/algarabía *s.* griterío confuso e insistente; **p. 72**

coax/convencer *v.* persuadir a una persona para que haga algo; **p. 716**

coerce/constreñir *v.* forzar; **p. 587**

coincide/coincidir *v.* ocurrir al un mismo tiempo; **p. 1270**

colossal/colosal *adj.* extraordinario en tamaño o intensidad; enorme; **p. 1156**

commensurate/proporcionado(a) *adj.* igual a; en proporción con; **p. 197**

commerce/comercio *s.* intercambio de ideas y opiniones; **p. 654**

commodity/mercancía *s.* producto o bien económico; artículo que se vende o compra; **p. 64**

compassion/compasión *s.* interés por el sufrimiento ajeno junto con el deseo de ayudar; **p. 76**

compel/compeler *v.* forzar; **p. 598**

compensation/remuneración *s.* paga; **p. 1166**

comprehension/comprensión *s.* acto de entender algo; **p. 896**

compromise/implicar *v.* comprometer la reputación o el interés; abrir a sospecha; **p. 1027**

conciliatory/conciliador *adj.* que trata de ganarse la buena voluntad con una actitud amistosa; **p. 1094**

congenital/congénito(a) *adj.* que existe al nacer, a consecuencia de herencia o influencias del ambiente; **p. 1287**

congregate/debris

congregate (kong′ gri gāt′) *v.* to bring or come together in a group, a crowd, or an assembly; **p. 1222**

congress (kong′ gris) *n.* a formal meeting; **p. 1218**

conjecture (kən jek′ chər) *v.* to form an opinion without definite evidence; to guess; **p. 484**

conjurer (kon′ jər ər) *n.* one who performs magic; sorcerer; **p. 25**

consecrate (kon′ sə krāt′) *v.* to set apart as sacred; to make or declare holy; **p. 388**

console (kən sōl′) *v.* to comfort; to cheer; **p. 1319**

consolidation (kən sä lə da′ shən) *n.* the process of uniting or merging; **p. 937**

constrained (kən strānd′) *v.* forced or limited; **p. 802**

contemplation (kon′ təm plā′ shən) *n.* the act of thinking about something long and seriously; **p. 1079**

contend (kən tend′) *v.* to argue; dispute; **p. 371**

contention (kən ten′ shən) *n.* verbal argument or struggle; quarreling; **p. 1028**

continuity (kon′ tə nōō′ ə tē) *n.* the state or quality of going on without interruption; **p. 1156**

contrivance (kən trī′ vəns) *n.* a cleverly designed device; **p. 771**

convalescent (kon və le′ sənt) *n.* a person who is recovering from an illness, an injury, or a surgical operation; **p. 404**

convene (kən vēn′) *v.* to come together; assemble; **p. 50**

copious (kō′ pē əs) *adj.* large in quantity; plentiful; **p. 70**

covet (kuv′ it) *v.* to desire, especially to an excessive degree, something belonging to another; **p. 1057**

crimson (krim′zən) *adj.* a bright purplish red; **p. 675**

curt (kurt) *adj.* rudely brief, or short; terse; **p. 986**

cynic (si′ nik) *n.* a person whose outlook is scornfully and often habitually negative; **p. 1288**

D

daunt (dônt) *v.* to overcome with fear; to intimidate; **p. 76**

debris (də brē′) *n.* large number of fragments or broken pieces; **p. 1005**

congregar/escombros

congregate/congregar *v.* juntarse o reunirse en un grupo, una masa o una asamblea; **p.1222**

congress/congreso *s.* reunión; **p. 1218**

conjecture/conjeturar *v.* formarse una opinión sin tener evidencia definitiva; suponer; **p. 484**

conjurer/mago *s.* que realiza magia; hechicero; **p. 25**

consecrate/consagrar *v.* declarar sagrado; santificar; **p. 388**

console/consolar *v.* alentar; tranquilizar; **p. 1319**

consolidation/fusión *s.* el proceso de unir o fusionar; **p. 937**

constrained/constriñov *v.* obligado o compeleidor; **p. 802**

contemplation/contemplación *s.* acto de pensar larga y seriamente; **p. 1079**

contend/contender *v.* disputar; pelear; **p. 371**

contention/contienda *s.* lucha o disputa verbal; pelea; **p. 1028**

continuity/continuidad *s.* estado o cualidad de seguir sin interrupción; **p. 1156**

contrivance/artificio *s.* instrumento diseñado con astucia; **p. 771**

convalescent/convaleciente *s.* persona que se recupera de una enfermedad, herida o cirugía; **p. 404**

convene/congregarse *v.* reunirse; **p. 50**

copious/copioso *adj.* grande en cantidad; abundante; **p. 70**

covet/codiciar *v.* desear de forma intensa algo ajeno; **p. 1057**

crimson/carmesí *adj.* de color rojo granate muy vivo; **p. 675**

curt/cortante *adj.* brusco y breve; seco; **p. 986**

cynic/cínico(a) *s.* persona que se burla o que ofende con ironía mordaz; **p. 1288**

D

daunt/acobardar *v.* intimidar; atemorizar; **p. 76**

debris/escombros *s.* gran número de fragmentos o piezas rotas; **p. 1005**

decimated (des′ ə māt′ əd) *adj.* destroyed or killed in large numbers; **p. 1292**

deduce (di dōōs′) *v.* to draw a conclusion from something known or assumed; **p. 253**

deferential (def′ə ren′shəl) *adj.* yielding to someone else's opinions or wishes; **p. 662**

degenerate (di jen′ ər it) *adj.* having declined in condition or character; deteriorated; **p. 501**

degrading (di grā′ ding) *adj.* tending to drag down in character or social status; **p. 1163**

deliberately (di lib′ ər it lē) *adj.* in a careful, thoughtful way; **p. 204**

deliberation (di lib′ ə rā′ shən) *n.* careful consideration; **p. 51**

delicious (di lish′ əs) *adj.* having a very pleasing taste; **p. 669**

delirium (di lēr′ ē əm) *n.* a temporary state of mental disturbance characterized by confusion and disorientation; **p. 1319**

delusion (di lōō′zhen) *n.* a false impression or belief; **p. 364**

depend (di pend′) *v.* to rely on; **p. 668**

depravity (di prav′ ə tē) *n.* the state of being morally bad or corrupt; **p. 339**

deprive (di prīv′) *v.* to take away from; to keep from enjoying or having; **p. 136**

desolation (des′ ə lā′ shən) *n.* devastation, misery, sadness; **p. 76**

detached (di tacht′) *adj.* not involved emotionally; aloof; indifferent; **p. 737**

detested (di test′ əd) *v.* greatly disliked or loathed; **p. 654**

diaspora (dī as′ pər ə) *n.* the scattering of a people; **p. 1331**

diffuse (di fūz′) *v.* to spread widely; to scatter in all directions; **p. 260**

digress (dī gres′) *v.* to depart from the main subject; to ramble; **p. 660**

dilapidated (di lap′ə dā′tid) *adj.* fallen into ruin or decay; shabby; **p. 484**

din (din) *n.* loud, continuous noise; **p. 212**

diplomatic (dip′ lə mat′ ik) *adj.* negotiating in a peaceful manner; **p. 970**

decimated/diezmado *adj.* destruido o liquidado en grandes cantidades; **p. 1292**

deduce/deducir *v.* sacar una conclusión de algo que se sabe o se asume; **p. 253**

deferential/deferente *adj.* que cede a las opiniones o deseos ajenos; **p. 662**

degenerate/degenerado(a) *adj.* que decae en calidad o condición moral; deteriorado; **p. 501**

degrading/degradantev *adj.* que se rebaja o disminuye en dignidad o privilegios; **p. 1163**

deliberately/deliberadamente *adv.* hecho con atención y detenimiento; **p. 204**

deliberation/deliberación *s.* consideración atenta y cuidadosa; **p. 51**

delicious/delicioso(a) *adj.* que tiene un sabor agradable; **p. 669**

delirium/delirio *s.* estado temporal de alteración mental que se caracteriza por confusión y desorientación; **p. 1319**

delusion/ilusión *s.* impresión o creencia falsa; **p. 364**

depend/depende *v.* basarse en algo; **p. 668**

depravity/depravación *s.* condición moral baja o corrupta; **p. 339**

deprive/privar(se) *v.* quitarle algo a alguien; dejar de tener o de disfrutar; **p. 136**

desolation/desolación *s.* devastación; miseria; **p. 76**

detached/indiferente *adj.* que no está involucrado emocionalmente; desinteresado; **p. 737**

detested/detestado(a) *v.* (part.) aborrecer, tener aversión; **p. 654**

diaspora/diáspora *s.* dispersión de grupos humanos; **p. 1331**

diffuse/difundir *v.* esparcir ampliamente; dispersar en todas las direcciones; **p. 260**

digress/divagar *v.* apartarse del tema principal; irse por las ramas; **p. 660**

dilapidated/dilapidado *adj.* que ha sido gastado o arruinado; muy usado; **p. 484**

din/estrépito *s.* ruido fuerte y continuo; **p. 212**

diplomatic/diplomático(a) *adj.* que negocia e interviene de manera cortés; **p. 970**

discern/enamored

discern (di surn´) *v.* to recognize as different and distinct; distinguish; **p. 77**

discord (dis´ kôrd) *n.* lack of agreement or harmony; conflict; **p. 230**

disdain (dis dān´) *v.* to look down on; to despise; **p. 1278**

disposition (dis´ pə zish´ ən) *n.* one's general way of thinking or feeling; **p. 49**

dissembling (di sem´ bling) *n.* the act of concealing one's true character, feelings, or intentions; **p. 771**

dissension (di sen´shən) *n.* disagreement or discord; **p. 564**

dissipate (dis´ə pāt´) *v.* to cause to scatter and gradually vanish; to break up and drive off; **p. 870**

diverse (di vurs´) *adj.* composed of different elements; **p. 832**

doggedly (dô´ gid lē) *adv.* in a stubbornly persistent manner; obstinately; **p. 521**

downy (dou´ nē) *adj.* soft and fluffy, like the feathers of young birds; **p. 1261**

dusk (dusk) *n.* the time of day just before nightfall; **p. 1264**

dusky (dus´ kē) *adj.* murky or dark in color; **p. 812**

dutiful (doo´ ti fəl) *adj.* careful to fulfill obligations; **p. 777**

dwell (dwel) *v.* to think about at length; **p. 1175**

E

ecclesiastical (i klē´ zē as´ ti kəl) *adj.* of or relating to the church; **p. 1293**

elusive (i loo´ siv) *adj.* difficult to explain or grasp; **p. 549**

embark (em bärk´) *v.* to set out on a venture; **p. 57**

emblem (em´ bləm) *n.* an object or a representation that functions as a symbol; **p. 1283**

emphatic (em fa´tik) *adj.* forceful; **p. 576**

enamel (i nam´ əl) *n.* a cosmetic or paint that gives a smooth, glossy appearance; **p. 708**

enamored (en am´ ərd) *adj.* inspired with love; charmed; captivated; **p. 949**

discenir/enamorado

discern/discenir *v.* reconocer como diferente; distinguir; **p. 77**

discord/discordia *s.* desacuerdo; conflicto; **p. 230**

disdain/desdeñar *v.* menospreciar, despreciar; **p. 1278**

disposition/disposición *s.* modo de pensar o sentir; **p. 49**

dissembling/encubrimiento *s.* acto de ocultar el verdadero carácter, sentimientos o intenciones; **p. 771**

dissension/disensión *s.* desacuerdo o discordia; **p. 564**

dissipate/disipar *v.* hacer que desaparezca gradualmente; disolver; **p. 870**

diverse/diverso(a) *adj.* compuesto de elementos distintos; **p. 832**

doggedly/obstinadamente *adv.* de manera persistente; firmemente; **p. 521**

downy/aterciopelado *adj.* suave y velloso, como las plumas de un pájaro recién nacido; **p. 1261**

dusk/anochecer *s.* tiempo en el que empieza a faltar la luz del día y se hace de noche; **p. 1264**

dusky/oscuro(a) *adj.* tan profundo o grande que no se puede poner en palabras; **p. 812**

dutiful/cumplidor *adj.* que cumple responsablemente sus obligaciones; **p. 777**

dwell/dilatarse *v.* pensar con calma; tomarse su tiempo **p. 1175**

E

ecclesiastical/eclesiástico *adj.* relativo a la iglesia; **p. 1293**

elusive/elusivo *adj.* difícil de explicar o entender; **p. 549**

embark/embarcar *v.* lanzarse a una empresa; partir en una aventura; **p. 57**

emblem/emblema *s.* un objeto o una representación que funciona como un símbolo; **p. 1283**

emphatic/enfático *adj.* enérgico; categórico; **p. 576**

enamel/esmalte *s.* cosmético o barniz que da un acabado liso y brillante; **p. 708**

enamored/enamorado *adj.* prendado; encantado; cautivado; **p. 949**

encircled (en sur′kəld) v. created a circle around; **p. 824**

endeavor (en dev′ ər) v. to make an effort to; to try; **p. 115**

engrossed (en grōst′) adj. fully attentive to; completely engaged in; absorbed; **p. 961**

enlighten (en līt′ ən) v. to give knowledge or wisdom to; **p. 1305**

enormity (i nor′ mə tē) n. outrageousness; state of being monstrous; **p. 1178**

ensure (en shoor′) v. to make certain; guarantee; **p. 1180**

entangled (en tan′gəld) adj. twisted together; caught; **p. 680**

enterprising (en′tər prī′zing) adj. showing energy and initiative, especially in beginning new projects; **p. 488**

enunciate (i nun′ sē āt′) v. to pronounce distinctly; **p. 1249**

ephemeral (i fem′ rəl) adj. lasting for a very brief time; short-lived; **p. 1156**

equanimity (ek′ wə nim′ ə tē) n. evenness of temper; calmness; **p. 508**

evacuate (i vak′ū āt′) v. to vacate or leave a place; **p. 1001**

evade (i vād′) v. to escape or avoid, as by cleverness; **p. 1040**

exalt (ig zôlt′) v. to lift up; to put in high spirits; **p. 793**

exalted (ig zôl′ təd) adj. elevated; **p. 549**

exclusively (iks′ klōo siv lē) adv. without the inclusion or involvement of any others; **p. 1305**

expedient (ək spē′ dē ənt) adj. convenient or efficient for a certain purpose; **p. 213**

exploit (eks′ ploit) n. notable, heroic deed; feat; **p. 125**

extraneous (ek strā′nē əs) adj. not intrinsically belonging; not forming a vital part; coming from outside; **p. 1213**

extricate (eks′ trə kāt′) v. to set free from; to remove; **p. 138**

F

fabled (fā′ bəld) adj. famous, well-known; told about in stories; **p. 1190**

encircled/ceñido(a) v. rodear o ajustar; **p. 824**

endeavor/empeñarse v. esforzarse; tratar; **p. 115**

engrossed/enfrascado adj. dedicado por completo a pensar en algo; ensimismado; absorto; **p. 961**

enlighten/ilustrar v. dar o revelar conocimientos o sabiduría; **p. 1305**

enormity/enormidad s. monstruosidad; atrocidad; **p. 1178**

ensure/garantizar v. asegurar; **p. 1180**

entangled/enredado(a) pp. liado; atrapado; **p. 680**

enterprising/emprendedor adj. que muestra dinamismo e iniciativa, especialmente al iniciar nuevos proyectos; **p. 488**

enunciate/enunciar v. pronunciar claramente; **p. 1249**

ephemeral/efímero adj. que dura muy poco tiempo; fugaz; **p. 1156**

equanimity/ecuanimidad s. igualdad y constancia de ánimo; calma; **p. 508**

evacuate/evacuar v. desalojar o desocupar un lugar; **p. 1001**

evade/evadir v. evitar algo de modo astuto; **p. 1040**

exalt/exaltar v. elevar; animar; **p. 793**

exalted/exaltado adj. elevado; **p. 549**

exclusively/exclusivamente adv. sin la participación de otros; **p. 1305**

expedient/conveniente adj. útil, oportuno, adecuado para un fin; **p. 213**

exploit/proeza s. acto heroico o notable; hazaña; **p. 125**

extraneous/extraño(a) adj. que no pertenece intrínsicamente; que no forma un parte vital; que previene del exterior; **p. 1213**

extricate/redimir v. liberar; sacar; **p. 138**

F

fabled/legendario(a) adj. famoso y popular; relacionado con las legendas; **p. 1190**

feigned (fānd) *adj.* fictitious; not genuine; **p. 64**

fetus (fē′təs) *n.* an unborn child that has been in utero for at least eight weeks; **p. 976**

fitfully (fit′fəl lē) *adv.* irregularly; in stops and starts; **p. 1271**

fondle (fond′ əl) *v.* to handle gently; **p. 1204**

fortitude (fôr′ tə tōōd′) *n.* strength, particularly strength of mind that enables one to encounter danger or bear adversity with courage; **p. 284**

fragrant (frā′grənt) *adj.* having a strong, pleasant smell; **p. 570**

fused (fūzd) *adj.* blended; **p. 832**

futile (fū′til) *adj.* serving no practical purpose; useless; worthless; **p. 903**

G

gape (gāp) *v.* to stare with the mouth open, as in wonder or surprise; **p. 1175**

garment (gär′mənt) *n.* a piece of clothing; **p. 1185**

garrulous (gar′ə ləs) *adj.* talkative; **p. 484**

gaunt (gônt) *adj.* thin, bony, and hollow-eyed, as from hunger or illness; **p. 915**

genial (jēn′ yəl) *adj.* mild or friendly; **p. 284**

ghetto (get′ō) *n.* neighborhood where a particular group of people are forced to live either by law, poverty, or social exclusion; **p. 1331**

glazed (glāzd) *adj.* covered with a smooth, glossy coating; **p. 668**

glisten (glis′ ən) *v.* to shine or to reflect light; **p. 691**

grapple (grap′əl) *v.* to struggle in hand-to-hand combat; to wrestle; **p. 959**

gratify (grat′ ə fī′) *v.* to satisfy or indulge; **p. 71**

grave (grāv) *adj.* dignified and gloomy; somber; **p. 892**

gravity (grav′ ə tē) *n.* seriousness; importance; **p. 1263**

grievous (grē′ vəs) *v.* causing or characterized by grief; extremely sad; **p. 1228**

grimace (grim′is) *n.* facial expression showing contempt, disgust, or pain; **p. 745** / *v.* to contort the face, especially to express pain or displeasure; **p. 1315**

grope (grōp) *v.* to feel about uncertainly with the hands; to search blindly; **p. 1174**

feigned/fingido *adj.* falso; que no es genuino; **p. 64**

fetus/feto *s.* bebé todavía no nacido que ha cumplido más de ocho semanas en el útero materno; **p. 976**

fitfully/intermitentemente *adv.* en forma irregular; que se interrumpe y prosigue; **p. 1271**

fondle/acariciar *v.* tratar con amor y ternura; **p. 1204**

fortitude/forteleza *s.* fuerza, particularmente fuerza mental que se permite encontrar peligro o tolerar adversidad con valor; **p. 284**

fragrant/fragante *adj.* que tiene o despide un aroma; **p. 570**

fused/fundido(a) *adj.* combinado; **p. 832**

futile/fútil *adj.* inútil; insignificante; **p. 903**

G

gape/boquear *v.* quedar boquiabierto por sorpresa o asombro; **p. 1175**

garment/vestido *s.* pieza de ropa; **p.1185**

garrulous/parlanchín *adj.* que habla mucho; locuaz **p. 484**

gaunt/enjuto *adj.* flaco y ojeroso por hambre o enfermedad; con aspecto enfermizo; **p. 915**

genial/simpático(a) *adj.* amable, amistoso; **p. 284**

ghetto/gueto *s.* barrio en que un grupo de gente están forzados de vivir a causa de la ley, la pobreza o exclusión social; **p. 1331**

glazed/glaseado(a) *adj.* cubierto con una capa brillante; **p. 668**

glisten/refulgir *v.* emitir fulgor o resplandecer; **p. 691**

grapple/forcejear *v.* luchar cuerpo a cuerpo; bregar; **p. 959**

gratify/gratificar *v.* satisfacer o complacer; **p. 71**

grave/grave *adj.* solemne y severo; sombrío; **p. 892**

gravity/gravedad *s.* seriedad; importancia; **p. 1263**

grievous/doloroso(a) *adj.* que causa o implica sufrimiento; profunda pena; **p. 1228**

grimace/gesticular *v.* hacer muecas con la cara, especialmente para expresar dolor o molestia; **p. 745, p. 1315**

grope/tantear *v.* palpar algo sin certeza; buscar a ciegas; **p. 1174**

guile (gīl) *n.* cunning, deceit, or slyness; **p. 565, p. 1078**

gunner (gun′ər) *n.* an airman or a soldier who operates a gun; **p. 976**

H

hallow (hal′ ō) *v.* to make or select as holy; to regard or honor as sacred; **p. 388**

haughty (hô′ tē) *adj.* conceited; arrogant; **p. 882**

heave (hēv) *n.* an upward motion, or an effort to raise; **p. 431**

hemorrhage (he′ mə rij) *n.* a severe discharge of blood; **p. 930**

holocaust (hol′ ə kôst′) *n.* great or complete destruction, especially by fire; **p. 1249**

hostile (host′əl) *adj.* feeling or showing hatred; antagonistic; **p. 903**

husky (hus′kē) *adj.* strong; burly; **p. 701**

hypocrisy (hi pok′ rə sē) *n.* an expression of feelings or beliefs not actually possessed or held; **p. 125**

hypothesis (hī poth′ə sis) *n.* an unproved explanation or assumption; **p. 511**

hysterical (his ter′ i kəl) *adj.* characterized by panic or other uncontrolled emotion; **p. 1241**

I

immaculate (i mak′yə lit) *adj.* unblemished; flawless; pure; **p. 1076**

immensity (i men′sə tē) *n.* greatness in size and degree; **p. 824**

immortality (im′ ôr tal′ ə tē) *n.* the condition of having eternal life; **p. 596**

impede (im pēd′) *v.* to slow or block progress or action; obstruct; **p. 253**

imperative (im per′ ə tiv) *n.* something absolutely necessary; an essential; **p. 1151**

imperial (im pēr′ ē əl) *adj.* of or relating to an empire or emperor; **p. 436**

imperially (im pēr′ē əl ē) *adv.* majestically; magnificently; **p. 569**

implementation (im′ plə mən tā′ shən) *n.* putting into effect; putting into use; **p. 1236**

guile/ardid *s.* engaño; astucia; trampa; **p. 565, p. 1078**

gunner/artillero(a) *s.* soldado de las fuerzas militares que sirve en la artillería; **p. 976**

H

hallow/consagrar *v.* santificar; honrar como sagrado; **p. 388**

haughty/altanero *adj.* presumido; arrogante; **p. 882**

heave/elevación *s.* movimiento hacia arriba, o esfuerzo para levantar algo; **p. 431**

hemorrhage/hemorragia *s.* pérdida grave de sangre; **p. 930**

holocaust/holocausto *s.* destrucción grande o total, especialmente debida al fuego; **p. 1249**

hostile/hostil *adj.* que siente o demuestra odio; adverso; **p. 903**

husky/corpulento(a) *adj.* fornido; grandote; **p. 701**

hypocrisy/hipocresía *s.* expresión de sentimientos o creencias que en realidad no se tienen; falsedad; **p. 125**

hypothesis/hipótesis *s.* explicación no comprobada; **p. 511**

hysterical/histérico(a) *adj.* caracterizado por pánico o alguna emoción sin freno; **p. 1241**

I

immaculate/inmaculado *adj.* sin mancha ni pecado; irreprochable; puro; **p. 1076**

immensity/inmensidad *s.* cantidad o número muy grande; **p. 824**

immortality/inmortalidad *s.* vida eterna; **p. 596**

impede/impedir *v.* detener o aminorar; obstaculizar; **p. 253**

imperative/imperativo *s.* algo absolutamente necesario; algo esencial; **p. 1151**

imperial/imperial *adj.* relativo al imperio o al emperador; **p. 436**

imperially/imperialmente *adv.* majestuosamente; magníficamente; **p. 569**

implementation/implementación *s.* suministro de los medios necesarios para llevar algo a cabo; **p. 1236**

implication (im′ plə kā′ shən) *n.* an effect or consequence; **p. 971**

impromptu (im promp′ too͞, -tū) *adv.* done on the spur of the moment; **p. 402** / *adj.* offhand; without preparation; **p. 818**

impropriety (im′ prə prī′ə tē) *n.* the quality of being improper; inappropriate behavior; **p. 507**

impudent (im′ pyə dənt) *adj.* cocky, bold; **p. 937**

impudently (im′ pyə dənt lē) *adv.* in an offensively bold manner; **p. 579**

inaudibly (in ô′ də blē) *adv.* in a manner not able to be heard; **p. 1263**

incessantly (in ses′ənt lē′) *adv.* continually; happening over and over without interruption; **p. 570**

incredulity (in′ krə doo͞′ lə tē, -dū′) *n.* disbelief; **p. 403**

indentured (in den′ chərd) *adj.* bound by contract to serve someone for a time; **p. 98**

indictment (in dīt′ mənt) *n.* a formal legal accusation, charging the commission or omission of an act, which is punishable by law; **p. 1098**

indifferent (in dif′ ər ənt) *adj.* lacking feeling or concern; having no marked feeling for or against; **p. 796, p. 1282**

induce (in doo͞s′) *v.* to lead by persuasion or influence; **p. 340**

ineffably (in ef′ ə blē) *adv.* to a degree that is impossible to express; indescribably; **p. 981**

ineptly (i nept′ lē) *adv.* incompetently; awkwardly; clumsily; **p. 1061**

inevitable (i nev′ə tə bəl) *adj.* incapable of being avoided or evaded; certain to happen; **p. 971, p. 1180**

infamy (in′ fə mē) *n.* a reputation as something evil or harmful; **p. 970**

infidel (in′ fə del′) *n.* an unbeliever; **p. 98**

infrastructure (in′ frə struk′ chər) *n.* the underlying base for an organization or a system; **p. 1237**

ingenious (in jēn′ yəs) *adj.* exhibiting creative ability; inventive; **p. 98**

ingenuous (in jen′ū əs) *adj.* lacking in sophistication; naïve; **p. 747**

ingenuously (in jen′ ū əs lē) *adv.* honestly; frankly; **p. 578**

implication/implicación *s.* efecto o consecuencia; **p. 971**

impromptu/improvisadamente *adv.* hecho espontáneamente, de improviso; **p. 402** / *adj.* espontáneo; sin preparación previa; **p. 818**

impropriety/impropiedad *s.* incorrección; indecencia; **p. 507**

impudent/insolente *adj.* atrevido, descarado; **p. 937**

impudently/descaradamente *adv.* de modo ofensivo y atrevido; sin decoro ni vergüenza; **p. 579**

inaudibly/inaudiblemente *adv.* de modo que no se puede escuchar; **p. 1263**

incessantly/incesantemente *adv.* de continuo; que no cesa ni se interrumpe; **p. 570**

incredulity/incredulidad *s.* descreimiento; **p. 403**

indentured/ligado por contrato *adj.* obligado por un contrato a servir a una persona por un tiempo determinado; **p. 98**

indictment/acusación *s.* denuncia legal y formal por la comisión u omisión de un acto que castiga la ley; **p. 1098**

indifferent/indiferente *adj.* que no demuestra sentimiento o preocupacion: **p. 796, p. 1282**

induce/inducir *v.* influir o persuadir; **p. 340**

ineffably/inefablemente *adv.* sin poderse explicar; de modo indescriptible; **p. 981**

ineptly/ineptamente *adv.* sin aptitud o destreza; torpemente; **p. 1061**

inevitable/inevitable *adj.* que no se puede evitar o eludir; irremediable; **p. 971, p. 1180**

infamy/infamia *s.* una reputación como algo funesto o dañoso; **p. 970**

infidel/infiel *s.* el que no cree; **p. 98**

infrastructure/infraestructura *s.* elementos o servicios necesarios para la creación o el funcionamiento de una organización o sistema; **p. 1237**

ingenious/ingenioso *adj.* que tiene habilidad creativa; talentoso; **p. 98**

ingenious/ingenioso *adj.* que tiene hablidad creativa; talentoso; **p. 747**

ingenuously/ingenuamente *adv.* de modo honesto; francamente; cándidamente; **p. 578**

iniquity (in ik′ wə tē) *n.* sin; **p. 269**

inquisitor (in kwi′ zə tər) *n.* one who asks questions; **p. 931**

inscrutable (in skrōō′ tə bəl) *adj.* mysterious, or not able to be interpreted or understood; **p. 287**

insidious (in sid′ē əs) *adj.* slyly dangerous; deceitful; deceptive; **p. 109, p. 658**

installment (in stôl′ mənt) *n.* one part of a payment that has been divided; **p. 1015**

intangible (in tan′ jə bəl) *adj.* not easily defined or evaluated by the mind; **p. 595**

integrate (in′ tə grāt′) *v.* to bring all parts together into a whole; **p. 180**

integrity (in teg′ rə tē) *n.* moral uprightness; honesty; **p. 184**

interminable (in tur′mi nə bəl) *adj.* seemingly endless; **p. 485**

interpose (in′ tər pōž′) *v.* to intrude, intervene, or to put oneself between; **p. 431**

intervene (in′ tər vēn′) *v.* to come or lie between; **p. 598**

intimation (in′ tə mā′ shən) *n.* a hint; a suggestion; **p. 932**

intimidated (in tim′ə dāt′ əd) *adj.* made timid or fearful; frightened into submission or inaction; **p. 960**

irreproachable (ir′ i prō′ chə bəl) *adj.* free from blame; faultless; **p. 274**

irrevocable (i rev′ ə kə bəl) *adj.* not possible to undo; **p. 1180**

J

jilt (jilt) *v.* to drop or reject as a sweetheart; **p. 779**

jostle (jo′ səl) *v.* to bump, push, or shove while moving, as in a crowd; **p. 737**

jubilant (jōō′bə lənt) *adj.* extremely happy; triumphantly joyful; **p. 961**

K

kin (kin) *n.* relatives, or a group of people with common ancestry; **p. 720**

iniquity/iniquidad *s.* pecado; maldad; **p. 269**

inquisitor/inquisidor *s.* el que hace preguntas; **p. 931**

inscrutable/inescrutable *adj.* misterioso, que no se puede interpreter o entender; **p. 287**

insidious/insidioso *adj.* engañoso; malicioso; **p. 109, p. 658**

installment/cuota *s.* parte proporcional en que se divide un pago; **p. 1015**

intangible/intangible *adj.* que no es fácil de definir o evaluar; **p. 595**

integrate/integrar *v.* unir todas las partes en un todo; **p. 180**

integrity/integridad *s.* rectitud moral; honestidad; **p. 184**

interminable/interminable *adj.* que parece no tener fin; **p. 485**

interpose/interponer *v.* meterse, mediar, poner algo entre cosas o personas; **p. 431**

intervene/intervenir *v.* tomar parte en un asunto; **p. 598**

intimation/insinuación *s.* sugerencia; indirecta; **p. 932**

intimidated/intimidado *adj.* atemorizado o asustado; reprimido; **p. 960**

irreproachable/irreprochable *adj.* libre de culpa; sin falta alguna; **p. 274**

irrevocable/irrevocable *adj.* que no se puede anular; **p. 1180**

J

jilt/dejar plantado *v.* rechazar; incumplir una cita; **p. 779**

jostle/empujar *v.* empellar mientras se camina, como en una multitud; **p. 737**

jubilant/jubiloso *adj.* dichoso; muy feliz por un triunfo; **p. 961**

K

kin/clan *s.* parientes o grupo de personas unidas por un vínculo familiar; **p. 720**

kinsmen (kinz′ men) *n.* someone who shares the same racial or cultural background as another; **p. 802**

L

lament (lə ment′) *v.* to express deep sorrow or grief; **p. 78**

latent (lā′ tənt) *adj.* present but not evident; hidden; **p. 183**

lattice (la′ təs) *n.* a structure of crisscrossed strips, commonly wood or metal, that forms a pattern of openings; **p. 246**

lean (lēn) *adj.* unproductive; lacking; **p. 828**

legacy (leg′ ə sē) *n.* an inheritance; **p. 520**

lethargy (leth′ ər jē) *n.* sluggish inactivity or drowsiness; **p. 255**

loiter (loi′ tər) *v.* to stand or linger idly or aimlessly about a place; **p. 960**

lopped (lopt) *v.* trimmed or chopped off, as the branches of a tree; **p. 1228**

lot (lot) *n.* way of life or purpose as determined by fate; fortune; **p. 198**

ludicrous (loo′ də krəs) *adj.* deserving laughter; foolish; false; **p. 196**

lull (lul) *v.* to soothe or cause to sleep; **p. 812**

lurch (lurch) *v.* to move suddenly and unevenly; **p. 735**

M

malevolence (mə lev′ ə ləns) *n.* a disposition to wish harm to others; ill will; **p. 508**

malinger (mə ling′ gər) *v.* to pretend incapacity or illness to avoid work; **p. 660**

manifest (man′ ə fest′) *adj.* apparent to the eye or the mind; evident; obvious; **p. 184**

marvel (mär′ vəl) *v.* to be filled with wonder; **p. 1271**

meager (mē′ gər) *adj.* deficient in quantity or completeness; **p. 943**

meandering (mē an′ dər ing) *adj.* following a winding course; **p. 1306**

kinsmen/parientes *s.* alguien quien es parte de la misma raza o experiencia cultural; **p. 802**

L

lament/lamentar *v.* expresar gran pena o dolor; **p. 78**

latent/latente *adj.* presente pero no evidente; oculto; **p. 183**

lattice/entramado *s.* conjunto de láminas entrecruzadas, de metal o material flexible, que forma aperturas; **p. 246**

lean/escaso(a) *adj.* improductivo; pobre; **p. 828**

legacy/legado *s.* herencia; **p. 520**

lethargy/letargo *s.* estado de sopor o inactividad; **p. 255**

loiter/holgazanear *v.* permanecer en un lugar sin hacer nada; estar ocioso; **p. 960**

lopped/podado(a) *v.* cortar y quitar, por ej. las ramas de un árbol; **p. 1228**

lot/destino *s.* lo que determina el modo de vida o los acontecimientos; fortuna; **p. 198**

ludicrous/absurdo(a) *adj.* disparatado; sin sentido; equivocado; **p. 196**

lull/arrullar *v.* tranquilizar o adormecer; **p. 812**

lurch/tambalearse *v.* caminar o moverse sin equilibrio; **p. 735**

M

malevolence/malevolencia *s.* deseo de lastimar a otros; mala voluntad; **p. 508**

malinger/fingirse enfermo *v.* hacerse el enfermo para no trabajar; **p. 660**

manifest/manifiesto *adj.* evidente o claro a la vista; obvio; **p. 184**

marvel/maravillar(se) *v.* ver con admiración y asombro; **p. 1271**

meager/exiguo *adj.* muy escaso; limitado; **p. 940**

meandering/tortuoso *adj.* que sigue un camino con muchas curvas; **p. 1306**

melancholy (mel′ ən kol′ ē) *adj.* depressing; dismal; gloomy; **p. 231**

mildewed (mil′ dyūd) *adj.* coated or partially coated with a fungus that causes spoilage; **p. 1218**

millennium (mi le′ nē əm) *n.* a period of great happiness, peace, or prosperity; **p. 818**

misanthropic (mis′ ən throp′ ik) *adj.* having hatred for humankind; **p. 284**

morose (mə rōs′) *adj.* bad-tempered, gloomy, and withdrawn; **p. 920**

mortification (môr′ tə fi kā′ shən) *n.* feeling of shame, humiliation, or embarrassment; **p. 98**

mount (mount) *v.* to ascend or to soar; **p. 675**

mundane (mun dān′) *adj.* ordinary; **p. 750**

mute (mūt) *adj.* silent; **p. 680**

myriad (mir′ ē əd) *adj.* countless; innumerable; **p. 205**

N

nobly (nō′ blē) *adv.* with superior morals or character; **p. 802**

nostalgia (nə stal′ jə) *n.* a bittersweet longing for things, persons, or situations of the past; **p. 1254**

O

oblige (ə blīj′) *v.* to make grateful or indebted; to do a favor or service for; **p. 356**

obliquely (ō blēk′ lē) *adv.* in a slanting or sloping direction; **p. 523**

oblivious (ə bliv′ ē əs) *adj.* without conscious awareness; unmindful; **p. 1263**

obscure (əb skyoor′) *adj.* little known or having an insignificant reputation; **p. 537**

occult (ə kult′) *adj.* beyond human understanding; mysterious; **p. 181**

ominous (om′ ə nəs) *adj.* like an evil omen; threatening; **p. 746, p. 1249**

ordeal (ôr dēl′) *n.* a circumstance or experience that is painful or difficult; a trial; **p. 1149**

melancholy/melancólico *adj.* deprimente; funesto; desconsolador; **p. 231**

mildewed/mohoso(a) *adj.* cubierto total o parcialmente con un hongo que puede causar daños; **p. 1218**

millennium/edad de oro *s.* periodo de felicidad, paz o prosperidad; **p. 818**

misanthropic/misantrópico(a) *adj.* que siente aversión o rechazo al trato humano; **p. 284**

morose/adusto *adj.* malhumorado; taciturno; **p. 920**

mortification/mortificación *s.* sentimiento de aflicción, humillación o vergüenza; **p. 98**

mount/montar *v.* subir o remontar; **p. 675**

mundane/mundano *adj.* ordinario; usual; terrenal; **p. 750**

mute/mudo *adj.* silencioso; falta de sonido; **p. 680**

myriad/innumerable *adj.* que no se puede contar; incalculable; **p. 205**

N

nobly/noblemente *adv.* con morales superiores o un carácter superior; **p. 802**

nostalgia/nostalgia *s.* tristeza melancólica por la ausencia o alejamiento de cosas, personas o recuerdos del pasado; **p. 1254**

O

oblige/agradecer *v.* hacer agradecido o adeudado por algo; hacerle un favor o un servicio; **p. 356**

obliquely/oblicuamente *adv.* de manera inclinada o sesgada; **p. 523**

oblivious/abstraído *adj.* distraído; ensimismado; **p. 1263**

obscure/obscuro(a) *adj.* no conocido; que tenga una reputación insignificante; **p. 537**

occult/sobrenatural *adj.* más allá de la comprensión humana; misterioso; **p. 181**

ominous/ominoso *adj.* que da mal presagio; siniestro; **p. 746, p. 1249**

ordeal/tribulación *s.* circunstancia o experiencia dolorosa o difícil; **p. 1149**

P

palpable (pal´pə bəl) *adj.* tangible; able to be touched or felt; **p. 680**

patronage (pā´ trə nij) *n.* business; trade; custom; **p. 816**

pepper (pe´pər) *v.* to shower with small objects; **p. 675**

perception (pər sep´ shən) *n.* an awareness; an insight; **p. 549**

perennial (pə ren´ ē əl) *adj.* continuing year after year; enduring; **p. 181**

perish (per´ish) *v.* to pass from existence; to disappear; **p. 388**

permeate (pur´ mē āt´) *v.* to penetrate, spread through, or diffuse; **p. 1212**

perpetual (pər pech´ oo əl) *adj.* lasting forever; eternal; **p. 180**

persistence (pər sis´ təns) *n.* stubborn or determined continuance; **p. 550**

persistent (pər sis´ tənt) *adj.* continuing or going forward, despite problems or obstacles; **p. 1190**

perturbation (pur´ tər bā´ shən) *n.* state of being perturbed, anxious, or uneasy; **p. 746**

perusal (pə roo´ zəl) *n.* the process of examining carefully; **p. 371**

pervade (pər vād´) *v.* to spread through every part; **p. 364**

petrified (pet´ rə fīd) *adj.* paralyzed with fear; stiff or like stone; **p. 125**

piety (pī´ ə tē) *n.* religious devoutness; goodness; **p. 781**

placid (pla´ səd) *adj.* calm; peaceful; undisturbed; **p. 247**

Plexiglas (plek´ si glas´) *n.* a light and very durable transparent plastic; **p. 976**

poignant (poin´ yənt) *adj.* sharp; severe; causing emotional or physical anguish; **p. 378**

pointless (point´ lis) *n.* making no sense; **p. 1184**

poise (poiz´) *n.* a state of balance; **p. 709**

poised (poizd) *adj.* having a calm, controlled, and dignified manner; composed; **p. 906**

ponder (pon´ dər) *v.* to think about thoroughly and carefully; **p. 1175**

P

palpable/palpable *adj.* tangible; que puede tocarse con las manos; **p. 680**

patronage/clientela *s.* conjunto de parroquianos de un negocio, oficio o establecimiento; **p. 816**

pepper/salpicar *v.* esparcir cosas como rociándolas sobre una superficie; **p. 675**

perception/percepción *s.* conocimiento; idea; **p. 549**

perennial/perenne *adj.* que continúa año tras año; duradero; **p. 181**

perish/perecer *v.* dejar de existir; desaparecer; **p. 388**

permeate/penetrar *v.* infiltrarse, introducirse o difundirse; **p. 1212**

perpetual/perpetuo *adj.* que dura por siempre; eterno; **p. 180**

persistence/persistencia *s.* perseverancia; continuación; **p. 550**

persistent/persistente *adj.* que continua a despecho de problemas o obstáculos; **p. 1190**

perturbation/perturbación *s.* agitación; ansiedad; inquietud; **p. 746**

perusal/escudriñamiento *s.* proceso de examinar cuidadosamente; **p. 371**

pervade/penetrar *v.* saturar; llenar por todos lados; **p. 364**

petrified/petrificado *adj.* paralizado de miedo; inmóvil como una piedra; **p 125**

piety/piedad *s.* devoción religiosa; bondad; **p. 781**

placid/plácido *adj.* quieto; apacible; sin perturbación; **p. 247**

Plexiglas/plexiglás *s.* material acrílico transparente y flexible; **p. 976**

poignant/punzante *adj.* agudo; lacerante; que causa angustia emocional o física; **p. 378**

pointless/inútil *s.* vano, sin sentido; **p. 1184**

poise/aplomo *s.* mesura, compostura; **p. 709**

poised/aplomado(a) *adj.* que tiene serenidad, seriedad y seguridad; con compostura; **p. 906**

ponder/ponderar *v.* pensar algo detenida y cuidadosamente; **p. 1175**

possessor (pə zes′ ər) *n.* one who has or takes control of something; owner; **p. 1184**

posterity (pos ter′ ə tē) *n.* generations of the future; all of one's descendants; **p. 50**

premeditated (prē med′ ə tāt′ əd) *adj.* thought about beforehand; **p. 971**

premonition (prē′ mə nish′ ən) *n.* a warning, or foreboding about the future; **p. 985**

presume (pri zo͞om′) *v.* to expect something without justification; to take for granted; **p. 660**

presumptuous (pri zump′ cho͞o əs) *adj.* going beyond what is proper; excessively bold; **p. 1292**

pretense (prē′ tens) *n.* a false show or appearance, especially for the purpose of deceiving; falseness; **p. 1033**

prevalent (prev′ ə lent) *adj.* widespread; **p. 230**

procure (prə kyoor′) *v.* to obtain by care or effort; **p. 64**

prosperous (pros′ pər əs) *adj.* wealthy or successful; **p. 536**

prostrate (pros′ trāt) *adj.* stretched out with face to the ground in humility, adoration, or submission; **p. 363**

protrude (prō tro͞od′) *v.* to stick out; to project; **p. 376**

providence (prov′ ə dəns) *n.* divine care or guidance; foresight; **p. 63**

proximity (prok sim′ ə tē) *n.* closeness in space, time, sequence, or degree; nearness; **p. 258**

prudence (pro͞od′ əns) *n.* exercise of good and cautious judgment; **p. 91**

R

racket (rak′ it) *n.* loud noise; clamor; din; **p. 356**

rampages (ram′ pāj′ iz) *v.* rushes wildly about; scurries; **p. 1228**

random (ran′ dəm) *adj.* lacking a definite pattern; haphazard; **p. 1249**

rank (rangk) *adj.* having a strong, offensive odor; **p. 1218**

ration (rā′ shən) *n.* fixed portion or share; **p. 56**

ravenous (rav′ ə nəs) *adj.* extremely hungry; **p. 918**

possessor/poseedor(a) *s.* persona que tiene en su poder el control de algo; dueño; **p. 1184**

posterity/posteridad *s.* generaciones del futuro; todos los descendientes; **p. 50**

premeditated/premeditado(a) *adj.* que se reflexionó con cuidado antes de realizar la acción; **p. 971**

premonition/premonición *s.* advertencia o presagio de que algo va a ocurrir; **p. 985**

presume/suponer *v.* esperar algo sin justicación; **p. 660**

presumptuous/atrevido(a) *adj.* que falta al respeto debido; insolente; **p. 1292**

pretense/simulación *s.* falsa apariencia, especialmente con el propósito de engañar; falsedad; **p. 1033**

prevalent/prevaleciente *adj.* frecuente; generalizado; **p. 230**

procure/procurarse *v.* obtener mediante esfuerzos; **p. 64**

prosperous/próspero(a) *adj.* rico o venturoso; **p. 536**

prostrate/postrado *adj.* agachado o arrodillado en señal de humillación, adoración o sumisión; **p. 363**

protrude/sobresalir *v.* resaltar; proyectarse; **p. 376**

providence/providencia *s.* cuidado o guía divina; disposición; **p. 63**

proximity/proximidad *s.* cercanía en espacio, tiempo, secuencia o grado; **p. 258**

prudence/prudencia *s.* ejercicio del buen juicio y la cordura; cautela; **p. 91**

R

racket/bulla *s.* gritería; clamor; barullo; **p. 356**

rampages/alborotar *v.* pasar saqueando; corretear; **p. 1228**

random/causal *adj.* que no sigue un patrón definido; fortuito; **p. 1249**

rank/fétido(a) *adj.* que tiene un olor repugnante; **p. 1218**

ration/ración *s.* porción definida; **p. 56**

ravenous/voraz *adj.* extremadamente hambriento; **p. 918**

reap (rēp) *v.* to gather, as in harvesting a crop; **p. 697, p. 828**

rear (rir) *v.* to lift upright; raise; **p. 1253**

recede (ri sēd´) *v.* to move back or away from a point, limit, or mark; **p. 1222**

recluse (rek´ lo͞os) *n.* someone who leads a secluded or solitary life; **p. 284**

recompense (rek´ əm pens´) *n.* something given in return for something else; compensation; **p. 85**

recourse (rē´ kôrs´) *n.* resorting to a person or thing for help; **p. 139**

rectitude (rek´ tə to͞od´) *n.* uprightness of moral character; honesty; **p. 116**

redress (rē´ dress´) *n.* compensation, as for wrong done; **p. 371**

rejuvenated (ri jo͞o´ və nāt´ əd) *adj.* restored to youthful vigor or appearance; renewed; **p. 1320**

remonstrate (ri mon´ strāt) *v.* to object; to protest; **p. 110**

render (ren´ dər) *v.* to reproduce or depict in verbal or artistic form; **p. 696**

repose (ri pōz´) *n.* relaxation; tranquility; eternal rest; **p. 501**

reprieve (ri prēv´) *n.* official postponement of the carrying out of a sentence; **p. 1095**

reprimand (rep´ rə mand´) *v.* to reprove or correct sharply; **p. 1047**

reproach (ri prōch´) *n.* an expression of disapproval; a reprimand; **p. 521**

repudiate (ri pū´ dē āt´) *v.* to refuse to accept as valid; to reject; to renounce; **p. 1151**

resign (ri zīn´) *v.* to make oneself accept; **p. 738**

resignation (rez´ ig nā´ shən) *n.* unresisting acceptance; submission; **p. 204**

resolution (rez´ ə lo͞o´ shən) *n.* firmness of purpose; **p. 125**

resolve (ri zolv´) *v.* to decide; determine; **p. 62**

respite (res´ pət) *n.* a period of rest or relief, as from work or sorrow; **p. 247**

retaliation (ri tal´ ē ā´ shən) *n.* the act of repaying an injury or a wrong by committing the same, or a similar, act; **p. 1095**

reap/cosechar *v.* recoger los cultivos cuando están maduros; **p. 697, p. 828**

rear/levantar *v.* alzar; subir; **p. 1253**

recede/retroceder *v.* recular o irse de un punto, un limite o una marca; **p.1222**

recluse/ermitaño(a) *s.* persona que vive recluida o en soledad; **p. 284**

recompense/recompensa *s.* algo dado en cambio de algo más; compensación; **p.85**

recourse/recurso *s.* ayuda; medio que, en caso de necesidad, sirve para conseguir lo que se pretende; **p. 139**

rectitude/rectitud *s.* buena condición moral; honestidad; **p. 116**

redress/desagravio *s.* compensación por un error o mala actitud; **p. 371**

rejuvenated/rejuvenecido *adj.* que ha recuperado el vigor o la apariencia joven; renovado; **p. 1320**

remonstrate/rezongar *v.* objetar; protestar; **p. 110**

render/producir *v.* causar; generar; **p. 696**

repose/descanso *s.* relax; tranquilidad; reposo eterno; **p. 501**

reprieve/aplazamiento *s.* demora oficial de una sentencia; **p. 1095**

reprimand/reprender *v.* regañar o corregir severamente; **p. 1047**

reproach/reproche *s.* expresión de desacuerdo; censura; **p. 521**

repudiate/repudiar *v.* negarse a aceptar como válido; rechazar; renunciar; **p. 1151**

resign/resignarse *v.* obligarse a aceptar; conformarse; **p. 738**

resignation/resignación *s.* aceptación; conformismo; sumisión; **p. 204**

resolution/resolución *s.* acción de decidir con firmeza; **p. 125**

resolve/resolver *v.* decidir; determinar; **p. 62**

respite/respiro *s.* rato de descanso o alivio, en medio de un trabajo o una pena; **p. 247**

retaliation/represalia *s.* acto de vengarse o devolver un mal acto cometiendo un acto similar o igual; **p. 1095**

retractable (ri trak′ tə bəl) *adj.* capable of being drawn back or in; **p. 930**

reverence (rev′ ər əns) *n.* a feeling of respect or deep affection; **p. 198**

revive (ri vīv′) *v.* to give new strength and vitality, or bring back to consciousness; **p. 56**

rouse (rouz) *v.* to awaken from sleep; **p. 56**

rudiment (roo′ də mənt) *n.* an imperfect or undeveloped part; **p. 205**

rue (roo) *v.* to regret; to be sorry for; **p. 922**

ruinous (roo′ i nəs) *adj.* causing ruin; destructive; **p. 502**

S

sagacious (sə gā′ shəs) *adj.* having or showing wisdom and keen perception; **p. 269**

salient (sāl′ yənt) *adj.* prominent or conspicuously noticeable; **p. 564**

sanction (sangk′ shən) *n.* approval or support; **p. 216**

scintillating (sin′ tə lā′ ting) *adj.* brilliant; sparkling; **p. 815**

score (skôr) *n.* a group of twenty items; **p. 388**

scorn (skôrn) *n.* contempt or disdain felt toward a person or an object considered despicable or unworthy; **p. 1254**

scorned (skôrnd) *v.* treated with open contempt; rejected something as worthless; **p. 570**

scruple (skroo′ pəl) *n.* moral principle that restrains action; **p. 72**

scuffle (skuf′əl) *v.* to move with a slow, heavy, shuffling gait; **p. 870**

sear (sēr) *v.* to char, scorch, or burn the surface with or as if with a sudden application of intense heat; **p. 1287**

seclusion (si kloo′ zhən) *n.* separation from others; isolation; **p. 511**

shtetl (shte′ təl) *n.* small Jewish town or community; **p. 1331**

sluggishly (slug′ ish lē) *adv.* slowly; without strength or energy; **p. 879**

sneer (snēr) *v.* to smile or laugh scornfully or critically; **p. 701**

retractable/retráctil *adj.* capaz de encogerse; **p. 930**

reverence/reverencia *s.* respeto o veneración; **p. 198**

revive/revivir *v.* dar nueva fuerza y vitalidad; hacer que recupere el conocimiento; **p. 56**

rouse/despertar *v.* dejar de dormir; **p. 56**

rudiment/rudimento *s.* parte imperfecta o sin desarrollar; **p. 205**

rue/deplorar *v.* lamentar; sentir; **p. 922**

ruinous/ruinoso(a) *adj.* que arruina; que destruye; **p. 502**

S

sagacious/sagaz *adj.* que tiene o demuestra astucia y agudeza mental; **p. 269**

salient/destacado(a) *adj.* prominente o notoriamente evidente; **p. 564**

sanction/ratificación *s.* aprobación o respaldo; **p. 216**

scintillating/chispeante *adj.* brillante; destellante; **p. 815**

score/veintena *s.* grupo de veinte objetos; **p. 388**

scorn/despreció *v.* desdén hacia una persona o un objeto que se considera desreciable o desmerecedor; **p. 1254**

scorned/despreciado *v.* tratar con desdén; despreciar; **p. 570**

scruple/escrúpulo *s.* principio moral que limita una acción; **p. 72**

scuffle/arrastrar los pies *v.* moverse con pasos rápidos y torpes; **p. 870**

sear/quemar *v.* calcinar, chamuscar o abrasar con fuego o algo muy caliente; **p. 1287**

seclusion/reclusión *s.* separación de otros; aislamiento; **p. 511**

shtetl/shtetl *s.* palabra de origen yiddish que significa pequeña ciudad o comunidad hebrea; **p. 1331**

sluggishly/perezosamente *adv.* lentamente; sin energía ni entusiasmo; **p. 879**

sneer/reírse socarronamente *v.* sonreír o reír despreciativamente o criticamente; **p. 701**

snicker (sni′ kər) *n.* a snide, partly suppressed laugh, often expressing disrespect; **p. 794**

solemn (sol′ əm) *adj.* serious; somber; **p. 896**

solidarity (sol′ ə dar′ ə tē) *n.* unity of a group that produces a sense of community; **p. 1166**

solitude (sol′ e tōōd′) *n.* the state of being alone; **p. 1326**

sown (sōn) *v.* planted; **p. 828**

speculate (spek′ yə lāt′) *v.* to engage in risky business ventures, hoping to make quick profits; **p. 236**

spurn (spurn) *v.* to reject with contempt or disdain; to scorn; **p. 110, p. 1278**

stark (stärk) *adj.* absolute; complete; **p. 788**

stately (stāt′ lē) *adj.* noble; dignified; majestic; **p. 919**

stature (stach′ ər) *n.* a level attained; standing; status; **p. 1150**

stigma (stig′ mə) *n.* mark or characteristic of disgrace; **p. 1239**

stipulate (stip′ yə lāt′) *v.* to require or demand as part of an agreement; **p. 1167**

stoically (stō′ ik lē) *adv.* calmly and unemotionally, especially despite pain or suffering; **p. 772**

stooped (stōōpt) *adj.* bent forward and downward; **p. 1175**

striking (strī′king) *adj.* impressive; attractive; **p. 1271**

stupor (stōō′ pər) *n.* a confused or dazed state of mind; **p. 538**

subjugation (sub′ jə gā′ shən) *n.* act of bringing under control; domination; **p. 109**

sublime (səb līm′) *adj.* of great spiritual or intellectual value; noble; **p. 204**

subsequently (sub′ sə kwent′ lē) *adv.* at a later time; **p. 403**

subservient (səb sur′ vē ənt) *adj.* useful, in an inferior capacity, to promote an end; submissive; **p. 1030**

subtle (sut′ əl) *adj.* barely noticeable; not open, direct, or obvious; **p. 788, p. 1060**

subverting (səb vurt′ ing) *v.* overthrowing and destroying; **p. 1228**

succumb (sə kum′) *v.* to give in or submit to; **p. 984**

snicker/risita burlona *s.* risa solapada que puede demostrar burla o falta de respeto; **p. 794**

solemn/solemne *adj.* serio; grave; **p. 896**

solidarity/solidaridad *s.* adhesión o apoyo a una causa ajena; **p. 1166**

solitude/soledad *s.* falta de compañía, estar solo; **p. 1326**

sown/sembrados *v.* (part.) plantados; **p. 828**

speculate/especular *v.* participar en negocios arriesgados con el deseo de obtener ganancias rápidas; **p. 236**

spurn/desdeñar *v.* rechazar con menosprecio o desdén; **p. 110, p. 1278**

stark/absoluto(a) *adj.* total; completo; **p. 788**

stately/majestuoso *adj.* noble; imponente; espléndido; **p. 919**

stature/estatura *s.* nivel alcanzado; posición; **p. 1150**

stigma/estigma *s.* marca o señal de mala fama; **p. 1239**

stipulate/estipular *v.* establecer o concertar de común acuerdo; **p. 1167**

stoically/estoicamente *adv.* de modo calmado y sin emoción, especialmente en momentos de dolor o sufrimiento; **p. 772**

stooped/encorvado *adj.* doblado hacia adelante y hacia abajo; **p. 1175**

striking/atractivo(a) *adj.* admirable; que atrae la atención; **p. 1271**

stupor/estupor *s.* disminución de las funciones intelectuales, aletargamiento; **p. 538**

subjugation/subyugación *s.* acto de someter o poner bajo control; dominación; **p. 109**

sublime/sublime *adj.* de gran valor espiritual o intelectual; noble; **p. 204**

subsequent/subsiguiente *adv.* que sigue inmediatamente; **p. 403**

subservient/subordinado *adj.* útil, en una capacidad inferior, para conseguir un fin; sumiso; **p. 1030**

subtle/sutil *adj.* que no es obvio ni directo; **p. 788, p. 1060**

subverting/subvirtiendo *v.* derrocar y destruir; **p. 1228**

succumb/sucumbir *v.* rendirse; ceder; **p. 984**

surmise (sər mīz´) *v.* to infer from little evidence; to guess; **p. 233**

susceptible (sə sep´ tə bəl) *adj.* easily influenced or affected; **p. 403**

swelter (swel´ tər) *v.* to suffer from oppressive heat; **p. 1222**

swindle (swin´ dəl) *v.* to cheat someone out of money or property; **p. 1017**

T

tactful (takt´ fəl) *adj.* able to speak or act without offending others; **p. 777**

taper (tā´ pər) *v.* to become progressively thinner or smaller; **p. 691**

temper (tem´ pər) *v.* to modify or moderate; soften; **p. 50**

tempest (tem´ pist) *n.* a violent storm; **p. 564**

tenure (ten´ yər) *n.* conditions or terms under which something is held; **p. 115**

terminus (tur´ mə nəs) *n.* one end of a travel route or the station placed there; **p. 1008**

token (tō´ ken) *n.* something serving as an indication, a proof, or an expression of something else; a sign; **p. 1283**

transformed (trans fôrməd´) *adj.* changed in a dramatic way; **p. 1205**

transfusion (trans fū´ zhən) *n.* the act of passing life-saving fluids from one to another; **p. 1205**

trepidation (trep´ ə dā´ shən) *n.* nervous anticipation; anxiety; dread; **p. 522, p. 986**

tribute (tri´ byüt) *n.* something given to show affection, gratitude, or respect; **p. 937**

tumultuously (too mul´ choo əs lē) *adv.* in an agitated manner; violently; **p. 549**

turret (tur´ it) *n.* a small, rotating domelike structure that is mounted with guns and attached to the body of an aircraft; **p. 976**

twinge (twinj) *n.* a sudden, sharp physical or emotional pain; **p. 938**

tyranny (tir´ ə nē) *n.* cruel use of authority; oppressive power; **p. 124**

surmise/suponer *v.* conjeturar con poca o ninguna evidencia; presumir; **p. 233**

susceptible/susceptible *adj.* sensible o capaz de recibir modificación; **p. 403**

swelter/achicharrar *v.* padecer de calor opresivo; **p. 1222**

swindle/estafar *v.* engañar a alguien para sacarle dinero o propiedad; **p. 1017**

T

tactful/discreto *adj.* capaz de hablar o actuar sin ofender a otros; **p. 777**

taper/reducir *v.* disminuir en tamaño o intensidad; **p. 691**

temper/atemperar *v.* modificar o moderar; suavizar; **p. 50**

tempest/tempestad *s.* tormenta con fuertes vientos; **p. 564**

tenure/tenencia *s.* condiciones o términos bajo los cuales se posee algo; **p. 115**

terminus/término *s.* final de un recorrido o el extremo de una línea de transporte público; **p. 1008**

token/muestra *s.* indicio, demostración o prueba de algo; un señal; **p. 1283**

transformed/convertido(a) *adj.* transformado en algo distinto de lo que era; **p. 1205**

transfusion/transfusión *s.* transferencia de sangre o plasma de una persona a otra; **p. 1205**

trepidation/perturbación *s.* anticipación nerviosa; ansiedad; **p. 522, p. 986**

tribute/tributo *s.* reconocimiento en muestra de afecto, gratitud o respeto; **p. 937**

tumultuously/tumultuosamente *adv.* de modo agitado; violentamente; **p. 549**

turret/torreta giravtoria *s.* pequeña torre acorazada, con forma de domo que rota y está montada en un avión, que sirve para sostener piezas de artillería; **p. 976**

twinge/punzada *s.* dolor repentino y agudo que puede ser físico o afectivo; **p. 938**

tyranny/tiranía *s.* abuso cruel de la autoridad; poder opresivo; **p. 124**

tyrant (tī′ rənt) *n.* a ruler who exercises power or authority in an unjust manner; one who has absolute power; **p. 137**

U

uncanny (un kan′ ē) *adj.* peculiarly unsettling in an eerie way; **p. 576, p. 1243**

undeviating (un dē′ vē āt′ ing) *adj.* not turning away from; **p. 1293**

unencumbered (ən in kəm′ bərd) *adj.* unhindered; unburdened; **p. 1327**

unique (ū nēk′) *adj.* unusual; **p. 832**

unorthodox (un ôr′ thə doks′) *adj.* not customary or traditional; **p. 1306**

unperturbed (un pər turbd′) *adj.* undisturbed; calm; **p. 1084**

unsheathed (un shēthd′) *adj.* removed from a protective case; **p. 832**

unutterable (un ə′ tə rə bəl) *adj.* too deep or great to be put into words ; **p. 788**

usurpation (ū′ sər pā′ shən) *n.* the act of seizing power without legal right or authority; **p. 114**

V

valedictory (val′ ə dik′ tə rē) *adj.* of or relating to an occasion or expression of farewell; **p. 1223**

vanity (van′ i tē) *n.* excessive pride, as in one's looks; **p. 779**

vanquish (vang′ kwish) *v.* to defeat; **p. 342**

vault (vôlt) *n.* an arched structure forming a roof or ceiling; **p. 24**

vehemently (vē′ə mənt lē) *adv.* in a strong or passionate manner; **p. 771**

venerable (ven′ ər ə bəl) *adj.* deserving respect because of age, character, or position; **p. 268**

vigorously (vig′ ər əs lē) *adv.* with power, energy, and strength; **p. 894**

vile (vīl) *adj.* evil, repulsive, or degrading; **p. 565, p. 1071**

vindicate (vin′ də kāt′) *v.* to justify; to prove correct in light of later circumstances; **p. 881**

tyrant/tirano(a) *s.* gobernante que abusa de su poder y autoridad de manera injusta; quien tiene el poder absoluto; **p. 137**

U

uncanny/espectral *adj.* inquietante y extraño; misterioso; **p. 576, p. 1243**

undeviating/recto *adj.* que no se desvía o extravía; **p. 1293**

unencumbered/aligerado(a) *adj.* aliviado o sin carga; **p. 1327**

unique/único(a) *adj.* fuera de lo común; **p. 832**

unorthodox/no ortodoxo *adj.* que no es usual ni tradicional; **p. 1306**

unperturbed/inalterado *adj.* que no se molesta o altera; calmado; **p. 1084**

unsheathed/desenvainado(a) *adj.* que se sacó que su vaina o funda; **p. 832**

unutterable/inefable *adj.* tan profundo o grande que no se puede ponerlo en palabras; **p. 788**

usurpation/usurpación *s.* acto de tomar el poder sin derecho o autoridad legal; **p. 114**

V

valedictory/de despedida *adj.* de una ocasión o una expresión de adiós; **p.1223**

vanity/vanidad *s.* orgullo excesivo, particularmente por la apariencia física; **p. 779**

vanquish/subyugar *v.* derrotar; conquistar **p. 342**

vault/bóveda *s.* estructura arqueada que forma un techo o cielo raso; **p. 24**

vehemently/vehementemente *adv.* de modo fuerte, intenso o apasionado; **p. 771**

venerable/venerable *adj.* que merece respeto debido a la edad, carácter o posición; **p. 268**

vigorously/vigorosamente *adv.* con poder, energía y fuerza; **p. 894**

vile/vil *adj.* malvado; bajo; repulsivo; degradante; **p. 565, p. 1071**

vindicate/vindicar *v.* justificar; demostrar que es correcto ante nuevas circunstancias; **p. 881**

vindictive (vin dik′ tiv) *adj.* desiring revenge; **p. 903**

virulent (vir′ yə lənt) *adj.* extremely poisonous or harmful; **p. 883**

vivid (viv′ id) *adj.* perceived as bright and distinct; brilliant; **p. 1282**

vogue (vōg) *n.* fashion; style; **p. 815**

volition (vō lish′ ən) *n.* act of choosing or deciding; **p. 1001**

W

wallowing (wol′ ō ing) *v.* moving in a clumsy manner or with difficulty; **p. 1204**

wane (wān) *v.* to decrease gradually; to decline; **p. 1294**

wanton (wont′ ən) *adj.* resulting from extreme cruelty or neglect; **p. 701**

warily (wār′ ə lē) *adv.* in a watchful or alert manner; cautiously; **p. 1249**

whimsically (hwim′ zik lē) *adv.* in a quaintly humorous manner; **p. 772**

withered (wi′ thərd) *adj.* shriveled; **p. 735**

woo (wōō) *v.* to tempt or invite; **p. 1253**

X

xenophobic (zen′ ə fō′ bik) *adj.* having an extreme fear of foreigners or strangers; **p. 1007**

Z

zealous (zel′ əs) *adj.* filled with enthusiastic devotion; passionate; **p. 274**

vindictive/vengativo *adj.* que desea venganza; **p. 903**

virulent/virulento *adj.* extremadamente nocivo o dañino; **p. 883**

vivid/vívido *adj.* auténtico; realista; distintivo; **p. 1282**

vogue/moda *s.* que está en boga; que se estila; **p. 815**

volition/volición *s.* acto de la voluntad de escoger y decidir; **p. 1001**

W

wallowing/andando pesadamente *v.* moverse torpemente o con dificultad; **p. 1204**

wane/declinar *v.* menguar o disminuir gradualmente; **p. 1294**

wanton/despiadado(a) *adj.* que es inhumano, cruel o sin piedad; **p. 701**

warily/cautelosamente *adv.* de modo cuidadoso o alerta; **p. 1249**

whimsically/caprichosamente *adv.* de modo extravagante; **p. 772**

withered/marchito *adj.* seco; arrugado; **p. 735**

woo/atraer *v.* tentar o buscar el apoyo de alguien; **p. 1253**

X

xenophobic/xenófobo *adj.* que siente hostilidad hacia los extranjeros; **p. 1007**

Z

zealous/fervoroso *adj.* lleno de entusiasmo y devoción; apasionado; **p. 274**

ACADEMIC WORD LIST

The lists of words that appear on this and the following pages represent a research-based collection of words that forms the core of academic literacy. The purpose of the lists is to present students with the basics of a working academic vocabulary, one that will prove useful in reading, writing, and research in many areas of study. Many of these words also appear throughout the Glencoe Language Arts program.

List One

analysis
approach
area
assessment
assume
authority
available
benefit
concept
consistent
constitutional
context
contract
create
data
definition
derived
distribution
economic
environment
established
estimate
evidence
export
factors
financial
formula
function
identified
income
indicate
individual

interpretation
involved
issues
labor
legal
legislation
major
method
occur
percent
period
policy
principle
procedure
process
required
research
response
role
section
sector
significant
similar
source
specific
structure
theory
variables

List Two

achieve
acquisition
administration

affect
appropriate
aspects
assistance
categories
chapter
commission
community
complex
computer
conclusion
conduct
consequences
construction
consumer
credit
cultural
design
distinction
elements
equation
evaluation
features
final
focus
impact
injury
institute
investment
items
journal
maintenance
normal

obtained
participation
perceived
positive
potential
previous
primary
purchase
range
region
regulations
relevant
resident
resources
restricted
security
select
site
sought
strategies
survey
text
traditional
transfer

List Three

alternative
circumstances
comments
compensation
components
consent
considerable

constant
constraints
contribution
convention
coordination
core
corporate
corresponding
criteria
deduction
demonstrate
document
dominant
emphasis
ensure
excluded
framework
funds
illustrated
immigration
implies
initial
instance
interaction
justification
layer
link
location
maximum
minorities
negative
outcomes
partnership

philosophy
physical
proportion
published
reaction
registered
reliance
removed
scheme
sequence
sex
shift
specified
sufficient
task
technical
techniques
technology
validity
volume

List Four

access
adequate
annual
apparent
approximated
attitudes
attributed
civil
code
commitment
communication
concentration
conference
contrast
cycle
debate
despite
dimensions
domestic
emerged
error

ethnic
goals
granted
hence
hypothesis
implementation
implications
imposed
integration
internal
investigation
job
label
mechanism
obvious
occupational
option
output
overall
parallel
parameters
phase
predicted
principal
prior
professional
project
promote
regime
resolution
retained
series
statistics
status
stress
subsequent
sum
summary
undertaken

List Five

academic
adjustment

alter
amendment
aware
capacity
challenge
clause
compounds
conflict
consultation
contact
decline
discretion
draft
enable
energy
enforcement
entities
equivalent
evolution
expansion
exposure
external
facilitate
fundamental
generated
generation
image
liberal
license
logic
marginal
medical
mental
modified
monitoring
network
notion
objective
orientation
perspective
precise
prime
psychology

pursue
ratio
rejected
revenue
stability
styles
substitution
sustainable
symbolic
target
transition
trend
version
welfare
whereas

List Six

abstract
accurate
acknowledged
aggregate
allocation
assigned
attached
author
bond
brief
capable
cited
cooperative
discrimination
display
diversity
domain
edition
enhanced
estate
exceed
expert
explicit
federal
fees
flexibility

furthermore
gender
ignored
incentive
incidence
incorporated
index
inhibition
initiatives
input
instructions
intelligence
interval
lecture
migration
minimum
ministry
motivation
neutral
nevertheless
overseas
preceding
presumption
rational
recovery
revealed
scope
subsidiary
tapes
trace
transformation
transport
underlying
utility

List Seven

adaptation
adults
advocate
aid
channel
chemical
classical

comprehensive
comprise
confirmed
contrary
converted
couple
decades
definite
deny
differentiation
disposal
dynamic
eliminate
empirical
equipment
extract
file
finite
foundation
global
grade
guarantee
hierarchical
identical
ideology
inferred
innovation
insert
intervention
isolated
media
mode
paradigm
phenomenon
priority
prohibited
publication
quotation
release
reverse
simulation
solely
somewhat

submitted
successive
survive
thesis
topic
transmission
ultimately
unique
visible
voluntary

List Eight

abandon
accompanied
accumulation
ambiguous
appendix
appreciation
arbitrary
automatically
bias
chart
clarity
conformity
commodity
complement
contemporary
contradiction
crucial
currency
denote
detected
deviation
displacement
dramatic
eventually
exhibit
exploitation
fluctuations
guidelines
highlighted
implicit
induced

inevitably
infrastructure
inspection
intensity
manipulation
minimized
nuclear
offset
paragraph
plus
practitioners
predominantly
prospect
radical
random
reinforced
restore
revision
schedule
tension
termination
theme
thereby
uniform
vehicle
via
virtually
visual
widespread

List Nine

accommodation
analogous
anticipated
assurance
attained
behalf
bulk
ceases
coherence
coincide
commenced
concurrent

confined
controversy
conversely
device
devoted
diminished
distorted
duration
erosion
ethical
format
founded
incompatible
inherent
insights
integral
intermediate
manual
mature
mediation
medium
military
minimal
mutual
norms
overlap
passive
portion
preliminary
protocol
qualitative
refine
relaxed
restraints
revolution
rigid
route
scenario
sphere
subordinate
supplementary
suspended
team

temporary
trigger
unified
violation
vision

List Ten

adjacent
albeit
assembly
collapse
colleagues
compiled
conceived
convinced
depression
encountered
enormous
forthcoming
inclination
integrity
intrinsic
invoked
levy
likewise
nonetheless
notwithstanding
odd
ongoing
panel
persistent
posed
reluctant
so-called
straightforward
undergo
whereby

INDEX OF SKILLS

Reading and Thinking

Speaking, Listening, and Viewing

Research and Study Skills

Interdisciplinary Activities

INDEX OF AUTHORS AND TITLES

INDEX OF AUTHORS AND TITLES

INDEX OF ART AND ARTISTS

ACKNOWLEDGMENTS

Unit 1

Excerpt from *The Way to Rainy Mountain* by M. Scott Momaday. Copyright 1969 © by the University of New Mexico Press. Reprinted by permission from the author.

"The Summer of the Black Widows" from *The Summer of the Black Widows,* copyright © 1996 by Sherman Alexie. Reprinted by permission of Hanging Loose Press.

Excerpt from "The Account: Álvar Núñez Cabeza de Vaca's Relación" is reprinted by permission from the publisher of *The Account: Álvar Núñez Cabeza de Vaca's Relación,* edited and translated José Fernández and Fatava (Houston: Arte Público Press – University of Houston, © 1993).

"To His Excellency George Washington" from *The Poems of Phyllis Wheatley,* edited and with an introduction by Julien D. Mason Jr. Copyright © 1966 by the University of North Carolina Press, renewed 1989. Used by permission of the Publisher.

"The Sky Tree" retold by Joseph Bruchac, from *Keepers of Life,* by Michael Caduto and Jospeh Bruchac. Copyright © 1994, Fulcrum Publishing, 350 Indiana St., Suite 350, Golden, CO 80401. (800) 992-2908.

From Lang, Amy Schranger, ed. "A True History of the Captivity and Restoration of Mary Rowlandson" in Andrews, William L., Sargent Bush Jr., Annette Kolodny, Amy Schranger Lang and Daniel B. Shea, eds. *Journeys in the New Worlds: Early American Women's Narratives.* Copyright 1990. Reprinted by permission of the University of Wisconsin Press.

Unit 2

"On the Eve of the Great Historic Dandi March" by Mohandas K. Gandhi from *Collected Speeches: 1909–1939, Volume I,* copyright © 1938 by New Directions Publishing Company. Reprinted by permission of New Directions Publishing Corp.

Long Walk to Freedom by Nelson Mandela. Copyright © 1994, 1995 by Nelson Rolihlahla Mandela. By permission of Little, Brown and Co., Inc.

In the Heart of the Sea: The Tragedy of the Whaleship Essex by Nathaniel Philbrick. Copyright © 2000. Reprinted by permission of Viking Penguin, a division of Penguin Putnam Inc.

Unit 3

Reprinted with the permission of Simon & Schuster Adult Publishing Group from *Lincoln at Gettysburg: The Words That Remade America,* by Garry Wills. Copyright © 1992 by Literary Research, Inc.

"Swing Low, Sweet Chariot" and "Go Down, Moses" from *Religious Folk-Songs of the Negro,* edited by R. Nathaniel Dett. Reprinted courtesy of AMS Press, Inc.

Excerpt from *Mary Chesnut's Civil War* edited by C. Vann Woodward. Copyright © 1986 by C. Vann Woodward, Sally Bland Metts, Barbara G. Carpenter. Sally Bland Johnson, and Katherine W. Herbert. Reprinted by permission of Yale University Press.

Poems #511, #303, #67, #435, #1624, #1732, #465, #1078, #712, #238, #441 reprinted by permission of the publishers and the Trustees of Amherst College from *The Poems of Emily Dickinson,* Thomas H. Johnson, ed., Cambridge, Mass: The Belknap Press of Harvard University Press, copyright © 1951, 1955, 1979, , 1983 by the President and Fellows of Harvard University Press.

"Frederick Douglass" copyright © 1966 by Robert Hayden, from *Collected Poems of Robert Hayden* by Frederick Glaysher, editor. Reprinted by permission of Liveright Publishing Corporation.

Unit 4

Gabriela Mistral, "Richness" from *Selected Poems: A Bilingual Edition,* translated and edited by Doris Dana (Baltimore: The Johns Hopkins Press, 1971). Copyright © 1961, 1964, 1970, 1971 by Doris Dana. Reprinted with the permission of Writer's House, LLC, New York, on behalf of the proprietors.

Unit 5

From *I: Six Nonlectures* by E.E. Cummings. Copyright 1953, © 1981 by the Trustees for the E.E. Cummings Trust. Used by permission of Liveright Publishing Corporation.

"The Negro Artist and the Racial Mountain" by Langston Hughes. Copyright © 1926 by Langston Hughes. Reprinted by permission of Harold Ober Associates Incorporated.

"Fireworks" and "Summer Rain" from *The Complete Poetical Works of Amy Lowell.* Copyright © 1955 by Houghton Mifflin Company. Copyright renewed © 1983 by Houghton Mifflin Company, Brinton P. Roberts, Esquire. Reprinted by permission of Houghton Mifflin Company. All rights reserved.

"Oread" by HD (Hilda Doolittle), from *Collected Poems, 1912–1944,* copyright © 1982 by the Estate of Hilda Doolittle. Reprinted by permission of New Directions Publishing Corp.

"In a Station of the Metro" by Ezra Pound, from *Personae,* copyright © 1926 by Ezra Pound. Reprinted by permission of New Directions Publishing Corp.

"The Red Wheelbarrow" by William Carlos Williams, from *Collected Poems: 1909–1939, Volume I,* copyright © 1938 by New Directions Publishing Company. Reprinted by permission of New Directions Publishing Corp.

"This is just to Say" by William Carlos Williams, from *Collected Poems: 1909-1939, Volume I,* copyright © 1938 by New Directions Publishing Corp. Reprinted by permission of New Directions Publishing Corp.

"Ars Poetica" from *Collected Poems, 1917–1982* by Archibald MacLeish. Copyright © 1985 by The Estate of Archibald MacLeish. Reprinted by permission of Houghton Mifflin Company. All rights reserved.

From the book *Letters to a Young Poet.* Copyright © 2000 by Rainer Maria Rilke. Reprinted with permission of the New World Library, Novato, CA. www.newworldlibrary.com Toll free 800/972-6657 ext. 52

"beware: do not read this poem" from the book *New and Collected Poems.* Copyright © 1989 by Ishmael Reed. Permission granted by Lowenstein-Yost Associates.

"Study of Two Pears" from *The Collected Poems of Wallace Stevens* by Wallace Stevens, copyright 1954 by Wallace Stevens and renewed 1982 by Holly Stevens. Used by permission of Alfred A. Knopf, a division of Random House, Inc.

"Eating Poetry" from *Selected Poems* by Mark Strand, copyright © 1979, 1980 by Mark Strand. Used by permission of Alfred A. Knopf, a division of Random House, Inc.

"anyone lived in a pretty how town" copyright 1940, © renewed 1968, 1991 by the Trustees of the E. E. Cummings Trust, from *Collected Poems: 1904–1962* by E. E. Cummings. Edited by George J. Firmage. Reprinted by permission of Liveright Publishing Corporation.

"somewhere i have never travelled,gladly beyond" Copyright 1931, © 1959, 1991 by the Trustees for the E.E. Cummings Trust. Copyright © 1979 by George James Firmage, from *Complete Poems: 1904-1962* by E.E. Cummings, edited by George J. Firmage. Used by permission of Liveright Publishing Corporation.

"Frederick Douglass." Copyright © 1966 by Robert Hayden, from *Collected Poems of Robert Hayden,* by Robert Hayden, edited by Frederick Glaysher. Used by permission of Liveright Publishing Corporation.

""Spotting by the Woods on a Snowy Evening," "Mending Wall," "Birches," and "The Death of a Hired Man" from *The Poetry of Robert Frost,* edited by Edward Connery Lathem. Copyright 1944, 1951, © 1956, 1958 by Robert Frost, © 1967 by Lesley Frost Ballantine, copyright 1916, 1923, 1928, 1930, 1939 © 1969 by Henry Holt & Co., Inc. Reprinted by permission of Henry Holt & Co., Inc.

"My City" copyright 1935 by James Weldon Johnson, renewed © 1963 by Grace Nail Johnson, from *Saint Peter Relates an Incident* by James Weldon Johnson. Reprinted by Viking Penguin, a division of Penguin Putnam Inc.

Excerpt from *Dust Tracks on a Road* by Zora Neale Hurston. Copyright © 1942 by Zora Neale Hurston. Copyright renewed 1970 by John C. Hurston. Reprinted by permission of HarperCollins Publishers, Inc.

"I, Too" copyright © 1994 by The Estate of Langston Hughes, "The Negro Speaks of Rivers," copyright © 1994 by The Estate of Langston Hughes, from *The Collected Poems of Langston Hughes* by Langston Hughes. Used by permission of Alfred A. Knopf, a division of Random House, Inc.

From *The Perfect Hour* by James L.W. West III, copyright © 2005 by James L.W. West III. Used by permission of Random House, Inc.

"In Another Country" reprinted by permission of Scribner, an imprint of Simon & Schuster Adult Publishing Group, from *Men Without Women* by Ernest Hemingway. Copyright © 1927 by Charles Scribner's Son. Copyright renewed 1955 by Ernest Hemingway.

"Soldiers of the Republic" by Dorothy Parker, from *The Portable Dorothy Parker* by Dorothy Parker, Introduction by Brendan Gill. Copyright 1928, renewed © 1956 by Dorothy Parker. Reprinted by permission of Viking Penguin, a division of Penguin Putnam Inc.

"Any Human to Another" from *On These I Stand* by Countee Cullen. Copyrights held by the Amistad Research Center, Tulane University, administered by Thompson and Thompson, Brooklyn, NY.

"The Jilting of Granny Weatherall" from *Flowering Judas and Other Stories,* copyright © 1930 and renewed 1958 by Katherine Anne Porter, reprinted by permission of Harcourt Brace & Company.

"A Black Man Talks of Reaping" by Arna Bontemps. Reprinted by Permission of Harold Ober Associates Incorporated. From Personals. Copyright © 1963 by Arna Bontemps.

Unit 6

"Breakfast" from *The Long Valley* by John Steinbeck. Copyright 1938, renewed © 1966 by John Steinbeck. Reprinted by permission of Viking Penguin, a division of Penguin Putnam Inc.

"A Rose for Emily" from *Collected Stories of William Faulkner* by William Faulkner. Copyright © 1930 and renewed 1958 by William Faulkner. Reprinted with permission of Random House, Inc.

"The Life You Save May Be Your Own" from *A Good Man is Hard to Find and Other Stories,* copyright © 1953 by Flannery O'Connor and renewed 1981 by Regina O'Connor, reprinted by permission of Harcourt Brace & Company.

"Upon Receiving the Nobel Prize for Literature" from *Essays, Speeches & Public Letters by William Faulkner* by William Faulkner, edited by James B. Meriwether. Copyright © 1950 by William Faulkner. Reprinted by permission of Random House, Inc.

Excerpt from *Black Boy* by Richard Wright. Copyright © 1937, 1942, 1944, 1945 by Richard Wright. Copyright renewed © 1973 by Ellen Wright. Reprinted by permission of HarperCollins Publishers, Inc.

"The Rockpile" © 1965 by James Baldwin is collected in *Going to Meet the Man,* published by Vintage Books. Copyright renewed. Used by arrangement with the James Baldwin Estate.

"The Magic Barrel" by Bernard Malamud, reprinted by the permission of Russell & Volkening, as agents for the author. Copyright © 1954, 1958 by Bernard Malamud, renewed 1986 by Bernard Malamud.

"The Second Tree from the Corner" from *The Second Tree from the Corner* by E. B. White. Copyright © 1947 by E. B. White. Copyright renewed. Reprinted by permission of HarperCollins Publisher, Inc.

"The Bean Eaters" and "To Don at Salaam" by Gwendolyn Brooks. Reprinted by consent of Brooks Permissions.

"A Worn Path" from *A Curtain of Green and Other Stories,* copyright 1941 and renewed 1969 by Eudora Welty, reprinted by permission of Harcourt, Inc., and Russell and Volkening as agents for the author.

"The Death of the Ball Turret Gunner" from *The Complete Poems* by Randall Jarrell. Copyright © 1969 by Mrs. Randall Jarrell. Reprinted by permission of Farrar, Straus & Giroux, Inc.

"The Portrait" is reprinted with permission from the publisher of *...And The Earth Did Not Devour Him* by Tomás Rivera (Houston: Arte Público Press-University of Houston, © 1992).

From *The Crucible* by Arthur Miller. Copyright 1952, 1953, 1954, renewed © 1980, 1981, 1982 by Arthur Miller. Used by permission of Viking Penguin, a division of Penguin Group (USA) Inc.

From *Hiroshima* by John Hersey, copyright © 1946 and renewed 1974 by John Hersey. Used by permission of Alfred A. Knopf, a division of Random House, Inc.

From *All Rivers Run to the Sea* by Elie Wiesel, copyright © 1995 by Alfred A. Knopf, Inc. Used by permission of Alfred A. Knopf, a division of Random House, Inc.

"Kubota" from *Volcano: A Memoir of Hawaii* by Garrett Hongo, copyright © 1995 by Garrett Hongo. Used by permission of Alfred A. Knopf, a division of Random House, Inc.

From *Maus I: A Survivor's Tale/My Father Bleeds History* by Art Spiegelman, copyright © 1973, 1980, 1981, 1982, 1984, 1985, 1986 by Art Spiegelman. Used by permission of Pantheon Books, a division of Random House, Inc.

Unit 7

From *Stride Toward Freedom* by Martin Luther King, Jr. Reprinted by arrangement with the Estate of Martin Luther King, Jr., c/o Writers House as agent for the proprietor of New York, NY. Copyright © 1958 Martin Luther King Jr., copyright renewed 1986 Coretta Scott King.

"Choice, A Tribute to Dr. Martin Luther King, Jr." from *In Search of Our Mothers' Gardens, Womanist Prose,* copyright © 1963 by Alice Walker, reprinted with permission of Harcourt, Brace & Company.

"A Fable for Tomorrow" from *Silent Spring* by Rachel Carson. Copyright © 1962 by Rachel L. Carson, renewed 1990 by Roger Christie. Reprinted by permission of Houghton Mifflin Company. All rights reserved.

"Roberto Acuna" from *Working* by Studs Terkel. Reprinted by permission of Donadio & Olson, Inc. Copyright © 1972, 1974 by Studs Terkel.

"Ambush" from *The Things They Carried.* Copyright © 1990 by Tim O'Brien. Reprinted by permission of Houghton Mifflin Company. All rights reserved.

"Snow" from *How the Garcia Girls Lost Their Accents.* Copyright © 1991 by Julia Alvarez. Published by Plume, an imprint of The Penguin Group (USA), and originally in hardcover by Algonquin Books of Chapel Hill. Reprinted by permission of Susan Bergholz Literary Services, New York. All rights reserved.

ACKNOWLEDGMENTS

"In Thai Binh (peace) Province" by Denise Levertov, from *The Freeing of the Dust,* copyright © 1975 by Denise Levertov. Reprinted by permission of New Directions Publishing Corp.

"Courage" from The *Awful Rowing Toward God,* by Anne Sexton. Copyright © 1975 by Loring Conant Jr., Executor of the Estate of Anne Sexton. Reprinted by permission of Houghton Mifflin Company. All rights reserved.

"My Father and the Figtree" from *Words Under the Words,* by Naomi Shihab Nye. Reprinted by permission of the author.

From *The Woman Warrior* by Maxine Hong Kingston, copyright © 1975, 1976 by Maxine Hong Kingston. Used by permission of Alfred A. Knopf, a division of Random House, Inc.

"El Olvido" by Judith Ortiz Cofer is reprinted by permission from the publisher of *Terms of Survival* (Houston: Arte Publico Press: University of Houston, 1997).

"The Names of Women" by Louise Erdrich. Copyright © 1992 by Louise Erdrich. Reprinted by permission of the Wylie Agency.

"Salvador Late or Early" from *Woman Hollering Creek.* Copyright © 1991 by Sandra Cisneros. Published by Vintage Books, a division of Random House, Inc., and originally in hardcover by Random House, Inc. Reprinted by permission of Susan Bergholz Literary Services, New York. All rights reserved.

"The Gift in Wartime" by Tran Mong Tu. Reprinted by permission of the author.

From *Stay Alive, My Son* by Pin Yathay. Copyright © 1987 by Pin Yathay. Forward by David Chandler copyright © 2000 Cornell University press. Used by permission of the publisher, Cornell University Press.

"The Fish" from *The Complete Poems 1927–1979* by Elizabeth Bishop. Copyright © 1979, 1983 by Alice Helen Methfessel. Reprinted by permission of Farrar, Strauss & Giroux, Inc.

"Root Cellar" copyright 1943 by Modern Poetry Association, Inc., from *Collected Poems of Theodore Roethke* by Theodore Roethke. Used by permission of Doubleday, a division of Random House, Inc.

"Nineteen Thirty-Seven" from *Krik? Krak!* By Edwidge Danticat. Copyright © 1991, 1992, 1993, 1994, 1995 by Edwidge Danticat. Reprinted by permission of Soho Press.

"Thoughts on the African-American Novel" by Toni Morrison, from *Black Women Writers (1950–1980)* by Mari Evans. Copyright © 1983 by Mari Evans. Reprinted by permission of Doubleday, a division of Random House, Inc.

"I Chop Some Parsley While Listening to Art Blakely's Version of 'Three Blind Mice'" from *Picnic, Lightning* by Billy Collins, copyright © 1998. Reprinted by permission of the University of Pittsburgh Press.

"Daisies" and "Cottonmouth Country" from *The Wild Iris* by Louise Gluck. Copyright © 1993 by Louise Gluck. Reprinted by permission of HarperCollins Publishers.

"Ending Poem" from *Getting Home Alive,* copyright © 1986 by Aurora Levins Morales and Rosario Morales. Reprinted by permission of Firebrand Books.

Content from The Academic Word List, developed at the School of Linguistics and Applied Language Studies at Victoria University of Wellington, New Zealand, is reprinted by permission of Averil Coxhead. http://language.massey.ac.nz/staff/awl/index.shtml.

Maps

Mapping Specialists Inc.

Photography

Cover (bkgd)Lorna Clark/Getty Images, (stars)Imtek Imagineering/Masterfile; **IN22** Terra Foundation for American Art, Chicago/Art Resource, NY; **IN23** Edward Hopper/AKG Images; **IN24** Richard Cummins/CORBIS; **IN25** SuperStock, Inc./SuperStock; **IN26** North Wind Picture Archive; **IN27** Bettmann/CORBIS; **IN28** Images.com/CORBIS; **IN29** Smithsonian American Art Museum, Washington, DC/Art Resource, NY; **IN30** CORBIS; **IN31** Christie's Images; **IN33** Smithsonian American Art Museum, Washington, DC/Art Resource, NY; **IN34** The Barnes Foundation, Merion Station, Pennsylvania/CORBIS; **IN36** Smithsonian American Art Museum, Washington, DC/Art Resource, NY; **IN37** UPI/CORBIS; **IN38** Bill Jacklin/Private Collection/Bridgeman Art Library; **IN39** Gayle Ray/SuperStock; **IN41** Bettmann/CORBIS; **IN42** SuperStock; **IN45** Mary Evans Picture Library; **IN46** Age Fotostock America Inc.; **IN49** Time Life Pictures/Getty Images; **IN50** David Turnley/CORBIS; **IN50** (l)David Turnley/CORBIS, (r)Getty Images; **3** (bkgd)Steven Allen/Getty Images, (b)PhotoDisc; **4–5** Asher Brown Durand/Brooklyn Museum of Art, New York, USA/Bridgeman Art Library; **6** (t)New York Historical Society, New York, USA/Bridgeman Art Library, (cl)Werner Forman/Art Resource, NY, (cr)George Henry Boughton/New York Historical Society, New York, USA/Bridgeman Art Library, (bl)Reich Lessing/Art Resource, NY, (br)Royalty Free/CORBIS; **7** (tl)Jean-Antoine Houdon/Musee des Beaux-Arts, Orleans, France, Roger-Viollet, Paris/Bridgeman Art Library, (tr)From the Collections of The Henry Ford Museum, (c) The Colonial Williamsburg Foundation, (b)NPS: Amer. Rev. War/Guilford Courthouse; **9** (tl)Art Archive/Musee de la Marine, Paris/Dagli Orti, (tr)Art Resource, NY, (b)Francis Guy/New York Historical Society, New York, USA/Bridgeman Art Library; **10** Bettmann/CORBIS; **13** Werner Forman/Art Resource, NY; **15** Museum of Fine Arts, Boston; **17** Geoffrey Clements/CORBIS; **19** Thomas Worthington/Century Association, New York, USA/Bridgeman Art Library; **20** (l)Getty Images, (r)Pat O'Hara/CORBIS; **21** Seattle Art Museum, Gift of John H. Hauberg; **24** Getty Images; **25** Peter Johnson/CORBIS; **27** Werner Forman/Art Resource, NY; **31** Joseph Sohm; Visions of America/CORBIS; **32** Bates Littlehales/Animals Animals; **33** (t)Danny Lehman/CORBIS, (tc)Seattle Art Museum/CORBIS, (bc)Owaki-Kulla/CORBIS, (b)Jim Bockowski/Animals Animals; **34** Robert Holmes; ns/CORBIS; **37** Seattle Art Museum, Gift of Katherine White and the Boeing Company; **39** Smithsonian American Art Museum, Washington, DC/Art Resource, NY; **40** Art Resource, NY; **42** courtesy of Historic Prophetstown; **44** Jerry Jacka Photography; **47** Getty Images; **51** CORBIS; **53** Thomas Smith/Worcester Art Museum, Massachusetts/Bridgeman Art Library; **54** Amanita Pictures; **56** (l, r)Richard T. Norwitz/CORBIS, (bkgd)The New York Public Library/Art Resource, NY; **58** Getty Images; **60** Bettmann/CORBIS; **62** Burstein Collection/CORBIS; **66** Royal Albert Memorial Musem, Exeter/Bridgeman Art Library; **68** SuperStock, Inc./SuperStock; **71** Burstein Collection/CORBIS; **74** Trustees of the Boston Library; **76** North Wind Picture Archives; **78** Daryl Benson/Masterfile; **81** Getty Images; **82** The Art Archive/St. Biddolph, Boston/Eileen Tweedy; **85** Victoria & Albert Museum, London/Art Resource; **88** Joseph Badger, Yale University Art Gallery; **90** Adam Woolfitt/CORBIS; **91** National Portrait Gallery, London/SuperStock; **94** Andrew Brookes/CORBIS; **95** SuperStock; **96** Christie's Images Ltd.; **98** Michael Sheldon/Art Resource, NY; **99** Benjamin Franklin-Printer, by John Ward Dunsmore, ca. 1928, oil on canvas, 28 x 36 inches, accession number 1938.312/Collection of The New York Historical Society; **104** (l)Getty Images, (r)Bettmann/CORBIS; **105** Frank Modell/The New Yorker/cartoonbank.com; **106** Getty Images; **108** Virginia Historical Society; **112** Bettmann/CORBIS; **114** Comstock/PunchStock; **115** Bettmann/CORBIS; **119** National Archives; **120** Archive Photos/NewsCom; **121** Andrew Brookes/CORBIS; **122 124** Bettmann/CORBIS; **126** North Wind Picture Archive; **129** Library of Congress; **130** Chateau de Versailles, France/ET Archive, London/SuperStock; **131** Bettmann/CORBIS; **134** Getty Images; **136** National Park Service, Adams National Historical Park; **138** White House Historical Association/Glencoe Stock; **139** Smithsonian Institution; **141** Getty Images; **142** National Park Service, Adams National Historical Park, (inset) AP Images; **146** Stockbyte; **148** Photodisc; **151** Photonica/Getty Images; **154** (t)Charles Gupton/CORBIS, (b)file photo; **156** CORBIS; **162–163** Smithsonian American Art Museum, Washington, DC/Art Resource, NY; **164** (t)British Museum, London, UK/Bridgeman Art Library, (cl)MPI/Getty Images, (cr)Bettmann/CORBIS, (bl)Carmen

Redondo/CORBIS; (br)Museum of London, UK/Bridgeman Art Library; **165** (t)Library of Congress, (cl)Heritage Coins, (cr)Archivo Iconografico, S.A./CORBIS, (b)George Frederick Watts/Trustees of the Watts Gallery, Compton, Surrey, UK/Bridgeman Art Library; **167** (tl)Boston Public Library, (tr)The New York Public Library/Art Resource, NY, (b)Josiah Wolcott /Massachusetts Historical Society, Boston, MA, USA/ Bridgeman Art Library; **168** ©Minnesota Historical Society/CORBIS; **171** Terra Foundation for American Art, Chicago/Art Resource, NY; **173** Art Resource, NY; **175** Bildarchiv Preussischer Kulturbesitz/Art Resource, NY; **177** Francis G. Mayer/CORBIS; **178** Bettmann/CORBIS; **181** Francis G. Mayer/CORBIS; **187** Bettmann/CORBIS; **190** James Schnepf; **191** (t)Bettmann/CORBIS, (b)Penny Gentieu; **192** Bettmann/CORBIS; **193** Getty Images; **194** Hulton-Deutsch Collection/CORBIS; **195 196** Bettmann/CORBIS; **200** (l)Getty Images, (r)Bettmann/CORBIS; **202** Hulton Archive/Getty Images; **203 204** Farrell Grehan/CORBIS; **206** Christie's Images; **210** (t)George Caleb Bingham/Private Collection/ Bridgeman Art Library, (c)Bildarchiv Preussischer Kulturbesitz/Art Resource, NY, (b)David Turnley/CORBIS; **212** Jean Miele/CORBIS; **213** The Pierpont Morgan Library/Art Resource, NY; **215** George Caleb Bingham/Private Collection/Bridgeman Art Library; **218** Bettmann/CORBIS; **220** David Turnley/CORBIS; **221** Louise Gubb/CORBIS SABA; **224** David Turnley/CORBIS; **225** Museum of Fine Arts, Boston; **226** (l) Getty Images, (r) Smithsonian American Art Museum, Washington, DC/Art Resource, NY; **227** Everett Collection; **228** Bettmann/CORBIS; **231** Photo Researchers, Inc.; **233** Cleveland Museum of Art. Mr. & Mrs. William H. Marlatt Fund, 1967.18; **234** The Ogden Museum of Southern Art, University of Nebraska; **237** The Fine Arts Museum of San Francisco. Gift of Mr. and Mrs. John D. Rockefeller III. 1979.7.84.; **242** Bettmann/CORBIS; **244** Scala/Art Resource, NY; **246** Erich Lessing/Art Resource, NY; **251** Scala/Art Resource, NY; **254** Giovanni Battista Piranesi/Hamburger Kunsthalle, Hamburg, Germany/Bridgeman Art Library; **257** Giraudon/Art Resource, NY; **261** Francisco Jose de Goya y Lucientes/Private Collection, Index/Bridgeman Art Library; **263** Scala/Art Resource, NY; **265** Charles Osgood/Peabody Essex Museum, Salem, MA/Bridgeman Art Library; **267** CORBIS; **270** Smithsonian American Art Museum, Washington, DC/ Art Resource, NY; **275** Lee Snider/Photo Image/CORBIS; **276** Gustave Courbet/Musee de la Vie Romantique, Paris, France, Lauros/Giraudon/ Bridgeman Art Library; **277** PhotoDisc; **279** Getty Images; **280** Bettmann/ CORBIS; **282** Paolo Curto/Getty Images; **284** Flip Nicklin/Getty Images; **286** Images.com/CORBIS; **289** James L. Amos/CORBIS; **291** Scala/Art Resource, NY; **292** William Page/Peabody Essex Museum, Salem, MA/ Bridgeman Art Library; **293 294 295** Courtesy of Nantucket Historical Association; **296** Stockbyte; **298** Royalty-Free/CORBIS; **303** Philip Marazzi; Papilio/CORBIS; **304** (t)Charles Gupton/CORBIS, (b)file photo; **306 307** Getty Images; **308** CORBIS; **314–315** Dennis Malone Carter/ The Bridgeman Art Library; **316** (t)Bettmann/CORBIS, (c)North Wind Picture Archives, (b)CORBIS; **317** (tl)Mary Evans Picture Library, (tr)Smithsonian Images, (c)New York Historical Society, New York, USA/ Bridgeman Art Library, (b)Mary Evans Picture Library/The Image Works; **319** (t)Currier & Ives/Art Resource, NY, (bl)CORBIS, (br)James Captain Hope/Art Resource, NY; **320** Alexander Gardner/CORBIS; **323** William Tolman Carlton/The Bridgeman Art Library; **325** Medford Historical Society/CORBIS; **327** George Luks/Private Collection, David Findlay Jr Fine Art, NYC/Bridgeman Art Library; **329** J. Eastman Johnson/The Bridgeman Art Library; **330** The Jacob and Gwendolyn Lawrence Foundation/Art Resource, NY; **332** Smithsonian American Art Museum, Washington, DC/Art Resource, NY; **333** Hampton University Museum, Hampton, Virginia; **334** Smithsonian American Art Museum, Washington, DC/Art Resource, NY; **336** (t)CORBIS, (c)Art Resource, NY, (b)David Muench/CORBIS; **337** National Portrait Gallery, Smithsonian Institution/ Art Resource, NY; **339** Hampton University Museum, Hampton, Virginia; **341** The Jacob and Gwendolyn Lawrence Foundation/Art Resource, NY; **347** Kaaria Mucherera/Private Collection/Bridgeman Art Library;

348 (l)Getty Images, (r)Library of Congress; **349** Mary Evans Picture Library/The Image Works; **351** Andy Snow; **352** (tl tr b)Taro Yamasaki, (c)courtesy National Underground Railroad Freedom Center; **353** Andy Snow; **354** Bettmann/CORBIS; **356** Smithsonian American Art Museum, Washington, D.C./Art Resource, NY; **358** Andrew Brookes/CORBIS; **359** Rick Reeves/United States National Guard; **360** Private Collection/ Art Resource, NY; **362 364 365** Bettmann/CORBIS; **367** Getty Images; **368** CORBIS; **370** SEF/Art Resource, NY; **373** Bettmann/CORBIS; **375** Lindy Powers/IndexStock Imagery; **376** Bettmann/CORBIS; **377** The Metropolitan Museum of Art, Gift of Mrs. John A. Rutherford 1914 (14:141) Photograph © 1980 The Metropolitan Museum of Art; **380** courtesy Rodrigue Studios; **382** G.E. Kidder Smith/CORIBS; **386** SuperStock, Inc./ SuperStock; **388** Reza Estakhrian/Stone/Getty Images; **390** Archival Research International/National Archives, (medallion)AP Images; **393** Smithsonian American Art Museum, Washington, DC/Art Resource, NY; **394** CORBIS; **396** (c) The St. Louis Art Museum; Art © T.H. Benton and R.P. Benton Testamentary Trusts/UMB Bank Trustee/Licensed by VAGA, New York, NY; **397** Photography Courtesy of Gwendolyn Knight Lawrence/Art Resource, NY; **399** William MacIlvaine the Younger/New York Historical Society/ Bridgeman Art Library; **400** Brooklyn Museum of Art, New York. Dick S. Ramsay Fund 59.9; **402** Christie's Images/CORBIS; **404** Chicago Historical Society/The Bridgeman Art Library: **406** Tony Craddock/Stone; **408** Columbus Museum of Art, Ohio: Museum Purchase, Howald Fund, 1942.083; **412** Brooklyn Museum, New York/Superstock; **413** AP Images; **416** Terra Foundation for American Art, Chicago/Art Resource, NY, (inset)Mark Lennihan/AP Images; **419** The New York Public Library/Art Resource, NY; **420** Hulton Archive/Getty Images; **421** CHIP EAST/ Reuters/CORBIS; **423** Hulton Archive/Getty Images; **425** Private Collection/ Christie's Images; **426** Clare Marie Leonard/CORBIS; **428** Images.com/ CORBIS; **429** Collection of the Birmingham Museum of Art, Birmingham, Alabama; Gift of John Meyer; **431** Caspar David Friedrich/Private Collection/ Bridgeman Art Library; **432** Patrick William Adam/Oldham Art Gallery, Lancashire, UK/Bridgeman Art Library; **434** Alinari/Art Resource, NY; **436** Vilhelm Hammershoi/Private Collection, Christie's Images/Bridgeman Art Library; **437** Christie's Images; **438** Caspar David Friedrich/Private collection/Bridgeman Art Library; **441** Christie's Images Ltd; **443** James Marshall/CORBIS; **444** Stockbyte; **447** Bettmann/CORBIS; **451** Courtesy of Vicksburg National Archive; **454** Charles Gupton/CORBIS; **456** (l)from the collection of Edith Hariton/Antique Textile Resource, Bethesda, (r)Hulton/ Archive; **457** (l r)Bettmann/CORBIS, (Lit. Library)file photo; **458** CORBIS; **464-465** National Gallery of Art, Washington, DC. Gift of the W.L. and May T. Mellon Foundation; **466** (t)Bettmann/CORBIS, (b)Imageworks; **467** (t)Library of Congress, (tc)Smithsonian Images, (bc)Hulton Archive/ Getty Images, (b)Bettmann/CORBIS; **469** (l)Bettmann/CORBIS, (c)CORBIS, (r)Snark/Art Resource, NY; **470** Currier & Ives/Art Resource, NY; **473** J. Eastman Johnson/New York Historical Society/Bridgeman Art Library; **475** Réunion des Musées Nationaux/Art Resource, NY; **477** CORBIS; **479** Smithsonian American Art Museum, Washington, DC/ Art Resource, NY; **480** (l)Getty Images, (r)Alfred Thompson Bricher/Butler Institute of American Art, Youngstown, OH/Bridgeman Art Library; **480** (t)Smithsonian American Art Museum, Washington, DC/Art Resource, NY, (b)Alfred Thompson Bricher/Butler Institute of American Art, Youngstown, OH/Bridgeman Art Library; **481 482** Bettmann/CORBIS; **484** Hirshhorn Museum and Sculpture Garden, Smithsonian Institution, Gift of Joseph H. Hirshhorn, 1966.; **485** Library of Congress; **486** CORBIS; **487** Bettmann/CORBIS; **490** Historical Picture Archive/ CORBIS; **491** Bettmann/CORBIS; **494 495 496 497** Diana Walker; **498** Steve Liss; **499** Bettmann/CORBIS; **501** Mary Evans Picture Library; **502** Art Resource, NY; **504** Bettman/CORBIS; **506** SuperStock, Inc./ SuperStock; **508** Roy Bishop/Stock Boston; **509** Columbus Museum of Art, Ohio: Bequest of Frederick W. Schumacher, [57] 1943.008; **511** Fine Art Photographic Library/CORBIS; **512** file photo; **517** Getty Images; **518** Bettmann/CORBIS; **520** The Heyden Collection, Museum of Fine

Arts, Boston; **522** David David Gallery/SuperStock; **527** National Portrait Gallery, Smithsonian Institution/Art Resource, NY; **529** ©1979 Howard Terpning ©The Greenwich Workshop® Inc. courtesy of The Greenwich Workshop Inc., Shelton, CT. For information on the limited edition fine art prints by Howard Terpning call 1-800-577-0666; **531** The Newark Museum/Art Resource, NY; **532** (l)Getty Images, (r) Photo Collection Alexander Alland, Sr./CORBIS; **533 534** Bettmann/CORBIS; **536** Private Collection, ©Connaught Brown, London/Bridgeman Art Library; **540** Hulton-Deutsch Collection/CORBIS; **543** Bildarchiv Preussischer Kulturbesitz/Art Resource, NY; **544** Andrew Brookes/CORBIS; **545** (t)Erich Lessing/Art Resource, NY, (c b)Scala/Art Resource, NY; **546** Missouri Historical Society; **548** The Butler Institute of American Art, Youngstown, OH; **552** Scala/Art Resource, NY; **554** Bildarchiv Preussischer Kulturbesitz/Art Resource, NY; **557** Scala/Art Resource, NY; **560** Christie's Images/CORBIS; **561** William Merritt Chase/National Gallery of Art, Washington DC, USA/Bridgeman Art Library; **562** Hulton Archive/Getty Images News Service; **564** Photograph Courtesy of Gwendolyn Knight Lawrence/Art Resource, NY; **565** Christie's Images/CORBIS/Romare Bearden Foundation/Licensed by VAGA, New York, NY; **567** Bettmann/CORBIS; **569** Smithsonian American Art Museum, Washington, DC/Art Resource, NY; **572** Bettmann/CORBIS; **577** Private Collection/Christie's Images; **581 584** Smithsonian American Art Museum, Washington, DC/Art Resource, NY; **587** DC Moore Gallery, NY; **589** Erich Lessing/Art Resource, NY; **590** Private Collection/Christie's Images; **593** Underwood & Underwood/CORBIS; **595** The Cavalry Club/E.T.Archives/SuperStock; **599** Berhard Otto/FPG; **603** Lynn Stone/Animals Animals; **604** Giraudon/Art Resource, NY; **607** Lynn Stone/Animals Animals; **608** Frank Krahmer/Masterfile; **610–611** Robert van der Hilst/CORBIS; **612** Brian A. Vikander/CORBIS; **614** Stockbyte; **617** Brand X Pictures; **620** Digital Vision/PunchStock; **624** Charles Gupton/CORBIS; **626 627** Getty Images; **628** CORBIS; **630** Bettmann/CORBIS; **634–635** Howard A. Thain/New York Historical Society, New York/Bridgeman Art Library; **636** (t)National Archives/John F. Kennedy Library, (c)Fotosearch/Comstock Royalty Free, (b)Imageworks; **637** (t)National Portrait Gallery, Smithsonian Institution/Art Resource, NY, (c)David J. & Janice L. Frent Collection/CORBIS, (b)Austrian Archives/CORBIS; **639** (tl b)Bettmann/CORBIS, (tr)Underwood & Underwood/CORBIS; **641** Library of Congress; **643** Terra Foundation for American Art, Chicago/Art Resource, NY; **645** National Gallery of Art, Washington, DC. Collection of Mr. and Mrs. Paul Mellon.; **647** Smithsonian American Art Museum, Washington, DC/Art Resource, NY; **649** The Museum of Modern Art/Licensed by SCALA/Art Resource, NY; **650** (l)Getty Images, (r) Réunion des Musées Nationaux/Art Resource, NY; **651** Ando Hiroshige/Art Resource, NY; **652** David Lees/CORBIS; **656** Bettmann/CORBIS; **658** Collection of the Newark Museum. Anonymous gift, 1929. (cat. No. 55)/Art Resource, NY; **661 663** San Diego Museum of Art. Gift of Anne R. and Amy Putnam; **666** Lisa Larsen/Time Life Pictures/Getty Images; **668** Smithsonian American Art Museum, Washington, DC/Art Resource, NY; **669** The Barnes Foundation, Merion Station, Pennsylvania/CORBIS; **671** Andrews Brookes/CORBIS; **672** Bettmann/CORBIS; **674** akg-images; **675** Images.com/CORBIS; **677** (t)V. Brockhaus/zefa/CORBIS, (tc)Royalty-Free/CORBIS, (b)Scot Frei/CORBIS, (bc)Images.com/CORBIS; **678** Oscar White/CORBIS; **682** Christie's Images/CORBIS; **684 685** Images.com/CORBIS; **686** Mary Iverson/CORBIS; **688** Brooklyn Museum of Art, New York, USA, Frank L. Babbott Fund/Bridgeman Art Library; **689** Bettmann/CORBIS; **691** Simon Fletcher/Private Collection/Bridgeman Art Library; **692** Estate of Pablo Picasso /Artists Rights Society (ARS), New York/Art Institute of Chicago; **694** Bettmann/CORBIS; **696** Konstantine Rodko/Private Collection, New York/Bridgeman Art Library; **697** Archivo Iconografico, S.A./CORBIS; **699** Yousuf Karsh/Woodfin Camp & Associates; **701** Bettmann/CORBIS; **702** CNAC/MNAM/Dist. Réunion des Musées Nationaux/Art Resource, NY; **704** Bettmann/CORBIS; **706** Yale University Art Gallery, New Haven, CT. Gift of Walter Bareiss, B.A. 1940; **708** Age Fotostock America Inc.; **711** Gerrit Greve/CORBIS; **713** Fine Art Photographic

Library/CORBIS; **716** CORBIS; **720** Collection of Harrison Young, Peking, China. Reproduced in "Spirit of Place" by John Arthur; **723** A. Corton/Visuals Unlimited; **725** Bob Krist/CORBIS; **726** Ted Streshinsky/CORBIS; **729** Butler Institute of American Art, Youngstown, OH/Bridgeman Art Library; **730** (l)Getty Images, (r)Edward Hopper/AKG; **731** University of South Carolina; **732** John Springer Collection/CORBIS; **734 736** Scala/Art Resource, NY; **741** Getty Images; **742** Bettmann/CORBIS; **744** Kirsten Soderlind/CORBIS; **746** Maude Martin Ellis/Private Collection/Bridgeman Art Library; **749** Visual Arts Library/Art Resource, NY; **750** Images.com/CORBIS; **753** Erich Lessing/Art Resource, NY; **755** Leon Dabo/Florence Griswold Museum, Old Lyme, Connecticut, Gift of the Hartford Steam Boiler Inspection & Insurance Co./Bridgeman Art Library; **760** PhotoEssentials/FotoSearch; **762** Bettmann/CORBIS; **763** Henri Lerolle/Musee des Beaux-Arts, Pau, France, Giraudon/Bridgeman Art Library; **764** Erich Lessing/Art Resource, NY; **765** Images.com/CORBIS; **768** Hulton Archive; **774** Bettmann/CORBIS; **776** Photograph courtesy of Hirschl & Adler Galleries, New York, NY; **777** ET Archive, London/SuperStock; **780** Christie's Images; **782** Photodisc; **785** Smithsonian American Art Museum, Washington, DC/Art Resource, NY; **786** CORBIS; **788** The Jacob and Gwendolyn Lawrence Foundation/Art Resource, NY; **790** CORBIS; **792** Philadelphia Museum of Art: The Louis E. Stern Collection; **795** Smithsonian American Art Museum, Washington DC/Art Resource, NY; **799** Andrews Brookes/CORBIS; **800** CORBIS; **802** Collection of Martin & Sondra Sperber, New York. Courtesy Heritage Gallery, Los Angeles.; **803** Private Collection/Superstock; **806** The Phillips Collection, Washington, D.C. **807** The Museum of Modern Art/Licensed by SCALA/Art Resource, NY; **808** The Phillips Collection, Washington, D.C.; **809** Robert W. Kelley/Time Life Pictures/Getty Images; **811** Colin Bootman/Private Collection/Bridgeman Art Library; **812** Leon Dabo/Indianapolis Museum of Art, USA, Gift of S. O. Buckner/Bridgeman Art Library; **815** Schomburg Center, The New York Public Library/Art Resource, NY; **817** Penguin/CORBIS; **819** Underwood & Underwood/CORBIS; **822** Schomburg Center/Art Resource, NY; **824** Images.com/CORBIS; **826** AP Images; **828** San Diego Museum of Art, San Diego, CA, Museum purchased with funds provided by Mrs. Leon D. Bonnet; Art © Estate of Robert Gwathmey/Licensed by VAGA, New York, NY; **830** National Portrait Gallery, Smithsonian Institution/Art Resource, NY; **832** Smithsonian American Art Museum, Washington, DC/Art Resource, NY; **834** Stockbyte; **837** Library of Congress; **839** Getty Images; **842** Charles Gupton/CORBIS; **845** (l)Jagarts/Photofest,(c)Getty Images, (R)AP Images, (Lit. Library)file photo; **846** CORBIS; **852–853** Smithsonian American Art Museum, Washington, DC/Art Resource, NY; **854** (t)Christie's Images, (cl)Bettmann/CORBIS, (cr)Mary Altaffer/AP Images, (b)U.S. Holocaust Memorial Museum; **855** (tl tr)David J. & Janice L. Frent Collection/CORBIS, (cl)Nobel Foundation, (cr)Getty Images, (b)Matthias Kulka/zefa/CORBIS; **857** (t bl)Bettmann/CORBIS, (br)CORBIS; **858** CORBIS; **861 863** Smithsonian American Art Museum, Washington, DC/Art Resource, NY; **865** CORBIS; **867** All rights reserved by the Estate of Nan Wood Graham/Licensed by VAGA, New York, NY; **868** Bettmann/CORBIS; **870 872** UPI/CORBIS; **875** Andrew Brookes/CORBIS; **876** Cofield Collection, Center for the Study of Southern Culture, University of Mississippi; **878** First Image; **880** John Atkinson Grimshaw/Leeds Museums and Galleries U.K/Bridgeman Art Library; **882** SuperStock; **883** Edward Hopper/Private Collection, James Goodman Gallery, New York/Bridgeman Art Library; **885** Bildarchiv Preussischer Kulturbesitz/Art Resource, NY; **887** Nobel Foundation; **890** Hulton Archive/Getty Images; **892 894 897** Eudora Welty/CORBIS; **900** CORBIS; **904** Smithsonian American Art Museum, Washington, DC/Art Resource, NY; **906** Lois Mailou Jones Pierre-Noel Trust; **909 911** Time Life Pictures/Getty Images; **912** Margaret Bourke-White/Time & Life Pictures/Getty Images; **913** Flannery O'Connor Collection, Ina Dillard Russell Library, Georgia College & State University; **915** Courtesy Hubert Shuptrine; **917** G. Kalt/zefa/CORBIS; **919** Martyn Goddard/CORBIS; **921** Dan Holmberg/CORBIS; **926** Getty Images; **927** Hulton Archive/Getty Images; **929** Julian Barrow/Private Collection/Bridgeman Art

Library; **931** Bill Jacklin/Private Collection/Bridgeman Art Library; **932** Jeff Greenberg/Photo Researchers; **935** Bettmann/CORBIS; **937** Art Resource, NY; **938** Cameraphoto Arte, Venice/Art Resource, NY; **940** David Lee/CORBIS; **942** Erich Lessing/Art Resource, NY; **944** The Jewish Museum of New York/Art Resource, NY; **947** The Newark Museum/Art Resource, NY; **948** North Wind Picture Archives; **952** Christopher Morris/Black Star Publishing/PictureQuest; **953** The Jewish Museum of New York/Art Resource, NY; **957** Bettmann/CORBIS; **959** The Jacob and Gwendolyn Lawrence Foundation/Art Resource, NY; **961** Smithsonian American Art Museum, Washington, DC/Art Resource, NY; **962** E.C. Stangler/Uniphoto; **963** Patti Mollica/CORBIS; **964** Smithsonian American Art Museum, Washington, DC/Art Resource, NY; **967** Collection of Whitney Museum of American Art, NY, Photography by Geoffrey Clements, NY; Art ©Jasper Johns/Licensed by VAGA, New York, NY; **968** Bettmann/CORBIS; **970** Bettmann/CORBIS SYGMA; **971** CORBIS; **973** Andrew Brookes/CORBIS; **974** AP Images; **976** Baldwin H. Ward/CORBIS; **978** (t)Bettmann/CORBIS, (c)CORBIS, (b)Aaron Horowitz/CORBIS; **979** AFP/Getty Images; **981** Nathan Benn/CORBIS; **983** Nathan Benn/CORBIS; **984** CORBIS; **987** Nathan Benn/CORBIS; **991** Richard Hutchings/PhotoEdit; **992** Collection of Michael D. Brown; **993** (l)Terry Ashe/The Liaison Agency, (r)Corry/Hulton Archive; **994 995** CORBIS; **996 997** From MAUS 1: A Survivor's Tale/My Father Bleeds History by Art Spiegelman, copyright 1973, 1980, 1981, 1982, 1984, 1985, 1986 by Art Spiegelman. Used by permission of Pantheon Books, a division of Random House.; **998** CORBIS; **999** Bettmann/CORBIS; **1001** Time Life Pictures/Getty Images; **1003** John Van Hasselt/CORBIS SYGMA; **1004** Hulton Archive/Getty Images; **1006** Time Life Pictures/Getty Images; **1008 1010** CORBIS; **1013** Photo of Tomás Rivera is reprinted with permission from the publisher—APP Archive Files (Houston: Arte Público Press—University of Houston); **1015** Scala/Art Resource, NY; **1016** Courtesy Robert C. Buitrón; **1020** (l) Getty Images, (R)CORBIS; **1021** Sal Veder/AP Images; **1022** Bettmann/CORBIS; **1024** (inset)20TH CENTURY FOX/THE KOBAL COLLECTION/Barry Wetcher, (bkgd)Daniel Root/Photonica/Getty Images; **1032** Daniel Root/Photonica/Getty Images; **1035** Nannette Carter; **1038** 20TH CENTURY FOX/THE KOBAL COLLECTION; **1042** Courtesy of SBC Communications; **1044** Solomon R. Guggenheim Museum, New York. 54.1408; **1048** ©2000 Willem de Kooning Revocable Trust/Artists Rights Society (ARS), NY/The Museum of Modern Art, New York; **1049** Mark Peterson/CORBIS; **1054 1056** 20TH CENTURY FOX/THE KOBAL COLLECTION; **1059** Courtesy Museum of Fine Arts, Boston/The Lane Collection. ©Estate of Ben Shahn/Licensed by VAGA, New York, NY; **1062** Albright-Knox Art Gallery, Buffalo, NY. Gift of Seymour H. Knox, 1957; **1064** Courtesy Robert Miller Gallery, NY/© 2000 Pollock-Krasner Foundation/Artists Rights Society (ARS), New York; **1065** Images.com/CORBIS; **1070** 20TH CENTURY FOX/THE KOBAL COLLECTION/Barry Wetcher; **1073** Nannette Carter; **1083** 20TH CENTURY FOX/THE KOBAL COLLECTION; **1085** Estate of Elaine DeKooning; **1087** Images.com/CORBIS; **1091** Robbie Jack/CORBIS; **1094** Gayle Ray/SuperStock; **1096** The Lane Collection. Courtesy Museum of Fine Arts, Boston; **1100** 20TH CENTURY FOX/THE KOBAL COLLECTION; **1102** 20TH CENTURY FOX/THE KOBAL COLLECTION/Barry Wetcher; **1104** Todd Davidson/Images.com; **1108** AP Images; **1109** Kobal Collection; **1110** Stockbyte; **1111** Brand X Pictures; **1112** Digital Vision; **1114** Getty Images; **1118** (t)Charles Gupton/CORBIS, (bl bc br)CORBIS; **1119** CORBIS; **1120 1121** Getty Images; **1122** CORBIS; **1128–1129** Louis K. Meisel Gallery, Inc./CORBIS; **1130** (t)Warner Bros./Photofest, (cl)Bettmann/CORBIS, (cr)W. Cody/CORBIS, (bl)Dave Bartruff/CORBIS, (br)Photodisc/Getty Images; **1131** (t)National Organization of Women, (cl)Reuters/CORBIS, (c)John Duricka/AP Images, (cr)Chris Trotman/Duomo/CORBIS, (bl)Reuters/CORBIS, (br)ROMEO RANOCO/Reuters/CORBIS; **1133** (l)John Nordell/

Getty Images, (c)Ralf-Finn Hestoft/CORBIS, (r)Nik Wheeler/CORBIS; **1134** Wally McNamee/CORBIS; **1137** Bettmann/CORBIS; **1139** Getty Images; **1141** Smithsonian American Art Museum, Washington, DC /Art Resource, NY; **1143** Hirshhorn Museum and Sculpture Garden, Smithsonian Institution; **1145** AP Images; **1146** Brian Lanker; **1147** Flip Schulke/CORBIS; **1149** Images.com/CORBIS; **1150** Culver Pictures, Inc.; **1151** Bettmann/CORBIS; **1153** Noah Berger/AP Images; **1155** *Stewart's Farm*, 1995, by Jonathan Green, Oil on Canvas, 47 5/8" x 59 5/8". From the collection of the Würth Museum, Künzelsau, Germany. Photography by Tim Stamm; **1158** Andrew Brookes/CORBIS; **1159** Bettmann/CORBIS; **1161** Leonard Nadel/National Museum of American History/Handout/Reuters/CORBIS; **1163 1164 1165** CORBIS; **1166** Peter Turnley/CORBIS; **1167** Bettmann/CORBIS; **1170** Getty Images; **1171** (t b)Tim Page/CORBIS, (c)Francis Bailly/The Liaison Agency; **1172** Miriam Berkley; **1174** Collection National Guard Bureau, Pentagon, Washington, DC. From the original painting by Mort Kunstler. ©1984 Mort Kunstler, Inc.; **1177** Francis Bailly/The Liaison Agency; **1178** Christine Spengler/CORBIS SYGMA; **1181** Steve Starr/CORBIS; **1182** Christopher Felver/CORBIS; **1184** Brenda Chrystie/CORBIS; **1188** New Directions/The Luce Photo/AP Images; **1192** Jacob Halaska/IndexStock; **1193** Library of Congress; **1194** Iconica/Getty Images; **1196** Jerry Schatzberg/CORBIS; **1198** Frank Driggs Collection/Getty Images; **1201** Bettmann/CORBIS; **1202** AP Images; **1204** Tate Gallery, London/Art Resource, NY; **1207** Andy Warhol Foundation/CORBIS; **1208** UPI/CORBIS; **1210** Francis G. Mayer/CORBIS; **1211** Private Collection/Bridgeman Art Library; **1212** The Museum of Modern Art/Art Resource, NY; **1213** Paul Anthony/CORBIS; **1216** Bettmann/CORBIS; **1218** Freyda Miller/CORBIS; **1220** Bettmann/CORBIS; **1222** Georgia O'Keeffe Museum, Santa Fe/Art Resource, NY; **1223** Didier Dorval/Masterfile; **1226** Betttmann/CORBIS; **1230** Royalty-Free/CORBIS; **1231** Bettmann/CORBIS; **1233** Copyright by Marian Wood Kolisch; **1235 through 1242** Images.com/CORBIS; **1246** Getty Images; **1247** Daniel Cima; **1251** courtsey Dorothy Alexander; **1253** Victoria & Albert Museum, London/Art Resource, NY; **1254** Mark Tomalty/Masterfile; **1257** Malcah Zeldis/Art Resource, NY; **1258** Doug Menuez/CORBIS; **1260** Zifen Qian SuperStock; **1263** Phil Schermeister/CORBIS;**1264** (t)Vince Streano/Getty Images, (b)North Wind Picture Archives; **1266** Vince Streano/Getty Images; **1268** Sophie Bassouls/CORBIS SYGMA; **1270** Ditz/Private Collection/Bridgeman Art Library; **1272** Paul Bullard/Private Collection, Agnew's, London, UK/Bridgeman Art Library; **1276** Miriam Berkley; **1278** Kactus Foto/SuperStock; **1280** Gerardo Somoza/CORBIS; **1282** PhotoCuisine/CORBIS; **1285** Christopher Felver/CORBIS; **1287** Gilbert Mayers/SuperStock; **1290** Christopher Little/CORBIS; **1292** (inset)courtesy Louise Erdrich, c/o Rembar and Curtis, (bkgd)John de Visser/Masterfile; **1293** Peter Harholdt/SuperStock; **1294** Richard B. Spencer/SuperStock; **1295** courtesy Louise Erdrich, c/o Rembar and Curtis; **1298** Cynthia Farah; **1299** Robert E. Daemmrich/Stone/Getty Images; **1300** Christie's Images; **1302** Erin Elder/SABA;**1304** Smithsonian American Art Museum, Washington, DC/Art Resource, NY; **1309** Andrew Brookes/CORBIS; **1310** (t)Getty Images, (b)Private collection, Christie's Images/Bridgeman Art Library; **1311** 2005 Marvel/CORBIS; **1312** Marion Ettlinger/CORBIS OUTLINE; **1315** Amanita Pictures; **1317** Collection of Jonathan Demme; **1318** Manu Sassoonian/Art Resource, NY; **1320** Yale University Art Gallery, New Haven, CT. Gift of Selden Rodman; **1324** Heather Conley Photographs; **1326** Franklin McMahon/CORBIS; **1329** Linda Haas; **1331** Elena Climent/Phoenix Art Museum, Arizona, Mr and Mrs Gene Lemon in honour of Clayton Kirking/Bridgeman Art Library; **1334** Stockbyte; **1335** BananaStock/PictureQuest; **1338** Getty Images; **1342** Charles Gupton/CORBIS; **1344** (l)Bettmann/CORBIS, (r)Richard Howard/Time & Life Pictures/Getty Images; **1345** (t)Aaron Haupt, (Lit. Library)file photo, (b)Reuters/CORBIS; **1346** CORBIS.